Need an eleven-letter word meaning "fear of open spaces"?
EASY.

Just look up "fear (of)" in the alphabetical listing. Go down the list of alphabetical subcategories to *open spaces*. And there it is—"agoraphobia."

The unique, convenient arrangement and design of this wonderful dictionary makes it fast and easy to find just the word you need to fill in those baffling spaces. The words you want are listed by number of letters. You'll also find variant spellings and subcategories, and it's all arranged alphabetically under clue words.

Make puzzle-solving more fun—and the results letter-perfect—with the best crossword dictionary you can buy!

WEBSTER'S NEW WORLD™ CROSSWORD PUZZLE DICTIONARY

SECOND EDITION

Compiled by

Jane Shaw Whitfield

POCKET BOOKS

New York   London   Toronto   Sydney   Singapore

POCKET BOOKS, a division of Simon & Schuster, Inc.
1230 Avenue of the Americas, New York, NY 10020

Webster's New World™ Crossword Puzzle Dictionary, Second Edition

Copyright © 1997 by Hungry Minds, Inc.

This edition is a major revision of *Webster's New World™ Crossword Puzzle Dictionary* copyright © 1983 by Jane Shaw Whitfield. All rights reserved.

Published by arrangement with Wiley Publishing, Inc.

ISBN: 0-671-00977-X

First Pocket Books printing July 2003

10 9 8 7 6 5 4 3 2 1

POCKET and colophon are registered trademarks of Simon & Schuster, Inc.

Manufactured in the United States of America

For information regarding special discounts for bulk purchases, please contact Simon & Schuster Special Sales at 1-800-456-6798 or business@simonandschuster.com.

Dictionary Editorial offices:
New World Dictionaries
850 Euclid Avenue
Cleveland, OH 44114

CONTENTS

FOREWORD

This new edition of *Webster's New World Crossword Puzzle Dictionary* represents a thorough revision and updating of the highly successful work originally compiled by Jane Shaw Whitfield. Thousands of new clue words and answer terms have been added from crossword puzzles published since the last revision. Biographical and geographical entries are now completely up to date. Tables have been introduced to provide a particularly effective and convenient way to locate large blocks of related terms in one place. In addition, a user's guide created especially for this edition will assist readers in finding precisely the words they want quickly and easily.

Crossword puzzle dictionaries and crossword puzzle solvers share, predictably, some special characteristics. Both are distinguished by their breadth of vocabulary and by their unique intellectual focus on the relationship between clues and answers. The editors of Webster's New World dictionaries wish to acknowledge the contributions to this edition of one very gifted crossword puzzle enthusiast, Mr. Joe Forest of Sharonville, Ohio, whose insightful suggestions have been invaluable.

This all-new second edition remains in one respect unchanged, namely, it is, as Jane Shaw Whitfield wrote in her foreword to the first edition, dedicated "to all enthusiasts of crossword puzzles and to their creators."

GUIDE TO THE USE OF THIS BOOK

1. **The Arrangement of Entries**—Each entry block has
   a clue word set in boldface type as its headword.
   All clue words, including single words, hyphenated and
   unhyphenated compounds, idioms, phrases, and proper
   names, are listed in strict alphabetical order:

   A . . .
   aa (Haw) . . .
   aal . . .
   Aani (Egypt) . . .
   abdominal limb (crustacean) . . .
   Abel's brother . . .
   aberration . . .

2. **Clue Words and Answer Terms**—Answer terms for each
   clue word are arranged by the count of letters in each
   word or phrase. Answer terms of varying parts of
   speech may be gathered together in a single entry block.
   Words in each group of answers with the same letter
   count are arranged in alphabetical order:

   abandon . . . **4.** quit **5.** cease, leave,
   remit, waive, yield **6.** abjure, depart, desert, disuse,
   give up, maroon, reject, resign, vacate
   7. cast off, discard, forsake, freedom, neglect
   8. abdicate, forswear, renounce
   9. surrender, turpitude **10.** relinquish
   11. abandonment, discontinue, unrestraint
   12. carelessness, heedlessness

3. **Variant Spellings and Forms**—When variants are some
   distance apart alphabetically, the full entry appears at the
   spelling or spellings most frequently used, and the other
   spellings are cross-referred to this entry:

   align, aline . . . **4.** true **5.** level, match **6.** equate,
   line up . . .

   . . .

   aline . . . see *align*

   Variants not alphabetically distant are given
   together in boldface type:

   harbor, harbour . . . **3.** bay **4.** cave, port
   5. haven **6.** covert, foster, . . .

narghile, nargile, nargileh . . . **4.** pipe
6. hookah

Variant spellings of answer words are given
immediately after the answer word in parentheses:

monument . . . **4.** tomb **5.** cairn, stele (stela),
tower, vault **6.** . . . .

4. *Labels, Abbreviations, and Explanatory Notes—*
Additional information for either clue words or answer
terms may appear abbreviated in parentheses. A list of
abbreviations used in this book appears below, p. x.

Aaru (Egypt Relig) . . . **12.** fields of Aaru
14. abode of the dead

monopoly . . . **5.** grant, right, trust . . .
10. possession (exclusive)

oomancy (divination by) . . . **4.** eggs

5. *Cross-references—*Cross-references to related terms are
introduced by "see" or "see also" and given in italics:

absence of . . . (see also *without*)

6. *Subcategories—*Answer terms may be divided into
informational subcategories related to the clue word.
They are introduced by the label "(pert to)":

cardinal (pert to) . . .
astrology . . **5.** nadir **6.** zenith
astronomy . . **10.** solstitial **11.** equinoctial . . .
compass point . . **4.** east, west **5.** north, south . . .
virtues (Theol) . . **4.** hope **5.** faith **7.** charity

7. *Variety Lists—*When the clue word is a general term
covering a variety of things, a list of those is supplied,
introduced by the label "(types of)":

flower (types of) . . . **3.** gul (rose) **4.** iris, ixia, lily,
pink, rose **5.** aster, calla, canna, . . .

8. *Tables—*Tables at the end of this book provide lists of
persons, things, or events in a particular category along
with a letter count for each item.

ABBREVIATIONS USED IN THIS WORK

Abbr Abbreviation
abdom abdominal
aborig aboriginal
Acad Academy
adj adjective
adm admitted
Afr African
Agric Agriculture
Alex Alexander
Am Ind American Indian
Anat Anatomy
anc ancient
Anglo-Ir Anglo-Irish
Anthrop Anthropology
Antiq Antiquity
Arab Arabian
Arch Architecture
Archaeol Archaeology
Astrol Astrology
Astron Astronomy
Austral Australia(n)

Babyl Babylonia(n)
Belg Belgium
Bib Bible, Biblical
Biol Biology
Bot Botany
Braz Brazil(ian)
Brit Britain, British
Brit Col British Columbia
Buddh Buddhism
Bus Business

Can Canada, Canadian
Capt Captain
Caucas Caucasian
Celt Celtic
Cent Central, Century
Cent Am Central America
Chem Chemistry
Chin Chinese
Chr Christian
coll colloquialism
comb form
    combining form
Confed Confederation
Constell Constellation
contemp contemporary
Criminol Criminology

Dan Danish
Dept Department
derog derogatory
dial dialectal
div division
Du Dutch

E East
East Ch Eastern Church

Eccl Ecclesiastical
Educ Education
Egypt Egyptian
Elec Electricity
Eng England, English
Episcop Episcopal
equiv equivalent
Esk Eskimo
est established
Eur Europe(an)
exclam exclamation
ext extinct

FDR Franklin D. Roosevelt
Fem Feminine
Finan Finance, Financial
Flem Flemish
Fr France, French

Gen General
Geog Geography
Geol Geology
Geom Geometry
Ger German
Gov Governor
Govt Government
Gr Greek
Gram Grammar
Gr Brit Great Britain

Haw Hawaiian
Heb Hebrew
Hem Hemisphere
Her Heraldry
Hind Hinduism
Hindu Hindustani
Hist Historical
Holl Holland
Horol Horology
Hung Hungarian

illeg illegal
Ind India, Indian
Indo-Chin Indo-China
Ins Insurance
Internat International
Ir Irish
irreg irregular
Isl(s) Island(s)
It Italian

Jap Japanese
Jew Jewish

L Latin
Legislat Legislature
Lit Literature
Log Logic

Maced Macedonia
Malay Malayan
Math Mathematics
MD Doctor of Medicine
Med Medical
Mex Mexican
Mil Military
Mohamm Mohammedan
Mt(s) Mountain(s)
Mus Music
Myth Mythology

Nat'l National
Naut Nautical
Nav Naval, Navy
neg negative
New Test New Testament
NZ New Zealand
No North
No Am North American

obs obsolete
Old Test Old Testament
opp opposite
Orient Oriental
Oxf Univ
    Oxford University

Penol Penology
Pers Persian
pert pertaining
Petrol Petrology
Pg Portuguese
Pharm Pharmaceutical
Philat Philately
Phil I Philippine Islands
Philol Philology
Philos Philosophy
Phonet Phonetics
Phys Physical
pl plural
PO Post Office
poet poetic
Polit Politics, Political
Polyn Polynesian
ppty property
pref prefix
P Rico Puerto Rico
Pros Prosody
pseud pseudonym

R Roman
RCCh
    Roman Catholic Church
Rd Road
ref referring
Relig Religion
R Estate Real Estate
Rev War Revolutionary War

x

Rhet Rhetoric
Riv River
Rom Roman
rr railroad
Rum Rumania
Russ Russian

S South
Scot Scotland, Scottish
Scand Scandinavian
Shaksp Shakespeare
sing singular
sl slang
Slav Slavonic
So Afr South Africa
So Am South America
Sp Spanish
Surg Surgical
sym symbol

Tag Tagalog
Tahit Tahiti
Terat Teratology
terr territory
Teut Teutonic
Theat Theatrical
Theol Theology
Theos Theosophy
triang triangular
TID Ter in die
Trop Tropical
Turk Turkish
TV Television

U Union
Univ University
USS United States Ship
USSR Union of Soviet
    Socialist Republics

Vet Veterinary

W West
WAC
    Women's Army Corps
W Indies West Indies
WWI World War I
WWII World War II

Yidd Yiddish
YMCA Young Men's
    Christian Association
yr year

Zool Zoology

WEBSTER'S NEW WORLD™ CROSSWORD PUZZLE DICTIONARY

SECOND EDITION

A

A . . . 5. alpha, first 7. article
A 1 . . . 5. prime 6. symbol 8. superior 10. first-class
aa (Haw) . . . 4. lava
aal . . . 8. morindin (dye), mulberry
aam (Du) . . . 7. measure (liquid) 11. water bucket
Aani (Egypt) . . . 3. ape (sacred) 6. baboon 12. cynocephalus
aardvark . . . 3. pig 6. farrow 8. anteater
aardwolf . . . 5. hyena 8. Proteles
Aaron (pert to) . . .
  ally (Bib) . . 3. Hur
  brother . . 5. Moses
  burial place . . 3. Hor
  leader (Jew) . . 9. Levitical 10. High Priest
  rod . . 4. wand (magic) 7. molding, mullein
  sister . . 6. Miriam
  son . . 5. Abihu, Nadab
Aaru (Egypt Relig) . . . 12. fields of Aaru 14. abode of the dead
aasvogel . . . 7. vulture
absca . . . 4. hemp 5. lupis 6. linaga
abacus . . . 4. slab 8. cupboard 10. calculator 11. compartment
Abaddon . . . 3. pit (bottomless) 4. Hell 5. Sheol 8. Apollyon (angel) 11. destruction
abaft . . . 3. aft 5. after 6. astern, behind
abalone . . . 5. awabi, ormer, uhllo (ullo) 6. sea ear 8. ear shell
abandon . . . 4. quit 5. cease, leave, remit, waive, yield 6. abjure, depart, desert, disuse, give up, maroon, reject, resign, vacate 7. cast off, discard, forsake, freedom, neglect 8. abdicate, forswear, renounce 9. surrender, turpitude 10. relinquish 11. abandonment, discontinue, unrestraint 12. carelessness, heedlessness
abandoned . . . 4. left, lost 7. disused, forlorn, given up 8. derelict, deserted, forsaken 9. desolated, discarded, neglected 11. surrendered 12. relinquished, unredeemable, unrestrained
abase . . . 5. lower, shame 6. bemean, depose, humble, reduce 7. degrade, mortify 8. cast down, disgrace 9. humiliate 10. depreciate
abash . . . 5. shame 6. appall, dismay 7. astound, confuse, disturb, mortify 8. bewilder, confound 9. discomfit, embarrass, humiliate 10. disconcert, put to shame
abate . . . 3. ebb 4. lull, wane 5. let up, relax, remit 6. deduct, lessen, reduce 7. abolish, nullify, qualify, slacken, subside 8. decrease, diminish, discount, moderate
abatement . . . 5. letup 6. myosis (miosis), rebate 8. decrease 9. lessening, reduction 10. diminution, mitigation,
moderation
abb . . . 4. wool, yarn 6. fleece (pert to)
Abba . . . 5. abbot, title 6. Father
abbe . . . 4. monk 6. cleric, curate, priest
abbess . . . 4. amma 15. spiritual mother
abbreviate . . . 7. abridge, curtail, shorten 8. compress, condense, contract, simplify 9. epitomize 11. make briefer
abbreviation . . . 5. brief, lapse 6. digest 8. abstract 9. reduction 10. abridgment, compendium, shortening 11. contraction 12. condensation
abdicate . . . 4. cede, quit 5. demit, leave 6. depose, disown, resign, retire 7. lay down 8. disclaim, renounce, withdraw 9. surrender 10. disinherit, relinquish
Abdiel (Heb) . . . 5. angel 12. servant of God
abdomen . . . 3. gut, pot (sl) 4. wame 5. belly, tharm (obs) 6. paunch, venter 7. stomach 8. potbelly 12. pelvic cavity
abdominal . . . 7. coeliac, gastric, ventral 11. ventricular
abdominal limb (crustacean) . . . 7. pleopod
Abel's brother . . . 4. Cain, Seth
aberration . . . 5. mania, wrong 6. lunacy, oddity 7. errancy, madness 8. dementia, insanity 9. departure, deviation, variation, wandering 10. alienation, digression, divergence 11. abnormality, derangement, distraction, peculiarity 12. eccentricity, irregularity 14. disorientation
abet . . . 3. aid, egg 4. back, help 5. egg on 6. assist, foment, incite, second, succor, uphold 7. connive, endorse, support, sustain 8. advocate 9. encourage, instigate 11. countenance
abeyance . . . 4. rest, stay 5. lapse, pause 7. waiting 9. inertness 10. expectancy, suspension
abhor . . . 2. ug 4. hate, shun 6. detest, loathe 7. despise, dislike 8. execrate 9. abominate
abhorrence . . . 5. odium 6. hatred, horror 7. dislike 8. aversion, loathing 9. antipathy, disliking, repulsion 10. repugnance
abide . . . 4. bide, live, stay, wait 5. await, dwell, pause, tarry 6. endure, remain, reside 7. sojourn 8. continue, submit to, tolerate 9. acquiesce, withstand
abide by . . . 3. own 4. avow, heed 5. admit, allow, yield 6. accept, follow, regard 7. concede, respect 8. adhere to 9. conform to 11. acknowledge
abiding . . . 7. durable, lasting 8. constant, enduring 9. permanent, steadfast 10. continuing, indwelling, persisting
Abies . . . 4. firs 5. pines 8. conifers 10. evergreens
abigail . . . 4. ayah, maid 5. bonne 7. servant 9. soubrette
Abijah's son (Bib) . . . 3. Asa

ability . . . 4. gift 5. force, might, power, skill 6. genius, talent 7. caliber, faculty, fitness, potency 8. aptitude, capacity, strength 10. capability, competence, efficiency 11. proficiency, sufficiency 13. qualification

abiosis . . . 11. without life

abject . . . 3. low 4. base, mean, meek, vile 6. humble, menial, supine 7. hangdog, ignoble, servile, slavish 8. beggarly, contrite, cringing, degraded, wretched 9. groveling, miserable 10. despicable, obsequious

abjuration . . . 6. denial 8. palinode (song), yielding 9. disavowal, rejection, surrender 10. abjurement, retraction, withdrawal 11. abandonment, forswearing, recantation, repudiation 12. disclamation 14. relinquishment

abjure . . . 4. deny, wave 6. disown, recant, reject, revoke 7. abandon, disavow 8. disclaim, forswear, renounce 9. disaffirm, repudiate

able . . . 3. can, fit 5. adept, smart 6. clever, fitted, suited 7. adapted, capable, learned, solvent 8. adjusted, literate, powerful, skillful (skilful), vigorous 9. competent, effective, efficient, qualified 10. omnipotent, proficient

able (pert to) . . .
suffix . . 7. capable, fitness
to pay . . 7. moneyed, solvent 8. affluent 10. prosperous
to read and write . . 8. lettered, literate 10. book taught

ablepsia . . . 9. blindness

ably . . . 7. capably 11. competently, effectively, efficiently

abnormal . . . 6. albino 7. erratic, unusual 8. aberrant 9. deviative, eccentric, irregular, unnatural 11. exceptional 13. extraordinary

aboard . . . 4. onto 6. across 7. athwart 9. alongside

abode . . . 3. dar, hut 4. cell, cote, Eden, home 5. delay, house, lodge 7. habitat, Olympus, sojourn 8. dwelling, tenement 9. apartment, residence 10. habitation

abode of the dead . . . 3. Dar 4. Aalu, Aaru, Hell 5. Aralu, Hades, limbo, Orcus, Sheol 6. Asgard, heaven, Naraka 7. Abaddon, Elysium, Nirvana 8. paradise, Valhalla 9. perdition, purgatory 11. Pandemonium

abolish . . . 4. undo 5. annul, quash 6. cancel, recall, repeal, revoke, vacate 7. destroy, nullify, rescind, retract, reverse 8. abrogate, withdraw 10. annihilate, invalidate 11. countermand

abominable . . . 4. base, dire, foul, vile 5. awful, gross 6. odious, wicked, woeful 7. beastly, hateful 8. dreadful, grievous, infamous, shocking, terrible, wretched 9. execrable, loathsome, obnoxious 10. despicable, detestable, outrageous, unpleasant 12. disagreeable, disreputable

Abominable Snowman . . . 4. Yeti

abominate . . . 4. hate 5. abhor 6. detest, loathe 8. execrate

abomination . . . 3. woe 4. evil 5. odium, wrong 6. hatred, horror, plague 7. disgust, outrage 8. aversion, loathing, vexation 9. grievance 10. abhorrence, defilement, odiousness, repugnance

aboriginal . . . 5. first, natal 6. binghi, native 7. ancient 8. original 9. beginning, primitive 10. autochthon, indigenous

aborigines . . . 4. Ainu (Aino), Toda 5. lubra, Sakai, Vedda 7. cave men, Indians, natives, savages 9. indigenes, old-timers 10. Dravidians 11. preadamites

abortion . . . 6. arrest 7. failure 11. embryoctomy, miscarriage, miscreation 13. misconception

abound . . . 4. flow, teem 5. swarm 8. overflow 9. exuberate, plentiful

abounding . . . 4. rife 5. ample, flush 7. copious, teeming 8. abundant 9. exuberant, luxuriant, plentiful

abounding in . . .
blossoms . . 7. flowery
forests . . 6. sylvan
grass . . 6. cressy
snow . . 5. nival

about . . . 2. of, on, re 3. amb (pref) 5. anent, astir, circa 6. almost, around, nearly 8. circiter 10. concerning 13. approximately

about to happen . . . 8. imminent

above . . . 2. on, up 3. o'er, sur (pref) 4. atop, over, upon 5. aloft, super, supra (pref)

abrade . . . 3. rub 4. file, fret, gall 5. chafe, grate 6. scrape 9. excoriate

Abraham (pert to) . . .
birthplace . . 2. Ur
concubine . . 5. Hagar
father . . 5. Terah
grandfather . . 5. Nahor
grandson . . 4. Esau
nephew . . 3. Lot
son . . 4. Shua (Shuah) 5. Isaac, Medan 7. Ishmael
wife . . 5. Sarah (Sara, Sarai) 7. Keturah

abrasion . . . 4. flaw, gall, hurt 5. scuff 6. lesion, scrape 8. limation 9. attrition

abrasive . . . 4. file, sand 5. emery 6. garnet, polish, pumice 7. erodent 8. abradant, corundum 9. attritive, sandpaper

abraxas . . . 3. gem 5. charm, stone

Abraxes (pert to) . . .
god (anc Gnostic) . . 12. Supreme Deity
source of mind . . 4. Nous
the Word . . 5. Logos

abreast . . . 4. even (with) 6. beside 8. opposite 9. alongside

abrege . . . 7. epitome 10. abridgment

abri . . . 4. shed 6. cavity, dugout 7. shelter

abridge . . . 5. brief, razee (rasee) 7. curtail, shorten 8. abstract, condense, diminish, retrench 9. epitomize 10. abbreviate

abridgment . . . 6. digest 7. compend, epitome, summary 8. abstract, syllabus, synopsis 9. lessening, reduction 10. compendium, diminution 11. deprivation

abroad . . . 4. away 5. forth 6. astray,

widely 7. at large, broadly, distant
8. away from 9. spread out 11. widely
apart

abrogate . . . 5. annul, quash 6. cancel,
repeal, revoke 7. abolish, rescind 8. set
aside 10. put an end to

abrogation . . . 8. quashing 9. annulling,
cessation 10. rescinding, rescission
11. dissolution

abrupt . . . 4. curt, rude 5. blunt,
hasty, quick, sharp, sheer, steep,
terse 6. broken, craggy, sudden
7. brusque 8. headlong, vertical
9. broken off, impetuous 10. unexpected
11. precipitous 12. disconnected
13. perpendicular, unceremonious

abruptly . . . 7. briefly, in brief 8. suddenly

Absalom (pert to) . . .
 father . . 5. David (King)
 host's captain . . 5. Amasa
 sister . . 5. Tamar
 slayer . . 4. Joab

abscond . . . 3. run 4. bolt, flee, hide
5. elope 6. decamp, desert, eloine,
levant 8. steal off

absence . . . 4. AWOL, lack, void, want
5. exeat, leave 6. vacuum 7. silence
10. deficiency, withdrawal
13. nonappearance, nonattendance

absence of . . (see also *without*)
 animal, plant . . 8. lipotype
 hair . . 6. acomia
 pain . . 8. anodynia
 pigment . . 9. alphosis
 self-worth . . 7. modesty
 taste . . 7. ageusia

absent . . . 3. off, out 4. away, gone, lost
6. dreamy, musing, truant 7. lacking
8. absorbed, engrossed 10. abstracted
11. preoccupied 12. nonattendant

absinthe . . . 5. green 6. ajenjo, liquor
8. wormwood

absolute . . . 4. alod, dead, pure, real, true,
very 5. freed, sheer, total, utter, whole
6. empery, simple 7. certain, elative,
perfect, plenary 8. absolved, complete,
positive 9. arbitrary, downright,
unlimited 10. autocratic, disengaged,
peremptory 11. categorical,
independent 13. unconditional
15. plenipotentiary

absolute (pert to) . . .
 dominion . . 6. empery
 property . . 4. alod 7. alodium
 sovereign . . 8. autocrat
 superlative . . 7. elative
 time . . 9. Greenwich, universal

absolutely . . . 3. yea, yes 5. stark
6. wholly 7. utterly 8. entirely
10. altogether, positively, thoroughly
13. unequivocally 15. unconditionally

absolution . . . 6. pardon, shrive
7. penance 9. acquittal, remission
11. exculpation, forgiveness

absolve . . . 4. free 5. remit 6. acquit,
finish, pardon 9. discharge, exonerate
10. accomplish

absonant . . . 8. contrary 10. discordant
12. unreasonable

absorb . . . 3. eat 4. soak, suck 5. drink,
eat up, learn, use up 6. corner,

digest, engulf, imbibe, soak up, sponge
7. consume, swallow 10. assimilate,
monopolize, understand 11. incorporate

absorbed . . . 4. deep, lost, rapt, sunk
6. buried, intent, lost in 7. bemused,
devoted, engaged 8. occupied
9. engrossed 11. monopolized,
preoccupied

absorbent . . . 5. fomes 6. spongy
7. blotter 9. adsorbent 10. imbibitory

absorption . . . 9. imbibition

abstain . . . 4. deny, fast, hold, shun
5. avoid, cease, forgo, waive 6. eschew
7. forbear, refrain 8. restrain, teetotal,
withhold

abstemious . . . 5. sober 7. sparing
8. moderate 9. abstinent, temperate
11. abstentious

abstinence . . . 6. disuse 7. encraty
8. sobriety 9. restraint, sacrifice
10. abstention, continence, desistance,
moderation, self-denial, temperance
11. abandonment, forbearance, self-
control 13. self-restraint
14. abstemiousness, discontinuance

abstract . . . 4. deed, part, take 5. brief,
steal 6. deduct, noetic (purely), remove
7. abridge, epitome, shorten, summary
8. argument, condense, syllabus,
withdraw 9. capsulize, statement
10. abridgment, compendium
12. nonobjective

abstract being . . . 3. ens 6. entity

abstruse . . . 4. deep 6. hidden 7. obscure
8. esoteric, profound 9. concealed,
recondite 10. acroamatic (acroatic)
16. incomprehensible

absurd . . . 4. wild 5. droll, inept, silly
6. stupid 7. asinine, foolish 8. fabulous,
farcical 9. ludicrous 10. impossible,
irrational, ridiculous 11. incongruous,
nonsensical 12. inconsistent,
unbelievable, unreasonable

absurdity . . . 5. farce 7. twaddle
8. nonsense 10. absurdness
11. foolishness 13. contradiction,
impossibility 14. ridiculousness
16. inconceivability

abundance . . . 4. mass, much, rife
5. ample 6. galore, plenty, riches,
volume 8. fullness (fulness), opulence,
overflow, quantity 9. affluence
10. exuberance 11. copiousness,
superfluity 12. extravagance,
generousness 13. plenteousness

abundant . . . 4. lush, much, rich, rife,
teem 5. ample 6. galore, plenty
7. copious, profuse 9. abounding,
exuberant, luxuriant, plentiful
10. sufficient

abundant, not . . . 5. spare 6. lenten,
meager (meagre)

abuse . . . 4. gall, harm, hurt, maul, rail,
rape 5. crime, curse, scold, snash
6. berate, ill use, injure, insult, malign,
misuse, ravish, revile 7. calumny,
deceive, obloquy, offense, pervert,
traduce, upbraid 8. dishonor, maltreat,
misapply, reproach 9. contumely,
disparage, invective, violation
10. opprobrium, revilement, scurrility

11. debauchment, malediction, objurgation 12. mistreatment, vituperation

abusive . . . 3. mud (throw) 10. scurrilous 12. catachrestic

abut . . . 4. butt, join 5. touch 6. adjoin, appose, border, rest on 7. conjoin, connect 8. adjacent, neighbor

abutment . . . 4. arch, pier, wall 6. alette 7. abuttal, sea wall 8. buttress, shoulder 13. fortification

abysmal . . . 4. deep 7. yawning 8. profound, unending 9. plumbless 10. bottomless, fathomless

abyss . . . 3. pit 4. Absu, gulf, hell, hole, void, well 5. abysm, chaos, chasm, cleft, shaft 6. cavity, vorago 15. infernal regions

Abyssinia, Ethiopia . . .
capital . . 10. Addis Ababa
city . . 5. Aduwa, Aksum (Axum) 6. Gondar 7. Ankober, Gambela, Magdala
dialect . . 4. Geez
Empire (old) . . 7. Axumite
Hamite . . 4. Afar
King . . 13. Haile Selassie
kingdom (former) . . 4. Shoa 5. Tigre 6. Amhara
river (famed) . . 5. Abdai (Blue Nile)
sea . . 3. Red
title (anc) . . 12. Negusa Nagast

Abyssinian (pert to) . . .
fly . . 4. zimb
gold (artificial) . . 5. talmi
lyre . . 6. kissar
tea leaves . . 3. kat
wolf . . 6. kaberu

academic . . . 4. moot 5. ideal, rigid 6. formal 7. classic, elegant 8. abstract, pedantic, Platonic 9. scholarly 10. Ciceronian, scholastic 11. educational, impractical, speculative, theoretical 12. conventional, hypothetical 13. institutional

academy . . . 5. école , lycée 6. lyceum, manège, school, Schule 7. college, escuela, society 8. academie, seminary 9. accademia, Gymnasium, institute 10. university 11. institution

Academy of Plato . . . 7. Academe

Acadia . . . 6. Acadie 10. Nova Scotia

acarpous . . . 7. sterile 9. fruitless

acaudal . . . 7. anurous 8. tailless

accede . . . 5. agree, enter, grant, yield 6. assent, attain, comply, concur, relent, submit 7. conform, consent 9. acquiesce 11. acknowledge

accelerate . . . 4. rush 6. hasten, step up 7. advance, forward, further, quicken, speed up 8. activate, dispatch, expedite

acceleration . . . 5. haste 6. pickup 8. velocity 9. catalysis, hastening 10. expedition, quickening 11. advancement

accelerator . . . 6. muscle 7. speeder 8. betatron, throttle 9. cyclotron, quickener 11. atom smasher, synchrotron

accent . . . 4. beat, mark, tone 5. breve,

ictus, pitch, twang 6. brogue, stress 7. cadence, dialect 8. emphasis 9. emphasize 10. accentuate, expression, inflection, modulation 12. accentuation

accent (pert to) . . .
Irish . . 4. blas 6. brogue
on last syllable . . 7. oxytone
Scot . . 4. birr
unaccented syllable . . 5. arsis

accept . . . 2. OK 3. buy, own 4. avow, fang, take 5. admit, adopt, agree, allow, grant, trust, yield 6. assent, comply, credit, expect, ratify 7. approve, believe, certify, condone, confess, consent, embrace, receive, swallow (coll) 8. accredit, tolerate, validate 9. undertake 11. countenance

accept (as one's own) . . . 12. nostrificate (of foreign degrees)

acceptable . . . 2. OK 6. worthy 7. welcome 8. eligible, passable, pleasant, pleasing, suitable 9. agreeable, allowable, desirable, expedient, qualified, tolerable 10. admissible 11. comfortable 12. satisfactory

accepted . . . 6. chosen, deemed 7. adopted, assumed, popular, reputed, trusted 8. admitted, approved, believed, credited, embraced, espoused, inferred, orthodox, received, standard, supposed 9. customary, prevalent 10. accredited, understood, undertaken 11. traditional 12. conventional, unquestioned 13. authoritative

access . . . 3. way 4. adit, door, gain 5. entry 6. avenue, entree, ingate, tunnel 7. ingress 8. approach, entrance, entryway, increase 9. accession, accretion, admission 10. admittance 11. entranceway 13. accessibility, attainability 15. approachability

accessible . . . 4. open 5. handy 6. open to, public 7. getable 8. amenable, pervious 9. admissive, available, permeable, reachable, receptive 10. attainable, obtainable, open-minded, penetrable, procurable 11. persuasible 12. approachable 13. communicative

accession . . . 6. access, assent, attack, growth 7. adjunct, consent, joining, uniting 8. addition, increase 9. accretion, agreement, increment 10. acceptance, affixation, annexation, attainment, compliance, concession, coronation 12. acquiescence 13. reinforcement 14. aggrandizement

accessory, accessary . . . 5. extra, party 7. abettor 8. addition, litigant 9. adjective, appendage, assistant, attendant, auxiliary, obligato 10. accomplish, additional, collateral, subsidiary 11. appurtenant, concomitant, participant 12. accompanying, appurtenance, contributory, nonessential, participator 13. accompaniment, supplementary

accident . . . 3. hap 4. luck 6. chance, hazard, mishap 8. calamity, casualty, disaster 9. adventure, befalling,

mischance 10. misfortune
11. catastrophe

accidental ... 6. casual, chance
9. unwitting 10. contingent, unforeseen, unintended

acclaim ... 4. hail, laud 6. praise
7. applaud 8. applause 11. acclamation, approbation

acclamation ... 3. cry, joy 5. shout
7. acclaim, ovation, plaudit 8. applause, approval 9. unanimity

acclimate ... 5. adapt, inure 6. adjust, season 8. accustom 9. condition, habituate 10. naturalize 11. acclimatize, familiarize

acclivity ... 4. bank, brow, hill, rise
5. climb, slope, talus 6. ascent
7. upgrade 9. ascendant (ascendent)
11. inclination

accolade ... 4. fold, rite 5. award, brace, clasp, Oscar 6. praise, reward
7. embrace, tribute 8. encomium
9. panegyric 10. enfoldment

accommodate ... 3. fit 4. help, lend, meet, suit 5. adapt, favor, lodge, shape, yield 6. adjust, afford, comply, invest, oblige, orient, settle, supply 7. conform, furnish 9. reconcile 10. correspond

accommodation ... 3. aid 4. loan, room 5. limit, space, terms 6. giving, volume 7. advance, lodging, service
8. capacity 9. advantage, provision
10. adaptation, adjustment, attunement, conformity, settlement 11. convenience, integration, orientation, subsistence
12. coordination 13. harmonization
14. reconciliation

accompaniment ... 7. adjunct, descant, support 8. ornament 9. attendant, obbligato 11. concurrence
12. concomitance

accompany ... 4. join 6. attend, convoy, escort, follow, squire 7. conduct
11. synchronize 12. contemporize

accomplice ... 3. pal 4. aide, ally, chum
6. stooge 7. abettor 9. accessory, assistant, associate 11. confederate, conspirator

accomplish ... 2. do 3. win 4. make, work 5. enact, equip 6. attain, effect 7. achieve, compass, execute, furnish, operate, perfect, produce, realize, succeed 8. contrive, engineer
9. negotiate 10. consummate, effectuate

accomplishment ... 4. deed, feat
5. dispatch 8. discharge, execution 10. attainment, completion
11. achievement, acquirement, fulfillment, performance, proficiency, transaction 12. effectuation

accord ... 5. award, grant, unity 6. accede, unison 7. comport, concede, concert, concord, harmony, rapport 8. diapason, symphony 9. agreement, harmonize, reconcile, unanimity 10. accordance, conformity, uniformity 11. concurrence

accordant ... 7. attuned 8. agreeing, suitable 9. agreeable, assenting, consonant 10. concordant, concurrent, consenting, consilient, consistent
11. conformable, homogeneous

13. corresponding

accordingly ... 2. so 4. then, thus
9. therefore 12. consequently

according to ... 3. a la, aux 4. alla, fact, true 5. datal 7. a la mode 8. pursuant

accost ... 4. hail, meet 5. greet, speak
6. halloo, salute 7. address 8. approach

accoucheuse ... 7. midwife

account ... 3. sum, tab 4. bill, cast, sake, tale, word 5. debit, honor, score, tally
6. assign, credit, esteem, profit, reckon, regard, report 9. compute, memoirs, recital 9. narration, reckoning, rehearsal, statement, summation 10. numeration, recitation 11. description, explanation, information 13. communication

accountable ... 6. liable 8. amenable, knowable 9. divinable, traceable
10. answerable, ascribable, assignable, calculable, explicable, fathomable
11. explainable, predictable, responsible
12. attributable, intelligible
13. apprehensible 14. comprehensible

accountant ... 5. clerk 7. actuary, auditor
8. reckoner 9. defendant, registrar
10. bookkeeper, calculator

accouter, accoutre ... 3. fit, rig 4. deck, gird, suit 5. array, dress, equip, habit
6. attire, fettle, outfit 7. appoint, costume, furnish, provide

accouterment, accoutrement ...
5. dress, sword 6. attire 8. trapping
9. equipment, haversack

accoy ... 4. tame 5. daunt 6. soothe, subdue

accredit ... 5. trust 6. accept, affirm, credit, depute, ratify 7. approve, ascribe, believe, certify, confirm, empower, endorse 8. deputize, sanction, validate
9. authorize 10. commission

accrete ... 3. add 6. attach

accretion ... 4. gain 6. growth 8. addition, adhesion, increase 9. coherence, increment 10. concretion
11. coagulation, enlargement
12. accumulation, augmentation
13. amplification

accrue ... 4. grow 5. arise, ensue, issue
6. mature, result 7. acquire, collect, redound 8. accresce 10. accumulate

accumulate ... 4. grow, heap, mass, save 5. amass, hoard, store 6. accrue, garner, gather, muster 7. advance, collect, store up 8. increase 9. aggregate

accumulation ... 4. fund, gain, mass
5. hoard, store 7. accrual 8. gleaning, increase, treasure 9. accession, accretion, extension, gathering
10. acervation, assemblage, collection
11. acquisition, serendipity
12. augmentation 13. amplification
14. aggrandizement

accuracy ... 6. nicety 9. exactness, fussiness, precision, rightness
11. correctness 14. meticulousness, scrupulousness

accurate ... 4. just, nice, prim 5. close, exact, right 6. proper, strict 7. correct, perfect, precise 8. faithful 9. syntactic
10. meticulous, particular
11. grammatical

accursed . . . 6. cursed, damned, doomed
9. execrable, execrated 10. detestable
13. anathematized

accusation . . . 5. blame 6. attack,
charge, taxing 7. calumny 8. reproach
9. complaint 10. imputation, indictment
11. impeachment 12. denunciation

accuse . . . 3. tax 5. blame 6. attack,
charge, delate, indict 7. arraign,
censure, impeach 8. denounce
9. criminate 11. incriminate, recriminate

accuser . . . 7. delator 8. accusant, libelant
(libellant) 9. plaintiff 10. prosecutor
11. complainant 12. incriminator

accustom . . . 3. use 4. wont 5. enure,
habit, inure, train 6. addict 7. educate,
toughen 9. habituate 11. familiarize

accustomed . . . 4. used, wont 5. usual
6. enured, inured 8. familiar
9. customary, sedentary (to sit)

ace . . . 3. jot, one, pip, tib 4. atom, card,
dole, dram, unit, whit 5. monad, pilot,
point, shark (sl) 7. aviator 8. particle,
pittance, superior 10. crackajack (sl),
proficient 11. crackerjack (sl)

ace (pert to) . . .
  ace-queen . . 6. tenace
  of clubs . . 5. basto

acedia (Gr) . . . 5. sloth 6. torpor

acedia (Sp) . . . 8. flatfish

Aceldama, Akeldama (Bib) . . . 12. Field
of Blood, potter's field

acemila . . . 8. pack mule

acephalous . . . 8. headless 10. leaderless

acephalus . . . 15. headless monster

acerb . . 4. sour 5. harsh, sharp 6. bitter,
unripe 7. acerbic, austere, pungent

acerbity . . . 7. acidity 8. acridity,
acrimony, asperity, mordancy,
pungency, severity 9. harshness
10. bitterness, causticity 11. astringency

acetic acid . . . 7. vinegar 8. vesicant
9. corrosive

Achaean, Achaian . . . 5. Greek (a)
6. Greece

ache . . . 4. burn, long, pain, pang
5. throb, yearn 6. grieve, sorrow,
twinge 7. agonize, longing 10. suffer
pain

achieve . . . 2. do 3. get, win 4. gain,
kill 6. arrive, attain, effect, finish
7. compass, execute, fulfill, perform,
produce, realize, succeed 8. complete,
conclude, contrive 10. accomplish,
consummate, effectuate

achievement . . . 3. act 4. deed, feat
5. doing, stunt 6. action, record
7. arrival, exploit 8. dispatch
9. adventure 10. attainment, escutcheon
(Her) 11. fulfillment, performance,
transaction 12. effectuation
14. accomplishment, implementation

Achilles (pert to) . . .
  advisor . . 6. Nestor
  dipped into . . 9. River Styx
  father . . 6. Peleus
  friend . . 7. Patroclus
  horse . . 7. Xanthus
  mother . . 6. Thetis
  slayer . . 5. Paris
  slayer of . . 6. Hector

son . . 7. Pyrrhus 11. Neoptolemus
vulnerable spot . . 4. heel

achromatic . . 4. gray 8. achromic
9. achromous, colorless, uncolored
13. free from color

achropsia . . . 14. color blindness

acid . . 4. keen, sour, tart 5. acrid, amino,
boric, malic, mucic, pyrol 6. acetic,
arabic, biting, bromic, nitric, oxalic,
tannic 7. acetose, caustic, chloric,
racemic, stearic, terebic, vinegar
8. carbolic, lysergic, sulfuric 9. corrosive
11. acrimonious 12. hydrochloric

acid, removing . . . 12. edulcoration

acidity . . . 4. acor, sour 8. acrimony,
mordancy, sourness, tartness, verjuice
9. sharpness 10. bitterness
13. acidulousness

acknowledge . . . 3. nod, own, pay, say
4. avow, sign 5. admit, allow, grant,
own up, reply, swear, thank, vouch,
yield 6. accede, accept, answer, assent,
attest, redeem 7. certify, concede,
confess, testify 8. disclose 9. recognize

acknowledgment . . . 5. favor, reply
6. answer, avowal, avowry, shrift,
thanks 7. apology, epistle, receipt,
voucher, warrant 8. rescript
9. admission 10. acceptance,
concession, confession, disclosure,
owning up to 11. recognition
12. thanksgiving

acme . . . 3. top 4. apex 5. limit 6. apogee,
climax, crisis, heyday, summit, tip-top,
vertex, zenith 7. ceiling, maximum
11. culmination 12. consummation

ecology, science of . . 8. remedies

acolyte . . . 7. patener 8. altar boy
9. assistant

acomia . . . 8. alopecia, baldness
12. hairlessness

aconite . . . 8. Cammarum, Eranthis
9. monkshood

acorn . . . 3. nut 4. duck 6. camata
10. meadowlark (color)

acosmic . . . 11. unorganized

acquaint . . . 4. tell 6. advise, impart,
inform 7. apprise 8. enlighten, introduce
11. familiarize

acquaintance . . . 3. ken 5. amigo 6. friend
7. privity 8. familiar, intimacy, intimate
9. companion, knowledge 10. fellowship
11. familiarity, information, sympathizer
15. familiarization

acquainted . . . 6. au fait 7. versant
8. familiar 9. cognizant 10. conversant

acquiesce . . . 3. bow 5. abide, agree,
chime, yield 6. accede, assent,
comply, concur, relent, resign, submit
7. conform, consent, succumb

acquire . . . 3. buy, get, win 4. earn,
gain, reap 5. adopt, catch, incur,
learn, steal 6. attain, effect, obtain,
secure 7. procure, receive 8. contract
9. cultivate

acquire (pert to) . . .
  beforehand . . 7. pre-empt
  feathers . . 6. fledge
  immunity . . 14. serum injection
  knowledge . . 5. clear, study 9. ascertain

acquit . . . 4. free 5. clear 6. excuse,

pardon, pay off **7.** absolve, fulfill, release, requite **9.** exculpate, exonerate

acquittal . . . **7.** freeing, payment, release **8.** clearing, requital **9.** clearance, discharge **10.** observance **11.** exculpation, fulfillment **12.** satisfaction

acquittance . . . **7.** payment, quietus, receipt **9.** discharge, quittance

acre . . . **5.** field **6.** arpent **7.** measure **8.** farmhold

acre (pert to) . . .
half . . **3.** erf (So Afr)
hundred . . **7.** hectare (metric)
quarter . . **4.** rood (Brit)

acres . . . **5.** lands **6.** estate, ground

acrid . . . **5.** acid, bask (dial), keen, sour, tart **5.** harsh, rough, sharp **6.** acetic, biting, bitter **7.** acetose, caustic, mordant, pungent, reeking **8.** unsavory, virulent **9.** acidulous, corrosive **10.** escharotic, irritating **11.** acrimonious

acrimonious . . . **4.** acid, keen **5.** acrid, angry, gruff, harsh, irate, sharp **6.** bitter **7.** caustic, stinging **9.** rancorous, resentful

acrimony . . . **5.** venom **6.** rancor **7.** ill will, vitriol **8.** acerbity, acidity, asperity, mordancy, pungency, rudeness, severity, sourness, tartness **9.** animosity, virulence **10.** bitterness, causticity, resentment **11.** astringency, crabbedness

acroamatic . . . **4.** oral **5.** parol **6.** arcane, occult, secret, verbal **8.** abstract, abstruse, anagogic, esoteric, profound **9.** recondite, unwritten **11.** nuncupative

acrobat . . . **7.** gymnast, tumbler **8.** balancer **9.** ropedancer, ropewalker **11.** funambulist **13.** contortionist, schoenobatist

acrochordon . . . **4.** wart (small)

Acrocorinth, Acrocorinthua . . . **9.** acropolis (Corinth) **12.** Pirene Spring (site)

acromegaly . . . **7.** disease **11.** enlargement (head, hands, feet)

acronical, acronichal (opp of cosmical) . . . **10.** rising star **11.** setting star

acronyx . . . **13.** ingrowing nail

acrophobia . . . fear of **7.** heights

acropolis . . . **6.** refuge **7.** citadel

Acropolis (pert to) . . .
Argos . . **7.** Larissa
Corinth . . **11.** Acrocorinth
Thebes . . **6.** Cadmea

across . . . **4.** over, span **5.** cross **6.** thwart **7.** athwart **8.** crossway, traverse **9.** crossways, crosswise **10.** crisscross, transverse

across (pref) . . . **3.** dia **4.** tran **5.** trans

acrostic . . . **4.** agla, game, poem **6.** puzzle **7.** erratic **8.** wordplay **9.** crosswise, jeu de mots, telestich

act . . . **2.** do **3.** jus, law, lex **4.** deed, feat, play, skit, turn, work **5.** actus, emote, favor, of God, stunt **6.** action, behave, demean, motion **7.** comport, measure, perform, pretend, process **8.** function,

kindness, simulate **9.** enactment, represent **10.** enterprise, exert power, theatrical **11.** impersonate, legislation, performance, transaction

act (pert to) . . .
a part . . **8.** simulate **9.** dissemble
causing ruin . . **11.** Kiss of Death
criminal . . **8.** villainy
detestable . . **11.** abomination
formal . . **10.** instrument
game . . **7.** charade
illegal . . **4.** tort **5.** crime **6.** delict
nonsense . . **10.** tomfoolery
planned . . **12.** premeditated
pompously . . **11.** pontificate
suffix . . **3.** ure

acting . . . **5.** doing **6.** action, posing **7.** playing, serving **8.** pretense **9.** dramatics, execution, operating **10.** masquerade, performing, simulating **11.** make-believe **13.** impersonating, impersonation

acting with force . . . **8.** vehement

action . . . **2.** re **3.** act, res **4.** deed, feat, play, stir, suit, work **5.** award, doing, order, works **6.** battle, decree, motion, praxis, ruling **7.** conduct, contest, lawsuit, verdict, working **8.** activity, behavior, demeanor, exercise, movement, sentence **9.** mechanism, operation **10.** automation, enterprise **11.** performance **13.** pronouncement

active . . . **4.** spry **5.** acute, agile, alert, brisk, quick, ready, smart, yauld **6.** breezy, dapper, lively, nimble, prompt, strong **7.** dynamic, intense, kinetic, vibrant **8.** animated, forceful, spirited, vigorous **9.** assiduous, effective, effectual, energetic, energized, operating, pragmatic, sprightly, vivacious **11.** industrious

active, not . . . **6.** static **7.** dormant **11.** inoperative

activity . . . **3.** ado, gog, pep, vir **4.** stir, work **5.** vigor **6.** action, energy **7.** agility, bristle **8.** business, movement **9.** athletics, briskness, operation, quickness **10.** activeness, employment, nimbleness, occupation

act of . . .
cutting . . **4.** kerf **8.** shearing
endearment . . **4.** kiss **6.** caress
God . . **8.** accident, disaster
kindness . . **5.** favor
leaving . . **6.** congee, egress
respect . . **6.** curtsy, homage
ruling . . **5.** regle
self-examination . . **13.** introspection
sharing . . **13.** participation
witnessing . . **11.** attestation
working together . . **13.** collaboration
worship . . **6.** prayer **8.** devotion

actor . . . **3.** ham **4.** doer, hero, mime, star, supe **5.** agent **6.** mummer, player, worker **7.** Roscius, trooper **8.** aisteoir, comedian, histrion, Thespian **9.** performer, portrayer, pretender, tragedian **10.** comedienne, dramatizer, pantomimic, personator **11.** barnstormer, entertainer, pantomimist, protagonist, tragedienne

12. impersonator

actor (personage) . . . 4. Lunt, Ward
5. Booth 7. Skinner 8. Warfield
9. Faversham

actors' group . . . 4. cast 6. troupe

actor's hint . . . 3. cue 12. teleprompter

actress (personage) . . . 5. Adams, Bates,
Hayes, Terry 6. Robson, Scheff
7. Marlowe, Russell 8. Fontanne,
Modjeska 9. Bernhardt

actual . . . 4. real, true 5. posit 7. factual,
genuine, present 8. absolute, positive,
tangible 9. practical, veritable
11. substantial

actual being . . . 4. esse

actuality . . . 4. fact 6. verity 7. reality
8. realness 9. existence 10. factuality
14. substantiality

actually . . . 5. quite, truly 6. indeed,
really, verily 8. actively 9. assuredly,
certainly

actuary . . . 5. clerk 9. registrar
10. accountant, bookkeeper, calculator
13. arithmetician, mathematician

actuate . . . 3. egg 4. move 5. force, impel,
rouse 6. arouse, induce, prompt, propel
7. animate 8. motivate 9. stimulate

acuate . . . 7. sharpen 12. needle-shaped,
sharp-pointed

acumen . . . 7. insight 8. gumption,
keenness, sagacity 9. acuteness,
sharpness 10. astuteness, perception,
shrewdness 11. discernment
12. perspicacity 14. discrimination

acute . . . 4. high, keen, tart, thin
5. canny, sharp, smart, vivid 6. accent,
biting, crafty, fierce, severe, shrewd,
shrill, subtle 7. crucial, cutting,
dynamic, intense, knowing, painful,
pointed, violent 8. critical, deep-felt,
forceful, incisive, piercing, poignant,
rigorous, stabbing, stinging, vigorous
9. energetic, ingenious, sensitive
11. sharp-witted 13. perspicacious
14. discriminating

acuteness of . . .
sight . . 7. oxyopia 10. oxyblepsia
taste . . 9. oxygeusia
touch . . 8. oxyaphia

A.D. . . . 10. Anno Domini

Adam (pert to) . . .
grandson . . 4. Enos
son . . 4. Abel, Cain, Seth
wife . . 3. Eve 6. Lilith (legend)

adage . . . 3. saw 5. maxim 6. saying
7. proverb

adamant . . . 4. hard 8. stubborn
10. unyielding

Adam's . . .
ale . . 5. water
apple . . 6. larynx 10. pomum Adami
herb . . 7. mullein
needle . . 5. yucca

adapt . . . 3. fit, set 4. suit 6. adjust,
attune, comply, modify, orient, season
7. arrange, conform, prepare, qualify
8. accustom, regulate 9. acclimate,
condition, habituate, harmonize,
reconcile 11. accommodate

adaptable . . . 7. elastic, pliable
9. tractable, versatile 10. adjustable,

responsive 11. conformable
13. accommodative

adaptation . . . 7. fitting 10. adjustment,
attunement, conformity, regulation
11. arrangement, habituation,
orientation 12. conditioning,
coordination, modification
13. accommodation, harmonization,
orchestration, qualification
15. familiarization

add . . . 3. eke, tot 4. foot, give, join,
plus, tote 5. affix, annex, sum up,
total, unite 6. append, attach, reckon
7. accrete, augment, compile, compute,
put with, subjoin 8. increase 9. calculate
10. supplement

adda . . . 5. skink (scink) 6. lizard 7. reptile

addax . . . 6. pygarg (Bib) 8. antelope

added . . . 3. and 4. plus 5. extra
6. joined, united 7. affixed, annexed
8. appended, attached 9. appendant
13. supplementary

adder . . . 3. asp 5. Bitis, krait, snake,
viper 6. nedder 7. machine, serpent
13. mathematician

addict . . . 4. buff 5. fiend 7. adjudge,
devotee, hophead 9. habituate 15. apply
habitually

addicted . . . 4. wont 5. prone 8. attached,
disposed, inclined 9. devoted to
10. accustomed, habituated 11. given
over to

addiction . . . 5. habit 9. surrender
10. attachment 16. enslavement

Addison, name for . . . 4. Clio (The
Spectator) 7. Atticus (by Pope)

addition . . . 3. and, ell, too 4. also,
gain, plus, wing 5. farse (Relig),
rider 6. addend, augend, lean-to
7. additum, adjunct, joining, uniting
8. addendum, additory, increase
9. accession, accretion, amendment,
appendage, extension, reckoning
10. annexation 11. calculation,
computation, enlargement
12. augmentation

additional . . . 3. new 4. else, more
5. added, extra, fresh, spare 7. another,
besides, further 9. auxiliary, extrinsic
12. supervenient, supplemental
13. supplementary

additional (pert to) . . .
explanation . . 10. epexegesis
11. elucidation
grant . . 3. ann 5. bonus
specimen . . 6. cotype

address . . . 3. air, wit, woo 4. call, hail,
mien, pray, tact, talk 5. abode, court,
grace, greet, guise, place, skill, speak
6. accost, direct, eulogy, salute, sermon,
speech 7. arrange, conduct, consign,
declaim, finesse, lecture, manners,
oration, prepare, prowess, request
8. behavior, demeanor, greeting,
harangue, inscribe, perorate, petition,
presence 9. dexterity, diplomacy,
direction, discourse, ingenuity,
readiness 11. comportment, destination,
inscription, savoir-faire
14. sophistication, superscription

addressee . . . 8. occupant 10. inhabitant

12. communicator 13. correspondent

adduce . . . 4. cite, name 5. argue, infer, offer, plead, quote 6. allege, assign 7. advance, mention, present, produce

Adelphi . . . 7. theater (Strand, London) 13. London Quarter

adeps . . . 4. lard 9. animal fat

adept . . . 3. ace, apt 4. deft, whiz (coll) 6. adroit, artist, expert, versed 7. capable, dabster, mahatma, skilled 8. skillful (skilful) 9. alchemist (formerly), occultist 10. conversant, proficient 11. crackerjack

adequate . . . 3. due, fit 4. able, full 5. ample, digne, equal 6. enough 7. capable 8. all right, equalize, suitable 9. competent, effective, effectual, sufficing, tolerable 10. sufficient 12. commensurate, satisfactory 13. proportionate

adhere . . . 4. cleg, glue, hold 5. cling, stick 6. cleave, cohere 7. accrete, observe, persist

adherent . . . 4. ally 6. adnate, sticky, votary 7. dangler, sequela 8. adhesive, clinging, disciple, faithful, follower, hanger-on, partisan, sticking, upholder 9. appendage, dependent, supporter

adherent to the Crown . . . 4. Tory

adhesive . . . 3. gum, wax 4. glue 5. paste 6. cement, mastic, sticky 8. adherent, mucilage 9. tenacious

adhesiveness . . . 4. stay 8. tenacity 12. cohesiveness 13. tenaciousness 16. stick-to-itiveness

adhibit . . . 3. use 5. admit, affix, apply 6. attach, devote 7. bring in 10. administer

adieu . . . 4. vale 5. adios, aloha 6. goodby, so long (sl) 7. cheerio, good-bye, good day 8. au revoir, farewell 11. leave-taking

adipose . . . 3. fat 4. oily 5. fatty, plump, pursy, squab 9. sebaceous

adit . . . 3. way 4. duct 5. entry, stulm 6. access, ingate, intake, tunnel 7. channel, conduit, haulage, ingress, passage 8. approach, drainage, entrance 10. admission 11. entranceway, ventilation

adjacent . . . 4. abut, near, nigh 5. close, handy 6. next to 7. meeting, nearest 8. abutting, touching 9. adjoining, bordering 10. contiguous, juxtaposed 11. neighboring 13. conterminous

adject . . . 3. add 4. join 5. annex

adjective . . . 3. the 6. adnoun 7. epithet (significant) 8. modifier 9. accessory, dependent

adjective (pert to) . . .
demonstrative . . 4. that, this 5. these, those
suffix . . 2. ic, il 3. ent, ial, ian, ile, ish, ist, ite, ive, ous
verbal . . 9. gerundive

adjoin . . . 3. add 4. abut, butt, join 5. unite 6. attach, border 7. conjoin 8. neighbor

adjourn . . . 3. end 5. close, defer, delay 6. recess 7. suspend 8. dissolve, postpone, prorogue 11. discontinue

adjudge, adjudicate . . . 3. try 4. deem, doom, find, hold, pass 5. award, judge, order 6. assign, decree, esteem, ordain, reckon, regard, settle 7. condemn 8. consider, sentence 9. determine

adjunct . . . 4. ally, word 5. added 6. device 7. additum, annexed, consort 8. addition, appanage (apanage) 9. appendant, associate, auxiliary, colleague, companion, component, qualifier 11. confederate 12. appurtenance, nonessential

adjuration . . . 4. oath, plea 6. appeal, avowal, charge 8. entreaty, swearing, vouching 10. deposition 11. beseechment, obsecration, obtestation

adjure . . . 3. ask, beg, bid 4. bind, pray 5. plead 6. appeal, charge 7. beseech, command, entreat, implore, swear in

adjust . . . 3. fit, fix, set 4. meet, size, suit, trim, true 5. adapt, align, amend, frame, group, match, right, shape 6. accord, attune, orient, remedy, settle, square 7. arrange, conform, correct, justify, mediate, rectify, redress 8. accustom, organize, regulate 9. condition, habituate, harmonize, reconcile 10. compromise, coordinate, straighten 11. accommodate, systematize

adjuster, adjustor . . . 6. fitter 8. arranger 11. coordinator

adjustment . . . 4. gear 5. means, terms 7. fitting, suiting 8. bearings, disposal 9. bundobust 10. adaptation, attunement, compromise, concession, conclusion, conformity, regulation, settlement 11. arrangement, disposition, habituation, orientation 12. assimilation, coordination, organization 13. harmonization, methodization, rectification 14. naturalization, reconciliation

adjutant . . . 4. aide, ally 6. helper 7. officer 9. assistant, auxiliary

adjutant bird . . . 5. stork 6. argala 7. hurgila, marabou

ad lib, ad libit, ad libitum . . . 6. make up 7. cadenza 9. extempore, impromptu, improvise 10. at pleasure 11. play it by ear 13. accompaniment

administer . . . 4. give 5. apply, issue 6. bestow, direct, govern, manage, supply, tender 7. adhibit, conduct, dispose, execute, fulfill, furnish, give out, husband, perform 8. dispatch, dispense, transact 9. discharge 10. distribute 12. administrate

administer extreme unction . . . 5. anele 6. anoint

administration . . . 3. use 4. rule 6. employ, giving, policy 7. conduct, regimen 8. bestowal, disposal, issuance, ministry 9. direction, execution 10. employment, government, management, regulation 11. application, directorate, disposition 12. dispensation, ministration 13. apportionment

administration of justice . . .

10. judicatory, judicature

administrator . . . 2. fu 5. dewan
7. alcalde, manager, provost, trustee
8. director, executor 9. dispenser,
executive 12. entrepreneur

admirable . . . 5. sweet 6. worthy
7. likable (likeable), winning, winsome
8. adorable, laudable 9. estimable,
excellent, marvelous, wonderful
10. creditable 11. commendable,
meritorious 12. praiseworthy

admiration . . . 6. esteem, liking, regard,
wonder 7. respect 8. surprise
9. adoration, amazement, reverence
10. wonderment 11. astoundment,
idolization 12. appreciation,
confoundment

admire . . . like, love 5. adore, honor
6. esteem, regard, revere 7. approve,
idolize, respect 8. venerate

admissible . . . 3. fit 4. just, sane 5. sound
6. worthy 7. apropos, germane, logical
8. apposite, eligible, rational, relevant,
suitable 9. admissory, agreeable,
allowable, desirable, pertinent,
qualified, receptive, tolerable
10. acceptable, applicable, legitimate,
reasonable 11. justifiable, permissible,
warrantable 12. satisfactory

admission . . . 4. adit 5. entry 6. access,
assent, avowal, entree, shrift
8. entrance 9. agreement, allowance,
inclusion, letting in, receiving,
reception, testimony 10. accordance,
admittance, allegation, avouchment,
compliance, concession, confession,
initiation, permission 11. affiliation,
affirmation, declaration
12. acquiescence, assimilation
14. acknowledgment, naturalization
15. enfranchisement

Admission Day holiday . . . 6. Nevada
(Oct 31) 7. Arizona (Feb 14)
10. California (Sept 9)

admit . . . 3. own 4. avow 5. adopt, allow,
enter, grant, let in, own up, trust,
yield 6. accept, credit, embody, permit
7. adhibit, believe, concede, confess,
embrace, include, profess, receive
8. initiate 9. affiliate 10. naturalize
11. acknowledge, incorporate

admittance . . . 6. access 8. entrance,
sanction 9. admission, letting in
10. initiation

admitted . . . 6. indeed 8. believed,
conceded 12. acknowledged

admixture . . . 5. alloy, blend 6. fusion
7. mixture 8. compound, infusion
7. mixture 8. compound, infusion
10. minglement 11. combination,
composition

admonish . . . 4. warn 5. chide, scold
6. advise, enjoin, exhort, preach,
rebuke, remind 7. caution, monitor,
reprove, upbraid 8. dissuade
9. reprimand 11. expostulate,
remonstrate, give warning

admonition . . . 6. advice 7. caution,
censure, reproof, warning 8. reminder
10. counseling (counselling), dissuasion
11. exhortation 12. remonstrance,

reprehension

ado . . . 4. fuss, stir 5. doing, hurry
6. bustle, flurry, hubbub, pother,
rumpus, tumult 7. trouble, turmoil
9. commotion 10. excitement
11. disturbance

adobe . . . 4. clay, silt 5. brick, house
(clay)

adolescent . . . 3. lad 5. minor, youth
6. nonage 9. pubescent, youngster
10. developing

Adonis (pert to) . . .
beloved by . . 9. Aphrodite
festival . . 6. Adonia
modern youth . . 6. a dandy
mother . . 5. Myrrh
slain by . . 8. wild boar

adopt . . . 4. take 5. admit, usurp
6. accept, assume, borrow, choose,
father, mother, select 7. embrace,
espouse, receive, welcome 9. affiliate
10. assimilate, naturalize 11. appropriate

adoption . . . 6. choice 8. espousal
9. admission, borrowing, reception
10. acceptance, assumption, conversion,
redemption, usurpation
11. embracement 13. appropriation
14. naturalization

adore . . . 4. love 5. enjoy, honor 6. esteem,
regard, revere 7. idolize, worship
8. venerate

adorn . . . 4. clad, deck, trim 5. array,
begem, drape, grace, primp, prink
6. attire, bedeck, clothe, enrich
7. bedight, bejewel, dignify, festoon,
garnish 8. beautify, decorate
9. embellish

adorn (with) . . .
color . . 4. gild 5. paint 7. emblaze
feathers . . 7. implume
needlework . . 9. embroider
ornaments . . 6. tinsel 7. imagery

adorned . . . 4. clad 6. ornate 7. clothed,
prinked 9. decorated
16. chryselephantine

adornment . . . 5. decor, frill 6. frills,
tinsel 10. decoration, embroidery
13. embellishment 14. beautification

ad patres . . . 4. dead 12. to his Fathers

Adriatic (pert to) . . .
city . . 5. Fiume 6. Venice 7. Lagosta,
Trieste 8. Brandisi
island . . 7. Lagosta
peninsula . . 6. Istria
wind (cold) . . 4. bora

adrift . . . 4. asea, free, lost 5. at sea,
loose 6. afloat, astray, aweigh, undone
7. aimless, unfixed 8. aberrant, derelict,
floating, insecure, straying, unmoored,
unstable 9. erroneous 10. bewildered,
unanchored, unfastened, without aim

adroit . . . 4. neat 5. quick, ready,
smart 6. clever, expert, habile,
nimble 7. cunning 8. skillful (skilful)
9. dexterous, ingenious

adroitness . . . 4. tact 5. knack, skill
7. address 9. dexterity, ingenuity,
readiness, smartness

adsorbent, absorbent . . . 6. spongy
7. osmotic, soaking 8. blotting
12. assimilative

adulation . . . 6. praise 8. flattery 9. adoration 10. compliment

adult . . . 6. mature, X-rated 7. grown up

adulterate . . . 3. mix 5. alter, taint 6. debase, defile 7. corrupt 8. denature 11. contaminate

adulterated . . . 6. impure 7. debased 8. spurious 9. denatured 11. counterfeit 12. contaminated

adust . . . 3. tan (color) 4. burn 5. burnt, dried, fiery 6. singed 7. parched 8. scorched 9. blistered

advance . . . 2. go 3. aid 4. gain, inch, loan, move, near, nose, pass, push, rise (in price) 5. ahead, boost, creep, march, raise 6. better, stride 7. elevate, process, promote, propose 8. approach, heighten, increase, progress 9. aforehand, elevation, promotion, upgrading 10. accelerate, beforehand, preferment 11. advancement, development, furtherance, improvement, progression

advanced . . . 3. old 4. aged 6. modern 7. elderly, forward 8. bettered, enhanced, enriched, foremost, unproved 9. venerable 10. in the front, precocious, senectuous 11. enlightened, progressive

advanced (pert to) . . .
   equally . . 7. abreast
   study . . 7. seminar
   time . . 6. modern 8. up-to-date 12. contemporary

advantage . . . 3. use 4. boot, bote (bot), edge, gain, good, hold, odds 5. avail, favor, start, stead 6. behalf, behoof, profit 7. benefit, further, promote, service, vantage 8. facility, interest, purchase 9. appliance 10. expedience 11. convenience, superiority 13. accommodation, vantage ground

advantageous . . . 5. handy 6. aidful, useful 7. helpful 8. edifying, salutary 9. expedient, favorable 10. auspicious, beneficial, convenient, profitable, propitious, worthwhile 11. encouraging

advent . . . 6. coming 7. arrival 8. approach 11. forthcoming

Advent (Eccl) . . . 14. Coming of Christ

adventitious . . . 4. rale 6. casual 8. acquired 9. extrinsic 10. accidental, incidental 12. nonessential

adventure . . . 3. act (heroic), hap 4. bout, dare, deed, feat, gest, risk 5. event, quest, stunt 6. action, hazard 7. episode, exploit, fortune, venture 8. escapade, incident (novel), maneuver, occasion 9. happening 10. enterprise, experience, occurrence 11. performance, undertaking 12. happenstance 13. striking event 14. accomplishment

adventurer . . . 4. goer 5. sport 7. bounder, gambler, Hessian, parvenu, soldier, upstart 8. gamester, hazarder, merchant, traveler 9. sportsman 10. speculator 16. soldier of fortune

adventuress . . . 7. demirep 10. gold digger

adventurous . . . 4. rash 5. risky 6. daring 8. reckless 9. dangerous, foolhardy,

hazardous, venturous 11. venturesome 12. enterprising, presumptuous

adversary . . . 3. foe 5. enemy, Satan 6. foeman 8. opponent 9. archfiend, assailant 10. antagonist, competitor, Philistine

adverse . . . 3. ill 4. anti 5. loath 7. opposed 8. contrary, converse, opposing, sinister, untoward 9. reluctant, unwilling 10. afflictive, calamitous, indisposed 11. conflicting, disinclined, unfavorable 12. antagonistic, unpropitious

adversity . . . 6. misery 7. trouble 8. calamity, distress, hardship 9. suffering 10. affliction, misfortune, opposition 11. destitution

advert . . . 5. recur, refer 6. allude, return

advertent . . . 7. heedful 9. attentive

advertise . . . 4. plug, warn 5. boast, boost 6. notify 7. promote, publish 8. announce, ballyhoo, proclaim 9. publicize 10. promulgate

advertisement . . . 2. ad 4. bill, copy, Neon, plug, sign 6. notice, poster, spread 7. placard 10. commercial (TV)

advice . . . 4. rede 5. aviso 6. caveat, wisdom 7. counsel, opinion, warning 8. prudence, reminder 9. knowledge 10. admonition, suggestion 11. exhortation, information, instruction 12. consultation, deliberation, intelligence 13. consideration 14. recommendation

advice, containing . . . 9. mentorial

advisable . . . 6. proper 7. prudent 9. befitting, desirable, expedient 11. commendable 13. recommendable

advise . . . 4. rede, tell, warn 5. coach 6. exhort, impart, inform, remind 7. apprise, bethink, caution, counsel, suggest 8. acquaint, admonish, advocate 9. enlighten, recommend 11. communicate, familiarize, take counsel

adviser, advisor . . . 5. guide 6. Egeria, nestor 7. monitor 8. appriser, kibitzer (sl) 9. counselor (counsellor), informant 10. admonisher

advisers, advisors . . . 7. Cabinet, Council 10. councilors, counselors, informants

advocate . . . 3. pro 4. urge 5. advise, backer, defend, deputy, lawyer 7. endorse, espouse, pleader, support 8. attorney, champion, defender, exponent, plead for 9. barrister, counselor, justifier, paraclete, proponent, recommend, solicitor, supporter 11. protagonist

advocate of the simple life . . . 14. simplicitarian

adytum . . . 6. shrine 7. chamber (inner), sanctum 9. sanctuary

Aeetes (pert to) . . .
   daughter . . 5. Medea
   keeper of . . 12. Golden Fleece
   king of . . 7. Colchis

Aegean islands . . . 5. Chios, Samos 6. Lesbos 8. Cyclades 10. Dodecanese

aegis, egis . . . 4. care 5. guard 6. screen, shield, symbol (anc) 7. backing, defense 8. guidance 9. fosterage, patronage 10. protection

Aello (Gr) ... 5. Harpy 7. monster

Aeneid ... 4. poem (Vergil)

aerage ... 11. ventilation

aerate ... 6. aerify 7. freshen, inflate, refresh 9. ventilate

aerial ... 3. ear 4. aery, airy, mast 5. aeric, lofty 6. unreal 7. airlike, antenna 8. ethereal, fanciful, vaporous 9. pneumatic 10. chimerical 12. aeronautical 13. unsubstantial

aerie, eyrie ... 4. nest 5. brood (birds) 6. family 9. penthouse

aeriform ... 6. unreal 7. gaseous

aeroplane ... 8. airplane

Aesir, Norse Gods ... 3. Tyr (Tiu), Ull 4. Odin (Woden), Thor (Donar), Vali 5. Bragi 6. Balder, Hoenir 7. Forseti 8. Heimdall

Aeson's son ... 5. Jason (Gr Myth)

Aesop (Gr) ... 5. fable, moral

affability ... 6. comity 8. civility, courtesy, urbanity 9. geniality 10. amiability, cordiality, politeness 11. sociability 12. conviviality 14. gregariousness 16. companionability 17. communicativeness

affable ... 4. mild 5. civil, suave 6. benign, fluent, social 7. amiable 8. gracious, sociable 9. convivial, courteous 10. accessible, gregarious 11. complaisant 13. communicative

affair ... 4. duel, love 5. fight, issue, thing, topic 6. action, gadget, matter, object, soiree 7. concern, problem 8. business, interest, question, sociable 9. gathering, reception, something 10. proceeding 11. get-together, transaction 12. circumstance

affect ... 4. melt, move, stir 5. feign, grate, haunt, touch 6. assume, excite, regale, relate, soften, thrill 7. concern, involve, operate, pretend, qualify 8. frequent, interest, simulate 9. influence 11. counterfeit, hypothecate

affectation ... 3. air 4. pose, sham 7. display, foppery, pietism 8. elegance, pretense 9. mannerism 12. affectedness 13. artificiality 14. grandiloquence 15. pretentiousness

affected ... 4. airy, sham 5. faked, moved, posey, put-on 6. fal-lal, formal 7. assumed, beloved, elegant, feigned, gushing, stilted 8. disposed, mannered 9. impressed, pretended, unnatural 10. artificial, euphuistic 11. pretentious 12. ostentatious 13. counterfeited, grandiloquent

affected by ...
  age .. 6. senile
  love .. 4. smit 7. smitten
  pain .. 4. pang 6. twinge
  paralysis .. 7. paretic
  wonder .. 6. marvel 9. convulsed

affectedly languid ... 13. lackadaisical

affectedly shy ... 3. coy, mim 4. prim 6. demure 10. coquettish

affection ... 4. amor, love 5. animus, defect, storge (animal) 7. disease, emotion, feeling, illness, leaning, passion 8. devotion, fondness, tendency 9. attribute, infirmity, sentiment

10. affliction, attachment, disability, proclivity, propensity, tenderness 11. disposition, inclination, temperament

affectionate ... 4. fond, soft, warm 6. ardent, loving, tender 7. adoring, devoted, earnest, zealous 8. attached, friendly, parental, romantic 10. headstrong 13. demonstrative

afferent ... 6. esodic (nerves), inward 7. sensory 11. centripetal

affiance ... 5. faith, troth, trust 6. belief, pledge, plight 7. betroth, promise 8. credence, reliance 9. assurance, betrothal 10. confidence, engagement

affiche ... 6. poster 7. placard

affidavit ... 4. oath 9. statement 10. deposition 11. affirmation, certificate, declaration

affiliation ... 4. body, sect 5. group, union 6. church, fusion, hookup, league 7. faction, lineage 8. adoption, alliance, espousal, relation 9. admission, alignment, coalition 10. connection, federation, fellowship, persuasion 11. association, cooperation 12. denomination, organization 13. confederation, consanguinity 14. naturalization

affinity ... 3. kin 6. accord, family, liking 7. kinship, rapport 8. relation, soul mate 9. agreement 10. attraction, connection, similarity 11. propinquity, resemblance 12. congeniality, relationship 13. compatibility, rapprochement

affirm ... 3. say 4. aver, avow 5. posit, state, swear, vouch 6. allege, assert, attest, avouch, ratify 7. assever, certify, confirm, declare, endorse, profess, testify, warrant 8. sanction, validate 9. predicate, pronounce 10. asseverate 12. authenticate, substantiate

affirmation ... 3. vow 4. amen, oath, word 5. basis 6. ground 7. premise 8. averment 9. admission, assertion, statement, testimony 10. affirmance, allegation, avouchment, deposition, foundation, profession 11. declaration, proposition 12. confirmation, ratification

affirmative ... 3. aye (ay), nod, yea, yes 8. dogmatic, positive, thumbs up (coll) 10. cataphatic (rare) 11. affirmation, declarative, predicative

affirmatory ... 9. assertive 11. affirmative, assertional

affix ... 3. add, fix, pen, tag 4. seal 5. annex, stamp 6. anchor, append, attach, fasten, impose 7. connect, subjoin 9. increment 11. superimpose

afflict ... 3. ail, try, vex 4. hurt, pain 5. upset, wound 6. grieve, harass, sicken 7. agitate, chasten, derange, disturb, oppress, torment, trouble 8. disorder, distress, lacerate 9. overthrow, persecute

afflicted ... 3. sad 5. ailed 6. pained 7. smitten, wounded 8. troubled 9. depressed, suffering 10. distressed

affliction ... 3. woe 4. airs, bane, evil, pain, pest 5. curse, grief 6. misery, plague 7. illness, scourge, torment, trouble 8. calamity, distress, hardship 9. adversity 10. misfortune, visitation 12. wretchedness

afflictive . . . 6. severe 11. causing pain, distressing

affluence . . . 4. ease, flow 6. afflux, influx, plenty, riches, wealth 8. opulence, richness 9. abundance, concourse, plenitude, profusion 10. prosperity

affluent . . . 4. rich 5. flush 6. fluent 7. copious, moneyed, opulent, wealthy 8. abundant, well-to-do 9. luxuriant, pecunious, plenteous 10. prosperous

afford . . . 4. bear, cost, give, lend 5. allow, endow, grant, spare, stand, yield 6. accord, confer, invest, supply 7. furnish, provide, support, undergo

affray . . . 3. war 4. feud, fray, riot 5. brawl, fight, melee, scrap (sl), set-to (coll) 6. battle, combat, tumult 7. assault, contest, quarrel, scuffle 9. encounter 11. disturbance

affright . . . 5. alarm, scare 6. appall (appal), dismay 7. confuse, startle, terrify 8. frighten

affront . . . 4. defy, face, meet, slap 5. abuse 6. harass, insult, offend, oppose 7. offense, outrage, provoke 8. confront, dishonor, envisage, illtreat, irritate 9. encounter, humiliate, indignity 11. provocation

afghan (pert to) . . .
fox . . 6. corsac
language . . 11. Afghanistan
prince . . 4. amir (ameer), emir (emeer)
rug . . 5. Herat 6. carpet
stitch . . 7. crochet
wrap . . 7. blanket (woolen)

Afghanistan . . .
capital . . 5. Kabul
city . . 5. Herat 8. Kandahar
language . . 6. Pushtu 7. Persian
mountain . . 9. Hindu Kush
Pass (famed) . . 6. Khyber
pony . . 4. yabu (yaboo)
religion . . 5. Islam
river . . 5. Indus

Africa . . . see also *African*
desert . . 6. Libyan, Sahara 8. Kalahari
gulf . . 4. Aden 5. Gabes, Sidra
island (largest) . . 10. Madagascar
lake . . 8. Nyassa 8. Victoria 10. Tanganyika
Mt. . . 5. Atlas, Kenya, Natal 7. Stanley 8. Cameroon 9. Ruwenzori 11. Kilimanjaro
river . . 4. Nile 5. Congo, Niger 7. Senegal, Zambezi
size (in world) . . 6. second

African (pert to) . . .
charm, fetish . . 4. juju 6. grigri
drum . . 8. bamboule
enclosure . . 4. boma 5. kraal
garment . . 4. haik, tobe 6. kaross
grass . . 7. esparto
grassland . . 4. veld (veldt) 8. bushveld
harp (Nubian) . . 5. nanga
hemp . . 3. ife
herb . . 4. ocra
instrument . . 4. gora (gorah) 5. nanga, rebab 6. balafo

language . . 3. Ibo 4. Zulu 5. Bantu, Sotho, Tonga 6. Somali, Yoruba 7. Ashanti (Ashantee)
palm . . 6. ronier 7. palmyra
secret society . . 4. Egbo 6. Mau Mau 8. Bachichi (cannibal)
soldier . . 5. spahi 6. askari
sorcery . . 5. obeah
spiritual power . . 4. ngai
thong (rawhide) . . 4. riem
tree . . 3. oak 4. akee, baku, cola (kola), etua, shea 5. artar, sassy, siris 6. baobab

African people (pert to) . . .
Islamitic sect . . 9. Almohades
Natal . . 4. Zulu 6. kaffir 7. Amazulu
people . . 3. Ibo 4. Arab, Boer, Copt, Hutu, Kefa (Kaffa), Zulu 5. Bantu, Fulah, Negro, Pygmy, Tutsi 6. Berber, Kabyle, Nubian, Semite, Somali, Yoruba 7. Ashanti (Ashantee), Bushman, Swahili 8. Bechuana 9. Hottentot

African wildlife (pert to) . . .
antelope . . 3. gnu 4. oryx 5. addax, eland, oribi 6. dik-dik, impala, rhebok 7. blaubok (small), blesbok, gemsbok 10. duikerbuck, hartebeest
bird . . 4. lory, taha 6. weaver 8. umbretti 9. beefeater, hammerkop
fly . . 4. kivu 6. tsetse
goat . . 5. Capra
horse disease . . 5. surra
mammal . . 8. anteater, pangolin
monkey . . 4. mona, waag 6. baboon, grivet, guenon 7. guereza 8. talapoin
peacock . . 5. paauw
rhinoceros . . 6. borele 7. keitloa
rodent . . 4. jird 5. ratel
sheep . . 4. zenu 5. oudad (udad)
squirrel . . 5. xerus
stork . . 6. simbil 7. marabou
toad . . 7. Xenopus
worm . . 3. loa

aft, after . . . 4. anon, past, rear 5. abaft, later, since 6. astern, behind 9. posterior 10. subsequent, succeeding

after (pert to) . . .
all . . 11. considering 12. nevertheless
awhile . . 4. anon 5. later
breast (Zool) . . 10. metathorax
date . . 8. postdate
dinner . . 12. postprandial
dinner coffee . . 9. demitasse
prefix . . 4. meta, post

aftermath . . . 4. crop 5. rowen 9. afterglow 12. consequences

aftermost . . . 4. last 7. aftmost 8. hindmost, rearmost

afterpiece . . . 3. act 4. heel 5. epode, exode 8. postlude 9. aftercome, afterpart, tailpiece

after song . . . 5. epode

afterthought . . . 6. regret, sequel 10. reflection 13. arrière-pensée, second thought

afterward, afterwards . . . 4. next 5. after, later, since 6. ensues 7. by and by 9. afterhand 10. thereafter 11. in the future 12. subsequently

aga, agha . . . 5. chief, title 9. commander

agacant, agacante . . . 8. exciting

11. provocative

agacella (Her) . . . 8. antelope

again . . . 2. re (pref) 3. yet 4. anew, anon, back, over, then 5. ditto, newly, often, recur 6. afresh, de novo, encore, rather 7. freshly 8. eftsoons (eftsoon), likewise, moreover, once more 9. twice over 10. repeatedly, second time 11. furthermore

against . . . 2. on, to, vs 3. con, non 4. agin (dial), anti, upon 6. contra, versus 7. counter, opposed, towards 8. averse to, converse, opposite

against the . . .
clock . . 4. race, time 7. in haste
current . . 8. upstream
grain . . 6. across 7. oblique 9. backwards 10. contrarily 11. unwillingly
law . . 7. illegal, illicit 8. wrongful 12. illegitimate
sun . . 16. counterclockwise

agal . . . 4. cord (Bedouin head wrap)

agalloch . . . 4. agar 5. aloes 7. linalon 8. calambac 9. eaglewood, lignaloes

agama, agamoid . . . 6. iguana, lizard

Agamemnon (pert to) . . .
brother . . 8. Menelaus
daughter . . 7. Electra 9. Iphigenia
father . . 6. Atreus
king of . . 7. Mycenae
rival . . 9. Aegisthus
son . . 7. Orestes
wife . . 12. Clytemnestra
wife's paramour . . 9. Aegisthus

agape . . . 4. agog, ajar 6. aghast, gaping 7. curious, yawning 8. open-eyed 9. expectant, love feast (Chr) 10. astonished, bewildered, breathless

agate . . . 3. taw 4. onyx, ruby, type 5. color 6. achate, marble (game), pebble, quartz 10. birthstone, chalcedony

agave . . . 4. aloe 5. datil, istle 6. maguey, mescal, pulque 8. henequen

age . . . 3. eon, era, old 4. aeon, date, eral, eval, time 5. cycle, epoch, major, minor, older, ripen 6. junior, mature, mellow, modern, period, remote, senior 7. century, grow old 8. eternity, lifetime, maturity 9. antiquate, senectude 10. generation

Age . . . 3. Air, Ice, Jet 4. Iron, Jazz, Yuga 5. Azoic, Kalpa, Space, Steel, Stone 6. Atomic, Bronze, Copper, Eocene, Gilded, Golden, Heroic, Silver 7. Glacial, Homeric, Miocene 8. Cambrian, Cenozoic, Mesozoic 10. Geological, Supersonic 11. Elizabethan

aged . . . 3. eld, old 5. anile, hoary, olden 6. feeble, infirm, senile 7. ancient, elderly, Ogygian 8. gerontic 9. Nestorian 10. senectuous

agency . . . 5. means 6. action, medium, office 8. function 9. operation 10. collection, commission, efficiency, management 14. intermediation 15. instrumentality

agenda . . . 5. slate 6. docket 7. agendum (sing), program 9. memoranda 14. memorandum book, things to be done

agent . . . 3. spy 4. doer, test, tool 5. actor, buyer, envoy, proxy 6. author, broker, deputy, factor, medium 7. creator, proctor, reagent, scalper 8. aumildar, emissary, operator, salesman 9. canvasser, comprador, consignee, go-between, operative 10. instrument, originator 11. facilitator 12. intermediary 14. representative

Age of Reason . . . 7. Diderot 8. Voltaire 9. d'Alembert 10. philosophe 12. Encyclopedia 13. Enlightenment

Ages . . . 4. Dark 6. Middle

aggrandize . . . 5. add to, exalt 6. extend 7. advance, enhance, enlarge, glorify, magnify, promote 8. increase 10. exaggerate

aggravate . . . 3. irk, nag, vex 4. miff, rile, twit 5. anger, annoy, chafe, pique, sting, taunt, tease, worry 6. nettle, pester, ruffle, worsen 7. bedevil, disturb, incense, magnify, provoke 8. heighten, increase, irritate 9. infuriate, intensify 10. exasperate

aggravation . . . 6. bother 7. anguish, torment, trouble 8. vexation 9. annoyance, worsening 10. affliction, excitement, irritation, resentment 11. displeasure, provocation 12. exasperation 15. intensification

aggregate . . . 3. all, sum 4. mass 5. total, whole 6. amount, volume 8. compound, ensemble 9. accretion 10. collection 11. combination 12. accumulation

aggregate (pert to) . . .
definable member . . 4. unit
fruit . . 7. etaerio
in the . . 7. en masse, totally 8. together 12. collectively
of plants . . 5. flock, flora 7. cluster

aggregation . . . 4. heap 5. group, union 9. congeries 10. assemblage, collection 11. combination 12. accumulation, amalgamation 13. consolidation

aggression . . . 6. attack, injury 7. assault, offense 8. invasion 9. hostility, intrusion, offensive 10. enterprise, initiative 11. provocation 12. encroachment 14. aggressiveness

aggressive . . . 7. hostile, pushing 9. assertive, attacking, bellicose, combative, offensive 10. assaulting, pugnacious 11. belligerent, contentious, provocative 12. enterprising

aggrieve . . . 4. pain 6. grieve 7. afflict, oppress, trouble 9. displease, persecute, tyrannize

aggrieved . . . 6. pained, woeful 7. doleful 8. mournful 9. sorrowful 10. displeased

aghast . . . 4. agog 5. agape 6. afraid 8. appalled, dismayed 9. astounded, horrified, terrified 10. astonished

agile . . . 4. fast, spry 5. alert, brisk, quick, ready, swift 6. active, lively, nimble, prompt, supple 7. lissome, springe 11. expeditious

aging . . . 6. doting, fading 8. maturing, ripening 9. mellowing, senescent 10. senescence

agio . . . 7. premium 8. discount, exchange 9. brokerage 13. money changing

agitate . . . 3. fan, jar, wey 4. fret, move, plot, rile, stir 5. alarm, churn, rouse, shake, upset 6. debate, devise, excite, foment, incite, ruffle 7. canvass, perturb, revolve, trouble 8. disquiet, distract, distress 10. discompose

agitated . . . 7. anxious, excited, ruffled 8. alarming, troubled 9. disturbed, perturbed, turbulent 10. distressed 11. discomposed, overwrought

agitation . . . 4. fury, rage, stir 5. alarm, storm 6. debate, dither, foment, frenzy, furore, hubbub, tumult, unrest, uproar 7. anxiety, flutter, shaking, turmoil 8. disorder, distress, upheaval, vexation 9. commotion, trepidity 10. discussion, excitement, incitement, turbulence 11. disturbance, fomentation, trepidation 12. deliberation, perturbation, restlessness

agnate . . . 3. sib 4. akin 6. allied 7. connate, kindred, related (father's side) 8. equiparent 11. correlative 14. consanguineous

agnomen . . . 4. name 5. alias, nomen 7. epithet, surname 8. nickname

agnus castus (Eccl) . . . 4. lamb 6. chaste 14. tree of chastity

Agnus Dei, Lamb of God . . . 4. disk 6. anthem, prayer 7. the Mass (part)

ago, agone . . . 2. by 4. erst, gone, over, past, yore 5. since 6. bygone, passed 7. extinct

agog . . . 4. avid, keen 5. agape, astir, eager 6. lively, wonder 7. all eyes, curious, excited, zestful 8. open-eyed, vigilant 9. expectant, impatient 10. astonished, breathless

agonize . . . 4. pain, rack 6. grieve, harrow, strive 7. crucify, torture 8. struggle 10. excruciate

agony . . . 4. pain, pang, rack 5. grief, gripe, panic, throe 7. anguish, torment, torture 8. distress 9. suffering 11. crucifixion

agrarian . . . 5. rural 6. rustic, sylvan (silvan) 7. bucolic, hoosier 8. agrestic, Arcadian, frontier, pastoral 10. campestral, hinterland, provincial 11. countrified 12. agricultural

agree . . . 3. fit 4. give, jive, make, rime, side 5. chime, ditto, grant, match, rhyme, tally 6. accede, accord, assent, commit, comply, concur, engage, submit 7. bargain, comport, concede, conform, consent, promise 8. coincide, contract 9. acquiesce, harmonize, stipulate 10. coordinate, correspond

agreeable . . . 4. nice 5. amene, sapid, suave 6. comely, dulcet, savory 7. amiable, likable, welcome, willing 8. charming, friendly, obliging, pleasant, pleasing 9. accordant, compliant, desirable, indulgent 10. acceptable, compatible, concordant, consenting, euphonious, harmonious 11. conformable, considerate 12. reconcilable, satisfactory

agreement . . . 4. mise, pact 5. terms 6. accord, assent, cartel, parity, treaty, unison 7. bargain, compact, concord, consent, entente, promise, rapport 8. contract, covenant, identity 9. accession, consensus 10. accordment, comparison, compliance, conformity, similarity 11. coincidence, concurrence, parallelism, stipulation

agrestic . . . 5. rural 6. rustic 7. bucolic 8. pastoral 10. provincial

agriculture . . . 7. culture, farming, tillage 8. agrology, agronomy 9. husbandry 10. agrotechny 11. cultivation 13. sharecropping

agriculture (pert to) . . .
goddess of . . 3. Ops 4. Gaea (Gaia) 5. Ceres, Flora 6. Pomona, Vacuna 7. Demeter
god of . . 4. Nabu, Nebo 6. Faunus 8. Dionysus
means of . . 3. hoe 4. plow (plough) 6. harrow, header, reaper, seeder 7. combine, planter, tractor 8. thrasher 10. cultivator 11. caterpillar
ref to . . 7. georgic
science, crop growing . . 11. arviculture
terms . . 5. arado, grove, ranch, thorp 6. garden, hamlet 7. cropper, orchard 8. haymaker, vineyard 9. homestead

agriculturist . . . 6. farmer 7. planter 10. agricolist, husbandman

Agrippina's son . . . 4. Nero

agrise . . . 5. abhor, dread 6. loathe 7. shudder, terrify, tremble 8. affright

agronomy, study of . . . 11. agriculture

aground . . . 5. stuck 6. ashore 7. swamped, wrecked 8. grounded, stranded 10. high and dry

agrypnia . . . 5. vigil 8. insomnia 13. sleeplessness

agua . . . 4. toad 5. water

aguacate . . . 7. avocado

ague . . . 5. chill, fever 7. disease, malaria, shaking, shivers 9. shivering

ague tree . . . 9. sassafras

agueweed . . . 7. boneset, gentian

Ahab (pert to) . . .
daughter . . 7. Athalie
king of . . 6. Israel
wife . . 7. Jezebel

ahead . . . 2. on 3. pre (pref) 4. fore 5. afore, early 6. before, onward 7. advance, forward, leading 10. successful, surpassing

ahoy . . . 4. hail, yo-ho 5. hello 8. ship ahoy 9. attention

ahu . . . 5. mound 7. gazelle 8. memorial

ai . . . 5. sloth 11. exclamation

aid . . . 4. abet, aide, help, pony 5. allay, devil (printer's), favor, serve 6. assist, helper, incite, relief, remedy, succor 7. benefit, service, stipend, subsidy, support 8. befriend, ministry 9. alleviate, allowance, assistant 10. assistance, benefactor 11. countenance 13. accommodation

aim . . . 3. end, fix, way 4. bent, goal, plan 5. point, scope 6. aspire, direct, intend, intent, object, strive 7. bearing, current, meaning, purpose 8. endeavor 9. direction, intention, objective 11. destination

aimful . . . 8. aspiring 10. purposeful
aimless . . . 4. idle 5. blind, loose
6. chance, random 8. drifting
9. desultory, orderless, senseless
10. designless, unarranged, undirected
11. meaningless, purposeless,
unorganized
aine . . . 5. elder 6. senior
air . . . 3. gas, oam, sky 4. aria, aura,
mien, tune, wind 5. draft, ether, ozone,
vapor 6. aerate, aerial, aspect, breath,
breeze, bubble, manner, melody,
oxygen 7. aerator, bearing, climate,
display, hyaline, posture, publish,
refresh 8. attitude, aviation, behavior,
buoyance, demeanor, hydrogen,
presence 9. lightness, publicize,
ventilate 10. appearance, atmosphere,
deportment, navigation 11. haughtiness
12. stratosphere
air (pert to) . . .
  disease . . 5. bends 7. caisson
  12. aeroembolism
  music . . 4. aria, lilt, solo, tune 6. melody
  7. arietta, sortita
  passage . . 4. duct, flue, vent 7. pharynx
  9. ventiduct
  pressure unit . . 8. millebar
  stone . . 8. aerolite 9. meteorite
  term . . 5. aural 6. flight, flying 9. jet
  stream, katabatic 11. aeronautics
  tight . . 5. close, proof 6. sealed
  7. compact 8. hermetic 9. resistant
  11. impermeable
  travel . . 6. jet lag 7. skyjack
aircraft . . . 3. jet 4. kite, link 5. avion,
blimp 6. bomber, glider 7. airship,
aviette, balloon, biplane, chopper
8. airplane, jetliner, triplane, turbojet,
zeppelin 9. amphibian, dirigible, fixed-
wing, monoplane, orthopter, simulator,
spaceship, transport, turboprop
10. helicopter, hydroplane, whirlybird
aircraft (pert to) . . .
  carrier . . 7. flattop
  designer . . 8. Sikorsky
  formation . . 5. fleet 7. echelon
  inventor . . 6. Wright (Brothers)
  motorless . . 6. glider
  part . . 3. fin, pod 4. keel, tail, wing
  5. rotor 6. cabane 7. aileron, cockpit,
  nacelle 8. fusilage 9. empennage (tail)
airily . . . 5. gaily 6. thinly 7. lightly, loftily
8. jauntily 10. delicately
13. pretentiously 14. ostentatiously
airiness . . . 6. rarity 7. tenuity 8. delicacy
9. gauziness, gustiness, lightness,
loftiness, unreality, windiness
10. breeziness, jauntiness
16. lightheartedness, unsubstantiality
airing . . . 4. walk 8. exposure
air mail . . . 8. par avion
airport (pert to) . . . 4. beam, dock, gate,
shed, taxi 5. apron, pylon, tower
6. hangar, runway, skycap 7. airpost,
fairway, jetport, taxiway 8. airfield,
airstrip, heliport 9. aerodrome
(airdrome), helidrome
airy . . . 3. gay 4. aery, cool, rare,
thin 5. foamy, light, lofty, merry,
windy 6. aerial, breezy, drafty, frothy,

jaunty, lively 7. gaseous, haughty,
soaring 8. animated, aspiring, delicate,
ethereal, fanciful, feathery, flippant,
towering, volatile 9. gossamery,
vivacious 10. chimerical, phantasmal
11. atmospheric 12. lighthearted,
ostentatious
aiseweed . . . 8. goutweed
aisle . . . 4. lane, nave 5. alley 6. artery,
avenue 7. passage 8. corridor
10. passageway
ait, eyot . . . 3. oat 4. holm, isle, reef
5. atoll, islet 6. island
aitu . . . 3. god 5. demon 6. spirit
Aix . . . 4. duck
aizle . . . 4. soot 5. ember, spark
Ajax (pert to) . . .
  called . . 11. Ajax the Less (next swiftest
  to Achilles)
  father . . 7. Telamen
  hero of . . 8. The Iliad (Homer)
ajonjoli . . . 6. sesame
a k a . . . 5. alias
akimbo . . . 4. bent 6. angled, hooked
7. angular, crooked
akin . . . 3. sib 4. like, near 5. close
6. agnate, allied 7. cognate, germane,
kindred, related, similar 9. connected
10. correlated 14. consanguineous
ala . . . 4. wing 8. winglike
a la . . . 2. so 4. thus 11. identically 13. in
the manner of
Alabama . . .
  capital . . 10. Montgomery
  Capitol, Confederate (2 months) . .
  10. White House (1st 1861)
  carnival . . 11. Azalea Trail
  city . . 6. Mobile 7. Gadsden
  10. Birmingham
  monument . . 11. Russell Cave
  museum . . 22. George Washington
  Carver
  native woman (famed) . . 11. Helen Keller
  President Confederate . . 5. Davis
  (Jefferson)
  State admission . . 12. Twenty-second
  State bird . . 12. yellowhammer
  State flower . . 8. camellia
  State motto . . 21. We Dare Defend Our
  Rights
  State nickname . . 12. Heart of Dixie
  statue (huge) . . 6. Vulcan
alabaster . . . 6. gypsum, marble
7. mineral
alacrity . . . 4. zest 7. avidity 9. briskness,
eagerness, immediacy, quickness,
readiness, swiftness 10. promptness
11. promptitude, punctuality,
willingness 13. sprightliness
Aladdin (pert to) . . .
  possessor of (magic) . . 4. lamp, ring
  spirit (of Magic) . . 4. jinn
  window . . 4. task (impossible)
  youth (character) . . 13. Arabian Nights
á la diable . . . 7. deviled (devilled)
8. seasoned
alameda . . . 4. mall, walk 5. prado
9. esplanade, promenade
Alamo . . . 6. poplar (tree) 7. Mission
(San Antonio, Tex)
a la mode . . . 4. mode 5. smart 6. modish,

spruce 7. fashion, stylish, voguish
8. up-to-date 9. stylishly 11. fashionably
12. with ice cream

alan ... 3. dog (Her)

alar (pert to) ... 4. wing 6. pteric
8. axillary, shoulder

alarm ... 3. din 4. call, fear, flap
5. alert, broil, clock, daunt, panic,
scare 6. alarum, arouse, dismay, fright,
terror, tocsin 7. startle, terrify, warning
8. affright, frighten 11. trepidation
12. apprehension 13. consternation

alarmist ... 6. scarer 9. pessimist, terrorist
10. frightener 11. scaremonger

alas ... 2. ah, ay, oh 3. ach, heu, och
4. oime 5. alack, ohone 6. dear me
7. woe is me 8. lackaday

Alaska ... see also Alaskan
capital .. 6. Juneau
city .. 4. Nome 5. Sitka 7. Skagway
9. Anchorage, Fairbanks, Ketchikan
discoverer .. 11. Vitus Bering
fish .. 6. salmon, wachna 7. inconnu
glacier .. 4. Muir
highway .. 5. Alcan 6. Alaska
island .. 6. Kodiak, Unimak 7. Diomede
(Little), Nunivak 9. Aleutians, Probilofs
mountain .. 3. Ada 7. Foraker 8. McKinley
(highest in N Am), Wrangell
northernmost point .. 11. Point Barrow
oil region .. 10. Prudhoe Bay
peninsula .. 5. Kenai 6. Seward
port (oil) .. 6. Valdez
rapids .. 10. Whitehorse
river .. 5. Yukon 9. Kuskokwim
State admission .. 10. Forty-ninth
State bird .. 9. (willow) ptarmigan
State flower .. 11. forget-me-not
State symbol .. 9. bald eagle
strait .. 6. Bering
volcano .. 6. Katmai 8. Wrangell

Alaskan (pert to) ...
boat .. 5. kayak, umiak 7. bidarka
(bidarkee)
codfish .. 6. wachna
liquor .. 9. hoochinoo
people .. 3. Aht 5. Aleut, Haida, Tinna
6. Ahtena, Eskimo 7. Tlingit 8. Aleutian
9. Tsimpsean 10. Athapascan

albacore ... 4. tuna 6. tunny 6. bonito,
germon

Albania ...
capital .. 6. Tirana
city .. 5. Berat 6. Durres, Valona 7. Scutari
8. Elbasani
dialect .. 4. Gheg, Tosk
lake .. 6. Prespa 7. Scutari
mountain .. 5. Koreb 6. Pindus
river .. 4. Drin 6. Bojana
soldier .. 7. palikar
tribe .. 4. Cham

albatross ... 5. nelly (sooty) 6. burden
7. pelican 9. mallemuck

albatross around the neck ... 6. burden
8. distress (cause of)

albe (anc) ... 5. album

albert (pert to) ...
jewelry .. 10. watch chain
medal .. 6. gold (for bravery)

Albion ... 7. England (Poet)

albumin ... 5. glair 7. protein

9. endosperm

alcazar ... 6. palace 8. fortress

alchemy ... 5. magic 6. change 7. sorcery
10. changeover, conversion

alcohol ... 5. drink 6. liquor 7. ethanol,
spirits, talitol, terpene 8. beverage
9. aqua vitae, firewater 10. intoxicant

alcoholic beverage ... 3. gin, rum
4. beer, brew, grog, malt, mead,
wine 5. booze, hooch, negus, punch,
vodka 6. arrack (arrak), brandy, mao-
tai, whisky (whiskey) 7. bourbon,
cordial, liqueur, tequila 8. champers
(Brit sl), cocktail, highball 9. applejack,
champagne, moonshine

alcoholism ... 9. addiction, oenomania
10. dipsomania 11. drunkenness
12. intoxication

Alcott character ... 2. Jo 3. Amy, Meg
4. Beth

alcove ... 3. bay 4. cove, nook 5. arbor,
bower, kiosk, niche, oriel 6. carrel,
recess 7. cubicle, dinette, pergola
8. alhacena

alder (pert to) ...
chief .. 5. ruler 6. prince
fishing .. 3. fly (artificial)
tree .. 8. sagerose (yellow)

ale ... 3. mum 4. beer, flip 5. stout
6. alegar, liquor (malt) 8. festival

alee ... 7. leeward (opp of windward)

Aleppo (pert to) ...
city .. 5. Syria
grass .. 7. Johnson
stone .. 3. gem 5. agate 8. eye agate

alert ... 4. keen, warn, wary 5. agile,
alarm, alive, aware, brisk, peart (pert),
quick, ready, sharp 6. active, bright,
lively, nimble, prompt 7. guarded
8. vigilant, watchful 9. attentive,
observant, sprightly, wide-awake
11. circumspect

Aleut ... 4. Atka 6. Eskimo 7. Unungun
8. Unalaska

Aleutians ...
islands (chain) .. 8. volcanic
native of .. 5. Aleut
site .. 6. Alaska 9. Bering Sea

alewife ... 4. fish 7. herring, pompano,
walleye 9. gaspereau

Alexander the Great (pert to) ...
birthplace .. 5. Pella (Macedonia)
conqueror of .. 6. Persia
expedition .. 10. Hellespont
horse .. 10. Bucephalus

Alexandria, Egypt ...
bishop .. 5. Arius 10. Athanasius
12. Eratosthenes
island .. 6. Pharos
obelisks .. 17. Cleopatra's Needles (now
in NY City & London)
ruler .. 7. Ptolemy
world wonder .. 10. Lighthouse (Pharos)

alfa ... 5. grass 7. esparto

alfalfa ... 3. hay 5. medic 6. clover,
fodder 7. lucerne (lucern)

alforja ... 3. bag 5. pouch 6. wallet
9. saddlebag

alfresco ... 4. airy 7. open-air, outside

alga, algae ... 4. cell, moss, nori
5. Dasya, fungi 6. Alaria, diatom, fungus

7. seaweed 8. plankton 9. spirulina, stonewort

Algeria . . .
capital . . 7. Algiers
Mohammedan saint . . 8. Marabout
monastery . . 5. ribat
mountain . . 5. Atlas (Range)
native . . 5. Arabs 7. Berbers, Kabyles
ruler . . 3. bey, dey
ship . . 5. xebec
soldier . . 5. spahi (spahee) 6. Zouave

algid . . . 3. icy 4. cold 5. brisk, crisp, nippy 6. frigid, frosty, wintry 7. ice-cold

algodon . . . 6. cotton

algology, study of . . . 5. algae 8. seaweeds

Algonquian spirit . . . 6. manito (manitou)

Algonquian people . . . 4. Cree, Sauk 5. Miami 6. Ottawa 7. Arapaho, Ojibway, Shawnee 8. Cheyenne, Delaware 9. Blackfoot

Alhambra (pert to) . . .
architecture . . 7. Moorish
palace, alcazar of . . 12. Moorish Kings
site . . 7. Granada (Spain)

alias . . . 6. anonym 7. epithet 8. cognomen, nickname 9. otherwise, pseudonym, sobriquet

Ali Baba (pert to) . . .
adventurer . . 4. cave (Forty Thieves)
password to cave . . 6. Sesame
tale . . 13. Arabian Nights

alien . . . 3. ger 5. fremd 6. exotic, remote 7. adverse, foreign, hostile, opposed, strange 8. outsider, stranger 9. foreigner, peregrine, unrelated 10. extraneous, unfriendly 11. incongruous

alianate . . . 4. part, wean 6. demise, detach, devest, divest, divide 8. disunite, estrange, separate

alienation . . . 4. outs 5. split 6. breach 8. disfavor 10. conveyance, falling-out, withdrawal 12. amortization, disaffection, estrangement

alienist . . . 12. psychiatrist

aliform . . . 8. winglike 10. wing-shaped

alight . . . 4. land, rest, stop 5. ditch, lodge, perch 6. settle 7. burning, descend, lighted 8. dismount

align, aline . . . 4. true 5. level, match 6. equate, line up 7. arrange, marshal 10. collineate, straighten 11. parallelize

alike . . . 3. iso (comb form) 4. akin, like, same, twin 7. similar, uniform 8. selfsame 9. duplicate, identical 10. homonymous 17. indistinguishable

aliment . . . 4. food, keep 5. broma, manna 7. nurture, pabulum, support 9. nutriment, nutrition, refection 10. sustenance 11. nourishment, refreshment

alimentary canal, part . . . 5. mouth 7. pharynx, stomach 9. esophagus, intestine

alimony . . . 7. stipend 8. estovers 9. allotment

aline . . . see *allgn*

alipin . . . 5. slave (Phil)

alipod . . . 3. bat 10. wing-footed

aliquid . . . 8. somewhat 9. something

aliquot . . . 4. part 5. prime 7. decimal, digital, divisor, partial 10. fractional, reciprocal 11. submultiple (opp of aliquant)

alive . . . 3. vif 4. keen 5. alert, awake, brisk, vital 6. extant, lively, loving, zoetic 7. animate, current, topical 8. animated, existent 9. breathing, conscious, sensitive, sprightly 11. clear-witted, unforgotten

alkali . . . 3. lye 4. salt, soda 8. saltwort

alkaline . . . 3. reh 4. usar 6. alkali 7. antacid, nonacid

alkaline forming . . . 10. kaligenous

alkaloid . . . 6. codein, conine, eserin 7. aricine, caffin, cocaine, codeine 8. atropine, morphine 10. strychnine 13. physostigmine

alkaloid (pert to) . . .
bark . . 7. aricine
bean . . 13. physostigmine
beverage . . 8. caffeine (caffin)
drug . . 7. cocaine, codeine, eucaine 8. morphine 10. strychnine
extract . . 6. curare (curari) 11. arrow poison
hemlock . . 7. coniine
ipecac . . 8. emetine
lupine . . 8. lupinine
mustard seed . . 7. sinapin

all . . . 3. pan (pref), sum 4. omni (pref), only, toto 5. alone, every, sum of, total, tutti, whole 6. entire, wholly 7. perfect 8. ensemble, entirely, totality 9. aggregate, everybody 10. altogether, completely, everything, thoroughly 11. exclusively

all (pert to) . . .
absorbing . . 4. main 5. chief, prime 6. ruling 7. capital, leading, primary 8. foremost 9. paramount, principal 11. controlling
around . . 5. handy 9. versatile
devouring . . 6. greedy 9. rapacious 10. gluttonous
in all . . 9. generally 10. on the whole
inclusive . . 6. global 7. omneity 8. catholic, ecumenic, pandemic 9. universal 12. cosmopolitan
knowing . . 4. wise 6. divine 10. omniscient
powerful . . 6. divine 7. all-wise, supreme 8. absolute, almighty 9. all-seeing 10. all-knowing, omnipotent, omniscient, ubiquitous
the same . . 9. identical 10. equivalent 12. nevertheless
together . . 7. en masse

Allah . . . 3. God 5. deity 12. Supreme Being

allay . . . 4. cool, ease 5. abate, check, slake 6. pacify, soothe, subdue 7. appease, assuage, compose, relieve, repress, satisfy 8. moderate 9. alleviate

allée . . . 4. mall, walk 5. aisle 6. avenue 7. passage

allege . . . 4. aver, cite 5. offer, plead, quote, state 6. adduce, affirm, assert, assign 7. advance, ascribe, declare, present, pretend, profess, propose 8. maintain 9. attribute

allegiance . . . 3. tie 4. bond 5. faith, liege 6. fealty, homage 7. loyalty 8. devotion, fidelity, firmness 9. adherence, constancy 12. faithfulness 13. steadfastness

allegory . . . 5. fable, story 6. emblem 7. parable 8. apologue

alleviate . . . 4. ease 5. abate, allay, erase, quiet, salve, slake 6. lessen, pacify, reduce, soften, solace, soothe 7. assuage, compose, lighten, relieve 8. mitigate, moderate, palliate 9. extenuate 11. tranquilize

alley . . . 3. mig (marble), way 4. lane, mall, path, slum 5. aisle, byway, tewer 6. arcade, artery, byroad 8. cul-de-sac

alliance . . . 4. pact 5. union 6. fusion, league, treaty 7. compact, entente 8. affinity, agnation, covenant 9. coalition 10. federation 11. association, combination, confederacy 13. confederation

allied . . . 4. akin 6. agnate, linked, united 7. cognate, germane, kindred, leagued, related, similar 10. associated, correlated

alligator . . . 5. gator, niger 6. Caiman, cayman, jacare (yacare) 7. lagarto 9. crocodile

alligator pear . . . 7. avocado 8. aguacate

alliteration . . . 4. rime 5. rhyme 6. jingle 9. assonance 10. repetition

allocate . . . 4. deal, mete 5. allot 6. assign, locate, ordain 7. appoint, arrange, consign, reserve 9. apportion 10. distribute

allocation . . . 8. disposal 9. billeting 11. collocation, disposition 12. distribution

allot . . . 3. fix 4. cast, dole, mete 5. grant 6. assign, billet, design, intend, ordain, ration, select 7. appoint, destine, specify 9. apportion, attribute, prescribe 11. appropriate

allotment . . . 5. cavel, share 6. ration 7. subsidy 10. allocation, assignment, ordainment 13. apportionment

allow . . . 3. let 4. bear, give 5. admit, think 6. endure, permit, rebate, suffer 7. approve, concede, suppose 8. consider, discount, tolerate 9. authorize 11. acknowledge

allowance . . . 3. fee 4. tare, tret 5. arras, grant 6. ration 7. pension, scalage, stipend 8. appenage (prince's), discount, granting, sanction 9. admitting, allotment, conceding, tolerance 10. permission 11. scholarship 13. authorization

allowing for . . . 2. if 8. provided

allow to pass . . . 5. lapse 6. expire, revert

alloy . . . 3. mix 4. asem 5. blend, mokum 6. billon, fusion, oroide 7. amalgam, bullion, corrupt, mixture 8. compound 9. composite 10. adulterate, amalgamate

alloys . . .
copper, aluminum . . 9. duralumin
copper, sulphur . . 6. niello
copper, tin . . 6. bronze
copper, white metal . . 6. oroide
copper, zinc . . 5. brass 6. tombac
copper, zinc, iron . . 4. Aich (Chin)
copper, zinc, nickel . . 4. iron 7. paktong (packtong)
copper, zinc, nickel, iron . . 7. rheotan
German silver . . 6. albata
gold, silver . . 4. asem
iron, carbon . . 5. steel
iron, nickel . . 6. Calite (trademark)
lead, tin . . 6. pewter, solder
nickel, steel . . 5. Invar

All Saints' Day . . . 4. Nov 1 10. Allhallows

allspice tree . . . 7. pimento

alitud . . . 5. alien, slave 9. foreigner

allude . . . 4. hint 5. get at, imply, point, refer 6. relate 7. mention, suggest 8. indicate, intimate 9. insinuate

allure . . . 3. win 4. bait, draw, lead, lure, tice, tole 5. charm, decoy, snare, tempt 6. entice, entrap, invite, seduce 7. attract, prevail 8. inveigle, persuade 9. captivate, fascinate, influence

allurement . . . 4. bait, lure 5. bride 7. glamour (glamor) 8. agacerie, coquetry 10. attraction, enticement, inducement, temptation 12. inveiglement

allusion . . . 4. clue, hint 7. inkling 8. innuendo, instance 9. reference 11. implication

alluvial deposit . . . 3. mud 4. silt 5. delta, geest 6. placer

ally . . . 3. pal 4. aide, join 5. union 6. fellow, friend, league 7. comrade, consort, kinsman, partner 8. adherent, relative 9. associate, attendant, colleague 10. accomplice 11. confederate 12. collaborator

Alma (It) . . . 4. soul 6. spirit 10. cherishing, nourishing

alma . . . 6. fabric (silk)

almacen . . . 4. shop 8. magazine 9. warehouse

Alma Mater . . . 6. school 7. college 9. goddesses 10. university

almanac . . . 5. fasti 6. record 7. calends (kalends) 8. calendar, register 9. ephemeris (obs)

almighty . . . 5. great 6. divine 10. omnipotent 11. all-powerful 12. irresistible

almond (pert to) . . .
confection . . 8. marzipan
dish with . . 8. amandine
liqueur . . 8. amaretto

almost . . . 4. most, nigh 5. anear, close 6. all but, nearly 8. well-nigh 9. nearabout 13. approximately

alms . . . 4. dole, mite 6. aumous, bounty, corban, relief 7. charity, handout 8. donation, gratuity, pittance 12. contribution, philanthropy

alms (pert to) . . .
box . . 4. arca 5. chest
giver . . 5. donor 7. almoner 11. contributor 14. philanthropist
man . . 5. donee 6. pauper 7. feoffee 9. pensioner

alodium . . . 4. land 6. tenure 8. freehold 10. real estate

aloe, aloes ... 4. drug 5. agave, plant 6. tambac 7. incense 8. agalloch

aloft ... 2. up 4. high, over 5. aloof 7. skyward 8. overhead

aloha ... 4. hail, love 7. good-bye 9. affection, greetings 11. salutations

Aloha State ... 6. Hawaii

aloin ... 4. drug 5. aloes 8. nataloin 9. barbaloin (Barbados) 12. isobarbaloin

alone ... 4. solo 5. apart, solus 6. single, singly, solely, unique 8. desolate, homeless, isolated, separate, solitary 9. exclusive, matchless 10. unassisted 12. single-handed 13. companionless, independently, unaccompanied

along ... 2. on 3. via 4. with 6. beside, onward 7. forward 8. together

alongside ... 2. by 4. near 6. beside 7. abreast 8. parallel

aloof ... 6. offish, remote 7. distant, haughty 8. reserved 10. unsociable 11. indifferent, standoffish 15. uncommunicative

aloofness ... 7. reserve 10. offishness, remoteness 11. haughtiness 12. indifference 13. unsociability

alopecia ... 6. acomia 8. baldness 12. hairlessness

aloud ... 4. oral 6. loudly 7. audibly, plainly

alp ... 3. tor 4. peak, pico, pike 6. summit 8. mountain 9. bullfinch

alp (Teut Folklore) ... 5. demon, witch 9. nightmare

alpaca ... 4. coat, paco 5. llama 7. garment

Alph ... 11. sacred river (Kubla Khan)

alpha ... 4. star 5. prime 6. letter 7. initial, numeral 9. beginning

alphabet ... 4. ABC's 6. Sarada (Kashmir) 9. abecedary 10. Davanagari (Sanskrit)

alphabet characters (Teut) ... 4. ogam, rune

alphabetize ... 4. file 5. group, index 6. codify, letter 8. classify, tabulate 9. catalogue (catalog) 10. categorize

alpha test (Army) ... 12. intelligence

alpine ... 5. alpen, hilly 6. knobby 10. alpestrine 11. mountainous

Alpine (pert to) ...
climber .. 10. alpestrian
dance .. 7. gavotte (gavot)
dress .. 6. dirndl
dwelling .. 6. chalet
goat .. 4. ibex
herdsman .. 4. senn
peak .. 5. Blanc 9. Monte Rosa 10. Matterhorn
plant .. 9. edelweiss
province .. 5. Tyrol
shelter .. 7. hospice
snowfield .. 4. firn, neve
tunnel .. 7. Simplon 10. St Gotthard
wind .. 4. bise 5. foehn

Alps ... 5. Blanc, Tirol (Tyrol) 6. Julian 7. Dinaric 8. Jungfrau 9. Dolomites, Monte Rosa (peak) 10. Matterhorn

already ... 3. ere, yet 5. afore 6. before 7. earlier 8. hitherto 10. heretofore 11. theretofore

also ... 2. as, et, so 3. and, too, yet 4. more, plus 7. besides, further 8. likewise, moreover 9. similarly 11. furthermore

altar (pert to) ...
boy .. 7. acolyte
cloth .. 6. dossal (dossel) 7. haploma 9. ependytes
constellation .. 3. Ara
curtain .. 6. riddel
end of church .. 4. apse 7. chancel
Greek .. 5. bomos 6. hestia 7. eschara
Latin .. 7. scrobis
ledge .. 7. retable
platform .. 8. predella
screen .. 7. reredos
shelf, table .. 6. gradin 7. retable 8. credence
step .. 8. predella
top slab .. 7. mensa

alter ... 4. geld, vary, veer 5. amend, emend, reset, shift 6. adjust, change, immute, modify, mutate, revise 7. falsify 8. castrate 9. transform

alteration ... 6. change 9. diversity, variation 10. castration, correction 12. modification 13. interpolation 15. diversification

altercation ... 3. row 4. feud, spat, tiff 5. fight, snarl 6. fracas, strife 7. dispute, quarrel, wrangle 8. squabble, vendetta 9. imbroglio 10. contention 11. controversy

alter ego ... 4. mate, self, twin 7. oneself 10. complement 11. counterpart

alternate ... 4. vary 5. proxy 6. change, deputy, rotate, seesaw 7. reverse, stand-in 8. delegate 9. oscillate 10. substitute 11. alternative, interchange, reciprocate

alternate writing mode (anc) ... 13. boustrophedon

alternative ... 2. or 3. nor 5. other 6. choice, either, option, switch 7. dilemma 8. election, loophole 9. secondary 10. nip-and-tuck, preference, substitute 11. replacement

although, altho ... 4. even, when 5. while 6. albeit, though 7. despite, whereas 15. notwithstanding

altimetry ... 6. height 10. hypsometry 11. measurement

altitude ... 6. height (highth) 7. heroics, stature 8. eminence, highness, tallness 9. elevation, loftiness

altogether ... 5. fully, quite 6. bodily, wholly 7. utterly 8. entirely, outright 9. generally 10. completely, thoroughly 12. collectively

alto horn ... 7. althorn, saxhorn 10. mellophone

altruism ... 7. charity, concern 8. kindness 11. beneficence, benevolence 12. philanthropy

aluminum ore ... 7. bauxite

alumnus (alumni) ... 4. grad 5. pupil 6. alumna (alumnae) 8. graduate, postgrad 12. postgraduate

alveary ... 4. hive 5. apiary 7. beehive

alveola ... 3. dip, pit 4. pore, sink 6. crater, pocket

alveolar ... 6. pitted, pocked 7. notched

8. indented 9. depressed

always . . . 2. ay 3. aye, e'er 4. ever
6. anyway, semper 7. forever
8. evermore 9. eternally, uniformly
10. constantly, invariably
11. continually, everlasting, perpetually,
universally

ama . . . 4. tree 5. amula (Bib) 6. vessel

amabile . . . 6. gentle, tender 9. agreeable

Amadis de Gaul (Arthurian) . . . 4. hero
5. lover

amadou . . . 4. punk 6. tinder 7. styptic

amah . . . 5. nurse 7. servant 9. nursemaid
11. maidservant

amain . . . 5. apace 7. hastily, quickly,
swiftly 9. posthaste

amalgamate . . . 3. mix 4. fuse, join,
weld 5. blend, merge, unite 6. commix
7. combine 8. coalesce, compound,
intermix 11. consolidate

amalgamation . . . 6. fusion, merger
7. mixture 11. combination

Amalkite . . . 4. Agag (King) 5. nomad
7. Bedouin

amant . . . 5. lover 6. amante

amaryllis . . . 4. bulb, lily 5. agave, plant
6. flower 8. mistress 10. sweetheart
11. shepherdess

amass . . . 4. save 5. hoard, stack, store
6. gather 7. collect 8. assemble
10. accumulate

amate . . . 5. daunt 6. subdue
10. dishearten

amateur . . . 3. ham 4. tyro 6. novice
7. dabbler, fancier 8. beginner, virtuoso
10. aficionado, apprentice, dilettante
15. nonprofessional

amateurish . . . 5. inapt 9. unskilled,
untrained, untutored 10. unfinished
15. nonprofessional

Amati . . . 6. family, violin

amatory . . . 4. fond 6. ardent, erotic,
loving, tender 7. amorous, philter
9. loverlike 10. passionate

amaze . . . 3. awe 4. stun 7. astound,
perplex, stagger, startle, stupefy
8. astonish, bewilder, confound,
surprise 9. dumbfound, overwhelm

amazement . . . 3. awe 5. alarm 6. wonder
8. surprise 10. perplexity
12. bewilderment 13. consternation

Amazon . . . 5. Queen (Myth), river
6. virago 9. androgyne 10. warrioress
11. Penthesilea

Amazon river (pert to) . . .
cetacean . . 4. Inia
discoverer . . 6. Pinzon (1500)
mouth . . 4. Para
rain forest . . 5. selva
tributary . . 3. Apa 4. Napo

ambary . . . 2. da 4. hemp 5. fiber 6. Nolita

ambassador . . . 5. envoy 6. legate,
nuncio 8. diplomat, emissary, minister
9. messenger 12. intermediary
14. representative 15. plenipotentiary

amber . . . 6. yellow 8. electrum

ambidextrous . . . 7. capable 8. two-faced
9. two-handed, versatile
11. ambidextral, treacherous 13. double-
dealing

ambiguous . . . 6. double 7. Delphic,

dubious 9. equivocal, uncertain,
unsettled 10. indefinite, indistinct,
mistakable 12. questionable
13. indeterminate

ambit . . . 5. orbit, scope 6. extent, sphere
7. circuit 8. precinct

ambition . . . 4. goal, spur 6. desire
10. aspiration

amble . . . 4. pace, rack, trot 7. piaffer

ambrosia . . . 4. food 5. honey, manna
6. nectar 7. perfume 8. delicacy, libation

ambulate . . . 4. hike, move, walk

ambush . . . 4. trap 5. snare 6. hiding,
waylay 7. mantrap 9. ambuscade
10. subterfuge 11. concealment

ameliorate . . . 4. ease, mend 5. emend
6. better 7. improve 8. progress
9. meliorate

amelioration . . . 10. betterment
11. improvement, restoration

amenable . . . 6. liable, pliant 7. movable
9. receptive 10. answerable, open-
minded, responsive 11. accountable,
persuadable, responsible

amend . . . 4. beat (dial), beet (beete)
5. alter, atone, emend 6. reform, repeal
7. convert, correct, improve, rectify,
redress, restore

amendment . . . 5. rider 8. addition
10. conversion, correction
11. improvement, reformation

amends . . . 7. redress 8. reprisal
9. atonement 10. recompense,
reparation 11. restitution

amenities . . . 5. mores 7. decorum,
manners 9. etiquette 10. civilities,
courtesies 11. formalities, gentilities,
proprieties

ament . . . 6. catkin 7. cattail

American (pert to) . . .
bear . . 7. musquaw (black)
buffalo . . 5. bison
cactus . . 4. bleo 7. saguaro
carnivore . . 4. puma
cataract . . 7. Niagara (Falls)
cedar (red) . . 5. savin
elk . . 6. wapiti
Japanese . . 5. Nisei 6. Kibbei
leopard . . 6. ocelot
marsupial . . 7. opossum
merganser . . 4. duck (fish-eating)
Mexican . . 6. gringo
mink . . 5. vison
moth . . 2. io
nickname . . 6. Yankee (Yank)
ostrich . . 4. rhea
palm . . 5. Sabal 8. palmetto
quail . . 5. colin
rail . . 4. sora
squirrel . . 5. chickaree (red)
vulture . . 5. urubu 6. condor

American, famed . . .
architect . . 3. Pei 6. Wright 7. Johnson,
Venturi 8. Sullivan
artist . . 4. Cole, West 5. Homer, Marsh,
Mount, Peale, Wyeth 6. Benton,
Demuth, Hopper, O'Keefe, Rivers,
Stuart, Warhol 7. Bellows, Bingham,
Gropper, Pollock, Sargent 8. Rockwell
9. Remington 10. Burchfield
chemist . . 6. Carver (G Washington)

composer.. 4. Ives, Kern 5. Grofé, Sousa 6. Barber, Foster 7. Copland, Rodgers (Richard) 8. Gershwin 9. Bernstein, Ellington

crusader (Temperance).. 12. Carrie Nation

doctor, surgeon.. 4. Mayo 6. Schick 7. Cushing

dramatist.. 4. Rice 5. Albee, Odets 6. Miller, O'Neill, Wilder 8. Williams (Tennessee)

educator.. 4. Hume, Mann 5. Eliot 10. Washington (Booker T)

explorer.. 4. Byrd 5. Boone, Clark, Lewis, Peary 6. Carson (Kit) 9. Ellsworth

naturalist.. 4. Muir 5. Beebe 7. Audubon, Burbank

patriot.. 4. Clay, Hale, Otis 5. Dawes, Henry (Patrick), Paine (Thomas) 6. Revere

physicist.. 6. Teller (H-bomb)

pianist.. 5. Blake (Eubie), Tatum 6. Duchin, Levant, Morton (Jelly Roll) 7. Cliburn (Van) 8. Horowitz, Liberace 10. Gottschalk

poet.. 5. Auden, Eliot, Frost, Pound 6. Kilmer, Lowell, Millay 7. Whitman 8. Cummings, Ginsberg, Sandburg, Teasdale 9. Dickinson 10. Longfellow

Red Cross organizer.. 6. Barton (Clara)

Scouts (Girl) organizer.. 3. Low (Juliette)

sculptor.. 6. Calder 7. Borglum

singer.. 4. Cole (Nat), Pons 5. Lanza, Sills, Torme 6. Callas, Crosby, Jolson 7. Garland, Holiday (Billie), Merrill, Presley, Robeson, Sinatra 9. Streisand 10. Fitzgerald (Ella)

writer.. 3. Poe 5. Crane, James (Henry), Lewis (Sinclair), Stowe, Twain (Clemens) 6. Cather, Cooper, Ferber, Irving, Mailer 7. Dreiser, Emerson, Thoreau, Wharton 8. Faulkner, Melville 9. Hawthorne, Hemingway, Steinbeck 10. Fitzgerald

American Indian (pert to)...
chief.. 5. brave 6. sachem
child.. 7. papoose
conference.. 6. powwow
girl.. 7. Nokomis (Myth) 9. Minnehaha, Sacagawea (Sakajawea) 10. Pocahontas
hero (Myth).. 8. Hiawatha
magician.. 6. shaman, wabeno (Ojibway)
shelter.. 4. tent 5. hogan, tepee (teepee) 6. wigwam 7. wickiup (wikiup)

American Indian people... see also
Indian 3. Fox, Oto (Otoe), Ree, Sac, Ute 4. Cree, Crow, Erie, Hopi, Iowa, Pima 5. Creek, Kansa, Osage, Piute, Sioux 6. Cayuga, Dakota, Mohawk, Oneida, Pueblo, Seneca 7. Arapaho, Choctaw, Mohican, Ojibway, Siksika 8. Cherokee, Chippewa, Iroquois, Onondaga, Seminole 9. Algonquin, Blackfoot, Chickasaw 10. Athapascan, Muskhogean

ami... 5. lover 6. friend (law)

amiable... 6. kindly 7. lovable 8. charming, friendly, pleasant, pleasing 9. agreeable, indulgent 10. hospitable

amicable... 4. kind 8. friendly, sociable 9. congenial, peaceable 10. harmonious

amicus curiae... 5. judge 6. deputy, lawyer 16. friend of the court

amid, amidst... 2. in 5. among 7. amongst, between

amigo... 6. friend 8. neighbor

amiss... 3. ill 5. badly, fault, wrong 6. astray, sinful 8. faultily, improper 10. disorderly 11. erroneously

amity... 4. love 5. peace 7. harmony 10. friendship 11. sociability 12. congeniality, friendliness

amma... 6. abbess, mother (spiritual)

ammonia... 9. hartshorn 10. fertilizer 11. refrigerant

ammoniac plant... 5. oshac

ammunition (pert to)...
box.. 9. bandoleer
chest.. 7. caisson
type.. 4. arms, bomb, shot 7. bullets 8. grenades, missiles, munition, shrapnel 10. explosives
wagon.. 7. caisson

amnesty... 6. pardon 8. oblivion 9. acquittal 13. forgetfulness

amoeba, ameba... 3. olm 4. cell 7. proteus 10. protoplasm 13. microorganism

among, amongst... 2. in 3. mid 4. amid, with 5. midst 6. amidst, imelle 7. between

among nations... 13. international

amontillado... 6. sherry

Amor... 4. Eros 5. Cupid

AMORC... 11. Rosicrucian

amorous... 4. fond 6. ardent, erotic, loving, tender 7. adoring, devoted 8. enamored 10. passionate 12. affectionate

amorous looks... 4. ogle 5. stare 8. coquetry 10. come-hither, flirtation

amorphous... 8. abnormal, formless 9. deviative, shapeless, subnormal 14. uncrystallized

amorphous mineral... 4. opal

amort... 8. dejected, lifeless 9. inanimate 10. spiritless

amortize... 5. clear 6. convey, payoff, settle 9. discharge, negotiate

amount... 3. lot, sum 4. cost, rate, rise, unit 5. chunk, price, ratal, store, total 6. ascend, degree 7. quantum, signify 8. quantity

amount (pert to)...
due.. 5. price 6. arrear 7. default, deficit
mean.. 7. average
realized.. 4. take 6. intake 8. proceeds
small.. 6. morsel 7. modicum
smallest.. 5. least
to.. 3. all 4. even 5. equal, match, total 10. correspond

amour... 6. affair 7. liaison, romance 8. intrigue, triangle 10. flirtation

ampere... 3. amp 4. unit 6. ohmage 7. current, voltage

ampersand... 3. and 4. also

Amphibia... 5. Anura, frogs, toads 7. Aglossa 8. tadpoles 9. Salientia 11. salamanders

amphibious... 5. mixed 9. adaptable 10. fifty-fifty 11. half-and-half, mixed nature (land and water)

amphibole . . . 7. edenite, mineral, uralite
 8. aluminum, nephrite
amphigory, amphigouri . . . 5. rhyme
 6. jingle, poetry 8. doggerel 9. rigmarole
amphilogism, amphilogy . . .
 9. ambiguity, duplexity (meaning)
 10. equivocacy
Amphion (pert to) . . .
 capturer of . . 6. Thebes
 husband of . . 5. Niobe
 son of . . 4. Zeus
 twin of . . 6. Zethus
amphitheater . . . 4. bowl 5. arena, cavea,
 scene, stage 6. circus, cirque 7. stadium
 8. coliseum, platform 10. hippodrome
amphora . . . 3. jar, urn 4. vase 5. diota,
 prize 7. measure 8. ornament
ample . . . 4. full, rich, wide 5. broad, large,
 roomy 6. enough, plenty 7. liberal
 8. abundant 9. bountiful, capacious,
 extensive, plenteous, plentiful,
 unstinted 10. munificent 12. satisfactory
ampliation . . . 5. flare 9. expansion,
 extension 11. enlargement
 12. postponement 13. amplification
 14. aggrandizement
amplify . . . 3. pad 5. widen 6. dilate,
 extend 7. develop, enlarge 8. increase
 9. aggravate, expatiate 10. exaggerate,
 overstress
amplitude . . . 4. size 6. amount 7. breadth
 8. fullness 9. greatness, plenitude
 12. spaciousness
amputate . . . 4. trim 5. prune, sever 6. cut
 off 8. mutilate, retrench, truncate
amuck, amok . . . 3. fit 4. rage 6. attack,
 frenzy, malady 12. corybantiasm
amulet . . . 3. gem 5. charm 6. fetish,
 scarab, voodoo 7. periapt 8. ornament,
 talisman 10. protection
amuse . . . 3. wow 6. divert, please, regale,
 tickle 7. beguile, gratify 8. recreate
 9. entertain, titillate 10. exhilarate
amusement . . . 3. fun 4. play 5. farce,
 mirth, sport 7. pastime 9. avocation,
 diversion 10. recreation, relaxation
 13. divertisement, entertainment
amusement place . . . 4. club, park
 6. casino, midway 7. cabaret, theater
ana . . . 5. books 6. events 8. analecta,
 excerpts 9. Americana 10. collection
 11. collectanea, compilation,
 memorabilia
anachronous . . . 8. misdated, mistimed
 10. beforehand, behindhand
anaglyph . . . 5. cameo, carve 6. chisel,
 plaque, relief 10. embossment
Anak (Eccl) . . . 5. giant (Canaan) 6. Anakim
analogous . . . 4. like 7. similar 8. parallel
 9. comparable, equivalent
 11. correlative
analogue . . . 8. parallel 11. resemblance
 13. correspondent 14. correspondence
analogy . . . 8. likeness, sameness
 9. agreement 10. accordance,
 comparison, similarity
 14. correspondence
analysis . . . 5. assay, logic 6. biopsy,
 theory 8. breakdown, diagnosis
 10. compendium, discussion, dissection
 11. examination 14. classification

analyze . . . 5. assay, parse, study
 7. discuss, dissect, examine 8. classify,
 describe, diagnose, separate
Ananias (Bib) . . . 4. liar 8. disciple
 (Damascus), Shadrack (Sidrack) 10. high
 priest 12. prevaricator
anarch, anarchist . . . 3. red 7. radical
 8. nihilist 9. socialist, terrorist
 13. revolutionist
anarchy . . . 4. riot 5. chaos 6. acracy
 7. license, misrule 8. disorder
 9. confusion, mobocracy, rebellion
 10. ochlocracy
anathema . . . 3. ban 5. curse 9. damnation
 11. abomination, imprecation,
 malediction
Anatolian rug . . . 4. Kurd 5. Tuzla
anatomy . . . 4. body 5. build, frame
 7. carcass 8. analysis, skeleton
 9. formation, structure 11. arrangement
anatomy of animals . . . 7. zootomy
ancestor . . . 4. Adam, sire 5. elder, stock
 6. atavus, family, parent 8. forebear
 9. patriarch, precursor 10. antecedent,
 forefather, forerunner, progenitor
 11. grandfather, predecessor
ancestral . . . 4. aval 6. avital, lineal
 7. atavism 9. maternal, paternal
 8. atavistic, primitive 10. hereditary
 11. patrimonial
ancestral spirits . . . 5. lares, manes
 7. lemures, penates
ancestry . . . 4. race, rank 5. birth, blood
 7. descent, lineage 11. antecedents
 14. progenitorship
anchor . . . 3. fix, tie 4. hook, moor, rest,
 stop 5. affix, clamp, kedge 6. attach,
 batten, fasten, secure 7. grapnel, killick
anchor (pert to) . . . 3. arm, cat, pee 4. cast,
 palm, tore (ring) 5. fluke 7. capstan
anchorite, anchoret . . . 6. hermit, shut-
 in 7. ascetic, eremite, recluse, stylite
 8. homebody
anchor-shaped . . . 8. ankyroid 10. hook-
 shaped
anchovy . . . 4. alec 5. sauce, sprat
 7. herring
ancienne noblesse . . . 5. elect, elite
 7. royalty 8. nobility 11. aristocracy
ancient . . . 3. eld, old 4. aged, auld, wise
 5. adept, early, hoary, olden 7. antique
 8. historic, obsolete, outdated, primeval,
 pristine 9. grandeval, primitive,
 venerable 10. aboriginal, antiquated,
 preadamite 12. antediluvian
ancient (pert to) . . .
 chariot . . 5. essed
 city . . 4. Elis, Tyre 5. Argos, Sedon
 6. Athens, Sparta, Thebes
 drink . . 5. morat
 empire . . 4. Gaul 5. Roman 6. Lydian
 7. Persian 8. Assyrian, Athenian,
 Chaldean, Hellenic 10. Babylonian,
 Phoenician
 god . . 4. Esus (Gaulish)
 isles . . 5. Chios, Crete, Samos 6. Aegina,
 Ionian, Ithaca, Lemnos, Lesbos, Rhodes
 7. Salamis 8. Cyclades
 language . . 4. Pali 5. Latin 6. Celtic,
 Gaelic 7. Cornish, Gaulish
 mariner . . 4. Rime (of) 5. rover 6. roamer,

sailor, seaman 8. seafarer, wanderer
9. navigator
soldier . . 7. peltast
theater . . 5. odeum
and . . . 2. et 4. also, plus 8. et cetera
9. ampersand, including 12. additionally
andante . . . 5. largo, tempo 6. slowly
Andean (pert to) . . .
beast . . 5. llama 6. alpaca, vicuña
7. guanaco
deer . . 4. pudu
region, wind . . 4. puna
term . . 5. grand, lofty
andiron . . . 3. dog 7. firedog, Hessian
and others . . . 4. et al
andrenid . . . 3. bee 10. Andrenidae
androgyny . . . 9. sissiness 10. effeminacy
11. unmanliness 15. hermaphroditism
android . . . 5. robot 9. automaton
anecdote . . . 4. tale, yarn 5. story
7. account 9. chronicle, narrative
anecdotes . . . 3. ana 7. sayings, stories
anemone . . . 7. actinia 10. windflower
anent . . . 2. of, on, re 4. upon, with
5. about 8. opposite 10. concerning
anesthesia, anaesthesie . . . 8. deadness,
numbness 13. insensibility
anesthetic . . . 3. gas 5. ether 8. freezing,
Novocain, procaine 9. pentothal
10. chloroform 13. refrigeration
anesthetize . . . 4. dull, numb, stun
6. benumb, deaden, freeze 7. stupefy
8. etherize, paralyze 9. narcotize
10. chloroform 11. desensitize
anew . . . 5. again, newly 6. afresh, de
novo 8. recently
angel . . . 6. cherub, genius, seraph (seraf)
7. Madonna, prophet
angel (pert to) . . .
Arab (apostate) . . 5. Eblis
archangel . . 5. Uriel 7. Gabriel, Michael,
Raphael
Biblical . . 6. bishop, pastor
Fallen . . 6. Belial, Mammon
financial . . 6. backer, patron 7. sponsor
8. promoter
fish . . 5. shark 9. spadefish
Hebrew . . 6. Abdiel 8. cherubim,
seraphim
Jewish . . 6. Azrael (of death) 7. Zadkiel
(of planet Jupiter) 8. Metatron
Mohammedan (Mus) . . 7. Israfil (Israfeel)
Moslem . . 5. Nakir (Repudiating)
6. Munkar (Unknown)
angelic . . . 5. godly 7. lovable, saintly
8. cherubic, heavenly, seraphic, virtuous
9. celestial 10. beneficent
angelica . . . 4. herb 6. lovely 7. liqueur
Angelus . . . 4. bell, call 6. prayer
8. devotion
anger . . . 3. ire, vex 4. fume, rage,
rile 5. annoy, chafe, wrath 6. choler,
dander, enrage, nettle, offend, temper
7. dudgeon, emotion, inflame, madness,
passion, trouble 8. vexation 9. infuriate
10. affliction, enragement, irritation,
resentment 11. displeasure, indignation
12. exasperation
angered . . . 3. mad 5. irate, wroth
8. incensed, wrathful 9. indignant,
irascible

angle . . . 3. ell, tee, zig 4. axil, coin, fish,
fork, hade, nook 5. acute, ancon, arris,
right, slant, story 6. akimbo, distal,
epaule, obtuse, octant 7. bastion,
outlook, ravelin, salient 8. attitude
9. incidence, rectangle, viewpoint
angler . . . 6. fisher 7. dibbler, trawler,
troller 8. piscator 9. fisherman,
Waltonian
angler's basket . . . 5. creel
Anglican . . . 7. English
Anglo-Celtic . . . 7. British 10. Anglo-
Saxon
Anglo-Indian (pert to) . . .
Empire founder . . 5. Clive
measure . . 3. ser 4. tola
pageant . . 7. tamasha
peasant . . 4. ryot
princess . . 5. begum
wealthy . . 5. nabob
Anglo-Saxon (pert to) . . .
armor . . 7. hauberk
assembly . . 4. moot 5. gemot (gemote)
attendant . . 5. thane
consonant . . 3. edh, eth
council . . 9. heptarchy
councilman . . 5. witan
epic (heroic) . . 7. Beowulf
native . . 7. English 11. Anglo-Celtic
prince (heir apparent) . . 8. atheling
slave . . 4. esne
tenant . . 5. geneat
warrior . . 5. thane
Angora . . .
capital of . . 6. Turkey
garment . . 5. shawl
goat . . 6. chamal
wool fabric . . 6. mohair
angry . . . 3. hot, mad 4. sore 5. cross,
grame, irate, irked, vexed 6. ireful,
stormy 7. enraged, painful, steamed
8. inflamed, wrathful 9. indignant,
irascible, resentful, ticked off, turbulent
10. passionate
anguish . . . 3. woe 4. bale, pain, pang
5. agony, dolor, grief, throe 6. misery
7. remorse, sadness, torment, torture
8. distress 9. heartache 10. desolation
11. lamentation
angular . . . 4. bent, bony, edgy 5. gaunt,
sharp 6. abrupt, akimbo, forked
7. crooked, pointed, scrawny
8. cornered, crotched
ani . . . 8. keelbill (keelbird) 9. blackbird
animadversion . . . 7. censure, comment,
obloquy 8. judgment, reproach
9. aspersion, criticism 10. imputation,
reflection 12. condemnation
animadvert . . . 4. note 5. watch 6. notice,
regard, remark 7. censure, comment,
observe 9. criticize (criticise)
anima humana . . . 4. mind, self, soul
5. heart, human 6. psyche, spirit
animal (pert to) . . .
anatomy . . 7. zootomy
back, spine . . 4. nota 5. chine
Biblical . . 8. Behemoth
body . . 4. soma
castrated . . 3. seg (segg)
coat . . 6. pelage
cud . . 5. rumen

disease . . 8. enzootic

enclosure . . 3. pen, sty 4. cage, coop, cote, reem, yard 5. hutch, kraal, stall 6. corral 7. pasture

fabulous . . 7. griffin

group . . 3. gam, pod 4. herd 5. drove, flock, pride 9. menagerie

hairless . . 5. pelon

hindleg part . . 4. crus

hornless . . 7. pollard

hybrid . . 4. mule 5. hinny

hypnosis . . 9. cataplexy

male . . 3. tom 4. bull, jack, stag 5. steer 8. stallion

many-egged . . 5. zooid

many-footed . . 7. polyped

molt . . 8. exuviate

mother . . 3. dam

no feet . . 4. apod

nose . . 5. snout

oar-footed . . 7. remiped

one-egged . . 4. zoon

one-footed . . 6. uniped

pet . . 4. cade

reference to . . 4. wild 6. carnal 7. bestial, fleshly, kingdom 8. domestic 12. ferae naturae 14. domitae naturae

regional . . 5. fauna

small . . 10. animalcule

symbolic . . 5. totem

track, trail . . 4. rack 5. piste, ꞓpoor

web-footed . . 8. pinniped

wing-footed . . 6. aliped

worship . . 8. zoolatry

young . . 3. cub, kid, pup 4. calf, colt, fawn, foal, lamb 5. filly, puppy 6. kitten

animal family . . .

bear . . 6. ursine

cat . . 6. feline

cow . . 6. bovine

deer . . 7. cervine

dog . . 6. canine

fox . . 7. vulpine

horse . . 6. equine

pig . . 7. porcine

sheep . . 5. ovine

wolf . . 6. lupine

animal stomach . . .

1st . . 5. rumen 6. paunch

2nd . . 5. tripe 9. honeycomb, reticulum

3rd . . 8. omasum 9. manyplies

4th . . 3. maw 4. read (reed) 8. abomasum

animate . . . 3. act 4. fire, live, move 5. alive, cheer, imbue, impel, liven 6. arouse, ensoul, spirit, vivify 7. enliven, inspire, organic, refresh 8. energize, vitalize 9. stimulate 10. exhilarate

animated . . . 3. gay 5. alive, brisk 6. active, lively, minded 7. disposed (in mind), prompted 9. energetic, refreshed

animated spirit . . . 6. animus

animation . . . 3. pep 4. brio, dash, life 5. ardor 6. energy, gaiety, spirit 8. airiness, buoyancy, vivacity 10. earnestness, liveliness, motivation 11. earnestness, inspiration 12. invigoration, vivification 13. sprightliness

animation suspended . . . 6. apathy,

torpor 8. dormancy, lethargy

animé . . . 6. bright 8. animated

animosity . . . 5. clash, spite 6. enmity, hatred, rancor 7. ill will 8. conflict 9. antipathy, hostility 10. antagonism, opposition, repugnance

animoso . . . 6. lively 8. animated 9. energetic

animous . . . 3. hot 8. resolute, vehement

animus . . . 4. mind, will 6. desire, hatred, spirit, temper 8. attitude, volition 9. intention 10. discretion 11. disposition, inclination

anise-flavored liqueur . . . 4. anis, ouzo 6. pastis 8. anisette

ankh (Egypt) . . . 3. tau 4. life 5. cross 6. emblem, symbol

ankle . . . 4. tali (pl) 5. joint, pivot, talus 6. tarsus 8. astragal 9. ginglymus 10. astragalus 11. diarthrosis

ankle cover . . . 4. spat 6. gaiter

ankylostoma . . . 7. lockjaw

annalist . . . 6. writer 8. recorder 9. historian 10. chronicler 11. memorialist 12. chronologist

annals . . . 5. diary 6. record 7. history, journal 8. register 9. chronicle 11. publication

Annam . . . 5. Hanoi 6. Tonkin (Tongking)

Annamese . . . 7. Chinese 8. Buddhist 9. Mongolian

anneal . . . 4. fuse, heat 6. harden, temper 7. inflame, toughen 8. indurate

Anne Hathaway's home . . . 8. Shattery

annelid . . . 3. lug 4. lurg, naid, worm 6. phylum 7. lugworm

annex . . . 3. add, ell 4. join, wing 5. affix 5. append, attach, fasten 7. acquire, subjoin 8. addition 9. extension

annexation . . . 7. adjunct 8. addition 9. accession 10. affixation 13. appropriation

Annie Oakley . . . 4. pass 6. ticket (free)

annihilate . . . 4. undo, void 5. erase, wreck 6. quench, reduce, stifle 7. abolish, destroy, expunge, nullify, smother 8. decimate 9. extirpate 10. extinguish, obliterate 11. exterminate

annihilation . . . 5. death 6. demise 7. passing 8. extinction 11. destruction, dissolution 13. extermination 14. extinguishment

anniversary . . . 5. cycle 6. course 7. jubilee, wedding 8. birthday 10. centennial, regularity 13. commemoration

annotation . . . 4. note 5. gloss 7. apostil, comment 8. exegesis, notation, rescript, scholium 9. reference 10. commentary

annotator . . . 6. critic 7. analyst 9. expositor, expounder, publicist, scholiast 10. glossarist 11. commentator

announce . . . 3. bid 4. call, tell 5. bruit 6. affirm, assert, herald, notify 7. declare, forerun, gazette, presage 8. proclaim 9. advertise, broadcast, pronounce 10. annunciate, promulgate

announcement . . . 4. fiat 5. blurb, edict 6. decree, notice 8. bulletin 9. manifesto 10. commercial 11. affirmation,

declaration 12. notification,
proclamation 13. advertisement

announcer . . . 4. page 5. crier, emcee
6. nuncio 9. harbinger, informant
10. newscaster, proclaimer
11. broadcaster

annoy . . . 3. irk, nag, try, vex 4. bore,
rile 5. anger, devil, harry, peeve,
spite, tease 6. bother, harass, molest,
offend, pester, ruffle 7. disturb, trouble
8. irritate 9. displease 13. inconvenience

annoyance . . . 4. bore, pest 8. nuisance,
vexation 10. resentment 11. molestation
13. inconvenience

annoying . . . 4. sore 7. galling 9. vexatious
11. distressing

annual . . . 4. book 5. plant 6. yearly
7. etesian 10. periodical 11. publication

annuity . . . 5. rente, trust 6. income (life)
7. pension, subsidy, tontine 9. allotment
10. investment, life income

annul . . . 4. cass, undo, void 5. avoid,
blank, quash 6. cancel, repeal, revoke
7. abolish, nullify, rescind 8. abrogate,
derogate, overrule, withdraw
9. disaffirm 10. invalidate, neutralize,
obliterate 11. countermand

annular . . . 6. banded, cyclic, ringed
8. cingular, circular

annulet . . . 4. ring (Her) 6. fillet 7. circlet,
ringlet

annulment . . . 6. repeal 7. erasure,
vacatur 9. abolition 10. abrogation,
defeasance, revocation 12. invalidation
14. neutralization

annunciate . . . 6. affirm, assert
8. announce, proclaim

annunciation . . . 11. affirmation
12. announcement, proclamation
13. pronouncement

anos . . . 2. ox (wild) 8. sapiutan

anode . . . 8. terminal (positive)
9. electrode (opp of cathode)

anodic . . . 12. turned toward

anodyne . . . 4. balm 6. opiate 7. soother
8. antalgic, narcotic, pacifier, sedative
9. analgesic 10. depressant, palliative

anoesia . . . 6. idiocy

anoint . . . 3. oil 4. balm, cere, nard
5. anele, bribe, smear 6. chrism,
grease, spread 7. moisten 8. medicate
9. embrocate, lubricate 10. consecrate

Anointing of the Sick . . . 9. last rites,
sacrament 14. Extreme Unction

anoli, anole . . . 6. lizard

anomalous . . . 3. odd 7. erratic, strange,
unusual 8. aberrant, abnormal, peculiar
9. eccentric, irregular 10. dissimilar
11. exceptional 13. unconformable

anomaly . . . 6. oddity, rarity
11. abnormality, nondescript
12. irregularity

anomy . . . 7. miracle

anon . . . 4. soon 5. again, later 6. mañana,
thence 7. by-and-by 8. tomorrow
10. eventually 11. straightway

anonymous (opp of onomatous) . . .
7. unknown 8. nameless, unavowed
9. undefined

anoöpsia . . . 10. strabismus (upward)

Anopheles . . . 10. mosquitoes

anophthalmia . . . 13. absence of eyes
(congenital)

anopia . . . 15. defective vision

anorak . . . 5. parka 12. hooded jacket
(Arctic)

anorexia . . . 10. no appetite

anorthopia . . . 15. distorted vision

anosmia . . . 11. loss of smell

another . . . 3. new 4. more 5. alias, extra,
other 6. second 7. further 10. additional

another time . . . 5. again 10. otherwhile

ansa . . . 4. loop 6. ansate, handle

anserine . . . 6. stupid 9. gooselike

answer . . . 2. do 3. say 4. echo
5. avail, reply, sauce, serve 6. oracle,
retort 7. defense, epistle, respond,
riposte 8. conclude, reaction, repartee,
response, solution 9. rejoinder
10. correspond, responsory
11. acknowledge 16. counterstatement

answerable . . . 6. liable 8. amenable,
solvable 11. responsible
12. commensurate 13. proportionate

answer the purpose . . . 2. so 3. fit 4. suit
5. avail, serve 6. become 7. benefit,
satisfy, suffice

ant (pert to) . . .
  family . . 10. Formicidae, Myrmicidae
    11. Formicoidea (super), Hymenoptera
  feeding on . . 13. formicivorous
  genus . . 6. Eciton, Termes 7. Formica
  killer . . 9. formicide
  male . . 8. macraner (large), micraner
    (small)
  nest . . 9. formicary
  ref to . . 6. formic
  type . . 5. emmet 7. formica, pismire
  white . . 4. anay (anai) 7. termite
  wingless . . 8. ergatoid
  worker . . 6. ergate 9. harvester

antacid . . . 6. alkali, remedy 8. medicine
9. absorbent 11. neutralizer
12. counteragent 13. counteractant

Antaeus, Antaios (Gr) . . . 5. giant
6. Libyan 8. wrestler

antagonism . . . 3. war 5. clash 8. conflict
9. antipathy, hostility 10. opposition,
repugnance 11. contrariety
12. disagreement 13. counteraction

antagonist . . . 3. foe 5. enemy, rival
6. foeman 8. opponent 9. adversary

antagonistic . . . 7. hostile, opposed
8. contrary, converse, inimical, opposite
9. repugnant 10. unfriendly
11. belligerent, disagreeing
13. counteractive

Antarctic . . .
  Circle . . 4. Pole 6. region
  Coast . . 6. Adélie
  continent . . 10. Antarctica
  explorer . . 4. Byrd, Ross
  islands . . 11. Archipelago
  rel to . . 8. subpolar 9. antipodal, South
    Pole
  sea . . 4. Ross 7. Weddell
  seal (brown) discoverer . . 7. Weddell
  volcano . . 6. Erebus

ante . . . 3. pay, pot 4. bank, fund, pool
5. kitty, stake 7. jackpot

anteater . . . 5. Manis 7. echidna
8. aardvark, edentate, pangolin,

tamandua
antebellum ... 6. prewar
antecede ... 4. head 5. front 6. prefix
7. outrank, precede, preface
antecedent ... 4. fore 5. prior, scout
6. former 7. pioneer 8. ancestor,
previous 9. foregoing, precedent,
preceding, precursor 10. forerunner,
precedence 11. voortrekker (Dutch)
12. avant-courier
antecedents ... 7. fathers 8. ancestors,
forebears 10. ascendants (ascendents)
11. forefathers 12. predecessors
13. prerequisites
antechamber ... 4. hall 5. lobby 6. lounge
7. chamber 8. anteroom 9. vestibule
antedate ... 7. precede, predate
8. datemark, pre-exist 10. anticipate
antelope ... 3. gau, gnu, goa, kob, nil
4. guib, koba, oryx, roan 5. addax,
bovid, eland, goral, oribi, peele, saiga,
serow 6. cabree, dik-dik, dzeren,
impala, nilgai, pygarg 7. blaubok,
blesbok, bubalia, chamois, gazella,
gazelle, gemsbok, sassaby 8. agacella,
bontebok, steinbok 9. duikerbok,
pronghorn 10. hartebeest
antenna ... 4. horn, mast, palp 5. clava
(Zool), tower 6. aerial, feeler 7. scanner
antepast ... 6. canape, repast 8. aperitif
9. antipasto, appetizer, foretaste
11. hors d'oeuvre, prelibation
anteroom ... 4. hall 5. lobby 6. lounge
7. chamber 9. vestibule
11. antechamber
anthem ... 3. lay 4. hymn, song 5. motet,
music, psalm 7. chorale 8. doxology
9. antiphony, offertory 10. responsory
anthill ... 5. mound 9. formicary
anthology ... 3. ana 5. album 6. corpus
7. omnibus, prayers 8. analects
9. potpourri 10. collection
11. collectanea, compilation
Anthozoa ... 6. corals, polyps
8. anemones
anthropoid ... 3. ape, lar, man 6. gibbon
7. gorilla, primate, siamang
9. orangutan (orangoutang)
10. chimpanzee, troglodyte
12. Anthropoidea (suborder)
anthropophagi ... 9. cannibals, man-
eaters
anti ... 6. contra 7. adverse, counter,
opposed 8. contrary, converse
13. contradictory
antibiotics ... 5. drugs 7. vaccine
10. penicillin 12. streptomycin
antic ... 4. dido 5. caper, prank, stunt
6. frolic, gambol 7. bizarre, buffoon,
gamboso 9. grotesque 11. merry-
andrew, monkeyshine
anticipate ... 4. hope 5. await, dread
6. expect 7. foresee, obviate, portend,
prevent 8. preclude 9. forestall,
foretaste, forethink 11. contemplate
anticipation ... 4. hope 9. foresight,
foretaste, intuition, prolepsis
10. foreboding 11. expectation,
forethought 12. presentiment
13. preoccupation
anticlimax ... 6. bathos 8. comedown,

decrease
antidote ... 6. remedy 10. corrective,
preventive 11. neutralizer
12. counteragent, prophylactic
13. counteractant
Antilles ...
   Greater .. 4. Cuba 7. Jamaica
10. Hispaniola, Puerto Rico
   Lesser .. 7. Leeward (Islands)
8. Windward (Islands)
Antioch ... 7. capital (Syria)
antipathy ... 6. hatred, nausea 7. dislike
8. aversion, loathing 9. disrelish,
hostility 10. abhorrence, antagonism,
opposition, reluctance, repugnance
11. contrariety, detestation, inimicality
13. counteraction 14. disinclination
antipodal ... 5. polar 7. counter (global)
8. contrary, opposite 14. contrapositive
antiquated ... 4. aged 5. passé 6. bygone,
voided 7. antique, archaic, elderly
8. absolute, medieval 9. Victorian
10. fossilized 12. antediluvian, old-
fashioned 13. superannuated
antique ... 3. old 5. hoary, relic
7. ageless, ancient 8. dateless,
outmoded 9. venerable 12. old-
fashioned
antiquities ... 5. codex, ruins 6. relics
7. fossils, papyrus, remains, tablets
9. archaisms, artifacts, monuments
11. manuscripts, palimpsests
antiquity ... 3. ago, eld 4. past, yore
7. oldness 9. paleology 11. ancientness,
elderliness 13. aboriginality,
primitiveness
antisepsis ... 7. asepsis 11. prophylaxis
12. disinfection, immunization
13. sterilization
antiseptic ... 5. Salol 6. cresol, iodine
(iodin), phenol 7. alcohol, aristol,
aseptic 8. creosote, peroxide
9. germicide 12. disinfectant,
formaldehyde, prophylactic
antispasmodic ... 7. anodyne 8. sedative
9. asadulcis (deadly carrot), asafetida
(asafoetida) 10. depressant
12. tranquilizer
antithesis (opp of thesis) ... 8. contrast,
opposite 9. antipodes 10. opposition
11. contrariety 14. contraposition
antitoxin ... 5. serum 7. vaccine
8. antibody 9. antivenin (antivenene)
10. antibiotic 11. antipyretic,
immunotoxin
antler ... 3. dag 4. horn, snag, tine
5. dague, point, prong, spike 6. bosset,
rights 8. advancer 10. caducicorn
Antony & Cleopatra characters ...
4. Eris, Iras 6. Caesar 7. Octavia
9. Demetrius
antonym (opp of synonym) ... 7. reverse
8. contrary, opposite
antrum ... 3. pit 5. sinus 6. cavern,
cavity, hollow 10. depression
Anu ... 3. god (sky, heavens)
Anubis ... 3. god (Necropolis) 6. Hermes
Anura ... 4. Rana 5. frogs, toads
9. Salientia 10. amphibians
anvil ... 5. block, incus, teest 6. stithy
7. bickern, incudes (pl) 8. beakiron

(horned)

anxiety . . . 4. care, fear 5. angst, dread, worry 7. concern, trouble 8. disquiet, distress, neurosis, suspense 9. eagerness, misgiving 10. foreboding, perplexity, solicitude, uneasiness 12. apprehension, restlessness

anxious . . . 4. cark 5. antsy, eager 6. uneasy 7. fearful, unquiet 8. watchful 9. concerned, disturbed, expectant, impatient 10. disquieted

any . . . 3. all, ary (dial), one, oni (dial) 4. some, that, this 5. aught, every 8. quantity 9. unlimited 10. unmeasured 12. undetermined

anybody . . . 3. any, one 5. aught 6. anyone 7. someone, whoever 15. no-account person

anything . . . 3. any 4. some 5. at all, aught 7. anywise 8. no choice, whatever 9. something 14. choicelessness

anything (pert to) . . .
existing . . 6. entity 8. quiddity
of value . . 5. asset
of value, least . . 5. plack
puzzling . . 4. crux 11. mind-boggler
remote . . 6. forane
small . . 3. tot 5. minim
spiral . . 4. gyre 5. helix
terrifying . . 5. ghost 9. scarecrow
true . . 4. fact 9. certitude
worthless . . 4. mean 7. useless 9. valueless

souded . . . 5. sheep 7. chamois

apa . . . 7. wallaba

Apache (pert to) . . .
French . . 4. thug 5. dance 8. assassin
Indian . . 5. nomad
Indian Chief (famed) . . 8. Geronimo
Indian jacket (deerskin) . . 6. bietle
State . . 7. Arizona

apart . . . 3. dis (pref) 4. away 5. alone, aloof, aside, solus, split 6. singly 7. asunder, distant 8. secluded, separate, unjoined 9. severally, unrelated 10. separately

apartheid . . . 4. bias 5. twist 7. bigotry 9. prejudice 11. segregation 13. provincialism 14. discrimination

apartment . . . 3. pad (sl) 4. flat 5. condo, suite 6. studio 7. chamber 8. tenement 11. compartment, condominium

apathetic . . . 4. dull 5. inert 6. torpid 7. passive 8. listless, sluggish 10. insouciant, phlegmatic 11. indifferent, unconcerned

apathy . . . 6. acedia (in a monastery), torpor 7. languor 8. neurosis 9. lassitude, unconcern 12. indifference, sluggishness 13. insensibility, unfeelingness

ape . . . 4. copy, dupe, fool, mine 5. mimic 6. alalus, mocker, monkey, parrot 7. barbary, copycat, emulate, imitate, portray 8. imitator, mimicker, simulate 10. anthropoid 11. impersonate

ape (pert to) . . .
anthropoid . . 6. pongid 10. chimpanzee, troglodyte
Egypt Relig . . 4. Aani
genus . . 5. Cebus, Simia

India . . 3. kra
kind . . 6. simian 7. macaque
largest . . 6. baboon 7. gorilla
Malay . . 3. lar 5. orang 6. gibbon 9. orangutan (orangoutang)
nocturnal . . 5. lemur

aperitif . . . 5. drink 6. canape 8. antepast 9. antipasto, appetizer 11. hors d'oeuvre

aperture . . . 3. gap, vue 4. hole, leak, pore, rift, rima, slit, slot, vent 5. chasm, chink, cleft, inlet, mouth, stoma 6. hiatus, window 7. fissure, foramen, opening, orifice, osteole 8. fenestra 10. passageway

apex . . . 3. tip, top 4. acme, cone, cusp, noon 5. point, spire 6. apogee, height, macron, summit, tittle, vertex, zenith 7. cacumen 8. pinnacle 11. culmination

apex ornament . . . 6. finial

aphid . . . 5. Aphis, louse 6. insect 7. puceron

aphorism . . . 3. saw 5. adage, axiom, gnome, maxim, moral 6. dictum, saying 7. proverb 8. apothegm

Aphrodite (pert to) . . .
consort . . 4. Ares 10. Hephaestus
father . . 4. Zeus
goddess of . . 4. love 6. beauty
Roman equivalent . . 5. Venus
sacred birds . . 5. doves 8. sparrows
statue . . 17. Aphrodite of Cnidus (by Praxiteles)
zoology . . 9. butterfly

apiarist . . . 9. beekeeper

apiary . . . 7. beehive

Apis . . . 4. bull (sacred)

aplomb . . . 5. poise 6. surety 7. balance 8. fastness, firmness, security, solidity 9. assurance, erectness, plumbness, restraint, soundness, stability 10. confidence, equanimity 11. equilibrium

apocalypse . . . 8. prophecy, teaching 9. discovery, scripture 10. revealment, revelation

a poco . . . 6. little, slowly 9. gradually

apocryphal . . . 4. mock, sham 5. bogus, false 6. mythic, unreal 8. doubtful, mythical, spurious 9. imitative 10. fictitious, unorthodox 11. counterfeit 15. unauthoritative

apod . . . 8. footless

Apodes . . . 4. eels 6. morays

apogee (opp of perigee) . . . 4. acme, apex, peak 6. climax, summit, zenith 11. culmination

apograph . . . 4. copy 5. tenor 7. tracing 8. transfer 9. recording 10. transcript 13. transcription

Apoidea . . . 4. Apis, bees 9. honeybees 11. Hymenoptera

Apollo (pert to) . . .
birthplace . . 5. Delos
father . . 4. Zeus
festival . . 5. Delia
god . . 3. sun (personified)
mother . . 4. Leto 6. Larona
oracle . . 8. Delphi
sage follower . . 6. Abaris
sister (twin) . . 5. Diana (Rom) 7. Artemis
son . . 3. Ion 5. Hymen, Linos

apologetic . . . 5. sorry 7. apology
8. excusing 10. excusatory, justifying,
remorseful 11. vindicative
12. propitiatory 13. justification

apologue . . . 4. myth 5. fable, story
6. legend 7. fantasy, parable 8. allegory

apology . . . 4. plea 6. excuse 7. pretext,
regrets 9. makeshift 11. explanation,
vindication 13. justification
14. acknowledgment

aport . . . 8. larboard, leftward 9. sinistrad

apostasy . . . 5. lapse 9. desertion,
recreancy 11. backsliding

apostate . . . 6. bolter 7. pervert, runaway,
seceder 8. deserter, recreant, renegade,
turncoat, turntail 10. unfaithful

apostle . . . 5. saint 8. disciple, follower
9. evangelist

Apostle (Bib) . . . 4. John, Jude 5. James,
Judas (Iscariot), Peter (Simon Peter),
Simon 6. Andrew, Philip, Thomas
7. Matthew 8. Matthias
11. Bartholomew (Nathanael)

Apostle of . . .
France (Gauls) . . 5. Denis
Franks . . 4. Remi
Gentiles . . 4. Paul
Germany . . 8. Boniface
Goths . . 7. Ulfilas
Indies . . 6. Xavier
Ireland . . 7. Patrick
Rome . . 4. Neri
Apostle to the Indians . . . 5. Eliot

apostolic . . . 5. faith, papal 6. gospel
8. Biblical 9. evangelic 10. pontifical,
scriptural

apostrophe . . . 8. squiggle 9. soliloquy

apothecary . . . 8. druggist, gallipot
9. dispenser 10. pharmacist, posologist
13. pharmaceutist 14. pharmacologist

apothecary measure . . . 4. dram, pint
5. minim, ounce

apothecary weight . . . 4. dram 5. grain,
ounce, pound 7. scruple

apothegm . . . 3. saw 4. dict 5. adage,
axiom, gnome, maxim 6. dictum,
saying 7. precept 8. aphorism

apotheosis . . . 5. ideal 10. exaltation
11. deification, ennoblement, idolization
12. resurrection 13. dignification,
glorification, magnification
14. aggrandizement

apotheosize . . . 5. deify, exalt 7. ennoble,
glorify, idolize 8. enshrine
11. immortalize

appall, appal . . . 3. awe 5. shock
6. dismay

appalling . . . 4. grim 5. awful 7. awesome,
fearful 8. dreadful, shocking, terrible,
terrific 9. frightful 10. remarkable

appalto . . . 8. monopoly

appanage . . . 7. adjunct, pendant
8. property 9. appendage, endowment
10. perquisite 11. prerogative
12. appurtenance

apparatus . . . 4. gear, tool 6. outfit
7. machine, rigging, trapeze 8. recorder
9. appliance, equipment, mechanism,
trappings 10. instrument
13. paraphernalia

apparatus (pert to) . . .

distillation . . 7. alembic
dyeing . . 4. ager
heating . . 4. etna 5. stove 6. boiler
7. furnace 8. radiator
hoisting . . 3. pry 4. jack 5. davit, lever,
lewis 7. capstan, derrick
planetarium . . 6. orrery
steering . . 4. helm 5. wheel 6. rudder,
tiller
water . . 4. pump 5. noria 6. faucet,
siphon, tremie

apparel . . . 3. alb 4. deck, duds, garb,
gear, togs, wear 5. dress, equip, habit
6. attire 7. clothes, costume, garment,
raiment, toggery, vesture 8. clothing,
fatigues 10. garmenture 11. habiliments

apparent . . . 4. open 5. clear, overt, plain
6. patent, visual 7. certain, evident,
obvious, seeable, seeming, visible
8. distinct, illusory, manifest, specious
9. notorious, plausible 10. ostensible
11. discernible, indubitable, perceivable,
superficial 12. recognizable

apparently . . . 7. visibly 9. evidently,
obviously, seemingly 10. manifestly,
presumably, speciously 11. perceptibly

apparition . . . 4. bogy, form 5. ghost,
shade, spook 6. shadow, spirit, sprite,
vision, wraith 7. eidolon, fantasy,
phantom, specter (spectre) 8. illusion,
phantasm, revenant 9. hobgoblin
10. appearance, phenomenon,
revelation

appassionato . . . 9. emotional
11. impassioned

appeal . . . 3. beg, cry 4. call, cite,
plea, pray, suit 5. charm, plead
6. avouch, invoke, prayer 7. address,
beseech, entreat, implore, request,
solicit 8. entreaty, petition 9. importune
10. lovability, loveliness, supplicate
11. winsomeness 12. supplication

appealing . . . 4. nice 7. winsome
8. alluring, charming, engaging,
pleasant 9. agreeable, glamorous,
imploring 10. attractive, beseeching,
bewitching, delightful, enchanting,
entreating 11. fascinating, interesting

appear . . . 4. loom, seem 5. occur
6. arrive, attend, emerge 11. materialize

appearance . . . 3. air 4. form, look, mien
5. front, guise, looks, phase 6. aspect,
format, manner, ostent 7. arrival,
feature, specter (spectre) 8. illusion,
presence, pretense 9. emergence,
semblance 10. apparition, disclosure,
revelation 11. resemblance
13. manifestation

appearance (pert to) . . .
book . . 6. format
brief . . 5. cameo
false . . 8. disguise
first . . 4. dawn 5. debut 8. premiere
frontal . . 6. facade
surface . . 6. patina
truth (appearance of) . . 14. verisimilitude
white . . 6. pallid

appease . . . 4. calm 5. allay, atone,
mease, quiet, salve 6. pacify, soothe
7. content, placate, relieve, satisfy
8. mitigate 10. conciliate 11. tranquilize

appeasement . . . 6. relief 7. salving
8. easement 10. compromise,
mitigation, palliation 12. pacification

appellation . . . 3. tag 4. name 5. label,
style, title 7. calling, epithet
8. cognomen, nickname 9. sobriquet
11. designation 12. denomination,
nomenclature 14. identification

append . . . 3. add 4. hang 5. affix,
annex 6. adjoin, attach 7. subjoin
11. superimpose

appendage . . . 3. arm, awn, cue, tab,
tag 4. barb, flap, lobe, tail 5. cauda,
queue 6. ligule (Bot), palpus 7. adjunct,
pigtail 8. addition, hanger-on, pendicle
9. accessory, tailpiece 10. dependency
12. appurtenance 13. accompaniment

appendix . . . 6. sequel 7. codicil, process
8. addendum, addition 9. accessory,
appendage 10. dependency
12. augmentation

appertain . . . 4. bear 5. apply 6. affect,
belong, regard, relate 7. involve, pertain

appetite . . . 4. zest 5. taste 6. desire,
hunger, orexis, thirst 7. longing, passion
8. cupidity 9. appetency 10. hungriness,
propensity

appetizer . . . 4. fish (sauce) 6. canape
8. antepast, aperitif 9. antipasto,
foretaste 11. hors d'oeuvre

appetizing . . . 6. savory 7. piquant
8. tempting 9. appealing, desirable
10. attractive 11. captivating,
provocative, tantalizing

applaud . . . 4. clap, hail, laud, root,
yell 5. cheer, extol, shout 6. hurrah,
praise 7. acclaim, approve, commend,
endorse 10. compliment

applauders (paid) . . . 6. claque 8. clappers
9. claqueurs

applause . . . 4. clap, hand 5. bravo, éclat,
huzza 6. encore, praise 7. acclaim,
ovation 8. plaudits 11. acclamation
12. commendation

apple . . . 3. May, Spy 4. crab, pome
6. annona, pippin, rennet, russet
7. Baldwin, codling (codlin), costard,
Newtown, Roxbury, winesap
8. Greening, Jonathan, Mandrake,
McIntosh, queening 9. astrachan,
Delicious 10. bellflower, Rome Beauty
11. Granny Smith, Gravenstein,
Northern Spy

apple (pert to) . . .
acid . . 5. malic
brandy . . 8. Calvados
crushed . . 6. pomace
dessert . . 6. brown betty
disease . . 7. stippen
genus . . 5. Malus
juice . . 5. cider 9. applejack
love . . 6. tomato
seed . . 3. pip
shaped . . 8. pomiform

Apple of Discord (Gr Myth) . . . 4. Eris

apple of one's eye . . . 3. pet 4. idol
5. jewel, pupil 7. darling, desired
8. favorite 10. preference

applesauce . . . 4. bunk, pooh 5. tripe
6. phooey 7. baloney, hogwash
8. malarkey, nonsense, tommyrot

12. fiddlesticks 13. horsefeathers

appliance . . . 3. dam (dental) 4. tool
6. device, gadget 7. utensil 8. facility
9. commodity, implement
10. instrument 11. application,
contraption, convenience

applicable . . . 3. apt, fit 6. usable
7. pliable 8. apposite, relative, relevant
9. compliant, pertinent 11. appropriate

application . . . 3. use 6. appeal, effort
7. bearing, concern, request 8. petition,
recourse 9. attention, constancy,
diligence, relevance, relevancy
10. connection, employment, pertinence
11. attribution, disposition,
engrossment, persistence, requisition
12. perseverance 14. administration

application (body) . . . 4. balm 5. salve,
stupe (hot) 7. plaster 8. cosmetic,
poultice

apply . . . 3. use 4. suit 6. appose,
bestow, comply, devote, employ, relate
7. solicit, utilize 9. associate, attribute
10. administer 11. appropriate

appoggiatura . . . 9. grace note
13. embellishment

appoint . . . 3. fix 4. name 5. equip
6. assign, decree, depute, detail, ordain
7. destine, prepare 8. delegate, deputize
9. designate, establish, prescribe
10. constitute

appointment . . . 4. date 5. order, tryst
7. command 8. position 9. direction,
equipment, ordinance 10. engagement
11. designation 13. establishment

appointments . . . 6. things 8. fittings,
fixtures 9. equipment, furniture
10. belongings, upholstery
11. acquirement, furnishings
12. accumulation, conveniences
13. accoutrements, paraphernalia

apportion . . . 3. fix, lot 4. deal, dele,
mete, part 5. allot, carve, share
6. assign, budget, divide 7. arrange,
dispose 8. allocate 9. collocate, partition
10. distribute

appose . . . 4. abut 5. audit, liken,
place 6. adjoin 7. compare, examine
9. juxtapose

apposite . . . 3. apt 4. like 5. close, match
6. timely 7. fitting, germane 8. position,
relative, relevant 9. pertinent
11. appropriate

appraise . . . 4. mark, rank, rate 5. assay,
gauge, judge, price, value 6. assess,
evalue, praise 7. apprise, commend,
measure 8. consider, estimate, evaluate
10. adjudicate, appreciate

appraiser (tax) . . . 5. rater 6. lister
8. assessor

appreciable . . . 3. any 8. tangible
9. estimable 11. perceptible

appreciate . . . 4. feel, grow, know
5. enjoy, prize, savor, value 6. admire,
esteem 7. advance, amplify, approve,
augment, realize, respect 8. estimate,
increase, treasure

appreciation . . . 7. respect 9. appraisal,
awareness, gratitude 10. estimation
11. realization, recognition, sensibility
12. gratefulness, thankfulness

apprehend ... 3. ken, see 4. know, take
5. dread, grasp, pinch (sl), savvy,
seize, sense 6. arrest 7. capture,
imagine, realize 8. conceive, perceive
10. anticipate, comprehend, understand

apprehensible ... 8. knowable
9. scrutable 10. explicable, fathomable
11. accountable 12. discoverable,
intelligible 14. comprehensible,
understandable

apprehension ... 4. fear, idea 5. alarm,
doubt, dread, qualm 6. arrest 7. anxiety,
capture, concern, opinion, seizure
8. distress, distrust, suspense
9. misgiving, suspicion 10. foreboding,
solicitude, uneasiness 11. fearfulness,
premonition 12. intelligence
13. understanding

apprehensive ... 5. smart 6. uneasy
7. alarmed, fearful, knowing, nervous,
worried 8. troubled 9. cognizant,
concerned, conscious, perturbed
10. perceptive, solicitous

apprentice ... 4. tyro 6. novice
7. amateur, trainee 8. beginner

apprize, apprise ... 4. rate, tell 5. price,
value 6. advise, assess, impart, inform,
reckon 8. acquaint, appraise 9. enlighten
11. communicate

apprized ... 5. aware 8. informed
9. cognizant

approach ... 3. way 4. adit, come, near,
road 5. stalk, verge 6. access, accost,
advent, impend 7. arrival, nearing, sea
gate 8. entryway, likeness, nearness,
overture, resemble 11. approximate,
entranceway

approachable ... 4. open 8. gettable,
passable 9. reachable 10. accessible,
attainable 13. communicative

approbation ... 5. favor, proof 6. praise
7. plaudit 8. applause, approval,
sanction 10. acceptance, admiration
12. commendation, confirmation

appropriate ... 3. apt, fit 4. akin,
meet, take 5. allot, steal, usurp
6. borrow, pirate, proper, timely,
worthy 7. condign, germane, related,
special 8. deserved, relevant, suitable
9. befitting, expedient, favorable,
opportune, pertinent 10. assimilate,
monopolize, plagiarize 11. conformable

appropriately ... 4. duly 5. aptly 6. timely

appropriation ... 5. theft 6. corner,
taking 8. monopoly 9. allotment
10. assignment, possession, usurpation

approval ... 6. assent 7. consent,
support 8. sanction 10. admiration
11. approbation, endorsement
12. ratification

approve ... 2. OK 4. like, okay, pass, sign,
test 6. attest, ratify 7. applaud, betoken,
certify, confirm, endorse (indorse),
signify 8. accredit, sanction, validate
9. authorize, undersign 10. appreciate
11. countenance 12. authenticate

approve of ... 5. favor 6. accept
7. endorse (indorse) 8. sanction
11. countenance

approximate ... 4. near 5. about, circa,
match 8. approach, draw near, parallel,

resemble 10. correspond

approximately ... 4. or so 5. about, circa
6. around, nearly 11. thereabouts

appui ... 4. prop, stay 6. bridle (manège)
7. support

appulse ... 6. syzygy 7. impinge
8. approach 9. collision 11. conjunction
(Astron)

appurtenance ... 4. gear 7. adjunct
8. addition 9. accessory, apparatus,
appendage, belonging, component

appurtenant ... 7. annexed 8. incident,
relevant 9. appendant, belonging
11. appropriate

après ... 5. after 10. afterwards

apricot (pert to) ...
   African .. 6. meebos (dried)
   beverage .. 7. cordial, liqueur, persico
   color .. 9. red-yellow
   confection .. 6. meebos (mebos)
   Japanese .. 3. ume 4. ansu
   vine .. 6. maypop

a priori (opp of posteriori) ... 9. deductive
11. conditional, presumptive
12. hypothetical 13. presumptively

apron ... 3. bib 4. boot, brat, tier 5. smock
6. barvel (barvell), runway 7. garment,
tablier 8. airstrip, lambskin (Masonic),
pinafore 9. appendage

apropos, à propos ... 3. apt, pat
7. germane, purpose 8. by the
way, relevant, suitably 9. pertinent
10. applicable, seasonable
11. appurtenant, opportunely
12. incidentally

apt ... 3. fit, pat 4. deft 5. adept,
prone, ready, smart 6. clever, expert,
likely, prompt, suited 7. capable,
elegant, subject 8. apposite, disposed,
inclined, skillful, suitable 9. competent,
dexterous, ingenious, masterful,
pertinent, qualified, teachable
10. proficient 11. appropriate

apteral ... 8. apterous, wingless

Apteryx ... 3. moa (extinct) 4. kiwi

aptitude ... 3. art 4. bent, gift, turn 5. flair,
skill 6. genius, talent 7. ability, aptness,
fitness, leaning 8. penchant, tendency
9. liability 10. likelihood, proclivity
11. inclination 12. suitableness
15. appropriateness

aptly ... 7. exactly, readily 8. suitably
11. pertinently

aptness ... 5. skill 7. fitness 8. tendency
9. smartness 11. suitability
12. teachability

aqua ... 3. eau 4. agua 5. water

aquatic ... 6. natant, wading, watery
8. natatory, swimming 12. grallatorial
13. water-dwelling

Aquila ... 6. eagles 13. constellation
(Milky Way)

aquiline ... 6. hanate, hooked 7. curving
8. aduncous, unciform 10. Roman-
nosed

ara ... 5. macaw 7. goddess (vengeance)
8. aracanga 9. screw pine
13. constellation

Arab ... 4. waif 5. gamin, horse,
nomad 6. Semite 7. Bedouin, Saracen
8. wanderer, Yemenite 9. Caucasian

araba . . . 3. cab 5. coach 6. monkey (howling)

Arabia . . . see *Saudi-Arabia*

Arabian (pert to) . . .
antelope . . 5. addax
beverage . . 4. boza (bosa) 5. leban (lebban)
bird . . 7. phoenix
chief . . 5. sheik
cloth (shoulder) . . 6. cabaan (caban)
demon . . 5. Eblis, jinni (jinnee) 6. afreet
father . . 3. Abu (Ab, Abou) 4. Abba
garment . . 3. aba 4. haik 8. burnoose
gazelle . . 4. cora, oryx 5. ariel
horse . . 4. Kohl 8. kadischi, palomino
jasmine . . 4. bela
judge . . 4. cadi
juniper (Bib) . . 5. retem
nomad . . 7. Saracen
peasant . . 6. fellah
people (anc) . . 3. Aus
physician . . 8. Avicenna
poet . . 5. Antar
prince . . 4. emir (amir) 5. emeer (ameer), sheik 6. sherif, sultan
ravine . . 4. wadi
romance . . 5. Antar (Antara)
ruler . . 6. caliph (calif)
Satan . . 5. Eblis 6. Azazel
scripture . . 7. Alcoran
seaport . . 4. Aden 5. Mocha
state of bliss . . 3. kef (kaif)
street urchin . . 5. gamin
tambourine . . 4. taar
vessel . . 4. dhow 6. boutre, sambuk
winds (hot) . . 6. simoom (simoon)

Arabic letter . . . 4. alif

arable land . . . 4. farm 5. arada, arado 6. plowed, tilled 10. cultivated

arachnid . . . 4. mite, tick 6. spider 8. scorpion 9. Arachnida

Aralu . . . 5. Hades

Aram . . . 6. Rimmon (deity) 7. Aramaic, Semitic 8. language

araneous . . . 4. thin 7. weblike 8. delicate 10. cobweblike

arapunga . . . 8. bellbird 9. campanero

Arawak . . . 5. Guana 6. Indian

arbeit . . . 4. work 8. research

arbiter . . . 3. ump 5. judge 6. umpire 7. arbiter, referee 8. mediator 9. moderator 10. arbitrator

arbitrary . . . 6. thetic 7. absolute, despotic, dogmatic 9. imperious, unlimited 10. autocratic, capricious, high-handed, peremptory, tyrannical 11. determinate, dictatorial 13. discretionary

arbitrate . . . 6. decide 7. bargain, mediate 9. determine, intervene, negotiate 12. intermediate

arbitrator . . . 5. judge 6. umpire 7. arbiter, referee 8. mediator 9. moderator 11. conciliator

arbor, arbour . . . 5. bower, kiosk 6. alcove, garden, pandal 7. pergola, retreat, trellis 11. latticework, summerhouse

arboreal . . . 6. ramous 8. branched, treelike 10. arboriform

arboreal mammal . . . 2. ai 4. unau 5. lemur, sloth 6. aye-aye, monkey

arc . . . 3. bow 5. curve 6. radian 7. azimuth, rainbow

arca . . . 3. box 5. chest, paten 9. reliquary

arcade . . . 3. orb 4. arch, hall 6. arches, avenue 7. gallery, portico 8. arcature, corridor 9. colonnade, peristyle 10. passageway

Arcadia . . .
composition . . 4. poem 5. prose 7. romance
district . . 6. Greece
huntress . . 8. Atalanta
pert to . . 5. rural 6. rustic 8. pastoral
poetic . . 6. Arcady
priestess . . 4. Auge
woodland spirit . . 3. Pan

arcanum . . . 6. elixir, enigma, remedy, secret 7. mystery

arch . . . 3. arc, sly 4. ogee 5. chief, hance (part), ogive, vault 6. fornix, instep 7. cunning, eminent, roguish 8. greatest, memorial, monument 9. principal 11. mischievous

arch (pert to) . . .
enemy . . 5. devil, Satan 9. adversary
inner curve . . 8. intrados
memorial . . 6. pailou (pailoo)
stone . . 8. keystone
title . . 4. duke 6. bishop, deacon 7. duchess

archaic . . . 3. old 8. obsolete, old-world 10. antiquated 13. old-fashioned

archangel (celestial) . . . 5. Uriel 7. Gabriel, Michael, Raphael

archangel plant . . . 4. mint 8. angelica

archbishop . . . 6. bishop (chief), exarch 9. patriarch

arched . . . 6. curved 7. embowed

Archer (Astron) . . . 11. Sagittarius

archery . . . 3. bow 4. vane 5. arrow, clout 6. quiver 8. fistmele, shooting 10. ballistics

archetype . . . 4. idea 5. model 7. pattern 8. standard 9. prototype

Archie (sl) . . . 3. gun 12. antiaircraft

Archipelago (pert to) . . .
Alaska . . 9. Alexander
Australia . . 8. Bismarck
Indonesia (largest) . . 5. Malay
Italy . . 6. Aegean

architect . . . 6. artist, author 7. builder, planner 8. designer 9. artificer, draftsman 11. constructor, enterpriser

architectural (pert to) . . .
arch . . 8. keystone, voussoir
base . . 5. socle 6. plinth
construction . . 8. tectonic
ornament (part) . . 5. gutta 6. bezant, finial, frieze 8. acanthus, dosseret, fretwork 10. chambranle
pier . . 4. anta
space (triang) . . 8. pediment
style . . 5. Doric, Greek, Ionic, Tudor 6. Gothic 7. Baroque, Cape Cod, Moorish, Spanish 8. Colonial, Etruscan, Georgian 9. Byzantine, Palladian 10. Corinthian, Romanesque 11. Renaissance 13. Mediterranean

archives . . . 6. annals 7. records 8. chancery, registry 9. documents, registers 10. chronicles

arch traitor . . . 6. Arnold (Benedict), Brutus 8. Quisling 13. Judas Iscariot

archway . . . 6. pailou (pailoo)

arctic . . . 5. polar 6. boreal, frigid, galosh 7. Alaskan 8. hibernal, Northern, Siberian 11. hyperborean

Arctic (pert to) . . .
  base . . 4. Etah (Greenland)
  bird . . 3. auk 4. skua, xema 6. falcon
  cetacean . . 7. narwhal
  current . . 8. Labrador
  dog . . 5. Husky (Siberian) 8. Malemute
  food . . 8. pemmican (pemican)
  jacket (hooded) . . 5. parka (parkee) 6. anorak
  native . . 5. Aleut 6. Eskimo, Indian
  polar . . 6. Circle
  sea . . 7. Barents 8. Beaufort

arctoid . . . 6. ursine 8. bearlike

Arctoidea . . . 4. bear 6. weasel 7. raccoon

ardent . . . 3. hot 4. avid, keen, warm 5. eager, fiery, rethe 6. fervid, fierce 7. amorous, cordial, fervent, flaming, glowing, intense, shining, violent, zealous 8. eloquent, vehement 10. passionate 12. affectionate, enthusiastic

ardilla . . . 8. squirrel

ardor . . . 4. élan, fire, heat, love, zeal 5. estro, flame, gusto, verve 6. fervor, fougue, spirit, warmth 8. fervency 9. affection, eagerness, eloquence, intensity 10. enthusiasm 11. impetuosity

arduous . . . 4. hard 5. steep 6. trying 7. onerous 8. toilsome 9. difficult, laborious, strenuous, wearisome 10. burdensome, exhausting

area . . . 4. belt, loci (pl), size, zone 5. areal, basin, field, locus, range, scope, space, tract 6. extent, locale, region, sector, sphere 7. circuit, compass, environ, expanse 8. province, vicinity 9. bailiwick, territory 12. neighborhood

Areca . . . 4. palm

arena . . . 4. bowl, oval, ring, rink 5. court, field 6. campus, circus 7. cockpit, stadium, theater 8. coliseum, platform 9. gymnasium 10. hippodrome 12. amphitheater

arenose . . . 5. sandy 6. grainy, gritty 8. sabulous

areola . . . 4. halo, ring 5. space 6. armlet, wreath 7. aureole, garland 10. interstice

Ares (pert to) . . .
  consort . . 9. Aphrodite
  father . . 4. Zeus
  god . . 3. war
  Roman name . . 4. Mars

argala . . . 7. marabou 8. adjutant (bird)

argent . . . 5. white 6. silver 7. shining, silvery 8. whiteness

Argentina . . .
  capital . . 11. Buenos Aires (1535)
  city . . 5. Lanus 6. Paraná 7. Cordoba, Mendoza, Rosario
  Indian . . 4. Lule
  mountain . . 5. Andes 9. Aconcagua (peak) 10. Cordillera (Range)
  native . . 7. Mestizo
  Plains . . 6. Pampas 9. Gran Chaco
  plateau . . 9. Patagonia

  poet . . 7. Andrade 10. Echeverria
  river . . 5. Plata 6. Chubut, Paraná

Argentine (pert to) . . .
  color . . 7. silvery 8. art brown
  cowboy . . 6. gaucho
  dance . . 5. tango

Argonauts (pert to) . . .
  destination . . 7. Colchis (anc)
  leader . . 5. Jason
  objective . . 12. Golden Fleece
  of '49 . . 6. miners (gold)
  ship . . 5. Argos
  sorceress . . 5. Medea

Argos . . . 3. dog (of Odysseus)

argosy . . . 4. ship 5. fleet 6. armada, vessel 8. flotilla

argot . . . 4. cant, jive 5. lingo, slang 6. jargon, patois 7. dialect 10. vernacular

argue . . . 3. rap 4. moot, spar 5. plead, prove 6. bicker, debate, evince, reason 7. contend, contest, discuss, dispute, wrangle 8. indicate, maintain, persuade 10. controvert 11. expostulate, ratiocinate, remonstrate

argument . . . 4. case, plea, spar 5. cavil, lemma, proof, theme 6. debate, hassle 7. defense, dispute, fallacy, polemic, premise, sophism 8. brouhaha, squabble 9. dialectic, discourse, enthymeme, pro and con 10. discussion 11. altercation, disputation 13. consideration, ratiocination

argumentative . . . 7. eristic 8. forensic 10. indicative, rhetorical 11. belligerent, contentious, presumptive, quarrelsome 12. disputatious 13. controversial

Argus (Gr Myth) . . . 7. monster (founder of Argos)

Argus-eyed . . . 8. vigilant 9. observant 11. hundred-eyed 12. sharpsighted

argute . . . 5. acute, sharp 6. astute, shrewd, shrill, subtle 9. sagacious

aria . . . 3. air, lay 4. solo, song, tune 5. canto 6. cantus, melody, strain 7. ariette, sortita

arid . . . 3. dry 4. dull 6. barren, jejune, vacant 7. parched, sterile, thirsty 9. anhydrous, waterless 13. unimaginative

Arid Austral zone . . . 7. Sonoran

Ariel . . . 5. angel, sylph 6. spirit 7. lioness 9. Jerusalem

ariel . . . 7. gazelle

Aries (Astron) . . . 3. ram 4. sign 6. meteor 13. constellation

aries . . . 12. battering-ram (anc)

aright . . . 4. fine, well 7. exactly 8. directly, straight 11. straightway

aril . . . 3. pod 7. arillus, coating 8. arillode (false), covering

Arion . . . 4. poet (of Lesbos) 5. horse (talking)

arioso . . . 7. melodic, tuneful 9. melodious

arise . . . 4. lift, rise, soar, stem, zoom 5. begin, issue, mount, occur, rebel, surge, tower, waken 6. appear, ascend, emerge, revolt, spring 7. emanate 8. originate

Aristarch . . . 6. critic 10. grammarian

Aristides . . . 7. The Just 9. statesman

(Athens)

aristocracy . . . 5. elite 7. peerage, royalty 8. nobility 10. government, patriciate, upper class

aristocrat . . . 4. lord, peer 5. noble 7. aristos, Brahman, Brahmin, grandee, parvenu 8. cavalier, eupatrid (Athens), nobleman 9. blueblood, patrician 12. silk-stocking

aristology, science of . . . 6. dining

Aristole (pert to) . . .
  birthplace . . 6. Thrace 7. Stagira (Macedonia)
  famed as . . 9. scientist 11. philosopher 12. The Stagirite
  school . . 6. Athens
  teacher . . 5. Plato
  wife . . 7. Pythias

arithmetic . . . 4. sums 7. numbers 11. computation, enumeration, mathematics

arithmetic terms . . . 5. prime 6. result 7. divisor, product 8. dividend, multiple, quotient 9. remainder 10. multiplier 12. multiplicand

Arizona . . .
  capital . . 7. Phoenix
  city . . 4. Yuma 5. Tempe 6. Bisbee, Tucson
  famed site . . 9. Hoover Dam 11. Grand Canyon 13. Painted Desert 15. Petrified Forest
  Indian . . 4. Hano, Hopi, Pima 6. Apache, Navaho (Navajo)
  river . . 4. Gila 8. Colorado
  State admission . . 11. Forty-eighth
  State bird . . 10. cactus wren
  State flower . . 6. cactus 7. saguaro
  State motto . . 9. Ditat Deus 11. God Enriches
  State nickname . . 11. Grand Canyon

ark . . . 3. vat 4. boat, ship 5. chest, haven 6. asylum, refuge, vessel 8. flatboat 9. broadhorn, sanctuary (Ararat)

Arkansas . . .
  capital . . 10. Little Rock
  city . . 8. El Dorado 9. Fort Smith
  famed for . . 8. diamonds (found in Murfreesboro)
  famed newspaper . . 7. Gazette (1819)
  mountain . . 6. Ozarks 9. Ouachitas
  river . . 5. White 11. Mississippi
  State admission . . 11. Twenty-fifth
  State bird . . 11. mockingbird
  State flower . . 12. apple blossom
  State motto . . 13. Regnat Populus 16. Let the People Rule
  State nickname . . 17. Land of Opportunity

arm . . . 4. limb 5. equip, saber, sword 6. branch, member, pistol, tappet, weapon 7. forearm, fortify, protect, quillon (of sword), support 8. revolver 9. appendage 10. projection 12. ramification

arm (pert to) . . .
  armpit . . 5. oxter 6. axilla
  bone . . 4. ulna 6. radius 7. humerus
  hole . . 4. scye (of sleeve)
  muscle . . 6. biceps 7. triceps 8. pronator

  9. supinator
  projection . . 6. tappet
  sea . . 4. gulf, mere 5. bayou, firth, inlet 7. estuary
  sundial . . 6. gnomon
  walk arm in arm . . 5. oxter

armada . . . 5. fleet 6. argosy 8. armament, flotilla, squadron, warships 10. escadrille

Armada (famed) . . . 7. Spanish (1588) 10. Invincible

armadillo . . . 4. apar, peba (peva) 5. apara, poyou, tatou (tatu) 6. mulita, peludo (giant) 7. tatouay 10. pichiciago, Tolypeutes 11. quirquincho (hairy)

Armageddon . . . 3. war 7. Megiddo (Bib) 8. conflict, world war

armed . . . 6. fitted, rigged 7. clothed, endowed 8. equipped, invested, prepared, provided, supplied 9. furnished, outfitted 10. laquearian (with noose)

armed (pert to) . . .
  conflict . . 3. war 6. combat 7. warfare 11. hostilities
  forces . . 4. army, host 5. ranks 6. troops 8. military 9. besiegers
  vessel . . 3. HMS, sub, USS 5. U-boat 9. destroyer, submarine 10. battleship 11. battlewagon

Armenia . . .
  anc name . . 9. Armenenak
  capital . . 6. Erivan
  founder . . 4. Haik
  herb . . 5. cumin 7. caraway
  highlanders . . 5. Gomer
  mountain . . 6. Ararat, Taurus
  river . . 3. Kur 5. Cyrus 6. Araxes, Tigris 9. Euphrates
  worshiper . . 7. Yesidio (Yesdi) 9. Gregorian

armistice . . . 5. peace, truce 9. cessation 12. pacification

armoire . . . 5. ambry 8. cupboard, wardrobe 10. repository

armor . . . 4. arms, bard (barde), egis, jamb, mail, tace 5. acton, aegis, plate, seton, tasse 6. cuisse, gorget, graith, greave, helmet, lorica, sconce, shield, tasset, tuille 7. ailette, cuirass, hauberk, jambeau, panoply 8. aventail, brassort, ordnance, pallette, solleret 9. cubitiere, epauliere, gardebras, mainferre, rerebrace 10. cataphract

armor-bearer . . . 6. squire 7. armiger, esquire

armored . . . 6. mailed 8. equipped, ironclad, mailclad 9. cuirassed, loricated, panoplied

armpit . . . 5. oxter 6. axilla

arms . . . 7. weapons 8. armament, ordnance 9. munitions

arms depository . . . 5. depot 6. armory 7. arsenal

army . . . 3. mob 4. host, unit 5. array, crowd, horde, posse 6. forces, galaxy, legion, rabble, throng, troops 9. multitude, Salvation

army (pert to) . . .
  brown . . 7. rosario
  commission (special) . . 6. brevet

trader .. 6. sutler
army unit ... 4. ROTC 5. corps, guard
(Nat), squad 7. brigade, cavalry,
company, militia, platoon, Sabaoth
(Bib) 8. division, infantry, Landwehr,
regiment, reserves 9. artillery, battalion,
minutemen 10. volunteers
Arnold's co-conspirator ... 5. Andre
(Maj)
aroma ... 4. musk, odor, tang 5. attar,
balmy, nidor, savor, scent, smell, spice
6. flavor 7. bouquet, feature, incense,
perfume 9. fragrance, muskiness,
redolence 11. peculiarity, singularity
aromatic ... 5. spicy 6. savory 7. odorous,
pungent 8. fragrant, redolent
11. fluorescent
aromatic (pert to) ...
gum .. 5. myrrh 12. frankincense
herb .. 4. mint 5. clary, nondo
oil .. 4. balm 6. balsam 9. sassafras
seed .. 4. anis 6. nutmeg 7. aniseed,
caraway
tree .. 5. aromo 6. balsam 7. champac
8. huisache
around ... 4. near, peri (pref) 5. about,
circa 9. bordering, somewhere
11. thereabouts 13. approximately
arouse ... 4. fire, stir, wake 5. alarm,
anger, evoke, pique, raise, rally, roust
6. awaken, elicit, excite, incite, kindle,
summon 7. animate
arpa ... 4. harp
arpeggio ... 5. chord 7. roulade
8. division, flourish
arraign ... 4. cite 6. accuse, charge, indict
7. impeach 8. denounce, reproach
9. prosecute
arrange ... 3. fix 4. cast, cite, file,
plan, plot, sort 5. adapt, aline, besee,
drape, ettle, frame, grade, preen,
range, stack 6. adjust, deploy, design,
devise 7. dispose, mediate, prepare,
provide, seriate 8. classify, contract,
contrive, laminate, organize, tabulate
9. catalogue (catalog), negotiate
10. distribute, paniculate
11. alphabetize, systematize
arranged ... 5. fixed, timed 6. ranked,
sorted 7. aligned, grouped, ordered,
orderly, planned, settled, uniform
9. regulated 10. contracted
arranged in ...
fives .. 7. quinate
fours .. 11. tetramerous
hours .. 9. staggered
rays .. 6. radial
threes .. 7. ternate
arrangement ... 3. art, rig (sails)
4. plan, rank 5. order, setup 6. series,
syntax, system 7. echelon (troops),
musical 8. disposal, neatness, trimness
9. agreement, condition, structure
10. adaptation, engagement, settlement
11. collocation, combination,
permutation, preparation
12. distribution
arrant ... 3. bad 6. wicked 8. rascally
9. confirmed, shameless
11. unmitigated 12. disreputable
array ... 3. don 4. deci, robe 5. adorn,

align, dress, order 6. clothe, muster,
series, throng 7. arrange, dispose,
envelop, marshal 8. clothing, garments
9. adornment 11. arrangement
arrears ... 3. due 4. debt 5. short
7. wanting 9. arrearage, deficient
10. behindhand, defaulting
arrest ... 4. halt, hold, stop 5. check,
delay, seize 6. detain, hinder, impede,
retard 7. custody, seizure 8. obstruct,
restrain, stoppage 9. apprehend,
hindrance, intercept, restraint
11. retardation
arrested ... 6. behind 7. checked, delayed,
impeded, stopped 8. detained, retarded
10. restrained 11. intercepted
arrested development ... 6. simple
7. dwarfed, idiotic, moronic
8. backward, retarded 10. half-witted
13. unintelligent
arrival ... 5. comer (anc) 6. advent,
coming 7. landing 8. approach,
reaching 10. attainment, homecoming
11. achievement
arrive ... 4. come 5. debus, reach 6. alight,
debark, happen 7. detrain 9. disembark
arrogance ... 5. pride 7. conceit,
disdain, hauteur 8. audacity, rudeness,
snobbery 9. brashness, insolence,
loftiness 10. effrontery 11. haughtiness
12. impertinence
arrogant ... 4. bold, pert 5. cocky, lofty,
proud 6. lordly, uppish 7. forward
8. impudent, insolent 9. audacious,
insulting, masterful, presuming
10. disdainful 11. domineering, highfalutin, impertinent, overbearing
12. contemptuous, contumelious,
presumptuous, supercilious
arrogate ... 5. seize, usurp, wrest
6. assume 11. appropriate
arrow ... 4. barb, dart, reed, vire
(feathered) 5. guide, shaft 6. finger
7. missile, pointer 10. guideboard
arrow (pert to) ...
astronomy .. 7. Sagitta
bows .. 6. bowyer (maker, seller)
case .. 6. quiver
end .. 4. nock 9. arrowhead
feather (to) .. 6. fletch
handle .. 5. stele
head .. 4. dart
poison .. 4. inee, upas 5. urali 6. curare,
uzarin
poisoned .. 6. sumpit 8. sumpitan
propeller .. 3. bow
shape .. 6. beloid 9. cuneiform, sagittate
stone .. 6. belemnite
variety .. 4. self 6. footed 7. chested
9. bobtailed
arrowroot ... 3. pia 5. araru 6. ararao,
starch 7. Maranta
arroyo ... 5. brook, creek 6. ravine,
stream 11. watercourse
arroz ... 4. rice
arse ... 4. butt, rump (vulgar) 8. buttocks
9. posterior
arsenal ... 4. dump 5. depot, plant
6. armory 7. factory 8. magazine
10. depository, storehouse
arsis ... 5. ictus 6. accent, stress (opp

of thesis), upbeat

arson . . . 7. burning, cautery 9. pyromania
12. incendiarism

art . . . 4. wile 5. cameo, craft, knack, skill,
taste, trade 6. design 7. calling, cartoon,
cunning, drawing, science 8. aptitude,
artifice, artistry, business, ceramics,
drafting, intaglio, painting, vocation
9. dexterity, duplicate, engraving,
ingenuity, readiness, sculpture,
sketching 10. adroitness, decoration,
profession 11. contrivance,
photography, portraiture
12. architecture

art (pert to) . . .
addict . . 8. aesthete (esthete)
decoration . . 9. sgraffito
design . . 7. graphic
fancier . . 10. dilettante
gallery . . 5. salon
grotesque . . 11. incongruous
mystic . . 6. cabala
of assaying . . 8. docimasy
of discourse . . 8. rhetoric
of embossing . . 9. toreutics
of government . . 8. politics
of horsemanship . . 6. manège
of imitation . . 7. mimicry
of manual craft . . 5. sloyd
of memory . . 10. mnemonics
of metal inlay . . 6. niello
primitive . . 9. artifacts
realistic . . 5. genre
rhyming . . 5. poesy 6. poetry
self-defense . . 6. boxing 7. fencing,
jujitsu (jiujitsu)
style, movement . . 3. pop 6. cubism,
rococo 7. baroque, Bauhaus, Dadaism,
Fauvism 8. futurism 9. modernism
10. surrealism 11. romanticism
13. expressionism, impressionism
theme . . 5. motif
tooling . . 10. diesinking
transmutation . . 7. alchemy

Artemis (pert to) . . .
brother (twin) . . 6. Apollo
epithet (Homeric) . . 6. Phoebe
father . . 4. Zeus
goddess of . . 4. moon 6. nature 7. the
Hunt 8. Olympian
Mother . . 4. Leto
religion . . 4. Upis
Roman equivalent . . 5. Diana

artery . . . 4. tube, vein 6. avenue, street,
vessel 7. channel, highway, passage
8. ligament 10. passageway

artery (Anat) . . . 4. tube, vein 5. aorta
6. vessel 7. anonyma, carotid, trachea
9. capillary, pulmonary 10. innominate

artery pulsation . . . 4. beat 5. ictus

artful . . . 3. sly 4. foxy, wily 5. cagey
6. adroit, clever, crafty, shrewd,
subtle, tricky 7. crooked, cunning,
knowing, politic 8. skillful, stealthy
9. deceitful, deceptive, designing,
dexterous, imitative 10. artificial

Artful Dodger . . . 3. fox 6. rascal 7. slicker
8. deceiver 11. John Dawkins (Dickens
tale) 12. crafty person

artfulness . . . 5. skill 7. finesse 8. artifice,
subtlety, wiliness 9. stratagem

10. cleverness, refinement, shrewdness

arthron . . . 5. hinge, joint, pivot
12. articulation

Arthurian abode . . . 6. Avalon
9. Lyonnesse (Leonnoys)

Arthurian character . . . 6. Arthur (King),
Elaine, Merlin 7. Geraint 8. Lancelot
9. Percivale

artichoke . . . 6. canada, Cynara
7. chorogi, thistle 9. Jerusalem

article . . . 3. mat 4. item, news, term
5. scoop, story, thing 6. belief,
clause, detail, gadget, object, treaty
7. camelot, feature (news), grammar,
integer 8. treatise 9. commodity
editorial 10. particular 11. composition,
stipulation

article (Gram) . . .
English . . 1. a 2. an 3. the
French . . 2. la, le, un 3. les, une
Spanish . . 2. el, un 3. las, los, una

article (of) . . .
agreement . . 8. contract
apparel . . 5. smock, tunic 6. duster,
gaiter, mantle 8. pinafore
faith . . 5. canon, creed, dogma, tenet
6. belief 7. precept
property . . 7. chattel
virtu . . 5. curio, relic 6. rarity 7. antique

articulation . . . 4. tone 5. hinge, joint,
sound, voice 7. voicing 8. locution,
sonation 9. phonation, utterance
11. enunciation 12. vocalization
13. pronunciation

artifact . . . 5. curio, relic, virtu 6. fossil
7. antique, remains 8. archaism

artifice . . . 3. plot, ruse, wile 5. blind,
chest, craft, dodge, fraud, guile, shift,
trick 6. deceit 7. cunning, evasion,
finesse, knavery, sleight 8. intrigue,
maneuver, trickery 9. chicanery,
collusion, deception, expedient,
imposture, stratagem 10. connivance,
imposition, subterfuge 11. contrivance,
machination, skulduggery

artificer . . . 5. smith 6. artist, framer
7. artisan, creator, deviser, workman
8. Daedalus, inventor, mechanic
9. architect, carpenter, craftsman,
goldsmith 11. coppersmith, silversmith

artificial . . . 4. fake, faux, mock, sham
5. bogus, dummy, false, phony
6. ersatz, forged, unreal 7. assumed,
bastard, elegant, feigned 8. affected,
fabulous, spurious 9. imaginary,
imitation, pretended, unnatural
11. adulterated, counterfeit, unauthentic
12. supposititious

artificial (pert to) . . .
butter . . 4. oleo 13. oleomargarine
channel . . 3. gat 4. leat 5. canal, flume
6. sluice
gum . . 7. dextrin
language . . 2. ro 3. Ido 5. Arulo
7. Volapuk 9. Esperanto 10. Occidental
silk . . 5. nylon, rayon
surface . . 4. rink
voice . . 8. falsetto

artillery . . . 4. army, guns 5. bombs
6. cannon, slings 7. cavalry, gunners,
gunnery, mortars 8. ordnance

9. arbalests, catapults 10. ballistics
artillery (pert to) . . .
emplacement . . 7. battery
fire . . 5. salvo 6. rafale
man . . 6. gunner 8. rifleman, topechee
9. cannoneer, musketeer 11. artillarist
wagon . . 7. battery
artiodactyl . . . (opp of perissodactyl) 2. ox
3. pig 4. deer, goat 5. camel, sheep
6. artiad 7. giraffe 12. hippopotamus
artisan . . . 6. artist, limner 7. painter,
workman 8. mechanic, virtuoso
9. artificer, craftsman
artist . . . 5. rapin (Fr pupil) 6. etcher,
limner, potter 7. artisan, painter
8. designer, sculptor 9. architect,
decorator 10. cartoonist, ceramacist
11. illustrator 12. photographer
artist (pert to) . . .
equipment . . 5. easel 7. palette
8. maquette
sleight of hand . . 4. mage 5. Magus
8. magician 9. alchemist
artiste . . . 5. actor, adept 6. dancer, singer
7. artisan 8. musician 9. performer
artistic . . . 4. pure 6. ornate 7. classic
8. graceful, skillful, tasteful 9. aesthetic
(esthetic), art-minded, beautiful,
exquisite
artistic (pert to) . . .
ardor . . 5. verve 6. spirit
dance . . 6. ballet
quality . . 6. virtue
symbol of the dead . . 5. orant
temperament . . 7. caprice, emotion
artless . . . 4. naif, open, rude 5. frank,
naive 6. candid, simple 7. natural,
sincere 8. ignorant 9. guileless,
ingenuous, unskilled 10. inartistic,
unaffected, uncultured 11. undesigning
15. unsophisticated
artlessness . . . 6. candor 7. naiveté
9. frankness, innocence 11. naturalness
13. ungenuousness
arts (pert to) . . .
liberal . . 7. trivium 10. quadrivium
quadrivium . . 5. music 8. geometry
9. astronomy 10. arithmetic
trivium . . 5. logic 7. grammar 8. rhetoric
aru . . . 6. indeed, really
arui . . . 5. oudad, sheep 7. chamois (Bib)
arum . . . 4. taro 5. calla (lily) 6. starch
9. arrowroot
arx . . . 7. citadel
Aryan (pert to) . . .
God of Fire . . 4. Agni
invader . . 4. Pict
people . . 4. Mede 5. Hindu 9. Caucasian
11. Indo-Iranian
as . . . 3. qua 4. como, than, thus 5. since,
while 7. because, equally, similar
9. similarly
Asa . . 11. King of Judah
asafetida . . . 8. medicine
13. antispasmodic
Asa's son . . . 11. Jehoshaphat
ascend . . . 3. fly 4. rise, soar, upgo
5. arise, climb, mount, scale, tower
6. aspire, uprise 7. clamber, upsurge
ascendancy . . . 4. sway 7. control,
mastery 8. dominion, prestige, priority

9. authority, influence, supremacy
10. domination 11. sovereignty,
superiority 12. predominance
13. preponderance
ascendant, ascendent . . . 5. elder
6. father 7. supreme 8. ancestor,
forebear, superior 9. governing,
patriarch 10. antecedent, decoration
(Arch)
ascended . . . 4. rose 5. arose, risen
6. uprose
ascending . . . 6. anodic, rising 7. scaling,
sloping 8. mounting, racemose
9. emanating
ascending signs . . . 5. Aries 6. Gemini,
Pisces, Taurus 8. Aquarius 9. Capricorn
ascenseur . . . 8. elevator
Ascension Day . . . 8. Thursday (Holy)
(40 days after Easter)
Ascension lily . . . 7. Madonna
ascertain . . . 4. find 5. learn, prove, solve
6. decide 7. certify 9. determine
ascetic . . . 4. yati, yoga, yogi 5. fakir,
stoic 6. Essene, hermit, strict 7. austere,
eremite, puritan, recluse 8. anchoret,
Diogenes, solitary 9. abstainer,
anchorite, mendicant 10. abstemious
asceticism . . . 4. Yoga 9. austerity,
nephalism 10. abstention, abstinence,
puritanism 11. anchoritism, teetotalism
ascribable . . . 3. due 9. traceable
10. assignable 11. attributive
12. attributable
ascribe . . . 5. count, refer 6. assign,
attach, credit, impute, reckon 7. ascribe
8. accredit 9. attribute
ascus fruit . . . 8. truffles
asepsis . . . 6. purity 7. clarity 9. sterility
13. taintlessness
ash . . . 4. sorb, tree 5. rowan 6. samara
(fruit) 8. Fraxinus
ashes . . . 4. dust, lava, lees, slag 5. dregs,
ruins 6. embers 7. cinders, residue
ash tree symbol (Norse Myth) . . .
10. Yggdrasil (horse of Yggr)
Asia . . . 4. East 5. Orient, region 7. Far
East 8. Old World 9. continent
Asia Minor . . .
city (anc) . . 4. Myra, Teos, Troy
5. Ilium, Issus, Lydia 6. Nicaea, Sardes
7. Ephesus
district . . 4. Aria 5. Ionia, Troad (The
Troad) 6. Aeolis
island . . 6. Lesbos
language (anc) . . 6. Lycian, Lydian
8. Etruscan
mountain . . 3. Ida
old name . . 8. Anatolia
sea . . 5. Black 6. Aegean 7. Marmosa
13. Mediterranean
Asiatic (pert to) . . .
barbarian (anc) . . 3. Hun 6. Vandal
cyclone . . 7. typhoon
desert . . 4. Gobi
gulf . . 4. Aden, Oman, Siam 6. Tonkin
7. Persian
island . . 4. Java 5. Luzon, Malay
7. Celebes, Diomede (Big), Formosa,
Sumatra 8. Japanese, Mindanao,
Sakhalin 11. Philippines
mountain . . 4. Ural 5. Altai, Sayan

7. Everest 8. Caucasus, Himalaya
9. Hindu Kush
native.. 4. Arab, Turk, Yuit 5. Tatar
6. Indian, Innuit (Esk), Syrian 7. Chinese,
Malayan 8. Annamese, Japanese
9. Mongolian
nomad.. 4. Arab
river.. 2. Ob 4. Amur, Lena, Yalu
5. Huang (Hwang), Indus 6. Ganges,
Tigris 7. Yangtze, Yenisei 9. Euphrates,
Irrawaddy 11. Brahmaputra
sea.. 4. Azov (Azof) 5. Black, China,
Japan 6. Bering, Yellow 7. Caspian,
Okhotsk
wind.. 7. monsoon
Asiatic animal ...
antelope.. 5. goral
ass.. 6. onager
camel.. 8. Bactrian 9. dromedary
carnivore.. 5. panda, tiger
cattle.. 4. zobo
deer.. 4. axis 10. chevrotain
elephant.. 7. Elephas
fox.. 6. corsac
gazelle.. 3. ahu
goat.. 5. serow
lemur.. 5. loris 6. macaco
lynx.. 7. caracal
mongoose.. 4. urva
monkey.. 6. langur (long-tailed)
ox.. 3. yak
rodent.. 4. pika
sheep.. 3. sha 5. uriel 6. argali
squirrel.. 8. jelerang 10. polatouche
Asiatic bird ...
finch.. 9. brambling
jay.. 7. sirgang
owl.. 4. utum
partridge.. 6. seesee
plover.. 8. dotterel
songless.. 5. Pitta
talking.. 4. myna (mynah)
Asiatic snake ... 3. asp 5. cobra
8. ringhals
Asiatic storm (pert to) ...
sand.. 6. simoom (simoon) 7. tebbard
snow.. 5. buran
wind.. 5. buran 7. monsoon
aside ... 4. away 5. apart, hence 6. aslant,
astray, beside 7. whisper 8. sidewise
9. alongside, privately, sotto voce
12. interjection
asinine ... 4. dumb 5. inane, inept, silly
6. mulish, stupid 7. doltish, foolish,
idiotic 9. obstinate
ask ... 3. beg 4. quiz 5. claim, exact,
query, speer 6. assess, demand, invite
7. beseech, entreat, implore, inquire,
request, require, solicit 8. petition,
question 9. catechize, obsecrate (Relig)
11. interrogate
askance ... 4. awry 5. askew 7. asquint,
crooked 8. sideways 9. obliquely
askew ... 4. agee, alop, awry 5. agley,
amiss 6. faulty 7. askance, asquint,
crooked 8. deranged 9. distorted,
obliquely 10. catawampus, disorderly
aslant ... 5. atilt 6. tilted, tipped
7. athwart, leaning, listing, pitched,
sloping 8. inclined 9. careening,
obliquely

asleep ... 4. dead, dull, numb 7. dormant,
unaware 8. deadened, sleeping,
unarisen 9. oblivious, senseless,
unruffled 10. motionless 11. inattentive,
insensitive, unconscious
Asoka's Empire (anc Ind) ... 5. Patna
asp ... 5. cobra, snake, viper 6. uraeus
(sacred sym)
aspect ... 3. air 4. look, mien, pose,
side, view 5. angle, decil, facet, guise,
phase, shape, sight, state 6. decile,
facies, status, visage 7. bearing,
posture, scenery 8. attitude 9. astrology,
component, influence, seaminess,
situation 10. appearance
11. countenance
aspen ... 4. tree, wood 6. poplar
7. quaking 9. quivering, shivering,
trembling, tremulous, vibrating
asperge ... 3. wet 4. damp 5. spray,
water 7. baptize 8. humidify, sprinkle
asperge ... 9. asparagus
Asperges ... 4. rite 6. anthem
10. sprinkling (altar)
aspergillum ... 5. brush 7. sprayer
8. baptizer 9. sprinkler
asperity ... 5. rigor 7. raucity 8. acerbity,
acrimony, hardship, severity, tartness
9. bleakness, roughness 10. causticity,
difficulty, inclemency, moroseness,
resentment
asperse ... 4. slur 5. abuse, decry,
libel 6. defame, malign, revile, vilify
7. blacken, slander, traduce 8. besmirch
9. bespatter, discredit 10. calumniate
aspersion ... 4. rite, slur 6. insult
7. affront, baptism, calumny, outrage,
wetting 8. innuendo 9. indignity
10. defamation, sprinkling
12. calumniating, calumniation
13. disparagement
asphalt ... 4. pave 5. pitch 7. bitumen,
mineral 8. blacktop, pavement, uintaite
9. gilsonite 10. macadamize
asphyxia ... 5. apnea (apnoea) 7. choking
11. suffocation 12. smotheration
aspic ... 3. asp (poet) 5. jelly 6. cannon
8. lavender 9. galantine
aspiration ... 3. aim 4. hope, wish
5. ideal 6. breath, desire 7. pumping,
sucking, suction 8. ambition, staccato
9. breathing 10. exhalation
11. inspiration
aspire ... 4. long, plan, rise, soar
5. tower 6. attain, desire, expect, intend
7. breathe, propose
ass ... 3. ono (comb form) 4. dolt, dope,
fool, jack 5. burro, jenny
assail ... 4. pelt 5. beset, stone 6. attack
7. assault 9. implicate 11. incriminate
assailant ... 3. foe 5. enemy 7. invader
8. assailer, attacker, opponent
9. adversary, aggressor 10. antagonist,
challenger
Assam ...
capital.. 8. Shillong
native.. 4. Ahom 8. Assamite 11. Indo-
Chinese
people.. 3. Aka 4. Garo, Naga
province of.. 5. India
river.. 11. Brahmaputra

tribe .. 2. Ao 3. Aka 4. Garo, Naga

assassin ... 4. Cain, thug 5. bravo
6. apache, cuttle, gunman, killer, slayer
7. gorilla, ruffian 8. murderer, sicarian
9. manslayer 11. slaughterer

assassination ... 6. purge 6. murder
7. killing 8. regicide 11. liquidation
12. manslaughter

Assassin Order ... 8. Ismalian
10. Mohammedan

assault ... 5. onset, storm 6. assail, attack,
charge 7. descent, seizure 8. invasion
9. incursion 13. incrimination

assay ... 3. try 4. test 5. prove, trial
6. accost 7. attempt 8. analysis,
docimasy (art), endeavor
10. experiment 12. verification

assay cup ... 5. cupel

assemblage ... 3. all 4. herd 6. throng
8. assembly, entirety 9. gathering
12. congregation

assemblage (pert to) ...
cattle .. 5. drove, rodeo 7. roundup
fashionable .. 5. salon
mob .. 4. rout 6. rabble
splendid .. 6. galaxy
tents .. 4. camp 10. encampment

assemble ... 3. pod 4. mass, meet
5. amass, piece, rally, unite 6. couple,
gather, muster 7. cluster, collect,
convene, convoke, recruit
10. congregate

assembly ... 4. bevy, diet, moot 5. agora,
gemot, group, synod, troop 6. assize,
sabbat 7. company, council, landtag,
meeting 8. auditory, conclave (secret),
folkmoot (Hist) 9. concourse, gathering
10. collection, convention
11. convocation 12. congregation

assent ... 3. aye, nod, yea, yes 4. amen
5. admit, agree, grant 6. accede,
accord, concur 7. consent 8. sanction
9. acquiesce, agreement 10. compliance
12. acquiescence

assert ... 3. say 4. aver, pose 5. claim,
plead, posit, state, voice 6. affirm,
allege, avouch, relate, uphold
7. contend, declare, profess, protest,
support 8. advocate 9. pronounce,
vindicate 10. asseverate

assertion ... 5. claim 6. remark, thesis
7. premise 8. averment 9. statement
10. assumption, hypothesis
11. affirmation, declaration,
maintenance, proposition, vindication

assertiveness ... 10. pragmatism
14. aggressiveness

assertor ... 8. affirmer, defender
9. supporter 10. vindicator

assess ... 3. ask, tax 4. cess, levy, mise,
rate 5. price, value 6. charge 7. measure
8. appraise, estimate

assessment ... 3. fee, tax 4. levy,
rate, scot 5. ratal, stock, value
6. surtax 7. pricing, scutage 8. estimate
9. appraisal, valuation 10. evaluation
11. measurement

assets ... 5. funds, means 6. wealth
7. capital 8. accounts, property
9. resources

asseverate ... 3. say, vow 4. aver

5. state, swear 6. affirm, allege, assert
7. contend, declare, profess, protest
8. maintain 9. pronounce

asseveration ... 3. vow 6. oath (solemn)
8. averment 9. assertion 11. affirmation,
declaration 13. pronouncement

assiduity ... 8. industry 9. diligence
11. painstaking, persistence
12. perseverance

assiduous ... 4. busy 6. active 7. intense,
zealous 8. diligent, sedulous
9. energetic, laborious, unwearied
11. industrious, perseverant
13. indefatigable, unintermitted

assign ... 3. fix, set 4. cast, cede, seal
5. allot, refer 6. allege, commit, detail
7. address, adjudge, appoint, ascribe,
consign, empower 8. accredit, allocate,
delegate, nominate, transfer 9. attribute
10. commission 11. appropriate

assignment ... 3. job 4. task 5. chore,
stint 6. lesson 7. mission 8. exercise,
transfer 9. allotment 10. allocation,
commission, commitment
11. attribution 13. specification

assimilate ... 5. adapt, learn, liken
6. absorb, digest, imbibe 7. convert
10. understand 11. approximate

assimilation ... 8. imbibing, learning
9. anabolism, digestion, ingestion,
reduction 10. absorption, adaptation,
comparison, conversion
14. naturalization

assist ... 3. aid 4. abet, back, help 5. avail,
boost, favor 6. attend, prompt, second,
succor 7. benefit, relieve, support,
sustain 8. befriend 9. accompany,
subsidize

assistance ... 3. aid 4. help 5. grant
6. relief, succor 7. service, subsidy,
support 10. logrolling (Polit)
11. furtherance

assistant ... 4. aide, ally 5. tutor
6. deputy, helper 7. abettor, famulus,
servant, teacher 9. associate, attendant,
auxiliary 11. subordinate 12. right-hand
man

assize ... 3. fix 4. rate 5. edict, trial,
value 6. assess, decree 9. ordinance
10. regulation 11. instruction,
measurement

associate ... 3. mix, pal 4. ally, chum,
mate 5. buddy, crony 6. fellow,
friend, hobnob, mingle 7. combine,
comrade, consort, partner 9. colleague,
companion 10. accomplice
11. concomitant, confederate

associated ... 6. allied, banded, joined,
united 7. coupled, leagued, related
9. connected 10. affiliated, concurrent

associates ... 4. crew 5. force, staff
7. retinue 9. personnel 12. constituency

association ... 4. body, club 5. artel,
cabal, guild, hanse (Hist), union
6. league, lyceum, symbol 7. company,
society 8. alliance, relation, sodality,
sorority 9. syndicate 10. fellowship,
fraternity 11. affiliation, combination,
comradeship, concurrence, corporation
13. communication, interrelation

assonance ... 3. pun 4. rime 5. rhyme

8. paragram 9. agreement
11. paronomasia, resemblance
12. alliteration

as soon as possible . . . 4. ASAP

assort . . . 4. sort, suit 5. adapt, class, grade, group 7. consort (with) 8. classify, separate 9. associate (with) 10. categorize, distribute

assortment . . . 3. mix, set 4. hash, mess, olio 5. class, group 6. jumble, medley 9. mélange, mixture, sorting 9. potpourri 10. collection, hodgepodge, miscellany 11. arrangement 14. conglomeration

assuage . . . 4. calm, ease 5. allay, slake 6. lessen, mellow, pacify, quench, soften, solace, soothe 7. appease, comfort, gratify, qualify, relieve, satisfy 8. mitigate, palliate 9. alleviate

assuasive . . . 5. balmy 6. easing 8. remedial, soothing 9. relieving, softening 10. mitigating, palliative 11. alleviative 13. tranquilizing

assume . . . 3. don 4. deem, sham, take 5. adopt, feign, guess, imply, infer, judge, think, usurp 6. affect, allege, betake, borrow, deduce 7. believe, imagine, premise, presume, pretend, suppose, surmise 8. arrogate, conclude, simulate 9. undertake 11. appropriate, counterfeit

assume (pert to) . . .
  character . . 11. impersonate
  different forms . . 7. protean
  unduly . . 5. usurp 8. arrogate
  without proof . . 11. theoretical
  12. hypothetical

assumed . . . 6. deemed 7. alleged, implied, thought 8. affected, inferred, presumed, supposed 9. fictional, pretended 10. fictitious, understood, undertaken 11. conjectured, make-believe, presumptive, presupposed, theoretical 12. appropriated, hypothetical, suppositious

assuming . . . 5. lofty 8. arrogant, superior 9. presuming 10. assumptive 11. overweening, pretentious 12. presumptuous

assumption . . . 8. adoption 9. arrogance, postulate, reception 10. usurpation 11. implication, proposition, supposition 13. appropriation, incorporation 14. presupposition

assurance . . . 4. hope, oath 5. poise, trust 6. aplomb, belief, pledge, surety 7. comfort, courage, promise 8. security, sureness 9. certainty, guarantee, impudence, insurance 10. confidence, steadiness 11. assuredness, intrepidity 12. cocksureness 14. self-confidence

assure . . . 4. aver 5. vouch 6. assert, avouch, depose, ensure, insure, secure 7. confirm, declare, protest, satisfy 8. convince, embolden, persuade, reassure 9. encourage, guarantee 10. asseverate

Assyria . . .
  capital . . 7. Nineveh
  city . . 5. Calab (Bib) 9. Khorsabad (ruins)
  empire (anc) . . 5. Assur (Ashur)

language . . 6. Semite 9. cuneiform (written)
people . . 6. Semite 7. Amorite (Bib)

Assyrian god . . .
  atmosphere . . 5. Hadad
  fire . . 5. Nusku
  hunt . . 7. Ninurta
  moon . . 3. Sin
  storm . . 2. Zu
  sun . . 7. Shamash
  war . . 6. Nergal 7. Ninurta
  winds . . 4. Adad 5. Hadad

Assyrian goddess . . . 5. Nanai 6. Allatu, Ishtar 9. Sarpanitu (Zirbanit)

Assyriology, science of . . . 8. language 11. antiquities

aster . . . 4. star 9. asterwort, karyaster 10. Carduaceae

asterisk . . . 4. mark (reference), star 6. accent, figure (star) 9. highlight 10. asteriskos (Eccl)

astern . . . 3. aft 4. baft, rear 5. abaft, after 6. behind 8. hindward, rearward, tailward

asteroid . . . 5. Ceres (largest) 6. planet 8. starlike 9. planetoid

Asteroidea . . . 8. starfish

astir . . . 2. up 5. about, afoot, eager 6. active, moving 8. stirring 11. forthcoming

as to . . . 7. apropos, suppose 9. regarding 10. concerning, respecting

astonish . . . 4. stun 5. amaze, appal 7. astound, stagger, startle 8. bewilder, confound, surprise 9. overwhelm

astonishing . . . 7. amazing 8. fabulous 9. appalling, marvelous, wonderful 10. incredible, remarkable

astound . . . 4. stun 5. abash, amaze, shock 6. appall (appal), dismay 7. stagger, stupefy 8. astonish, surprise 10. disconcert

astounding . . . 8. horrible, shocking 9. appalling, frightful 10. horrendous, horrifying 11. astonishing

astraddle . . . 7. astride 9. horseback, pickaback (piggyback) 10. straddling

astral . . . 6. spirit, starry 7. stellar 8. sidereal, starlike 9. celestial 11. star-studded

astray . . . 4. lost 5. amiss, wrong 6. adrift, afield, erring 8. aberrate, mistaken 9. erroneous 10. bewildered

astray, to go . . . 3. err, sin 4. mang, rove 5. drift, lapse, stray 6. wander 7. deviate, digress 8. miscarry 9. backslide 10. misbelieve

astriction . . . 4. bond 7. binding 8. thirlage 9. fastening 10. litigation 11. confinement, contraction 12. constipation

astride . . . 8. straddle 9. astraddle, horseback, pickaback (piggyback)

astringent . . . 4. acid, alum, sloe, sour 5. acerb, acrid, harsh, sapan, stern 6. tannin 7. austere, bitters, caustic, pungent, rhatany (root), styptic 9. vitriolic 10. antiseptic 11. acrimonious, argentamine 12. constrictive

astrologer . . . 8. Chaldean 9. stargazer

11. astrologian, astromancer,
Nostradamus
astrology (pert to) . . . 5. house, signs
6. aspect, zodiac 7. mansion, mundane
8. siderism 9. horoscope, planetary
11. horoscopist
astronaut . . . 7. Martian 8. spaceman
9. cosmonaut, rocketeer
astronomer . . . 9. stargazer
11. uranologist 12. uranographer
13. meteorologist, uranographist
astronomer, famed . . . 6. Kepler
7. Galileo 12. Eratosthenes
astronomical . . . 4. huge, vast 5. large
6. cosmic, uranic 7. immense,
mammoth, Uranian 8. colossal,
empyreal, heavenly 9. celestial
10. prodigious, stupendous,
tremendous
astronomy (pert to) . . . 4. coma (the)
5. apsis, saros (Bab) 6. syzygy
7. almanac, apsides, azimuth, gibbous
8. sidereal 9. idiometer, insulated
11. debilissima
astute . . . 3. sly 4. keen, wily 5. acute,
canny, smart 6. artful, clever, crafty,
shrewd 7. cunning, skilled 9. insidious,
sagacious 10. discerning
14. discriminating
asunder . . . 5. apart, cleft, rived (riven),
split 6. atwain, halved 7. divided
9. disjoined, separated
as yet . . . 8. hitherto
asylum . . . 3. ark 4. home, jail, port
5. haven 6. harbor, refuge 7. retreat,
shelter 9. hospitium, infirmary,
sanctuary 10. stronghold 11. institution
asymmetrical . . . 6. uneven, warped
7. twisted, unequal 9. contorted,
distorted 11. zygomorphic
16. disproportionate
at . . . 2. by, in 4. near, nigh 5. there
8. location, position 9. direction,
situation
at (pert to) . . .
great length . . 7. on and on 9. tediously
home . . 2. in 4. here 9. en famille
last . . 3. end 7. finally 9. extremely
10. ultimately
once . . 3. now 7. readily
the same . .
time . . 6. coeval 10. coetaneous
12. contemporary
atabal . . . 4. drum 5. tabor 10. kettledrum
atabeg . . . 5. title 6. vizier
Atalanta (pert to) . . .
defeated in romantic race by . .
10. Hippomenes 17. three golden
apples (Gr Myth)
famed . . 8. huntress
foe . . 9. Aphrodite
husband . . 8. Milanion
legend . . 8. Arcadian, Boeotian
atalaya . . . 10. watchtower
atap . . . 4. nipa, palm
atavism . . . 8. heredity 9. reversion
10. regression
ate . . . 5. dined, fared 6. dieted, gnawed,
supped
Ate . . . 7. goddess (of infatuation)
atelier . . . 5. easel 6. studio 8. workshop

a tempo . . . 4. time
Aten (Egypt) . . . 9. solar disk
ates . . . 8. sweetsop
athanasia . . . 8. athanasy 11. immortality
13. deathlessness 15. imperishability
athanor (Fr) . . . 7. furnace (alchemist's)
Athapascan Indian . . . 5. Tinne
6. Apache, Navaho (Navajo)
atheist . . . 5. pagan 7. heathen, infidel,
nastika 8. agnostic 10. unbeliever
11. disbeliever, unchristian
13. antichristian
Athena (pert to) . . .
attributes . . 3. owl 5. aegis 7. serpent
festival . . 11. Panathenaea
Rom equivalent . . 7. Minerva
shrine . . 9. Parthenon (Athens)
Athena, goddess of . . .
arts, crafts . . 6. Ergane
health . . 6. Hygeia
horses, tamer of . . 6. Hippia
light . . 4. Alea
maid of Athens . . 12. Pallas Athene
poetry . . 6. Pallas
victory . . 4. Nike
wisdom . . 8. Palladis
Athenian (pert to) . . .
assembly . . 4. Pnyx
Bee . . 5. Plato
general . . 8. Xenophon
lawgiver . . 5. Draco, Solon
sculptor . . 7. Phidias
statesman . . 8. Pericles 9. Aristides
(The Just) 10. Alcibiades
temple . . 11. Nike Apteros
Athens . . .
capital of . . 6. Attica (anc), Greece
citadel . . 9. Acropolis
magistrate . . 5. Draco, Solon
rival . . 6. Sparta (anc)
senate . . 5. boule
temple . . 9. Parthenon
Athens of . . .
America . . 6. Boston 9. Nashville (The
South)
Ireland . . 4. Cork 7. Belfast
North . . 9. Edinburgh 10. Copenhagen
Switzerland . . 6. Zurich
West . . 7. Cordoba
athlete . . . 7. acrobat, gymnast, tumbler
11. funambulist, palaestrian, pancratiast
13. contortionist
athlete (pert to) . . .
foot disease . . 15. dermatophytosis
of Christendom . . 10. Scanderbeg
portico (Gr, Rom) . . 6. xystus (xyst)
athletic . . . 5. lusty, thewy, yauld
6. brawny, robust, sinewy, strong
8. muscular, stalwart, vigorous
9. acrobatic, agonistic, gymnastic
10. palaestral (palestral) 15. broad-
shouldered
athwart . . . 6. across, aslant 8. sideways,
sidewise, traverse 9. crosswise,
obliquely 10. crisscross, perversely
atimon . . . 9. muskmelon
Atlantean . . . 6. strong 7. titanic
8. gigantic 9. Atlaslike 10. Gargantuan
atlantes (opp of caryatids) . . . 7. columns
(carved men) 9. telamones
Atlantic Sisters (Gr) . . . 8. Pleiades (stars)

Atlas (pert to) . . .
converted into . . 7. Mt Atlas
daughter . . 7. Calypso 8. Pleiades
famed as a . . 5. giant, Titan
king of . . 10. Mauretania
mother . . 4. Asia 7. Clymene
supporter of . . 5. earth 10. the heavens
Atman (Hind) . . . 3. ego 4. Self, Soul
6. Brahma
atmosphere . . . 3. air 4. aura, mood
5. ether, ozone 7. climate
10. aerosphere, background
11. environment, hydrosphere
atmosphere (pert to) . . .
condition . . 9. epedaphic
density . . 8. isostere, isoteric
disturbance . . 5. storm 6. static
9. tornadoes, whirlwind
pressure . . 10. barometric
shooting star . . 6. meteor
spectrum . . 7. rainbow
atole . . . 5. gruel 8. porridge
atoll . . . 4. belt, reef (coral) 6. island
atom . . . 3. ace, bit, ion, jot 4. gram,
iota, mite, whit 5. monad 8. particle
9. corpuscle
atom (pert to) . . .
central part . . 7. nucleus
charged . . 3. ion
energy . . 5. gluon 6. photon 7. quantum
particle . . 4. muon 5. boson, meson,
quark 6. baryon, lepton 7. fermion,
neutron 8. electron, neutrino
atomic . . . 3. Age, ray 4. beam, bomb, tiny
5. power 6. energy, minute, number,
radius, weight 7. nuclear 9. atomistic,
molecular, radiation 10. intangible
11. microscopic 13. infinitesimal
atomize . . . 4. fume 5. smash, spray
6. aerate, gasify 7. fission, perfume,
shatter 8. dissolve, fumigate, nucleize
9. carbonate, decompose, evaporate,
micronize, pulverize 11. disorganize
12. disintegrate
atom smasher . . . 11. accelerator
atomy . . . 4. atom, mote 5. dwarf,
pygmy 6. droich, midget 8. skeleton
10. micromorph
atonement . . . 6. amends 7. apology,
penance, redress 8. requital
10. recompense, redemption, reparation
11. reclamation, restitution
12. propitiation 15. indemnification
Atreus (pert to) . . .
brother . . 8. Thyestes
father . . 6. Pelops
king of . . 7. Mycenae
mother . . 10. Hippodamia
slayer of . . 12. Thyestes' sons
son . . 8. Menelaus 9. Agamemnon
wife . . 6. Aerope
atrium . . . 4. hall, room 5. court (inner)
6. cavity (Anat) 7. chamber 9. peristyle
atrocious . . . 4. rank, vile 5. awful,
cruel, grave 6. brutal, savage, sinful,
wicked 7. heinous, vicious, violent
8. dreadful, flagrant, horrible, infamous,
ruthless, shocking, terrible, wretched
9. monstrous, nefarious 10. abominable,
deplorable, detestable, outrageous
atrociousness . . . 8. baseness, vileness

12. dreadfulness, shamefulness
13. nefariousness 15. Schrecklichkeit
atrocity . . . 4. evil, harm 5. abuse, havoc,
wrong 7. misdeed, outrage 8. enormity
9. indignity 12. mistreatment
atrophy . . . 5. tabes 7. disease
8. marasmus 10. emaciation
11. attenuation
Atropos (Gr) . . . 7. goddess (Fate)
attach . . . 3. add, fix, pin, put, tag, tie
4. bind, glue, join, vest 5. affix, annex,
hitch, paste, seize, unite 6. append,
assign, fasten 7. ascribe, connect,
postfix, subjoin 9. associate, attribute
11. superimpose
attached . . . 4. fond 6. adnate, welded
7. annexed, devoted, engaged, sessile
(Bot), smitten 8. cemented, enamored
attachment . . . 4. bond, love 5. fancy
6. liking, regard 7. adjunct, fixture
8. addition, devotion, fidelity, fondness
9. accession, adherence, affection,
fastening, increment 10. annexation
11. attribution 12. augmentation
attack . . . 3. fit 4. pang, raid 5. beset, blitz,
drive, feint, foray, ictus, onset, sally,
siege, spasm 6. affret, assail, charge,
onrush, oppugn, sortie 7. aggress,
assault, bowling, descent, offense,
seizure 8. camisado (anc), paroxysm,
sickness 9. offensive, onslaught
10. aggression 11. enunciation
13. incrimination
attain . . . 2. do 3. get, win 4. earn, gain
5. enact, reach 6. accede, arrive, effect,
obtain 7. achieve, acquire, compass,
fulfill, perform, realize 9. discharge
10. accomplish, consummate
attainable . . . 8. gettable 9. available
10. achievable
attainment . . . 5. skill 7. arrival 8. learning
9. accession 11. acquirement
acquisition, cultivation, edification,
realization 14. accomplishment
attar . . . 4. otto 5. scent 6. parfum
7. essence, perfume, rose oil
attempt . . . 3. aim, jab (sl), try 4. dare,
seek, stab 5. assay, ensue, essay,
fling, offer, onset, siege, trial 6. attack,
effort, result 7. venture 8. endeavor
9. undertake
attend . . . 4. hark, heed, help, mind,
note, tend, wait 5. ensue, nurse, serve,
treat, visit 6. doctor, escort, follow,
foster, listen, result 7. conduct, hearken,
nurture, observe 9. accompany
attendance . . . 4. draw 5. court 7. service,
turnout 8. presence, tendance
9. following 13. accompaniment
attendant . . . 4. maid, page 5. nurse, staff,
usher 6. caddie, escort, gillie, porter,
waiter 7. bellboy, orderly 8. follower
9. associate, attending, companion
10. subsequent 11. concomitant,
ministering
attendants, train of . . . 5. suite
7. cortege, retinue 9. entourage
attention . . . 3. ear 4. care, heed, hist,
note 6. notice, regard 7. concern,
hearing, respect, thought 8. courtesy
11. mindfulness 13. concentration,

consideration

attentive ... 5. alert, awake, eared
6. intent 7. careful, heedful, mindful
8. obedient, vigilant, watchful
9. courteous, listening, observant,
wide-awake 10. meticulous, respectful
11. circumspect, considerate, surveillant

attenuated ... 3. cut 4. fine, rare, slim,
thin 6. svelte, wasted 7. diluted,
gracile, reduced, slender, thinned,
watered 8. lessened, rarefied, weakened
9. decreased, emaciated

attest ... 4. seal 5. vouch 6. adjure,
affirm, avouch, depose 7. certify,
testify, witness 8. evidence, indicate,
manifest 9. testimony 10. deposition
12. authenticate

attestation ... 4. oath (solemn) 5. proof
6. avowal 8. swearing 9. assertion
10. allegation 11. affirmation, certificate,
declaration, testimonial 13. testification
14. authentication

attic ... 3. top 4. dome, head, loft, wall
6. belfry, garret 8. cockloft

Attic ... 5. salty, witty 6. simple 7. elegant,
refined 8. academic, Athenian, tasteful
9. classical 10. Ciceronian

Attic (pert to) ...
Bee .. 9. Sophocles (poet)
bird .. 11. nightingale (Milton)
Muse .. 8. Xenophon
native .. 8. Athenian
school .. 9. sculpture

Attica (pert to) ...
capital of .. 6. Athens
state of .. 6. Greece (anc)
famed as .. 15. world's first city

Attila ... 3. Hun (leader) 5. Etzel (fabled)
12. Scourge of God

attired ... 7. arrayed, clothed, dressed

attitude ... 3. air, set 4. pose, view
5. angle, slant, stand 7. bearing, feeling,
opinion, outlook, posture, thought
8. position, reaction 9. arabesque
(dance), sentiment, viewpoint
10. estimation, impression

attitude (reverent) ... 6. salaam
8. kneeling 9. obeisance
12. genuflection (genuflexion)

attorney ... 6. lawyer 7. counsel, pleader
9. barrister, counselor (counsellor)
11. intercessor

attract ... 4. bait, draw, lure, pull
5. charm, tempt 6. appeal, beckon,
enamor, engage, entice, invite
8. interest 9. captivate, fascinate,
influence, magnetize

attraction ... 4. lure, pull, star 6. appeal
7. gravity 8. affinity, headline, interest,
penchant 9. magnetism, seduction
10. allurement 11. fascination

attractive ... 4. cute 6. lovely, pretty,
taking 7. winsome 8. alluring, engaging,
fetching, graceful, magnetic 9. allicient,
appealing, beauteous, beautiful,
desirable 10. attracting, delightful
11. captivating, interesting

attractive and repellent ...
10. ambivalent

attrahent ... 6. magnet 7. drawing
8. sinapism (Med) 10. attracting

attribute ... 3. owe 5. refer, trait
6. impute, nature, symbol 7. ascribe,
feature, quality 8. property 9. adjective,
qualifier, specialty

attrition ... 4. wear 5. grief (Theol)
7. massage 8. abrasion, friction,
limation 9. detrition 10. contrition

attune ... 4. tune 5. chime 6. accord,
adjust 7. concord, harmony, syntony
9. melodious 10. symphonize
11. concordance

atwain ... 7. asunder

atweel ... 5. truly 6. surely

aubade (Fr) ... 3. lay 4. poem, song
6. ballad 7. concert (morning)
8. serenade

auberge ... 3. inn

aubergiste ... 9. innkeeper

auction ... 3. bid 4. cant, roup, sale
5. block 6. vendue 7. bidding

auction (game) ... 4. pool 5. pitch
6. bridge, euchre, hearts 8. pinochle

audacious ... 4. bold 5. saucy 6. brazen,
daring 7. defiant 8. impudent, insolent,
intrepid, spirited 9. barefaced,
foolhardy, insulting 11. adventurous,
challenging, impertinent, presumptive,
venturesome

audacity ... 5. cheek, crust, nerve
6. daring 7. courage 8. defiance,
temerity 9. assurance, hardihood,
impudence, insolence, sauciness
10. effrontery, enterprise
11. presumption 12. impertinence
13. audaciousness, foolhardiness,
shamelessness

audible ... 5. aloud, clear 8. distinct,
hearable 10. articulate

audible respiration ... 4. sigh

audience ... 3. ear 5. house, trial
6. parley, tryout 7. hearing, theater
8. audition, auditory, congress
9. interview, listeners 10. conference
12. congregation

audit ... 5. check 6. reckon, verify
7. certify, collate 10. accounting
11. examination

audition ... 6. try out

auditor ... 5. clerk 6. censor, hearer
7. actuary, apposer 8. examiner,
listener 10. accountant, bookkeeper
11. comptroller

auditorium ... 4. hall, nave (anc)
5. house 7. theater 8. auditory, building
9. Guildhall

auditory ... 4. otic 5. audio, aural
6. phonic 7. hearers 8. audience
9. acoustic, auricular 12. congregation

au fait ... 4. able 5. expert 7. equal
to 8. informed, skillful 9. qualified
10. conversant (with)

au fond ... 9. basically, primarily
11. essentially 13. fundamentally

auger ... 3. bit 4. bore, tool 5. borer,
drill 6. gimlet, wimble 10. perforator

aught ... 3. any 4. none, some, zero
5. ought 6. cipher 7. nothing 8. anything

augment ... 3. add, eke 5. affix,
annex, exalt, swell 6. expand, extend
7. amplify, broaden, develop, enhance,
enlarge 8. increase 9. reinforce

Augsburg Church . . . 8. Lutheran
augur . . . 4. bode, omen, seer 5. sibyl, vates (Gauls) 6. oracle 7. betoken, presage 8. forebode, forecast, foretell, forewarn, haruspex (Rom), indicate, prophesy 10. anticipate, astrologer, conjecture, soothsayer 13. prognosticate 14. prognosticator
augury . . . 4. omen, rite 7. auspice, portent 8. ceremony
august . . . 5. awful, grand, novel, regal 6. sedate, solemn 7. courtly, eminent, stately 8. imposing, majestic 9. dignified, honorable, important, venerable 11. magnificent, ritualistic 12. aristocratic
August . . . 6. Lammas 8. Sextilis 10. First month (Rom year)
August meteor (11th of month) . . . 7. Perseid
auk . . . 4. Alca, Alle, bird (sea), falk 5. murre, noddy 6. auklet, rotche (rotch) 7. Alcidae, dovekie 9. guillemot, razorbill
Auk . . . 6. Indian 7. Alaskan, Tlingit 9. Koluschan
aula . . . 4. hall, room 5. court 6. emblic (E Ind tree) 8. ventricle
aulos . . . 5. flute 8. woodwind 9. woodwinds (collectively)
au naturel . . . 4. nude 5. naked
aura . . . 3. air 4. glow, halo, ring 6. astral, circle, fringe (Psychol), nimbus 7. aureola 9. effluvium, emanation 10. atmosphere, exhalation
aureole . . . 4. halo 5. glory 6. circle, nimbus
auricle . . . 3. ear 4. lobe 5. pinna 6. atrium (heart) 8. appendage
auricular . . . 3. otic 5. aural, eared 6. phonic 8. acoustic, auditory
aurifex . . . 9. goldsmith
aurochs . . . 3. tur 4. goat, urus 5. bison
aurora . . . 3. eos 4. dawn 5. sunup 7. sunrise 8. borealis, daybreak, daylight 9. australis 11. polar lights
aurora borealis . . . 14. northern lights
auroral . . . 4. dawn, eoan, rosy 7. eastern, radiant, roseate
auspices . . . 3. aid 4. care, sign, wing 5. aegis (egis) 6. charge 7. backing, custody 8. guidance 9. patronage 10. management, protection 11. sponsorship, supervision
auspicious . . . 4. good 6. timely 9. favorable, fortunate, opportune 10. convenient, propitious, prosperous, seasonable 12. advantageous
Aussie . . . 6. digger 10. Australian
Auster . . . 9. southland, south wind
austere . . . 4. dour, hard 5. acrid, harsh, rigid, rough, stern 6. bitter, severe, strict 7. ascetic, pungent 8. exacting 10. astringent
Australasia . . . 7. Oceania 15. South Sea Islands
Australasian bird . . . 8. lorikeet 9. pardalote
Australia . . . see also *Australian*
capital . . 8. Canberra
city . . 5. Perth 6. Sidney (largest)

8. Adelaide, Brisbane 9. Melbourne
desert . . 10. Great Sandy 13. Great Victoria
explorer . . 4. Cook
First Englishman (1688) . . 14. William Dampier
holiday . . 13. Foundation Day (Jan 26)
inlet . . 9. Botany Bay
island . . 8. Tasmania
mountain peak . . 9. Kosciusko
ocean . . 6. Indian
river . . 6. Murray
sea . . 5. Coral 6. Tasman
state . . 8. Victoria 10. Queensland 13. New South Wales
Tropic (southern) . . 9. Capricorn
Australian (pert to) . . .
bee . . 5. karbi
bedroll . . 6. bindle 7. matilda
candy . . 5. lolly
feast . . 10. corroboree
fish . . 4. mako (shark) 5. yabby
flag . . 13. Southern Cross
flower . . 7. waratah (tulip) 9. rhodanthe
hut . . 6. miamia
native . . 5. myall 6. Aussie, binghi 8. kangaroo, warragal 9. aborigine, Dravidian
reptile . . 6. elapid, goanna, lizard (barking, frilled)
soldier . . 5. Anzac 6. digger
Australian animal . . .
dog (wild) . . 5. dingo
horse (wild) . . 6. brumby
sheep dog . . 6. kelpie
mammal . . 7. daysure 8. duckbill, platypus 9. blind mole
marsupial . . 4. tait 5. koala 6. wombat 7. echidna 8. anteater, kangaroo 9. phalanger, teddy bear 10. kookaburra 14. Tasmanian Devil
Australian bird . . . 3. emu, owl 4. lory, titi 5. arara, ariel, galah 6. leipoa, petrel 7. boobook, bustard, corella (parrot), grinder, rosella (parakeet) 8. ganggang, lorikeet, lyrebird, morepork, nightjar, paradise 9. bowerbird, cassowary, pardalote 10. flycatcher, goatsucker 11. budgereegah (parakeet)
Australian tree . . . 4. teak, toon 5. belah, penda 6. jarrah, mallee, marara, she-oak, wattle 7. gunnung (mahogany) 8. Alstonia (dogbane), ironbark (eucalypt) 9. boobyalla (willow)
Austria . . .
alpine lake . . 8. Bodensee (Ger) 9. Constance
capital . . 4. Wien (Ger) 6. Vienna
city . . 4. Graz, Linz 8. Salzburg 9. Innsbruck
forest belt . . 10. Wiener Wald
monarchy . . 14. Austria-Hungary
mountain . . 4. Alps 6. Otztal 9. Dolomites
mountain peak . . 10. Wildspitze 13. Gross-Glockner
Pass (famed) . . 7. Brenner
river . . 3. Inn, Mur 6. Danube
Austrian (pert to) . . .
artist . . 5. Klimt
author . . 10. Schnitzler
botanist . . 6. Mendel

chemist, inventor.. 8. Welsbach
composer.. 4. Berg 5. Haydn 6. Mozart,
   Webern 7. Strauss (Johann) 8. Bruckner,
   Schubert
physicist.. 7. Doppler 11. Schrödinger
psychiatrist.. 5. Adler, Freud
ruler (former).. 6. kaiser
soldier.. 5. jäger
theaterman.. 9. Reinhardt (Max)
violinist.. 8. Kreisler
autarch... 6. despot, tyrant 8. autocrat
authentic... 4. pure, real, true 5. valid
   6. native 7. certain, correct, genuine,
   natural 8. bona fide, credible, official,
   original, orthodox, reliable 9. firsthand
   11. trustworthy 13. authoritative
authenticate... 6. affirm, attest, ratify
   7. certify, confirm, warrant 8. validate
   12. substantiate
authenticity... 11. genuineness,
   reliability 13. dependability
   15. trustworthiness
author... 4. doer, poet 5. ghost, maker
   6. parent, penman, writer 7. creator,
   inditer 8. annalist, begetter, compiler,
   composer, essayist, inventor, novelist,
   producer 9. dramatist, scribbler
   10. originator 13. encyclopedist
   (encyclopaedist)
authoritative... 4. wise 5. valid 6. potent,
   ruling, strong 7. weighty 8. approved,
   forceful, official, oracular, orthodox,
   positive, powerful 9. authentic,
   imperious 10. commanding, peremptory
   11. dictatorial, influential
   13. determinative
authoritative (pert to)...
   command.. 4. fiat 5. usage 6. decree,
   dictum 7. mandate
   example.. 9. precedent 10. antecedent
   letter.. 4. writ 5. breve
authority... 5. judge, power, right
   6. critic, expert, oracle, regent
   7. command, warrant, witness
   8. dominion, validity 9. influence,
   testimony 10. commission, competency
   11. connoisseur, prerogative 12. carte
   blanche, jurisdiction 13. authorization
authorize... 6. accept, permit, ratify
   7. certify, charter, empower, endorse,
   entitle, justify, license, warrant
   8. accredit, delegate, sanction, validate
   10. commission 11. enfranchise
   12. legitimatize
authorless... 8. nameless 9. anonymous
autobiography... 7. journal, letters,
   memoirs 11. memorabilia
autochthon... 6. binghi, native 8. indigene
   9. primitive 10. aboriginal
autocracy... 8. monarchy 9. despotism
   10. absolutism 15. totalitarianism
autocrat... 4. czar (tsar) 5. mogul
   6. despot 7. arbiter, monarch 8. dictator
   9. sovereign 10. taskmaster
autodidactic... 8. self-made 10. self-
   taught 12. self-educated
autograph... 4. seal, sign 5. cross
   9. signature 11. John Hancock
automatic... 7. machine 10. mechanical,
   self-acting 11. instinctive, involuntary,
   spontaneous

automatic device... 3. gun 4. gear
   5. drill, pilot, rifle, robot 6. pistol, switch
   8. computer, revolver 10. six-shooter
automaton... 5. golem, robot 6. puppet
   7. android, machine
automobile... 3. cab, car 4. auto, taxi
   5. coupe 6. jalopy 7. autocar, flivver,
   machine, taxicab, vehicle 8. motorcar
autosuggestion... 7. therapy 8. hypnosis
   9. hypnology, mesmerism
   10. psychology 14. self-suggestion
autumn... 4. fall 6. mature, old
   age, season (yearly) 7. equinox,
   harvest, October 8. maturity, November
   9. September
auxiliary... 4. ally, plus 5. extra 6. aiding,
   helper 7. adjunct, helping 9. accessory,
   ancillary, assistant, attendant, coadjutor,
   colleague, companion, secondary
   10. additional, subsidiary, supporting
   11. confederate, cooperating,
   subordinate, subservient
   12. nonessential, supplemental
   13. supplementary
auxiliary army... 6. relief 7. support
   8. Landwehr, recruits, reserves
   11. contingents 14. reinforcements
auxiliary verb... 3. can, had, has, may
   4. hast, have, will 5. could, shall,
   would 6. should
avail... 3. use 4. good, help 5. value
   6. inform, profit 7. benefit, service,
   utility 9. advantage, expedient
availability... 7. utility 9. usability
   10. usefulness 13. acquirability,
   attainability 14. serviceability
available (pert to)... 4. free, open 5. handy,
   ready, valid 6. on hand, usable, vacant
   8. unfilled 9. securable 10. accessible,
   attainable, convenient, obtainable,
   unoccupied
avalanche... 5. slide 7. descent (sudden)
   8. slippage
avant-garde... 3. van 8. vanguard
avant-propos... 7. preface
   12. introduction (remarks)
avarice... 4. lust 5. greed 7. avidity
   8. avidness, cupidity, grasping, rapacity,
   voracity 10. greediness
   12. covetousness
avarice demon... 6. Mammon
avaricious... 5. close 6. grabby, greedy
   7. miserly 8. covetous, grasping
   9. niggardly, penurious, rapacious,
   voracious 12. parsimonious
avatar... 7. epiphany 10. embodiment
   11. incarnation 14. transmigration
avatars of Vishnu (Hind Relig)...
   11. incarnation (deity to man)
avaunt... 4. away 5. allez, scram,
   vaunt 6. begone, depart 7. advance,
   vamoose
ave... 4. hail, viva, vive 8. farewell
avec (Fr)... 4. with
Ave Maria... 4. bead (rosary), song
   6. prayer 10. devotional
Avena... 4. oats 7. grasses
avenge... 7. requite 9. retaliate, vindicate
Avenging Angels... 8. nickname (Polit
   1858) 10. Danite Band (Mormons)
Avenging Spirit... 4. Fate, Fury 6. Erinys

7. Alastor, Atropos

avenue . . . 3. rue 4. land, pike, road, vent 5. alley 6. arcade, artery, defile, egress, outlet, street 7. channel, freeway, highway, opening 8. corridor, turnpike 9. boulevard, concourse 10. passageway 12. thoroughfare

aver . . . 3. say 5. state 6. affirm, allege, assert 7. declare, profess, protect 10. asseverate

average . . . 2. go 3. par, run 4. mean, rule 6. common, medial, medium, normal 7. balance 8. mediocre 10. generality

averment . . . 6. dictum, remark 7. witness 9. assertion, statement, testimony, utterance 10. allegation 11. affirmation, attestation 12. verification 13. pronouncement

Avernus . . . 4. lake (poison vapors) 5. Hades

averse . . . 5. loath 7. adverse 9. reluctant, unwilling 11. disinclined

aversion . . . 4. hate 5. odium 6. hatred, horror 7. disgust, dislike 9. antipathy, repulsion 10. abhorrence, repugnance 11. abomination 12. estrangement 13. indisposition, unwillingness

aversion to . . . see also *fear of*
novelty . . 9. neophobia
society . . 14. anthropophobia
strangers . . 10. xenophobia
wine . . 10. oenophobia

avert . . . 4. fend, save 5. check, deter, evade, repel 6. forbid, retard, switch, thwart 7. deflect, prevent 8. alienate, prohibit 9. forestall, sidetrack

aviary . . . 4. cage 5. house 7. dovecot (dovecote) 8. ornithon 9. birdhouse, columbary, enclosure 11. columbarium

aviation . . . 6. flight, flying 7. winging 9. skyriding 10. airplaning 11. aeronautics

aviation maneuver . . . 9. Immelmann (Ger)

aviator . . . 3. Ace 5. flier (flyer), pilot 6. airman, Icarus (fabled first) 7. wingman 8. aeronaut, aviatrix, operator 9. astronaut, birdwoman, Immelmann

avichi (Buddh) . . . 4. Hell 5. Hades 9. depravity, perdition 10. underworld

avid . . . 4. agog, keen 5. eager 6. grabby, greedy 7. anxious, craving, zestful 8. grasping 9. rapacious, voracious 10. avaricious

avidity . . . 4. lust 5. greed 7. avarice 8. cupidity, grasping 9. eagerness 10. greediness 12. covetousness

avion . . . 5. plane 7. airplane

avis . . . see *rara avis*

avisa . . . 4. news 6. advice, caveat 7. tidings, warning 11. information

Avis Indica (Astron) . . . 4. Apus 13. constellation

avital . . . 9. ancestral

avoid . . . 4. shun, snub 5. annul, dodge, elude, evade 6. escape, eschew, repeal, revoke, vacate 7. abstain, forbear 10. invalidate

avoidance . . . 6. outlet 7. evasion, removal 8. emptying, shunning,

vacating 9. annulment 10. withdrawal

avoirdupois . . . 4. beef 6. weight 7. gravity, tonnage 8. poundage 9. heaviness

avoirdupois weight . . . 3. ton 4. dram 5. grain, ounce, pound 13. hundred-weight

avow . . . 3. own, vow 5. admit, swear, vouch 6. allege, assert, pledge 7. confess, declare, profess, promise 10. avouchment 11. acknowledge

avulsion . . . 7. removal 9. severance 10. extraction, separation (ppty), withdrawal

awabi . . . 7. abalone

awaft . . . 6. adrift, afloat, wafted

await . . . 4. bide, come, heed, loom, pend, wait 5. abide, tarry, watch 6. ambush, attend, expect, impend, waylay 8. approach 10. forthcome

awake . . . 5. alert, alive, astir, rouse 6. arouse, excite, waking 8. open-eyed 9. attentive, conscious, sleepless, wide-awake

awaken . . . 5. awake 6. arouse, excite, stir up 8. roust out

award . . . 4. gift, give, meed, mete 5. allot, grant, medal, prize 6. reward, trophy 7. adjudge, present, verdict 8. accolade 9. medallion

award (pert to) . . .
book . . 4. Hugo 5. Edgar 6. Nebula
film . . 5. Oscar
television . . 4. Emmy
theater . . 4. Tony

aware . . . 3. hep 4. know 5. sense 7. mindful 8. apprized, sensible 9. cognizant, conscious 11. intelligent

awareness . . . 5. sense 7. feeling 9. sensation 10. impression, perception 11. mindfulness, sensibility 13. consciousness

away . . . 2. on 3. awa, far, fro, off, out 4. gone 5. aside, hence 6. abroad, absent, begone, onward, thence 7. escaped 8. vanished 9. elsewhere

away from . . .
body center . . 5. ectad 6. distal
mouth . . 6. aborad, aboral
wind . . 4. alee

awe . . . 3. cow 4. fear 5. dread 6. regard, terror, wonder 7. emotion, respect 8. astonish, frighten, surprise 9. reverence 10. admiration, veneration, wonderment 13. consideration

aweather (opp of alee) . . . 8. windward 11. weatherward

awe-inspiring . . . 5. eerie (eery) 7. awesome, ghostly 8. glorious, imposing, splendid, terrific 9. wonderful 10. impressive 11. magnificent

awe-struck . . . 4. awed 6. terrified 10. astonished, fear-struck, spellbound 12. wonder-struck 13. thunderstruck

awful . . . 4. awed, ugly 5. dread, great, gross 6. sacred, silent, solemn, woeful 7. awesome, fearful, hideous 8. dreadful, infamous, reverent, shocking, terrible 9. appalling, atrocious, deathlike, ludicrous, venerable, wonderful 10. deplorable,

impressive, outrageous, unpleasant
11. exceedingly
awkward . . . 5. gawky, inapt, inept
6. clumsy, gauche 7. froward, loutish,
unhandy 8. bungling, clownish,
lubberly, perverse, ungainly, unwieldy
9. graceless, inelegant, lumbering,
maladroit, ponderous 10. backhanded,
blundering, ungraceful
12. embarrassing, incommodious,
inconvenient
awkward age . . . 4. teen 5. teens
awkward fellow . . . 6. galoot
11. hobbledehoy
awless, aweless . . . 4. bald 6. brazen
8. fearless, unafraid 9. bold-faced,
dauntless 10. irreverent 11. unsurprised
12. unastonished
awn . . . 4. barb 5. beard (plant) 6. arista,
papous 7. bristle
awning . . . 6. canopy, screen, shield
7. shelter 8. velarium (anc)
AWOL . . . 5. hooky 7. truancy 9. truantism
11. absenteeism
awry . . . 4. agee 5. agley, amiss, askew
6. faulty 7. askance, asquint, crooked,
oblique 9. distorted 10. disorderly
11. disarranged 12. disorganized
ax, axe . . . 3. adz (adze), ask (dial) 4. tool
6. hammer, poleax (poleaxe) 7. hatchet
(small) 8. axhammer 9. discharge,
dismissal
ax (pert to) . . .
ancient . . 4. celt 6. chisel
blade . . 3. bit
execution . . 10. guillotine
handle . . 4. haft 5. helve
axial . . . 7. central, midmost, pivotal
axilla . . . 3. ala 4. axil 5. oxter 6. armpit
8. shoulder
axiom . . . 3. law, saw 4. rule 5. adage,
maxim, motto, truth 6. byword,
dictum, saying, truism 7. dictate,
precept, proverb, theorem
8. aphorism, apothegm 9. principle
11. proposition
axiomatic . . . 10. aphoristic, proverbial
11. self-evident, sententious

12. epigrammatic
axis . . . 3. hub 4. axle, bloc, nave,
stem 5. pivot, stalk 6. caulis, center,
league 7. fulcrum 8. alliance, vertebra
9. coalition
axle . . . 3. pin 4. axis 5. pivot, shaft
6. swivel 7. spindle 8. axletree
axle tooth . . . 5. molar
ayah . . . 4. amah, maid 5. mammy
9. governess, nursemaid
11. maidservant
aye . . . 2. ay 3. pro, yea, yes 4. ever, vote
5. voice 6. always, assent 8. thumbs
up, viva-voce
aye-aye . . . 5. lemur (Madagascar)
ayes . . . 10. all in favor
Azazel . . . 5. Eblis, Satan 9. scapegoat
Azerbaijanian . . . 4. Turk
14. Transcaucasian
azimuth . . . 3. arc 4. dial 6. circle
7. compass, horizon 8. distance,
magnetic 10. North point
Azores . . .
capital . . 5. Angra
city . . 5. Horta
group (islands) . . 6. St Mary 8. St
George 9. St Michael
locale . . 8. Atlantic (Ocean)
owner . . 8. Portugal
Aztec (pert to) . . .
calendar . . 7. Mexican
capital (anc) . . 12. Tenochtitlan
emperor . . 9. Montezuma
god . . 4. Xipe (sowing) 12. Quetzalcoatl
(peace)
hero . . 4. Nata (Myth) 6. Cortez
language . . 7. Nahuatl
locale (anc) . . 6. Aztlan
Noah (Mex) . . 6. Coxcox
people . . 7. Nahuatl (Nahuatlan)
stone . . 12. chalchihuitl
temple . . 8. teocalli
azure . . . 4. blue 7. celeste, sky-blue
8. bice blue, cerulean 9. blue vault,
cloudless 11. lapis lazuli
azygous . . . 3. odd 4. only, sole 6. single,
unique 8. singular 10. unrepeated
azymous . . . 10. unleavened

B

B . . . 4. beta 6. letter (2nd)
ba (Egypt) . . . 3. khu 4. soul
baa . . . 5. bleet
baehling . . . 4. lamb
Baal . . . 4. idol 5. deity 6. Baalim (pl)
7. Baalath 8. false god 9. fertility
baba (pert to) . . .
India . . 4. baby 5. child
Malaya . . 4. male
Slavic . . 5. nurse 7. midwife 8. old
woman
Turkey . . 5. title (of respect)
babacoote . . . 5. lemur (Madagascar)
Babber . . . 3. Utu (Utug) 6. sun god
babbo . . . 5. daddy 6. father

babel . . . 5. clang 6. jargon, tumult
7. discord 9. confusion
11. pandemonium
Babel (pert to) . . .
Bible . . 5. Tower 8. ziggurat
presently . . 14. Temple of Marduk
site (ancient) . . 6. Shinar (land of)
site (present) . . 7. Babylon
babirusa, babiroussa . . . 9. quadruped
(hoglike)
Babism (Persia) . . . 4. sect
baboon . . . 3. ape 5. Papio 6. chacma
7. babuina, monster 8. mandrill
babushka . . . 11. grandmother
baby . . . 4. babe, doll 6. coward, infant,

puppet, weanie 7. bambino, chicken **8.** juvenile, weakling **9.** miniature, youngling, youngster **10.** diminutive

baby carriage ... 4. pram **5.** wagon **6.** go-cart **8.** stroller **12.** perambulator

babyish ... 6. simple **7.** dollish, puerile **8.** childish **9.** childlike, infantile

Babylon ... see also *Babylonian*
capital of . . **9.** Babylonia
kingdom . . **4.** Elam **5.** Akkad (Accad)
meaning . . **9.** Gate of God
mountain . . **6.** Ararat
river . . **6.** Tigris **9.** Euphrates
World Wonder . . **14.** Hanging Gardens

Babylonian (pert to) ...
abode of the dead . . **5.** Aralu
chaos . . **4.** Apsu
deity . . **5.** Alalu (Alala), Siris
earth mother . . **6.** Ishtar
god . . **2.** Ea, Zu **3.** Anu, Bel **4.** Adad, Apsu, Irra **5.** Dagan, Enlil **6.** Nergal **7.** Shamash
goddess . . **3.** Aya **4.** Nina **5.** Belit (Beltis)
hero (Myth) . . **5.** Adapa, Etana **9.** Tilgamesh
king . . **6.** Sargon **9.** Habonidus, Hammurabi **10.** Nabonassar **14.** Nebuchadnezzar (Nebuchadrezzar)
temple, tower . . **8.** ziggurat

bacach ... 6. beggar **7.** cripple

bacalao ... 7. codfish, grouper

bacalao bird ... 3. auk **5.** murre **9.** guillemot

Bacardi ... 3. rum

bacca ... 5. berry

baccalaureate ... 6. degree (college), sermon **8.** bachelor

baccate ... 5. pulpy **9.** berrylike

bacchanal ... 7. reveler **8.** carouser

Bacchanalia ... 5. orgy **5.** feast **7.** debauch **9.** festival (Bacchus)

bacchante ... 6. maenad **7.** bacchae

Bacchus ... 4. wine **9.** god of wine

baccivorous ... 11. berry-eating

bachelor ... 4. male **6.** degree (Acad), garçon **8.** benedict, celibate **10.** misogamist

bacillus ... 9. bacterium

Bacis ... 2. Ra **4.** bull (sacred)

back ... 3. aft, aid, fro **4.** abet, hind, past, rear **5.** stern **6.** behind, second, uphold **7.** finance, sponsor, support, sustain **8.** extrados, intrados, resource **9.** encourage, posterior **10.** background

back (Anat) ... **4.** loin, nape **5.** notum **6.** dorsal, dorsum, lumbar, tergal, tergum **7.** occiput **8.** backbone, notalgia **10.** opisthenar (hand)

backbone ... 4. grit, guts **5.** nerve, pluck, spunk **6.** mettle, spirit **7.** courage, stamina, support **8.** firmness, gameness, mainstay **10.** dependence

backbone (Anat) ... **4.** axis **5.** brace, chine, spine **6.** column, spinal **7.** spinule, support **8.** ossicles **9.** vertebrae

backer ... 5. angel **6.** patron **7.** abettor, sponsor **8.** financer, promoter, upholder **9.** supporter, sustainer **10.** maintainer

background (opp of foreground) ...
4. rear **5.** stage **6.** offing **7.** horizon,

setting **8.** backdrop, distance, practice, training **9.** education **10.** experience **11.** savoir-faire

backhanded ... 6. clumsy **7.** awkward, devious **9.** insincere, insulting, sarcastic **10.** circuitous

backslider ... 8. apostate, deserter, recreant **10.** unfaithful

back-to-back ... 7. dos-à-dos

backward ... 4. back, dull, late **5.** arear, loath, tardy **6.** averse, modest, stupid **7.** bashful, belated, reverse **8.** arrested, dilatory, perverse, rearward, retarded, reticent, retrorse, reversed **9.** hindwards, recessive, reluctant, subnormal, unwilling **10.** behindhand, hesitating, regressive, retrograde **11.** unfavorable **13.** retrogressive, retrospective

bacon ... 4. lard, pork, side **5.** prize **6.** flitch, gammon, rasher **8.** Canadian, sowbelly

Bacon's Rebellion ... 6. revolt (Va 1676)

bacteria ... 5. cocci, germs **7.** aerobes, aerobia, bacilli **8.** microbes, spirilla **9.** organisms

bacteriologist culture ... 4. agar

Bactrian camel ... 9. two-humped

bad ... 3. ill, mal (pref) **4.** evil, fell, foul, poor, vile **5.** drole, fetid, nasty, wrong **6.** arrant, in pain, putrid, rotten, sinful, wanton, wicked **7.** corrupt, hurtful, naughty, noxious, spoiled, tainted, unlucky, unmoral, unsound, vicious **8.** annoying, criminal, improper, inferior, iniquity, sinister **9.** dangerous, defective, offensive, perverted, worthless **10.** iniquitous, malodorous, unsuitable **11.** inexpedient, inopportune **12.** disagreeable, inauspicious

bad (pert to) ...
blood . . **4.** feud **6.** enmity, rancor **7.** ill will **10.** bitterness, resentment
custom . . **9.** cacoethes
film . . **4.** bomb
legislation . . **7.** dysnomy
luck . . **5.** deuce **7.** ambsace
man's oatmeal . . **7.** hemlock (poison) **11.** wild chervil
writer . . **4.** hack

Baden ... 3. spa

badge ... 3. pin **4.** mark, sign, star **5.** index, token **6.** emblem, ensign, plaque, shield, symbol **7.** earmark **8.** insignia **14.** identification

badger ... 3. nag, rag **4.** bait **5.** harry, tease, worry **6.** bother, extort, harass, hawker, heckle, hector, pester **8.** huckster

badger (animal) ... **5.** Meles (anc), pahmi, ratel **6.** bauson, mammal, teledu, wombat **9.** bandicoot, mistonusk

Badger State ... 9. Wisconsin

badinage ... 4. fool **5.** joker, sport **6.** banter **8.** raillery **9.** badinerie, simpleton **10.** persiflage, pleasantry

badly ... 3. bad, ill **4.** sick **5.** amiss, wrong **6.** poorly, unwell **8.** faultily, wickedly **9.** viciously **11.** exceedingly, imperfectly **12.** disagreeably, unskillfully

13. unfortunately

badly off . . . 3. sad 7. hapless, unblest, unhappy, unlucky 8. luckless 11. impecunious, unfortunate 12. unprosperous 14. unprovidential

baff . . . 4. beat, blow, thud 6. strike, stroke (golf)

baffle . . . 4. balk, foil 5. cheat, elude, evade, spike 6. defeat, delude, muffle, puzzle, thwart 7. mystify, nonplus, perplex 8. bewilder, confound 9. bamboozle, frustrate 10. disconcert

baffling . . . 7. elusive, evasive 8. puzzling 9. bothering, confusing, dismaying 10. mystifying, perplexing, perturbing 11. frustrating 13. disconcerting

baft . . . 3. aft 4. baff 5. abaff, cloth, shaft 6. astern

bag . . . 3. net, pac, pot, sac, sag 4. etui, grip, load, poke, sack, trap 5. ascus, belly, catch, droop, pouch, purse, seize, snare, steal 6. entrap, sachet, valise 7. bladder, capture, distend, handbag, pannier, satchel 8. reticule, suitcase 9. Gladstone, haversack, sac de nuit 10. pocketbook 11. portmanteau

bag and baggage . . . 10. completely 11. impedimenta

bagatelle . . . 3. toy 4. game 6. bauble, geegaw, trifle 7. trinket 10. knickknack, triviality 12. fiddle-faddle

Bagdad, Baghdad . . .
capital of . . 4. Iraq
character . . 6. Sinbad (The Sailor)
founder (762) . . 8. Almanzor
kingdom (anc) . . 11. Mesopotamia
Oriental term . . 8. lambskin (raw)
river . . 6. Tigris
transportation (famed) . . 7. Railway

bagpipe, bagpipes . . . 5. drone, pipes 7. musette 9. Dudelsack 10. doodlesack, sordellina

bagpipe (pert to) . . .
music variations . . 7. pibroch
parts . . 4. lill, oboe 5. drone 7. chanter 9. chalumeau
player . . 5. piper
tube . . 6. drones 7. chanter
tune . . 4. port

Bahamas, Bahama Islands . . .
capital . . 6. Nassau
discoverer . . 8. Columbus
native . . 5. conch
naval base (US) . . 9. Mayaguana
San Salvador (now) . . 14. Watlings Island (Watling Island)

bahan . . . 6. poplar, willow (Bib)

bahay . . . 5. house

bahi . . . 7. fortune (gypsy)

bail . . . 3. dip 4. bond, hoop, lade, lave, ring, rynd 5. court, ladle, throw 6. bucket, dipper, handle, pledge, secure, surety 8. replevin, security 9. guarantee

bailiff . . . 5. agent, bobby, reeve, staff 6. deputy, staves (pl) 7. marshal, officer, sheriff, shrieve, steward 8. bluecoat, gendarme, overseer 9. constable 12. understeward

bailiwick . . . 6. canton, county, domain 7. commune, diocese 8. precinct,

province 12. municipality

bain . . . 4. near 5. lithe, ready, short 6. direct, limber, supple 7. forward, willing

bairn . . . 3. kid, tot 4. mite 5. child 6. urchin

bait . . . 3. fly 4. feed, hook, lure, trap 5. bribe, decoy, snare 6. badger, harass, hockle 7. fulcrum, torment 8. inveigle 9. persecute 10. enticement, exasperate, temptation

bait . . . 3. dap, dib 4. fish, hook 6. dibble

bakal (Orient) . . . 9. tradesman 10. shopkeeper

bake . . . 3. dry 4. cake, cook, fire, kiln 5. roast 6. anneal, harden 8. clambake 9. dehydrate

bakehead . . . 4. rail 5. guard, shack 6. stoker 7. fireman 8. trainman

baken . . . 4. buoy 6. beacon 8. landmark

baker's dozen . . . 4. long 6. devil's 7. inbread 8. thirteen

baksheesh . . . 3. sop, tip 5. bribe 7. largess (largesse) 8. gratuity 12. compensation

bal . . . 4. ball, mine, prom

balance . . . 4. even, rest, rule 5. poise, ratio, scale, weigh 6. adjust, aplomb, normal, offset, reason, rhythm, sanity 7. average, ballast, compare, euphony, measure, remains, surplus 8. equality, equalize, leftover, residual, saneness, serenity, symmetry 9. composure, equipoise, remainder, stability 10. equanimity, neutralize, proportion, symmetrize 11. equilibrium 12. counterpoise

balanced . . . 4. even, just 6. poised 7. equable 8. measured 9. equitable 10. euphonious 11. symmetrical 13. self-possessed

balancer . . . 7. acrobat, gymnast 10. ropedancer 11. equilibrist

balcony . . . 4. dais 5. stage 6. podium 7. estrade, gallery, rostrum 8. brattice, platform

bald . . . 4. bare, dull, mere, open 5. crude, naked, plain 6. simple 7. epilose 8. depilous, hairless 9. bald-pated 11. unconcealed

baldachin, baldaquin . . . 6. canopy (St Peter's, Rome), fabric

Balder (pert to) . . .
father . . 4. Odin
god of . . 5. light, peace
mother . . 5. Frigg
slain by . . 9. mistletoe (dart)
wife . . 5. Nanna

balderdash . . . 3. rot 4. bosh 5. trash 6. bunkum, jargon 7. bombast 8. buncombe, falderal, nonsense, tommyrot 9. poppycock

baldness . . . 6. acomia 8. alopecia 11. phalacrosis 12. hairlessness

baldric . . . 4. belt (ornament) 6. zodiac 7. support (sword)

bale . . . 3. woe 4. bind, load, pack 5. truss 6. ballot, bundle, burden, misery, packet, seroon 7. anguish, package 11. encumbrance

Balearic Islands . . . 5. Ibiza (Iviza), Palma

(capital) 7. Majorca (Mallorca), Minorca
10. Formentera

baleful . . . 3. bad, sad 4. dire 6. woeful
7. baneful, harmful, malific, noisome,
noxious 8. damaging 9. ill-omened,
malignant 10. pernicious
12. inauspicious

balk . . . 4. foil 5. check, ridge 6. baffle,
defeat, fallow, rafter, signal (fishing)
thwart 7. blunder, faux pas, stickle
9. frustrate, hindrance 10. bafflement,
disappoint 14. disappointment

Balkan Peninsula . . .
native. . 4. Serb
river. . 3. Une 4. Sava 6. Danube
sea. . 3. Black 6. Aegean 7. Marmosa
8. Adriatic 13. Mediterranean
State. . 6. Bosnia, Greece, Serbia, Turkey
(Eur) 7. Albania, Rumania 8. Bulgaria
10. Yugoslavia

balky . . . 7. restive 9. faltering, obstinate,
shrinking, stickling

ball . . . 3. bal, fly, hop, lob, orb 4. bead,
clew (yarn), pill, shot 5. dance, globe,
pearl, pinda (rice) 6. pellet, pelota,
sphere 7. rissole 8. conglobe, snowball
9. eight ball 10. cannonball 12. medicine
ball

ball (of games) . . . 4. golf, hand, polo,
soft 6. basket, tennis, volley 7. bowling,
cricket, croquet, jai alai 8. baseball,
billiard, ping-pong

ballad . . . 3. lay 4. lied, poem, song
5. derry, rhyme, verse 6. sonnet
7. ballade, canzone

ballast . . . 5. poise 6. aplomb, steady,
weight 7. balance 9. kentledge,
saburrate, stabilize 10. equanimity,
equivalent 14. counterbalance

balled up . . . 7. complex, mixed up,
muddled 8. confused, fouled up
9. befuddled, entangled, snarled up
10. disordered 11. complicated

ballet (pert to) . . .
arrangement. . 12. choreography
dance. . 6. adagio 9. pantomime
dancer. . 8. coryphee, danseuse
9. ballerina
jump. . 4. jeté 5. coupé
lover. . 11. balletomane
music. . 5. opera 6. comedy 7. d'action
14. divertissement
painter of. . 5. Degas
skirt. . 4. tutu

balloon . . . 3. bag 4. ball, tire 5. barge
(Siam), blimp, swell 6. aviate, ballon,
dilate, expand, gasbag 7. distend,
nacelle 8. aerostat, aircraft 9. dirigible

balloon (type) . . . 4. free, kite 5. pilot
7. captive 8. sounding 11. montgolfier,
observation

ballot . . . 4. bale, poll, vote 5. elect, slate,
voice 6. select, ticket 8. suffrage

ballyhoo . . . 4. plug 5. boost, noise
6. fracas, hoopla, hubbub, ruckus,
rumpus 7. promote 9. advertise,
publicity 10. hullabaloo

balm . . . 3. oil 4. bito, calm 5. cream,
salve 6. balsam, elixir, lotion, pacify
7. anodyne, cushion, Melissa, perfume,
relieve, unction, unguent 8. liniment,

mitigate, ointment 9. calmative,
fragrance, mitigator 10. palliative

balm (pert to) . . . 5. Vicks 6. arnica, zachun
7. camphor, lanolin, menthol 8. glycerin,
ointment, vaseline 10. petrolatum

Balm of . . . 6. Gilead

balmy . . . 4. mild 5. batty, daffy, dippy,
drunk, goofy, moony, spicy, sweet
6. dreamy, insane, savory 7. healing
8. aromatic, fragrant, lenitive, redolent,
soothing 9. ambrosial, assuaging,
emollient 10. palliative, refreshing
11. odoriferous 12. sweet-scented

balsam . . . 3. fir 4. riga, tolu 5. resin
6. embalm, poplar, storax 7. benzoin,
perfume 8. bdellium (Bib), medicine
9. oleoresin 12. Balsam of Peru, Balsam
of Tolu

Baltic States . . . 6. Latvia 7. Estonia
9. Lithuania

Baltimore . . .
Belle. . 4. rose
bird. . 6. oriole
butterfly. . 7. phaeton
city of. . 8. Maryland
hemp. . 4. flax
history of. . 18. Star Spangled Banner
(1814)

baluster . . . 4. post 7. support, upright
8. banister

bam . . . 4. fake, hoax, mock, sham
5. cheat, spoof, trick 6. deceit
7. wheedle 8. flimflam 9. deception,
imitation

bambino . . . 4. babe, baby, icon 5. child,
Pietà 6. infant (Christ)

bamboo (pert to) . . .
curtain. . 8. frontier
English. . 10. Philippine
genus. . 7. Bambuss
sacred. . 6. nandin
sprouts (pickled). . 5. achar
stems. . 4. cane
sugar. . 6. silica 9. tabasheer

bamboozle . . . 4. dupe, hoax 5. trick
6. baffle, cajole, humbug 7. beguile,
deceive, mystify, perplex 9. victimize

ban . . . 4. coin, tabu, veto 5. curse,
edict, taboo, title (anc) 6. muslin,
outlaw 7. embargo, exclude, kokumin
8. anathema 9. interdict, ostracism,
ostracize 10. injunction, kokumingun
11. malediction, prohibition
12. proscription 15. excommunication

banal . . . 4. flat 5. corny, stale, trite
6. cliché, common, old hat
11. commonplace, stereotyped
13. platitudinous

banana . . . 4. Musa, saba 6. ensete
8. Musaceae, plantain

banana (pert to) . . .
Bananaland. . 10. Queensland
bananalike. . 8. plantain
bird. . 4. quit 6. oriole
boa. . 5. snake
color. . 7. sunbeam
fish. . 8. ladyfish
freckle. . 7. disease
leaf. . 5. frond
oil. . 7. lacquer
Philippine. . 7. saguing

shrub .. 9. evergreen

bananas . . 5. crazy 7. excited

band . . 3. bar, tie 4. belt, body, crew, hoop, line, pack, ring, sash, zone 5. bunch, corps, group, patte, strap, stria, strip, tribe, unite 6. cohort, collar, fascia, fillet, girdle, ligula, outfit, pledge, radula (Zool), tether 7. bandage, company 8. cincture, encircle, ensemble, neckband, striping 9. frequency (radio), orchestra, striation

bandage . . 3. gag 4. bind, tape 5. sling, spica, truss 6. ligate, swathe 7. wrapper 8. compress, dressing, ligature 9. accipiter, blindfold 10. tourniquet

bandicoot . . 3. rat 9. Perameles

bandit . . 4. thug 5. thief 6. dacoit, outlaw, robber 7. bandido, brigand, footpad, ladrone 8. marauder, picaroon 9. bandolero 10. highwayman

bandmaster . . 5. Sousa 6. leader 7. maestro 8. choragus, director 9. conductor 13. Kapellmeister

bandolero . . 5. thief 6. robber 10. highwayman

bandy . . 4. beat, cart, game 5. bowed 6. curved, strive, stroke (tennis) 7. contend, embowed 8. carriage (Ind), exchange, to and fro 9. bowlegged 11. bandy-legged, reciprocate

bandy words . . 5. argue 6. bicker, parley 7. contend, wrangle 8. converse

bane . . 3. woe 4. evil, harm, kill, pest, ruin 5. curse, venom 6. injury, plague, poison, slayer 7. disease (sheep), scourge 8. murderer, vexation 9. grievance 10. affliction, pestilence, visitation

baneful . . 3. ill 4. vile 7. harmful, noxious 9. injurious 10. pernicious 11. detrimental

bang . . 3. hit, rap 4. beat, blow, dash, drub, kick, lift, shut, slam 5. crack, knock, pound, punch, smack, thump, verve, whack 6. energy, report, strike, thrash, thrill 7. collide 8. coiffure

bangle . . 5. charm 7. circlet 8. bracelet

banish . . 3. ban 4. oust 5. exile, expel 6. deport, dispel, outlaw, punish 7. condemn, dismiss, exclude 8. relegate 9. ostracize, proscribe 10. expatriate 13. excommunicate

banister . . 4. post, rail 8. baluster 10. balustrade

banjo . . 7. samisen

bank . . 3. row 4. brae, edge, heap, quay, ripa 5. brink, flock, hurst (sandy), marge, shoal, shore, slope, table 6. aviate, margin, quarry, rivage, series, stakes, strand 7. anthill, barrier, deposit, incline 8. buttress, treasury 9. acclivity, riverside 13. fortification

bank account . . 5. funds, means 6. assets, moneys 8. finances 9. exchequer

banker . . 4. game 6. broker, lender 9. financier 11. moneylender 12. money-changer

bankrupt . . 4. bust, ruin 5. broke, smash 6. failed, quisby (sl) 7. failure

---

9. destitute, insolvent, moneyless, penniless 12. impoverished

banner . . 4. fane, flag 6. ensign, poster 7. leading, pennant, placard 8. foremost, headline, standard, streamer 9. exemplary 10. surpassing

banns, marriage . . 6. notice 7. sibrede 12. proclamation

banquet . . 4. fete 5. diffa, feast, festa 6. fiesta, junket, regale, repast, spread 8. festival, jamboree 10. regalement

Banquo . . 9. character (Macbeth) *

banshee, banshie . . 4. shee 5. fairy, Geist, sidhe 6. spirit, sprite

banshee, banshie (pert to) . . 3. cry 4. keen, wail 5. death

bantam (pert to) . . .

   cock . . 3. fop 5. dandy, sport 7. peacock 8. strutter 9. swaggerer 12. swashbuckler

   Java . . 4. duck, fowl 5. breed 6. Brahma, Cochin

   slang . . 4. runt 6. peewee, shrimp

   sports . . 6. weight

bantamweight . . 5. boxer (118 lbs) 7. fighter 8. pugilist 9. contender 10. contestant

banter . . 4. jest, josh, mock, twit 5. borak, chaff, sport, tease, trick 6. delude, deride, satire 7. asteism, wheedle 8. badinage, raillery, ridicule 10. persiflage, pleasantry

Bantu, South Africa . . .

   language . . 3. Ila 8. Kongoese

   people . . 4. Vili, Zulu 5. Duala, Xhosa 6. Basuto, Damara 7. Swahili 8. Bechuana

banzai . . 4. hail 5. hello, hullo 6. attack, charge 9. greetings 11. salutations

baobab tree (pert to) . . .

   bark . . 4. rope 5. cloth, paper

   fruit . . 11. monkey bread

   genus . . 9. Adansonia

   pulp . . 8. beverage

baptism . . 4. rite 6. naming 9. wetting 8. ablution 9. aspersion, immersion, sacrament 10. initiation, sprinkling 11. christening 12. consecration, purification, regeneration (spiritual)

baptism (pert to) . . .

   cloth . . 7. chrisom

   dead (RCCh) . . 5. Blood 6. Desire

   fire . . 9. fuertaufe

   place . . 4. font 10. baptistery (anc)

   receptacle . . 5. basin 7. piscina

   water . . 5. laver

bar . . 3. ban, dam, fid, pry, pub, rod 4. bolt, deny, fess, joke, line, rack, rail, sess, type 5. betty (thieves' slang), block, court, deter, easer, estop, ingot, lever, shoal, space, staff 6. except, forbid, hinder, lounge, ripper, saloon, stitch, stripe, tavern 7. barrier, barroom, bass-bar, chevron, counter, crowbar, exclude, gin mill, prevent, railing, sandbar, trapeze 8. blockade, disallow, obstacle, obstruct, preclude, prohibit 9. barricade, hindrance, roadhouse 10. impediment, profession, singletree 11. obstruction, rathskeller, whippletree 12. underscoring, watering hole

barb ... 3. jag 4. clip, flue, harl, herl, seta 5. horse, point, ramus, scarf (nun's), speed 6. setula, striga 7. bristle, feather, pinnula 8. kingfish 9. arrowhead 10. projection

Barbados Island ...
capital .. 10. Bridgetown
drink .. 3. rum
government ... 7. British
location .. 8. Antilles (Lesser) 10. West Indies
native .. 3. Bim (nickname)

barbarian ... 3. hun 4. Goth, rude 5. beast, brute 6. savage, vandal 8. cannibal, man-eater 9. untutored, vulgarian 10. extraneous, Philistine, unlettered 11. uncivilized 15. anthropophagite

barbaric ... 5. cruel 6. brutal, Gothic, savage 7. foreign, inhuman, vicious 8. non-Greek, non-Latin, ruthless 9. barbarous, primitive 10. extraneous 11. uncivilized 12. non-Christian

barbarism ... 6. ferity 8. rudeness, solecism 9. barbarity, crudeness, Gothicism, ignorance, vulgarism 10. coarseness, corruption, foreignism 11. impropriety

Barbarossa ... 7. emperor (Rom) 8. red beard

Barbary ape ... 5. magot

Barbary State (former) ... 5. Tunis 7. Algiers, Morocco 12. Tripolitania

barbate ... 7. bearded, stubbly 9. whiskered 11. barbigerous

barbecue ... 5. feast, roast 6. animal (whole), picnic 7. brazier, hibachi 9. Dutch oven 10. shish kebab 13. entertainment (out-of-doors)

barber ... 5. shave 6. figaro, shaver, tonsor 7. tonsure 10. haircutter 12. tonsorialist

Barber of Seville character ... 6. Figaro, Rosina

Barcelona, Spain ...
building (famed) .. 6. palace (Kings of Aragon) 9. Cathedral (Gothic)
port .. 13. Mediterranean
street (famed) .. 6. Rambla

bard ... 4. muse, poet, scop (Hist) 5. druid, runer, vates 7. minstrel, musician (wandering) 10. Parnassian

Bard of ...
Avon .. 11. Shakespeare
Ayrshire .. 5. Burns
Rydal Mount .. 10. Wordsworth

bare ... 3. raw 4. bald, mere, nude, open 5. alone, empty, naked, plain, shear, sheer, stark, strip 6. barren, denude, divest, expose, reveal, simple, vacant 7. exposed, unarmed, uncover 8. desolate, disclose, stripped 9. destitute, unadorned, uncovered 10. stark-naked, threadbare 11. defenseless, unconcealed

barefaced ... 4. bare, bold 6. brassy, brazen 8. impudent 9. audacious, shameless 11. undisguised

barely ... 4. jimp, only 5. faint 6. hardly, merely, nudely, poorly, simply 7. nakedly 8. narrowly, scantily, scarcely

14. insufficiently

bargain ... 3. buy 4. deal, pact, prig, sell 5. trade 6. barter, chisel, dicker, haggle 7. chaffer, compact, mediate 8. contract, covenant, purchase 9. agreement, Bon Marché, cheapness, negotiate 10. engagement 11. stipulation, transaction

barge ... 3. ark, hoy 4. raft, scow, ship 5. ferry, float, praam, scold 6. berate, lumber, rebuke, tender 7. birlinn (birling), lighter 9. transport

barge in ... 5. enter 6. bungle, butt in, invade, push in 7. blunder, intrude

barghest ... 6. goblin

bargoose ... 4. duck 9. merganser, sheldrake

bark ... 3. bay, yap, yip 4. bang, bast, husk, peel, rind, ross, ship, skin, tapa, yelp 5. cough, niepa, shout, strip, youff 6. bowwow, clamor, cortex, outcry, packet, scrape 7. canella 8. ballyhoo, periderm 9. sassafras

barker ... 4. tout 6. pistol 7. spieler 9. solicitor 10. ballyhooer, theaterman

barking ... 7. latrant 8. hylactic

Barlaam and Josephet (Joasaph) ... 11. Buddha story (Christian version)

barley ... 4. bigg, food, seed 5. grain 6. ptisan, tsamba 7. Hordeum

barley (pert to) ...
bird .. 6. siskin 7. wagtail (yellow), wryneck 11. nightingale
bree .. 3. ale 6. liquor
shaped .. 10. hordeiform

barlow ... 9. jackknife (one-bladed)

barm ... 3. froth, yeast 6. leaven 7. ferment

barn ... 3. bay, mow 4. loft

barnacle ... 4. bray (Her) 5. acorn, goose, leech 6. animal, sucker 8. adherent, parasite 9. sycophant 10. Cirripedia, crustacean

barnstormer ... 5. actor 7. aviator 11. entertainer

baron ... 4. peer 5. mogul, noble 6. daimio, tycoon 7. freeman 8. nobleman, somebody 9. financier, personage 10. capitalist 13. industrialist

baroque ... 6. ornate, quaint, rococo 7. bizarre 9. irregular 11. extravagant

barracks ... 4. camp, huts 6. casern, laager 9. barracoon 10. encampment

barraclade ... 7. blanket (homemade)

barracuda ... 4. fish, spet 5. barry (Bahamas) 6. sennet

barrage ... 3. dam 4. weir 5. blitz 6. strafe 7. barrier, gunfire, milldaw 9. cannonade, roadblock 11. obstruction

barrage (military) ... 3. box 5. mines 6. normal 7. balloon 8. creeping, standing 9. emergency 12. anti-aircraft

barranca ... 4. bank 5. bluff 6. ravine

barratry ... 6. breach, simony 8. bad faith, mala fide 10. infidelity 11. dereliction

barred ... 6. cooped, fenced, grated, ribbed 7. striped 8. confined, debarred, excluded, streaked

barrel ... 3. box, keg, tun 4. cade, cask, drum, knag 5. quill, speed 6. runlet, tierce 7. calamus (Zool), rundlet

8. cylinder, hogshead 9. kilderkin

barrel (pert to) . . .
maker . . 6. cooper
miscellaneous . . 3. gun, pen 4. pipe
6. pencil
sling . . 9. parbuckle
stopper . . 4. bung

barren . . . 3. dry 4. arid, bare, dull 5. blank,
empty, heath, inane 6. desert, effete,
jejune, karroo, meager, Sahara, stupid
7. sterile 8. desolate, impotent, unpoetic
9. infertile 10. unfruitful, unprolific
12. unproductive, unprofitable

barricade . . . 3. bar 4. bolt, rail, seal, stop
5. block, close, fence 6. abatis 7. barrier,
padlock 8. blockade, obstacle, obstruct
11. obstruction 13. fortification

barrico . . . 3. keg 4. cask

barrier . . . 3. Alp, bar, dam 4. clog,
door, gate, wall, weir 5. block, fence,
hedge, panel 6. screen 7. parapet,
railing 8. blockade, boundary, fortress,
obstacle, stockade, stoppage
9. partition, restraint 10. impediment,
portcullis 11. obstruction

Barrie's boy . . . 8. Peter Pan

barrikin (Eng sl) . . . 6. jargon 9. gibberish

barrister . . . 6. lawyer 7. adviser, pleader
8. advocate, attorney 9. counselor
(counsellor), solicitor

barroom . . . 3. bar, pub, tap 6. lounge,
saloon, tavern 7. cantina, gin mill,
taproom 8. alehouse 9. roadhouse
11. rathskeller 12. watering hole

barrow . . . 3. hod, hog (male) 4. brae,
fell, hill, knap, moor 5. grave (anc),
mound 7. tumulus 8. mountain
11. wheelbarrow 12. Reihengräber

bartender . . . 5. mixer 6. barman, bistro
7. barkeep, tapster 8. publican

barter . . . 4. deal, sell, swap 5. trade,
truck 7. bargain, permute, traffic
8. commerce, exchange

Bartholomew (pert to) . . . 4. Fair, Play
(Shaksp) 5. Saint 6. martyr 7. Apostle
(one of 12) 8. Massacre

Bartimeus (Bib) . . . 6. beggar (blind)

barton . . . 4. farm 5. abode, manor
6. grange 7. demesne 8. farmyard,
hacienda 9. homestead

baru . . . 4. tree (fiber) 7. majagua

base . . . 3. bed, low 4. dado, evil, foot,
foul, mean, root, seat, site, sole
5. basis, basso, cause, petty, radix,
socle, voice 6. abject, bottom, center,
factor, patten, plinth, podium, singer,
sordid, vulgar, wicked 7. servile, station
8. basement, cosmetic, degraded,
infamous, inferior, pedestal, shameful,
standard 9. principle, worthless
10. despicable, foundation, villainous
12. contemptible, dishonorable,
headquarters

baseball (terms) . . . 3. bag, bat, box,
fan, fly, hit, lob, out, RBI, run 4. ball,
base, bunt, deck, foul, home, nine, pill,
sack, save, walk, wild 5. bench, clout,
coach, count, curve, drive, error, field,
first, force, glove, homer, liner, mound,
pitch, plate, pop-up, score, slide, sport,
swing, third 6. assist, batter, bungle,
double, dugout, fumble, ground, putout,
rubber, runner, screen, second, series,
single, sinker, stance, strike, string,
target, triple, windup 7. battery, bullpen,
diamond, fielder, floater, rhubarb (sl),
squeeze, stretch 8. backstop, grounder,
keystone, knuckler, outfield, pinch-
hit, powdered, spit ball 9. sacrifice,
strikeout 10. ballplayer

baseborn . . . 3. low 4. mean 5. lowly,
plain 6. common, humble 7. bastard,
ignoble, lowborn 8. plebeian, spurious
11. commonplace 12. illegitimate

based on . . .
evidence . . 7. damning 8. decisive
10. conclusive
experience . . 7. empiric 9. empirical
numbers . . 5. hexad 6. nonary, senary
7. tertial

baseness . . . 6. infamy 7. badness
9. servility, vulgarity 10. wickedness
11. inferiority 13. dastardliness,
subordination

bash . . . 3. bat, jab, lam 4. beat, belt, biff,
blow, conk, mash, slug, sock 5. clout,
paste, punch, smack, whack 6. bruise,
strike, wallop 7. clobber

Basham's King . . . 2. Og

bashful . . . 3. coy, shy 5. heioe, mousy,
timid 6. demure, modest 8. blushing,
retiring, sheepish, timorous, verecund
9. diffident 13. self-conscious

basic . . . 4. root 5. basal, basis 7. essence,
primary 8. alkaline, original 9. essential
10. underlying 11. fundamental

Basilian . . . 3. art 4. monk, rule 6. bishop
7. liturgy, St Basil (The Great)
8. precepts 10. Cappadocia

basilica . . . 5. major, minor, title
6. canopy, church, shrine, temple
11. patriarchal

Basilican (pert to) . . .
books . . 5. sixty 6. Digest
century . . 5. Tenth
empire . . 9. Byzantine
laws . . 9. Justinian

basin . . . 3. bed (water), cup, pit, tub
4. bowl, cock, font, hole, sink, tank
5. laver, plain, playa, stoup 6. cavity,
chafer, coulee, ground, lavabo, marine,
valley, vessel 7. lowland, piscina
8. curvette 9. washbasin 10. depression

basis . . . 4. base, fond, root 5. cause,
start 6. bottom, factor, motive, reason,
thesis 7. premise, warrant 9. assertion,
principle 10. foundation, groundwork
13. justification

bask . . . 3. sin, tub 4. warm 5. bathe,
revel 7. suffuse 8. apricate 9. luxuriate

basket . . . 3. bin, box, car (balloon), net,
ped, pod 4. caba, cage, kish, skep,
trug 5. cabas 6. dosser, gabion, vessel,
wisket 7. corbeil, hanaper, pannier,
scuttle, wattage 9. container

basket (pert to) . . .
coal mine . . 3. tub 4. corf
fig . . 5. frail 6. tapnet
fire . . 5. grate 7. cresset
fishing . . 3. pot 4. buck (eel), caul, weel
5. crail, crate, creel 6. hamper
making . . 5. slath 6. slarth

wicker . . 3. cob 5. cesta, osier 6. hamper
7. hanaper 8. bassinet
Basque (pert to) . . .
ancestors . . 8. Iberians
cap . . 5. beret
home . . 5. Spain 8. Pyrenees
bas-relief . . . 7. carving, relievo 12. basso-
relievo (basso-rilievo)
bass . . . 4. fish 5. fiber, voice (low)
6. singer 8. weakfish 13. basso profundo
bassoon . . . 4. oboe 6. fagott 7. fagotto
bast . . . 4. bass 5. fiber
Bast (Egypt) . . . 4. Ptah 7. goddess 10. lady
of life
bastard . . . 3. odd 4. heel (sl), sham
5. false, louse (sl) 7. bâtarde (Fr)
8. abnormal, bantling, spurious
9. scoundrel 10. adulterate
12. illegitimate 13. nullius filius
baste . . . 3. hit, sew 4. cook, lard, lash,
tack, whip 5. stitch, thrash 7. trounce
8. lambaste
bastion . . . 5. redan 8. fastness
10. stronghold 13. fortification
bat . . . 3. hit, jag, lam, rap 4. belt,
blow, clip, club, slug, sock, swat, wink
5. binge, clout, paste, smack, spree,
stick, whack 6. bender, cudgel, racket,
wallop 7. clobber
bat (mammal) . . . 6. aliped, fox bat, kalong
7. noctule, vampire 8. serotine 9. flying
fox, pipistrel (pipistrelle), reremouse
10. Chiroptera
batch . . . 3. lot 4. heap, lump, mess,
slew 5. bunch, group, stack 6. amount,
baking 7. mixture 8. quantity
10. collection
bath . . . 3. dip, tub 4. sitz 5. steam,
sweat, vapor 6. plunge, shower, sponge
7. Finnish, mineral, sulphur
bath (pert to) . . .
Eccl . . 8. ablution
house . . 6. bagnic, cabana 8. balneary
10. natatorium
photography . . 5. toner 9. developer
Roman . . 7. balneum 11. Warm Springs
sitz . . 5. bidet
warm . . 5. therm
bathe . . . 3. tub, wet 4. bask, lave, swim,
wash 5. flush 6. drench 7. immerse,
moisten, pervade, suffuse 8. medicate,
permeate
baton . . . 3. rod 4. mace, wand 5. staff,
stick 6. baston, cudgel, fasces
7. scepter, support 9. truncheon
Batrachia . . . 5. Anura, frogs, toads
7. Surinam 8. Salienta
Battalion of Death (Russ) . . . 13. legion
of women
batten . . . 5. close, gloat 6. fasten, fatten,
secure, thrive, timber
battered . . . 6. beaten, pasted 7. bruised
8. impaired 9. shattered, weathered
battery . . . 3. set 4. guns, pack 6. cohort,
series 7. assault, platoon 8. baseball
(term) 9. artillery
battery (Elec) . . . 4. cell, grid, pole
5. anode, plate 6. Leyden 7. storage,
voltaic 9. electrode
battle . . . 3. war 4. fray, meet, tilt 5. brush,
fight, joust, scrap 6. action, affray,

barney, combat, tussle 7. contest,
scuffle, warfare 8. conflict, skirmish,
struggle 9. challenge, encounter
10. engagement
Battle (pert to) . . .
Bib . . 8. Aceldama 12. potter's field
Civil War . . 7. Bull Run 15. Lookout
Mountain
formation . . 4. line 5. herse, order
Great . . 10. Armageddon
Hundred Years (1346) . . 5. Crecy
Revolution . . 10. Bunker Hill
slogan . . 8. aux-armes 9. battle cry
World War I . . 6. Verdun (1916)
World War II . . 11. Pearl Harbor (1941)
battologize . . . 6. repeat 7. iterate,
recount, restate 9. reiterate
12. recapitulate
bauble . . . 3. toy 4. gaud 6. doodad,
geegaw, trifle, trivia 7. bibelot, trinket
8. falderal (folderol) 9. bagatelle,
plaything 10. knickknack
bauxite product . . . 8. aluminum
Bavaria . . .
capital . . 6. Munich
city . . 8. Augsburg, Wurzburg
9. Nuremburg 12. Ludwigshafen
freeway . . 8. autobahn
king (former) . . 10. Maximilian
prince . . 6. Rupert
river . . 4. Eger, Isar
bawdy . . . 4. lewd 6. coarse, ribald, risqué
bawl . . . 3. cry, say, sob 4. bark, howl,
roar, wail, weep, yell 5. blare, shout
6. bellow, boohoo, plaint 8. proclaim
10. vociferate
bay . . . 3. ria 4. cove, howl, roan, wail
5. bight, horse, inlet, oriel, sinus
6. recess, window 7. ululate
bay (pert to) . . .
antler . . 9. stag's tine (2nd)
bird . . 5. snipe 6. curlew, godwit, plover
color . . 4. roan
tree . . 6. laurel
Bayard . . . 5. horse, steed (Rinaldo's)
bayonet . . . 5. lance, saber, spear, sword
6. dagger, weapon 7. poniard
bayou . . . 5. creek, marsh 6. slough,
stream 7. channel 11. watercourse
Bayou State . . . 11. Mississippi
Bay State . . . 13. Massachusetts
bazaar . . . 4. fair, shop 6. market
7. canteen (army) 10. exposition
be . . . 2. am 3. are 4. live 5. exist 7. prevail
beach . . . 5. coast, plage, playa, praya,
sands, shore 6. shilla, strand
9. waterside
beachcomber . . . 4. wave 6. loafer
8. vagabond
beach shelter . . . 6. cabana
beacon . . . 4. beam, flag, sign, vane
5. fanal, light, radar, radio 6. marker,
pharos, signal 7. cresset, lantern,
seamark 10. lighthouse, watchtower
bead . . . 4. ball, drop 5. bugle, pearl,
sight (firearm) 6. rondel 8. ornament
beads . . . 5. grain, sewan 6. rosary
7. chaplet, granose (antennae), jewelry,
prayers
beak . . . 3. neb, nib 4. bill, lora, nose,
peck, prow 5. judge, mouth, spout,

tutel 10. magistrate 11. stipendiary
beaker . . . 3. cup 6. vessel (Chem)
beakless . . . 9. erostrate
beam . . . 3. ray 4. emit, grin, sile, sill,
stud 5. caber, gleam, joist, shaft, shine,
smile, tonka, trave 6. girder, mantel,
rafter, timber 7. radiate, support,
trimmer 8. trabeate
bean . . . 3. buck, faba, gram, lima, mung,
navy, seed, snap, soya 5. black, coral,
pinto, Sieva 6. adzuki, castor, frijol
(frijole) kidney, legume, lentil, string
7. calabar 9. Phaseolus
bean (pert to) . . .
 eye of . . 5. hilum
 game . . 7. beanbag
 licorice seed . . 9. jequirity
 lima . . 4. haba
 seed (string bean) . . 7. haricot
 shaped . . 8. fabiform
 slang . . 4. buck, head 5. brain 6. dollar,
 noodle, trifle
bear . . . 3. aim, cub, lug 4. dubb, tote, turn,
ursa 5. bring, brown, bruin, carry, clack,
crank, koala, polar, press, short, sloth,
stand, ursus, yield 6. animal, endure,
grouch, harbor, Kodiak, stress, suffer,
Syrian, uphold 7. Ephraim (nickname),
furnish, grizzly, incline, musquaw,
produce, support 8. cinnamon, fructify,
maintain, Melursus, sorehead, tolerate
10. speculator 11. short seller (Finan)
bear (pert to) . . .
 cat . . 5. panda 9. binturong
 class . . 6. ursine 7. Ursidaw
 color . . 6. yellow
 constellation . . 9. Ursa Major, Ursa
 Minor
 flag . . 10. California (State)
 head . . 4. hure
 The . . 6. Russia
beard . . . 3. awn 6. arista, goatee
7. stubble, Vandyke 8. whiskers
bearded . . . 5. awned 7. barbate, pappose
8. aristate 9. whiskered
beards, science of . . . 10. pogonology
bearer . . . 3. boy 5. macer, usher 6. porter,
tender 7. carrier 8. cargador, conveyor,
escudero 9. attendant 10. khidmatgar,
pallbearer
bearing . . . 3. air 4. mien, port 5. poise
6. bel air, regard 7. concern, conduct,
dignity, meaning, posture 8. behavior,
carriage, demeanor, relation, tendency
9. direction, influence, relevance
10. connection, deportment, supporting
12. significance
bearing (Her) . . . 4. enté, orle 5. bevel,
pheon 6. billet
bear witness . . . 6. attest 7. testify
beast . . . 4. bête, game, lion, pard 5. brute,
camel, demon, fiend, horse, spado,
tiger 6. animal, cattle, dragon, savage
7. carrier, critter, leopard, monster
8. behemoth, creature 9. dromedary
beastly . . . 5. gross 6. animal, bloody,
carnal, odious 7. bestial, brutish,
hideous, inhuman, leonine, theroid,
ungodly 8. dreadful 9. execrable
10. abominable, disgusting
beat . . . 3. hit, lam, tan, taw, wap 4. bang,

bash, best, cane, drub, drum, flog,
lace, lash, maul, pelt, tund 5. baste,
excel, pound, pulse, route, scoop,
throb, thump 6. bruise, cudgel, defeat,
larrup, pommel, punish, rhythm,
strike, stroke, swinge, thrash, thresh
7. baffled, belabor, cadence, clobber,
conquer, flutter, musical, pulsate,
routine, surpass, trounce 8. chastise,
fatigued, lambskin, overcome, vanquish
9. exhausted, pulsation
beat (pert to) . . .
 back . . 7. repulse
 black and blue . . 9. suggilate
 down . . 6. haggle 7. cheapen
 into plate . . 8. malleate
 slang . . 4. blow 5. scoot, scram 6. beat
 it, skidoo 7. vamoose
 traverse . . 6. patrol
beatify . . . 5. bless, cheer, saint 6. hallow
7. gladden, glorify 8. enshrine, sanctify
beatnik . . . 8. Bohemian, maverick,
sulphite 13. nonconformist
beau . . . 3. fop 5. blade, dandy, flame,
lover, spark, swain 6. escort, squire
7. admirer, courter 9. caballero,
inamorato 10. beau-garçon
Beau Brummell . . . 3. fop 5. dandy
beaucoup (Fr) . . . 4. many, much
Beaumarchais comedy . . . 15. Barber
of Seville 16. Marriage of Figaro
beautiful . . . 4. fair, fine 5. bonny,
kalon (Gr) 6. comely, lovely, poetic,
pretty 7. elegant, Tempean 8. graceful,
handsome, stunning 9. aesthetic
(esthetic), exquisite 15. pulchritudinous
beautify . . . 4. deck, trim 5. adorn, grace
6. bedeck, doll up, enrich 8. decorate,
prettify 9. embellish, glamorize
beauty . . . 5. belle, charm, glory, grace
8. elegance 10. loveliness, prettiness
11. pulchritude
beauty, famed . . .
 Egypt . . 9. Cleopatra
 Greek . . 4. Hebe 6. Graces 9. Aphrodite
 11. Helen of Troy
 Historical . . 4. Lais
 Persian . . 4. peri 5. houri
 Norse . . 5. Freya
 Roman . . 5. Venus
Becken . . . 7. cymbals
beckon . . . 4. beck 5. court 6. invite,
summon 7. gesture 11. gesticulate
becloud . . . 5. bedim, cloud, shade, smoke
6. bemist, darken, opaque 7. conceal,
encloud, obscure 8. nubilate, overcast
9. adumbrate
become . . . 2. go 3. fit, get, wax 4. grow,
rise, suit 5. befit, grace 6. befall,
beseem, mature, mellow 7. behoove,
benefit 8. befuddle 9. originate
becoming . . . 3. fit 6. comely, decent,
fitted, likely, proper, seemly, suited
7. decorum, suiting 8. decorous,
pleasing, suitable, tasteful 9. befitting,
expedient 11. appropriate
Becquerel rays . . . 9. gamma rays
bec-scie . . . 4. duck 9. merganser
becuna . . . 9. barracuda
bed . . . 3. cot, kip, tye (feather) 4. bunk,
crib, doss, lair, nest 5. basin, berth,

couch, futon 6. billet, bottom, flower, litter, pallet 7. channel, feather, stratum 8. bassinet 9. stretcher 10. foundation

bed (pert to) . . .
canopy . . 4. ceil 6. tester
coverlet . . 5. quilt 6. spread 7. blanket 9. comforter 11. counterpane
famed . . 15. bed of Procrustes

bedaub . . . 3. dab 4. blur, daub, soil 5. paint, smear, stain 6. belaud, smudge 7. bedizen, besmear 8. besmudge, ornament

bedazzle . . . 4. daze, stun 5. blind, shine 6. dazzle 7. astound, confuse 8. astonish, bewilder

bedeck . . . 3. gem 4. trim 5. adorn, array, grace, prink 6. clothe, rag out 7. bedrape 8. ornament

bedevil . . . 3. hex 4. foul, ride 5. abuse, tease 6. befoul, muddle, needle, pester, plague 7. bewitch, confuse, torment 8. demonize 9. diabolize, tantalize 10. complicate

bedight . . . 5. adorn, array, equip

bedikah . . . 6. ritual

bedim . . . 3. dim, fog 4. blur, fade 5. blear, cloud 6. bemist, darken 8. bedarken

bedlam . . . 3. din 6. clamor, tumult, uproar 8. madhouse 9. charivari 11. pandemonium

Bedlam (London) . . . 6. priory (1247) 8. Hospital (St Mary of Bethlehem)

Bedouin . . . 4. Arab, Moor 5. gypsy, nomad 7. Saracen, vagrant

Bedouin head cord . . . 4. agal

bedroll . . . 6. bindle 7. matilda

bee . . . 3. dor 4. apis 5. drone, karbi, queen 6. insect, worker 8. andrenid, angelito, honeybee 9. bumblebee 12. carpenter bee

bee (pert to) . . .
fear of . . 9. apiphobia
glue . . 8. propolis
hive . . 4. butt, scap, skep (straw) 6. apiary 7. alveary 8. workshop
keeper . . 8. apiarist, skeppist
sociable . . 7. husking, raising 8. quilting, spelling
study . . 10. apiculture 11. melittology
wax . . 7. beeswax, ceresin, cerotic 9. cera flava

Beebe, William . . . 13. ichthyologist

beef . . . 4. heft, kine, thew 5. brawn, sinew, steer 6. buccan (dried), cattle, muscle 8. poundage 10. brawniness 11. muscularity

Beelzebub (pert to) . . .
Bible . . 5. deity 6. oracle 14. prince of demons
literature . . 5. demon (Prince), devil 11. fallen angel
zoology . . 6. monkey

beer . . . 3. ale 4. bock, flip, suds 5. lager, stout, weiss 6. liquor, porter, swipes 8. Pilsener (Pilsner)

beer (pert to) . . .
cask . . 4. butt
inventor . . 9. Gambrinus (Myth king)
making . . 4. hops, malt, wort
mug . . 4. toby 5. stein 8. schooner
vessel . . 6. tanker 9. blackjack

beet . . . 4. Beta 5. chard 6. mangel 8. beet root 9. sugar beet

Beethoven, Ludwig Van (pert to) . . .
birthplace . . 4. Bonn (Ger)
composed . . 6. Eroica 7. Fidelio 10. symphonies
famed as . . 7. pianist 8. composer

beetle . . . 3. bat, bug, dor, jut, ram 4. June, rose 5. Amara, gogga, Hispa, meloe, snout 6. chafer, elater, golach, goloch, hammer, masher, sawyer, scarab, weevil 7. ladybug, prionid 8. circulio, sharnbud, skipjack 9. cockroach, dorbeetle 10. cockchafer, Elateridae

beetlehead . . . 5. stupe 6. plover (bird), stupid 8. bonehead 9. blockhead 10. loggerhead

befall . . . 3. hap 4. come 5. occur 6. betide, chance, happen 9. eventuate, transpire

befit . . . 4. suit 5. serve 6. become, beseem, please

befitting . . . 3. fit 4. meet 6. filial, proper, seemly, timely 7. ethical, fitting, suiting 8. becoming, decorous, suitable 9. expedient 10. seasonable 11. appropriate

befog . . . 3. dim, fog 5. blind, cloud 6. bemist 7. becloud, conceal, confuse, mystify, obscure

before . . . 3. ere 5. afore, ahead, avant, early, prior 6. anteal, facing, openly, sooner 7. already, earlier, forward, yestern 8. anterior, foremost, formerly, hitherto 9. foregoing, preceding 10. beforehand, face to face, heretofore, previously 11. theretofore

before (pert to) . . .
birth . . 8. prenatal
long . . 4. soon
mentioned . . 4. said, same, such 5. named 6. former 10. aforenamed
others . . 5. first
this . . 3. ere 5. prior 6. erenow

before (pref) . . . 3. pre, pro 4. ante, prae

befoul . . . 4. soil 5. taint 6. bemire, defile, muddle 7. bedevil 8. entangle 10. complicate 11. contaminate

befriend . . . 3. aid 4. abet, help 5. favor 6. assist, foster, succor 7. benefit, support, sustain 11. countenance

befuddle . . . 3. fog 5. addle, besot 6. fuddle, muddle 7. becloud, confuse 9. inebriate 10. intoxicate

beg . . . 3. ask, sue, woo 4. pray, sorn 5. cadge, crave, mooch, plead, touch (sl) 6. appeal 7. beseech, entreat, implore, solicit 8. petition 9. importune 10. supplicate

beget . . . 3. ean 4. sire 5. breed, hatch, spawn 6. father 7. develop 8. engender, generate 9. procreate, reproduce

begetter . . . 4. sire 6. pater 7. author, father, mother, parent 7. creator 10. procreator, progenitor

beggar . . . 3. bum 4. hobo, waif 5. fakir (Muslim), gamin, lazar, rogue 6. loafer, pauper, wretch 7. almsman, dervish, vagrant, wastral 8. indigent, vagabond 9. mendicant, suppliant 10. panhandler, ragamuffin 14. tatterdemalion

beggarly ... 3. low 4. base, mean, poor, rank 5. petty 6. abject, meanly, paltry, vulgar 7. hangdog, ignoble 8. bankrupt, indigent, infamous, wretched 9. miserable, niggardly 10. despicably, obsequious 12. contemptible

Beggars, King of (Eng) ... 5. Carew

beggary ... 4. want 6. penury 9. indigence, mendicity, pauperism 10. mendicancy 11. destitution, panhandling

begin ... 4. open 5. enter, start 6. attack 8. commence, initiate, take rise 9. institute, introduce, originate 10. inaugurate

begin again ... 5. renew 6. resume 10. recommence

beginner ... 3. dub 4. tyro (tiro) 5. chela 6. infant, novice 7. amateur, entrant, recruit 8. begetter, freshman, neophyte 9. debutante, fledgling, initiator, novitiate 10. catechumen, originator, tenderfoot 11. inaugurator

beginning ... 4. head, rise, root 5. alpha, birth, debut, onset, start 6. origin, outset, source 7. genesis, infancy, opening 8. entrance, inchoate, nascency, outstart, starting 9. inception, threshold 10. derivation, foundation, incomplete, initiation 12. commencement, introduction

begone ... 3. out 4. away, scat, shoo 5. allez, scram 6. aroint, avaunt, depart 7. vamoose

begrudge ... 4. envy 5. covey, stint 6. grudge, refuse 7. grumble

beguile ... 4. dupe, lure, vamp 5. amuse, charm, cozen, elude, spend, trick 6. delude, divert, regale 7. bewitch, deceive, ensnare, mislead 8. enthrall, intrigue 9. bamboozle, captivate, deception, entertain, fascinate, victimize 11. double-cross 14. disappointment

begum (Hind) ... 5. queen 7. heiress 8. princess

begunk ... 4. jilt 5. trick

behalf ... 4. gain, good, part, sake, side 5. avail, stead 6. affair, matter, profit 7. benefit, defense, service, support, welfare 8. interest 9. advantage

behalf of ... 3. for 6. lieu of, rather 7. defense (of), instead

Behan Boy ... 7. Borstal

behave ... 2. do 3. act 4. bear 5. carry 6. demean, deport, manage 7. conduct 8. regulate, restrain

behavior, behaviour ... 3. air 4. mien 6. action, manner 7. actions, address, bearing, conduct, decorum, manners 8. carriage, demeanor, maintien 10. deportment 11. comportment

behavior (pert to) ...
good .. 7. decorum, P's and Q's
riotous .. 7. rampage
wicked .. 10. wrongdoing

behead ... 7. execute 9. decollate 10. decapitate, guillotine

Behemoth (Bib) ... 5. beast 12. hippopotamus

behest ... 3. vow 5. order 7. bidding, command, mandate, promise 10. injunction 11. commandment

behind ... 3. aft 4. late, past, rear, rump (vulgar), slow, tail 5. abaff, abaft, after, ahind, arear, later, tardy 6. astern 7. delayed, impeded 8. arrested, backward, retarded 9. in the past, posterior, remaining

behindhand ... 4. late 5. tardy 7. arrears, belated, overdue 8. backward, dilatory, misdated, mistimed 10. defaulting, delinquent

behind the times ... 5. passé

behold ... 2. lo 3. see 4. ahoy, ecce, ecco, espy, look, scan, view 5. voilà 6. descry, regard, retain 7. discern, observe, witness 8. maintain, perceive

beholden ... 5. bound 7. bounden, obliged 8. grateful, indebted, thankful 9. obligated

beholder ... 5. gazer 7. watcher, witness 8. looker-on, observer, onlooker 9. spectator

beige ... 4. ecru, hopi 5. grège 6. dorado 13. reddish-yellow

being ... 3. ego, ens, man, one 4. bion, body, esse, home, life, self 5. entia, gnome, human, thing, wight 6. actual, animal, entity, extant, mortal, person 7. Admaite, essence, present, reality 8. creature, existent, existing, organism, presence 9. actuality, existence, personage, something 10. individual 11. subsistence

being (pert to) ...
celestial .. 4. deva 5. angel 6. cherub, seraph
imaginary .. 4. pixy (pixie) 5. fairy, sylph
science of .. 8. ontology
supernatural .. 6. Garuda (Hind)
Supreme .. 3. God 7. Creator

Belarus (pert to) ...
capital .. 5. Minsk
name, former .. 10. Belorussia 11. Byelorussia, White Russia

belaud ... 4. laud 5. extol 6. praise 7. glorify

belay ... 4. halt, quit, stop 5. beset, cease, cover, halte 6. fasten, invest, waylay 7. besiege, silence 8. encircle

belch ... 4. burp, emit, vent 5. eject, eruct, erupt, spout, vomit 7. gush out 8. disgorge, eructate 9. small beer (vulgar) 10. eructation

beldam, beldame ... 3. cat, hag 4. fury 5. crone, frump, shrew, vixen, witch 6. virago 7. she-wolf, tigress 8. ancestor (fem), harridan 9. termagant 11. grandmother

Belgian (pert to) ... see also *Belgium*
anthem .. 13. La Brabanconne
artist .. 8. Magritte
hare .. 8. leporide
horse .. 9. Brabancon
marble .. 5. rance
resort .. 6. Ostend
sheep dog .. 8. Malinois 11. Groenendael
violinist .. 5. Ysaye

Belgian Congo ... see *Zaire*

Belgium ...
capital .. 8. Brussels

city . . 5. Ghent, Liege 6. Bruges
7. Antwerp, Louvain 9. Charleroi
commune . . 3. Ath
forest . . 8. Ardennes
king . . 6. Albert 7. Leopold 8. Baudouin
native . . 7. Fleming (of Flanders),
Flemish, Walloon
nickname . . 15. cockpit of Europe
World War I Battles of . . 5. Ypres
World War II Battle of . . 8. The Bulge
Belgravia (London) . . . 8. district (fashion)
Belial . . . 5. devil, Satan (New Test)
10. wickedness (Old Test) 11. Fallen
Angel
belie . . . 4. deny 6. belong, defame,
oppose, oppugn 7. besiege, falsify,
gainsay, pertain, slander 8. disclaim,
disprove, surround 9. encompass
10. calumniate 12. misrepresent
belief . . . 3. fay (anc), ism 4. cult, rule,
sect, view 5. credo, creed, dogma,
faith, maxim, tenet 7. opinion, precept
8. credence, doctrine, reliance, religion,
teaching 9. assurance, certainty,
principle 10. confidence, conviction,
persuasion 13. Apostles' Creed
believe . . . 3. buy 4. deem, feel, trow,
ween 5. think, trust 6. accept, credit,
reckon 7. suppose, swallow 8. conceive,
consider
believer (pert to) . . .
all religions . . 6. omnist
facts . . 7. realist
religion . . 5. deist 6. theist 9. Adventist,
Calvinist 13. particularist
Belit (Bab) . . . 7. goddess (wife of Bel)
belittle . . . 4. slur 5. decry, dwarf,
scoff, scorn 6. debase, demean,
deride, impugn 7. detract, run down
8. minimize 9. discredit, disparage,
underrate 10. depreciate
13. underestimate
bell . . . 4. gong 5. codon, knell 6. curfew,
tocsin 7. campana, cowbell 8. carillon,
doorbell 9. ship's bell 10. dinnerbell,
schoolbell 12. glockenspiel
13. tintinnabulum
bell, bells (pert to) . . .
bird . . 9. campanero 10. wood thrush
botany . . 7. corolla
evening . . 6. curfew 7. Angelus
flat . . 4. gong 6. tam-tam (Chin), tom-tom
funeral . . 5. knell
nautical . . 8. half hour
ringer . . 6. toller
ringing . . 7. peeling 14. tintinnabulism
science of . . 11. campanology
set of . . 6. chimes 8. carillon
shaped . . 11. campaniform
specialist . . 9. campanist
13. campanologist
tongue . . 7. clapper
tower . . 6. belfry 9. campanile
warning . . 6. tocsin
belle . . . 4. lady (fine) 5. toast 6. beauty
7. charmer 8. handsome 10. grande
dame
belles-lettres . . . 8. classics
10. humanities (The), literature
bellflower . . . 8. daffodil
belligerent . . . 7. hostile, scrappy, warlike

8. choleric, militant 9. bellicose,
irascible, litigious, offensive, wrangling
10. aggressive, pugnacious
11. contentious, quarrelsome
12. disputatious
belligerent's right (Internat law) . . .
6. angary
bellow . . . 3. cry, low, moo, say 4. bawl,
roar, wail, yawp 5. blare, shout
6. clamor 7. thunder 10. vociferate
bellows . . . 4. fish 5. gills, lungs 6. blower,
lights (Zool), rotary 8. ctenidia (Zool)
bellwether . . . 5. sheep 6. leader, wether
(with bell)
belly . . . 3. bag, pot 4. crap, wame
5. bulge, front, tummy 6. bottom,
paunch, venter 7. abdomen, stomach
8. potbelly, swell out 9. ingluvies
bellyache . . . 5. gripe 7. grumble
8. complain
belong (to) . . . 6. answer, inhere 7. pertain,
related 9. appendant, ingrained,
possessed (by) 10. correspond
belonging (to) . . .
collector, hobbyist . . 10. collection
11. collectible (collectable)
dean . . 7. decanal
era . . 8. epochal
Fall . . 8. autumnal
pencil, a . . 6. desmic
people . . 7. endemic
present, the . . 7. current
Spring . . 6. vernal
Summer . . 7. estival
Winter . . 6. hiemal
belongings . . . 4. duds, gear 5. goods,
traps 6. family, things 7. baggage,
effects, kinsmen 8. chattels, property
9. homefolks, relations, trappings
11. connections, perquisites,
possessions 13. accouterments,
appurtenances
beloved . . . 3. pet 4. dear 6. prized
7. darling 8. precious, truelove
9. cherished, inamorata
beloved physician . . . 6. St Luke
below . . . 4. alow, here, less 5. Hades,
neath, sotto, under 6. aneath, in hell
7. beneath, short of 10. downstairs
11. belowstairs
Belshazzar (Bib) . . . 11. crown prince
Bel's wife . . . 5. Belit (Beltis)
belt . . . 3. bar, bat, hit 4. area, band,
beat, blow, cest, mark, pelt, ring,
sash, sock, whip, zone 5. apron,
Libya, strap, whack, zonar 6. cestus,
cingle, cordon, fascia, fasten, fillet,
girdle, region, strait, streak, stripe
7. baldric, kurbash, sjambok, stratum,
terrain 8. cincture, encircle, surround
9. encompass 10. cummerbund
Belteshazzar (Bib) . . . 6. Daniel
belt of heaven . . . 6. zodiac 7. circuit
beluga . . . 5. whale (white)
Belus (pert to) . . .
father of . . 4. Dido
king of . . 4. Tyre 7. Assyria
son of . . 5. Libya
sons . . 7. Cepheus, Phineus 8. Aegyptus
belvedere . . . 5. cigar 7. cypress (mock)
10. watchtower 11. summerhouse

bema ... 8. platform 9. sanctuary
bemoan ... 4. pity, wail 5. mourn
  6. bewail, grieve, lament, regret, repine
  7. deplore 10. sympathize
bemuse ... 4. daze 5. addle, besot
  6. absorb, muddle 7. stupefy
  8. befuddle, distract 10. intoxicate
ben ... 2. in 3. oil, son 4. tree (Moringa)
  6. within
bench ... 3. pew 4. banc (judge's), seat
  5. chair, court, siege, staff, stand, stool,
  table 6. exedra, settee, settle 7. terrace
  8. platform, woolsack 9. committee
bend ... 3. bow, nod, ply, sag, sny
  4. bias, flex, genu, kink, knot, sway,
  turn, warp 5. crimp, crook, curve,
  drink, kneel, prone, squat, stoop,
  twist, yield 6. buckle, crouch, curtsy,
  direct, divert, humble, inflex, kowtow,
  pleach, relent, salaam, strain, swerve
  7. bendlet (Her), chevron (Her), incline,
  refract, retract 9. genuflect, introvert,
  sinuosity 10. inflection
bend (pert to) ...
  an ear .. 4. hear, heed 6. listen
  one's will .. 4. bias, move, sway
  the elbow .. 5. drink
  the knee .. 5. kneel 6. kowtow, salaam
    9. genuflect
  the mind .. 5. think
bends ... 7. caisson, disease 8. blackout
  (aeronaut)
beneath ... 4. alow 5. below, lower
  (than), neath, under 6. aneath, nether
  7. in Hades 11. underground
beneath one's dignity ... 8. infradig
  15. infra dignitatem
benedict ... 7. husband 10. bridegroom,
  married man (newly)
benediction ... 4. rite 6. praise, prayer,
  thanks 7. benison 8. blessing
  10. invocation 12. thanksgiving
benefaction ... 4. alms, boon, gift, good
  5. favor 7. benefit, present 8. courtesy,
  donation, gratuity, kindness 9. beau
  geste 11. beneficence, benevolence
benefactor ... 5. angel, donor 6. backer,
  helper, patron 8. promoter
  10. befriender
beneficence ... 7. charity 8. goodness,
  kindness 11. benefaction, benevolence
  12. philanthropy
beneficial ... 4. good 6. benign, useful
  7. helpful 8. edifying, salutary
  9. favorable, healthful, lucrative,
  wholesome 10. profitable, salubrious
  11. serviceable 12. advantageous,
  remunerative
beneficiary ... 4. heir 5. donee 6. vassal
  7. devisee, feoffee, grantee, legatee
  8. assignee 9. annuitant
benefit ... 3. aid, use 4. boon, gift, good,
  help, vail 5. avail, favor, trust 6. profit,
  relief, succor 7. advance, concert,
  improve, service, welfare 8. blessing,
  kindness 9. advantage 11. benefaction,
  convenience, performance
benevolence ... 3. tax 4. gift, good
  6. bounty, giving 7. charity 8. altruism,
  bestowal, blessing, donation, kindness
  10. generosity, liberality 11. munificence

  12. contribution, philanthropy
  14. charitableness
benevolent ... 4. free, good, king
  6. benign 7. liberal 8. generous, princely
  9. benignant, bountiful 10. altruistic,
  charitable, munificent 11. magnanimous
  13. philanthropic
Bengal, Indian State ...
  capital .. 8. Calcutta
  gentleman .. 5. baboo (babu)
  language .. 7. Bengali
  native .. 3. Kol (Kohl) 6. banian 7. Bengali
  river .. 6. Ganges 11. Brahmaputra
  river boat .. 7. bauleah
benign ... 4. mild 5. bland 6. genial,
  humane, kindly 7. benefic (Astrol),
  liberal 8. gracious, salutary
  9. benignant, favorable, healthful,
  wholesome 10. propitious, salubrious
benignity ... 5. favor 7. benefit
  8. blessing, goodness, mildness
  9. salubrity 10. kindliness
  11. benevolence 12. graciousness
benison ... 8. blessing 9. beatitude
  10. invocation 11. benediction
benjamin ... 6. jacket 7. benzoin
  8. overcoat 9. spicebush
Benjamin (Bib), (pert to) ...
  father .. 5. Jacob
  history .. 5. tribe
  mother .. 6. Rachel
Benjamin's mess ... 6. big end 10. lion's
  share
benjy (Brit sl) ... 3. hat (straw) 9. waistcoat
benne ... 6. sesame
bennet ... 4. herb 5. daisy 7. hemlock
bent ... 3. aim, way, wry 4. bias, turn,
  warp 5. drift, grass, slant, tenor,
  trend, twist 6. course, curved, desire,
  minded, nature, swayed 7. angular,
  aptness, crooked, heather, leaning,
  stooped 8. aptitude, penchant, tendency
  9. obliquity, prejudice, proneness
  10. propensity 11. disposition,
  inclination 12. idiosyncrasy, predilection
  13. prepossession 14. predisposition
Benthamism ... 9. welfarism
  14. utilitarianism
benthonic ... 7. benthal, deep sea
benthonic plant ... 6. enalid
benthos ... 5. deeps 6. depths 8. ocean
  bed 15. Davy Jones's locker
benumb ... 3. nip 4. drug, numb, stun
  5. chill 6. deaden, freeze 7. stupefy
  8. paralyze 11. anesthetize, desensitize
Beowulf ... 4. epic, poem (oldest in
  Teutonic language)
bequeath ... 4. give, will 5. endow, leave
  6. bestow, demise, devise, invest, will
  to 7. bequest 8. transmit
bequest ... 4. will 6. devise, legacy
  8. heritage 9. patrimony, testament
  10. birthright 11. inheritance
berate ... 3. jaw, nag 4. lash, rail 5. chide,
  scold, slate 7. censure, reprove, upbraid
Berber ... 4. Riff 6. Hamite, Kabyle,
  Tuareg
berceau ... 4. walk (leaf-covered) 5. arbor,
  bower 6. cradle
berceuse ... 10. cradlesong
  11. composition

bereave . . . 3. die, rob 5. leave, strip
6. divest, orphan, sadden 7. deprive,
despoil 10. disentitle, dispossess

bereavement . . . 4. loss 5. death
9. privation 10. divestment

bereft . . . 4. lorn 7. denuded, fleeced,
shorn of, witless 8. bereaved, divested,
orphaned, stripped 9. senseless
10. parentless, pauperized

Bereshith (Jew) . . . 7. Genesis
9. Beginning

beret . . . 3. cap, tam 7. biretta

bergamot . . . 4. pear 5. snuff 6. orange
7. essence 9. fragrance

beriberi . . . 5. kakke 7. disease

Berkeleianism (pert to) . . .
founder . . 8. Berkeley (Bishop)
science . . 10. philosophy
system . . 8. idealism 13. immaterialism

Berlin, Germany . . .
avenue . . 14. Unter den Linden
capital . . 7. Germany
garden (Zool) . . 10. Tiergarten
gate . . 11. Brandenburg
government . . 9. Reichstag

berm, berme . . . 4. mall, path 5. prado
6. runway 7. terrace 8. shoulder (road)

Bermuda . . .
capital . . 8. Hamilton
color . . 12. geranium pink
discoverer . . 8. Bermudez
government . . 7. British
grass . . 5. decil
ocean site . . 8. Atlantic

Bernardine Order . . . 11. Cistercians

Berne, Bern (Switz) . . . 7. capital

Bernstein musical . . . 13. West Side
Story

Bernoulli force . . . 8. calculus

berry . . . 3. haw 4. buck, seed 5. bacca,
cubeb, fruit, grain, money 6. acinus,
kernel

berry, fruit . . . 5. grape, salal 6. banana,
tomato 7. currant 8. bilberry, dewberry,
hagberry, mulberry 9. bearberry,
blueberry, cranberry, raspberry
10. blackberry, elderberry, gooseberry,
loganberry, strawberry 11. boysenberry,
huckleberry 12. checkerberry,
whortleberry

berserk . . . 4. amok, bunk, dock, post,
room 5. house, roost 6. billet, marina,
office, reside 8. quarters 9. situation
11. appointment

bertha . . . 4. cape 6. cannon, collar
7. Perchta (goddess) 9. Big Bertha
(Ger gun)

Besant belief . . . 9. theosophy

beseech . . . 3. beg, sue 4. pray 5. crave,
plead 6. obtest 7. entreat, implore,
solicit 9. obsecrate 10. supplicate

beset . . . 3. dun, ply, vex 4. stud 5. harry,
haunt, hem in, siege, worry 6. attack,
harass, infest, invade, obsess, plague,
ravage 7. besiege 8. blockade, surround
9. beleaguer, importune, infatuate

beset with danger . . . 5. risky 6. chancy
8. perilous 9. dangerous 10. jeopardous

beset with hairs . . . 7. barbate, bearded

beside, besides . . . 2. by 3. too, yet
4. also, else, near, nigh, para (pref)

5. about, along 6. nearby 8. likewise,
moreover 9. other than 11. furthermore
12. over and above

beside oneself . . . 3. mad 4. wild
5. crazy, rabid 6. beserk, raging,
raving 7. frantic, ranting 8. frenzied
9. desperate, overjoyed 10. distracted,
distraught 11. overwrought

besiege . . . 5. beset 6. attack, harass,
obsess, plague 7. torment 8. blockade,
surround 9. beleaguer

besmear . . . 3. dab 4. coat, daub, mark,
soil, spot 5. paint, smear, stain, taint
6. bedaub 7. tarnish 8. besmudge

besmirch . . . 4. blot, soil 5. smear,
sully 6. defile, smirch, smudge, vilify
7. besmear, blacken, tarnish 8. discolor

besom . . . 5. broom, hussy

besotted . . . 4. dull 5. drunk 7. muddled,
sottish 8. obsessed 9. senseless,
stupefied 10. infatuated 11. intoxicated

bespangled . . . 5. aglow 7. lighted,
studded, trimmed 8. spangled
9. decorated, garnished 10. glittering,
ornamented 11. embellished,
illuminated

bespatter . . . 3. wet 4. blot, spot 5. dirty,
slosh, smear, stain, sully 6. splash,
vilify 7. asperse, scatter, spatter,
tarnish 8. besmirch, splatter, sprinkle
9. denigrate 10. stigmatize

bespeak . . . 4. mean, show 5. imply 6. ask
for, attest, engage, evince 7. address,
betoken, connote, exhibit, suggest,
testify 8. foretell, indicate, manifest
11. demonstrate

Bessemer product . . . 5. steel

best . . . 4. aces, beat, most, tops 5. cream,
elite, queen 6. choice, finest 7. largest
8. champion, outstrip 9. nonpareil,
overmatch 11. superlative

bestial . . . 3. low 4. vile 5. cruel 6. brutal,
filthy, savage 7. beastly, brutish,
inhuman, sensual 8. depraved, ruthless
9. barbarous

bestow . . . 4. deal, give 5. allot, apply,
award, grant, spend 6. accord, confer,
convey, demise, devote, donate, impart,
render, tender 7. deposit, present
8. transmit 10. administer

bestow honor upon . . . 5. adorn, exalt,
grace 7. dignify, ennoble, glorify
10. aggrandize 11. distinguish

bestride . . . 4. pass 5. mount 7. climb
on, protect, support 8. straddle
10. bestraddle

bet . . . 3. bas (roulette), pot 4. play
5. stake, wager 6. gamble, hazard,
pledge

beta test (army) . . . 12. intelligence

bête . . . 5. beast, silly 6. stupid 7. foolish

betel (pert to) . . .
leaf . . 3. pan 4. buyo, paun (pan)
palm . . 5. areca
pepper . . 4. itmo (ikmo)

bête noire . . . 4. ogre 7. bugbear 10. black
beast, frightener, mumbo jumbo

bethel . . . 4. kirk 6. chapel, church
8. Bethesda (Jerusalem)
12. meetinghouse

bethink . . . 5. think 6. recall 7. reflect

8. cogitate, remember 9. cerebrate, recollect

betide . . . 3. hap 4. fall 5. occur 6. befall, happen 7. betoken, presage 9. come about, eventuate, transpire

betimes . . . 4. anon, soon 5. early 7. ere long, shortly 8. directly, speedily 9. forthwith, presently 10. beforehand, seasonably 12. occasionally

betise . . . 5. folly 9. asininity, silliness, stupidity 11. foolishness

betoken . . . 4. mark, mean, note 5. augur 6. denote, typify 7. bespeak, connote, express, portend, presage, purport, signify 8. evidence, indicate 9. foretoken, symbolize

betray . . . 4. blab, dupe, hoax, sell 5. bluff, peach, trick 6. reveal, seduce, tattle 7. beguile, deceive, divulge, mislead, sell out 8. disclose, inform on 9. bamboozle, victimize 11. double-cross

betrayal . . . 4. ruse 5. trick 7. sellout, treason 8. giveaway 9. Judas kiss, seduction, treachery 10. disclosure

betrayer . . . 5. Judas 6. Arnold, Brutus 7. seducer, traitor 8. derelict, informer, Quisling, turncoat 10. treasonist 13. double-crosser, Judas Iscariot

betroth . . . 4. affy, earl 5. tryst 6. engage, pledge, plight 7. espouse, promise 8. affiance, contract, espousal 10. engagement

better . . . 3. top 4. more 5. amend, emend, excel, raise (poker), safer, wiser 6. bigger, exceed, outwit, reform 7. advance, choicer, greater, improve, promote, surpass, victory 8. improved, superior 9. advantage, meliorate 10. ameliorate, preferable 11. superiority

betting term . . . 4. ante, odds, tout 6. exacta, parlay 7. pyramid 8. perfecta, quinella, trifecta 10. parimutuel 11. sweepstakes

between . . . 5. among, mesne 6. atween 7. average, betwixt

bevel . . . 4. edge, ream 5. angle, bezel, slant, slope, snape, splay 6. square 7. incline, oblique 9. obliquity

beverage . . . 3. ade, opo (comb form), pop, tea 4. coke, malt, maté, mead, milk, soda 5. cider, cocoa, drink, leban, morat (anc) punch, water 6. coffee, eggnog, frappé, nectar 7. Seltzer 8. Adam's ale, Coca-Cola, lemonade, root beer, sourdook 9. ginger ale, orangeade, phosphate 10. buttermilk, grape juice 12. sarsaparilla

beverage (alcoholic) . . . 3. ale, gin, rum 4. beer, brew, grog, kava, port, raki 5. booze, cider, hooch, julep, lager, negus, punch, smash, vodka 6. arrack, bishop, brandy, cognac, eggnog, kumiss, kummel, likker, porter, posset, sherry, tiswin, whisky (whiskey), zythum (anc) 7. Bacardi, bootleg, bourbon, cordial, liqueur, martini, tequila 8. absinthe, aleberry, Burgundy, cocktail, highball, muscatel, sauterne, vermouth 9. applejack, aqua vitae,

firewater, Manhattan 10. shandygaff, Tom Collins 11. Benedictine, boilermaker, grasshopper, mountain dew

bevy . . . 4. bund, gang, herd, host 5. covey, flock, group, party, troop 6. galaxy, throng 7. company 8. assembly 10. collection

bewail . . . 3. rue 4. keen, mean 5. mourn 6. bemoan, grieve, lament, regret, repine, sorrow 7. deplore

bewilder . . . 3. fog 4. daze 5. addle, amaze 6. baffle, dazzle, puzzle 7. buffalo, confuse, fluster, mystify, nonplus, perplex 8. astonish, confound, distract 9. bamboozle, embarrass

bewilderment . . . 3. awe, fog 4. maze 6. wonder 9. confusion 10. perplexity 11. distraction 12. perturbation 13. disconcertion, embarrassment

bewitch . . . 3. hex 5. charm, witch 6. enamor, entice, hoodoo, voodoo 7. beguile, delight, enchant 8. enthrall 9. captivate, enrapture, ensorcell, fascinate, infatuate

bewitching . . . 5. siren 6. hexing, lovely 7. magical 8. alluring, charming, enticing 10. enchanting 11. captivating, fascinating

bey (Turk) . . . 5. title 8. governor

Beyle's pseud . . . 8. Stendahl

beyond . . . 2. by 3. too, yet 4. meta (pref), past, plus, well 5. above, extra, ultra 6. yonder 7. besides, farther, further, yonside 8. moreover 9. exceeding, Hereafter (The) 11. furthermore 12. additionally, ultraliminal

beyond hope . . . 9. desperate

bezant (pert to) . . .
architecture . . 4. disc 8. ornament
coin (anc) . . 7. solidus (gold)
heraldry . . 4. disc (gold)
offering (Eng king) . . 4. gold

bezel . . . 4. edge 5. crown (gem), facet 6. chaton, flange 8. pavilion, template (templet) 9. obliquity

bezonian . . . 6. mucker, wretch 7. budmash, caitiff, recruit 8. blighter 9. pilgarlic, scoundrel

bhikshu . . . 6. gelong 7. ascetic 8. sannyasi 9. mendicant

bhut (Dravidian) . . . 5. demon, ghost 6. goblin

bias . . . 3. ply 4. awry, bent, turn, warp 5. amiss, slant, twist 6. desire 7. leaning, oblique 8. diagonal, slanting, tendency 9. obliquity, prejudice 10. favoritism, partiality, prepossess, transverse 11. disposition

biased . . . 4. bent 6. narrow, swayed 7. bigoted, partial 8. diagonal, partisan, slanting 10. prejudiced

bib . . . 3. sip, sup 4. swig 5. apron, drink, quaff 6. guzzle, imbibe, tipple, tucker 7. tablier 8. pinafore

bibacious . . . 6. toping 7. drunken, sottish 8. bibulous, drinking, tippling

Bible . . . 7. The Book, The Word, Vulgate 10. Scriptures, Testaments (Old, New) 11. The Good Book

Bible (pert to) . . .

battle site .. 10. Armageddon
city .. 2. Ur 5. Joppa, Sidon, Sodom
6. Hebron 9. Bethlehem, Jerusalem
coin .. 6. talent
Commandments .. 9. Decalogue
Holy Land .. 9. Palestine
interpretation .. 7. anagoge
introduction .. 9. Isagogics
kingdom .. 4. Elam 6. Basham, Canaan
7. Chaldea
land of plenty .. 6. Goshen
language .. 7. Aramaic
mountain .. 4. Ebol, Zion 5. Horeb,
Sinai 6. Ararat, Gilead, Moriah, Olives
(Olivet), Pisgah
pause .. 5. selah
pool .. 6. Siloam
precious stone .. 6. ligure (jacinth)
Promised Land .. 6. Canaan
sea .. 3. Red 4. Dead 7. Galilee
Sermon on the Mount .. 10. Beatitudes
sheep .. 7. chamois
town .. 4. Edar 5. Babel
Wells of .. 5. Hagar, Jacob
Bible character ...
archangel .. 7. Raphael
giant .. 4. Anak 7. Goliath
High Priest .. 3. Eli
hunter .. 6. Nimrod
liar .. 7. Ananias
patriarch .. 5. Jacob 6. Israel
prophet .. 4. Amos, Joel 5. Hosea,
Jonah, Micah, Nahum 6. Daniel,
Haggai, Isaiah, Joseph, Joshua,
Samuel 7. Ezekiel, Malachi, Obadiah
8. Habakkuk, Jeremiah 9. Zachariah,
Zephaniah
Bible version ... 5. Douay, Reims
6. Geneva 7. Bishop's, Luther's,
Revised, Targums, Vulgate
8. Cranmer's, Matthew's, Peshitta,
Tyndale's, Wartburg, Wycliffe
9. Jerusalem, King James, Maccabees
10. Great Bible, Septuagint
15. American Revised
bicker ... 5. argue, cavil 6. hassle,
quiver, strife 7. dispute, flicker, flutter,
quarrel, quibble, rhubarb (sl), wrangle
8. argument, pettifog 9. scrimmage,
tremulous 10. contention 11. altercation
bicuspid ... 5. bifid, tooth, valve
6. cuspid 8. premolar 10. two-pointed
13. double-pointed
bid ... 3. beg 4. pray 5. offer, order,
utter 6. charge, direct, enjoin, invite,
reveal, tender 7. command, declare,
entreat, offered, summons 8. overture,
proclaim 9. quotation 12. presentation
biddy ... 3. hen 4. dame 5. skirt
6. female 7. chicken, Partlet 8. bedmaker
11. maidservant
bide ... 4. bear, stay, wait 5. abide,
await, tarry 6. endure, remain, suffer
8. continue, tolerate 9. encounter,
withstand
bield ... 3. den 4. cozy 7. comfort,
courage, hearten, shelter 8. boldness,
embolden 9. sheltered 10. confidence,
habitation
bien ... 4. fine, good, snug
bienseance ... 7. decorum, manners

9. propriety 11. correctness, proprieties
(the) 12. mannerliness
17. conventionalities
bier ... 6. coffin, litter 10. catafalque
Bier ... 4. beer
biff ... 4. bash, blow, slug, sock 5. paste,
punch
bifold ... 4. dual 5. duple 6. binary,
binate, double 7. twofold
bifurcate ... 3. wye (letter) 4. fork
7. forking, furcate 8. biforked, branched,
forklike 9. two-forked
big ... 4. huge 5. bulky, grand, great,
grown, jumbo, large 6. august,
famous, mighty 7. massive, pompous,
teeming 8. boastful, powerful, pregnant,
swelling 9. momentous 10. tremendous
11. magnanimous, pretentious
big (pert to) ...
shot .. 3. VIP
stick .. 5. power (T Roosevelt)
toe .. 6. hallux
top .. 6. circus
wig .. 3. VIP (humorous)
Big (pert to) ...
Ben .. 5. clock 13. Tower of London
Bend State .. 9. Tennessee
Bertha .. 3. gun 6. Krupp (factory)
Blue .. 3. IBM
Board .. 4. NYSE 13. stock exchange
Easy .. 10. New Orleans
House .. 3. pen 6. prison (State)
12. penitentiary
Push (WWI) .. 5. Somme
Bigfoot ... 9. Sasquatch
bight ... 3. bay 4. bend, gulf, loop
5. angle, noose, point 6. corner, hollow
7. estuary
bigot ... 3. bug, nut 6. zealot 7. fanatic
9. dogmatist, hypocrite, illiberal
10. enthusiast, opinionist, positivist
bigoted ... 5. petty 6. little, narrow
10. intolerant, prejudiced 12. narrow-
minded
bijou ... 5. jewel 7. trinket
bilbi, bilby ... 5. kangaroo
bilbo ... 5. sword 6. rapier
bilingual ... 6. diglot 12. linguistical
bilious ... 3. ill 8. choleric, liverish
9. dyspeptic, jaundiced 11. ill-tempered
bilk ... 2. do 3. gyp 4. balk, hoax, sell
5. cheat, cozen, trick 6. delude, fleece,
illude 7. deceive, defraud, swindle
8. flimflam 11. hornswoggle
bill ... 3. dun, nab, nib, pee, tab, Vee
($5) 4. beak, deed, list, menu, sign
5. carte, money 6. docket, pickax,
poster, ticket 7. account, invoice,
mattock, placard, program, receipt,
statute, voucher 8. billhook, schedule
9. publicize, statement 10. prospectus
11. legislative 13. advertisement
billet ... 3. bar, log 4. note, pass
5. berth, stick, strap 6. assign, docket,
letter, notice, ticket 7. bearing (Her),
epistle, missive, molding 8. dispatch,
document, insignia, position, quarters
11. appointment
billiard shot ... 5. carom, masse
6. cannon
Billingsgate ... 4. Gate (London) 10. fish

market 12. vituperation
billow . . . 3. sea 4. roll, toss, wave
   5. eagre, heave, surge, swell 6. dilate
   7. distend 10. undulation
billowy . . . 4. wavy 5. surgy 7. surging
   8. swelling 10. undulating
bin . . . 3. box 4. crib, loft, vina 5. frame,
   kench, pungi (Hind flute) 6. manger
   8. elevator
binary . . . 4. dual 6. bifold, binate, double,
   duplex 9. duplicate
bind . . . 3. jam, tie 4. ally, frap, gird,
   gyve, hold, lace, lash, rope, tape
   5. chain, leash, stick, truss, withe
   6. engage, fasten, fetter, pinion, pledge,
   secure 7. confine, shackle 8. obligate
   10. constipate
binding . . . 4. tape 5. valid 6. binder,
   edging 7. girding, joining, liaison
   8. trimming, trussing, wrapping
   9. bordering, fastening, stringent
   10. astringent, compulsory, obligatory
   11. restraining, restrictive
binding (agreement) . . . 4. bond, pact
   7. bargain, promise 8. contract
binding (book) . . . 4. yapp 5. cover
   6. jacket 10. bibliopegy
binge . . . 4. bout 5. spree 6. bender
   8. carousal 11. celebration
bingo . . . 3. pop 4. bang, keno 5. lotto,
   socko 6. brandy 7. tombola
biographer . . . 8. annalist 9. historian
   10. chronicler 11. biographist,
   memorialist
biography . . . 4. life 6. memoir 7. history,
   memoire, recount 8. memorial
   11. hagiography
biological . . . 4. gene 5. class, genus,
   order, vital 6. biotic, family 7. animate,
   organic, paracme, species
biology, science of . . . 6. botany
   7. ecology, zoology 8. eugenics,
   genetics 9. bionomics, organisms
   10. embryology, morphology,
   physiology
biopsy (Med) . . . 8. analysis (tissue)
   9. diagnosis 11. examination
   (microscopic)
biped . . . 3. man 9. two-legged
birch . . . 4. flog 5. stick 6. switch
birch tree (pert to) . . .
   family . . 10. Betulaceae
   genera . . 5. alder, birch, hazel
   order . . 7. Fagales
   product . . 16. oil of wintergreen
   variety . . 5. paper, river, sweet, white
   6. cherry, yellow
bird (pert to) . . .
   best swimmer . . 4. loon 6. gannet
   cage . . 6. aviary 7. paddock 8. dovecote
   Class . . 4. Aves
   crested . . 7. hoatzin 9. stinkbird
   extinct . . 3. moa 4. dodo
   fabled, sacred . . 3. roc 4. ibis
   fastest flyer . . 4. hawk 5. eagle, swift
   6. falcon
   fastest runner . . 7. ostrich
   feathers . . 4. remix (sing) 7. remiges
   first . . 13. archaeopteryx
   footless . . 4. apod
   greatest traveler . . 4. tern

   greatest wingspread . . 9. albatross
   halcyon . . 10. kingfisher
   highest flyer . . 5. goose
   immortal . . 7. phoenix
   killing . . 7. avicide
   largest . . 6. condor 7. ostrich
   13. whooping crane
   Latin . . 4. avis
   life . . 5. ornis
   longest-lived . . 5. macaw
   lover . . 12. ornithophile
   most dangerous . . 9. cassowary
   naked hatched . . 11. gymnogenous
   of prey (prized) . . 6. falcon
   oldest known . . 13. archaeopteryx
   one year old . . 8. annotine
   Order . . 7. Rasores 8. Raptores
   smallest . . 14. bee hummingbird
   smartest . . 4. crow
   study . . 6. oology
   young . . 4. eyas 8. birdikin, nestling
   9. fledgling
bird, anatomy (pert to) . . .
   beak . . 3. neb, nib 4. bill, lora 5. ceral
   7. rostrum
   eye process . . 6. pecten
   head . . 4. lore 6. pileum
   jaw . . 4. mala
   leg (featherless) . . 9. cnemidium
   wing part . . 5. alula
bird, Arctic . . . 3. auk 4. gull, skua 5. brant
   6. dunlin, fulmar, jaeger 7. penguin
   9. ptarmigan
bird, colorful . . . 3. kea 5. egret, macaw
   6. magpie, parrot, trogon 7. peacock,
   quetzal (quezal) 8. lyrebird 10. kingfisher
   14. bird of paradise
bird, common . . . 3. ani, daw, owl
   4. chat, dove, lark, pisk, wren 5. finch,
   pipit, robin, vireo 6. dunlin, linnet,
   martin, oriole, phoebe, pigeon, shrike,
   siskin, thrush, towhee 7. blue jay,
   bunting, catbird, cowbird, flicker,
   grackle, kinglet, sparrow, swallow,
   tanager, warbler, waxwing 8. blackcap,
   bluebird, bobolink, cardinal, grosbeak,
   kingbird, redstart, starling, titmouse
   9. chickadee, goldfinch, nighthawk,
   sandpiper 10. flycatcher, meadowlark,
   turtledove, woodpecker
   11. hummingbird, mockingbird,
   nightingale, pyrrhuloxia
   12. whippoorwill, yellowhammer
   14. scarlet tanager
bird, crow family . . . 4. crow, rook
   5. crake, raven 6. chough, magpie
   7. corvine, jackdaw
bird, duck family . . . 4. clee, coot, lory,
   smew, teal, wood 5. eider, goose
   6. scoter 7. gadwall, mallard, Muscovy,
   pintail, pochard 8. baldpate, redshank,
   shoveler 9. merganser 10. bufflehead,
   canvasback
bird, flightless . . . 3. emu, moa 4. dodo
   (ext), kiwi, rhea, weka 7. apteryx,
   ostrich, peacock, penguin 8. Notornis
   9. cassowary
bird, foreign
   Africa . . 4. taha 5. crane 6. cuckoo
   7. ostrich 8. umbrette 10. weaverbird
   Arctic . . 3. auk 4. gull, skua 5. brant

6. dunlin, falcon, jaeger 7. penguin
8. grayling 9. gyrfalcon, ptarmigan
Asia . . 4. myna 5. pitta 6. bulbul,
linnet 7. boobook, peacock, sirgang
8. dotterel, leaf bird 9. brambling,
muted swan
Australia . . 3. emu 4. kiwi, lory
5. lowan 6. leipoa 7. boobook,
grinder 8. ganggang, lorikeet, lyrebird,
morepork, parakeet, platypus
9. bowerbird, cassowary, pardalote
Central America . . 6. barbet, toucan
7. quetzal (quezal) 8. puffbird
Cuba . . 6. trogon 8. tocororo 14. bee
hummingbird
England . . 4. kite, rook 9. cormorant
11. carrion crow
Europe . . 4. merl 5. pipit, stilt (3-
toed), stork (white), swift, tarin
6. godwit, hoopoe, merlin, roller, siskin
7. bittern, ortolan, skylark, starnel 8. bee
eater, dotterel, garganey, nuthatch,
redstart 9. brambling, chaffinch,
gallinule, sheldrake 10. lammergeir,
turtledove 11. nightingale, wallcreeper
12. capercaillie (grouse)
Hawaii . . 2. io, o-o 3. ava, iwa, poe
4. iiwi, mamo 6. parson 7. frigate
India . . 5. shama 8. amadavat, pheasant
11. red hornbill
Java . . 7. sparrow 8. rice bird 9. fruit
dove
New Guinea . . 9. cassowary 14. bird
of paradise
New Zealand . . 3. ihi, kea, moa, tui
4. kuku, weka
So America . . 4. guan 5. macaw
6. barbet, motmot, toucan 7. jacamar,
tinamou, warrior 8. boatbill, caracara
9. trumpeter 11. scarlet ibis
bird, game . . . 4. teal 5. brant, goose,
quail, snipe 6. grouse, pigeon,
plover, turkey (wild) 7. bustard,
gadwall, mallard 8. bobwhite, pheasant,
woodcock 9. partridge, ptarmigan
10. canvasback 14. prairie chicken
bird, group . . .
partridge . . 5. covey
pheasant . . 3. nye 4. nide
quail . . 4. bevy
bird, long-legged . . . 4. ibis, rail, sora
5. crane, egret, heron, stilt, stork
6. avocet, curlew, jacana 7. seriema
8. flamingo 9. sandpiper 10. demoiselle
Bird of . . .
Freedom . . 9. bald eagle
Jove . . 5. eagle
June . . 7. peacock
Minerva . . 3. owl
Wonder . . 7. phoenix
bird, pet . . . 4. myna (mynah) 6. canary,
parrot 8. cockatoo, lovebird, parakeet
bird, poultry . . . 4. duck 5. goose
6. pigeon, turkey 7. chicken 8. pheasant
bird, shore . . . 4. swan 5. egret, heron,
stork 6. avocet, curlew, plover, willet
7. frigate, pelican 8. dotterel, killdeer
10. demoiselle
bird, sky . . . 4. erne (ern), gier (Bib),
hawk, kite 5. Buteo, eagle, saker
6. condor, falcon, gannet, jaeger,

merlin, osprey 7. buzzard, harrier,
kestral, vulture 8. caracara, ringtail
9. Accipiter 10. lammergeir
bird, water . . . 3. auk 4. coot, gull,
ibis, loon, rail, shag, skua, swan
5. cahow, crane, grebe, heron, stork
6. curlew, cygnet, gannet, jabiru,
jacana, petrel, plover 7. bittern, bustard,
dovekie, pelican, seriema, skimmer
8. dabchick, flamingo, umbrette
9. albatross, cormorant, gallinule,
guillemot, phalarope, spoonbill
10. kingfisher, yellowlegs
biretta . . . 8. skullcap 9. headdress
birl . . . 4. spin 6. rattle 7. resolve
birler . . . 10. lumberjack
Biro . . . 9. ballpoint
birth . . . 3. nee 4. line 5. blood,
breed 6. origin 7. descent, genesis,
lineage 8. heritage, nativity, nobility
9. beginning 10. derivation, extraction,
renascence 11. inheritance, Renaissance
birthday (pert to) . . .
astrology . . 7. casting, lineage (the gods)
nativities . . 9. genethlic 10. genethliac
poems . . 12. genethliacon
birth flower (by months) . . .
Jan . . 9. carnation
Feb . . 8. primrose
Mar . . 6. violet
Apr . . 5. daisy
May . . 15. lily of the valley
June . . 4. rose
July . . 8. sweet pea
Aug . . 9. gladiolus
Sept . . 5. aster
Oct . . 6. dahlia
Nov . . 13. chrysanthemum
Dec . . 5. holly 10. poinsettia
birthmark . . . 4. mole 5. nevus (naevus)
birthright . . . 6. rights 8. heritage
9. privilege 10. possession
11. inheritance
birth seniority . . . 9. first-born
13. primogeniture
birthstone (by days) . . .
Sun . . 5. topaz 7. diamond
Mon . . 5. pearl 7. crystal
Tues . . 4. ruby 7. emerald
Wed . . 8. amethyst 9. loadstone
Thurs . . 8. sapphire 9. carnelian
Fri . . 7. cat's eye, emerald
Sat . . 7. diamond 9. turquoise
birthstone (by months) . . .
Jan . . 7. garnet
Feb . . 8. amethyst
Mar . . 10. aquamarine, bloodstone
Apr . . 7. diamond
May . . 7. emerald
June . . 5. pearl 11. alexandrite
July . . 4. ruby
Aug . . 7. peridot 8. sardonyx
Sept . . 8. sapphire
Oct . . 4. opal 10. tourmaline
Nov . . 5. topaz 7. citrine
Dec . . 6. zircon 9. turquoise
bis . . . 5. again, ditto, twice 6. encore,
repeat 7. replica 8. repetend 9. duplicate
10. repetition
biscuit . . . 3. bun, doe 4. rusk 5. bread,
cooky, scone, wafer 6. pommel

7. cracker 8. biscotin, zwieback

bise . . . 4. wind (cold) 6. winter 7. Norther

bisect . . . 4. fork 5. cross, halve, split
6. cleave, divide

bishop . . . 4. Abba 7. pontiff, prelate
8. chessman, director, overseer
9. churchman, clergyman, inspector
14. superintendent

bishop (pert to) . . .
Bible . . 10. Great Bible
cap . . 4. hura 5. miter
revenue . . 7. annates
staff . . 7. baculus, crosier (crozier)
throne . . 3. see 4. apse
vestment . . 4. cope 5. stole 6. rochet
7. gremial, pallium 8. dalmatic
10. omophorion

bishopric . . . 3. see 4. seat 7. diocese
10. episcopacy, episcopate

Bismark . . . 14. Iron Chancellor

bison . . . 2. ox 4. gaur, urus 6. catalo
(hybrid) 7. aurochs, buffalo
9. quadruped

bisque (pert to) . . .
ceramics (unglazed) . . 7. biscuit
color . . 9. red-yellow
food . . 4. soup 8. ice cream
term (sports) . . 4. turn 5. point 6. stroke

bissext (pert to) . . .
calendar . . 6. Julian (Rom)
day . . 5. sixth (intercalary)
year . . 8. Leap Year

bistro . . . 4. cafe 6. tavern 7. barroom
8. wine shop 10. restaurant

bit . . . 3. ace, jot, ort 4. atom, bite, coin,
iota, mite, mote, part (acting), role, snip,
tool, tube, whit 5. check, crumb, hitch,
money, piece, scrap, speck 6. morsel,
smidge, tittle 7. portion, smidgen,
traneen 8. someone 9. something

bit (harness) . . . 4. curb 6. bridle, Pelham
7. snaffle 9. Liverpool

bit (money) . . .
two bits . . 7. quarter 9. ninepence
(Bahamas)
four bits . . 10. half dollar

bitch . . . 4. female (animal) 8. slattern,
strumpet 9. complaint

bite . . . 3. cut, eat, nip, zip 4. food, gnaw,
grip, hold, knap, pang, tang, zest
5. champ, smart, snack, sting, taste
6. morsel, nibble, pierce 8. pungency

biting . . . 4. acid, tart 5. acerb, acrid, sharp
6. bitter, rodent 7. caustic, cutting,
mordant, nipping, painful, piquant,
pungent 8. piercing, poignant, scathing,
stinging 9. sarcastic, trenchant, vitriolic,
withering 10. astringent, irritating
11. acrimonious, penetrating

biting nails . . . 12. phaneromania

bito (pert to) . . .
bark . . 10. fish poison
seeds . . 6. zachun (oil)
tree . . 7. hajilij

bitter . . . 4. acid, cold, keen, sore, sour
5. acerb, acrid, irate, sharp 6. severe
7. cutting, hostile, pungent 8. grievous,
stinging, virulent 9. rancorous, resentful
10. embittered, unpleasant
11. acrimonious, distressful, reproachful

bitter (pert to) . . .

apple (herb) . . 9. colocynth
chemical . . 4. alum
earth . . 8. magnesia
gentian . . 9. baldmoney
grass . . 9. colicroot
herb . . 3. rue 4. aloe 5. aloin 8. centaury
plant . . 10. bitterroot 11. bittersweet
(poisonous)
prefix . . 5. picro
salts . . 5. Epsom
suffix . . 6. picrin
vetch . . 3. ers
waters (Bib) . . 5. Marah
wintergreen . . 10. pipsissewa
wormwood . . 8. de Gaulle (said of)

bitterness . . . 3. rue 5. venom 6. rancor
7. remorse 8. acerbity, acrimony,
tartness, wormwood 9. animosity,
poignancy, virulence 10. causticity,
resentment

bivalve . . . 4. clam, spat, Unio 5. pinna
6. Anomia, mussel, oyster, Teredo
7. mollusk, pandora, scallop
10. brachiopod (fossil form)

bivocal . . . 9. diphthong (dipthong)

bivouac . . . 4. camp 6. encamp, laager
7. camping, leaguer (Hist)
10. encampment

biwa . . . 6. loquat

bizarre . . . 3. odd 5. dedal, outré, queer
6. absurd, exotic, quaint, rococo
7. baroque, fanciful 8. eccentric,
fantastic, grotesque, highflown
11. extravagant, sensational

Bizen . . . 7. pottery (unglazed)

Bizet opera . . . 6. Carmen

bizzarro (Mus) . . . 7. bizarre 9. whimsical

blab . . . 6. gossip, reveal, snitch, tattle,
tell on 7. blabber, chatter 8. informer,
squealer, telltale 10. taleteller, tattletale
11. taletelling

blabber . . . 4. blab 6. babble, gabber,
gossip, tattle 7. chatter, twaddle
8. informer, nonsense

black . . . 3. ink, jet 4. ebon, evil, foul,
inky, noir 5. color, cruel, ebony, murky,
niger (L), raven, sable, tarry 6. dismal,
filthy, gloomy, pitchy, somber, sullen,
wicked 7. hateful, melanic, nigrine,
nigrous, ominous, unclean 8. atrament,
menacing, mournful, sinister
9. atrocious, lightless, nigricant
10. calamitous, disastrous, forbidding

black (pert to) . . . see also *Black*
African . . 10. blackamoor
alloy . . 6. niello
and blue . . 5. livid 7. bruised
10. discolored, ecchymosed,
ecchymosis 11. bluish-black, lead-
colored
art . . 5. magic 7. alchemy 8. wizardry
10. black magic
ball . . 7. exclude 9. ostracize
bird . . 2. Zu (Myth) 3. ani, daw, pie
4. crow, merl, rook 5. amsel, ouzel,
raven 6. thrush 7. grackle, jackdaw
10. Melanesian, Polynesian
bottom . . 9. clog dance
coffee . . 8. café noir
diamond . . 4. coal
duck . . 6. Cayuga

earth . . 4. mold 9. chernozem (Russ)
face . . 4. type 5. sheep 8. minstrel
fish . . 6. tautog
garnet . . 8. melanite
gibbon . . 7. siamang
guard . . 5. drole, gamin, knave, rogue, scamp 6. rascal 7. vagrant, villain 8. criminal, scalawag, scullion, vagabond 9. scoundrel 11. rapscallion
Harry . . 7. sea bass
jack . . 4. flag (pirate) 6. coerce, cudgel, hijack 9. strong-arm 10. Jolly Roger
partridge . . 9. francolin
rhinoceros . . 7. borelle
sheep . . 10. scapegrace
smith . . 5. smith 6. forger, smithy 7. farrier
spruce . . 7. yewpine
strap . . 8. molasses
widow spider . . 6. pokomo

Black (pert to) . . .
Bess . . 4. mare (Dick Turpin's)
Current . . 5. Japan
Death . . 6. Plague (bubonic)
Foot . . 6. Indian (Siksika) 10. Algonquian
Friar . . 4. monk 9. Dominican (mendicant Order)
Friday . . 4. Fisk 5. Gould, panic 10. Good Friday
Hand . . 7. anarchy, Camorra, Society (secret) 9. blackmail
Hawk . . 3. War (1831) 11. Indian Chief
Hole . . 8. Calcutta
Jack (General) . . 5. Logan (Civil War) 8. Pershing (WWI)
Maria . . 7. vehicle (prisoner's) 14. explosive shell
Monday . . 12. Easter Monday (1630)
Monk . . 11. Benedictine
Plague . . 7. bubonic
Prince . . 6. Edward
Republic . . 5. Haiti
Rood . . 8. crucifix, Holy Rood (anc)
Sea . . 6. Euxine (anc), Odessa (port) 8. Bosporus (Bosphorus) (strait)
Shirt . . 7. Fascist 9. Mussolini
Watch . . 16. Royal Highlanders
Water State (nickname) . . 8. Nebraska
blacken . . 5. sully 6. defame 9. denigrate
bladder . . 3. bag, sac 4. sack 5. pouch 6. bubble, pocket 7. blister, globule
blade . . 3. arm, bit, fop 4. beau, dude, edge, epee, foil, leaf, vane 5. blood, dandy, frond, knife, spark, spear, spire, sport, sword 6. cutter, rafter (roof), runner, Toledo (sword) 7. gallant, sabreur, scapula, traneen 9. swordsman
blague . . 6. humbug 8. claptrap
blah . . 4. bunk 8. contempt, nonsense
blain . . 4. bleb, sore 5. bulla 7. blister, inflame, pustule 8. swelling 9. chilblain
blame . . 5. chide, curse, shend 6. accuse, charge, revile 7. accusal, censure, obloquy, reproof, reprove 8. denounce, reproach 9. criticism, damnation, reprehend 10. accusation, imputation 11. attribution, reprobation 12. condemnation, denunciation, reprehension 14. responsibility
blameless . . 7. sinless 8. innocent 9. faultless, guiltless 12. sans reproche

blame taker . . . 4. goat 9. scapegoat
blameworthy . . . 8. culpable 10. censurable, reprovable 11. impeachable 13. reprehensible
blanch . . . 4. fade, pale 5. gloss, scald 6. whiten 8. etiolate 9. whitewash
blanc mange . . . 7. dessert, pudding
bland . . 4. glib, mild, oily, smug, soft, tame 5. suave 6. gentle, smooth 7. affable 8. soothing (manner), unctuous 9. temperate 10. flattering 12. hypocritical, ingratiating, mealy-mouthed, smooth-spoken
blandishment . . . 7. amenity, coaxing, palaver 8. cajolery, flattery 9. wheedling 10. allurement, inducement
blank . . . 4. arid, bare, dash, dull, form, nude, null, void 5. empty, naked, verse 6. closed, hollow, jejune, poetry, stupid, vacant, vacuum 8. bull's-eye, document, spotless (domino) 9. fruitless, unadorned, untrimmed 10. instrument (law), tabula rasa 11. empty-headed, thoughtless 13. unembellished, unintelligent 14. expressionless
blank book . . . 5. album 6. tablet 8. memo book, notebook 10. memorandum, pocketbook
blanket . . . 3. rug 4. robe 5. bluey, cloak, cotta, cover, manta, spread, throw 6. afghan, shroud, spread 7. lap robe 8. covering, coverlet 10. barraclade (homespun)
blankness . . . 7. vacancy, vacuity 8. negation 9. emptiness
blare . . . 4. bawl, blow, bray, honk, peal, toot 5. blast, blaze, glare 6. bellow 7. fanfare, tantara 9. tantarara
blarney . . . 6. bunkum 7. wheedle 8. buncombe, cajolery, flattery, soft-soap 9. adulation
Blarney Stone site . . . 13. Blarney Castle (Cork, Ir)
blart . . . 4. blab, roar 5. bleat 6. bellow
blasé . . . 5. bored, sated 6. casual 9. easygoing, sans souci, surfeited 10. hard-boiled, nonchalant 11. indifferent, self-assured, unconcerned, worldly-wise 12. disenchanted 13. disillusioned, disinterested, lackadaisical
blaspheme . . . 4. damn 5. abuse, curse, swear 6. revile, vilify 10. calumniate
blasphemy . . . 7. cursing, impiety 8. anathema, swearing 9. profanity, sacrilege 10. execration 11. desecration, imprecation, irreverence, malediction
blast . . . 3. jet, pop 4. bang, blow, gust, ruin, shot, toot 5. curse, stunt 6. blight, flurry, onrush, wither 7. blowout, explode 9. discharge, explosion, explosive, frustrate 10. detonation, propulsion 11. fulmination
blasted . . . 5. blown 6. blamed, cursed, danged (sl), darned, ruined 7. wrecked 8. blighted 10. confounded
blatant . . . 5. crude, noisy 6. garish, puling, vulgar 7. flaring, glaring, howling, ululant, wailing 8. brawling 9. clamorous, turbulent 10. blustering,

uproarious, vociferous 12. obstreperous

blate . . . 4. blab, dull, slow 5. bleat, blunt, prate, timid 7. bashful 8. sheepish 9. diffident 10. spiritless

blaw . . . 4. blow, brag 5. boast

blaze . . . 4. fire, gash, mark (trail), sign 5. flame, flare 6. luster 7. bonfire, flare-up 8. eruption, outburst, radiance, splendor 9. explosion, firebrand 10. effulgence 11. resplendent

blazer . . . 6. jacket

blazon . . . 4. deck, show 5. adorn, blaze, grace, paint 6. enrich, shield 7. display, étalage, exhibit, furbish 8. proclaim 9. embellish 10. coat of arms, exhibition 11. publication

blazoning arms . . . 8. bearings, heraldry

bleach . . . 3. lye, sun 4. lime 6. blanch, purify, whiten 7. decolor, lighten 8. chemical, chlorine, etiolate, peroxide 9. whiteness 10. dealbation, decolorant 11. decolorizer

bleaching vat . . . 4. kier 5. kieve

bleak . . . 3. dry, raw 4. arid, bare, cold, pale 5. gaunt, sharp 6. bitter, desert, dismal, dreary, frigid, pallid, severe 7. cutting, exposed 8. desolate, rigorous 9. cheerless, wind-blown, wind-swept 10. depressing

blear . . . 3. dim, fog 4. blur, dull, film 6. bleary 7. blurred 10. indistinct

bleat . . . 3. baa 4. blat 5. blate, whine 7. blather

bleb . . . 5. bulge, bulla 6. bubble 7. bladder, blister, globule, pustule, vesicle

bleed . . . 3. cup, tap 4. milk, soak 5. drain 6. fleece, grieve, let out, suffer 7. agonize, despoil, exploit, overtax 8. let blood, transude 9. surcharge 10. hemorrhage, overcharge

bleeding . . . 7. cupping 9. hemorrhea 10. hemorrhage, phlebotomy 11. venesection 12. bloodletting

blemish . . . 3. mar 4. blot, blue, dent, flaw, mole, mote, pock, rift, scar, spot, wart 5. crack, fault, nevus, sully, taint 6. breach, macula, macule, stigma 7. failing, fissure, freckle, lentigo 8. cicatrix, pockmark 9. birthmark, cicatrice, deformity, disfigure 10. defacement, deficiency 12. imperfection 13. disfigurement

blench . . . 4. duck, pale, wile 5. blink, dodge, quail, trick, wince 6. bleach, cringe, flinch, recoil, shrink, whiten 9. stratagem 10. disconcert

blend . . . 3. mix 4. fuse, melt 5. merge, shift, unite 6. fusion, mingle 7. combine, mixture, scumble 8. coalesce, compound, tincture 9. commingle, composite, harmonize 10. amalgamate 11. combination, incorporate

blended . . . 5. fondu, mixed 6. merged 7. mingled 9. confluent

blending . . . 6. crasis 11. inheritance

blessing . . . 4. boon, gift, good, luck, rite 5. favor, grace 7. benefit, benison, fortune, godsend, service, welfare 8. good turn, kindness 9. advantage 10. benedicite, good

wishes 11. benediction, benevolence 12. felicitation 13. beatification

Bligh's ship . . . 6. Bounty

blight . . . 3. mar, nip 4. dash (hope), ruin, rust, seer, smut 5. blast, crush, spoil 6. freeze, mildew, wither 7. destroy, shatter 9. frustrate 10. disappoint

blighter . . . 4. chap 6. beggar (anc), fellow

blimp . . . 6. ballon 7. airship, balloon 8. potbelly, zeppelin 9. dirigible 10. bureaucrat 12. Graf Zeppelin, stuffed shirt

blind . . . 3. dim 4. ante (poker), mask, peed, ruse, seel, slat, veil, wile 5. ciego, guise, trick 6. ambush, scheme, screen 7. benight, conceal, dim-eyed, eyeless, gimmick, obscure, pretext, shutter 8. artifice, hoodwink, jalousie, purblind, unseeing 9. dead-drunk, senseless, sightless 10. ableptical, dim-sighted, subterfuge 11. inattentive 12. undiscerning 13. stalking-horse

blind (pert to) . . .
   alley . . 7. impasse 8. cul-de-sac
   fear . . 5. panic
   girl (of Pompeii) . . 5. Nydia
   gut . . 6. caecum, window 10. persiennes
   one eye . . 4. peed
   printing for . . 7. braille

blindness . . . 7. anopsia, meropia (part) 8. ablepsia 9. achropsia, amaurosis 10. bleariness, nyctalopia 11. gutta serena, hemeralopia 13. achromatopsia

blink . . . 4. wink 5. light, quail, wince 6. cringe, flinch 7. flicker, glimmer, glimpse, glitter, nictate, shimmer, twinkle 9. nictitate 10. bat the eyes

blink at . . . 6. accept, ignore 7. condone 8. overlook, tolerate 9. be blind to, disregard

bliss . . . 3. joy 4. Eden 6. heaven 7. delight, harmony, rapture 8. felicity, gladness 9. beatitude, happiness 11. blessedness 12. spirituality 14. blithesomeness

blissful . . . 4. holy 5. seely 6. Edenic 7. blessed, Elysian, Utopian 8. ecstatic 9. beatified, glorified

blister . . . 4. bleb, blob, burn, flay 5. blain, bulge, bulla, roast 6. beat up, bubble, oyster, scorch (with words), thrash 7. bladder, blemish, pustule, trounce, vesicle 9. criticize 10. vesicatory

blistered . . . 6. seared, singed 7. parched 8. scorched 9. vesicated

blithe . . . 4. airy, glad 5. merry 6. cheery, joyous 7. jocular 8. cheerful 10. blithesome

blitz . . . 5. shell 6. strafe 7. bombard 10. blitzkrieg

blizzard . . . 4. blow, wind 5. purga 7. tornado 9. snowstorm 10. snow squall 11. white squall

Blizzard State . . . 11. South Dakota

bloated . . . 5. cured (herring), proud, tumid 6. sodden, turgid 7. dilated, pompous, swollen 8. inflated, puffed up, tumefied 9. distended, flatulent, plethoric 10. incrassate 13. emphysematous

bloated plutocrat . . . 9. bourgeois

10. capitalist

blob ... 3. wen 4. bleb, blot, daub, drop, lump, mark 5. bulge 6. bubble, pimple 7. blister, globule, pustule, splotch

bloc (political) ... 4. axis 5. cabal, union 6. league 7. faction 8. alliance 9. coalition 11. combination

block ... 3. bar, dam, set 4. cake, clog, cube, mass, peck, plot, stop 5. check, parry, shape, solid 6. hamper, hinder, impede, oppose, shares, stymie 7. auction, barrier, outline 8. blockage, obstacle, obstruct 9. barricade 10. impediment 11. obstruction

block (pert to) ...
architecture .. 5. socle 6. dentil, mutule, plinth 7. tessera
blacksmith's .. 5. anvil
coal (Eng) .. 3. jud
executioner's .. 10. guillotine
falconry .. 5. perch
finance .. 6. shares
football .. 4. clip
glacier .. 5. serac
insulating .. 6. taplet
land .. 4. city 5. tract 7. section
medicine .. 10. anesthesia
railroad .. 6. signal
sandstone (Eng) .. 6. sarsen

blockade ... 3. bar, dam 5. hem in, siege 6. shut in 7. closure, exclude, fortify 8. obstacle, obstruct 9. exclusion 11. obstruction

blockhead ... 3. oaf 4. dolt, fool, mome (anc) 5. dunce, idiot 7. half-wit, tomfool 8. bonehead, lunkhead 11. knucklehead

blockhouse ... 4. fort 7. shelter 8. log cabin 10. stronghold

bloke ... 3. man 4. bird, chap, tuff 6. fellow 9. personage

blond, blonde ... 4. fair 5. color, light 6. flaxen 10. goldilocks

blood ... 4. cell, clot, type, vein 5. aorta, fluid, group, grume, hemad (haemad), hemal, hemic, ichor (gods'), lymph, serum 6. artery, factor, fibrin, haemal, plasma, Rhesus (type) 7. blister, carotid 8. platelet 9. corpuscle, hemamoeba, leucocyte 10. hemachrome, hemoglobin, hemorrhage, phlebotomy 11. erythrocyte, transfusion 12. bloodletting

blood (pert to) ...
classification .. 3. ABO
clotted .. 4. gore 5. cruor 8. thrombus
color .. 7. crimson, para red 8. blood red, sanguine 11. sanguineous 13. sanguinaceous
disease .. 6. anemia 8. leukemia (leukaemia, leucemia)
feud .. 8. vendetta
flower .. 5. hippo 9. blood lily
horse .. 7. blooded 12. thoroughbred
hound .. 4. lyam (lyme)
money (anc) .. 3. cro 5. eric 7. galanas, wergild 9. bloodwite
particle (foreign) .. 7. embolus
poisoning 6. pyemia (pyaemia)
pressure .. 12. hypertension
pudding .. 7. sausage
relationship .. 3. sib 6. agnate 7. cognate,

kinship, kinsman, progeny, sibship
shed .. 6. murder 7. killing, slaying 9. slaughter
stone .. 10. chalcedony
sucker .. 5. leech 8. parasite 10. sanguisuge
thirsty .. 5. cruel 8. sanguine 9. ferocious, murderous 10. sanguinary 11. ensanguined
vessel .. 3. vas 4. vein 6. artery 9. capillary

blood, kinship ... 4. race, ties 5. birth, breed, stock 6. strain 7. descent, kinsman, lineage, royalty, sibship 8. heredity, nobility, relation 9. blue blood, lifeblood, life force 10. extraction 13. consanguinity

bloodless ... 4. pale 5. ashen, faint 6. anemic (aenemic) 7. ghastly, inhuman 8. lifeless, peaceful 9. unfeeling 11. cold of heart

bloody ... 4. gory 5. cruel, wound 6. cruent (obs), cursed 7. smeared 8. infamous 9. murderous 10. sanguinary 11. ensanguined 12. bloodstained, bloodthirsty

Bloody (pert to) ...
Angle .. 11. battlefield (Spotsylvania, 1860)
Mary .. 5. Queen (Eng) 8. cocktail

bloom ... 3. dew 4. glow, posy 5. blush, flush, youth 6. beauty, flower, health, heyday, thrive 7. blossom 11. healthiness

bloomer ... 5. boner, error 6. bobble, boo-boo 7. blooper, blunder, failure, faux pas, mistake, trouser

blossom ... 4. bell, blow, grow, posy 5. bloom, ripen 6. floret, flower, mature, thrive 7. develop, prosper 8. flourish, floweret, progress 10. effloresce 13. efflorescence

blossoming ... 4. rise 6. growth 8. anthesis, blooming 9. flowerage, flowering 10. florescent, unfoldment 11. development, florescence, flourishing, progressing 13. efflorescence, inflorescence

blot ... 3. dry, mar 4. blur, soil, spot 5. erase, error, fleck, smear, speck, stain, sully 6. absorb, blotch, damage, impair, smutch, soak up, sponge, stigma 8. blacken, blemish, erasure, expunge 9. bespatter 10. obliterate, stigmatize 11. obliteration

blot out ... 3. fix 4. dele, kill 5. purge 6. absorb, cancel, delete, efface, excise, rub out 7. bump off, destroy, expunge, obscure, wipe out 8. black out 10. obliterate

blotch ... 4. bleb, mark, soil, spot 5. patch, stain 6. macula, mottle, stigma 7. blemish

blotched ... 4. pied 5. pinto 6. spotty 7. mottled 8. speckled

blouse ... 4. blou, sark 5. bluey, middy, shift, shirt, smock, tunic, waist 6. basque 7. casaque 10. shirtwaist

blow ... 3. dab, hit, rap, tap 4. brag, bump, coup, gust, pant, puff, slap, toot, waft, wind 5. bloom, devel,

feint, impel, knock, shock, sound, utter
6. expand, puff up 7. beating, bluster,
whiffle 8. calamity, disaster, disclose,
lambskin (obs) 14. disappointment

blow . . . 4. flee, over, rant, slog 5. boast,
clout, scram 6. beat it, betray, buffet,
depart, wallop 8. squander 10. blow
me down

blow (pert to) . . .
hard . . 6. blower 7. windbag 8. braggart
11. braggadocio
hot and cold . . 4. vary 5. shift, waver
6. seesaw 7. quibble 9. fluctuate,
vacillate 12. shilly-shally
out . . 5. douse, snuff 10. extinguish

blower . . . 4. blow, gale, wind 5. whale
6. puffer (fish), squall 7. bellows,
bloomer, blowgun, boaster, monsoon,
tornado 8. braggart 9. hurricane,
whirlwind, windstorm 11. braggadocio

blow up . . . 4. fail, rage 5. blast, bloat,
burst, fluff 6. berate, dilate, excite,
expand, forget, praise 7. blow out,
enlarge, explode, inflate 8. demolish,
detonate, disprove 9. fulminate
10. exaggerate

blowzy . . . 5. dowdy, ruddy, tacky
6. coarse, frowzy, sloppy, untidy
7. unkempt 8. careless, frumpish,
slovenly 10. disheveled, slatternly

blubber . . . 3. fat 4. weep 5. bubble
7. whimper 8. whale fat

blubbery . . . 3. fat 7. swollen 9. quivering
10. gelatinous

bludgeon . . . 3. bat, hit 4. beat, club,
mace 5. billy, bully, stick 6. coerce,
cudgel, menace 8. browbeat, bulldoze,
threaten 9. truncheon 10. intimidate,
shillelagh (shillalah)

blue . . . 4. anil, baby, bice, bleu,
navy 5. azure, beryl, Ching, email,
king's, merle, perse, royal, smalt
6. cobalt, cyanic, French, indigo, powder
7. aniline, azarite, cesious, Dresden,
Dumont's, gobelin, lobelia, mesange,
peacock, Persian 8. caesious, calamine,
cerulean, Coventry, electric, lavender,
midnight, pavonine, sapphire, wisteria
9. turquoise 10. aquamarine, cornflower

blue (pert to) . . . see also *Blue*
baby . . 8. cyanotic
bonnet . . 3. cap 4. Scot 6. flower (Texas
State) 8. Scotsman, titmouse
china . . 7. Nanking
circle (archery) . . 6. target
day . . 6. Monday
emblem of . . 6. Oxford 9. Cambridge
grass . . 3. poa
ground . . 10. kimberlite
hero . . 9. Bluebeard
melancholy . . 3. sad 6. gloomy
7. pensive, wistful 8. tristful
9. cheerless, depressed, penseroso
10. atrabiliar 11. atrabilious,
melancholic 13. hypochondriac
nose . . 4. snob 5. prude 7. Puritan
10. goody-goody 11. Nova Scotian
pencil . . 4. dele, edit 6. delete, excise,
revise
print . . 4. plan, plot 5. graph 6. layout
7. diagram, program 8. schedule

9. cyanotype 10. master plan,
photograph, photoprint
ribbon . . 5. award, badge 10. cordon
bleu, decoration
skin . . 5. livid
sky . . 5. ether, vault 6. caelum, heaven,
welkin 7. the blue 8. empyrean
9. firmament 10. blue yonder, the
heavens
stocking . . 4. blue 6. pedant 7. bas
bleu 8. Gamaliel (Bib) 9. formalist,
pedagogue 10. Parliament

Blue (pert to) . . .
Boy . . 8. painting (Gainsborough)
Grass State . . 8. Kentucky
Grotto site . . 5. Capri
Law State . . 11. Connecticut

Bluebeard's wife . . . 6. Fatima
blue-gray . . . 7. cesious (caesious)
blue-green . . . 8. calamine

bluff . . . 4. bank (steep), crag, curt,
dupe, fool, rude, wall 5. brash,
cliff, frank, gruff, krans, sheer, short
6. abrupt, crusty 7. beguile, blinder,
blinker, bluffer, bluster, brusque,
deceive, pretend, uncivil 8. impolite
9. bamboozle, blusterer, charlatan,
falseness, four-flush, precipice 11. four-
flusher 13. unceremonious

bluffer . . . 5. quack 9. blusterer, charlatan
10. mountebank 11. four-flusher

bluffness . . . 6. candor 9. bluntness
10. abruptness 11. brusqueness

blunder . . . 3. err, mix 4. bull, goof, slip
5. boner, botch, error, misdo 6. boo-
boo, bungle, fumble 7. faux pas,
mistake, stumble 8. flounder, solecism
(speech) 9. mismanage

blunt . . . 4. curt, dull, open 5. bluff, frank,
gruff, plain 6. benumb, candid, deaden,
obtund, obtuse, snippy, stupid, weaken
7. artless, brusque, sincere 8. hebetate
9. ingenuous 13. unceremonious

blur . . . 3. bog, dim, hum 4. blob, blot,
film, mist, soil, spot 5. blear, cloud,
smear, stain 6. blotch, darken, mackle
7. blemish, dimness, obscure, splotch
9. disfigure

blurb . . . 2. ad 4. plug 5. boost, brief
6. notice 7. write-up 8. ballyhoo
9. publicity 12. announcement,
commendation 13. advertisement

blurt out . . . 4. blab, bolt 7. blunder
9. ejaculate

blush . . . 4. glow, look 5. bloom,
color, flush 6. glance, mantle, redden
7. modesty, redness 9. suffusion

blushing . . . 4. meek 5. ruddy 6. modest
7. roseate 8. flushing, sheepish
9. reddening, rubescent 10. erubescent

bluster . . . 4. blow, bray, fume, rage,
rant, roar 5. broil, bully, furor,
noise 6. flurry, hoopla, hubbub,
squall, tumult 7. roister, swagger,
turmoil 8. boasting, bullying, threaten
9. agitation, confusion 10. swaggering,
turbulence 11. rodomontade

blusterer . . . 5. bully 7. boaster
8. blowhard, braggart 9. roisterer,
swaggerer 11. braggadocio
12. swashbuckler

bo . . . 4. hobo 5. buddy, tramp 9. sundowner 10. landlouper 11. bindle stiff

bo, boh (Burma) . . . 5. chief 6. leader 7. captain

boa . . . 5. aboma, scarf (feather), snake 8. anaconda

boar . . . 3. hog, sus 4. apex, hure (head) 5. swine 6. barrow, hogget (2-year) 9. hoggaster (3-year)

board . . . 4. deal, doll, feed, lath, side, slat, wood 5. curia (anc), enter, forum, meals, plank, table 6. border, lumber, timber 7. binding (book), council, lodging 8. approach, exchange (Finan), tribunal 9. committee, provision 11. accommodate, bed and board, directorate, refreshment 14. accommodations

boast . . . 4. brag, crow 5. extol, exult, glory, pride, vapor, vaunt 6. menace 7. bluster, swagger 8. braggart, flourish 9. gasconade

boastful . . . 4. vain 8. bragging 9. conceited, overproud, presuming 11. thrasonical 12. vainglorious 13. self-important

boat . . . 3. ark, bac, gig, tub, tug 4. brig, dhow, dory, junk, punt, saic, scow, ship, trow, yawl 5. aviso, balsa, barge, canoe, craft, dandy, dhoni, dingy, ferry, kayak, ketch, liner, oolak, praam, scull, skiff, U-boat, umiak, xebec, yacht 6. argosy, baidak, bateau, convoy, cutter, dinghy, dogger, launch, mistic, oomiac, packet, randan, sampan, settee, tanker, vessel, whaler 7. bidarka, caravel, coracle (anc), cruiser, gondola, masoola, piragua, pirogue, rowboat, scooter, shallop, trawler, tugboat, warship 8. dahabeah, man-of-war, palander, sailboat, seaplane 9. catamaran, destroyer, steamship, submarine 10. brigantine, windjammer 11. side-wheeler, treckschuyt

boat (pert to) . . .
boatswain . . 5. bosun 6. serang
captain . . 4. rais (reis) 6. master 7. skipper
deck . . 4. poop 6. flight 9. promenade
man . . 5. rower 6. bargee 7. ferrier, oarsman 9. gondolier, yachtsman
sail . . 3. jib 4. main, reef 6. lateen, mizzen
shaped . . 9. navicella, navicular
side . . 7. gunwale
song . . 7. chantey 9. barcarole

bob . . . 3. bow, cut, nod, rap, tap 4. bend, jeer, jerk, jest 5. cheat, filch, float, flout, plumb, shake, taunt, trick 6. bobble, curtsy, delude, hairdo, kowtow, sinker, weight 7. haircut 8. coiffure, greeting, shilling 9. obeisance, oscillate

bobac . . . 5. pahmi 6. marmot

bobber . . . 4. duck (ruddy) 5. float 6. bobfly 7. dropper 8. deadhead

bobbin . . . 3. pin 4. coil, cord, pirn, reel 5. braid, spool 7. spindle

bobble . . . 3. bob, dib (angling) 4. muff 5. shake 6. boggle, bungle, fumble 7. blunder 9. oscillate

bobby . . . 6. peeler 9. policeman

Boccaccio's tales . . . 9. Decameron

Boche . . . 6. German (a)

bodach . . . 5. churl, clown 7. bugaboo

bodacious . . . 4. bold 8. insolent, reckless 9. audacious, bumptious, insulting 12. contumelious

bode . . . 5. augur 6. divine 7. portend, presage 8. forebode, foreshow, foretell 13. prognosticate

bodhisattva . . 8. Buddhism 13. Enlightenment

bodice . . . 4. belt 5. stays, waist 6. basque, girdle 7. corsage, garment

bodily . . . 6. carnal 7. fleshly, somatic 8. corporal, material, physical 9. corporeal 10. completely

boding . . . 7. ominous 10. foreboding, portentous, prediction, prognostic 12. apprehension

bodkin . . . 3. awl 6. dagger, needle 7. hairpin, poniard 8. stiletto 9. eyeleteer

body . . . 3. man 4. deha (Theos), homo, soma 5. being, human, trunk 6. corpse, entity, licham, mortal, person 7. carcass 8. creature, organism 9. substance 10. individual 13. corpus delicti 14. substantiality

body (pert to) . . .
armed . . 5. corps, posse
business . . 7. company 11. cooperation 12. organization
celestial . . 3. sun 4. luna, star 5. comet 6. meteor, planet
church . . 4. nave
dead . . 6. corpse 7. cadaver
division (mollusk) . . 7. prosoma
injury . . 6. mayhem, trauma
petrified . . 6. fossil
political . . 4. weal 6. senate 7. cabinet 11. legislature
small . . 6. nanoid 8. dwarfish

body of . . .
people . . 3. mob 4. band, bevy, gang, host 5. bunch, crowd, flock, group, horde 6. rabble, throng 9. multitude
singers . . 5. choir 6. chorus
soldiers . . 4. file 5. corps, squad, troop 7. brigade, company, platoon 8. division
water . . 3. bay, sea 4. lake, pond, pool 5. fiord (fjord), inlet, ocean 6. lagoon 9. reservoir

Boeotian (pert to) . . .
city . . 5. Ionia (Dist) 6. Thebes
figurine . . 7. Tanagra
king (Myth) . . 6. Ogyges

Boer (pert to) . . .
General, statesman . . 5. Botha
language . . 4. Taal 9. Afrikaans
War site . . 9. Ladysmith (So Afr)

bog . . . 3. bug, fen 4. blei, bold, holm, mire, moor, moss, ooze, quag, sink 5. jheel, marsh, saucy, swamp 6. morass, slough 8. quagmire 9. everglade

bogey, bogie, bogy . . . 3. par 5. Devil 6. goblin 7. bugaboo, bugbear

boggle . . . 3. shy 4. foil, quip 5. botch, cavil, demur, parry, pause, start 6. bicker, bungle, falter, object, shrink 7. dispute, quibble, scruple 8. hesitate,

sidestep 9. dissemble, objection
10. difficulty, equivocate
bogglebo . . . 5. bogle 7. bugaboo, specter
9. hobgoblin, scarecrow
bogus . . . 4. fake, mock, sham 5. phony,
queer 8. spurious 10. apocryphal,
factitious, fictitious 11. counterfeit
bohawn . . . 3. hut 5. cabin 7. cottage
Bohemia . . .
    capital . . 6. Prague
    city . . 5. Praha 6. Aussig, Pilsen
        7. Budweis, Teplitz 11. Reichenberg
    dance . . 6. redowa
    measure . . 5. stopa 6. merice
    mineral . . 6. egeran
    reformer . . 7. Huss
    river . . 4. Elbe, Iser 6. Moldau
    vagabond . . 5. gypsy (gipsy)
bohunk . . . 6. Slovak 7. laborer
        8. Bohemian, Croatian (formerly)
boil . . . 3. sty (styr) 4. buck, cook, fume,
stew 5. churn, steam 6. bubble, pimple,
seethe 7. bristle 8. furuncle
boiling . . . 3. angry 7. cooking, flushed,
stewing 8. seething, sizzling 9. agitating,
ebullient 10. smoldering
bois (Fr) . . . 4. wood
boisterous . . . 4. loud 5. noisy, rough,
rowdy 6. stormy 7. blatant, excited,
furious, roaring, violent 8. brawling
9. clamorous, turbulent 10. blustering,
roisterous, tumultuous, unyielding
12. obstreperous
Bokhara (pert to) . . .
    fur . . 9. astrakhan, broadtail
    rug . . 8. Turkoman
    sheep . . 7. karakul (caracul)
    site . . 4. Asia (Russ)
bola . . 4. tree (fiber) 6. weapon
bold . . . 4. deep, pert, rash, rude, snug
5. steep, stout 6. abrupt, brazen, daring,
heroic, raised 7. dashing, defiant,
eminent, forward, salient, valiant
8. fearless, immodest, impudent, in
relief, intrepid, powerful, repoussé,
stalwart 9. audacious, confident,
dauntless, shameless, unabashed
10. courageous 11. lionhearted,
outstanding, precipitous, venturesome
12. presumptuous, stouthearted
boldness . . . 5. valor 6. defial, virtue
7. bravery, courage 8. audacity,
defiance, salience, temerity
9. assurance, gallantry, hardihood,
immodesty, impudence 10. brazenness,
confidence, effrontery, prominence,
resolution 11. forwardness, intrepidity,
obviousness 12. protuberance
13. dauntlessness 14. courageousness
bolero . . . 5. dance, music, waist 6. jacket
boliche . . . 3. inn 5. bowls
Bolivia . . .
    capital . . 5. La Paz (Polit), Oruro (anc),
        Sucre (law)
    hero . . 5. Sucre 7. Bolivar, Pizarro
    Indian . . 3. Uro 4. Iten, Moxo
    lake . . 8. Titicaca (world's highest)
    mountain . . 5. Andes 6. Sorata 8. Illimani
    product . . 3. tin 8. tungsten
    river . . 4. Beni 6. Blanco
bolo . . . 5. knife 7. machete 8. pacifist

(Bolo Pasha, traitor) 9. defeatist
Bolshevik, bolshevik . . . 5. Lenin
7. Marxian, radical (Bolsheviki)
9. Communist (1918), Socialist
13. revolutionist 14. Social Democrat
18. Third International
bolster . . . 3. pad 4. bear, hold 5. boost
6. pillow 7. cushion, support, sustain
8. maintain
bolt . . . 3. bar 4. dart, flee, lock, roll,
sift 5. arrow, rivet, scram, screw,
shaft, speed 6. decamp, devour,
faster, flight, pintle, secede, staple,
toggle 7. missile, padlock 8. firebolt,
separate 10. projectile 11. eat greedily,
fulgration, thunderbolt
bolus . . . 4. bite, clay, clod, food (chewed),
mass, pill 6. tablet, troche 8. mouthful
bomb . . . 3. dud, egg 5. shell 6. petard
7. grenade, missile 8. divebomb,
fireball, surprise 9. bombshell,
pineapple 10. projectile
bomb (type of) . . . 4. time 5. stink 6. aerial,
atomic, rocket 7. nuclear, tear gas
8. hydrogen 10. demolition
bombard . . . 3. zap 5. blitz, shell 6. assail,
attack, strafe 8. atomize, barrage
9. cannonade
bombardier . . . 5. jager 6. bomber,
gunner 9. cannoneer, musketeer
12. artilleryman
bombast . . . 4. blow, brag, rage, rant, rave
5. boast 7. fustian 8. boasting, inflated,
stuffing (hist) 9. bombastic, turgidity
11. rodomontade 12. magniloquent
13. grandiloquent
bombastic . . . 5. tumid 7. orotund,
pompous, stilted 8. boastful, inflated
12. high-sounding 13. grandiloquent
Bombay . . .
    capital of . . 11. Maharashtra (state)
    college . . 11. Elphinstone
    duck . . 10. lizard fish
    hemp . . 4. sunn 6. ambary
    merchant . . 4. Arab
    seaport of . . 5. India
bombed . . . 5. drunk
bomber . . . 5. stuka 10. bombardier
Bombyx . . . 4. eria, moth 8. silkworm
bona fide . . . 4. real 7. genuine
9. authentic 10. constantly, faithfully,
legitimate
bona mano . . . 3. tip 8. gratuity
bon ami . . . 5. lover 6. friend 10. good
friend, sweetheart
bonanza . . . 6. riches 8. El Dorado (Myth),
gold mine (US)
Bonanza State . . . 7. Montana
Bonaparte . . . see *Napoleon I*
bond . . . 3. tie, vow 4. duty, gyve, link,
mise, pact, yoke 5. chain, nexus,
rente 6. fetter, league 7. entente,
manacle, shackle 8. contract, covenant,
relation, security (Finan) 9. agreement,
captivity 10. allegiance, connection
11. association, certificate
bondage . . . 4. yoke 6. chains 7. serfdom,
slavery 9. captivity, restraint, servitude,
thralldom 11. enslavement, subjugation
bondman, bondsman . . . 4. esne, serf
5. churl, helot, slave 6. thrall, vassal

7. servant 8. bailsman 9. guarantor

bone . . . 2. os 4. chip 5. boner 6. dollar, osteon 7. blunder, counter (game), ossicle 8. skeleton, wishbone 9. funny bone (humerus), pygostyle (bird's), whalebone

bone (Anat) . . . 3. rib 4. ulna 5. femur, ilium, incus (ear), malar, skull, spine, talus, tibia 6. carpus, coccyx, fibula, tarsus 7. humerus, maxilla, patella, scapula, sternum 8. astragal, clavicle, mandible, phalange, vertebra 9. calcaneus, occipital 10. metacarpus, metatarsus

bone (pert to) . . .
bonelike . . 6. osteal 7. osteoid
cell . . 10. osteoblast
china . . 7. English
curvature . . 8. lordosis
divination . . 10. osteomancy
fish . . 9. operculum
marrow . . 7. medulla
process . . 7. mastoid 8. alveolar 9. apophysis
science . . 9. osteology
surgery . . 9. osteotomy 11. osteoclasis 12. osteoplastic
tissue . . 6. ossein
tumor . . 7. osteoma

bones . . . 4. body, dice, form, ossa 5. cubes, frame, money, torso, trunk 6. end man, refuse 7. carcass, ivories 8. skeleton 11. rattlebones

boneyard . . . 4. bank (game) 8. golgotha 9. graveyard 10. necropolis 11. polyandrium

Bonheur subject . . . 6. animal

bonhomie . . . 8. pleasant 9. good humor 10. affability, amiability

Bonhomme Richard . . . 4. ship 8. man-of-war (1779) (opponent of Serapis)

bonito, bonita . . . 4. nice 6. pretty 8. mackerel, skipjack

bon mot . . . 9. witticism 10. jeu d'esprit 11. smart saying

bonne . . . 5. mammy 9. nursemaid 10. baby sitter 11. maidservant

bonnet . . . 3. cap, hat 4. coif, hood, poke 5. toque 7. chapeau 9. headdress

bonnetman . . . 10. Highlander

bonny, bonnie . . . 3. bon 4. good 5. plump 6. comely, lively, pretty 7. healthy, très bon 8. handsome 9. beautiful

Bontok . . . 7. Malayan (Luzon) 10. Indonesian

bonus . . . 3. tip 4. cash, gift 5. batta, bribe, extra, share, stock (Finan) 7. cumshaw, douceur, premium, rake-off, subsidy 8. dividend, gratuity 9. Trinkgeld 10. honorarium

bon vivant . . . 7. epicure, gourmet 8. gourmand, hedonist, sybarite 10. boonfellow, good fellow, voluptuary 12. Heliogabalus (anc)

bony . . . 4. hard, thin 6. osteal, skinny 7. osseous 8. rawboned, skeletal

bonze (Far East) . . . 2. bo 4. monk

boo . . . 4. hoot, jeer, razz 7. catcall, feather (ostrich) 9. raspberry 10. Bronx cheer

boob . . . 4. dupe, fool, goon, jerk

5. chump, dunce 6. nitwit 7. fathead 9. schlemiel, simpleton

boobook . . . 3. owl 8. morepork

booby hatch . . . 3. can, jug 4. jail 6. asylum, cooler, prison 8. hoosegow, madhouse 11. institution (mental)

boodle . . . 3. sop 4. loot, swag 5. booty, bribe, bunch, crowd, graft, money (hush) 6. spoils 8. caboodle 10. pork barrel 11. counterfeit

boohoo . . . 3. rob 4. bawl, hoot, weep 5. shout 8. sailfish

book . . . 2. mo (abbr) 3. day 4. hire, opus, tome 5. album, atlas, Bible, canto, diary, folio, liber, novel 6. agenda, engage, ledger, manual, missal, primer, record, sign up, volume 7. diurnal, journal, mystery 8. brochure, libretto, register, schedule, songbook, whodunit 9. paperback, storybook 10. literature, memorandum 11. publication

book (pert to) . . .
announcement . . 5. blurb
back . . 5. spine
binder . . 12. bibliopegist
binding devise . . 7. trindle
collector . . 9. bibliothec 12. bibliomaniac 14. bibliothecaire
cover . . 5. recto 6. jacket
destroyer . . 11. biblioclast
division . . 7. chapter
lore . . 10. bibliology
lover . . 11. bibliophile
one versed in . . 11. bibliognost
page . . 5. folio
seller . . 10. bibliopole (rare books)
sheath . . 5. forel
size . . 6. quarto
stealer . . 11. biblioklept
style . . 6. Aldine 8. Etruscan 9. Arabesque
treatise . . 8. isagogue
worshiper . . 11. bibliolater
writer . . 13. bibliographer

book (religious) . . . 4. Ordo 5. Bible, Kells, Tobit 6. Esdras, Mormon 7. Psalter 8. Holy Writ 9. Apocrypha, Catechism, Testament 10. Pentateuch, Scriptures

Book of . . .
award (Harvard) . . 5. detur
Concord . . 8. Lutheran
Discipline . . 12. Presbyterian
Hours . . 5. Horae
Moses (Laws) . . 10. Pentateuch
Psalms . . 7. Psalter
the Dead . . 12. Pyramid Texts

boom . . . 3. hum 4. gain, peal, raft, roar, spar, zoom 5. boost, cable, speed, sprit, withe 6. thrive, upturn 7. pontoon, resound, thunder 8. bowsprit, flourish, increase 9. cannonade, Golden Age, outrigger 10. navigation, prosperity

boomerang . . . 6. resile 7. rebound 8. backfire, ricochet

Boomer State . . . 8. Oklahoma

boon . . . 3. gay 4. bene, gift, good, nice 5. favor, jolly 6. jovial, kindly 7. benefit, gleeful, godsend, present 8. blessing 9. convivial 11. benefaction

boor . . . 3. cad, oaf 4. hick, lout 5. churl, clown, yokel 6. rustic 7. bumpkin, cauboge, peasant, ruffian 9. roughneck,

vulgarian 10. clodhopper; husbandman
boorish . . . 4. rude 5. gawky, surly
6. clumsy, rustic, sullen 7. awkward,
crabbed, loutish, uncouth 8. churlish,
inurbane, lubberly, ungainly
9. farmerish, unrefined 11. countrified
boost . . . 4. help, hike, lift, plug, push
5. heist, raise, shove 6. assist,
thrust 7. commend, hearten, inspire,
promote, upswing 8. advocate, increase
9. promotion, publicize 10. assistance
11. advancement 12. commendation
boot . . . 3. pac 4. kick, pack, sack, shoe
5. armor, bonus, jemmy, kamik, wader
6. buskin, fumble, rookie, sheath
7. dismiss, recruit, trainee 8. balmoral,
enlistee, inductee, napoleon
9. discharge
booth . . . 3. hut, pew 4. crib, loge 5. stall,
stand, store 6. manger 11. compartment
booty . . . 4. gain, loot, pelf, swag 5. graft,
prize, spoil 6. spoils 7. pillage, plunder
booze . . . 4. bout 5. drink, spree 6. liquor
8. potation
boozer . . . 3. pub, sot 5. toper 6. barfly,
bibber, saloon 7. guzzler, reveler, tippler
8. drunkard 9. alcoholic, inebriate
11. dipsomaniac
borax . . . 4. salt 5. cheap
Bordeaux, France . . .
capital . . 7. Gironde
entrance gate . . 16. Porte de Bourgogne
Roman name . . 9. Burdigala
wine . . 5. Cotes, Medoc, Palus 6. claret
(best-known), Graves
border . . . 3. hem, rim, tip 4. abut,
brow, dado, edge, line, rand, rund
5. bound, brink, flank, limit, marge,
shore, skirt, touch, verge, wings
6. adjoin, fringe, margin, ruffle
7. bordure, confine, flounce, selvage,
valance 8. boundary, frontier, neighbor
9. periphery 10. borderland, sidepieces
border (pert to) . . .
heraldry . . 4. orle 7. bordure
lace . . 5. picot 9. hemstitch
picture . . 3. mat 4. orle
stamps (PO) . . 8. tressure
wall . . 4. dado
Border Country (Russ) . . . 6. Latvia,
Poland 7. Estonia, Finland, Romania
9. Lithuania
bordering . . . 4. near 6. edging 7. binding
8. abutting, adjacent, marginal, skirting,
trimming 9. adjoining, immediate
10. contiguous
Border State (Civil War Era) . . .
8. Arkansas, Delaware, Kentucky,
Maryland, Missouri, Virginia
9. Tennessee 13. North Carolina
bore . . . 3. irk, tap 4. drip, hole, pest,
pill, ream 5. auger, drill, eagre (tidal
wave), weary 6. bother, cavity, pierce
7. caliber, carried 8. diameter, nuisance,
ordnance (anc), puncture, terebate
9. penetrate, perforate, tidal wave,
worriment 10. capability 11. perforation
boreal . . . 8. northern
boredom . . . 5. ennui 6. tedium
Borglum work . . . 8. Rushmore
boring . . . 3. dry 5. yawny 6. tiring

7. irksome, tedious 8. piercing,
tiresome, wearying 11. penetrating
boring tool . . . 3. awl, bit 4. rime (Eng)
5. auger, drill 6. gimlet, reamer, wimble
born . . . 3. ean, nee 4. bred, foal, lamb
5. calve, hatch, issue 7. hatched,
quicken 9. originate
born (pert to) . . .
after father's death . . 10. posthumous
again (Theos) . . 7. renewed
high . . 8. imperial 11. to the purple
14. porphyrogenite
in the country . . 10. rurigenous
well . . 7. eugenic
yesterday . . 5. naive 6. simple 8. gullible
borne . . . 4. held 6. eolian, upheld
7. aeolian, carried, endured 8. produced
9. cherished, supported 10. maintained
borné . . . 6. narrow 7. limited 12. narrow-
minded
Borneo . . .
aborigine . . 4. Dyak (Dayak), Iban
5. Dusun, Malay
ape . . 9. orangutan (orangoutang)
island of . . 11. Archipelago (Malay)
mountain . . 8. Kinibalu
pirate people (anc) . . 5. Bajau 9. Samal
Laut
protectorate . . 6. Brunei 7. Sarawak
river . . 6. Rejang
rubber . . 9. gutta susu
sea . . 4. Java, Sulu 10. South China
tree (antproof) . . 7. billian
borough . . . 4. burg, town, ward 5. burgh,
manor 6. suffix 8. precinct, township
10. municipium 11. corporation
12. municipality
borrow . . . 4. copy, take 5. adopt,
steal, touch 8. simulate 10. plagiarize,
substitute 11. appropriate
borscht, borsch . . . 4. soup (beet juice)
6. ragout
borscht belt . . . 6. resort 9. Catskills
borzoi . . . 9. wolfhound
Bos . . . 2. ox 3. cow 4. beef, calf, neat
6. cattle 8. ruminant 9. quadruped
bosh . . . 4. bull, bunk 5. trash 6. humbug,
piffle 7. baloney 8. buncombe, falderal,
nonsense 9. poppycock 10. balderdash
bosky . . . 5. braky, bushy, shady, tipsy,
woody 6. woodsy 7. fuddled, shadowy
8. intoxicated (Eng)
Bosnia . . .
capital . . 8. Sarajevo
site . . 10. Yugoslavia (formerly)
15. Balkan Peninsula
bosom . . . 4. bust 5. chest 6. breast,
dickey, spirit 7. cherish, embrace
8. inner man, interior 9. enclosure
(loving), innermost 10. affections
12. heartstrings
boss . . . 4. dean 6. manage, master
7. foreman 8. director 9. supervise
14. superintendent
boss (pert to) . . .
architecture . . 4. knob, stud
12. protuberance
politics . . 4. whip 6. leader 7. cacique
(W Indies) 8. dictator
sculpture . . 5. chase, raise 6. emboss,
relief 7. relievo 8. ornament

shield . . 4. umbo
bosthoon (Anglo-Ir) . . . 4. boor, dolt
5. clout
Boston . . .
building (Hist) . . 11. Faneuil Hall 14. Old
North Church
capital of . . 13. Massachusetts
famed men . . 6. Holmes, Lowell
7. Emerson 8. Whittier 9. Hawthorne
10. Longfellow
hero . . 10. Paul Revere
history . . 8. Massacre (1770), Tea Party
(1773)
Puritan leader . . 8. Winthrop (Gov)
river . . 7. Charles
botany (pert to) . . .
development (plant) . . 7. peloria
10. craticular
research terms . . 7. ecology 8. cytology,
taxonomy 9. pathology 10. morphology
science . . 7. biology 9. plant life
Botany Bay . . .
colony (original) . . 5. penal
discoverer . . 4. Cook (1770)
settlers . . 8. convicts (Eng)
site . . 9. Australia
botch . . 3. fix, mar 4. hash, mend, mess,
mull 5. patch, spoil 6. boggle, bungle,
fiasco, goof up, muddle 7. blunder,
failure
both . . . 3. two 4. duad, pair 5. twain
6. as well 7. equally
bother . . . 3. ado, ail, nag 4. fuss,
to-do 5. annoy, tease 6. badger,
bustle, harass, molest, pester, pother
7. concern, confuse, fluster, torment,
trouble 8. bewilder, distress, irritate,
nuisance 9. commotion
10. discommode, excitement, perplexity
11. botheration, disturbance
13. inconvenience
bothersome . . . 6. trying 7. galling,
irksome, onerous 8. annoying
9. difficult, worrisome 10. disturbing
11. troublesome
both sexes . . . 7. epicene, sexless
10. effeminate
bo tree (Buddh) . . . 5. pipal 6. sacred
(at Buddh Gaya)
Botticelli masterpiece . . . 12. Birth of
Venus
bottle . . 3. pig 4. lota, vial 5. cruet,
flask, gourd, phial 6. carafe, carboy,
flagon, lagena, matara, vacuum
7. ampoule (ampule), ampulla (anc),
costrel, enclose 8. borachio, calabash,
decanter, preserve 9. aryballus (anc)
bottom . . . 3. bed (water) 4. base, glen,
hulk, less, root, rump, vale, vlei
5. basin, fanny, floor, marsh, nadir
6. coulee, hopper (RR) 7. bedrock,
channel 9. underside 10. nethermost
bottomless . . . 7. abysmal, abyssal
8. baseless 9. plumbless, soundless
10. fathomless 12. unfathomable
boudoir . . . 7. bedroom, cabinet, chamber
10. bedchamber
bouffant . . . 4. full 7. bulging 9. puffed
out
bough . . . 4. fork, limb, spur, twig 5. shoot,
spray, sprig 6. branch 8. offshoot

bought . . . 8. boughten (dial) 9. purchased
(see also *buy*)
bouillabaisse . . . 7. chowder (fish)
boulangerie (Fr) . . . 6. bakery
boulevard . . . 4. pike 7. highway
8. highroad, turnpike 12. thoroughfare
bounce . . . 3. hop 4. bang, brag, bump,
jump, kick, leap, snap 5. bound, burst,
carom, eject, shake, thump, verve
6. levity, recoil, spring 7. bluster,
bravado, rebound 8. buoyancy,
outburst, ricochet 9. discharge,
lightness 10. resilience 11. fanfaronade,
ostentation, springiness
16. lightheartedness
bouncer . . . 4. liar 5. bully 6. fibber,
ouster 7. boaster, chucker, whopper
8. braggart, fanfaron 9. falsehood
bound . . . 3. hop, run 4. jump, leap,
skip, tied 5. ambit, limit, speed,
taped, tiled (secrecy), vault, verge
6. border, bounce, bourne, domain,
hurdle, spring, sprint 7. barrier, certain,
confine, cramped, limited, obliged,
pledged, rebound, secured, trussed
8. beholden, boundary, confined,
enclosed, frontier, precinct, promised,
resolved, surround 9. committed,
duty-bound, encompass (incompass)
10. borderland, determined, restrained,
restricted 11. termination
12. circumscribe
boundary . . . 3. end, rim 4. edge, mere
(obs), mete, term, wall 5. ambit,
bourn, fence, limit, march, verge
7. barrier 8. terminus 9. perimeter
11. conterminal, termination
13. circumference
bounder . . . 3. cad 4. snob 6. rotter
7. epicier, parvenu, upstart
bounding (Mus) . . . 8. saltando
boundless . . . 4. vast 7. endless 8. infinite,
termless 9. limitless, unlimited
10. unconfined 11. illimitable
12. interminable, unfathomable
bounds . . . 4. pale 5. frames, limits,
skirts 7. borders, margins 8. confines,
outlines 9. outskirts 10. delineated
11. limitations
bounteous . . . 5. ample 6. freely, lavish
7. liberal 8. generous, prodigal
9. bountiful, plentiful 10. munificent
11. extravagant
bountiful . . . 4. rich 7. copious, fertile,
liberal, teeming, uberous 8. abundant,
fruitful, generous, prolific 9. bounteous,
exuberant, luxuriant, plentiful
bounty . . . 3. fee 4. gift 5. bonus
6. reward 7. largess, premium,
subsidy 8. gratuity, solatium, sportula
9. pourboire 10. generosity, liberality
11. beneficence 12. compensation
bouquet . . . 4. odor, posy 5. aroma,
cigar, spray 7. corsage, flowers,
incense, nosegay, perfume 9. fragrance,
redolence 10. compliment
Bourbon, bourbon . . .
ancient . . 7. Reunion (Isl)
dynasty . . 5. Spain 6. France, Naples
famed personage . . 4. Duke 13. French
General

famed ruins .. 7. castles (Dukes')
liquor .. 6. whisky (whiskey)
rose .. 9. Le Phoenix
bourd ... 3. fun 4. jest 7. mockery
bourdon ... 4. stop (organ) 5. baton, music (bagpipe), spear, staff 6. burden (Fr), cudgel
bourgeois ... 4. type (size) 8. commoner 9. common man, plutocrat 10. capitalist 11. middle-class, proletarian
bourn, bourne ... 3. aim 4. goal, port 5. bound, brook, limit, realm 6. arroyo, stream 7. rivulet 8. boundary 11. destination
bourock ... 3. hut 4. heap (stone) 5. crowd, mound 7. cluster
Bourse ... 5. Board 8. Exchange 13. Stock Exchange
bouse ... 3. cup 4. haul (Naut), swig, tope 5. booze, drink, heave 6. beaker 7. carouse
bouser ... 5. toper 6. boozer, bursar 7. fuddler, swigger
bout ... 2. go 3. act, war 4. coup, fray, game, spar, turn 5. cycle, fight, match, revel, round, scrap, set-to, spree, trial 6. fracas, inning, series, stroke 7. attempt, circuit, contest, exploit 8. conflict, maneuver, rotation 9. encounter 10. enterprise, prize fight 11. celebration
boutade ... 4. whim 5. dance, prank 7. caprice 8. outbreak 11. composition (Mus)
boutonniere ... 6. flower 7. bouquet, nosegay 8. incision 10. buttonhole
bovine ... 2. ox 3. Bos, cow, yak 4. bull, dull, goat, kine, zebu 5. bison, dogie, steer, stirk, zebus 6. catalo, cattle, oxlike, stolid, stupid 7. bullock, cattalo, taurine, vaccine 8. maverick, sluggish 10. complacent 11. beef-brained
bow ... 3. arc, bob, nod 4. arch, beak, bend, knot, node, prow 5. bulge, curve, debut, embow, kneel, stoop, yield 6. assent, convex, curtsy, encore, kowtow, salaam, submit, weapon 7. curtain (Theat), incline, rainbow 8. crossbow, greeting 9. obeisance 11. fiddlestick 12. bow and scrape
bow (out) ... 4. exit 6. depart 7. concede, dismiss
Bow Bells (pert to) ...
area .. 10. cockneydom
bells of .. 9. Bow Church (St Mary le Bow)
city .. 6. London
bowels ... 3. pit 4. guts 5. abyss, chasm, depth 7. innards, insides, viscera 8. entrails, interior (earth) 10. compassion (Shaksp), tenderness
bower ... 5. abode, arbor, cards (game), kiosk 6. alcove, pandal 7. retreat, shelter 11. summerhouse
Bowery denizen ... 4. wino
bowfin ... 4. Amia 7. mudfish
bowhead (Arctic) ... 10. Right whale
Bowie, bowie (pert to) ...
instrument .. 5. knife
knife inventor .. 5. Bowie (James)
Scottish .. 3. tub 4. cask 6. milk pail

State nickname .. 8. Arkansas
bowkail ... 4. kale (kail) 7. cabbage
bowl ... 3. cup, jug 4. ball, roll, vase 5. arena, basin, kitty (poker), mazer, rogan 6. cavity, crater, hollow, patina (anc), vessel 7. stadium 8. washbowl 9. washbasin 10. hippodrome, receptacle 12. amphitheater
Bowl (sports) ...
Abilene .. 5. Pecan
Atlanta .. 5. Peach
Dallas .. 6. Cotton
El Paso .. 3. Sun
Honolulu .. 4. Hula
Houston .. 10. Bluebonnet
Jacksonville .. 5. Gator
Memphis .. 7. Liberty
Miami .. 6. Orange
Mobile .. 6. Senior
New Orleans .. 5. Sugar
Orlando .. 9. Tangerine
Pasadena .. 4. Rose
Sacramento .. 8. Camellia
bowlegged ... 6. valgus
bowler ... 3. hat 5. derby 6. kegler 7. trundle
bowling ... 4. ball, rink 5. alley, green, spare 6. strike 7. rolling, tenpins 8. ninepins 10. greensward, playground
Bowling Green ... 4. Park (Ky, NY)
bowsprit ... 3. jib 4. boom 6. steeve
box ... 2. ro (Jap) 3. bin, pew, pyx 4. arca (alms), cage, case, cist (anc), cuff, kist, kite, loge, safe, spar, tray 5. brace (faro), caddy (tea), cheat, crate, stall, vault 6. buffet, carton, casket, coffin, encase 7. confine, enclose 8. bungalow 9. fisticuff 11. compartment
box (pert to) ...
alms .. 4. arca
bed .. 7. springs
cosmetic .. 4. inro
floating .. 3. car (for fish)
lifesaving .. 9. faking box
railroad .. 6. boxcar 8. box wagon
resistance .. 8. rheostat
sewing .. 5. plait, pleat
sleigh .. 4. pung
sports .. 5. score
tea .. 5. caddy 8. canister
theater .. 4. loge, seat
tree .. 8. Buxaceae
boxer ... 3. dog, pug 5. champ 6. miller 7. bruiser, fighter, sparrer 8. derby hat, pugilist 11. fisticuffer 12. prizefighter 13. militia member (Chin)
boxer weight ... 4. bantam, middle, welter 7. feather 10. light heavy
boxing ... 4. bout 5. match, set-to 7. contest, crating 8. pugilism, sparring 10. encasement, fisticuffs 12. shadowboxing
boy ... 2. bo 3. bat, bus, lad, tad, tot 4. nino, page, puer 5. child, gamin, knave, rogue, water, youth 6. garcon, laddie, master, rascal, shaver, urchin, varlet 7. callant, gossoon 8. muchacho
boy (pert to) ...
book author .. 5. Alger, Henty
errand .. 4. page 9. messenger

friend . . 4. beau 10. sweetheart
interjection . . 5. Oh boy
organization . . 6. Scouts
Scout founder . . 11. Baden-Powell
street . . 4. Arab 6. urchin
boycott . . 3. ban 6. oppose, strike
9. blackball, ostracize
Boz (pseud) . . 7. Dickens
brace . . . 3. leg, tie, two 4. bind, cord,
gird, pair, prop, span, stay, yoke
5. spale, staff, stave, strut 6. couple
7. bandage, bracket, fulcrum, refresh,
rigging, support 8. encircle 9. reinforce,
stimulate 10. invigorate, recuperate,
strengthen
bracelet . . . 5. armil, armor, chain
6. sankha 7. armilla 8. handcuff,
vambrace 10. calombigas
bracer . . . 4. prop 5. tonic 7. reviver,
support 8. pick-me-up, roborant
9. stimulant
bracing . . . 5. crisp, tonic 10. salubrious
11. stimulating 12. invigorating
bracken . . . 4. fern 5. brake, plaid
bracket . . . 4. mark 5. ancon, angle,
group, strut 6. corbel, sconce 7. fixture
11. electrolier
brackish . . . 4. foul 5. salty 7. saltish
8. nauseous 13. distasteful
bract . . . 4. leaf 5. glume, palea, palet
6. spathe 8. bractlet 9. bracteole
brad . . . 3. pin 4. nail 5. sprig
brae . . . 4. bank, down, hill, moor 5. slope
6. valley 8. hillside
brag . . . 4. crow 5. bluff, boast, vaunt
6. flaunt 7. blow off, bluster, deceive,
roister, swagger 8. braggart
9. gasconade 11. braggadocio
braggart . . . 4. brag 6. crower 7. boaster
8. boastful, fanfaron 9. blusterer,
swaggerer 11. braggadocio
12. swashbuckler
bragging . . . 11. thrasonical
Brahma . . . 3. God 4. fowl 5. Hindu
Brahman (pert to) . . .
learned . . 6. pundit
precept . . 5. sutra 8. netineti
sacred book . . 4. Veda
Sanskrit scholar . . 6. pundit
Supreme soul . . 6. Brahma
title . . 3. Aya
Trinity . . 4. Siva 6. Brahma, Vishnu
woman created by . . 6. Alalya
Brahmin . . . 4. prig, snob 7. egghead
8. highbrow 10. high-hatter
12. intellectual
braid . . . 3. cue 4. cord, gimp, hair, plat,
trim 5. lacet, orris, plait, pleat, queue,
tress, twist, weave 6. oxreim, sennit
7. entwine, outline, pigtail, topknot
8. ornament, soutache 9. interlace
10. interweave
brain . . . 4. head, mind, nous 6. psyche,
reason 9. intellect, mentality
10. encephalon, vital organ
brain (pert to) . . .
canal . . 4. iter
case . . 3. pan 5. skull 7. cranium
child . . 4. idea 5. storm
division . . 8. cerebrum 10. cerebellum
11. pons Varolii 16. medulla oblongata

matter . . 4. alba, dura, tela
operation . . 6. trepan 8. trephine
term . . 4. lobe, lura
6. sulcus 7. fissure 9. ventricle
11. convolution
tumor . . 6. glioma
X-ray . . 14. encephalograph
brainless . . . 4. dumb 5. dizzy, giddy,
silly 6. unwise 7. asinine, foolish,
witless 9. senseless 10. unthinking
11. thoughtless 14. scatterbrained
brainy . . . 5. smart 6. bright, clever
9. brilliant
brake . . . 4. cage, curb, drag, fern,
reef, skid, trap 5. check, delay, snare
6. bridle, retard 7. dilemma, thicket
9. canebrake 10. decelerate
bramble . . . 4. burr 5. berry, brier, shrub
(prickly), thorn 6. nettle 7. prickle,
thicket 9. brierbush 10. blackberry
12. brambleberry
branch . . . 3. arm, set 4. axil, fork, limb,
rame, stem, twig, wing 5. bough,
class, frond, ramus, shoot, spray,
sprig, vimen, withe 6. divide, member,
ramify, sprout, stolon, stream, switch
7. descent, diverge, lineage 8. category,
division, offshoot 9. affiliate, bloodline,
filiation 10. department, descendant,
triskelion (three branches)
Branchiata (Group) . . . 6. fishes
9. Crustacea 10. Amphibians
brand . . . 4. burn, iron, kind, mark, sear,
smit 5. label, stamp, sword, torch
6. smirch, stigma 7. earmark, feature,
hot iron, quality 8. gridiron (Hist),
hallmark 9. trademark 10. stigmatize
brandish . . . 5. shake, swing, wield
6. flaunt 7. flutter, glitter, flourish
brandy . . . 4. marc 6. cognac, grappa,
kirsch 8. Armagnac, eau de vie (Fr)
9. applejack, slivovitz
brash . . . 4. dash, rain, rash 5. gruff,
saucy, storm 6. scurry 7. brittle (lumber)
8. impudent, tactless 9. impetuous
brass . . . 4. cash, gall 5. alloy, braze,
cheek, money, nerve, plate 6. latten,
ormolu, platen 8. brass hat, officers,
sisterce (anc coin) 9. impudence
10. instrument (wind)
brass (wind instrument) . . . 5. bugle
6. cornet, lituus (anc) 7. althorn,
brasses, clarion, saxhorn, trumpet
8. trombone 9. saxophone
10. flügelhorn, French horn
brasserie . . . 6. saloon 7. brewery 8. beer
shop
brassy . . . 4. bold 6. aerose, brazen
8. impudent
brat . . . 3. bib, elf, imp 4. film, minx,
scum 5. apron, bairn, child, cloak,
minor 6. mantle 7. garment 8. clothing
9. offspring 14. enfant terrible,
whippersnapper
brattice . . . 7. support 9. partition (mining)
10. breastwork
bravado . . . 4. bounce, daring, defial
7. bluster, bombast, bravery, bravura
8. defiance 11. braggadocio
brave . . . 4. bold, buck, dare, game,
hero, meet 5. boast, bravo, bully,

front, manly, showy, stout 6. daring,
endure, heroic, Indian 7. Amerind,
gallant, soldier, spartan, valiant,
warrior 8. confront, fearless, intrepid,
valorous 10. courageous, untimorous
12. stouthearted

bravery . . . 5. valor 7. bravado, bravura,
courage

bravo . . . 3. mug 4. good, thug 5. rough,
tough 6. bandit 7. gorilla, ruffian
8. assassin 9. blusterer, cutthroat,
roisterer, roughneck, swaggerer
11. exclamation

bravura . . . 4. dash 5. macho 6. daring
7. bravado, bravery 10. brilliance (Mus)
confidence

brawl . . . 3. row 4. fray, fury, rage, riot
5. broil, fight, furor, melee, scold
6. affray, clamor, fracas, hubbub,
rumpus, shindy, tumult, uproar
7. dispute, quarrel, rampage, turmoil,
wrangle 10. hullabaloo, turbulence
11. altercation, embroilment

brawny . . . 5. beefy, burly, lusty, thewy
6. fleshy, robust, sinewy, strong,
sturdy 7. callous 8. muscular, powerful,
stalwart 9. corpulent

bray . . . 4. beat 5. blare, bleat, grind, neigh
6. heehaw, powder, thrash, whinny
9. pulverize, triturate 12. disintegrate

braze . . . 4. weld 5. plate (with metal)
6. solder

brazen . . . 4. bold, pert 5. brass, brave,
harsh 6. brassy, cheeky, harden
7. aweless, callous 8. immodest,
impudent, indurate, insolent, metallic
9. bold-faced, shameless, unabashed
10. unblushing 13. bronze-colored,
harsh-sounding

brazier . . . 5. grill 6. brazer 7. hibachi
8. barbecue, gridiron 10. money chest
(anc)

brazil . . . 3. red 4. wood (hard) 8. dyestuff

Brazil . . . see also *Brazilian*
capital . . 8. Brasilia 12. Rio de Janeiro
(old)
city . . 5. Bahia, Belem 6. Recife, Santos
8. Sao Paulo 9. Horizonte 11. Porto
Alegre, Sao Salvador
discoverer . . 6. Cabral (1500)
Falls (world wonder) . . 6. Iguacu
lake . . 12. Lago dos Patos
product . . 6. coffee
river . . 5. Negro 6. Amazon, Branco,
Paraná 7. Madeira, Orinoco 8. Paraguay
9. Tocantins

Brazilian (pert to) . . .
aborigine . . 5. Carib
ant (powerful) . . 9. tucandera
bird . . 3. ani, ara 5. arara, macaw
6. cuckoo, darter, tiribo 7. maracan,
sierema
crab (land) . . 8. horseman
dance . . 5. samba 6. maxixe
drink . . 5. assai
flycatcher . . 5. yetapa
indien . . 4. Anta 5. Arara, Araua, Guana
6. Tupian 8. Araquayu, Arawakan
mammal . . 5. tapir
parrot . . 3. ara 5. macaw 6. tiriba
plant . . 4. yaje 5. caroa 7. ayapana

(Med)
tree . . 3. apa 4. anda (oil), jara 5. assai
(palm) 6. embuia, satiné 7. araroba,
gomavel, seringa (rubber), wallaba
8. bakupari 10. barbatimao
weight . . 4. onza 5. libra 6. arroba
7. quintal

breach . . . 3. gap 4. rent, rift 5. break,
burst, chasm, cleft, split 6. schism
7. caesura, dispute, quarrel, rupture
8. fracture, solecism 9. violation
10. disruption, falling-out, infraction,
separation 12. infringement,
interruption 16. misunderstanding

bread . . . 3. rye 4. naan, pita, rusk
5. matzo, quick 6. simnel 7. anadama,
challah, chapati, hoecake 8. baguette,
hardtack, tortilla, zwieback 9. sourdough
12. pumpernickel

bread (pert to) . . .
basket . . 7. stomach
bread and butter . . 5. plate 6. letter
(of thanks), pickle, staple 7. prosaic
8. juvenile
fruit . . 3. nut 4. tree 6. simnel 7. castana
8. chestnut
winner . . 6. earner, toiler, worker
7. workman 8. provider 10. wage
earner

break . . . 3. gap 4. dash, knap, luck,
lull, rent, rift, ruin, rush, slip, snap,
stop 5. blank, burst, cleft, lapse,
letup, pause, smash, train 6. breach,
chance, change, depose, escape,
hiatus, injury, lacuna, market (Finan),
recess, subdue, weaken 7. blunder,
caesura (cesura), disrupt, getaway,
respite, rupture, shatter, violate 8. bad
break, bankrupt, breakage, breather,
fracture, interval 9. interlude, jail break,
violation 10. depreciate, falling-out,
infraction, suspension 11. fragmentize
12. intermission, interruption
13. discontinuity

break down . . . 3. cry, sob 4. bawl,
raze, weep 5. crush 6. boohoo,
divide, master, reduce, revolt, subdue
7. analyze, crack up, dissect, resolve,
unnerve 8. classify, collapse, separate
9. decompose, overwhelm, subdivide

breakdown . . . 7. debacle, failure
8. analysis 9. cataclysm 10. dissection,
impairment, revolution

breakfast . . . 6. brunch (late) 8. dejeuner
10. chota hazri

break in . . . 4. open, tame 5. enter,
force, train 6. butt in, subdue 7. barge
in, intrude, prepare 9. interrupt
10. housebreak

break up . . . 4. cure, rift, ruin 5. decay,
leave, smash, spall, split, upset
7. adjourn, atomize, crumble, disband,
relieve, scatter, shatter 8. disperse,
dissolve, separate, unsettle
9. decompose 10. demobilize,
dispersion, disruption 11. disorganize,
dissolution 12. disintegrate

breakwater . . . 4. dike, mole, pier
5. jetty, jutty 6. refuge, riprap 7. sea
wall 8. buttress 10. embankment
11. obstruction

bream ... 4. fish, scup 5. clean (Naut)
breast ... 4. bust, soul, teat 5. bosom,
cheat, gland (mammary), heart 6. spirit,
thorax 8. inner man 9. encounter
breast (pert to) ...
absence of .. 7. amastia
bone .. 6. ratite 7. sternum
breastlike .. 7. mastoid
plate .. 4. Urim 5. armor, ephod
6. gorget, lorica 7. poitrel
12. breastsummer
works .. 7. defense, parapet, railing
(Naut), ravelin 8. mantelet 9. banquette
breath ... 3. air 4. fume, life, odor,
pant, puff, wind 5. draft, pause,
prana, scent, smell, touch, vapor, whiff
6. breeze, caress, flatus, pneuma, spirit
7. halitus, respite, whisper 8. breather
9. emanation, ozostomia, utterance
10. exhalation 11. respiration
breathe ... 3. say, tip 4. gulp, live, mean,
pneo (comb form), rest, sigh, tell
5. exist, imbue, imply, scent, smell,
snuff 6. evince, exhale, infuse, inhale,
let out, reveal 7. bespeak, divulge,
emanate, instill (instil), pervade, respire,
suspire, whisper 8. aspirate, indicate
breathe (pert to) ...
comb form .. 4. pnea, pneo
convulsively .. 4. sigh
hard .. 4. pant
one's last .. 3. die 6. expire, perish
7. decease, succumb
vengeance .. 9. retaliate
breather ... 4. lull, rest 5. break, pause,
truce 6. recess 7. interim, respite
9. interlude 12. intermission
breathing ... 5. alive, vital 6. living,
zoetic 7. animate, panting, respite
8. animated 9. conscious, phonation,
utterance 10. aspiration 11. respiration,
respiratory, ventilation 12. articulation
breathing (pert to) ...
apertures .. 5. stoma 8. spiracle
morbid .. 4. rale 7. stridor 8. rhonchus
painful .. 8. dyspnoea
pause .. 7. caesura
smooth .. 4. lene
breathless ... 4. awed, dead, gone, keen
5. eager 6. ardent, fervid, winded
7. airless, demised, fervent 8. deceased,
lifeless, windless, wordless 9. impatient
10. astonished, speechless, spellbound
bred ... 6. hybrid, inbred, reared, tablet
(compressed) 7. lowbred, mongrel
8. exogamic, purebred 9. autogamic,
crossbred, endogamic, half-caste,
interbred 11. half-blooded,
impregnated, inseminated
12. thoroughbred
bree ... 4. brow 5. broth, scare 6. liquor
7. eyebrow 9. commotion
11. disturbance
breech ... 4. doup, rump, tall 5. fanny,
stern 6. bottom 8. buttocks 9. posterior,
underside
breeches ... 5. chaps, jeans, pants,
trews 8. britches, jodhpurs, trousers
10. pantaloons 12. galligaskins (jocular)
breed ... 3. ilk 4. kind, race, rear, sort
5. beget, brood, caste, class, mixed,

raise, stock, train, tribe 6. family
7. descent, educate, lineage, mongrel,
produce 8. engender, generate, instruct
9. originate, posterity, procreate,
propagate 10. crossbreed
breeding ... 6. polish 7. culture, decorum,
exogamy, manners, raising, rearing
8. autogamy, endogamy, hatching,
training 9. education, fostering, gentility
10. deportment, upbringing
11. instruction, procreation, propagation
breeding place ... 4. nest 5. nidus
7. brooder 8. hatchery 9. incubator
10. birthplace
breeze ... 3. air, row 4. aura, pirr, snap,
stir, wind 5. cinch, rumor 6. squall,
zephyr 7. ill wind, whisper 8. duck soup,
pushover 9. commotion 11. disturbance
breezy ... 4. airy, spry 5. blowy, brisk,
gusty, windy 6. drafty, jaunty, lively
7. squally 8. animated, blustery, spirited
9. vivacious 12. lighthearted
Brehon Law ... 4. eric (anc) 10. Senchus
Mor 12. Book of Aicill
breve ... 4. note (Mus), writ 5. brief,
order 7. compose
brevet ... 4. fiat 5. ukase 6. decree
7. warrant 10. commission 11. certificate
(teaching)
breveté ... 8. patented
breviary ... 6. manual, ritual 7. compend,
epitome
brevity ... 9. briefness, shortness,
terseness 11. conciseness, transcience
12. succinctness
brew ... 3. ale, mix 4. grog, plot 5. hatch,
steep 6. cook up, foment, gather,
menace, scheme 7. concoct, distill
(distil) 8. contrive, threaten 9. aqua
vitae
brewer's grain ... 4. corn, malt 6. barley
brewer's yeast ... 4. barm 6. leaven
bribe ... 3. oil, sop 5. bonus 6. boodle,
buy off, grease, suborn 9. hush money
bric-a-brac ... 6. curios 7. artware
8. antiques, trinkets 9. artifacts, objet
d'art 11. knickknacks
bric-a-brac cabinet ... 7. étagère,
whatnot
brick ... 3. bat 4. dobe, tile 5. adobe,
stone 6. pament (pamment) 7. clinker
8. hardness
brick (pert to) ...
color .. 3. red 7. Saravan
kiln .. 5. clamp
layer .. 3. cad (helper) 5. mason
laying .. 8. toothing
slang .. 3. pip 4. lulu 5. dilly, peach
6. corker, winner 8. jim-dandy
10. sweetheart 11. crackerjack
12. lollapaloosa
unburned .. 5. samel
brickbat ... 4. rock 5. stone 7. affront,
missile, offense 9. indignity
bridal (pert to) ...
chest .. 9. trousseau
flower .. 13. orange blossom
ode, song .. 9. Brautlied 11. Epithalamon
(anc)
portion .. 3. dot 5. dower, dowry
(dowery)

rite.. 7. wedding 8. marriage, nuptials

bridge ... 3. tie 4. arch, bond, link, pons, pont, span 5. unite 7. connect, passage (Mus), ponteon, viaduct 9. structure 13. steppingstone

bridge (pert to) ... 4. deck, game, nose 5. magas, truss 6. phoebe (bird) 7. bascule, trestle 9. dentistry 10. ponticello (Mus)

bridge, historic ...
Bridge of Boats .. 10. Hellespont
Bridge of Sighs .. 6. Venice (Doge's Palace) 7. Al Sirat (Muslim, over infernal fire)
Norse Myth .. 7. Bifrost (rainbow)
Old Bridge .. 12. Ponte Vecchio (Florence It, 1345)

Bridge game ... 3. bid 4. pass, ruff, slam 5. Goren (expert) 6. honors, points, renege, tenace 7. finesse 9. part-score

bridle ... 3. bit 4. cord (kite), curb, rein 5. check, guide, smirk 6. fetter, govern, halter, master, simper, subdue 7. harness, manacle, repress, shackle, snaffle 8. cavesson, headgear, noseband, restrain, suppress 9. hackamore, headstall, restraint

brief ... 4. curt, plan, writ 5. breve, charm, pithy, short, terse 6. report 7. compact, concise, laconic, summary 8. fleeting, instruct, succinct 9. condensed, ephemeral, summarize, transient 10. compendium, short-lived, transitory 11. compendious 14. inconsiderable

brier, briar ... 4. burr, pipe 5. heath, shrub, spine, thorn 7. bramble, bruyère, clotbur, prickle, sticker, thistle 8. adherent 11. French brier

brig ... 4. boat 6. vessel 10. guardhouse

brigade ... 4. unit 6. troops 7. company 8. regiment

brigand ... 5. rover, thief 6. bandit, dacoit, pirate, robber 7. bedouin, cateran, ladrone 8. picaroon 10. highwayman

bright ... 3. apt, gay 4. naif, rosy 5. alert, beamy, fresh, lucid, nitid, palmy, sleek, smart, sunny, vivid, witty 6. brainy, clever, florid, garish, golden 7. halcyon, radiant, shining, unfaded 8. cheerful, colorful, flashing, gleaming, luminous, lustrous, splendid 9. brilliant, effulgent, refulgent, sparkling 10. auspicious, epiphanous, glistening, glittering, optimistic 11. intelligent, resplendent

brightness ... 5. sheen 6. luster 7. sparkle 8. radiance, splendor 9. alertness, clearness, smartness 10. brilliance 12. cheerfulness, colorfulness, pleasantness

brilliance, brilliancy ... 5. éclat, glory 6. luster 7. glitter, oriency, success 8. radiance, splendor 9. smartness, vividness 10. brightness, cleverness

brilliant ... 5. smart, vivid, witty 6. bright 7. eminent, radiant, shining 8. gorgeous, meteoric, splendid 9. refulgent, sparkling 10. glittering 11. illustrious

brilliant group ... 6. galaxy

brim ... 3. hem, lip, rim 4. edge 5. brink, marge, verge 6. border, margin

7. selvage

brine ... 3. sea 4. main, salt 5. brack, ocean, tears 6. pickle 7. the deep 12. preservative

bring ... 3. get 4. bear, cost, haul, lead 5. carry, fetch, go get, yield 6. convey, entail, induce, obtain 7. contain, involve, require 8. comprise 9. transport

bring about ... 2. do 4. make 5. cause 6. create, effect 7. achieve, produce 8. generate 9. instigate 10. accomplish, consummate, effectuate

bring around ... 4. cure, heal, ween 5. renew, sober 6. revive 7. convert, restore, win over 8. persuade 10. rejuvenate

bring back ... 5. fetch 6. recall, return, revive 7. restore 8. rekindle, remember, retrieve 9. recollect, resurrect

bring forth ... 5. ean 6. bear, rise 5. beget, breed, cause, educe, hatch, spawn, yield 6. adduce, elicit, reveal 7. develop, produce 8. disclose, fructify, generate, manifest

bring forward ... 4. cite 5. offer 6. adduce, broach, submit 7. advance, improve, promote, propose 8. manifest 9. introduce

bring into ...
bondage .. 7. enslave
court .. 7. arraign
harmony .. 6. attune
position .. 5. align, aline
union .. 9. correlate

bring together ... 5. amass, group 6. gather 7. cluster, compile, reunite 8. assemble 9. harmonize, reconcile 10. accumulate

bring to light ... 4. find 5. trace 6. elicit, expose, reveal 7. uncover, unearth 8. disclose, discover

bring to mind ... 6. recall, remind 8. look like, remember, resemble

bring to pass ... 2. do 5. cause 6. author, father 9. originate 10. accomplish, effectuate

bring up ... 4. rear, spew 5. drill, raise, train, vomit 6. foster, muster 7. advance, educate, nurture, propose 9. challenge, condition, cultivate 10. discipline 11. regurgitate

bring up to date ... 4. post 6. update 9. modernize 10. streamline

brink ... 3. lip, rim 4. bank, brow, edge, near 5. ditch, marge, skirt, verge 6. border, margin

briny ... 3. sea 4. salt 5. salty 6. saline 8. brackish

Brisbane, capital of ... 10. Queensland (Austral)

Brisbane tree ... 3. box 8. quandong

brisk ... 3. gay 4. cold, fast, keen, racy, spry, yern 5. agile, alert, alive, crisp, fresh, peart, quick, sharp, tangy, zippy 6. breezy, lively, nimble, snappy 7. caustic, pungent 8. animated, forceful, spirited, vigorous 9. energetic, sprightly, vivacious 11. stimulating

bristle ... 4. barb, hair, seta 5. anger, seton 6. chaeta, palpus, ruffle, rumple, see red, setula, setule 7. acicula, prickle,

stubble
bristling . . . 5. angry 6. horrid (anc)
7. horrent 9. offensive
bristly . . . 5. rough, setal 6. hispid, setose,
thorny 7. prickly, scopate, unshorn
8. acicular, echinate 9. setaceous
11. bristlelike
Bristol . .
church (England's finest) . . 15. St Mary
Redcliffe
fashion . . 6. ataunt 9. shipshape
library . . 6. oldest (British Isles)
milk . . 6. sherry
Britain . .
name, ancient . . 6. Albion
name, modern . . 12. British Isles,
Commonwealth, Great Britain
13. United Kingdom
name, Roman . . 9. Brittania
native . . 5. Iceni, Jutes, Picts, Scots
6. Angles 7. Britons, Silures
native (sl) . . 5. limey (limy), tommy
7. Blighty
sea . . 5. Irish, North 8. Atlantic, Hebrides
British (pert to) . . see also English
battle . . 8. Hastings
boat (anc) . . 7. coracle
cavalry . . 8. yeomanry
emblem . . 4. lion
fish . . 8. dragonet (gobylike)
oak . . 5. robur
Order of . . 9. The Garter
prison . . 4. gaol
pudding . . 4. suet 9. Yorkshire
tavern . . 3. pub 9. beerhouse, jerry shop
thief (wharf) . . 6. tosher
Z (letter) . . 3. Zed
British people . . .
buccaneer . . 4. Kidd 5. Drake 6. Morgan
explorer . . 4. Cook, Ross 6. Baffin
7. Stanley 10. Livingstone
hero (sea) . . 6. Nelson
king (legend, Myth) . . 3. Lud 4. Beli,
Bran, Brut 7. Belenus
soldier . . 7. Redcoat (Hist)
Brittany . . 7. Armoric 8. Bretagne
brittle . . 4. weak 5. brash, candy, crisp,
frail 6. feeble, infirm, slight 7. fragile,
friable 8. delicate, insecure 9. breakable,
frangible 11. shatterable
broad . . 4. free, girl, lake (Eng), wide
5. ample, large, roomy, thick, wench
7. breadth, diffuse, general, liberal
8. spacious, strumpet, sweeping,
tabulate, tolerant 9. expansive,
extensive 10. collective, commodious,
indefinite, voluminous
13. comprehensive
broad (pert to) . . .
arrow . . 5. pheon (Her) 6. stigma
8. insignia
footed . . 8. platypod
hearted . . 8. generous 11. magnanimous
minded . . 7. liberal 8. tolerant
9. receptive
broaden . . . 5. swell, widen 6. dilate,
expand, extend, spread 7. augment,
enlarge, ennoble 8. increase
broadly . . . 3. far 6. widely 10. far and
wide 11. extensively 12. indefinitely,
right and left

broadside . . . 4. guns, side 6. folder
7. gunfire, quarter, surface 8. enfilade,
sideways 10. broadsheet, floodlight
11. breadthwise
broadsword . . . 7. cutlass, Ferrara
8. claymore, scimitar
Brobdingnagian . . . 5. giant, titan
8. colossal, gigantic 10. gargantuan
brocade . . 6. broché, fabric 8. baudekin
9. baldachin
brochan . . 7. oatmeal 8. porridge
brochure . . . 5. tract 6. folder 7. booklet,
leaflet 8. chapbook, pamphlet
brod . . . 3. awl 4. goad, pike, urge 5. thorn
6. sprout 9. incentive
brode, brodee . . . 11. embroidered
brodyaga . . . 7. vagrant 8. vagabond
brogan, brogue . . . 4. shoe
brogue . . . 4. burr 5. twang 6. accent
7. dialect
broil . . . 4. cook, fray, fume 5. brawl,
grill, melee 6. affray, braise (braize),
scorch 7. contest, discord, dispute,
quarrel 8. conflict, grillade, scramble
10. contention, dissension, turbulence
11. altercation, embroilment
broke . . . 4. flat 6. busted, ruined
8. bankrupt, strapped 9. destitute,
insolvent, penniless
broken . . . 4. tame 5. broke, bumpy,
burst, rough, tamed 6. chined, ruined,
shaken, uneven, zigzag 7. crushed,
décousu, severed, subdued 8. bankrupt,
detached, impaired, ruptured, sporadic,
weakened 9. conquered, dispersed,
irregular, shattered, unsettled
10. incoherent, incomplete
11. fragmentary, housebroken,
interrupted 12. disconnected,
domesticated, intermittent
13. discontinuous
broken pottery (anc) . . . 5. shard (sherd)
8. potsherd
broker . . . 5. agent 6. dealer, jobber
7. cambist, scalper (ticket) 8. marriage
9. go-between, insurance, middleman,
schatchen 10. pawnbroker, real estate
11. internuncio, stockbroker
12. intermediary
brokerage . . . 3. fee 4. agio 6. charge
8. agiotage, business 9. exactment
10. commission
brolly . . . 5. chute 8. umbrella 9. brollyhop,
parachute
bromide . . . 4. corn 5. trite 6. Babbit,
cliché, halide, old hat 8. banality,
sedative 9. conformer, criticism,
platitude 10. conformist, Philistine
15. conventionalist
bronco, broncho . . . 4. pony 5. horse
6. cayuse 7. mustang 10. broomstick
bronco, bucking . . . 9. estrapade
broncobuster, bronchobuster . . .
6. cowboy 7. trainer, vaquero
Brontë (pert to) . . .
Charlotte . . 7. Shirley 8. Jane Eyre,
Villette 10. Currer Bell (pseud)
Emily . . 16. Wuthering Heights
Bronx cheer . . . 3. boo 4. hiss, razz
9. raspberry
bronze . . . 3. aes (anc), tan 5. alloy, color

    6. ormolu, patina, suntan 9. sculpture

Bronze Age . . . 6. Aegean 9. Neolithic 11. Aeneolithic

Bronze Plaques (pert to) . . .
called . . 14. Eugubine Tables (Iguvine Tables, 1444)
number . . 5. Seven
site . . 6. Gubbio (It)

brooch . . . 3. bar, pin 4. boss, ouch 5. cameo, clasp 6. fibula (anc), shield 8. pectoral 9. breastpin

brood . . . 3. fry, nye, set 4. kind, mope, mull, muse, nide, race 5. breed, covey, folks, hatch, pride (lions), young 6. clutch, family, farrow (pigs), litter, ménage, people, strain 7. lineage, progeny, reflect 8. cogitate, incubate, meditate, ruminate, soredium 9. household, offspring 11. contemplate

brood over . . . 4. fret, mope 5. hover 6. grieve, ponder 7. agonize 8. remember

brook . . . 3. run 4. bear, beck, burn, rill, sike 5. abide, bourn, creek, crick 6. arroyo, endure, rillet, runlet, suffer 7. freshet, rivulet 8. brooklet 9. arroyuelo, streamlet

broom . . . 5. besom, shrub, spart, sweep, whisk

broth . . . 4. soup 5. stock 6. brewis 8. bouillon, consommé

brother . . . 3. fra 4. mate, monk 5. friar, title 6. frater, friend, member, oblate 8. alter ego, relative 9. associate 11. counterpart

brotherhood . . . 5. lodge 7. kinship, society 8. sodality 10. fellowship, fraternity 11. association 12. fraternalism 13. confraternity

brotherly . . . 4. kind 6. tender 8. friendly 9. fraternal 11. sympathetic 12. affectionate

Brothers . . . 7. Danites (Mormon) 9. Christian (RCCh)

brothers and sisters (same family) . . . 8. siblings

brow . . . 3. cap, rim, tip, top 4. brae 5. brink, crest, crown 6. border, summit, tiptop, visage 7. eyebrow, feature 8. boldness, forehead 9. gangplank 10. effrontery 11. countenance

browbeat . . . 3. cow 5. bully 6. hector 7. buffalo, henpeck 8. bulldoze, domineer 10. intimidate

brown . . . 4. dark 5. cheat, dusky 6. august, braise, tanned 9. red-yellow (class)

brown . . . 3. bay, dun, nut, tan 4. ecru, faon, fawn, roan, rust, seal 5. acorn, cocoa, hazel, henna, khaki, mocha, olive, otter, sepia, snuff, sumac, tawny, tenné, toast, topaz 6. auburn, bister, bronze, burnet, coffee, copper, loutre, oriole, russet, sienna, sorrel, titian, walnut 7. asphalt (smoke), gazelle, perique, rosario (army) 8. chestnut, cinnamon, mahogany 9. buckthorn, chocolate 10. café au lait, terra cotta

brown (pert to) . . .
Bess . . 6. musket
betty . . 5. daisy 7. pudding

    10. coneflower
earth . . 5. umber
ebony . . 6. wamara 10. coffeewood

browned in deep fat . . . 7. rissole

Brownian movement (Bot) . . . 7. pedesis

brownie . . . 3. elf 4. cake 5. dwarf, gnome, nisse, pixie, Scout, urisk 6. camera, goblin 9. sandpiper

Brownism (Eng) . . . 17. Congregationalism

browze . . . 4. brut (obs), read, scan 5. graze 6. nibble

bruckle . . . 5. frail 7. brittle 9. breakable 10. changeable, inconstant

bruin . . . 4. bear

bruise . . . 4. bash, beat, hurt, maul 5. abuse, crush, dinge, pound, wound 6. batter, buffet, injury 7. contuse 8. abrasion, black eye 9. contusion, pulverize, triturate

bruiser . . . 3. mug, pug 5. boxer, bravo, tough 7. fighter, ruffian, sparrer 8. pugilist 11. fisticuffer

bruit, bruit about . . . 3. din 4. fame, hawk, tell 5. bandy, noise, rumor 6. clamor, report 9. advertise

brujo . . . 8. magician, sorcerer 11. witch doctor

brumal . . . 4. cold 6. hiemal, wintry 8. hibernal 10. winterlike

brune . . . 6. brunet (brunette) 11. Melanochroi

Brunhild . . . 5. Queen (wife of Siegfried) 8. Valkyrie (Myth)

brunt . . . 3. rub 4. crux 5. pinch, shock 6. stress 7. squeeze

brush . . . 3. art 4. bush, comb, tail (fox), tuft 5. besom, briar, broom, clash, graze, groom, sweep, touch 6. artist, forest, pappus, stroke, teazel 7. painter, scuffle, thicket 8. conflict 9. brushwood, encounter 10. paintbrush 11. undergrowth

brush aside . . . 5. spurn 6. reject 7. dismiss 8. shrug off 9. disregard

brush wolf . . . 6. coyote

brusque . . . 4. curt 5. bluff, blunt, brash, brusk, frank, gruff, rough, sharp, short 6. abrupt, candid, snippy

brutal . . . 5. cruel, gross 6. animal, carnal, coarse, savage 7. bestial, inhuman 8. ruthless 9. barbarous

brutality . . . 7. cruelty 9. barbarian, carnality 12. ruthlessness

brute . . . 5. beast, gross, harsh, rough 6. animal 7. beastly, bestial, sensual, varment 8. soulless 9. barbarian, inanimate 10. unpolished 11. uncivilized

brutish . . . 4. rude 5. cruel, gross 6. brutal, carnal, fierce, savage, stupid 7. bestial, inhuman, sensual, vicious 9. barbarous, ferocious, insensate, unfeeling 10. insensible, irrational

Brutus . . . 3. wig 4. hairdo, peruke 7. traitor (Julius Caesar) 13. chrysanthemum

Bryan's speech (1896) . . . 11. Cross of Gold 13. Crown of Thorns

bryology, science of . . . 6. mosses 10. bryophytes, liverworts

Brython . . . 4. Celt 6. Briton 8. Welshman

Brythonic god . . . 3. Ler 4. Bran
Brythonic goddess . . . 9. Arianrhod
bubble . . . 4. bead, bleb, blob, boil, foam
  5. bulge, empty, fancy, tumor 6. burble,
  gurgle, murmur, ripple, scheme,
  trifle 7. chimera (chimaera), globule,
  trickle 8. bubbling, delusive, illusion
  9. ephemeron, intumesce, lightness
  10. effervesce 16. unsubstantiality
buccal . . . 4. oral 5. cheek, mouth
buccaneer . . . 4. Kidd (Capt) 5. rover
  6. Morgan, pirate, rifler, viking
  7. corsair, Lafitte, spoiler 8. marooner,
  picaroon 9. privateer 10. Blackbeard
  (Capt Teach), freebooter
Bucephalus . . . 5. horse, steed 7. charger
  8. war horse (Alex the Great)
buck . . . 3. man, ram, rat 4. bunt, butt,
  deer, goat, hare, jump, male, sore (4-yr
  deer) 5. fight, sasin 6. animal, combat,
  dollar, Indian, oppose 7. contest,
  launder, pricket 8. antelope, sawhorse
  10. fallow deer
buckaroo . . . 6. cowboy 7. trainer,
  vaquero 8. horseman 12. broncobuster
  (bronchobuster)
bucket . . . 3. tub 4. bail, bowk, pail, ship
  5. chest, cozen, scoop, skeel 6. bailer,
  bushel, drench, sityla 10. bucket shop
Buckeye State . . . 4. Ohio
Buckingham Palace . . . 9. residence
  11. St James Park (London)
buckle . . . 3. bow 4. bend, curl, kink,
  warp 5. tache 6. fasten 8. marriage
  9. fastening
buckthorn . . . 4. tree 5. brown, shrub
  7. cascara, Rhamnus
buckwheat . . . 4. cake, coal, herb, seed,
  titi 5. flour
bucolic . . . 4. idyl, poem, poet 5. idyll,
  local, rural 6. farmer, poetic, rustic
  7. eclogue, georgic 8. agrestic, pastoral
  9. bucoliast
bud . . . 3. deb 4. bulb, cion, germ, grow,
  knop, stem 5. brier, buddy, gemma,
  graft, plant, shoat, youth 6. embryo,
  sprout 7. blossom, brother, burgeon,
  develop 8. rudiment, soredium
  9. debutante, germinate
Buddha (Gautama) . . . 2. Fo 4. sage
  (Shakya) 5. amita, deity 7. ascetic,
  teacher 8. Daibutsu 10. Blessed One
Buddhism (pert to) . . .
  church . . 4. tera
  city (sacred) . . 5. Lassa (Lhasa)
  evil spirit . . 4. Mara
  fate . . 5. Karma
  festival . . 3. Bon
  friar, monk . . 2. Bo 5. arbat, bonze
    6. bhikku, gelong 7. Mahatma
    8. poonghia 9. Dalai Lama
  goal . . 13. Enlightenment
  hell . . 6. Naraka
  language (sacred) . . 4. Pali 5. sutra
    9. Tripitaka
  liberation . . 7. Nirvana
  monk . . 4. lama (Tibet)
  mountain (sacred) . . 4. Omei (Chin)
  paradise . . 4. Jodo 8. gokuraku
  sect . . 3. Zen
  shrine (Ind) . . 4. tope 5. stupa 6. dagoba

  temple . . 4. rath, Tera 6. vihara
  temple column . . 3. lat
  term . . 6. nidana
buddy . . . 3. pal 4. chum, mate 5. crony
  7. brother, comrade 8. tentmate
  9. bedfellow, companion
budge . . . 3. fur (lambskin) 4. grog, move,
  stir 5. booze, brisk, stiff 6. guzzle,
  jocund, liquor, solemn, tipple 7. austere,
  pompous 8. movement 11. nervousness
budget . . . 3. bag 4. bulk, plan, sack
  5. funds, pouch, purse, store 6. agenda,
  assets, bundle, moneys, packet,
  parcel, ration, wallet 7. program,
  stipend 8. finances, quantity, schedule
  9. allowance, statement
  12. accumulation
Buenos Aires (pert to) . . .
  avenue (famed) . . 13. Avenida de Mayo
  bourse . . 5. Bolsa
  capital . . 9. Argentina
  river . . 7. La Plata
buff . . . 3. rub 4. hide (animal) 5. color,
  scour 6. polish 7. burnish, leather
buffalo (animal) . . .
  American . . 5. bison
  Asian, African . . 2. ox 4. arna, Cape,
    gaur 8. seladang
  European . . 7. aurochs
  hybrid . . 7. cattalo (catalo)
  Indian . . 4. arna
  Philippines . . 7. carabao, timarau
buffalo (pert to) . . .
  grass . . 5. grama 6. guinea 11. St
    Augustine
  pea . . 4. plum 5. vetch 10. bluebonnet
  slang . . 3. cow 5. bully 7. perplex
    8. bulldoze, confound
Buffalo Bill . . . 11. William Cody
buffer . . . 4. buff 5. guard, wheel
  6. bumper 7. bulwark, cushion
  8. backstop, polisher
buffet . . . 3. bar, box, hit 4. beat,
  blow, cuff, slap, toss, whip 5. abuse,
  smite, stool 6. bruise, oppose, strike
  12. chastisement 14. disappointment
buffet . . . 6. supper 7. counter, hassock
  8. cupboard 9. sideboard
buffo . . . 7. buffoon 10. bass singer
  (comic opera), buffo-basso
buffoon . . . 4. fool, mima (fem), mime,
  zany 5. actor, clown, droll, mimer
  6. jester, mummer 8. humorist,
  ridicule 9. Hanswurst, harlequin
  12. Eulenspiegel (Tyll) 13. pickel-herring
  (pickle-herring)
buffoonery . . . 6. japery, pranks 7. fooling
  8. clownery, drollery, trickery
  9. slapstick 10. buffoonism
  12. harlequinade
bug (insect) . . . 3. fly, sow 4. flea,
  gnat, moth, pill, tick 5. Anasa,
  aphid, Aphis, cimex, louse 6. beetle,
  cicada, earwig, locust, mantis, needle,
  scarab, slater, spider, weevil 7. firefly,
  hexapod, katydid, ladybug, Ranatra,
  termite 8. chilipod, diplopod, mosquito,
  myriapod 9. arthropod (jointed),
  centipede, cockroach, lightning,
  millipede, tarantula 10. silverfish
  11. grasshopper

bug (slang) . . . 3. nut 4. bogy, flaw, rage
5. craze, fault, manis 6. defect, zealot
7. bugaboo, bugbear, fanatic, passion
9. energumen
bugaboo . . . 4. bogy, ogre, trap (golf)
bugan . . . 5. ghost 6. spirit (evil)
9. hobgoblin
bugger . . . 3. guy, rat 4. chap, heel
6. booger, jasper, wretch
buggy . . . 3. bus 4. ga-ga, shay 5. wagon
6. cuckoo 7. caboose, foolish, haywire,
vehicle 8. carriage, demented, infested,
stanhope 9. insectile 10. insectlike
bug juice . . . 6. liquor (strong), whisky
(inferior)
bugle . . . 3. iva (ragweed) 4. bead,
call (mating), honk, horn, nose,
toot 7. clarion, trumpet 9. schnozzle
10. instrument
bugle call . . . 4. taps 6. alerte, sennet
(Hist) 7. retreat, tantara 8. last post,
reveille
build . . . 4. form, rear 5. edify, erect,
found, frame, raise, shape 6. create,
evolve, figure, nidify 7. fashion, stature
8. increase, physique 9. construct,
establish
building . . . 4. barn, casa, crib, shed,
wing 5. annex, tower 6. casino, castle,
lean-to, making, museum 7. edifice,
factory, forming, rookery, rotunda,
theater 8. creation, dwelling, erecting,
erection, tenement 9. apartment,
structure 10. fashioning, production,
skyscraper, storehouse 11. fabrication
build-up . . . 5. boost 9. promotion
11. advertising 12. commendation
built . . . 4. made 6. formed, shaped
7. crested, erected 8. fashioned
10. fabricated 11. constructed
bulb . . . 3. bud 4. corm, lily, root,
sego, stem 5. onion, swell, tuber,
tulip 6. bulbil, camass, crocus, dahlia
7. bulblet, globule, rhizome 8. earthnut
bulbous . . . 5. round 7. bulbose, bulging
8. swelling, tuberous
Bulgaria . . .
capital . . 5. Sofia
city . . 5. Varna 6. Plevna, Sliven
7. Ruschuk
native . . 6. Bulgar
origin . . 4. Slav 9. Mongolian
river . . 6. Danube, Marica (Maritsa),
Struma
bulge . . . 3. bow 4. bump, edge, hump,
jump, knob, odds 5. bilge, bloat,
flash, pouch, swell 6. convex, wallet
7. vantage 9. advantage 10. projection
12. protuberance
bulk . . . 3. sum 4. loom, mass, most, size
6. extent, staple, volume 7. bigness,
quantum 8. majority, quantity
9. dimension, largeness, substance,
thickness 11. massiveness
12. accumulation 13. preponderance
bulky . . . 5. heavy, hulky, stout, thick
6. clumsy 7. awkward, lumpish, massive
8. unwieldy 9. corpulent, policemen
(Eng sl) 10. cumbersome,
unwielding 11. substantial
bull . . . 4. fiat, seal 5. edict, error,

large, ukase 6. brevet, decree, firman,
humbug, letter (papal), market (Finan),
rising, Taurus 7. blunder 8. nonsense,
solecism 9. Irish bull, policeman
10. speculator
bull (male animal) . . . 2. ox 3. cow 4. Apis
(sacred), stot, toro, zebu 5. moose,
steer, whale 6. walrus 7. bullock
8. elephant, Minotaur, terrapin
bull (slang) . . . 4. blah, bosh, bunk
5. hokum 6. hot air 7. baloney
8. buncombe, flimflam
bulla . . . 4. bleb, boss, case (leather), knob,
seal (papal), stud 6. button 7. blister,
globule, pendant, vesicle 8. ornament
bulldog . . . 3. ant 4. pipe 5. leech
7. courage, forceps 8. barnacle,
stubborn, tenacity 9. newspaper (early),
tenacious
bulldoze . . . 3. cow 5. bully, grade, level
6. coerce, harass 7. buffalo 8. browbeat
10. intimidate
bullet . . . 4. ball (cannon), shot, slug
6. dumdum, pellet, sinker (angling),
tracer 7. missile
bulletin . . . 5. brief, flash 6. notice,
record 7. account, message 8. newsbill
9. statement 10. newsletter, periodical
11. publication 12. announcement
bullfighting (pert to) . . .
assistant . . 9. cuadrilla
bullfighter . . 6. torero 7. matador, picador
8. toreador
dart . . 10. banderilla
final thrust . . 8. estocada 13. moment
of truth
maneuver . . 4. pase 5. faena 8. veronica
matador, famed . . 8. Belmonte, Manolete
10. El Cordobés
matador's tool . . 4. capa 6. muleta
music . . 9. pasodoble
parade . . 5. paseo
program, series . . 7. corrida
shout . . 3. olé
bullfinch . . . 3. alp 4. nope 5. hedge
11. pyrrhuloxia 12. gray grosbeak
Bull Moose . . . 16. Progressive Party
bullpen (pert to) . . .
camp . . 8. barracks 9. enclosure
ice hockey . . 5. bench (penalty)
ring cell . . 5. toril
Western US . . 6. corral
Bull Run (battle) . . . 8. Manassas
bully . . . 4. beef 6. hector, jovial
7. gleeful, ruffian 8. browbeat, bulldoze
9. bulldozer, tormentor 10. browbeater,
intimidate
bulwark . . . 4. bank 6. buffer, sconce
7. barrier, parapet, rampart 8. abutment,
buttress 10. protection 13. fortification
bum . . . 3. beg 5. idler, revel, rummy,
souse, spree 6. beggar, loafer,
tipple, wretch 7. budmash, moocher,
wastrel 8. blighter, drunkard, vagabond
9. lazzarone, schnorrer 10. panhandler
bump . . . 3. hit, jog 4. bang, clop, jolt,
lump, meet, push, thud 5. bulge, cahot,
crash, crump, knock, lower, plunk,
tumor 6. demote, impact, reduce, strike
7. collide 8. demotion, dilation, swelling
9. air pocket, collision, downgrade

bumpkin . . . 4. boor, clod, gawk, hick, lout, rube, tike 5. yokel 6. farmer, rustic 7. cauboge, hayseed, hoosier, lumpkin 9. chawbacon 10. clodhopper
bumptious . . . 8. insolent 9. audacious, insulting 12. contumelious
bunch . . . 3. bob, lot, mop, set 4. pack, tuft, wisp 5. batch, clump, covey, crowd, flock, grist, group 6. bundle 7. cluster, company 8. assemble, quantity 9. multitude 10. congregate
bundle . . . 3. lot, wad 4. bale, bolt, hank, pack, send 5. bluey, bunch, fagot, sheaf, shook 6. bindle, fardel, fascis, packet, parcel, seroon 7. fascine, package, rouleau 10. collection
bung . . . 3. tap 4. cork, plug, stop 5. spile 6. bruise 7. contuse, stopper, stopple, tampeon, tampoon 8. bankrupt, bunghole 9. falsehood
bungle . . . 3. err 4. muff 5. botch, fudge 6. bobble, foozle, fumble, tailor (hunting) 7. blunder
bungling . . . 5. fudgy 6. clumsy 7. awkward, unhandy 8. botchery 9. unskilled 10. blundering, unskillful
bunion . . . 12. hallux valgus
bunk . . . 3. bed, kip, rot 4. blah, brag 5. abide, berth, couch, dwell, hokum, hooey, sleep 6. humbug, kibosh 7. baloney, hogwash 8. nonsense, tommyrot 9. cross-beam (logging)
Bunker Hill (Mass) . . . 6. battle (1775)
bunkum . . . see *buncombe*
Bunsen . . . 4. cell, disk 5. flame, valve 6. burner 9. Professor (Ger)
bunt . . . 3. bat, dig, jab, jog, tap 4. blow, bump, butt, pike, push, tail (Scot) 5. knock, shove 6. bunting 10. propulsion
bunting . . . 4. flag, hood 5. flags 6. banner, pennon 7. pennant 8. streamer
bunting (bird) . . . 3. red 4. cirl, corn, crow, lark, pape (Creole) 5. finch 6. indigo, towhee 7. cowbird, ortolan 8. bobolink 12. yellowhammer
Bunyan (John) **work** . . . 16. Pilgrim's Progress
Bunyan (Paul) **ox** . . . 4. Babe, blue
buoy . . . 3. dan 4. bell 5. float 6. marker 7. can buoy, nunbuoy 8. bell buoy, deadhead, life buoy, spar buoy 11. mooring buoy 12. breeches buoy 13. whistling buoy
buoyance, buoyancy . . . 4. hope, snap 5. verve 6. bounce 7. flotage 9. lightness 10. levitation, resilience 12. floatability 16. lightheartedness
buoyant . . . 5. light 7. elastic 8. cheerful, floating, levitate, volatile 11. supernatant 12. lighthearted, recuperative
bur, burr . . . 3. nut 5. thorn 8. adherent (see also *burr*)
burble . . . 6. muddle 7. confuse, trouble 8. disorder
burbot . . . 4. ling, Lota 7. eelpout
burden . . . 3. key, tax 4. birn, care, cark, clog, lade, load, note, onus, task, tone 5. cargo, cross, music, tenor, voice

6. charge, cumber, hamper, saddle, weight 7. bourdon, freight, oppress, payload, refrain 8. capacity, overload, pressure 10. impediment, imposition 11. encumbrance
burdensome . . . 5. heavy 7. arduous, massive, onerous, weighty 8. unwieldy 9. difficult, laborious, ponderous 10. cumbersome, oppressive 11. troublesome 12. impedimental
bureau . . . 4. desk, shop 6. office 7. dresser 8. chambers 10. chiffonier, department
bureaucracy . . . 10. government 11. directorate, officialdom, officialism
burgeon . . . 3. bud 4. grow 5. gemma, shoot, sprit 6. sprout
burglar . . . 4. yegg 5. thief 9. cracksman 11. safecracker 10. housebreaker
burglary . . . 5. theft 6. burgle 7. larceny, robbery 8. stealage 13. housebreaking
burgle . . . 3. rob 8. burglary 10. burglarize
burgomaster . . . 5. mayor 7. alcalde 10. magistrate 11. burghmaster
burgoo, burgout . . . 4. stew 5. gruel 7. pudding (oatmeal) 8. porridge
burial . . . 5. inurn 7. funeral 8. interment, sepulture 10. engulfment, inhumation, submersion 11. concealment, submergence
burial ground . . . 4. pyre 5. grave 6. barrow 7. tumulus 8. bone yard, catacomb, cemetery, golgotha 9. graveyard 10. churchyard, necropolis 11. polyandrium 12. potter's field
burlesque . . . 3. fun 4. jest 5. farce, comic 6. parody, review, satire 7. mimicry, mockery, overact, take-off 8. burletta, doggerel, ridicule, travesty 9. charivari, imitation, travestie 10. caricatura, caricature 13. entertainment
Burlingame Treaty . . . 11. Immigration (Chin 1868)
burly . . . 3. fat 5. bulky, large, noble, obese, stout 6. brawny 7. stately 8. imposing, stalwart 9. corpulent, excellent
Burma, Burmese . . .
alphabet . . 4. Pali
capital (anc) . . 3. Ava 4. Pegu
capital, modern . . 6. Yangon 7. Rangoon
city . . 8. Mandalay
dagger . . 3. dah (dhao)
gibbon . . 3. lar
girl . . 4. mima
monk . . 2. bo
native . . 3. Lai
people . . 3. Mon, Tai 4. Laos, Shan 7. Siamese
relation . . 5. Thais (Tais) 6. Malays 7. Chinese 8. Tibetans 10. Mongolians
religion . . 8. Buddhism
robber . . 6. dacoit
shed (public) . . 5. zayat
viol . . 4. turr (3-stringed)
Burma Road . . . 6. Lashio (to China, 1938–1942, replaced by Ledo Rd)
burn . . . 3. dry, tan 4. char, fire, glow, hurt, pain, sear, sere 5. blaze, brand, brook, cense, flame, scald, singe 6. ignite, injury, scorch 7. cremate, encauma,

flicker, sunburn, swelter, torrefy
9. cauterize, sacrifice 10. incandesce,
incinerate

burner . . . 3. jet 4. lamp 5. torch
6. Bunsen, candle, censer (incense)
7. cresset 9. blowtorch 10. lucubrator
11. incinerator

burning . . . 3. hot 4. fire, pain, sore
5. afire, angry, ardor, arson, blaze, fiery,
flame 6. ablaze, ardent, fervid 7. blazing,
cautery, excited, fervent, flaming,
glowing, shining, zealous 8. eloquent,
feverish, inustion 9. cremating,
cremation, execution 10. combustion,
ustulation 13. conflagration

burning place . . . 4. ghat 9. crematory
10. cinerarium

burnish . . . 3. rub 4. buff 5. glaze, gloss,
shine 6. patina, polish

burnt . . . 3. red 5. dried 6. burned,
seared, singed 7. charred 8. hardened,
scorched, sunburnt 9. blistered,
sunburned

burnt (pert to) . . .
 art . . 11. pygrography, pyrogravure
 color . . 4. rose 5. ocher, topaz 6. almond,
 orange, russet, sienna 8. amethyst
 sugar . . 7. caramel

burn with anger, excitement . . . 4. fume
5. smoke 6. seethe, simmer, sizzle
7. smolder

burp . . . 5. belch, eruct 8. eructate

burr . . . 3. cut, hem 4. buzz, whir
5. brier, drone, gnarl, knurl, thorn
6. brogue, corona (moon), meatus (ear)
7. bramble, clotbur, prickle, silique,
sticker 8. excavate, follicle 9. cocklebur,
whetstone

burro . . . 3. ass 4. jack 5. cuddy, neddy
6. dickey, donkey 7. jackass

burrow . . . 3. dig 4. abri, hide, hole,
lair, mine 5. couch (otter's), lodge
(beaver's) 6. search, tunnel 7. shelter

burrowing . . . 9. effodient, fossorial
11. lithodomous (in rock)

burrowing animal . . . 4. mole, peba
5. poyou 6. peludo 8. suricate
9. armadillo

burst . . . 3. pop 4. bang, rend 5. blast,
blaze, break, broke, erupt, flare, flash,
shots, spurt 6. volley 7. explode,
flare-up, gunfire, implode 8. outbreak,
outburst, ruptured 9. discharge,
explosion, fractured 10. detonation
11. dissiliency

burst (forth) . . . 4. grow 5. erupt, sally
6. sprout

burst (pert to) . . .
 applause . . 5. éclat, hands 7. ovation,
 plaudit 8. clapping
 cheers . . 5. salvo
 gunfire . . 6. rafale
 laughter . . 3. fit 4. peal, roar
 10. convulsion
 temper . . 4. rage 5. scene, storm
 7. passion 9. explosion

bursting . . . 4. full 7. brimful, crammed,
excited, replete 8. overfull, thrilled,
volcanic 9. explosive, surfeited
10. detonating 11. impassioned,
overflowing, overwhelmed

bury . . . 4. hide, sink 5. cache, cover, inter,
inurn, plant, stash 6. engulf, entomb,
inhume 7. conceal, embosom, repress,
secrete 8. submerge 9. overwhelm,
sepulture

bus . . . 6. jitney 7. omnibus 10. motor
coach

bush . . . 3. tod 4. shag (hair) 5. brush,
plain, shrub, wahoo, wilds 6. branch,
lining 7. boscage, bushing 8. bushveld,
woodland 10. hinterland

bushed . . . 4. beat 5. all in 6. pooped
7. baffled 8. dog-tired 9. exhausted,
nonplused, perplexed, played out
10. nonplussed

bushel . . . 3. foo 4. full 6. basket, vessel
7. measure (dry) 8. imperial, standard
10. Winchester

Bushido (Jap) . . . 11. code of honor

bushing . . . 4. bush 6. lining, sleeve
(mach) 7. bearing, padding (piano)

Bushman . . . 3. San 4. Saan 5. nomad,
pygmy 6. Abatua, rustic 8. woodsman
9. aborigine

bushmaster . . . 5. snake

bushwhacker . . . 7. pioneer 8. guerilla
10. forerunner 11. bushfighter,
voortrekker 12. frontiersman

bushy . . . 5. hairy, thick, woody
6. dumose, shaggy, woodsy 7. hirsute,
scrubby, shrubby

business . . . 3. job 4. firm, game, line,
work 5. craft, house, trade 6. affair,
career, matter, racket 7. calling,
company, concern, pursuit
8. commerce, industry, interest,
practice, vocation 10. enterprise,
occupation, proceeding, profession
11. transaction 13. establishment

business (pert to) . . .
 agreement . . 6. cartel
 businesslike . . 11. pragmatical
 customer . . 6. patron
 cycle . . 9. recession 10. depression,
 prosperity 11. liquidation
 deal . . 4. turn 9. operation
 11. negotiation, transaction
 Exchange . . 4. bank 5. Bolsa 6. Bourse
 11. stock market
 man . . 6. tycoon 8. salesman 9. solicitor
 place . . 4. mart, shop 5. store 6. office,
 shoppe 8. Exchange

bust . . . 4. bang, fail, hand (Bridge), tame
(bronco) 5. burst, chest, crash, flunk,
spree 6. breast, figure 7. degrade,
explode, failure 8. collapse, demotion,
fracture 9. sculpture 10. bankruptcy

bustard . . . 4. bird (Old World), kori, Otis
5. goose, paauw 6. curlew 8. Otididae

busted . . . 4. flat 5. broke 6. broken, failed,
ruined 7. severed 8. bankrupt, ruptured,
strapped 9. insolvent, penniless
10. stone-broke

bustle . . . 3. ado 4. fuss, stir, to-do
5. haste, whirl 6. flurry, hubbub,
hustle, pother, scurry, tumult 7. bluster,
ferment, fluster, scamper, turmoil
8. activity 9. agitation, commotion
10. excitement, hurly-burly
11. disturbance

bustling . . . 6. active 7. hurried, rushing

8. eventful, stirring

busy ... 4. nosy, work 5. drive 6. active, devote, employ, engage, occupy 7. engaged, on the go, operose 8. diligent, employed, meddling, occupied, on the run, sedulous 9. assiduous, attentive, laborious, officious 10. meddlesome 11. industrious, inquisitive, persevering

busy ... 4. dick 6. gossip 7. gumshoe, meddler 8. busybody, flatfoot 9. detective

busybody ... 6. gossip 8. quidnunc 9. pragmatic

but ... 2. ma 3. yet 4. even, just, mere, save 5. hence, outer, still 6. except 7. however, without 10. regardless 12. nevertheless 15. notwithstanding

butcher ... 3. fly (angling), mar 4. kill, slay 5. botch, spoil 6. killer, vendor 7. croaker, meatman 8. merchant, train-boy 9. slaughter 11. slaughterer 12. bloodshedder

butchery ... 6. murder 7. carnage 8. business, massacre, shambles 9. slaughter 14. slaughterhouse

butt ... 3. aim, end, jut, pit, ram, tun, tup 4. buck, bunt, cart, cask, goat, rump, stub 5. cigar, hinge, joint, mound, piece, stump 6. target (archery), thrust (fencing) 7. buttock, parapet, project 8. flatfish 9. cigarette 13. laughingstock

butter ... 3. pat 4. coat, ghee (ghi), oleo 5. smear 6. bedaub, spread 7. butyric 8. flattery 9. margarine, suaveness 10. semiliquid 13. oleomargarine

butter-and-eggs ... 8. flaxweed, ranstead, toadflax

buttercup fruit ... 6. achene 7. crowtoe

butterfingered ... 6. clumsy 7. awkward, unhandy 8. bungling, careless 9. all thumbs 10. blundering

butterflies (slang) ... 6. nerves 7. fidgets, jitters

butterfly (pert to) ...
 American .. 7. viceroy
 family .. 10. Agapetidae 11. Rhopalocera
 genus .. 7. Lycaena 11. Lepidoptera
 large .. 7. monarch
 larva .. 11. caterpillar
 lily .. 4. sego 8. mariposa
 peacock .. 2. io 7. buckeye
 swallowtail .. 5. black, tiger, zebra
 type .. 4. moth 5. satyr 10. fritillary, silverspot

buttocks ... 4. butt (vulgar), hips, rear, rump, seat 5. fanny, podex 6. bottom 8. haunches, maneuver (wrestling) 9. backsides, posterior

buttress ... 4. pier, pile, prop, stay 5. brace, tower 7. shelter, support 8. abutment 10. projection, strengthen 11. counterfort 13. fortification

buttress (Arch) ... 4. pier 6. flying 7. hanging

buxom ... 3. gay 4. boon, rosy 5. jolly, plump 6. blithe, jocund, jovial 7. gleeful

buy ... 5. bribe 6. accept, redeem 7. bargain, expiate 8. purchase

buy back ... 6. redeem

Buyer Beware ... 12. Caveat Emptor

buzz ... 3. hum, saw 5. rumor, snore 6. bustle, murmur, rumble 7. ferment, whisper 9. fricative, murmuring 10. sibilation

buzzard ... 4. aura (turkey), hawk, pern 5. buteo 6. osprey, stupid 7. harrier 9. dorbeetle, senseless 10. cockchafer

buzz bomb ... 9. doodlebug 10. bumblebomb 14. Chase-Me-Charlie

bwana (Afr) ... 4. boss 6. master

by ... 2. at, in, on 3. ago, bei, par, per, via 4. away, gone, near, over, pass (bridge), past, with 5. after, aside 6. beside, beyond, nearby, toward 7. abreast, close by, through 9. in reserve

by-and-by ... 4. anon, soon 5. later, sweet 6. mañana 7. betimes, bientôt, ere long, shortly 8. directly 9. presently 11. tout à l'heure

by birth ... 3. nee

bygone ... 3. ago 4. lost, over, past 6. buried, bypast, gone by, passed 7. elapsed, extinct 8. departed, preterit (preterite)

byname ... 6. eponym 7. babyism, epithet, surname 8. cognomen, monicker, nickname 9. sobriquet 10. patronymic 11. appellation

bypass ... 4. go by, miss 5. byway, elude 6. byroad, detour, escape 7. deviate, digress 8. side path 10. circumvent, roundabout

By the Grace of God ... 9. Dei Gratia

byword ... 3. mot, saw 5. adage, maxim 6. byname, phrase, saying, slogan 7. adagium, parable, proverb 8. aphorism, nickname, reproach 9. catchword, sobriquet 10. shibboleth

by word of mouth ... 4. oral 5. parol (parole)

Byzantine Empire ...
 architecture .. 7. St Marks (Venice) 9. elaborate
 bookbinding .. 9. unadorned (earlier) 10. bejewelled (later)
 church .. 7. Eastern
 city .. 14. Constantinople (Istanbul)
 creator .. 11. Constantine (the Great)
 historian .. 9. Procopius 11. Anna Comnena
 poetry .. 5. hymns
 scepter .. 6. ferula
 writer .. 6. Prazes 7. Priscus, Romanus

Byzantium ... 14. Constantinople (Istanbul)

C

C ... 4. clef 7. cedilla, century, hundred, keynote

caama ... 3. fox 4. asse 10. hartebeest

cab ... 4. pony, taxi 7. measure, purloin, shelter, taxicab, vehicle 8. carriage (anc) 9. cabriolet 10. locomotive (part) 11. translation

cabal ... 4. clan, plot 5. group, junta, party 7. chatter, complot, coterie, dispute, faction 8. intrigue 9. camarilla, collusion, Committee 10. complicity, conspiracy

cabala ... 7. mystery 9. mystic art, occultism

cabaissou ... 9. armadillo (giant)

cabalistic ... 6. occult 7. cabalic 8. abstract, anagogic, esoteric, mystical 10. mysterious

caballeria ... 7. measure (land) 8. chivalry 10. knighthood

caballero ... 5. lover, rider 6. knight 8. cavalier, horseman 9. chevalier, gentleman 10. equestrian

caballo ... 5. horse

cabaret ... 3. inn 4. cafe 6. hostel, posado, tavern 7. barroom 9. night club, roadhouse 11. café dansant 13. entertainment

cabbage ... 3. kos (cos) 4. cole, kale, palm 5. colza, savoy 7. collard 8. colewort, kohlrabi 11. cauliflower 15. Brussels sprouts

cabbage (pert to) ...
curly leaf.. 5. savoy
daisy.. 11. globeflower
fermented.. 5. kraut
headless.. 4. kale
salad.. 4. slaw
seed.. 5. colza
slang.. 4. crib, fool 6. pilfer 7. fathead, purloin 9. numbskull 11. cabbagehead, knucklehead
species.. 8. Brassica
tree.. 4. palm 7. angelin 8. palmetto
white.. 9. butterfly
yellows.. 7. disease (destructive)

caber ... 4. apar, beam, pole 6. rafter, timber

cabin ... 3. hut 4. shed 5. booth, coach (Naut), house, hovel, lodge, shack 6. cabana, saloon 7. caboose 10. blockhouse

cabinet ... 3. box, den 4. Body, buhl, case 6. bureau, closet, office 7. almirah, boudoir, council, étagère, whatnot 8. cellaret, cupboard, ministry 9. committee

cable ... 4. boom, cord, rope, wire 5. chain, twine 6. fasten, hawser 7. coaxial, measure, molding, ropeway 8. telegram 9. cablegram

cable (pert to) ...
car.. 7. telpher
holder (Naut).. 7. wildcat 10. cable wheel

post.. 4. bitt

cabling ... 9. rudenture

cabochon ... 5. jewel, stone (uncut), style (convex cut) 8. ornament

caboodle ... 3. all, kit, lot 5. bunch, whole 10. collection 14. kit and caboodle

caboose ... 3. car (RR) 5. buggy 6. galley 7. kitchen 9. deckhouse

cabotin ... 5. actor (strolling) 9. charlatan

cachaca ... 3. rum (white)

cache ... 4. hide, hole 5. stash, store 7. conceal, hide-out, retreat 8. hideaway 10. storehouse

cachet ... 4. seal 5. sigil, stamp, wafer 6. signet 7. capsule

cachila ... 8. white man

cachot ... 7. dungeon

cackle ... 3. gab 4. cank, chat, crow, talk 5. clack, laugh, prate 6. babble, gabble, giggle, gossip, jabber 7. chatter, prattle 8. laughter

cacodemon ... 4. deva 5. devil, fiend, Indra 10. evil spirit

cacology ... 10. bad diction, corruption (speech) 16. mispronunciation

cacophonous ... 7. raucous 8. jangling, strident 9. diaphonic, dissonant 10. discordant 11. unmelodious

cacophony ... 5. clash 6. jangle 7. discord 8. diaphony (Mus) 9. harshness 10. dissodence

cactus ... 4. bleo 5. agave 6. chaute, cholla, mescal 7. Opuntia, saguaro 8. fishhook 9. Turk's-head 11. prickly pear 12. Echinocactus

cad ... 4. boor, chum, heel, hick 5. yokel 6. mucker 7. bounder, servant 8. townsman 9. scoundrel, vulgarian

cadaver ... 4. body (dead) 5. stiff 6. corpse 7. carcass 8. skeleton

cadaverous ... 4. pale 5. gaunt, lurid 6. sickly, wasted 7. ghastly, haggard 9. emaciated 10. attenuated, corpselike

caddis (pert to) ...
bait.. 3. fly 4. worm 5. cadew
material.. 4. yarn 5. twill 6. crewel 7. worsted
worm.. 5. larva (aquatic)

caddle ... 4. fuss 5. annoy, worry 6. gossip 7. confuse, trouble 8. disarray 9. confusion

cade ... 3. keg, oil (Med), pet 4. cask, lamb (orphan) 6. barrel, coddle, petted

cadeau ... 4. gift

cadence ... 4. beat, lilt, tone 5. meter 6. rhythm 7. balance 9. free verse, vers libre 10. modulation

cadence ... 4. half 5. trill 6. plagal 7. perfect 9. authentic, deceptive, imperfect, suspended 11. interrupted

cadency (Her) ... 4. rose 5. label 6. mullet 7. annulet, martlet 8. crescent 10. fleur-de-lis 11. cross moline

cadenza ... 7. cadence 8. flourish

cadet ... 3. son 4. pleb 5. color (blue),

youth 6. junior 10. midshipman
cadge ... 3. beg 4. hawk 5. fakir, mooch
6. beggar, hawker, mumper, peddle,
sponge, vendor 7. carrier, moocher,
sponger 8. huckster, sannyasi
cadgy ... 6. wanton 7. lustful 8. cheerful,
mirthful
Cadmus (pert to) ...
daughter .. 3. Ino 6. Semele
father .. 6. Agenor
founder of .. 6. Thebes (Boetia)
sister .. 6. Europa
wife .. 8. Harmonia
cadre ... 4. list, unit 5. frame, panel 6. line-
up, roster, scheme 8. cadastre, register,
schedule, skeleton 9. framework
caduceus (Gr Antiq) .. 4. wand (Hermes')
5. staff 6. symbol 8. insignia (Med
Corps)
Caesar (pert to) ...
betrayer .. 6. Brutus
colleague .. 7. Bibulus
death site .. 4. Nola
Emperor, Dictator of .. 4. Rome
fatal day .. 4. Ides (of March) 11. Ides
of March
language .. 5. Latin
rival .. 6. Pompey
river .. 7. Rubicon
sister .. 4. Atia
uncle .. 11. Caius Marius
wife .. 8. Cornelia
caesura, cesura ... 4. rest 5. break,
colon, comma, pause 8. interval
12. interruption
cafard ... 5. bigot, blues 6. humbug
9. hypocrite 10. depression
café ... 5. coffe 6. coffee 10. restaurant
11. coffeehouse
café (pert to) ...
au lait .. 5. brown 6. alesan 10. French
nude
creme .. 5. suede (color)
noir .. 4. musk (color) 11. black coffee
parfait .. 8. beverage
cafetière ... 9. coffeepot 10. percolator
caffeine ... 6. coffee, theine (in tea)
8. alkaloid 9. stimulant
cafila ... 7. caravan (camel)
cage ... 3. mew, pen 4. coop 6. corral
7. confine, goal net, impound 8. goal
post
cagey ... 3. sly 4. foxy, wary, wily
5. canny, leery 6. artful, crafty, shifty,
shrews 7. cunning, evasive, knowing
Cain (pert to) ...
brother .. 4. Abel
founder of .. 5. Enoch (1st city)
Land of .. 3. Nod
slayer of .. 4. Abel
son .. 5. Enoch
cairn ... 4. heap (stones) 6. menhir
8. catstone (catstane), landmark,
memorial, monument
Cairo ...
capital .. 5. Egypt
city gate (famed) .. 9. Bab-el-Nasr
mosque .. 12. Sultan Hassan
resident .. 7. Cairene
river .. 4. Nile
seaport .. 10. Alexandria

tomb .. 10. Mehemet Ali
warrior .. 9. Rameses II
caisson ... 3. box 4. case 5. chest, wagon
7. chamber
caitiff ... 4. base, mean, vile 6. coward,
wicked, wretch 7. budmash, captive
10. despicable
cajole ... 4. coax, urge 5. cheat, jolly
6. delude 7. flatter, palaver, sweeten,
wheedle 8. blandish 9. importune
10. honeyfogle
Cajun (pert to) ...
descent .. 6. French (Canadian)
dialect .. 5. Cajun
home (present) .. 9. Louisiana
native of .. 6. Acadia (Nova Scotia)
cake ... 3. bun, wig 4. bake, food, lump,
mass, wigg 5. batty, block, crust,
solid, torte, wafer 6. gateau, harden
7. bannock, congeal, oatcake, pancake
8. corn pone, solidify 9. charlotte,
simpleton 10. griddle-cake
cake (pert to) ...
almond paste .. 7. ratafia
corn .. 4. pone
flat .. 7. placent
fried .. 7. cruller 8. doughnut
Lenten .. 6. cimbal, simnel
Scotch .. 4. farl (farle) 5. scone
unleavened .. 8. tortilla
Cake Day (Scot) ... 8. hogmanay (New
Year's)
calabar bean ... 6. myotic, ordeal
7. eserine 8. alkaloid 13. physostigmine
calabash ... 5. gourd 6. baobab, bronze
(color)
calaboose ... 4. gaol, jail 5. choky, clink
6. bagnio, lockup, prison 8. bastille,
calabozo 9. Bridewell
calamitous ... 3. sad 4. dire, evil 5. black
6. tragic, woeful 7. adverse, baleful,
ruinous, unhappy 8. grievous, tragical,
wretched 10. afflictive, deplorable,
disastrous 11. cataclysmic, destructive,
distressful, unfortunate 12. catastrophic
calamity ... 4. blow, evil, ruin 5. wrack
6. mishap 7. tragedy 8. casualty,
disaster, distress, fatality 9. adversity
10. affliction, misfortune
11. catastrophe, direfulness,
unhappiness 12. wretchedness
calathiform ... 9. cup-shaped
calcarea ... 5. coral 7. sponges
calceiform ... 10. orchidlike 13. clipper-
shaped
calcitrant ... 8. stubborn 12. recalcitrant
calcitrate ... 4. boot, kick 6. oppose
calculate ... 3. aim 4. deem, rate, tell
5. allow, count, frame, judge, score,
tally, think 6. cipher, deduce, figure,
gather, number, reckon 7. average,
compute, suppose 8. conclude, estimate
9. determine, enumerate
calculated ... 7. advised, studied,
weighed 8. measured 10. considered,
deliberate 11. intentional
12. contemplated
calculating ... 8. plotting, scheming
9. computing, designing, judicious
10. estimating, numerative, reflecting,
thoughtful 11. circumspect, considerate

14. discriminative
calculator . . . 5. table 6. abacus 7. suan
pan (swan pan, Chin) 8. computer
9. estimator, tabulator 10. parimutuel
11. Comptometer, totalizator

caldron, cauldron . . . 3. pot, red (color),
vat 6. boiler, kettle, mortar, retort
7. alembic 8. crucible

Caleb (pert to) . . .
daughter . . 7. Achsaph
literally . . 3. dog
son . . 3. Hur, Iru
spy of . . 6. Canaan

calèche . . . 7. vehicle (Quebec)

Caledonia (anc) . . . 8. Scotland

Caledonia bird . . . 4. kagu

Caledonian . . . 5. brown 6. Scotch
8. Scotsman, Scottish

calefacient . . . 4. warm 6. remedy
7. heating 11. calefactory

calendar . . . 4. list, Ordo 5. index, slate
6. docket, line-up, record 7. almanac,
calends (kalends), program 8. register,
schedule 9. catalogue, ephemeris
10. chronology, prospectus

calendar (type) . . . 5. Roman, Swiss
6. Jewish, Julian 7. Chinese
9. Cotsworth, Gregorian, perpetual
13. International (fixed)

calenture . . . 4. glow 5. ardor, fever
7. passion, pyrexia 9. febrility, sunstroke

calepin . . . 4. book (ref) 7. lexicon
10. dictionary

calf . . . 3. leg (part) 4. dolt, fool, skin
6. bovine, island, weaner 7. iceberg,
leather 9. youngling

calf (pert to) . . .
flesh . . 4. veal
hide . . 3. kip
leg (part) . . 5. sural
motherless . . 5. dogie 8. maverick
sweetbread . . 9. ris de veau
time . . 5. youth

Caliban (pert to) . . .
character . . 5. brute, slave (The Tempest)
deity . . 7. Setebos
mother . . 9. Sycorax (witch)

caliber, calibre . . . 4. bore 7. ability

calico . . . 4. dame 5. cloth 6. salloo
8. goldfish 12. multicolored

calico (pert to) . . .
bird . . 9. turnstone
bush . . 6. laurel
horse, pony . . 5. pinto 7. piebald
printing . . 4. teer 7. topical

calid . . . 3. hot 4. mild, warm 6. genial
7. burning, thermal

California . . .
bay . . 8. Monterey
capital . . 10. Sacramento
city . . 6. Fresno 7. Oakland 8. San Diego,
Stockton 9. Long Beach 10. Los Angeles
12. San Francisco, Santa Barbara
desert . . 6. Mojave 8. Colorado
discoverer . . 6. Cortez (1535)
fault . . 10. San Andreas
flower . . 5. poppy
history . . 8. Gold Rush (1848), Missions
11. Sutter's Mill
lake . . 5. Tahoe 8. Elsinore 9. Salton
Sea

lowest point . . 11. Death Valley
missionary . . 5. Serra
mountain . . 6. Lassen, Shasta 7. Whitney
river . . 4. Kern 7. Feather, Russian
10. Sacramento
pageant . . 10. Rose Parade
17. Tournament of Roses
State admission . . 11. thirty-first
State motto . . 6. Eureka
State nickname . . 6. Golden
State tree . . 7. redwood
wine region . . 4. Napa

caliph, calif . . . 3. Ali (4th) 4. Imam
(Imaum), Omar 6. Othman 7. Abu Bekr
8. Islamite

Caliph Ali's descendants . . . 5. Alids
(Alides)

caliphate . . . 7. Omniads, Shiites
(Sectaries) 8. Idrisids 9. Fatimites

calk, caulk . . . 4. copy, plug, stop 5. close,
sleep (Naut sl) 6. calque, catnap,
chinse, plug up, stop up 7. occlude

call . . . 3. bid, cry, dub, hip, nod 4. ahoy,
beck, dial, name, plea, ring, soho,
sook (hog), taps, term, yell 5. alarm,
basis, cause, clepe, rally, rouse,
shout, style, visit, waken 6. appeal,
beckon, demand, ground, invoke,
motive, muster, option, reason, sennet,
signal, slogan, summon 7. appoint,
bidding, collect, convoke, fanfare,
summons, trumpet 8. assemble,
nominate, occasion, reveille 9. battle
cry, challenge, designate, induction,
telephone, watchword 10. denominate,
invitation 11. recruitment, requisition
12. conscription 13. justification

call (pert to) . . .
attention . . 6. direct, remind 8. point
out
back . . 6. recall, recant, repeal, revive,
revoke 7. retract 8. remember
9. recollect
down . . 6. invoke 7. bawl out, reprove,
tell off
evil upon . . 8. execrate
forth . . 5. evoke, rouse 6. elicit, excite,
induce, prompt, summon
names . . 4. cite 5. abuse, curse 6. insult,
revile, vilify 8. besmirch 10. vituperate
together . . 6. muster, summon
7. convoke
to mind . . 4. cite 8. remember 9. visualize

callant, callan . . . 3. boy, lad 4. chap
5. youth 6. fellow, garcon, laddie
8. customer, muchacho
11. hobbledehoy

calle . . . 6. street

called . . . 5. named 6. dubbed, y-clept,
yermed 7. y-cleped

calling . . . 3. art, nod 4. beck, lure,
name, work 5. trade 6. career, metier,
naming, outcry 7. bidding, mission,
pursuit, styling, summons 8. biddance,
business, labeling (labelling), practice,
vocation 9. condition, evocation
10. employment, invitation, occupation,
profession 13. circumstances

calling crab . . . 7. fiddler

calling hare . . . 4. pika

Calliope . . . 4. Muse (poet) 5. organ

8. asteroid
Calliope's son ... 7. Orpheus
callous, calloused ... 4. horn, sear
5. horny, inure 6. harden, seared
8. hardened 9. heartless, indurated,
unfeeling 10. impervious
11. hardhearted 12. thick-skinned
14. pachydermatous
callow ... 5. crude, green 6. tender,
unripe, vernal 7. budding 8. immature,
unformed 9. unfledged 10. unseasoned
11. undeveloped 15. unsophisticated
callus ... 6. tyloma
calm ... 3. lay 4. cool, dill, fair, lull, mild
5. allay, balmy, peace, quiet, sober,
still 6. becalm, hushed, pacify, placid,
sedate, serene, smooth, soothe, steady
7. appease, compose, halcyon, orderly,
pacific, placate, restful, unmoved
8. peaceful, tranquil 9. quiescent,
unruffled 10. phlegmatic 11. tranquilize,
undisturbed 13. dispassionate,
imperturbable
calmant, calmative ... 7. anodyne,
soother 8. lenitive, pacifier, sedative,
soothing 10. depressant, palliative
11. alleviative 12. tranquilizer
calmato (Mus) ... 4. calm 8. tranquil
calmness ... 4. calm, lull 5. peace, poise,
quiet 6. repose 8. quietude, serenity
9. composure, placidity 10. equanimity,
quiescence 11. restfulness, self-control
calor ... 4. heat 5. therm 7. thermal
calorifics ... 4. heat 7. heating
calumet ... 9. peace pipe
calumniate ... 4. slur 5. belie, libel
6. accuse, malign, revile 7. asperse,
slander, traduce 9. blaspheme
calumnious ... 7. abusive 8. derisive,
insolent, libelous 9. insulting
10. defamatory, derogatory, slanderous
11. maledictory, opprobrious
calumny ... 5. abuse 7. lampoon, slander
9. contumely 10. detraction, scurrility
11. malediction 12. vilification
calvary ... 8. crucifix
Calvary (Bib) ... 8. Damascus, Golgotha
9. Jerusalem
Calvinism (pert to) ...
author .. 6. Calvin
doctrine .. 5. Grace 9. Atonement,
Depravity (total) 12. Perseverance (of
Saints) 14. Predestination
site .. 6. Geneva
Calvinistic Methodist ... 5. Welsh
10. Whitefield 14. Lady Huntingdon
Calypso ... 6. Ogygia (home) 8. Cytherea,
sea nymph (The Odyssey)
calyx ... 3. cup 4. husk 5. galea, sepal
6. corona 7. corolla 8. epicalyx, perianth
camarada ... 7. comrade, partner
9. companion
camaraderie ... 8. good will
11. familiarity 14. good-fellowship
camarilla ... 5. cabal 6. clique 7. council
camato ... 6. acorns 8. oak fruit
cambist ... 6. banker, broker 9. financier
11. moneylender 12. money-changer
Cambodia ...
capital .. 6. Angkor 8. Pnom-Penh
king .. 8. Sihanouk

language .. 5. Khmer 9. Cambodian
name, former .. 9. Kampuchea
religion .. 8. Buddhism
Cambria ... 5. Wales
Cambridge University (pert to) ...
English examination .. 6. tripos
English student .. 5. sizar 6. optime
(honor)
Massachusetts .. 3. MIT 7. Harvard
camel ... 4. oont 5. llama 6. deloul,
mammal, vicuna 7. Camelus 8. Bactrian
(2-humped) 9. Camelidae, dromedary
camel hair shawl ... 8. cashmere
camelopard ... 7. giraffe 13. constellation
Camelot ... 6. legend 10. King Arthur,
palace site, Round Table
cameo ... 4. onyx 7. relievo 8. anaglyph
camera type ... 5. Kodak 7. Brownie
10. Rollieflex
Cameroon ...
capital .. 7. Yaounde (Afr)
native .. 4. Sara
people .. 3. Abo 5. Bantu
river .. 5. Shari
seaport .. 6. Douala
Camino Real (Calif) ... 9. Royal Road
12. El Camino Real, King's Highway
Camorra (It) ... 12. organization (secret)
camouflage ... 7. falsify 8. disguise
9. dissemble 10. false front
12. misrepresent
camp ... 4. clan, tent 5. abode, etape,
junto, tabor 6. campoo, clique, laager
7. bivouac, faction 10. encampment
campaign ... 7. serve 7. crusade
9. operation
camphorated tincture of opium ...
9. paregoric
campus ... 4. quad 5. field (academic)
can ... 3. jar, may, tin 6. hopper,
vessel 7. capable 8. canister, conserve
9. competent 10. receptacle
can ... 5. skill 7. ability 9. competent
10. receptacle
can (sl) ... 3. jug, tin 4. boot, bump,
fire, jail, john, kick 6. bounce, cooler,
toilet 7. dismiss 9. discharge 11. give
the gate
Canaan ... 9. Palestine 12. Promised
Land
Canada ... see also *Canadian*
capital (Federal) .. 6. Ottawa
city .. 7. Toronto 8. Hamilton, Montreal,
Winnipeg 9. Vancouver
discoverer .. 9. John Cabot (1497)
Hudson's Bay Co. .. 8. fur trade
native .. 6. French 7. English
nickname .. 6. Canuck
park .. 6. Jasper
peninsula .. 5. Gaspé
police .. 8. Mounties 12. Royal Mounted
(7,000)
river .. 5. Peace, Slave 6. Fraser, Nelson,
Ottawa 8. Gatineau 9. Athabasca,
Churchill, Mackenzie 10. St Lawrence
Canadian (pert to) ...
flour .. 6. Shorts (milling) 8. canaille
jay .. 9. moose bird 10. whisky jack
lynx .. 5. pishu
plum .. 6. cheney
porcupine .. 5. urson 7. cawquaw

squaw .. 6. mahala
canaille ... 3. mob 4. ruck 6. rabble,
   ragtag, Shorts 8. riffraff 10. roughscuff
canal ... 4. duct, iter (brain), pipe, tube
   5. drain 6. meatus 7. acequia, channel
   10. waterspout 11. watercourse
Canal ... 4. Erie, Kiel, Suez 6. Panama
   8. Sault Ste Marie (Soo)
Canal Zone Lock ... 5. Gatun
   10. Miraflores
canard ... 4. duck, hoax 5. rumor
   6. humbug 9. falsehood
canary ... 6. yellow 8. song-bird, songster,
   weakling
Canary Islands ...
   capital .. 9. Santa Cruz (Teneriffe)
   city .. 9. Las Palmas (Grand Canary)
   commune .. 4. Icod
   owner .. 5. Spain
cancel ... 4. blot, dele, kill, omit, undo
   5. annul, erase 6. delete, excise, recall,
   repeal, revoke 7. abolish, destroy,
   nullify, rescind, retract 8. write off
   10. invalidate, neutralize, obliterate
   11. countermand
cancellation ... 6. repeal 7. erasure
   8. deletion, write-off 10. moratorium
   12. obliteration
cancer ... 4. evil 5. tumor 6. canker,
   growth 7. sarcoma 8. neoplasm
   9. carcinoma
Cancer ... 4. crab 7. mansion (moon)
   10. zodiac sign 13. constellation
cancion ... 4. song 5. lyric
Candia ... 5. Crete (Isl)
candid ... 4. fair, just, open, frank
   6. direct, honest 7. sincere 9. guileless,
   impartial, ingenuous 10. impersonal
   13. dispassionate 15. straightforward
candidate ... 6. seeker 7. aspirer,
   electee, nominee 8. aspirant, selectee
   9. applicant, appointee, postulant
   10. solicitant
candidate list ... 4. leet 5. slate 6. roster
Candide (pert to) ...
   hero, title .. 5. novel
   novel, author .. 8. Voltaire
   philosophy .. 8. optimism
candied ... 5. sweet 7. honeyed
   9. congealed, incrusted, preserved
   10. flattering, granulated 12. crystallized
candied sea holly ... 6. eryngo (eringo)
candle ... 3. dip, wax 5. light, power,
   taper 6. bougie, cierge, tallow, votive
   7. paschal 8. bayberry 9. chandelle
candlestick (pert to) ...
   Bib .. 6. lampad
   branched .. 9. girandole
   ornamental .. 10. candelabra
   Scot .. 6. crusie
   spike .. 7. pricket
   three-branched .. 9. tricerion
   torch type .. 8. flambeau
   wall .. 6. sconce
candlewood ... 6. flower 8. ocotillo
candor ... 8. fairness, openness
   9. frankness, sincerity, unreserve
   10. directness 11. artlessness,
   unrestraint 13. outspokenness
candy ... 5. sweet 6. penide (pulled),
   sweets 7. sweeten 8. crystals

9. granulate, sweetmeat 10. confection
   11. crystallize 13. confectionary
candy (type) ... 4. mint 5. fudge, taffy
   6. bonbon, nougat, toffee 7. brittle,
   caramel, fondant, panocha, penuche,
   praline 8. licorice, lollipop 9. chocolate
   11. marshmallow
candytuft ... 6. iberis
cane ... 3. rod 4. beat, club, reed, stem,
   whip 5. crook, sorgo, staff, stick, sugar
   6. bamboo, rattan 7. bagasse, bourdon,
   sorghum, sucrose 9. handstaff,
   truncheon 12. swagger stick
canescent ... 5. hoary, white 7. grizzly,
   silvery, whitish 9. snow-white
Canfield ... 9. solitaire
canine ... 3. cur, dog, fox, pug, pup
   4. lobo, mutt, tike 5. dingo, pooch,
   puppy, whelp 6. animal, coyote
   7. Canidae, doggish, laniary, mastiff,
   mongrel, reynard 8. dogtooth, eyetooth
canis ... 3. dog
Canis Majoris ... 13. Constellation (with
   Dog Star, Sirius)
cannibalism ... 9. barbarity, endophagy
   10. perversion 11. blood thirst
   13. anthropophagy
cannon ... 3. gun 5. crash 6. mortar
   7. firearm, robinet 8. dog of war,
   howitzer, ordnance 9. artillery, collision
cannon (pert to) ...
   ball .. 6. pellet 7. missile
   bore .. 6. breech
   fire .. 7. barrage
   handle .. 4. anse
   nautical .. 5. chase
   part .. 8. cascabel
   pivot .. 8. trunnion
   platform .. 10. terreplein
   plug .. 7. tampion
   shot .. 5. grape
   shoulder part .. 7. rimbase
cannonade ... 4. boom, peal, roar 5. blitz,
   shell 6. rumble, strafe 11. bombardment
canny ... 3. sly 4. foxy, wary, wily 6. artful,
   frugal, shrewd, subtle 7. cunning,
   knowing, prudent, thrifty 8. cautious
   9. sagacious
canoe ... 4. kiak, pahi, proa, waka
   5. bongo, bungo, kayak, umiak, waapa
   6. corial, dugout, oomiak, pitpan
   7. almadia, buckeye (bugeye), coracle,
   piragua, pirogue 12. pambanmanche
canon ... 3. law 4. code, list, rule,
   type 5. model, nodus (Mus) 6. belief,
   clergy, decree, ritual 7. measure,
   precept 8. decision 9. catalogue,
   criterion 10. regulation 11. composition
   12. constitution
canonical ... 4. None (hour), Sext
   (hour) 5. Lauds, Prime 6. Matins
   7. creedal 8. dogmatic, orthodox
   9. doctrinal 10. scriptural 11. theological
   14. ecclesiastical
canonization ... 8. sainting
   10. ordainment, ordination
   12. consecration, enshrinement
canopy ... 3. sky 4. ceil, cope, dais,
   tent 5. cover, shade, vault 6. awning,
   tester 7. blanket, marquee, shelter
   8. caponier (caponiere), ciborium,

pavilion 9. baldachin, firmament

canorous . . . 5. clear 8. sonorous
9. melodious 10. euphonious

cant . . . 3. tip 4. lean, list, sing, song,
sway, tack, tilt 5. angle, argot, chant,
lingo, pitch, slang, slope, whine
6. careen, intone, jargon, patois,
snivel 7. auction, incline, mummery
8. pretense 9. hypocrisy 10. intonation,
sanctimony 17. sanctimoniousness

cantabank . . . 6. singer (ballad)

cantador . . . 6. singer (folk songs)

cantankerous . . . 8. perverse 9. malicious
10. contention, ill-natured 12. cross-
grained

cantata . . . 5. motet 8. serenata
9. pastorale

canter . . . 4. gait, lope 6. gallop
(Canterbury) 8. vagabond

Canterbury . . .
archbishop . . 7. Cranmer, Primate
13. Thomas à Becket (murdered)
capital (Eng) . . 14. ecclesiastical
famed building . . 9. Cathedral
gallop . . 5. aubin 6. canter
Tales, author . . 7. Chaucer

canticle . . . 3. lay, ode 4. hymn, lied,
song 5. carol, ditty 6. Te Deum

Canticle of Canticles (Bib) . . . 11. Song
of Songs 13. Song of Solomon

cantilena . . . 6. legato, melody 8. graceful

cantina . . . 3. bag 6. pocket, saloon
7. canteen

cantle . . . 4. nook, part 5. crown, slice
6. corner, saddle (part) 7. segment
11. cornerpiece

canto . . . 4. book, song 5. poems (div
of), tenor, verse 6. cantus, melody,
poetry 7. descort

canton . . . 3. Uri (Switz) 6. county
6. commune, quarter 8. district, insignia
(Her), mofussil (Ind) 9. bailiwick,
partition

cantor . . . 6. leader, singer 7. soloist
8. melodist, vocalist 9. precentor

cantoria . . . 7. balcony, gallery (choir)

cantrip . . . 5. charm, magic, spell, trick

canty . . . 6. lively 7. chipper 8. cheerful
9. sprightly

Canuck . . . 8. Canadian

canvas . . . 4. sail, tent, tuke (tewke)
5. cloth 6. circus 7. picture, tentage
8. covering, likeness, pavilion
9. tarpaulin 14. representation

canvasback . . . 6. duck

canvass . . . 4. poll 5. study 6. survey
7. examine, inquiry, solicit 8. campaign,
consider 10. scrutinize 11. electioneer
12. solicitation 13. questionnaire

canyon, cañon . . . 4. abra (mouth)
5. chasm, dalle (wall), gorge, gulch
6. arroyo, coulee, ravine, violet
7. couloir

canzone, canzonetta . . . 4. poem, song
6. ballad, melody 8. canzonet, madrigal

caoba . . . 8. mahogany, muskwood

caoutchouc . . . 3. ule 6. caucho, rubber

cap . . . 3. fez, hat, lid, taj, tam 4. atef,
coif, hood, kepi 5. beret, boina, busby,
shako, toque 6. barret, biggin, bonnet,
calpac, cloche, pileus, turban 7. biretta

(beretta), calotte, calpack, chapeau
8. Balmoral, havelock 9. headdress,
headpiece, shtreimal, sou'wester,
zucchetto 10. cervelière
11. mortarboard, tam-ó-shanter

cap (outer part) . . . 3. lid, tip, top 4. dome,
fuze, peak, type 5. cover, crown, excel,
match, spire, trump 6. summit, top
off 7. capital (Arch), overlie, patella
8. complete 9. copestone, detonator

capa . . . 5. cloak 6. mantle 7. tobacco

capability . . . 5. power, skill 6. genius
7. ability, caliber, faculty, potency
8. ableness, adequacy, capacity
10. competence 13. qualification

capable . . . 3. apt, can, fit 4. able 5. adept
6. expert 7. equal to, skilled 8. adequate
9. competent, effective, efficient,
qualified 10. proficient 12. accomplished

capable of . . .
boring . . 10. zylotomous
carrying . . 9. portative
flying . . 6. volant
growing . . 6. viable
living in harmony . . 10. compatible
penetration . . 8. pervious
suffering . . 8. passible 9. sensitive

capable of being . . .
ascertained . . 12. determinable
cultivated . . 6. arable
cut . . 7. sectile
defended . . 7. tenable
done . . 10. effectible
heard . . 7. audible
prevented . . 9. avertible
proved . . 8. testable 12. demonstrable
regulated . . 12. controllable
separated . . 9. divisible
spread . . 10. infectious 12. communicable
thrown . . 7. missile
uttered . . 7. effable

capacious . . . 4. full, much, wide 5. ample,
broad, large, roomy 8. generous,
spacious 9. expansive, extensive
10. commodious, voluminous
12. considerable 13. comprehensive

capacitance unit . . . 5. farad

capacity . . . 4. role, room, size 5. limit,
power, skill, space 6. extent, spread,
status, talent, volume 7. caliber,
content, faculty, fitness, measure
8. adequacy, aptitude, function,
position, relation, strength 9. character
10. capability, efficiency 11. capacitance
(Elec) 12. intelligence
13. accommodation

capacity for knowing . . . 9. intellect

cap and bells . . . 6. bauble, comedy
(symbol), motley 7. costume, marotti
9. headdress

caparison . . . 3. rig 4. tack 5. armor, dress,
get-up 6. livery 7. harness, housing,
panoply 10. horsecloth 12. horse
blanket

cape . . . 3. ras 4. hood, mino, naze, ness,
spur 5. amice, capra, cloak, fichu, orale,
point, sagum, talma 6. mantle, sontag,
tippet 8. pelerine (fur) 9. Inverness

cape (pert to) . . .
gooseberry . . 4. poha
hen . . 4. skua 6. petrel

pigeon . . 7. pintado
polecat . . 5. zoril
ruby . . 6. garnet, pyrope
sheep . . 9. albatross (Naut term)
Cape Cod turkey . . . 7. codfish (humor)
Cape Dutch . . . 9. Afrikaans (language)
Cape of Good Hope discoverer . . .
   4. Diaz (1488)
Capek play . . . 3. RUR
caper . . . 3. tea 4. dido, leap, romp,
   skip 5. antic, berry, dance, frisk,
   prank 6. cavort, frolic, gambol, prance
   8. capriole, marigold 9. privateer (Hist)
capercaille . . . 6. grouse 13. cock of the
   wood
caper herb family . . . 6. Cleome
   8. Capparis 9. Polanisia
   10. clammyweed 13. Capparidaceae
capias . . . 4. writ 6. caveat 7. process,
   warrant 8. mandamus 9. nisi prius
capillary . . . 4. fine, tube 6. minute,
   vessel 7. slender 8. hairlike, trichoid
capilliform . . . 7. thready 8. hairlike
capillus . . . 4. hair
capistrate . . . 6. cowled, hooded
capital . . . 3. top 4. city, main, rare,
   seat, type 5. chief, crest, crown, funds,
   major, means, prime, vital 6. assets,
   letter, ruling, supply 7. leading, primary,
   serious, weighty 8. cardinal, dominant,
   foremost, splendid 9. excellent,
   financial, important, paramount,
   principal, prominent 10. commanding,
   preeminent, shoestring
capitalism . . . 8. politics 10. government
   11. bourgeoisie 14. free enterprise
capitalist . . . 5. baron 6. tycoon 7. rich
   man 8. investor 9. bourgeois, financier,
   plutocrat
capital letter . . . 6. uncial 9. majuscule
capital punishment . . . 5. noose
   7. gallows, hanging 8. shooting,
   the chair 9. beheading, execution,
   fusillade 10. guillotine 12. decapitation
   13. electrocution
capitano . . . 3. don 4. capo 5. chief
   7. captain, headman
capitate . . . 7. globose 8. enlarged,
   headlike
Capitol (pert to) . . .
   Federal . . 10. Washington (DC)
   State . . 10. Statehouse
capitulate . . . 4. cede, fall 9. surrender
capitulation . . . 6. resumé, review, treaty
   7. recount, summary 9. agreement,
   reckoning, rehearsal, statement,
   summation, surrender 10. compendium
   11. enumeration, stipulation
   14. relinquishment
capon . . . 3. hen 4. cock, fowl 6. pullet,
   rabbit (castrated) 7. chicken, poulard,
   poultry, rooster
caporal . . . 4. boss 7. foreman, tobacco
   8. overseer
capote . . . 4. hood 5. cloak 6. bonnet,
   mantle, piquet 8. overcoat
capped . . . 7. crested, pileata, pileate
Capri . . .
   beverage . . 4. wine (white)
   color . . 4. blue 9. blue-green
   island site . . 11. Bay of Naples

ruins (famed) . . 7. palaces (Tiberius)
   8. grottoes 10. Blue Grotto
caprice . . . 3. fad, toy 4. kink, mood,
   whim 5. fancy, freak, humor, prank,
   quirk 6. vagary 7. whimsey (whimsy)
   8. crotchet, escapade, flimflam
capricious . . . 5. moody 6. fickle, fitful
   7. erratic, wayward 8. fanciful, freakish,
   humorous, notional, sporadic, unsteady
   9. arbitrary, crotchety, eccentric,
   fantastic, whimsical 10. inconstant
   12. inconsistent 13. temperamental
Capricorn . . . 4. goat 7. mansion (of
   Saturn) 10. zodiac sign 13. constellation
capriole . . . 4. leap 5. caper 6. cavort,
   curvet, gambol
capsicum . . . 4. herb 5. chili 6. pepper
capsize . . . 5. spill, upset 7. subvert, tip
   over 8. overturn 9. overthrow 10. turn
   turtle
capsule . . . 3. sac 4. pill 5. ascus, brief,
   theca, wafer 6. précis, sheath 7. enclose,
   epitome 8. abstract, envelope, pericarp,
   seedcase, synopsis 10. compendium
capsulize . . . 5. brief 7. abridge, outline
   8. abstract, condense 9. epitomize,
   summarize
captain . . . 4. skip 5. chief, ruler
   6. leader, master, patron, police
   7. headman, officer, skipper 8. overlord
   9. commander 10. shipmaster
Captain Kidd . . . 6. pirate
Captains Courageous (pert to) . . .
   author . . 7. Kipling
   setting . . 9. Grand Bank (Newfoundland)
   tale of . . 7. romance
caption . . . 5. title 6. legend, rubric
   7. capture, seizure 8. headline, subtitle
captious . . . 6. severe 7. carping, cynical,
   peevish 8. caviling, critical 9. bickering,
   paltering, quibbling 12. equivocatory,
   faultfinding 13. hypercritical
captivate . . . 4. lure, vamp 5. charm,
   snare 6. allure, enamor, ravish, seduce
   7. attract, becharm, beguile, bewitch,
   capture, delight, enchant 8. enthrall
   9. enrapture, fascinate, infatuate,
   transport
captive . . . 4. bond, serf 5. helot
   6. détenu, thrall, unfree, vassal
   7. hostage 8. conquest, enslaved,
   prisoner 10. subjugated
captivity . . . 6. duress 7. bondage,
   durance, serfdom, slavery 9. detention,
   servitude, thralldom 10. internment,
   subjection 11. confinement,
   impoundment 12. imprisonment
   13. incarceration
captor . . . 5. taker 7. catcher 8. capturer
capture . . . 3. beg, nab, net, win 4. gain,
   haul, take 5. catch, pinch, raven, snare
   6. arrest, collar 7. caption, seizure
   9. apprehend, detention
   12. apprehension
capuche (Eccl) . . . 4. cowl, hood
capuchin . . . 3. sai 5. Cebus 6. monkey,
   pigeon
caput . . . 3. cap, top 4. head 5. crest,
   crown 7. chapter, section 9. paragraph
car . . . 4. auto, cart, jeep, tram 5. coupe,
   motor, sedan, truck, wagon 6. hot rod,

jalopy, wheels (sl) 7. caboose, chariot, clunker (sl), compact, flivver, machine, Pullman, vehicle 8. carriage 9. dune buggy, hatchback 10. automobile, subcompact

carabao . . 5. mango 7. buffalo

carabinieri . . . 9. policeman 10. carabineer

caracal . . . 3. fur 4. lynx, pelt

caracara . . . 4. hawk 8. carancha

caracole . . . 5. caper (manège) 9. staircase

caract . . . 5. charm 6. symbol (magic)

carafe . . . 6. bottle

carafon . . . 8. decanter

carapace . . . 5. plate, shell (turtle) 6. chitin, lorica, shield 7. carapax

caravan . . . 3. van 5. wagon 6. cafila (camel) 8. cavalcade, motorcade 10. expedition, procession

caravansary . . . 3. inn 4. khan (chan) 5. hotel, serai 6. hostel, imaret, posada 8. hostelry 9. resthouse, roadhouse

carbine . . . 5. rifle 6. musket 7. escopet

carbohydrate . . . 5. sugar 6. starch 7. dextrin, glucose, lactose, maltose, sucrose 8. dextrose, glycogen, nutrient 9. cellulose 10. saccharide, saccharose

carbon . . . 4. coke, copy, fuel, lead, soot 7. diamond, residue 8. graphite

carbonate . . . 3. ore 5. trona 6. aerate, natron 9. carbonize 11. chemicalize

carbon dioxide . . . 3. gas 6. dry ice 7. seeding (cloud) 11. refrigerant

Carborundum . . . 5. emery 8. abrasive 14. silicon carbide

carcass . . . 4. body 5. bones, kreng (whale) 6. corpse 7. cadaver, remains 8. skeleton

carcer . . . 5. stall (Rom circus) 6. prison

card . . . 3. map, turn 4. comb, menu, post, rove 6. docket, domino, oddity, postal, record, ticket 7. calling, program 8. calendar, schedule 9. character 13. communication

card game . . . 3. gin, hoc, loo, pan 4. bank, faro, keno, skat 5. cinch, comet, monte, pitch, poker, rummy, stuss, tarot, whist 6. bridge, casino, écarté, hearts, piquet, rounce 7. auction, bezique, canasta, cassino, cayenne 8. baccarat, contract, cribbage, pinochle 9. solitaire 10. panguingui

card game term . . . 3. ace 4. meld, pass, pone, slam, trey, vole 5. joker, pedro, tarot 6. cathop, misère, tenace, tricon 7. declare 9. mistigris

cardinal . . . 3. red 4. bird, fish, main 5. chief 6. bishop, deacon, number, priest, ruling 8. crowning, dominant, foremost 9. paramount, principal 10. preeminent

cardinal (pert to) . .
astrology . . 5. nadir 6. zenith
astronomy . . 10. solstitial 11. equinoctial
biology . . 7. maximum, minimum, optimum
compass point . . 4. east, west 5. north, south
number . . 7. primary (one, two, three)
office . . 6. datary 7. dataria
virtues . . 7. justice 8. prudence 9. fortitude 10. temperance

virtues (Theol) . . 4. hope 5. faith 7. charity

cardinal's hat . . . 3. red 4. rank 6. office

care . . . 4. duty, fret, heed, reck, task, tend, wish 5. aegis, worry 6. desire, regard 7. anxiety, caution, cherish, concern, custody, keeping 9. attention, patronage 10. affliction, protection, solicitude 11. carefulness, heedfulness, supervision, thriftiness 12. jurisdiction 13. consideration

careen . . . 3. tip 4. cant, heel, keel, lean, list, tilt 5. slant, slope

career . . . 3. set 4. flow, flux, line, work 6. course, stream 7. calling, mission, passage, pursuit 8. business, practice, progress, vocation 10. occupation, profession

care for . . . 4. help, like, love, mind, reck, tend 5. fancy, guard, nurse, prize, watch 6. attend, dote on, foster, mother, relish, wait on 7. nurture 10. appreciate

carefree . . . 5. happy 6. jaunty 8. debonair 10. insouciant 12. lighthearted

careful . . . 4. wary 5. canny, chary, exact 7. anxious, guarded, heedful, mindful, prudent, thrifty 8. cautious, discreet, gingerly, vigilant 9. advertent, attentive 10. meticulous, scrupulous, solicitous, thoughtful 11. circumspect, considerate, painstaking, punctilious

careless . . . 3. lax 5. loose 6. rakish, remiss, sloppy 8. heedless, mindless, reckless, slipshod, slovenly 9. impulsive, negligent, unheeding, unmindful 10. nonchalant, regardless, unthinking 11. inadvertent, thoughtless, unconcerned 13. inconsiderate

carelessness . . . 8. bungling, disorder 9. disregard, unconcern 10. blundering, negligence 11. nonchalance 12. heedlessness, indifference, recklessness 13. impulsiveness 15. inconsideration, thoughtlessness

caress . . . 3. pat, pet 4. bill, kiss 5. touch 6. coddle, cosset, dandle, fondle, pamper, stroke 10. endearment

caressing . . . 7. hugging, kissing 8. fondling 9. endearing

cargo . . . 4. load 5. goods 6. burden, charge, lading 7. carload, freight 8. boatload, shipload 9. truckload

cargo (pert to) . . .
afloat . . 7. flotsam
cast overboard . . 6. jetsam
loader, unloader . . 9. stevedore

Carib . . . 6. Indian

caribou . . . 4. deer 8. reindeer

caricature . . . 5. comic 6. overdo, parody 7. cartoon, lampoon, picture 8. satirize, travesty 9. burlesque 10. caricatura, distortion 12. exaggeration

caricaturist . . . 6. artist 8. humorist, parodist 10. burlesquer

caries . . . 5. decay (Dent) 10. ulceration

carillon . . . 4. lyra 5. bells (fixed) 6. chimes 12. glockenspiel

cark . . . 3. vex 4. care, heed, load 5. pains, worry 6. burden, charge, harass 7. trouble 8. distress

carl, carlot . . . 4. boor 5. churl 6. rustic
7. peasant, villein 8. bondsman
10. husbandman, pinchpenny
Carmelite . . . 3. nun 4. monk 5. friar
8. White Nun 10. White Friar
carmen . . . 4. poem, song 11. incantation
Carmen . . . 5. gypsy, opera (1875)
7. heroine, romance
carmine . . . 3. red 5. color, stain
7. crimson, scarlet
carnage . . . 8. butchery, massacre
9. bloodshed, slaughter 10. decimation
carnal . . . 4. lewd 6. bodily, fleshy
7. earthly, mundane, sensual, worldly
9. corporeal 11. unspiritual
12. bloodthirsty
carnation . . . 3. red 4. pink, self 7. bizarre,
picotee 8. Dianthus
carnelian . . . 4. sard 9. copper red
10. chalcedony
carnival . . . 4. fair, show 6. circus
7. revelry 8. feasting, festival
9. amusement, Mardi Gras
11. merrymaking 12. masquerading
carnivore . . . 3. cat, dog 4. bear, lion,
puma, seal 5. civet, coati, genet, hyena,
otter, panda, ratel, sable, tiger, ursus
6. badger, mammal, marten, weasel
7. meerkat, raccoon 8. mongoose
9. ichneumon 10. cacomistle
carnivorous . . . 10. meat-eating,
predaceous 11. omophageous
carol . . . 3. lay 4. lied, lilt, noel, sing,
song 5. dance (anc) 6. ballad, warble
7. rejoice
Caroline Islands (coral) . . . 3. Yap
5. Parao 6. Ponape
carom . . . 4. bump 6. bounce, cannon,
strike 8. ricochet
carousal . . . 4. lark, orgy, romp 5. binge,
feast, fling, revel, spree 6. frolic
7. banquet, carouse, revelry, wassail
carouse . . . 4. birl 5. bouse, drink, spree,
toast 9. dissipate
carpet . . . 3. mat, rug 4. Agra, Kali,
Kuba 5. Herat (Herati), namda,
tapis 6. nammad, Wilton 7. drugget
8. Brussels, flooring, moquette
9. Axminster, broadloom
11. Baluchistan
carpetbagger . . . 8. swindler 10. politician
carriage . . . 3. air 4. mien, pose 7. bearing,
posture 8. attitude, demeanor, presence
10. deportment
carriage (pert to) . . .
English . . 6. waggon 7. growler
8. dormeuse, stanhope
French . . 6. fiacre 7. caliche, voiture
general . . 3. bus, cab, car, gig, rig,
van 4. baby, hack, pram, shay, trap
5. buggy, coach, wagon 6. calssh,
chaise, cision, dennet, go-cart, hansom,
landau, surrey, tandem 7. cariole,
chariot, omnibus, phaeton, tallyho,
vehicle 8. carryall, clarence, dearborn,
rockaway, victoria 9. kittereen, landaulet
10. conveyance, shandrydan
12. perambulator
history . . 7. tumbrel, vis-à-vis, whiskey
8. curricle
Indian . . 4. okka 5. tonga 6. gharry

7. hackery
Italian . . 7. vettura
one-horse . . 3. gig 4. shay 5. sulky
Orient . . 4. sado 10. jinrikisha
Philippines . . 9. carromata
Russia . . 5. araba 6. troika 7. droshky
9. tarantass
carried . . . 5. borne, giddy, toted
6. carted, lugged 8. conveyed, ravished
11. transported
carrier . . . 3. boy 4. mail, mule, rail,
ship, wave 5. crate 6. bearer,
coolie, pigeon, porter, redcap, runner,
vessel 7. courier, drayman, express
8. cargador, conveyor, teamster
9. messenger, stevedore
carrier (pert to) . . .
disease . . 3. fly, rat 7. typhoid
8. mosquito
Indian . . 5. Tinne (Brit)
staff . . 5. macer
carrion . . . 4. vile 6. corpse, rotten
7. carcass, corrupt 9. loathsome
carrion (pert to) . . .
bug . . 6. beetle
buzzard . . 4. hawk 7. vulture 8. caracara
flower . . 5. morel
fungus . . 9. stinkhorn
carrot . . . 5. drias (deadly) 6. Daucus (Old
World) 9. Ammiaceae 10. nivernaise
(glazed), umbellifer
carrousel . . . 9. whirligig 10. roundabout,
tournament 12. merry-go-round
carry . . . 3. lug 4. bear, cart, hold, take,
tote, wart 5. ferry 6. convey 7. conduct,
publish 8. transfer, transmit 9. transport
carry away, off . . . 3. win 6. abduct,
eloign, enamor, remove 7. succeed
9. fascinate 10. accomplish
carry on . . . 4. rage, wage 6. endure,
frolic, manage 7. conduct, operate
8. continue 9. misbehave, persevere
carry out, through . . . 2. do 5. apply
6. ravish 7. execute, perform, sustain
8. complete, continue, transact
10. accomplish
cart . . . 4. dray, wain 5. carry, sulky,
wagon 6. convey, reckla, telega
7. morfrey (morphrey), tumbrel (anc),
vehicle (2-wheeled)
carta, Charta . . . 4. deed 5. Magna (Eng)
7. charter 9. parchment
cartage . . . 7. drayage, portage 8. carriage,
teamster, truckage 10. expressage
14. transportation
carte . . . 3. map 4. card, list, menu
5. chart 7. diagram 10. bill of fare
cartel . . . 4. bloc (Polit), defy, pact,
pool 5. paper, truce, trust 6. letter
7. compact, entente 8. covenant
9. agreement, challenge, syndicate
10. convention 11. arrangement
Carthage . . . see also *Carthaginian*
capital . . 13. Vandal Kingdom
destroyer . . 6. Romans
queen . . 4. Dido
rebuilt by . . 8. Augustus
Carthaginian (pert to) . . .
apple . . 11. pomegranate
foe . . 4. Cato
general . . 6. Xerxes 8. Hannibal

god.. 6. Moloch 8. Melkarth
language.. 5. Punic
Lion.. 8. Hannibal
magistrate.. 7. suffete
name (later).. 15. Justinianopolis
wars (three).. 5. Punic
Carthusian Order (pert to) ...
founder.. 7. St Bruno
monastery.. 7. Certosa (It, 1396)
site.. 8. Grenoble (Fr)
cartilage ... 4. bone (ossified) 6. tissue
7. gristle
cartload ... 6. fother
cartograph ... 3. map 4. plat 5. chart
cartoon ... 6. design, sketch 7. pattern,
picture 10. caricature
cartoonist ... 4. Arno, Capp, Ding, Nast
6. Disney
cartouche ... 5. shell 6. corbel, design,
shield (Her), tablet 7. console
9. cartridge 10. cantilever (Arch)
cartwheel ... 4. coin 6. dollar 8. somerset
10. handspring, somersault
carve ... 3. cut, hew 4. form, make
5. chase, grave, sever, shape 6. chisel,
cleave, furrow, incise 7. engrave,
fashion 9. apportion, fabricate,
sculpture
carving ... 5. cameo 6. diaglyph, intaglio
9. anaglyphy, embossing, sculpture
11. anaglyptics
caryatid ... 6. column, figure (fem)
8. pilaster 11. priestesses (temple)
casa ... 5. adobe, cabin, house 8. building
cascade ... 4. fall, linn 5. Falls, Sault
7. Niagara 8. cataract 9. waterfall
case ... 3. box 4. etui, file 5. cover,
crate, crush (sl), event, folio 6. carton,
coffer, pillow, sheath, victim 7. attaché,
cabinet, example, holster, lawsuit
8. argument, covering, cupboard,
instance 9. condition, portfolio
10. receptacle 12. circumstance
case (in any) ... 3. yet 4. even
6. anyhow, anyway 7. anywise,
however 8. possibly, provided
10. regardless 15. notwithstanding
case (pert to) ...
arrow.. 6. quiver
book.. 5. forel
bottle (liquor).. 8. cellaret
cigar.. 7. humidor
conscience (Sci).. 9. casuistry
grammar.. 6. dative 8. ablative, genitive,
vocative 10. nominative
history (disease).. 6. record 9. anamnesis
image (Bib).. 5. ephod
jewel, relics.. 3. tye 4. apse
spore.. 5. ascus
surgeon's.. 7. trousse
cash ... 4. coin, dust (gold) 5. darby,
funds, money 6. silver, specie 7. capital,
coinage, mintage 8. currency
9. spondulix
cashmere ... 4. goat, wool 5. shawl
6. fabric
casino ... 6. tavern 7. cabaret, cassino
(game) 8. ballroom, gambling
9. roadhouse 11. summerhouse
cask ... 3. tun 4. butt, case, drum, pipe
5. terce 6. bareca, barrel, casket, firkin,

tierce 8. puncheon 9. kilderkin
cask (pert to) ...
amt when not filled.. 6. ullage
bulge.. 5. bilge
oil.. 4. rier
part.. 3. lag 4. hoop 5. stave
rim.. 5. chime (chimb)
support.. 8. stillage
casket ... 3. box, pyx, tye (jewel)
4. cist, kist, tomb 5. chest 8. cassette
11. sarcophagus
casserole ... 4. dish, mold 5. brown
(color) 6. vessel 8. saucepan
cassine ... 4. game (card)
cast ... 3. hue 4. form, hurl, kind,
look, mold, role, shed, tone, toss,
type 5. eject, fling, heave, model,
pitch, sling, throw 6. glance, matrix,
squint, troupe 7. pattern 8. template
9. facsimile 10. impression, strabismus
16. dramatis personae
cast (pert to) ...
aside.. 4. jilt, junk, shed 5. scrap 6. reject
7. discard
away.. 5. eject, wreck 6. unmoor
9. shipwreck
blame.. 6. accuse 7. censure 8. reproach
9. reprehend
off.. 4. doff, knit, molt, shed 5. untie
6. unmoor 7. discard 9. eliminate
castaway ... 6. pariah 7. outcast
8. derelict 9. reprobate
caste ... 4. race, rank 5. breed, class,
stock 6. status 7. lineage, society
8. standing
caste (Ind) ... 3. Dom, Meo 4. Ahir, Jati,
Koli, Magi, Mali, Pasi, Teli 5. Gaddi,
Sudra, Varna 6. banian, pariah, Vaisya
7. Brahman 9. Kshatriya
caster, castor ... 4. vial 5. cruet, horse
(old), wheel 6. roller, vessel (condiment)
castigate ... 5. emend 6. punish, revise,
strafe 7. chasten, correct, reprove
8. chastise, penalize 9. criticize
10. discipline
Castile ... 4. soap 7. kingdom
Castilian ... 7. Iberian, Spanish
castle ... 4. fort, keep, rook (chess)
5. house, tower, villa 6. donjon
7. chateau, citadel 8. fortress
10. stronghold 13. fortification
Castor (pert to) ...
brother (twin).. 6. Pollux
constellation.. 6. Gemini
mother.. 4. Leda
stars.. 6. Castor, Pollux
castrate ... 4. geld, spay 5. alter, prune
10. emasculate
castrated (pert to) ...
bull.. 5. steer
cat.. 3. gib
horse.. 7. gelding
man.. 6. eunoch
rooster.. 5. capon
casual ... 5. stray 6. chance, random
9. offhanded 10. contingent, fortuitous,
incidental, occasional, unforeseen
11. indifferent 14. unpremeditated
casual observation ... 6. remark
casualty ... 6. chance, hazard, injury,
mishap 7. payment, tragedy 8. accident,

calamity, disaster, fatality 9. mischance
10. misfortune 11. contingency,
contretemps 12. misadventure

casus (pert to) . . .
act of God . . **14.** casus fortuitus
common law . . **12.** casus omissus
conscience . . **17.** casus conscientiae
Latin . . **4.** case 5. event 8. occasion
treaty . . **13.** casus foederis
war . . **10.** casus belli

cat . . . **3.** gib 4. balu, eyra, lynx, pard,
puma 5. alley, civet, Felid, Felis,
genet, hyena, manul, ounce, tabby,
tiger 6. caffre, cougar, feline, jaguar,
margay, ocelot, pajero, rasset, serval
7. cheetah, dasyure, leopard, panther,
wildcat 9. catamount, grimalkin

cat (pert to) . . .
cartoon . . **5.** Felix 8. Krazy Kat
fear of . . **12.** ailurophobia
fictional . . **8.** Cheshire 9. Mehitabel
fish . . **4.** pout, raad 6. hassar, tandan
7. eelpout
game . . **6.** tipcat
gut . . **5.** tharm 6. string (violin)
slang . . **6.** hepcat
term . . **3.** tom 5. kitty, pussy, tabby
6. feline, kitten, mouser 9. grimalkin
wild . . **4.** lion, lynx, puma 5. tiger
6. bobcat, cougar, jaguar, ocelot, tiglon
7. cheetah, leopard, panther, wildcat

cat (breed) . . . **3.** Rex 4. Manx 5. korat
6. Angora, Birman, Bombay 7. Burmese,
Maltese, Persian, Siamese, Turkish
(Van) 8. Egyptian (Mau) 9. shorthair
10. Abyssinian

cataclysm . . . **4.** ruin 6. deluge 7. debacle
8. calamity, disaster, The Flood,
upheaval 10. convulsion, inundation,
revolution 11. catastrophe

catacomb . . . **4.** tomb 5. crypt, vault
6. grotto, locule 8. cemetery
(underground) 9. Appian Way

catalepsy . . . **6.** trance 8. hypnosis
9. cataplexy 10. thanatosis

catalogue . . . **4.** book, file, list 5. index,
tally 6. codify, digest, record
8. calendar, classify, pamphlet, register,
schedule, tabulate 11. enumeration

catamaran . . . **4.** boat, raft 5. balsa, float
6. vessel 7. jangada

catamount . . . **3.** cat 6. cougar
12. catamountain

catapult . . . **4.** hurl 5. shoot, sling
6. engine, onager 7. robinet 8. arbalest,
ballista, scorpion 9. slingshot

cataract . . . **4.** fall, linn 5. Falls, flood,
sault (soo) 6. deluge 7. cascade,
disease, Niagara, opacity (eye), torrent
8. downpour, Victoria 9. cachoeira,
waterfall

cataria . . . **6.** catnip

catasta . . . **5.** stage (slave traffic) 6. stocks
8. scaffold

catastrophe . . . **4.** doom, ruin 6. finale,
mishap, payoff 7. tragedy 8. calamity,
disaster, dénouement 11. termination

catastrophic . . . **4.** dire 5. black 7. ruinous
10. calamitous, deplorable, disastrous

catawba . . . **4.** wine 5. color (red), grape

6. Indian

catch . . . **3.** get, nab 4. draw, hear, hold,
hook, take, trap 5. fault, ketch, prize,
reach, rondo, seize, snare, trick, troll
6. detent (clock), engage, entrap, ignite
7. attract, capture, seizure 8. overtake
9. intercept

catch (pert to) . . .
a likeness . . **4.** draw 6. depict 7. portray
a ride . . **4.** hook 5. hitch, thumb
9. hitchhike
sight of . . **3.** see 4. espy 6. behold,
descry 7. discern, glimpse

catchword . . . **3.** cry, cue 6. byword,
phrase, slogan 7. formula 10. shibboleth

cate . . . **4.** food 6. viands 8. dainties
10. delicacies, provisions (bought)

catechism . . . **5.** guide 6. belief, manual
9. questions (set of) 11. instruction
(oral)

catechumen . . . **5.** chela, pupil 6. layman,
novice 7. convert 8. disciple, neophyte

categoric, categorical . . . **6.** direct
7. crucial, logical 8. absolute, explicit,
positive 9. arbitrary, pragmatic
10. convincing 11. dictatorial,
unequivocal, unqualified

category . . . **4.** head 5. class, genre,
genus, group, order, state 6. branch,
family, specie 7. bracket, species
8. division 12. denomination
14. classification

catena . . . **5.** chain 6. series 8. sequence
10. continuity

catenary . . . **5.** curve (Math) 9. chainlike

cater, cater to . . . **4.** feed 5. favor, humor,
serve, toady 6. oblige, pander, please,
purvey 7. indulge, procure, provide,
satisfy 10. minister to 11. diagonalize
13. cater-cornered

caterpillar . . . **4.** grub, weri 5. aweto,
eruca, larva 7. tractor

caterwaul . . . **3.** woo (derog) 4. meow,
wail 5. court, miaow 7. screech

cathedral . . . **3.** dom 4. fane (anc)
5. duomo 6. church 8. official 10. ex
cathedra 13. authoritative

Cathedral . . .
England . . **6.** Durham 9. Salisbury
10. Canterbury
France . . **5.** Reims (Rheims) 6. Amiens
8. Chartres 9. Notre Dame
Istanbul (Constantinople) . . **8.** St Sophia
Italy . . **7.** Lateran, St Mark's 8. St Peter's
Scotland . . **7.** St Giles

cathedral (pert to) . . .
chair (Bishop's) . . **8.** cathedra
chapter member . . **10.** capitulary
part . . **4.** apse, nave 5. choir 6. chapel
7. chancel, narthex 8. sacristy, transept
10. baptistery (baptistry)
style . . **6.** Gothic

catholic . . . **4.** wide 5. broad 6. church,
global 7. general, liberal 8. orthodox,
pandemic 9. Christian, universal
10. ecumenical 12. cosmopolitan

Catholic Church (Roman) . . .
Bible books . . **16.** deuterocanonical
calendar . . **4.** ordo
clergy . . **4.** monk 5. friar 6. bishop,
Jesuit, priest 8. cardinal 9. monsignor

head .. 4. pope 7. pontiff
papal residence, state .. 7. Vatican
rite .. 4. Mass 7. baptism, penance
  9. Communion, Eucharist, matrimony,
  sacrament 10. Holy Orders
  12. confirmation
seat of authority .. 7. Holy See
catkin ... 5. ament, spike 7. cattail
catlike ... 5. catty 6. feline 8. stealthy
  9. noiseless
catling ... 3. cat (little) 6. kitten, string
  (violin)
Cato (pert to) ...
author of .. 13. De Agri Cultura
famed as .. 7. General 9. statesman
  10. ambassador (to Carthage)
nickname .. 8. The Elder 11. Cato of
  Utica
Catoism ... 9. austerity, harshness
cats ... 8. Kilkenny
cat's cradle ... 3. hei 4. game 7. ribwort
cat's-paw ... 4. dupe, gull, loof, pawn,
  tool 5. cully, hitch (knot) 6. breeze
  (Naut), puppet, stooge 10. instrument
cattail ... 4. musk, reed, tule 5. ament,
  raupo, teree 6. catkin, totora 7. matreed
  9. Typhaceae
cattle ... 3. Bos 4. cows, kine, neat,
  oxen, stot, yaks 5. asses, goats, mules,
  sheep, stock, swine 6. bovine, camels,
  horses, llamas, niatas, rabble , Taurus
  7. banteng, chattel 8. bullocks, property
  9. livestock
cattle (breed) ... 4. Zebu 5. Angus,
  Devon, Kerry, Niata, Welsh 6. Brahma,
  Durham, Jersey, Sussex 7. Dishley
  8. Guernsey, Hereford, Holstein,
  Longhorn 9. Charolais, Leicester,
  Shorthorn 14. Santa Gertrudis
cattle (pert to) ...
collection .. 4. herd 5. drove
disease .. 7. murrain 10. rinderpest
driver .. 6. drover
food .. 6. fodder, forage, silage
herder .. 6. cowboy, drover
hybrid .. 4. Zobo 7. cattalo 9. cattleyak
motherless .. 6. dogies
pen .. 4. crew 5. barth, reeve
shed .. 6. hemmel
stealer .. 7. abactor, abigeus, rustler
unbranded .. 9. mavericks
catty ... 6. feline, weight 7. catlike, cattish
  8. spiteful, stealthy 11. treacherous
cauboge ... 4. boor 7. bumpkin
Caucasian ... 4. race, Slav, Svan,
  Turk 5. gypsy, Latin, Norse, Osset,
  Pshav, white 6. Hebrew, Semite,
  Teuton, Viking 8. Armenian, Bohemian,
  Georgian, White Man 10. Anglo-Saxon
  11. Xanthochroi
Caucasian (pert to) ...
blond .. 6. Teuton 8. Estonian
  11. Xanthochroi
brunette .. 7. Iberian 8. Armenian
  11. Melanochroi
Chinese .. 4. Lolo, Nosu
dialect .. 4. Andi, Avar, Svan
European .. 8. Japhetic
goat (wild) .. 3. tur
liquor .. 5. kefir
Moslem .. 3. Laz (Laże, Lazi) 7. Sunnite

mountain .. 8. Caucasus
peak .. 6. Elbrus (Elbruz), Kazbek
cauchemar ... 9. nightmare
caucus ... 7. meeting (Polit), primary
  8. assembly
cauda ... 4. scut, tail 9. appendage
caudata ... 5. newts 8. Amphibia
  11. salamanders
caught ... see also *catch* 5. treed
  7. latched 8. cornered
caught (pert to) ...
napping .. 7. unready 8. unprimed
  10. unprepared
sight of .. 3. saw 6. espied 8. descried
up in .. 4. tied 7. engaged, tangled
  8. absorbed, intent on, involved
  10. implicated
caul ... 3. net 6. basket 7. netting,
  network, omentum 8. membrane
cause ... 5. aetio (comb form), agent,
  basis, drive, greed 6. create, factor,
  ground, induce, motive, reason,
  source 7. crusade, produce, provoke
  8. campaign, etiology, movement,
  occasion 9. originate 10. mainspring
  13. justification
cause (pert to) ...
approach .. 7. attract
be done .. 4. writ 11. fieri facias
bring about .. 6. effect
buy and sell .. 7. whipsaw
coagulate .. 4. curd 6. curdle 7. congeal,
  thicken
contract unevenly .. 6. pucker
face East .. 6. orient
harm .. 4. bane
irritate .. 6. rankle
raise in relief .. 6. emboss
remember .. 6. remind
roll .. 7. trundle
speed up .. 10. accelerate
take root .. 8. radicate
causerie ... 4. chat, talk 6. parley 7. article
  8. converse, treatise 9. paragraph
  10. discussion 12. conversation
causes, science of ... 8. etiology
causeuse ... 4. sofa 8. tête-à-tête
causeway ... 4. dike 7. highway
  10. embankment
causing ...
destiny .. 5. fatal
emotion .. 7. emotive
forgetfulness .. 8. nepenthe
laughter .. 8. risorial
motion .. 6. motile
caustic ... 4. acid, tart 5. acrid, curve
  (optic), sharp 6. biting, bitter, severe
  7. acerbic, burning, cutting, erodent,
  mordant, pungent, pyrotic 8. snappish,
  stinging, virulent 9. corrosive, satirical,
  vitriolic 10. astringent, escharotic
  11. acrimonious, penetrating
caustic agent ... 3. lye 4. alum, lime
  7. erodent 9. quicklime
cautel ... 5. trick 7. caution 8. prudence
  9. direction (Eccl) 10. precaution
cauterize ... 4. burn, char, sear 5. brand,
  singe 7. torrefy
cautery ... 7. burning, searing 8. inustion
  10. instrument 13. cauterization
caution ... 4. card (coll), care, heed, warn

5. aviso 6. advice, caveat, notice, oddity
7. anxiety, counsel, precept, proviso,
warning 8. forecast, prudence, wariness
9. chariness, vigilance 10. admonition,
providence, solicitude 11. exhortation,
forethought, mindfulness
12. cautiousness, notification,
watchfulness 14. circumspection

cautious . . . 4. wary 5. canny, chary
6. Fabian 7. careful, guarded, heedful,
mindful, prudent 11. circumspect

cautiously . . . 6. cagily, warily 7. cannily,
charily 8. gingerly 9. carefully,
guardedly, heedfully, mindfully, prud-
ently 10. discreetly 13. circumspectly

cavalcade . . . 4. raid, ride 5. march
6. parade, review 7. caravan, pageant
9. motorcade 10. procession

cavalier . . . 3. gay 4. coin (Fr), curt
5. brave, frank, lover, rider 6. escort,
knight, squire 7. admirer, brusque,
esquire, gallant, haughty, soldier
8. horseman, Royalist 9. caballero,
cavaliere, chevalier, Roundhead
10. disdainful, equestrian 12. high-
spirited, supercilious

cavalry . . . 4. army 6. horses, yellow
(color) 8. horsemen 10. knighthood

cavalry (pert to) . . .
horse . . 6. lancer
man . . 5. spahy, uhlan 6. Hussar, lancer
7. dragoon, trooper
unit . . 5. troop
weapon . . 5. lance, saber 9. demilance

cave . . . 3. den, mew 4. abri, cove,
grot, hole, lair 5. antre, cover, lodge
(beaver), speos 6. antrum, cavern,
cellar, covert, dugout, grotto, subway,
tunnel 7. chamber, shelter, spelunk
10. subterrane

cave (pert to) . . .
fish . . 9. blindfish
man . . 9. Paleolithic
nature of . . 9. speluncar
study of . . 10. speleology

cave canem . . . 11. Beware of Dog
cave dweller . . . 10. troglodyte
Cave of Adulam . . . 9. Seceeders (1866)
caviar, caviare . . . 3. roe 5. garum
6. relish 8. delicacy, fish eggs

cavil . . . 4. cark, carp, marl, quip 5. dodge,
evade, parry, shift 6. bicker, boggle,
haggle, palter 7. quibble, shuffle
9. criticize, pussyfoot 10. equivocate

caviler . . . 5. momus 6. critic, hedger
8. frondeur, quibbler 10. criticizer
11. equivocator, faultfinder

cavity . . . 3. dip, pit, sac, vug (voog)
4. aula, bore (gun), cava, hole, sink,
well 5. abyss, antra, atria, bursa, chasm,
fossa, fosse, geode, lumen, shaft,
sinus 6. antrum, areole, atrium, caries,
coelom, crater, hollow 7. cochlea,
loculus 10. depression 11. compartment

cavort . . . 4. dido, romp, skip 5. antic,
caper, cut up, frisk, prank 6. curvet,
gambol, prance 7. flounce, gambade,
gamboid

cavy . . . 3. pig 4. paca 5. stray 6. agouti,
rodent 8. capybara (capibara) 9. guinea
pig

caw . . . 3. cry 5. croak, quark, quawk
11. exclamation

cay . . . 3. kay 5. islet

cease . . . 3. end 4. quit, rest (law), stop
5. avast, pause, stint 6. desist, perish
7. abandon, fade out, refrain 8. intermit,
leave off, shutdown 9. disappear,
pretermit 11. discontinue

ceaseless . . . 7. endless, nonstop
8. constant, unbroken, unending
9. continued, incessant, perennial,
perpetual, unceasing 10. continuous
12. interminable 13. round the clock,
uninterrupted

ceaselessness . . . 9. constancy
10. continuity, incessancy, perpetuity
11. endlessness 14. successiveness

cease to be . . . 3. die 6. expire, perish
8. dissolve 9. disappear

cease to please . . . 4. pall

Cebus . . . 3. sai 6. monkey 8. capuchin

cecils . . . 10. croquettes

cecity . . . 9. blindness

Cecrops (pert to) . . .
daughter . . 5. Herse 8. Aglauros
founder of (tradition) . . 6. Athens
king of . . 6. Attica
symbol . . 7. half man 10. half dragon

cedar (pert to) . . .
bird . . 7. waxwing
class . . 7. conifer
fruit . . 6. cedron
genus . . 5. Thuja, Toona 6. Cedrus
9. Juniperus
green . . 5. cedre
moss . . 8. hornwort
type . . 5. savin 6. deodar, sabine
7. incense, juniper, Lebanon (Bib),
Spanish 10. arborvitae
11. cryptomeria

cede . . . 5. grant, waive, yield 6. assign,
confer 7. abandon 8. renounce
9. surrender 10. capitulate, relinquish

cedula . . . 3. tax 6. permit 8. schedule,
security (Finan) 10. obligation
11. certificate

ceil . . . 4. line 5. cover 7. overlay
8. wainscot

ceiling . . . 4. acme, roof 5. astel, limit,
price, trave 6. apogee, lining, screen,
utmost 7. curtain, lacunar, maximum,
plafond 8. covering 9. lacunaria
10. planchment, visibility
12. consummation

celebrant . . . 6. priest (Eucharist)
9. worshiper (worshipper)
11. communicant

celebrate . . . 4. keep, laud, sing 5. extol,
honor, revel 6. herald, praise 7. glorify,
maffick, observe, roister 8. emblazon,
proclaim 9. solemnize
11. commemorate, memorialize

celebrated . . . 5. famed, noted 6. famous
7. feasted, honored, popular 8. far-
famed, observed, renowned
9. distingué, well-known 11. illustrious
13. distinguished

celebration . . . 4. bout, fete, rite 5. fling,
revel, spree 6. bender 7. fanfare, jubilee
8. ceremony, function 9. epinicion,
festivity, rejoicing 10. observance

13. commemoration

celebrity . . . 3. VIP 4. fame 5. éclat, glory 6. notary 7. notable 8. luminary, somebody 10. famousness, popularity 11. recognition

celerity . . . 5. haste, speed 8. dispatch, rapidity, velocity 9. swiftness 10. speediness

celery . . . 4. ache 8. smallage (wild) 9. Ammiacaea

celestial . . . 6. astral, divine, uranic 7. angelic, sky blue 8. ethereal, heavenly 12. paradisaical

Celestial (pert to) . . .
being . . 5. angel 6. cherub, seraph
body . . 4. star 5. comet 6. nebula
city . . 6. heaven, utopia 9. Jerusalem
empire . . 7. Chinese, Tien Chu
equator . . 8. meridian
mind elevation . . 7. anagoge
teacher . . 6. Taoist

celibate . . . 4. monk 6. single 8. bachelor, monastic, Platonic, spinster 9. abstinent, continent, unmarried

cell . . . 3. egg, kil 4. cyst, germ, ovum 5. cnida, crypt 6. cytode, prison 7. alveola, cellule, dungeon 11. compartment

cell (pert to) . . .
animal . . 6. amoeba (ameba) 7. rotifer 8. protozoa
biology . . 7. energid, meiosis, mitosis, nucleus, spireme
cell-like . . 9. celliform
division . . 5. linin 7. spireme 8. amitosis
eating . . 9. cytophagy
Egyptian (tomb) . . 6. serdab
honeycomb . . 8. alveolus
Irish . . 3. kil (kill)
locomotive . . 5. sperm, zooid
Roman . . 4. alla, naos
study . . 8. cytology
substance . . 5. linin
walls . . 9. cellulose

cellaret . . . 4. case 8. tantalus 9. sideboard

Celt . . . 4. Erse, Gael, Manx, Scot 5. Welsh 6. Breton 7. Cornish

Celtic (pert to) . . .
abbot . . 5. coarb
bard . . 6. Ossian
cattle . . 2. ox
church . . 9. Christian
deity . . 7. Taranis
foot soldier . . 4. kern
horse . . 4. pony (Shetland)
island . . 4. Manx
king . . 4. Bran
language . . 4. Erse
minstrel . . 4. bard
Mother of Gods . . 3. Ana (Anu)
mountain . . 3. ben
Neptune . . 3. Ler
nickname . . 10. Turtleback
Order . . 5. Druid
people . . 5. Gauls, Irish, Scots, Welsh 7. Bretons, Britons
perfume . . 4. nard 9. spikenard
sun god . . 3. Lug (Lugh)

cembalo . . . 8. dulcimer 11. harpsichord 12. clavicembalo

cement . . . 4. bind, fuse, glue, join,

paar, pave 5. putty, stick, unite 6. cohere, fasten, mastic, mortar, solder 8. adhesive, concrete, pavement, solidify

cemetery . . . 6. litten 7. Calvary 8. boneyard, catacomb, Golgotha, lich gate (entrance), mortuary 9. graveyard, mausoleum 10. churchyard, necropolis 11. polyandrium 12. potter's field

cenobite . . . 4. Monk 5. Order (anc) 6. Essene 7. recluse

cenotaph . . . 4. tomb (empty) 7. memento 8. memorial, monument

censer bearer . . . 7. acolyte 8. altar boy, thurifer

censor . . . 5. judge 6. critic 7. monitor 8. censurer, reviewer, superego 11. faultfinder

censure . . . 4. flay 5. blame, chide, slate, targe 6. accuse 7. chasten, condemn, impeach, inveigh, reprove, slating 8. reproach 9. damnation, expurgate, reprimand 11. reprobation 12. condemnation, denunciation, reprehension

cent . . . 4. coin, game (old) 5. penny 6. copper, trifle 7. hundred, red cent

centaur (Myth) . . . 4. race (Thessaly) 6. Nessus 8. Lapithae, man-horse (half man) 9. bucentaur, Centaurus (Astron)

centennial . . . 4. game (dice) 9. hundredth, red-yellow 11. anniversary

Centennial State . . . 8. Colorado

center . . . 3. cor, hub 4. base, core, nave 5. axial, focus, heart, midst 6. kernel, marrow, middle 7. midmost, nucleus, pivotal, seaport 8. emporium

center (pert to) . . .
away from . . 6. distal
bull's-eye . . 5. clout 6. target
line . . 6. axiate, cesura

center of . . .
attention . . 8. cynosure
earth . . 9. epicenter
gravity . . 6. kernel 7. centrum
nervous system . . 5. brain
sail . . 4. bunt
target . . 3. eye 8. bull's-eye

centerpiece . . . 4. bowl 7. epergne

centipede . . . 5. rope (Naut) 6. earwig, insect 8. chilipod, myriapod

central . . . 3. mid 4. arch, main 5. axial, basic, chief, focal, prime 6. master, middle 7. capital, centric, leading, midmost, pivotal, primary 8. cardinal, dominant, foremost 9. principal 11. equidistant

Central America . . .
bird . . 7. jacamar 8. puffbird
boat . . 6. cayuco, pitpan
country . . 6. Panama 8. Honduras 9. Costa Rica, Guatemala, Nicaragua 10. El Salvador
Indian . . 4. Maya 5. Carib
monkey . . 4. mono
rodent . . 4. paca
snake . . 10. bushmaster
tree . . 3. ebo, ule 5. amate 9. sapodilla

Central Asia (pert to) . . .
gazelle . . 3. ahu

wild horse .. 6. tarpan
wind storm .. 5. buran
Central State ... 6. Kansas
centuries (ten) .. 7. chiliad
century ... 3. Age 4. aeon (eon) 7. centred (anc), hundred 8. eternity 9. centenary 10. centennial
century plant ... 4. aloe 5. agave 6. maguey
ceorl (Eng Hist) ... 5. churl, thane 7. freeman, villein
cepa ... 5. onion
cephalon ... 4. head (Zool)
cephalopod ... 3. ink (secretion) 5. sepia 6. cuttle 7. octopus 10. cuttlefish
ceramics ... 4. tile 5. china, delft, spode 6. mosaic 7. pottery, Satsuma 8. crockery, majolica, Wedgwood 9. porcelain
ceramics (pert to) ... 4. clay, kiln, laun 5. adobe, stove, wheel 6. sleeve (silk) 7. furnace 8. ceramist 10. ceramicist 12. ceramography
ceratoid ... 5. horny 8. hornlike 10. horn-shaped
cere ... 3. wax 4. wrap (dead body) 6. anoint 12. protuberance (bird's)
cereal ... 4. bran, mush, rice 5. grits, gruel, maize, wheat 6. farina, hominy 7. granola, oatmeal 8. porridge 10. corn flakes
cereal grass ... 3. oat, rye 4. ragi 5. grain, maize, wheat 6. barley, millet, raggee
cereal spike ... 3. ear
cerebellum ... 5. brain (part)
cerebral (pert to) ... 4. lobe 5. brain 6. speech 8. arteries, peduncle 9. consonant (Phonet) 11. crus cerebri, hemispheres
cerebrum ... 5. brain 10. encephalon
cere cloth ... 7. wrapper (corpse) 8. cerement, chrismal 12. grave clothes
ceremonial ... 4. prim 5. stiff 6. custom, formal, ritual 7. precise, service, studied 8. ceremony, function, liturgic 9. formality 11. punctilious 12. conventional
ceremonial (pert to) ...
   chamber .. 4. kiva
   departure .. 6. congee
   splendor .. 9. pageantry
ceremonious ... 6. formal, polite 7. precise 8. gracious 9. attentive, courteous 10. ceremonial, respectful 11. deferential, ritualistic
ceremony ... 4. form, pomp, rite, show 6. parade, review, ritual 8. function 9. formality, solemnity 10. observance 11. performance
ceremony, without ... 6. humbly, meekly, simply 7. quietly 8. casually, modestly 9. sans façon 10. informally 15. unceremoniously
Ceres, Rom (pert to) ...
   astronomy .. 8. asteroid (1st found)
   father .. 6. Saturn
   Feast .. 8. Cerialia (Apr 19)
   Goddess of .. 4. Corn 5. Grain 9. Fertility 11. Agriculture
   Greek name .. 7. Demeter
   mother .. 3. Ops

Cereus ... 6. cactus 7. saguaro 13. night-blooming
cerise ... 5. color 7. blue-red, fuchsia 10. cherrylike
ceroplastics ... 8. modeling, waxworks
certain ... 3. one 4. sure 5. clear, exact, fixed, plain 7. assured, decided, insured, precise 8. absolute, definite, positive 9. certified, confident, exclusive, indubious, undoubted, warranted 10. guaranteed, inevitable, undeniable, undoubting 11. determinate, trustworthy 14. unquestionable 16. incontrovertible
certainly ... 3. yea, yes 4. amen 5. truly 6. indeed, really, surely, verily 7. clearly, in truth, utterly 8. actually, of course 9. assuredly, precisely 10. absolutely, by all means, definitely, inevitably, positively
certainty ... 5. cinch 6. pledge, shoo-in, surety 8. sureness 9. assurance, certitude 13. inevitability, infallibility
certificate ... 5. check, money 6. ticket 7. diploma, voucher 10. credential 11. testimonial
certificate (pert to) ...
   financial .. 5. IOU 5. draft, scrip 9. debenture
   India .. 5. hundi
   medical (Eng college) .. 8. aegrotat
certification ... 2. OK 3. fix 5. proof 8. sanction 10. validation 11. affirmation, attestation, certificate, endorsement 12. confirmation, ratification 13. ascertainment, authorization 14. substantiation
certify ... 5. prove, swear, vouch 6. assure, attest, avouch, ratify, verify 7. approve, confirm, endorse, witness 8. accredit, validate 9. ascertain, determine, establish, guarantee 11. acknowledge, corroborate
cerulean ... 4. blue 5. azure 7. sky-blue
cerumen ... 6. earwax
cervine ... 8. deerlike
cess ... 3. bag, tax 4. cede, duty, levy, toll 5. yield 6. assess, impost, tariff 7. revenue 9. surrender 10. assessment
cessation ... 3. end 4. lull, stay 5. letup, truce 7. respite 8. abeyance, desition 9. interlude 10. suspension 12. intermission, interruption 14. discontinuance
cetacea, cetacean ... 3. orc 4. apod, orca, susu (blind) 5. whale 6. whales 7. cowfish, finback, grampus, narwhal (narwal), rorqual
Cete ... 5. whale 10. The Cetacea
Cetus ... 8. The Whale 13. constellation (Equator)
Ceylon ...
   capital .. 7. Colombo
   city .. 5. Galle, Kandy (famed Buddhist Temple) 6. Jaffna
   mountain peak .. 14. Pidurutalagala
   new name .. 8. Sri Lanka
   ocean .. 6. Indian
   old name .. 9. Taprobane
   people .. 5. Tamil 6. Malays, Veddas 8. Malabars 10. Singhalese

Ceylon (pert to) . . .
boat . . 5. dhoni (doni)
canoe . . 5. balsa
Festival . . 8. Perahera
garment . . 6. sarong
hill dweller . . 4. Toda
monkey . . 4. maha 6. langur, rillow
moss . . 4. alga 6. Jaffna 7. gulaman
8. agar-agar
palm . . 7. talipot
rat . . 9. bandicoot
sand (sea bottom) . . 4. paar
tree . . 4. doon

chabouk, chabuk (Ind) . . . 4. whip
9. horsewhip

chacma . . . 6. baboon

chafe . . . 3. cut, irk, rub, vex 4. fret,
fume, fuss, gall, heat, rage, skin, warm
5. anger, annoy, grate, grind, pique,
scuff, worry, wound 6. abrade, banter,
excite, harass, injure, nettle, rankle
7. inflame 8. irritate

chaff . . . 3. hay 4. bran, husk, quiz, twit
5. dregs, fluff, husks, palea, straw,
trash, waste 6. banter, cobweb, glumes,
refuse, scraps 7. remains, residue,
tailing 8. raillery, ridicule, riffraff

chaffer . . . 5. trade, wares 6. buying,
dicker, haggle, higgle, market
7. bargain, chaffer, chatter, selling
9. negotiate 11. merchandise

chafing dish . . . 7. cresset

chagrin . . . 7. anxiety, mortify 8. distress,
troubles, vexation 13. mortification

chain . . 4. bind, bond, boom, gyve, reef,
torc 5. cable, range 6. catena, fasten,
fetter, secure, series, tether, torque
7. creeper, sorites 15. contravallation
(fort series)

chair . . 4. seat, sill 5. bench, sedan
6. rocker, throne 7. enchair, speaker

chair (pert to) . . .
back . . 5. splat 7. upright
collegiate . . 10. fellowship
13. professorship
cover . . 4. tidy 12. antimacassar
India . . 6. musnud
Japan . . 4. kago
maker . . 5. caner 6. reeder

chair (type of) . . . 4. camp, deck, easy,
high, lawn, wing 6. lounge, Morris,
swivel 7. contour, folding, steamer,
Windsor 8. armchair, captain's, electric,
fauteuil, straight 10. ladder-back
11. overstuffed

chairman . . . 7. officer, speaker 8. director
9. moderator

chalcedony . . . 4. onyx, opal, sard
5. agate 6. jasper, quartz 7. opaline
9. carnelian, chrysoprase

Chaldean (pert to) . . . 2. Ur 4. seer
6. Semite 10. astrologer, soothsayer
13. Neo-Babylonian (language)

chalice . . . 3. ama, cup 5. amula (anc),
calix, grail 6. goblet 8. daffodil

chalice pall . . . 4. veil 8. animetta

chalk . . . 4. draw, mark, pale, tick 5. score
6. blanch, bleach, crayon, credit,
pastel, whiten 7. account, drawing
9. limestone, reckoning

chalker . . . 7. milkman (Eng sl)

chalklike . . . 10. calcareous

chalky . . . 5. white 7. crumbly, friable,
powdery 10. cretaceous

challenge . . . 4. dare, defy, gage 5. claim,
doubt, query 6. accost, cartel, defial,
demand, impugn 7. dispute, protest
8. question, reproach 10. accusation,
controvert 11. questioning

chamal . . . 4. goat (Angora)

chamber . . . 4. cave, hall, kiva, room
5. court 6. camera, cavity 7. bedroom,
boudoir, cabinet, chambre, cubicle
10. bedchamber 11. compartment

chamber (pert to) . . .
harem . . 3. oda
heart . . 7. auricle 9. ventricle
King's . . 9. camarilla
music . . 14. sonata da camera

chambers . . . 4. flat 5. suite 6. office
9. apartment, bicameral (Legis) 14. Inns
of Chancery (Eng)

chameleon . . . 6. lizard 10. vacillator
13. changeability, constellation

chamfer (to) . . . 5. bevel, carve, flute,
score 6. chisel, groove

chamois . . . 5. Gemse, izard 8. antelope

champ . . . 4. bite, chew, mash 5. gnash
6. victor 7. trample 11. battlefield

champagne . . . 4. wine 9. red-yellow
13. chrysanthemum

champaign . . . 5. field, plain 7. expanse
11. battlefield

champion . . . 3. Ace 4. best, hero
5. champ 6. defend, expert, victor,
winner 7. espouse, fighter, titlist
8. advocate, defender 9. combatant,
conqueror 10. unexcelled

champion (pert to) . . .
Christian (anc) . . 3. Cid
constellation . . 7. Perseus
knight (legend) . . 7. Paladin
Spanish . . 12. conquistador

chance . . . 3. die, hap, lot 4. fate, luck,
odds, risk, turn 6. casual, gamble,
happen, mishap, tossup 7. fortune,
lottery, tychism 8. fortuity, Lady Luck,
occasion 9. happening, mischance
10. likelihood 11. opportunity,
possibility, probability 12. happenstance

chancel (pert to) . . .
part . . 4. bema
screen . . 4. jube
seats . . 7. sedilia

change . . . 4. flux, move, turn, vary,
veer 5. alter, amend, break, coins,
money, shift 6. modify, mutate, switch
7. caprice, convert, deviate, variety
8. transfer 9. diversity, transform,
transmute, variation 10. alteration,
fickleness, modulation 11. inconstancy,
vicissitude 12. substitution
13. metamorphosis 14. transformation
15. diversification

change (pert to) . . .
color . . 3. dye, wan 4. fade, pale 5. blush
6. blanch, redden
medicine . . 11. heterotopia
mind . . 6. repent 12. tergiversate
music . . 4. muta
order of . . 9. metabolic, rearrange,
transpose

changeable ... 6. fickle, fitful, mobile
7. erratic, flighty, mutable, protean
8. freakish, notional, unstable, variable,
volatile, weathery 9. alterable,
chameleon, metabolic, uncertain,
unsettled, whimsical 10. capricious,
inconstant 15. interchangeable

changeling ... 3. oaf 4. dolt 5. idiot
7. waverer 8. imbecile, renegade,
turncoat 9. simpleton 10. substitute
(child)

channel ... 3. bed, cut, gat, way 4. dike,
duct, gate, gurt, lane, leat, pass, vein
5. basin, canal, ditch, drain, flume,
flute, fosse, radio, river, sinus, stria
6. alveus, avenue, coulee, groove,
gutter, outlet, sluice, trench, trough
7. conduit, tideway 8. aqueduct, tailrace
9. broadcast 10. passageway

Channel Islands ... 4. Sark (Sercq)
6. Jersey 8. Alderney

chanson ... 4. song 5. lyric 6. ballad

chant ... 3. say 4. sing 6. intone, melody,
warble 7. introit, singing 8. canticle
10. intonation 11. composition

chanter ... 6. cantor, singer 7. bagpipe
(part), intoner, sparrow (hedge)
8. songster, vocalist 9. chanteuse,
chorister

chanticleer ... 4. cock 7. rooster 11. cock-
a-doodle 14. cock-a-doodle-doo

chaos ... 2. Nu (Egypt) 3. pie (type) 4. gulf,
mess 5. abyss, babel, chasm 7. anarchy
8. disorder 9. confusion, imbroglio
10. unruliness 13. orderlessness

Chaos (pert to) ...
　daughter .. 3. Nox, Nyx
　parent of .. 5. earth 6. heaven 8. Creation
　son .. 6. Erebus

chaotic ... 6. muddle 8. confused,
formless 12. disorganized

chap ... 3. boy, buy, guy, lad, man 4. kibe
(sore) 5. buyer, chink, cleft, crack, scout,
split, youth 6. barter, choose (Scot),
fellow, galoot 7. chapman 8. customer

chapeau ... 3. cap, hat, lid 5. beret

chapel ... 4. cape, cope, cowl, hood
5. altar, choir 6. bethel 7. chantry,
galilee, oratory, service, Sistine
8. sacellum (anc) 9. reliquary

chaperon ... 4. hood 6. attend, duenna,
escort 8. guardian 9. attendant
10. gooseberry

chaplet ... 4. band 5. beads 6. anadem,
wreath 7. garland, prayers 8. beadroll,
insignia, necklace

chappaul ... 9. squawfish

chaps ... 8. overalls 10. chaparajos

chapter ... 4. Sura 5. topic 6. clause
7. council, meeting, passage, section,
Society 8. division 9. capitular
10. fraternity 12. organization

chaptrel ... 6. impost

char ... 4. burn 5. trout 6. scorch
8. charcoal, sandbank

character ... 4. hero, kind, mark, role,
sign, star 5. trait 6. cipher, letter,
nature, repute, status, symbol 7. quality
8. function 9. reference 10. reputation
11. temperament 14. characteristic

character (pert to) ...

giver .. 5. toner
Hebrew .. 3. Tav, Taw
Irish .. 5. Ogham
musical .. 3. bar 4. clef, rest 5. neume
of people .. 5. ethos
real .. 7. essence
science of .. 8. ethology
Teutonic .. 4. rune

characteristic ... 4. mark 5. habit, trait
7. feature, impress, quality, typical
8. peculiar, symbolic 9. attribute,
character, idiopathy, lineament,
specialty 11. distinctive, peculiarity,
singularity, symptomatic
13. individualism

characteristic (pert to) ...
descent .. 5. racial
peculiar .. 9. idiopathy
spirit .. 5. ethos
tone (Mus) .. 7. seventh

characterization ... 4. role 5. drama
9. depiction, portrayal 11. description,
distinction 13. impersonation
14. identification, representation

characterize ... 4. mark, name 5. enact
7. engrave, imprint, portray 8. describe,
inscribe 9. delineate, designate,
epitomize, represent 11. distinguish

characterized by ...
abstinence .. 7. ascetic
bacteria exclusion .. 7. asepsis
cruelty .. 7. Neronic
exact thinking .. 13. ratiocinative
melody .. 6. ariose
poison (bloodstream) .. 6. sepsis
pomposity .. 13. grandiloquent

characterless ... 5. inane 9. colorless,
pointless

charcoal ... 4. coke, fuel, lave, peat
5. black, chark 6. carbon, fusain
7. drawing, residue 9. boneblack,
briquette

charge ... 4. bill, cost, dues, fill,
load, onus, rate, task, toll, ward
5. blame, chore, debit, onset, order,
price, trust 6. accuse, advice, advise,
allege, amount, attack, client, commit,
credit, demand, dictum, impute,
indict 7. assault, command, concern,
custody, expense, impeach, keeping,
mandate, precept, primage, protégé
8. guidance, insignia, instruct, tutelage
9. dependent, electrify, exactment
10. accusation, commission, imposition,
impregnate, injunction, management
11. arrangement, attribution,
instruction, supervision
13. incrimination 14. responsibility

charged atom ... 3. ion

charge of affairs ... 8. diplomat
15. chargé d'affaires

charge off ... 5. debit 6. forget 7. dismiss,
forgive 8. discount

charges (law) ... 4. dues, fees 5. costs
9. retainers

charge with ...
crime .. 6. indict 7. impeach
　11. incriminate
debt .. 5. debit
gas .. 6. aerate
offense .. 6. accuse

to .. 5. blame 7. ascribe 9. attribute
charily .. 6. cagily, warily 8. frugally
9. carefully, thriftily 10. cautiously
12. economically, suspiciously
chariness ... 7. caution 8. caginess,
distrust, wariness 9. frugality
11. heedfulness, thriftiness
chariot ... 3. car 4. biga, cart, rath (ratha),
wain 5. essed (anc), wagon 7. vehicle
8. quadriga
charioteer ... 6. Auriga (Astron), Ben
Hur
charitable ... 3. big 4. kind 5. kindly
7. lenient, liberal 8. generous, tolerant
9. forgiving, indulgent 10. altruistic,
benevolent, bighearted 11. beneficient
12. eleemosynary, humanitarian
13. compassionate, philanthropic
charity ... 4. alms, dole 6. bounty, virtue
7. handout, largess 8. lenience, pittance
9. tolerance 10. almsgiving, liberality
11. benevolence 12. philanthropy
charity dispenser ... 7. almoner
charivari ... 5. babel 6. medley, uproar
8. serenade (mock) 10. callithump
charlatan ... 5. faker, fraud, phony, quack
6. humbug 7. empiric 8. impostor
9. pretender 10. medicaster,
mountebank
Charlemagne, Emperor (pert to) ...
brother .. 8. Carloman
emperor of .. 7. The West
father .. 5. Pepin (the Short)
name also .. 15. Charles The Great
nephew .. 7. Orlando
charm ... 3. obi 4. lure, mojo, play,
song 5. grace, magic, oomph, spell
6. allure, amulet, appeal, beauty,
enamor, entice, fetish, glamor, scarab
7. beguile, bewitch, cantrip, delight,
enchant, glamour, periapt 8. breloque,
elegance, entrance, ornament, talisman
9. captivate, fascinate, sex appeal,
sweetness 10. allurement, attraction,
brimborion (brimborium), lovability
11. captivation, conjuration, incantation,
pulchritude, winsomeness
12. antinganting 14. attractiveness,
delightfulness
charmer ... 5. siren 6. beauty 7. enticer
8. exorcist, magician, sorcerer
9. bewitcher
charming ... 7. winsome 8. alluring,
pleasing 10. bewitching, delightful
11. captivating, fascinating
Charon's river ... 4. Styx
chart ... 3. map 4. list, plat, plot
7. diagram
charter ... 4. hire 5. carta, grant 6. charta,
firman, treaty 7. license 9. privilege
(special), purwannah
chartreuse ... 4. mold (cookery) 5. color
7. liqueur
Chartreuse ... 9. monastery 18. La
Grande Chartreuse (Grenoble)
chary ... 4. wary 5. cagey 6. frugal,
skimpy 7. thrifty 8. cautious
10. suspicious 12. parsimonious
Charybdis ... 6. Scylla 8. Galoforo
9. whirlpool (Messina)
chase ... 3. gun (Naut), set (gem) 4. hunt,

park, race 5. chevy (chivy), raise,
sport, track 6. emboss, follow, furrow,
groove, hasten, pursue, shikar, stroke
(tennis) 7. engrave, pursuit, repulse
8. ornament 12. steeplechase
Chase (The), **goddess of** ... 5. Diana
chasm ... 3. gap, pit 4. gulf, hole, rift,
well 5. abyss, cleft, shaft 6. breach,
canyon, cavity, hiatus 7. fissure,
opening 8. crevasse
chasma ... 7. yawning
chasse ... 4. step (dance) 6. shrine
9. reliquary
chaste ... 4. pure 6. modest, simple
8. innocent, virtuous 9. continent,
uncorrupt, undefiled, unmarried
10. immaculate
chasten ... 4. rate 5. smote 6. punish,
refine 7. correct 8. chastise, penalize,
restrain 9. castigate 10. discipline
chastened ... 4. meek 5. smote
7. subdued 8. punished, purified,
tempered 10. restrained
chastise ... 4. beat, slap, whip 5. amend,
blame, scold, spank, taunt 6. punish,
rebate, rebuke, swinge 7. correct,
reprove 9. castigate 10. discipline
chastity ... 6. purity, virtue 9. cleanness
10. chasteness 12. virtuousness
chat ... 3. gab, rap, yak 4. chin, coze, jist,
talk, tove 5. prate 6. babble, confab,
gabble, gibber, gossip, jabber 7. chatter,
prattle 8. causerie, chitchat, converse
12. conversation 14. chitter-chatter
chatelaine ... 3. pin 4. etui, hook 5. clasp,
purse, watch 6. brooch, torque
chattels ... 4. naam 5. goods, money,
wares 6. estate 7. effects 8. holdings,
property 9. livestock, principal
11. possessions
chatter ... 3. gab, yap 5. clack, prate
7. clatter, prattle
chatterer ... 3. jay, mag 4. bird, piet
6. magpie 10. chatterbox
chatty ... 3. pot (earthen) 4. glib 5. gabby
7. affable 8. sociable 9. garrulous,
prattling, talkative 14. conversational
Chaucer (pert to) ...
author of .. 15. Canterbury Tales
Inn .. 6. (The) Tabard
pilgrimage city .. 10. Canterbury
style of work .. 7. novella
chauvinist ... 5. jingo 6. Rajput
7. chauvin, patriot 8. jingoist
9. warmonger 10. militarist
cheap ... 3. low 5. small, tacky, tinny, trade,
value 6. cheesy, paltry, plenty, sleazy
7. abashed, bargain, chintzy, cut-
rate, reduced, schlock 9. niggardly
11. inexpensive
cheapen ... 3. cut 4. trim 5. lower, slash
6. debase, reduce 7. degrade 8. mark
down
cheat ... 2. do 3. ban, con, fob, gyp
4. bilk, fake, flam, hoax, liar, rook,
scam, sell, sham 5. cozen, elude, guile,
phony, scalp 6. deceit, fleece, humbug,
hustle, illude, rip-off 7. deceive,
finesse, sharpen, swindle 8. artifice,
impostor 9. bamboozle, overreach,
stratagem, victimize 10. thimblerig

13. bait-and-switch
check . . . 3. nip, tab 4. balk, curb, damp, mark, rein, stem, stop, test 5. agree, brake, count, delay, limit, money, plaid, repel, stunt, tally 6. bridle, cheque, detain, detent, impede, oppose, rebuff, retard, ticket, verify 7. counter, examine, inhibit, measure, monitor, pattern, repress 9. hindrance, restraint 12. verification
check (pert to) . . .
  in . . 3. die 6. arrive 8. register
  out . . 3. die 5. croak, leave 6. assess 8. withdraw
  pattern . . 11. houndstooth
  game, term . . 5. chess 8. gambling
checkered . . . 4. vair 5. diced, plaid 6. mosaic, tartan, varied 7. checked 10. changeable, tesserated, variegated 11. diversified
checkers, chequers . . . 4. game 8. draughts (Brit)
cheek . . . 4. gall, gena, jowl 5. brass, bucca, crust, malar, nerve 8. audacity, chutzpah 9. impudence 10. buccinator
cheer . . . 3. rah 4. yell 5. bravo, elate, huzza, liven, mirth, salvo 6. gaiety, hurrah, regale, repast, salute, solace 7. animate, applaud, console, gladden, hearten, jollity, refresh, rejoice 8. applause, inspirit, pleasure, vivacity 9. encourage, merriment 10. exhilarate 12. conviviality
cheerful . . . 3. gay 4. gleg (Scot), rosy 5. happy, peart, sunny 6. blithe, cheery, genial, hearty, jocund, joyful 8. gladsome, homelike 9. contented, lightsome 12. lighthearted
cheerfulness . . . 3. joy 4. glee 5. cheer, mirth 6. gaiety 7. jollity 8. gladness, hilarity 9. happiness, merriment 12. exhilaration
cheerio . . . 5. adios, aloha, skoal, toast 6. hurrah, prosit 8. au revoir, farewell, Godspeed 9. greetings
cheerless . . . 3. sad 4. cold, drab 5. drear 6. dismal, dreary, gloomy 7. forlorn, joyless, unhappy 8. dejected 9. unsmiling 10. depressing, melancholy 11. dispiriting 12. disconsolate
cheese . . . 4. blue (bleu), brie, Edam, feta, jack 5. cream, Gouda, Swiss 6. chevre, Romano 7. Cheddar, cottage, fromage (Fr), Gruyère, havarti, ricotta, sapsago, Stilton 8. American, Monterey (jack), Muenster, Parmesan 9. Camembert, Jarlsberg, Limburger, Roquefort 10. Gorgonzola, Neufchâtel
cheese dish . . . 6. fondue, omelet, quiche, strata 7. rarebit, soufflé
cheesy . . . 3. bad 6. paltry 8. inferior 9. worthless 12. disreputable
cheetah . . . 3. cat 5. youse (youze) 7. guepard (gueparde)
cheilos . . . 3. lip
chela . . . 4. claw 6. novice 8. disciple
Chelonia . . . 7. reptile, turtles 9. tortoises
chemical (pert to) . . .
  analysis . . 5. assay
  cleanser . . 6. kryton
  etching . . 11. chemigraphy

  strength . . 5. titer (titre)
  term . . 3. gas 4. acid, atom, base, salt 5. imine 6. alkali, eluate 7. hormone, nonacid, organic, radical, valence 8. catalyst, compound 10. bathoflore 11. bathochrome
  vessel . . 4. etna 6. aludel, retort 7. alembic 8. crucible, reductor
chemical suffix . . . 2. ac, el, yl 3. ane, ene, ile, ine, ole, ose 4. enoi, olic, osan
chemin de fer . . . 7. railway 8. baccarat, railroad
chemise . . . 4. slip 5. shift
chemist . . . 7. analyst 8. druggist 9. alchemist 10. apothecary, biochemist 12. iatrochemist (anc)
cherish . . . 3. aid, hug, pet, woo 4. love 5. adore, cheer, nurse, prize 6. caress, faddle, fondle, foster 7. care for, comfort, nourish, nurture, protect, support 8. enshrine, remember, treasure 9. cultivate, encourage, entertain
cheroot . . . 5. cigar
cherry . . . 3. pin 4. Bing, bird, gean, ming 5. black 6. egriot, Prunus 7. capulin, marasca, mazzard, Morello, oxheart 8. Napoleon 9. amarelles, bigarreau, Queen Anne 11. chokecherry, Montmorency
cherub . . . 5. angel, child, saint 6. seraph, spirit 7. darling, eudemon 8. cherubim, seraphim
chess (pert to) . . .
  chessman . . 4. king, pawn, rook 5. piece, queen 6. bishop, castle, knight
  Italian . . 7. scacchi
  term . . 4. dual, move 5. debut 6. chassé, fidate, gambit 7. endgame, opening, problem 9. checkmate, en passant, roo k's tour, stalemate 10. fianchetto
chesslike . . . 8. scacchic
chest . . . 3. ark, box 4. arca, cist, kist 5. bahut 6. breast, cajeta, coffer, coffin, locker 7. highboy, wanigan (wangan) 10. chiffonier 11. gardeviance
chest (pert to) . . .
  ammunition . . 7. caisson
  animal . . 7. brisket
  human . . 6. thorax 7. midriff
  sound . . 4. rale
  sepulchral . . 6. larnax
Chester (Eng), **inhabitant** . . . 8. Cestrian
chesterfield . . . 4. sofa 5. divan 8. overcoat 9. cigarette, davenport
chestnut . . . 4. ling, rata 5. horse, water 6. marron 7. buckeye 8. Aesculus, Castanea 10. breadfruit, chinquapin
chestnut . . . 4. joke 6. cliché 7. bromide 8. banality
chestnut color . . . 4. roan 5. brown 6. sorrel 12. reddish-brown
chevalier . . . 5. cadet (nobility), noble 6. knight 7. gallant 8. cavalier, horseman 10. greenshank (bird)
chevron . . . 4. beam 5. glove 6. rafter, stripe, zigzag 8. insignia
chevrotain . . . 4. napu 7. deerlet, kenchil, meminna 9. Tragulina
chevy . . . 3. cry (hunting) 4. game, hunt

5. chase 6. flight, harass, pursue
7. torment

chew . . . 3. cud 4. bite, chaw, gnaw,
quid 5. champ, chomp, grind, munch
6. chavel, ponder 8. meditate, ruminate
9. masticate

chiasma . . . 11. decussation
12. intersection

chiasmus . . . 9. inversion (of words)

chib (Gypsy) . . . 6. tongue 8. language

chic . . . 4. trig, trim 5. natty, smart
6. modish, spruce 7. stylish

Chicago's nickname . . . 9. Windy City

chicanery . . . 4. ruse, wile 5. feint, trick
6. deceit 7. knavery 8. artifice, trickery
9. stratagem 11. skulduggery

chickadee . . . 8. titmouse 10. Pebthestes

chicken . . . 3. hen 4. cock, fowl,
girl 5. biddy, capon, chick, deedy,
fryer, poult, young 6. coward, pullet
7. broiler, rooster 8. cockerel, weakling
9. youngling 11. chanticleer,
milquetoast

chickenhearted . . . 5. timid 8. cowardly
12. fainthearted

chicory . . . 6. endive 7. succory
12. Cichoriaceae

chickpea . . . 8. garbanzo

chide . . . 4. rate 5. blame, scold 6. berate,
rebuke 7. censure, reprove, wrangle
8. admonish, reproach 9. reprimand

chief . . . 3. dux, top 4. arch, head,
main, rais (reis) 5. first, forte, major,
mogul 6. leader, primal, staple, syndic
7. kingpin, supreme 9. directing,
governing, paramount, potentate,
principal, prominent 11. predominant

chief (pert to) . . .
African . . 3. dey 4. kaid 5. negus
6. induna
Am Indian . . 6. sachem 7. Osceola
8. sagamore
Arab . . 5. sheik
Chinook . . 4. tyee
Cossack . . 6. ataman, hetman
Egypt . . 3. Min (Panopolis)
Europe . . 6. syndic
Germany . . 6. Führer (Fuehrer), Kaiser
Iran . . 9. ayatollah
Italy . . 4. doge, duce
Japan . . 6. mikado, shogun
Mexico . . 7. cacique
Nepal . . 4. Rais
Oriental . . 4. kahn 6. sirdar
Persia . . 4. shah
Russia . . 4. czar (tsar)
Spain . . 7. alcalde
Tibet . . 9. Dalai Lama
Turkey . . 3. aga (agha) 6. vizier

chilblain . . . 6. pernio

child . . . 3. imp, kid, tad, tot 4. babe,
baby, bata, brat, teen, tike, waif
5. bairn, cupid, elfin, fetus 6. cherub,
childe (anc), infant, urchin 7. adoptee,
nestler, preteen, progeny 9. offspring,
youngster 10. descendant

childish . . . 4. weak 5. naive, petty,
young 6. senile, simple 7. babyish,
kiddish, puerile, unmanly 8. immature
9. infantile, kittenish

children (pert to) . . .

doctor . . 12. pediatrician
mythology . . 6. Titans
Patron Saint . . 5. Santa
slain by Herod . . 12. The Innocents
study of . . 8. pedology 10. pediatrics

Chile . . . see also *Chilean*
cape . . 4. Horn
capital . . 8. Santiago (1541)
city . . 4. Lota 5. Arica 8. Valdivia
10. Concepcion, Valparaiso (1543)
conqueror . . 7. Pizarro 8. Valdivia
desert . . 7. Atacama
explorer . . 8. Magellan (1520)
mountain . . 5. Andes
poet . . 6. Neruda
river . . 3. Loa 6. Biobio
settlement (southernmost) . . 8. Navarino
(Isl) 14. Puerto Williams

Chilean (pert to) . . .
coconut . . 7. coquito
evergreen . . 6. pepino 10. arborvitae
shrub (poison) . . 5. lithi
wind . . 5. sures 11. sures pardos
workman . . 4. rote

chiliad . . . 8. thousand 9. millenium
13. thousand years

chill . . . 3. ice, raw 4. ague, cold, damp
5. algor, frost, rigor 6. damper, formal,
shiver 7. malaria 8. coldness, coolness,
dispirit 10. depressing 11. refrigerate

chilly . . . 3. raw 4. ague, cold 5. gelid
6. aguish, freeze, frosty 12. refrigerated

chiloplasty . . . 10. lip surgery 12. mouth
surgery

chime . . . 4. bell, peal, ring, suit 5. agreé,
bells, prate, rhyme 6. accord, concur,
cymbal, jingle 7. harmony

chimera . . . 5. dream, fancy, vapor
6. bubble, utopia 7. monster 8. illusion,
paradise (fool's)

chimerical . . . 4. vain 7. utopian
8. delusive, fanciful, romantic
9. fantastic, imaginary, unfounded

chimney . . . 3. lum 4. flue 5. cleft, stack,
tewel 10. smokestack

chimpanzee . . . 6. gibbon, nohega
7. gorilla

chin . . . 4. talk 5. genio (comb form)
6. mentum, weight (Chin) 8. converse
10. chew the rag 11. genioplasty (Surg),
mentoplasty (Surg)

china . . . 7. Dresden, pottery 8. crockery
9. porcelain 11. earthenware

China . . . see also *Chinese*
Buddha . . 2. Fo
capital . . 7. Beijing
capital, old name . . 7. Peiping (Peking)
city . . 4. Amoy, Tsin, Wuhu 6. Canton,
Hankow, Ningpo 7. Foochow, Nanking,
Soochow 8. Hangchow, Shanghai,
Tientsin
Communist leader . . 3. Mao 4. Deng
dynasty . . 3. Han, Kin, Sui 4. Chou,
Hsia (BC), Ming, Tsin, Yuan 5. Ching
6. Manchu, Mongol (Kublai Khan's)
island . . 5. Matsu 6. Quemoy, Taiwan
(Formosa)
magistrate . . 5. tupan 6. tuchun
8. mandarin
Mainland . . 15. People's Republic
Military Academy . . 7. Whompoa

Mongol .. 3. Hun
mountain .. 7. Kuen-lun 9. Himalayas
Nationalist leader .. 13. Chiang Kai-shek
nickname .. 14. Flowery Kingdom
philosopher .. 6. Laotse 9. Confucius
poet .. 4. Li Po 7. Li Tai Po
race .. 9. Mongoloid
religion .. 6. Taoism 8. Buddhism
  9. Confucian 12. Confucianism
revolutionary leader .. 9. Sun Yat-sen
river .. 5. Chang (formerly Yangtze)
  7. Huang He (formerly Hwang Ho)
sea .. 5. China 6. Yellow
treaty port .. 4. Amoy
Chinese (pert to) ...
antelope .. 6. dzeren
boat .. 4. junk 5. tanka 6. sampan
cabbage .. 7. pakchoi
card game .. 6. fantan
carpet .. 6. Khotan 7. Kashgar, Yarkand
  9. Samarkand, Turkestan
Catholic Church .. 11. Tien Chu T'ang
  12. Tien Chu Chiao
chestnut .. 4. ling
confection .. 8. chowchow
deer .. 8. elaphure
defense .. 4. Wall (2,000 mi long)
desert .. 4. Gobi 5. Shamo
dragon .. 6. chi-lin
fabric .. 3. sha 7. nankeen
festival (Spring) .. 9. Ch'ing Ming
flute .. 4. tche (che)
fruit .. 6. litchi (nut)
game .. 6. fantan
ginger .. 9. galingale
God .. 4. Shen (Chr) 7. Shangti, Tien
  Chu (RCCh)
gong .. 6. tam-tam, tom-tom
grass .. 5. ramee
idol .. 4. joss 6. pagoda (pagod)
instrument .. 3. che, kin 4. tche 5. sheng
  (cheng)
jade .. 2. yu
jute .. 7. chingma
laborer .. 6. coolie
lily .. 9. narcissus
liquor .. 6. samshu (rice)
literary degree .. 8. hsiu tsai
monkey .. 4. douc
nurse .. 4. amah
officer .. 4. kwan
oil .. 4. tung
ox .. 4. zebu
pagoda .. 3. taa
paradise (Buddh) .. 4. Jodo 7. Ching-tu
  8. Gekuraku
philosophy .. 10. Yang and Yin
religion .. 6. Taoism 8. Buddhism
  12. Confucianism
residence (official) .. 5. yamen
screen (folding) .. 10. Coromandel
silkworm .. 4. sina 9. ailanthus
silver ingot .. 5. sycee
sky .. 4. tien
society (secret) .. 3. hui (hoey) 4. tong
vessel .. 4. junk 6. lorcha
chink ... 4. rent, rift, rima, rime, ring
  5. cleft, crack 6. cranny, furrow
  7. bunting (bird), fissure 10. interstice
chinook ... 4. herb, wind 6. salmon
  7. quinnat

Chinook (pert to) ...
chief .. 4. tyee
people .. 8. Flathead
State (nickname of) .. 10. Washington
chinquapin ... 3. oak 6. bonnet (water)
  8. chestnut
chip ... 3. cut, hew 4. coin 5. break, carve,
  flake, piece, scrap, token 6. chisel,
  gallet (stone) 7. counter
chipmunk ... 6. hackee
chipped stone (instrument) ...
  9. paleolith
chipper ... 5. chirp 6. babble, chisel,
  hammer, lively 7. chirrup, twitter
  8. cheerful
chirognomy ... 9. palmistry
  10. chiromancy
chironomy ... 7. gesture (hands)
  9. pantomime
chiropter ... 3. bat 6. aliped
chirp ... 3. pew (pue) 4. peep 5. cheep,
  chirl, tweet 7. chirrup, twitter
chisel ... 3. cut, gad, hew 4. celt (anc),
  form, pare 5. bruzz, burin, carve, cheat,
  drove, gouge, grave 6. furrow, jagger,
  mallet, peeker, pommel 7. engrave,
  swindle 9. sculpture
chit ... 4. note, runt, wisp 5. child,
  shoot 10. sprout 10. memorandum
  14. recommendation
chitarra, chitarrine ... 6. guitar
chiton ... 7. garment (anc), mollusk
chivalrous ... 5. brave 6. gentle,
  heroic 7. gallant, valiant 8. knightly
  9. courteous 11. magnanimous
chive ... 4. stab 5. onion, plant 6. garlic
chloride ... 3. ore 4. salt 5. ester
  7. calomel
chlorine ... 2. Cl 7. bromine, halogen,
  radical 8. cyanogen, fluorine
chloroform ... 4. dope, kill 6. poison
  7. stupefy 9. narcotize 11. anesthetize
chlorophyll ... 5. ester, green 7. etiolin
  9. deodorant
chocolate ... 5. brown, cacao, candy,
  cocoa, color 6. pinole 6. beverage
  13. Sterculiaceae
choice ... 4. beat, rare, will 5. prime
  6. dainty, option, select, tidbit
  8. election, free will, uncommon
  9. recherché, selection 10. preference,
  well-chosen 11. alternative
choir ... 6. chorus 7. singers
choir leader ... 6. cantor 9. precentor
choke ... 3. gag, jam, ram 4. clog 5. burke,
  check 6. hinder, impede, muffle, stifle
  7. garrote, repress, smother 8. obstruct,
  strangle, throttle 9. constrict, suffocate
choler ... 3. ire 4. bile, foam, gall, rage
  5. anger, wrath 6. spleen 10. resentment
  11. biliousness 12. irascibility
choleric ... 5. angry, testy 7. bilious,
  enraged, iracund 8. wrathful
  9. dyspeptic, irascible 10. passionate
chololith ... 9. gallstone
choose ... 4. opt 6. cull, like, list, pick,
  want 5. elect 6. desire, optate, prefer,
  select
choosing ... 6. optant 8. eclectic, elective
  9. selecting
chop ... 3. axe, cut, hew, jaw, lop

4. dice, fell, hack, jowl, meat, raze,
seal 5. cheek, mince, prune, sever,
stamp 7. griskin 8. noisette (eye of)

choppy . . . 5. bumpy, rough 6. uneven
7. jolting 8. unstable, variable
9. irregular 10. changeable, incoherent
13. discontinuous

chord . . . 4. rope 6. radius, secant,
string, tendon 7. concord, harmony
8. arpeggio, concento, filament

chord (terms) . . . 5. major, minor, tonic,
triad 6. broken, common, tetrad
7. seventh 8. dominant, unbroken
10. enharmonic

chords . . . 4. tune 7. cadence, cantata

chore . . . 3. job (odd) 4. task, work 5. stint
10. assignment

chorography . . . 5. chart 7. diagram
10. topography 11. cartography,
description (region), ichnography

chortle . . . 5. laugh, snort 7. chuckle,
snortle

chorus . . . 4. echo 5. choir 6. accord,
outcry, unison 7. refrain, singers
8. chanters 9. unanimity

chorus (pert to) . . .
girl . . 7. chorine, chorist
leader . . 8. choragus 9. conductor
small . . 7. octette

Chosen (Jap) . . . 5. Korea

Chosen People . . . 10. Israelites

chrism . . . 7. unction, unguent
10. anointment 12. confirmation

christen . . . 4. name 6. launch 7. baptize
10. denominate, inaugurate
12. Christianize

Christian (pert to) . . .
Eastern . . 5. Uniat
feast . . 5. agape (anc) 8. Epiphany
9. Christmas
martyr (first) . . 7. Stephen
philosopher (anc) . . 6. Jesuit
9. Schoolman 10. Scholastic
sect . . 7. Docetae
symbol . . 9. orant (fem)

Christie detective . . . 10. Jane Marple
13. Hercule Poirot

Christmas (pert to) . . .
bag . . 6. piñata
carol . . 4. Noel
decoration . . 6. crèche
feast . . 4. Yule
hymn . . 13. Adeste Fideles
mummer . . 6. guiser
plant . . 5. holly 9. evergreen, mistletoe
term . . 4. Noel, Xmas 8. Nativity, Yuletide
11. Weihnachten
time before . . 6. Advent

Christ's-thorn . . . 4. nabk

chromosome . . . 2. id 5. idant 8. biophore,
germ cell

chronic . . . 7. abiding 8. constant,
enduring, habitual 9. confirmed
10. continuous, inveterate, persistent
14. valetudinarian

chronicle . . . 4. sard 5. annal, diary
6. record 7. account, archive, history
8. register 9. narrative 10. chronology

chronicler . . . 6. writer 8. annalist,
compiler, recorder 9. historian
12. chronologist

chronology error . . . 9. prolepsis

chronometer . . . 5. clock, timer, watch
6. ghurry 7. sundial 9. hourglass,
metronome, timepiece

chrysolite . . . 5. green (color) 7. olivine,
peridot

chthonian . . . 4. gods (underworld)
7. hellish, worship 9. diabolist
11. demonolater

chub . . . 4. bass, dace, doit, fool, lout
6. shiner, tautog 8. fallfish 9. hornyhead,
squawfish

chubby . . . 3. fat 5. plump, pudgy, round
6. stocky, stubby 9. corpulent

chuck . . . 4. beef, cast, food, hurl, jerk,
toss 5. fling, heave, pitch, throw
9. eliminate

chuckle . . . 5. cluck, laugh 6. cackle,
wabble 7. chortle

chuff . . . 3. fat 4. boor 5. churl,
clown, cross, proud, sulky, surly
6. chubby, elated, rustic 9. conceited
11. ill-tempered

chum . . . 3. pal 4. bait, pard 5. buddy,
crony 6. fellow, hobnob 7. company,
comrade, consort, partner 8. playmate,
roommate 9. associate, classmate,
colleague, companion

chump . . . 3. ass 4. doit, dupe, fool, head
5. block, booby 8. endpiece

chunk . . . 3. dab, gob, pat, wad 4. hunk,
junt, lump, slug (metal) 5. stick, stump,
throw 8. fragment

chunky . . . 3. fat 4. game (Am Ind), junt
5. lumpy, stout, tubby 6. chubby, portly,
stocky, stodgy, stubby 8. thickset

church . . . 3. dom 4. fane (anc), kirk,
sect 5. abbey 6. bethel, temple
7. Lateran, minster, templet 8. basilica,
conclave 9. cathedral 10. House of
God, worshipers 11. Christendom
12. denomination

church (pert to) . . .
assistant . . 5. Elder
attendant . . 5. usher 6. sexton, verger
calendar . . 4. ordo
Court . . 10. Consistory
dignitary . . 4. dean 6. bishop, priest
7. prelate, primate 8. benefice, cardinal,
minister 9. monsignor
dissenter . . 7. sectary 10. anti-Nicean,
anti-Nicene
doctrine (State, church) . . 8. Erastian
dominion . . 10. sacerdotum
doorkeeper . . 7. ostiary
Elder . . 9. Presbyter
feast . . 4. utas (octave of) 6. Easter
governing body . . 7. classis
law . . 5. canon, synod 7. council
part . . 4. apse, bema, nave 6. altar,
canon 7. chancel, narthex 8. transept
10. clerestory
peace device . . 8. irenicon
property . . 5. glebe
receptacle . . 10. monstrance
Roman . . 7. Lateran 8. basilica
screen . . 4. rood
seats . . 4. pews 5. sedilia
service (part) . . 3. pax 4. Mass 5. crede
7. epistle, introit, sanctus 8. Agnus
Dei, blessing 9. communion

stipend . . 7. prebend
traffic (preferments) . . 6. simony
vessel . . 3. ama, pyx (pix) 6. lavabo
  7. chalice 8. ciborium
vestry . . 8. sacristy
churl . . 3. cad, oaf 4. boor, carl, hind,
  lout, serf 5. ceorl, knave 6. rustic
  7. bondman, freeman, peasant, villain
  9. vulgarian 10. countryman
churlish . . 4. mean 5. gruff, rough,
  surly 6. rustic, sordid, sullen, vulgar
  7. boorish, crabbed, knavish
  9. gruffness, niggardly 10. ill-humored
  11. countrified
churn . . 4. beat, kirn, stir, whip 5. mixer,
  shake 6. beater, seethe, vessel 7. agitate
  8. agitator, emulsify
chute . . 4. tube 5. flume, scarp, slide
  6. trough 7. channel, incline, passage
  9. parachute
cibol . . 5. chive, onion 7. shallot
ciborium . . 3. pyx 6. canopy, coffer,
  vessel
cicada . . 6. dog-day, locust 9. Cicadidae
cicatrix . . 4. mark, scar 7. blemish
Cid . . 3. Ruy 4. hero, poem 5. Chief
  6. leader (Christian) 7. Rodrigo
cider (weak) . . 6. perkin
Cid's sword . . 6. colada
cienaga . . 5. marsh, swamp
cigar . . 4. rope, toby 5. claro 6. corona,
  Havana, maduro, stogie 7. cheroot
  8. panatela 9. cigarillo
cigarette . . 3. fag 4. pill 5. cubeb, smoke
  6. gasper, reefer 9. cigarillo 10. coffin
  nail
cilium . . 4. hair, lash 7. eyelash
  8. barbicel, ciliolum, filament
  9. eyewinker
cimarron . . 6. marron 7. bighorn, wild
  dog 8. district (Okla)
cimex . . 6. bedbug
Cimmerian, Homer Myth . . 4. dark
  5. Nomad (anc) 6. gloomy (abode)
  8. Cimmeria
cinch . . 4. game (cards), grip, sure
  5. girth 6. fasten 7. harness (part)
  9. certainty, sure thing
cinders . . 3. ash 4. lava, slag 5. ashes,
  dross 6. embers 7. residue 8. clinkers
cinerarium . . 8. mortuary
cinerator . . 7. furnace 9. crematory
  11. crematorium, incinerator
cingular . . 7. annular 8. circular
cinnamon . . 5. brown, spice 6. cassia
  8. ishpingo (So Am) 10. Cinnamomum
cinque . . 4. dice, five
cipher . . 3. nil 4. code, zero 5. aught
  6. figure, nobody, number, symbol
  7. compute 9. calculate, character,
  nonentity
circa . . 5. about 6. around
  13. approximately
Circe (pert to) . . .
brother . . 6. Aeetes
father . . 6. Helios
Island abode . . 5. Aeaea
role, Odyssey . . 7. siren 7. charmer
  9. sorceress, temptress
sister . . 5. Medea
circle . . . 3. orb 4. halo, hoop, loop, ring

  5. ambit, orbit, rhomb, rigol, round,
  wheel 6. clique, cordon, girdle, rotate,
  sphere 7. annulus, aureole, circuit,
  compass, enclose, revolve 9. circulate,
  encompass 13. circumference
circle (pert to) . . .
astronomy . . 6. tropic
celestial . . 6. colure 10. almucantar
Japan . . 4. maru
luminous . . 6. corona
of hell (8th) . . 9. Malebolge
of monoliths . . 8. cromlech 9. cyclolith
part . . 3. arc 6. areola, octant, radius,
  sector 7. sextant 8. diameter
circuit . . . 3. lap, orb 4. bout, gyre,
  loop, tour, zone 5. ambit, cycle, orbit,
  relay, round, route 6. circle, detour
  7. compass 9. round trip 10. revolution
circuit court . . . 4. eyre
circuitous . . . 4. mazy 6. curved
  7. crooked, devious, sinuous, twisted,
  vagrant, winding 8. circular, flexuous,
  indirect, tortuous 9. deceitful, deviating,
  underhand, wandering 10. roundabout,
  serpentine 12. disingenuous,
  labyrinthine 14. circumlocutory
circular . . . 5. round 6. ringed 7. annular,
  discoid, program 8. cingular, coronary,
  ringlike 9. crownlike, orbicular
  10. circuitous, roundabout
  13. advertisement
circular (pert to) . . .
enclosure . . 3. lis (liss)
indicator . . 4. dial
letter . . 10. encyclical
ornament . . 8. patera
circulate . . . 4. pass 5. issue 6. circle,
  rotate, spread 7. diffuse, publish
  8. monetize 9. propagate
  11. disseminate
circumference . . . 4. girt 5. ambit, bound,
  girth 6. bounds 7. circuit, compass
  8. encircle, surround 9. outskirts,
  perimeter, periphery
circumscribe . . . 5. bound, fence, limit
  6. define 7. enclose, environ 8. encircle,
  restrict 9. encompass
circumscribed . . . 6. finite, narrow
  9. definable 10. restricted
circumspect . . . 4. wary 5. chary
  7. careful, politic, prudent 8. cautious,
  discreet 9. judicious 10. thoughtful
  11. considerate
circumstance . . . 4. fact, item, pomp
  5. event, state 7. proviso 8. incident,
  occasion, position 9. condition,
  provision, situation 10. occurrence,
  particular 11. arrangement, opportunity,
  stipulation
circumstantial . . . 5. exact 6. minute
  7. precise 8. detailed 10. evidential,
  incidental, particular 11. conditional
  12. nonessential
circumvent . . . 5. cheat, evade 6. delude,
  entrap, outwit, thwart 7. capture, circuit,
  deceive 8. surround 9. encompass,
  frustrate
circus . . . 4. hawk, ring, show 5. arena
  6. big top, circle, cirque 7. harrier,
  theater 8. carnival, side show
  12. amphitheater

circus (pert to) . . .
 concessionaire . . **7.** grifter
 hawk . . **15.** circus assimilis
 rider . . **8.** desultor
 Roman . . **13.** Circus Maximus
 sideshow . . **6.** freaks
 superintendent . . **10.** ringmaster
cirque . . **6.** circle, corrie **7.** circlet
cis (pref) . . **8.** this side
cist . . **3.** box, pit **5.** chest **7.** chamber
 8. cistvaen (kistvaen)
Cistercian . . **4.** monk, Rule (Benedictine)
 5. Order **8.** Trappist
cistern . . **3.** bac, sac, tub, vat **4.** back,
 tank, well **7.** cuvette, raintub
 9. impluvium, reservoir
citadel . . **3.** arx **4.** fort **5.** Alamo, tower
 6. castle **7.** bastion, bulwark **8.** fastness,
 fortress **9.** acropolis **10.** stronghold
 13. fortification **14.** propugnaculum
citation . . **5.** honor **6.** eulogy, notice
 7. mention, summons **8.** subpoena
 9. quotation **11.** enumeration
 12. verification
cite . . **5.** quote **6.** adduce, allege, repeat,
 summon **7.** extract **8.** indicate
citizen . . **3.** cit **6.** native **7.** citoyen,
 denizen (of beasts), dweller **8.** civilian,
 townsman **10.** inhabitant
citizenship . . **10.** citizenism
 15. enfranchisement
citron . . **5.** melon **6.** cedrat (cedrate),
 citrus, yellow
citrus fruit . . **4.** lime **5.** lemon **6.** orange
 7. kumquat **8.** citrange, shaddock
 10. grapefruit
cittern, cithern . . **4.** lute (anc) **6.** zither
 7. cithara, gittern
city . . **4.** town **8.** township **10.** metropolis
 12. municipality
city (parts) . . **4.** ward **5.** civic, urban
 8. district, precinct
City of . . .
 Bells . . **10.** Strasbourg
 Bridges . . **6.** Bruges
 Brotherly Love . . **12.** Philadelphia
 Churches . . **8.** Brooklyn
 David . . **9.** Jerusalem
 Dead (The) . . **8.** cemetery **10.** Necropolis
 Elms . . **8.** New Haven
 Gods . . **6.** Asgard (Asgarth)
 Golden Gate (The) . . **12.** San Francisco
 Great King . . **9.** Jerusalem
 Hundred Towers . . **5.** Pavia
 Kings . . **4.** Lira
 Lilies . . **8.** Florence
 Magnificent Distances . . **10.** Washington
  (DC)
 Masts . . **6.** London
 Palms (Bib) . . **7.** Jericho
 Prophet (The) . . **6.** Medina
 Rams . . **6.** Canton
 Saints . . **8.** Montreal
 Seven Hills . . **4.** Rome
 Straits . . **7.** Detroit
 Sun (the) . . **7.** Baalbek **10.** Heliopolis
 Victory . . **5.** Cairo
 Violated Treaty . . **8.** Limerick
 Violet Crown . . **6.** Athens
civet . . **5.** fossa, genet, rasse **6.** foussa,
 musang **7.** nandine **10.** paradoxure

civic . . **5.** civil, urban **6.** public **7.** burghal,
 oppidan **9.** municipal **12.** metropolitan
civil . . **4.** hend (hende) **5.** suave **6.** decent,
 polite, public, urbane **7.** affable,
 courtly, elegant, secular **8.** discreet,
 gracious, obliging, polished, well-bred
 9. courteous, political **10.** respectful
 11. complaisant **13.** condescending
civil (pert to) . . .
 dress . . **5.** mufti **7.** civvies
 fraud (Rom) . . **11.** stellionate
 process . . **4.** writ
 strife . . **6.** stasis
 wrong . . **4.** tort
civility . . **6.** comity **7.** amenity
 8. courtesy, urbanity **9.** attention,
 etiquette, gentility **10.** affability,
 politeness
civilization . . **6.** kultur, polish **7.** culture
 10. refinement **11.** cultivation
civilize . . **4.** tame **6.** polish **8.** humanize,
 urbanize **9.** cultivate **11.** domesticate
clad . . **5.** robed **6.** decked, garbed
 7. arrayed, attired, clothed, dressed
 9. appareled, garmented
claim . . **3.** hak (hakh) **4.** case, lien,
 name **5.** right, title **6.** assert, demand
 7. preempt, profess, require **8.** arrogate,
 maintain, pretense (pretence), proclaim
 9. postulate **10.** pretension
claimant . . **7.** claimer **9.** applicant,
 plaintiff, pretender **10.** solicitant
clairvoyance . . **3.** ESP **7.** insight
 8. lucidity, sagacity **9.** intuition
 10. divination **11.** penetration
clairvoyant . . **4.** seer **7.** prophet, seeress
 9. sagacious **12.** clearsighted
clam . . **3.** Mya **5.** Chama, razor, Solen
 6. gweduc, Mactra, quahog **7.** mollusk
 10. veneriform (shape)
clam destroyer . . **6.** winkle
 10. periwinkle
clammy . . **4.** cool, damp, dank, soft
 5. moist, mucid **6.** sticky, sweaty
clamor . . **3.** cry, din, hue **4.** roar, wail
 5. decry, noise, vocal **6.** hubbub, outcry,
 racket, uproar **10.** hullabaloo
clamorous . . **4.** loud **5.** noisy **7.** blatant,
 clamant, excited **8.** brawling
 9. demanding, insistent, turbulent
 10. blustering, uproarious, vociferous
clamp . . **4.** vise **6.** fasten **9.** appliance
clan . . **3.** set **4.** camp, club, cult, gens,
 race, sept **5.** group, party, tribe **6.** circle,
 clique, family **7.** coterie, society
clan (quarrel) . . **4.** feud **8.** vendetta
clandestine . . **3.** sly **5.** privy **6.** covert,
 secret **7.** furtive, illicit **8.** stealthy
 9. concealed, underhand **10.** frandulent,
 undercover **11.** unobtrusive
 13. surreptitious
clang . . **4.** ding, ring **5.** clank, sound
 6. jangle **7.** ringing
clang color . . **6.** timbre **8.** tonality
clangor . . **3.** din **4.** ring **5.** clang, noise
 6. fracas, hubbub, jangle, racket, ruckus,
 rumpus, tumult, uproar **7.** discord,
 ringing
clank . . **4.** ring **5.** clang **7.** ringing
clapper . . **4.** bell, clap **5.** bones (minstrel)
claque . . **8.** chaqueur, opera hat

9. applauder

clarify . . . 5. clear 6. filter, purify, refine, render, strain 7. cleanse, explain, rectify

clash . . . 3. jar 4. bang, bump 5. crash 6. impact, jangle, tussle 7. collide, scuffle 8. conflict, disagree, skirmish 9. collision, encounter, hostility 10. dissonance

clasp . . . 3. hug 4. belt, grip, hasp, hold, ouch (anc), tach 5. grasp, morse (priest's), seize, stick, tache (anc) 6. buckle, enwrap, fasten, secure 7. agraffe (agrafe), embrace, tendril 8. fastener 10. chatelaine

class . . . 3. ilk 4. rank, sect 5. caste, genus (pl genera), grade, order, tribe 6. brevet (mil), status 7. station 8. category, classify, division 9. catalogue 14. classification

class (learned) . . . 8. literate, literati 14. intelligentsia

classical . . . 4. pure 5. Attic 6. chaste 7. classis, elegant 8. academic, literary, tasteful 10. Ciceronian

classification . . . 4. rank, sort 5. genus, grade 6. rating, system 7. species 8. analysis, category, grouping 12. distribution

classify . . . 4. list, rank, rate, sort, type 5. grade, label, range 6. assort, digest, ticket 7. aggroup, arrange 8. register 9. catalogue

clatter . . . 3. din, jar 5. noise, rumor 6. babble, gabble, hubbub, racket, rattle, rumpus, tattle, uproar 7. chatter, prattle 9. commotion 11. disturbance

clause . . . 5. rider 6. phrase 7. passage, proviso, section

claustral . . . 9. cloistral 10. cloistered

claw . . . 4. hand, nail, unce 5. chela, cloof, clufe, talon 6. nipper, unguis

claw . . . 3. dig 4. grab, grip, pull, tear 5. grasp, seize 6. clutch, scrape, snatch 7. grapple, scratch

clay . . . 3. mud 4. marl, mire, soil 5. argil, earth 6. corpse, kaolin

clay (pert to) . . .
baked . . 4. tile 5. brick
box . . 6. sagger
covered . . 6. lutose
mix . . 3. pug
mold . . 3. dod
molded . . 7. fictile
nodule . . 10. eaglestone
pipe . . 2. TD 10. meerschaum
plug . . 4. bott
polish . . 5. rabat
softening . . 8. malaxage
variety . . 4. bole, loam, marl 5. gault, ocher, tasco 8. petuntse

clayey . . . 4. soft 5. adobe, bolar 6. earthy 12. argillaceous

clean, cleanse . . . 4. dust, swab, wash, wipe 5. brush, purge, rinse, scrub 6. kosher, purify, refine 7. cleanse, deterge, launder 8. absterge, depurate, renovate 9. disinfect, elutriate, expurgate

cleanness . . . 6. purity (of life) 7. clarity 8. chastity, elegance, neatness, pureness, tidiness 10. immaculacy

13. impeccability

clear . . . 3. net, rid 4. free, gain, over, pure 5. clean, lucid, plain 6. acquit, excuse, exempt, hurdle, limpid, pardon, purify 7. absolve, concise, crystal, evident, explain, graphic, lighten, release 8. apparent, distinct, incisive, luculent 9. cloudless, exonerate, extricate, vindicate

clear land . . . 7. thwaite (Eng)

clearsighted . . . 4. keen 10. discerning 13. perspicacious

cleat . . . 4. bitt 5. level, strip, wedge 7. joinery

cleave . . . 3. cut 4. part, rend, rive, tear 5. clave, cling, clove, crack, sever, shear, split 6. adhere, bisect, cohere, divide, pierce 7. dispart 8. separate

cleek . . . 5. marry, pluck, seize 6. clutch, snatch

clef . . . 1. C, F, G 4. alto, bass 6. treble 7. descant, soprano 9. character

cleft . . . 3. gap 4. reft, rent, rift, rima 5. chasm, chink, crack, notch, riven, split 6. chappy, cranny, gaping, recess 7. crevice, fissure 8. scissure

cleft palate operation . . .
13. staphyloraphy (staphylorrhaphy)

clemency . . . 5. favor, grace, mercy 6. lenity 7. quarter 8. kindness, leniency, mildness 10. compassion, indulgence 11. forbearance

Clemens (Samuel) **pen name** . . . 9. Mark Twain

clench . . . 4. fist, grip, grit, hold 5. grasp 6. clinch, clutch 8. purchase 9. interlock

Cleopatra (pert to) . . .
attendant . . 4. Iras
downfall . . 3. asp
lover . . 6. Antony (Marc), Caesar
obelisk (two) . . 6. Needle
queen of . . 5. Egypt
river . . 4. Nile

clepe . . . 3. bid 4. call, name 6. invite, invoke 7. address 8. christen

clergy . . . 5. cloth 6. pulpit 9. clergymen, clericals 10. priesthood

clergyman . . . 4. abbé, dean 5. canon, vicar 6. cleric, curate, divine, parson, pastor, priest, rector 7. dominie, prelate 8. minister, preacher, sky pilot 9. presbyter 12. ecclesiastic

clergywoman . . . 3. nun 8. minister 9. parsoness, priestess 10. religieuse

cleric, non . . . 4. laic

clerical . . . 7. scribal 11. ministerial

clerical (pert to) . . .
attire . . 3. alb 5. amice, cloth, fanon, orale, stole
collar . . 5. rabat
hat . . 7. biretta

clerk . . . 3. nun 4. monk 5. write 6. cleric, hermit, layman, scribe 7. scholar (anc) 8. salesman 9. assistant, clergyman 12. ecclesiastic

cleronomy . . . 8. heritage 11. inheritance

clever . . . 3. apt 4. able, cute, deft 5. handy, slick, smart, witty 6. adroit, astute, brainy, bright, expert, habile, nimble 7. amiable, cunning, parlous 8. pleasing, skillful, talented 9. brilliant,

dexterous, ingenious 11. good-natured
cleverness . . . 4. tact, wits 5. skill 6. esprit
7. cunning 9. ingenuity, smartness,
wittiness 10. adroitness, astuteness,
shrewdness
clew, clue . . . 3. key 4. ball, loop (Naut)
rope 5. globe 6. cocoon, tackle (see
also *clue)*
cliché . . . 3. joke 5. banal, trite 6. old
saw 7. bromide 8. banality, chestnut
9. Joe Miller, platitude
click . . . 3. rap 4. snap 5. clack 6. go
over 7. prosper, succeed
click beetle . . . 3. dor (dorr) 6. elater
cliff . . . 3. gat 4. crag, klip, rock, wall
5. bluff, cleve, crest, scarp, slope
6. rocher 7. clogwyn 8. palisade
9. precipice 10. escarpment
climax . . . 3. cap, epi (Arch) 4. acme, near,
peak, shut 5. tight 6. apogee, result,
summit 7. heights 11. culmination
12. consummation
climb . . . 3. fly, gad 4. shin 5. grimp, scale,
speel 6. ascend, ascent 7. clamber,
upgrade 9. acclivity
climbing . . . 7. scaling 8. scandent
10. scansorial
climbing plant . . . 3. hop, ivy 4. bine,
nito, vine 5. betel, liana 6. bryony
clime . . . 4. zone 5. realm, tract 6. region
7. climate
clinch . . . 4. bind, grip, hold, seal
5. grasp, prove, seize 6. clutch, fasten,
secure 7. confirm, grapple 8. conclude,
purchase 9. establish
cling . . . 4. hold 5. stick 6. adhere, cohere
clingfish . . . 6. testar
clink . . . 4. rime, slap 5. rhyme 6. jingle,
lockup, prison, strike 9. assonance
clinquant . . . 4. gold, sham 6. tinsel
8. frippery, tinseled 10. glittering
clip . . . 3. bob, lop, mow 4. barb, blow,
dock, gaff, snip, trim 5. clasp, prune,
shear 6. clutch, fasten 7. curtail, scissor,
shorten 8. ornament 10. instrument
clique . . . 3. set 4. cell, clan, club, ring
5. group, Junta, junto 6. circle (people)
7. coterie
Cloaca Maxima (anc Rome) . . . 5. sewer
10. repository
cloak . . . 3. aba 4. cape, mask, pall,
wrap 5. cover, grego, jelab, manta,
sagum 6. abolla, capote, dolman,
mantle, mantua, screen, serape, shield
7. chlamys (anc), conceal, galabia,
manteau, paenula (anc), paletot, pelisse,
pretext, protect 8. disguise 9. dissemble,
new-market 10. witzchoura
clobber . . . 3. hit 4. beat, conk, poke,
swat 5. clout, punch, whack 6. defeat,
strike, wallop
clock . . . 3. nef (ship's) 4. dial, time
5. knock 6. record 7. digital 8. recorder,
sidereal 9. clepsydra, metronome,
timepiece 10. isochronon
11. chronometer
clockwise . . . 6. deasil (dessil)
11. withershins 14. dextrorotation,
dextrorotatory
clog . . . 4. stop 5. choke, dance 6. daggle,
hamper, impede 8. encumber, obstruct,

restrain
clog shoe . . . 4. geta 5. sabot 6. chopin,
cobcab (Orient), patten 7. chopine
cloister . . . 4. stoa 5. abbey 6. arcade,
friary, immure, priory 7. confine,
convent, nunnery, retreat 9. anchorage,
hermitage, monastery, peristyle
10. passageway
cloistered . . . 7. recluse 8. enclosed,
monastic 11. sequestered
clone . . . 4. copy, twin 7. replica
close . . . 2. at, by 3. end 4. near, nigh,
seal, shut, slam 5. dense, finis, stivy
6. finale, finish, period, secret, stingy,
sultry 7. airless, extreme, occlude,
related 8. complete, conclude, familiar,
imminent, intimate, stifling 9. extremity,
secretive, terminate 11. approximate,
termination 13. juxtaposition
close (pert to) . . .
eyes (the) . . 4. seel 5. blink
fasten . . 6. batten
of day . . 8. eventide 9. nightfall
poetic . . 4. nigh 5. anear
tightly . . 3. bar 4. bung, seal 6. clench,
enseal 9. obturate
closely . . . 4. just 6. almost, barely, nearly
8. narrowly
closely allied . . . 6. chummy 7. germane
8. intimate
closeness . . . 7. density, secrecy
8. fidelity, intimacy, likeness, nearness,
sameness 9. tightness 10. chumminess,
narrowness, similarity, stinginess,
strictness, sultriness 11. airlessness,
compactness, conciseness, familiarity,
resemblance 14. oppressiveness
closet . . . 5. ambry, cuddy, emery
6. locker, pantry 7. cabinet 8. cupboard,
wardrobe 9. cloakroom, storeroom
closing device . . . 3. key 4. lock, snap
5. clasp, hinge, latch 6. Velcro (tm),
zipper
closing measure (Mus) . . . 4. coda
clot . . . 4. lump, mass 5. grume 7. thicken
8. coagulum, concrete 9. coagulate
12. crassamentum
cloth . . . 3. net, tat 4. brin, crea, drap,
felt, lamé, silk, tapa, wool 5. adati,
baize, bezan, bluet, carda, crash,
crepe, denim, khaki, linen, manta,
nylon, orlon, rayon, satin, scrim,
surat, tamis, terry, tulle, twill, voile
6. alpaca, burlap, calico, canvas, chintz,
cotton, damask, dimity, dowlas, duffel,
faille, jersey, madras, mohair, muslin,
nankin, pongee, poplin, samite (gold),
sateen, velour 7. acetate, baracan,
brocade, bunting, cambric, challis,
chiffon, drap d'or, flannel, foulard,
gingham, nankeen, organdy, organza,
percale, sacking, spandex, taffeta,
ticking, worsted 8. cashmere, chambray,
corduroy, cretonne, drilling, nainsook,
Shantung 9. crinoline, gabardine,
polyester, sailcloth, tarpaulin, tricotine
10. broadcloth, seersucker
11. cheesecloth, drap d'argent (silver),
marquisette
cloth (pert to) . . .
checkered . . 5. plaid

dealer . . 6. draper
finisher . . 7. beetler
measure . . 4. nail
piece . . 4. bolt 5. scrap
ridge . . 4. wale
selvage . . 4. roon 6. border 7. listing
twilled . . 5. denim, serge
weaving . . 4. warp, weft, woof
clothe . . . 3. tog 4. deck, garb, gird, robe,
   vest 5. array, drape, dress, endue, indue
   6. afford, enrobe, invest 7. empower,
   provide, sheathe 8. accouter
clothes . . . 3. rig 4. duds, garb, togs
   5. guise, habit, jeans, Levis 6. attire,
   bikini, briefs 7. apparel, costume,
   raiment, regalia, threads (sl) 8. clothing,
   garments, leotards, swimsuit
   9. dungarees 10. bedclothes,
   garmenture 11. habiliments, investiture
cloud . . . 3. fog, low 4. dust, film, haze,
   mist, rack, scud 5. nepho (comb
   form), nubia, stain, sully, taint, vapor
   6. cirrus, damage, darken, defame,
   defect, nebule, nimbus, shadow, stigma
   7. blacken, blemish, cumulus, nubilus,
   obscure, pea-soup, stratus, tarnish,
   tornado 8. cat's-tail, cocktail, overcast
   10. horizontal
clouds (pert to) . . .
astronomy . . 4. coma 9. nubeculae
kind . . 6. cirrus, nimbus 7. cumulus,
   fractus, stratus 9. mare's-tail
luminous . . 5. nimbi
Magellanic . . 5. Major, Minor
photography . . 9. nephogram
science of . . 9. nephology
seeding . . 10. nucleation
vapory . . 9. rack
cloudy . . 4. dark, hazy 5. filmy, foggy,
   misty, murky, shady, vague 6. gloomy,
   lowery, opaque 7. nebular, obscure
   8. confused, overcast, vaporous
   9. cloudlike 10. indistinct, lackluster
clout . . . 3. hit, jab, rag 4. blow, bump,
   clod, mend, nail, swat 5. patch,
   power, shred, smack 9. influence
   12. handkerchief
clove . . . see also *cleave* 5. spice
clover . . . 3. red 4. bush 5. lotus, snail,
   white 6. alsike 7. crimson, melilot,
   prairie, spotted 9. Melilotus
clown . . . 3. oaf 4. boor, fool, lout,
   mime, mome, zany 5. comic, Kelly
   (Emmet), mimer, yahoo 6. jester, rustic
   7. buffoon 9. harlequin 10. countryman
   11. merry-andrew
clownish . . . 4. rude 5. gawky, rough
   6. clumsy, coarse, rustic 7. awkward,
   boorish, ill-bred, loutish, uncivil
   8. churlish, ungainly 9. untutored
   10. buffoonish 11. countrified
cloy . . . 4. clog, glut, pall, sate 5. gorge,
   stuff 6. accloy 7. satiate, satisfy, surfeit
club . . . 3. bat, hit 4. beat, join, mace
   5. billy, clout, staff, unite, yokel
   6. cudgel, league, weapon 7. society
   8. bludgeon, spontoon 9. boomerang,
   espantoon 10. nulla-nulla, pogamoggan
   11. association
club (pert to) . . .
actors . . 6. Friars

historic . . 5. Whigs 8. Jacobins
   10. Cordeliers
Service . . 7. Kiwanis
Women's (first) . . 7. Sorosis
clubfoot . . . 7. talipes 9. deformity, pes
   valgus 13. talipes valgus
club-shaped . . . 7. clavate
clue, clew . . . 3. key, tip 4. data, hint
   5. scent 6. thread 7. inkling 8. evidence
   9. suspicion 11. fingerprint
clump . . . 3. tod 4. heap, lump, thud,
   tuft 5. bunch, chunk, group, motte
   (mott), patch, stamp 6. growth, trudge
   7. cluster, thicket
clumsy . . . 4. ugly 5. bulky, gawky,
   inapt, inept, unfit 6. gauche, oafish
   7. awkward, uncouth, unhandy
   8. slipshod, ungainly, unwieldy
   9. inelegant, lumbering, maladroit,
   misshapen 10. blundering,
   cumbersome, left-handed
   13. inappropriate
clumsy person . . . 4. gawk 5. jumbo,
   staup 7. bungler
clupeoid fish . . . 7. herring
cluster . . . 4. crop, cyme, gang, tuft
   5. bunch, clump, group 6. huddle
   8. fascicle 9. glomerule
cluster (pert to) . . .
bean . . 4. guar 6. legume
fibers . . 3. nep
flowers . . 6. raceme 7. rosette
   8. anthemia, panticle
fruit . . 6. grapes
spores . . 5. sorus
stars . . 8. Globular, Pleiades (The)
clustery . . . 8. racemose
clutch . . . 3. nab 4. claw, grip, hold, nest
   5. brood, catch, clasp, grasp, seize
   6. clench, cletch, crisis
clyster . . . 5. enema 6. lavage 9. injection
Clytemnestra's mother . . . 4. Leda
cnemis . . . 4. shin 5. tibia
coach . . . 3. car, rig 5. prime, stage,
   train, tutor 6. direct, fiacre, jarvey
   7. adviser, prepare, tallyho, teacher
   8. carriage, equipage, instruct, preparer
   9. charabanc 10. instructor
coach dog . . . 9. Dalmatian
coachman . . . 3. fly (angling) 4. fish,
   jehu, whip 6. driver
coagulate . . . 3. gel, jel, set 4. cake, clot,
   curd, lump 6. curdle, posset 7. congeal
   8. solidify
coagulator . . . 6. enzyme, rennet
coagulum . . . 4. clot, curd 5. grume
   7. clabber
coal . . . 4. fuel 5. black, ember 6. carbon,
   cinder 7. lignite, residue
coal (pert to) . . .
bin . . 6. bunker
car . . 3. dan 4. corf, tram 6. hopper
dust . . 4. coom (coomb), culm, smut
gas . . 7. Pintsch 9. acetylene
miner . . 7. collier
miner's disease . . 11. anthracosis
oil . . 8. kerosene
residue . . 4. coke
tar . . 5. lysol, pitch 6. cresol, decane,
   phenol 7. toluene
tunnel . . 4. adit

type . . 3. egg, nut, pea 4. dant, hard,
peat, soft 6. broken, cannel 8. charcoal,
chestnut 9. buckwheat 10. anthracite,
bituminous
coalition . . . 4. bloc 5. trust, union
6. fusion, hookup, league, merger
7. society 8. alliance 10. federation
11. affiliation, combination,
confederacy, conjunction
coalition advocate . . . 9. fusionist
coals . . . 5. gleed 6. embers 7. cinders
coarse . . . 3. fat, low 4. dank, lewd,
rude, vile 5. broad, crass, gross, thick
6. carnal, earthy, impure, ribald, rustic,
vulgar 7. goatish, obscene, sensual
8. granular, immodest, indecent,
inferior, unchaste 9. inelegant,
offensive, unrefined 10. unfinished,
unpolished
coarse (pert to) . . .
grain . . 4. meal
grass . . 4. reed 5. sedge 6. quitch
hominy . . 4. corn, samp
coast . . . 4. sail 5. beach, glide, shore,
slide 6. rivage 7. seaside 8. seaboard,
seashore
coast (pert to) . . .
dweller . . 7. orarian
live oak . . 6. encina
projection . . 4. cape, ness
coat . . . 4. jupe 5. cloak, frock, parka,
tunic 6. blazer, capote, duster, jacket,
raglan, reefer, trench, tuxedo, ulster
7. cassock, cutaway, paletot, slicker
8. gossamer, Mackinaw, tegument
9. newmarket, redingote
coat (pert to) . . .
fastener . . 4. frog 6. zipper
of animal . . 3. fur 4. pelt, wool 6. pelage
8. feathers
of arms . . 5. crest 8. blazonry
10. escutcheon
of mail . . 6. byrnia 7. hauberk
of the eye (inner) . . 6. retina
coati . . . 5. Nasua 6. narica 7. raccoon
coating (pert to) . . .
cake . . 5. glacé, icing 8. frosting
copper, bronze . . 6. patina
grain . . 4. bran
medical . . 9. collodion
metal . . 5. plate
seed . . 5. testa 6. tegmen 10. endopleura
tin, lead . . 5. terne
vitreous . . 6. enamel
coax . . . 3. beg, ply 4. lure, urge 5. press,
tease 6. cajole, entice, exhort 7. beguile,
flatter, implore, wheedle 8. blandish,
inveigle, persuade 9. importune
10. manipulate
cob . . . 4. axis, blow, gull, loaf, mole, pier,
swan 5. block, chief, horse 6. basket,
leader, muffin, spider 7. beating,
corncob 8. dumpling 10. breakwater
cobbler . . . 3. pie 5. coler, sutor 6. bungle,
repair, souter 7. botcher, crispin
9. fortescue (fortesque), shoemaker
cobbra . . . 4. head 5. skull
cobby . . . 5. stout 6. hearty, lively, stocky
10. headstrong
cobra . . . 3. asp 4. Naga (Myth), Naja
5. mamba, snake, viper 8. ringhals

cobweb . . . 3. net 4. trap 5. snare,
wevet 7. fiction, network 8. filament,
gossamer 9. intricacy
cobweblike . . . 8. araneous 9. arachnoid
cocaine . . . 4. coca, snow (sl) 8. narcotic
9. mydriatic 10. anesthetic
coccus . . . 4. cell 5. spore 9. bacterium,
cochineal
cochleate . . . 6. spiral 11. shell-shaped
cock . . . 3. nab, tap 4. bird, heap, kora,
pile, vane (weather) 5. strut, valve
6. faucet, grouse, leader, muckna
7. rooster, swagger
cockade . . . 4. knot 7. rosette
Cockade State . . . 8. Maryland
cockatoo . . . 3. ara 5. arara (palm), galah
6. parrot 8. ganggang
cockle . . . 4. boat, gith, kiln, oast 5. shell,
stove 6. pucker 7. mollusk, wrinkle
cockpit . . . 3. pit 4. well 5. arena, cabin
(airplane) 7. gallera
cockscomb (coxcomb) . . . 5. crest, plant
cocktail . . . 5. cloud, drink, horse 6. beetle
9. appetizer
cocky . . . 4. pert 5. saucy 6. jaunty
7. stuck-up 9. conceited
cocoa . . . 5. broma, cacao 8. beverage
9. chocolate 11. theobromine
coconut (pert to) . . .
fiber . . 4. coir, kyar
India . . 6. nargil (narghile)
meat . . 5. copra
tree . . 4. palm
cocoon . . . 3. pod 4. bave (silk), clew,
kell, pupa 9. chrysalis
cod . . . 3. bib, cor 4. fish, ling 5. scrod,
sprag 6. burbot, cultus, gadoid
7. bacalao
coddle . . . 3. pet 4. baby, cock 5. humor,
spoil 6. caress, fondle, pamper
11. mollycoddle
code . . . 3. law 5. canon, codex, Morse,
salic 6. digest, cipher, signal, symbol
7. pandect, precept 12. Commandments
codfish (pert to) . . .
Alaska . . 6. wachna
genus . . 5. Gadus
ready for cooking . . 5. scrod
type . . 3. cod, red 4. cusk, rock 6. Murray,
tomcod 7. buffalo
codger . . . 5. crank, miser 6. oddity
codicil . . . 4. will 5. rider 6. sequel
8. addition, appendix 10. instrument
Cody (William) . . . 11. Buffalo Bill
coerce . . . 4. curb 5. force 6. compel
7. dragoon, enforce, repress
9. blackjack, strong-arm, terrorize
10. intimidate
coercion . . . 5. force 6. duress 8. violence
10. compulsion, constraint
coffee (pert to) . . .
bean . . 3. nib
container . . 8. canister
cup holder . . 4. zarf
drink . . 8. espresso 10. café au lait,
cappuccino
extract . . 8. caffeine
kind . . 3. Rio 4. Java, Kona 5. Kenya,
Milds, Mocha 6. Bogota, Brazil, Santos
7. Sumatra, Turkish 8. Medellin
9. Maracaibo

mix . . 7. chicory
pot . . 6. biggin 10. percolator
coffin . . 3. box, urn 4. bier, case, kist, mold 5. chest, crust 6. basket, casing, casket 11. sarcophagus

coffin (pert to) . . .
cloth . . 4. pall 5. cloak
litter . . 4. bier
nail . . 9. cigarette
prehistoric . . 4. cist 5. chest
structure . . 10. catafalque

cog . . . 3. cam 4. boat (fishing), gear 5. catch, cheat, cozen, tenon, tooth 7. ratchet, wheedle 8. sprocket 9. deception

cogent . . . 5. valid 6. potent, strong 7. telling 8. powerful 9. effective 10. compelling, conclusive, convincing, persuasive

cogitate . . . 4. mull, muse, plan 5. think 6. ponder 8. meditate 9. cerebrate

cognizance . . . 3. ken 4. heed, plea 5. badge (knight's) 9. knowledge 11. recognition 12. apprehension

cognizant . . . 5. aware 7. knowing 8. sensible 9. conscious 10. perceptive 11. intelligent

cognomen . . . 4. name 5. title 6. y-clept 7. surname 8. nickname 10. patronymic 11. appellation

coheir . . . 5. joint 8. parcener

cohere . . . 5. agree, cling, serry, stick, unite 6. adhere, cleave 9. glutinate

coherence . . . 5. cling 8. adhesion, cohesion, sticking 9. adherence, connected 11. consistency

coil . . . 4. ansa, clew, curl, loop, mesh, wind 5. querl, twine, twist 6. spiral 7. haycock 8. encircle 11. convolution

coiled . . . 7. tortile, twirled

coin . . . 3. rin, sou, yen 4. cash, cent 5. money, penny, stamp 6. specie

coin (pert to) . . .
Bib . . 6. talent
brass . . 13. Rosa Americana (1722)
gold . . 3. lev 4. ryal (rial) 5. daric, eagle 6. guinea
minor . . 4. doit
parts of . . 4. flan 5. field, tails, verso 6. legend 7. exergue, obverse (front), reverse
silver . . 4. batz, obol, ryal (rial) 5. crown, ducat, sceat 6. tester
tester . . 6. shroff (saraf)

coincide . . . 5. agree, check, chime, match, tally 6. concur 7. consent 10. correspond 11. synchronize

coincident . . . 9. consonant 10. concurrent 12. contemporary

coiner . . . 8. inventor 9. neologist (words) 10. fabricator 13. counterfeiter

coins (pert to) . . .
roll of . . 7. rouleau
science of . . 11. numismatics
specialist . . 11. numismatist

colander . . . 5. sieve 6. filter, sorter 8. strainer

Colchis King . . . 6. Aeetes

cold . . . 3. icy, nip, raw 4. dank, dead, drow, dull, frio, sure 5. algid, bland, bleak, frore (anc), gelid 6. chilly, frigid,

frosty 7. chilled, cinched 8. chilling, reserved, unheated 9. heartless 10. lackluster 11. indifferent, passionless, unconscious

cold (pert to) . . .
blooded . . 9. heartless, unfeeling 13. dispassionate, heterothermal 14. poikilothermal
feet . . 9. cowardice
infection . . 4. post 5. rheum 6. coryza 7. catarrh
sore . . 6. herpes 7. simplex, vesicle 14. herpes labialis
steel . . 5. sword 7. bayonet, weapons
term . . 8. frigoric
wind . . 4. bise

Coleoptera . . . 7. beetles, insects

Coleridge (Samuel Taylor) (pert to) . . .
place . . 6. Xanadu
poem . . 9. Kubla Khan
Rime of the . . 14. Ancient Mariner
river . . 4. Alph

colewort . . . 4. kale 7. cabbage

colic . . . 4. pain 5. gripe, spasm 7. tormina 10. enteralgia 11. stomachache

coliseum . . . 4. bowl 5. arena 6. circus 7. stadium, theater 9. Colosseum 10. hippodrome 12. amphitheater

collaborate . . . 3. aid 6. co-work 8. coauthor 9. cooperate 10. fraternize

collage . . . 6. gluing 7. montage 8. abstract, adhesive 9. cyclorama

collapse . . . 4. cave, fail, fall 5. crash, slump 6. cave-in, defeat 7. crack-up, debacle, deflate, failure 8. downfall 9. breakdown, shrinking 10. bankruptcy, exhaustion 11. prostration

collar . . . 4. band, grab, ruff 5. chain, rabat, ruche 6. arrest, bertha, rabato, tackle, torque 7. barghan, capture, harness (part), shackle 8. carcanet, neckband 10. pickadilly

collard . . . 4. kale

collate . . . 5. audit, check 6. verify 7. certify, compare, examine

collateral . . . 5. extra 6. margin 7. related 8. indirect, relation (folks), security 9. accessory, secondary 10. contingent, obligation, subsidiary 11. subordinate 12. nonessential

collation . . . 3. tea 4. meal 5. lunch 6. repast, sermon 7. address, reading 8. luncheon, treatise 10. collection, comparison, conference 12. consultation, contribution

colleague . . . 6. fellow 7. compeer, comrade, consort, partner 8. camarada, confrere 9. associate, companion 11. confederate

collect . . . 3. bag, tax 4. levy, mass 5. amass, glean, raise, rally 6. deduce, forage, garner, gather, muster, prayer, sheave 7. compile, procure 8. assemble, mobilize 9. aggregate 10. accumulate, congregate

collection . . . 3. ana, bag, set 4. book, olio 5. group, hoard, store 6. rosary, sorite 8. assembly, donation, offering 9. aggregate, congeries, gathering, repertory 10. assemblage, repertoire 11. acquisition

collection (pert to) . . .
 anecdotes . . 3. ana 4. data 8. analecta
 animals (wild) . . 3. zoo 9. menagerie
 bubbles . . 4. foam
 curiosities . . 6. museum
 documents . . 4. Veda 6. corpus 7. dossier
 fruit . . 7. syncarp
 implements (Surg) . . 7. trousse
 of four . . 6. tetrad
 of twenty-four . . 5. quire
 poems . . 5. sylva 9. anthology
 proper names . . 11. onomasticon
 type . . 4. font
 writing . . 10. literature
collector (pert to) . . .
 bird eggs . . 8. oologist
 books . . 10. bibliothec 11. bibliophile
  12. bibliomaniac
 coins . . 11. numismatist
 rent . . 8. landlord
 stamps . . 11. philatelist
colleen . . 4. girl, lass, maid 6. damsel,
  maiden 7. girleen
college . . . 6. school 7. academy, society
  9. Alma Mater, institute 10. université,
  university 11. corporation, institution
college (pert to) . . .
 campus . . 4. lawn, quad 7. grounds
 graduate . . 6. alumna 7. alumnus
 license for absence . . 5. exeat
 official . . 4. dean 5. prexy 6. beadle,
  bursar, regent 7. proctor
collegiate . . . 8. academic 9. collegian,
  scholarly 11. college-bred
collide with . . . 3. hit, ram 5. clash, crash
  6. hurtle, strike 7. contend 8. conflict,
  disagree
collier . . . 5. miner 6. plover
colloshangie . . 3. row 7. quarrel
  8. squabble 9. disturbance (noisy)
collision . . . 4. bump 5. clash, crash
  . impact 7. smashup 8. accident
  9. hostility 11. composition,
  impingement 12. interference
colloquial . . . 6. common 8. everyday,
  familiar, informal 9. unstudied
  10. vernacular 11. undignified
  14. conversational
colloquy . . . 4. chat, talk 6. parley
  9. discourse 10. conference
  12. conversation
Cologne Kings (legend) . . . 4. Magi
  6. Gaspar 8. Melchior 9. Balthasar
Colombia . . .
 capital . . 6. Bogota (1538)
 city . . 4. Cali 5. Pasto 8. Medellin
  9. Cartagena 10. Santa Marta
 Falls . . 10. Tequendama
 Liberator . . 7. Bolivar (Simon)
 mountain . . 5. Andes 11. Cordilleras
 river . . 9. Magdalena
colonize . . . 6. gather, people, settle
  8. populate 9. establish
colonizer . . . 3. ant 6. oecist 7. planter,
  settler
colonnade . . . 3. row (columns) 4. stoa
  6. arcade 7. columns, pillars, portico
  8. cloister 9. peristyle
colony . . . 4. body 5. group, swarm
  8. dominion 9. community
  10. dependency, settlement

colophon . . . 4. logo 6. emblem
  9. bookplate 11. inscription (book)
color . . . 3. dun, dye, hue 4. tint, tone
  5. blush, paint, shade, stain, terne,
  tinge 6. flaxen, nuance, pastel, sallow,
  timbre 7. piebald, pigment 8. tincture
  (Her) 10. complexion
color (pert to) . . .
 application (paste) . . 7. impasto
 blending . . 4. teer 5. fondu 9. scumbling
 blind . . 13. achromatopsia
 clouded . . 9. nebulated
 colorful . . 9. chromatic
 colorless . . 4. drab, dull, pale 6. pallid
  7. whitish 8. blanched 10. achromatic
 irregularity . . 5. fleck 6. streak
  10. rivulation
 material . . 5. eosin, morin, smalt
  7. pigment 11. chlorophyll
 off color . . 6. risqué 8. improper
 organ . . 8. clavilux
 paint, rouge . . 6. ruddle 7. blusher
 science of . . 10. chromatics
  11. spectrology
 variegated . . 7. rainbow, The Flag,
  vibgyor 8. spectrum 11. iridescence
Colorado . . .
 canyon . . 5. Black 10. Royal Gorge
 capital . . 6. Denver
 city . . 5. Aspen, Lamar 6. Pueblo
  7. Boulder, Manassa, Manitou
 Indian . . 7. Arapaho
 lake (highest) . . 10. Frozen Lake
 Mt peak . . 6. Elbert 9. Pike's Peak
 park . . 5. Estes 15. Garden of the Gods
 river . . 4. Gila 6. Platte 8. Arkansas
 State admission . . 12. Thirty-eighth
 State bird . . 11. lark bunting
 State flower . . 9. columbine
 State motto . . 13. Nil Sine Numine
  (Nothing Without God)
 State nickname . . 10. Centennial
colossal . . . 4. huge 5. great, large
  6. absurd, superb 7. mammoth
  8. gigantic 9. monstrous
colossal beast . . . 8. behemoth (Bib)
colt . . . 3. gun 4. foal 5. filly, horse
  8. yearling
Columbus (pert to) . . .
 birthplace . . 5. Genoa (It)
 companion . . 5. Ojeda
 discoverer . . 7. America (1492)
 landing site . . 11. San Salvador
 sailing site . . 5. Palos (Sp)
 vessel . . 4. Nina 5. Pinta 10. Santa
  Maria
column . . . 3. lat (Buddh) 4. anta 5. pylon,
  shaft, stele (stela) 6. pillar 7. telamon
  8. baluster, caryatid, pilaster
column (pert to) . . .
 base . . 5. socle 6. plinth 9. stylobate
 military . . 4. unit 9. formation
 Order (Arch) . . 5. Doric, Ionic 6. Tuscan
  9. Composite 10. Corinthian
 ref to . . 5. train 7. cortege 8. cylinder,
  memorial, monument 10. procession
 shaft . . 4. fust 5. scape 8. apophyge
 term . . 5. bague, galbe, shank 7. capital,
  entasis
coma . . . 4. daze, tuft 5. carus, sleep,
  sopor 6. stupor, trance 9. catalepsy

12. sluggishness 13. insensibility
15. unconsciousness

comatose . . . 6. drowsy, torpid
9. apathetic, lethargic 10. cataleptic,
insensible 11. unconscious

comb . . . 4. card, wave 5. cock's, crest,
curry, groom, scour, tease 6. search
7. rummage 8. caruncle

combat . . . 3. war 4. cope, duel, fray, tilt
5. fight, joust (anc) repel 6. action,
battle, karate, kung fu, oppose, strife
7. contest, jujitsu, scuffle 8. argument,
conflict 9. withstand 10. antagonize,
contention, engagement

combat (pert to) . . .
challenge . . 6. cartel 8. gauntlet
code . . 6. duello
scene . . 5. arena 8. coliseum

combatant . . . 6. dueler 7. battler, fighter
8. disputer 9. contender 10. competitor,
contestant

combative . . . 8. militant 9. agonistic,
bellicose 10. aggressive, pugnacious
11. belligerent, contentious

combination . . . 4. gang, pact, pool
5. blend, combo, party, trust, union
6. clique, fusion, hookup, league,
merger 7. amalgam, combine, faction,
mixture 8. alliance, coalesce, ensemble,
junction 9. camarilla, coalition,
synthesis 10. embodiment
11. aggregation, association,
confederacy, unification
12. undergarment 13. incorporation

combine . . . 3. add, mix 4. join, pool
5. merge, unite 6. concur, mingle
7. machine 10. synthesize

combining form . . .
above, beyond . . 3. sur 5. ultra
across . . 4. tran 5. trans
bad . . 3. dys, mal
black . . 4. mela
earth . . 3. geo 5. terra
equal . . 3. iso 4. homo, pari
far . . 3. tel 4. tele
good . . 2. eu
hundred . . 4. cent
inner, within . . 4. ento (ent)
kidney . . 4. reni
middle . . 4. medi 5. medio
mountain . . 3. oro
needle . . 3. acu
new . . 3. neo
not . . 2. un 3. non
old, ancient . . 5. paleo
one . . 3. uni 4. mono
outside, without . . 3. ect, ext 4. ecto
personal . . 4. idio
soft . . 4. leni
stone . . 4. lith
thought . . 4. ideo
thrice . . 3. ter
tooth . . 6. odonto
touch . . 3. tac
up, upward . . 3. ano
watery . . 4. sero

comblike . . . 7. ctenoid 8. pectinal

combustible . . . 5. fiery, quick 7. piceous
8. volcanic 9. flammable, irascible
10. accendible 11. hot-tempered,
inflammable

combustion . . . 4. fire 6. tumult 7. blazing,
flaming 8. ignition 9. agitation,
confusion, cremation 12. inflammation
13. conflagration

come . . . 3. hop 4. near 5. issue, occur
6. appear, arrive, happen 8. approach
9. transpire

come (pert to) . . .
across . . 3. pay 4. meet 7. confess
10. contribute
back . . 6. answer, retort, return
7. rebound, recover 8. remember,
repartee
before . . 4. lead 7. precede, prevene
8. antecede, antedate
between . . 6. divide 8. estrange, interlie
9. interpose, intervene
by . . 3. get 4. gain 6. obtain 7. acquire,
inherit, receive
forth . . 3. jet 4. gush, spew 5. hatch,
issue, occur 6. appear, emerge, spring
7. emanate 9. originate
together . . 4. join, knit, meet 5. clash,
merge 7. collide, convene 8. assemble,
converge

come (to) . . .
light . . 7. develop
maturity . . 5. ripen
pass . . 5. occur 6. befall, betide, happen
9. eventuate
rest . . 3. sit 5. light 6. settle

comedian, comedienne . . . 3. wit 4. buff
5. actor, comic 6. player 7. farcist
8. funnyman 9. dramatist

comedy . . . 5. drama, farce, revue
7. comedie, stand-up 8. travesty
9. burlesque, slapstick

comestibles . . . 4. food 5. manna
8. eatables, victuals

comet (pert to) . . .
cloud . . 4. Oort
famous . . 7. Halley's 8. Kohoutek
part . . 4. coma, tail 7. nucleus

comfort . . . 4. ease 5. cheer, quilt 6. relief,
solace, soothe, succor 7. confirm,
console, enliven, fortify, refresh, relieve,
support, sustain 8. inspirit, nepenthe
(drug) 9. enjoyment 10. invigorate,
strengthen 11. consolation
12. satisfaction

comfortable . . . 4. cozy, easy, snug
5. scarf 8. adequate, cheerful, homelike,
wristlet 9. contented, endemonic
10. complacent, prosperous
11. consolatory, encouraging

comforter . . . 5. quilt 6. tippet 7. solacer
8. pacifier 9. Paraclete

comfortless . . . 7. forlorn 8. desolate
9. cheerless, heartsick 10. despairing
11. distressing 12. disconsolate,
inconsolable

comic, comical . . . 3. odd 5. cutup, droll,
funny, queer, witty 6. absurd, quaint
7. cartoon, risible 8. comedian, farcical,
humorous 9. burlesque, laughable,
ludicrous, quizzical, whimsical
10. capricious, outlandish

coming . . . 3. due 6. access, advent, future
7. arrival, forward, looming 8. eventual,
expected, imminent 9. imminence
11. approaching, forthcoming

coming into being ... 7. genesis, nascent

comity ... 7. amenity, suavity 8. civility, courtesy, urbanity 10. affability

command ... 3. bid, gee, haw, hup 4. bade, beck, fiat, hest, rule, sway 5. evast, check, edict, exact, grasp, order, power, ukase 6. behest, charge, compel, decree, direct, enjoin, govern 7. control, dictate, mandate, mastery 8. dominion, restrain 9. authority, prescribe 10. domination 11. commandment 12. jurisdiction

commander ... 3. cid 5. chief, ruler 6. leader 7. admiral, captain, skipper 8. dictator, governor, myriarch, overlord

commander, Eastern ... 3. ras 4. amir, emir, Imam, khan, rani 5. ameer, begum, dewan, emeer, nawab, Nizam 6. caliph, regent, Sultan

commanding ... 8. dominant 9. imperious 10. imperative 13. authoritative

commandments ... 4. laws 6. orders, tables 8. mandates, precepts 9. Decalogue (Ten)

comme il faut ... 8. properly 9. correctly 10. decorously 12. as it should be

commemoration ... 7. service 8. Encaenia (Oxford Univ) 10. observance 11. anniversary, celebration, remembrance 13. solemnization

commence ... 4. open 5. arise, begin, start 6. spring 8. initiate 9. originate

commencement ... 4. rite 6. source 8. ceremony, nascency 9. beginning, formality, inception, novitiate 10. initiation

commend ... 4. plug 5. boost, extol, offer 6. assign, commit, praise, remand, resign 7. approve, deliver, entrust 8. advocate, delegate 9. recommend 10. compliment

commendation ... 4. hype, plug, puff 5. boost, kudos 8. approval 10. assignment, commitment, compliment, delegation 11. approbation, consignment, entrustment

comment ... 4. note, talk 6. gossip, postil, remark, report 7. descant, discuss, explain, mention 8. annotate, critique 9. criticism, discourse

commentary ... 5. gloss 6. memoir 7. remarks 8. treatise 9. memoranda 10. annotation 11. explanation

commerce ... 5. trade 7. traffic 8. dealings 9. communion 11. interchange 13. communication

commis ... 5. agent, clerk 6. deputy

commiserate ... 4. pity 7. condole, console 10. sympathize

commiseration ... 4. pity, ruth 5. mercy 6. sorrow 7. empathy, feeling 8. sympathy 10. compassion, condolence

commission ... 4. duty, task 5. allot, board, share, trust 6. brevet, depute, office, ordain 7. empower, mandate, mission, payment, rake-off, warrant 8. delegate 9. authority 10. assignment, constitute, delegation, deputation

11. performance 12. perpetration

commissioned ... 8. allotted, assigned, breveted 9. delegated 10. accredited, authorized

commissioner ... 5. envoy 6. dubash, legate 7. steward 8. delegate, emissary, official 9. commissar

commissure ... 4. seam 5. cleft, joint, mitre, raphe 6. stitch, suture 7. closure 8. juncture 10. interstice

commit ... 2. do 3. con 4. game (cards) 5. refer 6. remand 7. confide, consign, entrust, promise 8. memorize, relegate 10. commission, perpetrate

commode ... 3. cap 5. chest 8. fontange 9. washstand 10. chiffonier

commodious ... 3. fit 5. ample, roomy 6. proper 8. suitable 9. capacious, expansive, opportune 10. convenient 11. comfortable, serviceable 13. accommodating

commodity, commodities ... 5. goods, wares 6. profit 7. staples

common ... 4. park 5. cheap, plain, stale, trite, usual 6. mutual, paltry, vulgar 7. average 8. familiar, frequent, mediocre, ordinary, plebeian 9. customary, household, universal 11. commonplace

common (pert to) ...
ancestor .. 4. Adam 10. progenitor
funds .. 4. pool 7. tontine
gender .. 6. unisex 7. epicene
informer .. 7. delator
people .. 3. mob 5. demos, gente 6. vulgus 7. demotic 8. populace

commonly accepted ... 7. vulgate

commonly thought ... 8. putative

commonplace ... 5. banal, daily, stale, theme, trite, usual 6. truism 7. humdrum, prosaic 8. ordinary, workaday 9. platitude

commonwealth ... 5. group, State 7. society 8. Kentucky, Virginia 9. Australia, community 12. Pennsylvania 13. Massachusetts

commotion ... 3. ado 4. fray, riot, stir, to-do, whir 5. flare, tizzy 6. flurry, fracas, hubbub, rumpus, tumult, unrest 7. turmoil 8. foofaraw, uprising 9. agitation, confusion 10. concussion (med), excitement, turbulence 12. perturbation

commune ... 4. area, soil 5. realm, share 6. confer, impart 7. kibbutz 8. converse 9. communion 10. commonalty 11. intercourse (spiritual) 12. conversation

Commune of Paris (1871) ... 10. government

communicate ... 3. say 4. give, join 5. share 6. bestow, impart, inform 7. apprize 8. converse, transmit 9. communion

communication ... 4. word 5. radio 6. letter, report 7. account, contact, epistle, message 8. buzzword, feedback 9. statement 10. communique, connection 11. computerese, impartation, information, intercourse 12. body language 14. word processing

communion . . . 5. share 6. church 7. concord, rapport 8. converse 9. agreement 11. intercourse 12. denomination 13. participation

Communion . . . 4. host 9. Eucharist, Sacrament 10. intinction, Last Supper

communion (pert to) . . .
bread (blessed) . . 4. host 5. wafer 7. eulogia 9. antidoron
cloth . . 8. corporal, corporas
plate . . 5. paten 12. processional
table . . 5. altar
vessel . . 3. ama, pyx

communique . . . 4. word 7. message 8. dispatch 13. communication

comose . . . 5. hairy 6. tufted

compact . . . 3. etui, firm, pact, plot, snug, trim 5. brief, close, dense, pithy, press, solid, terse, tight 6. treaty, united, vanity 7. concise, crowded, entente, leagued, serried 8. alliance, compress, contract, covenant, succinct 9. agreement, condensed 10. compressed, conspiracy 11. compendious, sententious, stipulation

companion . . . 3. pal 4. ally, fare, mate, twin 5. amigo, crony 6. fellow, shadow 7. Achates, compeer, comrade, consort 8. alter ego, co-worker 9. associate 11. confederate, counterpart

companionship . . . 5. amity 7. society 10. fellowship, fraternity 11. comradeship, sociability 13. accompaniment

company . . . 3. set 4. band, bevy, body, crew, gang, ging, host 5. crowd, flock, group, party, troop 6. circle, cohort, throng, troupe 9. concourse, gathering

company (pert to) . . .
detachment . . 5. posse
people, players . . 4. bevy, crew, gang, team 5. troop 6. galaxy, guests, troupe 9. cavalcade
ships . . 5. fleet 6. armada 8. squadron
soldiers . . 5. corps, squad 7. brigade, phalanx, platoon 9. battalion
travelers . . 7. caravan 8. pilgrims, tourists 9. merchants

comparative . . . 5. equal, rival 8. relative 10. comparable, relational

compare . . . 4. even 5. liken 6. confer, semble 7. collate, examine 8. contrast

comparison . . . 6. simile 7. analogy, parable 8. likening, metaphor 10. accordance, similarity 11. parallelism

compartment . . . 3. bin 4. cell, part 5. stall 6. alcove 7. cellule, chamber, quarter 8. district, division 10. department

compass . . . 3. arc 4. area, plot, ring 5. guide, range (Mus) reach, solar, sweep 6. attain, bounds, circle, curved, degree, extent 7. circuit, divider, enclose, imagine 8. circular, distance, surround

compass (pert to) . . .
housing . . 8. binnacle
part . . 3. pen 6. needle
point . . 4. airt 5. rhumb 7. azimuth
sight . . 4. vane
suspender . . 6. gimbal

compassion . . . 4. pity, ruth (anc) 5. mercy 8. humanity, sympathy 10. condolence 13. commiseration

compassionate . . . 6. gentle, humane 7. clement, pitiful 8. merciful 11. sympathetic, warmhearted 12. sympathizing

compatible . . . 8. affinity, suitable 9. accordant, agreeable, congruous 10. consistent, harmonious 12. congeniality

compeer . . . 4. mate, peer 5. equal, match, rival 7. comrade 9. companion

compel . . . 4. urge 5. drive, force, impel, press 6. coerce, incite, oblige, obsess 7. actuate, dragoon, require 9. constrain, influence, instigate

compelling . . . 6. urgent 7. driving 8. pressing 9. insistent, necessary, obsessing 10. compulsory, motivating, obligatory, persuasive

compelling assent . . . 6. cogent

compelling attention . . . 9. insistent

compendious . . . 5. brief, short, terse 7. compact, concise 8. abridged, succinct 9. condensed 10. summarized

compendium . . . 5. brief 6. abrégé, digest 7. capsule, epitome, medulla, pandect, summary 8. abstract, syllabus, synopsis 9. comprisal 10. abridgment 11. compilation, contraction 12. abbreviation

compensate . . . 3. pay 5. atone, repay 6. reward 7. redress, requite 9. indemnity 10. recompense, remunerate 14. counterbalance

compensation . . . 3. pay 4. hire 5. bonus, wages 6. manbot (manbote), reward, salary 7. penalty, stipend 8. gratuity, pittance, requital, solatium 9. atonement, indemnity 10. reparation 12. remuneration, satisfaction 15. indemnification

compete . . . 3. vie 4. cope 5. match 6. outvie, strive 7. contend, contest, emulate

competence . . . 5. means, skill 7. ability, fitness 8. adequacy, capacity, property 10. capability, efficiency 11. proficiency, sufficiency, suitability 13. effectiveness, qualification

competent . . . 3. apt, can, fit 4. able 5. capax, smart 7. capable 8. adequate, suitable 9. effective, effectual, efficient, qualified 10. catechumen, sufficient 12. appertaining (to)

competition . . . 5. match, trial 6. strife 7. contest, rivalry 8. ambition, concours 9. emulation 10. corrivalry

compilation . . . 5. cento 6. digest 9. Americana 10. collection

compile . . . 3. add 4. edit 5. amass 6. gather 8. assemble

complacent . . . 4. smug 6. bovine 7. fatuous 9. contented, satisfied 11. considerate 13. self-satisfied

complain . . . 4. beef, carp, fret, kick, pule, wail 5. gripe, growl, whine 6. accuse, bewail, grieve, grouse, lament, murmur, mutter, repine, squawk, yammer 7. deplore, grumble,

protest 9. bellyache
complaint . . . 4. beef 6. charge, lament, malady 7. ailment, disease, illness, protest 8. disorder, repining, reproach 9. grievance, murmuring 10. accusation, imputation 11. declaration, lamentation
complaisance . . . 6. regard 7. amenity, concern, suavity 8. civility, courtesy, urbanity 10. indulgence, solicitude, submission, toleration 13. consideration
complaisant . . . 4. easy, kind 5. civil 6. polite 7. lenient 8. gracious, obliging 9. compliant, courteous
complement . . . 4. crew 7. adjunct 8. addition, complete 10. correspond, supplement 11. counterpart
complete . . . 3. all, end 4. dead, fill, full, sole 5. stark, total, utter, whole 6. effect, entire, finish, intact, mature 7. achieve, execute, germane, perfect, plenary, realize 8. absolute, conclude, detailed, outright 9. terminate 10. accomplish, complement, consummate 11. unqualified
completely . . . 3. all 5. fully, quite, stark 6. in toto 7. solidly, totally, utterly 8. entirely
completeness . . . 9. entelechy, integrity
complex . . . 4. mazy 5. mixed 6. knotty 7. twisted 8. involute, involved 9. entangled, intricate, perplexed 10. interlaced 11. complicated
complexion . . . 4. blee, mode, tone 5. color, guise, tinge 10. appearance
compliance . . . 6. assent 7. consent 9. accession, obedience 10. concession, conformity, observance, submission 11. willingness 12. acquiescence
compliant . . . 6. docile 7. duteous, dutiful, willing 8. obedient 10. submissive 11. acquiescent, complaisant, conformable
complicated . . . 6. daedal 7. complex, Gordian, snarled, tangled 8. involved 9. difficult, embroiled, intricate 11. embarrassed 12. labyrinthine
complication . . . 4. node (drama) 5. nodus 7. illness 9. complexus 10. complexity 11. combination
compliment . . . 6. praise 7. adulate, commend, flatter 8. encomium, flattery 12. blandishment, commendation 14. congratulation
comply . . . 4. obey 5. agree, yield 6. accede, accord, assent, submit 7. conform, observe 9. acquiesce
compone . . . 6. settle 7. arrange, compose 8. compound
component . . . 3. ion 4. part 5. basis 6. factor 7. element 8. integral 10. ingredient 11. constituent
comport . . . 3. act 6. accord, behave 7. conduct 10. correspond
comportable . . . 8. suitable 10. consistent
compose . . . 3. pen 4. calm, form, make 5. order, score, write 7. arrange, fashion, prepare 8. compound, melodize 9. reconcile 10. constitute 11. orchestrate, tranquilize
composed . . . 4. calm, cool 5. quiet, sober, wrote 6. sedate, serene 7. consist

8. arranged, tranquil 9. collected 11. unflappable
composed of . . . flat plates . . 9. lamellate lobes . . 6. lobate
composer . . . 6. author 7. idylist (idyllist) 10. compositor, typesetter
composer of . . . *Aida* . . 5. Verdi *Carmen* . . 5. Bizet *Faust* . . 6. Gounod *La Boheme* . . 7. Puccini *Merry widow* . . 5. Lehar *Mikado* . . 8. Sullivan *Naughty Marietta* . . 7. Herbert *Stars and Stripes Forever* . . 5. Sousa
composition . . . 4. opus 5. piece, theme 6. make-up 7. melange 8. formation, synthesis 12. constitution, construction
composition (pert to) . . . *literature* . . 5. cento, essay, poesy, prose 6. poetry, satire, thesis 8. treatise 10. brainchild
music . . 2. op 4. aria, glee, hymn, opus 5. drama, étude, motet, nonet, opera, rondo, suite 6. anthem, septet (septuor), sextet (sestet), sonata 7. duetino, quartet 8. concerto, oratorio, postlude, symphony
composure . . . 6. repose 8. calmness, coolness, serenity 9. placidity 10. equanimity, quiescence, sedateness 11. tranquility
compound . . . 3. mix 4. olio 5. agree, amide, ester, oxide, pyran, unite 6. anisil, elixir, iodide, ketone 7. ammonia, combine, farrago, metamer 8. tincture 9. composite
comprehend . . . 4. know 5. grasp, sense 6. embody, fathom 7. enclose, imagine, include, involve, realize 8. comprise, conceive 10. understand
comprehensible . . . 8. exoteric, included, knowable 9. comprised 11. conceivable, discernible, perceptible 12. intelligible
comprehensive . . . 4. full, wide 5. large 7. generic, knowing 8. thorough 9. extensive, inclusive, universal 11. compendious
compress . . . 4. firm 5. cling, crowd, pinch, press, stupe 6. compact, densify, embrace, squeeze 8. astringe, condense, contract, decrease
comprise, comprize . . . 5. imply 6. number 7. contain, embrace, enclose, include, involve 8. perceive 10. comprehend, constitute
compromise . . . 4. bind 6. adjust 8. compound, trade-off 9. agreement 10. adjustment, concession, settlement 11. appeasement, arbitration
compulsion . . . 5. drive, force 6. duress, urging 7. impulse 8. coaction, coercion 9. necessity, obsession 10. compelling
compulsory . . . 7. driving 9. mandatory, necessary 10. compelling, imperative, obligatory 11. involuntary
compunction . . . 3. rue 5. guilt, pangs, qualm 6. regret 7. remorse 8. pricking 9. penitence 11. impenitence 13. regretfulness

compute ... 5. count, score, tally
6. cipher, figure, number, reckon
8. estimate 9. calculate, enumerate
computer terms ... 3. bit, LAN, RAM,
ROM 4. byte, GIGO 5. BASIC,
COBOL, coder, e-mail, input, modem
6. access, analog, glitch, laptop,
Pascal, server 7. digital, FORTRAN,
monitor 8. database, download,
gigabyte, Internet, megabyte, printout,
software, terminal 9. mainframe,
videodisc 10. cyberspace, floppy disc
11. computerese 12. minicomputer
13. microcomputer, word processor
comrade ... 3. pal 4. ally, chum, mate,
peer 5. buddy, crony 6. fellow, frater
7. compeer 8. camarada, sidekick
9. associate, colleague, companion
con ... 2. no 3. nay 4. know, read,
scam 5. cheat, learn, steer, study
6. peruse 7. convict, deceive, swindle
8. memorize, negative 10. understand
13. confidence man
conceal ... 4. dern, hide, mask, palm,
veil 5. cloak, cover, derne, eloin, feign
6. eloign, pocket, screen 7. secrete
8. bescreen, disguise, enshield
concealed ... 5. doggo 6. covert, hidden,
latent, perdue, secret, veiled, velate
7. covered, larvate, obscure, unknown,
velated 9. disguised, incognito,
insidious 11. clandestine
concede ... 3. own 5. admit, agree,
allow, grant, yield 6. accord 7. confess,
consent 8. consider 9. surrender
11. acknowledge
conceit ... 3. ego 4. idea 5. fancy,
pride 6. vagary, vanity 7. caprice,
egotism, foppery, tympany 8. priggery
12. boastfulness
conceited ... 4. smug, vain 5. proud
7. foppish 8. arrogant, boastful, priggish
9. egotistic, pragmatic 11. egotistical,
opinionated 12. stuffed shirt
conceivable ... 7. tenable 8. credible
9. plausible 10. believable, imaginable
12. intelligible
conceive ... 5. dream, fancy, think
6. create, devise, ideate 7. imagine,
produce, realize, suppose, suspect
9. originate 10. understand
concentrate ... 4. mass 5. focus
6. center 7. compact, densify, extract
8. condense, converge 9. intensify
10. centralize 11. consolidate
concept ... 4. idea 5. image 7. opinion,
thought 8. category
conception ... 4. idea 5. image, savvy
6. notion 7. conceit, opinion
9. pregnancy 12. apprehension
13. comprehension, understanding
concern ... 4. care, firm, sake 5. event,
grief 6. affair, affect, import, matter
7. anxiety, pertain 8. business, interest,
salience 9. relevance 10. importance
11. consequence 12. significance
13. consideration
concerning ... 3. for 4. as to, over,
upon 5. about, anent 9. regarding
10. respecting
concert ... 6. aubade 7. recital

9. agreement, unanimity 11. co-
operation, performance
concert hall ... 5. odeum (odeon)
6. lyceum 7. theater 9. music hall,
playhouse
concession ... 5. grant 6. market
7. consent 8. discount 10. compromise,
confession 13. qualification
concierge ... 6. porter, warden 7. ostiary
8. chokidar 10. doorkeeper
conciliate ... 4. ease 6. pacify 7. appease,
mollify, placate 9. reconcile
10. propitiate
conciliatory ... 6. assent, irenic 8. irenical
9. appeasing, forgiving 10. mollifying
concise ... 4. curt, neat 5. brief, crisp,
pithy, terse 6. précis 7. laconic,
pointed, serried, summary 8. succinct
11. compendious, sententious
13. comprehensive
conclude ... 3. end 4. rest 5. close,
infer 6. deduce, endeth, finish, settle
7. arrange, presume, resolve, suppose
8. complete 9. determine, terminate
conclusion ... 3. end 4. last 5. close,
finis 6. finale, finish, result 8. decision,
epilogue 9. deduction, diagnosis,
inference 10. completion
13. determination
conclusive ... 5. final, valid 8. decisive,
ultimate 9. mandatory 10. convincing,
evidential 11. irrefutable, sockdologer
(answer) 12. unanswerable
concoct ... 3. mix 4. brew, cook, make
6. devise, digest, invent, scheme
7. perfect, prepare 9. fabricate
concoction ... 4. dish, plan, plot 6. device
7. mixture 8. compound 9. falsehood,
invention 11. combination, fabrication,
preparation
concomitant ... 9. accessory, attendant,
co-operant 10. coincident, concurrent
11. synchronous 12. accompanying,
simultaneous
concord ... 4. tune 5. chord, peace
6. accord, treaty, unison 7. concert,
harmony, rapport 8. symphony
9. agreement, unanimity
Concorde ... 3. SST
concordant ... 8. agreeing, harmonic,
unisonal 9. consonant, unanimous
10. harmonious 11. conformable
13. correspondent
concrete ... 4. hard, pave 5. béton,
solid 6. cement 7. congeal, plaster
8. hardness, pavement, solidify
11. substantial
concur ... 5. agree, chime, unite
6. accede, assent 7. approve, combine,
consent 9. acquiesce, co-operate
11. synchronize
concurrence ... 6. united 7. joining
9. adherence, concourse, unanimity
11. coincidence, conjunction,
convergence, co-operation, parallelism
concurrent ... 5. joint 6. united
7. meeting, uniting 8. parallel,
syndrome 9. unanimous 10. associated,
coincident, synergetic 11. co-operative,
synchronous 12. accompanying,
simultaneous

concussion ... 5. clash, shock, smash, wound 6. injury, trauma 9. collision

condemn ... 3. ban 4. doom 5. blame, decry 7. adjudge, censure, convict 8. penalize, sentence

condense ... 3. mix 5. unite 6. absorb, decoct, deepen, harden, lessen, narrow, reduce 7. abridge, combine, compact, densify, enhance, shorten, squeeze, thicken 8. compress, contract, diminish, heighten, solidify 9. constrict, intensify 11. concentrate, consolidate

condensed ... 7. compact, concise, cramped, tabloid 9. shortened 10. compressed, contracted 12. concentrated

condenser (anc) ... 9. Leyden jar

condescend ... 5. deign, stoop 6. submit, unbend 7. concede, descend 9. patronize, vouchsafe

condign ... 3. fit 4. just 6. severe, worthy 7. fitting 8. adequate, deserved, suitable

condiment ... 3. soy 4. dill, mace, mint, sage, salt 5. chili, clove, curry, sauce, spice 6. catsup, garlic, ginger, nutmeg, pepper, relish 7. cayenne, ketchup, mustard, paprika, vinegar 9. seasoning 10. peppermint

condition ... 2. if 4. case, haze, rank, term 5. covin, limit, stage, state 6. estate, fettle, health, plight, status 7. posture, proviso, quality, station 8. capacity, position, standing 9. requisite, situation 10. limitation 11. predicament 12. circumstance

condition (pert to) ...
favorable .. 4. odds
flushed .. 4. rosy
habitual .. 5. tenor
hypnotic .. 4. daze 6. stupor, trance 7. narcose
made .. 7. premise
murk .. 3. fog 4. haze, mist 5. gloom
proper .. 6. kilter
stipulation .. 7. proviso

conditionally ... 2. if 8. provided 11. tentatively 13. provisionally

condone ... 5. remit 6. accept, excuse, pardon 7. absolve, forgive 8. tolerate 11. countenance

condor ... 6. falcon 7. vulture

conduce ... 4. lend, tend 5. serve 6. effect 7. advance, dispose, incline, redound 10. contribute

conducive ... 6. useful 7. helpful 11. implemental, serviceable 12. instrumental

conduct ... 2. act, run 4. lead, mien, rule 5. guide, usage, usher 6. action, convey, convoy, direct, escort, govern, manage 7. bearing, comport, control, manners 8. behavior, demeanor, regulate 9. operation, supervise 10. deportment, management 11. comportment, superintend

conduct (pert to) ...
a cause .. 5. plead
breach .. 5. guilty
doctrine of .. 6. morals
one's self .. 6. behave, demean 7. comport

conducting inward ... 9. afference

conductor ... 5. guide 6. escort, leader 7. cathode, maestro, manager 8. cicerone, director, operator, trainman

conduit ... 3. way 4. adit, duct, pain, pipe, tube 5. canal, sewer 6. course 7. channel 8. aqueduct

cone (pert to) ...
conelike .. 5. conic 6. pineal 7. conical
pine .. 8. strobile
silver .. 4. pina
tree .. 5. larch 7. conifer

confab, confabulation ... 4. chat, talk 7. palaver, prattle 8. chinfest, talkfest 12. conversation

confection ... 3. jam 5. candy, dulce, icing, jelly 6. cimbal, comfit, nougat, sweets 7. caramel, fondant, praline, succade 8. preserve 9. sweetmeat 11. bittersweet, marshmallow

confederacy ... 5. cabal, hanse, union 6. fusion, league 8. alliance, covenant 9. coalition 10. complicity, conspiracy, federation 11. affiliation, association, combination 13. consolidation

confederate ... 3. pal, reb 4. ally 5. stall 7. abettor 9. accessory, assistant, associate, auxiliary 10. accomplice

confer ... 4. give 6. advise, bestow, invest, parley 7. collate, commune, consign, consult, counsel 8. ordinate (knighthood) 10. deliberate

conference ... 5. trust 6. huddle, parley, powwow 7. council, palaver 9. interview 10. discussion 12. consultation

conferring respect ... 9. honorific

conferring title ... 9. ennobling

confess ... 3. own, rue 4. avow 5. admit, own up 6. regret, repent, reveal, shrive 7. concede 11. acknowledge

confession ... 5. credo (of faith), creed 6. avowal, shrift 7. admission, communion 10. profession 14. acknowledgment (acknowledgement)

confetti ... 5. paper 6. ribbon 7. bonbons 9. cascarons (in eggshells) 10. sweetmeats 11. confections

confidant ... 6. friend 8. intimate

confide ... 4. hope, rely 5. trust 6. commit, depend, repose

confidence ... 5. faith, poise 6. aplomb, belief, morals, secret 7. courage 8. credence, sureness 9. assurance, impudence 10. effrontery 12. impertinence

confident ... 4. smug, sure 6. secure 7. assured, certain, hopeful, reliant 8. cocksure, positive, sanguine, unafraid 9. convinced 10. determined

confidential ... 5. privy 6. secret 7. private 8. esoteric, intimate 9. auricular 10. unquotable 11. trustworthy

confidentially ... 7. sub rosa

configuration ... 4. form 5. shape 6. figure 7. contour, Gestalt, pattern 8. asterism 13. constellation

confine ... 3. dam, hem, mew, pen, sty, tie 4. bind, cage, coop, jail, lock 5. bound, limit, stint 6. border, immure,

intern, secure, strain 7. compass
8. imprison, restrain 9. enclosure
11. incarcerate, restriction
12. circumscribe

confined ... 4. pent 5. bound, caged
6. shut-in 7. cribbed, endemic,
limited 8. esoteric, impended, interned
9. bedridden, impounded, invalided,
parochial

confinement ... 5. limbo 7. durance,
lying-in 9. detention, isolation, restraint
10. cabin fever, childbirth
12. accouchement, imprisonment
13. incomm unicado 15. circumscription

confirm ... 4. seal 5. prove 6. assure,
attest, ratify, settle, verify 7. approve,
fortify, sustain 8. convince, sanction,
validate 9. establish 11. corroborate
12. substantiate

confirmed ... 6. proved 7. chronic
8. habitual, ratified 10. encouraged,
inveterate 11. established

confiscate ... 5. seize, usurp 7. impound
11. appropriate

conflagrant ... 5. afire 6. ablaze, aflame
7. blazing, burning

conflagration ... 4. fire 5. blaze, fever
8. wildfire 9. holocaust 12. inflammation

conflict ... 3. war 4. bout, duel, fray
5. clash, fight, run-in 6. action,
battle, combat, oppose, strife, tussle
7. contend, contest, discord 8. clashing,
struggle 9. antipathy, collision,
encounter, hostility 10. contention,
donnybrook, opposition 11. competition

confluence ... 4. flow 5. crowd 6. stream
7. flowing (together), meeting
8. junction 10. assemblage
11. concurrence, convergence
12. assimilation

conform ... 2. go 3. fit 4. lean, obey,
suit 5. adapt, agree 6. adjust, concur,
settle 7. compose, consent, observe
8. coincide, fine-tune 9. reconcile
11. accommodate

conformity ... 6. dharma 7. harmony
8. legality, symmetry 9. agreement,
congruity 10. compliance
15. conventionality

confound ... 3. mix 5. abash, amaze
6. baffle, dismay, puzzle, thwart
7. astound, buffalo, mystify, nonplus,
perplex 8. astonish, bewilder
9. dumbfound, embarrass, frustrate
10. complicate, contradict, disconcert
11. intermingle

confront ... 4. face, meet 5. front
6. oppose 7. compare 9. encounter

confrontation ... 6. crisis 7. face-off
8. showdown 9. encounter
10. opposition

confuse ... 3. mix 4. maze 5. abash,
addle, upset 6. baffle, flurry, garble,
jumble, muddle 7. derange, fluster
8. befuddle, bewilder, disorder, distract,
entangle 9. embrangle 10. complicate,
disarrange, discompose, disconcert

confused ... 4. asea 6. addled 7. chaotic,
jumbled, rattled 8. deranged
9. chagrined, flustered, perplexed,
uncertain 10. indistinct

confusion ... 3. ado, din 4. mess, moil
5. babel, chaos 6. jumble, pother, welter
7. anarchy, clutter, turmoil 8. disarray,
disorder 9. abashment, agitation
10. perplexity 11. derangement
12. bewilderment 13. embarrassment

confute ... 4. deny 5. rebut 6. answer,
expose, refute 7. dismiss 8. confound,
overcome, redargue 9. overwhelm (by
argument)

congeal ... 3. gel, ice, set 4. rime 6. freeze
7. pectize, thicken

congenial ... 4. boon 7. kindred 8. friendly
9. accordant, agreeable 10. affinitive,
compatible 11. sympathetic

congenital ... 6. inborn, innate
7. connate, genetic, natural
14. constitutional

conger ... 3. eel 8. cucumber
13. Leptocephalus

congeries ... 4. heap 9. amassment
10. collection 11. aggregation

congestion ... 3. jam 4. heap 8. fullness,
stoppage 9. gathering 11. obstruction
12. accumulation

Congo ...
capital .. 11. Brazzaville
city .. 6. Makoua 7. Louboma
port .. 11. Pointe Noire
river .. 5. Congo (Zaire) 6. Sangha

congratulate ... 4. laud 5. bless 6. salute
7. rejoice 8. macarize 10. compliment,
felicitate

congregate ... 4. herd, mass, meet
5. group, troop 6. gather, muster
7. collect 8. assemble 9. forgather

congregation ... 4. mass 5. house,
laity 7. council 8. assembly, audience
9. gathering 10. collection
11. churchgoers

congress ... 4. diet 5. synod 6. durbar,
indaba, soviet 7. council, meeting
8. assembly, conclave 9. Sanhedrin
10. convention, parliament
11. convergence, convocation,
legislature 12. congregation

congruous ... 3. fit 4. meet 6. proper
7. fitting 8. agreeing, becoming, suitable
9. consonant

conic, conical ... 8. parabola
9. pyramidal 10. cone-shaped, funnellike

conifers ... 4. yews 5. pines 6. cedars
7. larches, Pinales, Sabines, spruces,
Torreys 8. hemlocks, Soledads
9. Coniferae, Corsicans 10. evergreens

conjecture ... 3. aim 5. ettle, guess,
opine, think 6. divine 7. conjoin,
imagine, presume, suppose, surmise,
suspect 8. supposal 9. inference
10. assumption, hypothesis
11. supposition

conjoin ... 4. join, link, yoke 5. hitch,
unite 6. adjoin, concur 7. combine,
connect 8. correlate 9. correlate

conjoined parts ... 6. adnexa

conjointly ... 10. hand-in-hand

conjugal ... 7. marital, nuptial
9. connubial 11. matrimonial

conjugate ... 4. join 5. yoked 6. couple,
united 7. coupled, related 8. bijugate,
combined 10. paronymous

12. etymological

conjugation . . . 5. union 6. fusion
7. duality, joining, uniting
10. assemblage 11. combination
13. juxtaposition

conjunct . . . 6. united 8. combined
9. conjoined, corporate

conjunction . . . 2. as, et, if, or 3. and,
but, nor 4. than, that 5. since,
union 6. casual, though 7. whether
10. connection 11. adversative,
association, combination, concurrence,
correlative

conjure . . . 4. pray 5. charm 6. adjure,
enjoin, invoke, juggle, summon (magic)
7. beseech, enchant, entreat, implore
10. supplicate

conjure (up) . . . 5. raise 6. call up
8. exorcise (exorcize), remember
9. visualize

conjurer, conjuror . . . 4. mage 6. voodoo,
wizard 7. juggler 8. exorcist, magician

conk . . . 4. head, nose 5. decay (tree)

conk out . . . 4. fade, fail 5. stall 6. fizzle,
perish, weaken

connate . . . 4. akin 6. allied 7. cognate,
related, similar 9. congenial
10. congenital

connect . . . 3. tie 4. ally, join, link, meet
5. unite 6. adjoin, attach, couple,
enlink, fasten, relate 7. bracket, succeed
9. associate, hyphenate

connected . . . 3. met 5. telic 6. adnate,
joined 7. serried, similar 8. coherent,
inlinked, syndetic 10. continuous,
correlated

Connecticut . . .
capital . . 8. Hartford
city . . 6. Darien, Mystic 7. Meriden
8. Hartford, New Haven 9. Waterbury
10. Bridgeport
college (famed) . . 4. Yale (1701)
historic site . . 10. Charter Oak (1687,
Hartford)
museum . . 6. Barnum (P T)
river . . 6. Thames 9. Naugatuck
10. Hoosatonic 11. Connecticut
State admission . . 5. Fifth
State Motto . . 21. Qui Transtulit Sustinet
(He Who Transplants Sustains)
State nickname . . 6. Nutmeg
12. Constitution

connecting link . . . 3. tie 4. bond
6. connex 7. kiaison 8. ligament,
vinculum 11. intermedium
12. intermediary

connection . . . 4. bond 5. nexus, union
6. clevis, family, series 7. kinship,
passage 8. alliance, commerce,
junction, relation 9. coherence, go-
between, relevance 10. continuity
11. association, intercourse
12. intermediary, relationship
13. communication, juxtaposition

conner . . . 5. pilot 6. balker, tester
7. peruser 8. examiner 9. inspector

connive . . . 4. plot, wink 5. blink 6. scheme
7. collude, complot, finagle 8. conspire,
contrive, maneuver, overlook

conniving . . . 8. scheming 9. collusive,
deceitful 10. conspiring 11. calculating

connoisseur . . . 5. judge, maven 6. expert
7. epicure, gourmet 8. gourmand
11. cognoscente, connaisseur

connotation . . . 5. sense 6. import,
intent 7. meaning, purport 8. overtone
10. denotation 11. implication
12. significance 13. comprehension

connubial . . . 7. martial, nuptial
8. conjugal 11. matrimonial
12. epithalamium (song)

conquer . . . 3. win 4. beat, best 5. crush
6. defeat, humble, master, reduce,
subdue 7. subject 8. overcome,
overturn, surmount, vanquish
9. discomfit, overpower, overthrow,
subjugate

conqueror . . . 4. hero 6. captor, Cortez,
victor, winner 7. subduer 10. subjugator
12. conquistador

conquest . . . 6. Norman (1066) 7. mastery,
triumph, victory

consanguinity . . . 5. nabob 7. kinship,
sibship 8. affinity, relation (blood)
12. relationship

conscience . . . 4. mind, self 6. psyche
8. superego 9. casuistry

conscientious . . . 7. dutiful, servile
8. faithful 10. fastidious, meticulous,
scrupulous 11. punctilious

conscientious objection . . . 7. scruple

conscious . . . 4. keen 5. alive, awake,
aware, vital 7. animate, feeling
8. sensible, sentient 9. breathing,
cognizant 10. self-conscious

consecrate . . . 4. sain 5. bless, exalt
6. anoint, devote, hallow, ordain
7. glorify 8. dedicate, sanctify

consecrated (pert to) . . .
bread . . 4. host 5. wafer
oil . . 6. chrism
thing . . 6. sacrum

consent . . . 4. give 5. agree, grant, yield
6. accede, accord, assent, concur,
permit 8. approval 9. acquiesce
10. compliance, permission
11. concurrence 13. understanding

consequence . . . 3. end 5. event 6. course,
effect, result, weight 7. dignity,
outcome 8. pursuant (in), sequence
9. aftermath, inference, influence,
loftiness, outgrowth 10. importance,
notability 11. distinction

consequential . . . 7. pompous 8. eventual
9. important 13. self-important

consequently . . . 2. do 4. ergo, then
5. hence 9. as a result, therefore,
wherefore 12. subsequently
13. consecutively

conservative . . . 4. Tory 5. staid 7. die-
hard, fogyish, old-line 8. moderate
10. long-haired 11. reactionary
12. preservative 13. unprogressive

conserve . . . 3. jam 4. save 5. guard,
uvate 6. defend, secure, shield,
uphold 7. protect, sustain 8. maintain
9. preserves, sweetmeat

consider . . . 3. ain, see 4. care, deem,
heed, muse, rate 5. judge, think, treat,
weigh 6. esteem, intend, ponder,
regard 7. discuss, examine, reflect,
revolve 8. cogitate, meditate, ruminate

10. deliberate 11. contemplate

considerable . . . 5. great, large 7. notable, several 8. numerous 9. important 10. noteworthy, remarkable 13. authoritative

considerate . . . 4. kind 6. gentle 7. careful, heedful, prudent, serious 8. obliging 9. attentive, judicious 10. deliberate, reflective, solicitous, thoughtful

consideration . . . 4. self 5. study 6. esteem, regard 7. respect, thought 9. attention, deference, incentive, influence 10. cogitation, importance, meditation, reflection, reputation, rumination 11. examination 12. compensation, deliberation

considering . . . 2. if 5. since 8. after all, inasmuch, in view of

consign . . . 5. allot 6. assign, commit, devote, remand, resign 7. deliver, entrust 8. transfer 11. subscribe to

consignee . . . 6. factor 7. awardee 8. assignee 9. committee

consign to . . .
a place . . 8. allocate
prison . . 6. commit, send up
ruin . . 4. doom
unimportance . . 8. relegate

consistent . . . 5. equal, solid, stiff 7. equable, logical, uniform 8. coherent 9. agreement, consonant, steadfast 10. persisting

consisting of . . .
cavities . . 9. cellulose
layers (thin) . . 8. laminate
names . . 8. onomatic
one word . . 7. monepic
pages . . 7. paginal
three measures . . 8. trimeter
three spots . . 4. trey
three styles (Bot) . . 10. tristylous
two parts . . 6. binary

consist of . . . 5. imply 6. embody 7. contain, embrace, enclose, involve 8. comprise (comprize)

consolation . . . 6. solace 7. comfort 10. condolence

console . . . 4. desk 5. cheer, organ, table 6. solace, soothe 7. bracket, cabinet, comfort, support, sustain 9. alleviate, encourage

consolidate . . . 4. knit, mass 5. merge, unify, unite 7. combine, densify 8. coalesce, compress, organize, solidify 9. intensify 10. strengthen

consonant . . . 4. lene, surd 5. lenis, nasal, velar 6. dental, labial 7. lingual, palatal, spirate 8. gutteral 9. accordant, congruous 10. compatible, concordant, consistent

consonant (pert to) . . .
hissing . . 8. sibilant
rustling . . 9. fricative
voiceless (breathed) . . 6. atonic 7. spirate

consort . . . 4. Devi (of Siva), mate, wife 5. group, Sakti 6. mingle, spouse 7. husband, partner 9. associate, colleague, companion, harmonize 11. combination, confederate, conjunction

conspicuous . . . 6. famous, signal

7. eminent, glaring, obvious, salient, visible 8. distinct, lionized, manifest, striking 9. important, prominent 10. celebrated, noticeable, remarkable 11. illustrious, outstanding 13. distinguished

conspiracy . . . 4. plot 5. cabal, unite 6. scheme 8. intrigue 9. collusion 10. connivance 11. confederacy, machination

conspire . . . 4. plot 5. unite 6. concur, scheme 7. collude, complot, finagle 9. fainaigue 11. confederate

constable . . . 3. cop 5. staff 6. beadle, keeper, warden 7. bailiff 8. tipstaff 9. policeman

constabulary . . . 6. bureau (police) 10. constables

constancy . . . 4. zeal 5. ardor, faith, truth 6. fealty, garnet (symbol) 7. honesty, loyalty 8. devotion, fidelity 9. adherence, continual, eagerness, integrity, stability 10. allegiance, attachment, permanence, perpetuity, uniformity 11. devotedness, earnestness 12. faithfulness

constant . . . 4. firm, true 5. fixed 7. regular, uniform 8. faithful, resolute 9. continual, invariant, parameter (Math), perpetual, steadfast 10. continuous, invariable, persistent 12. unchangeable

constant desire . . . 4. itch 9. hankering

Constantine (pert to) . . .
birthplace . . 4. Nish (Nis) 7. Naissus (now Yugoslavia)
known as . . 8. The Great
title . . 7. Emperor (Rome)

Constantinople . . .
official name . . 8. Istanbul
patriarch . . 9. Nestorius
site . . 6. Turkey (Eur)

constellation . . . 5. stars 6. galaxy 8. asterism 10. luminaries 13. configuration (stars)

Constellations (partial list) . . .
arrow . . 7. Sagitta
bears (Dipper) . . 9. Ursa Major, Ursa Minor
Bird of Paradise (S Pole) . . 4. Apus
bull . . 6. Taurus
crab . . 6. Cancer
crane . . 4. Grus
crow . . 6. Corvus
dog . . 5. Canis
dragon . . 5. Draco
eagle . . 6. Aquila
fishes . . 6. Pisces
goat . . 9. Capricorn
goldfish . . 6. Dorado
hunter . . 5. Orion (most conspicuous)
lion . . 3. Leo
Noah's Ark . . 4. Argo
Northern Crown . . 14. Corona Borealis, Northern Lights
peacock . . 4. Pavo
scorpion . . 7. Scorpio
serpent (sea) . . 5. Hydra
Southern Cross . . 4. Crux
swan . . 6. Cygnus
Twins . . 6. Gemini

virgin .. 5. Virgo
water bearer .. 8. Aquarius
whale .. 6. Cestus
winged horse .. 7. Pegasus
wolf .. 5. Lupus

Constellations' brightest star .. 3. Cor
Constellations of the Zodiac .. 3. Leo
5. Aries, Libra, Virgo 6. Cancer, Gemini,
Pisces, Taurus 7. Scorpio 8. Aquarius
11. Capricornus, Sagittarius

constituent ... 5. voter 6. factor,
matter 7. elector, element, essence
8. elective 9. component 10. ingredient
11. determinant (Math)

constituent of ...
blood serum .. 7. opsonin
coal .. 6. carbon
coffee, tea .. 8. caffeine
hair, nails .. 7. keratin
oil of cloves .. 7. eugenol

constitute ... 4. form 5. enact, found
6. create, depute 7. appoint, compose
8. legalize 9. determine, establish

constitution ... 3. law 6. crasis, custom
7. passage 8. creation 9. enactment,
essential, ordinance, structure
11. composition, institution
12. organization

Constitution (ship) ... 12. Old Ironsides

constitutional ... 5. legal, valid 6. innate
9. essential, healthful 12. governmental
13. dispositional

constitutional (pert to) ...
health .. 4. walk 6. stroll 8. exercise
right .. 9. franchise
temperament .. 6. crasis
vigor .. 5. nerve

Constitution State ... 11. Connecticut

constrain ... 4. curb, urge 5. chain, check,
drive, force, impel, press 6. compel,
oblige 7. confine, repress 8. restrain
11. necessitate

constrained ... 6. forced, modest
7. cramped 8. moderate, reserved
9. obligated

constraint ... 4. bond, urge 5. force
6. duress, stress 7. modesty, reserve
8. coercion, pressure 9. restraint,
stiffness 10. compulsion, moderation
11. confinement

constrict ... 3. tie 4. bind 5. cramp
6. narrow, shrink 7. squeeze, tighten
8. astringe, condense, contract
10. constringe

constriction ... 9. narrowing, stricture,
tightness 11. contraction
13. strangulation

constrictor ... 3. boa 5. snake 7. serpent,
styptic 9. sphincter 10. compressor

construct ... 4. make, rear 5. build,
erect, frame 6. create 7. compose
9. establish, fabricate, originate

constructive ... 7. virtual 8. creative,
implicit 9. anabolism 10. suggestive
14. interpretation, interpretative

construe ... 5. parse 6. deduce, render
7. explain 9. interpret, translate

consuetude ... 5. habit, usage 6. custom

consuetudinary ... 6. manual (customs),
ritual 9. customary

consult (with) ... 6. advise, confer, take

up 7. discuss 10. deliberate

consultation ... 7. counsel 8. audition,
congress 9. interview 10. conference,
discussion 12. deliberation

consume ... 3. eat, use 4. burn 5. spend,
waste 6. absorb, devour, expend
7. destroy (fire) 8. squander 9. dissipate
12. disintegrate

consumed ... 3. pau

consummate ... 3. end, top 4. ripe
5. ideal 6. finish, utmost 7. achieve,
perfect 8. complete 10. accomplish

consumption ... 3. use 4. loss 5. decay,
waste 6. eating 7. disease, using up
8. phthisis 11. destruction
12. tuberculosis 13. deterioration

contact ... 4. meet 5. touch, union
6. impact, syzygy (Astron) 7. meeting,
oscnode (Math) 8. junction, tangency,
touching 10. contiguity
13. communication

contain ... 4. have, hold, keep 5. cover
6. embody, number, retain 7. embrace,
enclose, include, involve, subsume
8. comprise, restrain 9. divisible (by)
10. comprehend

container ... 3. bag, bin, box, can, cup,
jar, jug, lug, pan, pod, pot, tin, tub,
urn, vat 4. case, crib, ewer, pail, sack,
vase 5. crate, cruet, pouch 6. basket,
bottle, carboy, carton, hamper, hatbox
7. capsule, hanaper 8. canister, decanter

containing ...
air .. 9. pneumatic
antimony .. 8. stibiate
boron .. 5. boric 7. boracic
carbon .. 7. organic 13. carboniferous
copper .. 6. cupric
fire .. 7. igneous
gold .. 4. doré 5. auric
iron .. 6. ferric
silver .. 5. lunar
slag .. 6. drossy
ten .. 6. denary
tin .. 7. stannic

containing maxims ... 6. gnomic

contaminate ... 4. slur, soil 5. stain,
sully, taint 6. befoul, defile, infect,
poison 7. corrupt, debauch, degrade,
pollute, vitiate 8. dishonor 9. desecrate
10. adulterate

contemn ... 4. defy, hate 5. scorn, spurn
6. reject 7. despise, disdain

contemplate ... 4. muse, plan, scan,
view 5. study 6. design, expect, intend,
ponder 7. examine, foresee, propose
8. consider, envision, meditate

contemplation ... 5. study 6. musing
7. theoria, thought 8. scrutiny
9. foresight, intuition 10. expectancy,
reflection 11. examination, expectation,
speculation

contemplative ... 6. sedate 7. pensive
10. meditative, reflective, ruminative,
thoughtful 11. speculative
13. retrospective

contemporary ... 6. coeval 7. present
10. coetaneous, coexistent, coincident
11. concomitant, synchronous
12. simultaneous 15. contemporaneous

contempt ... 4. fico, geck 5. scorn, shame,

sneer 7. despect, disdain 8. defiance, derision, ridicule 9. arrogance, contumely 10. disrespect 12. disobedience

contemptible ... 3. low 4. base 5. cheap, petty, sorry 6. abject, paltry, sordid 7. pitiful 8. beggarly, inferior, unworthy 9. groveling, worthless 10. despicable 13. insignificant

contemptuous ... 6. sneery 7. haughty 8. insolent, scornful 10. disdainful 12. contumelious, supercilious

contemptuous action ... 9. indignity 10. incivility

contend ... 3. vie, war 4. cope, deal, race 5. argue, fight 6. assert, bicker, insist, strive 7. compete, contest, grapple, quarrel, wrangle 8. contrive, maintain, militate

content, contents ... 4. list, room 5. index, space 6. amount, please, volume 7. filling, gratify, makings, satisfy, suffice 8. capacity 9. contented, happiness, satisfied 10. components, dimensions 11. ingredients

contention ... 3. war 4. feud 6. combat, debate, strife 7. quarrel, rivalry 8. argument, conflict, struggle, variance 9. emulation 10. dissension, litigation 11. altercation, competition, controversy 12. disagreement

contentious ... 7. peevish 8. perverse 9. combative, litigious, wrangling 10. pugnacious 11. belligerent, dissentious, quarrelsome 13. argumentative

contentment ... 4. ease 5. bliss 8. pleasure 11. peace of mind 12. satisfaction 13. contentedness, gratification

conterminous ... 4. next 8. abutting, adjacent, proximal 9. adjoining

contest ... 3. sue, vie 4. agon, bout, cope, deny, game, race, tilt 5. argue, set-to, trial 6. debate, oppose, strife, strive, tryout 7. contend, dispute, tourney, wrangle 8. argument, disclaim, litigate, skirmish, struggle 9. emulation 10. engagement 11. altercation, competition

contest (pert to) ...
art of .. 10. agonistics
draw .. 9. stalemate
log hurling .. 5. roleo
prize .. 5. stake
undecided .. 4. draw

contestant ... 5. rival 6. player 7. athlete, entrant 8. opponent 9. candidate, combatant, contender 10. competitor

contiguous ... 4. near, next 8. adjacent, touching 9. adjoining, immediate, proximate 11. neighboring

continent ... 4. Asia 6. Africa, Europe 7. Eurasia, Lemuria 8. Atlantis (lost), Cascadia, landmass 9. Australia, Greenland 10. Antarctica 12. North America, South America

contingency ... 4. case 5. event 6. chance 8. accident, casualty, exigency, juncture 9. emergency, liability 11. eventuality, possibility, uncertainty

contingent ... 6. casual 8. eventual 9. dependent (law), provisory 10. accidental, fortuitous, incidental 11. conditional, provisional

continual ... 7. endless, eternal, regular, undying, uniform 8. constant, enduring, frequent, unbroken 9. ceaseless, connected, continued, incessant, perennial, permanent, perpetual, unceasing 10. continuous, invariable 11. everlasting, intermitted, unremitting 12. imperishable 13. uninterrupted

continually ... 3. aye 4. ever 5. often 7. eternal 9. eternally 10. constantly 11. perpetually, unceasingly 12. continuously

continuation ... 6. sequel 8. addition, sequence 10. continuity 11. continuance, propagation, protraction 12. postponement, prolongation

continue ... 3. run 4. go on, last, stay 5. abide 6. endure, extend, remain, resume 7. perdure, persist, proceed, sustain 8. protract 9. persevere, steadfast (be)

continuing ... 5. still 7. chronic, durable, lasting 9. permanent 10. continuous 11. persevering

continuous ... 7. chronic, endless, uniform 8. unbroken 9. continued, perpetual 13. uninterrupted

contorted ... 3. wry 4. bent 6. coiled, warped 7. garbled, gnarled, twisted, wristed 8. deformed 9. perverted

contour ... 4. form, line 5. curve, graph 6. figure 7. isobase, outline, profile 9. lineament, periphery 13. configuration

contra ... 6. offset 7. against, counter, reverse 8. contrary, opposite 9. vice versa 10. conversely 12. contrariwise

contraband ... 7. bootleg, illegal, illicit 8. unlawful 9. moonshine 10. prohibited

contract ... 4. hale, knit, pact 5. incur, lease 6. cartel, engage, pledge, reduce, shrink 7. bargain, compact, promise, shorten, shrivel 8. covenant 9. agreement, constrict, indenture 10. convention, obligation, straighten 11. arrangement 13. understanding

contraction ... 3. tic 4. coup, fist 5. spasm 7. elision, systole 8. decrease 9. reduction, short-hand, stricture 11. compression

contrada ... 3. way 4. ward 6. street 7. quarter

contradict ... 4. deny 5. belie, rebut 6. impugn, negate, oppose, refute 7. gainsay 10. counteract

contradiction ... 6. denial 7. paradox 10. opposition, refutation 11. contrariety 13. counteraction

contradictory ... 7. denying 8. contrary, opposite 10. refutatory 12. inconsistent

contrary ... 7. adverse, counter, froward, opposed, reverse 8. captious, inimical, opposite, perverse, refutive 9. different, repugnant 10. discordant, unorthodox 12. antagonistic

contrast ... 7. compare 8. opposite

11. contrariety

contravene . . . 4. defy 6. hinder, oppose, refute, thwart 7. violate 8. infringe 9. disregard

contravention . . . 6. denial 9. violation 10. opposition, refutation

contribute . . . 3. aid 4. give 6. donate 7. benefit, conduce, provide 9. subscribe

contribution . . . 3. tax, tip 4. boon, gift, scot 6. tariff 7. payment, tribute 8. donation 12. subscription 13. participation

contrite . . . 6. abject, humble 8. penitent 9. repentant, sorrowful 10. remorseful 11. penitential

contrition . . . 7. remorse 9. attrition, penitence 11. compunction

contrivance . . . 3. art 5. means, shift 6. design, devise 7. coinage, machine, measure, project 8. artifice, intrigue 9. expedient, invention, makeshift 11. contraption

contrive . . . 4. plan, plot 5. frame, hatch, weave 6. design, devise, invent, manage, scheme 7. fashion, project 9. fabricate

control . . . 4. hold, rein, rule, sway, test 5. check, gripe, guide, leash, power, wield 6. direct, govern, manage, subdue 7. conduct, mastery, preside, regimen 8. dominate, dominion, ironhand, regulate, restrain 9. direction, influence, regulator, restraint 10. management, regulation 11. self-control, superintend

controller, comptroller . . . 7. auditor 8. governor 9. dominator, regulator

controversial . . . 7. eristic, polemic 9. eristical, polemical, pro and con 11. contentious 12. disputatious, questionable 13. argumentative

controversy . . . 6. debate 7. dispute, quarrel, wrangle 8. argument 10. contention 11. altercation 12. disagreement, disputatious

controvert . . . 4. deny, moot 5. argue 6. debate, oppose, refute 7. discuss, dispute 10. contradict

contumacious . . . 6. unruly 7. riotous 8. mutinous, perverse 9. seditious 10. headstrong, rebellious, refractory, unyielding 11. disobedient, intractable 12. ungovernable 13. insubordinate

contumelious . . . 7. haughty 8. insolent 9. insulting 10. derogatory, despiteful, disdainful 12. contemptuous

contumely . . . 5. scorn 8. contempt 9. indignity, insolence 10. revilement 11. humiliation, malediction

contusion . . . 4. blow 6. bruise, injury 8. black eye 13. discoloration

conundrum . . . 5. rebus 6. enigma, puzzle, riddle 7. charade

convalesce . . . 5. rally 7. recover, recruit 10. recuperate

convene . . . 3. sit 4. come, meet 5. unite 6. summon 8. assemble 10. congregate, foregather

convenient . . . 5. handy, ready 6. fitted, nearby, suited, timely 7. adapted 8. suitable 9. agreeable, available, opportune 10. accessible, commodious,

seasonable 11. comfortable

convent . . . 4. meet 6. concur, friary, priory 7. convene, nunnery 8. cloister, lamasery 9. monastery, sanctuary

convention . . . 4. rule 5. usage 6. accord, custom 7. meeting 8. assembly 9. gathering, tradition 10. assemblage, compliance, conformity

conventional . . . 5. fixed, nomic, usual 6. formal, modish 7. correct 8. accepted, orthodox 9. customary 10. ceremonial 11. established, traditional

converge . . . 4. meet 5. focus, unite

conversant (with) . . . 5. adept 6. expert, versed (in) 7. skilled 8. familiar 9. practiced 10. acquainted, proficient

conversation . . . 4. chat, talk 5. trialog 8. causerie, converse, dialogue 9. communion, discourse 10. conference 11. association 13. conversazione, interlocution

conversationalist . . . 6. talker 9. converser 10. discourser 12. confabulator

converse . . . 4. chat, talk 8. contrary, opposite

convey . . . 4. cede, deed, pass, send 5. bring, carry, eloin, grant 6. assign, convoy, demise, devise, impart, import 7. dispone 8. transfer, transmit 9. transport 10. commission 11. communicate

conveyance . . . 3. bus, car, van 4. auto, sled, taxi, tram 5. plane, train 6. demise, litter 7. cession, norimon, trailer, vehicle 8. airplane, carriage 10. automobile

conveyer, conveyor . . . 6. bearer, coolie, pigeon (homing), porter 7. bheesty, carrier 8. cargador 9. stevedore

convict . . . 4. damn 5. felon, lifer 6. refute, termer, trusty 7. condemn, culprit 8. criminal, prisoner 10. malefactor

conviction . . . 4. hope 6. belief 7. opinion 9. certainty 10. persuasion 12. condemnation

convince . . . 6. assure, subdue 7. confute, jawbone 8. overcome, persuade 9. overpower

convincing . . . 5. proof 6. cogent, potent 7. telling 8. assuring 10. conclusive, persuasive, satisfying

convivial . . . 3. gay 4. gala 5. jolly, merry 6. festal, jovial, joyful, joyous, social 7. festive, jocular 8. hilarious

convocation . . . 4. diet 5. synod 7. bidding, council, meeting, summons 8. assembly, congress 10. convention 12. congregation

convoke . . . 4. call 6. summon 7. convene 8. assemble

convoy . . . 5. guard, guide 6. attend, escort 7. conduct 8. navigate 9. accompany, conductor

convulse . . . 5. amuse, shake 8. regale 7. agitate, disturb, torture 9. entertain 10. discompose

convulsion . . . 4. cramp, spasm, throe 6. tumult, uproar 8. laughter, paroxysm 9. agitation, commotion 10. revolution 11. disturbance

cony, coney . . . 3. das, fur 4. dupe, hare, pika 5. daman, hyrax 6. burbot, rabbit

cony catcher . . . 5. cheat 7. sharper 8. swindler

coo . . . 4. bill (and), curr 5. chirr 6. murmur, mutter

cook . . . 4. bake, boil, chef, stew 5. broil, roast, sauté, spoil (chess), steam, trill 6. braise, seethe 7. parboil, stir-fry 8. barbecue, magirist 9. charbroil, cuisinier

cookie . . . 5. scone 7. biscuit, brownie 8. macaroon 10. gingersnap, ladyfinger, shortbread

cooking (pert to) . . .
art . . 8. magirics
device . . 3. wok 4. etna, olla 5. grill, plate, stove 6. spider 7. griddle 9. autoclave, microwave (oven)
room . . 6. galley 7. cuisine, kitchen 8. scullery 11. kitchenette
scent . . 4. reek 5. nidor

cool . . . 3. fan, ice 4. calm 5. chill, fresh, nervy, sober, tepid 6. chilly, freeze, sedate, serene, temper 7. unmoved 8. careless, composed, impudent, mitigate, reserved, tranquil 9. apathetic, collected, unruffled 10. nonchalant, unfriendly, unsociable 11. indifferent, levelheaded, unconcerned 13. dispassionate, imperturbable, self-possessed

cooler . . . 4. icer, jail 6. icebox, lockup, prison 7. chiller 10. ventilator 11. refrigerant 12. refrigerator

coolness . . . 4. cold 5. nerve 6. aplomb 7. reserve 12. indifference 14. unfriendliness

coop . . . 3. mew, pen 4. cage, cote, yard 5. court, hutch 7. confine 9. enclosure

cooper . . . 5. drink 6. vessel 8. grogshop (floating) 11. barrel maker 12. wine retailer

Cooper, (James Fenimore) (pert to) . . .
hero . . 10. Deerslayer, Natty Bumpo, Pathfinder
tales . . 15. Leatherstocking

cooperate . . . 4. join, tend 5. agree, coact 6. concur 7. combine, conduce, connive 8. conspire 9. interface, synergize 10. contribute 11. collaborate

coordinate . . . 5. talky 6. adjust 7. syntony (radio) 8. classify, equalize, organize, regulate 9. harmonize, integrate 10. proportion 11. systematize

copious . . . 4. full, rich 5. ample 7. diffuse, profuse 8. abundant, numerous 9. exuberant, plenteous, plentiful 11. overflowing

copper . . . 2. Cu 3. aes 4. cent, coin 5. metal, penny 6. cuprum 9. policeman 12. reddish-brown

copper (pert to) . . .
alloy . . 5. brass 6. bronze, oroide
brass . . 6. chalco
cup . . 3. dop
engraving . . 9. mezzotint
film . . 6. patina
kettle (anc) . . 5. lebes
pewter . . 7. rheotan

Copperfield characters . . . 4. Dora 6. Dartle 8. Micawber 9. Uriah Heep 11. Little Emily

coppice . . . 4. bosk, holt 5. copse, grove 6. growth 7. boscage, thicket 9. brushwood, underwood

Coptic (pert to) . . .
church . . 8. Egyptian
color . . 7. oxblood
title . . 4. anba

copy . . . 3. ape 4. news 5. clone, model, Xerox (tm) 6. ectype, follow 7. edition, estreat, imitate, pattern, replica, reprint, tracing 8. protocol, revision 9. duplicate, imitation 10. transcribe, transcript 11. counterfeit 12. reproduction

coquet, coquette . . . 4. vamp 5. flirt 7. amorous 11. hummingbird

coquille . . . 5. shell 7. ruching

Coquille . . . 6. Indian 10. Athapascan

coquin . . . 5. knave, rogue 6. rascal

coral . . . 3. red 6. polyps, porite 8. Anthozoa 9. madrepore, millepore

coral (pert to) . . .
branch . . 7. ramicle
division . . 7. Aporosa
formation . . 5. palus
island . . 3. key 5. atoll
ridge . . 4. reef 5. shoal
snake . . 5. Elaps 6. garter 7. Micurus
worm . . 6. palolo

corbie (Scot) . . . 4. crow. 5. raven

cord . . . 3. guy, rib 4. lace, line, rope, welt, wood 5. sinew, twine 6. lariat, sennet, spinal, string, tendon 7. measure (cubic), skirreh 8. corduroy, shoelace 9. hamstring 11. clothesline

cordage . . . 5. ropes 7. rigging 8. ropework

Corday's victim . . . 5. Marat

cordelle . . . 6. hauler 7. towline, towrope

cordial . . . 4. real, warm 6. ardent, elixir, genial, hearty, liquor 7. fervent, liqueur, sincere, zealous 8. friendly, vigorous 9. unfeigned 10. hospitable

cordial (liqueur) . . . 5. shrub 6. kummel 8. anisette, periscot 9. Cointreau 11. Benedictine, crème de moka 13. crème de menthe

cordiality . . . 4. zeal 5. ardor 6. fervor 7. ardency 8. kindness, warmness 9. geniality 11. hospitality 12. empressement, friendliness

corduroy feature . . . 4. wale

core . . . 3. ame, hub, nub, nut 4. gist, nave, pith 5. heart, nowel 6. center, kernel, matrix 7. nucleus 9. substance

Corinthian (pert to) . . .
Age . . 5. plush 11. extravagant
color . . 3. red 4. pink 6. purple
Epistles (Bib) . . 12. New Testament
General (Rom) . . 9. Flaminius
King . . 8. Polybius
Spring . . 14. Pirene Fountain
Temple . . 5. Doric 7. Minerva

cork . . . 3. ork 4. bark, bung, plug 5. float, shive, suber (oak) 7. blacken, stopgap, stopper, stopple

corm . . . 4. bulb (flower)

cormorant . . . 4. bird, shag 5. norie, scart, urile 8. ravenous 9. snakebird, voracious 13. Phalacrocorax

corn ... 4. joke 5. grain, grist 6. cliché, kaffir, kernel, liquor

corn (pert to) ...
  bread .. 4. pone 8. dumpling 10. corndodger
  goddess .. 5. Ceres
  hulled .. 4. samp 6. hominy
  Indian .. 3. Zea 5. maize
  lily .. 4. Ixia 8. bindweed 10. wandflower
  liquor .. 6. whisky (whiskey)
  meal .. 4. masa 7. hoecake
  porridge .. 5. atole
  salad .. 8. fetticus

Corn Belt ... 4. Iowa, Ohio 6. Dakota, Kansas 7. Indiana 8. Illinois, Missouri, Nebraska 9. Minnesota

Corncracker State ... 8. Kentucky

corner ... 2. in 4. nook, pose, trap, tree 5. angle, coign (coigne), herne, ingle, niche, quoin

cornered ... 5. cater (diagonal), sharp, treed 7. angular, up a tree 10. cornerwise

cornerstone ... 4. coin 5. quoin 8. keystone 10. foundation

Cornhusker State ... 8. Nebraska

cornice ... 4. drip, eave 7. antefix 8. astragal

Cornish ... 3. elm 4. fowl 5. heath 7. dialect, diamond (Cornwall)

Cornwallis surrender site ... 4. York (Va)

corolla ... 5. galea (Her), petal 8. perianth

corollary ... 6. effect, porism, result 7. adjunct 8. addition 9. deduction 11. proposition

corona ... 4. coin, halo 5. cigar, crown 6. circle, aureole, circlet, garland, scyphus 8. Borealis 11. corona lucis

Corona Australis ... 13. Southern Crown

Corona Borealis ... 13. Northern Crown

coronet ... 5. crown, tiara 6. anadem, circle, diadem, wreath 8. insignia, ornament

Corot subject ... 9. landscape

corporate ... 5. joint 6. united 7. leagued 8. conjoint 10. associated

corporeal ... 5. hylic, somal 6. bodily 7. fleshly, somatic 8. corporal, material, physical, tangible

corpse ... 4. body 7. cadaver, carcass 9. endowment (Eccl)

corpulent ... 3. fat 5. bulky, obese, stout 6. fleshy

corpus ... 4. body, mass 9. principal 10. collection

corpuscle ... 11. poikilocyte, schistocyte 12. erythroblast

corral ... 3. mew, pen, sty 4. coop, herd 5. atajo, pound, tambo 7. impound 8. stockade 9. enclosure, inclosure

correct ... 2. OK 4. edit, okay, true 5. amend, emend, right 6. better, proper, punish, reform, remedy, revise, strict 7. chasten, improve, perfect, rectify, regular, retouch 8. accurate, definite, orthodox, rigorous 9. faultless 10. particular, scrupulous 11. grammatical, punctilious 12. conventional

correlative ... 2. or 3. nor 6. mutual 7. similar 8. conjoint 10. reciprocal 11. conjunction, counterpart 13. corresponding

correspond ... 3. fit 4. suit 5. agree, equal, match, tally 6. accord 7. comport 8. assonate (sound), coincide, parallel 9. analogous, harmonize 11. parallelize

correspondence ... 4. mail 8. homology (Biol), identity, symmetry 10. conformity, epistolary, similarity 11. equivalence, intercourse

corresponding ... 8. balanced 9. analogous, homologic, isometric 10. coinciding 11. paralleling

corrida sound ... 3. olé

corridor ... 4. hall 5. aisle 6. airway, arcade 7. gallery 10. passageway

corrige (obs) ... 6. punish 7. correct

corrigible ... 8. amenable 10. submissive 11. rectifiable

corroborate ... 5. prove 7. certify, confirm, support 8. calidate, roborate 9. establish 12. adminiculate, substantiate

corroborative ... 11. adminicular

corrode ... 3. eat 4. bite, etch, gnaw, rust 5. erode, waste 11. deteriorate 12. disintegrate

corrosive ... 4. acid 7. caustic, erodent, erodine, mordant 9. corroding 10. escharotic 14. disintegrative

corrugate ... 5. crimp 6. rugate 7. crumble, wrinkle 8. crumpled, furrowed, wrinkled

corrupt ... 3. rot 5. bribe, taint, venal 6. Augean, debase, putrid, rotten 7. attaint, crooked, defiled, deprave, putrefy, vitiate 8. polluted 9. dishonest 11. adulterated 12. contaminated

corruption ... 5. taint 6. pidgin (language) 8. impurity 9. chicanery, pollution 10. debasement, defilement, distortion 11. depravation, putrescence 12. adulteration 13. contamination

corsage ... 5. waist 6. bodice 7. bouquet (boquet), flowers

corsair ... 5. rover 6. pirate 7. Saracen 8. picaroon, rockfish 9. buccaneer, privateer 10. freebooter

Corsica ...
  capital .. 7. Ajaccio
  birthplace of .. 8. Napoleon
  feud (blood) .. 8. vendetta
  seaport .. 6. Bastia

cortege ... 5. train 6. parade 7. funeral, retinue 10. procession

Cortes palace site ... 8. Coyoacan (Mexico)

cortex ... 4. bark, peel, rind

corundum ... 3. gem 5. emery 7. mineral 8. abrasive

corundum colors ...
  blue .. 5. white 8. sapphire
  brown .. 14. adamantine spar
  green .. 7. emerald
  purple .. 8. amethyst
  red .. 4. ruby
  topaz .. 6. yellow

coruscate ... 5. gleam, shine 7. glitter, radiate, sparkle 11. scintillate

cosmetic ... 5. cream, henna, paint, rouge 6. enamel, lotion, make-up 7. blusher, mascara 8. lipstick, toiletry 11. beautifying

cosmic ... 4. vast 5. great 7. orderly 8. catholic, infinite 9. grandiose, universal 10. harmonious

Cosmic Order ... 4. Rita (Vedic law)

Cossack (pert to) ...
chief .. 6. ataman, hetman
district .. 6. Voisko
native .. 5. Tatar 7. Russian
squadron .. 6. sotnia
village .. 8. stanitsa (stanitza)
whip (knotted) .. 5. knout

cosset ... 3. pet 4. lamb 6. caress, coddle, cuddle, fondle, pamper

cost ... 4. loss, rate 5. price 6. amount, charge, figure, outlay, rental 7. expense 9. detriment, suffering 11. deprivation, expenditure

costa ... 3. rib 4. vein (Bot) 5. ridge 6. border, midrib

Costa Rica ...
capital .. 7. San José
crater (world's greatest) .. 4. Poas
discovered .. 8. Columbus (4th visit)
export .. 6. coffee 7. bananas
port .. 5. Limon 10. Puntarenas

costate ... 6. ribbed (Bot)

costermonger ... 6. coster, hawker 7. peddler 9. costerman 11. apple seller

costly ... 4. dear, rich 8. gorgeous, splendid 9. expensive, sumptuous 10. high-priced 11. extravagant

costume ... 3. rig 4. garb, suit 5. dress, habit 6. attire, tights 7. apparel, raiment 8. clothing

cot ... 3. bed, hut, pen, set 4. boat (Ir), coop, cote 5. cabin, cover, house 6. cabana 7. charpoy, cottage, shelter 8. bedstead

cote ... 3. hut, pen 4. coop 5. house 7. cottage, shelter 9. sheepfold

Côte d'Azur ... 7. Riviera

coterie ... 3. set 4. clan, club, ring 5. cabal, group, junto 6. circle, clique 9. camarilla (secret)

cotillion ... 4. ball 5. belle, dance 9. debutante, petticoat, quadrille

cottage ... 3. cot, hut 4. shed 5. cabin, house, villa 6. cabana 7. shelter 8. bungalow

cottager ... 6. cottar (cotter) 7. cottier, laborer, peasant

cotton (pert to) ...
cloth .. 4. jean, lawn 5. denim, khaki, scrim, surat, terry 6. calico, dimity, madras, nettle 7. batiste, percale
fiber .. 4. lint 6. staple 7. viscose
gin inventor .. 7. Whitney (Eli)
knot .. 3. nep
layer .. 7. batting
medical .. 5. gauze 6. sponge
raw .. 5. bayal
roll .. 4. slub
seed .. 4. bole, boll
seed sugar .. 9. raffinose
staple .. 6. upland (short) 8. Egyptian (long) 9. Sea Island (long)

thread .. 5. lisle

Cotton State ... 7. Alabama

couch ... 3. bed, cot 4. lair, sofa 5. divan 6. canapé, canopy, litter, lounge, pallet, phrase 8. loveseat 9. embroider (with gold), stretcher

cougar ... 3. cat 4. lion, puma 7. panther 9. catamount

cough ... 4. bark (sl), hack 6. tussis

council ... 4. diet, rede 5. cabal, synod 6. senate 7. cabinet 8. assembly, conclave, tribunal 10. conference, parliament 12. consultation 15. League of Nations

council table cover ... 5. tapis

counsel ... 4. rede 6. advice, advise, confer, lawyer 8. guidance 9. recommend 10. suggestion 11. instruction 12. deliberation

counselor, counsellor ... 4. sage 6. lawyer, mentor, nestor 7. adviser, advisor, counsel 8. attorney 9. barrister, solicitor

count ... 3. sum, tot 4. tale, tell 5. check, judge, relay, tally 6. number, reckon, rely on 7. compute, summary 8. nobleman, quantify 9. calculate, enumerate, reckoning, summation 12. capitulation

Count (pert to) ...
Mayence .. 3. Gan 7. Ganelon
Monte Cristo .. 6. Dantes
Rousillon .. 7. Bertram

countenance ... 3. aid 4. abet, brow, face, mien 6. aspect, permit, visage 7. approve, endorse, support 8. approval, sanction, tolerate 9. composure, encourage 10. appearance, permission

counter ... 4. chip 5. table, token 7. adverse 9. computer, contrary, opposite 9. retaliate 10. calculator

counteract ... 6. offset, oppose, thwart 7. nullify 8. antidote 10. neutralize 11. countermand

counter current ... 4. eddy 5. swirl 6. vortex 9. whirlpool 12. counterforce

counterfeit ... 4. base, fake, mock, sham 5. bogus, false, feign, forge, phony, queer 6. assume, forged, unreal 7. falsify, forgery, imitate 8. simulant, spurious 10. artificial, fictitious 11. unauthentic

counterirritant ... 4. móxa 5. seton 6. arnica, iodine, pepper 7. mustard

countermand ... 5. annul 6. cancel, forbid, recall, revoke 7. abolish, reverse 8. prohibit 9. frustrate 10. counteract 12. counterorder

counterpane ... 5. quilt 8. bedcover, coverlet 9. comforter 10. counterpin 11. comfortable

counterpart ... 4. copy, like, twin 5. image 6. double, eponym (name) 8. parallel 9. duplicate 10. complement, equivalent

counterpoise ... 6. offset 8. equalize 10. compensate, counteract 12. counterforce 14. counterbalance

countersign ... 4. sign 6. signal 7. tessera 8. password 9. signature, watchword

10. mot de passé, open sesame
12. counterstamp
countersink . . . 4. ream 5. bevel
6. deepen 7. chamfer
countertenor . . . 4. alto (male) 8. falsetto
counterthrust (fencing) . . . 7. riposte
(ripost) 12. return thrust
countless . . . 8. infinite 10. numberless,
unnumbered 11. innumerable
12. incalculable
countrified . . . 5. rural 7. boorish, hickish,
uncouth 8. inurbane 10. unpolished
country . . . 4. land, pais (law), vale
5. rural, state, weald 6. nation,
region 9. territory 10. fatherland
12. commonwealth
country (pert to) . . .
alien . . 7. enclave, exclave
ancient . . 4. Aram, Elis, Gaul
bumpkin . . 4. clod, jake, rube 5. churl,
yokel 9. greenhorn
gallant . . 5. swain
mythical . . 2. Oz
native (earliest) . . 9. aborigine
Roman . . 8. campagna
term . . 5. rural, urban 6. rustic 8. agrestic,
pastoral, praedial (predial)
countryman . . . 4. rube 5. yokel 6. rustic
7. hayseed, patriot, peasant
10. compatriot, home towner
county . . . 4. seat 5. shire 6. domain,
parish 8. district
coup . . . 3. buy 4. blow, move (games)
5. scoop, upset 6. barter, strike,
stroke (master) 8. overturn, strategy
9. overthrow, trump card
coup de grâce . . . 9. deathblow
coup de main . . . 6. attack (sudden)
8. strategy 9. stratagem
coup d'état . . . 6. stroke (political)
8. strategy 9. overthrow
couple . . . 3. duo, tie, two 4. bond, dyad,
join, link, mate, pair, span, team, twin,
yoke 5. brace, marry, twain, unite
6. Gemini 8. bracket
coupled . . . 5. gemel, mated 6. braced,
joined, linked, paired, teamed, united
7. leagued, married
couplet . . . 3. two 4. pair 5. brace, verse
7. distich, doublet
coupon . . . 5. scrip, stock, token 6. ticket
11. certificate (Finan)
courage . . . 4. grit, sand, will 5. heart,
metal, moxie, nerve, pluck, spine,
valor 7. bravery, heroism, prowess
8. audacity, backbone, boldness,
firmness 8. fortitude, gallantry,
hardihood 11. intrepidity
12. fearlessness 13. dauntlessness
courageous . . . 4. bold, game 5. brave,
hardy, manly, stout 6. daring, heroic,
spunky 7. gallant, spartan, valiant
8. fearless, intrepid, knightly, resolute,
stalwart, valorous 11. adventurous
12. enterprising, stouthearted
courant . . . 4. romp 5. caper 6. letter
7. gazette, running (Her) 9. messenger,
newspaper
courier . . . 5. guide 8. dragoman,
horseman 9. attendant, messenger
course . . . 3. run 4. flow, line, mode, path,

road, rote, tack 5. route, study, trend
6. career, manner, method, policy,
series, stream 8. progress 9. direction,
procedure 10. succession
course (pert to) . . .
college . . 7. seminar
direct . . 7. beeline
golf . . 5. links
regular . . 4. rote 6. regime 7. routine
roundabout . . 6. detour 11. indirection
course of . . .
action . . 5. habit 7. routine 9. procedure
eating . . 4. diet
instruction . . 6. lesson
procedure . . 4. rule
thought . . 5. tenor
courser . . . 5. horse, steed 6. hunter,
plover 7. charger 8. war horse
court . . . 3. see (papal), woo 4. area, eyre,
fawn (upon), rota 5. atria, curia, dairi,
gemot, patio, spark 6. palace, parvis,
street 7. council, tribune 8. tribunal
10. attendance, curry favor, quadrangle
court (Eng) . . . 3. soc 4. eyre, leet
8. woodmate 10. court-baron
court (pert to) . . .
assistant . . 5. staff 6. elisor
crier, cry . . 4. hear, oyez (oyes) 6. beadle
criminal . . 6. assize
exemption, excuse . . 6. essoin
game . . 6. tennis 8. badminton
hearing . . 4. oyer
minutes . . 4. acta
order . . 4. writ 5. arret 6. capias
7. summons 8. subpoena
public . . 5. forum 8. forensic
sitting . . 7. session
courteous . . . 5. civil 6. gentle, polite,
urbane 7. affable, gallant 8. debonair,
gracious 9. attentive 10. respectful
courtly . . . 4. hend (hende) 5. aulic, civil
7. elegant, gallant, stately 9. dignified
10. obsequious 11. ceremonious
courtship . . . 4. suit 6. plight, wooing
7. romance 8. courting
covenant . . . 4. bond, pact 6. engage
7. bargain, compact, entente, promise
8. contract 9. agreement, stipulate,
testament 11. undertaking
Covenant of God to Noah . . . 7. rainbow
Coventry equestrienne . . . 6. Godiva
cover . . . 3. cap, lap, lid 4. coat, cozy,
hide, mask, pale, pave, roof, span, veil
5. blind, crust, drape, tapis 6. canopy,
mantle, purdah, screen, shield, thatch
7. elytron, overlay, shelter 8. chrismal,
coverlet 9. tarpaulin 10. overspread
cover (pert to) . . .
alloy . . 5. terne
cork . . 9. corticate
crumbs . . 5. bread
dots . . 7. stipple
figures (Her) . . 4. seme
straw . . 6. thatch
turf . . 3. sod
up . . 4. bury 5. inter 7. conceal
8. submerge 10. camouflage
with wax . . 4. cere
covering . . . 3. mat, rug 4. caul, film,
hull, tile 5. apron, armor, shell, testa
6. awning, carpet, cestus, lorica,

pelage, screen, shroud 7. epeiric, shelter, tegumen, wrapper 8. lineolum, pericarp 9. caparison 10. integument, protection 11. smoke screen

covering (head) ... 3. cap, hat, wig 4. hood 5. beret, scarf, snood 6. bonnet, peruke, toupee 7. chapeau 10. fascinator

coverlet ... 3. quilt 6. afghan, spread 7. blanket, lap robe 11. counterpane

covert ... 3. den, lie 4. abri, lair 6. hidden, refuge, secret 7. covered, private, thicket 9. concealed, disguised, insidious, sheltered

covet ... 4. envy 5. crave, yisse (obs) 6. aspire, desire, grudge, hanker 7. long for 8. begrudge

covetousness ... 5. greed 7. avarice

covey ... 4. bevy, pack 5. brood, flock, hatch 6. flight 7. company 9. multitude

cow ... 3. awe 5. abash, daunt 7. overawe, terrify 8. browbeat, frighten 10. intimidate

cow (animal) ... 3. Bos 4. calf, kine, moil 5. Angus, bossy, brock (obs), Kerry, vache 6. bovine, heifer 7. pollard 8. Ayrshire, maverick, moulleen

cow (pert to) ...
  barn .. 4. byre, shed 5. reeve, stall
  6. stable 7. vaccary, vachery
  food (chewed) .. 3. cud 5. rumen
  hornless .. 6. mulley 7. pollard
  8. moulleen
  sea .. 6. dugong, walrus 7. manatee, Sirenia 8. hippopotamus
  tether .. 4. rope 6. baikie
  unbranded .. 8. maverick
  young .. 4. calf 6. heifer

coward, cowardly ... 3. shy 5. sneak 6. afraid, craven, scared, yellow 7. caitiff, chicken, dastard, milksop 8. poltroon, recreant, weakling 9. dastardly, fraidy-cat, jellyfish 12. uncourageous 13. pusillanimous

cowboy ... 5. roper, waddy 6. herder 7. llamero, puncher, vaquero 8. jackaroo, neatherd 12. broncobuster (sl)

cowboy garb ... 5. chaps 7. Stetson 8. jodhpurs

cower ... 4. fawn 5. crawl, quail, stoop 6. cringe, crouch, grovel

cowfish ... 3. ray 4. toto 7. dolphin, grampus, manatee 8. porpoise

cowled ... 9. cucullate

coxcomb ... 3. fop 4. dude, fool 5. cleat (Naut), dandy 8. popinjay

coy ... 3. shy 4. arch 5. timid 6. demure, modest 7. bashful 10. coquettish 13. self-conscious

coyote ... 4. wolf (prairie)

Coyote State ... 11. South Dakota

coypu ... 6. nutria, rodent

cozen ... 5. cheat, trick 7. beguile, deceive, defraud

cozy ... 4. easy, snug 6. chatty 8. cheerful, familiar, homelike, sociable 9. contented, talkative 11. comfortable

crab ... 3. Uca 4. king, Maia (genus) 5. ayuyu (Guam) 6. nebula, partan, spider 7. fiddler, limulus, mollusk,

Ocypode 8. Lithodes 9. horseshoe 10. crustacean

crabbed ... 5. cross 6. bitter, crusty, morose, trying 7. bilious, peevish 8. abstruse, liverish 9. difficult, fractious, irascible, irregular 10. perplexing

crab claw ... 5. chela 6. metope, nipper

crab walk ... 5. sidle

crachoir ... 8. cuspidor, spittoon

crack ... 4. blow, chap, clap, flaw, kibe, leak, quip, rift, rime, snap 5. brack, break, chink, craze, spang, split 6. breach, cleave, cranny 7. crackle, crevice, fissure, rupture 8. fracture

Cracker State ... 7. Georgia

crackle ... 4. snap 5. craze (art), crink 9. crepitate

crackman ... 4. yegg 7. burglar

cradle ... 4. slee (ship's) 7. infancy, nursery 8. bassinet, cunabula 10. beginnings, incunabula

cradle book ... 11. incunabulum

Cradle of Liberty ... 11. Faneuil Hall (Boston)

cradle song ... 7. lullaby 8. berceuse 13. Schlummerleid

craft ... 3. art 4. boat 5. skill, trade 6. device, tender 7. cunning, finesse, know-how, prowess 8. aptitude, vocation 9. dexterity 10. employment, handicraft, occupation, watercraft 12. skillfulness

craftsman ... 6. artist, writer 7. artisan, workman 9. artificer

crafty ... 3. sly 4. foxy, slim, wily, wise 6. artful, astute, shifty, shrewd, subtle, tricky 7. cunning 8. skillful (skilful) 9. deceitful, ingenious, underhand 10. fraudulent 13. Machiavellian 15. Mephistophelean

crag ... 3. tor 4. spur 5. arête, cliff 7. nunatak 9. precipice

craggy ... 5. rough 6. cliffy, clifty, jagged, knotty, rugged

cram ... 4. fill 5. choke, crowd, drive, force, gorge, press, study, stuff 9. overstuff 10. gluttonize

cramp ... 4. pain 5. stunt 6. hamper 7. confine, seizure 8. compress, restrict 9. hindrance, paralysis (muscle) 11. restriction

cranberry ... 3. red 9. sourberry

cranberry center of trade ... 10. Barnstable (Mass)

crane ... 3. gib, jib 5. davit, jenny, titan 7. derrick, machine

crane ... 4. Grus 5. heron, sarus 7. Gruidae 9. cormorant 10. Gruiformes 13. constellation

cranial nerve ... 5. radix, vagus

cranium ... 5. skull 8. cerebrum

crank ... 3. wit 4. bear, crab 5. crook, winch 6. griper, grouch, handle 7. fanatic, growler, hothead 8. frondeur, grumbler, sorehead 9. eccentric 10. bellyacher, crosspatch, monomaniac

cranny ... 4. hole, nook 5. chink, cleft, crack 6. corner, furrow 7. crevice, fissure 8. crevasse

crash ... 4. bank, fail 5. smash 7. debacle, failure, intrude, shatter 8. accident

9. collision 10. bankruptcy

crate . . . 3. box 4. case 6. basket, cradle, encase, hamper 8. airplane 9. container 10. automobile

crater . . . 3. pit 6. cavity 7. caldera 13. constellation (The Cup)

cravat . . . 3. tie 4. teck 5. ascot, stock 7. bandage, bolo tie, necktie 9. neckcloth 10. four-in-hand

crave . . . 3. ask, beg 4. long, seek 5. covet, yearn 6. desire, hanker 7. beseech, entreat, implore, request, solicit 10. supplicate

craven . . . 6. afraid, coward 7. caitiff, dastard 8. cowardly, poltroon, recreant 12. fainthearted 13. pusillanimous

craving . . . 4. pica 6. desire, thirst 7. longing 8. appetite, yearning

craw . . . 3. maw 4. crop 6. gebbie 7. gizzard, stomach 9. ingluvies

crawfish . . . 5. yabby (yabbie) 7. back out, crawdad, lobster, retreat 8. crayfish

crawl . . . 4. fawn, inch, shug 5. creep 6. cringe, grovel, recant

crayon . . . 5. chalk 6. pastel, pencil 8. charcoal

craze . . . 3. fad 4. flaw, maze 5. crack (ceramics), crush, furor, mania, vogue 6. defect, whimsy 7. crackle, fashion 9. infirmity 11. infatuation

craze (for) . . . see also *madness, mania*
foreign customs . . 9. xenomania
freedom . . 14. eleutheromania
love (erotic) . . 10. erotomania
music . . 9. melomania
setting fires . . 9. pyromania
shopping . . 9. oniomania
single subject . . 9. monomania
stamps (postage) . . 11. timbromania
stealing . . 11. kleptomania
wandering . . 10. dromomania
wealth . . 10. plutomania

crazed . . . 4. amok 6. insane, marked (with crazes) 7. severed 8. deranged 10. distraught

crazy . . . 3. mad 4. amok, daft, loco 5. batty, loony, nutty, silly 6. dottle, insane 7. damaged, foolish, unsound 9. deficient

cream . . . 4. best, ream 5. elite 6. lotion 8. sillabub (with wine)

cream of tartar . . . 5. argol

crease . . . 4. fold, ruck 5. crimp, pleat 7. wrinkle 9. plication

create . . . 4. make 5. build, cause, clone, hatch 6. invent 7. fashion, produce 8. generate 9. originate

creation . . . 3. art 5. virtu, world 6. cosmos, making 7. classic, fantasy, forming, product 8. artifact, universe 9. objet d'art 10. providence 11. composition, fabrication, manufacture, masterpiece

creator . . . 5. maker 6. author 8. designer, inventor, producer 10. originator

Creator . . . 3. God 5. Maker 7. Jehovah 8. Almighty, Demiurge 11. King of Kings

creature (pert to) . . .
civetlike . . 3. cat
duplicate . . 5. clone

elflike . . 4. peri 6. hobbit
evil . . 7. helicat 8. hellicat
fire . . 10. salamander
folklore . . 3. elf 4. Yeti 5. dwarf, fairy, pixie 9. sasquatch
ghost . . 11. poltergeist
minute . . 10. animalcule
outer space . . 5. alien
sentient . . 6. animal
timid . . 4. deer 5. sheep
underground . . 5. gnome
water . . 5. sylph 6. undine
winged (Myth) . . 6. wivern 10. cockatrice

crèche figure . . . 4. Magi 6. Infant 8. shepherd

credence . . . 5. trust 6. belief, credit 8. affiance, reliance 10. acceptance, confidence, dependence 15. trustworthiness

credential . . . 7. voucher 11. certificate, testimonial 14. recommendation

credible . . . 6. likely 7. tenable 8. probable 9. plausible 10. believable 11. well-founded

credit . . . 5. faith, honor, trust 6. belief, esteem, impute 7. account, believe 8. accredit, credence 10. estimation, regulation 15. trustworthiness

creditor . . . 5. agent (collection) 6. debtee, dunner, usurer 7. Shylock (greedy)

creed . . . 5. credo, dogma, tenet 6. belief, Nicene 8. Apostles' 9. Catechism 10. Athanasian, confession

creek . . . 3. rio 4. burn, slue, wick 6. arroyo, estero, slough, spruit, stream

creel . . . 4. rack, trap 6. basket (fish)

creep . . . 5. crawl, prowl, skulk, slink, sneak, steal (away) 6. grovel 8. scramble 9. pussyfoot

creeping . . . 4. slow 7. reptant 8. crawling 10. slithering 11. reptatorial

Cremona, famed name . . . 5. Amati 8. Guarneri 10. Stradivari

crena . . . 4. gash, kerf, nick 5. cleft, notch 7. scallop 10. depression 11. indentation

creole . . . 6. French 7. mestizo 9. half-breed, janissary

Creole State . . . 9. Louisiana

crepitate . . . 4. snap 7. crackly

crescent . . . 4. cusp, horn, lune 5. curve 8. meniscus

crescent-shaped . . . 4. horn, lune 6. bicorn, lunate 7. lunular 8. lunulate 9. horseshoe, meniscate, semilunar

crest . . . 3. top 4. comb, peak, tuft 5. arête, crown, ridge 6. copple, crista, height, summit 7. panache, topknot, wave top 8. feathers, insignia, pinnacle 9. cockscomb 11. mountaintop

crested . . . 6. capped, topped, tufted 7. coppled, cristed, crowned, pileate

creta . . . 5. chalk

Crete
capital . . 5. Canea
city . . 6. Candia, Khanis
civilization (anc) . . 6. Aegean, Minoan
king (anc) . . 5. Minos (Gr)
monster . . 8. Minotaur (man, bull)
mountain . . 3. Ida 9. Theodoros
priests . . 7. Curetes

cretin . . . 5. idiot 8. imbecile

crevice . . . 3. gap 4. rift 5. chink,
cleft 6. cranny 7. fissure, opening
8. peephole 10. interstice

crew . . . 3. men 4. band, body, gang, pack
5. force, staff 7. company 9. employees,
personnel

crib . . . 3. bed, bin, den (gambling)
5. cheat, stall, steal 6. Cratch (stars),
manger, pilfer 7. brothel 8. Praesepe

cricket . . . 4. game, grig 6. acheta,
cicada, locust 7. katydid 9. footstool
10. Orthoptera 11. grasshopper

cricket (pert to) . . .
game term . . 3. bye, run 6. yorker
noise . . 5. chirp 7. stridor
symbol (Myth) . . 4. tice 5. ashes

cried . . . 4. wept 6. bawled, called, wailed,
yelled 7. shouted, uttered 8. lamented,
screamed, shrieked 9. exclaimed
10. proclaimed

crime . . . 3. sin 4. evil 5. guilt, wrong
6. delict, felony, mayhem 7. offense
8. delictum, iniquity 9. violation
10. illegality, wickedness, wrongdoing
11. malfeasance

crime (pert to) . . .
benefice (Eccl) . . 6. simony
goddess (Myth) . . 3. Ate
of 1873 . . 12. Silver Dollar
scene . . 5. venue

Crimea . . .
city . . 5. Kerch, Yalta 6. Odessa
10. Sevastopol
isthmus site . . 8. Black Sea
Russian . . 4. Krim
sea (Russ) . . 4. Azof

criminal . . . 4. thug, yegg 5. crook,
felon, thief 6. nocent 7. convict,
yeggman 8. swindler 9. desperado,
dishonest, felonious 10. malefactor,
recidivist 11. blameworthy, disgraceful
13. reprehensible

criminal refuge . . . 7. Alsatia
11. Whitefriars (London)

criminology . . . 8. penology

crimp . . . 4. curl, fold 5. frizz, notch, plait
6. ruffle, thwart 7. crinkle, wrinkle
8. Shanghai

cringe . . . 4. fawn 5. cower, quail, sneak,
wince 6. flinch, grovel, shrink, submit
7. truckle

crinkle . . . 4. curl, kink, turn, wind 5. twist
6. rustle 7. wrinkle

crinose . . . 5. hairy 7. hirsute
11. barbigerous

cripple . . . 4. halt, hock, lame, maim
6. injure, weaken 7. amputee, disable
8. handicap 9. hamstring
12. incapacitate

crisis . . . 5. cycle, peril 8. exigency,
juncture 9. criterion, emergency
11. climacteric

crisp . . . 4. cold 5. curly, flaky, sharp,
short, spalt 7. brittle, concise, crackle,
crinkle, friable 8. clear-cut 9. frangible

criterion . . . 4. norm, rule, test, type
5. canon, model 7. measure 8. standard
9. yardstick

critic . . . 5. judge, Momus (Myth)
6. censor, slater, Zoilus 8. collator,
reviewer 9. literator 11. connoisseur,

criticaster, faultfinder

critical . . . 4. edgy 7. carping, crucial,
cynical, Zoilean 8. captious, caviling,
exacting 10. censorious, particular
12. faultfinding 13. hairsplitting
14. discriminating

Critical system of philosophy . . .
10. Kantianism

criticism . . . 3. rap 5. cavil, roast 6. report,
review 7. censure, Zoilism 8. critique,
judgment 9. aspersion 10. commentary

criticize, criticise . . . 3. pan 4. carp, flay
5. cavil, judge, knock, slate 6. review
7. censure, comment 9. castigate
10. animadvert

Croatian capital . . . 6. Zagreb

crock . . . 3. ewe (old), jug, pot, urn
4. smut, soil, soot 5. horse (old)
7. ceramic 8. potsherd 11. earthenware

crocodile . . . 3. goa 5. nakoo 6. gavial,
mugger 7. reptile, sophism 9. Niloticus
10. Crocodilia, Crocodilus

crocus . . . 4. bulb, herb, iris 6. flower,
yellow 7. saffron

croft . . . 5. crypt, field, vault 6. carafe,
cavern 7. hillock

cromlech . . . 6. dolmen 8. monument

crone . . . 3. ewe (old), hag 5. witch
6. beldam (beldame)

Cronus (pert to) . . .
god of . . 8. Harvests
father . . 6. Uranus
son . . 4. Zeus
wife . . 4. Rhea

crony . . . 3. pal 4. chum 5. buddy 6. friend
9. companion 10. playfellow

crook . . . 4. bend, warp 5. angle, curve,
staff, thief 6. akimbo 7. crosier
8. criminal, insignia 10. camshachle

crooked . . . 3. wry, zag 4. agee, awry,
bent 5. agley, askew, false 6. aslant,
curved, hooked, zigzag 7. angular,
askance, asquint, oblique 8. deformed
9. dishonest, distorted 10. circuitous,
fraudulent 12. dishonorable

crooked legs . . . 8. rhebosis (rhaebosis)
10. tortuosity

croon . . . 3. hum 4. boom, sing, wail
5. whine 6. bellow, lament, murmur
8. complain

crop . . . 3. lop, maw 4. clip, craw,
dick, reap, whip 5. belly, shear,
yield 6. gebbie, growth, sheave
7. harvest, produce, soilage, stomach
11. cultivation

cross . . . 2. go 3. tau 4. crux, ford,
rood 5. bless, corse, croix (Fr),
irate, staff 6. oppose, thwart, touchy
7. athwart, fretful, oblique, peevish,
pettish 8. crucifix, insignia, monument
obstruct, petulant, snappish, swastika,
traverse 9. hybridize, intersect, irritable
10. disappoint, transverse 11. crucifixion

cross (pert to) . . .
archaeology . . 4. ankh
astronomy . . 13. Southern Cross
barred . . 11. trabeculate
beam . . 5. spale, trave 6. girder
bow . . 8. arbalest
breed . . 5. Husky (dog) 6. hybrid
British . . 6. Celtic

Egypt . . 10. life symbol
eye . . 9. esotropia 10. strabismus
heraldry . . 6. pattée 7. erminee, patonce
Latin . . 12. crux commissa
palm . . 5. bribe (gypsy)
St Anthony's . . 3. tau
stroke . . 5. serif
tau-shaped . . 10. crux ansata
crossing . . . 6. voyage 7. chiasma, fording, passage 8. cheating, opposing 9. hybridism 10. traversing 13. crossbreeding
crossing (famed) . . .
Alps . . 8. Hannibal, Napoleon
Hellespont . . 6. Xerxes
Pyrenees . . 8. Hannibal
Rubicon . . 6. Caesar
crouch . . . 4. bend, fawn 5. cower, squat, stoop 6. cringe, grovel, hunker
crow . . . 3. daw 4. brag, rook 5. aylet, boast, crake, raven, vaunt 6. chough, Corvus, Indian (Sioux) 7. corvine, jackdaw 8. laughter 13. constellation
crowbar . . . 5. jimmy, lever 7. gablock
crowberry . . . 5. shrub 8. bilberry 9. cranberry
crowd . . . 3. jam, mob 4. bike (Scot), cram, host, pack, push, ruck, urge 5. crush, drive, drove, horde, press, serry, swarm, three, wedge 6. galaxy, hasten, legion, masses, throng 7. squeeze 8. compress 9. multitude 10. assemblage
crowded . . . 6. packed 7. compact, crammed, serried, teeming 8. numerous, populous 9. congested, jampacked
crown . . . 3. cap, top 4. atef, coin, pate, peak, poll, tiar 5. crest, miter (mitre), tiara 6. anadem, circle, corona, diadem, fillet, reward, summit, trophy, wreath 7. chaplet, coronet, garland, glorify, install 8. coronate, enthrone, ornament, pinnacle, surmount
crowning glory . . . 8. last word
crucial . . . 5. final 6. severe, trying, urgent 7. crossed 8. critical, decisive 9. cruciform 13. demonstrative
crucible . . . 3. pot 4. etna, test 6. retort, vessel 10. conversion
crucifix . . . 3. pax 4. rood 5. cross 6. emblem
crucifixion . . . 5. death (on a cross) 7. torture 9. execution, suffering 11. persecution
crude . . . 3. raw 4. rude 5. crass, green, rough 6. callow, coarse, common, garish, savage, vulgar 8. unseemly 9. inelegant, rough-hewn, tasteless, uncourtly, unrefined 10. outlandish, unpolished 13. inexperienced
crudity . . . 7. rawness 9. crassness, harshness, roughness, vulgarity 10. immaturity
cruel . . . 4. fell, hard 5. harsh 6. brutal, savage, severe, unkind 7. inhuman, painful, unhuman 8. dreadful, fiendish, pitiless, ruthless, sadistic, tyrannic 9. ferocious, heartless, merciless, murderous, truculent 11. remorseless
cruelty . . . 9. brutality 10. inclemency,

inhumanity 12. ruthlessness 13. heartlessness 15. remorselessness
cruelty, lover of . . . 6. sadist 9. masochist
cruet . . . 3. ama 4. vial 6. bottle, caster (castor), vessel 7. ampulla, urceole
cruller . . . 7. olycook (olykoek) 8. doughnut 9. friedcake
crumb . . . 3. bit 5. break, piece 6. little 8. fragment
crumble . . . 5. decay 6. molder, powder 7. friable 9. pulverize 12. disintegrate
crumple . . . 4. ruck 6. crease, raffle, rumple 7. wrinkle 9. corrugate
cruor . . . 4. gore 5. blood, ichor
crusade . . . 5. cause, drive, issue, jihad (jehad) 7. crusado 8. campaign 10. expedition
Crusades . . . 8. Holy Land 9. Children's (1212)
crush . . . 3. jam 4. bray, mash, sink 5. crash, crowd, grind, press, smash 6. bruise, crunch 7. conquer, mortify, oppress, shatter, squeeze 8. compress, suppress 9. humiliate, pulverize 11. infatuation
crushed sugar cane . . . 7. bagasse
Crusoe's creator . . . 5. Defoe
crust . . . 4. rind 5. shell 8. dumpling, exterior 9. impudence 11. lithosphere 14. aggressiveness
crustacean . . . 4. crab 5. prawn 6. huitre, isopod, limpet, mussel, oyster, shrimp 7. limulus, lobster, scallop 8. barnacle, crawfish, starfish 9. shellfish, trunkfish 10. coquillage, periwinkle
crustacean (pert to) . . .
extinct . . 5. Eryon
footless . . 4. apod, apus
fossil . . 9. trilobite
genus . . 5. Hippa 6. Triops 7. Caridea (Carida) 8. Copepoda, Decapoda 10. Notostraca
larva . . 5. alima
limb . . 6. endite, podite
crutch . . . 5. brace, staff, stave 6. crotch 7. support
cry . . . 3. baa, caw, cri, hue, mew, olé, sob 4. alas, barr, call, evoe, home, hoot, mewl, pish, pule, wail, weep, yell, yelp 5. alack, avast, bleat, crook, miaou, yoick 6. bellow, boohoo, clamor, outcry, scream, shriek, slogan, snivel, squawk 7. tantivy (hunting), trumpet, weeping 8. entreaty, jeremiad, lackaday, proclaim 10. shibboleth 11. lamentation
cry (out) . . . 5. crake, decry, shout 6. accuse, clamor, object, scream, suffer 7. censure, exclaim 8. complain, denounce 10. vociferate
crying . . . 6. puling, urgent 7. clamant, heinous, howling, sobbing, weeping 9. insistent, notorious
crying bird . . . 6. Aramus 7. courlan, limpkin 8. raillike
crypt . . . 4. tomb 5. vault 6. cavity, recess 7. chamber
cryptic . . . 4. Rite (Freemasonry) 6. hidden, occult, secret 8. puzzling 9. concealed, enigmatic 10. mysterious 11. problematic 12. hieroglyphic
cryptogram . . . 4. code 5. agama

7. writing (secret) **8.** symbolic
crystal ... **4.** dial **5.** clear, glass, lucid
6. argent (Her), quartz **7.** diamond
8. pellucid **9.** glassware, snowflake
11. crystalline, transparent
crystal (pert to) ...
diamond .. **7.** glassie
gazer .. **4.** seer **7.** diviner **8.** presager
10. soothsayer **13.** fortuneteller
gazing .. **4.** scry
twin .. **5.** macle
crystalline ... **4.** pure **8.** pellucid
11. transparent **12.** crystal-clear
crystalline (pert to) ...
colorless .. **7.** orcinol
compound .. **5.** oscin **6.** anisil, dulcin
mineral .. **4.** spar **7.** apatite **8.** elaterin,
feldspar
rock .. **7.** diorite, greisen
salt .. **5.** borax **8.** analgene (analgen)
cub ... **3.** bin, box, fox, pen, pup **4.** bear,
coop, crib, lion, shed **5.** shark, stall,
tiger, whale, whelp **8.** boy scout,
cupboard **9.** youngling
Cuba ...
capital .. **6.** Havana
castle .. **5.** Morro
city .. **8.** Santiago **10.** Bahia Honda,
Guantánamo
discoverer .. **8.** Columbus (1492)
island .. **11.** Isle of Pines (Isla de Pinos)
mountain .. **8.** Camaguey **9.** Las Villas
12. Pico Turquino
nickname .. **18.** Pearl of the Antilles
province .. **7.** Oriente
Cuban (pert to) ...
asphalt .. **9.** chapapote
bird .. **6.** trogan **8.** tocororo
dance .. **5.** rumba
fish .. **4.** bobo
rodent .. **5.** hutia (jutia) **6.** pilori
rum .. **7.** Bacardi
cube ... **3.** die **4.** dice **5.** solid **6.** triple
7. tessera (marble) **10.** third power
cubic (pert to) ...
body .. **3.** die **4.** dice
decimeter .. **5.** litre
math .. **9.** isometric
measure .. **4.** cord
meter .. **5.** stere
shape .. **6.** cuboid **8.** cubiform
cubicle ... **4.** cell, room, tomb
7. bedroom, chamber, roomlet
9. cubiculum
cuckoo ... **5.** mimic **8.** imitator, songbird
cuckoo (pert to) ...
ally .. **3.** ani
American .. **8.** Coccyzus
bees .. **9.** Nomadidae
bird (Orient) .. **4.** coel (koel)
cap .. **9.** monkshood
family .. **9.** Cuculidae
fool .. **7.** wryneck
pint .. **4.** arum **10.** cuckoo spit
cucullate (Bot) ... **6.** cowled, hooded
cucumber ... **4.** cuke, pepo **6.** pedata
(sea), pepino
cucurbit ... **5.** flask, gourd **7.** matrass
cud ... **4.** bite, quid **5.** rumen **6.** merycism
cuddle ... **3.** hug, pet **6.** fondle, nestle
7. snuggle

cudgel ... **3.** bat, hit **4.** beat, club, drub
5. baste, staff, stave, stick **6.** alpeen
7. belabor **9.** fustigate, shillalah
(shillelagh)
cue ... **3.** nod, rod, tip **4.** ball, clue,
hint, role, tail **5.** braid, queue, twist
6. prompt **8.** billiard (term), function
9. catchword **10.** intimation
cuerpo ... **4.** body, hulk **5.** naked, torso
10. dishabille (in)
cuff ... **3.** hit **4.** band, blow, slap **5.** clout
6. strike **8.** chastise, gauntlet, handcuff
12. chastisement
cuirass ... **4.** mail **5.** armor **6.** lorica
11. breastplate
cul-de-sac ... **5.** alley (blind) **7.** impasse
14. pouch of Douglas
cull ... **4.** pick **6.** assort, choose, gather,
select **8.** separate
culmination ... **3.** end **4.** acme, apex,
auge, noon **6.** ascent, climax, result,
vertex, zenith **10.** perfection
12. consummation
culpability ... **5.** blame, fault, guilt
11. criminality **15.** blameworthiness
culpable ... **6.** faulty, guilty **7.** immoral
8. criminal **9.** accusable, imputable
10. censurable, indictable
11. blameworthy **12.** reproachable
13. reprehensible
cult ... **4.** sect **9.** following
cultivate ... **3.** ear (dial), hoe **4.** farm,
grow, plow, teel, till **5.** court, train
6. excite, foster, harrow, plough, refine
7. educate, improve **8.** approach, civilize
9. tend
cultivated ... **4.** grew, hoed **6.** seeded,
tilled, urbane **7.** genteel, refined
8. cultured, polished, well-bred
cultivation ... **5.** tilth **7.** culture, farming,
tillage **9.** husbandry **10.** refinement
12. civilization
culver ... **4.** dove **6.** pigeon **10.** wood
pigeon
cumbersome ... **5.** bulky **6.** clumsy
8. cumbrous, unwieldy **10.** burdensome
cummer ... **4.** lass **5.** witch **6.** friend (girl)
7. midwife **9.** companion, godmother
cummerbund ... **4.** band, belt, sash
6. cestus, girdle
cumshaw ... **3.** tip **5.** bonus **6.** thanks
7. present **8.** gratuity
cunning ... **3.** sly **4.** cute, foxy, wile,
wily **5.** sharp, skill **6.** artful, clever,
crafty, dainty, shrewd, subtle, tricky
7. politic, shyness **8.** dextrous,
foxiness, skillful, stealthy, trickery
9. designing, dexterity, ingenious,
ingenuity, insidious **13.** Machiavellian
cunningly formed ... **6.** daedal (dedal)
cup ... **3.** ama, can, dop, mug, tyg
4. tass, teet, Toby **5.** calyx, chark,
cruse, cupel, cylix, grail, jorum, ladle,
stein **6.** beaker, goblet, noggin, trophy
7. chalice, tumbler
cupbearer ... **4.** Hebe, saki **8.** Ganymede
cupboard ... **3.** kas **5.** ambry (anc)
6. buffet, closet, larder, pantry
7. armoire, dresser **8.** aparador
9. sideboard
Cupid ... **3.** boy, Dan **4.** amor, Eros, Kama,
love **5.** Freya **7.** Amorino, cupidon

Cupid (pert to) . . .
mother . . 5. Venus
sweetheart . . 6. Psyche
title . . 3. Dan
cupidity . . . 4. lust 5. greed 6. desire
7. avarice, avidity, longing 8. appetite,
avidness, rapacity
cuplike (pert to) . . .
calyx . . 9. calicular
stone . . 5. geode
vessel . . 4. zarf
cupola . . . 4. dome, kiln 5. tower 6. concha
(Arch) 7. ceiling, furnace (foundry)
cur . . . 3. dog 4. mutt 7. gurnard (fish),
mongrel 9. goldeneye
curare, curari . . . 5. urali 7. extract
9. Strychnos 11. arrow poison
curate . . . 4. abbé 6. cleric, parson, pastor,
priest 7. dominie 9. clergyman
curator . . . 6. keeper 7. manager, steward
8. guardian 9. custodian, librarian,
treasurer
curb . . . 3. bit 4. rein 5. check, limit
6. arrest, border, bridle, market (Finan)
7. control, inhibit, repress 8. restrict
9. hindrance, restraint
curd . . . 4. crud 6. casein
curds and whey . . . 7. clabber
cure . . . 4. balm, heal, salt 5. smoke
6. elixir, remedy, rizzor 7. nostrum,
panacea, restore, therapy 8. preserve
10. corrective
curio . . . 8. artifact 9. bric-a-brac, curiosity
curiosity . . . 5. curio 6. gabion (rare),
oddity, prying, wonder 8. interest
9. exception, spectacle
14. meddlesomeness 15. inquisitiveness
curious . . . 3. odd 4. rare 5. nosey (nosy),
outre, queer 6. prying, quaint 7. careful,
strange, unusual 8. cautious, meddling,
singular 9. inquiring, intrusive
10. meticulous 11. inquisitive
curl . . . 4. coil, kink, lock, roll 5. crimp,
crisp, frizz, tress, twirl, twist 6. marcel,
spiral 7. crinkle, frizzle, ringlet
8. curlicue 9. corkscrew 11. convolution
curled . . . 5. curly, spiry 6. coiled
7. crimped, savoyed, twisted 8. wrinkled
(Bot)
curlew . . . 4. bird, fute 5. kioea, snipe,
whaup 6. marlin 7. bustard 8. whimbrel
curlewlike . . . 6. godwit 9. sandpiper
curly . . . 4. wavy 5. kinky, oundy (obs)
6. crispy, frizzy, kinked 8. crinkled
curmudgeon . . . 4. crab 5. churl, miser
7. niggard 8. tightwad 9. skinflint
currant . . . 3. red 5. berry, Ribes 6. raisin,
rizzar (rizzart)
currency . . . 5. money, scrip 6. dinero
9. publicity 10. greenbacks, popularity,
prevalence 15. fashionableness
current . . . 4. eddy, flow, race (water),
rife, tide 5. draft, going, rapid, trend,
usual 6. course, stream 7. present,
topical 8. existent 9. direction, prevalent
11. fashionable
current regulator . . .
electric . . 9. rheometer 12. galvanometer
physiology . . 11. hematometer
curriculum . . . 7. courses, studies, Three
R's 8. curricle

curry . . . 4. comb, cook, drub 5. dress,
groom 6. cajole 9. condiment
curry favor . . . 6. cajole 7. flatter,
smoodge (smooge), wheedle
curse . . . 3. ban 4. bane, damn, oath
5. swear 7. bewitch, malison
8. anathema, execrate 9. blaspheme
10. affliction 11. imprecation,
malediction 13. excommunicate
cursed . . . 6. damned, odious, wicked
7. hateful 8. damnable, shrewish
9. execrable 12. cantankerous
Cursores . . . 5. birds (long-legged)
7. spiders (wolf)
Cursoria . . . 6. mantes (mantis)
10. Orthoptera 11. cockroaches
cursory . . . 5. hasty 6. fitful, roving,
slight 7. passing 8. careless, rambling
9. desultory, irregular 10. evanescent
12. disconnected, unmethodical
curt . . . 4. buff 5. bluff, brief, brusk,
gruff, short, terse 6. abrupt 7. brusque,
concise, curtate, laconic 9. condensed
curtail . . . 3. lop 4. crop, dock, pare,
slip 5. short 6. lessen, reduce
7. abridge, shorten 8. compress,
decrease, diminish, retrench
curtain . . . 4. mask, veil 5. drape, shade
6. coster (altar), encore, purdah, riddel,
screen, shadow, shield 7. drapery,
secrecy, shelter, vitrage 8. portiere
curtsy, curtsey . . . 3. bow, nod 4. bend
6. kowtow, salaam 12. genuflection
curvature . . . 3. arc, bow 4. arch,
bend 5. plane, sinus 6. camber
7. arching, curving, evolute 8. aduncity,
cyrtosis, lordosis, vaulting 9. curvation
11. convolution
curve . . . 3. arc, bow, ess 4. arch,
bend, ogee, turn 5. crook, polar
6. spiral, toroid 7. cissoid, evolute,
flexure 8. extrados, parabola, sinusoid
9. curvature, sinuosity
curved (pert to) . . .
arch . . 8. arciform, arcuated
glass . . 4. lens
inward . . 5. adunc 8. aduncous
molding . . 4. ogee
planking (ship's) . . 3. sny
process . . 5. hamus (Zool)
roundabout . . 10. circuitous
staircase . . 8. caracole
wedge . . 3. cam
curvet . . . 4. leap 5. bound, caper, frisk,
prank 6. frolic, gambol
cush . . . 3. cow 5. money 7. cookery,
sorghum
Cush (pert to) . . .
father . . 3. Ham
land of . . 8. Ethiopia 10. land of Cush
son . . 4. Seba 6. Nimrod
cushion . . . 3. pad 4. mute, seat 6. ignore,
pillow, sachet 7. brioche, conceal,
dashpot, muffler 8. plantula, pulvinus,
suppress, swelling (Queen Mary's)
9. pulvillus 10. pincushion
cusk . . . 4. fish (codlike), tusk 5. torsk
6. burbot
cusp . . . 3. end, tip 4. apex, peak 5. crown,
point 6. cantle, corner 8. peracone
custard . . . 4. flan 7. charlet, pudding

custard apple . . . 4. tree 5. papaw
8. sweetsop
custodian . . . 5. guard 6. bailee, jailer,
keeper, warden, warder 7. curator,
janitor 8. curatrix, guardian
custody . . . 4. care, keep 5. trust
6. charge 8. guidance 10. protection
12. guardianship, jurisdiction
custom . . . 3. fad, law, mos, use 4. mode,
wont 5. habit, mores, usage, vogue
7. fashion 8. practice 9. patronage,
tradition 10. consuetude, consuetudo
customary . . . 5. usual 6. wonted
7. general, usitate 8. habitual, orthodox
11. traditional 12. conventional
customs . . . 4. duty 5. mores, taxes
cut . . . 3. bob, lob, lop, mow, nip,
rip 4. blow, chop, crop, dock, edit,
fell, gash, hack, make, mode, nick,
open, pain, pare, reap, slit, snee,
snip, snub, trim 5. canal, carve,
cleft, lance, notch, piece, plate, scarp,
sever, share, shear, shorn, slash, slice,
slish (Shaksp), snick, split, vogue
6. dilute, furrow, injury, mangle, reduce,
trench 7. affront, curtail, engrave,
offense, sectile, serrate, truancy,
whittle 8. discount, excision, incision
9. engraving, indignity, reduction
10. adulterate
cut (pert to) . . .
  and furrow . . 7. chamfer
  and polish . . 8. lapidate
  and weave . . 5. plash
  back . . 6. polled 7. shorten
  capable of being . . 7. sectile
  down . . 5. razee
  fine . . 5. mince
  in . . 7. intrude 9. interpose, interrupt,
  introduce
  in half . . 9. dimidiate
  in squares . . 4. dice
  into . . 6. incise
  jaggedly . . 4. snag
  out . . 6. excide, excise
  up . . 6. frolic, grieve 9. apportion,
  misbehave
  vertically . . 5. scarp, slice
  with shears . . 4. snip 5. shirl
cutaneous . . . 4. skin 6. dermal, dermic
cute . . . 4. keen 5. peart, sharp 6. brainy,
clever, dainty, pretty, shrewd 7. cunning
10. attractive 11. picturesque
cuticle . . . 4. skin 5. cutin, cutis
8. membrane, pellicle 9. epidermis,
scarfskin 10. integument
cut of beef . . . 4. loin, ribs, rump 5. chine,
roast, steak 6. corned, cutlet, rosbif,
saddle 7. brisket, icebone 8. shoulder
9. aitchbone, roundbone
cut off . . . 3. bob 4. crop, dock, drib,
snip 5. elide, pared, roach (Naut)
6. bereft, bobbed, divest, lopped, screen
7. abscind, abscise, clipped, deprive,
severed 8. amputate 9. amputated,
apocopate, intercept 10. disinherit
cut off (pert to) . . .
  by bits . . 4. drib
  edges (coins) . . 3. nig
  on slant . . 4. bias 5. bevel, miter
  short . . 3. bob 4. crop

  syllable . . 5. elide
  with die . . 4. dink
  wool . . 3. dod (dodd)
cut short . . . 3. bob, lop 4. crop, dock,
halt, stop 5. check 6. arrest 7. clipped,
cropped, curtail, shorten 9. terminate
cutter . . . 4. boat 5. knife, sloop, tooth
6. sleigh, vessel 7. incisor
cutting . . . 4. cold, slip, tart 5. piece,
scion, sharp 6. biting, secant, severe
7. caustic, incisal, satiric, sectile
8. chilling, piercing 9. sarcastic,
severance, trenchant 10. separating
11. penetrating 12. adulteration
cutting (pert to) . . .
  diamonds (imperfect) . . 4. bort
  edge . . 5. blade
  in two . . 6. secant
  last letter of word . . 7. apocope
  off . . 7. apocope 10. abscission,
  amputation
  tool . . 3. axe (ax), bit 4. adze 5. razor
  6. chisel
  wit . . 6. satire
cuttle . . . 4. thug 5. knife 7. ruffian
8. assassin 9. swaggerer
cuttlebone . . . 7. osselet
cuttlefish . . . 5. Sepia, squid 7. mollusk,
octopus
cuttlefish secretion . . . 3. ink (black)
cuttyhunk . . . 11. fishing line
Cuzco native . . . 4. Inca
Cyclades Islands (Gr) . . . (200 in all)
3. Ios 5. Delos (smallest), Melos,
Naros, Paros, Tenos, Thera 6. Andros
7. Amorgos, Myconus
cycle . . . 3. Age, eon, era 4. aeon
5. orbit, recur, saros (Astron), wheel
6. course, period, series 7. bicycle,
circuit 8. electric, tricycle 9. Arthurian
10. revolution 12. Carlovingian
(Charlemagne)
cyclone . . . 5. storm 6. baguio 7. tornado,
twister, typhoon 9. hurricane
cyclopean . . . 4. huge, vast 7. massive,
one-eyed 8. gigantic
Cyclops (pert to) . . .
  assistant of . . 6. Vulcan (Fire God)
  father . . 6. Uranus
  forger of . . 12. thunderbolts
  home . . 6. Sicily (Mt Etna)
  oddity . . 7. one-eyed
  race (Myth) . . 6. giants
cygneous . . . 8. swanlike
cygnet . . . 4. swan
cylinder . . . 4. drum, pipe, roll, tube
5. inker, stele 6. barrel, gabion,
platen, record, roller, rounce, terete
10. cylindroid
cylindrical . . . 5. conic 6. terete 7. tubular
cymbal, cymbals . . . 3. tal, zel 6. Becken,
piatti 7. potlids 8. doughnut
Cymric . . . 5. Welsh 9. Brythonic
Cymric (pert to) . . .
  bard . . 6. Merlin 7. Aneurin
  god of the dead . . 5. Pwyll
  god of the sky . . 7. Gwydion
  god of the sun . . 4. Lleu
  god of the waves . . 5. Dylan
cynic . . . 5. Timon 7. ascetic, doglike,
egotist, snarler 9. pessimist

11. misanthrope
Cynic (pert to) . . .
  pupil . . 8. Socrates
  school . . 10. Philosophy
  teacher . . 8. Diogenes
  teaching . . 6. virtue
cynical . . . 7. currish 8. captious,
  snarling 9. sarcastic 11. pessimistic
  12. misanthropic
cynosure . . . 5. guide 8. lodestar
  (loadstar), polestar 9. celebrity, North
  Star 13. constellation
cyprinoid (fish) . . . 2. id 3. ide, orf
  (orfe) 4. bass (black), carp, chub,
  dace 6. chevin, shiner 7. herring
  (lake) 8. fallfish 9. hornyhead,
  squawfish
Cyprus . . .
  capital . . 7. Nicosia (Sicily)
  colonizer (anc) . . 11. Phoenicians
  history . . 11. New Stone Age
  mountain . . 7. Troodos
  port . . 7. Lorcana 8. Limassol
    9. Famagusto
Cyrenaic (pert to) . . .
  city . . 6. Cyrene
  country . . 9. Cyrenaica (Afr)
  division of . . 5. Libya

harbor . . 6. Tobruk 7. Bengazi
philosophy . . 8. hedonism, pleasure
Cyrene . . . 4. city (anc) 5. nymph
  7. goddess
cyrus . . . 5. crane, sarus
Cyrus the Elder (pert to) . . .
  conqueror of . . 7. Babylon
  founder of . . 6. Persia (Empire)
  king of . . 5. Lydia, Media
  subduer of . . 9. Palestine
cyst . . . 3. box, sac, wen 5. chest, pouch
  7. vesicle
Czar . . . 4. Ivan, tsar, tzar 5. Peter
  8. Nicholas
Czechoslovakia . . .
  capital . . 6. Prague (Praha)
  city . . 6. Pilsen 7. Ostrava 10. Bratislava
  divided (1993) . . 8. Slovakia 13. Czech
    Republic
  empire (anc) . . 7. Bohemia, Moravia
    8. Slovakia
  forest . . 12. Great Bohemia
  mountain, peak . . 3. Ore 6. Tatras
    11. Carpathians
  people . . 6. Czechs 7. Slovaks
  river . . 4. Elbe (Labe), Iser, Oder 6. Vltava
  statesman . . 7. Masaryk
czigany . . . 5. gypsy

D

D . . . 3. 500 6. letter (4th)
dab . . . 3. hit, tap 4. blow 5. paint, smear
  6. expert, lizard, smooth 7. dabster
  8. flatfish
dabble . . . 4. mass 5. dally 6. befoul,
  meddle, paddle, potter, splash, tamper,
  trifle 7. spatter 8. sprinkle
dabbler . . . 7. trifler 8. sciolist
  10. dilettante
dabchick . . . 5. grebe 9. gallinule
dab hand . . . 6. expert
dacha (Russ) . . . 5. villa 12. country house
dacoit . . . 6. bandit, robber
dacry, dacryo (comb form) . . . 5. tears
dactyl . . . 3. toe 4. foot 6. finger
  8. dactylus
dactyliomancy . . . 17. divination by rings
  (finger)
dactylogram . . . 11. fingerprint
dactylology . . . 12. sign language
Dadaism . . . 4. cult 8. negation
daddy longlegs . . . 5. stilt 6. curlew,
  spider, Tipula 7. spinner 10. harvestman
daedal, dedal . . . 4. rich 6. varied
  8. artistic, skillful (skilful) 9. ingenious,
  intricate 10. variegated
Daedalus (Gr Myth) . . . 9. artificer
daemon (Gr Myth) . . . 6. spirit 8. guardian
daffodil . . . 6. yellow 9. narcissus
  10. bellflower
daffy, daft . . . 3. gay, mad 4. wild 5. batty,
  crazy, giddy, goofy, loony 6. insane
  7. foolish, idiotic
Dagda (pert to) . . .
  children . . 6. Aengus (Angus), Brigit

famed as . . 7. harpist
Gaelic name . . 7. Jupiter
god of . . 10. pagan Irish
dagger . . . 4. dirk, kris, snee 5. kalar
  6. anlace, bodkin, creese 7. bayonet,
  poniard 10. misericord
Dahomey . . . 5. Benin
Daibutsu (pert to) . . .
  famed image . . 8. Buddha
  Japanese Bronze . . 11. Great Buddha
  site . . 8. Kamakura (near Tokyo)
daikon . . . 6. radish
daily . . . 4. a day 7. diurnal, journal
  9. hodiurnal, newspaper, quotidian
  11. day in day out
daily food . . . 4. fare 5. bread
  10. livelihood 11. subsistence,
  substance
dainties . . . 5. cates, estes 7. titbits
  (tidbits)
dainty . . . 4. fair, fine, rare 5. frail, small
  6. choice, pretty, select 8. elegance
  9. exquisite, toothsome 10. fastidious
dairy . . . 4. farm 8. creamery 9. lactarium
dairymen caste (Ind) . . . 4. Ahir
dais . . . 5. stage, table 6. podium
  7. estrade 8. platform
daisy . . . 5. gowan, oxeye 6. morgan,
  Shasta 7. Gerbera 9. Whiteweed
dale . . . 4. dell, dene, vale 5. spout
  6. dingle, ravine, trough, valley
dalles . . . 5. dells 11. canyon walls
dalliance . . . 4. chat 5. delay 6. gossip,
  trifle 8. fondling, trifling 10. flirtation
dally . . . 3. toy 5. tarry 6. dawdle, linger

13. procrastinate

Dalmatia . . .
capital . . 7. Spalato (Yugoslavia)
cherry . . 7. marasca
coast . . 8. Adriatic
dog . . 5. coach 8. carriage
home of . . 10. Diocletian
people . . 5. Serbs 8. Adriatic 9. Yugoslavs
product . . 4. lace

dam . . . 4. stay, stem, stop, weir 5. Aswan, block, check, choke, Gatun (CZ) 6. Hoover (Boulder), mother, Norris, parent 7. barrier 8. millpond, obstruct, Oroville, restrain 9. Roosevelt 10. Bull Shoals, Glen Canyon 11. Grand Coulee

damage . . . 3. mar 4. harm, hurt, loss, maim, noxa 6. impair, injury, mayhem, scathe, strafe 8. disserve, sabotage 9. detriment, vandalism 10. impairment

daman . . . 4. cony (Bib) 5. Hyrax 6. mammal 8. Procavia

Damascus, Syria (pert to) . . .
Bib scene . . 20. Street Called Straight
division . . 6. Jewish, Moslem 9. Christian
history . . 16. world's oldest city (inhabited)
mosque (renowned) . . 7. Ommiade
river . . 5. Abana 6. Barada

damask . . . 3. red (color) 5. cloth, steel (Damascus) 8. to deface (the Great Seal, Eng)

dame . . . 4. lady, Miss 5. Madam, title 6. matron, Nature, parent

damn . . . 4. cuss, ruin 5. abuse, curse 6. revile, shucks 7. accurse, condemn, swear at

damp . . . 3. wet 5. moist

dampen . . . 3. wet 6. dismay 7. depress, moisten

damsel . . . 4. girl, lass 5. Rhoda (Bib), wench 7. colleen 10. damoiselle

dance . . . 4. jazz, prom, skip, trip 5. frisk, glide 6. cavort, frolic, gambol 7. flicker, flutter, rejoice, saltate 10. tripudiate

dance (pert to) . . .
art . . 12. choreography
clumsily . . 6. balter
mimetic (Rom) . . 5. Salii 7. Luperci 8. Curetics
movement . . 6. chassé, gestic 7. saltant 9. pirouette
step . . 3. pas 5. coupe 6. chassé 7. gambado (gambade), shuffle 8. glissade 9. arabesque, grapevine 10. pigeonwing

dance (type) . . . 3. bal, hop, jig, tap, toe 4. ball, clog, haka, kolo, polo, reel, shag 5. gavot (gavotte), gigue, pavan, polka, tango, twist, waltz 6. althea, apache, ballet, bolero, cancan, cha-cha, corant, maxixe, minuet, morris, redowa, rhumba (rumba), shimmy, square, watusi 7. beguine, coranto (old), courant, foxtrot, gavotte, hoedown, mazurka, one-step, ridotto, tempete, two-step 8. bunny hug, cakewalk, courante, fandango, flamenco, halliard (anc), hornpipe, lanciers, rigadoon, saraband 9. allemande (anc), butterfly, farandole, polonaise, quadrille 10. Charleston,

tarantella 11. schottische (schottish)

dancer . . . 6. hoofer 7. danseur 8. coryphee, danseuse, stripper 9. ballerina, ecdysiast, jitterbug 11. terpsichore 13. choreographer

dancer (pert to) . . .
Bib . . 6. Salome
Egyptian . . 4. alme (almeh) 7. ghawazi 8. Baramika
Japanese . . 6. geisha (girl)
Oriental . . 6. hula 6. nautch 8. bayadere

dancing (pert to) . . .
arrangement . . 12. choreography
Muse of . . 11. Terpsichore
term . . 6. ballet, chassé, gestic 7. hoofing, saltant

dandelion . . . 4. herb 5. plant 6. yellow 9. Taraxacum

dander . . . 3. ire 5. anger 6. temper

dandified . . . 7. foppish

dandify . . . 6. spruce 7. adonize, smarten 8. titivate (tittivate)

dandy . . . 3. fop 4. beau, dude, good, toff 5. daisy 6. Adonis 7. coxcomb 9. exquisite 11. Beau Brummel

dangerous . . . 3. bad 4. dire 5. feral, risky 6. chancy 7. ominous, parlous 8. alarming, critical, insecure, menacing, perilous 9. hazardous 10. jeopardous, precarious

dangle . . . 3. lop 4. hang, loll, yawl 5. droop, swing 6. flaunt, mizzen

Daniel (pert to) . . .
Bib . . 4. Book (Old Test) 7. prophet (Heb)
form of verse . . 7. lyrical, sestina
verse adopted by . . 5. Dante 8. Petrarch

Danish . . . see also *Denmark*
capital . . 10. Copenhagen
council (anc) . . 8. Rigsraad
country . . 7. Denmark
doctor . . 6. Finsen
export . . 6. cryolite
fiord . . 3. Ise
flag . . 9. Dannebrog
island . . 3. Als (Alsen) 5. Faroe 9. Greenland
King (anc) . . 6. Canute
native . . 4. Dane 12. Scandinavian
parliament . . 7. Rigsdag
prince (legend) . . 6. Hamlet
settlers in Ireland . . 6. Ostmen
storyteller . . 8. Andersen (Hans Christian)

dank . . . 3. wet 4. damp 5. humid, moist, muggy

Dan McGrew . . . 11. Hound of Hell

danseuse . . . 7. danseur 8. coryphee 9. ballerina

Dante (pert to) . . .
birthplace . . 8. Florence
famed as . . 4. poet 6. lyrist
famed poem . . 12. Divine Comedy
poem's companion . . 6. Vergil (Virgil)
poem's division . . 4. Hell 6. Heaven 9. Purgatory
poem's love . . 8. Beatrice

Danube River (pert to) . . .
end . . 8. Black Sea
source . . 11. Black Forest
tributary . . 4. Isar, Raab 5. Drava 6. Morava

D

Danubian (pert to) ...
  color .. 5. green
  fish .. 6. huchen (huch)
  goose .. 10. Sevastopol

Danzig ...
  Polish name .. 6. Gdansk
  river site .. 7. Vistula
  Sea .. 6. Baltic
  territory of (now) .. 6. Poland

dap ... 3. bob, dab, dib, dip 6. bounce, dibble, guddle 7. rebound

Daphne (pert to) ...
  Bib .. 4. Park (Antioch, Syria)
  father .. 5. Ladon 6. Peneus
  lover .. 6. Apollo
  transformation .. 10. laurel tree

dapper ... 4. braw, neat, pert, trim 5. natty, sleek 6. jaunty, little, lively, spruce 7. dashing, finical

dappled ... 6. dotted 7. flecked, piebald, spotted

dare ... 4. daze, defy, face, osse, risk 5. brave 6. assume, dazzle 7. venture 8. confront, defiance, paralyze 9. challenge, undertake

daring ... 4. bold, rash 5. brave, manly 8. boldness, defiance 9. audacious, foolhardy 11. adventurous, venturesome 12. enterprising

dark ... 3. dim, mum, sad 4. ebon 5. black, blind, dense, faint, mirky, murky, night, unlit, vague 6. closed, gloomy, occult, opaque, secret, wicked 7. joyless, melanic, obscure, stygian 8. abstruse, darkling (poet), ignorant, moonless 9. ambiguous, atrocious, Cimmerian (realm), lightless, nightfall, tenebrous, uncertain 10. foreboding, indistinct

dark (pert to) ...
  Ages .. 6. Middle 8. Medieval 9. Neolithic
  Continent .. 6. Africa (formerly) 10. unexplored
  horse .. 7. unknown 9. candidate
  hue .. 5. dusky, swart 6. somber 7. swarthy
  moon area .. 4. mare

darken ... 3. dim 4. dull 5. blind, umber 6. darkle, sadden, shadow 7. becloud, blacken, confuse, eclipse, enshade 8. bewilder 9. obfuscate

darkness ... 4. dark, dusk, mirk, murk 5. shade 6. Erebus, shadow 7. dimness, tenebra 9. blackness, blindness, ignorance, obscurity 10. opaqueness

darling ... 2. jo 3. pet 4. dear, idol, lief 5. cheri, sweet 6. minion 7. acushla, beloved 8. favorite 9. mavournin 10. mavourneen, sweetheart 13. cushlamochree (cushlamachree)

darnel ... 4. tare, weed 5. grass 6. Lolium

dart ... 4. barb, bolt, flit, leap, vire 5. arrow, bound, lance, scoot, shoot, start, throw 6. dartle, elance, glance, spring, weapon 7. javelin, missile, stinger 8. jaculate

Darwinism ... 9. Evolution (theory, 1858) 12. Evolutionism

das, dasse ... 6. badger

dash ... 4. code, élan, gift, race, ruin, rush, slam 5. ardor, crash, haste, onset,

plash, smash, speed, swash 6. energy, obelus (anc), spirit, sprint, strike, stroke 7. bravura, spatter, splurge 8. confound, gratuity 9. animation 11. punctuation

dashing ... 3. gay 4. fast 5. showy 6. dapper, jaunty, sporty 7. stylish

dastardly ... 4. base, foul 6. craven 8. cowardly

data ... 5. facts, logic 7. grounds (for facts) 11. information

date ... 3. age 4. line (newspaper), time 5. fruit, tryst 6. person 10. engagement 11. appointment

date (pert to) ...
  birth .. 5. natal
  coin line .. 7. exergue
  error .. 11. anachronism
  fruit of .. 4. palm
  plum .. 6. sapote

dated ... 8. outmoded 10. antiquated 12. old-fashioned

daub ... 3. dab 4. blob, gaum, soil, teer 5. paint, smear, stain, sully 6. bedaub 7. besmear, picture (art), plaster 8. scribble

daughter ... 5. child 7. cadette 9. offspring 10. descendant

daughter of ...
  Inachus (river god) .. 2. Io
  Night .. 7. Nemesis
  the moon .. 7. Nokomis
  the Spanish king .. 7. infanta

daunt ... 3. awe, cow 4. faze 5. amate (anc) 6. dismay, subdue 7. overawe, repress 10. discourage, dishearten, intimidate

dauntless ... 4. bold 7. aweless (awless) 8. fearless, intrepid, resolute 9. dreadless 11. unfaltering

davenport ... 3. bed 4. desk, sofa 5. divan 12. Chesterfield

David (Bib) ...
  daughter .. 5. Tamar
  father .. 5. Jesse
  helpers .. 4. Igal 5. Abner 7. Shammah
  king of .. 6. Israel (40 years)
  slayer of .. 7. Goliath
  son .. 7. Solomon
  wife .. 7. Abigail

davit ... 4. spar 5. crane

dawdle ... 3. lag 4. idle, poke, toit 5. dally 6. linger, loiter, potter, trifle 9. vacillate 10. dillydally 13. procrastinate

dawn ... 2. eo (comb form) 3. Eos (goddess), red 4. morn 5. sunup 6. appear, aurora, sink in 7. sunrise 8. daybreak 9. beginning, penetrate

day (pert to) ...
  Athenians, Jews .. 6. sunset
  Babylonians .. 7. sunrise
  blindness .. 10. nyctalopia 11. hemeralopia
  divisions .. 5. lunar, solar 8. sidereal
  dream .. 4. muse 5. fancy 7. fantasy, reverie 8. phantasy
  Egyptians, Romans .. 8. midnight
  god .. 5. Horus
  nursery .. 6. crèche
  scholar .. 7. externe

Day of ...
  Atonement .. 9. Yom Kippur

Brahma .. 9. Maha Yugas
doom .. 8. Judgment
day's march ... 5. étape
day's work ... 4. darg (dargue)
daze ... 3. fog 4. asea, maze, stun
5. sopor, swoon 6. benumb, dazzle,
stupid, trance 7. confuse, stupefy
8. bewilder 9. dumbfound 12. razzle-
dazzle
dazzling ... 6. bright, garish 7. glaring
8. blinding, gorgeous 9. beautiful,
brilliant 11. bewildering
dead ... 3. fey 4. flat, numb, obit
5. amort, blind, inert, napoo, passé
6. active, barren, lapsed 7. defunct,
expired, insipid, tedious 8. ad patres,
complete, deceased, inactive, lifeless,
obsolete 9. apathetic, inanimate
10. lusterless, motionless, spiritless,
unexciting 11. nonexistent
dead (pert to) ...
Dead Sea apple .. 12. Apple of Sodom
Dead Sea country .. 4. Moab 5. Sodom
8. Gomorrah
language .. 5. Latin
rise from the .. 7. resurge 9. reanimate,
resurrect
set (slang) .. 8. full tilt, hell-bent
tree .. 7. rampike (rampick)
deaden ... 4. damp, dull, mute, numb
6. muffle, obtund, opiate, weaken
7. relieve, repress 8. enfeeble
10. devitalize
deadly ... 4. dire, mort 5. fatal 6. lethal,
mortal 7. deathly 8. venomous
10. implacable, lifelessly 11. destructive,
internecine
dead ringer ... 9. look-alike
deaf ... 4. surd 7. earless 10. intolerant
11. inattentive, preoccupied
deaf alphabet ... 11. dactylology 12. sign
language
deaf and dumb ... 9. surdomute
10. deaf-mutism 11. surdimutism
deafness ... 6. amusia (tone) 7. surdity
13. insensibility
deafness operation ... 8. fenestra
deal ... 3. lot 4. dole, give, mede,
mete, sale, sell 5. allot, share, trade,
treat 6. parcel 7. dispose, portion,
wrestle 8. business, dispense, quantity
9. apportion, entertain 10. administer,
distribute
dealer (pert to) ...
cattle .. 6. drover, herder
cloth .. 6. draper, mercer
drug .. 8. druggist 10. apothecary,
pharmacist 14. pharmacopolist
retail .. 6. grocer, monger 8. merchant
9. tradesman
stock exchange .. 6. broker, jobber,
trader 11. stockbroker
dean, dene ... 4. dell 6. valley
dean ... 4. head, Inge 5. decan, doyen
6. fellow (Educ), master, senior, verger
7. officer 9. churchman, principal
dear ... 5. chere, cheri, deary, lover, sugar,
sweet 7. beloved, darling 8. precious
9. expensive 10. sweetheart
dearth ... 4. want 6. famine, rarity
7. paucity, poverty 8. rareness, scarcity,

sparsity
death ... 4. doom, mort, obit 5. sleep
(eternal) 6. demise 7. decease, passing,
quietus, release 10. euthanasia (mercy),
expiration 11. evanishment
death (pert to) ...
after .. 10. posthumous
eternal .. 9. perdition
foreboding .. 6. funest 7. doleful
lawless .. 8. lynching
notice .. 4. obit 5. orbit 8. obituary
of a deity .. 4. Mors
rattle .. 4. rale
stoning (by) .. 8. lapidate
deathlessness ... 9. athanasia
11. immortality 15. everlastingness
debacle ... 4. rout 5. crash, flood
7. washout 8. collapse, stampede
9. breakdown, cataclysm
11. catastrophe, destruction
debar ... 3. bar 4. deny 5. estop 6. forbid,
hinder, refuse 7. exclude 8. obstruct,
preclude, prohibit
debark ... 4. land 6. go ashore
9. disembark
debase ... 5. abase, alloy, lower
6. demean, demote, reduce 7. corrupt,
degrade, deprave 8. disgrace
10. adulterate, depreciate 11. deteriorate
debasement ... 8. demotion
9. abasement, abjection, reduction,
vitiation 11. degradation
13. deterioration
debatable ... 4. moot 9. refutable
10. disputable 11. contestable
13. controversial
debate ... 4. agon (anc), moot 5. argue,
forum, plead, weigh 6. reason
7. analyze, closure, cloture, dispute,
wrangle 8. argument, consider, forensic,
militate 9. quodlibet 10. deliberate,
discussion 11. controversy
12. deliberation, dissertation
13. argumentation
debauch ... 4. bout, orgy 5. broil, spree,
taint 6. defile, seduce, splore 7. mislead
8. carousal, escapade 9. disaffect,
dissipate 11. contaminate
debauchee ... 4. rake, roué 5. satyr
7. rounder 9. libertine 10. profligate
debenture (Finan) ... 4. bond 5. claim
6. pledge 7. voucher 10. instrument
11. certificate
debilitated ... 4. weak 5. seedy 6. feeble,
infirm, sapped, sickly 7. languid
8. asthenic, impaired, weakened
9. enfeebled, langorous 11. devitalized
debility ... 5. atony 7. languor
8. adynamia, asthenia, cachexia,
weakness 9. infirmity, lassitude
10. feebleness, sickliness
debit ... 4. debt 5. entry 6. charge
debonair, debonaire ... 4. airy 5. suave
6. breezy, jaunty, urbane 7. affable,
buoyant 8. carefree
debris ... 4. junk 5. attle, ruins, scrap,
talus, trash 6. litter, refuse, rubble
7. deposit, remains, rubbish 8. detritus
10. clamjamfry
debt ... 3. due, IOU, sin (Bib) 7. arrears,
default 8. trespass 9. arrearage, liability

10. obligation

debut . . . 3. bow 8. entrance (formal) 9. coming out 12. introduction, presentation

debutante . . . 3. bud, deb 6. subdeb 9. socialite

decade . . . 3. ten 9. decennium

decadence . . . 5. decay 7. decline 13. deterioration, retrogression

Decalogue . . . 15. Ten Commandments

Decameron author . . . 9. Boccaccio

decamp . . . 4. flee 6. depart 7. abscond, vamoose 12. absquatulate

decanter . . . 4. ewer 5. croft 6. bottle, carafe, vessel (liquors)

decapitate . . . 6. behead 10. guillotine

decapod . . . 4. crab 5. prawn 6. shrimp 7. Homarus, lobster 8. Decapoda 10. crustacean

decay . . . 3. rot 4. blet, doty 5. spoil, waste 6. caries, wither 7. crumble, mortify, putrefy 8. spoilage 9. decadence, decompose 11. deteriorate, dissolution 13. decomposition, deterioration

deceased . . . 4. dead, gone, late 6. at rest 7. defunct, demised 8. decedent, departed

deceit . . . 5. covin, craft, fraud, guile, guise 7. cunning 8. artifice, cozenage, intrigue, subtlety, trickery, wiliness 9. chicanery, deception, duplicity, imposture, mendacity, sophistry, treachery 10. craftiness, sneakiness 13. deceitfulness, dissimulation 14. tergiversation 15. treacherousness

deceitful . . . 4. wily 5. false 6. artful, crafty, sneaky, tricky 8. guileful, scheming, trickish 9. deceptive, gnathonic, insincere 10. fraudulent 11. treacherous 13. Machiavellian

deceive . . . 3. cog, lie 4. bilk, dupe, flam, fool, gull, hoax, sile 5. cheat, cozen, elude, hocus, trick, troil 6. baffle, delude, illude, seduce 7. beguile, mislead 8. hoodwink

deceiver . . . 3. gay 5. cheat 6. hoaxer, trepan (trapan) 8. betrayer, impostor 9. trickster

decency . . . 7. decorum, fitness, modesty 8. chastity, niceness 9. propriety 10. seemliness 12. tastefulness

decent . . . 4. kind 5. comely, kindly, proper, seemly 7. clothed 8. adequate, gracious, suitable, tasteful 9. tolerable

deception . . . 3. lie 4. hoax, wile 5. cheat, fraud, guile 6. deceit, misled 7. fallacy 8. artifice, deceived, flimflam, illusion 9. duplicity, imposture

deceptive . . . 5. vague 8. illusive, illusory 9. deceiving, sirenical (sirenic) 10. fallacious

decide (upon) . . . 3. opt 4. vote 5. adapt, elect, judge 6. choose, settle 7. referee, resolve 8. arbitrate, ascertain, determine, influence

decided . . . 8. clear-cut, definite 10. determined

decima . . . 4. stop (organ) 5. tenth, tithe 8. interval

decimal . . . 3. ten 5. tenth 7. tenfold 8. repetend

decimate . . . 3. few 4. kill, slay 5. burke, tenth 6. divide 7. destroy 8. subtract 9. devastate, slaughter

decipher . . . 4. read 5. crack 6. decode, detect 7. unravel 8. discover 9. translate

decision . . . 4. grit 5. arret, nerve, pluck 6. mettle, report 7. verdict 8. firmness 10. conclusion, resolution, settlement 12. announcement 13. determination

decisive . . . 3. end 5. final 7. certain, crucial 8. critical, resolute 9. mandatory 10. conclusive, convincing

decisive moment . . . 6. crisis

deck (ship's) . . . 3. gun 4. main, poop 5. orlop, upper 6. bridge 7. scupper (gutter) 8. hatchway, platform 9. promenade 10. forecastle

deck . . . 4. gild 5. adorn, array, cards (playing), equip, floor 6. blazon, clothe, enrich 7. bedizen, dress up 8. emblazon 9. knock down

declaim . . . 4. rant, rave 5. orate, spiel, spout 6. herald, recite 8. denounce, harangue, perorate 9. discourse 11. declamation

declamation . . . 7. lecture 9. elocution 10. recitation

declaration . . . 3. vow 4. oath 6. avowal, decree, oracle 8. pleading (law) 9. assertion, manifesto, testimony 10. confession (of faith) 11. affirmation 12. proclamation 13. pronouncement

declare . . . 3. say 4. aver, avow, meld 5. bruit, state 6. affirm, allege, assert, blazon, herald, spread 7. publish 8. announce, indicate, maintain 9. advertise

declare (pert to) . . .
against . . 6. indict
as fact . . 5. posit
innocent . . 6. acquit

declension . . . 4. drop, fall 5. slope 7. decline, descent, refusal 10. inflection 13. deterioration

decline . . . 3. dip, ebb, set 4. fade, fail, fall, flag, sink, wane 5. droop, repel, slope, slump, stoop 6. refuse, reject, weaken 7. dwindle 8. decrease, downhill 9. decadence, declivity, repudiate 10. retrograde 12. depreciation

declivity . . . 3. dip 4. drop, hill 5. scarp, slope 7. descent 8. downgate 9. downgrade

decoction . . . 4. sapa (sape) 6. apozem, cremor, tisane 7. boiling 10. extraction 11. preparation

décolleté . . . 6. low-cut 8. plunging 9. revealing

decompose . . . 3. rot 4. frit 5. decay 7. resolve 10. photolysis 12. disintegrate

decorate . . . 4. deck, trim 5. adorn, honor 6. emboss 7. bedizen, brocade, miniate 8. beautify, ornament 9. scrimshaw

decorated . . . 5. fancy 6. ornate 7. adorned 8. nielloed 9. sigillate (pottery) 11. embellished

decoration . . . 4. buhl 5. gutta (anc), medal 6. plaque, purfle, ribbon 7. epergne, festoon, garnish 8. gold star, ornament, trimming 9. adornment, garniture, sgraffito 10. cordon bleu, emblazonry, embroidery

decorous . . . 4. calm, prim 5. grave, quiet, staid 6. decent, demure, modest, proper, sedate, seemly, serene 7. fitting, regular, settled 8. becoming, composed, suitable, tasteful 9. unruffled 12. conventional

decorticate . . . 4. bark, flay, husk, pare, peel, skin 5. strip 9. excoriate

decoy . . . 4. bait, lure, tole 6. capper, entrap 8. by-bidder 9. come-on man 11. stool pigeon

decrease . . . 3. ebb 4. drop, sink, wane 5. abate, waste 6. decess, lessen, reduce, shrink 7. decline, dwindle, shorten, slacken, subside 8. compress, diminish, moderate 9. abatement, deduction, deflation, lessening 10. diminution 11. contraction 12. depreciation

decree . . . 3. act, law 4. bull, fiat, rede (anc), will 5. arret, canon, edict, enact, irade, order, ukase 6. dictum, ordain 7. command, mandate, verdict 8. decision, rescript 9. ordinance

decree beforehand . . . 7. destine

decree nisi . . . 7. divorce

decrepit . . . 3. old 4. aged, lame, weak 6. infirm, senile, wasted (with age) 7. worn out 8. unstable, unsturdy

decry . . . 3. boo 4. slur 5. lower 7. condemn, degrade, detract 8. belittle, denounce, derogate 9. discredit, disparage, underrate 10. depreciate, undervalue

dedal . . . see *daedal*

de͏ ͏ate . . . 6. devote, hallow 7. address ͏ ͏ scribe 10. consecrate

͏ . . ͏ se . . . 5. infer 6. deduct, derive, elicit, evolve 7. suppose

dedu͏t . . . 4. bate, fa͏k, take 6. ͏ ͏ ͏ 8. di͏count, ͏ ͏rench, separa͏ ͏ ͏act

deduction . . . 6. rebate 7. reprise 8. discount, illation 9. allowance, corollary, induction, inference, reasoning, syllogism

deed . . . 3. act, ado 4. feat, fiat, gest (geste) 5. actum, actus, stunt, title 6. action, doings 7. exploit 8. contract, tenendum 11. achievement, malefaction, performance

deem . . . 5. judge, opine, think 6. esteem, regard 7. believe, presume, suppose 8. conclude, consider 10. adjudicate

deemed . . . 7. assumed, reputed 8. adjudged, inferred, presumed, supposed 10. considered

deep . . . 3. low, pit 4. rich, wide, wise 5. great 6. hidden, remote, solemn 7. learned, obscure, serious 8. immersed, involved, powerful, profound 9. engrossed, entangled, sagacious 10. deep-seated, mysterious

deep (pert to) . . .
  dish pie . . 7. cobbler
  sea . . 5. depths
  seated . . 8. habitual 9. ingrained 11. established
  sleep . . 5. sopor
  sound . . 4. bell, gong

deepen . . . 5. lower 6. dredge 7. broaden,

enhance 9. aggravate, intensify 10. strengthen

deer . . . 3. elk, red, roe 4. buck, fawn, hart, hind, maha, stag 5. eland, moose, ratwa 6. fallow, sambar, wapiti 7. caribou, deerlet, roebuck 8. reindeer, ruminant

deer (pert to) . . .
  antler . . 3. dag 4. snag 8. tres-tine (royal)
  Asiatic . . 6. sambar
  barking . . 7. muntjac (muntjak)
  deerlike . . 10. chevrotain
  female . . 3. doe, roe 4. hind
  genus . . 4. Dama 6. Cervus 8. Cervidae
  Japanese . . 4. sika
  Java . . 4. napu 7. muntjac (muntjak)
  Lapland . . 8. reindeer
  male . . 4. buck, hart, stag 6. havier 7. brocket (brok), pricket
  meat . . 7. venison
  mouse . . 7. plandok
  Oriental . . 4. axis, Rusa 5. kakar 6. chital, rativa, sambar 7. kanchil, muntjac (muntjak)
  Russian . . 4. olen
  S American . . 4. pita 6. guemal (guemul) 7. brocket, spitter
  Tibet . . 4. shou
  tiger . . 6. cougar
  tracks . . 3. run 4. slot 5. spoor
  type . . 3. red, roe 4. mule 6. fallow 11. black-tailed, white-tailed

deface . . . 3. mar 4. ruin, scar 5. spoil 6. damage, injure 7. blemish, distort 9. discredit, disfigure

defalcate . . . 8. embezzle

de͏ ͏ation . . . 5. libel 7. calumny, sl͏nder, spatter 8. disgrace, dishonor 9. aspersion 1͏ ͏lement, detraction

de͏ ͏e . . . 5. libel 6. accuse, ͏ ͏arge, in͏ ͏y, malign, vilify 7. asperse, blacken, d͏ ͏ ͏t, sl͏ ͏ 8. dishonor 10. calumniate

default . . . 4. fail, lack, loss, mora 7. deficit, failure, neglect 9. deficient, denigrate, oversight 10. nonpayment 11. delinquency 14. nonfulfillment

defeat . . . 4. beat, best, lose, rout 5. worst 6. baffle, derout, master, refute 7. beating, clobber, confute, conquer, failure, mastery, repulse, triumph (over), undoing 8. Waterloo 9. frustrate, overthrow 10. disappoint 11. subjugation 12. discomfiture 14. disappointment

defeating . . . 7. beating, routing 10. anarreptic, conquering 11. vanquishing

defeatism . . . 6. malism 7. Boloism 10. retreatism

defect . . . 4. flaw, lisp, lock, quit, want 5. fault 7. blemish, forsake 8. withdraw 9. discredit 10. deficiency, inadequacy 12. imperfection, irregularity

defection . . . 4. loss 7. failing, failure 9. desertion 10. abjuration 11. abandonment

defective . . . 3. bad 4. lame 5. idiot 6. cretin, faulty 7. half-wit, lacking 8. crippled 9. deficient, imperfect, subnormal 10. incomplete

defective vision . . . 6. anopia, myopia

defend . . . 4. save, ward 5. guard, plead, shend, watch 6. screen, secure, shield, uphold 7. contest, justify, protect, shelter, support, sustain 8. enshield, preserve 10. controvert

defendant . . . 4. reus 7. accused, libelee, suspect 8. appellee 10. respondent

defender . . . 8. advocate, champion 9. justifier, protector 10. vindicator

defense . . . 4. boma, fort, plea 5. alibi, guard 6. abatis (abattis), glacis (slope) 7. bastion, bulwark, rampart, ravelin 8. estacade (dike), sepiment, stockade 10. protection 12. counterscarp 13. justification, machicolation

defenseless . . . 7. aidless, forlorn, unarmed 8. helpless 9. unarmored, unguarded 10. undefended, unshielded 11. unfortified, unprotected

defer . . . 3. bow 4. wait 5. delay 6. retard 7. adjourn, suspend 8. postpone, protract, stave off 13. procrastinate

defer (to) . . . 5. yield 6. admire, regard, submit 7. concede, respect 9. recognize 11. acknowledge

deference . . . 5. honor 6. esteem, fealty, homage, regard 7. respect 8. courtesy 9. reverence 10. politeness, submission 12. complaisance 13. consideration

deferential . . . 8. obeisant 9. attentive, courteous 10. respectful, submissive 11. ceremonious

defiance . . . 6. defial 8. audacity, boldness 9. challenge, disregard, insolence

deficiency . . . 4. lack, want 6. dearth, ullage 7. aneuria, deficit 8. scarcity, shortage 10. inadequacy 13. insufficiency 14. incompleteness

deficient . . . 5. minus, short 6. faulty, meager (meagre) 7. scarce 7. lacking, missing, wanting 8. inferior 9. defective, imperfect 10. inadequate, incomplete 12. insufficient

defile . . . 4. file, pass (Mt) soil 5. dirty, gorge, notch, sully, taint 6. befoul, debase, ravine, vilify 7. corrupt, debauch, deprave, pollute, tarnish 8. dishonor 10. passageway

define . . . 3. fix 4. name 5. bound, limit 6. decide 7. delimit, explain, outline 8. boundary 9. delineate, determine, stipulate 11. distinguish 12. characterize, circumscribe

defined (sharply) . . . 8. clear-cut 9. trenchant

defined track . . . 3. rut 4. slot

definite . . . 4. sure 7. certain, limited, precise 8. absolute, distinct, explicit, manifest, positive 10. undeniable 11. determining, unqualified 12. unmistakable 14. unquestionable

definitely . . . 10. explicitly, positively 12. conclusively, unmistakably

definition . . . 6. naming 7. clarity, meaning 9. sharpness 11. description, explanation 12. delimitation, distinctness 14. interpretation

deflation . . . 7. decline 8. collapse 9. reduction 10. cheapening 11. devaluation, humiliation

12. depreciation

deflect . . . 4. bend, warp 5. avert 6. divert 7. deviate

Defoe character . . . 6. Crusoe, Friday, Roxana 12. Moll Flanders

deformed . . . 5. varus 7. taliped 8. formless 9. amorphous, distorted, grotesque, loathsome, malformed, misshapen, monstrous 10. clubfooted

defraud . . . 3. gyp, rob 4. bilk, gull 5. cheat, cozen 6. fleece 7. swindle

deft . . . 3. apt, fit, pat 4. meet, trim 5. adept, handy, quick 6. adroit, clever, expert 8. skillful (skilful) 9. dexterous, masterful

defunct . . . 3. die 4. dead, gone 6. depart, finish 7. extinct 8. deceased 11. nonexistent

defy . . . 4. dare 5. beard, brave, stump 6. cartel 7. disdain, disobey 9. challenge

degenerate . . . 6. debase, wicked, worsen 7. atrophy, corrupt, degrade, deprave 8. decadent 10. retrogress 11. deteriorate

degeneration . . . 7. decline 9. decadence, turpitude 10. degeneracy 11. degradation 13. deterioration, retrogression

degradation . . . 5. shame 7. censure, decline 8. demotion, disgrace, ignominy 9. reduction, turpitude 10. debasement, punishment 11. humiliation 13. deterioration

degrade . . . 5. abase, lower 6. debase, demean, demote, depose, humble 7. corrupt 8. disgrace, dishonor 9. humiliate 10. depreciate

degrade (socially) . . . 8. déclassé

degree . . . 4. rank, step, tate 5. class, grade, order, point, scope, shade, stage, stair 6. extent 7. station 8. capacity, relation 9. intensity

degree (pert to) . . .
academic . . 8. bachelor 9. doctorate, masterate 11. engineering 13. baccalaureate
slight . . 5. shade 9. gradation
to what . . 9. howsoever 10. howsomever
with honors . . 8. cum laude

dehydrate . . . 3. dry 5. dry up 6. wither 8. preserve 9. anhydrate, dessicate, evaporate, exsiccate

deify . . . 5. exalt 7. ennoble, glorify, idolize 8. enshrine 11. apotheosize, immortalize

deign . . . 7. consent 9. vouchsafe 10. condescend

deity . . . 2. El 3. Dea, God 4. Deus, deva 5. numen 6. Elohim 7. goddess, godhead, godhood 8. Almighty, Divinity, Immortal 12. Supreme Being

deity (aboriginal) . . . 4. mana, Zemi 5. huaca, wakan 6. manito (manitou), nagual, orenda, pokunt 8. tamanoas

deity (pert to) . . .
avenging . . 6. Erinys 7. Alastor, Anteros
destroying . . 4. Siva (Shiva)
evil . . 5. Sebek (crocodile-headed)
hearth . . 5. Vesta
household . . 3. Lar 7. Penates
human sacrifice . . 6. Moloch

judge of the dead .. 4. Yama
love .. 4. Amor, Eros 5. Cupid
mockery .. 5. Momus
music .. 6. Apollo
solar .. 5. Mentu (Ment, falcon-headed)
sun .. 2. Ra
supreme .. 6. Ormazd
two-faced .. 5. Janus
underworld .. 3. Dis 4. Gwyn 5. Pluto
   6. Osiris
war .. 4. Ares
woodland .. 3. Pan 4. faun 5. satyr
   7. silenus
dejected ... 3. sad 5. amort 6. abased,
   droopy 7. à la mort, lowered
   8. downcast 9. depressed, prostrate
   10. despondent 11. downhearted,
   low-spirited
dejection ... 7. lowness, sadness
   10. depression, melancholy
   11. despondency
déjeuner ... 5. lunch
Delaware ...
beach .. 8. Rehoboth
capital .. 5. Dover
church (oldest Prot) .. 9. Old Swedes
city .. 5. Lewes 9. New Castle
   10. Wilmington (Fort Christina, 1638)
corporation .. 6. DuPont
product .. 9. chemicals 13. Blue Hen
   chicks
river .. 8. Delaware 10. Brandywine
State admission .. 5. first
State motto .. 22. Liberty and
   Independence
State nickname .. 5. First 7. Diamond
delay ... 3. lag 4. halt, mora, stay, wait
   5. block, check, daily, defer, demur,
   pause, tarry 6. arrest, detain, hinder,
   impede, loiter, retard 7. confine,
   setback 8. lateness, obstruct, postpone,
   reprieve, slow-down 9. detention,
   hindrance 10. cunctation, moratorium
   13. procrastinate 15. procrastination
delayed ... 4. late, slow 5. tardy
   7. belayed, overdue 10. behindhand
delectable ... 6. savory 8. luscious,
   pleasing 9. ambrosial, delicious
   10. delightful 11. scrumptious
delegate ... 4. name, send 6. assign,
   commit, depute, deputy, legate
   7. appoint, consign, entrust 8. deputize
   9. authorize 10. commission
   12. commissioner 14. representative
delete ... 4. dele 5. erase 6. cut out,
   excise, remove 7. edit out, expunge
   9. eradicate 10. obliterate
deleterious ... 7. harmful, hurtful,
   noxious 9. injurious 10. pernicious,
   prejudiced 11. destructive, detrimental,
   prejudicial
deletion ... 4. stet 7. apocope 8. excision
   9. expunging
delf, delft ... 3. pit 4. mine 6. quarry
Delhi ... 7. capital (Ind)
deliberate ... 4. cool, muse, pore, slow
   5. study, think, weigh 6. ponder
   7. discuss, reflect, studied 8. consider,
   measured, prepense 9. calculate,
   leisurely, speculate, unhurried,
   voluntary 11. contemplate, intentional,

   premeditate 12. premeditated
   13. dispassionate
deliberately ... 6. slowly 7. tardily 8. by
   design 9. expressly, purposely, willfully
   13. intentionally
delicacy ... 4. cate, tact 5. snack, taste
   6. caviar, luxury, nicety, tidbit 7. finesse,
   frailty, tenuity 8. fineness, niceness,
   softness, subtlety 9. exactness, fragility,
   precision 10. daintiness, refinement,
   slightness 11. sensitivity
delicate ... 3. sly 4. fine, lacy, nice, soft
   5. frail, light 6. dainty, mignon, petite,
   pretty, queasy, subtle, tender 7. elegant,
   fragile, minikin, refined, tenuous
   8. araneous, graceful, luscious, tasteful
   9. exquisite, sensitive 10. fastidious,
   meticulous, scrupulous 11. considerate
delicious ... 5. tasty 8. luscious
   9. ambrosial, nectarean 10. delightful,
   nectareous
delight ... 3. joy 4. glee 5. amuse,
   bliss, charm, exult, mirth 6. divert,
   please, ravish, regale, relish 7. enchant,
   gratify, overjoy 8. pleasure 9. delectate,
   enrapture, happiness 13. gratification
delightful ... 6. lovely, savory 7. amusing,
   winsome 8. charming, engaging,
   pleasant 9. appealing, delicious,
   enjoyable 10. enchanting 11. fascinating
delineate ... 3. map 4. draw, limn, line
   5. trace 6. define, depict 7. outline,
   picture, portray 8. describe 9. represent
delinquency ... 7. default, failure
   8. omission 9. violation 10. nonpayment
   11. malfeasance, misdemeanor,
   misfeasance 13. nonobservance
deliquesce ... 4. give, melt 6. ramify
   7. liquefy 8. diminish, dissolve
delirious ... 6. insane, raving 8. frenzied
   9. wandering (mental) 14. disorientation
delirium ... 4. fury, rage 6. frenzy,
   lunacy 7. madness, passion 8. insanity
   9. phrenitis 10. aberration, excitement,
   unsaneness 11. derangement
   13. hallucination
deliver ... 4. free, give, save 5. speak
   6. commit, impart, ransom, redeem,
   render, resign 7. consign, release,
   relieve 8. transfer 9. discharge,
   enunciate, extradite, surrender
deliver of evil spirits ... 8. exorcise
deliver oration ... 7. declaim
dell ... 4. dale, dene, vale 5. slade 6. dalles
   (pl), dingle, ravine, valley
Delos ...
famed for .. 5. ruins 10. Stone Lions
island group .. 8. Cyclades
sea .. 6. Aegean
Delphi, Delphoi (Gr) ...
god .. 6. Apollo
modern name .. 6. Kastri
mount .. 9. Parnassus
oracle .. 7. Delphic 8. Delphian
priestess .. 6. Pythia
delude ... 3. jig 4. dupe, flam, fool, hoax
   5. elude, trick 6. befool 7. beguile,
   deceive, mislead 9. bamboozle,
   frustrate, victimize 11. double-cross
deluge ... 5. flood 6. drench 7. freshet,
   Niagara, torrent 8. cataract, flooding,

inundate, overflow, submerge, The Flood 9. cataclysm, overwhelm 10. oversupply 14. superabundance

delusion . . . 4. ruse 6. mirage 7. fallacy, fantasm 8. illusion, phantasm 9. deception 10. misleading 13. hallucination

delve . . . 3. dig 4. mine, till 5. gouge, scoop, spade 6. exhume 8. excavate

demand . . . 3. ask, COD, cry, dun, fee 4. call, need 5. claim, query 6. elicit 7. require 8. exaction, question 9. requisite, ultimatum 11. requirement, requisition

demandant . . . 9. plaintiff

demeanor, demeanour . . . 4. mien 7. bearing, conduct, posture 8. behavior, carriage 11. comportment

demented . . . 3. mad 4. daft, loco, luny 5. crazy, loony 6. crazed, insane 7. cracked, deranged 10. unbalanced 11. disoriented

demesne . . . 4. land 6. estate 10. possession

Demeter . . . 7. goddess (Agric)

demigod . . . 4. hero 5. satyr (sylvan) 6. Triton 7. godling, half-god 10. semidivine

demise . . . 5. death, lease 6. convey 7. decease 8. bequeath 10. alienation, conveyance

demit . . . 4. quit 5. leave 6. resign, vacate 8. abdicate 10. relinquish 11. resignation

demiurgic . . . 8. creative 9. formative

demivolt . . . 4. jump 5. vault (half) 6. curvet 8. capriole

Democrat (Polit slang) . . . 6. Hunker

demoded . . . 5. passe 6. passed 10. out of style

demolish . . . 4. rase, raze, ruin, undo 5. level, wreck 7. destroy, shatter 9. devastate, dismantle, overthrow 11. disassemble

demon, daemon . . . 3. hag, imp, nat 4. atua, jinn, Mara, ogre, Rahu 5. asura, devil, Eolis, fiend, genie, jinni (jinnee), lamia, Satan 6. afreet 7. Amaimon, villain 8. Asmodeus 9. cacodemon (cacodaemon)

demoniac . . . 8. devilish, fiendish

demons (pert to) . . .
adjurers . . 9. exorcists
assembly of . . 6. sabbat
charm against . . 10. demonifuge
possessed of . . 8. demoniac
theory of . . 10. demonology
worship of . . 11. demonolatry

demonstrate . . . 4. show 5. prove 6. evince, typify 7. display, explain, portray 8. manifest 9. exemplify

demonstrative . . . 7. gushing 8. effusive 9. emotional 10. indicative 11. explanatory 12. affectionate, illustrative

Demosthenes (Gr) . . . 6. orator (greatest)

demotic . . . 6. common 7. popular 8. everyday 10. vernacular

demur . . . 4. stay 5. delay, pause, tarry 6. linger, object (to) 7. scruple 8. demurrer, hesitate 9. objection

12. irresolution

demure . . . 3. coy, mim, shy 4. prim, smug 5. grave, staid, timid 6. sedate, solemn, stuffy 7. bashful, prudish, serious 8. decorous

den . . . 4. cave, dell, lair, nest, room 5. cavea (anc), group (scouts), haunt, study 6. cavern, grotto, hollow, ravine 7. retreat 8. hideaway

denial . . . 5. cross 7. refusal 8. demurrer, negation 9. disavowal, disowning, rejection 10. refutation 11. deprivation 12. disallowance 13. disaffirmance

denizen . . . 3. cit 6. native 7. citizen, dweller, hellion (of hell) 9. indweller 10. inhabitant 11. cosmopolite

Denmark . . . see also *Danish*
anc name . . 5. Thule
capital . . 10. Copenhagen
city . . 6. Nyborg (Fyn Isl), Odense 7. Aalborg 8. Elsinore
founder . . 7. Absalon (Axel)
Hamlet's grave . . 8. Elsinore
island possession . . 6. Faroes 9. Greenland
peninsula . . 7. Jutland
river . . 5. Guden
ruler (anc) . . 6. Canute (Kanute)

denomination . . . 3. ism 4. cult, name, sect 5. class, party, value 6. church, number, school 7. society 8. category 10. persuasion 11. appellation, designation, stipulation

denote . . . 4. mark, mean, note, show 5. imply 6. convey 7. bespeak, betoken, connote, express, purport, signify 8. indicate 10. denominate

denoting (pert to) . . .
equal pressure . . 8. isobaric
final end (Gram) . . 5. telic
usual action . . 9. usitative

denouement . . . 3. end 5. issue 6. result 7. outcome (plot) 8. solution 10. revelation

denounce . . . 4. damn, rail (at, against) 6. accuse, assail, scathe 7. arraign, censure, condemn, upbraid 9. reprobate 10. denunciate, stigmatize

de novo . . . 3. new 4. anew 5. fresh, newly 6. afresh

dense . . . 4. dewy, firm 5. close, crass, gross, heavy, solid, thick 6. opaque, stupid 7. compact, crowded 8. populous, thickset 11. thickheaded

density . . . 4. dord (Chem) 8. dumbness 9. stupidity 11. compactness

dent . . . 3. pit 4. dint 5. dinge, notch, tooth 6. batter, hollow, indent 7. imprint 10. depression, impression 11. indentation

dentagra . . . 7. forceps 9. dentalgia, toothache

dental (pert to) . . .
appliance . . 3. dam 6. scaler 7. forceps
drill . . 8. cavitron
filling . . 5. inlay
measure . . 10. dentimeter
toothache . . 8. dentagra 9. dentalgia

dentate . . . 7. serried, toothed

dentine . . . 7. ivory

dentist . . . 10. exodontist 12. orthodontist

14. prosthodontist

denude ... 4. bate 5. scalp, strip 6. divest, expose, unrobe 7. uncover

denunciation ... 6. menace, threat 7. inveigh 8. reproach 10. accusation 11. arraignment

deny ... 4. nego 5. debar 6. abjure, impugn, negate, recant, refuse, renege 7. confute, disavow, dispute, gainsay 8. disclaim, forswear, traverse 9. repudiate 10. contradict, contravene, controvert

deodar (species) ... 5. cedar

depart ... 2. go 3. die 4. exit, quit 5. leave, mosey 6. decamp, demise, egress, perish 7. abscond, vamoose 8. separate (Chem), withdraw

depend ... 4. rely 5. hinge

depraved ... 4. evil, vile 6. shrewd, wicked 7. corrupt, immoral, vicious 8. vitiated 9. debauched, dissolute, perverted 10. degenerate

depravity ... 8. depraved 9. turpitude 10. corruption, wickedness 15. incorrigibility

depreciate ... 4. fall 5. lower, slump 6. debase, lessen, reduce, shrink 7. cheapen, deflate 8. belittle, discount, pejorate, vilipend 9. disparage 10. undervalue

depreciation ... 8. decrease, discount 9. deflation 10. cheapening, pejoration 12. belittlement 13. disparagement 14. undervaluation

depredator ... 5. thief 6. looter, robber 7. spoiler 8. marauder, ravisher 9. despoiler, plunderer

depress ... 4. dent, sink 5. lower 6. dampen, deepen, deject, indent, reduce, sadden 7. flatten, imprint, oppress 8. dispirit, enfeeble 10. discourage

depressed ... 3. low, sad 4. dire, sunk 6. dismal, oblate 8. dejected, downcast 9. debruised (Her), flattened (vertically) 10. dispirited 11. downhearted 12. disheartened

depressing ... 5. chill 6. dismal, dreary, gloomy, somber 7. joyless 9. saddening 10. melancholy

depression ... 3. col, dip, pit 4. dent, fall 5. blues, fossa (Anat), gloom, gully 6. cavity, crater, ravine, trough, vapors 10. melancholy 11. despondency, humiliation

deprivation ... 4. loss, want 7. deposal, ousting, removal 9. privation, unseating 10. divestment 11. bereavement

deprive ... 3. rob 4. take 5. debar, mulct, strip 6. divest, remove 7. bereave, despoil 10. dispossess

deprived of ...

authority .. 9. dethroned

life .. 5. slain 6. killed 12. exterminated

limb .. 6. maimed

natural qualities .. 9. denatured

possessions .. 12. expropriated

professional standing .. 8. laicized

rank .. 7. deposed

reason .. 8. demented

vigor .. 6. sapped 8. deadened, unnerved

9. enervated, enfeebled

depth ... 5. abyss, midst 6. extent 9. intensity 10. profundity

depths ... 3. sea 5. adyta (spiritual), ocean 16. Davy Jones's locker

depute ... 6. assign, devote 7. appoint 8. delegate, deputize

deputy ... 5. agent, envoy, proxy, vicar 6. legate 8. alter ego 9. alternate 10. substitute

deracinate ... 6. evulse, unroot, uproot 7. extract (forcibly)

deride ... 3. pan 4. dupe, geck, gibe, jeer, mock, razz 5. cheat, fleer, flout, scoff, scorn, trick 6. insult 8. ridicule

derision ... 5. fleer, scorn 7. asteism, mockery 8. contempt, ridicule

derivation ... 6. effect, origin, source 7. descent, lineage 9. deduction, education, evolution 10. derivative 12. transmission

derivation of ...

descent .. 7. lineage 8. pedigree 9. genealogy

name (race, tribe) .. 7. eponymy

word .. 9. etymology

derivative of ...

bauxite .. 8. aluminum

benzine .. 6. phenol

coal tar .. 8. creosote

flax .. 5. linen

mercury .. 11. quicksilver

milk .. 6. lactic

morphine .. 6. heroin

pitchblende .. 6. radium 7. uranium

sorrel .. 10. oxalic acid

derogate ... 5. annul, decry 6. repeal 7. detract 8. restrict, withdraw 9. disparage

derogatory ... 10. detracting, detractory, pejorative 11. deprecatory, disparaging 12. depreciatory

derrick ... 3. rig 4. spar 5. crave, hoist, tower 6. lifter, steeve, tackle 7. hangman, staging

dervish ... 4. monk 5. fakir, friar 6. beggar, fakeer 7. ascetic 11. religionist

dervish cap ... 3. taj 4. atef

dervishes ...

howling .. 8. Rufaiyah

wandering .. 12. Kalandariyah

whirling, dancing .. 10. Maulawiyah

Descartes (pert to) ...

geometry .. 8. analytic 10. coordinate

system .. 9. Cartesian

tenet .. 13. cogito ergo sum

descend ... 4. fall, sink 5. deign, stoop 6. alight, unbend 7. decline 9. gravitate 10. condescend

descendant ... 3. son 5. child, scion 8. daughter, offshoot 9. offspring

descendants ... 5. breed 7. progeny 9. posterity

descent ... 4. drop, fall, root 5. birth, issue, scarp, slope, stock 7. assault, decline, lineage 8. ancestry, downfall, invasion (sea), pedigree 9. declivity, incursion, posterity 10. extraction 11. degradation

describe ... 4. name 5. paint, parse, state 6. define, depict, relate 7. explain, express, narrate, outline 9. delineate, designate, represent 12. characterize

description . . . 4. idyl, kind, sort 5. idyll 7. account, version 8. features, relation 9. discourse, narration, narrative, portrayal 10. definition 11. delineation, explanation 14. representation 18. descriptio personae

descry . . . 3. see 4. espy, view 6. behold, detect, reveal 7. discern, observe, witness 8. discover 9. determine 11. distinguish

Desdemona's husband . . . 7. Othello

desecrate . . . 5. abuse 6. misuse 7. profane, violate 8. misapply

Deseret . . . 4. Utah (1849)

desert . . . 3. due 4. bolt, fail 5. merit, oasis 6. defect, renege, reward 7. abandon, forsake 8. desolate 10. apostatize, relinquish, wilderness

desert (pert to) . . .
Africa . . 5. El Erg 6. Karroo, Sahara 8. Kalahari
Algeria . . 3. Erg
Australia . . 10. Great Sandy 13. Great Victoria
beast . . 5. camel
dweller . . 4. Arab
Mongolia (Asia) . . 4. Gobi
phenomenon . . 6. mirage
prospector . . 3. rat
ship . . 5. camel
shrub . . 5. ratem 6. Alhagi 7. juniper (Bib)
train, travelers . . 7. caravan
US . . 6. Mojave (Mohave) 7. Painted 11. Death Valley
wind (hot) . . 6. simoom (simoon) 7. sirocco

deserter . . . 3. rat 6. bolter 8. apostate, recreant, renegade, turncoat, turntail

deserved . . . 3. due 4. fair, just 5. rated 6. earned, worthy 7. condign, merited 8. rightful 9. justified, warranted 11. appropriate

deserving . . . 6. worthy 8. laudable 10. creditable, entitled to 11. commendable, meritorious 12. praiseworthy

desiccated . . . 3. dry 4. arid, sere 5. dried 6. seared 7. parched 9. preserved 10. dehydrated, exsiccated

design . . . 3. aim, art, end 4. draw, form, idea, mean, plan, plot 5. ettle 6. intent, layout, motive, object, scheme, sketch 7. destine, drawing, meaning, outline, pattern, propose 8. artifice, artistry, contrive 11. arrangement

design (pert to) . . .
carved . . 4. seme 5. cameo 8. intaglio
metal glass . . 4. etch 6. niello
ornamental . . 9. medallion 10. needlework
pattern . . 5. batik 6. mosaic
skin . . 6. tattoo

designate . . . 3. fix, set 4. call, mark, name, show 5. state, style, title 6. select 7. appoint, entitle, specify 8. describe, indicate, nominate 9. determine, stipulate 10. denominate 11. distinguish 12. characterize

designation . . . 4. name 7. meaning 9. selection 10. indication 12. denomination 13. signification

desire . . . 3. yen 4. care, urge, want, wish 5. covet, crave, yearn 6. aspire, hunger, prefer, thirst 7. craving, longing, passion, request 8. appetite 9. appetency, eagerness 10. desiderium 11. inclination

desire (pert to) . . .
expectant . . 4. hope
greatly . . 6. aspire
liquid . . 6. thirst
ungovernable . . 5. mania

desirous . . . 4. avid 5. eager 6. ardent 7. envious, lustful, willing 8. covetous, spirited 9. ambitious 10. solicitous

desist . . . 2. ho 3. end 4. don't, halt, quit, stay, stop 5. cease 6. lay off 7. forbear, refrain 8. cut it out 11. discontinue

desk . . . 4. ambo, dais 5. board, table 6. pulpit 7. lectern, rostrum 8. kneehole 9. monocleid (monocleide), secretary 10. escritoire

desolate . . . 3. sad 4. arid, lorn, ruin 5. alone, bleak, drear, gaunt 6. barren, dismal, gloomy, lonely, ravage 7. forlorn 8. deserted, forsaken, solitary, wretched 9. destitute 10. depopulate 11. comfortless, uninhabited

desolation . . . 3. woe 4. ruin 5. gloom, grief, havoc, waste 6. ravage 7. sadness 10. gloominess, loneliness, melancholy 11. destitution, destruction, devastation, forlornness 12. depopulation, solitariness, wretchedness

despair . . . 11. desperation, despondency, forlornness 12. hopelessness

desperado . . . 5. brave 6. outlaw 7. ruffian 8. criminal 10. lawbreaker

desperate . . . 3. mad 4. rash, wild 7. frantic, furious 8. headlong, heedless, hopeless, reckless 10. despairing, desponding, distraught, infuriated 11. extravagant, precipitate 13. irretrievable

despicable . . . 4. base, vile 6. odious, shabby 8. terrible, unworthy, wretched 9. miserable 12. contemptible, contemptuous, disreputable, vilipendious

despise . . . 4. defy, hate 5. scorn, scout, spurn 6. detest, slight 7. contemn, disdain 8. vilipend 9. disregard

despised being . . . 6. pariah 7. outcast

despoil . . . 3. rip, rob 4. riot 5. reave, rifle, strip 6. divest, fleece, injure, ravage, ravish 7. bereave, debauch, deprive, disrobe, pillage, plunder 9. depredate

despondency . . . 7. despair 10. depression 11. desperation 13. heartlessness

despot . . . 4. czar (tsar), lord 6. master, satrap, tyrant 8. autocrat, dictator 9. patriarch

despotic . . . 8. arrogant 9. arbitrary, tyrannous 10. autocratic, tyrannical 11. dictatorial, patriarchal 12. governmental

dessert . . . 3. ice, pie 4. cake 5. fruit,

glacé, sweet 6. mousse, pastry, sweets
7. parfait, pudding, sherbet, strudel
8. ice cream 10. shoofly pie

destination . . . 3. end 4. goal, port
5. bourn (bourne) 7. address, destiny
9. objective

destine . . . 4. doom, fate 5. allot 6. design,
devote, intend, ordain 7. appoint 8. set
apart 9. designate 10. foreordain,
predestine 12. predetermine

destiny . . . 3. end, lot, ure (anc) 4. bahi,
doom, eure, fate, goal 5. karma, stars
6. Kismet 7. fortune 11. destination

destitute . . . 4. void 5. needy 6. bereft,
devoid 7. forlorn, lacking 8. bankrupt,
forsaken, homeless 9. abandoned,
penniless 10. down-and-out

destitution . . . 6. penury 7. poverty
11. deprivation 12. helplessness

destroy . . . 3. end 4. kill, rase, raze,
root, ruin, sack, slay, undo 5. abash,
annul, erase 6. ravage 7. abolish,
consume, nullify, unbuild 8. decimate,
demolish, overturn 9. dismantle,
eradicate 10. annihilate, neutralize
11. exterminate

destroyer . . . 3. hun 6. ruiner, vandal
7. marplot, wrecker 8. nihilist, saboteur
9. iconclast (of images) 11. torpedo
boat

destroying angel . . . 6. Danite
7. Abaddon, Amanita (fungus)
8. Apollyon

destruction . . . 4. loss, ruin 5. havoc,
waste 7. killing 8. downfall, genocide,
ravaging, sabotage, shambles
9. holocaust, overthrow, perdition,
ruination 10. decimation, demolition,
desolation, extinction, subversion
11. devastation, dissolution, extirpation
13. extermination

destructive . . . 5. fatal 6. deadly, mortal
7. baleful, fateful, ruinous 8. aneretic
(anaeretic), ravaging 10. calamitous,
catawampus, pernicious, subversive

desuetude . . . 6. disuse, nonuse
9. cessation 12. obsolescence
13. nonemployment 14. discontinuance

desultory . . . 4. idle 5. hasty 6. roving,
wanton 7. aimless, cursory, wayward
8. rambling, unsteady, wavering
9. deviative, orderless, unsettled
10. discursive, inconstant

detach . . . 4. part, wean 5. sever 7. disjoin,
isolate 8. disunite, separate, withdraw
9. disengage

detached . . . 4. free 5. alone, aloof, scarp
7. detaché, retired, severed 8. isolated,
secluded, separate, solitary 9. unrelated,
withdrawn 11. unconnected
12. disconnected

detachment . . . 8. disunion 9. aloneness,
aloofness, isolation, seclusion,
unconcern 10. separation
11. disjunction 14. demobilization

detail . . . 4. item, unit 6. assign 7. appoint,
itemize, minutia, narrate, specify
9. enumerate, narrative 10. particular
12. technicality

details . . . 6. trivia 8. minutiae 10. ins
and outs 11. particulars

detain . . . 4. hold, keep, stop 5. check,
delay 6. arrest, hinder, intern, retard
8. imprison, restrain, withhold

detect . . . 3. see, spy 4. show, spot, tail
6. accuse, descry, reveal 7. discern,
find out, uncover 8. discover, perceive
9. recognize

detective . . . 4. dick 6. beagle, sleuth,
tailer, tracer 7. gumshoe, spotter
8. exposing, flatfoot, Hawkshaw,
mouchard 9. operative 12. investigator

detent . . . 3. dog 4. pawl 5. catch, click,
fence 6. tongue 7. ratchet

detention . . . 5. delay 6. duress 7. detinue
9. captivity, hindrance 10. detainment,
internment 11. restraining, retardation,
withholding 12. imprisonment

deter . . . 5. daunt, delay, repel 6. divert,
hinder 7. prevent 8. restrain
10. discourage, disincline

deterge . . . 5. purge 6. purify 7. cleanse
8. depurate 9. elutriate

detergent . . . 4. soap 7. cleaner, purging,
saponin (saponine), smectic, solvent
8. cleanser, medicine, purifier
9. cleansing 10. abstergent, lixiviator

deteriorate . . . 4. wear 6. impair, weaken,
worsen 10. degenerate, retrogress

deterioration . . . 5. decay 7. decline
9. decadence 10. debasement,
declension, impairment, perversion
11. degradation 12. degeneration
13. retrogression

determinate . . . 5. fixed 6. cymose
7. certain, special 8. definite, resolute,
resolved, specific 9. arbitrary
10. definitive, invariable 11. established,
unqualified

determination . . . 4. will 5. limit,
proof 6. choice 7. purpose, resolve,
verdict 8. decision, firmness, judgment
9. impulsion 10. conclusion, definition,
discussion, resolution, settlement
11. disputation, measurement,
termination 12. decisiveness,
dijudication, resoluteness
13. specification

determine . . . 3. end 5. impel, learn,
prove, state 6. assess, choose, decide,
define, direct, ordain, settle 7. delimit,
resolve, specify 8. conclude, discover
9. arbitrate, ascertain, stipulate,
terminate, variously 10. dijudicate,
foreordain

determined . . . 3. set 4. sure 5. fixed
6. mulish 7. assured, cinched, decided,
settled 8. foregone, perverse, resolute,
stubborn 9. obstinate, pigheaded

detest . . . 4. hate 5. abhor 6. loathe
8. execrate 9. abominate

detestable . . . 6. odious 7. hateful
8. accursed, terrible 9. abhorrent,
execrable, loathsome, obnoxious
10. abominable 12. contemptible

dethrone . . . 6. depose, disbar, divest
7. uncrown 8. disbench

detonation . . . 4. bang, boom 5. blast
7. blowout 8. backfire 9. discharge,
explosion 10. combustion

detract . . . 6. deduce, deduct, vilify
7. asperse, traduce 8. belittle, derogate,

distract, subtract, withdraw 9. disparage
10. depreciate
detraction . . 5. delay 7. calumny,
slander 9. aspersion 10. belittling
11. distraction, subtraction
detriment . . 4. hurt, loss 6. damage,
injury 8. mischief, weakness
10. impairment, impediment
12. disadvantage
detrimental . . . 7. baleful, baneful,
harmful, hurtful, noxious 9. injurious
10. pernicious 11. deleterious,
mischievous, prejudicial
15. disadvantageous
Deus Fidius . . . 7. Jupiter
Deus vobiscum . . . 12. God be with you
Deus vult . . . 8. God wills (anc cry)
deuterogamy . . . 6. digamy
Deuteronomy (pert to) . . .
comprising . . 10. law of Moses
Fifth Book of . . 10. Pentateuch
meaning . . 11. repeated law (of Moses)
devastate . . . 4. rape, ruin, sack 5. havoc,
strip, waste 6. ravage 7. destroy,
pillage, plunder, scourge 8. demolish,
desolate 10. depopulate
devastation . . . 4. ruin 5. havoc, waste
6. ravage 7. scourge
develop . . . 4. grow 5. arise, ripen, train
6. appear, detect, evolve, expand,
mature, reveal 7. advance, convert,
enlarge, expound, further, improve,
perfect, promote 8. discover, generate
9. elaborate (details)
developed . . . 4. ripe, zoon 5. adult
6. mature, mellow 7. grownup
8. improved 9. perfected 10. precocious
development . . . 6. growth 7. changes,
endysis 8. increase, maturity
9. evolution, expansion, formation,
unfolding 10. maturation
11. elaboration, improvement,
ontogenesis 12. phylogenesis
devest . . . 5. strip 6. denude, divest
7. deprive, undress 8. alienate
Devi (Hind) . . . 3. Uma 4. Kali 5. Durga,
Gauri 6. Chandi, Shakti 7. heroine,
Parvati 8. divinity 9. Haimavati
deviate . . . 3. err, yaw 4. hade, miss, slew,
vary, veer 5. sheer, stray 6. change,
depart, swerve, wander 7. deflect,
digress, diverge
deviation . . . 3. yaw 5. lapse 6. change
7. circuit, synesis 8. aberrant
9. aberrance, deformity, departure,
diverging, obliquity, variation
10. deflection, difference, digressing,
digression, distortion, divergence
11. abnormality 12. eccentricity
device . . . 4. plan, tool 5. motto,
shift, trick 6. design, desire, dingus,
gadget, scheme 7. adjunct, compass,
project, purpose 8. artifice, insignia
9. appliance, expedient, implement,
invention, stratagem 10. instrument
11. contrivance
device (pert to) . . .
bark peeling . . 8. stripper
clamping . . 4. vise 7. pincers
distilling . . 7. alembic
fabric stretching . . 7. stenter

heating . . 4. etna 5. stove
hoisting . . 5. crane, davit, lewis 6. garnet
7. derrick 8. elevator 9. parbuckle
leveling . . 6. gimbal
measuring . . 4. gage, tape 5. chain,
gauge, meter, ruler 9. ergometer,
yardstick 10. micrometer
nautical . . 4. bitt 5. cleat, otter 6. becket
8. paravane
regulating . . 5. valve 9. remontoir
spraying . . 8. atomizer 9. sprinkler
steering . . 4. helm 5. wheel 6. rudder,
tiller
stopping . . 5. brake, sprag
devil . . . 3. imp 4. deil, deva, evil, haze
5. annoy, demon, error, fiend, grill,
ruler (of Hell), Satan, tease 7. hellion,
serpent, tempter, torment 8. printer's
9. archenemy, daredevil, dust devil
devil (pert to) . . .
dog . . 6. marine
bird . . 3. owl 5. swift 10. goatsucker
fish . . 3. ray 5. manta, whale (gray)
7. octopus
grass . . 7. Bermuda
lore . . 10. demonology
tree . . 4. dita
Devil, the . . . 5. Deuce, Eblis, Satan
6. Azazel, Belial, Diablo, Teufel
7. Ahriman, Amaimon (Amammon),
diavolo, Evil One, Lucifer, Old Nick,
Sammael, Shaitan (Sheitan)
8. Apollyon, Asmodeus, Diabolos
9. Archenemy, Archfiend, Beelzebub
11. Auld Clootie 14. Mephistopheles
devilish . . . 5. cruel 6. daring, rakish,
wicked 7. extreme, hellish, satanic
8. fiendish, infernal 9. chthonian
10. demoniacal 11. mischievous
deviltry . . . 6. malice 7. cruelty, devilry
8. mischief 9. diablerie, diabolism
10. black magic, wickedness
12. fiendishness
devious . . . 6. errant, erring, roving,
sinful 7. oblique, vagrant, winding
8. rambling, tortuous 9. deviative,
eccentric 10. circuitous 11. out-of-the-
way 14. unconventional
devise . . . 3. aim 4. form, plan 5. array,
build, frame 6. create, divide, evolve,
invent, scheme, will to 7. appoint,
arrange, bequest, concoct, fashion
8. bequeath, contrive 9. fabricate
10. distribute, excogitate 11. distinguish
deviser of IQ test . . . 5. Binet
devitalize . . . 3. sap 6. weaken
devoid . . . 4. free, void 5. empty
6. faulty, vacant 7. without 9. destitute
11. nonexistent
devoid of . . .
feeling . . 9. apathetic, insensate
interest . . 6. jejune
devote . . . 3. use, vow 5. apply 6. employ,
hallow, resign 7. address, consign,
destine 8. dedicate, set apart
10. consecrate 11. appropriate
devoted . . . 5. loyal, pious, vowed
6. doomed, loving 7. betaken, zealous
8. addicted, constant, faithful, friendly,
obedient 9. dedicated, engrossed,
patriotic

devotee ... 3. fan, ist, nun 4. monk
6. votary 7. epicure, fanatic, Pietist
8. aesthete (esthete), partisan

devotion ... 4. love, zeal 5. ardor, piety
6. novena, prayer 7. pietism, worship
8. idolatry 9. addiction, adoration,
constancy 10. attachment, dedication,
devoutness, friendship 11. devotedness,
earnestness, engrossment
12. consecration 13. appropriation,
religiousness

devour ... 3. eat 4. bolt, gulp, wolf
5. gorge, use up, waste 6. absorb,
engulf 7. consume, engorge, swallow
(up) 8. prey upon 9. devastate
10. annihilate

devout ... 4. holy, warm 5. godly, pious
6. hearty, solemn 7. cordial, devoted,
saintly, sincere, zealous 8. reverent
9. religious, righteous 10. worshipful

dew ... 4. rime 5. bedew, bloom, roris

dewy ... 5. roral, roric

dexterity ... 3. art 4. knack, magic,
skill 7. ability, address, aptness,
finesse, sleight 8. aptitude, deftness,
facility 9. smartness 10. adroitness
15. right-handedness

dexterous ... 3. apt 4. deft, yare 5. adept,
handy, quick, ready 6. adroit, artful,
clever 7. skilful 8. skillful 11. right-
handed

dextral ... 5. right (to the) 9. favorable

diabolical ... 5. cruel 6. wicked 7. beastly,
demonic, hellish, satanic, ungodly
8. damnable, demoniac, devilish,
fiendish, infernal

diacritic ... 4. mark 5. point 7. symptom
10. diagnostic 14. distinguishing

diacritical mark ... 5. breve, tilde 6. tittle
9. diaeresis (dieresis)

diadem ... 5. crown, tiara 6. anadem,
circle, emblem, empire, fillet 7. coronet
8. headband, insignia, ornament
11. sovereignty

diaeresis, dieresis ... 4. mark 5. break
8. division 10. resolution

diagnose ... 7. analyze 8. construe
9. interpret

diagnosis ... 8. analysis, decision,
nosology 9. prognosis 14. interpretation

diagonal ... 6. bias 7. oblique 8. bendwise
(Her) 10. transverse 11. cater-corner
13. cater-cornered

diagram ... 4. draw, icon, plan, plot,
tree 5. chart, epure, gamut, graph
6. design 7. drawing 9. blueprint

dial ... 4. disk 5. plate 8. horologe
9. indicator, timepiece 11. chronometer

dialect ... 5. idiom, lingo 6. patois,
speech 7. diction 8. language, locution,
parlance 10. vernacular

dialect (pert to) ...
Afrikaans .. 4. Taal
Aramaic .. 6. Syriac
Aryan .. 4. Pali
provincial .. 6. patois
Semitic .. 4. Geez

diameter ... 2. pi (3.1416) 4. bore 5. width
6. module, radius 7. breadth, caliber
(calibre) 9. thickness

diametric, diametrical ... 6. averse

7. adverse 8. antipode, opposite
9. antipodal, diametral

diamond ... 3. gem, ice 5. cards, field
(baseball), jager, jewel, plane 6. carbon
7. adamant, infield, lozenge, rhombus
8. treasure

diamond (pert to) ...
base .. 5. culet
crystal .. 7. glassie
cutting .. 4. bort
cutting cups .. 3. dop
famed .. 4. pitt 5. Sancy 6. Orloff
7. Lesotho (601 carat) 8. Cullinan, Koh-
i-noor 9. Excelsior 10. Great Mogul
14. Star of the South
surface .. 5. facet
weight .. 5. carat (karat)

Diamond State ... 8. Delaware

diaphanous ... 4. fine, thin 5. filmy,
gauzy, lucid, sheer 6. flimsy
9. gossamery 11. translucent,
transparent

diaphragm ... 4. wall 6. middle, septum
7. midriff 9. partition

diary ... 3. log 6. record 7. journal
8. register 9. chronicle
13. autobiography

diaskeuast ... 6. editor 7. reviser

diatribe ... 6. screed, tirade 7. lecture
8. berating, harangue 9. invective,
philippic 10. discussion (prolonged)

dice ... 3. cog, die (sing) 4. cube, game,
sice (6's) 5. bones, craps, cubes
7. ivories, tessera

Dickens characters ... 3. Tim 4. Dora,
Nell 5. Fagin, Miggs, Sikes 6. Cuttle
7. Barnaby, Scrooge 9. Pecksniff
10. Chuzzlewit 11. Oliver Twist

Dickens pseudonym ... 3. Boz

dictate ... 3. law 4. rule 5. maxim,
order, utter 6. advise, dictum, enjoin,
impose 7. command, deliver, require,
suggest 9. prescribe 10. injunction

dictatorial ... 5. bossy 6. lordly
7. pompous 8. absolute, arrogant,
despotic, dogmatic, oracular, positive
9. imperious, masterful, pragmatic
10. autocratic, dogmatical, imperative,
peremptory 11. categorical,
domineering, magisterial, opinionated,
overbearing 13. authoritative

diction ... 5. style 8. language, parlance,
phrasing 9. elocution 10. vocabulary
11. enunciation, phraseology
14. expressiveness

dictionary ... 5. words 7. calepin, lexicon
8. wordbook 9. reference 10. vocabulary
11. terminology

dictionary compiler ... 7. Webster
(Noah) 13. lexicographer

dictum ... 3. saw 5. adage, maxim
6. saying 7. opinion, precept, proverb
8. aphorism, apothegm 11. declaration

didactic ... 8. teaching 9. mentorial
10. preceptive, instructive

dido ... 5. antic, caper, prank, trick 6. frolic

Dido (also Elissa) ... 5. Queen (of
Carthage) 8. Princess (Tyrian)

die ... see also *dice* 4. fade, mold, pass,
seal, wane 5. stamp 6. expire, perish,
recede, vanish, wither 7. decease,

succumb 8. languish 12. extinguished (to be)

die-hard . . . 4. Tory 11. British Army 12. Conservative

dies . . . 3. day

dies atri . . . 9. black days

dies faustus . . . 13. favorable omen (day of)

diet . . . 4. fare 5. board 6. Hoftag, ration, viands 7. Council, Landtag, regimen 8. assembly, Kreistag 9. allowance, nutrition, Reichstag 10. Parliament

Diet (of) . . . 5. Worms (1521) 6. Speyer (1529), Spires 8. Augsburg (1530)

dietetics . . . 8. sitology 9. nutrition 12. biochemistry, dietotherapy

differ . . . 4. vary 5. clash 7. dispute, dissent, quarrel 8. disagree

difference . . . 3. sum 5. shade 6. nuance 8. variance 10. inequality, unlikeness 11. contrariety, distinction, distinguish 12. disagreement, discriminate 13. differentiate, dissimilarity

different . . . 4. many 5. novel, other 6. divers, sundry, unlike 7. diverse, several, unequal, unusual, variant 8. assorted, contrary, distinct, manifold, opposite, separate, variform 9. divergent, otherwise 10. dissimilar, variegated 11. diversified 13. heterogeneous

different place . . . 9. elsewhere 10. otherwhere

difficulty . . . 3. bar, rub 4. clog, crux, knot, snag 5. cavil, check, demur, nodus 6. plight, scrape, strait 7. barrier, problem, trouble 8. obstacle 9. hindrance 10. impediment, ruggedness 11. obstruction 12. disagreement

difficulty in swallowing . . . 9. dysphagia

diffidence . . . 5. doubt, qualm 7. anxiety, modesty 8. distrust, humility, timidity 10. hesitation 11. bashfulness 12. apprehension

diffident . . . 3. coy, shy 5. timid 6. modest 7. anxious 8. doubtful, reserved, retiring 9. shrinking, unwilling 11. distrustful 12. apprehensive

diffuse . . . 4. full, shed 5. strew 6. expand, extend, prolix 7. copious, perplex, pervade, publish, radiate, refract, verbose 8. disperse 9. redundant 10. widespread

diffused . . . 5. loose 6. sparse 7. flowing 9. dispersed

diffusion . . . 7. osmosis 9. pervasion, radiation 10. dispersion, refraction

dig . . . 3. jab 4. find, grub, mine, open, pion, pod, root 5. delve, dwell, spade 6. exhume, loosen, pierce, plunge, search, thrust 7. extract, unearth 8. excavate 10. understand

digamy . . . 11. deuterogamy 12. twice married (legally)

digest . . . 4. code 5. brief 6. abrégé, codify 7. epitome, Pandect 8. abstract, classify, synopsis 10. assimilate, compendium

digestion . . . 6. pepsis 8. eupepsia 9. dyspepsia, ingestion 10. absorption 12. alimentation, assimilation

digestive secretions . . . 4. bile, gall 6. pepsin, rennin 7. chalone, gastric, glucase, hormone, maltase 8. salivary, thyroxin 9. endocrine 10. intestinal, pancreatic

digestive tract . . . 7. enteron 15. alimentary canal

digger . . . 3. loy, pal 4. plow, wasp 5. spade 6. Indian, sapper 7. comrade, soldier 8. Levelers 9. excavator 12. New Zealander

digit . . . 3. toe 4. unit 5. thumb 6. finger, number (under 10) 7. dewclaw, integer, measure

digits repeated . . . 8. repetend

digitus . . . 6. finger, tarsus 8. dactylus

dignified . . . 5. grand, lofty, manly, sober, staid 6. august, graced, sedate 7. courtly, pompous, togated 8. decorous, ennobled, imposing, majestic 9. venerable 11. ceremonious 12. aristocratic

dignify . . . 5. exalt, grace, honor 7. elevate, ennoble 9. solemnize 11. distinguish

dignitary . . . 3. don 4. rank 5. mogul 6. priest, sachem 7. magnate, notable, prelate 9. clergyman

dignity . . . 4. rank 5. grace, honor 6. status 7. decorum, majesty 8. nobility, prestige, standing 9. loftiness, nobleness 10. excellence, sedateness

diagraph . . . 8. ligature 9. diphthong

digress . . . 4. veer 5. shift 6. swerve, wander 7. deviate 9. turn aside 10. transgress

digression . . . 4. loop 6. ecbole 7. circuit, episode 8. excursus 9. deviation, excursion, obliquity 10. discussion

digressive . . . 8. rambling 9. deviative, excursive, wandering 10. circuitous, discursive

dike, dyke . . . 3. bar, dig, gap 4. bank, gulf, ha-ha, mole, pond, pool 5. ditch, levee, mound 7. barrier, channel 8. causeway, estacade 9. earthwork 10. embankment 11. watercourse 13. fortification

diked land . . . 6. polder

dike rock . . . 7. odinite

dik-dik . . . 8. antelope

dilapidation . . . 4. ruin 5. decay, waste 7. breakup 9. disrepair 10. impairment 11. dissolution 13. decomposition 14. disintegration

dilate . . . 5. bulge, swell, widen 6. expand 7. distend, enlarge, inflate 9. expatiate

dilation . . . 7. ectasia, ectasis 8. swelling 9. expansion 10. dilatation, distension

dilatory . . . 3. lax 4. slow 5. slack, tardy 6. fabian, remiss 8. backward, delaying, inactive, sluggish 10. behindhand 13. lackadaisical 15. procrastinating

dilemma . . . 4. trap 5. brike (obs) 6. snare 8. argument, quandary 10. perplexity 11. alternative, predicament

dilettante . . . 7. amateur, dabbler, devotee, esthete (aesthete)

diligence . . . 4. care, heed 6. effort 7. caution 8. industry, sedulity 9. assiduity, attention, constancy

10. stagecoach 11. application, earnestness, painstaking 12. heedlessness, perseverance, sedulousness 15. industriousness

diligent ... 4. busy 6. active 7. operose 8. sedulous 9. assiduous, attentive, laborious 11. industrious, persevering

dill, dill seed ... 4. anet, herb 5. anise (Bib) 6. fennel

dillydally ... 3. lag 6. linger, loiter, trifle 9. vacillate 12. shilly-shally 13. procrastinate

dilute ... 3. cut 4. thin 6. debase, rarefy, reduce, weaken 8. lengthen 9. attenuate 10. adulterate 12. denaturalize

diluted ... 4. thin, weak 7. reduced, thinned, watered 10. attenuated

dim ... 4. dull, fade, pale 5. bleak, blear, faint 6. darken 7. darkish, dimness, eclipse, obscure 8. overcast 10. caliginous, indistinct, mysterious

dimension ... 4. size 6. extent, height, length 7. breadth 9. magnitude, thickness 11. measurement 13. circumference

diminish ... 3. ebb 4. bate, fade, pare, ploy, wane 5. abase, abate, taper, peter, taper 6. lessen, recede, reduce, weaken 7. curtail, dwindle 8. decrease, subtract 9. disparage

diminution ... 5. abate, taper 7. litotes 8. decrease, lowering 9. decrement, lessening, reduction 10. moderation

diminutive ... 3. wee 4. runt, slip 5. minny, small 6. bantam, little, peewee, petite 7. bendlet

diminutive suffix ... 2. el, ie 3. ole, ule 4. ette

dimmer ... 6. rheostat

din ... 4. ding 5. clang, noise 6. clamor, hubbub, racket, rattle, tumult, uproar 7. clatter, turmoil 9. commotion

diner ... 5. eater

dingle ... 4. dale, dell, glen, ring, vale 6. jingle, tingle, tinkle, valley 7. tremble 9. storm door

dining room ... 4. hall 5. salon 6. spence 7. cenacle 8. mess hall 9. refectory 12. salle à manger

dining science ... 10. aristology

dinosaur ... 7. reptile 8. sauropod 9. Sauropoda 10. Diplodocus, Morosaurus 11. Ornithopoda, Stegosaurus 12. Brontosaurus, Ceratosaurus, Megalosaurus, Palaeosaurus 13. Atlantosaurus, Tyrannosaurus

diocese ... 3. see 6. parish 8. district, province 9. bishopric 12. jurisdiction

Diocletian martyr (Rome) ... 5. Agnes

Dionysian ... 4. wild 5. frenzied, sensuous 9. orgiastic

Dionysus (pert to) ...
 birthplace .. 6. Thebes
 father .. 4. Zeus
 festival .. 8. Dionysia
 god of (Gr) .. 4. wine (Bacchus, later) 10. vegetation
 lover .. 6. Selene
 mother .. 6. Semele

Dioscuri, The (Gr Myth) ... 4. cult

5. twins (Castor and Pollux) 8. Castores 10. Polydeuces

dip ... 3. dap, dib, sop 4. bail, dunk, lade 5. merge, merse, pitch, rinse, scoop, slope, souse 6. candle, plunge 7. baptize, immerse 9. declivity 10. pickpocket 11. hors d'oeuvre

diphthong, dipthong ... 5. sound 7. digraph 8. ligature

diploma ... 8. testamur 9. sheepskin 10. credential 11. certificate, testimonial

diplomacy ... 4. tact 5. address, cunning 9. dexterity 10. artfulness, discretion 11. arbitration, diplomatism, negotiation, savoir-faire

diplomat ... 5. doyen (head), envoy 6. consul 7. attaché 8. emissary, minister 10. ambassador, politician 15. chargé d'affaires, plenipotentiary

diplomatic ... 6. crafty 7. cunning 8. consular 11. mediatorial

diplomatic corps, staff ... 7. embassy 8. legation 17. corps diplomatique

dipsomania ... 9. addiction, oenomania, potomania 10. alcoholism 15. delirium tremens

dipthong ... see *diphthong*

dire ... 3. bad 4. base, evil, rank, want 5. awful, fatal, needy 6. deadly, dismal, funest, odious 7. baneful, doleful, fearful, ghastly 8. dreadful, horrible, terrible, ultimate 10. oppressive 12. inauspicious, overpowering

direct ... 3. ain, bid, con 4. bend, boss, head, lead, turn 5. order, pilot, refer, steer, teach 6. govern, manage 7. avigate, command, conduct, marshal 8. instruct, straight 9. influence

direction ... 3. way 4. airt, bent, care, east, west 5. avast, belay, north, route, south, trend 6. advice, course 7. address, command, pointer 8. guidance 10. management 11. instruction 15. superintendence

directly ... 4. soon 6. pronto 7. shortly 8. as soon as, promptly 9. forthwith, instantly, presently 11. immediately

directly opposite ... 9. antipodal, diametric 10. antipodean

director ... 4. boss 5. aimer (gunner) 6. conner, leader 7. manager, teacher 8. governor, producer 14. superintendent

director's cry ... 3. Cut!

direful ... 4. dire 6. woeful 8. dreadful, terrible 10. calamitous

dirge ... 4. keen, Mass, song 5. psalm, rites 6. lament 7. requiem 8. coronach

dirigible ... 4. Roma 5. blimp 7. balloon 10. Shenandoah 12. Graf Zeppelin

Dirigo ... 5. I Lead 7. I Direct (Maine motto)

dirk ... 4. snee, stab 5. knife, sword 6. dagger

dirt ... 3. mud 4. dust, foul, land, muck, soil 5. earth, filth, grime, stain 6. gossip, refuse 7. scandal, slander 9. obscenity

dirty ... 4. foul, mean 5. dingy, foggy, gusty, mucky, nasty 6. bemire, filthy, soiled, stormy, untidy 7. clouded, muddied, squalid, sullied

dis (pert to) . . .
Greek . . 5. Pluto
Norse . . 5. Freya 7. spirits 9. Valkyries 11. superhumans
prefix . . 5. twice 6. double
Roman . . 3. Dis 8. Dis pater 12. realm of Pluto

disable . . . 4. maim 5. unfit 6. impair, weaken 7. cripple 9. disparage, hamstring 10. disqualify 12. incapacitate

disadvantage . . . 3. out 4. harm, hurt 6. damage, injury 7. penalty, trouble 8. drawback, handicap 9. detriment, liability, prejudice 12. inexpedience 13. inconvenience

disagreeable . . . 4. edgy 5. cross, nasty 7. fulsome 8. unsavory 9. dissonant, invidious, irritable, offensive, repugnant 10. ill-humored, unpleasant 11. displeasing, ill-tempered, incongruous 13. uncomfortable

disagreement . . . 5. clash 7. detente, discord, dispute, dissent, wrangle 8. variance 9. diversity 10. contention, difference, dissension, unlikeness 11. contrariety, controversy, discrepancy, incongruity 13. nonconformity 16. misunderstanding

disappear . . . 3. die 4. face, pass 5. cease 6. be lost, perish, vanish 7. dwindle 8. evanesce 9. evaporate

disappoint . . . 4. balk, bilk, fail, fall, foil 6. baffle, thwart 7. let down 9. frustrate 10. disenchant, dissatisfy 11. disillusion

disappointment . . . 3. rue 6. defeat 7. failure 10. bafflement 11. frustration 15. dissatisfaction

disapprobation . . . 5. odium 11. disapproval 12. condemnation 13. disparagement

disapproval . . . 3. boo 4. hiss, veto 7. censure, protest 9. objection, rejection 12. condemnation 14. disapprobation

disarrange . . . 4. muss 5. upset 6. foul up, jumble 7. disturb 8. disorder, unsettle 10. discompose 11. disorganize

disarray . . . 5. strip 6. unrobe 7. despoil, undress, unkempt 8. disorder 9. confusion, ungarment 10. disarrange, dishabille 12. discomposure, dishevelment

disaster . . . 4. evil, ruin 6. mishap 8. accident, calamity, casualty, fatality 9. cataclysm, mischance 10. misfortune 11. catastrophe 12. misadventure

disastrous . . . 4. dire 7. unlucky 8. ill-fated 9. ill-boding 10. calamitous 11. destructive, unfortunate 12. unpropitious

disavow . . . 4. deny 6. abjure, disown, recant, refuse 7. decline, retract 8. disclaim, renounce 9. disaffirm, repudiate

disbeliever . . . 5. pagan 7. atheist, heathen, heretic, infidel 8. agnostic

disburse . . . 5. spend 6. defray, expend, pay out

disbursement . . . 5. outgo 6. outlay 7. payment 8. spending 11. expenditure

disc . . . see also *disk* 3. man 4. dial, puck 5. medal, plate, quoit, wheel 6. circle, record 7. discoid 8. artifact 9. gyroscope, medallion

discard . . . 4. drip, shed 5. scrap, sluff 6. disuse, reject, remove 7. abandon, cast off, dismiss, forsake 9. eliminate, eradicate, throw away

discern . . . 3. see, spy 4. espy, know, read, view 5. sight 6. behold, descry, detect 7. witness 8. discover, perceive 10. understand 11. distinguish 12. discriminate 13. differentiate

discernible . . . 7. evident, obvious, visible 8. apparent, distinct, knowable, manifest 11. conspicuous, perceptible 15. distinguishable

discerning . . . 4. sage 5. acute, sharp 6. astute, shrewd 9. sagacious 14. discriminating, discriminative

discernment . . . 4. tact 5. taste 6. acumen 7. insight 8. sagacity 9. sharpness 10. astuteness, perception, shrewdness 12. perspicacity 14. discrimination

discharge . . . 2. do 4. bang, cass, fire, sack, shot 5. blast, egest, eject, erupt, expel, exude, flash, salvo, shoot, speed 6. acquit, bounce, defray, exempt, pay off, report, unload, volley 7. dismiss, execute, explode, payment, quietus, release 8. emission, eruption 9. acquittal, dismissal, excretion, execution, explosion, fusillade 10. accomplish, detonation, observance 11. performance

disciple . . . 5. chela, Judas, pupil 7. apostle, convert, learner, scholar, student 8. adherent, believer, follower

disciples (Bib) . . . 6. twelve (72, Vulgate) 10. Christians

disciplinarian . . . 7. Puritan, teacher, trainer 8. martinet

discipline . . . 4. rule, whip 6. govern, punish 7. chasten, control, culture, educate, penance, scourge 8. training 9. education, restraint 10. correction, punishment 11. castigation, instruction, self-control 12. chastisement 13. regimentation

disclaim . . . 4. deny 6. abjure, cry out, disown, recant, refuse, reject 7. disavow 8. abnegate, disallow, renounce 9. repudiate

disclose . . . 4. bare, open, show, tell 5. utter 6. expose, impart, reveal, unmask, unveil 7. divulge, uncloak, unclose 8. discover, indicate

disclosure . . . 6. exposé 8. exposure 9. discovery, revealing, unmasking, unveiling 10. appearance, revealment, revelation

discolor . . . 4. spot 5. stain 6. bruise 7. distain (anc) tarnish 9. ecchymose (by blood)

discolored . . . 4. doty (by decay) 5. faded 7. altered 8. ustulate 10. variegated

discomfit . . . 4. balk, rout 5. upset 6. baffle, defeat, dismay 7. confuse 9. embarrass, frustrate, overthrow 10. disconcert

discomfiture . . . 4. rout 6. defeat, flurry

7. letdown 9. confusion, overthrow
10. bafflement 11. frustration
13. embarrassment, inconvenience
14. disappointment

discomfort . . . 4. pain 6. sorrow
7. misease 8. distress 9. annoyance
10. uneasiness 11. displeasure
13. embarrassment, inconvenience

discommode . . . 6. bother, molest,
put out 7. trouble 9. incommode
13. inconvenience

discompose . . . 4. fret 5. upset 6. excite,
flurry, rubble 7. agitate, confuse,
derange, disturb, fluster 8. unsettle
9. embarrass 10. disarrange, disconcert

disconcert . . . 5. abash, alarm 6. rattle,
thwart 7. confuse, disturb, fluster,
nonplus 8. bewilder 9. discomfit,
embarrass 10. disarrange

disconnect . . . 5. sever 6. detach, unyoke
7. disjoin 8. disunite, separate, uncouple

disconnected . . . 6. broken 8. detached,
rambling 9. desultory, scattered
10. disjointed, incoherent
11. unconnected

disconsolate . . . 3. sad 6. gloomy,
woeful 7. forlorn 8. desolate, hopeless
9. sorrowful 10. despairing, despondent,
melancholy 12. inconsolable

discontent . . . 6. misery, unrest
8. disquiet 9. unquietude, uneasiness
11. displeasure, unhappiness
14. discontentment 15. dissatisfaction

discontinue . . . 3. end 4. drop, quit, stop
5. cease 6. desist, give up 7. abandon,
refrain 8. intermit 9. terminate

discord . . . 3. din 5. noise 6. strife
7. dissent 8. disunity, variance
9. cacophony, Discordia, harshness
10. antagonism, contention, difference,
discordant, disharmony, dissension,
dissonance 11. altercation
12. disagreement

discord (goddess of) . . . 3. Ate 4. Eris

discordant . . . 5. harsh 7. grating, jarring
8. contrary, jangling 11. cacophonous,
disagreeing, incongruous, quarrelsome,
unmelodious 12. inconsistent,
inharmonious 14. irreconcilable

discordant (pert to) . . .
music . . 8. scordato
serenade . . 9. charivari 10. callithump
sound . . 8. jangle

discount . . . 3. cut 4. agio 6. rebate,
reduce 8. mark down 9. abatement,
allowance, reduction 10. concession,
percentage

discourage . . . 4. damp 5. check, daunt,
deter 6. deject, dismay, oppose
7. depress 8. dispirit, dissuade
10. dishearten

discourse . . . 3. talk, tell 5. essay,
paper (written), prose, speak, spiel
6. homily, lesson, screed, sermon
7. account, address, article, declaim,
discant, dissert, expound, lecture,
narrate, oration 8. converse, treatise
9. expatiate, narrative 10. exposition,
recitation 12. conversation, dissertation

discourteous . . . 4. rude 7. uncivil
8. impolite, insolent 9. ungallant

10. ungracious 13. disrespectful

discover . . . 3. see 4. espy, find 5. learn
6. descry, detect, expose 7. exhibit, find
out, uncover, unearth 9. apprehend,
ascertain

discoverer . . . 3. spy 5. scout

discoverer of . . .
America . . 4. Eric (the Red) 7. Vikings
8. Columbus (1492)
blood circulation . . 6. Harvey
electric light . . 6. Edison
North Pole . . 5. Peary (1909)
radium . . 5. Curie (Madame)
South Pole . . 8. Amundsen (1911)
telegraph . . 5. Morse (Samuel)
telephone . . 4. Bell (Alexander)
vaccination . . 6. Jenner

discovery, logic of . . . 8. heuretic

discredit . . . 5. doubt 7. asperse, falsify,
scandal 8. disgrace, dishonor, disprove,
distrust 9. disbelief, disparage,
disrepute, misgiving, suspicion
10. invalidate 11. discredence

discreet . . . 4. wary 5. civil 6. polite
7. careful, mindful, politic, prudent
8. cautious 9. judicious, selective
11. circumspect 12. noncommittal
13. discretionary

discrepancy . . . 8. variance 9. disaccord,
disparity, diversity 10. difference
11. contrariety 12. disagreement
13. inconsistency 15. incompatibility

discretion . . . 4. tact, will 6. option
7. caution, reserve 8. judgment,
prudence, wariness 11. disjunction
12. cautiousness, discreetness
13. discontinuity, judiciousness,
secretiveness 14. circumspection,
discrimination

discretionary . . . 7. politic, prudent
8. discreet 9. arbitrary, judicious,
voluntary 10. prudential 11. considerate
14. discriminating

discriminate . . . 6. divide, screen, secern
8. separate, set apart 11. distinguish
13. differentiate

discrimination . . . 5. taste 6. acumen,
option 9. prejudice 10. discretion
11. discernment, distinction,
penetration, segregation

discursive . . . 6. roving 7. cursory
9. desultory, diffusive, wandering
10. circuitous, digressive

discus . . . 4. disk 5. plate, quoit

discuss . . . 3. air, rap 4. moot 5. argue,
treat 6. confer, debate, parley
7. bargain, canvass, dispute, dissert,
mention 8. talk over 9. discourse,
thrash out

discus thrower . . . 10. discobolus

disdain . . . 5. pride, scorn 7. askance,
contemn, despise 8. contempt
9. arrogance 11. haughtiness
16. contemptuousness

disease . . . 6. malady 7. ailment, illness,
trouble 8. disorder, sickness 9. affection,
infirmity 10. affliction, disability
11. derangement

disease (of) . . .
animals (Afr) . . 5. nenta
apoplexy . . 4. esca

apples . . 7. stippen 9. bitter pit
blood . . 6. anemia 8. leukemia
  (leukaemia, leucemia)
cattle . . 5. hoose (hooze) 6. nagana,
  wheeze 7. anthrax
chickens . . 3. pip 4. roup
diet . . 7. rickets 8. pellagra, rachitis
divers . . 5. bends 7. caisson
dog . . 5. lyssa 6. rabies 11. hydrophobia
eye . . 6. caligo 7. pinkeye 8. cataract,
  glaucoma, trachoma 9. amaurosis
  14. conjunctivitis
fungus . . 6. mildew 9. elm blight
Oriental . . 8. beriberi
painful . . 7. lumbago 9. arthritis
plant . . 4. rust, smut 5. ergot, scald
  6. Panama (banana) 7. erinose (grape)
potato, tomato . . 8. dartrose
skin . . 5. hives, psora 6. eczema, herpes,
  tetter 7. scabies 8. impetigo, shingles
  9. psoriasis, urticaria 10. erysipelas
stonecutter's . . 9. silicosis
sugar cane . . 5. sereh
disease (pert to) . . .
  classification . . 8. nosology
    10. nosography
  decline . . 9. catabasis
  determination of . . 9. diagnosis
  germ transfer . . 7. vection
  native to . . 7. endemic
  outlook . . 9. prognosis
  science of . . 8. etiology, medicine
  spread of . . 8. epidemic
  suffix . . 4. itis, osis
  treatment . . 7. therapy 12. kinesiatrics
disembark . . . 4. land 6. alight, debark
  7. deplane, detrain, pile out (sl)
disembowel . . . 3. gut 10. eviscerate
disengage . . . 5. clear 6. detach, loosen
  7. release 8. liberate, unfasten
  9. extricate 11. disencumber,
  disentangle 12. disembarrass
disentangle . . . 4. card, comb 5. clear,
  loose, ravel, solve 6. evolve, sleave,
  sleeve 7. unravel, unsnare, untwine,
  untwist 8. simplify 9. disengage,
  extricate 10. disinvolve, unscramble
disfavor . . . 7. dislike 8. distaste
  9. detriment, disrepute 10. alienation
  11. disapproval, displeasure
  14. discountenance
disfigure . . . 3. mar 4. scar 6. deface,
  deform, injure, mangle, uglify
  7. blemish 8. mutilate
disgorge . . . 4. barf (sl), spew, vent
  5. eject, eruct, erupt, expel, heave,
  vomit 7. exhaust 9. discharge
  10. relinquish 11. regurgitate
disgrace . . . 5. abase, odium, shame,
  shend, sully 7. attaint, degrade, distain,
  obloquy, upbraid 8. dishonor, ignominy,
  reproach 9. discredit, disesteem,
  disrepute, humiliate 10. opprobrium
  11. abomination, humiliation
  13. disparagement
disguise . . . 3. mum (mumm) 4. mask,
  veil 5. cloak, feign 6. covert, masque
  7. conceal, costume, falsify, pretend
  9. dissemble, incognito, inebriate
  10. camouflage, masquerade
  11. dissimulate 12. misrepresent

disgust . . . 6. nausea 7. offense, quarrel
  8. aversion, loathing, nauseate
  9. animosity, annoyance, antipathy,
  revulsion 10. abhorrence, repugnance
  11. abomination
disgusting . . . 5. gross, nasty 6. filthy,
  odious 9. loathsome, obnoxious,
  offensive, repellent, repulsive, revolting,
  sickening
dish . . . 3. jar, pot 4. boat (gravy) 5. cruse,
  nappy, paten, plate 6. patera, saucer,
  tureen 7. charger (anc), platter, ramekin
  9. casserole
dish (food) . . . 5. kibbe (kibbeh), pilaf,
  pilau, salmi 6. hachis, haslet, omelet,
  potage, ragout 7. bok choy, chowder,
  falafel (felafel), pudding, soufflé 10. egg
  foo yong, shish kabob 11. ratatouille
dishabille . . . 6. kimono 7. négligé,
  undress 8. bathrobe, negligee, peignoir
  9. housecoat, nightgown
dishearten . . . 5. amate (anc), appal,
  daunt, deter, unman 6. deject, dismay
  7. depress, unnerve 8. dispirit
  10. disconcert, discourage
disheveled . . . 5. tousy 6. frowzy,
  mussed, shaggy, untidy 7. ruffled,
  tousled, tumbled, unkempt 8. deranged,
  uncombed 10. disarrayed, disordered
  11. disarranged
dishonest . . . 4. base 5. false, lying
  6. crafty, unjust 7. corrupt, crooked,
  knavish 8. rascally, scheming
  9. deceitful, truthless 10. fraudulent,
  mendacious, perfidious, untruthful
  12. dishonorable
dishonor . . . 5. shame 6. defame,
  infamy 7. debauch, degrade, obloquy
  8. disgrace, ignominy, reproach
  9. desecrate, disrepute, improbity
  10. disrespect, opprobrium
  13. disparagement
dishonorable . . . 7. ignoble 8. infamous,
  shameful 9. dishonest 10. inglorious
  11. disesteemed, disgraceful
  12. disreputable
disillusion . . . 10. disquixote
disillusioned . . . 8. thwarted
  12. disappointed, disenchanted
disinclination . . . 7. dislike 8. aversion,
  distaste 10. reluctance, repugnance
  12. disaffection 13. indisposition
disinclined . . . 6. averse 8. indolent
  9. reluctant, unwilling 10. indisposed
disinfectant . . . 5. Lysol 6. cresol,
  iodine, phenol 7. alcohol 9. germicide
  10. antiseptic 12. formaldehyde
disintegrate . . . 5. decay, erode 7. break
  up, corrode, crumble, disband, resolve
  8. dissolve 9. decompose
  11. disorganize
disinter . . . 5. dig up 6. exhume, reveal
disjoin . . . 4. part, undo 5. sever,
  untie 6. detach, sunder, unhook
  7. unhitch 8. disunite, separate,
  unbutton 9. disengage 10. disconnect,
  dissociate
disk, disc . . . 4. puck 5. medal, paten,
  plate, quoit, wafer, wheel 6. harrow,
  record, sequin 7. discoid, medalet
  9. faceplate, gyroscope, medallion

dislike ... 4. mind 5. odium 6. detest
8. aversion, distaste 9. antipathy,
disrelish 12. disaffection

dislike of children ... 9. misopedia

dislike of home ... 9. ecophobia

disloyal ... 5. false 6. fickle, untrue
9. faithless 10. inconstant, perfidious,
unfaithful 11. treacherous

dismal ... 3. sad, wan 4. dark 5. black,
bleak, drear, lurid 6. dreary, gloomy,
somber 7. doleful, joyless, Stygian,
unhappy, unlucky 8. dolorous, dreadful,
funereal, lonesome, mournful, overcast,
sinister 9. ill-omened, sorrowful
10. calamitous, depressing, lugubrious
11. pessimistic, unfortunate

dismantle ... 4. raze, undo 5. strip
6. divest 7. deprive, destroy, disrobe,
uncloak 8. demolish 11. disassemble

dismay ... 4. fear 5. alarm, daunt
6. appall, fright, terror 8. affright,
bewilder 9. dejection 10. depression,
disconcert 12. apprehension
13. consternation 14. discouragement

dismiss ... 4. drip, fire 5. amand, amove,
eject, exile, remue 6. acquit, bounce,
depose, recall, refute, shelve 7. forgive,
release 8. relegate 9. discharge,
disregard 11. relinquish

dismount ... 6. alight 7. descend,
unhorse, unmount 11. disassemble

disobedient ... 7. forward, froward,
wayward 8. mutinous 10. rebellious,
refractory 11. intractable
12. contumacious

disorder ... 3. tic 4. mess, riot 5. chaos,
deray, snarl 6. malady, tumult
7. ailment, anarchy, derange, illness,
misdeed 8. disarray, paranoia, sickness
9. confusion, craziness, distemper,
paranomia 10. discompose, revolution
11. lawlessness, misdemeanor
12. irregularity 13. indisposition
14. disarrangement 15. disorganization

disorderly ... 3. bad 5. mussy, rowdy
6. unruly 7. chaotic, naughty, violent
8. confused, rowdyish, slipshod
9. irregular, offensive, turbulent
12. ungovernable, unmanageable

disorganization ... 5. decay 7. anarchy,
breakup, split-up 8. disorder
10. separation 11. destruction,
dissolution 13. disbandment
14. disarrangement, disintegration

disown ... 4. deny 5. expel 6. recant,
reject 7. disavow 8. disclaim, renounce
9. disaffirm, repudiate 10. disinherit

disparage ... 3. dis 4. slam, slur 5. decry,
lower 6. lessen, slight 7. degrade,
detract, run down 8. bad-mouth,
belittle, dishonor, minimize 9. discredit
10. depreciate, disapprove, disrespect,
undervalue

disparagement ... 7. diasyrm 8. disgrace
9. indignity 10. detraction
12. depreciation

disparaging ... 8. decaying
10. defamatory, pejorative
11. unfavorable

disparity ... 3. gap 7. deficit 8. shortage
10. deficiency, difference, inequality

dispart ... 4. open, rend, rive 5. break,
sever, split 6. cleave, divide

dispassionate ... 4. cool, fair 6. serene
8. composed, moderate 9. collected,
impartial, temperate, unruffled
11. unemotional 12. unprejudiced

dispatch ... 4. kill, mail, post, send,
slay 5. haste, speed 6. hasten
7. message 8. celerity, conclude,
expedite 9. diligence 10. accelerate,
accomplish, promptness

dispatch boat ... 5. aviso 6. packet

Dis pater (Rom) ... 3. god (underworld)
5. Pluto (Gr) 12. realm of Pluto

dispel ... 6. vanish 7. scatter 8. disperse
9. dissipate

dispensation ... 6. scheme 7. economy
9. exemption, remission 10. dispersion,
management, misericord (misericorde)
11. arrangement 12. distribution
13. apportionment 14. administration

dispense ... 4. deal, dole, give, vend
6. effuse, excuse, exempt 7. absolve
8. disperse 9. apportion 10. administer

dispenser of alms ... 7. almoner

disperse ... 3. sow 4. rout 5. strew
6. branch, spread, vanish 7. diffuse,
refract, scatter 9. apportion, dissipate
10. distribute 11. disseminate

dispirit ... 3. cow 4. damp 5. daunt
6. deject 7. depress 10. discourage,
dishearten, intimidate

displace ... 6. depose, mislay, remove
8. misplace 9. discharge, dislocate,
supersede 10. substitute

display ... 3. air 4. pomp, show,
wear 5. array 6. evince, flaunt,
parade, set out 7. exhibit, pageant,
splurge 8. emblazon 9. advertise
10. appearance 11. demonstrate,
ostentation 13. manifestation

display (pert to) ...
case .. 10. show window
in public .. 5. stage
of emotion .. 10. enthusiasm
of force (distant) .. 9. telenergy
of temper .. 5. scene 9. spectacle

displease ... 3. vex 4. miff, roil 5. anger,
annoy, pique 6. offend 7. provoke
8. irritate 10. dissatisfy

displeasure ... 5. anger 7. disgust,
dislike, offense, trouble 8. disfavor,
distaste 10. resentment, uneasiness
11. indignation, unhappiness
14. disapprobation 15. dissatisfaction

dispose (of) ... 3. set 4. give, mind, sell,
tend 5. order, place 6. adjust, assign,
bestow, settle 7. arrange, destroy,
discard, testate 8. give away, regulate
9. eliminate 10. distribute, relinquish

disposed ... 5. prone 7. settled, willing
8. arranged, assigned, inclined
11. distributed

disposed (pert to) ...
favorably .. 7. propend
to cling together .. 8. clannish
to doubt .. 9. skeptical
to please .. 11. complaisant

disposition ... 3. use 4. bent, bias,
mood, turn 6. animus, giving, morale,
nature, temper 7. control 8. tendency

9. character 10. management, settlement 11. arrangement, elimination, temperament 12. organization 13. apportionment

dispossess . . . 5. eject, evict 6. divest, refute 8. disseize

dispossessed . . . 6. bereft, ousted 7. ejected, evicted 8. deprived, divested 9. ejected, evicted 8. deprived, divested

disproof . . . 6. answer, denial 8. negation, rebuttal 10. refutation 11. confutation 12. invalidation

disprove . . . 5. belie, rebut 6. refute 7. confute 9. discredit 10. invalidate

disputation . . . 6. debate 7. polemic 8. argument 10. contention 11. controversy 12. conversation

disputatious . . . 7. eristic, polemic 11. contentious, quarrelsome 13. argumentative, controversial

dispute . . . 4. deny, feud, moot, spar 5. brawl, broil 6. bicker, debate, haggle, higgle, naggle 7. contest, dissent, protest, quarrel, wrangle 8. argument, squabble 11. altercation, controversy

disqualify . . . 5. debar 9. indispose 10. invalidate 12. incapacitate

disquiet . . . 3. vex 4. fret 5. alarm 6. excite 7. agitate, concern, disturb 8. distress, frighten 12. apprehension

disquisition . . . 7. essay 10. discussion 12. dissertation

disregard . . . 4. snub 6. ignore, slight 7. neglect 8. defiance 9. unconcern 11. inattention

disreputable . . . 3. low 4. base 5. seamy 7. raffish 8. shameful, unworthy 13. discreditable 15. persona non grata

disrespect . . . 7. affront 9. disesteem, insolence 10. incivility 11. discourtesy

disrespectful . . . 7. uncivil 8. impudent, insolent 10. irreverent 12. discourteous

disrupt . . . 4. part (forcibly), rend, tear 5. upset 6. thwart 11. disorganize

dissatisfaction . . . 8. vexation 10. discontent 11. displeasure, unsatisfied

dissect . . . 3. cut 6. divide 7. analyze 8. separate 9. anatomize

disseize (law) . . . 4. oust 5. evict 6. depose 10. dispossess 11. expropriate

dissemble . . . 4. hide 5. cloak, feign 7. conceal 8. disguise 9. disregard 11. counterfeit

disseminate . . . 3. sow 6. effuse, spread 7. publish, scatter 8. disperse 9. circulate, propagate

dissension . . . 7. discord 8. brouille, friction 10. dissidence 12. disagreement

dissent . . . 3. nay 8. apostasy, disagree 10. separation 12. disagreement, nonagreement 13. nonconformity 14. nonconcurrence

dissenter . . . 7. heretic, Sectary 8. apostate, recusant 9. protester 10. Protestant 13. nonconformist

dissertation . . . 5. essay, tract 6. debate, thesis 7. article, lecture 8. treatise 9. discourse 10. discussion, exposition 12. disquisition

dissidence . . . 7. dissent 8. variance 9. cacophony 10. difference, dissension

12. disagreement

dissimilarity . . . 7. variety 9. disparity, diversity 10. difference, unlikeness, unsameness 13. dissimilation, heterogeneity 17. heterogeneousness

dissipate . . . 5. spend, waste 6. dispel, expend 7. consume, scatter, shatter 8. dispense, dissolve, squander 9. disappear

dissipation . . . 4. loss 9. decrement, diffusion 10. dispersion, profligacy 11. consumption, prodigality 12. intemperance 13. disappearance, dissoluteness 14. disintegration

dissolute . . . 3. lax 4. lewd, wild 5. loose 6. loosed, rakish, wanton, wicked 7. lawless, vicious 8. reckless, uncurbed 9. abandoned, debauched, unbridled 10. dissipated, licentious, profligate 11. demoralized 12. unrestrained

dissolve . . . 4. fuse, melt 5. solve 7. adjourn, liquefy 9. decompose, disappear 11. disorganize 12. disintegrate

dissolved . . . 6. solute 7. soluble

dissonant . . . 5. harsh 7. grating, jarring 8. jangling 9. deviative, different, differing 10. discordant, discrepant 11. disagreeing, unmelodious 12. inconsistent, inharmonious 13. contradictory

dissuade . . . 5. deter 6. advise, dehort, divert 8. admonish 10. discourage, disincline 11. expostulate

distaff side . . . 5. women 6. female

distain . . . 5. stain, tinge 6. define 7. tarnish 8. discolor

distance . . . 4. step, yond 5. depth, range, space 6. offing 7. mileage, reserve, yardage 8. coldness, outstrip 9. aloofness, antiquity, dimension 10. remoteness

distant . . . 3. far, tel, yon 4. afar, cold, tele (pref) 5. aloof 6. remote, utmost, yonder 7. foreign 8. ulterior

distaste . . . 7. disgust 8. aversion 9. disrelish 10. repugnance 11. displeasure 14. disinclination 15. dissatisfaction

distasteful . . . 7. hateful 8. nauseous, unsavory 9. loathsome, offensive 10. disgusting, unpleasant 11. displeasing, unpalatable 12. disagreeable

distemper . . . 3. vex 4. soak 5. anger, color, steep 6. dilute, malady, ruffle 7. ailment, disease, disturb 8. painting (process), sickness 13. indisposition

distend . . . 4. grow 5. bulge, swell 6. dilate, expand, spread 7. enlarge, inflate, stretch 8. lengthen

distended . . . 5. tumid 7. bloated, swollen 8. inflated, patulous, puffed up

distich . . . 7. couplet 8. two lines

distill, distil . . . 4. leak 6. decoct, infuse 7. extract, squeeze, trickle 8. vaporize

distilling device . . . 5. flask 6. retort 7. alembic 10. distillery

distinct . . . 4. fair 5. clear 7. audible, obvious, precise, several 8. explicit, manifest 9. different 10. individual

13. distinguished

distinction ... 4. rank 5. honor 6. repute
8. nobility 9. clearness, greatness,
variation 10. difference
14. discrimination 15. differentiation

distinctive ... 7. typical 8. peculiar
9. prominent 14. characteristic,
discriminative

distinctive mark ... 4. sign 5. badge
6. cachet, emblem, symbol

distinctive quality ... 6. genius, talent
9. specialty

distinguish ... 6. secern 7. discern
8. perceive, separate 9. recognize
12. discriminate 13. differentiate

distinguished ... 5. great, noted
6. famous, marked 7. defined, eminent,
honored, special 8. laureate, renowned,
superior 9. different, egregious,
prominent 10. celebrated
11. conspicuous, illustrious
13. extraordinary 14. characteristic

distort ... 4. skew, warp 5. screw, twist,
wrest 6. deform 7. contort, falsify,
pervert 10. camshackle 12. misrepresent

distorted ... 4. awry 6. rubato 7. twisted

distortion ... 5. loxia 6. perversion
12. malformation

distract ... 5. craze 6. divert, harass,
madden, puzzle 7. confuse, perplex
10. distraught

distracted ... 3. mad 7. frantic 8. distrait,
diverted, rambling 9. disturbed
10. distraught 11. overwrought

distraction ... 6. frenzy, tumult 7. despair,
madness 8. disorder 9. agitation,
confusion, diversion 10. dissension,
perplexity 11. derangement,
disturbance, inattention 12. perturbation

distrain ... 5. seize

distress ... __in 5. agony, annoy,
grief, worry 6. danger, grieve, harrow,
misery 7. anguish, anxiety, perplex,
poverty, trouble 8. distrain, vexation
9. necessity 10. affliction, discomfort

distress call ... 3. SOS

distribute ... 3. dot, sow 4. deal, dole,
mete 5. allot, share 6. assign, assort,
divide, spread 7. deal out, prorate,
scatter 8. allocate, classify, dispense,
disperse 9. apportion, broadcast
10. administer

distribution ... 8. disposal 9. allotment
10. dispersion 11. arrangement,
disposition 12. dispensation
13. apportionment 14. classification

distribution of favors ... 9. patronage
11. benefaction

distributor ... 5. agent 6. agency
8. merchant 11. broadcaster

district ... 4. pale, slum, ward 5. realm
6. canton, domain, ghetto, region
7. circuit, demesne, quarter 8. province
9. bailiwick, territory

District of Columbia ... see *Washington,
DC*

distrust ... 5. doubt, qualm 8. jealousy,
mistrust, wariness 9. misgiving,
suspicion, treachery

disturb ... 3. vex 4. riot, roil 5. alarm,
annoy, rouse, roust, upset 6. excite,

molest, ruffle 7. agitate, derange,
fluster, perturb, trouble 8. disorder,
distract 9. interrupt 10. discompose,
disconcert

disturbance ... 5. alarm, brawl 6. hubbub,
rumpus, static, tumult, uproar
7. anxiety, clatter 8. stramash
9. agitation, annoyance, commotion,
confusion 10. excitement, turbulence
11. derangement 12. perturbation

disturbed ... 6. uneasy 7. annoyed,
excited, inquiet, unquiet 8. agitated
10. bewildered 12. disconcerted

disunion ... 9. severance 10. alienation,
detachment, dissension, separation
11. disjunction 13. disconnection

disunite ... 3. rip 4. part 5. sever, untie
6. divide, sunder, unteam, unyoke
7. discerp, disjoin, unravel 8. alienate,
separate 9. dismember

disuse ... 6. misuse, nonuse 7. abandon,
discard 8. disusage 9. desuetude
11. antiquation, discontinue
12. obsolescence

ditch ... 3. sap 4. dike, hole, moat,
rine 5. canal, evade, fossa, fosse,
rhine 6. escarp, furrow, relais, trench
7. abandon, acequia, channel

dithyramb ... 3. ode 4. hymn 6. poetry
7. epithet (of Dionysus)

ditty ... 3. lay 4. poem, sing, song 5. carol
6. saying 7. canzone 8. canticle

diurnal ... 5. daily 8. everyday
9. quotidian

divan ... 4. sofa 5. couch 6. leewan,
settee 9. davenport 12. Chesterfield

diva's forte ... 4. aria

dive ... 4. swim 6. plunge, resort, saloon
7. brothel, descend, descent, explore
8. submerge

divergence ... 7. theorem 9. deviation,
obliquity 10. difference, separation
12. disagreement, divarication

divers ... 5. cruel 6. sundry 7. several,
various 8. perverse 9. different

diver's disease ... 5. bends 7. caisson

diverse ... 6. sundry, unlike 7. several,
various 8. distinct, separate 9. different,
multiform

diver's gear ... 8. flippers
12. respirometer

diversify ... 4. vary 6. change 7. variate
9. variegate 10. distribute
13. differentiate

diversion ... 4. game, play 5. hobby,
sport 6. change 7. pastime 8. apostasy
9. amusement 10. deflection, recreation
11. distraction 13. entertainment

diversity ... 7. variety 10. difference
11. variegation 12. multiformity

divert ... 5. amuse, avert, parry 7. deflect,
delight 8. dissuade, distract, recreate
9. entertain 10. disincline

divest ... 4. doff, reft, tirl 5. strip
6. debunk, depose 8. unclothe
10. dispossess

divide ... 3. lot 4. fork, part 5. cleft,
halve, sever, share, slice, space, split
6. bisect, cleave, septum, sunder
7. prorate 8. alienate, classify, separate
9. apportion, bifurcate, calculate,

dismember, partition, segregate,
watershed 11. distinguish
divide (pert to) . . .
areas (small) . . 8. areolate
feet . . 4. scan
four parts . . 4. paly (Her) 7. quarter
many parts . . 8. fraction 9. multisect
seven parts . . 9. septimole
steps . . 8. graduate
transversely . . 12. cross-section
two parts . . 6. bisect
divided . . 4. enté (Her), reft 5. bifid,
split, zoned 6. halved, parted 7. partial,
partite, septate 8. aerolate, bifidate,
unjoined 9. alienated, disunited
11. distributed
dividend . . 5. bonus, share 6. number
7. payment
divination . . . 3. art (magic) 4. omen,
sors 6. augury, sortes 7. presage
9. intuition
divination by . . .
ashes (sacrificial) . . 11. tephromancy
cards . . 10. cartomancy
dead spirits . . 10. necromancy
dreams . . 11. oneiromancy
eggs . . 7. oomancy
fig leaf . . 9. sycomancy
figures . . 8. geomancy
fire . . 9. pyromancy
footprints . . 10. ichnomancy
forehead . . 11. metapomancy
fountains . . 9. pegomancy
letters of a name . . 7. nomancy
8. onomancy
mice . . 8. myomancy
moon . . 10. seleomancy
neighing horse . . 10. hippomancy
oracles . . 9. theomancy
palmistry . . 10. chiromancy
pebbles . . 9. thrioboly
romantic medium . . 5. daisy
salt . . 9. halomancy
serpents . . 10. ophiomancy
smoke (sacrificial) . . 10. capromancy
stars . . 11. sideromancy
straws (burning) . . 11. sideromancy
sword . . 13. machairomancy
verses . . 9. rhapsodomancy
wands, rods . . 11. rhabdomancy
water . . 9. hydromancy
weather . . 9. aeromancy
wild animals . . 11. theriomancy
wine . . 9. oenomancy
divine . . 5. divus, guess, pious 6. priest,
sacred, superb 7. foresee, godlike,
predict 8. forebode, foretell, heavenly,
minister, prophecy 9. beautiful,
celestial, clergyman, religious
10. anticipate, superhuman, theologian
12. supernatural
divine (pert to) . . .
being . . 4. deva
breath . . 4. soul
force . . 5. deity, numen 6. spirit
gift . . 8. blessing
inspiration . . 8. afflatus
messenger . . 7. apostle
opinion . . 14. theologoumenon
power . . 7. entheos (obs)
utterance . . 8. prophecy

wisdom . . 8. theogamy
word . . 5. grace, logos
work . . 7. theurgy
divining rod . . 4. wand 6. dowser
9. doodlebug
divinity . . . 3. God, Ler 4. Deus,
Lord 5. Allah, deity, Khuda, Mazda
6. Brahma, Christ 7. Jehovah, Saviour,
Taranis, Trinity 8. Almighty
division . . . 4. part, sect, unit 5. share
6. schism, sector 7. faction, section
8. cleavage, disunion, variance
9. allotment, bisection, partition
10. alienation, department, separation
11. compartment, disjunction
12. distribution 13. apportionment,
disconnection, dismemberment
14. classification
division (pert to) . . .
center (Biol) . . 9. centriole
city . . 4. ward 5. block 8. precinct
French . . 6. canton 7. Commune
10. department 14. arrondissement
mankind . . 4. race
poem . . 5. canto, verse 6. stanza
time . . 3. Age, Eon (Aeon), Era 6. Eogaea
(Zool)
zone (earth) . . 6. frigid, torrid, tropic
9. temperate
divorce, Mohammedan law . . . 5. talak
divot . . . 3. sod 4. clod, turf
divulge . . . 4. tell 6. expose, impart, reveal
7. confide, publish, uncover 8. disclose,
discover, proclaim 11. communicate
Dixie, Dixieland . . . 4. song 6. utopia
7. Sunbelt 8. The South (US)
dizziness . . . 5. whirl 7. vertigo
9. giddiness 10. fickleness
dizzy . . . 5. crazy, giddy, tipsy 6. fickle,
stupid 7. foolish 8. confused,
swimming, unsteady 9. delirious
10. capricious 11. vertiginous
Djibouti, east Africa . . .
city . . 5. Obock 6. Dikkil
gulf . . 4. Aden
do . . . 2. ut (Mus) 3. act, pay 4. dost, fare,
make, suit, work 5. avoid, cause, cheat,
exert, serve, solve 6. answer, effect,
finish 7. achieve, deceive, execute,
perform, produce, prosper, suffice
8. transact 9. discharge 10. administer
docile . . . 4. calm, tame 6. gentle
7. duteous 9. compliant, teachable,
tractable
dock . . . 4. clip, pier, slip 5. basin,
jetty, plant, wharf 6. cut off, deduct,
hangar 7. curtail, shorten 8. waterway
9. anchorage 12. witness stand
docket . . . 4. list, mark 6. record, ticket
8. calendar, schedule 11. certificate
docking post . . . 7. bollard
dock worker . . . 6. loader 7. laborer
9. stevedore 12. longshoreman
doctor . . . 3. cut, fly (angling) 4. dose
5. spike, title, treat 6. degree, dilute,
healer, intern (interne) 7. surgeon,
teacher 9. physician 10. adulterate,
veterinary 12. psychiatrist
doctrine . . . 3. ism, ist 4. rule 5. credo,
creed, dogma, logic, maxim, tenet
6. gospel 7. article, opinion, precept

8. position 9. principle
doctrine (pert to) . . .
   existence (Philos) . . 6. henism
   finality (Theol) . . 11. eschatology
   good . . 8. agathism
   inevitability . . 8. fatalism
   philosophy . . 10. pragmatism
   secrecy . . 6. cabala 8. esoteric
   selfishness . . 6. egoism
doctus . . . 7. learned
document . . . 4. deed, writ 5. paper,
   proof, scrip 6. escrow 7. archive
   11. corroborate
document (pert to) . . .
   copy (true) . . 5. Xerox 7. estreat
      8. syngraph 9. duplicate, photostat
   depository . . 8. archives
   file, report . . 7. dossier
   hamper . . 7. hanaper
dodecade . . . 5. dozen 6. twelve (series)
dodge . . . 4. duck, jouk, snub 5. avoid,
   cheat, elude, evade, parry, trick
   6. escape, palter 7. deceive 8. artifice
   9. expedient
dodger . . . 7. biscuit, shirker 8. deceiver,
   handbill
dodo . . . 3. moa 4. bird (extinct)
doe . . . 3. tag, teg 4. deer, hind
doer . . . 5. actor, agent, maker 6. author,
   factor, worker 7. manager 8. attorney,
   executor, producer 9. performer
doff . . . 4. shed, vail 5. strip 6. divest,
   remove 7. take off, undress
dog . . . 3. cur, pug 4. foot, lyam
   (lyme) 5. canis, hound, pooch,
   whelp 6. canine, fallow, shadow,
   wretch, yelper 7. mongrel 9. carnivore
   13. constellation
dog (breed) . . . 3. pom 4. chow, Dane
   5. boxer, husky 6. basset, beagle, collie,
   lucern, nootka, poodle, Saluki, setter,
   Sussex 7. bulldog, griffon, mastiff,
   pointer, Samoyed, Shih Tzu, spaniel,
   terrier, whippet 8. Airedale, Doberman,
   Keeshong, Labrador, Malemute, Pekinese,
   Sealyham, shepherd 9. Chihuahua,
   dachshund, Dalmatian, greyhound,
   Pekingese, retriever, schnauzer, St
   Bernard, wolfhound 10. bloodhound,
   Pomeranian, schipperke 11. Skye terrier
   12. gazelle hound 13. Boston terrier
dog (pert to) . . .
   Buster Brown . . 4. Tige
   Cape (hunting) . . 8. cynhyena
   days . . 8. canicule
   F D R's . . 4. Fala (Falla)
   ferocious . . 7. agouara
   fictional . . 4. Asta, Toby 6. Lassie 9. Rin
      Tin Tin
   heroic . . 5. Balto
   house . . 6. kennel
   howl . . 9. ululation
   like . . 6. cynoid
   mythical . . 7. Cerebus
   part . . 5. flews 7. dewclaw
   short-eared (Her) . . 4. alan (aland)
   star . . 6. Sirius 8. Canicula
   Victor records . . 6. Nipper (His Master's
      Voice)
   wild . . 5. dhole, dingo 6. bandog, kolsun
      8. cimarron

Doge's barge . . . 9. Bucentaur
dogfish . . . 5. shark 6. burbot 9. blackfish
   10. nursehound
dogma . . . 4. code 5. tenet 6. belief,
   dictum (pl dicta), ritual 7. precept
   8. doctrine 9. Levitical, principle
dogmatic . . . 7. certain 8. absolute,
   positive 9. assertive, canonical,
   doctrinal, pragmatic 11. dictatorial,
   doctrinaire, magisterial, opinionated
dogmatism . . . 10. pragmatism
   11. intolerance
dogwood . . . 5. osier 6. cornel 7. boxwood
do it again . . . 5. itero
dole . . . 4. alms, mete 5. grief 6. sorrow
   8. pittance 9. allotment 10. distribute,
   misfortune 12. distribution
doleful . . . 3. sad 4. dree 5. drear
   6. dismal, dreary, rueful, woeful
   8. doloroso, dolorous, grievous,
   jeremiad, mournful 10. lugubrious,
   melancholy
doll . . . 3. toy 4. baby (toy), girl 6. moppet,
   puppet 9. miniature, plaything
dolmen . . . 8. cromlech
dolphin . . . 4. fish, inia 5. bouto 6. dorado,
   dugong, sea pig 8. Cetacean, porpoise
   9. goosebeak 10. bottlenose
dolt . . . 3. ass, oaf 4. clod, dope,
   loon, lout, moke 5. dunce, idiot
   7. dullard, half-wit 8. clodpate,
   dumbbell, numskull 9. blockhead, dumb
   bunny 10. ignoramous
domain . . . 5. realm 6. empery, empire,
   sphere 7. country, demesne 8. dominion
dome . . . 4. arch, head, roof (Astron)
   5. spire, tower 6. cupola, turret
Domesday, doomsday . . . 4. Book (Eng
   Hist) 11. Judgment Day 13. Great
   Domesday 14. Little Domesday
   17. Domesday of St Paul's
domestic . . . 4. tame 5. domal 7. servant
   9. enchorial, home-grown, intestine
   (not foreign)
domestic establishment . . . 6. ménage
   9. household
domicile . . . 5. abode, house 7. habitat
   8. dwelling 9. residence 10. habitation
dominant . . . 5. chief, chord 6. ruling
   7. regnant, supreme 8. superior
   9. ascendant, governing, imperious,
   paramount, principal 10. pre-eminent,
   prevailing 11. influential, outweighing,
   overtopping 12. preponderant
   13. authoritative, overbalancing
dominate . . . 4. boss, rule, sway 5. reign
   6. govern 7. command, control, overtop,
   possess 11. predominate
domineering . . . 6. lordly 7. haughty
   8. arrogant, blustery 9. imperious,
   masterful 10. oppressive
   11. overbearing
Dominican Republic . . .
   capital . . 12. Santo Domingo
   city . . 14. Ciudad Trujillo
   discoverer . . 8. Columbus
   island site . . 10. Hispaniola
   oldest city (W Hem) . . 12. Santo Domingo
      (1496)
dominion . . . 4. rule, sway 5. realm
   6. empery, empire, sphere 7. control

9. authority, hierarchy (celestial)
12. jurisdiction
domino ... 3. pip (spot) 4. game (in pl), hood, mask 5. amice, cloak, ivory 7. costume
dominoes, galloping ... 7. vories
donate ... 3. tip 4. give 6. bestow 7. present
done ... 4. fini 5. baked, ended, finis 6. agreed, cooked 7. through 8. finished, tired out 9. completed, concluded, exhausted
done (pert to) ...
by stealth .. 13. surreptitious
by word of mouth .. 5. parol
for pay .. 9. mercenary
with effort .. 5. labor
Don Juan's lover ... 6. Haidee
donkey ... 3. ass 4. moke 5. burro, neddy 6. onager
donna ... 4. Dona, lady, wife 5. madam, woman 8. mistress
Don Quixote's steed ... 9. Rosinante
doom ... 3. fey, lot 4. fate, ruin 5. death 7. condemn, destine, destiny 8. sentence 11. destruction
doomed ... 3. fey 5. death, fated, goner 9. sentenced
doomsayer ... 9. Cassandra
doomsday ... 8. Ragnarok 11. Judgment Day (see *Domesday*)
door ... 4. gate 6. portal 7. doorway, opening, passage, postern 11. entranceway 12. porte-cochere
doorframe ... 3. dar 4. jamb, rail, sash, sill 5. janua, panel, stile 6. lintel 9. threshold
doorkee:.:. ... 4. hasp 5. tiler 6. porter 7. du: .um, ostiary 8. chokidar 9. concierge
... 3. hop, LSD 4. hemp 6. me:::!, opiate, peyoti (peyote) 7. fathead 8. narcotic 9. marijuana
Dorian Festival (Sparta) ... 6. carnea (carneia)
Dorian magistrates ... 6. ephors
Doric Order (Gr Arch) ...
capital .. 6. abacus
frieze fillet .. 6. taenia
frieze space .. 6. metope
history .. 6. oldest 8. simplest
dormant ... 5. inert 6. asleep, latent, torpid 7. resting 8. inactive, sleeping 9. quiescent
dormer window ... 5. oriel 6. gablet 7. dormant (obs), lucarne
dormeuse ... 5. couch 8. carriage (sleeping), nightcap
dormouse ... 4. Glis, loir 5. lerot 6. rodent
dorsal (pert to) ...
back .. 5. notal, notum 6. dorsum, lumbar, neural, tergal, tergum
column .. 6. spinal
dose ... 5. bolus, draft, treat 6. potion 7. portion
Dos Passos trilogy ... 3. USA
dot ... 3. jot 4. clot, code, lump 5. dowry, fleck, point, speck, telia (fungus) 6. period 7. stipple
dote ... 3. rot 5. decay, dowry 6. babble, dotage, dotard, drivel, stupor 7. portion

(marriage) 8. imbecile
dotted ... 5. pinto 7. piebald, specked, studded 8. stippled 9. sprinkled 11. diversified
lotty ... 5. crazy 6. feeble, senile
Douay Bible ... 4. Aree
double ... 2. di (pref) 4. dual, fold, twin 5. duple, plait, twice 6. binary, binate, duplex, folded 7. twofold 8. artifice, two-faced 9. deceitful, duplicate, insincere, intensify 11. counterpart
double (pert to) ...
bars (Her) .. 5. gemel
cross .. 7. deceive, two-time
dagger .. 6. diesis
edged .. 9. ancipital
ghost (live person) .. 11. counterpart 12. Doppelgänger, doubleganger
meaning .. 9. equivocal
doubt ... 5. demur, waver 8. hesitate, mistrust, question 9. misgiving, suspicion 10. Pyrrhonism, skepticism 11. uncertainty
doubter ... 5. cynic 6. Humist 7. skeptic 10. Pyrrhonist
doubtful ... 7. dubious 8. wavering 9. ambiguous, equivocal, uncertain, undecided 10. hesitating, improbable, precarious 11. distrustful, vacillating 12. questionable, unbelievable, undetermined 13. problematical
doubtful authority ... 6. mythic, unreal 10. apocryphal
dough ... 4. cash, mash 5. money, paste 6. leaven, noodle
doughnut ... 6. sinker 7. cruller, simball 9. friedcake
dour ... 5. .arsh, stern 6. gloomy, severe 9. obstinate 10. inflexible
dove ... 3. nun 4. blue (color), Inca 5. color 6. culver, pigeon 7. Columba, tumbler 8. pacifist, peacenik
Dove, the ... 6. symbol (Relig) 10. Holy Spirit
dovefoot ... 8. geranium (wild)
dovekey, dovekie ... 3. auk 4. Alle 6. rotche 9. guillemot
dowdy ... 3. pie (deep-dish) 6. pastry, shabby, untidy 7. pudding 8. slovenly 10. slatternly
dowel ... 3. pin 4. coak 5. tenon 6. fasten, pintle
dower ... 3. dos 5. dowry, endow, grant 6. dotate 7. bequest 8. dotation, jointure
down ... 2. de (pref) 3. nap 4. fuzz, hair 5. adown, below, floor 7. descent 8. softness
downcast ... 3. low, sad 7. lowered 8. dejected 9. bowed down, depressed 10. despondent, dispirited 11. discouraged, downhearted
downright ... 4. flat 5. blunt, plain, sheer, stark, utter 6. arrant, candid 8. positive, thorough 10. absolutely, forthright 11. unqualified 13. unceremonious
down source ... 5. eider
downy ... 4. soft, warm 5. nappy, pilar, quiet 6. placid 7. villous 8. feathery 10. flocculent, lanuginose, lanuginous
dowry ... 3. dos, dot 4. gift 5. dower, sulka 6. talent 9. endowment

dowser's tool ... 4. wand 6. willow
Doxology ... 4. hymn 6. praise 7. Kaddish
doze ... 3. nap, nod 5. sleep 6. catnap, drowse, snooze 7. stupefy (obs)
Dracula (pert to) ...
actor .. 6. Lugosi (Bela)
author .. 6. Stoker (Bram)
film (Murnau) .. 9. Nosferatu
homeland .. 12. Transylvania
inspiration for .. 4. Vlad (Tepes) 14. Vlad the Impaler
draft, draught ... 3. map, nip 4. dose, dram, draw, plan, pull, swig 5. drink, epure 7. current, diagram, drawing, outline 8. protocol, recruits, traction 9. conscript 10. money order
drag ... 3. lag, lug, tow, tug 4. clog, draw, hale, haul, pull, sing, tump 5. drawl, scent (hunt), smoke, trail 6. drogue, harrow 7. grapnel 8. dragrope, linger on, obstacle 10. conveyance
dragoman ... 11. interpreter (official)
dragon ... 4. lung 5. drake, Rahab (Bib) 6. animal, duenna, lizard, musket (anc), pigeon 7. dragoon, monster (Her), serpent 10. earthdrake 14. Dragon of Komodo
drain ... 3. gaw, sap 4. lade, loss, sink, sump 5. ditch, dreen, empty, rhine, sewer, siver 6. filter, trench 7. acequia, alberca, channel, consume, exhaust, outflow 11. watercourse
dram ... 3. nip 4. mite, slug 5. draft, drink 6. drachm 8. potation 11. indifferent
drama (pert to) ...
beginning .. 8. Dyonysia (anc)
form .. 4. play 5. opera 6. comedy 7. tragedy 10. peripeteia 11. composition
parts .. 8. epitasis, protasis 12. introduction
scenery .. 7. diorama
dramatic ... 4. wild 5. stagy, vivid, vocal 6. poetic, scenic 8. thespian 10. histrionic, theatrical 11. pretentious, spectacular 12. melodramatic
dramatic piece ... 4. skit
drastic ... 5. stern 6. fierce, severe 7. intense, radical 8. rigorous
draught ... see draft
Dravidian (pert to) ...
country (anc) .. 5. India
ghost .. 4. bhut
language .. 5. Tamil 8. Kanarese 12. Dravido-Munda
native .. 5. Croat 8. Croatian
people .. 4. Nair 6. Slavic
soldier .. 8. Croatian
draw ... 3. lug, tie, tow, tug 4. drag, etch, haul, limn, lure, plot, pull, tole 5. draft, smoke 6. allure, arroyo, convey, entice 7. attract, conduct, extract, lottery 9. delineate 10. attraction
draw (pert to) ...
away .. 6. abduce, divert 7. detract
close .. 4. loom, near 5. hover 8. approach
forth .. 5. educe 6. elicit, ferret 7. extract
off .. 6. siphon 7. extract 8. abstract, withdraw
through an eye .. 4. rove

together .. 4. coul, frap, lace, rake 8. assemble
drawback ... 5. fault, wince 6. defect, resile, retire 8. obstacle 9. objection 12. disadvantage
drawing ... 3. art 5. draft 7. diagram, hauling, picture, pulling 8. doodling 9. animation 10. attracting, extracting
drawing back ... 9. retrahent
drawing room ... 6. parlor, saloon
drayage ... 6. charge 7. cartage, haulage 8. truckage 14. transportation
dread ... 3. awe 4. fear 5. timor 6. dismay, horror, terror 7. anxiety 8. affright, disquiet 9. reverence 12. apprehension
dreadful ... 4. dire 6. horrid 7. awesome, fearful, hideous 8. horrible, terrible, terrific 9. frightful 10. formidable, outrageous
dreadnaught, dreadnought ... 5. cloth 7. garment 8. fearless 10. battleship, fearnought
dream ... 4. muse, rêve 5. fancy 6. bubble, vision 7. imagine, reverie, romance, suppose 8. illusion, stargaze 11. contemplate
dream (pert to) ...
interpretation .. 10. oneirology
interpreter .. 12. oneirocritic
tranquility .. 3. kef (keef) 7. reverie
dreamer ... 4. seer 7. fantast 8. idealist, puffbird 9. visionary 11. romanticist 13. castle-builder
dreamy ... 3. kef (keef) 6. poetic 7. languid 8. soothing 9. visionary 11. imaginative
dreary ... 3. sad 4. dull, gray 5. bleak, ourie 6. dismal, elenge, gloomy, remote 7. doleful, tedious 9. cheerless 10. depressing, foreboding, melancholy, monotonous 11. comfortless
dredge ... 4. tong (for oysters) 5. scoop 6. burrow, deepen, grains, tunnel 8. excavate
dregs ... 4. faex, lees, marc, silt 5. draff, dross, magma 6. refuse, scoria, sludge 7. grounds, hogwash, residue 8. riffraff, sediment 9. settlings 10. faex populi
drench ... 4. hose, soak 5. douse, draft, imbue, purge, scour, souse 6. potion 7. immerse 8. inundate, permeate, saturate, submerge
drenched ... 4. asop 5. asoak 6. doused, soaked 9. saturated
dress ... 3. rig, tog 4. deck, garb, gown, suit, trim 5. getup, mufti, preen 6. attire, clothe, enrobe, livery, toilet 7. apparel, threads (sl) 8. clothing, decorate, negligee 10. habiliment 13. mother hubbard
dress (pert to) ...
flax .. 3. ted
gaudily .. 5. prank 7. bedizen, spangle
leather .. 3. taw, tew 5. curry
of Mecca pilgrims .. 5. ihram
riding .. 5. chaps, habit 7. hacking (jacket) 10. chaparajos
stone .. 3. dab, nig 5. nidge
surgically .. 5. dight, panse 7. bandage 8. ligature
up .. 4. dude 5. preen, primp 6. spruce 8. titivate

dressed loosely ... 8. discinct, ungirded
dressing ... 4. lint 5. sauce 7. bandage,
pledget, raiment, reproof 8. attiring,
scolding 9. condiment, neatsfoot
(leather) 11. castigation
draw ... see *draw*
Dreyfus defender ... 4. Zola
dried ... 4. sere 5. wiped 6. seared,
wasted 7. drained, parched, wizened
9. shriveled 10. dehydrated, desiccated,
exsiccated
dried meat ... 7. biltong (biltongue),
charqui 8. pemmican 10. jerked beef
dried tubers (orchids) ... 5. salep
drift ... 3. aim, sag 4. idle, pile, sail, soar,
tide, tool 5. float, stray, tenor, trend
6. course, intent 7. deposit, impetus,
meaning 8. crescent (sidewise),
movement, seaweeds, tendency
9. deviation
drill ... 3. gad, row (seeds), tap 4. bore
5. auger, borer, train 6. baboon, pierce
7. machine 8. excavate, exercise,
practice, rehearse 9. perforate
drilling ... 5. denim 7. nurture 8. training
11. inculcation
drink ... 3. ade, ale, bib, lap, nip, pop,
rum, sip, tea, tot 4. flip, fram, grog,
shot, slug, soda, soma, swig, tope
5. bouse, draft, julep, negus, posca,
punch, quaff, skink, toast, toddy, water
6. caudle, coffee, imbibe, liquor, mai
tai, mao-tai, posset, potion, ptisan,
tipple 8. beverage, cocktail, highball,
sillabub 9. decoction 10. intoxicant,
mixed drink
drink (pert to) ...
ancient .. 5. morat
Arabian .. 4. boza
English .. 7. wassail 8. champers
fond of .. 8. bibulous
frozen .. 6. frappé
gods (of the) .. 6. nectar
honey .. 4. mead 5. morat
hot .. 5. salep, toddy 6. posset, saloop
Irish .. 10. shandygaff
Japanese .. 4. sake
mix .. 5. setup 8. vermouth 9. grenadine
rum .. 5. bumbo
Russian .. 5. vodka 6. kumiss (koumiss)
Spanish .. 7. tequila
together .. 9. symposium
tropical .. 7. sangria 8. sangaree
Turkish .. 4. raki 5. airan, arrak
drinking salutation ... 5. skoal, toast
6. prosit 7. propine, slainte
drinking vessel ... 3. mug 4. bowl,
tass 5. cylix (anc), glass, gourd,
jorum, mazer, stein 6. goblet, rhyton
7. tankard 8. schooner 10. Vaphio cups
(gold)
drip ... 4. bore, drop, leak 5. droop
7. dribble, falling, trickle
drive ... 3. caa 4. herd, ride, slog, urge
5. force, guide, impel, pilot, press,
rouse 6. attack, compel, energy, propel,
thrust 7. crusade, operate 8. campaign
10. compulsion
drive (pert to) ...
away .. 4. rout 5. chase, exile, expel,
repel 6. banish, dispel, rebuff 7. repulse

8. disperse
down .. 4. tamp
frantic .. 4. loco 6. madden 7. bedevil
obliquely .. 3. toe 5. slice
stakes .. 4. camp, park 6. locate, settle
drivel ... 4. dote 5. drool 6. slaver
7. slobber, twaddle 8. nonsense
driveler ... 4. fool 5. doter, idiot 6. dotard,
prater 8. jabberer 9. blatherer, chatterer
driver ... 4. club (golf), jehu 6. drover,
hammer, mahout, sarwan 7. speeder
8. coachman, engineer, motorist,
operator, overseer, reinsman
9. propeller 10. charioteer, taskmaster
drizzle ... 4. mist, rain, smur 6. mizzle
(misle)
droll ... 3. odd 4. zany 5. comic, merry,
queer, witty 6. jester 7. amusing,
buffoon, waggish 8. farcical, humorous
9. diverting, laughable, whimsical
10. ridiculous 11. merry-andrew
drollery ... 3. wit 4. jest 5. farce, humor
6. puppet 9. absurdity 10. buffoonery
dromedary ... 4. oont 5. camel (one-
hump) 6. hageen 7. Camelus 8. Bactrian
(two-hump)
drone ... 3. bee, dor, hum 4. male (bee)
5. idler, snail 6. loafer 7. bagpipe,
humming, slacker 8. sluggard 9. non-
worker, slow mover
drool ... 6. drivel, slaver 7. dribble,
slabber, slobber
droop ... 3. lop, sag 4. flag, hang, loll,
pine, sink, tire, wilt 6. nutate, slouch
7. decline 8. languish
drooping ... 4. alop, weak 5. loose
7. hanging, nodding, sinking
8. dejected, fatigued 11. languishing
drooping eyelids ... 6. ptosis
drop ... 4. bead, blob, dose, dram,
drib, drip, fall, omit, shed, sink, slot,
stop, tear 5. candy, dreep, droop,
gutta, lower, minim, remit 6. letter,
plunge 7. abandon, descent, distill
(distil), earring, globule, pendant, trickle
8. ornament, trapdoor 9. declivity
10. relinquish
drop (pert to) ...
anchor .. 4. moor
by drop .. 7. guttate 9. guttation
measure .. 7. pipette 11. stactometer
nautical .. 5. hance
serene .. 9. amaurosis (Med)
vowel .. 5. elide
dropsy ... 5. edema 8. hydropsy, swelling
dross ... 4. lees, scum, slag 5. chaff,
dregs, scobs, sprue, waste 6. refuse,
scoria, sinter (iron)
drove ... 4. herd 5. crowd, drive,
flock
drover ... 4. boat 6. dealer (cattle), driver
8. herdsman
drowse ... 3. nid, nod 4. doze 5. dover
(Eng), sleep 6. snooze
drowsiness ... 7. languor 8. dullness,
lethargy 9. lassitude, oscitance
10. narcolepsy, sleepiness
12. listlessness, sluggishness
drowsy ... 4. logy 6. sleepy 8. oscitant,
soothing 9. somnolent, soporific
drudge ... 3. fag 4. grub, hack, mail,

plod, toil 5. labor, slave 6. toiler
7. plodder

drug . . . 4. alum, dope, dull, numb
6. opiate 7. stupefy 8. narcotic, sedative
10. medication 11. anesthetize

drug (pert to) . . .
action . . 7. synergy
addict . . 6. junkie
analgesic . . 6. Anacin 7. aspirin
10. acetanilid, phenacetin
anesthesia . . 3. gas 5. ether 8. Novocain
10. chloroform
dangerous . . 11. thalidomide
emetic . . 6. ipecac 11. ipecacuanha
eye . . 8. atropine 10. belladonna
forgetfulness . . 8. nepenthe
narcotic . . 3. hop, kif 4. hemp 5. bhang,
daggo, opium 6. codein 7. cocaine
9. marijuana
sedative . . 7. bromide, Seconal, Veronal
8. barbital, Nembutal 11. scopolamine
13. phenobarbital

drugget . . . 3. mat, rug 5. cloth

druggist . . . 8. gallipot 10. apothecary,
pharmacist

Druids (anc) . . . 5. Order (Relig)
9. conjurers 12. philosophers

drum . . . 4. beat, naker, snare, tabor,
tombe 6. atabal, barrel, tambor
(tambour), tom-tom, tympan 7. taboret,
timbrel, timpany 8. cylinder, tympanum
(ear)

drum (pert to) . . .
call . . 4. dian (diana) 6. rappel, tattoo
8. rataplan
Indian . . 6. nagara
nautical term . . 7. capstan
Oriental . . 6. tom-tom 7. anacara

drumming fingers . . . 12. devil's tattoo

drunkard . . . 3. sot 4. soak, wino
5. souse, toper 6. addict, barfly, boozer
7. guzzler, tippler 9. alcoholic, inebriate
11. dipsomaniac

dry . . . 3. sec, ted 4. arid, blot, brut,
dull, keen, seco, sere, wipe 5. drain,
parch, vapid 6. aerify, barren, jejune,
shrewd 7. insipid, sterile, thirsty, xerotic
8. solidify, tiresome 9. dehydrate,
fruitless, pointless 12. unprofitable
13. uninteresting

dryad . . . 5. deity, Napea, nymph, oread

duck . . . 3. dip 4. flee, fowl 5. dodge,
douse 6. plunge 7. bob down

duck (breed) . . . 4. Anas, coot, pato,
skua, smee, smew, teal 5. Anser, eider,
scaup 6. Aythya, Nyroca, Peking, scoter
7. mallard, Muscovy, pintail, pochard,
Spatula, widgeon 8. Anatinae, bluebill,
shoveler (shoveller) 9. harlequin,
merganser, sheldrake 10. bufflehead,
canvasback, ring-necked

duck (pert to) . . .
baby . . 8. duckling
class . . 3. sea 5. river 7. Muscovy
crested . . 4. smew
disabled . . 4. lame
ducklike . . 5. decoy 8. duckbill
fabric . . 5. cloth
flock (mallards) . . 4. sord
flower . . 12. lady's slipper
game . . 6. tenter

hawk . . 6. falcon 7. harrier
litter . . 4. team
male . . 5. drake
ruddy . . 5. noddy

duct . . . 3. vas 4. main, pipe, race, tube
5. canal 7. channel, passage, trachea
8. aqueduct

ductile . . . 6. docile, facile, pliant 7. elastic,
plastic, tensile 8. flexible, tractile,
yielding 9. compliant, complying,
malleable, tractable 10. manageable

dude . . . 3. fop 5. dandy 7. coxcomb,
Johnnie 10. tenderfoot

dudeen . . . 4. pipe (tobacco)

due . . . 4. debt, duty, just, meed, owed
5. owing 6. charge, lawful 7. exactly
8. adequate, directly, expected, rightful
9. appointed 10. ascribable, sufficient

duel . . . 4. tilt 5. fence 6. combat
7. contest 8. conflict 9. monomachy
12. satisfaction

duelist's aide . . . 6. second

duet . . . 3. duo 8. duettino

dug . . . see *dig*

dugong . . . 7. manatee, Sirenia 8. Halicore

dugout . . . 4. abri, cave, shed 5. canoe
6. cavity 7. pirogue, shelter

dulcet . . . 5. sweet 6. ariose 7. tuneful
8. pleasant, soothing 9. agreeable,
melodious 10. harmonious

dulcimer . . . 6. citole 7. bagpipe, cembalo
8. psaltery 10. instrument

dull . . . 3. dim, dry, dun 4. dead, drab,
gray, logy, poky 6. barren, cloudy,
deaden, dismal, dreary, drowsy,
jejune, leaden, muffle, obtund, obtuse,
sleepy, somber, stupid 7. doltish,
irksome, prosaic, tedious 8. lifeless,
listless, overcast, sluggish, stagnant,
tiresome 9. apathetic, inanimate,
saturnine, unfeeling 10. insensible,
lackluster, melancholy, slow-witted
13. unimaginative

dull (pert to) . . .
finish . . 3. mat (matte)
heavy . . 4. logy 5. leady 6. stodgy
of cloth . . 6. starry (Eng)
statement . . 9. platitude

dullard . . . 3. oaf 4. dope, mope 5. dunce
8. dumbbell, numskull 9. dumb
bunny

dumb . . . 4. mute 6. aphony, silent,
stupid 7. aphonia 8. ignorant, taciturn
9. inanimate, irregular 10. speechless
12. inarticulate

dumbfounded . . . 6. amazed 7. crabbed
9. staggered, surprised 10. astonished,
bewildered 11. overwhelmed
13. flabbergasted

dummy . . . 3. pel 4. copy, dolt, mort
(cards), sham 5. model 6. pontic, silent
9. imitation, mannequin, nonentity
10. figurehead, substitute 11. counterfeit

dump . . . 3. tip 4. bump, game (Eng),
jail, sell, thud, tune 5. empty,
hovel 6. plunge, unload 7. discard
10. rendezvous

dumpling . . . 7. biscuit, gnocchi
10. appleberry

dupe . . . 3. fox 4. bilk, cull, tool
5. cheat, fraud, trick 6. delude, sucker

7. cat's-paw, deceive, mislead

duplicate . . . 4. copy, game (cards), twin 6. double, duplex 7. estreat, mislead, replica, twofold 8. likeness 9. analogous, facsimile, identical, replicate 10. transcript 11. counterpart 12. reproduction

duplicated . . . 7. dittoed 8. repeated 10. repetitive

duplicity . . . 5. fraud, guile 6. deceit 7. duality 9. deception, duplexity, falsehood, treachery 13. dissimulation, double-dealing

durable . . . 4. firm 5. stout, tough 6. staple 7. lasting 8. constant, enduring 9. permanent 10. continuing, persistent 11. everlasting, substantial

duration . . . 3. age 4. date, span, term, time 6. period 8. eternity, lifetime 10. durability, permanence 11. continuance

during . . . 4. time 5. while 6. whilst 7. pending, through 10. throughout

dusk . . . 4. dark 5. dusky, gloom, slate (color) 8. gloaming, twilight

dusky . . . 3. dim, sad 4. dark, dusk 5. murky, tawny, umbra 6. gloomy, somber 7. swarthy 8. blackish 10. melancholy

dust . . . 4. cash, coom (coomb), dirt, gold, pilm, soil 5. briss, brush, chaff, clean, color, earth, money, stive, stour (dial), trash 6. corpse, pollen, powder 7. dryness, turmoil 9. commotion, confusion, sweepings

dust (pert to) . . .
flax . . 5. pouce
flour . . 5. stive
glacier . . 10. kryokonite
reduce to . . 4. mull
speck . . 4. mote

Dutch (pert to) . . . see also _Netherlands_
cheese . . 4. Edam 7. cottage
country . . 7. Germany, Holland 11. Netherlands
man . . 10. Hogen-Mogen
news agency . . 5. Aneta
painter . . 3. Dou 4. Hals 7. van Gogh, van Eyck, Vermeer 8. Mondrian, Ruisdael (Ruysdael) 9. Rembrandt (van Rijn)
poet . . 7. Da Costa
pottery . . 4. delf (delft) 9. delftware
river . . 3. Eem 4. Maas 5. Meuse
scholar . . 7. Erasmus (Humanist)
woman, wife . . 4. frow
uncle . . 3. eme (dial), oom

Dutch East Indies (Indonesia) . . .
capital . . 7. Batavia (former), Jakarta (Djakarta)
islands (3,000), largest . . 4. Bali, Java 6. Borneo (part) 7. Celebes, Sumatra 8. Malaysia (part) 9. New Guinea (part)
renamed . . 9. Indonesia

Dutch Guiana (Netherlands Antilles) . . .
capital . . 10. Paramaribo
mountain . . 10. Tumuc Humac
renamed . . 7. Surinam

dutiful . . . 6. devout, docile 7. duteous 8. obedient, reverent 9. compliant

10. respectful, submissive 11. deferential, reverential

duty . . . 3. job, tax 4. care, onus, rite, task, toll 5. chore, stint, trick 6. devoir, dharma, excise, heriot (anc), impost, tariff 7. payment, respect 9. reverence 10. imposition, obligation

duvet . . . 9. comforter

dwale . . . 5. sable (Her) 6. opiate, potion 9. soporific 10. belladonna, nightshade

dwarf . . . 3. elf, urf 4. grig, puny, runt 5. crile, gnome, midge, pygmy (pigmy), small, stunt, troll 6. droich, durgan, midget 7. manikin, Pacolet, stunted 9. dandiprat, micrander 10. diminished, homunculus

dwarfish . . . 6. nanoid

dwarfishness . . . 6. nanism

Dwarfs, The Seven . . . 3. Doc 5. Dopey, Happy 6. Grumpy, Sleepy, Sneezy 7. Bashful

dweeb . . . 4. nerd

dwell . . . 4. bide, harp, live, stay 5. abide, delay, lodge, pause, tarry 6. linger, remain, reside

dwelling . . . 3. hut 4. flat 5. abode, hotel, house, hovel 6. duplex, shanty 7. trailer 8. abidance, domicile, tenement 9. apartment, residence 10. habitation

dwelling (pert to) . . .
house (law) . . 8. messuage
in field . . 10. arvicoline
in groves . . 10. nemoricole
of dead (Bab) . . 5. Aralu
of souls (Polyn) . . 2. Po
Oriental . . 3. dar

dwindle . . . 4. melt, wane 5. taper, waste 6. lessen, shrink, sicken 8. decrease, diminish 10. degenerate

dyad . . . 3. two 4. duad, pair 6. couple, dyadic

Dyak, Dayak . . . 6. Borneo 7. blowgun 8. sumpiter 9. aborigine

dye . . . 4. anil 5. color, imbue, stain, tinge 7. pigment 8. colorant

dyeing method . . . 5. batik

dye stuff (pert to) . . .
blue . . 4. woad (wad, wade)
brown . . 5. erika, sumac
indigo . . 4. anil
mulberry . . 3. aal
red . . 4. chay 5. aurin, eosin, henna 6. isatin, madder, relbun 7. annatto, magenta 8. morindin 9. rhodamine 10. orseilline
violet . . 5. murex 6. archil
yellow . . 7. xanthic 8. luteolin, orpiment 10. quercitron

dyke . . . see _dike_

dynamic . . . 4. keen 5. acute, vivid 6. potent 7. intense, kinetic 8. forceful, forcible 9. energetic, strenuous

dynamite inventor . . . 5. Nobel (1866)

dynamo (pert to) . . .
attachment . . 10. commutator
inventor . . 7. Faraday
machine . . 9. generator
part . . 5. rotor 8. armature

dynast . . . 5. ruler 6. prince 8. governor

dynasty . . . 4. race 8. dominion, lordship 10. succession 11. sovereignty
dynasty (pert to) . . .
 Chinese . . 2. Fo 3. Han, Yin 4. Isin,

Ming, Sung, Tang
 Spanish . . 6. Ommiad
dysphoria . . . 7. illness 8. debility
dyvour . . . 6. beggar 8. bankrupt
dzeren . . . 8. antelope

E

E . . . 7. Epsilon (Gr)
Ea (Bab) . . . 3. God 5. deity
each . . . 3. all, per 5. alike, every 6. apiece, singly 10. separately 12. individually 14. distributively
eager . . . 3. apt 4. agog, avid, keen, yare 5. agasp, sharp 6. ardent, greedy, intent 7. anxious, burning, excited, thirsty, willing, zealous 8. desirous, spirited 9. strenuous
eager beaver . . . 7. hustler 8. go-getter 10. enthusiast
eagerness . . . 4. élan, zeal 5. ardor 6. fervor 7. avidity 8. alacrity, cupidity, fervency 9. alertness, readiness 10. enthusiasm, impatience 13. impetuousness
eagle . . . 4. erne (ern), gier (Bib), seal 5. bergut, eaglet, emblem 8. standard (Rom) 13. constellation (Milky Way)
eagle (pert to) . . .
 American . . 4. bald
 brood . . 5. aerie, eyrie
 coin . . 4. gold
 European . . 3. sea 5. harpy 6. golden 8. imperial
 genus . . 6. Aquila
 heraldry . . 8. allerion
 male . . 6. tercil
 sacred to Jupiter . . 9. Jove's bird
 S America . . 9. eagle hawk
 scout badge . . 5. merit
Eagles . . . 14. Fraternal Order
eagre (acker) . . . 4. bore, flow, wave 5. flood (tidal)
ear . . . 4. head 5. auris 7. auricle, hearing 8. orillion 9. appendage, attention, orecchion (obs)
ear (pert to) . . .
 anvil . . 5. incus
 bone . . 6. stapes, tegman 7. stirrup
 canal . . 7. cochlea 9. labyrinth 10. Eustachian, scala media
 drum . . 8. tympanum
 external . . 6. concha
 grain . . 3. epi 5. spica 6. mealie, rizzom (ressum)
 hammer . . 7. malleus
 inflammation . . 6. otitis
 part . . 5. helix, pinna 6. tragus
 science . . 7. otology
 shell . . 5. ormer 7. abalone
 specialist . . 6. aurist 9. otologist
 stone . . 7. otolith
 term . . 4. otic 5. aural 9. auricular
 wax . . 7. cerumen
earache . . . 6. otalgy 7. otalgia

early . . . 4. soon 7. ancient, betimes, matinal 9. premature, primitive 10. beforehand, beforetime
earn . . . 3. get, win 4. gain 5. ettle, merit 7. acquire, deserve
earnest . . . 5. arles (pledge), grave, sober, staid 6. ardent, hearty, pledge, sedate, solemn 7. handsel (money), serious, sincere, zealous 8. resolute 9. heartfelt, important 10. thoughtful 12. wholehearted
earnestly . . . 8. solemnly 9. intensely, zealously 10. resolutely
earphone . . . 7. trumpet (double) 8. otoscope 9. auriphone, topophone (double) 11. stethoscope
earring . . . 4. hoop 6. earbob, pendle 7. earstud, pendant 9. girandole (girandola)
earth . . . 3. erd 4. clay, clod, dirt, land, marl, muck, sand, soil, vale 5. geest, loess, sloam, terra 6. ground, planet, rideau 7. topsoil 8. alluvium
earth (pert to) . . .
 center . . 10. geocentric 12. centrosphere
 comb form . . 3. geo
 deformation . . 10. epeirogeny
 formed beneath . . 8. hypogene, plutonic
 formed by ores . . 9. supergene
 formed on surface . . 7. epigene
 god (Egypt) . . 3. Geb (Keb)
 goddess . . 4. Erda, Gaea (Gaia), Tari 6. Semele 7. Demeter
 produced by . . 6. mortal 11. terrigenous
 satellite . . see *satellite*
 volcanic . . 5. trass
earthdrake . . . 6. dragon
earthly . . . 7. mundane, secular, terrene, worldly 8. temporal 11. terrestrial, universally, unspiritual 13. materialistic
earthmover . . . 6. digger 7. backhoe, leveler 9. bulldozer, excavator 11. steam shovel
earth pig . . . 8. aardvark
earthquake . . . 5. quake, seism 7. temblor 12. diastrophism
earthstar . . . 6. fungus 7. Geaster
earthworm . . . 7. annalid, dew worm, ipokoea 9. Lumbricus
earthy . . . 3. low 5. gross, marly 6. coarse 7. worldly 8. material 9. unrefined
ease . . . 4. calm, rest 5. abate, allay, peace, quiet, relax 6. pacify, relief, repose, soothe 7. assuage, comfort, content, leisure, relieve, slacken 8. facility, mitigate 9. alleviate, disburden, enjoyment 10. prosperity,

E

relaxation, solicitude 11. informality,
tranquilize 12. tranquillity (tranquility)

easily ... 4. eath (eith) 6. gently,
slowly, softly 7. readily 8. smoothly
11. comfortably, dexterously
12. effortlessly

easily (pert to)...
broken.. 6. shelly 7. fragile, friable
frightened.. 8. skittish
managed.. 6. docile
moved.. 6. mobile
offended... 9. sensitive
split.. 8. schistic
understood.. 5. lucid

east .. 4. Asia, dawn 6. Levant, Orient
7. sunrise 8. eastward

East Africa ...
hartebeest.. 4. tora
house (mud).. 5. tembe
republic.. 5. Kenya 7. Somalia
island.. 8. Zanzibar
people.. 3. Luo 4. Embu, Teso 5. Bantu,
Masai 6. Kikuyu, Mau Mau 7. Nilotes
vessel.. 4. dhow

East India ... see also East Indian
drink.. 4. nipa
fan.. 6. punkah (punka)
gateway (temple).. 5. toran (torana)
hat, helmet.. 5. topee (topi)
money of account.. 4. anna
mountain pass.. 4. ghat (ghaut)
musical instrument.. 4. vina 5. ruana,
saron
police station.. 5. thana (tanna)
sailing vessel.. 5. dhoni (doni)
7. patamar
sugar, molasses.. 3. gur 10. massecuite
water vessel (brass).. 4. lota (lotah)

East Indian animal ...
antelope.. 5. bongo, takin 6. impala,
nilgai 8. axis deer
cattle.. 4. gaur, zebu 5. gayal, tsine
7. banteng
civet.. 6. musang 10. paradoxure
goat (wild).. 4. tahr 7. markhor
lemurlike.. 7. tarsier
raccoonlike.. 3. wah 5. panda
rat.. 9. bandicoot
swine.. 8. babirusa (babiroussa)

East Indian bird ...
broadbill.. 4. raya
bulbul.. 4. kala
falcon.. 5. besra
fruit pigeon.. 6. treron
thrush.. 5. shama
weaverbird.. 4. baya

East Indian people ...
boatswain.. 6. serang
chief.. 6. sirdar
groom.. 4. syce
harem.. 6. zenana
native sailor, soldier.. 5. sepoy 6. lascar
nurse.. 4. amah, ayah
peasant.. 4. ryot
poet.. 6. Tagore
princess.. 4. rani (ranee)
robber.. 6. dacoit
title.. 4. raja 5. rajah, sahib
warrior.. 5. singh

East Indian tree, plant ...
bark.. 4. lodh 5. niepa

cedar.. 6. deodar
cotton.. 5. simal
fiber.. 4. jute
fruit.. 3. bel 6. lanseh (lansa)
gum.. 4. kino
herb.. 5. tikor 6. sesame 7. roselle
mahogany.. 4. toon
mulberry.. 4. tapa
palm.. 3. tal (fiber) 4. nipa (thatch)
5. sural (juice), toddy 7. palmyra
pea.. 4. dhak 5. Butea
rubber.. 3. saj
shade.. 6. banyan
timber.. 3. saj, sal (saul) 4. poon, teak
5. siris 6. sissoo
walnut.. 6. lebbek

east wind ... 5. Eurus

easy ... 4. calm, slow 5. loose, suave
6. cinchy, facile, gentle, simple
7. natural 8. gullible, informal,
moderate, tranquil, unforced
9. leisurely, unhurried 10. manageable,
nonchalant, unaffected 11. comfortable,
complaisant, unconcerned

easy-going ... 4. calm 11. unflappable

easy job ... 8. sinecure

easy mark ... 4. dupe, gull 6. sucker,
victim 7. cat's-paw

eat ... 3. sup 4. dine, etch, feed, gnaw
5. board, erode 6. devour, ravage
7. consume, corrode, destroy

eat (pert to)...
between meals.. 4. nosh 5. bever,
snack
by rule.. 4. diet
earth, clay.. 8. geophagy
12. chthonophagy
greedily.. 3. lab 4. glut 5. gorge, scarf
(down) 6. gobble, pig out (sl) 7. edacity
8. voracity

eatable ... 6. edible 8. esculent, gustable
10. comestible

eater ... 5. diner 7. epicure, glutton,
gourmet 8. gourmand

eating (pert to)...
alone.. 5. monophagy
comb form.. 7. phagous
decay.. 5. saprophagous
fish.. 11. piscivorous 13. icthyophagous
flesh, raw.. 9. omophagia
flesh-eating.. 9. creophagy
10. zoophagous 11. carnivorous
man-eating.. 12. androphagous
13. anthropophagy
nuts.. 10. nucivorous 11. nuciphagous
plants, herbs.. 11. herbivorous
12. phytophagous
roots.. 12. rhizophagous

eavesdrop ... 3. bug 4. drip 6. harken,
listen 7. wiretap 10. stillicide 14. listen
secretly

ebb ... 3. low 4. neap, sink, tide, wane
5. abate, decay 6. recede, reflux, retire
7. decline, dwindle, shallow, subside
8. decrease

ebb and flow ... 5. surge 6. aestus
(estus) 11. alternation

ebb tide ... 8. low water

ebullition ... 7. boiling, ferment
8. bubbling 9. agitation, commotion
12. fermentation 13. effervescence

eccentric . . . 3. cam (shaft), odd 5. flaky, kinky 6. weirdo 7. erratic, strange 8. abnormal 9. erratical, irregular 13. nonconformist 15. idiosyncratical

eccentricity . . . 6. oddity 9. queerness 10. aberration, erraticism 11. abnormality, peculiarity, strangeness 12. idiosyncrasy, irregularity 13. nonconformity 17. unconventionality

Ecclesiastes . . . 8. Koheleth (Gr)

echidna . . . 7. monster (Gr Myth) 8. anteater

echinoderm . . . 8. starfish 9. sea urchin

echo . . . 4. mute, stop (organ) 5. nymph (Myth), reply 6. repeat 7. imitate, resound, respond 8. resemble, response 9. duplicate 10. repetition 13. reverberation

echoism . . . 12. onomatopoeia

Eciton . . . 4. ants (legionary)

eclipse . . . 5. cloud, sully 6. darken 7. obscure, surpass 10. extinguish

ecliptic term . . . 5. lagna, orbit 6. circle 9. penumbral

ecology, oecology . . . 4. sere 6. botany 7. biology 9. bionomics, sociology 10. bioecology

economical . . . 5. canny, chary 6. frugal, saving 7. careful, thrifty 8. domestic 9. provident 12. parsimonious

economics terms . . . 5. T-bill 7. bailout 8. bankable, cash flow, rollover 9. plutology 10. monetarism, production (wealth)

economize . . . 4. save 5. skimp, stint 6. scrimp 7. husband, utilize 8. retrench

economy . . . 4. care 6. saving, thrift 7. cutback 8. prudence 9. canniness, husbandry 10. providence

ecru . . . 3. tan 5. beige

ecstasy . . . 5. bliss 6. trance 7. emotion, rapture

ecstatic . . . 4. rapt 7. rapture 9. rapturous, rhapsodic

ectad . . . 7. outward

ecto (comb form) . . . 7. outside, without 8. external

Ecuador (pert to) . . .
capital . . 5. Quito
export . . 7. bananas
hat . . 6. Panama 8. 'Jipijapa'
island . . 9. Galapagos
mountain . . 5. Andes
reptile . . 6. iguana 8. tortoise
volcano . . 10. Chimborazo

ecumenical . . . 7. general, liberal 8. catholic, tolerant 9. universal, world-wide 12. cosmopolitan

eczema . . . 6. herpes, tetter 8. eruption 9. salt rheum

edacity . . . 5. greed 7. avarice 8. appetite, gulosity, voracity 10. greediness

eddy . . . 4. bore, gulf 5. gurge, surge, swirl, whirl 6. vortex 7. current, wreathe 9. whirlpool

Edentate (Zool) . . . 6. sloths 7. mammals 9. aardvarks, anteaters 10. armadillos

edge . . . 3. hem, jag, lip, rim 4. brim, brow, side 5. arris, brink, crest, marge, sharp, sidle (to), splay, verge 6. border, flange,

labrum, margin 7. ambitus, selvage 8. acrimony, pungency, selvedge 9. advantage, sharpness 10. escarpment

edged . . . 5. erose 7. crenate 8. bordered, invected (Her)

edging . . . 3. hem 4. lace, welt 5. frill, ruche 6. border, fringe, ruffle 7. binding, bordure (Her), flounce, tatting

edgy . . . 5. sharp 7. angular, nervous 8. critical, snappish 9. excitable, impatient 13. sharp-cornered

edict . . . 3. act, ban 4. Bull (Pope's), fiat 5. arret, dicta (pl), irade, order, ukase 6. assize, decree, dictum, firman 7. command, mandate 8. decretal 9. ordinance 12. proclamation

edification . . . 8. learning 9. knowledge 11. improvement, instruction

edifice . . . 5. house 6. church, palace, temple 7. Capitol 8. building 9. structure 10. tabernacle

edify . . . 5. build, teach 7. educate, improve 8. instruct, organize 9. construct, enlighten, establish

Edinburgh . . .
burgh . . 5. Leith
capital of . . 8. Scotland
county . . 10. Midlothian
famed street . . 9. Royal Mile
Gaelic name . . 7. Dun Edin (Dunedin)
nickname . . 16. Athens of the North
site . . 12. Firth of Forth

Edison's workplace . . . 9. Menlo Park

edit . . . 5. emend 6. direct, excise, redact, revise, reword 7. arrange, correct, prepare

edition . . . 4. copy 5. issue 6. number 7. version

editions (Bib) . . .
eight texts . . 7. octapla
four texts . . 8. tetrapla
six texts . . 7. hexapla
style and type . . 7. Elzevir (1583)

editor . . . 7. analyst, newsman, reviser 8. arranger, redactor 9. annotator, gazetteer 10. journalist, supervisor 11. commentator 12. newspaperman

editor's word . . . 4. dele, stet

Edom . . . 5. Teman (Bib) 7. Idumaea

Edomite . . . 4. Esau 5. Isaac, Jacob 8. Idumaean

educate . . . 4. rear 5. teach, train 6. inform 7. develop 8. instruct 9. cultivate, enlighten 10. discipline 12. indoctrinate

educated . . . 6. taught 7. erudite, learned, trained 8. cultured, informed, lettered, literate 11. enlightened

education . . . 8. breeding, literacy, training 9. opsimathy (late in life), schooling 10. discipline

educe . . . 4. draw 6. deduce, elicit, evolve, obtain, secure

eel (pert to) . . .
colorful . . 5. moray 7. Muraena
genus . . 8. Anguilla 13. Leptocephalus
marine . . 5. elver 6. conger
mud . . 5. siren
sand . . 4. grig
young . . 5. elver

eellike . . . 4. lant, ling 7. eelpout, lamprey 8. Ophidion 10. anguilloid

11. Lepidosiren

eels, fishing for . . . 7. sniggle

eels, migration of . . . 7. eelfare

eelworm . . . 4. nema 8. Nematoda
9. roundworm 10. vinegar eel

eerie, eery . . . 5. scary, timid, weird
6. gloomy, spooky 7. awesome,
fearful, uncanny 9. deathlike, unearthly
10. frightened

efface . . . 5. erase 6. cancel, delete 7. blot
out, expunge 10. obliterate

effect . . . 4. does 5. close, éclat,
force, mneme 6. mirage, obtain,
result 7. achieve, compass, conjure,
execute, fulfill, meaning, operate,
outcome, perform, reality, realize
8. complete 9. discharge, execution,
influence 10. accomplish, appearance,
consummate, impression
11. consequence, performance

effective . . . 4. able 6. active, actual,
cogent 7. capable, telling 8. adequate,
eloquent, equipped, striking 9. brilliant,
competent, effectual, efficient,
operative, trenchant 11. efficacious,
influential

effects . . . 5. goods, wares 8. movables,
property

effeminate . . . 3. sop 5. sissy 6. female,
tender 7. cockney, epicene, womanly
8. feminine, womanish 9. Sybaritic
11. mollycoddle 12. overdelicate
13. overemotional

effervescent . . . 5. fizzy 6. bubbly,
lively 7. boiling, hissing 8. bubbling,
mousseux 9. ebullient, sparkling
10. boisterous

effete . . . 4. aged, idle 5. spent 6. barren
7. worn out 9. exhausted, fruitless
11. ineffectual

efficacious . . . 4. able 5. valid 6. potent
9. effective, effectual, operative
11. influential

efficacy . . . 4. dint 5. force, power
6. virtue 7. ability, potency 10. efficiency

efficiency . . . 5. power, skill 7. ability,
utility 8. efficacy 10. capability,
competence 11. proficiency
12. productivity 13. effectiveness
15. efficaciousness

efficient . . . 4. able 7. capable, operant
9. competent, effective, effectual,
operative 10. productive
12. businesslike

effigy . . . 4. copy, icon 5. image 8. likeness
9. facsimile, jackstraw, semblance
11. resemblance

effluvium . . . 4. aura, fume, odor
9. ectoplasm, emanation

efflux . . . 3. end 6. expiry, runoff
7. outflow 8. effusion 9. effluence,
emanation

effodient . . . 9. burrowing, fossorial

effort . . . 3. try, tug 4. dint, jump, toil,
will, work 5. assay, burst, labor, nisus,
pains, trial 6. strain 7. attempt, conatus,
trouble 8. endeavor, exertion, struggle
11. application

effrontery . . . 5. brass 8. audacity,
boldness 9. arrogance, impudence,
sauciness 11. presumption

effulgence . . . 5. aglow, glory 6. luster
8. radiance, rutilant, splendor
10. brightness, brilliance

effusive . . . 7. gushing 9. exuberant,
rhapsodic 13. demonstrative

eft . . . 4. evet, newt 6. lizard, triton
7. urodele 10. salamander

egest . . . 4. emit, void 7. excrete
9. discharge, ejaculate, eliminate

egg . . . 3. nit, ova (pl), ove 4. goad,
ovum, prod, urge 5. ovule 6. incite
9. instigate

egg (pert to) . . .
bird's . . 7. chalaza (white of), treadle
(embryo)
case . . 6. ovisac
comb form . . 2. oo 3. ovi
part . . 7. latebra
shaped . . 4. ooid, oval 5. ovate, ovoid
6. ooidal 9. ovaliform
shell . . 5. shard 6. ovisac
undeveloped . . 5. addle
white . . 5. glair 7. albumen
yolk, yelk . . 7. liaison 8. lecithin

eggplant . . . 9. melongena

eggs (pert to) . . .
feeding on . . 9. ovivorous
fish . . 3. roe 5. berry, spawn
preserved . . 5. pidan
tester of . . 7. candler
two at a time . . 8. ditokous

egis, aegis . . . 4. care 5. guard 6. shield,
symbol (anc) 7. backing, defense
8. advocacy, auspices, guidance,
tutelage 9. fosterage, patronage
10. protection 11. sponsorship

ego . . . 3. man 4. self 5. atman (Hind)
6. psyche, spirit 7. conceit, jivatma
(Hind) 11. selfishness

egress . . . 4. exit 5. issue 6. outlet
8. issuance 9. departure

egret . . . 5. heron, plume 8. aigrette

Egypt, UAR . . . see also *Egyptian*
capital . . 5. Cairo
Christian . . 4. Copt
city (ruined) . . 5. Luxor, Tanis 6. Karnak,
Thebes
dam . . 5. Aswan
desert . . 5. Dakla
gulf . . 4. Suez 5. Aqaba
king . . 6. Farouk (Faruk)
language (anc) . . 6. Coptic
lighthouse (anc) . . 6. Pharos
mother . . 3. Mut
peninsula . . 5. Sinai
philosopher . . 8. Plotinus
port . . 4. Said, Suez 10. Alexandria
president . . 5. Sadat 6. Nasser
queen . . 9. Cleopatra
river . . 4. Nile
ruler . . 5. pasha 6. caliph 7. khedive
ruler . . 7. Busiris (Myth), Pharaoh,
Ptolemy, Rameses
sea . . 3. Red 13. Mediterranean

Egyptian (pert to) . . .
abode of dead . . 4. Aaru (fields of)
6. Amenti
antelope . . 7. bubalis
ape (sacred) . . 4. Aani
beetle . . 6. scarab
bird (crocodile) . . 6. sicsac

bird (sacred) .. 4. Benu, ibis 7. phoenix
bull .. 4. apis
cobra .. 4. haje
cross .. 3. tau 4. ankh (emblem of life)
   10. crux ansata
crown .. 4. atef
dancing girl .. 4. alma (alme, Almeh)
   7. ghawazi 8. Baramika
dog .. 6. saluki (gazelle hound)
headdress of ruler .. 6. Uraeus
heaven .. 4. Aaru
lizard .. 4. adda 5. skink
lute .. 5. nable
paper .. 7. papyrus
solar disk .. 4. aten
soul .. 2. Ba 4. khet, sahu
stone (famed) .. 7. Rosetta
symbol .. 3. asp 6. scarab (beetle)
tomb .. 6. serdab (cell) 7. mastaba
watchman .. 6. ghafir (ghaffir)
writing .. 13. hieroglyphics
Egyptian god of ...
day .. 5. Horus
earth .. 3. Geb, Keb
life .. 4. Ptah
pleasure .. 3. Bes
primeval fluid .. 2. Nu
sea .. 5. Aegir
sun .. 2. Ra 3. Tem (Tum) 4. Atmu
   5. Mentu (Ment) 7. Khepera
   11. Harpocrates
supreme .. 4. Amon (Amun) 6. Amon-Re
underworld .. 6. Osiris 7. Hershef
unknown .. 2. Ka
wisdom .. 5. Thoth 6. Dhouti
Egyptian goddess of ...
arms .. 4. Anta
fertility .. 4. Isis
gods .. 4. Sati
motherhood .. 4. Apet
sea .. 3. Ran
truth .. 4. Maat
eidolon .. 5. image 7. phantom 8. illusion
   10. apparition
eight, eighth (pert to) ...
day (every) .. 5. octan
feast day .. 4. utas
group .. 5. octad, octet 6. octave
   7. octette
heaven .. 5. stars (fixed)
number .. 4. ocho 6. ogdoad
philosophy .. 8. Diagrams
sided .. 9. octagonal
tone, note .. 4. unca 6. quaver (8th)
   8. diatonic
eighteen inches ... 5. cubit
Eire ... 4. Erin 7. Ireland
ejaculate ... 4. emit, oust, void 5. blurt,
   eject, evict, expel 7. exclaim 8. dislodge
eject ... 4. emit, oust, spew, void 5. evict,
   expel, spout, spurt 6. banish 7. extrude
   9. discharge, eliminate
ejection ... 6. ouster 8. eviction
   9. expulsion 11. elimination
eke (out) ... 3. add, imp, tab 4. also, etch
   8. addition, appendix (dial), increase,
   piece out 10. postscript
El ... 3. God 5. deity
elaborate ... 6. ornate, refine 7. develop,
   improve, perfect, studied 9. embellish,
   perfected, superfine 11. complicated,

high-wrought
Elam capital ... 4. Susa (anc)
élan ... 4. dash 5. ardor 6. spirit
   9. eagerness 10. enthusiasm
elapse ... 2. go 3. die, fly, run 4. flit,
   pass, slip 5. lapse 6. expire
elastic ... 6. pliant, rubber 7. buoyant,
   ductile, springy 8. flexible, stretchy
   9. expansive, resilient 12. recuperative
elasticity ... 4. give 6. elater, spring
   7. pliancy, rebound 9. ductility
   10. resilience
elated ... 6. jovial 7. gleeful 8. exultant,
   jubilant 9. overjoyed
Elbe tributary ... 4. Eger, Iser
elbow ... 5. ancon, joint, nudge 6. jostle
   8. chelidon (hollow of)
El Camino Real ... 9. Royal Road
   12. King's Highway (Pac Hwy)
elder ... 3. iva 4. ainé, blue (color)
   5. berry, judge, ruler 6. Mormon, senior
   7. ancient 8. ancestor 10. forefather
eldest ... 5. eigne 6. oldest 8. earliest
   9. firstborn
eldritch ... 4. wild 5. eerie (eery), weird
   9. frightful
Eleatic philosopher ... 4. Zeno
   10. Parmenides
elect ... 3. ort 4. name 5. elite 6. choose,
   select 9. designate
election ... 6. choice 11. alternative
   13. determination 14. discrimination
Electra (pert to) ...
brother .. 7. Orestes
father .. 9. Agememnon
mother .. 12. Clytemnestra
electric (pert to) ...
atom .. 8. electron
condenser (anc) .. 9. Leyden jar
conductor .. 6. ohmage
current .. 2. AC, DC 7. circuit
force .. 4. elod
generator .. 6. dynamo
light .. 3. arc 4. neon 12. incandescent
meter .. 7. ammeter 9. voltmeter,
   wattmeter
particle .. 3. ion 6. cation (kation)
power .. 7. wattage
safety device .. 4. fuse
unit .. 3. ohm, rel 4. volt, watt
   5. farad, henry, joule 6. ampere, proton
   7. coulomb, oersted 8. kilowatt
electricity ... 5. juice, power
   10. illuminant
eleemosynary ... 4. alms, free 7. charity
   10. almsgiving
elegance ... 5. charm, grace, taste
   6. beauty, polish 9. propriety
   10. ornateness, politeness, refinement
   13. sumptuousness
elegant ... 4. rich 6. dressy, ornate,
   soigné, urbane 7. courtly, genteel,
   refined 8. graceful, handsome, polished,
   tasteful 9. admirable, beautiful,
   excellent 10. fastidious 11. fashionable
   13. grandiloquent
element ... 3. air 4. fire 5. earth, water
elementary ... 5. basic 6. simple
   7. primary 8. inchoate, original
   9. beginning 11. fundamental
elephant ... 3. cow 4. bull, calf 5. hathi,

rogue 6. tusker 8. behemoth
9. pachyderm
elephant (pert to) ...
  apple .. 7. Feronia
  boy .. 4. Sabu
  call, cry .. 4. barr 7. trumpet
  enclosure, trap .. 6. keddah
  extinct .. 7. mammoth
  goad .. 5. ankus
  keeper .. 6. mahout
  seat .. 6. howdah
  tusk .. 5. ivory 9. scrivello
  young .. 4. calf
elevate ... 4. lift, rear 5. elate, exalt, raise
6. refine, uplift 7. advance, dignify,
ennoble, glorify, inspire, promote
10. exhilarate
elevated ... 2. el 5. lofty, risen 6. elated
7. exalted, sublime 8. eminence
elevation ... 4. hill 6. height (highth)
9. promotion 10. exaltation
11. composition (Eccl), distinction
13. glorification
elevation of the mind ... 7. anagoge
elevator ... 3. bin 4. cage, lift, silo
9. ascenseur
elevator name ... 4. Otis
eleven ... 7. hendeca (comb form)
elf ... 3. fay, hob, imp, nix 4. peri 5. fairy,
gnome, ouphe, pixie 6. goblin, sprite
7. brownie
elfish ... 5. elfin 6. elvish, impish 7. elflike,
tricksy 8. eldritch 11. mischievous
Elgin Marbles ... 10. sculptures (by
Phidias)
Elia ... 4. Lamb (Charles)
Eli alma mater ... 4. Yale
elicit ... 3. get 4. draw, pump 5. claim,
educe, evoke, exact, wrest, wring
6. deduce, demand, entice, extort,
induce, obtain 7. extract
elide ... 4. dele, omit 5. annul 6. ignore
7. destroy, nullify, shorten 8. demolish,
suppress 9. eliminate
eligible ... 3. apt, fit 4. meet 6. worthy
8. entitled, suitable 9. competent,
desirable, qualified 10. acceptable,
admissible
Elijah ... 7. prophet 8. oratorio 14. John
the Baptist (Bib)
eliminate ... 3. rid 4. kill 5. erase, expel
6. detach, remove 7. discard, divulge,
exclude, excrete, release 8. evacuate,
separate 9. segregate 11. exterminate
Eliot, George (pseud) ... 12. Mary Ann
Evans
Elisha ... 7. prophet 8. disciple (of Elijah)
elision ... 7. syncope 9. severance
10. abridgment, shortening
11. suppression (vowel)
elite ... 5. stars 6. flower, galaxy
7. fashion, society 9. beau monde
10. upper crust
elixir ... 6. remedy 7. cure-all, essence,
extract, heal-all, panacea 8. medicine,
tincture 10. catholicon 12. quintessence
elixir of life ... 11. elixir vitae
Elixir of Love ... 13. L'Elisir d'Amore
elk ... 4. deer 5. Alces, eland, moose
6. sambar, wapiti
ellipse ... 5. curve, focus (foci), ovoid

ellipsis ... 4. dots 6. points 8. omission
elliptical ... 5. ovoid, vague 7. obscure
10. incomplete
elm (pert to) ...
  borer .. 6. beetle, lamiid
  fruit .. 6. samara
  genus .. 5. Ulmus
  rock, wing (kinds) .. 5. wahoo
Elm City ... 8. New Haven
Elmo ... 11. patron saint (sailors)
elocution ... 7. oratory 8. rhetoric
9. eloquence 10. expression
elocutionist ... 6. reader 7. reciter
11. elocutioner 13. recitationist
eloge ... 6. eulogy 7. address, oration
8. encomium, eulogism
eloign ... 6. convey, remove 7. conceal
elongate ... 6. extend, remove 7. stretch
8. continue, lengthen, protract
elongated ... 6. lank, long 6. linear,
oblong 7. prolate, slender 8. extended
9. stretched 10. attenuated
elope ... 6. decamp 7. abscond, skip out
8. slip away
eloquence ... 7. fluency, oratory
9. discourse, elocution
14. expressiveness
eloquence, teacher of ... 6. rhetor
eloquent ... 7. vivid 10. Ciceronian,
expressive, meaningful, oratorical
11. significant
else ... 2. or 4. ense (ens) 5. if not,
other 9. otherwise 10. additional
12. accompanying
elsewhere ... 4. away 5. alibi (law)
elucidate ... 5. clear, lucid 7. clarify, clear
up 8. simplify 9. interpret 10. illustrate
elude ... 4. flee, foil, mock, shun 5. avoid,
dodge, evade 6. baffle, befool, escape
10. circumvent
elusive ... 4. eely 6. subtle 7. elusory,
evasive 8. baffling 9. equivocal
10. impalpable
elves ... see *elf*
Elysium (Myth) ... 8. paradise
em ... 2. en (half) 4. unit (Elec)
emaciated ... 4. lean 5. gaunt 6. peaked,
wasted 7. pinched 10. attenuated,
cadaverous
emanation ... 4. aura, odor 5. light,
niton (radium), vapor 7. outcome
8. creation, effluvia 9. ectoplasm,
radiation 10. exhalation, generation
11. consequence
emancipation ... 6. rescue 7. freedom,
release 10. liberation 11. manumission
15. enfranchisement
emancipator, famous ... 7. Lincoln
emasculate ... 4. geld, spay 5. unman
6. soften 8. castrate 9. expurgate,
sterilize 10. effeminize
embalmer ... 5. cerer 9. mortician,
preserver 10. undertaker
embankment ... 3. dam 4. bund, dike
5. levee, revet, shore 7. barrier, pilapil
(rice field) 8. buttress 10. breakwater
13. fortification
embargo ... 5. edict, order 7. exclude
8. blockade, prohibit, stoppage
9. exclusion 10. impediment
11. prohibition, requisition

embark . . . 4. sail, ship 5. begin 6. depart,
invest, set off (out), unmoor 7. cast
off, entrain

embarrass . . . 5. abash, shame 6. hamper,
hinder, impede 7. confuse, fluster,
involve, mortify, nonplus 8. bewilder,
confound, encumber, handicap
9. discomfit, dumbfound 10. complicate,
disconcert

embarrassed . . . 8. red-faced

embarrassment . . . 5. shame
9. abashment, confusion
11. involvement, predicament
12. discomfiture, entanglement
13. inconvenience, mortification

embellish . . . 3. gem 4. deck, gild
5. adorn, array, dress, gouge, grace
6. bedeck, enrich 7. bedrape, enhance,
garnish 8. beautify, emblazon, furbelow,
ornament 9. embroider 10. exaggerate

embellishment . . . 9. garniture
10. decoration, furbishing
12. exaggeration 13. ornamentation

ember . . . 3. ash 4. coal (live), izle 5. gleed
6. cinder 7. residue

embers . . . 5. ashes 8. emotions (past),
memories

embezzle . . . 5. steal, swipe 6. lessen,
thieve, weaken (obs) 7. purloin
8. peculate, squander 9. dissipate
11. appropriate

embitter . . . 4. sour 5. anger 7. envenom
8. acerbate 10. antagonize, exacerbate

emblazon . . . 4. laud 5. color, extol
6. praise 7. display, exhibit, glorify
9. celebrate, embellish

emblem . . . 3. rue 4. mace, sign, type
5. badge, crown, image, token, totem
6. device, figure, symbol 7. balance
(justice), coronet, sceptor 9. prototype

emblematic . . . 5. typal 7. typical
8. symbolic 10. figurative
14. characteristic

embodiment . . . 4. Apis 6. avatar, matter
7. epitome 9. inclusion 10. enfoldment
11. combination, composition,
incarnation 12. organization
13. incorporation 14. representative
15. personification

embolden . . . 5. nerve 6. assure 7. hearten
8. reassure 9. encourage

embosom . . . 6. foster 7. cherish,
embrace, enclose 8. surround

embrace . . . 3. hug 4. fold, gain, hold,
love, wrap 5. adopt, clasp, cling,
grasp, inarm, seize 6. accoll (obs),
caress, enfold 7. cherish, contain,
enclose, espouse, include, involve,
welcome 8. comprise, encircle, greeting,
surround 9. encompass

embroider . . . 7. falsify 8. decorate,
ornament 9. embellish 10. exaggerate

embroidery . . . 8. appliqué 9. hardanger

embroidery frame . . . 7. taboret
(tabouret)

embroil . . . 4. upset 6. jumble 7. agitate,
disturb, perplex, trouble 8. convulse,
disorder, distract 9. commingle,
implicate 10. complicate, discompose

emcee . . . 4. host

eme . . . 5. uncle 6. friend, gossip

amend . . . 4. edit, mend 5. amend, right
6. better, remedy, revise 7. correct,
improve, rectify

emerald . . . 5. beryl, color, green
7. smaragd

Emerald isle . . . 4. Erin 7. Ireland

emerge . . . 3. dip 4. pend, rise 5. hatch,
issue 6. appear 7. debouch, emanate
10. disembogue

emergency . . . 5. pinch 6. clutch, crisis,
strait 8. exigency, juncture 9. extremity,
necessity 10. substitute

emery . . . 6. pumice 8. abradant, abrasive,
corundum 9. sandpaper

emesis . . . 6. puking 7. spewing
8. vomiting 12. disgorgement
13. regurgitation

emeute . . . 4. riot 6. Putsch 8. outbreak
10. insurgence 12. insurrection

emigrant . . . 6. emigré 7. migrant,
outgoer, settler 8. colonist, stranger
9. immigrant, migratory (of birds)

eminence . . . 4. hill 5. title 6. height,
rideau 7. dignity 8. authority, elevation,
greatness, loftiness 10. famousness,
importance, projection 11. superiority
13. transcendency

eminent . . . 4. arch, high 5. great,
lofty, noted 6. famous, marked,
signal 8. renowned, superior, towering
9. important 10. celebrated, protruding
11. illustrious 13. distinguished

emissary . . . 3. spy 5. agent, scout
8. delegate, diplomat

emit . . . 4. glow, reek, shed 5. eject, eruct,
exude, issue, pluff, voice 6. exhale
7. distill (distil), emanate, publish,
radiate 8. opalesce (colors), transmit
9. discharge, irradiate

emmet . . . 3. ant 7. pismire 8. formicid

emollient . . . 4. balm 5. ointment,
soothing 9. lubricant, softening

emolument . . . 4. fees, gain 5. wages
6. profit, salary 7. stipend, tribute
9. allowance 12. compensation

emotion . . . 5. agony, stoic 6. pathos
7. feeling, passion 9. agitation,
gratitude, sensation, sentiment
10. excitement 11. disturbance,
sensibility

emotional seat . . . 5. bosom

emotionless . . . 9. apathetic, impassive,
unfeeling 10. spiritless 11. unemotional
12. unresponsive

emperor . . . 4. czar, tsar 5. Mogul
7. monarch 9. commander, imperator,
sovereign

emphasis . . . 6. accent, stress 7. cadence
8. salience 10. insistence
14. impressiveness

emphasize . . . 6. accent, insist, stress
7. point up 9. punctuate 10. accentuate

emphatic . . . 7. earnest 8. forcible,
positive, striking 9. energetic, insistent
10. expressive 11. significant

empire . . . 4. rule, sway 5. green (color),
reign, state 6. domain 7. control,
country

Empire (pert to) . . .
of the Rising Sun . . . 5. Japan
State . . 7. New York

State of the South . . 7. Georgia

empiric . . . 4. fake 5. cheat, quack
8. impostor 6. charlatan 10. mountebank

employ . . . 3. use 4. busy, coax,
hire 5. apply, exert 6. devote,
occupy 7. concern, entrust, service
10. occupation

employees . . . 4. crew, gang, help 5. force,
hands, staff 9. personnel 10. associates

employer . . . 4. user 5. hirer 6. master
8. consumer 12. entrepreneur

employment . . . 3. use 4. work 5. trade
7. calling, purpose, service 8. business,
vocation 10. occupation, profession

emporium . . . 4. fair, mart 5. store
6. bazaar, market 10. exposition

empower . . . 6. enable 7. entitle
8. delegate, deputize 9. authorize
10. commission

empty . . . 4. idle, toom, vain, void 5. blank,
clear, drain, inane 6. hollow, hungry,
jejune, vacant, vacate 7. deplete,
foolish, vacuous 8. evacuate, unfilled
9. insincere 10. unburdened,
unoccupied

empusa (Gr Myth) . . . 5. fungi 7. specter
9. hobgoblin

empyrean . . . 3. sky 5. ether 6. Caelus,
welkin 7. heavens, the blue

emulate . . . 5. equal, outdo, rival
7. compete, imitate, vie with
11. competition

emulsion . . . 9. demulcent 10. semiliquid,
suspension

enable . . . 5. equip 6. clothe 7. empower,
qualify 9. authorize 10. capacitate

enact . . . 4. pass, play 6. decree,
enjoin, ordain, record 7. actuate,
appoint, perform 9. legislate, represent
10. constitute 11. impersonate

enactment . . . 3. law 4. veto 5. canon,
edict, usage 6. decree 7. statute
9. ordinance 11. legislation

encamp, encampment . . . 4. camp, tent
5. siege 7. bivouac, camping

enchant . . . 5. charm 6. delude 7. bewitch,
delight 8. ensorcel 9. captivate,
enrapture, fascinate

enchantment . . . 5. charm, magic, spell
7. sorcery 8. witchery 10. allurement,
necromancy, witchcraft
11. bewitchment, fascination,
incantation

enchantress . . . 5. Circe, Medea
7. charmer 8. bewitcher, sorceress,
temptress

encina . . . 7. live oak

encircle . . . 3. orb 4. gird, ring, zone
5. belay, inorb, twist 6. enfold
7. besiege, circuit, enclose, environ,
include, wreathe 8. surround
12. circumscribe

encircled . . . 4. girt 5. orbed, paled,
zoned 6. belted, forded, hooped, ringed
7. enlaced 8. enclosed, enfolded,
wreathed 10. surrounded

enclose . . . 3. hem, mew 5. bound, fence
6. corral, encase, engulf 7. enclave,
envelop, harness, include 8. imprison,
surround 9. encompass
12. circumscribe

enclosed . . . 4. pent, sept (area)
7. encased 8. confined 10. surrounded

enclosure . . . 3. pen 4. bawn, cage, yair
(yare), yard 5. carol (cloister), kraal
(craal), sekos 6. corral 8. contents,
poundage, stockade

encomium . . . 4. hymn 5. eloge 6. eulogy,
praise 7. tribute 8. accolade 9. panegyric

encompass . . . 4. ring 5. hem in 6. begird,
effect 7. besiege, circuit, compass,
contain, enclose, environ, include
8. encircle, surround 10. accomplish
12. circumscribe

encompassing . . . 7. ambient
13. circumambient

encore . . . 3. bis 4. echo, over 5. again
8. applause, once more

encounter . . . 4. bout, meet 5. brave,
brush, fight, incur, onset 6. attack,
breast, oppose 7. collide, meeting
8. conflict 10. engagement, experience

encourage . . . 4. abet, urge 5. boost,
cheer, impel, nerve, rally 6. assure,
exhort, foster, incite 7. advance,
comfort, console, hearten, inspire,
promote 8. embolden, inspirit
9. instigate, stimulate 11. countenance

encouragement . . . 3. aid 7. comfort
9. fosterage, incentive 10. inducement
11. emboldening

encroach upon . . . 5. poach 6. invade,
trench 7. impinge, intrude 8. infringe,
overstep, trespass

encumber . . . 4. clog, load 5. check
6. burden, hamper, hinder, retard,
saddle 7. involve, oppress 8. entangle,
handicap, obstruct, overload
9. embarrass 10. overburden

encumbrance . . . 5. alien (law), claim
6. burden 9. dependent 10. impediment

encyclic . . . 6. letter 7. pandect 8. circular,
treatise 10. encircling
13. comprehensive

encyclopedic learning, person of . . .
10. polyhistor 13. encyclopedist

end . . . 3. aim, neb, tip, toe 4. fate,
kill, ruin, tail 5. amend, close, death,
finis, limit, omega, point, telos, upend
6. expire, finale, finish, result, thirty
7. destroy, purpose 8. complete,
conclude, dissolve 9. cessation,
determine, extremity, intention,
objective, terminate 10. completion
11. termination

end (pert to) . . .
arrow . . 4. nock
boundary . . 5. bourn 7. abuttal
cloth . . 7. remnant
game . . 4. goal
man . . 8. minstrel
news . . 5. thirty
timber . . 5. tenon

endanger . . . 4. risk 6. expose, hazard
7. imperil 10. compromise, jeopardize

endeavor . . . 3. aim, try, vie 4. seek
5. essay, ettle, nisus, tempt 6. effort,
strive 7. attempt 8. struggle

endemic . . . 6. native 10. indigenous
14. characteristic

ending . . . 5. death 6. result 9. cessation,
desinence 10. completion, conclusion

    11. destruction, termination

endless ... 4. many 6. eterne 7. eternal,
    undying 8. eternity, infinite, numerous,
    unending 9. boundless, continual,
    incessant, perpetual, unceasing,
    unstinted 10. continuous 11. everlasting
    12. interminable 13. uninterrupted

endorse, indorse ... 4. sign 6. attest,
    second 7. approve, support 8. sanction
    9. authorize, guarantee

endorsement ... 4. fiat, visa (vise)
    8. approval, sanction 9. provision,
    signature 10. acceptance, validation
    12. ratification 14. authentication

endow ... 3. dow, due 4. dote, vest
    5. dower, endue, indue 6. bestow,
    clothe, enrich, invest to, invest
    7. empower, furnish, provide

endowment ... 4. gift 5. dower, grant
    7. talents 8. appanage (apanage)
    9. insurance, provision
    11. empowerment, instruction
    (Mormon)

endue ... 5. endow, teach 6. clothe,
    digest, invest, supply 7. empower

endurable ... 8. bearable 9. tolerable
    10. sufferable 11. supportable

endurance ... 7. stamina 8. patience,
    strength 9. fortitude, suffering
    10. durability, permanence, sufferance
    11. continuance, resignation
    12. perseverance

endure ... 4. bear, bide, dree, last, live,
    tide, wear 5. abide, allow, brook, stand
    6. afford, remain, suffer 7. condone,
    persist, sustain, undergo 8. continue,
    tolerate 9. persevere, withstand

enduring ... 7. durable, lasting, patient
    9. permanent 11. persevering,
    substantial, unforgotten 13. long-
    suffering

enemy ... 3. foe 5. devil, force, fremd
    (frenne), hater, rival, Satan 6. foeman
    8. opponent 9. adversary 10. antagonist

energetic ... 5. fresh 6. active 8. forceful,
    forcible, vigorous 9. strenuous
    11. industrious

energy ... 2. go 3. erg, pep, vim
    4. bent 5. force, nerve, power, vigor
    6. spirit 7. potency, sthenia 8. strength
    9. animation

energy (pert to) ...
    lack of .. 5. atony 6. anergy 7. aneuria,
      inertia 8. asthenia
    mental .. 8. psychurgy
    personified .. 6. Shakti
    potential .. 5. ergal
    unit .. 3. erg 5. ergon

enervate ... 3. sap 5. drain, unman
    6. weaken 7. exhaust, unnerve
    8. enfeeble 10. debilitate

enfeeble ... 4. numb 6. sicken, soften,
    weaken 7. depress 8. enervate
    9. attenuate 10. debilitate

enfilade ... 4. rake 5. vista 7. barrage
    9. broadside 11. arrangement (in rows)

enfold, infold ... 4. fold, wrap 5. clasp,
    cover 6. infold 7. embrace, envelop
    8. surround

enforce ... 5. drive 6. assail, compel
    7. execute, inspire 9. constrain,

    encourage, intensify, reinforce
    10. invigorate

enfranchise ... 4. free 5. admit 7. deliver,
    set free 8. liberate 10. emancipate

engage ... 4. bind, draw, hire, rent
    5. lease 6. absorb, embark, employ,
    enlist, induce, occupy, pledge 7. attract,
    betroth, engross, involve, promise
    8. contract, entangle 9. interlock,
    intermesh

engaged ... 4. busy 5. hired 6. bonded,
    meshed 7. earnest, entered, pledged,
    versant 8. embedded, employed,
    involved, occupied, promised
    9. affianced, betrothed, engrossed
    10. contracted

engaged in controversy ... 9. disputant

engagement ... 4. date 6. battle
    7. promise 9. betrothal, encounter
    10. attachment 11. appointment,
    involvement

engaging ... 5. sapid 6. taking 8. alluring,
    duelling 10. attractive, delightful
    11. interesting

engender ... 3. sow (seeds) 5. beget,
    breed, cause 6. excite 7. develop,
    produce 8. generate, occasion 9. call
    forth, procreate, propagate

engine ... 3. gin, ram 5. mogul, motor
    6. onager 7. machine, robinet, turbine
    10. locomotive

engine (type) ... 3. gas 5. motor, solar,
    steam 6. Diesel, rocket 8. gasoline
    10. combustion

engineer ... 4. plan 7. manager
    8. computer, contrive, designer,
    inventor, maneuver, operator, therblig
    9. construct 11. constructor, superintend

engineer (type) ... 5. civil, corps, sales
    6. driver, mining 7. planner 8. chemical,
    geodetic, military, railroad, research,
    sanitary 9. hydraulic 10. electrical,
    industrial, mechanical, structural
    11. electronics 12. aeronautical,
    construction 14. administrative

engird ... 6. begird, circle, girdle
    7. envelop 8. encircle, ensphere

England ... see also *English*
    called .. 6. Albion (anc) 7. Britain
      9. Britannia
    capital .. 6. London
    city .. 3. Ely 4. Hull, York 5. Derby,
      Leeds 6. Exeter 7. Bristol, Croydon
      8. Brighton, Coventry, Hastings,
      Plymouth 9. Liverpool, Sheffield
      10. Birmingham, Epsom Downs,
      Manchester, Nottingham, Portsmouth
      11. Southampton
    college (famed) .. 6. Oxford
      9. Cambridge, Sandhurst (military)
    conqueror .. 5. Danes 6. Angles, Saxons
      7. Normans
    constitution .. 10. Magna Carta (1215)
      12. Bill of Rights (1688)
    county .. 4. Kent 5. Devon, Essex
      6. Dorset, Sussex 9. Yorkshire
    emblem .. 4. lion, rose
    House of .. 4. York 5. Blois, Tudor
      6. Stuart 7. Hanover, Windsor
      8. Normandy 9. Lancaster
      11. Plantagenet

island .. 5. Wight 6. Scilly, Virgin
7. Bahamas, Bermuda, Channel,
Solomon 8. Falkland, Windward 9. Isle
of Man
king (anc) .. 6. Arthur (legend), Egbert
8. Ethelred 9. Ethelwulf
native (anc) .. 4. Celt, Dane, Jute
5. Saxon 8. Anglican 9. Sassenach
10. Anglo-Saxon
river .. 3. Exe 4. Avon, Ouse 5. Trent
6. Thames
royal residence .. 7. Windsor
school .. 4. Eton 5. Rugby 6. Harrow
street (London) .. 10. Piccadilly
12. Threadneedle
English (pert to) ...
bride's gift .. 3. dos
court .. 4. eyre (circuit), leet (anc)
dislike of .. 11. Anglophobia
district .. 4. Soho
estate (feudal) .. 4. fief
excuse (legal) .. 6. essoin
festival (country) .. 3. ale
field .. 5. croft
forest .. 5. Arden 8. Sherwood
freeman .. 5. ceorl, thane, thegn
hamlet .. 4. dorp
heather .. 4. ling
lawyer .. 9. barrister, solicitor
leave of absence (school) .. 5. exeat
lover of .. 10. Anglophile
Marbles .. 6. Oxford 7. Arundel
money of account .. 3. ora
news agency .. 6. Reuter
Parliament process .. 7. Hansard
political party .. 4. Tory, Whig 8. Laborite
12. Conservative
porcelain .. 5. Spode 8. Wedgwood
prehistoric site .. 8. Piltdown
race course .. 5. Ascot 9. Newmarket
10. Epsom Downs
races (famed) .. 5. Derby 7. The Oaks
sheep (blackface) .. 4. Lonk
song (mock) .. 12. lillibullero
stolen article (on thief) .. 7. mainour
subway .. 4. tube 11. underground
symbol .. 4. bull, lion, rose
thicket .. 5. copse 7. spinney
tract (sandy) .. 4. dean (dene)
trolley .. 4. tram
uplands .. 5. downs
wren .. 6. tomtit
English Channel ... 8. La Manche
English, famed ...
architect .. 4. Wren
composer .. 4. Arne, Byrd 5. Elgar
6. Handel, Tallis 7. Dowland, Stainer
15. Vaughan Williams
diarist .. 5. Pepys
dramatist .. 6. Jonson, Pinter 7. Marlowe
8. Sheridan
engraver .. 3. Pye 7. Hogarth
essayist .. 4. Elia (Charles Lamb), Lang
6. Arnold, Steele 7. Addison
explorer .. 4. Ross 5. Cabot 6. Baffin,
Beatty, Hudson 7. Raleigh
10. Shackleton
financier .. 7. Gresham
historian .. 4. Bede 7. Spelman, Toynbee
8. Macaulay
humorist .. 4. Lear (Edward)

navigator .. 4. Cook 5. Drake 6. Nelson
painter .. 6. Turner 7. Millais 8. Reynolds,
Rossetti 9. Constable 12. Gainsborough
philosopher .. 7. Russell, Spencer
poet .. 4. Pope 5. Byron, Keats
6. Dryden 7. Bridges, Chaucer, Shelley,
Skelton, Southey, Spenser 8. Browning,
Tennyson 9. Wordsworth
printer .. 6. Caxton
reformer .. 4. Owen 6. Spence
saint .. 6. George (patron saint)
7. Alphege, Swithin
satirist .. 5. Swift
scientist .. 4. Davy 5. Boyle 6. Dalton,
Darwin, Halley, Harvey, Huxley, Jenner,
Kelvin, Lister, Newton 7. Faraday,
Fleming 9. Cavendish, Priestley
10. Rutherford
spy (in Am Rev) .. 5. André
statesman .. 4. Peel, Pitt 7. Baldwin,
Balfour, Walpole 8. Cromwell, Disraeli,
Thatcher 9. Churchill 11. Chamberlain,
Lloyd George
theologian .. 5. Booth 6. Becket 7. Tyndall
8. Wycliffe 10. Whitefield
thesaurus compiler .. 5. Roget
writer .. 5. Hardy, Woolf 6. Austen,
Barrie 7. Boswell, Dickens, Johnson
8. Fielding, Lawrence, Trollope
9. Thackeray
engrave ... 3. cut 4. etch, rist 5. carve,
chase, hatch, infix 6. chisel, incise
7. enchase, impress, imprint, stipple
9. sculpture
engraver's tool ... 5. burin
engraving ... 3. cut 5. print 7. etching,
chasing, tooling 8. celature, incising,
intaglio 9. stippling 10. xylography
(wood) 11. lithography 12. glyptography
engross ... 6. absorb, engage
10. monopolize 11. concentrate
engrossed ... 4. busy, rapt 6. intent
8. absorbed, employed 10. interested
engulf ... 4. gulf, gulp 5. swamp 6. absorb
7. swallow 8. inundate, submerge
9. overwhelm
enhance ... 4. lift 5. exalt, extol, raise
7. advance, augment, elevate, enlarge,
magnify 8. increase 9. aggravate
10. exaggerate
enigma ... 3. why 5. rebus 6. puzzle,
riddle 7. charade, mystery
9. conundrum 11. mind-boggler
enigmatic ... 6. arcane, mystic 8. puzzling
12. inexplicable
enjoin ... 3. bid 5. order 6. advise, charge,
decree, direct, forbid 7. command
8. admonish, prohibit
enjoy ... 4. bask, have 5. savor 6. relish
10. appreciate
enjoyment ... 4. ease, zest 6. relish
7. delight 8. felicity, fruition, pleasure
9. amusement, happiness
enlarge ... 3. eke 4. ream 5. swell 6. dilate,
expand, extend, spread 7. amplify,
augment, develop, distend 8. increase
9. expatiate 10. exaggerate
enlargement ... 8. increase 9. expansion,
extension 10. augmentation
13. amplification
enlighten ... 5. teach 6. inform 7. educate,

explain 8. enkindle, instruct
10. illuminate 11. disillusion

enlightened person . . . 10. illuminate

enlist . . . 4. join, list 6. engage, enroll,
induce, muster

enliven . . . 5. amuse, cheer, rouse
7. animate, comfort, inspire, refresh
8. brighten, energize, inspirit
9. encourage, stimulate 10. exhilarate,
invigorate

enmity . . . 3. war 4. feud 6. hatred,
malice, rancor 7. discord 8. aversion
9. antipathy, disaccord, hostility
10. antagonism, repugnance
11. malevolence 14. unfriendliness

ennead . . . 4. gods (nine), nine 18. Ennead
of Heliopolis (famed)

ennoble . . . 5. exalt, honor, raise 6. uplift
7. elevate, glorify, promote

ennui . . . 4. bore 5. bored 6. tedium
7. boredom, fatigue, languor
9. weariness 15. dissatisfaction

enormous . . . 4. huge, vast 5. great
6. wicked 7. immense, massive,
titanic 8. abnormal, colossal, gigantic,
infamous 9. atrocious, excessive,
monstrous 10. inordinate, prodigious,
stupendous

Enos' father . . . 4. Seth

enough . . . 4. enow 5. ample, basta, fully,
quite 6. plenty 8. adequate 9. amplitude
10. sufficient 12. satisfactory

enounce . . . 5. state, utter 8. proclaim
9. enunciate, pronounce

enow . . . 9. presently

enrage . . . 5. anger 6. madden 7. incense,
inflame 9. infuriate

enraged . . . 5. irate 7. angered
8. maddened 10. infuriated

enraptured . . . 6. enrapt 8. ecstatic
9. delighted, entranced 10. enravished

enravished . . . 9. rapt 9. enchanted,
entranced, rapturous 10. enraptured

enrich . . . 4. lard 5. adorn, endow 6. fatten
7. improve 8. increase, ornament
9. embellish, fertilize

enroll . . . 4. coil, join, list, roll 5. enter
6. enlist, induct, unfurl, wrap up
7. engross, impanel 8. initiate, register
11. matriculate

ens . . . 5. being 6. entity 7. essence

ensconce . . . 4. hide 5. cover 6. settle
7. conceal, protect, shelter 9. establish
10. costume

enshroud . . . 4. wrap 6. clothe, swathe
7. conceal, enclose 8. enshrine

ensiform . . . 12. xiphisternum

ensign . . . 4. flag 6. banner 7. officer
8. gonfalon, standard 9. oriflamme
(oriflamb, anc)

ensign of Othello . . . 4. Iago

enslave . . . 8. enthrall

ensnare . . . 3. web 4. trap 5. benet,
catch, innet, noose 6. allure, enmesh,
entrap, seduce 7. involve

ensorcell, ensorcel . . . 7. bewitch,
enchant

ensue . . . 6. follow, pursue, result
7. imitate, succeed 8. come next

ensuing . . . 4. next 9. resultant

10. subsequent, succeeding

ensure . . . 6. assure, insure, secure
7. protect, warrant 9. guarantee

entad . . . 6. inward (opp of ectad)

ental . . . 5. inner (opp of ectal)

entangle . . . 3. mat, web 4. mesh, mire
5. afoul, ravel, snarl, twist 6. enlace,
enmesh, puzzle, raffle 7. confuse,
ensnare, involve, perplex 8. bewilder
9. embarrass 10. interweave

entanglement . . . 4. knot 5. snare, snarl
6. abatis 7. obstacle 9. barricade,
imbroglio 10. barbed wire, complexity
11. involvement

enter . . . 4. join, list 5. begin, start, train
6. come in, engage, enlist, enroll, insert,
record 8. initiate, inscribe, register
9. introduce, penetrate 11. participate

enter (pert to) . . .
career . . 6. incept
legal objection . . 5. demur
with hostility . . 6. invade
without permission . . 7. intrude
8. encroach, infringe

enterprise . . . 4. firm 5. essay 6. daring
7. attempt, crusade, exploit, venture
10. initiative 11. undertaking

enterprising . . . 4. bold 6. daring
9. energetic 11. up-and-coming

entertain . . . 4. fete 5. amuse, treat
6. divert, regale 7. beguile, cherish
8. interest

entertainer . . . 5. actor 6. dancer,
singer 7. actress, speaker 8. magician
9. performer 11. pantomimist
12. impersonator

entertainment . . . 4. play 5. party, revue,
sport 6. kermis (kermess), repast
7. pastime, ridotto, theater 8. entr'acte,
musicale 9. amusement, diversion,
reception, wayzgoose 10. recreation
12. Roman holiday

enthralled . . . 10. captivated, fascinated,
spellbound

enthusiasm . . . 4. élan, fire, zeal, zest
5. ardor, craze, estro, furor (furore),
mania, verve 6. fervor 7. ecstasy
8. interest 9. animation, eagerness,
transport 10. exaltation

enthusiast . . . 3. fan 5. bigot 6. rooter,
zealot 7. devotee, fanatic

enthusiastic . . . 5. eager, nutty, rabid
6. active, ardent 7. zealous
10. interested

entice . . . 4. bait, coax, lure, tole 5. decoy,
tempt, allure, cajole, incite, seduce
7. attract, wheedle 8. inveigle, persuade

enticement . . . 9. seduction
10. allurement, attraction, incitement,
inducement, persuasion, temptation
12. inveiglement

entire . . . 3. all 5. cover (Philat),
sound, total, utter, whole 6. intact
7. perfect, sincere, upright 8. complete,
faithful, stallion 9. integrate, undivided
10. unimpaired 11. unqualified
12. undiminished

entirely . . . 3. all 5. clean, fully, stark
6. solely, wholly 7. totally 9. every inch,
perfectly, sincerely 10. completely

entitle . . . 3. dub 4. call, name, term

5. style 6. assign, enable, impute
7. empower, qualify 9. authorize,
designate 10. denominate

entity . . . 3. ens 4. soul, unit 5. being,
entia, thing 7. integer 8. infinity (Math)
9. existence

entomb . . . 4. bury 5. inter, inurn
6. hearse, inhume 7. confine
9. sepulture

entourage . . . 5. suite, train 7. retinue
10. associates, attendants
12. surroundings

entr'acte . . . 3. act 5. dance, music
7. interim 9. interlude

entrails . . . 4. guts 6. bowels 7. insides,
viscera 8. interior 10. intestines

entrance . . . 3. way 4. adit, door,
gate 5. entry, inlet 6. access, portal
7. gateway, ingress, postern
9. admission, insertion, threshold,
vestibule 10. admittance

entrance (pert to) . . .
church (Eastern) . . 5. Great 6. Little
formal . . 5. debut 12. introduction
hostile . . 9. incursion
temple (Buddh) . . 5. toran (torana)

entranced . . . 4. rapt 7. charmed
8. dreaming 9. delighted, overjoyed
10. fascinated, hypnotized, spellbound
11. overpowered

entrap . . . 3. net 4. trap 5. catch, decoy,
noose, snare 6. tangle 7. beguile,
ensnare 8. entangle, inveigle

entreat . . . 3. ask, beg, woo 4. pray
5. crave, halse (obs) plead 6. adjure,
appeal 7. beseech, implore, solicit
8. petition 9. importune 10. supplicate

entreaty . . . 4. plea, suit 6. appeal, prayer
7. request 8. petition 10. invitation
11. importunity 12. solicitation,
supplication

entree, entrée . . . 4. dish 6. access
7. ingress, opening 9. admission
10. permission (to enter)

entrench . . . 6. invade 7. enter on,
fortify, intrude 8. encroach, trespass
9. establish

entrenchment . . . 7. defense, parapet
9. intrusion 10. protection
12. encroachment, infringement
13. establishment

entrepot . . . 5. depot, store 9. warehouse
10. depository

entrepreneur . . . 7. provost 9. executive
10. impresario 13. administrator

entrust . . . 6. commit 7. confide, consign
8. delegate 10. commission

entry . . . 4. hall, item, lane, post 7. ingress
8. entrance, register 9. admission,
vestibule 10. contestant, memorandum
12. introduction

entwine . . . 4. lace 5. clasp, twine, twist,
weave 6. enlace 7. wreathe 9. interknit

enumerate . . . 4. list, tell 5. count 6. detail,
number, reckon, relate 7. compute
8. estimate, name over, rehearse
9. calculate, catalogue (catalog)
12. recapitulate 13. particularize

enumeration . . . 4. list 5. count 6. census
10. numeration 14. recapitulation

enunciate . . . 3. say 5. utter 6. affirm

7. declare 8. announce, proclaim
9. postulate, pronounce 10. articulate

enunciation . . . 9. statement, utterance
11. affirmation, attestation, declaration
12. announcement 13. pronouncement,
pronunciation

envelop . . . 4. case, wrap 5. cover
6. clothe, encase, enwrap, infold,
invest, sheath, shroud 7. conceal,
enclose, sheathe 8. encircle, surround
9. encompass, enwreathe
10. integument

envelope . . . 3. bur (burr) 5. cover, curve
6. jacket 7. conceal, rampart, vesicle,
wrapper 8. membrane 10. integument

enveloped . . . 6. amidst 7. covered
10. surrounded

envenom . . . 5. taint 6. poison 8. embitter

envious . . . 7. jealous 8. covetous,
grudging, spiteful 9. green-eyed
10. begrudging

environ . . . 3. hem 6. suburb 7. compass,
envelop, hedge in, involve, purlieu
8. encircle, outskirt, surround
9. encompass

environment . . . 4. area 6. medium,
milieu 7. setting, suburbs, terrain
8. environs 10. background
12. neighborhood, surroundings
13. encompassment

environmental . . . 10. ecological

envisage . . . 4. face 8. confront 9. visualize
11. contemplate 12. meet squarely

envision . . . 5. dream 7. picture
9. visualize 11. contemplate 12. meet
squarely

envoy . . . 5. agent 6. legate, l'envoi
stanza 7. refrain 8. ambjate, delegate,
diplomat 9. messenger 10. ambassador,
postscript 12. commissioner

envy . . . 5. covet 6. grudge 8. jealousy
12. covetousness

enwrap, inwrap . . . 4. roll wrap 5. clothe,
enfold, infold 7. engross 8. surround

enzyme . . . 3. ase (suff) 5. bread (Eccl)
6. lotase, olease, pepsin, rennin,
urease 7. amylase, ferment, laccase,
ptyalin, trypsin 8. diastase, protease
9. digestant

enzyme activator . . . 11. biocatalyst

eoan . . . 7. auroral 8. daybreak, easterly

eon, aeon . . . 3. age, era 4. time 5. cycle
8. eternity 10. generation

ephemeral . . . 7. diurnal 9. chickweed,
deciduous, transient 15. short-lived

ephemeris . . . 5. diary 7. almanac, journal
8. calendar 10. periodical 11. publication

Ephesus (pert to) . . .
city of . . 6. Greece (anc)
famed for . . 5. ruins 12. Christianity
site . . 9. Aegean Sea
temple . . 7. Artemis
visitor (early) . . 6. St Paul

Ephraim . . . 4. bear (grizzly) 5. tribe
8. fruitful

epi . . . 6. finial

epic . . . 3. cid 4. epos, -poem, saga
5. epode 6. Aeneid (by Vergil), epopee,
heroic 9. narrative

epicene . . . 7. neutral, sexless
10. effeminate

epicure . . . 6. friand (obs) 7. glutton, gourmet 8. gourmand, Sybarite 9. bon vivant 10. gastronome, voluptuary 11. connoisseur

epidemic . . . 4. pest 6. plague 8. pandemic 9. prevalent, spreading 10. contagious, pestilence

epidermis . . . 4. skin 7. cuticle 8. ectoderm 9. scarfskin

epigram . . . 3. mot, saw 4. poem, quip 5. adage, maxim 6. dictum, saying 7. distich 11. inscription (obs)

epigraph . . . 5. motto, title 9. quotation 11. inscription

Epiphany (Eccl) . . . 5. Feast (Jan 6)

Epirus, oracle of . . . 6. Dodona (Mt Tomarus, Gr)

episode . . . 3. event, story 8. incident 10. digression (Mus), occurrence

epistle . . . 4. note, post 6. billet, lesson, letter 7. message, missive, writing 8. dispatch, rescript 13. communication

epitaph . . . 7. writing (monument) 8. hic jacet 11. inscription

epithet . . . 4. name, term 5. label 6. byname 7. agnomen 9. sobriquet 11. appellation (significant)

epitome . . . 6. digest 7. summary 8. abstract 9. comprisal 10. abridgment, compendium

epitomize . . . 7. abridge, curtail 8. abstract, compress, condense, contract, diminish 9. capsulize

epoch . . . 3. age, day, eon, era 4. date, time 5. event 6. period

epopee . . . 4. epic, epos, poem 5. genre (epic) 6. poetry (epic)

epoptic . . . 6. mystic, secret

Epstein-Barr . . . 4. mono 5. virus

equable . . . 4. even 6. steady 7. uniform

equal . . . 3. iso (pref), par, tie 4. both, even, fere (obs), just, pari (pref), peer, same 5. match, rival 7. compeer, emulate, equable, uniform 8. adequate, parallel 9. equitable, identical 10. coordinate, equivalent, substitute 11. counterpart 12. commensurate 13. proportionate

equal day and night . . . 11. equidiurnal, equinoctial

equal density (atmospheric) . . . 8. isoteric

equality . . . 3. par, tie 6. equity, owelty (payment), parity 7. egalite, isonomy (law) 8. adequacy, evenness, fairness, identity, sameness 10. uniformity 12. impartiality

Equality State . . . 7. Wyoming (first with Woman Suffrage)

equalize . . . 4. even 5. equal, level, match 6. equate, smooth 7. balance 10. symmetrize

equally . . . 2. as 4. equi (pref) 5. alike 6. evenly, justly 11. identically 15. correspondingly

equanimity . . . 5. poise 6. aplomb 7. balance 8. calmness, evenness, serenity 9. assurance, composure 10. confidence, equability 11. tranquility 12. tranquillity

equilibrium . . . 5. poise 6. stasis 7. balance 8. equality 9. stability

10. equanimity

equine . . . 3. ass 4. colt, foal, mare 5. filly, horse, steed, zebra 6. donkey

equine cry . . . 5. neigh 6. whinny

equip . . . 3. arm, fit, imp, rig 4. deck, gear, gird 5. dress, endow 7. costume, furnish, qualify 8. accouter

equipment . . . 4. gear 5. armor 6. outfit, tackle, traits (personal) 7. ability, panoply (warriors) 8. equipage 9. apparatus 11. preparation 12. accoutrement, accouterment

equitable . . . 4. fair, just 5. right 6. honest 7. upright 9. impartial 10. bonitarian (Rom law), reasonable

equity . . . 4. laws 6. rights 7. honesty, justice 8. fairness 9. rectitude 11. uprightness

equivalence . . . 3. par 7. valence 8. equality, sameness 10. relativity 11. correlation

equivalent . . . 5. alike, equal 9. identical 10. tantamount

equivocal . . . 7. dubious, obscure 8. doubtful, puzzling 9. ambiguous, enigmatic, uncertain 10. amphibolic, mysterious, perplexing 11. problematic 13. indeterminate

equivocate . . . 3. lie 5. dodge, evade, fence, shift 6. palter, trifle 7. quibble, shuffle 11. prevaricate 12. tergiversate

era . . . 2. AD, BC 3. age, eon 4. date, time 5. cycle, epoch 6. period 10. Anno Domini 12. Before Christ

eradicate . . . 4. dele, root, weed 5. annul, erase 6. remove, uproot 7. abolish, destroy, epilate, extract, root out 9. eliminate, extirpate 10. annihilate 11. exterminate

erase . . . 4. dele, kill 5. arase (obs) 6. cancel, delete, efface, excise 7. expunge, relieve 10. obliterate

Erasmus satire . . . 16. The Praise of Folly

Erastus (Swiss) . . . 9. physician 10. theologian

ere . . . 4. also, soon 5. early, prior 6. before, erenow, sooner 7. earlier, ere long 8. erewhile, formerly 10. before long, previously, sooner than

Erebus (pert to) . . .
 brother . . 3. Nox
 father of . . 3. Day 6. Aether
 Greek myth . . 8. darkness (nether)
 native of . . 5. Hades
 son . . 5. Chaos

erect . . . 4. lift, rear, stay 5. build, found, raise, stand, upend 6. raised 7. elevate, upright 8. uplifted, vertical 9. construct, establish, institute 13. perpendicular

eremite . . . 6. hermit 7. recluse 8. anchoret, solitary 9. anchorite

erenow . . . 5. prior 8. erewhile, formerly 10. heretofore

ergo . . . 5. hence 9. therefore

Erin . . . 4. Eire 7. Ireland

Eritrea, Africa . . .
 capital . . 6. Asmara
 formerly part of . . 8. Ethiopia
 site . . 6. Red Sea

ermine . . . 3. fur 4. robe (emblem)

5. stoat (stot) 6. clothe, lasset, weasel 7. ermelin

erode ... 3. eat 4. gnaw, wear 7. corrode, decline, destroy 11. deteriorate 12. disintegrate

erotic ... 6. loving, sexual 7. amative, amatory, amorous, sensual

err ... 3. sin 4. miss, slip 5. stray 6. bungle 7. blunder, deviate 10. transgress 12. miscalculate, misinterpret

Er Rai ... 5. stars 8. shepherd

errand ... 4. task, trip 7. journey, mission 8. business (special) 10. commission

errand boy ... 4. page 7. bellboy, bellhop, courier 9. messenger

errant ... 6. erring, roving 7. peccant 8. fallible 9. deviating, erroneous, itinerant, wandering 10. journeying

erratic ... 5. queer, rogue 6. whacky 7. nomadic, strange 8. abnormal 9. eccentric, irregular, planetary, wandering 10. capricious, changeable

erroneous ... 5. false, wrong 6. untrue 7. peccant 8. illusory, mistaken 9. wandering

error ... 3. sin 4. flub, muff, slip 5. boner, lapse 6. errata (pl) 7. miscue 7. blunder, falsity, misstep, mistake 8. iniquity 11. anachronism, misjudgment 14. miscalculation

ersatz ... 5. proxy, token 9. vicarious 10. equivalent, substitute 11. alternative, replacement 12. substitution

Erse ... 5. Irish 6. Celtic, Gaelic

erst, erstwhile ... 4. also, once 5. first 6. former, sooner 8. earliest, formerly 10. heretofore, previously

erudite ... 4. wise 7. learned 8. cultured, educated, literate 9. scholarly

erudition ... 4. lore 6. finish, wisdom 7. letters 8. learning, pedantry 9. knowledge

eruption ... 4. rash 6. geyser 7. volcano 8. ejection, outbreak, outburst 9. commotion, exanthema 10. nettlerash 13. efflorescence

Esau (pert to) ...
Bible ref .. 7. Genesis
brother .. 5. Jacob
father .. 5. Isaac
home .. 4. Seir
mother .. 7. Rebekah
name (later) .. 4. Edom

escape ... 4. flee 5. dodge, elope, elude, evade, vent 7. evasion 9. avolation 13. circumvention

escargot ... 5. snail

escarpment ... 5. cliff, slope 9. precipice 13. fortification

eschar ... 4. scab, sore 5. crust 6. slough

escharotic ... 7. caustic, mordant 8. stinging 9. corrosive

escheat ... 4. fall 5. lapse 6. revert (land) 7. forfeit 9. reversion 10. forfeiture

eschew ... 4. shun 5. avoid 7. abstain, refrain

escolar ... 4. fish 8. mackerel (like)

escort ... 3. see 4. beau 5. guard (honor), usher 6. attend, convoy, gigolo, squire 7. conduct, retinue 8. chaperon 9. accompany 13. accompaniment

escritoire ... 4. desk 6. bureau 7. dresser 9. secretary 10. secretaire

escrow ... 4. bond, deed (deposit) 9. muniments

esculent ... 6. edible 7. eatable 8. gustable 10. comestible

escutcheon ... 4. fess (band), orle (voided) 5. crest 6. shield

esker, eskar ... 2. os 4. osar (pl) 5. drift, hills, mound, ridge

Eskimo ... 3. Ita 4. Yuit 5. Aleut 6. Innuit 10. skraelling 11. Yikirgaulit (Diomede Isles)

Eskimo (pert to) ...
boat, canoe .. 5. kayak, umiak (oomiac)
boot (sealskin) .. 5. kamik
coat (bird skin) .. 5. parka 6. temiak
color .. 5. brown (rustic)
dog .. 5. Husky 6. Malemute
family .. 9. Eskimauan
fish .. 4. Atka 8. mackerel
hut, house .. 5. igloo, tupek (tupik)
jacket .. 6. temiak
knife (woman's) .. 3. ulu
memorial post .. 3. xat
settlement .. 4. Etah
totem .. 4. pole, post 6. symbol

esne ... 4. serf 5. slave 8. hireling

esophagus, oesophagus ... 4. crop, gula 6. gullet, throat 7. pharynx

esoteric ... 5. inner 6. occult, secret 7. private 8. abstruse, initiate, personal 9. recondite 12. confidential

esoteric doctrine ... 6. cabala

esoteric wisdom ... 6. gnosis

espalier ... 7. epaulet, railing, trellis

Español ... 7. Spanish

especial ... 5. chief 7. special 8. peculiar, uncommon

Esperanto ... 3. Ido 8. language (Internat)

espionage ... 4. espy 6. spying 11. observation (secret) 14. reconnaissance

esplanade ... 4. walk 5. drive, level, Prado, praya 6. strand 7. walkway

espousal ... 7. wedding 8. adoption, ceremony 10. acceptance 11. embracement

espouse ... 3. wed 4. bind, mate 5. adopt, marry 6. defend, pledge 7. betroth, embrace, support 8. maintain, plead for

esprit de corps ... 3. wit 6. spirit 8. devotion 10. enthusiasm, fellowship 11. partisanism

esprit fort (Relig) ... 11. freethinker

espy ... 3. see 5. watch 6. behold, descry, detect 7. discern 8. discover 9. look about

esquire ... 5. title 6. escort, gentry 7. armiger 8. escudero, nobleman 11. armor-bearer 12. shield-bearer

essay ... 3. try 4. test 5. assay, chris (Rhet), paper, theme, tract, trial 6. effort, thesis 7. attempt 8. endeavor, treatise 11. composition 12. disquisition, dissertation

esse ... 5. being (real) 9. existence

essence ... 3. ens 4. core, gist, odor, pith 5. attar, being, scent 6. kernel, nature 7. element, extract, perfume

9. principle, substance 12. quintessence
essential ... 5. vital 6. mortal 7. needful
8. existent, inherent 9. necessary,
necessity 13. indispensable
essential oil ... 8. volatile 12. attar of
roses
essential part ... 4. core, crux, gist, pith
7. element 8. inherent 10. inwardness
establish ... 3. fix 4. base, seat 5. build,
enact, erect, found, plant, prove, set
up 6. create, ground, locate, ordain,
settle 7. confirm, pre-empt 8. ensconce,
legalize, radicate (rare) 9. ascertain,
originate
established ... 5. fixed 6. proved, rested,
stable 11. naturalized, traditional
12. conventional
established (pert to) ...
    church .. 9. Episcopal (Eng)
    rule .. 8. standard
    thing .. 4. fact
    truth .. 8. verified
establishment ... 4. mill 5. plant
6. custom, menage 7. factory
9. structure 12. organization
establishment of cordial relations ...
13. rapprochement
establishment of new plant home ...
6. ecesis
estate ... 4. alod, fief (feudal), rank
(social) 5. manor, title 6. assets,
equity 7. alodium, demesne, fortune
8. freehold, interest, property
9. situation
esteem ... 4. dear 5. adore, honor, judge,
pride, value 6. admire, regard, repute,
revere 7. respect 8. appraise, venerate
10. appreciate 13. consideration
ester of ...
    silicic acid .. 8. silicate
    stearic acid .. 7. stearin 8. stearate
    tropic acid .. 7. tropate
    vinegar .. 7. acetate
esthetic, aesthetic ... 6. essene
8. artistic, tasteful 9. beautiful
estimable ... 6. worthy 8. valuable
9. admirable, honorable, reputable,
venerable 10. measurable
12. praiseworthy
estimate ... 3. aim, set 4. gage, rank,
rate 5. audit, gauge, guess, prize, think
6. assess, repute 7. adjudge, compute,
measure, opinion 8. appraise, judgment
9. calculate, statement, valuation
Estonia ...
    capital .. 5. Revel 7. Tallinn
    industry .. 3. oil
    island .. 5. Oesel
estop ... 3. bar 4. fill, halt, plug, stay
6. impede, stop up 7. prevent 8. prohibit
estrange ... 4. part, wean 6. divert,
divide 8. alienate, disunite, separate
estreat ... 4. copy 6. amerce, sconce
7. extract 9. duplicate, penalties (law)
estuary ... 3. bay 4. Pará 5. firth, frith,
Plata
etch ... 3. cut 4. bite 5. infix 7. corrode,
engrave, impress (upon)
eternal ... 6. eonian 7. aeonian, ageless,
endless, lasting 8. enduring, immortal,
timeless 9. boundless, ceaseless,

immutable, incessant, unceasing
10. unchanging 11. everlasting
12. imperishable, interminable,
unchangeable
Eternal City ... 4. Rome
eternal death ... 9. perdition
eternal home ... 6. heaven 12. The
Hereafter
eternity ... 3. eon 4. aeon, ages, olam
8. Olam haba
etesian ... 4. wind (Aegean Sea) 6. annual
8. seasonal 10. periodical
Ethan Frome author ... 7. Wharton
ether ... 3. air, sky 5. ester, space
6. anisol, heaven (anc) 8. empyrean
10. anesthetic
ethereal ... 4. rare 5. aerie (aery), light
7. fragile, slender, tenuous 8. delicate,
heavenly, vaporous 9. celestial
10. atmosphere (earth's), spiritlike
11. phantomlike 13. unsubstantial
ethereal (pert to) ...
    being .. 5. sylph
    color .. 7. sky blue
    fluid .. 5. ichor (icor)
    poetic .. 4. aery
    salt .. 5. ester
ethical ... 5. moral, right 7. upright
8. virtuous
ethics ... 6. morals 8. hedonics
10. principles (moral) 11. highest good,
summum bonum 12. Magna Moralia
(Aristotle)
Ethiopia (Abyssinia) ...
    capital .. 10. Addis Ababa
    city .. 5. Adowa
    empress .. 7. Zauditu
    king (Myth) .. 5. Negus 6. Memnon
    people .. 6. Hamite 10. Abyssinian
    people (anc) .. 5. Bejas, Galla 6. Hamite,
    Semite
    river .. 3. Omo 4. Juba 5. Abbai (Blue
    Nile)
    ruler .. 7. Menelik 13. Haile Selassie
    tribes (anc) .. 5. Bejas, Galla 7. Hamites,
    Semites
Ethiopian (pert to) ...
    ape .. 6. gelada
    banana .. 6. ensete
    dialect .. 4. Geez
    lily .. 5. calla
    Torah .. 5. tetel
ethnic ... 5. pagan 6. racial 7. gentile,
heathen
ethnology ... 5. races (Man)
ethology ... 7. manners 9. bionomics,
character
ethos (opp of pathos) ... 9. attitudes
(moral), esthetics
etiquette ... 4. form 5. label, mores
6. ticket 7. decorum, manners
9. amenities, propriety 10. civilities
etiquette, breach of ... 8. solecism
Etruria, Italy ... see *Etruscan*
Etruscan (pert to) ...
    bookbinding (anc) .. 9. classical
    deity .. 3. Lar, Uni
    pottery .. 8. bucchero (black)
    race .. 7. Rasenna 8. Tursenoi, Tyrrheni
    soothsayer .. 8. haruspex (a)
    soothsayer's function .. 8. extispex

ettle ... 3. try 4. plan 6. aspire, design, intent 8. consider, endeavor
etui, etwee ... 4. case 7. trousse
etymology ... 10. word origin
eucalyptus ... 4. lerp (laap, juice) 7. gum tree 8. eucalypt
eucalyptus eater ... 5. koala
Eucharist (pert to) ...
 administer to .. 6. housel 8. viaticum (dying)
 plate .. 5. paten
 rite .. 9. Communion (Holy) 11. Lord's Supper
 wafer .. 4. host
 wafer vessel .. 8. ciborium
 wine .. 5. krama
 wine vessel .. 3. ama 5. amula
Euclid (Gr) ... 8. geometer (BC)
eulogist ... 9. encomiast 10. panegyrist
eulogize ... 4. laud 5. boost, extol 6. praise 7. commend, glorify 9. celebrate 10. panegyrize
eulogy ... 5. eloge 6. hesped (Heb), praise 7. oration 8. citation, encomium 9. laudation, panegyric
euphony ... 5. meter 6. melody, rhythm, speech (ease of) 7. harmony
Eurafrica ... 5. Egypt 6. Europe 7. Algeria 9. Abyssinia (anc)
Eurasia ... 4. Asia 6. Europe 7. Scythia (anc)
Eurasian (pert to) ...
 herb .. 6. yarrow 7. gosmore
 mint .. 6. Nepeta
 people .. 5. Finns 7. Ugrians 9. Armenians, Turanians
eureka ... 3. aha 11. exclamation 12. I Have Found It (Calif motto)
Euripedes (Gr) ... 4. poet (BC)
Europe ... see also *European*
 basin (coal) .. 4. Saar
 battlefield .. 5. Marne 6. Verdun 8. Normandy, Waterloo 11. Belleau Wood
 capitals .. 4. Bonn, Oslo, Riga, Rome 5. Berne, Paris, Sofia 6. Athens, Berlin, Dublin, Lisbon, London, Madrid, Moscow, Prague, Warsaw 8. Belgrade, Brussels, Budapest, Helsinki 9. Amsterdam, Bucharest, Stockholm 10. Bratislava, Copenhagen, Monte Carlo
 country (anc) .. 4. Elis (Gr) 7. Etruria (It)
 country (modern) .. 5. Italy, Spain 6. France, Greece, Latvia, Monaco, Norway, Poland, Russia, Sweden 7. Belgium, Denmark, England, Finland, Germany, Hungary, Ireland, Rumania 8. Bulgaria, Portugal, Slovakia 10. Yugoslavia 11. Netherlands, Switzerland 13. Czech Republic 14. Czechoslovakia
 economic union .. 7. Benelux
 gulf .. 4. Riga 7. Bothnia
 invaders .. 4. Huns 5. Arabs, Turks 7. Mongols
 kingdom (anc) .. 5. Arles 6. Aragon 8. Burgundy
 lancer .. 5. uhlan 6. hussar
 mountain region .. 4. Alps 5. Tirol (Tyrol)

 8. Pyrenees 9. Apennines
 race (anc) .. 5. Goths 7. Teutons 9. Visigoths 10. Ostrogoths
 river .. 4. Elbe, Isar 5. Loire, Meuse, Rhine, Rhone, Seine, Volga 6. Danube 7. Dneiper, Moselle
 sea .. 4. Azov 5. North 6. Baltic
 strait .. 8. Bosporus
 valley .. 4. Ruhr
 volcano .. 4. Etna 8. Vesuvius 9. Stromboli
European (pert to) ...
 antelope .. 7. chamois
 bat .. 8. serotine
 bird .. 3. ani, daw, mew (gull) 4. kite, stag 5. glede, mavis, ousel, serin 6. godwit, linnet, marten, merlin (falcon) 7. bittern, jackdaw, ortolan, starnel 8. dotterel, garganey 9. brambling, gallinule 10. turtledove 11. lammergeier 12. capercaillie
 bison .. 7. aurochs
 clover .. 6. alsike
 dog .. 7. griffin
 fish .. 3. gar 4. dace, rudd, spet, tope (shark) 5. sprat 6. allice, barbel, brasse, morgay, turbot
 grape .. 6. muscat
 linden .. 4. teil
 mint .. 6. hyssop 9. horehound
 mouse .. 4. loir, vole
 polecat .. 7. fitchew
 rodent .. 3. erd 4. loir 6. leriot 7. hamster
 sandpiper .. 4. ruff 5. terek
 squirrel .. 5. sisel 10. polatouche
 tree .. 4. cade (juniper), sorb (apple) 5. carob 6. terebinth
 weasel .. 5. stoat
 wheat .. 5. emmer (speltz) 7. einkorn
evacuant ... 6. emetic 8. diuretic 9. cathartic, purgative
evacuate ... 4. void 5. empty, expel 6. depart, vacate 7. deprive, exhaust 8. withdraw 9. discharge
evade ... 3. gee 4. duck, foil, shun 5. avoid, dodge, elude, parry, shirk, shunt 6. baffle, escape, illude 7. beguile, quibble 8. sidestep, slip away 10. circumvent
evaluate ... 5. judge, weigh 6. assess 8. appraise
evanescent ... 8. fleeting 9. ephemeral, transient, vanishing 11. impermanent 12. disappearing 13. infinitesimal
evangelical ... 7. Gospels 8. orthodox 10. Protestant, scriptural
Evangeline (pert to) ...
 home .. 6. Acadia
 lover .. 7. Gabriel
 poem by .. 10. Longfellow (1847)
evangelist ... 6. Graham, Sunday (Billy) 7. apostle, Roberts 9. McPherson
evaporate ... 3. dry 5. steam 6. escape, exhale 7. avolate 8. vaporize 9. cease to be, dehydrate, disappear
evasion ... 5. dodge, shift 6. escape 8. avoiding 9. avoidance, quibbling, shuffling 12. equivocation 13. circumvention, secretiveness
evasive ... 3. sly 4. eely 6. shifty 7. elusive, elusory 9. deceitful,

quibbling, secretive

eve . . . 3. iva (herb), wet 4. dusk, thaw 6. sunset 12. on the brink of, on the verge of

even . . . 3. e'en, tie 4. just, tied 5. equal, exact, level, match, plane 6. placid, smooth, square, steady 7. abreast, balance, equable, neutral, regular, uniform 8. directly, parallel 9. impartial, precisely 11. symmetrical

even (if) . . . 8. although 12. nevertheless 15. notwithstanding

even (so) . . . 3. yes 12. nevertheless

evener . . . 9. equalizer 10. doubletree

evenglow . . . 3. red (color) 8. twilight

evening . . . 5. Abend 6. sunset

evening dress . . . 4. gown 6. jewels, tuxedo 8. slippers (high heel) 9. full dress, headdress 10. dinner coat 11. tie and tails 15. swallow-tailed coat

event . . . 4. fate (obs), game 5. drama, issue 6. result 7. contest, episode, scandal 8. incident 9. adventure, happening, milestone 10. conclusion, occurrence 11. consequence, termination 12. circumstance

event (pert to) . . .
  extraordinary . . 10. phenomenon
  supernatural . . 7. miracle
  theater . . 6. opener 8. premiere
  turning point . . 6. crisis 8. decision, landmark

eventide . . . 4. dusk 6. sunset, vesper 7. evening, sundown 8. twilight 9. nightfall

eventually . . . 3. yet 6. lastly 7. finally 10. ultimately

ever . . . 3. e'er 4. anon 5. at all 6. always 7. forever 10. constantly 11. perpetually

Everest peak . . . 6. Lhotse (28,100 ft)

evergreen shrub . . . 4. ilex, moss, Olax, titi 5. heath, holly, savin, toyon 6. laurel 7. baretta, jasmine 9. perennial 12. rhododendron

evergreen tree . . . 3. fir, yew 4. pine 5. carob, cedar, larch, olive, Taxus 6. balsam, deodar, spruce, tarata 7. conifer, hemlock, madrona, redwood

everlasting . . . 6. eterne 7. aeonian, agelong, durable, endless, eternal, forever, lasting, tedious 8. enduring, evermore, immortal, infinite 9. continual, incessant, perpetual, unceasing, wearisome 10. immortelle, indefinite 11. never-ending, strawflower 12. Eternal Being, imperishable 13. unintermitted, uninterrupted

every . . . 3. all, any, ilk 4. each, ilka 6. entire 8. complete

every one, everyone . . . 3. all 4. each 9. everybody 10. individual

everything . . . 3. all, sum 4. total

evict . . . 4. oust 5. eject, expel, prove 6. remove 7. confute 8. force out

eviction . . . 6. ouster 9. ejectment 11. dislodgment 13. dispossession

evidence . . . 4. clue, sign 5. proof, token 6. attest, evince 7. constat (law), probate, support 8. argument, manifest, rebuttal 9. testimony 10. indication 15. circumstantiate

evident . . . 5. clear, plain 6. patent 7. obvious, visible 8. apparent, manifest, palpable 9. notorious 11. indubitable

eviscerate . . . 3. gut 10. disembowel

evil . . . 3. bad, ill, mal (pref) 4. bane, vile 6. injury, sinful, wicked 7. adverse, baleful, corrupt, hurtful, immoral, malefic, misdeed, satanic, unsound, vicious 8. depraved, iniquity, sinister 9. injurious, malignant, offensive 10. calamitous, malevolent, pernicious, wrongdoing 12. unpropitious

evil (pert to) . . .
  child . . 3. imp
  deed . . 3. sin 4. harm
  devil (little) . . 9. deevilick (Scot)
  doer . . 5. cheat 9. miscreant, wrongdoer 10. malefactor
  omen . . 5. knell
  spirit . . 5. bugan, demon, devil, ghoul, Satan 6. Belial 7. Ahriman, Amaimon 8. Asmodeus 9. cacodemon, demonkind, lost souls

evile . . . 4. ills, mala

evince . . . 4. show 7. display, exhibit, express, provoke 8. convince, evidence, indicate, manifest

evoke . . . 4. call (out) 5. educe, voice 6. elicit, prompt, summon 7. conjure

evolution . . . 7. biogeny, cosmism 8. heredity, maneuver, movement 9. Darwinism, phylogeny, unfolding, unrolling 10. evolvement 11. development 13. manifestation, Spencerianism

evolve . . . 4. emit 5. educe 6. create, deduce, derive, unfold, unroll 7. develop, grow out 9. disengage, expatiate, extricate 11. disentangle

ewe . . . 3. keb 4. lamb 5. crone (old), sheep 6. theave

ewer . . . 3. jug 5. crock 7. pitcher

exacerbate . . . 5. anger 6. incite 8. embitter, irritate 9. aggravate

exact . . . 4. just, levy, nice 6. assess, demand, elicit, extort, formal, minute, oblige, strict 7. careful, correct, literal, precise, regular, require 8. accurate 10. methodical, meticulous

exact (pert to) . . .
  opposite of . . 8. antipode 9. antipodal
  penalty . . 4. fine 7. estreat
  thinking . . 13. ratiocination
  vengeance . . 6. avenge

exacting . . . 6. severe, strict 7. arduous 8. critical 9. demanding, elicitory 10. fastidious 12. extortionate

exacting devotion (exclusive) . . .
7. jealous

exactly . . . 3. due 5. spand 6. nicely 7. quite so 8. as you say 9. precisely 10. accurately

exaggerated . . . 5. outré 7. enhanced, enlarged, overdone, romanced 9. excessive, increased, magnified 10. overstated 11. exceptional 13. overestimated 14. misrepresented

exaggerated comedy . . . 5. farce

exalt . . . 5. elate, extol, raise 6. praise 7. elevate, ennoble, glorify, inspire, promote, worship 8. enthrone, increase, sanctify 10. aggrandize

exalted . . . 5. grand, noble, sheen 6. elated 7. refined, sublime 8. elevated, extolled 9. dignified 11. illustrious

examination . . . 4. test 5. audit, trial 7. inquiry 8. research, scrutiny, specimen 10. discussion, inspection 11. inquisition 13. investigation

examine . . . 3. pry, spy, try (law) 4. pore, scan, sift, test 5. audit, probe, quest 6. censor, debate, ponder 7. analyze, collate, discuss, explore, inspect 8. consider 10. scrutinize 11. interrogate

examiner . . . 6. censor, conner, tester 7. auditor, officer (court) 9. inspector

example . . . 4. case, norm, type 5. bysen (obs), model 6. sample 7. pattern, warning 8. instance, paradigm, specimen 9. exemplify, precedent 12. illustration 15. exemplification

ex animo . . . 9. sincerely 12. from the heart

Excalibur . . . 5. sword

excavate . . . 3. dig 4. cave, mine 5. dig up, scoop, stope 6. dredge, exhume, quarry 9. hollow out

excavation . . . 3. pit 4. hole, mine 5. stope 6. cavity, dugout 7. digging 8. opencast

exceed . . . 3. top 4. pass 5. excel, outdo 6. outvie, overdo 7. eclipse, outrank, surpass 8. outstrip, overstep 9. overshoot, transcend 11. predominate

exceedingly . . . 4. many, very 9. extremely 13. extraordinary

excel . . . 3. cap, top 4. beat, best 5. outdo, outgo, rival 6. better, exceed, precel 7. surpass 8. dominate, outshine 9. transcend

excellence . . . 4. meed 5. merit 6. desert, virtue 7. classic, probity 9. supremacy 13. inimitability

excellent . . . 4. A-one, best, fine, good 5. bravo, prime, super 6. choice, select, tiptop, worthy 7. capital, corking, stellar 8. skillful (skilful), stunning, valuable 9. admirable, exquisite, first-rate 12. transcendent

except . . . 3. bar, but 4. omit, save 6. exempt, reject, unless 7. besides 9. eliminate, other than

exception . . . 4. plea 5. cavil, doubt 6. oddity 7. dissent 8. demurrer 9. condition, exclusion, exemption, objection, rejection 11. restriction

exceptional . . . 4. rare 7. notable, unusual 8. superior, uncommon 9. exclusive, wonderful 10. remarkable 11. outstanding 13. extraordinary

excerpt . . . 4. cite 5. quote, scrap 6. choice 7. extract, passage (selected) 9. selection

excess . . . 3. too 4. over, plus 5. luxus 7. nimiety, overage, profuse, surplus 10. indulgence (undue), redundancy 11. superfluity 12. intemperance 14. immoderateness, superabundance

excess (solar over lunar month) . . . 5. epact

excessive . . . 3. too 5. undue 6. overly 7. extreme, profuse 8. overmuch 9. fanatical, plethoric 10. exorbitant, immoderate, inordinate, redundancy 11. exaggerated, extravagant 12. unreasonable

excessive (pert to) . . . *development* . . 11. hypertrophy *fear* . . 5. panic 6. phobia *gushing* . . 8. effusion *waste* . . 12. extravagance

excessively . . . 3. too 5. enorm 6. unduly 12. exorbitantly, inordinately 13. intemperately

exchange . . . 4. swap 5. bandy, trade 6. barter, resale, rialto 7. dealing, traffic 9. transpose 10. substitute 11. interchange, reciprocate

exchange (pert to) . . . *discount* . . 4. agio *for money* . . 4. cash, sell *letters* . . 10. correspond *place* . . 4. mart 5. store 6. bourse, market, shoppe *premium* . . 4. agio *visits* . . 3. gam

exchequer . . . 4. fisc (fisk) 5. funds, purse 8. finances, treasury 11. possessions (money)

excise . . . 3. tax 4. toll 6. impost

exciseman . . . 5. gager 7. officer 8. revenuer

excision . . . 7. erasure, removal 10. cutting off, cutting out, mutilation 11. destruction, extirpation

excite . . . 4. fire, roil, spur, stir, urge 5. elate, impel, rouse 6. arouse, awaken, bestir, incite, kindle, prompt, stir up 7. agitate, animate, inflame, provoke, psych up 8. energize, interest 9. electrify, impassion, instigate, stimulate

excited . . . 4. agog 6. hoopla 7. aroused, fevered, keyed up 8. agitated, startled 10. interested 11. impassioned

excited, not easily . . . 6. stolid 7. stoical 9. impassive

excitement . . . 3. ado 4. stir 5. fever 6. furore 7. emotion, ferment 9. agitation, commotion 10. incitement, irritation 11. disturbance, stimulation

exciting . . . 5. kicky 6. gung-ho, hectic 7. parlous 8. alluring 9. desirable, thrilling 10. delightful 11. interesting, provocative

exciting compassion . . . 7. piteous

exclamation . . . 2. ah, lo, oh, so 3. aha, bah, boo, fic, hep, oho, tut, ugh, yah 4. ahem, alas, drat, egad, evoe, phew, pish, rats, yech 5. bravo, humph, pshaw 6. indeed, shezam 7. kerwham 8. alackaday 11. ejaculation 12. interjection

exclude . . . 3. bar 4. omit 5. debar, eject, expel 6. banish 7. shut out 8. disallow, preclude, prohibit 9. eliminate 13. excommunicate

exclusive . . . 5. aloof, ritzy 6. select 7. special 8. limiting, snobbish 9. seclusive 10. definitive, unsociable 11. prohibitive, restrictive

exclusive right ... 6. patent
   10. concession 11. restriction
excoriate ... 4. flay, gall, peel 5. strip
   6. abrade 9. criticize
excrescence ... 4. boss (Arch), lump
   6. growth, nodule 9. appendage,
   outgrowth 10. protrusion
excrete ... 5. egest 9. discharge, eliminate
excruciating ... 7. painful, racking
   9. agonizing, torturing 11. distressing
excursion ... 3. row 4. ride, sail, tour,
   trek, trip 5. jaunt, sally 6. junket, outing,
   ramble 7. circuit, journey, outlope
   8. circuity 10. expedition
excusable ... 6. venial 9. allowable,
   justified 10. defensible, exemptible,
   pardonable, remissible 11. justifiable
excuse ... 4. plea 5. alibi, remit 6. acquit,
   essoin, pardon 7. absolve, apology,
   condone, forgive, pretext 8. overlook
   9. exonerate, extenuate
execrate ... 4. hate 5. abhor, curse
   6. detest, loathe 8. denounce
execute ... 2. do 3. act 4. hang, kill,
   vest 6. direct, effect, finish, manage
   7. conduct, enforce, perform 8. carry
   out, complete, transact 10. accomplish,
   administer
execution ... 4. writ 7. hanging
   10. production, punishment
   11. achievement, performance,
   transaction 14. accomplishment
exegete ... 3. leader 7. adviser
   8. dragoman 11. interpreter
exegesis ... 7. explain 9. interpret
   10. exposition, expounding
exemplar ... 5. ideal, model 7. example,
   paragon, pattern 8. specimen
   9. archetype
exemplary ... 8. laudable, monitory
   11. commendable 12. exemplifying,
   praiseworthy 14. representative
exemplify ... 4. copy 6. typify 7. explain
   10. illustrate, transcribe
exempt ... 4. exon 5. clear 6. immune
   7. absolve, release 8. dispense,
   excepted, excluded, released, set apart
   10. privileged
exemption ... 6. essoin 7. freedom
   8. immunity, impunity, navicert
   12. dispensation
exercise ... 3. ply, ure (anc) 4. use
   4. task, yoga 5. drill, étude, exert,
   train 6. action, employ, lesson, praxis,
   school, tai chi 7. display, jogging,
   problem, workout 8. activity, aerobics,
   ceremony, practice, training 9. athletics
   10. exhibition, gymnastics, isometrics
exertion ... 5. essay, trial 6. effort
   7. attempt 9. endeavor
exhalation ... 4. aura, fume 5. steam
   6. breath 7. halitus 8. effluvium,
   emanation 10. expiration
   11. evaporation 12. vaporization
exhale ... 4. emit 6. vanish 7. exhaust,
   respite 9. transpire 10. breathe out
exhaust ... 3. fag, sap 4. emit, jade, tire
   5. drain, empty, spend, waste, weary
   6. exhale, overdo, weaken 7. consume,
   deplete, fatigue 9. discharge
   10. impoverish

exhausted ... 4. done, worn 5. spent,
   tired 6. used up 7. emptied, petered
   (out) 8. dog-tired, forspent
exhaustion ... 6. effete 7. burnout, fatigue
   9. depletion, lassitude 11. prostration
   14. impoverishment
exhibit ... 3. air 4. fair, shew (anc)
   show, wear 5. stage, state 6. evince,
   expose, flaunt, parade, reveal 7. display
   8. disclose, evidence, manifest
   9. spectacle 11. demonstrate
   15. circumstantiate
exhibit (pert to) ...
   colors (change of) .. 8. iridesce, opalesce
   pleasure .. 5. gloat, revel (in)
   taste (refined) .. 6. ostent 7. elegant
exhibition ... 4. fair, show 9. spectacle
   10. exposition 11. ostentation
   13. manifestation
exhibition room ... 10. panopticon
exhilaration ... 6. gaiety 7. jollity
   8. gladness, hilarity 9. animation,
   merriment 10. excitement, joyousness
   11. gleefulness, refreshment
   12. cheerfulness, invigoration
exhort ... 4. urge, warn 6. advise, dehort,
   incite, preach 7. caution 9. encourage,
   stimulate
exhume ... 3. dig 5. delve 7. unearth
   8. disinter, exhumate
exigeant ... 8. exacting 11. importunate
exigency ... 4. need, urge 6. crisis
   7. demands, urgency 8. juncture,
   pressure 9. emergency, extremity,
   necessity 12. requirements
exigent ... 4. writ 6. strict, urgent
   8. critical, exacting, pressing
   9. demanding, necessary 10. compelling
   13. indispensable
exile ... 6. banish, deport 7. outcast
   8. outlawry, relegate 9. expulsion
   10. banishment, expatriate
   12. expatriation, proscription
exist ... 2. am, be, is 3. are 4. live
   5. alive 6. abound 9. be present
existence ... 3. ens 4. esse, life 5. actus,
   being, entia 6. extant 7. essence, reality
   8. presence 9. actuality
   13. manifestation
existing (pert to) ...
   fancifully .. 9. imaginary 10. transitory
   name only (in) .. 7. nominal, titular
   now .. 6. extant 7. current, present
   9. immediate
   same time .. 15. contemporaneous
   way of .. 9. lifestyle
exit ... 3. die 4. door, gate, vent 5. going,
   go out, issue 6. egress, outlet 7. leaving,
   passage (out), walkout 9. departure
exitus ... 5. death, issue 6. exodus, outlet
   7. outcome
exlex ... 6. outlaw
ex libris ... 8. colophon 9. bookplate
exodus ... 4. Book (Bib), exit 5. going
   6. flight, hegira 7. departure
Exodus author ... 4. Uris
exonerate ... 4. free 5. clear 6. acquit
   7. absolve, release, relieve 9. disburden
   (obs), exculpate
exorbitant ... 5. undue 9. excessive
   10. high-priced

exorbitant interest ... 5. usury
exorcism ... 5. spell 7. formula
8. expulsion (of evil spirits)
11. conjuration, incantation
exordium ... 5. proem 7. preface, prelude
8. overture 9. beginning 12. introduction
exoteric ... 8. exterior, external, outsider
14. comprehensible
exotic ... 5. alien 7. foreign, strange
8. colorful, ulterior 9. not native,
peregrine, unrelated 10. extraneous,
outlandish
expand ... 4. grow, open 5. sheet, splay,
tract 6. dilate, spread 7. broaden,
develop, distend, enlarge 9. expatiate,
intumesce
expanse ... 3. sea 4. main (broad)
5. ocean, plain, reach, tract 6. desert,
extent, spread 7. stretch 8. eternity
(time) 9. expansion
expansion ... 4. size 6. extent, growth,
spread 8. dilation, increase
10. distention 11. development,
enlargement, expatiation
expansive ... 4. wide 5. broad, large
7. elastic, liberal 8. effusive, spacious
9. bombastic, grandiose 11. extensional,
sympathetic 12. unrestrained
13. comprehensive
expatiate ... 5. dwell 6. dilate 7. descant,
enlarge 10. widespread
expatriate ... 5. exile, expel 6. banish,
outlaw 7. exclude, outcast 9. ostracize
13. excommunicate
expect ... 4. deem, hope, wait 5. await,
think 6. intend 7. suppose 10. anticipate
expectation ... 4. hope 9. imminence,
intention 12. anticipation
expedience ... 6. wisdom 7. fitness
10. adaptation, timeliness 11. suitability
expedient ... 4. wise 5. shift 6. timely
7. fitting, politic, ressort, stopgap
8. artifice, resource 9. advisable
10. profitable 12. advantageous
expedite ... 3. hie 4. easy, free 5. hurry,
light, speed 6. hasten 7. further, quicken
8. dispatch 10. accelerate, facilitate
expedition ... 5. drave, foray, haste,
speed 6. safari 7. Crusade, entrada,
journey 8. Crusades 9. excursion,
hastening
expel ... 4. oust, void 5. eject, evict,
exile 6. banish, exhale 7. extrude
9. discharge, eliminate 10. dispossess
expend ... 3. pay, use 5. spend, waste
7. consume 8. disburse 10. distribute
expenditure ... 5. outgo, price 6. outlay
7. expense, payment 11. consumption
12. disbursement
expense ... 4. cost 5. price 6. outlay
9. allowance 11. consumption
12. disbursement
expensive ... 4. dear, high 5. fancy, steep
6. costly, lavish 7. liberal 10. high-priced
11. extravagant
experience ... 3. see, try 4. feel, have,
know, test 5. maxim, sense, skill
6. ordeal, suffer, wisdom 7. emotion,
undergo 8. facility 9. knowledge,
sensation 10. occurrence
experience (pert to) ...

pleasure .. 5. enjoy
regret .. 6. repent
suffering .. 7. calvary
worldly .. 14. sophistication
experiment ... 3. try 4. test 5. essay,
proof, prove, trial 6. verify
11. observation
expert ... 3. ace 4. deft, whiz (whizz)
5. adept 6. adroit, clever, habile,
master 7. casuist (in conscience), dab
hand 8. artistic, skillful 10. proficient
11. connoisseur, experienced
12. professional
expiate ... 5. atone, purge 6. purify,
shrive (anc)
expiation ... 4. rite 6. amends 7. redress
8. piacular 9. atonement 10. redemption
12. compensation, propitiation
expire ... 3. die, end 4. pass 5. cease,
lapse 6. elapse, perish 7. breathe (out)
9. terminate
explain ... 5. clear, solve 6. define
7. expound, premise 8. describe
9. elucidate, interpret 10. demonstrate
explanation ... 6. theory 7. meaning
8. exegesis, scholium, solution
10. exposition 11. description,
explication 13. clarification
14. interpretation 15. exemplification
expletive ... 3. gee 4. egad, gosh,
oath 5. curse, there, voilà 6. behold
8. addition 9. added word
11. exclamation
explicit ... 4. open 5. exact, fixed
6. candid 7. express, precise 8. absolute,
distinct, implicit, manifest, positive
9. outspoken 11. unambiguous,
unequivocal, unqualified
13. unconditional 14. discriminating
explode ... 3. pop 4. fail 5. blast, burst
6. blow up 7. implode 8. backfire,
detonate
exploit ... 3. act (heroic) 4. dare,
deed, feat, gest, milk 5. bleed
7. heroism 9. advantage 10. overcharge
11. achievement
explore ... 4. look, view 5. probe 6. search
7. examine 8. discover 9. penetrate
11. investigate
explorer ... 5. diver 7. pioneer
10. discoverer
explorer ... 4. Byrd, Cook, Dias, Polo
(Marco), Ross 5. Cabot, Drake, Peary,
Scott 6. Balboa, Cortes (Cortez), De
Soto, Hudson, Pinzón 7. Cartier,
Pizarro, Raleigh (Ralegh) 8. Columbus,
Coronado, Magellan 9. Champlain
10. Shackleton 11. Ponce de León
explosion ... 3. pop 4. bank 5. blast,
noise 6. report 7. failure 8. outburst
10. detonation
explosive ... 3. cap, TNT 4. mine
5. niter, shell 6. amatol, petard,
powder, tittle, tonite 7. cordite, grenade,
lyddite 8. dynamite 9. cartridge,
cellulose, fulgurite, guncotton, pyroxylin
11. firecracker 13. nitroglycerin
15. trinitrotoluene
exponent ... 4. note 5. index 7. symptom
9. explainer, expounder 10. explaining
11. interpreter

expose ... 3. air 4. bare, open 6. divest, reveal, unmask 7. exhibit, unearth 8. disclose, discover, endanger 9. ventilate 10. exposition

expose to danger ... 11. periclitate

expose to scorn ... 6. satire 7. pillory

exposition ... 4. fair 6. bazaar, expose, lesson 7. display 8. exposure, treatise 9. discourse, spectacle 10. disclosure, exhibition 11. abandonment, explanation 12. dissertation 14. interpretation

expostulate ... 5. orate 6. advise, demand 7. call for, discuss, protest 8. complain, dissuade 11. remonstrate

exposure ... 8. disproof, jeopardy, openness, snapshot 9. liability 10. appearance, disclosure, exposition, visibility

express ... 3. say 4. mean, show 5. exude, speak, state, train, utter, voice 6. depict, evince, extort, phrase 7. betoken, carrier, declare, exhibit, expound, extract, signify, testify 8. describe, dispatch, indicate, intimate, manifest 9. delineate, messenger, posthaste, utterance 11. declaration

express (pert to) ...
censure .. 10. animadvert
disapproval .. 9. deprecate
fervor .. 7. enthuse
gratitude .. 5. thank
indirectly .. 5. imply
in words .. 6. phrase
numerically .. 8. evaluate
regard .. 6. praise 10. compliment
regret .. 9. apologize
sympathy .. 7. condole, console 10. grieve with 11. commiserate

expressing ...
doubt .. 10. dubitative
extra phrase (Gram) .. 12. periphrastic
feeling .. 7. emotive
past tense .. 11. preteritive
pique .. 5. pouty
praise .. 9. laudatory

expression ... 4. grin, show, term 5. scowl, smile 6. aspect, oracle, phrase 7. diction, meaning 8. locution 9. statement, utterance 10. extraction, indication 11. delineation 13. manifestation 14. representation

expression (pert to) ...
mathematics .. 8. equation
of approval .. 4. clap 7. ovation 8. applause
of contempt .. 3. fie 5. pshaw, sneer
of disapproval .. 6. rebuke
of ideas .. 4. mode 5. style 7. fashion
of politics .. 4. vote
of weariness .. 4. sigh
peculiar .. 5. idiom
without .. 7. deadpan

expressive motion ... 7. gesture 13. gesticulation

expulsion ... 5. exile 10. banishment, expiration 11. elimination

expunction ... 4. blot 7. erasure 10. effacement 12. obliteration

expunge ... 4. dele 5. erase 6. cancel, delete, efface, excise, rub out 7. blot

out, destroy 9. strike out 10. annihilate, obliterate

expurgate ... 5. bathe, purge 6. censor, excise, purify 7. cleanse

exquisite ... 4. fine, rare 6. dainty, superb 7. perfect, refined 8. delicate 9. beautiful, delicious, matchless 10. delightful, fastidious

exsanguine ... 6. anemic 9. bloodless

exsiccate ... 3. dry 4. arid, sear 5. dry up, parch 7. exhaust 9. evaporate

extant ... 5. being 7. in vogue, present, visible 8. existent, existing

extempore ... 7. offhand 8. ad-libbed 9. impromptu 10. improvised 14. unpremeditated

extend ... 2. go 3. eke, jut, lie, run 4. give, span 5. bulge, reach, renew, steal, widen 6. deepen, deploy, expand, spread 7. amplify, broaden, draw out, proffer, prolong, radiate, stretch 8. continue, increase, lengthen, postpone, protract, protrude 10. exaggerate, straighten

extended ... 4. open 5. broad 6. valued 7. assured, diffuse 8. expanded, spacious 10. lengthened 12. outstretched

extended view ... 8. panorama

extension ... 4. area 5. range, scope 6. extent 8. addition, duration, increase, sequence 9. expansion 10. denotation 11. continuance, enlargement, lengthening 12. augmentation 13. extensiveness

extension of time ... 4. stay 7. respite

extensive ... 4. vast, wide 5. broad, large 7. immense, titanic 8. expanded, spacious 9. expansive, wholesale 10. widespread 11. far-reaching

extent ... 4. area, bulk, room, side, writ 5. areal, range, reach, scope 6. amount, degree, length 7. breadth, compass, expanse, measure 8. distance, frontage 9. dimension 10. assessment (Hist), denotation, proportion

extenuate ... 4. thin 6. excuse, lessen, reduce, sicken, weaken 7. justify 8. diminish, palliate 9. attenuate

extenuating ... 10. justifying, qualifying

exterior ... 5. ectad (toward), ectal, outer 7. outside 8. external 10. extraneous

exterminate ... 4. kill 5. expel 7. abolish, destroy 8. get rid of 9. eradicate, extirpate 10. annihilate

extermination ... 9. expulsion 11. destruction, eradication

extern ... 7. outward 8. exterior, external 9. extrinsic

external ... 4. ecto 5. outer, outre 6. nonego 7. outside 8. cortical 10. extraneous

external appearance ... 5. guise, image, looks 6. aspect 8. features 9. semblance

extinct ... 4. dead, past 5. passé 7. defunct, died out, expired 8. quenched 11. nonexistent 12. extinguished

extinct bird ... 3. moa 4. dodo

extinction ... 5. death 9. quenching

11. destruction 12. annihilation
extinct reptile . . . 11. pterodactyl
extinguish . . . 5. annul, choke, douse,
quell 6. put out, quench, stifle 7. destroy
8. suppress
extirpate . . . 4. dele, root, stub 5. erase,
expel 6. excise, uproot 7. destroy
9. eradicate 11. exterminate
extol . . . 4. laud 5. exalt, kudos 6. praise
7. applaud, commend, elevate, glorify
8. emblazon 9. celebrate
extort . . . 5. bleed, exact, steal, wrest,
wring 6. compel, elicit, wrench
7. extract 10. overcharge
extortion . . . 7. robbery, seizure
8. exaction, rapacity 10. extraction,
oppression, overcharge
extortionist . . . 5. harpy 7. vampire,
vulture 9. profiteer 11. blackmailer
extra . . . 3. bye 4. over 5. added, spare,
super 7. surplus 8. superior 9. accessory
10. additional
extra cache . . . 5. stock, store 7. reserve
9. reservoir
extract . . . 4. cite, pull 6. deduce, elicit,
select 7. essence, estreat, excerpt
8. withdraw
extract (pert to) . . .
balsam . . 7. toluene
Bible . . 7. passage 8. pericope
forcibly . . 6. evulse
newspaper . . 8. clipping
orchid (climbing) . . 7. vanilla
extraction . . . 5. birth, stock 6. origin
7. essence, excerpt 8. tincture
9. parentage 10. withdrawal
extraneous . . . 5. outer 6. exotic 7. foreign
9. extrinsic, separated, unrelated
11. unessential
extraordinary . . . 3. odd 4. rare, unco
5. great 7. notable, special, unusual
8. singular 9. irregular, marvelous,
wonderful 10. noteworthy, remarkable
11. exceptional 13. distinguished
extravagance . . . 5. waste 6. excess
8. wildness 9. abundance 10. fanaticism,
lavishness 11. exorbitance, prodigality
12. exaggeration, intemperance,
recklessness
extravagant . . . 3. E la 4. ee la (Mus), high
(priced) 5. outré 6. absurd 7. baroque,
bizarre, diffuse, fanatic 8. boastful,
prodigal, wasteful 9. excessive,
fanatical, fantastic, luxurious, plentiful
10. digressive 11. intemperate
12. unrestrained
extreme . . . 3. end 4. last, sore 5. final,
great, ultra 6. excess, severe, utmost
7. drastic, intense, outward, radical
8. farthest, greatest, ultimate
9. excessive, extremity, fanatical,
outermost 10. conclusive, immoderate
extreme degree . . . 3. nth
extreme fear . . . 5. panic 6. horror
extreme unction . . . 5. anele 9. last
rites, sacrament

extremist . . . 7. radical 8. ultraist
extremity . . . 3. end, tip 4. foot, limb
(body), pole 5. verge 6. border,
crisis, summit 8. terminal 9. necessity
11. termination
extricate . . . 4. free 5. loose 6. evolve,
rescue, wangle 7. extract 8. liberate
9. disengage 10. disembroil
11. disentangle 12. disembarrass
extrinsic . . . 7. foreign, outward
8. external 9. objective 10. accidental
(Log), contingent, extraneous, incidental
12. adventitious, nonessential
extrovert . . . 11. personality (opp of
introvert)
exuberance . . . 6. excess, plenty
8. overflow, rankness, vivacity
9. abundance, animation, profusion
10. friskiness, liveliness, luxuriance
11. copiousness 14. superabundance
exuberant . . . 6. frisky, lavish 7. fertile,
profuse 8. effusive, fruitful, thriving
9. luxuriant, plentiful 11. overflowing
13. superabundant
exudation . . . 3. gum, lac, tar 5. pitch,
resin 6. oozing 8. emission, sweating
9. discharge, excretion
exude . . . 4. emit, ooze, reek 5. sweat
7. excrete, give out 9. discharge
exult . . . 3. joy 4. crow, leap (obs), rave
5. boast, elate, ovare, pride 7. rejoice
8. jubilate
exultant . . . 5. ovant 6. elated
exultation . . . 3. joy 7. delight 8. boasting
9. jubilance, rejoicing 10. jubilation
exults . . . 5. leaps 7. glories, springs
9. jubilates
eye . . . 2. ee 3. orb, see 4. auge, glim, hole,
ogle 5. optic, organ (human), sight,
watch 6. look at, peeper 7. observe,
witness 10. scrutinize
eye (pert to) . . .
absence of pupil . . 6. acorea
black . . 5. mouse 6. shiner
brow . . 4. arch 6. eebree 11. supercilium
cavity . . 5. orbit 6. hippus, socket
disease . . 8. cataract, glaucoma,
hypopyon, trachoma 9. amblyopia
14. conjunctivitis
disorder . . 6. squint 7. walleye
9. exotropia 10. strabismus
dropper . . 7. pipette
glass . . 4. lens 7. lorgnon, monocle
8. pince-nez 10. spectacles
inflammation . . 6. ititis 7. uveitis
lash, lashes . . 5. cilia (pl) 6. cillum
lid . . 8. palpebra
part . . 4. iris, uvea 5. pupil 6. cornea,
retina
to blind (falconry) . . 4. seel
eyelet . . . 7. cringle, grommet, ocellus
8. loophole, peephole
eyetooth . . . 6. cuspid 8. dogtooth
eyot . . . 3. ait 4. holm 5. islet
eyra . . . 7. wildcat
eyrie, eyry . . . 4. nest 5. aerie, nidus

F

F . . . 6. letter (6th)

fabes . . . 10. gooseberry

fabian . . . 7. caution 8. dilatory, inaction 15. procrastination

Fabian . . . 7. General (Rom), Society

fable . . . 3. lie 4. myth 5. story 6. legend 7. fabliau, fantasy, fiction, Marchen, parable 8. allegory, apologue, folk tale 9. falsehood

fable (pert to) . . .
being . . 5. troll
king . . 3. Log
monster . . 4. ogre 7. centaur
narrator . . 10. parabolist
writer . . 5. Aesop

fabric . . . 5. build, cloth 6. tissue 7. texture 8. erection, material 9. framework 11. workmanship 12. construction

fabric (types of) . . . 3. rep 4. alma, duck, felt, gros, jean, lamé, lawn, leno, silk 5. baize, batik, beige, crash, crepe, denim, linen, nylon, pekin, rumal, satin, scrim, serge, suede, toile, tulle, tweed, twill, voile, wigan 6. agaric, alpaca, burlap, calico, canvas, chintz, cotton, damask, dimity, étoile, madras, mohair, moreen, muslin, penang, pongee, poplin, ratiné, sateen, tricot 7. batiste, brocade, bunting, challis, chiffon, delaine, elastic, etamine, flannel, galatea, gingham, hernani, paisley, percale, satinet, ticking, worsted 8. cashmere, chambray, chenille, corduroy, cretonne, drilling, prunella, sarcenet, Shantung, sheeting, whipcord 9. bombazine, crinoline, gabardine, grenadine, lansdowne, matelassé, paramatta 10. broadcloth, seersucker, terry cloth

fabric (pert to) . . .
dealer . . 6. mercer
ornamental . . 4. lace 8. fagoting
silk, watered . . 5. moiré
silk and gold . . 4. acca (anc) 7. brocade
twill . . 6. caddis (cadis)
velvet . . 5. panne, terry 6. velure 7. velours
waste . . 5. mungo
window shade . . 7. Holland
woven . . 6. tricot

fabricate . . . 4. coin, form, make, mint 5. build, frame, weave 6. create, devise, invent, scheme 7. falsify, fashion, produce, trump up 9. construct 11. manufacture

fabrication . . . 3. lie, web 5. guile 6. cogger, deceit, making 7. fiction, forging, untruth 9. falsehood, invention 12. construction

fabulist . . . 4. liar 5. Aesop 11. storyteller

fabulous . . . 6. absurd 7. feigned 8. mythical 9. fictional, imaginary, legendary 10. fictitious, remarkable 11. astonishing 12. mythological

fabulous (pert to) . . .

facade . . . 4. face 5. facia, front 7. frontal

face . . . 3. mug 4. dare, defy, dial, line, meet, moue, phiz 5. brave, cover, front 6. answer, obvert, oppose, phizog, visage 7. grimace 8. boldness, confront, envisage, exterior, features, pretense 9. encounter, impudence 10. effrontery 11. countenance, physiognomy, self-respect

face (pert to) . . .
bone . . 6. zygoma (cheek) 7. maxilla (jaw)
card . . 4. jack, king 5. queen
east . . 9. orientate
gem . . 5. facet
lifting . . 13. rhytidoplasty
masonry . . 5. revet
nose . . 11. rhinoplasty
pains . . 4. ague 13. tic douloureux
surgery . . 14. blepharoplasty (eyelid)
to face . . 6. afront 7. vis-à-vis 8. opposite
value . . 3. par

faces (twelve) . . . 12. dodecahedron

facet . . . 4. face 5. bezel, culet 6. aspect, collet 8. exterior

facetious . . . 5. droll, funny, witty 6. facete, jocose 7. comical, jesting 8. laughter 9. whimsical

facia . . . 5. plate 6. tablet

facial pain . . . 3. tic 4. ague 9. neuralgia 13. tic douloureux

facient . . . 4. doer 5. agent 10. multiplier

facile . . . 4. easy 5. quick, ready 6. expert, fluent, gentle, pliant 7. affable, lenient, pliable 9. compliant, teachable

facilitate . . . 3. aid 4. ease, help 6. assist

facility . . . 3. art 4. ease, help 5. éclat, means, skill 7. address, pliancy 8. easiness 9. readiness 10. adroitness, expertness, pliability 11. convenience, furtherance 13. accommodation

facing . . . 6. lining, veneer 7. coating, surface 8. opposite

facing (pert to) . . .
glacier direction . . 5. stoss
inward . . 8. introrse
outward . . 8. extrorse

facsimile . . . 4. copy 5. match 7. replica 9. duplicate 11. counterpart

fact, facts . . . 4. data, deed, feat, fiat 5. datum, event, posit, truth 6. really 7. keynote, lowdown, paradox 9. actuality

fact collector . . . 7. statist 12. statistician

faction . . . 4. bloc, camp, sect, side 5. cabal, junto, party 6. clique 7. machine (Polit) 11. combination, partisanism

factious . . . 9. demagogic, seditious, turbulent

factitious... 4. made (by art), mock, sham 5. phony 9. unnatural 10. artificial 11. make-believe

factor... 4. ager, gene 5. agent, cause 6. detail 9. component 11. constituent

factotum... 4. maid 5. do-all 7. servant 8. busybody

faculties... 4. wits 6. senses 7. talents 9. abilities, aptitudes 12. capabilities

faculty... 3. art 4. body, ease, gift 6. talent 7. ability, know-how 8. aptitude, teachers 9. endowment (mental) 12. professorate

fad... 4. rage, whim 5. craze, fancy, hobby, mania 6. custom 7. caprice, fashion

faddist... 10. monomaniac

fade, fade out... 3. age, dim, dow, wan 4. flat, pale, wilt 5. daver, decay, peter 6. perish, vanish, weaken, wither 7. decline, insipid 8. discolor, dissolve, languish 9. disappear 11. deteriorate

faded... 3. dim 4. dull, pale 5. faint, passé 8. impaired

Faerie Queene (pert to)...
author.. 7. Spenser
character.. 3. Ate, Una 5. Guyon, Truth 7. Acrasia 8. Gloriana
theme.. 8. chivalry 10. knighthood
type work.. 4. poem 8. allegory

fag... 4. flag, hack, jade, tire, toil, work 5. droop, slave, weary 6. drudge, menial 7. exhaust, fatigue, untwist (rope end) 8. drudgery 9. cigarette

fag end... 3. end 4. tail 6. scraps, tag end 7. remnant 8. last part, leavings

Fagin... 3. Jew (Oliver Twist)

Fagin's pupil... 12. Artful Dodger (John Dawkins)

fagot, faggot... 4. bind 5. bunch 6. bundle, emblem (Her) 8. firewood, slattern

fail... 3. ebb, err 4. flop, lack, miss, sink 5. decay, flunk, lapse 6. defect, desert, weaken 7. decline, exhaust 8. unbetide 9. fall short 10. disappoint, go bankrupt 11. deteriorate

failed admission... 11. blackballed

failed to follow suit... 7. reneged

failure... 3. dud 4. flop, foil, lack, lose, miss 5. decay, fault, lapse 6. defeat, fiasco 7. default 10. bankruptcy, deficiency, insolvency, nonsuccess, suspension 11. delinquency

faint... 3. dim, ill 4. pale, soft, weak 5. swelt, swoon, timid 6. feeble, sickly 7. languid 8. cowardly, fatigued, listless, timorous 10. indistinct, oppressive

faintness... 5. qualm (sudden) 7. dimness, syncope 8. paleness, weakness 10. feebleness

fair... 4. just, mart 6. bazaar, blonde, comely, honest, kermis 8. festival, mediocre, rainless, unbiased 9. impartial 10. auspicious, reasonable 12. unprejudiced 13. dispassionate

fairy, faery... 3. elf, fay 4. peri, pixy 5. genie, magic, nymph, ouphe, pixie 6. elfkin, sprite 7. brownie, gremlin 8. illusion

fairy (pert to)...

abode (Scot).. 4. shee (sidhe)
death spirit.. 7. banshee
evil.. 4. ogre, puck 9. hobgoblin
fort.. 3. lis (liss)
German.. 6. kobold
Irish.. 10. cluricaune, leprechaun
king.. 6. Oberon
Persian.. 4. peri
queen.. 3. Mab, Una 7. Titania
Scandinavian.. 5. nisse
tale.. 3. fib 7. Marchen 8. allegory 9. narrative

faith... 4. hope 5. creed, piety, troth, trust 6. belief, credit, verily, virtue 7. loyalty 8. credence, fidelity 9. assurance, authority, orthodoxy 10. confidence 11. credibility

faithful... 4. fast, feal, leal, true 5. liege, loyal, pious 6. devout, steady, trusty 7. devoted, sincere, staunch 8. constant, obedient, reliable 9. believers, steadfast, veracious

faithful friend... 7. Achates (Vergil's Aeneid)

faithless... 5. false, punic 6. fickle, untrue 8. apostate, disloyal, shifting 9. deceptive, mercurial, skeptical 10. perfidious, unfaithful 11. incredulous, irreligious, treacherous, unbelieving 12. falsehearted

fake... 3. rob 4. faux, sham 5. cheat, fraud, trick 6. ersatz 7. trump up 8. doctor up 9. deception, fabricate, imitation 10. artificial 11. counterfeit

faker... 5. cheat, fraud 7. bluffer 8. impostor 9. hypocrite, pretender

fakir... 4. sect (Muslim, Islam), yogi 7. dervish 9. mendicant

falcon... 4. hawk 5. besra, saker 6. laggar, lanner, luggar, merlin, shahin (shaheen), sorage, tercel 7. kestrel, sakeret 8. lanneret, Raptores 9. gyrfalcon (gerfalcon), peregrine

falcon, military... 8. ordnance

falconry term... 4. hood, jess, lure, seel 6. rebate 7. hawking

fall... 3. ebb 4. bang, drop, plop, ruin, sink, slip 5. crash, spill 6. autumn, defeat, perish, plunge, tumble 7. descend, descent, devolve, failure, plummet, relapse 8. collapse, commence, downfall, rainfall 9. abatement, overthrow, surrender, waterfall 10. depreciate, subversion 11. degradation, precipitate

fall (pert to)...
asleep.. 6. nod off
back.. 6. recede, recoil 7. relapse, retreat 10. retrogress
behind.. 3. lag 4. lose 7. regress
guy.. 5. patsy
in.. 4. cave 5. agree, lapse 6. concur, line up 8. collapse 9. terminate
rhythmical.. 6. cadent
short.. 4. lack, want 10. disappoint

fallacious... 4. wily 5. false 6. crafty, untrue 8. delusive, guileful 9. deceitful, deceptive, erroneous, illogical, insidious 10. fraudulent, misleading 13. disappointing

fallacy... 5. error 6. idolum 7. sophism

9. deception, falseness, sophistry
13. deceitfulness

false . . . 4. sham, tale 5. bogus, paste
6. betray, impugn, pseudo, untrue
7. mislead 8. apostate, spurious
9. deceitful, deceptive, erroneous,
faithless, incorrect, insincere,
pretended, unfounded 10. fictitious,
mendacious, traitorous, unfaithful,
unreliable, untruthful 11. counterfeit
12. illegitimate

false (pert to) . . .
  friend . . 5. Judas 7. traitor
  front . . 8. disguise 11. affectation
  fruit . . 10. pseudocarp
  god . . 4. idol
  hearted . . 9. deceitful 10. perfidious
    11. treacherous
  items . . 6. spuria
  jewelry . . 5. paste 6. strass
  reasoning . . 10. paralogism
  report . . 5. rumor 6. canard 7. slander
  show . . 6. tinsel
  wing (bird's) . . 5. alula

falsehood . . . 3. lie 4. tale 7. falsity,
fiction, perjury, untruth 9. imposture,
mendacity 11. counterfeit, fabrication
12. exaggeration

falseness . . . 5. error 8. illusion
9. deception, falsehood 10. infidelity

falsetto . . . 5. voice (false) 10. artificial
11. high-pitched

falsify . . . 3. lie 5. belie, forge 7. distort,
pervert 8. disprove 10. adulterate
11. counterfeit 12. misrepresent

Falstaff . . . 5. opera (Verdi) 9. character
(Shaksp)

falter . . . 3. lag 4. fail 5. demur,
pause, waver 6. flinch, quaver, totter
7. stagger, stammer, stumble, tremble
8. hesitate, lose hope

fame . . . 4. note 5. éclat, glory, kudos
6. renown, repute 9. celebrity

famed . . . 7. eminent, honored, popular
8. renowned 9. notorious 10. celebrated

familiar . . . 4. easy 5. usual 6. common,
versed 7. affable 8. domestic, frequent,
friendly, habitual, informal
9. companion, customary, well-known
10. accustomed, colloquial, conversant
12. domesticated, presumptuous
13. unconstrained

familiarity . . . 8. intimacy 9. awareness,
knowledge, liberties 10. affability
12. acquaintance (close), friendliness

familiarize . . . 6. inform 8. accustom
9. habituate

family . . . 3. ilk, kin 4. clan, line, race
5. class, group, house, tribe 6. stirps
7. kindred, lineage 9. community,
household, posterity 10. kith and kin

family (pert to) . . .
  bees . . 5. apina 7. Apoidea
  favoritism . . 8. nepotism
  herbs . . 7. Ranales
  Italians (famed) . . 4. Este
  kings . . 7. dynasty
  name . . 7. surname

famous . . . 5. named, noted 7. eminent,
namable, notable 8. renowned
9. excellent, notorious 10. celebrated,

remarkable 13. distinguished

famous murderer . . . 4. Aram, Cain
9. Bluebeard

famous pirate . . . 4. Kidd (Capt)

fan . . . 4. blow, cool, vane, whip
5. punka (punkah) 6. blower, foment,
incite, rooter, spread, thresh, winnow
7. admirer, devotee, refresh
9. stimulate, strike out (baseball),
ventilate 10. enthusiast

fanatic, fanatical . . . 3. mad 5. bigot,
crank, crazy, rabid 6. maniac, zealot
7. devotee, frantic, lunatic 8. frenzied
9. energumen, phrenetic 10. enthusiast,
unbalanced 11. extravagant,
overzealous 12. enthusiastic
13. nonconformist, overreligious

fanatical partisan . . . 6. zealot

fancied . . . 6. unreal 7. dreamed, ideated
8. favorite, imagined 9. well-liked
10. ornamental

fanciful . . . 3. odd 5. queer 7. bizarre,
strange 8. romantic 9. fantastic,
grotesque, visionary, whimsical
10. capricious, chimerical
11. imaginative 13. grandiloquent

fancy . . . 3. fad 4. idea, like, love, ween,
whim 5. dream, freak 6. design, desire,
devise, humour, ideate, megrim, notion,
ornate, vagary 7. caprice, conceit,
fantasy, imagine, impulse, suppose,
thought 8. illusion, phantasy, superior
9. expensive 10. conception, impression
11. extravagant, imagination, inclination
12. ostentatious

fandango . . . 3. hop 4. ball, prom 5. dance
7. cantico

fandango bird . . . 7. manakin

Faneuil Hall (1742) . . . 4. hall 6. market
(Boston) 15. Cradle of Liberty

fanion . . . 4. flag 6. guidon, marker

fanon . . . 4. cape (Pope's) 5. orale
6. banner 7. manipie

fan-shaped . . . 10. flabellate

fan sticks (radiating) . . . 4. brin
7. panache

fantastic . . . 3. odd 5. outré, queer
6. absurd, rococo, unreal 7. baroque,
bizarre, caprice, foppish, unusual
8. fanciful, freakish, illusory 9. eccentric,
grotesque, visionary 10. capricious,
chimerical, irrational 11. extravagant,
imaginative 12. phantastical

fantastic imitation . . . 6. parody
8. travesty

fantasy . . . 5. dream, fancy, story 6. vision
7. caprice, phantom, romance 8. illusion
10. apparition 13. hallucination

far . . . 3. tel (pref) 4. afar, long, tele
(pref) 6. marked, remote 9. separated
10. abstracted

farce . . . 4. mime, play 5. drama
(humorous), exode, humor, stuff
6. comedy 7. mockery 8. stuffing
9. burlesque, forcemeat

farceur . . . 5. joker 8. comedian
9. dramatist

fare . . . 3. eat 4. diet, food, rate 5. crowd,
going, swarm, table 7. conduct, journey,
passage, prosper, succeed 9. passenger
10. expedition

farewell ... 3. ave 4. vale 5. adieu, adios, aloha, congé (formal) 7. good-bye, leaving, parting 8. au revoir, Godspeed 9. bon voyage 11. leave-taking

farinaceous drink ... 6. ptisan

farinaceous food ... 4. sago 5. flour, grain, salep, wheat 7. cereals

farm ... 4. plot, till, torp 5. croft, ranch 6. grange, rancho 7. acreage, cotland 9. cultivate

farm (pert to) ...
English .. 6. barton
laborer .. 4. hind 6. farmer, tiller
prefix .. 4. agro
repairer .. 10. plowwright
Spanish .. 8. hacienda
steward .. 7. granger
tenant .. 6. cotter

farmer ... 4. ryot 5. kulak 6. grower, tiller 7. cropper, metaver, peasant, planter, rancher 10. agronomist, cultivator 13. agriculturist

faro term ... 4. bank 5. monte, stuss 6. cathop, layout

Faroe (Faeroe) Islands ...
called also .. 12. Sheep Islands
capital .. 9. Thorshavn
magistrate .. 4. foud
rule .. 5. Norse (anc) 7. Denmark
whirlwind .. 2. oe

far-reaching ... 4. deep, long 5. scope 7. intense 9. extensive

farrow ... 3. pig 6. litter

farsighted ... 6. shrewd 9. provident, sagacious 10. presbyopic 11. foresighted 12. clearsighted

farther, further ... 4. also 7. thither 8. moreover 10. additional

farthest ... 5. final 6. inmost, utmost 7. endmost, extreme, longest

farthest point ... 6. apogee

fascia ... 4. band, sash 6. fillet, ribbon 7. bandage

fascinate ... 5. charm 6. allure, enamor, thrill 7. bewitch, delight, enchant 8. entrance, interest 9. captivate, enrapture

fascinating ... 5. siren 8. alluring, charming 10. attractive, bewitching, delightful 11. interesting

Fascist (1919) ... 6. Pareto 9. Mussolini 10. Black Shirt

fashion ... 3. fad, fit, ton, way 4. make, mode, mold, rage 5. adapt, carve, craze, feign, forge, frame, guise, model, shape, style, vogue 6. create, custom, invent 7. compose 8. contrive 9. construct, fabricate, smartness 10. appearance

fashionable ... 5. smart 6. formal, modish 7. a la mode, in vogue, stylish 8. up-to-date 10. conforming 13. well-appearing

fast ... 5. agile, fixed, fleet, hasty, quick, rapid, sound, space, stuck, swift 6. lively, speedy, staple 7. abiding, soundly 8. enduring, securely 10. profligate, stationary, unyielding 11. expeditious

fasten ... 3. bar, pin, tie 4. bind, clip, lace, lash, moor, nail, rope, seal, tack,

wire 5. affix, belay, chain, clamp, clasp, latch, paste, rivet 6. attach, secure, solder, staple, tether, toggle 7. padlock

fastening ... 5. desmo (comb form)

fastest (pert to) ...
animals ... 6. coyote 7. cheetah
8. antelope
birds .. 5. eagle, goose 7. ostrich

fast horse ... 6. pelter

fastidious ... 4. nice 6. dainty 7. elegant, finical, precise 8. critical, delicate, exacting, overnice 9. squeamish 10. meticulous, particular, scrupulous

fastness ... 4. fort 6. fixity 7. citadel 8. celerity, firmness, velocity 9. stability 10. profligacy, stronghold

fat ... 4. lard, oily, suet 5. adeps, fatty, lipin, obese, olein, stout 6. axunge (goose), grease, portly, steato (pref), stocky, tallow 7. adipose, lanolin, opulent, paunchy, stearin, wealthy 9. corpulent, plentiful 10. profitable

fatal ... 5. fated 6. deadly, doomed, lethal, mortal 7. fateful, ominous 8. destined 9. condemned, prophetic 10. calamitous, disastrous 11. destructive

fatality ... 4. fate 5. death 8. disaster 10. deadliness

fatally ... 8. mortally 9. ruinously

fate ... 3. end, lot 4. doom, luck, ruin 5. karma 6. chance, kismet 7. destiny, fortune 8. disaster, downfall 13. inevitability

fateful ... 5. fated 6. deadly 9. momentous 10. inevitable, portentous 11. destructive, predestined

Fates (Gr) ... 6. Clotho, Moirae (group of Three) 7. Atropos 8. Lachesis

Fates (Norse) ... 4. Urth 5. Norns (group of three), Skuld 9. Verthandi

Fates (Rom) ... 4. Fata, Mona 5. Morta 6. Decuma, Parcae (group of three)

father ... 2. pa 3. Abu, dad 4. abba, papa, père, sire 5. adopt, friar, padre, pater, vater 6. priest, senior 7. creator 8. generate 9. confessor, procreate 11. acknowledge

Father (of) ...
Ajax .. 7. Telamon
Christmas .. 10. Santa Claus
English learning .. 4. Bede
engraving .. 3. Pye
Evil .. 5. Satan
his country .. 6. Cicero (Rom), Medici (It) 10. Washington (US)
history .. 9. Herodotus
Mankind (Myth) .. 7. Iapetus
New York .. 13. Knickerbocker
Ocean .. 7. Neptune
the Gods .. 6. Amen-Ra
Time .. 10. Methuselah
Waters .. 11. Mississippi

father (pert to) ...
land .. 6. native
land, love of .. 10. philopater
term .. 6. agnate 8. paternal
wise .. 6. mentor

fatherless ... 6. orbate 7. forlorn 8. helpless, orphaned

fathom ... 3. try 4. test 5. delve, plumb,

solve, sound 7. measure, plummet 8. encircle 9. penetrate 10. understand 13. take soundings

fatigued . . . 5. bored, faint, jaded, spent, tired, weary 6. fagged 7. languid, wearied 9. exhausted

Fatima (pert to) . . .
character in . . 13. Arabian Nights
father . . 9. Mohammed
husband . . 9. Bluebeard

fatten . . 4. feed 6. batten, enrich 7. improve, prosper 8. pinguefy

fatty . . . 5. suety 6. greasy 7. adipose 9. aliphatic

fatty (pert to) . . .
acid . . 6. adipic 7. valeric
degeneration . . 8. adiposis
substance, sheep . . 5. suint
tumor . . 6. lipoma

fatuous . . . 4. vain 5. inane, silly 6. vacant 7. foolish, idiotic, witless 8. demented, illusory, imbecile 9. insensate 11. thoughtless

faucet . . . 3. peg, tap 4. cock 6. spigot 7. fixture, hydrant, petcock

fault . . . 4. hade, lode, slip, vice 5. cavil, cleft, culpa (law), error, lapse, tache (anc) 6. defect, foible 7. blemish, blunder, demerit, failing, frailty, misdeed, offense 8. fracture 10. peccadillo 11. delinquency 12. imperfection

faultfinder . . . 6. carper, nagger 7. caviler 10. complainer, criticizer

faultfinding . . . 7. carping, nagging 8. captious, caviling, critical 9. censorial

faultless . . . 4. pure 5. right 7. correct, paragon, perfect 8. flawless, innocent 9. blameless 10. impeccable 13. unimpeachable 14. irreproachable

faultlessness . . . 8. accuracy 9. innocence 10. perfection 11. preciseness

faulty . . . 3. ill 5. amiss, unfit 6. guilty 8. culpable 9. blemished, defective, deficient, erroneous, imperfect 11. blameworthy

faun . . . 3. Pan 5. deity, satyr 6. Faunus 10. Praxiteles

Faust . . . 4. hero 5. drama (Goethe), opera

faux pas . . . 4. slip 5. error, gaffe 6. booboo, slip-up 7. blunder, misstep, mistake

favor, favour . . . 3. aid 4. boon, gift, help 5. bless, grace, token 6. esteem, letter, regard 8. good will, kindness, leniency, resemble 9. patronage, patronize, privilege 10. assistance, concession, favoritism, partiality, permission 11. approbation

favorable . . . 4. good, kind, rosy 6. benign, timely 7. helpful, hopeful, popular 8. friendly, gracious, pleasing 9. approving, opportune 10. auspicious, beneficial, propitious 11. complaisant 12. advantageous

favorite . . . 3. pet 4. lamb (pet) 6. minion 7. darling 10. preference

favoritism . . . 4. bias 7. leaning 8. nepotism 10. partiality 12. predilection

fawn . . . 3. doe 4. buck, coax, deer, faon (color) 5. color, cower, crawl, creep, toady 6. cringe, grovel, shrink 7. truckle 10. ingratiate

fawning . . . 7. servile 8. toadyish 9. truckling 10. obsequious 11. bootlicking, sycophantic

fawnskin (classic art) . . . 6. nebris

fay . . . 3. elf 5. fairy 6. sprite

fealty . . . 4. duty 6. homage 7. loyalty, respect 8. fidelity 9. constancy 10. allegiance, obligation

fear . . . 3. awe 5. alarm, dread, panic 6. dismay, fright, horror, phobia, terror 7. anxiety 8. venerate 9. apprehend, cowardice, reverence 11. nervousness 13. consternation

fear (of) . . .
animals . . 9. zoophobia
bees . . 9. apiphobia
being alone . . 10. autophobia, monophobia
blood . . 10. hemophobia
cats . . 12. aelurophobia
crossing streets . . 11. dromophobia
crowds . . 11. ochlophobia
darkness . . 11. nyctophobia, scotophobia
death . . 11. necrophobia
disease . . 10. nosophobia
enclosures . . 14. claustrophobia
fire . . 10. pyrophobia
food . . 10. cibophobia
heights . . 10. acrophobia 11. hypsophobia
holy things . . 11. hagiophobia
men . . 11. androphobia
new things . . 9. neophobia
open spaces . . 11. agoraphobia
pain . . 10. algophobia
places (certain) . . 10. topophobia
poison . . 10. toxiphobia
reptiles . . 13. herpetophobia
sea . . 14. thalassophobia
strangers . . 10. xenophobia
sunlight . . 11. heliophobia
thirteen . . 13. tridecaphobia
weeds . . 11. runcophobia

fear (pert to) . . .
for fear that . . 4. lest

fearful . . . 4. dino (pref), dire 5. awful, pavid, timid 6. afraid, craven 7. anxious, nervous 8. dreadful, horrible, timorous 9. appealing, frightful 11. distressing, frightening 12. apprehensive

fearless . . . 4. bold 5. brave 6. daring 7. impavid 8. harmless, intrepid 9. audacious, confident, dauntless, undaunted 10. courageous

feast . . . 4. fete, meal 5. agape, epulo, revel 6. junket, picnic, regale, repast 7. banquet, gratify 8. carousal, festival 9. carrousel

Feast (of) . . .
Lanterns (Jap) . . 3. Bon
Lots . . 5. Purim
Nativity . . 9. Christmas
Pentecost (weeks) . . 8. Shabuoth
Tabernacles . . 7. Succoth

feasting . . . 6. dining 9. epulation

feat . . . 3. act 4. deed 5. stunt 7. exploit 11. achievement, performance

14. accomplishment
feather . . . 4. deck, flaw (jewel), tuft
   5. adorn, penna, plume, quill 6. clothe,
   fletch, hackle, trifle 7. plumage
   9. lightness
feather (pert to) . . .
  an arrow . . 6. fledge, fletch
  barb . . 7. pinnula 8. barbicel
  bird (area) . . 7. pteryle
  featherlike . . 7. pinnate
  filament . . 4. dowl
  key (machine) . . 6. spline
  molt . . 3. mew
  repair (falconry) . . 3. imp
  shaft . . 5. scape
feathered . . . 5. swift 6. plumed, winged
   7. fledged 8. pennated, plumaged
   10. ornamented
feature . . . 4. face 5. motif, trait
   6. aspect 7. special 8. headline,
   resemble 9. component, lineament
   10. appearance, comeliness
   11. countenance 14. characteristic
features . . . 3. mug 4. face 5. looks
   6. visage 7. outline 9. geography
February birthstone . . . 8. amethyst
federal agent . . . 4. G-man, T-man
Federalist Papers . . . 3. Jay 7. Madison
   8. Hamilton
federation . . . 5. union 6. league
   8. alliance 10. government 11. affiliation
   13. confederation
fed up . . . 5. bored, jaded 7. wearied
   8. satiated 9. surfeited
fee . . . 3. feu, tip 4. fief, rate, wage
   5. bribe 6. charge, estate (law)
   8. gratuity, retainer 8. emolument
   10. honorarium
feeble . . . 4. aged, lame, puny, weak
   5. dotty 6. infirm 10. indistinct
   11. debilitated
feeble-minded . . . 5. anile 9. infirmity
   10. irresolute, weak-willed
   11. vacillating
feed . . . 4. dine, meal, sate 5. stoke
   6. fodder, gavage 7. engorge, foldage,
   furnish, indulge, nourish, nurture,
   pannage (swine) 9. encourage,
   provision
feel . . . 3. ail, air 4. palp 5. grope, sense,
   touch 6. handle, suffer 7. examine,
   explore, quality, texture 8. perceive
   10. atmosphere, experience
feel (pert to) . . .
  compunction . . 6. repent
  dejection . . 6. repine
  fear . . 2. ug
  melancholy . . 6. grieve
  worth of . . 10. appreciate
feeler . . . 4. palp, test 6. barbal, palpus
   7. antenna 8. question, tentacle
feeling . . . 4. feel, tact, view 5. hunch,
   touch 7. emotion, opinion, passion
   8. attitude 9. sensation, sentiment
   10. atmosphere, experience,
   perception 11. sensibility
   13. consciousness
feeling (pert to) . . .
  capable of . . 5. emote 8. sentient
   9. sensitive
  displeasure . . 9. resentful

hostility . . 6. animus 9. animosity
ill . . 7. malaise 10. discomfort
impassive . . 8. stoicism
joyful . . 6. jocund
offense . . 5. pique
superiority . . 9. arrogance
without . . 6. apathy, steely 7. callous
   8. numbness 9. unfeeling
   13. insensibility
feet . . . see also *foot*
  designating . . 5. podal
  having . . 6. pedate
  number . . 7. footage
  two (Pros) . . 6. dipody 7. dimeter
   9. ditrochee
  without . . 4. apod 6. apodal 8. footless
feign . . . 3. act 4. sham 5. fable 6. affect,
   assume, gammon, garble, invent
   7. connive, imagine, pretend 8. malinger
   (illness), simulate 9. dissemble
   11. counterfeit, make-believe
feint . . . 5. appel (fencing), blind, shift,
   trick 6. attack (mock), thrust 7. mislead,
   pretext 8. artifice, pretense
Felicia . . . 7. thistle 9. happiness
felicitate . . . 4. laud 5. bless 8. macarize
   10. compliment 12. congratulate
felicity . . . 5. bliss, grace 7. aptness,
   success 8. aptitude 9. happiness,
   well-being 11. achievement (happy),
   blessedness 12. blissfulness
Felidae . . . 4. cats, lion, lynx, pard, puma
   5. tiger 6. jaguar 7. cheetah, leopard,
   wildcat
feline . . . 3. sly 5. Felis 6. animal 7. catlike,
   furtive 8. stealthy 11. treacherous
Felis . . . 3. cat
fell . . . 3. cut, hem, hew 4. beat, hill,
   kill, pelt, ruin, skin 5. cruel, level
   6. fierce, fleece, lay low, mighty,
   savage 7. brutish, tumbled
   9. barbarous, ferocious, overthrow,
   prostrate
fellow . . . 3. lad, man 4. beau, chap,
   peer 5. equal 6. member, person
   7. comrade 8. neighbor 9. associate,
   companion 10. sweetheart
   11. confederate
fellow (pert to) . . .
  accomplice . . 7. abettor 9. accessory
   11. confederate
  awkward . . 4. boor, gawk
  clumsy . . 3. oaf 4. lout, pleb 5. yahoo
   7. bumpkin
  coward . . 3. cad, fop 4. drip 7. bounder
   8. spalpeen
  droll . . 3. wag 4. card
  old . . 6. geezer 7. callant
  small . . 6. shaver
  smart . . 5. aleck
  young . . 4. chap 5. blade, youth
   7. younker 9. stripling
fellowman . . . 7. brother 11. fellow being
fellowship . . . 4. sect 5. guild, union
   7. company 8. alliance, sodality
   9. communion 10. membership
   11. affiliation, comradeship, partnership,
   scholarship 12. friendliness
   13. companionship
felon . . . 3. bum 4. wild 5. cruel 6. wicked
   7. convict, culprit, outcast, villain,

whitlow 8. criminal, disloyal 9. infection,
malignant, murderous 10. malefactor,
paronychia, traitorous

felony . . . 3. sin 5. crime, wrath 6. daring,
deceit 8. baseness, burglary, outlawry
9. treachery 10. illegality, wickedness
11. misdemeanor

female . . . 4. bibi, dame, doña, girl, gyne,
lady, miss 5. donna, femme, rhyme,
squaw, woman 6. maiden, matron
7. distaff, dowager, fair sex, Sahibah
8. mistress 9. weaker sex

female (pert to) . . .
architecture . . 8. Caryatid
comb form . . 5. gyneo, thely
erudite . . 10. pedantress
fox . . 5. vixen
government . . 8. gynarchy
hormone . . 8. estrogen
monster . . 6. gorgon
prayerful . . 5. orant
spirit . . 7. banshee 8. succubus
suffix . . 4. ette
term . . 7. distaff 8. gynecoid
warrior . . 6. Amazon

feminine . . . 4. soft, weak 6. female,
gender, tender 7. womanly 8. maidenly
10. effeminate

femme fatale . . . 4. vamp 5. siren
7. Lorelei, vampire

femur . . . 3. hip (bone) 4. bone (thigh),
coxa

fen . . . 3. bog 4. moor, pool 5. marsh,
swale 7. The Fens

fence . . . 3. aha 4. bank, duel, ha-ha,
pale, rail, wall 5. close, ditch, fight,
hedge, stile 6. paling, picket, secure
7. barrier, confine, enclose, fortify,
protect, railing 8. palisade, prohibit
9. enclosure, swordplay 11. self-defense

fencing (pert to) . . .
breastplate . . 8. plastron
defense . . 5. carte, parry, prime, sixte
6. octave, quinte, tierce 7. seconds,
septime
master . . 7. lanista
position . . 9. pronation 10. supination
sword . . 4. epee, foil, tuck 5. extoc
6. rapier
term . . 4. volt 7. corrida 8. estocado
thrust . . 7. remise 9. riposte

fend . . . 4. ward 5. avert, parry, shift
6. defend, resist 7. prevent, repulse,
ward off

fender . . . 5. guard 6. buffer, bumper,
shield, sluice 7. cushion 9. fireguard
10. firescreen 11. splashboard

fenestra (Ir) . . . 6. window 7. foramen,
opening, orifice

Fenian (Ir) . . . 4. hero 11. nationalist

fennel . . . 4. herb 6. Seseli 7. Azorian,
Nigella

feral . . . 4. wild 6. deadly, ferine, savage
7. bestial, untamed 8. funereal,
unbroken 9. malignant 12. uncultivated

feretory . . . 4. bier 6. chapel, shrine
(saint's) 8. feretrum

ferment . . . 4. barm, brew, fret, sour,
stum, zyme 5. anger, fever, yeast
6. enzyme, foment, leaven, rennin,
seethe, uproar 7. glucase, maltase

8. diastase, disorder 9. agitation
10. effervesce, turbulence

fermentation . . . 6. unrest 9. agitation,
chemistry, leavening 10. ebullition
13. effervescence

fermented drink . . . 3. ale 4. beer, mead
6. kumiss (koumiss) 9. hard cider
10. malt liquor

fermenting vat . . . 4. gyle

fern . . . 4. tara 5. brake, heath, holly
6. osmund, spider 7. bracken
8. polypody 10. maidenhair
11. elephant-ear

fern (pert to) . . .
family . . 12. pteridophyte
genus . . 6. Anemia
leaf . . 5. frond
scale . . 8. ramentum
seedlike part . . 5. spore

ferocious . . . 4. grim, wild 5. cruel,
feral 6. bloody, brutal, fierce, savage
7. acharne, inhuman 8. pitiless,
ravenous, ruthless 9. barbarous,
malignant, merciless, murderous,
rapacious, truculent 10. implacable,
malevolent, relentless, sanguinary
11. remorseless 12. bloodthirsty

ferret . . . 3. hob 4. hunt, jill, tape 5. worry
6. badger, harass, search, weasel
7. polecat

ferrotype . . . 7. tintype 10. photograph

ferrum . . . 2. Fe (sym) 4. iron

ferry . . . 7. traject 9. transport 10. sail
across

ferryboat . . . 3. bac 4. pont 6. wherry

ferryman . . . 6. Charon (River Styx)
7. ferrier

fertile . . . 4. rank, rich 7. teeming
8. abundant, fruitful, prolific
9. exuberant, inventive, plenteous,
plentiful 10. productive

fertilizer . . . 4. marl 5. guano 6. pollen
7. compost, nitrate 8. bone meal,
dressing 9. phosphate

ferule . . . 3. rod 5. ruler 6. fennel
10. punishment

fervency . . . 4. heat, keen, zeal 5. ardor,
eager, fiery, gusto, verve 6. fervor,
warmth 7. ardency, passion
9. eloquence, vehemence
12. empressement 15. impassionedness

fervent . . . 3. hot 4. keen, warm 5. eager,
fiery 6. ardent, fervid 7. excited,
intense, zealous 8. eloquent, vehement
10. passionate 11. impassioned

fervid . . . 3. hot 5. fiery 6. ardent, tropic
7. boiling, fervent, zealous 8. vehement
11. impassioned

fervor . . . 4. rage, zeal, zest 5. ardor
7. ecstasy, passion 11. earnestness

fester . . . 6. rankle 7. abscess, pustule,
putrefy 9. suppurate

festival . . . 3. ale, bal 4. fete, gala
5. Delia (Apollo), feast, revel, Seder
6. Easter, Kermis 7. holiday, uphelya
8. apodosis (Church) 9. Christmas,
Mardi gras 10. Parentalia, Saturnalia

festive . . . 3. gay 4. gala 5. merry 6. joyous
8. mirthful, sportive 9. convivial

festivity . . . 3. joy 4. fete, gala 5. mirth,
revel 6. gaiety 7. jollity, whoopee

8. festival, jamboree 10. joyfulness
11. celebration, merrymaking
12. conviviality

festoon ... 4. loop 5. adorn 6. wreath
7. garland

fetch ... 3. get 5. bring, reach 6. attain,
deduce, revive 7. achieve 8. go and
get, retrieve

fetching ... 8. alluring, charming,
pleasing 10. attractive, delightful
11. fascinating

fete ... 4. gala 5. feast, party 6. fiesta
8. carnival, festival 10. Saturnalia
13. entertainment

fetid ... 4. olid, rank 5. fusty 6. noisome
10. maladorous 11. ill-smelling

fetish ... 3. obi 4. idol, joss, juju 5. charm,
image, totem 6. amulet, avatar, mascot
7. Dahoman 8. talisman

fetter ... 4. band, bond, gyve, iron
5. chain 6. hamper, hobble, hopple,
thrall 7. enchain, manacle, shackle

feud ... 4. fief, fray 5. broil 6. affray,
estate, strife 7. contest, dispute, quarrel
8. vendetta 9. hostility

feudal (pert to) ...
estate .. 3. fee 4. fief, soke
French .. 4. feod
lord .. 6. tenure 8. overlaid, suzerain
payment .. 6. socage
service .. 5. banal
tenant .. 4. ieud 6. vassal
tribute .. 6. heriot

fever ... 4. ague 5. ardor 6. frenzy
8. delirium, sickness 9. calenture
10. excitement

fever (pert to) ...
heat .. 9. sunstroke
intermittent .. 6. octan 7. quartan
malarial .. 4. ague
marsh .. 6. elodes 7. helodes
subsidence .. 12. defervescent
term .. 7. febrile, pyretic
tropical .. 6. dengue 9. calenture

feverish ... 5. hasty 7. excited, febrile,
fervent, fevered 8. restless 9. delirious,
overeager 10. disordered

fey ... 4. dead 5. dying, elfin, fatal, spell
9. enfeebled, visionary 12. otherworldly

fez ... 3. cap 5. busby, shako 8. tarboosh
9. headdress

fiat ... 3. act 5. edict, order 6. decree
7. command 8. decision, sanction

fiber ... 3. nap, nep, tal 4. bast, eruc,
hemp, imbe, jute, lint, pile, pita, silk,
yarn 5. datil, istle, kapok, linen, nerve,
rayon, sisal 6. fibril, raffia, staple,
thread 7. filasse, texture 8. fibrilla,
filament

fiber plant ... 4. hemp, imbe, palm
5. abaca, agave 6. ambary, cotton,
linaga

fibers ... 5. hairs 7. strands 9. filaments

fibula ... 4. bone (arm) 5. class 6. brooch
(anc), buckle 9. safety pin

fickle ... 5. false 6. mobile 7. mutable
8. unstable, unsteady, variable,
wavering 9. changeful, deceitful,
faithless, unsettled 10. capricious,
changeable, inconstant, irresolute,
unfaithful 11. vacillating

fiction ... 4. tale 5. false, fancy,
novel, story 6. legend 7. coinage,
figment, forgery, romance 9. falsehood,
invention 11. fabrication

fictitious ... 5. false 6. poetic, pseudo
(pref) 7. assumed, feigned 8. chimeric
9. imaginary, imitative, pretended
10. artificial

fictitious name ... 5. alias 6. anonym
7. pen name 8. nickname
9. pseudonym, stage name 10. nom
de plume 11. nom de guerre

Fidel (eg) ... 8. caudillo

Fidelio (eg) ... 5. opera

fidelity ... 5. topaz, troth, truth 6. fealty
7. honesty 8. accuracy, devotion,
veracity 9. adherence, constancy,
exactness 10. allegiance 12. faithfulness

fidget ... 4. fuss 5. worry 6. twitch
9. dysphoria 10. uneasiness
12. restlessness

fidgety ... 5. jerky 6. uneasy 7. nervous,
restive, twitchy 8. bustling, restless
9. excitable, impatient

fiducial ... 4. firm 5. solid, sound
6. secure, stable 7. trusted 8. trustful
9. confident 11. trustworthy

fiduciary ... 4. held (in trust) 5. trust
7. founded, holding, in trust, trustee
12. confidential

fief ... 3. fee 4. feud 6. estate

field ... 3. lea, lot 4. acre, ager, land,
mead, rand 5. croft, glebe, range,
tract 6. campus, ground, meadow,
sphere 7. compass, diamond, expanse,
pasture, savanna (savannah), terrain
8. clearing, gridiron 11. battlefield

field (pert to) ...
athletic .. 4. oval 5. arena, court, track
6. course, sphere 7. diamond, stadium
8. gridiron
bloodshed .. 8. Aceldama (Akeldama)
13. Ager Sanguinis
duck .. 7. bustard
god of .. 4. Faun
mouse .. 4. vole
snow .. 4. neve
stubble .. 5. rowen
term .. 5. agral 8. agrarian 10. campestral

fiend ... 3. foe 5. demon, devil, enemy,
Satan 6. addict, wizard 7. Amaimon
(Amamon) 9. archfiend 10. evil spirit

fiendish ... 5. cruel 6. wicked 7. Avernal,
demonic 8. demoniac, devilish, diabolic

fierce ... 4. grim 5. cruel, eager 6. raging,
savage 7. furious, racking, violent
9. ferocious, impetuous, truculent
10. catawampus, forbidding, passionate
11. belligerent, overwrought
12. overpowering

fierceness ... 7. cruelty 8. violence
10. truculence

fiery ... 3. hot, red 4. sore 5. angry
6. ardent 7. burning, excited, fervent,
flaming, glowing, igneous, parched,
violent 8. choleric, feverish, inflamed,
spirited, vehement 9. impetuous,
irascible 10. mettlesome, passionate
11. hot-tempered, inflammable

fiery cross ... 5. alarm 6. emblem, signal,
symbol 8. crantara 10. call to arms

fiesta . . . 5. color 7. holiday 8. festival 9. festivity

fifish . . . 6. cranky 9. half crazy

fig . . . 4. fico 5. eleme, gruit 6. Carica, Fiscus, Smyrna, trifle

fig basket . . . 5. cabas, seron

fight . . . 3. row, war 4. bout, duel, fray, meil, tilt 5. brawl, melee, scrap, set-to 6. affray, attack, barney, battle, combat, oppose, strife, strike, strive 7. contest, quarrel, warfare 8. conflict, struggle 9. pugnacity 13. combativeness

fighter . . . 7. battler, duelist, soldier, warrior 8. champion, pugilist, scrapper 9. combatant

fighting . . . 3. war 4. game 6. plucky 7. warlike 8. militant 10. contention, pugnacious 11. belligerent

fig leaf . . . 6. symbol (modesty) 8. clothing (Bib), covering

figment . . . 5. fancy 7. fiction 9. falsehood, invention

figurative . . . 6. florid 7. flowery, typical 8. allusive 9. numerical 12. emblematical, metaphorical

figure . . . 4. body, dash, dope, form, nude, rank, type 5. digit, image, judge, price, shape, solve 6. aspect, emblem, entail, number, symbol 7. diagram, numeral, outline, pattern 8. ornament, phantasm 9. calculate, celebrity, character, personage 10. appearance, impression, similitude 11. distinction

figure (pert to) . . .
    column . . 6. elamon 7. telamon 8. Atlantes, Caryatid, pilaster
    geometric . . 4. cone, lune 5. prism, rhomb 6. isagon, isogen, isogon (rare) 7. ellipse, rhombus 8. pentagon, triangle 13. parallelogram, quadrilateral 16. parallelepipedon
    praying . . 5. orant
    repeated digits . . 8. repetend
    speech . . 5. trope 6. aporia, simile 8. metaphor
    star-shaped . . 8. pentacle

figured . . . 4. rich 6. ornate 7. façonné 10. ornamented

figurine . . . 4. doll 7. carving, tanagra 9. sculpture, statuette

Fiji island, Viti Levu . . .
    capital . . 4. Suva
    export . . 5. sugar
    mountain . . 8. Victoria
    people . . 11. Melanesians
    ruler . . 7. British

filament . . . 4. barb, dowl (dowle), hair 5. fiber (fibre), harle 6. strand, thread

filament lamp . . . 12. incandescent

filbert . . . 3. nut 5. brown, hazel 7. Corylus 8. hazelnut

filch . . . 3. nim, rob 4. beat 5. steal, theft 6. pilfer 7. purloin

file . . . 3. row 4. list, rasp, rate 5. enter, march, store 6. abrade, smooth 7. sharpen 8. classify 9. catalogue 10. pickpocket 11. triggerfish (filefish)

file (combmaking) . . . 5. grail (graille) 6. carlet 7. quannet

fillbeg . . . 4. kilt 5. skirt

filibuster . . . 6. pirate 7. impeder

8. thwarter 9. legislate 10. freebooter, obstructer 14. obstructionist

filicide . . . 6. murder (child by parent)

filigree . . . 4. lace 5. adorn (with) 7. pattern 8. fanciful 10. decorative 13. unsubstantial

Filipino, Filipina (pert to) . . .
    homeland (mostly) . . 5. Luzon
    people . . 5. Bikol (Bicol) 7. Malayan (Christian), Tagalog (Tagal), Visayan (see also *Philippine*)

fill . . . 3. pad 4. calk, feed, glut, hold, plug 5. block, close, gorge, stuff 6. occupy, stop up 7. execute, fulfill, pervade, satiate, satisfy, suffuse 8. complete, compound, permeate 10. accomplish 11. superabound

fille . . . 4. girl 8. daughter

filled . . . 5. dated, laden 7. replete 8. suffused 9. saturated

filled with crevices . . . 7. areolar

fillet . . . 4. band, orle, ring, tape 5. snood, tiara 6. anadem, border, ribbon, taenia 7. bandage 8. headband, insignia 9. lemniscus, scantling 10. tenderloin

fillet (Arch) . . . 5. stria 6. cimbia, listel, reglet, regula, taenia 7. chaplet, molding (part)

filly . . . 4. colt, foal, girl, mare

film . . . 4. brat, haze, scum, skin, veil 5. cover, layer 6. lamina, patina 7. coating 8. pellicle 10. photograph

film fan . . . 8. cinéaste

filmy . . . 3. dim 4. fine 5. gauzy, misty 6. cloudy, opaque 7. clouded 9. laminated 10. indistinct

fils . . . 3. son

filter . . . 4. ooze 5. clean, drain 6. purify, strain 7. trickle 8. colature 9. percolate

filth . . . 6. vermin 7. squalor 9. excrement, obscenity, scoundrel

filthiness . . . 8. cenosity 9. fetidness, obscenity 10. odiousness

filthy . . . 3. low 4. foul, vile 5. dirty, fetid, gross 6. impure, odious, putrid 7. obscene, squalid, unclean 9. polluting 10. licentious

filthy lucre . . . 4. gain (shameful) 5. money

fimbriated . . . 5. edged 7. fringed 8. bordered (Her), margined

fin . . . 3. arm 4. five, keel

fin (pert to fish) . . .
    median . . 4. anal 6. caudal, dorsal
    paired . . 6. pelvic 7. ventral 8. pectoral

final . . . 3. end 4. last 5. be-all, telic 7. dernier 8. decisive, definite, eventual, ultimate 9. mandatory, ultimatum 10. conclusive, definitive 11. unqualified 13. determinating

final argument . . . 11. ultima ratio

finale . . . 3. end 4. coda 5. close 6. result 8. swan song 10. completion, conclusion 11. termination

finality . . . 5. finis 6. finale, finish, windup 10. conclusion 11. termination 12. decisiveness 14. conclusiveness

finally . . . 10. eventually, ultimately 12. conclusively

final notice . . . 4. obit

final outcome ... 5. issue 6. upshot
10. denouement
financial ... 6. fiscal 8. monetary
9. pecuniary
finch ... 4. moro 5. Junco, serin, spink,
tarin 6. burion, linnet, siskin, towhee
7. chewink, redpoll 9. brambling,
chaffinch, Fringilla
find ... 3. get 4. gain 5. learn 6. detect,
locate, summon, supply 7. procure,
provide 8. discover, meet with, perceive
9. determine, discovery, good thing
10. experience 11. acquisition
find fault ... 4. beef, carp 5. cavil
8. complain 9. criticize
finding ... 7. verdict 8. solution
9. discovery 11. serendipity
find out ... 5. learn, solve 6. detect
8. discover 9. ascertain
fine ... 3. fit 4. good, lacy, pure, rare, thin
5. dandy, filmy, frail, gaudy, noble,
sharp, sheer 6. ornate, slight, smooth
7. elegant, fragile, healthy, perfect,
powdery, precise, slender 8. absolute,
ethereal, handsome, polished, skillful,
superior 9. beautiful, excellent, sensitive
10. fastidious, pulverized, surpassing
finery ... 6. beauty 7. clothes, gaudery,
gewgaws 8. elegance, fineness,
frippery, ornament 10. decoration,
lavishness 11. refinements
finesse ... 5. skill 6. purity, serene
7. cunning 8. artifice, card play,
subtlety, thinness 9. clearness, good
taste, stratagem 10. refinement
14. discrimination (subtle)
finger ... 3. toy (with) 4. hook 5. digit,
touch 6. dactyl, handle, pilfer
7. measure, purloin 8. identify
finger (pert to) ...
alphabet .. 11. dactylology
cymbal .. 8. castanet
fish .. 8. starfish
flower .. 8. foxglove
foods .. 12. hors d'oeuvres
fore .. 5. index 7. pointer
little .. 6. pinkie 7. minimus 9. auricular
middle .. 6. medius
ring .. 7. annular
stall .. 3. cot
term .. 7. digital
Finger Lakes ... 6. Cayuga, Seneca
fingernail moon ... 6. lunule
fingernail overgrowth ... 10. onychauxis
fingerprint (term) ... 4. arch, loop
5. whorl 9. composite 11. dactylogram
12. dactyloscopy
finial ... 3. epi, tee
finical ... 4. nice 5. fussy 6. dainty,
dapper, jaunty, spruce 7. finicky,
foppish, mincing, prudish 8. delicate
9. finicking, squeamish 10. fastidious,
meticulous 11. overprecise
14. overscrupulous
finis ... 3. end 4. goal 6. finale 8. finality
10. conclusion 11. culmination
finish ... 3. end 4. kill 5. chare, close,
matte (mat), style 6. enamel, polish
7. destroy, perfect, surface, texture
8. complete, conclude 9. terminate
10. completion, consummate, perfection

finished ... 3. o'er 4. done, fine, over, ripe
5. ended 6. closed 7. refined, stopped
8. climaxed, complete, lustered,
polished 9. completed, concluded,
perfected 10. terminated
finite ... 7. fleshly, limited 9. definable
10. restricted, terminable 11. conditional
fink ... 3. spy 4. scab 5. finch 8. informer
13. strikebreaker
Finland ... see also *Finnish*
capital .. 8. Helsinki (Helsingfors)
Finnish for Finland .. 5. Suomi
government .. 8. republic
island .. 5. Aland
language .. 6. Magyar 7. Swedish
8. Estonian
legislature .. 7. Eduskunta
port .. 3. Abo 5. Turku 9. Mariehamn
Finnish (pert to) ...
bath .. 5. sauna
dramatist .. 4. Kivi 7. Waltari
people .. 5. Finns, Suomi 9. Karelians
10. Tavastians
fire ... 4. heat, zeal 5. blaze, fever,
flame 6. excite, fervor, igneus,
ignite, incite, kindle 7. barrage,
explode, inspire 8. detonate, illumine
9. discharge, eloquence 11. inspiration
12. inflammation 13. conflagration
fire (pert to) ...
basket .. 5. grate 7. cresset
comb form .. 4. igni
cracker .. 6. petard
dog .. 7. andiron
fear of .. 10. pyrophobia
god .. 6. Vulcan
opal .. 7. girasol (girasole)
power over .. 10. ignipotent
worshiper .. 5. Parsi 9. pyrolater
10. ignicolist
firearm ... 3. BAR, gat, gun, rod,
Uzi 4. heat 5. luger, piece, rifle
6. musket, pistol 7. handgun, shotgun,
sidearm 8. ordnance, petronel, repeater,
revolver, tommy gun 9. flintlock,
harquebus (arquebus) 10. six-shooter
11. Springfield (rifle)
firearms discharge ... 9. fusillade
firearms maker ... 4. Colt 7. Beretta
8. Browning 9. Remington
10. Winchester 14. Smith and Wesson
fired ... 3. lit 4. shot 5. baked 6. on
fire (Her) 7. excited 8. inspired
10. discharged
fireman ... 4. vamp 6. fueler, stoker
8. trainman 9. fire-eater 11. firefighter
fireplace ... 5. fogon, forge, ingle
6. hearth 9. inglenook 13. Franklin
stove
fireside (home) ... 11. hearthstone
firewood ... 8. billet
fireworks ... 4. caps, gerb 6. flares
7. fizgigs, gunfire, rip-raps, rockets
8. serpents 9. pinwheels, sparklers,
torpedoes 10. girandoles
12. firecrackers, Roman candles
firm ... 4. fast, hard, safe, sure, trig
5. dense, fixed, rigid, solid, sound,
stout, tight 6. secure, stable, stanch,
steady, strict, strong 7. compact,
company, decided, devoted, staunch

8. faithful 9. immovable, steadfast
10. determined, unslipping, unyielding
11. substantial

firmament . . . 3. sky 5. vault 6. Caelus,
welkin 7. heavens 8. empyrean

firmly set . . . 5. fixed, solid 6. rooted
10. inveterate

firmness . . . 8. fidelity, rigidity, solidity,
strength, tenacity 9. constancy, stability
10. immobility, steadiness 11. reliability
15. indissolubility

firmness, want of . . . 5. loose 6. laxity
8. weakness 11. instability, vacillation

firn . . . 3. ice 4. neve, snow

firs . . . 5. Abies, pines

first . . . 5. chief, front, prime 6. maiden,
primal, primus 7. highest, initial,
leading, primary 8. earliest, foremost,
original 9. beginning, elemental,
principal 10. primordial

first (pert to) . . .
appearance . . 5. debut 8. premiere
born . . 5. eigne 6. eldest
Christian martyr . . 7. Stephen
coin (silver) . . 8. sesterce
days of Rom month . . 7. calends
(kalends)
fruits (Eccl) . . 7. annates
letter . . 4. Alif 5. Aleph
stages . . 8. inchoate 9. rudiments
world navigator . . 8. Magellan

fish . . . 3. dib 4. food 5. angle, drail,
seine, troll 6. Pisces 13. constellation

fish (types of) . . . 2. id 3. cat, cod, gar, ray
4. bass, carp, char, chub, cusk, dace,
goby, hake, ling, opah, parr, peto, pike,
ruff, scup, shad, sisi, sole, tuna, ulua
5. bream, cisco, fluke, guppy, perch,
porgy, shark, skate, smelt, snook, sprat,
trout, tunny, wahoo 6. barbel, bonito,
bowfin, burbot, conger, darter, marlin,
minnow, puffer, redfin, salmon, shiner,
sucker, tarpon, tautog, turbot 7. alewife,
anchovy, catfish, crappie, croaker,
dogfish, garfish, grouper, haddock,
halibut, herring, hogfish, jewfish,
lamprey, mudfish, oquassa, pollack,
pompano, redfish, sardine, sawfish,
sunfish, torpedo, walleye 8. albacore,
blue fish, bluegill, bonefish, bullhead,
chimaera, filefish, flatfish, flounder,
goldfish, grayling, kingfish, lumpfish,
mackerel, menhaden, pickerel, pilchard,
sailfish, sergeant, sting ray, sturgeon,
toadfish, weakfish 9. barracuda,
cigarfish, devilfish, jellyfish, namaycush,
sheatfish, whitefish 10. barramunda,
butterfish, candlefish, hammerhead,
yellowtail 11. muskellunge (see also
mammal)

fish (pert to) . . .
adhering . . 4. pega 6. remora
ascending rivers . . 7. anadrom
10. anadromous
bait . . 4. chum 5. chack 6. minnow
9. killifish (killy)
basket . . 4. caul 5. creel, slath (slarth)
bivalve, mollusk . . 4. clam, slug 5. snail,
whelk 6. limpet, mussel, oyster
7. abalone, Ocypode (crab), scallop
caviar-yielding . . 7. sterlet

climbing, jumping . . 5. saury 6. anabas
7. skipper
club . . 6. muckle
codfish . . 4. cusk 5. torsk 7. bacalao,
buffalo
comb form . . 7. ichthyo
crustacean . . 3. Uca 4. crab 6. shrimp
7. lobster 8. Decapoda
devil . . 3. ray 5. manta
eaters . . 12. ichthyophagi
eating . . 11. piscivorous
14. ichthyophagous
fabled (Pers) . . 4. Mahi (Mah)
gaff (through ice) . . 5. ching
game . . 4. tuna 5. chiro, sword, trout
6. marlin, salmon, tarpon 8. grayling
11. muskellunge
genus . . 4. Amia (bowfin), Mola
(sunfish) 5. Elops (tarpon), Perca
(perch) 8. Haliotis (abalone), Octopoda
(octopus)
hook . . 5. Kirby, snell (part) 8. Aberdeen,
barbless, Carlisle, Limerick
largest (freshwater) . . 8. arapaima
like . . 8. ichthyic
line . . 6. nossel (norsel) 7. spillet
living by . . 9. piscatory
living on . . 12. ichthyophagy
man-eating . . 6. caribe 7. piranha
mollusk . . see *bivalve*
nest building . . 5. acara
net . . 4. fyke 5. seine, snell, trawl
7. boulter, spiller
pond . . 7. piscina 8. aquarium
roe . . 6. caviar
salmon . . 3. fog 4. masu, parr 5. sprod
6. alevin 7. gilling
sauce . . 4. alec
spear . . 3. gig
taboo . . 13. ichthyophobia
treatise . . 11. ichthyology
worship . . 12. ichthyolatry
young brood . . 3. fry

fisherman . . . 6. angler 8. piscator

fishery . . . 7. piscary

fishing . . . 4. chug (through ice) 8. snelling
9. halieutic, piscation

fishing vessel . . . 5. smack 6. seiner
7. trawler

fishy . . . 4. dull 6. vacant 8. fishlike
9. deceptive, dishonest 10. improbable,
lusterless, suspicious, unreliable
11. extravagant 14. expressionless

fissure . . . 3. gap 4. leak, lode, open,
rent, rift, rima, seam, slit, vein 5. break,
chasm, chine, chink, cleft, crack, sever,
split 7. crevice

fissured . . . 5. cleft 6. rimate, rimose

fist . . . 4. duke, hand (closed) 5. nieve
6. clench 8. tightwad 11. handwriting

fit . . . 3. due, fay, pat 4. able, gear,
meet, mesh, ripe, suit, whim 5. adapt,
equip, fancy, ready, spasm, train
6. attack, enmesh, frenzy, proper,
stroke, suited 7. adapted, caprice,
conform, healthy, prepare, tantrum
8. disposed, dovetail, eligible, outbreak,
suitable 9. competent, qualified
11. accommodate, appropriate

fit (pert to) . . .
an arrow (archery) . . 4. nock

fury.. 4. rage
groove (Arch).. 4. dado
resentment.. 4. huff, mood 5. pique
7. tantrum
to eat.. 6. edible
to till.. 6. arable
fitchew... 5. skink, zoril 7. foumart,
polecat
fitful... 8. restless, unstable, variable
9. impulsive, irregular, orderless,
spasmodic 10. capricious, convulsive
12. intermittent
fitly... 4. duly 5. right 6. timely
8. properly, suitably 10. decorously
fitness... 7. decorum 9. congruity
10. expedience, timeliness 11. eligibility,
suitability 12. preparedness
fitting... 3. apt, pat 4. just, meet
6. proper, seemly, timely 8. adapting,
suitable 9. expedient 11. appropriate
five (pert to)...
Books of Moses.. 10. Pentateuch
children (born at once).. 11. quintuplets
Civilized Tribes (Ind).. 5. Creek
7. Choctaw 8. Cherokee, Seminole
9. Chickasaw
comb form.. 5. penta
cornered.. 11. pentagonous
divided by.. 11. quinquesect
dollar bill.. 1. V 3. fin 5. fiver
feet.. 10. pentameter
five-year period.. 6. pentad 7. lustrum
(census) 12. quinquennial
fold.. 9. quintuple
group.. 6. pentad 8. fivesome
lines (nonsense).. 8. limerick
Nations (Ind Confed).. 7. Cayugas,
Mohawks, Oneidas, Senecas
9. Onondagas
trump card (auction pitch).. 5. pedro
fix... 3. peg, pin, set 4. mend, moor,
nail 5. amend, brace, bribe, imbed,
limit, stamp 6. adjust, anchor, cement,
define, fasten, ossify, punish, repair,
settle 7. arrange, confirm, delimit,
dilemma, prepare, rectify 8. organize,
solidify 9. condition, establish, stabilize,
stipulate 10. prearrange
fixed... 3. set 4. firm 5. rigid 6. formal,
intent, nailed, static 7. assured, limited,
settled, special 8. arranged, habitual
9. immovable, permanent, unwinking
11. established, prearranged, traditional
fixed (pert to)...
allowance.. 4. diet 6. ration 7. stipend
10. remittance
beforehand.. 13. predetermined
by choice.. 8. elective
idea.. 8. idée fixe 9. obsession
manner.. 8. immovably
routine.. 4. rote
star.. 4. Veda
time.. 3. era 4. date, fast
fizgig... 9. fireworks, whirligig
flabellate... 9. fan-shaped
flabrum... 3. fan 9. flabellum
flaccid... 4. limp, weak 6. flabby
8. yielding
flag... 3. sag 4. fail, fane, iris, pave,
pine, sign, weak, wilt 5. Roger
(pirate) 6. banner, burgee, colors,

cornet, ensign, fanion, flower, guidon,
pennon, signal 7. bunting, calamus,
decline, pennant 8. gonfalon, masthead,
standard, streamer, vexillum
9. banderole 16. Quincunx of Heaven
flagging... 4. weak 7. languid
8. pavement 10. flagstones, spiritless
11. languishing
flagging in energy... 9. lassitude
flagitious... 6. wicked 7. corrupt, heinous
8. criminal, flagrant 10. scandalous,
villainous
flag maker... 9. Betsy Ross
flagon... 3. jug 4. ewer 5. stoup 6. bottle,
carafe 7. canteen 8. demijohn
flagpole standard... 7. bracket
9. bracciale
flagrant... 4. rank 5. great 6. absurd,
wanton, wicked 7. glaring, hateful,
heinous, obvious, scarlet, violent
8. infamous, terrible 9. abandoned,
atrocious, monstrous, nefarious
10. profligate, villainous
flail... 4. beat, flag, whip 6. thrash,
weapon (anc) 7. swingle
flam... 4. hoax 5. cheat, spoof, trick
6. cajole 7. pretext 8. drumbeat,
flimflam 9. deception, falsehood
flambeau... 5. torch (flaming) 7. cresset
11. candlestick
flamboyant... 4. wavy (Arch) 6. florid,
ornate 9. brilliant, flamelike
11. resplendent
flame... 3. arc 4. beam, burn, fire,
glow, leye (obs), love, zeal 5. ardor,
blaze, flare, flash, glare, ingle, light,
lover 6. redden 7. scarlet 8. flemmule
(small) 10. brightness, sweetheart
flamen... 6. priest (anc)
flamenco... 5. dance (gypsy)
Flaminian Way... 4. Rome
Flanders, Belgium...
brick.. 4. Bath
capital.. 5. Ghent (East) 6. Bruges
(West)
city.. 5. Alost 6. Ostend 7. Dixmude
(Dixmuide)
people (anc).. 5. Celts 6. Franks
11. Burgundians
poppy.. 9. corn poppy
flâneur... 5. idler
flap... 3. tab 4. blow, slap, sway,
wave 5. skirt 6. dangle, lappet, stroke
7. flapper, flutter 9. appendage
flare... 5. blaze, flame, flash, fusee,
glare, light 6. signal, spread 7. display,
flicker 8. outburst 10. illuminate
flaring... 5. gaudy, spread 7. burning,
glaring 8. dazzling, flashing
flash... 4. show 5. blaze, burst, gleam,
glint, shine, spark 6. glance, signal
7. display, glimmer, glisten, glitter,
instant, shimmer, sparkle 8. dispatch
9. telegraph
flashing... 5. showy 6. flashy 8. meteoric,
snapping 9. transient
flashy... 3. gay 5. fiery, gaudy, showy
6. frothy, garish, sporty 7. raffish
8. vehement 9. flaunting, impetuous
13. grandiloquent
flask... 4. ewer, olpe 5. betty 6. flagon

7. ampulla, canteen 9. aryballus
(aryballas, anc)
flask-shaped . . . 10. lageniform
fiat . . . 3. low 4. palm 5. banal, blunt,
level, molle, plain, plane, prone, stale,
suite, tract, vapid 6. boring, dreary,
wholly 7. insipid, uniform 8. tenement,
unbroken 10. horizontal
flat (pert to) . . .
boat . . 3. ark 4. punt, scow 5. barge
breastbone . . 6. ratite
canopy . . 6. tester
flatfoot . . 9. pes planus 13. talipes planus
iron . . 7. sadiron
nosed . . 6. simous
piece . . 4. slab
surface . . 4. area 6. pagina 7. tabular
worm . . 9. planarian, trematode
flatfish . . . 3. dab 4. sole 5. brill, fluke
6. acedia, turbot 7. halibut 8. flounder
flatten . . . 4. even 5. level 6. deject,
smooth 7. depress 8. dispirit
9. prostrate 10. discourage, dishearten
flattened . . . 6. evened, oblate 7. leveled
8. smoothed 9. applanate
flatter . . . 3. oil 4. coax, palp 5. charm,
float 6. cajole, caress, please, praise,
smooge, soothe 7. adulate, beguile,
blarney, flutter 8. blandish 9. encourage
10. compliment, ingratiate
flatterer . . . 6. flunky, glozer 7. Jenkins
8. adulator, courtier, parasite
9. sycophant
flattering . . . 9. adulatory, gnathonic,
insincere 10. obsequious
13. complimentary
flattery . . . 5. gloze, taffy 6. praise
7. blarney, eyewash, fawning, palaver
8. cajolery 9. adulation 10. compliment,
sycophancy 14. obsequiousness
flaunt . . . 4. wave 5. boast, vaunt
6. parade 7. display, flutter 8. brandish
Flavian, House of Flavius, Emperors . . .
5. Titus 8. Domitian 9. Vespasian
Flavian Amphitheater . . . 8. Colosseum
(Rome)
flavor . . . 4. gust, odor, tang, zest
5. aroma, imbue, sapid, sapor,
sauce, savor, scent, taste 6. season
7. perfume 8. piquancy 9. flavoring
14. characteristic
flaw . . . 3. gap, mar 4. rase, rift
5. cleft, fault 6. breach, defect
7. blemish, fissure, sophism 8. fracture
12. imperfection
flawless . . . 5. ideal 7. perfect 8. unmarked
11. unblemished
flax . . . 3. lin, tow 5. linen
flax (pert to) . . .
capsule . . 4. boll
dust . . 5. pouce
filaments . . 4. harl
process plant . . 7. rettery
refuse . . 3. pob, tow 5. hurds
seed . . 7. linseed
soak . . 3. ret
weed . . 8. toadflax
flaxweed . . . 8. toadflax
flay . . . 4. peel, skin 6. fleece 7. censure,
reprove, scarify 9. criticize, excoriate
flea . . . 4. puce 5. pulex 6. beetle,

chigoe 7. chigger, cyclops 8. reminder
13. Ctenocephalus
fleam . . . 6. lancet, stream 10. millstream
fleck . . . 4. flea, mark, spot 5. flake
6. blotch, dapple, streak, stripe
7. freckle, speckle, stipple 8. particle
9. variegate
flection, flexion . . . 7. bending, turning
flee . . . 3. fly, run 4. shun 5. avoid, elope,
evade, speed 6. vanish 7. abandon,
forsake 9. disappear
fleece . . . 3. abb, nap 4. flay, pile,
skin, wool 5. fleck, mulct, sheer,
strip 6. divest 7. despoil, swindle
10. overcharge
fleer . . . 4. gibe, jeer, mock 5. flout, scoff,
sheer, taunt
fleet . . . 4. fast, flit, flow, navy, sail,
swim 5. drift, group, quick, rapid, swift
6. armada, hasten, nimble, speedy
9. transient 10. evanescent, transitory
fleeting . . . 7. passing 9. transient
10. evanescent, transitory
Fleet Street . . . 5. Fleta (book written in
prison) 6. prison (London) 11. London
press
Flemish painter . . . 5. David 6. Rubens
7. Van Dyke
flesh . . . 3. kin 4. body, meat, pink,
pulp, race (human) 6. family, fatten,
muscle 7. kindred, kinsmen, mankind
8. humanity 9. mortality 10. sensuality
flesh (pert to) . . .
eating . . 8. omophagy (raw)
9. omophagia 10. omophagous,
zoophagous 11. carnivorous,
creophagous
fond of . . 12. sarcophilous
like . . 7. carnose
lust for . . 9. carnality
resembling . . 7. sarcoid
slain animals . . 7. carnage
fleshpots . . . 6. plenty, wealth 10. high
living, prosperity 12. fat of the land
fleshy . . . 3. fat 5. beefy, human, obese,
plump, pulpy, stout 6. carnal 7. adipose,
carnose 9. corpulent
fleshy fruit . . . 4. pear, pome 5. bacca,
berry, drupe
fleur-de-lis . . . 3. lis (Her) 4. iris, lily,
luce 6. emblem
flew . . . see fly
flexible . . . 4. limp 5. lithe 6. limber,
pliant, supple 7. elastic, lissome
flexion, flection . . . 9. anaclasis
flexure . . . 4. genu 5. crook 7. bending
flick (sl) . . . 4. film 5. movie
flicker . . . 4. burn, flit 5. blaze, glare,
waver 7. flutter, high-hoe
10. woodpecker
flickering . . . 7. burning, lambent
8. flickery 9. irregular
flier, flyer . . . 3. ace 4. bird 5. pilot,
train 6. airman, gamble, insect
7. aviator, speeder, sunfish, venture
11. speculation
flight . . . 3. hop 4. rout 5. arrow
(volley), flock, skein (wild fowl), speed
6. exodus, fletch (arrows), speed,
hegira, perron, stairs, throng 7. soaring
8. escapism, mounting, stampede,

swarming 9. excursion, formation,
migration 10. volitation

flightless bird ... see *bird, flightless*

flighty ... 5. barmy, swift 6. fickle, fitful
7. foolish 8. fanciful, freakish, volatile
9. frivolous 10. capricious

flimflam ... 5. freak, hocus, trick
6. humbug 7. caprice, swindle
8. nonsense, trifling 9. deception,
deceptive 11. nonsensical

flimmer ... 7. flicker, glimmer

flimsy ... 4. limp, rare, thin, vain, weak
5. frail 6. feeble, paltry, sleazy, slimsy
7. flaccid, shallow, trivial 9. illogical
11. superficial 13. unsubstantial

flinch ... 4. game 5. quail, start, wince,
wonde 6. blench, cringe, falter, flense,
recoil, shrink, swerve

fling ... 3. shy 4. dart, dash, gibe, hurl,
toss 5. cheat, dance, flock (sandpipers),
revel, sling, sneer, throw 6. baffle,
spirit 7. cast off, sarcasm 9. prostrate

flint ... 5. chert, clint, silex 6. quartz
7. lighter 8. hardness 9. firestone,
skinflint

flip ... 3. hop, tap 4. flap, glib, snap, toss
5. drink (spiced), flick, flirt, throw 6. fillip
8. flippant, turn over 10. somersault
11. impertinent

flippant ... 4. flip, glib, pert 5. cocky
6. chatty, fluent 8. impudent
10. persiflate 11. impertinent

flipper ... 3. arm, fin, paw 4. hand
5. panel 8. flapjack

flirt ... 3. toy 4. dart, fike, flip, jerk, jilt,
mash, play, toss 5. dally 6. coquet,
fillip, masher, trifle 7. trifler 8. coquette
9. philanderer

flirtation ... 5. dance 8. coquetry, trifling
10. love affair

flit ... 3. fly 4. dart 5. glide, hover
6. nimble 7. flicker, flutter, migrate

flitter ... 3. rag 5. hover, piece 6. tatter
7. flicker, flutter, fritter 8. fragment

flittermouse ... 3. bat

float ... 4. buoy, cork, hove, lure, raft,
ride, sail, soar, swim, waft 5. balsa,
drift, hover, ladle 6. launch 7. support
8. navigate, undulate 9. transport
10. inaugurate

floating ... 4. free 5. awash, loose
6. adrift, natant 7. buoyant, movable,
rumored 8. changing, drifting, shifting
9. launching, wandering

floating herb ... 7. frogbit
16. Hydrocharitaceae

flock ... 4. bevy, fold, herd, pack,
raft 6. flight, hirsel 7. company
9. multitude 10. assemblage, collection
11. aggregation

flock (pert to) ...
bees .. 4. hive 5. swarm 6. colony
cattle .. 4. herd
fish .. 5. shoal
geese .. 5. skein 6. gaggle
herons .. 5. sedge
insects .. 5. swarm
like .. 6. gregal
lions .. 5. pride
partridge .. 5. covey
pheasants .. 4. nide (nid)
sandpipers .. 5. fling
walrus .. 3. pod

flocks, god of ... 3. Pan

floe ... 3. ice 4. berg

flog ... 3. cat, tan 4. beat, cane, goad,
lash, wale, welt, whip 6. larrup, punish,
strike, thrash 8. chastise

flogging ... 4. toco (toko) 7. beating
8. whipping 9. threshing 10. punishment
12. chastisement

flood ... 3. sea 5. eagre, spate 6. deluge,
drench, excess 7. freshet, torrent
8. cataract, inundate, overflow
9. cataclysm 10. oversupply
14. superabundance

flood (pert to) ...
disaster .. 9. Galveston (1900),
Johnstown (1889)
gate .. 4. gool, lock, slow 6. sluice
8. penstock
lights .. 5. klieg
tidal .. 5. eagre

floor ... 4. base, pave, sill 5. chess
(pontoon), story 6. baffle, bottom,
defeat 7. coaming, silence 9. overthrow
10. substratum

floor leader ... 4. whip

flora ... 6. plants 11. florilegium

flora and fauna ... 5. biota

Florence gallery ... 5. Pitti 6. Uffizi

Florentine (pert to) ...
color .. 7. scarlet
family (famed) .. 6. Medici
lily .. 6. giglio
school .. 6. Tuscan
sculptor .. 8. Ammanati, Ghiberti

florid ... 3. red 5. ruddy 6. ornate, rococo
7. flowery, flushed 8. enriched, rubicund
9. figurative, melismatic, rhetorical
11. embellished 13. grandiloquent

Florida ...
cape .. 9. Canaveral
capital .. 11. Tallahassee
city .. 5. Miami, Tampa 7. Daytona, Key
West, Orlando 8. Sarasota 9. Pensacola
11. St Augustine (1565) 12. Jacksonville,
St Petersburg 14. Fort Lauderdale
discoverer .. 11. Ponce de Leon (1513)
fish .. 6. mullet, shrimp, tarpon, testar,
tetard 8. blue crab
flower .. 13. orange blossom
Indian .. 8. Seminole
lake .. 10. Okeechobee
museum .. 10. Circus Hall (Ringling)
plant .. 7. coontie
river .. 8. Suwannee
State motto .. 22. Liberty and
Independence
State nickname .. 8. Sunshine
swamp, park .. 10. Everglades
trail .. 7. Tamiami

flounce ... 4. flap, fold, jerk, trim 5. caper,
frill, twist 6. edging, frolic 8. flounder,
struggle

flounder ... 4. roll 6. bungle, muddle,
welter 7. stumble 8. struggle 9. fluctuate

flounder (fish) ... 3. dab 5. fluke 6. plaice,
turbot 8. flatfish

flour ... 4. bran, meal 6. farina, pinole,
powder 9. middlings, pulverize

flour (pert to) ...

diabetic .. 9. aleuronat
gravy .. 4. roux
maker .. 6. miller
pudding .. 4. duff

flourish .. 4. grow, show, wave 5. vaunt
6. flaunt, paraph (signature), thrive
7. display, fanfare, prosper, roulade
8. arpeggio, brandish, ornament
9. embellish, luxuriate 11. ostentation

flout .. 4. defy, gibe, jeer, mock 5. fleer,
scoff, scout, sneer, taunt 6. insult
8. ridicule

flow ... 3. jet, run 4. bore, flow, flux,
gush, ooze, pour, roll, teem 5. glide,
issue, river, spout 6. abound, afflux,
course, stream 7. current, fluency,
flutter 9. streaming 10. outpouring

flow (pert to) ...
along .. 4. lave
back .. 7. redound
jet .. 4. gush 5. spurt
out .. 5. exude, issue, spill
over .. 5. slosh, spill 6. deluge, engulf
8. inundate 9. overwhelm
tide .. 3. ebb 4. flow, neap

flower ... 3. bud 4. best, blow 5. bloom
6. unfold 7. blossom, develop, essence,
produce 8. choicest, ornament 11. Four
Hundred (Society)

flower (types of) ... 3. gul (rose) 4. iris,
ixia, lily, pink, rose 5. aster, calla,
canna, daisy, pansy, peony, phlox,
poppy, stock, tulip 6. azalea, cosmos,
crocus, dahlia, lupine, maypop, orchid,
oxalis, violet, zinnia 7. arbutus,
begonia, fuchsia, gentian, passion,
petunia, rhodora, verbena 8. amaranth,
arethusa, camomile, cyclamen, daffodil,
geranium, hepatica, hyacinth, larkspur,
magnolia, marigold, Mariposa (lily),
primrose, sweet pea 9. amaryllis,
calendula, carnation, edelweiss,
gladiolus, hollyhock, mayflower,
narcissus, water lily 10. cornflower,
delphinium, fleur-de-lis, marguerite,
mignonette, nasturtium, periwinkle,
poinsettia, snapdragon 11. forget-me-
not, strawflower 13. chrysanthemum
15. lily of the valley

flower (pert to) ...
arranging .. 7. ikebana
bed, garden .. 8. floretum, parterre
bloom (full) .. 8. anthesis
bud (sauce) .. 5. caper
bunch .. 4. posy 7. bouquet, corsage,
nosegay
bursting into .. 12. efflorescent
cluster, clustered .. 4. cyme 5. umbel
6. racemose 9. glomerule 10. paniculate
largest .. 9. rafflesia (3-ft diameter)
like .. 7. anthoid
meadow-grown .. 6. pratal
part .. 4. stem 5. bract, calyx, petal,
sepal, spike, torus 6. carpel, pistil,
stamen 7. corolla, petiole 8. epicalyx,
peduncle, perianth
poet's .. 8. asphodel 9. narcissus
sacred .. 5. lotus
seed .. 5. ovule
shaped .. 7. fleuron
small .. 7. fleuret

stand .. 7. epergne
flower, shrub ... 5. lilac 6. azalea,
laurel 7. dogwood, heather, jasmine,
spiraea, syringa 8. bayberry, hawthorn
9. jessamine, mistletoe, sagebrush
10. bitterroot 12. rhododendron

flower, vine ... 8. clematis, wisteria
11. honeysuckle 12. morning glory

flower, wild ... 5. bluet, daisy 6. cactus,
clover, myrtle, pasque 7. anemone,
cowslip 8. bluebell, camellia
9. buttercup, goldenrod, mayflower,
sunflower 10. bluebonnet 12. lady's-
slipper

flowering again ... 9. remontant
flowers ... 9. flowerage
flowers, goddess of ... 5. Flora (Rom)
Flowery Kingdom ... 5. China
flowing ... 5. fluid 6. afflux, fluent
7. copious, cursive, emanant, fluxing
8. coursing, eloquent 9. streaming
10. transitive

flowing (pert to) ...
from source .. 6. rising 9. emanating
together .. 9. confluent
veil .. 5. colet (anc)
well .. 6. gusher

fluctuate ... 4. roll, vary, veer 5. waver
7. vibrate 8. intermit, undulate,
unsteady 9. oscillate, vacillate
10. irresolute 12. undetermined

flue ... 4. barb 5. fluke 6. funnel, tunnel
7. chimney

fluent ... 4. glib 5. fluid, ready 6. facile,
smooth, solute 7. copious, elegant,
flowing, gliding, verbose, voluble
8. eloquent 9. talkative 10. loquacious

fluff ... 4. down, girl, lint, yarn 5. floss
6. bungle 8. softness 9. lightness

fluffy ... 4. soft 5. downy, drunk,
fuzzy, linty 8. feathery 9. forgetful
12. undependable

fluid ... 3. gas, ink, oil 4. bile, milk
5. ichor, serum, water 6. fluent, liquid,
plasma, watery 7. flowing 8. floating,
nonsolid

fluke ... 4. fish, worm 5. blade (whale)
8. accident, flatfish, flounder

flume ... 5. shoot 6. raving, sluice
7. channel, conduit

flummox ... 7. confuse, perplex

flunk ... 4. fail, miss, slip 5. shirk 6. flinch
7. back out

flunky, flunkey ... 4. snob 5. toady
6. cookee, lackey 7. footman, servant
8. henchman 9. stagehand

flurry ... 3. ado 4. fret, gust 5. haste,
hurry 6. bustle, squall 7. bluster,
fluster, flutter 8. snowfall 9. agitation,
commotion, confusion 10. excitement

flush ... 3. hot, jet 4. full, glow, gush,
rush 5. blush, cards, color, drunk, fever,
rinse, ruddy 6. drench, lavish, redden,
thrill 7. healthy, wealthy 8. abundant,
affluent, prodigal, rosiness, squarely,
unbroken 10. prosperous

flushed ... 3. hot, red 4. ruby 5. aglow,
drunk 6. elated, florid 7. excited,
fervent 8. blushing, exultant, feverish,
reddened

fluster ... 4. move 5. shake 6. bustle,

excite, flurry, pother 8. distract
10. excitement 11. distraction
flute . . . 5. crimp, twill 6. furrow, groove
7. magadis 9. organ stop, wineglass
10. instrument
flute (pert to) . . .
bagpipe part . . 7. chanter
nose . . 3. bin 5. pungi
player . . 6. aulete 7. tootler
shrill . . 7. piccolo
stop . . 7. ventage
transverse . . 4. fife
fluting . . . 5. strix 7. gadroon, shading
10. decoration
flutter . . . 4. flap, flit, wave 5. float, haste,
hover, waver 6. bustle, ruffle 7. agitate,
pitapat 8. disorder 9. agitation,
confusion, palpitate
flux . . . 4. flow, fuse, melt 5. flood, purge,
resin, rosin, smelt, smear 6. course
7. flowing, liquefy, outflow, solvent
fly . . . 3. hop 4. flee, flit, leap, melt,
soar, wave, whir, wing 5. alate, float,
glide, speed 6. aviate, elapse, escape,
insect, spring, vanish 7. avigate, avolate
8. fishhook 9. cease to be, disappear
fly (types of) . . . 3. bot 4. gnat 5. cadew,
horse, house, midge 6. Asilus, caddis,
gadfly, punkie, tsetse 7. Diptera, nosee-
um 8. dipteron, lacewing, mosquito
11. caterpillar
fly (pert to) . . .
African . . 4. zimb (zebub) 6. tsetse
agaric . . 8. mushroom (poisonous)
artificial . . 4. harl 5. alder, sedge 6. Cahill,
claret 7. grannom
blow . . 4. eggs 5. larva
catcher . . 4. tody 6. peewee (pewit),
phoebe 8. kingbird
flying . . . 5. a-wing, brief, hasty, yarak
(falcon) 6. volant, waving 7. fleeing
8. fleeting, floating 9. temporary,
transient 12. aeronautical
flying (pert to) . . .
adder . . 9. dragonfly
boat . . 8. airplane, seaplane 9. amphibian
cat . . 5. lemur 6. marmot
Dutchman . . 5. opera 7. mariner (fabled)
8. wanderer
fox . . 3. bat 6. kalong
island . . 6. Laputa (Gulliver's Travels)
machine . . 9. gyroplane, orthopter
foal . . . 4. colt 5. filly 8. Equuleus (Astron)
9. youngling
foam . . . 4. barm, boil, fume, rage, scum,
suds 5. froth, spume, yeast 6. trivia
7. bubbles
foaming . . . 7. spumous 8. bubbling
10. fermenting, infuriated
11. overwrought
fob . . . 4. sham 5. cheat, trick 6. impose,
pocket 7. palm off 8. ornament
focal point . . . 8. omphalos
focus . . . 6. center 8. converge, omphalos
10. adjustment 11. concentrate
fodder . . . 3. hay 4. corn, feed 5. straw,
vetch 6. forage, silage, stover 7. stubble
8. ensilage 9. pasturage, provender
fodder (pert to) . . .
pit . . 4. silo
storage . . 6. haymow

store . . 6. ensile
stored . . 6. silage
foe . . . 4. army 5. enemy, rival 8. opponent
9. ill-wisher
fog . . . 4. blur, daze, haar, haze, mist,
roke, smog 5. brume, cloud, vapor
6. nebula, opaque, stupor 7. aerosol,
confuse, pogonip (Sierras) 9. confusion
fogdog . . . 5. stubb 8. fogeater
foggy . . . 3. dim 4. dull, hazy, roky
5. dense, misty, vague 6. cloudy,
opaque 7. muddled, obscure
8. confused, nubilous 9. beclouded,
uncertain 10. indistinct
12. muddleheaded
foghorn . . . 5. siren, voice (hoarse)
6. signal
fogle . . . 12. handkerchief (thieves')
fogy . . . 4. dull, slow 6. dotard, fogram,
Hunker 8. mossback 10. Barnburner
12. conservative, old-fashioned
16. overconservative
foible . . . 5. blade (part), fault 7. failing,
frailty 8. weakness 9. infirmity
12. imperfection
foil . . . 4. balk 5. actor, metal, sheet,
stump, sword 6. defeat, offset, outwit,
stooge, thwart, weapon 7. failure,
repulse 9. frustrate 10. disappoint
11. frustration
Foism . . . 8. Buddhism
foist . . . 4. palm 5. cheat 7. intrude
9. interpose 11. interpolate
fold . . . 3. end, lap, pen, ply 4. coil
(serpent), fail, furl, loop, pile, reef, ruga,
sile, tuck, wrap 5. clasp, close, crimp,
drape, laity, plait, pleat, plica 6. crease,
dewlap, double, infold, lamina, lappet,
rimple, suffix 7. entwine, envelop,
plicate (fanlike) 8. collapse 9. plicature
10. go bankrupt
folded, not . . . 8. eplicate
folder . . . 7. booklet, leaflet 8. pamphlet
13. advertisement
foliage . . . 5. spray 6. leaves, ramage
7. bouquet, leafage, umbrage
8. ornament (Arch)
folio . . . 4. case, leaf 5. paper (folded)
6. folder, number (serial)
folk . . . 4. race 5. tribe 6. nation, people
8. servants 9. followers, relatives,
retainers 11. aggregation
folk (pert to) . . .
learned . . 7. pedants
lore . . 6. legend 9. mythology, tradition
12. superstition
song . . 4. fado, lied 7. art song, lullaby
9. Kunstlied, Volkslied
tale . . 4. myth, saga 5. fable, Nancy
6. legend, mythos, mythus 7. fantasy,
parable
follow . . . 3. dog, tag 4. heed, heel, next,
nose, obey, seek, tail 5. after, ensue,
trace, trail 6. pursue, result, shadow
7. conform, draggle, emulate, imitate,
observe, replace, succeed 8. come
next, practice, supplant 9. persevere,
supervene 10. understand
follower . . . 3. fan, ist (suff), ite (suff), son
4. aper 5. lover (of) 6. copier, ensuer,
votary, zealot 7. devotee, pursuer,

sequent 8. adherent, believer, disciple,
henchman, partisan 9. Christian,
dependent, satellite 10. enthusiast
11. cuadrillero

follower of . . .
Arius . . 5. Arian
Buddha . . 8. Buddhist
Confucius . . 9. Confucian
Falstaff . . 3. Nym
Mohammed . . 6. Moslem 8. Islamite

following . . 4. next, sect 5. suant
7. ensuing, pursuit, sequent 8. trailing
9. resultant 10. subsequent, succeeding,
successive 13. accompaniment

following (pert to) . . .
exact words . . 7. literal
one's death . . 10. posthumous
stories . . 6. sequel, series

folly . . . 3. sin 5. crime 6. levity,
lunacy 7. blunder, foolery, madness
8. lewdness, unwisdom 9. silliness
10. desipience, imprudence,
wantonness 11. foolishness
12. indiscretion

foment . . . 3. egg 4. abet, brew, spur
5. bathe, rouse 6. arouse, excite,
incite 7. agitate, cherish 9. encourage,
instigate

fomentation . . . 6. lotion, stupes
10. excitement 11. instigation
13. encouragement

Fomoriana (Celt Myth) . . . 10. sea robbers
(race of)

fonda . . . 3. inn 5. hotel 6. fonduk

fondle . . . 3. pet 4. neck 5. ingle 6. caress,
coddle, cosset, foster, pamper 7. cherish
8. blandish

fondling . . . 3. pet 4. fool 5. ninny
9. caressing, simpleton 10. love-making

fondly . . . 6. dearly 8. tenderly
14. affectionately

fondness . . . 3. gra 4. love 6. desire,
doting, liking, relish 8. appetite
9. affection 10. attachment, propensity

fond of . . .
hunting . . 7. venatic
sea . . 15. thalassophilous
wife (overly) . . 8. uxorious

font . . . 3. jet 4. fons, lava 5. stoup
6. source, spring 7. piscina 8. fountain
9. reservoir

food . . . 3. cud, pap 4. cate, chow, diet,
eats, fare, grub, junk (food), meat,
tofu 5. bread, manna, scran 6. bulgur
(wheat), cereal, gluten, quiche, snacks,
Tex-Mex, viands 7. aliment, cuisine,
edibles, tapioca 8. chili dog, fast-
food, kreplach, munchies, victuals
9. nutriment, nutrition, provender
10. sustenance 11. charcuterie,
comestibles, nourishment

food (pert to) . . .
animal . . 6. forage 9. provender
bit . . 4. bite 6. morsel 7. munchie
devotee . . 7. epicure, gourmet
digestant . . 5. chyle
digested (partly) . . 5. chyme
dislike of . . 9. sitomania 10. cibophobia
element . . 7. protein, vitamin
fasting (Lenten) . . 9. xerophagy
gods, the . . 6. amrita 8. ambrosia

heavenly . . 5. manna
impure . . 4. tref
provide . . 5. cater, scaff 6. tucker
room . . 6. pantry, spence
7. butlery, pantler

fool . . . 3. ass, toy 4. butt, dolt, dupe,
jerk, nerd, nizy, raca (Bib), simp
5. clown, idiot, moron, ninny 6. dotard,
jester, noodle, trifle, turkey 7. buffoon,
deceive, dingbat, fathead 9. ignoramus,
simpleton

foolhardy . . . 4. rash 7. Icarian 8. reckless
11. adventurous

fool hen . . . 6. grouse

foolish . . . 3. mad 4. daft, raca, rash,
zany 5. inane, inept, silly 6. absurd,
harish 5. palty 6. simple, stupid,
unwise 7. asinine, fatuous, idiotic,
puerile, witless 9. brainless, desipient,
imprudent, ludicrous, senseless
10. illadvised, irrational, ridiculous
12. preposterous 13. insignificant

foolish fancy . . . 7. chimera (chimaera)

foolishness . . . 5. folly 6. levity
9. absurdity, stupidity 10. triviality

fool's bauble . . . 7. marotte

fool's gold . . . 6. pyrite

foot . . . 3. pad 6. pew pes (pref) 4. base,
hoof, inch (part), sole, step, walk
5. sum up, tread 6. reckon 7. residue
8. calculate, extremity

foot (pert to) . . .
bone . . 6. tarsus 10. metatarsus
care of . . 8. pedicure, podiatry
9. chiropody 11. chiropodist
combining form . . 4. pede, pedi
lever . . 5. pedal 7. treadle
like . . 8. pediform
measure . . 4. inch
part . . 3. toe 4. arch, heel, sole
prefix . . 4. pedi
race course (anc) . . 7. diaulos
reference to . . 5. pedal, podal
rest . . 4. rail 7. cricket, hassock, ottoman,
support 8. footrail 9. footstool
sole . . 7. plantar
unstressed part (Pros) . . 5. arsis

foot, feet (metric) . . . 4. iamb, mora, unit
6. dactyl, dipody, iambus 7. anapest,
dimeter, pyrrhic, spondee, tripody
8. trimeter 9. hexameter 10. heptameter,
pentameter

footed . . . 5. biped 7. bipedal, megapod
(large), metered

footing . . . 4. lace, rank 5. basis, dance,
tread 6. status 7. support 8. foothold,
progress, standing 9. condition
11. calculation

footlike part . . . 3. pes

footman . . . 6. varlet, walker 7. servant
9. attendant 10. pedestrian

footprint mold . . . 7. moulage

footway . . . 7. catwalk (Naut)

fop . . . 3. nob 4. Adon, buck, dude
5. dandy, puppy, sport, swell 6. Adonis,
masher 7. coxcomb, gallant 9. exquisite,
pretender 12. boulevardier

foppish . . . 6. dapper, spruce 7. finical,
foplike 8. dandyish 9. conceited,
dandified

for . . . 2. to 3. pro 5. spite 7. because,

instead 8. behalf of 9. intending
10. indicating 11. preparation

for (pert to) . . .
  each . . 3. per
  example . . 2. as, eg 4. vide 13. exempli
gratia
  fear . . 4. lest
  most part . . 6. mostly 7. chiefly, usually
9. generally
  nothing . . 6. gratis, naught 9. lagniappe
(lagnappe)
  this reason . . 4. ergo 5. hence

forage . . 4. food, mast, raid 5. spoil
6. browse, ravage 7. plunder
9. pasturage

foramen . . . 4. pore 7. opening, orifice,
passage 8. fenestra

foray . . . 4. raid 6. ravage, sortie 7. pillage
9. incursion

forbear . . . 4. lose, shun 5. avoid 6. desist,
endure 7. abstain, decline, refrain
8. part with 9. be patient

forbearance . . . 5. mercy 6. disuse,
lenity 8. leniency, mildness, patience
9. tolerance 10. abstinence, temperance
11. forgiveness, placability

forbid . . . 3. ban 4. deny, tabu, veto
5. debar, taboo 6. disbar, hinder,
impede, oppose 7. exclude, inhibit,
prevent 8. disallow, preclude, prohibit
9. interdict, proscribe 11. countermand

forbiddance . . . 3. ban 4. veto
11. unallowable 12. illiberality,
interdiction, proscription

forbidden city . . . 5. Lhasa (Tibet), Pekin
(walled)

forbidden food (Bib) . . . 4. tref
8. teraphah

forbidding . . . 4. grim, ugly 5. plain,
stern 6. fierce, odious 9. offensive,
revolting 10. prevention, unpleasant
11. displeasing, prohibitive

force . . . 3. vim, vis 4. dint, make, urge
5. drive, impel, power, press, repel,
staff, vigor 6. coerce, compel, effect,
energy, extort, hasten, strain 7. impetus,
meaning 8. eloquent, momentum,
pressure, validity, violence 9. constrain,
influence, puissance 10. compulsion,
constraint 11. necessitate

force (pert to) . . .
  alleged . . 2. od
  armed . . 4. army 5. posse
  by seizure . . 5. usurp
  down . . 7. detrude
  full . . 5. amain
  substance . . 8. catalyst
  unit . . 4. dyne 5. staff, tonal 7. poundal

forced . . . 7. labored 9. reluctant, unwilling
10. artificial, compulsory, farfetched
11. constrained

forced feeding . . 6. gavage

forceful . . . 5. valid 6. mighty, potent,
strong 7. dynamic 8. eloquent,
emphatic, vigorous 9. effective,
energetic 10. compulsory

forces . . . 4. army 5. armed 6. troops

forcible . . . 6. cogent, mighty, potent
7. violent, weighty 8. emphatic, positive, puissant 9. energetic
10. compulsory, impressive

11. influential

forcible entry . . . 10. effraction

forciform . . . 6. forked 7. furcate
11. forficulate 14. scissors-shaped

ford . . . 4. wade 5. cross 6. stream

fore . . . 3. way 5. front, prior, track
6. former 7. journey

forebear . . . 4. sire 5. elder 6. parent
8. ancestor 10. antecedent, forefather,
progenitor

forebode . . . 5. augur 6. betoken,
portend, predict, presage 8. foretell
15. prognostication

foreboding . . . 6. augury 8. croaking,
sinister 11. pessimistic, presagement
12. apprehension, presentiment

forecast . . . 4. bode, plan 6. scheme
7. foresee, fortune, predict 8. foretell,
prophecy 9. calculate, foresight,
foretoken 10. foreordain, prediction
12. predetermine

forecaster . . . 4. seer 5. vates 6. oracle
7. diviner, palmist, prophet 8. dopester,
presager 10. astrologer, soothsayer
11. Nostradamus 13. meteorologist
14. prognosticator

foreclose . . . 5. debar 6. hinder 7. prevent,
shut out 8. preclude 10. dispossess

foredoom . . . 4. doom 7. predict
12. predestinate

foredoomed . . . 3. fey 5. fatal 8. accursed

forefather . . . 4. sire 5. elder 6. parent
8. ancestor, forebear 10. progenitor

forefinger . . . 5. index

foregather . . . 4. meet 7. convene
8. assemble 9. encounter

forego, forgo . . . 6. pass by 7. neglect,
precede 8. renounce

foregoing . . . 4. past 5. above 6. former,
prefix 7. leading 10. antecedent

foregone . . . 4. past 8. previous
11. predestined, preordained,
preresolved 13. predetermined

foregone conclusion . . . 9. certainty

forehead . . . 4. brow 8. calvaria, glabella,
sinciput 9. assurance 10. effrontery

forehead, divination by . . .
11. metopomancy

forehead, frontal . . . 7. metopic

foreign . . . 4. xeno (comb form) 5. alien,
fremd 6. exotic, remote 7. distant,
outside (of country), strange 8. excluded
9. extrinsic, peregrine, unrelated
10. extraneous, outlandish
11. incongruous 12. adventitious

foreign (pert to) . . .
  accent . . 4. burr 6. brogue, patois
7. dialect
  crystals (Geol) . . 7. epigene
  disease . . 7. ecdemic
  insertion . . 13. interpolation
  place . . 6. forane
  quarter . . 4. Para 5. Latin 6. French
7. enclave
  service residence . . 9. consulate

foreigner . . . 5. alien 6. gringo 8. outsider,
stranger 9. outlander, uitlander
10. tramontane 12. ultramontane

foreland . . . 8. headland 10. promontory

forelock . . . 4. bang 7. cowlick, fetlock
8. linchpin 9. cotter pin, fastening

(armor)

foreman . . . 4. boss 5. chief 6. leader 7. juryman, overman 10. supervisor 14. superintendent

foremost . . . 5. chief, first, front 7. leading, supreme 8. headmost 13. most important

forensic . . . 10. rhetorical 13. argumentative

foreordain . . . 7. destine 9. predicate, preordain 12. foreordinate, predestinate, predetermine

forerun . . . 6. herald 7. advance, prelude, presage 8. announce, antecede 9. forestall, introduce, prefigure 10. anticipate, foreshadow

forerunner . . . 4. omen, sign 6. augury, herald 8. ancestor 9. harbinger, messenger, precursor 10. forefather, foreganger, progenitor, prognostic 11. predecessor

foreshadow . . . 6. shadow (beforehand) 7. presage 8. adumbrate, prefigure

foresight . . . 8. sagacity 9. prevision 10. precaution, prediction, prescience, prevoyance, providence 11. omniscience 13. foreknowledge

forest . . . 4. wold, wood 5. grove, woods 6. jungle, timber 8. woodland 9. greenwood 10. timberland, wilderness

forest (pert to) . . .
  deity . . 3. Pan 7. Aegipan
  fire . . 5. crown, stand 6. ground 7. surface
  fire-finding instrument . . 7. alidade
  . . . 6. camass (camass, cammas)
  . . . lover of . . 9. nemophile, nemophily
  regarding . . 6. sylvan 7. nemoral
  tilion . . 7. thwaite
  warden . . 6. ranger

forestall . . . 6. hinder 7. exclude, head off, prevent 9. intercept 10. anticipate, monopolize

foretell . . . 4. bode, spae 5. augur, insee 7. portend, predict, presage 8. forebode, forecast, prophesy 10. vaticinate 13. prognosticate

foretelling . . . 6. augury 7. fatidic 9. fatidical, prophetic 10. vaticinant

forethought . . . 8. prepense, prudence 9. foresight, provident 10. deliberate, precaution 12. aforethought, anticipation 13. premeditation

foretoken . . . 4. omen 7. presage 8. foreshow, indicant 10. presignify 13. preindication, prognosticate

foretooth . . . 5. biter 6. cutter 7. incisor 9. milk tooth

forever . . . 3. ake (Maori), aye (ay) 4. olam, ever 6. always, eterne 7. endless 8. infinity 9. continual, perpetual 10. constantly, invariably 11. ceaselessly, continually, incessantly, perpetually, unceasingly 12. interminably, unchangeably 13. everlastingly

forewarning . . . 4. omen 7. caution, portent 9. informing 10. admonition, foreboding

foreword . . . 5. proem 7. preface, prelude 8. exordium, preamble, prologue 12. introduction

forfeit . . . 4. fine, lose, loss 5. forgo, mulct 6. forego, pledge 7. deodand, penalty

forfeiture . . . 4. fine, loss 5. dédit, mulct 7. penalty 10. amercement

forfend . . . 5. avert 6. forbid 7. prevent, protect 8. preserve, prohibit

forfex . . . 6. shears

forgather . . . 4. meet 7. consort, convene 8. assemble 9. encounter 10. fraternize

forge . . . 4. coin, form, mint 5. feign 6. create, smithy, stithy, swinge 7. falsify, imitate 8. bloomery, smithery 11. counterfeit

forgery . . . 4. sham 7. fiction 9. falsehood, invention 11. counterfeit, fabrication 13. falsification

forget . . . 4. omit 5. lapse, remit 6. slight 7. neglect 9. disregard 11. disremember

forgetfulness . . . 5. Lethe (Myth), lotus (legend) 7. amnesia, amnesty 8. Manassah, oblivion 12. carelessness, heedlessness 13. obliviousness

forgive . . . 5. remit, spare 6. acquit, excuse, pardon 7. condone

forgiveness . . . 6. pardon 9. remission 10. absolution 11. condonation, exoneration, magnanimity

forgiving . . . 6. humane 8. merciful, placable 9. remissive 11. magnanimous

forgo . . . 4. quit 5. leave, waive 6. give up, resign 7. abstain, forbear, forfeit, forsake, neglect, refrain 8. overlook, renounce 9. do without 10. relinquish

forsake . . . 7. abandon, despise

fork . . . 6. expand, out 7. dilemma, diverge 10. divaricate, divergence, headstream 11. bifurcation

fork (pert to) . . .
  feature . . 4. tine 5. prong
  garden . . 5. graip
  pickle . . 13. runcible spoon
  table . . 5. salad 6. dinner, oyster 7. dessert 8. ice-cream

forked . . . 5. bifid 6. horned, ramous 7. divided, furcate 8. branched, crotched 9. ambiguous, equivocal 10. bifurcated, branchlike

forlorn . . . 4. reft 5. alone 6. abject, bereft 8. deserted, desolate, forsaken, helpless, pitiable 9. abandoned, destitute, miserable 10. friendless 12. disconsolate

form . . . 4. body, cast, idea, mold, rite 5. build, guise, model, shape 6. beauty, create, figure, invent, ritual 7. compose, contour, formula, outline, pattern, profile, species, variety 8. ceremony, conceive, document 9. establish, formality 10. appearance 11. arrangement 12. conformation 13. configuration, questionnaire 15. conventionality

form (pert to) . . .
  bust . . 6. taille
  chainlike . . 8. catenate
  deceptive . . 5. ghost 7. specter 8. phantasm

display . . 4. rack
good . . 4. chic 6. fettle
government . . 6. polity
hollow . . 5. shell
into fabric . . 4. knit, spin 5. weave
primitive . . 7. prototype
spiral . . 5. helix
suffix . . 5. shape 10. resembling

formal . . 4. prim 5. exact, stiff 6. solemn 7. orderly, outward, precise, regular, stilted 8. affected, apparent, starched 9. formative 10. ceremonial, methodical 11. pharisaical, ritualistic, superficial 12. conventional

formal introduction . . . 5. debut 12. presentation

formalities . . . 5. rites 9. etiquette 10. ceremonies

formal warning . . . 5. alarm 6. caveat 12. caveat emptor

format . . . 4. size 5. shape, style

formation . . . 4. form 5. order 9. structure 11. arrangement, composition 12. construction

formation (pert to) . . .
chain (twisted) . . 9. torquated
geologic . . 7. terrain, terrane
military . . 4. line 5. herse 7. echelon
sand . . 4. dene, dune

formed . . . 4. made 6. built 7. created, decided, matured, settled 8. arranged 9. fashioned, organized 11. constructed

formed (pert to) . . .
by law . . 9. corporate
by lips . . 6. labial
mountain foot . . 8. piedmont
on earth's surface . . 7. epigene
plates (two) . . 11. bilamellate

formed into . . .
chain . . 8. catenate 9. torquated
fabric . . 5. spun 6. woven 7. knitted
mass (hard) . . 4. iced 5. caked 6. frozen 9. congealed
mosaic . . 9. tessellar 11. tessellated

former . . . 2. ex 3. old 4. erst, late, once, past 5. front, prior 6. passed, whilom 7. ancient, earlier 8. previous 9. erstwhile, foregoing, preceding 10. antecedent

former days . . . 3. eld, old 4. yore

formerly . . . 3. nee 4. erst, once, then 6. before, whilom 7. one-time 8. sometime 9. aforetime, erstwhile 10. heretofore, previously

formicary . . . 7. anthill 8. ant's nest

formicid . . . 3. ant 5. emmet 7. Formica

formidable . . . 7. fearful 8. alarming, dreadful, menacing, terrible 9. difficult 11. redoubtable, threatening

formless . . . 5. arupa 7. anidian, chaotic 9. amorphous, shapeless 3. indeterminate

Formosa, Taiwan . . .
capital . . 6. Taipei
city . . 6. Tainan 7. Hualien, Keelung 9. Kaohsiung
group . . 6. Penghu (64 Isls)
island . . 5. Matsu 6. Quemoy

formula . . . 3. law 4. form, rule 5. axiom, creed, lurry, maxim, model 6. method, recipe, ritual 12. prescription

forsake . . . 4. deny, quit, shun 5. avoid, leave 6. depart, desert, refuse, reject 7. abandon 8. renounce, withdraw 9. surrender

forsaken . . . 4. lorn 6. vacant 7. forlorn 8. deserted, lovelorn, rejected 9. abandoned

forspeak . . . 5. curse 6. forbid 7. asperse, bewitch 8. renounce 10. relinquish

fort . . . 5. redan, tower 6. abatis, castle, escarp, glacis (bank of) 7. bastion, bulwark, castlet 8. bastille, fastness, fortress 10. stronghold 13. fortification, propugnaculum

Fort (Fr Ind War) . . . 9. Necessity

forte . . . 4. loud 5. skill 8. strength 10. strong suit

forth . . . 3. out 4. away 6. abroad, onward 7. forward, outward

forthright . . . 5. ahead 7. frankly 8. forwards 9. downright 11. immediately, straightway 13. straightforth

forthwith . . . 3. now 6. pronto 8. promptly 9. summarily 11. immediately, straightway

fortification . . . 4. wall 5. redan 6. abatis 7. bastion, citadel, defense, parados, ravelin, redoubt 8. barbette (part), fortress 10. stronghold 13. corroboration, strengthening

fortify . . . 3. arm, man 4. gird 5. add to, spike, stank 6. defend, secure 7. confirm, refresh 8. embattle 10. adulterate (drink), invigorate, strengthen, vitaminize 11. corroborate

fortitude . . . 6. virtue 7. bravery, courage 8. strength 9. endurance 10. resolution 12. resoluteness 14. impregnability

fortress . . . see fort

fortuitous . . . 3. hap 6. chance 10. accidental 12. unexpectedly

fortunate . . . 5. happy, lucky 6. timely 7. favored 10. auspicious, prosperous, successful 12. providential

fortune . . . 3. hap, lot 4. doom, fate, luck 6. chance, estate, riches, wealth 7. destiny, success 8. accident 10. prosperity 13. circumstances

fortune (pert to) . . .
gypsy . . 4. bahi
ill . . 9. mischance
place . . 6. cookie
planet (Astrol) . . 5. Venus 7. Jupiter
teller . . 4. seer 5. sibyl, Tyche 6. oracle 7. spaeman

fortuneteller's deck . . . 5. tarot (cards)

forum fashion . . . 4. toga

forward . . . 2. on, to 3. aid 4. abet, bold, fore, help, pert, send, ship, vain 5. ahead, along, eager, front, impel, ready, relay, saucy, ultra 6. active, bright, hasten, onward 7. deliver, earnest, extreme, further, radical, willing 8. advanced, immodest, impudent, transmit 9. audacious, encourage 10. precocious 11. progressive 12. presumptuous

forward moving (Zool) . . . 5. proal (digestion) 11. mastication

fosse, foss . . . 3. pit 4. moat 5. canal,

ditch, fossa, grave 6. cavity, trench
10. depression

fossil, fossils ... 5. relic, stone 7. antique,
remains

fossil (pert to) ...
egg .. 7. ovulite
footprint .. 7. ichnite
resin .. 5. amber
shell .. 6. dolite 8. ammonite
site .. 8. Badlands
study of .. 12. paleontology
toothlike .. 8. conodont
worm track .. 7. nereite

foster ... 4. rear 5. breed, nurse 7. cherish,
gratify, indulge, promote 9. cultivate

fosterage ... 7. nurture 11. development

foster child ... 4. dalt 5. norry (nurry)
7. stepson 8. nursling 12. stepdaughter

fought ... see *fight*

foul ... 3. bad 4. olid, ugly 5. dirty,
fetid, grimy, nasty, reeky, spoil,
sully 6. defame, filthy, malign,
odious, putrid, rotten, thwart, unfair
7. abusive, confuse, noisome, obscene,
profane, unclean 8. entangle, indecent,
infamous, shameful, stagnant, stinking
9. dishonest, obnoxious 10. complicate,
malodorous, scurrilous 11. contaminate,
ill-smelling, unfavorable
12. inauspicious, unpropitious

foul play ... 6. murder, unfair (play)
7. perfidy 8. violence 9. deception,
treachery 10. unfairness

found ... 3. fix 4. base, cast 5. endow,
set up 6. attach, create 9. establish,
institute, originate

foundation ... 3. bed 4. base, plot,
sill 5. basal, basis 6. legacy, riprap
7. bedding, charity, premise, support
8. cosmetic, creation, donation, pedestal
9. placement 11. corporation
13. justification

found by chance (thing) ...
11. serendipity

founded on ...
base .. 10. predicated
evidence .. 10. evidential
experience .. 7. empiric 9. empirical
imagination .. 7. Utopian

founder ... 4. fail, fall, sink 6. author
7. capsize, creator, stumble 8. miscarry
9. break down, organizer 10. originator

foundling ... 3. oaf 4. waif 5. child
(unclaimed) 6. orphan 8. derelict,
nursling

fountain ... 3. jet, spa 4. font, head, well
6. spring 9. reservoir 11. scuttlebutt
(ship's) 12. fountainhead

fountain (pert to) ...
god of .. 4. Fons
Muse (Gr) .. 8. Aganippe
nymph .. 5. naiad 6. Egeria
of Lions .. 8. Alhambra (Spain)

four (pert to) ...
bits .. 7. quarter (silver)
Books .. 8. Classics (Chin)
footed .. 8. tetrapod
genii, of Amenti .. 13. Horus' children
group .. 6. tetrad
Hundred .. 5. elect, elite 7. society
letters, word of .. 9. tetragram

seas .. 13. Great Britain's
senses (Bib) .. 15. interpretations

four-flusher ... 5. cheat, fraud 7. bluffer
8. impostor 9. pretender

four-in-hand ... 3. tie 4. team (horses)
6. cravat 7. necktie

fourth (pert to) ...
Caliph .. 3. Ali
century martyr .. 8. St Blaise
estate .. 5. press 10. newspapers
part .. 6. fardel 7. quarter
stomach (cow) .. 8. abomasum

fowl ... 3. hen 6. bantam, Gallus 7. Blue
Hen, broiler, chicken, Dorking, leghorn,
Minorca, poultry, rooster, seafowl
8. pheasant 9. guinea hen, waterfowl
11. chanticleer

fox ... 3. cub, tod 4. stag 5. vixen

fox (pert to) ...
African .. 4. asse
Asian .. 5. adive 6. corsac
fabled .. 7. Reynard
female .. 5. vixen
genus .. 6. Vulpes
hedge (hunter's) .. 4. oxer
foot .. 3. pad
Indian .. 10. Algonquian
Russian .. 6. corsac 7. karagan

foxglove ... 9. digitalis

foxy ... 3. sly 4. sexy, wily 6. artful,
crafty 7. cunning, vulpine

foyer ... 5. lobby 8. anteroom, entrance
9. greenroom

fracas ... 3. row 5. brawl, melee, set-
to 6. uproar 7. quarrel 8. commotion
11. disturbance

fraction ... 3. bit 4. part 5. piece, scrap
6. sector 7. element, ruction 8. division,
fragment 9. commotion

fractious ... 4. ugly 5. cross 6. unruly
7. peevish, waspish 8. perverse,
snappish 9. irritable 10. ill-humored
11. disobedient

fracture ... 4. rend 5. break, cleft, crack
6. breach, injury 7. rupture

fragile ... 4. weak 5. brash, frail 6. frough
(obs), infirm, slight 7. brittle 8. delicate,
slattery 9. frangible

fragment ... 3. bit, ort 4. chip, grot, part,
snip 5. groat, piece, relic, scrap, shard,
sherd, shred, torso (art) 6. morsel,
sippet 7. flinder 8. fraction

fragments ... 3. ana 6. fardel, groats,
rubble 8. buttings, excerpts, flinders
10. miscellany 11. smithereens

fragrance ... 4. odor 5. aroma, elemi,
smell 7. incense, perfume 9. redolence

fragrant ... 4. nard 5. balmy, olent,
spicy, sweet 7. odorous 8. aromatic,
redolent 9. ambrosial 11. odoriferous
12. sweet-scented 13. sweet-smelling

frail ... 4. girl, thin, weak 5. woman
6. basket (fig), feeble, sickly, slimsy
7. brittle, fragile 8. strumpet, unchaste
10. weak-willed 12. destructible

frailty ... 5. fault 6. defect 7. failing
8. thinness, weakness 9. fragility,
infirmity 12. imperfection

frame ... 4. body, make, plan, rack, sess,
sill 5. build, easel, grate, herse, knape
6. abacus, border, charge (falsely),

direct, tenter 7. carcass, chassis,
cresset (torch), fashion, prepare,
setting, taboret 8. conceive, skeleton
9. construct 10. prearrange

framework . . . 4. rack, sill 5. cadre,
shell 6. cradle 7. trestle 8. skeleton
11. scaffolding

France . . . see also *French*
anc name . . 4. Gaul 6. Gallia
Bay . . 6. Biscay
Botanical Gardens . . 16. Jardin des
Plantes
capital . . 5. Paris
city . . 4. Nice 5. Lyons 7. LeHavre
8. Bordeaux, Toulouse 9. Marseille
10. Strasbourg
dread of . . 11. Gallophobia
12. Francophobia
island . . 6. Comoro (Afr), Tahiti
7. Corsica, Réunion 10. Guadeloupe
(Leeward), Martinique (Windward)
12. New Caledonia
lover of . . 10. Gallophile 11. Francophile
mountain . . 4. Alps, Jura 5. Pelat
8. Pyrenees 9. Mont Blanc 11. Pic
Montcalm
port . . 4. Caen 5. Brest 6. Calais, Toulon
7. Dunkirk (Dunkerque), Le Havre
8. Bordeaux
resort . . 3. Pau 5. Vichy 6. Cannes,
Menton (Mentone) 7. Riviera 9. Côte
d'Azur 11. Aix-les-Bains (anc)
river . . 3. Lys 4. Yser 5. Aisne, Eiser,
Loire, Meuse, Rhône, Seine
Southern . . 4. Midi
Verdun battle site . . 4. Vaux
wine region . . 8. Bordeaux, Burgundy

franchise . . . 4. vote 5. right 6. patent
7. freedom, license 8. immunity,
suffrage 9. exemption

frank . . . 4. free, mail, open 5. blunt,
naive, plain 6. candid, direct, honest
7. artless, liberal, sincere 8. generous
9. ingenuous, outspoken 10. unreserved
11. frankfurter 15. straightforward,
unsophisticated

frankincense . . . 4. thus 8. gum resin,
olibanum 9. fragrance

Frankish (pert to) . . .
dynasty . . 11. Carolingian, Merovingian
king . . 5. Pepin 6. Clovis
law . . 5. Salic
people (anc) . . 6. Salian
site . . 4. Gaul

Franklin, Benjamin . . . 11. Poor Richard

frantic . . . 3. mad 4. mang 5. moved,
rabid 7. furious 8. frenetic, frenzied
9. delirious, desperate, turbulent
10. distracted, distraught
11. overwrought

frappé . . . 3. ice 5. chill 6. freeze 7. dessert,
mixture (sweet) 8. beverage

fraternal . . . 4. kind 5. order, twins
7. society 8. friendly 9. brotherly

fraud . . . 4. fake, sham, wile 5. cheat,
covin, craft, guile 6. deceit, ringer
7. defraud, roguery 8. artifice, cozenage,
impostor, subtlety, swindler, trickery
9. deception, imposture, stratagem
10. imposition 13. circumvention

fraudulence . . . 9. improbity

10. subreption

fraudulent . . . 4. fake, wily 5. snide
6. crafty, quacky 7. cunning, knavish
8. cheating, guileful, spurious
9. deceitful, deceiving, deceptive,
designing, dishonest, insidious
10. fallacious 11. counterfeit,
treacherous

fraught . . . 4. lade, load 5. cargo, equip,
laden 6. burden, filled 7. freight
9. freighted, transport

fray . . . 4. fret (cloth), wear 5. broil,
dread, melee, panic, ravel 6. affray,
combat, fright, hassle, terror, tumult
7. contest, frazzle, ruction 9. commotion
12. apprehension

freak . . . 4. flam, lune, whim 5. fancy,
prank, sport 6. streak, vagary 7. caprice,
checker, crochet, monster 8. eccentric,
variegate 11. monstrosity
12. whimsicality

freakish . . . 7. curious 9. eccentric,
fantastic, whimsical 10. capricious,
changeable

freck . . . 4. bold, hale 5. eager, frack,
lusty, ready, stout 6. strong 7. forward
8. desirous

freckle . . . 4. mark, spot 7. blemish,
ephelis, lentigo, speckle 10. ferntickle

free . . . 3. rid 4. easy, open 5. clear,
frank, loose 6. acquit, candid, exempt,
gratis, immune, vacant 7. absolve,
inexact, manumit, not busy, release,
relieve, unbound 8. liberate 9. extricate,
footloose, voluntary 10. autonomous,
gratuitous, unconfined, unhampered
11. emancipated 12. uncontrolled,
unrestrained, unrestricted

free (pert to) . . .
bacteria . . 7. aseptic, sterile
difficulty . . 9. extricate
doubt . . 7. resolve
flesh (dietary) . . 6. maigre
knots . . 7. enodate, unravel
reproach . . 9. blameless
slavery . . 7. manumit 10. emancipate
suspicion . . 5. clear, purge 6. acquit
7. absolve 9. exculpate, exonerate
sweetness . . 3. sec

freebooter . . . 5. rover 6. pirate 8. pillager
9. plunderer 10. filibuster

freed . . . 3. rid 6. loosed, spared, untied
8. released 9. delivered, liberated
10. manumitted 11. emancipated

freedom . . . 6. candor 7. leisure, liberty,
license 8. latitude 9. exemption,
privilege 11. manumission
12. emancipation, independence

freedom (pert to) . . .
abused . . 7. liberty (excess), license
from doubt . . 9. assurance, certitude
from sepsis . . 7. asepsis

Freedom Our Rock (motto) . . .
7. Tammany (1789)

free enterprise . . . 6. policy 8. commerce
10. capitalism 15. noninterference

freely . . . 6. gratis 7. largely, readily
9. bountiful, copiously, liberally,
willingly 10. abundantly, generously
11. bounteously, plenteously,
plentifully, voluntarily 12. gratuitously

freeze . . . 3. ice 5. be-ice, chill 6. steeve
7. congeal, terrify 8. preserve, solidify
9. stabilize 11. anesthetize, refrigerate

freezing, science of . . . 10. cyrogenics

freight . . . 4. load, ship 5. cargo,
laden, train 6. burden, charge, lading
7. fraught, rattler 8. shipment
9. transport 14. transportation

freight boat . . . 5. barge 9. freighter

freit, freet . . . 4. omen 5. charm

fremd (obs) . . . 5. alien 7. foreign, hostile
9. unrelated

French (people) . . .
  artist . . 4. Dore 5. Corot, David, Degas,
  Leger, Manet, Monet, Rodin 6. Braque,
  Gerome, Greuze, Renoir, Seurat
  7. Courbet, Gauguin, Matisse, Watteau
  8. Daubigny, Pissarro, Rousseau
  9. Delacroix, Fragonard
  author . . 4. Hugo, Loti, Zola 5. Camus,
  Dumas, Verne 6. Balzac, Proust
  8. Flaubert, Rabelais
  cardinal, famed . . 7. Mazarin 9. Richelieu
  caricaturist . . 7. Daumier, Gavarni
  chemist . . 7. Gautier, Holbach, Pasteur
  composer . . 4. Lalo 5. Bizet, D'Indy,
  Ravel, Satie 6. Gounod 7. Berlioz,
  Debussy, Delibes, Poulenc 8. Couperin
  conqueror (anc) . . 7. Clovis
  crusader . . 7. Godfrey (of Bouillon)
  dramatist . . 6. Favart, Racine 7. Molière
  8. Quinault 12. Beaumarchais
  dynasty . . 5. Caput 6. Valois 7. Bourbon
  emperor . . 8. Napoleon (Bonaparte)
  encyclopedist . . 7. Diderot 9. D'Alembert
  film director . . 6. Renoir 8. Truffaut
  film star . . 6. Bardot 7. Deneuve
  9. Depardieu
  Foreign Legion creator, 1831 . . 8. Philippe
  (Louis)
  historian . . 5. Renan, Taine 7. Braudel
  8. Michelet 9. Froissart
  marshal . . 3. Ney 4. Foch, Niel, Saxe
  5. Murat
  naturalist . . 8. Audebert
  navigator . . 9. Freycinet
  officer, famed . . 7. Dreyfus
  pantomimist . . 7. Pierrot
  patron saint . . 5. Denis 6. Martin
  philosopher . . 5. Bayle 6. Pascal,
  Sartre 7. Abelard 8. Rousseau,
  Voltaire 9. Descartes, Montaigne
  11. Montesquieu
  physician . . 7. Laveran
  physicist . . 5. Binet 6. Ampere
  poet . . 6. Villon 7. Mistral, Rimbaud
  10. Baudelaire
  radical . . 7. Jacobin
  revolutionary . . 5. Marat 6. Danton
  11. Robespierre
  scientist . . 5. Curie 7. Pasteur
  statesman . . 4. Coty 5. Laine, Laval,
  Morny 6. Carnot 7. Briande, Herriot
  8. DeGaulle 9. Lafayette

French (pert to) . . .
  academic rank . . 6. agrégé
  Academy . . 12. The Institute
  and . . 2. et
  annuity . . 5. rente
  anthem . . 12. Marseillaise
  article . . 2. la, le, un 3. les, une

beast . . 4. bête
bread . . 4. pain
calender (Rev) . . 6. Nivose 7. Ventose
cathedral . . 8. Chartres 9. Notre Dame
champagne . . 2. Ay
cheese . . 4. Brie 6. Chevre 9. Camembert
chorus (male) . . 7. orpheon
coach . . 6. fiacre
coat-of-arms . . 10. fleur-de-lis
coffee (black) . . 8. café noir
company (Bus) . . 3. cie
crown (gold coin) . . 3. ecu
cult (art) . . 7. Dadaism
daisy . . 10. marguerite
dance . . 3. bal 5. gavot 6. cancan
decree, edict . . 5. arrêt
dialect . . 6. patois
dugout . . 4. abri
father . . 4. père
fortification . . 7. parados
friend . . 3. ami 4. amie
fugitive . . 6. émigré
God . . 4. Dieu
hairdresser . . 7. friseur
hat . . 5. beret 7. chapeau
here . . 3. ici
inn . . 6. hostel
king . . 3. roi
lace . . 5. Cluny
language (Provence) . . 9. Provençal
laugh . . 3. ris
legal code . . 10. Napoleonic
liquor . . 8. absinthe (banned 1915)
love . . 5. amour
lover . . 5. amant
mask . . 4. loup
morning . . 5. matin
mountain peak . . 3. pic
museum . . 6. Louvre
narcissus . . 10. polyanthus
native . . 8. Gallican
nursemaid . . 5. bonne
ornaments (set of) . . 6. parure
outcast . . 5. Agote, Cagot 6. pariah
pancake . . 6. crepe
parliament . . 5. Sénat
pastry . . 7. dariole, galette
plane . . 5. avion
poem, poetry . . 3. dit 6. aubade, rondel
police . . 6. Sûreté 8. gendarme
political club . . 7. Jacobin
porcelain . . 6. Sèvres 7. Limoges
priest . . 4. abbe, père
prison, famed . . 8. Bastille
racecourse . . 7. Auteuil
restaurant . . 4. café 6. bistro
revolutionary government . . 7. Commune
sauce . . 8. ravigote 9. allemande
school . . 5. école, lycée
school of painting . . 8. Barbizon
securities . . 6. rentes
smoking room . . 9. estaminet
soldier . . 5. poilu 6. Zouave
stable . . 6. écurie
state . . 4. état
stock exchange . . 6. Bourse
storm . . 5. orage
street . . 3. rue
summer . . 3. été
theater . . 16. Comédie Française
university . . 8. Sorbonne

uprising . . 6. Fronde
verse . . 3. lai 4. alba 6. rondel 7. ballade, virelay
wall . . 3. mur
water . . 3. eau
wind . . 7. mistral
wine . . 5. Medoc 6. Barsac, brandy, claret, Cognac, masdeu 8. Bordeaux, Burgundy, sauterne 10. Beaujolais
world . . 5. monde
Frenchy . . 6. Gallic
frenzied . . . 4. amok 5. rabid 7. enraged, frantic, madding 8. maddened 9. turbulent 11. overwrought
frenzy . . . 3. mad 5. furor, mania 7. frantic, madness 8. delirium 9. agitation 10. excitement, turbulence
frequent . . . 3. oft 5. haunt, often, usual 6. common 7. current 8. familiar, habitual, intimate (with) 9. recurrent 10. persistent
frequenter . . . 7. habitué, visitor 8. attender
frère . . . 5. friar 7. brother
fresh . . . 3. new 4. good, lush 5. relay, ruddy, sound, sweet 6. florid, lively, strong, unused 7. healthy, unfaded, untried 8. impudent, original 10. additional, refreshing, unimpaired 13. inexperienced
freshen . . . 4. cool 5. renew 6. revive 7. refresh, sweeten
freshet . . . 4. gush 5. flood, spate 6. stream 7. outflow, torrent 10. inundation (sudden)
freshman . . . 5. frosh 6. novice 7. student
freshness . . . 7. newness, novelty 8. verdancy 9. impudence 11. originality
freshwater fish . . . 2. id (ide) 4. chub, dace, inid (porpoise) 6. anabas 7. herring 8. drumfish
fret . . . 3. eat, nag, orp, rub, vex 4. fray, fume, gall, gnaw, stew 5. adorn, annoy, chafe, grate, tease, worry 6. abrade, grieve, harass, plague, strait 7. agitate, consume, disturb, network, roughen 8. diminish, irritate, ornament
fretful . . . 5. angry 6. repine 7. peevish, pettish 8. captious, petulant 9. impatient, irascible, irritable, plaintive, querulous 10. ill-humored, ill-natured
Freud (pert to) . . .
birthplace . . 6. Vienna
complex . . 7. Electra, Oedipus
concept . . 2. id 3. ego 8. superego
topic . . 3. sex 5. dream 7. anxiety 8. hysteria, neurosis 9. sexuality 10. repression 11. unconscious 12. subconscious 14. psychoanalysis
friable . . . 5. crisp, frail, mealy, short 7. brittle 8. fragible
friar . . . 3. fra 4. fish (small), monk 5. abbot, Minor 6. lister (obs) 7. brother 8. cenobite, Minorite, Teresian (anc) 9. Carmelite, Dominican 10. Franciscan 11. Augustinian
friction . . . 7. erasure, rubbing 8. clashing 9. attrition, disaccord 10. resistance 12. disagreement 13. counteraction
friend . . . 3. ami, pal 4. ally, amie, chum,

kith, sect 5. amigo, crony 7. comrade 8. promoter 9. associate, attendant, companion, supporter 10. benefactor, sweetheart, well-wisher
Friend . . . 6. Quaker
friendless . . . 5. alone 7. forlorn 8. helpless 9. destitute (friends)
friendly . . . 3. sib 4. kind 7. affable 8. amicable, homelike, sociable 9. favorable 10. harmonious, hospitable 11. comfortable
Friendly Islands . . . 5. Tonga
friendship . . . 4. kelt 5. amity 7. harmony 8. good will, relation 9. affection, right hand 10. attachment 12. friendliness
frieze . . . 4. band (sculptured) 5. adorn, chase 6. taenia (Doric) 8. ornament, trimming 10. decoration, embroidery
Frigga, Norse Myth (pert to) . . .
goddess . . 3. sky
maid . . 5. Fulla
named for . . 6. Friday
wife of . . 4. Odin
fright . . . 3. awe 4. fear, ogre 5. alarm, panic, scare, shock 6. terror 7. eyesore 13. consternation
frighten . . . 3. cow 5. alarm, appal, scare 7. startle, terrify 10. intimidate
frightened . . . 3. rad 5. eerie, timid 6. afraid 8. skittish
frightful . . . 5. awful, great 6. horrid 7. hideous 8. alarming, dreadful, horrible, shocking, terrible, terrific 11. frightening
frightfulness . . . 13. atrociousness 15. Schrecklichkeit
frigid . . . 3. icy 4. cold 5. stiff 6. formal 8. freezing, impotent, reserved
frijol, frijole . . . 4. bean
frill . . . 4. purl 5. jabot, ruche (rouche) 6. border, edging, ruffle 8. furbelow 9. frillback (pigeon) 11. superfluity
fringe . . . 4. lace, loma, tuft 5. thrum 6. border, edging, margin 8. ciliella, trimming
frisk . . . 4. skip 5. brisk, caper 6. frolic, gambol, lively, search 7. disport, rejoice
frisky . . . 3. gay 6. lively 7. playful 8. sportive 10. frolicsome
frisson . . . 5. chill 6. quiver, shiver, thrill 7. shudder 10. excitement
frivolous . . . 5. giddy, petty 6. fickle, slight 7. fatuous, trivial 9. worthless 13. shallow-witted
frock . . . 4. gown, wrap 5. dress, tunic 6. jersey, kirtle (anc), mantle 7. garment, soutane
frog . . . 3. pad (horse's) 4. Rana, toad 5. Anura 6. peeper 7. croaker, paddock, tadpole 8. Amphibia, pollywog 9. Batrachia, Frenchman, Salientia 10. hoarseness
froglike . . . 6. ranine
frogman . . . 5. diver 6. seaman 7. swimmer 9. Frenchman
frog pond . . . 8. ranarium
frolic . . . 3. fun 4. lark, ogle, play, ramp, romp 5. binge, caper, frisk, prank, spree, trick 6. gambol, shindy 7. disport, marlock, shindig, wassail 8. carousal
frolicsome . . . 3. gay 5. merry 6. frisky

7. playful, waggish 8. sportive

from . . . 2. at, de (pref), of 3. apo (pref)
4. away 5. above, out of 6. source
8. away from, downward

from (pert to) . . .
  beginning to end . . 4. over 7. through
  egg to apple . . 16. ab ovo usque ad
    mala
  head to foot . . 7. cap-a-pie
  slang . . 10. soup to nuts 11. stem to
    stern

front . . . 3. bow, van 4. face, fore 5. aface,
afore, blind (false), forne (obs) 6. before,
facade 7. obverse 8. confront, mediator
9. forefront 10. appearance, figurehead
11. affectation 12. intermediary

frontier defense . . . 11. arcifinious

frontiersman . . . 5. Boone 6. Carson
(Kit)

frost . . . 3. ice, mat 4. cold, foam, hoar,
rime 5. chill 6. freeze, whiten 7. failure
8. severity (manner) 14. unfriendliness

frosty . . . 3. icy 4. cold, gray, rimy 5. chill,
hoary, white 6. frigid 8. freezing,
inimical 10. unfriendly

froth . . . 4. foam, scum, suds 5. spume,
yeast 6. lather 7. bubbles

frothy . . . 5. foamy, light, sudsy
7. spumous 8. sillabub

frow . . . 4. froe (tool), wife 5. woman
6. maenad 8. slattern

froward . . . 5. cross 7. peevish, wayward
8. perverse, petulant, scolding,
shrewish, untoward 9. obstinate
10. refractory, unyielding
11. disobedient 12. ungovernable

frowl . . . 9. guillemot

frown . . . 5. gloom, lower, scowl 6. glower

frowsey, frowzy . . . 5. musty 7. unkempt
8. slovenly 9. offensive 10. discordant,
disordered

frozen . . . 4. cold 5. frore (anc), froze,
gelid, glacé 6. chilly, mousse 7. chilled
9. congealed, terrified, unfeeling,
unmovable 10. unyielding
11. coldhearted 12. refrigerated

frugal . . . 5. chary 6. meager, saving
7. careful, sparing, thrifty 9. provident
10. economical, unwasteful
11. inexpensive 12. parsimonious

frugality . . . 6. thrift 7. economy
9. parsimony

fruit (types of) . . . 3. fig 4. lime, pear,
plum, pome 5. apple, berry, drupe,
grape, guava, lemon, mango, melon,
olive, peach, pomum 6. banana,
cherry, orange, papaya, pawpaw,
pomelo 7. apricot, azarole, genipap,
tangelo 8. shaddock 9. persimmon,
tangerine 10. grapefruit, watermelon
11. pomegranate

fruit . . . 4. diet, food 5. yield, young
7. benefit, product 9. offspring,
outgrowth, posterity 11. consequence

fruit (pert to) . . .
  aggregate . . 7. etaerio
  astringent . . 4. sloe
  basket . . 4. pottle
  buttercup . . 6. achene 8. achenium
  class . . 6. simple 9. aggregate
    10. collective

  cordial . . 7. ratafia (ratafee)
  decay . . 4. blet
  dried . . 6. raisin 7. apricot
  drink . . 3. ade 6. nectar
  Goddess . . 6. Pomona
  gourd . . 4. pepo 7. chayote
  grapefruit . . 6. pomelo
  imperfect . . 6. nubbin
  jelly substance . . 6. pectin
  Jove's . . 9. persimmon
  part . . 7. epicarp 8. mesocarp, pericarp
    9. sarcocarp
  preserve . . 7. compote 9. marmalade
  pulpy . . 3. uva
  rose . . 3. hip
  study of . . 9. carpology
  tree . . 4. date, nuts 5. regma 6. camato,
    samara (winged)
  tropical . . 3. fig 4. date 5. guava, mango,
    papaw (pawpaw) 6. papaya

fruitful . . . 7. fertile, uberous 8. abundant,
prolific 9. plenteous

fruitfulness, goddess of . . . 7. Demeter

fruitless . . . 4. vain 6. barren 7. sterile,
useless 10. profitless 11. ineffectual
12. unprofitable, unsuccessful

frump . . . 3. vex 4. mock, snub 5. crone,
flout, shrew 6. gossip, insult 7. provoke
8. irritate

frustrate . . . 4. balk, bilk, foil 5. block,
cross, elude 6. baffle, blight, defeat,
outwit, thwart 7. nullify 8. confound
9. checkmate 10. circumvent,
disappoint, disconcert

frustrater . . . 7. marplot 8. thwarter

frustration . . . 4. balk 6. defeat, fiasco
13. circumvention 14. disappointment
15. disillusionment

fry . . . 4. cook 5. brood (fish), group,
saute, young 7. stir-fry 9. offspring

frying pan . . . 6. spider 7. skillet

fubsy . . . 5. plump, short 6. chubby

fuddle . . . 4. bout (drinking) 5. drink
(strong), spree 6. muddle, tipple
7. confuse 9. confusion, inebriate

fudge . . . 4. fake 5. candy, cheat
6. bungle, humbug 7. trump up
8. nonsense 9. makeshift 10. substitute
11. counterfeit

Fuegian . . . 3. Ona 6. Indian, Yakgan
8. Alikuluf 14. Tierra del Fuego (pert
to)

fuel . . . 3. gas, log, oil 4. coal, coke, peat
6. butane, diesel, elding 7. gasohol,
nuclear, synfuel 8. gasoline, kerosene
9. petroleum 11. combustible

fugie . . . 4. cock (nonfighter) 6. coward

fugient . . . 7. fleeing 8. retiring

fugitive . . . 5. exile 6. outlaw, roving
7. fleeing, refugee, roaming, runaway
8. fleeting, unstable, vagabond, volatile
9. fugacious, strolling, uncertain
10. evanescent

fugue . . . 5. theme, tonal 7. amnesia,
stretto (stretta) 9. psychosis, ricercare

fulcrum . . . 4. axis, bait, prop 5. pivot,
scale (fish), thole 7. support

fulfill . . . 4. meet 6. finish, redeem
7. execute, satisfy 8. complete
10. accomplish, effectuate

fulfillment . . . 8. fruition 9. execution,

flowering 10. completion
11. performance 14. accomplishment
full . . 3. fat 4. fill 5. drunk, sated 6. entire,
filled, rotund 7. perfect, plenary,
replete, satiety 8. abundant, adequate,
complete, occupied, resonant, satiated,
thorough 9. satisfied
full (pert to) . . .
authority . . 12. carte blanche
blooded . . 4. pure, rich 5. lusty 6. virile
7. genuine 8. purebred, vigorous
9. authentic
bloom . . 8. anthesis, blooming, maturity
bodied . . 4. rich 5. large 6. robust
control . . 7. mastery 10. domination
force . . 5. amain
house . . 3. SRO
full of . . .
cracks . . 6. rimose
hollows . . 8. lacunose
love . . 7. amative, amatory
meaning . . 7. pithy 10. meaningful
openings (tiny) . . 6. porous
sand . . 7. arenose 8. sabulous
substance . . 5. meaty
suffix . . 3. ose
thorns . . 6. briary
vigor . . 5. lusty
fulness, fullness . . . 4. much 7. orotund,
pleroma, satiety, surfeit 9. abundance,
greatness, plenitude, repletion,
resonance 10. perfection
12. completeness
fulsome . . 3. bad, fat 4. base, foul, full
5. nasty, plump, suave 7. copious,
overfed 8. abundant 9. offensive,
overgrown, repulsive 10. disgusting
Fulton's Folly . . 8. Clermont
fumble . . 5. grope 6. bungle, huddle,
mumble 7. confuse
fume . . . 4. odor, rage, rant, reek 5. anger,
smoke, steam, vapor 8. outburst
10. excitement, exhalation
fun . . 4. gell, jest, joke, play 5. chaff,
sport 9. amusement, merriment
function . . . 3. act, use 4. duty, rite,
role, work 5. party 6. office 7. calling,
operate, purpose, service 8. ceremony,
province 10. providence
function (pert to) . . .
math . . 4. sine 6. cosine
mind . . 8. ideation
social . . 3. tea
functional . . . 8. official 9. operative
11. ceremonious, utilitarian
fund . . . 5. basis, money 6. bottom,
supply 7. capital, provide, revenue
10. foundation, groundwork
fundamental . . . 4. tone 5. basal, basic,
vital 7. basilar, organic, primary, radical
8. original, rudiment 9. elemental,
essential, principle 10. elementary
Fundamental Orders (US Hist) . . .
8. document (1639) 12. Constitution
(first, 1639 Conn)
funds . . 5. means 6. assets, moneys
8. finances
funeral . . . 5. rites 6. burial 8. exequies
9. obsequies 10. procession
funeral (pert to) . . .
bell . . 5. knell

ceremony . . 6. exequy
hymn, song . . 5. dirge, éloge, elogy
7. requiem 8. threnody
oration, poem . . 5. elegy
pile . . 4. pyre
procession . . 6. exequy 7. cortege
vase . . 3. urn
funereal . . . 3. sad 4. dark 6. dismal,
solemn 8. exequial, mournful
9. dirgelike
fungi . . . 5. rusts, Uredo 6. mildew
7. Boletus
fungoid . . . 6. fungal, fungus
fungus . . . 4. bunt, mold, rust, smut
5. ergot, morel, uredo 6. agaric, lichen,
mildew 7. aminita, blewits, boletus,
geaster, truffle 8. mushroom, puffball
9. toadstool
fungus, edible . . . 5. morel 7. truffle
8. mushroom
funguslike . . . 6. agaric
funk . . . 4. kick, odor, rage 5. panic, smell
(bad), smoke, spark 6. flinch, fright,
shrink, terror 8. frighten 9. cowardice,
touchwood
funnel . . . 4. cone, flue, pipe, tube
6. hopper 7. channel
funnel-shaped . . . 8. choanoid
funny . . . 3. odd 5. comic, droll, queer,
witty 7. comical, rowboat (Eng), strange
8. humorous 9. eccentric, laughable
fur . . . 3. fox 4. mink, pelt, seal, vair
5. coypu, fitch, genet, otter, sable,
skunk 6. badger, ermine, martin, nutria
7. miniver (anc) 8. squirrel 9. chinchilla
fur (pert to) . . .
collective . . 6. peltry
cover . . 4. pelt 6. pelage
garment . . 4. robe 5. stole 6. tippet
7. pelisse
tippet . . 8. palatine
furbish . . . 3. rub 4. vamp 5. clean,
scour 6. polish 7. burnish, touch up
8. renovate 9. embellish
Furies . . 5. Dirae 6. Alecto, ghosts,
Semnae 7. Erinyes (Erinys), Magaera,
spirits (avenging) 9. Eumenides,
Tisiphone
Furies, The Three . . . 6. Alecto
7. Magaera 9. Tisiphone
furious . . . 5. angry, hasty 6. fierce
7. frantic, violent 8. frenzied, vehement
9. impetuous, turbulent 10. boisterous,
passionate, tumultuous
11. overwrought
furl . . . 4. roll, wrap 6. bundle, inroll
furlough . . . 5. leave 14. leave of absence
furnace . . . 4. etna, kiln, oven 5. forge,
stove 6. boiler 7. caldron, reactor,
rotator, smelter
furnish . . . 3. fit 4. bear, give, lend
5. adorn, cater, endow, equip, indue
6. afford, fit out, render, supply
7. appoint, provide
furnishing . . . 7. fitting 8. fixtures,
ornament 9. adornment, apparatus,
furniture, provision 10. enrichment
furnish with . . .
funds . . 5. endow
meals . . 5. board, cater
Mil equipment . . 8. accoutre

tapestry .. 5. arras
wings .. 3. imp
furniture ... 4. Adam 5. Eames, Louis,
Phyfe, suite (matched set) 6. Empire,
graith (obs) 7. mission 8. Sheraton,
Stickley 9. Queen Anne 10. Directoire
11. Chippendale, Hepplewhite
13. Mediterranean 16. French
Provincial
furor ... 4. fury, rage 5. anger, craze
6. fervor, flurry, frenzy, furore, tumult
7. madness 10. excitement, turbulence
furrow ... 4. plow 6. groove,
gutter, trench 7. channel, wrinkle
furrowed ... 5. rutty 6. rivose 7. grooved
further ... 3. aid, and, new, yet 4. abet,
more 7. advance, develop, improve,
promote, remoter, thither 10. additional
furtherance ... 3. aid 4. help 6. relief,
succor 8. progress 9. promotion
11. advancement, development
furtherer ... 7. abettor 8. promoter
furthermore ... 3. and, yet 4. then
5. again 7. au reste, besides
8. moreover 10. in addition
12. additionally
furtive ... 3. sly 4. wary 6. covert, secret,
sneaky, stolen 8. skulking, stealthy
9. deceitful 11. clandestine
fury ... 3. ire 4. rage 5. anger, wrath
6. frenzy 7. madness 8. violence
10. excitement, turbulence
13. desperateness

Fury ... 6. Erinys, Spirit (avenging)
7. Atropos
furze ... 4. Ulex, whin 5. gorse, shrub
fuse ... 4. flux, frit (partly), melt
5. blend, smelt, unite 6. anneal, mingle,
solder 7. combine, liquefy 8. dissolve
9. detonator
fusee ... 5. flair, torch 6. signal
fusion ... 5. alloy, blend, union 7. melting,
mixture, nuclear 8. fluidity 9. coalition
fuss ... 3. ado 4. spat, to-do 5. busle
6. bother, bustle, pother, tumult
7. bombast, dispute, quarrel, trouble
8. brouhaha 9. confusion
fussy ... 7. finical 8. overnice
10. fastidious, meticulous
fustian ... 4. rant 5. cloth, tumid
7. bombast, pompous 8. claptrap,
inflated 9. bombastic, worthless
fustic ... 3. dye 5. amber, morin
7. dyewood
futile ... 4. idle, vain 6. otiose 7. trivial
8. hopeless 11. ineffectual
futility ... 6. nugacity 10. invalidity
11. uselessness 12. bootlessness
future ... 3. yet 4. to be 5. later, still,
tense 6. fiancé 8. expected, intended
9. hereafter 11. prospective
fuzzy ... 5. downy, hairy 6. fluffy
7. blurred, frizzly 9. imperfect
10. indistinct
fyke ... 3. net 6. bag net
fylfot ... 8. swastika 9. gammadion

G

G ... 4. tone (scale) 6. letter (7th)
gab ... 3. lie 4. mock, talk 5. boast,
mouth, prate, scoff, taste 6. tongue
7. chatter, deceive 9. utterance
gabardine ... 6. cotton, woolen
gabble ... 4. chat 6. babble, jabber,
mumble 7. chatter 8. nonsense
gabelle ... 3. tax 5. likin (imports)
6. excise, impost
gaberdine ... 4. gown 5. frock 6. mantle
7. garment (loose) 8. covering, pinafore
9. gabardine
gable ... 4. roof (part) 7. aileron (half)
8. pediment
gablock ... 4. gaff, spur 5. spear 6. gaffle
7. crowbar 8. gavelock
Gabon, Africa ...
capital .. 10. Libreville
Gabriel (pert to) ...
astrology .. 10. moon spirit
New Test .. 6. herald 11. good tidings
Old Test .. 5. angel
tradition .. 9. archangel (one of seven),
messenger
gaby ... 4. fool 9. simpleton
gad ... 3. bar, God (oath), rod 4. goad,
roam, rove, whip 5. ingot, spear, staff
6. billet, chisel, wander 7. on the go,
run wild, traipse (trapes) 8. gadabout

9. gallivant
Gad (pert to) ...
Bib .. 7. prophet
deity (Bib) .. 7. Fortune
father .. 5. Jacob
tribe .. 6. Gadite, Israel (one of seven)
gadabout ... 3. gad 6. roving 7. dogcart,
gadding, on the go
Gaddang, Gaddan ... 7. Malayan
8. language (Indonesia)
gadfly ... 6. botfly, insect 8. horsefly
gadget ... 6. device, jigger 7. gimmick
8. gimcrack 11. contrivance,
thingumajig
Gadsden Purchase (1853) ... 5. tract
7. Arizona 9. New Mexico
gadwall ... 4. duck
Gaea, Gaia ... 12. Earth Goddess
Gael ... 4. Celt, Kelt, Manx, Scot
10. Highlander
Gaelic (pert to) ...
for John .. 3. Ian
hero .. 6. Ossian
language .. 4. Erse
native .. 4. Erse 5. Irish 6. Celtic, Keltic,
Scotch
pagan god .. 5. Dagda (harpist)
sea god .. 3. Ler
spirit .. 7. banshee

warriors .. 7. Fenians

gaff ... 4. hoax, hook, scam, spar, spur, talk 5. fraud, spear, trick 6. deceit, fleece, gamble 7. chatter, prating 8. trickery 9. spearhead

gaffer . . . 4. hick, rube 6. old man 11. electrician (TV)

gag ... 4. hoax, joke 5. choke, retch 7. closure, prevent, shackle 8. obstruct, one-liner, restrain, silencer 9. imposture 10. instrument 13. interpolation

gage, gauge ... 4. rule, test 5. scale 6. device, pledge 7. measure 8. capacity, defiance, diameter (firearm), mortgage, security 9. challenge 11. measurement

gaggle ... 5. flock (geese), group (women) 6. cackle

gaiety, gayety ... 4., glee, show 5. mirth 6. finery 7. jollity 8. vivacity 9. festivity, merriment, showiness 10. liveliness 12. colorfulness, conviviality

gain ... 3. get, net, win 4. earn, pelf, reap 5. booty, clear, lucre, reach 6. attain, come by, obtain, profit, secure, trover 7. acquire, benefit, procure, realize 8. addition, arrive at, increase 9. advantage 11. acquisition 12. accumulation 13. amplification

gainsay ... 4. deny 6. forbid, impugn, oppose, refute 7. dispute 10. contradict, controvert

gait ... 3. run, way 4. lope, pace, trip, trot, walk 5. amble, order, strut, tread 6. canter, gallop 8. slowness, velocity

gaiter ... 4. boot, spat 5. strad 6. puttee 7. legging 8. overshoe 11. galligaskin

gala ... 4. fete, pomp 5. festal, fiesta, gaiety 8. festival 9. festivity 11. celebration

Galago ... 5. lemur

Galahad's quest ... 9. Holy Grail

Galatea ... 7. heroine 8. sea nymph 9. Pygmalion (sculptor) 11. shepherdess

galaxy ... 6. throng 8. Milky Way 10. assemblage 11. celebrities

gale ... 4. gust, wind 5. storm 8. outburst 9. hurricane

galea ... 6. helmet

galeate ... 12. helmet-shaped

Galen (Gr) ... 9. physician

Galilean (pert to) ...
province .. 9. Palestine
religion .. 9. Christian
town .. 4. Cana 8. Tiberias

gall ... 3. vex 4. bile, fret 5. annoy, chafe, grate, spite 6. bitter, harass, rancor 8. irritate 9. impudence, secretion, virulence

gallant ... 4. hero 5. dandy, lover, noble, spark, swain 6. escort, suitor 7. stately 8. cavalier, cicisbeo 9. attentive, courteous 10. chivalrous, courageous

gallantry ... 7. bravery, courage, display 8. courtesy 9. courtship 11. intrepidity

galleon ... 6. vessel (sailing)

gallery ... 3. poy 4. hall 5. salon 6. dedans, loggia, museum 7. passage, veranda 8. audience, corridor, platform 9. promenade 10. ambulatory 11. observatory

galley ... 4. boat, tray 6. vessel 7. caboose, caravel (caravelle), dromond, kitchen 8. cookroom

galley, Roman ...
one-bank oared .. 7. unireme
two-bank oared .. 6. bireme
three-bank oared .. 7. trireme
six-bank oared .. 7. hexeris
slave .. 5. rower 6. drudge

Gallic ... 4. Gaul 6. French

Gallic chariot ... 5. essed

gallimaufry ... 4. hash, olio, stew 6. jumble, medley, ragout 9. potpourri 10. hodgepodge

gallipot ... 6. vessel (Medit) 8. druggist

gallo ... 7. rooster 12. fighting cock

gallop ... 3. run 4. lope, ride 5. canter 7. tantivy

gallopade ... 5. dance, galop 6. curvet

gallows humor, like ... 6. morbid

gam ... 3. leg 4. herd 5. visit 6. school

Gambia, Africa ...
capital .. 6. Banjul

gambit ... 4. move 7. comment, opening (chess) 8. maneuver 9. launching 10. concession

gamble ... 3. bet 4. dice, game, risk 5. stake, wager 6. chance, exacta, hazard, plunge 7. perfecta 9. speculate, totalizer 10. parimutuel, superfecta 11. daily double, uncertainty

gambler ... 5. shill 7. sharper

gambol ... 3. hop 5. bound, caper, prank 6. cavort, curvet, frolic

Gambrinus (King) ... 6. brewer (1st)

game ... 4. lark, play, prey 5. brave, dodge, prank, sport 6. frolic, gamble, gritty, plucky, quarry 7. contest, pastime 8. resolute 9. amusement, diversion 10. courageous

game, ball ... 4. golf, polo, pool 5. rugby 6. hockey, pelota, soccer, squash, tennis 7. cricket, croquet 8. baseball, football 11. racquetball

game, beans ... 6. fan-tan 8. beanbags

game, board ... 4. keno 5. bingo, chess, lotto 7. pachisi (parchesi) 8. checkers, cribbage, Monopoly 10. backgammon

game, card ... 3. gin, pam 4. bank, faro, skat 5. pitch, poker, rummy, whist 6. bridge, canasta, cassino, old maid, seven-up

game, club ... 4. golf 6. hockey 7. cricket

game, court ... 6. pelota, squash, tennis 7. jai alai 9. badminton

game, parlor ... 5. jacks 7. marbles 8. charades, dominoes 11. tiddlywinks

game plan ... 6. scheme 8. strategy

game, ring ... 6. quoits

gamin ... 3. tad 4. serf 6. urchin 7. mudlark 10. street Arab

gamut ... 5. orbit, range 6. extent 7. compass

gamy ... 4. game 7. lustful 8. sporting 12. high-flavored

gander ... 5. goose 6. stroll 9. simpleton

Gandhi (Hind) ... 6. Indira, leader 7. Mahatma (Mohandus)

gang ... 3. mob, set 4. band, crew, pack, team, walk (cattle) 5. group, horde, sheet (Print), shift 6. clique 7. company

9. pasturage

gangling ... 5. lanky 9. spindling

gangrene ... 5. decay 6. slough
8. necrosis 9. sphacelus
13. mortification

gangster ... 4. thug 5. thief 6. bandit
7. mobster 8. criminal, hireling
9. racketeer

gannet ... 4. ibis, Sula 5. booby, goose,
solan 6. gander

gap ... 4. hole, pass 5. break,
chasm, cleft, fault, meuse, shard, space,
split 6. breach, hiatus, lacuna, lacune,
ravine 7. opening

gaping ... 5. agape 6. chappy 7. ringent,
yawning 9. expectant

garb ... 5. array, dress, habit, mufti
(civilian), style 6. attire, clothe
7. apparel, costume, fashion, raiment,
uniform 8. clothing 10. appearance,
habiliment

garbage ... 5. trash, waste 6. refuse

garbanzo ... 8. chickpea

garbed ... 4. clad 7. attired, dressed,
habited

garble ... 5. alloy 6. mangle 7. distort,
falsify, pervert 8. mutilate
12. misinterpret, misrepresent,
sophisticate

garden ... 3. bed 4. yard 5. hardy, patch
6. jardin, verger 7. topiary 8. outfield
9. arboretum, cultivate, enclosure,
herbarium

garden (pert to) ...
Berlin .. 10. Tiergarten
Bible .. 4. Eden
city .. 4. Kent 6. Sicily 7. Chicago
8. Touraine
colony .. 5. Natal
Colorado .. 9. of the Gods
Kansas .. 9. of the West
kind of .. 5. truck 8. kaleyard 9. botanical
10. zoological
State .. 9. New Jersey

garden implement ... 3. hoe 4. fork,
rake 5. graip, mower 6. scythe, sickle,
trowel, weeder

Garfield's assassin ... 7. Guiteau

Gargantua (pert to) ...
character .. 4. King (Rabelais romance)
son .. 10. Pantagruel (giant)

gargantuan ... 4. huge 7. titanic

garish ... 5. gaudy, showy 7. flighty,
glaring 8. dazzling

garland ... 3. lei 6. anadem, circle,
corona, fillet, rosary, trophy, wreath
7. chaplet, coronal, festoon 8. headband
9. anthology 11. compilation

garlic ... 4. herb, moly 5. clove 6. ramson

garment ... 4. cape, coat, gown, robe,
suit, vest, wrap 5. cloak, dress,
frock, shift, simar, smock, stole, tunic
6. coatee, duster 7. pelisse, raiment,
surcoat, topcoat 8. overcoat, vestment

garment (pert to) ...
African .. 6. kaross
ancient .. 5. burel
Arab .. 3. aba
clerical .. 3. alb 5. amice 6. chimer
7. cassock, zimarra 8. surplice
cover .. 5. apron 8. overalls, pinafore

9. coveralls
Eskimo .. 5. parka
Jewish .. 5. ephod
knight's .. 6. tabard
patchwork .. 5. cento
thin .. 8. gossamer

garner ... 4. reap 5. amass, store 6. gather
7. collect 10. accumulate

garnet ... 3. gem, red 5. color 6. aplome,
pyrope 7. olivine (green) 8. cinnamon
(stone), essonite (yellow), melanite
(black) 9. almandine (almandite, dark
red), uvarovite (green)

garnish ... 4. trim 5. adorn 6. attach,
bedeck 7. fetters 8. decorate, ornament

garnishment ... 4. lien 7. summons
8. ornament 10. attachment, decoration

garret ... 4. loft 5. attic 6. turret 8. cockloft
10. watchtower

garrot ... 9. goldeneye (duck)
10. tourniquet

garrote, garrotte ... 8. strangle
9. execution 10. throttling
13. strangulation

garrulous ... 5. gabby, wordy 6. chatty
7. diffuse 9. talkative 10. loquacious

gas ... 4. brag, talk 5. vapor 6. poison
7. chatter 8. gasoline, nonsense
10. anesthesia, asphyxiate, illuminant
11. anesthetize

gas ... 3. air 4. neon 5. argon,
ether, ozone, radon, xenon 6. arsine,
butane, ethane, helium, ketene, nebula
(luminous), oxygen 7. methane
8. chlorine, cyanogen, etherion,
hydrogen, nitrogen 9. butadiene

gascon ... 7. boaster 8. braggart
11. braggadocio 12. swashbuckler

gasconade ... 4. brag 5. boast 7. bluster,
bravado 11. fanfaronade, rodomontade

gaseous ... 4. smog, thin 5. smoke
7. tenuous 8. vaporous
13. unsubstantial

gash ... 3. cut 5. cleft, notch, sever,
slash 6. furrow, gossip, injury, tattle
8. incision

gasp ... 3. say 4. pant, yawn 5. utter
7. breathe

gasping ... 5. agasp 7. panting

gastropod ... 4. slug 5. Harpa, Murex,
Oliva, snail, whelk 6. Nerita, volute
7. abalone, mollusk 8. sea snail

gat ... 3. gun, rod 7. channel, passage
8. revolver

gate ... 3. dar 4. door, hole, pass 5. start
(racing), toran, valve 6. defile, portal
7. barrier, opening, postern 8. Lion-
Gate 9. floodgate, turnstile 10. Needle's
Eye (Jerusalem), portcullis

gateau ... 4. cake

gather ... 4. bale, brew, fold, meet, reap
5. amass, glean, pleat, rally, shirr
6. bundle, deduce, garner, muster,
pucker 7. acquire, collect, compile,
convene, convoke, harvest, procure,
suppose 8. assemble 10. accumulate

gatherer, collector of ...
coins .. 11. numismatist
money .. 5. miser
news .. 8. reporter 10. journalist
stamps .. 11. philatelist

gathering . . . 3. sum 4. stag 5. crowd,
party, troop 6. galaxy, smoker
7. abscess, meeting 8. swelling
10. assemblage, harvesting
11. contraction 12. accumulation,
congregation 14. conglomeration
gaucho . . . 8. cowboy (pampas)
8. herdsman, horseman
gaucho weapon . . . 4. bola
gaud . . . 4. jest, joke 5. adorn, fraud, paint,
sport, trick 6. finery, flashy, gewgaw
7. trinket 8. artifice, ornament
gaudy . . . 4. fine, loud 5. cheap, feast,
showy 6. flashy, flimsy, garish, tawdry,
tinsel 7. glaring, trinket 9. flaunting
11. pretentious 12. meretricious,
ostentatious 13. overdeveloped
gaufre . . . 4. iron (waffle) 6. waffle
gauge, gage . . . 4. norm, rate, rule,
size 5. judge, scale, value 6. assess
7. measure 8. estimate
gauge (pert to) . . .
airplane . . 10. tachometer
distance . . 10. micrometer
miles . . 8. odometer
pointer . . 3. arm
rain . . 8. udometer
velocity . . 11. speedometer
wind . . 10. anemometer
Gaul . . . 5. Aedui 6. France, Gallia
9. Frenchman
Gauls . . . 4. Remi 5. Celts, Cymry
gaunt . . . 4. bony, lank, lean, thin, ugly
5. spare 7. haggard 8. desolate
gauntlet . . . 4. cuff 5. armor (part), glove
7. bandage
gaur . . . 2. ox 5. gayal 7. buffalo
gauss . . . 4. unit (Elec)
Gauss . . . 13. mathematician
Gaussian curve, like a . . . 10. bell-shaped
gauze . . . 4. haze, leno 5. crape, lisse,
marli (marly) 6. barege, filter, tissue
8. dressing
gauze film on wine . . . 8. beeswing
gavage . . . 7. feeding
gave . . . see *give*
Gavia . . . 4. loon
gavial . . . 11. crocodilian
gaw . . . 4. gape 5. drain 6. trench
gawk . . . 4. dolt, gowk, left, lout 5. booby,
stare 9. simpleton
gawky . . . 6. clumsy, cuckoo, stupid
7. awkward, foolish 8. clownish
gay . . . 4. airy, glad 5. drunk, gaudy,
jolly, merry, riant, showy 6. blithe,
cheery, jovial, joyful, joyous, lively
7. dashing, festive, gleeful 8. cheerful,
colorful, rory-tory, sportive 9. convivial,
sprightly, vivacious 10. frolicsome,
profligate 12. lighthearted
gay time . . . 4. lark 5. spree 8. jamboree
gazabo, gazebo . . . 4. cony 6. rabbit,
turret 7. balcony, blunder, whopper
11. summerhouse
gaze . . . 3. con, eye 4. gape, look, moon,
peer, pore, scan 5. glare, gloat, stare
6. glower, regard
gazelle . . . 3. ahu, goa 4. admi, cora,
dama, kudu, mohr, oryx 5. ariel, brown,
korin 7. chikara (4-horn), corinne,
dibatag 8. antelope 9. springbok

gazette . . . 7. journal, publish 8. announce
9. newspaper 15. Arkansas Gazette
(1819)
gazetteer . . . 7. newsman 9. newspaper
10. dictionary
gear . . . 3. cam, rig 5. equip, goods,
tools, wheel 6. things 7. baggage,
conform, harness, rigging 8. adjust
to, clothing, cogwheel, garments
9. equipment, mechanism, trappings,
vestments 10. appliances, implements
gecko . . . 6. lizard 7. tarente
geese . . . 5. brant, quink, solan
geese (pert to) . . .
fat . . 6. axunge
flock . . 4. raft 6. gaggle
formation . . 3. vee
genus . . 4. Chen 5. Anser 6. Branta
gecko . . . 6. lizard
Geisel . . . 7. Dr Seuss (pseud)
gelatin, gelatine . . . 4. agar, food, jell
5. jelly 6. collin 7. protein 8. agar-agar
gelid . . . 3. icy 4. cold 6. frozen
gem . . . 4. jade, onyx, opal, ruby, sard,
type 5. agate, beryl, bijou, jewel,
pearl, stone, topaz 6. garnet, ligure,
spinel, zircon 7. cat's-eye, diamond,
emerald, jacinth 8. amethyst, hawk's-
eye, sapphire 9. carnelian, moonstone
10. aquamarine 11. alexandrite, lapis
lazuli 12. star sapphire
gem (pert to) . . .
artificial . . 5. paste
base . . 5. culet
carver . . 8. lapidary
Egyptian . . 6. scarab
flaw . . 8. gendarme
food . . 6. muffin
imperfect . . 5. loupe
semiprecious . . 5. cameo 8. intaglio
six rays . . 5. asteria
surface . . 5. bezel, facet
weight . . 5. carat
with many facets . . 9. brilliant
gemel . . . 4. bars (Her), twin 6. paired
7. coupled, doubled
gemsbok . . . 4. goat, oryx 7. chamois
Gem State . . . 5. Idaho
gendarme . . . 4. blue, flaw (gem) 5. guard
6. police 7. officer, soldier, trooper
9. policeman 10. cavalryman
gender . . . 3. sex 5. breed, genus
7. grammar (term) 8. engender
genealogy . . . 4. tree 5. order (of descent)
6. family 7. account, history, lineage,
peerage, progeny 8. pedigree, register
9. offspring
genealogy of the gods . . . 8. theogony
gener . . . 8. son-in-law
general . . . 5. gross, usual, vague, whole
6. common, public 7. officer 8. catholic,
communal 9. extensive, prevalent,
universal, well-known 10. encyclical,
indefinite 13. approximate
general (pert to) . . .
agreement . . 5. chief, court
aspect . . 6. facies
chief . . 6. Führer, Il Duce 9. president
10. Grand Mogul 13. Generalissimo
court . . 5. Synod
direction . . 5. tenor, trend 6. course

favor . . 7. popular 10. popularity
feature . . 5. motif
group . . 8. ensemble
orders . . 7. routine
rule . . 5. canon
summary . . 8. synopsis
type . . 7. average
generalize . . 5. widen 6. extend, reason, spread 7. broaden 12. universalize
General Sherman (pert to) . . .
  Civil War march . . 15. Atlanta to the Sea
  giant trees . . 8. sequoias
  tree . . 10. eucalyptus
generate . . 5. beget, breed, cause 6. create 7. develop, produce 8. engender 9. originate, procreate, propagate
generation . . 3. age 7. descent 8. lifetime 9. epigonous (later), formation, genealogy 10. production 11. abiogenesis, procreation
generosity . . 10. liberality 11. hospitality, magnanimity, munificence
generous . . 4. free 5. large 7. liberal 8. tolerant 9. indulgent, plentiful, unstinted 10. hospitable 11. magnanimous
genesis . . 4. Book 5. birth 6. origin (of races) 8. nascency 9. beginning, ethnology, etymology, inception 10. generation
genet . . 3. fur 5. civet
genethliac . . 5. stars (influence) 9. birthdays
genetics term . . 3. DNA, RNA 4. gene 8. dominant, heredity 9. recessive 10. chromosome, hereditary 11. recombinant
Geneva Cross . . 8. Red Cross
genial . . 4. warm 5. bland 6. jovial, kindly 7. amiable, festive, nuptial 8. cheerful, friendly, pleasant 9. expansive 10. enlivening
geniculate . . 5. kneel
genie . . 4. jinn 6. genius
genius . . 5. deity, jinni 6. talent 7. ability, prodigy 9. endowment (supreme) 11. inspiration 12. intelligence
Genoa lace . . 4. tape 6. bobbin 7. macramé 13. gold and silver
genos . . 4. clan, gens, race
genre . . 3. art (style) 4. kind, sort 5. genus 6. gender 7. species 8. category
genteel . . 6. polite 7. refined 8. wellborn, well-bred
Gentiles . . 6. goyims 10. Christians, non-Moslems 14. non-Mohammedans
gentle . . 4. calm, easy, meek, mild, soft, tame 5. bland, quiet 6. docile, humane, kindly, tender 7. amabile (Mus), clement, genteel, refined, subdued 8. moderate, peaceful, soothing, tranquil, wellborn 9. courteous, honorable, temperate, tractable 10. chivalrous 11. considerate 13. compassionate
gentleman . . 3. sir 6. knight 7. esquire, shoneen (would-be), younker 8. nobleman
gentleness . . 6. lenity 8. elegance,

leniency, meekness, softness 9. lightness 10. kindliness, moderation 11. genteelness
genuflect . . 5. kneel 6. curtsy
genuine . . 4. pure, real, true 5. frank, pucka (pukka) 7. germane, sincere 8. existent 9. authentic, simon-pure, unalloyed, veritable 10. unaffected 13. unadulterated
genus . . 4. kind, sort 5. class, order
genus, animal life . . .
  animals (one-celled) . . 6. Amoeba 8. Protozoa 9. Rhizopoda
  ants . . 6. Eciton
  apes . . 5. Simia
  armadillos . . 9. Glyptodon
  auks . . 4. Alle
  bears . . 5. Ursus
  bees (honey) . . 4. Apis
  beetles . . 10. Coleoptera
  birds . . 7. Ratitae
  bivalve mollusks . . 6. Anomia 8. Estheria
  bugs (long-legged) . . 5. Emesa
  cats . . 5. Felis
  cattle . . 3. Bos
  crabs . . 4. Maia
  dogs . . 5. Canis
  ducks . . 3. Aix 4. Anas 7. Harelda 8. Clangula
  elks . . 5. Alces
  fish . . 6. Cybium, Remora 7. Girella, Muraena
  flies . . 6. Asilus 8. Glossina (tsetse)
  frogs . . 4. Rana 5. Anura 8. Amphibia 9. Batrachia
  geese . . 4. Chen 5. Anser
  goats . . 5. Capra
  gulls . . 4. Xema
  herons . . 7. Egretta
  hogs . . 3. Sus
  horses . . 5. Equus
  insects . . 10. Coleoptera
  lemurs . . 6. Galago
  lizards . . 3. Uta 5. Agama
  mammals . . 4. Homo
  Man . . 11. Homo sapiens
  marten . . 7. Mustela
  mice . . 5. Mus
  monkeys (spider) . . 6. Ateles
  moose . . 5. Alces
  moths . . 5. Tinea
  oysters . . 6. Ostrea
  peacocks . . 4. Pavo
  pigeons (crowned) . . 5. Goura
  porcupines . . 7. Hystrix
  porpoise . . 4. Inia
  rats . . 6. Spalax
  roadrunners . . 9. Geococcyx
  scorpions . . 4. Nepa
  seabirds . . 5. Sula
  sloths . . 11. Megatherium
  slugs . . 5. Arion
  snails . . 5. Mitra 6. Nerita, Triton 8. Geophila
  snakes . . 4. Eryx (sand) 7. Ophidia
  spiders . . 7. Agalena
  squirrels . . 7. Sciurus
  swans . . 4. Olar 6. Cygnus
  ticks . . 6. Ixodes
  tortoises . . 4. Emys
  turkeys . . 9. Meleagris

wasps.. 5. Vespa
whales.. 4. Orca 5. Areta 9. Sibbaldus
  (blue)
genus, plant life...
  algae (blue-green).. 10. Gloeocapsa
  apple trees.. 5. Malus
  cabbage.. 3. Cos
  currant.. 5. Ribes
  elms.. 5. Ulmus
  evergreen, heaths.. 5. Erica
  fern.. 6. Anemia
  fungi.. 7. Boletus 10. geoglossum
  grasses.. 3. Poa (blue) 5. Avena
  6. Elymus 7. Setaria
  herbs.. 4. Arum 6. Asarum, Asitis
    (mustard), Cassia, Seseli 7. Hedeoma,
    Linaria 8. Solidago
  holly.. 4. Ilex
  ipecac.. 4. Evea
  ivy.. 11. Hedera helix
  lily.. 7. Bessera
  maples.. 4. Acer
  olives.. 4. Olea
  orchids.. 5. Vanda 7. Listera
  palms.. 5. Areca, Assai 6. Bacaba
  poplar.. 5. Alamo
  rhubarb.. 5. Rheum
  vines (woody).. 6. Hedera
geode.. 3. vug (vugg, vugh, voog)
  5. druse 6. nodule
geological (pert to)...
  division.. 3. eon, era
  era.. 6. Eocene 7. Miocene 8. Cenozoic,
    Mesozoic 9. Paleozoic 11. Archaeozoic
  period.. 4. Dyas, Lias 5. Trias
  prelife.. 5. Azoic
  zone (fossil).. 6. assise
geologist... 6. Strabo (anc Gr)
  8. geognost 12. mineralogist
geometric (pert to)...
  angle.. 9. incidence
  axis.. 8. abscissa
  contact.. 10. osculation
  curve.. 6. spiral 7. evolute
  pottery.. 7. Dipylon (anc)
geometric figure... 4. cone, cube,
  lune 5. prism 6. gnomon, oblong,
  square 7. hexagon, octagon, polygon,
  rhombus 8. heptagon, pentagon,
  triangle 9. rectangle, trapezoid
  10. quadrangle 13. parallelogram
geometric proposition (pert to)...
  ratio.. 2. pi (3.1416)
  surface.. 4. tore 5. nappe
  term.. 4. sine 5. locus 6. secant
  7. tangent 11. asses' bridge
geometry (pert to)...
  figure.. 6. conoid 9. ellipsoid
  10. paraboloid
  mathematician.. 6. Euclid, Pascal
  proposition.. 6. porism
geoponic... 5. rural 6. rustic
Georgia...
  capital.. 7. Atlanta
  city.. 5. Macon 7. Augusta 8. Columbus,
    Marietta, Savannah 9. Brunswick
  holiday.. 10. Georgia Day (Feb 12)
  memorial.. 11. Warm Springs 16. Little
    White House (FDR)
  mountain.. 7. Lookout 9. Blue Ridge
    11. Alleghenies

peak.. 9. High Point 13. Brasstown Bald
river.. 8. Savannah, Suwannee
settler (1st).. 10. Oglethorpe
State admission.. 6. Fourth
State nickname.. 5. Peach 7. Cracker
  16. Empire of the South
swamp.. 10. Okefenokee
Georgian of the Caucasus... 4. Svan
georgic... 4. poem (rural)
geosphere... 5. earth
Geraint, Sir... 6. Knight (Round Table)
germ... 3. bud 4. ovum, seed 5. spore
  6. embryo, origin 7. microbe 8. bacteria
  (pl) 9. bacterium 13. microorganism
germ (free).. 7. aseptic 10. antiseptic
German (pert to)... see also Germany
  air force.. 9. Luftwaffe
  art.. 5. kunst
  art movement.. 13. Sturm und Drang
  article.. 3. das, der, ein
  battleship.. 8. Graf Spee
  beverage.. 5. lager
  book.. 4. buch, heft
  cake.. 5. torte
  castle.. 7. schloss
  Christmas.. 11. Weihnachten
  dance.. 9. allemande
  deity.. 5. Donar (thunder)
  drinking salute.. 6. prosit
  folklore.. 5. gnome 6. kobold
  guild member.. 13. Meistersinger
  gun.. 9. Big Bertha
  hail.. 4. heil
  highway.. 8. autobahn
  language.. 7. Deutsch
  league.. 4. Bund 6. Verein 9. Hanseatic
  10. Turnverein
  letter.. 4. rune
  lyric poems.. 6. lieder
  mister.. 4. Herr
  ox (wild).. 4. urus
  parliament.. 9. Bundestag, Reichstag
    (formerly)
  people.. 5. Goths, Quadi 6. Franks,
    Saxons 7. Teutons, Vandals
    8. Lombards 9. Prussians
    10. Herminones
  police.. 7. Gestapo
  prison camp.. 6. stalag
  ruler.. 6. kaiser
  society.. see league (above)
  song.. 4. lied
  teacher.. 6. docent 12. privatdocent
  title.. 3. Von 4. Graf, Herr 6. Ritter
  tribal group.. 3. gau
  vowel change.. 6. umlaut
  wheat.. 5. spelt
  wine.. 4. hock, wein 5. Rhine 7. Moselle
    (Mosel) 8. Riesling 11. Niersteiner
  woman.. 4. frau 8. fraulein
  yes.. 2. ja
germane... 4. akin 6. allied 7. kindred
  8. relevant 11. appropriate
Germanic language... 5. Dutch
  6. Danish, German, Gothic 7. English,
    Frisian, Swedish, Yiddish 8. Old Norse
  9. Icelandic, Norwegian
German people (famed)...
  actor.. 8. Jannings (Emil)
  archaeologist.. 10. Schliemann
  artist.. 5. Dürer, Ernst, Grosz 8. Kollwitz

9. Friedrich
astrologer.. 5. Faust
astronomer.. 5. Galle 6. Kepler
author.. 4. Böll, Mann 5. Grass,
Grimm, Hesse, Kafka, Zweig 6. Goethe
7. Fontane, Wieland 8. Brentano
auto engineer.. 4. Benz 5. Bosch
6. Diesel 7. Daimler, Porsche
bacteriologist.. 4. Koch (Nobel Prize,
1905)
chemist.. 5. Haber 6. Bunsen, Liebig
composer.. 4. Bach 5. Gluck, Weber
(Carl Maria) 6. Handel, Schütz,
Wagner 8. Schumann 9. Beethoven
11. Stockhausen
dramatist.. 6. Brecht, Kleist 7. Lessing
8. Schiller 9. Hauptmann, Sudermann
Egyptologist.. 5. Ebers
general.. 6. Moltke, Rommel 7. Steuben
(Rev War) 10. Hindenburg, Ludendorff
geographer.. 6. Ritter
Gestapo chief.. 7. Himmler
goldsmith (anc).. 5. Faust
hero.. 8. Arminius
historian.. 4. Dahn 5. Ranke 7. Meineke,
Mommsen 8. Spengler
industrialist.. 5. Krupp
leader.. 7. Bismark, Wilhelm (William)
9. Frederick (the Great) 10. Hindenburg
mathematician.. 5. Gauss
military expert.. 10. Clausewitz
mystic.. 5. Bohme 7. Eckhart (Meister)
naturalist.. 8. Humboldt 9. Ehrenberg
neurologist.. 11. Krafft-Ebing
pathologist.. 6. Eberth
philologist.. 5. Grimm, Heyne
philosopher.. 4. Kant, Marx 5. Hegel
6. Engels, Fichte, Herder 7. Liebniz
8. Schlegel 9. Feuerbach
12. Schopenhauer
physicist.. 3. Ohm 5. Weber (Wilhelm)
6. Planck 10. Fahrenheit
poet.. 5. Heine, Rilke 6. Goethe
9. Holderlin
president (first).. 5. Ebert
socialist.. 10. Liebknecht
sociologist.. 5. Weber (Max)
teller of tall tales.. 10. Munchausen
(Baron)
theologian.. 6. Luther
Germany...
capital.. 6. Berlin
capital, former.. 4. Bonn (W Ger)
6. Berlin (E Ger)
city.. 5. Essen, Halle, Mainz 6. Bremen
7. Cologne, Dresden, Hamburg, Leipzig,
Munster 9. Frankfurt, Nuremberg,
Stuttgart
coal region.. 4. Ruhr, Saar
lake.. 8. Konstanz (Constance)
mountain range.. 4. Harz
mountain region.. 11. Black Forest
(Schwarzwald)
Nazi state.. 10. Third Reich
region, annexed.. 7. Sudeten
(Sudetenland)
region, state.. 6. Anhalt, Saxony
7. Bavaria, Hanover, Prussia 8. Saarland
9. Rhineland, Thuringia 10. Palatinate,
Westphalia
republic.. 6. Weimar

river.. 4. Elbe, Main, Oder 5. Rhine,
Weser 6. Danube, Neisse 7. Moselle
(Mosel)
secondary school.. 9. gymnasium
germicide... 6. iodine (iodin), phenol
10. antiseptic 12. disinfectant
germinate... 3. bud 4. grow 5. beget
6. sprout 7. develop 8. vegetate
10. effloresce
Geronimo... 6. Apache (Chief)
gerrymander (Polit)... 6. divide (unfairly)
10. manipulate
gesticulation... 6. motion 7. gesture
gesture... 3. act 4. gest (geste), sign
5. sanna 6. beckon, behave, motion
7. perform, pretext 8. carriage (body)
11. gesticulate 13. gesticulation
get... 3. pen, win 4. earn, hear, pain,
take, trap 5. beget, fetch, incur, learn
6. attain, become, derive, induce,
obtain, profit, secure 7. achieve,
acquire, capture, prepare, procure,
receive 8. contract, contrive, discover
9. ascertain, determine 10. understand
get along... 3. age 4. fare 5. hurry
6. begone, depart, manage, move on
7. advance, prosper
get around... 5. evade 6. cajole,
outwit, spread 7. deceive 9. circulate
10. circumvent
get off... 5. start, utter 6. alight, depart,
escape, go free 8. dismount
get out... 4. exit 5. scram 6. elicit,
escape, reveal 7. draw out, leak out,
publish 8. evacuate 9. extricate
get over... 4. move 5. cover 6. bridge,
finish 7. recover 8. surmount 9. make
clear
Ghana, capital of... 5. Accra (Gold
Coast)
ghastly... 3. wan 4. grim, pale
5. lurid 6. dismal, grisly, pallid
7. deathly, hideous 8. gruesome,
horrible, shocking, terrible 9. deathlike,
frightful 10. cadaverous
ghost... 3. Ker 5. larva (Rom Relig),
lemur, shade, spook 6. daemon,
spirit, wraith 7. banshee (banshie),
eidolon, phantom, specter 8. phantasm,
revenant 10. apparition, glimmering,
substitute 11. ghostwriter, poltergeist
ghostly... 5. eerie (eery) 6. spectral
9. spiritual
giant... 4. huge, ogre 5. Titan 6. afreet,
nozzle, thurse 7. monster 8. colossus
9. monstrous 10. gargantuan,
prodigious, tremendous
giant (pert to)...
Biblical.. 7. Goliath, Rephaim
crafty.. 5. Cacus
Greek.. 5. Atlas, Mimas, Titan
7. Antaeus, cyclops
hundred-armed.. 9. Enceladus
land, country.. 9. Utgarthar
10. Jotunnheim 11. Brobdingnag
Norse.. 4. Ymir (Ymer) 5. Mimir
6. Jotunn (Jotun) 12. Utgartha-Loki
one-eyed.. 5. Arges 7. Brontes, Cyclops
10. Polyphemus
primeval.. 4. Ymir 12. Utgartha-Loki
Rabelais'.. 9. Gargantua 10. Pantagruel

sea god.. 5. Aegir
seer.. 5. Mimir
strong.. 6. Samson, Targan 7. Antaeus
  8. Hercules
Teutonic.. 4. Wade 5. Aegir
thousand-armed.. 4. Bana
three-hundred handed, many-handed..
  8. Briareus
giantess (Teut Myth) ... 4. Norn
gibbed ... 9. castrated (cat)
gibber ... 4. chat, hump, talk (rapid)
  5. stone (loose) 6. mumble 7. boulder,
  chatter 8. swelling
gibberish ... 4. talk 5. lingo 6. jargon,
  patois, patter 8. nonsense
gibbet ... 3. jib 4. hang 7. gallows
  9. execution
gibbon ... 3. ape, lar 6. wou-wou
  7. hoolock, siamang 10. anthropoid
gibe ... 4. jape, jeer, jibe, quip 5. fleer,
  flirt, flout, scoff, sneer, taunt 6. heckle
Gibraltar ...
  named for (legend).. 5. Gobir
  ruled by.. 12. Great Britain
  site.. 5. Spain (coast)
giddy ... 4. reel 5. dizzy, tipsy, whirl
  6. fickle 7. flighty 8. gyratory, heedless
  9. delirious 14. scatterbrained
gift ... 4. alms, bent, boon, dole, free
  5. bribe, grant, knack, token 6. legacy,
  talent 7. aptness, faculty, largess
  (largesse), present 8. aptitude, blessing,
  donation, gratuity 9. endowment,
  lagniappe (lagnappe), readiness
  11. serendipity 12. contribution
gifted ... 7. endowed 8. talented
gigantic ... 4. huge 5. giant, large, titan
  7. immense, mammoth 8. colossal,
  enormous 9. colossean, monstrous
  10. prodigious
giggle ... 5. laugh (silly) 6. tee-hee
  titter 7. chuckle, snicker, snigger
Gila monster ... 4. Gila 6. lizard
glid ... 4. coat, lure 6. adorn, paint,
  tempt 7. aureate, falsify 8. brighten
  9. embellish
gilding ... 4. gilt, gold 6. ormolu
  7. coating 8. ornament, painting
gill ... 5. brook, leach, organ, penny
  6. tipple, valley, wattle 7. measure
  10. sweetheart
gimcrackle ... 3. fob, toy 5. showy
  6. bauble, gewgaw, paltry, trifle
  7. trinket 8. trumpery, whimwham
  15. Jack-of-all-trades
gimlet ... 3. awl 4. tool 5. drink (mixed)
  6. wimble
gimp ... 5. orris (upholstery) 6. fabric,
  thread 7. galloon 8. fishline, trimming
gin ... 4. game, sloe, tool, trap, whim
  5. snare, trick 6. device, liquor, scheme,
  thresh 7. machine 8. artifice, schnapps
  11. contrivance
ginger ... 3. pep 5. color 6. Asarum,
  energy, lively, mettle, spirit
  8. pungency, Zingiber 9. rootstalk
gingerbread ... 4. cake 5. money
  6. flimsy, frills, wealth 8. ornament
  (tawdry) 11. superfluity
gingerly ... 6. warily 7. charily 9. carefully,
  finically, guardedly 10. cautiously

  12. fastidiously
gingham ... 5. cloth 8. umbrella (cheap)
gipsy ... see *gypsy*
giraffe ... 5. okapi 6. mammal, spinet
  10. cameloparal 13. constellation
girasol, girasole ... 4. opal 9. artichoke,
  sunflower
gird ... 4. belt, bind, gibe, girt, sill 5. brace,
  equip, scoff, sneer 6. fasten, girdle,
  secure 7. enclose, environ 8. surround
  10. strengthen
girder ... 4. beam 5. truss 6. timber
  7. support
girdle ... 3. obi 4. band, belt, cest, ring,
  sash 6. cestus, cingle, circle, corset
  8. cincture, encircle 10. cummerbund
girdle bone ... 12. sphenethmoid
Girdle of Venus (pert to) ...
  bridal.. 11. power of love
  palmistry line.. 8. hysteria
  11. nervousness
girl ... 3. sis 4. bint, chit, dame, lass,
  minx, miss 5. filly, sissy, skirt 6. damsel,
  female, giglet, hoyden (holden), lassie,
  maiden, shiver, thrill, tomboy 7. colleen,
  damosel, fillock, ingénue, roebuck
  10. sweetheart 11. maidservant
girlish ... 4. pert 5. sissy 7. artless
  8. immature, maidenly 10. flapperish
girt ... 4. band 6. fasten, saddle 7. besiege
  9. encircled
girth ... 4. band, hoop, size 5. brace,
  strap 6. girdle, saddle 7. measure
  8. encircle 13. circumference
gist ... 3. nub 4. core, crux, meat, pith
  5. heart, point (main) 7. essence,
  meaning
give ... 3. gie 4. hand 5. endow, grant,
  yield 6. accord, afford, bestow, confer,
  devote, donate, impart, remise, render,
  supply 7. present, proffer, provide
  9. attribute, vouchsafe 10. administer,
  elasticity
give (pert to) ...
  and take.. 11. reciprocity
  authority.. 7. empower
  away.. 5. break, grant, marry, yield
  6. bestow, betray 7. discard, divulge,
  succumb 8. disclose 9. sacrifice
  10. relinquish
  back.. 4. echo 5. remit 6. recede,
  remand, remise, retire, return
  7. replace, restore, retreat
  birth to.. 4. foal 5. calve 6. farrow,
  mother 9. originate
  expectation.. 7. promise
  forth.. 4. emit 5. blaze 6. afford, exhale
  7. publish
  information.. 4. tell 6. inform, report
  7. divulge, publish 8. disclose
  9. advertise
  out.. 4. deal, emit 5. exude, issue,
  print, utter (publicly) 6. report, weaken
  7. declare, publish, release 8. allocate,
  announce 9. apportion, circulate
  10. distribute
  prominence.. 4. star 7. feature
  8. headline
  up.. 4. cede, emit, fail, quit 5. demit,
  waive, yield 6. betray, disuse, resign,
  vacate 7. abandon, despair, succumb

8. abdicate, part with, renounce, swear off **9.** sacrifice, surrender **10.** capitulate, relinquish

given . . . **5.** dated, datum, fixed **6.** stated **7.** assumed, granted **8.** accorded, addicted, bestowed, inclined, set forth **10.** determined, disposed to

given (pert to) . . .
by word of mouth . . **4.** oral **5.** parol
name . . **7.** surname
particularly . . **9.** specified

given (to) . . .
experiment . . **7.** empiric
expression . . **13.** demonstrative
meditation . . **13.** contemplative
suspicion . . **9.** querulent

giving . . . **6.** ceding **7.** largess (largesse) **9.** bestowing **10.** conferring, liberality **12.** philanthropy, presentation **13.** administering

giving up . . . **8.** yielding **10.** abandoning, despairing **11.** sacrificing **12.** surrendering **13.** relinquishing

glacial (pert to) . . .
deposit . . **6.** placer **7.** moraine
direction . . **5.** stoss (opp to lee)
drift . . **8.** diluvium
dust . . **10.** kryokonite
erosion wall . . **6.** cirque
mill . . **6.** moulin
ridge . . **2.** os (pl osar) **4.** kame (Scot) **5.** esker (eskar)
snow . . **4.** neve

glaciarium . . . **4.** rink (skating)

glacis . . . **5.** slope **7.** incline **13.** fortification

glack . . . **4.** fork (road) **6.** defile, ravine, valley

glad . . . **3.** gay **4.** fain **5.** merry **6.** elated, joyful, joyous **8.** animated, cheering, pleasing **9.** animating, beautiful, delighted, gratified **11.** exhilarated, well-pleased **12.** exhilarating

gladden . . . **5.** cheer, elate **6.** please **7.** gratify

gladdy . . . **12.** yellowhammer

glade . . . **4.** dell, nemo (comb form), vale **5.** laund **6.** valley **8.** clearing **9.** everglade, open space

gladiator . . . **6.** fencer **7.** lanista

gladiator's arena . . . **4.** ludi

gladly . . . **4.** fain, lief **5.** fitly **6.** freely **7.** eagerly, readily **8.** joyfully, properly **9.** willingly **10.** cheerfully, preferably

gladsome . . . **4.** glad **6.** blithe, joyful **7.** festive, jocular, pleased **8.** cheerful

Gladstone . . . **3.** bag (travel) **4.** wine **7.** Liberal (Party) **8.** carriage, Irishman **11.** portmanteau

glad tidings . . . **3.** joy **6.** gospel **7.** evangel

glamorous . . . **8.** alluring, charming **10.** bewitching **11.** fascinating

glance . . . **3.** eye **4.** hint, leer, look, ogle, scry, skew **5.** flash, gleam, glint, touch **6.** allude, signal **7.** glimpse

gland . . . **5.** gonad, liver, lymph, ovary **6.** spleen, thymus **7.** adrenal, carotid, parotid, thyroid **8.** pancreas, salivary **9.** pituitary **10.** suprarenal

gland (pert to) . . .
enlargement . . **6.** ademia
full of . . **7.** adenose

glandlike . . **7.** adenoid **9.** glandular
inflammation . . **8.** adenitis
secretion . . **7.** hormone
tumor . . **7.** adenoma

glaring . . . **5.** clear, plain **6.** bright, garish **7.** evident, flaring, obvious, staring, visible, vividly **8.** apparent, distinct, flagrant, manifest **9.** barefaced **11.** conspicuous

glass . . . **4.** lens, pony **5.** glaze, purex **6.** goblet, liquor, mirror, seidel **7.** binocle, crystal, reflect, tumbler **9.** barometer, binocular, hourglass, telescope **10.** microscope, opera glass **11.** stactometer, thermometer

glass (pert to) . . .
blue . . **5.** smalt
cabinet . . **7.** vitrine
component . . **6.** silica
French for . . **5.** verre
furnace, oven . . **4.** lehr (leer) **5.** bocca, siege, tisar **7.** drosser (part)
jeweler's . . **5.** paste **6.** strass
like . . **6.** vitric **7.** hyaline, hyaloid **8.** vitreous
material . . **4.** frit (fritt)
mineral . . **7.** hyalite **8.** feldspar
molten . . **7.** parison
mosaic . . **7.** tessera
red . . **7.** schmelz (schmelze)
scrap . . **6.** cullet
sheet . . **4.** pane **5.** slide **7.** platten
showcase . . **7.** vitrine
volcanic . . **6.** pumice **8.** obsidian
worker . . **7.** glazier

glass (type of) . . . **3.** cut **4.** milk, spun **5.** crown, plate, Pyrex **6.** ground, safety **7.** Corning, frosted, Lalique, stained, Steuben, Tiffany **8.** Sandwich, Venetian **9.** Waterford **10.** Depression

glass blowing (pert to) . . .
annealing term . . **4.** fuse, heat
glass content . . **4.** sand, zinc **6.** potash, temper **7.** soda ash
oven . . **4.** lehr (leer)
rod . . **5.** punty (pontil)

glass container . . . **3.** jar **4.** vial (phial) **5.** ampul (ampoule, ampule), flask **6.** beaker, bottle, carboy **7.** matrass **8.** test tube

glazier's diamond . . . **5.** emery (emeril)

glazing machine . . . **8.** calender

gleam . . . **3.** ray **4.** glow **5.** flash, glint, gloze, light **7.** glimmer, shimmer **8.** radiance **9.** coruscate **10.** brightness

glean . . . **4.** reap **5.** sheaf (of hemp) **6.** bundle, deduce, gather **7.** collect, harvest, procure

glee . . . **3.** joy **4.** club, song **5.** mirth **7.** delight **8.** pleasure **9.** merriment **12.** cheerfulness

glen . . . **4.** dale, dell, vale **6.** dingle, ravine, valley **10.** depression

glib . . . **4.** easy, oily **5.** suave **6.** facile, fluent, smooth **8.** castrate, flippant, slippery **9.** talkative **10.** loquacious

glide . . . **4.** sail, skid, slip, soar **5.** coast, slide

gliding over . . . **7.** lambent **10.** slithering

glimmer . . . **3.** bit **4.** hint, leam **5.** blink, flash, gleam, glint **7.** glimpse, glitter

10. perception (slight)

glimpse ... 4. view (quick) 5. flash, tinge, trace 6. glance, luster 7. glimmer, inkling

glisten ... 5. flash, shine 7. glister, sparkle 9. coruscate

glitter ... 5. glare, gleam, shine 7. glimmer, glisten, sparkle 9. coruscate, showiness 14. attractiveness

glooming ... 4. dusk 8. twilight 9. darkening 11. candlelight

globe ... 3. map, orb 4. ball, moon 5. earth 6. sphere 10. hemisphere (half)

Globe, The ... 7. Theater (London, first to play Shakespeare)

globular ... 5. beady 7. globose 9. orbicular, spherical 10. orbiculate 11. globe-shaped

globule ... 4. bead, blob, drop, pill, tear 5. minim 6. bubble 8. spherule

glochis ... 4. hair (barbed) 7. bristle

glockenspiel ... 4. lyra, stop (organ) 8. carillon 10. instrument

gloom ... 5. cloud, frown, scowl 7. dimness, sadness 8. darkness 9. dejection, heaviness, obscurity 10. cloudiness, depression, melancholy, sullen look

gloomy ... 3. dim, sad, wan 4. dark, dour, glum 5. drear, eerie, lurid, moody, murky 6. cloudy, droopy, lowery, morose 7. obscure 8. darkling, dejected, dolesome, downcast 9. darkening, depressed, tenebrous 10. depressing, foreboding, tenebrific 11. pessimistic 12. disheartened

Gloomy Dean ... 4. Inge

gloomy person ... 7. killjoy

Gloria ... 4. rite 8. doxology

glorification ... 6. praise 7. worship 8. doxology, honoring 9. festivity 10. apotheosis 13. jollification 14. sanctification

glorify ... 4. laud 5. adore, bless, exalt, extol, honor 6. praise 7. elevate, worship 8. beautify, sanctify 9. celebrate

glorious ... 3. sri 5. grand, noble 6. elated, superb 7. eminent, radiant 8. ecstatic, renowned, splendid 9. beautiful, hilarious 10. celebrated, delightful 11. illustrious, magnificent, resplendent 12. praiseworthy

glory ... 4. fame, halo 5. bliss (celestial), boast, éclat, honor 6. heaven, nimbus (cloud of), praise, renown 8. grandeur 10. admiration, brilliancy, effulgence 11. distinction 13. glorification

gloss ... 4. glow, note 5. color, sheen, shine 6. enamel, luster, polish, remark 7. burnish, comment, pretext 8. glossary, palliate 9. extenuate 10. annotation, brightness, commentary 14. interpretation

gloss over ... 4. fard (obs) 5. wink 5. blink, color 6. excuse 8. palliate

glossy ... 5. glacé, nitid, shiny, sleek 6. luster, sheeny, smooth 7. radiant, shining 8. lustrous, polished 10. reflecting

glove ... 3. mit 4. mitt 5. trank (shaped) 6. boxing, ceatus, mitten 7. gantlet

8. gauntlet 12. mousquetaire

glow ... 4. burn 5. ardor, flame, flush, glean, shine 6. beauty, redden 7. redness 9. eloquence 10. luminosity 13. incandescence

glower ... 4. gaze 5. glare, scowl, stare

glowing ... 3. red 4. warm 5. drunk 6. ardent, cadent 7. burning, excited, fervent, flushed 8. eloquent, luminous 9. beautiful 12. enthusiastic

glucose ... 5. rutin, sugar 8. dextrose

glue ... 3. fix 4. join 5. paste, stick 6. adhere, cement, fasten, sizing 7. gelatin 8. adhesive, fastener 9. viscosity

glum ... 3. sad 5. moody 6. dismal, gloomy, sullen 8. frowning

glut ... 4. cloy, fill, sate 5. gorge, stuff 6. pamper 7. engorge, satiate, satisfy, surfeit 8. overfill, overload, plethora, saturate

gluten ... 3. gum 4. glue 6. fibrin 7. gliadin 8. adhesive

glutinous ... 4. sizy 5. gluey 6. viscid 8. adhesive

glutton ... 6. rascal, wretch 7. epicure 8. gourmand 9. cormorant, scoundrel, wolverine 11. gormandizer, greedy eater

gluttony ... 5. greed 7. edacity 8. voracity 12. intemperance 13. voraciousness

glycerine machine man ... 8. effetman

gnar, gnarr (of dogs) ... 5. growl, snarl

gnarl ... 4. knot 5. growl, snarl, twist 6. tangle 7. contort, distort, roughen 10. contortion 12. protuberance (tree)

gnarled ... 5. rough 6. knotty, rugged 7. complex, knotted, twisted 12. cross-grained

gnash ... 4. bite 5. grate, grind (teeth)

gnat ... 3. fly 5. nidge 6. insect 8. mosquito

gnaw ... 3. eat 4. bite, chew 5. grind, waste 6. rankle 7. corrode 8. wear away

gnede ... 6. scanty 7. lacking, miserly, sparing

gnib ... 5. ready, sharp 6. clever

gnome ... 3. elf, imp, saw 5. bodie, bogey, dwarf, maxim, nisse 6. goblin, kobold, sprite 8. aphorism

gnomic ... 8. didactic 10. aphoristic

gnomic poets (Gr) ... 5. Solon 8. Theognis (of Megara) 10. Phocylides (of Miletus)

gnostic ... 4. wise 6. shrewd 7. knowing 9. sagacious

Gnostic ... 6. Ophite 7. Abraxas (Abrasax), Sethite

gnu ... 6. kokoon 8. antelope

go ... 3. act, die, gee, run 4. fail, fare, game, move, pass, turn, walk, wane, wend, work 5. leave, sally 6. betake, decamp, depart, elapse, embark, energy, extend, result, retire, travel, weaken 7. advance, entrain, journey, proceed 8. continue, diminish, withdraw 9. eventuate, harmonize

go (pert to) ...
around ... 6. detour 7. circuit 8. surround
ashore ... 4. land 9. disembark

astray .. **3.** err
at .. **6.** attack **8.** undertake
away .. **4.** exit, scat, shoo **5.** scoot,
   scram **6.** begone, depart **9.** disappear
back .. **3.** ebb **5.** recede, repass, retire,
   return, revert
   7. regress, retrace
before .. **7.** precede **8.** antecede
   11. participate
down, under .. **4.** fail, sink **7.** capsize,
   descend, founder, succumb, undergo
   8. submerge **11.** deteriorate
easily .. **4.** lope **5.** amble
furtively .. **5.** steal **6.** tiptoe
over .. **5.** renew **6.** revise **7.** retrace
   8. rehearse, traverse **9.** backtrack,
   re-examine
through .. **4.** pass **5.** spend **6.** suffer
   7. exhaust (fortune), persist, undergo
   9. persevere **10.** experience
up .. **4.** fail, rise **5.** arise, raise **6.** ascend
with .. **4.** suit **5.** agree, court **6.** accord
   8. coincide **9.** accompany
   10. understand
goa .. **8.** antelope (Tibet)
goad .. **3.** egg **4.** poke, prod, prog, spur,
   urge **5.** ankus (elephant), decoy, impel,
   prick, sting, thorn, valet (manège)
   6. incite **7.** inflame **8.** irritate, stimulus
   9. incentive
goal .. **3.** aim, end **4.** base, fate, home,
   mark **5.** bourn (bourne), Mecca, reach,
   score, Thule (Myth) **6.** object **7.** purpose
   9. objective **11.** destination
goanna .. **6.** iguana, lizard **7.** monitor
goat .. **4.** buck, dupe **5.** brown **6.** engine,
   lecher **9.** scapegoat **13.** laughingstock
goat (pert to) ...
   astronomy .. **9.** Capricorn
   fig .. **8.** caprifig
   fish .. **6.** mullet
   get one's .. **3.** irk, vex **4.** rile **5.** pique
     6. nettle
   god .. **3.** Pan
   haircloth .. **5.** Tibet (Thibet) **6.** camlet
   hair cord (Bedouin) .. **4.** agal
goat (type of) .. **3.** kid, ram, tur, zac
   4. ibex, tahr, urus **5.** Capra, goral,
   pasan (pasang), serow, takin **6.** Alpine,
   Angora, chamal, Jemlah, mammal
   7. aurochs, markhor **8.** Cashmere,
   ruminant
goatsucker .. **4.** bird **7.** dorhawk, grinder
   9. nighthawk **12.** whippoorwill
gob .. **4.** lump, mass **5.** choke, mouth
   6. sailor **7.** mouthful, quantity
goby .. **4.** fish, mapo
go-by .. **4.** snub **7.** evasion, passing
   13. circumvention
god (Myth, Relig) ...
   Babylonian .. **2.** Zu **3.** Anu, Sin **4.** Adad,
     Enzu, Nama, Nebo (Nebu) **5.** Aruru,
     Cirru, Dagan, Nintu **8.** Ningirsu
     10. Ninkhursag **11.** Ningishzida
   Celtic .. **6.** Aengus
   Cymric .. **4.** Lleu (Llew)
   Egyptian .. **2.** Ra **3.** Bes, Dis, Geb
     (Keb), Min, Seb **4.** Amen, Amon, Ptah
     5. Horus, Thoth **6.** Dhouti, Osiris
   false .. **4.** Baal, idol **6.** Mammon
   Greek .. **4.** Ares, Zeus **5.** Comus, Hymen,

Momus, Pluto **6.** Hermes, Somnus
     7. Bacchus **8.** Dionysus
   Hebrew .. **6.** Yahweh (Jahveh, Jahweh,
     Yahveh)
   Hindu .. **4.** Agni, Deva, Kama, Siva
     (Shiva) **6.** Varuna
   household .. **3.** Lar **5.** Lares **6.** Penate
   Irish .. **5.** Dagda (pagan)
   love of, for .. **5.** piety **6.** bhakti
     9. theophile
   Muslim .. **5.** Allah
   Norse .. **2.** Er, Ve **3.** Tyr, Ull, Van
     4. Loki, Odin, Thor, Ymir **5.** Aesir,
     Donar, Vanir, Wodin
   Roman .. **4.** Jove **5.** Comus, Janus, Orcus
     7. Bacchus, Mercury **8.** Dis pater
   Semitic .. **5.** Hadad **6.** Nergal
   Supreme .. **3.** Dei, Deo, Dio **4.** Deus,
     Soul, Zeus **6.** Elohim, Spirit **12.** Infinite
     Mind, Supreme Being
   Teutonic .. **3.** Tiu **4.** Hoth
god (of) ...
   agriculture .. **4.** Nebo **6.** Faunus
   beauty .. **6.** Aengus (Oengus)
   beginnings, creation .. **4.** Ptah, Zeus
     5. Janus **6.** Varuna
   commerce .. **5.** Vanir **7.** Mercury
   darkness, evil .. **3.** Set, Sin **6.** Nergal
   day .. **5.** Horus
   dead .. **5.** Orcus **6.** Osiris
   discord .. **4.** Loki
   earth .. **3.** Geb (Keb), Seb **5.** Dagan
   east wind .. **5.** Eurus
   evil .. **2.** Zu **3.** Set, Sin **6.** Nergal
   fate .. **5.** Moira (Moera)
   fire .. **4.** Agni **5.** Girru **6.** Vulcan
   flocks .. **3.** Pan
   January .. **5.** Janus
   joy .. **5.** Comus
   justice .. **7.** Forseti (Forsete)
   law .. **4.** Zeus
   lightning .. **4.** Agni
   love .. **4.** Amor, Ares, Eros, Kama
     5. Bhaga, Cupid **6.** Aengus (Oengus)
   March .. **4.** Mars
   marriage .. **5.** Hymen
   medicine .. **11.** Ningishzida
   mountains .. **5.** Atlas **7.** Olympus
   music .. **6.** Apollo
   Northmen .. **5.** Aesir
   oceans .. **7.** Oceanus
   poetry .. **5.** Bragi
   ridicule .. **5.** Momus
   sea .. **7.** Neptune, Proteus
   sky .. **3.** Anu
   sleep, dreams .. **6.** Somnus **8.** Morpheus
   storm .. **2.** Zu **6.** Teshup
   sun .. **2.** Ra (Re) **3.** Apollo, Nergal
   thunder .. **4.** Thor **7.** Jupiter
   Thursday .. **4.** Thor
   Tuesday .. **3.** Tiu, Tyr
   underworld .. **3.** Dis **5.** Pluto **6.** Osiris
     7. Serapis **8.** Dis pater **11.** Ningishzida
   war .. **3.** Ira, Tyr **4.** Mars **5.** Woden
     8. Ningirau
   wealth .. **5.** Bhaga **6.** Plutus
   Wednesday .. **5.** Woden
   wind .. **4.** Adad **5.** Eolus, Eurus, Hadad
     6. Aeolus, zephyr **8.** Favonius
   wine .. **7.** Bacchus **8.** Dionysus
   wisdom .. **4.** Nebo **5.** Thoth **6.** Dhouti

woods .. **7.** Silenus
youth .. **6.** Apollo
goddess ... **3.** Ate, Dea, Eir, Eos, Nox,
Nyx, Ops, Pax, Uni **4.** Apet, Eris, Fury,
Gaea, Hera, Isis, Leda, Maat, Nike, Nina,
Sati **5.** Aruru, Damia, Diana, Doris,
Epona, Freya, Hygea, Irene, Pakht,
Salus, Venus, Vesta **6.** Allatu, Athena,
Aurora, Cybele, Hecate, Hestia, Ningal,
Pietho, Selene, Semele, Tellus, Vacuna
7. Artemis, Demeter, Minerva, Parvati
9. Aphrodite, Eumenides, Mnemosyne
10. Persephone, Proserpina
goddess of ...
agriculture .. **3.** Ops **7.** Demeter
arts .. **6.** Athena, Pallas
beauty .. **3.** Sri **5.** Freya, Venus
7. Lakshmi
dawn .. **3.** Eos **5.** Ushas **6.** Aurora,
Matuta
destiny .. **4.** Fate **5.** Moira, Parca
discord .. **3.** Ate **4.** Eris
earth .. **4.** Gaea **5.** Aruru **6.** Ishtar, Tellus
Eskimos .. **5.** Sedna
fertility .. **4.** Isis **7.** Demeter
fire .. **6.** Hestia
fortune .. **5.** Tyche
freedom .. **7.** Feronia
fruit .. **6.** Pomona
grain, harvest .. **3.** Ops **5.** Ceres
Hawaiians .. **4.** Pele
healing .. **3.** Eir **4.** Gula
health .. **5.** Damia, Hygea, Salus
hearth .. **5.** Vesta
history .. **4.** Saga
horses .. **5.** Epona
hunt .. **5.** Diana **6.** Vacuna
infatuation .. **3.** Ate
justice .. **7.** Nemesis
light .. **6.** Lucina
love .. **5.** Venus **6.** Ishtar **9.** Aphrodite
magic, witchcraft .. **6.** Hecate
marriage .. **4.** Hera
maternity .. **4.** Apet
mischief .. **3.** Ate **4.** Eris
moon .. **4.** Luna **5.** Diana **6.** Phoebe,
Selene (Selena)
mother of the gods .. **4.** Rhea
nature .. **4.** Rhea **5.** Nymph **6.** Cybele
night .. **3.** Nox, Nyx
peace .. **3.** Pax **5.** Irene **6.** Athena
poetry .. **5.** Erato
rainbows .. **4.** Iris
sea .. **5.** Doris
seasons .. **5.** Horae
summer .. **6.** Aestus
sun .. **5.** Pakht (Pacht)
trees .. **6.** Pomona
truth .. **4.** Maat
underworld .. **4.** Fury **6.** Allatu
10. Persephone, Proserpina
vengeance .. **3.** Ara, Ate **7.** Nemesis
victory .. **4.** Nike
virtue .. **5.** Fides
war .. **5.** Anath, Bella
wealth .. **3.** Sri **7.** Lakshmi
wisdom .. **6.** Athena **7.** Minerva
youth .. **4.** Hebe
Godforsaken ... **6.** vacant **7.** forlorn
8. desolate, wretched **9.** neglected
godly ... **5.** pious **6.** devout, divine

7. saintly **9.** religious, righteous
godmother ... **6.** cummer (kimmer)
7. sponsor
God's ...
abode .. **7.** Olympus
acre .. **10.** churchyard
board .. **14.** communion table
country .. **4.** home **8.** homeland
9. Vaterland **10.** fatherland
cupbearer .. **8.** Ganymede
fluid (vein) .. **5.** ichor (icor)
food .. **8.** ambrosia
gods, The (pert to) ...
death of .. **9.** theoktony
marriage of .. **8.** theogamy
messenger of .. **6.** Hermes
mother of .. **4.** Rhea
Twilight of .. **8.** Ragnarok
worship of .. **9.** theolatry
Goetae ... **7.** wizards (anc) **9.** sorcerers
14. thaumaturgists
Goethe (pert to) ...
home .. **6.** Weimar (Ger)
masterpiece .. **5.** Faust
talent .. **4.** poet **8.** novelist **9.** dramatist
goffer, gauffer ... **5.** crimp, flute, plait
(lace, paper)
gog ... **3.** bog **4.** stir **9.** agitation
Gog (Bib) ... **5.** Ruler (of Magog)
goggle ... **3.** eye **4.** roll **5.** state **6.** squint
11. roll the eyes
goggler ... **4.** fish (oceanic)
goggles ... **6.** screen **7.** glasses **8.** blinkers,
eyeshade **10.** spectacles
going ... **6.** moving, travel **7.** current,
working **9.** departure **10.** obtainable
11. in operation
gola ... **7.** granary **9.** storeroom **11.** Indian
caste
golach, goloch ... **6.** beetle, earwig
9. centipede
Golconda ... **6.** wealth **8.** rich mine
gold ... **2.** Au **3.** oro **4.** gelt, gilt **5.** aurum,
color, lucre, metal, money **6.** riches,
wealth **7.** bullion
gold (pert to) ...
alloy .. **4.** asem **6.** oroide
artificial .. **8.** Mannheim
assayer cup .. **5.** cupel
bar .. **5.** ingot
braid, lace .. **5.** orris
brick .. **7.** swindle
coin .. **5.** eagle **10.** Krugerrand (So Afr)
compound .. **6.** auride
containing .. **6.** doré
discoverer (US) .. **6.** Sutter (1849)
field (Bib) .. **5.** Ophir
fish .. **9.** shubunkin
fool's .. **6.** pyrite
gilding .. **6.** ormolu **9.** imitation
Heraldry .. **2.** or
King (Myth) .. **5.** Midas
land of (Bib) .. **5.** Ophir
like .. **5.** auric **7.** aureate
measure .. **5.** carat
Rush .. **8.** Klondike (1897) **10.** California
(1849)
seekers (Calif) .. **9.** Argonauts (1849)
11. Forty-Niners
symbol .. **2.** Au
vein .. **4.** lode

washing pan .. 5. cupel
gold and silver .. 11. noble metals
golden ... 4. gilt 5. auric, blest 6. blonde,
    yellow 7. aureate, aureous, halcyon
    8. metallic, precious, valuable
    9. Pactolian 10. auspicious
    11. flourishing
golden (pert to) ...
    Age .. 9. Saturnian, siècle d'or
    apple .. 3. bel 4. Eris (goddess) 5. Paris
        (giver) 6. tomato
    bird .. 6. oriole
    bough .. 9. mistletoe
    Fleece seeker .. 5. Jason 8. Argonaut
    Fleece ship .. 5. Argos
    rod .. 8. solidago
goldenrod (pert to) ...
    genus .. 8. Solidago
    State Flower of .. 7. Alabama
        8. Kentucky, Nebraska
goldfish ... 4. carp 9. shubunkin
Goldfish (Astron) ... 6. Dorado
golf (pert to) ...
    club .. 4. iron, wood 5. baffy, spoon,
        wedge 7. brassie, midiron, niblick
    hazard .. 4. trap 5. stymy 6. bunker
        11. restriction
    score .. 3. par 4. bogy (bogie) 5. eagle
        6. birdie
    stroke .. 4. baff, chip, fade, hook, loft,
        putt 5. drive, slice 8. approach, mulligan
    term .. 3. ace, par, tee 4. baff, fore
        5. bogey, divot, eagle, green, links,
        rough, slice 6. birdie, dormie, sclaff,
        stymie (stimy) 7. fairway, gallery
Golgotha ... 7. Calvary 8. cemetery
goliath ... 4. frog 5. crane, giant, heron
Goliath (pert to) ...
    Bib .. 5. giant (Philistine)
    death site .. 4. Elah
    home .. 4. Gath
    slayer .. 5. David
Gomorrah (Bib) ... 5. Sodom 13. wicked
    country
Gomuti palm ... 5. areng
gondola race (Venice) ... 7. regatta
gone ... 3. ago, off 4. dead, left, lost,
    past, yore 5. since 6. absent, passed,
    ruined 8. departed, past hope, vanished
    9. forgotten 10. infatuated
goober ... 6. peanut
good ... 2. eu (pref) 3. bon, fit 4. able,
    full, gain, just, kind 5. ample, godly,
    moral, nifty, pious, sound, valid
    6. benign, devout, expert, profit, savory
    7. genuine, helpful, liberal, trained,
    upright 8. decorous, interest, pleasing,
    salutary, suitable, virtuous 9. admirable,
    competent, enjoyable, estimable,
    excellent, favorable, honorable,
    indulgent, reputable 10. auspicious,
    beneficial, courageous, gratifying,
    profitable, sufficient 11. commendable,
    well-behaved 12. considerable,
    satisfactory, stouthearted
good (pert to) ...
    bye .. 4. ta-ta 5. adieu, adios, ciaou
        6. so long 7. cheerio 8. farewell
    for nothing .. 4. mean 5. idler 6. wretch
        7. useless 8. indolent 9. worthless

11. rapscallion
    health .. 5. skoal 6. prosit
    management .. 6. eutaxy
    mighty .. 7. skookum
    ordinarily .. 8. mediocre
    spirit .. 6. daemon 8. Eudaemon
        12. agathodaemon
    tidings .. 6. gospel 7. evangel
    will .. 5. favor 9. affection, readiness
        11. benevolence 12. friendliness
Good Book ... 5. Bible
goodness ... 5. piety 6. virtue 8. kindness,
    validity 9. godliness, propriety
    10. excellence, generosity, savoriness
goods ... 5. wares 7. ability 8. chattels,
    property 11. information, merchandise
goods cast overboard, sunk ... 5. lagan
    (lagend) 6. jetsam 7. flotsam
    10. contraband
goose ... 4. bean, dupe, fool, gull, iron,
    snow, tule 5. Anser, brant, solan
    6. Canada, gander, gannet, goslet
    7. gosling, graylag (greylag) 8. barnacle
    12. white-fringed
goose (pert to) ...
    egg .. 4. zero
    grease .. 6. axunge
    group .. 6. gaggle
    pygmy .. 6. goslet
    relating to .. 8. anserine
    story character .. 5. ganza
gooseberry ... 5. fabes (color) 6. escort,
    groser (groset), thapes 8. chaperon,
    feaberry
gopher ... 5. snake 6. rodent 7. burglar
    8. squirrel, tortoise 10. salamander
Gopher State ... 9. Minnesota
gore ... 3. mud 4. dirt, dung, stab 5. blood,
    cloth (triang), filth, slime 6. pierce
    8. heraldry 9. bloodshed, penetrate
gorge ... 3. eat 4. bolt, glut, sate 5. chasm,
    gully 6. canyon, coulee, defile, nullah,
    ravine, valley 7. choke up, overeat,
    pitcher, satiate 8. overfill
gorgeous ... 5. grand, showy 8. colorful,
    dazzling 9. beautiful 10. delightful
    11. magnificent, resplendent
gorgon ... 4. ogre, ugly 7. Jezebel (Bib),
    monster
Gorgons (Gr Myth) ... 6. Medusa, Stheno
    7. Euryale 9. sentinels
gorilla ... 3. ape 4. thug 5. brute
    6. monkey 8. assassin
gorilla man ... 9. Du Chaillu (brought
    ape from Africa)
gormandizer ... 9. chowhound
    11. trencherman
gorse ... 5. furze 7. juniper
goshawk ... 5. Astur 6. tercel
gospel ... 5. faith, truth 6. belief 7. epistle,
    evangel 8. doctrine 9. orthodoxy,
    selection (Bib) 10. revelation 11. glad
    tidings 12. proclamation
Gospels (Four) ... 11. diatessaron
gossip ... 3. cat, eme, gup 4. chat, news,
    talk 5. on-dit 6. claver, gabble, norate,
    report, tattle 7. clatter 8. idle talk,
    quidnunc 9. chatterer 10. newsmonger,
    talebearer
gossoon ... 3. boy, lad (serving) 5. youth
    6. garçon

got ... see *get*
Gotham ... 9. Newcastle (Eng) 11. New York City
Gothamite ... 9. New Yorker
Gothic (pert to) ...
  alphabet .. 11. Moeso-Gothic
  architecture .. 6. French
  design .. 7. writing 12. architecture
  era .. 10. Middle Ages
  people .. 4. rude 5. Goths 6. fierce 7. Teutons
  printing type .. 5. Doric 9. square-cut
gouge ... 4. tool 5. cheat 6. chisel, groove 7. defraud, swindle 8. impostor 10. imposition
Gounod's opera ... 5. Faust
gourd ... 4. pepo 5. color, flask, melon 6. squash 8. calabash, cucurbit 9. Cucurbita 11. calabazella
gourmand ... 5. eater (luxurious) 6. taster 7. epicure, glutton, gourmet 10. fastidious, gluttonous, voluptuary 11. connoisseur
gourmet ... 7. epicure 8. gourmand 11. connoisseur
gout ... 4. clot, drop 6. blotch 7. disease 9. arthritis
govern ... 3. run 4. curb, lead, rein, rule 5. reign 6. bridle, direct, manage 7. conduct, control, preside 8. dominate, regulate, restrain 9. influence, supervise
governess ... 4. ayah 5. nurse 6. abbess, duenna 8. guardian 12. instructress
government ... 4. rule, sway 6. polity 7. control, regimen 10. management 12. jurisdiction 14. administration
government (pert to) ...
  absence of .. 6. acracy 7. anarchy
  centralized .. 12. totalitarian
  church .. 9. hierarchy 10. heirocracy
  science of .. 8. politics
  system .. 6. regime
government by ...
  church, clergy .. 9. theocracy 10. hierocracy
  few .. 9. oligarchy
  God .. 8. theonomy
  holy body .. 9. hagiarchy 10. hagiocracy
  law .. 9. nomocracy
  men .. 9. andocracy
  mob .. 10. ochlocracy
  no one .. 6. acracy
  rich .. 10. plutocracy
  seven .. 9. heptarchy
  six .. 12. sextumvirate
  slaves .. 10. doulocracy
  ten .. 8. decarchy (dekarchy)
  three .. 8. triarchy 11. triumvirate
  women .. 8. gynarchy 11. gynecocracy
  worst men .. 12. kakistocracy
governor ... 4. woon 5. chief, nabob, ruler 6. dynast, regent 7. alcalde, decarch (of 10 men), viceroy 8. decurion, director 9. mechanism 10. magistrate
gown ... 4. robe, toga 5. cloak, dress, frock 6. chiton, clothe, cyclas, invest, kimono, mantle 7. cassock, college, garment, matinee, soutane (Eccl), sultane 8. negligee, peignoir 9. nightgown
gozeli, gozili ... 10. gooseberry

gozzard ... 9. gooseherd
gra ... 4. love 5. agrah 6. liking 8. fondness 10. sweetheart
grab ... 3. nab 4. game (cards), take 5. grasp, seize 6. arrest, clutch, snatch, vessel
grabble ... 4. feel 5. grope 6. grovel, sprawl 7. harvest 11. appropriate
grace ... 4. fate, luck, note, tact 5. adorn, charm, favor, honor, mercy, title 6. beauty, become, bedeck, polish, prayer, virtue 7. dignify, enhance 8. clemency, easiness, elegance, kindness, reprieve 10. comeliness, refinement, seemliness 12. graciousness, thanksgiving
graceful ... 4. airy, easy, feat 6. comely, seemly 7. elegant, fitting, tactful 8. charming, debonair 9. beautiful, courteous, sylphlike 11. appropriate
Graces, The Three (Gr Myth) ... 5. Aegle (Mother) 6. Aglaia (Brilliance), Thalia (Bloom) 10. Euphrosyne (Joy)
gracile ... 4. slim, thin 6. slight 7. slender
gracious ... 4. kind 5. suave 6. benign, urbane 7. affable 8. generous 9. courteous, favorable
grackle ... 3. daw 4. bird, myna 7. jackdaw 9. blackbird
gradation ... 4. step 5. scale, steps 6. ablaut, nuance, series, stages 7. degrees 10. graduation, succession
grade ... 4. even, rank, rate, size, sort, step 5. level, order 6. assort, degree, school, smooth 7. arrange, incline 8. classify, gradient, graduate
gradual ... 4. easy, slow 6. gentle 9. leisurely
graduate ... 4. pass, size 5. grade, taper 6. alumna 7. alumnus, promote, student 8. shade off
graffito (scratched crudely) ... 7. drawing 10. scratching 11. inscription
Graf Spee blown up ... 7. Uruguay (1939)
graft ... 3. dig 4. cion (scion), join, toil, work 5. ditch, fraud, labor, spade, unite 6. boodle, fasten, inarch, trench 7. bribery, implant, joining
grafted (Her) ... 4. enté
Grail ... see *Holy Grail*
grain ... 3. jot, rye 4. atom, bran, corn, dram, food, grit, iota, malt, meal, mite, oats, rice, whit 5. fiber, maize, scrap, spark, trace, wheat 6. barley, millet, sesame 8. particle
grain (pert to) ...
  Bible .. 4. ador
  bundle .. 5. sheaf 7. sheaves
  chaff .. 4. bran, grit
  cracked .. 6. groats
  ear of .. 5. spike 6. ressum (rizzom)
  exchange (Finan) .. 3. pit
  feeding on .. 11. granivorous
  fungus, disease .. 4. rust, smut 5. ergot 6. mildew
  goddess of .. 5. Ceres
  ground .. 4. meal 5. flour, grist
  husks .. 4. bran 5. straw
  measure .. 6. thrave
  mill .. 5. quern

mixture.. 6. fodder 7. farrage
9. bullimong
small.. 7. granule
spike.. 3. ear 6. rizzom
stack.. 4. rick
storage, warehouse.. 3. mow 4. silo
5. hutch 8. elevator
grammar (pert to)... 5. parse 6. gender,
simile, syntax 7. diction, parsing,
prosody, synesis, wordage 8. enallage,
language, metaphor, paradigm
9. accidence, etymology, phonology
10. conformity, declension, inflection
11. conjugation
grammatical case... 6. dative
8. ablative, genitive, vocative
9. objective 10. accusative, nominative
grampus... 3. arc 4. orca 5. whale
6. killer 7. dolphin 8. cetacean
granada... 11. pomegranate
Granada Moorish Castle site...
8. Alhambra (Sp)
granary... 3. bin 6. grange 8. cornloft
10. repository, storehouse (grain)
grand... 4. epic 5. great, large, lofty,
money, noble, piano 6. august, epical,
famous, superb, swanky 7. eminent,
sublime 8. gorgeous, majestic, splendid,
thousand 9. dignified, grandiose,
important, sumptuous 11. illustrious,
magnificent
Grand Canyon State... 7. Arizona
grandchild... 2. oe, oy
grandchild, great... 5. ieroe
grandee... 7. magnate 8. nobleman
10. clarissimo
grandeur... 5. glory 7. dignity, majesty
8. elegance, eminence, vastness
9. greatness, immensity, sublimity
10. augustness 11. stateliness
grandeval... 4. aged 7. ancient
grandfather... 4. aiel (obs), avus
6. atavus 8. gudesire
grandiloquent... 5. grand, lofty 6. turgid
7. pompous 8. bombastic
12. magniloquent
grandiose... 4. epic 5. grand 6. turgid
8. imposing 9. bombastic, flaunting
12. ostentatious
Grandma Moses... 17. Anna Mary
Robertson
grandmother... 6. beldam (beldame),
granny, gudame 7. grandam
(grandame), grandma 8. babushka
grandparent (pert to)... 4. aval
grandson... 6. nepote
Grand Teton peak... 7. Wyoming
grange... 4. farm 7. granary 9. farmhouse
11. association (1867) 18. Patrons of
Husbandry
granite... 4. rock 5. stone 6. aplite,
marble, quartz 8. feldspar 9. pegmatite
Gran Quivira... 5. ruins (mission)
16. National Monument (N M)
grant... 4. cede, deed, enam, gift,
give, lend, loan, mise 5. admit, allow,
bonus, jagir (jaghar), spare 6. accord,
bestow, confer, demise, permit,
remise 7. appease, concede, confess,
subsidy 8. appanage, sanction, transfer
10. conveyance 11. acknowledge

granulated... 5. rough 6. coarse
7. grained 8. granular, hardened
12. crystallized
grape... 3. fox, uva 5. Tokay 6. Malaga,
Muscat 7. Catawba, Concord, Hamburg,
Mission, Niagara 8. Delaware, grenache,
Isabella, Thompson 9. Chasselas,
muscadine 10. sweetwater
11. scuppernong
grape (pert to)...
cluster.. 6. raceme
color.. 7. blue-red 9. cathedral
conserve.. 5. uvate
cultivation.. 11. viticulture
dried.. 4. pasa 6. raisin
family, genus.. 5. Vitus 8. Vitaceae
juice.. 4. dibs, must, sapa, stum
military.. 4. shot
pomace.. 4. marc, rape
preserve.. 7. raisine
residue.. 4. marc, rape 6. pomace
seed.. 6. acinus
sugar.. 7. maltose 8. dextrose
grapefruit... 6. pomelo 8. shaddock
12. Citrus Maxima
grapevine... 4. caro 5. rumor 6. canard,
report 8. maneuver (wrestling), pipeline
9. dance step 11. information,
underground
graph... 5. chart 7. contour, diagram,
drawing
graphic... 5. clear, drawn, vivid 7. written
8. engraved 9. pictorial 11. descriptive,
picturesque, significant
12. diagrammatic
grasp... 4. grip, hent (obs), hold,
take 5. catch, clasp, gripe, seize
6. clinch, clutch, gowpen (gowpin)
7. control 8. handgrip 9. apprehend
10. comprehend, understand
grasping... 4. avid 5. close 6. greedy
7. holding, miserly 8. covetous
9. rapacious 10. avaricious, prehensile
11. acquisitive 13. comprehending,
understanding
grass... 3. eel, hay, Poa, rye 4. cane, Coix,
crab, gama, herb, oats, reed, rice, rush,
tare, wire 5. ankee, Avena, Briza, brome,
chess, goose, grain, grama, hedge,
otate, spart, spear 6. bamboo, barley,
darnel, fescue, marram, millet, redtop,
sesame, switch 7. alfalfa, Bermuda,
buffalo, esparto, Hordeum, Poeceae,
timothy 8. mesquite 9. blue-grass,
Boutelous
grasshopper... 4. grig 6. cicada, locust
7. katydid
grassland... 3. lea, sod 4. mead, veld
(veldt) 5. llano, range, sward 7. pasture,
prairie, savanna (savannah)
grasslike plant... 5. sedge
grate... 3. rub 4. fret, grid, grit, rasp
5. annoy, chafe, grind 6. abrade, scrape
7. network 8. irritate
grateful... 7. cumshaw (beggar's
phrase), welcome 8. pleasing, thankful
10. gratifying 12. appreciative
gratification... 6. relish, reward
8. gratuity, pleasure 10. indulgence,
recompense
gratified... 4. glad 7. pleased

gratify . . . 5. favor, grace, humor 6. arride, foster, pamper, please 7. appease, delight, flatter, indulge, requite, satisfy 10. remunerate

grating . . 4. grid 5. grate, grill, harsh, raspy 6. grille 7. lattice, network 8. strident 9. partition 10. irritating 11. latticework 12. nerve-racking

gratis . . . 4. free 6. freely 9. on the cuff 10. for nothing, gratuitous, on the house 12. gratuitously

gratitude . . . 5. grace 6. praise, thanks 12. appreciation, gratefulness, thankfulness

gratuitous . . . 4. free 5. given 6. gratis, wanton 7. assumed 8. baseless, needless 9. voluntary 10. groundless 11. superfluous, unwarranted

gratuity . . . 3. fee, tip 4. dole, gift, give, vail 5. bonus, bribe 6. bounty 7. cumshaw, pension, present 9. baksheesh (bakshish), buonamano, lagniappe (lagnappe), pourboire

grave . . . 3. pit, urn 4. bier, tomb 5. fosse (foss), sober, staid 6. sedate, solemn, trench 7. earnest, engrave, serious 8. sermonic 9. important, momentous, ponderous, sculpture, sepulcher

grave (pert to) . . .
cloth . . 6. shroud 8. cerement 9. cerecloth
coffin . . 4. pall
comb form . . 5. serio
mound (anc) . . 6. barrow 7. hillock, tumulus
person . . 10. sobersides
robber . . 5. ghoul

gravel . . . 5. geest, grain, stone 6. baffle, defeat, refute 7. calculi, erratic (boulder), pebbles 10. meerschaum (color)

graven . . . 6. etched 7. infixed 8. engraved 10. sculptured

gravestone . . . 5. stele (stela) 6. cippus, marker, pillar 8. monument 9. tombstone 11. sarcophagus

gravitation . . 7. descent, gravity 10. attraction

gravity . . . 6. weight 7. dignity, sadness 8. enormity, grimness, sobriety 9. formality, solemnity 10. attraction, importance 11. earnestness, seriousness, weightiness 12. significance 13. momentousness

gravity law, discoverer . . . 6. Newton

gray, grey . . . 3. dim, old, sad 4. aged, dark, dull, gris, obex 5. dingy, hoary, polio (comb form), sober 6. animal (gray), dismal, somber 7. hueless, neutral, silvery 9. cheerless 10. achromatic

gray, grey (color) . . . 3. ash, bat, dun 4. ashy, dove, iron, lead, mole, zinc 5. acier, ashen, dusty, mouse, pearl, slate, smoke, steel, taupe 6. French, Oxford, Quaker, reseda, silver 7. cesious, dappled, grizzle 8. charcoal, cinereal, gunmetal 10. battleship, dapple-gray 11. pepper-and-salt

graze . . . 3. eat, rub 4. drab, rase, skim 5. brush, shave 6. browse, feed on, scrape 7. scratch

grease . . . 3. fat, oil, tip 4. daub, lard, mort, saim, soil 5. bribe, smear, suint 6. axunge 7. fatness, fawning, lanolin 8. flattery 9. lubricate

greasy . . . 4. oily 5. dirty, gross, thick 6. smooth 8. slippery, unctuous 10. indelicate

great . . . 3. big 4. good, huge, vast 5. ample, chief, large, major, stout, whole 6. famous, grande 7. drastic, eminent, extreme 8. intimate, numerous 9. elaborate, important 11. magnanimous 12. considerable 13. distinguished

great (comb form) . . . 5. macro, megal

Great (pert to) . . .
Barrier (NZ) . . 4. Otea (Isl) 9. coral reef
Beyond . . 5. grave 9. afterlife, hereafter 10. after world, The Unknown 11. eternal home 14. beyond the grave
Cham of Literature . . 13. Samuel Johnson (Dr)
Circle sailing . . 10. orthodromy
Commoner . . 4. Clay, Pitt 7. Stevens (Thaddeus) 9. Gladstone
Divide . . 7. Rockies 8. Rocky Mts 9. watershed (US) 14. Rocky Mountains 17. Continental Divide
Fire . . 6. London (1666) 7. Chicago (1871)
Lakes . . 4. Erie 5. Huron 7. Ontario 8. Michigan, Superior
Mogul . . 5. Akbar (Hind) 7. diamond
Names . . 6. Hector 8. Hercules, Lysander 9. Alexander
Pyramid . . 6. Cheops
Spirit (Ind) . . 4. Mana, Zemi 5. Wakan 6. Manito (orenda), Pokunt
White Way . . 8. Broadway (NY)

Great Britain . . . 5. Wales 7. England 8. Scotland 12. Commonwealth 13. United Kingdom 15. Northern Ireland

greatest . . . 6. utmost 7. extreme, noblest

greatness . . . 9. largeness 10. importance 11. magnanimity

Greco, Graeco (comb form) . . . 5. Greek 7. Grecian

Greece . . . see also *Greek*
ancient . . 4. Elis 5. Argos, Doris, Ionia 6. Attica, Epirus, Hellas 7. Argolis, Boeotia 8. Thessaly
cape . . 5. Melea 7. Matapan
capital . . 4. Elis (anc) 6. Athens
citadel . . 9. Acropolis
city . . 6. Patras, Sparta 7. Corinth, Piraeus 8. Salonika
island . . 5. Chios, Corfu, Crete, Samos 6. Ithaca, Lesbos, Patmos, Rhodes 10. Dodecanese (group), Samothrace
mountain . . 3. Ida 5. Athos 6. Peleon, Pindus 7. Olympus 9. Parnassus
peninsula . . 6. Balkan
river . . 4. Arta 7. Hellada 9. Archelous
sea . . 6. Aegean, Ionian
seaport . . 4. Enor, Volo 5. Corpu, Pylos 8. Salonika

Greek, Grecian (pert to) . . .
abbess . . 4. amma
alphabet . . see *Greek alphabet*
altar . . 7. eschara

architecture .. 5. Doric, Ionic 6. xystus
  (part) 10. Corinthian
assembly .. 4. pynx 5. agora
avenging spirit .. 3. Ate, Ker 6. Erinys
boat .. 6. caique
bowl (golden) .. 5. depas
breath .. 6. pneuma
chariot .. 4. biga
church section .. 6. andron, bemata
citadel .. 9. Acropolis
city (Greek for) .. 5. polis
commander (anc) .. 7. navarch
commune .. 4. deme, nome
contest .. 4. agon (anc) 6. Delian
  7. Pythian, Olympic 8. marathon
courtesan (Athen) .. 5. Thais
culture, literature .. 7. classic 9. classical
cup, bowl .. 5. depas 6. cotula
cupid .. 4. Eros
dance (anc) .. 6. hormos 7. pyrrhic,
  strophe 9. dithyramb
department .. 8. nomarchy
dessert .. 7. baklava
dish .. 8. moussaka 9. souvlakia
early .. 5. Arius 6. oecist
epic .. 5. Iliad 7. Odyssey
female worshipper .. 5. orant
garment .. 5. tunic 6. chiton, peplos
gravestone .. 5. stele
horse (talking) .. 5. Arion
hospitality .. 5. zenia
judge .. 6. dicast
language .. 6. Romaic
lawgiver .. 5. Minos, Solon
magistrate .. 6. archon, eparch
  7. nomarch
mistress .. 7. hetaera (hetaira)
monster .. 8. Minotaur, Typhoeus
  (100-headed)
note .. 4. nete 5. neume 6. pneuma
  9. hexachord 10. tetrachord
Old Testament .. 10. Septuagint
platform .. 4. bema 7. logeion
poem .. 5. Iliad 7. Odyssey
portico .. 5. stoa, xyst
sacred enclosure .. 5. sekos
sacred object .. 6. sacrum
sacrificial offering .. 6. hiera 8. sphagion
sandwich .. 4. gyro
school .. 7. Eleatic
serpent .. 4. seps 6. Python
slave .. 5. Baubo, helot, iambe 6. penest
soldier .. 7. hoplite
song .. 5. melos
sorceress .. 5. Circe
spirit .. 5. Momus (evil)
temple .. 4. naos 5. cella (part)
theater .. 5. odeon
war cry .. 5. alala
youth (would-be citizen) .. 7. ephebus
Greek alphabet ... 2. Mu, Nu, Pi, Xi
  3. Chi, Eta, Phi, Rho, Tau 4. Beta,
  Iota, Zeta 5. Alpha, Delta, Gamma,
  Kappa, Omega, Sigma, Theta 6. Lambda
  7. Digamma (obs), Epsilon, Omicron,
  Upsilon
Greek Furies ... 6. Alecto, Erinys
  7. Magaero 9. Tisiphone
Greek god of ...
  atmosphere .. 5. Hadad
  chief .. 4. Zeus

dreams .. 8. Morpheus
fire .. 6. Vulcan
flocks .. 3. Pan
heavens .. 6. Uranus
love .. 4. Eros
lower world .. 5. Hades
ridicule .. 5. Momus
river .. 8. Eridanus
sea .. 6. Nereus
storm .. 6. Teshup 7. Hittite
sun .. 6. Apollo, Helios 7. Phoebus
vegetation .. 8. Dionysus
war .. 4. Ares 8. Enyalius
winds .. 5. Eurus 6. Aeolus
youth .. 6. Apollo, Pothos (winged)
Greek goddess of ...
  agriculture .. 7. Artemis, Demeter
  beauty .. 9. Aphrodite
  chase .. 7. Artemis
  clouds .. 5. Niobe
  dawn .. 3. Eos 7. Alcmene, Ariadne
  discord .. 4. Eris
  earth .. 2. Ge 4. Gaea
  fate .. 5. Moira
  fortune .. 5. Tyche
  heaven .. 4. Hera
  infatuation .. 3. Ate
  magic .. 6. Hecate (3-headed)
  memory .. 9. Mnemosyne
  moon .. 2. Io 5. Diana 6. Selene
  nature .. 7. Artemis
  night .. 3. Nyx 4. Leto 6. Hecate
  peace .. 5. Irene
  phallus .. 5. Baubo
  retribution .. 7. Nemesis
  underworld .. 6. Hecate (Hekate)
  vengeance .. 3. Ara 7. Nemesis
  victory .. 4. Nike
  wisdom .. 6. Pallas 7. Minerva
  youth .. 4. Hebe
Greek Myth ...
  character .. 5. Niobe, Sinon 6. Adonis,
  Gorgon, Rhesus 7. Calchus, Icarius,
  Pandora, Phrixos 8. Atalanta,
  Endymion, Meleager, Tantalus
  12. Erichthonius
  deity .. 5. Satyr, Titan 6. Cronus
  enchantress .. 5. Circe, Medea
  giant .. 7. Antaeus 9. Enceladus
  (100-armed)
  huntress .. 8. Atalanta
  monster .. 8. Typhoeus (100-headed)
  nymph .. 5. Oread 6. Nereid
  serpent .. 6. Python
  spirit (evil) .. 5. Momus
Greek personalities ...
  astronomer .. 12. Eratosthenes
  biographer .. 8. Plutarch
  counselor .. 6. Nestor
  dramatist .. 9. Aeschylus, Euripides,
  Sophocles 12. Aristophanes
  fabulist .. 5. Aesop
  geographer .. 6. Strabo
  hero .. 4. Ajax 5. Talos 6. Nestor
  7. Cecrops, Theseus 8. Achilles,
  Odysseus 10. Hippolytus
  historian .. 8. Xenophon 9. Dionysius,
  Herodotus 10. Thucydides
  mathematician .. 6. Euclid
  10. Archimedes
  painter .. 7. Apelles

patriarch . . 5. Arius
philosopher . . 4. Zeno 5. Galen,
  Plato, Timon 6. Nestor 8. Diogenes,
  Epicurus 10. Aristotle 10. Heraclitus,
  Parmenides, Pythagorus, Xenophanes
  11. Anaximander
physician . . 5. Galen
poet . . 5. Arion, Homer 6. Hesiod, Pindar
  7. Thespis 8. Anacreon 9. Aeschylus
poetess . . 6. Erinna, Sappho 7. Corinna
sage . . 6. Thales
satirist . . 6. Lucian
sculptor . . 5. Myron 7. Phidias
statesman . . 8. Pericles 9. Aristides
green . . . 3. raw 4. vert 5. fresh, mossy
  6. callow, praseo (comb form), unripe
  7. emerald, verdant 8. malachite,
  unskilled, untrained 11. flourishing
  13. inexperienced 15. unsophisticated
green (pert to) . . .
  back . . 4. frog 11. legal tender (US)
  blue . . 4. cyan, saxe 7. sistine
  comb form . . 6. praseo
  eyed . . 7. jealous
  famous . . 6. Gretna (Scot)
  film . . 6. patina
  gray . . 5. olive 6. reseda
  pale . . 7. celadon
  pigment . . 10. terre-verte
  quartz . . 5. prase
  sickness . . 9. chlorosis
  tea . . 5. Hyson
green-back herring . . . 5. cisco
Greenland . . .
  Bay . . 6. Baffin
  capital . . 8. Godthaab
  Danish word . . 8. Crönland
  explorer . . 9. Frobisher (1576) 10. Eric
    the Red
  natives . . 6. Eskimo (mostly)
  settlement . . 4. Etah
  strait . . 5. Davis
  whale . . 5. right
Green Mt Boys' leader . . . 10. Ethan
  Allen (1775)
Green Mt State . . . 7. Vermont
greenness . . . 5. color 8. sourness
  9. ignorance 10. immaturity
  11. gullibility 12. inexperience
Greenwich time (London) . . . 8. absolute,
  standard 16. Royal Observatory
Greenwich Village . . . 9. Manhattan
  11. New York City
greeting . . . 3. ave, how 4. hail 5. hallo
  6. accoil, halloa, salute 7. address,
  welcome 8. saluting 9. reception
  10. compliment, salutation
  14. correspondence
gregarious . . . 6. common, social
  7. affable 8. sociable 12. social-minded
  13. communicative
grego . . . 5. cloak 6. jacket 9. greatcoat
Gregory . . . 4. Code (Rom law), Pope,
  year 5. chant, staff (Mus) 6. church
  8. calendar
grenier . . . 5. attic
grey . . . see *gray*
grid . . . 5. grill 7. grating, griddle, network
  8. gridiron 13. football field
grief . . . 3. rue, woe 4. care, pain,
  ruth 5. abuse, dolor, trial 6. mishap,

sorrow 7. anguish, offense, remorse,
  sadness 8. disaster, distress, document
  9. grievance, suffering 10. affliction
  11. bereavement, lamentation
grieve . . . 3. cry, rue 4. erme, pain
  5. mourn, wound 6. lament, sorrow
  7. afflict 8. complain, distress
  10. discomfort
grievous . . . 4. sore 6. bitter, severe
  7. doleful, heinous, intense 8. terrible
  9. sorrowful 10. disastrous, oppressive
  11. distressing, gravaminous
griff . . . 4. claw, glen 6. griffe, ravine
griffe . . . 4. spur (Arch) 7. mulatto
griffin, griffon . . . 6. charge (Her)
  7. monster 10. decoration
grig . . . 3. eel 5. annoy, dwarf 7. cricket,
  heather 8. irritate 9. tantalize
  11. grasshopper
grill . . . 4. cook 5. broil 7. griddle, network,
  torture 8. gridiron 10. restaurant
  11. interrogate 12. cross-examine
grille . . . 6. window (ticket) 7. grating,
  network
grilse . . . 6. salmon 7. botcher
grim . . . 4. dour, sour 5. gaunt, harsh,
  stern 6. grisly, horrid, savage, sullen
  7. ghastly, hideous 8. horrible, pitiless,
  ruthless, sinister 9. ferocious, frightful,
  merciless, repellent 10. forbidding,
  inexorable, relentless, unyielding
grimace . . . 3. mop, mow, mug 4. face,
  mock, moue, pout, sham 8. pretense
  10. distortion 11. affectation
grimalkin . . . 3. cat 5. vixen 6. feline
  8. old woman
grime . . . 4. dirt, smut, soot 5. sully
  9. blackness
grin . . . 5. fleer, smile, smirk
grind . . . 3. dig, rub, vex 4. bray, grit,
  mull, whet 5. crush, gnash, grate,
  study 6. abrade, drudge, harass,
  polish, powder, satire, school, squash
  7. operate, routine, sharpen 8. drudgery
  9. comminute, masticate, pulverize,
  triturate
grinder . . . 5. molar, tooth, tutor
  8. sideshow 9. announcer 10. flycatcher,
  goatsucker
grinding . . . 6. boning 7. grating
  9. attrition 10. burdensome, irritating,
  tyrannical 12. excruciating
grinding (pert to) . . .
  mental . . 6. boning 8. cramming,
    studying
  stone . . 4. mano 6. metate, muller
    9. millstone
  substance . . 5. emery 8. abrasive
gringo . . . 5. alien 8. American 9. foreigner
  10. Englishman
grip . . . 3. bag 4. hold 5. clasp, cleat,
  ditch, drain, grasp, seize, spasm
  6. clench, clutch, furrow, grippe, handle,
  obsess, trench, valise 7. control, illness
  8. gripsack, handfast
gripe . . . 4. grip, hold, pain 5. annoy,
  brake, colic, grasp, pinch, spasm
  6. clutch, harass 7. afflict, control,
  mastery, vulture 8. complain, distress
  9. complaint 10. affliction, oppression
griskin . . . 4. chop, loin 5. steak

grisly . . . 4. grim 5. harsh 7. ghastly, hideous 8. gruesome, terrible 9. deathlike 10. forbidding

grist . . . 3. lot 4. malt 5. grain, grind 8. quantity (bees)

grit . . . 4. sand 5. nerve, pluck 6. gravel 7. bravery, courage, Liberal 9. sandstone 11. persistence 12. perseverance

grivet . . . 4. tota, waag 6. monkey

grizzly bear . . . 7. Ephraim (hunter's) 15. Ursus horribilis

groats . . . 5. grain, wheat (cracked) 6. cereal

grog . . . 3. rum 5. rumbo 8. beverage 9. firewater

groggy . . . 5. dazed, drunk, shaky, tipsy 8. unsteady, wavering 9. tottering

groin . . . 4. lisk 6. inguen

groom . . . 4. syce, tidy 5. brush, curry, dress, preen, train 7. hostler, servant, shopboy 9. assistant, stableman 10. bridegroom, manservant

groove . . . 3. rut 4. dado 5. chase, croze, flute, scarf, stria, track 6. furrow, rabbet, raggle, scrobe, sulcus 7. channel, rifling, routine 8. philtrum 10. excavation 11. canaliculus

grooved . . . 6. fluted 7. striate, sulcate 11. canalicular 12. canaliculate

grope . . . 4. feel 6. fumble, search 7. grabble, grubble

groper . . . 4. fish 7. grouper

grosbeak . . . 5. finch 8. hawfinch

gros point . . . 4. lace (Venetian) 6. stitch (Aubusson) 8. tapestry (Gobelin) 11. cross-stitch

gross . . . 3. fat 5. obese 6. brutal, coarse, earthy, greasy, impure, vulgar 7. brutish, massive, obscene, sensual, witless 8. flagrant, indecent, receipts 9. aggregate, unrefined 10. indefinite, indelicate, scurrilous

grotesque . . . 3. odd 5. antic, clown, freak 6. unique 7. awkward, baroque, bizarre 8. deformed, fanciful 9. fantastic 11. incongruous

grotesque figure (Chin) . . . 5. magot

grotto . . . 3. den 4. blue, cave, grot 5. crypt, speos, vault 6. cavern, recess 8. catacomb

ground . . . 3. bog 4. acre, area, base, clay, clod, farm, land, moor, park, plot, root, soil 5. basis, cause, earth, field, hurst, marsh, ridge, solum, swale, train 6. belief, bottom, milled, region 7. country, gritted, opinion, premise, terrain (terrane) 8. initiate, instruct 9. establish, territory, viewpoint 10. background, foundation, substratum

ground (pert to) . . .
  beetles . . 5. Amara
  berry . . 9. cranberry 12. checkerberry
  grain . . 4. bran, meal 5. flour, grist
  nut . . 5. chufa, gobbe 6. goober, peanut
  squirrel . . 5. Xerus 6. gopher, hackee, rodent 8. chipmunk 11. spermophile

groundhog (pert to) . . .
  American . . 6. marmot
  day . . 9. Candlemas (Feb 2)
  home . . 8. Puxatori

termed . . 6. marmot, rodent 8. aardvark, whistler 9. woodchuck 10. whistlepig

groundless . . . 4. idle 5. false 8. baseless 9. unfounded 11. unwarranted 13. unsubstantial

grounds . . . 4. lees, park 5. basis, dregs 7. residue 8. scruples

group . . . 3. set 4. band, bevy, clan, crew, gang, herd, pack, sect, sept, team, unit 5. batch, bunch, class, clump, corps, flock, genus, order, panel, shift, tribe 6. legion, troupe 7. arrange, bracket, cluster, company, species 8. assemble, category, classify, division 10. assemblage 11. aggregation

group (pert to) . . .
  actors . . 6. troupe
  animal . . 3. gam (whales), pod (seals, whales) 4. herd, pack 5. drove, flock, pride (lions)
  beautiful women . . 4. bevy
  birds . . 4. bevy, nest, nide (pheasants) 5. covey (quail), flock 6. clutch (eggs), flight, gaggle (geese)
  celebrities . . 6. galaxy
  church . . 5. laity 6. clergy, parish 12. congregation
  fish . . 6. school
  followers . . 4. cult, sect
  insects . . 4. hive 5. swarm 6. colony
  musicians . . 3. duo 4. band, trio 5. combo, nonet (nonette), octet (octette) 7. septet (septette), sextet (sextette) 7. quartet (quartette), quintet (quintette) 9. orchestra
  offspring . . 5. brood 6. clutch, litter
  political . . 4. bloc, ring 5. junta, party 7. machine
  secret . . 5. cabal
  singers . . 3. duo 4. trio 5. choir 6. chorus 7. quartet (quartette)
  trees . . 4. tope 5. copse, grove, woods 7. alameda, orchard, pinetum (pines)
  witches . . 5. coven

group (quota of) . . .
  eight . . 5. octad, octet (octette)
  five . . 6. pentad 7. quintet (quintette)
  four . . 6. tetrad 7. quartet (quartette)
  nine . . 6. ennead
  seven . . 6. heptad, septet (septette)
  six . . 6. sextet (sextette)
  ten . . 6. decad 6. decade
  three . . 4. trio 5. triad, trine 7. Trinity
  two vowels . . 6. digram 7. digraph 9. diphthong

grouped . . . 7. classed 8. agminate, arranged, gathered 9. assembled, collected, organized 10. classified

grouper . . . 4. fish 5. guasa 6. groper 8. rock hind

grouse . . . 4. bird 6. repine 7. grumble 8. complain 9. ptarmigan 12. capercaillie

grouse (pert to) . . .
  courtship . . 3. lak
  red . . 7. Lagopus
  ruffed . . 6. Bonasa

grouty . . . 5. cross, sulky 6. crabby, grumpy 7. grouchy

grove (pert to) . . .
  living in . . 7. nemoral

mango . . 4. tope
pine . . 7. pinetum
poplar . . 7. alameda
sacred . . 5. Altis (Gr), Nemus (to Diana)
small trees . . 5. copse
grovel . . . 4. fawn, roll 5. crawl, creep
6. cringe, crouch, shrink, tumble,
wallow, welter 7. debauch, truckle
8. flounder
groveling, grovelling . . . 6. abject
7. fawning 9. prostrate, truckling
11. bootlicking
grow . . . 3. bud, wax 4. come 5. raise
6. accrue, expand, mature, thrive
7. augment, develop, enlarge, improve,
produce 8. increase, vegetate
9. cultivate
grow (pert to) . . .
dark . . 6. darkle
dim . . 5. blear
intense, profound . . 6. deepen
thin . . 8. emaciate
tiresome . . 4. bore, pall
together . . 7. accrete
worse . . 11. deteriorate
growing (pert to) . . .
angry . . 8. irascent
from without . . 9. ectogenic
10. ectogenous
in . . 6. linose
on trees . . 10. epidendral, epidendric
11. xylophilous (fungus)
out from . . 3. bud 4. stem 5. enate
6. sprout
spontaneously . . 9. adventive
together . . 7. accrete, joining 8. adhering
growing in . . .
clusters . . 8. racemose
fields . . 8. agrestal 9. agrestial
10. campestral
ground . . 9. geogenous
mud . . 9. uliginose
pairs . . 6. binate
rubbish . . 7. ruderal
snow . . 5. nival
water . . 7. aquatic
growl . . . 4. girn, gnar, rome 5. snarl
6. mutter 7. grumble 8. complain
growler . . . 3. cab, can 4. bass (black)
7. iceberg, pitcher 8. clarence
growth . . . 3. bud, wen 4. rise 5. felon,
shoot, tumor 6. effect, result 8. increase,
swelling 9. expansion 10. vegetation
11. consequence, development,
enlargement 12. augmentation
growth (pert to) . . .
from within . . 8. endogeny
from without . . 9. ectogenic
10. ectogenous
fungus . . 4. mold, moss 6. mildew
marine . . 7. seaweed
of wood . . 5. copse 7. coppice
9. brushwood
premature . . 9. precocity
process of . . 8. nascency
retarding . . 9. paratonic
grub . . . 3. dig 4. food, plod, root, spud
5. larva, mathe, slave, stump 6. assart,
drudge, maggot, search 7. plodder
8. victuals
grubby . . . 5. dirty, grimy, small

8. dwarfish, infested, slovenly, toadfish
grudge . . . 4. envy 5. covet, spite 6. hatred
7. grumble 8. begrudge 10. resentment
grudging spender . . . 8. tightwad
gruel . . . 4. diet 6. cereal, liquid 7. disable
8. porridge
grueling, gruelling . . . 6. trying
9. demanding, punishing, weakening
10. exhausting
gruesome . . . 4. ugly 6. grisly, horrid,
sordid 7. ghastly, hideous, macabre
9. deathlike
gruff . . . 4. deep, rude, sour 5. bluff,
harsh, surly 6. clumsy, hoarse, morose,
severe 7. austere, bearish, brusque
grum . . . 4. glum, sour 6. sullen 8. guttural
13. harsh-sounding
grumble . . . 4. fret, hone, kick 5. growl,
snarl 6. grouse, mumble, mutter, repine,
rumble 7. maunder 8. complain
guacharo . . . 6. owlish 7. oilbird
10. goatsucker
Guam . . .
capital . . 5. Agana
discoverer . . 8. Magellan (1521)
idol, fetish . . 5. anito
island . . 7. Mariana
mountain peak . . 6. Lamlam
port . . 4. Apra
guanaco . . . 5. llama (like) 6. alpaca
guarantee . . . 6. avouch, ensure, insure,
surety 7. endorse, promise, warrant
8. guaranty, security, warranty
9. agreement
guaranty . . . 4. bond 6. pledge 8. security,
warranty 9. agreement, assurance,
guarantee
guarapucu . . . 5. wahoo
guard . . . 3. van 4. care, curb, keep, tend,
tile 5. tiler, watch 6. bantay, bridle,
convoy, defend, escort, fender, gaoler,
jailer, keeper, patrol, picket, police,
sentry, shield, warden 7. defense,
protect 8. restrain, sentinel, watchman
9. attention, protector 10. cowcatcher,
precaution, protection
guarded . . . 4. wary 7. careful 8. cautious,
defended, discreet, vigilant, watchful
9. protected 10. restrained
11. circumspect, sentinelled
guardhouse . . . 4. brig
guardian . . . 5. angel, tutor 6. helper,
keeper, patron, warden 7. trustee
8. defender, tutelary 9. custodian,
protector 10. mystagogue (Church
relics)
guardian (Gr) . . . 5. Argus (100-eyed)
8. Cerberus (3-headed)
guardianship . . . 4. care 6. charge
7. custody, tuition 8. guidance, tutelage
13. protectorship
Guatemala . . .
ant . . 5. kelep
bird (sacred) . . 7. quetzal (quezal)
capital . . 13. Guatemala City
coin (gold) . . 7. quetzal
fruit (avocadolike) . . 4. anay
Indian people . . 4. Inca
port . . 7. San José 10. Champerico
13. Puerto Barrios
ruins . . 5. Mayan

volcano . . **4.** Agua **5.** Fuego

gudgeon . . . **4.** bait, dupe, goby **9.** killifish **10.** allurement

gue . . . **5.** rogue **7.** sharper

guenon . . . **6.** monkey (long-tailed)

guerdon . . . **5.** crown, prize **6.** reward **8.** requital **10.** recompense

guereza . . . **6.** monkey

Guernsey . . . **6.** brandy, cattle, Island (Channel) **7.** garment

guess . . . **5.** fancy, think **6.** divine **7.** imagine, presume, surmise, suspect **8.** estimate **10.** conjecture

guest . . . **6.** caller, inmate, lodger, patron **7.** visitor **9.** inquiline (insect)

Guiana . . .
  British capital . . **10.** Georgetown
  Dutch (Surinam) capital . . **10.** Paramaribo
  French capital . . **7.** Cayenne

guide . . . **3.** con, key **4.** clew, clue, lead, rein, sign, sley **5.** order, pilot, steer, teach, tutor, usher **6.** advise, beacon, direct, dirigo, govern, guidon **7.** adviser, conduct, courier, marshal **8.** Baedeker (book), cicerone, director, polestar, regulate **9.** regulator

Guido (scale) . . . **2.** ut **3.** alt, A re, B mi, E la (highest) **5.** E la mi, gamut **7.** alamire

guild . . . **5.** hanse **7.** society **10.** fellowship **11.** association, brotherhood

Guildhall statue (London) . . . **3.** Gog **5.** Magog (1708)

guile . . . **5.** craft **6.** deceit **9.** duplicity, falseness, treachery **11.** furtiveness

guileless . . . **5.** naive **6.** simple **7.** artless, natural, sincere **8.** innocent

guillemot . . . **3.** auk **4.** coot **5.** murre

guilt . . . **3.** sin **4.** sake **5.** culpa **8.** iniquity, peccancy **10.** guiltiness, wickedness **11.** criminality, culpability **14.** impeachability

guilty . . . **6.** nocent **8.** culpable

Guinea, W Afr . . .
  capital . . **7.** Conakry (Konakri)
  city . . **4.** Boke, Labe
  export . . **7.** bananas **10.** pineapples
  government . . **8.** republic
  mineral . . **4.** gold **7.** bauxite **8.** diamonds
  people . . **6.** Fullah **7.** Malinke, Soussou
  tree . . **4.** akee

guinea fowl . . . **3.** hen **4.** keet **6.** turkey **7.** pintado **8.** pheasant

guinea pig . . . **4.** boar, cavy **5.** Cavia **8.** capybara

guise . . . **3.** way **4.** form, garb, mask, mien, mode **5.** cloak, cover **6.** aspect, custom **7.** fashion, pretext **8.** behavior **9.** semblance **10.** appearance

guitar (pert to) . . .
  Hindu . . **4.** vina
  like . . **4.** lute **7.** bandore
  octaves . . **5.** three
  Oriental . . **5.** sitar
  pitch (term) . . **5.** dital
  ridge . . **7.** samisen
  small . . **7.** ukulele

gula . . . **4.** cyma, neck, ogee **6.** gullet **7.** cavetto, molding

gulch . . . **5.** cleft, gorge **6.** arroyo, coulee, ravine

gulf . . . **3.** bay, pit, sea (landlocked) **4.** eddy **5.** abyss, basin, chasm, cleft, inlet **6.** vorago **7.** opening **9.** whirlpool **10.** separation (wide)

gull . . . **4.** dupe, fool, gray **5.** brick, cheat, cully, fraud **7.** cheater, deceive, defraud, mislead **8.** impostor

gull (bird) . . . **3.** cob (cobb), mew **4.** Lari, pirr, skua, tern, Xema **5.** pewit (laughing) **7.** Larinae **8.** seedbird **9.** kittiwake

gullet . . . **3.** maw **4.** tube **5.** gully **6.** throat **7.** channel, harness (part) **9.** esophagus

gullible one . . . **4.** dupe, fool **8.** easy mark

Gulliver, Lemuel (pert to) . . .
  brutes . . **6.** Yahoos (race of)
  character, story by . . **5.** Swift
  voyage . . **6.** Laputa **8.** Lilliput **9.** Houyhnhnm **11.** Brobdingnag

gully . . . **3.** gut **4.** wadi (wady) **5.** drain, gorge, gulch **6.** arroyo, gutter, ravine **7.** couloir **11.** watercourse

gum . . . **3.** ase **4.** chew, lerp (larp, laarp) **5.** elemi, myrrh, xylan **6.** acacia, arabic, chicle, conima, thwart, tupelo **7.** camphor, deceive, elastic, gingiva **8.** bdellium (Bib), mucilage **12.** frankincense

gum (pert to) . . .
  Africa . . **4.** kino **7.** catechy
  Asia . . **6.** Storax **8.** galbabum
  Australia . . **5.** tuart
  Central America . . **6.** chicle
  Egypt . . **5.** kikar
  India . . **5.** amrad
  Philippines . . **8.** galagala
  United States . . **5.** Nyssa **6.** tupelo

gumbo . . . **3.** mud **4.** okra (ocra), sail, soup **6.** patois

gumboil . . . **7.** abscess, parulia

gummy . . . **5.** lumpy **6.** viscid **7.** viscous **8.** adhesive, resinous

gumption . . . **8.** sagacity **10.** enterprise, initiative, shrewdness

gums . . . **3.** ula **6.** resins **8.** gingivae

gun . . . **3.** gat, rod **4.** iron, pump, roer **5.** Maxim, rifle, thief, tommy **6.** ack-ack, Archie, barker, Bertha, cannon, mortar, pistol, Rodman **7.** bazooka, carbine, firearm, Gatling, machine, shotgun **8.** amusette, ordnance, revolver

gun (pert to) . . .
  blow . . **8.** sumpitan
  caliber . . **4.** bore
  case (leather) . . **7.** holster
  chamber . . **5.** gomer
  cleaner . . **6.** ramrod
  cotton . . **5.** nitro **9.** explosive, pyroxylin
  mount . . **6.** turret
  platform . . **11.** emplacement

gunfire . . . **5.** salvo **6.** strafe **8.** enfilade

gunner . . . **10.** bombardier **12.** artilleryman

guppy . . . **6.** minnow **8.** Lebistes **9.** killifish

gurnard . . . **4.** fish **6.** rochet, Trigla **8.** dragonet, sea robin

guru (Ind) . . . **7.** teacher

gush . . . **3.** jet **4.** flow, pour, spew **5.** emote, spurt **7.** chatter **10.** outpouring **14.** sentimentalize

gushing . . . **7.** flowing **8.** diffused, effusive,

spurting 9. exuberant 11. sentimental 13. demonstrative

gusset ... 4. gore 7. bracket 9. abatement (Her)

gust ... 4. blow, gale, scud, wind 5. berry, blast, storm 6. flurry, squall 8. outburst 10. excitement

gusto ... 4. élan, zest 5. savor, taste 6. fervor, liking, relish 9. eagerness 12. appreciation

gut ... 3. sac (silkworm) 5. gully 6. bowels, catgut, defile, strait 7. destroy, plunder 8. entrails 9. intestine 10. disembowel, eviscerate

guts ... 5. belly, force, pluck 6. vitals 7. courage, insides, stamina, stomach 8. backbone, gluttony 10. intestines

gutta ... 4. drop, spot 5. latex 7. campana, marking 8. ornament

guttate ... 7. spotted 8. droplike

gutter ... 4. rone 5. brook, ditch, drain, eaves, gully, siver 6. cullis, groove 7. channel, conduit, scupper 11. watercourse

gutteral ... 3. dry 4. burr 5. husky, velar 6. hoarse 7. rasping, throaty

guttersnipe ... 4. Arab 5. gamin 6. poster 9. ragpicker, sandpiper, vulgarian

guy ... 3. rod 4. flee, rope, stay, vang 5. chaff, chain, guide 6. banter,

decamp, effigy (Guy Fawkes), fellow, person

Guy Fawkes Day ... 13. Gunpowder Plot (Eng, Nov 5, 1605)

guzzle ... 3. tun 4. tope 5. drain, drink, spree 6. gutter, liquor, throat, tipple 7. debauch, swallow

gymnast ... 7. acrobat, athlete, teacher

gymnastics ... 9. exercises 10. acrobatics 12. calisthenics

gypsy (pert to) ...
book .. 3. lil
devil .. 5. theng
Dutch .. 8. Heidenen
horse .. 3. gri (gry)
Hungarian .. 7. Czigany
husband .. 3. rom
India .. 7. Bazigar
language .. 6. Romany
man .. 4. chal
sea .. 6. Selung
Spanish .. 5. gitano 7. Zincalo
Syrian .. 5. Aptal
term .. 4. calo 5. nomad
woman .. 4. chai (chi)

gyrate ... 4. spin 5. twirl, whirl 6. rotate 7. revolve

gyre ... 5. demon, whirl 10. revolution

gyves ... 5. irons 6. chains 7. fetters 8. shackles

H

H ... 5. aitch, zygal (shaped) 6. letter (8th), symbol 8. aspirate

haab ... 8. calendar (Mayan)

haar ... 3. fog

haba ... 4. bean 8. lima bean

Habakkuk ... 4. Book (Old Test) 7. prophet

habble ... 5. brawl 6. gabble, hobble, uproar 9. confusion 10. difficulty

habeas corpus ... 4. writ 7. summons (you have the body)

habile ... 3. apt, fit 4. able 6. adroit, clever, expert 8. skillful (skilful), suitable 9. dexterous

habiliment ... 4. garb 5. dress, habit 6. attire 7. apparel, costume, raiment 8. clothing, vestment 11. furnishings

habilitate ... 5. dress, equip 6. clothe, fit out 7. entitle, quality (for teaching)

habit ... 3. rut, use 4. garb, suit, vice, wont 5. array, dress, haunt, usage 6. attire, clothe, custom, joseph (riding), nature 7. costume 8. clothing, habitude, practice 9. mannerism 10. deportment, habiliment

habitat ... 4. home 5. abode, house, hovel 6. harbor, reside 7. exhibit (museum), lodging, station

habitation ... 4. ecad, home 5. hovel 6. ghetto, warren (rabbit) 7. lodging 8. domicile, dwelling, tenement 9. occupancy, residence

habitual ... 5. usual 6. common, wonted

7. orderly, regular 9. customary 10. accustomed, inveterate

habituate ... 5. enure, inure 6. addict, inborn, season, settle 8. accustom, frequent, inherent 9. acclimate 11. acclimatize, familiarize

habitué ... 8. attender 10. frequenter

hacendero ... 6. farmer 10. proprietor

hache ... 2. ax 7. hatchet

hacienda ... 4. farm 5. abode, croft 6. estate 7. revenue 13. establishment

hack ... 3. cut, hew 4. chop, jade, rent 5. coach, cough, devil, horse (rented), sever 6. drudge, mangle, mutilate 8. carriage, mutilate 9. mercenary 11. chronometer

hackberry ... 6. Celtis 8. hapberry, oneberry 10. sugarberry

hackee ... 8. chipmunk

hackle ... 3. fly (angling) 4. comb, hack 6. shiner, temper 7. feather, hatchel, plumage 11. stickleback

hackneyed ... 3. saw 5. banal, corny, stale, trite 6. cliché 8. timeworn 10. threadbare 11. commonplace, stereotyped 13. platitudinous

Hades ... 3. pit 4. hell 5. abyss, limbo 7. inferno 9. perdition 10. lower world, underworld 11. netherworld

Hades (pert to) ...
Babylonian .. 5. Aralu
capital .. 11. Pandemonium
ferryman .. 6. Charon

god .. 5. Pluto
guide .. 6. Hermes
Hebrew .. 5. Sheol 7. Abaddon, Gehenna 8. Apollyon
Hindu .. 6. Naraka
mother .. 4. Rhea
region, lowest .. 8. Tartarus
river .. 4. Styx 5. Lethe 7. Acheron
Roman .. 3. Dis 5. Orcus
hadj, hajj ... 10. pilgrimage (Mecca)
haft ... 4. ansa, grip, hold 6. handle 8. dwelling
hag ... 4. Fury, goad 5. crone, ghost, Harpy, vixen, witch 6. beldam (beldame), goblin 8. harridan, old woman 9. hobgoblin
hageen, hagein ... 9. dromedary
hagfish ... 5. borer 6. Mysine 7. lamprey (lowest existing craniate vertebrate)
haggard ... 4. bony, lank, lean, pale, thin, wild 5. gaunt, spare 6. wanton 7. anxious, untamed 8. harrowed, unchaste, wild-eyed 9. deathlike, suffering, untrained 10. cadaverous 11. intractable, overwrought
haggle ... 3. cut, hew 4. hack, prig 5. cavil 6. chisel, dicker, higgle, palter 7. bargain, chaffer, stickle, wrangle
Hague, The ... 7. capital (Neth)
Haida (pert to) ...
famed for .. 6. totems 7. carving 10. seamanship
people .. 11. Skittagetan
hail ... 3. ave, ice 4. ahoy, call 5. avast, greet, skoal 6. accost, health, signal 7. acclaim, address, graupel, pellets
hair ... 3. cue, fur, mop 4. lock, mane, seta, shag 5. pilus, plume, tress 6. thread 7. bristle 8. filament 10. narrowness
hair (pert to) ...
accessory .. 3. net, pin 8. barrette
Angora .. 6. mohair
band .. 5. snood 6. fillet
braid .. 3. cue 4. fall 5. queue 7. pigtail
cell .. 12. Organ of Corti
cloth .. 3. aba 5. shirt 6. cilice
comb form .. 4. pilo
curly .. 10. cymotrichy
disease .. 8. dandruff, psilosis
dresser .. 7. friseur (Fr), stylist
dryness .. 7. xerasia
excessive growth .. 7. pilosis
flaxen .. 5. linus
horse's foot .. 7. fetlock
intestinal .. 6. villus
liquid for .. 3. set 5. spray 6. lotion 7. relaxer
lock .. 5. tress 7. earlock, ringlet 8. lovelock 9. dreadlock
loss of .. 8. alopecia, baldness
of the .. 6. crinal
remover .. 9. decalvant, epilatory 10. depilatory
straight .. 10. leiotrichy
style .. 4. set 4. Afro, tete, updo 6. hairdo 7. chignon, cornrow 8. coiffure
tuft .. 4. coma 5. beard 6. goatee 7. cirrose, Galways, Vandyke 8. whiskers 9. sideburns
wave .. 4. perm 6. marcel

wig .. 6. peruke 7. periwig
wooly .. 9. ulotrichy
hairiness ... 7. villous 9. villosity
hairless ... 4. bald 5. acoma 7. acomous, epilose 8. depilous, glabrous
hairpin ... 6. bodkin 8. bobby pin
hairsplitting ... 9. quibbling 11. distinction 13. hypercritical 14. hypercriticism, overparticular
hairy ... 4. noil 5. pilar 6. comate, comoid, comose, crinal, pilose, shaggy 7. bristly, crinose, hirsute 8. trichoid
Haiti, Haitian ...
bandit .. 4. caco
capital .. 12. Port-au-Prince
dance .. 5. mambo
dictator .. 7. Papa Doc 8. Duvalier
discoverer .. 8. Columbus (1492)
evil spirit .. 4. baka (boko)
island .. 10. Hispaniola 15. Greater Antilles
language .. 6. Creole, French, patois
liberator .. 9. Toussaint
product .. 6. coffee
sweet potato .. 6. batata
hake ... 4. fish 5. idler, tramp 6. loiter 7. handgun 8. kingfish
halberd ... 4. bill 5. frame (flogging) 6. glaive, weapon (Mil)
halcyon ... 4. bird, calm 8. peaceful, tranquil 10. auspicious, kingfisher
Halcyone (pert to) ...
changed to .. 10. kingfisher
daughter of .. 6. Aeolus
wife of .. 4. Ceyx (Gr)
hale ... 3. tug 4. drag, draw, haul, pull, well 6. hearty, robust, strong 7. healthy 8. vigorous 9. strapping
half ... 4. demi, hemi, part, semi, term 5. share 6. moiety 7. divided, partial 8. division, semester 9. equal part, bisection 11. imperfectly
half (pert to) ...
and half .. 5. equal, mixed 6. halved 7. neutral
boot .. 3. pac (pack) 6. buskin
man, half bull .. 8. minotaur
man, half horse .. 7. centaur
mask .. 6. domino
moon-shaped .. 9. semilunar
nelson (wrestling) .. 4. hold
stem to stern .. 8. midships
turn (manège) .. 8. caracole (caracol)
wit .. 4. dolt 5. dunce 9. blockhead
Half Moon ship (pert to) ...
captain .. 11. Henry Hudson
country .. 11. Netherlands
first to sail .. 11. Hudson River (1609)
Halicarnaseus, famed for ...
Historians (Gr) .. 9. Dionysius, Herodotus
monument .. 9. Mausoleum (Tomb of Mausolus, 325 BC)
hall ... 4. aula, room, sala 5. entry, foyer, odeum (odeon) 6. atrium, lyceum 7. hallway, passage, theater 8. corridor 9. vestibule 10. auditorium, passageway
hallow ... 5. bless 8. dedicate, sanctify, venerate 9. celebrate 10. consecrate
hallowed place ... 4. fane, holy 5. altar 6. bethel, church, shrine, temple 9. cathedral, synagogue

H

hallucination . . . 4. trip 6. mirage 7. chimera, fantasy 8. delusion 9. nightmare

hallucinogen . . . 3. LSD 4. acid 6. mescal, peyote 9. mescaline 10. psilocybin 12. lysergic acid

hallux . . . 3. toe 5. digit

halo . . . 3. arc 4. aura, glow, nimb, ring 5. glory, light 6. areola, brough, circle, corona, nimbus 7. aureole (aureola) 8. encircle, halation

halt . . . 3. end 4. camp, lame, limp, stop 5. cease, check, pause, stand 6. arrest, desist, hold up, maimed 7. limping 8. blockage, crippled, lameness 9. mutilated 10. standstill

halter . . . 4. hang, rope 5. noose, strap 6. hamper 7. shackle 8. cavesson, restrain 9. hackamore

halting . . . 4. lame 6. maimed 7. limping 8. spavined 10. hesitating, stammering

halting place . . . 4. camp 5. étape 7. bivouac 10. encampment

halved . . . 9. dimidiate

Hamburg, Germany . . .
color . . 5. white 6. yellow 7. carmine 11. carmine base
fowl . . 11. Leghornlike
fruit . . 5. grape
lace . . 6. edging
root (edible) . . 7. parsley
steak . . 4. beef

hamiform . . . 6. curved, hooked 7. hamulus 8. aquiline 10. hook-shaped

Hamilton (pert to) . . .
killed by . . 4. Burr
party . . 10. Federalist
secretary (lst) . . 8. Treasury

Hamite (No Afr) . . . 5. Fulah 6. Berber, Somali (Somal)

hamlet . . . 4. dorp, vill 5. aldea (aldee), casal (casale), thorp (thorpe) 7. grouper (fish), village

Hamlet (pert to) . . .
author . . 11. Shakespeare
country . . 7. Denmark
friend . . 7. Horatio
site . . 8. Elsinore

hammer . . . 4. beat, claw, jack, maul, peen, tack, tamp 5. gavel, kevel, madge, pound 6. beetle, martel, oliver, sledge, strike, swinge 7. belabor 8. malleate

hammer (pert to) . . .
bird . . 8. umbrette
blacksmith's . . 6. fuller, oliver
bricklayer's . . 6. scutch
end . . 4. poll
face . . 4. trip
head . . 4. peen 5. shark
medical . . 6. plexor 7. plessor
out . . 5. anvil, forge
smite . . 5. skite
stone . . 5. kevel, spall

hamper . . . 3. ped 4. clog, curb, load, slow 5. cramp, crate, maund 6. basket, burden, fetter, hinder, hopple, impede, seroon 7. confine, hanaper, manacle, shackle, trammel 8. encumber, restrain, restrict 9. container, embarrass 10. impediment

Ham's son . . . 4. Cush

hamster . . . 6. rodent 8. Cricetus

hamus . . . 4. hook 7. process (Zool)

hanaper . . . 6. basket, hamper

hand . . . 3. paw 4. fist, give, mano, palm, part, pass, side, till 5. claut, grasp, index, manus, power, share, skill 6. agency, worker 7. ability, pointer, workman 8. applause, tendency, transmit 9. craftsman, handiwork, signature 10. metacarpus 11. handwriting, performance 15. instrumentality

hand (pert to) . . .
back of . . 10. opisthenar
bag . . 4. etui, grip 5. cabas, purse 8. reticule
book . . 4. tome 5. codex 6. manual 9. vade mecum
cuffs . . 7. darbies 8. manacles 9. bracelets
handful . . 4. kirn 6. gowpen 7. maniple 8. quantity
measure . . 8. fistmele
me-down . . 4. used, worn 5. cheap 9. ready-made 10. secondhand
of the . . 6. chiral, manual
palm . . 4. loof 6. thenar
picked . . 5. eleme 6. choice 8. selected
script . . 6. Neskhi (Neski)
stone (grinding) . . 4. mano
without . . 7. amanous
writing . . 11. chirography
writing on walls . . 4. doom, mene (Bib), omen 8. graffito

handicap . . . 3. lisp, race 6. burden, hamper, hinder, impede 8. encumber, equalize, penalize 9. advantage 10. impediment, stuttering 11. encumbrance 12. disadvantage

handicraftsman . . . 7. artisan

handkerchief . . . 7. malabar 8. mouchoir 9. neckcloth 11. neckerchief

handle . . . 3. ear, paw, ply, use 4. ansa, bail, deal, feel, haft, hilt, knob, maul, name, toat, tote 5. helve, pilot, snath, swipe, title, touch, treat, wield 6. deal in, direct, manage, rounce, second, sneath, tiller 7. control, operate

handle (pert to) . . .
awkwardly . . 6. fumble, mumble
carelessly . . 6. cajole 7. tweedle
roughly . . 4. maul 6. bruise, injure, mangle
shaped . . 6. ansate
skillfully . . 6. manage 7. control 10. manipulate

hands (pert to) . . .
nautical . . 4. crew, gang
off . . 4. don't, quit, stop 5. taboo 6. desist 9. interdict
on hips . . 6. akimbo
without . . 7. amanous

handsome . . . 5. ample 6. comely, heppen (dial) 7. elegant, gallant, liberal 8. generous, gracious, pleasing, suitable 9. agreeable, beautiful 10. jimpricute 11. appropriate, magnanimous 12. considerable

handwriting on the wall . . . 4. mene (Bib) 8. graffito, upharsin

handy . . . 4. deft 5. adept, ready

6. adroit, heppen, nearby, wieldy
8. skillful (skilful) 9. dexterous, versatile
10. accessible, convenient
hang ... 3. sag 4. pend, rest, sway 5. cling,
drape, droop, hover, knack 6. cleave,
dangle, depend 7. execute, meaning,
suspend
hang (pert to) ...
around .. 4. loaf, wait 6. loiter 8. frequent
back .. 3. lag 5. demur, loath 6. falter
9. reluctant
down .. 3. lop 4. lave 5. droop 6. depend
loosely .. 3. lop 4. flag, loll 6. bangle,
dangle
on, onto .. 5. cling 6. adhere, depend
9. persevere
over .. 6. impend
together .. 4. loin 6. cohere 9. co-operate
hanger-on ... 3. bur 5. toady 6. heeler
8. follower, loiterer, parasite
9. appendage, dependent, sycophant,
toadeater (menial) 10. blackguard
hanging ... 5. arras, drape, loose
7. curtain, pendant (pendent), pensile,
valance 8. downcast, pendency
9. execution, suspended
hanging (pert to) ...
Eccl .. 6. dorsal, dossal (dossel)
Gardens of Babylon, builder ..
14. Nebuchadnezzar (Nebuchadrezzar)
ornament .. 6. bangle 7. pendant
stage .. 7. scenery
hangmen ... 8. carnifex 9. Jack Ketch
11. executioner
hangman's noose ... 4. rope 6. hempen
hangnail ... 6. agnail 7. whitlow
hangout ... 5. joint 10. rendezvous
hank ... 3. ran (twine) 4. coil 5. skein
hanker after ... 5. crave, yearn 6. aspire,
desire, hunger 7. long for
Hannibal (pert to) ...
accomplishment .. 8. Punic War (2nd)
father .. 13. Hamilcar Barca
native of .. 8. Carthage
rank .. 7. General (genius)
victory at .. 8. Cannae
Hanover, House of ... 8. Victoria
Hanukkah, Hanukka ... 7. holiday (Jew)
16. Festival of Lights (Bib) 17. Feast
of Dedication (Jew)
haphazard ... 6. chance, random
8. accident, careless 9. orderless
haply ... 9. perchance
happen ... 4. come, fall, fare 5. evene
(obs), occur 6. arrive, befall, betide,
chance, mayhap 9. eventuate, transpire
happening ... 4. fact 5. event (chance)
6. tiding 7. episode 8. incident, periodic,
sporadic 10. occurrence
happily ... 5. fitly, haply 6. gladly
9. tactfully, willingly 10. blissfully,
cheerfully, gracefully 11. contentedly,
opportunely 12. auspiciously,
felicitously, prosperously, successfully
13. appropriately
happiness, science of ...
11. eudaemonics
happy ... 3. apt 4. cosh, glad 5. blest,
faust, lucky, ready, seely, sunny
6. joyful, timely 7. blessed, content,
fitting 8. cheerful 9. contented,

fortunate, pertinent 10. auspicious,
felicitous, propitious, prosperous
Happy Valley ... 8. paradise (of Rasselas,
Andrew Jackson)
hara-kiri (Jap) ... 7. seppuku, suicide
harangue ... 3. nag 4. rant 5. orate,
spiel, spout 6. screed, speech, tirade
7. address, declaim, expound, lecture,
oration
harass ... 3. din, fag, nag, try, vex
4. bait, fret, gall, haze, jade, raid, tire
5. annoy, beset, bully, chafe, grind,
harry, tease, weary, worry 6. badger,
bother, heckle, hector, molest, pester,
plague 7. agitate, disturb, hagride,
perplex, provoke, torment, trouble
8. distress, irritate 9. persecute, tantalize
harbinger ... 4. host, omen 5. usher
6. herald 7. presage, shelter 8. fourrier,
harborer 9. informant, messenger,
precursor 10. forerunner
harbinger of Spring ... 5. robin, tulip
6. crocus
harbor, harbour ... 3. bay 4. cave,
port 5. haven 6. covert, foster, refuge
7. lodging, outpost, retreat, shelter
hard ... 3. fit 4. cold, dour, firm, iron,
mean 5. close, harsh, rigid, stern, stony
6. knotty, robust, steely, stingy, strict,
strong 7. callous, onerous 8. diligent,
rigorous, toilsome 9. difficult, heartless,
intricate, strenuous, stringent,
wearisome 10. inflexible, relentless,
unyielding 12. impenetrable,
incorrigible 13. unsympathetic
hard (pert to) ...
boiled .. 4. hard 5. tough 6. strict
7. callous 8. hardened 10. solidified
13. sophisticated
coal .. 10. anthracite
money .. 6. silver 8. metallic
prefix .. 3. dys
question .. 5. poser
rubber .. 7. ebonite 9. vulcanite
shell .. 6. lorica
stone .. 7. adamant (diamond)
wood .. 4. mabi, teak 5. maple 6. walnut
8. mahogany
harden ... 3. gel, set 4. cake, kern
5. enure, inure, steel 6. freeze, ossify,
temper 7. toughen 8. indurate, solidify
9. habituate 10. strengthen
hardened ... 4. hard 5. caked 6. frozen,
wicked 7. callous, steeled 8. indurate,
obdurate, ossified 9. heartless,
reprobate, unfeeling 10. impenitent,
impervious, inveterate, solidified
12. impenetrable
hardening of the arteries ...
16. arteriosclerosis
hardening of the eyeball ... 8. glaucoma
hardheaded ... 6. shrewd, strict
9. obstinate, sagacious
hardhearted ... 4. mean 5. cruel
7. callous 8. pitiless 9. unfeeling
13. unsympathetic
hardship ... 5. rigor 6. injury 7. trouble
8. hardness 9. adversity, privation
hardtack ... 5. bread 7. galette 10. sea
biscuit
hardwood ... 3. ash, oak 4. ipil, mabi,

teak 5. maple 6. walnut 8. mahogany

hardy ... 4. bold, hale, rash 5. brave, lusty, stout 6. daring, strong 7. healthy, spartan 8. intrepid, resolute 9. audacious, confident 10. courageous

Hardy heroine ... 4. Tess

hare ... 3. doe, wat (watt) 4. buck, cony, pika (tailless) 5. lapin, Lepus 6. rabbit, rodent, tapeti 7. leveret

hare (pert to) ...
constellation .. 5. Lepus
harelike .. 6. agouti 8. leporine
tail .. 4. scut
track .. 4. slot
type .. 10. cottontail, jack rabbit

harem ... 5. serai 6. purdah, zenana 8. seraglio 9. gynaeceum

harem room ... 3. oda (odah)

harem slave ... 9. odalisque (odalisk)

hark ... 4. heed, hist 6. listen 7. hearken, whisper 9. attention

harkened ... 5. heard 6. heeded 8. listened 9. hearkened

harlequin ... 4. duck (sea) 5. clown, color 7. buffoon 9. fantastic, trickster 11. masquerader 12. multi-colored, parti-colored

Harlequin (comedy) ... 11. pantomimist

harm ... 3. mar 4. bane, dere, evil, hurt, pain 5. grief, wrong 6. damage, impair, injure, injury, scathe (scath) sorrow 8. misfortune, wickedness 12. disadvantage

harmful ... 3. bad 4. evil, upas 6. nocent 7. baneful, hurtful, malefic, noisome, noxious 8. damaging, sinister 9. injurious 10. pernicious 11. deleterious, detrimental 12. insalubrious

harmless ... 5. seely 6. unhurt 8. dehorned, unharmed 9. innocuous, undamaged, uninjured 11. unoffending

harmonious ... 6. syntax 7. harmony, musical, orderly, spheral, tuneful 9. accordant, agreeable, congruous, consonant, eurythmic (eurhythmic), melodious 10. compatible, concordant, euphonious 11. conformable, symmetrical

harmonize ... 2. go 3. gee 4. tone 5. agree, blend, chime 6. attune 7. conform, consist 9. reconcile 10. correspond, symmetrize, sympathize

harmony ... 4. tone, tune 5. music, order, triad, unity 6. accord, cosmos, melody, unison 7. concord, euphony 8. symmetry 9. agreement, harmonics 10. conformity, consonance

harness ... 4. gear 5. armor, equip 6. graith, tackle 7. uniform 8. accouter, ornament 9. caparison, parachute

harness part ... 3. tug 4. hame, rein 5. trace 6. collar, halter, terret 7. apparel 8. hackamore 10. breastband, martingale

harp ... 4. arpa, koto, lyre, Lyra (Astron) 5. nanga 8. Irishman 11. clairschach

harp (pert to) ...
key .. 5. C Flat
octaves (number) .. 11. six and a half
pedals .. 5. seven

star .. 12. Harp of Arthur
strings .. 8. forty-six

harping ... 7. humdrum, tedious 9. iterating, repeating 11. repetitious

harpoon ... 5. spear 7. javelin 8. lily iron

harpsichord ... 6. spinet 8. clavecin 9. lyrichord 12. clavicembalo

harpy ... 3. bat 5. eagle, fiend 9. plunderer 12. extortionist

Harpy (Myth) ... 5. Aello, ghoul 7. Celaeno, monster (part bird, woman), Ocypete, Podarge (The Iliad)

harridan ... 3. hag 5. vixen, witch 6. virago 7. Jezebel 8. strumpet 9. termagant

harrier ... 3. dog 4. hawk 5. bully, hound 7. heckler 8. badgerer 9. tormentor

harrow ... 4. dish, pain 5. harry, herse (Hist), wound 7. oppress, torment, torture 8. distress, lacerate 9. cultivate, formation (geese), implement

harrowing ... 7. painful, racking, tilling 9. agonizing, torturous 11. cultivating, distressing 12. heart-rending

harry ... 3. vex 4. sack 5. annoy, hound, worry 6. harass, plague, ravage, ravish 7. agitate, besiege, pillage, plunder, violate 8. lay waste 9. persecute

Harry ... 5. Devil (Shaksp)

harsh ... 3. raw 4. dure, grim 5. acerb, acrid, asper, crude, gruff, raspy, stern, stiff 6. bitter, coarse, severe, unkind 7. drastic, painful, pungent, rasping 8. clashing, gutteral, jangling, rigorous, strident 9. inclement, offensive, repellent 10. discordant, relentless 11. acrimonious, disagreeing

harshness ... 5. rigor 7. raucity 8. acrimony, pungency, severity 9. gruffness 11. raucousness

hart ... 4. deer, stag 5. spade

hartebeast ... 4. asse, tora 5. caama (kaama) 6. lecama 7. bubalis 8. antelope 10. Alcelaphus

Harvard College honor ... 4. book 5. detur 12. let it be given

harvest ... 4. crop, gain, rabi, reap 5. fruit, yield 6. autumn, gather, reward 7. acquire, produce

harvest (pert to) ...
god .. 6. Cronus, Saturn
goddess .. 3. Ops 5. Ceres
home .. 4. kirn, mell 6. hockey
moon .. 4. full 15. autumnal equinox
second .. 9. aftermath
tick .. 6. acarid

hash ... 4. food 5. mince 6. jumble, medley, ragout 7. mixture 10. hodgepodge 11. gallimaufry, olla podrida

hashish ... 4. hemp 5. bhang (bang) 8. cannabis, narcotic

hassle ... 4. fray 5. brawl, melee

hasten ... 3. hie 4. scud, urge 5. amain, apace, hurry, scamp, speed 7. further 8. expedite 10. accelerate 11. precipitate

hastened ... 3. ran 4. hied, sped 5. raced 6. rushed 7. hurried, scooted 8. galloped 9. expedited 11. accelerated

12. precipitated

hasty ... 4. fast, rash 5. brash, eager,
fleet, quick, swift 6. speedy, sudden,
urgent 7. cursory, hurried 8. reckless
9. impetuous, impulsive, premature
11. expeditious, precipitate

hasty pudding ... 4. mush 9. stirabout

hat ... 3. fez, tam, top 4. felt, hood, silk
5. beret, derby, gibus, opera, straw,
terai, toque 6. bonnet, cloche, cocked,
fedora, Panama, sailor, topper, turban
7. chapeau, picture, pillbox, porkpie,
tricorn 8. sombrero 9. headdress,
sou'wester, stovepipe, ten-gallon
11. mortarboard 13. three-cornered

hat (pert to) ...
  antique .. 7. bycoket (bycocket), petasos
    (petasus)
  covering .. 8. havelock
  crown .. 4. poll
  defensive .. 4. coif
  Eccl .. 7. biretta 9. Cardinal's
  military .. 5. shako
  opera .. 4. tile 5. gibus 6. topper
  pess (the hat) .. 10. collection
  slang .. 4. plug 5. dicer
  stovepipe .. 8. caroline
  under one's .. 6. secret 9. to oneself

hatch ... 4. door, gate, line (art),
plot 5. breed 6. invent 7. concoct,
produce 8. contrive, hatchway, incubate
9. floodgate, originate 10. bring forth,
sluice gate

hatchet ... 2. ax (axe) 3. adz (adze)
4. mogo 8. tomahawk

hate ... 4. miso (comb form) 5. abhor,
odium 6. detest, hatred, loathe, rancor
7. despise, dislike 9. abominate,
antipathy

hateful ... 6. odious 7. heinous 8. terrible
9. abhorrent, execrable, invidious,
loathsome, malicious, obnoxious,
offensive, revolting 10. abominable,
detestable, disgusting 11. distasteful
12. disagreeable

hater of ...
  children .. 10. misopedist
  mankind .. 11. misanthrope
  marriage .. 10. misogynist
  mathematics .. 8. misomath
  newness .. 9. misoneist
  sights .. 11. misoscopist
  strangers .. 8. misoxene
  work .. 11. ergophobiac

hatred ... 5. odium 6. animus, enmity,
rancor 8. aversion, loathing
9. animosity, malignity 10. abhorrence,
repugnance 11. detestation,
malevolence

hatred of ...
  argument .. 8. misology
  change .. 9. misoneism
  children .. 9. misopedia
  God, gods .. 10. misotheism
  mankind .. 11. misanthropy
  marriage .. 8. misogamy
  strangers .. 9. misoxeny 10. xenophobia
  war .. 9. polemical 11. misopolemic
  wisdom .. 9. misosophy
  women .. 9. misogyny

hauberk ... 5. armor 9. habergeon

haughty ... 4. airy, bold, high 5. lofty,
noble, proud 6. snooty 7. fatuous,
stately 8. arrogant, cavalier, orgulous,
scornful 10. disdainful, hoity-toity
11. domineering, highfalutin
12. contemptuous, supercilious

haul ... 3. lug, tow, tug 4. cart, drag,
draw, pull 5. booty, bouse, catch,
check, shift 9. reprimand, transport

haul down a flag ... 6. strike

haunch ... 3. hip 4. huck 10. leg and
loin 12. hindquarters

haunch bone ... 10. innominate

haunt ... 3. den 4. dive, nest 5. ghost,
habit 6. infect, obsess, resort 7. torment
8. frequent, practice

hautboy ... 4. oboe

have ... 3. get, hae, own 4. hold, keep,
know 5. beget, trick 6. accept, effect,
retain 7. cherish, perform, possess,
swindle 10. experience, understand,
suffer from

have (pert to) ...
  ambition .. 6. aspire
  charge .. 4. tend
  on .. 4. wear
  thoughts of .. 6. ideate
  to do with .. 4. deal
  weight .. 8. militate

haven ... 3. bay 4. port 5. hithe (small),
inlet 6. asylum, harbor, recess, refuge
7. shelter 9. sanctuary

havier ... 4. deer

having (pert to) ...
  blind end .. 6. caecal
  branches .. 6. ramose
  clamp, pincers .. 7. chelate
  dignity .. 8. majestic
  equal sides .. 9. isosceles
  eyes .. 7. oculate
  faith .. 8. trusting
  featherlike petals .. 7. pinnate
  feelers .. 9. antennate
  fingers .. 8. digitate
  foreknowledge .. 9. prescient
  four feet .. 11. quadrupedal
  harmful quality .. 9. innocuous
  leaves .. 6. foliar 7. foliate
  limits .. 6. finite
  local designation .. 7. topical
  lumps .. 7. noduled
  more than one mate .. 9. polyandry
  no angles .. 6. agonic
  no interest .. 6. supine
  no teeth .. 7. edental 8. edentate
  nothing to do .. 6. otiose
  one foot .. 6. uniped
  pits, depressions .. 7. foveate 9. foveolate
  plane surfaces .. 7. faceted
  pointed end .. 6. peaked 7. cuspate
    8. aristate
  power over fire .. 10. ignipotent
  power to believe .. 9. creditive
  reflecting surface .. 8. specular
  same ending .. 11. conterminal
  same parents .. 7. germane
  sawlike edge .. 7. serrate
  scales .. 8. perulate
  scalloped edge .. 7. crenate
  taste .. 5. sapid
  thorns .. 7. spinate

three broods yearly .. 11. trigoneutic
two feet .. 5. biped 7. bipedal
two horns .. 6. bicorn
two meanings .. 9. ambiguous
unequal sides .. 7. scalene
web feet .. 8. pinniped
wings .. 4. alar

having a ...
backbone .. 10. vertebrate
beak .. 8. rostrate
beard .. 8. aristate
handle .. 6. ansate
large nose .. 6. nasute
shield .. 9. clypeated
stem .. 9. petiolate
tail .. 7. caudate
tuft .. 6. comose
veil .. 6. velate
will .. 7. testate

havoc ... 4. harm 5. botch, waste
7. destroy 11. destruction, devastation
12. annihilation

haw .. 4. sloe 5. fence, hedge 6. eyelid
(3rd) 7. stammer 8. hawthorn,
messuage, turn left 9. enclosure
11. exclamation

Hawaii ... see also *Hawaiian*
capital .. 8. Honolulu
city .. 4. Hilo 7. Wailuku
district .. 7. Lahaina
explorer .. 4. Cook (Capt)
harbor .. 5. Pearl (bombed 12/7/41)
islands (major) .. 4. Maui, Oahu 5. Kauai,
Lanai 6. Hawaii, Niihau 7. Molokai
9. Kahoolawe
lake .. 5. Waiau
native .. 10. Polynesian
old name .. 15. Sandwich Islands
peak .. 8. Mauna Kea, Mauna Loa
9. Waialeale
resort .. 7. Waikiki
Southernmost point (US) .. 5. Ka Lae
State admission .. 8. Fiftieth
State bird .. 13. Hawaiian goose
State flower .. 8. hibiscus
State nickname .. 5. Aloha 20. Paradise
of the Pacific
volcano .. 7. Kilauea 8. Mauna Loa
(largest active)

Hawaiian ... 6. Kanaka 10. Melanesian,
Polynesian 16. South Sea islander

Hawaiian (pert to) ...
banquet, feast .. 7. ahaaina
basket .. 2. ie
beverage .. 4. kava 8. kavakava
bird .. 2. io, o-o 3. iwa 4. iiwi, mamo
(ext), noio, o-o-a-a 6. olomao (thrush)
8. drepanis
canoe .. 5. waapa
chant .. 4. mele
cloth, clothes .. 4. kapa, tapa
coffee .. 4. kona
dance .. 4. hula
fern .. 4. pulu
fibre (pine) .. 2. ie
fish .. 4. awa 4. ulua 5. akule, lania
flower wreath, garland .. 3. lei
food .. 3. poi 4. kalo, taro
garment .. 6. holoku, muumuu
god .. 5. Wakea 7. Kanaloa (Pantheon)
goddess .. 4. Pele (volcanoes, fire)

gooseberry .. 4. poha
grass .. 6. emoloa
greeting .. 5. aloha
herb .. 3. pia (starch root)
king (first) .. 10. Kamehameha
lava .. 2. aa 8. pahoehoe
loincloth, girdle .. 4. malo
musical instrument .. 7. ukulele
newcomer .. 8. malihini
pepper .. 3. ava 4. kava 8. kavakava
precipice .. 4. pali
Queen .. 8. Kamamalu
royalty .. 4. alii
seaweed (edible) .. 4. limu
shampoo, massage .. 8. lomi-lomi
shrub .. 3. pia 4. akia, pulu 5. olona
temple .. 5. heiau
tern .. 4. noio
tree .. 3. koa
veranda .. 5. lanai
windstorm .. 4. kona
woman .. 5. haole 6. wahine
yam .. 3. hoi

hawfinch ... 8. grosbeak

hawk .. 3. cry 4. hunt, sell, vend
6. peddle 7. canvass 9. plunderer,
warmonger

hawk (bird) ... 2. io 3. hen 4. eyas,
kahu, kite, nyas, seel (blind) 5. Astur,
Buteo 6. falcon, osprey, tercel (tiercel)
7. buzzard, Cooper's, goshawk, harrier,
kestrel, puttock, sparrow, vulture
8. caracara 9. Accipiter, red-tailed

hawker of fruit (Eng) ... 6. coster
12. costermonger

hawk-eyed deity ... 2. Ra

Hawkeye State ... 4. Iowa

hawking .. 7. hunting, vending
8. falconry

haw ... ... 3. maw

haw ... ... 2. sphinx 8. sphingid

haw ... ... awl 6. turtle 8. tortoise

haw ... raw ... 6. sleuth 8. detective
11. sleuthhound

hawk's nest ... 5. aerie (aery)

hawk's opposite ... 4. dove

hawser .. 4. line, rope

hawser post ... 4. bitt 7. bollard

hawthorn ... 3. may 5. hazel (fruit) 6. red
haw 7. haw tree 9. mayflower

Hawthorne's ...
adultress .. 6. Hester (Prynne)
House of .. 11. Seven Gables
Letter .. 7. Scarlet
reverend .. 10. Dimmesdale

hay ... 6. fodder 7. timothy

hay (pert to) ...
bird .. 7. hay jack 8. black cap
9. sandpiper (pectoral)
bundle .. 3. mow 4. bale, cock, rick
5. stack
fork .. 5. pikel (pikle), pitch
herb .. 8. sainfoin
mown .. 5. swath
second cutting .. 5. rowen
spreader .. 6. tedder
stack .. 4. rick 7. hayrick
storage site .. 3. mow 4. barn, loft, silo

haywire ... 4. awry 5. crazy

hazard ... 3. fog 4. dare, game, jump,
risk 5. peril 6. gamble, sanger, stroke

7. imperil, jeopard, presume, venture
8. cabstand, casualty, endanger, jeopardy 11. restriction

hazardous . . . 5. hairy (sl), jumpy, risky 6. chancy, queasy, unsafe
7. unsound 8. perilous 9. uncertain, venturous 10. fortuitous 11. speculative, venturesome

haze . . . 3. fog 4. beat, film, glin (at sea), mist, smog 5. scold, smoke, vapor
7. dimness, drizzle 8. frighten

hazy . . . 3. dim 5. filmy, foggy, misty, smoky, thick, vague 6. cloudy, opaque, stupid 7. muddled, nebular, obscure
8. overcast 9. invisible, uncertain
10. indistinct

he . . . 2. il 3. man 4. ipsi, male 6. any one, letter 7. pronoun

head . . . 3. aim, nob 4. lead, pate, poll, tête (Fr) 5. caput, chief, skull 6. noggin, noodle (sl), source 7. cranium

head (pert to) . . .
abbey . . 5. abbot 6. abbess
back of . . 7. occiput
bald . . 6. acomia 9. pilgarlic
bone . . 8. parietal 9. occipital
Gorgon . . 6. Medusa (Myth)
hard . . 5. boche
of hair . . 5. crine
pert to . . 8. cephalic
proportion . . 14. mesitacephalic
shaven . . 7. tonsure
shrunken . . 7. tsentsa

headache . . . 6. megrim 8. migraine
11. cephalalgia

head covering . . . 3. cap, hat, tam, wig
4. hair, hood, veil 5. beret, miter, scalp
6. bonnet, peruke, toupee, wimple
7. biretta 8. sombrero 10. fascinator

headdress . . . 3. wig 4. pouf, tête
5. busby, miter, shako, tiara 6. coiffe, diadem, hennin, peruke, pinner
7. bandore, buzz wig, coronet, periwig
8. coiffure, headtire

headdress (Egypt) . . . 6. uraeus (with sacred asp)

headhunters (Luzon) . . . 7. Igorots

heading . . . 3. top 5. front, title, topic
6. pillow 7. bolster, caption 8. headline
9. direction 12. decapitation

headland . . . 4. cape, mull, ness 5. morro, ridge 10. promontory

headless . . . 6. stupid 7. acephal, topless
9. acephalus (monster) 10. acephalous

headline . . . 6. banner 7. caption, display, heading 8. streamer

headliner . . . 4. star 7. feature 8. composer

headlong . . . 4. rash 5. hasty, steep
6. head-on, sudden 8. reckless
9. headfirst, impetuous, impulsive
10. recklessly 11. impulsively, precipitate, precipitous

headpiece . . . 3. cap, hat, top 4. atef
5. crown 6. halter, helmet, lintel
7. fitting 8. covering, ornament, skull cap 9. headboard, headdress, headstall

head-shaped . . . 8. capitate

headstrong . . . 4. rash 6. entêté, unruly
7. violent, wayward 9. obstinate
11. intractable, opinionated
12. contumacious, ungovernable

heal . . . 4. cure, knit, mend 6. doctor, pacify, remedy, repair 7. correct, restore
9. cicatrize

healing (pert to) . . .
agent . . 6. balsam
compound . . 4. balm
goddess . . 3. Eir
magic . . 6. powwow
plant . . 4. aloe (vera)
process . . 4. scar 8. cicatrix
remedy . . 8. curative, sanative
science . . 9. iatrology
suffix . . 7. iatrics

health (pert to) . . .
care . . 7. welfare
comb form . . 4. sani
conditions . . 8. sanitary
goddess . . 5. Salus 6. Hygeia 7. Minerva
Latin . . 5. salus
neurotic . . 13. hypochondriac
resort . . 3. spa 7. springs
symbol . . 5. pansy

healthful . . . 7. healthy 8. curative, salutary, sanatory 9. medicinal
10. salubrious

healthy . . . 4. hale, sane, well 6. hearty, robust 8. salutary, vigorous 9. healthful, wholesome 10. salubrious

heap . . . 3. cop 4. dess, load, lump, pile, pyre, raff, raft 5. amass, cairn, crowd, stack 6. plenty, sorite, throng
7. cumulus 9. multitude 10. accumulate

heaped . . . 5. piled 7. stacked 8. acervate
9. collected

hear . . . 3. see 4. feel, heed, oyez (oyes)
5. favor, judge, learn 6. attend, listen
7. hearken (harken) 8. listen to, perceive
9. attention 10. adjudicate

hearer . . . 7. audient, auditor 8. disciple, listener 9. hearkener (harkener)
12. eavesdropper

hearing (pert to) . . . 3. act, aid, ear
4. otic, oyer 5. aural, sense (special), sound, trial 6. otosis, tryout 7. earshot
8. audience, audition, auditory
9. attention, auricular, interview, knowledge

hearken, harken . . . 4. hear, heed
6. attend, listen 7. give ear, inquire

hearsay . . . 4. talk 5. bruit, rumor
6. gossip, report 8. evidence

heart . . . 3. cor 4. card, core, gist, life, love, mood, soul 5. cheer, organ 6. center, depths, kardia, middle, spirit, vitals
7. courage, emotion, essence, feeling
9. affection, substance 10. conscience
11. temperament

heart (pert to) . . .
ache . . 5. grief 6. sorrow 7. anguish
active . . 7. sthenic
artery . . 5. aorta
beat . . 5. pulse, throb 7. systole
8. diastole 9. pulsation 10. palmoscopy
bleeding (flower) . . 8. dicentra
burn . . 4. envy 6. enmity 7. burning, pyrosia 8. jealousy 10. cardialgia, discontent, heartscald (heart-scaud)
cavity . . 6. atrium
chamber . . 6. atrium 7. auricle 9. ventricle
11. ventriculum
contraction . . 7. systole

disease . . 14. angina pectoris
Egypt . . 2. Ab 4. hati
expansion . . 8. diastole
felt . . 4. dear, deep, real, true 7. genuine,
sincere
shaped . . 7. cordate
valve . . 6. mitral 8. bicuspid 9. tricuspid
hearten . . . 5. cheer 7. comfort
8. embolden, inspirit, reassure
9. encourage
hearth . . . 4. home 5. ingle 6. astrer (pert
to) 8. fireside 9. fireplace
hearth goddess . . . 5. Vesta 6. Hestia
hearty . . . 4. hale, real, rich, warm
5. heavy, lusty 6. active, robust,
stanch 7. cordial, earnest, fervent
8. friendly, vigorous 9. convivial,
energetic, unfeigned 10. nourishing
11. substantial
heat . . . 4. fire, race, warm, zeal
5. ardor, calor, cauma, fever, tepor
6. degree, warmth 7. inflame, passion
10. excitement 11. temperature
heat (pert to) . . .
heating . . 9. calorific
measure . . 5. therm (therme) 7. calorie
(calory), Celsius 10. centigrade,
Fahrenheit
pert to . . 7. thermic
plaster . . 4. mull 7. steatin
principle . . 7. caloric
white . . 13. incandescence
heater . . . 4. etna, kiln, oven 5. forge,
stove, tisar 6. boiler, retort 7. brazier,
furnace 8. annealer, register 12. electron
tube
heath . . . 4. moor 5. Erica, plain, savin,
waste 8. tamarisk 10. underbrush
heathen . . . 5. pagan 6. ethnic, paynim
7. gentile, godless, infidel 10. unbeliever
11. irreligious 13. unenlightened
heathen deity . . . 4. idol 5. image
6. symbol
heather . . . 5. color, Erica, plant
9. crowberry 12. poverty plant
heaume . . . 6. helmet (armor)
heave . . . 4. cast, draw, hurl, lift, toss
5. fling, hoist, pitch, raise, retch, scena,
throw 11. rise and fall
heaven . . . 3. sky 4. ciel, Eden 5. ether
6. utopia, welkin 7. arcadia, Elysium,
Nirvana 8. empyrean, Paradise, Valhalla
(Valhall) 9. firmament
heavenly . . . 5. godly 6. divine, sacred
7. angelic, blessed, uranian 8. supernal
9. beautiful, celestial 10. delightful
heavenly (pert to) . . .
being . . 5. angel, saint 6. cherub, seraph
7. Madonna 8. cherubim, Dei Mater,
seraphim
belt . . 6. galaxy, zodiac
body . . 3. sun 4. luna, moon, star
5. comet 6. planet 8. luminary
city . . 4. Zion 12. New Jerusalem
food . . 5. manna
path . . 5. orbit
solar apparatus . . 6. orrery
sphere . . 8. empyrean
twins (Gemini) . . 6. Castor, Pollux
heavens . . . see heaven
heaves . . . 9. emphysema

heavy . . . 3. sad 4. deep, dull, hard, role
5. actor, dense, grave, great, inert,
massy 6. coarse, gloomy, leaden,
sleepy, strong, viscid 7. doleful,
onerous, serious, villain, violent,
weighty 8. burdened, grievous,
overcast, pregnant, profound 9. difficult,
ponderous 10. afflictive, burdensome,
encumbered, oppressive 11. substantial
13. consequential
heavy (pert to) . . .
handed . . 6. clumsy 7. awkward, unhandy
8. bungling 9. maladroit 10. oppressive
headed . . 4. dull, logy 6. drowsy, stupid
hearted . . 3. sad 10. despondent,
melancholy
laden . . 6. loaded 8. careworm
9. oppressed 12. weighted down
with moisture . . 6. sodden
Hebrew . . . 3. Jew 4. Zion 6. Habiri,
Habiru, Semite 7. Semitic
Hebrew (pert to) . . .
abode of the dead . . 5. Sheol
acrostic . . 4. agla
amulet . . 4. agla
demon . . 8. Asmodeus
eternity . . 4. Olam 8. Olam haba
excommunication form . . 5. herem
festival . . 5. Purim, Seder 8. Passover
flute (Bib) . . 8. nehiloth
forbidden . . 4. tref
God . . 2. El 5. Eloah 6. Adonai, Elohim,
Yahweh (Yahveh) 7. Jehovah
grammar . . 7. stative
greeting . . 6. Shalom
instrument (lyrelike) . . 4. asor
kinsman . . 4. goel
law book . . 5. Torah (Tora) 6. Talmud
7. Mishnah (Mishna) 8. Tosephta
10. Pentateuch
lesson (Nebiim) . . 9. haphtarah
marriage custom . . 8. levirate
month (Spring) . . 4. Abib 5. Nisan
Order (Cenobite) . . 6. Essene
plural ending . . 2. im
prayer shawl . . 7. tallith
proselyte . . 3. ger
psalm of praise . . 6. hallel
quarters . . 6. ghetto
rabbis, teachers . . 6. sabora 7. amoraim,
tannaim 8. saboraim
sacred objects . . 4. Urim 7. Thummin
school . . 5. heder (cheder)
spice (anc) . . 6. stacte
town . . 6. Mizpah (Mizpeh)
trumpet . . 7. shophar (shofar)
underworld . . 5. Sheol
Hebrew alphabet . . . 2. he, pe 3. mem,
nun, sin, tav, vau 4. ayin, beth, caph,
koph, resh, shin, yodh 5. aleph, cheth,
gimel, sadhe, zayin 6. daleth, lamedh,
samekh
Hebrides, New . . .
administrators . . 6. French 7. British
church . . 6. Celtic (early)
islands . . 4. Iona, Skye 5. Banks 6. Torres
people . . 10. Melanesian
type rule . . 11. Condominium
hecatomb . . . 9. sacrifice 11. hundred
oxen
hecco . . . 8. hickwall 10. woodpecker

heckle ... 4. gibe 6. badger, hackle, harass

hectic ... 5. fever, flush 7. excited 8. feverish, restless 9. reddening 11. consumptive

hector ... 5. bully, worry 6. harass 7. bluster, swagger 8. browbeat 9. roisterer 10. intimidate

Hector (pert to) ...
character in .. 5. (The) Iliad
companion .. 8. Diomedes
father .. 5. Priam
mother .. 6. Hecuba
slain by .. 8. Achilles
wife .. 10. Andromache

heddle ... 4. loom 5. blade (with eyelet) 7. weaving

hedge ... 3. bar, haw, hem, pen 4. boma 5. fence 6. hinder, raddle 7. barrier, enclose, quibble 8. boundary, obstruct, sidestep, surround

hedgehog ... 6. animal, tenrec, urchin 7. dredger, echidna, echinus, pudding (fruit) 8. herisson, hurcheon 9. porcupine 11. transformer

hedge trimmer ... 7. plasher, topiary

hedonism (pert to) ...
advocate .. 8. Cyrenaic 9. Epicurean
doctrine of .. 8. pleasure

heed ... 3. ear 4. care, hear, mind, note, obey 6. attend, listen, notice, regard 7. caution, observe 8. consider 9. attention, be careful, diligence 10. cognizance, solicitude 11. observation

heedful ... 4. wary 5. alert 6. attent 7. careful, mindful 8. cautious, vigilant 9. advertent, attentive 11. considerate

heedless ... 6. remiss 8. careless 9. desperate, impulsive, negligent 10. insouciant, regardless 11. improvident, inadvertent, inattentive, thoughtless, unobservant, without heed 13. inconsiderate

heehaw ... 4. bray

heel ... 3. cad, tip 4. knob, tilt 5. stern 6. careen, follow 7. bounder, deviate, incline 9. scoundrel 12. protuberance

Heidi author ... 12. Johanna Spyri

heifer ... 3. cow 4. quey 5. stirk, woman 6. bovine 8. terrapin (fem) 10. colpindach

height ... 3. alt, top 4. apex 5. crest, pitch 6. summit 7. stature 8. altitude, eminence, highness 9. elevation 10. The Heavens

heighten ... 5. raise 7. augment, elevate 8. increase 9. aggravate, intensify 10. exaggerate

height of action, drama ... 10. catastasis

heimlich ... 11. reticently 12. mysteriously

Heimweh ... 9. nostalgia 12. homesickness

heinous ... 3. bad 6. odious, wicked 7. beastly (Brit), hateful 8. flagrant, infamous, terrible 9. atrocious, malicious 10. outrageous

heir ... 5. scion 7. heritor, legatee 8. atheling (apparent), parcener (joint) 9. firstborn, inheritor, successor

11. beneficiary

Hejaz ...
city .. 5. Islam, Mecca 6. Medina
monument .. 14. Tomb of Mohammed (Mosque of the Prophet)
district of .. 11. Saudi Arabia
shrine .. 5. Kaaba

helcos ... 5. ulcer

helcos (pert to) ...
repair .. 11. helcoplasty
science .. 9. helcology
ulceration .. 8. helcosis

held ... see hold

Helen of Troy (pert to) ...
abductor, lover .. 5. Paris
brother-in-law .. 9. Agamemnon
famed for .. 6. beauty
husband .. 8. Menelaus (King)
mother .. 4. Leda
sister of .. 11. The Dioscuri

helical ... 5. helix (formed) 6. spiral

helical year ... 6. Sothic

helicoid ... 6. curved, ear rim (like) 10. snail shell (like)

helicon ... 4. tuba

helicopter (pert to) ... 5. rotor 7. chopper 8. autogiro (autogyro), heliport 9. eggbeater 10. whirlybird

helicopter developer ... 8. Sikorsky

heliophobia ... 14. fear of sunlight 16. sensitivity to sun

Heliopolis ... 12. City of the Sun (Egypt)

Helios ... 3. Sol 6. sun god 16. Colossus of Rhodes

helix ... 4. coil 5. snail 6. spiral

hell ... 7. dungeon, inferno 9. perdition, purgatory 10. underworld 11. nether world

hell (pert to) ...
bottomless pit .. 9. barathrum
capital of .. 11. Pandemonium
Greek .. 5. Hades 8. Tartarus
Hebrew .. 5. Sheol
Hindu .. 6. Naraka
Jewish .. 6. Tophet 7. Gehenna
Norse .. 7. Niflhel (Neflheim)
Queen .. 3. Hel
Roman .. 3. Dis 5. Orcus

hellbent ... 7. dead set, like mad 8. full tilt, reckless 10. determined, recklessly 12. determinedly

Hellene ... 5. Greek

Hellenistic school (Sculp) ... 9. Pergamene

Hellespont ...
city .. 6. Abydos (legend), Sestos
legend .. 4. Hero 7. Leander (swimmer)
modern name .. 11. Dardanelles (The)
peninsula .. 9. Gallipoli
port .. 8. Gelibola (Gallipoli)
sea .. 6. Aegean 7. Marmara

helm ... 5. wheel 6. helmet, rudder, summit, tiller 7. control 10. management 12. steering gear

helmet ... 5. armet, armor, galea, topee (topi) 6. casque, heaume, morion, sallet, sconce 7. basinet, hard hat

helmet (pert to) ...
flap .. 8. aventail
lower part .. 6. beaver
nose guard .. 5. nasal

opening . . 3. vue
part . . 4. bell 5. crest, visor (vizor)
   7. ventail 8. aventail
shaped . . 7. galeate
helminth . . . 4. worm
helmsman . . . 5. pilot 6. conner, guider
   8. coxswain 9. steersman
helot . . . 4. esne, serf 5. slave 6. thrall,
   vassal 7. servant
help . . . 3. aid 4. abet, back, cure 5. avail,
   boost, serve, stead 6. assist, relief,
   remedy, succor 7. benefit, forward,
   further, improve, prevent, relieve,
   servant, serving, subsidy, support,
   sustain
helper . . . 3. aid (aide) 8. teammate
   9. assistant, paramedic 10. apprentice,
   benefactor
helpful . . . 6. useful 7. helping 8. salutary
   10. beneficial, tiding over
   12. contributory, instrumental
helpless . . . 4. limp, weak 7. forlorn
   8. impotent, unaiding 9. destitute,
   powerless, spineless 10. bewildered,
   unsupplied 11. defenseless, unprotected
   12. irremediable
helpmate . . . 4. wife 6. helper, spouse
   7. husband 8. helpmeet 9. assistant,
   companion
Helsinki, Finland . . . 7. capital
helter-skelter . . . 5. haste, hurry 7. hastily
   8. disorder 9. confusion 10. carelessly,
   recklessly
helve . . . 5. lever 6. handle
hem, hem in . . . 3. pen 4. edge 5. beset
   6. border, margin 7. environ, stammer
   8. hesitate, surround 9. hem and haw
   11. exclamation 12. circumscribe
hemal, haemal (pert to) . . . 5. blood
   12. blood vessels
hemeralopia . . . 12. day blindness (opp
   of nyctalopia)
hemi . . . 4. half, semi (pref)
hemiplegia . . . 9. paralysis (body half)
hemlock . . . 3. kex 5. Tsuga 6. conium
   (fruit) 9. evergreen, poisoning
hemophilia . . . 8. bleeding
   10. hemorrhage (uncontrollable)
hemp . . . 3. ife, kef 4. flax, keef, kief,
   rine, sunn 5. abaca, bhang, istle, sisal
   (sizal) 6. fennel, Manila 7. hashish,
   lhiamba (liamba) 8. cannabis
hemp (pert to) . . .
   bagasse . . 6. linaga
   cannabis . . 5. ganja (smoking)
   fabric . . 6. burlap
   filament . . 4. harl
   leaves . . 5. sabzi
   like . . 9. cannabine
   loose . . 5. oakum
   resin (narcotic) . . 6. charas
   seed . . 6. rogue, scamp
   short . . 3. tow
hen . . . 4. fowl, wife 6. pullet
hen (pert to) . . .
   clam . . 4. surf 5. pismo
   hawk . . 7. buzzard, harrier
   heath . . 4. gray 6. grouse (black)
   of Reynard the Fox . . 7. Partlet
   poison . . 7. hebenon, henbane
   water . . 9. gallinule

hence . . . 2. so 4. away, ergo, thus
   8. away from 9. therefore
henchman . . . 4. page 5. groom 6. gillie,
   squire 7. mafioso 8. follower, hanger-on
   9. attendant, supporter 12. right-hand
   man
hend, hende . . . 4. fair, kind, near
   5. civil 6. clever, comely, gentle, kindly
   8. gracious, pleasant, skillful (skilful)
   9. dexterous 10. convenient
Henley event . . . 7. Regatta
henpeck . . . 3. nag
heortology, science of . . . 14. liturgical
   year
hepar . . . 5. liver 8. compound (Chem)
hepatitis . . . 12. liver disease
Hephaestus (Gr Relig) . . . 9. god of Fire
Hepplewhite . . . 9. furniture
heptad . . . 5. seven (group of)
Hera (pert to) . . .
   husband . . 4. Zeus
   mother of . . 4. Ares, Rhea
   rival . . 2. Io 4. Leto
herald . . . 5. crier 6. tabard 7. presage,
   usher in 8. announce, point man,
   proclaim 9. harbinger, messenger
   10. forerunner
heraldic (pert to) . . .
   balls . . 5. palle (6 balls of Medici)
   band . . 3. bar 4. fess, fill
   barnacle . . 4. brey
   bearing . . 4. ente, gore, orle 5. pheon
      6. charge 8. tressure
   boss . . 5. rumbo
   charge . . 5. fusil, gyron 7. bearing,
      humetty (humettee)
   circle (gold) . . 6. bezant
   cross . . nowy, paty, urde 6. cleche,
      pattée (patté), raguly 7. patonce, saltier
      (saltire)
   decoration . . 4. seme 5. crest
   design (fur) . . 4. pean, vair
   division . . 4. ente, paly 5. barry 6. canton
      7. compone 11. counterpaly
   embattled . . 8. bretesse
   end (metal) . . 7. boterol (boteroll)
   large . . 5. pavis
   lozenge (voided) . . 6. mascle
   opening . . 6. rustre
   panel . . 7. hatchment (death)
   sardonyx . . 8. sanguine
   scalloped, edged . . 8. invected
   segment . . 6. flanch
   ship . . 7. lymphad
   star . . 6. mullet 7. estoile
   stripe . . 4. pale
   swallow . . 10. hirondelle
   winged . . 4. aile
   wreath . . 5. torse 7. chaplet, garland
heraldic (pert to animals) . . .
   head . . 8. caboshed (cabochED)
   bear . . 5. grise
   beast, running . . 7. courant
   beast, sitting . . 5. assis 6. sejant
   beasts . . 6. enurny
   beast's leg . . 4. gamb (gambe)
   bird . . 7. issuant (half visible), martlet
      9. half eagle
   duck (footless) . . 6. cannet (cannette)
   fish, swimming . . 6. naiant
   headless . . 5. etète

heraldic (pert to color) . . .
   black . . **5.** sable
   blue . . **5.** azure
   brown . . **5.** tenne
   gold, yellow . . **2.** or
   green . . **4.** vert
   purple . . **7.** purpure
   red . . **5.** gules
heraldic shield (pert to) . . .
   back . . **8.** aversant
   back to back . . **8.** addorsed
   bent . . **9.** debruised
   broken . . **5.** rompu
   Danes . . **5.** raven
   England . . **14.** lilies of France
   facing each other . . **8.** affronté
   savages . . **6.** tattoo
   toward spectator . . **4.** gaze **7.** gardant
   tribe of Judah . . **4.** lion
herb . . **3.** pia, rue **4.** aloe, anet
   balm, dill, hemp, mint, moly, sage,
   woad, yamp **5.** anise, basil, nondo,
   sedge, senna, tansy, thyme **6.** arnica,
   borage, catnip, cicely, clover, endive,
   fennel, hyssop, jacoby, madder,
   yarrow **7.** boneset, caraway, chervil,
   chicory, figwort, gentian, ginseng,
   henbane, parsley, ragwort **8.** abelmosk,
   licorice, marjoram, rosemary, samphire,
   tarragon **9.** coriander, digitalis,
   spikenard **10.** elecampane, pennyroyal,
   turtlehead
herb (pert to) . . .
   bitter . . **3.** rue **4.** aloe **5.** tansy **7.** boneset
   8. centaury **9.** snakehead **10.** turtlehead
   dill . . **4.** anet
   genus . . **3.** Iva **4.** Arum, Ruta **5.** Galax,
   Inula, Lemna, Rubia **6.** Cassia, Mentha,
   Oxalis, Sagina **7.** Alpenia, Anemone,
   Freesia, Hedeoma, Tellima, Tovaria
   8. Hepatica, Psorales **9.** Grundelia
   living on . . **11.** herbivorous
   12. phytophagous
   mythical . . **4.** moly
   narcotic . . **4.** hemp
   onionlike . . **5.** chive
   poisonous . . **4.** loco **6.** conium
   7. hemlock, henbane **9.** hellebore
   salad . . **6.** endive **7.** chicory
   10. watercress
Hercules (pert to) . . .
   captured . . **8.** Cerberus
   father . . **4.** Zeus
   hero of . . **8.** strength **12.** twelve labors
   killed . . **5.** Hydra
   mother . . **7.** Alcmene
   stables . . **6.** Augean
   statue . . **7.** Farnese
   stone . . **9.** loadstone
   sweetheart . . **4.** Iole
   wife . . **4.** Hebe
herd . . **3.** mob **5.** crowd, drive, drove,
   flock, guard **6.** gregis, rabble **7.** shelter
   11. aggregation
herd's grass . . **7.** timothy
herdsman . . . **4.** senn **6.** drover **7.** vaquero
   (vaciero) **8.** Damoetas, ranchero,
   wrangler
herdsman's god . . . **5.** Pales
here . . . **3.** ici, now **6.** hereat, hither
   7. present **8.** vicinity **9.** this place

   11. in this place
here and now . . . **8.** thisness **9.** haecceity
   11. specificity
here and there . . . **5.** about **6.** passim
   10. everywhere
hereditary . . . **6.** inborn, innate, lineal
   8. heirship **9.** ancestral, descended,
   lineality **11.** inheritable, inheritance,
   patrimonial
heredity . . . **4.** gene **5.** birth **7.** atavism
   8. heritage **10.** Mendel's law
   11. inheritance
heretic . . . **9.** dissenter, sectarian
   10. schismatic **13.** nonconformist
heretofore . . . **6.** erenow **7.** prior to
   8. formerly, hitherto, previous
heritage . . . **3.** lot **9.** cleronomy
   10. birthright **11.** inheritance
heritrix, heretrix . . . **7.** heiress
herl, harl . . . **3.** fly (angling) **4.** barb
hermeneutics . . . **14.** interpretation
   (Scriptures)
Hermes (pert to) . . .
   birthplace . . **7.** Cyllene
   character . . **6.** herald **9.** messenger
   father . . **4.** Zeus
   god of . . **5.** youth **7.** science **9.** eloquence,
   invention
   mother . . **4.** Maia
   Roman equivalent . . **7.** Mercury
   shoes (winged) . . **7.** talaria
hermetic . . . **6.** closed, sealed **7.** magical
   8. airtight **10.** alchemical
hermetic art . . . **7.** alchemy
hermit . . . **4.** monk **5.** cooky **7.** ascetic,
   eremite, recluse, stylite (Hist)
   8. headsman **9.** anchorite, pillarist
   11. hummingbird
hermitary . . . **3.** hut **4.** cell
hern, herne . . . **4.** hers, hook **5.** heron
   6. corner
hero . . . **4.** idol, star **5.** model **7.** demigod,
   warrior **8.** champion **9.** celebrity,
   conqueror **11.** protagonist
hero (pert to) . . .
   American . . **5.** Allen (Ethan), Bowie
   6. Bonham, Travis **8.** Crockett
   Babylonian . . **5.** Etana
   deified . . **7.** demigod
   genealogy . . **9.** heroogony
   Greek . . **3.** Ion **4.** Ajax
   legendary . . **6.** Amadis, Roland
   7. Paladin, Tancred
   lore . . **9.** heroology
   Persian . . **6.** Rustam (Rustum)
   romantic . . **4.** Erec **6.** Amadis **7.** Leander
   Russian . . **4.** Igor
heroic . . . **4.** bold, epic, huge **5.** brave,
   great, noble **6.** epical, poetic, viking
   7. extreme, gallant, valiant **8.** fearless,
   intrepid, powerful **10.** courageous
   11. magnanimous, venturesome
heroic poem, story . . . **4.** epic, epos
   6. epopee
heroine . . . **4.** Tess **5.** actor **6.** Esther,
   Europa **8.** Atalanta **9.** celebrity
   11. demigoddess
heroism . . . **5.** valor **7.** bravery, courage
   9. fortitude **11.** magnanimity
   13. unselfishness
heron . . . **5.** Ardea, crane, egret, herle

7. Bittern 8. Ardeidae, heronsew
9. Great Blue 10. Great White, Little
Blue
heron flock ... 5. sedge
herpes ... 6. eczema 8. cold sore, shingles
herring ... 3. cob 4. alec, brit, raun (fem),
sile 5. cisco, matie, sprat 7. alewife,
anchovy, shadine 8. scuddawn
herring (pert to) ...
barrel .. 4. cade, cran
bone .. 7. pattern 11. arrangement
fry .. 4. sile
herringlike .. 5. cisco 7. anchovy
young .. 4. brit 5. sprat (sprot)
Herse (Gr) ... 7. goddess (dew)
Hersey setting ... 5. Adano 9. Hiroshima
Hershef (Egypt) ... 5. deity (tutelary)
hesitate ... 3. haw, hem 4. wait 5. delay,
demur, pause, stall 6. falter, loiter
7. stammer 13. procrastinate
hesitation ... 5. doubt, pause, waltz
9. faltering, hesitancy 10. reluctance,
stammering 11. uncertainty, vacillation
15. procrastination
hesped (Heb) ... 6. eulogy 7. funeral
Hesperides (pert to) ...
group name .. 10. Atlantides
guards of .. 12. golden apples (Hera)
nymph .. 4. Aegle 6. Hestia 7. Hespera
8. Arethusa, Erytheia
Hesperus ... 4. poem (Wreck of the
Hesperus) 5. Venus 6. Hesper
11. evening star
Hessian ... 3. fly 5. boots, Hesse
6. German 9. mercenary 10. adventurer
hest ... 6. behest 7. command, precept,
promise 10. injunction
Hestia (pert to) ...
goddess of .. 6. hearth
guard of .. 12. golden apples
mother .. 4. Rhea
hetaera, hetaira (Gr) ... 4. Lais 6. Phryne
8. mistress, paramour
hetaerocracy, governed by ...
8. hetaerae 10. college men
Heterodontus ... 5. shark
heterodox ... 9. heretical 10. unorthodox
11. nonorthodox
heterogeneous (opposed to
homogeneous) ... 5. mixed 6. unlike
7. diverse 9. different 10. dissimilar
11. diversified 13. miscellaneous
hew ... 3. cut 4. chop, fell, hack 5. carve,
sever
hex ... 3. hag, six 4. jinx 5. lamia, spell
6. bewitch 9. sorceress, witchwife
hexad ... 3. six 6. sestet
hexameter verse ...
meter .. 7. six feet
terms .. 4. iams 8. dipodies, trochees
9. anapaests
hexapod ... 7. six feet 9. six-footed
hexarchy ... 9. six States (group)
hexastich, poem or stanza ... 8. six
lines 9. six verses
heyday ... 3. joy 4. acme 8. wildness
11. high spirits 12. highest vigor
14. frolicsomeness
heyrat ... 8. kinkajou (obs)
Hezekiah (pert to) ...
Biblical .. 4. King (12th)

kingdom .. 5. Judah
mother .. 3. Abi
hiatus ... 3. col, gap 5. break, chasm,
pause, space 6. lacuna 7. fissure,
opening 8. interval 12. interruption
Hiawatha (pert to) ...
character, poem by .. 10. Longfellow
grandmother .. 7. Nokomis
mother .. 7. Wenonah
people .. 8. Iroquois
hibernate ... 6. hole up (summer in
torpor), winter 8. estivate 10. latibulize
Hibernia ... 4. Erin 7. Ireland
Hibernian (pert to) ...
color .. 5. green
native .. 8. Irishman
secret society (US 1832) .. 24. Ancient
Order of Hibernians
hickory ... 4. cane 5. Carya, pecan
6. switch 8. kiskatom 9. shellbark
hidalgo ... 5. title 8. nobleman (lower
class)
hidden ... 4. dern, lurk 5. inner, perdu
6. arcane, buried, cached, closed,
covert, latent, masked, occult, secret
7. covered, cryptic, obscure, unknown
8. abstruse, screened, secluded,
secreted 9. concealed, latescent
10. mysterious 11. clandestine
hide ... 3. kip 4. bury, cyst, dern
(derne), lurk, mask, pelt, skin, veil
5. cache, cloak, cover, skulk 6. screen,
shroud 7. conceal, eelskin, rawhide,
secrete 8. carucate, disguise, ensconce,
suppress 9. dissemble 10. camouflage
hidebound ... 5. bound, petty 6. little,
narrow 7. bigoted 9. barkbound
10. restrained (opinion) 11. strait-
laced 12. conventional, narrow-minded
13. hyperorthodox
hideous ... 4. grim, ugly 6. grisly, horrid,
odious 7. ghastly 8. scabrous, terrible
9. frightful, revolting 10. detestable,
terrifying
hiding place ... 3. mew 4. lair 5. cache
9. latibulum
hi-fi devotee ... 10. audiophile
high ... 3. alt, dry, ela (note) 4. tall
5. aloft, drunk, great, noble, steep
6. costly, shrill 7. eminent, haughty
8. elevated, foremost, stranded,
towering 9. excessive, expensive
high (pert to) ...
and mighty .. 8. arrogant 9. imperious
brow .. 4. snob 7. Brahmin, egghead,
high-hat, learned 12. intellectual
14. intelligentsia
flown diction .. 8. euphuism
flying .. 7. Icarian 9. visionary
11. extravagant, pretentious
12. ostentatious 13. grandiloquent
handed .. 9. arbitrary 10. autocratic,
imperative 11. domineering,
overbearing
hat .. 8. snobbish 12. aristocratic
priest .. 3. Eli (Israel) 11. Melchezedek
(Mormon)
sounding .. 4. loud 7. fustian 8. high-
toned 13. grandiloquent
spirited .. 4. edgy 5. fiery 6. lively
9. excitable 10. mettlesome 11. high-

mettled
strung . . 4. taut 5. tense 7. nervous
9. excitable
time . . 3. fun 5. binge, spree 8. carousal
11. opportunity
toned . . 5. tense 7. stylish 8. elevated
9. dignified 11. fashionable
highest . . . 3. top 4. best 6. utmost
7. maximum, supreme, topmost
8. bunemost, dominant 9. nth degree,
uppermost
highest (pert to) . . .
comb form . . 4. acro
dice number . . 3. six 4. sise (sice)
point . . 3. top 4. acme, apex 5. crest
6. apogee, climax, summit, vertex,
zenith 7. ceiling, noonday 8. meridian,
noontide, pinnacle 11. ne plus ultra
Highlands, the (pert to)
heavy pole . . 5. caber
inhabitant . . 4. Scot
sword . . 8. claymore
highway . . 3. via, way 4. bahn, iter, path,
pike, road, toby 6. artery, course, street
7. beltway, freeway, parkway, thruway
(throughway) 8. arterial, autobahn,
turnpike 9. boulevard, concourse
10. expressway 12. thoroughfare
highwayman . . . 5. thief 6. bandit, robber
7. brigand, footpad, ladrone 8. hijacker
9. bandolero 10. bushranger, highjacker
hike . . . 4. jerk, toss, walk 5. hitch,
march, raise, throw, tramp 8. backpack,
increase
hilarious . . 3. mad 5. merry, noisy
7. festive 8. mirthful 9. ludicrous
hilarity . . 4. glee 5. mirth 6. gaiety,
levity 7. jollity, whoopee 8. laughter
9. joviality 10. jocularity, joyousness
12. cheerfulness, exhilaration
hill . . . 3. kop, tor 4. dene, dune, heap,
holt, kame, knob, loma, mesa, paha,
rath 5. bargh, butte, esker, morra,
mound 6. barrow, summit 9. acclivity,
elevation, monadnock
hill myna . . 8. starling
hillside . . 4. bank, brae, hill, knop, ramp
5. cleve (cleeve), cliff, knoll, scarp,
slope 6. glacia
hilt . . . 4. haft 6. handle
hilum . . 3. eye (bean) 5. hilar, notch
7. opening (kidney)
Himalaya (pert to) . . .
antelope . . 4. goral, serow
bear . . 5. bhalu
bearcat . . 5. panda
bird . . 5. monal (pheasant) 6. chough
(crow)
cat . . 5. ounce
country . . 5. Nepal
dweller . . 8. Nepalese
formations . . 7. Siwalik
goat . . 4. ibex, kail, tahe
kingdom . . 5. Hunza
mountain peak . . 3. Api 7. Everest, The
Hump
pass . . 7. Nathula
plant . . 4. nard (Med)
sheep (wild) . . 6. bharal, nahoor
swamp . . 5. Terai
tree . . 3. fir (silver) 5. Neoza (pine)

6. Bhutan, deodar (cedar)
himself . . . 4. ipse
hind . . . 3. doe 4. back, deer, rear, stag
6. caudal, haunch, rustic 7. peasant,
servant 8. domestic 9. posterior
11. hindquarter
hind (red fish) . . . 7. grouper 8. cabrilla
hinder . . . 3. bar 5. block, check, cramp,
debar, delay, deter, embar 6. cumber,
hamper, impede, retard 7. prevent
8. restrain 9. posterior
hindrance . . . 3. bar, rub 4. clog, snag,
stop 5. check, delay 8. obstacle
9. deterrent, restraint, stricture
10. impediment 11. obstruction
12. interruption
Hindu, Hindoo . . . 4. Koli, Sikh 5. Tamil
6. Indian 9. Hindustan
Hindu (pert to) . . .
alphabet . . 6. Sarada
apartment . . 5. mahal
ascetic . . 4. yati, yogi 5. fakir, sadhu
atheist . . 7. nastika
author of law . . 4. Manu (Code)
bird . . 5. Munia 6. garuda
Buddha's mother . . 4. Maya
caravansary . . 8. choultry
carriage . . 6. gharry (gharri)
caste . . 4. Bhil 5. Palli, Sudra, Tamil
7. Brahman
ceremony . . 7. sraddha
city (sacred) . . 5. Mecca 7. Benares
9. Allahabad
coin . . 4. anna
cymbals . . 3. tal
dancing girl . . 8. bayadere
darkness (spiritual) . . 5. tamas
deity . . 4. Devi, Rama, Siva (Shiva),
Yama 5. Ahura, Asura 6. Brahma,
Vishnu 7. Krishna 8. Trimurti
deity consort . . 5. sakti
dialect . . 5. Tamil
division . . 5. Patti, Taraf 6. zillah
7. Pargana
Dravidian . . 5. Tamil
drink (sacrificial) . . 4. soma
evil spirit . . 4. Mara 5. asura 6. yaksha
festival . . 4. Holi, tali 6. Dewali, Pongal
9. Dashahara
first mortal to die . . 4. Yama
flute . . 3. bin 5. pungi
garment . . 4. sari (saree)
Gautama's wife . . 6. Ahalia
gentleman (Mr) . . 5. baboo (babu), sahib
giant . . 4. Bana (thousand-armed)
government . . 6. sircar
guitar . . 4. vina 5. sitar
hero . . 4. Nala
incarnation . . 4. Rama 5. asura 6. yaksha
jackal . . 4. kola
king . . 5. Rajah
language (oldest) . . 5. Tamil
language (sacred) . . 4. Pali
loincloth . . 5. dhoti
magic . . 4. jadu (jadoo), maya
magician . . 4. yogi 5. fakir
meal (wheat) . . 4. atta (ata)
mendicant . . 4. naga 8. sannyasi
merchant . . 6. banian (banya) 7. goladar
mind . . 5. manas
monkey god . . 7. Hanuman

mountain . . 4. Meru
mystic . . 4. yogi
nursemaid . . 4. ayah
paradise . . 7. Nirvana
patriarch . . 5. Pitri
peasant . . 4. ryot
philosophy . . 4. yoga, Yuga 5. tamas
physicist . . 5. Raman (Nobel 1930)
pillar . . 3. lat
poet . . 5. rishi 6. Tagore (Nobel 1913)
prince . . 4. raja
reign . . 3. raj
sacred river . . 6. Ganges
sage . . 5. rishi 6. Dharma 7. Gautama,
   Mahatma
savant . . 5. swami
scarf . . 4. sari (saree)
serpent (semi-human) . . 4. Naga
servant . . 5. hamal
slave . . 4. dasi (fem)
soldier . . 4. sikh 5. sepoy
supernatural being . . 6. Garuda
swan . . 5. hansa
syllable of assent . . 2. om
Taraf ruler . . 9. tarafdar
title . . 3. Sri 4. Raja, Rana, Rani 5. Rajah,
   Ranee 6. sirdar 8. maharaja (maharajah)
tree (sacred) . . 5. pipal 6. bo tree
tunic . . 4. jama (jamah)
underworld (series) . . 6. Patala
village . . 5. abadi
virtue . . 5. sharma
widow (cremation) . . 6. suttee
woman (first) . . 6. Ahalya
Hindu Ages, Yoga . . .
1st . . 5. Krita
2nd . . 5. Treta
3rd . . 7. Dvapara
4th . . 4. Kali
end . . 7. Pralaya
total . . 4. Maha 10. Manvantara
Hindu goddess . . . 3. Sri, Uma 4. Devi,
   Kali 5. Durga, Gauri 6. Chandi, Shakti
   7. Lakshmi, Parvati 9. Haimavati (Durga)
Hindu god of . . .
ancestors . . 5. Pitri
dead . . 4. Yama
fire . . 4. Agni
love . . 4. Kama
spirit . . 5. Asura
unknown . . 2. Ka
wisdom (elephant-headed) . . 6. Ganesa
   (Ganesha)
Hindu religion . . .
abode of gods . . 4. Meru
call to prayer . . 4. azan (adan)
ceremony, rite . . 7. araddha
congregation . . 5. samaj
convert (to Islam) . . 6. shaikh
creator . . 6. Brahma
cremation . . 4. sati 6. suttee
doctrine, destiny . . 5. karma
first human to die (deified) . . 4. Yama
hell . . 6. Naraka
Hinduism . . 5. Agama 6. Tantra
   7. Jainism 8. Buddhism 10. Brahmanism
holy man . . 5. Sadhu (Sadh)
image worship . . 5. arati
incarnation . . 4. Rama 6. avatar
   11. Ramachandra
literature (sacred) . . 4. Veda 7. Shastra

lord of the world . . 9. Jagannath
   (Jagannatha)
monastery . . 4. math
philosophy (life) . . 5. artha, atman, prana
   6. tattva
prayer, call to . . 4. azan (adan)
prayer rug . . 5. asana, Melas
religion . . 5. Agama 6. Tantra 7. Jainism
   8. Buddhism 10. Brahmanism
scripture . . 4. Veda 5. Agama 6. Tantra
   7. Shastra
sect . . 4. Jain (Jaina), Sikh 6. tantra
Shastra (4 parts) . . 5. aruti 6. purana,
   smriti, tantra
Siva worshiper . . 5. Saiva
Supreme Spirit . . 5. atman 7. jivatma
teacher . . 4. guru 5. swami
Trimurti (Triad) . . 4. Siva 6. Brahma,
   Vishnu
trinity, triad . . 8. Trimurti (Siva, Brahma,
   Vishnu)
unorthodox . . 7. Jainism
widow (cremation) . . 6. suttee
Hindustan (pert to) . . .
dialect . . 4. Urdu 10. Hindustani
people . . 9. Dravidian
poet . . 5. Siraj (Beng)
rice . . 7. aghanee
hinge . . . 3. pan (part) 4. axis, axle,
   hang, knee, turn 5. joint, pivot, stand
   6. depend, fasten, lamina, pintle
hint . . . 3. cue 5. imply, refer, trace
   6. allude, glance 7. eyewink, inkling,
   suggest 8. allusion, innuendo, intimate,
   reminder 9. insinuate 10. intimation,
   suggestion 11. insinuation, supposition
hip . . . 3. hop, pod 4. coxa, limp, miss,
   skip 6. haunch 8. greeting
hip, hips (pert to) . . .
bone . . 4. coxa 5. ilium 7. os coxae
   10. innominate
muscle . . 9. iliopsoas
nerve . . 7. sciatic (largest)
rose fruit . . 10. pseudocarp
Hippocrates (pert to) . . .
drug . . 5. mecon (possibly opium)
famed as . . 9. physician (Gr)
oath . . 11. Hippocratic
hippopotamus . . . 5. hippo 6. seacow,
   zeekoe 8. behemoth (Bib)
hippopotamus, thong of hide . . .
   7. chicote
Hiram . . . 9. most noble 10. King of Tyre
   (Bib)
hire . . . 3. let, use 4. hack, rent 5. bribe,
   lease, price, wages 6. employ, engage,
   reward, salary 7. charter, stipend
   9. allowance 12. compensation
hireling . . . 4. esne, serf 5. slave, venal
   8. employee 9. mercenary
hirmos . . . 4. hymn 8. canticle 9. troparion
hirondelle (Her) . . . 7. swallow
hirsel . . . 4. herd 5. flock 7. pasture
hirsute . . . 5. hairy, rough 6. coarse,
   shaggy 7. boorish, bristly, uncouth
Hispania (anc) . . . 16. Spain and Portugal
Hispanic . . . 6. Latino 7. Spanish 13. Latin
   American 15. Spanish American
hispid . . . 5. rough 7. grooved 8. strigose
hiss . . . 3. boo, tst 4. fizz 7. condemn
   8. derision, sibilate 10. effervesce,

sibilation
historian ... 5. actor 6. writer 8. annalist
  10. chronicler
history ... 5. drama 6. annals, events,
  memoir 7. account 8. relation, treatise
  9. chronicle, narrative
history (pert to) ...
  Father of .. 9. Herodotus
  muse of (Gr Myth).. 4. Clio
  period .. 3. era
  personal .. 7. memoirs 9. biography,
  genealogy 13. autobiography
histrio ... 5. actor
histrion ... 5. actor
histrionics ... 6. acting, actors 9. theatrics
  11. theatricals
hit ... 3. bop, lob, rap, tap 4. blow, bunt,
  slam, slap, slog, suit, swat 5. flick,
  knock, shoot, smite 6. buffet, larrup,
  please, strike 7. succeed, success
  9. collision
hitch ... 3. hop, tie, tug 4. halt, jerk, knot,
  limp, pull, yoke 5. catch, cling, crick,
  marry, unite 6. enlist, fasten, hobble
  8. obstacle 9. hindrance 10. enlistment
hitherto ... 3. ago, yet 5. as yet 7. prior
  to 8. formerly, until now
hit or miss ... 6. casual 8. at random,
  by chance, careless 9. haphazard
Hittite (pert to) ...
  ancestor (Bib).. 4. Heth
  city.. 6. Hamath, Pteria (ruins)
  country.. 6. Khatti (Asia Minor)
  people (anc).. 8. Hittites 10. aborigines
  storm god.. 6. Teshup (Teshub)
hoagie, hoagy ... 3. sub 4. hero
hoar ... 4. aged, gray, rime 5. hoary,
  white 7. ancient 9. hoarfrost, venerable
hoard ... 5. amass, lay up, store 6. garner,
  supply 7. husband 8. treasure, treasury
  10. accumulate, collection
hoarder ... 5. miser 6. storer 9. treasurer
hoarfrost ... 3. rag 4. hoar, rime
  7. needles (ice) 9. Jack Frost
hoarse ... 3. old 4. aged, gray 6. remote
  (in time) 7. ancient 9. canescent
hoatzin, hoactzin ... 4. anna 5. hanna
  8. pheasant 9. stinkbird 11. Opisthocomi
  (group)
hoax ... 3. bam 4. bilk, ruse, sham
  5. bluff, cheat, spoof, trick 6. canard
  7. deceive 8. artifice 9. deception
hob ... 3. elf, hub, peg, pin 4. game,
  mark 5. clown, fairy, havoc 6. ferret,
  rustic, sprite 7. hobnail 8. mischief
  9. fireplace, hobgoblin
hobble ... 4. clog, gait (unequal), halt,
  limp 5. dance 6. fetter, tether,
  wabble 7. dilemma, pastern, shackle
  11. predicament
hobbledehoy ... 4. gawk 5. youth
hobbler ... 5. pilot 7. boatman, hoveler,
  laborer, soldier 8. retainer
hobby ... 3. fad, nag 5. dolly, horse
  6. falcon 7. bicycle, pastime
  9. avocation, plaything 10. hobbyhorse
  12. rocking horse
hobgoblin ... 5. elf, imp 4. bogy, pixy,
  Puck 5. scrat 6. sprite 7. bugaboo
  9. coltpixie 10. apparition 15. Robin
  Goodfellow

hobnob ... 9. associate (with), drink with,
  hit or miss
hobo ... 3. bum 5. tramp 6. beggar
  7. vagrant 8. vagabond
hock ... 3. ham 4. pawn, wine 5. ankle,
  joint, thigh (man) 6. pledge 7. disable
  9. hamstring
hockey (pert to) ...
  ball, disk.. 3. nur 4. knur, puck
  cup.. 7. Stanley (prize)
  goal.. 4. cage
  stick.. 6. shinny 7. cammock
  team number.. 5. seven
hocus ... 4. drug 5. cheat 6. liquor
  (drugged) 7. deceive, falsify 8. cheating,
  trickery 10. adulterate
hocus-pocus ... 5. cheat, trick 6. bunkum,
  humbug 7. juggler 8. flimflam,
  nonsense, quackery 9. deception,
  trickster 11. incantation 12. charlatanism
  13. sleight of hand 15. juggler's formula
hod ... 3. tub 4. hide 6. barrow, trough
  7. scuttle
hodgepodge ... 4. hash, mess, olio, stew
  5. cento 6. jumble, medley 7. mélange,
  mixture 10. miscellany 11. gallimaufry,
  olla-podrida
hog ... 3. pig, sow, Sus 4. bene, boar, galt,
  gilt 5. sheep (unshorn), shoat, swine
  6. barrow 8. babirusa (babiroussa),
  javelina 9. boschvark, razorback
hog ... 6. corner (the market) 7. glutton
  8. slattern 9. take it all 10. locomotive,
  monopolist
hog (pert to) ...
  breed.. 5. Essex 9. Hampshire
  food.. 4. mast
  ground.. 6. marmot
  hoglike.. 7. porcine
  salted side.. 5. bacon 6. flitch
  shears (snout).. 7. snouter
  thigh (cured).. 3. ham
hogfish ... 7. capitan, pigfish 8. scorpene
hoggerel ... 5. sheep 6. hogger
hoggery ... 4. hogs 5. greed
  11. beastliness 14. hoggish manners
hoggish ... 6. filthy, greedy 7. porcine,
  selfish, swinish 10. gluttonous
hogshead ... 4. cask 6. barrel 7. measure
hogwash ... 5. swill, waste
hoi polloi ... 3. mob 5. herde 6. masses,
  rabble 7. the many 8. populace
  9. multitude
hoist ... 4. lift, sail 5. boost, heave,
  hoise, raise 7. elevate 8. elevator
hoisting device ... 3. gin 4. jack
  5. crane, davit, lewis 7. capstan, derrick
  8. elevator, windlass 9. parbuckle
hoity-toity ... 5. giddy, proud 6. snooty
  7. flighty, haughty 8. arrogant
  11. exclamation, harum-scarum,
  patronizing, thoughtless
  13. irresponsible
hold ... 3. own 4. bind, have, keep,
  lien, seat, stow 5. avast, cling,
  delay, grasp, judge 6. adhere, arrest,
  cleave, clench, defend, detain, endure,
  harbor, regard, retain 7. contain,
  control, custody 8. consider, foothold,
  maintain, thurrock (ship's), treasury
  9. anchorage, constrain, entertain,

prosecute 11. compartment
hold (pert to) . . .
  back . . 3. dam 4. last, stem 5. delay,
    deter, stint 6. detain, hinder, refuse,
    retard 7. abstain, inhibit, repress
    8. restrain
  belief . . 7. suppose
  dear . . 7. cherish
  fast . . 5. cling 6. adhere 9. persevere
  forth . . 5. offer, speak 7. declaim,
    descant, exhibit, expound 8. continue,
    maintain, propound
  off . . 5. avert, delay 7. repulse, ward
    off 8. stay aloof, temporize
  on . . 4. stop, wait 6. endure, retain
    7. forbear 8. continue
  opinion . . 4. deem
  out . . 4. last 6. endure, refuse, resist
    7. exclude 8. continue
  session . . 3. sit 7. convene 8. assemble
  together . . 5. adhere, cohere 8. be joined
    9. co-operate
  up . . 3. rob 4. buoy, halt, lift, rein
    5. check, delay, raise 6. hinder, resist,
    retard 7. display, exhibit, pillory (to
    scorn), robbery, support, sustain
  water . . 5. sound 10. consistent
holder . . 3. cop (yarn) 4. file 5. owner,
  payee 6. bearer, binder, lienor, tenant
  7. trustee 8. endorsee 9. mortgagor,
  possessor, recipient 10. receptacle
hold in . . .
  check . . 4. curb, rein 6. arrest, bridle
    7. control 8. restrain
  custody . . 4. jail 6. detain, intern
    7. bottoms, low land
  hand . . 6. assure 7. control, promise,
    toy with
  mind . . 6. harbor 7. cherish 9. entertain
holding . . 5. asset, claim, stake, tenet,
  title, trust 6. belief, equity, estate,
  tenure 8. interest, property 9. retention
  10. possessing, possession, supporting
holding fast . . 9. tenacious 10. persistent
holding sway . . 7. regnant 8. dominant,
  reigning
hole . . 3. den, pit 4. bore, cave, cove,
  dive, flaw, gulf, lair, nook, slot,
  vent 5. abyss, chasm, fault, hovel,
  place, shaft 6. burrow, cavern, cavity,
  cellar, hollow, prison 7. impasse,
  opening, orifice, ostiole 10. excavation
  11. predicament
hole (pert to) . . .
  bowling ball . . 4. grip
  cable (ship's) . . 5. hawse
  enlarger . . 6. reamer
  implement . . 3. awl, eye 4. bore 5. drill
    8. stiletto
  metal mold . . 5. sprue
  mud . . 6. wallow
  wall . . 5. niche
  water . . 5. oasis
  whirlpool . . 5. gourd (obs)
Holi (or Hoolee) . . 8. festival (Hind)
holia . . 6. salmon (humpback)
holiday . . 4. fete 5. feria, merry 6. fiesta,
  jovial, outing 7. festive, playday
  8. festival, vacation 9. convivial, festivity
  10. recreation
holiness . . 5. piety, title (Pope) 8. sanctity
  9. godliness 10. sacredness

11. saintliness 13. righteousness
Holland . . 11. Netherlands (which see)
Holland . . .
  capital . . 8. The Hague (Court)
    9. Amsterdam
  city . . 3. Ede 5. Doorn 6. Leyden
    9. Amsterdam, Rotterdam
  government . . 8. monarchy
  liquor . . 3. gin 8. schnapps
  oddity . . 5. dikes 6. canals, tulips
  painter . . 6. Rubens 7. Van Eyck
  people . . 5. Dutch
  port . . 4. Edam
  pottery . . 5. delft (delf)
  province . . 4. Edam 7. Drenthe, Zeeland
  river . . 3. Ems, Lek 5. Meuse, Rhine
    7. Scheldt (Schelde)
  sea . . 5. North
  village . . 3. Ede
hollow . . 3. den, pit 4. thin, void
  5. bight, empty, false, gaunt, sinus
  6. cavern, cavity, cirque, corrie,
  groove, hungry, socket, sunken, vacant
  7. concave, unsound 8. capsular,
  specious 9. cavernous, depressed,
  faithless, insincere, worthless
  10. sepulchral 12. unsatisfying
hollowed . . 6. cavate 7. concave, glenoid
holly . . 4. holm, hull, ilex 5. yapon
  6. hulver, laurel 8. Eryngium
  9. blackjack, Ilicaceae 10. Sapindales
hollyhock . . 5. color 7. Althaea, blue-red
  9. perennial
holm . . 3. oak 5. holly, islet, marsh
  7. bottoms, low land
holobaptist . . 12. immersionist
holocaust . . 9. sacrifice (by fire)
  11. destruction 13. burnt offering
holy . . 5. godly, pious 6. chaste, devout,
  sacred 7. epithet (Relig), sainted
  8. hallowed 9. venerated
Holy, holy (pert to) . . .
  Alliance name . . 10. Metternich
  Bottle (Rabelais) . . 6. Bacbuc
  carpet . . 5. kiswa (kiswah)
  comb form . . 5. hagio
  Communion . . 9. Eucharist
  cow (smoke, Toledo, etc.) . . 3. wow
  Father . . 4. Pope
  Island . . 11. Lindisfarne
  Joe . . 8. sky pilot 9. clergyman
  Land . . 9. Palestine
  oil . . 6. chrism 7. unction
  Ones . . 9. Innocents (slain by Herod)
  orders . . 10. ordination
  Roman Empire name . . 4. Otto 7. Francis
    9. Frederick (Barbarossa)
    11. Charlemagne
  Scripture(s), Writ . . 5. Bible
  water, et al . . 11. sacramental
  water sprinkler . . 11. aspergillum
  war . . 5. jihad
  Willie's Prayer . . 4. poem 5. Burns
Holy Grail (pert to) . . .
  castle . . 9. Monsalvat (Mt)
  guardian . . 8. Amfortas
  knight . . 7. Galahad
  legend . . 8. Sangraal (Sangreal)
  quest by . . 4. Bors 7. Galahad 9. Percivale
  terms . . 7. platter, wine cup
homage . . 5. dulia, honor, liege 6. fealty,

latria 7. loyalty, ovation, respect,
worship 9. deference, obeisance,
reverence 10. allegiance
12. commendation

homard . . . 7. Homarus, lobster

hombre . . . 3. man 4. homo, male 6. fellow

home . . . 4. care, goal (games), kern
(kirn), nest 5. abode, astre, grave,
heart 6. asylum, estate, hearth
7. habitat, village 8. domicile, dwelling
9. residence 10. fatherland, habitation

home (pert to) . . .
base . . 3. den 5. plate
dislike . . 9. ecophobia
Home Sweet Home author . . 5. Payne
(John Howard 1823)
Irish King's . . 4. Tara
of the gods . . 7. Olympus
of the Golden Fleece . . 7. Colchis

homely . . . 4. ugly 5. plain 6. humble,
kindly, simple 7. plainly 8. domestic,
homelike, informal, plebeian, uncomely
9. unsightly 10. intimately
11. comfortable 13. unpretentious

homemade . . . 5. plain 6. simple
8. domestic, handmade, homespun

Homer (pert to) . . .
birthplace . . 5. Chios (claimed)
book . . 5. Iliad 7. Odyssey
burial place . . 3. Ios (Isl)
hero . . 6. Aeneas

Homer's poems (pert to) . . .
rhapsodists . . 9. Homeridae
student, reciter of . . 7. Homerid
8. Homerist
study of . . 10. Homerology
style . . 7. Homeric

homesickness . . . 7. Heimweh 9. mal
du pays, nostalgia

homespun . . . 5. cloth, plain, rough
6. coarse, russet 8. domestic,
homemade 10. not elegant, unpolished
(person)

homicide . . . 5. morth 6. murder 7. killing
12. manslaughter

homily . . . 5. adage 6. sermon
8. assembly, converse 9. communion,
discourse

homing pigeon . . . 13. carrier pigeon

hominy . . . 4. samp 5. maize 10. hulled
corn

Homo sapiens . . . 3. man 4. homo
9. anthropos

Honduras . . .
capital . . 10. Tegucigalpa
city . . 4. Tela 6. Roatan 8. Trujillo
12. Puerto Cortes
discoverer . . 8. Columbus
gulf . . 7. Fonseca
Indian people . . 5. Lenca
language . . 7. Spanish
river . . 4. Ulua 5. Negro 8. Patuca

hone . . . 4. long, pine 5. delay, dress,
stone (sharpening), strop, yearn
6. lament 7. grumble, sharpen
8. oilstone 9. whetstone

honest . . . 4. open 5. frank 6. candid,
chaste 7. genuine, up and up, upright
8. faithful, suitable, virtuous 9. guileless,
honorable, ingenuous, integrity
10. creditable 13. unadulterated

15. straightforward

honesty . . . 5. honor 6. equity 7. justice
8. fairness 9. integrity, rectitude
11. genuineness, uprightness
12. truthfulness 15. trustworthiness

honey . . . 3. mel 5. melli (comb
form), sweet 6. nectar 7. sweeten
10. endearment

honey (pert to) . . .
bear (sloth) . . 8. Melursus
bearing . . 11. melliferous
bee . . 4. Apis 6. dingar 7. deseret
9. mellifera
bird . . 3. iao 6. manuao 10. honey eater
brew . . 4. mead
buzzard . . 4. kite, pern
comb . . 4. raat 5. favus 8. alveolus
drink . . 4. mead 5. morat
flowing . . 11. mellifluent, mellifluous
pert to . . 8. melissic
sucking . . 11. mellisugent, mellivorous
yellow . . 6. dorado 10. melichrous

Hong Kong . . .
capital . . 8. Victoria
government . . 11. Crown Colony
island . . 12. Stonecutters
peninsula . . 7. Kowloon

Honolulu . . .
capital of . . 6. Hawaii
island site . . 4. Oahu
port . . 11. Pearl Harbor
suburb . . 3. Ewa

honorable, honourable . . . 5. moral, title
7. upright 8. honorary 9. estimable,
reputable, venerable 10. creditable
11. commendable, illustrious,
meritorious, respectable

honorably . . . 5. nobly 6. fairly, justly
8. worthily 9. equitably, reputably,
uprightly

honorarium . . . 7. douceur

honored . . . 5. famed, feted 6. graced
7. awarded, revered 8. knighted
9. accoladed

hood . . . 4. corf, cowl, hide, mail (armor)
5. amice, blind, cloak 6. bonnet,
camail, capote 7. capuche (capouch)
8. babushka, burnoose (burnous),
capsheaf, covering, liripipe, mozzetta,
tapadera 12. strong-arm man

hood (suff) . . . 9. condition

hooded . . . 9. cucullate

hooded seal . . . 11. bladdernose

hoodwink . . . 4. dupe, fool, hide, wile
5. blear, blind, cheat, cover, cozen
6. befool, delude 7. deceive, mislead
9. blindfold

hooey . . . 4. blah, bunk 5. tripe 7. baloney,
hogwash 8. buncombe, malarkey,
nonsense 13. horsefeathers

hoof . . . 4. clee, frog, walk 5. cloof (clufe,
cluve) 6. ungula 7. pastern (part)
8. periople (part), pododerm

hoof-paring tool . . . 8. butteris

hoof-shaped . . . 8. ungulate

hoof track . . . 5. piste

hook . . . 4. gaff, lure 5. catch, chape,
cleek, crome, curve, hamus, snare,
steal 6. anchor, clevis, fasten, hangle,
tenter 8. hamulus

hookah, hooka . . . 4. pipe 8. narghile

hooked ... 6. curved, hamate 7. angular, cleeked 8. aduncous (adunc), anchoral, aquiline, uncinate

Hooker (Thomas) .. 9. clergyman 18. Luther of New England

hooks (group) ... 5. Party (Neth) 9. pulldevil, scrodgill 10. Kabbeljaws (Nobles)

hookworm ... 7. Necator 9. Uncinaria

hooligan ... 6. loafer 7. gorilla, hoodlum, ruffian 8. larrikin

hoop ... 4. bail, band, ring 5. clasp 6. circle, wicket 7. circlet 8. surround

hoop skirt ... 9. crinoline 11. farthingale

Hoosier poet ... 5. Riley (J Whitcomb)

Hoosier State ... 7. Indiana

hop ... 3. fly 4. drug, halt, jump, leap, limp, trip, vine 5. bound, caper, dance, frisk, opium 6. flight, gambol, spring 8. narcotic

hope ... 3. bay 4. opal, spes, Spes (Goddess) 5. haven, inlet, trust 6. aspire, desire, expect 7. cherish, promise 8. optimism, reliance 11. expectation 12. anticipation

hoped for ... 7. sperate

hopeful ... 8. probable, sanguine 9. confident, expectant 10. propitious

hopeless ... 4. vain 6. futile 7. forlorn, useless 8. downcast 9. desperate, incurable 10. despairing, despondent 11. ineffectual 12. disconsolate, irremediable 13. irrecoverable, irretrievable

hopelessness ... 7. despair 8. futility 13. impossibility

hop kiln ... 4. oast (ost)

hoplite ... 7. soldier

hopper ... 3. box 5. chute 6. dancer, jumper, leaper 9. penguin (rock) 10. receptacle 11. grasshopper

hopscotch ... 6. pebble, peever 7. pallall

Horace ... 4. poet 10. Ars Poetica

Horae (Gr Relig) ... 4. dike (justice) 6. Eirene (peace) 7. Eunomia (wisdom) 9. goddesses 11. Book of Hours

horal ... 6. hourly

horde ... 4. army, camp, clan, pack 5. crowd, swarm, tribe, troop

Horde, Golden ... 6. Tatars (Mongol)

Horde, Great (Anthrop) ... 5. Kazak 7. Kirghiz

horizon ... 4. blue 5. limit, range 6. circle, sea rim 7. azimuth, sea line, sky line 8. junction (earth and sky), boundary

horizon glass ... 7. sextant

horizontal ... 4. flat 5. level 8. parallel (to horizon)

hormone ... 8. estrogen 9. cortisone

horn ... 4. Cape, cusp, gore, peak, tuba 5. alarm, bugle, cornu, keras, siren 6. antler, beaker, cornet, vessel 7. buccina, process (animal), trumpet 8. tentacle 9. appendage

horn (pert to) ...
blare .. 4. toot 7. fanfare, tantara 9. tantarara
comb form .. 5. kerat 6. kerato
crescent moon .. 4. cusp
drinking (anc) .. 6. rhyton
insect's .. 7. antenna
Jewish .. 7. shophar (shofar)
player .. 6. bugler 9. cornetist, trumpeter
producing .. 11. keratogenic
trumpet .. 6. kerana (kerrana)
unbranched (antler) .. 3. dag 7. pricket

hornbeam ... 8. ironwood

hornbill ... 4. bird, tock 6. homrai, toucan 7. Buceros

horned animal (Myth) ... 7. Unicorn 9. Monoceros

horned rattlesnake ... 3. asp 5. viper 8. cerastes 10. sidewinder

horned toad ... 6. lizard 9. Iguanidae

hornet ... 4. wasp 5. Vespa 6. crabro

horny tissue ... 7. keratin 8. keratoid (ceratoid), keratose (ceratose)

horologe ... 4. dial 5. clock, watch

horoscope ... 3. map 5. chart 6. scheme 7. diagram

horrendous ... 7. fearful 8. horrible

horrible ... 4. dire, grim 6. grisly, horrid, odious 7. ghastly, hideous 8. dreadful, shocking, terrible 9. atrocious, frightful, revolting 10. detestable, horrendous

horror ... 3. awe 4. fear 5. dread 6. aghast, terror 8. aversion, distress 10. abhorrence 11. abomination, detestation 13. consternation

hors d'oeuvre ... 6. canapé, relish 8. aperitif 9. antipasto, appetizer

horse ... 3. cob, nag 4. colt, foal, mare, mule, plug, pony, prad, race, stud 5. beast, burro, draft, filly, genet (jennet), hobby, mount, pacer, steed 6. bronco (broncho), cheval, dobbin, donkey, equine, garran, hippos, maiden, pelter, rouncy 7. caballo, cavalry, charger, courser, Equidae, gelding, hackney, harness, mustang, prancer, quarter, stepper, trotter 8. roadster, stallion, trotting 9. broomtail

horse (pert to) ...
ankle .. 4. hock
arena .. 10. hippodrome
Australian .. 5. dingo, myall 8. warragal, yarraman
blanket .. 5. manta
breastplate .. 7. poitrel (peytrel)
broken-down .. 6. garran, gleyde
buyer (of nags) .. 5. coper 7. knacker
calico .. 5. pinto
collar .. 7. bargham
comb form .. 4. hipp 5. hippo 6. hippus
command .. 3. gee, haw, hup 4. whoa 6. giddap
covering .. 9. caparison
cry .. 5. neigh 6. whinny
dealer .. 7. chanter, scorser
disease .. 5. surra (surrah) 6. heaves, lampas, spavin 7. founder, lampers
draft .. 9. Percheron
family .. 7. Equidae 9. Miohippus, Orohippus
fast .. 6. pelter
feed box .. 6. manger
female .. 4. mare, yaud 5. filly
fly .. 4. cleg (clegg) 6. botfly
foot .. 4. frog, hoof 7. fetlock, pastern
forehead .. 8. chanfrin
gait .. 3. run 4. lope, pace, trot, walk 6. canter, gallop

genus . . 5. Equus
giant (Norse) . . 7. Goldfax
goddess . . 5. Epona
gray . . 8. schimmel
hide . . 8. cordovan
hired . . 4. hack
hoof (part) . . 7. caltrop 8. periople
laugh . . 5. snort 6. guffaw, heehaw
leap . . 6. curvet, hurdle 9. ballotade
lover . . 10. hippophile
mackerel . . 5. atule, tunny 6. bonita
male . . 4. stud 7. gelding 8. stallion
manège term . . 5. longe, mount
   6. pesade 7. piaffer, saccade 8. caracole
   9. estrapage
measure . . 4. hand
miracle (Myth) . . 5. Arion
monster (fabled) . . 11. Hippocampus
old . . 4. jade, yaud 5. skate 8. harridan,
   old paint
opera . . 7. Western
pace . . 4. lope, trot 5. amble 6. canter
pack . . 7. sumpter
pair . . 4. span, team
pasturage right . . 9. horsegate
piebald . . 5. pinto
pole . . 5. poler, wheel
prehistoric . . 8. Eohippus
   10. Mesohippus, Pliohippus
   13. Protorohippus
racer . . 4. pony 6. mudder, plater, staker
ref to . . 6. equine, equoid, hippic
   9. caballine
relay (remounts) . . 6. remuda
riding . . 3. cob
rope . . 5. longe 6. halter
roundup . . 5. rodeo
saddle . . 3. cob 5. mount 7. palfrey
shoer . . 7. farrier 10. blacksmith
slang . . 3. nag 4. hack, plug 6. dobbin
   8. bangtail
small . . 3. cob, tit 4. pony 5. bidet,
   genet (jennet) 8. Galloway, Shetland
sorrel . . 4. roan 8. chestnut
spirited . . 4. Arab 5. steed 6. rearer
   7. courser
stable of . . 6. string
study of . . 9. hippology
swift . . 6. pelter 7. Pacolet
talking (Myth) . . 5. Arion
three (harnessed) . . 7. tandem 7. unicorn
track, arena . . 10. hippodrome
trappings . . 5. manta 6. tackle 7. harness
   9. caparison
trotting . . 6. Morgan
turn . . 7. passade
war . . 5. steed 7. charger 8. destrier
   (anc)
white-streaked face . . 4. shim
wild . . 6. bronco, tarpan 7. mustang
   8. warragal (warrigal)
winged . . 7. Pegasus
horse, breed . . 4. Arab, Barb 5. Shire,
   Waler 6. Cayuse, Morgan 7. Arabian,
   Belgian, Hackney, Mustang, Suffolk
   8. Galloway, Normandy, Palomino,
   Shetland 9. Appaloosa, Miohippus,
   Percheron 10. Clydesdale
horse, color . . 3. bay, tan 4. pied,
   roan 5. cream, pinto 6. calico, sorrel
   7. brindle, dappled, piebald 8. chestnut,

palomino, schimmel, skewbald 10. flea-
   bitten
horse, famed (and rider) . . . 4. Tony
   (Tom Mix) 5. Grani (Sigurd) 6. Bayard
   (Rinaldo), Rienzi (Gen Sherman),
   Silver (Lone Ranger), Trojan (legend),
   Whitey (Zachary Taylor) 7. Alborak
   (Mohammed), Morengo (Napoleon),
   Pegasus (Gr Myth), Trigger (Roy
   Rogers), Xanthus (Achilles)
   8. Comanche (Gen Custer), Sleipnir
   (Odin), Soapsuds (Will Rogers) 9. Black
   Bess (Dick Turpin), Houyhnhnm
   (Gulliver's Travels), Incitatus (Caligula),
   Rosinante (Don Quixote), Traveller
   (Gen Robt E Lee) 10. Bootlegger
   (Will Rogers), Bucephalus (Alexander
   the Great), Cincinnati (Gen Grant),
   Copenhagen (Wellington at Waterloo),
   King Philip (Gen Forrest) 11. Black
   Beauty (legend), Vegliantino (Orlando)
   12. Little Sorrel (Stonewall Jackson)
horseman . . 5. rider 6. cowboy
   7. centaur, vaquero 8. buckaroo
   10. cavalryman, equestrian
   12. broncobuster
horsemanship . . . 6. manège
horseradish tree . . . 3. ben (oil) 5. behen
   (behn) 7. Moringa
Horus (pert to) . . .
   bird . . 6. falcon
   father . . 6. Osiris
   hawk-headed god of . . 3. day
   mother . . 4. Isis
   slayer of . . 4. Seth
hospice . . . 3. inn 6. asylum, imaret
   9. hospitium, infirmary
hospitable . . 6. kindly 7. cordial
   8. friendly, gracious 9. receptive,
   welcoming 10. neighborly
hospital . . . 6. crèche, refuge
   9. ambulance (mobile), infirmary
   10. nosocomium, sanatorium,
   sanitarium 11. institution, xenodochium
   12. ambulatorium
hospitality . . . 7. accueil, welcome 8. open
   door 9. open house, xenodochy
   10. cordiality 13. receptiveness
host . . . 3. sum (obs) 4. army 5. swarm
   6. legion, throng 8. assemble, landlord
   9. multitude, sacrifice 11. entertainer
hostel . . . 3. inn 5. hotel, motel 6. tavern
   8. lodgings 9. residence (student)
hostelry . . . 3. inn 5. hotel 6. hostel,
   tavern 11. caravansary
hostile . . . 5. enemy 7. adverse (law),
   opposed 8. contrary, inimical
   10. malevolent, unfriendly
   11. belligerent 12. antagonistic
   13. unsympathetic
hostilities . . . 3. war 5. feuds, raids
hostility . . . 5. anger 6. animus, enmity,
   hatred, rancor 7. ill will, warfare
   8. opponent 9. animosity, antipathy
   10. antagonism, bitterness, opposition,
   resentment 11. contrariety
   13. antisocialism 14. unfriendliness,
   vindictiveness
hostler . . . 5. groom 7. equerry
   9. innkeeper, stableboy, stableman
Host vessel . . . 3. pyx 5. paten

10. monstrance

hot . . . 3. red 5. calid, eager, fiery
6. fervid, raging, recent, torrid, urgent
7. burning, calidus, excited, fervent,
glowing, peppery, violent 8. feverish,
sizzling, vehement 10. hot-blooded,
passionate

hot cakes . . . 8. kneepads (army sl)

hotel . . . 3. inn 5. lodge 6. hostel, tavern
7. albergo 11. caravansary

hot-tempered . . . 5. angry, breth, fiery
7. enraged, iracund 8. choleric, wrathful
10. hot-blooded

Hottentot, S Africa (pert to) . . .
cloak . . 6. kaross
hut . . 5. kraal
language . . 7. Khoisan
mixed native . . 6. Griqua
musical instrument . . 4. gora (gorah)
nickname . . 9. Khoi-Kholn (Koi-Koin)
(men of men)
people . . 5. Bantu 7. Bushman

hound . . . 4. hunt 5. chase, track 6. follow,
pursue 7. devotee 9. scoundrel

hound (animal) . . . 4. alan 6. Afghan,
basset, beagle, setter 7. harrier, skirter
8. Cerberus (Myth), elkhound, foxhound
9. boarhound, dachshund, deerhound,
greyhound, staghound, wolfhound
10. bloodhound, otterhound

hounds, relay of . . . 8. avantlay

hour (pert to) . . .
astrology . . 7. inequal 9. planetary
by the . . 5. horal 6. horary
Eccl . . 4. sext 9. canonical
Latin . . 4. hora 5. Horae (Book of Hours)
measure . . 9. hourglass
term . . 4. time 6. period 7. measure
8. interval

houri . . . 5. nymph (Muslim)

Hours, Book of . . . 5. Horae

house . . . 3. eco (comb form) 4. casa,
firm, home 5. abode, cover, lodge,
tribe 6. billet, family 7. cottage,
enclose, lineage, mansion, quarter,
shelter, theater 8. audience, bungalow,
Congress, domicile, dwelling
9. playhouse, residence, workhouse
10. habitation, Parliament

house (pert to) . . .
astrology . . 7. mansion, mundane
9. planetary
boarding . . 3. inn 5. hotel 6. tavern
9. dormitory
comb form . . 3. eco 4. oeco, oiko
correction . . 9. Bridewell (Eng)
11. reformatory
dog . . 6. kennel
government . . 5. Lords 7. Commons
15. Representatives
ranch . . 4. casa 6. casita 8. hacienda
roof . . 9. penthouse
small . . 3. hut 4. nest 5. cabin, shack
stately . . 5. villa 6. palace 7. mansion
summer . . 6. casino, gazebo 9. belvedere
warming . . 6. infare

household (pert to) . . .
deity . . 5. Lares 7. Penates
domestic . . 6. family, menage
fairy . . 4. Puck
linen . . 6. napery

housekeeping . . . 8. oikology
10. management 11. hospitality

House of . . . 4. Keys (Isle of Man) 5. David,
Lords, Peers 7. Bishops, Commons,
Windsor 11. Seven Gables

housewarming . . . 6. infare
11. merrymaking

Houston, Texas . . .
capital . . 8. Republic (Texas, 1837)
college . . 4. Rice
named for . . 10. Sam Houston (Gen)
nickname . . 12. Space City USA
site . . 11. Ship Channel
site of . . 4. NASA

hovel . . . 3. den, hut 4. shed 5. cabin,
hutch, shack 6. dugout 7. shelter

hover . . . 4. flit, soar 5. brood, drift,
float 6. linger 7. shelter 9. hang about
12. be irresolute

however . . . 3. but, how, tho, yet
6. anyhow, though 7. at least
8. although 11. at all events
12. nevertheless 15. notwithstanding

howl . . . 3. bay, cry 4. wail, yell, yowl
6. lament 7. ululate

howling monkey . . . 5. araba

hoyden, holden . . . 4. rude 5. a romp
6. tomboy 9. ill-bred

Hoyle's forte . . . 5. cards, games

hub . . . 3. hut 4. axle, nave 5. center
(centre) 7. hummock 12. protuberance
(rough)

Hub (The) . . . 6. Boston

hubbub . . . 3. ado, din 4. game (US Ind),
stir 6. bustle, clamor, outcry, racket,
rumpus, tumult, uproar 8. rowdy-dow
9. agitation, commotion, confusion
10. turbulence

hubristic . . . 8. arrogant, insolent
12. contemptuous

huck . . . 3. hip 4. hook, howk 6. haunch,
higgle, hollow 7. bargain

Huck Finn (pert to) . . .
con man . . 4. Duke 7. Dauphin
creator . . 5. Twain 7. Clemens
friend . . 9. Tom Sawyer
feud family . . 7. Granger
11. Shepherdson
raft mate . . 3. Jim

huckleberry . . . 5. bacca 9. blueberry
12. Vacciniaceae

huckleberry endocarp . . . 6. pyrene

huckster . . . 6. broker, hawker, vendor
7. peddler 8. pitchman, retailer
9. middleman

huddle . . . 3. hug 5. crowd 6. bustle,
confer, jumble, mingle 7. confuse
8. assemble, disorder, grouping
(football) 9. confusion, skinflint
10. conference 14. conglomeration

Hudson (pert to) . . .
boat . . 8. Half Moon (Henry Hudson's)
explorer . . 11. Henry Hudson
River School . . 8. Painters (19th Cent)
River seal . . 7. muskrat

hue . . . 4. form, tint, tone 5. color, guise,
shade, shout, swart, tinge 6. outcry
7. swarthy 8. shouting 10. complexion

huff . . . 4. puff 5. anger, bully, swell
6. offend 7. inflate

hug . . . 4. hold, clasp, seize 6. adhere

7. embrace, welcome 8. greeting

huge . . . 3. big 4. vast 5. giant, great, large 7. immense, mammoth, massive, monster, titanic 8. colossal, enormous, gigantic 9. monstrous 10. gargantuan

Huguenot . . . 10. Protestant

Huguenot leader . . . 6. Adrets (Baron)

hui (Chin) . . . 4. firm 5. guild 7. society (secret) 11. partnership

huisache . . . 4. wabe (wabi) 5. shrub 7. popinac

huissier . . . 5. usher 7. bailiff, sheriff 10. doorkeeper

huitre . . . 5. oyster

hulky . . . 5. bulky, large 6. clumsy 7. hulking, loutish

hull . . . 3. pod 4. free, husk 5. calyx, frame (ship), shell, shoot, strip 8. covering

hullabaloo . . . 3. din 6. clamor (clamour), hubbub, outcry, racket, tumult, uproar 9. confusion

hulled corn . . . 4. samp 5. maize 6. hominy

hulver . . . 5. holly

hum . . . 4. buzz, sing (with closed lips) 5. croon, drone 6. murmur 7. deceive

human . . . 3. man 4. homo, kind 6. humane, mortal 7. Adamite 8. merciful

human (pert to) . . .
being . . . 3. man 6. mortal, person 7. Adamite 8. creature
bondage . . 7. slavery
race . . 3. man 7. mankind
skull . . 10. death's-head
structure . . 7. anatomy
trunk . . 5. torso

humble . . . 3. low 4. mean, meek, mild, poor 5. abase, abash, demit, lower, lowly, plain 6. modest, simple, subdue 7. degrade, mortify 8. chastise, deferent, disgrace, plebeian, reverent 9. humiliate 10. unassuming 12. unpretending

humbug . . . 4. bosh, fake, flam, guff, hoax, sham 5. cheat, fraud, guile, trick 7. deceive, mislead 8. pretense 9. deception, imposture, stratagem

humid . . . 4. damp, dank 5. moist 6. sultry 8. vaporous

humiliate . . . 5. abase, abash, shame 6. humble, nither 7. affront, degrade, mortify 8. disgrace

humiliation . . . 7. subdual 9. abasement 11. disgraceful 13. mortification

humility . . . 6. humble (spirit) 7. modesty 8. meekness, mildness 9. lowliness (mind) 10. humbleness

hummingbird . . . 3. ava 4. star 5. sylph, topaz 6. rufous, Sappho 7. colibri, Lucifer 8. calliope 9. sheartail, thornbill, thorntail 10. rackettail 11. Trochilidae

humor, humour . . . 3. fun, wit 4. baby, mood, whim 5. blood, cater, fancy, fluid, freak, quirk 6. comedy, levity, nature, please 7. caprice, gratify, indulge 8. drollery 10. comicality 11. inclination, temperament

humorist . . . 3. wag 5. comic, droll 8. comedian 11. entertainer

humorist (famed) . . . 3. Ade, Nye 4. Cobb, Ward (Artemus) 5. Dunne (Peter

Finley), Twain (Clemens) 6. Rogers (Will) 7. Lardner, Leacock, Thurber 8. Benchley, Perelman 9. Wodehouse

humorous . . . 5. funny, humid, moist, witty 6. jocose 7. amusing, jocular 9. facetious, laughable, whimsical 10. capricious

hump . . . 4. arch, hunk, lump 5. bulge, exert, hurry, mound, sulks 7. hummock 8. shoulder 12. protuberance

humpbacked . . . 6. humped, kyphos 8. deformed, kyphosis 9. camel back 11. hunchbacked

humpbacked fish . . . 5. whale 6. salmon, sucker 9. whitefish

humus . . . 4. mold, soil 5. humin, mulch

Hun . . . 3. Attila, vandal 7. soldier 9. barbarian 10. Ephthalite

hunch . . . 4. bend, hump, lump 5. crook, fudge, shove 6. chilly, crouch, frosty, thrust 9. intuition 12. protuberance

Hunchback of Notre Dame (pert to) . . .
actor . . 6. Chaney 8. Laughton
author . . 4. Hugo
character . . 8. Esmeralda (gypsy), Quasimodo (The Hunchback)
French name . . 16. Notre Dame de Paris

hunched . . . 7. gibbous

hundred (pert to) . . .
comb form . . 5. centi, hecto 7. hecaton
eyed being . . 6. Argus
fold . . 8. centuple 12. centuplicate
historian (of centuries) . . 11. centuriator
Latin . . 6. centum
men, soldiers . . 7. century 12. centumvirate
number . . 7. ten tens 9. five score
symbol . . 1. C
victim sacrifice . . 8. hecatomb
weight . . 6. cental 7. centner
years . . 7. century 9. centenary, centurial

Hundred Days (pert to) . . . 8. Napoleon, Waterloo (Battle 1815)

hundred percent . . . 5. quite 8. entirely 10. altogether 14. unquestionable

hundredth of a right angle . . . 4. grad

Hundred Years War . . . 5. Crécy (Cressy)

hung . . . see hang

Hungarian (pert to) . . . see also *Hungary*
army . . 6. Honvéd 9. Honvédség
cavalryman . . 6. hussar
Communist leader . . 4. Nagy 5. Kádár
composer . . 5. Lehár, Liszt 6. Bartók, Kodály
dance . . 7. czardas
ethnic group . . 6. Magyar
gypsy . . 7. tzigane
hash . . 7. goulash
hero . . 5. Arpad 7. Kossuth
Hungarian name . . 12. Magyarország
language . . 6. Magyar, Uralic 10. Finno-Ugric
legislature . . 8. Felsohaz
measure . . 5. antal, itcze
partridge . . 6. Perdix
Pretender to the throne . . 4. Otto
turnip . . 8. kohlrabi
wine . . 5. Tokay
writer . . 6. Molnár

Hungary . . .
capital . . 8. Budapest

city . . 6. Szeged 8. Debrecen
lake . . 7. Balaton
plain . . 6. Alfold
river . . 6. Danube
hunger . . . 4. long, want 6. acoria, desire,
famine, thirst 7. craving 8. appetite,
coveting, voracity 9. esurience
hungry . . . 4. avid, poor 5. eager 6. barren,
hollow, jejune 7. starved 8. esurient,
famished, indigent 10. avaricious
Hung Society (secret) . . . 5. Tried (Man,
Earth, Heaven) 6. Deluge
hunt . . . 3. dig 4. seek 5. chase, delve,
hound, probe, quest, track, trail 6. ferret,
follow, pursue, search, shikar
hunter . . . 3. dog 5. green, horse, jager,
Jason, Orion 6. cuckoo, Nimrod
7. shikari (shikaree), stalker, trapper,
venerer 8. huntsman
hunting (pert to) . . .
act of . . 6. venery 7. pursuit
10. cynegetics
coyotes . . 7. wolfing
dog . . 5. dhole 6. basset, beagle, setter
7. pointer
Dogs (Astron) . . 13. Canes Venatici
expedition . . 6. safari
fond of . . 7. venatic
horn . . 5. bugle
leopard . . 7. cheetah
hurdy-gurdy . . . 4. lire, rota 5. organ
(street) 7. sambuke 10. instrument
(lutelike), waterwheel
hurl . . . 4. cast, pelt, rush, toss 5. fling,
pitch, sling, throw 6. elance (dart),
hurtle 9. overthrow
hurlbarrow . . . 11. wheelbarrow
hurled . . . 4. cast, sent 5. flung, slung,
threw 6. pelted, tossed 7. hurtled,
twisted 8. betossed
hurly-burly . . . 5. storm 6. tumult, uproar
9. agitation, confusion 10. excitement
huron . . . 6. grison (animal) 9. black bass
Huron . . . 4. lake 6. Indian 9. Iroquoian
hurrah . . . 3. joy 4. viva 5. cheer,
huzza, shout 7. triumph 8. applause
10. hallelujah 11. exclamation
13. encouragement
hurricane . . . 5. storm 6. baguio
7. cyclone, Hurakan (god), tornado,
typhoon (in China Sea)
hurry . . . 3. hie 4. rush, scud 5. chase,
haste, impel, sessa, speed 6. hasten,
scurry, tumult, urge on 7. quicken
8. dispatch, expedite 9. agitation,
commotion 10. expedition
11. disturbance, precipitate
hurst . . . 4. hill, wood 5. copse, grove,
knoll 7. hillock (wooded)
hurt . . . 4. harm, maim, pain 5. lesed,
parry 6. damage, grieve, impair, injure,
injury, offend 8. distress, mischief
9. detriment 10. impairment
hurtful . . . 6. malign, nocent 7. baneful,
harmful, malefic, nocuous, noisome,
noxious, painful 9. injurious
10. pernicious 11. destructive,
detrimental, prejudicial
15. disadvantageous
hurtle . . . 4. dash, push 5. clash, fling
6. assail, jostle 7. collide, resound

8. brandish
husband . . . 3. eke 4. mate, save 5. marry,
store 6. direct (frugally), farmer, spouse,
tiller 7. espouse, granger, manager,
steward 8. conserve 9. cultivate,
economize 10. husbandman
husbandry . . . 6. thrift 7. economy,
farming, tillage 10. management
(domestic) 11. agriculture, cultivation
husband's brother . . . 5. levir
hush . . . 3. tut 4. calm, hist, lull 5. allay,
quiet, still 6. soothe 7. appease, silence
10. keep secret
husk . . . 4. bran, leam, rind 5. shood,
shuck, straw
husky . . . 3. dry 5. burly, harsh 6. hoarse,
strong 7. raucous 8. powerful
Husky . . . 3. dog 6. Eskimo 8. Malemute
huss . . . 7. dogfish
hussar . . . 4. fish (banded) 6. dolman
(jacket) 10. cavalryman, skirmisher
hussy . . . 4. girl, jade 8. strumpet
9. housewife
hustings . . . 5. court 8. platform
(Guildhall)
hut . . . 3. cot 4. cote, isba, shed, skeo
(fisherman's) 5. cabin, hogan, hovel,
igloo, jacal, scale 6. lean-to, shanty,
wigwam
hutch . . . 3. bin, box, car, hut, pen
4. coop 5. chest, hoard, hovel 6. coffer,
humped, shanty, warren
hyacinth (pert to) . . .
color . . 5. tenne 7. blue-red
genus . . 10. Hyacinthus
mineral . . 6. zircon
myth . . 4. iris, lily (Turk's cap)
of Peru . . 9. Cuban lily
precious stone . . 8. sapphire (legend)
wild . . 6. camass
hybrid . . . 7. mongrel 9. half-breed
hybrid (pert to) . . .
buffalo . . 7. cattalo
dog . . 5. Husky 7. mongrel
fruit . . 7. plumcot, tangelo 8. citrange
horse . . 4. mule 5. hinny, jenny
vegetable . . 6. pomato
zebra . . 7. zebrass, zebrula 8. zebrinny
hydra . . . 4. evil 6. polyps 11. thermometer
Hydra (Gr) . . . 6. island 7. serpent
13. constellation
hydraulic (pert to) . . .
brake . . 8. cataract
element . . 5. water
engine . . 3. ram 6. tremie
product . . 5. power
hydria . . . 3. jar 6. kalpis
hydrocarbon . . . 5. tolan (tolane)
6. ethane, octane, pinene, pyrene,
tolane, toluol 7. benzene, methane,
terpene 9. acetylene
hydrocarbon radical . . . 4. amyl 6. pentyl
hydrocyanic acid . . . 7. cyanide, prussic
8. fumigant
hydrogen . . . 1. H 3. gas 7. element
(univalent)
hydroid . . . 9. polyplike
hydrophobia . . . 5. lyssa 6. rabies
Hydrus . . . 12. water serpent (fabled)
13. constellation
hyena . . . 6. mammal 8. aardwolf

9. earthwolf 13. Tasmanian wolf
hygienic . . . 7. sterile 8. sanitary
  9. healthful 10. uninfected
  12. prophylactic
hylophagous . . . 10. wood-eating
hymenopter, hymenopteron . . . 3. ant,
  bee, fly 4. wasp 9. ichneumon
hymn . . . 3. ode 4. song (of praise)
  5. dirge, music, paean (pean) 6. anthem,
  hirmos, Te Deum 7. chorale 8. doxology
  9. Trisagion 11. recessional
hymn (pert to) . . .
  book . . 6. hymnal
  composer . . 7. hymnist
    12. hymnographer
  science of . . 9. hymnology
  singing of . . 7. hymnody
  victory . . 9. epinicion
hypnotic . . . 6. opiate, sleepy 8. mesmeric,
  narcotic, sedative 9. soporific
  12. somnifacient 13. sleep-inducing
hypnotist . . . 6. Mesmer 9. mesmerist
  10. hypnotizer
hypnotize . . . 5. charm 6. dazzle
  8. entrance 9. fascinate, mesmerize,
  spellbind
hypochondriac . . . 4. hypo 6. insane
  7. invalid (imaginary) 8. dejected,
  neurotic 9. depressed, psychotic
  10. nosomaniac

hypocrisy . . . 4. cant 6. deceit 8. feigning
  9. falseness 10. sanctimony, simulation
  11. outward show
hypocrite . . . 4. fake 5. cheat 7. tartufe
  (tartuffe) 8. deceiver 10. dissembler
hypocritical . . . 5. false 8. specious,
  two-faced 9. insincere 10. Janus-faced
  11. pharisaical 13. sanctimonious,
  self-righteous
hypodermic glass vessel . . . 7. ampoule
  (ampule)
hypodermic injection . . . 4. shot
  11. inoculation
hypothesis . . . 3. ism 6. theory 7. premise,
  theorem 8. proposal 9. condition,
  postulate 10. assumption
  11. proposition, supposition
hypothetical . . . 8. academic
  11. conditional, conjectural, speculative,
  theoretical
hypothetical (pert to) . . .
  being . . 3. ens 5. entia (pl) 6. entity
  biological unit . . 2. id
  force . . 2. od
  medium . . 5. ether
hyrax . . . 8. procavia
hyssop . . . 4. mint 11. aspergillum
hysteria . . . 7. anxiety 12. emotionalism
hysterical . . . 7. frantic 8. frenzied,
  wild-eyed 9. emotional 12. uncontrolled

I

I . . . 2. me 3. eye 4. iota (Gr), self 6. letter
  (9th), myself 7. pronoun
I (pert to) . . .
  big . . 3. ego
  excessive . . 8. iotacism
  love . . 3. amo
Iago . . . 7. villain (Othello)
iambus . . . 4. foot, iamb
iatrics (comb form) . . . 11. treatment of
iatrology . . . 7. healing 8. treatise
Iberia . . . 5. Spain 7. Georgia (anc)
ibex . . . 3. sac, tur, zac 4. kail (kyl)
  6. sakeen 8. antelope
ibid . . . 6. lizard 7. monitor
ibidem . . . 4. ibid 9. same place
ibis . . . 5. guara, stork 9. gourdhead
Ibsen drama . . . 6. Ghosts 8. Peer Gynt
  11. A Doll's House, Hedda Gabler
ice . . . 4. rime 5. frost, glacé, glaze
  6. freeze 7. congeal, diamond, jewelry
  11. refrigerant, refrigerate
ice (pert to) . . .
  bartender's . . 5. rocks (sl)
  cream dish . . 4. cone, soda 6. frappé,
  mousse, sundae 7. parfait
  dessert . . 5. glacé 6. frappé 7. sherbet
  fine, slushy . . 4. grue, hail, sish, snow
  5. flake, frost, sleet
  fishing . . 4. chug
  glacier . . 4. neve 5. serac
  mass . . 4. berg, calf, floe 5. serac
  6. icecap 7. glacier, growler
  pendent . . 6. icicle

  sea . . 6. sludge
Iceland . . .
  airport . . 9. Kopavogur
  assembly . . 7. Althing
  bird . . 4. gull 6. falcon 10. gyrofalcon
  capital . . 9. Reykjavik
  city . . 3. Hof 8. Akureyri
  dramatist . . 12. Siguryonsson
  epic . . 4. Edda
  first discoverer . . 8. Norseman (about
  870)
  giant . . 4. Atli
  glacier . . 6. Jökull 11. Orafajökull
  god . . see *Norse god(s), goddess*
  government . . 8. republic (1944)
  legends . . 5. Eddas, Sagas 12. Volsunga
  Saga
  Parliament . . 7. Althing (world's oldest)
  product . . 7. herring
  sculptor . . 9. Sveinsson
  volcano . . 5. Askja, Hekla, Katla
ichneumon . . . 3. fly 8. mongoose
  9. Herpestes 12. hymenopteron
ichor . . . 5. fluid (of the gods)
ichthus . . . 4. fish 6. amulet, symbol
  8. talisman
ichthyophagy . . . 10. fish eating
icicle . . . 7. shoggle 10. stalactite,
  stalagmite
icing . . . 8. frosting, meringue
icterus . . . 6. oriole 7. disease 8. jaundice
  10. yellowness
ictus . . . 4. beat (rhythm), blow 6. accent,

stress, stroke

icy . . . 4. cold 5. algid, gelid 6. frigid, frosty, frozen 7. glacial 8. chilling

id . . 4. idem, unit 5. idant 6. libido, psyche, suffix 7. the same

Idaean (pert to) . . .
dweller of . . 5. Mt Ida
goddess . . 4. Rhea (Crete) 6. Cybele (Asia Minor)
nature goddess . . 6. Cybele 11. Great Mother

Idaho . . .
capital . . 5. Boise
city . . 7. Orofino 9. Pocatello
crop (famed) . . 8. potatoes
dam . . 5. Oxbow 8. Brownlee
famed citizen . . 5. Borah (Sen)
monument . . 16. Craters of the Moon
mountain . . 8. Sawtooth 11. Bitterroots
river . . 5. Snake
salmon (landlocked) . . 7. kokanee
State admission . . 10. Forty-third
State bird . . 8. bluebird
State flower . . 7. syringa
State motto . . 11. Live Forever 12. Esto Perpetua
State nickname . . 8. Gem State

ide (id) . . . 3. orf (orfe) 4. fish 7. the same

idea . . . 4. clue, idée, ideo (comb form) 5. ethic, motif 6. belief, notion 7. concept, meaning, opinion, wrinkle 10. impression 11. supposition

ideal . . . 4. type 5. dream, model, Thule (Myth) 6. unreal 7. paragon, pattern, perfect, typical, Utopian 8. complete, exemplar, fanciful 9. faultless, imaginary, visionary 10. conceptual, consummate, idealistic 11. mental image, theoretical 12. intellectual

idealist . . 7. dreamer 8. romancer 9. visionary 11. illusionist

idealistic . . . 9. fictional, visionary 10. starry-eyed 13. philosophical

ideate . . 5. think 6. invent 7. imagine 8. conceive 9. prefigure

identical . . . 4. same, self, twin 5. alike, equal 10. equivalent, tantamount

identification . . . 3. tag 4. disk, sign 5. badge, brand 6. naming 7. earmark 11. recognition, unification

identify . . . 4. name 5. place, prove 8. coalesce 9. designate, establish 13. associate with

identity . . . 5. unity 7. oneness 8. equality, sameness 9. exactness 11. homogeneity 13. individuality

ideologist . . . 7. dreamer 8. theorist 9. visionary

idiocy . . . 7. amentia, anoesia, fatuity, idiotry 10. deficiency (mental) 11. foolishness

idiograph . . . 9. trademark

idiom . . . 6. phrase 7. diction 8. language 11. peculiarity

idiosyncrasy . . . 9. mannerism 11. peculiarity 12. eccentricity 14. characteristic

idiot . . . 3. oaf 4. dolt, fool 5. booby, dunce, moron 6. cretin, nitwit 7. dullard, half-wit 8. imbecile 9. blockhead, simpleton

idiotic . . . 4. daft 5. crazy 7. foolish 9. senseless 12. feeble-minded

idle . . . 4. laze, lazy, loaf, sorn, vain 5. drone, empty, inert 6. loiter, otiose, tiffle, truant, unused, vacant 7. leisure, loafing, trivial, useless 8. baseless, inactive, indolent, slothful, trifling 9. unfounded, worthless 10. groundless, unemployed, unoccupied 11. ineffectual, unwarranted

idleness . . . 5. folly, sloth 6. vanity 7. inertia 8. delirium, faniente, laziness 9. silliness 10. inactivity, triviality 15. lightheadedness

idler . . . 4. hobo 5. drone 6. loafer 7. dawdler, lounger 8. loiterer

idol . . . 3. god (sacred) 4. Baal, icon, zemi 5. afgod, deity (heathen), eikon, satyr 6. effigy, fetish, idolum, statue 7. darling, fallacy, phantom, picture 8. impostor 9. pretender

idolater . . . 5. pagan 6. adorer 7. admirer, Baalist, Baalite, heathen 8. idolizer 9. worshiper

idolize . . . 5. adore 6. esteem, revere 7. worship 10. idolatrize

idyl, idyll . . . 4. poem 5. image 7. bucolic, eclogue, picture 8. pastoral

i.e. . . . 5. id est 6. that is

if . . . 2. si 3. gif 8. granting, provided 9. supposing

if ever . . . 4. once

if not . . . 4. else, nisi (law) 6. unless

igneous rock . . . 4. boss, dike, trap 5. magma 6. basalt 7. peridot 10. granophyre 11. molten magma

ignis . . . 4. fire

ignite . . . 4. burn, fire, heat 5. light 6. kindle 7. blaze up, flare up 9. set fire to

ignoble . . . 3. low 4. base, mean, vile 6. menial 7. plebeian, shameful 11. disgraceful 12. dishonorable, disreputable

ignoramus . . . 4. dolt, fool 5. dunce 6. nitwit, no bill (law) 11. know-nothing

ignorance . . . 5. tamas (Hind) 9. nescience 12. inexperience

ignorant . . . 7. unaware 8. nescient 9. unknowing, untutored 10. illiterate, unlettered 13. inexperienced, unintelligent

ignore . . . 3. cut 4. omit, snub 7. condone, disobey, neglect 8. overlook 9. disregard, eliminate

Igorot . . . 6. Bontok 7. Nabaloi 8. Kankanai 10. Indonesian

iguana . . . 6. goanna (goana), lizard 7. monitor, tuatara 9. Iguanidae 10. lace lizard

I Have Found It . . . 6. Eureka (Calif motto)

ihi (Maori) . . . 7. skipper 8. halfbeak 10. stitchbird

IHS . . . 5. Jesus 6. symbol 10. in hoc signo

iiwi . . . 4. bird

ikbal . . . 7. arrival 8. prestige 10. prosperity

Iknaton . . . 9. Amenhotep, Amenophis (IV)

ikona ... 9. greenhorn, simpleton

ileum ... 9. intestine (small)

ilex ... 5. holly 7. holm oak 11. Paraguay tea

Iliad (pert to) ...
  founder (anc) .. 4. Troy 5. Ilium
  poem author .. 5. Homer
  poem character .. 4. Ajax 6. Hector
    7. Stentor 8. Achilles, Brisseis
    9. Agamemnon, Cassandra

ilium ... 4. bone (pelvic)

Ilium ... 4. Troy (anc)

ilk .. 4. kind, sort, type 6. nature
    9. character

ill ... 3. bad, mal (comb form) 4. evil,
    hard, poor, rude, sick 5. badly, wrong
    6. ailing, malice, poorly, savage,
    unkind 7. noxious, painful, unlucky
    9. dangerous, difficult 10. disastrous,
    indisposed, iniquitous, malevolent,
    unpolished, unskillful 11. unfavorable,
    unfortunate, unwholesome
    12. disagreeable, inauspicious

ill (pert to) ...
  at ease .. 7. awkward 9. graceless,
    maladroit
  bred .. 4. rude 7. uncivil 8. impolite
    9. bourgeois
  hap .. 10. misfortune
  humored .. 5. cross, moody
  natured .. 4. dour 5. cross, moody,
    surly 6. morose, sullen 7. crabbed
    10. crosspatch
  tempered .. 7. bilious 8. choleric
  timed .. 5. inapt 8. untimely 9. premature
    10. malapropos 11. inexpedient,
    inopportune
  will .. 8. enmity, malice
    11. malevolence

illegal ... 4. foul 7. illicit 8. outlawry,
    unlawful, wrongful 10. contraband,
    unofficial 12. illegitimate, unauthorized

illegal entry ... 6. ringer

illimitable ... 4. vast 8. infinite
    9. boundless 11. measureless
    12. immeasurable, unrestricted

Illinois ...
  airport .. 5. O'Hare
  capital .. 8. Vandalia (first) 11. Springfield
  city .. 5. Elgin 6. Peoria 7. Chicago,
    Decatur 8. Evanston, Waukegan
    9. Centralia
  lake .. 8. Michigan
  slogan .. 13. Land of Lincoln
  State admission .. 11. Twenty-first
  State nickname .. 7. Prairie

illiterate ... 6. unread 8. ignorant,
    untaught 9. inerudite, unlearned,
    unrefined, untutored, unwritten

ill-mannered ... 4. rude 7. boorish

illness ... 6. malady 8. cachexia, sickness
    9. complaint, distemper 10. affliction
    13. indisposition

illuminant ... 3. gas 4. lamp 9. petroleum
    10. Kleig light

illuminate ... 5. adorn, color, light
    6. illume 7. explain, lighten, miniate
    8. emblazen, illumine 9. elucidate,
    enlighten, irradiate, rubricate
    10. illustrate

illumination, unit of ... 3. lux 4. phot

illusion ... 5. fancy 6. mirage 7. chimera,
    fallacy, mockery, phantom 8. delusion,
    phantasy 9. deception, false show
    10. apparition 13. hallucination,
    misconception

illusive ... 5. false 6. unreal 8. spectral
    9. deceitful, deceptive, imaginary
    10. phantasmal, transitory

illusory ... 5. false 8. delusory, illusive
    9. deceptive, erroneous, imaginary,
    unfounded 10. fallacious

illustrate ... 4. cite, draw 5. adorn
    7. explain, picture 8. beautify
    9. elucidate, exemplify, represent
    10. illuminate

illustrious ... 5. noble, noted 6. famous,
    heroic 7. eminent, exalted, radiant
    8. glorious, luminous, renowned,
    splendid 9. brilliant, honorable
    10. celebrated

image ... 3. god 4. copy, icon, idea,
    idol, ikon, type 6. airaun, aspect,
    effigy, idolon, mirror, recept, sphinx,
    statue, typify 7. eidolon, phantom,
    picture, portray 8. illusion, likeness,
    phantasm 9. semblance 10. apparition,
    conception, simulacrum 11. counterpart
    12. reproduction

imaginary ... 5. ideal 7. fancied 8. fanciful,
    illusory, mythical 10. fictitious

imaginary disease ... 9. nosomania

imagination ... 5. dream, fancy
    8. phantasy, poetical

imagine ... 5. dream, fancy, opine, think
    6. ideate 7. suppose 8. conceive
    10. conjecture

imam ... 6. caliph, priest (Muslim)

imbecile ... 4. dolt, weak 5. anile,
    idiot, inane, moron 6. cretin, dotard,
    feeble, stupid, witlet 7. fatuous, idiotic,
    witling 9. driveling 10. half-witted
    12. feeble-minded

imbed ... 5. embed, inset 6. cement
    9. establish

imberbe ... 9. beardless

imbibe ... 4. soak 5. drink, imbue,
    learn 6. absorb, inhale 8. saturate
    10. assimilate

imbroglio ... 5. brawl 11. embroilment,
    predicament 16. misunderstanding

imbrue ... 3. fig, wet 4. soak 5. color,
    stain (with blood), steep 6. defile,
    drench 7. moisten 8. saturate

imbue ... 3. dye 5. steep, teach,
    tinge 6. infuse, leaven 7. ingrain,
    inspire 8. permeate, saturate, tincture
    9. inculcate 10. impregnate

imitant ... 9. imitation 11. counterfeit

imitate ... 3. ape 4. copy, mime,
    mock 5. mimic 6. borrow 7. emulate
    8. pastiche, resemble, simulate
    9. dissemble, reproduce

imitation ... 4. copy, echo, sham 5. apery,
    apism, paste 6. ectype, olivet (pearl),
    parody 7. mimesis, mimicry 8. travesty
    9. burlesque 10. caricature, simulation
    12. onomatopoeia

imitative ... 5. apish 8. apatetic
    9. emulative, imitation 10. simulative
    11. counterfeit

immaculate ... 4. pure 5. clean 6. chaste

8. spotless, unsoiled 9. faultless, undefiled, unstained, unsullied

immanence . . . 7. inbeing 9. inherence 10. indwelling, innateness

immanent . . . 5. inner 6. inward 8. internal 9. intrinsic 10. indwelling

immaterial . . . 6. slight 8. trifling 9. spiritual 10. impalpable, intangible 11. disembodied, incorporeal, unimportant 12. supernatural 13. insignificant, unsubstantial

immature . . . 5. crude, green 6. callow, unripe 7. untried 8. untimely, youthful 9. premature 10. unfinished 11. undeveloped

immeasurable . . . 7. endless 8. infinite 9. boundless, unlimited 10. indefinite 11. illimitable, innumerable 12. immeasurable, incalculable, unfathomable 13. indeterminate 16. incomprehensible

immediacy . . . 9. awareness, closeness 10. directness 11. punctuality

immediate . . . 4. next, stat 6. direct, prompt 7. instant, nearest, present 10. continuous, succeeding

immediately . . . 3. now 4. anon 7. closely 8. directly, promptly 9. instantly, therewith 11. straightway 12. without delay

immemorial . . . 3. old 7. ageless, ancient 8. dateless 9. out of mind 11. prehistoric, traditional

immense . . . 4. huge, vast 5. grand, great 6. superb 7. mammoth, titanic 8. enormous, infinite 9. monstrous 10. prodigious, unmeasured

immerge . . . 3. dip 4. sink 5. merge 6. engulf, plunge 7. immerse 8. inundate, submerge

immerse . . . 3. dip 4. bury, dunk, sink 5. douse, souse 6. absorb, plunge 7. baptize, engross 9. overwhelm

imminent . . . 7. nearing 8. menacing, upcoming 9. impending 10. near at hand 11. approaching, forthcoming, overhanging, threatening

immobile . . . 3. set 5. fixed, inert 6. stable 8. moveless 9. immovable, obstinate, unfeeling 10. inflexible, motionless, stationary

immoderate . . . 5. ultra, undue 7. extreme 9. excessive 10. exorbitant, inordinate 11. extravagant, intemperate 12. unreasonable

immolation . . . 8. oblation, offering 9. sacrifice

immoral . . . 3. bad 6. wicked 7. corrupt, vicious 8. depraved, indecent 9. dissolute 10. licentious, misconduct

immortal . . . 6. divine 7. abiding, endless, eternal, godlike, undying 8. enduring 9. ambrosial, ceaseless, celebrity, perpetual 10. superhuman 11. amaranthine, everlasting 12. imperishable 13. incorruptible

Immortal (Taoism) . . . 8. Chang Kuo

immortality . . . 4. fame 6. amrita (conferring) 9. anathasia 11. lasting fame 13. deathlessness 15. everlastingness

immovable . . . 3. pat 4. fast, firm 5. fixed, rigid 6. stable 7. adamant 8. immobile, obdurate 9. obstinate, unfeeling 10. inflexible, stationary

immunity . . . 7. freedom 8. impunity 9. exemption 10. resistance (power of) 11. unrestraint

immure . . . 4. wall 6. entomb 7. confine 8. imprison, surround 9. encompass 11. incarcerate

immutable . . . 4. firm 6. stable 7. eternal 8. constant 9. obstinate 10. inflexible, invariable 12. unchangeable 13. unadulterated

imp . . . 3. bud, elf, fay 4. brat, cion, pixy, slip 5. child, demon, devil, fairy, graft, rogue, scion, shoot, youth 6. repair (falconry), spirit, sprite 7. progeny 9. offspring

impact . . . 4. pack, slam 5. brunt, force, shock, wedge 6. effect, stroke 7. contact, impulse, meaning 8. striking 9. collision, fix firmly, impinging

impair . . . 3. mar 4. harm, hurt, ruin, rust, wear 5. break, spoil 6. damage, debase, injure, lessen, reduce, weaken 7. vitiate 8. decrease, enfeeble 11. deteriorate

impale . . . 4. edge, gore, join (Her), spit, stab 5. hem in, spike 6. border, pierce, punish 7. confine, torture 8. encircle, surround

impalement . . . 5. calyx 8. stabbing 10. punishment 11. coats of arms (united)

impalpable . . . 4. fine 10. immaterial, intangible 13. infinitesimal

impart . . . 3. say 4. give, lend, tell 5. grant, share, yield 6. confer, convey, inform, reveal 7. divulge 8. disclose, discover 9. partake of 10. distribute 11. communicate

impartial . . . 4. even, fair, just 7. neutral 8. unbiased 9. equitable 12. unprejudiced 13. disinterested, dispassionate

impartiality . . . 7. justice 8. fairness 10. neutrality 11. unprejudice 17. disinterestedness

impassable . . . 6. stolid 9. impassive 10. impervious, unpassable 11. impermeable, unnavigable 12. impenetrable

impasse . . . 8. cul-de-sac 9. stalemate 10. blind alley

impassible . . . 9. impassive, unfeeling

impassioned . . . 6. ardent 7. amorous, zealous 8. eloquent, vehement 10. passionate

impassive . . . 4. calm 5. stoic 6. serene 7. passive 8. apathetic 10. impassable 12. invulnerable 13. insusceptible

impatient . . . 5. eager, testy 6. uneasy 7. anxious, fretful, itching, peevish, restive 8. choleric, petulant, restless 9. impetuous, irascible, irritable 10. intolerant

impavid . . . 8. fearless

impeach . . . 4. harm 6. accuse, charge, hinder, impair, impede, indict 7. arraign, censure, prevent 9. challenge, criminate, discredit, disparage

impeccable ... 8. flawless, innocent 9. faultless 10. immaculate

impede ... 3. bar, let 4. clog 5. block, debar, estop 6. hamper, hinder, retard, stymie (stimy) 8. encumber, obstruct, restrict

impediment ... 3. bar, rub 4. snag 5. hitch 6. defect, malady 7. baggage, barrier 8. obstacle 9. hindrance 10. difficulty 11. encumbrance, obstruction

impel ... 3. put 4. move, urge 5. drive, force, forge 6. compel, incite, induce, obsess, prompt, propel 7. actuate 9. constrain, influence

impel a boat ... 3. oar, row 4. pole 5. scull

impelling force ... 7. impetus 8. momentum

impending ... 7. nearing 8. awaiting, imminent, menacing 9. hindering 11. overhanging, threatening

impenetrable ... 5. dense 10. impervious 11. impregnable, inscrutable 12. inaccessible, unfathomable 13. unimpressible 14. unintelligible

impenitent ... 8. obdurate 10. uncontrite 11. unrepentant, unrepenting

imperative ... 4. mood (Gram) 6. needed, urgent 7. binding 8. pressing 9. directive, imperious, mandatory, necessary 10. compulsory, obligatory, peremptory 13. authoritative

imperceptible ... 6. subtle 9. invisible 10. insensible 13. inappreciable, indiscernible, infinitesimal 14. unintelligible

imperfect ... 3. mal (pref) 4. cull 5. frail 6. faulty, second 7. errable 8. fallible, immature, impaired 9. blemished, defective 10. inadequate, incomplete

imperfection ... 4. flaw, vice 5. fault 6. defect 7. blemish, failing 8. frailty, weakness 10. deficiency 11. shortcoming 14. incompleteness

imperfectly ... 8. slightly 12. inadequately

imperial ... 5. regal, royal 6. kingly, lordly, purple 8. majestic 9. imperious, masterful, monarchal, sovereign

imperial (pert to) ...
Academy .. 6. Han-lin (Chin)
blue .. 5. smalt
cap .. 5. crown
city (anc) .. 4. Rome
domain .. 6. empire
legislature .. 7. Diet (Jap)
officer .. 8. palatine

imperil ... 4. risk 6. expose 8. endanger 10. jeopardize

imperious ... 6. lordly 7. haughty 8. arrogant, despotic, dominant, pressing 10. commanding, compelling, tyrannical 11. dictatorial, domineering, overbearing

imperishable ... 7. eternal, undying 8. enduring, immortal 11. everlasting 14. indestructible

impermanent ... 8. fleeting, temporal, unstable 9. ephemeral, momentary, temporary, transient 10. evanescent, short-lived

impersonate ... 3. ape 4. pose 6. pose

as, typify 7. portray 9. exemplify, personate (law), personify, represent, symbolize

impertinence ... 4. sass 9. impudence, insolence, unfitness 10. incivility 11. impropriety, irrelevance

impertinent ... 4. rude 5. saucy 7. ill-bred 8. impudent, insolent 9. frivolous, officious 10. inapposite, irrelevant 12. inapplicable, inconsequent 13. disrespectful

imperturbability ... 8. ataraxia (ataraxy), serenity

imperturbable ... 4. calm, cool 6. placid, serene, steady 8. tranquil 9. impassive 10. phlegmatic 13. dispassionate

impervious ... 5. tight 6. opaque 7. callous 10. impassable 12. impenetrable, inaccessible

impetuosity ... 5. ardor 6. fougue 8. rashness

impetuous ... 3. hot 4. rash 5. eager, hasty, heady, sharp 6. ardent, bensel (motion), fervid, sudden 7. furious, violent 8. forcible, headlong, reckless, vehement 9. impulsive 10. passionate 11. precipitate

impetus ... 4. birr 7. impulse 8. momentum, stimulus 9. incentive

impi (Zulu) ... 8. armed men, warriors

impignorate ... 4. pawn 6. pledge 8. mortgage

impious ... 7. godless, profane 9. nefandous, undutiful 10. irreverent 11. irreligious

impish ... 5. elvan 6. elfish 7. puckish 9. malignant 11. mischievous

implacable ... 6. enmity 11. immitigable 12. unappeasable 14. uncompromising

implant ... 4. root 5. infix, inset, plant 6. enroot, infuse, insert 7. enforce, engraft, impress, inspire, instill 9. establish, inculcate, inoculate, insinuate, introduce

implement ... 3. kit 4. peel, tool 5. dolly, knife, means, scoop, tongs 6. pestle, petard 7. fulfill, utensil 8. carry out, complete, material, scissors 9. equipment 10. accomplish, instrument

implement (pert to) ...
ancient .. 4. celt 6. eolith 9. paleolith (stone)
cleaning .. 3. mop 5. broom, brush 6. vacuum 7. sweeper
hide flesher .. 9. slater
holding .. 5. tongs 6. pliers 8. tweezers
lifting .. 3. pry 5. crane, lever, tongs
lumbering .. 4. tode 6. peavey (peavy)
nap .. 6. teasel
printing .. 5. biron, press 6. brayer
reaping .. 5. mower 6. reaper, scythe, shears, sickle
surgical .. 7. scalpel 9. tenaculum
threshing .. 5. flail

implicate ... 5. imply 7. embroil, entwine, involve 8. entangle 10. interweave 11. incriminate

implicit ... 5. tacit 7. implied, virtual 8. complete, inherent 9. entangled, potential 11. unqualified

12. constructive 13. unquestioning

implied . . . 5. tacit 11. inferential 12. not expressed

implore . . . 3. ask, beg 4. pray 5. crave 7. beseech, entreat, solicit 8. petition 10. supplicate

imply . . . 4. hint, mean 5. argue 6. infold 7. connote, involve, suggest, suppose 9. predicate

impolite . . . 4. rude 5. crude, rough 7. uncivil 10. ill-behaved, mannerless, ungracious, unmannerly, unpolished 12. discourteous 13. disrespectful

impolitic . . . 8. unwise 9. untactful 10. indiscreet 11. inexpedient 12. undiplomatic

import . . . 5. drift, sense, value 6. denote, weight 7. betoken, meaning, signify 8. commerce, indicate 9. introduce, of concern 10. importance 11. consequence, implication, importation, merchandise

importance . . . 6. moment, stress, weight 8. prestige 9. influence 10. famousness 11. consequence, importunity 12. solicitation

important . . . 3. key 5. grave 6. famous, urgent 7. pompous, weighty 8. material 9. momentous 11. considerate, influential, significant, substantial 12. considerable, ostentatious 13. consequential

import tax . . . 4. duty 6. tariff

importune . . . 3. beg, ply, tax, woo 4. coax, push, urge 5. beset, impel, plead, press 6. appeal, cajole 7. entreat, press on

importunity . . . 11. importunate, pertinacity 12. solicitation

impose . . . 3. tax 4. duty, levy 6. burden, entail 7. command, confirm (Eccl) exploit, inflict, intrude, obtrude, penalty, presume 10. discommode

imposing . . . 5. noble, regal 6. august 7. stately 8. dignified, grandiose 10. commanding, impressive 11. ceremonious 13. grandiloquent

impossible . . . 6. absurd 8. hopeless, terrible 9. insoluble 10. outlandish 11. unthinkable 12. unimaginable 13. contradictory, impracticable

impost . . . 3. tax 4. levy, task, toll 5. abwab 6. custom, excise, surtax, tariff, weight 7. tribute 8. handicap

impostor . . . 4. fake 5. fraud, phony, quack 6. humbug 7. empiric 9. charlatan, pretender 10. mountebank

imposture . . . 5. fraud, trick 8. delusion, quackery 9. deception 10. imposition

impotent . . . 4. weak 6. barren 7. cripple, sterile 9. deficient, incapable, powerless 13. uninfluential

impound . . . 5. pen in, seize, store 6. freeze 8. collect 8. imprison 9. reservoir 10. confiscate 11. appropriate

impoverish . . . 4. ruin 6. beggar 7. despoil, exhaust 8. bankrupt, make poor 11. make sterile

imprecation . . . 4. oath 5. curse 8. anathema 9. execration

11. malediction

impregnable . . . 4. hard 10. inviolable 12. inexpugnable, invulnerable 13. unconquerable

impregnate . . . 5. imbue 6. infuse 8. fructify 9. fertilize, inculcate

impresa . . . 5. maxim, motto 6. device, emblem

impresario . . . 7. manager 9. conductor, projector (opera) 12. entrepreneur

impress . . . 3. awe, fix 4. bite, dent, levy, mark, seal 5. press, print, stamp 6. affect, effect, enlist, indent 7. engrave, imprint 8. printing, shanghai 9. conscript, engraving, inculcate 10. commandeer, impression 11. indentation 14. characteristic

impressed . . . 4. awed 7. infixed, stamped 8. affected, engraved 9. imprinted

impression . . . 4. form, idea, mark 5. hunch, print, stamp 6. macule, signet 7. emotion, opinion 8. printing 9. engraving, sensation 10. appearance 11. inculcation, indentation, supposition

impressionable . . . 6. pliant 7. plastic 9. sensitive, teachable 10. responsive 11. suggestible, susceptible

impressive . . . 6. solemn 8. dramatic, eloquent 9. arresting, grandiose 10. convincing

imprint . . . 3. fix 4. dint 5. infix, press, stamp 6. indent 7. edition, engrave 8. printing 9. engraving

imprison . . . 4. bond, cage, gaol, jail 5. limit 6. arrest, detain, immure, intern, lock up 7. confine, impound 8. restrain 11. incarcerate

imprisonment . . . 4. band 6. duress 8. coercion 9. restraint 10. constraint, immurement, internment 11. confinement, impoundment 13. incarceration

impromptu . . . 6. extemp 7. offhand 11. extemporary 13. improvisation 14. extemporaneous 15. autoschediastic

improper . . . 3. ill, pah 4. evil 5. amiss, wrong 6. vulgar 7. illegal, naughty 8. indecent, unseemly, unsuited, untoward 9. incorrect, inelegant 10. inaccurate, indecorous, indelicate, unbecoming, unsuitable

impropriety . . . 5. wrong 8. solecism 9. indecency, vulgarity 11. malapropism, misbehavior

improve . . . 4. mend 5. amend, edify, emend, moise, train 6. better, employ, uplift 7. advance, augment, correct, enhance, perfect, promote, recover, rectify, upgrade 9. cultivate, get better, intensify, meliorate 10. ameliorate, recuperate

improvident . . . 4. rash 8. prodigal, wasteful 9. negligent 10. thriftless 11. thoughtless

improvise . . . 5. ad lib 6. invent 7. ad libit 9. ad libitum 11. extemporize 13. autoschediaze

imprudence . . . 5. brass 8. rashness 9. hardihood 12. indiscretion, recklessness

impudence . . . 5. cheek 8. rudeness

9. flippancy, indecency, insolence
10. brazenness, disrespect
12. impertinence 13. shamelessness
impudent . . 4. bold, pert, rude 5. brash,
saucy 6. brazen 8. flippant, insolent,
malapert 9. audacious, shameless
11. impertinent 13. disrespectful
impugn . . . 4. deny 5. blame 6. assail
(by words), oppose, refute 7. asperse,
censure, gainsay
impulse . . . 3. ate 4. rush, urge 5. force
6. motive 7. impetus 8. instinct
9. incentive 11. instigation
impulsive . . . 5. hasty, quick 6. moving
9. impellent, impetuous 10. motivating
11. instinctive 13. ill-considered
impure . . . 4. foul, lewd 5. dirty,
mixed 6. filthy, unholy 7. bastard,
defiled, obscene, unclean 8. unchaste
10. inaccurate, unhallowed
11. adulterated, unwholesome
impure metal . . 5. alloy, matte 6. speiss
impure rock . . . 5. chert 9. flintlike
imputation . . . 7. censure 8. charging
9. aspersion, criticism 10. accusation,
ascription 11. attribution, insinuation
impute . . . 6. accuse, charge, credit,
impart, reckon, regard 7. arraign,
ascribe 8. consider 9. attribute
impy . . . 11. mischievous
in . . . 2. at 4. amid, into 5. among 6. at
home, inside, within
in (pert to) . . .
abundance . . 5. store 6. galore
accordance . . 8. pursuant
addition . . 3. too, yet 4. also, more,
plus 11. furthermore
all directions . . 8. everyway
12. everywhither
an undertone . . 9. sotto voce
as much as . . 3. for 5. since 6. seeing
7. because, insofar
back . . 3. aft 5. arear 6. astern 7. postern
behalf of . . 3. for, pro 7. favor of
camera . . 9. in private 10. in chambers
common . . 4. same 5. alike
concert . . 8. together
contact . . 7. touching 9. attingent
current style . . 3. a la 7. alamode,
popular
existence . . 6. extant
fact . . 5. truly 6. indeed 7. de facto
favor of . . 3. aye, pro, yea
good health . . 3. fit 4. hale 7. healthy
love . . 7. smitten 9. enamoured
name only . . 7. nominal, titular
need . . 7. straits 8. distress
open air . . 7. outdoor 8. al fresco
passing . . 9. en passant
place of . . 3. for 5. stead 7. instead
possession . . 5. title 6. seizin
private . . 8. in camera
regard to . . 5. anent
rows . . 4. arow 6. serial 7. aligned
(alined)
so far as . . 3. qua
spite of . . 6. mauger 7. despite, however
11. nonetheless
standing position . . 7. statant
store . . 5. ready 7. waiting 8. awaiting
straight lines . . 8. e regione

succession . . 6. series 8. serially, seriatim
the future . . 5. hence, later 6. mañana
12. subsequently
the know . . 3. hep
the same place . . 4. ibid 6. ibidem
the year of . . 4. anno
truth . . 6. certes, indeed, verily
8. forsooth
what way . . 3. how 7. quo modo
inability . . . 9. impotence 10. inadequacy,
incapacity 12. incapability,
incompetence
inability to . . .
articulate . . 7. inaudia
chew . . 8. amasesis
comprehend . . 11. acatalepsia
move . . 7. apraxia
name objects . . 9. paranomia
read . . 6. alexia
stand erect . . 7. estasia
swallow . . 7. aphagia
inaccessible . . . 8. reserved
10. unsociable 11. out-of-the-way
12. unattainable 14. unapproachable
inaccurate . . . 5. loose 6. faulty 7. inexact
9. defective, erroneous, imperfect,
incorrect 13. ungrammatical
inaction . . . 6. torpor 7. inertia
8. abeyance, idleness 9. inertness
10. suspension
inactive . . . 4. idle 5. inert 7. abeyant,
neutral, not busy 8. sluggish
9. sedentary 10. indisposed
inadequacy . . . 9. inability 10. deficiency,
inequality 11. inferiority
12. incompetence 13. insufficiency
14. incompleteness
inadvertence . . . 5. error 7. neglect
11. inattention 12. carelessness,
heedlessness 15. thoughtlessness
inadvertent . . . 9. negligent, unwitting
11. inattentive
inadvertently . . . 10. heedlessly
11. unwittingly 12. neglectfully
inane . . . 4. vain, void 5. empty,
inept, silly 6. famous 7. fatuous,
foolish, puerile, trivial 8. trifling
9. frivolous 11. ineffectual, thoughtless
13. characterless
inappropriate . . . 5. inept, undue
8. untimely 10. irrelevant, unsuitable
11. inexpedient
inapt . . . 5. inept 10. unsuitable
inattentive . . . 3. lax 6. absent, remiss
8. careless, heedless 9. negligent,
unheeding, unmindful 10. distracted,
regardless 11. inadvertent
inaugurate . . . 5. admit, begin, start
6. induct 7. install, instate, usher
in 8. initiate 9. auspicate, institute,
introduce 10. consecrate
inauspicious . . . 7. adverse, ominous,
unlucky 8. sinister, untimely 9. ill-
omened 12. unpropitious
inborn . . . 6. allied, inbred, innate,
native 7. cognate, natural 8. inherent
10. connatural
inbred . . . 6. inborn, innate 9. endogamic
10. bred within 15. to the manner
born
Inca (pert to) . . .

descent.. 6. the sun
empire.. 4. Peru (11th cent)
government.. 11. communistic
king.. 9. Atahualpa (15th cent)
prince.. 7. Huascar (16th cent)

incalculable ... 8. infinite 9. boundless, uncertain, very great 11. illimitable 12. immeasurable 13. unforeseeable

incandescent ... 5. clear, light, white 7. glowing, shining

incantation ... 5. magic, spell 6. powwow 7. sorcery 8. exorcism 10. hocus-pocus, mumbo jumbo

incapable ... 6. unable 8. impotent 11. incompetent, inefficient, unqualified 12. disqualified

incapacitate ... 7. cripple, disable, invalid 10. disqualify 11. render unfit

incapacitated ... 8. crippled, disabled 9. hamstrung, paralyzed 11. invalidated 12. disqualified 13. superannuated (retired)

incarcerate ... 5. hem in 6. immure, intern, lock up, retire 7. confine, impound 8. imprison 10. disqualify

incarnate ... 4. rosy 6. embody 9. enshrined 11. incorporate, personified 12. impersonated

incarnation ... 6. avatar, Christ 10. embodiment

Incarnation of Vishnu (eight) ... 4. Apis, Rama 7. Krishna (8th)

incase ... 3. box, can 4. pack 5. box up, cover, crate 6. carton 7. enclose, package 8. surround

incaution ... 4. rash 6. unwary 8. careless, heedless, reckless 9. impolitic, imprudent 10. indiscreet

incendiarism ... 5. arson 9. pyromania

incendiary ... 7. firer 7. exciter 8. agitator, arsonist, incitive 9. seditious 10. instigator 12. inflammatory

incense ... 3. ire 5. anger 6. arouse, enrage, incite 7. inflame, provoke 8. irritate 9. instigate

incense (pert to) ...
burner.. 6. censer 8. thurible 9. incensory
carrier.. 8. thurifer
Hebrew for.. 7. keturah
pert to.. 5. aroma, spice 7. perfume 9. fragrance, redolence
product.. 5. matti, myrrh 6. storax 7. linaloa 8. gum resin, olibanum, pastille, thurible 9. lignaloes, tacamahac 12. frankincense
sacrifice.. 8. oblation
spice.. 8. balsam, stacte
tree bearing.. 7. linaloa 8. agalloch, calambac 9. Boswellia
vessel.. 6. censer 7. navette

incensed ... 3. mad 5. angry, irate, vexed, wroth 6. peeved, piqued 7. angered, enraged, nettled 8. wrathful 11. exasperated

incentive ... 4. brod, call, goad, spur, urge, whet 5. spark 6. motive 7. impulse, rousing 8. inciting, stimulus 9. influence 10. incitement, inducement 11. provocation, stimulative 13. encouragement

inception ... 6. origin, source 9. reception 10. inchoation, initiation 12. commencement 15. intussusception

inceptive ... 9. beginning 10. inchoative

incessant ... 7. endless 8. constant 9. ceaseless, continual, perpetual 10. continuous 11. unremitting 13. unintermitted

inch (pert to) ...
barometric.. 6. degree
forward.. 4. edge 7. crowhop
inch by inch.. 9. gradually, piecemeal
meal.. 9. gradually
three parts.. 11. barleycorns (anc)
twelve parts.. 5. lines
twelve seconds.. 6. a prime (anc)
verb.. 5. creep 7. measure

inches ... 4. hand (4), nail (2 1/4), span (9)

inchoate ... 6. partly 8. initiate, recently 9. beginning, incipient 10. incomplete

inchpin ... 10. sweetbread

incident ... 5. event 7. episode, subject 8. accident, casualty 9. befalling, happening 10. incidental, occurrence 11. contingency 12. circumstance, slight matter

incidental ... 3. bye 6. casual, chance, liable 8. episodic 9. accessory, extrinsic 10. accidental, contingent, fortuitous, occasional 11. subordinate 12. nonessential 13. parenthetical

incidentally ... 6. obiter 8. by chance, by the way 9. en passant, in passing

incinerate ... 4. burn 7. consume, cremate

incipient ... 4. seat 6. induct 7. initial 8. inchoate 9. beginning, embryonic 10. commencing, inaugurate 11. rudimentary

incise ... 3. cut 4. open 5. carve, lance, sever 6. furrow 7. engrave

incised ... 7. carved 8. notched 8. engraved, furrowed 9. laciniate 10. laciniated

incision ... 3. cut 4. gash, slit 5. cleft 6. furrow, injury 7. cutting 8. engraving 10. laceration, separation 11. penetration

incisor ... 5. tooth

incite ... 3. egg, tew 4. abet, fire, goad, prod, spur, urge 5. impel, sting 6. arouse, foment, stir up, suborn 7. agitate, animate, inflame, provoke 9. encourage, stimulate

inclement ... 4. foul 5. harsh, rough 6. severe, stormy 9. merciless

inclination ... 3. dip, nod 4. bent, bias, love, urge 5. fancy, grade, slant, slope, taste, trend 6. animus, bowing, desire, liking, nature 8. aptitude, penchant, tendency 9. affection, attention, deviation, direction, intention, obeisance, proneness 10. attachment, proclivity, propensity 11. disposition 12. predilection 13. prepossession

incline ... 3. dip, tip 4. bend, cant, heel, lean, tend, tilt 5. alist, bevel, grade, slant, slide, slope, trend 9. be willing, gravitate

inclined ... 3. apt, dip 4. wont 5. prone

6. sloped 7. leaning, pronate, willing
8. disposed 11. predisposed
inclined (pert to) . . .
plane . . 4. ramp 7. oblique
to believe . . 9. credulous
to droop . . 3. sag
to sin . . 13. transgressive
inclose . . . see also enclose 3. hem, pen,
pin 4. case, mure 5. embar 6. encase,
encave, incase 7. enclose, environ
inclosure . . . 3. pen, ree, sty 4. cage, cote,
sept 5. hutch, kraal 6. corral 8. sepiment
9. enclosure 10. impalement
include . . . 6. shut up 7. confine, contain,
embrace, enclose, inclose, involve
8. comprise 9. encompass
including . . . 8. covering 10. comprising,
containing 12. encompassing
13. comprehensive
incognito . . . 6. veiled 7. feigned
8. disguise, not known 10. camouflage
incoherent . . . 5. loose 6. broken
8. detached, inchoate 9. delirious,
illogical 11. incongruous
12. disconnected, inconsequent,
inconsistent
income . . . 4. gain 5. rente, wages
6. profit, return, usance 7. annuity,
pension, produce, revenue, tontine
8. interest, proceeds, receipts
9. emolument
incommensurate . . . 7. unequal
12. insufficient 14. unsatisfactory
16. disproportionate
incommode . . . 3. vex 5. annoy 6. molest,
plague, put out 7. disturb, trouble
8. disquiet 13. inconvenience
incomparable . . . 7. eminent, unalike
8. peerless 9. matchless, unrivaled
10. surpassing 11. superlative
12. transcendent, without equal
incompatible . . . 9. differing 10. intolerant
11. disagreeing 12. inconsistent,
inharmonious 13. contradictory,
unsympathetic 14. irreconcilable
incompetence . . . 9. inability, unfitness
10. disability, inadequacy
13. insufficiency 15. unqualification
incompetent . . . 5. inept, unfit 7. wanting
8. impotent 9. incapable 10. unskillful
11. inefficient 12. disqualified,
insufficient 14. incommensurate
incomplete . . . 5. crude 6. undone
7. lacking 8. immature, inchoate
9. defective, deficient, imperfect,
partially 10. unfinished
incomprehensible . . . 8. infinite
9. wonderful 10. miraculous,
mysterious, unreadable 11. unthinkable
12. unfathomable, unimaginable
13. inconceivable, unconceivable
14. unintelligible
incongruity . . . 9. inharmony
10. dissonance 11. incoherence
12. disagreement, inexpedience
13. inconsistency 14. unsuitableness
incongruous . . . 5. alien 6. absurd,
motley 8. off-color 9. differing,
illogical 10. solecistic, unsuitable
12. disagreeable, inconsistent,
inharmonious 13. inappropriate

inconsequent . . . 7. invalid 8. unproved
9. illogical 10. irrelevant 11. impertinent,
unimportant 12. inconsistent
13. inconsecutive
inconsiderate . . . 4. rash 5. hasty
6. unkind 8. careless, heedless
9. imprudent, impulsive 10. ill-advised,
incautious, indiscreet, neglectful
11. improvident, injudicious,
thoughtless
inconsistent . . . 9. differing, dissonant,
fanatical, illogical 10. discordant,
discrepant, incoherent, inconstant
11. incongruous 12. incompatible,
inharmonious 13. contradictory
14. irreconcilable
inconspicuous . . . 9. unseeable 10. out
of sight, unapparent 12. not prominent
13. imperceptible, indiscernible
incontestable . . . 7. certain
10. undeniable 11. indubitable,
irrefutable 13. unimpeachable
14. unquestionable
inconvenience . . . 6. bother 8. disquiet
9. incommode 10. uneasiness
11. awkwardness, disturbance
12. disadvantage, untimeliness,
unwieldiness
inconvenient . . . 5. unfit 7. unhandy
8. annoying, improper, unwieldy
10. unsuitable 11. inexpedient,
inopportune, troublesome
12. unreasonable 15. disadvantageous
incorporate . . . 3. mix 4. fuse 5. blend,
merge, unite 6. embody 7. combine,
include 8. embodied 10. assimilate
incorporation . . . 5. union 9. inclusion
10. embodiment 11. affiliation,
association, combination, composition,
incarnation 12. assimilation
incorporeal . . . 7. phantom 8. bodiless
9. spiritual 10. immaterial
13. unsubstantial
incorrect . . . 5. wrong 6. faulty
8. improper, erroneous, inelegant
10. inaccurate, solecistic, unbecoming
13. ungrammatical
incorrect naming of objects . . .
9. paranomia
incorruptible . . . 4. just 7. upright
8. immortal 11. trustworthy
14. indestructible
increase . . . 3. add, eke, wax 4. gain,
grow, rise 5. add to, amass, raise, swell
6. accrue, dilate, enrich, expand, extend
7. accrete, advance, augment, enhance
(inhance), inflate, promote, upswing
8. heighten, multiply 9. accession,
aggravate, crescendo, expansion,
extension, increment, intensify
10. accelerate 11. aggravation,
enlargement 13. amplification
15. intensification
incredible . . . 8. fabulous, unlikely
9. fantastic, marvelous, wonderful
10. improbable, remarkable
12. unbelievable
increment . . . 6. growth 8. addition,
increase 11. enlargement
12. augmentation
incriminate . . . 6. accuse 7. involve

9. implicate, inculpate

incubator . . . 8. couveuse, isolette

incubus . . . 4. ogre 5. demon, dream 6. burden 8. nightmare 10. evil spirit 13. hallucination

inculcate . . . 5. imbue, infix 7. implant, impress, instill (instil) 12. indoctrinate

incumbent . . . 5. vicar 6. rector 8. resident 9. clergyman, impending, overlying 10. burdensome, obligatory (upon) 11. threatening 12. superimposed

incumbents . . . 3. ins

incunabula . . . 7. infancy 10. beginnings

incur . . . 5. bring 6. accrue, entail 7. bring on 8. be liable, contract, fall into 10. be involved

incurable . . . 8. hopeless 9. apathetic 11. inattentive, indifferent, unconcerned, uninquiring 12. uninterested 13. uninquisitive

incur hostility . . . 10. antagonize 11. contend with

incursion . . . 4. raid 5. foray 6. attack, influx, inroad 8. invasion 9. intrusion

incus . . . 4. bone (ear) 5. anvil 6. hammer

indecency . . . 8. impurity 9. immodesty, indecorum, obscenity, vulgarity 10. indelicacy, unchastity

indecent . . . 5. gross 6. impure, vulgar 7. obscene 8. immodest, improper, uncomely 9. offensive 10. ill-looking, indecorous, indelicate 11. inexpedient

indecision . . . 5. doubt 10. hesitation 11. uncertainty, vacillation 12. irresolution

indecisive . . . 7. dubious 8. formless 9. uncertain 10. hesitating, indefinite, indistinct, irresolute 11. unsupported, vacillating 12. inconclusive

indecorous . . . 4. rude 5. wrong 6. coarse, vulgar 7. uncivil 8. impolite, improper, indecent, unseemly 9. inelegant 10. out of place, unbecoming 11. inexpedient

indefatigable . . . 6. active 8. sedulous, tireless, untiring 9. unwearied, weariless 10. unwearying 11. persevering

indefinite . . . 5. loose, vague 7. general, inexact, neutral 8. formless 9. ambiguous, equivocal, uncertain 10. inexplicit, unmeasured 12. undetermined 13. indeterminate

indefinite amount . . . 3. any 4. some 5. about 10. more or less

indehiscent (pert to) . . .
fruit . . 3. uva 4. pepo (gourd) 5. apple, grape 6. orange, samara 9. sunflower
legume . . 3. pea 4. bean 6. loment
vegetable . . 5. melon 6. squash, tomato 7. pumpkin 8. cucumber

indelible . . . 4. fast 5. fixed 8. deepfelt 9. permanent 10. inerasable 12. ineffaceable, ineradicable, inexpungible 13. unforgettable

indelicate . . . 5. gross 6. coarse, vulgar 7. fulsome 8. impolite, improper, indecent, unseemly 9. offensive, unrefined 10. indecorous, unbecoming

indemnification . . . 9. atonement 10. recompense 11. restitution 12. compensation 13. reimbursement

indemnify . . . 3. pay 6. recoup, secure

8. make good 9. reimburse 10. compensate, recompense

indent . . . 3. cut, jag 4. dent 5. inlay, notch, press, stamp, tooth 6. emboss, furrow, recess, zigzag 7. impress, imprint, press in 8. contract, covenant, draw upon 9. indenture 11. requisition

indentation . . . 3. jab 4. dint, nick 5. choil, notch 6. crenel, furrow, hollow, recess 7. imprint 8. crenelet 10. depression, impression

indented . . . 6. dented, jagged, milled 7. notched, sinuous 8. serrated (Her) 9. impressed 10. undulating

indenture . . . 4. dent 5. notch 8. contract, document 9. agreement 10. depression 11. indentation

independence . . . 7. freedom 9. exemption 10. competency, neutralism, Urania blue 13. unrelatedness 14. nonpartisanism 15. self-subsistence

independent . . . 4. free 5. Party (Polit) 7. neutral, wealthy 8. separate 9. competent, exclusive, free-lance, isolative, sovereign, uncoerced, unrelated 12. irrespective, uncontrolled, unrestricted 13. self-governing

independent land . . . 7. alodium (law)

indescribably . . . 9. ineffably 11. wonderfully

indeterminate . . . 5. vague 7. apeiron, general, neutral, obscure 8. formless, infinite

index . . . 4. face, file, fist, list 5. guide, ratio, table 6. gnomon 7. pointer 8. exponent 9. indicator 10. forefinger, indication

India . . . see also *Indian*
anc . . 9. Hindustan
Bay . . 6. Bengal
Cape . . 7. Comorin
capital . . 4. Agra (anc) 5. Simla (summer) 8. New Delhi
city . . 4. Agra, Gaya 5. Delhi, Poona, Surat 6. Bombay, Jaipur, Madras, Madura, Mysore, Nagpur 8. Calcutta, Kolhapur, Mandelay, Mirzapur, Shahpura 9. Bangalore 10. Darjeeling
city, sacred . . 5. Nasik 7. Benares
Coast . . 7. Malabar
kingdom . . 5. Asoka, Nepal
mountain . . 5. Ghats 8. Sulaiman (Throne of Solomon) 9. Himalayas, Hindu Kush 12. Vindhya Hills
Persian name (anc) . . 9. Hindustan
region . . 3. Goa 5. Assam, Surat 6. Baroda, Bengal 7. Benares, Kashmir
relics (famed) . . 8. Taj Mahal (Agra) 10. Kutab Minar 11. Ajanta Caves
river . . 6. Ganges 7. Krishna (Kristna)
State . . 4. Rewa 5. Delhi 6. Baroda, Indore, Jaipur, Madras, Marwar, Punjab, Rampur, Sakkim 7. Manipur

Indian (pert to) . . .
aeon . . 5. kalpa
animal . . 4. gaur, zebu 5. sasin 6. nilgai
apartment . . 6. zenana
army officer . . 4. naik (naig) 7. jemadar
attorney . . 6. muktar
bandit . . 6. dacoit

bard . . 4. bhat
bird . . 4. baya, kala, koel, kyak 5. sarus,
   shama 6. seesee, shahin 8. amadavat
boat . . 5. dhoni (doni)
book (sacred) . . 6. Avesta
bracelet . . 6. sankha
bread (unleavened) . . 4. naan 7. chapati
breakfast . . 5. hazri
buffalo . . 4. arna (arnee)
carpet . . 4. Agra
carriage . . 4. ekka 5. tonga 6. gharry
   (gharri)
caste . . 3. Jat, Meo 4. Ahir 5. Sudra,
   Varna 6. Lohana, Rajput, Vaisya
   7. Brahman (Brahmin) 9. Kahatriya
cavalryman . . 5. sowar 7. ressala
charm . . 6. mantra
chief . . 4. Raja 5. Rajah 6. sirdar
   7. Gaekwar
cigarette (cheap) . . 4. biri
claim (legal) . . 3. hak (hakh)
college (Sanskrit) . . 3. tol
Court, Supreme . . 6. Sudder
crocodile . . 6. gavial, mugger (muggar,
   muggur)
cymbal . . 3. tal
dagger . . 5. katar
dam . . 6. anicut (annicut)
dancer (fem) . . 8. bayadere
dancing girls . . 6. nautch
deer . . 4. axis 5. kakar 6. sambur
deity . . 4. Deva
demon . . 4. bhut 5. asura 6. daitya
devil's tree . . 4. dita
dialect . . 4. Urdu 5. Hindi, Tamil 7. Prakrit
disciple . . 5. chela
dog . . 5. dhole 6. pariah
drama . . 6. nataka
drink . . 4. soma 5. bhang (bang) 6. arrack
dust storm . . 7. peesash, shaitan
   (sheitan)
elephant . . 5. hathi
elephant driver . . 6. mahout
elephant trappings . . 5. jhool
epic . . 8. Ramayana 11. Mahabharata
falcon . . 6. shahin (shaheen)
father . . 4. babu
festival . . 4. Holi, Mela 6. Dewali
   10. Rathayatra
fig tree (sacred) . . 5. pipal 6. banian,
   banyan
garment . . 4. sari 7. luhinga
gateway . . 5. toran
ghost . . 4. bhut
god . . 4. Deva, Yama 5. Shiva
goddess . . 4. Amma
governor . . 5. nazim
grove . . 5. Sarna
guard . . 7. daloyet
hall . . 6. durbar
handkerchief . . 7. malabar
harem . . 5. serai 6. zenana 8. seraglio
heiress . . 5. Begum
herb . . 6. sesame 7. curcuma, tumeric,
   zeodary
holy . . 3. sri (shri)
holy powder . . 4. abir (perfumed)
hunt . . 6. shikar
intoxicant . . 4. soma
jungle . . 6. shola
king . . 4. Shah

king of serpents (Myth) . . 6. Shesha
   (Sesha)
king's son . . 8. shahzada
knife . . 3. dah 5. kukri
lady . . 7. sahibah
language . . 4. Urdu 5. Hindu, Tamil
   8. Sanskrit (anc)
leader . . 13. Mahatma Gandhi
legal claim . . 3. hak (hakh)
leopard . . 7. cheetah
licorice . . 9. jequirity (bean)
loincloth . . 5. dhoti
lover of . . 9. Indophile
mahogany . . 4. toon
mail . . 3. dak (dawk)
medicine man . . 6. Shaman
mendicant . . 5. fakir
merchant . . 8. soudagar
midwife . . 4. dhai
Minister of Finance . . 5. Dewan
mountain pass . . 4. ghat
musical instrument . . 5. ruana
narcotic . . 4. bang 5. bhang 7. hashish
native . . 5. Hindu, Sepoy, Tamil
   8. Assamese 10. Hindustani
ox . . 4. gaur
palanquin (conveyance) . . 6. palkee
   (palhi)
palm . . 7. Calamus, malacca
peasant . . 4. ryot
pheasant . . 5. monal (monaul)
philosopher . . 4. Yogi
pillar . . 3. lat
pipe . . 6. hookah
police . . 4. peon 5. sepoy
police station . . 5. thana
priest . . 5. mobed 6. shaman
prince . . 4. rana
princess . . 4. rani (ranee) 5. Begum
queen . . 4. rani (ranee) 8. maharani
religious body . . 5. samaj 7. ajivika (anc)
resort . . 3. Abu 5. Mt Abu
rope dancer . . 3. nat
rubber . . 10. caoutchouc
ruler . . 4. rana 5. nabob, nawab, nizam
sage . . 6. pundit
sailor . . 6. lascar
sarsaparilla root . . 7. nunnari
servant . . 3. par 4. amah, maty
sheep . . 5. urial 6. nahoor
shrine . . 6. dagoba
silkworm . . 3. eri
snake . . 5. krait 6. bongar, katuka
soldier . . 4. peon 5. sepoy, singh
split pea . . 3. dal
steps (to a river) . . 4. ghat
study of . . 8. Indology
sugar (crude) . . 3. gur 9. tabasheer
   (bamboo)
Supreme Court . . 6. Sudder
sword (short) . . 5. kukri
syllable of assent . . 2. om
tapir . . 8. saladang
tariff . . 6. zabeta
teacher . . 5. mullah (mulla)
temple . . 4. rath 12. Seven Pagodas (of
   Madras)
title of respect . . 3. sri (shri) 4. mian
tower . . 5. minar, sikar 7. sikhara
tree . . 3. saj 4. dita, teak 5. dhava
   6. banyan, sissoo

umbrella.. 6. chatta
water carrier.. 7. bheesty (bheestie)
wheat.. 4. suji
wine.. 5. shrab
yellow (color).. 5. piuri 7. majagua
Indian, American (pert to)...
  chief.. 5. Logan 6. Joseph, Philip,
    sachem 7. Cochise, Pontiac
    8. Geronimo, Red Cloud, Tecumseh
    9. Massasoit 10. Crazy Horse 11. Sitting
    Bull, Spotted Tail
  dance.. 7. cantico
  festival.. 8. potlatch
  hatchet.. 8. tomahawk
  hero.. 4. Rama (So Am)
  lodge.. 5. hogan, igloo, tepee 6. wigwam
    7. wickiup
  married.. 5. squaw (fem) 6. sannup
    (male)
  Mexico.. 4. Maya 5. Aztec 7. Tehueco
  money.. 5. sewan (beads) 6. wampum
  Newfoundland.. 6. Micmac
  pipe (peace).. 7. calumet
  pony.. 6. cayuse
  richest tribe.. 5. Osage
  S America.. 3. Ona 4. Cara (anc), Inca,
    Peru, Tupi 5. Carib 6. Arawak, Aymara
    7. Quechua
  Spirit, Great.. 6. Manito 7. Manitou
    12. Gitchi Manito
  squaw.. 6. mahala
  symbol.. 5. totem
  tax, impost.. 5. abwab
  village.. 6. pueblo
  water lily.. 5. wokas (wocas)
Indiana...
  capital.. 12. Indianapolis
  city.. 4. Gary 6. Muncie 7. Hammond
    9. Vincennes 10. Terre Haute
  industrial region.. 7. Calumet
  monument (Hist).. 7. Lincoln 12. Indian
    Mounds 13. Wyandotte Cave
  post office (famed).. 10. Santa Claus
  river.. 6. Maumee, Wabash
    10. Tippecanoe
  State admission.. 10. Nineteenth
  State bird.. 8. cardinal
  State flower.. 5. peony
  State motto.. 19. Crossroads of America
  State nickname.. 7. Hoosier
Indian people... 3. Aht, Fox, Oto (Otoe),
  Ree, Sac, Ute 4. Cree, Crow, Erie, Hano,
  Hopi, Iowa, Maya, Mono, Sauk, Yuma,
  Zuni 5. Aleut, Cadoo, Carib, Coree,
  Creek, Haida, Huron, Miami, Moqui,
  Omaha, Osage, Piute, Ponca, Sioux,
  Sooke, Teton, Yazoo 6. Ahtena (Alaska),
  Apache, Biloxi, Cayuga, Dakota,
  Eskimo, Isleta, Lenape, Mohawk,
  Mojave, Navaho, Nootka, Oneida,
  Paiute (Piute), Pawnee, Santee, Seneca,
  Siwash 7. Amerind, Bannock, Catawba,
  Chinook, Ojibway, Tlingit, Yavanai
  8. Arapahoe, Cherokee, Chippewa,
  Comanche, Iroquois, Kickapoo, Nez
  Percé, Onondaga, Sagamore, Seminole,
  Shoshone 9. Algonquin, Athabasca,
  Blackfoot, Chickasaw, Winnebago
  10. Muskhogean 12. Narragansett
Indicate... 4. cite, hint, mark, mean,
  show 5. point 6. denote, evince,

reveal, sketch 7. bespeak, betoken,
connote, declare, display, signify,
specify 8. disclose, evidence, intimate,
manifest, point out, register
9. designate, foretoken
indicated... 6. marked, signed
7. denoted, implied 8. presumed
9. betokened, portended, suggested
indicating succession... 7. ordinal
indication... 4. clue, hint, mark, note,
omen, sign 5. proof, token, trace
6. signal 7. reading (a) 8. evidence
10. suggestion 13. manifestation
indicative... 7. ominous 10. evidential,
indication, meaningful, suggestive
11. connotative 13. significative
indicator... 4. dial, hand, sign, vane
5. arrow, gauge, index, level 6. gnomon
7. indices (pl), pointer 9. grape fern
(belief) 10. instrument 11. annunciator,
thermometer 15. telethermometer
indicia (sing indicium)... 5. marks,
signs 6. tokens 8. markings (PO)
11. appearances, indications, metered
mail
indict... 6. accuse, charge, decree
7. arraign, impeach 8. proclaim
indictive... 8. declared 9. appointed
10. proclaimed
indictment... 6. charge 10. accusation,
imputation 11. arraignment
indifference... 5. shrug 6. apathy
7. inertia 8. coldness 9. unconcern
10. mediocrity, negligence, neutrality
12. carelessness, heedlessness,
unimportance 13. insensibility
14. insignificance
indifferent... 3. ill 4. cold, cool,
sick 5. blasé 6. casual, poorly
7. neutral, stoical, uneager 8. careless,
heedless, listless, mediocre 9. apathetic
10. nonchalant, regardless
11. adiaphorous, unimportant
12. nonessential, uninterested
indigence... 4. lack, need, want 6. penury
7. poverty 10. deficiency
indigene... 6. native 8. habitant
9. primitive 10. autochthon
indigenous... 6. inborn, innate, native,
rooted 7. edaphic, endemic, natural
8. endemism, inherent
13. autochthonous
indigent... 4. free, poor, void 5. needy
6. bereft 7. lacking, wanting 8. beggarly
9. destitute, penniless 10. pauperized
11. impecunious, necessitous
15. poverty-stricken
indigestion... 8. disorder, phthisis
9. dyspepsia 10. immaturity
indignant... 3. hot 5. angry, irate,
wroth 7. annoyed 8. incensed, wrathful
9. resentful 11. exasperated
indignation... 3. ire 4. base, fury
5. anger, wrath 7. disdain 8. contempt
indignity... 7. affront, dudgeon
10. uncivility
indigo... 3. dye 4. anil, blue
indigo (pert to)...
  bale of.. 6. seroon
  compound.. 6. isatin
  plant.. 4. anil

source . . 7. indican 9. indigotin
  wild . . 8. Baptisia
indirect . . . 7. devious, oblique
  9. deceitful, dishonest 10. circuitous,
  contingent, misleading, roundabout
indirect expense . . . 8. overhead
indiscreet . . . 4. rash 5. hasty, silly
  6. unwise 7. foolish, witless 8. careless,
  heedless 9. imprudent 10. incautious
  11. injudicious 12. undiscerning
  13. inconsiderate
indiscriminate . . . 5. mixed 7. mingled
  9. extensive, haphazard, orderless,
  wholesale 13. heterogeneous
indispensable . . . 5. basic, vital 6. needed
  7. exigent 8. integral 9. essential,
  requisite, right-hand 10. imperative
  13. irreplaceable
indisposed . . . 3. ill 4. sick 6. averse
  9. unwilling 10. disordered, unfriendly
  11. disinclined
indisposition . . . 7. ailment, illness,
  malaise 10. averseness, reluctance
  13. unwillingness
indisputable . . . 4. sure 7. certain,
  evident 8. positive 10. undeniable
  11. indubitable 12. irrefragable
  13. incontestable
indistinct . . . 3. dim 4. hazy 5. vague
  7. blurred, obscure, unclear 8. confused
  9. ambiguous, undefined 10. indefinite
  16. undiscriminating
  17. indistinguishable
indite . . . 3. pen 5. write 6. phrase
  7. compose 8. describe, inscribe
individual . . . 3. man, one 4. bion, idio
  nb form), self, sole, unit, zoon
  goist, person, single 7. special
   organism, selfsame 9. identical
  11. inseparable, personality
individuality . . . 5. being, seity 6. nature
  7. oneness 8. ethology, identity,
  selfness
individually . . . 9. severally 10. personally
  12. each by itself 14. distributively
Indo-Aryan (pert to) . . .
  deity . . 5. Indra
  native of . . 5. India
  speech . . 5. Aryan
  type . . 4. Jats 7. khatris, Rajputs
Indochina . . . 4. Laos 5. Burma 6. Malaya
  7. Myanmar (formerly Burma), Vietnam
  8. Cambodia, Thailand
indoctrinate . . . 5. coach, edify, imbue,
  teach 8. instruct 12. rehabilitate
indolence . . . 5. scorn, sloth 7. inertia,
  languor 9. inaction, laziness
  10. ergophobia 11. lotus-eating, spring
  fever 13. indisposition
indolent . . . 4. idle, lazy 5. inert
  6. otiose 8. inactive, slothful, sluggish
  10. unemployed
indomitable . . . 10. invincible
  11. intractable, "never say die"
  13. unconquerable
Indonesia . . .
  capital . . 7. Jakarta (Djakarta)
  formation . . 11. archipelago (once
    world's largest)
  former name . . 7. Batavia 15. Dutch
    East Indies

  government . . 8. Republic (1950)
  islands (3,000 in all) . . 4. Bali, Java
    7. Sumatra 8. Sulawesi (Celebes)
    9. New Guinea (W half) 10. Kalimantan
    (W Borneo)
  president . . 7. Sukarno
  race . . 5. Dyaks (Dayaks) 7. Battaks
    (Bataks), Igorots 8. Balinese, Javanese
  religion . . 6. Moslem
  shrine . . 6. dagoba
indorse, endorse . . . see *endorse*
indorsement, endorsement . . . 4. visa,
  visé (passport)
Indra (Hindu) . . . 3. God 5. Deity, Sakra
  (Sakka)
indubitable . . . 4. fact, sure 7. evident
  10. infallible, undeniable 11. irrefutable
  12. irrefragable, unanswerable
  13. incontestable 14. unquestionable
  16. incontrovertible
induce . . . 4. lead, move, urge 5. cause,
  impel, infer 6. allure, elicit, entice, incite
  8. persuade 9. influence, instigate,
  prevail on
inducement . . . 6. motive, reason
  8. stimulus 9. incentive, influence
  10. persuasion 13. consideration
induct . . . 6. enroll 7. bring in, install
  8. initiate 9. conscript, introduce
inductance unit . . . 5. henry
inductile . . . 10. inflexible, unyielding
induction . . . 5. logic 7. causing
  8. entrance 9. accession, beginning,
  deduction 10. conclusion, initiation,
  production 12. commencement,
  conscription, installation, introduction
indue . . . 5. endow 6. assume, clothe,
  draw on, invest, supply (spiritual)
  7. furnish
indulge . . . 3. pet 5. grant, humor, yield
  6. pamper 7. cherish, gratify
indulgences . . . 8. excesses 10. tolerances
indulgent . . . 4. easy 7. lenient, patient
  8. tolerant, yielding 9. compliant
  10. permissive 11. considerate,
  intemperate
indurate . . . 6. harden 7. callous
  10. solidified
indurated . . . 3. set 5. fixed 9. calloused
  10. solidified
industrial magnate . . . 6. shogun, tycoon
industrious . . . 4. busy 6. active 7. zealous
  8. diligent, sedulous 9. assiduous
  11. intentional, painstaking
  13. indefatigable
industry . . . 4. toil, work 5. labor, trade
  7. concern 8. commerce 9. diligence
  12. perseverance, sedulousness
indweller . . . 6. native 7. denizen
  8. indigene
indwelling . . . 7. inbeing 8. immanent,
  inherent 9. immanence, inherence
  10. inhabiting
inearth . . . 5. inter 6. inhume
inebriacy . . . 11. drunkenness
  12. intemperance
inebriate . . . 3. sot 5. addle, drunk,
  toper 7. stupefy, tippler 8. drunkard
  10. exhilarate (by liquor), intoxicate
ineffable . . . 4. surd 6. sacred 9. wonderful
  11. unspeakable, unutterable

13. indescribable, inexpressible
15. unpronounceable

ineffaceable . . . 9. indelible 10. inerasable
12. ineradicable

ineffectual . . . 4. vain, weak 6. futile
7. useless 9. fruitless 10. unavailing
11. inefficient 12. unsuccessful
13. inefficacious, uninfluential

inefficient . . . 6. unable 10. indisposed
11. incompetent 12. unproficient

inelegant . . . 6. clumsy, vulgar 8. indecent
9. deficient (in beauty) 11. unbeautiful

inept . . . 4. null, void 5. silly, unfit
6. absurd, clumsy 7. foolish 8. unsuited
10. out of place, unbecoming, unskillful,
unsuitable 11. inexpedient

inequality . . . 9. disparity, diversity
10. inadequacy, unevenness
12. disagreement, variableness
13. disproportion

ineradicable . . . 7. lasting 9. indelible,
permanent 10. ineffaceable

inerrant . . . 8. unerring 10. infallible

inert . . . 4. dead, lazy 6. latent, stupid,
supine, torpid 7. passive 8. inactive,
lifeless, listless, slothful, sluggish
9. apathetic, inanimate, lethargic
10. motionless, phlegmatic

inertia . . . 9. indolence, inertness
10. immobility

inesculant (rare) . . . 9. indelible

inestimable . . . 9. priceless 10. invaluable
12. incalculable

inevitable . . . 3. due 5. fated 7. nemesis
9. necessary 11. unavoidable

inexorability . . . 5. rigor 9. obstinacy
10. strictness

inexorable . . . 6. strict 9. obstinate
10. inflexible, relentless, unyielding

inexpedience, inexpedient . . . 6. unwise
8. untimely 9. ignorance, impolitic,
imprudent, unfitting 10. indiscreet,
unwiseness 11. inadvisable
15. disadvantageous

inexperience . . . 6. unwise 9. ignorance,
imprudent 10. immaturity, indiscreet
11. inadvisable 12. unprofitable
14. unskillfulness 15. disadvantageous

inexperienced . . . 3. raw 4. naif 5. green,
naive 6. callow 8. ignorant, immature,
prentice 9. unskilled 10. amateurish
11. unpracticed

inexplicable . . . 11. undefinable
12. supernatural 13. preternatural,
unaccountable, unexplainable

inextricable . . . 4. mazy 5. stuck
8. involved 9. intricate 10. insolvable

infallible . . . 4. sure, true 6. gospel
7. certain 8. inerrant, unerring
9. inerrable 11. indubitable

infamous . . . 4. base 6. odious, wicked
8. shameful, terrible 9. nefarious
10. detestable 11. ignominious
12. contemptible, disreputable

infamy . . . 5. shame 8. disgrace, dishonor,
ignominy, reproach 9. disrepute
10. opprobrium 11. abomination

infancy . . . 8. babyhood, minority
9. beginning

infant . . . 4. babe, baby 5. child, minor
6. novice 8. bantling 9. foundling

infantryman . . . 6. Zouave 7. dog-face
8. chasseur 9. musketeer
11. footslogger, foot soldier 14. gravel
agitator

infatuated . . . 7. foolish, smitten
8. enamored, obsessed 9. bewitched
10. captivated, enraptured
12. enthusiastic

infatuation . . . 3. ate, mad 4. love 5. craze,
folly 10. enthusiasm 11. foolishness

infeasible . . . 8. unlikely 10. improbable,
unsuitable 13. impracticable

infect . . . 5. taint 6. defile, excite,
poison 7. corrupt, deprave, pollute
11. contaminate

infection . . . 7. disease 8. epidemic
9. pollution 11. implication (law),
inspiration 13. contamination

infelicity . . . 6. misery 9. inaptness
10. misfortune 11. unhappiness
12. inexpedience, untimeliness,
wretchedness

infer . . . 4. hint 5. drive, guess, imply
6. deduce 7. presume, suppose, surmise
8. conclude, construe

inference . . . 5. truth 8. illation
9. corollary, deduction 10. assumption,
conclusion 11. implication, proposition

inferential . . . 8. illative 9. deductive,
inducible 10. deductible, suggestive
15. inconsequential

inferior . . . 3. bad 4. less, poor 5. baser,
lower, minor, petit, petty 6. lesser,
menial, nether 7. humbler, unequal
8. anterior, mediocre 10. inadequate,
low-blooded 11. subordinate

inferior lawyer . . . 9. leguleian
11. pettifogger

infernal . . . 6. cursed, plaguy, wicked
7. hellish, satanic 8. damnable, devilish
9. chthonian, execrable, malignant,
Tartarean 10. demoniacal, detestable,
outrageous

inferno (pert to) . . .
Bib . . 4. Hell 5. abyss, limbo
Buddah . . 6. Naraka
Egypt . . 6. Amenti
ferry to . . 4. Styx
Hebrew . . 5. Sheol 7. Abaddon, Gehenna
myth . . 5. Aralu, Hades, Orcus
7. Acheron, Niflhel 8. Tartarus

infest . . . 3. vex 5. annoy, beset 6. assail,
molest, plague 7. overrun, torment
8. frequent

infidel . . . 5. deist, pagan 7. atheist,
Saracen, skeptic 8. agnostic
10. unbeliever 11. freethinker 12. non-
Christian 13. non-Mohammedan

infidelity . . . 6. deceit 7. perfidy 8. unbelief
9. misbelief, treachery 10. disloyalty
11. incredulity 13. faithlessness

infinite . . . 4. vast 5. vague 6. divine
7. endless, eternal, immense, perfect
9. boundless, limitless, unlimited
10. indefinite 11. illimitable, interminate,
omnipresent, The Absolute 12. all-
embracing, interminable, undetermined
13. inexhaustible, The Omnipotent
16. all-comprehensive

Infinite Being . . . 3. God

Infinite knowledge . . . 11. omniscience

infinitesimal ... 5. small 7. minimum
9. invisible 10. evanescent
11. microscopic

infirm ... 4. weak 5. anile, frail 6. senile
7. fragile 8. decrepit 9. doddering
10. irresolute 11. vacillating

infirmity ... 4. defect, foible, malady, old
age 7. disease, failing, frailty, illness
8. debility, weakness 10. feebleness

inflame ... 4. burn, fire 5. anger 6. arouse,
enrage, excite, ignite, kindle, madden,
rankle, redden 7. incense 8. irritate
10. exasperate

inflammable ... 5. fiery 6. tinder
7. piceous 8. burnable 9. excitable,
irascible, irritable 10. accendible
11. combustible

inflammable substance ... 6. ethane,
tinder 7. acetone, bitumen

inflammation ... 8. ignition, soreness
10. congestion, excitement, incitement

inflammation (pert to) ...
bladder .. 8. cystitis
bone .. 7. rickets 8. osteitis
13. osteomyelitis
ear .. 6. otitis
eye .. 6. iritis 7. uveitis
joints .. 4. gout 9. arthritis
10. rheumatism
spinal cord .. 13. poliomyelitis
stomach .. 8. gastritis
suffix .. 4. itis
vein .. 9. phlebitis

inflect ... 3. bow 4. bend 5. curve
7. decline, deflect 8. modulate

inflection, inflexion ... 4. tone 5. angle,
curve 7. bending 8. paradigm
9. accidence 10. modulation

inflexible ... 4. iron 5. rigid, stiff 6. strict
8. obdurate, rigorous 9. immovable,
immutable, obstinate, unbending
10. implacable, inexorable, relentless,
unyielding 11. unalterable
14. uncompromising

inflict ... 3. add 4. deal 5. wreak
6. impose, punish

inflorescence ... 4. cyme 5. whorl
6. cymose 7. budding, flowers
8. racemose 9. flowerage, flowering
10. unfoldment 13. efflorescence

inflow ... 6. influx 9. inpouring
11. inspiration

influence ... 3. win 4. lead, move, pull,
sway 5. aegis (egis), bribe, force,
impel, lobby 6. affect, effect, induce,
influx, leaven, obsess 7. control,
inspire, mastery 8. dominate, effusion,
persuade, prestige 9. authority,
determine

influence (world-wide) ... 8. ecumenic

influenced ... 6. biased 7. induced,
pliable (easily) 8. affected 10. prejudiced

influential ... 6. potent, strong 7. weighty
8. momentus, powerful 9. effective
13. authoritative

influx ... 4. tide 5. firth, mouth (river)
6. import, inflow 7. estuary, illapse
9. influence, inpouring
11. debouchment

infold ... see *enfold*

inform ... 4. tell 5. teach, train 6. advise,

notify, report 7. animate, apprise,
inspire 8. instruct 9. enlighten

informal ... 7. offhand 9. irregular

information ... 3. air, tip 4. data, lore,
news 5. aviso, datum, facts 6. digest
7. advices, tidings 9. knowledge
10. annotation 11. instruction
12. intelligence

informed ... 2. up 3. hep 4. up on,
wise 5. aware 6. posted 8. apprised,
educated, versed in, well-read
10. instructed 11. enlightened

informer ... 3. spy 4. tout 6. gossip,
snitch, teller 7. delator 8. affirmer,
betrayer, mouchard, reporter, telltale
9. informant, spokesman 10. talebearer,
tattletale

informer (sl) ... 4. fink, nark 6. canary,
snitch 7. stoolie 8. snitcher, squealer
9. blabberer 11. stool pigeon
12. blabbermouth

infraction ... 6. breach 8. fracture,
trespass 7. intrusion, violation
12. encroachment, infringement,
overstepping 13. transgression

infrequency ... 6. rarity 7. fewness
8. rareness, solitude 9. isolation
12. uncommonness

infrequent ... 4. rare 6. scarce, seldom,
sparse 8. uncommon 9. spasmodic
10. occasional

infrequently ... 6. rarely, seldom 8. not
often, sparsely

infringe ... 6. defeat, refute 7. confute,
destroy, violate 8. encroach, overstep,
trespass 9. frustrate

infringement ... 6. breach, piracy
(copyright) 9. intrusion, violation
10. infraction 12. overstepping
14. nonfulfillment

infundibulum ... 4. cone, lura 10. gray
matter (brain)

infuriate ... 5. anger 6. enrage, incite,
madden 8. irritate 10. antagonize

infuscate ... 6. darken 7. obscure

infuse ... 4. fill, shed 5. steep 6. drench
7. implant, instill 9. insinuate, introduce

infusion ... 3. tea 4. wort 5. affusion,
tincture 9. admixture, decoction,
inpouring 12. instillation

ingang ... 5. porch 8. entrance
10. intestines

ingenious ... 5. sharp, smart, witty
6. adroit, clever, daedal, gifted, shrewd,
subtle 8. skillful, talented 9. Daedalian,
deviceful 11. intelligent, resourceful

ingenuity ... 5. skill 6. candor, genius
10. adroitness 11. originality
13. inventiveness

ingenuous ... 4. naif, open 5. frank, naive,
noble, plain 6. candid, innate 7. artless,
sincere 8. freeborn, innocent 9. guileless
10. unreserved 15. unsophisticated

ingest ... 3. eat 5. learn 6. take in
7. consume, swallow

ingot ... 3. gad, pig 4. mold 5. metal,
sycee 7. bullion

ingratiate ... 4. fawn 7. commend, flatter
9. insinuate, introduce

ingredient ... 6. factor 7. element
9. component 11. constituent

ingress . . . 4. go in 5. entry 6. access, portal 8. entrance 9. reception 11. entranceway

ingrowing nail . . . 7. acronyx

inhabitant . . . 3. cit 6. inmate, people, tenant 7. citizen, denizen 8. resident

inhabitant (pert to) . . .
  Alaska . . 9. sourdough
  desert . . 4. Arab 5. nomad
  earliest . . 9. aborigine
  foreign . . 5. alien
  Maine . . 10. down-easter
  moon . . 8. selenite
  northern . . 6. Yankee 11. Septentrion (Lowell)

inhabitants, equator's other side . . . 8. antiscii 10. antiscians

inhabited . . . 5. lived 7. dwelled, peopled 8. occupied, tenanted 9. populated

inhabiting (pert to) . . .
  caves . . 8. spelaean (spelean) 10. troglodyte
  ground . . 9. terricole 11. terricolous
  groves . . 7. nemoral 10. nemoricole
  islands . . 7. nesiote
  lakes . . 9. lacustral
  sea . . 7. pelagic 15. thalassophilous
  seashore . . 8. littoral

inhale . . . 4. suck 5. smell, smoke, sniff 7. breathe, inspire, respire

inharmonious . . . 7. jarring 9. differing, dissonant, unmusical 10. discordant 11. conflicting, disagreeing

inherent . . . 6. inborn, innate 7. infixed 8. immanent 9. immanence, intrinsic 10. indwelling, subsistent 11. instinctive 13. indispensable

inheritance . . . 6. legacy 7. bequest, legitim 8. heirship, heredity, heritage, Salic law 9. cleronomy 10. birthright

inheritance diminisher . . . 6. abator

inheritor . . . 4. heir 6. coheir 7. heiress, legatee 10. coparcener 11. beneficiary

inhibit . . . 5. check 6. forbid, hinder 8. prohibit, restrain 9. interdict

inhibition . . . 3. ban, bar 4. writ 7. embargo 8. checking 9. hindrance, restraint 10. impediment 11. prohibition 12. interdiction

inhuman . . . 4. fell 5. cruel 6. brutal, savage 7. bestial, brutish 8. devilish, nonhuman 9. barbarous, ferocious 10. demoniacal, diabolical

inhumation . . . 6. burial 9. arenation, interment

inhume . . . 4. bury 5. inter, inurn 7. deposit, inearth

inimical . . . 7. adverse, hostile, opposed 8. contrary 10. unfriendly 11. belligerent, unfavorable

iniquity . . . 3. sin 4. evil, vice 5. crime 7. misdeed 9. injustice 10. immorality, wickedness

initial . . . 6. paraph 9. incipient 11. large letter 12. commencement

initiate . . . 4. open 5. admit, begin, epopt (anc) 6. induct 7. install, instate 8. inchoate 10. inaugurate 11. preinstruct

initiation . . . 8. ceremony 9. admission 10. admittance 12. inauguration,

introduction

injection . . . 4. hypo 5. enema 7. clyster 9. immission

injudicious . . . 4. rash 6. unwise 9. impolitic, imprudent 11. inexpedient

injunction . . . 3. ado 4. writ 5. order, union 6. behest 7. mandate, precept 9. direction 11. prohibition

injure . . . 3. mar 4. harm, hurt, lame, maim 5. wound, wrong 6. assail, damage, grieve, impair, scathe 7. affront, slander, tarnish

injurious . . . 3. bad 4. evil 7. abusive, harmful, hurtful, noxious 10. defamatory, slanderous 11. detrimental, mischievous

injury . . . 3. ill, mar 4. dere (obs), evil, harm, hurt, loss, pain, tort 5. wound, wrong 6. damage, lesion, mayhem, trauma 7. slander 9. detriment, indignity, injustice 10. impairment

injustice . . . 5. wrong 6. injury 7. umbrage 8. hardship, inequity, iniquity 10. imposition, unfairness

ink . . . 3. jet 5. black 7. blacken 8. atrament, blacking

ink (pert to) . . .
  bag . . 3. sac (fish)
  berry . . 5. holly 6. indigo
  black . . 10. atramental 11. atramentous
  cap . . 8. mushroom
  fish . . 5. squid 6. cuttle
  pad . . 7. tompion (tampion)
  ref to . . 10. atramental
  source . . 7. inkweed, oak gall 8. inkstone, pokeweed 9. gallberry
  spreader . . 6. brayer

inkle . . . 4. hint, tape, yarn 5. braid, twist 6. thread 8. intimate

inkling . . . 4. hint 5. rumor 6. desire, report 9. intimation 11. supposition

inlaid . . . 6. mosaic 7. adorned, set into 9. champlevé, decorated

inlay . . . 4. buhl, line 5. inset 6. insert, mosaic, niello, tarsia 7. filling, implant 8. buhlwork, intarsia 9. champleve

inlet . . . 3. bay, ria, voe 4. cove, slew, sump 5. admit, bayou, bight, creek, fiord (fjord), firth , inlay 6. estero, recess, strait 7. estuary, orifice 8. entrance, waterway

inn . . . 3. pub 4. khan 5. abode, fonda, hotel, motel, serai 6. hostel, imaret, posada, tavern 7. albergo, cabaret, hospice, locanda, osteria, pension, shelter 8. alehouse, hostelry 9. roadhouse 11. caravansary

innate . . . 4. born 6. inborn, inbred, native 7. natural 9. ingrained, inherited, intrinsic 10. congenital, hereditary, inveterate 11. instinctive 14. constitutional

innate ability . . . 6. genius, talent

innate idea (Philos) . . . 11. immortality

inn courts . . . 11. Inner Temple

inner . . . 4. ento (comb form) 5. ental 6. inside, inward, secret 7. obscure 8. esoteric, interior, internal 9. intestine 10. indistinct 14. intramolecular

inner circle . . . 3. set 4. clan, club, ring 5. group, junta, junto 6. clique

inner man . . . 4. mind, self, soul 6. psyche
7. stomach

innermost coating . . . 6. intima

Inner Temple . . . 11. Inns of Court

Innisfail . . . 4. Eire, Erin 7. Ireland
15. Island of Destiny

innocence . . . 6. purity 7. diamond
11. sinlessness 12. harmlessness
13. guiltlessness, innocuousness

innocent . . . 4. Holy, pure 5. idiot, naive,
seely 6. benign, lawful 7. artless,
sinless, upright 8. spotless 9. destitute,
guiltless, ingenuous, permitted,
simpleton, stainless, unsullied
10. unblamable 12. simple-minded
13. free from guilt

innocuous . . . 8. harmless, hurtless,
innocent 9. innoxious 11. inoffensive,
unoffending

innovation . . . 3. new 6. change 7. novelty
13. prolification

Inns of Court name . . . 4. Gray 7. Lincoln

innuendo . . . 4. hint, slur 6. change
7. meaning 9. aspersion 10. intimation
11. implication, indirection, insinuation

Innuit . . . 4. Yuit (Eskimo)

innumerable . . . 6. legion, myriad
7. umpteen 8. infinite, numerous
9. countless 10. numberless

inodorous . . . 8. odorless 9. scentless

inopportune . . . 8. ill-timed, untimely
10. malapropos, unsuitable
11. contretemps, inexpedient
12. embarrassing, unseasonable

inordinate . . . 5. undue 9. excessive,
fanatical 10. disordered, disorderly,
exorbitant, immoderate 11. unregulated
12. unrestrained

inorganic . . . 7. mineral 9. inanimate
13. nonbiological

inquest . . . 4. jury 5. quest, trial 6. assize,
search 7. inquiry 11. examination
13. investigation

inquire . . . 3. ask 4. seek 5. query
7. examine 8. question 11. interrogate,
investigate

inquirer . . . 6. seeker 7. querier, student,
zetetic 8. searcher

inquiry . . . 5. query 6. examen, tracer
7. examine, seeking 8. question,
research 11. examination
13. investigation

inquisition . . . 5. trial 6. search 7. inquiry
8. tribunal 11. examination
13. investigation

inquisition figure . . . 10. Torquemada

inquisitive . . . 4. nosy 5. peery 6. prying
7. curious 8. meddling 10. meddlesome

inquisitor . . . 6. tracer 7. coroner, sheriff
8. examiner

in re . . . 10. concerning 13. in the matter of

inroad . . . 4. raid 5. foray 8. invasion,
trespass 9. incursion, intrusion,
irruption 12. overstepping
13. transgression

insane . . . 3. mad 4. daft, loco, luny
5. batty, crazy, loony 6. crazed
7. cracked, foolish, frantic, rammish,
touched, witless 8. demented, deranged
9. non compos 15. non compos mentis

insane urge to steal . . . 11. kleptomania

insanity . . . 5. mania 6. frenzy, lunacy,
trance 7. madness 8. delirium, dementia
10. alienation 11. derangement
16. mental deficiency

inscribe . . . 4. draw, etch 5. infix, stamp,
write 6. blazon, enroll 7. address,
engrave, impress 8. dedicate, depencil

inscribed . . . 5. runed 7. written
8. engraved, recorded 10. registered,
rupestrian (on rocks)

inscription . . . 4. text 5. motto, title
6. legend 7. epitaph, writing
8. colophon, epigraph, graffito
9. lettering, sgraffito 10. dedication
14. superscription

inscrutable . . . 6. secret 8. abstruse
10. mysterious 12. impenetrable,
inexplorable, unfathomable
16. incomprehensible

insect . . . 3. ant, bee, bug, dor, fly
4. flea, gnat, lerp, lice, mite, moth, tick,
wasp 5. aphid, borer, cadew, emmet,
leech, louse, roach, Vespa 6. acarid,
beetle, cicada, earwig, hornet, locust,
mantis, sawfly, scarab, spider 7. ant
lion, chigger, firefly, gallfly, katydid,
ladybug, pismire, termite 8. bullhead,
glowworm, mosquito, stinkbug, turicata
9. bumblebee, butterfly, caddis fly,
centipede, cockroach, dragonfly,
ichneumon, tsetse fly, tumblebug
10. silverfish 11. caterpillar,
grasshopper 12. yellow jacket

insect (pert to) . . .
adult . . 5. imago
aquatic . . 7. Ranatra
arboreal . . 7. katydid
back . . 5. notum
Bible . . 7. ant lion
butterfly . . 11. Lepidoptera
egg . . 3. nit
eyes . . 6. ocelli 7. stemmas
feelers . . 5. palps 8. antennas 9. tentacles
fly . . 4. zimb 7. Diptera
hymenopterous . . 3. ant, bee 4. wasp
6. sawfly 7. gallfly
immature . . 4. grub, pupa 5. larva
6. maggot 9. chrysalis
immature covering . . 6. cocoon
leg . . 6. proleg
like . . 8. entomoid
long-legged . . 5. emesa 10. harvestman
13. daddy-longlegs
mature . . 5. imago
molting . . 6. instar 7. ecdysis
parasitic . . 4. lice 5. louse
plant . . 5. aphid, aphis , borer, thrip
plate . . 6. scutum
praying . . 6. mantis
reference to . . 11. entomologic
relationship to host . . 7. metochy
10. parasitism
science . . 10. entomology
sound . . 5. chirr 7. stridor
stage . . 4. pupa 5. imago, larva 6. instar
9. chrysalis
stinging . . 3. ant, bee 4. wasp 6. hornet
7. sciniph (Bib) 12. yellow jacket
wingless . . 4. flea 6. aptera
wing vein . . 5. media

Insectivora (mammals) . . . 5. moles

6. shrews 7. desmans, tenrecs
9. hedgehogs

insecure . . . 5. risky, shaky 6. infirm,
unsafe, unsure 7. dubious, rickety,
unsound 8. unstable 9. dangerous,
hazardous 10. precarious

insensate . . . 5. blind, harsh 6. brutal,
unwise 7. fatuous, foolish 8. lifeless
9. inanimate, unfeeling, untouched
10. insensible, insentient 11. insensitive
13. unintelligent

insensibility . . . 4. coma 8. neurosis
9. analgesia 13. lack of feeling

insensible . . . 4. numb, slow 7. gradual,
unaware 8. apathetic, inanimate,
insensate, senseless 11. indifferent,
unconscious 13. inappreciable

insert . . . 4. gore 5. foist, graft, immit,
inset, panel, wedge 7. ingraft 8. interact,
ornament 9. interface, interpose,
introduce 11. intercalate, interpolate

insertion . . . 5. inset 9. injection
10. embroidery, needlework

insertion (pert to) . . .
cords in cloth . . 5. shirr
day in calendar . . 13. intercalation
newspaper . . 2. ad 13. advertisement
phrases, words . . 11. parenthesis
sound in a word . . 9. anaptyxis
10. epenthesis

inset . . . 5. panel 6. inflow, influx
10. phenocryst

inside out, turning . . . 5. evert 8. aversion
9. evertible

insidious . . . 4. deep, wily 7. cunning
8. guileful 9. deceitful, dishonest 11. full
of plots, treacherous

insight . . . 3. ken 6. acumen, aperçu
9. intuition 11. discernment, penetration
12. clairvoyance 13. understanding

insignia . . . 3. bar 4. ankh, flag 5. badge,
cross, crown 6. banner, emblem,
symbol 7. chevron, regalia, scepter
8. caduceus, swastika 15. hammer and
sickle

insignificance . . . 6. trifle 9. smallness
10. slightness 12. unimportance

insignificant . . . 4. puny 5. minor, petit,
petty, small, zilch 6. paltry 7. trivial
8. inferior 9. senseless 11. meaningless,
unimportant 12. contemptible
13. inconsiderate

insignificant object . . . 8. molehill

insincere . . . 5. false 6. affected
9. deceptive 12. hypocritical

insinuate . . . 4. hint 5. enter, imply
6. allude, infuse 8. intimate 9. penetrate
10. ingratiate

insinuation . . . 4. hint 5. sneer
8. innuendo 9. aspersion, insertion,
intrusion 10. intimation 12. ingratiation,
interjection

insipid . . . 3. dry 4. dead, dull, flat, tame
5. heavy, prosy, stale, vapid, wimpy (sl)
6. jejune 7. prosaic 8. lifeless, mediocre
9. tasteless 10. monotonous, namby-
pamby, spiritless, unanimated, wishy-
washy 11. indifferent 13. uninteresting

insisted . . . 5. urged 6. held to 7. pressed
8. demanded 9. persisted
10. maintained, stipulated

insnare . . . see ensnare

insolence . . . 5. serve 6. insult 8. defiance
9. arrogance, contumely, impudence
11. haughtiness

insolent . . . 4. pert, rude 7. abusive,
defiant 8. arrogant, impudent
9. insulting 10. disdainful
11. extravagant, impertinent,
overbearing 12. contemptuous,
contumelious 13. disrespectful

insolvent . . . 8. bankrupt

insouciant . . . 8. carefree 11. indifferent,
unconcerned

inspect . . . 3. pry, spy 4. view 5. grade
7. examine 10. scrutinize

inspector . . . 4. ager 6. conner, grader,
police, sealer, tester 8. examiner,
overseer

inspiration . . . 6. sprite 8. afflatus,
hiccough 9. influence, intuition
10. exhalation, inhalation, motivation

inspire . . . 4. fire 5. cheer, exalt 6. infuse,
inhale 7. animate, breathe, enliven
8. motivate 9. encourage, infatuate
11. communicate (to the spirit)

inspired power . . . 7. entheos

inspiring . . . 8. cheering, eloquent
11. provocative

inspiring (pert to) . . .
awe . . 4. fear 5. awful, eerie
confidence . . 11. encouraging
favor . . 13. prepossessing
horror . . 6. grisly

inspirit . . . 5. cheer, elate, rouse
7. animate, enliven, hearten, inspire,
quicken 9. encourage 10. ingratiate,
invigorate

instability . . . 8. weakness 10. changeable,
insecurity, mutability, unsafeness
11. inconstancy 12. irresolution,
unsteadiness 13. changeability,
unreliability

install . . . 4. seat 6. induct, ordain
7. instate 8. initiate 9. establish
10. inaugurate

instance . . . 4. case, suit 6. motive
7. example, request, urgency
8. occasion 10. suggestion
11. instigation

instant . . . 3. pop 4. time, urge 5. flash,
trice 6. direct, minute, moment,
second, urgent 7. current, solicit
8. pressing 9. immediate, importune
11. importunate

instantly . . . 3. now 8. directly, in a flash,
in a trice

instate . . . 5. admit, endow 6. invest
7. install 9. establish

instead of . . . 4. else 5. stead 6. in lieu,
rather 10. equivalent, substitute

instigate . . . 3. egg 4. abet, goad, move,
prod, spur, urge 5. impel 6. foment,
incite, suborn 7. provoke 8. motivate
9. stimulate

instigator . . . 5. urger 7. abettor, exciter,
inciter 8. agitator, fomenter, inflamer,
provoker 10. ringleader

instill, instil . . . 5. imbue 6. impart,
infuse, pour in 7. pervade 9. inculcate,
insinuate

instinct . . . 5. knack 6. libido, talent

7. impulse 8. aptitude 11. instigation, orientation

instinctive ... 6. innate 7. natural 8. inherent, original 9. automatic, intuitive 11. involuntary, spontaneous

institute ... 5. erect, found 6. create, ordain, school 7. academy, college, precept, society 8. initiate, organize, seminary 9. originate, principle 10. inaugurate 12. organization

Institute (The) ... 5. Gaius 6. France 8. Politics 10. Technology

institute a suit ... 3. sue 7. go to law 8. litigate 9. prosecute

Institution, international (maritime) ... 7. Veritas 13. Bureau Veritas

instruct ... 4. show 5. coach, edify, order, teach, train 6. advise, direct, inform 7. command, confirm, educate, nurture 9. enlighten 10. discipline 12. indoctrinate

instruction ... 3. act 4. lore, news 6. lesson, report 7. precept, tuition 8. pedagogy, teaching, tutorage 9. paideutic 11. information 13. propaedeutics

instructive ... 8. didactic, sermonic 10. commanding, preceptive 11. educational, informative 12. propaedeutic

instructor ... 5. tutor 6. mentor 7. adviser, teacher, trainer 8. lecturer 9. preceptor, professor

instrument ... 4. barb, bill, deed, tool, writ 5. agent, means 6. medium 7. utensil, writing 8. document 9. implement 11. contrivance

instrument, musical (pert to) ...
ancient .. 4. asor, lyre 5. rebab, rocta, shawn 7. bandore, cithern, theorbo 8. penorcon, psaltery
brass .. 4. horn 6. cornet 7. helicon
keyboard .. 5. organ, piano 6. spinet 7. celesta (celeste), cembalo 8. virginal 10. clavichord 11. harpsichord
percussion .. 4. drum, gong 5. bells, conga 6. bongos, chimes, claves 7. cymbals, marimba 8. carillon 9. castanets, xylophone 10. vibraphone 12. glockenspiel
sacred (Mormon) .. 4. Urim 7. Thummim
stringed .. 4. asor, harp, lute, lyre, rota 5. banjo, cello, dobro, ribec (ribeck), sitar, viola 6. fiddle, guitar, violin 7. ukulele 8. dulcimer, mandolin 9. hurdy-gurdy
wind .. 3. sax 4. horn, oboe, reed, tuba 5. flute, organ 6. cornet 7. althorn, bassoon, ocarina, piccolo, trumpet 8. clarinet, trombone 9. accordion, flageolet, harmonica, saxophone 10. concertina

instrument, others (pert to) ...
astronomical .. 5. armil
Biblical .. 4. Urim
butcher's .. 5. steel 7. cleaver
communication .. 9. telegraph, telephone 10. hydrophone
cooking (eggs) .. 7. oometer
cutting .. 5. knife, razor 6. scythe, shears, sickle 7. cutlery 8. scissors, strickle

drawing .. 10. pantograph
gripping .. 4. vise 5. clamp, tongs 7. pincers 8. tweezers
legal .. 4. deed, writ 6. escrow
mathematics .. 6. abacus 8. mesolabe
measure .. 7. ammeter 8. odometer, otoscope, rheostat 9. barometer, koniscope, rheometer 11. pyronometer
medical .. 6. trocar (trochar) 7. dilator, levator, ligator, scalpel 8. trephine
mining .. 6. jumper
music .. 4. bell 9. ergograph, metronome
navigating .. 7. pelorus, sextant
optical .. 7. alidade (alidad) 9. periscope, telescope
pointed .. 3. awl 5. stylet, stylus 8. stiletto
time .. 11. chronometer, chronoscope
two-pronged .. 6. bident

instrumental ... 6. useful 7. helpful 9. conducive, promoting, symphonic 10. orchestral 11. implemental, serviceable

instrumental (pert to) ...
composition .. 5. fugue, rondo 6. sonata 7. cantata 8. symphony
grammar .. 4. case
introduction .. 7. intrada

instrumentality ... 5. means 6. agency, medium 7. organon 9. mechanism

insubordinate ... 8. mutinous 10. unresigned 11. disobedient 12. contumacious, unsubmissive

insubstantial ... 5. frail 6. flimsy 9. illogical 10. unreliable 12. apparitional

insufficient ... 5. short 6. scanty, scarce 7. unequal, wanting 9. deficient 10. inadequate 14. incommensurate, unsatisfactory

insular ... 5. alone 6. narrow 7. neslote 8. detached, islander, isolated, secluded 9. illiberal, insulated, sclerosis, separated, unrelated 10. contracted 12. Island of Reil (Anat)

insulated ... 5. isled, taped 8. isolated 9. separated 10. segregated

insulating material ... 4. tape 5. kapok 6. balata, Kerite 7. okonite 10. fiber glass 12. friction tape

insult ... 3. cag 4. mock, slur 5. flout 6. offend, revile 7. affront, assault, offense, outrage 8. contempt 9. contumely, indignity

insulting ... 8. arrogant, insolent 9. offensive 10. affrontive 13. disrespectful

insurance ... 4. risk 7. annuity, promise 8. guaranty, security, warranty 9. assurance 10. protection

insurance group ... 7. tontine

insurance personnel ... 5. agent 6. broker 7. actuary 8. adjuster

insurgent ... 5. rebel 8. agitator, mutineer, revolter 10. rebellious 13. insubordinate

insurmountable ... 10. impassable, invincible 11. insuperable 13. beyond control

insurrection ... 4. riot 6. mutiny, revolt 8. sedition, uprising 9. rebellion 10. insurgence, revolution

intact . . . 5. sound, whole 9. unchanged, undefiled, undivided, uninjured, untouched 10. unimpaired

intaglio . . . 3. die, gem 6. relief 7. carving 9. engraving

intangible . . . 5. vague 7. phantom 10. immaterial, impalpable 13. imperceptible, insubstantial, unsubstantial

integer . . . 3. one 5. whole 6. entity, number 8. integral

integral . . . 3. all 5. inner, whole 8. totality 9. component, essential

integration . . . 5. whole 10. adjustment 11. unification 12. coordination, equalization 13. accommodation

integrity . . . 5. unity 6. purity, virtue 7. honesty, probity 9. innocence, soundness 12. completeness

integument . . . 4. aril, coat, derm, skin 5. testa 8. covering, envelope 10. investment

intellect . . . 3. wit 4. mind, nous 5. inwit, mahat 6. genius, noesis, reason 7. noetics, wise man 9. mentality 12. intelligence 13. understanding

intellectual . . . 6. brainy, mental, noetic, sophic 7. egghead, learned 8. highbrow 11. intelligent

intelligence . . . 4. mind, news 5. sense, spies 6. acumen, spirit 8. capacity 9. intellect, knowledge 11. information 13. understanding

intelligent . . . 3. apt 4. sane 5. acute, aware, smart 6. astute, bright, versed 7. knowing, skilled 8. rational, sensible 9. cognizant 13. understanding

intelligentsia . . . 8. literati 10. illuminati 11. the educated 13. intellectuals

intelligible . . . 5. clear, plain 8. knowable 10. cognizable, conceptual, explicable, fathomable 11. perspicuous 13. suprasensuous 14. comprehensible, understandable

intelligibly . . . 6. simply 7. clearly, lucidly, plainly 13. unequivocally 14. comprehensibly, understandably

intemerate . . . 4. pure 9. inviolate, undefiled

intemperance . . . 6. excess 8. bibacity, gluttony, severity, tippling 10. debauchery, inclemency 11. drunkenness 12. inabstinence, incontinence

intemperate . . . 6. Frigid (Zone), severe, Torrid (Zone) 7. extreme 8. addicted, bibulous 9. excessive, inclement, indulgent 10. gluttonous, immoderate, inordinate 11. ungovernable, unrestrained

intend . . . 3. aim 4. mean, plan 5. serve 6. design, direct, expect, regard, set out, strive 7. proceed, propose 8. aspire to, attend to, consider

intended . . . 5. meant 8. designed, purposed, remedial 9. affianced, betrothed, meditated 10. calculated, considered 11. deliberated, intentional 12. contemplated

intense . . . 4. deep 5. great, vivid 6. strong 7. violent 8. powerful 9. energetic

10. high degree

intensely . . . 4. very 5. quite 7. acutely

intensify . . . 6. deepen 7. enhance 8. condense, heighten, increase 9. aggravate

intensity . . . 5. ardor, depth 6. deepen, degree, energy 7. density 8. loudness, softness, strength 9. greatness, vehemence 12. colorfulness

intent . . . 4. rapt 5. eager, tense 6. design 7. earnest, meaning, purpose 9. intention

intention . . . 3. aim, end 4. will 6. animus, design, motive, object 7. concept, healing, meaning, purpose 8. intentio 13. determination

intentional . . . 5. aimed, meant 7. knowing 8. designed, intended 9. voluntary 10. calculated, deliberate 12. contemplated

intently . . . 7. eagerly, fixedly 9. earnestly, zealously 10. diligently, sedulously 11. attentively, steadfastly

inter (pref) . . . 5. among, intra 6. mutual, within 7. between 10. reciprocal

inter (verb) . . . 4. bury 5. inurn 6. entomb, inhume 7. inearth

intercalary month . . . 6. Veadar 8. leap year 10. bissextile

intercalate . . . 6. insert 11. interpolate

intercede . . . 6. umpire 7. bargain, mediate, referee 9. arbitrate, go between, interpose, intervene

intercessor . . . 5. agent, front 6. bishop, Christ 8. mediator 9. middleman 10. interceder 11. internuncio

interchange . . . 5. trade 6. barter 7. permute 8. commerce, exchange 9. alternate 10. transposal 11. alternation, reciprocate, retaliation

intercourse . . . 7. dealing 8. commerce 10. connection, fellowship 12. conversation 13. communication

interdependence . . . 9. mutuality 13. interrelation 16. interaffiliation

interdict . . . 3. ban 4. veto 5. debar, taboo (tabu) 7. forbid 7. inhibit 8. prohibit 9. proscribe

interest . . . 4. hold, weal 5. savor, share, usury 6. behalf, engage 7. attract, concern 9. entertain

interested . . . 4. rapt 7. partial 8. a party to, involved, partisan 9. attentive 10. prejudiced

interesting . . . 8. exciting 10. attractive 11. provocative

interfere . . . 5. clash 6. hinder, meddle, molest, tamper 7. intrude 9. interpose, intervene 11. intermeddle

interim . . . 7. respite 8. interval, meantime 9. interlude, meanwhile 12. intermission

interior . . . 5. inner 6. center, inland, inside, secret 8. internal 9. enclosure

interjection . . . 2. eh, lo 3. bah 4. ahem, alas, egad, haha, whew 7. heavens 11. ejaculation, exclamation

interlace . . . 3. mix 5. braid, unite 9. alternate, interlink 10. intertwine, interweave 11. interpolate, intersperse

interlock . . . 4. knit, mesh 5. unite, weave 6. device, engage 7. connect

9. interjoin, interlace 11. interrelate

interlope . . . 6. insert 7. intrude, obtrude
9. interfere, intervene 11. intermeddle,
interpolate

interloper . . . 8. intruder 10. trespasser
11. gate crasher

interlude . . . 5. farce, pause, truce
6. verset 7. interim, respite 8. entr'acte,
overture, versicle 10. intermezzo
11. performance 13. entertainment

intermediary . . . 5. agent 6. medium,
middle 8. mediator 9. go-between
10. interagent 11. intervening,
mediatorial

intermediate . . . 5. mesne 6. grades,
medial, medium, middle 7. aniline
(dye), mediate 8. mediator 9. naphthols
11. interjacent, intervening
12. intermediary

interminable . . . 4. aeon, long 7. endless,
eternal 8. infinite, unending
9. boundless, limitless, perpetual,
unlimited 10. continuous, protracted

intermission . . . 4. rest 5. pause 6. recess
7. respite 8. entr'acte, interval
9. cessation 10. suspension
12. interruption

intermit . . . 4. stop 5. cease, recur
7. suspend 9. interpose, interrupt
11. discontinue

intermittent . . . 6. broken, fitful
8. periodic 9. irregular, recurrent,
spasmodic 11. alternating

internal . . . 5. inner 6. inside, inward,
mental, within 7. revenue 8. domestic,
esoteric, interior 9. intrinsic, spiritual

internal organs . . . 6. vitals 7. viscera

international (pert to) . . .
agreement . . 4. pact 6. accord, treaty
7. entente 8. suzerain
business combine . . 6. cartel
fixed calendar . . 9. Cotsworth
language . . 2. Ro 3. Ido 5. Arulo
7. Volapük 9. Esperanto 10. Occidental
11. Interlingua

interpolate . . . 5. alter 6. insert 7. corrupt,
implant 11. intercalate

interpose . . . 7. intrude, mediate
9. intercede, interfere, interject,
intervene, introduce

interpret . . . 4. read, rede, scan 6. define
7. explain, expound 8. construe
diagnose, exegesis 9. elucidate,
translate

interpretation . . . 5. sense 8. solution
9. rendering 10. definition
11. explanation, translation

interpretation, science of . . . 7. anagoge
(Bib) 8. exegesis 9. dittology
12. hermeneutics

interpreter . . . 5. ulema 6. gnomon
7. exegete, latiner 8. dragoman,
exponent 9. catechist, exegetist,
explainer, go-between, hermeneut
10. oneirocritic (dreams)

interrogate . . . 3. ask 4. pump, quiz,
test 5. grill, query 7. examine, inquire
8. question 9. catechize

interrogation . . . 7. eroteme (question
mark) 8. erotisis, question, quizzing
11. examination, questioning

interrupt . . . 4. stop 5. break, check
6. arrest, hinder, thwart 7. break
in, intrude 8. obstruct 9. intercept
11. interpolate

interrupter (electric) . . . 8. rheotome

interruption . . . 3. gap 5. pause 6. hiatus
7. interim 8. interval 9. cessation,
hindrance 10. suspension
11. obstruction 12. intermission,
intervention 13. interposition

intersect . . . 3. cut 4. meet 5. cross
6. divide, pierce 9. decussate
10. intercross

intersperse . . . 6. insert, thread 7. scatter
9. diversify

interstice . . . 4. mesh, pore 5. chink, crack,
space 6. areola 7. crevice 8. interval
10. interspace

intertwine . . . 5. unite, weave 8. entangle
9. interknit, interlace 10. intertwist

interval . . . 3. gap 4. rest 5. break, lapse,
pitch, space 6. degree, period, recess
7. diastem, interim, respite 8. diastema,
distance, half step 10. interspace
12. intermission, interruption

intervals, at . . . 8. brokenly, fitfully
11. haphazardly, irregularly
12. occasionally 14. intermittently
15. longo intervallo

intervene . . . 6. step in 7. intrude, mediate
9. interlude, interpose 10. lie between
11. come between

intervening (pert to) . . .
between, among . . 11. interjacent
law . . 5. mesne
space . . 8. distance
time . . 7. interim 9. interlude

interweave . . . 3. mat 4. plat 5. braid,
plait, plash 6. enlace, raddle, splice,
wattle 8. intermix 9. interlace 13. twist
together

intestinal . . . 7. enteric 8. visceral

intestine (pert to) . . .
coating . . 4. caul
comb form . . 6. entero
part . . 5. colon, ilium, large, small
6. caecum, rectum 7. jejunum
8. appendix, duodenum 15. alimentary
canal

intestines . . . 4. guts 6. bowels 8. entrails

intimacy . . . 9. closeness 10. connection,
friendship 11. association, familiarity,
sociability

intimate . . . 3. sib 4. hint, near 6. friend,
united 8. familiar, friendly, informal,
personal, sociable 9. confidant,
innermost 12. confidential

intimation . . . 3. cue 4. clue, hint 5. trace
7. inkling 9. reference 10. foreboding,
indication, suggestion 11. supposition
12. announcement, notification

intimidate . . . 3. awe, cow 5. abash,
bully, daunt, deter 7. overawe, terrify
8. browbeat, frighten, threaten

intolerance . . . 7. bigotry 9. dogmatism,
prejudice 10. impatience, narrowness
12. illiberality

intolerant . . . 6. narrow 7. bigoted
8. dogmatic 9. impatient 10. prejudiced
11. not enduring

intolerant person . . . 5. bigot 7. fanatic

intone ... 4. sing 5. chant, croon, sound 7. introit

intoxicated ... 3. lit, sot 4. tosy 5. drunk, heady, tipsy 6. boiled 7. fervent, fuddled, maudlin 8. besotted, temulent 9. befuddled 10. inebriated

intractable ... 5. tough 6. sullen, unruly 7. restive, willful (wilful) 8. indocile, perverse, stubborn 9. obstinate, unbending, unpliable 10. headstrong, inflexible, refractory 11. unteachable 12. ungovernable

intransitive ... 6. neuter, verbal 8. confined 10. in transitu

intrenchment ... 2. pa (pah) 4. fort 7. defense, parapet 8. stockade 12. encroachment, infringement

intrepid ... 4. bold 5. brave 6. heroic 7. doughty, valiant 8. fearless, resolute 9. dauntless, undaunted 10. courageous

intrepidity ... 5. nerve, valor 7. courage, prowess 8. boldness, valiancy 9. gallantry

intricacy ... 9. sinuosity 10. complexity, involution, perplexity 11. complexness 12. complication, entanglement

intrigue ... 4. plot 5. amour, cabal 6. brigue, scheme 8. artifice, cheating 9. fascinate 10. conspiracy 11. machination

intrinsic ... 4. real, true 5. inner 6. inborn, inbred, inward, native 7. genuine, natural 8. immanent, implicit, inherent 9. essential, necessary 11. inseparable 13. indispensable

intrinsically ... 5. truly 6. really 10. internally 11. essentially

intrinsic being ... 7. essence

introduce ... 5. immit, start, usher 6. broach, herald, infuse, insert, submit 7. bring in, preface, present, sponsor 8. acquaint, approach, initiate, innovate 10. inaugurate 11. preinstruct

introduced from foreign country ... 6. exotic 10. extraneous

introduced serum ... 10. inoculated

introduction ... 5. debut, guide, proem 7. introit, isagoge, preface 8. exordium, foreword, preamble 9. insertion 10. innovation 11. instruction, preparation 12. inauguration, presentation

introduction (pert to) ...
Biblical .. 9. isagogics
drama (anc) .. 8. protasis
new words .. 7. neology
spurious matter .. 13. interpolation

introductory ... 9. prefatory, prelusive 11. preliminary

introit ... 4. hymn, rite 5. psalm 8. entrance 12. introduction

introrse ... (opp of extrorse) 12. facing inward

introversion ... (opp of extroversion) 9. inversion, reticence

intrude ... 5. enter 6. invade, meddle 8. encroach, infringe, overstep, trespass 9. interfere, interlope

intruder ... 7. invader 8. outsider 9. buttinsky 10. interloper, trespasser

intrust, entrust ... 6. commit 7. confide,

consign 8. delegate 10. commission

intuition ... 5. hunch 6. noesis, regard 7. insight 9. knowledge, reference 13. contemplation

intuitive ... 6. noetic, seeing 7. sensing 10. perceiving 11. instinctive

inulase ... 6. enzyme

inunction ... 7. unguent 8. inunctum, ointment

inundate ... 3. dip 4. dunk 5. douse, drunk, flood 6. deluge, engulf 7. baptize, immerse 8. overflow, submerge 9. overwhelm 10. oversupply

inure ... 6. harden, season 7. benefit, callous, toughen 8. accustom 9. habituate

inurn ... 4. bury 5. inter 6. entomb

invade ... 4. raid 5. enter (foeman), usurp 6. attack, infest 7. intrude, overrun, violate 8. encroach, trespass

invader ... 4. Pict 8. attacker, intruder 9. aggressor, assailant 10. trespasser

invalid ... 4. null, sick, void, weak 5. frail 6. feeble, infirm, sickly 8. nugatory 11. ineffectual 14. valetudinarian

invalidate ... 4. undo 5. annul, quash 7. abolish, nullify, vitiate 8. disprove 10. disqualify, neutralize

invalidism ... 13. indisposition 17. valetudinarianism

invaluable ... 6. useful 8. precious 9. priceless, worthless 11. inestimable

invariable ... 7. uniform 8. constant 10. unchanging 12. unchangeable

invasion ... 4. raid 5. foray 6. attack, breach, inroad 8. entrance (hostile) 9. incursion, intrusion, irruption 10. infraction 11. infestation

invective ... 5. abuse, curse 6. tirade 7. inveigh, railing 8. diatribe 10. revilement 11. malediction 12. vituperation

inveigle ... 4. lure, rope 5. snare 6. allure, entice, entrap, seduce 7. deceive, wheedle 10. lead astray

invent ... 4. coin 5. frame 6. create, design, devise 7. concoct 8. discover 9. fabricate (mentally), originate

inventive ... 6. adroit 7. fertile 8. creative, original 9. ingenious

inventor ... 7. creator 8. imaginer 10. discoverer, originator

inventor, discoverer of ...
adding machine .. 9. Burroughs
air brake .. 12. Westinghouse
airplane .. 6. Wright (Bros)
automobile (gasoline) .. 7. Daimler
ballpoint pen .. 4. Biro
baseball (reputed) .. 9. Doubleday
bifocal lens .. 8. Franklin
brake (safety) .. 4. Otis
calculating machine .. 7. Babbage
camera .. 4. Land 7. Eastman
cotton gin .. 7. Whitney
dynamite .. 5. Nobel
electric light .. 6. Edison
elevator .. 4. Otis
frozen food .. 8. Birdseye
gun .. 4. Colt 5. Maxim 7. Gatling 8. Browning 9. Remington
harp (Bib) .. 5. Jubal

helicopter .. 8. Sikorsky
lamp (safety) .. 4. Davy
lightning rod .. 8. Franklin
lock, cylinder .. 4. Yale
locomotive .. 6. Cooper 10. Stephenson
phonograph .. 6. Edison
printing .. 9. Gutenberg
radio .. 8. De Forest
reaper .. 9. McCormick
safety razor .. 8. Gillette
sewing machine .. 4. Howe
sleeping car .. 7. Pullman
steamboat .. 5. Fitch 6. Fulton
steam engine .. 4. Watt 8. Newcomen
telegraph .. 5. Morse
vulcanized rubber .. 8. Goodyear
wireless .. 7. Marconi
X-ray .. 8. Roentgen
inventory ... 4. list 5. index, stock
   6. supply 7. account , catalog
   (catalogue) 8. register 10. tally sheet
inverse .. 8. inverted, opposite, reversed
inversely club-shaped ... 9. obclavate
inversely oval ... 7. obovate
inversion ... 8. overturn, reversal
   9. overthrow, reversion 10. conversion
   12. introversion
invert ... 7. capsize, convert, pervert
   (obs), reverse, tip over 8. overturn
   9. transpose 10. turn turtle
invertebrate ... 5. polyp 6. insect, sponge
   7. mollusk 9. spineless 10. weak-willed
invest ... 3. don 4. vest, wrap 5. array,
   dress, endow, indue, spend 6. clothe
   7. empower, envelop, instate
   8. surround
invest (pert to) ...
   authority .. 8. accredit, sanction
   ministry .. 6. ordain
   sovereignty .. 8. enthrone
investigate ... 3. pry 4. sift 5. probe,
   study, track 6. excuse, search 7. discuss,
   explore 8. indagate 10. scrutinize
investigation ... 6. examen 7. inquiry,
   zetetic 8. research 9. discovery, heuristic
   10. discussion 11. examination
investiture ... 7. clothes, vesture
   8. clothing, covering 9. induction
   10. holy orders, investment (money),
   ordination 11. instatement
   12. installation 15. enfranchisement
investment ... 5. siege 7. finance,
   garment 8. blockade, clothing, covering,
   purchase, vestment 9. endowment
   11. empowerment
investment list ... 9. portfolio
inveterate ... 3. old 6. rooted 7. chronic
   8. habitual, hardened 9. confirmed,
   ingrained 10. deep-rooted
   11. established, traditional 15. long-
   established
invidious ... 6. odious, ornery 7. envious,
   hateful 9. malignant 14. discriminating
   (unjustly)
invigorate ... 3. pep 5. brace, cheer,
   nerve, renew 6. vivify 7. animate,
   enliven, fortify, refresh 8. energize
   9. stimulate 10. exhilarate, strengthen
invigorating ... 4. cool 5. tonic
   8. cheering 10. energizing, life-giving,
   refreshing 11. stimulating

invincible ... 10. unbeatable
   11. indomitable 13. unconquerable
inviolate ... 6. sacred, secret 8. faithful,
   unbroken 9. unchanged, undefiled,
   unstained 10. inviolable, unimpaired,
   unprofound 13. incorruptible
invisible ... 3. hid 6. hidden 10. indistinct,
   unapparent 13. infinitesimal,
   undiscernible, unperceivable
invisible, The ... 3. God 11. Rosicrucian
   16. German Protestant
invisible emanation ... 4. aura
invitation ... 3. bid 4. call 7. bidding,
   summons 10. allurement, inducement
   12. solicitation
invite ... 3. ask, beg, bid, try 4. bade
   5. court, order, tempt 6. allure, entice,
   induce 7. request, solicit 9. encourage
invocation ... 4. call, plea, rite 6. appeal,
   prayer, sermon 7. summons 8. entreaty
   11. conjuration, incantation
   12. supplication
invoice ... 4. bill 7. account (written)
   8. manifest 9. reckoning 12. bill of
   lading
invoke ... 3. beg 4. pray 6. appeal
   7. address, conjure, entreat, implore,
   solicit 8. draw down 10. supplicate
involuntary ... 9. not willed, reluctant,
   unwilling, unwitting 11. instinctive,
   spontaneous 13. unintentional
involve ... 3. lap 4. coil, wind, wrap
   5. imply 6. employ, entail, evince, infold
   7. concern, ensnare, entwine, envelop,
   include 8. interest 9. embarrass,
   implicate 10. complicate 11. incriminate
involved ... 7. complex, implied
   8. involute, tortuous 9. engrossed
   10. implicated
involving punishment ... 8. punitive
invulnerable ... 10. invincible
   11. impregnable, insuperable
   12. impenetrable, unassailable
inward ... 4. into 5. entad, inner 6. inside
   7. ingoing, muffled 8. interior, internal
   9. spiritual 10. internally
inwards ... 8. entrails 10. intestines
Io ... 7. goddess (Gr) 9. butterfly, satellite
   (of Jupiter)
iodine, iodin (pert to) ...
   comb form .. 3. iod 4. iodo
   compound .. 6. iodide
   containing .. 5. iodic 6. iodous
   poisoning .. 6. iodism 9. iododerma
   source .. 4. kelp 8. sea water 9. salt
   peter 12. thryoid gland
   standard .. 9. idiometry
   substitute .. 7. Aristol
ion ... 5. anion 6. cation (kation)
   8. electron, particle (Elec)
Ionian (pert to) ...
   city .. 4. Teos (birthplace of Anacreon)
   islands .. 5. Greek 9. Asia Minor
   mode (Mus) .. 6. Lydian
Ionic (pert to) ...
   architecture .. 5. Order
   dialect .. 5. Greek
   poetry .. 4. foot 5. meter
   printing .. 4. type
iota ... 3. ace, jot 4. atom, mite, star
   (9th brightest), whit 6. letter (Gr), tittle

8. particle

Iowa . . .
capital . . 9. Des Moines
city . . 4. Ames 8. Waterloo 9. Davenport,
Fort Dodge, Marquette, Sioux City
10. West Branch 11. Cedar Rapids
famed attractions . . 10. Hoover home
12. Effigy Mounds 17. Little Brown
Church
famed first . . 12. apple orchard (1799)
famed names . . 6. Joliet 7. Dubuque
9. Marquette
flower . . 8. wild rose
locale . . 8. farm belt (Midwest)
river . . 8. Missouri 11. Mississippi
State admission . . 11. twenty-ninth (1846)
State nickname . . 7. Hawkeye

ipecac . . 4. evea 6. emetic 7. emetive
9. purgative

irade . . . 6. decree (Turk)

Iran . . . see also *Iranian, Persia*
capital . . 6. Tehran (Teheran)
city . . 6. Abadan, Shiraz 7. Isfahan
conqueror . . 6. Darius 9. Alexander
lake . . 7. Rezaieh
mountain . . 6. Elburz, Zagros
8. Damavand (peak)
old name . . 6. Persia
parliament . . 6. Majlis (Mejlis)
people (anc) . . 5. Medes 6. Aryans
8. Persians
ruins . . 10. Persepolis (Shiraz)

Iranian (pert to) . . .
almond . . 5. badam
Ayatollah . . 8. Khomeini
books . . 5. Koran, Yasma 6. Avesta
country . . 4. Elam 5. Media
demigod . . 4. Yima
demon . . 7. Ahriman
diadem . . 3. taj
dynasty . . 6. Safavi, Seljuk 8. Sassanid
fire worshiper . . 5. Parsi (Parsee)
god . . 6. Ormazd (Supreme) 7. Mithras
Koran student . . 5. hafiz
language . . 5. Farsi 7. Avestan, Pehlevi
(Pahlavi), Persian
poet . . 4. Omar 5. Saadi
Relig founder . . 9. Zoroaster
Shah . . 7. Pahlavi
tapestry . . 7. susanee
tentmaker . . 4. Omar

Iraq, Mesopotamia . . .
capital . . 6. Bagdad (Baghdad)
culture (anc) . . 8. Sumerian
historic city . . 2. Ur 5. Eridu 7. Babylon,
Nineveh
historic Valley . . 15. Tigris-Euphrates
port . . 5. Basra (Busrah)
product . . 3. oil 4. date 5. sheep
river . . 6. Tigris 9. Euphrates 11. Shatt-
al-Arab

irascibility . . . 3. ire 6. choler 9. crossness,
testiness 10. perversity 11. waspishness
12. churlishness, irritability

irate . . . 3. hot 5. angry, wroth 7. enraged
8. incensed 9. irascible

ire . . 5. anger, wrath 7. madness
8. vexation 9. vehemence
10. enragement, resentment
12. exasperation

ireful . . . 5. angry, wroth 7. iracund

9. irascible 10. passionate

Ireland . . 4. Eire, Erin 5. Irena 6. Old
Sod, Ulster 8. Hibernia 9. Innisfail
11. Emerald Isle, Erin go brath
14. Ireland Forever

Ireland (pert to) . . . see also *Irish*
Bay . . 6. Bantry, Dingle, Galway
7. Donegal
capital . . 4. Tara (old) 6. Dublin
channel . . 5. North 9. St George's
city . . 4. Cork, Tara 6. Galway, Tralee,
Ulster 7. Belfast, Donegal, Kildare,
Wexford 8. Kilkenny, Limerick
9. Tipperary
county . . 4. Cork, Mayo 5. Kerry,
Sligo 6. Dublin, Galway 7. Wicklow
8. Kilkenny, Limerick
islands . . 4. Aran
legislature . . 4. Dail
mountain . . 7. Errigal 13. Carrantuohill
northern province . . 6. Ulster
river . . 3. Lee 4. Erne, Suir 6. Liffey
7. Shannon
sea . . 5. Irish
seat of archbishops . . 6. Armagh

irenic . . . 7. henotic 8. peaceful
11. harmonizing 12. conciliatory

iridescent . . . 7. opaline 9. prismatic
10. opalescent

iris . . . 4. flag 6. flower 7. rainbow

iris (pert to) . . .
astronomy . . 8. asteroid (7th)
color . . 11. reddish-blue
eye part . . 4. uvea 5. irian
Florentine . . 5. orris (orrice)
inflammation . . 6. iritis
mineral . . 6. quartz (iridescent)

iris, goddess . . . 7. rainbow

Irish (pert to) . . .
alphabet (early) . . 4. ogam (ogham)
battle cry . . 3. abu (aboo) 9. To Victory
11. Erin go brath
cattle . . 5. Kerry
Celtic, chief's heir . . 6. tanist
churchman . . 7. erenach (herenach)
club, cudgel . . 10. shillalagh (shillalah)
convention (anc) . . 4. Feis 10. Feis of
Tara
cordial . . 10. usquebaugh
dagger (anc) . . 5. skean
dance . . 3. jig 4. rink 10. rinkafadda
emblem . . 8. shamrock
exclamation . . 3. aru 5. arrah
fairy, spirit . . 4. shee (sidhe) 7. banshee
(banshie) 10. leprechaun
festival . . 4. feis
goblin . . 5. pooka
god . . 3. Ler (sea)
goddess . . 4. Dana
hero, warrior . . 9. Cuchulain (Cuchullin)
king's home . . 4. Tara
landholding . . 7. rundale
legislature . . 10. Oireachtas (House)
11. Dail Eireann (Chamber) 13. Seanad
Eireann (Senate)
liquor house (illegal) . . 7. shebeen
love, sweetheart . . 3. gra
moss . . 9. carrágeen
peasant . . 4. kern (lerne)
pig . . 5. bonav
policeman . . 8. spalpeen

potato city .. **7.** Youghal
queen (folklore) .. **4.** Medb
Society (secret) .. **6.** Fenian
soldier .. **4.** kern (kerne) **10.** galloglass
tenant .. **4.** saer
theatre, famed .. **5.** Abbey
verse .. **4.** rann
whisky, whiskey (illegal) .. **6.** poteen
    (potheen)

Irish (people) ...
ancestor (fabled) .. **3.** Mil **6.** Miledh
author .. **5.** Behan, Joyce, Synge, Yeats
    6. O'Casey **7.** Beckett
chemist .. **5.** Boyle
clan subdivision .. **4.** sept
composer .. **7.** Herbert
family .. **5.** cinel
Irishman .. **4.** Aire, Celt, Gael **6.** Teague
    8. Milesian **9.** Hibernian, Orangeman
    10. Eireannach
lawyer .. **6.** brehon
Nuns (Order) .. **15.** Ladies of Loretto
patriot .. **5.** Emmet, Tandy **6.** Oakboy
refugee .. **7.** fuidhir
saint .. **7.** Columba, Patrick
Saxon .. **8.** Sasanach
sea robbers (Myth) .. **9.** Fomorians
surgeon .. **6.** Colles

irk ... **3.** vex **4.** bore, tire **5.** annoy,
    weary **6.** nettle **7.** disgust, trouble
    10. exasperate
irksome ... **5.** vexed, weary **7.** operose,
    painful, tedious **8.** annoying **9.** fatiguing,
    vexatious, wearisome **10.** burdensome,
    exhausting, monotonous
    12. disagreeable
iron ... **2.** Fe (symbol) **5.** harsh, metal,
    power, press **6.** ferrum, fetter, mangle,
    pistol, severe **7.** firearm, manacle,
    shackle, sideros **8.** firmness, handcuff,
    hardness, strength **10.** inflexible,
    unyielding **11.** unrelenting

iron (pert to) ...
casting .. **5.** mitis
comb form .. **5.** ferro **6.** sidero
compound .. **5.** steel
containing .. **6.** ferric
dog .. **7.** firedog
dross .. **6.** sinter
herb .. **8.** Vernonia **9.** ironweeds
lump .. **3.** pig
magnet .. **8.** armature
meteoric .. **8.** siderite
ore .. **7.** turgite **8.** hematite, siderite
    11. sesquioxide
ref to .. **6.** ferric **7.** ferrous **8.** siderous
rod .. **5.** punty (puntee)
salts of .. **10.** chalybeate
sand .. **7.** iserine
science of .. **10.** siderology
symbol .. **2.** Fe
tailor's .. **5.** goose
tool .. **6.** lifter
vessel, basket .. **7.** cresset

ironclad ... **6.** severe **7.** armored, Monitor
    (ship) **8.** exacting, rigorous **9.** stringent
ironic, ironical ... **3.** dry **7.** cynical,
    satiric **9.** sarcastic **10.** figurative
    11. Rabelaisian
irons ... **5.** gyves **6.** chains **7.** fetters
    8. manacles, shackles **9.** handcuffs

Ironsides ... **7.** cavalry (Cromwell's)
    8. Cromwell
ironwood ... **4.** acle **5.** olive **6.** colima
    7. breakax **8.** hornbeam **9.** stavewood
irony ... **6.** banter, satire **7.** lampoon,
    sarcasm **8.** ridicule
Iroquoian Indian ... **4.** Erie **5.** Huron
    6. Cayuga, Mohawk, Oneida, Seneca
    7. Wyandot **8.** Cherokee, Onondaga
    9. Conestoga, Tuscarora
Iroquois (pert to) ...
Five Nations .. **6.** Cayuga, Mohawk,
    Oneida, Seneca **8.** Onondaga
native of .. **7.** New York **9.** Wisconsin
irrational ... **6.** stupid **9.** fanatical,
    illogical, senseless **10.** ridiculous
    11. impractical **12.** preposterous,
    unreasonable **13.** unintelligent
irregular ... **4.** wild **5.** erose, rough
    6. fitful, rugged, uneven **7.** atactic,
    crooked, devious, erratic, mutable,
    styptic, unequal **8.** aberrant, abnormal,
    atypical, informal, variable
    9. anomalous, desultory, distorted,
    eccentric, haphazard, orderless,
    unsettled **10.** changeable, immoderate,
    inconstant **11.** intemperate
    12. unsystematic
irregularity ... **6.** ataxia (muscular)
    7. anomaly **8.** disorder **9.** deviation
    10. distortion **11.** abnormality,
    informality **12.** eccentricity
irrelevant ... **7.** foreign **9.** unrelated
    10. extraneous **11.** impertinent,
    unessential **12.** inconsequent
    13. insignificant
irreligious ... **5.** pagan **7.** godless,
    impious, profane **11.** unreligious
irreparable ... **4.** gone, lost **6.** ruined
    11. irrevocable **12.** incorrigible,
    irremediable **13.** irrecoverable,
    irretrievable
irrepressible ... **7.** Homeric (laughter)
    12. ungovernable, unrestrained
irrepressible conflict ... **8.** civil war
irreproachable ... **7.** perfect **9.** blameless
    10. impeccable, inculpable
irresolute ... **6.** fickle, unsure **8.** doubtful,
    unstable **9.** uncertain, undecided
    10. capricious, changeable, inconstant
    12. undetermined
irresolution ... **10.** fickleness, indecision
    11. fluctuation, uncertainty, vacillation
    14. capriciousness
irresponsible ... **6.** fickle **7.** lawless
    8. carefree **9.** insolvent
    12. independable **13.** unaccountable,
    untrustworthy
irretrievable ... **8.** hopeless **9.** incurable
    11. irreparable **12.** irremediable,
    unchangeable **13.** irrecoverable
irreverence ... **7.** impiety **8.** dishonor
    9. profanity **10.** disrespect
irrevocable ... **3.** end **4.** past **5.** final
    10. inevitable, past recall **11.** unalterable
    12. beyond recall, unchangeable
irrigate ... **3.** wet **5.** water **6.** dilute,
    sluice **7.** moisten, refresh
irritable ... **4.** edgy **5.** cross, techy, testy
    6. cranky, ornery, touchy **7.** fretful,
    iracund, peevish, tempery, twitchy

8. snappish

irritate ... 3. irk, nag, vex 4. fret, gall, rasp, rile 5. anger, annoy, chafe, cross, grate, peeve, pique, rouse, sting, tease 6. excite, incite, madden, needle, nettle, rankle 7. incense, provoke 10. exacerbate, exasperate 14. rub the wrong way

irritated ... 4. sore 5. afret, testy 6. peeved 7. annoyed, nettled, rankled 8. provoked

irritation ... 4. itch 5. pique 6. temper 9. annoyance 10. resentment 12. exasperation

irruption ... 5. foray 6. inroad 8. invasion 9. incursion

Irving pseudonym ... 13. Knickerbocker (Diedrich)

is ... 6. exists 10. represents 11. personifies

Isaac (pert to) ...
Bib .. 9. patriarch (Heb)
father of .. 4. Esau 5. Jacob
grandfather of .. 4. Edom
husband of .. 7. Rebekah
son of .. 5. Sarah 7. Abraham

Ishmael (pert to) ...
ancestor .. 11. Ishmaelites
Bib .. 6. pariah 7. outcast
father of .. 8. Nebaioth
son of .. 5. Hagar 7. Abraham

isinglass ... 4. huso, mica 7. gelatin 8. agar-agar

Isis (pert to) ...
daughter of .. 3. Geb, Nut
goddess of .. 9. fertility 10. motherhood
identified with .. 7. Dog Star
mother of .. 4. Sept (Horus)
represented (at times) .. 9. cow-headed
shrine of .. 5. Iseum (Iseium)
wife of .. 6. Osiris

Islam, Islamic (pert to) ...
adherent .. 6. Muslim (Moslem) 10. Mohammedan
convert .. 5. ansar
founder, prophet .. 8. Mohammed (Mahomet)
God .. 5. Allah
holy city .. 5. Mecca 6. Medina
holy war .. 5. jihad (jehad)
leader .. 9. ayatollah
mosque .. 6. masjid
praying position .. 6. kiblah
rules for living .. 5. Sunna
sacred place .. 5. Kaaba (Caaba) 10. Black Stone
sacred text .. 5. Koran
scholarly group .. 5. ulema
teacher .. 4. alim 6. mullah (mulla)

Islamic (pert to) ...
convert .. 5. ansar
holy city .. 5. Mecca 6. Medina
mosque .. 6. masjid
pilgrimage .. 5. Kaaba (Caaba) 10. Black Stone
Supreme Being .. 5. Allah
teacher .. 4. alim 5. ulema 6. mullah (mulla)

island ... 3. ait, cay, ile, key 4. calf, cayo, eyot, holm, isle, reef 5. atoll, islet 7. isolate 8. insulate

island (pert to) ...
city .. 8. Montreal
coral .. 5. atoll 8. Zanzibar
enchanted .. 4. Bali
fabled .. 4. Meru 6. Avalon, Bimini 8. Atlantis
fabulous .. 7. Zangbar
group .. 8. Antilles, Marshall 11. archipelago
inhabitant, native .. 7. nesiote 8. islander
universe (Astron) .. 6. galaxy

island of ...
Langerhans .. 8. pancreas
Odysseus .. 6. Ithaca
Saints .. 4. Erin

Isle of Man ...
Celtic name .. 4. Manx
city .. 4. Peel 6. Ramsey 7. Douglas
division .. 5. Treen
judge .. 8. deemster (dempster)
legislature .. 7. Tynwald
mountain peak .. 8. Snaefell
Northern point .. 4. Ayre
site .. 8. Irish sea

Isle of Wight ...
Queen's summer home .. 12. Osborne House
site .. 10. English Sea
sport (famed) .. 9. yacht race
town .. 7. Newport
watering place .. 4. Ryde

Isles of Galway Bay .. 4. Aran

ism ... 4. cult 5. dogma, ideal, tenet 6. belief, school, system 8. doctrine, practice 11. abnormality

isochromatic ... 9. same color

isochronal ... 9. equal time 11. uniform time

isocracy ... 9. equal rule 10. equal power

isodont (Zool) ... 10. alike teeth

isogonal ... 11. equal angles

isolate ... 4. isle 6. enisle 7. seclude 8. insulate, separate 9. segregate, sequester 10. quarantine

isolation ... 8. escapism, solitude 9. seclusion 10. insulation, loneliness, separation 11. segregation

isomer ... 7. metamer 8. compound (Chem)

isonomy ... 11. equal rights

isonym ... 7. paronym 8. same name

isosceles ... 10. equal sides (triangle)

Israel (Bib) ... 4. Jews 5. Jacob, Zions 13. Hebrew Kingdom

Israel (pert to) ... see also *Israelite*
appellation .. 8. Jeshurun
capital .. 9. Jerusalem
city .. 4. Acre 5. Elath, Haifa, Jaffa 7. Galilee, Jericho, Tel Aviv
desert .. 5. Negev
dust storm .. 7. khamsin
lawgiver .. 5. Moses
Plain of .. 6. Sharon
priest .. 3. Eli
river .. 6. Jordan
sea .. 4. Dead 7. Galilee
song (Zionist) .. 8. Hatikvah
statesman .. 4. Meir 5. Begin

Israelite (pert to) ...
hero .. 6. Gideon

judge . . 4. Elon 8. Jephthah
king . . 4. Ahab, Jehu, Saul (1st) 5. David
  (2nd) 7. Solomon
lawgiver . . 5. Moses
priest . . 3. Eli
tribe . . 3. Dan 5. Asher 6. Reuben
tribe, priestly . . 4. Levi
issue . . 3. son 4. come, emit, flow, gush
  5. arise, child, sally, spout, stock, topic,
  utter 6. effect, emerge, escape, sortie,
  source, upshot 7. edition, emanate,
  proceed, product, progeny 8. question
  9. emergence, offspring, posterity
  11. consequence, publication
Istanbul (Constantinople) . . .
  ancient name . . 9. Byzantium
  capital of . . 6. Turkey (to 1923)
  foreign quarter . . 4. Pera
  Greek quarter . . 5. Fanar
  site . . 8. Bosporus 10. Golden Horn
isthmus (pert to) . . .
  American . . 6. Panama
  anatomy . . 6. fauces
  Greek (anc) . . 7. Corinth
  Siam . . 3. Kra
it . . . 5. charm, thing 6. itself, person
  7. egotist, pronoun
Ita . . . 4. Acta 6. Negrito
Italian (pert to) . . . see also Italy
  card game . . 5. tarot
  carriage . . 7. vettura
  cathedral . . 5. duomo
  cheese . . 6. Romano 8. Parmesan
  10. mozzarella
  condiment . . 6. tamara (tamarind)
  deity . . 4. faun
  dish . . 5. pizza 7. calzone 8. braciola
  11. saltimbocca
  dome, peak . . 4. cima
  entertainment . . 5. festa 7. ridotto
  food . . see pasta
  grape . . 6. verdea
  hamlet . . 5. casal
  house . . 4. casa 6. casino (summer)
  inlay . . 6. tarsia
  inn . . 7. locanda
  innkeeper . . 7. padrone
  lady . . 5. donna 7. signora
  lake . . 4. lago
  law . . 6. Latium 8. Jus Latii
  lover . . 7. amoroso
  magistrate (anc) . . 8. podestra
  marble . . 4. Neri 7. carrara, cipolin
  marsh . . 7. maremma
  opera house . . 7. La Scala (1778)
  peasant . . 7. paesano 9. contadino
  photographers . . 9. paparazzi (press)
  porridge . . 7. polenta
  pottery . . 8. majolica
  secret society . . 5. Mafia (Maffia)
  7. Camorra
  sheep . . 6. merino
  unification . . 12. Risorgimento
  vessel . . 9. trabacolo
  wind (hot) . . 7. sirocco
  wine . . 4. Asti 5. Capri, Soave 6. Barolo
  7. Chianti, Orvieto 9. Bardolino 12. Asti
  Spumante, Valpolicella
Italian (pert to people) . . .
  anti-Fascist . . 6. Sforza
  architect . . 7. Bernini 8. Bramante

artist . . 6. Titian 7. Cellini, da Vinci,
  Raphael 9. Donatello 10. Botticelli,
  Caravaggio, Tintoretto, Modigliani
  12. Michelangelo
astronomer . . 6. Secchi 7. Galileo
author . . 5. Dante 9. Boccaccio
  11. Machiavelli
biographer (artists) . . 6. Vasari
composer . . 5. Verdi 7. Puccini, Rossini,
  Vivaldi 9. Scarlatti 10. Palestrina
deity . . 6. Faunus
dictator . . 9. Mussolini
educator . . 10. Montessori
explorer . . 8. Columbus, Vespucci
  9. Marco Polo
family (princely) . . 4. Este 5. Doria
  6. Medici
family (violin) . . 5. Amati
friend (outside) . . 10. Italophile
geographer . . 8. Amoretti
goddess . . 3. Ops 4. Juno 5. Diana
hero . . 7. Orlando
historian . . 4. Dion 5. Cantu
king . . 7. Umberto
naturalist . . 4. Poli
noblewoman . . 8. Marchesa
  11. Marchioness
people . . 5. Aequi (anc) 7. Italici
  8. Umbrians 9. Etruscans, Ligurians
philosopher . . 4. Vico 5. Croce 7. Aquinas
physician . . 5. Abano 9. Eustachio
physicist . . 5. Volta 7. Galvani, Marconi
poet . . 4. Redi 5. Dante, Tasso 7. Manzoni
  8. Annunzio, Casanova, Petrarch
  9. Boccaccio
saint . . 4. Neri 7. Aquinas (Thomas)
sculptor . . 5. Dupre, Leoni 8. Ammanati
  12. Michelangelo
singer . . 5. Patti 6. Caruso
statesman . . 5. Rossi 8. Gioberti
  11. Machiavelli
theologian . . 7. Peronne
violinist . . 8. Paganini
Italy . . .
  Alps . . 5. Cozie 6. Carnac, Julian
  7. Atesine, Letiche, Pennine 8. Maritime
  9. Lepontine
  capital . . 4. Rome
  city . . 4. Lodi, Pisa 5. Anona, Fiume,
  Genoa, Milan, Padua, Pavia, Trent,
  Turin 6. Mantua, Modena, Naples,
  Spezia, Venice, Verona 7. Messina,
  Palermo, Pompeii, Ravenna,
  Trieste 8. Brindisi, Florence,
  Sorrento
  commune . . 6. Rivoli (Hist) 7. Trieste
  country (anc) . . 7. Etruria, Lucania,
  Tuscany
  gulf . . 7. Salerno
  historical site . . 10. Blue Grotto
  18. Leaning Tower of Pisa
  island . . 4. Elba 5. Capri, Leros 6. Eschia,
  Sicily 8. Sardinia
  lake . . 4. Como 6. Albano, Lugano
  8. Maggiore
  mountain . . 4. Alps, Rosa 5. Blanc
  12. Gran Paradiso
  port (fishing) . . 6. Amalfi
  resort . . 4. Lido 5. Capri 6. Agnone
  7. Riviera
  river . . 2. Po 4. Arno 5. Tiber

sea .. 6. Ionian 8. Apennine
10. Tyrrhenian
strait .. 7. Messina, Obranto
volcano .. 4. Etna 8. Vesuvius
9. Stromboli
itch ... 4. reef, riff 5. mange, psora
6. desire, eczema 7. scabies, sycosis
9. cacoethes, hankering, psoriasis,
sensation 10. irritation
ite ... 8. adherent, disciple, follower
item ... 3. bit 4. news 5. asset, entry,
scrap, topic 6. detail 7. article, integer
9. commodity 10. memorandum
11. information
iter ... 4. eyre, road (Rom) 7. circuit
iterate ... 6. recite, repeat, retell, review
7. recount 8. rehearse
iteration ... 5. recap 10. repetition
11. restatement
ithand ... 8. constant, diligent
14. unintermittent
itinerant ... 5. mover, nomad 6. roamer
7. nomadic 8. gadabout 9. traveling,
unsettled, wandering, wayfaring
itinerary ... 4. gest (royal), plan 5. route
6. prayer, record 8. register, roadbook
9. directory, guidebook

Ivanhoe (pert to) ...
author .. 5. Scott
character .. 5. Boeuf 6. Cedric, Rowena,
Ulrica
hero .. 7. Ivanhoe
ivories (pert to) ...
anatomy .. 5. teeth
game .. 4. dice
piano .. 4. keys
ivory (pert to) ...
anatomy .. 5. tooth 7. dentine
block .. 4. dice 7. tessera
carving .. 9. toreutics
color .. 5. white (off)
Latin .. 4. ebur
mixture (dust, cement) .. 7. eburine
plum .. 11. wintergreen
tower .. 7. retreat
ivy ... 5. Rheus, sumac 11. Hedera helix
iwa ... 11. frigate bird
IWW ... 6. wobbly
izar (Hind) ... 4. star 7. garment 9. loin
cloth
izle ... 4. root 5. ember, spark
Izmir ... 5. Smyrna
izzat ... 5. honor 6. credit 8. prestige
10. reputation

J

J ... 3. Jay 6. letter (10th)
ja (Ger) ... 3. yes
jaal goat ... 4. ibex 5. beden
jab ... 3. dig, hit, jag 4. poke, prod, stab
5. punch 6. strike, thrust
jabber ... 4. chat 5. prate 6. babble,
gabble, jargon 7. chatter, twaddle
8. nonsense 9. gibberish
Jabberwock ... 6. Jubjub 7. monster
(Through the Looking Glass)
Jabberwocky ... 4. poem 6. prolix
8. nonsense 10. double talk
jabble ... 6. splash 7. dashing 8. rippling
9. agitation, confusion, splashing
jabiru ... 5. stork
jack ... 3. can, jug, man 4. card, coat, flag,
male, pump 5. hoist, knave, money
6. lifter, sailor 7. mariner 8. nickname
jackal ... 3. dog (wild) 4. dieb, kola,
Thos 7. cat's-paw 8. henchman
jackass ... 3. ass 4. deer (mule), dolt,
fool, hare, nerd 6. clover, donkey,
rabbit 7. morwong, penguin, witling
9. blockhead
jackdaw ... 3. daw, kae 4. crow 7. grackle
jacket ... 4. coat, Eton, pelt 5. cover
(book) 6. blazer, blouse, bolero, casing,
jerkin, jumper, reefer 7. garment, Mae
West, wrapper
jacket (pert to) ...
Arctic .. 6. anorak
armor .. 6. acton
Eskimo .. 6. temiak
horseback riding .. 7. hacking (jacket)
knitted .. 6. jersey, sontag 7. sweater
8. cardigan
Levant .. 5. grego
Scottish .. 6. jupe
Spanish .. 8. chaqueta
jack-in-the-pulpit ... 4. arum
Jack Ketch ... 7. hangman (Eng)
11. executioner (public)
jackknife ... 6. barlow 8. penknife
11. toadstabber, toadsticker
jack-of-all-trades ... 8. handyman
jackstones ... 4. dibs, game 7. pebbles
Jacob ... 6. Israel 9. patriarch
Jacob (pert to) ...
brother .. 4. Edom, Esau
daughter .. 5. Dinah
father-in-law .. 5. Laban
parents .. 5. Isaac 7. Rebekah
retreat .. 5. Haran
son .. 3. Gad, Dan 4. Levi 5. Asher,
Judah 6. Reuben (oldest)
wife .. 4. Leah 6. Rachel
Jacobin ... 4. Club 5. Friar (Dominican)
7. plotter, radical, Society 8. Democrat
(Fr 1789)
Jacob's ladder ... 4. herb 8. hyacinth
10. belladonna 11. bittersweet
12. Solomon's seal
jade ... 4. bore, tire 5. green, horse,
stone, wench 7. fatigue 8. strumpet
jaded ... 6. fatigued, shopworn
9. dissolute 10. bedraggled
jaeger (jager) ... 4. gull (like), skua
6. teaser
jager ... 6. hunter 7. diamond
8. huntsman, rifleman

jagged . . . 5. erose, rough, sharp
  6. barbed, pinked, ragged, rugged
  7. cutting, notched, pointed, slashed
  8. serrated 10. saw-toothed
jague . . . 4. palm 7. genipap
jaguar . . . 3. cat 4. puma 5. ounce
  6. cougar 7. panther 11. snow leopard
Jah (Heb) . . . 3. God 7. Jehovah
jai alai . . . 4. game 5. cesta 6. pelota
  7. fronton
jail . . . 3. jug 4. brig, gaol 5. clink
  6. cooler, lockup 7. slammer (sl)
  8. hoosegow 9. Bridewell (London),
  calaboose 11. incarcerate
jailer, jailor . . . 5. guard 6. gaoler, keeper,
  warden 7. alcaide, turnkey
jail sentence . . . 3. rap
jalousie . . . 5. blind 7. shutter
Jamaica . . .
  beverage . . 3. rum 4. jake
  capital . . 8. Kingston
  cucumber . . 7. gherkin
  ebony . . 10. crocuswood
  island . . 10. West Indies
  pepper . . 8. allspice
  tree (drug) . . 7. quassia
jangle . . . 5. brawl, chide, noise, prate
  6. babble, gossip 7. chatter, grate on,
  quarrel, ringing, whimper
Janizary (anc) . . . 5. slave 7. soldier
Janus (Rom) . . . 3. god (two-faced)
Japan . . . 3. Jipun (Chin), Nihon, Nisei
  6. Nippon 7. Cipango (of Marco Polo)
Japan . . . see also *Japanese*
  capital . . 4. Nara (anc) 5. Kyoto (anc),
  Tokyo
  city . . 4. Kobe 5. Sapporo 8. Kawasaki,
  Kumamoto, Nagasaki, Yokohama,
  Yokosuka 9. Hiroshima 10. Kitakyushu
  current . . 8. Kuroshio
  islands . . 6. Honshu, Kyushu 7. Shikoku
  9. Haikkaido (Yezo)
  mountain . . 8. Fujiyama
  naval base . . 8. Yokosuka
  port . . 4. Kobe 5. Osaka 6. Nagoya
  8. Yokohama
  protectorate . . 9. Manchukuo
  river . . 4. Yalu (Annock)
  shrine . . 7. Toshogu (at Nikko)
  spring (hot) . . 6. Hakone
  volcano . . 9. Asamayama
Japanese (pert to) . . .
  airplane . . 4. Zero
  annals, chronicles . . 7. Nihongi
  apricot . . 3. ume
  army (conscription) . . 6. geneki
  army officer . . 7. samurai
  art of self-defense . . 4. judo 7. jujitsu
  (jujutsu, jiujutsu)
  badge (family) . . 3. mon
  banjo . . 7. samisen
  battle cry . . 6. banzai
  brazier . . 7. hibachi
  button (carved) . . 7. netsuke
  cape . . 4. mino
  cedar . . 4. sugi
  chess . . 5. shogi
  church (Buddhist) . . 4. tera
  circle, ship (suffix) . . 4. maru
  deer . . 4. sika
  dog . . 4. tanate

  drama . . 2. no 6. no-gaku
  drink . . 4. sake (saki)
  entertainer . . 6. geisha
  festival . . 3. Bon 15. Feast of Lanterns
  fish . . 3. ayu, tai 4. fugu
  flower arranging . . 7. ikebano
  flower design . . 10. Shin, Soe, Tai
  (Heaven, Man, Earth)
  game (forfeits) . . 3. ken
  gateway . . 5. torii
  girdle . . 3. obi
  girdle box . . 4. inro
  greeting . . 6. banzai
  herb (edible) . . 3. udo
  legislature . . 4. Diet
  litter (covered) . . 7. norimon
  monster (film) . . 8. Godzilla
  news agency . . 5. domei
  newspaper (Tokyo) . . 12. Asahi Shimbun
  outlaw . . 5. ronin
  pagoda . . 3. taa
  painting school . . 4. Kano
  palanquin, litter . . 4. pago 7. norimon
  paper-folding art . . 7. origami
  partition . . 5. shoji
  persimmon . . 4. kaki
  plant . . 3. udo (edible) 6. sugamo
  porgy . . 3. tai (fish)
  pottery . . 7. Satsuma
  prefecture . . 2. fu
  radish . . 6. daikon
  religion . . 6. Shinto 8. Buddhism
  9. Shintoism
  robe . . 6. kimono
  sash . . 3. obi
  salmon . . 4. masu
  screen (partition) . . 5. shoji
  seaweed . . 4. nori
  self-defense, art of . . 4. judo 7. jujitsu
  (jujutsu, jiujutsu)
  ship suffix . . 4. maru
  shout (greeting) . . 6. banzai
  shrine . . 7. Toshogu (at Nikko)
  silk . . 7. habutai 8. chirimen (crepe)
  silkworm . . 4. eria 7. yamamai
  sock (separate big toe) . . 4. tabi
  song . . 3. uta
  suicide . . 7. seppuku 8. hara-kiri
  (hari-kari)
  tree . . 5. akeki, kiaki 7. camphor, hinooki
  verse . . 5. hokku, tanka 6. haikai
  wrestling . . 4. sumo
Japanese people . . .
  aborigine . . 4. Ainu (Aino)
  admiral . . 3. Ito 4. Togo
  admirer . . 11. Japanophile
  American-born . . 5. Issei, Nisei
  army officer . . 7. samurai
  baron . . 6. daimio
  Buddha, Great . . 8. Daibutsu
  caste (nobility) . . 7. kwazoku
  clan . . 7. Satsuma 8. Fujiwara, Minamoto
  deity . . 5. Amita (Amida) 8. Amitabba
  Emperor . . 8. Hirohito
  Emperor, founder . . 5. Jimmu (660 BC)
  Emperor, title . . 5. Tenno 6. Mikado
  God of Happiness . . 7. Jurojin 10. Fuku-
  roku ju
  governor . . 6. shogun
  nobility (caste) . . 7. kwazoku
  outlaw . . 5. ronin

J

paradise (of Amita) .. 4. Jodo
race .. 4. Ainu

jape ... 4. fool, jeer, jest, jipe, mock
5. fraud, trick 6. banter, deride

japery ... 4. jest, joke 7. jesting 8. trickery
10. buffoonery

jar ... 4. jolt, grate, shake 6. incase,
rattle 7. startle, vibrate 8. preserve
9. vibration

jar ... 3. jug, urn 4. ewer, lute (rubber),
olla 5. cadus (anc), crock, cruse
6. dolium, goglet, hydria 7. amphora,
terrine 10. jardiniere

jararaca ... 7. serpent 10. fer-de-lance
11. jararacussu

jardiniere ... 3. jar, jug, urn 4. vase
5. stand (plant) 8. flowerpot

jargon ... 4. cant 5. argot, idiom, lingo,
slang 6. drivel, patois, patter, zircon
7. Chinook, Yiddish 8. nonsense
9. gibberish 10. vocabulary (secret)

jasmine, jasmin ... 4. bela 5. color,
papaw 7. jessamy 9. jessamine

Jason (pert to) ...
friend, sweetheart .. 5. Medea
heroes .. 9. Argonauts
quest .. 12. Golden Fleece
ship .. 4. Argo
son .. 5. Aeson
uncle .. 6. Pelias

jaundice ... 7. disease, icterus 8. jealousy
9. prejudice 10. yellowness

jaunt ... 4. ride, trip 6. ramble 7. journey
9. excursion

jaunty ... 4. airy 5. perky, showy, smart
6. dapper, rakish 7. finical, stylish
12. lighthearted

Java ... see also Javanese
city .. 7. Batavia, Jakarta (Djakarta)
8. Samerang, Surabaya 9. Surakarta
island group .. 10. East Indies
Java Man (anc) .. 15. Pithecanthropus
(erectus)
location .. 7. equator 16. Malay
Archipelago

Javanese (pert to) ...
arrow poison .. 4. upas
badger .. 5. ratel 6. teledu
carriage .. 4. sado (sadoo)
cotton .. 5. kapok
dancers .. 6. bedoyo
dog (wild) .. 5. adjag
ox (wild) .. 7. banteng
pantomime .. 6. topeng
plum .. 5. jambo (jambul) 6. lomboy
puppet show .. 6. wajang (wayang)
rice field .. 5. sawah
squirrel .. 8. jelerang
temple .. 6. chandi (candi)
tree .. 4. upas 5. ligas 7. gondang

javelin ... 3. bat 4. dart, pike 5. lance,
spear 6. jereed (jirid) 7. assagai
(assegai)

javelina ... 4. boar 7. peccary

jaw ... 3. maw 4. chop 5. scold 6. berate,
splash 7. chatter, orifice 8. scolding

jaw (pert to) ...
angle of .. 6. gonion
bone .. 7. maxilla 8. mandible
comb form .. 6. gnatho
disease .. 7. lump jaw 13. actinomycosis

formation .. 8. gnathism
Greek for .. 7. gnathos
muscle .. 8. masseter
ref to .. 5. malar 7. gnathic
without .. 8. agnathic

jawab ... 5. reply 6. answer, mosque
(false Arch)

jay ... 3. gae 4. bird, blue, dupe
9. chatterer

jayhawker ... 6. Kansan, spider 7. soldier
8. guerilla

Jayhawker State ... 6. Kansas

jazz ... 4. jive 5. dance, music, swing
9. syncopate 11. syncopation

jealous ... 7. envious, zealous 8. doubtful,
grudging, vigilant, watchful 9. jaundiced
10. solicitous 11. distrustful
12. apprehensive

jealousy ... 4. envy 5. doubt 7. rivalry
8. distrust, jaundice, mistrust
12. covetousness

jeans ... 8. overalls, trousers

jeer ... 4. gibe, hoot, jape, mock 5. flout,
scoff, sneer, taunt 6. deride 8. ridicule

Jehovah ... 3. God, Jah 4. Lord 6. Yahweh
(Yahwe) 8. Almighty (The) 12. Supreme
Being

Jehovah's comfort ... 8. Nehemiah

jehu (humorous) ... 8. coachman 10. fast
driver

Jehu's father (Bib) ... 11. Jehoshaphat

jejune ... 3. dry 4. arid 5. banal, empty,
stale, trite 6. barren, hungry, meager
7. insipid 8. foodless 12. unproductive

jelly ... 3. jam, rob (rhob) 4. food, sapa
5. aspic 6. pectin 7. gelatin 8. gelatine,
Kei Apple 10. semiliquid

jellyfish ... 5. quarl 6. coward, medusa
7. acaleph 8. weakling 9. Acalephae

jellyfish (pert to) ...
class .. 9. Acalephae
group .. 10. discophora
part .. 6. pileus 8. umbrella
10. exumbrella
stinging .. 9. sea nettle
swim organ .. 5. stene

jemmy ... 4. boot (riding) 5. jimmy, lever
7. crowbar 9. greatcoat

Jena (Ger) ... 5. glass 6. battle (1806)

jenna ... 8. Paradise (Muslim)

jennet ... 3. ass 5. horse 6. donkey

jenny ... 3. ass 5. crane (moving)
6. female 8. airplane 13. spinning
wheel

jenny (pert to) ...
billiards .. 6. hazard
folklore .. 4. wren
howlet .. 3. owl 5. owlet
machine .. 13. spinning wheel
spinner .. 3. fly (angling)

jeopardize ... 4. risk 6. expose, hazard
7. imperil 8. endanger

jeopardy ... 4. risk 5. peril 6. hazard,
menace

jeremiad ... 3. woe 6. lament, plaint,
tirade 9. complaint

jerk ... 3. tic 4. flip, jolt, push, yank
5. shake, tweak 6. chorea, thrust, twitch
7. charqui

jerkin ... 4. coat 6. jacket, salmon
9. gyrfalcon, waistcoat

jeroboam ... 4. bowl 6. battle, goblet
Jeroboam ... 4. King (of Israel)
jerry ... 5. aware 6. flimsy, Geremy,
German 7. knowing 9. beer house,
conscious
jersey ... 5. cloth 6. cattle, jacket
Jersey Red ... 5. swine 11. Duroc-Jersey
Jersey tea ... 11. wintergreen
12. checkerberry
Jerusalem ... 5. Ariel, Salem 8. Holy
City 11. City of David
Jerusalem (pert to) ...
  artichoke .. 7. girasol 10. topinambou
  capital of .. 6. Israel
  corn .. 5. durra
  Garden .. 10. Gethsemane
  haddock .. 4. opah
  hill .. 6. Olivet 13. Mount of Olives
  historic site .. 11. Wailing Wall
    12. Mosque of Omar 13. Mount
    of Olives (Olivet) 18. Garden of
    Gethsemane
  mosque .. 4. Omar
  pool .. 6. Siloam 8. Bethesda
  region .. 5. Perea 6. Gilead
  Relig .. 7. Judaism 12. Christianity
    13. Mohammedanism
  spring .. 5. Gihon 6. Siloam
  star .. 7. salsify
  Sunday .. 11. Refreshment
  thorn .. 7. catechu 12. Christ's-thorn
  willow .. 8. oleaster
jess ... 5. strap (hawk's leg) 6. ribbon
jessamy ... 3. fop 5. dandy 7. jasmine
jessant (Her) ... 7. issuing 9. lying over
jessur ... 5. viper (Russell's)
jest ... 3. fun, mot, wit 4. fool, jape, jeer,
joke, quip 5. droll, prank, sport, taunt,
trick 6. banter, rail at, trifle 8. ridicule
jester ... 4. fool, mime 5. clown
7. buffoon, goliard 8. humorist
11. merry-andrew
jester's cap ... 7. coxcomb
Jesuit ... 5. Order 7. casuist, sectary
8. explorer 9. intriguer 10. missionary
14. Society of Jesus (S J)
jet ... 3. jut 4. gush, spew 5. black,
ebony, ladle, raven, spout, spray, spurt
6. burner, nozzle, stream 7. mineral,
outpour 9. spouting 9. black onyx
jet coal ... 6. cannel
jetty ... 4. mole, pier 5. wharf 8. buttress
Jew ... 6. Essene, Hebrew, Semite
9. Israelite
jewel ... 3. gem 4. naif, opal, ruby 5. beryl,
stone 6. garnet 7. bearing, diamond,
emerald 8. ornament 9. bespangle,
brilliant 10. rhinestone 13. precious
stone, precious thing
jewel cutter ... 10. lapidarist
jeweled headdress ... 5. tiara 7. coronet
jeweler's glass ... 5. loupe
jeweler's weight ... 4. tola 5. carat
(karat, kerat)
jewelry ... 3. ice 4. ring 5. paste 6. parure,
strass 7. costume 10. bijouterie
Jewish ... 6. Hebrew 7. Yiddish 9. Israelite
Jewish (pert to) ...
  academy (Talmudic) .. 8. Yeshinah
  adherent .. 7. Zionist
  benediction .. 5. Shema

  Bible .. 5. Torah (Tora) 6. Gemara,
    Talmud 7. Haggada, Halakah
    10. Pentateuch
  calendar .. 4. Adar, Ahab, Elul, Iyar
    5. Nisan, Sivan, Tebet 6. Kislev, Shebat,
    Tammuz, Tishri, Veadar (leap year)
    7. Heshvan
  Day of Atonement .. 9. Yom Kippur
  Dispersion .. 8. Diaspora
  divorce .. 3. get (gett)
  doctrine .. 7. Mishnah (Mishna)
  enemy (Bib) .. 5. Haman
  faction .. 7. Zealots
  father, patriarch .. 7. Abraham
  festival .. 5. Purim, Seder (Sedar)
    7. Sukkoth
  greeting, peace .. 6. Shalom
  high priest .. 3. Eli 4. Ezra 5. Aaron,
    Annas 8. Caiaphas
  high priest costume .. 4. urim 5. abnet
    7. petalon, tallith, yamilke
  historian .. 8. Josephus
  holiday .. 7. Sukkoth 8. Hanukkah
    (Hannukka), Tishabov 11. Rosh Hashana
    (Rosh Hashonoh)
  horn .. 7. shophar (shofar)
  lawgiver .. 5. Moses
  leader .. 8. Nehemiah
  liturgy .. 6. minhah (PM) 9. shaharith
    (AM)
  loaves (unleavened) .. 9. shewbread
    (showbread)
  mystical writing .. 6. atbash
  patriots .. 9. Maccabees
  prayer book .. 6. siddur
  prophet .. 6. Elijah
  psalms of praise .. 6. hallel
  quarter (living) .. 6. ghetto
  ram's horn .. 7. shophar (shofar)
  slaughter (Relig) .. 8. shehitah
  song (Zionist anthem) .. 8. Hatikvah
    (Hattikvah)
jew's harp ... 8. guimbard 9. crembalum
Jezebel (pert to) ...
  epithet .. 5. vixen 6. virago 8. strumpet
  father .. 7. Ethbaal
  husband .. 4. Ahab (King)
  murdered (caused to be) .. 6. Naboth
jib ... 3. gib, jaw 4. balk, boom, sail,
spar, tack 5. crane, shift 6. fleece
8. underlip
jibe ... 3. fit 4. gibe 5. agree, shift
9. harmonize
jiff, jiffy ... 5. trice 6. moment 7. instant,
quickly 9. instantly, twinkling
jig ... 4. jerk, jolt 5. dance 6. ballad,
twitch 8. fishhook
jigger ... 4. club, dram
jiggle ... 5. sauce, shake
jimmy ... 3. pry 5. handy, smart
6. spruce 7. coal car, crowbar, pry
open 10. sheep's head
jimson weed ... 6. dature
10. stramonium, thorn apple 11. apple
of Peru
jingle ... 4. poem, rime 5. clink, rhyme
6. tinkle 13. two-wheeled car
jinn, jinnee ... 5. demon, Eblis, genie
6. afreet 8. jenniyeh
jinx ... 3. hex 5. Jonah 6. hoodoo,
whammy

jitters . . . 6. nerves 7. dithers, fidgets
  8. trembles

jittery . . . 4. edgy 5. jumpy 7. nervous

jivatma (Hind) . . . 4. soul 9. life force
  10. life energy 11. human spirit

Joan of Arc's appellation . . . 7. pucelle
  13. Maid of Orleans

job . . . 3. act 4. hire, task 5. chare, chore,
  stint 8. position, sinecure

Job (pert to) . . .
  Book . . 9. patriarch 12. Old Testament
  friend . . 6. Zophar
  home . . 2. Uz
  literally . . 9. afflicted 10. persecuted

jockey . . . 3. pad 5. cheat, racer, rider
  6. outwit 7. cushion 8. cavalier,
  horseman, minstrel, vagabond 9. Earl
  Sande (famed)

jocose . . . 3. dry 5. droll, lepid, merry
  7. jocular 8. humorous 9. facetious

jocular . . . 3. gay 4. airy, loco 5. droll,
  funny, merry, witty 6. elated, jocund,
  lively, ribald 7. comical, festive,
  gleeful, jesting, playful, waggish
  8. animated, mirthful 9. convivial,
  facetious, hilarious, laughable,
  vivacious 10. frolicsome

jocund . . . 3. gay 4. airy 5. merry 6. lively
  7. jocular 8. cheerful, sportive

jog . . . 4. gait, jolt, lope, plod, push, trot,
  walk 6. canter, notify, remind, trudge
  8. slow pace 9. suggest to

John . . . 3. Ian 4. Ivan, Jack, Juan
  8. Chinaman, Johannes 9. policeman

John (pert to) . . .
  Bull . . 10. Englishman
  Company . . 9. East India
  Crow . . 7. buzzard (turkey)
  Doe (law) . . 7. unknown 9. false name
  Hancock . . 9. autograph, signature
  Q Public . . 6. people 8. populace

johnnycake . . . 4. pone 7. hoecake 9. corn
  bread

join . . . 3. add, mix, pin, tie, wed
  4. ally, fuse, link, lock, meet, pair,
  seam, team, weld, yoke 5. annex,
  blend, enter, graft, group, hitch,
  marry, merge, unite 6. adjoin, attach,
  cement, concur, couple, engage, enlist,
  fasten, mingle, solder, splice, suture,
  syzygy 7. combine, conjoin, connect
  8. assemble, coalesce, compound
  9. associate 11. incorporate

joint . . . 3. ell, hip 4. dive (sl), knee,
  node, seam 5. alula, elbow, hinge,
  miter, nexus, tenon, wrist 6. rabbet,
  resort 7. hangout, pastern 8. coupling,
  dovetail 12. articulation

joint (pert to) . . .
  cavity . . 5. bursa
  firs . . 7. ephedra
  fluid . . 7. synovia 8. synovial
  grass stem . . 4. culm
  pert to . . 5. nodal 9. articular
  put out of . . 6. lucate 9. dislocate
  without . . 10. acondylous

joke . . . 3. fun, gag, pun 4. fool,
  hoax, jape, jest, quip 5. prank, rally,
  sport 6. banter, humbug 7. bromide
  8. chestnut, one-liner

joker . . . 3. dor, wag, wit 4. card

7. buffoon, farceur, gagster 8. humorist
  9. mistigris

jollity . . . 4. jest 5. mirth 6. gaiety
  8. hilarity 9. enjoyment, festivity,
  joviality, merriment 12. conviviality

jolly . . . 6. banter, jovial, joyful, mellow
  7. flatter, jocular 9. make merry

Jolly Roger . . . 5. Roger 10. pirate flag

jolt . . . 3. jar, jig, jut 4. blow, butt,
  stun 5. shake, shock 6. jostle, jounce
  7. startle 8. astonish, jail term (thieves)

Jonah (pert to) . . .
  Bib . . 7. prophet (Heb)
  Book . . 12. Old Testament
  slang . . 4. jinx
  swallowed by . . 5. whale

Jordan . . .
  capital . . 5. Amman
  city . . 7. Jericho, Samaria 9. Bethlehem
  historic trove . . 14. Dead Sea Scrolls
  official name . . 9. Hashemite (The)
  people (anc) . . 7. Essenes
  region . . 5. Perea 6. Basham
  river . . 6. Jordan

Jorth (pert to) . . .
  goddess . . 5. Earth
  husband . . 4. Odin
  named also . . 6. Forgyn
  son . . 4. Thor

Joseph (pert to) . . .
  Bib . . 9. patriarch
  buyer of . . 8. Potiphar
  coat of . . 10. many colors
  father . . 5. Jacob
  mother . . 6. Rachel
  son . . 5. Jesus 7. Ephraim

josh . . . 3. guy, kid 5. chaff, spoof, tease
  6. banter

Joshi (Ind) . . . 10. astrologer, astronomer

Joshua (pert to) . . .
  associate . . 5. Caleb
  Book . . 12. Old Testament
  burial place . . 5. Gaash
  successor to . . 5. Moses
  tree . . 5. yucca

jostle . . . 4. jolt, push, rush 5. crowd,
  elbow, joust, shake, shove 6. hustle,
  joggle, jounce, thrust

jot . . . 3. ace, bit 4. atom, iota, item, mite,
  whit 5. minim, point, speck 6. tittle
  7. smidgen 8. particle

jouk . . . 4. dart, duck, fawn, hide 5. cheat,
  dodge, evade, perch, roost, skulk
  6. cringe 9. obeisance

Joule, James P . . . 9. physicist

journal . . . 3. log 5. diary, paper 6. record
  7. daybook, diurnal, logbook, support
  8. magazine, register 9. chronicle
  10. periodical 11. account book

journalist . . . 6. editor, legman
  7. newsman 8. reporter 9. columnist,
  gazetteer 11. interviewer
  13. correspondent

journey . . . 3. run 4. fare, iter, ride, tour,
  trek, trip, wend 5. jaunt 6. travel, voyage
  7. odyssey 8. traverse 9. excursion
  10. expedition, pilgrimage
  13. peregrination

journey (pert to) . . . 4. eyre (circuit)
  6. viatic 8. anabasis (upward)
  9. itineracy, itinerary, traveling

10. travelling

joust . . . 4. bout, spar, tilt 6. combat
10. tournament

Jove . . . 7. Jupiter

jovial . . . 5. jolly, merry 6. elated,
joyous 7. festive, jocular 8. Jovelike
9. convivial, hilarious 14. mirth-inspiring

jowl . . . 3. jaw 4. chop 5. cheek 6. dewlap,
wattle 7. jawbone

joy . . . 4. glee 5. bliss, exult, gelid 6. gaiety
7. delight, ecstasy, rapture, rejoice
8. felicity, gladness, hilarity, pleasure
9. beatitude, happiness, merriment,
transport 10. exultation 12. exhilaration

joyous . . . 3. gay 4. glad 5. happy, merry
6. blithe, elated, festal, joyful 7. festive,
gleeful, jocular 8. cheerful, mirthful

jubilant . . . 6. elated 8. exultant, exulting
9. overjoyed, rejoicing 10. triumphant

Judah (pert to) . . .
ancestry . . 7. tribe of Judah
brother . . 4. Levi 6. Reuben, Simeon
father . . 5. Jacob
kingdom . . 9. Palestine
son . . 2. Er 6. Shelah
translation (Heb) . . 10. celebrated

Judas (pert to) . . .
Bible . . 7. apostle, traitor 8. betrayer,
deceiver, disciple
called . . 8. Iscariot
historic . . 13. Paschal candle
kiss . . 8. betrayal 11. double-cross,
treacherous
priest . . 4. oath
suicide site . . 8. Aceldama

Judea (pert to) . . .
governor . . 6. Pilate
king . . 3. Asa 5. Herod 7. Jehoram
11. Jehoshaphat
location . . 5. Berea
people . . 4. Jews
province of . . 9. Palestine

judge . . . 3. try 4. deem, rate 5. opine,
think 6. critic, puisne 7. arbiter,
referee, suppose 8. deemster, estimate,
mediator, sentence 9. arbitrate, criticize
10. adjudicate, magistrate
11. connoisseur

judge (pert to) . . .
bench . . 4. banc (bancus)
chamber . . 6. camera
circuit . . 4. iter
gavel . . 4. mace
group . . 5. bench 9. judiciary
of the dead . . 6. Osiris
opinion . . 12. obiter dictum
sittings . . 7. assizes
summary . . 6. postea

judgment . . . 4. doom 5. arrêt, award,
sense, taste 7. censure, opinion
8. decision, judicium, sentence
9. criticism 10. conclusion, discretion,
persuasion (Relig), punishment
11. arbitration, sensibility

judgment (pert to) . . .
creditor . . 13. quasi contract
day . . 7. last day 8. Dies Irae, doomsday
left to one's . . 13. discretionary
note . . 10. promissory
seat . . 3. bar 5. mercy 8. tribunal,
woolsack

judicial . . . 5. legal 8. critical 9. judicious
10. judicatory

judicial (pert to) . . .
council . . 5. cabal, junta, junto 7. coterie
hearing . . 5. trial
order . . 4. writ 6. elegit, venire 7. precept
security . . 7. custody

judicious . . . 4. wise 7. politic, prudent
8. cautious, discreet 9. sagacious
10. discerning 11. circumspect, well-
advised

jug . . . 4. ewer, jail, olpe, toby 5. askos,
buire, cruse, gotch 6. flagon, gomlah,
lockup, prison, tinaja, urceus 7. pitcher
13. Schnabelkanne

Juggernaut . . . 6. Vishnu (Hind)

juggler . . . 5. cheat, trick 7. buffoon
8. deceiver 13. sleight of hand
14. legerdemainist

Jugoslavia, Yugoslavia . . .
area . . 6. Kosovo 8. Dalmatia
brandy . . 5. rakia 9. slivovitz
capital . . 8. Belgrade
language . . 7. Slovene 10. Macedonian,
Serbo-Croat
leader . . 4. Tito
monarch . . 5. Peter
money . . 5. dinar
organization . . 9. Comitadji
people . . 4. Serb 5. Croat 7. Slovene

juice . . . 3. rob, sap 4. milk (plant),
must, stum 5. fluid, latex, syrup
(sirup) 7. essence, hebenon, moisten
10. succulence 11. electricity

jujitsu, jiujitsu . . . 11. self-defense

juju . . . 5. charm, magic 6. amulet, belief,
fetish, voodoo

jujube . . . 3. ber 5. fruit, jelly 7. lozenge
8. Zizyphus

Jules Verne's captain . . . 4. Nemo (the
Nautilus)

Julian Emperors (first Five) . . . 4. Nero
8. Augustus, Caligula, Claudius, Tiberius

jumble . . . 2. pi 3. mix 4. cake, hash, heap,
mess, raff, stir 5. blend, botch, chaos,
shake 6. medley, muddle 7. agitate,
confuse, mixture 8. disorder, riffraff

jumble type . . . 3. pie (pi)

jump . . . 3. hop, lep 4. leap, move
(checkers) 5. bound, caper, halma, salto,
scold, start, vault 6. chorea, escape,
hurdle, spring, twitch 7. saltary, saltate
8. increase 9. advantage 10. transition

jumping (pert to) . . .
adjective . . 7. saltant
Frog, tale by . . 9. Mark Twain
music . . 7. saltato
rodent . . 5. mouse 6. jerboa 11. kangaroo
rat
stick . . 4. pogo, pole

junction . . . 4. axil, seam 5. union
6. suture 7. joining, meeting
11. combination, concurrence

juncture . . . 4. pass 5. joint, pinch 6. crisis,
strait 8. exigency, quandary
9. emergency 10. connection
11. conjuncture, predicament
12. articulation

June bug . . . 3. dor 6. beetle, May bug
8. figeater

jungle . . . 4. camp 7. thicket 8. woodland

11. dense growth 12. complication
jungle (pert to) . . .
dweller . . 5. beast 6. savage
fever . . 7. malaria
grass . . 3. poa
ox . . 4. gaur 5. gayal 7. timarau
sheep . . 7. muntjac
junior . . . 5. cadet, petty 6. puisne, recent 7. student, younger 8. inferior 9. unskilled
juniper . . . 4. cade, puny 5. cedar, gorse, retem (raetem), savin
junket . . . 4. dish (milk), food, meal 5. feast 7. banquet 8. festival 9. excursion, sweetmeat
Juno (pert to) . . .
consort . . 7. Jupiter
goddess (Rom) . . 3. sky 5. light
identified with . . 4. Hera
messenger . . 4. Iris
junta, junto . . . 5. cabal 6. circle, clique 7. coterie, council, faction 8. intrigue 11. combination
jupe . . . 4. coat 5. jupon, shirt, skirt, tunic 6. bodice, jacket
Jupiter (pert to) . . .
angel . . 7. Zadkiel
astronomy . . 6. planet (largest)
daughter . . 4. Bura
deity . . 4. Jove 9. Father Sky
festival . . 14. Vinalis sustica
god of . . 7. Heavens
heraldry . . 5. azure
lover . . 2. Io
son . . 6. Castor, Pollux
triad . . 4. Juno 7. Minerva
wife . . 4. Juno
Jupiter, god of . . .
law . . 6. Fidius 10. Dius Fidius
lightning . . 6. Fulgur
rain . . 7. Pluvius
thunder . . 6. Tonans
jurat . . . 5. juror 8. recorder 10. magistrate (Channel Isis)
jure . . . 3. jus (ius), law 5. right 13. jurisprudence
jurisprudence . . . 3. law, soc 4. soke

5. power (legal) 6. charge, sphere 7. control, custody, emirate 9. authority, consulate 10. government, judicature, patriarchy
juror . . . 6. dicast 7. assizer, juryman 9. venireman
jury . . . 5. panel, tales (additions) 6. venire
jus . . . 3. law 5. gravy, juice 10. legal power, legal right
just . . . 4. fair, tilt 5. equal, exact, valid 7. logical, upright 8. provided, unbiased 9. equitable, righteous 10. legitimate
just begun . . . 8. inchoate
justice . . . 4. doom 5. right 6. equity, virtue 8. fairness, fair play, justness 9. rectitude 10. judicature 11. give and take 12. rightfulness
justice of the peace . . . 6. squire 10. magistrate
justification . . . 7. apology, defense 11. vindication
justify . . . 5. clear 6. defend, excuse 7. absolve, support, warrant 8. maintain, sanction, underpin 9. authorize, exculpate, vindicate 12. substantiate
justly . . . 5. truly 6. fairly 7. equally 8. honestly 9. equitably 10. deservedly
justness . . . 7. fitness, justice 8. accuracy, validity 9. exactness 11. correctness
Justus . . . 4. just
jute . . . 5. fiber, gunny 6. burlap 7. sacking
Jute . . . 4. Dane 9. Jutlander
jutty . . . 4. mole, pier 5. jetty 7. project 8. buttress, protrude
juvenile . . . 5. actor, young, youth 8. immature, youthful 9. youngling, youthlike 11. undeveloped
juvia . . . 9. Brazil nut
juxta . . . 4. near 6. nearby
juxtaposition . . . 5. touch 7. contact 8. nearness 9. proximity 10. contiguity, side by side
jynx . . . 5. charm, spell 7. wryneck 10. woodpecker
Jynx . . . 11. woodpeckers
J'y suis, j'y reste . . . 18. I am here; here I remain

K

K . . . 5. kappa (Gr) 6. letter (11th)
Ka . . . 3. God (Hind)
Kaaba, Caaba (pert to) . . .
content . . 10. Black Stone (of Mecca)
location . . 11. Great Mosque (Mecca)
pilgrimage . . 7. Islamic
praying direction . . 6. Kiblah
shape . . 7. cubical
kaama . . . 10. hartebeest
kachina worshipper . . . 4. Hopi, Zuni 6. Pueblo
Kaddish . . . 8. Doxology
Kadiak, Kodiak, bear . . . 5. brown

7. Alaskan
Kaiser brown . . . 6. ginger
Kaiser's residence . . . 5. Doorn
keka . . . 6. parrot
kakapo . . . 6. parrot 9. owl parrot
kaker . . . 7. muntjac
kakariki . . . 6. lizard
keki . . . 5. stilt (bird) 9. persimmon
kakkak . . . 5. heron 7. bittern
kakke . . . 8. beriberi
kala . . . 6. bulbul (bird)
kale . . . 4. cole 5. money 7. cabbage, collard 8. colewort, corecole

kaleidoscopic ... 7. varying
   10. changeable, variegated
Kali (pert to) ...
   Hindu .. 10. evil genius
   Persian .. 6. carpet
   Vedic Myth .. 12. tongue of Agni
   (fire-god)
kallah ... 5. bride (Jew)
kamavachara ... 6. heaven (Buddh)
Kamchatka ...
   capital .. 13. Petropavlovsk
   peninsula .. 7. Siberia
   people .. 7. Russian 9. Mongolian
   sea .. 6. Bering 7. Okhotsk
Kamehameha Day ... 7. holiday (Haw)
Kamerad .. 7. comrade 9. surrender
kamik ... 7. sealskin boot
Kammerspiel ... 5. drama 7. theater
Kanaka ... 3. man 8. Hawaiian
   10. Melanesian, Polynesian 16. South
   Sea islander
Kanaloa ... 3. God (Pantheon)
kangaroo (pert to) ...
   class .. 9. marsupial
   family .. 12. Macropodidae
   female .. 3. doe, gin, 'roo
   giant .. 8. forester
   leaping .. 6. jeroba 7. bettong (bettonga)
   male .. 5. bilby (bilbi)
   rat .. 7. pototoo
   reference to .. 7. wallaby
   11. macropodine
   small .. 7. wallaby
   young .. 4. joey
kangaroo court ... 9. mock court, moot
   court 14. irregular court
Kansas ...
   capital .. 6. Topeka
   city .. 5. Dodge 7. Abilene, Wichita
   10. Hutchinson, Kansas City
   11. Leavenworth
   Eisenhower home .. 7. Abilene
   military post .. 9. Fort Riley
   penitentiary .. 11. Leavenworth
   State admission .. 12. Thirty-fourth
   State motto .. 16. Ad Astra per Aspera
   (To the Stars Through Difficulties)
   State nickname .. 9. Sunflower
kapok tree ... 7. God tree 9. Ceiba tree
   10. silk-cotton
kappa ... 1. K (Gr) 4. star 6. letter (10th)
karakul, karakule ... 5. sheep
   9. astrakhan, broadtail
karma ... 4. fate 7. destiny 8. casualty
Kartvelian people ... 4. Svan (Svane)
   9. Georgians 10. Imeritians, Svanetians
kasha ... 4. mush (Russ)
Kashmir, India ...
   alphabet .. 6. Sarada
   capital .. 8. Srinagar
   deer .. 6. hangul
   official .. 6. pundit
Kashyapa (Vedic Myth) ... 8. tortoise
Kaskaskia ... 5. epoch 6. Indian
   10. Algonquian
kat ... 5. shrub 8. narcotic
katar ... 6. dagger
katchung ... 6. peanut
katogle ... 8. eagle owl
kava, kavakava ... 6. Kawaka, pepper
kayak ... 5. canoe

kea ... 6. parrot
Keat's poem ... 8. Endymion, Hyperion
keek ... 3. spy (of rival fashions) 6. peeper
keel ... 4. cool, seel, ship, skeg, tilt
   6. careen, ruddle, timber (ship's)
   7. capsize 8. overturn, red ocher, turn
   over 10. guinea fowl
keelbill, keelbird ... 3. ani
keeling ... 7. codfish
keel-shaped ... 6. carina 7. carinal
keen ... 4. avid, cute, gare, good, nice,
   tart 5. acute, alert, eager, sharp, smart,
   snell, vivid, witty 6. astute, bitter,
   clever, shrewd, shrill 7. caustic, fervent
   9. sensitive, trenchant 11. acrimonious,
   penetrating
keenness ... 4. edge 5. acies (of sight),
   nifty 6. acuity, acumen 8. acrimony,
   pungency 9. acuteness, eagerness,
   sharpness, smartness, wittiness
keep ... 4. save 6. detain, retain
   7. confine, custody, fulfill, husband,
   reserve 8. conserve, maintain, preserve,
   restrain, withhold 14. accommodations
keep (pert to) ...
   account .. 5. score
   afloat .. 4. buoy
   apart .. 7. seclude 8. separate
   back, out .. 3. bar, dam 4. save 5. debar,
   delay 6. detain, except, hinder, retard
   7. exclude, reserve 8. restrain, withhold
   from .. 5. avoid, delay 7. abstain, boycott,
   prevent
   hidden .. 7. secrete
   in .. 6. retain
   off .. 4. fend 7. prevent, repulse, ward
   off
   on .. 6. endure 9. persevere
keeper ... 5. guard 6. warden 9. constable,
   custodian, possessor 10. maintainer
keeper of ...
   birds .. 8. aviarist
   borders .. 8. margrave
   door .. 5. tiler
   elephant .. 6. mahout
   golden apples (Myth) .. 6. Ithunn (Ithun)
   parks .. 6. ranger
   prison .. 6. gaoler, jailer, jailor, warden
   7. turnkey
keeping ... 4. care 5. board, guard, trust
   7. custody 8. tutelage 9. retention
   10. caretaking, conformity, possession,
   preserving, protection 11. maintenance
   12. guardianship
keeve ... 3. tub 4. tuft 5. knoll, plume
   8. haystack
kef ... 6. dreamy 7. languor 12. tranquillity
   (tranquility)
keg ... 3. tun, vat 4. cade, cask 6. firkin
kelly ... 5. derby, killy (fish)
kelp ... 4. game 5. sight, wrack 7. insight,
   seaweed 9. water lily
ken ... 4. lore 9. recognize 10. cognizance,
   prescience 13. understanding
Kentish freedman ... 4. laet
Kentucky ...
   bluegrass .. 3. poa
   capital .. 9. Frankfort
   city .. 7. Paducah 9. Lexington
   10. Louisville 12. Bowling Green
   famed road .. 15. Wilderness Trail

K

famed sights.. 7. Obelisk (J Davis)
   8. Fort Knox, Log Cabin (Lincoln)
   11. Federal Hill (My Old Ky Home),
   Mammoth Cave
famed sport.. 13. Kentucky Derby
   (Churchill Downs)
mountain.. 4. Pine 10. Cumberland
pioneer.. 11. Daniel Boone
river.. 4. Ohio 10. Cumberland
State admission.. 9. Fifteenth
State name meaning (Indian)..
   8. tomorrow
State nickname.. 9. Bluegrass
Kenya...
   capital.. 7. Nairobi
   leader.. 3. Moi 8. Kenyatta
   mountain, volcano.. 5. Kenya
   people.. 5. Masai 6. Kikuyu
   secret society.. 6. Mau Mau
kept... see keep
ker (Gr)... 4. doom, fate 5. ghost 6. spirit
kermis, kermess... 4. fair 8. festival
kernel... 3. nut 4. core, gist, meat, pith,
   seed 5. grain, heart 6. acinus, nutmeg
   7. nucleus
ketch... 4. Jack, saic, ship 6. vessel
ketone... 5. irone 6. carone 7. acetone,
   camphor 8. deguelin
kettle... 3. pot 4. drum, pail 6. kibble
   7. caldron 8. cauldron 9. teakettle
   10. kettledrum
kettledrum... 4. drum 5. naker, tabor
   6. atabal 7. anacara 8. tympanon
key... 4. clue, crib, isle, quay, reef,
   tone 5. islet, pitch, tasto 6. clavis,
   cotter, fasten, island, opener, switch,
   tapper 7. digital 8. mainstay, solution
   11. explanation, fundamental,
   translation
keyed up... 4. agog 5. eager, fired
   7. aroused, stirred 8. hopped up,
   worked up 10. stimulated
Keys, House of... 9. Isle of Man, officials
Keystone State... 12. Pennsylvania
khan... 3. inn 4. lord 6. prince
   9. resthouse 11. caravansary
kiang... 4. diver 6. onager 7. wild ass
kick... 4. blow, boot, funk, punt
   6. energy, object, thrill 7. grumble,
   protest 8. complain, pungency, sixpence
   9. complaint 10. calcitrate, enthusiasm
Kickapoo... 6. Indian 10. Algonquian
kickshaw... 3. toy 6. trifle 7. trinket
   8. delicacy
kid... 3. guy 4. fool, goat, hoax, joke,
   josh, twit 5. child, jolly, suede 6. banter,
   humbug 8. antelope (young), yeanling
   9. youngling
kidang... 4. deer 7. muntjac
kidney... 4. neer 5. gland, reins
   7. nephros
kidney (pert to)...
   comb form.. 6. nephro
   disease.. 7. nephria 9. nephritis
   pyramid.. 9. reniculus
   reference to.. 4. reni 5. renal 6. vitals
   7. nephric
   shaped.. 8. reniform
   stone.. 6. pebble 8. nephrite
kiki... 14. castor oil plant
kill... 4. slay, veto 5. blast, creek 6. defeat,

murder 7. channel, destroy, execute,
   silence 8. dispatch, immolate, lapidate,
   massacre, overbeat 9. slaughter
   11. assassinate, exterminate
killer... 4. Cain 6. gunman, slayer
   7. butcher 8. cannibal, man-eater,
   mongoose, murderer 9. cutthroat
   12. assassinator
killer whale... 3. orc 4. orca 7. grampus
killing... 5. fatal 6. deadly, murder
   7. amusing, carnage, cleanup
   (speculation), garrote 8. homicide
   9. execution 10. euthanasia
   11. captivating 12. overpowering
killing of...
   brother.. 10. fratricide
   cats.. 8. felicide
   father.. 9. patricide
   man.. 8. homicide
   mother.. 9. matricide
   old men (tribal).. 8. senicide
   self.. 7. suicide 9. martyrdom
   sister.. 10. sororicide
   wolf.. 8. lupicide
kiln... 4. oast, oven 5. clamp, stove,
   tiler 7. furnace
kilo (pref)... 8. thousand
kind... 3. ilk 4. good, race, sort, type
   5. class, genre, genus, order, seely,
   style 6. benign, gender, humane,
   loving, strain 7. kindred, lenient, species
   8. gracious 9. benignant 10. benevolent
   11. sympathetic 12. well-disposed
kindle... 4. burn, fire 5. brood, light,
   rouse, young 6. excite, ignite, incite,
   litter 7. animate, inflame, provoke
kindly... 4. mild 6. benign, blithe, genial,
   humane 7. natural 8. benignly, heartily
   9. agreeably, benignant, indulgent
   10. beneficent, legitimate, pleasantly
   11. sympathetic
kindness... 5. favor 8. clemency,
   goodness, humanity, mildness
   9. benignity 10. compassion, generosity,
   gentleness, indulgency, tenderness
kindred... 3. sib, tie 4. akin, clan, kith
   5. blood 6. allied, family 7. cognate,
   descent, kinship, kinsmen, related
   8. kinsfolk 9. relations 12. relationship
   14. consanguineous
kine... 4. cows 5. cattle
kinetic... 6. active, moving
king... 3. rex, rey, roi 4. rank 5. chief,
   ruler 6. master 7. regulus 8. chessman
   9. potentate, sovereign
king (pert to)...
   beasts.. 4. lion
   birds.. 5. eagle
   chamber.. 9. camarilla
   cheeses.. 4. Brie
   child.. 6. prince 8. princess
   dwarfs.. 8. Alberich (Ger)
   fairies.. 6. Oberon
   family.. 7. dynasty
   gods.. 7. Jupiter
   heaven.. 3. God 6. Christ
   herrings.. 4. opah 7. oarfish 8. chimaera
   mackerel.. 4. cero
   March (The).. 5. Sousa
   metals.. 4. gold
   monkeys.. 7. guereza

murder of.. 8. regicide
myth.. 4. Atli 5. Midas
myth (classical).. 4. Zeus 7. Jupiter
rivers.. 6. Amazon
serpents (race of).. 6. Shesha (Sesha)
symbol.. 7. scepter (sceptre)
vultures.. 4. papa
waters.. 7. Neptune, Pacific
Woods (The).. 13. Rex Nemorensis
King Arthur (pert to)...
  abode.. 6. Avalon 7. Camelot
  battleground (fatal).. 6. Camlan
  father.. 5. Uther (Pendragon)
  home.. 8. Caerleon (on the Usk)
  Knights of the Round Table.. 3. Kay
    6. Galahad 7. Galahad 8. Lancelot,
    Tristram (Tristan) 9. Percivale
  Lady of the Lake.. 6. Vivian
  magician.. 6. Merlin
  Queen.. 9. Guinevere
  quest of.. 9. Holy Grail (The)
  shield.. 7. Pridwin
  sister.. 11. Morgan le Fay
  son.. 7. Mordred (Modred)
  sword.. 9. Excalibur
kingdom... 5. realm 6. empire, estate
    8. dominion, kingship, monarchy
kingdom (pert to)...
  ancient.. 4. Elam, Moab
  Asia.. 5. Nepal
  between Spain, France.. 7. Navarra
    (Navarre)
  confusion.. 5. Babel
  divisions.. 6. animal 7. mineral
    9. vegetable
  Indo-China.. 5. Annam (Anam)
kingfish... 4. cero, haku, opah 7. kingpin,
    pintado 8. big wheel 9. threadfin
kingly.. 5. grand, noble, regal, royal
    6. august 7. leonine 8. imperial,
    majestic, princely 9. dignified, sovereign
    11. monarchical
King of ...
  Albania.. 3. Zog
  Bashan.. 2. Og
  Bulgaria.. 5. Boris
  Greece (anc).. 9. Agamemnon
  Israel.. 4. Ahab, Jehy, Saul 5. David
    7. Solomon 8. Jeroboam
  Judea.. 3. Asa
  Kings.. 3. God 6. Christ
  Men.. 4. Odin, Zeus 7. Jupiter
  Oriental.. 11. King of Kings
  Persia (Iran).. 5. Cyrus 6. Xerxes
  Troy.. 5. Priam
  Tyre.. 5. Hiram
  Visigoths.. 6. Alaric
Kipling, Rudyard (pert to)...
  award.. 10. Nobel Prize (1907)
  birthplace.. 6. Bombay
  book.. 3. Kim 10. Jungle Book
  poem (for Queen Victoria)..
    11. Recessional
kissing, science ... 13. philematology
knee (pert to) ...
  bend.. 9. genuflect
  bent.. 10. geniculate
  bone.. 6. rotula 7. kneepan, patella
  britches.. 6. smalls 8. knickers
  on bended.. 7. humbled 8. obeisant
    10. submissive, worshipful

    12. supplicatory
kneeling desk ... 8. prie-dieu
knew ... see know
Knickerbocker, Father ... 9. New Yorker
    (Hist)
knickknack ... 3. toy 6. bauble, gewgaw,
    trifle 7. trinket 8. gimcrack
knife ... 4. bolo, snee, stab 5. corer,
    prune 6. cutter, weapon
knife (pert to) ...
  Burmese.. 3. dah
  Hindu.. 5. kukri
  Irish.. 5. skean 8. skean dhu
  Malay.. 4. kris 6. barong, creese
  New Zealand.. 4. patu
  one-bladed.. 6. barlow
  Scottish.. 4. dirk
  Spanish.. 7. machete
  surgical.. 7. scalpel 10. greffotome
  Turkish.. 8. yataghan (yatagan)
  US Navy.. 7. cutlass
knife maker ... 6. cutler
knife-throwing game ...
    11. mumbletypeg 12. mumble-the-peg
knight (pert to) ...
  adventure.. 8. errantry
  adventurer.. 8. cavalier 9. caballero,
    chevalier
  cloak.. 6. tabard
  combat.. 5. joust
  ensign.. 8. gonfalon, gonfanon
  errant.. 7. Paladin
  hero.. 7. Paladin
  servant.. 4. page 6. varlet
  title.. 3. Sir 8. banneret
  wife.. 4. Dame, Lady
  wreath (with crest).. 4. orle
Knight of the Round Table ... 3. Kay
    6. Gawain 7. Galahad 8. Lancelot,
    Tristram (Tristan) 9. Percivale
Knight of the Rueful Countenance ...
    10. Don Quixote
knit ... 4. bind, heal, join, seam 5. plait,
    unite, woven 6. cement, couple, fasten
    7. conjoin, connect, wrinkle 8. contract
    9. interlace 11. consolidate
knitting machine guide ... 4. sley
knitting stitch ... 4. knit, purl
knob ... 3. nub 4. boss, head, hill, lump,
    node, stud, umbo 5. bulge, knur!
    6. croche (antler), pommel 8. tubercle
    12. protuberance
knobkerrie ... 4. club, kiri 5. stick
knock ... 3. hit, rap, tap 4. bang, bash,
    beat, bump, dash, glow, hill, pass,
    slay, snop 5. pound, thump 6. hammer,
    jostle, strike 7. collide 9. criticism,
    criticize, disparage 12. faultfinding
knock (pert to) ...
  about.. 6. travel, wander
  down.. 4. fell, raze 6. deject, strike
    8. vanquish
  off.. 3. die 6. deduct, recess 9. improvise
  out.. 2. KO 4. kayo
knocking ... 6. rat-tat 7. rapping, tapping
    9. rat-tat-tat
knock-knee ... 6. in-knee
knoll ... 4. bank, clod, hill, knap, knob,
    lump 5. bunch, hurst, knell, mound
    7. hillock
knot ... 3. bow, nep, tie 4. burl, knar,

knob, knur, lump, node, noil, snag
5. gnarl, noose 6. clique, nodule,
tangle 7. dilemma, lanyard, problem,
rosette 9. sandpiper 10. sheepshank
12. complication, protuberance

knotted . . . 3. nep 5. noded, nowed (Her)
6. knotty 7. clotted, complex, gnarled,
knitted, nodated 8. abstruse, puzzling
9. difficult, entangled

knotty . . . 5. nodal, rough 7. gnarled,
knarred, knobbed, knurled, nodular
9. difficult, entangled, intricate
10. perplexing

know . . . 3. ken, wis, wot 5. sense
6. regard, reveal 8. perceive
9. apprehend, be certain, recognize
11. be cognizant, distinguish

knowing . . . 3. hep 6. artful, crafty,
scient, shrewd 7. cunning 8. informed
9. cognitive, conscious, wide-awake
10. perceptive 11. intelligent,
intentional 12. familiar with
13. comprehension

know-it-all . . . 6. gossip 8. quidnunc,
wiseacre

knowledge . . . 3. ken 4. kith, lore
5. ology 6. wisdom 7. science
8. learning, scientia 9. erudition
11. familiarity, information, instruction
12. acquaintance

knowledge (pert to) . . .
acquisition of . . 7. organon
ancestral . . 9. tradition
epithet of Muses . . 7. Pierian
exhibition of . . 6. pedant
instrument . . 7. organon
lack of . . 9. ignorance, nescience
object of . . 7. scibile
pert to . . 7. gnostic 8. instinct
9. epistemic, intuition, sciential
12. epistemology
pretender to . . 7. aeolist (eolist) 8. sciolist
seeker of . . 10. philonoist
slight . . 7. inkling, smatter 10. smattering
summarized . . 12. encyclopedia
(encyclopaedia)
superficial . . 9. sociology
system . . 7. science
universal . . 9. pantology
without . . 8. atechnic

know-nothing . . . 5. dunce 8. agnostic
9. ignoramus

kobird . . . 6. cuckoo

kobold . . . 3. elf, imp 5. gnome 8. folklore
9. hobgoblin

Kodiak, Kadiak bear . . . 7. Alaskan

Kohinoor . . . 7. diamond (700 carats)

kohl . . . 5. horse 8. antimony, cosmetic

kola . . . 3. nut 6. jackal

kooky . . . 7. offbeat

kopje . . . 5. mound 7. hillock

Koran, Alcoran (pert to) . . .
author . . 8. Mohammed
division . . 4. Sura (chapter)
learned man . . 5. ulema
recording angel . . 6. sijill (sijil)
scriptures . . 10. Mohammedan
teacher . . 5. ulema 7. alfaqui (alfaquin)

Korea . . .
capital . . 5. Seoul (South) 9. Pyongyang
(North)
city . . 6. Gensan
dynasty . . 2. Yi
leader . . 9. Kim Il-Sung (North)
11. Syngman Rhee (South)
mountain peak . . 6. Paekdu
old name . . 6. Chosen 13. Hermit
Kingdom
peninsula . . 6. Ongjin
province . . 5. Fusan (Fuzan)
river . . 4. Yalu 5. Tuman 7. Naktong

Korean dish . . . 6. kimchi

Krakatoa, et al . . . 7. volcano

kosher . . . 5. clean 6. kashruth
10. sanctioned

kra . . . 3. ape (long-tailed)

krimmer . . . 8. lambskin

Krishna (Hind) . . . 5. deity (of Vishnu)
6. avatar (8th), Goloka

Krupp steel works, site . . . 5. Essen
(Ger)

kudu . . . 8. antelope 9. gray-brown

kusimansel . . . 6. mangue 8. mongoose

kvetch . . . 3. nag

Kwantung capital . . . 6. Dairen

kwazoku (Jap) . . . 8. nobility (modern)

kyah . . . 9. partridge

kyaung . . . 9. monastery

kymatology, science of . . . 5. waves
10. wave motion

kyphosis . . . 8. humpback 9. hunchback
15. spinal curvature

kyte . . . 5. belly 7. stomach

Kyushu (Jap) . . . 6. Island (southernmost)

L

L . . . 5. fifty (Rom num) 6. lambda, letter
(12th) 7. lammedh

laager, lager . . . 4. camp

laagte . . . 6. bottom, valley 8. riverbed

Laban (pert to) . . .
daughter . . 4. Leah 6. Rachel
father . . 7. Bethuel
son-in-law . . 5. Jacob

label . . . 3. tab, tag 4. band, name
6. fillet, lappet, tassel, ticket 8. insignia
9. designate

labellum . . . 3. lip 6. labium, labrum

labia . . . 4. lips

labial stop . . . 9. organ stop

labial teeth . . . 6. canine 7. incisor

labile . . . 8. shifting, unstable

labium . . . 3. lip

La Boheme . . . 4. Mimi 7. Puccini

labor, labour . . . 4. moil, task, toil, work
5. sweet 6. strive 7. travail, work
for 8. drudgery, endeavor, exertion,
industry

labored . . . 5. heavy 6. forced, strove
7. not easy, operose 8. strained
9. difficult, elaborate, laborious
11. painstaking
laborer . . . 4. hind, peon, toty 5. navvy
6. coolie, toiler, worker 7. bracero,
wetback, workman
laborious . . . 4. hard 7. arduous, operose
8. toilsome 9. difficult 11. hard working,
industrious, painstaking
labor leader . . . 5. Hoffa, Lewis, Meany
7. Gompers (1st), Reuther 8. Petrillo
labor letters . . . 3. AFL, CIO, ILO, UAW
Labrador (pert to) . . .
  Arctic flow . . 7. Current
  dog . . 9. retriever 10. Newfoundland
  missionary . . 8. Grenfell (Dr)
  part . . 12. Newfoundland
  tea . . 5. Ledum 8. gowiddie
labyrinth . . . 4. maze 7. circuit, cochlea
10. perplexity 12. complication
labyrinths . . . 7. complex 8. involved
9. intricate 10. circuitous
11. complicated
lac . . . 4. milk 5. resin 7. lacquer, shellac
lace . . . 3. net, tat, tie, web 4. band, beat,
cord, flog, lash, line, trim 5. braid, filet,
lacis, snare 6. fasten, string, tissue
7. network 9. embroider 10. intertwine,
shoestring 13. dash of spirits
lace (pert to) . . .
  Antwerp . . 7. pot lace
  bobbin . . 3. val 12. Valenciennes
  cape, scarf . . 8. mantilla
  edge . . 5. picot
  Flemish . . 7. malines, Mechlin
  French . . 5. filet 7. guipure
  frill . . 5. ruche
  front . . 5. jabot
  gold, silver . . 5. orris
  make . . 3. tat 5. weave 7. crochet,
    entwine
  needlepoint . . 7. Alencon
  opening . . 6. eyelet
  patterned . . 7. guipure
lacerate . . . 3. cut, rip 4. pain, rend, tear
6. harrow, injure, mangle 7. afflict,
torture
lachryma . . . 4. tear 5. fluid 8. teardrop
lachrymal, lachrymose . . . 5. teary,
weepy 7. tearful 8. tearlike
lack . . . 4. need, want 6. dearth 7. absence,
lacking, missing, require 8. have
need, scarcity 9. fall short, neediness
10. deficiency
lack (pert to) . . .
  blood cells (red) . . 6. anemia
  correspondence . . 13. nonconformity
  energy . . 5. atony, tepid 6. energy
    7. aimless, sapless
  feeling . . 10. insensible 13. insensibility
  firmness . . 4. limp 8. boneless
    9. spineless
  interest . . 6. apathy 9. apathetic
  knowledge . . 9. ignorance, nescience
  melody . . 6. atonic 9. atonality
  preparation . . 8. unfitted
  reasoning . . 7. idiotic
  refinement . . 5. gross 9. grossness,
    inelegant 10. inelegance
  vigilance . . 6. unwary

lackadaisical . . . 7. languid 8. listless
10. spiritless
Laconia (anc) . . .
  capital . . 6. Sparta
  clan . . 3. obe
  inhabitant . . 5. Lacon
  location . . 12. Peloponnesus
  race . . 6. Dorian
laconic . . . 5. brief, pithy, short, terse
7. concise, pointed, summary
8. succinct, taciturn
lacquer . . . 3. lac, red (color) 5. japan,
resin 6. enamel 7. shellac, varnish
lacrimando . . . 9. lamenting, plaintive
lactarium . . . 5. dairy
lacteal . . . 5. milky
lacune, lacuna . . . 3. gap, pit 5. break
6. hiatus 7. opening (small)
10. depression
ladder . . . 3. run, sty 5. scale 7. scalade
8. escalade 10. stepladder
lade . . . 3. dip 4. bail, draw, fill, load,
ship 5. drain, ladle 6. burden
laden . . . 6. loaded 8. burdened
9. freighted
lading . . . 4. load 5. cargo 6. burden
7. freight
ladle . . . 3. dip 4. bowl 5. scoop, spoon
6. dipper
lady . . . 4. burd (anc), dame 5. donna
6. domina, female, senora 7. signora
8. ladylove 13. harlequin duck
lady (pert to) . . .
  bird . . 6. beetle 7. Vedalia
  fish . . 6. wrasse
  killer . . 4. wolf 5. shiek 7. Don Juan
    8. Casanova
  like . . 6. female, polite 7. genteel
    8. feminine
Lady Godiva's town . . . 8. Coventry
Lady of the Lake character (legend) . . .
6. Merlin, Vivian
Lady's Book author . . . 5. Godey
lady's-slipper . . . 6. balsam, orchid
8. Noah's ark 9. nerveroot
lady's-thumb . . . 5. peachwort, persicary
lag . . . 4. slow 5. delay, tardy 6. dawdle,
linger, loiter 7. belated 10. dillydally,
fall behind
lagarto . . . 9. alligator 10. lizard fish
laggard . . . 4. slow 5. idler 7. lagging
8. backward, dilatory, indolent, loiterer,
sluggish 9. loitering, straggler
La Gioconda . . . 8. Mona Lisa
lagniappe, lagnappe . . . 5. pilon
7. largess (largesse), present (trifling)
8. gratuity
lagoon . . . 4. lake, pond, pool 5. atoll
laic . . . 3. lay 5. civil 6. layman 7. secular
8. temporal
lair . . . 3. bed, den, pen 4. cave, shed, trap
5. abode, couch 6. cavern 7. retreat
Lais (Gr) . . . 7. hetaera (of Corinth)
8. mistress 14. beautiful woman
laissez faire, laisser faire . . . 5. let
go 7. let pass 8. inaction, letup
9. do-nothing, passivism, unconcern
12. indifference 15. noninterference
Laius' son . . . 7. Oedipus (of Thebes)
lake . . . 4. loch, mere, pond, pool, tarn
5. lacus 6. lagoon 7. carmine (color)

L

lake (pert to) . . .
bass . . 4. rock 6. calico
deposit . . 5. trona
duck . . 5. scaup 7. mallard
dweller . . 10. lacustrian
dwelling . . 7. crannog
growing in . . 10. lacustrine
Hades (of) . . 7. Avernus
highest . . 8. Titicaca
pert to . . 9. lacustral
poet (Eng) . . 6. lakist 7. Southey
  9. Coleridge 10. Wordsworth
State . . 8. Michigan
lama . . 4. monk 5. Dalai
Lamaism . . 8. Buddhism
Lamaism, Buddhist (pert to) . . .
convent . . 8. lamasery
dignitary . . 8. hutukhtu
palace site . . 5. Lhasa
priest, monk . . 4. lama 6. Getsul 9. Dalai
  Lama, Grand Lama
reliquary, stupa . . 7. chorten
lamb . . 3. ean, ewe 4. cade, yean 5. gigot,
  sheep 6. cosset 7. eanling, lambkin
  8. yearling 9. youngling 10. endearment
Lamb, Charles . . 4. Elia (pen name)
lambaste . . 4. beat, whip 6. thrash
  7. reprove
lambent . . 7. glowing, radiant
  8. wavering 10. flickering 11. gliding
  over
Lambeth (London) . . . 6. palace (of
  Archbishops) 15. religious center
Lamb of God . . . 7. paschal 8. Agnus
  Dei
lame . . 4. halt 7. halting, limping
  8. crippled, disabled, hobbling
  9. defective 11. inefficient
lame (pert to) . . .
brains . . 9. balminess, daffiness,
  goofiness, wackiness
duck . . 7. session 9. insolvent
  10. politician, speculator
Lamech (pert to) . . .
descendant of . . 4. Cain
father of . . 5. Jabal, Jubal 9. Tubal-cain
lament . . 3. rue 4. keen, moan, sigh,
  wail, weep 5. mourn 6. bemoan, bewail,
  grieve, plaint, regret, repine, yammer
  7. condole, deplore, elegize, weeping
  8. jeremiad
lamentation . . . 3. cry, woe 5. dolor, grief,
  tears 6. sorrow 7. anguish, wailing
Lamentations . . . 4. Book (Old Test)
lamia . . 5. witch 7. monster, vampire
  (Myth) 8. cub shark 9. sorceress
lamina . . . 4. obex (brain) 5. blade, flake,
  hinge, layer
lamp . . 4. davy, etna 5. light, torch
  6. crusie 7. lantern, lucigen 9. veilleuse
lamp (pert to) . . .
black . . 4. soot
holder . . 11. candelabrum
lighter . . 5. spill
safety . . 4. davy 7. Geordie
slang . . 6. look at
waving of . . 5. arati
lampadedromy (Gr) . . . 8. foot race (with
  torch)
lampoon . . 4. skit 5. squib 6. iambic
  8. ridicule, satirize 10. pasquinade

lampoon writer . . . 8. satirist
lamprey . . 3. eel 6. ramper
Lamps of the Lord . . . 5. yucca (blooms)
Lancashire (Eng) . . . 6. Eccles
lance . . 3. cut 4. dart, hurl, stab 5. blade,
  spear 6. incise, launch, pierce, weapon
  7. javelin
lance (pert to) . . .
battle . . 5. joust
head . . 5. morne
knight . . 10. lansquenet (Hist)
officer . . 4. Jack
surgical . . 6. lancet
Lancelot . . 6. Knight 13. Lancelot du
  Lac
Lancelot's beloved . . . 6. Elaine
lancer . . 5. uhlan 6. Hussar 7. cossack,
  soldier, spearer
land . . 3. lot 4. acre, farm 5. arada,
  downs, field, range, tilth 6. alight,
  debark, ground, region 7. country,
  pasture 9. disembark
land (pert to) . . .
absolute ppty . . 4. alod 7. alodium
alluvial . . 5. delta
ancestral . . 5. ethel
assessor . . 8. cadastre (cadaster)
church . . 5. glebe
heritable . . 4. odal, udal
holding . . 6. tenure 9. leasehold
leasehold . . 5. feoff
locked in . . 13. mediterranean
mythical . . 4. Eden 6. Utopia 9. Shangri-
  La
northernmost . . 5. Thule (Greenland)
open . . 4. moor, wold 5. heath
pile . . 5. cairn
prefix . . 4. agro
reversion . . 7. escheat
sandy . . 4. dene
surveyor . . 9. arpenteur
Sussex tract (Eng) . . 5. laine
treeless . . 5. llano 6. steppe 7. prairie
verb . . 3. win 4. gain 5. catch 6. secure
  7. capture
waste . . 5. heath
landed estate . . . 5. manor 7. demesne
landing place . . 4. deck, dock, pier, quay
  5. field, levee, strip, wharf 7. airport
  8. platform 9. staircase
landmark . . . 4. copa, tree 5. senal
Land of (the) . . .
bondage . . 5. Egypt
Cush . . 8. Ethiopia
Eden (East of) . . 3. Nod
Enchantment . . 9. New Mexico
Leal . . 6. Heaven
Little Sticks (Canada) . . 19. Barren Islands
  border
Midnight Sun . . 6. Alaska, Norway
O'Cakes . . 8. Scotland
Opportunity . . 8. Arkansas
Plenty . . 6. Goshen
Promise . . 6. Canaan
Regrets . . 5. India
Rising Sun . . 5. Japan
Rose . . 7. England
Shamrock . . 4. Eire 7. Ireland
sleep . . 3. Nod
Steady Habits . . 11. Connecticut
Thistle . . 8. Scotland

Thousand Lakes .. 7. Finland
White Elephant .. 4. Siam
landscape ... 7. paysage, scenery, topiary
landslide ... 9. avalanche 10. éboulement
Landsmaal, Landsmal ... 8. language (Norway)
Landstag ... 4. Diet 8. assembly 11. legislature
lane ... 4. path, road 5. alley, route, track 6. airway, course, gullet, throat 7. channel, red land 8. footpath 10. passageway
language ... 6. langue, speech, tongue 7. dialect, diction 8. parlance 9. utterance 11. linguistics
language (pert to) ...
acquiring .. 12. chrestomathy
ancient .. 4. Pali 5. Aryan, Greek, Latin 6. Hebrew 7. Chinese 8. Sanskrit
artificial .. 2. Od, Ro 3. Ido 7. Volapük 9. Esperanto
classical .. 5. Greek, Latin
conversant in .. 9. pantoglot
dead .. 4. Pali
deaf-mute .. 11. dactylology
expression, peculiar .. 5. idiom, lingo 6. jargon 7. dialect 13. colloquialism
international .. 2. Od, Ro 3. Ido 7. Volapük 9. Esperanto
pert to .. 8. semantic
pretentious .. 7. bombast 11. highfalutin
Romance .. 5. Latin 6. French 7. Catalan, Italian, Spanish 9. Provencal 10. Portuguese
sacred .. 4. Pali
sign .. 11. dactylology
thieves .. 5. argot
languid ... 4. slow, weak 5. faint, inert, weary 6. dreamy, feeble, sickly, supine, torpid 7. passive 8. careless, drooping, flagging, heedless, indolent, sluggish 9. apathetic 10. spiritless
languish ... 3. die 4. fade, fail, flag, pine, wilt 5. droop, faint 6. repine, sicken, weaken, wither 7. decline
languor ... 3. kef (kief) 7. fatigue 8. dullness, weakness 9. indolence, lassitude 10. dreaminess, drowsiness, stagnation 12. listlessness, sluggishness
lanky ... 4. lean, tall, thin 5. gaunt, spare 12. loose-jointed
lanner ... 6. falcon
Lanterns, Feast of (Jap) ... 3. Bon
Laodicean ... 8. lukewarm 9. apathetic 11. indifferent
Laos ...
aborigine .. 3. Kah
capital .. 9. Vientiane 12. Luang Prabang
native .. 7. Chinese 14. Thai-Indonesian
religion .. 8. Buddhism
river .. 6. Mekong
lap ... 3. sip 4. fold, lick, wrap 5. drink 6. ripple, tipple 7. circuit
lapel ... 4. fold 5. rever 6. facing, lappet
lapicide ... 11. stonecutter
lapidary's forte ... 4. gems
lapin ... 6. rabbit
lapis lazuli ... 4. blue 5. stone 6. lazurite, sapphire 10. azure stone
Lapland ...
people .. 5. Lapps 10. Laplanders

11. Ural-Altaics 12. tent-dwellers
sledge (traveling) .. 5. pulka (pukk)
sledge puller .. 8. reindeer
town .. 6. Kiruna
waterfalls .. 11. Harspranget
lappet ... 4. flap, fold, lobe 5. lapel 6. wattle 9. appendage
lapse ... 3. err 4. fall, slip 5. error, fault, pause 6. expiry 7. decline, misstep, relapse 8. apostasy 9. reversion
lapsus ... 4. slip 5. error 12. inadvertence
lapsus calami ... 10. lipography 12. slip of the pen
lapsus linguae ... 15. slip of the tongue
lapwing ... 4. gull 5. pewee, pewit 6. plover
larceny ... 5. theft 7. robbery 8. burglary, stealage 10. scrounging
larch ... 5. Larix 8. tamarack
lard ... 3. fat 4. line, pork 5. adeps, bacon, baste, enarm 6. axunge, cerate, enrich, fatten, grease 7. garnish 8. saindoux 9. lubricate
larder ... 6. pantry 7. buttery 8. cupboard 12. commissariat
lares (Rom) ... 4. gods (household) 7. spirits
large ... 3. big, nth 4. bold, huge, much, vast 5. ample, bulky, burly, giant, great, loose, scads 7. copious, immense, leonine, liberal, massive, titanic, weighty 8. colossal, enormous, gigantic, spacious 9. excessive, extensive, plentiful 11. exaggerated 12. considerable 13. comprehensive
large (pert to) ...
artery .. 5. aorta
comb form .. 5. macro
fish .. 4. opah, tuna 9. swordfish
intestine .. 5. colon 6. caecum, rectum
knife .. 4. bolo, snee
lettered .. 6. uncial
number .. 4. slew 6. myriad
pulpit .. 4. ambo
volume .. 4. tome
largess, largesse ... 4. gift 6. bounty 7. charity, present 10. generosity, liberality 11. beneficence
largest bird ... 6. condor 7. ostrich 13. whooping crane
largest fish (freshwater) ... 8. arapaima
larghetto ... 9. slow tempo
larghissimo ... 8. very slow
lariat ... 4. rope 5. honda (part), lasso, noose, reata, riata
lark ... 5. ghost (anc), prank, revel 6. frolic 7. skylark, titlark 8. songbird 9. adventure, Alaudidae, parchment (color)
larrigan ... 8. moccasin
larrikin ... 5. rough, rowdy 6. loafer 10. street Arab
larrup ... 3. hit 4. beat, blow, flog, whip
larva ... 3. bot (bott) 4. grub, pupa 5. redia 6. embryo, maggot 7. atrocha 8. cercaria 9. chrysalis, doodlebug 11. caterpillar
lascivious ... 4. lewd 5. bawdy 6. erotic, wanton 7. lustful, sensual 9. lecherous, salacious 10. libidinous, licentious
laser ... 9. light beam

lash ... 3. tie 4. beat, bind, flag, whip 5. scold, smite 6. splice, strike 7. scourge

lass ... 4. girl 6. lassie, maiden 7. colleen 11. maidservant

lassitude ... 7. languor 8. debility, lethargy, weakness 9. weariness

lasso ... 4. lash, rope 5. noose, reata (riata), snare 6. lariat 8. cabestro

last ... 3. end 5. final, omega 6. endure, latest, lowest, newest, penult, ultima, utmost 7. extreme, supreme 8. eventual, rearmost, terminal, ultimate 9. penultima 10. antepenult, conclusive, most recent

last (pert to) ...
at last .. 6. Eureka
but one .. 6. penult
cry .. 10. dernier cri
evening .. 9. yesterday
long .. 7. outwear, perdure 9. perendure
month .. 3. ult 6. ultimo
offer .. 9. ultimatum
person in contest .. 4. mell
shoe .. 5. block
syllable but one .. 6. penult
syllable but two .. 10. antepenult

Last (pert to) ...
Assize .. 11. Last Inquest 12. Last Judgment
Days of Pompeii character .. 4. Ione 5. Nydia 7. Glaucus
Gospel .. 4. Mass
of the Gothic Kings .. 8. Roderick
of the Mohicans .. 5. Uncas (Chief)
Supper .. 6. Christ 9. disciples

lasting ... 4. long 6. stable 7. abiding, durable, eternal 8. constant 9. continual, lingering, permanent, steadfast 11. substantial, unforgotten

lasting briefly ... 9. ephemeral, temporary

lat ... 6. column, pillar

latchet ... 3. tap 4. lace (leather) 5. strap, thong 9. fastening

late ... 3. neo (comb form), new 4. sero 5. tardy 6. former, recent 7. belated, overdue 8. neoteric 10. behindhand

latent ... 5. inert 6. hidden 7. dormant 9. disguised, potential, quiescent, suspended 10. underlying

later ... 4. anon, soon 5. after 6. future, mañana, puisne 9. posterior, presently 12. subsequently

lateral ... 5. flank, raphe 8. indirect, sideward

lath ... 4. slat 9. wood strip

lathe ... 4. tool 7. mandrel

lather ... 4. foam, suds 5. froth

Latin (pert to) ...
alphabet letters .. 9. twenty-one
and .. 2. et
bath .. 7. balneum
behold .. 4. ecce
booth .. 7. taberna
bowl .. 6. patina
bronze .. 3. aes
church .. 8. Catholic
couch .. 9. accibutum
country .. 6. French 7. Italian, Spanish
dish .. 4. lanx 6. patina

foot .. 3. pes
God .. 3. Dei, Deo 4. Deus 7. Mercury
goddess .. 3. Dea
grammar (case) .. 6. dative 8. ablative, genitive, vocative 10. accusative, nominative
historian .. 6. Justin
holidays .. 5. feria
hymn .. 13. Adesti Fideles
javelin .. 5. aclys, pilum
land .. 4. ager
law .. 3. lex 6. Latium
life .. 4. vita
people .. 6. Romans
poet .. 4. Ovid 6. Horace
pronoun .. 2. tu 3. ego, hic 4. ille, ipse, iste
quarter (section) .. 5. Paris 10. New Orleans
ram .. 5. aries
rite .. 4. orgy 5. sacra
seat .. 5. sella
trumpet .. 4. tuba 7. buccina
Way .. 9. Via Latina

latite ... 4. lava

latitude ... 4. zone 5. scope, width 6. extent 7. breadth, freedom 8. distance 10. liberality

latrant ... 7. barking

latter ... 4. last 5. final 6. latest 9. foregoing 10. more recent

Latter-day Saint ... 6. Mormon

lattice ... 6. grille 7. trellis 8. cancelli 9. crossbars, framework 12. crossed slats

latticelike ... 7. grating 8. espalier 9. clathrate 10. cancellate

Latvia ...
capital .. 4. Riga
city .. 6. Dvinsk, Libava (Libau)
money unit .. 3. lat (gold)
people .. 4. Lett 7. Lettish
river .. 2. Aa

laud ... 4. sing 5. extol 6. praise 7. applaud, commend, glorify, magnify 8. eulogize

laudable ... 9. admirable, estimable 11. commendable, meritorious 12. praiseworthy

laudatory ... 9. panegyric 10. flattering 11. approbatory, encomiastic 12. commendatory

laugh ... 4. roar 5. fleer, smile, snort 6. cackle, deride, giggle, guffaw, hawhaw, tee-hee 7. chortle, chuckle 8. ridicule 10. cachinnate

laughable ... 3. odd 5. droll, funny, merry, queer, witty 7. amusing, comical, jocular, risible, strange, waggish 8. humorous, sportive 9. burlesque, diverting, facetious, ludicrous 10. ridiculous

laughing ... 3. gay 5. merry, riant 6. rident

laughing (pert to) ...
bird .. 4. loon 10. woodpecker
falcon .. 4. hawk
gas .. 12. nitrous oxide
jackass .. 10. kingfisher, kookaburra
pert to .. 9. gelastic

laughter ... 4. gelo (comb form) 5. gelos, mirth, risus 6. guffaw 12. cachinnation

launch . . . 4. hurl 5. begin, float, lance, shove, start, throw 6. plunge 7. descant 9. undertake 10. inaugurate

laureate . . . 4. poet 6. decked (with laurel) 7. drowned, honored 13. distinguished

laurel . . . 3. bay, ivy, oak, oil 6. daphne, Kalmia, salmon 8. magnolia 9. sassafras, spoonwood

laurel wreath . . . 7. iresine

lava . . 2. aa, oo 3. ash 5. ashes 6. coulee, latite, scoria 8. lapillus, pahoehoe

lava field . . 8. pedregal

lavaliere, lavalier . . 7. pendant 8. ornament

lavatory . . . 5. basin 7. piscina 8. washroom 9. washbasin

lave . . . 4. lade, pour, wash 5. bathe, rinse 6. drench 8. absterge

lavender . . . 4. mint 6. purple 7. blue-red, perfume 9. fragrance

laver . . . 4. bowl 5. basin 6. trough, vessel 7. cistern, seaweed

Lavinia (pert to) . . .
father . . 7. Latinus
husband . . 6. Aeneas
mother . . 5. Amata
myth . . 5. Roman

lavish . . . 4. free, lush, rank, wild 5. spend 7. profuse 8. abundant, generous, prodigal, reckless, squander 9. bountiful, exuberant, impetuous, luxuriant, plentiful, unstinted 10. immoderate 11. extravagant 12. unrestrained 13. superabundant

law . . . 3. act, jus, lex 4. bill, code, jure, nisi, rule 5. axiom, canon, droit, edict, mercy, mesne 6. decree, equity, Latium, police 7. justice, precept, statute 8. enactment 12. constitution 13. jurisprudence

law (pert to) . . .
action . . 3. res 4. suit 5. actus 6. trover 7. impeach, implead 8. gravamen, replevin 9. ademption
Bible . . 6. Mosaic 12. Old Testament
claim . . 6. lien
code . . 8. Napoléon 9. Hammurabi 10. codex juris 16. Codex Justinianus
decree . . 4. nisi 5. edict
degree . . 3. LLD
divine . . 11. commandment
document . . 4. deed, writ 6. capias, elegit
drafting . . 10. nomography
evidence . . 7. constat
expert (US) . . 5. Moore (John B)
for fourth offender (NY) . . 6. Baumes
German Franks . . 5. Salic
goddess . . 4. Maat (Egypt)
heredity . . 5. Gresham's
Manu . . 5. sutra
mathematics . . 7. formula
morals . . 7. conduct
Moses . . 5. Torah (Tora) 10. Pentateuch
offender . . 5. felon 6. sinner 8. criminal 9. wrongdoer
offense . . 4. tort 5. crime, malum 6. delict
pert to . . 3. res 9. judiciary
philology . . 6. Grimm's
science . . 8. nomology 13. jurisprudence
student . . 8. stagiary

thought . . 7. noetics
warning . . 6. caveat
within the . . 5. licit 8. judicial
wrong . . 4. tort

lawful . . . 3. due 5. legal, licit, valid 9. permitted 10. legitimate 11. permissible

lawgiver . . . 5. Moses

lawless . . . 4. lewd 6. unruly 7. illegal 10. anarchical, disorderly

lawlessness . . . 4. riot 6. mutiny 7. anarchy, license 12. disobedience

lawmaker . . . 5. solon 7. senator 10. legislator 11. congressman

lawn . . . 5. green 7. batiste 9. grassplot 12. village green

lawyer . . . 5. agent 6. jurist, legist 7. abogado, shyster 8. advocate, attorney, lawgiver 9. barrister, counselor (counsellor), leguleian, solicitor 11. intercessor, pettifogger

lawyer group . . . 3. ABA

lax . . . 4. dull, free, limp, open, slow 5. loose, slack, tardy 6. remiss 7. lenient 8. backward, dilatory, inactive, indolent, not tense 9. dissolute, scattered 10. licentious, unconfined 12. unrestrained

lay . . . 3. bet, put 4. lair, pave, poem, song 5. allay, ditty, place, quiet, stake, still 6. ballad, hazard, impose, impute, pacify 7. appease, ascribe, deposit, relieve, store up 9. direction 10. profession

lay (pert to) . . .
aside . . 5. table 6. remove, shelve 7. dismiss, reserve 8. postpone 9. segregate
away . . 4. heap, hive 5. amass, cache, hoard, store 7. husband 8. treasure 10. accumulate
bare . . 5. strip 6. denude, expose, reveal 7. uncover
down . . 3. bet, set 5. level 6. give up 7. declare, deposit 9. postulate, prescribe, stipulate, surrender
off . . 4. don't, stop 5. cease 6. recess 7. dismiss, measure
out . . 4. plan 5. set up 6. design 7. pattern
waste . . 6. ravage 7. destroy 8. desolate 9. deprecate, devastate

layer . . . 3. bed 4. coat, derm, tier, uvea 5. sloam (earth) 6. lamina 7. stratum (strata, pl) 10. substratum

lazar . . . 5. leper 9. loathsome

lazaretto, lazaret . . . 8. hospital 9. pest house 10. lazar house

laziness . . . 5. sloth 7. inertia 8. oisivity, vagrancy 9. indolence 10. ergophobia, remissness 12. slothfulness 13. shiftlessness

lazy . . . 3. lax 4. idle, slow 5. slack 6. otiose, remiss 7. dronish, laggard 8. dilatory, inactive, indolent, slothful, sluggish 9. shiftless 13. lackadaisical

lazy man . . . 3. bum 4. lusk 5. drone, idler 6. rotter 9. lazybones 11. Weary Willie

lea . . . 4. mead 5. haugh 6. meadow 7. pasture 9. grassland

leach . . . 3. wet 7. moisten 9. lixiviate,

percolate

lead . . . 3. cue, key, van 4. cart, clue, head, lode 5. begin, guide, pilot, plumb, usher 6. direct, entice, escort, govern, induce 7. conduct, pioneer, precede 8. antecede, guidance 9. direction, influence, precedent 10. precedence

lead (mineral) . . . 4. came (rod), gray, shot 6. ceruse, fother, galena, leaden, strass (glass) 7. bullets, plummet 8. graphite, litharge, plumbago

lead astray . . . 4. lure, mang 6. allure, delude, entice, induce 7. deceive, pervert 8. inveigle

leader . . . 4. head 5. chief, guide, sinew 6. cantor, tendon 7. special 8. choragus, director 9. chieftain, conductor 10. forerunner

leader (Eccl) . . . 3. fra 4. pope 5. rabbi 6. bishop, priest 8. cardinal, minister, preacher 10. evangelist

leading . . . 5. chief, first 6. ruling 7. guiding 8. foremost, in the van 9. directing, governing 11. controlling

leaf . . . 3. ola 4. gear, page 5. blade, frond, petal, sepal 6. areola, ligula, spathe 7. tendril

leaf (pert to) . . .
book . . 5. folio
bud . . 5. gemma
curvature . . 8. epinasty (down) 9. hyponasty (upward)
floating . . 3. pad
green . . 11. chlorophyll
heart-shaped . . 9. obcordate
mold . . 5. humus
network . . 6. areola
part . . 5. bract, costa, stoma 6. pagina, stipel 7. petiole 8. petiolule
point, pointed . . 5. mucro 9. mucronate 13. mucroniferous
pore . . 8. lenticel
secretion . . 4. lerp
stalk . . 7. petiole 8. petiolus
vein . . 3. rib 5. costa

leafless . . . 9. aphyllous

leaflet . . . 5. pinna, tract 6. folder 7. booklet 8. pamphlet 13. advertisement

league . . . 4. band, Bund 5. Hanse, union 7. combine 8. alliance 9. coalition 10. federation 11. affiliation, combination 13. confederation

League of Nations site . . . 5. Paris (1920) 6. Geneva (Secretariat)

League of the Iroquois . . . 11. Five Nations

Leah (pert to) . . .
Bible book . . 7. Genesis
sister . . 6. Rachel
son . . 4. Levi
wife of . . 5. Jacob

leak . . . 4. drip, hole, seep 5. crack 6. escape, run out 7. crevice, fissure 10. be revealed

leal . . . 4. just, real, true 5. legal, loyal 6. lawful 7. correct, genuine 8. accurate, faithful

lean . . . 4. bare, cant, lank, poor, rely, slim, tend 5. gaunt, slope, spare 6. barren, meager 7. scraggy, slender 8. not plump 9. deficient, gravitate

lean (pert to) . . .
animal, person . . 4. ribe (Scot)
emaciated . . 6. marcid
make . . 8. macerate
towards . . 6. prefer

Leander's love . . . 4. Hero

leaning . . . 5. slope 6. desire 7. pronate, tending 8. aptitude, enclitic, penchant, tendency 9. prejudice 10. partiality

Leaning Tower . . . 4. Pisa 6. Venice 7. Bologna 8. Zaragoza

lean-to . . . 4. roof, shed, wing 5. shack 9. extension (bldg)

leap . . . 4. dive, jump, ramp, skip 5. bound, caper, lunge, salto, spang, vault 6. spring 7. saltary 8. capriole

leaping . . . 7. jumping, salient, saltant 8. bounding, salience 9. saltation

learn . . . 4. lere (anc) 6. master 8. memorize 9. ascertain, determine

learned . . . 3. wot 4. read, sage 6. legist 7. erudite 8. lettered, literate, schooled 9. scholarly 12. well-informed

learned person . . . 6. master, pundit 7. scholar, teacher 9. professor

learning . . . 3. art, ken, wit 4. lore 7. culture 8. pedantry 9. education, erudition, knowledge, philology (love of), philomath 11. scholarship

lease . . . 3. let 4. hire, rent 5. weave 6. demise, remise, tenure 8. contract

leasehold . . . 6. rental, tenure

leash . . . 4. bind, cord, lash, lune (hawking) 5. reins, thong 6. fasten, string, tierce 9. restraint 11. subjugation

leash hound . . . 6. limer

least . . . 5. grain 6. little, lowest, merest 7. minimum 8. minority, shortest, simplest, smallest 9. slightest

leather . . . 4. hide, skin 5. aluta, leder (old spelling) 6. vellum 7. canepin 8. cheveril (cheverel) 9. toughness

leather (kinds) . . . 3. kid, kip 4. calf, napa, vici 5. Mocha, suede 6. patent, saddle, skiver 7. chamois, Morocco 8. cordovan 9. sheepskin

leather (pert to) . . .
artificial . . 7. keratol
bookbinding . . 4. roan 6. levant
bottle . . 4. olpe 6. matara
cuirass . . 6. lorica
glove . . 5. suede, trank 8. capeskin
pare . . 5. skive
patch . . 5. clout
piece of . . 5. strap, thong 6. latigo
pouch (Highlander's) . . 7. sporran
process . . 3. tan, taw
strap . . 5. thong 6. latigo
term . . 8. efflower
tool . . 6. skiver
worker . . 6. chamar, tanner 8. chuckler

leatherneck . . . 6. marine

leave . . . 2. go 4. quit 6. depart, retire, vacate 7. liberty 9. allowance 10. permission

leave (pert to) . . .
desolate . . 7. bereave
empty . . 6. vacate
isolated . . 6. desert, maroon
of absence . . 5. exeat 8. furlough

off . . **4.** don't, stay **5.** cease **6.** desist

out . . **4.** omit, skip **5.** elide **8.** pass over

taking . . **5.** adieu **6.** congee **7.** vamoose **9.** departure

leaven . . . **4.** barm **5.** imbue, yeast **6.** enzyme **7.** corrupt (implied), ferment, pervade **10.** impregnate

leaves . . . **5.** pages, shaws **6.** sepals **7.** foliage

leaves, feeding on . . . **13.** phyllophagous

leavings . . . **4.** left, orts, rest **5.** culls, dregs, dross, waste **6.** refuse **7.** remains, residue **8.** remnants

leban, lebban . . . **5.** drink **8.** beverage, sour milk

Lebanon city . . . **5.** Sidon **6.** Beirut (capital) **7.** Tripoli

lech (anc) . . . **4.** slab **8.** capstone, monument

lecher . . . **7.** glutton **8.** gourmand, parasite **9.** debauchee, libertine

lectern . . . **4.** ambo, desk **6.** pulpit **10.** escritoire

lecture . . . **4.** jobe, rate **5.** scold **6.** lesson **7.** declaim, expound, lection, reproof, reprove **8.** instruct, scolding **9.** discourse **10.** admonition

lecturer . . . **6.** docent, reader **7.** teacher **9.** prelector

Leda (pert to) . . .

geology . . **4.** clay (marine)

husband . . **9.** Tyndareus

lover . . **4.** Zeus (swan)

mother of . . **6.** Castor, Pollux **11.** Helen of Troy **12.** Clytemnestra

zoology . . **7.** mollusk

ledge . . . **4.** berm, edge, lode, reef, sill **5.** shelf **7.** retable, stratum

leechlike . . . **8.** bdelloid

lees . . . **5.** draff, dregs **8.** sediment

leeward . . . (opp of windward) **9.** protected, sheltered

Leeward Islands . . . **5.** Nevis **7.** Antigua, Barbuda, Redonda **8.** Anguilla, Sombrero **10.** Montserrat **13.** St Christopher

Leeward Islands group . . . **6.** Virgin **7.** Society

leeway . . . **4.** room **5.** drift

left . . . see also *leave* **3.** haw, kay **8.** departed, larboard **9.** abandoned, remaining

left (pert to) . . .

aground . . **6.** neaped **8.** beneaped

animal (motherless) . . **4.** cade **5.** dogie

comb form . . **8.** sinistro

hand (Mus) . . **8.** sinistra

hand page . . **5.** verso

hand pitcher . . **8.** southpaw

out . . **7.** omitted **8.** excluded **10.** eliminated

spirally . . **11.** sinistrally

to one's judgment . . **13.** discretionary

toward . . **5.** aport **9.** sinistrad, sinistral **12.** levorotatory (Chem)

left-handed . . . **6.** clumsy, gauche **7.** oblique **8.** southpaw **9.** insincere, insulting **14.** sinistromanual **16.** counterclockwise

left-handed marriage . . . **10.** morganatic

leftist . . . **7.** liberal, radical **10.** left-winger,

liberalist **11.** progressive

leg (pert to) . . .

armor . . **4.** jamb **6.** greave **7.** jambeau

bone . . **4.** shin **5.** tibia **6.** fibula

calf . . **5.** sural

insect . . **4.** coxa

joint . . **4.** hock, knee **5.** thigh

longest bone . . **5.** femur

of lamb (cooked) . . **5.** gigot

term . . **4.** crus **5.** jambe **6.** crural

legacy . . . **4.** gift, will **6.** devise **7.** bequest, codicil **9.** testament **10.** bequeathal

legal . . . **4.** leal **5.** licit, valid **6.** lawful **10.** authorized, legitimate

legal (pert to) . . .

abstract . . **6.** précis

act, thing . . **5.** actus

action . . **3.** res **4.** case **7.** detinet, lawsuit, summons

case, postponed . . **7.** remanet

claim . . **4.** lien

confirmation . . **10.** validation

contestant . . **6.** suitor **8.** litigant **9.** plaintiff

critic . . **6.** censor

decree, divorce . . **10.** decree nisi

defense . . **5.** alibi

delay . . **4.** mora

denial, stoppage . . **8.** estoppel

extract . . **7.** estreat

matter . . **3.** res

order . . **4.** writ

paper . . **4.** deed, writ **5.** lease **6.** escrow

possession . . **6.** seizin (seisin)

power (to take) . . **7.** prender (prendre)

process . . **6.** caveat **7.** detinet

right, by . . **6.** ex jure

security . . **4.** bond

surrender . . **6.** remise

legally competent . . . **5.** capax

legate . . . **5.** envoy **8.** bequeath, delegate **10.** ambassador, diplomatic

legend . . . **4.** Edda, myth, saga, tale **5.** fable **7.** history **9.** narrative, tradition **11.** inscription

legendary . . . **8.** fabulous **9.** imaginary, narrative **11.** traditional **12.** mythological

legendary (pert to) . . .

goddess (slave) . . **5.** Baube, lambe

primate . . **6.** Dubric

water sprite . . **6.** undine

legendry . . . **7.** legends (collectively)

leggings . . . **5.** chaps, spats **6.** strads **7.** gaiters, greaves, puttees **8.** gamashes, gambados **10.** galligaskins

legislate . . . **3.** act **5.** elect, enact **8.** pass laws **10.** put through

legislative (pert to) . . .

agent . . **8.** lobbyist

assembly . . **4.** diet **6.** assize, senate **8.** congress **10.** parliament

group . . **4.** bloc

legislator . . . **5.** solon **7.** senator **8.** lawgiver, lawmaker **9.** statesman **11.** congressman **14.** representative

legislature . . . **4.** Diet **5.** House **6.** Senate **8.** Congress **9.** bicameral (2 branches)

legitimate . . . **4.** real, true **5.** legal, licit, valid **6.** cogent, lawful **7.** genuine **9.** permitted **11.** efficacious, justifiable legman ... 8. newshawk

legume ... 3. pea, pod, uva 4. bean, soya 6. clover, lentil, loment 7. alfalfa

leisure ... 4. ease, time, toom 5. otium 6. otiose 7. freedom 9. spare time 11. convenience, opportunity

lemming ... 4. maki, vari 5. mouse 6. rodent

lemur ... 5. indri, loris, makis, potto 6. anguid, aye-aye, colugo, galago, macaco, monkey 7. tarsier 8. Anguidae, mongoose 10. angwantibo

Lenape ... 6. Indian (Del)

lend ... 4. loan 5. grant 6. devote (to) 7. advance

length (pert to) ...
measure .. 4. area 5. gauge 6. linear, volume
ten meters .. 9. decameter
three-quarters inch .. 5. digit
time .. 3. age, eon, era 6. moment, period
two and one-quarter inches .. 4. nail
unit .. 6. micron, parsec (Astron)

lengthen out ... 7. prolong, stretch 8. continue, elongate, protract

lengthwise ... 5. along 12. horizontally 14. longitudinally

lenient ... 3. lax 4. easy, mild 7. clement, patient 8. merciful, relaxing, tolerant 9. assuasive, emollient, softening

Lenin (pert to) ...
leader of .. 10. Bolsheviks
real name .. 7. Ulyanov (Ulianov)
Revolution .. 7. October, Russian

Leningrad (Russ) ... 9. Petrograd 12. St Petersburg 15. Window on the West

lenis ... 4. soft 6. gentle, smooth

lenitive ... 4. mild 6. gentle 8. mitigant, ointment, remedial 9. assuasive, emollient, mitigator, relieving, softening 10. palliative, qualifying

lens ... 5. toric 7. bifocal, lentoid 8. meniscus, sunglass 9. lenticula 10. anastigmat 13. apochromatism

Lent ... 6. carême 9. Forty days, Great Fast 12. Quadragesima

lentamento ... 6. slowly

lentando ... 9. retarding 14. becoming slower

lenticula ... 7. freckle, lentigo (freckly)

lento ... 4. slow

Leo constellation star ... 7. Regulus, the Lion

leopard ... 4. pard 5. ounce 6. jaguar, ocelot 7. cheetah, panther

leper ... 5. lazar, mesel 6. Naaman (Bib)

lepidopteran ... 4. moth 9. butterfly

Lepontine Alps ... 10. Monte Leone (peak)

lepra ... 7. leprosy 14. Hansen's disease

Lesbos ... 5. Assos (Aristotle's) 6. Island (Sappho's) 8. Mytilene

Les Misérables author ... 4. Hugo (Victor)

lessen ... 4. bate, wane 5. abate, lower, peter, relax 6. impair, minify, narrow, reduce, shrink, weaken 7. cut down, relieve 8. decrease, diminish, mitigate, moderate, palliate 11. deteriorate

lesser ... 4. less 5. minor (Mus) 7. smaller

Lesser Bear (Astron) ... 9. Ursa Minor

Lesser Dog (Astron) ... 10. Canis Minor

Lesser Lion (Astron) ... 8. Leo Minor

let ... 4. hire, rent 5. allow, lease, leave 6. hinder, impede, permit 7. prevent

let (pert to) ...
down .. 5. lower 8. comedown, drawback, relaxing 10. slackening 14. disappointment
fall .. 4. drop, slip 5. spill 7. mention
in .. 5. admit, enter 6. insert
it be given .. 5. detur
it stand .. 3. sta (Mus) 4. stet
up .. 4. rest 5. cease, pause, relax 6. slow up 7. slacken 8. decrease

lethal ... 5. fatal, feral 6. deadly, mortal 7. deathly, killing 11. destructive 12. death-dealing

lethargic ... 4. dull 5. heavy, inert 6. drowsy, sleepy, torpid 8. comatose, listless 9. apathetic

lethargy ... 4. coma 5. sleep, sopor 6. apathy, stupor, torpor 7. languor 8. hebetude, neurosis 9. lassitude 10. drowsiness (morbid)

Lethe ... 5. abyss, Hades, river 8. oblivion 13. forgetfulness

lethiferous ... 6. deadly 11. destructive

Leto (pert to) ...
mother of .. 6. Apollo 7. Artemis
Roman name .. 6. Latona
wife of .. 4. Zeus

letter ... 4. note, type 7. epistle, message 9. character 13. communication

letter (pert to) ...
bright star .. 4. Beta
carrier .. 6. correo 7. mailman, postman
cross stroke .. 5. serif
first .. 7. initial
letter for letter .. 9. literatim
marks .. 5. brave
of advice .. 11. lettre d'avis
of challenge .. 6. cartel
representation .. 10. literation
short .. 4. line, note 6. billet
sloping .. 6. italic
sound loss (last) .. 7. apocope
two letters (one sound) .. 7. digraph 9. diphthong
writer .. 13. correspondent

letters (pert to) ...
decorate with .. 7. miniate 10. illuminate
man of .. 9. literatus
ref to .. 8. literary

lettuce ... 3. cos 4. head 7. Lactuca, romaine

leukocyte ... 6. corpuscle (white)

Levant ... 4. East 6. Orient 7. leather (Morocco) 8. East wind

Levantine (pert to) ...
country .. 13. Mediterranean
garment .. 6. caftan
herb .. 6. madder
ketch .. 3. bum 4. jerm, saic 5. xebec 6. settee 8. levanter
valley .. 4. wadi (wady)
wind .. 7. Morocco

levee ... 4. bank, dike, pier, quay 5. ridge 6. durbar, trench 8. assembly 9. reception 10. embankment

level ... 4. even, fell, flat, just, raze
5. equal, grade, plane, plani (comb
form), point 6. peavey (peavy), smooth,
steady, topple 7. flatten, terrace,
uniform 8. demolish, equalize, parterre
12. well-balanced

lever ... 3. bar, lam, pry 5. crank, jimmy,
pedal, prise 6. peavey (peavy), tappet,
tiller 7. crowbar, treadle

leveret ... 4. hare

leviathan (pert to) ...
animal (Bib) .. 5. whale 6. dragon
9. crocodile
embroidery .. 6. canvas 11. cross-stitch
political .. 12. (the) commonwealth
size .. 4. huge 11. titanic 10. formidable

Levi's father (Bib) ... 5. Jacob

levitate ... 4. rise 8. float

Levite ... 5. tribe 10. descendant

Levitical ... 7. Aaronic 9. Aaronical
10. priesthood (Mormon)

Leviticus ... 10. Pentateuch

levity ... 6. gaiety 8. buoyancy 9. frivolity,
lightness 10. triviality, volatility

levy ... 3. tax 4. fine, wage (war) 5. rally,
stent 6. assess, impose 7. collect,
estreat 9. recruital

lex ... 3. law 7. statute

lexicon ... 4. book (of words)
10. dictionary, vocabulary

lex loci ... 13. law of the place

lex non scripta ... 12. unwritten law

liability ... 4. debt 5. debit 8. cessavit
9. proneness 10. likelihood, obligation
11. possibility 15. responsibility

liable ... 3. apt 5. bound 6. likely
7. exposed, subject 10. answerable,
chargeable 11. responsible

liable (pert to) ...
likely to .. 3. apt 5. prone 11. predisposed
not liable .. 6. exempt
to objection .. 13. exceptionable
to penalty .. 6. guilty

Lia Fail ... 12. Stone of Scone
15. Coronation Stone (Ir)

liaison ... 4. link 7. joining 8. intimacy,
intrigue 11. co-operation
18. intercommunication

liana ... 4. cipo 6. vines (woody) 9. wild
grape

liar ... 5. cheat 6. fibber 7. Ananias,
wernard (obs) 8. deceiver, fabulist,
perjurer 12. prevaricator

Lias system ... 8. Jurassic

libation ... 5. drink 8. oblation, offering,
potation

libel ... 4. bill 6. defame 7. lampoon,
request, slander 8. circular (obs),
handbill, roorback 10. defamation
11. certificate, declaration
12. supplication

liberal ... 4. free, Whig 5. ample,
frank 7. copious, profuse 8. eclectic,
generous 9. bountiful, extensive,
plentiful 10. hospitable, munificent
11. broad-minded, magnanimous
12. uncontrolled

liberate ... 4. flee, free 5. loose 6. redeem
7. deliver, manumit, release 8. separate,
unfetter 9. disengage 10. emancipate

Liberia ...

capital .. 8. Monrovia
city .. 8. Buchanan 10. Greenville
gulf .. 5. Sidra
language .. 3. Vai (Vei)
people ... 3. Vai (Vei)

libertine ... 4. rake, roué

liberty ... 4. ease, free 5. leave
7. freedom, license 9. exemption,
privilege 10. permission 11. opportunity

librarian ... 7. bookman 10. bibliosoph,
bibliothec 13. bibliothecary

Libya, Africa ...
astronomy .. 4. Mars (portion)
capital .. 7. Tripoli 8. Benghazi
district .. 6. Fezzan 9. Cyrenaica
12. Tripolitania
language .. 7. Hamitic
oasis (saline) .. 6. Sebkha (Sebka)
people .. 5. Arabs
sea .. 13. Mediterranean

Libya, Gr (pert to) ...
children .. 5. Belus 6. Agenor
heroine of .. 5. Libya
husband .. 8. Poseidon

license ... 5. right 6. bandon, permit
7. dismiss, freedom, liberty 8. sanction
9. approbate, authority, authorize,
privilege 10. permission 11. lawlessness
13. authorization

licentious ... 3. lax 4. lewd 5. loose
7. immoral, lawless 9. debauched,
dissolute 10. lascivious, profligate
12. uncontrolled, unrestrained

licet ... 6. lawful 7. granted 12. it is
conceded

lichens (pert to) ...
abounding in .. 9. lichenose
derivative .. 4. moss 5. usnic 6. litmus
genus .. 5. Usnea 7. Evernia
study of .. 11. lichenology

licit ... 3. sue 4. just 5. legal 6. lawful
9. permitted

lick ... 3. lap, win 4. flog, whip 5. lap
up, taste 6. baffle, defeat, thrash
7. conquer 8. overcome, vanquish

licorice ... 5. abrin 9. jequirity

licorice-flavored liqueur ... 7. sambuca

lid ... 3. cap, hat 4. bred, case,
roof 5. cover 6. eyelid 7. stopper
9. operculum

lid, put on the ... 3. end 6. hush up
7. license 8. complete, suppress

lie ... 3. fib 4. rest 7. falsify, falsity,
recline, untruth 9. deception, falsehood,
mendacity 10. equivocate
13. prevarication

lie (pert to) ...
at ease .. 4. loll 5. droop 6. dangle
face down .. 7. pronate
hidden, in ambush .. 4. lurk, plot 6. in
wait 9. insidiate 11. concealment
in warmth .. 4. bask 9. luxuriate
low .. 6. abased 9. prostrate
prostrate .. 4. flat 5. creep 6. grovel

Liebestraum composer ... 5. Liszt

Liechtenstein, Europe ...
capital .. 5. Vaduz
government .. 12. principality
language .. 6. German
religion .. 8. Catholic

lief (anc) ... 4. dear, fain, glad 7. willing

8. disposed 9. agreeably, favorably
lieutenant . . . 6. deputy 10. substitute
11. locum tenens
life . . . 3. vie 4. bios 5. being 6. always,
energy, spirit 8. vitality, vivacity
9. animation, existence
life (pert to) . . .
after death . . 8. Olam-haba
animal . . 4. bios 5. biota (flora, fauna)
biology . . 4. bios
comb form . . 3. bio
giving . . 9. animative 11. procreative
god of . . 6. Faunus
insurance . . 7. tontine
jacket (sl) . . 7. Mae West
later, older . . 8. autumnal
lifelike . . 5. alike, vital 6. biotic 9. realistic
plant . . 4. bios 5. biota
principle . . 5. atman, prana, tenet 6. spirit
prolonger . . 6. elixir
science of . . 7. anatomy, biology, zoology
12. paleontology
sea . . 5. coral 8. plankton
staff of . . 5. bread
without . . 4. dead 5. azoic 8. lifeless
9. inanimate
lifeless . . . 4. abio (comb form), dead, dull,
flat 5. amort, azoic, heavy, inert, vapid
6. jejune, torpid 8. inactive, listless
9. bloodless, exanimate, inanimate,
powerless, tasteless 10. lackluster,
spiritless, unanimated
lifetime . . . 3. age, day, eon (aeon)
6. always 8. duration 10. generation
lift . . . 3. aid, pry 4. jack, perk 5. boost,
exalt, heave, hoist, raise, steal,
theft 6. puff up, thrill 7. derrick,
elevate, improve, inspire 8. elevator
11. inspiration
lifting device . . . 4. jack, pump 5. crane,
davit, lever, tongs 7. capstan, derrick,
erector 8. elevator, heighten, windlass
lifting muscle . . . 7. erector, levator
ligament . . . 4. bond, cord 6. tendon
7. bandage
ligan, lagan . . . 6. debris, jetsam
7. flotsam
ligature . . . 3. tie 4. band, bond, cord, note
6. amulet, binder, taenia 7. bandage
light . . . 3. arc, gay, sun 4. dawn,
easy, glim, lamp, lume, mild, pale,
soft 5. flare, flood, klieg, laser, taper
6. alight, aspect, blonde, bright,
candle, gentle, ignite, illume, medium,
window 7. cresset, fragile, glimmer,
glowing, trivial 8. buoyancy, daylight,
delicate, illumine, lambency, radiance,
trifling 9. effulgent 10. brightness,
luminosity, weightless 11. information
12. incandescent
light (pert to) . . .
apparatus . . 9. holophote
circle . . 4. halo, nimb 6. corona, nimbus
7. aureola, aureole
cloud . . 6. nimbus
coating . . 4. film
footed . . 4. fast 5. agile
globe . . 4. bulb
god . . 6. Balder (Baldr)
handed . . 4. deft
headed . . 5. dizzy 6. fickle 9. beeheaded

image . . 8. spectrum
leading . . 8. luminary
reflector . . 4. lens 6. mirror
refractor . . 5. prism
science . . 6. optics
source . . 3. sun
touch . . 3. dab
unit . . 3. lux, pyr 4. phot, watt 5. lumen
6. carcel, Hefner
without . . 4. dark 7. aphotic, obscure
8. starless 9. pitch-dark 10. caliginous
yellow . . 5. amber
light and airy . . . 7. tenuous 8. delicate,
ethereal
light and quick . . . 6. nimble, volent
light dress fabric . . . 6. merino
8. cashmere 9. bombazine, paramatta
(parramatta)
lighten . . . 4. ease 5. allay, cheer, clear
6. reduce 7. gladden, relieve 8. brighten,
illumine, jettison 9. alleviate, disburden
10. illuminate
lighter . . . see also *light* 4. scow 5. barge
7. gabbard, igniter, pontoon 8. chopboat
(Chin)
lighthearted . . . 3. gay 6. upbeat
7. buoyant 8. carefree, cheerful, jubilant
9. vivacious
Light Horse Harry . . . 3. Lee (Gen Henry
Lee)
lighthouse . . . 5. tower 6. beacon, pharos
7. seamark 10. watchtower
lightness . . . 6. gaiety, levity 8. airiness,
buoyancy, sobriety 9. flippancy,
frivolity, giddiness 10. fickleness,
triviality, volatility, wantonness
11. flightiness, inconstancy, instability
12. unsteadiness 14. weightlessness
15. thoughtlessness
lightning . . . 4. lait 5. flash, levin 6. stroke
8. flashing 9. discharge
lightning (pert to) . . .
bug . . 6. beetle 7. firefly
discharge . . 4. bolt 11. thunderbolt
form . . 4. fork 5. chain, sheet
reference to . . 8. fulgural
rod . . 8. arrester
stone . . 9. fulgurite
war . . 10. blitzkrieg
lightsome . . . 3. gay 4. airy 5. agile, clear,
light, lucid, merry 6. fickle, nimble
7. lighted 8. cheerful, cheering, graceful,
luminous, unsteady 9. frivolous
12. lighthearted
lights out . . . 4. taps
ligneous . . . 5. woody 6. wooden, xyloid
8. firewood
lignite . . . 4. coal
like . . . 2. as 4. copy, love 5. enjoy, equal,
liken, savor 6. admire, desire 7. similar
10. comparable 11. counterpart,
homogeneous
like (pert to) . . .
bone . . 6. osteal
fern . . 8. frondose, frondous
gland . . 7. adenose
gold . . 7. aureate
house, dome . . 5. domal
kneecap . . 7. rotular 10. rotuliform
sea lion . . 7. otarian, otarine
suffix . . 2. ar, ic 3. ine, oid, ose

likeable, likable ... 6. genial 8. charming, pleasant

likelihood ... 8. prospect 10. good chance 11. possibility, probability 14. apparently true

likely ... 3. apt, fit 5. prone 6. comely 8. credible, feasible, probable, suitable 9. promising 11. verisimilar

likeness ... 4. copy, icon, twin 5. clone, guise, image 6. effigy, statue 7. parable, picture, replica 8. parallel, portrait 9. imitation, semblance 10. comparison, photograph, similarity 11. counterfeit 12. reproduction 14. representation

likewise ... 3. too 4. also 5. ditto 8. moreover 11. furthermore

liking ... 4. like, love, lust 5. fancy 6. comely 7. delight 8. pleasing 10. preference 12. predilection

lilac ... 5. lilas, mauve 6. purple 7. syringa

lilac throat ... 11. hummingbird

Lilliputian ... 4. tiny 5. dwarf, minim 6. midget 7. dwarfed 10. diminutive

lilt ... 3. air 4. song, tune 5. swing 6. poetic, rhythm 7. rejoice

lily ... 2. ti 3. lis 4. aloe, ixia, sego 5. calla, lotus, onion, water, wokas (wocas), yucca 6. Allium, Nuphar 8. daffodil, mariposa, martagon, soaproot 9. narcissus

lily (pert to) ...
family, genus .. 4. aloe 6. Tulipa 7. Bessera 9. Liliaceae 10. Hyacinthus
grass .. 10. cuckoopint
iron .. 7. harpoon
of France .. 10. fleur-de-lis
shaped .. 7. crinoid 9. crinoidal
water .. 8. Castalia, Nymphaea

lily of the valley (pert to) ...
bud .. 3. pip
Cape Cod .. 13. barney-clapper
English .. 6. mugget
family .. 15. Convallariaceae
liliaceous plant .. 5. yucca
shrub .. 10. fetterbush
tree .. 6. sorrel

lima bean disease ... 6. mildew 9. yeast spot

liman ... 5. marsh 6. lagoon

limb ... 3. arm, fin, imp, leg 4. wing 5. bough, scamp 6. branch, member 7. flipper 9. anaclasis

limber ... 4. limp, weak 5. agile, lithe, loose 6. flabby, pliant, supple 7. flaccid, lissome 8. flexible, yielding

limbo ... 4. hell, jail 6. prison 9. purgatory

limbs, absence of ... 6. amelia 7. acolous

lime ... 4. calx 5. color, fruit 8. chlorine, fumigant 9. deodorant, quicklime 11. green-yellow 12. linden yellow

limen ... 9. threshold

limestone ... 4. calp, malm 5. chalk 6. marble, oolite 8. pisolite

lime tree ... 6. linden, tupelo

limey ... 6. sailor 7. soldier

limit ... 3. end, fix, ori (comb form) 4. term 5. allot, bourn 6. summit 7. confine 8. boundary, capacity, restrain, restrict, terminal 11. restriction, termination 12. consummation

limited ... 3. few 5. local, scant 6. finite,

narrow, scanty 7. bounded, topical 8. confined, reserved 9. astricted, parochial 10. restricted 11. conditional, topopolitan 13. circumscribed

limiting ... 7. hedging 10. qualifying, relational 11. restraining, restricting, restrictive

limn ... 4. draw 5. paint 6. depict 7. portray 8. decorate 9. delineate 10. illuminate

limp ... 3. hop, lax 4. halt, soft, thin, weak 5. loose 6. flabby, limber 7. flaccid 8. drooping, flexible 9. inelastic 13. unsubstantial

limpid ... 4. pure 5. lucid 6. bright 7. crystal 8. pellucid 11. translucent, transparent 12. intelligible

Lincoln, Abraham (pert to) ...
assassin .. 15. John Wilkes Booth
birthplace .. 8. Kentucky (1809)
debater .. 7. Douglas (Stephen A)
dog .. 4. Fido
mother .. 10. Nancy Hanks
Secy of State .. 6. Seward
Secy of War .. 7. Stanton
son .. 10. Robert Todd
wife .. 8. Mary Todd

Lincoln (pert to) ...
color .. 9. Carthamus 11. yellow-green
sheep (breed) .. 7. English

Lindbergh, Charles A (pert to) ...
birthplace .. 7. Detroit (1902)
flight field .. 9. Roosevelt (LI)
flight to (1927) .. 5. Paris (1st)
retreat .. 10. Illiec Isle (Fr)
wife .. 10. Anne Morrow

linden ... 3. lin 4. lime, teil 5. Tilia

line ... 3. row 4. arow, axis, cant, ceil, clew, cord, face, mark, race, rail, rein, rule, seam, side 5. agone, align, raphe, ridge, route, stria, track 6. crease, isobar, policy, series, streak, stripe 7. engrave, outline 8. boundary, vocation, wainscot 9. delineate

line (pert to) ...
adjusting .. 9. alinement
central .. 4. axis
comb form .. 4. lino
conceptual, geological .. 6. agonic, isotac, tropic 7. equator 8. isothere, isotherm, latitude, meridian 9. longitude
equidistant .. 8. parallel
fine (type) .. 5. leger, serif
fishing .. 5. snell 7. ratline (ratlin)
imaginary .. 7. equator, Maginot
mathematics .. 4. sine 5. agone 6. secant 7. tangent
measure .. 3. gry 4. rule
meteoric .. 6. isobar
nautical .. 6. earing 7. halyard, hawsing
poetic .. 6. stich, verse
racing .. 4. wire
raised .. 4. weal, welt 5. ridge
selling .. 11. merchandise
soldiers .. 4. file, rank 6. cordon
transport .. 5. stage 7. carrier 8. carriage
type .. 5. agate, serif
up, lineup .. 4. plan 5. align 6. muster 7. arrange 8. schedule 9. formation 11. arrangement, parallelize

lineage ... 3. kin 4. race 5. birth, blood,

stock, tribe 6. family, strain 7. descent 8. pedigree 9. offspring 10. extraction, progenitor

lineal ... 6. racial 10. continuous, delineated 12. genealogical

lineman ... 3. end 5. guard 6. center, tackle 9. wireman 11. electrician

linen ... 4. crea, duck, lawn, lint 5. crash, gulix, inkle (tape), toile 6. barras, damask, dowlas, napery, sheets 7. cambric, Holland, lockram

ling ... 4. fish, hake 5. heath 6. burbot 7. eelpout, Gidadae, heather 8. chestnut

linger ... 3. lag 4. drag, idle, wait 5. dally, defer, delay, dwell, hover, tarry 6. dawdle, go slow, loiter, remain 8. continue, hesitate 13. procrastinate

lingerie ... 9. underwear 11. underthings 14. unmentionables

lingering ... 5. delay 7. chronic 8. dilatory, slowness 10. protracted

lingo ... 4. cant 5. jargon, lingua, patois, patter, tongue 8. language

lingua ... 5. lingo 6. jargon, tongue 11. hypopharynx

lingual ... 7. glossal 9. lingulate 10. linguiform, tonguelike

linguistics ... 6. syntax 7. grammar 8. language 9. phonology, semantics 10. lexicology

link ... 3. tie 4. bond, join, loop, yoke 5. annex, nexus, torch, unite 6. couple, member, relate 7. connect, liaison, passage 8. catenate 12. intermediary

linkage ... 5. tie-up, union 6. hookup 7. joinder, joining 8. junction 11. conjunction

linking ... 7. liaison 9. annectent

links in a chain ... 7. hundred

linseed ... 8. flaxseed

lion ... 3. cat, cub, leo 4. puma 5. simba 6. cougar, Lionel, lionet 8. Felis leo 9. celebrity 12. King of Beasts

Lion (pert to) ...
England .. 8. heraldry
God .. 3. Ali
Lucerne .. 11. Switzerland (Sculpture)
St Mark .. 6. Venice (winged)
the North .. 6. Sweden (King Adolphus)

lionlike ... 6. feline 7. catlike, leonine

lip ... 3. jib, rim 4. edge, kiss, talk 5. cheil, words 6. flange, labium, labrum, speech 7. cheilos 8. labellum 10. mouthpiece 12. impertinence

lip (pert to) ...
comb form .. 5. chilo, labio
formed .. 6. labial
inflammation .. 9. cheilitis
ornament .. 6. labret
service .. 4. kiss 7. hypocrisy 10. sanctimony 12. unctuousness
surgery .. 9. chilotomy 11. chiloplasty
tumor .. 7. chiloma

lipped ... 6. labial 7. labiate

liquefy ... 4. fuse, melt, thaw 6. reduce 8. dissolve, fluidify 10. deliquesce

liqueur ... 4. anis, ouzo 5. crème, noyau, sirup 6. cognac, genepi, kummel, Pernod 7. cordial, curaçao, ratafia 8. absinthe, anisette, Drambuie 9. Cointreau 11. Benedictine

liquid ... 5. clear, fluid 6. watery 7. flowing 8. beverage, manifest, not solid

liquid (pert to) ...
assets .. 4. cash 5. money 9. resources
chemical .. 7. acetone 8. furfural
inflammable .. 3. gas 5. ether 7. alcohol 8. gasoline
oily .. 5. olein 7. aniline, picamar
soap .. 6. napalm
thick .. 3. tar 4. dope 5. syrup (sirup)
weak .. 5. blash

liquidate ... 4. kill 6. depose, pay off, settle 8. amortize 9. discharge 11. exterminate

liquor ... 3. ale, dew, gin, rum, rye 4. beer, brew, grog, lush, sake, wine 5. hooch, kefir, punch, stout, vodka 6. arrack (arak), arrope, elixir, whisky (whiskey) 8. cocktail, highball 9. applejack, moonshine 10. chasse-café

liquor container ... 3. keg 5. flask 6. barrel, bottle 8. cellaret, decanter

liquor maker ... 6. abkari (Ind), brewer 7. vintner 9. distiller

liquor server ... 6. barman 7. barmaid, skinker (anc), tapster

liquor shop ... 3. bar 6. saloon, tavern 7. barroom, cabaret, shebeen (Scot), taproom 8. alehouse 9. groghouse, honky-tonk 11. rathskeller (ratskeller)

liripipe, liripoop (Hist) ... 4. hood 5. scarf 6. dotard, tippet

lissom ... 5. layer 7. stratum 8. platform 12. strand of rope

lissome ... 5. agile, lithe 6. limber, nimble, supple 7. willowy 8. flexible

list ... 3. tip 4. edge, file, roll, rota, rote 5. index, limit, panel, table 6. careen, edging, enlist, record, roster, stripe 7. catalog, incline 8. calendar, classify, manifest, register, schedule, tabulate 9. catalogue, enclosure, inventory, repertory 10. repertoire 11. enumeration

list (pert to) ...
actors .. 4. cast
competitors .. 5. entry, slate
foods .. 4. menu 5. carte
investments .. 9. portfolio
memoranda .. 5. scrip
officers .. 6. roster
references .. 5. index

listen ... 3. ear 4. hear, heed 6. attend 7. give ear, hearken (harken) 8. overhear 9. eavesdrop

listening ... 7. audient 9. attentive

listing ... 4. list 6. strips 7. selvage 10. enlistment, enrollment

listless ... 4. dull 6. abject, drowsy, moping, supine 7. languid 8. careless, heedless, sluggish 9. apathetic 10. spiritless 11. unconcerned 13. uninteresting

litchi nut ... 7. rambutan

literary ... 6. versed 8. lettered 9. classical 11. book-learned

literary (pert to) ...
composition .. 5. cento, essay, opera 8. rhetoric
criticism .. 9. epicrisis
drudge .. 4. grub, hack
extracts .. 9. anthology

fragments.. 3. ana 5. notes 8. analecta, analects

laws.. 9. copyright

piracy.. 10. plagiarism

selection.. 7. excerpt

style.. 5. prose 6. purism 8. pedantic

literature.. 4. book, epic, Veda 5. drama, lyric, novel 6. ballad, poetry 7. fiction, writing 10. nonfiction 13. belles-lettres

lithe.. 4. slim 6. limber, supple, svelte 7. lissome, slender 8. flexible

Lithuania...

  capital.. 5. Vilna (Vilnius) 6. Kaunas (Kovno)

  Jew.. 6. Litvak

  people.. 5. Balts, Letts 6. Aestii

  port.. 8. Klaipeda (Memel)

  river.. 6. Niemen

litigant... 6. suitor 9. defendant, disputant, litigator, plaintiff

litigation.. 4. suit 7. contest, dispute, lawsuit 10. contention, discussion

litigious... 10. disputable 11. belligerent, contentious

litten... 7. lighted 8. cemetery 10. churchyard

litter.. 3. bed, hay 4. bier, mess 5. couch, dooly (doolie), mulch, straw, young 6. coffin, jumble 7. clutter, rubbish 8. palanquin, stretcher

litter of pigs... 6. farrow

little... 3. sma, wee 4. puny, tiny, weak 5. brief, petit, petty, scant, short, small 6. dapper, petite, slight 7. not much 8. trifling 9. niggardly 11. unimportant 12. narrow-minded 14. inconsiderable

little (pert to)...

  bethel.. 6. chapel (seaman's), church

  by little.. 6. slowly 7. peu à peu 9. piecemeal, poco a poco

  comb form.. 5. steno

  devil.. 3. imp 4. minx 5. rogue 7. ruffian 13. mischief-maker

  fellow.. 6. shaver

  finger, toe.. 7. minimus

  flag.. 9. banderole

  music term.. 4. poco

  ring.. 7. annulet

Little Rhody... 11. Rhode Island

Little Women, author... 6. Alcott (Louisa)

littoral... 4. zone (marine) 5. shore 7. coastal 9. bordering

liturgical... 10. ceremonial 11. ritualistic

liturgy... 4. rite 6. ritual 8. ceremony 14. consuetudinary

live... 5. dwell, exist 6. reside 7. breathe 8. continue, have life

live (pert to)...

  by sponging.. 5. cadge

  by stratagems.. 5. shark

  by wits.. 5. cheat 7. deceive, falsify 13. Machiavellize

  earlier.. 8. pre-exist

  in.. 7. inhabit

  in tents.. 5. nomad 7. scenite

  in the country.. 9. rusticate

live... 5. alert, alive, vital, vivid 6. bright, lively, living, virgin (mineral) 7. charged, not dead 8. vigorous 9. energetic 11. electrified

lively... 3. gay, vif 4. airy, grig, keen, pert, spry, yare 6. active, blithe, bright, snappy 7. animate, buoyant, pungent, tittupy (tittuppy) 8. spirited 9. energetic, sprightly, vivacious 10. enlivening, rebounding 11. interesting 12. effervescent

liver (pert to)...

  comb form.. 6. hepato

  disease.. 9. cirrhosis, hepatitis

  duct.. 4. bile

  pert to.. 5. hepar 7. hepatic

  resembling.. 8. hepatoid

Liverpool native... 12. Liverpudlian

liverwort... 6. Riccia 8. agrimony, hepatica 9. bryophyte

living... 4. life 5. alive, being, quick 6. extant 7. animate, organic, topical 8. benefice, existent, lifelike 10. livelihood 11. subsistence

living (in, on, near)...

  currents.. 5. lotic

  ground.. 7. epigeal

  holes.. 11. latebricole

  leaves.. 13. phyllophagous

  oxygen.. 7. aerobic

  plane (same).. 8. coplanar

  poverty.. 11. necessitous

  river bank.. 9. riparious

  rivers, streams.. 9. rheophile

  seas (deep).. 8. bathybic

  shores.. 8. littoral

  solitude, seclusion.. 10. eremitical 11. eremiticism

  tents.. 7. scenite

  together.. 11. contubernal

living (pert to)...

  again.. 6. Buddha 7. revived 8. Hutukhtu 9. redivivus

  being.. 5. wight 6. animal 8. organism

  capable of.. 6. viable

  dull.. 10. vegetation

  individual.. 4. bion

  near the ground.. 7. epigeal

  together.. 8. intimate 11. contubernal (contubernial)

lixivium... 3. lye 6. bleach 8. cleanser

lizard... 3. dab, eft 4. adda, gila, newt, seps, uran 5. agama, anoli, gecko, skink, varan 6. dragon, hardim, iguana, moloch 7. monitor, saurian, tuatera 8. basilisk 9. chameleon 10. chuckwalla, salamander

llama... 6. alpaca, vicuna 7. guanaco

load... 3. jag 4. fill, lade, onus 5. cargo 6. burden, charge, weight 7. fraught, freight, oppress, prepare 8. contents, encumber 10. imposition 11. encumbrance

loaded... 5. drunk, flush, laden, ready 7. charged, fraught 8. burdened, weighted 10. in the chips

loader of vessels... 9. stevedore

loadstone, lodestone... 6. magnet 8. terrella 9. magnetite

loaf... 4. idle, lump 5. bread 6. loiter, lounge 9. Eucharist

loafer... 5. idler 6. beggar 7. lounger 8. vagabond

loam... 3. rab 4. clay, lime, malm, silt, soil 5. chalk, loess, regur

loan ... 4. lend 6. borrow 7. advance
10. provisions 13. accommodation

loath ... 6. averse 7. hostile 9. disliking,
reluctant, unwilling

loathe ... 4. hate 5. abhor 6. detest
7. despise, dislike 9. abominate

loathsome ... 4. foul, vile 5. nasty
6. odious 7. cloying, hateful
9. abhorrent, offensive, repellant
10. abominable, disgusting

lob ... 3. box, cop 4. step, till, toss, vein
5. stair, throw 7. lugworm, pollack
9. chandelle

lobby ... 4. hall, room 5. foyer
8. anteroom, corridor, coulisse
9. enclosure, vestibule 10. wirepuller
13. pressure group

lobe ... 5. alula 6. earlap, lappet, lobule
7. pendant

lobster (pert to) ...
claw .. 5. chela 6. nipper, pincer
eggs .. 3. roe 5. coral
French .. 6. homard
genus .. 7. Homarus, Macrura
8. Nephrops
part .. 6. thorax
tail .. 6. telson
trap .. 3. pot 4. corf 5. creel 6. bow
net

local ... 7. edaphic, topical 8. regional
9. parochial 10. epichorial (epichoric)
13. autochthonous

local court ... 5. gemot (gemote)

locale ... 4. site 5. place, scene, venue

locality ... 4. area, spot 5. place, situs
7. endemic, habitat 8. position

locate ... 4. find, spot 6. settle 7. situate
9. establish

locatio ... 7. leasing, letting

location ... 4. seat, site, spot 5. locus,
place, situs 6. ubiety 7. habitat 8. district
9. situation 12. neighborhood

locator of forest fires ... 7. alidade

loch ... 3. bay 4. lake, pond 5. inlet,
lough

lock ... 4. bolt, hasp, hold 5. Gatun,
latch 6. cotter, detent, fasten, fetter
8. fastener 9. floodgate

lockjaw ... 7. tetanus, trismus
11. ankylostoma

lockman ... 8. summoner (Isle of Man)
11. executioner

lock of hair ... 4. curl 5. tress 6. berger
7. daglock, ringlet 8. lovelock, spit
curl

lockup ... 3. jug 4. jail 5. clink 6. cooler
8. hoosegow (hoosgow) 9. calaboose

loco ... 3. mad 4. daft 5. craze, crazy
6. crazed 7. disease 10. moonstruck
15. non compos mentis

locomotion ... 6. lation (Astrol), moving,
travel 7. transit 8. progress

locomotive ... 3. hog 5. dolly, mogul
6. diesel, dinkey, engine, mikado 9. iron
horse

locomotive cowcatcher ... 5. pilot

locus ... 4. area, drug, site 5. place
8. locality

locus (pert to) ...
in quo .. 5. where 12. place in which
sigilli .. 14. place of the seal

locust ... 4. weta 6. beetle, cicada,
cicala, kowhai 7. Locusta 9. wetapunga
11. grasshopper

locust (pert to) ...
berry .. 5. drupe 9. glamberry
bird .. 4. dial 7. grackle 8. starling
10. white stork
like .. 6. mantis
plant .. 5. senna
sound .. 7. stridor 10. stridulate
tree .. 5. carob, honey 6. acacia

lode ... 3. vug (vugg) 4. path, road,
vein 5. canal, drain, ledge 6. course
7. deposit 8. waterway

lodestar ... 8. cynosure, polestar
11. guiding star

lodestone, loadstone ... 6. magnet
8. terrella 9. magnetite

lodge ... 3. hut, lie 4. camp, tent
5. cabin, hovel 6. billet, encamp, reside
7. deposit, quarter 11. brotherhood

lodge doorkeeper ... 5. tiler

lodging ... 3. inn 4. gite, room 5. abode,
hotel, roost 6. billet, harbor (harbour),
tavern 8. barracks, dwelling, hosteiry,
quarters 9. dormitory, harborage
(harbourage) 10. habitation

loess ... 4. loam, silt, soil

lof ... 6. praise 7. measure

loft ... 3. bin 4. balk 5. attic

loftiness ... 6. height 7. dignity
8. eminence 9. eloquence
11. distinction, magnanimity

Lofting's doctor ... 8. Dolittle

lofty ... 4. high, tall 5. proud 6. aerial,
Alpine, Andean 7. eminent, exalted,
haughty, stately, sublime 8. arrogant,
elevated, eloquent, majestic, towering
9. dignified 11. magisterial,
magnanimous 13. distinguished

lofty place ... 4. peak 5. aerie, eyrie
(eyry) 6. summit 8. eminence, pinnacle

log ... 4. birl, slab 5. diary 6. record
8. firewood, mountain, puncheon,
register 11. speedometer

log (pert to) ...
cock .. 10. woodpecker
gin .. 6. jammer
hauler (sled) .. 4. tode
implement .. 6. nigger, peavey (peavy),
rosser
measure .. 7. scalage
noser .. 6. sniper
rolling .. 7. birling
section .. 5. spalt
support .. 3. nog

logarithmic terms ... 3. bel 4. base
5. power 8. mantissa 14. characteristic

logarithm inventor ... 6. Napier

loge ... 3. box 5. booth, stall

loggerhead ... 4. tool 6. turtle 7. fathead
8. bonehead, numskull 9. blockhead
10. thickskull

loggerheads, be at ... 8. disagree

loggia ... 7. gallery

logging (pert to) ...
boots .. 4. pacs
rock .. 6. loggan
sled .. 4. tode 7. travois (travoise)
wheels .. 7. katydid

logic ... 9. reasoning 13. argumentation

logic (pert to) . . .
 fallacy . . 6. idolum
 induction . . 7. epagoge
 proposition . . 5. lemma 7. ferison
  9. enthymeme, obvertend
 specious . . 7. sophism
 term . . 5. Darii, Ferio 8. Celarent
logical . . . 4. sane 5. sound, valid
  8. coherent, credible, rational
  9. plausible 10. consistent, reasonable
logician . . . 8. reasoner
logogriph . . . 5. rebus 6. riddle 7. anagram
  8. logogram
logy . . . 4. dull 6. drowsy 8. sluggish
Lohengrin (pert to) . . .
 character . . 4. Elsa 8. Parsifal
 composer . . 6. Wagner (1850)
 Knight . . 15. Knight of the Swan
loin (pert to) . . .
 beef . . 10. tenderloin
 mutton . . 4. rack 5. chump
 pork . . 7. griskin
loincloth . . . 5. dhoti, pagne 7. G-string
  11. breechcloth
loir . . . 8. dormouse
Loire, France . . .
 Dept capital . . 12. Saint Etienne
 river's old name . . 5. Liger
 town . . 6. Nantes
 tributary . . 5. Indre
loiter . . . 3. lag 5. dally, delay, tarry
  6. dawdle, linger 7. saunter
loiterer . . . 4. slug 5. drone, idler 6. lagger
  7. dawdler, laggard 8. sluggard
Loki (pert to) . . .
 god . . 7. Discord 8. Mischief
 wife . . 5. Sigyn
loll . . . 4. hang 5. droop 6. dangle,
  frowst (froust), lounge, repose, sprawl
  7. recline
loma, lomita . . . 4. hill
Lombard (pert to) . . .
 ancient . . 6. cannon
 historic . . 4. bank, loan
 King . . 6. Alboin (legend)
 school . . 11. Renaissance
 street . . 6. London
Lombardy province . . . 4. Como
lomboy . . . 8. Java plum
lomilomi (Haw) . . . 3. rub 7. massage,
  shampoo
London, England . . .
 art gallery . . 4. Tate
 bank . . 27. Old Lady of Threadneedle
  Street
 borough . . 6. Ealing 11. Westminster
 bridge . . 5. Tower 6. London 7. Chelsea
  8. Waterloo
 bridle path . . 9. Rotten Row
 brown . . 9. carbuncle
 cathedral . . 7. St Paul's
 clock . . 6. Big Ben
 club (Whigs) . . 6. Kit-Kat
 concert hall . . 11. Royal Albert
 district . . 7. Chelsea, Mayfair
  8. Vauxhall 9. Southwark
  10. Bloomsbury, Kensington,
  Marylebone
 hawker . . 6. coster
 monument (Guildhall) . . 3. Gog 5. Magog
 Opera Company . . 12. Sadler's Wells

 palace . . 10. Buckingham
 park . . 4. Hyde 7. Regent's
  10. Kensington
 porter . . 6. George
 press . . 11. Fleet Street
 prison . . 7. Newgate 9. Bridewell
 quarter . . 8. Vauxhall
 roisterer (Hist) . . 3. mum
 Roman name . . 6. Agusta
 square . . 9. Trafalgar
 stables . . 4. mews
 stock exchange . . 17. Throgmorton Street
 street . . 5. Fleet 6. Strand 8. Pall Mall
  9. Cheapside, Whitehall 10. Piccadilly
  11. Throgmorton 12. Threadneedle
 subway . . 4. tube 11. underground
 train station . . 6. Euston 9. Victoria,
  Waterloo 9. St Pancras 10. King's
  Cross, Paddington
Londoner . . . 7. Cockney
Londres . . . 5. cigar
lone . . . 3. one 5. alone 6. lonely, single
  7. forlorn 8. solitary 9. unmarried
  12. unfrequented
loneliness . . . 8. loneness, solitude
  9. aloneness, dejection, isolation
  10. depression, desolation
  12. lonesomeness
lonely . . . 4. lorn 6. dreary 8. desolate,
  lonesome, secluded, solitary
  10. friendless 11. sequestered
  12. unfrequented
Lone Star State . . . 5. Texas
long . . . 3. yen 4. pine 5. crave, wordy,
  yearn 6. aspire, prolix, thirst 7. lengthy,
  tedious 8. tiresome 9. prolonged,
  wearisome 10. protracted
long (pert to) . . .
 ago, since . . 3. eld 4. yore
 beard . . 9. graybeard 10. bellarmine
  (jug)
 discourse, speech . . 6. screed, tirade
  7. descant 9. philippic, rigmarole
 dog . . 9. dachshund, greyhound
 dozen . . 8. thirteen
 established . . 8. habitual 10. inveterate
  11. traditional
 for . . 4. hope, pine 5. covet, crave
 horn . . 6. cattle (Tex)
 inlet . . 3. ria
 journey . . 4. trek 7. odyssey
 jump . . 5. halmo
 letters . . 7. screeds
 life . . 9. longevity
 limbed . . 5. rangy
 lived . . 9. macrobian
 periods . . 4. ages, eons
 scarf . . 4. sari
 suffering . . 7. patient 10. forbearing
 Tom . . 3. gun 8. titmouse
 windedness . . 9. garrulity, prolixity
  13. longiloquence
longing . . . 3. yen 6. desire, pining
  7. craving, wistful 8. yearning
  9. hankering, nostalgia
longitudinal . . . 6. euthytatic (stress),
  lengthwise
longshoreman . . . 6. docker, loader,
  lumper, stower 9. stevedore
  10. roustabout
loo . . . 3. pam 4. game

look ... 3. con, ken, pry, see 4. haze, heed, leer, peep, scry, seek, seem 5. point, stare, watch 6. appear, expect 7. examine, inspect, observe 8. indicate, perceive 9. search for

look (pert to) ...

after .. 4. tend 5. serve 6. follow 7. care for 9. keep vigil, supervise

at .. 3. eye 4. face, scan, upon 6. regard 7. examine

back .. 6. recall 7. retrace 8. remember 9. recollect 10. call to mind

down upon .. 4. leer, snub 5. fleer, gloat 7. askance, despise

forward to .. 5. await 6. expect 7. foresee 10. anticipate

like .. 8. resemble

obliquely .. 4. skew

slyly .. 4. leer, ogle, peer

sullen .. 5. frown, lower 6. glower

toward .. 4. face

upon .. 2. at 4. deem 6. behold 11. contemplate

lookout ... 4. view 5. guard, watch 6. conner 7. outlook 9. vigilance

looks ... 4. cons, face, kens, sees 5. peers, pores, pries, seeks, seems 6. visage 8. features 9. resembles 10. appearance 11. countenance

loom ... 3. auk 4. loon, tool 6. appear, puffin, vessel, weaver 7. machine 9. guillemot, implement 10. receptacle

loom part ... 3. lam 4. caam, leaf, sley 5. easer, lathe, lever 6. heddle

loon ... 5. diver (great Northern), Gavia, grebe, wabby 10. Gavia immer

loon ... 4. dolt 6. menial (anc), rascal 7. lunatic

loony ... 3. mad 4. daft 5. crazy, silly 8. demented

loop ... 3. eye, tab 4. ansa, clew, kink 5. bight, bride, honda, noose, picot, sling, wootz (iron) 6. becket 7. folding 8. doubling

loophole ... 4. hole, plea 5. mense, oilet 6. escape, eyelet, outlet 7. opening, pretext 8. aperture

loop-shaped ... 9. fundiform 11. sling-shaped

loose ... 3. lax 4. free, limp 5. slack 6. detach, remiss, unlash, wanton, wobbly 7. escaped, immoral, movable, relaxed, slacken, unbound, unleash 8. insecure, unstable 9. discharge (gun, arrow) 10. unconfined 11. improvident 12. loose-moraled 14. unconventional

loose (pert to) ...

ends .. 4. dags 5. slack 7. tagrags 8. restless

garment .. 5. simar 6. banion, chimar, kimono 7. zimarra 8. peignoir

jointed .. 5. lanky, rangy 6. wobbly 7. rickety 10. ramshackle

loosely dressed ... 8. discinct

loosen ... 4. ease, free, undo 5. pried, relax 6. soften 7. slacken

looseness ... 7. laxness 8. limpness 9. slackness, vagueness 10. remissness, wantonness

loot ... 3. rob 4. gelt, haul, sack, swag 5. booty 6. spoils 7. pillage, plunder,

seizure 10. contraband

looter ... 6. rifler, sacker 7. ravager, spoiler 8. marauder, pillager

lop (off) ... 3. bob, cut 4. oche, sned, trim 5. droop, prune 6. cut off, snathe 8. truncate

lopsided ... 4. alop 7. leaning 8. top-heavy 10. unbalanced 13. unsymmetrical

loquacious ... 4. glib 6. chatty 7. voluble 9. garrulous, talkative 10. chattering

loquacity ... 7. fluency, leresis 8. glibness 9. gabbiness, garrulity 12. effusiveness

lord ... 3. aga (agha), bey, God 4. earl, peer, rule, tsar 5. liege, ruler, title 6. master, prince 7. Jehovah, marquis, Saviour 8. governor, nobleman, seignior, suzerain, viscount 10. proprietor 11. Jesus Christ

Lord (pert to) ...

Buddhism .. 6. Buddha

Jacobite .. 3. Mar

of Heaven .. 7. Tien Chu (Chin)

of Lords .. 8. Demiurge (Plato) 11. King of Kings 13. Prince of Peace

of Wisdom .. 5. Mazda 6. Ormazd

Lord have mercy upon us ... 12. Kyrie eleison 14. Christe eleison

lordly ... 6. uppish 8. arrogant, despotic 9. dignified, masterful 10. tyrannical 11. domineering, overbearing

Lord's Prayer ... 11. Pater Noster

lore ... 4. lear 6. advice, wisdom 7. counsel 8. learning 9. erudition, mythology, tradition 12. superstition

lorgnette ... 7. lorgnon 8. eyeglass 10. opera glass

lorica ... 5. shell 7. cuirass 11. Breastplate (St Patrick's)

lorikeet ... 6. lories, parrot

loris ... 5. lemur

lorn ... 6. bereft 7. forlorn 8. deserted, desolate, forsaken 9. abandoned 11. Godforsaken

loro ... 10. monk parrot, parrot fish

lose ... 4. fail, miss, omit 5. leese (obs), spill, waste 6. forget, mislay, perish 7. forfeit, let slip 8. estrange, squander 9. incur loss 10. wander from

lose (pert to) ...

balance .. 4. trip 7. stumble

courage .. 7. despair, despond

flesh .. 8. emaciate

freshness .. 4. fade, wilt 6. wither

ground .. 7. regress 8. slow down 9. fall short 10. fall behind

luster .. 7. tarnish

vigor .. 3. fag, sag 4. fail, flag, pine 6. weaken 7. decline

loser ... 6. victim 7. also ran 8. defeatee, underdog

loss ... 4. ruin, weak 6. damage, injury 9. decrement, detriment, privation 10. forfeiture 11. bereavement, destruction

loss of ...

commodities .. 6. ullage

eyebrows, lashes .. 9. madarosis

feeling .. 7. agnosia 10. anesthesia (anaesthesia)

hair .. 8. alopecia

loved one .. 11. bereavement

memory.. 7. amnesia
reason.. 7. amentia
smell.. 7. anosmia
speech.. 4. mute 6. alalia 7. aphasia
  10. laloplegia
voice.. 7. aphonia
willpower.. 6. abulia
lost... 4. asea, gone, lorn 5. unwon
  6. hidden, ruined, sinful, wasted
  7. mislaid 8. absorbed, confused,
  defeated, obscured, vanished
  9. abandoned, forfeited, forgotten,
  perplexed, reprobate, subverted
  10. abstracted, bewildered, dissipated,
  overthrown, parted with
  11. preoccupied 13. irreclaimable,
  irretrievable
lost (pert to)
cause.. 8. Civil War
color.. 5. faded, paled
consciousness.. 7. fainted, swooned
life fluid.. 4. bled
to view.. 5. perdu
tribes (ten).. 10. Israelites
lot... 3. tax 4. doom, fate, luck, much,
  plat 5. share 6. chance, hazard, studio
  7. destiny, fortune, portion 9. allotment,
  great deal 13. apportionment
Lot (pert to)...
father.. 5. Haran
penalty.. 12. pillar of salt
sister.. 6. Milcah
son.. 4. Moab
uncle.. 7. Abraham
lots, divination by... 9. sortilege
lottery... 4. game 5. bingo, lotto
  6. chance, raffle 7. Genoese, grab bag
  11. sweepstakes
lottery prize... 4. tern (from three
  numbers)
lotus... 7. nelumbo 10. chinquapin
lotus (pert to)...
bird.. 6. jacana
eaters.. 9. indolents, Lotophagi
  11. daydreamers
tree.. 4. sadr 6. jujube, nettle
  9. persimmon
loud... 5. crass, gaudy, noisy, showy
  6. coarse, flashy, garish, vulgar
  7. blatant, booming 8. vehement
  9. clamorous, turbulent, unrefined
  10. blustering, boisterous, tumultuous,
  vociferous 11. stentorious
  12. obstreperous
loudmouthed... 10. scurrilous, stentorian
  11. thersitical
Louise de la Remée (novelist)... 5. Ouida
  (pen name)
Louisiana...
bird.. 7. pelican
capital.. 10. Baton Rouge
city.. 10. New Orleans, Shreveport
county.. 6. parish
dialect.. 6. Creole
dish (cooked).. 9. jumbalaya
flower.. 8. magnolia
hero.. 6. De Soto, de Vaca, Pineda
  7. La Salle
native.. 5. Cajun 6. Creole, French
  7. Acadian, Spanish
purchased from.. 8. Napoleon (1803)

river.. 5. Pearl 6. Sabine 11. Mississippi
State admission.. 10. Eighteenth
State motto.. 22. Union, Justice,
  Confidence
State nickname.. 7. Pelican
tradition.. 10. pirate lore
Louis Viaud (author)... 10. Pierre Loti
  (pen name)
lounge... 4. loaf, loll, sofa 5. divan
  6. frowst, repose 7. recline
louse... 5. aphis 6. cootie, insect, slater
  8. Anoplura, arachnid 9. Hemiptera,
  scoundrel
lout... 3. oaf 4. boor, clod, dolt 6. lubber,
  rustic 7. bumpkin
loutish... 4. rude 7. awkward, boorish,
  ill-bred 8. clownish 11. countrified
lovable... 7. amiable 8. adorable,
  charming 9. desirable, endearing
love... 3. amo, gra, woo 4. like 5. adore,
  amore, fancy 6. liking 7. charity
  8. fondness, good will 9. affection
  10. endearment, sweetheart
love (pert to)...
affair.. 7. liaison, romance 10. flirtation
apple.. 6. tomato
bird.. 6. parrot
call.. 3. coo
feast.. 5. agape
flower.. 4. lily
full of.. 4. dote 6. doting, erotic
  7. amative 9. idolizing
god of.. 4. Amor, Ares, Eros, Kama
  5. Bhaga, Cupid
goddess of.. 5. Athor, Freya (Freyja),
  Venus 6. Ishtar 9. Aphrodite
intrigue.. 5. amour
knot, token of.. 6. amoret
meeting.. 5. tryst 10. rendezvous
of.. 5. phile (comb form)
parental.. 6. storge
potion.. 7. philter
science.. 9. erotology
song.. 6. serena (evening) 8. madrigal
lover... 4. beau 5. amant, Romeo
  6. minion 7. amorist, Don Juan
  8. paramour 9. enamorato
  10. sweetheart
lover of... see also craze for
animals.. 10. zoophilist
beauty.. 8. aesthete (esthete)
wealth.. 9. plutocrat
work.. 9. ergophile
Lover's Leap... 10. Cape Ducato
Lovers' Quarrels... 12. amantium irae
loving... 4. fond 5. phile (comb
  form) 6. ardent, erotic 7. adoring,
  amative, amatory, amorous, devoted
  8. charming, enamored, romantic
  11. sentimental 12. affectionate
loving cup... 3. tyg (tig)
low... 3. bas, moo 4. base, deep,
  neap, orra 5. faint 6. humble, menial,
  sneaky, vulgar, wicked 8. dejected,
  indecent, infamous, inferior, plebeian
  9. inelegant 11. unfavorable
low (pert to)...
born.. 4. rude 5. lowly 6. common
  7. lowbred 8. plebeian
bred.. 5. crude 6. coarse, vulgar
brow.. 9. ignoramus

church.. 11. evangelical
comedy.. 8. travesty
country.. 7. Belgium, Holland
9. Luxemburg 11. Netherlands
German.. 5. Saxon 8. Frankish
12. Plattdeutsch
in spirits.. 4. blue 6. megrim 8. dejected,
downcast 10. dispirited, melancholy
11. crestfallen
Roman wall.. 5. spina
shrubs, plants.. 4. moss 5. Erica
syllable (Mus).. 2. ut
tide.. 3. ebb 4. neap 8. low water
wall.. 7. parapet
lower.. 3. dip 4. vail, vase 5. abase,
demit, frown, neath 6. bemean,
debase, deepen, demean, demote,
humble, lessen, meaner, nether, reduce
7. cheapen, degrade, depress, descent
8. diminish, inferior 10. depreciate
lower (pert to)...
case letter.. 5. small
Empire.. 9. Byzantine
geology.. 5. Chalk (Eng) 6. strata
7. stratum
most.. 6. bottom, lowest 7. bedrock
10. nethermost
world.. 4. hell 5. earth, Hades, limbo,
orcus, Sheol 7. Abaddon, Gehenna
8. Cerberus 9. perdition, purgatory
lowering.. 4. dark 6. gloomy, sullen
7. ominous 8. frowning 9. deepening
10. cheapening 11. threatening
lowery.. 5. cloudy, gloomy 8. lowering
lowest (pert to)...
animal life.. 6. amoeba (ameba)
deck.. 5. orlop
least.. 5. minim 6. bottom 7. minimum
pedestal member (Arch).. 6. plinth,
quadra
peer (ranking).. 5. baron
point.. 5. depth, nadir 6. bottom
10. nethermost
point, planet.. 7. perigee
lowing.. 6. mooing 7. mugient
9. bellowing
lowland.. 4. flat, holm, spit 5. plain,
terai 6. bottom 8. molehill
lowly.. 4. mean, meek 6. humble,
humbly, meekly, menial, modest
8. inferior, modestly, plebeian
12. unpretending
loxia.. 7. wryneck 9. crossbill
loy.. 5. slick (tool), spade
loyal.. 4. feal, leal, true 5. liege 6. stanch
7. staunch 8. constant, faithful, obedient
loyalty.. 5. faith 6. fealty, homage
8. devotion, fidelity 9. constancy
10. allegiance, stanchness (staunchness)
12. faithfulness 13. steadfastness
Loyolite.. 6. Jesuit
lozenge.. 5. candy, facet 6. jujube,
tablet, troche 7. diamond, molding
8. pastille (pastil, pastale) 11. perforation
lubber.. 4. boor, dolt, gawk, lout
5. churl, drone, idler, thick 6. sailor
8. landsman 11. grasshopper
lubricity.. 8. lewdness 10. smoothness
12. slipperiness
lubricous.. 4. lewd 6. tricky, wanton
7. elusive 8. unstable 10. lascivious

lucban... 8. shaddock
luce.. 4. pike 10. fleur-de-lis
lucent.. 5. clear 6. bright 7. shining
11. translucent, transparent
lucern.. 3. dog 4. lynx
lucerne.. 4. herb 6. fodder 7. alfalfa
8. purple medic
lucet, luce.. 4. pike (fish)
Lucia's home... 10. Lammermoor
lucid... 4. sane 5. clear, vivid 6. bright,
lucent 7. shining 8. luminous, pellucid
11. translucent 12. intelligible
Lucifer... 5. Satan
luck.. 3. hap 4. cess 5. deuce 6. chance
7. ambsace 8. fortuity 11. good fortune
lucky... 5. canny, happy 6. timely
9. fortunate 10. auspicious 11. good
fortune
lucky animal... 6. mascot
lucky token... 4. mojo 5. charm
6. amulet 7. periapt 8. talisman
9. alectoria 10. rabbit foot
12. antinganting
lucrative... 3. fat 6. paying 7. gainful
10. productive, profitable, worthwhile
12. remunerative
lucre... 4. gain, pelf 6. profit, riches
9. emolument 11. acquisition
lucubrate... 18. burn the midnight oil
ludicrous... 5. antic, comic, droll,
funny 6. absurd 7. amusing, comical,
jesting, risible 9. burlesque, laughable
10. ridiculous
Ludolphian... 2. pi (3.14159)
14. Ludolph's number
Luftpost... 7. airmail, air post
lug.. 3. box, ear, hug 4. drag, hale,
haul, loop, pull, tote 5. carry 6. basket
9. container
luge... 4. sled
luge... 4. airs 7. clothes (showy), tobacco
10. affections
lugubrious... 3. sad 6. woeful 7. doleful
8. grievous, mournful 9. plaintive
10. lamentable
lugworm... 3. lob 7. annelid 9. Arenicola
luhinga... 9. petticoat
lukewarm... 4. cool 5. tepid 6. tepefy
8. tepidity 9. not ardent 10. irresolute
11. indifferent
lumber... 4. wood 6. bungle, litter, refuse,
rumble, timber, trudge 7. lombard
9. rough wood 10. pawnbroker
11. impedimenta
lumberman... 6. logger, sawyer, scorer
9. timberman 10. lumberjack,
woodcutter
lumberman's half boot... 3. pac
lumberman's sled... 4. tode 7. go-devil,
travois (travoise)
luminary... 3. sun 4. fire, star 5. light
7. wise man 9. celebrity 12. illumination,
leading light
luminescence... 7. foxfire
12. fluorescence 15. phosphorescence
luminous... 5. clear, lucid 6. bright
7. shining 9. brilliant 11. enlightened,
illuminated, intelligent, transparent
14. phosphorescent
luminous circle... 4. halo
luminous impression... 9. phosphene

10. afterimage

lummox ... 3. oaf 4. boor, dolt,
lout 5. yahoo 7. bumpkin, bungler
12. clumsy fellow

lump ... 3. gob, lob, wad 4. beat, blob,
clot, hunk, loaf, mass 5. bulge 6. nodule,
nubble, nugget, thresh 7. cluster
8. swelling 12. protuberance

lump (pert to) ...
butter .. 3. pat
clay .. 4. clag, clod
metal .. 3. pig 5. ingot

lumpish ... 4. dull 5. bulky, inert
6. clumsy, stolid, stupid 7. boorish
8. sluggish 9. heaviness, inertness,
ponderous 11. countrified
13. shapelessness

lumpy ... 5. drunk, rough 6. choppy
7. gnarled, nodular

lumpy jaw ... 6. big jaw
13. actinomycosis

luna ... 6. silver 11. moon goddess

lunacy ... 4. moon 5. mania 7. madness
8. insanity 9. craziness
11. derangement, foolishness

lunar ... 5. orbed 6. lunate 8. crescent,
moonlike 9. celestial, satellite 10. moon-
shaped

lunar (pert to) ...
appulse .. 7. eclipse
bone .. 7. lunatum
cycle .. 7. Metonic 9. Callippic
deity .. 6. Selene (Selena)
halo .. 6. corona, nimbus 7. aureola
surface feature .. 6. crater

lunatic ... 3. mad 5. crazy, idiot, loony
6. insane, madman 8. demoniac
10. moonstruck

lunatic asylum ... 9. Bethlehem (London)

lunch ... 5. snack 6. brunch, repast, tiffin
8. brown-bag, luncheon, nuncheon
9. collation 11. refreshment

lunchroom ... 6. eatery 10. coffee shop,
restaurant 12. luncheonette

lundyfoot ... 5. snuff (by Lundy Foot)

lunge ... 3. cut, jab 4. grab, pass, stab
5. feint, swing 6. thrust

lungs (pert to) ...
ailment .. 9. emphysema 10. chalicosis
12. tuberculosis
having .. 9. pulmonate
part .. 5. lobes 6. lights 7. bronchi,
trachea
sound .. 4. rale 6. rattle

lunula ... 8. crescent, half moon

lurch ... 4. joll, roll, sway 5. lunge
6. careen, topple 7. deceive 8. flounder
10. disappoint

lure ... 4. bait, trap 5. decoy, snare,
tempt 6. allure, entice, invite 7. attract,
beguile, trumpet, tweedle
10. enticement

lurid ... 3. wan 4. dark, pale 5. color,
vivid 6. dismal, gloomy 7. ghastly,
obscene 9. deathlike 11. sensational

lurk ... 4. hide, lote (obs) 5. creep,
prowl, skulk, slink, sneak 9. lie in wait,
pussyfoot

luscious ... 4. rich 5. sweet 6. creamy,
wanton 7. cloying, honeyed 8. sensuous
9. delicious 10. lascivious, voluptuous

lush ... 4. soft 5. drink, drunk, juicy
6. lavish, limber, liquor, mellow
7. verdant 8. flexible 9. luxuriant,
succulent 11. intoxicated

lusory ... 7. playful 8. sportive

lust ... 5. greed 6. desire, libido
7. craving, longing, passion 8. virility
14. lasciviousness

luster, lustre ... 4. naif 5. glory,
gloss, sheen, shine 6. beauty, polish
7. glitter, lustrum 8. radiance, schiller,
splendor 10. brightness 11. distinction,
iridescence

lusterless ... 3. dim, mat 4. dead, dull,
flat 14. expressionless

lustful ... 4. lewd 5. randy 9. lecherous
10. lascivious

lustrous ... 4. naif 5. nitid 6. agleam,
bright 7. radiant, shining 11. illustrious,
transparent

lustrous mineral ... 4. spar

lustrum (Roman) ... 6. census, luster
12. purification (5 yrs), quinquennium

lusty ... 6. active, robust, strong, sturdy
7. healthy 8. vigorous 9. corpulent

lute ... 4. clay, ring (rubber), seal
6. cement

lute, lutelike ... 4. asor 6. guitar
7. bandore, pandore, theorbo, ukulele
8. archlute (archilute)

lute tablature ... 7. lyraway

lutjanoid fish ... 4. sesi 7. snapper

Luxembourg ...
capital .. 10. Luxembourg
government .. 10. Grand Duchy
language .. 6. French, German
13. Letzeburgesch
river .. 7. Moselle

luxuriant ... 4. lush, rank, rich 6. ornate,
uberty 7. fertile, opulent, profuse,
teeming 8. abundant, prolific
9. bounteous, Sybaritic

luxuriate ... 4. bask 5. revel 8. flourish

luxurious ... 5. plush, ritzy 6. ornate,
superb 8. imposing 9. expensive,
grandiose, sumptuous 10. impressive
11. extravagant

luxury ... 4. lust 7. lechery 8. elegance,
pleasure, richness 10. prosperity,
sensuality 11. superfluity
12. extravagance 13. gratification,
sumptuousness 14. voluptuousness

luxury lover ... 7. reveler 8. Sybarite

Luzon ...
dialect .. 6. Itaves
mountain .. 3. Iba 6. Pagsan (Sicapoo)
people .. 5. Malay 6. Igorot (Igorrote)
7. Tagalog 8. Tinggian (Tinguian)
seaport .. 5. Vigan 6. Aparri, Cavite
volcano .. 5. Mayon

lyam ... 5. leash (Her) 10. bloodhound

lycanthrope ... 8. werewolf 9. loup-garou

Lycia (pert to) ...
citizen .. 6. Lycian
city .. 4. Myra
district of .. 9. Asia Minor
language .. 5. Greek 6. Lycian

Lydia ...
capital .. 6. Sardis
dynasty of .. 5. Gyges 7. Croesus
13. Cyrus the Great

name, later .. 6. Persia
name, old .. 5. Ionia
queen .. 7. Omphale
river .. 8. Pactolus
ruins .. 6. temple
lye ... 4. buck 6. bleach, potash
8. lixivium
lying ... 5. false 6. deceit 7. fudging
9. decumbent, mendacity, reclining,
recumbent 10. untruthful
lying (pert to) ...
across .. 10. transverse
at mountain base .. 8. piedmont
hidden .. 6. latent 11. delitescent
in .. 12. accouchement
near earth's axis .. 5. polar
on the back .. 5. prone 6. supine
7. passive
lymph ... 3. sap 5. chyle, fluid, serum,
water 6. plasma 7. cassein
lynch ... 4. hang 6. murder, punish
(lawlessly) 7. execute
lynx ... 6. bobcat, lucern 7. caracal,

wildcat 8. carcajou 13. constellation
lynx-eyed ... 7. oxyopia
lyre ... 4. asor, harp 6. kissar, sabeca,
trigon, zither 7. cithara, cittern, testudo
8. phorminx
lyre (pert to) ...
bird .. 6. Menura 8. lyretail, pheasant
shaped .. 6. lyrate
tree .. 5. tulip
turtle .. 11. leatherback
lyric (pert to) ...
Arabic .. 5. gazel
Muse .. 5. Erato 10. Polyhymnia
music, poetry .. 3. lay, ode 4. epic, poem
5. epode, melic, rhyme (rime), verse,
vocal 6. epopee, poetic 7. canzone,
musical, rondeau 8. operatic, palinode
9. dithyramb
poet .. 5. odist
lyrical ... 6. epodic
lyrichord ... 11. harpsichord
lyssa ... 6. rabies 11. hydrophobia
lyssophobia ... 17. fear of hydrophobia

M

M ... 2. Mu (Gr) 6. letter (13th) 8. thousand
Ma (Ma Bellona) ... 7. goddess (fertility)
maarib (Jew) ... 7. liturgy
Maat (Egypt) ... 7. goddess (justice)
Mab (Queen Mab) ... 4. poem 10. fairy
queen
mabolo ... 4. plum 7. camagon
macabre ... 4. grim 5. lurid, weird
6. grisly 7. ghastly 8. gruesome
12. Dance of Death
macaco ... 5. lemur 6. Macaca
7. macaque 10. Barbary ape
macan ... 4. rice
macao ... 4. game (gambling)
Macao ... 6. island 7. seaport
macaque ... 6. machin, monkey
Macassar ... 7. seaport (Celebes)
macaw ... 3. ara 5. arara 6. parrot
7. maracan 8. aracanga (blue and red),
ararauna (blue and yellow)
Macbeth (pert to) ...
author .. 11. Shakespeare (1605)
character .. 4. Duff, Ross 5. Angus
6. Banquo, Hecate, Lennox 7. Macduff
murder victim .. 6. Duncan
play type .. 7. tragedy
rival .. 7. Macduff
McBurney's Point (Med) ...
13. abdominal wall
Maccabees ... 11. Hasmonaeans
14. fraternal order, Jewish patriots
maccaboy ... 5. snuff
mace ... 4. maul 5. baton, gavel, spice
(nutmeg), staff 6. ensign, mallet
7. scepter (sceptre)
mace bearer ... 5. macer 6. beadle
Macedonia, Balkans ...
capital (anc) .. 5. Pella
city .. 5. Berea 6. Edessa 8. Salonika

people .. 6. Greeks 8. Serbians
9. Albanians 10. Bulgarians
ruler .. 6. Philip 9. Alexander (the Great)
site .. 15. Balkan Peninsula
macerate ... 3. ret, vex 4. soak 5. steep
6. soften 7. mortify, oppress, torture
8. emaciate 9. waste away
machete ... 4. bolo, fish 5. knife 6. guitar
11. cutlass fish
Machiavellian, Machievelian ... 4. wily
6. crafty 7. cunning 8. guileful,
scheming 9. deceitful 12. falsehearted
machila ... 7. hammock
machin ... 6. monkey 7. macaque
machinate ... 4. plan, plot 6. scheme
8. contrive, maneuver
machination ... 6. design, device, scheme
7. machine 8. intrigue 9. stratagem
10. conspiracy
machine ... 3. car 4. auto 6. device,
engine 7. vehicle 9. apparatus,
automaton 10. automobile
11. association, standardize
machine (pert to) ...
cloth maturing .. 4. ager
cloth stretching .. 6. tenter
cotton .. 3. gin 4. mule 5. baler
glazing .. 8. calender
hay .. 5. baler 6. tedder
hoisting .. 3. gin, pry 4. pump 5. crane,
davit, lever, tongs 7. derrick
humming .. 5. awner
hydraulic .. 8. telemotor
imitating .. 9. automaton
military .. 3. ram 6. onager
mixing .. 9. malaxator
ore .. 6. vanner
planing .. 8. surfacer
planting .. 6. seeder

political . . 5. party 6. system 7. faction

reckoning . . 6. abacus 9. tabulator
10. calculator

rubber shaping . . 8. extruder

stage effect . . 13. deus ex machina

tool . . 5. drill, lathe

machine gun . . . 4. nest (hidden place)
5. Maxim 6. cannon 7. Gatling
9. Hotchkiss 10. chatterbox

machine-made . . . 11. stereotyped

machine power, energy . . . 5. input
6. output

machinist . . . 7. artisan 8. mechanic

mackerel . . . 5. atule, spike, tunny
6. sierra, tinker

mackerel (pert to) . . .

bait . . 9. jellyfish

bird . . 7. wryneck 9. kittiwake

genus . . 7. Scomber

goose . . 9. phalarope

like . . 4. cero 6. bonito 7. escolar

net . . 7. spiller

shark . . 9. porbeagle

sky . . 6. clouds 9. striation

small (allowable size) . . 5. spike 6. tinker
7. blinker

mackle . . 5. blur, spot 6. blotch, macule

macrobiotic . . . 9. long-lived

mad . . . 3. vain, wild 5. angry, crazy,
irate, rabid, vexed 6. insane, maniac
7. enraged, foolish, frantic, furious
8. demented, frenetic, maniacal,
reckless 9. hilarious, turbulent
10. distraught, infatuated, infuriated
12. arreptitious

Madagascar, Malagasy . . .

animal . . 5. indri, lemur 6. aye-aye,
tenrec (tendrac) 9. babacoote

capital . . 10. Tananarive

cattle . . 4. zebu (humped)

city . . 7. Majanga 8. Tamatave

civet . . 7. fossane

government . . 8. Republic (1960)

language . . 16. Malayo-Polynesian

native . . 4. Hova 8. Sakalava

palm . . 6. raffia

religion . . 7. Animist 9. Christian

Madam . . . 3. Mrs 4. Frau, lady, Ma'am
5. donna, hussy 6. Madame, Señora
8. goodwife, mistress 9. courtesan

madcap . . . 3. wag 4. rash, wild
5. blood 6. madman 7. hotspur, violent
8. reckless 9. daredevil, foolhardy

madden . . . 3. vex 5. craze 6. enrage, incite
7. incense 9. infuriate 10. antagonize

madder . . . 2. al 3. aal, red 4. herb, rose
(color) 5. brown, Rubia 6. orange,
violet, yellow 7. crimson, xanthin
9. turkey-red

made . . . 5. built 7. created, trained
8. invented, prepared, produced,
rendered 10. artificial, successful
11. constructed 12. enfranchised,
manufactured

made (pert to) . . .

accurate . . 5. trued

believe . . 7. feigned 9. pretended,
simulated

blind . . 6. seeled

clear . . 9. explained 10. elucidated

destitute . . 6. bereft

fun of . . 6. jeered, mocked 7. derided
9. ridiculed

hard, obdurate . . 7. steeled

light of . . 7. dwarfed 9. belittled
10. disparaged

over . . 8. reformed, revamped
9. remodeled

plain . . 9. evidenced, exhibited
10. manifested

public . . 5. aired 7. accused, delated
8. reported

scalloped edges . . 6. pinked

sound . . 7. bleated, rumbled, swished

tart . . 7. euchred

up . . 9. composite 10. artificial, fabricated
12. manufactured

up mind . . 7. decided

valid . . 6. proved 9. confirmed
13. authenticated

whole again . . 7. renewed 10. reconciled
13. redintegrated, re-established

Madeira Islands . . .

capital . . 7. Funchal

embroidery . . 6. eyelet

nut . . 6. walnut

owner of Islands . . 8. Portugal

wind . . 5. leste

wine . . 4. bual 5. tinta (red) 7. malmsey,
sercial 8. verdelho

wood . . 8. ironwood (white), mahogany

madhouse . . . 5. chaos 6. asylum, bedlam
8. nuthouse

madman . . . 3. nut 4. coot, loon 6. maniac
7. lunatic 9. phrenetic

madness . . . 3. ire 4. fury, rage 5. anger,
mania 6. frenzy, lunacy 8. insanity
9. agitation, theomania (Relig)
11. foolishness, inspiration

Mad Parliament (1258) . . . 18. Provisions
of Oxford

Madras, India . . .

capital . . 6. Madras

city . . 5. Adoni, Arcot 7. Calicut

export . . 4. lace 7. fabrics 9. kerchiefs
(for turbans)

government . . 10. presidency

madrepore . . . 5. coral 6. fossil, marble
8. Acropora 12. Madreporaria

Madrid, Spain . . .

architecture . . 7. Moorish

boulevard . . 5. Prado 12. Salon de Prado

noted buildings . . 7. Armeria 11. Prado
Museum, Royal Palace

madrigal . . . 3. ode 4. glee, poem 5. lyric,
music 6. verses

maduro . . . 5. cigar 6. mature 11. dark-
colored

maelstrom . . . 5. churn 6. foment
7. turmoil 9. whirlpool (Norway)

maestro . . . 6. master 7. teacher
8. composer, musician 9. conductor
13. Kapellmeister

maestro-di-cappela . . . 11. choirmaster

Mae West . . . 8. life belt

Mafia . . . 9. syndicate 10. Cosa Nostra,
underworld 12. organization (Sicilian)

maffle . . . 6. muddle, mumble 7. confuse,
stammer 8. squander

mafoo, mafu (Chin) . . . 5. groom 9. stable
boy

mag . . . 6. magpie 7. chatter 8. titmouse

M

9. halfpenny

magadis . . 5. flute 9. monochord

magazine . . . 4. shop 5. depot, store
6. review 7. arsenal, chamber (gun),
tabloid 9. ephemeris, reservoir,
warehouse 10. periodical, repository,
storehouse

magazine rifle . . . 6. Mauser 8. repeater

mage . . 5. Magus 6. Merlin 7. Houdini
8. conjurer, magician

magenta . . . 3. dye 7. fuchsia

maggot . . . 4. grub, mawk 5. larva,
mathe 6. notion 7. caprice, Diptera
12. eccentricity

Magi (Three Wise Men) . . . 6. Gaspar
8. Melchior 9. Balthasar

magic . . 3. art 4. juju, mana, maya, rune,
show 5. charm, fairy, spell 6. voodoo
10. necromancy 11. conjuration,
enchantment, legerdemain

magic (pert to) . . .
art (black) . . 7. demonry 9. diablerie,
diabolism
art (white) . . 5. turgy 7. theurgy
ejaculation . . 2. om (um) 6. sesame
goddess . . 5. Circe 6. Hecate
image . . 5. sigil 8. sigillum
lantern . . 11. epidiascope
12. stereopticon
lantern slide . . 6. tinter
staff, wand . . 6. rhabdo 8. caduceus
symbol . . 5. charm 6. caract, fetish
8. pentacle 9. pentalpha
word . . 2. om (um) 5. voilà 6. presto,
sesame 10. abacadabra

magical . . . 6. goetic (goety) 8. charming

magician . . . 4. mage 5. magus 6. Merlin,
wizard 7. Houdini, juggler 8. conjurer,
mandrake, sorcerer 9. archimage,
charlatan, enchanter 11. entertainer,
necromancer, thaumaturge
13. thaumaturgist 15. prestidigitator

magician (pert to) . . .
attendant . . 7. famulus
command . . 6. presto 11. abracadabra
manual . . 8. grimoire

magirics . . . 7. cookery

magirist . . 4. cook

magisterial . . . 5. lofty, proud 6. august,
lordly 7. haughty, stately 8. arrogant,
dogmatic, judicial, official 9. dignified,
imperious, masterful 10. commanding
11. dictatorial, domineering,
overbearing 13. authoritative

magistrate . . . 4. cadi, doge 5. ephor,
judge 6. aedile (edile), archon, bailli,
puisne, syndic 7. alcaide (alcaid),
alcalde, bailiff

magistrate's orders . . . 4. acta

magma . . . 5. dregs 8. sediment
10. molten rock, suspension (Pharm)

magna cum laude . . . 14. with great
honor

magnanimous . . . 4. free 5. lofty,
noble 7. exalted, liberal 8. generous
9. honorable, unselfish, unstinted
10. high-minded 11. great of mind
13. disinterested

magnate . . . 4. lord 5. baron, mogul, noble
6. bashaw, bigwig, tycoon 7. grandee,
richman 9. personage 11. millionaire

magnesium (pert to) . . .
limestone . . 8. dolomite
nitrate . . 9. saltpeter
silicate . . 4. talc
sulphate . . 10. Epsom salts

magnet . . . 7. terella 8. solenoid
9. loadstone, lodestone

magnet (type) . . . 3. bar 9. horseshoe
10. artificial

magnetic . . . 10. attractive, electrical
14. attractiveness

magnetism . . . 5. oomph 8. polarity

magnificence . . . 4. pomp 5. glory
8. grandeur, splendor
15. superexcellence

magnificent . . . 5. grand, regal 6. lavish,
superb 7. exalted, pompous, sublime
8. imposing, palatial, splendid, striking
9. brilliant, grandiose, sumptuous
10. munificent

magnify . . . 4. laud 5. exalt, extol
6. expand, praise 7. enlarge, glorify,
worship 8. increase 9. intensify,
overstate 10. exaggerate

magnitude . . . 4. size 6. extent 7. bigness
8. grandeur, nobility 9. extension,
greatness

Magnolia State . . . 11. Mississippi

magnum . . . 4. bone (wrist) 6. bottle
9. capitatum

magnum opus . . . 9. great work
11. achievement

magpie . . . 3. daw, mag, pie 4. Pica,
piet (pyet) 5. madge, scold 6. pigeon,
talker 9. chatterer 10. chattermag

magpie type . . .
diver . . 4. smew
shrike . . 7. tanager

maguari . . 5. stork

magus . . . 8. magician 9. one of Magi

Magyar . . . 3. Hun 9. Hungarian

Mah (Persian) . . . 9. moon angel

maha . . . 10. sambar deer

Mahabharata (blind king, Hind) . . .
13. Dhritarashtra

mahajan, mahajun (Ind) . . . 8. great man
11. moneylender

mahal . . . 3. Taj Mahal 9. residence
(summer) 10. apartments, Natal brown

mahala . . . 5. squaw

maharaja, maharajah . . . 5. ruler
6. prince

maharani, maharanee . . . 5. queen

mahatma . . . 4. sage 7. wise man
9. great soul, occultist 21. Great White
Brotherhood (member)

mahi-mahi . . . 7. dolphin

mah-jongg piece . . . 4. tile

mahogany . . . 3. roe (burl) 4. toon, wood
5. brown 6. totara 7. ratteen

maholi . . . 5. lemur

Mahomet . . . see *Mohammedan*

Mahound . . . 5. Devil 8. Mohammed

mahout . . . 6. driver (elephant), keeper

Mah to Mahi . . . 10. Fish to Moon

Maia (pert to) . . .
mountain nymph . . 7. Arcadia
son . . 6. Hermes
star . . 8. Pleiades

maid . . . 4. girl, lass 5. bonne, woman
6. damsel, maiden, virgin 7. abigail,

servant 8. spinster 9. tirewoman
Maid (of) . . .
   Astolat . . 6. Elaine
   Athens . . 12. Theresa Macri
   Lydia . . 7. Arachne (changed to a spider)
   Orléans . . 9. Joan of Arc
   Zeus . . 2. Io (changed to heifer)
maidenhair . . . 4. fern 8. Adiantum
   10. Venus's hair
maidenhair tree . . . 6. gingko
maidenly . . . 6. gentle, modest 7. girlish
   9. unmarried
maigre . . . 4. diet, fish
mail . . . 3. dak (dawk) 4. post 5. armor
   7. consign, letters, plumage 8. dispatch
mail, coat of . . . 5. armor 6. byrnie
   (brinie) 7. broigne, cuirass (part),
   hauberk, panoply
mail boat . . . 6. packet
maim . . . 6. injure, mangle, mayhem
   7. disable 8. mutilate 9. tear apart
main . . . 3. sea 4. duct 5. chief, first, great,
   prime, sheer, utter 6. mighty, potent
   7. chiefly, conduit, leading 8. foremost
   9. conductor, essential, principal 10. on
   the whole 11. essentially 13. most
   important
main (pert to) . . .
   act (drama) . . 8. epitasis
   beam . . 6. girder 7. walking
   part . . 4. body
   point . . 3. jet, nub 4. crux, gist, pith
   post . . 9. sternpost
   sea (poet) . . 11. Spanish Main (Caribbean
   Sea)
Maine . . .
   bay . . 5. Casco 13. Passamaquoddy
   capital . . 7. Augusta
   city . . 4. Saco 5. Hiram, Orono 6. Bangor
   8. Lewiston, Portland 11. Millinocket
   college . . 5. Bates, Colby 7. Bowdoin
   Easternmost city . . 8. Eastport
   Easternmost point . . 19. West Quoddy
   Head Light
   Easternmost town . . 5. Lubec
   lake . . 6. Sebago 9. Moosehead
   mountain . . 5. Kineo 8. Cadillac, Katahdin
   resort . . 9. Bar Harbor
   resort island . . 8. Mt Desert
   river . . 8. Kennebec 9. Penobscot
   State admission . . 11. Twenty-third
   State motto . . 6. Dirigo 7. I Direct
   State nickname . . 8. Pine Tree
   trout . . 7. oquassa
Maine, The . . . 10. battleship (Sp-Am
   War)
maintain . . . 4. aver, hold, keep 5. claim
   6. affirm, allege, assert, avouch, defend,
   endure, insist, retain 7. justify, support,
   sustain 8. continue, preserve
maintainable . . . 7. tenable
maintenance . . . 3. aid 6. upkeep
   7. alimony, defense, support
   9. retention 10. livelihood, sustenance
   11. continuance 12. conservation,
   preservation, sustentation
maison . . . 5. house
Maison Carrée . . . 12. Norman Temple
   (Nimes)
maison de santé . . . 6. asylum 8. hospital
   10. sanatorium

maître d'hôtel (famed) . . . 5. Oscar
maize . . . 3. Zea 4. corn 7. mealies
maja, majo . . . 5. belle, dandy
majestic . . . 5. grand, great, lofty,
   noble, regal, royal 6. august, kingly
   7. stately, sublime 8. elevated,
   eloquent, imperial, splendid 9. dignified,
   grandiose 11. ceremonious, magnificent
majesty . . . 5. title 7. crowned (Her),
   dignity 8. grandeur 9. eloquence,
   greatness, loftiness, sceptered (Her)
major . . . 3. dur (Mus) 6. course (study),
   ditone 7. greater, officer 8. legal age,
   majority
major-domo . . . 6. butler 7. bailiff, steward
   9. seneschal
majority . . . 3. age 4. most 6. quorum
   7. greater 8. maturity 9. majorship,
   plurality, seniority 12. more than half
make . . . 2. do 4. earn, form, gain, kind
   5. shape 6. compel, create, induce,
   render 7. compose, execute, produce
   8. contrive, generate 9. structure
   10. accomplish 11. composition,
   manufacture
make (pert to) . . .
   affidavit . . 4. affy
   allowance . . 5. abate, admit 7. concede
   allusion to . . 7. mention
   amends . . 5. atone 7. redress
   as if . . 7. pretend 8. as though
   bare . . 5. strip 6. balden, denude
   believe . . 4. sham 5. feign 7. pretend
   8. pretense
   better . . 5. widen 6. soften 7. broaden,
   improve 9. meliorate 10. ameliorate
   book . . 10. record bets
   buoyant . . 8. levitate
   calm . . 5. allay, quiet 6. serene
   7. appease, compose
   certain . . 6. assure, ensure
   cheerful . . 6. solace 7. comfort, console
   choice . . 3. opt 4. cull 6. choose, select
   7. pick out
   clean breast of . . 7. confess 8. disclose
   clear . . 7. explain 9. elucidate
   coins . . 4. mint
   counterchange . . 11. recriminate
   crisp . . 9. embrittle
   deduction . . 6. rebate
   desolate . . 5. strip 7. bereave
   diminutive . . 9. bantamize
   do . . 3. eke 5. get by 6. manage 8. piece
   out 9. improvise
   eccentric . . 8. decenter
   edging . . 3. tat 7. crochet
   effective . . 6. compel 7. enforce
   enduring . . 6. anneal, temper
   equal . . 6. equate
   evident . . 6. evince
   familiar . . 8. accustom
   famous . . 8. eternize 11. immortalize
   fast . . 4. snub 5. belay 6. batten, secure
   faulty . . 6. impair 7. vitiate
   11. contaminate
   firm . . 3. fix 5. brace 6. cement
   fit . . 4. suit 5. adapt 6. adjust 7. conform
   foolish, stupid . . 4. daff 8. stultify
   10. ridiculous
   fun of . . 3. rib 5. scoff 8. ridicule
   glass . . 7. platten

good .. 7. absolve, justify, succeed 9. indemnify, vindicate

happy .. 5. elate 7. beatify 8. felicify (obs)

hard, harsh .. 5. steel 6. freeze 7. roughen

harmonious .. 6. attune

headway .. 4. gain 7. advance 8. progress

holy .. 5. bless 6. hallow 10. consecrate

honorable .. 5. exalt 6. uplift 7. ennoble

ineffective .. 4. void 5. annul

insensible to pain .. 11. anesthetize (anaesthetize)

into law .. 5. enact 9. legislate

known .. 6. impart, reveal 7. divulge, publish, uncover 8. disclose, discover, proclaim

lace .. 3. tat 7. crochet

less dense .. 4. thin 6. rarefy

less smooth .. 7. roughen

level .. 4. true

light .. 6. jetsam 8. illumine, jettison

like .. 7. imitate 11. impersonate

lively .. 8. energize

love .. 3. coo, woo 5. court

merry .. 5. laugh 6. banter 7. disport

mild .. 8. mitigate, modulate

moral .. 8. ethicize

much of .. 6. praise 7. enthuse, lionize 10. exaggerate

muddy .. 4. roil

notes .. 8. annotate

off with .. 5. steal

out .. 4. know 5. solve 6. decode, draw up 7. analyze, discern 8. contrive, decipher 10. understand

over .. 4. redo 6. revamp 7. convert 8. renovate, transfer 9. refashion, reproduce

pale, sickly .. 8. etiolate

possible .. 6. enable

pottery .. 7. spattle

precious .. 6. endear

pretentious .. 7. buckram

public .. 3. air 5. bruit, noise 6. delate 7. publish 9. divulgate 11. acknowledge

ready .. 4. gear 5. coach, prime 7. prepare

reparation .. 5. atone

resistance .. 5. rebel 6. mutiny, revolt

secure .. 3. fix, pin 4. nail, snub 5. belay 6. batten, fasten

shift .. 9. temporary

short work of .. 6. hasten 7. destroy 10. accomplish

shrill noise .. 10. stridulate

smooth .. 4. buff, iron 5. sleek, slick 6. scrape

spruce .. 4. perk 7. smarten

strong .. 7. stouten

thin .. 8. attenuate

three-cornered .. 11. triangulate

unhappy .. 8. embitter 10. exacerbate

up .. 5. atone, build 6. invent, settle 7. compose, concoct, prepare 8. assemble, cosmetic 9. construct, improvise, reconcile 10. compensate

use of .. 5. apply 6. borrow, employ 7. utilize 11. appropriate

waste (law) .. 7. estrepe

watertight .. 4. calk, seal

white .. 6. blanch, bleach

worse .. 9. aggravate

zealous .. 7. enthuse

maker of ...

arrows .. 8. fletcher

barrels .. 6. cooper

bundles .. 5. baler

infusion .. 7. steeper

knives .. 6. cutler

pottery .. 6. potter 8. ceramist

makeshift ... 7. stopgap

maki ... 5. lemur

mal (comb form) ... 3. bad, ill 5. badly 7. disease 8. sickness

Malabar (pert to) ...

bark .. 5. ochna

nutmeg .. 10. Bombay mace

palm .. 7. talipot

rat .. 9. bandicoot

Malacca ... 7. seaport (Malaya)

Malachi ... 4. Book (Old Test) 7. prophet

malachite ... 4. bice 5. green 6. copper 7. pigment

maladroit ... 6. clumsy 7. awkward, unhandy 8. bungling 9. all thumbs, graceless 10. blundering, left-handed, ungraceful

maladventure ... 6. mishap 8. escapade 12. ill adventure

malady ... 4. amok 7. ailment, disease, illness 8. disorder, sickness 9. complaint, distemper 13. indisposition

mala fide ... 10. in bad faith

Malaga ... 4. city (Sp), wine 10. oxblood red

Malagasy lemur ... 6. aye-aye

Malagasy region ... 10. Madagascar

malaise ... 4. pain 10. discomfort, uneasiness

malapert ... 4. bold, pert 5. saucy 8. impudent

malaria ... 5. miasm 6. miasma 10. strophulus

malaxation ... 7. massage 9. softening

Malay Archipelago ...

animal .. 4. mias 5. tapir, tsine 6. gibbon, taguan 7. banteng

apparel .. 4. baju 5. banju 6. sarong

buffalo .. 4. gaur 7. carabao, seldang

canoe .. 4. proa 5. prahu

chief (tribal) .. 4. dato (datto)

crane .. 5. sarus

dagger, knife .. 6. creese (kris), parong

disease (jumping) .. 4. Lata (Latah)

gentleman .. 3. sir 4. tuan

island .. 4. Bali, Java 5. Timor 7. Celebes, Sumatra 9. New Guinea 11. Philippines

isthmus .. 3. Kra

language .. 7. Tagalog

native .. 5. Bajau 6. Ifugao 8. Filipino 9. Samal Laut 10. sea gypsies

palm .. 6. Arenga, gomuti (gomuto) 8. Saguerus

pygmy .. 4. Aeta

rice field .. 5. sawah

seaport .. 7. Malacca

state .. 5. Kedah, Perak 6. Jahore

tree .. 4. upas 5. kapur, niepa, terap 6. durian (fruit)

vessel .. 4. toup 6. lugger

Malaysia ...

capital .. 11. Kuala Lumpur
malcontent ... 5. rebel 6. Fenian,
uneasy 7. repiner 8. agitator, grumbler
10. rebellious 12. discontented
male ... 2. he 3. cob, him, tom 4. bull,
dude, galt, jack, stud 5. andro (comb
form), macho, manly 6. tercel, virile
7. rooster 8. stallion 9. masculine
male (pert to) ...
column (Arch) .. 7. Telamon 8. Atlantes
One Hundred eyes .. 5. Argus
malediction ... 5. curse 6. threat
7. malison, slander 8. anathema
11. imprecation 12. denunciation
malefaction ... 5. crime 7. offense
9. malum in se
malefactor ... 5. felon 7. culprit
8. criminal, evildoer 9. wrongdoer
malevolence ... 4. hate 5. pique, spite
6. grudge, malice, rancor 7. ill will
8. inimical 9. animosity, malignity
10. bitterness
malevolent ... 4. evil 6. hating 7. envious,
hateful 8. spiteful 9. malicious,
rancorous 11. ill-disposed
malfeasance ... 7. misrule 8. impolicy
10. wrongdoing 11. evil conduct, illegal
deed
malfeasant ... 6. criminal, evildoer
malgré ... 9. in spite of
15. notwithstanding
malheur ... 10. misfortune
Mali, Africa ...
capital .. 6. Bamako
malice ... 4. envy, evil 5. malum,
pique, spite, wrong 6. rancor 7. ill
will 9. animosity, malignity, malintent
10. bitterness 11. malevolence
malicious ... 4. evil, mean 6. bitter,
malign, ornery 7. hateful 8. sinister,
spiteful 9. rancorous, resentful, vitriolic
11. ill-disposed 12. cantankerous,
unpropitious
malicious (pert to) ...
destruction .. 5. arson 8. sabotage
9. vandalism
gossip .. 4. dirt 7. scandal, slander
intention .. 6. animus
maliform ... 11. apple-shaped
malign ... 4. evil 5. abuse, libel 6. deadly,
defame, revile, vilify 7. asperse, baleful,
harmful, slander, traduce 8. badmouth,
virulent 10. calumniate 12. unpropitious
malignancy ... 6. malice 9. virulence
10. deadliness 11. harmfulness,
noxiousness
malignant ... 3. ill 4. evil 5. felon
6. deadly, wicked 7. harmful, heinous,
vicious 8. spiteful, virulent 9. felonious,
invidious, malicious, poisonous,
rancorous 10. rebellious 11. deleterious
maligner ... 8. libelist 9. slanderer
malignity ... 4. evil, hate 5. spite, venom
11. harmfulness, heinousness
maline(s) ... 3. net 11. Mechlin lace
malingerer ... 6. truant 7. quitter, shirker,
slacker, welsher
malison ... 5. curse 11. malediction
malkin ... 3. cat, mop 4. drab, hare
6. sponge 8. slattern 9. scarecrow
mall ... 4. gull, walk 5. alley, plaza,

prado 6. arcade, mallet 7. alameda
8. assembly 9. esplanade, promenade
14. shopping center
mallangong ... 8. duckbill
mallard ... 4. Anas, duck 5. drake
malleable ... 4. soft 6. pliant 7. ductile,
plastic 9. teachable
mallemuck ... 6. fulmar, petrel
9. albatross
mallet ... 3. tup 4. club, mace, maul
5. gavel, madge 6. beater, beetle,
driver, hammer
malm ... 4. marl 5. chalk
malmsey ... 4. wine
malodorous ... 4. foul, rank 5. fetid
6. rotten, smelly 7. noisome, odorous
11. ill-smelling, odoriferous
malt (pert to) ...
froth .. 4. barm
ground .. 5. grist
infusion .. 4. wort 9. sweetwort
kiln .. 4. oast
liquor .. 4. beer, suds 6. Scotch (whisky)
mixture .. 6. zythum 7. maltate
source .. 5. grain 6. barley
vinegar .. 4. wort 6. alegar
Malta, Mediterranean Isle ...
capital .. 8. Valletta
fever .. 8. undulent
group island .. 4. Gozo 6. Comino
Maltese ... 3. cat 5. cross 6. Knight,
native (of Malta)
maltreat ... 5. abuse 6. misuse 8. ill
treat 9. do wrong by
malty ... 5. drunk
malum ... 4. evil 5. wrong 7. offense
malversation ... 9. extortion (in office)
10. corruption 11. evil conduct,
fraudulence, misbehavior
mammal ... 3. ape, man 4. homo 5. whale
10. vertebrate
mammal ... 2. ai, ox 3. ape, bat, cat,
cow, dog, hog, orc, pig, rat, yak
4. bear, bull, deer, lion, mink, mole,
paca, seal, tait, zebu 5. camel, coati,
daman, koala, lemur, llama, moose,
mouse, okapi, otter, ounce, panda,
ratel, rhino, sable, shark, sheep, swine,
tapir, tayra, whale 6. alpaca, badger,
desman, dugong, marten, monkey,
ocelot, rytina (ext), tenrec (tendrac),
walrus, weasel 7. dolphin, manatee,
opossum, peccary, raccoon 8. aardvark,
anteater, antelope, elephant, kangaroo,
mongoose, reindeer 10. chevrotain,
rhinoceros 12. hippopotamus
mammal (pert to) ...
coat .. 4. hide, skin 6. pelage
cud-chewing .. 8. ruminant
edentate .. 8. anteater, pangolin,
tamandua (anteater)
extinct .. 6. rytina 8. mastodon
9. Glyptodon
flying .. 3. bat
largest .. 5. whale
man .. 6. Bimana (group)
meat-eating .. 9. carnivore
nipple .. 4. teat 8. mammilla
omnivorous .. 3. hog, pig 5. swine
Order .. 7. Cetacea 8. Edentata, Rodentia
Order, highest .. 7. Primata 8. Mammalia

Order, lowest . . 9. Marsupial
plantigrade . . 7. raccoon
primate (except Man) . . 10. Quadrumana
scaled . . 8. pangolin
shelled . . 9. armadillo
smallest . . 5. shrew
snake-eating . . 8. mongoose
toothless . . 8. edentate
web-footed . . 6. aliped
wing-footed . . 6. aliped
zebralike . . 6. quagga
mammock . . . 4. tear 5. break, scrap
    8. fragment
mammon . . . 5. money 6. riches, wealth
    11. fallen angel (Bib) 15. demon of
    cupidity
mammoth . . . 5. giant, large (very)
    7. titanic 8. behemoth, elephant,
    gigantic, mastodon 9. pachyderm
    11. Dinotherium 12. hippopotamus
man . . . 3. arm, fit, rig 4. homo, male
    5. adult, equip, fit up, human, staff
    6. outfit, person 7. fortify, furnish,
    mankind, prepare, someone 9. human
    race 10. human being
man (of) . . .
    all work . . 4. mozo 6. Friday 8. factotum
        9. assistant
    Blood and Iron . . 8. Bismarck
    Destiny . . 9. Bonaparte (Napoleon)
    Galilee . . 11. Jesus Christ
    God . . 5. saint 6. priest 9. clergyman
        12. ecclesiastic
    law . . 6. lawyer 7. counsel 8. attorney
        9. counselor (counsellor)
    learning . . 6. pundit, savant 7. scholar
        9. literatus 11. litterateur
    quackery . . 7. buffoon 9. trickster
        10. mountebank
    the sea . . 3. tar 6. merman, sailor
    the signs . . 12. homo signorum
    the woods . . 6. rustic 8. silvanus,
        woodsman 9. orangutan
    the world . . 6. layman 11. cosmopolite
        12. sophisticate
    war . . 7. frigate, soldier, warrior
man (pert to) . . .
    aged . . 3. vet 9. patriarch
        12. octogenarian
    bachelor . . 4. stag 8. celibate
    bald . . 9. pilgarlic
    conceited . . 7. coxcomb
    cunning . . 5. rogue 6. rascal 7. shyster
        10. mountebank
    dissolute . . 4. roué
    eccentric, elderly . . 4. sire 5. uncle
        6. codger, gaffer 11. grandfather
    effeminate . . 9. androgyne
    entire (soul and body) . . 3. ego
    fashionable . . 3. fop 4. dude 5. dandy
        11. Beau Brummel 12. boulevardier
    fungus . . 9. earthstar (the)
    handsome . . 6. Adonis
    hardheaded . . 5. Boche
    hard-pressed . . 3. Job
    important . . 4. hero, lion 5. chief, nabob
        6. tycoon 7. mugwump
    isle of, capital . . 7. Douglas
    lady's . . 4. beau 6. fiancé
    lawless . . 7. ruffian
    learned . . 6. pundit, savant 7. erudite,

scholar 9. literatus 11. philologist
    little . . 6. mankin, shrimp, squirt
        10. homunculus
    loud-voiced . . 7. stentor
    lowbred . . 4. serf 5. churl 6. rustic
        7. peasant 8. plebeian
    medicine, magic . . 6. shaman
    millionaire . . 7. Croesus 10. capitalist,
        Corinthian
    newspaper . . 6. editor 8. reporter
        10. journalist
    old . . 5. elder 7. veteran 12. octogenarian
    prehistoric . . 4. cave 6. Ice Age 8. eolithic,
        Grimaldi, Piltdown 9. neolithic
        11. paleolithic
    red . . 6. Indian
    strong . . 6. Samson 8. ironside
    wise . . 4. sage, seer 5. solon 6. nestor
        7. Solomon
    without a country . . 5. Nolan (Philip)
manacle . . . 4. gyve, iron 5. chain 6. fetter
    7. shackle 8. handcuff 9. restraint
manada . . . 4. herd 5. drove, flock
manage . . . 3. man, run 4. boss, head,
    lead, tend 5. cater, dight, guide, pilot,
    wield 6. direct, govern 7. control,
    husband, operate 8. contrive, engineer
    10. administer, manipulate
manageable . . . 4. easy, tame, yare
    6. docile, wieldy 7. ductile 9. compliant,
    tractable 10. governable 12. controllable
management . . . 4. care 6. charge,
    menage 7. conduct, control, gestion
    9. direction 10. government
    11. negotiation
manager . . . 4. boss 6. gerent 7. steward
    8. director, governor, operator, overseer
    9. economist 12. entrepreneur
    13. administrator
managery . . . 7. cunning 8. artifice
    9. frugality, husbandry 10. management
    12. manipulation 14. administration
mañana . . . 8. tomorrow 10. before long
manas (Hind) . . . 3. ego 4. mind
Manasseh . . . 5. tribe (Israel) 11. King
    of Judah
Manchuria . . .
    capital . . 6. Mukden (old) 9. Changchun
    government . . 5. China
    Japanese name . . 9. Manchukuo
    native . . 9. Mongolian
    river . . 4. Amur, Liao, Yalu
manciple . . . 5. slave 7. servant, steward
    8. purveyor
mandarin (pert to) . . .
    bird . . 4. duck
    city . . 9. Chungking
    color . . 3. red
    dialect . . 7. Chinese
    figure in Chinese dress, seated . .
        9. grotesque
    fruit . . 6. orange 9. tangerine
    official . . 8. governor 10. bureaucrat
    residence . . 5. yamen
    ware . . 9. porcelain
mandate . . . 5. edict, order 6. behest,
    charge, decree, mandat 7. bidding,
    command, precept 9. direction
    10. injunction, referendum
mandatory . . . 10. imperative, obligatory,

preceptive
mandible . . . 3. jaw 4. beak 5. chops,
molar (part) 9. chelicera
mandrel, mandril . . . 3. hob 4. axle, pick
(miner's) 5. arbor 7. spindle
mandriarch . . . 3. monk ruler
mandrill . . . 6. baboon
mane . . . 4. hair, juba, shag 6. thatch
manege . . . 6. school (riding) 7. academy
(riding) 8. cavesson (halter)
manes (Rom) . . . 4. gods (lower world)
7. spirits
maneuver, manoeuvre . . . 4. ruse
5. trick 6. device, jockey, scheme,
tactic 7. operate 8. artifice, intrigue,
strategy 9. stratagem 10. manipulate
13. Immelmann turn
mangabey . . . 6. monkey
manger . . . 3. bin 4. crib, meal, rack
6. bunker, trough 7. banquet
mangle . . . 3. cut, mar 4. hack, maim
5. press 6. bruise, injure, ironer
8. calender, demolish, lacerate, mutilate
9. dismember
mango (pert to) . . .
  bird . . 6. oriole 11. hummingbird
  fish . . 9. threadfin
  fruit . . 5. amini, bauno, drupe, melon
  9. muskmelon
  grove . . 4. tope
mangy . . . 4. mean 5. itchy, seedy
6. ronyon, scurvy, shabby 7. squalid
12. contemptible
manhandle . . . 4. maul 5. abuse 7. rough
up 8. maltreat, mistreat
mania . . . 4. rage 5. craze, furor
6. frenzy, furore, lunacy 7. madness,
passion 8. delirium 10. alienation
11. fascination, infatuation
mania (for) . . .
  buying . . 9. oniomania
  drink . . 9. potomania 10. dipsomania
  foreign customs . . 9. xenomania
  narcotics . . 10. narcomania
  religion . . 9. theomania
  stealing . . 10. erotomania
  11. kleptomania
  wandering . . 10. dromomania
  work . . 9. ergomania
manifest . . . 4. list, open, show 5. clear,
index, overt 6. evince, liquet, patent
7. declare, evident, express, obvious,
visible 8. apparent, disclose
11. indubitable 12. indisputable,
unmistakable
manifestation . . . 4. aura 5. phase
7. display 8. evidence 10. appearance,
disclosure, exhibition, indication,
revelation 13. demonstration
manifestation of . . .
  deity . . 4. Apis 7. serapis
  divinity . . 6. Christ 8. Epiphany
  Vishnu . . 6. avatar
manifesto . . . 5. edict 6. decree
8. evidence, rescript 11. declaration
(public) 12. announcement
13. demonstration
manikin . . . 5. dwarf, model, pygmy
6. figure 7. phantom 9. mannequin
Manila . . .
  boat . . 6. bilalo

  capital of . . 11. Philippines
  hemp . . 5. abaca
  hero . . 5. Dewey (Adm)
  island site . . 5. Luzon
  native . . 7. Chinese, Tagalog 9. Filipinos
manioc . . . 7. cassava
maniple . . . 5. fanon, orale 7. handful,
phalanx, platoon
manipulate . . . 3. rig, use 4. work
5. pilot, treat, wield 6. handle, manage
7. operate
manipulation . . . 5. using 8. handling,
intrigue 9. operation, stratagem
10. management, use of hands
Manitoba, Canada . . .
  capital . . 8. Winnipeg
  Indian . . 4. Cree
  lake . . 8. Manitoba
  river . . 3. Red
mankind . . . 3. man 4. Adam, folk
7. menfolk 8. humanity 9. human race
mankind (pert to) . . .
  division . . 4. race 5. tribe
  group (kindred) . . 6. ethnos, socius
  hater . . 11. misanthrope
  science . . 9. ethnogeny, ethnology
  12. anthropology
manly . . . 4. bold 5. adult, brave, hardy,
noble 6. daring 8. resolute 9. honorable,
masculine, undaunted 10. courageous
manna . . . 4. food (miracle), ierp (leap,
laarp) 7. godsend 8. gazangabin
manner . . . 3. air, way 4. kind, mien,
mode, sort 5. guise, style 6. aspect,
custom, method 7. fashion 8. behavior
10. appearance, deportment
manner (pert to) . . .
  frenzied . . 4. amok 5. amuck, huffy
  7. haughty
  law . . 5. modus
  like . . 4. thus 6. in kind 8. parallel
  meddlesome . . 9. officious
  meditative . . 13. contemplative
  rough . . 7. brusque 10. irreverent
mannerism . . . 4. mode 8. elegance
11. affectation
mannerly . . . 4. nice 5. moral, suave
6. seemly 8. decorous, politely
9. courteous 10. well-spoken
12. ingratiating
manner of . . .
  making something . . 7. facture
  pronouncing . . 6. accent, brogue
  speaking . . 7. grammar
manners . . . 5. mores 8. behavior
9. amenities, etiquette
Mannheim gold . . . 5. brass
mano (comb form) . . . 4. hand
manoc . . . 4. fowl (jungle) 7. chicken,
rooster
manor . . . 4. hall 5. abode 6. estate
7. demesne, mansion
manred . . . 6. homage 9. vassalage
10. leadership (in war)
mansion . . . 4. seat 5. house, manor,
manse 8. dwelling 9. astrology
manta . . . 3. ray (fish) 4. wrap 5. cloak,
cloth 7. blanket 8. mantelet (mantlet)
9. devilfish
mantilla . . . 4. cape, veil 5. cloak
mantis . . . 4. Cagn (deity) 6. insect

7. mantoid 9. rearhorse

mantis crab . . . 7. squilla

mantle . . . 4. cape, cope, robe 5. cloak, cover 6. capote, kittel 7. garment 8. filament, insignia, mantelet, mantling (Her), vestment 10. witzchoura 11. mantelletta

manto . . . 3. ore 4. gown 5. cloak 6. mantle, mantua

mantoid . . . 6. mantis

Mantua (pert to) . . .
birthplace of . . 6. Vergil (Virgil)
capital . . 7. Mantova
walled by . . 11. Charlemagne

Manu (Myth) . . .
laws . . 8. creation, religion
progenitors of . . 3. Man
Seventh Age, author of . . 10. Code of Manu (Hind laws)

manual . . . 4. book 7. clavier (Mus), didache, exercise, handbook 14. consuetudinary

manual (pert to) . . .
alphabet (deaf) . . 11. dactylology
arts . . 6. crafts
crafts . . 5. sloyd (sloid, slojd) 10. handicraft
digit . . 3. toe 5. thumb 6. finger 8. dactylar
ritual . . 7. rituale 8. breviary 9. formulary

manufacture . . . 4. make 6. invent 7. produce, trump up 9. fabricate

manufacturer of drugs, liquors . . . 6. abkari (abkary)

manumission . . . 7. freeing 10. liberation (slave) 12. emancipation

manumit . . . 4. free 5. let go 6. unhand 7. dismiss, release 8. liberate

manuscript (Ms, Mss) . . . 4. copy (author's), opus 5. codex, folio 7. writing 8. document 11. composition, handwriting 13. written by hand

manuscript (pert to) . . .
back . . 5. dorso
blank space . . 6. lacuna
copier . . 6. scribe
mark (old) . . 6. obelus

many . . . 6. divers 7. diverse, several, various 8. frequent, manifold, numerous 9. different, multitude 10. multiplied

many (pert to) . . .
footed . . 8. multiped
prefix . . 4. poly, vari 5. multi
sided . . 9. versatile 12. multilateral
times . . 5. often 10. frequently

manyplies . . . 12. third stomach (ruminant)

Manx cat characteristic . . . 6. no tail 8. tailless

mao . . . 7. peacock

Maori (pert to) . . .
Adam, ancestor . . 4. Tiki
bird . . 3. tui 4. weka (flightless)
canoe, raft . . 4. moki, waka
charm (grotesque) . . 7. heitiki
compensation . . 3. utu
fish . . 4. hiku 7. rainbow 9. trumpeter
hero . . 4. Maui
people . . 3. Ati 4. Hapu
priest . . 7. tuhunga
sect . . 7. Ringatu

tatooing . . 4. moko
tree . . 5. mapau
village . . 4. kaik (kaika)
weapon . . 4. mere, patu, rata 5. marree

Maoriland . . . 10. New Zealand

map . . . 4. plat 5. chart, image 6. charte, design, isobar (weather line), sketch, survey 7. diagram, epitome, explore, picture 9. delineate 10. embodiment 14. representation

maple (pert to) . . .
bowl . . 5. mazer, rogan (sap)
flowering . . 8. abutilon
genus . . 4. Acer 9. Aceraceae
insect scale . . 10. pulvinaria
seed . . 6. samara
sugar tube . . 5. stile
tree . . 8. box elder 9. moosewood

map maker . . . 4. Eric (Father) 7. charter 8. Mercator 12. cartographer

mapo . . . 4. goby (fish)

mar . . . 4. ruin, scar 5. botch, spoil 6. damage, deface, impair, mangle 7. blemish 8. mutilate 9. disfigure

Mar . . . 4. Lord (Jacobite)

marabou, marabout . . . 5. stork 6. argala, covert 8. adjutant

maracan . . . 5. macaw

maranon . . . 6. cashew

marasca, maraschino . . . 6. cherry

marasma . . . 5. waste 7. disease 10. emaciation 12. malnutrition

maraud . . . 3. rob 4. loot, raid, rove, sack 6. forage 7. brigand, cateran, pillage, plunder 10. plundering

marble . . . 3. mib, mig, taw 4. cold, hard 5. agate, white 6. basalt, marmor 7. pattern (mottled) 8. dolomite 9. limestone, sculpture, unfeeling

marble (pert to) . . .
Belgian . . 5. rance
Catalonia . . 8. brocatelle (brocatelle)
cork (tree) . . 9. tambookie
famous . . 6. Parian 7. Carrara 8. Pentelec
game . . 3. taw 5. alley
group (famed) . . 5. Elgin (Marbles)
made of . . 9. marmoreal
mosaic . . 7. tessera
Roman . . 7. cipolin
slab . . 5. dalle, stele

marbled . . . 9. marmorate

Marbles . . . 5. Elgin 7. Arundel

marc . . . 6. refuse, spirit 7. residue 14. eau de vie de marc

marcato (Mus) . . . 6. marked 8. accented, emphatic

march . . . 4. fill, hike, step, trek 5. troop 6. border, parade 7. advance, proceed 8. boundary, drumbeat, frontier, lockstep, movement, progress, smallage 9. cavalcade, quickstep

March King . . . 5. Sousa (John Philip)

marcid . . . 4. weak 7. decayed, tabetic 8. withered 9. exhausted 10. emaciating

Marcobrunner . . . 4. wine (White Rhine)

Mardi Gras . . . 8. carnival 10. fat Tuesday (literal) 13. Shrove Tuesday

Mardi Gras King . . . 3. Rex

mare . . . 4. yaud 5. filly, horse 6. goblin, grasni (gypsy) 7. incubus, specter, trestle 8. the blues 9. nightmare 10. blue devils, melancholy

marge, margent . . . 3. rim 4. brim, edge,
side 5. brink, shore 6. border, fringe,
margin 8. marginal

margin . . . 3. rim 4. brim, edge, rand,
room, side 5. brink, limit 6. amount,
border, reward 10. collateral

margin (pert to) . . .
  business . . 5. gross
  notched . . 5. erose
  note . . 7. apostil 8. scholium
    10. annotation
  scalloped . . 7. crenate
  set in . . 6. indent
  straighten (to) . . 5. align

marginal note . . . 4. kere (kri, keri)
7. apostil 8. scholium 10. annotation

marigold . . . 7. aster, boots, caper,
finch 6. orange (cadmium) 7. cowslip,
Tagetes

marijuana . . . 3. hay 4. hemp 6. reefer
7. tobacco (wild) 8. locoweed
9. cigarette

marikina . . . 7. tamarin 8. marmoset

marimba . . . 9. xylophone

marina . . . 4. dock 5. basin 9. esplanade,
promenade (seaside)

marinal . . . 6. marine, sailor, saline

marine . . . 3. tar 5. jolly, naval 7. mariner,
oceanic, pelagic 8. maritime, nautical
11. leatherneck

marine (pert to) . . .
  animal . . 3. orc 4. brit, seal 5. coral,
polyp 6. dugong, Otaria, teredo, walrus
7. manatee, mollusk, octopus
  clam . . 8. shipworm
  crustacean . . 4. brit 8. barnacle
  fauna, flora . . 7. benthos
  fish . . 5. shark 8. menhaden
  gastropod . . 5. conus (snail), murex
7. terebra
  growth . . 4. kelp 5. algae 6. enalid
7. seaweed 10. ditch grass
  individual . . 6. merman 7. mermaid
  skeleton . . 5. coral
  slogan . . 6. gung-ho

mariner . . . 3. gob, tar 4. salt 5. Jacky
6. sailor, seaman 8. waterman

mariner's card . . . 5. chart

mariner's compass points . . . 6. rhumba

marionette . . . 4. doll, duck 6. figure,
puppet

maritime . . . 5. naval 6. marine 7. oceanic
8. nautical

marjoram . . . 3. dot 4. mint 6. origin
8. origanum 9. flavoring

mark . . . 3. aim, tee 4. heed, line, note, rist,
seal, sign 5. brand, label, notch, score,
stain, stamp, trait 6. denote, symbol,
target 7. betoken, blemish, earmark,
engrave, impress, imprint, insigne
8. evidence, identify, insignia, landmark
9. emphasize, objective, punctuate,
signature, trademark 10. indication
11. distinction, distinguish
14. characteristic

mark (pert to) . . .
  bad . . 7. demerit
  bounds . . 7. delimit 9. demarcate
  contest (in a) . . 5. bogey (bogie)
  critical . . 6. obelus

  diacritical . . 5. hacek, tilde 6. tittle,
umlaut 7. cedilla
  disgrace . . 6. stigma
  fingerprint . . 5. whorl
  logic . . 11. differentia
  misconduct . . 7. demerit
  off . . 4. plot 6. assign 7. measure
12. characterize, circumscribe
  of homage . . 7. ovation
  of whip . . 4. wale, welt
  on a seed . . 5. hilum (pl hila)
  out . . 6. cancel 10. obliterate
  possessive . . 10. apostrophe
  printing . . 4. dele, stet 5. caret 6. dagger,
diesis, obelus 7. obelisk 10. apostrophe
  pronunciation . . 5. breve 6. macron
  proofreading . . 4. dele 5. caret
  prosody . . 7. caesura, triseme
9. diaeresis, tetraseme
  punctuation . . 4. dash 5. colon, comma
6. period 8. diaeresis (dieresis),
semicolon 10. apostrophe
  question . . 7. eroteme (erotema)
  reference . . 4. star 6. dagger, diesis
8. asterisk
  with bars . . 5. grill
  with dots, spots . . 6. dapple 7. stipple
  with pointed instrument . . 6. scrive
  with ridges . . 3. rib

marked by . . .
  dispute . . 13. controversial
  maneuvering . . 8. tactical
  nicety . . 7. elegant
  small areas . . 9. areolated
  time . . 5. dated

marked with . . .
  colors . . 7. mottled 10. variegated
11. psychedelic
  depressions . . 7. dimpled
  furrows . . 6. rivose
  grooves . . 6. lirate
  lines . . 5. ruled 6. linear, notate
  sables (Her) . . 8. pelleted
  spots . . 6. notate 7. mottled
  stripes . . 7. lineate
  zones . . 6. zonate

marker . . . 4. buoy 5. pylon 6. scorer,
signal 7. brander, counter, monitor
8. bookmark, marksman, monument,
recorder 9. indicator

market . . . 4. mart, sale, sell, shop
5. forum, trade 6. rialto, square
9. clientele

market (pert to) . . .
  bonds . . 5. float
  day (Rom) . . 7. nundine
  French . . 8. débouché
  place . . 4. sook 5. agora, plaza, store
6. bazaar, rialto 8. emporium, exchange

marketable . . . 6. staple 7. salable 8. in
demand, vendible 12. merchantable

markhor . . . 4. goat

marking (crescent) . . . 6. lunula, lunule
7. lunulet 9. engraving

markings . . . 7. rasceta

marksman . . . 4. shot 6. gunner, sniper
7. shooter 9. Orangeman

Mark Twain (pert to) . . .
  character . . 7. Tom Sawyer
15. Huckleberry Finn
  pseud of . . 13. Samuel (Langhorne)

Clemens
tale . . 9. Gilded Age 10. Roughing It
15. Innocents Abroad

marl . . . 4. malm 5. earth, fiber 6. manure
7. deposit (earthy), marlite 9. greensand
10. fertilizer, overspread

marli . . . 4. lace 5. gauze, tulle 6. border
(raised on dish)

marlin . . 6. curlew, godwit 8. sailfish
9. spearfish

marlinspike . . . 3. fid 4. bird, tool 6. jaeger
8. skua gull

marmalade . . . 3. jam 6. Achras, sapote
8. plum tree, preserve 12. mammee
sapota

marmit . . . 6. kettle 7. soup pot

marmite (Mil) . . . 4. bomb (soup kettle)
5. shell

marmor . . 6. marble

marmoset . . . 4. mico (black-tailed)
6. monkey, sagoin 7. tamarin

marmot . . . 5. bobac 6. rodent 7. Marmota
8. Arctomys, whistler 9. ground hog,
woodchuck

maroon . . . 5. slave 7. abandon, cast off,
forsake, isolate 8. chestnut 13. leave
helpless

marquee . . . 4. tent 6. canopy

Marquis, infamous . . . 4. Sade

marriage . . . 5. union 7. wedding,
wedlock 8. matrimony 10. nuptiality
11. espousement

marriage (pert to) . . .
absence of . . 5. agamy
age . . 6. mature, nubile
broker . . 9. schatchen 10. matchmaker
forswearer . . 8. celibate
god . . 5. Hymen
goddess . . 4. Hera
hater . . 10. misogamist
late in life . . 8. opsigamy
more than one . . 6. bigamy, digamy
8. polygamy 9. polyandry, tetragamy
(4th) 11. deuterogamy
notice . . 5. banns
of the gods . . 8. theogamy
outside the tribe . . 7. exogamy
pert to . . 7. marital, spousal 8. hymeneal
9. connubial, endogamic
portion . . 3. dot 5. dotal, dowry
promise . . 7. betroth 8. affiance
secret . . 7. elopement

married . . . 5. wived 6. wedded
8. espoused 9. connubial

married (pert to) . . .
more than once at a time . . 9. polyandry
(woman)
once at a time . . 8. monandry
person . . 4. wife 6. spouse 7. husband
8. benedict
twice . . 6. bigamy, digamy
11. deuterogamy

marrow . . . 4. pith 6. center 7. essence,
medulla 9. substance

Mars . . . 3. god (of War) 4. Ares 6. planet,
war-god

Mars (pert to) . . .
altar . . 13. Campus Martius (field of
Mars)
constellation . . 3. Ara
festival . . 5. March 7. October

pert to . . 5. Arean 7. Martian
priests . . 5. Salii
red . . 5. totem
satellites . . 6. Deimos, Phobos
ship . . 8. moon ship 9. spaceship
sons (twin) . . 5. Remus 7. Romulus
spot . . 5. oasis

Marseillaise . . . 4. song (1792)

Marseille, France . . .
capital of Dept . . 14. Bouches du Rhone
church . . 9. Notre Dame
fort . . 11. Rue Noailles 13. Rue
Cannebière
old name . . 8. Massilia
seaport site . . 13. Mediterranean

marsh . . . 3. bog, fen 4. meer, mire, moor,
slue 5. bayou, liman, swale, swamp
6. morass, saline, slough 7. maremma

marsh (pert to) . . .
bird . . 4. rail, sora 5. crane, snipe, stilt
7. bittern
crocodile . . 3. goa
elder . . 3. Iva
fever . . 7. helodes
gas . . 7. methane 8. firedamp
grass . . 5. sedge, spart
hawk . . 5. harpy 7. harrier
hen . . 4. rail
inhabiting . . 12. limnophilous
mallow . . 5. altea
marigold . . 6. boots, calla 7. cowslip
pert to . . 8. paludine
shrub . . 4. reed 5. sedge 7. bulrush,
cattail 8. moorwort 12. pickerelweed

marshal . . . 3. Ney (Fr) 4. lead 5. align,
aline, array, groom, guide, range,
usher 6. direct, parade 7. farrier, officer
8. official

Marshall Islands . . .
chains (two) . . 6. Ralick (eleven isls)
7. Rattach (13 isls)
government . . 11. trusteeship
WWII scene . . 6. Bikini 8. Eniwetok
9. Kwajalein

marshberry, marshwort . . . 9. cranberry

marshy . . . 3. wet 5. boggy, fenny, liman
7. moorish 8. morassey, paludine

marsupial . . . 4. frog, tait 5. kaola
6. wombat 7. opossum, wallaby
8. kangaroo 9. bandicoot, phalanger,
tapoatafa 10. Diprotodon
11. Marsupialia

marsupium . . . 5. pouch

martel (Hist) . . . 6. hammer

martel-de-fer . . . 6. weapon 12. hammer
of iron

marten . . . 3. fur 4. pelt 5. sable
6. mammal 7. Mustela

martial . . . 4. Mars (pert to) 5. brave
7. warlike 8. fighting, militant, military

Martinique . . .
capital . . 8. St Pierre (former) 12. Fort
de France
formation . . 8. volcanic
mountain peak . . 9. Mont Pelée

martyr . . . 4. kill 5. title 7. Stephen
(Christian), torture 8. sufferer

marvel . . . 4. gape 6. wonder 7. miracle,
portent, prodigy 8. astonish

marvelous . . . 6. superb 7. strange
9. wonderful 10. improbable, incredible,

remarkable 11. astonishing
13. extraordinary
Maryland . . .
bay . . 10. Chesapeake
capital . . 9. Annapolis
city . . 9. Baltimore
Hist site . . 8. Antietam 10. State House
(nation's oldest) 11. Fort Mc Henry
mountain . . 8. Backbone, Piedmont
11. Appalachian
race (famed) . . 9. Preakness
12. Steeplechase
race track . . 5. Bowie 6. Butler, Laurel
7. Pimlico
school . . 9. Annapolis (Acad) 12. Johns
Hopkins
settler . . 7. Calvert (Leonard)
State admission . . 7. Seventh
State motto . . 22. Manly Deeds,
Womanly Words
State nickname . . 4. Free 7. Old Line
mash . . . 4. feed, ogle, pulp 5. crush, flirt,
press, smash, steep 6. jumble, soften
7. mixture 9. pulverize 11. infatuation
mashal . . . 7. parable, proverb
masher . . . 5. dandy, flirt, ricer 7. utensil
10. pulverizer 11. philanderer
masjid . . . 6. mosque
mask . . . 4. ball, loup, veil 5. cloak,
cover, dance, drama, onkos 6. domino,
screen 7. conceal, pretext 8. disguise
10. subterfuge
masked . . . 6. comedy, cowled, hidden,
veiled 7. larvate, obscure 8. shrouded
9. concealed, disguised
masker . . . 5. mimer 6. mummer
11. masquerader
maslin . . . 5. brass 6. kettle 7. mixture
(grain) 9. potpourri
Masonic doorkeeper . . . 5. tiler
Mason, Perry (pert to) . . .
actor . . 4. Burr (Raymond, TV) 6. Larkin
(John, radio) 7. William (Warren, film)
author . . 18. Erle Stanley Gardner
detective . . . 5. Drake (Paul)
secretary . . 6. Street (Della)
title words . . 9. The Case of
masonry . . . 6. ashlar 9. revetment
mass . . . 3. cob, dab, gob, mop, pat, wad
4. blob, body, bulk, load, loaf, lump,
roll, size 5. solid 8. quantity 9. large
part, magnitude 11. large amount
12. accumulation, congregation
mass (pert to) . . .
book . . 6. missal
collection . . 9. aggregate
directory (RCCh) . . 4. ordo
for dead . . 7. requiem
matter . . 5. molar
molten glass . . 7. parison
nerve tissue . . 8. ganglion
tangled . . 3. mop 4. shag
vestment (Eccl) . . 5. amice
Massachusetts . . .
capital . . 6. Boston (1630)
city . . 5. Salem 7. Concord 8. Plymouth
9. Cambridge, Lexington 10. Gloucester,
New Bedford 12. Provincetown
college (oldest, US) . . 7. Harvard
explorer . . 5. Cabot 7. Gosnold 9. Capt
Smith (John)

hero . . 10. Paul Revere
island . . 9. Nantucket 15. Martha's
Vineyard
mountain . . 3. Tom 8. Greylock
10. Berkshires
river . . 10. Housatonic 11. Connecticut
school (first free) . . 6. Dedham (1649)
settlers . . 8. Pilgrims, Puritans
State admission . . 5. Sixth
State nickname . . 8. Bay State 9. Old
Colony
massacre . . . 5. havoc 6. pogrom
7. carnage 8. butchery, decimate,
genocide 9. slaughter
massage . . . 3. rub 5. knead 6. stroke
7. therapy
masses, the . . . 4. folk 6. rabble 9. hoi
polloi, multitude 11. proletariat, rank
and file 12. common people 13. great
unwashed
massive . . . 3. big 4. bold 5. bulky,
large, massy 7. weighty 8. imposing
9. ponderous 10. impressive
11. substantial
mast . . . 3. cue, fid 4. pole, spar 5. stick,
stuff (oneself)
master . . . 3. man, rab 4. lord, mian, rule
5. chief, judge, rabbi, tutor 6. expert,
humble, subdue 7. captain, conquer,
maestro, padrone, subject, teacher
8. dominate, overcome, regulate,
surmount, vanquish 9. commander,
conqueror, craftsman, preceptor,
subjugate
master (pert to) . . .
African . . 5. bwana
Eton . . 4. beak
fencing . . 7. lanista
hard . . 6. despot
Indian . . 5. sahib
music . . 7. maestro
of a house . . 13. paterfamilias
of ceremonies . . 2. M C 5. emcee
of Heaven . . 16. Celestial Teacher
of the horse . . 7. equerry
stroke . . 4. coup
masterful . . . 6. lordly 7. haughty
8. arrogant, skillful 9. arbitrary,
imperious 10. commanding
11. dictatorial, domineering, magisterial,
overbearing 13. authoritative
masterpiece . . . 10. magnum opus
11. chef d'oeuvre 17. pièce de
résistance
mastery . . . 4. gree 5. power, skill
7. control, victory 8. dominion
10. ascendancy 11. proficiency
12. vanquishment
mastic . . . 3. asa, gum 5. resin 6. liquor
8. adhesive 9. red-yellow
masticate . . . 4. chew 5. crush, grind
8. macerate
mastiff . . . 3. dog 5. burly, matin
7. massive
mastodon . . . 5. giant 6. animal, Mammut
7. mammoth 8. behemoth 9. dinothere
10. Dinotheres, Mammutidae
11. Dinotherium
mat . . . 3. rug 4. dull (finish) 5. doily,
platt, twist 7. webbing 8. entangle,
material 10. interweave, lusterless

matador ... see *bullfighting*

matagasse ... 11. butcherbird

match ... 3. pit 4. copy, game, mate, pair, peer, sort 5. equal, fusee, marry, tally, vesta 7. compare, contest, lighter, lucifer 8. coincide, marriage, parallel 10. correspond 11. counterpart

matched ... 5. mated 6. paired, pitted, teamed 7. equaled (equalled)

matchless ... 5. alone 6. unlike 7. unequal 8. peerless 9. unequaled 10. inimitable 12. incomparable

matchlock ... 3. gun 7. gunlock

mate ... 4. pair, wife 5. equal, marry, match 6. seaman, spouse 7. comrade, husband, mariner, partner 9. companion 11. confederate, counterpart

matelassé ... 6. fabric 8. quilting (imitation) 13. ornamentation

material, materiel ... 4. data 5. goods, stuff 6. fabric, matter, plasma, staple, swatch 7. weighty 8. relevant, supplies, tangible 9. apparatus, corporeal, equipment, essential 11. substantial 12. nonspiritual 13. materialistic

material (pert to) ...
building .. 4. frit, lime, tile, wood 5. adobe, brick, rabat, tapia 6. cement, thatch 7. plywood 8. asbestos, Masonite 9. wallboard
discard .. 4. slag 5. scrap 6. refuse 7. rubbish
dress .. 4. silk, wool 5. crepe, linen, satin, surah, tulle, tweed 6. baleen, faille, sennit, tricot, velvet 8. corduroy
household .. 5. scrim 6. carpet, damask, lampas, mohair, napery 7. drapery 8. tapestry
needlework .. 4. lace, yarn 6. thread 8. arrasene, chenille
paper .. 3. wax 4. bond, news, note, rice 6. letter, tissue, vellum 7. drawing, writing 8. wrapping 9. cardboard, onionskin, parchment 11. papier-mâché
polishing .. 11. rottenstone

materia medica ... 7. acology 10. leechcraft

maternal ... 7. enation 8. motherly 10. motherlike

math ... 6. mowing 9. aftermath, monastery

mathematician ... 6. Euclid 7. actuary 9. physicist, Whitehead

mathematics (pert to) ...
abbreviation .. 7. QED
arbitrary .. 5. radix 9. parameter
deduction .. 8. analysis
diagram .. 5. graph
element .. 4. cube, root 6. factor 7. decimal, divisor, formula, minuend 8. dividend, fraction, quotient, repetend 10. multiplier, subtrahend 12. multiplicand
equation .. 2. pi 4. cosh, sine, surd 6. cosine
factor .. 10. quaternion
instrument .. 6. sector 7. compass 8. arbalest
number .. 5. digit
operation, operator .. 5. nabla 6. scalar

7. operand 10. quaternion
proposition .. 7. theorem
quantity .. 6. addend, augend, scalar
sheets of .. 4. cone 5. nappe
symbol .. 5. digit 7. facient, operand 12. multiplicand
type .. 4. pure 6. higher 7. algebra, physics 8. abstract, calculus, geometry 10. arithmetic, elementary, quadratics 12. trigonometry

mathemeg ... 7. catfish

matie ... 7. herring

matin ... 6. aubade (song) 7. morning, service 8. watchdog 11. morning song 13. morning prayer

matinee ... 5. levee, party, salon 6. soiree 8. negligee 9. reception 13. conversazione, entertainment

matipo ... 4. wood (fuel) 5. napau

matka, matkah ... 5. seal

matlow ... 6. sailor

matrass ... 4. tube 5. flask 6. bottle, carafe 8. boithead

matriculate ... 4. list 5. admit, adopt, enter 6. enroll 8. register 10. naturalize

matrimonial ... 7. marital, nuptial, spousal 8. conjugal, hymeneal 9. connubial

matrimony ... 7. wedlock 8. marriage

matrix ... 3. bed 4. cast, form, mold, womb 5. cutis 6. gangue 10. foundation, impression

matron ... 4. dame, wife 5. widow 11. housekeeper

matter ... 3. gas, pus 4. body, gear, malm, pith 5. atoms, fluid, vapor 6. affair, amount, solids 7. problem, trouble 8. business, elements, material 10. importance 11. constituent 12. circumstance

matter (pert to) ...
alluvial .. 5. geest
celestial .. 6. nebula
coloring .. 5. eosin 10. endochrome
fatty .. 5. sebum
noxious .. 6. miasma
of doubt .. 7. dubiety
of fact .. 7. literal, prosaic 9. practical, pragmatic
of law .. 3. res
of note .. 8. notandum
particle .. 4. atom
perfume .. 7. essence
spinal cord .. 4. alba
uniform (physics) .. 7. inertia
volcanic .. 2. aa, oo 4. lava

mattress ... 3. bed, pad 5. futon 7. cushion

mature ... 3. age, due, old 4. ripe 5. adult, grown, ripen 6. digest, mellow, season 7. develop, fall due, grow old, perfect 8. complete 9. full-grown, perfected, ratheripe

maturity ... 8. ripeness 9. adulthood, readiness 10. falling due 11. development

matutinal ... 5. early, matin 7. morning 12. antemeridian

maty ... 7. servant

maud ... 3. rug 5. plaid, shawl

maudlin ... 5. beery, drunk, silly, tipsy

7. tearful, weeping 10. lachrymose
11. sentimental (overly)

maul, mall ... 4. beat, bung, club, mace,
mall, moth 5. abuse, gavel, staff
6. beetle, bruise, mallet

maumet ... 3. god (false), guy 4. doll,
idol 5. image 6. puppet 9. scarecrow

maund, maun ... 3. beg 6. basket,
hamper 7. begging, measure

Maundy ... 4. alms 8. ceremony 10. Last
Supper

Maundy Thursday (Bib) ... 8. Holy Week
13. washing of feet

Mauritius, Ile de France ...
  capital .. 9. Port Louis
  government .. 7. British
  product .. 5. coral, sugar
  site .. 11. Indian Ocean

Mauser ... 5. rifle 7. firearm

mauve ... 5. lilac 6. mallow, purple,
violet 10. atmosphere (color)

maven ... 6. expert 11. connoisseur

maverick ... 4. calf (unbranded) 5. dogie
(dogy), stray 11. independent
13. nonconformist

mavis, mavie ... 6. thrush

maw ... 4. craw, crop 6. gullet, mallow
7. gizzard, stomach

mawk ... 6. maggot

mawkish ... 5. vapid 6. sickly 8. nauseous
9. squeamish 10. disgusting
11. sentimental

maxilla ... 7. jawbone

maxim ... 3. saw 4. dict, rule 5. adage,
axiom, gnome, motto, tenet, truth
6. saying 7. precept, proverb
8. aphorism, apothegm 10. apophthegm

maxims ... 5. logia 9. moralisms

maximum ... 4. most 5. limit 7. highest,
supreme 8. greatest 12. consummation

maximus ... 7. largest

may ... 3. can 6. be able 9. be allowed
11. in one's power, opportunity

May (pert to) ...
  apple .. 8. mandrake
  bird .. 6. thrush
  cock .. 5. melon 6. plover
  curlew .. 8. whimbrel
  Duke .. 6. cherry
  festival .. 7. Beltane (anc)
  First .. 7. Beltane 14. May-day festival
  fish .. 9. killifish
  flower .. 7. arbutus 8. hawthorn,
  marigold 9. calla lily 10. stitchwort
  12. cuckooflower
  fly .. 3. dun 7. shad fly 9. ephemerid
  goddess .. 4. Maia
  gowan .. 5. daisy

Maya ... 3. Mam (people) 6. Indian
8. Pokonchi

Mayan calendar ...
  five added days .. 5. uayeb
  no leap year .. 5. solar
  twenty-day month .. 5. uinal
  year .. 4. haab

Mayan underworld ... 7. xibalba

maybe ... 2. if 7. perhaps 8. possibly
9. perchance 11. conceivably,
possibility, uncertainty

Mayday ... 3. SOS 4. help 8. distress

Mayfair ... 6. London (fashionable)

Mayflower (pert to) ...
  boat of .. 8. Pilgrims (1620)
  Compact .. 9. agreement (1620)
  sister ship .. 9. Speedwell

mayhap ... 7. perhaps 12. peradventure

mayor ... 5. maire 7. alcalde
10. magistrate 11. burgomaster

mazarine ... 4. blue (color from Cardinal
Mazarin)

maze ... 5. fancy 7. stupefy 8. confound,
delirium, delusion 9. confusion,
deception, labyrinth 12. bewilderment,
complication

mazed ... 4. lost 7. in a maze 9. stupefied
10. bewildered

mazuma ... 5. money

mead ... 5. drink 6. meadow 8. hydromel
9. metheglin

meadow ... 3. lea 4. mead 5. field, haugh,
pampa, swale 7. pasture, savanna
(savannah) 9. grassland 10. agostadero

meadow (pert to) ...
  chicken .. 8. sora rail
  crocus .. 7. saffron
  crowfoot .. 9. buttercup
  hen .. 4. coot, rail 7. bittern
  mouse .. 4. vole 8. arvicole
  part .. 5. swale
  sage .. 6. salvia
  saxifrage .. 6. seseli
  sweet .. 7. Spiraea

meager, meagre ... 4. arid, bare, lank,
poor, slim 5. gaunt, scant, spare
6. barren, jejune, lenten, narrow, sparse
7. starved, sterile, trivial 9. emaciated
10. inadequate

meal ... 3. tub 4. bran, dune, mess
5. feast, grout, salep, snack 6. bucket,
fodder, powder, ration, repast, tiffin
7. banquet 8. sandbank 9. collation,
pulverize

mealy ... 4. pale 7. friable, powdery
10. soft-spoken 11. farinaceous
12. mealymouthed

mealy (pert to) ...
  Amazon .. 6. parrot
  back .. 6. cicada
  bird, duck .. 5. squaw
  bug .. 4. pest 5. scale 10. pear blight
  mouth .. 7. warbler
  tree .. 9. arrowwood, wayfaring

mealy-mouthed ... 5. suave 10. flattering
12. hypocritical 13. sanctimonious

mean ... 3. low 4. base 5. petty,
small, snide, solar (time), sorry
6. common, denote, design, humble,
intend, medium, menial, middle,
midway, paltry, shabby, sordid, stingy
7. average, ignoble, purport, purpose,
servile, squalid 8. beggarly, ordinary,
plebeian, shameful, wretched
9. difficult, malicious, niggardly,
penurious 10. despicable, ill-humored,
spiritless 11. closefisted, disgraceful
12. contemptible, dishonorable, narrow-
minded, parsimonious

mean clef (Mus) ... 5. C clef

meander ... 4. wind 6. ramble, wander

meaning ... 4. null (without) 5. sense
6. import, intent, spirit 7. purport
8. semantic 9. intending, intention,

knowledge 10. understand
12. significance 13. signification
14. interpretation

meaningless . . . 4. rote 5. banal, derry
7. aimless 8. senseless 10. designless
11. purposeless 13. insignificant

meanness . . . 6. infamy, malice
8. baseness, ill-humor 9. servility
10. humbleness, paltriness, sordidness,
stinginess 11. inferiority

means . . 5. funds 7. capital 8. averages
9. resources 11. wherewithal

means of . . .
access . . 4. adit 5. inlet 7. ingress
8. aperture
communication . . 4. note 5. flags, phone,
radio, smoke 6. letter, postal, tom-tom
8. telegram 9. telegraph, telephone
livelihood . . 4. work 5. labor, trade
8. vocation 10. profession
outlet . . 4. door, exit 6. egress 8. aperture
support . . 5. funds 6. assets 7. aliment
11. maintenance

meantime . . . 5. while 7. interim
8. interval, same time 9. meanwhile

measles . . . 7. rubella, rubeola 8. morbilli

measure (pert to) . . .
area . . 2. ar 3. are, rod 4. acre, area, mile,
rood 6. square 7. geodesy, hectare,
section 8. township
Bible . . 3. cab (kab), kor, log 4. epha
5. cubit, homer
gauge . . 3. erg, lea (yarn) 5. ergon,
level, plumb, scale, stone 6. denier,
square 7. calorie (calory), compass,
sextant 8. calipers, quadrant
length . . 3. ell, mil, rod 4. foot, hand,
inch, knot, mile, nail, pace, rule, tape,
yard 5. chain, cubit, meter 6. league
7. furlong 9. kilometer, yardstick
10. centimeter, micrometer, millimeter
nautical . . 4. knot 5. fathom, league
paper . . 4. page, ream 5. quire, sheet
poetry . . 6. dipody, iambic, rhythm,
sestet 7. anapest, couplet, distich,
tripody 8. quatrain 9. hexameter
10. ottava rima, pentastich, tetrameter,
tetrastich 11. Alexandrine
printer . . 2. em, en 4. pica 5. agate
volume, weight . . 3. ton, tun (wine)
4. bale, butt, cord 5. carat, liter,
minim, ounce, pound, quart 6. barrel,
bushel, finger, gallon, magnum, pottle
8. hogshead, teaspoon 9. kiloliter
10. tablespoon

measurement . . . 4. size 6. amount,
alnage, extent, metage 7. azimuth
8. abscissa, capacity, quantity
9. substance 11. calculation,
mensuration

measuring instrument . . . 6. stadia
7. alidade, caliper 8. odometer
12. perambulator (surveyor)

meat . . . 4. beef, fish, food, lamb, pork
5. flesh 6. fillet, kernel, mutton, quarry
7. brisket 9. aitchbone (icebone),
spareribs

meat (pert to) . . .
ball . . 7. rissole 9. croquette, hamburger
cured, dried . . 3. ham 5. bacon
6. flitch, jerked 7. biltong (biltongue)

8. pemmican
jellied . . 5. aspic
minced, roll . . 7. rissole
roasted . . 5. cabob (kabob) 9. barbecued
slaughterhouse . . 8. abattoir
smoking place . . 6. buccan (bucan)
stew . . 8. mulligan 9. lobscouse

meatus . . . 4. burr (ear) 5. canal
7. opening, passage

meaty . . . 5. pithy, solid 11. substantial

Mecca, Arabia . . . 8. Holy City 16. City
of the Prophet

Mecca (pert to) . . .
birthplace of . . 8. Mohammed
capital . . 5. Hejaz
color . . 11. Tuscan brown
famed for . . 5. Kaaba (Caaba, Kaabeth)
10. Black Stone 11. Great Mosque
governor . . 6. sherif (shereef)
pilgrimage . . 4. hadj
pilgrim's dress . . 5. ihram
rug . . 6. Shiraz

mechanic . . . 7. artisan, workman
8. operator 9. artificer, craftsman,
machinist, operative

mechanical . . . 8. machinal 9. automatic,
practical, technical 11. involuntary,
stereotyped

mechanical (pert to) . . .
adjustment . . 9. tentation
drawing . . 8. drafting
law, motion . . 8. dynamics, kinetics
lever . . 6. tappet
part . . 5. rotor 6. stator

mechanics . . . 9. technique
11. mechanology

mechanism . . . 4. gear, tool 5. means
6. tackle 7. control, rigging 9. apparatus,
machinery, technique

medal . . . 4. coin, disk (disc) 5. badge
6. plaque 9. medallion 10. decoration

medallion . . . 4. coin 5. cameo, medal,
panel 6. tablet 9. ornament

meddle . . . 3. pry 4. nose 5. dabble,
tamper 8. obtrude 9. interfere

meddler . . . 8. busybody 9. pragmatic

meddlesome . . . 7. Paul Fry 8. meddling
9. officious 11. inquisitive, pragmatical

Mede . . 6. Median 7. Persian

medial, median . . . 4. mean 5. mesne,
raphe (valve) 6. medium, middle
7. average 11. intervening
12. intermediate

Median . . . 4. Magi, Mede 5. Medic

mediate . . . 5. opine 9. intercede,
interpose, reconcile

mediator . . . 5. muser 7. arbiter 9. go-
between 10. interagent 11. intercessor

medic . . . 3. doc 6. clover, doctor, median,
medico 9. physician

medical (pert to) . . .
comb form . . 3. oma 4. itis 6. iatric
7. iatrics
compound . . 5. hepar
fluid . . 5. blood, lymph, serum
man . . 5. medic 6. shaman, voodoo
monster . . 5. teras
officer . . 7. coroner
practitioner . . 2. MD 6. doctor, intern
(interne) 7. surgeon 8. sawbones
system . . 7. therapy 9. allopathy

10. homeopathy, psychiatry
term .. 8. curative 9. medicinal
medical terms ...
  chicken pox .. 9. varicella
  flat feet .. 9. pes planus
  headache .. 11. cephalalgia
  heartburn .. 7. pyrosis
  hives .. 9. urticaria
  measles .. 7. rubella, rubeola
  mumps .. 9. parotitis
  whooping cough .. 9. pertussis
medicinal (pert to) ...
  agent .. 3. tea 6. tisane 9. decoction
  bark .. 6. cartex
  dropper .. 7. pipette
  equal parts .. 3. ana
  herb, plant .. 3. rue 4. aloe 5. ergot,
    jalap, orris, senna, tansy 6. arnica,
    cohosh, ipecac 7. boneset, chirata,
    comfrey 8. licorice, valerian
  pain allaying .. 7. anodyne 8. sedative
    9. goofballs, paregoric 11. barbiturate
  patent .. 7. nostrum
  remedy .. 5. drops, salve 6. elixir, iodine
    7. panacea 8. antidote, ointment
  science .. 7. biology 10. physiology,
    psychology
  tablet .. 4. pill 6. troche 7. lozenge
  term .. 4. drug 11. therapeutic
mediety ... 6. loiety 10. moderation,
  temperance
medieval, mediaeval ... 7. archaic
  10. Middle Ages
medieval (pert to) ...
  contest .. 4. tilt 5. joust 10. tournament
  empire .. 9. Holy Roman 11. Carolingian
  emperor .. 4. Otto 11. Charlemagne
  estate .. 4. fief 5. manor
  freeholder .. 7. franklin
  galley (ship's) .. 3. nef 5. xebec 6. bireme,
    galiot (galliot) 7. dromone (dromon),
    trireme, unireme
  garment .. 6. tabard
  headdress .. 6. abacot, wimple
  helmet .. 5. armet
  holy wars .. 8. Crusades
  instrument (stringed) .. 5. rebec (rebeck)
  knights' system .. 8. chivalry
  land system .. 9. feudalism
    11. manorialism
  legend .. 9. Holy Grail 12. Wandering
    Jew
  merchant guild .. 5. hanse
  money of account .. 3. ora
  musical form .. 7. organum 9. plainsong
    (plainchant), polyphony 14. Gregorian
    chant
  musical instrument .. 4. rote 5. rebec
    (rebeck), shawm 7. clarion, sackbut
  papal seat (temporary) .. 7. Avignon
  peasants' overseer .. 5. reeve
  philosopher .. 9. alchemist, Schoolman
    (Scholastic)
  pilgrim .. 6. palmer
  plague .. 10. Black Death (1347)
  poem .. 3. lay 7. fabliau (pl fabliaux)
    14. chanson de geste (epic)
  poet, singer .. 7. gleeman 8. jongleur,
    minstrel, trouvère 9. troubador
  preacher .. 8. pardoner
  secular movement .. 8. Humanism

shield .. 3. ecu 5. pavis (pavise) 6. scutum
tax .. 8. Danegeld
title, teacher .. 8. magister
wandering student .. 7. goliard
weapon .. 4. mace 5. oncin 8. falchion
Medina, Saudi Arabia (pert to) ...
  anc name .. 9. Lathrippa
  Mohammed supporters .. 6. ansars
  sacred city of .. 5. Islam
  tombs .. 4. Omar 6. Fatima
    8. Mohammed
mediocre ... 4. mean, so-so 6. medium
    7. average 8. middling, ordinary,
    passable 9. tolerable 11. indifferent
meditate ... 4. muse, plan, pore 5. brood,
    study, watch, weigh 6. ponder
    7. purpose, reflect, revolve 8. cogitate,
    consider 11. contemplate
meditation ... 4. yoga 7. thought
    8. devotion 10. rumination
    11. thanatopsis 13. contemplation
    14. omphaloskepsis
mediterranean ... 6. inland 7. midland
    10. landlocked
Mediterranean (pert to) ...
  boat .. 3. nef 4. saic 5. xebec (zebec)
    6. galiot (galliot), mistic (mistico),
    settee (setee) 7. felucca, hexeris
  cat .. 5. genet
  coast .. 7. Riviera
  falcon .. 6. lanner
  fish .. 6. remora
  fowl .. 7. leghorn
  fruit .. 5. olive 7. azarole
  gulf .. 5. Tunis
  herb .. 4. Ammi
  inland .. 3. sea
  island .. 4. Elba, Gozo 5. Crete, Malta
    6. Candia, Cyprus, Ebusis, Sicily
    7. Majorca 8. Belearic (group), Sardinia
  island, volcanic .. 6. Lipari, Salina
    7. Vulcano 9. Stromboli
  port .. 5. Tunis 7. Tunisia
  region .. 6. Levant
  storm .. 7. borasca (borasco, borasque)
  tree .. 5. carob 7. azarole
  wind .. 6. solano 7. etesian, gregale,
    mistral, sirocco 8. levanter
    10. euroclyden
medium ... 4. agar (cultured), doer, mean
    5. color, organ 6. degree, medial,
    oracle 7. average, psychic 8. mediator,
    mediocre 10. instrument, interagent
    11. environment 12. intermediary,
    spiritualist
medium's meeting ... 6. séance
medley ... 4. olio 5. relay 6. jumble
    7. ferrago, mélange, mixture 8. fantasia,
    mingling 9. potpourri 10. hodgepodge,
    salmagundi
medrick ... 4. gull (Bonaparte's), tern
    (Wilson's)
medulla ... 4. pith 6. marrow 7. summary
    9. oblongata 10. compendium
Medusa (Myth) ... 6. Gorgon, Stheno
    (sister) 9. gorgoneum
Medusa's head (pert to) ...
  constellation (cluster) .. 7. Perseus
  star .. 5. Algol
  vegetable .. 8. mushroom
  Zool .. 10. basket fish

meed ... 5. bribe, merit, repay, share
6. desert, reward 7. bribery
10. recompense

meek ... 4. mild 6. docile, gentle, humble,
modest 7. pacific, patient 8. moderate,
yielding 10. spiritless, submissive

meerkat ... 6. monkey

meerschaum ... 4. pipe 6. gravel (color)
7. seafoam 9. sepiolite

meet ... 3. fit 4. face, game, join 5. equal,
match, touch 6. battle, combat, concur
7. collide, conform, contact, contest,
convene, fulfill, satisfy 8. assemble,
confront 9. encounter 10. congregate,
experience, rendezvous

meet halfway ... 7. mediate
10. compromise

meeting ... 4. mall, race 5. court,
gemot (gemote), joint, synod, tryst,
union 6. caucus, powwow, séance
7. contact, joining 8. assembly,
conclave, junction 9. encounter,
gathering, in contact 10. conference,
convention, converging, rendezvous
11. convergence 12. congregation,
intersection

mega, meg (comb form) ... 5. great
6. mighty

megalith ... 5. stone (huge) 6. dolman
7. boulder 8. monument (Prehist)

megapode, megapod ... 6. leipoa
9. mound bird 10. jungle fowl 11. brush
turkey

megascope ... 12. magic lantern

megaseism ... 10. earthquake

megrim, megrims ... 4. whim 5. fancy,
freak, humor 8. headache 9. dizziness
12. hypochondria

Mehitabel, Mehetabel ... 3. cat

Mekong River people ... 3. Moi (Asian)

mel ... 5. honey

melancholia ... 7. sadness 8. neurosis
9. nostalgia, psychosis 10. depression

melancholy ... 3. sad 4. blue, dark, glum
5. drear, gloom 6. sombre, sorrow
7. doleful, sadness 8. atrabile, liverish,
tristful 9. dejection 10. depressing,
depression, dispirited, lamentable
11. despondency, downhearted,
pensiveness 12. hypochondria,
mournfulness

Melanesia ... 14. Pacific Islands

Melanesian (pert to) ...
island .. 4. Fiji 7. Solomon 11. New
Hebrides
native .. 4. Fiji 6. Papuan 10. Polynesian
superbeing .. 5. adaro

mélange ... 4. olio 6. jumble, medley
7. mixture 9. pasticcio 10. miscellany
14. conglomeration

melee ... 3. row 4. fray 5. fight
6. affray 7. contest, diamond (small
cut) 8. skirmish 9. commotion

melicocca ... 5. genip 9. soapberry

melicratum ... 4. mead 8. beverage,
hydromel

melilotus ... 7. clover

meliorate ... 6. soften 7. improve
10. ameliorate

melisma ... 6. melody 7. cadenza

Melissa ... 4. balm 12. Old World mint

mell ... 3. mix 4. maul 5. grain (last
cut), honey 6. beetle, hammer, mallet,
meddle, mingle

mellow ... 4. rich, ripe, soft 5. drunk
6. genial, jovial, mature, tender
7. amiable, matured 9. melodious

melodic ... 6. ariose 7. cadenza, melisma
9. melodious

melodious ... 6. ariose, arioso, dulcet
7. musical, tunable, tuneful
10. harmonious

melodist ... 6. singer 8. composer,
musician 9. harmonist

melodramatic ... 8. dramatic, romantic
11. sensational

melody ... 3. air 4. aria, tune 5. canto,
charm, dirge, melos, music 6. rhythm,
strain 7. harmony, melisma, rosalia
9. cantilena, cantilene 11. tunefulness

melon ... 4. musk, pepo 6. casaba
7. Persian 8. honeydew 9. muskmelon,
red-yellow 10. cantaloupe, paddymelon,
watermelon

melon (pert to) ...
financial .. 4. plum 8. dividend
like .. 5. gourd
pear .. 6. pepino
political .. 5. graft 6. spoils

melongena ... 7. brinjal (brinjaul)
8. eggplant

melos ... 4. song 6. melody

melt ... 4. frit, fuse, thaw 5. smelt,
swale 6. render, soften 7. liquefy
8. diminish, dissolve 9. disappear
12. disintegrate

Melville (pert to) ...
character .. 4. Ahab, Babo 5. Billy (Budd)
6. Cereno (Benito), Delano 7. Ishmael
8. Bartleby, Queequeg, Starbuck
work .. 4. Omoo 5. Typee 6. Pierre
8. Moby Dick

member ... 4. limb, part 5. organ
6. branch, fellow, joiner 7. section
8. belonger, district, enlistee, enroller
9. associate

member (pert to) ...
boy's club .. 3. cub 5. scout
Caliph dynasty .. 6. Omniad
chapter (Eccl) .. 9. capitular
crew .. 4. hand
diplomatic staff .. 6. consul 7. attaché
8. minister 10. ambassador
Jewish brotherhood .. 6. Essene
laity .. 6. layman
literary club .. 9. academist
11. academician
oldest .. 4. dean
regiment .. 8. legioner 9. grenadier,
legionary 11. legionnaire
religious sect .. 5. Amish 6. Quaker,
Shaker
Roman Catholic society .. 6. Jesuit
State .. 7. citizen
swing band .. 6. hepcat 7. swinger

membrane ... 4. caul, skin, tela 5. lemma
6. lamina 8. ectoderm, striffin

membrane (pert to) ...
brain .. 13. meninges mater
diffusion .. 7. osmosis
ear .. 7. eardrum
fold .. 5. plica

optical . . **6.** retina

weblike . . **4.** tela

memento . . . **5.** relic, token **6.** trophy **8.** keepsake, memorial, souvenir **11.** remembrance

Memnon (pert to) . . .

famed statue . . **11.** vocal Memnon

father . . **8.** Tithonus

Greek name . . **8.** Amenhotep

king of . . **8.** Ethiopia

mother . . **3.** Eos (Aurora)

war hero . . **6.** Trojan

memoir . . . **4.** hint, note **5.** éloge, essay **6.** record, report **7.** account, history **9.** biography, narrative, reminding **10.** memorandum **12.** dissertation **13.** autobiography

memorabilia . . . **3.** ana **5.** notes **6.** record **7.** memoirs **8.** memories

memorable . . . **7.** namable, notable **9.** reminding **11.** reminiscent

memorandum . . . **4.** chit, note **5.** diary **6.** minute, record **7.** tickler **8.** protocol, reminder

memoria . . . **4.** tomb **6.** chapel, church, shrine **8.** monument **9.** reliquary

memorial . . . **6.** memoir, memory, record, trophy **8.** mnemonic, monument **10.** memorandum **11.** celebrative, remembrance **12.** recollection **13.** commemorative

memorial mound . . . **5.** cairn (stone), totem (carved)

memory . . . **4.** mind **5.** recall **9.** retention **11.** remembrance **12.** recollection, reminiscence **13.** commemoration

memory (pert to) . . .

aid . . **8.** mnemonic **10.** anamnestic

book . . **5.** diary **9.** scrapbook

jog . . **6.** remind

loss of . . **5.** lethe **7.** amnesia, aphasia (partial) **13.** forgetfulness

term . . **6.** mnesic **8.** mnemonic

Memphis, Egypt (pert to) . . .

deity . . **2.** Ra (Re) **3.** Shu, Tem

dynasty . . **8.** Memphite

god, chief . . **4.** Ptah

men (pert to) . . .

armed body . . **5.** posse

gymnasts . . **8.** acrobats

learned . . **8.** erudites, literati

mechanical . . **6.** robots

of same tongue . . **6.** langue

old . . **7.** gaffers **10.** patriarchs

party of . . **4.** stag **6.** smoker

section, Gr Church . . **6.** andron

single . . **5.** stags **9.** bachelors, celibates

slang . . **6.** blokes

Three Wise . . **4.** Magi (Gaspar, Melchior, Balthazar)

wild . . **7.** savages **9.** cannibals

menace . . . **6.** threat **8.** forebode, threaten **10.** intimidate **11.** fulmination

menacing . . . **7.** ominous **8.** imminent **11.** threatening

menage . . . **4.** club **7.** society **9.** homestead, household, husbandry **10.** management **12.** housekeeping

menagerie . . . **3.** zoo **10.** collection, Tiergarten

menald (said of horses) . . . **8.** speckled

10. variegated

Menaspis . . . **5.** shark (crescent-shaped)

mend . . . **3.** fix, sew **4.** cure, darn, heal, knit **5.** alter, amend, botch, emend, moise, patch **6.** better, cobble, reform, repair **7.** correct, improve **9.** reconcile **10.** ameliorate

mendacious . . . **5.** false, lying **6.** untrue **7.** in error **9.** truthless **10.** fallacious

mendacity . . . **3.** lie **5.** lying **6.** deceit **7.** falsity, fibbery, untruth

mendicant . . . **5.** fakir **6.** beggar **7.** begging

mendicant order . . . **10.** Carmelites, Dominicans **11.** Franciscans **12.** Augustinians

mendole . . . **4.** fish **8.** cackerel

Menelaus' wife . . . **11.** Helen of Troy

menhaden . . . **4.** pogy **7.** sardine **8.** bonyfish **10.** mossbunker

menhir . . . **5.** stone (standing) **8.** monolith

menial . . . **6.** flunky, varlet **7.** servant, servile, serving, slavish

meninges membrane . . . **8.** pia mater **9.** arachnoid, dura mater

meniscus . . . **4.** lens **8.** crescent **12.** crescent moon

Mennonite leader . . . **11.** Menno Simons

Mennonite sect . . . **5.** Amish

meno . . . **4.** less **5.** month (comb form)

menology (Eccl) . . . **8.** calendar, register

Menominee, Menomini . . . **5.** Falls (Wis), river **6.** Indian **9.** whitefish

Menorah . . . **11.** candelabrum (Jew) **12.** organization

mensk . . . **5.** adorn, favor, grace, honor **6.** credit **8.** ornament **9.** reverence **12.** graciousness

mental . . . **7.** phrenic **9.** of the mind, psychotic **11.** intelligent **12.** intellectual

mental (pert to) . . .

alienation . . **8.** insanity

deficiency, deficient . . **5.** ament, idiot, moron **6.** idiocy **8.** imbecile

discipline . . **8.** mathesis

disorder . . **7.** aphasia **8.** insanity, neurosis, paranoia **9.** psychosis **11.** megalomania **12.** hypochondria **13.** forgetfulness, schizophrenia

faculties . . **4.** mind, wits

feeling . . **7.** emotion

image, picture . . **4.** idea **6.** idolus **8.** phantasm **10.** conception

peculiarity . . **12.** idiosyncracy

science, study . . **10.** New Thought, psychiatry

state . . **6.** morale **7.** doldrum (doldrums) **8.** euphoria

strain . . **7.** tension

mentality . . . **4.** mind **5.** sense **6.** acumen, sanity **9.** endowment, intellect **11.** mental power **12.** intelligence

mention . . . **4.** cite, mind, name **5.** refer, speak, trace **6.** denote, notice, record, remark **7.** specify, vestige **8.** citation, indicate **9.** make known, statement **10.** indication

mentor . . . **7.** adviser, teacher, wise man **10.** instructor

mentum . . . **4.** chin

menu . . . **4.** card, list **5.** carte **8.** schedule

10. bill of fare

Mephistopheles ... 5. devil, Faust, Satan

mephitis ... 4. odor 5. skunk, smell 6. stench 7. polecat 10. exhilation (earth)

mercantile ... 5. trade 7. trading 10. commercial, industrial

mercenary ... 4. hack 5. hired, venal 6. sordid 7. Hessian 8. hireling, salaried, vendible

merchandise ... 4. ware 5. goods, wares 7. effects 9. vendibles 10. emporeutic (pert to) 11. commodities 12. stock in trade

merchant ... 5. buyer 6. trader 7. vintner 10. shopkeeper, trafficker 11. storekeeper

merchant (pert to) ...
  group .. 5. guild, hanse 6. cartel
  Indian .. 4. seth
  League .. 9. Hanseatic
  ship .. 6. argosy 8. Indiaman
  wine .. 7. vintner

Merchant of Bagdad ... 7. Sindbad

Merchant of Venice character ... 6. Portia 7. Antonio, Shylock

merci ... 6. thanks

merciful ... 4. kind, mild 6. humane, tender 7. clement, lenient 9. benignant 10. charitable 13. compassionate

merciless ... 5. cruel 8. pitiless 9. unsparing 10. relentless 13. unsympathetic

mercurial (pert to God Mercury) ... 4. fast 5. swift 6. active, clever, fickle 8. metallic 9. saturnine 11. money-making

mercurous chloride ... 7. calomel

mercury ... 5. azoth, guide, metal 7. chibrit, element 9. barometer 11. quicksilver, temperature, thermometer

Mercury (pert to) ...
  astronomy .. 6. planet (smallest)
  god of .. 8. commerce
  Greek name .. 6. Hermes
  staff .. 8. caduceus
  statue, image .. 5. herma
  winged cap .. 7. petasos (petasus)
  winged shoes .. 7. talaria

mercy ... 4. pity, ruth 5. grace 6. blithe, lenity 7. charity 8. clemency, lenience, leniency 9. tolerance 10. compassion, indulgence 11. forbearance

mercy killing ... 10. euthanasia

mercy seat ... 5. bench 11. golden plate (on the Ark), Throne of God 12. judgment seat 13. seat of justice

mere ... 3. sea 4. bare, lake, only, pool, sole, such, wisp 5. bound, limit, sheer, small 6. divide, simple 8. absolute, boundary, landmark, only this

mero ... 6. mother

merely ... 4. also, just, only 5. quite 6. barely, purely, simply, singly, solely 7. utterly 8. entirely, scarcely 9. unmixedly 10. absolutely

mere show ... 4. airs 5. front 8. pretense 9. formality 10. pretension 11. affectation

mere taste ... 3. nip, sip 4. gulp

7. draught

merganser ... 3. nun 4. duck, smee, smew 6. Mergus 7. bec-scie 8. Merginae 9. goosander

merge ... 4. sink 5. blend, unite 6. mingle 7. combine, immerse 8. coalesce 11. consolidate

merger ... 4. pool 5. union 6. cartel, fusion 8. monopoly 10. absorption 12. amalgamation

meridian ... 3. top 4. apex, noon 5. plane 6. midday, summit, zenith 8. latitude, southern 9. celestial 11. culmination 12. highest point

meringue ... 5. icing 8. egg white, frosting

Merino ... 4. wool, yarn 5. sheep

merit ... 4. earn, meed 5. worth 6. desert, reward 7. deserve 10. excellence

merited ... 3. fit 4. just 6. worthy 8. adequate, deserved, suitable 9. warranted

meritorious ... 5. valid 6. worthy 7. merited 9. deserving, honorable 12. praiseworthy

merlin ... 6. falcon

Merlin ... 7. prophet, romance 8. magician

mermaid ... 5. siren 6. merrow 7. Oceanid, swimmer 8. sea nymph 9. sea spirit 14. marine creature

mermaid's hair ... 4. alga

mero ... 4. fish 5. guasa 7. grouper 8. rock hind

merogenesis ... 12. segmentation

meropia ... 9. blindness (partial)

meros ... 5. thigh 6. meropodite

merriment ... 3. fun 4. glee 5. mirth 6. gaiety (gayety) 8. laughter 9. amusement, diversion 11. merrymaking

merrow ... 7. mermaid

merry ... 3. gai, gay 4. glad 5. funny, happy 6. blithe, bonnie, jocose, jovial, joyous 7. comical, festive, gleeful, jocular 8. cheerful, mirthful, sportive 9. favorable, hilarious, sprightly 13. sweet-sounding

merry-andrew ... 4. mime, zany 5. antic, clown, joker 6. jester 7. buffoon 8. merryman

merry-go-round ... 8. carousel (carrousel) 17. revolving platform

merrymaking ... 4. reel 5. momus, revel 7. festive, wassail 9. festivity, merriment 12. conviviality

merrythought ... 8. wishbone

merrytrotter ... 5. swing 6. seesaw

merrywing ... 4. duck 9. goldeneye 10. bufflehead

merse ... 3. dip 5. marsh 6. plunge 7. immerse

merycism ... 7. chewing 10. rumination

mesa ... 5. butte 7. mesilla, oakwood (color), plateau, terrace 9. tableland 14. flat-topped hill

mescal ... 6. cactus, liquor, peyote

mesel ... 5. leper

mesh ... 3. net, web 5. catch 6. areola 7. complex, ensnare, netting, network 10. crisscross 11. interaction

mesial plane ... 5. meson (Zool) 6. median, middle

mesmeric . . . 11. fascinating, hypnotizing 12. irresistible, spellbinding
mesmeric force . . . 2. od
Mesopotamia . . .
  ancient city . . 2. Ur 5. Eridu 7. Babylon, Ninevah
  city . . 5. Basra, Mosul 6. Edessa
  colloquialism . . 6. Mespot
  culture . . 8. Sumerian
  export . . 3. oil
  language . . 6. Arabic
  people (anc) . . 8. Aramaean (Aramean)
  river . . 6. Tigris 9. Euphrates
  wind . . 6. shamal
Mesopotamian . . . 5. Iraqi
Mesozoic era . . . 7. reptile 8. dinosaur 10. evergreens, ganoid fish
mesquin . . . 4. mean 6. shabby, sordid
mesquita . . . 6. mosque
mesquite . . . 5. pacay 7. thicket 8. Prosopis 9. algarroba
mesquite bean flour . . . 6. pinole
mess . . . 4. meal 5. batch, share, spoil 6. bungle, jumble, litter 7. eyesore, failure, mixture 8. disorder 9. confusion 11. predicament 12. kettle of fish
mess (up) . . . 5. botch, spoil 6. muss up 7. clutter, derange, shuffle 10. disarrange
message . . . 4. news, note, wire, word 5. cable 6. brevet, letter, notice 7. epistle, evangel, tidings 8. dispatch, telegram 10. communiqué 13. communication
message medium . . . 5. Ouija
messenger . . . 4. Iris, page, sand, toty 5. angel, envoy 6. herald, nuncio, Revere (Paul) 7. apostle, carrier, courier, prophet, totyman 8. delegate, minister 9. estafette (estafet) 10. forerunner
messenger bird . . . 9. secretary
Messenger of the Gods . . . 6. Hermes (Gr) 7. Mercury (Rom)
Messiah . . . 6. Christ 7. Saviour (Savior) 8. Oratorio (Handel) 9. deliverer
Messina Rock . . . 6. Scylla
messy . . . 5. dirty 6. untidy 7. jumbled 8. slovenly 10. disordered
mestive . . . 8. mournful
mesto . . . 3. sad 7. pensive
met . . . 3. sat 7. equaled, measure 11. measurement (see also *meet*)
metabolism . . . 9. anabolism 10. catabolism 12. assimilation 13. dissimilation, metamorphosis 14. transformation
metacarpus . . . 4. bone
metad . . . 3. rat
metagnomy . . . 10. divination
metagnostic . . . 10. unknowable
metal . . . 3. tin 4. gold, iron, lead, zinc 5. steel 6. cobalt, copper, erbium, nickel, radium, silver, sodium 7. cadmium, calcium, element, gallium, iridium, lithium, mercury, terbium 8. cast iron 9. potassium 11. quicksilver
metal . . . 6. mettle, spirit 8. material 9. substance
metal (pert to) . . .
  bar . . 3. gad 5. ingot
  cake . . 4. slag

casting . . 3. pig
cement . . 6. solder
clippings . . 7. scissil
coarse . . 5. matte
coat . . 6. patina
color . . 9. pearl blue
content . . 3. ory
crude . . 5. matte
deposit . . 4. lode
disc . . 5. paten
dross . . 4. slag
electric . . 6. magnet
filings . . 5. lemel
forging term . . 5. sprue
goldlike . . 6. oroide
impurity . . 7. regulus
layer . . 4. seam, vein 5. stope
lightest . . 7. lithium
lump . . 3. pig 4. slug 6. nugget
patch . . 6. solder
plate . . 4. foil, shim
rare . . 6. erbium 7. iridium, terbium, yttrium 8. platinum
refuse . . 4. slag 5. dross 6. scoria
rock . . 3. ore
science of . . 10. metallurgy
tag . . 5. aglet (aiglet)
test . . 5. assay
tool . . 5. swage 7. stemmer
ware . . 4. tole 6. Revere
worker . . 6. welder 7. riveter 9. goldsmith 11. silversmith
metamerism . . . 12. segmentation (Zool)
metamorphosis . . . 6. change 9. oxidation 10. hydrolysis 12. degeneration, ossification 14. transformation
metaphor . . . 5. trope 6. simile 10. comparison 11. tralalition
metaphysics . . . 5. being 6. nature 8. ontology, theology 9. cosmology 10. psychology
mete . . . 4. dole, give, goal 5. allot, award 7. measure 8. boundary 9. apportion 10. distribute
meteor . . . 5. bolis 6. Bielid, bolide, Leonid, Lyraid 7. Arietid, Perseid 8. fireball 9. Andromede
meteorite (pert to) . . .
  iron . . 10. siderolite
  shower . . 6. Leonid 9. Andromede (Andromedid)
  stony . . 8. aerolite
meteor mark . . . 6. crater
meteorology . . . 9. astronomy 10. atmosphere 11. climatology
meter, metre . . . 5. gauge 6. rhythm 7. cadence, measure 8. measurer
meter (pert to) . . .
  cubic . . 5. stere
  measure . . 5. litre
  millionth . . 6. micron
  prosody . . 4. mora
  square . . 7. centare
  ton . . 5. tonne
  unit term . . 3. are 6. decare 9. decameter, decastere
  weight . . 4. gram
methane . . . 8. paraffin
metheglin . . . 4. mead 8. beverage
mether . . . 3. cup
method . . . 3. way 4. mode, plan, rule

5. means, order, usage 6. course,
manner, system 7. fashion, process
9. procedure 11. arrangement
14. classification
methodic, methodical . . . 6. formal
7. orderly, regular 10. systematic
Methuselah (pert to) . . .
  Bib . . 7. aged man 9. Patriarch
  father . . 5. Enoch
metic . . . 5. alien 7. settler 9. immigrant
meticulous . . . 4. nice, prim 5. fussy
7. careful, fearful, precise 8. exacting
9. selective 10. fastidious, scrupulous
14. discriminating
métier . . . 4. line 7. calling 8. business
10. occupation, profession
metis, metisse . . . 7. mulatto 8. octoroon
9. half-breed
Metis . . . 8. asteroid 9. Zeus's wife
metrical . . . 8. measured, poetical,
rhythmic
metrical composition . . . 4. poem
5. poesy 6. poetry
metrical foot . . . 4. iamb 6. iambus
7. anapest, spondee, trochee
8. choriamb
metrical stress . . . 4. scan 5. arsis, ictus
6. thesis
metronome (Maelzel's) . . . 5. timer
metropolis . . . 4. city, seat, town 6. center
8. district 9. metropole
metropolitan . . . 5. chief, urban 6. bishop,
center 7. leading 9. principal
mettle . . . 5. ardor, honor, nerve, pluck,
spunk, spirit 7. courage 9. fortitude
11. temperament
meuse, muse . . . 3. gap 4. hole 7. opening
8. loophole
Meuse River . . . 4. Maas
mew . . . 3. cob, den 4. cage, cast, coop,
gull, molt, shed 5. miaow, miaul
6. change 7. seagull, stables 8. spicknel
11. concealment, confinement
mewl . . . 3. cry, mew 6. squall 7. whimper
Mexican (pert to) . . . see also *Mexico*
  agave . . 5. datil 6. zapupe 8. henequen
  almond . . 7. malabar
  American . . 6. gringo
  ancient . . 4. Maya 5. Aztec, Nahua
    6. Mixtec, Toltec 7. Zapotec
  antelope . . 9. pronghorn
  asphalt . . 9. chapapote
  bean . . 6. frijol 7. frijole
  bedbug . . 8. conenose
  beverage (alcoholic) . . 6. mescal, pulque
    7. tepache, tequila
  bird . . 6. jacana, towhee 7. jacamar,
    tinamou 8. zopilote
  blanket . . 6. serape
  brigand . . 7. ladrone
  bull . . 6. toro
  cactus . . 6. chaute, mescal
  cape . . 6. serape
  cat . . 6. margay
  cherry tree . . 7. capulin
  cheif . . 4. jefe 12. jefe politico
  cloak . . 6. manta
  cockroach . . 9. cucaracha
  common land (law) . . 6. ejidos
  coral drops (lily) . . 7. Bessera
  cottonwood . . 5. alamo

  dance (solo) . . 8. guaracha
  dish . . 4. taco 5. atole, chili (chile)
    6. tamale 7. burrito 8. frijoles, tortilla
    9. enchilada 13. chili con carne
  dog . . 9. Chihuahua
  dollar . . 4. peso 5. adobe
  dove . . 4. Inca
  drug . . 6. damiana
  elm . . 6. mezcal 8. Ulmaceae
  estate, farm . . 8. hacienda
  fever . . 10. tabardillo
  fish (food) . . 6. salema 7. totuava
  game (card) . . 4. frog
  grass . . 3. mat 5. otate 6. petate
    8. henequen
  herdsman . . 8. ranchero
  hog . . 7. peccary
  hut, house . . 5. jacal
  insect . . 8. turicata
  labor system . . 7. peonage
  landmark . . 5. senal
  masonry . . 5. adobe
  moon god (Aztec) . . 6. Meztli
  mullet . . 4. bobo
  musical instrument . . 6. clarin (anc)
    7. maracas
  Noah . . 6. Coxcox
  onyx . . 6. tecali
  orange . . 7. Choisya
  peasant . . 4. peon
  persimmon . . 7. chapote
  phlox . . 6. cobaea
  plant, shrub . . 4. pita 5. agave, amole,
    datil, istle, sisal, sotol, yucca 6. maguey
    8. ocotillo 10. candlewood, Dasylirion
  rose . . 9. portulaca
  saloon . . 7. cantina
  sandal . . 8. huaracho (huarache)
  sauce . . 7. Tabasco
  scarf . . 6. tapalo
  shawl . . 6. serape
  stirrup . . 7. estribo
  stirrup hood . . 8. tapadera (tapadero)
  sugar . . 7. panocha
  tea . . 6. basote 7. apasote
  thong . . 5. romai
  throwing stick . . 6. atlatl
  tree . . 3. ule 5. alamo, ocote 6. colima,
    poplar 7. capulin 10. cottonwood
  war god . . 7. Mexitli
  yucca . . 6. izote (isote)
Mexican people . . .
  artist . . 6. Orozco, Posada, Rivera
  composer . . Chavez
  conqueror . . 6. Cortés (Cortez)
  dictator . . 4. Díaz 9. Santa Anna
  emperor . . 10. Maximilian
  president . . 6. Huerta, Juárez, Madero
    7. Obregón 8. Cárdenas, Carranza
  revolutionary . . 6. Madero, Zapata
    11. Pancho Villa
  writer . . 3. Paz 6. Azuela 7. Fuentes
Mexican War (1846) . . .
  battle site . . 11. Chapultepec
  general . . 5. Scott (Winfield) 6. Taylor
    (Zachary) 9. Santa Anna (Mex)
  president . . 4. Polk
Mexico . . .
  battleground . . 6. Puebla
  capital . . 10. Mexico City
  city . . 6. Merida, Puebla 7. Durango,

Tampico 8. Mazatlan, Monterey, Vera
Cruz 11. Guadalajara
conqueror . . 6. Cortes (Cortez)
hero . . 6. Juarez 11. Poncho Villa
lake . . 7. Chapala
mountain . . 12. Popocatepetl
peninsula . . 4. Baja 7. Yucatan
people . . 5. Mayas 6. Aztecs 7. Toltecs
10. Cuitlateco
river . . 9. Rio Grande
volcano . . 6. Colima 7. Jorullo, Orizaba
12. Ixtaccihuatl, Popocatepetl
mezzanine . . 8. entresol, low story
miaow, miaou . . . 3. mew
mias . . . 9. orangutan
miasma . . . 4. fume 6. poison 7. malaria,
malodor 9. contagion
mib . . . 7. a marble
mica . . . 4. talc 5. glist 7. biotite 8. chlorite,
silicate 9. damourite, hydromica,
isinglass, muscovite 10. lepidolite
Micah . . . 4. Book (Old Test) 7. prophet
mice . . . 3. Mus 5. voles 7. rodents
miche . . . 5. skulk, sneak 6. lie hid
7. conceal
micher . . . 5. sneak, thief 6. truant
Michigan . . .
capital . . 7. Lansing
city . . 5. Flint 6. Detroit, Lansing 8. Ann
Arbor 9. Marquette
explorer . . 7. Jolliet, Nicolet 9. Marquette
13. Sault Ste Marie
river . . 4. Cass 5. Huron
State admission . . 11. Twenty-sixth
State motto . . 6. Tuebor 11. I Will
Defend
State nickname . . 9. Wolverine
mickey finn . . . 5. drink 8. narcotic
mico . . . 6. monkey 8. marmoset
micraner . . . 3. ant (small)
micro (comb form) . . . 4. moth 5. petty,
small
microbe . . . 4. germ 5. virus 8. organism
9. bacterium 13. microorganism
microcosm . . . 4. body (humerous)
5. world (small) 8. universe
microscopic (pert to) . . .
algae . . 6. amoeba, diatom
anatomy . . 9. histology
size . . 5. small 6. minute 9. very small
13. infinitesimal
microspores . . . 6. pollen
microwave (sl) . . . 4. nuke
Midas (Gr) . . . 13. King of Phrygia
midday . . . 4. noon 7. noonday
8. meridian, noontide
midday nap . . . 6. siesta
middle . . . 5. mesne, midst 6. center,
centry, median, medium, mesial
7. central 8. interior 11. intervening
13. intermediator
middle (pert to) . . .
Age . . 8. Medieval
class . . 9. bourgeois 11. proletarian
comb form . . 3. mes 4. medi, meso
finger . . 6. medius 10. third digit
ground . . 4. mean 7. average 9. mid-
course
man . . 5. agent 6. broker, medium
8. mediator 9. go-between
11. intercessor 12. intermediary

middling . . . 4. fair 6. medium, middle
7. average, between, midland
8. mediocre, moderate, ordinary
10. middle-aged
midge . . . 3. fly 4. gnat 6. midget, punkie
7. minutia
Midi . . . 8. The South (France)
Midian king . . . 3. Evi 4. Reba
Midian priest . . . 6. Jethro
midriff . . . 9. diaphragm
midshipman . . . 5. cadet 6. reefer
8. toadfish
Midsummer Night's Dream (play) . . .
4. Puck, Snug 6. Bottom, Oberon
7. Titania
midwife . . . 4. baba, dhai 6. cummer
(kimmer) 11. accoucheuse
mien . . . 3. air, eye 4. look 5. guise
6. aspect, manner, ostent 7. bearing,
posture 8. behavior, carriage, demeanor
10. appearance, deportment
miff . . . 3. vix 4. tiff 5. anger 6. offend
7. dudgeon, quarrel 9. displease,
sulkiness 10. sullenness
mig . . . 4. duck 7. a marble
might . . . 3. arm 5. force, power 7. ability
8. efficacy, strength 9. greatness
mighty . . . 4. huge, vast, very 6. potent,
strong 7. eminent, violent 8. enormous,
forcible, powerful, puissant 9. extremely
10. omnipotent 11. efficacious
13. authoritative
migniard . . . 6. dainty, minion 7. mincing
8. delicate, mistress
mignon . . . 5. small 6. dainty, petite
7. blue-red 8. delicate, graceful
mignonette (pert to) . . .
color . . 5. green 6. reseda
emblem of . . 6. Saxony
herb . . 6. reseda
tree . . 5. henna
vine . . 7. Madeira, tarweed
migraine . . . 6. megrim 8. headache
10. hemicrania
migrate . . . 4. move, trek 8. resettle,
transfer 12. transmigrate
migration . . . 4. trek 5. exode 6. exodus
7. passage 8. shifting (Chem)
10. relocation
migratory . . . 6. moving, roving
7. nomadic 9. peregrine, wandering
migratory (pert to) . . .
ant . . 6. driver
cell . . 9. leucocyte
thrush . . 5. robin
mihrab . . . 4. slab 5. niche 7. chamber
(mosque)
Mikado . . . 5. dairi, opera, title 9. red-
yellow, sovereign
Mikado character . . . 4. Ko-Ko 6. Yum-
Yum 7. Pooh-Bah
Mikania . . . 7. dogbane, thistle
11. Willugbaeya (Willugheia)
12. Ancylocladus
mike . . . 4. loaf 6. loiter 10. microphone
mil . . . 5. mille 8. thousand
milady . . . 5. woman 6. madame
10. noblewoman 11. gentlewoman
Milan (pert to) . . .
hat . . 5. straw
opera house . . 7. La Scala

point . . 10. bobbin lace 12. point de
Milan
mild . . . 4. calm, kind, meek, soft, warm
5. balmy, bland 6. benign, gentle
7. clement, insipid, lenient 8. benedict,
favonian, gracious, lenitive, moderate,
soothing, tranquil 9. assuasive,
indulgent, temperate 10. mollifying
11. considerate
mild (pert to) . .
attack . . 5. touch (flu)
burn . . 11. first-degree
cheese . . 9. mozzarella
cigar . . 5. claro
illness . . 7. ailment
nausea . . 5. butterflies
oath . . 4. darn, drat, heck 5. shoot
6. shucks
reproof . . 10. admonition
mildew . . . 4. mold, must, rust, smut
6. blight, fungus 8. honeydew
mild expression . . . 9. euphemism
mild offense . . . 6. delict
mile (term) . . . 3. sea 7. statute 8. nautical
9. Admiralty 12. geographical
Miledh . . . 8. ancestor (fabled)
Milesian . . . 4. Celt 8. Irishman
10. Miledh's son
milestone . . . 5. stele 7. waymark
8. landmark, milepost
milfoil . . . 4. herb 6. yarrow
milieu . . . 7. ecology 8. ambience
11. environment 12. surroundings
militant . . . 7. hawkish, warlike 8. battling,
fighting 9. combating, combative
11. contentious
military . . . 7. martial 8. soldiers
military (pert to) . . .
advance . . 8. anabasis
aide . . 7. attaché
base . . 4. camp 5. depot, field 7. billets
8. barracks, firebase, quarters
10. encampment
call . . 6. tattoo 8. reveille
cap . . 4. kepi 5. busby, shako
cap, hat cover . . 8. havelock
cloak . . 5. sagum (anc)
commission . . 6. brevet
defense . . 4. fort 6. abatis
depot . . 4. base
division . . 4. unit 5. corps, squad
7. company, platoon 8. regiment
engine . . 6. onager 7. robinet
expedition to Holy Land . . 7. Crusade
force . . 4. army 5. ranks, troop 6. legion
7. reserve 8. soldiery
guard . . 6. patrol
horsemen . . 7. cavalry, hussars
infraction . . 4. AWOL
inspection . . 5. drill 6. parade, review
instrument . . 5. bugle 7. althorn
landing point . . 9. beachhead
maneuver . . 6. tactic
messenger . . 7. estafet
night attack . . 8. camisade
obstruction . . 6. abatis
officer . . 5. major 7. captain, colonel,
general 8. corporal, sergeant
9. brigadier, subaltern 10. lieutenant
operations . . 8. campaign, strategy
order . . 7. command

organization . . 5. cadre
pit . . 10. trou-de-loup
police . . 2. MP 9. gendarmes
12. constabulary
punishment . . 4. brig 9. strappado
quarters . . 4. camp 7. billets 8. barracks
10. cantonment
salute (artillery) . . 5. salvo
science . . 3. war 7. war game 8. warcraft
9. logistics
service stripes . . 9. hashmarks
signal . . 7. chamade (anc)
staff . . 5. cadre
storehouse . . 5. étape 7. arsenal
supplies . . 8. materiel, ordnance
survey . . 11. reconnoiter
testament, will . . 11. nuncupative
tool (hook-shaped) . . 4. croc (anc)
truck (cannon) . . 6. camion
vehicle . . 4. jeep, tank 6. camion
7. caisson
militate . . . 5. fight 6. debate, rebuff
7. contend 8. conflict

milk . . . 3. lac 5. cream, drain, fluid
6. elicit, suckle 7. despoil, draw out,
exploit, extract 8. beverage
milk (pert to) . . .
beverage . . 4. whig 10. buttermilk
coagulator . . 4. ruen 6. rennet
curd . . 5. zeiga 6. casein
curdled . . 6. yogurt 7. clabber
fermented . . 5. kefir 6. kumiss (koumiss)
7. matzoon
fish . . 3. awa 6. Chanos, sabalo
food (fasting) . . 10. lacticinia
glass . . 7. opaline 8. cryolite
mouse . . 6. spurge
pail . . 5. bowie, eshin
pert to . . 6. lactic 7. lactary, lacteal
product . . 6. cheese, yogurt
sap . . 5. latex
sop . . 5. sissy 11. mollycoddle
sour . . 4. curd, whey, whig 6. blinky
store . . 5. dairy 9. lactarium
strainer . . 6. milsey (milsie)
sugar . . 7. lactose
watery part . . 4. whey
with (milk) . . 6. au lait
milkweed . . . 6. spurge 7. dogbane
10. sow thistle 14. Asclepiadaceae
milkwood . . . 8. Moraceae 9. paperbark
milky . . . 4. mild, tame, weak 5. timid,
white 6. gentle, liquid 7. lacteal
8. emulsion, emulsive, lactesce (to
become), timorous 10. effeminate
Milky Way . . . 6. Galaxy 9. Via Lactea
14. galactic circle
Milky Way black spaces . . . 9. Coalsacks
mill . . . 3. box 4. beat, coin (to) 5. crush,
dress, fight, grind, knurl, quern, shape
6. finish, powder, thrash 7. factory,
machine, serrate 8. arrastra, snuffbox,
vanquish, workshop 9. comminute,
pulverize, transform 10. move around
12. housebreaker
mill (pert to) . . .
beetle . . 9. cockroach
bill . . 3. adz
clapper . . 10. chatterbox
course . . 4. lade 8. millrace, tailrace
end . . 7. remnant

grain .. 5. grist
run of .. 7. average 8. millrace, ordinary
millefleurs ... 7. perfume
millenarian ... 8. chiliast
millennium ... 6. period, utopia
  9. millenary 13. thousand years
millepede ... 6. insect 8. myriapod
millepore ... 5. coral 9. madrepore
miller ... 3. ray 4. moth 5. boxer 7. harrier
  8. pugilist 10. flycatcher
miller's thumb ... 4. bird, fish 7. warbler
  8. titmouse (long-tailed) 9. goldcrest
millesimal ... 10. thousandth
millet ... 4. moha 5. bajra, grass, hirse,
  milly 8. cenchrus 9. broomcorn 10. hirse
  grass 14. non-Moslem group
millimeter ... 6. micron 14. thousandth
  part
millions, one thousand ... 7. billion
millions of millions ... 9. trillions
Mills grenade ... 4. bomb
Milne character ... 6. Eeyore (donkey),
  Piglet, Winnie (the Pooh)
  16. Christopher Robin
milo ... 5. durra 12. grain sorghum
Milvus ... 4. kite
mime ... 3. ape 4. aper, copy 5. actor,
  clown, mimic 6. jester, mummer
  7. buffoon, imitate
mimesis ... 7. mimicry 9. imitation
mimic ... 3. ape 4. aper, copy, mime,
  mimo, mock 5. actor 6. mummer, parrot
  7. buffoon, copying, imitate, mimetic
  8. imitator 9. imitative 11. counterfeit
mimicry ... 5. apery, apism 7. mimesis,
  mockery 8. parrotry
mimic thrush ... 11. mockingbird
Mimidae, Miminae ... 7. catbird
  8. thrasher 11. mockingbird
Mimir ... 5. giant
mimsey ... 4. prim 7. prudish
min ... 5. ruler 6. memory, prince, remind
  8. remember 11. remembrance
Min (Egypt) ... 3. god (procreation)
  5. deity
Minar ... 4. myna 5. Kutab (Delhi), tower
minaret ... 4. lamp 5. tower 10. lighthouse
minaway ... 6. minuet
mince ... 3. cut 4. chop, dice, hash
  5. slash 8. diminish, prim step
  9. subdivide 10. short steps
minced meat ... 7. rissole
minced oath ... 4. drat, egad
minchen ... 3. nun
minchery ... 7. nunnery
minchiate ... 5. tarot
mind ... 4. care, heed, mens, obey,
  reck, tend, will 6. desire, memory,
  psyche 7. opinion 9. intellect, intention
  11. remembrance 12. intelligence
mind (pert to) ...
  development .. 13. psychogenesis
  peace of .. 8. ataraxia, calmness
    16. imperturbability
  picture .. 4. idea 5. image
  reader .. 8. telepath
  set .. 8. attitude
  split .. 13. schizophrenic
Mindanao ...
  language .. 3. Ata
  people .. 3. Ata 4. Moro 5. Lutao

  6. Bagobo, Ilano
  site .. 11. Philippines
  town .. 4. Dapa 5. Davao 9. Zamboanga
  volcano .. 3. Apo 9. Malindany
mindful ... 8. disposed 9. observant,
  regardful 11. remembering
mine (pert to) .. 2. my 3. bal, dig, mio, pit, sap
  4. meum 5. stope 6. cavity, quarry
  7. gallery, passage 10. excavation
  12. entrenchment
mine (pert to) ...
  basket, tub .. 4. corf
  ceiling .. 5. astel
  coal .. 3. rob
  deviation (lode) .. 4. hade
  device (sweeper) .. 3. gad 8. paravane
  entrance, passage .. 4. adit 5. stulm
  excavation .. 5. stope
  floor .. 4. sill
  guardian (Myth) .. 5. gnome
  holes .. 7. gophers
  prop .. 5. sprag, stull
  reservoir .. 4. sump 8. standage
  shack .. 3. doe
  shaft .. 4. sump 6. upcast
  signalman .. 5. cager 7. cageman
  step .. 7. stemple (stempel)
  surface .. 6. placer
  thrower .. 6. minnie 11. minenwerfer
  tunnel .. 5. stulm
  vein .. 4. lode
  waste .. 3. gob 4. goaf
  worker .. 5. cager, miner 8. onsetter
miner (pert to) ...
  disease .. 8. phthisis
  instrument .. 4. dial
  lamp .. 4. davy
  pick .. 3. gad 7. mandrel
  sieve .. 6. dillue
  worm .. 8. hookworm
mineral ... 3. ore, tin 4. alum, iron
  5. pitch 6. barite, egeran, gangue,
  iolite, pinite, quartz 7. apatite, asphalt,
  ataxite, bullion, epidote, felsite, felspar
  8. danalite, edentite, misenite
  9. uraninite
mineral (ore)
  black .. 3. jet 6. cerine, yenite (Elba)
    7. niobite 8. graphite 10. minguetite
  blue-green .. 5. beryl
  brittle .. 7. euclase
  brown .. 6. cerine, egeran, rutile
    9. elaterite
  calcium, plus .. 7. calcite 8. calespar,
    diopside
  crosslike .. 10. staurolite
  dark .. 7. minette
  fibrous .. 8. asbestos (abeston)
  flaky .. 4. mica
  gray white .. 5. trona
  green .. 7. alalite, erinite 9. malachite
  gunpowder .. 7. niter 7. thorite
  hard .. 4. ruby 6. spinel (spinelle)
    7. adamant
  jelly .. 8. vaseline
  jewelry .. 8. diopside
  lustrous .. 4. spar 7. blendes
  magnetic .. 9. lodestone (loadstone)
  nonmetallic .. 5. boron 6. iodine
  plaster of Paris .. 6. gypsum
  rare, brittle .. 7. euclase, thorite

red .. 4. ruby 6. garnet
soft .. 4. talc
waxlike .. 9. ozocerite 11. hatchettine
white, colorless .. 6. barite, gypsum
yellow .. 5. topaz 6. pyrite 7. epidote
mineral (pert to) ...
cavity .. 3. vug (vugg, vugh, voog)
dark spot .. 5. macle
deposit .. 4. lode 6. placer
greasy .. 7. atopite
oil .. 5. colza
pitch .. 7. asphalt
pocket .. 4. nest
salt .. 4. alum
spring .. 3. spa 4. well
tallow, wax .. 9. ozocerite 11. hatchettine
tar .. 6. maltha
water .. 6. lithia 7. Seltzer 8. alkaline
Minerva (pert to) ...
feast .. 11. Quinquatrus
flower, plant .. 6. azalea
goddess of .. 5. civic 6. health
11. handicrafts
shield .. 5. aegis (egis)
temple site .. 9. Aventine (Rome)
ming ... 6. remind 7. mention, recount
8. remember
Ming (Chin) ... 7. dynasty
mingle ... 3. mix 4. fuse, meld 5. admix,
blend, merge, unite 7. combine, concoct
8. coalesce, intermix 9. associate
10. amalgamate 11. consolidate
mingle-mangle ... 6. jumble, medley
7. mixture 9. potpourri 10. hodgepodge,
miscellany
minhag (Jew) ... 6. custom, manner
7. liturgy
miniate ... 5. paint 8. decorate, luminate
9. rubricate
minikin ... 4. type 5. baize 6. dainty
7. elegant, mincing 8. affected, delicate
10. diminutive
minim ... 3. jot 4. drop 5. Order (RCCh)
6. minute 8. smallest 11. small amount
minimize ... 6. reduce 7. detract
8. belittle 9. disparage 10. depreciate
13. underestimate
minimum ... 3. jot 5. least 6. lowest
minion, minionette ... 4. idol, neat
5. lover 6. dainty, pretty 7. darling,
elegant 8. delicate, favorite, ladylove,
mistress, paramour
minister ... 4. tend 5. angel, cater, serve
6. afford, attend, curate, parson, pastor,
priest, supply 7. furnish 8. diplomat,
executor, preacher 9. clergyman,
officiate
ministerial ... 7. serving 9. executive
12. instrumental 14. administrative,
ecclesiastical
minister's home ... 5. manse
9. parsonage
Minnesota ...
capital .. 6. St Paul
city .. 6. Duluth 11. Minneapolis
hero .. 14. Father Hennepin
lake .. 3. Red 10. Minnewaska
land of .. 16. Ten Thousand Lakes
mountain .. 6. Cayuna, Mesabe
9. Vermilion
river .. 3. Red 10. St Lawrence

11. Mississippi
State admission .. 12. Thirty-second
State motto .. 13. L'Etoile du Nord
14. Star of the North
State nickname .. 6. Gopher 9. North
Star
Minoan ... 6. Cretan 7. culture (Prehist)
8. language
minor ... 3. key 4. less, mode 5. friar
(Franciscan), petit, petty, scale, youth
6. course, infant, league, lesser
7. smaller 8. inferior, interval, underage
9. youngling
minority ... 3. few 6. nonage 7. smaller
8. underage 10. immaturity
11. inferiority
Minos (pert to) ...
daughter .. 7. Ariadne
father .. 4. Zeus
king of .. 5. Crete
mother .. 6. Europa
Minotaur (Gr) ... 7. monster (half man,
half bull)
minster ... 6. church 9. monastery
minstrel ... 3. lay 4. bard, poet, show
6. end man, troupe 7. gleeman, goliard
8. jongleur, musician 9. troubador
11. entertainer
minstrel show (pert to) ...
end man .. 5. bones
middleman .. 12. interlocutor
part .. 4. olio
mint ... 3. aim 4. blow, coin, sage 5. basil,
feint, money 6. hyssop, intend, invent,
mentha, ramona 7. attempt, purpose,
venture 8. endeavor 9. fabricate
mint (pert to) ...
charge, levy .. 8. brassage
11. seigniorage
drink .. 5. julep
family .. 5. basil 6. catnip 8. calamint
9. Lamiaceae
genus .. 6. Ramona 7. Melissa
geranium .. 8. costmary
hog .. 8. shilling
sauce .. 5. money
minuet ... 5. dance 7. scherzo
minus ... 4. lack, less 6. absent, bereft,
defect 7. short of, without 8. subtract
10. deficiency
minuscule ... 4. type 5. petty, small
6. letter (lower case) 10. diminutive
minute ... 3. jot, wee 4. mite, note,
tiny 5. draft, petty, small 6. atomic,
little, moment, period, record, slight,
tittle 7. instant 8. atomical, trifling
10. memorandum 11. unimportant
12. sixty seconds 14. circumstantial
minute (pert to) ...
animal .. 10. animalcule
details .. 11. particulars
difference .. 5. shade
glass .. 9. hourglass
Jack .. 10. timeserver
opening .. 4. pore 5. stoma
organism .. 5. monad, spore 8. zoospore
part .. 6. tittle
particle .. 4. atom, iota, mote
record .. 8. protocol
minutely ... 9. continual, unceasing
11. every minute

minutes . . . 4. acta 6. record

minutia . . . 6. detail, minute 11. minor detail, petty matter

minx . . . 4. brat, doll, miss 6. pet dog 7. colleen 8. pert girl 9. saucy girl, saucy jade 13. mischief-maker

minyan . . . 6. quorum 7. pottery

Miohippus . . . 5. horse

miqra . . . 9. Bible text (Heb)

mir (Pers) . . . 4. head 5. chief, title 9. president

miracle . . . 4. feat, play 5. anomy 6. marvel, wonder 10. occurrence, phenomenon 17. supernatural event

miracle drug . . 6. elixir 7. cure-all, panacea

miracle scene . . . 4. Cana

miracle wheat . . . 7. poulard

miracle worker . . . 8. magician 11. thermaturge

miraculous . . . 9. marvelous, wonderful 12. supernatural 13. wonder-working

mirador . . . 5. brown, oriel 6. loggia, turret 7. balcony 9. bay window 10. watchtower

mirage . . . 5. serab 7. chimera, reflect 8. illusion 10. phenomenon

mire . . . 3. bog, mud, wet 4. glar, moil, ooze, slud 5. addle, dirty, marsh, slush, stall 7. sludder

mirror . . . 5. glass 7. crystal, paragon, pattern, reflect 8. exemplar, speculum 9. reflector 11. image worker 12. looking glass

mirror iron . . . 12. spiegeleisen

mirth . . . 3. fun, joy 4. glee 6. gaiety (gayety), levity, spleen 7. delight, jollity 8. gladness, hilarity 9. happiness, merriment, rejoicing 10. joyousness 12. cheerfulness

mirthful . . . 3. gay 5. happy, jolly

miry . . . 4. oozy 5. boggy, muddy, slimy 6. filthy, lutose

mis (comb form) . . . 5. amiss, wrong

misadventure . . . 6. mishap 8. accident, calamity, casualty, disaster 9. mischance 10. misfortune

misandry (opp of misogyny) . . . 12. dislike of man (by woman)

misanthrope . . . 5. cynic, Timon (Shaksp) 8. man hater 9. pessimist 12. mankind hater

misapply . . . 5. misdo 6. misuse 12. misinterpret

misapprehend . . . 7. mistake 8. misapply 11. misconceive 13. misunderstand

misbegotten . . . 8. deformed 12. illegitimate

miscalculate . . . 3. err 8. misjudge 9. misreckon, overshoot

miscall . . . 5. abuse 6. revile 7. misname 9. read amiss 12. mispronounce

miscarriage . . . 5. lapse 6. mishap 7. failure, misdeed, mistake 8. abortion 9. mischance 11. misdemeanor 13. mismanagement 14. premature birth

miscellaneous . . . 5. mixed 6. medley, varied 7. blended, diverse, mingled 8. combined 12. conglomerate 13. heterogeneous 14. indiscriminate

miscellany . . . 6. medley 7. mixture 8. excerpts 9. anthology 10. collection 11. odds and ends

mischance . . . 6. mishap 8. calamity, disaster 10. misfortune 12. misadventure

mischief . . . 3. ill 4. evil, harm 5. wrack 6. damage 7. trouble 9. devilment

mischief (pert to) . . .
   god . . 4. Loki
   goddess . . 3. Ate 4. Eris
   maker . . 8. agitator 12. troublemaker

mischievous . . . 4. arch 6. elfish (elvish), impish 7. harmful, mocking, naughty, parlous, roguish, waggish 8. sportive

misconduct . . . 7. offense 10. wrongdoing 11. delinquency, misbehavior, misdemeanor 13. mismanagement

miscreant . . . 6. rascal, wretch 7. heretic, villain 8. polisson 9. reprobate 10. unbeliever, villainous 11. fallen angel, misbeliever 12. unscrupulous

miscue . . . 3. err 4. miss, slip 5. error 6. bungle 7. mistake

misdeed . . . 5. crime, wrong 7. offense 8. wrongful 11. misdemeanor

misdemeanor . . . 3. sin 4. tort 5. crime 7. misdeed, offense 10. illegality, wrongdoing 11. misbehavior

mise . . . 4. levy 5. grant 6. layout, treaty 8. expenses (law), immunity 9. privilege

miser . . . 5. hunks, Nabal (Bib) 6. nipper, wretch 7. boarder, niggard

miserable . . . 3. sad 6. abject, paltry 7. forlorn, pitiful, unhappy 12. disconsolate, disreputable

misericord, misericorde . . . 4. hall, pity 5. mercy 6. dagger 9. refectory 10. compassion 12. dispensation

miserly . . . 4. mean 5. close, tight 6. stingy 7. chintzy (sl) 8. churlish, covetous 9. niggardly, penurious 10. avaricious 12. parsimonious

misery . . . 3. woe 5. grief 7. anguish, avarice, poverty, sadness 8. calamity, distress 9. heartache, privation 10. affliction, misfortune 11. despondency, Pandora's box, unhappiness 12. covetousness, wretchedness 13. niggardliness

misfeasance . . . 5. wrong 8. trespass 10. wrongdoing

misfortune . . . 3. ill 4. evil, harm 6. mishap 7. bad luck, reverse, setback 8. calamity, disaster 9. adversity, holocaust, mischance 11. catastrophe 12. misadventure

misgiving . . . 5. doubt, qualm 7. anxiety 10. foreboding 12. apprehension

mishap . . . 4. slip 8. accident, casualty 10. misfortune 11. contretemps, miscarriage 12. misadventure

Mishnah, Mishna . . . 4. Moed 5. tenet 6. Nashim 7. Nezikim 8. doctrine, Halakoth, Kodashim, Tohoroth 9. tradition

misinterpret . . . 3. err 4. warp 7. distort, misread 8. misjudge

misjudge . . . 3. err 11. misconstrue 12. miscalculate

misky . . . 5. foggy, misty

mislay . . . 4. lose 8. displace, misplace

misle . . . 4. mist, rain 6. mizzle 7. drizzle

mislead . . . 4. fool 5. blear 6. delude, seduce 7. deceive 8. misguide 9. deception, misbehave, misinform

misleading . . . 5. false 7. crooked 8. illusory 9. deceptive 10. fallacious, fraudulent 12. misinforming 14. misinformation

mislippen . . . 6. delude 7. neglect, suspect 10. disappoint

mismanage . . . 5. blunk, misdo 6. bungle, misuse 9. mishandle

misogynist . . . 8. celibate 10. woman hater

misplace . . . 4. lose 6. mislay, misset 8. displace 9. dislocate, mislocate 11. anachronism

misplay . . . 3. err 5. error 6. renege 7. mismove 9. wrong play

misprise, misprize . . . 5. scorn 6. slight 7. despise, disdain, mistake 8. contempt 9. underrate 10. misprision, undervalue 13. underestimate

misprision . . . 5. scorn 7. mistake 8. contempt, misprize 10. misconduct 11. misdemeanor 12. depreciation 16. misunderstanding

mispronunciation . . . 8. cacology 10. bad diction

misrepresent . . . 5. belie 7. deceive, distort, falsify 8. disserve

miss . . . 2. Ms. 3. err 4. chit, fail, girl, lack, lose, omit, skip 5. evade, lapse, title 7. failure, mistake 8. mistress 9. fall short 10. prostitute 12. mademoiselle

missal . . . 4. book (Eccl) 8. breviary

missel . . . 9. mistletoe

misshapen . . . 4. ugly 8. deformed 9. distorted, monstrous, unshapely

missile . . . 2. MX 4. ICBM, Nike, Thor 5. Atlas, Snark, Titan 6. rocket 7. grenade, matador 8. Redstone 9. Minuteman

missing . . . 3. out 4. gone, lost 6. absent 7. lacking, wanting 8. vanished 11. nonexistent

missing part . . . 3. gap 4. void 5. space 6. hiatus, lacuna 8. omission

mission . . . 3. job 4. body, duty, task 5. Alamo 6. charge, church, errand 7. calling, embassy 8. legation, outreach 10. assignment, commission, delegation, deputation, missionary

missionary . . . 7. apostle 8. emissary, preacher 10. evangelist

Missionary Ridge . . . 11. Chattanooga (Tenn)

Mississippi . . .
capital . . 7. Jackson
city . . 6. Biloxi 7. Natchez 8. Gulfport 9. Vicksburg 13. Pass Christian
explorer, colonizer . . 6. De Soto 9. Iberville
festival . . 9. Mardi gras (Biloxi)
king crop . . 6. cotton
kite (bird) . . 9. everglade
mountain . . 6. Woodal
river . . 5. Yazoo 11. Mississippi
State admission . . 9. Twentieth
State bird . . 11. mockingbird
State flower . . 8. magnolia
State motto . . 14. Virtute et Armis (By Valor and Arms)
State nickname . . 5. Bayou

Mississippian (Geol) . . .
15. Eocarboniferous (system)

Mississippi River head . . . 10. Lake Itasca (Minn)

Mississippi River nickname . . . 10. Great River 14. Father of Waters

missive . . . 4. note 6. billet, letter 7. message, missile 8. document

Missouri . . .
capital . . 13. Jefferson City
city . . 7. Sedalia, St Louis 8. Hannibal, St Joseph
famed native . . 6. Carver (G W), Truman (Pres) 9. Mark Twain 10. Jesse James
gourd . . 11. calabazilla
mountains . . 6. Ozarks
river . . 8. Big Muddy, Missouri 11. Mississippi
skylark . . 13. Sprague's pipit
State admission . . 12. Twenty-fourth
State bird . . 8. bluebird
State flower . . 8. hawthorn
State nickname . . 6. Show Me
sucker (fish) . . 10. black horse

misspelling . . . 10. cacography

misspend . . . 4. lose 5. waste 8. squander 10. spend amiss

misstep . . . 4. slip, trip 7. faux pas

mist . . . 3. dim, fog 4. blur, film, gray, haze, rain, smur 5. bedim, brume, cloud 7. droplet 9. obscurity 11. uncertainty

mistake . . . 3. err 4. bull, goof, slip 5. boner, botch, error, fault, folly 7. blooper, blunder, erratum, violate 8. miscount, solecism 11. anachronism 12. inadvertence 13. misconception 15. misapprehension

mistaken . . . 5. wrong 9. erroneous 12. misconceived 13. misunderstood 14. judging wrongly

mistletoe . . . 6. emblem (Okla), missel, Viscum 9. Loranthus

mistonusk . . . 6. badger

mistreat . . . 5. abuse, wrong 6. ill-use

mistress . . . 4. bibi (beebee) 5. title, woman 6. matron 7. control, teacher 8. Dulcinia, ladylove 9. concubine, governess, patroness 10. proprietor, sweetheart

Mistress of . . .
Adriatic . . 6. Venice
Charles II . . 4. Nell
Seas . . 12. Great Britain
World . . 4. Rome (anc)

misty . . . 3. dim 4. hazy, roky 5. foggy, rouky, vague 6. blurry, cloudy, hoarse 7. obscure, shadowy 10. indistinct 13. unenlightened, unilluminated

misuse . . . 5. abuse 6. revile 7. pervert 8. maltreat, misapply, wrong use 9. misemploy 12. misrepresent

misuse of words in speech . . .
11. heterophemy, malapropism

mite . . . 3. bit, jot 4. atom, coin, mote 5. child, speck 6. acarus, insect 7. bdellid, chigger, smidgen (smidge) 8. acaridan, particle

miter, mitre . . . 4. belt 5. frank, joint, tiara 6. fillet, girdle, gusset, tavern 7. petalon (Eccl) 8. dovetail, headband, insignia 9. headdress

mithridate . . . 8. antidote 9. electuary 12. alexipharmic

mitigate . . . 4. ease, tone 5. abate, allay, mease, relax, remit, slake 6. lessen, reduce, soften, temper 7. appease, mollify, qualify, relieve 8. diminish, lenitive, moderate, palliate 9. alleviate, extenuate, meliorate

mitigation . . . 6. relief 9. abatement 10. diminution, moderation 11. extenuation 13. mollification

mix . . . 3. pug (clay) 4. ease, join, meng, stir 5. addle, blend, cross, knead, unite 6. jumble, mingle, muddle 7. combine, fluster 8. coalesce 9. associate 10. complicate

mixable . . . 8. miscible

mixed (pert to) . . .
bag . . 6. medley 10. assortment, hodgepodge, miscellany
breed . . 7. mongrel
type . . 2. pi
with water . . 6. slaked
with yeast . . 6. barmed, frothy

mixer . . . 5. whisk 6. beater 7. mingler 9. eggbeater, (food) processor

mixture . . . 4. hash, mash, olio 5. blend, chaos, mixed 6. batter, medley, miscue 7. amalgam, mélange 8. compound, solution 9. admixture, potpourri 10. hodgepodge 11. combination, preparation

mixture (pert to) . . .
beverage . . 5. clary 10. shandygaff
cement . . 5. putty
medicinal . . 5. hepar 6. potion 12. prescription
metallic . . 6. speiss
sand and clay . . 4. loam

mix-up . . . 5. melee, snafu 6. muddle, tangle 8. conflict 9. confusion

Mizar . . . 4. Zeta (Great Dipper)

mizmaze . . . 9. confusion 12. bewilderment

mizzenmast . . . 9. aftermast, third mast

mizzle . . . 4. mist, rain 5. misle 6. decamp 9. slink away

mizzy . . . 3. bog 8. quagmire

Mnemosyne (pert to) . . .
ancestor . . 5. Titan
goddess . . 6. memory
mother of . . 8. The Muses

moa . . . 6. ratite (flightless) 8. Dinornis

moab . . . 3. hat (anc)

Moabite (pert to) . . .
dwelling (Bib) . . 7. Dead Sea
language . . 7. Semitic
mountain . . 4. Nebo
people . . 4. Emim
stone (Bib) . . 11. black basalt

moan . . . 3. cry 4. suum, wail 5. groan, sough 6. bemoan, bewail, grieve, lament, suffer 9. complaint 11. lamentation

moat . . . 4. foss (fosse) 5. ditch 6. trench 13. fortification

mob . . . 3. set 4. gang, herd, mass 5. crowd, drove, flock, group, Mafia, taunt 6. clique, rabble, throng 7. company 8. canaille, populace

mobile . . . 7. movable 8. not fixed 9. versatile 10. changeable

Mobile Bay hero . . . 8. Farragut (Adm)

mobile home . . . 3. van 6. camper 7. caravan (Brit), trailer

mob member . . . 6. rioter 7. Mafioso 8. criminal, mobocrat 9. roisterer

mobocracy . . . 7. mob rule

Moby Dick (pert to) . . .
author . . 8. Melville (Herman)
character . . 4. Ahab 7. Ishmael 8. Queequeg, Starbuck
ship . . 6. Pequod

moccasin . . . 3. pac 4. shoe 5. snake 6. Flower (Minn State), orchid 8. larrigan 10. argus brown 11. cottonmouth

moch . . . 4. moth

mocha . . . 4. bark, town (Arab) 6. coffee, dollar 7. leather 9. moss agate

mock . . . 3. ape 4. defy, gibe, jape, jibe, sham 5. feign, fleer, flout, mimic, scoff, sneer, taunt 6. delude, deride 7. imitate, mockery, pretend 8. ridicule 10. disappoint 11. counterfeit

mock (pert to) . . .
brawn . . 10. headcheese
cucumber . . 11. balsam apple
duck . . 4. meat 8. pork chop
hero . . 5. comic
jewelry . . 5. logie, paste 9. imitation
lead, ore . . 10. sphalerite
moon . . 10. paraselene
nightingale . . 7. warbler 8. blackcap
olive . . 9. axbreaker 12. cherry laurel
orange . . 7. syringa (seringa)
plane . . 8. sycamore
sun . . 9. parhelion
turtle . . 9. calf's head

mockage . . . 7. mimicry, mockery 9. imitation

mocker . . . 5. mimic 7. scoffer 8. deceiver 11. mockingbird

mockernut . . . 7. hickory

mockery . . . 5. farce 6. satire 7. mimicry, sarcasm 8. derision 9. imitation 11. counterfeit

mockingbird . . . 5. Mimus

mode . . . 3. fad, way 4. form 5. flair, style, vogue 6. manner, method 7. fashion, variety

mode (pert to) . . .
expression . . 10. vernacular
government . . 6. regime, system
logic . . 7. Ferison (3rd figure)
procedure . . 5. order 6. system
speech . . 8. parlance 11. phraseology
standing . . 4. pose 6. stance 7. posture 8. position

model . . . 3. act 4. form, idea, mold, norm, plan, plat, pose 5. ideal, image, shape 7. example, manikin, measure, paragon, pattern, templet 8. ensample, paradigm, standard, template 9. archetype, mannequin, precedent 11. meritorious 12. reproduction

model (of) . . .
a word . . 8. paradigm

a work .. 9. archetype
excellence .. 7. paragon 8. exemplar
solar system .. 6. orrery 11. planetarium
moderate ... 4. bate, ease, slow, some
5. abate, lower, slake 6. frugal,
lessen, soften, temper 7. control,
lenient, mediate, modesto 8. mediocre,
modulate, slow down 9. temperate
10. reasonable 11. inexpensive
12. conservative 14. inconsiderable
moderation ... 7. control 9. abatement,
restraint 10. diminution, governance,
limitation, mitigation 11. restriction
13. temperateness
moderator ... 5. judge 6. umpire 7. arbiter
8. mediator 10. arbitrator, controller
modern ... 3. neo (pref), new 4. late
6. latter 7. present 8. neoteric
modernize ... 6. update 10. streamline
Modern School of Art ... 4. Dada
7. Dadaism (1920)
modern Syriac script ... 5. serta
8. peshitta
modest ... 3. coy, mim, shy 6. chaste,
demure, humble, seemly 8. reserved,
retiring, virtuous 9. diffident 11. well-
behaved 13. unpretentious
14. inconsiderable
modesty ... 7. decency, reserve, shyness
8. chastity, humility, pudicity
10. diffidence, humbleness 11. self-
control
modicum ... 3. bit 4. drop 5. minim, share
6. little 11. small amount 12. small
portion
modification ... 4. tone 6. change,
umlaut 9. variation 10. adaptation,
alteration, limitation 13. qualification
15. differentiation
modify ... 4. vary 5. alter, limit 6. change,
master, temper 7. assuage, qualify
8. attemper, mitigate, moderate,
quantify 9. influence 13. differentiate
modish ... 4. chic, trim 5. smart 7. in
vogue, stylish 8. vogueish (voguish)
11. fashionable
modiste ... 8. milliner 9. couturier
10. couturière, dressmaker
modulated ... 5. toned 6. merged
7. adapted, attuned, changed, intoned
8. softened, tempered 9. inflected,
regulated
modulation ... 4. tone 6. change
8. shifting 9. tempering 10. alteration,
inflection, moderation
moggan ... 8. stocking 10. knit sleeve
moggy ... 3. cat, cow 4. calf 7. pet name
8. slattern 9. scarecrow
mogo ... 7. hatchet
mogul ... 4. lord 5. nabob 6. tycoon
7. magnate 8. autocrat 9. dignitary
10. locomotive, panjandrum 14. great
personage
Mogul ... 6. Empire, Mongol 7. dynasty
9. Mongolian
Mohammed (pert to) ...
birthplace .. 5. Mecca
daughter .. 6. Fatima
flight to Mecca .. 6. hegira
horse .. 5. Fadda (white mule) 7. Alborak
names .. 7. Mahomet, Mahound

son-in-law .. 3. Ali
Mohammedan (pert to) ...
angel of death .. 6. Azrael
ascetic .. 4. Sufi 5. fakir (fakeer)
8. Marabout
caliph .. 3. Ali 4. Omar 6. Othman 7. Abu
Bekr
chief .. 3. aga (agha) 4. dato (datto)
5. sayid 6. Caliph
crier (for prayer) .. 7. muezzin
crusader's enemy (Muslim) .. 7. Saracen
deity .. 5. Allah 9. Termagant
demon .. 6. afrit, eblis, jinni (jinnee)
7. Shaitan (Sheitan)
Malay (Javanese) .. 6. Sassak
Moslem .. 5. hanif 9. Mussulman
noble .. 4. amir (ameer), emir
nymph .. 5. houri
officer .. 3. aga 5. diwan 6. vizier (vizir)
princess, queen .. 5. begum
saint .. 3. pir 6. santon
scholars, body of .. 5. ulema
sect .. 6. Wahabi (Wahabee, Wahhabi)
student (Theol) .. 5. softa
successor .. 6. Caliph (Calif)
teacher .. 5. mufti 6. mullah (mollah)
Mohammedanism (pert to) ...
Bible, book .. 5. Koran 7. Alcoran
bier, tomb .. 5. tabut
cap .. 3. taj
caravansary .. 6. imaret
crusade .. 5. jihad (jehad)
custom, tradition .. 8. sunnah
divorce .. 5. talak 7. mubarat
dome, over tomb .. 6. turbeh
Easter .. 3. Eed
Fast (annual) .. 7. Ramadan
festival .. 6. Bairam
garment .. 4. izar 6. jubbah
house (men's part) .. 8. selamlik
instrument .. 5. rebab
marriage custom .. 5. iddat
marriage settlement .. 4. mahr
Messiah, priest .. 4. Imam (Imaum)
5. Mahdi
monastery .. 5. ribat
platform, porch .. 7. mastaba
prayer .. 4. azan (adan) 5. namaz
property (law) .. 6. mushaa
religion .. 6. Moslem 8. Islamism
saber .. 8. yataghan (yatagan)
salutation .. 6. salaam (salam)
shrine (Mecca) .. 5. Kaaba (Caaba,
Kaabeh) 10. Black Stone
veil .. 7. yashmak (yashmac)
war (Relig) .. 5. jihad (jehad)
moho ... 4. rail 9. gallinule 10. honey
eater
mohr ... 7. gazelle
molder ... 4. toil 5. crowd, worry
6. wander 7. smother 8. bewilder,
encumber
molety ... 4. half, part (small) 7. portion
moil ... 4. spot, tire, toil 5. labor, taint
6. seethe 7. torment, trouble, turmoil
8. drudgery 9. confusion 10. defilement
molré ... 7. clouded, watered
moist ... 3. wet 4. damp, dank, dewy,
uvid 5. humid, rainy 7. tearful
moisten ... 3. wet 4. hose, moil 5. bedew,
spray 6. anoint, dampen, sparge

8. humidify, sprinkle

moisture . . . 3. dew, fog 5. vapor, water
6. liquid 8. dampness, dankness,
dewdrops, humidity

moisture (pert to) . . .
body . . 6. humors 9. exudation
condensed . . 4. drip, drop
excess, swelling . . 5. edema
expose to . . 3. ret
remove . . 4. wipe 5. wring

mojo . . . 4. Moxo 5. charm (voodoo)
6. amulet 7. majagua

moke . . . 4. dolt, mesh 5. horse 6. donkey
7. network 8. minstrel 9. performer

moki . . 4. raft

moko . . . 9. tattooing

moky . . 5. foggy, misty

molar . . . 5. tooth 6. molary 7. chopper,
grinder 8. grinding

molarimeter . . . 11. thermometer

molasses . . . 5. sirup 7. treacle 8. theriaca

mold, mould . . . 3. die 4. cast, form,
must 5. humus, knead, nowel, plasm,
sprue 6. blight, growth (fungus),
matrix, mildew 7. moulage 9. sculpture
12. reproduction

Moldavia, Rumania . . .
balm . . 4. mint
capital . . 5. Balta 8. Tiraspol
govt . . 9. Socialist

molding . . . 3. ess 4. bead, beak, cyma,
ogee, reed, tori 5. conge, gulla,
ovolo, splay, torus 6. fascia, fillet,
listel, raglet, scotia 7. cavetto, cornice,
reeding, shaping 8. astragal, bezantee
12. reproduction

molding (pert to) . . .
convex . . 5. torus
decoration . . 4. dado
egg and dart . . 9. arrowhead
series . . 7. surbase
suit of . . 8. ledgment (ledgement)

moldy, mouldy . . . 5. fusty, mucid, musty,
stale 8. mildewed

mole (rat) . . . 4. gray 5. fault, nevus
(naevus), shrew, snake, Talpa, taupe
6. rodent 7. blemish, Nesokia
9. birthmark 12. imperfection

molecule . . . 3. ion 4. atom, unit 6. steric
8. particle

molest . . . 4. harm 5. annoy, tease
6. bother, harass, pester 7. disturb
8. mistreat 9. incommode 13. interfere
with

Molière (pert to) . . .
author of . . 5. drama, Miser, plays
6. comedy, satire 8. Tartuffe
11. Misanthrope
character (story) . . 5. Damis 6. Eraste,
Scapin 7. Dorante

mollify . . . 4. calm 5. allay, relax,
sleek 6. pacify, relent, soften, temper
7. appease, lighten, qualify, relieve
9. alleviate 10. conciliate

molitious . . . 8. sensuous 9. luxurious,
softening

mollusk . . . 3. asi 4. clam, pipi, slug,
spat 5. chama, snail, squid, whelk
6. cockle, limpet, mussel, oyster
7. abalone, bivalve, octopus, scallop,
veliger 8. univalve 10. cuttlefish

mollusk . . . 5. Anoma, Chama, Murex
6. Chiton 7. Astarte, Etheria
8. Buccinum, Mollusca, Nautilus

mollusk (pert to) . . .
bait . . 6. limpet
eight-armed . . 7. octopus
freshwater . . 7. etheria
marine . . 7. abalone, scallop 8. nautilus
shell . . 4. test 5. testa 6. cockle, cowrie
(cowry)
shell, without . . 4. slug
shell concretion . . 5. pearl
teeth . . 6. radula
ten-armed . . 5. squid
young . . 4. spat

mollycoddle . . . 6. coddle, pamper
8. weakling 12. spoiled child
13. effeminate boy

Moloch (pert to) . . .
Bible . . 5. deity
doctrine . . 4. evil
zoology . . 6. agamid, lizard

Molotov cocktail . . . 4. bomb

molt, moult . . . 3. mew 4. cast, mute,
shed 7. ecdysis 8. exuviate

molten rock . . . 2. aa

Moluccas, Spice islands . . .
capital . . 7. Amboina
island . . 5. Banda
product . . 5. spice
site . . 9. Indonesia

moly . . . 4. herb (fabled) 6. garlic

momble . . . 6. jumble, tangle

mome (anc) . . . 4. fool 7. buffoon
9. blockhead

moment . . . 4. time 5. avail, flash, nonce,
point, trice, value 7. crisis, minute,
second, weight 7. impetus, instant
9. influence, twinkling 10. importance
11. consequence 13. consideration,
signification

momentary . . . 9. ephemeral, transient
10. transitory 13. instantaneous

momentous . . . 7. weighty 8. eventful
9. important 11. influential
13. authoritative

momo . . . 3. owl

Momus (Gr) . . . 3. god (of ridicule) 6. critic
11. faultfinder

mon . . . 5. badge (imperial) 7. kikumon
13. chrysanthemum

monachal . . . 8. celibate, monastic
9. claustral

monad . . . 3. one 4. atom, unit 5. deity,
monas 8. particle 10. individual
12. Supreme Being

monadnock . . . 4. hill 8. mountain (NH)

Mona Lisa (pert to) . . .
famed for . . 5. smile (subtle)
named also . . 10. La Gioconda
painter . . 7. da Vinci
site (of picture) . . 6. Louvre

monandry . . . 10. one husband (at a
time)

monarch . . . 4. czar, king, shah 5. chief,
queen, ruler 6. dynast, kaiser, sultan
7. czarina, emperor 9. potentate,
sovereign 13. royal highness

monarch . . . 9. butterfly 13. constellation

monastery . . . 5. abbey 6. friary, priory
7. convent, hospice, nunnery 8. cloister

monastery (pert to) . . .
head . . 3. dom 5. abbot
Pavia . . 10. Carthusian
room . . 4. cell
Tibet . . 8. lamasery

monastic . . . 4. monk 5. friar 7. monkish
8. celibate 9. claustral

monde . . . 5. globe, world (fashion)
6. circle (fashion) 7. coterie, société,
society 9. beau monde

monetary . . . 7. coinage 8. currency
9. financial, pecuniary

monetary unit (sl) . . . 3. bob (Brit), fin
4. buck 7. sawbuck, smacker, ten spot
8. simoleon

money . . . 3. wad 4. cash, coin, grig, mina,
pelf 5. frank, funds, lucre, maneh, uhllo
(ullo) 6. mazuma, talent, wampum,
wealth 8. currency 10. spondulics
(spondulix) 11. legal tender

money (pert to) . . .
ancient . . 3. aes
bank (Eur) . . 5. banco
box, chest . . 4. arca, safe, till, tray
5. chest 6. drawer 7. brazier 8. register
changer . . 6. banker, broker, shroff
(saraf), usurer 7. cambist
coinage . . 4. mint
English slang . . 7. ooftish (oof)
found . . 5. trove
gamblers' . . 6. barato
gift . . 4. alms 7. bequest 9. endowment
lender . . 6. banker, usurer 7. Shylock
10. pawnbroker
luck . . 6. barato 7. handsel
maker . . 6. coiner, minter
13. counterfeiter
manual . . 7. cambist
matters . . 6. fiscal 9. economics
of account . . 3. ora
paper . . 4. bill, kale 7. lettuce
pledge . . 5. arles
premium . . 4. agio
roll (coins) . . 7. rouleau
shell . . 5. uhllo (ullo) 6. cowrie (cowry)
slang . . 4. gilt, jack, lour 5. rhino
6. boodle, wampum
spinner . . 6. usurer 10. speculator
substitute . . 5. scrip
to coin . . 4. mint
wildcat . . 9. yellow dog
worthless . . 4. pelf 11. shinplaster

moneyed . . . 4. rich 5. flush 7. opulent,
wealthy 8. affluent, well-to-do
10. prosperous, well-heeled

monger . . . 6. dealer, mercer, trader,
vendor 7. peddler 8. merchant
9. tradesman

mongler . . . 9. sandpiper

Mongol . . . see also *Mongolian* 5. Asian,
Tatar 9. yellow man

Mongolian (pert to) . . .
ass (wild) . . 8. chigetai
capital . . 4. Urga
conjurer . . 6. shaman
conqueror . . 9. Tamerlane
desert . . 4. Gobi
dynasty . . 4. Yuan
monk, priest . . 4. lama
people . . 3. Lai 4. Lapp 5. Ordos
7. Khalkas, Tsakter 9. Ouryantai

religion . . 9. Shamanism, Shintoism
12. Confucianism
river . . 3. Pei 4. Onon

mongoose . . . 4. urva 5. lemur
9. ichneumon

mongrel . . . 3. cur 5. mixed 6. hybrid
10. crossbreed 14. stilt sandpiper

mongrel fish . . . 5. skate (angelfish)
8. tullibee (whitefish)

moniel . . . 3. nun

moniker . . . 4. name 8. nickname

monition . . . 6. advice, notice
7. summons, warning 10. admonition,
dissuasion, intimation 11. forewarning

monitor . . . 4. ship (Civil War), uran
5. varan 6. lizard, manual, mentor,
nozzle 7. adviser, student, warning
8. conenose (bug), director, recorder,
reminder 9. informant

monk . . . 3. fra 4. bede, lama, saki 5. fakir,
friar, padre 6. ferret, monkey 7. ascetic,
caloyer, dervish 8. anchoret, capuchin,
celibate, cenobite 9. anchorite, bullfinch,
touchwood

monkey (pert to) . . .
African . . 4. waag 5. potto 6. grivet,
vernet
American . . 4. saki 5. acari 7. ouakari
8. marmoset 9. beelzebub
bearded . . 8. entellus
bonnet . . 4. zati 5. toque
bread . . 6. baobab
chimpanzee . . 6. nchega
crying . . 4. kaha
cups . . 9. nepenthes 12. pitcher plant
family . . 10. Catarrhina
flower . . 7. mimulus (herb)
genus . . 5. Cebus 6. Ateles 7. Colobus,
Saimiri, Tarsius 8. Alouatta
handsome . . 4. mona
house . . 9. apery
howling . . 4. mono 5. araba 7. stentor
8. alouatte
large . . 5. sajou
Madagascar . . 8. mangabey (mangaby)
organ grinder . . 5. Cebus 8. capuchin
Oriental . . 7. macaque
puzzle . . 5. piñon
small . . 8. marmoset
South American . . 4. titi 6. grison
9. beelzebub
spider . . 7. sapajou
squirrel . . 7. saimiri
tailless . . 3. ape
wrench . . 7. spanner

monk's hood . . . 4. cowl

monkshood . . . 4. atis 7. aconite
9. dandelion

monoceros . . . 4. fish (one-horned)
7. sawfish, Unicorn 9. swordfish
13. Constellation

monochord . . . 7. concord, harmony
9. sonometer 10. clavichord, instrument

monocle . . . 8. eyeglass

monocleid, monocleide . . . 4. desk (one
key) 7. cabinet

monocracy . . . 9. autocracy 13. undivided
rule

Monodelphia . . . 7. mammals 8. Eutheria

monody . . . 3. ode 4. poem (lament),
song 5. dirge 6. melody 9. homophony

monogamy . . . 11. one marriage
monogram . . . 6. cipher, sketch 7. outline
8. initials 9. character
monolith . . . 5. stone 6. menhir, pillar,
statue 8. monument
monologue . . . 6. speech 9. soliloquy
monomachy . . . 4. duel 6. combat
monopoly . . . 5. grant, right, trust
6. corner 7. charter, control 9. privilege,
syndicate 10. possession (exclusive)
monotonous . . . 4. dead, drab, dull
5. drone, thrum 6. dreary, samely
7. humdrum, tedious 8. singsong
9. wearisome 11. repetitious
monotony . . . 6. tedium 8. sameness
9. wearisome 10. sameliness, uniformity
15. repetitiousness
monoxylon, monoxyle . . . 4. boat
5. canoe
monseigneur . . . 5. title 6. My Lord
monster . . . 4. ogre 5. fiend, harpy,
teras 6. dragon, ellops, geryon,
gorgon, sphinx 8. behemoth, Cerberus
11. monstrosity
monster (pert to) . . .
abode (Scot) . . 8. Loch Ness
actor . . 6. Chaney 7. Karloff
classic . . 8. minotaur
comb form . . 6. terato
desert . . 4. Gila
eight-headed . . 6. Scylla
fabled . . 5. harpy 6. kraken, sphinx
7. centaur 9. bucentaur
flame-breathing . . 7. chimera (chimaera)
half man, half bull . . 8. minotaur
headless . . 9. acephalus
like . . 8. teratoid
man-eating . . 4. ogre 5. lamia
medical . . 5. teras
Shelley's . . 12. Frankenstein
three-bodied . . 6. Geryon (slain by
Hercules)
Tokyo's . . 8. Godzilla
twin . . 10. xiphopagus
two-bodied . . 7. disomus
two-headed . . 10. dicephalus,
opodidymus
winged . . 5. harpy
monstrous . . . 4. huge, ugly, vast
5. enorm (anc) 6. absurd, wicked
7. strange, titanic 8. deformed, gigantic,
infamous 9. fantastic, monstrous,
unnatural 10. prodigious, stupendous
12. overpowering, overwhelming
13. extraordinary
Montaigne (pert to) . . .
translator . . 6. Florio
writer of . . 6. essays
Montana . . .
capital . . 6. Helena
city . . 5. Butte 8. Anaconda, Billings
10. Great Falls
Historic site . . 14. Custer Cemetery
lake . . 8. Flathead
mountain . . 7. Rockies 17. Continental
Divide
park . . 7. Glacier 11. Yellowstone
peak . . 7. Granite
reservation (Ind) . . 4. Cree, Crow 5. Sioux
8. Cheyenne, Chippewa 9. Blackfeet
State admission . . 10. Forty-first

State motto . . 13. Gold and Silver
State nickname . . 8. Treasure
montanto . . . 6. rising 10. broadsword
Monte Cristo, Count of (pert to) . . .
author . . 5. Dumas (Alexandre)
hero . . 6. Dantès
Montenegro . . . 10. Yugoslavia
montero . . . 3. cap (hunter's) 6. ranger
8. forester, huntsman, mountain
Montezuma (pert to) . . .
Chief of . . 6. Aztecs
cypress . . 9. ahuehuete
hero of . . 6. Mexico
prisoner of . . 6. Cortez
ruins, site of . . 6. Pueblo
month (pert to) . . .
astronomy . . 5. lunar, solar
half . . 9. fortnight
revolution . . 8. sidereal 9. synodical
term . . 5. epact 6. ultimo 7. proximo
twelfth part . . 8. calendar
monticule . . . 4. cone (volcano) 5. mount
7. hillock 10. prominence (small)
montilla . . . 6. sherry
Montmorency . . . 6. cherry
monture . . . 5. frame, horse (saddle),
mount
monument . . . 4. tomb 5. cairn, stele
(stela), tower, vault 6. bilith, dolmen
7. obelisk 8. cenotaph, cromlech,
monolith 9. sepulcher 10. gravestone
11. commemorate, remembrance
monumental . . . 4. high 5. great
7. mammoth, massive, notable
8. colossal 10. impressive, sculptural,
stupendous
Monumental City . . . 9. Baltimore
moo . . . 3. low (of a cow) 6. lowing
mooch . . . 4. loaf 5. skulk, sneak, steal
6. loiter, pilfer 7. vagrant
moocha . . . 6. girdle 9. loincloth
mood . . . 3. tid 4. tone, vein, whim
5. freak, humor 6. nature 7. caprice
11. disposition
moody . . . 3. sad 4. glum 5. sulky
6. gloomy, sullen 7. pensive
9. whimsical 10. capricious
mool . . . 4. bury, mold, soil 5. earth,
grave 6. mingle 7. crumble
mools . . . 10. chilblains
moon . . . 4. idle, Luna 5. Diana 6. Phoebe,
wander 7. Cynthia 8. crescent 9. satellite
13. celestial body
moon (pert to) . . .
age (first of year) . . 5. epact
area . . 4. mare
Astrol . . 6. Cancer (mansion), planet
autumn . . 7. harvest
beam . . 3. ray 9. pearl blue
bird . . 11. goldencrest
blindness . . 10. nyctalopia
calf . . 4. dolt 7. monster 8. born fool,
imbecile
comb form . . 5. selen
fern . . 8. moonwort
festival . . 8. neomenia
fish . . 4. opah 6. minnow 7. sunfish
9. spadefish
flower . . 10. oxeye daisy
gazing . . 16. absent-mindedness
geographer . . 13. selenographer

god . . 3. Sin 6. Nannar
heraldry . . 6. argent
inhabitant . . 8. Selenite
instrument . . 11. selenoscope
lighter . . 9. serenader 10. moonshiner
  11. night worker
lily . . 10. moonflower
mad . . 7. lunatic
mock . . 10. paraselene
month . . 5. lunar
new . . 6. phasis
phase . . 7. gibbous, horning
picture of . . 11. selenograph
point . . 4. cusp, horn 5. apsis 6. apogee
  7. perigee
position . . 6. octant
raker . . 10. stupid lout 12. woolgatherer
stone . . 3. gem 8. feldspar 10. hecatolite
struck . . 7. lunatic 8. obsessed
Uranus's . . 5. Ariel
valley . . 4. rill (rille) 5. cleft
moon goddess . . .
  Greek . . 6. Hecate, Phoebe 7. Artemis,
  Cynthia
  Italian . . 5. Diana
  Phoenician . . 6. Tanith (Tanit) 7. Astarte
  Roman . . 3. Dea 5. Virgo 9. Caelestis
moonish . . . 7. flighty 10. capricious
moonshine . . . 6. empty 6. liquor, poteen,
  whisky (whiskey) 7. bootleg 8. egg
  sauce, nonsense 10. balsamweed
moony . . 5. round 6. dreamy
  9. moonlight 10. abstracted
  14. crescent-shaped
moor . . . 3. bog, fen 4. hill, root 5. heath,
  marsh, swale 6. anchor, fasten, secure
  9. fix firmly
Moor . . . 6. Berber, Moslem 7. Moorman,
  Othello (Shaksp), Saracen 8. goldfish
  (black), Moroccan
moor (pert to) . . .
  berry . . 9. cranberry
  bird . . 6. grouse
  blackbird . . 5. ouzel
  buzzard . . 5. harpy 7. harrier
  cock . . 5. blackcock
  dance . . 7. morisco
  grass . . 5. heath 6. sundew
  hen . . 4. coot 9. gallinule
  monkey . . 7. macaque
  stone . . 7. granite
Moorish . . . 6. Moslem 8. Moresque
Moorish (pert to) . . .
  garment . . 5. jupon
  horse . . 4. barb (Barbary)
  judge . . 4. cadi
  kettledrum . . 5. tabor 6. atabal
  Order . . 7. Alcazar 8. Alhambra
  9. horseshoe, Saracenic
  palace . . 7. Alcazar
moose . . . 3. elk 4. alce 5. eland 7. society
  (Loyal Order)
moose bird . . . 9. Canada jay
moot . . . 4. pose 5. argue, plead, speak
  6. debate 7. discuss, propose
mop . . . 4. swab, wipe 5. scrub 6. merkin
  7. drink up, grimace 9. blindfold,
  implement
mope . . 5. sulk 6. dumps, idler 6. grieve
moppet . . . 3. tot 4. baby, doll, tike
  7. darling, toddler 9. youngster

mora . . . 4. tree (Trinidad) 5. delay,
  stool 7. default 8. syllable 9. footstool
  11. Spartan army 12. postponement
moral . . . 4. good, pure 5. maxim 6. lesson
  7. epimyth, ethical, upright, virtual
  8. likeness, virtuous 9. righteous
moral (pert to) . . .
  excellence . . 6. virtue
  fault . . 4. vice
  law . . 9. Decalogue
  obligation . . 4. duty
  poem . . 3. dit
  principle . . 7. precept
  story . . 5. fable 7. parable 8. apologue
morale . . . 4. hope, zeal 6. morals, spirit
  8. morality 10. confidence
moralist . . . 4. prig 7. teacher 9. moralizer
  10. sermonizer
morality . . . 6. amoral, ethics, virtue
  13. righteousness
morals . . 8. morality 10. ethography
morass . . . 3. bog, fen 4. moor 5. marsh,
  swamp 6. slough 8. quagmire
  9. everglade
moratorium . . . 5. delay 10. suspension
Moravia, capital . . . 5. Brünn (Brno)
Moravian . . . 9. Christian 10. Herrnhuter
  13. Unitas Fratrum 19. Church of the
  Brethren
moray . . . 3. eel 6. hamlet 7. Muraena
  8. food fish 10. Muraenidae
morbid . . . 4. sick 6. gloomy 7. ghastly,
  unsound 8. diseased 9. unhealthy
  11. unwholesome
morbid (pert to) . . .
  appetite . . 10. adephagous
  complex . . 11. inferiority
  condition . . 8. ochlesis
  desire for music . . 9. melomania
  displacement . . 7. ectopia
morbus . . . 7. disease, illness
morceau . . . 3. bit (Mus) 6. morsel
mordant . . . 4. acid, keen 6. biting
  7. burning, caustic, pungent 8. scathing
  9. corrosive, sarcastic 11. acrimonious
more . . . 3. yea 4. also, mair, plus, some
  5. again, extra 6. plural 7. greater
  10. additional 13. approximately
more (pert to) . . .
  cunning . . 5. slyer 6. tricky
  difficult . . 6. harder
  distant . . 8. ulterior
  mature . . 5. older, riper
  miserly . . 6. closer, meaner, nearer
  not any . . 4. dead, past 8. vanished
  11. nonexistent
  or less . . 4. some 8. somewhat
  13. approximately
  over . . 3. and 4. also, else 7. besides,
  further, thereto
  precious . . 6. dearer
  relative . . 11. comparative
  severe . . 7. sterner
  so . . 3. yea
  than . . 4. over 5. above 6. beyond
  9. exceeding 10. in excess of
  than enough . . 3. too
  than one . . 4. many 6. plural 7. several
  than this . . 3. yes
  unusual . . 5. rarer
  vapid . . 6. staler

morel ... 6. fungus 8. mushroom
morello ... 4. ruru 6. cherry 7. boobook 8. morepork, mulberry (color)
morena ... 8. brunette
mores ... 7. customs, manners 9. etiquette 11. conventions
Moreton Bay ... 9. Australia
Morgan ... 5. horse 10. sea dweller
morganatic marriage ... 10. left-handed (royal)
morgay ... 7. dogfish
morglay ... 5. sword
morgue ... 8. mortuary 9. deadhouse, stolidity 11. haughtiness, impassivity
Morgue (The) ... 17. Library of Congress
moribund ... 4. sick 5. dying 9. near death
moriform ... 14. mulberry-shaped
morindin dye ... 2. al
morion ... 6. helmet, quartz 8. cabasset
Mormon Church (pert to) ...
Band (Polit) .. 6. Danite (1837)
cricket .. 11. grasshopper
emblem .. 3. bee
Indian .. 8. Lamanite
instrument .. 4. Urim 7. Thummin
officer .. 5. Elder
official name .. 36. Church of Jesus Christ of Latter Day Saints
patriarch .. 11. Joseph Smith 12. Brigham Young
prophet .. 6. Moroni
State .. 4. Utah
tea plant .. 7. Brigham
tree .. 11. black poplar
morning (pert to) ...
clouds .. 4. velo
coat .. 7. cutaway
concert .. 6. aubade
glory .. 3. nil 7. ipomoea 14. Convolvulaceae
goddess .. 3. Eos
performance .. 7. matinee
prayer .. 5. matin
reception .. 5. levee
star .. 4. Mars 5. Venus 6. Saturn 7. Daystar, Jupiter, Lucifer, Mercury 8. Phosphor
term .. 2. AM 4. dawn 5. matin, wight 6. Aurora 7. sunrise 9. matutinal
moro ... 5. finch
moro (comb form) ... 6. stupid
Moro ... 6. Muslim
Morocco ...
capital .. 5. Rabat
city .. 3. Fez 5. Tangier 9. Marrakech (Marrakesh) 10. Casablanca
color .. 3. red
enclave .. 4. Ifni
famed site .. 5. Casba
hat .. 3. fez
island .. 7. Madeira
Jewish quarter .. 2. El Millah
language .. 6. Arabic
leather imitation .. 4. roan
military expedition .. 5. harka
millet .. 12. Johnson grass
mountains .. 5. Atlas
people .. 4. Arab, Moor 6. Berber
plateau .. 6. mesata
ruler .. 4. king 5. malek 6. sultan

soldier .. 5. askar
morology ... 5. folly 8. nonsense
moron ... 4. dull 5. ament, idiot, zombi 6. nitwit, stupid 8. imbecile, sluggish 12. stupid person
morose ... 4. blue, dour, glum, grum, sour 5. moody, surly 6. crusty, gloomy, sullen 7. crabbed, unhappy 9. splenetic 10. embittered
Morpheus (Gr) ... 10. god of Sleep 11. god of Dreams
morphine ... 6. heroin 8. hypnotic 9. analgesic, calmative
morphology ... 7. anatomy 8. cytology 9. histology 10. embryology 12. organography
morris ... 4. game 5. chair, dance
morro ... 4. hill 6. Castle (Havana) 7. hillock 11. point of land
Mors (Rom) ... 5. Death, deity
Morse ... 4. code, lamp 8. alphabet
morsel ... 3. ort 4. bite, chip 5. piece, scran (sl), scrap, snack 6. tidbit, titbit 7. morceau 8. delicacy, fragment 11. small amount
mort ... 4. dead, lard 5. death, fatal 6. deadly, grease, salmon 9. abundance
mortacious ... 4. very 9. extremely
mortal ... 5. fatal, human 6. deadly, lethal 10. perishable
mortally ... 5. amort 6. deadly 7. à la mort, deathly, fatally 9. extremely 10. grievously
mortar ... 3. rab 4. bowl 5. putty 6. cannon 7. mortier 10. night light (Hist)
mortarboard ... 3. cap (Acad)
mortgage ... 4. bond, pawn 6. pledge
mortician ... 8. embalmer 10. undertaker 15. funeral director
mortification ... 5. decay, shame 7. chagrin 8. gangrene, vexation 11. humiliation
mortify ... 5. abase, abash, abuse, shame, spite 6. ashame, deaden, humble 7. chagrin 9. embarrass, humiliate
mortis causa ... 15. by reason of death
mortise, mortice ... 6. cavity, insert 8. amortize 10. foundation
mortuary ... 5. gift (burial) 6. morgue 7. funeral 8. funereal 9. deadhouse, sepulcher 10. cinerarium 12. corsepresent (offering, Hist)
mosaic ... 5. virus 6. design 7. ceramic, picture 10. decoration, variegated 11. tessellated
mosaic (pert to) ...
apply .. 7. incrust
gold .. 6. ormolu
law .. 5. Torah (Moses)
piece .. 7. tessera
Moscow ...
capital of .. 6. Russia
citadel .. 7. Kremlin
river .. 6. Moskva
shrine .. 9. Lenin Tomb, Red Square
Third Internat .. 9. Comintern
Moselle ... 4. Saar, wine 5. river, Ruwer 9. Rhine wine
Moses (pert to) ...
Bible .. 7. prophet 8. lawgiver

brother.. 5. Aaron
emissary.. 5. Caleb
father.. 5. Amram
father-in-law.. 6. Jethro
law.. 5. Torah (Tora) 10. Pentateuch
mother.. 8. Jochebed
mountain.. 4. Nebo
sister.. 6. Miriam
successor.. 6. Joshua
wife.. 8. Zipporah
mosey... 6. depart, stroll 7. shuffle
Moslem... see *Muslim*
mosque... 4. Omar 5. Kaaba (Caaba)
    6. masjid 11. Great Mosque
mosque tower... 7. minaret
mosque warden... 5. nazir
mosquito (pert to)...
bite preventive.. 10. culicifuge
coast.. 8. Honduras 9. Nicaragua
comb form.. 6. culici
destroyer.. 8. culicide
disease.. 7. malaria 11. yellow fever
family.. 9. Culicidae
fish.. 8. gambusia
genus.. 5. Aedes, Culex 7. Diptera
    8. Mansonia 9. Anopheles, Culicidae
    10. Psorophora
hawk.. 9. dragonfly, nighthawk
Indian drink.. 6. mushla
larvae.. 8. wigglers
plant.. 4. mint 10. pennyroyal
shaped.. 10. culiciform
term.. 7. culicid 11. gallinipper
moss... 3. bog, rag 4. agar 5. Maium,
    money, Musci, swamp 6. lichen, morass
    7. skeeter 8. agar-agar 9. treebeard
moss (pert to)...
back.. 4. dodo, fogy (fogey) 9. old turtle
    10. fuddy-duddy, Southerner (1861)
    12. conservative
berry.. 9. cranberry
capsule.. 9. operculum
color.. 5. green
coral.. 8. bryozoan
duck.. 7. mallard 8. moss-head
    9. merganser
fish.. 8. menhaden 10. mossbunker
grown.. 10. antiquated
kind.. 4. peat 7. Spanish
like.. 6. mnioid
mossy... 4. dull 5. boggy, downy
    6. marshy, stupid 9. crumbling
most... 7. highest, maximum 8. greatest,
    main part, majority 9. nearly all
most favorable... 7. optimum
Most High... 3. God 12. Supreme Being
most northerly land... 5. Thule
mot... 5. adage, maxim, motto 7. opinion
    9. witticism
mote... 4. atom, hill, iota 5. match,
    speck, squib 6. barrow, height, trifle
    7. tumulus 8. eminence, particle
mote nut... 5. carap
motet... 4. hymn 6. anthem, choral
moth... 2. io 5. egger, tinea 6. lappet,
    miller 7. noctuid, Tineina 8. forester
    (8-spotted), Tineidae 9. Tineoidea
    11. Lepidoptera
moth (pert to)...
hawk.. 10. goatsucker
kind.. 5. gypsy 6. carpet 9. browntail

spot (Med).. 8. chloasma
spot (wing).. 8. fenestra
mother... 2. ma 3. dam 4. amma
    5. adopt, mamma, mater 6. abbess,
    parent 7. care for, creator 8. ancestor,
    begetter, genetrix, producer
    10. procreator
mother (pert to)...
church.. 9. cathedral 16. Christian
    Science
goddess.. 6. matris 7. Shaktis 10. sapta-
    matri (7 mothers)
goddess of motherhood (Egypt).. 4. Isis
godmother.. 4. Rhea 6. cummer
    (kimmer) 9. Brigantia
Goose character.. 5. Simon, Sprat
    6. Bo-peep
Govt.. 10. matriarchy, metrocracy
house.. 7. convent 9. monastery
Hubbard.. 4. gown 5. dress
lode.. 3. ore
Maid.. 10. Virgin Mary
Mother Carey's chickens.. 7. petrels
    (stormy)
Myth (Gr).. 5. Niobe
related.. 6. enatic
spiritual.. 4. amma
Tagalog.. 3. Ina
motherly... 8. maternal
mother of...
Castor.. 4. Leda
gods.. 4. Rhea 9. Brigantia
Graces.. 5. Aegle
Nature.. 6. Cybele
Night.. 3. Nox, Nyx
pearl.. 5. nacre 7. abalone
presidents.. 8. Virginia
States.. 8. Virginia
the month.. 4. Moon
motif... 5. theme, topic 6. edging
    7. subject
motion... 3. bob 4. lipe, move 5. impel,
    trend 6. seesaw, travel, tremor, unrest
    7. gesture, propose, request, suggest
    8. kinetics, mobility, movement, petition
motionless... 5. inert, rigid, still 6. static
    8. immobile, stagnant 10. stationary,
    stock-still
motion picture terms... 4. film,
    show 5. flick, klieg (light), movie,
    rerun 6. cinema 7. cartoon, feature
    9. filmstrip, videotape 11. golden oldie
    12. silver screen
motivate... 4. move 5. force, impel
    6. compel, incite, induce, propel
    7. actuate, animate, promote, trigger
    9. stimulate
motive... 4. sake, spur 5. cause,
    motif, topic 6. reason 7. pretext
    8. stimulus 9. incentive, influence,
    intention 10. incitement, inducement
    11. instigation 13. consideration
motley... 5. mixed 6. fabric 7. diverse,
    mixture, mottled 9. checkered, diversity
    10. variegated 12. parti-colored
    13. heterogeneous
motor... 5. mover, rotor 6. Diesel,
    dynamo, engine 7. turbine 8. motor
    car 9. locomotor 10. automobile
motor speed control... 8. governor,
    rheocrat

mottled ... 3. roe 4. pied 5. pinto 6. calico
   7. dappled, marbled, piebald, spotted
   13. pepper-and-salt
mottled soap ... 7. castile
motto ... 3. mot 5. adage, axiom, gnome,
   maxim 6. advice 7. empresa (impresa),
   precept 8. aphorism 9. principle
   11. inscription
motto of ...
   Boy Scouts .. 10. Be Prepared
   Coast Guard .. 11. Always Ready
   13. Semper paratus
   Order of the Garter .. 20. Honi soit qui
   mal y pense
   Queen Elizabeth .. 11. Semper Eadem
   13. Always the Same
mouche ... 5. patch (black)
mouchoir ... 12. handkerchief
mouflon, moufflon ... 5. sheep
mould, mold ... 5. knead 6. matrix
moulrush ... 7. pollack (food fish)
mound ... 3. dam, dun, tee 4. bank, dene,
   doon, dune, heap, hill, terp, tomb,
   tump 5. knoll 6. bounds 7. barrier,
   bulwark, rampart, tumulus 8. boundary
   9. elevation 10. embankment
   13. fortification
mound (pert to) ...
   bird .. 8. megapode
   City .. 7. St Louis
   lily .. 5. yucca
   memorial .. 5. cairn
   of light .. 8. Kohinoor (diamond)
   Polynesian .. 3. ahu
   prehistoric .. 5. matte
   Scottish .. 5. toman
mount ... 3. fly, set (jewel) 4. glue, hill,
   lift, pony (polo) rise 5. arise, climb,
   horse, paste, steed 6. ascent 7. elevate
   8. increase, mountain 10. promontory
Mount (pert to) ...
   Etna city .. 7. Catania
   Everest peak .. 6. Lhotse
   Parnassus fountain, spring .. 8. Castalia
   S Dakota .. 8. Rushmore
mountain ...
   Africa .. 11. Kilimanjaro
   Alaska .. 8. McKinley
   Asia .. 7. Everest 9. Himalayas
   Babylonia .. 6. Ararat
   California .. 6. Shasta 7. Whitney
   Crete .. 3. Ida
   Europe .. 4. Ural 8. Pyrenees
   fabled .. 4. Meru
   Greek (Myth) .. 7. Helicon
   Japan .. 8. Fujiyama
   legendary .. 3. Kaf, Qaf (Muslim) 4. Meru
   Mexico .. 12. Popocatepetl
   Montana .. 6. Tetons
   South America .. 5. Andes
   Switzerland .. 4. Alps 10. Matterhorn
   Thessaly .. 4. Ossa 6. Pelion
   U S Chain .. 5. Rocky 7. Sawback,
   Sierras 9. Blue Ridge 11. Appalachian
   Yukon .. 5. Logan
mountain (pert to) ...
   ash .. 5. rowan
   badger .. 6. marmot
   balsam .. 3. fit
   banana .. 3. fei
   barometer .. 8. orometer

   beaver .. 8. sewellel
   blackbird .. 5. ouzel
   cat .. 4. lynx 6. bobcat, cougar
   10. cacomistle
   comb form .. 3. oro
   cowslip .. 8. auricula
   crest, spur .. 5. arête
   curassow (pheasant) .. 10. oreophasis
   defile .. 3. gap 4. gate, ghat (ghaut),
   pass 5. gorge
   depression .. 3. col
   dew .. 6. whisky
   eagle .. 6. golden
   goat .. 4. ibex
   highest .. 7. Everest
   ice .. 4. berg 7. glacier
   ivy .. 6. laurel
   lake .. 4. tarn
   lion .. 4. puma 6. cougar
   lodge .. 4. gite
   low .. 5. butte
   nymph .. 5. oread
   oak .. 8. chestnut
   peak .. 3. tor
   raspberry .. 10. cloudberry
   rose .. 6. laurel
   sheep .. 7. bighorn 13. Rocky Mountain
   shrub .. 10. fetterbush
   sickness .. 7. soroche
   State .. 7. Montana
   sunset .. 9. alpenglow
   Tatars .. 5. Tauli
   witch .. 9. quail dove
mountaineer ... 7. climber 11. backsettler
mountains, science of ... 7. orology
   9. orography
mountant ... 6. raised, rising 8. mounting
   9. ascendant
mountebank ... 4. gull 5. cheat, quack
   7. buffoon, empiric 8. impostor
   9. charlatan, pretender 11. quack doctor
mounted men ... 7. knights
mounting ... 6. ascent 7. rimbase,
   seating, setting 9. adjusting, equipment
   13. embellishment
mourn ... 3. rue 4. erme, long, sigh,
   wail, weep 6. bemoan, bewail, grieve,
   lament, murmur, repine, sorrow
   7. deplore
mourner ... 6. keener, wailer 7. griever
   8. lamenter
mournful ... 3. sad 6. repine 7. elegiac
   8. grievous 9. elegiacal, plaintive,
   saddening, sorrowful, threnodic,
   woebegone
mournful poem ... 5. elegy
mourning ... 3. sad 4. garb 5. crape,
   weeds (dress) 6. lament, sorrow
   7. drapery 9. sorrowing 10. black badge
   11. lamentation
mourning dress ... 5. weeds 6. sables
mouse ... 3. erd, Mus 4. buck, vole
   5. prowl, shrew 6. jerboa, migale
   7. harvest, toy with
mouse (pert to) ...
   bird .. 4. coly 6. shrike
   color .. 4. gray
   deer .. 7. plandok 10. chevrotain
   ear .. 8. hawkweed 9. bloodwort,
   chickweed 11. forget-me-not
   fish .. 9. sargassum

hare.. 4. pika
hound.. 6. weasel
kind.. 6. pocket 7. harvest, jumping
leaping.. 6. jerboa
milk.. 6. spurge
mouselike.. 6. murine
web.. 6. cobweb, phlegm 8. gossamer
mousse... 7. dessert 9. moss green
  12. gelatine dish
moutan... 5. peony
mouth... 2. os 3. mow, mun 4. boca,
  dupe, lade, lick 5. inlet, stoma 6. cavity,
  rictus 7. declaim, opening, orifice
  8. aperture, lorriker 9. impudence
mouth (pert to)...
away from.. 6. aboral
deformity.. 7. harelip
disease.. 6. canker 10. stomatitis
furnace.. 5. bocca
glands.. 8. salivary
muscle.. 7. caninus
organ.. 4. harp 7. Pandean 8. jew's-harp
  9. crembalum, harmonica
part.. 3. lip 5. uvula 6. palate 7. pharynx
pert to.. 4. oral 6. rictal, stomal
  8. stomatic
piece (Mus).. 10. embouchure
through the.. 7. peroral
tissue.. 3. gum
toward.. 4. orad
wide, gaping.. 6. rictus
mouthed, loud... 11. thersitical
mouton... 5. sheep 9. prison spy
movable... 6. mobile 10. changeable
  12. transferable
movable property... 8. chattels
move... 3. act, gee, mog, say 4. goad,
  sell, spur, stir 5. budge, cause,
  impel, rouse, shift 6. excite, incite,
  induce, kindle, motion, prompt, travel
  7. actuate, advance, animate, propose,
  provoke 9. instigate, recommend,
  stimulate
move (pert to)...
about.. 8. locomote
along.. 5. mosey, scram 7. maunder
back.. 3. ebb 6. recede, retire, revert
  7. retreat 10. retrogress
back and forth.. 6. teeter, wigwag
  7. shuttle 9. oscillate
clumsily.. 4. joll
false.. 4. balk 5. feint
forward.. 4. edge, scud 5. drive
  7. advance 8. progress
furtively.. 5. slink, sneak
heavily.. 3. lug 6. fidget, lumber, trudge
in circles.. 4. purl
place to place.. 7. migrate 8. emigrate
quickly.. 3. ply 4. dart, dash, scud,
  shot 5. scoot, spank 6. bustle, gallop,
  hurtle
restlessly.. 6. kelter
rhythmically.. 5. dance
sideways, sidewise.. 4. slue 5. sidle
slowly.. 3. jog, lag 4. edge, inch, pant
smoothly.. 4. slip 5. glide, skate, slide
spasmodically.. 6. twitch
to and fro.. 3. wag 4. flap, sway
together.. 5. unite 8. converge
towards each other.. 8. converge
towards the east.. 9. orientate

unsteadily.. 4. reel 6. wabble 7. stagger
up and down.. 3. bob 6. teeter
with exertion.. 5. heave
with measured tread.. 5. march
moved by entreaty... 8. exorable
moved easily... 5. loped 6. mobile
  8. affected 9. emotional
movement... 5. cause, trend 6. action,
  motion, rhythm, travel 7. emotion,
  gesture, impulse 8. activity, maneuver,
  progress
movement (pert to)...
backwards.. 13. retrogression
dance step.. 4. lilt 6. chassé 9. pirouette
music.. 4. moto 7. con moto
of ships.. 5. heave, pitch, scend
of waves.. 4. roll, toss 5. surge
  6. tumble, welter
vibratory.. 6. tremor
moving... 6. active, motile 7. nomadic
  8. eloquent, exciting, pathetic
  9. affecting, impelling, traveling
  10. motivating
moving stairway... 9. escalator
mow... 3. cut, lay, mew 4. dess, fell,
  heap, mass, math, mock, raze, stow
  5. mouth, stack 6. garner, smooth
  7. cut down, grimace, harvest, shorten
  9. cornfield
mowana... 6. baobab
mowing... 7. cutting, mockery 8. derision
  9. grimacing 10. harvesting,
  meadowland
mowing machine... 5. mower 6. scythe,
  sickle
moxieberry... 9. snowberry
moy... 4. mild 6. demure, gentle
  8. affected
moyen... 3. way 5. means 6. agency,
  course 8. property 9. influence
Mozambique...
Bay.. 8. Mossuril
capital.. 15. Lourenco Marques
native.. 3. Yao
port.. 10. Mozambique
mozo... 10. manservant
Mrs... 5. madam 8. goodwife, Mistress
mucaro... 3. owl
much... 3. lot 4. high, many 5. great
  7. greatly 8. abundant, uncommon
  9. great deal 10. indefinite
  12. considerable
muchacha... 4. girl, lass
muchacho... 3. boy, lad 7. servant
mucid... 5. musty, slimy 6. clammy,
  mucous 8. muculent
mucilage... 3. gum 5. paste 6. mucago
  8. adhesive 9. lubricant
mucilaginous... 5. moist 6. sticky, viscid
muckender... 12. handkerchief
mucker... 4. fall (from a horse),
  mess 6. muddle, wretch 8. disorder
  9. confusion, vulgarian
muckle... 4. club, fret 5. bother, putter
muckraker... 7. defamer 8. vilifier
  9. slanderer
mud... 4. mire, muck, silt, slop 5. abuse,
  gumbo, limus, shine 6. gobbet, sludge
  12. offscourings 14. abusive charges
mud (pert to)...
bath.. 10. illutation

dab . . 8. flounder
dauber . . 4. wasp
devil . . 10. hellbender
eel . . 5. siren
hole . . 6. puddle 8. quagmire
lark . . 5. gamin, horse 6. magpie, urchin
like . . 7. luteous
living in . . 10. limicolous
peep . . 9. sandpiper 11. meadow pipit
pike . . 5. saury
puppy . . 10. hellbender, salamander
rake . . 5. cleut
shoveler . . 13. spoonbill duck
snipe . . 8. woodcock
sunfish . . 4. bass 8. warmouth
teal . . 9. greenwing
volcano . . 5. salse

Mudcat State . . 11. Mississippi
muddle . . 3. mix 4. daze, mess, soss,
    stir 5. addle, botch, snafu 6. bemuse,
    bollix, jumble 7. confuse, perplex,
    stupefy 8. befuddle, bewilder, confound,
    disorder, squander 10. intoxicate
    11. predicament
muddled . . 3. ree 5. drunk, muzzy,
    tipsy 7. burbled, fuddled 8. confused
    9. befuddled, entangled
muddlehead . . 5. dolt 9. blockhead
muddy . . 4. base, miry 5. dingy, dirty,
    roily, slaky 6. lutose, opaque, slushy,
    turbid 7. clouded, obscure 8. confused
    9. besmeared
muddy places . . 7. wallows
muezzin . . 4. azan (adan) 5. crier
    (Muslim)
muff . . 5. beard, cover 6. bungle
    7. bungler, failure 8. feathers
    11. mollycoddle, whitethroat
muffed . . 5. vexed 7. crested 9. irritated
muffet . . 11. whitethroat
muffetee . . 7. muffler 8. wristlet
muffin . . 3. cob, gem 5. bread, hazel,
    plate, scone 7. biscuit, crumpet, English,
    popover
muffle . . 3. gag 4. damp, dull, mute,
    wrap 6. deaden, mumble, shroud,
    stifle 7. conceal 8. decorate, envelope
    9. blindfold, soft-pedal
muffler . . 3. gag 4. mute 5. scarf
    6. muzzle, tippet 8. silencer
    10. suppressor
mufflin . . 8. titmouse
mufti . . 5. dress (civilian)
mufti (Muslim) . . 4. alim 5. judge
    6. priest 8. assessor, official
mug . . 3. cup 4. cram, dupe, face, fool,
    Toby 5. mungo, pulse, sheep, study
    6. noggin 7. drizzle, grimace 8. quantity
    10. photograph
muga . . 4. moth, silk 11. caterpillar
mugger . . 3. goa 6. robber, tinker
    7. peddler 9. crocodile
mugget . . 8. woodruff 15. lily of the
    valley
muggins (game) . . 5. cards 7. penalty
    8. dominoes
muggy . . 4. damp, warm 5. humid,
    moist, moldy 6. sticky, stuffy, sultry
    10. sweltering 11. whitethroat
mug house . . 6. tavern 7. barroom
    8. alehouse, pothouse

mugient . . 6. lowing 9. bellowing
mugwump . . 5. chief 8. apostate,
    objector 11. independent, nonpartisan
    16. Republican bolter
Muhammed . . see *Mohammed*
muir . . 4. wall
muirfowl . . 9. red grouse
muishond . . 5. zorii 6. weasel
mujer . . 4. wife 5. woman
mulberry . . 2. al 5. Morus 6. murrey
    10. blackberry 12. thimbleberry
mulberry (pert to) . . .
    bark (paper) . . 4. tapa (tappa)
    beverage . . 5. morat
    bird . . 8. starling
    dye . . 3. aal 8. morindin
    fig . . 8. sycamore
    purple . . 7. blue-red 8. camerier
    tree . . 5. Morus
    wild . . 7. yawweed
mulch . . 5. straw 6. ground, leaves
    7. sawdust
mulct . . 4. fine, scot 6. amerce, defect,
    punish 7. blemish, deceive, penalty,
    swindle 10. amercement
mulcter . . 7. amercer
mule . . 4. mewi, mool, mute 5. coble,
    hinny, jenny 6. acemia, hybrid
    7. slipper, tractor 9. chilblain
    10. crossbreed, locomotive 15. obstinate
    person
mule (pert to) . . .
    chair . . 7. cacolet
    driver . . 7. skinner 8. muleteer
    drove . . 5. atajo
    killer . . 8. mantis
    leading . . 8. cencerro
    skinner . . 6. driver
    untrained . . 9. shavetail
muleteer . . 4. peon 6. driver
mulga . . 6. acacia, shield
muliebria . . 8. feminine
muliebriety . . 9. womanhood
    10. femininity 11. womanliness
muller . . 4. wife 5. woman 6. mother
mulish . . 6. hybrid, sullen 7. asinine,
    sterile 8. stubborn 9. obstinate
mull . . 3. cow 4. crag, dust, heat,
    mess, mold 5. crush, grind, snout,
    spice 6. fumble, muddle, muslin,
    muzzle, ponder 7. failure, rubbish,
    squeeze, steatin, sweeten 8. cogitate,
    consider, ointment, ruminate, snuffbox
    9. pulverize 10. promontory
    11. contemplate
mullah . . 6. priest 7. teacher (Muslim)
mullet . . 4. bobo, fish, star 6. puffin
mullet hawk . . 6. osprey
mulligan . . 4. stew
mulligatawny . . 4. soup
mulligrubs . . 5. blues, colic, sulks
mullock . . 5. spoil, waste 6. refuse
    (mine) 7. rubbish
mulloway . . 7. jewfish
multi (comb form) . . 4. many
multifarious . . 8. manifold 9. multifold,
    multiplex 10. multiphase
multifold . . 7. diverse 8. manifold,
    multiple, numerous
multilingual . . 8. polyglot
multiped . . 10. many-footed

multiplier . . . 6. bulbil 7. facient
8. operator
multiply . . . 5. breed 6. spread 7. amplify,
magnify 8. increase 9. calculate,
pluralize, procreate
multitude . . . 3. mob 4. host, many,
mass, much 5. crowd, horde, shoal,
swarm 6. legion, throng 7. myriads
8. populace 9. profusion 11. bourgeoisie
12. numerousness
multitudinous . . . 6. myriad
mum . . . 3. ale 4. mute 6. silent 8. taciturn
11. not speaking
mumble . . . 4. chew, mump 6. chavel,
fumble, mutter, patter
mumbo jumbo . . . 6. genius 7. bugaboo
12. superstition 13. awesome person
mummer . . . 5. actor 6. guiser 7. buffoon
9. performer
mummy . . . 5. brown, Congo (color), relic
6. corpse, mother 7. cadaver, carcass
mummy apple . . . 6. papaya
mump . . . 3. beg 5. cheat, sulks
6. mumble, sponge 7. deceive, grimace
10. impose upon
mumpish . . . 4. dull, glum 5. sulky
6. sullen
mumruffin . . . 8. titmouse
mundane . . . 6. cosmic 7. earthly, horizon,
secular, terrene, worldly 8. temporal
11. unspiritual
mundatory . . . 9. cleansing 11. purificator
mundil . . . 6. turban (embroidered)
mungo . . . 4. herb, wool (reclaimed)
8. mongoose, mung bean
13. mongoose plant
municipal . . . 5. civic, urban 7. oppidan
9. political 10. municipium
munificence . . . 6. bounty 7. largess
(largesse) 10. generosity, liberality
13. bounteousness, unselfishness
muniment . . . 6. record 7. defense
8. evidence, writings 9. valuables
10. furnishing 13. fortification
munity . . . see *immunity* 9. privilege
munshi (Hind) . . . 6. writer 7. teacher
9. secretary 11. interpreter
muntjac, muntjak . . . 5. kakar, ratwa
6. kidang
mura (Jap) . . . 7. village 9. community
Mura . . . 6. Indian
mural . . . 4. wall (pert to) 5. crown
8. painting
murder . . . 4. kill, slay 7. carnage
8. homicide 9. slaughter 11. assassinate
12. manslaughter
murder of . . .
brother . . 10. fratricide
father . . 9. patricide
king . . 8. regicide
mother . . 9. matricide
own child . . 9. prolicide
parent . . 9. parricide
prophet . . 8. vaticide
sister . . 10. sororicide
spouse (by the other) . . 10. mariticide
wife . . 9. uxoricide
woman . . 8. femicide
murderous . . . 4. gory 5. cruel 6. bloody,
deadly, savage 7. killing 10. sanguinary
12. bloodthirsty

mure . . . 4. meek, soft, wall 6. gentle,
immure, modest 8. imprison
murk, mirk . . . 3. fog 4. dark, mist
5. gloom 6. opaque 7. blacken
8. darkness 9. dark color 11. dark-
colored
murky, mirky . . . 4. dark 5. dense,
foggy, thick 6. gloomy, opaque
7. obscure, stained 11. dark-colored
12. impenetrable
murmur . . . 3. coo, hum 4. blow, curr,
fret, purl 6. babble, mutter, repine
7. trickle, whisper 9. complain
muscle . . . 4. beef, thew 5. brawn, sinew,
teres 6. flexor, lacert, tensor 8. lacertus,
retentor
muscle (pert to) . . .
affection . . 5. crick 6. ataxia
bending . . 6. flexor
chemistry . . 6. inosic 8. inosinic
chest . . 8. pectoral
column . . 10. sarcostyle
contracting . . 7. agonist
expander . . 7. dilator
extending . . 8. extensor
eyeball . . 6. rectus
lifting . . 7. levator
loin, tenderloin . . 5. psoas
lower . . 9. depressor
raising . . 7. deltoid, erector, levator
recording . . 8. ergogram 9. ergograph
round . . 5. teres
segment . . 8. myocomma
sense . . 11. kinesthesia
separating . . 11. divaricator
spasm . . 5. cramp, tonus 12. charley
horse
stretching . . 6. tensor
sugar . . 8. inositol
thigh . . 10. quadriceps
trapezius . . 10. cucullaris
triangular . . 7. deltoid
turning . . 7. evertor, rotator
two-headed . . 6. biceps
muscovite . . . 4. mica 11. yellow-green
Muscovite . . . 7. Russian
muscular . . . 4. wiry 5. beefy, thewy
6. brawny, mighty, sinewy, strong,
torose 8. athletic, stalwart, vigorous
muscular (pert to) . . .
contraction (involuntary) . . 3. tic 5. spasm
co-ordination . . 7. synergy
in-co-ordination . . 6. ataxia 15. locomotor
ataxia
non-co-ordination in walking . . 6. abasia
spasm . . 5. tonus
stomach . . 7. gizzard
muse . . . 4. mull, poet, rune 5. dream
6. ponder 7. bagpipe, reverie 8. cogitate,
consider, meditate, ruminate
Muse of . . .
astronomy . . 6. Urania
choral song . . 11. Terpsichore
comedy . . 6. Thalia
dancing . . 11. Terpsichore
eloquence . . 8. Calliope
history . . 4. Clio
joy . . 4. Tara
music . . 7. Euterpe
poetry . . 5. Erato (lyric) 6. Thalia (bucolic)
8. Calliope (heroic)

tragedy . . 9. Melpomene
Muses . . . 4. Clio 5. Erato 6. Thalia,
  Urania 7. Euterpe 8. Calliope, Polymnia
  (Polyhymnia) 9. Melpomene
  11. Terpsichore
Muses (pert to) . . .
  epithet . . 7. Pierian
  fountain . . 8. Aganippe (near Thebes)
  mother of . . 9. Mnemosyne
  mountain . . 6. Pierus 7. Helicon
    9. Parnassus
  number . . 4. nine
  sacred place . . 5. Aonia (Boeotia)
  spring . . 7. Pierian
  The Muses (Gr) . . 8. Pierides
musette . . 3. air, bag 4. oboe 7. bagpipe,
  gavotte
museum, famed . . .
  Florence . . 6. Uffizi
  London . . 4. Tate 14. Madame Tussaud's
  Madrid . . 5. Prado
  New York . . 4. MOMA 10. Guggenheim
    12. Metropolitan
  Oxford . . 9. Ashmolean
  Paris . . 6. Louvre
  St Petersburg (Russia) . . 9. Hermitage
  Washington, DC . . 9. Hirshhorn
    11. Smithsonian
museum keeper . . 7. curator
    9. custodian
mush . . . 3. cut 4. call, face, pulp 5. atole,
  march (over snow), notch 6. cereal,
  indent, sepawn 8. flattery, umbrella
  12. hasty pudding 14. sentimentality
mushroom . . . 5. morel, plant 6. agaric,
  anchor, fungus 7. parvenu, upstart
  8. umbrella 11. beaver brown
mushroom (pert to) . . .
  circle . . 9. fairy ring
  disease . . 5. flock
  edible . . 5. morel 11. chanterelle
  poisoning . . 8. mycetism
  poisonous . . 7. amanita 9. toadstool
  stem . . 5. stipe
  umbrella top . . 6. pileus
music (pert to) . . .
  abridgment . . 7. ridotto
  accompaniment . . 9. obbligato
  aftersong . . 5. epode
  all voices . . 5. tutti
  as written . . 3. sta
  chapel . . 9. a cappella
  character . . 3. bar, key 4. clef, rest, slur
    5. cleft, neume, segno
  chord . . 8. arpeggio
  clear-cut . . 8. staccato
  closing measure . . 4. coda
  comic . . 6. bouffe
  do . . 2. ut
  drama . . 5. opera
  duet . . 3. duo
  encore . . 3. bis
  flourish . . 7. cadenza
  half note . . 5. minim
  half tone . . 8. semitone
  impassioned, emotional . .
    12. appassionato
  interlude . . 6. verset
  interval . . 6. octave 7. tritone
  introduction . . 7. prelude
  it proceeds . . 2. va

knowledge . . 10. musicology
lead cue . . 5. presa
left-handed . . 8. sinistra
light notes . . 6. ottava
low pitch . . 5. grave
lutelike . . 10. hurdy-gurdy
major . . 3. dur
major third . . 6. ditone
melodious . . 6. arioso
melody . . 5. melos
nine-piece composition . . 5. nonet
one performer (choral) . . 4. soli
opera (comic) . . 6. bouffe
organization . . 4. band 5. Ascap, choir
    6. chorus 8. symphony 9. orchestra
organ stop . . 6. dulcet, tromba 7. celesta
pause . . 4. rest
performance . . 7. recital
phrase . . 9. leitmotiv (leitmotif)
pick . . 8. plectrum
pitch C . . 2. du
pompous . . 7. orotund
refrain . . 5. epode 8. repetend
repetition . . 5. rondo
scale . . 5. gamut
sestet . . 7. sestuor
sextuplet . . 7. sestole (sestolet)
soprano part . . 5. canto
speaking part . . 8. parlando
study . . 5. étude
tenor part . . 5. canto (original)
theme . . 4. tema
third . . 6. tierce
three-chord note . . 5. triad
thrice . . 3. ter
time . . 4. temp 6. giusto
timing device . . 9. metronome
twice . . 3. bis
variations, set of . . 7. partita
whimsical . . 8. bizzarro 9. capriccio
musical direction (pert to) . . .
  accented . . 8. sforzato 9. sforzando
  bold . . 6. audace
  brisk . . 5. tanto 7. animato
  detached . . 8. spiccato, staccato
  dying away . . 7. calendo
  emphatic . . 7. marcato
  evenly . . 10. egualmente
  fantastic . . 11. carpiccioso
  fast . . 4. vivo 5. tosto 6. presto, vivace
    10. tostamente
  faster . . 7. stretto
  fluctuating . . 6. rubato
  gay . . 7. giocoso 10. brilliante
  gentle . . 5. dolce
  half . . 5. mezzo
  held firmly . . 6. tenuto
  high . . 3. alt
  hurried . . 7. agitato
  less . . 4. meno
  let it stand . . 3. sta
  lightly . . 10. con agilita
  little by little . . 9. poco a poco
  lively . . 6. vivace 7. allegro, animato
  loud . . 5. forte 10. fortissimo
  louder . . 9. crescendo
  lutelike . . 10. hurdy-gurdy
  more rapid . . 7. stretto (stretta)
  movement (with) . . 7. con moto
  muted . . 5. sorda, sordo
  narrating . . 8. narrante

one by one . . 7. uno a uno
quick . . 6. presto
quickening . . 11. affrettando
quicker than . . 7. andante 9. andantino
repeat . . 3. bis 6. da capo 7. ripresa
sadly . . 7. dolente 8. doloroso
shake . . 5. trill
silent . . 5. tacet
sliding . . 9. glissando
slow . . 5. largo, lento, molto, tardo
  6. adagio 7. andante
slow (very) . . 5. molto
slowing . . 9. allentando 10. ritardando
  11. rallentando
smooth . . 6. legato
soft . . 5. dolce, piano
softer . . 10. diminuendo
spirited . . 7. con moto
strict tempo . . 6. giusto
sustained . . 6. tenuto 9. sustenuto
tenderly . . 10. affettuoso, con affetto
turn . . 5. verte 9. gruppetto
vivacious . . 7. con brio

musical form . . . 3. jig, ode, pop, rap
  4. aria, folk, jazz, jive, olio, opus, punk
  (rock), scat, song, soul 5. derry, dirge,
  disco, elegy, fugue, melos, motet,
  opera, salsa 6. arioso, ballad, fusion,
  hip-hop, medley, melody, minuet,
  New Age, reggae, sonata 7. ragtime,
  toccata 8. carillon (bells), hornpipe,
  operetta, oratorio, serenade, symphony
  9. barcarole, bluegrass, interlude,
  polonaise 10. heavy metal, rockabilly
  11. rock and roll 12. boogie woogie
musical instruments . . . 3. sax 4. asor,
  drum, fife, harp, horn, lute, lyre,
  oboe, pipe, reed, tuba, viol 5. banjo,
  bugle, cello, Dobro, flute, organ, piano,
  rebec (rebeck), rocta, tabor, vibes,
  viola 6. atabal, cither, citole, cornet,
  fiddle, guitar, spinet, tabret, violin,
  zither 7. althorn, bagpipe, bandore,
  bassoon, celesta, clarion, clavier,
  gittern, helicon, marimba, musette,
  ocarina, pandora, piccolo, theorbo,
  timpani (tympani), trumpet, ukulele
  8. castanet, clarinet, dulcimer, keyboard,
  mandolin, trombone 9. flageolet,
  saxophone 10. concertina, pianoforte,
  sousaphone (tuba), tambourine
  11. harpsichord, synthesizer, violoncello
musical instruments (foreign) . . .
Africa . . 5. nanga 7. kalimba (thumb
  piano), sistrum
China . . 3. kin
E Indies . . 4. bina
Egypt . . 7. sistrum
Greece . . 7. cithara (anc)
Hindu . . 4. vina (anc)
India . . 5. ruana
Italy . . 6. tromba
Japan . . 7. samisen (shamisen)
  10. shakuhachi
Java . . 8. gamelang (gamelan)
Mexico . . 6. clarin 7. maracas
Spain . . 6. atabal 7. castanets
musician . . 4. bard 5. piper 6. hepcat,
  lyrist, singer 7. chorist, crooner,
  drummer, fiddler, flutist, harpist,
  pianist, reedman, yodeler 8. bandsman,

composer, minstrel, organist
  9. conductor, serenader, troubador,
  violinist 10. prima donna, trombonist
  11. clarinetist, keyboardist, minnesinger,
  saxophonist 12. interlocutor
  13. Kapellmeister, percussionist
musicians' group . . . 4. band, duet, trio
  5. nonet 6. septet, sextet 7. nonetto,
  quartet 8. ensemble, septette, sextette,
  symphony 9. orchestra, quartette
musicians' patron saint . . . 7. Cecilia
musk . . . 4. deer 7. perfume
musk (pert to) . . .
beaver . . 7. muskrat
cat . . 5. civet
cattle . . 4. oxen
cucumber . . 11. cassabanana
deer . . 10. chevrotain
duck . . 7. Muscovy
hog . . 7. peccary
melon . . 10. cantaloupe
okra . . 8. abelmosk
shrew . . 6. desman
weasel . . 5. civet
muskellunge . . . 4. fish, pike
musket . . . 4. hawk 5. rifle 7. firearm
  9. flintlock
Musketeers, Three . . . 5. Athos 6. Aramis
  7. Porthos 9. D'Artagnon
muskmelon . . . 6. atimon, casaba
  10. cantaloupe
muskrat . . . 5. shrew 6. desman 7. ondatra
Muslim . . . 5. Hanif, Islam, Salar
  7. Saracen 9. Mussulman
  10. Mohammedan
Muslim (pert to) . . .
ablution . . 4. wudu (widu, wuzu)
cap . . 3. fez, taj
capturer of Jerusalem . . 4. Omar
caste . . 5. mopla (moplah)
chief . . 4. dato (datto), rais
city (holy) . . 5. Mecca
college, school . . 8. madrasah (madrasa,
  madrasseh)
dagger . . 7. khanjar
deity . . 5. Allah, Eblis
devil . . 5. Eblis
devotee . . 6. santon 7. dervish
Easter . . 3. Eed
guide (spiritual) . . 3. pir
interpreter . . 5. ulema
invocation . . 9. bismillah
javelin . . 6. jereed
judge . . 4. cadi
lawyer . . 5. mufti
market, booth . . 4. sook
monastery . . 5. ribat 7. khankah
mosque . . 6. masjid
noble . . 4. amir (ameer), emir
officer . . 5. dewan (diwan)
people . . 4. Moro
pilgrimage to Mecca . . 4. hadj
prayer . . 4. azan (adan)
priest . . 4. imam (imaum)
saint . . 3. pir 6. santon 8. Marabout
sect . . 6. Senusi (Senousi, Senussite)
shrine, Mecca . . 5. Kaaba (Caaba,
  Kaabeh)
teacher . . 4. Alim 8. mujtahid
title . . 3. Sid 5. Sayid (Said)
tradition . . 7. Al Sirat (Bridge to Paradise)

Turkish .. 5. Salar
university .. 8. madrasah (madrasa)
viceroy .. 7. Saracen
muslin ... 3. ban, cap 4. mull 5. doria,
shela 6. canvas, gurrah 7. organdy
8. nainsook, sheeting, tarlatan
muss ... 4. mess, soil 5. chaos, dirty
6. bitter, muddle, rumple, tousle
7. confuse, wrinkle 8. dishevel,
scramble, squabble 10. disarrange
mussel ... 4. food, naid, unio 5. horse,
moule, naiad 6. byssus, mucket, nerita
7. mollusk, Mytilus
Musselman ... 6. Moslem 7. Saracen
10. Mohammedan
must ... 4. mold, musk, sapa, stum
5. juice, ought, shall 6. blight,
mildew, refuse 7. malodor 9. necessity
10. obligation
mustang ... 5. horse, pinto 6. bronco,
sphinx
mustard ... 5. nigra, senvy 7. sinapis
8. charlock
mustard (pert to) ...
chemistry .. 8. sinapine
gas .. 7. yperite
genus .. 7. Sinapis 8. Brassica
plaster .. 8. sinapism
Mustelidae ... 5. minks 7. badgers,
martens, weasels
muster ... 4. levy 5. erect 6. gather,
summon 7. collect, marshal
8. assemble, comprise 10. assemblage
muster out ... 7. disband
musty ... 3. bad, old 4. damp, hoar,
rank 5. fetid, fusty, moist, moldy, rafty,
stale, trite 6. rancid 7. pungent
mutable ... 6. fickle 7. erratic 8. variable
9. alterable, changeful
mute ... 3. mum 4. dumb, lene, surd
6. muffle, silent 8. deadener, silencer,
taciturn 9. voiceless 10. speechless
mutilate ... 3. mar 4. geld, hack, maim
6. deface, deform, garble, injure,
mangle 7. cripple, destroy 8. castrate
9. dismember, tear apart
mutinous ... 6. unruly 9. seditious,
turbulent 10. rebellious, refractory
11. intractable
mutiny ... 6. Putsch (Swiss), revolt,
strife, tumult 9. commotion, rebellion
12. insurrection 15. insubordination
mutter ... 5. growl 6. murmur, patter,
plaint 7. grumble, maunder 8. complain
9. mussitate
mutton ... 4. meat 5. cabob (kabob),
gigot, sheep 6. candle
muttonfish ... 4. sama 5. pargo
7. abalone, eelpout, mojarra, snapper
mutual ... 4. plan 5. joint 6. common
8. intimate 9. symbiotic 10. reciprocal,
responsive 15. interchangeable
mutual understanding ... 9. agreement,
unanimity 12. consentience, coordination 13. interrelation
17. interrelationship
mux ... 4. mess 5. batch
muy ... 4. very 7. greatly
muzhik, muzjik ... 7. peasant
muzzle ... 3. gag 4. cope, maul, nose
5. mouth, snout 6. clevis, thrash

7. shackle, sheathe, silence 8. restrain
10. respirator
my ... 3. mes, mon 4. mine 7. due to
me 11. exclamation
myall ... 4. wild, wood (fragrant) 6. acacia
11. uncivilized
Myanmar ... see *Burma, Burmese*
mycoderma ... 5. fungi 6. mother (formed
on wine) 8. membrane (ferment)
mycophagy ... 11. eating fungi 15. eating
mushrooms
myna, mynah ... 4. bird 7. grackle
8. starling
Mynheer ... 8. Dutchman
myo (comb form) ... 6. muscle
myomancy, divination by ... 14. muscle
movement
myopic ... 11. nearsighted
myriad ... 11. innumerable, ten thousand
13. multitudinous
myriapod ... 9. centipede
myrmicid ... 3. ant
myrtle ... 8. ramarama 10. periwinkle
11. candleberry
mysterious ... 4. dark 6. arcane,
mystic, occult, secret 7. cryptic
8. abstruse, esoteric 9. recondite,
sphinxian 10. cabalistic 12. inexplicable,
unfathomable
mystery ... 4. cult, rune 6. arcane, cabala,
enigma, puzzle, secret 7. arcanum,
esotery, miracle 8. whodunit
9. sacrament 13. inexplainable
19. incomprehensibility
mystery writer's award ... 5. Edgar
mystic ... 4. seer, yogi 5. magic, runic
6. occult, orphic, secret 7. cryptic
Mahatma 8. cabalist, esoteric, symbolic
9. enigmatic, recondite 10. cabalistic,
mysterious
mystic (pert to) ...
cry .. 4. evoe
doctrine .. 5. cabal 7. esotery 8. esoteric
initiate .. 5. epopt (Gr Antiq)
ocean isle .. 6. Avalon
theosophy .. 6. cabala
word .. 2. om 7. abraxas 11. abracadabra
mystical ... 6. muddle, puzzle 7. confuse,
cryptic, furtive, obscure 9. enigmatic,
obfuscate
mystical (pert to) ...
character (Teut Myth) .. 8. Eckehart
meaning .. 7. anagoge
word .. 11. abracadabra
mystify ... 5. befog 6. muddle, puzzle
7. becloud, confuse, perplex
8. befuddle, bewilder 9. bamboozle,
obfuscate
myth ... 4. tale 5. fable, fancy, story
6. legend 7. figment, parable
8. apocrypha, falsehood
mythical ... 7. fancied 8. fabulous
9. fictional, imaginary, legendary
10. fictitious 12. mythological
mythical (pert to) ...
being .. 6. Garuda, Icarus 7. centaur,
griffin
bird .. 3. roc
deity .. 6. Moloch (tyrant)
demon .. 4. Rahu (tail called Kehu)
hero .. 4. Ajax 8. Achilles

heroine . . 4. Leda 6. Europa
8. Atalanta
hunter . . 5. Orion
island . . 8. Atlantis
king (Hind) . . 4. Nala
monster . . 4. ogre 7. chimera
mother . . 5. Niobe

river . . 4. Styx
serpent . . 5. Apepi
winged creature . . 7. Alborak
woman . . 6. Gorgon, Medusa, Stheno
7. Euryale
mythogony, science of . . . 5. myths
mythologist . . . 9. mythmaker

N

N . . 2. en, Nu 8. nitrogen (symbol)
nab . . . 4. grab 5. catch, seize 6. arrest,
nibble, snatch 7. capture 9. apprehend
Nabal's wife (Bib) . . . 7. Abigail
nabob . . . 5. nawab 6. bigwig, tycoon
7. viceroy 8. governor 9. plutocrat
10. viceregent
Nabokov nymphet . . . 6. Lolita
nacelle . . . 4. boat 7. shelter
nacket . . . 3. boy 4. cake 5. lunch 6. caddie
8. saucy boy
nacre . . . 9. shellfish 10. conchiolin
13. mother-of-pearl
Nadab (Bib) . . . 12. King of Israel
nadir . . . 4. pole 11. lowest point (opp
zenith)
nag . . . 4. pony, twit 5. annoy, cobra,
horse, scold, snake, tease 6. heckle,
hector, peck on, pester, plague
7. henpeck 8. harangue
nagor . . . 8. antelope, reedbuck
nahoor . . . 5. sheep 6. bharal
naiad . . . 5. nymph 6. mussel, Nereid
7. limniad, Oceanid
nail . . . 3. cut, hob 4. brad, claw,
spad, stud, tack, wire 5. clout, spike,
sprig, talon 6. fasten, secure, unguis,
ungula 7. capture, measure 8. sparable
9. finishing, intercept 12. upholstering
nail (pert to) . . .
headless . . 5. sprig
ingrowing . . 7. acronyx
marking, fingernail . . 6. lunule
size . . 8. tenpenny
slanted . . 4. toed
naissance . . . 5. birth 6. origin
naive . . . 5. frank 6. simple 7. artless,
ingenue 8. childish, gullible, untaught
9. guileless, ingenuous, unworldly
10. simplicity 13. unphilosophic
15. unsophisticated
naked . . . 4. bald, bare, mere, nude,
open 5. clear, plain 6. barren,
meager 7. exposed, literal, obvious
8. manifest, stripped 9. unadorned,
uncovered 11. defenseless, unprotected,
unsupported
nakoo . . . 6. gavial 9. crocodile
namaycush . . . 5. togue, trout
namby-pamby . . . 5. inane, silly, vapid
7. insipid 10. wishy-washy
11. sentimental
name . . . 3. dub, nom 4. call, cite, term
5. clepe, nomen, style, title 6. y-
clepe 7. appoint, entitle, mention

8. cognomen, identify 9. celebrity,
enumerate, personage 10. denominate,
reputation 11. appellation, designation
12. denomination
name (pert to) . . .
added . . 7. agnomen
assumed . . 3. pen 5. alias 7. John Doe
9. incognito, pseudonym, sobriquet
10. nom de plume
bad . . 7. caconym
binomial . . 8. teutonym
by location . . 7. toponym
derivation . . 7. eponymy
family (father's) . . 7. eponymy
9. patronymy
fictitious . . 9. pseudonym
first . . 9. baptismal, Christian, praenomen
Japanese . . 4. maru
known . . 9. onomatous
nickname . . 7. moniker (monicker)
8. cognomen
nominate . . 9. designate
secret . . 9. cryptonym
spelled backwards (real name) . .
6. ananym
surname . . 7. eponymy
technical . . 4. onym
unknown . . 9. anonymous
wrong . . 8. misnomer
name as agent . . . 6. depute
named . . . 5. cited 6. called, y-clept
(y-cleped)
named for a god . . . 11. theophorous
nameless . . . 7. bastard, obscure 8. not
known 9. aforesaid, anonymous,
unnamable 10. unrenowned
12. illegitimate 13. indescribable,
inexpressible 15. undistinguished
namelessness . . . 9. anonymity
namely . . . 5. to wit 9. expressly,
nominally, videlicet (viz)
names, divination by . . . 8. onomancy
names, science of . . . 11. onomatology
namesake . . . 6. eponym 9. homonym
nanga . . . 4. harp
nanism . . . 12. dwarfishness (opp of
gigantism)
Nanking . . .
capital . . 5. China (1932--1937)
color . . 12. Naples yellow
province . . 7. Kiangsu
river site . . 7. Yangtze
nanoid . . . 8. dwarfish
nanpie . . . 6. magpie
naos . . . 5. cella 6. shrine, temple

Naos . . . 4. star

nap . . . 3. nod 4. doze, pile, shag, wink
5. fluff, grasp, seize, sleep, steal
6. duffel, siesta, snooze

nape . . . 5. nucha, nuque, scrag 6. scruff,
turnip 7. niddick 8. auchenium

napellus . . . 9. monkshood

napery . . . 5. linen (table)

napiform . . . 12. turnip-shaped

napkin . . . 5. doily, towel 6. diaper
8. kerchief 9. serviette 11. neckerchief

Naples . . .
　biscuit . . 7. ladyfinger
　famed building . . 9. Cathedral (Gothic,
　　1272)
　red . . 5. ochre 6. Indian
　site . . 11. Bay of Naples

napoleon . . . 4. game 6. pastry 7. top
boot 11. reddish-blue, sweet cherry
13. crimson clover

Napoleon I (pert to) . . .
　birthplace . . 7. Ajaccio (Corsica)
　brother-in-law . . 5. Murat
　death site . . 8. St Helena
　exiled to . . 4. Elba
　father . . 7. Charles
　island . . 5. Capri
　marshal . . 3. Ney (executed)
　title . . 7. Emperor (of France)
　warfare site . . 5. Ligny, Malta 7. Marengo
　　8. Waterloo 10. Alexandria, Austerlitz

napped (short) . . . 3. ras

nappy . . . 3. ale 4. dish 5. downy,
heady, wooly 6. liquor, shaggy, sleepy
7. foaming 10. inebriated

napu . . . 10. chevrotain

Naraka (Hind) . . . 4. hell

Narcissus (Gr) . . . 6. egoist 14. beautiful
youth

narcosis . . . 5. sleep 10. drowsiness

narcotic . . . 4. dope, drug, hemp,
junk 5. bhang (bang), ether, opium
6. heroin 7. anodyne, cocaine, hashish
8. hypnotic, mandrake, morphine
9. soporific 10. belladonna,
hyoscyamus, stramonium

narcotic (pert to) . . .
　dose . . 3. fix 5. locus
　package . . 6. bindle
　seller . . 6. pusher 7. peddler
　user (group) . . 6. love-in 9. snow party

nard . . . 6. anoint 8. matgrass, ointment,
rhizomes

nardoo, nardu . . . 6. clover

nares . . . 8. nostrils

narghile, nargile, nargileh . . . 4. pipe
6. hookah

nargil . . . 7. coconut

nark . . . 3. spy 5. annoy 8. informer
11. stool pigeon

Narragansett . . . 3. Bay 5. horse 6. Indian,
turkey

narrate . . . 4. tell 6. detail, recite, relate
7. recount 8. describe

narration . . . 4. tale 5. drama (acted), story
6. detail 7. account, recital 8. relation
9. discourse, narrative, rehearsal

narrative . . . 4. epic, epos, myth, poem,
saga, tale 5. conte, drama, fable,
story 6. legend 7. account, episode,
history, parable 8. allegory, anecdote

9. narration, statement

narrator . . . 9. raconteur 11. storyteller

narrow . . . 4. mean, poor 5. inlet,
scant, taper 6. linear, strait 7. closely,
slender 8. strictly 9. confining, illiberal,
niggardly 10. restricted, straighten
11. reactionary 12. parsimonious
13. circumscribed

narrow (pert to) . . .
　comb form . . 4. sten 5. steno
　leather strip . . 5. thong
　minded . . 5. petty 6. biased 7. bigoted
　　10. intolerant, prejudiced
　opening . . 4. rima, slot 9. stenopaic
　souled . . 10. ungenerous

narrowly incised . . . 9. laciniate

narrows . . . 5. sound 6. strait

narthex . . . 7. portico 9. asafetida
(asafoetida)

narwhal, narwal . . . 5. whale 8. cetacean

nasab (Muslim Law) . . . 7. kinship
13. consanguinity

nasal . . . 4. nose 5. sound 6. narine,
rhinal, twangy 11. inspiratory

nascency . . . 5. birth 6. origin 7. genesis
9. beginning

naseberry . . . 9. sapodilla

Nasi . . . 6. prince 8. Gamaliel 9. patriarch

Nasicornia . . . 10. rhinoceros

Naso, famed . . . 4. Ovid

nasology . . . 9. nose study

Nassau . . .
　capital . . 7. Bahamas
　hamlet . . 7. grouper
　sports . . 4. golf

nastika . . . 7. atheist

nasty . . . 4. foul, mean 5. dirty 6. filthy,
odious 7. obscene 8. indecent,
unsavory 9. offensive 12. disagreeable,
dishonorable

Nasua . . . 5. coati 6. coatis

nasute . . . 10. large-nosed

nasutiform . . . 8. noselike

natal . . . 6. inborn, native 7. gluteal,
nascent 9. from birth

Natal . . . 7. seaport (Braz) 8. Province
(So Afr)

natator . . . 7. swimmer

natatorium . . . 4. pool 6. plunge
12. swimming hole

natchbone . . . 9. aitchbone

Natchez . . . 4. city (La) 6. Indian

nation . . . 4. host, race 5. caste, class,
state 6. people, polity 7. country
9. community, multitude

national . . . 4. blue 6. racial 7. citizen,
federal

nationality . . . 4. race 6. nation 8. nativity
9. statehood 11. nationalism

national salute . . . 13. Twenty-one guns

native . . . 3. ite, son 5. natal 6. innate,
normal, simple 7. genuine, natural,
primary 8. inherent, original, primeval
9. unbranded 10. aboriginal,
indigenous, unaffected 11. not acquired

native (pert to) . . .
　agent . . 9. comprador (compradore)
　bear . . 5. koala
　cat . . 7. dasyure
　dog . . 5. dingo
　Indian . . 4. Arab

juniper.. 9. blueberry
Madagascan.. 4. Hova
naturalized person.. 7. denizen
plant, animal.. 8. indigene
salt.. 6. halite
nativity... 5. birth 9. beginning, horoscope, sculpture
Nativity, The... 8. festival 9. Christmas 13. birth of Christ
natterjack... 4. toad
natty... 4. chic, neat, tidy, trim 6. spruce 10. fastidious
Natty Bumppo's alias... 7. Hawkeye 10. Deerslayer, Pathfinder 15. Leatherstocking
natural... 3. raw 4. born 5. flesh, usual 6. common, cretin, expert, inborn, inbred, innate, normal 7. genuine, regular, typical 8. informal, inherent, lifelike, ordinary 9. character (Mus), dice throw, unassumed, unfeigned 10. unaffected
natural (pert to)...
capacity.. 9. endowment
condition.. 4. norm
group.. 4. race 6. ethnic, family
location, position.. 4. site 5. situs
not (natural).. 5. alien 8. acquired 10. artificial
philosophy.. 7. physics
science.. 10. physiology
voice (Mus).. 7. dipetto
naturalist... 4. Muir (John) 7. Burbank (Luther)
naturalize... 5. adapt 8. accustom 9. acclimate 11. domesticate, familiarize
nature... 4. kind, self, sort, soul, type 6. cosmos 7. essence 8. tendency, universe 11. naturalness, temperament 14. characteristic
nature (pert to)...
concealed.. 7. latency
divinity of.. 5. dryad, naiad, nymph
god.. 3. Pan
goddess.. 6. Cybele 7. Artemis
in the raw.. 6. nudity
of the case.. 8. ipso facto
worship.. 11. physiolatry
natue... 4. born
nausea... 4. pall 5. qualm 8. loathing, mal de mer 10. queasiness 11. seasickness
nauseous... 7. fulsome, mawkish 9. loathsome, offensive, sickening, squeamish 10. disgusting
nautical... 5. naval 6. marine 7. oceanic 8. maritime
nautical (pert to)...
almanac.. 9. ephemeris
direction.. 5. avast, belay
hail.. 4. ahoy
instrument.. 3. aba 7. compass, pelorus, sextant
measure.. 3. ton 4. knot 6. fathom 7. sea mile
nautilus... 7. mollusk 8. argonaut 9. submarine 10. diving bell
Navaho, Navajo... 5. hogan 6. Indian 7. blanket 9. red-yellow
naval... 6. marine 8. nautical
naval (pert to)...
brigade.. 7. militia

commander.. 7. navarch
depot.. 4. base
device.. 6. dolter
officer.. 5. bosun 6. ensign, yeoman 7. admiral, captain 9. boatswain (bosun), commander 10. lieutenant
nave... 3. hob, hub, nef 4. apse, fist 5. nieve 7. apsidal
navel... 6. middle, orange 8. omphalos 9. umbilicus 10. depression
navigate... 4. keel, sail 7. avigate 11. ship science
navigator... 5. navvy 12. third command (or 4th)
navy (fleet)... 7. tankers 8. cruisers, flattops, gunboats 10. destroyers, submarines 11. battleships 12. mine sweepers 13. hospital ships 16. aircraft carriers
navy (pert to)...
bean.. 6. kidney
coffee.. 3. mud
color.. 4. blue 10. marine blue
drinking fountain.. 11. scuttlebutt
fleet.. 6. armada 13. combat vessels
plug.. 7. tobacco
ships, collectively.. 5. fleet 6. armada
song.. 13. Anchors Aweigh
training camp.. 8. boot camp
underwear.. 8. skivvies
nawab, nabob... 5. ruler, title 7. viceroy
nay... 2. no 4. deny 5. flute, never 6. denial, naysay, refuse 7. refusal 8. negative 11. prohibition
nayaur... 5. sheep
nayword... 6. byword 7. proverb (of reproach) 9. watchword
Nazarene (pert to)...
artist.. 8. Overbeck (of Rome)
disciple.. 9. Christian
native.. 11. Jesus Christ
native of.. 8. Nazareth
Nazi... 9. Hitlerite
Nazi emblem... 6. fylfot 8. swastika
nchega... 6. monkey 10. chimpanzee
neanic... 8. immature, youthful
neap... 4. tide 6. tongue (vehicle) 7. low tide 8. low water
Neapolitan (pert to)...
dance.. 9. tarantella
fever.. 8. undulent
Italian.. 6. Naples
medlar.. 5. fruit 7. azarole
music.. 5. chord (6th)
ointment.. 9. mercurial
yellow.. 6. Naples
near... 2. at 4. nigh 5. about, close, handy 6. around, within 7. closely, related 8. adjacent, approach, imminent, intimate 11. approximate 13. propinquitous
nearby, near-by... 3. gin 4. nigh 5. anent, handy 6. beside, nearly 7. close by, close to, vicinal 8. adjacent 9. adjoining 10. convenient
Nearctic... 9. Greenland, Holarctic 11. Palaearctic 13. Arctic America
Near East... 7. Balkans 12. Balkan States
Near East valley... 4. wadi (wady) 5. oasis 6. ravine
nearest... 4. next 7. closest 9. proximate

nearly ... 5. about 6. almost 7. closely
8. narrowly 10. similarity
13. approximately

nearness ... 8. affinity, intimacy, likeness,
relation 9. closeness 11. propinquity

near of kin ... 7. germane

nearsighted ... 6. myopic 8. purblind
12. narrow-minded, shortsighted,
undiscerning

neat ... 3. pat 4. prim, smug, snod, tidy,
trig, trim 5. natty 6. adroit, dapper,
spruce 7. orderly, perjink, precise
9. shipshape 10. meticulous, perjinkety
12. spick-and-span

neatherd ... 7. cowherd 8. herdsman

neathmost ... 6. lowest

neb ... 3. tip 4. beak, bill, face, kiss,
nose 5. point, snout

Nebo, Nebu ... 8. mountain (Bib) 11. god
of wisdom

Nebraska ...
   capital .. 7. Lincoln
   city .. 5. Omaha 8. Hastings
    11. Scottsbluff
   Indian .. 4. Otoe 5. Omaha 6. Pawnee
   meaning .. 11. water valley
   railroad (1865) .. 12. Union Pacific
   river .. 6. Nemaha, Platte 8. Missouri
   State admission .. 13. Thirty-seventh
   State motto .. 20. Equality Before the
    Law
   State nickname .. 4. Beef 10. Cornhusker

nebula ... 3. sky 4. mist 5. cloud, vapor
10. atmosphere

Nebula of ... 4. Lyra 5. Orion
9. Andromeda

nebulous ... 4. hazy 5. misty, vague
6. cloudy 7. clouded, nebular
8. nebulose

nebulous envelope ... 4. coma
9. chevelure

necessarily ... 8. perforce
11. unavoidably 12. consequently
13. indispensably

necessary ... 5. vital 7. needful
9. essential, mandatory, requisite
11. requirement, unavoidable
13. indispensable

necessitate ... 5. force, impel 6. compel,
entail, oblige 7. require 9. constrain

necessity ... 4. food, need, want
5. drink 7. aliment, poverty, urgency
9. neediness 10. constraint
14. inevitableness

neck ... 4. hals (halse) 5. crane, scrag,
swire 6. cervix, fondle, strait 7. channel,
embrace, isthmus

neck (pert to) ...
   armor .. 6. gorget 8. gorgerin
   artery .. 7. carotid
   back of .. 4. nape 5. nucha, nuque
    6. scruff
   frill .. 5. jabot, ruche 6. wimple
   land .. 6. strake 9. peninsula
   muscle .. 8. scalenus
   pendant .. 6. locket 9. lavaliere
   piece .. 3. boa 5. amice, rabat, scarf,
    stole 6. collar
   water .. 6. strait
   zoology .. 4. gula 6. wattle 7. withers

neckcloth ... 6. cravat 7. muffler

9. barcelona 11. neckerchief

neckerchief ... 7. belcher 8. kerchief
12. handkerchief

necklace ... 5. beads 6. torque 7. baldric,
chaplet, rivière 11. shark's-teeth

neckpiece ... 3. boa 5. ascot, rabat,
scarf, stole 6. collar 8. kerchief

necktie ... 3. tie 4. band 5. ascot, scarf
6. cravat 10. four-in-hand

necrology ... 9. death roll 13. death
register 14. obituary notice

necromancy ... 5. goety, magic 7. sorcery
9. sortilege 11. conjuration,
enchantment

necropolis ... 8. cemetery

necropsy ... 7. autopsy 10. post-mortem

nectar ... 3. red 5. drink, honey
8. beverage

nectar of the gods ... 8. ambrosia

neddy ... 6. donkey 13. life preserver

need ... 4. lack, poor, thar, want
7. poverty, require, urgency 8. exigency
9. extremity, necessity 10. compulsion,
deficiency 11. requirement

needle ... 3. sew 4. acus, goad,
sail 5. tease, thorn 6. bodkin,
pierce 7. darning, obelisk 9. astatizer
10. upholstery

needle (pert to) ...
   bath .. 3. jet 9. sprinkler
   bird .. 9. phalarope 10. needlebill
   bug .. 4. Nepa 7. Ranatra
   case .. 4. etui (etwee)
   fish .. 3. gar 8. pipefish
   gun .. 11. Dreyse rifle
   kind .. 5. blunt, sharp 7. between,
    crochet, darning 8. knitting
   long-eyed .. 10. embroidery
   medical .. 10. hypodermic
   needlelike body .. 7. spicule
   needlework .. 7. crochet, sampler
    8. knitting 10. embroidery
   record .. 10. phonograph
   shaped .. 6. acuate 7. acerose 8. acicular
   under the skin .. 5. seton

needy ... 4. poor 7. almoner 8. indigent
9. necessary, penniless, requisite
10. distressed

neel-bhunder ... 8. wanderoo 10. blue
monkey

neep ... 6. turnip

ne'er-do-well ... 5. idler 6. wretch
8. poltroon 9. schlemiel 14. good-for-
nothing

nef ... 4. nave 5. clock (ship-shaped)

nefarious ... 6. wicked 7. heinous,
impious 8. horrible, infamous, terrible
9. atrocious 10. detestable, iniquitous,
villainous

nefas ... 6. sinful

negate ... 4. deny 6. refuse, refute
7. nullify 8. disprove 10. counteract

negative ... 2. ir, ne, no 3. nay, non,
nor, not 4. deny, film, veto 5. minus
6. refuse 7. neutral 8. disprove, negation
9. privative 13. contradiction

negative (pert to) ...
   electrode, pole .. 7. cathode (kathode)
   eyepiece .. 8. Campani's 9. Huygenian
   ion .. 5. anion
   sign .. 5. minus

neglect ... 4. fail, omit, slip, snub
5. shirk 6. slight 7. failure 8. omission
9. disregard, negligent, pretermit
11. inattention

negligee ... 4. gown, robe 6. attire
8. peignoir

negligence ... 7. laxness 9. oversight,
unconcern 10. remissness
11. inattention 12. carelessness,
inadvertence

negligent ... 3. lax 4. lash 6. remiss,
supine 8. careless, heedless
10. neglectful 11. unconcerned

negotiate ... 4. deal, pass 5. treat
6. manage, treaty 7. bargain, mediate
8. transact

Negrito (pert to) ...
African .. 4. Akka 5. Batwa, Pygmy
7. Bambute, Bushman
Dutch New Guinea .. 6. Tapiro
Indonesian .. 3. Ata 4. Aeta (Ita)
Malay .. 6. Semang

neigh ... 4. akin 6. whinny 7. whicker

neighborhood ... 7. purlieu 8. environs,
vicinity 9. proximity 10. thereabout

neither right nor wrong ...
11. adiaphorous, indifferent

Nemesis ... 7. avenger, goddess, penalty

nemoral ... 6. sylvan 14. living in a
grove

neology ... 8. new words 9. neologism
11. new doctrine 14. new expressions

neonate ... 7. new baby, newborn

neophobia (fear of) ... 6. the new

neophyte ... 4. tyro 6. novice 7. convert
8. beginner 9. proselyte 10. catechumen

neoplasm ... 5. tumor

neosology (study of) ... 10. young birds

neoteric ... 3. new 4. late 6. modern,
recent

nep ... 6. catnip

Nepal ...
aborigines .. 10. Mongolians
capital .. 8. Katmandu
district .. 7. Mustang
mountain .. 7. Everest 9. Himalayas
ruler .. 9. Maharajah

nepesh ... 4. soul 10. animal soul
12. divine breath

nephew ... 4. neve 6. nepote

nephrite ... 4. jade 7. mineral 11. kidney
stone

nephroid ... 8. reniform 12. kidney-
shaped

nephros ... 6. kidney

nepote ... 6. nephew 8. grandson

nepotism ... 9. patronage 10. favoritism,
preference

Neptune ... 3. sea 5. ocean 6. sea god

Neptune (pert to) ...
Astron .. 6. planet (3rd largest)
Celtic .. 3. Ler
consort .. 7. Salacia
emblem .. 7. trident
Greek .. 8. Poseidon
Roman .. 6. sea god
son .. 6. Triton
wife .. 6. Medusa

Nereid (Gr) ... 8. sea nymph

Nero (pert to) ...
excesses .. 7. cruelty 13. burning of

Rome (64 AD)
mother .. 9. Agrippina
Roman title .. 7. Emperor
wife .. 6. Sabina 7. Octavia

nerve ... 4. pulp 5. cheek, fiber, pluck,
sinew 6. aplomb, energy, tendon,
tissue 7. courage, nervure 8. audacity,
coolness, strength 10. resolution

nerve (pert to) ...
action .. 9. neurergic
cell .. 4. axon 6. neuron
center .. 8. ganglion
comb form .. 5. neuro
fiber .. 5. motor 7. sensory 8. afferent,
efferent
force .. 7. neurism
gray matter .. 7. cinerea
inflammation, medical .. 8. neuritis,
neurosis 9. neurotomy 10. neurectasy,
neurolysis, neuropathy 11. neurologist
13. tic douloureux
network .. 4. rete 6. plexus
of Wrisberg .. 6. facial
operation .. 10. neurolysis
passage .. 4. rete 5. hilum 8. ganglion
ref to .. 6. neural, neuric 7. neuroid
8. neurotic
root .. 5. radix
science .. 9. neurology
sheath .. 9. medullary
tissue .. 7. cinerea, neurine 9. neuroglia
tumor .. 6. glioma 7. neuroma

nerveless ... 4. dead 5. inert 9. foolhardy,
powerless 10. courageous

nervous ... 5. tense, timid 6. neural,
touchy 7. fearful, jittery 8. eloquent,
neurotic, timorous 9. excitable, sensitive
10. high-strung 12. apprehensive

nervous (pert to) ...
affliction .. 3. tic 6. ataxia, chorea
7. aphasia 8. neurosis
energy deficiency .. 7. aneuria
seizure .. 4. amok (amuck)
system, center .. 5. brain, spine
system, description .. 11. neurography
system, name .. 9. neuronymy
system, science .. 9. neurology
system, specialist .. 12. neuropathist,
psychiatrist
tissue tumor .. 11. neurocytoma

ness ... 4. cape 8. headland
10. promontory

nest ... 3. bed, den, nye, web 4. inro
5. abode, aerie, eyrie, group, haunt,
nidus 6. cuddle, series (graduated)
7. lodging, retreat 9. residence
10. nidificate 13. breeding place

nest (pert to) ...
boxes .. 4. inro
eagle's .. 5. aerie, eyrie (eyry)
pheasant's .. 4. nide
spider's .. 3. web
squirrel's .. 4. dray (drey)
swallow's .. 9. nidus avis
to build .. 6. nidify

nestle ... 3. pet 4. nest 6. cuddle, pettle,
settle 7. protect, shelter, snuggle

nestling ... 4. bird 5. child 9. fledgling,
youngling

Nestor (pert to) ...
famed for .. 6. wisdom

King of . . 5. Pylos
known as . . 4. sage 7. adviser 8. The
    Elder 9. Patriarch
net . . . 3. gin, web 4. mesh, toil, trap,
    weir 5. clear, lacis, score, seine, snare,
    weave 6. profit 7. enclose, network,
    trammel 8. receipts 9. reticulum
net (pert to) . . .
fishing . . 4. fyke 5. seine, trawl
    7. trammel
hair . . 5. snood
lacemaking . . 5. lacis
silk . . 5. tulle 6. maline
winged (lacy) . . 12. neuropteroid
Netherlands . . . see also *Dutch, Holland*
capital . . 9. Amsterdam
cheese . . 4. Edam
city . . 5. Delft 7. Utrecht 9. Eindhoven,
    Rotterdam
gin . . 8. schnapps
government . . 8. monarchy
government seat . . 8. The Hague
inhabitant . . 5. Dutch 7. Flemish
lake . . 7. Haarlem
legislative body . . 4. Raad
low land . . 6. polder
port . . 9. Rotterdam
possession . . 7. Surinam (Dutch Guiana)
    8. Antilles (W Ind)
river . . 3. Eem 6. Meuse, Rhine 6. Ijssel
    (Yssel), Kromme
sea (inland) . . 9. Wadden Sea, Zuider
    Zee 10. Ijssel Lake, Ijsselmeer
nettle . . . 3. vex 4. fret, herb, line,
    whip 5. anger, annoy, pique, rouse
    6. incite, Urtica 7. provoke 8. irritate
    10. Parietaria, Urticaceae
nettle (pert to) . . .
bird . . 11. whitethroat
geranium . . 6. coleus
rash . . 5. hives, uredo 9. urticaria
sea . . 5. cnida
network . . . 3. web 4. caul, fret, kell, lace,
    mesh, moke, rete 5. chain 6. cobweb,
    plexus, reseau, sagene 7. webwork
neume . . . 5. neuma 6. pneuma
neurad . . . 12. to neural side
neural . . . 6. dorsal, nerval 7. ventral
    9. posterial
neuralgia . . . 3. tic 4. pain 8. face ague
    13. tic douloureux
neuter . . . 6. gender 7. neither, neutral,
    sexless 9. impartial
neutral . . . 7. antacid 8. mediocre,
    middling, negative, unbiased
    10. achromatic 11. indifferent,
    nonpartisan 12. noncombatant,
    noncommittal
neutral equilibrium . . . 7. astatic
neutralize . . . 5. annul 6. offset 7. nullify,
    vitiate 9. frustrate 10. counteract
    11. countervail 14. counterbalance
Nevada . . .
capital . . 10. Carson City
city . . 3. Ely 4. Elko 6. Sparks 7. Boulder
    8. Las Vegas
lake . . 4. Mead 6. Mohave 7. Pyramid
mine (famed) . . 12. Comstock Lode
    (1859)
mountain . . 7. Rockies, Wasatch
    13. Sierra Nevadas

native Indian . . 6. Digger
resort . . 4. Reno 8. Las Vegas (The
    Meadows) 9. Lake Tahoe
State admission . . 11. Thirty-sixth
State motto . . 16. All For Our Country
State nickname . . 6. Silver 9. Sagebrush
neve . . . 4. firn, snow 6. nephew 7. glacier
nevel, nevell . . . 9. fisticuff
never . . . 4. nary 6. nowise 7. not ever
    8. at no time, not at all 9. by no
    means, nevermore
nevertheless . . . 3. but, yet 5. still
    6. anyhow 7. however
    15. notwithstanding
nevus . . . 4. mark, mole 5. tumor
    7. blemish 9. birthmark
new . . . 3. neo (pref) 4. anew, late,
    nova (star) 5. fresh, novel 6. growth,
    modern, recent 8. neoteric, original,
    untested 9. recreated, renovated
    12. unaccustomed 13. inexperienced
New Brunswick . . .
capital . . 11. Fredericton
city . . 6. St John
gulf . . 10. St Lawrence
new but yet old . . . 10. novantique
Newfoundland . . .
city . . 7. St John's 9. Grand Bank
discoverer . . 9. John Cabot (1497)
gulf . . 10. St Lawrence
New Guinea, Papua Island . . .
capital . . 6. Rabaul
hog (wild) . . 4. bene
island size (world) . . 5. third
native . . 6. Papuan
parrot . . 4. lory
port . . 4. Daru 7. Moresby
region . . 10. Melanesian
river . . 3. Fly
New Hampshire . . .
capital . . 7. Concord
city . . 6. Durham 7. Hanover 8. Merrimac
    10. Manchester, Portsmouth
cog rail (first) . . 12. Mt Washington
lake . . 13. Winnipesaukee
mountains . . 5. White
Our Town . . 13. Grover's Corner
park . . 13. Crawford Notch, Dixville
    Notch
range . . 12. Presidential
river . . 8. Merrimac 11. Connecticut
sculpture . . 14. Great Stone Face (Profile
    Peak)
State admission . . 5. Ninth
State motto . . 13. Live Free or Die
State nickname . . 7. Granite
New Jersey . . .
capital . . 7. Trenton
city . . 6. Camden, Newark 7. Raritan
    9. Montclair 12. Fort Monmouth, New
    Brunswick
college . . 9. Princeton (1746)
inventor . . 6. Edison
naval air station . . 9. Lakehurst
poet . . 11. Walt Whitman
resort . . 7. Cape May 8. Wildwood
    9. Ocean City 10. Asbury Park
    12. Atlantic City
river . . 7. Raritan
State admission . . 5. Third
State motto . . 20. Liberty and Prosperity

State nickname . . 6. Garden
New Mexico . . .
  capital . . 7. Santa Fe
  city . . 4. Taos 7. Roswell 11. Albuquerque
  Fort . . 5. Tejon
  Indian Reservation . . 5. Acoma (Sky
    City) 11. Chaco Canyon
  peak . . 7. Wheeler
  river . . 4. Gila 5. Pecos 8. Canadian
  space center . . 6. Sandia 8. Holloman,
    Kirtland 9. Los Alamos 10. White Sands
  State admission . . 12. Forty-seventh
  State bird . . 10. road runner
  State flower . . 6. yucca
  State motto . . 12. Crescit Eundo 15. It
    Grows as it Goes
  State nickname . . 17. Land of
    Enchantment
  State wonder . . 15. Carlsbad Caverns
new moon festival . . 8. neomenia
news . . . 5. flash, scoop 6. report
    7. courier, evangel, tidings
news agency . . . 2. AP 3. DNB, UPI
    4. Tass 5. Aneta, Domei 7. Reuters
    9. syndicate
newspaper (pert to) . . .
  editor . . 7. reviser 8. redactor
  file . . 6. morgue
  popular name . . 7. gazette
  writer . . 8. reporter 9. columnist
    10. newscaster 13. correspondent
newsstand . . . 5. booth, kiosk, stall
new star . . . 7. nova
newt . . . 3. eft 6. lizard, triton
    10. salamander
New Testament . . . 6. Gospel 8. Epistles
    15. Pauline Epistles
new wine . . . 4. must
new word, usage . . . 7. neology
    9. neologism, neoterism
New York . . .
  borough . . 5. Bronx 6. Queens
    8. Brooklyn, Richmond (formerly)
    9. Manhattan 12. Staten Island
  buyer (for $24) . . 11. Peter Minuit
  capital . . 6. Albany
  city . . 5. Utica 7. Buffalo, New York
    8. Saratoga 9. Rochester
    11. Schenectady 12. Poughkeepsie
  college . . 7. Colgate, Cornell 8. Columbia
    9. West Point
  Falls . . 7. Niagara
  Indian . . 6. Oneida, Seneca 8. Iroquois
  Irving's home . . 9. Tarrytown
  island . . 6. Staten 9. Manhattan
  monument . . 7. Obelisk 10. Grant's
    Tomb 15. Statue of Liberty
  mountains . . 9. Catskills
  name, old . . 12. New Amsterdam
  nickname . . 6. Gotham 8. Big Apple
  river . . 4. East 6. Harlem, Hudson
  river channel . . 8. Hell Gate
  section (famed) . . 4. SoHo 16. Greenwich
    Village
  State admission . . 8. Eleventh
  State bird . . 8. bluebird
  State flower . . 4. rose
  State motto . . 9. Excelsior 10. Ever
    Upward
  State nickname . . 6. Empire
New Yorker . . 8. Dutchman 9. Gothamite

    13. Knickerbocker
New Zealand . . .
  capital . . 10. Wellington
  city . . 7. Dunedin 8. Auckland, Hamilton
    12. Christchurch
  discoverer . . 6. Tasman
  explorer . . 4. Cook (Captain James)
  location . . 12. South Pacific
  native . . 3. Ati 5. Maori 10. Polynesian
  peak . . 6. Mt Cook
  sect . . 7. Ringatu
  soldier . . 5. Anzac
  volcano . . 7. Ruapehu
New Zealand (pert to) . . .
  bird . . 3. kea, moa, poe 4. titi, weka, kiwi
    7. apteryx, boobook, wrybill, Xenicus
  caterpillar . . 5. aweto
  club, weapon . . 4. mere
  mahogany . . 6. totara
  mollusk . . 4. pipi
  myrtle . . 8. ramarama
  morepork . . 4. peho, ruru
  palm . . 5. nikau
  parrot . . 6. kakapo 9. owl parrot
  pigeon . . 4. kuku
  reptile . . 7. tuatara
  white pine . . 5. kauri (kaury)
next . . . 4. then 5. aware, neist 7. closest,
    nearest, proximo 9. adjoining,
    immediate 10. contiguous, succeeding
next to . . . 6. almost, beside, nearly
    8. adjacent
next to last syllable . . . 6. penult
    11. penultimate
nexus . . . 3. tie 4. bond, link 5. group
    6. series 10. connection
    15. interconnection
Nez Percé . . . 6. Indian 11. pierced nose
Niagara . . . 5. flood, grape (green)
Niagara Falls (pert to) . . .
  cataract . . 8. American, Canadian
    9. Horseshoe
  division between . . 10. Bridal Veil, Goat
    Island
  point of interest . . 14. Cave of the Winds
nib . . . 3. end 4. beak, bill 5. point (pen),
    prong 6. tongue
nibble . . . 3. eat, nab, nip 4. gnaw, peck
    5. champ, munch 6. browse
Nicaragua . . .
  capital . . 7. Managua
  city . . 7. Granada
  lake . . 7. Managua
  mountain range . . 10. Cordillera
  river . . 4. Coco, Tuma 7. San Juan
nice . . . 4. fine, good, kind, neat
    6. dainty, proper, queasy, subtle, tickle
    7. elegant, finical, genteel, prudish,
    refined 8. exacting, pleasant, pleasing,
    suitable 9. agreeable, squeamish
    10. appetizing, delightful, fastidious,
    particular, scrupulous 11. considerate,
    punctilious, well-behaved
    13. hypercritical 14. discriminating,
    discriminative
Nicene Creed . . . 10. Confession
nicety . . . 7. finesse, modesty 8. accuracy,
    delicacy 9. precision 11. preciseness
    13. squeamishness
niche . . . 4. apse, nook 5. space (recessed)
    6. alcove, covert, recess 7. retreat,

secrete 10. tabernacle
nick . . 3. gap 4. dent, dint, slit 5. notch, steal 7. swindle
Nick Charles . . . see *Thin Man*
nickel (pert to) . . .
  alloy . . 5. Invar
  bronze . . 11. cupranickel
  coin . . 13. five-cent piece
  color . . 4. gray 6. nimbus
  compound . . 8. argenton 11. maillechort
  silver . . 6. German
  symbol . . 2. Ni
nickelodeon . . . 4. juke 7. jukebox, theater (5-cent)
nickname . . . 3. pun 6. monica 7. agnomen, epithet, misname, moniker (monicker), pet name 8. cognomen, misapply 10. soubriquet
nicknaming pun . . . 12. prosonomasia
nictate . . . 4. wink 5. blink 7. twinkle 9. nictitate
nid . . . 3. nod 6. bend and bob
nide . . . 4. nest 5. brood
nidge . . . 3. nig 5. shake 6. quiver
nidificant . . . 12. nestbuilding
nidology, science . . . 8. birds' nests
nidor . . . 5. aroma, scent
nidus . . . 4. nest 5. abode 7. nucleus 13. breeding place
Nietzsche . . . 11. philosopher
nieve . . . 4. fist, hand
niffer . . . 7. bargain 8. exchange
niffy-naffy . . . 7. finical 8. trifling
Niflheim, Nifelheim (Norse Myth) . . . 8. Universe (division of) 10. Nine Worlds
nifty . . . 5. smart 7. stylish 8. very good
Nigeria . . .
  capital . . 5. Abuja, Lagos (formerly)
  city . . 3. Ede 6. Ibadan
  people . . 3. Ibo 6. Yoruba
  plains . . 5. Bornu
niggardly . . . 5. scant 6. paltry, sordid, stingy 9. penurious, scrimping 10. avaricious 12. parsimonious
nigh . . . 2. at 3. nei 4. left, near 5. about, anear, close 6. almost, direct, nearly 8. adjacent 10. contiguous 11. neighboring
night . . . 4. nuit 5. death 7. evening 8. darkness, wee hours 9. adversity, nightfall 11. concealment
night (pert to) . . .
  bird . . 5. potoo 8. nightjar 9. nighthawk 10. goatsucker, nightchurr, owl swallow, shearwater 11. nightingale
  blindness . . 6. nyctalopia
  cap . . 6. biggin
  club . . 4. café 5. disco 6. bistro 7. cabaret 11. discotheque
  goddess . . 3. Nox, Nyx
  jasmine . . 10. hursinghar
  Norse . . 4. Nott
  sight (only) . . 11. hemeralopia
  wandering . . 11. noctivagant
nightfall, at . . . 6. sunset 9. acronical (achronical) (opp of cosmical)
nightingale . . . 6. thrush 8. philomel 9. bed jacket
night jar . . . 5. potoo 10. goatsucker
nightmare . . . 3. alp 4. Mara, ogre

5. dream 7. incubus 9. cauchemar 13. hallucination
nightshade . . . 5. morel (moril) 7. henbane 10. belladonna 11. bittersweet
nigrescent . . . 8. blackish
nihil . . . 7. nothing, no value
nihil debet . . . 13. he owes nothing
nihil ex nihilo . . . 7. nothing (comes) 11. from nothing
Nihilist . . . 9. anarchist, Socialist
Nile (pert to) . . .
  bird . . 4. ibis 7. wryneck
  boat . . 5. baris 6. nuggar 8. dahabeah
  branch . . 4. Blue 5. White
  city . . 7. Rosetta
  color . . 3. boa 5. green
  dam . . 5. Aswan
  Falls . . 5. Ripon
  fish . . 5. bagre 8. mormyrid (sacred)
  god . . 4. Hapi
  headstream . . 6. Kagera
  houseboat . . 8. dahabeah
  island . . 4. Roda (Rhoda)
  waste . . 4. sudd
nilgai . . . 8. antelope
nimble . . . 4. deft, fast, flit, gleg, lish, spry 5. agile, alert, brisk, fleet, quick, smart, swift 6. active, adroit, clever, lively, prompt, volant
nimbose . . . 6. cloudy, stormy 7. clouded 8. nebulous, nubilous, overcast
nimbus . . . 4. disk, halo 5. cloud, vapor 6. fabric, gloria, nickel 7. aureole 10. atmosphere
nimiety . . . 6. excess 10. redundancy
niminy-piminy . . . 7. mincing, refined 10. effeminate
nimmer . . . 5. thief
Nimrod (Bib) . . . 5. ruler 6. hunter 8. Cush's son
nimshi . . . 4. fool 7. half-wit 11. silly person
Nimshi's son (Bib) . . . 11. Jehoshaphat
nine (pert to) . . .
  angles . . 7. nonagon
  banded armadillo . . 4. peba
  based on . . 8. novenary
  Books of nine chapters . . 7. Enneads
  comb form . . 6. ennead
  composition for nine . . 5. nonet
  days' devotion . . 6. novena
  eyes . . 7. lamprey
  gems . . 7. Vikrama
  gods . . 9. Etruscans
  group . . 6. ennead, nonary 18. Ennead of Heliopolis
  headed monster . . 5. Hydra
  inches . . 4. span
  number . . 5. ennea, nueve
  pert to . . 8. enneadic
  players . . 8. baseball
  poetic . . 8. ninefold
Nineteenth amendment . . . 14. Woman's Suffrage
Nineveh (Bib) . . .
  capital . . 7. Assyria
  famed for . . 11. excavations (1814)
Nine Worlds (Norse) . . . 3. Hel 6. Asgard 7. Alfheim, Midgard 8. Niflheim, Vanaheim 10. Jotunnheim

12. Muspellsheim 13. Svartalfaheim

Nine Worthies ... 5. David, Judas
6. Arthur, Caesar, Hector, Joshua
7. Godfrey 9. Alexander
11. Charlemagne

ninny ... 4. clod, dolt, fool, nerd
9. blockhead, simpleton

ninth ... 5. nones (day before Ides)
8. enneatic, ninefold 11. ennea-eteric
(year)

Ninth of Ab (Jew) ... 7. fast day

ninut ... 6. magpie

Niobe (pert to) ...
changed by Zeus to .. 5. stone
father.. 8. Tantalus
husband.. 12. King of Thebes

nip ... 3. bit, cut, sip 4. bite, clip, dram,
peck 5. blast, cheat, check, chili, clamp,
draft, drink, hurry, pinch, seize, sever,
steal, thief 6. benumb, blight, catnip,
cut off, freeze, snatch, tipple 7. shorten,
squeeze 8. compress 10. pickpocket

nipa (pert to) ...
drink.. 9. alcoholic
mat.. 6. thatch
palm.. 4. atap
palm sap.. 5. sugar 7. alcohol

nipcheese ... 5. miser 6. purser

nipper ... 3. boy, lad 4. claw, grab 5. biter,
drink, miser, thief 6. cunner, mitten,
urchin 7. gripper, incisor, pincers
12. costermonger

nippers ... 6. pliers 7. pincers 8. leg
irons, pince-nez 9. handcuffs

nipple ... 3. pap 4. teat 7. mamelon,
papilla 8. mammilla 10. projection
12. protuberance

nippy ... 4. cold 5. brisk 6. active,
biting 7. nipping, pungent 8. grasping,
vigorous

Nirvana ... 4. rags 5. heaven 8. oblivion
12. emancipation

Nisan (Jew calendar) ... 10. first month
(Mar-Apr)

nisi ... 5. if not 6. unless

nissen ... 4. goblin, kobold 7. brownie

nisus ... 7. impulse 8. endeavor, striving

nit ... 3. egg 4. mite 8. parasite

nitency ... 6. luster 10. brightness

niter, nitre ... 6. natron 9. saltpeter
13. sodium nitrate 16. potassium nitrate

nither ... 5. blast 6. debase, shiver
7. oppress, tremble 9. humiliate

nithing (anc) ... 6. coward 7. niggard

nitid ... 3. gay 6. bright 8. lustrous

nitric acid ... 10. aqua fortis

nitrogen ... 3. azo (comb form), gas
5. azote 8. element 10. atmosphere

nitrogen compound ... 7. ammonia

nitroglycerin, nitroglycerine ...
8. dynamite (1846) 9. explosive,
guncotton

nitrous oxide ... 3. gas 10. anesthetic
11. laughing gas

nitty-gritty ... 4. base, crux, gist
7. essence

Niue, Pacific island ...
territory of .. 10. New Zealand

niveau .. 5. level

niveous ... 5. snowy, white (shining)

nix ... 2. no 5. no one 6. forbid, nobody,

sprite 7. nothing

Njorth, Njord (Norse) ... 3. god (fertility)
5. Vanir

Njorth's daughter ... 5. Freya (Freyja)
7. goddess (love and beauty)

Njorth's son ... 3. god 4. Frey

no ... 3. naw, nay, nit 4. baal, dead, gone,
none 5. not so 6. denial, no-gaki, not
any 8. not at all

Noah, Bib (pert to) ...
boat.. 3. Ark
dove.. 7. Columba
father.. 6. Lamech
flood.. 6. Deluge
Genesis.. 9. patriarch
grandson.. 4. Aram
landing, the Ark.. 6. Ararat
raven.. 6. Corvus
son.. 3. Ham 4. Shem 7. Japheth

nob ... 4. head, nave 6. hobnob
8. nobleman 9. personage

nobby ... 4. boat 5. smart 7. stylish

Nobel powder ... 10. Ballistite

noble ... 4. epic, fine, peer 5. ducal,
grand, lofty, manly 6. epical 7. eminent,
grandee, liberal, stately, sublime
8. elevated, generous, imposing,
renowned, splendid 9. dignified,
high birth, honorable 10. impressive
11. illustrious, magnanimous,
magnificent 12. aristocratic

nobleman ... 3. sir 4. duke, earl, lord,
peer 5. baron 6. barony, flaith,
thakur 7. baronet, grandee, marquis
8. margrave, optimate, viscount
9. blueblood, patrician 10. aristocrat,
chess piece

nobleness of birth ... 6. eugeny

noblewoman ... 4. lady 5. begum
7. duchess, peeress 8. baroness,
contessa, countess, marquise
11. marchioness

nobody ... 4. none 5. no one 7. nebbish
8. no person 9. jackstraw, nonentity
10. not anybody

nocent ... 6. guilty 7. harmful, hurtful
8. criminal (opp of innocent)

nocturnal ... 5. night 7. nightly
8. darkness, nocturne

nocturnal (pert to) ...
animal.. 3. bat 4. coon 5. lemur, ratel
6. possum 7. opossum
astronomy.. 9. astrolabe
bird.. 3. owl
signs.. 8. zodiacal

nocturne ... 7. lullaby 8. serenade
10. night scene (art)

nocuous ... 7. hurtful, noxious

nod ... 3. bow 4. bend, bock, doze,
tend, wink 6. beckon, signal 7. bidding
8. greeting

Nod (Bib) ... 9. Land of Nod 10. East
of Eden

nodding ... 6. nutant 7. annuent, weeping
(as a willow) 8. cernuous, drooping

noddy ... 3. auk 4. fool 6. drowsy, fulmar,
noodle, sleepy 7. foolish, hackney
9. simpleton

node ... 4. knob, knot, knur, plot
5. joint, nodus 7. dilemma 8. swelling
10. difficulty 12. complication,

protuberance

nodule ... 4. auge, bump, knot, lump, mass 5. geode 7. granule, nablock 8. tubercle 12. complication

nodus ... 4. knot, node 10. difficulty 12. complication

noel ... 5. carol (Xmas), shout 9. sign of joy

Noel ... 6. Natale 9. Christmas

noeud ... 3. bow 4. knot

nog ... 3. peg, pin 5. block 6. eggnog, noggin 8. treenail 9. brickwork

nogada ... 10. pecan candy

nogal ... 5. pecan

noggin ... 3. cup, mug 4. head, pate

noise ... 3. din, pop, rap 4. bang, boom, klop, roar, rout 5. blare, blast, bruit, chang, clang, click, rumor, sound 6. clamor, outcry, racket, report, strife, uproar 7. brattle, chortle, discord, quarrel, rapping 9. shoutings

noise (pert to) ...

ghost .. 11. poltergeist

harsh .. 4. bray 7. stridor 9. caterwaul

respiration .. 4. rale

rustling .. 5. swish

Scotch .. 5. chang

water .. 5. plash 6. ripple, splash

whirring .. 4. burr

noised ... 6. dinned 7. rumored 8. reported

noisemaker ... 4. horn 5. siren 6. rattle 7. clacker, whistle 8. whiz-bang

noisome ... 3. bad 4. foul 5. fetid, nasty 7. harmful, noxious 8. stinking 9. offensive 10. malodorous, pernicious 11. destructive, unwholesome 12. insalubrious

noisy ... 4. loud 7. blatant 8. brawling, clattery 9. clamorous, turbulent 10. blustering, boisterous, vociferous 12. obstreperous, rattley-bang

nom ... 4. name

nomad ... 4. arab 5. gypsy 6. roamer, Romany 7. Bedouin, Saracen, scenite, zingaro 8. wanderer

nomadic ... 9. itinerant

nomarchy (Gr) ... 4. nome 8. province 10. department

nom de plume ... 7. pen name 9. pseudonym

nomen ... 4. gens, name 7. agnomen 8. cognomen 9. praenomen

nomenclature ... 4. name 5. onymy 8. glossary, onymatic, register 10. dictionary, Latin names, vocabulary 11. designation, terminology

nominal ... 3. par 6. unreal 7. not real, titular, topical 8. so-called

nominal recognizance (law) ... 3. Doe

nonage ... 6. neanic 8. immature, minority, pupilage, youthful

nonary ... 9. nine group 10. base of nine 11. group of nine

nonbeliever ... 5. pagan 7. atheist, heathen, infidel 8. agnostic 11. disbeliever 12. non-Christian

nonce ... 3. now 8. meantime 11. temporarily

nonchalant ... 4. cool 6. casual 8. careless 10. insouciant 11. indifferent,

unconcerned 13. imperturbable

noncompliance ... 7. refusal 12. disobedience 13. recalcitrance

non compos mentis ... 7. unsound 8. demented, deranged 11. disoriented

nonconformist ... 7. heretic, sectary 8. objector, recusant 9. dissenter, protester

nondescript ... 11. exceptional 13. indescribable 14. indeterminable

none ... 2. no 4. nary 5. nones, no one 6. nobody, not any, not one 10. nobody else

nonentity ... 7. a nobody, nullity 8. nihility, nonbeing 9. res nihili 11. nothingness 12. nonexistence

nonessential ... 8. needless 9. extrinsic 10. adiaphoron, incidental, irrelevant 11. superfluous 12. adventitious

non licit ... 8. unlawful

nonmetallic ... 4. spar 5. argon, boron 6. carbon, helium, iodine, oxygen 7. bromine 8. chlorine, nitrogen

nonpareil ... 4. type 7. paragon 8. nonesuch, peerless 9. unrivaled 11. unsurpassed 14. painted bunting

nonplus ... 4. stop 5. blank, stump 6. baffle, puzzle, thwart 9. mystify, perplex 8. quandary

nonproductive ... 6. barren 7. sterile 9. fruitless

nonprofessional ... 3. ham, lay 4. laic 5. laity 7. amateur 10. apprentice

nonsense ... 3. bah 4. bosh, bunk, tosh 5. folly, stite 6. drivel, humbug, jargon 7. blarney, foolery, rubbish, trifles, twaddle 8. falderal, flimflam, tommyrot, trumpery 9. absurdity, frivolity, poppycock, silliness 10. balderdash, tomfoolery, triviality

nonsense verse ... 9. amphigory (amphigouri), rigmarole

non tanto (Mus) ... 9. non troppo, not as much

noodle ... 4. fool, head 5. brain, ninny 9. blockhead, simpleton 12. stupid person

nook ... 4. cant, cove 5. angle, herne, niche 6. corner, cranny, recess 7. crevice 10. promontory

noon ... 6. midday, summit 8. meridian, noontide 9. ninth hour 11. noon of night (poet)

noonday rest ... 6. siesta

noose ... 3. tie 4. bond, hang, loop 5. snare 6. circle, halter 7. laniard (lanyard) 7. hangman's rope

Nootka ... 3. Aht, dog 6. Indian

norati ... 5. noise 6. gossip

Norbertine ... 12. Premonstrant

Nordic ... 8. Germanic 12. Scandinavian

norie ... 9. cormorant

norm ... 4. rule, type 5. model, norma 7. average, measure, pattern 8. standard, template

norma ... 4. rule 5. gauge, model 6. square 7. pattern 8. standard, template 13. constellation

normal ... 3. par 4. just, mean, sane 5. usual 6. common 7. average, logical, natural, orderly, regular, typical

8. everyday, ordinary 9. customary

Norman ... 6. French 7. crimson
8. Northman 10. Romanesque
17. conquest of England (1066)

Normandy ...
beach .. 5. Omaha
capital .. 4. Caen 5. Rouen (old)
city .. 5. Havre 6. Dieppe 7. Alençon
8. Cherbourg
conqueror .. 5. Rollo 8. William I
governed by .. 6. France (1940)
Viking duke (anc) .. 5. Rollo

Norn (Teut Myth) .... 4. Urth, Wyrd
5. Skuld 9. Verthandi

Norse ... 9. Norwegian 12. Scandinavian

Norse (pert to) ...
abode of gods .. 6. Asgard 8. Valhalla
alphabet .. 6. runics
ash tree, universe .. 10. Yddrasill
bard .. 5. scald (skald) 7. sagaman
collected songs, myths .. 4. Edda
demon (Fire) .. 4. Surt (Surtr)
earth .. 7. Midgard
epic .. 4. saga
explorer .. 11. Leif Ericson
first man .. 4. Askr
giant .. 4. Loki, Ymir (Ymer) 5. Jotun
6. Fafnir
horse .. 8. Brimfaxi 9. Skinfaksi
horse (Odin's) .. 10. Yggdrasill
king .. 4. Atli
language (old) .. 9. Icelandic
maidens (Odin's) .. 8. Valkyrie
man .. 8. Northman
monster .. 6. kraken 7. Midgard
patron saint .. 4. Olaf
poem .. 4. rune
toast .. 5. skoal
warrior .. 9. berserker
watchdog (Hel's) .. 4. Garm (Garmr)
wolf .. 6. Fenrir

Norse goddess of ...
death, underworld .. 3. Hel, Ran
fate .. 4. Norn, Urth, Wyrd
flowers .. 5. Nanna
giantess .. 4. Nott
love, beauty .. 5. Freya
peace, healing .. 3. Eir
sky .. 5. Frigg (Frigga)

Norse God of ...
day .. 3. Dag
evil .. 4. Loki
fertility .. 4. Frey (Freyr) 6. Njorth (Njord)
giants .. 4. Ymir
justice .. 4. Frey 7. Forseti
light .. 6. Balder
night .. 4. Nott
poetry .. 4. Odin 5. Bragi
primeval (the world) .. 4. Ymir (Ymer)
sea .. 5. Aegir
thunder .. 4. Thor
war, wisdom .. 4. Odin (Wodin)
watchfulness .. 8. Heimdall

Norse gods, chief ... 3. Tyr (Tiu) 4. Frey,
Jarl, Loki, Odin (Othin, Wodin), Thor
(Donar), Vali, Ymir 5. Aesir (group)
6. Balder, Njorth 7. Asynjur (group),
Forseti 8. Heimdall

North (far) ... 6. Arctic

North Africa ... see also Africa
country .. 7. Algeria, Tunisia

fruit .. 3. fig 4. date
people .. 4. Moor 6. Berber, Hamite,
Libyan
port .. 4. Sfax

North America ... see also America
Indian blanket .. 6. stroud
mountain, highest .. 8. McKinley
orchid .. 8. arethusa
owl .. 7. wapacut
rail .. 4. sora
reindeer .. 7. caribou
river, longest .. 5. Yukon 8. Missouri
11. Mississippi
snake .. 5. adder

North Atlantic (pert to) ...
cape .. 5. Sable
island .. 7. Britain, Iceland, Ireland
9. Greenland, Manhattan
sea gull .. 4. skua

North Carolina ...
cape .. 4. Fear 7. Lookout 8. Hatteras
capital .. 7. Raleigh
city .. 6. Durham 9. Asheville, Charlotte
12. Winston-Salem
explorer .. 6. De Soto 9. Verrazano
famed person .. 12. Virginia Dare 16. Sir
Walter Raleigh
first flight .. 9. Kitty Hawk
mountain .. 10. Mt Mitchell
pine .. 8. loblolly
river .. 3. Tar 5. Neuse 6. Peedee (Yadkin)
State admission .. 7. Twelfth
State bird .. 8. cardinal
State flower .. 7. dogwood
State motto .. 14. Esse Quam Videri
20. To Be Rather Than To Seem
State nickname .. 7. Tarheel 8. Old
North

North Dakota ...
capital .. 8. Bismarck
city .. 5. Fargo, Minot
fort .. 6. Mandan 7. Lincoln
11. Abercrombie
historic site .. 24. International Peace
Garden
mountain .. 10. White Butte
reservoir .. 8. Garrison
State admission .. 8. Fortieth (or
Thirty-ninth)
State bird .. 10. meadowlark
State flower .. 11. prairie rose
State nickname .. 5. Sioux 11. Flickertail

northeaster .. 4. gale, wind 5. storm

Northern ... 6. boreal 11. hyperborean
13. septentrional

Northern constellation ... 3. Cor 4. Lyra
9. Andromeda

northernmost world (inhabitable) ...
5. Thule 9. Trondheim

North Pole ... 10. boreal pole

North Sea ... 6. Baltic, German

North Sea arm ... 8. Kattegat
9. Skagerrak (Skager-Rak)

North Sea canal ... 4. Kiel

North Star ... 7. Polaris 8. Cynosure,
lodestar (loadstar), polestar

north wind ... 6. Boreas 10. tramontane

Norway ... see also Norwegian
capital .. 4. Oslo 11. Christiania (old)
city .. 6. Bergen 7. Drammen
9. Trondheim

county . . 5. fylke
inlet . . 5. fiord (fjord)
mountain . . 6. Kjolen
parliament . . 8. Storting (Storthing)
patron saint . . 4. Olaf (Olaus)
phenomenon . . 11. midnight sun
   14. Northern Lights
plateau . . 5. fjeld
river . . 2. Oi 4. Tana 7. Glommen
Norwegian (pert to) . . .
  bird . . 4. rype 9. ptarmigan
  cart . . 11. stolkjaerre
  dance . . 7. halling
  duck . . 7. widgeon
  embroidery . . 9. hardanger
  goblin . . 5. Nisse 6. kobold
  guardian spirit . . 6. fylgia 8. hamingja
  haddock . . 8. rosefish
  language . . 5. Norse 8. Rigsmaal
   9. Landsmaal
  liquor . . 7. akevitt
  sea monster . . 6. kraken
  tales . . 4. Edda
Norwegian people . . .
  author . . 6. Hamsun, Undset
  composer . . 5. Grieg
  dramatist . . 5. Ibsen
  explorer . . 6. Nansen (Nobel Prize)
   8. Sverdrup
  king . . 6. Harold (The Fairhaired)
   15. Harold Hardraade
  philologist . . 5. Assen
  raiders . . 7. Vikings
  saint . . 4. Olaf (Olaus)
  violinist . . 7. Ole Bull
  zoologist . . 5. Sars
nose . . . 3. neb, pry 4. conk, prow
  5. nasus, scent, smell, snout 6. meddle,
  muzzle, nuzzle 8. olfactor 9. detective,
  proboscis 11. investigate
nose (pert to) . . .
  ailment . . 6. coryza 8. rhinitis
  bees, birds . . 4. lore 5. lorum
  bleeding . . 9. epistaxis
  cartilage . . 6. septum
  glasses . . 8. pince-nez
  large . . 6. nasute
  muscle . . 7. nasalis
  opening . . 5. naris (nares, pl) 7. nostril
  partition . . 5. vomer
  plug . . 12. rhineurynter
  relating to . . 5. nasal 6. narial, rhinal
  snub . . 6. simous
  surgery . . 11. rhinoplasty
noseband (bridle) . . 6. misrol
nosegay . . . 4. posy 7. bouquet, perfume
  9. fragrance 10. frangipani (tree)
nosh . . . 3. eat
nosocomium . . . 8. hospital
nosography, nosology (science of) . . .
  7. disease
nostalgia . . . 8. yearning 11. wistfulness
  12. homesickness 14. sentimentality
nostology (study of) . . . 8. senility
  10. geriatrics 11. gerontology
Nostradamus . . . 4. seer 7. prophet
  10. astrologer
nostril . . . 5. naris (nares, pl) 6. narial
  9. olfactory
nostril-shaped . . . 8. nariform
nosy . . . 5. nasal 6. prying 7. curious

  8. fragrant 10. malodorous
  11. inquisitive
Nosy, Old (nickname) . . . 16. Duke of
  Wellington
not (pert to) . . .
  any . . 2. no 4. nane, nary, none 7. no
  trace
  at all . . 5. nohow 6. nowise
  easy . . 7. labored
  either . . 7. neither
  feral . . 4. tame
  harmed . . 9. unscathed
  having a will . . 9. intestate
  hollow . . 5. solid
  in motion . . 5. fixed 6. stable, static
  7. stabile 10. stationary
  in the least . . 6. nowhit
  moral . . 6. amoral 7. immoral
  open (fruit) . . 11. indehiscent
  prefix . . 2. il, im, in, ir, un 3. non
  professional . . 4. laic 7. amateur
  qualified . . 5. unfit
  running (stream) . . 8. stagnant
  separable . . 11. indivisible
  settled . . 4. moot
  subjugated . . 7. unbowed
  suitable . . 5. inept
  the same . . 5. other 9. different
  to know . . 5. unken 10. unfamiliar
notable . . . 6. famous 8. historic
  9. celebrity, important, memorable,
  notorious 10. noteworthy, remarkable
  13. distinguished, extraordinary
notandum . . . 4. note 5. entry
  10. memorandum
notary . . . 5. notar 8. attestor, notebook,
  official 9. scrivener 12. notary public,
  stenographer
notation . . . 4. memo, note 5. entry
  7. comment, marking 9. etymology
  10. annotation
notator . . . 5. noter 8. recorder
  9. annotator
notch . . . 3. gap, jap 4. dent, dint,
  kerf, nick, nock 5. cleft, crena, score
  6. defile, dentil (Her), indent 7. passage
  8. undercut 9. indenture 11. indentation
notched bar (door) . . . 4. risp
notched opening (Anat) . . . 5. hilum
note . . . 2. ut 3. jot 4. chit, head,
  mark, memo, sign, sole, song, tone,
  tune 5. breve, gloss, sound, token
  6. billet, notice, postil, record, remark,
  report 7. apostil (apostille), comment,
  epistle 8. dispatch, eminence, indicate,
  marginal, scholium 9. character
  10. annotation, importance, indication,
  memorandum, reputation 11. certificate,
  observation
note (pert to) . . .
  death sound . . 4. mort
  explanatory . . 5. gloss 8. scholium
  half . . 5. minim
  high . . 3. alt, E la
  marginal . . 6. postil 7. apostil (apostille)
  musical . . 5. breve 6. ecbole 7. punctus
  stem of . . 5. filum
notebook . . . 6. street 7. estreat
  8. ratebook 10. adversaria,
  memorandum
noted . . . 4. seen 5. famed 6. famous,

marked 7. eminent, notable 8. far-famed, renowned 9. distingué, prominent, well-known 10. celebrated

notes . . . 5. duole 6. strain 7. tiralee 11. solmization

nothing . . . 3. nil, nox 4. luke, rien, void, zero 5. nihil 6. naught, nichil, nought, trifle 7. a nobody 9. nonentity 11. empty-handed 12. nonexistence

nothing doing . . . 4. calm 6. hushed, no dice, no soap, placid 7. I refuse 9. by no means, God forbid, quiescent

notice . . . 2. ad 3. see 4. heed, idea, mark, mind, news, note, sign 5. blurb, edict, quote 6. advice, espial, notion, regard, remark 7. affiche, mention, observe, warning 8. bulletin, citation 9. attention 10. commentary 11. information, observation 12. announcement, intelligence 13. advertisement

notice (pert to) . . .
advance . . 8. ballyhoo
death . . 4. obit 8. obituary
marriage . . 4. bans 5. banns

notify . . . 4. cite, page, tell, warn 6. inform, remind 7. apprise, declare, publish 8. announce

notion . . . 4. idea, view, whim 5. freit 6. belief, theory, vagary 7. caprice, impulse, opinion 9. intention 10. conception, denotation, knickknack 11. supposition

notionable . . . 8. fanciful 9. whimsical

notional . . . 6. unreal 9. imaginary, visionary, whimsical

notions . . . 5. goods, wares 11. commodities, merchandise

notoriety . . . 4. fame, plug 5. éclat 8. ballyhoo 9. limelight, publicity, spotlight

notorious . . . 5. known, noted 6. arrant, famous, notour 8. flagrant, infamous, talked of 10. recognized 11. conspicuous

notorious character . . . 5. James (Jesse) 7. Cochise, Younger 8. Geronimo, Jennings, Murietta 9. Jack Ketch, Wyatt Earp 11. Billy the Kid, Poncho Villa, Sitting Bull 12. Calamity Jane 13. John Dillinger 14. Wild Bill Hickok

notum . . . 4. back

notus . . . 4. back (comb form)

notwithstanding . . . 3. but, yet 5. still 6. mauger (maugre), though 7. despite, however 8. although 9. in spite of 12. nevertheless

nought, naught . . . 3. bad, nil 4. zero 5. wrong 7. nothing, useless 9. worthless

noughty . . . 3. bad 9. worthless

noumenal . . . 4. real 5. ontal (opp of phenomenal)

noun . . . 7. subject

noun (pert to) . . .
gender, common . . 7. epicene
indeclinable . . 6. aptote
irregular . . 5. pecus 11. heteroclite
suffix . . 2. et, ia 3. ent, ery, ier, ion, ior, ist, ite 4. ence
verbal . . 6. gerund

nourish . . . 4. feed, grow 5. nurse 6. foster, suckle, supply 7. support, sustain

9. cultivate 13. promote growth

nourishing . . . 6. alible 8. nutrient 9. nutritive 10. alimentary

nourishment . . . 3. aid 4. food 5. manna, meats 7. aliment, pabulum 9. nutriment, nutrition 10. sustenance 13. nutritiveness 14. nutritiousness

nous . . . 4. mind 8. ready wit 9. intellect 11. world spirit

Nova . . . 4. star

Nova Scotia . . .
bay . . 5. Fundy 10. Chedabucto
cape . . 5. Canso
capital . . 7. Halifax
greens . . 11. sea plantain
island . . 10. Cape Breton
lake, salt . . 7. Bras d'Or
native . . 7. Acadian 8. Bluenose
poetic name . . 6. Acadia (Acadie)
settlement, first . . 9. Port Royal

novel . . . 3. new 4. book, rare 5. fresh, story 7. fiction, romance, strange, unusual 8. original

novelty . . . 3. fad 7. newness 9. freshness 10. innovation, recentness 11. originality

novice . . . 3. nun 4. tyro (tiro) 5. chela 6. rookie, tyrone 7. amateur, learner 8. beginner, freshman, initiate, neophyte, newcomer 9. fledgling, greenhorn, postulant 10. apprentice, catechumen 11. abecedarian

novitiate . . . 6. novice 9. probation 14. apprenticeship

now . . . 3. noo 4. hora 6. at once 7. present 9. at present, forthwith, instantly 10. very lately 12. at this moment

nowhere . . . 5. limbo 6. absent 7. no place 8. oblivion 9. nowhither 11. nonexistent, not anywhere, nullibicity

nowhere else . . . 5. there

nowise . . . 8. not at all

Nox (pert to) . . .
brother . . 6. Erebus
daughter . . 10. Hesperides
goddess (Rom) . . 5. Night
husband . . 5. Chaos

noxious . . . 4. evil 5. nasty, yucky (sl) 6. nocent, odious 7. baneful, harmful, hurtful, noisome 8. injurious, miasmatic 10. corruptive, pernicious 11. destructive, unwholesome 12. insalubrious

nozzle . . . 3. tew 4. nose, vent 5. giant, snout 6. nuzzle, outlet, tuyère 7. conduit 9. sprinkler

nuance . . . 5. shade 9. gradation, variation 10. refinement

nub . . . 4. gist, knob, knot, knub, lump, neck, snag 9. main point 12. protuberance

Nubia (pert to) . . .
afterglow . . 14. second twilight
animal . . 4. goat 5. horse
autonym . . 6. Berber 7. Barabra
harp . . 5. nanga
people . . 4. Nuba

nubia . . . 4. wrap 5. cloud

nucha . . . 4. nape, neck

nuclear complex . . . 7. Oedipus

nuclear energy (terms) ... **4.** mass
 6. fusion, ionize **7.** fission, neutron,
 reactor, tokamak **8.** hydrogen,
 meltdown
nuclear network fiber ... **5.** linin
nucleus ... **4.** core **5.** cadre, focus, umbra
 6. center, kernel **8.** rudiment
nude ... **4.** bare **5.** color, naked **6.** Season
 (color) **7.** denuded **8.** stripped, undraped
 9. unadorned, unclothed, undressed
nudge ... **3.** jog, nog **4.** knub, lump, poke,
 prod, push **5.** block, elbow **6.** jostle,
 remind, signal
nudibranch ... **7.** mollusk
nugatory ... **4.** vain **7.** invalid, trivial
 8. trifling **9.** worthless **11.** ineffectual
nuisance ... **4.** bane, bore, harm, hurt,
 pest **6.** injury **9.** annoyance
nuit ... **5.** night
null ... **4.** void **6.** vacant **7.** invalid
 8. nugatory **11.** nonexistent
 13. inefficacious, insignificant
nullifidian ... **7.** skeptic **9.** nullibist,
 skeptical **10.** unbeliever **11.** disbeliever
nullify ... **4.** undo, void **5.** annul **6.** cancel,
 negate **7.** abolish, destroy **8.** abrogate
 10. counteract, neutralize
numb ... **6.** clumsy, freeze, stupid, torpid
 8. benumbed, deadened, helpless
 9. apathetic, incapable, rigescent
 10. insensible **12.** anesthetized
number ... **3.** sum **5.** count, digit,
 limit **7.** integer, numeral **8.** quantity
 9. aggregate, enumerate
 10. complement **11.** information
number (pert to) ...
 added .. **6.** encore
 again .. **10.** renumerate
 by tens .. **10.** decimal
 cardinal .. **7.** primary (one, two)
 consecutively .. **5.** folio
 copies (printed) .. **7.** edition
 describable .. **6.** scalar
 irrational .. **4.** surd
 least whole .. **4.** unit
 lucky .. **5.** seven
 many .. **4.** herd **6.** myriad **7.** several
 9. multitude **12.** considerable
 ordinal .. **5.** first **6.** second (etc)
 third power .. **4.** cube
 votes .. **4.** poll
 whole .. **7.** integer
numbles, nombles ... **6.** umbles
 7. inwards **8.** entrails
numbness ... **6.** torpor **10.** rigescence
numeral ... **5.** Roman **6.** Arabic, figure
 9. character
numerous ... **4.** lots, many **7.** copious,
 crowded **8.** abundant, measured,
 thronged **9.** plentiful
Numidia (pert to) ...
 city .. **5.** Hippo
 crane .. **10.** demoiselle
 language (written) .. **5.** Punic **6.** Tuareg
 7. Hamitic
 modern kingdom .. **7.** Algeria
numskull ... **4.** dolt, nerd **5.** dunce
nun ... **4.** moth, smew **5.** Clare
 (Franciscan), Vesta **6.** monial, pigeon,
 sister **8.** titmouse, votaress **9.** priestess
 13. Lady of Loretto

nun bird ... **6.** Monasa **8.** puffbird
nunciate ... **9.** announcer, messenger
nuncio ... **6.** legate **8.** delegate
 9. messenger **11.** internuncio
nuncupate ... **7.** declare **8.** dedicate,
 inscribe, proclaim **9.** designate
nuncupative ... **4.** oral **9.** unwritten (will)
 11. designative
nun headdress ... **6.** wimple
nunnari root ... **12.** sarsaparilla
nunnery ... **5.** abbey **7.** convent **8.** cloister
nunnery head ... **6.** abbess
nunni ... **7.** blesbok (blesbuck) **8.** antelope
Nuphar ... **11.** spatterdock
nuptial ... **6.** bridal **7.** marital **9.** connubial
 11. matrimonial
nurse ... **4.** amah, ayah, feed, rear, tend
 5. bonne, mammy **6.** caress, suckle
 7. care for, cherish, nourish, nurture,
 nutrice **9.** nursemaid
nursed ... **3.** fed **6.** tended **7.** cradled,
 suckled **8.** nurtured **9.** nourished
nursery ... **6.** crèche, school **7.** day care
 (center)
nurse shark ... **4.** gata
nurture ... **3.** aid **4.** feed, rear **5.** nurse
 6. foster **7.** care for, cherish **8.** breeding,
 training **9.** education, encourage,
 nutriment
nut ... **4.** anta, kola (cola) **5.** acorn,
 betel, pecan, piñon **6.** almond, Brazil,
 cashew, litchi, peanut, walnut **7.** filbert,
 hickory, maranon **8.** beechnut, chestnut
 9. butternut
nut (pert to) ...
 bearing .. **10.** nuciferous
 brown .. **5.** hazel **6.** walnut **8.** chestnut
 coal .. **10.** anthracite
 collectively .. **4.** food **5.** shack
 9. beechnuts
 confection .. **8.** marzipan
 cracker .. **4.** crow
 eating .. **10.** nucivorous **11.** nuciphagous
 edible part .. **5.** kernel
 grass .. **5.** sedge
 Med .. **4.** kola **5.** bichy **9.** gourounut
 odd .. **9.** eccentric
 palm .. **5.** betel, lichi **7.** coconut
 ref to .. **5.** nucal
 shell .. **4.** case, hull **6.** trifle
Nut (pert to) ...
 consort of .. **3.** Geb
 daughter .. **4.** Isis **8.** Nephthys
 goddess of .. **5.** earth
 son .. **2.** Ra
nutation ... **3.** nod **7.** nodding
nuthatch ... **4.** bird **5.** sitta **6.** xenops
 8. titmouse **9.** nutpecker
nutmeg ... **4.** mace **5.** drupe **6.** beaver
 (color)
nutmeg (pert to) ...
 bird, finch .. **5.** cowry **10.** weaverbird
 family .. **13.** Myristicaceae
 tree .. **6.** camara
Nutmeg State ... **11.** Connecticut
nutpecker ... **8.** nuthatch
nut quad ... **6.** en quad
nutria ... **3.** fur **5.** grège **10.** beaverlike
nutria fur bearer ... **5.** coypu
nutrice ... **5.** nurse
nutriment ... **4.** food **7.** aliment, pabulum

9. nutrition 11. nourishment
nutritious ... 9. alimental 10. alimentary, nourishing
nuts ... 4. food, mast 5. shack
9. beechnuts
nut's partner ... 4. bolt
nutty ... 4. gaga, zest 5. queer, smart, spicy 7. amorous, piquant
10. unbalanced 11. fascinating
14. cracker-brained
nuzzle ... 5. nurse 6. burrow, cuddle, foster, nestle 7. cherish 8. make snug
nyctalopia ... 14. night blindness
nye ... 4. eyas, nest, nide 5. brood
nymph ... 4. nais 5. deity, dryad, naiad, oread, siren, sylph 6. Nereid 7. Oceanid
9. hamadryad
nymph (pert to) ...
Arcadian .. 6. Syrinx
beloved of Narcissus .. 4. Echo
color .. 4. pink
Cretan .. 8. Cynosura
fountain, river .. 4. nais 5. naiad 6. Egeria
German legend .. 7. Lorelei
Greek .. 4. Echo 6. Daphne 8. Arethusa
Hesperides (one of) .. 5. Aegle
7. Hespera

hills, mountain .. 5. oread
laurel tree .. 6. Daphne
Messina Strait .. 6. Scylla
monster .. 6. Scylla
Mt Ida .. 6. Oenone
Muslim paradise .. 5. houri
ocean .. 5. siren 6. Nereid 7. Galatea, Oceanid 10. Callirrhoe
pursued by Apollo .. 6. Daphne, Syrinx
8. Arethusa
Queen .. 3. Mab
sea bird .. 6. Scylla
tree .. 5. Dryad 9. Hamadryad
water .. 5. Naiad 6. Undine 7. Hydriad
woods .. 5. Dryad 8. Arethusa
9. Hamadryad
young .. 7. nymphet
Nymphaea ... 8. Castalia 11. water lilies
nymphs ... 10. Atlantides, Hesperides
nystagmus ... 14. eyeball disease
Nyx, Nox (pert to) ...
daughter .. 4. Eris
father .. 5. Chaos
goddess of .. 5. Night
mother of .. 11. Day and Night
Nzambi ... 7. goddess (Afr) 11. earth mother

O

O (pert to) ...
interjection .. 11. exclamation
letter .. 5. tenth
mathematics .. 4. zero 6. cipher
pref (family) .. 5. Irish
oaf ... 4. boor, dolt, lout 5. idiot, ouphe, yokel 9. blockhead, simpleton
10. changeling
oafish ... 6. simple, stupid
oak ... 4. club 5. brave, color, oaken, stout 6. strong 7. Quercus 8. hardness, strength 13. artificial fly
oak (pert to) ...
apple .. 4. gall 10. she-oak cone
beauty .. 4. moth
California .. 5. roble 6. encina
comb form .. 6. querci
evergreen .. 4. holm, ilex 5. holly
family .. 8. Fagaceae
fern .. 8. polypody
fruit .. 5. acorn 6. camata
fungus .. 10. armillaria
gall .. 8. oak apple
Jerusalem .. 7. ambrose
kinds .. 3. bur, red 5. black, white
6. ground, poison, willow 8. chestnut
10. canyon live
plantation .. 9. quercetum
resembling .. 9. roboreous
tannin .. 7. quercic 9. quercinic
thicket .. 9. chaparral
Turkey .. 6. cerris
web .. 10. cockchafer
young .. 8. flittern
oam ... 5. steam 7. warm air

Oannes (Bab) ... 5. deity (part man, part fish)
oar ... 3. row 5. blade, remus, rower, scull 6. paddle, propel 7. oarsman
oar (pert to) ...
blade .. 4. palm, peel
feather .. 5. remex
fulcrum, lock .. 5. pivot, thole
lop .. 6. rabbit
shaft .. 4. loom
shaped .. 7. remiped 8. remiform
oars (pert to) ...
collective .. 6. oarage, sculls
one bank .. 7. unireme
reverse .. 5. sheave
three banks .. 7. trireme
two banks .. 6. bireme
oasis ... 3. ojo 4. wadi (wady) 5. Gafsa
6. Dakhla 11. fertile spot
oast ... 4. kiln, oven
oat (pert to) ...
cake .. 5. caper
ear (Old World) .. 4. bird 7. wagtail
fowl .. 11. snow bunting
genus .. 5. Avena 6. oathay
grass .. 4. ulla 9. chaparral
husks .. 5. shood (shude)
like .. 10. avenaceous
rent (paid as) .. 7. avenage
oath ... 3. God 4. aith, drat, egad 5. bedad, curse 6. pledge 7. serment 9. affidavit, holy smoke, profanity 10. deposition
11. affirmation
Obadiah (Bib) ... 6. Quaker 7. prophet
obbligato ... 8. required

13. accompaniment, indispensable

obduction ... 7. autopsy 8. covering

obdurate ... 4. firm, hard 5. rough, stony
6. mulish, rugged 7. adamant, callous
8. stubborn 9. heartless, obstinate,
unbending, unfeeling 10. impenitent,
inflexible, insensible, unyielding
11. hardhearted, intractable

obedient ... 6. docile 7. duteous,
dutiful, orderly 8. amenable, yielding
9. attentive, compliant 10. submissive
11. conformable

obeisance ... 3. bow 5. binge, congé
6. curtsy, fealty, homage 9. deference
10. respectful 14. obsequiousness

obeisance, to make ... 3. bow 6. congee,
curtsy, salaam

obelisk ... 5. pylon 6. guglia (guglio),
needle, obelus, pillar 16. Cleopatra's
Needle

Oberon (pert to) ...
  Astron .. 9. satellite
  character of .. 11. Shakespeare
  classic .. 4. poem 5. opera
  husband of .. 7. Titania
  Myth .. 13. King of Fairies

obese ... 3. fat 5. puffy, pursy, squab,
stout 6. fleshy, turgid 8. liparous
9. corpulent

obey ... 3. ear 4. hear, mind 5. yield
6. comply, submit

obfuscate ... 3. dim 6. darken, opaque
7. confuse, perplex 8. bewilder

obi ... 4. sash 6. girdle

obit ... 4. rest 5. death 6. notice
7. decease, release 8. obituary
9. obsequies 10. necrologue
11. Requiem Mass 12. mortuary roll

obiter ... 9. in passing 12. incidentally

obiter dictum ... 7. opinion (of judge)

object ... 3. aim, end 4. goal, hulk 5. cavil,
demur, scoff, thing 6. appose, expose,
motive, oppose 7. article, grammar,
protest, purpose 9. intention

object (pert to) ...
  bulky .. 4. hulk
  circular .. 7. trundle
  cloudlike .. 6. nebula
  illustrative .. 6. realia (pl)
  rare .. 5. curio 7. antique
  rational .. 8. noumenon
  sacred .. Urim 7. Thummim
  small .. 4. mite

object for ...
  devotion, worship .. 4. icon, idol 5. totem
  6. fetish
  dread .. 5. bogey (bogie) 6. goblin 8. the
  Devil
  going and coming .. 6. errand
  greed .. 5. lucre, money 6. wealth
  knowledge .. 7. scibile

objection ... 3. bar 5. cavil 7. protest,
quarrel 8. demurrer, obstacle
9. exception 11. disapproval

objectionable ... 9. offensive
11. exceptional, inexpedient
13. uncommendable

objective ... 3. aim, end 4. goal 6. motive,
target 7. purpose

objector, conscientious ... 6. conchy

objects (Bib) ... 4. Urim 7. Thummim

objects (floating) ... 7. flotsam

objurgate ... 5. abuse, chide, scold
6. rebuke 7. reprove, upbraid
9. reprimand

oblate ... 5. oblat 7. devoted 9. dedicated,
flattened (opp of prolate)

obligated ... 5. bound 6. in debt
7. obliged 8. beholden 9. obstringe

obligation ... 3. tie, vow 4. bond, debt,
duty, oath, onus 7. promise 8. civility,
contract 9. agreement, necessity
10. compulsion 11. obstriction

obligatory ... 7. binding 8. imposing,
required 9. mandatory, necessary
10. compulsory

oblige ... 4. bind, pawn 5. favor
6. compel, engage 7. gratify 8. obligate
9. constrain, obstringe
11. accommodate

obliged ... 7. favored 8. beholden,
grateful 9. duty bound

obliging ... 4. kind 7. helpful 8. agreeable,
courteous, indulgent 11. complaisant,
considerate 13. accommodating

oblique ... 4. cant, skew 5. bevel, slant,
slope 7. obscure, scalene 8. inclined,
perverse, sidelong, sidewise, sinister,
slanting 9. underhand 10. circuitous,
collateral, transverse 12. disingenuous

oblique angle ... 5. acute 6. obtuse

obliquely ... 4. skew 6. aslant 7. askance
8. sideways, sidewise 9. on the bias
10. slantingly

obliterate ... 4. blot, dele 5. erase
6. cancel, delete, efface, sponge
7. expunge

obliteration ... 6. rasure 7. erasure
8. deletion 10. extinction

oblivion ... 7. nirvana, silence 9. unfeeling
13. forgetfulness 15. unconsciousness

oblivion, producing ... 8. nepenthe

oblivion, river of ... 5. Lethe

oblivious ... 6. asleep 8. heedless
9. forgetful, unfeeling 10. abstracted
11. unconscious

oblong ... 8. elliptic 9. elongated
11. rectangular 12. quadrangular

obloquy ... 5. abuse 6. infamy 7. calumny
9. criticism 11. malediction
12. reprehension

obnoxious ... 4. vile 5. nasty 6. odious,
rancid 7. hateful 8. amenable, infamous,
terrible 9. offensive 13. objectionable

oboe ... 4. reed 5. shawm (anc)
7. hautboy, musette 8. schalmei
(schalmey) 9. chalumeau

obscene ... 4. lewd 6. vulgar 8. indecent,
prurient 9. offensive, repulsive
10. disgusting 12. pornographic

obscuration ... 7. eclipse 9. darkening,
vagueness

obscure ... 3. dim, fog 4. dark, hazy, slur
5. bedim, blind, mirky, misty, murky
6. cloudy, darken, delude, mystic,
opaque, remote 7. becloud, conceal,
eclipse, shadowy, unknown 8. darkling,
formless, nameless, nubilous, obstruse,
oversile (obs) 9. enigmatic, undefined
10. indistinct, unrenowned

obscurity ... 3. fog 5. gloom 7. dimness,
opacity, unknown 8. darkness

9. nonentity, vagueness
12. formlessness 13. imperspicuous
14. insignificancy, uncomprehended

obsecrate . . . 7. beseech, entreat
10. supplicate

obsequies . . . 5. wakes 8. funerals 9. last
rites

obsequious . . . 5. slick 6. abject
7. devoted, dutiful, fawning, servile,
slavish 8. cringing, funereal, obedient,
toadying 9. attentive, compliant
11. subservient

observance . . . 3. act 4. form, rite
6. custom 8. behavior, ceremony,
practice 9. attention, deference,
sacrament, vigilance 10. conformity
11. celebration

observant . . . 7. careful, heedful, mindful
8. faithful, vigilant, watchful 9. attentive,
regardant, regardful

observation . . . 4. idea 6. espial, remark
7. opinion 9. attention

observatory . . . 4. Lick 6. Yerkes
7. lookout, Palomar 8. Mt Wilson
11. planetarium

observe . . . 2. lol 3. eye, see, spy 4. espy,
heed, keep, nark, note, obey, tout
6. behold, notice, remark 7. conform,
examine, witness 8. preserve
9. celebrate, solemnize

observed, to be . . . 8. notandum
10. memorandum

observer . . . 4. eyer, nark 7. aviator,
student, witness 8. beholder, informer,
looker-on, onlooker 9. spectator
11. stool pigeon

obsess . . . 5. beset, haunt 6. harass
7. bewitch, possess 8. demonize
9. influence, preoccupy

obsession . . . 5. mania 8. impelled
11. bewitchment 13. spirit control

obsignate . . . 4. seal 5. stamp 6. ratify

obsolete . . . 3. old 5. passé 6. effete
7. archaic, disused, effaced, outworn,
worn out 9. out of date 10. antiquated
12. old-fashioned

obstacle . . . 3. dam 4. snag 6. hurdle
9. hindrance 10. difficulty, impediment
11. obstruction

obstetrician . . . 6. doctor 10. accoucheur

obstetrix . . . 7. midwife

obstinate . . . 4. set 5. balky, tough
6. dogged, mulish, sullen 7. willful
8. perverse, stubborn 9. pigheaded
10. determined, headstrong, self-willed
11. opinionated

obstreperous . . . 5. noisy 6. unruly
7. blatant 8. clamorous, turbulent
10. vociferous 11. disobedient
12. ungovernable

obstruct . . . 3. bar, dam, dit 4. clog, ditt,
stop 5. beset, block, check, choke,
delay 6. arrest, hamper, oppose, stop
up 7. occlude 9. barricade, embarrass,
interfere, interrupt

obstruction . . . 3. ban, dam 4. clog, reef,
snag 7. barrier 8. obstacle 9. hindrance
10. difficulty, filibuster, impediment
11. retardation

obtain . . . 3. buy, eke, get, win 4. earn,
fang, gain 5. fetch, reach 6. attain,

derive, elicit, secure 7. achieve, acquire,
capture, prevail, procure, receive

obtain (pert to) . . .
by intimidation . . 9. blackmail
by threats . . 6. extort
control of . . 6. corner 8. overcome
equivalent . . 6. recoup

obtest . . . 6. beg for 7. beseech
10. supplicate

obtrude . . . 5. eject, expel 6. impose
7. intrude

obtrusive . . . 7. forward, pushing
9. intrusive, officious

obtund . . . 4. dull 5. blunt, quell 6. deaden
8. moderate

obtuse . . . 4. dull, slow 5. blunt,
crass, dense 6. stupid 9. unfeeling
11. insensitive

obvelation . . . 7. veiling 10. concealing

obverse . . . 5. front 8. converse
10. complement 11. counterpart

obviate . . . 7. head off, rule out
8. preclude 9. forestall 10. anticipate

obvious . . . 5. clear, gross, plain
7. evident, patient 8. apparent, distinct,
manifest, palpable 11. conspicuous,
open and shut

obvolute . . . 7. twisted 9. contorted,
convolute 11. overlapping

occasion . . . 4. sele, time 5. cause, event,
nonce 6. excuse, motive 7. pretext
8. ceremony, exigency, function,
incident 9. condition, happening
11. opportunity 12. circumstance

occasional . . . 3. odd 4. orra 5. stray
6. casual 10. incidental, infrequent

occasionally . . . 7. at times 9. sometimes
10. now and then 11. at intervals
12. sporadically

occasive . . . 8. westward 10. setting sun

Occident . . . 4. West 6. sunset 17. Western
Hemisphere (opp of Orient)

Occidental . . . 6. ponent 7. The West,
Western 9. Hesperian

occiput . . . 10. back of head 11. back
of skull

occlude . . . 3. dam 4. shut 5. close 6. shut
up 8. obstruct

occult . . . 5. magic 6. hidden, mystic
7. alchemy, cryptic 8. esoteric
9. concealed, recondite 10. mysterious,
necromancy 11. supernormal
12. supernatural

occultation . . . 4. gone, lost 7. eclipse
11. concealment

occultism . . . 6. cabala 7. mystery

occult science . . . 9. esoterics

occupant . . . 6. inmate, tenant
10. inhabitant

occupation . . . 3. job 4. call, note,
work 5. hobby, trade 6. career,
tenure 7. calling, pursuit 8. business,
vocation 9. avocation 10. employment,
habitation, possession, profession
11. engrossment

occupied . . . 3. sat 4. busy, held 6. filled
7. engaged 8. employed, pervaded
9. engrossed, inhabited

occupy . . . 3. use 4. fill, hold 6. employ,
engage, expend, invest 7. engross,
inhabit, oversit, pervade, possess

8. interest
occur... 4. come, fall, meet 5. clash
6. appear, befall, betide, happen
occurrence... 3. hap 5. event 8. incident,
presence, scenario 9. existence,
happening 10. appearance
11. eventuality 12. circumstance
occurring (pert to)...
after death.. 10. posthumous
at nightfall.. 9. acronical
often.. 8. frequent 10. frequently
ocean... 3. sea 4. brim, deep, main
5. brine 6. depths, pelago 8. great sea
ocean (pert to)...
approach.. 7. sea gate
bottom.. 3. bed
crop cultivation.. 11. mariculture
deep.. 7. bathyal
deepest, lowest.. 5. hadal 8. bathybic
12. bathypelagic
division.. 6. Arctic, Indian 7. Pacific
8. Atlantic 9. Antarctic
floating matter.. 5. algae 7. flotsam
geography.. 12. oceanography
mammal.. 4. seal 5. whale
on (the ocean).. 4. asea
periodic motion.. 4. tide
person.. 8. aquanaut, oceanaut 9. skin
diver 10. scuba diver
ref to.. 7. pelagic 9. Neptunian
route.. 4. lane
sealing.. 7. pelagic
vessel.. 6. Sealab 9. submarine
10. bathyscaph 11. bathysphere
Oceania, Oceanica... 9. Melanesia,
Polynesia 10. Micronesia 12. Pacific
lands
Oceanids (Gr Myth, pert to)...
father.. 7. Oceanus
mother.. 6. Tethys
nymphs.. 13. three thousand
Oceanus (Gr Myth, pert to)...
children.. 5. Doris 8. Eurynome
(goddess), Oceanids
god of.. 6. rivers
wife.. 6. Tethys
ocellus... 3. eye 6. stemma 7. eyespot
ocelot... 3. cat 7. leopard
ocher, ochre (pert to)...
red.. 5. tiver 7. almagra 8. hematite
9. faded rose
yellow.. 3. sil 7. Chinese 8. limonite
9. ochrolite
ochlocracy... 7. mob rule
ochlophobia (fear of)... 6. crowds
ocotillo... 5. shrub 10. candlewood
ocracy... 9. group rule
octad... 5. eight (group)
octaemeron... 12. eight-day fast
octagon... 8. octangle 11. eight angles
octahedron... 10. eight faces
octameter... 8. octapody 9. eight feet
octarchy... 11. rule by eight
octastich... 6. octave 10. eight lines
11. eight verses
Octateuch (Old Test)... 10. Eight Books
(1st)
octave... 4. utas 5. eight 6. eighth
8. wine cask 10. eight notes
Octavia (pert to)...
sister of.. 8. Augustus

wife of.. 10. Mark Antony
Octavian... 7. Library (Rome's 1st)
16. committee of eight (one of)
octet, octette... 7. huitain 12. group
of eight
October (pert to)...
bird.. 8. bobolink
birthstone.. 4. opal 5. beryl
Club.. 9. political
drink.. 3. ale
month.. 5. tenth
octogenarian... 13. eighty-year-old
octopod... 9. eight arms, eight legs
Octopoda (Roder)... 8. mollusks (8-
armed) 9. argonauts, octopuses
octopus... 5. poulp (poulpe)
octroi, octroy... 3. tax 9. privilege
10. concession
ocular... 3. eye (pert to) 5. optic, sight
6. visual 10. ophthalmic
oculus... 3. eye 14. Corona Borealis
odd... 4. orra, rare 5. droll, extra, outré,
queer 6. uneven, unique 7. azygous,
bizarre, strange, unequal, unusual
8. unpaired 9. eccentric, remaining,
unmatched 10. occasional
oddity... 9. queerness 11. peculiarity,
singularity 12. eccentricity, idiosyncrasy
odds... 6. gamble 7. dispute, quarrel
8. gambling, variance 9. advantage
10. difference, dissension, inequality
11. probability 12. disagreement
13. probabilities
odds and ends... 4. orts 6. refuse,
scraps 7. mixture, remains 8. remnants
10. miscellany
ode... 4. like (suff), poem 5. psalm
8. canticle, serenata
ode (type)... 7. Lesbian, regular
8. Horatian, Pindaric 9. irregular
odeon... 4. hall 7. gallery, theater
Odin (pert to)...
attendants.. 9. Valkyries
god of.. 3. war 6. poetry, wisdom
hall.. 8. Valhalla
horse.. 8. Sleipner
son.. 3. Tyr 4. Thor 6. Balder
Teutonic name.. 5. Woden (Wotan)
wife.. 5. Frigg (Frigga)
odious... 4. foul, vile 5. nasty 7. hateful
8. infamous, terrible
odium... 6. hatred, infamy 9. antipathy
10. abhorrence, opprobrium
11. detestation
odontist... 7. dentist
odontology (science of)... 5. teeth
9. dentistry
odor, odour... 4. fume, funk, nose
5. aroma, fetor, nidor, scent, smell
6. flavor 7. essence, malodor, perfume
9. fragrance, redolence
odor, meat cooking... 5. fumet
(fumette)
odorous... 8. aromatic, fragrant, redolent,
smelling
Odysseus (pert to)...
chieftain.. 8. Trojan War
dog.. 5. Argos
father.. 7. Laertes
hero of.. 10. The Odyssey (Homer)
king of.. 6. Ithaca (Gr)

magic herb . . 4. moly
modern name . . 7. Ulysses
wife . . 8. Penelope
oecist . . . 9. colonizer
oecodomic . . . 13. architectural
Oedipus (pert to) . . .
daughter . . 8. Antigone
father . . 5. Laius (King of Thebes)
mother . . 7. Jocasta
oeno (comb form) . . . 4. wine
oenomancy . . . 12. wine prophecy
oenophilist . . . 9. wine lover
oenopoetic . . . 10. wine making
oestrus . . . 4. fury 5. sting 6. desire,
frenzy 7. impulse 8. stimulus
of . . 2. in, on 4. over, upon, with 5. about,
avent 10. indication
of (pert to) . . .
a chamber . . 7. cameral
a class (related) . . 7. generic
a father . . 6. agnate
a flock . . 6. gregal
a forefather . . 9. ancestral
a grandfather . . 4. aval
all . . 3. ava
a mother . . 7. cognate
an epoch . . 4. eral
an order . . 7. ordinal
a wife . . 7. uxorial
common gender . . 7. epicene
each . . 3. ana
earth . . 4. geal
equal value . . 10. comparable
French . . 2. du 3. des
great importance . . 7. capital
9. momentous
high standing . . 8. sterling
little importance . . 5. petty 7. trivial
morning . . 5. matin 7. matinal
New Stone Age . . 9. Neolithic
no avail . . 6. futile
nostrils . . 6. narine
old age . . 3. gerontal
planet's path . . 7. orbital
recent times . . 6. lately 9. latter-day
reign . . 6. regnal
river banks . . 8. riparian
same family . . 7. cognate, germane
sound . . 5. tonal
summer . . 7. estival
tears . . 8. lacrimal
the country . . 5. rural
the ear . . 4. otic
the eys . . 6. ocular
the mouth . . 4. oral
the skin . . 6. dermal
the third degree . . 7. cubical
the throat . . 5. gular
the tongue . . 7. glossal
the wrist . . 5. carpal
this day . . 9. hodiernal
thread color . . 7. ficelle
winter . . 6. hiemal
yore . . 5. olden
off . . . 3. ill 4. agee, away, doff 5. aside
6. begone, insane, remote 7. distant,
tainted 9. dissonant, erroneous,
imperfect, right-hand 10. unemployed
offal . . . 5. filth 6. ordure, refuse 7. carrion,
garbage, rubbish
offbeat . . . 14. unconventional

off-color . . . 6. risqué 7. dubious
8. inferior
offend . . . 3. cag, sin, vex 4. miff 5. anger,
annoy, pique, wound 6. assail, insult,
revolt 7. affront, do wrong, mortify
9. displease
offender . . . 6. sinner 8. criminal
9. wrongdoer 10. malefactor
12. transgressor
offense . . . 3. sin 5. crime, delit, fault,
grief, malum 6. delict, felony, insult
7. outrage, umbrage 8. trespass
9. indignity 10. resentment
11. delinquency, misdemeanor,
stellionate
offensive . . . 4. foul, ugly 6. attack,
odious, ribald, vulgar 7. abusive,
eyesore, fulsome, harmful, obscene
8. invading, shocking 9. assailant,
attacking, insulting, obnoxious,
repugnant, revolting 10. aggressive,
malodorous, scurrilous 11. approbrious,
displeasing, distasteful 12. disagreeable
13. transgressive
offer . . . 3. bid 6. adduce, tender 7. proffer,
propine, propose 8. immolate, overture
9. ultimatum
offering . . . 4. gift 6. corban 7. deodate,
present 8. oblation 9. sacrifice
offering resistance . . . 8. renitent
offhand . . . 8. careless, informal, slapdash
9. extempore, impromptu 10. carelessly,
nonchalant 11. extemporary
12. nonchalantly 15. autoschediastic
office . . . 4. duty, post, rite, wike (obs)
5. place, trust 7. station 8. ceremony,
function, position 9. situation
11. appointment
office (pert to) . . .
chief . . 7. manager
divine . . 9. akoluthia
for the dead . . 7. trental
holder . . 8. placeman
of a datary (Roman Curia) . . 7. dataria
of a ruler . . 7. regency
relinquish (to) . . 5. demit
third hour . . 6. tierce
officer . . . 6. tindal 7. bailiff, command,
conduct, general, manager, marshal,
sheriff 8. adjutant, avigator, director
9. constable, policeman, president
officer (pert to) . . .
assistant . . 4. aide
Brit Royal Guard . . 4. exon
chief executive . . 3. dey 4. czar
5. mayor 7. emperor, monarch, premier
8. governor 9. president 10. chancellor
church . . 5. elder 6. sexton
civil law . . 6. notary, police 7. bailiff,
marshal, sheriff 9. constable, policeman
10. magistrate
club . . 7. steward
corrupt . . 7. grafter
despotic . . 6. satrap
diplomatic . . 7. attaché
Jewish Relig . . 6. parnas
King's stables . . 6. avener
monastic . . 5. prior
naval . . 6. ensign, yeoman
parish . . 6. beadle, bedral
ship's . . 9. boatswain (boson)

weights, measures .. 6. sealer
official ... 6. formal 9. authentic
10. functional 13. authoritative
official (pert to) ...
  command .. 5. edict
  despotic .. 6. satrap
  game .. 5. judge 6. umpire 7. referee
  government .. 10. bureaucrat
  insurance .. 7. actuary 8. adjuster
  intinerant (Hist) .. 6. missus
  mark .. 5. stamp
  order (RCCh) .. 8. rescript
  proclamation .. 5. ukase 6. decree
  record .. 5. actum
  state .. 8. governor 9. secretary
officious ... 4. cool, pert 5. saucy
  6. formal 8. arrogant, impudent,
  official 9. pragmatic 10. meddlesome
  11. efficacious, impertinent, pragmatical
  12. contemptuous
officiousness ... 10. pragmatism
offing ... 10. background
offshoot ... 3. rod 5. scion 6. branch,
  member 8. addition 9. by-product
  10. descendant 12. organization
offspring ... 3. son 4. brat, seed 5. child,
  fruit, issue, sprig 6. origin, result
  7. produce, product, progeny 8. fountain
  9. posterity 10. descendant
oficina ... 5. works 6. office 7. factory
  10. laboratory
often ... 3. oft 9. many times
  10. frequently, repeatedly 11. over and
  over 13. time after time
ogdoad ... 5. eight 10. eight group
ogee ... 4. gula 5. talon 7. molding
  9. cyma recta 11. cyma reversa
ogle ... 3. eye 4. gaze, leer 5. stare
  7. examine
Ogpu ... 8. Gay-Pay-Oo (Russ secret
  service)
O Henry ... 6. Porter (Wm Sydney)
Ohio ...
  capital .. 8. Columbus
  city .. 5. Akron 6. Dayton, Toledo
    9. Cleveland 10. Cincinnati
  first settlement .. 8. Marietta
  hero .. 12. Anthony Wayne (Gen)
  lake .. 4. Erie
  name meaning (Indian) .. 14. Beautiful
    River
  State admission .. 11. Seventeenth
  State motto .. 27. With God All Things
    are Possible
  State nickname .. 7. Buckeye
oil ... 3. ben, fat 4. balm, ghee 5. bribe,
  oleum 6. aceite, anoint, asarum, grease,
  olanin 8. flattery, medicate, painting
  9. lubricant, lubricate, petroleum
  10. illuminant
oil (pert to) ...
  beetle .. 5. meloe
  berry .. 5. olive
  bird .. 8. guachare
  cartel .. 4. OPEC
  cask .. 4. rier
  class .. 5. fatty, fixed 6. animal 7. mineral
    8. volatile 9. essential, vegetable
  cloth .. 8. linoleum
  coal .. 8. photogen
  comb form .. 2. ol 3. ole

fish .. 7. escolar
flask .. 4. olpe
gauge .. 9. oleometer
glands (birds) .. 9. uropygial
  11. elaeodochon
lamp .. 7. lucigen
mineral .. 7. naphtha
plant .. 6. sesame 9. castor-oil
prefix .. 2. ol
rock .. 5. shale 9. limestone
seed .. 3. til (teel) 6. sesame 7. linseed
  8. rapeseed 10. castor bean, cottonseed
skin .. 5. sebum
stone .. 4. hone 9. whetstone
term .. 5. oleic
tree .. 4. eboe (ebo), tung 5. mahua
  6. illupi 7. oil palm 9. candlenut,
  castor-oil
tube .. 5. vitta
whale .. 5. sperm
oil of ...
  cloves .. 7. eugenol
  myrcia .. 6. bay oil
  orange blossoms .. 6. neroil
  roses .. 4. otto 5. attar (atar)
  salt .. 7. bittern
oils ... 10. elaeoptene (elaeopten) (opp
  of stearoptene)
oily ... 3. fat 4. glib 5. bland, oleic, suave
  6. olease, supple 7. pinguid 8. unctuous
  9. compliant, plausible 10. flattering,
  oleaginous 11. insinuating, subservient
  12. hypocritical
oily liquids ... 3. tar 6. cresol, octane
  7. aniline, picamar 8. creosote
oily tissue ... 3. fat
ointment ... 4. balm, cere, lard, nard
  5. salve 6. balsam, carron, cerate,
  ceroma, grease 7. pomatum, unguent
  8. liniment 9. spikenard, xeromyron
  10. petrolatum 11. embrocation
Oise (France) ... 5. Aisne (tributary), river
  10. department
Ojibway secret order ... 4. mide (meda)
  9. midewiwin
ojo ... 5. oasis
OK ... 6. righto 7. correct
Okinawa ...
  capital .. 4. Naha
  island group (64) .. 6. Ryukyu
  prefecture of .. 5. Japan
Oklahoma ...
  capital .. 12. Oklahoma City
  city .. 3. Ada 4. Enid 5. Tulsa 6. Lawton
    8. Muskogee 9. Claremore
    12. Bartlesville
  Five Civilized Tribes .. 5. Creek
    7. Choctaw 8. Cherokee, Seminole
    9. Chickasaw
  lake .. 6. Texoma
  migrant from .. 4. Okie
  mountain .. 5. Ozark 8. Ouachita
  museum .. 6. Indian 8. Woolaroc
  native son (famed) .. 10. Will Rogers
  old name .. 15. Indian Territory
  State admission .. 11. Thirty-third
  State bird .. 10. flycatcher
  State flower .. 9. mistletoe
  State motto .. 16. Labor Omnia Vincit
    (Labor Conquers All)
  State nickname .. 6. Sooner

okra ... 5. bendy, gumbo 6. mallow

old .. 3. ald, eld 4. aged 5. anile 6. infirm, senile 7. ancient, antique, archaic 8. obsolete 9. doddering, senescent, venerable 10. antiquated

old (pert to) ...

age .. 6. senile 7. geratic 8. gerontic, senility 10. geriatrics (Med), senescence 11. gerontology

ancient (very) .. 7. Ogygian

billy, granny .. 5. squaw

fashioned .. 4. fogy 7. antique 9. primitive 12. conservative

hat .. 5. trite 9. out-of-date

maid .. 5. prude 10. fussbudget

man .. 5. elder 6. codger, gaffer, geezer, Nestor 7. oldster 8. old-timer 10. fuddy-duddy

sailor .. 3. tar 4. salt

saying .. 3. saw 5. adage, maxim

time .. 3. eld 4. syne

woman .. 3. hag 5. crone 6. dotard, gammer

womanish .. 5. anile

Old (pert to) ...

Bailey .. 12. English court

Bay State .. 13. Massachusetts

Dominion .. 8. Virginia

Empire .. 4. Maya

English alphabet .. 10. Anglo-Saxon

Faithful .. 6. geyser

Franklin State .. 9. Tennessee

Gentleman Harry .. 5. Devil

Gooseberry .. 5. Devil, Satan

Glory .. 15. Stars and Stripes

Guard (Waterloo) .. 9. Napoleon's

Hickory .. 13. Andrew Jackson

Ironsides .. 15. USS Constitution

Kingdom .. 7. Memphis (Egypt)

Lady of Threadneedle Street .. 13. Bank of England

Line State .. 8. Maryland

Man of the Mountain .. 7. Profile (The)

Noll .. 14. Oliver Cromwell

North Church .. 12. Christ Church

North State .. 13. North Carolina

Rough and Ready .. 13. (Gen) Zachary Taylor

Serpent .. 5. Satan

Sod .. 4. Erin 7. Ireland

Sol .. 3. sun

Stone Age .. 11. Paleolithic

Three Stars .. 5. (Gen) Grant

World .. 7. Eastern

olden ... 6. bygone

older ... 5. elder 6. senior 8. ancestor

oldest ... 4. dean 6. eldest 7. stalest

Old Testament (pert to) ...

Books (number) .. 10. Thirty-nine

Elohim .. 3. God (The Hexateuch)

Hexateuch .. 13. first Six Books

Land of riches .. 5. Ophir

objects (sacred) .. 4. Urim 7. Thummim

Pentateuch .. 10. Law of Moses 14. first Five Books

writer .. 7. Elohist (The Hexateuch)

Old World (pert to) ...

ape .. 7. Primate 10. Catarrhina

carnivore .. 5. genet

falcon .. 5. saker

herb .. 5. tansy

lizard .. 5. Agama

shrub .. 4. Olax

oleaginous ... 4. oily 5. oleic 8. unctuous

oleander ... 6. Nerium 11. rhododaphne 12. rhododendron

oleoresin ... 5. anime, elemi 6. balsam 7. copaiba

oleum ... 3. oil

olfaction ... 7. osmesis 8. smelling 12. sense of smell

olfactory organ ... 4. nose 8. olfactor

olid ... 4. foul 5. fetid 6. rancid, smelly 10. malodorous 11. strong smell

oligarchy ... 10. rule by a few

olinda bug ... 6. weevil

olio ... 4. olla, stem 6. medley 7. mixture 8. chowchow 9. burlesque, potpourri 10. collection, hodgepodge 11. olla-podrida

oliphant ... 8. elephant 9. ivory horn

oliprance ... 4. romp, show 7. jollity 11. merrymaking, ostentation

olive (pert to) ...

branch .. 5. child, peace 6. symbol (peace)

color .. 11. yellow-green

dun .. 3. fly (fishing)

enzyme .. 6. olease

family .. 8. Oleaceae

fly .. 3. dun 4. gnat 5. quill

gray .. 10. Scotch gray

gum .. 6. olivil

overripe .. 5. drupe

stuffed .. 6. pimola

true .. 4. Olea

wild .. 8. oleaster

yard .. 6. olivet

yellow .. 9. moss green 10. chartreuse

olla ... 3. jug, pot 4. olio 8. palm leaf (palmyra) 11. olla-podrida

olla-podrida ... 4. hash, olio 6. medley 10. hodgepodge

oloroso ... 6. sherry

olpe ... 5. flask 8. oenochoë 11. wine pitcher

olycook, olykoek ... 7. cruller 8. doughnut

Olympia ... 4. ship 7. capital (Wash) 8. heavenly 9. sanctuary (anc)

Olympiad ... 14. four-year period

Olympian god ... 4. Ares, Zeus 6. Apollo, Hermes 8. Dionysus, Hercules, Poseidon 10. Hephaestus

Olympian goddess ... 4. Hera 6. Athena, Hestia 7. Artemis, Demeter 9. Aphrodite

Olympic cupbearer ... 8. Ganymede

Olympic Games (pert to) ...

honor of .. 4. Zeus

period .. 14. four years apart

revival site .. 6. Athens (1896)

site (first) .. 4. Elis 7. Olympia

time of games .. 4. Olympia 8. four days

Olympieion, Olympium ... 6. temple (Athens)

Olympus (Gr) ... 3. sky 5. Mount 6. heaven 8. mountain

Olympus (Hind) ... 4. Meru

Omaha ... 4. city (Neb) 5. Sioux 6. Indian

Omar Khayyam (pert to) ...

country .. 4. Iran 6. Persia

fish (fabled) .. 3. mah

poem . . 8. Rubaiyat
omasum . . . 9. manyplies 10. psalterium
   12. third stomach
ombro (comb form) . . . 4. rain
ombrometer . . . 9. rain gauge
omega . . . 3. end 4. last 5. final 6. letter
   (Gr)
omen . . . 4. bode, sign 5. abode,
   knell, token 6. augury 7. auspice,
   portent, presage 8. forebode, foreshow
   9. abodement 10. divination
   15. prognostication
omer . . . 5. ephah, sheaf 9. fifty days
   (Passover to Pentecost)
ominous . . . 4. dour, trim 8. sinister
   9. ferocious 10. inexorable, portentous
   12. inauspicious
omission . . . 4. want 5. caret, error
   7. neglect 9. oversight 10. deficiency,
   leaving out 13. nonobservance
omission of end syllables . . . 7. apocope
omission of words . . . 8. ellipsis
omit . . . 4. dele, pass, skip 5. elide
   6. delete, ignore 7. exclude 11. leave
   undone
omitting . . . 7. elision 9. excepting,
   excluding 10. precluding
omneity . . . 7. allness 16. all-
   comprehensive
omnipotent . . . 6. divine 8. almighty
   9. unequaled, unlimited 11. all-powerful
omniscient . . . 4. wise 6. divine 7. learned
   10. all-knowing
omnitude . . . 7. allness 8. totality
   12. universality
omnivorous . . . 6. greedy 9. all-eating
   10. gluttonous
omoplate . . . 7. scapula
omphalos . . . 3. hut 4. knob 5. altar,
   navel 6. center 9. umbilicus
on . . . 2. at 4. atop, upon 5. above, ahead,
   along 6. toward 7. against, forward
   10. concerning 13. juxtaposition
On (Bib) . . . 7. Baalbek 8. holy city
   10. Heliopolis (Egypt) 12. City of the
   Sun
on (pert to) . . .
   account of . . 3. for
   all sides . . 5. about 6. around
   and on . . 7. forever, tedious 9. tediously
   behalf of . . 3. for
   dit . . 5. rumor 6. report
   going . . 7. forward 10. proceeding
   grand scale . . 4. epic
   hand . . 4. here 7. present 9. available
   high . . 5. aloft
   other side . . 4. over 6. across
   sheltered side . . 4. alee
   this side . . 3. cis (pref) 9. cisalpine
   10. cismontane, cispontine
   windward side . . 8. aweather
onager . . . 3. ass 5. kiang 8. catapult
once in a while . . . 9. erstwhile 10. now
   and then 12. occasionally
once upon a time . . . 6. one day 7. the
   past, time was 8. formerly 10. the
   long ago
Oncorhynchus . . . 6. salmon
ondoyant . . . 4. wavy (art)
one . . . 2. an, un 3. ace, ain, ein 4. unit
   5. alone, unity, whole 6. person, single

   9. unmarried 10. individual
one (pert to) . . .
   after the other . . 8. serially, seriatim
   12. successfully
   bearing heraldic arms . . 7. armiger
   behind the other . . 6. tandem
   born in serfdom . . 4. neif
   bringing good luck . . 6. mascot
   by one . . 6. apiece, singly 10. one at
   a time 12. individually
   comb form . . 3. uni 4. mono
   curious . . 6. gossip 8. quidnunc
   despondent in views . . 9. pessimist
   fond of women . . 11. philogynist
   footed . . 6. uniped
   frantic for freedom . .
   15. eleutheromaniac
   gigantic in size . . 5. giant, titan
   happy in views . . 8. optimist
   horse . . 5. petty 6. little 8. inferior
   10. second-rate 13. insignificant
   in a thousand . . 6. oddity 7. paragon,
   prodigy
   in second childhood . . 6. dotard
   instructed in secret system . . 5. epopt
   8. initiate
   living on another . . 8. parasite
   moving stealthily . . 7. prowler
   sided . . 5. askew 7. partial 10. prejudiced,
   unilateral
   thousand . . 3. mil
   time . . 7. quondam 8. formerly
   undergoing change . . 6. mutant
oneberry . . . 9. hackberry
   14. partridgeberry
one devoted to . . .
   deviltry . . 7. hellion
   fast driving . . 4. jehu 7. speeder
   indolence . . 10. daydreamer, lotus-eater
   own opinion . . 5. bigot
   physical feats . . 7. athlete
   pursuit . . 3. ist (suff)
   table delicacies . . 7. epicure
onefold . . . 6. simple, single 7. sincere
   9. guileless
onegite . . . 8. amethyst
Oneida . . . 6. Indian 8. Iroquois
   9. Community (NY)
oneiros . . . 5. dream
oneirotic . . . 6. dreams (pert to)
oneism . . . 6. egoism, monism
oneness . . . 5. union, unity 7. concord
   8. identity, sameness 9. agreement,
   aloneness, constancy 10. loneliness,
   singleness, uniformity, uniqueness
   11. singularity 13. undividedness
one of . . .
   ancient race . . 4. Mede 7. Iberian
   Buddhist precepts . . 6. nidana
   Persian dynasty . . 8. Sassanid
   religious sect . . 10. Anabaptist
   the Bears . . 4. Ursa
   the Greek Wise Men . . 6. Thales
   the initiated . . 5. epopt
   twins . . 5. gemel (Her)
onerous . . . 4. load 5. heavy 6. burden
   7. onerose 9. difficult, laborious,
   ponderous 10. burdensome, oppressive
   12. impedimental
one versed in . . .
   children's diseases . . 12. pediatrician

law . . 6. legist
literature . . 6. savant 9. literatus
memory . . 9. mnemonist
politics . . 9. statesman
religious law . . 8. canonist
resources, wealth . . 9. economist
one who . . .
  absconds . . 6. eloper 8. decamper, deserter
  appropriates . . 9. pre-emptor
  attacks . . 9. aggressor
  believes in all religions . . 6. omnist
  believes in personal God . . 5. deist
  believes in self . . 9. solipsist
  beseeches . . 7. pleader
  brings meat to royal table . . 7. dapifer, steward
  cherishes . . 8. fosterer
  collects voluntary taxes . . 6. tither
  conveys property . . 7. alienor
  dies for a cause . . 6. martyr
  differs . . 4. anti 9. dissenter, dissident
  disowns . . 10. repudiator
  displays learning . . 6. pedant
  disposes by will . . 7. devisor
  edits . . 7. reviser
  feigns illness . . 10. malingerer
  fights for cause . . 8. crusader
  forsakes faith principles . . 8. apostate
  frustrates a plan . . 7. marplot
  gives up . . 9. abnegator
  grants by deed . . 7. remiser
  hates argument . . 10. misologist
  hates people . . 11. misanthrope
  holds office . . 2. in 9. incumbent
  inculcates . . 7. infuser 9. instiller
  inflicts retribution . . 7. nemesis
  misuses authority . . 6. satrap
  plunders . . 6. sacker 8. pillager
  practises palmistry . . 11. chiromancer
  prevents entrance . . 5. hajib
  quarrels . . 5. rowdy
  removes nuisance . . 6. abator
  rules, manages . . 6. gerent
  sells provisions to troops . . 6. sutler
  shoots from ambush . . 6. sniper
  sponges . . 6. cadger 8. parasite
  stays . . 5. bider
  summons spirits . . 8. evocator
  testifies . . 8. deponent
  transfers property . . 7. alienor
ongall . . 5. onset 6. attack
onion . . . 3. set (bulbs) 4. boll, bulb, cepa, leek 5. chive, cibol, pearl, rareripe 6. Allium 7. Bermuda, onionet, shallot 8. eschalot, rareripe, scallion
onkos (Gr) . . . 7. topknot
only . . . 4. just, lone, mere, sole 5. chief 6. lonely, merely, simple, simply, single, singly, solely 8. uniquely 11. exclusively 13. companionless 14. above all others
onocentaur . . . 3. ape 5. demon (fabled)
onomasticon . . . 7. lexicon 10. dictionary, vocabulary (Gr)
onomatology (science of) . . . 5. names 11. terminology
onomatopoeic . . . 6. echoic 9. imitative (of natural sound)
onset, onslaught . . . 6. attack 7. assault 11. rushing upon, setting upon
Ontario . . .

Bay . . 6. Hudson
capital . . 7. Toronto
city . . 6. Ottawa 7. Timmins 8. Hamilton
lake . . 9. Great Lake (one of five)
province . . 6. Canada
river . . 6. Ottawa, Thames 7. Niagara 10. St Lawrence
ontogeny . . . 9. evolution
ontology (science of) . . . 5. being 7. reality
onus . . . 4. duty, load 6. burden, charge 10. impediment, imposition, obligation
onus probandi . . . 13. burden of proof
onward, onwards . . . 5. ahead, forth 6. future, moving 7. forward 8. forwards, progress 9. in advance
onychauxis . . . 14. nail overgrowth
onyx . . . 6. nicolo (niccolo), tecali
ooid . . . 9. egg-shaped
oology (science of) . . . 8. bird eggs
oomancy (divination by) . . . 4. eggs
oont . . . 5. camel 13. beast of burden
oop . . . 4. join 5. unite
oopak, oopack . . . 3. tea (black)
oorial . . . 3. sha 5. sheep, urial
ooze . . . 3. bog 4. drip, leak, seep, sipe, soak 5. exude, marsh 6. be damp 7. leather 8. transude 9. percolate
oozy . . . 4. miry 5. muddy, slimy
opah . . . 4. fish, soko 8. kingfish 9. Lampridae
opal . . . 3. gem 4. blue 5. stone 7. hyalite 10. pearliness
opal, variety of . . . 4. wood 5. black, noble, pitch, resin 6. common 7. girasol, hyalite 8. menilite, precious 9. cacholong, geyserite, harlequin 10. chalcedony
opalescent . . . 6. pearly 7. opaline 8. irisated 10. iridescent
opaque . . . 4. dark 6. obtuse, stupid 7. obscure 8. eyeshade 10. not shining 13. unilluminated 14. not transparent
open . . . 3. ope 4. ajar, bare, free, undo 5. agape, begin, clear, frank, overt, plain, start, untie 6. candid, honest, patent, public, reveal, unbolt, unfold, unfurl, unlock, unseal, unstop, vacant 7. artless, evident, exposed, natural, obvious, sincere, unbosom, unclose 8. apparent, commence, disclose, expanded, initiate, patulous, revealed, unclosed, unfasten 9. spreading, uncertain, uncovered, unfeigned 10. accessible, unreserved 11. unprotected 12. questionable
open (pert to) . . .
  acknowledgment . . 6. avowal
  air . . 8. alfresco
  and shut . . 7. assured, obvious 11. prearranged
  bursting . . 10. dehiscence
  cabinet . . 7. étagère
  country . . 5. veldt, weald
  court . . 4. area 5. patio
  door . . 6. policy 11. hospitality
  eyed . . 7. curious 8. vigilant 9. attentive, expectant
  for discussion . . 4. moot
  fully . . 4. wide 9. dehiscent, full-blown
  land . . 4. moor 5. heath 6. desert, plains
  out . . 6. deploy (Mil)

partly.. 3. mid 4. ajar
passage in forests.. 5. glade
to scorn.. 9. derisible
to view.. 5. overt
opening... 2. os 3. bay, gap 4. door,
gate, hole, loop, pore, rift, slot,
vent 5. cleft, mouth, sinus, start
6. breach, eyelet, hiatus, outlet,
portal 7. display, foramen, initial,
orifice, vacancy 8. aperture, fenestra,
position 9. admission, beginning
10. passageway, unfoldment
11. entranceway, opportunity
opening (pert to)...
chess.. 6. gambit
ear.. 4. burr
enlarge.. 4. ream
from third ventricle (Anat).. 4. pila
having.. 10. fenestrate
in a mold.. 6. ingate
minute.. 5. stoma
narrow.. 4. rima, slot 7. crevice
9. stenopaic
nasal.. 4. nare
small.. 4. pore 5. chink 6. cranny, eyelet,
lacuna 7. foramen, orifice, pinhole
wide (Bot).. 9. dehiscent
openings... 3. ora 7. stomata
openwork... 6. eyelet 7. Madeira, tracery
10. decoration
opera (pert to)...
comic (singer).. 5. buffa, buffo
7. buffoon
glass.. 7. binocle 8. binocular, lorgnette
hat.. 5. crush, gibus 6. topper
kind.. 4. soap 5. horse 8. burletta
singer.. 4. bass, diva 5. buffa, buffo,
tenor 7. buffoon, soprano 10. basso
buffo, coloratura
solo.. 4. aria 5. scena
star.. 4. diva 10. prima donna
text.. 8. libretto
opera, composer... 5. Bizet, Gluck,
Haydn, Verdi 6. Glinka, Gounod,
Handel, Mozart, Wagner 7. Puccini,
Rossini 9. Donizetti, Meyerbeer
11. Deems Taylor 14. Rimski-Korsakov
(Korsakoff)
opera, drama... 4. Aida 5. Boris,
Faust, Orfeo, Thais, Tosca 6. Bohême,
Carmen, Coq d'or, Daphne, Isolde
7. Alceste, Fidelio 9. Lohengrin,
Pagliacci, Rigoletto 10. Magic Flute,
Prince Igor, Tannhäuser 11. Don
Giovanni, Il Travatore 13. Peter Ibbetson
14. Tales of Hoffman 15. Hansel and
Gretel, Madame Butterfly 16. Marriage
of Figaro
operation... 6. action, agency 7. surgery
8. creation 9. influence 11. functioning,
transaction
Operation Overlord... 4. D-Day
16. Normandy invasion
operation, surgical... 6. trepan
8. excision 9. resection 10. amputation,
castration 11. exploratory
12. appendectomy, hysterectomy
13. tonsillectomy
operative... 6. worker 7. artisan, working
8. mechanic 9. detective
operative, become... 5. inure (enure)

operator... 5. agent, quack 6. dealer,
worker 7. creator, handler, surgeon
10. mountebank, speculator
operculum (Bot)... 3. cap, lid 7. stopper
8. covering
operose... 4. busy 8. diligent 9. difficult,
laborious 11. painstaking
Ophidia... 6. snakes 8. reptiles, serpents
9. Serpentes
ophidian... 5. snake, viper 7. serpent
ophiolatry... 12. snake worship
ophthalmic... 6. ocular 7. optical 9. eye
region
ophthalmology, science... 6. the eye
opiate... 4. drug, hemp, snow 5. opium
6. heroin 7. anodyne, cocaine, hashish
(hasheesh), soother 8. narcotic
9. analgesic, paregoric 11. somniferous
12. somnifacient
opine... 4. deem 5. judge, think 6. remark
7. opinion, suppose 10. conjecture
opinion... 4. idea, view 6. belief, esteem,
notion, report 7. feeling 8. judgment,
two cents 9. sentiment 10. estimation,
impression, ober dictum, reputation
opinion (pert to)...
expert.. 9. expertise
expression, common... 5. theme
expression, formal.. 4. vote
religious, unorthodox.. 6. heresy
opinions (pert to)...
collection.. 9. anthology, symposium
professed.. 5. credo
opium... 4. drug 8. narcotic 10. intoxicant
opium (pert to)...
concentrate.. 6. heroin
derivative (Chem).. 7. meconic
Egyptian.. 8. thebaine
extract.. 6. chandoo (chandu), codeine
8. morphine 9. narcotine 10. papaverine
overuse.. 8. opiumism
poppy seed.. 3. maw
source.. 5. poppy
tincture.. 9. paregoric
variety.. 6. Indian, Smyrna, Turkey
7. Chinese, Persian
opodeldoc... 7. plaster 8. liniment
opodidymus... 7. monster (two-headed)
opossum... 7. Marmosa 9. didelphid,
marsupial, phalanger
opossum (pert to)...
S America.. 5. quica 7. sarigue
variety.. 5. mouse, water, wooly
water.. 5. yapok (yapock)
wood.. 10. silver bell
opponent... 3. foe 4. anti 5. enemy, rival
7. adverse 8. opposite 9. adversary,
combatant 10. antagonist
opportune... 3. fit, pat 5. ready
6. timely 7. apropos 8. suitable
9. expedient, well-timed 10. convenient
11. appropriate
opportunist... 10. politician, vacillator
opportunity... 4. turn 6. chance
7. opening 8. occasion 12. circumstance
16. suitable occasion
oppose... 3. bar 4. deny, face 5. fight,
rebel 6. expose, oppugn, refute, resist
7. contest, exhibit, gainsay 8. confront
10. antagonize, contradict, contravene,
counteract

opposed ... 3. met 4. anti, vied
5. coped 6. averse, pitted 7. adverse,
fronted 8. contrary, renitent, resisted
9. contested, withstood 12. oppositional

opposed (pert to) ...
against . . 6. pitted
lee . . 5. stoss
to change . . 7. die-hard 11. reactionary
12. conservative
to entad (inward) . . 5. ectad
zenith . . 5. nadir

opposite ... 5. polar 6. facing 7. adverse,
antonym, hostile, opposed, reverse
8. contrary, converse 9. different,
repugnant 10. opposition
12. antagonistic 13. contradictory
14. contrapositive

opposite (pert to) ...
directly . . 10. antipodean
exact . . 8. antipode
in action, in nature . . 5. polar 7. inverse
prefix . . 6. contra
science . . 3. art
to spring tide . . 4. neap

opposition ... 9. hostility, opponency
10. antagonism, antithesis, refutation,
resistance 11. contrariety, disapproval
13. contradiction

oppress ... 4. rape 5. crush 6. burden,
harass, nither (Scot), ravish 7. depress,
swelter 8. distress, macerate, suppress
9. overpower, overwhelm, persecute,
tyrannize 10. extinguish

oppressive ... 5. harsh 6. severe,
stuffy, sultry 7. onerous 8. rigorous
9. ponderous 10. burdensome,
depressing, tyrannical

oppressor ... 4. czar (tsar), Nero
6. despot, tyrant 8. autocrat, burdener
11. Simon Legree

opprobrious ... 7. abusive 8. despised,
infamous 9. insulting, offensive
10. scurrilous 11. disgraceful
12. contumelious

opprobrium ... 5. odium 6. infamy
8. disgrace 11. malediction

oppugn ... 6. assail, oppose
10. controvert, counteract

oppugnant ... 7. hostile, opposed
8. contrary 12. antagonistic
13. counteractive

Ops (pert to) ...
called also . . 10. Ops Consiva
consort of . . 6. Consus, Saturn
Festival . . 6. Opalia
Greek counterpart . . 4. Rhea
Roman goddess of . . 7. Harvest

opsigamy ... 14. old-age marriage

opt ... 4. pick 5. elect 6. choose 11. make
a choice

optic ... 6. ocular, visual 11. optological

optical (pert to) ...
device . . 9. stenopaic
glass . . 4. lens
illusion . . 6. mirage
instrument . . 5. prism 7. alidade, reticle
9. eriometer, optometer 10. microscope
membrane . . 6. retina
organ . . 3. eye

optic defect ... 6. myopia

optimistic ... 4. rosy 7. hopeful, roseate

8. cheerful, sanguine 9. expectant
10. auspicious

optimum ... 4. best 7. maximum 13. most
favorable

option ... 6. choice, future (Finan)
7. refusal 8. free will 11. alternative
13. right to choose

optional ... 8. elective 9. voluntary
10. permissive 13. not compulsory

opulence ... 6. plenty, riches, wealth
9. abundance, affluence, amplitude,
profusion

opulent ... 4. rich 6. lavish 7. profuse,
wealthy 8. abundant, affluent
9. luxuriant

opulus ... 11. guelder-rose 13. cranberry
tree

opus ... 3. art 4. work 5. étude 10. embroidery,
needlework 11. composition

oquassa ... 5. trout

oracle ... 4. seer 5. sibyl 6. Dodona,
medium, mentor 7. prophet, wise man
8. Delphian (Delphic) 10. revelation

oracular ... 4. wise 5. vatic (vatical)
9. prophetic 10. predictive
11. forecasting

orage ... 5. storm 7. tempest

oral ... 5. parol, vocal 6. spoken, verbal
10. not written 11. nuncupative

orang ... 9. orangutan (orangutang)

orange (pert to) ...
Bowl site . . 5. Miami
bird . . 7. tanager
color . . 5. ocher, peach 6. carrot 7. apricot
8. mandarin
covering . . 4. rind
flower oil . . 6. meroli
genus . . 6. Citrus
heraldry . . 6. tenné
kind . . 4. mock 5. hedge, navel, Osage
8. bergamot, mandarin, Valencia
9. tangerine
leaf . . 6. karamu
marigold . . 9. tangerine
membrane . . 4. zest
mock . . 7. seringa
seed . . 3. pip

Orangeman ... 14. North Irelander

orangutan ... 4. mias 5. orang, Pongo,
satyr, Simia

orate ... 5. plead, speak, spiel 8. harangue

oration ... 5. éloge 6. eulogy, prayer,
sermon, speech 7. lecture 8. encomium,
petition 9. discourse

orator ... 6. rhetor 7. speaker 9. perorator
10. petitioner 11. rhetorician,
spellbinder

orator, famed ... 5. Bryan (Wm Jennings)
6. Cicero 9. Churchill 11. Demosthenes

oratory ... 6. chapel 7. chantry
9. elocution, eloquence

orb ... 3. eye, sun 4. ball, moon, star
5. earth, globe, world 6. bereft, circle,
planet, sphere 7. enclose 8. encircle,
insignia, surround

orbed ... 5. lunar, round

orbit ... 4. path 5. globe, route 6. sphere
7. circuit 9. trajectory

orbit (pert to) ...
cavity . . 9. eye socket
curve . . 10. trajectory

of a planet .. 7. ellipse
point .. 5. apsis 6. apogee (farthest)
     7. perigee (nearest)
orc, Orca ... 5. whale 7. grampus
orchestra (pert to) ...
bells .. 12. glockenspiel
circle .. 7. parquet 8. parterre
small .. 11. symphonette
orchestra instrument group ...
brass .. 4. horn, tuba 6. cornet 7. trumpet
     8. trombone
percussion .. 4. drum 7. cymbals, timpani
     (tympani) 8. triangle
strings .. 5. cello, viola 6. violin
     10. contrabass 11. violoncello
wind .. 4. oboe 5. flute 7. bassoon
     8. clarinet
orchid .. 4. Disa 5. vanda 6. Ophrys
     7. Listera, lycaste, pogonia 8. arethusa,
     Cattleya, Oncidium 9. cymbidium,
     puttyroot 10. letterleaf
orchid (pert to) ...
appendage .. 8. caudicle
handsomest .. 4. Disa
largest .. 10. letterleaf
meal .. 5. salep
petal .. 8. labellum
tuber, root .. 5. salep 7. cullion
Orcus .. 3. God (Rom) 5. Hades, Pluto
     (Gr) 10. lower world
ordain .. 4. plan 5. allot, enact,
     equip 6. decree 7. appoint, arrange,
     command, destine, install 8. canonize
     9. institute 10. predestine
ordeal ... 4. gaff, test 5. trial 7. sorcery
     8. judgment 10. experience (painful)
order ... 3. bid 4. fiat, ordo, rank,
     rule, sect, will 5. array, class, edict,
     genus, money 6. cosmos, decree,
     direct, enjoin, genera (pl), manage,
     system 7. arrange, command, dispose,
     mandate, prepare, verdict 8. regulate,
     sequence 9. condition, procedure
     10. injunction 11. arrangement
order (pert to) ...
back .. 6. remand
connecting .. 6. in turn 8. seriatim
cosmic .. 3. tao 4. rita
for writ .. 7. precipe
good .. 6. eutaxy
grammar .. 5. taxis
judicial .. 4. fiat, writ 7. summons
proper .. 6. kilter
written .. 6. billet
Order, architecture ... 5. Doric, Ionic
     6. Tuscan 8. Etruscan 10. Corinthian
Order, association ... 4. Club 5. Guild
     7. DeMolay, Society, St Clare
     8. Sodality, Sorority 9. The Garter,
     Trappists 10. Fellowship, Fraternity,
     Sisterhood 11. Brotherhood, Eastern
     Star, Purple Heart 12. The Rising Sun
ordered ... 4. bade, trim 7. regular
     8. arranged, measured, ordained
     9. regulated
orderly ... 4. neat, tidy, trim 7. regular,
     uniform 8. obedient, peaceful
     9. attendant, regularly, shipshape
     10. methodical, systematic
order of ...
amphibians .. 5. Anura

aquatic animals .. 7. Cetacea
holy beings .. 9. hierarchy
insects .. 7. Diptera
mammals .. 8. Edentata, Primates
mites .. 6. acarid
the day .. 8. schedule 12. instructions
whales .. 4. Cete
ordinal ... 6. number, ritual, serial
     10. succession 11. Book of Rules (Eccl),
     categorical
ordinance ... 3. law 4. rite 5. bylaw, edict
     6. assize, decree 7. control, statute
     8. decretum 9. allotment, direction,
     enactment, sacrament 10. management,
     regulation
ordinarily ... 7. plainly, usually
     8. commonly 9. generally, naturally
     11. customarily
ordinary ... 4. ruck, so-so 5. judge,
     nomic, plain, prosy, usual 6. common,
     normal, tavern 7. average, natural,
     prosaic, vulgate 8. everyday, habitual,
     mediocre, plebeian, workaday 9. of
     the Mass 10. table d'hôte
ordinate ... 6. ordain 7. appoint, orderly,
     regular 8. moderate 9. harmonize
     10. co-ordinate
ordination ... 5. order 11. appointment,
     arrangement, disposition
     12. organization
ordnance ... 4. guns 5. armor, orgue
     7. petards, rabinet, weapons
     8. armament, firearms, supplies
     9. artillery, torpedoes 10. ammunition
     14. apparatus belli
ordo ... 5. order 11. publication
ore ... 3. tin 4. gold, iron, lead, paco
     5. brass, metal, ochre 6. copper,
     silver, speiss 7. mercury, mineral,
     seaweed, uranium 8. cinnabar, tungsten
     9. loadstone (lodestone) 11. quicksilver
ore (pert to) ...
box .. 6. sluice
deposit .. 4. lode, mine 7. bonanza
fuser .. 7. smelter
horizontal layer .. 5. stope
impure .. 6. speiss
iron .. 5. ocher 8. hematite 9. magnetite
lead .. 6. galena
loading platform .. 4. plat
machine separator .. 6. vanner
refuse .. 6. scoria 8. tailings
roller .. 9. edgestone
silver .. 5. noble (metal)
sluice .. 5. trunk
stirrer .. 5. dolly
tin .. 5. scove
trough .. 6. strake
vein .. 4. lode 5. scrin, stope
worthless .. 5. matte
oread ... 5. nymph 7. seamaid
Oregon ...
capital .. 5. Salem
caves .. 11. Marble Halls
city .. 6. Eugene 7. Astoria, Medford
     8. Portland 12. Klamath Falls
crab apple .. 7. powitch
emigrant route .. 11. Oregon Trail
famed persons .. 4. Gray (Capt) 5. Astor,
     Clark, Lewis
Indian .. 5. Modoc 7. Chinook, Klamath

8. Nez Percé
mountain . . 4. Hood 5. Coast 8. Cascades
native nickname . . 7. webfoot
river . . 5. Rogue 7. Klamath 8. Columbia
  10. Willamette
State admission . . 11. Thirty-third
State motto . . 8. The Union
State nickname . . 6. Beaver 13. Sawdust
  Empire
wind . . 7. chinook
oremus . . . 9. let us pray
Oreortyx . . . 5. quail
Orestes (pert to) . . .
father . . 9. Agamemnon
friend . . 7. Pylades
mother . . 12. Clytemnestra
sister . . 7. Electra
wife . . 8. Hermione
orf, orfe . . . 3. ide 4. fish
orfevrerie . . . 7. jewelry 9. gold plate
organ (pert to) . . .
anatomy . . 3. ear, eye 4. lung, nose
  5. brain, heart, liver 6. kidney, syrinx,
  tongue, tonsil 7. viscera (pl)
bristlelike . . 4. seta
desk . . 7. console
fish . . 8. drumfish
honey-secreting . . 7. nectary
plant . . 5. stoma 7. tendril
motion . . 6. muscle
respiratory . . 4. lung
secretion . . 5. gland
spider's spinner . . 9. spinneret
stop (music) . . 8. register
tactile . . 6. feeler 8. tentacle
organic . . . 5. state, vital 6. innate
  8. inherent 9. organized 10. structural
  11. fundamental 14. constitutional
organic (pert to) . . .
compound . . 5. amine, ester 6. enzyme,
  ketone
disease . . 11. organopathy
memory . . 5. mneme
radical . . 5. ethyl
remains . . 5. azoic
soil . . 5. humus
organism (pert to) . . .
bacterial . . 4. germ 7. microbe
body of . . 4. soma
elementary . . 5. monad
minute . . 5. spore 6. amoeba
pelagic . . 6. nekton
plant . . 5. spore
potential . . 7. idorgan
sea . . 6. nekton 7. benthos 8. plankton
type . . 5. plant 6. animal 9. vegetable
vegetable . . 4. tree 5. plant
organization . . . 4. bloc, sect, unit
  5. cadre, guild, party, setup 6. empire
  11. association, corporation
  12. constitution 13. establishment
  14. classification
organized body . . . 5. corps, posse
organized matter . . . 5. fauna, flora
  6. living, nekton 7. animate, benthos
  8. plankton
organology, science . . . 10. phrenology
  13. splanchnology
organoscopy . . . 10. phrenology
orgueil . . . 5. pride 11. haughtiness
orgy . . . 4. lark, romp 5. binge, revel,

rites (anc), spree 6. frolic, ritual,
  shindy 7. debauch, revelry, shindig,
  wassail 8. carousal 11. celebration,
  merrymaking
oribi . . . 7. bleebok, Ourebia 8. antelope
oriel . . . 3. bay 6. recess, window
  7. balcony, gallery, portion 8. corridor
  10. moucharaby 11. meshrabiyeh
  (Muslim)
orient . . . 4. dawn 7. eastern, shining,
  sunrise 8. oriental, pellucid
  11. resplendent
Orient . . . 4. Asia, East 6. Levant
oriental (pert to) . . .
abode, gateway . . 3. dar
animal . . 4. zebu
archangel . . 5. Uriel
beverage . . 6. arrack
building . . 6. pagoda
burden bearer . . 5. hamal
cap (sheepskin) . . 6. calpac (calpack)
caravansary . . 4. khan 5. serai 6. imaret
carpet . . 4. kali
carriage . . 10. jinrikisha (jinricksha)
cart, wagon . . 5. araba
chief . . 4. Khan 6. Mikado
Christian . . 5. Uniat
corn . . 4. para
cosmetic . . 4. kohl
council . . 5. Divan
cymbals . . 4. zels
deity . . 3. Bel
destiny . . 6. Kismet
disease . . 8. beriberi
dish . . 4. rice 5. pilau (pilaw) 6. pilaff
  8. chop suey, chow mein
drug . . 5. opium 6. heroin 7. hashish
  (hasheesh)
drum . . 6. tom-tom
dulcimer . . 6. santir
fan . . 3. ogi
food . . 4. rice 5. salep
garment . . 3. aba 6. sarong
guitar . . 5. sitar
head cover . . 6. turban
hospice . . 6. imaret
inn . . 5. serai
instrument (Mus) . . 7. samisen
laborer . . 6. coolie (cooly)
leader . . 4. amir (ameer)
liquor . . 4. sake, saki
litter . . 5. dooly (doolie) 9. palanquin
lute . . 3. tar
maid . . 4. amah, ayah, eyah
manservant . . 5. hamal 6. coolie
marketplace . . 6. bazaar
monkey . . 7. macaque
nurse . . 4. amah, ayah (governess)
obeisance . . 6. salaam (salam)
pagoda . . 3. taa
people . . 4. Sere (anc) 5. Asian, Malay
  6. Indian 7. Chinese, Eastern, Tartars
  (Tatars) 8. Japanese 10. Mohammedan
pipe . . 8. narghile
rice paste . . 3. ame
rug . . 8. sedjadeh 11. Baluchistan
ruler . . 4. Khan, Shah 5. sahib (saheb)
  6. caliph (calif), sultan
sabre . . 8. scimitar
sailor . . 6. lascar
sash . . 3. obi

tambourine .. 5. daira
taxi .. 7. ricksha (rickshaw) 10. jinrikisha
trousers (women) .. 9. shaksheer
vessel (sailing) .. 4. dhow, saic
wagon .. 5. araba
warehouse .. 6. godown
wind .. 7. monsoon
worker .. 6. coolie (cooly)
orifice ... 4. hole, lura, pore, vent 5. inlet,
mouth, porus, stoma 6. outlet, porule
7. chimney, opening, ostiole 8. aperture,
bunghole, spiracle
origin ... 3. nee 4. germ, rise, root,
seed 5. alpha, birth, cause, start
6. nature, parent, source 7. genesis
9. beginning, etymology, inception,
parentage 10. inconabula, provenance
11. provenience 12. commencement,
fountainhead
original ... 3. new 5. basic, first, novel
6. fontal, native, primal, primer,
unused 7. genuine, pattern, primary
8. pristine 9. aborigine, beginning,
inventive, primitive 10. inimitable
11. fundamental, origination
12. commencement
original copy ... 6. ectype
originate ... 4. coin, open, rise, stem
5. arise, begin, breed, start 6. author,
create, derive, invent 7. emanate,
produce 8. generate, initiate
11. etymologize
originator ... 5. cause, maker 7. creator
8. inventor, producer 9. contriver
10. discoverer
oriole ... 5. pirol 6. golden, hooded,
loriot, Mimeta 7. orchard 8. Bullock's
9. Baltimore, Icteridae
Orion (pert to) ...
 Astron .. 7. Dog Star 10. Canis Major
 11. Orion's Hound 13. constellation
 color .. 11. Holland blue
 Gr Myth .. 6. hunter
 Jacob's Staff .. 10. Yard and Ell
 13. Golden Yardarm
 slain by .. 7. Artemis
 star .. 5. Rigel
orison ... 6. prayer
Orkney Islands, Scotland ...
 capital .. 8. Kirkwall
 Firth .. 8. Pentland
 fishing grounds .. 4. haaf
 island, largest .. 6. Pomona
 President, Supreme Court .. 4. foud
 stone tower (Prehist) .. 5. broch
orle (Her) ... 6. border, fillet, wreath
7. bearing, chaplet 10. escutcheon
(voided)
Orloff ... 5. horse 7. diamond (Russ,
194 3/4 carats)
orlop ... 4. deck (lowest)
Ormazd (Pers) ... 5. deity (supreme)
ormer ... 7. abalone 8. ear shell
ornament (pert to) ...
 apex .. 6. finial
 ball .. 6. pompon

bell-shaped .. 9. clochette
Bible .. 4. Urim
boat-shaped .. 3. nef
brilliant .. 4. gaud 5. spang 6. sequin,
 tinsel 7. spangle
circular .. 7. rosette
delicate .. 7. tracery
diamond-shaped .. 11. epigonation
dress .. 5. jabot 8. stomacher
 10. embroidery
egg-shaped .. 3. ove
hair, head .. 4. comb 5. tiara 8. barrette
indented .. 5. chase
Japanese girdle .. 4. inro
leaves and grapes .. 6. pampre
magical .. 6. amulet
mantel .. 7. bibelot, trinket
pendant .. 6. bangle, tassel 7. earring
 9. lavaliere (lavalier)
pretentious .. 6. rococo
protuberant .. 4. boss
raised design .. 7. brocade
scroll-like .. 6. volute
set of .. 6. parure
setting in .. 5. inlay 7. emblema
silverware .. 7. gadroon
spiral .. 5. helix
terminal .. 6. finial
wall .. 6. plaque, sconce
ornamental (pert to) ...
 bottle .. 8. decanter
 button .. 4. stud
 description .. 5. fancy 10. decorative
 lace edge .. 5. picot 7. tatting
 metal .. 6. niello
 raised .. 7. brocade
 stand .. 7. étagère
 vase .. 3. urn
ornamented ... 6. chased, etched, tooled
8. engraved
ornate .. 3. gay 5. fancy 6. florid, tawdry
7. adorned 9. decorated
ornery ... 8. perverse, stubborn
9. malicious 11. ill-tempered
ornithoid ... 8. birdlike
ornithology (study of) ... 5. birds
ornithon ... 6. aviary
oro ... 4. gold 5. money
Oro ... 3. God (Tahiti)
oro (comb form) ... 5. month, serum
8. mountain
orology (science of) ... 9. mountains
orotund ... 7. pompous 9. bombastic
orp ... 4. fret, weep
Orpheus (pert to) ...
 astronomy .. 6. Cygnus
 eighteenth century .. 6. Handel
 father .. 6. Apollo
 mother .. 8. Calliope
 poet .. 8. Thracian
 reference .. 6. Orphic
 river .. 6. Hebrus
 wife .. 8. Eurydice
Orphic ... 3. egg (Creation's) 5. hymns
7. tablets (gold) 13. Book of the Dead
(rites)
orphrey ... 10. embroidery (gold)
orpit (Scot) ... 7. fretful
orra ... 3. odd 5. oddly 10. not
matched, occasional, unemployed
13. miscellaneous

ort . . . 3. end 4. bits 5. scrap 6. refuse, scraps 7. remnant 8. leavings, leftover

orthodox . . . 7. Trinity 8. accepted, approved, believer, standard 9. canonical, customary 12. conventional

Orthodox Moslem . . . 5. hanif

orthography . . . 8. spelling

ortolan . . . 7. bunting 8. bobolink, sora rail, wheatear

Oryx . . . 5. beisa 7. gazelle, gemsbok 8. antelope, leucoryx

os . . . 4. bone 5. mouth, osker (Geol) 7. opening

Osage . . . 5. river 6. Indian (Sioux)

Osaka, Japan . . . 7. capital 10. prefecture 10. orange tree

oscillate . . . 3. wag 4. rock, sway, vary 5. swing, waver, weave 7. vibrate 9. fluctuate

Oscines . . . 12. singing birds

oscitancy . . . 6. gaping 7. yawning 8. dullness, lethargy 10. drowsiness

oscitant . . . 4. dull 6. drowsy, gaping, sleepy 7. yawning 8. careless, sluggish 9. apathetic

osculate . . . 4. buss, kiss

osier . . . 3. rod 4. wand 6. sallow, willow 7. dogwood

Osiris, Egypt (pert to) . . .
brother . . 3. Set (Seth)
crown . . 4. atef
enemy . . 3. Set 7. brother
father . . 3. Geb
god . . 9. fertility 10. underworld
god (Gr) . . 8. Dionysus
husband of . . 4. Isis
king of . . 5. Egypt
mother . . 3. Nut
seat . . 6. Abydos
son . . 5. Horus 6. Anubis

Osmanli . . . 4. Turk 8. language

osmesis . . . 8. smelling 9. olfaction

osmosis . . . 10. absorption 12. infiltration

osprey . . . 4. hawk 7. feather (hat) 8. fish hawk 9. ossifrage 10. breakbones

ossature . . . 8. skeleton 9. framework (Arch)

osse . . . 4. dare 7. attempt, presage, promise 8. prophecy

osseous . . . 4. bony, hard 10. ossiferous

ossifrage . . . 5. eagle 6. osprey 11. lammergeier

ossuary . . . 3. urn 4. tomb 10. depository 12. charnel house 13. burial chamber

ostend . . . 6. reveal 7. exhibit 8. manifest 11. demonstrate

ostensible . . . 5. shown 6. avowed 7. alleged, seeming 8. apparent, declared, specious 9. exhibited, plausible, professed

ostent . . . 3. air 4. mien 5. token 7. portent 10. appearance

ostentatious . . . 4. arty, vain 5. dashy 6. sporty 8. pompous 11. conspicuous, pretentious

ostiole . . . 4. pore 5. stoma 7. orifice 8. aperture

ostler . . . 7. hostler 9. stableman

ostracize . . . 5. exile, expel 6. banish, deport 7. cast out, exclude 9. extradite 10. expatriate

ostrich . . . 3. emu 4. Rhea 5. nandu 8. Struthio 9. cassowary

ostrichlike . . . 11. struthiform

ostrich tail feather . . . 3. boo

Otaheite . . . 5. Tahiti

otalgia . . . 7. earache

Othello (pert to) . . .
opera by . . 5. Verdi
tragedy by . . 11. Shakespeare
villain . . 4. Iago
wife . . 9. Desdemona

other . . . 2. or 5. alter, ither 6. either, second 8. one of two 9. different 10. additional

others . . . 7. the rest 9. remaining

otherwise . . . 2. or 5. alias, ossia, other 6. or else 9. different 10. contrarily 11. differently

Othman . . . 4. Turk 5. Osman 6. sultan 7. Osmanli, Ottoman, Turkish

Othman's successor . . . 3. Ali

otiant . . . 4. idle 8. in repose 10. unemployed

otiose . . . 4. idle 6. at ease, futile 7. sterile, useless 8. indolent 12. functionless

otium . . . 7. leisure

otkon . . . 4. okee (oki) 5. demon (Iroquois)

otologist . . . 6. aurist 9. ear doctor

ottava . . . 6. eighth, octave

ottava rima . . . 15. eight-line stanza

ottavino . . . 7. piccolo

ottoman . . . 4. seat 5. couch, stool 7. cricket 9. footstool

Ottoman (pert to) . . . see also *Othman*
color . . 9. vermilion
court . . 5. Porte 12. Sublime Porte
Empire . . 7. Turkish
fabric . . 6. ribbed 10. corded silk
governor . . 3. bey, dey 5. pasha
leader . . 5. Osman
native . . 4. Turk
poetry (couplet) . . 4. beyt
province . . 6. eyalet (former) 7. vilayet
Turkish . . 7. Osmanli

oubliette . . . 7. dungeon (top opening)

ouch . . . 5. bezel, clasp, jewel 6. brooch 8. ornament 11. exclamation

ought . . . 4. duty, must, zero 5. at all, aught, owned 6. cipher, should 7. behoove, nothing 8. anything, in need of 9. possessed 10. obligation

Ouija board . . . 10. planchette

ouk . . . 4. week

ouphe . . . 3. elf 6. goblin

Our (pert to) . . .
Father . . 11. Lord's Prayer
French . . 5. notre
Lady . . 10. Virgin Mary
Lady's-mint . . 9. spearmint
Lady's Wand (Astron) . . 10. Orion's Belt
Lady's Way . . 6. Zodiac

ourie . . . 4. cold 5. dingy 6. dreary

ousia . . . 6. nature 7. essence 9. substance, true being

oust . . . 3. bar 5. eject, evict 6. depose, remove, unseat 7. turn out

out . . . 3. odd 4. away 5. drunk 6. absent, beyond, excuse, issued, outlet 9. published 10. dislocated, extinguish 11. unconscious

12. extinguished, not available

out and out ... 6. arrant 8. absolute, complete, outright, thorough 9. downright 13. thoroughgoing

outbreak ... 4. rash, riot 5. burst, spurt 6. emeute, tumult 7. outcrop, ruction 8. eruption, hysteria, outburst 12. insurrection 13. recrudescence

outburst ... 4. gale 5. blast, flare, flash 8. ejection, eruption 9. explosion 10. ebullition

outcast ... 5. exile, leper, ronin 6. pariah 7. quarrel 8. castaway, derelict, vagabond 9. expatriate

outclass ... 5. excel, outdo 6. outvie 7. outrank, surpass 8. outshine 10. outperform

outcome ... 5. issue 6. effect, outlet, result, sequel, upshot 7. emanate, product 8. solution 10. denouement 11. consequence

outcry ... 4. wail, yell 5. alarm, shout 6. clamor, plaint 7. suction 8. proclaim 11. exclamation

outdated ... 7. archaic 8. obsolete 10. antiquated 12. old-fashioned

outdo ... 5. excel 6. defeat, exceed, outwit

outdoor game ... 4. polo 6. hockey, tennis 7. cricket, croquet

outer ... 5. ectad, ectal 7. outside, outward 8. exterior, external 9. objective 10. extraneous

outer (pert to) ...
boundary .. 9. perimeter
coat .. 4. coat, hull 5. testa 6. extine, jacket 8. tegument
garment .. 4. suit, wrap 5. cloak, dress 7. paletot, sweater 8. mackinaw, mantilla, overcoat, raincoat
layer of roots .. 7. exoderm
opposed to .. 5. ental
shell .. 4. test
skin .. 9. epidermis

Outer Mongolia ...
capital .. 4. Urga 14. Ulan Bator Khoto
desert .. 4. Gobi

outermost ... 6. utmost 7. extreme, outmost 8. far-flung, farthest

outfit ... 3. kit, rig 4. gear, suit, unit 5. equip, group 7. company, costume 8. wardrobe 12. organization 13. paraphernalia

outflow ... 4. gush, teem 6. deluge, efflux 7. freshet, outflux, outpour 8. effusion 10. ebullience

outgate ... 4. exit, vent 6. egress, outlet 7. outcome

outknee ... 6. bowleg

outlander ... see *outsider*

outlandish ... 3. odd 6. remote 7. bizarre, foreign, strange, uncouth 8. freakish 9. barbarous, inelegant, unrelated 10. extraneous, impossible, tramontane

outlaw ... 5. horse, ronin 6. bandit, banish 7. brigand, outcast 8. criminal, fugitive 9. ostracize, proscribe

outlet ... 4. exit, vent 5. bayou 6. stream 7. culvert, opening, outcast, passage

outline ... 3. map 5. chart, draft, frame, shape 6. sketch 7. contour, drawing, summary 8. scenario 9. adumbrate, delineate, lineament, perimeter, summarize 10. compendium 11. delineation 13. configuration

outlook ... 5. scope, vista, watch 7. purview 8. frontage, prospect 9. viewpoint 10. perception 11. probability 12. watchfulness

outmoded ... 6. passé 7. offbeat 8. outdated 10. superseded

outmost ... 5. final, utter 6. remote, utmost 8. farthest 9. extremest, outermost, uttermost 15. farthest outward

out of ...
agreement .. 6. dehors
danger .. 4. safe
date, style .. 3. old 5. passé 10. antiquated
place .. 5. inept
sorts .. 5. nohow 7. peevish
the ordinary .. 7. unusual
the question .. 10. impossible
the way .. 5. aside 6. afield

outpeer ... 5. excel 7. surpass

output ... 3. cut 5. expel, power, yield 6. amount, energy 7. turnout 10. production

outraged ... 6. abused, harmed 8. insulted, offended 9. affronted 10. infuriated, mistreated

outrageous ... 6. absurd 7. furious, heinous, obscene 8. flagrant 9. atrocious, excessive, monstrous 10. exorbitant, scandalous 11. disgraceful, unwarranted

outré ... 3. odd 6. absurd 7. bizarre 10. immoderate 11. extravagant

Outre-Mer ... 13. Book of Travels (Longfellow, 1835)

outremer ... 12. beyond the sea, foreign parts

outrigger ... 4. proa, spar 5. canoe

outright ... 8. thorough 10. completely 11. unqualified 12. unreservedly

outrival ... 5. excel 6. outvie 7. eclipse, outrank 8. outclass, outshine, outsmart, outstrip

outside ... 3. exo (pref) 4. ecto (comb form) 8. exterior, external, outdoors 10. extraneous 11. superficial

outsider ... 5. alien 8. stranger 9. auslander, foreigner, Uitlander

outspoken ... 4. free 5. blunt, frank 6. candid, direct 10. unreserved 13. communicative

outstanding ... 3. due 5. famed, noted 6. famous, unpaid 7. eminent, obvious 8. exterior 9. important, principal, prominent 10. projecting 11. conspicuous, uncollected

outstrip ... 4. best, lead 5. excel, outdo 7. surpass 8. outrival

outward ... 5. ectad, evert, outer, overt 8. formal, spiral 9. apparent, exterior, external, manifest 9. extrinsic 11. superficial

outwit ... 4. balk, best, foil 5. block, check, cross 6. baffle, thwart 9. checkmate, frustrate 10. circumvent, disappoint

outwork (Fort) ... 7. ravelin 8. tenaille

(tenail)

ouvrage . . . 4. work

ouzel, ousel . . . 4. piet 6. thrush 8. whistler 9. blackbird

oval . . . 5. ovate, ovoid 6. circle 7. ellipse 10. elliptical 11. ellipsoidal

ovale . . . 3. egg

ovate . . . 4. bard, oval 7. obovate (inversely)

oven . . . 3. umu 4. kiln, oast (oste) 7. furnace 8. hot place 9. microwave 12. brick chamber

oven (pert to) . . .
  glass annealing . . 4. lehr (leer)
  hop drying . . 4. oast
  mop . . 6. scovel

over . . . 3. o'er, too 4. also, anew, atop 5. above, again, ended, super, supra 8. finished

overact . . . 3. haw 5. emote, spout

overalls . . . 5. chaps 8. trousers 10. chaparajos

overbearing . . . 7. haughty 8. arrogant, cavalier, snobbish, subduing 9. imperious 10. highhanded 11. domineering 12. overpowering

overcast . . . 3. dim 4. dark 6. cloudy, darken, gloomy 10. overturned (Geol)

overcoat . . . 5. benny, parka 6. capote, raglan, slip-on, ulster 7. paletot, surtout, topcoat 9. greatcoat, inverness (sleeveless)

overcome . . . 3. awe, win 4. beat 5. crush 6. beaten, defeat, exceed 7. conquer 8. outstrip, overbear, overturn, persuade, surmount, unnerved, vanquish 9. overpower, overthrow, overwhelm, prostrate

overcrowded . . . 9. congested

overdue . . . 4. late 5. tardy 7. belated 8. mistimed

overfeed . . . 4. glut 6. agrote, pamper 7. satiate, surfeit 8. overfill 9. crapulate, overstuff

overflow . . . 4. teem 5. spate 6. abound, deluge, outlet 7. copious, overrun 8. inundate, opulence, overload, plethora, teem with 9. abundance, pour forth 10. ebullience

overfond of . . . 4. dote 5. silly

overfull . . . 8. inflated, satiated 9. plethoric 10. overloaded

overhang . . . 3. jut 6. beetle 7. project, suspend 9. advantage 11. over and over

overlapping . . . 8. obvolute 9. imbricate, syphering

overloaded . . . 6. turgic 8. inflated, overfill 9. bombastic, plethoric

overlook . . . 4. face, miss, scan, skip, snub 6. acquit, excuse, ignore, slight, survey 7. absolve, condone, forgive, neglect, overtop 9. disregard, oversight, rise above, supervise

overlord . . . 6. master 8. domineer, governor 9. tyrannize

overly . . . 3. too 8. careless 9. negligent 11. overbearing, superficial 12. supercilious

overmodest . . . 7. prudish 8. priggish 11. puritanical, strait-laced

overnice . . . 5. fussy 6. purist 7. elegant, finicky 8. affected 10. fastidious

overpower . . . 3. awe 4. rout, stun 5. crush 6. dazzle, defeat, master, subdue 7. conquer 8. overbear, overcome, vanquish 9. overthrow, overwhelm

overpowering . . . 6. fierce 8. exciting 12. overwhelming

overreach . . . 4. dupe 5. cheat 6. exceed, nobble, outwit, overgo, strain 7. deceive 10. circumvent

overrun . . . 5. crush, swarm 6. abound, desert, exceed, infest, outrun, ravage, spread 7. destroy, pervade, run over, trample 8. overflow 9. overwhelm 11. superabound

overscrupulous . . . 7. prudish 9. overexact 10. overstrict 14. overfastidious

overshadow . . . 5. excel 6. darken 7. eclipse, obscure, shelter 8. dominate 9. overcloud

overshoe . . . 3. gum 6. arctic, galosh (galoshe)

oversight . . . 4. care 5. error, lapse, watch 6. charge 7. control, neglect 8. omission 9. direction 10. inspection 11. supervision 12. guardianship, surveillance 13. nonobservance

overskirt . . . 7. pannier (anc) 11. upper skirt

oversleeve . . . 6. armlet

overspread . . . 5. cover 6. infest 7. overrun, pervade 8. disperse, suffused

overt . . . 4. open 6. patent, public 7. obvious 8. apparent, manifest 10. open to view

overtake . . . 5. catch, reach, seize 6. detect, rejoin 7. ensnare 9. apprehend, captivate

overthrow . . . 4. down, rout, ruin 5. worst 6. defeat, depose, refute, unseat 7. conquer, deposal, destroy, ruinate, unhorse 8. demolish, disprove, overcome, overturn, vanquish 9. prostrate 10. revolution

overthrown . . . 6. fallen, ruined 8. defeated 9. disproved

overtones . . . 5. tones 8. partials 9. harmonics

overtop . . . 5. dwarf, excel 7. obscure, surpass 8. go beyond, overhead, override 9. transcend 10. tower above

overture . . . 5. offer, proem 7. opening, prelude 8. aperture, proposal 11. composition, proposition 13. peace offering

overturn . . . 3. tip 4. tilt 5. throw, upset 6. topple 7. capsize, conquer, destroy, overset, reverse, subvert 9. overthrow, overwhelm

overweight . . . 7. obesity 11. overbalance 13. preponderance

overwhelm . . . 4. bury, rout 5. crush 6. defeat, deluge, engulf 7. confute, conquer, engross, immerse, oppress 8. submerge 9. overpower, overthrow

Ovidae, Ovinae . . . 5. goats, sheep

oviparous ... 11. ovoviparous 12. egg producing (opp of viviparous)
ovoid, ovoidal ... 7. egglike 9. egg-shaped
ovule ... 3. egg 4. seed 6. embryo, ovulum
ovum ... 3. egg 4. seed 5. spore 6. gamete 8. germ cell
owe ... 3. due, own 7. possess 9. be obliged 10. be indebted
ower ... 6. debtor
owl (pert to) ...
  barn .. 4. lulu 5. padge
  breed .. 6. pigeon
  eagle .. 7. katogle 14. Tiger of the Wood
  eye .. 4. disc
  family .. 9. Strigidae
  female .. 3. hen
  genus .. 4. Bubo 5. Ninox, Strix 7. Syrnium
  horned .. 4. Bubo 6. aziola (small) 8. Hush-wing
  light .. 4. dusk
  like .. 4. owly 8. strigine
  parrot .. 6. kakapo
  Puerto Rican .. 6. mucaro
  short-eared .. 8. marsh owl
  tawny .. 8. billywix
  term .. 4. hoot 11. bird of night 13. bird of Minerva
  white .. 7. wapacut
  young .. 4. utum 5. owlet
own ... 4. have 5. admit 7. confess, possess 11. acknowledge
owner ... 6. master 7. planter (plantation) 8. landlady, landlord 10. proprietor
ownership ... 4. oadl (anc law) 5. claim 7. tenancy 8. dominium, interest, property 10. possession 11. seigniorage 12. seignioralty 14. proprietorship
ox ... 5. beeve, steer 6. bovine 8. strength 13. beast of burden
ox (pert to) ...
  Celebes .. 4. anoa

  genus .. 3. Bos
  harness .. 4. yoke
  horned .. 4. reem
  India .. 4. gaur
  like .. 5. bison 6. bovine 7. taurine
  stall .. 5. boose
  Tibetan .. 3. yak
  type .. 4. zebu
  wild .. 4. urus 7. banteng
  working .. 4. aver
  yoke .. 4. span
oxeye ... 4. boce (fish) 5. daisy 6. dunlin, plover
oxford ... 4. gray, shoe 5. cloth
Oxford (pert to) ...
  college accts .. 6. battel
  color .. 4. blue, gray
  Marbles .. 7. Arundel
  Museum .. 9. Ashmolean (1683)
  officer .. 6. beadle (bedel at Oxford) (bedell at Cambridge)
  scholarship .. 6. Rhodes
  school .. 10. University (1570)
  sheep (hornless) .. 4. Down
oxide of iron ... 4. rust
oxide of sodium ... 4. soda
oxidize ... 4. rust 5. erode 9. sulphuret (Philat)
oxter ... 3. arm 6. armpit 7. embrace
oxtongue ... 5. plant 7. biltong, bugloss
oxwort ... 9. butterbur
oxygen ... 3. gas 5. oxide, ozone 7. element
oxyopia ... 10. extra sight
oyez, oyes ... 6. hear ye
oyster ... 6. huitre 7. bivalve, mollusk
oyster (pert to) ...
  gatherer .. 7. tongman
  rake .. 5. tongs
  shell .. 4. husk, test 5. shuck
  spawn .. 6. cultch
  type .. 9. bluepoint
  young .. 4. spat
Ozark State ... 8. Missouri
Oz author ... 4. Baum (L Frank)
ozone ... 3. air 6. oxygen

P

P ... 2. Pi 6. letter (16th)
pa ... 4. Papa 6. father
pa, pah ... 4. fort 7. village 10. settlement (fortified)
paauw ... 7. bustard
pabulum ... 4. food, fuel 7. aliment, support 9. nutriment 10. sustenance 11. nourishment
pac, pack ... 8. half boot, moccasin
paca ... 6. rodent 9. Cuniculus
pace ... 3. run 4. gait, lope, rate, step, trot, walk 5. speed 7. measure 8. movement, velocity
pace (L) ... 5. peace
Pace ... 5. Pasch 6. Easter
pachyderm ... 8. elephant 10. rhinoceros 12. hippopotamus, Pachydermata

pachydermous ... 11. thick-walled 12. thick-skinned
pacific ... 4. calm 6. irenic, serene 8. irenical, peaceful, tranquil 9. peaceable, quiescent 12. conciliatory
Pacific (pert to) ...
  Coast tree .. 7. madrona 8. knob pine
  Highway .. 10. Camino Real
  island bird .. 4. kagu
  island shark .. 4. mako 11. blue pointer
  island tree .. 4. ipil
  islands .. 4. Guam, Wake 5. Samos 7. Oceania 8. Caroline, Tasmania 9. Melanesia, Polynesia 10. Micronesia
  shrub .. 5. salal
  States .. 6. Oregon 10. California, Washington

stepping stones . . 9. Aleutians (Russia to America)
Pacific Ocean discoverer . . . 6. Balboa
pacifier . . . 3. sop 4. ring (baby's) 6. nipple 7. soother 8. sedative 10. peacemaker
pacify . . . 4. calm, ease, lull 5. abate, allay 6. soften, soothe 7. appease, assuage, mollify, placate 8. mitigate, palliate 9. alleviate 10. conciliate, propitiate 11. tranquilize (tranquillize)
pack . . . 3. ram, set, wad 4. cram, fill, load, stow, tamp 5. carry, flock, horde, steve, truss 6. bundle, embale 8. assemble, encumber, quantity, send away
pack (pert to) . . .
animal . . 3. ass 5. burro, camel, llama 6. donkey
back . . 8. knapsack
horse . . 7. sumpter
horse bag . . 5. kyack 7. pannier
of hounds . . 6. kennel
package . . . 3. pad 4. bale 5. fadge 6. bundle, packet, parcel, robbin (peppers), seroon 11. combination
packing . . . 4. lute, seal 7. stowage 9. packaging 10. rubber ring
paco . . . 3. ore 6. alpaca
Pacolet . . . 10. swift horse
pact . . . 6. pactum 7. bargain 8. contract 9. agreement
Pactolian . . . 6. golden
Pactolus, Myth (pert to) . . .
famed for . . 5. Midas 11. gold-bearing
river (Asia Minor) . . 5. Lydia
pad . . . 3. mat, paw 4. fill, foot, frog, line, path, walk 5. quilt, stuff, track, tramp 6. tablet, trudge 7. bedding, bolster, cushion, footpad 8. notebook, protract, saturate 9. footprint, pulvillus 10. highwayman
pad (pert to) . . .
cloth . . 7. housing 11. saddlecloth
hair . . 3. rat
harness, part . . 5. panel 6. terret 7. housing 10. horsecloth
perfume . . 6. sachet
padding . . . 6. lining 7. wadding 8. softness, stuffing 11. superfluity
paddle . . . 3. oar, row 4. beat, stir, wade, whip 5. blade, board, scull, spank, spoon 6. dabble, propel 7. flipper 8. lumpfish
paddle (pert to) . . .
English . . 6. trample 8. lumpfish 9. tread upon 10. paddlecock
Scotch . . 3. hoe 4. spud
paddock (pert to) . . .
paddockstool . . 9. toadstool
piper . . 9. horsetail
stone . . 10. greenstone
paddy . . . 4. rice, soft 7. padlike 8. cushiony 9. rice field 10. hod carrier
Paddy . . . 7. Patrick 8. Irishman
paddymelon . . . 7. wallaby
Paddy's hurricane (Naut) . . . 4. calm
paddywhack . . . 4. beat, blow 6. temper 9. ruddy duck, thrashing
padge . . . 7. barn owl
padmasana . . . 11. cross-legged (Buddha style), lotus-shaped
padre . . . 4. monk 6. Father, priest

8. chaplain, minister
padrona . . . 8. landlady, mistress
padrone . . . 6. master, patron 8. landlord 9. innkeeper
paedarchy . . . 14. rule by children
pagan . . . 6. ethnic, paynim 7. heathen 10. heathenism, idolatrous, unbeliever 11. irreligious
Paganalia . . . 8. festival (Rom)
pagan god . . . 4. idol
page . . . 3. boy 4. leaf 5. child, folio 6. summon 9. attendant, messenger
page (pert to) . . .
beginning . . 7. flyleaf
book . . 5. folio 6. cahier, sheets
lady's . . 7. esquire 8. escudero
left-hand . . 5. verso
number . . 5. folio
right-hand . . 5. recto
title . . 5. unwan 6. rubric 12. frontispiece
pageant . . . 4. pomp, show 5. drama 6. parade 7. tableau 8. aquacade 9. spectacle 10. exhibition 11. ostentation
pages . . . 7. paginal 8. paginate
Pagliacci . . . 5. opera 9. character
pagne . . . 9. loincloth, petticoat
pagoda . . . 2. ta 3. taa 4. idol 5. booth 6. temple 11. summerhouse
pagoda (pert to) . . .
finial . . 7. tee
sleeve . . 12. funnel-shaped
stone . . 12. Agalmatolite
tree . . 6. banyan 10. frangipani
paha . . . 4. hill 5. ridge (glacial)
pahi . . . 4. ship 5. canoe (seagoing)
pahmi . . . 5. bobac 6. marmot
paho . . . 7. pahutan 11. prayer stick
pahutan . . . 5. mango
paid . . . 5. hired 6. cashed 7. content, settled, yielded 9. satisfied 10. discharged
paideutics . . . 8. pedagogy, teaching
paid office (without work) . . . 8. sinecure
paid out . . . 5. spent 8. expended 9. disbursed
paigle . . . 7. cowslip 8. crowfoot 10. stitchwort 12. cuckooflower
pail . . . 3. can, pan 4. beat 6. bucket, harass, situla, thrash, vessel 8. cannikin
paillasse, palliasse . . . 3. bed (masonry) 8. mattress (straw)
pailles . . . 6. straws (cookery)
paillou, pailoo . . . 7. archway (memorial)
pain . . . 3. ail 4. ache, agra, pang 5. agony, labor, thraw, throb, wound 6. grieve, stitch 7. afflict, ailment, gnawing, torture, trouble 8. disquiet, distress 9. suffering 10. affliction, punishment
painful . . . 4. sore 7. careful 8. diligent 9. difficult, laborious 10. afflictive, unpleasant 11. industrious, painstaking
painkiller . . . 7. anodyne 8. medicine, sedative 9. analgesic, calmative 10. depressant
painstaking . . . 5. fussy 7. careful, labored 8. diligent, thorough 9. assiduity, assiduous, laborious
paint . . . 4. coat, draw, limn 5. adorn, color, rouge, stain 6. depict, parget, sketch 7. picture, pigment, portray

8. cosmetic, describe 9. delineate, embellish 11. application (Med)

paint (pert to) ...
blue, green . . 4. bice
comb form . . 5. picto
face . . 4. fard
glossy . . 6. enamel
Latin . . 6. pinxit
spreader . . 7. spatula
through pattern . . 7. stencil
with vermilion . . 7. miniate

paintbrush ... 8. hawkweed 10. painted cup 11. St John's wort

painted ... 6. coated 7. colored, feigned 9. disguised, portrayed 10. artificial, variegated

painted (pert to) ...
bat . . 11. Vespertilio
beauty . . 9. butterfly
bunting . . 5. finch
duck . . 8. mandarin 9. harlequin
enamel . . 7. Limoges
hyena . . 4. Cape hunting dog
lady . . 7. thistle 8. sweet pea 9. butterfly
process . . 7. scumble
trillium . . 9. wake-robin
turtle . . 8. carapace

painter ... 4. puma 6. cougar 7. panther
painter ... 4. Dali 5. Monet 6. Millet, Rubens 7. da Vinci, El Greco, Picasso, van Gogh 8. Reynolds, Whistler 9. Rembrandt 12. Gainsborough, Grandma Moses, Michelangelo

Painter's Easel ... 6. Pictor (constellation)

painting ... 3. oil 5. genre, mural, Pietà (sacred), secco 6. fresco, marine 7. impasto, tempera 9. encaustic, grisaille, landscape 10. cerography 11. portraiture 12. illustration

pair ... 3. duo, two 4. dyad, mate, span, team, yoke 5. brace, unite 6. couple

paired ... 5. gemel (Her) 7. coupled, leagued

pairs, growing in ... 6. binate, double

paisano ... 7. peasant 10. countryman, road runner

pal ... 4. chum, pard 5. buddy, crony 6. cobber 7. partner 9. companion 10. accomplice

palace ... 4. court, Doges, house (Astrol) 6. palais 7. palazzo 10. praetorium (pretorium)

paladin ... 4. hero 6. knight (Round Table)

Paladins of France ... 9. The Twelve

palais ... 6. palace 10. courthouse

Palamedes ... 4. hero (Trojan War)

palampore ... 7. hanging (cotton) 8. bedcover

palanquin, palankeen ... 4. kago 5. dooly (doolie), palki 6. litter, palkee 10. conveyance

palanquin bearer ... 5. hamal 6. sirdar

pales ... 4. dhak, tree (yellow dye)

palatable ... 5. sapid, tasty 6. savory 8. pleading, seasoned 10. acceptable

palate ... 4. cion 5. taste, uvula, velum 6. relish 10. epipharynx

palatine ... 4. bone 6. artery, county 8. palatial

Palatine Confession ... 10. Heidelberg

palaver ... 4. talk 6. confer 7. chatter 8. converse, flattery 10. conference 12. conversation

pale ... 3. dim, wan 4. ashy, fade, lily 5. ashen, fence, lurid, pasty, stake, white 6. blanch, bounds, paling, pallid, pallor, sallow, sickly, sphere 7. haggard, obscure, whitish 8. palisade 9. deathlike 10. indistinct

pales, palet ... 4. fold 5. bract, scale 6. dewlap 8. ramentum

paleo (comb form) ... 3. old 7. ancient

paleolithic culture ... 8. Stone Age

Paleozoic ... 10. Appalachia

Palestine (pert to) ...
ancient name . . 6. Canaan
animal . . 4. cony (Bib) 5. daman
conqueror . . 5. David, Turks 11. Constantine
country (anc) . . 4. Edom 5. Endor (Indur) 8. Nazareth 9. Philistia
lake . . 7. Dead Sea, Galilee
language . . 7. Aramaic
mountain (Bib) . . 4. Zion 6. Carmel, Gilead, Hermon 13. Mount of Olives
plain, steppe . . 5. Negeb 6. Sharon
river . . 6. Jordan
town, district . . 4. Gaza 5. Haifa 7. Samaria 9. Jerusalem

paletot ... 4. coat 8. overcoat

pali ... 9. precipice 10. steep slope

pali (comb form) ... 5. again 8. backward

Pali ... 7. dialect (anc) 12. dead language

palimpsest ... 9. parchment, rewritten 10. re-engraved 15. codex rescriptus

palindrome (same backward, forward) ... 8. wordplay 9. inversion

paling ... 5. fence, limit, palis, stake 6. fading, picket 7. fencing 9. enclosure

palisade ... 5. cliff, fence, stake 6. picket 7. defense, enclose, fortify 8. espalier, palisado, surround 9. precipice 10. impalement 13. fortification

pall ... 4. pale 5. cloak, cover, faint, qualm 6. coffin, mantle, nausea 7. secrecy 12. graveclothes

pallall ... 9. hopscotch

palle ... 5. balls 8. six balls (Medici)

pallet ... 3. bed 4. pate 5. quilt 7. blanket 8. mattress 9. headpiece, paillasse

palliard ... 6. beggar, lecher, rascal 8. vagabond

palliate ... 4. hide 5. abate, cloak, cover, gloss 6. excuse, lessen, soften 7. conceal, qualify, relieve, shelter 8. disguise, mitigate, moderate 9. alleviate, extenuate

pallid ... 3. wan 4. gray, pale 5. pasty, white 6. anemic, sallow

Pallu ... 10. Reuben's son (Bib)

palm ... 4. hand (part) 5. areca, bribe, steal 6. bacaba, handle, rattan, stroke, trophy

palm (pert to) ...
civet . . 6. musang
cockatoo . . 5. arara
down . . 7. pronate
drink . . 5. assai
drink (alcoholic) . . 4. beno, nipa
hand . . 6. palmus, thenar
handlike . . 7. palmate

house .. 8. palmetum
lily .. 2. ti
mat .. 6. petate
off .. 5. foist
ref to .. 10. palmaceous
sap (fermented) .. 5. toddy
starch .. 4. sago
sugar .. 7. jaggery
thatch .. 4. nipa
palm (tree) ...
  African .. 7. palmyra (sugar, wine)
  Arab .. 4. doum (doom)
  Asiatic .. 4. atap, nipa
  betel .. 5. areca, bonga 6. pinang
  book .. 4. tara 7. taliera
  Brazil .. 7. urucuri (urucury)
  bussu, thatching .. 7. troolie (trooly)
  cabbage .. 5. Sabal 8. palmetto
  Ceylon .. 5. tala 7. talipot (fanleaf)
  climbing, flexible .. 6. rattan
  dwarf .. 5. Sabal
  E Indies .. 4. atap, nipa 7. jaggery
    (sugar), tokopat (hat)
  fan .. 7. talipot 8. palmetto
  fiber .. 3. tal 6. raffia 8. piassava
    (piassaba)
  Florida .. 5. royal
  gingerbread tasting .. 4. doum (doom)
  leaf .. 3. tal 4. olla (ola) 12. chiquichiqui
  Malayan, feather .. 4. irok 6. gomuti
  palmyra .. 4. brab, olla 6. ronier
  Philippine (coconut) .. 4. niog
  pinnate .. 5. assai, nikau 7. calamus,
    feather
  S America .. 5. bussu, datil 6. tooroo
    12. chiquichiqui
  spiny .. 6. grugru
palmate ... 6. antler, webbed 10. hand-
  shaped
palmer ... 6. ferule 7. pilgrim (Holy Land)
  8. date palm 15. prestidigitator
Palmetto State ... 13. South Carolina
palmistry ... 10. chirognomy, chiromancy
palmodic (Med) ... 5. jerky
palp ... 6. feeler, palpus 8. tentacle
palpable ... 5. plain 6. patent 8. manifest,
  tangible 9. touchable 10. noticeable,
  ponderable
palpebra ... 6. eyelid
palpebrate ... 4. wink
palpitate ... 4. beat, drum 5. throb
  7. flutter, pulsate
palpitation ... 7. flutter, tremble
  9. pulsation, quivering, throbbing
  10. excitement
palsied ... 5. shaky 9. paralyzed, tottering
palter ... 5. shift 6. babble, haggle,
  mumble, parley 7. bargain, chatter,
  quibble 9. vacillate 10. equivocate
  11. prevaricate
paltry ... 4. mean, vile 5. petty, trash
  6. trashy 7. pitiful, rubbish 8. picayune,
  trifling 9. worthless 10. despicable
  12. contemptible
pampas ... 5. Pampa 6. plains (treeless)
pamper ... 3. pet 4. cram, glut 5. humor,
  spoil 6. caress, coddle, cosset, cuddle,
  dandle, posset 7. gratify, indulge
  11. mollycoddle
pamphagous ... 10. omnivorous
pamphlet ... 5. tract 6. folder 7. booklet,

  leaflet 8. brochure
pan ... 3. tab 4. part, tina (mining),
  wash 5. basin, roast, title (nobility)
  6. frying, lappet, spider, vessel
  7. cranium, hardpan, portion, skillet,
  subsoil 8. ridicule, saucepan 9. criticize
  10. acetabulum
pan (comb form) ... 3. all 5. every
Pan (pert to) ...
  animal .. 3. ape 10. chimpanzee
  god (Gr) .. 6. flocks
  instrument .. 4. pipe, reed
  music .. 7. Pan's pipes
  Pipes of .. 6. syrinx 8. Panpipes
  Roman identity .. 6. Faunus
  seat of worship .. 7. Arcadia
  son .. 7. Silenus
panacea ... 4. cure 6. elixir, remedy
  7. allheal (plant), cure-all 8. nepenthe
  10. catholicon 11. panchreston
panache ... 4. tuft (feathered) 5. plume
  7. swagger
Panama ...
  bay .. 5. Limon
  capital .. 10. Panama City
  city .. 5. Colon 6. Balboa 9. Cristobal
  engineer .. 8. Goethals
  gulf .. 6. Darien
  Indian .. 4. Cuna
  isthmus of .. 6. Darien (old name),
    Panama 7. San Blas
  redwood .. 5. quira
  river .. 7. Chagres
Panama Canal Lock ... 5. Gatun
  10. Miraflores
panarchy ... 13. universal rule
panaris ... 5. felon 7. whitlow
  10. paronychia
panary ... 5. bread 11. breadmaking
panatela ... 5. cigar
pancake ... 6. froise (fraise) 7. fritter
  8. flapjack 10. griddlecake
Pancake Day ... 13. Shrove Tuesday
pancreas ... 5. gland 10. sweetbread
  16. Isle of Langerhans
panda ... 7. bearcat
pandemonium ... 4. hell 5. noise
  6. tumult, uproar
Pandemonium (pert to) ...
  abode of .. 6. demons
  capital of .. 4. Hell
  palace of .. 5. Satan
  pert to .. 15. infernal regions
pander ... 4. bawd, pimp 5. cater, serve
  7. toady to 12. administer to
pandle ... 7. a shrimp
Pandora's Box ... 6. plague 9. human
  ills
Pandora's husband ... 10. Epimetheus
panegyric ... 5. éloge, elogy 6. eulogy
  7. oration, writing 8. encomium
  9. discourse, laudation
pang ... 3. fit 4. pain 5. throe 6. twinge
  8. paroxysm
pangolin ... 5. Manis 8. anteater
  9. Pholidota
panhandle ... 3. beg
Panhellenic ... 5. games (Isthmian)
  6. Greece 10. fraternity (Greek-letter)
panic ... 4. fear, fray 5. alarm, chaos,
  scare 6. fright 8. stampede

pannier ... 6. basket, dosser (dorser)
   7. corbeil 9. overskirt
panoply ... 7. defense 11. suit of armor
panorama ... 4. view 5. scene 7. picture,
   scenery 9. cyclorama
pant ... 4. beat, gasp 5. heave, throb
   7. breathe, pulsate 11. palpitation
Pantagruel (pert to)...
   character (romantic) .. 5. giant
   companion .. 7. Panurge
   father .. 9. Gargantua
pantaloon, pantaloons ... 5. pants
   6. dotard, old man 8. breeches, trousers
   11. Patron Saint (Venice)
Pantheon (pert to) ...
   aggregate .. 4. gods 7. deities
   builder .. 7. Hadrian (120 AD)
   building .. 6. shrine, temple 10. le
     Pantheon (Paris) 16. Westminster Abbey
   Rome .. 15. Temple of the Gods
panther, painter ... 4. pard, puma
   6. cougar, jaguar, ocelot 7. leopard
pantler ... 6. butler 7. servant
pantry ... 5. ambry 6. larder 7. buttery,
   pannier, pantler 8. cupboard
pants ... 5. chaps 7. drawers 8. trousers
   10. chaparajos (chaparejos), pantaloons
panuelo ... 6. collar 8. kerchief
   9. neckcloth
pap ... 4. teat 6. nipple 8. mammilla,
   soft diet
papa ... 3. dad 4. clay, Pope 6. baboon,
   father, potato, priest 7. vulture
papal ... 9. apostolic 10. pontifical
papal (pert to) ...
   book of decrees .. 8. decretal
   chancery .. 6. datary
   Court .. 3. See 5. Curia
   envoy .. 8. ablegate
   legate .. 6. nuncio
   letter .. 4. bull
   reformer .. 7. Gregory
   residence .. 7. Vatican
   seal .. 5. bulla
   vestment .. 5. fanon, orale
paper (pert to) ...
   absorbent .. 7. blotter
   broken .. 5. casse
   brown .. 6. manila
   coated .. 6. charta
   collection .. 7. dossier
   copy .. 6. carbon
   crinkled .. 5. crepe
   crisp .. 6. pelure
   currency .. 5. scrip
   cutlet wrap .. 8. papilote
   damaged .. 5. casse, salle 6. retree
   design .. 9. watermark
   fine .. 5. linen 6. vellum 9. parchment
   flower .. 11. strawflower
   folded .. 6. folio
   for pounding gold sheets .. 7. cutches
   gummed .. 5. label, stamp 7. plaster,
     sticker
   legal .. 4. writ 5. title
   measure .. 4. page, ream 5. quire, sheet
   nautilus .. 8. argonaut
   official .. 5. targe 8. document
   pad .. 6. tablet
   postage stamp .. 6. pelure
   size .. 3. cap 4. copy, demy, pott, quad

     5. atlas, crown, folio, legal 6. octavo
     8. foolscap, imperial 9. colombier
   small piece .. 5. scrip
   thin .. 4. rice 6. pelure, tissue 9. onionskin
   transfer .. 12. decalcomania
   untrimmed .. 6. deckle (deckel) 10. deckle
     edge 11. deckle-edged
   writing size .. 3. cap
paper chase ... 13. hare and hounds
papilla ... 6. nipple 10. projection
papule ... 6. papula, pimple
papyra (comb form) ... 5. paper
papyrus ... 4. pith, reed 5. paper, sedge
   6. scroll
par ... 2. by 5. value 7. average, by
   way of, strokes, through 8. equality,
   superior
parable ... 4. myth, tale 5. fable, story
   8. allegory, apologue 10. comparison,
   similitude
parabola ... 5. curve
parade ... 4. pomp, show 5. march
   6. flaunt 8. flourish, grandeur, splendor
   9. pageantry, promenade, spectacle
   10. pretension, procession
   11. ostentation 12. magnificence
   13. formal display
paradigm ... 5. model 7. example, pattern
paradisaic ... 6. Edenic
Paradise ... 4. Eden 5. Jenna 6. Aidenn,
   heaven, Utopia 7. Elysium
Paradise (pert to) ...
   apple .. 5. dwarf
   Arabic form .. 6. Aidenn
   Buddhist, Western .. 4. Jodo
   fool's .. 5. limbo
   grosbeak .. 9. cutthroat (bird)
   Mohammedan .. 5. Jenna
   plumage .. 14. bird of paradise
   poem (Milton) .. 12. Paradise Lost
     16. Paradise Regained
   river .. 5. Gihon (Bib)
   tree .. 9. China tree
paragon ... 4. type 5. ideal, match,
   model 7. diamond (100 carats), paladin,
   pattern 8. parallel 9. nonpareil
paragram ... 3. pun
Paraguay ...
   capital .. 8. Asunción
   city .. 9. Paraguari 10. Concepcion,
     Villarrica
   language .. 7. Guarani, Spanish
   river .. 6. Paraná 8. Paraguay
   tea .. 4. maté 5. yerba 11. yerba de
     maté
parakeet ... 5. green 6. parrot, puffin
   11. budgereegah (budgerygah)
paralysis ... 5. palsy 7. paresis
   10. hemiplegia, paraplegia 11. loss of
   power
paralyze ... 5. scram 6. benumb, deaden
   7. astound, terrify, unnerve
paramount ... 3. top 5. chief, liege
   6. ruling 7. supreme 8. dominant,
   superior 9. principal 10. preeminent
   13. most important
paramour ... 5. amour, leman, lover,
   wooer 8. mistress 9. gallantry
   10. sweetheart
paranoia ... 9. catatonia, monomania,
   nosomania

parapet . . . 5. redan 7. barrier, bulwark, rampart
parasite . . . 3. bur, sug 5. drone, toady
  6. Gnatho, insect, sponge 7. entozoa
  8. hanger-on 9. entophyte, sycophant
parasite (pert to) . . .
  animal . . 6. cuckoo 7. cowbird, entozoa
  external . . 12. ectoparasite
  internal . . 7. entozoa
  marine . . 6. remora, sponge
  plant . . 9. entophyte
  slang . . 6. flunky
  trout . . 3. sug
parasitic (pert to) . . .
  fish . . 6. remora
  fungus . . 4. rust 6. lichen
  worm . . 8. trichina (larva)
parcel . . . 3. lot 4. mete, part 5. piece, solum (law) 6. bundle, packet
  7. package, portion 8. fragment
parch . . . 3. dry 4. burn 5. dry up, roast, toast 6. scorch 7. shrivel, torrefy
parched . . . 4. sere 5. burnt, dried
  7. thirsty 8. withered
parchment (pert to) . . .
  bookcover . . 5. forel (forrel)
  fine . . 6. vellum
  manuscript . . 10. palimpsest
  roll . . 4. pell 6. scroll
  school . . 7. diploma
pard . . . 4. chum 5. tiger 7. comrade, leopard, panther, partner
  10. camelopard 11. confederate
pardesi (Hind) . . . 9. foreigner, outlander
pardie, parde, pardi (anc) . . . 4. oath
  6. indeed, surely, verily 9. certainly
pardon . . . 5. mercy, remit, spare
  6. acquit, excuse 7. absolve, amnesty, condone, forgive 8. tolerate 9. acquittal, remission 10. absolution, indulgence (Eccl) 11. forgiveness
pardonable . . . 6. venial 8. expiable
  9. excusable 10. forgivable
pardon chair, stall . . . 12. confessional
pare . . . 3. cut 4. peel, skin 5. shave
  6. cut off, remove, resect
parent . . . 3. dad 4. sire 5. pater 6. father, mother, source 7. genitor 8. begetter
  10. progenitor
parental affection (animal) . . . 6. storge
parget . . . 4. coat 5. paint 7. plaster
  8. decorate, ornament 9. whitewash
parhelion . . . 3. sun (mock)
pariah . . . 3. dog (half-wild) 7. outcast
  8. commoner, low caste
parian . . . 5. marble, market
Parian . . . 5. Paros 8. marble (sculptural)
  9. porcelain
parimutuel machine . . . 9. totalizer
  11. totalizator
Paris (pert to) . . .
  blue . . 6. cobalt 8. Prussian
  daisy . . 10. marguerite
  Garden (London) . . 10. bear garden
  green . . 11. insecticide
Paris, France . . .
  anc name . . 7. Lutetia (Lutice)
  airport . . 4. Orly
  capital of . . 6. France
  criminal . . 6. apache
  famed sites . . 6. Louvre 8. Pantheon

  9. Notre Dame 10. Montmartre 11. Eiffel Tower 13. Champs Elysées, Napoleon's Tomb
  native . . 8. Parisian
  patron saint . . 5. Denis (Denys)
  racecourse . . 7. Auteuil
  river . . 5. Seine
  subway . . 5. Metro
Paris, Gr legend . . .
  brought about . . 9. Trojan War 10. Fall of Troy
  father . . 5. Priam (King of Troy)
  killer of . . 8. Achilles
  mother . . 6. Hecuba
  wife . . 6. Oenone
parish . . . 5. laity 7. diocese 8. district
  9. parochial
parishioner . . . 6. tonsil
park . . . 4. area (enclosed) 5. place, tract
  6. claire, common, settle 7. pasture (Eng) 8. woodland 9. grassland, pleasance 10. playground
  11. reservation, set and leave
Park, Highway . . .
  Avenue . . 9. Manhattan
  Lane . . 6. London
  Row . . 9. Manhattan
Park, Historical . . . 6. Shiloh 8. Pea Ridge, Saratoga 9. Minute Man
  10. Gettysburg, Morristown 12. Harper's Ferry, Independence
Park, US . . . 4. Zion 7. Glacier, Olympic (rain forests) 8. Sequoyah (Sequoja), Yosemite 9. Haleakala, Mesa Verde
  10. Everglades, Mt McKinley, Shenandoah 11. Grand Canyon, Kings Canyon, Yellowstone 12. Harper's Ferry
  15. Petrified Forest
parlay, parley . . . 4. chat 5. parle, treat 6. confer 7. discuss 8. converse
  10. conference, discussion
  11. arbitration
parliament . . . 4. Diet 8. Congress
  11. legislature
parlous . . . 4. keen 5. risky 6. shrewd
  7. cunning 8. shocking 9. dangerous
Parnassian . . . 4. muse, poet 9. butterfly
  10. Parnassius
Parnassus, Greece . . .
  mountain . . 6. Phocis
  site of . . 6. Delphi 8. Castalia (fountain) 13. Delphic Apollo
  symbol of . . 6. poetry
parody . . . 5. farce 6. satire 7. mockery, take-off 9. burlesque, imitation
  10. caricature
paroemia . . . 7. proverb
parol, parole . . . 4. oral, word 6. speech
  7. freedom, promise, release 8. pleading 11. word of mouth
paronomasia . . . 3. pun 7. punning
  8. wordplay 9. assonance
  12. agnomination
paroxysm . . . 3. fit 4. pang 5. throe
  6. access, attack, frenzy 7. illness
  9. agitation 10. fit of anger
  12. exacerbation
paroxysm of grief . . . 5. agony
parricide (murder of) . . . 7. kinsman
parrot . . . 3. ara, hia, kea 4. jako, kaka, loro, lory 5. arara, cagit, macaw,

polly 6. kakapo, tiriba 7. corella,
lorilet 8. cockatoo, lorikeet, lovebird,
parakeet 9. Psittacus (Old World)
14. Psittaciformes
parrot (pert to) . . .
disease . . 11. psittacosis
genus . . 6. Nestor 9. Psittacus
gray . . 4. jako
green . . 5. cagit
hawk . . 3. hia
long-tailed . . 5. macaw
monk . . 4. loro
New Zealand . . 4. kaka
owl . . 6. kakapo
parrot fish . . 4. loro, scar 5. lauia 6. scarid
7. labroid 8. Labridae, Scaridae
parrotlike (tongued) . . 12. anthropoglot
sheep-killing . . 3. kea
short-tailed . . 7. lorilet
parry . . . 4. fend, ward 5. avert, avoid,
elude, evade, shift 6. refute, thwart
pars . . . 4. part
Parsee Bible . . . 10. Zend Avesta
Parsai, Parsi . . . 6. Gheber (Ghebre)
11. Zoroastrian 13. fire worshiper
Parsifal (pert to) . . .
character . . 6. Knight
healer or . . 8. Amfortas
son . . 9. Lohengrin
parsimonious . . . 4. near 5. close
6. frugal, meager, skimpy, sordid,
stingy 7. miserly, sparing 8. covetous,
grasping 9. illiberal, mercenary,
penurious 10. avaricious
parsley . . . 4. herb 5. cumin 7. garnish
9. Ammiaceae, flavoring
parsley camphor . . . 6. apiole
parson . . . 6. rector 8. minister, preacher,
reverend 9. clergyman
parsonage . . . 5. gleve, manse, tithe
7. rectory 8. benefice, vicarage
9. pastorate 10. presbytery
parson bird . . . 3. tui
part . . . 3. cut, die 4. open, role, twin
5. allot, break, piece, sever, share
6. depart, divide, member, sunder
7. analyze, disband, disjoin, divorce,
portion, section, segment 8. dissever,
disunite, division, fragment, function,
separate 9. component
part (pert to) . . .
basic . . 4. core, pith 7. essence, nucleus
choice . . 5. cream, elite 6. marrow
coarse . . 5. dregs
composite . . 7. section
corresponding . . 7. isomere
essential . . 4. core, gist, pith 5. heart
extra . . 5. spare
greater . . 4. bulk
hardest . . 5. brunt
infinitesimal . . 4. atom, mite
insignificant . . 3. bit 4. iota 6. trifle
kept . . 6. retent
main . . 4. body 5. trunk
narrow . . 4. neck
proportional . . 5. quota
rootlike . . 7. radicle
sawlike . . 5. serra
segment . . 5. tmema
small . . 3. bit, jot 4. iota 6. detail
7. snippet

smallest . . 4. whit 5. minim
solo accompaniment . . 9. obbligato
tenth . . 5. tithe
unpaid . . 6. arrear 9. arrearage
uppermost . . 3. top 4. peak 6. upside
7. topside
winglike . . 3. ala
with . . 7. discard 10. relinquish
partage . . . 4. part 5. share 7. portion
8. division
partake . . . 3. eat 5. share 7. receive
11. participate
partan . . . 4. crab
parted . . . 5. cleft 6. cloven 7. divided,
severed 9. separated 11. apportioned
parterre . . . 10. level space 12. theater
boxes, theater space 17. ornamental
gardens
parthogenesis . . . 7. apogamy
10. thelyotoky 12. reproduction
partial . . . 6. biased, unfair, unjust
7. limited 8. not total, one-sided,
partisan 9. imperfect 10. fractional,
incomplete, prejudiced 11. predisposed
13. foolishly fond
partiality . . . 4. bias 6. desire 9. injustice,
prejudice 10. preference 11. inclination,
partisanism 12. partisanship,
predilection
participant . . . 6. sharer 7. entrant
8. partaker 9. accessory, colleague
12. participator
particle . . . 3. ace, bit, ion, jot 4. atom,
drop, iota, mite, mote, whit 5. grain,
piece, shred, spark 6. tittle 7. glob,
granule, smidgen
particle (pert to) . . .
electric . . 3. ion 5. anion 6. proton
least possible . . 5. minim
minute . . 3. jot, ray 4. atom, iota 5. grain,
speck 7. granule
negative . . 3. nor, not
nuclear . . 5. gluon, meson, quark
6. baryon, hadron
parti-colored . . . 4. pied, roan 5. pinto
6. motley 7. piebald 9. harlequin
10. variegated 11. polychromic
particular . . . 4. item, nice, part, sole
5. event, fussy 6. detail 7. precise,
special, topical 8. detailed, especial,
peculiar, separate, specific 9. attentive
[   ]tidious, individual, overminute
10. fasu[   ]kety 12. circumstance,
11. persnic[   ]
technicality
partisan, partizan . . . [   ]4. pike 5. staff
[   ]herent, advocate,
6. zealot 7. partial 8. adhe[   ]ctional,
follower 9. supporter 10. fra[   ]
prejudiced
partition . . . 4. wall 5. allot 6. divide,
screen, septum 7. scantle 8. set apart
9. apportion, severance 10. distribute,
separation 13. apportionment
partitioned . . . 7. septate
partly . . . 6. in part 9. partially
partly illuminated . . . 6. shaded
8. adumbral 9. penumbral
partly open . . . 4. ajar
partner . . . 3. pal 4. ally, mate, wife
6. sharer, spouse 7. comrade, husband
9. associate, coadjutor, colleague
10. accomplice 11. confederate,

participant

partnership . . . **4.** firm **7.** cahoots, co-mated **8.** business, contract **10.** fellowship **11.** affiliation **13.** participation

part of . . .
anchor . . **4.** palm
bird wing . . **5.** alula
cannon . . **5.** chase
church . . **4.** apse, nave **5.** altar **7.** chancel **8.** transept
circle . . **3.** arc **6.** degree **7.** segment
compass . . **6.** needle
ear . . **4.** lobe **5.** pinna **6.** tragus **8.** tympanum **9.** labyrinth
eye . . **4.** iris, uvea **5.** pupil **6.** cornea, retina
flower . . **4.** stem **5.** calyx, petal, sepal
foot lever . . **5.** pedal **7.** treadle
fort . . **5.** redan **7.** bastion
head . . **4.** pate **5.** scalp, skull **7.** cranium
minstrel show . . **4.** olio **5.** bones **6.** end man **12.** interlocutor
newspaper . . **3.** ear **4.** item, page **6.** by-line **9.** editorial
optical measure . . **7.** alidade
printing press . . **6.** platen
rifle (anc) . . **4.** tige
ship . . **3.** bow **4.** brig, deck, helm, keel, mast **5.** stern, wheel **6.** anchor, bridge, rudder **8.** steerage
step . . **5.** riser, tread **6.** nosing
theater . . **3.** box **4.** loge **5.** foyer, stage **7.** balcony, curtain, gallery, parquet **8.** parterre **9.** orchestra
turtle . . **7.** calipee **8.** calipash

partridge . . . **4.** hill, snow, yutu **5.** covey (flock) **6.** bamboo, chukar (chukor), Perdix, seesee **7.** cinerea, tinamou **8.** raw umber **9.** francolin **11.** Francolinus **12.** ruffed grouse

party . . . **3.** tea **4.** ball, drum, sect, side **6.** clique, fiesta, person **7.** company, faction **8.** sociable **9.** reception **10.** detachment **11.** association, combination **12.** participator

party (pert to) . . .
deserter . . **6.** bolter
evening . . **6.** soiree
lawn . . **4.** fete
man . . **8.** partisan
member . . **8.** Democrat, Federate **9.** Communist, Dixiecrat, Greenback (Hist), Socialist **10.** Republican **11.** Independent
men's . . **4.** stag

Parvati (pert to) . . **6.** smoker
consort . . **4.** Siva(?)
father . . **6.** Siva
. . . . **7.** Himavat
goddess . . **8.** mountain

parvenu . . . **5.** snob **7.** upstart **12.** nouveau riche

Pasch, pasch . . **4.** lamb, moon **6.** candle, Easter, supper **8.** Passover **12.** Good Friday **11.** candlestick, celebration

pascual . . . **8.** pascuage, pastures

pasear . . **4.** walk **6.** parade, stroll **9.** promenade **11.** perambulate

pasha, pacha . . **3.** dey **4.** emir **5.** title **6.** bashaw (early) **8.** nobleman **10.** magistrate

pashalik (pashalic) . . . **9.** territory (pasha's) **12.** jurisdiction

pashm . . **6.** fleece (Tibetan goat)

pasigraphy . . . **6.** system (Universal) **7.** symbols **8.** language

Pasiphae (pert to) . . .
mother of . . **7.** Ariadne
son . . **8.** minotaur (monster)
wife of . . **5.** Minos

pasquinade . . . **5.** squib **6.** satire **7.** lampoon, pasquil

pass . . . **2.** go **3.** die, end, gap **4.** ghat, hand, lane, pace, step **5.** canto, enact, gorge, lapse, occur, relay, spend, throw **6.** convey, crisis, defile, elapse, exceed, happen, passus, perish, permit, ratify, ticket **7.** excrete, passage **8.** hand over, passport, surmount, transfer **10.** permission **11.** Annie Oakley **13.** complimentary

pass (pert to) . . .
Alpine . . **3.** col
around . . **5.** skirt **6.** detour
as genuine . . **5.** cheat, foist **11.** interpolate
away . . **3.** die, end **6.** perish, vanish **9.** cease to be, disappear, obsolesce
by . . **4.** cote, omit, skip, snub **5.** elapse, forego, ignore **7.** proceed **8.** overlook **9.** disregard
hurriedly . . **7.** scamper, skitter **9.** skim along
into . . **5.** glide, merge **6.** become **7.** get to be **9.** penetrate
judgment . . **4.** rule **6.** decree, ordain **8.** sentence
on . . **3.** die **6.** confer, ratify **7.** advance **8.** bequeath, continue
out . . **3.** die **4.** exit **5.** faint **7.** be dazed **9.** disappear **11.** be dead drunk **13.** be unconscious
over . . **4.** omit, skip **5.** cross **6.** elapse, excuse, exempt, ignore, slight **7.** condone, exclude, neglect **8.** overlook, transfer, traverse
sudden . . **5.** lunge
through . . **5.** cross, reeve (cringle) **6.** pierce **7.** pervade, undergo **8.** traverse **9.** penetrate **10.** comprehend, experience
up . . **4.** snub **5.** evade **6.** reject **7.** decline **9.** disregard
without touching . . **5.** clear

passable . . . **5.** so-so **7.** current **8.** mediocre, moderate, traveled **9.** navigable, tolerable, traversed **10.** acceptable, accessible, admissible **12.** satisfactory

passado (fencing) . . . **6.** thrust

passage . . . **4.** adit, exit, flue, ford, gang, hall, iter **5.** aisle, allay, allée, canal, death **6.** atrium, avenue, egress, travel, voyage **7.** channel, excerpt, journey, transit **8.** corridor, incident, progress, sanction **9.** enactment, migration **10.** transition **11.** altercation, negotiation, preterition **12.** thoroughfare

passage (pert to) . . .
book . . **7.** excerpt
brain . . **4.** iter
closed end . . **7.** impasse **8.** cul-de-sac

covered .. **4.** pawn
history .. **5.** alure
mine .. **4.** sill **5.** stope
narrow .. **3.** gut **5.** aisle, alley, gully, slype **6.** defile, strait
river .. **7.** estuary
passageway ... **4.** hall, lane, ramp, slip **5.** aisle, alley, lumen **6.** access, arcade, avenue, defile, outlet, strait, tunnel **7.** gangway **8.** corridor
passant ... **7.** cursory, walking (Her) **8.** passer-by **9.** ephemeral, excelling **10.** surpassing, transitory
passé ... **4.** aged, past, worn **5.** faded **6.** gone by **8.** obsolete **10.** antiquated **13.** superannuated
passed (pert to) ...
by .. **6.** bygone, former **8.** preterit (preterite)
over .. **7.** fleeted **11.** preterition
through pores .. **7.** osmosed **8.** dialyzed **9.** permeated, transuded
passenger ... **4.** fare **6.** pigeon, trekku **7.** pilgrim, tourist **8.** commuter, traveler, wayfarer **9.** sightseer, transient
passerine bird ... **5.** finch **7.** sparrow **8.** songbird
passing ... **7.** cursory **8.** elapsing, fleeting **9.** departing, enactment, ephemeral, exceeding, happening, transient, vanishing **10.** surpassing, transitory **11.** preterition
passion ... **3.** ire, yen **4.** love, lust, rage, zeal **5.** anger, craze, wrath **6.** desire **7.** emotion, feeling **9.** eloquence, martyrdom **10.** enthusiasm, excitement
passion (pert to) ...
flower .. **6.** maypop **11.** passionwort
flower family .. **10.** Passiflora
for doing great things .. **11.** megalomania
music .. **8.** oratorio
Play .. **14.** Christ's Passion (Oberammergau)
Week .. **8.** Holy Week
passionate ... **3.** sad **5.** angry **6.** ardent **7.** amorous, excited, fervent, pitiful, violent **8.** agitated, eloquent, vehement **9.** emotional, irascible **10.** passionato **11.** hot-tempered, impassioned
passionless ... **4.** calm **8.** painless **9.** heartless, unfeeling **10.** spiritless **11.** unemotional **13.** dispassionate
passive ... **5.** inert, quiet, stoic **6.** stolid **7.** languid, patient **8.** inactive **9.** apathetic **10.** submissive **11.** acquiescent, indifferent, unresisting
Passover (pert to) ...
festival .. **5.** Seder **6.** Jewish
lamb .. **7.** paschal
psalm .. **6.** hallel **14.** Egyptian Hallel
sacrifice .. **11.** paschal lamb
The (Passover) .. **5.** Pasch
passport ... **4.** pass, visa (vise) **5.** congé **6.** congee, permit **8.** document **11.** safe conduct
passus ... **5.** canto
password ... **9.** watchword **10.** mot de passé, open sesame **11.** countersign
past ... **2.** by **3.** ago **4.** date, dead, gone, over, yore **5.** after, since **6.** beyond, ultimo **7.** elapsed, outworn **9.** foregoing,

yesterday
pasta ... **7.** gnocchi, lasagna, ravioli **8.** linguini, macaroni **9.** fettucini, manicotti, spaghetti **10.** vermicelli
paste ... **3.** pap, poi **4.** glue, sham **5.** dough, stick **6.** mastic, strass **8.** adhesive, frippery, mucilage **10.** confection **13.** stick together
pastel ... **5.** light **6.** crayon, sketch **9.** pale color
pastille ... **6.** troche **7.** lozenge
pastime ... **4.** game **5.** hobby, sport **9.** amusement, diversion **10.** recreation **13.** entertainment
pastor ... **5.** rabbi **6.** curate, divine, keeper, parson, priest, rector **8.** chaplain, guardian, minister, Reverend, shepherd
pastoral ... **4.** poem **5.** drama, rural **6.** poetic **7.** romance **14.** ecclesiastical
pastoral (pert to) ...
cantata .. **8.** serenata
crook, staff .. **5.** pedum **7.** crosier
god .. **3.** Pan
oboe .. **7.** musette
pert to .. **6.** rustic **8.** agrestic, herdsman, shepherd
pipe .. **3.** oat **4.** reed
poem .. **5.** idyll (idyl) **7.** bucolic, eclogue
pastry ... **3.** pie **4.** tart **6.** Danish, éclair **7.** dariole, strudel **8.** napoleon, pandowdy, turnover **9.** cream puff, shortcake **10.** pâtisserie
past tense ... **8.** preterit (preterite)
pasturage, right of ... **9.** horsegate
pasture ... **3.** ham, lea **4.** feed, food **5.** agist, grama, grass, graze **6.** meadow **9.** grassland **10.** agostadero
pasture bird ... **6.** plover **7.** sparrow
pat ... **3.** dab, fit, paw, tap **4.** blow, lump **5.** fixed, impel, known, throw **6.** caress, smooth, stroke **7.** flatten **8.** immovable **10.** seasonable
Patagonia (So Am) ...
city .. **11.** Punta Arenas
deity .. **7.** Setebos
Indian people .. **9.** Tehuelche
nearby island .. **5.** Tierra del Fuego
race (said of) .. **6.** giants **7.** Big Feet, tallest **9.** Patagones
rodent .. **4.** cavy **8.** capybara, Caviidae
strait .. **8.** Magellan (Magallanes)
patamar (pattamar) ... **6.** vessel (Naut) **7.** courier **9.** messenger
patata ... **6.** potato **11.** sweet potato
patch ... **4.** mend, vamp **5.** bodge, botch, clump, cover, field **6.** blotch, cobble, parcel **8.** addition, appliqué **9.** reconcile
patch (pert to) ...
cloth .. **5.** clout
imprinting .. **5.** friar
metal .. **6.** solder
of trees .. **4.** mott
patcher (humorous) ... **6.** sartor
patchwork ... **5.** quilt **6.** jumble, pillow, scraps **7.** mixture **9.** checkered, fancywork, fragments **10.** hodgepodge
pate ... **3.** pie, top **4.** head **5.** brain, crown, pasty, patty **6.** badger
patella ... **3.** pan **4.** bone, dish, vase **7.** kneecap, kneepan

paten ... 4. disc, dish, disk 5. plate
7. patener (bearer of)
patent ... 4. open 5. berat (Turk), right
7. license, warrant 8. document,
manifest 9. available, copyright,
privilege, trademark 10. accessible,
protection, university 12. unobstructed
pater ... 6. father, priest
Pater Noster ... 11. Lord's Prayer
Paternoster Row ... 6. street (London)
Pater Patriae ... 18. Father of his country
(Cicero, Marius, Trajan, Washington,
etc)
path ... 3. way 4. lane, line 5. piste,
route, swath, track, trail 6. course
7. footway
path (pert to) ...
  along a slope .. 4. berm (berme)
  animal .. 5. piste, spoor 6. roddin
  7. rodding
  of energy .. 7. ergodic
  of moving parts .. 5. locus
  of planets .. 5. orbit
  Spanish .. 6. camino, comino
pathetic ... 3. sad 5. teary 8. dolorous,
grievous, stirring 9. affecting
10. lamentable
pathological ... 6. morbid 9. unhealthy
pathological reaction ... 7. allergy
patience ... 3. endurance, fortitude,
solitaire, tolerance 10. submission,
sufferance 11. forbearance, resignation
12. acquiescence, perseverance
patient ... 4. calm, meek 6. client
8. tolerant 9. unsettled 11. persevering
13. long-suffering
patio ... 5. court 9. courtyard
patriarch ... 4. Noah, sire 5. elder,
pater 6. bishop, father 7. aged man,
veteran 9. churchman 10. Methuselah
13. paterfamilias
patrimonial ... 9. inherited 10. hereditary
patrimony ... 8. heritage 10. birthright
11. ancient rite, inheritance
patriot ... 4. Cato (Rom), Otis (Am)
5. jingo 7. chauvin 9. flag-waver
10. chauvinist, countryman
patriotism ... 10. chauvinism
11. nationalism 13. love of country
patrol ... 5. guard 7. protect 8. traverse
9. keep guard 13. perambulation
patron ... 5. buyer, guest 6. backer,
seller, trader 8. customer, guardian
9. financier, protector, supporter
10. benefactor
patronage ... 5. aegis (egis), favor
6. defend 7. support 8. auspices
9. clientele, fosterage 10. assistance
13. condescension, encouragement
patronizing ... 8. deigning 9. financing,
revealing 10. sponsoring
13. condescending
patrons (group) ... 7. backers, masters
9. clientele, customers
Patron Saint of ...
  beggars .. 5. Giles
  boys .. 8. Nicholas
  England .. 4. Anne 6. George
  fishermen .. 5. Peter
  France .. 5. Denis
  Ireland .. 7. Patrick
  lawyers .. 4. Ives
  motherhood .. 6. Gerard
  musicians .. 7. Cecilia
  Pueblo Indians .. 7. Stephen
  sailors .. 4. Elmo
  Scotland .. 6. Andrew
  shoemakers .. 7. Crispin
  swineherds .. 7. Anthony
  Venice .. 4. Mark 9. Pantalone
  Wales .. 5. David
patten ... 4. clog 5. skate 8. footgear,
overshoe, snowshoe
pattern ... 4. norm, seme 5. habit, model
6. design, format 7. diagram, paragon
8. paradigm, parterre, template
pavilion ... 4. tent 5. cover, kiosk
6. canopy 8. covering 9. gloriette
10. tabernacle
pavis ... 5. cover 6. screen, shield
7. protect
paw ... 3. pad, pud 4. foot, hand 5. patté,
pedal 6. handle, stroke 7. foreleg (Her)
8. forefoot 10. manipulate
pawl ... 4. bolt, sear, trip 5. click 6. detent,
pallet, tongue 7. ratchet 9. mechanism
pawn ... 4. gage, hock, tool 6. pledge
7. counter, peacock 8. chessman,
guaranty, hockshop 9. put in pawn
10. pawnbroker
Pawnee ... 6. Indian
pawnie ... 7. peacock
pay ... 3. aby (abye), fee, tip 4. ante,
meet, wage 5. remit, repay 6. defray,
reward, salary, suffer 7. requite, satisfy
9. indemnify, reimburse, retaliate
10. compensate, punishment,
recompense, remunerate 11. retribution
12. compensation
pay (pert to) ...
  attention .. 4. heed 6. listen
  back .. 6. rebate, refund 9. reimburse,
  retaliate
  dirt .. 3. ore
  envelope .. 5. wages 6. salary 7. stipend
  extra .. 5. bonus 8. kickback
  for .. 3. aby (abye) 5. atone 6. suffer
  off .. 6. punish 7. requite 9. pay in full,
  retribute 10. compensate
  out .. 5. spend 6. expend, settle
  7. hand out 8. disburse 10. distribute
  12. exorbitantly 14. through the nose
  up .. 4. ante 6. settle 9. liquidate
paymaster ... 6. burser, purser 7. cashier
payment ... 3. cro, fee 4. dues,
mail 6. return 8. defrayal, requital
10. punishment, recompense
12. chastisement, compensation
payment (pert to) ...
  for homicide, murder .. 3. cro 4. eric
  (Brehon Law) 7. galanas (Welsh),
  wergild (weregild)
  immediate .. 4. cash
  upon delivery .. 3. COD 14. cash on
  delivery
paynim ... 5. pagan 7. heathen, infidel
8. Pagandom 10. Mohammedan
peyong ... 8. umbrella (golden)
paysage ... 7. picture (landscape)
9. landscape
pea (pert to) ...
  bird .. 6. oriole

chick . . 4. gram 5. Cicer
everlasting (Bib) . . 9. vetchling
family . . 8. Fabaceae
flour (seasoned) . . 9. Erbswurst
heath . . 7. carmele
pigeon . . 3. dal 5. arhar
sausage . . 9. Erbswurst
shaped . . 8. pisiform
soup . . 3. fog (dull yellow)
split . . 3. dal
tree . . 8. laburnum
tropical . . 4. dove 7. Zenaida
　　12. mourning dove
vine . . 8. earthpea

peace . . . 3. pax 5. amity, quiet, truce
　　6. accord, repose 7. harmony, Nirvana,
　　silence 8. ataraxia (ataraxy), serenity
　　9. stillness 10. quiescence 11. tranquility
peaceable . . . 5. quiet, still 6. irenic,
　　silent 7. henotic, pacific 8. amicable,
　　tranquil 9. quiescent 10. concordant,
　　harmonious 11. undisturbed
peaceful . . . 4. calm 5. irene 6. irenic,
　　placid, serene 7. halcyon, pacific
　　8. tranquil 11. comfortable
peace pipe . . . 7. calumet
peach . . 5. fruit 6. accuse, betray, brandy,
　　indict, inform 7. impeach 8. quandong
　　9. red-yellow
peach (pert to) . . .
　cordial . . 7. persico 8. persicot
　family . . 12. Amygdalaceae
　French . . 8. persicot
　grafted (quince) . . 9. melocoton
　like . . 6. almond
　origin . . 5. China
　stone . . 7. putamen
　variety . . 7. Elberta 8. Crawford
　　9. freestone, nectarine 10. clingstone
peacock . . . 3. mao 4. Pavo (Astron),
　　pawn, pose 5. strut 9. swaggerer
peacock (pert to) . . .
　blue (color) . . 4. paon
　butterfly . . 2. io
　fan . . 9. flabellum
　feather part . . 4. marl
　female . . 6. peahen
　fish . . 6. wrasse
　flower . . 9. poinciana
　heron . . 7. bittern
　ref to . . 7. peafowl 8. pavonine
　tail spot . . 3. eye
peak . . . 3. alp, epi, pic, top, tor 4. acme,
　　apex, cone, crag, cusp, dent, dolt
　　5. crown, piton, slink, sneak, steal
　　6. finial, shrink, summit 8. headland,
　　mountain 9. simpleton 10. promontory
Peak . . 5. Borah, Logan 7. Everest,
　　St Elias 8. McKinley 9. Mont Blanc
　　10. Matterhorn 11. Kilimanjaro
　　12. Popocatepetl
peal . . . 4. boom, clap, echo, ring, toll
　　6. appeal, shovel 7. resound, summons,
　　thunder 8. carillon
peanut . . . 5. pinda (pindal, pindar)
　　6. goober, trifle 8. earthnut, earthpea,
　　katchung
pear (pert to) . . .
　alligator . . 7. avocado
　cider . . 5. perry
　Latin . . 5. pirum

prickly . . 4. tuna 5. nopal 7. Opuntia
shaped . . 8. pyriform
shaped vessel . . 6. aludel
squash . . 7. chayote
type . . 4. Bosc 8. Bartlett
pearl . . . 3. gem 4. drop 5. nacre, tooth,
　　white 9. margarite
pearl (pert to) . . .
　bird . . 10. guinea fowl
　color . . 4. blue 13. mother-of-pearl
　eye . . 8. cataract
　imitation . . 6. olivet
　of great luster . . 6. orient
　opal . . 9. cacholong (opaque)
　oyster . . 7. Avicula
　seed . . 7. aliofar (obs)
　vegetable . . 5. onion
pearly . . . 5. milky, quick, smart 7. opaline,
　　whitish 8. pellucid 10. opalescent
　　11. flourishing
Pearly Gates (Bib) . . . 6. heaven, twelve
peasant . . . 4. boor, hind, peon, serf
　　5. clown, knave, swain 6. carlot,
　　cotman, cottar, rascal, rustic
　　10. countryman
peasant (pert to) . . .
　Arab, Syria . . 6. fellah
　cropsharer . . 7. metayer
　English . . 4. hind 5. churl
　Indian . . 4. ryot
　Irish . . 4. kern (kerne) 7. cottier
　like . . 4. base, rude 8. clownish
　Russian . . 5. kulak (rich)
　Scottish . . 4. tyke (tike) 6. cotter (cottar)
pease . . . 5. quiet 6. pacify 7. appease
　　9. reconcile
peasecrow . . . 4. tern
peat . . . 3. bog, pet 4. coal, fuel, moor,
　　moss, turf 6. minion 7. darling
　　8. favorite 11. combustible
peat (pert to) . . .
　cutter . . 5. piner
　moss . . 8. sphagnum
　turf spade . . 5. slave
　wood . . 11. loosestrife
peau . . . 4. skin (silks) 6. fabric
peba . . . 9. armadillo
pebble . . . 5. scree, stone, talus 6. quartz
　　7. chuckie (chucky), crystal, psephos
　　11. gravelstone, pebblestone
peccadillo . . . 4. slip 5. error, fault, lapse
　　12. indiscretion
peccant . . . 3. bad 5. wrong 6. guilty,
　　morbid, wicked 7. corrupt, sinning,
　　spoiled 9. incorrect, unhealthy
　　12. insalubrious
peccary . . . 6. mammal (piglike)
　　7. Tagassu, Tayassu 8. javelina
pech . . . 4. pant 11. breathe hard
pecht (Scot) . . 5. fairy, gnome, pygmy
peck . . . 3. dab, dot, eat, nag 4. food,
　　hole, jerk, kiss 5. pitch, prick, throw
　　6. peggle, stroke 7. measure 8. quantity
　　11. large amount
peck at . . . 3. nag 4. carp, twit 5. tease
　　6. attack, harass
pectase . . . 6. enzyme
peculiar . . . 3. odd 4. idio (comb form)
　　5. queer 6. oddish, unique 7. curious,
　　special, strange, typical 8. distinct,
　　separate, singular 9. different, eccentric

10. particular 14. characteristic
peculiar expression ... 5. idiom
peculiarity ... 4. kink 5. quirk, trait
6. oddity 7. oddness 8. mannerism
10. partiality 11. singularity
12. eccentricity 14. characteristic
peculiar to a district ... 7. endemic
pecuniary ... 6. fiscal 8. monetary
9. financial
pedagogue ... 5. tutor 6. pedant
7. teacher 12. schoolmaster
pedal ... 4. foot 5. lever 6. driver 7. treadle
9. propeller
pedant ... 4. prig 5. tutor 6. dorbel, purist
9. formalist, pedagogue 10. conformist
12. bluestocking, precisionist,
schoolmaster
peddle ... 4. hawk, sell, vend 6. piddle,
retail 11. disseminate
peddler, pedlar ... 6. cadger, coster,
hawker, mugger, sutler 7. chapman
8. huckster 9. vivandier
12. costermonger
peddler's French ... 6. jargon (thieves')
9. gibberish
pedestal ... 7. support 10. foundation
pedestal part ... 3. die 4. base, dado
5. socle 6. plinth, quadra
pedestrian ... 3. ped 4. dull, slow 5. hiker
6. hoofer, walker 11. commonplace
12. foot traveler 13. unimaginative
pedicel ... 3. ray (of an umbel) 4. stem
5. stalk 8. peduncle
pediculosis ... 9. lousiness
Pediculus ... 4. lice
pedigree ... 6. stemma 7. descent, lineage
8. ancestry, register 9. genealogy
10. family tree
pedio (comb form) ... 4. sole 6. instep
pedology ... 9. soil study 10. child study
pedometer ... 5. watch 8. odograph
10. instrument, passometer
pedregal ... 9. lava field
pedum ... 5. crook, staff (pastoral)
peduncle ... 4. stem 5. scape, stalk
7. pedicel, pedicle, sessile
peek ... 3. pry 4. peep 5. chirp, flash
6. glance 7. glimpse 9. look slyly
peekaboo ... 4. game 6. bopeep
peel ... 4. bark, pare, rind, skin 5. slipe,
stake, strip 6. cut off, lamina, shovel
8. car blade, palisade, stockade
peel (off) ... 4. harl, pare, tear 7. come
off 8. get loose 11. decorticate
peeler ... 4. crab (shedding), yarn 5. corer
7. hustler 8. pillager 9. policeman
peep ... 3. pry 4. peek, peer, pule, skeg
5. cheep, chirp, pipit, sight (firearms)
6. glance, squeak 7. crevice 8. peephole
9. sandpiper
peephole ... 5. hole 6. eyelet 8. aperture
9. sighthole
peer ... 4. duke, earl, fere, gaze, mate
5. baron, equal, match, noble, stare,
stime (styme) 7. marquis 8. nobleman,
superior, viscount
Peer Gynt (pert to) ...
drama, poem by ... 5. Ibsen
mother ... 3. Ase
music suite by ... 5. Grieg
peerless ... 9. matchless, nonpareil,

paper size, unequaled, unmatched
10. unexcelled 11. ne plus ultra,
superlative
peesweep, peeaweep ... 7. lapwing
10. greenfinch
peetweet ... 9. sandpiper (spotted)
peeved ... 4. sore 7. annoyed, nettled
9. irritated
peevish ... 3. coy 4. sour 5. cross, sulky,
techy, testy 6. crusty, morose, touchy
7. fretful, pettish, spleeny, waspish
8. captious, choleric, contrary, perverse,
petulant, snappish 9. irascible, irritable,
querulous, splenetic
peg ... 3. hob, leg, nob, nog, pin 4. dram,
skeg 5. drink, stake, tooth 6. drudge,
fasten, reason 7. pretext, support
9. persevere, recognize
peg (pert to) ...
cribbage .. 4. game
iron .. 5. piton
out .. 7. croquet
shoe .. 5. cleat
wood .. 5. spill, thole 8. treenail
pega ... 5. shark 6. remora
Pegasus ... 5. horse (winged), steed
13. constellation
Pegasus's rider ... 11. Bellerophon
pegomancy, divination by ... 7. springs
9. fountains
peho ... 8. morepork
peignoir ... 8. negligee 12. dressing
gown, dressing sack
pejorative ... 11. disparaging
12. depreciatory
Peking, Pekin ... 4. blue, city, duck
7. spaniel
pelagic ... 6. marine 7. oceanic
9. underseas
pelagic organism ... 6. nekton 7. benthos
8. plankton
Pele ... 7. goddess (volcanoes)
pêle-mêle ... 8. pellmell
Peleus (pert to) ...
father .. 6. Aeacus
King of .. 9. Myrmidons
son .. 8. Achilles
wife .. 6. Thetis
pelf ... 3. fur, rob 4. gain 5. booty,
lucre, money, spoil, trash 6. pilfer,
profit, refuse, riches, wealth 7. rubbish
10. ne'er-do-well
Pelias (pert to) ...
daughter .. 5. Medes
King of .. 6. Iolcus
nephew .. 5. Jason
son .. 7. Acastus
pelican (pert to) ...
heraldry .. 10. in her piety
symbolic of .. 6. Christ 7. charity
Pelican State ... 9. Louisiana
pell ... 3. fur 4. hide, pelt, skin 5. hurry
6. hasten 13. parchment roll
pellagra ... 5. zeism
peliar, peller ... 6. wizard 8. conjurer
pellet ... 4. ball, pill 6. bullet 7. granule,
missile, pallion
pellicle ... 4. film, scum 6. lamina
7. coating 8. membrane
pell-mell, pellmell ... 10. vehemently
12. furious haste 13. helter-skelter

pellock ... 8. porpoise
pellucid ... 5. clear 6. bright, limpid
8. luminous 11. translucent, transparent
12. intelligible
pelmet ... 7. valance (short)
Peloponnesus ...
capital .. 7. Corinth
city .. 7. Argolis
League .. 11. Confederacy
peninsula (Gr) .. 5. Morea
12. Peloponnesos (old), Peloponnesus
(modern)
race (anc) .. 6. Dorian 7. Spartan
School .. 6. Dorian 9. Sculpture
War .. 12. Athens-Sparta (BC)
Pelops (pert to) ...
father .. 8. Tantalus
son .. 6. Atreus 8. Thyestes
wife .. 10. Hippodamia
pelota .. 4. ball, game 5. cesta 7. fronton,
jai alai
pelt .. 3. fur 4. blow, fell, hide, push,
skin 5. stone 6. hurl at, pelage, refuse,
strike, thrust 7. apparel (of skins),
rubbish 8. woolfell
peltry ... 4. furs, pelt 5. skins
peludo ... 9. armadillo (six-banded)
pelvic bone ... 5. ilium 7. ischium 8. seat
bone
pelvic-shaped ... 11. basin-shaped
pemmican ... 4. meat (dried) 7. buffalo,
venison
pen .. 3. cot, sty 4. bolt, coop,
gaol 5. abode, hutch, quill, write
6. fasten, indite 7. confine 9. enclosure
12. penitentiary
pen (pert to) ...
like .. 7. styloid
name .. 6. anonym 9. pseudonym
10. nom de plume
point .. 3. neb, nib 4. stub
text .. 5. ronde
penalize ... 4. fine 5. mulct 6. punish
8. handicap
penalty .. 4. fine, loss 7. forfeit
8. handicap, hardship 10. punishment,
repentance
Penang Island capital ...
10. Georgetown
penchant ... 4. bent 6. desire, liking
7. leaning 8. tendency 10. attraction
11. inclination 12. decided taste
pendant ... 3. bob, tag 4. tail 5. aglet
(aiglet), queue 6. tassel 7. eardrop,
earring, hanging 8. appendix, pendulum
9. lavaliere 10. chandelier
pendent ... 3. lop 4. pend 7. hanging
8. appended 9. impending, pendulous
11. jutting over, overhanging
pendent cone (limestone) ... 10. stalactite
pendulous fold, skin ... 6. dewlap
Penelope (pert to) ...
father .. 7. Icarius
husband .. 7. Ulysses 8. Odysseus
island .. 7. Ithaca
suitor .. 9. Agelaus
penetrate ... 4. bore, gore, stab 5. delve,
elbow, enter 6. pierce 7. pervade
8. permeate 9. perforate 10. move
deeply
penetrating ... 4. cold, deep 5. acute,

sharp 6. shrill, subtle 7. caustic, odorous
8. incisive 9. pervading, sagacious,
searching
penetration ... 6. acumen 7. ingress,
insight 9. acuteness, sharpness
11. discernment, perforation
14. discrimination
Peneus (pert to) ...
father of .. 6. Daphne
genus of .. 6. prawns
god of .. 11. Peneus River (Thessalia)
penguin ... 3. auk 6. Johnny 10. rock
hopper
penguin (pert to) ...
aviation .. 13. training plane
duck .. 12. Indian Runner (duck)
genus .. 8. Eudyptes
nest .. 7. rookery 10. penguinery
type .. 4. king 6. Adelie 7. emperor,
jackass
peninsula ... 4. neck 6. penile
10. chersonese
Peninsula ...
Asia .. 5. Malay
Cimbrian, Cimbric .. 7. Jutland
Iberia .. 5. Spain
Seward .. 6. Alaska
Tauric .. 6. Crimea
Thracian .. 9. Gallipoli
penitent ... 5. sorry 8. contrite
9. repentant
penitential discipline ... 7. penance
penitential period ... 4. Lent
pennant ... 4. fane, flag, whip 6. banner,
burgee (yacht), ensign, pennon, pinion
9. banderole
pennant fish ... 11. cobblerfish
pennate ... 6. winged 7. pinnate
9. feathered, penniform
pennon ... 4. flag, wing 6. banner, pinion
9. streamer
Pennsylvania ...
capital .. 10. Harrisburg
city .. 4. Erie 7. Reading 8. Scranton
10. Pittsburgh 12. Philadelphia
famed site .. 10. Gettysburg 11. Liberty
Bell, Valley Forge 16. Independence
Hall
founder .. 11. William Penn
mountain .. 5. Davis 11. Alleghenies
named, first .. 10. Penn's Woods
river .. 4. Ohio 8. Delaware 10. Schuylkill
11. Susquehanna
State admission .. 6. second
State motto .. 28. Virtue, Liberty, and
Independence
State nickname .. 8. Keystone
penny ... 4. cent, coin 5. pence 6. copper,
stiver 8. denarius (Bib)
penologist, famed ... 5. Lawes
penology, study of ... 11. criminology
18. punishment for crime
pensive ... 3. sad 5. mesto, sober
6. dreamy, musing 7. wistful
10. meditative, melancholy, reflective,
thoughtful 13. contemplative
pentastich ... 4. poem 6. stanza
7. strophe 11. five verses
Pentateuch ... 5. Torah (Tora) 10. Law
of Moses 14. First Five Books (Old
Test) 16. Five Books of Moses

Pentecost . . . 8. festival 10. Whitsunday
Pentheus (pert to) . . .
  grandson of . . 6. Cadmus
  King of . . 6. Thebes
  mother . . 5. Agave
penthouse . . . 6. lean-to 7. leaning,
  pentice 9. apartment (roof)
  11. overhanging
penury . . . 4. want 7. poverty 9. indigence,
  privation 10. scantiness 11. destitution,
  miserliness
peon . . . 4. pawn (chess), serf 7. laborer,
  peasant, soldier 9. attendant, constable,
  messenger, policeman
peony . . . 4. piny 6. moutan 7. Paeonia
  11. Burmese ruby
people . . . 3. kin, men 4. folk, ones, race,
  Rais 5. demos, laity 6. family, nation,
  public 7. kinsmen, persons 8. populace,
  subjects 9. citizenry 10. population
people (pert to) . . .
  Am Indian, Eskimo . . 7. Amerind
  ancient . . 5. Medes 6. Greeks, Romans
    7. Sabines 9. Egyptians, Etruscans
  class, lowest . . 8. canaille
  common . . 6. vulgar 7. tilikum (tilicum)
  headless (Myth) . . 8. Acephali
  old-fashioned . . 6. prudes 7. squares
    13. antediluvians
  ref to . . 4. laic 6. ethnic 7. demotic
  Spanish . . 5. gente
  wild young . . 10. rantipoles
people (of) . . .
  culture (earliest) . . 8. Grecians
  gentle birth . . 6. gentry
  one government . . 6. nation
  rank . . 11. aristocracy, aristocrats
  the people . . 8. ethnic
peopled . . . 5. abadi (Ind village)
  8. occupied, populous 9. populated
pep . . . 2. go 3. vim 4. dash 6. energy
  7. quicken 9. stimulate 10. initiative,
  liveliness
pepper . . . 4. pelt 5. shoot 6. energy
  7. bombard 8. sprinkle 9. condiment
pepper (pert to) . . .
  betel . . 4. siri (sirih)
  black . . 11. Piper nigrum
  box . . 5. tower 8. spitfire
  Capsicum, source of . . 7. cayenne, chilies
    (chili), paprika
  climbing . . 5. betel 6. nigrum
  condiment . . 7. cayenne, paprika
  dulse . . 7. seaweed (red)
  genus . . 8. Capsicum
  grass . . 5. crass 8. pillwort
  sauce . . 7. Tabasco
  turnip . . 15. jack-in-the-pulpit
pepper (pert to country) . . .
  Australia . . 4. kava (cava) 8. kavakava
  Borneo . . 4. kava (cava)
  Guinea . . 5. chili 8. Capsicum
  Malay . . 4. siri (sirih)
  Spain . . 7. paprika, pimento 8. allspice,
    pimiento
pepper-and-salt . . . 4. gray 17. harbinger-
  of-spring
peppermint . . . 3. oil 4. herb 6. spirit
  7. essence, gum tree, lozenge, menthol
  (camphor)
peppery . . . 5. fiery 7. piquant, pungent

  8. choleric, spirited, stinging
  10. passionate 11. hot-tempered
per . . . 2. by 7. for each, through 9. by
  means of 11. according to
peradventure . . . 3. hap 5. doubt 7. it
  may be 8. possibly 11. uncertainty
perambulate . . . 4. walk 6. ramble, stroll
  8. traverse 9. promenade, walk about
perceive . . . 3. see 4. hear, know, note
  5. sense 6. behold, descry, detect,
  divine, notice, remark 7. discern,
  observe, sensate 9. apprehend
  10. comprehend, understand
  11. distinguish 12. discriminate
perceptible . . . 5. faint 7. tactile, visible
  8. knowable, manifest, tangible
  10. cognizable 11. appreciable,
  discernible, perceivable
perception . . . 3. ear 4. tact 5. sense,
  taste 6. acumen, seeing 8. sagacity
  9. awareness, sensation 10. cognizance
  11. discernment 13. consciousness
  14. discrimination
perceptive . . . 7. knowing 8. sensible
  9. sagacious 14. discriminative
perch . . . 3. bar, peg, rod, sit 4. fish,
  pole 5. aerie, barse, roost, sit on,
  staff 6. alight, aviary, sauger, settle,
  weapon 7. measure 9. trumpeter
Percheron . . . 5. horse 15. Percheron
  Norman
perchers . . . 5. birds 7. candles 8. Passeres
  10. Insessores
percolate . . . 4. ooze, seep, sift, silt, sipe
  5. exude, leach, steep 6. filter, strain
  7. trickle 8. permeate, transude
percussion . . . 9. collision 10. concussion,
  detonation
percussion instrument . . . 4. drum, gong
  5. bells, bones, conga, snare, traps
  6. Becken, bongos, chimes, tom-tom
  7. celesta, cymbals, marimba, potlids,
  timpani (tympani) 8. carillon, clappers,
  triangle 9. castanets, xylophone
  10. kettledrum, tambourine, vibraphone
  12. glockenspiel
perdition . . . 4. hell, loss (soul), ruin
  5. wreck 9. damnation 11. destruction
peregrinate . . . 6. travel, wander 7. go
  about, migrate, sojourn
peregrine . . . 5. alien 6. exotic, falcon
  7. foreign, pilgrim, strange 8. foreigner
perempt . . . 5. quash 6. defeat 7. destroy
peremptory . . . 5. final 7. express
  8. absolute, arrogant, decisive,
  dogmatic, positive, resolute 9. arbitrary,
  mandatory 10. compulsory, conclusive,
  imperative, obligatory 11. dictatorial
  13. authoritative 16. incontrovertible
perennial . . . 7. lasting 8. constant,
  enduring 9. continual, evergreen,
  permanent, perpetual, unceasing
  10. continuous 12. never-failing
perennial (pert to) . . .
  climbing . . 5. liana (liane)
  grass . . 4. lyme 6. Elymus (genus) 7. wild
    rye
  herb . . 4. Geum 5. avens
  weed . . 8. toadflax
perfect . . . 4. holy, pure, sole 5. ideal,
  model, teleo (comb form), whole

6. entire 7. correct, develop, improve
8. finished 9. blameless, faultless,
inviolate, righteous 10. consummate,
satisfying 11. unqualified

perfection . . . 4. acme 5. ideal 7. paragon
8. accuracy, maturity 10. completion,
excellence 13. faultlessness

perfectly . . . 5. quite 7. ideally, rightly,
utterly 9. correctly 10. absolutely,
accurately, altogether, completely,
flawlessly, thoroughly

perfecto . . . 5. cigar (tapering)

perficient . . . 6. actual 9. effective,
effectual

perfidious . . . 6. shifty 8. disloyal
9. faithless 11. disaffected, treacherous
12. falsehearted

perfidy . . . 7. treason 8. apostasy
9. duplicity, treachery 10. disloyalty
13. faithlessness

perforate . . . 4. bore, dock 5. drill, punch
6. pierce, pounce, riddle 9. penetrate
10. umbilicate

perforated . . .
block . . 3. nut
initials (Philat) . . 10. stamp marks
nozzle . . 4. rose
space . . 5. brain
sphere . . 4. bead

perforation . . . 4. bore, hole 6. eyelet
8. aperture, piercing, punching

perform . . . 2. do 3. act 4. play 5. enact,
exert 6. effect 7. execute, fulfill, produce
8. complete, transact 9. officiate
10. accomplish, bring about, perpetrate

performance . . . 3. act 4. test, work
6. action 7. exploit 8. ceremony
9. operation 10. completion, exhibition,
observance, production
12. consummation 14. accomplishment

performance (pert to) . . .
clumsy . . 6. bungle
daytime . . 7. matinee
for one . . 4. solo
notable . . 4. feat
of duty . . 8. feasance

performer . . . 4. doer 5. actor 6. dancer,
worker 8. magician, musician, thespian
9. pretender 15. prestidigitator

perfume . . . 4. balm, odor 5. aroma, attar,
orris, savor, scent, smell 7. bouquet,
cologne, essence, rose oil 9. fragrance,
redolence 10. frangipani

perfume (pert to) . . .
base . . 4. musk 9. ambergris
cherry . . 7. mahaleb
essence . . 5. attar 8. bergamot
medicated . . 8. pastille (pastil)
musky . . 5. civet
oriental . . 5. myrrh 7. incense
12. frankincense
scent . . 7. jasmine 8. lavender
10. heliotrope
toilet . . 6. bay rum 12. eau de Cologne
unguent . . 6. pomade
violet . . 5. irone

pergola . . . 5. arbor, bower, kiosk
6. pandal 7. balcony, trellis 9. colonnade
11. summerhouse

perhaps . . . 5. maybe 6. ablins (Scot),
belike, mayhap 8. doubtful, possibly,

probably 9. perchance 10. contingent

peri . . . 3. elf 5. about (pref), fairy 6. beauty

periapt . . . 5. charm 6. amulet

pericarp . . . 3. pod 5. berry, shell
8. seedcase

Pericles (Gr) . . . 9. statesman

periculum (Rom law) . . . 4. risk 5. peril
6. danger

perigee (Astron) . . . 12. nearest earth
(opp of apogee)

peril . . . 4. risk 6. danger, hazard, menace
8. jeopardy

perilously high . . . 7. Icarian (flying)

perimeter . . . 5. ambit 6. border 7. outline
8. boundary 9. periphery

period . . . 3. age, day, dot, end, eon,
era, eve 4. stop, term, time, year
5. cycle, epoch, limit, spell 6. degree,
moment, season 8. duration, sentence
10. conclusion 11. termination

period (pert to) . . .
historical . . 4. eral 6. Eocene 7. Neocene
penitential . . 4. Lent
statutory . . 10. limitation
Tertiary . . 6. Eocene 7. Miocene, Neocene
8. Pliocene

periodic . . . 4. eral 6. annual 7. etesian
8. seasonal 9. recurrent 10. rhythmical
12. intermittent

periodic (pert to) . . .
sea motion . . 4. tide
wind . . 2. oe 7. chinook, etesian,
monsoon
windstorm . . 2. oe 7. tornado
9. whirlwind

periodical . . . 5. paper 6. review
7. etesian, journal 8. magazine
9. recurring 11. publication

periodical cicada . . . 6. locust (17 yrs)

period of . . .
delay . . 10. moratorium
dryness . . 7. drought
evolution . . 6. hemera
fifty days . . 13. quinquagesima
five years . . 6. pentad
holding . . 6. tenure
instruction . . 7. session
possession . . 5. lease
probation . . 6. parole
prosperity . . 4. boom 6. golden
recovery . . 13. convalescence
14. reconstruction
sleep . . 11. hibernation
ten years . . 6. decade
time . . 3. age, day, eon 4. span
work . . 4. turn 5. shift, spell, watch
youth . . 6. nonage

peripatetic . . . 7. walking 8. rambling

Peripatetic (pert to Aristotle) . . . 6. school
8. disciple 10. Philosophy

peripheral . . . 6. distal 7. outmost
8. external 9. outlinear 10. round about

periphery . . . 3. lip, rim 4. brim
5. ambit 6. areola, border 8. confines
9. perimeter 10. borderland
13. circumference

perique . . . 7. tobacco (strong) 10. otter
brown

perish . . . 3. die, rot 4. fade 5. decay,
waste 6. pass away, squander 9. cease
to be, disappear 11. be destroyed

perissodactyl ... 15. odd-numbered toes
peristyle ... 7. columns (range of)
  8. corridor 9. colonnade 10. peripteral
peritoneum fold ... 7. omentum
periwig ... 3. wig 6. frizzy, peruke
  9. shellfish 10. periwinkle
periwinkle ... 4. blue 5. snail, vinca
  6. mussel, myrtle 9. evergreen
perjink ... 4. neat, nice 7. precise
perjure ... 7. violate 8. forswear
perjury ... 9. violation 12. breech of oath
  13. false swearing
perk ... 5. preen, prink 7. smarten
  9. percolate 10. parquisite
perkin ... 5. cider
perk up ... 7. cheer up, improve, raise
  up, refresh 10. recuperate
permanent ... 5. fixed 6. innate, stable
  7. abiding, durable, lasting 8. constant,
  enduring, inherent 9. perpetual
  10. changeless, continuing
  12. unchangeable
permeate ... 5. imbue 7. pervade
  8. saturate
permission ... 5. grace, leave 7. consent,
  license 9. allowance 10. sufferance
  13. authorization
permissive ... 8. optional 9. allowable,
  permitted, tolerated 10. consenting,
  permitting 13. power of choice
permit ... 3. let 4. leve 5. allow, grant,
  leave 6. suffer 7. consent, license,
  warrant 8. tolerate 9. authorize
  10. permission
permit to live ... 5. spare 8. reprieve
permutate ... 6. change 9. rearrange
  11. interchange
permutation ... 6. barter 11. interchange
  13. transmutation 14. transformation
pern ... 6. Pernis 7. buzzard (honey)
pernicious ... 4. bane 5. fatal 6. anemia,
  deadly, malign, wicked 7. baleful,
  baneful, harmful, hurtful, noisome,
  noxious, ruinous, vicious 10. villainous
  11. deleterious
pernio ... 9. chilblain
perorate ... 5. speak (at length) 7. declaim
  8. harangue 9. expatiate
perpendicular ... 4. sine 5. erect, plumb,
  sheer, steep 7. apothem, upright
  8. binormal, vertical 9. rectitude
  10. standing up 11. precipitous
perpetrate ... 6. commit 7. perform
  12. carry through
perpetual ... 7. endless, eternal
  8. constant, unending 9. continual,
  perennial, permanent, unceasing
  10. continuous 11. everlasting
perpetually ... 9. endlessly, eternally
  11. ceaselessly 12. interminably
perpetuity ... 7. annuity 8. eternity
  11. endless time
perplex ... 3. vex 4. cark 5. amaze
  6. puzzle, riddle 7. confuse 8. bewilder,
  entangle 9. obfuscate 10. complicate
perplexity ... 3. fog 6. tangle 7. anxiety,
  dilemma, problem 8. question
  9. confusion, situation 10. complexity
  11. distraction 12. bewilderment,
  complication
perquisite ... 3. tip 4. gain 6. boodle

  8. appanage, gratuity
perquod ... 7. whereby
Perry Mason ... see *Mason, Perry*
per se ... 6. itself 8. directly 11. essentially
  13. intrinsically
perse ... 4. blue
persecute ... 5. annoy, harry, hound
  6. harass 7. afflict, oppress, torment
  8. hunt down 9. martyrize
persecution ... 9. treatment
  10. harassment, oppression
  12. mistreatment
Persephone (pert to) ...
  abductor .. 5. Hades
  Attica, name .. 4. Kore (Cora)
  deity of .. 11. agriculture
  father .. 4. Zeus
  Greek name .. 11. Persephassa
  mother .. 7. Demeter
  Orphic literary name .. 8. Despoina
  queen of .. 15. infernal regions
  Roman name .. 10. Proserpine
    (Proserpina)
Perseus (pert to) ...
  Astron .. 13. Constellation
  father .. 4. Zeus
  mother .. 5. Danae
  slayer of .. 6. Medusa
perseverance ... 8. patience, tenacity
  9. constancy 10. resolution, steadiness
  11. persistence, pertinacity
  13. steadfastness
persevere ... 5. abide 6. endure, insist,
  keep on 7. carry on, persist 8. continue
Persia (Iran, Irani) ... see also *Persian*
  capital .. 6. Tehran (Teheran)
  city .. 5. Niriz 6. Abadan, Shiraz, Tabriz
    7. Hamadan, Ispahan
  country (anc) .. 4. Elam 7. Chaldea
  gulf .. 4. Oman 7. Persian
  gulf port .. 7. Bushire 9. Mohamerah
  gulf province .. 6. Kuwait
  gulf wind .. 6. shamal
  lake .. 7. Rezaieh, Urumidh (Salt)
  mountain .. 6. Ararat, Elburz, Zagros
    9. Hindu Kush
  pert to .. 6. Persic
  river .. 5. Safid 9. Euphrates
  ruins .. 10. Persepolis (Shiraz)
Persian (pert to) ... see also *Iranian*
  blue .. 10. regimental
  calendar reformer .. 9. Jalalaean
    (Jalalian)
  carpet, rug .. 4. kali 5. Herat (Herati),
    Senna 6. Kerman, Tabriz 11. Baluchistan
  cushion .. 6. musnud
  diadem .. 3. taj
  door .. 3. dar
  evergreen .. 4. olax
  grass .. 6. millet
  gum .. 10. tragacanth
  hat .. 3. fez 6. turban
  idiom .. 7. persism
  javelin .. 6. jereed (jerid)
  rose .. 3. gul
  rug .. see *carpet (above)*
  screen .. 6. purdah
Persian animals, birds, fruit ...
  apple .. 6. citron
  bird .. 6. bulbul
  cat .. 6. Angora

deer.. 5. maral 6. fallow
gazelle.. 4. cora
lamb.. 9. astrakhan, broadtail
lynx.. 7. caracul
tick (venomous).. 8. Miana bug
Persian Myth, Religion...
angel.. 3. Mah
deity.. 6. Ormazd (Supreme)
demigod, hero.. 4. Yima
demon.. 7. Apaosha
fairy.. 3. elf, fay 4. peri
fire worshiper.. 5. Parsi (Parsee)
god of light.. 7. Mithras
mystic.. 4. sufi
nymph.. 5. houri
religion founder.. 9. Zoroaster
religious doctrine.. 6. Babism (Babiism)
sacred books (Zoroastrian).. 6. Avesta
scriptures (Muslim).. 5. Koran
spirit.. 7. Ahriman
Persian people, government...
assembly (1906).. 6. Majlis (Mejlis)
caste (priestly).. 4. Magi 7. Wise Men
chief.. 3. mir 4. Shah
chief's wife, lady.. 4. bibi
civil officer.. 4. khan
dynasty.. 5. Kajar 7. Arsacid 8. Selencid
  10. Sassanidae (Sassanid)
governor (anc).. 6. satrap
King.. 4. Shah 5. Cyrus (the Great)
  6. Darius, Xerxes
language (anc).. 4. Zend 7. Pahlavi
  (Pahlevi)
New Year's Day.. 7. Nowroze
people.. 4. Leks, Lurs 5. Arabs,
  Kurds, Medes, Mukri, Perse 6. Aryans
  7. Gypsies, Hadjemi, Iranics 8. Baluchis,
  Iranians
poet.. 4. Omar 5. Hafiz, Saadi
ruler.. 4. Shah 6. atabeg (atabek), Sultan
student (Koran).. 5. hafiz
trader.. 4. Sart
Wise Men.. 4. Magi
persiflage... 6. banter 8. raillery
persimmon... 4. kaki 7. chapote
persist.. 4. last, urge 6. endure 7. prevail
  9. persevere
persistent... 7. durable 8. constant,
  habitual 10. determined, inveterate
  11. persevering 13. indefatigable
persistently opposed... 8. renitent
  9. obstinate 10. recalcitrant
person.. 3. one 4. body, soul 5. being,
  wight 6. figure 8. creature 9. character
  10. individual
person (pert to)...
  accuser, challenger.. 9. appellant
  acting for another.. 5. proxy 9. alternate
  baptized (anc).. 11. illuminatus
  base.. 7. caitiff, hangdog
  bringing bad luck.. 4. jinx 5. Jonah
  bringing good luck.. 6. mascot
  canonized.. 5. saint
  careless.. 7. trifler 11. pococurante
  charged with high mission.. 7. apostle
  charitable.. 9. samaritan
  cheerful.. 8. optimist
  clumsy.. 3. oaf 5. staup 6. lummox
    7. bungler
  common.. 3. lay 8. roturier
  conceited.. 4. prig

contemptible.. 3. cad 4. heel, toad
  7. bauchle (Scot)
crazed.. 6. maniac 10. monomaniac,
  psychopath
credulous.. 5. Simon
cruel.. 5. fiend
dishonorable.. 6. rotter
dissolute.. 4. roué
drunken.. 4. lush
dull.. 4. dolt 5. dunce, moron, stock
  6. dorbel 9. blockhead
dwarf.. 5. shurf
educated.. 6. pedant, pundit, savant
  7. erudite, learned, student 8. cultured,
  highbrow 9. literatus 12. intellectual
emitting smoke.. 7. whiffer
enterprising.. 8. go-getter
fabulously rich.. 5. Midas
foolish.. 3. sop 4. zany 5. clown, idiot,
  nutty 6. dotard 7. bonkers, buffoon
  9. simpleton
gigantic.. 5. giant, titan 7. monster
gloomy.. 7. killjoy 10. crosspatch
good luck.. 6. mascot
grotesque.. 9. golliwogg
guilty.. 7. culprit 12. transgressor
held as pledge.. 7. hostage
image of.. 4. doll, idol 5. clone 6. poppet,
  puppet
impatient.. 6. fidget 7. hotspur
important.. 3. VIP 5. mogul 7. magnate,
  notable 9. personage
indifferent.. 5. stoic
inexperienced.. 9. greenhorn
insignificant.. 5. sprat 6. little, nobody
lazy.. 5. drone 8. sluggard
learned.. see *educated (above)*
left-handed.. 6. clumsy 8. sinister
  9. portsider
loud-voiced.. 7. stentor 8. blowhard
low-bred.. 3. cad 6. vulgar
miserly.. 5. skinflint 10. curmudgeon
non-Jewish.. 5. Aryan 7. Gentile
overmodest.. 5. prude 8. bluenose
perfidious.. 5. snake 7. traitor 9. faithless
rapacious.. 4. wolf 5. harpy
relaxed.. 4. calm 8. laid-back
representing another.. 5. proxy 7. stand-
  in 9. alternate
respondent to appeal.. 8. appellee
rich.. 7. wealthy 9. plutocrat 10. capitalist
  11. millionaire
rude, ill-mannered.. 4. boor 5. yahoo
scatterbrained.. 6. madcap
self-centered.. 6. egoist 7. egotist
  9. extrovert, introvert
self-righteous.. 8. pharisee
sharp-eyed.. 5. alert, Argus
sick.. 9. aegrotant, bedridden
skilled.. 6. artist, master 7. artisan
  8. mechanic
staff (Mil).. 10. aide-de-camp
stupid.. 3. ass 4. dolt, gump, nerd
  5. moron, stock
supercilious.. 4. snob 9. conceited
thankless.. 7. ingrate
unclassified.. 11. nondescript
unique.. 4. oner
unknown.. 7. inconnu 8. inconnue
unmarried.. 6. maiden, single
  8. bachelor, celibate, spinster

untidy . . 5. messy 6. grungy 8. slipshod, slovenly 9. litterbug
valorous . . 4. hero 8. champion
violent-tempered . . 6. tartar
wealthy . . 5. nabob, pluto (comb form) 10. capitalist 11. millionaire
who reads, writes . . 8. literate
witty . . 3. wag 7. punster 8. comedian 10. comedienne
worthless . . 5. lorel, losel
writ serving . . 6. elisor
young . . 9. stripling 14. whippersnapper

personage . . . 5. image, mogul 7. bearing, stature 8. great man, one's body, portrait 13. impersonation

persona grata . . 13. welcome person 16. acceptable person

personal (pert to) . . .
appearance . . 8. presence
comb form . . 4. idio
history . . 6. memoir
ornament . . 6. parure
ownership, land . . 6. estate 7. demesne 8. chattels, property

personality . . 3. ego 5. being 6. person 8. identity 13. individuality 15. distinctiveness

persona non grata . . . 18. unacceptable person

personate . . 5. enact 7. feigned 9. represent 10. personated 11. counterfeit

personification . . . 3. Una (truth) 10. embodiment 11. attribution 14. representation

person of . . .
age . . 5. major
courage . . 7. Spartan
eighty years . . 12. octogenarian
encyclopedic learning . . 10. polyhistor
fifty years . . 15. quinquagenarian
forty years . . 14. quadragenarian
great intellect . . 6. genius
nervous disorders . . 8. neurotic
ninety years . . 12. nonagenarian
one hundred years . . 11. centenarian
seventy years . . 14. septuagenarian
sixty years . . 12. sexagenarian
skill . . 6. master, talent 7. magnate

persons of . . .
a familiar set . . 7. coterie
a family tree . . 6. stirps
groups . . 4. army, band, team 6. chorus, troupe 7. company 8. assembly 9. orchestra
organized bodies . . 5. corps, posse

perspicacity . . . 6. acumen, vision 8. sagacity 9. acuteness 11. discernment, penetration

perspicuity . . . 8. lucidity, sagacity 12. translucency, transparency

perspiration . . . 5. sudor, sweat 7. sudoric 8. hard work 11. evaporation, saline fluid 13. transpiration

persuade . . . 4. coax, sway, urge 6. entice, induce, reason 7. convert, suasion 8. convince, inveigle 9. influence, plead with, stonewall

persuasible . . . 6. pliant 11. persuadable 14. open-mindedness

persuasive . . . 8. eloquent 9. impelling

10. convincing, persuading

pert . . . 3. gay 4. bold, keen 5. brash, sassy, saucy 6. clever, comely, dapper daring, lively, nimble 7. forward 8. handsome, skillful 9. exquisite, officious, sprightly 11. impertinent 12. presumptuous

pert (girl) . . . 4. chit, minx

pertain . . . 5. belie 6. belong, relate 7. adjunct 8. function, peculiar 9. accessory, appendage, appertain, attribute

pertaining to . . .
act of rising . . 6. ortive 7. eastern
agriculture . . 7. georgic
ancestral type . . 9. atavistic
ancient Nile city . . 4. Sais (Saite)
ancient Troy . . 5. Iliac
anything remote . . 6. forane
apostles . . 7. Petrine
Asiatic (old) . . 8. Chaldean
Asiatic mountain . . 6. Altaic
Athens . . 5. Attic
authorized doctrine . . 8. dogmatic 10. dogmatical
birthmark . . 6. nevoid (naevoid)
body . . 5. somal
body of land . . 11. continental
book description . . 13. bibliographic
both ears . . 8. binaural
both sexes . . 6. unisex 7. epicene
breadmaking . . 6. psnary
breastbone . . 7. sternal
bristles . . 5. setal
bunch . . 5. comal
canonical hours . . 7. matinal
carving . . 6. glypic 7. glyptic
cheek . . 5. malar
church, part . . 7. apsidal
city . . 5. civic, urban
cod family . . 6. gadoid
coins . . 12. numismatical
colors . . 9. chromatic
construction . . 8. geodesic, tectonic
cork . . 7. suberic
cough . . 7. tussine
court . . 5. aulic 9. judiciary
crown . . 7. coronal
dance . . 6. gestic 13. terpsichorean
daughter . . 6. filial
dawn . . 4. eoan
day (ordinary) . . 6. ferial
desert wastes . . 6. eremic
diaphragm . . 7. phrenic
dogma . . 9. levitical
doves . . 9. columbine
downward air . . 9. katabatic
downy . . 5. dotal
dreams . . 7. oneiric 9. oneirotic
ducks . . 7. anatine
early church . . 9. patristic
early culture . . 8. eolithic
earth . . 4. geal 5. terra 7. teluric 9. planetary
earthquake . . 7. seismic
east . . 4. dawn, eoan 7. auroral
elms . . 9. ulmaceous
engraving . . 7. glyptic
equal rights . . 3. ERA 6. libber
essence . . 5. basic
exhaustion . . 7. burnout 9. tiredness

fallow deer.. 6. damine
fashion.. 5. modal 6. preppy, trendy
fasting.. 8. anorexic 9. abstinent
fats.. 6. adipic, sebaic 9. cellulite
feet.. 5. pedal
fields.. 8. agrarian
fine arts.. 9. aesthetic (esthetic)
fingers.. 7. digital
first principles.. 9. elemental
fissure.. 5. rimal
flood.. 8. diluvian
flowers.. 9. floscular 10. florescent
forehead.. 7. metopic
frogs.. 6. anuran, ranine
funeral music.. 10. threnodial
funerals.. 8. exequial
gospel.. 9. evangelic
gulls.. 6. larine
gums (Anat).. 8. gingival
hair.. 5. pilar 7. blow-dry
hands.. 6. chiral, manual
head.. 8. cephalic
heaths.. 8. ericetal
holiday.. 6. ferial (Eccl), festal
honey.. 10. melaginous
horse.. 6. equine
house.. 5. domal (Astrol)
hypothetical force.. 4. odic
infernal regions.. 7. avernal
ink.. 10. atramental
insects.. 11. entomologic
intellect.. 6. noetic
iron.. 6. ferric
islands.. 7. insular
jaw.. 10. mandibular
kidney.. 6. renal
knots.. 5. nodal
land.. 8. praedial (predial)
language meaning.. 8. semantic
laughter.. 8. risorial
leg.. 6. crural 7. fibular
lips.. 6. labial
liver.. 7. hepatic
living organism.. 13. parasitologic
lockjaw.. 7. tetanic
love.. 6. erotic 7. amatory 8. erotical
male.. 5. macho, manly 7. agnatic
marriage.. 7. marital 8. hymeneal
marsh.. 8. paludine
meaning, in language.. 8. semantic
medicine.. 6. iatric 8. iatrical
medulla oblongata (brain).. 6. bulbar
memory.. 6. mnesic 7. mnestic
　　8. mnemonic 13. retrospective
midday.. 8. meridian
milk.. 7. lactary, lacteal
mind.. 6. mental 7. phrenic
money matters.. 5. T-bill 7. bailout
　　8. economic
morning.. 5. matin, sunup 7. matinal
　　9. matutinal
motion.. 7. kinetic
mouth.. 4. oral 7. oscular, palatal
　　8. stomatic
mustard family.. 11. cruciferous
nephew.. 7. nepotal
north wind.. 6. boreal
nose.. 5. nasal 6. narial, rhinal
nut.. 5. nucal
ocean.. 7. pelagic
old age.. 6. senile 7. geratic 8. gerontic

9. geriatric
Old World.. 13. gerontogenous
peacock.. 8. pavonine
people.. 4. laic 7. demotic
pigs.. 7. porcine
pleasure.. 7. hedonic
priests.. 10. sacerdotal
prophecy.. 9. vaticinal
public.. 7. cameral
public prayer.. 8. liturgic 10. liturgical
punishment.. 5. penal 8. punitive
queen.. 7. reginal
rainbow.. 6. iridal
reason.. 6. noetic
region without earthquakes..
　　11. peneseismic
rhubarb.. 7. rheumic
river.. 5. amnic
river bank.. 8. riparian
rock.. 7. petrean
royal court.. 5. aulic
salvation.. 8. soterial 9. soterical
sarcasm.. 8. ironical
school of philosophy.. 7. Eleatic
sea.. 6. marine 7. oceanic, pelagic
　　9. thelassic
seacoast.. 8. littoral
sense of taste.. 9. gustatory
sepulchral mound.. 7. tumular
shin, shinbone.. 7. cnemial
ship's sails.. 5. velic
singing birds.. 6. oscine
skull.. 5. inial
sole of foot.. 7. plantar
spring.. 6. vernal
stars.. 6. astral 7. stellar 8. sidereal
state affairs.. 9. pragmatic
stepmothers.. 8. novercal
storks.. 7. pelagic
summer.. 7. estival (aestival)
　　8. festival
sun.. 5. solar 6. heliac
tail.. 6. caudal
teaching.. 9. pedagogic
tears.. 8. lacrimal
tempo.. 6. agogic
the plague.. 6. loimic
the skin.. 5. deric 6. dermic
thread.. 5. filar
tile.. 7. tegular
time.. 7. chronic
tin.. 7. stranic
tissue.. 5. telar
tongue.. 7. glossal, lingual
tortoises.. 9. chelonian
touch.. 7. tactile
travel.. 6. viatic
trees.. 8. arboreal
verse stress.. 5. ictic
walls.. 5. mural 8. parietal
wax.. 5. ceral
weight.. 5. baric 8. ponderal
whales.. 5. rotal
wife.. 7. uxorial
wine.. 5. vinic
wine making.. 10. oenopoetic
wings.. 5. alary
winter.. 6. hiemal
womanhood.. 9. muliebral
woods.. 6. sylvan
wrist.. 6. carpal

pertaining to country ...
Asiatic .. 8. Chaldean
Asiatic mountain .. 6. Altaic
Athens .. 5. Attic
Carthage .. 5. Punic
Celts .. 4. Erse
Cretan language .. 6. Minoan
Dissenters meeting house .. 7. pantile
  (from the roofing)
England .. 8. Anglican
Ethiopian religion .. 6. Coptic
France .. 6. Gallic
Franks .. 5. Salic
Gentiles .. 6. ethnic
German State .. 8. Bavarian
Greek epic .. 9. Homerical
Greek philosophy .. 7. Eleatic 8. Platonic
Greek race (anc) .. 6. Aeolic
Greek valley .. 6. Nemean 8. Argolian
Hindu books, writing .. 5. Vedic 7. Tantric
Hindu philosophy, inertia .. 5. tamas
Irish .. 6. Celtic, Gaelic
Isle of Man .. 4. Manx
Mars .. 5. Arean
Mediterranean .. 6. Levant
Moses .. 6. Mosaic
Nile city (anc) .. 4. Sais (Saite)
Norse poem .. 5. runic
Passover .. 7. Paschal
Red Sea colony .. 8. Eritrean
Rhine .. 7. Rhenish
Scotch Highlander .. 6. Gaelic
Spice Islands .. 7. Molucca
Troy (anc) .. 5. Illac 6. Trojan
Vulcan .. 11. Mulcibirian
West Indies .. 9. Antillean
pertenencia ... 10. concession 11. mining
  claim
Perth .. 6. Atholl (Athole) 7. Ontario
  9. Australia
pertinacious ... 4. firm 8. adhering,
  resolute 9. tenacious 10. determined,
  inflexible, persistent, unyielding
  11. persevering
pertinacity ... 9. obstinacy
  11. persistency
pertinent ... 3. fit 6. timely 7. germane
  8. apposite, relevant
perturb ... 5. alarm 6. excite 7. agitate,
  derange, disturb, fluster, trouble 8. bewilder, disorder, distress 9. confusion
perturbation ... 5. alarm 7. anxiety,
  fluster 9. agitation, confusion
  10. excitement 11. fearfulness
  12. bewilderment, irregularity
pertusion ... 8. piercing, punching
  11. perforation, punched hole
pertussis ... 5. cough 13. whooping
  cough
Peru ... see also *Peruvian*
  capital .. 4. Lima 5. Cuzco (Inca) 14. City
    of the Kings
  hero .. 7. Bolivar, Pizarro
  lake .. 8. Titicaca
  mountain .. 9. Andes 10. Cordillera
  port .. 6. Callao 7. Iquitos 8. Mollendo
  river .. 4. Sama 5. Santa 6. Amazon
    7. Maranon, Ucayali 8. Urubamba
  ruins .. 4. Inca 5. huaco (relics)
Peruvian (pert to) ...
  animal .. 4. paco 5. llama 6. alpaca

bark .. 8. cinchona
goddess of fertility .. 4. Mama
inn, tavern .. 5. tambo
king (petty) .. 7. cacique
plant .. 3. oca
rodent .. 10. chinchilla
tinamou .. 4. yutu
tree .. 8. cinchona
university .. 9. San Marcos
volcano .. 7. El Misti
wind (cold) .. 4. puna
pervade ... 4. fill 5. imbue 6. extend
  8. permeate, traverse 9. penetrate
pervading ... 9. prevalent, universal
perverse ... 3. awk 4. awry, wogh
  5. wrong 6. cranky, erring 7. corrupt,
  forward, froward, wayward, willful
  (wilful) 8. contrary, petulant 9. obstinate
  10. ill-humored
perversion ... 5. error 6. misuse
  8. apostasy 9. sophistry 10. corruption,
  distortion 13. falsification
  17. misinterpretation, misrepresentation
perversion of taste ... 7. malacia
pervert ... 4. ruin 5. upset 6. divert,
  misuse 7. corrupt, distort, falsify,
  heretic 8. apostate, overturn, renegade
  9. turn aside 10. degenerate, lead
  astray 12. misinterpret, misrepresent
pervulgate ... 7. publish
Pesach, Pesah ... 8. Passover (Feast)
pesante ... 5. heavy 10. impressive
peshkash ... 3. tax 7. present, tribute
  8. offering
peskar ... 5. agent 7. steward 8. minister
  10. accountant
pesky ... 6. plaguy 7. teasing 9. harassing
  10. tormenting
pes planus ... 8. flatfoot 13. talipes
  planus
pess ... 7. hassock (church)
pessimist ... 5. cynic 6. malist 9. defeatist,
  worrywart
pessimistic ... 6. gloomy 7. cynical
  8. cowardly, hopeless 10. despairing,
  foreboding, uncheerful
pest ... 3. nag 4. bane 6. plague
  7. ragweed 8. epidemic, nuisance
  9. annoyance 10. pestilence
pester ... 3. nag, rib 5. annoy, tease,
  worry 6. badger, harass, impede, infest
  7. torment 8. entangle 9. importune
  10. overburden
pestilence ... 4. bane 7. disease, scourge
  8. epidemic 13. bubonic plague
pestilent ... 6. deadly 7. noxious
  8. annoying 9. pestering, poisonous
  10. contagious, infectious, pernicious
  11. mischievous, troublesome
pestle ... 4. club 6. muller 7. crusher,
  pounder
pes valgus ... 9. bowlegged 13. talipes
  valgus
pet ... 4. dear, tiff 5. humor 6. caress,
  coddle, cosset, dandle, fondle, pamper
  7. darling, dudgeon, indulge 8. cade
  lamb, favorite 10. endearment
petals (pert to) ...
  flower .. 7. corolla
  having .. 8. petalous
  orchid .. 8. labellum

ref to .. 5. whorl 8. petaline, petaloid
without .. 9. apetalous
petard ... 9. explosive 11. firecracker
peteman (thieves' sl) ... 5. thief 7. burglar
8. peterman 9. cracksman, fisherman
(Hist) 10. safeblower
Peter (pert to) ...
Bell .. 4. poem
Bible .. 5. Simon (also called) 7. epistle
(New Test)
the Great .. 4. Czar
the Great's father .. 6. Alexis
the Hermit .. 8. Crusader (1st)
peter out ... 4. fade, fail, tire, wane
6. weaken 7. dwindle 9. cease to be
Peter Pan (pert to) ...
author .. 6. Barrie
children .. 4. John 5. Wendy 7. Michael
fairy .. 10. Tinker Bell
family .. 7. Darling
Indian princess .. 9. Tiger Lily
pirate .. 11. Captain Hook
place .. 14. Never-Never Land
petiole ... 4. stem 5. stalk 8. peduncle
9. leafstalk 10. mesopodium
petit ... 4. mean 5. petty, small 6. little
13. insignificant
petite ... 5. small 6. demure, little
petition ... 3. ask, beg, sue 4. plea, pray
5. apply, plead 6. prayer 7. entreat,
relator, request, solicit 8. entreaty
10. supplicate
peto ... 5. wahoo
petrified ... 8. hardened 9. terrified
15. carved from stone
petrified body ... 6. fossil
petrify ... 4. numb 5. deaden, harden
7. astound, stupefy 8. paralyze
11. become stone
petroglyph ... 11. rock carving 15. rock
inscription
Petrograd ... 9. Leningrad 12. St
Petersburg
petroleum product ... 6. butane, diesel
7. naphtha, propane 8. gasoline
petrology (science of) ... 5. rocks
petrosal ... 4. bone 5. sinus, stony
7. petrous 8. ganglion
petticoat ... 4. girl, kilt 5. jupon,
pagne, woman 6. kirtle 8. basquine
9. undercoat, waistcoat 10. fustanella,
underskirt
petticoat tails ... 7. teacake 9. shortcake
pettifogger ... 4. tyro 5. quack 6. lawyer
7. shyster 8. attorney
pettish ... 7. fretful, peevish 9. irritable
pettle ... 6. cuddle, nestle, potter
7. cherish
petto ... 12. in one's breast 15. in
contemplation
petty ... 4. mean, orra 5. minor,
small 6. paltry 7. trivial 8. childish,
inferior, nugatory, trifling 9. miniscule
10. diminutive 11. small-minded,
subordinate, unimportant 12. narrow-
minded 13. insignificant
14. inconsiderable
petty (pert to) ...
captain .. 9. centurion
fault .. 10. peccadillo
larceny .. 10. scrounging

mullein .. 7. cowslip
objection .. 5. cavil
prince .. 6. satrap
petulance ... 8. ill humor, pertness
9. insolence, sauciness 10. wantonness
11. peevishness, pettishness
petulant ... 4. pert 5. cross, huffy, saucy,
testy 6. wanton 7. forward, fretful,
peevish, wayward, willful 8. contrary,
immodest, insolent 9. querulous
peu à peu ... 9. by degrees 14. little by
little
pewee ... 5. pewit 6. phoebe 8. woodcock
10. flycatcher
pewit ... 5. pewee 7. lapwing 12. laughing
gull
Pfefferkuchen ... 11. gingerbread
Phaëthon, Class Myth (pert to) ...
bird .. 4. swan
car .. 3. sun
father .. 6. Helios
sun god .. 6. Helios
phagomania ... 8. insanity 16. insatiable
hunger
Phalacrocorax ... 5. coots 10. cormorants
phalacrosis ... 8. alopecia, baldness
phalanger ... 5. tapoa 9. marsupial
phalanx ... 4. bone 5. pawns 6. troops
7. company (Mil) 8. infantry
phalera ... 4. boss 5. cameo
phantasm ... 5. dream, fancy, ghost
6. idolum, spirit 7. eidolon, fantasy,
phantom, specter (spectre) 8. delusion,
illusion 10. apparition
phantasy, fantasy ... 5. fancy, image
6. autism 8. daydream 11. imagination
phantom ... 5. fairy, ghost 7. eidolon,
specter (spectre) 10. simulacrum
Pharaoh (Bib) ... 4. faro, king
Pharaoh (pert to) ...
ancestor .. 2. Ra
chicken, hen .. 7. vulture (Egypt)
fig .. 8. sycamore
mouse .. 9. ichneumon
pharos ... 6. beacon, pharos 10. lighthouse
pharisee ... 7. pietist 9. hypocrite
pharmacology ... 5. drugs 13. materia
medica
pharos ... 5. cloak 6. beacon
10. chandelier (Eccl), lighthouse,
watchtower
phase ... 5. facet, stage 6. aspect
7. caprice, chapter, horning (moon)
phases, having many ... 11. Hydra-
headed
phasm ... 6. meteor 7. phantom
pheasant ... 5. cheer, monal 6. pukras
7. kallege 8. tragopan 12. ruffed grouse
pheasant (pert to) ...
brood .. 3. nye 4. nide (nid) 5. flock
cuckoo .. 6. coucal
duck .. 7. pintail 9. merganser
finch .. 7. waxbill
genus .. 10. Oreophasis
wren .. 7. emu wren
pheasant species ... 5. argus, blood
6. golden, silver 7. kallege 8. curassow
9. Mongolian 10. ring-necked 12. Lady
Amherst's
phenomenal ... 7. unusual 8. eventful,
sensible 9. objective, wonderful

13. extraordinary
phenomenon... 4. fact 5. event (unusual) 7. prodigy
phial... 3. cup 4. bowl, vial 6. bottle, vessel
phiale... 5. laver 6. vessel 8. fountain (Eccl)
Phi Beta Kappa (pert to)...
 badge.. 8. watch key
 founding.. 21. William and Mary College (1776)
 meaning.. 24. Philosophy the guide of life
 society.. 11. Greek-letter (oldest)
philabeg (filibeg)... 4. kilt
Philadelphia...
 City of.. 13. Brotherly Love
 fleabane.. 7. skevish
 lawyer.. 6. shrewd
 ref to.. 12. Philadelphus (Ptolemy II)
 sport team.. 6. Eagles 8. Phillies
philander... 5. flirt, lover 7. opossum
 10. flirtation, love-making, lover of men
philanthropic... 6. humane
 10. benevolent 12. eleemosynary
philanthropist... 5. donor 8. altruist, do-gooder 9. Robin Hood 10. benefactor, benevolist, Montefiore, Rothschild 12. humanitarian
philanthropy... 7. charity 8. good will 10. almsgiving 11. beneficence, benevolence (opp of misanthropy)
philatelist's concern... 5. stamp (postage)
Philippic... 6. screed, tirade 7. oration 8. diatribe 9. Philippus
Philippine, Philippines...
 archipelago.. 4. Sulu 5. Malay
 bay.. 6. Manila
 capital.. 6. Baguio (summer), Manila 10. Quezon City
 city.. 5. Albay, Davao 6. Cavite 7. Dagupan
 district.. 7. Lepanto
 fort.. 4. Gota 10. Corregidor
 island.. 4. Cebu 5. Leyte, Luzon, Panay, Samar, Ticao 6. Negros 7. Palawan, Paragua 8. Mindanao
 mountain.. 3. Apo, Iba 5. Mayon
 river.. 4. Abra, Agno 5. Pasig 8. Mindanao, Pampanga
 university.. 10. Santo Tomas (1611)
 volcano.. 3. Apo 5. Mayon
Philippine (pert to)...
 animal.. 5. civet, lemur
 ant, termite.. 4. anay (anai)
 barracks.. 7. cuartel
 boat, canoe, raft.. 5. balsa, banca
 breadfruit.. 7. camansi
 buffalo.. 7. carabao, timarau (timerau)
 chair (on poles).. 7. talabon
 dagger.. 4. itac
 drink.. 4. beno 5. bubud
 fabric.. 4. pina 9. pineapple
 fetish, idol.. 5. anito
 food.. 3. poi 4. Musa, saba, taro
 hemp.. 5. abaca 6. Manila
 house.. 5. bahay
 knife.. 4. bolo
 litter, pole chair.. 7. talabon

 lizard.. 4. ibid (monitor)
 mango.. 5. bauno 7. pahutan
 market day.. 7. tiangue
 melon.. 6. atimon
 mudfish.. 5. dalag
 palm.. 4. nipa 6. anahau (anahao)
 parrot (green).. 5. cagit
 reptile.. 6. python
 rice.. 4. paga 5. macan
 rice field bank.. 7. pilapil
 river.. 4. ilog
 shrub.. 4. alem
 sweetsop.. 4. ates
 town.. 4. agoa
 tree.. 3. tui 4. ipil (ypil) 5. asana, ligas, narra, yacal 6. molave 7. Eugenia, tindalo 8. macaasim
 turnip.. 7. cincoma
 vehicle (public).. 9. carromata
 water jar.. 5. banga
 wood.. 4. teak 5. ebony 6. sandal 8. mahogany
Philippine people (pert to)...
 discoverer.. 8. Magellan (1521)
 farmer.. 3. tao
 headman.. 4. datu
 language.. 4. Moro 7. Tagalog (Tagal) 8. Pilipino
 Muslim, Moslem.. 4. Moro
 native worker.. 7. polista
 Negrito.. 3. Ati 4. Aeta
 patriot.. 5. Rizal
 peasant.. 3. tao
 people.. 3. Ati, Lao 4. Aeta, Moro, Sulu 5. Bikol (Chr) 7. Tagalog, Visayan
 president.. 5. Roxas 6. Aquino, Marcos, Quezon
 priest (Moro).. 7. pandita
 servant.. 4. bata 5. alila
Philistine... 5. enemy 7. prosaic 9. philister 10. conformist, uncultured 12. antagonistic 13. prosaic person, unenlightened
Philistine (pert to)...
 anc name.. 9. Palestine, Philistia
 assimilated by.. 7. Semites
 city.. 4. Gaza 5. Ekron (Bib)
 god.. 4. Baal 5. Dagon
philo (comb form)... 6. fond of, loving
philogeant... 12. lover of earth
philogyny... 11. love of women
philology... 11. linguistics 14. love of learning
Philomela (pert to)...
 father.. 7. Pandion (King of Athens)
 sister.. 6. Procne
 turned into.. 7. swallow 11. nightingale
philosopher...
 American.. Dewey, James (William), Royce 6. Peirce 9. Santayana
 Arab.. 8. Averreos (Averrhoes)
 Chinese.. 6. Lao-tzu 9. Confucius
 Christian.. 7. Abelard, Aquinas 9. Augustine
 Danish.. 11. Kierkagaard
 Dutch.. 7. Spinoza
 English.. 4. Mill 5. Bacon, Locke 6. Hobbes 7. Bentham, Russell, Spencer 9. Whitehead
 French.. 6. Pascal 8. Rousseau, Voltaire 9. Descartes

German.. 4. Kant 5. Hegel 9. Heidegger, Nietzsche 12. Schopenhauer
Greek.. 4. Zeno 5. Plato 8. Epicurus, Socrates 9. Aristotle
Indian.. 6. Buddha
Italian.. 5. Bruno
Scottish.. 4. Hume
Seven Sages (7 Wise Men of Greece).. 4. Bias 5. Solon 6. Chilon, Thales 8. Pittacus 9. Cleobulus 10. Epimenides (or Periander)

Philosopher of...
Farney.. 8. Voltaire
Malmesbury.. 6. Hobbes
Sans Souci.. 17. Frederick the Great
Syracuse.. 4. Dion
Wimbledon.. 14. John Horne Tooke

philosopher's school... 7. Eleatic
philosophical... 5. wise 7. erudite, logical, sapient 8. rational 9. temperate, unruffled
philosophical being... 6. entity
philosophy (pert to)...
choice of.. 11. eclecticism
of law.. 13. jurisprudence
of pantheists.. 5. Stoic
sublimated.. 17. Transcendentalism
theory.. 4. yoga 9. pantheism, Platonism, solipsism 12. epistemology
phlegmatic... 4. calm, dull, slow 5. inert 6. mucous, watery 7. viscous 8. sluggish 9. apathetic
phlogistic... 5. fiery 6. heated 7. burning 11. impassioned 12. inflammatory
Phoebad... 7. seeress 9. priestess (Delphian) 10. prophetess
Phoebe (pert to)...
daughter.. 4. Leto
epithet of.. 7. Artemis
mother.. 4. Gaea (earth goddess)
poetic.. 4. moon
phoebe.. 4. fish 5. craps, pewit 6. peewee 9. satellite (Saturn) 10. flycatcher
Phoebus... 3. Sol 6. sun god
Phoenicia...
capital city.. 4. Tyre 5. Sidon
Colony.. 5. Hippo 8. Carthage
deity.. 4. Baal
famed for.. 9. purple dye 10. navigation
goddess of fertility.. 5. Baltis 7. Astarte
god of healing.. 6. Eshmun (Eshmoun)
king.. 6. Agenor
region.. 5. Syria
Phoenix... 4. bird (fabled), palm 7. capital (Ariz)
phonetic (pert to)...
science.. 9. phonology
sound.. 7. phoneme
stop.. 9. occlusive
system.. 5. romic
phonic... 6. spoken, voiced 7. sounded 8. auditory 9. accoustic, vibration
phony (comb form)... 5. sound, voice
phony.. 4. fake 9. contrived, simulated 11. counterfeit
photograph... 4. film 5. image, photo 7. picture 8. likeness, portrait 9. ferrotype, pictorial, portrayal 10. centerfold, heliograph 12. photogravure

photographic bath... 5. toner 7. reducer 9. developer
photography, science of... 5. light 6. optics 7. photics
photography inventors... 4. Land 6. Niepce, Talbot 8. Daguerre
photometric unit... 3. pyr, rad
phrase... 5. idiom 6. remark, saying, slogan 7. diction, epigram, epithet, passage 8. flattery 9. catchword 10. expression 11. phraseology
phraseology... 5. style 6. jargon 7. diction, wording 8. parlance
phratry (Hist)... 4. clan 5. group
phrenetic... 3. mad 5. crazy 6. madman 7. fanatic, frantic, violent 9. delirious 10. passionate
phrenology, science of... 5. skull 10. craniology
Phrygia, Asia Minor...
cap (comical).. 10. liberty cap
deity.. 5. Attis
Eccl Hist.. 9. Montanist
founder.. 7. Gordius (800 BC)
King.. 5. Midas
marble (anc).. 9. pavonazzo (pavonazzetto)
music.. 4. mode
river.. 7. Meander
phylactery (Eccl)... 4. case 5. charm, chest, miter 6. amulet, infula, record, scroll
phylarchy... 12. rule by tribes
phyletic... 6. racial 7. descent, species 12. phylogenetic
phyllophagous... 15. feeding on leaves
physical... 6. bodily 7. natural, somatic 8. material 9. corporeal
physical force... 10. attraction
physical unit... 3. erg
physician... 5. medic 6. doctor, healer, intern 7. coroner 8. restorer
physician (pert to)...
ancient.. 5. Galen
comb form.. 5. istro
French Nobel Prize.. 7. Laveran
Greek (anc).. 5. Galen 11. Asclepiades
quack.. 10. medicaster
symbol.. 8. caduceus
physicist... 4. Bohr, Mach, Rabi 5. Fermi, Pauli 6. Dalton, Pascal, Teller 7. Feynman, Hawking, Marconi, Maxwell 8. Chadwick, Einstein, Sakharov 11. Oppenheimer, Schrödinger
physiognomy... 3. mug 4. face 11. countenance 14. external aspect, interpretation
physique... 4. body 6. figure
physis (Gr)... 6. nature
phytology, science of... 6. botany, plants
piacle... 3. sin 5. crime, guilt 7. offense 15. sacrificial rite 17. expiatory offering
pian... 5. tumor 9. frambesia
piano (pert to)...
direction.. 10. pianissimo (softly)
duet, upper part.. 5. primo
dumb keyboard.. 10. digitorium
early.. 6. spinet
Italian.. 10. Cristofori

keyboard . . 7. clavier 8. pedalier
pedal . . 7. celeste
pianolike . . 7. celesta
player . . 7. pianola
slang . . 11. eighty-eight
small . . 8. pianette
piatti . . 7. cymbals
piazza . . 5. campo, porch 6. square
7. gallery, portico, veranda
pic . . 4. peak 8. picayune
picacho . . 4. hill 5. butte
picador . . 3. wit 6. jester 7. debater
8. horseman (with lance), toreador
11. bullfighter
picaro . . 5. knave, rogue 7. sharper
8. vagabond 10. picaresque
picaroon . . 5. rogue, thief 6. pirate,
rascal 7. brigand, corsair 8. prey upon
pick . . 4. cull, gaff, peck, sort 5. elect,
pluck, strum 6. assort, choose, indent,
pickax, pierce, select 7. diamond (card),
harvest, the best 8. plectrum, the elite
9. toothpick
pick (pert to) . . .
flaws . . 5. cavil
out . . 6. pilfer, select 7. acquire,
procure, specify 9. eliminate, segregate
11. distinguish
pick-me-up . . 5. tonic 6. bracer
9. kittiwake, stimulate 11. restorative
up . . 4. tidy 6. arrest 7. improve
9. stimulant 10. recuperate
picked . . 4. trim 5. piked, spiny 6. choice,
chosen, culled, dainty, peaked, spruce
7. adorned, plucked, pointed 8. stripped
10. fastidious
pickerel . . 4. fish, pike 9. Esox niger
12. walleyed pike
picket . . 3. peg 4. pale, post, tern
5. fence, guard, stake 6. bullet, fasten,
paling, sentry, tether 7. enclose, fortify,
shackle 8. sentinel 10. go on strike
pickle . . 4. alec, peck 5. achar, brine
6. dawdle, nibble, piddle, pilfer, trifle
7. chutney, vitriol
pickled . . 5. drunk 6. soused
9. marinated
pickled pig's feet . . . 5. souse
pickle fork . . . 8. runcible
pickle-herring . . . 7. buffoon 11. merry-
andrew 12. Pickelhering
pickpocket . . 4. wire 5. thief 6. bulker
picnic . . 3. fun 4. camp, play 6. junket,
outing 9. festivity
Pict (anc) . . . 4. Scot 5. Aryan 9. aborigine
Pictland . . . 8. Scotland
pictorial . . . 8. painting 11. illustrated,
picturesque
Pict's house (Archaeol) . . . 8. dwelling
(subterranean)
picture . . 3. oil 4. copy, draw, icon
5. image, print, scene 6. chromo,
depict, pastel 7. diorama, etching,
portray, porture, tableau 8. describe,
likeness, painting, portrait 9. engraving,
paintings, represent, visualize
10. photograph 11. description
14. representation
picture (pert to) . . .
mounting, border . . 3. mat 5. frame
8. kakemono, makimono (scroll)

moving . . 4. film 5. movie 6. cinema
positive . . 5. print
puzzle . . 5. rebus
small . . 5. cameo 9. miniature
stand . . 5. easel
viewer . . 11. alethoscope, stereoscope
12. magic lantern, stereopticon
picturesque . . . 5. vivid 6. scenic
7. graphic 9. pictorial
picuda . . . 9. barracuda (great), picudilla
(small)
picudo . . . 6. weevil 10. boll weevil
piddle . . . 3. toy 4. pick, play 6. putter,
trifle 9. waste time
pie . . 4. food, mess 5. chaos, patty
6. jumble, magpie, pastry 7. cobbler,
dessert, measure 9. confusion
piebald . . 4. pied 5. mixed, pinto
6. motley 7. mongrel, mottled, pintado
10. variegated 13. heterogeneous
piece . . 3. bit 4. join, part, role
5. crumb, drama, piece, scrap, shred
6. sample 7. measure, portion, writing
8. chessman, fragment, specimen,
treatise
piece (pert to) . . .
armor . . 5. tasse (tace) 8. corselet
de résistance . . 6. entrée 8. main dish
door, jamb . . 6. lintel
eccentric . . 3. cam
fastening . . 3. gib
fitted . . 4. shim 5. tenon
flat . . 4. slab, slat 5. flake, strip
meal . . 9. by degrees, fragments
12. piece by piece 14. little by little
metal . . 3. sow
neck . . 3. boa 5. rabat, scarf, stole
8. kerchief
of one's mind . . 6. rebuke 7. reproof
13. candid opinion
out . . 3. eke 6. cantle
preventing slippage . . 5. cleat
short . . 5. skit
side . . 3. rib 5. stave
split off . . 6. sliver, splint 8. splinter
tapering . . 4. gore 6. gusset
work (art) . . 4. pavé 6. mosaic, niello
pieces of . . .
eight . . 6. dollar, escudo
meat . . 5. cabob
silk waste . . 4. noil
pied . . 4. foot 5. pinto 7. colored (2
or more colors), dappled, piebald
10. variegated 12. parti-colored
pied (pert to) . . .
blackbird . . 6. thrush
brant . . 5. goose
diver . . 4. smew
duck . . 8. Labrador
Friar (Eccl Hist) . . 9. mendicant
monk . . 10. Bernardine, Cistercian
Piper of Hamelin . . 8. musician 10. rat
charmer
widgeon . . 8. garganey 9. goldeneye
Piedmont, Italy . . . 7. capital (Turin)
pieplant . . . 7. rhubarb
pier . . 4. anta, dock, mole, quay 5. groin,
wharf 6. pillar 7. landing 8. buttress,
gatepost 9. promenade 10. breakwater
pierce . . . 4. bore, cold, gore, pain, tart
5. enter, gride, lance, probe, spear,

spike, sting, wound 6. riddle, tunnel
7. discern 8. puncture 9. penetrate,
perforate 10. comprehend

piercing . . . 4. keen, loud 5. acute 6. shrill
7. caustic, clearly, painful, piteous,
pungent, sharply, shrilly, spiking,
violent 8. deep-felt, poignant, spearing,
stabbing 9. searching.

Pieria, Macedonia (pert to) . . .
epithet of . . 5. Muses
native . . 7. Pierian
reference to . . 6. poetry 9. knowledge
seat of . . 5. Muses

piet . . . 5. ouzel 6. magpie 7. piebald
10. chatterbox, chattering 11. saucy
person

Pietà (It) . . . 9. sculpture 10. Virgin Mary

pietose (Mus) . . . 11. sympathetic
13. compassionate

piety . . . 4. pity, zeal (worship) 6. filial
8. devotion, holiness, religion
9. reverence 10. compassion,
devoutness, sanctimony 11. dutifulness

pig . . . 3. car (RR), ham, hog, sow
4. boar, pork 5. bacon, crosk, flask,
swine 6. farrow 7. casting, dogboat,
glutton 8. pressman, sixpence, slattern
9. policeman 10. stoolpigeon

pig (pert to) . . .
bed . . 3. pen, sty 5. reeve 6. pigsty
female . . 3. sow 4. gilt
guinea . . 4. cavy
headed . . 6. stupid 9. obstinate
iron . . 5. ingot
iron, ballast (Naut) . . 9. kentledge
iron, cast . . 5. kentle (Mil)
last of litter . . 4. runt
lead, weight . . 6. fother
litter . . 6. farrow
piglike . . 7. hoglike, porcine, suiform
piglike animal . . 7. peccary 8. babirusa
potato . . 7. cowbane
rat . . 9. bandicoot
skin . . 6. saddle 8. football
yoke . . 7. sextant 8. quadrant
young . . 5. grice, shoat 6. farrow, piglet
9. gruntling

pigdan . . . 8. spittoon

pigeon . . . 3. nun 4. barb, dove, dupe,
fowl, girl, gull, ruff 5. heart, piper,
pluck, sweet 6. coward, fleece, pouter,
roller, turbit 7. fantail, jacobin, pintail,
tumbler 9. trumpeter

pigeon, pidgin (pert to) . . .
Australia . . 5. wonga 10. wonga-wonga
berry . . 7. dogwood 9. Juneberry, wild
elder
blood . . 6. garnet
carrier . . 5. homer 6. homing
10. scandaroon
extinct . . 4. dodo
food . . 7. saltcat
genus . . 5. Goura 7. Columba
hawk . . 5. falcon, merlin
house . . 7. dovecot 9. columbary
ref to . . 12. peristeronic
short-beaked . . 4. barb
wood . . 6. cushat 8. ringdove
young . . 5. piper

pigment . . . 3. red 4. blue, gray, pink
5. black, brown, color, green, ocher

(ochre), paint, white 6. orange, purple,
yellow 8. colorant

pigment (pert to) . . .
arsenic, yellow . . 8. orpiment
black . . 3. tar 5. sepia 7. melanin
blue . . 5. smalt
blue-green . . 4. bice
brown . . 5. sepia, umber 6. bister (bistre),
sienna (burnt) 7. cypress
brownish yellow . . 6. sienna
calico yellow . . 7. canarin (canarine)
coal tar . . 7. aniline
cuttlefish . . 5. sepia
madder root . . 7. rubiate
orange red . . 7. realgar
oxide of lead . . 8. massicot
red . . 7. turacin
yellow . . 5. ocher (ochre) 7. etiolin

pigmy . . . see pygmy

pignus . . . 4. pawn 6. pledge

pig's feet . . . 9. pettitoes

pigtail . . . 5. braid, queue 7. tobacco
(rolled) 8. rope's end (Naut)

pika . . . 6. rodent

pike . . . 3. ged (gedd) 4. fish, luce, pick
6. beacon, pickax

pike (pert to) . . .
North American . . 11. muskellunge
perch . . 6. sauger
pikelike . . 3. gar 4. luce 5. lucet 6. robalo
8. robalito 9. barracuda
walleyed . . 4. doré

pikel, pikle . . . 7. hayfork 9. pitchfork

pikelet . . . 7. crumpet

piker . . . 5. thief, tramp 6. coward
7. gambler, quitter, shirker, vagrant
8. tightwad

pilar . . . 5. downy, hairy

pilaster . . . 4. anta 5. alette (part), column

Pilate (Bib) . . . 10. procurator (Judean)

pilchard . . . 7. sardine

pile . . . 3. awn, mow, nap 4. heap, load,
mole, pier, rick, shag 5. amass, slack,
spile, stake 6. heap up, pillar, wealth
7. fortune, store up, texture

pile (pert to) . . .
burning . . 4. pyre
defense . . 8. estacade
driver . . 7. fistuca
of hay . . 3. mow 4. dess, rick 5. stack
up . . 4. heap 7. smashup, store up
9. shipwreck 10. exaggerate

pilfer . . . 3. rob 4. lift, loot 5. filch, steal,
swipe 6. rustle (cattle), snitch 7. purloin

pilgrim . . . 5. exile (Relig) 6. palmer
8. crusader, newcomer, traveler,
wanderer, wayfarer 9. immigrant,
sojourner 10. tenderfoot
12. peregrinator

Pilgrim (pert to) . . .
father . . 9. John Alden
Fathers . . 11. Separatists (1620)
garment . . 5. ihram (Mecca)
landing . . 12. Plymouth Rock (1620)
Scotch . . 6. palmer
ship . . 9. Mayflower, Speedwell

pilgrimage to Mecca . . . 4. hadj

Pilgrim's bottle . . . 7. ampulla, costrel

Pilgrim's Progress . . . 8. allegory
(Bunyan)

pill . . . 3. rob 4. ball, bore, pare, pell, pool

5. bolus, creek 6. bullet, pellet, pilule
8. medicine 9. cigarette 11. decorticate

pillage ... 4. flay, loot, prey, sack
5. booty, harry, spoil, strip 6. rapine,
ravage 7. despoil, plunder, robbery
9. depredate, extortion 10. spoliation

pillar ... 4. post, slab 5. shaft, stele
(stela), tower 6. column 7. support
8. mainstay, monument, pedestal

pillar (pert to) ...
  airfield .. 5. pylon
  Buddhist .. 3. lat
  carved .. 7. totem pole
  little .. 8. pillaret
  of society .. 9. personage
  pillarlike .. 6. stelar
  saint .. 7. recluse, stylite
  tall, slender .. 7. obelisk
  with front figure .. 7. osiride

Pillars of Hercules site ... 5. Abila,
Calpe 17. Strait of Gibralter

pillbox ... 3. cap, hat 8. brougham,
fortress 13. fortification

pillory ... 4. yoke 5. stock, trone
6. cangue, punish

pillow ... 3. pad 5. block 7. cushion,
support

pillow (pert to) ...
  case, cover .. 4. sham, slip
  long .. 7. bolster
  stuffing .. 5. kapok 8. feathers

pilose ... 5. hairy 6. pilous

pilot ... 4. lead 5. flyer, guide, steer
6. aviate, direct, leader 8. director,
helmsman, preacher 9. clergyman,
navigator 10. cowcatcher

pilot (pert to) ...
  bird .. 6. plover
  expert .. 3. ace
  fish .. 6. remora 9. amberfish, whitefish
  house .. 10. wheelhouse
  jacket .. 9. pea jacket
  sky .. 8. preacher 9. clergyman
  snake .. 10. copperhead
  weed .. 9. rosinweed
  whale .. 9. blackfish

pilotless plane ... 5. drone

Piltdown, England (pert to) ...
  Hist yield .. 7. Dawn Man, fossils
  Prehist station .. 6. Sussex

piltock ... 8. coalfish

pilum ... 6. pestle 7. javelin

pilus ... 4. hair

Pima ... 5. Opata

pimento ... 6. pepper 7. paprika
8. allspice, pimiento

pin ... 3. hob, peg, pen 4. axle, bolt,
coak (coag), join 5. affix, badge,
dowel, rivet, thole 6. brooch, cotter,
fasten, secure, trifle 7. confine, enclose,
gudgeon, jewelry, spindle, stopper,
trenail 8. linchpin, ornament, transfix
10. chatelaine

pin (pert to) ...
  axle .. 8. linchpin
  dial .. 5. style
  fish .. 11. stickleback
  game .. 7. skittle
  grass .. 8. alfilaria (forage)
  jackstraw (game) .. 8. spilikin (spillikin)
  meat fastener .. 6. skewer

  quoits .. 3. hob
  sailmaker's .. 3. fid
  small .. 3. peg 4. lill
  with looped head .. 7. eyebolt

pinafore ... 5. apron, smock 7. tablier
8. sun dress

Pinafore ... 5. opera (Gilbert & Sullivan)

pinag ... 4. lake (rain season)

piñata ... 5. globe (swinging, with gifts)

pinax ... 4. dish 5. table 6. plaque,
scheme, tablet 7. picture 9. catalogue

pinbone ... 7. hipbone

pince-nez ... 7. glasses, nippers
10. eyeglasses

pincers ... 3. tew 5. chela, tongs 6. pliers
7. forceps, pinette

pinch ... 3. nip, rob 4. pain, raid 5. cramp,
gripe, pugil (anc), steal, stint, tweak
6. arrest, crisis, extort, scrimp, snatch,
snitch, strait, twinge 7. afflict, confine,
squeeze, urgency 8. compress, contract,
exigency, straiten

pinchbeck ... 4. sham 5. alloy (cheap
jewelry) 8. frippery, spurious
11. counterfeit

pinched ... 4. poor, thin 8. squeezed
10. compressed, contracted, distressed,
straitened

pinchem ... 8. titmouse

pinda ... 6. peanut

Pindar ... 4. poet (lyric)

pindaric ... 3. ode 9. irregular
12. unrestrained

pine ... 4. flag 5. waste, yearn 6. grieve,
lament, needle, repine, sicken, weaken,
wither 8. languish 11. deteriorate

pine (pert to) ...
  Brazil .. 6. paraná
  chemical .. 5. pinic
  exudation .. 5. resin, rosin
  family .. 3. fir 5. larch, piñon 6. spruce
  finch .. 6. siskin
  fir .. 6. balsam 12. Balm of Gilead
  fruit .. 4. cone
  genus .. 5. Pinus
  gum .. 8. sandarac
  knot .. 7. dovekie
  leaf .. 6. needle
  low-growing .. 5. piñon
  mahogany .. 6. totara
  New Zealand .. 5. kauri (kaury)
  Pacific coast .. 8. knobpine
  Philippine .. 7. Amboina 8. galagala
  screw .. 3. ara 6. pandan
  tar extract .. 6. retene
  tulip .. 10. pipsissewa

pineal ... 5. brain, gland 8. pine cone

pineapple ... 4. bomb, pina 5. fiber, fruit
6. ananas 8. pine cone 12. Bromeliaceae

pineapple (pert to) ...
  cheese .. 7. Cheddar
  cloth .. 4. pina
  segment .. 3. pip
  weed .. 8. marigold

Pine Tree State ... 5. Maine

pinguescent ... 9. fattening

pinguid ... 3. fat 4. oily, rich 5. fatty
8. unctuous

pinguitude ... 7. fatness, obesity
8. oiliness 10. greasiness

pink ... 3. cut, Red 4. deck, rose, stab

5. adorn, blink, color, coral, smart, wound **6.** flower, indent, minnow, pierce, salmon, vessel **7.** radical, serrate **8.** decorate, grayling **9.** carnation **11.** fashionable

pink (pert to) . . .
coat . . **10.** foxhunter's
eye . . **4.** duck **14.** conjunctivitis
family . . **7.** Campion **9.** Carnation **15.** Caryophyllaceae
fish . . **8.** gobylike
genus . . **6.** Silene
lady . . **3.** fly (fishing) **8.** cocktail
needle . . **9.** alfilaria
Pearl . . **6.** azalea
pill . . **7.** cure-all
root . . **8.** wormroot

pinkeen . . . **6.** minnow **19.** insignificant person

pinna . . . **3.** fin **4.** wing **7.** auricle, feather, leaflet

pinnace . . . **4.** boat **5.** woman **6.** tender (Naut) **9.** procuress **10.** prostitute

pinnacle . . . **3.** epi, tee, top **4.** acme, apex, peak **5.** crest, crown, serac, spire **6.** finial, needle, summit

pinnate . . . **11.** featherlike

pinniped . . . **4.** seal **6.** walrus

pinochle term . . . **3.** dix **4.** meld

piñon . . . **4.** pine, seed **8.** pignolia **12.** monkey puzzle

pintado . . . **4.** cero, fish, sier (fish) **5.** pinto **6.** chintz, pigeon, sierra

pintail (pert to) . . .
duck . . **4.** smee **5.** river, ruddy
grouse . . **4.** sand **11.** sharp-tailed

pinto (horse) . . . **4.** pied **6.** calico **7.** mottled, painted, piebald, spotted

pinwing . . . **7.** penguin

pioneer . . . **4.** lead **5.** guide, miner **6.** digger, open up **7.** settler **8.** colonist, explorer **9.** excavator **10.** forerunner

Pioneer's Day . . . **4.** Utah (July 24) **5.** Idaho (June 15)

pious . . . **5.** godly, loyal **6.** devout, worthy **9.** excellent, religious **11.** reverential **13.** sanctimonious

pip . . . **3.** ace **4.** paip, peep, roup, seed, spot, trey **7.** disease **12.** officer's star

pipe . . . **2.** TD **3.** see, tee **4.** blow, clay, duct, reed, tube **5.** spout, voice **6.** convey, dudeen, hookah (hooka), outlet **7.** channel **9.** brierwood

pipe (pert to) . . .
connection . . **3.** ell, tee **5.** cross, elbow
dream . . **8.** illusion **10.** bemusement
end . . **4.** taft **5.** nozzle
line . . **9.** grapevine
Oriental . . **8.** narghile (nargile)
pastoral, shepherd's . . **3.** oat **4.** reed **7.** larigot **9.** flageolet
peace . . **7.** calumet
player . . **5.** fifer **8.** shepherd
short . . **5.** dudeen
smoke . . **5.** tewel
steam . . **5.** riser
tobacco . . **10.** meerschaum
wood . . **5.** brier (briar) **9.** brierwood
wrench . . **8.** Stillson

pipette . . . **6.** taster, tubule **7.** dripper

pipit . . . **7.** titlark

piquancy . . . **4.** zest **5.** spice **8.** pungency, raciness, tartness **11.** conciseness

piquant . . . **4.** racy, tart **5.** salty, sharp, spicy, zesty **7.** concise, cutting, pungent **11.** interesting, provocative

pique . . . **4.** dive, fret, goad **5.** anger, annoy, sting, tempt **6.** grudge, incite, nettle, offend **7.** dudgeon, offense, provoke, umbrage **8.** irritate **9.** displease **10.** irritation, resentment **11.** displeasure

pir (Muslim) . . . **4.** tomb **5.** guide, saint

pirate . . . **6.** robber **7.** corsair, mariner **8.** marauder, picaroon **9.** buccaneer **10.** freebooter **11.** appropriate

pirate (famed) . . . **4.** Kidd **6.** Morgan **7.** Lafitte **10.** Blackbeard (Capt Teach)

pirate (pert to) . . .
base, famed . . . **7.** Barbary (Coast)
bird . . **10.** jaeger gull
flag . . **10.** Jolly Roger
gallows . . **7.** yardarm
perch . . **8.** Xenarchi
ship . . **5.** rover **7.** corsair **8.** picaroon
weapon . . **4.** snee

piraya . . . **6.** caribe (fish) **7.** piranha

pirogue . . . **5.** canoe **7.** piragua

pirol . . . **6.** oriole

Pisa, Italy . . .
capital of . . **7.** Tuscany
famed for . . **9.** campanile **12.** Leaning Tower
river . . **4.** Arno

pis aller . . . **10.** last resort

piscary . . . **7.** fishery **12.** fishing place **13.** fishing rights

piscatology (science of) . . . **7.** angling, fishing **10.** halieutics

Pisces . . . **4.** fish **6.** fishes **13.** constellation

piscina . . . **4.** tank **5.** basin (Eccl) **8.** fishpond **9.** reservoir

Piscis Volans . . . **10.** flying fish **13.** constellation

Pisgah (pert to) . . .
site . . **4.** Nebo **8.** mountain (top)
view . . **12.** Land of Canaan **13.** Land of Promise
viewer . . **5.** Moses

pismire . . . **3.** ant **5.** emmet

pistachio . . . **3.** nut **5.** green

piste . . . **4.** path **5.** spoor, track, trail **10.** racecourse

pisteology, pistiology . . . **5.** faith **6.** belief

pistil . . . **5.** ovary **6.** carpel **9.** gynoecium

pistol . . . **3.** dag **7.** firearm **9.** derringer

pistol (pert to) . . .
case . . **7.** holster
lock . . **5.** rowet
slang . . **3.** gat, rod **6.** barker, cannon, heater

pistology (Theol) . . . **5.** faith

piston . . . **7.** plunger

pit . . . **4.** cave, hole, mine, pool, sump, tomb, trap, well **5.** abyss, arena, grave, sluig, snare **6.** cavity, slough **7.** alveola, cockpit, dungeon **8.** audience **9.** waterhole **10.** excavation **13.** Stock Exchange

pit (pert to) . . .
anatomy . . **5.** fossa, fovea
botany . . **7.** alveola, pitamen **8.** endocarp
bottomless . . **7.** Abaddon

fodder .. 4. silo
Hades .. 4. hell
Hawaiian .. 3. imu
theater .. parquet
viper .. 9. Viperidae 11. rattlesnake
pitch . . . 3. key, tar 4. camp, hurl, tilt,
tone, toss 5. black, color, erect, fling,
heave, lurch, resin, sense, slope, throw
6. degree, encamp, plunge, settle,
topple 7. incline 8. flounder 9. sales
talk
pitch (pert to) . . .
high .. 6. shrill
identity .. 6. unison
inflammable .. 7. piceous
mineral .. 4. flat 6. accent, stress
music .. 4. flat 6. accent, stress
8. paranete 9. tonometer
pitchlike .. 7. piceous
pitchblende . . . 6. radium 7. uranium
pitched ball, curving away . . .
8. outshoot
pitcher . . . 3. jug 4. ewer, olla, olpe,
toby 5. gorge 8. cruisken (cruiskeen),
oenochoe (wine), southpaw (left-
handed)
pitcher (pert to) . . .
plant, genus .. 9. Nepenthes
10. Cephalotus, Sarracenia
plus catcher .. 7. battery
shaped .. 8. urceolate
shaped vessel .. 8. aiguière
piteous . . . 5. pious 6. devout, paltry,
tender 7. pitiful, pitying 8. pitiable
13. compassionate
pitfall . . . 3. pit 4. lure, trap 5. decoy,
snare 6. danger 10. difficulty
pith . . . 3. jet, nub 4. gist, meat, pulp
6. center, kernel, marrow 7. essence,
meaning, nucleus 9. substance
pith helmet . . . 3. cap, hat 5. topee (topi)
pith tree (Nile) . . . 7. ambatch (ambash)
pithy . . . 4. soft 5. crisp, meaty, pulpy,
terse 7. laconic 10. meaningful
12. epigrammatic
pithy (pert to) . . .
expression .. 7. epigram
saying .. 3. mot
sentence .. 5. motto
pitiable . . . 3. sad 6. woeful 7. piteous
8. grievous, terrible 9. miserable,
sorrowful 10. lamentable
pitiful . . . 4. mean 6. paltry 7. piteous
8. pathetic, shameful 10. despicable
12. contemptible 13. compassionate,
tenderhearted
pitiless . . . 5. cruel 8. ruthless 9. merciless
10. relentless 13. unsympathetic
pitpit . . . 8. guitguit 12. honey creeper
Pitri, Hindu (pert to) . . .
ancestor of .. 4. gods 6. demons 10. four
castes
Prajapatis, one of .. 10. progenitor
(human race)
semidivine .. 6. father 9. patriarch
10. forefather
pittance . . . 4. alms, dole, gift, scat
7. bequest 8. donation 9. allowance
11. small amount
pity . . . 4. ruth 5. mercy, yearn 7. remorse
8. clemency, sympathy 10. compassion,

condolence, repentance
13. commiseration
pivot . . . 3. toe 4. slew, slue, turn 5. hinge
6. pintle, swivel
pivotal . . . 4. crux 5. polar 7. turning
pixy, pixie . . . 3. elf, imp 5. fairy 6. goblin,
sprite 13. mischief-maker
Pizarro (pert to) . . .
adventurer .. 7. Spanish
conqueror of .. 4. Peru
founder of .. 4. Lima (capital)
placable . . . 8. peaceful 9. agreeable,
forgiving, peaceable 10. appeasable
placard . . . 4. bill, post 5. edict 6. notice,
poster 7. affiché 9. manifesto,
stomacher 12. proclamation
placate . . . 4. calm 5. pacify, soothe
7. appease 10. conciliate 11. tranquilize
place . . . 3. put 4. lieu, site, spot 5. abode,
locus, posit, situs, stead 6. locale,
locate, region, street 7. arrange,
demesne, deposit 8. classify, location,
position 9. recognize, situation
place (of) . . .
amusement .. 4. park 6. casino, midway
bliss .. 4. Eden 8. paradise
confinement .. 3. pen 4. brig, cage,
coop, gaol, jail, stir 6. asylum, corral,
prison 7. dungeon 9. calaboose
12. penitentiary
confusion .. 5. Babel
content .. 7. Arcadia
darkness .. 6. Erebus
exit .. 6. egress
honor .. 9. right hand
origin .. 6. cradle, source
refuge .. 3. ark 4. port 5. haven
resort .. 7. purlieu
rest .. 3. bed, den 4. lair, nook 5. chair,
couch, grave, niche
sleep .. 3. bed 4. doss 5. berth, couch
6. pallet 7. hammock
suffering .. 10. Armageddon,
Gethsemane
trial .. 5. venue
place (pert to) . . .
apart .. 6. enisle 7. isolate 9. sequester
beneath .. 9. infrapose
between .. 9. interpose
burial .. 5. grave 8. catacomb, cemetery
9. graveyard 10. necropolis
by itself .. 7. isolate
camping .. 5. étape
confidence in .. 7. entrust
different .. 10. otherwhere
for boats .. 7. portage
for candles .. 9. chandlery
forest (open) .. 5. glade
for keeping animals .. 3. zoo 4. barn
7. pasture 9. menagerie
frequented .. 4. dive 5. haunt 6. resort
from which jury is taken .. 5. venue
hallowed .. see sacred (below)
hiding .. 3. mew 4. lair 5. niche
high .. 7. eminent 8. eminence
horse training .. 4. ring 5. longe
in a row .. 5. align, aline
in bondage .. 7. enslave
in order .. 7. arrange 11. systematize
in statu quo .. 7. put back, replace,
restore

interpretation on . . 8. construe
landing . . 4. dock, pier 5. wharf 7. airport
market . . 4. mart 5. agora 6. rialto
meeting . . 5. tryst
of . . 4. lieu 5. stead
on mound . . 3. tee
opposite . . 6. appose
over . . 11. superimpose
sacred . . 4. fane 5. altar 6. chapel,
church, shrine, temple 9. synagogue
10. tabernacle
side-by-side . . 9. collocate, juxtapose
sleeping . . 3. bed 4. bunk 5. berth,
couch 6. pallet 7. hammock
under . . 9. infrapose
under restraint . . 6. arrest, intern
value upon . . 5. price 6. assess
8. appraise, estimate
wet . . 4. slew 5. marsh 6. slough
wrestling . . 5. arena 9. palaestra
(palestra)
placed . . . 3. put 7. located 8. arranged,
situated 10. classified
placed in lodgings . . . 6. roomed
8. billeted
placid . . . 4. calm 5. quiet, suant
6. demure, gentle, serene 8. composed,
peaceful 9. agreeable, quiescent,
unruffled 11. undisturbed
pladaroma . . . 5. tumor (eyelid)
plafond . . . 7. ceiling 14. contract bridge
plage . . . 5. beach
plagiarism . . . 6. piracy 8. cribbing,
stealing 10. purloining 13. appropriation
plague . . . 3. dun, vex 4. bane, pest, twit
5. harry, tease, worry 6. harass, hector,
infest 8. scourge, torment 9. epidemic,
nuisance 10. Black Death, pestilence
11. infestation
plaguy . . . 6. vexing 8. annoying
9. difficult, harassing 10. tormenting
11. troublesome
plaice . . . 8. flatfish, flounder
plaid . . . 4. maud 6. tartan
plain . . . 3. lea 4. chol, mesa, moor, wold
5. blunt, camas, clear, frank, heath
6. lenten 7. artless, evident, genuine,
legible, obvious, prairie 8. apparent,
distinct, explicit, ordinary 9. downright,
primitive, unadorned 10. unaffected
plain (pert to) . . .
clothes . . 10. unofficial
dealing . . 4. open 5. frank
knitting . . 12. garter stitch
of Mars . . 9. palmistry
spoken . . 15. straightforward
Plains (pert to) . . .
Arctic . . 6. tundra
Europe . . 6. steppe
Florida . . 7. savanna (savannah)
Italy . . 8. campagna
Russia . . 6. steppe, tundra
S African . . 6. pampas
Sp American . . 4. vega 5. llano 6. salada
(salt-covered)
Plains Indians . . . 6. Kiowan, Siouan
7. Caddoan 10. Algonquian,
Athapascan, Uto-Aztecan
plainsman . . . 6. cowboy 7. llanero
8. herdsman
Plains of Abraham . . . 10. Quebec City

plaint . . . 6. bewail, lament 9. complaint
11. lamentation
plaintiff . . . 4. suer 6. orator 7. accuser
8. claimant, libelant (libellant)
10. complainer 11. complainant
plaintive . . . 3. sad 5. cross 7. elegiac,
fretful, peevish, pettish, wailful, wistful
8. mournful, petulant, repining
9. lamenting, sorrowful 10. melancholy
11. complaining 12. discontented
plait . . . 4. fold, hair, knit, lace, plat
5. braid, pleat, weave 6. pleach, wimple
9. corrugate, interlace 10. interweave
plaited . . . 5. Milan (straw) 6. folded,
kilted, sennit (palm leaves) 8. pleached
10. interlaced 11. intertwined
plan . . . 3. map, way 4. form, idea, line,
plat, plot 5. chart, draft, ettle, frame,
setup 6. design, devise, intend, layout,
method, scheme 7. arrange, diagram,
outline, pattern, project 8. engineer,
strategy 9. calculate, procedure
11. arrangement, contemplate,
preconceive, premeditate
plan (pert to) . . .
architecture . . 5. draft, épure
frustrator of . . 7. marplot
preliminary . . 4. idea 6. map out
8. proposal
secretly . . 4. plot 7. connive 8. conspire
planate . . . 5. plane 9. flattened
plancher . . . 3. bed 5. board (occult), floor,
plank 6. pallet 8. planking, platform
plancier . . . 6. soffit 7. cornice
plandok . . . 9. mouse deer
plane . . . 3. fly 4. even, flat, ramp, scar, tool
5. level 6. degree, smooth 7. jointer,
surface 8. airplane 10. smoothness
plane (pert to) . . .
block . . 5. stock
boundary . . 9. perimeter
four-angled . . 6. square 7. rhombus
8. tetragon 10. quadrangle
handle . . 4. tote (bench plane)
inclined . . 4. ramp 5. chute
iron . . 5. blade
kind . . 3. mig 5. stuka 6. router
measure . . 10. planimeter
smoothing, chamfering . . 5. howel
tree . . 6. chinar (Orient) 8. Platanus
type . . 5. bench, block, stock 6. trowel
7. jointer, routing
planet . . . 4. Mars, star 5. Earth, Pluto,
Venus 6. Saturn, Uranus 7. Jupiter,
Mercury, Neptune 8. wanderer
planet (pert to) . . .
astrology . . 9. alfridary
brightest . . 5. Venus
cone . . 8. strobile
course . . 5. orbit
minor . . 9. satellite
nearest sun . . 7. Mercury
orbit . . 7. ellipse
red . . 4. Mars
remotest . . 5. Pluto (1930)
resembling . . 8. asteroid
ringed . . 6. Saturn
satellite . . 4. moon
shadow . . 5. umbra
small . . 8. asteroid
sphere . . 6. oblate

planet (solar system) **by size** . . . 7. Jupiter 6. Saturn 7. Neptune 6. Uranus 5. Earth, Venus, Pluto 4. Mars 7. Mercury

planetarium . . . 5. Zeiss 6. orrery

planetary . . . 7. earthly, erratic 9. celestial, wandering, worldwide

planetology (study of) . . . 7. planets 10. satellites

plangor . . . 4. wail 11. lamentation

planisphere . . . 7. sextant 9. astrolabe

plank . . . 3. sny 4. deal, slab 5. board, shole, stone 6. timber 7. pay down 8. planking 10. gravestone

plank down . . . 3. pay 7. advance, deposit

planner . . . 8. designer, engineer, gardener 9. architect, projector

plant . . . 3. fix, sow, spy 4. ache, bury, herb, seed, trap 5. cache, decoy, shrub 6. clover 7. falsify 8. colonize, workshop 9. deception, detective, equipment, vegetable

plant (pert to) . . .
abnormal environs . . 4. ecad
adjustment . . 6. ecesis
air . . 8. epiphyte
appendage . . 7. stipula
biggest . . 10. Aspidistra
body . . 6. cormus 7. thallus
bud . . 4. cion 5. scion
climbing . . 4. vine 5. liana
coloring matter . . 11. chlorophyll
crossbred . . 6. hybrid
cross-fertilization . . 9. phytogamy
disease . . 4. gall, rust, smut 5. ergot 7. blister 8. ramentum
embryo . . 8. plantule
enchantment-proof . . 7. haemony (Milton's Comus)
flowerless . . 4. fern 6. lichen 9. cryptogam 11. Cryptogamia (opp of phanerogam)
growing on rock . . 6. lichen
growing on sea bottom . . 6. enalid
growing wild . . 9. agrestial
history . . 12. phytogenesis
legendary, forgetfulness . . 5. lotus
male . . 3. mas
mosslike . . 6. orpine
mushroom type . . 6. fungus
native . . 8. indigene
orifice . . 5. stoma
pigment lacking . . 6. albino
poisonous . . 4. atis 6. datura 7. amanita 8. oleander
poisonous to cattle . . 4. loco 8. locoweed
pore . . 8. lenticel
round-leaved . . 9. pennywort
science of . . 6. botany
seedless . . 6. agamic
stem, stalk . . 4. bine 5. haulm 6. caulis
tequila-yielding . . 5. agave
tissue . . 7. tapetum
without chlorophyll . . chlorophyll 6. albino
without petals . . 9. apetulous
woody . . 6. xyloid

plant (type of) . . .
aconite . . 4. bikh
agave, century plant . . 4. aloe, pita 9. amaryllis
ammoniac . . 5. oshac

anise . . 4. dill
aquatic . . 6. sugamo 7. frogbit 8. plankton
aromatic . . 4. mint, nard 5. basil, tansy, thyme 8. tarragon
arum . . 4. sago 6. starch 9. arrowroot
aster family . . 5. daisy 8. fleabane
bitter . . 3. rue
bitter vetch . . 3. ers
box . . 5. Buxus 7. boxwood
broom . . 5. spart 6. Canary 7. genista
bryophytic . . 4. moss
burdock . . 5. elite 8. Xanthium
burning bush . . 5. wahoo
butter-and-eggs . . 8. ranstead
cactus . . 5. dildo 6. cereus, chaute, mescal 7. saguaro 9. xerophyte
century . . 4. aloe 5. agave 6. maguey
dill . . 4. anet
evergreen . . 3. ivy 5. holly 6. laurel 8. conifers 9. mistletoe
everlasting . . 6. orpine 11. live-forever
furze . . 4. ulex 5. gorse
garlic (wild) . . 4. moly
leguminous . . 3. pea 4. bean 6. Cassia, clover, lentil
lilaceous . . 4. aloe, iris, leek 5. lotus, onion, tulip, yucca
linen . . 4. flax
medicinal . . 4. alem, aloe 5. anise, wahoo 6. arnica, cacoon, catnip, ipecac 7. aconite, boneset, gentian, lobelia, rhatany 8. camomile
pea family . . 7. Cytisus
perennial . . 4. Geum 5. avens 10. sneezewort
poisonous . . 6. datura 8. oleander
poisonous to cattle . . 8. locoweed
poisonous to fowl . . 7. henbane
prickly, thorny . . 5. brier 6. cactus, nettle, teasel 7. thistle
satinpod (transparent) . . 7. honesty
soap . . 5. amole
tapioca . . 7. cassava
thorny . . see *prickly* 6. fatsia
trifoliate . . 6. clover 8. shamrock

plant, typical of . . .
Africa . . 5. argel (arghel)
Alps . . 9. edelweiss
Arabia . . 3. kat (stimulant)
Australia . . 5. Hakes, lilac 6. Correa 7. columba, fuchsia 8. Rutaceae
China . . 5. ramie
Egypt . . 5. anise, cumin 7. aniseed 8. nepenthe
Hawaii . . 5. olona
Japan . . 3. tea 5. acuba 6. quince 7. cydonia 8. japonica
Japan (vine) . . 8. Bignonia 14. trumpet creeper
Mexico . . 4. chia 5. datil 6. salvia 9. sabadilla
Peru . . 3. oca 7. rhatany
Philippines . . 4. alem (Med) 6. agamid
Spain . . 3. aji 6. pepper 8. Capsicum
Syria . . 5. cumin
tropical vine . . 8. redwithe 10. tillandsia
tropics . . 4. arum, palm, taro 5. agave, zamia 7. dasheen, hamelia 8. mangrove

plantain . . . 6. banana

plantation pines . . . 7. pinetum

plantation trees ... 4. holt 6. forest
7. nopalry (cactus), orchard
planters, Govt of ... 11. plantocracy
plantigrade mammal ... 5. panda
plaque ... 5. medal, patch 6. brooch,
tablet 8. ornament, platelet (Anat)
plash ... 4. plop, pool 5. swash 6. puddle,
ripple, splash
plasm ... 4. mold 6. matrix
plasma ... 4. cell, whey 5. blood (fluid)
10. protoplasm
plaster ... 4. teer 5. gesso, grout, salve
6. gypsum, parget, stucco 8. adhesive,
poultice 9. inebriate
plastered ... 5. drunk 7. crocked, smeared
8. mortared
plasterer ... 5. mason
plaster of Paris ... 5. gesso 6. gypsum
15. calcium sulphate
plastic ... 3. pug 5. gesso, vinyl 6. slurry
7. ductile, fictile, pliable, viscose
8. creative 9. compliant, formative,
teachable 14. impressionable
plastic, commercial ... 6. Lucite
7. Formica 8. Bakelite, Vinylite
9. Plexiglas
plasty (pert to) ...
  comb form .. 7. molding
  eyelid .. 14. blepharoplasty
  face lift .. 13. rhytidoplasty
  nose .. 11. rhinoplasty
platanist ... 4. fish, susu
plate ... 3. gib 4. disc, dish, shoe (horse)
5. paten 6. lamina, patera 7. coating,
denture, overlay 9. bookplate,
engraving 10. receptacle
plate (pert to) ...
  armor .. 6. cuisse (cuish)
  battery .. 4. grid
  bone (Anat) .. 7. scapula
  cooking .. 4. grid
  culture .. 8. bacteria
  Eccl .. 5. paten 6. patina
  graduated .. 4. dial
  holder .. 8. cassette
  horny .. 6. scute
  horse .. 6. plater
  insect (bony) .. 6. scutum
  mark .. 8. hallmark 9. engraving
  numbered .. 4. disc
  of glass .. 5. slide
  perforated metal .. 3. dod
  ship-shaped .. 3. nef
plateau ... 4. dish, mesa, puna 5. plain
6. plaque, salver 9. tableland
platform ... 3. map 4. dais, deck, k'ang,
plan 5. arena, chart, plank, stage
6. lissom, lyceum, podium, policy,
pulpit, scheme 7. estrade, outline,
rostrum, soapbox, tribune 8. hustings
9. bandstand 14. public speaking
platform (pert to) ...
  fort .. 8. barbette
  gun .. 11. emplacement
  mining .. 6. sollar (soller)

  nautical .. 7. foretop, maintop
  9. gangplank
  scaffold (funeral) .. 10. catafalque
  wheeled .. 5. float
platic (Astrol) ... 8. not exact 9. imperfect
plating ... 5. armor 6. lamina 7. shoeing
platinum wire ... 4. oese
platitude ... 6. cliché, old hat, truism
7. bromide 8. banality 9. staleness,
triteness 11. commonplace
15. commonplaceness
Plato (pert to) ...
  famed for .. 9. Dialogues 10. philosophy
  founder of .. 7. Academe, academy
  name, real .. 10. Aristocles
  pupil of .. 8. Socrates
platoid ... 4. flat 5. broad
Platonic (pert to) ...
  idea .. 5. eidos
  love .. 4. pure 5. ideal 6. chaste
  8. virtuous 10. idealistic
  11. comradeship
  philosophy .. 8. idealism 9. Platonism
  11. theoretical
  solids .. 10. hexahedron, octahedron
  11. icosahedron, tetrahedron
  12. dodecahedron
platoon ... 3. set 4. unit 5. squad
7. company, coterie 11. subdivision
platoon school ... 4. Gary (Ind)
platter ... 4. dish, lanx 5. grail, plate
6. record 9. scutellum
platter-shaped ... 10. scutellate
platyfish ... 8. moonfish
platypus ... 8. duckbill
plaudit ... 5. cheer, éclat 6. encore
8. applause, approval, clapping,
encomium 10. plaudation
11. acclamation, approbation
plausible ... 8. credible, probable,
specious 10. applausive, believable,
ostensible, plauditory, reasonable
11. conceivable
plausible excuse ... 5. alibi
play ... 3. act, fun, toy 4. game, jest,
romp 5. dally, drama, enact, feign,
sport, wager 6. affect, frolic 7. disport,
operate, pretend 9. amusement,
diversion, melodrama, pantomime
10. recreation 11. impersonate
13. entertainment
play (pert to) ...
  exhibit a .. 5. stage
  for time .. 5. stall
  house .. 5. movie 6. cinema 7. theater
  9. dollhouse
  musical .. 5. opera 8. burletta, operetta
  outline .. 8. scenario
  part .. 4. role 7. prelude 8. epilogue,
  epitasis, prologue
  pranks .. 4. haze
  silent .. 9. pantomime
  story .. 8. scenario
  stupid .. 5. boner
  the bagpipe .. 5. skirl 6. doodle
  the buffoon .. 5. droll
  the coquette .. 5. flirt
  tricks .. 4. hoax, shab
  truant .. 5. miche
  unskillfully .. 5. strum
  upon words .. 3. pun 11. paronomasia

playa . . . 5. beach, shore 7. salt pan
playboy . . . 4. fool 5. clown, cutup
7. buffoon, reveler 8. carouser
10. merrymaker 12. Jack of Trumps
(Spoilfive)
player . . . 3. dub 4. star 5. actor, idler,
piper 7. gambler, trifler 8. gamester,
musician, stroller, thespian 9. frolicker,
performer 11. barnstormer
player on words . . . 7. punster
playful . . . 3. gay 6. lusory 7. jocular
8. humorous, playsome, sportive
9. facetious, kittenish 11. mischievous
playing cards . . . 4. deck, pack 6. tarots
playlet . . . 4. skit 9. short play
plaything . . . 3. die, toy 4. dupe 6. bauble
7. cat's-paw
plea . . . 4. suit 5. claim 6. abater, appeal,
excuse, prayer 7. apology, defense,
pretext 8. argument, entreaty, pretense
10. advocation, allegation 13. nolo
contendre
plead . . . 3. beg, sue 5. argue 6. adduce,
allege 7. entreat, implore
plead (for) . . . 7. entreat, justify, solicit
10. supplicate
pleader . . . 4. suer 6. lawyer 8. advocate
9. entreater, justifier 11. intercessor
pleading . . . 4. oyer 8. advocacy,
demurrer, entreaty 9. imploring,
objection 10. litigation 12. intercession,
supplication
pleasant . . . 3. fun, gay 4. nice 5. merry,
sweet 6. genial 7. affable, amusing,
leesome, winsome 8. cheerful, friendly,
humorous, pleasing, sportive
9. agreeable, diverting, laughable,
sprightly
pleasant (pert to) . . .
manners . . 9. amenities
sound . . 6. dulcet 8. euphonic
9. melodious 10. harmonious
to peruse . . 8. readable
weather . . 4. fair, fine 6. bright 8. rainless
9. cloudless
please . . . 4. like, suit 5. fancy 6. arride
7. appease, content, delight, gratify,
indulge, placate, satisfy 9. vouchsafe
pleased . . . 4. fain, game, glad 5. happy
9. contented, gratified
pleasing . . . 4. cool, lief, nice 5. sooth
6. comely, eesome, savory 7. amiable,
roseate, welcome 8. pleasant
9. agreeable, desirable 10. delectable
11. pleasureful
pleasurable . . . 7. hedonic 8. pleasant
10. gratifying
pleasure . . . 3. joy 4. gree, will, wish
5. mirth, sport 6. choice, gaiety
7. delight, purpose 8. gladness,
hedonism, hilarity 9. amusement,
diversion, enjoyment, happiness,
merriment 11. delectation
12. satisfaction 13. gratification
pleasure (pert to) . . .
god . . 3. Bes
ground . . 4. park 9. pleasance
pert to . . 7. hedonic
philosophy . . 8. Hedonism
seeker . . 5. sport 7. epicure, playboy
8. hedonist

pleat . . . 4. fold 5. braid, plait
pleater . . . 8. plicator
plebeian . . . 4. pleb (Rom) 6. common,
vulgar 7. ignoble, ill-bred, lowborn
8. ordinary
plebiscite . . . 4. vote 6. decree
10. referendum
pleck . . . 4. plot (ground), spot 5. speck,
stain 9. enclosure
plectrum . . . 4. pick 5. uvula 6. tongue
7. malleus 8. plectron
pledge . . . 3. bet, vas, vow 4. bond,
gage, gate, oath, pawn, seal, wage
5. swear, toast, troth 6. engage, parole,
plight 7. chattel, earnest, promise
8. guaranty, mortgage, obligate,
security 9. assurance 10. collateral
11. impignorate
pledget . . . 4. swab 8. compress
Pleiad (pert to) . . .
Alexandria . . 10. Seven Poets
French . . 10. The Pléiade
lost Pleiad . . 6. Merope 7. Electra
philosophical (Gr) . . 12. Seven Wise
Men
Pleiades (pert to) . . .
Seven Daughters of Atlas . . 10. Atlantides
star . . 4. Maia 7. Sterope 8. Asterope
star cluster . . 8. in Taurus (Constellation)
plenary . . . 4. full 5. great 6. entire
7. perfect 8. absolute, complete
9. unlimited 11. unqualified
plenipotentiary . . . 5. envoy 8. diplomat,
minister 10. ambassador
plenteous . . . 6. plenty 7. copious, fertile,
liberal 8. abundant, fruitful, generous
9. bounteous, bountiful, plentiful
10. productive
plentiful . . . 4. full, rich, rife 5. ample
6. lavish 7. copious, fertile, liberal,
opulent, profuse 9. abounding,
bounteous, bountiful 13. superabundant
plentifully . . . 6. galore 9. abounding,
abundance
plenty . . . 4. enow 6. enough, galore,
uberty 8. fullness 9. abundance,
plenitude 10. perfection 11. copiousness
12. completeness, considerable
14. superabundance
plenum . . . 5. space 8. assembly, fullness
(of space) (opp of vacuum)
pleon . . . 6. telson 7. abdomen
pleonasm . . . 8. fullness 10. redundancy
11. diffuseness, reiteration
plethora . . . 4. glut 6. excess 9. repletion
14. superabundance
plethoric . . . 6. turgid 8. inflated, overfull
9. bombastic 10. overloaded
plexiform . . . 4. rete 7. network
11. complicated
plexus . . . 4. rete 5. solar 7. network
pliable . . . 4. limp 6. limber, pliant,
supple 7. plastic 8. flexible, suitable
9. compliant, teachable
pliant . . . 7. bending, pliable, tensile,
willowy 8. flexible, workable, yielding
9. adaptable, compliant
plicate . . . 4. fold 5. pleat 6. folded
7. plaited
plight . . . 4. fold 5. braid, plait 6. status
7. embrace, promise 8. position

9. condition, situation (bad)
11. predicament

plinth ... 4. orlo 7. subbase

Pliosaurus (extinct) ... 7. reptile

plod ... 3. dig, mog 4. slog, toil, tore
6. drudge, trudge

plodder ... 3. fag 4. grub, hack 5. slave
6. drudge

plot ... 3. lot, map 4. acre, area, brew,
burn, pack, plan, plat 5. cabal, frame,
tract, trick 6. design, scheme, scorch,
secret 7. diagram, project 8. conspire,
intrigue 10. conspiracy, prearrange
11. machination

plot (of ground) ... 3. lot 4. acre, area,
plat 5. grave, tract 7. terrain

Plotinus ... 11. philosopher (Alexandrian
School)

plotted ... 7. charted, hatched 8. lineated
9. conspired 10. delineated
11. prearranged

plotter ... 5. Haman 7. Jacobin, planner,
schemer 8. agitator 9. contriver
11. conspirator

ploughshare (plowshare) **part** ... 6. colter
(coulter)

plover ... 4. dupe 5. piper, sandy
7. lapwing 9. courtesan, sandpiper,
shorebird

plover (pert to) ...
crab .. 5. drome
crested .. 7. lapwing
egg .. 11. darning ball
genus .. 12. Charadriidae
Old World .. 8. dotterel, killdeer
page .. 6. dunlin 9. sandpiper
quail .. 13. plain wanderer
ring .. 5. pandy

plow ... 4. rove, till 5. break, miner,
scaut 6. furrow, turn up 7. break up
8. reinvest 9. cultivate

plow (pert to) ...
fish .. 3. ray
gang .. 6. oxgang 7. measure
light .. 10. Plow Monday 13. hoggler's
light
man .. 6. rustic 10. countryman,
husbandman
part .. 4. buck, chip, hale 5. share, slade,
stilt 6. clevis, colter
type .. 5. sulky 8. mole plow

plowed land ... 5. arada, arado

pluck ... 3. pug, rob, tug 4. grab, jerk,
pick, pull 5. nerve, spunk, steal, strip,
strum 6. avulse, divest, fleece, gather,
twitch 7. courage, harvest, pick off,
plunder, strip of, swindle 10. resolution,
straighten (wool)

plucky ... 4. game 5. brave, nervy
6. spunky, sticky 8. adhesive, resolute,
spirited 11. courageous

plug ... 3. tap, top 4. blow, bung
5. horse, knock, punch, shoot, spile,
wedge 7. commend, hydrant, stopper,
stopple, tobacco 9. persevere, publicity,
publicize 12. commendation

plug (pert to) ...
board .. 11. switchboard
cannon muzzle .. 7. tampion (tampeon,
tampoon)
dentistry .. 7. filling

hat .. 4. tile 5. gibus 6. topper
medical .. 4. clot 6. fibrin, tampon
7. embolus
slender .. 5. spill
up .. 4. calk (caulk)

plum ... 5. drupe, money, prune 6. Prunus
8. dividend 9. good thing, sugarplum

plum (pert to) ...
beetle .. 8. curculio
bitter .. 4. sloe
California (wild) .. 5. islay
coco .. 5. icaco
England .. 6. damson
Europe .. 7. bullace
hybrid .. 7. plumcot
India .. 7. hog plum
Java .. 7. jambool (jambul) 8. jambolan
type .. 4. gage 6. damson 9. greengage,
wild-goose 11. Reine Claude

plumage ... 4. down 6. hackle 7. floccus
(first down) 8. feathers, ornament

plumb ... 4. seal, true 5. delve, gauge,
sound, utter 6. adjust, fathom, sinker,
weight (lead) 7. examine, measure,
plummet 8. absolute, complete, vertical
9. downright 13. perpendicular

plumbago ... 8. leadwork

plumbog ... 9. raspberry (dwarf)

plumcot ... 6. hybrid 11. plum apricot

plume ... 5. crest, egret, preen, pride
6. plumet 7. feather, panache
8. decorate, plumelet

plummet ... 4. dive, drop, fall, lead, plop,
test 5. pitch, sound, swoop 6. fathom,
plunge, weight 9. criterion

plump ... 3. fat 4. drop, dull, fall, plop,
rude, sink, tidy 5. blunt, buxom, flock,
fubsy, obese 6. chubby, dilate, fatten,
flatly 7. distend 8. blurt out, straight
9. corpulent, filled out 10. vertically
11. well-rounded

plumpness of person ... 9. stoutness
10. embonpoint

plunder ... 3. rob 4. boot, loot, pelf,
prey, raid, rape, sack 5. booty, poach,
raven, reave, rifle, strip 6. boodle,
fleece, maraud, profit, rapine, ravage,
spoils 7. despoil, pillage 8. spoliate
9. depredate

plundered ... 4. reft 6. looted, robbed

plunderer ... 5. thief 6. looter, pirate,
preyer, raider, robber 7. spoiler, stealer
8. pillager 10. freebooter

plunge ... 3. bet, dip 4. dash, dive,
fall, pool, risk, sink 5. douse, drive,
lunge, plumb, souse 6. gamble,
thrust 7. baptize, immerse 8. flounder
9. gravitate, overwhelm, speculate

plunge (into) ... 4. clap, dive 5. begin
7. immerge, immerse 9. set to work,
undertake

plunger ... 5. diver 6. risker 7. gambler
10. speculator

plunk ... 4. blow, drop, pull, push, sink,
thud 5. drive, plump, strum, throw
7. a dollar 10. play truant

plurality ... 8. majority 9. multitude
11. greater part, large number

plural marriage ... 8. polygamy

Plutarch (Gr) ... 10. biographer

Pluto (pert to) ...

Astron.. 6. planet (most remote)
god of.. 10. lower world
Greek name.. 5. Hades
kingdom.. 5. Hades
Roman name.. 3. Dis 5. Orcus
wife.. 10. Proserpina
plutocracy... 13. rule by wealthy
17. dominion of the rich
Plutus (pert to)...
god of.. 6. wealth
son of.. 6. lesion 7. Demeter
pluvia... 4. rain 9. pluviosus
pluviometer, pluvioscope... 9. rain
gauge
pluvious... 5. rainy 7. pluvial
ply... 4. bend, fold, mold, sail, urge
5. exert, plait, wield 6. employ, handle,
lamina 8. navigate 9. importune,
thickness
pneuma... 4. soul 5. neume 6. breath,
spirit 9. breathing, life force, vital soul
pneumology (science of)... 5. lungs
17. respiratory organs
poach... 3. mix, ram 4. poke, push,
sock, stir 5. drive, force, shirr (egg),
steal 6. thrust 7. trample 8. encroach,
trespass
poacher... 7. lurcher, stalker, widgeon
Poblacht... 8. Republic
Pocahontas (pert to)...
father.. 8. Powhatan (Chief)
husband.. 9. John Rolfe
Indian title.. 8. Princess
name.. 12. Rebecca Rolfe
rescuer of.. 9. John Smith (Capt)
pocket... 3. bag, bin, cly, fob, sac
4. poke, sack, take 5. money, pouch,
purse 6. cavity, hollow 7. conceal,
confine, enclose 8. envelope
pocketbook... 3. bag, lil 5. pouch,
purse 6. income, wallet 8. notebook
9. resources
pod... 3. bag, kid, sac 4. aril, boll 5. belly,
carob, chili, pouch, shuck 6. legume
poem... 3. dit, lay, ode 4. Edda, epic,
epos, hymn, rune, saga 5. elegy,
epode, idyll, psalm, verse 6. ballad
(ballade), jingle, rondel (roundelle),
sonnet 7. eclogue, erotics, rondeau
8. limerick, rondelet 9. dithyramb
10. villanelle 11. acatalectic
poem (pert to)...
bad.. 8. doggerel
division.. 5. canto, epode, verse
6. stanza 7. refrain
eight lines.. 7. triolet
foot.. 6. iambic 7. anapest, pyrrhic
imitation.. 6. parody
Japanese.. 5. haiku
line.. 5. stich 6. octave, septet, sestet,
tercet 7. couplet, triplet 8. cinquain,
quatrain 11. alexandrine
meter.. 6. iambic 8. spondaic, trochaic
9. dactyllic, hexameter 10. anaepestic
(anapestic), pentameter
ref to.. 5. meter, rhyme, verse
7. cadence, helicon 8. feminine,
scansion 9. masculine
religious.. 4. hymn 5. psalm
rhythmic break.. 7. caesura
satirical.. 3. dit 6. parody

poem, famed...
Homer.. 5. Iliad 7. Odyssey
Khayyám.. 8. Rubáiyát
Milton.. 12. Paradise Lost
Ovid.. 13. Metamorphoses
Poe.. 8. The Raven
Poem in Marble.. 8. Taj Mahal
poem of declaration.. 8. Invictus
Shakespeare.. 7. Macbeth
Spenser.. 12. Faerie Queene
poems... 5. poesy, sylva 6. poetry
poet... 4. bard 5. odist, rimer 6. lyrist
7. dreamer 8. laureate 9. poetaster,
rhymester, versifier
poetic word... 3. ere, 'tis 4. ne'er, 'twas
5. 'twere, 'twixt
Poet Laureate (a few)... 6. Dryden
7. Spenser 8. Tennyson 9. Ben Jonson,
Masefield 10. Wordsworth
poetry (pert to)...
Muse of.. 5. Erato 6. Thalia 8. Calliope
Norse god of.. 5. Bragi
School of (anc).. 9. Parnassus
type.. 4. epic 5. lyric 6. ballad 8. didactic
9. free verse, narrative 10. blank verse
pogoniate... 7. bearded
pogonip... 3. fog (Sierras)
pogonology (study of)... 6. beards
pogrom... 8. massacre
poi... 4. food, taro, then (Mus)
poignant... 4. keen 5. acute 6. biting,
bitter 7. cutting, pungent
point... 3. aim, dot, jab, jot, neb, nib, pin
4. apex, barb, cape, gaff, gist, node,
peak, stop, tack 5. focus, prong, quill,
spike 6. bodkin, direct, needle, period,
summit, zenith 7. apicula, punctum
10. breakwater, promontory
point (pert to)...
antler, branch.. 4. snag
astronomy.. 5. apsis 6. syzygy
central, pivotal.. 4. crux
farthest from earth.. 6. apogee
focal.. 9. epicenter
geometry.. 6. acnode 7. crunode
highest.. 4. acme, apex, peak 6. summit,
zenith 8. meridian, pinnacle
lace.. 10. petit point 11. needlepoint
law.. 3. res 5. locus
lowest.. 5. nadir 6. bottom
mathematics.. 5. unode
nearest earth.. 7. perigee
of contact.. 5. focus
of debate.. 5. issue, topic
of honor.. 7. scruple
of view.. 5. angle, slant 8. attitude
opposite zenith.. 5. nadir
reference to.. 6. apical
salient.. 7. feature
starting, golf.. 3. tee
strong.. 5. forte
utmost.. 7. extreme
weak.. 4. flaw 5. fault 6. foible
pointed... 5. aimed, noded, piked,
sharp, terse 6. acute, marked, peaked
7. angular, concise, conical 8. aculeate,
piercing, poignant, spicated, stinging
9. acuminate, pertinate, spiculate
10. emphasized 11. conspicuous,
significant 12. epigrammatic
pointed (pert to)...

architecture .. 5. ogive 6. Gothic
end .. 4. cusp
fox .. 3. red
instrument .. 3. awl, gad 4. prod
  6. gimlet, stylet
rod .. 4. goad
pointer ... 3. arm, dog, tip 4. sign 5. index
  6. fescue, gnomon
pointless ... 4. dull 5. blunt, inane, silly,
  vapid 6. stupid 7. insipid, witless
poise ... 6. aplomb 7. balance, ballast
  8. carriage 9. composure, equipoise,
  stability
poison (pert to) ...
  arrow .. 4. inee, upas 5. urari 6. curare
  (curari)
  deadly .. 4. bane, upas 5. arrow
    7. arsenic, cyanide, hemlock
    10. strychnine
  study of .. 10. toxicology
poissarde ... 8. fishwife, low woman
poisson ... 4. fish
poisson bleu ... 7. catfish 8. bluefish,
  grayling
poitrel ... 5. armor, plate 9. stomacher
  11. breastplate
poke ... 3. bag, jab, jog, pry 4. bore,
  goad, prod, root, sack 5. grope, nudge,
  probe, purse 6. dawdle, potter, search,
  thrust, wallet 7. project, tobacco
poker ... 3. rod 6. beadle 7. bugbear,
  pochard 9. hobgoblin
poker (pert to) ...
  face .. 8. immobile
  form of .. 4. draw, stud
  painting .. 10. pyrography
  picture .. 11. pyrogravure
  stake .. 3. pot 4. ante 6. roodle
poky, pokey .. 3. dull, mean, slow
  5. dowdy, small 6. bonnet, narrow,
  shabby 7. cramped, tedious
Poland ... see also *Polish*
  ancestors .. 5. Lakha, Slavs
  ancient name .. 7. Polonia
  capital .. 6. Warsaw
  city .. 4. Lodz 6. Gdynia, Krakow, Lublin
  river .. 7. Dnieper, Vistula
Poland China ... 5. swine
polar ... 5. curve 6. Arctic 7. guiding
  8. opposite 9. Antarctic, magnetism
Polar base (exploration) ... 4. Etah
Polaris ... 5. Alpha 9. North Star
  11. guiding star
Polaroid inventor ... 4. Land
pole ... 3. bar, car, pew, poy, rod, xat
  4. axle, beam, mast, prop, spar 5. shaft,
  sprit, staff, stool, totem
pole (pert to) ...
  bad end .. 7. raw deal
  burn .. 7. disease (tobacco)
  cat .. 5. skunk, zoril 6. ferret, musang
    7. fitchew 8. Putorius 9. scoundrel
  cat weed .. 12. skunk cabbage
  electric .. 5. enode, pitch 7. cathode
    8. magnetic 9. electrode
  Gaelic .. 5. caber
  head .. 7. tadpole
  Spanish .. 4. pale, palo
  star .. 5. guide 7. polaris 8. lodestar
    9. North Star 13. l'Etoile du Nord
  vehicle .. 4. cope, crab 5. thill

well .. 5. sweep
polemic ... 9. disputant 11. contentious
  13. argumentative, controversial
polenta ... 8. porridge
poles of cold ... 7. Siberia (Verkhoyansk)
  12. Grinnell Land (Fort Conger)
police (pert to) ...
  badge .. 6. buzzer, shield
  club .. 8. spontoon
  man .. 3. cop 5. guard 6. bobbie, copper,
    peeler, Ranger 7. officer, sheriff, trooper
    9. constable, detective, N W Mounted
    11. carabinière (carabineer)
  station .. 5. thana 6. lockup 8. bargello
policy ... 3. wit 4. plan 6. wisdom
  8. regulate, sagacity 9. insurance
  10. government, management,
  shrewdness 11. contrivance
  13. judiciousness 14. administration
policy of segregation ... 9. apartheid
polish ... 3. rub 4. buff 5. glaze, gloss,
  rabat, scour, shine 6. finish, luster,
  smooth 7. burnish, culture, furbish
  8. brighten, civilize, elegance, lapidate,
  levigate, urbanity 10. refinement
Polish (pert to) ...
  Bull .. 13. Constellation
  cake .. 4. baba
  carriage .. 7. britska
  composer, pianist .. 6. Chopin
    10. Paderewski
  dance .. 7. mazurka 9. polonaise
    11. cracovienne (krakowiak)
  nobleman .. 7. starost
  premier .. 10. Paderewski (pianist)
  president (1st) .. 10. Philsudski
  scientist .. 5. Curie (Madame)
polishing material ... 5. emery, rabat,
  rouge 6. pumice 11. rottenstone
polite ... 4. neat, tidy 5. civil, suave,
  urban 6. gentle, smooth, urbane
  7. gallant, genteel, refined 8. polished
  9. courteous, debonaire (debonair,
  debonnaire) 10. cultivated
  11. complaisant
politesse ... 10. politeness (formal)
  11. cleanliness, courtliness
  12. decorousness
politic ... 4. wary 7. cunning, tactful
  8. cautious, discreet 9. judicious,
  political, politique, provident
  10. diplomatic
political (pert to) ...
  boss .. 7. cacique
  district .. 4. city, ward 5. State 6. canton,
    county, parish 7. borough 10. palatinate
  economy .. 9. economics
  faction .. 4. bloc, ring 5. junta, party
    7. machine
  hanger-on .. 6. heeler 10. ward heeler
  influence .. 5. lobby, rally 6. caucus
  party (old) .. 4. Tory, Whig 9. Politique
politician ... 7. schemer 9. intriguer,
  statesman 11. gerrymander
  12. politicaster
politics ... 7. cunning 8. scheming
  10. government, profession 15. partisan
  rivalry 16. political affairs
Polizei ... 9. the police
poll ... 3. cut, tax 4. clip, head, roll,
  vote 5. shear, skull 6. fleece, survey

7. despoil 8. election, schedule
pollan . . . 9. whitefish
polled . . . 5. shorn 6. shaved 8. hornless
pollen . . . 4. seed 6. anther 8. fine dust
 11. microspores 13. fertilization
pollen brush (bee's) . . . 5. scopa
pollenization . . . 5. xenia 13. fertilization
pollent . . . 6. strong 8. powerful
poller . . . 5. voter 6. barber 9. plunderer
 11. extortioner, taxgatherer
pollex . . . 5. thumb 11. bastard wing
 (bird) 13. dactylopodite
pollex impression . . . 10. thumbprint
polliwog . . . 7. tadpole
pollute . . . 4. soil 5. taint 6. befoul, defile,
 ravish 7. corrupt, debauch, profane
 9. desecrate, inebriate 11. contaminate
pollution . . . 8. impurity 9. infection
 10. corruption, defilement
 13. contamination
Pollux (pert to) . . .
 brother (twin) . . 6. Castor
 father . . 4. Zeus
 mother . . 6. Leda
 protector of . . 7. sailors
 star . . 13. Beta Geminorum
Polly's request . . . 7. cracker
Polonius . . . 8. courtier (Shaksp)
polony . . . 7. sausage
poltergeist (folklore) . . . 5. ghost 6. spirit
poltfoot . . . 8. clubfoot
poltroon . . . 4. idle, lazy 6. coward,
 craven, wretch 7. buffoon, dastard
 8. cowardly 9. dastardly 10. ne'er-do-
 well, scaramouch
polverine . . . 6. potash (of Levant)
 8. pearlash
polyandrium (Gr) . . . 8. cemetery
polyandry . . . 8. polygamy 14. plural
 husbands (Tibet)
polychromatic . . . 10. variegated
polyglot . . . 6. jargon 9. languages
 (confusion of) 10. dictionary
 11. philologist 21. Complutensian
 Polyglot (Bib)
polygon . . . 6. isagon 7. decagon,
 hexagon, nonagon, octagon
 8. heptagon 9. dodecagon
polygyny . . . 8. polygamy 11. plural wives
polyhedron . . . 5. solid 6. figure
 14. trisoctahedron 17. triakisoctahedron
polymny . . . 10. sacred song
Polynesia . . .
 native . . 5. Maori 6. Kanaka 8. Hawaiian
 10. Melanesian
 ocean . . 7. Pacific
 origin (probable) . . 7. Savaiki (Isl)
 South Sea Island group . . 5. Samoa
 6. Hawaii, Tahiti 7. Savaiki 10. New
 Zealand
Polynesian (pert to) . . .
 butterfly . . 2. io
 chestnut . . 4. rata
 cloth . . 4. tapa
 demon . . 4. atua
 dragon . . 3. ati
 goddess of volcanoes . . 4. Pele
 god of forests . . 4. Tane
 hero . . 4. Maui
 homeland (fabled) . . 7. Havaiki
 loincloth . . 5. pareu

 memorial . . 3. ahu
 oven . . 3. umu
 people . . 3. Ati
 social tradition . . 6. tattoo
 wages, reward . . 3. utu
polyp . . . 5. coral, Hydra, tumor 10. sea
 anemone 12. invertebrate
polyphone . . . 4. lute
polytropic . . . 9. versatile
pomade . . . 6. anoint 7. pomatum,
 unguent 8. ointment
pome . . . 4. pear 5. apple, fruit 6. quince
 11. pomegranate
pomelo . . . 8. shaddock 10. grapefruit
Pomerania (pert to) . . .
 animal . . 3. dog
 capital . . 7. Stettin
 formerly . . 5. duchy (Prussia)
 river . . 4. Oder
pomme de terre . . . 6. potato
Pomona . . . 4. city (Calif) 7. college,
 goddess (of fruit)
pomp . . . 5. pride, state 6. parade
 7. cortege, display, pageant 8. grandeur
 9. pageantry, spectacle 10. ceremonial
 11. ostentation 12. magnificence
pompano . . . 7. alewife
Pompeii, Italy (pert to) . . . 10. earthquake,
 excavation, Mt Vesuvius (site)
pompous . . . 5. budge 6. august,
 stilty 7. Podsnap (Dickens), stilted
 9. bombastic, grandiose
 11. ceremonious 12. high-sounding,
 ostentatious, stuffed shirt
Ponce de Leon (pert to) . . .
 discoverer of . . 7. Florida 15. Fountain
 of Youth
 famed as . . 8. explorer
 landing site, America . . 11. St Augustine
pond . . . 4. pool 5. ocean (humorous)
 6. lagoon 7. lakelet
pond (pert to) . . .
 apple . . 9. evergreen
 crow, hen . . 4. coot
 dogwood . . 10. buttonbush
 duck . . 7. mallard
 fish . . 7. sunfish
 frog . . 8. ranarium
 glass . . 8. aquarium
ponder . . . 4. mull, muse, pore 5. brood,
 opine, weigh 7. perpend, reflect
 8. appraise, cogitate, consider, evaluate,
 meditate, ruminate
ponderous . . . 4. dull, huge 5. bulky,
 heavy 7. weighty 8. ungainly
 9. important, momentous
 11. elephantine
pongee . . . 4. silk 6. tussah 8. shantung
poniard . . . 4. dirk, kill 5. sword 6. dagger,
 pierce
ponica . . . 8. gardener
pont . . . 5. ferry, float 6. bridge 7. caisson,
 pontoon 9. ferryboat
Pontiac . . . 4. city (Mich) 5. Chief (Ottawa
 Indian) 6. Indian
pontiff . . . 4. pope 6. bishop 8. pontifex
pony . . . 3. cab, nag 4. crib 5. glass, horse,
 pinto 6. bronco 7. Express (mail, 1860),
 piebald 8. Shetland 11. translation
pooch . . . 3. dog 5. pouch
pooka . . . 6. goblin 7. specter

pool ... 3. lin, pot 4. carr, fund, game, linn, mere, pond, tank, tarn 5. kitty, stake 6. cartel, lagoon, league, puddle 7. alberca, plashet 9. billiards, reservoir, resources 10. natatorium 11. aggregation

pool ball ... 3. cue 4. spot 6. ringer

poon tree ... 5. domba, keena

poor ... 3. bad 4. mean, thin 5. needy 6. feeble, humble, meager, paltry, shabby, sickly 7. hapless, unlucky 8. indigent, inferior 9. destitute, illogical, imperfect, infertile 10. unskillful (unskilful) 11. impecunious, unfavorable, unfortunate 12. impoverished, inauspicious, insufficient 14. unsatisfactory

poor (pert to) ...
creature .. 9. pilgarlic
joe .. 5. heron
John .. 3. cod 4. hake 8. mean fare
man's remedy .. 8. valerian
Richard .. 8. Saunders (Richard)
section of city .. 4. slum 6. ghetto 7. skid row 10. shantytown
soldier .. 9. friarbird

poorly ... 3. ill 5. badly 8. abjectly, meagerly, shabbily 10. indisposed 11. defectively 13. disparagingly

pop ... 3. bang, snap, soda 5. bulge, burst, crack 6. bubble 7. concert 8. beverage

popadam ... 5. water (fried) 10. popper cake

popdock ... 8. foxglove

pope ... 3. fin 4. ruff 6. bishop, puffin, shrike, weevil 8. beverage 9. bullfinch 14. painted bunting

Pope (pert to) ...
cathedral .. 7. Lateran
collar .. 5. orale
court officer .. 6. datary
crown .. 5. tiara 6. triple
first .. 5. Peter
headdress .. 5. miter (mitre)
name .. 4. Pius 5. Ratti 7. Gregory
palace .. 7. Vatican
scarf .. 5. fanon

Pope, Alexander (pert to) ...
essay .. 10. Essay on Man
poem .. 13. Rape of the Lock
satire .. 7. Dunciad
translation .. 5. Iliad 7. Odyssey

popeler ... 7. sea gull 9. spoonbill

popinac ... 8. huisache

popinjay ... 6. parrot

poplar ... 3. abele, alamo, aspen, bahan, white 10. cottonwood 12. balm of Gilead

poplar (pert to) ...
Arabic .. 5. bahan, garab
balsam .. 9. tacamahac
Fr black .. 4. liar 10. cottonwood
N. American .. 7. Populus 8. Lombardy
white .. 5. abele, bolle

poppy ... 3. maw 7. Papaver (opium), ponceau 8. foxglove

poppycock ... 3. rot 4. bosh 8. nonsense

populace ... 3. mob 4. mass 5. demos, plebs 6. people 11. inhabitants 12. common people

popular ... 3. lay, pop 5. cheap,

liked, usual 6. famous, simple, vulgar 7. crowded, demotic, secular 8. accepted, epidemic, favorite, populous 9. prevalent, well-known, well-liked 11. fashionable, proletarian 12. nontechnical

popular belief ... 4. lore 7. opinion 9. tradition 12. old wives' tale, superstition

popularity ... 4. fame 5. vogue 10. reputation 15. fashionableness

popular success ... 3. hit

population study ... 10. larithmics

porcelain ... 4. frit 5. china 6. kaolin 7. ramekin (mold)

porcelain (kind) ... 5. Spode 6. Sèvres 7. celadon, Dresden, Limoges 8. Haviland

porch ... 4. door, stoa 5. stoop 6. harbor, loggia 7. galilee, gallery, portico, veranda 8. entrance 9. colonnade

porcine animal ... 3. hog, pig, sow 5. shoat, swine 6. porker 7. peccary 8. babirusa (babiroussa) 9. razorback

porcupine (pert to) ...
anteater .. 7. echidna
Canada .. 5. urson 7. cawquaw
disease .. 10. ichthyosis
grass .. 5. stipa
species .. 6. rodent, tenrec (tendrac) 8. hedgehog, quill pig

pore ... 3. con 4. duct, gaze, vent 5. stare, stoma, study 6. ponder 7. eporose (without), opening, orifice, ostiole 8. lenticel

porgy ... 4. fish, scup 5. bream, pargo 6. pagrus, red tai

pork (pert to) ...
barrel .. 4. fund (Polit) 6. boodle
chop .. 7. griskin
fish .. 4. sisi

porker ... 3. hog, pig 5. swine, sword (obs)

porpoise ... 4. inia 6. seahog 7. dolphin, pellock 8. cetacean, Phocaena

porr ... 4. cram, kick, poke, push, stir 5. poker 6. thrust

porrect ... 6. tender 7. present

porridge ... 3. pob 4. pobs, samp 5. atole, brose, grout, gruel 6. cereal 7. oatmeal, polenta, pottage 9. stirabout

port ... 4. gate, left, mien, wine 5. armor, haven 6. harbor, portal 7. airport, bearing, opening, posture 8. carriage, demeanor, larboard, porthole, portside 10. deportment 11. destruction

portable ... 6. mobile 7. movable

portable altar ... 10. altar stone, superaltar (Hist)

portal ... 4. door, gate 5. porch 7. gateway 8. entrance 9. vestibule 12. porte-cochere

portcullis ... 3. bar 4. shut 5. herse 7. barrier, grating, lattice (Her) 13. fortification

Porte ... 12. Ottoman court (anc), Sublime Porte

porte-bonheur ... 5. charm 6. amulet

porte-cochere ... 5. porch (carriage) 7. gateway

portefeuille ... 9. portfolio

portend . . . 4. bode 5. augur 7. betoken,
predict, presage 8. forebode, foreshow,
foretell, prophecy 9. foretoken

portent . . . 4. omen, sign 6. marvel,
ostent 7. prodigy 11. forewarning

portentous . . . 4. dire 5. fatal, grave
6. solemn 7. fateful, ominous 8. sinister
9. monstrous, wonderful 10. impressive
13. extraordinary

porter . . . 3. ale 4. beer 5. hamal
(hammal), stout (drink) 6. bearer
7. carrier, janitor 9. attendant
10. doorkeeper

Porter's pseudonym . . . 6. O Henry

Portia (pert to) . . .
character (Merchant of Venice)..
7. heiress
husband.. 8. Bassanio
husband's friend.. 7. Antonio
maid.. 7. Nerissa

portico . . . 4. stoa 6. atrium, xystus (xyst)
7. pteroma, veranda 9. colonnade,
peristyle, vestibule

portion . . . 3. bit, cut, dab, lot 4. dole,
dose, dunt, fate, half, mete, part,
some 5. piece, share, whack 6. moiety,
parcel 7. section, segment 8. quantity
9. allotment, apportion, partition

portion (pert to) . . .
curve.. 3. arc 7. segment
detached.. 6. coupon
inheritance.. 7. legitim 9. dead's part
marriage.. 7. dowry
sectional.. 5. curve
widow's.. 5. dower

Portland (pert to) . . .
arrowroot, sago.. 4. arum
beds (Eng).. 11. Upper Oolite 13. Upper
Jurassic
city of.. 5. Maine 6. Oregon
stone.. 6. cement 8. concrete
vase.. 9. Barberini (Rom palace)
10. cameo glass

portmanteau . . . 3. bag 4. word (blended)
5. cloak 6. mantle, valise

portoise . . . 7. gunwale 8. portlast

Porto Rico . . . see *Puerto Rico*

portrait . . . 4. copy 5. image 7. picture
8. likeness, painting 10. similitude
11. description, portraiture
12. lifelikeness 14. representation

portrait on dollars . . .
fifty.. 5. Grant
five.. 7. Lincoln
five hundred.. 8. McKinley
five thousand.. 7. Madison
one.. 10. Washington
one hundred.. 8. Franklin
one hundred thousand.. 6. Wilson
one thousand.. 9. Cleveland
ten.. 8. Hamilton
ten thousand.. 5. Chase
twenty.. 7. Jackson
two.. 9. Jefferson

portray . . . 3. act 4. draw, form,
limn 5. enact, frame, image, paint
6. depict 7. fashion, picture 8. describe
9. delineate, represent

portrayal . . . 3. act 5. drama 7. process
8. portrait 9. depiction 11. delineation,
description

portreeve . . . 5. mayor 7. bailiff

Port Royal . . . 15. Cistercian abbey
(Versailles)

Portugal . . . see also *Portuguese*
bridge.. 7. Salazar
capital.. 6. Lisbon
city.. 5. Braga 6. Aveiro, Guarda, Oporto
7. Granada
island.. 6. Azores 7. Madeira 8. Principe
mountain.. 15. Serra da Estrella
peninsula.. 7. Iberian
port.. 6. Aveiro
province.. 3. Goa 5. Macao, Timor
9. Cape Verde 10. Mozambique
resort.. 7. Estoril
river.. 5. Tagus (Tajo)

Portuguese (pert to) . . .
author.. 9. de Lobeira
bird, fish.. 8. man-of-war
ceremonial (Inquisition).. 8. auto de fe
coin (gold).. 6. escudo 7. milreis (old)
lady.. 4. dona
legislature.. 6. Cortes 12. Cortes Geraes
money of account.. 4. reis
navigator.. 6. da Gama 8. Magellan
wine.. 5. porto

Portunus (Rom Relig) . . . 10. god of
gates

posada . . . 3. inn 5. hotel

posaune . . . 8. trombone 9. organ stop

posca . . . 5. drink (Hist)

pose . . . 3. put, sit 5. model 6. baffle,
puzzle, stance 7. nonplus, posture,
pretend, propose 8. attitude, position,
pretense, propound 9. postulate
11. affectation, impersonate

Poseidon (pert to) . . .
attributes.. 5. horse 7. dolphin, trident
cult site.. 7. Corinth
father.. 6. Cronus
god of.. 3. sea 6. waters
mother.. 4. Rhea
Roman name.. 7. Neptune
wife.. 10. Amphitrite

poser . . . 5. facer 6. puzzle 7. problem,
sticker 14. attitudinarian

posh . . . 5. smart 6. spruce 7. elegant
9. luxurious

position . . . 3. job, lie 4. pose, rank, seat,
site 5. coign (coigne), place, situs,
stand, state 6. manner, stance, ubiety
7. opinion, posture, premise 8. attitude,
location, prestige, proposal 9. viewpoint
11. affirmation, supposition

position (pert to) . . .
anchorlike.. 5. apeak
fencing.. 7. septime
finder (gun).. 13. triangulation
golf.. 6. stance
inescapable.. 7. impasse
of affairs.. 6. status
relative.. 8. standing
secure.. 7. footing
with no responsibility.. 8. sinecure

positive . . . 4. plus, sure 5. exact 6. actual,
thetic 7. certain 8. dogmatic, emphatic
9. assertive, convinced, downright
11. dictatorial

positive (pert to) . . .
charge (Elec).. 8. positron
evidence.. 7. constat

pole .. 5. anode

saying .. 6. dictum

school, criminology .. 10. Lombrosian (by Lombroso)

positivism ... 7. Comtism 9. certainty, dogmatism 10. confidence 11. materialism

posture ... 7. posture 11. arrangement, disposition 13. configuration

posnet ... 3. pot (3-footed) 8. saucepan

poss ... 4. beat, dash, push 5. drive, knock, pound, stamp 6. thrust

posse ... 5. crowd 6. throng 7. company 9. armed band 10. detachment (police)

possess ... 3. own 4. have, know, take 5. haunt 6. inform, occupy 7. bewitch, inhabit 8. convince, demonize, persuade

possessed ... 5. hadst, owned 6. insane 7. haunted 8. demoniac, obsessed 9. bewitched

possessing (pert to) ...

feeling .. 6. souled

flavor .. 5. sapid, tasty

land .. 5. acred

pincer claws .. 6. chelated

power .. 11. plenipotent

sensation .. 8. sentient

special ability .. 6. gifted 8. talented

possession ... 4. hold 5. asset 6. taking, wealth 7. control, country, mastery 8. dominion, property 9. obsession, ownership 10. equanimity 11. bewitchment

possession (pert to) ...

again .. 6. revest

law .. 6. seizin (seisin)

not in (*possession*) .. 6. devoid

suffix .. 3. ose

possessions ... 6. assets, estate, wealth 7. effects 8. property

posset ... 4. turn 6. curdle, pamper 8. beverage, infusion 9. coagulate

possibility ... 4. bare 7. latency 9. liability, potential 10. good chance, likelihood 11. contingency 13. improbability 16. prospective value

possible ... 6. latent, liable, likely 8. feasible 9. plausible, potential 11. practicable

possibly ... 5. maybe 7. perhaps 9. perchance 11. conceivably

post ... 3. bet, dak (dawk), xat. 4. bitt, fort, list, mail, trot 5. enter, newel, opium, place, stake, totem 6. alette, assign, hasten, inform, marker, office, pillar, pledge 7. bollard, placard, station, upright 8. dispatch, position 9. messenger, sternpost 12. enter account

post (pert to) ...

adverb .. 5. after, later 9. afterward

boat .. 4. mail 5. stage 6. packet

boy .. 7. courier 9. postilion (postillion)

dance (*army sl*) .. 8. struggle

goal (*anc*) .. 4. meta

Indian memorial .. 3. xat 5. totem

meridian .. 5. afternoon

mortem .. 7. autopsy 8. necropsy 10. after death

office .. 6. correo

prefix .. 5. after 6. behind 10. subsequent

stair .. 5. newel

postage stamp paper (pert to) ...

design .. 8. spandrel

paper .. 6. pelure

pattern .. 6. burele 8. burelage

poster ... 4. bill, card 7. placard, sticker 8. bulletin 9. messenger 10. billposter

posthumous ... 5. after 10. after death, post-mortem

postiche ... 9. false hair 10. artificial 11. counterfeit

postilion ... 5. guide 7. postboy 9. postrider

postimpressionist ... 6. cubist, Derain 7. Cezanne, Matisse

postpone ... 4. wait 5. defer, delay, remit, table 6. put off, shelve 7. adjourn, reserve, suspend 8. hold over, prorogue 10. pigeonhole 11. subordinate 13. procrastinate

postponement ... 7. remanet, respite 8. deferral, reprieve 9. deferment 11. prorogation

postprandial ... 11. after dinner

postulate ... 6. assume 7. prelude, premise 9. condition, predicate, stipulate 10. hypothesis 11. stipulation, supposition

posture ... 4. pose 6. stance 8. attitude, position, pretense 9. viewpoint 11. frame of mind

pot ... 3. jug, pan 4. olla 5. belly, crock, cruse 6. aludel, kettle, liquor, teapot 7. amphora (anc), caldron 9. flowerpot 10. jardiniere

potash ... 6. potass, saline 7. potassa 8. pearlash 18. potassium carbonate

potassium (pert to) ...

bitartrate .. 13. cream of tartar

bromide .. 8. sedative

carbonate .. 6. potash

compound .. 4. alum

dichromatic .. 6. chrome

iodide .. 8. medicine

nitrate .. 5. niter 9. saltpeter

permanganate .. 8. oxidizer

sulphate .. 4. alum

potate ... 9. liquefied

potation ... 5. draft, drink 6. liquor 8. beverage, tippling 12. drinking bout

potato ... 3. oca, yam 4. papa, spud 5. tuber

potato (pert to) ...

beetle .. 9. hardback

bogie .. 9. scarecrow

French .. 12. pomme de terre

French style .. 9. lyonnaise

genus .. 10. Solanaceae

Indian .. 4. yamp

moss .. 9. pondgrass

So Am .. 7. Uruguay

sweet .. 6. patata

potator ... 5. poter 7. tippler

potboiler ... 4. book 6. writer 8. painting (for quick money) 9. potwaller

potdar ... 7. assayer, cashier, weigher

potence, potency ... 3. vis 4. élan 5. cross, power 6. energy, gibbet 7. gallows 8. virility 9. authority, influence

potent . . . 4. able 6. cogent, mighty, strong, virile 7. dynamic, warrant (Mil) 8. forcible, heraldry, powerful, puissant, virulent 9. effective, efficient 11. efficacious, influential 13. authoritative

potentate . . . 4. amir (ameer), emir (emeer) 5. mogul, ruler 6. dynast, prince 7. emperor, monarch 8. syzerain 9. sovereign

potential . . . 4. mood (Gram) 5. ergal 6. latent, mighty 8. possible 11. influential, in the making, possibility, undeveloped

potentiality . . . 5. power 7. latency 11. possibility

poter . . . 5. toper 7. drinker

potgun . . . 5. rumor 6. cannon, mortar, pistol 8. braggart

pothead . . . 7. dullard 8. terminal (Elec) 9. blackfish

pother . . . 3. ado, row 4. fuss, stir 5. worry 6. bother, bustle, harass 7. fluster, perplex, trouble 9. commotion 10. excitement, perplexity 11. disturbance 12. perturbation

potherb . . . 4. mint 6. greens 7. spinach

pothook . . . 3. rod 4. hook (S-shaped) 5. crook 6. scrawl, stroke (S-like) 8. pot lifter 10. iron collar (penalty)

pothouse . . . 3. bar, low 6. saloon, tavern, vulgar 7. barroom 8. alehouse, grogshop, mughouse 11. public house

potiche . . . 4. vase 7. ceramic

potion . . . 4. dose, dram, drug 5. draft, drink 7. draught, philter 8. nepenthe

potlatch . . . 4. gift 5. feast 8. Festival

pot mender . . . 6. tinker

potomanie . . . 10. dipsomania 15. delirium tremens

potong . . . 5. crown 6. wreath 9. head cloth

potoroo . . . 11. rat kangaroo

potpourri . . . 4. olio, stew 6. medley 7. mixture, perfume 9. anthology 11. olla-podrida, salamagundi

potrero . . . 4. farm 7. pasture 10. cattle farm

pottage . . . 4. soup 6. brewis 8. porridge

pottah . . . 5. lease 6. tenure 9. title deed

potter . . . 3. pry 4. mess, poke, push 6. dawdle, doodle, meddle, putter, tamper, trifle 7. saunter 8. ceramist

potter's clay, earth . . . 4. slip 5. argil 6. galena, kaolin 8. aiquifou 10. terra cotta

potter's wheel . . . 4. disk 5. lathe, throw 6. jigger, pallet (palet)

pottery . . . 5. Delft 6. Samian 7. celadon (Chin), keramos (Gr) 8. Arretine (It), ceramics, Majolica (It) 9. delftware (Holland), keramikos (Gr) 11. earthenware 14. terra sigillata (anc)

pottery (pert to) . . .
black . . 6. basalt
broken . . 5. shard (sherd)
decorate . . 6. stamps 9. sigillate
decoration . . 11. sigillation
firing box . . 6. sagger
glasslike . . 8. vitreous
glaze . . 6. enamel

mineral . . 8. feldspar
oven . . 4. kiln
paste . . 9. barbotine
red . . 7. aretine

pottle . . . 3. pot 6. basket, vessel 7. tankard

potty . . . 3. pot 5. crazy 7. foolish, haughty 8. trifling 12. supercilious 13. insignificant

pot-valiant . . . 10. courageous (when drunk)

pouch . . . 3. bag, pod, sac 4. cyst, poke, sack 5. bulge, bursa, purse 6. gipser (Hist), pocket 7. bladder, mailbag, silicle, sporran (sporan) 10. pocketbook

pouch bone . . . 9. marsupial

pouched (pert to) . . .
dog . . 9. thylacine 13. Tasmanian wolf
frog . . 9. marsupial
gopher . . 6. pocket
mouse . . 9. marsupial
rat . . 8. kangaroo
rodent (cheek-pouched) . . 11. spermophile
stork . . 8. adjutant

poultry . . . 4. fowl, hens 5. cocks, ducks, geese 6. capons 7. Bantams, peahens, pigeons, turkeys 8. chickens, peacocks, roosters, volaille 9. cockerels, pheasants 10. guinea fowl

poultry (breeds) . . . 6. Ancona, Bantam, Brahma 7. Cornish, Dorking, Hamburg, Leghorn, Minorca 9. Wyandotte 12. Plymouth Rock 14. Rhode Island Red

poultry (pert to) . . .
disease . . 3. pip 4. roup, tick
dish . . 9. galantine
farm . . 7. hennery

pounamu . . . 5. jade 6. weapon 8. nephrite 10. greenstone

pound . . . 3. hit, ram 4. beat, ding, drum, maul, pond, quid (Brit money), tamp 5. money, pen up, thump 6. bruise, hammer, kennel, prison 7. impound 9. enclosure, pulverize

pounding instrument . . . 6. hammer, pestle

Pound of poetry . . . 4. Ezra

pounds (100) . . . 6. cental 13. hundredweight

pour . . . 4. flow, gush, rain, teem, vent, well 5. flood 6. abound, effuse, stream 7. niagara, radiate, torrent 8. downpour 9. discharge 11. extravasate

pour (pert to) . . .
molten glass . . 7. dagrade
molten steel . . 4. teem
off . . 5. drain 6. decant
oil upon . . 6. anoint, pacify
out . . 11. extravasate
sacrificial liquid . . 6. libate

pouring hole (mold) . . . 5. sprue

pout . . . 3. bib, mop 4. fish, moue, sulk 5. pique 7. catfish, eelpout, grimace 9. sulkiness

poverty . . . 4. lack, need, want 5. ilith (opp of wealth) 6. dearth, penury 8. leanness, poorness, scarcity 9. indigence, pearlweed 11. destitution

powder . . . 4. dust, talc 5. boral 6. pollen,

yttria 7. crumble 8. cosmetic, sprinkle
9. explosive, pulverize
powder (pert to) ...
antiseptic .. 6. formin 7. aristol
bag .. 6. sachet
festival (Ind) .. 4. abir (perfumed)
goa .. 7. araroba
heater, melter .. 6. sinter
insecticide .. 9. hellebore
medical .. 8. tannigen
perfumed .. 6. empasm
polishing .. 5. emery 7. tripoli
smokeless .. 6. poudre 8. amberite
stamping .. 6. pounce
powdered (Her) ... 4. semé
power ... 3. arm, art, can, jet, vis
4. dint, gift, iron, sway, will 5. force,
magic, might, steam, vigor 6. degree,
energy 7. control, faculty, magnate,
potency 8. capacity, efficacy, strength
9. authority, eloquence, influence,
magnetism, puissance 10. efficiency,
government 11. mathematics (term)
power (pert to) ...
creative .. 6. Shakti
device .. 9. telemotor
hammer .. 4. trip
inherent .. 6. energy
of attorney .. 5. agent 10. procurator
of feeling .. 7. sensate
of mind .. 4. wits
of resistance .. 7. stamina
persuasive .. 6. rhetoric 9. political
sovereign .. 6. throne
spiritual .. 8. divinity
superior .. 10. prepotency
under one's .. 10. subjugated
unit .. 3. erg 4. dyne 8. kilowatt
powerful ... 4. loud 5. great 6. cogent,
mighty, potent, strong 7. drastic,
intense, leonine, skookum 8. eloquent,
forcible, puissant 9. effective, effectual,
efficient 10. armipotent, convincing
11. efficacious, influential
13. authoritative
powerful force ... 6. libido
powerful man, businessmen ... 5. titan
6. tycoon 7. magnate
powerless ... 4. weak 8. impotent
pownie ... 7. peacock
powwow ... 6. frolic, priest 7. meeting
8. assembly, ceremony, congress,
conjurer 9. gathering 10. conference,
convention
poyou ... 9. armadillo
prabble ... 7. chatter, quarrel 8. squabble
practic ... 6. artful, shrews 7. cunning,
skilled 9. difficult, practical, practiced
11. experienced
practicable, practical ... 5. utile
6. usable, useful 7. virtual, working
8. feasible, possible, workable
9. available, expedient, operative,
pragmatic, realistic 11. pragmatical,
utilitarian
practical (pert to) ...
Christianity .. 10. New Thought
example .. 6. praxis
joke .. 4. hoax 5. trick 6. humbug
judgment .. 7. ethical (Kant)
practically ... 9. virtually 11. essentially

13. approximately
practice, practise ... 2. do 3. ply,
ure, use 4. plot, rite 5. drill, habit,
train, usage 6. action, addict, custom,
scheme, tryout 7. perform 8. ceremony,
exercise, intrigue, rehearse, training,
vocation 9. procedure 10. experience,
experiment, observance
practice (pert to) ...
corrupt .. 5. abuse
established .. 5. canon 6. custom
fraud .. 5. cheat, shark 8. trickery
specific .. 6. praxis
voice .. 8. intonate
witchcraft .. 3. hex
practicer of evasions ...
13. tergiversator
practicer of palmistry ...
11. chiromancer
prad ... 5. horse
pragmatic ... 7. meddler, skilled
8. busybody, dogmatic, meddling
9. conceited, officious, practical
10. systematic 11. opinionated
pragmatical ... 8. dogmatic 9. officious,
practical 10. meddlesome
11. commonplace
Prague, Praha ...
capital of .. 14. Czechoslovakia
famed bldg .. 10. University (1st in Cent
Eur, 1348)
famed teachers (anc) .. 4. Huss 6. Jerome
founder .. 14. Duchess Libussa (722)
prairie ... 3. bay 5. llano, plain 6. camass
(camas, cammas), meadow, steppe
7. quamash (camass) 9. grassland
10. prairillon
prairie (pert to) ...
anemone, crocus .. 12. pasque flower
antelope .. 9. pronghorn
apple .. 9. breadroot
artichoke .. 9. sunflower
berry .. 9. trompillo
chicken .. 6. grouse
dog .. 6. marmot
mud .. 5. gumbo
pigeon .. 6. plover 9. sandpiper
rose .. 14. Baltimore belle
schooner .. 12. covered wagon
squirrel .. 11. spermophile
tree (clump) .. 5. motte
weed .. 10. cinquefoil
wolf .. 6. coyote
Prairie State ... 8. Illinois
praise ... 4. laud 5. bless, extol, honor,
kudos, eulogy 6. acclaim, applaud,
commend, glorify, magnify, plaudit
8. applause, encomium, eulogize,
macarize 9. adulation, celebrate,
panegyric 11. approbation
12. commendation
praise (pert to) ...
continual .. 5. chant
high .. 5. extol 8. encomium
hymn of .. 8. doxology
insincere .. 4. bull 7. flatter 8. flattery
of another's blessing .. 8. macarism
9. Beatitude
to God .. 7. Laus Deo
Ye The Lord .. 8. Alleluia (Alleluiah)
10. Hallelujah (Halleluiah)

praiseworthy ... 8. laudable
11. commendable, meritorious

prana (Hind) ... 6. spirit 9. life force
10. life breath

prance ... 4. gait 5. caper, dance 6. cavort,
spring 7. swagger

prank ... 3. jig 4. fold, joke, prat 5. antic,
caper, pleat, shine, trick 6. frolic,
prance 7. caprice, dress up 8. escapade
11. monkeyshine

prankish ... 9. facetious 10. frolicsome
11. mischievous

prate ... 3. gab 4. chat, talk 6. gossip
7. chatter, twaddle 8. nonsense

prattle ... 3. gab 4. chat, talk 5. clack,
prate 6. babble 7. blather 12. impudent
talk, trifling talk

prawn ... 6. shrimp 10. crustacean,
shrimp pink

pray ... 3. ask, beg, sue 7. entreat,
implore, request, worship 8. devotion
10. supplicate

praya ... 4. bund, road 5. beach 6. strand

prayer ... 3. ave 4. bead, bene, plea, suit
5. credo, grace, matin 6. litany, orison,
vesper 7. request, worship 8. petition
12. intercession, supplication

prayer (pert to) ...
book .. 4. ordo 6. missal 7. portass
(portas) 8. breviary
call (Muslim) .. 4. azan (adan)
call tower .. 7. minaret
cloak .. 8. zizith (fringed) 7. tallith
desk, ledge .. 8. prie-dieu
evening .. 7. complin (compline) 9. night
song
figure .. 5. orant
incarnation .. 7. Angelus 11. Angelus
Bell
liturgical .. 6. litany 7. complin
Lord's (prayer) .. 11. Paternoster
morning .. 5. matin
nine days' devotional .. 6. novena
response .. 8. antiphon
short .. 5. grace
stick .. 4. paho

praying ... 8. entreaty 9. precation
12. supplication

praying cricket ... 6. mantis

praying figure ... 5. orant

preach ... 6. exhort 7. expound, lecture
8. advocate, homilize 9. discourse,
sermonize

preacher ... 6. parson, rector 7. evangel,
teacher 8. homilist, lecturer, minister
9. clergyman, pulpiteer

preaching ... 6. sermon 7. kerygma
(kerugma) 10. preachment
11. exhortation

preaching friar ... 9. Dominican

Preaching of Peter ... 9. Apocrypha

preamble ... 5. proem 7. preface, prelude
11. preliminary 12. introduction

prebellum ... 7. antewar 12. before the
war

prebend ... 7. stipend 8. benefice
9. allowance

precarious ... 7. assumed, dubious
8. insecure, unstable 9. hazardous,
uncertain, unsettled 10. unreliable

preceded ... 3. led 8. prefaced, was prior

9. anteced, antedated 10. introduced,
went before 13. had precedence,
occurred first

precedence ... 3. pas 4. lead, rank
8. priority 12. anteposition

precedent ... 4. sign 5. model, usage
7. example, leading 8. anterior,
decision, standard 10. antecedent,
forerunner 11. going before

preceding others ... 5. first 7. leading,
ternary (by threes) 10. antecedent

precept ... 4. rule, writ 5. adage, axiom,
maxim, order, sutra (sutta), torah
(tora) 6. belief 7. command 8. doctrine
9. direction 11. commandment,
instruction

preceptor ... 4. guru 5. guide, tutor
6. master, mentor, mullah, pundit
7. teacher 8. educator 10. instructor

precinct ... 5. ambit, space 6. region
8. boundary, district, environs

precious ... 4. dear, rare 5. great 6. costly,
valued 7. beloved, elegant, perfect
8. complete, esteemed, overnice,
valuable 9. downright 10. beloved one,
fastidious, particular

precious (pert to) ...
Blood (RCCh) .. 5. Feast (July 1)
garnet .. 6. pyrope
stone .. 3. gem 4. opal, ruby 5. pearl,
topaz 6. garnet, ligure 7. diamond,
emerald, jacinth (Bib) 8. hyacinth,
sapphire
stone, sometimes .. 7. cat's-eye
11. alexandrite

precipice ... 4. crag, linn, pali 5. bluff,
cliff 9. declivity

precipitancy ... 5. haste 8. rashness

precipitation ... 3. gel 4. fall, hail, mist,
rain, snow 5. haste, sleet 8. downpour
9. hastening 11. prematurity
12. acceleration, condensation,
recklessness

precipitous ... 4. rash 5. hasty, steep
6. abrupt, sudden 7. rushing (headlong)
9. very rapid 11. precipitate

précis ... 6. sketch 7. epitome, pandect,
summary 8. abstract, synopsis
9. summarize

precise ... 4. prim 5. exact 7. correct,
literal, special 8. accurate, definite,
detailed, overnice 10. meticulous,
overminute, particular, scrupulous
11. ceremonious, punctilious

preciseness ... 9. exactness 10. strictness
12. definiteness 14. fastidiousness

precision ... 6. nicety 8. accuracy
9. exactness, formality 11. preciseness
12. definiteness

preclude ... 3. bar 4. omit, stop 5. avert,
debar, estop 6. hinder, impede 7. head
off, prevent, shut out 8. prohibit

precocious ... 7. forward 8. advanced
9. premature

preconceive ... 6. ideate, precox
7. presume 8. foreknow, prejudge
9. predecide 10. presuppose

predatory ... 7. looting 9. marauding,
pillaging, piratical 10. plundering,
predaceous (predacious) 11. destructive

predatory bird ... 3. owl 4. hawk, kite

6. falcon
predatory raid ... 5. foray
predestine ... 4. doom, fate 6. decree,
ordain 7. appoint 9. determine,
foretoken 10. foreordain
predetermine ... 4. bias 7. destine
8. prejudge 9. prejudice, preordain
10. prepossess 11. premeditate
predicament ... 3. fix 4. pass 5. state
6. plight, scrape 7. dilemma, impasse
8. quandary 9. condition, situation
predicator ... 4. seer 5. friar 7. prophet
8. preacher 9. predicter
predict ... 4. bode, dope, omen 7. foresee,
portend, presage 8. forecast, foretell,
prophecy 13. prognosticate
prediction ... 6. augury 8. prophecy
9. foresight 10. foreboding
11. foretelling 15. prognostication
predilection ... 4. bias 6. desire
8. tendency 9. prejudice 10. favoritism,
partiality, preference, propensity
11. disposition 13. preconception
14. predisposition
predominant ... 5. chief 6. ruling
8. reigning, superior 9. hegemonic
11. controlling, influential, outstanding
predominate ... 5. excel 7. prevail
8. dominate 10. be superior
12. preponderate
pre-eminent ... 3. top 4. only, star
5. chief 7. palmary, ranking 8. superior
9. excellent, principal 11. outstanding
pre-emption ... 8. monopoly, purchase
10. prior right 13. appropriation
preen ... 3. pin, sew 4. perk 5. clasp,
dress, groom, plume, primp 6. bodkin,
brooch, stitch 9. make sleek
preface ... 5. front, proem 6. herald,
prayer 7. prelude, problem 8. exordium,
foreword, preamble, prologue
10. paraphrase 12. introduction
prefect, praefect ... 4. dean (Jesuit)
6. chin fu 7. monitor, officer 8. director,
minister, official 9. president
10. magistrate
prefecture ... 7. eparchy
prefer ... 5. elect, offer 8. choose, select
7. outrank, present, proffer, promote
9. be partial 12. give priority
preference ... 6. choice 8. favorite,
priority 9. advantage 10. favoritism
11. alternative, prior choice
12. predilection
prefiguration ... 4. omen 9. foretoken,
prototype 12. typification
13. preindication
prefigure ... 7. imagine, suggest
8. foretell 10. foreshadow
prefix for ...
about .. 3. amb 4. peri
above .. 3. epi, sur 5. hyper, super,
supra
across .. 3. dia 4. tran 5. trans
again .. 2. re
against .. 4. anti
ahead .. 3. pre
all .. 4. omni
alongside .. 3. par 4. para
an .. 2. al
apart .. 2. se 3. dia, dis

appearing to .. 5. quasi
around .. 4. peri
away .. 3. aph, apo
back .. 2. re 3. ana
backward .. 5. retro
bad .. 3. dys, mal
badly .. 3. mis
beauty .. 5. calli (kalli)
before .. 2. ob 3. pre, pro 4. ante, prae
beside .. 3. par 4. para
between .. 3. dia 4. meta 5. inter
beyond .. 4. para 5. ultra
black .. 4. atra
blood .. 4. haem, hemo
bone .. 4. oste 5. osteo
both .. 4. ambi
Chinese .. 4. Sino 5. Chino
clear .. 4. delo
dawn .. 2. eo
difficult .. 3. dys
distant .. 3. tel 4. tele
double .. 2. di
down .. 2. de 4. cata
ear .. 3. oto
earnest .. 5. serio
earth .. 3. geo
eight .. 3. oct 4. octa, octo
English .. 5. Anglo
equal .. 3. iso
equally .. 4. equi
evil .. 3. mal
far .. 3. tel 4. tele
faulty .. 3. mis
fictitious .. 6. pseudo
fire .. 3. pyr
five .. 3. penta
for .. 3. pro
former .. 2. ex
four .. 5. tetra 6. quadri
from .. 2. ab, de, ec
from away .. 3. apo
gas .. 4. aero
good .. 3. eu
half .. 4. demi, hemi, semi
hard .. 3. dys 6. stereo
ill .. 3. mal, mis
in, into .. 2. en 4. endo
iron .. 5. ferro
lizard .. 5. saura, sauro
many .. 4. mult, poly 5. multi
middle .. 4. meso 5. medio
modern .. 3. neo
mountain .. 3. oro
nail .. 4. helo
negative .. 2. il, ir, un 3. mon
new .. 3. neo
not .. 2. il, im, ir, un 3. non
numerical .. 3. uni
one .. 3. uni 4. mono
oneself .. 4. auto
out of, outer .. 2. ec, ex 3. ect, epi,
exo 4. ecto
over .. 3. epi, sur 5. super, supra
possession .. 3. ose
pray .. 3. ora
priority .. 3. pre
recent .. 3. neo
release .. 2. un
reversed .. 2. di
same, equal .. 3. iso 4. equi, homo
separation .. 2. di 3. dis

shoulder . . 6. humero
single . . 4. mono
son of . . 3. Mac
ten . . 3. dec 4. deca
this side of . . 3. cis
three, thrice . . 3. ter, tri 4. tris
through . . 3. dia, per
to . . 2. ap
together . . 3. com, con, cor, syn
toward . . 2. ob, oc
turning . . 4. roto
twice . . 2. bi, di
twofold . . 2. bi, di 3. dua
under . . 3. sub
upon . . 2. ep 3. epi
upward . . 3. ana, ano
very much . . 3. eri
well . . 2. eu
with . . 3. col, com, pro, syl, syn
within . . 3. eso 4. endo, ento 5. intra
without . . 2. se 3. ect 4. ecto
wood . . 4. xylo
wrong . . 3. mis

pregnant . . . 7. fertile 8. fruitful
9. expecting, with child 10. parturient

prehistoric (pert to) . . .
animal . . 7. reptile 8. dinosaur, mastodon
9. phytosaur
continent . . 8. Atlantis (Atalantis)
man . . 4. cave, Dawn 11. lake dweller
ref to . . 9. primitive
tool . . 6. eolith

prejudiced . . . 6. biased 7. partial
8. partisan 11. opinionated
12. prepossessed

prejudicial . . . 9. injurious 11. detrimental
15. disadvantageous

prelate . . . 4. head, pope 5. abbot, chief
6. bishop, priest 7. primate, red-blue
8. minister, superior 9. Monsignor
(Monsignore)

prelector, praelector . . . 6. reader
7. teacher 8. lecturer 9. professor

preliminary . . . 6. prior 7. preface,
prelude 8. entrance, previous, proemial
9. precedent, prefatory, threshold
10. antecedent 11. preparatory
12. introduction, introductory

preliminary memo . . . 8. protocol

preliminary plan . . . 4. idea

prelude . . . 5. proem 6. verset 7. preface
8. overture, ritornel (ritornelle)

premature . . . 6. infant 8. too early,
untimely 10. precocious

premier . . . 3. bet (gambling) 5. chief
7. leading 8. earliest 9. principal
13. prime minister

premiere . . . 4. show 10. first night
12. presentation 16. first performance

premium . . . 4. agio 5. bonus, prize,
stake 6. reward 8. gratuity, interest
10. recompense

premonition . . . 5. hunch 6. notice
7. warning 8. forecast 10. foreboding
11. forewarning, information
12. presentiment

preoccupied . . . 4. lost 6. absent, filled
8. absorbed, observed 9. engrossed
10. abstracted, pre-engaged 13. lost
in thought

preparation . . . 8. training 9. equipment,

study hour 10. groundwork 11. making
ready 12. introduction

preparation (pert to) . . .
of a dress . . 7. fitting
place . . 10. laboratory, paratorium
sugar, for candy . . 7. fondant
without . . 5. ad lib 9. impromptu

prepare . . . 3. fit, fix, get 4. cook, gird,
make, pave, yark 5. adapt, equip,
ready, train 6. adjust 7. arrange

prepare (pert to) . . .
by boiling . . 6. decoct
for golf game . . 3. tee
for melting glass . . 4. frit
for publication . . 4. edit
for seasoning . . 8. marinate
skins . . 3. taw

prepared . . . 5. armed, ready 7. adapted,
groomed, skilled, trained 8. equipped,
provided

prepared instruction . . .
13. propaedeutics

preponderance . . . 6. weight 8. dominion,
majority 9. influence 11. outweighing,
superiority

prepose . . . 6. prefix 7. preface 11. place
before

preposition . . . 2. at, by, ex, in, of, on,
to, up 3. off, out, tae 4. into, onto,
over, unto, upon, with

prepossession . . . 4. bent, bias
9. obsession, prejudice 10. preference
11. inclination 12. predilection
13. appropriation, preconception
14. predisposition

presage . . . 4. bode, omen, osse, sign
5. token 6. augury, betide, divine
7. portend, predict 8. forebode,
foretell 10. prediction, prognostic
11. preindicate 13. foreknowledge

presager . . . 7. prophet 9. foreboder

presbytery . . . 6. church, clergy 7. council
8. ministry 9. parsonage 10. presbyters

prescribe . . . 3. set 5. allot, guide, limit,
order 6. advise, bestow, direct, ordain
7. control, dictate 9. designate

presence . . . 4. mien, port 7. bearing,
posture, specter 8. phantasm
9. existence, proximity 10. apparition,
appearance, attendance 11. personality

present . . . 3. now 4. boon, gift, give
5. grant, nonce, offer 6. bestow, bounty,
donate 7. largess (largesse) 8. donation,
gratuity 9. introduce 10. contribute
11. benefaction

present (pert to) . . .
for acceptance . . 6. tender
pupil to teacher . . 8. mineral
time . . 3. now 5. nonce, today 7. current
8. juncture
to customers . . 7. freebie, premium
8. giveaway 9. lagniappe (lagnappe)
to foreign ambassador . . 6. xenium

presentation . . . 4. gift, plan 5. debut,
offer 7. present 8. bestowal, donation,
offering 10. appearance, exhibition
12. introduction

presently . . . 4. anon, soon 6. at once
7. shortly 8. nowadays 9. forthwith
10. before long 11. immediately

preservation . . . 6. saving 9. retention,

safeguard 10. protection
11. maintenance, safekeeping
12. conservation, perpetuation
preservative . . . 4. salt 5. spice 7. alcohol,
vinegar 10. protective 14. sodium
benzoate
preserve . . . 3. can, jam, tin 4. corn,
cure, keep, salt, save 5. guard, jelly,
spare, store 6. defend, pickle, retain,
secure, shield, uphold 7. compote,
protect, sustain 8. conserve, maintain
9. freeze-dry, safeguard
preserve (pert to) . . .
by drying . . 9. desiccate
fruit . . 7. compote 9. marmalade
grape . . 5. uvate (conserve)
in brine . . 4. corn, cure, salt
in oil . . 8. marinate
president . . . 4. head 5. ruler 8. governor
14. chief executive
President (US) . . . 4. Ford, Polk, Taft
5. Adams (John), Adams (John Q),
Grant, Hayes, Nixon, Tyler 6. Arthur
(Chester), Carter, Hoover, Monroe,
Pierce, Reagan, Taylor, Truman, Wilson
7. Harding, Jackson, Johnson (Andrew),
Johnson (L B), Kennedy, Lincoln,
Madison 8. Buchanan, Coolidge,
Fillmore, Garfield, Harrison (Benj),
Harrison (Wm Henry), McKinley,
Van Buren 9. Cleveland, Jefferson,
Roosevelt (Theo), Roosevelt (F D)
10. Eisenhower, Washington
President (pert to) . . .
place . . 10. Oval Office, White House
power . . 4. veto
press . . . 3. dun 4. cram, iron, urge
5. crowd, force, wedge 6. compel,
hasten, smooth, throng, thrust
7. impress, squeeze 8. compress,
condense, insist on 9. extractor,
importune 10. compulsion, journalism,
newspapers 12. conscription
press (pert to) . . .
ancient . . 6. Aldine
bookbinder . . 7. smasher
corrector . . 11. proofreader
critic . . 6. censor 8. reviewer
ranks . . 5. serry
pressed (pert to) . . .
amber . . 8. amberoid
cheese . . 7. cheddar
grapes, residue . . 4. marc (mark)
into a mass . . 7. kneaded
together . . 5. dense 6. mashed
7. compact, crowded, serried
pressing . . . 6. urgent, urging 7. exigent
8. insistent 10. compelling, extraction,
motivating 11. importunity
pressure . . . 4. urge 5. force 6. compel,
stress, weight 7. squeeze, urgency
8. exigency, instancy 9. authority,
influence 10. compulsion, constraint,
harassment 11. compression
pressure (pert to) . . .
barometer . . 7. mesobar
boiler, cooker . . 9. autoclave
instrument (for liquids) . . 9. manometer
10. piezometer 11. Bourdon tube
of necessity . . 7. urgency
resisting . . 8. renitent

unit . . 5. barad
prestidigitation . . . 8. juggling
11. legerdemain 13. sleight of hand
prestige . . . 4. bias, face, sway 5. clout,
éclat 6. renown, repute 7. sorcery
8. illusion 9. authority, deception,
influence 10. importance 11. superiority
presto . . . 5. magic 7. command, passing,
quickly 8. suddenly 9. instantly
10. rapid tempo 11. immediately
13. instantaneous
presumably . . . 7. no doubt 8. probably
10. ostensibly, supposedly
presume . . . 4. dare, hope 5. imply, judge,
think 6. assure, impose 7. suppose,
venture 10. presuppose 11. preconceive
14. take for granted
presumption . . . 4. hope 6. daring
7. opinion 8. audacity 9. arrogance,
impudence, insolence 10. effrontery
11. implication, probability, supposition
presumptive . . . 5. brash 7. assumed,
Icarian 8. arrogant, inferred, probable
10. evidential
presumptuous . . . 5. undue 7. forward,
haughty 8. arrogant, insolent
9. foolhardy 11. venturesome
pretend . . . 3. act, aim 4. fake, sham
5. claim, feign, feint 6. affect,
allege, assume, pose as 7. presume,
pretext, profess 8. disguise, simulate
11. impersonate, make believe
pretended . . . 4. sham 7. alleged
8. affected, intended, proposed,
so-called 10. ostensible
pretended omission (Rhet) . . .
9. apophasis 11. paraleipsis (paralepsis)
pretender . . . 4. idol, snob 5. cowan,
quack 6. seemer 7. Aeolist (Eolist)
8. claimant, impostor 9. charlatan
10. mountebank 11. fourflusher
pretense, pretence . . . 3. act 4. flam,
ruse, sham, show 5. claim, cloak,
cover, feint, horse, study 6. excuse,
tinsel 7. pretext 8. artifice, stalking
10. appearance, masquerade
subterfuge 11. affectation, fabrication,
ostentation
pretentious . . . 4. arty 5. showy 6. rococo
7. elegant, pompous 8. affected,
boastful 9. high-flown 12. ostentatious
13. grandiloquent
pretentious words, use of . . .
9. bombastic 10. lexiphanic
pretermit . . . 4. omit 6. pass by
7. neglect, suspend 8. intermit, pass
over 9. interrupt
pretext . . . 4. flam, plea 5. cloak, cover,
trick 6. excuse 8. pretense (pretence)
9. deception, semblance
pretty . . . 3. toy 4. cute, fair, joli, very
5. bonny (bonnie) 6. clever, comely,
lovely, rather 7. dollish, finical, foppish
8. handsome 9. ingenious, tolerably
10. attractive, knickknack 11. good-
looking, interesting 15. pulchritudinous
prevail . . . 3. win 5. exist 6. induce,
subdue 7. succeed, triumph
8. dominate, frequent 9. prevalent
11. predominate
prevailed . . . 3. got, won 5. urged

9. succeeded, triumphed

prevailing . . . 4. rife 5. chief, usual
6. common 7. current, general
8. abundant, dominant 9. prevalent
10. widespread 11. predominant

prevail upon . . . 4. urge 6. induce
8. persuade

prevalent . . . 4. rife 6. potent 7. current
8. dominant, powerful 9. extensive
10. prevailing, successful, victorious,
widespread 11. efficacious, influential

prevaricate . . . 3. lie 5. evade 7. deviate,
quibble, shuffle

prevene . . . 7. prevent 9. forestall
10. anticipate

prevent . . . 4. warn 5. avert, debar,
deter, estop 7. ward off 8. preclude
9. forestall, frustrate 10. circumvent

preventative, preventive . . . 8. antidote
9. deterrent 12. prophylactic

previous . . . 4. past 5. prior 6. before,
former 7. earlier 8. untimely
9. foregoing, preceding, premature
11. unwarranted

previously . . . 4. erst 6. before 7. earlier
8. formerly 9. aforesaid 10. heretofore

prey . . . 3. rob 5. booty, spoil 6. quarry,
victim 7. plunder

prey (to seize) . . . 9. raptorial

prey upon . . . 3. eat 4. feed 5. ravin
(raven) 7. plunder, torment 9. predacity

Priam (pert to) . . .
  daughter . . 8. Polyxena 9. Cassandra
  grandfather . . 4. Ilus
  King of . . 4. Troy
  servant . . 7. Agelaus
  son . . 5. Paris 6. Hector 7. Troilus
  wife . . 6. Hecuba

price . . . 3. sum 4. cost, fare, odds,
rate 5. offer, value, worth 6. charge
7. expense 10. estimation, excellence,
recompense 12. preciousness

priceless . . . 7. amusing 8. precious
10. high-priced, invaluable, not salable

prick . . . 4. goad, pain, pang 5. sting,
wound 6. pierce 7. prickle, remorse
8. distress

pricked . . . 6. dotted, pinked 7. pointed
9. punctured

prickle . . . 4. burr, prod, seta 5. spike,
thorn 6. pierce, tingle 7. acantha
8. stinging

prickly . . . 6. tingly 7. pointed 8. echinate

prickly (pert to) . . .
  flower . . 4. burr
  pear . . 4. tuna 5. nopal 6. cactus
  7. Opuntia
  plant . . 3. ash 5. briar, elder 6. teasel
  7. juniper, lettuce, thistle 12. Hercules-
  club

pride . . . 6. vanity 7. conceit, egotism
9. arrogance, proudness 11. self-respect

priest . . . 3. Eli, fra 4. abbé, curé, lama,
père 5. clerk, druid, padre 6. cleric,
father 7. prester 9. oratorian

priest (pert to) . . .
  assistant . . 7. acolyte
  Brit order (anc) . . 5. Druid
  cap . . 5. miter (mitre) 7. biretta
  fish . . 8. rockfish
  mantle . . 4. cope

priest-in-the-pulpit . . 10. cuckoopint
relating to . . 10. sacerdotal
tribe (Israel) . . 4. Levi
vestment . . 3. alb 5. amice, ephod (Jew),
stole 7. cassock, maniple 8. chasuble,
surplice

priestly caste . . . 4. Magi 7. wise men

prig . . . 3. beg, fog, pan 4. buck, snob
5. dandy, filch, plead, prink, prude,
steal, thief 6. haggle, pilfer, purist, tinker
7. bargain, entreat, pitcher 8. pilferer

priggish, prim . . . 7. prudish 8. snobbish,
thievish

prim . . . 4. fish, neat, smug 5. primp,
smelt 6. demure, formal 7. precise,
prudish 8. decorous

prima donna . . . 4. diva 6. singer

prima facie . . . 7. at sight 9. first view
10. apparently

primal . . . 5. basic, chief, first 7. primary
8. original 9. elemental, primitive

primary . . . 5. basic, color, first 6. primal
7. initial 8. election, primeval, pristine
9. elemental, essential, firsthand,
primitive, principal 10. elementary
11. fundamental

primary (pert to) . . .
  armament . . 6. cannon
  circles . . 7. equator, horizon 8. ecliptic,
  galactic
  colors . . 3. red 4. blue 5. yellow

primate, bishop . . . 10. Archbishop

Primates (Order of) . . . 3. ape, man
5. lemur 6. mammal, monkey
8. marmoset 9. orangutan
(orangoutang)

prime . . . 4. best, dawn 5. first, paint
7. primary, the best 8. original, primeval
9. primitive

prime minister . . . 7. premier

primer . . . 5. paint 8. hornbook, textbook,
type size 9. detonator 10. battledore

primeval . . . 6. primal 7. primary
8. original, pristine

primeval deity . . . 5. Titan

primitive . . . 5. basic, first 6. embryo,
native, quaint 7. ancient, priscan
8. pristine 10. aboriginal, antiquated
11. fundamental

primitive (pert to) . . .
  area . . 5. Idaho 8. Colorado
  art objects . . 9. artifacts
  group . . 6. ethnos
  self . . 2. id 8. instinct

primness . . . 8. neatness, niceness
9. stiffness 11. preciseness

primo . . . 5. chief, first 12. leading tenor

primordial . . . 7. primary 8. original
9. elemental, primitive 10. prototypal
11. rudimentary 12. first created

primrose (pert to) . . .
  called . . 10. an innocent 13. flower of
  youth
  color . . 6. yellow 10. snapdragon
  genus . . 7. Primula 11. Primulaceae
  green . . 5. color
  League . . 13. Conservatives (Eng)
  path . . 8. sensual

prince . . . 4. knez 5. prinz 7. dynasty,
monarch 8. archduke 9. potentate,
princekin, sovereign 10. princeling

prince (pert to) . . .
  Albert . . 9. frock coat
  allowance . . 8. appenage
  petty . . 6. satrap
princely . . . 5. noble, regal, royal 6. kingly
  10. munificent 11. magnificent
princely Italian family . . . 4. Este
Prince of . . .
  Afghanistan . . 4. amir
  apostate angels . . 5. Eblis
  Apostles . . 6. St Paul 7. St Peter
  darkness . . 5. devil, Satan 7. Ahriman
  demons . . 5. devil 9. Beelzebub
  destruction . . 9. Tamerlane
  evil spirits . . 7. Sammael
  liars . . 5. Pinto
  Peace . . 7. Messiah 11. Jesus Christ
  Spanish poetry . . 4. Vega
  the Church . . 8. cardinal
  the ode . . 7. Ronsard
  the sonnet . . 6. Bellay 15. Joachim du
    Bellay
  this world (Bib) . . 5. Satan
  Tunis . . 3. bey
princess (pert to) . . .
  literally . . 5. Sarah
  loved by Cupid . . 6. Psyche
  loved by Zeus . . 6. Europa
  Mohammed . . 5. begum
  mythical . . 5. Danae 8. Atalanta
  royal . . 14. eldest daughter
  Tyrian . . 4. Dido (Elissa)
principal . . . 3. top 4. arch, head, main
  5. chief, major, prime 6. Führer, leader,
  master, origin, source 7. captain,
  leading, palmary, primary 8. foremost
  9. important, organ stop, preceptor
  10. capital sum 11. outstanding
principality . . . 6. Monaco
principal meal (Rom) . . . 4. cena
principle . . . 4. rule 5. axiom, canon,
  prana, tenet 6. dictum 7. precept,
  theorem 9. essential 10. foundation
principle (pert to) . . .
  active in tobacco . . 8. nicotine
  distance . . 11. perspective
  Hindu . . 5. Sakti
  life, theosophy . . 5. prana, tenet
  musical . . 8. tonality
  vital . . 4. soul 5. anima
principles . . . 5. creed 9. generalia
  10. essentials 12. generalities
princox, princock . . . 7. coxcomb 9. pert
  youth
prink . . . 4. deck, wink 5. adorn, preen,
  primp 6. bedeck, glance 7. dress up
print . . . 5. stamp 7. edition, engrave,
  impress, picture, publish 11. indentation
printed (pert to) . . .
  defamation . . 5. libel
  fabric . . 4. silk 6. calico 7. percale
  sheets . . 8. pamphlet
printer . . . 8. pressman 9. publisher
  11. typographer 12. lithographer
printer (pert to) . . .
  aid . . 5. devil 10. apprentice
  dauber . . 5. biron
  direction . . 4. stet
  hand ink roller . . 6. brayer
  ink pad . . 6. dabber
  manuscript . . 4. copy

  mark . . 4. dash, stet 5. caret, serif, tilde
    8. asterisk
  measure . . 2. em, en 4. pica
  type, mixed . . 3. pie (pi)
printing (pert to) . . .
  blur . . 6. mackle, macule
  cylinder . . 6. rounce
  error . . 7. erratum
  form . . 3. die
  for the blind . . 7. braille
  mark . . 4. dele 6. diesis 8. ellipsis
  measure . . 2. em, en 5. agate
  metal block . . 4. quad
  press part . . 6. platen, rounce 7. frisket
prion . . . 6. petrel 7. sea bird
prior . . . 3. ere 4. fore, past 6. before,
  former 8. previous, priorate
  9. preceding 10. antecedent
priority . . . 10. precedence 11. order of
  time
priory . . . 5. abbey 8. cloister
priscan . . . 9. primitive
Priscian . . . 7. grammar 10. grammarian
Priscilla (pert to) . . .
  Bib . . 16. Christian convert
  color . . 7. fog blue
  Hist . . 7. Puritan
  husband . . 9. John Alden
  tale . . 24. Courtship of Myles Standish
prism (optical device) . . . 5. Porro
prismatic . . . 10. iridescent, variegated
prison . . . 4. jug 4. brig, gaol, jail, keep,
  quod 5. clink 6. carcer 10. guardhouse
  12. penitentiary
prison (pert to) . . .
  courtyard . . 4. quad
  English (old) . . 7. Newgate 9. Bridewell
  French . . 8. Bastille
  guarded . . 10. panopticon
  keeper . . 5. guard 6. gaoler, jailer,
    keeper, warden 7. turnkey
  Russian . . 5. gulag
  slang . . 3. jug 4. quod, rock 5. clink,
    limbo 6. cooler 7. slammer 8. big
    house, hoosegow
  spy . . 6. canary, mouton
Prisoner of . . .
  Chillon . . 16. Francois Bonivard
  Vatican . . 4. Pope
prisoner's release . . . 6. parole
pristine . . . 7. primary 8. original
  9. primitive
prittle-prattle . . . 7. chatter, prattle
  8. chitchat 9. chatterer, empty talk
privacy . . . 7. privity, retreat, secrecy
  8. solitude 9. seclusion
private . . . 5. privy 6. covert, secret
  7. one's own 8. esoteric, eyes-
  only, hush-hush, personal, secluded,
  separate, solitary 11. sequestered
  12. confidential 15. uncommunicative
privateer . . . 4. Kidd (Capt) 5. caper
  6. pirate 7. corsair, soldier (not enlisted)
  9. freelance
privately . . . 5. aside 6. secret 8. in secret
  10. personally, unofficial 12. unofficially
privation . . . 4. loss, want 6. misery
  7. poverty 8. hardship 10. divestment
  11. destitution
privilege . . . 3. soc, use 5. favor, right
  7. charter 8. easement 9. advantage

10. concession 12. carte blanche
privileged . . . 6. exempt 8. licensed
privileged ones . . . 5. haves
prix . . 5. prize
prize . . . 3. cup 5. award, booty, Detur
(Harvard), medal, plate, price, purse,
stake, value 6. assess, esteem, ribbon,
trophy 7. premium, respect 8. treasure
prize fight . . . 2. go, KO 3. TKO 4. bout,
spar 6. boxing 7. contest 8. knockout,
pugilism 10. fisticuffs
pro . . . 3. aye, for 6. before 8. behalf of
9. in front of 12. professional
probability . . . 4. odds 6. chance, shoo-in
(sl) 7. vantage 9. liability 10. conclusion,
good chance, likelihood, likeliness
11. credibility
probe . . . 3. dig 4. prod, tent 5. sound
6. feeler, pierce, search, stylet
7. examine, explore, feel out, inquiry
10. instrument, scrutinize
probity . . . 6. virtue 7. honesty 9. integrity,
rectitude 11. uprightness
problem . . . 3. nut 4. crux, knot
6. enigma, riddle 7. theorem 8. question
9. situation
pro bono publico . . . 16. for the public
good
proboscis . . . 4. beak, nose 5. snout,
trunk
procaccia . . . 4. cart (carrier's) 7. carrier
procacious . . . 4. pert 8. insolent, petulant
procacity . . . 8. pertness 9. insolence,
petulance
Procavia . . . 4. cony 5. hyrax 6. rabbit
procedure . . . 4. step 5. order 6. custom,
method, policy, system 7. process
8. behavior 11. continuance
proceed . . . 2. go 4. fare, move,
pass, wend 5. arise, issue 6. derive
7. emanate 8. continue, progress
9. originate
proceed (pert to) . . .
hastily . . 5. speed
leisurely . . 5. amble, mosey (mosy)
on one's way . . 4. wend
rapidly . . 4. zoom 6. gallop
proceeding . . . 4. step 5. actum 6. course
7. conduct, measure, process 8. activity,
behavior 9. procedure 11. transaction
proceeding (pert to) . . .
by threes . . 7. ternary
from earth . . 8. telluric
from the sun . . 5. polar
proceedings . . . 4. acta 5. trial 6. doings
7. affairs, lawsuit, minutes 8. activity
proceeds . . . 4. gain, goes 6. income
7. marches, profits, returns
procerity . . . 6. height 8. tallness
process . . . 4. cook, writ 5. lapse (of time),
order 6. course, notice 7. advance,
mandate, summons 8. progress
9. emanation, operation, outgrowth,
procedure, sterilize
process (pert to) . . .
beak (small) . . 9. rostrulum
electroplating, steeling . . 8. acierage
fabric coloring . . 5. batik
fish (winglike) . . 3. fin
in ornaments . . 6. moisis
of development . . 7. nascent

pointed . . 3. awn
steel making . . 8. Bessemer
11. cementation
surveying . . 13. triangulation
transferring pictures . . 5. decal
12. decalcomania
procession . . . 4. file 5. train 6. parade
7. cortege 8. sequence 9. formation
prochein, prochain . . . 4. next 7. nearest
proclaim . . . 4. nype (sl) 5. tout 5. blaze,
voice 6. herald 7. declare, enounce,
presage, publish 8. announce
10. promulgate
proclamation . . . 4. fiat 5. bando, banns
(bans), blaze, edict, ukase 6. decree,
notice 9. manifesto 12. announcement,
promulgation
proclivity . . . 4. bent 6. desire 7. leaning
8. tendency 10. propensity
11. disposition, inclination
procrastinate . . . 5. defer, delay, stall
7. soldier 8. postpone
procrastination . . . 5. delay, stall
7. laxness 10. hesitation 11. vacillation
12. dilatoriness
procrastinator . . . 7. delayer, trifler
8. deferrer
procreant . . . 8. fruitful 9. producing
10. generating 11. propagative
Procrustes (Gr legend) . . .
10. highwayman (Attica)
14. Procrustean bed
procurator . . . 5. agent 6. lawyer
7. proctor, steward
procure . . . 3. get 4. gain 5. bring, fetch
6. effect, elicit, induce, obtain 7. acquire
8. contrive, purchase
prod . . . 3. egg, jab 4. goad, poke, urge
6. thrust
prodigal . . . 4. cloy 6. lavish 7. spender
9. plentiful 10. squanderer
11. extravagant, intemperate,
spendthrift, squandering
prodigality . . . 5. waste 9. abundance
12. extravagance, intemperance
13. superabundant
prodigious . . . 4. huge 5. great 7. amazing,
immense 8. enormous 9. marvelous,
monstrous, wonderful 10. miraculous,
portentous, tremendous 11. astonishing
13. extraordinary
prodigy . . . 4. omen, sign 6. genius,
marvel, oddity, wonder 7. miracle
prodition . . . 7. treason 8. betrayal
produce . . . 2. do 4. bear, make, show,
wage 5. carry, cause, stage, yield
6. author, create, effect 7. exhibit,
product 8. engender, generate, receipts
9. originate 10. accomplish
11. merchandise
produce (pert to) . . .
copy of . . 4. type
effect . . 3. act
ideas . . 6. ideate
noise . . 5. sound
produced . . . 8. extended 9. elongated,
prolonged
produced (pert to) . . .
by heat . . 7. igneous 8. volcanic
by kitchen gardens . . 7. olitory
8. potherbs

by wind . . 7. aeolian
regularly . . 6. staple
producer . . . 4. doer 6. farmer, parent
7. creator 10. theaterman
12. manufacturer
producing (pert to) . . .
cold . . 7. algific
fire . . 8. sparking
illusions . . 15. phantasmagorial
poison . . 6. septic
product . . . 3. sum 4. crop 5. fruit
6. result 7. hormone 8. artifact, creation
9. commodity, outgrowth
production . . . 3. hit 4. book, work 5. fruit
7. produce 8. creation 9. execution,
extension 14. accomplishment
productive . . . 4. rich 7. fertile, gainful
8. creative, fruitful 9. inventive
10. generative
proem . . . 7. preface, prelude 8. foreword,
preamble 12. introduction
profane . . . 6. misuse, unholy, wicked
7. godless, impious, ungodly, wicked
8. temporal 9. desecrate 10. unhallowed
11. blasphemous, unspiritual
12. unsanctified
profess . . . 4. avow 5. claim, feign
6. affirm, allege 7. declare
11. acknowledge
profession . . . 5. claim, faith, trade
6. avowal, career, metier 7. calling,
pretext 8. vocation 9. testimony
10. occupation 11. affirmation
14. acknowledgment
professional . . . 4. paid 5. hired 6. expert
7. skilled, trained 8. finished
professional, non . . . 3. lay 4. laic
7. amateur 9. unskilled
proffer . . . 3. bid 4. give 5. offer 6. tender
proficient . . . 3. apt 5. adept 6. expert,
versed 7. skilled 12. accomplished
profile . . . 4. draw, form 7. contour,
diagram, outline, picture 9. biography
14. representation
profit . . . 3. net 4. boot, gain, good,
mend 5. avail 6. return 7. benefit, rake-
off, results 8. interest 9. advantage
11. share of gain 12. remuneration
profitable . . . 6. paying, useful 7. helpful
8. repaying 9. expedient, lucrative
10. beneficial 12. remunerative
profligate . . . 6. wicked 7. corrupt,
spender, vicious 8. depraved, prodigal,
wasteful 9. abandoned, dissolute,
reprobate 10. overthrown
11. extravagant
profound . . . 4. deep, wise 5. heavy
7. abysmal, intense, learned 8. abstruse,
complete, deep-felt, poignant
9. downright, recondite, sagacious
11. far-reaching 12. encompassing,
unfathomable 13. thoroughgoing
profundity . . . 5. depth 6. wisdom
8. deepness 12. abstruseness
profuse . . . 6. galore, lavish 7. diffuse,
liberal, palaver 8. abundant, generous,
numerous, prodigal, wasteful
9. bountiful 10. munificent
11. extravagant, overflowing
profusion . . . 6. plenty 8. abundance
11. diffuseness, prodigality

12. extravagance, lavish supply
progenitor . . . 4. sire 6. parent 8. ancestor
9. precursor 10. forefather
progenitor of giants (Norse Myth) . . .
4. Ymir 8. rime-cold
progeny . . . 3. son 4. race 5. issue
6. family 7. outcome 8. children,
daughter, outbirth 9. offspring,
parentage, resultant 11. descendants
prognosis . . . 7. outlook 8. forecast
9. diagnosis 10. prediction
14. interpretation
prognosticate . . . 4. bode, omen
7. betoken, predict, presage 8. forebode,
foreshow, foretell, prophecy
9. foretoken
program, programme . . . 4. bill (printed),
card, plan 5. edict 6. notice, policy
7. outline 8. bulletin, platform,
schedule, syllabus 9. broadcast,
catalogue, programma 10. prospectus
12. proclamation, prolegomenon
13. advertisement
programma . . . 5. edict 6. decree, notice
7. preface 12. prolegomenon
progress . . . 4. fare, tour, wend 5. march
6. course, travel 7. advance, journey
10. expedition 11. progression
progress (pert to) . . .
chart . . 5. Gantt
clumsily . . 8. scramble
intelligently . . 6. egress 7. telesis (telesia)
laborious . . 4. plod, wade
outward . . 6. egress
weakly . . 6. feebly
progressive . . . 6. modern, onward
7. forward, gradual, liberal
9. advancing, improving 11. consecutive
12. enterprising
prohibit . . . 3. ban, bar, bid 5. debar,
estop, taboo (tabu) 6. enjoin, forbid,
hinder 7. prevent 9. interdict
prohibited . . . 7. illegal, illicit 8. unlawful
prohibition . . . 3. ban 7. embargo
8. estoppel 9. exclusion 10. prevention,
temperance 11. forbiddance
12. interdicting
project . . . 3. jet, jut 4. abut, cast, idea,
plan 5. shoot 6. beetle, design, device,
scheme 7. pattern, problem 8. contrive,
proposal, protrude 9. intention
10. conception 11. undertaking
projectile . . . 4. bomb 5. shell 6. bullet,
rocket 7. missile, torpedo 8. parabola
9. cartridge
projection . . . 3. arm, ear, fin, jag,
toe 4. barb, cape, lobe, ness, prop,
snag 5. apsis, bulge, ledge, prong,
redan, socle, tenon 6. lobule, tappet
8. headland
prolific . . . 6. fecund 7. fertile, teeming
8. fruitful 9. inventive 10. generative
11. propagative 12. reproductive
prolix . . . 5. wordy 6. diffuse, verbose
8. tiresome 9. prolonged, rigmarole,
wearisome 10. long-winded, pleonastic,
protracted
prolocutor . . . 6. orator 7. speaker,
teacher 8. chairman 9. spokesman
10. mouthpiece 11. Lord Speaker (Eng)
prolong . . . 4. spin 7. draw out 8. continue,

lengthen, postpone, protract
prolonged . . . 7. chronic, delayed
8. extended 9. continued, postponed
10. lengthened, protracted
promenade . . . 4. mall, walk 6. airing,
marina, pasear 7. alameda, gallery
Prometheus (pert to) . . .
famed as . . 5. Titan (a)
poem (Shelley) . . 17. Prometheus
Unbound
tale, tragedy . . 15. Prometheus Bound
16. Prometheus Loosed 24. Prometheus
the Fire Bringer
prominence . . . 4. cusp 6. height
8. eminence, prestige, salience
9. greatness 10. famousness,
importance 11. distinction, obviousness,
prosiliency 12. distinctness,
protuberance
prominent . . . 4. high, star 5. great
6. famous, marked 7. obvious, salient
8. distinct, manifest 9. important
10. celebrated, noticeable, prosilient,
protruding 11. conspicuous, distinctive,
outstanding 13. distinguished
promiscuous . . . 5. mixed 8. careless
9. haphazard, orderless
14. indiscriminate
promise . . . 3. vow 4. hope, oath 5. swear
6. engage, parole, pledge, plight, votive
(by vow) 7. betroth, predict 8. affiance,
contract, give hope 9. assurance, ray
of hope 11. declaration
Promised Land . . . 6. heaven, utopia
8. Paradise 9. millenium, Shangri-la
11. Happy Valley 13. Celestial City
promontory . . . 3. tor 4. cape, naze
(nase), ness, scaw 5. mount, point
8. headland 10. projection
promote . . . 4. help 5. exalt, nurse
6. extend, prefer 7. actuate, advance,
dignify, elevate, finance, further,
improve 8. increase 9. advertise,
encourage, patronize
promoter . . . 5. agent 6. backer 7. planner
8. lobbyist 9. financier, publicist
promotion . . . 6. brevet 7. advance
10. preferment 11. advertising,
furtherance, improvement
prompt . . . 3. cue 4. easy, hint, soon,
tell, yare (anc) 5. alert, early, quick,
ready 6. advise, remind 7. animate,
suggest 8. punctual 11. expeditious
prompter . . . 3. aid 4. cuer 6. pit man,
reader 7. inducer, reciter 8. reminder
promptly . . . 4. tite (anc) 6. at once
7. quickly 9. willingly
promulgate . . . 7. declare, publish
8. proclaim 10. make known
prone . . . 3. apt 4. bent, flat 5. apish
6. supine 7. willing 8. downward
9. prostrate, recumbent
13. ventricumbent
prone to sin . . . 8. peccable
prong . . . 3. nib, peg 4. fang, fork, tine
5. spike, tooth 6. branch
pronghorn . . . 6. cabree (cabrie) 9. prong
buck, springbok
prong key . . . 7. spanner
pronoun . . . 2. he, it, me, my, us, we, ye
3. her, him, one, she, thy, who, you

4. that, thee, them, they, thou, what,
your 5. these, those 6. itself, myself
7. herself, himself, oneself, ourself
8. one's self, yourself 9. ourselves
10. themselves
pronoun (possessive) . . . 2. my 3. her,
his, its, our, 4. hers, mine, one's, ours,
your 5. their, yours 6. theirs
pronounce . . . 3. say 5. bless (holy),
speak, utter 6. affirm, assert 7. adjudge,
declare, deliver 8. announce
9. enunciate 10. adjudicate, articulate,
assibilate
pronouncement . . . 6. decree 8. judgment
9. manifesto 11. affirmation, declaration
12. announcement
pronto . . . 5. quick 7. quickly 8. promptly
11. immediately
pronunciation . . . 4. burr 8. orthoepy
9. utterance (clear) 11. enunciation
pronunciation mark . . . 5. tilde 7. cedilla
8. dieresis
proof . . . 4. test 5. trial 6. result 7. outcome
8. evidence 9. testimony 11. galley
proof 12. confirmation, verification
13. certification
proofreader's mark . . . 4. dele, stet
5. caret, space
prop . . . 3. beg, gib, nog 5. brace, shore,
sprag, staff, stell 6. shorer 7. fulcrum,
support 9. stanchion
propagate . . . 5. breed 6. extend,
spread 7. diffuse, publish 8. disperse,
engender, generate, increase, multiply,
transmit
propel . . . 3. row 4. pole, push, urge
5. drive, impel 7. project
propeller . . . 3. fan, gun, oar 4. vane
5. screw 6. driver 9. plane part
propensity . . . 4. bent 6. desire 7. leaning
8. aptitude, tendency 9. proneness
10. proclivity 11. disposition, inclination
proper . . . 3. fit 4. fine, just, meet,
prim, smug 5. exact, right 6. chaste,
decent, goodly, honest, kilter 7. correct
8. decorous, inherent, orthodox,
suitable 9. excellent, expedient
11. appropriate, grammatical,
respectable 12. conventional
properly . . . 5. fitly 7. rightly, utterly
8. decently, strictly, suitably 9. correctly
11. expediently 14. conventionally
proper sense of worth . . . 5. pride
property . . . 3. res 4. bona, gear
5. asset, goods, trait 6. estate, nature,
realty, wealth 8. holdings 9. attribute,
copyright, ownership 10. real estate
11. peculiarity, possessions
14. characteristic
property (pert to) . . .
act to regain . . 8. replevin (repleven)
destruction of . . 8. sabotage 9. vandalism
landed property . . 9. cadastral
light without heat . . 15. phosphorescence
movable . . 8. chattels
no private ownership . . 11. aspheterism
of matter . . 7. inertia
one's own . . 7. alodium
right . . 4. lien
stolen . . 4. loot, pelf 5. lucre, spoil
suit for recovery . . 6. trover

transferrer . . 7. alienor, grantor
wife to husband . . 3. dos
woman's (Hindu) . . 9. stridhana
  (stridhan)

prophecy . . . 6. oracle 9. utterance
  10. divination, prediction 11. foretelling

prophesy . . . 4. osse 5. augur 6. divine
  7. predict, presage 8. forecast,
  foreshow, foretell 10. vaticinate
  11. preindicate 13. prognosticate

prophet . . . 4. seer 6. medium, oracle
  7. psychic 8. Mohammed, preacher,
  preseger 9. John Smith, predictor
  10. soothsayer 11. Joseph Smith
  (Mormon)

prophet (Bib) . . . 4. Amos 5. Cyrus, Hosea
  6. Elijah (Elias) 7. Malachi, Obadiah

prophet, murder of . . . 8. vaticide

prophetess . . . 5. sibyl 7. seeress
  9. Cassandra (of evil)

prophetic, prophetical . . . 5. vatic
  6. mantic 7. fateful, vatical 8. oracular
  9. vaticinal 10. divinatory, presageful
  11. predicative

propinquity . . . 7. kinship 8. nearness
  9. proximity 12. neighborhood,
  relationship 13. consanguinity

propitiate . . . 5. atone 6. pacify 8. atone
  for 10. conciliate

propitiation . . . 9. atonement, expiation
  12. pacification, satisfaction
  14. reconciliation

propitious . . . 4. rosy 5. happy, lucky
  6. benign, timely 7. helpful 9. favorable,
  opportune, promising 10. auspicious,
  benevolent, prosperous
  12. advantageous, well-disposed

proponent . . . 8. advocate 10. propounder

proportion . . . 4. part, rate 5. quota, ratio,
  share 6. adjust, extent 7. analogy,
  compare, euphony, prorate 8. equalize,
  symmetry 9. apportion

proportional . . . 4. rate 8. relative
  10. comparable, respective
  11. dimensional

proportionate . . . 5. equal 8. adequate,
  relative 9. analogous 10. respective
  11. comparative 13. corresponding

proposal . . . 3. bid 4. plan 5. offer
  6. feeler, motion 8. marriage 9. intention
  10. nomination, suggestion
  11. proposition, supposition

propose . . . 5. image, offer, state,
  toast 6. intend, submit 7. purpose
  8. nominate, propound 9. postulate

proposed (pert to) . . .
for consideration . . 9. suggested
for debate . . 6. mooted
international language . . 2. Ro 3. Ido
  9. Esperanto

proposition . . . 4. plan 5. axiom, lemma
  6. porism, thesis 7. project 8. empirema,
  proposal 9. corollary 11. supposition,
  undertaking

proposition, proof of . . . 18. reductio
  ad absurdum

propound . . . 6. submit 7. propose 8. set
  forth 9. postulate

proprietary . . . 5. owner, title 8. interest,
  medicine (secret) 9. ownership
  10. proprietor 12. landed estate

propriety . . . 7. decency, decorum,
  fitness 8. standard 9. ownership
  10. convention, expedience, properness
  11. correctness, suitability
  12. tastefulness 13. possessorship

propugnaculum . . . 7. bulwark, defense
  8. fortress

prorogue . . . 5. defer 6. extend 7. adjourn,
  prolong 8. postpone, protract

prosaic . . . 4. drab, dull, flat 5. plain,
  prosy 6. prolix, stupid 7. humdrum,
  insipid, tedious 8. ordinary, tiresome
  10. unexciting 11. commonplace
  12. matter-of-fact 13. unimaginative

proscribe . . . 3. ban 6. forbid, outlaw
  7. condemn (to death) 8. prohibit,
  restrain 9. interdict, ostracize

proscription . . . 5. exile 8. outlawry
  11. prohibition 12. interdiction

prosecute . . . 3. sue 4. urge 5. chase
  6. intend (law), pursue 7. carry on,
  enforce, execute

prosecutor . . . 6. lawyer 7. accuser,
  relator 8. attorney

proselyte . . . 3. ger (to Judaism)
  7. convert

proseuche, proseucha . . . 7. oratory
  9. synagogue 13. place of prayer

prosody . . . 13. versification

prospect . . . 4. view 5. buyer, scene, vista
  6. survey 7. explore, foresee, outlook
  8. customer 9. applicant, candidate,
  foresight, intention 10. contestant
  11. probability 12. anticipation

prosper . . . 4. fare 5. cheve, speed
  6. thrive 7. succeed 8. flourish

prosperity . . . 3. hap, ups 4. boom, weal
  6. thrift 7. success, welfare 9. well-being
  11. good fortune

Prospero (pert to) . . .
character . . 9. Ferdinand
daughter . . 7. Miranda
servant . . 5. Ariel
slave . . 7. Caliban
The Tempest . . 11. Duke of Milan

prosperous . . . 4. weal 5. lucky, palmy,
  sonsy (sonsie) 7. wealthy 8. thriving
  9. favorable, fortunate 10. auspicious,
  successful 11. flourishing

prostitute . . . 4. drab 5. venal 6. harlot
  7. corrupt 8. infamous 12. street walker

prostrate . . . 4. flat, raze 5. abase, prone
  6. fallen, grieve, supine 7. exhaust
  8. helpless, supinate 9. flattened,
  recumbent 10. obsequious, submissive

prosy . . . 3. dry 4. dull 6. jejune
  7. prosaic, tedious 11. commonplace
  13. plain-speaking

protagonist . . . 4. hero, lead (theater)
  5. actor 6. leader 8. advocate,
  champion, defender 9. contender,
  principal, spokesman 11. participant

Protagoras (Gr) . . . 7. Sophist, teacher
  11. philosopher

protasis . . . 5. maxim 9. drama part
  11. proposition 12. introduction

protect . . . 3. arm 4. save 5. guard
  6. defend, insure, police, screen, sheath,
  shield 7. cherish, shelter 8. enshield,
  preserve 9. safeguard

protected . . . 5. armed 6. shaded

7. aproned, guarded 8. shielded
12. invulnerable

protection . . . 3. bib, lee 4. coat, fort,
moat 5. aegis (egis), apron, armor,
guard, shade, shell, smock 6. glacis,
refuge, safety 7. defense, parapet,
shelter 8. havelock, passport, security
11. safekeeping 12. preservation

protector . . . 6. patron, regent
8. defender, guardian 10. safekeeper

protector of vineyards (Gr) . . . 7. Priapus

protégé . . . 4. ward 6. charge 9. dependent

Proteida . . . 7. Proteus 10. amphibians
11. salamanders

protein . . . 6. casein 7. albumin, mucedin,
peptone 8. globulin, lecithin, nutrient
9. protamine 11. chlorophyll

protein (pert to) . . .
    blood . . 6. fibrin 8. globulin
    castor oil bean . . 5. ricin (poison)
    egg . . 7. albumin
    milk . . 6. casein
    muscles . . 8. creatine
    seeds . . 7. edestin 8. aleurone, prolamin

Proteles . . . 8. aardwolf

protest . . . 4. aver, beef, deny 6. assert
7. declare 9. objection, stipulate
10. asseverate 11. expostulate
13. expostulation

protestation . . . 6. avowal (public)
7. protest 11. affirmation, obtestation
12. asseveration, supplication

Proteus (pert to) . . .
    biology . . 3. olm 6. amoeba 8. bacteria
        10. salamander
    Gr Myth . . 6. sea god
    Shakespeare . . 17. Gentleman of Verona

protocol . . . 5. rules (official) 7. compact
8. schedule 9. agreement, etiquette
10. memorandum (diplomatic)
12. original copy

protograph . . . 9. holograph
12. illustration (of species)

protoplasm . . . 5. spore 7. nucleus
9. archetype, cytoplasm 10. primordium
11. basis of life

protoplasmic (pert to) . . .
    body . . 8. ectosark 9. ectoplasm,
        endoplasm
    cell . . 6. amoeba (ameba)
    cell contents . . 9. metaplasm
    substance . . 3. gel

protozoan . . . 6. amoeba (ameba),
Lobosa, phylum 11. unicellular

protract . . . 4. spin 5. defer, delay
6. extend 7. prolong, stretch 8. continue,
elongate, lengthen, postpone, protrude
9. expatiate

protrude . . . 3. jut 5. bulge 6. exsert
7. project 9. thrust out

protuberance . . . 3. jag, nub, wen 4. boss,
bump, cere, hump, knob, knot, lobe,
lump, node, snag, wart 5. bulge,
caput, inion, knurl, torus 8. eminence,
swelling 9. extrusion 10. projection

proud . . . 4. vain 5. grand, lofty, noble
6. elated, lordly 7. haughty, pleased,
stately, valiant 8. arrogant, boastful,
imposing, splendid 9. conceited,
gratified 10. impressive
11. independent, magisterial,

magnificent 12. presumptuous,
supercilious

prove . . . 3. try 4. test 5. check, nurse
6. evince, try out, verify 7. confirm,
justify, probate 8. identify, manifest
9. ascertain, establish 11. corroborate,
demonstrate

prove false . . . 6. refute

Provencal dialect . . . 9. langue d'oc

provender . . . 3. hay 4. food 5. grain
6. fodder 8. ensilage

proverb . . . 3. saw 5. adage, axiom
6. byword, enigma, saying 8. aphorism,
link verb, paroemia

proverbial . . . 10. aphoristic
11. sententious 12. epigrammatic

provide . . . 4. give 5. cater, endow, endue,
equip, stock, treat, yield 6. afford,
ration, supply 7. care for, finance
9. make ready 10. contribute

provided . . . 2. if, so 5. boden 6. sobeit
8. afforded, equipped, prepared,
supplied 11. on condition
13. conditionally

Providence founder . . . 13. Roger
Williams (1636)

provident . . . 4. wise 6. frugal, saving
7. prudent, thrifty 9. judicious
10. economical 11. precautious,
preparatory

providential . . . 5. lucky 7. prudent
9. opportune, provident 10. miraculous
11. foresighted

province . . . 4. area, beat, nome 5. arena,
range, shire, tract 6. colony, domain,
empire, eparch, region, sphere 7. circuit,
diocese, kingdom 8. district 9. territory
10. palatinate (royal) 12. jurisdiction

provincial . . . 4. rude 5. crude, local,
rural 6. narrow 7. insular, limited
8. suburban 10. restricted, uncultured
11. countrified 12. narrow-minded
15. unsophisticated

provincialism (diction) . . . 6. patois
10. patavinity

provision . . . 4. fare, food 5. board, stock,
store 6. vivres 7. proviso 9. condition
11. preparation

provisional . . . 9. makeshift, temporary,
tentative 10. promissory, substitute
11. conditional, preparatory
12. experimental 14. circumstantial

provision seller (Mil) . . . 6. sutler

proviso . . . 5. salvo 6. clause

provocative . . . 9. desirable, provoking
10. appetizing, stirring up, suggestive
11. interesting

provoke . . . 3. ire, vex 4. bate, goad,
move, rile, spur, stir 5. anger, annoy,
start 6. arouse, induce, incite, invite,
invoke, nettle, offend, stir up, summon
7. incense 8. irritate 9. challenge
10. antagonize, exasperate

provoking . . . 8. annoying, exciting
10. suggestive 11. interesting
12. antagonizing

provoking laughter . . . 7. risible

prow . . . 3. bow 4. beak, duty, good, proa,
stem 5. brave, honor, prore 6. steven
7. courage, gallant, gun deck

prowess . . . 5. valor 9. gallantry

proximal ... 9. immediate (opp of distal)
proximate ... 4. next 6. direct 7. closest, nearest 9. immediate 10. succeeding
proximity ... 8. nearness, nighness, relation, vicinity 9. adjacence, closeness 11. propinquity
proxy ... 5. agent, power 6. agency, ballot, deputy 7. proctor 9. authority 10. procurator, substitute
prudence ... 6. virtue, wisdom 7. caution, economy 8. sagacity 9. foresight 11. calculation, forethought 13. judiciousness 14. circumspection
prudent ... 4. wary, wise 5. canny 6. frugal 8. cautious, discreet 9. judicious, penny-wise, provident 10. economical 11. circumspect, considerate
prudish ... 4. prim 8. priggish
prune ... 3. cut, lop 4. clip, food, frog, plum, trim, weed 5. dress, plume, preen, purge, shape 6. anoint 7. cut down, tonsure 9. simpleton
prunelike fruit ... 9. myrobalan
pruning knife ... 8. serpette
prurient ... 7. itching, longing, lustful 10. lascivious
Prussia ...
  bay.. 4. Kiel 6. Danzig 10. Pomeranian
  cathedral city .. 5. Essen 7. Cologne 10. Düsseldorf
  city .. 6. Aachen
  color .. 4. blue 12. gold pheasant
  Knight .. 8. Noachite
  lagoon .. 4. haff 12. Frisches Haff
  lancer .. 5. Uhlan
  land aristocracy .. 6. Junker
  legislature .. 7. Landtag
  mountain .. 4. Harz
  resort .. 3. Ems
  river .. 3. Ems 4. Elbe, Oder, Saar
  seaport .. 4. Kiel 5. Emden 7. Stettin
  State .. 6. German
pry ... 4. nose, peek 5. lever, mouse, snoop 6. meddle, search
prying ... 7. curious, peeking, peeping, peering 8. snooping 9. searching 10. meddlesome 11. inquisitive
psalm (pert to) ...
  book .. 7. Psalter
  Fiftieth, Vulgate .. 8. Miserere
  Mass opening .. 7. introit
  Ninety-fourth, Vulgate .. 6. Venite
Psalms (Old Test) ... 7. Psalter
psalterium ... 4. lyra 6. omasum 7. stomach 9. manyplies
psammite ... 4. rock 9. sandstone
psephology ... 7. pebbles (study of)
psephomancy ... 19. divination by pebbles
pseudatoll ... 9. coral reef
pseudo ... 4. sham 5. bogus, false 6. untrue 7. feigned 8. spurious 9. deceptive, imitation, pretender
pseudologist ... 4. liar (humorous)
pseudology ... 5. lying 9. falsehood
pseudonym ... 5. alias 6. anonym 7. pen name 10. nom de plume
pseudonym (famed) ...
  C L Dodgson .. 12. Lewis Carroll
  Mary Ann Evans .. 11. George Eliot

  Samuel Clemens .. 9. Mark Twain
  W S Porter .. 6. O Henry
psychagogic ... 9. inspiring 10. attractive, persuasive
psyche ... 4. mind, self, soul 6. spirit
psychedelic psychologist ... 5. Leary
psychic ... 6. mental 9. spiritual 10. Gnosticism 11. incorporeal 12. spiritualist, supernatural 13. psychological
psychic (pert to) ...
  emanation .. 4. aura
  devotion .. 6. autism
  monism .. 10. one reality
psychotic ... 3. mad 6. insane 8. neurotic 12. psychopathic
Ptah (pert to) ...
  Egypt Relig .. 8. chief god (of Memphis)
  father of .. 3. men 4. gods
  representation .. 5. mummy
  symbolic of .. 4. life 8. strength
ptarmigan ... 4. rype 6. grouse
pterodactyl ... 7. reptile (extinct) 9. pterosaur 11. ornithosaur
pterography (description of) ... 8. feathers
pteroid ... 8. fernlike, winglike
pteropod ... 6. Clione (Arctic) 7. mollusk
ptilosis ... 7. plumage 9. madarosis 10. loss of hair 15. loss of eyelashes
ptisan ... 3. tea 5. drink 6. coddle 9. decoction
Ptolemy (pert to) ...
  author of .. 8. Almagest
  birthplace .. 5. Egypt (130 AD)
  famed as .. 10. astronomer, geographer
public ... 3. inn 4. open 5. state 6. people, vulgar 8. communal 9. clientele, community
public (pert to) ...
  assembly .. 4. Diet
  conveyance .. 3. bus, cab, car 4. taxi, tram 5. train 10. jinrikisha (jinricksha)
  display .. 10. exhibition 13. exhibitionism
  edict .. 3. ban 12. proclamation
  entertainment .. 7. ridotto
  hangman (Eng) .. 9. Jack Ketch
  lands .. 4. ager (Hist) 6. domain
  official .. 6. notary
  position .. 8. official
  storehouse .. 5. étape
  walk .. 4. mall 7. alameda 9. esplanade, promenade
publication ... 4. book 8. pamphlet, printing 12. notification, proclamation, promulgation
publication (pert to) ...
  article .. 7. feature
  condensed .. 7. tabloid
  make-up .. 6. format
  prelim .. 9. prodromus
publicist ... 5. solon 6. Gallup, lawyer, writer 10. journalist, publicizer 11. commentator
publish ... 4. edit, vent 5. issue, print 6. blazon, delate 7. divulge 8. proclaim 10. promulgate 11. disseminate
publish (pert to) ...
  abroad .. 8. promulge
  after death .. 10. posthumous
  banns .. 7. betroth 8. marriage

far and wide .. 6. blazon
without authority .. 6. pirate
    10. plagiarize
publisher's description (book) ...
    5. blurb 13. advertisement
publisher's inscription (book) ... 5. facts
    8. colophon
Puccini heroine ... 4. Mimi
pucker ... 4. fold 5. bulge, purse 6. crease
    7. anxiety, fluster, wrinkle 8. contract
puckered ... 7. bullate 8. wrinkled
    10. contracted
puckish ... 6. impish 8. Pucklike
    10. mysterious 11. mischievous
pud ... 3. paw 4. hand 8. forefoot
pudding ... 4. duff, mush, plum, sago
    6. junket 7. custard, dessert, tapioca
    8. roly-poly, softness, stuffing (game)
    9. Yorkshire
puddle ... 3. mud 4. mess, pond, pool
    5. plash, swamp 6. muddle 7. plashet,
    pollute
puddle duck ... 7. mallard
puddock ... 4. kite, toad 7. buzzard
    9. enclosure (paddock)
pueblo ... 4. town 7. village
Pueblo (pert to) ...
    ceremonial chamber .. 4. kiva
    Indian (American) .. 4. Hopi, Piro, Tano,
    Zuni 5. Acoma 7. Keresan 12. cliff
    dweller
    water jar .. 4. olla
puerile ... 4. weak 5. young 7. babyish,
    trivial 8. childish, juvenile, youthful
    12. simple-minded
Puerto Rican (pert to) ...
    bark, beverage .. 4. mabi
    dove .. 4. rola
    fish .. 4. sama, sisi 8. porkfish
Puerto Rico ... see also *Puerto Rican*
    capital .. 7. San Juan
    city .. 5. Ponce 7. Arecibo
    discoverer .. 8. Columbus
    first settlement .. 7. Caparra
    government .. 12. Commonwealth
    Indian name .. 9. Borinquen
    island (off shore) .. 4. Mona 7. Culebra
    island group .. 15. Greater Antilles
    politically .. 12. Commonwealth
    program (Polit) .. 18. Operation Bootstrap
    sea .. 9. Caribbean
puff ... 3. blow, blub, chug, flam, pant,
    pegh (Scot), pouf, waff 5. elate 7. efflate
puffbird ... 6. barbet 8. barbacou
pug ... 3. dog, elf 4. moth, puck, snub
    5. chaff, dwarf 6. harlot, refuse (grain),
    sprite 8. bargeman, mistress, pugilist
    9. footprint, hobgoblin
pugging ... 8. grasping, thieving
pugilistic ... 6. fistic 10. pugnacious
pugnacious ... 9. combative
    11. belligerent, quarrelsome
pugnacious man ... 12. fighting cock
pug-nosed ... 5. camus (camuse)
puisne ... 4. puny 5. judge, later,
    petty 6. feeble, junior 9. associate,
    unskilled 10. law student, subsequent
    11. subordinate
puissance ... 5. force, might, power
    8. strength 9. authority
puissant ... 6. mighty, potent 7. mastery

    8. forcible, powerful 13. authoritative
pulchritude ... 5. grace 6. beauty
    10. comeliness, loveliness
pule ... 4. peep 5. cheep, whine 7. ululate,
    whimper
pulicat ... 8. bandanna (bandana)
puling ... 6. sickly 7. babyish, howling,
    whining 8. childish, delicate
Pulitzer prizes ... 6. awards
    10. journalism, literature
pull ... 2. pu 3. lug, tow, tug 4. drag,
    draw, haul, yank 5. bouse, drink,
    tweak 6. effort, strain 7. attract, extract
    9. influence 10. attraction
pull (pert to) ...
    apart .. 4. rend, tear 7. destroy
    8. demolish, enfeeble, separate
    back .. 5. demur 6. recoil 7. retract
    8. withdraw
    down .. 4. fell, raze 9. dismantle
    off .. 3. pug 6. avulse, commit 8. carry
    out 10. accomplish
    one's leg .. 4. hoax, joke 7. deceive,
    flatter 8. hoodwink 9. make fun of
    out .. 5. leave 6. secede 7. extract
    9. eradicate
    up .. 4. stop 5. elate 6. aviate 7. arraign,
    extract
pullet ... 4. fowl 5. child 7. bivalve
    8. poullard
pulley (pert to) ...
    groove .. 5. gorge
    grooved .. 5. fusee (fuzee)
    part .. 4. arse
    wheel .. 4. sheave (grooved)
pulp ... 3. pap 4. marc, mash, mass
    5. chyme 8. magazine 10. fleshy part
pulpit ... 4. ambo, bema, dais, desk
    5. stage 6. clergy 7. rostrum 8. platform,
    scaffold
pulpy ... 5. mushy 7. squashy
pulpy (pert to) ...
    dregs .. 5. magma
    fruit .. 3. uva 4. pome 6. sidder (siddow)
    state .. 4. mash, soft 6. fleshy
pulsate ... 4. beat, drum 5. throb
    7. vibrate
pulsation ... 5. ictus 6. moving, rhythm
    7. impulse, systole 8. acrotism (failure),
    vitality 9. throbbing, vibrating
pulsatory ... 8. rhythmic, systolic
    9. throbbing
pulse ... 3. dal (split) 5. seeds (edible),
    throb 6. rhythm 7. beating 8. resonate
    9. pulsation, throbbing
pulse family ... 3. pea 8. Fabaceae
pulverize ... 4. bray, mull 5. crush,
    grind 6. abrade, powder 7. atomize
    8. levigate 9. triturate 12. disintegrate
pulverulent ... 5. dusty 7. crumbly
    8. powdered
puma ... 6. cougar 7. Quechua (Kochua)
pummel ... 4. beat, maul 5. thump
    6. batter, buffet, hammer, pommel,
    strike
pump ... 3. gin, ram 4. draw, emit, quiz
    5. eject 6. elicit, propel 7. extract
    8. interrogate
    10. pulsometer 11. interrogate
pumpernickel ... 5. bread (Westphalian)
pump handle ... 5. sweep, swipe
pumpkin (pert to) ...

head . . 4. dolt 7. Puritan 9. blockhead, Roundhead

seed . . 7. sunfish 8. sailboat

yam . . 11. sweet potato

pun . . . 4. yoke 8. paragram 9. assonance, equivoque (equivoke), witticism 11. paronomasia

punch . . . 3. die 4. blow, poke, prod, tool 5. douse, drink, negus, paste 6. liquor, pierce 7. mattoir (etcher's) 8. beverage, puncture 9. perforate 11. punch cattle

Punch and Judy dog . . . 4. Toby

Punch Bowl . . . 6. crater 9. graveyard (Honolulu), hot spring (Yellowstone)

puncheon . . . 3. die 4. cask 5. punch, stamp 6. dagger

puncher . . . 6. cowboy 10. cowpuncher, perforator

punching . . . 8. piercing 9. pertusion

punctilious . . . 4. nice 5. exact 6. formal, strict 7. correct, precise 8. exacting 9. observant 10. meticulous, scrupulous

punctuation mark . . . 3. dot 4. dash, star 5. brace, breve, colon, comma, tilde 6. dagger, hyphen, period, tittle, umlaut 8. brackets, ellipsis 9. ampersand, semicolon 10. apostrophe, circumflex 11. exclamation 12. question mark

pundit . . . 6. nestor, savant 7. Brahmin, scholar, teacher 10. learned man

pung . . . 4. sled 6. sleigh

pungent . . . 4. keen, racy, sour, tart 5. acrid, acute, sharp, smart, snell 6. biting, bitter 7. caustic, odorous, painful, peppery, piquant 8. piercing, poignant, stabbing 11. stimulating

pungent herb . . . 6. Asarum

punish . . . 4. fine 5. mulct, spank, wreak 6. amerce 7. chasten, correct 8. chastise, penalize 9. castigate 10. discipline

punishment (pert to) . . .

Brehon law . . 4. eric

by torture . . 5. strappado

church . . 15. excommunication

condign . . 11. retributive

law . . 5. peine

term . . 5. penal 7. penalty, revenge 8. punitive

Turk, Chin . . 9. bastinade

Welsh law (anc) . . 3. cro 7. galanas

punitive . . . 5. penal 10. revengeful, vindictive 11. castigatory

Punjab, India . . .

capital . . 6. Lahore (West) 8. Amritsar (East)

language . . 7. Panjabi

name meaning . . 10. Five Rivers

soldier . . 4. Sikh

summer capital . . 5. Simla

punk . . . 3. bad 5. child 6. amadou 7. lighter 8. inferior 9. touchwood

punto . . . 3. hit 5. joint (fencing) 6. stitch (needle)

puny . . . 4. weak 5. frail, petty 6. little, meager, puisne, sickly 8. delicate 14. inconsiderable

pupa . . . 5. shell 9. chrysalis

pupil . . . 3. eye, son 4. tyro 5. élève, youth 7. écolier, learner, scholar 8. disciple, neophyte

puppet . . . 3. guy 4. doll 5. image 6. maumet 9. miniature, nonentity 10. figurehead, marionette

puppeteer, famed . . . 4. Sarg

puppy . . . 3. dog, fop 5. shark, whelp

purblind . . . 10. dim-sighted 11. partly blind 12. narrow-minded, undiscerning

purchasable . . . 5. venal 8. bribable, hireling 9. mercenary 11. corruptible

purchase . . . 3. buy, win 4. earn, hold 5. bribe 6. buying, obtain 7. acquire, bribery, procure 8. barratry, foothold, leverage

purchaser . . . 5. buyer 6. patron, vendee 8. customer 9. acquéreur 13. adjudicataire

purdah (Ind) . . . 4. veil 6. screen 7. curtain

pure . . . 4. neat, real 5. clean, fresh, godly, sheer, utter 6. candid, chaste, simple, vestal 7. genuine, perfect, refined, unmixed 8. absolute, filtered, innocent 9. downright, faultless, inviolate, stainless, undefiled, unsullied 11. pure-blooded, uncorrupted, unqualified 13. unadulterated

purga (Russ) . . . 8. blizzard 9. snowstorm

purgative . . . 5. jalap 6. physic 8. absterge 9. catharsis, cathartic, cleansing

purgatory . . . 4. hell 5. limbo 6. erebus 7. torment

purified . . . 10. elutriated

purified wool fat . . . 7. lanolin (lanoline)

purify . . . 5. clean, purge 6. filter, refine, spurge 7. cleanse, epurate 8. lustrate, renovate, sanctify 9. elutriate

purifying . . . 7. smectic 8. depurant 9. cathartic, cleansing 10. distilling

Purim . . . 7. holiday 8. festival (Jew) 11. Feast of Lots

puritan . . . 5. prude 7. ascetic 9. precisian 10. Separatist

puritan clergyman . . . 10. Cartwright

puritanical . . . 6. strict 7. ascetic 11. strait-laced 15. hyperorthodox

purity . . . 8. chastity 9. innocence

purl . . . 4. eddy 5. frill 6. murmur, ripple 7. trickle

purloin . . . 5. filch, steal, swipe 6. finger 11. appropriate

purple . . . 4. bice, lake, plum, puce 5. lilac, mauve, pansy, regal, showy 6. damson, orchid, ornate, Tyrian, violet 7. Cassius, magenta, mollusk, pigment 8. amaranth, Burgundy, imperial, mulberry 9. brilliant, cathedral 11. sovereignty

purple (pert to) . . .

bottle . . 4. moss

cactus . . 8. Missouri

death adder . . 10. black snake

emperor . . 9. butterfly

Forbidden City . . 5. Lhasa

granadilla . . 13. passion flower

haw . . 7. capulin (Mex) 8. bluewood

Heart, Order of . . 5. medal (Mil) (est by Washington, re-est. 1932)

laurel . . 12. rhododendron

lily . . 8. Turk's cap

martin . . 7. swallow

navy . . 10. marine blue

nightshade . . 9. trompillo

purport ... 4. feck, gist, mean 5. sense, tenor 6. allege, import, intent 7. meaning 9. substance

purpose ... 3. aim, end 4. goal, idly, main, plan, sake 5. avail 6. design, intend, intent, motive 7. meaning, resolve 8. function 9. determine, discourse, intention, objective, predesign

purposive ... 5. telic

purse ... 3. bag, cly 5. pouch 6. pucker, wallet 7. wrinkle 8. crumenal (obs) 10. pocketbook 12. porte-monnaie

purser ... 5. clerk (ship's) 6. bursar 7. boucher, cashier 9. paymaster

purse rat ... 12. pocket gopher

pursue ... 3. run 4. hunt, seek, tack 5. chase, court 6. follow 7. carry on, proceed 9. persecute 10. specialize

pursuit ... 3. chase, quest, scent 9. objective 10. occupation

purvey ... 5. cater 6. supply 7. foresee, provide

purveyor of untruth (Bib) ... 7. Ananias

purview ... 4. body (statute) 5. field (law), range, scope 7. compass 8. province

push ... 2. go 4. bunt, butt, gang, ping, pole, prod, urge 5. crowd, elbow, impel, nudge, press, shove 6. attack, energy, propel, thrust 9. importune, offensive (Mil) 10. forge ahead, propulsion 12. press forward

pusillanimous ... 4. base, weak 5. timid 6. craven 8. cowardly 12. fainthearted, mean-spirited

put ... 3. set 4. butt, dupe, fool, sail 5. place, throw 6. impose, option, phrase, repose, rustic 7. deposit 8. invest in 9. attribute

put (pert to) ...
an end to .. 5. quash (law)
away .. 4. kill 5. store 6. murder
back .. 6. demote 7. replace, restore
before .. 6. appose
down .. 6. humble 7. degrade, deposit, depress 8. suppress
forth .. 5. exert 7. propose 9. circulate
off .. 4. doff, haft, sail 5. defer, delay, evade 8. postpone
on alert .. 5. alarm 6. alarum
out .. 3. vex 4. oust 5. eject 9. ostracize 10. expatriate
over .. 6. bilk 5. cheat, trick 7. deceive

put in, into ...
action .. 6. excite
holy place .. 8. enshrine
motion .. 6. arouse
opposition .. 3. pit
order .. 4. trim 5. mense 6. settle 7. arrange 8. organize 11. systematize
rapture .. 8. entrance
relation to .. 9. correlate 10. coordinate, co-ordinate
rhythm .. 7. meter
scabbard .. 7. sheathe

putrefaction ... 3. rot 5. decay 13. decomposition 14. disintegration

puttee ... 6. gaiter 9. legging

put to ...
flight .. 4. rout
strain .. 3. tax
trouble .. 10. discommode

use .. 5. apply
wrong use .. 8. misapply

put up ... 3. pay 4. ante, hang 5. build, offer 6. pledge 7. install 8. nominate 9. construct

put up with ... 4. bear 5. stand 6. endure, permit 7. stomach 8. tolerate

puzzle ... 3. cap 4. crux, pose 5. griph (griphus), poser, rebus 6. enigma, riddle 7. anagram, confuse, mystify, nonplus, paradox, perplex, problem 8. entangle 9. conundrum 10. complicate, disconcert

puzzle (pert to) ...
monkey .. 5. piñon
picture .. 5. rebus
word .. 7. charade 9. crossword 10. anacrostic

puzzling ... 6. knotty 10. perplexing 11. enigmatical, paradoxical

pygarg, pygargus ... 5. addax 8. sea eagle 9. quadruped (Bib)

Pygmalion (pert to) ...
color .. 5. brown
endowed with life .. 7. Galatea (statue)
king of .. 6. Cyprus
sister .. 4. Dido
talented as .. 8. sculptor

pygmy, pigmy ... 3. elf 4. Akka, Doko, pixy 5. atomy, Batwa, dwarf, gnome, minim, short 6. Abongo, Achuas 7. manikin 9. dandiprat

pygmy (pert to) ...
hog .. 7. Porcula
musk deer .. 10. chevrotain
owl .. 8. gnome owl
rattlesnake .. 10. massasauga
squirrel (smallest known) .. 9. Sciuridae

pyic ... 8. purulent, virulent

pyknic ... 3. fat 5. round, stout

pylon ... 4. post 5. tower 6. marker 7. gateway 10. monumental mass

pyosis ... 3. pus 4. boil 11. suppuration

pyramid ... 4. cone, heap, pile, tomb 5. tower 8. monument 9. speculate

pyramid (pert to) ...
builder, largest .. 6. Cheops (khufu)
Egypt .. 9. The Sphinx 12. Great Pyramid, Tomb of Cheops
group .. 5. Gizeh 7. Menkare 8. Chephren 9. Mycerinus
kidney (Anat) .. 7. Perrein 10. Malpighian
Mexico .. 7. Benares
site of Cheops .. 4. Giza (Gizeh)
texts .. 12. inscriptions 13. Book of the Dead
world wonder .. 12. Great Pyramid, Tomb of Cheops

pyramidal ... 4. huge 7. angular, conical 8. enormous, imposing

pyre ... 4. bier, heap, pile 9. cremation, death fire

Pyrenees (pert to) ...
bandit .. 8. Miquelet
mountain chain .. 11. France-Spain
peak .. 9. Pic d'Aneto 11. Pic de Méthou
resort .. 3. Pau
State .. 7. Andorra (Fr)

pyriform ... 10. pear-shaped

pyrology (study of) ... 4. heat

pyromaniac ... 7. firebug 8. arsonist

10. incendiary

pyrope ... 3. red 6. garnet 7. mineral
pyrophobia ... 11. dread of fire
pyrotechnics ... 7. oratory, science
   9. fireworks
pyrrhic ... 4. foot (Pros) 5. dance
Pyrrhic victory ... 11. at great cost
pyrrho (comb form) ... 3. red 5. tawny
Pyrrho (Gr) ... 7. teacher (Pyrrhonism)
pyrrhotist ... 7. redhead
Pyrrhulexia ... 5. finch 8. grosbeak
Pythagorus (Gr) ...
   birthplace .. 5. Samos
   daughter .. 4. Camo
   famed as .. 11. philosopher
   friend .. 5. Damon
   teacher of .. 8. theorems 18. influence
   of numbers
Pythian (pert to) ...
   contests .. 6. Delphi

Festival .. 11. Panhellenic
   patron .. 6. Apollo
   term .. 8. ecstatic 9. phrenetic
python (pert to) ...
   home .. 11. Mt Parnassus
   myth .. 14. monster serpent
   slaver .. 6. Apollo
   survivor of .. 10. muddy earth (anc)
pythonic ... 4. huge 6. Pythia
   (Delphi), python 8. oracular
   9. monstrous
pythonism, art of ... 8. prophecy
   10. divination
pyx, pix ... 3. box 4. test, veil 5. chest
   6. coffer, vessel (Eccl) 8. binnacle,
   ciborium 10. tabernacle
pyxie ... 5. shrub 9. evergreen
pyxis ... 3. box 4. Argo (Astron), vase
   9. jewel case

Q

Q ... 5. queue 6. letter (17th)
QED ... 21. Quod Erat Demonstrandum
Q-ship (Eng) ... 11. mystery ship
qua, quabird ... 10. night heron
quachil ... 12. pocket gopher
quack ... 3. cry (duck) 5. faker 7. empiric
   8. impostor 10. charlatan, pretender
   10. medicaster, mountebank
quack medicine ... 6. patent 7. nostrum
quad (pert to) ...
   printing .. 5. crown 7. quadrat
   school .. 4. yard 6. campus
   10. quadrangle
   slang (Brit) .. 5. horse
quadra ... 6. fillet, listel, plinth
quadragenarian ... 12. forty-year-old
   (person)
Quadragesima ... 4. Fast, Lent 6. Sunday
   (1st in Lent) 7. Holy Day 9. Forty Days
quadrangle ... 5. plane (four-angles)
   6. square 7. rhombus 8. tetragon
quadrant ... 4. gill 6. fourth 7. measure,
   quarter 8. farthing, six hours
   10. instrument, semicircle
quadrate ... 4. suit 5. adapt, agree,
   ideal 6. square 7. conform, perfect,
   squared 8. balanced 10. correspond
   13. correspondent
quadriga ... 3. car 7. chariot (4-horse)
   10. four horses
quadrumane ... 3. ape 6. mammal
   7. gorilla, Primate (except Man)
   10. chimpanzee 13. feetlike hands
quadruped ... 3. ass, cat, cow, dog
   4. bull, calf, colt, foal, lion, mule
   5. burro, horse, jenny, panda, tiger
   6. badger, donkey, mammal 7. bullock
   10. four-footed
quaff ... 5. draft, drink 6. tipple
quag ... 5. quake 6. quiver 8. quagmire
quagga ... 5. zebra 7. wild ass
quaggy ... 6. boggy, fenny 6. spongy
   7. queachy 8. yielding

quagmire ... 3. bay, fen 4. lair 5. marsh,
   swamp 6. morass 11. predicament
quahog ... 4. clam
quail ... 3. cow 4. bird 5. colin,
   cower, quake, shake 6. blench,
   curdle, flinch, shrink, tremor, Turnix
   7. massena, tremble 8. bobwhite,
   Coturnix 9. coagulate, courtesan, eddish
   hen
quail (pert to) ...
   button .. 6. Turnix
   call .. 4. pipe
   color .. 9. hair brown
   flock .. 4. bevy
   French .. 6. caille
   hawk .. 7. falcon
   quailhead .. 11. lark sparrow
   snipe .. 9. dowitcher
quaint ... 3. odd 4. wise 5. proud
   6. expert, pretty, proper 7. curious,
   prudent, refined, strange, uncouth
   8. fanciful, peculiar
quake ... 5. shake 6. quiver, shiver,
   tremor 7. shudder, tremble, vibrate
   10. earthquake
Quaker (pert to) ...
   bird .. 9. albatross (sooty)
   city .. 12. Philadelphia
   colonizer .. 4. Penn (Wm)
   color .. 4. drab, gray 5. acier
   poet .. 6. Barton 8. Whittier
   sect .. 16. Society of Friends
   sect founder .. 9. George Fox
   State .. 12. Pennsylvania
   word .. 4. thee
qualified ... 3. fit 4. able 6. fitted
   7. adapted, capable, enabled, limited
   8. eligible, entitled, equipped, modified,
   prepared, tempered 9. competent
   10. restrained, restricted 11. conditional
qualify ... 3. fit 4. name 5. abate, adapt,
   be fit, equip, limit, train 6. enable,
   modify, soften, temper 7. assuage,

prepare 8. diminish, mitigate, modulate, quantify, regulate, restrain, restrict

quality . . . 5. prime, trait, value 6. nature, pathos, strain 7. caliber, texture 8. accident, capacity, inferior, nobility, property 9. attribute, character, specialty 10. difference, excellence 14. characteristic

quality of heredity . . . 9. lineality

qualm . . . 4. pall 5. demur, doubt, spasm 6. nausea, regret 7. scruple 9. faintness, misgiving 11. compunction 12. apprehension

quandary . . . 3. fix 6. pickle, plight, strait 7. dilemma 10. perplexity 11. predicament

quandy . . . 9. squaw duck

quant . . . 11. punting pole

quantity . . . 3. ace, any, gob, lot, sea, sum 4. bulk, dose, drop, mass, much, raff, raft, scad, size, some 5. batch, scads, store 6. amount, cupful, degree, extent, hatful, number, oceans 7. handful

quantity (pert to) . . .
fixed . . 8. quota 9. constant
mathematics . . 4. surd 5. graph 6. scalar, vector
minute . . 4. atom, dram, iota, mill
standard . . 4. unit 9. allotment
time unit . . 4. rate

quantum . . . 4. body 5. share 6. amount, energy, theory 7. atomics, portion 9. quantity

quap . . . 5. heave, throb 6. quaver 9. palpitate

Quapaw . . . 5. Sioux 8. Arkansas

quarantine . . . 7. confine, isolate 8. pratique (marine) 9. forty days (law), isolation, segregate 11. confinement

quarantine flag . . . 6. yellow 7. warning 10. yellow jack

quarenden . . . 5. apple (deep red)

quarentene . . . 4. rood 7. furlong

quark . . . 3. caw 5. croak, quawk

quarl, quarle . . . 4. sour, tile 5. brick 6. cundle, medusa 9. jellyfish

quarred . . . 6. soured 7. curdled (beer)

quarrel . . . 3. row 4. spat, tiff, tile 5. arrow, brawl, broil, cavil, flite (flyte), gnarr, scene, scrap 6. affray, bicker, chisel, dustup, hassle 7. diamond, wrangle 8. argument, squabble 9. complaint 10. accusation, Donnybrook, free-for-all 11. altercation 12. disagreement 16. misunderstanding

quarrel (pert to) . . .
hereditary . . 4. feud 8. vendetta
noisy . . 6. fracas, jangle, uproar
over . . 6. bicker 7. contend, dispute
petty . . 4. miff, spat, tiff

quarrelsome . . . 8. choleric, petulant 9. irascible, irritable, litigious 10. discordant, pugnacious 11. belliferent, contentious 13. argumentative

quarry . . . 4. delf, game, heap, mine, prey 6. victim 8. entrails, excavate 12. object hunted

quart . . . 5. gills (eight) 6. fourth 7. measure 8. schooner

quarter . . . 4. coin, side 5. house 6. fourth,

region 7. measure, two bits 8. insignia, semester 9. direction, dismember 10. quadrature (Astron), quadrisect

quarter (pert to) . . .
acre . . 4. rood
animal . . 5. horse
astronomy . . 10. quadrature
fathom . . 6. fourth
military . . 8. clemency (to enemy)
music . . 4. note 8. crotchet
nautical . . 4. deck, lift 6. galley
pint . . 4. gill
sports . . 4. back 11. quarterback

quartered . . . 8. billeted 12. quartersawed (wood)

quarters (living) . . . 4. camp, room 5. abode 7. housing, lodging, shelter 8. barracks, diggings, lodgings, lodgment 9. dormitory

Quartodeciman . . . 10. paschalist

quartz . . . 4. onyx, sard 5. flint 6. silica 7. mineral

quartz (pert to) . . .
banded, spotted . . 4. onyx 5. agate 6. jasper 8. sardonyx
blue-red . . 10. bloodstone, heliotrope
brown . . 5. smoky 6. cairngorm
brownish-red . . 7. sinople
chalcedony . . 4. sard 9. carnelian 11. chrysoprase
flint . . 9. hornstone 10. touchstone
glass . . 6. silica
green . . 5. prase (dull) 6. plasma (bright) 11. chrysoprase
hard . . 5. flint
opaque . . 6. jasper
purple . . 8. amethyst
red . . 4. sard 9. carnelian
ruby-red . . 7. rubasse
silica . . 5. silex
transparent . . 11. rock crystal
violet . . 8. amethyst
yellow . . 5. topaz (false) 7. citrine

quash . . . 4. cass, void 5. abate, annul, crush, quell, shake 6. hush up, subdue 7. shatter 8. suppress 9. overthrow 10. extinguish

quasi . . . 4. as if 6. pseudo 8. as it were, as though 9. seemingly

Quasimodo . . . 9. Hunchback (Notre Dame), Low Sunday (first after Easter)

quatern . . . 8. fourfold 10. quadrangle 12. four quarters (having)

quaver . . . 5. shake, trill 6. quiver 7. tremble, tremolo, vibrate 11. trepidation 13. tremulousness

quawk . . . 3. caw 5. heron (night) 7. screech 8. quagmire

quay, key . . . 4. pier 5. levee, wharf 7. landing

queachy . . . 5. boggy, bushy, fenny 6. marshy, swampy

quean . . . 4. girl, jade, slut 5. vixen, wench 6. harlot

queasy . . . 4. sick 8. delicate, qualmish, ticklish, troubled 9. hazardous, ill at ease, nauseated, squeamish, uncertain, unsettled

Quebec . . .
battle site . . 15. Plains of Abraham
capital . . 6. Quebec (province)

city .. 6. Verdun 8. Montreal 11. Three Rivers
founder .. 9. Champlain (1608)
river .. 10. St Lawrence
vehicle .. 7. calèche (2-wheeled)
quebrada ... 3. gap 5. brook, gorge 7. fissure
qued, quede ... 3. bad 4. evil 8. The Devil
queen ... 3. ant, bee, cat 7. empress, goddess, monarch 8. chessman, honeybee 9. sovereign 10. chess piece 11. playing card
queen (pert to) ...
bee .. 8. honeybee
cactus .. 7. Mexican 10. ornamental
conch .. 5. shell
fern .. 5. royal
pigeon .. 7. crowned
Queen (pert to) ...
Bernice's Hair (Astron) .. 13. Coma Berenices
City of the Lakes .. 7. Buffalo
City of the West .. 10. Cincinnati
Mab .. 11. Fairie Queen (Rom/Juliet)
Victoria .. 14. Widow of Windsor (nickname by Kipling)
Queen Anne's ...
lace .. 6. carrot (wild)
melon .. 6. dudaim
War .. 17. Spanish Succession
War treaty .. 14. Peace of Utrecht
queen of ...
chess .. 4. fers
fairies .. 3. Mab 7. Titania 8. Gloriana
gods .. 4. Hera (Gr), Juno (Rom)
Hearts .. 9. Elizabeth
heaven .. 10. Virgin Mary
Isles (Brit) .. 6. Albion
night .. 4. moon
Scots .. 4. Mary
Sheba .. 6. Balkis (Koran)
Spades (solo) .. 5. basta
the Adriatic .. 6. Venice
the Antilles .. 4. Cuba
the East .. 7. Antioch (Syria), Batavia (Java), Zenobia
the tides .. 7. the moon
the underworld .. 3. Hel
queen's (pert to) ...
arm .. 6. musket
flower .. 9. bloodwood
hub .. 7. tobacco
July flower .. 8. damewort
ware .. 9. Wedgewood
Queensland (Austral) ...
animal .. 8. kangaroo 9. koala bear (teddy bear)
bean .. 8. snuffbox
capital .. 8. Brisbane
fire tree .. 5. tulip
fish .. 9. trumpeter
hemp .. 4. sida 6. lucern 9. jellyleaf 11. paddy lucern
plum .. 8. Burdekin
tree (timber) .. 3. box 4. pine 5. beech, ebony 10. sandalwood 12. Dundathu pine
queer ... 3. odd, rum 4. sham 5. false, funny 6. insane, thwart 7. strange 8. peculiar, singular, spurious

9. eccentric, fantastic, interfere
10. disconcert, suspicious
11. counterfeit 12. questionable
queer fellow ... 4. coot, goop 6. galoot, geezer 9. character
queersome ... 3. odd 7. strange 8. abnormal
Queer Street ... 9. imaginary
queest ... 8. ringdove
queet ... 4. coot 5. ankle
quell ... 3. end 4. calm 5. allay, crush, quash, quiet 6. pacify, reduce, soothe, stifle, subdue 7. destroy, repress 8. suppress 9. overpower 10. extinguish
quench ... 4. cool, damp, sate 5. allay, check, slake, still 6. stifle, subdue 7. assuage, gratify 8. suppress 10. discourage, extinguish 11. clamp down on
quenelle ... 8. meatball
Quercus ... 4. oaks
queriman ... 4. fish 6. mullet
quern ... 4. mill (grain)
quernal ... 5. crown (oak leaves)
querulous ... 7. fretful, peevish 9. plaintive 11. complaining 12. faultfinding
query ... 5. doubt 6. murmur 7. inquire, inquiry, whining 8. question
quest ... 3. bay (dog's) 4. hunt, seek 6. desire, pursue, search 7. inquest, request 8. seek alms 9. adventure 12. solicitation
question ... 3. ask 4. quiz 5. cavil, doubt, grill, poser, query, scout, topic 6. riddle 7. dispute, inquire, inquiry, problem 8. erotesis 9. catechize (catechise) 11. interrogate, uncertainty 12. interpellate (formally) 13. interrogation
question, out of the ... 6. absurd 7. refused 8. hopeless, rejected 10. impossible, prohibited 11. unthinkable
questionable ... 4. moot 7. dubious 8. doubtful 9. debatable, dishonest, uncertain 10. disputable, improbable 12. unbelievable 13. problematical
questioning (prolonged) ...
11. inquisition
question mark ... 7. erotema, eroteme
quet ... 3. auk 5. murre 9. guillemot
quethe ... 3. say 4. call, tell, will 5. quoth, speak 6. clamor 8. bequeath 9. testament
quetzal, quezal ... 6. trogon 14. national emblem (Guatemala)
Quetzalcoatl ... 10. god of winds (Aztec)
queue ... 3. cue 4. hair, line (waiting) tail 7. pigtail 9. lance rest
quey ... 6. heifer
quia-quia ... 9. cigarfish
quib, quibble ... 3. pun 4. carp, quip 5. argue, cavil, cheta, evade 7. shuffle
Quiche, Indian ... 5. Mayan
quick ... 3. apt 4. deft, fast, yare 5. agile, alert, brisk, fiery, fleet, hasty, rapid, ready, smart, swift 6. lively, nimble, presto, prompt, pronto, speedy, sudden 7. animate 9. dexterous, impatient, impulsive, sprightly, vital

part 10. passionate 11. expeditious,
hot-tempered
quicken ... 5. hurry, rouse, speed
6. excite, hasten, incite, revive, vivify
7. animate, further, refresh, sharpen
8. energize, expedite 9. stimulate
10. accelerate 11. resuscitate
12. reinvigorate
quickly ... 4. cito, fast, soon 5. apace
6. presto, pronto 7. briefly, hastily,
rapidly 8. promptly, speedily, vigorous
quickness ... 4. nous (humor) 5. haste
6. acumen 7. acidity, agility 8. alacrity,
celerity, dispatch, pungency, rapidity
9. acuteness, briskness, fleetness,
sharpness, smartness 10. expedition,
promptness 13. impulsiveness
quicksand ... 3. bog 4. syrt 6. Syrtis
quickset ... 4. hedge 7. thicket
8. hawthorn
quicksilver ... 5. metal 7. mercury
quid ... 3. cud, fid 6. guinea 7. essence,
tobacco 9. sovereign
quidam ... 8. somebody 10. one unknown
quidnunc ... 6. gossip 7. what now
11. inquisitive
quid pro quo ... 9. tit for tat
10. equivalent, substitute
11. interchange
quiescent ... 5. quiet, still 6. at
rest, latent, silent, static 8. sleeping
10. motionless
quiet ... 2. sh 3. pet 4. calm, ease,
hush, lull, mild 5. peace, sober,
still 6. gentle, hushed, modest,
placid, smooth, soothe 7. halcyon,
restful, silence 8. peaceful, tranquil
9. contented, peaceable, quiescent,
reposeful, unruffled 10. unmolested
11. undisturbed
quietist ... 6. mystic (Quietism)
quietive ... 8. sedative
quietly ... 6. calmly, gently, simply
8. modestly, silently 9. patiently,
peaceably, privately 10. composedly
11. noiselessly 16. unostentatiously
quietude ... 4. rest 5. peace 6. repose
7. silence 10. quiescence 12. tranquillity
(tranquility)
quietus ... 4. mort, obit 5. death 6. defeat
7. release 9. acquittal, deathblow,
discharge (of debt)
quiff ... 4. coif, puff 5. whiff
quilkin ... 4. frog, toad
quill ... 3. cop, pen 5. remex 6. bobbin
7. spindle
quilt ... 3. pad 4. flog, gulp 5. duvet
6. caddow 7. swallow 8. coverlet
9. patchwork 11. comfortable,
counterpane
quin ... 7. scallop
quincentenary ... 11. anniversary
13. commemoration 16. five hundred
years
quindecemvir (Rom) ... 10. custodians
(Sibylline Books), fifteen men
quink ... 5. brant, goose
quinoa ... 6. cereal 7. pigweed
Quinquagesima Sunday ... 10. before
Lent 12. Shrove Sunday
quinque (comb form) ... 4. five

quinsy ... 10. sore throat 11. tonsillitis
quint ... 3. tax (one 5th) 7. E string
8. interval, schooner (5-masted)
9. organ stop
quintal ... 13. hundredweight
quintessence ... 3. col 5. elite 6. elixir
7. essence, the best 10. perfection
quip ... 3. mot 4. gibe, jest 5. sally, taunt
6. oddity 7. caprice, quibble 8. gimcrack
9. witticism 12. equivocation
quires, twenty ... 4. ream 6. sheets (20)
quirk ... 4. quip, turn 5. clock, shift, twist
7. caprice, evasion, quibble 8. flourish
9. deviation, mannerism, witticism
12. eccentricity
quirt ... 4. whip 5. romal
quis ... 8. woodcock
quisby ... 5. idler, queer 8. bankrupt
10. down and out
quit ... 3. rid 4. free, stop 5. cease, clear,
leave, pay up, repay, yield 6. depart,
resign 7. abandon, discard, forsake,
release, relieve, requite 8. abdicate,
liberate, renounce 9. surrender
10. relinquish 11. discontinue
quitclaim ... 6. acquit 7. release
12. convey a claim 13. deed of release
14. relinquishment
quite ... 3. all, yes 4. very 5. stark, truly
6. really, wholly 7. totally 8. entirely,
somewhat 10. absolutely, completely,
positively
quite so ... 8. that is so, very true, very
well
quite some ... 12. considerable
quittance ... 5. repay 6. return 7. requite
8. reprisal, requital 9. atonement,
departure, repayment 10. recompense
11. acquittance
quitter ... 5. piker 6. coward, truant
7. shirker, welsher
quiver ... 4. case 5. quake, shake
6. quaver, sheath, shiver, tremor
7. flicker, tremble, tremolo, vibrate
11. trepidation
quiver leaf ... 5. aspen
Quivira (pert to) ...
famous for .. 6. wealth
sought by .. 8. Coronado (1541)
town site .. 6. Kansas
Quivira, Gran ... 12. mission ruins
16. National Monument (N Mex)
qui vive ... 5. alert 7. excited 9. challenge
12. who goes there
quixotic ... 7. utopian 9. visionary 10. Don
Quixote (like) 11. impractical
quiz ... 4. hoax, jest, joke, mock 5. coach
6. banter 8. ridicule 11. examination,
inquisitive, interrogate, questioning
quizzical ... 3. odd 7. amusing, teasing
9. bantering, eccentric, inquiring,
perplexed
quizzing ... 6. banter 11. questioning
quizzing glass ... 7. monocle 8. eyeglass
quod ... 3. jug 6. prison 8. imprison
quoddies ... 7. herring
quod erat demonstrandum ... 3. QED
24. which was to be demonstrated
quodlibet ... 6. medley 8. fantasia,
subtlety 13. what you please
quoit ... 4. disc 6. discus

quoit pin . . . 3. hob
quoits . . . 4. game 8. cromlech 10. stone cover
quo modo . . . 5. means 6. manner, method
quondam . . . 6. former 8. formerly, sometime
quorum . . . 7. council 8. majority 10. select body
quota . . . 4. part 5. share 6. ration 10. proportion
quotable . . . 7. citable
quotation . . . 5. chria, cital, motto, price, stock 7. passage 8. citation 10. memorandum, repetition

quotation mark . . . 9. guillemet
quote . . . 4. cite, name 5. price 6. adduce, repeat 7. extract 9. quotation, reference
quoth . . . 4. said 5. spoke
quotha . . . 6. indeed 8. forsooth
quotidian . . . 5. daily 8. day by day, every day, ordinary 9. recurring 11. commonplace
quotient . . . 6. number, result
quotity . . . 5. group, quota 7. integer 10. collection
quotum . . . 5. quota, ratio
quo vadis . . . 16. whither goest thou
Quo Vadis tyrant . . . 4. Nero

R

R . . . 3. rho (Gr) 6. letter (18th)
Ra, Egypt Relig (pert to) . . .
  atmosphere . . 5. Shu
  god of . . 3. sun
  morning sun . . 7. Chepera, Khepera
  night sun . . 7. Sokaris
  representation . . 3. cat 4. lion 5. Bacis (bull) 6. falcon 9. solar disk
  rising sun . . 5. Horus 9. Marmachis
  setting sun . . 3. Tem
  solar disk . . 4. Aten
  son . . 6. Khonsu
  son of . . 3. Nut (the sky)
  wife . . 3. Mut
raad . . . 15. electric catfish
raad . . . 7. council (So Afr) 9. volksraad
raadzaal . . . 11. council hall (So Afr)
rab . . . 5. mixer (mortar) 6. beater
Rab . . . 5. title 6. master, rabban 7. teacher 8. Gamaliel
rabato, rebato . . . 4. ruff 6. collar 9. piccadill
rabbet . . . 4. weld 5. miter 6. groove, recess 7. channel 8. dovetail
rabbi . . . 4. lord 5. rabat, title 6. master 7. teacher 9. clergyman 11. breastpiece
rabbi (pert to) . . .
  examiners . . 8. sabaraim (saboraim)
  interpreters . . 7. amoraim
  teachers . . 7. tannaim
rabbit . . . 4. cony (coney), hare, tyro 5. bunny, lapin 6. animal, novice, rodent 10. cottontail 11. Belgian hare
rabbit (pert to) . . .
  breeding ground . . 6. warren 8. rabbitry
  ear . . 7. antenna 8. toadflax
  female . . 3. doe
  fever . . 9. tularemia
  fiction . . 6. Harvey
  fish . . 8. chimaera 9. globefish, porcupine
  foot . . 5. charm 8. talisman
  fur . . 4. cony (coney) 5. lapin
  genus . . 5. Lepus
  male . . 4. buck
  mouthed . . 10. harelipped
  rat . . 9. bandicoot
  S America . . 6. tapeti

  shelter . . 5. hutch
  stew . . 12. hasenpfeffer
  tail . . 3. fud 4. scut
rabbitry . . . 5. hutch 6. warren
rabble . . . 3. mob 4. herd, raff, rout, skim, stir 5. crowd 6. ragtag, tumult 7. bobtail 8. canaille, riffraff 9. confusion, rigmarole, the masses 12. accumulation (chaotic)
rabble rouser . . . 6. ragtag
Rabelais (Fr) . . . 6. author 8. satirist 9. Gargantua (1st work)
rabid . . . 3. mad 6. raging 7. frantic, furious, rampant, violent 8. frenzied 9. fanatical 10. infuriated
rabies . . . 5. lyssa 11. hydrophobia
raccoon, ally of . . . 5. coati, panda
race . . . 3. cut, hie, run 4. flow, lane, line, rush, slit, sort, stem 5. breed, caste, flume, relay, speed 6. course, family, nation, people, strain 7. contest, regatta, running, scratch 10. passageway 11. competition, watercourse
race (pert to horses) . . .
  chariot . . 13. Circus Maximus
  gait . . 4. lope, pace, trot
  horse . . 4. pony 5. racer 6. maiden, mantis, plater 8. bangtail
  handicap . . 6. impost
  open . . 10. Donnybrook, free-for-all
racecourse, racetrack (pert to) . . .
  3. lap 4. heat, oval, tout, turf 5. track 6. circus (anc), colors 7. raceway, tipster 8. dopester
Rachel (pert to) . . .
  daughter of . . 5. Laban
  mother of . . 6. Joseph 8. Benjamin
  sister of . . 4. Leah
  wife of . . 5. Jacob
racing colors . . . 6. silks
rack . . . 3. gin 4. gait, gear, pain, ruin 5. agony, frame 6. punish, strain, wrench 7. agonize, support, torment, torture 9. framework 10. excruciate
rack (pert to) . . .
  barrel . . 3. job
  comb . . 9. toothcomb

corn . . 4. crib
floating . . 5. vapor
plate . . 5. creel
skin of . . 6. rabbit

racket . . . 3. bat, din 5. fraud, noise, revel 6. bustle, clamor, crosse, outcry, scheme 8. vocation 9. commotion 15. illicit business

rackety . . . 5. noisy 8. clattery, exciting 9. turbulent 10. boisterous

racy . . . 5. brisk, fresh, naive, smart, spicy 6. lively, risqué 7. piquant, pungent, zestful 8. eloquent, spirited, stirring 11. interesting 12. exhilarating, full-flavored

rad . . . 4. unit 5. eager, quick, ready 6. afraid, elated 11. exhilarated

radar (pert to) . . .
beacon . . 4. buoy 5. racon 6. ramark
navigation . . 5. navar
range (Navig) . . 5. loran 6. shoran
sight . . 5. scope 6. radome, screen 7. display
signal . . 3. pip 4. beam, blip 5. pulse 11. transceiver, transponder
sounding . . 5. rawin 9. ionosonde
television . . 7. teleran

raddle . . . 3. rod 4. beat, twig 5. cheat, color, fence, hedge 6. branch, hurdle, ruddle, thrash 7. wheedle 10. interweave

radeau . . . 4. raft 5. gloat

radial . . . 3. ray 8. quadrant 9. diverging

radiance . . . 5. beamy, glare, light, nitor, sheen 6. beauty, luster 7. beaming, glitter, glowing, lambent, shining 8. splendor 9. brilliant, radiation 10. brilliancy, effulgence 12. cheerfulness

radiant . . . 5. aglow, beamy, sheen 7. beaming, glowing, lambent, shining 8. glorious 9. beautiful, diverging, effulgent 11. resplendent

radiate . . . 4. beam, emit, shed 5. gleam, shine 7. diffuse, diverge, emanate 9. irradiate 10. illuminate

radiation . . . 5. alpha (particle), light, polar (point) 10. divergence 12. illumination 13. radiant energy

radiation unit . . . 4. rad, rem 8. roentgen

radical . . . 3. red 4. atom, left, root, surd 5. basic, radix, ultra, vital 7. capital, drastic, extreme 8. cardinal, reformer 9. extremist 10. foundation 11. fundamental

radicated . . . 6. rooted 11. established

radicle . . . 4. root 5. radix 6. etymon 7. rootlet

radio (pert to) . . .
activity . . 7. fallout 9. radiation
antenna . . 6. aerial
detector . . 5. radar 11. transceiver
frequency . . 5. audio
interference . . 5. static
operator . . 2. CB 3. ham (amateur) 11. dit-da-artist 12. citizens' band
rays . . 5. beams
receiver, interfering . . 7. blooper
tube . . 4. grid 5. diode

radium (pert to) . . .
discoverer . . 5. Curie (1898)

emanation . . 5. niton, radon
paint . . 8. luminous
source of . . 7. uranite 9. carnotite

radius . . . 4. area, bone 5. spoke 6. circle, extent 8. diameter

radix . . . 4. root 6. etymon, source 7. radical, radicle

raff . . . 4. heap, rake, scum 5. sweep, trash 6. jumble, litter 7. rubbish 8. leavings, riffraff

raffia . . . 4. palm 5. fiber 6. jupati

raffish . . . 3. low 6. common, flashy, frowsy 7. unkempt 9. worthless 12. disreputable

raffle . . . 5. chance, rabble, tangle 7. confuse, crumple, lottery, perplex, serrate 8. entangle, plucking, riffraff 9. stripping 10. plundering

raft . . . 3. lot 4. spar 5. balsa, float 6. rafter 7. to flock 10. collection (large)

raft-breasted (Ornith) . . . 6. ratite

raft duck . . . 5. scoup 7. redhead 8. bluebill

rag . . . 3. fog 4. mist, sail 5. cloth, scold, shred 6. berate, catkin, lichen, tatter 7. ragtime, remnant 8. farthing 9. hoarfrost 11. syncopation

rag (pert to) . . .
bag . . 10. depository
doll . . 3. toy 6. moppet, puppet 10. marionette
fish . . 10. Icosteidae
rag picker . . 5. tramp
weed . . 3. Iva
wool . . 5. mungo 6. shoddy

ragamuffin . . . 8. titmouse 9. ragged boy 14. tatterdemalion

rage . . . 3. fad 4. fume, fury, gret, ramp, rant, tear 5. anger, chafe, craze, furor (furore), storm, wrath 6. fervor, frenzy 7. bluster, passion 8. violence 9. vehemence 10. excitement

ragged . . . 5. harsh, rough 6. jagged, raguly (Her), scoury, shabby, uneven 7. shreddy 9. defective, dissonant, irregular 10. straggling 11. dilapidated

raging . . . 4. grim 5. rabid 7. acharne 8. storming 9. ferocious, turbulent 10. blustering, infuriated 11. overwrought

raglan . . . 8. overcoat 11. sleeve style

Ragnarok, Norse (pert to) . . .
leader . . 4. Loki
meaning . . 16. world destruction
repeopler of the world . . 3. Lif 10. Lifthrasir

ragout . . . 4. beef, stew 5. civet, salmi 6. mutton 7. goulash, haricot

rahdar . . . 14. tollroad keeper

raid . . . 4. tata 5. foray, seize 6. inroad 8. invasion 9. incursion

rail . . . 3. bar, jaw 4. coot, jest, rant, sora, weka 5. cloak, crake, dress, scoff, scold 6. banter, revile, septum (altar) 7. courlan, garment, inveigh, limpkin, ortolan 8. reproach

railbird . . . 9. spectator 12. horse watcher

railing . . . 5. fence, rails 7. barrier, parapet 10. balustrade

raillery . . . 5. chaff, sport 6. banter 7. asteism (Rhet) 8. badinage, ridicule

10. persiflage

railroad (pert to) . . .
 flare . . 5. fusee
 signal . . 9. semaphore
 sleeper . . 3. tie 7. pullman
 switch . . 4. frog
 torpedo . . 9. detonator
 worker . . 6. dinger 8. strapper 11. gandy
  dancer

Rail Splitter . . . 14. Abraham Lincoln

raiment . . . 4. garb 5. amice, dress
 7. apparel, clothes, vesture 8. clothing,
 garments

rain (pert to) . . .
 cloud . . 6. nimbus
 coat . . 3. mac 4. mino 6. poncho 7. slicker
  10. mackintosh
 comb form . . 5. hyeto, ombro 6. pluvio
 fine . . 4. mist 5. serein
 fowl . . 6. cuckoo 10. woodpecker
  11. channelbill
 gauge . . 8. udometer 10. hyetometer
 glass . . 8. barometer
 icy . . 4. hail 5. sleet
 protection . . 9. ombrifuge
 short . . 6. shower
 storm . . 5. spate 13. precipitation
 study . . 9. hyetology, ombrology
 sudden . . 5. plash, spate 6. deluge
  7. torrent 10. downpour

rainbow . . . 3. arc 4. arch, iris, omen

rainbow (pert to) . . .
 bridge (Norse Myth) . . 7. Bifrost (to
  Asgarth)
 chaser . . 9. visionary 11. doctrinaire
 flower . . 4. iris
 goddess . . 4. Iris
 term . . 6. iridal
 tree . . 5. saman 8. genisaro
 unit . . 4. inch
 worm . . 8. nematode 9. earthworm

rainy . . . 3. wet 7. showery

rais, reis (Muslim) . . . 5. chief, title
 7. captain (ship's)

Rais . . . 10. Mongoloids

raise . . . 3. end 4. grow, levy, lift, rear,
 stir 5. boost, breed, erect, exalt,
 heave, hoist, rouse 6. awaken, excite,
 gather, leaven, muster, remove, uplift
 7. collect, elevate, enhance, lighten,
 present, produce, provoke, recruit
 8. heighten, increase 9. construct,
 cultivate, promotion, propagate
 10. aggrandize

raise (pert to) . . .
 a nap . . 5. tease 6. teasel
 Cain . . 3. Ned 4. hell 5. cut up 7. be
  noisy 10. vociferate
 the dead . . 13. lift the anchor
 vegetables . . 12. olericulture

raised . . . 4. bred, hove 6. buoyed,
 enlève, hefted, lifted, reared 7. hoisted
 8. elevated, leavened, produced,
 promoted

raised (pert to) . . .
 spirits . . 6. elated
 to 3rd power . . 5. cubed
 troops . . 6. levied 7. drafted
  11. conscripted
 type . . 7. braille
 uproar . . 6. rioted

 with a bar . . 7. levered

raisin . . . 4. pasa 5. grape, lexia

raja, rajah . . . 4. king, rana 5. title 6. prince
 9. dignitary

raja's consort . . . 4. rani (ranee)
 8. princess

Rajmahal hemp . . . 5. fiber 9. jiti fiber

Rajput . . . 5. caste 9. Kshatriya

rake . . . 3. rut 4. comb, path, raff,
 roué 5. slope, teeth, track 6. lecher
 7. debauch, seducer 8. enfilade,
 Lothario 9. cultivate, implement,
 libertine

rakehell . . . 4. free, rake 9. debauched,
 debauchee, dissolute 10. dissipated,
 licentious, profligate

rakh . . . 3. hay 5. hayfield 9. grassland

raki, rakee . . . 7. spirits (distilled)

rale . . . 6. rattle 8. rhonchus 11. morbid
 sound

rallentando . . . 9. direction (Mus)
 10. ritardando, slackening

Rallidae . . . 5. birds, coots, rails, wekas
 6. crakes 10. gallinules

rally . . . 6. banter 7. recover, reunite
 8. assemble, recovery, ridicule
 10. assemblage, call to arms

rallying cry . . . 4. call 6. slogan 9. battle
 cry, bugle call

ralph . . . 5. raven

ram . . . 3. hit, pun, tup 4. buck, butt,
 tamp 5. Aries, crash, sheep 6. rancid,
 wether 7. collide

Rama . . . 11. Ramachandra (7th of fame)
 19. incarnation of Vishnu

ramada . . . 5. arbor 7. pergola

Ramadan (Muslim) . . . 7. fasting 10. ninth
 month (for fasting)

ramage . . . 4. wild 5. rough 6. branch
 (tree), unruly 7. untamed 8. frenzied

ramage hawk . . . 8. brancher

ramass . . . 6. gather 7. collect

ramberge . . . 6. galley (swift)

ramble . . . 3. gad 4. roam, rove, walk
 5. jaunt, prowl, range 6. stroll, wander
 7. deviate, digress, saunter 8. straggle

rambling . . . 7. devious 9. desultory,
 deviation, deviative, wandering
 10. circuitous, discursive, distracted
 14. discursiveness

rambunctious . . . 4. wild 6. unruly
 10. rampageous 12. obstreperous
 14. uncontrollable

rementum . . . 5. palea (palet) 6. scales
 8. a shaving, particle (minute)

Rameses Dynasties (pert to) . . .
 famed for . . 5. ruins 7. papyrus
 kings . . 6. twelve
 site . . 5. Egypt

ramex . . . 6. hernia 10. varicocele

ram-headed goat . . . 5. Ammon

ramie . . . 4. hemp, rhea 5. plant (fiber)
 7. garment 9. Boehmeria 10. China
 grass

ramification . . . 3. arm 5. ramus 6. branch
 8. offshoot 9. branching 10. divergence
 12. embranchment

rammack . . . 4. gawk, romp 5. scamp

rammel . . . 4. hard 6. coarse 7. new milk,
 raw milk 9. brushwood 11. undergrowth

Ramona (pert to) . . .

heroine .. 9. half-breed (Ind)
novel by .. 7. Jackson (Helen Hunt)
shrub .. 4. mint

ramp ... 3. rob 4. rage, romp, walk
5. bound, climb, crawl, creep, storm
6. dupery, unruly 7. incline, rampage,
swindle 8. gradient, platform
9. helicline, impetuous 10. cuckoopint

rampant ... 6. fierce, unruly, vallum (anc)
7. ramping 8. abundant, reared up (Her)
9. exuberant, prevalent, unchecked
10. rampageous 12. high-spirited,
unrestrained 13. perpendicular

rampart ... 4. wall 5. agger, mound, redan
6. escarp 7. barrier, bulwark, defense,
parapet, ravelin 8. buttress 9. earthwork
10. embankment 13. fortification

ram's horn (Heb) ... 7. shophar (shofar)

ran ... 4. fled, sped 6. flowed 7. coursed,
managed, trotted 8. operated

ran (pert to) ...
aground .. 8. decamped, levanted,
stranded
away .. 4. fled 6. eloped 9. absconded
out .. 5. spilt 7. petered, spilled

rana (Ind) ... 5. title 6. prince
Rana ... 5. frogs 10. amphibians (tailless)
ranarium ... 8. frog pond
rance ... 4. prop 6. marble 7. support
ranch ... 4. casa, farm 6. estate
8. estancia, hacienda
ranchero ... 6. cowman 7. vaquero
8. herdsman 9. cattleman
rancid ... 4. rank 5. musty, stale 6. reechy
9. obnoxious, offensive 10. unpleasant
rancor, rancour ... 3. ire 4. gall 5. spite
6. enmity, hatred, malice, rankle 7. ill
will 9. animosity 10. resentment
rand ... 4. edge, rant 5. ridge, storm
6. border, margin
random ... 5. stray 6. casual, chance
7. aimless 8. casually 9. at liberty,
haphazard, orderless 10. accidental,
fortuitous 11. haphazardly
randy ... 4. wild 5. revel, spree 6. beggar,
coarse, frolic, virago 7. canvass
8. carousal 9. festivity 10. disorderly
11. ill-mannered 12. unmanageable
rang (pert to) ... see also *ring*
loudly ... 7. clanged
mournfully .. 6. tolled 7. knelled
slowly .. 6. tolled
range ... 3. row 4. area, line, rank,
roam, size 5. align, gamut, orbit,
scope 6. limits, ramble, region, series,
wander 7. arrange, compass, earshot,
habitat, pasture 8. classify, mountain
9. cookstove
range (pert to) ...
finder .. 9. mekometer, telemeter
10. trekometer
man .. 5. rider 6. warden
of hills .. 5. ridge
of knowledge .. 3. ken
of stables .. 4. mews
rangle ... 5. stray 6. wander 8. entangle,
straggle
rani, ranee (Hind) ... 4. wife 5. queen
7. empress 8. princess
rani (Romany) ... 4. lady, wife
Ranier, Mt ... 10. Washington (State)

ranine ... 5. frogs 7. Raninae 8. mink
frog
rank ... 3. bad, row 4. file, foul, line, rate,
size, tier 5. caste, class, grade, gross,
order, range 6. degree, estate, rancid,
status, wicked 7. arrange, glaring,
tainted 8. absolute, abundant, classify,
eminence, flagrant, indecent, infamous,
nobility, palpable, position, prestige,
unsavory 9. downright, formation,
luxuriant, plentiful 10. malodorous
11. distinction

rank (pert to) ...
and file .. 4. army 8. regulars
10. commonalty 11. third estate
celestial .. 9. hierarchy
exalted .. 8. eminence
military (old) .. 8. banneret
noble .. 5. patriciate
rider .. 8. reckless 10. highwayman
social .. 5. caste

rankle ... 5. chafe 6. fester 7. putrefy
8. make sore 9. suppurate 10. be
inflamed
rann ... 5. verse 6. stanza, strain
ransack ... 4. rake, sack 5. rifle 6. search
7. plunder, rummage
ransom ... 4. fine 6. redeem, rescue
7. expiate 8. recovery
ranstead ... 8. toadflax (yellow)
13. butter-and-eggs
rant ... 4. rage, rail, rave 5. boast 6. steven
7. bluster, bombast, declaim 9. gay
frolic 10. get excited
rantipole ... 4. wild 6. rakish, unruly
9. termagant
ranula ... 4. cyst
Ranunculaceae ... 7. anemone
8. aconitum, clematis, crowfoot
10. delphinium, ranunculus
rap ... 3. bop, hit 4. bang, blow,
gibe, grab, knap, tirl 5. knock, steal
6. rascal, snatch, trifle 8. betrayal,
sentence (prison) 9. criticism, reprimand
10. punishment 11. skein of yarn
rapacious ... 6. greedy, rapine
8. grasping, ravenous 9. devouring,
voracious 10. avaricious, predacious
rapacity ... 5. greed, ravin (raven)
6. rapine 8. appetite 9. predacity
rapid ... 4. fast 5. fleet, quick, swift
7. stretto (stretta)
rapidity ... 5. haste, speed 8. celerity,
velocity 9. fleetness, quickness
rapidly ... 5. amain, apace 7. quickly,
swiftly 8. snappily
rapids ... 5. rifts 6. dalles
rapier ... 5. bilbo, sword 6. verdun
7. ricasso (part)
rapine ... 7. pillage, plunder 8. spoiling
10. ravishment, spoliation
rapport ... 6. accord 7. empathy,
harmony 8. relation 9. agreement
11. co-operation (hypnotism)
rapt ... 8. absorbed, ecstatic
10. enraptured, interested
11. preoccupied, transported
rapture ... 3. joy 4. love 5. bliss
6. trance 7. delight, ecstasy 8. rhapsody
9. transport 10. exultation
rapturous ... 8. ecstatic

rara avis ... 6. rarity 8. rare bird

rare ... 3. odd, raw 4. thin 6. scarce, seldom, sparse 7. notable, unusual 8. rarefied, uncommon 10. infrequent 11. undercooked

rare (pert to) ...

  bird .. 8. rara avis

  earth .. 6. cerium 7. terbium, yttrium

  metallic element .. 7. yttrium

  object .. 5. curio 6. oddity 7. antique

Rare Ben, inscription ... 15. tomb of Ben Jonson (Westminster Abbey)

rarebit ... 10. cheese dish 11. Welsh rabbit

rarefy ... 4. thin 6. dilute, expand 9. attenuate

rarely ... 6. finely, seldom 8. not often, scarcely 9. extremely, unusually 11. beautifully 12. infrequently

rarity ... 6. oddity 7. fewness, tenuity 8. scarcity, thinness 9. infrequency

ras ... 4. cape 6. prince 11. short-napped 13. Fascist leader

rasa ... 3. sap (tree) 5. fluid, taste 6. amrita, flavor 7. essence 11. living water

rascal ... 3. cad, imp 5. knave, rogue, scamp 6. varlet 9. miscreant

rascally ... 4. mean 6. impish 7. knavish, roguish 8. scampish 11. mischievous

rase ... 3. cut, rub 4. tear 5. graze, level 6. scrape 7. scratch

rash ... 3. mad 4. wild 5. giddy, hasty, heady, hives, scamp 6. unwary, wanton 7. Icarian 8. careless, eruption, heedless 9. desperate, exanthema, impetuous 10. headstrong, incautious, indiscreet 11. temerarious, thoughtless

rasher ... 5. piece, slice 7. portion 9. thin slice

rashness ... 6. acrisy 7. acrisia 8. temerity 9. hastiness

rasion ... 6. filing 7. erasing, rasping, shaving 8. scraping

Rasores ... 4. fowl 5. birds 6. quails 7. turkeys 8. Columbae, Gallinae 9. pheasants 10. partridges

rasp ... 3. rub 4. file 5. belch, chafe, erupt, grate 6. abrade, offend, scrape 8. irritate 9. raspberry

raspberry ... 3. red 5. apple, Rubus 6. raspis 7. plumbog 8. blackcap

rasping ... 5. harsh 7. chafing, grating, raucous 8. grinding, scraping, very fast 9. offensive 10. irritating

raspings ... 6. refuse 7. filings, remains

rasse ... 5. civet

rasure ... 3. cut 5. shave 7. erasure, polling, scratch, tonsure 8. scraping 12. obliteration

rat ... 3. rut 4. scab, snob, wart 5. track 6. desert, ratton, rodent 7. scratch, traitor 8. deserter 9. hairpiece, scoundrel

rat (pert to) ...

  fish .. 8. chimaera

  goose .. 11. common brant

  hare .. 4. pika

  kangaroo .. 7. Potorus 9. marsupial

  pineapple .. 7. pinguin

  poison .. 8. ratsbane

ratlike .. 4. vole

rhyme .. 6. jargon 13. doggerel verse

ratafia ... 7. biscuit (almond), curacao, liqueur (Danzig)

ratchet ... 4. pawl 5. click 6. bobbin, detent

rate ... 4. fare, pace 5. price, ratio, style, tempo, value 6. assess, berate, charge, reckon, regard 7. account, deserve, premium, reprove 8. appraise, classify, estimate, evaluate, interest

rate (of exchange) ... 4. agio 5. batta

rath (anc) ... 4. hill, home (walled)

rath, ratha ... 3. car 6. temple (Seven Pagodas, Madras) 7. chariot

Rathaus ... 8. town hall

rathe, rath ... 4. soon 5. eager, quick, speed 7. betimes, quickly 8. speedily

rather ... 3. ere, yes 6. before 7. earlier, however, instead 8. somewhat 9. more truly, tolerably 10. especially, preferably 11. immediately 14. on the other hand

ratification ... 4. amen 5. logic 8. sanction 9. reasoning 11. endorsement 12. confirmation

ratify ... 4. amen, pass, seal 6. enseal, verify 7. approve, confirm, consent, endorse 8. roborate, sanction 9. authorize

ratio ... 2. pi 4. rate, sine 5. share 6. cosine, ration 7. portion 10. proportion

ratiocination ... 5. logic 7. thought 9. reasoning

ration ... 5. share 6. budget 8. relation 9. allotment, allowance, provision 11. calculation

rational ... 4. sane, wise 5. sober 7. logical 8. sensible 9. reasoning 10. reasonable 11. philosophic

rationale ... 6. reason 11. explanation 12. the how and why

ratio scripta ... 13. written reason

ratite ... (opp of carinate)7. Ratitae 8. unkeeled 14. flat breastbone

ratite bird ... 3. emu (emeu), moa 7. ostrich 9. cassowary

ratoon ... 5. shoot, stalk 6. spring, sprout

rattan, ratan ... 4. cane, palm, sega, whip 6. switch 8. calamus

ratteen ... 8. mahogany

rattle ... 3. toy 4. herb, rale, rick, tirl 5. annoy, clack 6. assail, prison (Nav), racket, uproar 7. agitate, chatter, clapper, clatter, confuse, fluster, maracas, prattle 8. nonsense 9. chatterer, rapid talk 10. disconcert, noisemaker

rattle (pert to) ...

  bones .. 8. clappers, snappers 9. castanets

  headed .. 8. confused 11. empty-headed 13. rattlebrained

  mouse .. 3. bat

  nut .. 10. chinquapin

  pate .. 3. ass

  root .. 7. bugbane

rattlesnake ... 7. rattier 8. belltail, Crotalus, pit viper 9. Sistrurus

rattlesnake (pert to) ...

  bean .. 6. cedron

bite . . 9. meadow rue
fern . . 9. chain fern, sporangia
flag (Maine) . . 13. Don't Tread on Me (Hist)
herb . . 9. baneberry
leaf . . 8. plantain
pilot . . 10. copperhead
plantain . . 6. orchid
variety . . 3. red 6. banded, timber 7. prairie 11. diamondback
venom . . 8. crotalus

rattletrap . . 6. gewgaw 7. rickety 8. claptrap, the mouth 10. knickknack, ramshackle

ratton . . 3. rat

ratwa . . 7. muntjac

raucous . . 3. dry 4. bray, loud 5. harsh, noisy 6. hoarse, raucid, rauque 8. strident 11. cacophonous

rauk, roke . . 4. poke, stir 5. vapor 7. scratch

raun . . 3. roe 4. fish 5. spawn

ravage . . 4. loot, ruin, sack 5. havoc, spoil, waste 6. damage, infest 7. debauch, destroy, overrun, pillage, plunder 9. devastate 10. desolation 11. despoilment, devastation, infestation

ravages of time . . 13. deterioration 14. disintegration

rave . . 4. rage, rant 5. crush, storm 7. bluster, declaim, enthuse 8. be insane, harangue

ravel . . 4. fray 6. runner, slough, unwind 7. involve, unravel, untwist, unweave 8. entangle, separate 11. disentangle, loose thread

ravelin . . 7. railing 8. demilune, half-moon 13. fortification

Ravel opus . . 6. Bolero

raven . . 4. bird, crow 6. Corvus 8. standard (vikings) 10. raven-black 11. Corvus corax

Raven (The) . . 4. poem (Edgar Allan Poe)

ravening . . 3. mad 5. rabid 6. greedy, prying 8. desirous 9. rapacious, turbulent

ravenous . . 6. greedy 8. edacious 9. rapacious, voracious 10. gluttonous 11. catawampous

ravine . . 3. gap 4. dell, linn (lin), wadi (wady) 5. chine, gorge, gulch, slade, strid 6. arroyo, clough, gulley, nullah 8. barranca

ravish . . 3. rob 4. rape 5. seize 7. corrupt, debauch, delight, despoil, plunder, violate 8. deflower, entrance 9. enrapture, transport

raw . . 4. cold, sore 5. bleak, crude, naked 6. chilly, unripe, vulgar 7. natural, not spun, untried 8. immature, indecent, uncooked 9. inclement, unskilled, windswept 10. unprepared 11. undeveloped, unprocessed 13. inexperienced

rawboned . . 4. lank 5. gaunt 7. angular 8. skeletal

rawbones . . 5. Death 8. skeleton

raw-flesh-eating . . 9. omophagia

rawhide . . 4. skin (untanned), whip

rawhide whip . . 5. knout, quirt, thong

7. sjambok

raw sugar . . 9. cassonade

rax . . 5. reach 6. become, strain 7. stretch

ray . . 4. beam, dorn, soil, X-ray 5. array, dress, gamma, order, skate (fish) 6. defile, radius, stripe, vision 7. besmear, raiment 8. particle, radiance, stingray 11. arrangement, irradiation

raya . . 9. broadbill

rayless . . 4. dark 5. blind

rayon . . 3. ray 5. fiber 6. radius 14. postal district (Switz)

raze, rase . . 3. cut 4. fell, ruin 5. erase, graze, level, shave 6. efface, scrape 7. destroy 9. demolish 9. dismantle, prostrate 10. obliterate

razee . . 3. cut (Naut) 5. prune 7. abridge

razor (pert to) . . .
back . . 3. hog 4. boar 5. ridge 10. roustabout (circus)
bill . . 3. auk 7. skimmer
billed auk . . 4. falk 5. murre, noddy
clam . . 5. Solen 11. chopa blanca
grinder . . 10. goatsucker
sharpen . . 4. hone 5. strop
stone . . 9. whetstone 10. novaculite
strap . . 5. strop
type . . 6. safety 7. rattler

razz . . 5. chaff, tease 6. banter, deride 8. ridicule 9. raspberry

razzle-dazzle . . 5. cinch (game), spree 6. dazzle 7. confuse 8. bewilder 9. commotion 10. noisemaker

re . . 4. back (pref) 5. about, again, anent, tone D (Mus) 8. syllable (Mus) 10. concerning

Re . . 2. Ra (Egypt) see also *Ra*

reach . . 4. come, gain, hawk, ryke, spar, spit 5. equal, retch 6. advene, arrive, attain, extend, length 7. achieve, compass, earshot, expanse, possess, stretch 9. distance, overtake 9. influence 10. understand

reach (pert to) . . .
across . . 4. span
for applause . . 9. captation
high point . . 9. culminate
out . . 6. extend 7. stretch
under . . 7. subtend
up . . 6. aspire

reaction . . 4. kick 6. change (Chem) 7. tropism 8. response 9. influence 10. opposition

reactionary . . 4. Tory 10. malcontent 12. conservative, recalcitrant

read . . 3. con 4. pore, scan, skim, tell 5. guess, solve 6. advise, browse, peruse, recite, relate 7. counsel, declare, discern, foresee, prelect (praelect), stomach 8. decipher, describe, foretell 9. interpret 10. understand

readable . . 7. legible 12. decipherable

reader . . 6. lector, lister, primer (McGuffey) 7. browser, license, reciter, speaker, teacher 8. anagnost (anagnostes), literate, textbook 9. churchman, prelector (praelector) 10. pocketbook 11. proofreader 12. elocutionist

readily . . 6. at once, easily 7. quickly

8. probably 9. willingly 10. very likely

readjust . . . 7. readapt, restore
9. rearrange 11. reconstruct
12. rehabilitate

ready . . . 3. apt, fit, fix 4. bain, free,
here, ripe, yare 5. alert, apert, eager,
handy, point, quick 6. facile, fitted,
prompt 7. willing 8. cheerful, disposed,
inclined, prepared, skillful 9. dexterous
12. unhesitating

ready acceptance . . . 11. embracement

ready for . . . 6. awaits 8. liable to 10. in
store for 11. prepared for

ready-to-wear . . . 12. haute couture

real . . . 4. true, very 5. pucka (pukka)
6. actual 7. factual, genuine, sincere
8. absolute, existent, handmade,
tangible 9. authentic, veritable
10. unaffected 11. substantial

real (pert to) . . .
being . . 6. entity
estate . . 5. lands 6. domain, houses,
realty 7. demesne 8. easement,
freehold, property 9. tenements
13. hereditaments
map . . 4. plot
name (backwards) . . 6. ananym
school . . 10. Realschule

realistic . . . 5. vivid 6. lifelike 9. practical
11. descriptive

reality . . . 5. truth 7. realism
11. genuineness

reality, non-existent . . . 8. nihilism

realize . . . 3. get, win 4. gain, know
5. sense 7. convert 8. conceive
10. accomplish

realm . . . 6. domain, empire, region,
sphere 7. country, demesne, kingdom
8. division, province 10. department
12. jurisdiction

realm (of) . . .
darkness (Myth) . . 2. po
Jamshid . . 6. Persia
perfection . . 7. Utopia

ream . . . 4. bore, foam, scum 5. widen
6. bundle 7. enlarge 8. bevel out
11. countersink 14. enormous amount

reanimate . . . 5. rally 6. revive 7. refresh
11. resuscitate 12. reinvigorate

rear . . . 3. aft 4. back, grow, hind, lift,
loom, rise, rump 5. breed, build, erect,
raise, stern, train 6. behind, foster
7. arriere, educate, elevate, produce
8. instruct 9. construct, establish,
posterior 10. background

rear (pert to) . . .
admiral . . 7. two bars (silver)
commodore, yacht club . . 7. officer
end . . 6. breech 7. hind end 9. afterpart,
posterior
horse (insect) . . 6. mantis
most . . 4. last
toward . . 3. aft 5. abaft 6. astern
8. backward, rearward

rearing up (horse) . . . 5. stend 6. pesade

rearrange . . . 4. sort 8. readjust
10. reordinate, reorganize

reason . . . 5. argue, cause, logic, sense,
think 6. deduce, ground, motive, sanity
7. discuss 8. argument, conclude,
judgment, question, solution

9. discourse, intellect 11. explanation,
ratiocinate, rationalize 13. justification,
understanding

reason (pert to) . . .
discursively . . 11. ratiocinate
doctrine of, author . . 10. Anaxagoras
higher . . 4. mind, nous 5. logic
Latin . . 5. causa
ostensible . . 7. pretext
pert to . . 6. noetic
proof of . . 8. argument
want of . . 7. amentia
why . . 5. cause 6. motive

reasonable . . . 4. fair, just, sane 6. proper
7. logical 8. rational 9. equitable,
plausible, practical 10. fair-minded
11. inexpensive, intelligent, justifiable

reasoning (pert to) . . .
basis of . . 7. premise
delusive . . 7. fallacy
exact . . 5. logic
harmonize . . 11. rationalize
plausible . . 9. specious

reassure . . . 6. assure, solace 7. comfort,
console, hearten 8. embolden, give
hope

reata . . . 4. rope 5. lasso, riata 6. lariat

reave . . . 3. rob 4. rend, tear 5. break,
burst, seize, split 7. plunder

reb . . . 5. rebel

rebate . . . 5. check 6. reduce, weaken
8. diminish, discount 9. abatement,
deduction, remission

rebato (Hist) . . . 4. ruff 6. collar, rabato
9. piccadill

Rebekah (pert to) . . .
husband . . 5. Isaac
sister . . 5. Laban
son . . 4. Esau 5. Jacob

rebel . . . 3. reb 4. rise 6. resist, revolt
8. renounce, turncoat 9. insurgent
13. revolutionist

rebellion . . . 5. Great (Eng 1642-49)
6. mutiny, revolt 8. American (Civil
War 1861-65) 10. resistance, revolution
12. insurrection, renunciation

rebellious . . . 8. mutinous 9. insurgent
10. refractory 12. contumacious
13. insubordinate, revolutionary

rebirth . . . 7. revival 9. salvation
10. conversion 11. renaissance
13. reincarnation

rebound . . . 4. stot 5. carom 6. bounce,
recoil, re-echo, spring 7. resound
8. rebounce, ricochet 11. reverberate

rebuff . . . 4. slap, snub 5. chide, scold
6. defeat, lesson, recoil, refuse, reject,
resist 7. censure, refusal (brusque),
reprove, repulse 9. reprimand

rebuke . . . 3. nip 4. slap 5. check,
chide 6. rebuff 7. repress, reproof,
reprove 8. admonish, reproach, restrain
9. criticize, reprehend, reprimand
11. comeuppance

recalcitrant . . . 5. rebel 9. renitent
9. obstinate, recoiling, resistant
10. rebellious, refractory 11. disobedient
12. ungovernable

recall . . . 5. annul 6. encore, recant,
remind, repeal, revoke, summon
7. retract 8. remember, withdraw

9. recollect, reminisce 11. recantation
12. recollection

recant . . . 6. abjure, revoke 7. disavow, retract 8. renounce, withdraw 9. repudiate 10. contradict

recapitulate . . . 5. essay, sum up 6. repeat, review 7. restate 8. argument 9. reiterate, summarize

recapture . . . 6. recall, regain, retake 7. recover

recede . . . 3. ebb 4. wane 6. depart, retire 7. deviate, regress, retreat 8. withdraw 10. retrograde

receipt . . . 5. axiom 6. acquit, answer, recipe 7. formula 12. prescription 14. acknowledgment

receipts . . . 7. the take

receive . . . 3. get 4. hold, take 5. admit, greet, learn, reset 6. accept, assent, derive, obtain, take in 7. acquire, contain, procure 9. apprehend

receive (pert to) . . .
a confession . . 6. shrive
a reward . . 4. reap
stolen property . . 5. reset

receiver . . . 5. donee, fence 7. catcher 8. believer 9. recipient, treasurer 10. receptacle

receiver (pert to) . . .
fixed income . . 7. rentier
profits (law) . . 6. pernor
property in trust . . 6. bailee
stolen property . . 5. fence

recension . . . 6. review 8. revising, revision 9. reviewing 11. enumeration, examination

recent . . . 3. new 4. late, past 5. fresh 6. former, modern 7. current, newborn 8. neonatal, neoteric

receptacle . . . 3. bag, bin, box, can, cup, pan 4. case, cask, cyst (anc), etui, pail, tank, tray, vase 5. basin, crock 6. basket, bottle, bucket, carton, holder, hopper 7. compote, hanaper, platter 8. canister, catchall 9. container 10. repository

receptacle (pert to) . . .
assayer's, stonecutter's . . 7. sebilla
botany . . 5. torus
coal . . 3. bin
corporal (RCCh) . . 5. burse
grain . . 3. bin 8. elevator
holy water . . 5. stoup
vote . . 6. situla

reception . . . 3. tea 5. levee, salon 6. infare, soiree 7. accueil, ovation, receipt, welcome 8. ceremony, sociable 9. admission, interview, intuition 12. housewarming 13. entertainment

reception hall, room . . . 5. salon 6. atrium, parlor 9. vestibule

receptionist . . . 4. host 7. hostess 8. landlord

receptive . . . 6. pliant 8. sensible 9. acceptant, admissive, teachable 10. hospitable, open-minded 11. persuasible

receptor . . . 5. basin 8. receiver 10. dispositor (Astron), sense organ

recess . . . 3. ala, bay, pan (leaf) 4. apse, nook, rest 5. crypt, niche, pause,

sinus, space 7. adjourn, respite, retreat 9. recession, seclusion 11. indentation 12. intermission

recipe . . . 5. axiom 7. formula, receipt 12. prescription

recipient . . . 4. heir 5. donee 7. legatee 8. receiver

reciprocal . . . 5. joint 6. mutual, shared 8. exchange 9. alternate 11. convertible, correlative, retaliatory 15. interchangeable

reciprocate . . . 5. bandy 6. accord, concur 8. exchange 9. alternate, retaliate 10. correspond 11. interchange

recision . . . 6. repeal 7. pruning 9. canceling (cancelling) 10. rescinding

recital . . . 4. tale 5. story 6. lesson, speech 7. account, concert (exhibition) 8. musicale 9. narration, narrative, rehearsal 10. recitation, repetition 11. enumeration, reiteration

recitation . . . 6. lesson, speech 7. reading 10. exhibition

recite . . . 4. tell 5. quote, speak, state 6. relate, repeat 7. declaim, narrate, recount 8. rehearse, tell over 9. enumerate, pronounce 12. recapitulate

recite (pert to) . . .
in monotone . . 6. intone
metrically . . 4. scan
rhetorically . . 7. declaim
to music . . 5. chant 10. cantillate

reciter . . . 4. book (of extracts) 5. roter 7. relator, speaker 8. narrator

reck . . . 4. care, deem, heed, mind 6. regard 7. concern 8. estimate

reckless . . . 4. rash 5. perdu (perdue) 6. madcap 7. hotspur 8. careless, heedless 9. desperate, hotheaded, imprudent 10. neglectful, regardless 11. indifferent, thoughtless, unconcerned 13. inconsiderate

reckon . . . 4. aret (arette), date, deem, tell 5. class, count, judge, tally, think 6. impute, number, regard, repute 7. account, compute, include, suppose 8. consider, estimate, evaluate 9. calculate, enumerate

reckoning . . . 3. sum 4. bill, shot 5. score, tally 6. esteem 7. account, verdict 8. counting 9. summation 10. estimation 11. calculation

reckoning instrument . . . 6. abacus 9. tabulator 10. calculator

reclaim . . . 4. tame 5. renew, train 6. ransom, recall, redeem, revoke 7. convert, recover, restore 8. civilize 10. regenerate 12. rehabilitate

recline . . . 3. lay, lie, sit 4. lean, loll, rest 6. repose 9. incline, lie down

reclining . . . 4. flat 5. prone 6. supine 7. lolling 8. couchant, reposing 9. prostrate, recumbent

recluse . . . 3. fra, nun 4. monk 6. hermit, hidden, secret, shut up 7. ascetic, eremite, retired (from world) 8. anchoret, isolated, solitary 9. anchorite 10. cloistered 11. sequestered

recognition . . . 4. fame 6. recall

9. detection 10. cognizance
11. discernment 14. acknowledgment
recognize... 3. see 4. know 5. admit
6. detect 7. consent 8. identify,
perceive 10. appreciate, recognosce
11. acknowledge
recoil... 3. shy 4. funk 5. quail 6. flinch,
resile, shrink 7. rebound, retreat
8. reaction, withdraw
recollect... 6. recall, revive 7. think of
8. remember 10. call to mind
recollection... 5. mind 6. memory
9. anamnesis 11. remembrance
12. reminiscence
recommence... 5. renew 6. resume
8. return to 9. begin anew
recommend... 4. tout, urge 6. advise,
commit, denote, praise 7. commend,
consign, entrust 8. advocate
recompense... 3. fee, pay 4. meed
5. repay 6. reward 8. requital
9. indemnify, reimburse
10. compensate, remunerate
11. reciprocate
recompense (pert to)...
Brehon Law.. 4. eric
Germanic law.. 7. wergild
Scot law.. 3. cro
Welsh law.. 7. galanas
reconcile... 4. suit, wean 5. atone
6. adjust, pacify, settle 7. cleanse
(Eccl), conform, reunite 9. harmonize
10. conciliate, propitiate
reconciliation... 7. harmony, reunion
10. adjustment, conformity
12. pacification 13. reconcilement
reconciliator... 10. arbitrator, reconciler
13. intermediator
recondite... 4. dark, deep 6. hidden,
mystic, occult 7. cryptic 8. abstract,
abstruse, esoteric 9. concealed
reconnaissance... 6. survey 8. scouting
11. examination
reconnoiter... 5. scout 6. survey
reconstruct... 6. recast, remake
7. rebuild, remodel 9. reproduce
11. reestablish
record... 3. log, tab 4. disc, file, list,
memo 6. annal, diary, enter, entry,
score 6. agenda, legend, memoir,
postea 7. archive, estreat, history
8. memorial, register 9. chronicle
10. chronology, transcribe, transcript
record (pert to)...
criminal investigation.. 7. dossier
document.. 8. protocol
earth tremor.. 11. seismograph
formal.. 4. vita 8. register
historic.. 6. annals 7. rotulet
keeper.. 9. registrar 10. chartulary
of events.. 5. annal, fasti 7. history
official.. 5. actum
pictorial.. 5. graph
ship's voyage.. 3. log
year's.. 5. diary 8. calendar
recording terms... 2. LP 4. reel, tape
5. album, Dolby 6. needle, stereo, stylus
7. capstan 8. cassette 9. cartridge,
videotape
recount... 3. min 4. tell 5. sum up
6. reckon, relate, repeat, retail 7. narrate

8. rehearse 9. enumerate, reiterate
12. recapitulate
recoup... 4. gain 7. recover 8. retrieve
9. indemnity, reimburse 10. compensate
recourse... 3. use 5. recur 6. access,
betake, refuge, resort, return, revert
7. retreat
recover... 3. get 4. cure, gain, heal
5. rally, reach, upset 6. obtain, recoup,
redeem, regain, rescue, resume 7. get
well, reclaim, recruit 8. overcome,
retrieve 9. repossess 10. convalesce,
recuperate
recovery... 6. return 7. salvage
9. retrieval 11. reclamation, reformation,
restoration
recreant... 6. coward, wretch 7. dastard,
knavish 8. apostate, betrayer, cowardly,
deserter 9. reprobate 10. unfaithful
recreation... 4. food, game, meal,
play 5. sport 7. holiday, renewal
8. vacation 9. amusement, diversion
11. refreshment 12. reproduction
14. reconstruction
recrement... 5. dross 6. refuse, scoria
recruit... 5. raise 6. enlist, gather, muster,
novice, revive, rookie 7. recover,
refresh, restore 8. assemble, inductee,
newcomer 9. conscript, reinforce,
replenish 12. reinvigorate
rectangle... 10. quadrangle
13. parallelogram
rectangular... 6. oblong
12. quadrangular
rectify... 5. amend, emend, right
6. adjust, better, reform, remedy
7. correct, justify 8. emendate, regulate,
set right 10. straighten
rector... 5. chief 6. leader, master
(Oxford), pastor 8. director, governor
9. churchman, clergyman
10. headmaster
rectory... 8. benefice 9. personage
recumbent... 4. idle 5. lying, prone
7. leaning, resting 8. inactive, reposing
9. reclining
recuperate... 4. rest 6. recoup, regain
7. improve, recover, restore 9. get
better, reimburse
recur... 5. again 6. repeat, return
7. persist, reoccur 8. reappear
recurrent... 10. repetitive
recurring (pert to)...
continually.. 8. constant 10. habitually,
repeatedly
ninth day.. 5. nonan
seventh day.. 6. septan
third day.. 7. tertian
red... 4. rosy 5. color, ruddy 7. radical
8. blushing, inflamed, rutilant, sanguine
9. bloodshot 12. bloodstained
13. revolutionary
red (color)... 4. fire, lake, pink, puce,
rose, ruby, tile, wine 5. blood,
brick, canna, coral, flame, flesh,
henna, poppy 6. auburn, cerise,
cherry, claret, damask, maroon,
minium, raddle, salmon, titian, Turkey
7. anemone, annatto, carmine, Chinese,
crimson, lobster, magenta, nacarat,
scarlet, stammel 8. cardinal, cinnabar

9. carnation, carnelian, vermilion

red (pert to)...
cap (Turk).. 8. tarboosh
cell.. 11. erythrocite
corpuscle.. 10. hemoglobin (source of)
dog.. 4. game 8. banknote
dye.. 3. aal, lac 4. chay (choy) 5. aurin
  (aurine), eosin (eosine) 8. morindin
gum.. 10. strophulus
hair.. 6. titian
herring.. 4. ruse 9. diversion
minded.. 7. radical
planet.. 4. Mars
race.. 7. Indians
robbin.. 14. scarlet tanager
truffle.. 12. melanogaster
viper.. 10. copperhead

Red (pert to)...
Book.. 7. Austria 13. Royal Kalendar
Crescent.. 8. Red Cross (Turk)
Cross.. 9. St George's (Eng)
Friar.. 13. Knight Templar
Guard.. Army 7. Russian
Hand.. 13. Badge of Ulster
Horse.. 10. Kentuckian
Planet.. 4. Mars
Polled.. 6. cattle (hornless)
Prince.. 7. Russian (Frederick Charles)
Ribbon.. 14. Order of the Bath
Rose.. 16. House of Lancaster
Russian.. 9. Bolshevik
Sea.. Erythraean main
Sea city.. 9. Leningrad
Sea colony.. 7. Eritrea
Sea gulf.. 5. Aqaba
Square.. 8. Moscow
The Red.. 4. Eric (Scand)
Triangle.. 4. YMCA (symbol)

redact... 4. edit 5. draft, frame 6. revise
7. defense, ravelin
redactor... 6. editor 7. reviser
9. redacteur
reddish (pert to)...
blue.. 5. smalt 9. damascene
brown.. 3. bay 4. roan 5. henna
  6. auburn, russet, sorrel 8. chestnut
dye.. 7. annatto
yellow.. 5. amber 6. orange
rede... 6. advice, relate 7. counsel,
explain, predict 9. interpret
redeem... 3. pay 6. ransom, regain,
rescue 7. convert, fulfill, reclaim,
recover 8. liberate 9. repurchase,
substitute
redeemer... 4. goel (Heb) 7. saviour
  (savior) 9. deliverer, liberator
11. emancipator
Redeemer, The... 8. Son of God 10. The
Messiah, The Saviour 11. Jesus Christ
redintegrate... 5. renew, unite 7. restore
9. reconcile 11. re-establish
redness... 4. glow 8. blushing
10. erubescent, rubescence
redolence... 4. odor 5. aroma, scent
9. fragrance, sweetness
redolent... 5. balmy 7. odorous, scented
8. aromatic, fragrant 11. impregnated,
reminiscent
redouble... 6. re-echo, repeat 7. reflect,
reprise (fencing) 9. intensify
10. ingeminate, repetition
11. reduplicate

redoubt... 4. fear 5. doubt 6. reduit
7. defense, ravelin
redound... 5. surge 6. abound, return
7. conduce, resound 8. flow back,
overflow 10. contribute (to)
11. reverberate
redpoll... 5. finch 6. linnet 7. warbler
Red Polled cattle... 8. hornless
redress... 4. help 5. amend, emend
6. reform, remedy 7. correct, relieve
8. atone for, reprisal 9. atonement
10. correction, recompense, reparation
11. reformation, restitution
reduce... 3. cut 4. bant, bate, pare,
thin 5. abase, abate, lower, razee
6. demote, derate, humble, lessen,
subdue, weaken 7. abridge, analyze,
cheapen, conquer, curtail, deplete,
qualify, relieve, shorten 8. decrease,
diminish, discount, minimize, moderate
9. subjugate 10. impoverish, slenderize
reduce in flesh... 8. emaciate
reduce in rank... 6. demote
reduce to...
ashes.. 7. cremate
average.. 4. mean 6. equate
bondage.. 7. enslave
common measure.. 12. commensurate
half.. 9. dimidiate
lower grade.. 6. demote 7. degrade
mean time.. 6. equate
spray.. 7. atomize
reduction... 6. rebate 7. subdual
8. decrease, demotion, discount,
lowering 9. weakening 10. abridgment,
cheapening, conversion, moderation
reduction (pert to)...
in value.. 12. depreciation
to absurdity.. 18. reductio ad absurdum
to common level.. 15. standardization
to compactness.. 12. condensation
to standard.. 15. standardization
redundancy... 6. excess 7. profuse
8. pleonasm, verbiage 9. prolixity,
talkative, tautology, verbosity
10. repetition 11. periphrasis
13. diffusiveness 14. circumlocution
redundant... 6. lavish 7. copious, diffuse,
verbose 9. excessive, exuberant,
plethoric 10. pleonastic 11. overflowing,
repetitious, superfluous
13. superabundant
ree... 3. dam 4. sift, wild 5. crazy, drunk,
river 6. harbor, riddle 7. channel,
fuddled 8. coalyard 9. enclosure,
sheepfold
re-echo... 7. resound 11. reverberate
reechy... 5. fetid 6. rancid
reed... 4. stem, tube 5. arrow, straw
6. thatch 10. instrument
reed (pert to)...
bird.. 4. wren 7. babbler, warbler
  8. bobolink
buck.. 5. bohor, nagar 8. antelope
bunting.. 7. sparrow 8. reedling
instrument.. 4. oboe 7. bagpipe
  8. clarinet 9. accordion, saxophone
loom.. 4. sley
mace.. 7. cattail, matreed
measure (Jew).. 9. six cubits
pipe.. 5. kazoo 8. mirliton

reef ... 3. bar, cay (cayo), key (quay)
4. itch, lode, sail, vein 5. islet, mange,
shoal 6. island 7. shorten 8. eruption

reef (pert to) ...
coral .. 3. key
knot .. 6. square
mining .. 4. lode, vein
nautical .. 5. sails
sand .. 3. bar

reefer ... 5. miner 6. jacket, oyster
9. cigarette 10. midshipman

reek ... 3. fug, rig 4. fume 5. equip,
exude, smell, smoke, steam 7. malodor,
seaweed 8. fetid air, smell bad, vaporize
10. exhalation

reel ... 3. eddy, pirn, rock, sail, sway,
wind 5. dance, lurch, spool, swift
(yarn), swing, waver, wince 6. tatter
7. scrieve, stagger 8. flounder, titubate,
windlass 12. Virginia reel

reeling ... 5. drunk 7. swaying, winding
8. rotating

reem (Bib) ... 6. animal (horned), wild
ox 7. unicorn

re-embody ... 7. combine, reshape
10. reorganize 11. reincarnate
13. reincorporate

reeve ... 3. pen 4. ruff 5. strip 6. thread
8. official (Eng Hist) 9. enclosure,
sheepfold

refect ... 7. refresh, restore

refectory ... 6. frater (monastery) 8. mess
hall 10. dining hall

refer ... 4. cite 5. apply, recur 6. allude,
appeal, charge, impute, relate, return
7. ascribe 8. appertain, attribute

refer (to) ... 4. harp 6. advert 7. consult,
mention

referee ... 5. judge 6. umpire 7. arbiter
8. attorney 9. moderator 10. arbitrator

reference ... 6. regard 7. respect
8. allusion, relation 9. character,
relevance 10. connection, pertinence
14. recommendation

reference (pert to) ...
book .. 5. atlas 8. handbook, syllabus
9. thesaurus 10. dictionary
12. encyclopedia

referendum ... 4. vote 7. mandate
8. politics 10. plebiscite

refine ... 5. smelt 6. rarefy 7. clarify,
elevate, improve, sublime 9. elaborate,
sensitize, sublimate

refined ... 4. fine, nice, pure, rare
5. urban 6. chaste 7. elegant, smelted
8. cleansed, highbred, purified, well-
bred 9. clarified, courteous, perfected
10. cultivated, fastidious, meticulous

refined spirit ... 5. grace 6. elixir

refinement ... 5. taste 6. polish 7. finesse
8. delicacy, elegance, fineness
9. gentility 11. cultivation, rarefaction
13. clarification

refinery (ore) ... 7. smelter

refining cup ... 5. cupel

reflect ... 3. say 4. muse, pore 5. radar,
think 6. divert, mirror, ponder 7. deflect
8. cogitate, consider, meditate,
ruminate, turn back 9. reproduce
11. reverberate

reflecting ... 6. musing 9. judicious

10. reflective, ruminating, thoughtful
11. insinuating 13. reverberatory
15. casting reproach

reflection ... 4. idea 5. image, light
6. musing 7. bending, thought
8. reaction, thinking 10. cogitation,
meditation, rumination 12. afterthought,
recollection 13. consideration,
contemplation

reflex ... 4. bent 6. turned 8. allusion,
reaction, reversed 9. duplicate, reflected
13. introspection

reflux ... 3. ebb 6. ebbing, reflow
8. backflow, reaction 9. refluence,
returning

reform ... 4. mend 5. amend, emend,
renew 6. better, remake, remass, repair
7. convert, rebuild, reclaim, rectify,
restore 9. amendment 10. regenerate
11. reformation

reformation ... 7. rebirth 10. conversion,
emendation 12. regeneration,
reproduction 15. re-establishment

Reformation leaders (Hist) ... 4. Knox
6. Calvin, Luther, Ridley 7. Cranmer,
Latimer, Zwingli 8. Campbell
11. Melanchthon

reformer ... 7. amender, reviser
9. reformado, reformist 10. politician

refraction ... 7. rebound 9. diop트rics
10. deflection, dispersion 11. anaclastics

refractor ... 7. prism 9. telescope

refractory ... 7. restive 8. indocile,
stubborn 11. disobedient
12. ungovernable

refrain ... 4. curb, shun 5. avoid,
cease, derry, epode 6. chorus, govern
7. abstain, forbear 8. response, restrain

refrain from using ... 5. spare 7. boycott

refresco ... 4. food 5. drink
11. refreshment

refresh ... 3. air, dew 4. cool 5. cheer,
renew, slake 6. repose, revive
7. freshen, relieve 8. recreate, renovate
9. reanimate, replenish 10. invigorate,
strengthen 11. refreshment
12. reinvigorate

refreshing ... 5. balmy 7. bracing
8. regaling 10. heartening
11. stimulating 12. exhilarating

refrigerant ... 3. ice 6. cooler 7. ammonia,
coolant, cryogen

refrigeration ... 7. cooling 8. cryogeny
10. anesthetic, cryogenics
12. preservation

refuge ... 3. ark 4. plea 5. haven
6. asylum, covert, excuse 7. retreat,
shelter 8. hospital, recourse, resource
9. sanctuary 10. protection, safety zone

refugee ... 5. exile, fleer 6. émigré
7. escapee, evacuee 8. fugitive,
renegade

refulgence ... 6. luster 8. radiance,
splendor 10. brilliancy

refund ... 5. repay 6. rebate 9. reimburse

refurbish ... 4. vamp 5. renew 8. brighten,
renovate 11. recondition

refusal ... 3. nay 6. denial 9. rejection
11. declination

refuse ... 3. cot (wool), ort 4. balk, coom
(coomb), culm, deny, junk, marc, scum

5. attle, chaff, dregs, dross, repel, scrap, trash, waste, weeds 6. debris, give up, litter, midden, naysay, reject, renege, scoria, scraps 7. abandon, bagasse, cast off, decline, garbage, hogwash, repulse 8. disclaim, leavings, oddments, renounce, withhold 9. excrement, repudiate 11. odds and ends

refuse to . . .
accept . . 6. reject
acknowledge . . 7. disavow 9. repudiate
comply . . 12. recalcitrant
proceed . . 4. balk

refutation . . . 6. answer 8. disproof, elenchus, rebuttal 11. confutation

refute . . . 4. deny, meet 5. rebut, refel 6. assoil 8. disprove, elenctic, redargue 9. overthrow 10. contradict

regain . . . 6. recoup 7. get back, recover 8. retrieve 9. get back to 10. reach again

regal . . . 5. royal 6. groove, kingly 7. channel, stately 8. imperial, majestic, splendid 9. dignified, sovereign

regale . . . 4. dine, fete 5. amuse, feast, treat 7. gratify, refresh 9. entertain 11. refreshment

regalia . . . 6. finery 7. costume, emblems, symbols 8. insignia 11. decorations 12. special dress 13. paraphernalia

regard . . . 3. air, awe 4. care, deem, gaze, heed, hold, look, love, mind, obey (law), rate, sake, view 5. honor, judge, think, treat 6. aspect, behold, esteem, remark, repute 8. attitude, consider, estimate, hold dear, listen to 9. attention, relevance, viewpoint 10. appearance, estimation 11. contemplate, observation 13. consideration

regard (pert to) . . .
for others . . 8. altruism
for other's wish . . 9. deference
highly . . 6. admire 7. lionize
with approval . . 6. admire
with deference . . 5. honor 7. respect
with veneration . . 6. revere

regardful . . . 7. careful, mindful 8. cautious 9. attentive, observant 10. altruistic, respectful, thoughtful 11. considerate

regarding . . . 2. re 4. as to 5. anent 10. concerning, respecting

regardless . . . 6. anyhow 8. careless, heedless, slighted 9. negligent 10. neglectful 11. inattentive, indifferent, unconcerned, unobservant 15. notwithstanding

regards . . . 8. respects 9. greetings 11. compliments

regatta cup . . . 5. Platt 8. Carnegie, Grimoldi

regency . . . 4. rule 8. dominion 10. government

regenerate . . . 5. shape 6. redeem, reform, revive 7. convert, restore 8. re-create 9. reproduce 11. fashion anew

regeneration . . . 7. renewal, revival 9. reversion 10. re-creation 11. reformation 12. reproduction 14. divine function

regent . . . 5. ruler 6. deputy, ruling 7. regnant 8. governor

Regent diamond, 137 carats (pert to) . . .
included in . . 11. State jewels (France)
named for . . 14. Regent of France
placed in . . 6. Louvre
sold (1717) to . . 4. Pitt (Gov of Madras, Ind)

regime, regimen . . . 4. diet, rule 6. system 7. therapy 10. government, regulation 14. administration

regiment . . . 4. unit, wing 6. outfit 8. organize 11. systematize

regiment, framework of . . . 5. cadre

regina . . . 5. queen

region . . . 4. area, belt, zone 5. clime, place, realm, space, tract 6. sphere 7. climate, cockpit, country, demesne, kingdom, section 8. district, province

region (pert to) . . .
beyond Jordan . . 5. Perea 6. Basham
blissful . . 4. Eden
comb form . . 5. nesia
desert . . 3. erg 5. waste
indefinite . . 5. tract
infernal . . 7. Avernal 8. Tartarus
meteorological . . 6. pleion
wooded . . 4. wold
woodless . . 5. weald

region of . . .
contentment . . 6. Arcady
dead (Egypt Myth) . . 6. Amenti
fabled wealth . . 8. Eldorado
nether darkness . . 6. Erebus
opposite side earth . . 9. Antipodes
Solomon's gold (Bib) . . 5. Ophir

register . . . 3. act 4. list, roll 5. annal, entry, index 6. docket, enlist, enroll, record 7. rotulet 8. archives, recorder, schedule 9. catalogue, chronicle, necrology, registrar 11. account book, matriculate

registrar . . . 8. recorder 9. accounter

regius . . . 5. royal 13. professorship

regret . . . 3. rue 4. ruth 5. grief, sorry 6. repent, repine, sorrow 7. deplore, remorse 9. penitence 10. repentance 11. compunction 12. self-reproach

regretful . . . 5. sorry 8. repining 9. repentant

regular . . . 4. even 5. usual 6. formal, normal, smooth, stated 7. correct, orderly, typical, uniform 8. constant, habitual, ordinary, ordinate, rhythmic, standard 9. isometric 10. systematic

regularity . . . 5. order 8. symmetry 9. constancy 10. smoothness, uniformity

regularly . . . 6. always 7. usually 8. properly, smoothly 9. correctly 10. constantly, habitually 12. methodically, periodically 13. symmetrically

regulate . . . 3. set 4. rule 6. adjust, direct, govern, manage, ordain, remedy 7. arrange, control, dispose 8. organize 9. influence, methodize 11. standardize

regulation . . . 3. law 4. rule 5. bylaw, order 6. system 7. control, precept 9. direction, principle

regulator ... 7. control 8. governor, rheostat 9. rheometer

Regulus .. 4. king, star 5. Alpha 8. warblers 9. Cor Leonis (star)

rehabilitate ... 7. restore 9. reeducate, reinstall

rehash ... 7. restate 9. réchauffé

rehearse .. 3. say 4. tell 5. speak, sum up, train 6. detail, recite, relate, repeat, try out 7. mention, narrate, recount 8. describe, rehearse 9. enumerate, reiterate 12. recapitulate

rehoboam ... 3. hat 4. bowl 6. flagon 8. jeroboam

Rehoboam (Bib) ... 11. King of Judah (1st) 12. King of Israel (last)

reif ... 7. plunder, robbery

reign .. 3. raj 4. rule, sway 5. guide, realm 6. empire 7. kingdom, prevail 8. dominion, flourish 11. sovereignty 12. supreme power

Reign of Terror (Fr Hist) ... 7. anarchy 9. bloodshed, despotism 12. confiscation

reimburse ... 3. pay 5. repay 6. refund 7. pay back, replace 9. indemnify 10. recompense

Reims, Rheims (pert to) ...
  capital (anc) .. 4. Remi
  famed building .. 9. Cathedral (Gothic)
  famed site .. 15. crowning of kings (Fr)

rein ... 4. curb, stop 5. check, leash 6. direct, retard 7. control 8. reindeer, restrain 9. hindrance 10. bridle part

reina ... 8. rockfish

reindeer ... 6. tarand 7. caribou 13. constellation

reindeer (pert to) ...
  age, epoch .. 11. Paleolithic
  flower .. 9. buttercup (white)
  genus .. 8. Rangifer

reinforce ... 4. back 5. add to, brace, reman 7. restore, support 9. intensify, replenish 10. strengthen

reinforcement ... 7. adjunct, support 8. addition 13. replenishment, strengthening

reins ... 5. loins 7. harness, kidneys 9. restraint

reis ... 6. escudo 7. milreis 14. money of account

reit ... 5. sedge 7. seaweed

reiterate ... 4. drum, harp 6. repeat 8. rehearse 12. recapitulate

reject ... 5. repel, spurn 6. disown, recuse (law) refuse 7. decline, discard, dismiss 8. athetize, disallow 9. repudiate

rejectamenta .. 5. wrack 6. refuse, reject 7. rubbish 8. excrement

rejection ... 6. heresy 7. discard, refusal 8. ejection 9. exclusion, objection 11. disapproval, repudiation

rejoice ... 5. cheer, elate 7. delight, gladden 8. jubilate

rejoinder ... 5. reply (law) 6. answer, retort, return 8. comeback

rejuvenate ... 6. revive 7. restore 9. stimulate 12. reinvigorate

relâche ... 10. relaxation 12. intermission 13. no performance (Theat)

relapse ... 4. sink 5. lapse 7. subside

8. slip back 9. backslide, reversion 10. recurrence, regression 11. falling back 12. recidivation

relate ... 4. tell 5. state 6. assert, detail, recite, report 7. narrate, pertain, recount 8. describe, rehearse 9. appertain, associate

related (pert to) ...
  by blood .. 3. sib 4. akin 7. cognate
  on father's side .. 6. agnate 7. cognate 8. agnation
  on mother's side .. 5. enate 6. enatic 7. cognate, enation 9. umbilical
  story .. 7. sidebar
  to land .. 8. praedial (predial)

relating to ...
  bread .. 6. panary
  Chinese .. 7. Sinitic
  dancing .. 7. gestic 13. choreographic
  fruit jelly .. 7. pectous
  grandparents .. 4. aval
  Hindu literature .. 5. Vedic
  life .. 5. vital
  morn .. 7. matinal 8. forenoon
  motion .. 7. kinetic 9. kinematic
  realities .. 7. factual 9. entelechy
  soft palate .. 5. velar
  vascular fluid .. 5. hemic

relation ... 3. kin 4. mode, tale 6. status, ubiety 7. account, analogy, kinship, kinsman, recital, telling 8. relative 9. character, narration, reference, rehearsal, rishtadar (Hind law) 10. connection 13. consanguinity

relationship ... 4. outs 7. kinship, kinsman, metochy 8. affinity, relative 13. consanguinity

relative ... 3. eme, kin, sib, son 4. aunt 5. niece, uncle 6. allied, cousin, father, mother, nephew, sister 7. brother, kindred 8. apposite, daughter, kinsfolk 9. pertinent 11. comparative, correlative 13. corresponding, proportionate

relative (pert to) ...
  favor to .. 8. nepotism
  rank .. 6. degree
  to .. 7. apropos 12. in proportion

relax ... 4. ease, open, rest 5. abate, loose, remit 6. divert, loosen, soften, unbend 7. detente, slacken 8. mitigate, slow down

relaxed ... 4. calm, cool 6. casual 8. laid-back 9. easygoing

relay ... 3. dak (dawk) 4. race 5. shift 6. remuda 7. relieve 8. avantlay 10. television (station)

release ... 4. drop, free, trip, undo 5. death, let go, loose, undam, unpen, untie 6. acquit, escape, exempt, loosen, parole, remise 7. deliver, freedom, manumit, receipt, relieve, unleash, unloose 8. liberate 9. discharge 10. liberation, relinquish 11. acquittance, deliverance

relegate ... 5. exile, refer 6. assign, banish, commit, deport, depute, remove 7. ascribe, consign, discard, dismiss, exclude 8. delegate

relent ... 5. abate, yield 6. regret, soften, submit 7. slacken

relentless ... 6. strict 9. merciless

10. inflexible, unyielding
11. persevering, unremitting

relevant ... 7. germane 9. pertinent
10. sufficient 11. referential

reliable ... 4. safe, sure 5. tried
6. stable, trusty 7. solvent 8. true-blue
11. trustworthy

reliance ... 4. hope 5. trust 6. belief
8. mainstay 10. confidence, conviction,
dependence

relic ... 5. curio, huaca, huaco, ruins
7. antique, memento, remains
8. artifact, fragment, memorial,
souvenir, survival 9. antiquity

relic cabinet ... 7. étagère, whatnot

relict ... 5. widow 7. widower 8. survivor

relied ... 6. banked 7. counted, reposed,
trusted 8. confided, depended, reckoned

relief ... 3. aid 4. bote (bot), dole,
ease, fret (Arch), help 5. spell
6. remedy, succor 7. comfort, outline,
redress, relieve, welfare 8. easement
10. assistance, embossment, mitigation,
substitute, sustenance 11. alleviation,
deliverance 15. indemnification

relieve ... 3. aid 4. cure, ease, free,
help 5. abate, allay, clear, raise, spell
6. assist, remedy, remove, succor
7. assuage, lighten, redress, refresh,
support, sustain, unloose 8. diminish
10. substitute

religion (pert to) ... 4. sect 5. creed,
deism, faith, piety, trust 6. belief,
hermit, schism, theism, voodoo
8. monastic, theology 9. solipsism
10. conformity, persuasion

religion, type ... 5. Islam 6. Taoism
7. Jainism, Judaism 8. Buddhism,
Hinduism 9. Mormonism, Moslemism,
Muslimism, Shintoism 11. Anglicanism,
Catholicism 12. Christianity,
Confucianism 13. Mohammedanism,
Protestantism

religious ... 4. holy 5. exact, godly, pious,
rigid 6. devout, sacred 7. devoted,
fervent, zealous 8. born-again,
pharasaic, spiritual 10. devotional,
meticulous, scrupulous 11. theological
13. conscientious

religious (pert to) ...
assembly .. 12. congregation
belief .. 5. deism 6. omnist
10. monotheism
brotherhood .. 8. sodality 9. ecumenism
10. fellowship 11. ecumenicism
center .. 7. Lambeth (Eng)
composition .. 5. motet
cult, sect .. 5. fakir 6. Shaker, Shinto
7. Pietism, Sikhism 8. cenobite
9. anchorite 11. Hare Krishna
devotee .. 5. fakir
devotion .. 6. novena
division .. 6. schism
expedition (Mil) .. 7. crusade
fasting .. Lent 9. Ember Days
10. Ember Weeks
festival .. 4. mela (Ind) 5. Purim (Jew)
image .. 4. icon
madness, mania .. 9. theomania
metaphysics .. 7. gnostic
musical .. 6. anthem

offering .. 7. deodate 8. oblation
Order member .. 6. Marist 7. Templar
poem .. 5. psalm
psalm .. 4. hymn, poem, song
publication (RCCh) .. 4. ordo

relinquish ... 3. let 4. cede, quit
5. forgo, leave, waive, yield 6. desert,
desist, forego, give up, remise, resign
7. abandon, forsake, release 8. abdicate,
renounce 9. surrender 11. leave behind
12. withdraw from

relinquishment ... 9. surrender
11. abandonment 12. renunciation

reliquary, reliquiae (pl) ... 3. box 4. arca,
tomb 5. chest 6. casket, chasse, shrine
8. monument

relish ... 4. gust, tang, zest 5. achar,
enjoy, gusto, sauce, taste 6. canape,
caviar, degust, flavor, liking 8. pleasure
9. condiment, degustate, enjoyment,
flavoring, seasoning 11. hors d'oeuvre
13. gratification

relucent ... 5. lucid 6. lucent 7. radiant,
shining 8. lightish 9. refulgent

reluctance ... 8. aversion 10. repugnance
13. indisposition, unwillingness
14. disinclination

reluctance unit (Elec) ... 3. rel

reluctant ... 5. chary, loath 6. averse
8. hesitant, not ready 9. resisting,
unwilling 11. disinclined

reluctate ... 5. repel 6. oppose
9. repudiate

rely ... 4. hold, lean, rest 5. count, trust
6. cleave, depend, reckon, repose
7. confide

rely on, upon ... 4. hope 5. trust
6. depend, lippen 7. believe

remain ... 3. lie 4. bide, last, rest,
stay 5. abide, tarry 6. endure, reside
8. continue

remainder ... 4. rest, stub 5. relic, stump
6. estate 7. balance, remnant, residue,
surplus 8. fragment, leavings, residual,
residuum

remaining ... 4. left, over 6. ledger (leger)
7. durable, remnant, staying, surplus
8. residual 9. permanent

remaining stationary ... 6. static
7. waiting 8. awaiting

remains ... 5. ashes, ruins, stays
6. corpse, relics 7. cadaver, fossils
9. remainder

remanent ... 4. left 7. further, lasting,
remains, remnant, residue 8. enduring,
leftover, residual 9. permanent,
remainder 10. additional
13. supplementary

remark ... 3. say, see 4. heed, note
5. gloss, state 6. notice, regard
7. comment, observe 8. perceive,
point out 9. statement 10. annotation,
commentary, indication 11. observation
12. interjection

remark (pert to) ...
amusing, witty .. 3. gag 4. quip
clever .. 3. mot
commonplace .. 9. platitude
smarting .. 7. sarcasm, stinger
upon .. 7. explain
witless .. 5. boner

remarkable ... 5. great 7. notable, strange, unusual 8. uncommon 9. wonderful 10. noteworthy, noticeable, observable 11. conspicuous 13. extraordinary

Rembrandt (pert to) ...
birthplace .. 6. Leyden (Neth)
color .. 5. brown
famed as .. 6. etcher (Dutch) 7. painter
style .. 14. Rembrandtesque

remedial ... 6. remedy (pert to) 7. healing 8. curative, panacean 10. corrective 11. therapeutic

remedy ... 3. aid, fix 4. bote (bot), cure, gain, help 5. amend 6. doctor, relief 8. antidote, medicine 10. assistance, reparation

remedy (pert to) ...
cure-all .. 6. elixir
mysterious (of Paracelsus) .. 7. arcanum
quack .. 7. nostrum
soothing .. 4. balm 6. balsam
universal .. 7. panacea

remember ... 3. min 9. recollect, reminisce 10. keep in mind

remembrance ... 4. fame 5. token 6. memory, Minnie, trophy 7. memento 8. allusion, memorial, reminder, souvenir 12. recollection 13. commemoration

remex ... 12. quill feather

remind ... 6. prompt, recall 9. remember 13. call attention

reminder ... 4. memo, twit 7. memento 8. souvenir 10. memorandum 11. remembrance

reminiscence ... 3. act 4. fact 5. power 6. memory 8. anecdote 10. experience 11. memorabilia 12. recollection

remise ... 6. giving, return 7. release, replace, respite 8. granting 9. remission, surrender

remiss ... 3. lax 5. slack 7. lenient 8. careless, dilatory, heedless 9. negligent 10. neglectful 11. inattentive, thoughtless

remissness ... 7. neglect 9. indolence 10. negligence 12. improvidence

remit ... 3. pay 5. relax 6. acquit, assign, cancel, excuse, pardon, reduce, resign 7. absolve, forgive, release, restore, suspend 8. abrogate, liberate, mitigate, recommit 9. surrender

remnant ... 3. ash, end, ort, rag 4. dreg, left, rest, stub 5. piece, relic, scrap, shred, trace 7. oddment, remains, yet left 8. fragment 9. remainder, remaining 10. suggestion

remolade ... 5. sauce 8. dressing, ointment

remonstrate ... 5. plead 7. protest 8. point out 11. expostulate

remontant ... 14. flowering again

remora ... 4. fish, pega (pegora)

remord ... 5. taint 6. ponder, rebuke 7. afflict, censure, remorse

remorse ... 4. pity 6. regret, sorrow 8. distress 9. penitence, repentent 10. compassion 11. compunction

remorseful ... 5. sorry 7. pitiful 8. contrite, merciful, penitent, pitiable 9. regretful 13. compassionate

remorseless ... 8. pitiless 9. merciless, unpitying 10. implacable, inflexible, relentless, unmerciful 11. unregretful

remote ... 3. far, off 5. alien, vague 6. elenge, forane, ultima 7. distant, foreign 8. abstruse, reserved, secluded, ulterior 10. farfetched, unsociable 11. out-of-the-way

remote control ... 10. pushbutton, tele-action

remote region ... 5. Thule (Greenland)

remotest ... 7. endmost, very end 8. farthest 14. ghost of a chance

removal ... 8. ejection 9. deduction 10. divestment, evacuation, extraction 11. elimination 12. transference

remove ... 3. rid 4. dele, doff, move, void, weed 5. erase, evict, expel, strip 6. change, debunk, delete, depose, divest, eloign (law) 7. dismiss, extract, relieve 8. abstract, displace, evacuate, put aside, transfer 9. eliminate, eradicate, translate 11. assassinate

remove (pert to) ...
cover .. 5. uncap
from office .. 6. oust 6. depose, recall
moisture .. 3. dry 5. wring 9. dehydrate
point of origin .. 6. distal
seed from flax .. 6. ribble
seeds .. 3. gin, pit
stalk .. 5. strig
to another place .. 8. transfer 9. translate
whole blubber .. 6. flense

removed ... 4. took 5. apart 6. betook, remote 7. distant, far away 8. reserved, secluded 9. separated, unrelated 10. unsociable

remover ... 6. porter 7. carrier, drayman, solvent 9. scavenger 10. contractor, eradicator

remunerate ... 3. pay 5. repay 6. reward 7. requite, satisfy 9. reimburse 10. compensate, recompense

remuneration ... 3. pay 6. reward 7. payment 8. pittance, requital 9. emolument 10. recompense 12. compensation, satisfaction 13. reimbursement

Remus (pert to) ...
brother .. 7. Romulus
father .. 4. Mars
legendary founder of .. 4. Rome (with brother)
slayer .. 7. Romulus

renable ... 4. glib 5. ready 6. fluent 8. eloquent

renaissance ... 7. rebirth, revival

Renaissance (pert to) ...
Archit .. 12. Roman classic
art .. 10. neoclassic
associated with .. 8. Petrarch
furniture .. 6. carved 7. English, Flemish
Italian reference .. 12. Resorgimento (new arising)
lace .. 10. Battenburg

renal ... 6. kidney 7. nephric

renascence ... 7. rebirth, revival 14. The Renaissance

rencounter ... 4. duel 5. clash 6. action, combat, flight 7. contest, meeting

8. conflict 9. collision

rend . . . 3. rip 4. rive, tear 5. break, burst,
sever, split, wrest 7. extract, rupture
8. fracture

render . . . 3. pay, put 4. give, make,
melt 6. return 7. clarify, convert,
deliver, execute, extract, narrate,
present, requite 8. transmit 9. translate
10. understand 11. communicate

render (pert to) . . .
accessible . . 6. open
agreeable . . 7. dulcify
angry, choleric . . 6. enrage
conformable to Eng . . 7. Anglify
9. Anglicize
divine . . 5. deify
dull . . 8. hebetate
enduring . . 6. anneal
fat . . 3. try 6. try out
fertile . . 6. enrich
free from bacteria . . 9. sterilize
ineffective . . 4. void 5. annul
10. invalidate
intelligible . . 9. elucidate
less pliant . . 7. stiffen
muddy, turgid . . 4. roil
oblique . . 5. splay
obscure . . 6. darkle 9. obfuscate
sharp . . 9. acuminate
unconscious . . 4. stun

rendezvous . . . 5. tryst 6. refuge
7. meeting, retreat 11. appointment

rendition . . . 7. account 8. delivery
9. surrender 10. extraction
11. performance, translation
14. interpretation

renegade . . . 3. rat 5. rebel 7. pervert,
traitor 8. apostate, deserter, fugitive,
turncoat

renege . . . 4. deny 6. desert, revoke
7. decline 8. renounce

renew . . . 6. resume, revamp, revive
7. convert, refresh, restore 8. renovate
10. invigorate, regenerate
12. redintegrate

renewal . . . 10. conversion, renovation,
resumption 11. restoration

renitent . . . 7. opposed 9. reluctant,
resistant 12. recalcitrant

rennet . . . 3. lab 5. apple 6. curdle, rennin
7. extract 9. coagulate

rennin . . . 6. enzyme

renommé . . . 8. renowned 10. celebrated

Renommist . . . 8. braggart, renowner
9. swaggerer

renounce . . . 4. cede, deny 5. forgo
(forego), waive 6. abjure, desert,
disown, recant, reject, renege, resign
7. abandon, forsake, retract 8. abnegate,
forswear, swear off 9. repudiate,
surrender 10. relinquish
12. abrenunciate

renouncement . . . 9. rejection
10. temperance 11. abandonment,
recantation

renovate . . . 5. renew 6. repair, resume,
revive 7. restore 10. regenerate

renown . . . 4. fame, note 5. éclat, glory
10. reputation

renowned . . . 5. famed, noted 6. famous
10. celebrated 11. illustrious

13. distinguished

rent . . . 3. let, pay 4. dues, hire, hole,
slit, tear, toll, tore, torn 5. break, cleft,
lease, share, split 6. reward 7. revenue,
rupture, slitted, tribute 8. tattered

rent (pert to) . . .
asunder . . 5. rived
harvest . . 7. onstand
in oats . . 7. avenage
paid . . 3. tac

renter . . . 6. lessee, lodger, tenant

renunciation . . . 6. denial 9. disavowal,
rejection, surrender 10. abjuration,
disclaimer, temperance
11. abandonment, recantation,
withdraw 14. relinquishment

repaid in kind . . . 10. retaliated

repair . . . 3. fix 4. darn, heal, mend
5. amend, patch, renew 6. doctor,
remedy, resort 7. correct, rebuild,
restore 8. atone for 9. condition
13. betake oneself

reparation . . . 6. amende, amends,
remedy, repair, reward 7. damages,
redress 8. reprisal, requital
9. atonement, indemnity
10. recompense 11. restitution
12. compensation, satisfaction

repartee . . . 3. wit 5. reply 6. retort
7. riposte

repast . . . 3. tea 4. feed, meal 5. feast,
lunch, treat 6. tiffin 8. mealtime,
prandial 9. collation

repatriate . . . 5. exile 6. banish
10. expatriate

repay . . . 4. meed 6. answer, avenge,
refund, return 7. requite, restore
9. reimburse, retaliate 10. compensate,
recompense, remunerate

repeal . . . 5. annul, emend, forgo (forego)
6. appeal, cancel, recall 7. abandon,
abolish, rescind, retract, reverse
8. abrogate, renounce, withdraw

repeat . . . 4. copy, echo, rame 5. recur
7. iterate, restate 8. remember
9. duplicate, reiterate

repeat (pert to) . . .
mathematics . . 8. repetend
mechanically . . 6. parrot
noisily . . 7. din
performance . . 6. encore
twice (pref) . . 3. bis

repeating . . . 4. rote 10. repetitive
11. repetitious

repel . . . 5. avert, check 6. offend, oppose,
rebuff, refuse, reject, resist, revolt
7. disgust, repulse 9. drive back, force
back

repellent . . . 5. harsh 6. odious
9. repulsive, resistant, revolting

repent . . . 3. rue 4. reform, regret 9. do
penance

repentance . . . 4. ruth 5. shame 6. regret
9. penitence 10. contrition
11. compunction

repercussion . . . 4. blow 6. impact
9. afterclap, aftermath 10. reflection

repertory . . . 4. list 5. index, store
8. calendar, magazine, treasure
9. catalogue 10. collection, repertoire,
storehouse

repetition ... 4. rote 5. troll 6. encore
  8. iterance 9. iteration 11. reiteration
  14. recapitulation
repetition (pert to) ...
  biology .. 6. merism
  music .. 5. rondo 7. tremolo
  rhetoric .. 8. anaphora 9. tautology
  sound .. 4. echo
  sounds (slight) .. 6. patter
repetitive ... 8. habitual 9. redundant
  11. repetitious
repine ... 4. fret 6. lament, regret
  7. grumble 8. complain
replace ... 4. stet 5. reset, stead 6. repone
  7. restore 8. supplant 9. discharge,
  supersede 10. substitute
replaceable ... 10. expendable
replenish ... 4. feed, fill 5. store 6. refill
  7. perfect, provide 8. complete
replete ... 3. fat 4. full 5. sated
  6. filled, gorged 7. bloated 8. abundant
  9. surfeited
replevin ... 4. bail, writ 8. recovery
replica ... 3. bis 4. copy 6. repeat
  9. duplicate, facsimile
reply ... 4. echo 5. rebut 6. answer,
  oracle, rejoin, retort 7. defense, epistle,
  respond 8. reaction, repartee, response
  9. rejoinder 11. retaliation
report ... 3. cry, pop 4. bang, note 5. bruit,
  rumor, sound, state, story 6. delate,
  recite, relate, repute 7. account,
  hearsay, recital, verdict 8. describe
  9. narration, narrative, statement
  10. accounting, commentary,
  responsory 11. information, publication
report (pert to) ...
  common .. 6. gossip
  false, absurd .. 5. rumor 6. canard
  7. slander
  following lightning .. 7. thunder
  for duty .. 14. present oneself
  official .. 7. hansard
  of proceedings .. 6. cahier
reporter ... 3. cub 6. legman, pistol
  7. newsman 8. newshawk 9. informant
  12. newspaperman
reporter's rounds ... 8. newsbeat
reporter's sign off ... 6. thirty
repose ... 3. lie, sit 4. ease, rely, rest
  5. peace, place, sleep 7. deposit, recline
  9. quiescent, quietness 10. quiescence,
  relaxation
repository ... 3. ark 4. file 5. vault
  6. chapel (RCCh), museum 8. treasury
  9. confidant, sepulcher 10. depository,
  storehouse 11. auction room
reposoir ... 5. altar
repoussé ... 7. art work
reprehensible ... 8. blamable, culpable
  9. accusable, obnoxious 10. censurable,
  reprovable 11. blameworthy
reprehension ... 5. blame 7. censure,
  reproof 9. reprimand 11. reprobation
  12. condemnation, denunciation
represent ... 5. enact 6. denote, depict,
  typify 7. betoken, exhibit, portray,
  produce 8. describe 9. delineate
representation ... 3. art 4. copy, icon,
  idea, idol, show 5. drama 6. avowal,
  symbol 7. picture 9. depiction,

  enactment, portrayal, spectacle
  10. exhibition, profession
  11. delineation, description, portraiture
  12. reproduction
representation (pert to) ...
  by characters (Mus) .. 8. notation
  graphic .. 5. chart
  Medusa's head .. 9. gorgoneum
  mental .. 5. image 7. eidolon, phantom
  of scene .. 7. tableau
  of solar system .. 6. orrery
  of star .. 7. estoile
  small .. 5. model 9. miniature
representative ... 4. heir, type 5. agent,
  envoy 6. deputy, legate 7. example,
  tribune, typical 8. delegate, exponent,
  symbolic 9. successor 10. ambassador,
  legislator, lieutenant, substitute
  12. illustrative
repress ... 4. curb, rein, stop 5. check,
  crush, quell 6. hush up, muffle, stifle
  7. put down 8. restrain, suppress
  9. overpower
reprieve ... 5. delay 6. pardon, relief
  7. relieve, respite 8. postpone
reprimand ... 5. chide, scold, slate
  6. rebuke 7. censure, reprove
reprisal ... 7. revenge, revenue 8. requital
  11. retaliation
reproach ... 4. taca, twit 5. abuse, blame,
  chide, shend, taunt 6. accuse, revile,
  vilify 7. censure, condemn, reproof,
  sarcasm, upbraid 8. disgrace, dishonor
  9. disrepute, invective 10. accusation,
  opprobrium 12. vilification
reproach, free of ... 9. blameless
reprobate ... 6. disown, reject, wicked
  7. abandon, corrupt, knavish, vicious
  8. depraved, hardened, recreant
  9. condemned, miscreant, reprehend,
  scoundrel 10. black sheep
  12. unprincipled 13. reprehensible
reproduce ... 4. copy 6. recite, remake,
  repeat 8. multiply 9. duplicate,
  propagate
reproduction ... 4. copy 6. ectype,
  recall 7. picture, replica 8. likeness
  10. repetition 11. counterpart,
  duplication 14. representation
reproductive ... 5. gamic, spore
  10. recreative 12. regenerative
reproof ... 5. roast 6. rebuke 7. chiding
  8. disgrace, reproach 9. reprimand
  10. admonition, censurable, refutation
  11. blameworthy, confutation
  12. reprehension 13. reprehensible
reprove ... 4. rate 5. blame, chide,
  scold 6. berate, rebuke 7. censure,
  correct, upbraid 8. admonish, reproach
  9. objurgate, reprehend, reprimand
reproving ... 10. admonitive
reptile ... 4. toad, worm 5. snake,
  viper 6. dragon, iguana, lizard, turtle
  7. monitor, serpent 8. creeping, Reptilia
  9. scoundrel
reptile (pert to) ...
  class .. 8. Reptilia
  crocodile .. 6. mugger
  extinct .. 9. pterosaur 10. diplodocus
  11. pterodactyl, Pterosauria
  group .. 6. Sauria

hard-shelled .. 6. iguana, turtle
8. terrapin, tortoise
iguanalike .. 7. tuatara
large .. 3. boa 9. alligator, crocodile
10. salamander
lizard .. 3. eft 4. adda, newt, seps 5. skink
(scink) 6. Anolis, iguana, moloch
7. monitor 9. chameleon 10. chuckwalla
11. Gila monster
Mesozoic .. 8. dinosaur
myth .. 6. dragon 8. basilisk
10. cockatrice, salamander
oldest .. 9. sea turtle
salamander .. 3. eft 4. newt
scale .. 5. scute
snake .. 3. asp 5. adder, cobra,
krait 6. garter, python 8. anaconda,
Squamata 10. copperhead
reptilian .. 7. saurian
Reptilian Age ... 8. Mesozoic
Republic ... 5. State 6. France 7. Andorra
(Andorre) 9. San Marino
10. commonweal, government
12. United States
Republican Party ... 3. GOP
7. mugwump (bolter 1884)
Republic of Plato ... 4. Book (famed)
8. dialogue 10. ideal State
repudiate ... 4. deny 6. abjure, disown,
recant, reject 7. disavow, discard,
exclude 8. renounce
repugnance ... 4. hate 5. odium 6. nausea
7. disgust, opposed 8. aversion,
loathing 9. antipathy, hostility
10. abhorrence, antagonism, opposition,
reluctance 12. disagreement
repugnant ... 6. odious 7. adverse,
hostile, opposed 8. inimical 9. offensive,
repellent, repulsive 10. refractory
11. distasteful 12. incompatible
14. irreconcilable
repulse ... 5. repel 6. denial, rebuff
7. refusal 9. rejection
repulsive ... 4. ugly, vile 5. nasty
6. odious 7. fulsome 9. offensive,
repellent, resistant, revolting
10. disgusting, forbidding, malodorous
repurchase ... 6. redeem
reputable ... 6. worthy 9. estimable,
honorable 10. creditable 11. respectable
reputation ... 4. fame, name, note
5. glory, honor 9. celebrity, notoriety
11. distinction 13. consideration
repute ... 4. hold, word 5. éclat, honor
6. credit, esteem, regard, report, revere
8. prestige 9. reputable 10. popularity,
reputation
reputed ... 6. deemed 7. assumed
8. accepted, presumed, putative,
supposed 10. understood
request ... 3. ask, beg 4. plea, pray, suit
6. appeal, behest, demand 7. entreat,
solicit 8. entreaty, petition, rogation
12. supplication
requiescat in pace ... 11. rest in peace
requiescence ... 8. repose
requin ... 5. shark 8. man-eater
require ... 3. ask 4. need 5. claim, exact,
force 6. charge, compel, demand,
enjoin, entail, oblige 8. obligate
11. necessitate

requisition ... 5. order 6. demand
11. application, requirement
requital ... 7. payment, revenge
8. reprisal 10. recompense
11. retaliation, retribution
12. compensation
requite ... 3. pay 5. atone, repay
6. avenge, return, reward 7. revenge,
satisfy 9. retaliate 10. compensate,
recompense 11. interchange
reredos ... 4. wall 6. screen 8. back-plate
(armor), partition
reremouse ... 3. bat
res ... 5. point, thing 6. matter
rescind ... 6. annul 6. cancel, recall,
recant, repeal, revoke 7. abolish
8. abrogate
rescue ... 3. aid 4. free, save 6. ransom,
redeem, repair 7. deliver, reclaim,
recover, release 8. delivery, liberate
9. extricate 11. deliverance
rese ... 4. rage, rush 5. hurry, onset,
quake, shake 7. impulse, tremble
8. rashness
resemblance ... 6. ringer 7. analogy
8. affinity, likeness 9. agreement,
semblance 10. similarity, similitude
resembling (pert to) ...
bark .. 11. corticiform
comb .. 8. pectinal
goose .. 8. anserine
gypsum .. 11. alabastrine
horse .. 6. equoid
man .. 7. android
minute animals .. 11. animalcular
rind .. 8. cortical
salt .. 6. haloid
seed .. 8. ovular
snakes .. 7. elapine 8. viperine
star .. 7. stellar 8. stellate 9. stellated
turf .. 5. soddy
wall .. 5. mural
resentment ... 3. ire 5. pique, spite
6. choler, enmity, hatred, malice, rancor
7. dudgeon, umbrage 9. animosity,
malignity 11. displeasure, indignation
reservation ... 5. tract 8. preserve
9. reticence 10. engagement, limitation
11. withholding 13. qualification
reserve ... 4. bank, fund, keep, save
5. allot, spare, stock, store 6. engage,
refuge 7. backlog, modesty, shyness
8. coldness, distance, postpone,
withhold 9. exception, restraint,
retention, reticence, sanctuary
10. constraint, diffidence, limitation,
substitute 11. self-control, taciturnity
reserved ... 3. coy 4. cool, kept,
unco 5. aloof, saved, staid, taken
6. modest, sedate 7. distant 8. reticent
15. uncommunicative
reservoir ... 4. font, pool, sump 5. store
6. cavity, cenote, supply 7. piscina,
reserve 8. fountain
reservoir of Pecquet (Anat) ... 12. lymph
channel 13. cisterna chyli
res gestae ... 5. deeds, facts 8. exploits
10. things done
resiant ... 7. present 8. resident
reside ... 4. bide, live, room, stay 5. abide,
dwell, lodge 6. remain 7. sojourn

8. habitate

residence . . . 4. home, seat, stay 5. abode
6. palace 7. deanery 8. domicile,
dwelling 9. consulate, residency
10. habitation

residencia . . . 5. court, trial

resident . . . 3. cit 6. intern, tenant
7. burgess, citizen 8. diplomat, occupant
10. inhabitant

residual . . . 7. remnant 8. residuum
9. remainder

residue . . . 3. ash, ort 4. coke, dreg, marc,
rest, silt, slag 5. ashes 6. pomace,
relics 7. balance, remains, remnant
8. leavings, sediment 9. remainder

residuum . . . 7. residue 8. hangover,
leavings 9. remainder

resign . . . 4. cede, quit 5. demit,
waive, yield 6. give up, submit
7. abandon, consign 8. abdicate,
renounce 9. surrender 10. relinquish

resignation . . . 5. demit 8. patience
9. demission, endurance 10. abdication,
submission 12. renunciation
14. relinquishment

resigned . . . 9. contented 10. submissive
11. acquiescent 13. uncomplaining

resilient . . . 7. buoyant, elastic 8. cheerful
9. recoiling 10. rebounding 11. returning
to 12. recuperative

resin . . . 3. gum, lac 4. aloe, tolu 5. amber,
anime, copal, jalap, rosin 6. dammar,
mastic

resin (pert to) . . .
  aromatic . . 4. balm 5. elemi, myrrh
    6. balsam 7. acouchi, camphor, copaiba
    8. sandarac 12. frankincense
  Bib . . 8. bdellium
  bitter . . 8. labdanum (ladanum)
  brown (mineral) . . 9. elaterite
  Chian turpentine . . 8. alk
  fossil . . 5. amber 8. retinite
  gum . . 5. gugal (googul)
  hard . . 5. rosin
  medicinal . . 7. aroeira 9. asafetida
    (asafoetida)
  narcotic . . 6. charas
  pine . . 7. galipot
  soft . . 5. animé, copal, elemi
  translucent . . 8. sandarac
  tropical . . 5. copal
  varnish ingredient . . 6. dammar
  yellowish . . 5. amber 7. gamboge

resinous substance . . . 3. gum, lac
5. copal 7. shellac

resist . . . 4. fend, stem 5. rebel, repel
6. defeat, oppose 7. prevent, ward off
8. outstand 9. withstand 10. counteract

resistance . . . 6. rebuff 7. defense
8. rheostat 9. hostility 10. opposition

resistance unit . . . 3. ohm

resistant . . . 5. tough 8. obdurate
9. resisting 10. unyielding
13. counteractive

resisting . . . 7. hostile 8. opposing
9. oppugnant, tenacious
12. antagonistic

resisting (pert to) . . .
  description . . 11. indefinable
  power . . 4. wiry
  pressure . . 8. renitent

pressure bar . . 5. strut

resolute . . . 4. bold, firm 5. fixed, stern
6. gritty, steady 7. decided 8. constant,
positive, resolved, unshaken
9. desperado, obstinate, steadfast
10. determined, inflexible, unyielding
11. perseverant, persevering

resolution . . . 4. firm 5. nerve 6. motion,
steady 7. courage, purpose, resolve,
verdict 8. analysis, decision, resolved,
strength 9. assurance, constancy,
fortitude 10. conversion, conviction,
relaxation, separation 11. persevering
12. perseverance 13. determination,
steadfastness 15. disentanglement

resolve . . . 4. melt 5. lapse (law), parse,
relax, solve 6. assure, decide, dispel,
inform, reduce, settle 7. analyze,
explain, purpose, unravel 8. convince,
dissolve, separate 9. determine,
transform 11. disentangle

resonance . . . 8. sonority, vibrance
10. resounding

resonant . . . 7. echoing, ringing, vibrant
8. sonorous, sounding 10. resounding
11. reverberant

resort . . . 3. spa 4. dive 5. haunt
6. betake, casino, refuge 7. finagle,
purlieu 8. frequent, recourse, resource
9. expedient, fainaigue, honky-tonk

resound . . . 4. echo, peal, ring 6. be loud,
re-echo 8. proclaim 11. reverberate

resounding . . . 4. loud 13. reverberating

resource . . . 5. means, skill 6. refuge,
resort, supply 9. expedient
10. capability 11. contrivance

resourceful . . . 5. sharp 9. Daedalian,
ingenious

resources . . . 5. funds, means, money
6. assets, supply 7. resorts
10. expedients 12. contrivances

respect . . . 3. awe 4. heed 5. defer,
favor, honor 6. aspect, detail, esteem,
homage, regard, repute, revere
7. concern, observe, regards 8. attitude,
venerate 9. attention, deference,
relevance, reverence, viewpoint
10. politeness 13. consideration

respectable . . . 6. decent 9. estimable,
honorable, reputable, tolerable
11. presentable

respectful . . . 5. civil 6. polite 7. careful,
duteous, heedful 8. reverent
11. deferential

respective . . . 6. mutual 7. careful,
heedful, several, special 9. attentive,
regardful 10. particular 12. distributive

respiration . . . 4. rale, sigh 7. eupnoea
9. breathing

respire . . . 7. breathe

respite . . . 4. rest 5. delay, first, pause
6. breath 7. leisure 8. postpone, reprieve
9. extension (time) 10. suspension
11. opportunity, short shrift
12. intermission

resplendent . . . 5. grand 7. aureate,
radiant, shining 8. lustrous, splendid
9. beautiful, brilliant, refulgent
10. epiphanous 11. illustrious

respond . . . 4. echo 5. react, reply
6. accord, answer, retort 8. response

10. correspond 11. reciprocate

response . . . 4. echo 5. reply 6. answer, anthem, chorus 7. rapport, refrain 8. antiphon (Mus), reaction

responsibility . . . 4. care, duty, onus 6. charge 8. solvency 15. reliability 14. accountability 15. trustworthiness

responsible . . . 6. liable 7. solvent 8. amenable, reliable 10. answerable 11. accountable, respectable, trustworthy

responsive . . . 6. pliant 7. elastic 8. reactive 9. answering, sensitive, teachable 10. open-minded 11. persuasible, sympathetic

res publica . . . 5. state 8. republic 10. commonweal 12. commonwealth

rest . . . 3. lay, set, sit 4. base, calm, ease, lair, lean, prop, seat, slip, stay, stop 5. cease, death, found, pause, peace, quiet, relax, renew 6. depend, desist, ground, repose, settle 7. balance, leisure, recline, refresh, remains, remnant, reposal, respite, silence, support, surplus 8. at anchor, interval, lodgment, residuum 9. cessation, quietness, remainder, stillness 10. quiescence, remain idle 12. intermission, peacefulness, tranquillity

rest (pert to) . . .
assured . . 9. be certain, believe me
at rest . . 4. abed, dead 6. otiose 11. comfortable
day . . 7. Sabbath
foot . . 4. rail 7. hassock, ottoman
house (Orient) . . 5. serai
reading . . 7. caesura (cesura)

restaurant . . . 4. café, deli (sl) 5. diner 6. eatery, automat, beanery, tearoom 8. fast-food, pizzeria, snack bar 9. cafeteria 10. coffee shop 11. rathskeller 12. luncheonette

resting . . . 4. abed 7. dormant 8. drowsing 9. quiescent

resting place . . . 4. tomb 5. étape, roost 6. hearth 7. lairage, landing, support 8. quarters

restitution . . . 6. return 9. atonement, repayment 10. recompense, reparation 12. compensation 13. reinstatement

restless . . . 5. antsy, hyper, itchy 6. roving, uneasy 7. agitato, fidgety, fretful, unquiet, restive, wakeful 8. agitated 9. impatient, sleepless, unceasing, unrestful, unsettled, wandering 10. changeable, reposeless 12. discontented

restoration . . . 6. repair, return 7. renewal, revival 8. recovery 10. renovation, reparation 11. improvement, restitution 14. redintegration 15. reestablishment

restorative . . . 6. acopon 7. anodyne 8. remedial 10. reparative

restore . . . 4. cure, heal 5. renew, repay 6. redeem, refund, repone, revive 7. rebuild, recover, replace 8. renovate 9. reinstate 11. reconstruct, reestablish 12. redintegrate, rehabilitate

restore (pert to) . . .
after cancelling . . 4. stet

certainty, confidence . . 8. reassure
to former position . . 9. reinstate
to original condition . . 9. refurbish
to proper position . . 5. right

restrain . . . 3. dam 4. bate, bind, curb, rein, stay 5. check, cramp, deter, limit, stint 6. arrest, bridle, fetter, halter, hinder, tether 7. abridge, confine, control, inhibit, overawe, qualify, repress 8. restrict, suppress, withhold 9. constrain, detention

restraint . . . 3. bit 4. curb, stop 5. check, force 7. durance, modesty, reserve 9. condition, hindrance, reticence 10. abridgment, constraint, inhibition, limitation, moderation, repression, temperance 11. confinement, deprivation, self-control 12. tastefulness

restraint, lack of . . . 9. looseness

restrict . . . 3. tie 4. bind, curb 5. bound, cramp, limit, scant, stint 6. censor, coerce, modify 7. confine, qualify, repress 10. specialize 12. circumscribe

restricted . . . 5. local 6. narrow 7. limited, topical 9. exclusive 10. restrained 11. specialized

restriction . . . 5. stint 9. restraint 10. limitation, narrowness, regulation, tightening 11. reservation 12. constriction 13. qualification

resty . . . 5. quiet 7. restive 8. sluggish

result . . . 3. end, sum 4. rise 5. arise, ensue, event, fruit, issue, total 6. accrue, answer, effect, follow, sequel, spring, upshot 7. proceed, product 8. solution 9. aftermath, deduction, eventuate, terminate 10. conclusion 11. achievement, consequence, termination

resume . . . 5. recur, renew 6. reopen 7. recover 8. reoccupy 9. epitomize, reiterate, summarize 10. recommence

résumé . . . 8. abstract 10. compendium 11. work history

resurrection . . . 6. rising 7. revival 10. apotheosis 11. restoration

resuscitate . . . 6. revive 7. restore 8. revivify

ret . . . 3. rot 4. soak 5. steep 6. expose, impute 7. ascribe

retable . . . 5. ledge, shelf 6. gradin (gradine) 8. predella

retail . . . 4. sale, sell 6. repeat 8. dispense, disperse

retain . . . 4. hold, keep, save, stet 6. employ 8. maintain, preserve, remember 9. recollect

retainer . . . 3. fee 4. cage 6. menial, minion, vassal, yeoman 7. servant 9. attendant, bodyguard

retaining wall . . . 9. revetment

retaliate . . . 5. repay 6. avenge 7. requite 12. make requital

retaliation . . . 6. talion (Mosaic law, eye for eye, tooth for tooth) 7. revenge 8. reprisal, requital 10. punishment 11. comeuppance, retribution

retard . . . 4. clog, drag, slow 5. defer, delay, laten 6. belate, deaden, detain, hinder, impede 7. keep back, obstruct, postpone, slow down

retardant ... 4. clog, drag 6. remora 8. obstacle

retardate ... 6. impede 8. retarded

retch ... 3. gag 4. barf (sl), hawk, spit 5. reach, vomit 6. expand, extend, strain 7. stretch, upchuck

rete ... 3. net 6. plexus 7. network

retention ... 6. memory 7. custody, holding, keeping 8. tenacity 11. maintenance, self-control

retentive ... 6. memory 7. keeping 9. tenacious 13. recollective

retenue ... 7. reserve 10. discretion 11. self-control 13. self-restraint

rethe ... 5. cruel 6. ardent, fierce, severe

retiary ... 6. spider 7. netlike 9. gladiator, retiarius

reticence ... 7. reserve, silence 9. restraint 13. secretiveness

reticulated ... 7. web 6. meshed, netted 7. network 12. intercrossed

reticule ... 3. bag 4. etui 5. cabas (caba) 7. handbag, reticle, workbag

reticulum ... 7. network, stomach (2nd) 9. neuroglia

retinue ... 4. crew 5. harem, suite, train 6. escort 7. cortege, service 8. equipage 9. entourage, retainers 10. attendants

retire ... 6. depart, depose, pay off, recede, vanish 7. go to bed, retreat 8. withdraw 9. disappear, discharge

retired ... 4. abed, left, lone, paid 7. receded 8. departed, emeritus, recessed, resigned, secluded, solitary, vanished, withdrew 9. pensioned 10. disengaged 11. disappeared, sequestered

retirement ... 7. deposal, payment, privacy, retreat 8. solitude 9. departure, recession, reticence 10. withdrawal 11. resignation 13. disemployment

retiring ... 3. shy 6. modest 8. reserved, reticent 9. diffident 10. not forward, retreating 11. unobtrusive

retort ... 3. mot 4. quip 5. reply 6. answer 7. riposte (ripost) 8. repartee 9. retaliate 11. retaliation

retract ... 6. abjure, disown, draw in, recent, repeal 7. disavow, rescind, swallow 8. take back 9. repudiate

retraction ... 6. repeal 8. palinode 10. revocation, withdrawal 11. recantation

retrad ... 8. backward 11. posteriorly

retral ... 8. backward 9. posterior 10. retrograde

retreat ... 3. den 4. abri, lair, nest, nook, rout 6. asylum, recede, recoil, refuge, retire 7. privacy, retiral, sanctum, shelter 8. fallback, solitude 9. departure, katabasis, seclusion 10. retirement, withdrawal

retrench ... 6. cut off, excise, lessen, reduce 7. abridge, curtail, cut down 8. decrease, diminish 9. economize, intercept

retrenchment ... 3. cut 8. excision 9. lessening, reduction 10. abridgment 11. curtailment, economizing

retribution ... 3. pay 6. return, reward 7. nemesis 8. reprisal, requital

9. vengeance 10. punishment 11. restitution 12. Last Judgment

retrieve ... 5. fetch 6. redeem, regain, rescue, revive 8. make good

retrograde ... 4. slow 6. recede, retral, revert 7. regress 8. backward, decadent, rearward 10. regressive 11. deteriorate 12. reversionary

retroussé ... 6. pugged (nose) 8. turned up

retund ... 4. beat, dull 5. blunt 6. refute, subdue 8. attenuate, drive back 10. render weak

return ... 5. recur, repay, reply 6. answer, render, repeat, report, revert 7. regress, relapse, requiet, respond, restore 9. repayment 11. restitution, retaliation

return (pert to) ... day .. 12. answer to writ evil for evil .. 7. revenge 9. retaliate tennis term .. 3. lob thrust (fencing) .. 7. riposte (ripost) to .. 6. resume 7. relapse, revisit to first theme (Mus) .. 7. reprise

returns ... 5. gains, polls 8. receipts

reune ... 3. join 7. reunite 10. reassemble

reunion ... 7. joining 8. sociable 14. reconciliation

re-up ... 8. re-enlist

reus ... 9. defendant

Reuter's News Agency ... 6. London

reveal ... 3. bid 4. bare, jamb, open, tell, wray 6. impart, unveil 7. divulge, exhibit, uncover 8. disclose, discover, evidence, indicate, manifest 11. communicate

reveal (in trust) ... 7. confide

reveal intentionally ... 4. tell 6. betray, expose 7. divulge, mislead

reveille ... 4. call 5. levet 6. signal (sunrise)

revel ... 3. joy 4. orgy, riot, wake 5. feast, spree, watch 6. frolic 7. carouse, delight, rejoice, revelry, wassail 8. carousal, festival 10. celebration, merrymaking 12. conviviality

revelant ... 5. clear 8. manifest 12. intelligible

revelation ... 6. oracle, vision 8. The Bible 9. discovery 10. appearance, disclosure 13. communication, manifestation

Revelation (Bib) ... 10. Apocalypse

revelry ... 3. joy 4. orgy, riot 6. revels 8. carnival, carousal 9. revelment, revelrout 11. merrymaking

revenant ... 5. ghost 7. eidolon, specter (spectre) 9. recurring 10. apparition

revendicate ... 7. reclaim, recover 10. real action

revenge ... 6. avenge 7. requite 8. reprisal, requital 9. retaliate, vengeance 10. punishment 11. retribution

revenue ... 3. tax 5. yield 6. income, profit 7. annates

reverberate ... 4. echo, ring 5. repel, reply 6. return 7. rebound, reflect, resound

reverberation ... 4. echo 9. reboation 10. reflection, resounding

revere ... 4. love 5. adore, honor

6. esteem, regard, repute 7. respect, worship 8. venerate

reverence ... 3. awe 5. dread, honor, piety 7. respect, worship 8. venerate 9. adoration, deference 10. veneration

reverent ... 5. pious 6. devout 7. dutiful 10. respectful, worshipful

reverie ... 4. muse 5. dream 6. notion, trance, vision 7. fantasy

reversal ... 6. defeat, repeal 9. inversion, reversion 14. tergiversation

reverse ... 4. back 5. upset 6. back up, defeat, invert, repeal, revert, revoke 7. relapse 8. contrary, converse, opposite, overturn 9. transpose 10. misfortune

reversion ... 6. estate 7. revival 8. transfer 9. inversion 10. regression 11. inheritance

reversion (pert to) ...
ancestral .. 7. atavism 9. atavistic
insurance .. 7. annuity
land .. 7. escheat

revert ... 5. react, recur 6. advert, return 7. regress, relapse 11. antistrophe

revest ... 4. robe 5. dress 6. attire, clothe 8. reinvest 9. reinstate

review ... 4. edit 6. parade, relate, survey 8. critique, remember 9. criticism, criticize, re-examine 10. certiorati, commentary, compendium, discussion, inspection, periodical, reconsider 11. examination, reiteration 12. recollection 15. reconsideration

reviewer ... 6. critic, writer 11. commentator

revile ... 4. rail 5. abuse, curse 6. berate, debase, vilify 7. asperse 8. reproach, ridicule

revise ... 4. edit 5. amend, emend 6. redact 7. correct, rewrite 8. readjust

revision ... 7. revisal 10. correction, emendation 11. rebeholding 13. re-examination

revival ... 7. rebirth, renewal 10. quickening 11. reanimation, renaissance, restoration 12. resurrection

revive ... 4. stum (wine) 5. rally, renew, rouse 6. come to 7. enliven, recover, refresh, respire, restore 8. rekindle, remember 11. resuscitate

revocate ... 6. recall, revoke 7. repress

revocation ... 6. repeal 8. reversal 10. retraction, withdrawal 11. recantation

revoke ... 5. adeem, annul 6. abjure, cancel, recall, recant, renege, repeal, revive 7. abolish, retract 8. abrogate 9. fainaigue 11. countermand

revolt ... 5. rebel 6. mutiny, offend, strike 8. nauseate, sedition, uprising 9. rebellion 10. revolution 12. insurrection

revolting ... 4. ugly 7. hideous 8. shocking 9. offensive, repellent 10. disgusting, nauseating

revolution ... 4. gyre, turn 5. cycle, epoch, orbit, round 6. revolt 7. circuit 8. disorder, rotation 9. rebellion

revolutionary ... 3. new 7. radical 12. catastrophic 15. insurrectionary

Revolutionary hero ... 5. Allen (Ethan), Gates 6. Revere 8. Burgoyne 10. Cornwallis, Washington 15. Lighthorse Harry (Gen Lee)

revolve ... 4. pirl, roll, spin, turn 5. recur, wheel, whirl 6. circle, gyrate, ponder, rotate 7. trundle 8. meditate 9. circulate 10. deliberate

revolver ... 3. gat, gun, rod 6. pistol 7. firearm 10. six-shooter

revolving ... 3. orb 4. cowl (metal cap) 6. rotary

revolving (pert to) ...
in thought .. 8. perusing
light .. 10. lighthouse
part .. 3. cam 5. rotor
storm .. 7. cyclone

revue ... 6. medley, review 9. burlesque 13. musical comedy

reward ... 3. pay, utu 4. meed 5. award, bonus, merit, Oscar, yield 6. hallow (to hounds) 7. guerdon 8. reprisal 10. recompense, remunerate 11. retribution 12. compensation, remuneration

reword ... 5. alter 7. restate 8. rephrase 9. reiterate 10. paraphrase

rex ... 4. king

rey ... 4. king

Reynard ... 3. fox (epic character)

rezai ... 8. coverlet (quilted)

rhamn ... 7. Rhamnus 9. buckthorn

rhapontic ... 7. rhubarb 8. knapweed, pieplant

rhapsodic ... 6. poetic 8. ecstatic

rhapsodist ... 4. poet 8. minstrel 9. visionary 10. enthusiast

rhapsody ... 6. jumble, medley 9. utterance (ecstatic) 10. recitation 11. composition

rhea ... 3. emu (emeu) 5. nandu 7. ostrich

Rhea (pert to) ...
called .. 15. Mother of the Gods
father .. 6. Uranus
home .. 5. Mt Ida (Crete)
mother .. 4. Gaea
mother of .. 4. Hera, Zeus 5. Hades 8. Poseidon
wife of .. 6. Cronus

rhebok ... 5. peele 8. antelope

Rheims ... see *Reims*

rhema ... 4. term, verb, word

rheophile ... 15. living in streams

rhetoric ... 7. diction, oratory 9. eloquence 11. composition

rhetorical term ... 6. aporia, simile 10. antithesis, oratorical 11. catachresis

rhetoric digression ... 6. ecbole

rheumatism root ... 7. wild yam

rheumatism weed ... 10. Indian hemp, pepsissewa

rhexis ... 7. rupture

rhinal ... 5. nasal 6. narial

rhine ... 5. ditch, drain 6. runnel

Rhine (pert to) ...
breed .. 7. rabbits
native .. 11. Rhinelander
nymph .. 7. Lorelei
ref to .. 7. Rhenish
tributary .. 4. Ruhr 6. Neckar
wine .. 7. Moselle

rhino ... **4.** cash, nose (comb form)
5. money **10.** rhinoceros
rhinoceros (pert to) ...
Bib .. **4.** reem
bird .. **8.** hornbill **9.** beefeater
black .. **6.** borele **7.** keitloa
Malay .. **5.** abada
viper .. **5.** snake (poisonous)
rhizopod ... **6.** amoeba **8.** Protozoa
Rhoda ... **4.** rose
Rhode Island ...
bay .. **12.** Narragansett
capital .. **10.** Providence
city .. **7.** Newport **9.** Pawtucket
10. Woonsocket
famed cotton mill .. **6.** Slater
first U.S. synagogue .. **5.** Touro
founder .. **13.** Roger Williams (1636)
Rebellion .. **5.** Dorr's (1842)
resort .. **7.** Newport **11.** Block Island
river .. **9.** Pawtucket **10.** Blackstone
settlers .. **8.** Puritans
State admission .. **10.** Thirteenth
State motto .. **4.** Hope
State nickname .. **11.** Little Rhody
Rhode Island Red ... **4.** fowl
Rhodesia ... see Zimbabwe
rhododaphne ... **8.** oleander
Rhoeadales ... **7.** poppy **11.** Papaverales
rhomb ... **7.** rhombus **10.** magic wheel
11. spinning top
rhomboid ... **13.** parallelogram
rhombus ... **5.** rhomb **13.** parallelogram
(equilateral)
Rhone tributary ... **5.** Isere
rhubarb ... **5.** clash, Rheum **6.** hassle
7. citrine, dispute, yawweed
8. argument, pieplant **9.** rhapontic
10. discussion
Rhus ... **5.** sumac **7.** wax tree
rhyme, rime ... **4.** poem **6.** poetry,
rhythm **7.** measure **9.** assonance
rhythm ... **4.** beat, lilt **5.** meter, pulse,
swing, tempo **6.** poetry **7.** cadence,
euphony, measure, pattern
8. movement, rhythmus, symmetry
rhythmical break ... **7.** caesura
ria ... **5.** creek, inlet
rial ... **4.** coin, king **5.** great, noble, royal
6. prince **8.** splendid **9.** excellent, stag's
horn **11.** magnificent
rialto ... **4.** mart **6.** Bridge (Venice),
market **7.** theater **8.** exchange
riant ... **3.** gay **6.** blithe, bright **7.** smiling
8. laughing
riata ... **4.** rope **5.** lasso **6.** lariat
rib ... **4.** bone, meat, vein **5.** costa, ridge
6. lierne
ribald ... **3.** low **4.** lewd **6.** coarse,
erotic, harlot, risqué, vulgar **7.** obscene
10. scurrilous **11.** blasphemous
12. ribble-rabble
riband ... **6.** ribbon
ribbed ... **3.** rep **5.** piqué **6.** corded,
ridged **7.** costate
ribble-rabble ... **6.** gabble, rabble, ribald
7. chatter **10.** incoherent
ribbon ... **3.** bow **4.** band, sash **5.** strip
6. cestus, fillet, riband **10.** decoration
ribbon (pert to) ...
badge .. **6.** cordon

band .. **5.** corse **9.** banderole
fish .. **7.** oarfish **8.** dealfish
inked .. **10.** typewriter
knot .. **7.** rosette
ribbonlike .. **8.** taenioid
snake .. **6.** garter
Society .. **7.** Ireland
worm .. **8.** tapeworm **9.** nemertine
ribwort ... **8.** plantain
rice (pert to) ...
bird .. **4.** rail, sora **8.** bobolink
dish .. **5.** pilaf (pilau, pilaw) **7.** risotto
8. kedgeree **9.** jambalaya, ricetable
drink .. **5.** bubud
feeding on .. **11.** oryzivorous
field .. **5.** paddy
hen .. **9.** gallinule
inferior .. **4.** chit, pago
paste .. **3.** ame
rat .. **8.** Oryzomys
refuse .. **5.** shood (shud)
Spanish .. **5.** arroz
wild .. **4.** reed
wine .. **4.** sake
rich ... **3.** fat **5.** opime **6.** creamy, fecund,
fruity, mighty, ornate, potent **7.** copious,
fertile, moneyed, opulent, wealthy
8. abundant, affluent, colorful, powerful,
resonant, valuable **9.** bountiful,
expensive, luxuriant, sumptuous **10.** in
the chips **13.** grandiloquent
rich (pert to) ...
English slang .. **4.** oofy **6.** oofier
man .. **5.** Dives (Bib), Midas, nabob
7. Croesus **9.** plutocrat **10.** capitalist
11. millionaire
richard ... **9.** plutocrat
riches ... **5.** lucre, means **6.** mammon
(Bib), wealth **7.** bonanza **8.** big bucks
(sl), opulence **9.** affluence, megabucks
(sl) **10.** prosperity
riches, demon of ... **6.** Mammon
rick ... **4.** heap, pile **5.** noise, scold,
stack, twist **6.** pile up, rattle, sprain,
wrench **7.** chatter
rickets ... **7.** disease **8.** rachitis
rickety ... **4.** weak **5.** crazy, shaky **6.** senile
7. unsound **8.** unstable, unsteady
9. tottering **10.** ramshackle
rickle ... **4.** heap, pile, rick **5.** stack
6. jingle, rattle
rickrack ... **5.** braid **6.** edging **9.** insertion
ricksha, rickshaw ... **10.** jinrikisha
ricochet ... **5.** carom **7.** rebound
10. bounce back
rid ... **4.** doff, free, kill **5.** clear, empty
6. remove, rescue **7.** deliver, destroy,
discard **9.** dispose of, drive away,
eliminate **11.** disencumber
riddance ... **6.** escape **7.** discard
11. elimination **14.** disencumber
riddle ... **3.** ree **4.** crux, sift **5.** rebus,
sieve **6.** enigma, pierce **7.** perplex
8. separate **9.** conundrum, perforate
ride ... **4.** twit **5.** drive, float **6.** pester,
travel **7.** be borne, journey, overlap
8. domineer, ridicule **9.** carrousel
(carousel), cavalcade, excursion
10. forest road **12.** merry-go-round
13. roller coaster
ride (pert to) ...

herd . . 9. guard over
off . . 4. polo (term)
roughshod over . . 9. tyrannize
shank's mare . . 4. walk
to hog, pig . . 11. boar hunting
to line . . 4. herd
rident . . . 5. riant 7. smiling 8. laughing
rider . . . 5. ryder 6. clause, knight
   7. allonge, codicil 8. addition, horseman
   9. performer 10. freebooter,
   highwayman 11. endorsement,
   mosstrooper
Rider Haggard's novel . . . 3. She
ridge . . . 3. aas, rib 4. hill, rand, weal,
   weal, welt 5. arête, bulge, chine, crest
   7. wrinkle
ridge (pert to) . . .
   anatomy . . 4. ruga 6. carina
   barrier . . 5. parma
   between furrows . . 7. porcate 8. porcated
   coral . . 4. reef
   glacial . . 2. os 5. esker (eskar)
   military . . 6. rideau
   mountain . . 4. loma 5. arête 6. sierra
   narrow, raised . . 4. wale
   oak . . 9. blackjack
   raised by stroke . . 5. wheal, whelk
   short . . 4. kame
   sloping . . 6. cuesta
   steep . . 7. hogback
   stony . . 4. rand
   zoology term . . 5. varix
ridicule . . . 3. guy, pan 4. butt, gibe, jeer,
   mock, quiz, twit 5. chaff, irony, sneer,
   taunt 6. banter, deride, satire 7. asteism,
   mockery, sarcasm 8. derision, raillery
   9. burlesque
ridiculous . . . 5. funny 6. absurd
   7. amusing 8. farcical 9. grotesque,
   laughable, ludicrous 10. impossible,
   outrageous 12. preposterous,
   unbelievable
ridiculous failure . . . 6. fiasco
riding (pert to) . . .
   bitts . . 11. anchor cable
   breeches . . 8. jodhpurs
   dress, costume . . 5. habit
   knot . . 8. slipknot
   rhyme . . 7. couplet
   school . . 6. manège
   whip . . 4. crop 5. quirt
rife . . . 7. replete, rumored 8. abundant
   9. abounding, plentiful, prevalent
   10. prevailing, widespread
riff . . . 6. rapids, riffle, ripple 7. midriff
   9. diaphragm 13. improvisation
riffle . . . 7. shallow, shuffle, wavelet
riffraff . . . 3. mob 4. mean 5. offal
   6. rabble, refuse, trashy 7. rubbish
   9. sweepings
rifle . . . 3. rob 5. reeve, steal, strip
   6. Mauser, search, snider 7. carbine,
   despoil, firearm, pillage, plunder,
   ransack
rifle (pert to) . . .
   accessory . . 6. ramrod
   ball . . 5. Minié 6. bullet
   bird . . 14. bird of paradise
   bomb . . 7. grenade
   French . . 9. chassepot
   old form . . 4. tige

rifler . . . 4. hawk 6. robber
rift . . . 3. gap, lag 4. rima, rive 5. break,
   cleft, split 6. cleave, divide 10. falling
   out
rig . . . 3. fit 4. gear, suit 5. dress, equip
   6. lateen 7. bedizen, costume, rigging,
   vehicle 9. Bermudian (Naut)
Riga (pert to) . . .
   balsam . . 5. resin (Swiss pine)
   capital of . . 6. Latvia
   native . . 4. Lett 7. Latvian
   rine . . 4. hemp
rigging (ship) . . . 4. gear, rope, spar
   6. tackle 9. equipment
right . . . 3. fit, pat 4. fair, true 6. adjust,
   dexter, proper, remedy 7. correct,
   justice, upright 8. becoming, suitable
   9. equitable, faultless, franchise,
   privilege, propriety 10. put in order
   11. appropriate, prerogative
   13. justification
right (pert to) . . .
   angled . . 10. orthogonal
   comb form . . 6. dextro
   exclusive . . 6. patent 10. concession
   hand . . 6. dexter
   hand page . . 5. recto
   law . . 5. droit
   neither right nor wrong . .
     11. adiaphorous
   of belligerent (Naut) . . 6. angary
   of ownership . . 5. title
   of procedure . . 3. pas
   real estate . . 8. easement
   royal . . 7. regalia
   time . . 3. tid
   to choice . . 6. option
   to pasture . . 6. eatage
   turn . . 3. gee
righteous . . . 4. holy, just 5. godly,
   moral, pious 6. worthy 7. upright
   8. virtuous 9. believers, blameless,
   equitable, guiltless
righteousness . . . 6. equity, virtue
   8. holiness 9. godliness, rectitude
   11. uprightness
rightful . . . 4. just, true 5. legal, right
   6. honest, lawful, proper 7. fitting,
   genuine 9. equitable 11. appropriate
rigid . . . 3. set 4. firm, hard 5. exact,
   stern, stiff, tense 6. formal, narrow, not
   lax, severe, strict 7. ascetic, austere
   8. rigorous 9. obstinate, stringent,
   unbending 10. inflexible, meticulous,
   unyielding
rigidity . . . 7. tensity 8. hardness, severity
   9. exactness, obstinacy, stiffness
rigol . . . 4. ring 6. circle, groove 7. channel
Rigoletto . . . 5. dance, opera (Verdi)
rigor, rigour . . . 4. cold, fury 7. cruelty
   8. asperity, rigidity, severity, violence
   9. exactness, harshness, rigidness
   10. shuddering, strictness
   13. inflexibility
rigor mortis . . . 10. stiffening (death)
   12. rigor of death
rigorous . . . 4. cold 5. exact, harsh, rigid,
   stern, stiff 6. severe, strict 7. austere,
   drastic, violent 8. accurate 9. inclement,
   obstinate, puritanic 10. inexorable,
   inflexible, relentless

rikk . . . 10. tambourine
rile . . . 3. vex 4. roil 5. anger, muddy
6. offend 7. agitate 8. irritate 9. turbidity
rill . . . 5. brook 6. course, runnel 7. rillock,
rivulet 9. streamlet
rim . . . 3. lip, web 4. band, brim, edge,
orle, tire 5. bezel, brink, felly (felloe),
verge 6. border, flange, margin, shield
7. enclose, horizon, rimrock 8. boundary
9. perimeter
rima . . . 5. cleft 7. fissure 8. aperture
10. breadfruit
rima oris . . . 16. space between lips
rim ash . . . 9. hackberry
rimate . . . 8. fissured
rime . . . 4. hoar, poem, rent 5. chink,
cleft, crack, frost, rhyme 6. poetry
7. fissure 8. aperture 9. assonance,
hoarfrost 10. ladder step
rime-cold giant (Norse) . . . 4. Ymir
(Ymer)
rimple . . . 4. fold 6. ripple, rumple
7. wrinkle
rimption . . . 3. lot 9. abundance
Rinaldo's steed . . . 6. Bayard
rind . . . 4. bark, husk, peel, skin 5. crust
6. cortex 7. epicarp 9. hoarfrost
rindle . . . 5. brook 6. runnel 7. rivulet
ring . . . 3. rim, set 4. band, halo,
hoop, peal, toll 5. arena, bague,
chime, group, knell 6. circle, clique,
collar 7. annulus, circlet, coterie,
resound 8. encircle, insignia, ornament,
surround 9. encompass 11. association
ring (pert to) . . .
    around . . 7. environ
    around the sun . . 6. corona
    barrel . . 4. hoop
    bill . . 4. duck
    bird . . 11. reed bunting
    comb form . . 4. gyro
    dove . . 6. cushat
    finger . . 5. third
    fruit jar . . 4. lute
    gem crown . . 5. bezel
    gem setting . . 6. chaton
    gun carriage . . 7. lunette (lunet)
    harness part . . 6. terret
    horse training . . 5. longe
    Latin . . 7. annulus
    leader . . 6. rouser 9. demagogue
    12. rabble-rouser
    little . . 7. annulet, circlet
    ornament (metal) . . 3. bee (angling)
    ouzel . . 6. thrush
    rope . . 7. grommet
    sail . . 4. hank 8. ringtail
    tail . . 3. cat 4. coon 5. lemur 6. godwit,
    marlin 10. cacomistle 11. golden eagle
    (young)
ringed boa . . . 5. aboma
ringed worm . . . 7. annelid
ringhals . . . 5. snake (spitting)
ringing . . . 5. clangor, orotund, pealing,
tolling 8. clanging, resonant
10. resounding
ringle-eye . . . 7. walleye
ringlet . . . 4. curl, lock 5. tress 6. circle
7. circlet 9. fairy ring
ringworm . . . 5. tinea 6. tetter 7. disease,
serpigo 9. millepede

rink . . . 4. hero, race, ring 6. circle,
course 7. warrior 8. encircle, ice sheet
(skating) 9. encounter
rinse . . . 4. lave, sind, wash 5. flush
6. sluice 7. cleanse 8. absterge
rinthereout, rintherout (Scot) . . .
5. tramp 7. vagrant 8. vagabond
rio . . . 5. river 6. coffee, stream
Rio de Janeiro . . . 7. capital (old, Braz)
Rio Grande . . . 5. river 7. disease (lettuce)
riot . . . 3. din 5. brawl, melee 6. clamor,
excess, pogrom, revolt, tumult, uproar
7. dispute, quarrel, revelry 8. carousal,
disorder, violence 9. commotion
riotous . . . 4. raid 5. aroar 6. wanton
7. violent 9. dissolute, luxuriant,
seditious 10. profligate, tumultuous
12. unrestrained
riotous jollity . . . 9. dissolute
11. saturnalian
rip . . . 3. cut 4. rend, rent, tear 5. break,
horse (old) 7. riptide 9. debauchee,
libertine, reprobate 10. fish basket,
laceration
ripe . . . 3. fit 5. ready, rifle 6. mature,
mellow 7. plunder 8. finished, prepared,
rareripe 9. developed, full-grown,
perfected 10. consummate
ripen . . . 3. age 5. addle 6. digest, mellow,
nature 7. develop, perfect, prepare
8. complete, grow ripe
riposte, ripost . . . 5. reply 6. answer,
retort, thrust 8. repartee
ripping . . . 5. bully, grand, swell
9. admirable, hunky-dory 12. fine and
dandy
ripplt . . . 9. fist fight
ripple . . . 3. cut, lap 4. fret, purl, riff, tear,
wave 5. acker, eagre, graze 6. dimple,
murmur 7. crinkle, disturb, scratch,
trickle, wavelet 11. corrugation
ripple grass plantain . . . 7. ribwort
ris de veau . . . 10. sweetbread
rise . . . 4. grow, soar, well 5. arise,
begin, climb, get up, mount, raise,
reach, rebel, start, surge, tower
6. ascend, ascent, attain, be high,
emerge, growth, height, revolt, spring,
thrive 7. succeed 8. eminence,
flourish, increase, levitate, reaction
9. acclivity, ascension, beginning,
elevation, originate 11. development
rise (pert to) . . .
    above . . 4. loom 8. surmount 11. triumph
    over
    again . . 7. resurge 11. resurrected
    and fall of the sea . . 5. scend, tidal
    6. welter
    by buoyancy . . 8. levitate
    gradually . . 4. loom
    hawk's . . 5. mounty
    high . . 5. tower
risible . . . 5. funny 6. absurd 9. laughable
rising . . . 6. ascent, ortive, revolt
7. growing, montant, sloping, surgent
8. elevated, emergent, gradient (by
degrees), swelling 9. acclivity,
advancing, ascending, ascension
rising and falling . . . 5. tidal 7. surging
8. undulant
risk . . . 4. dare 5. peril 6. chance, danger,

expose, gamble, hazard, injury, plight
7. venture 8. endanger 10. investment
12. disadvantage
risky . . . 6. risqué 9. hazardous
11. venturesome
risp . . . 3. rub 4. file, rasp, tirl 5. stalk
7. bulrush, scratch
risper . . . 11. caterpillar
risqué . . . 4. racy 5. risky, salty 8. off-color
9. hazardous 10. suggestive
rissle . . . 4. pole 5. staff, stick
rieus . . . 5. laugh 8. laughter
rit (rare) . . . 3. cut, rip 4. slit, tear 5. split
6. pierce 7. scratch
ritardando . . . 9. direction, retarding
10. slackening 11. rallentando
rite . . . 4. cult, form 6. ritual, sacrum
7. formula, liturgy, tonsure 8. ceremony
9. solemnity 10. ceremonial, initiation,
observance 12. patriarchate
ritratto . . . 7. picture 8. portrait
Ritter . . . 6. knight
ritual . . . 4. book, code, cult, form,
rite 5. feast, salat 6. novena, prayer
7. liturgy 8. ceremony 10. ceremonial
ritus . . . 5. usage 6. custom
ritzy . . . 5. smart (vulgarly), swank
6. swanky 11. pretentious 16. ultrafashionable
rivage . . . 4. bank, duty 5. coast, green,
shore
rival . . . 3. foe, vie 4. even, peer 5. excel,
match 7. compete, emulate 8. emulator,
opponent 10. antagonist, competitor
11. compete with
rivalry . . . 4. feud 9. emulation
11. competition
rive . . . 3. rip 4. bank, open, rent, rift, tear
5. cleft, sever, shore, split 6. cleave
8. lacerate
rive droite . . . 9. Right Bank (Seine)
rive gauche . . . 8. Left Bank (Seine, Paris,
including Latin Qtr)
rivel . . . 6. shrink 7. shrivel, wrinkle
river . . . 2. ea 3. ria, rio, run 4. ilog
5. amnis, brook, creek 6. stream
7. rivulet, torrent 8. riverlet 9. streamlet
river (pert to) . . .
arm (of sea) . . 7. estuary
bank . . 4. ripa 5. levee
bank, pert to . . 8. riparian
bed . . 4. holm 6. alveus, bottom
7. channel
bend . . 5. oxbow
boat . . 3. ark
delta branch . . 5. bayou
dog . . 10. hellbender
dragon . . 9. crocodile
duck . . 4. teal
fish (spawning, from sea) . .
10. anadromous
horse . . 5. hippo 12. hippopotamus
inlet . . 4. slew 5. fiord (fjord) 6. slough
islet . . 3. ait 4. holm
mouth . . 4. lade 5. delta 7. estuary
mussel . . 4. unio
Near East . . 4. wadi (wady)
Nile measure . . 9. Nilometer
nymph . . 4. nais 5. naiad
rat . . 5. thief
ref to . . 5. amnic

region (near) . . 8. riverine
siren . . 7. Lorelei
thief . . 3. rat 6. ackman
winding . . 3. ess
river in . . .
Africa . . 4. Nile, Tana 5. Niger
Austria . . 4. Iser 5. Drava
Bavaria . . 4. Eger, Isar
Belgium . . 4. Yser
Bohemia . . 4. Elbe, Iser
Brazil . . 3. Rio
Bulgaria . . 5. Mesta
China . . 3. Wei 6. Yellow 7. Hwang Ho
England . . 4. Isis 6. Thames
France . . 5. Seine
Germany . . 6. Danube
Italy . . 4. Arno 5. Tiber
Netherlands . . 3. Eem 4. Maas (Meuse)
S America . . 6. Amazon
Siberia . . 2. Ob 4. Lena
Switzerland . . 3. Aar 5. Reuss
river of . . .
Annie Laurie . . 4. Nith
Caesar . . 7. Rubicon
lower regions . . 4. Styx 5. Lethe
7. Acheron
woe . . 7. Acheron
rixy . . . 4. tern
road . . . 3. via, way 4. iter, path, raid
5. agger 7. estrada, highway, journey,
passage 8. pavement 9. incursion,
roadstead 10. expedition
road (pert to) . . .
block . . 3. dam 4. weir
goose . . 5. brant
hog . . 8. motorist 10. monopolist
horse . . 6. saddle (horse)
impassable . . 7. impasse
man . . 7. drummer, peddler 8. salesman
9. canvasser
map . . 5. chart, globe 9. directory
master . . 10. supervisor 11. trackmaster
nautical . . 9. roadstead
no outlet . . 8. cul-de-sac
paving . . 5. Tarmac 7. ballast, macadam
runner . . 6. cuckoo
scraper . . 4. harl
weed . . 8. plantain
roam . . . 2. go 3. err, gad 4. rove
5. prowl, range 6. ramble, stroll, wander
7. meander 9. gallivant
roan . . . 5. horse (bay, gray, chestnut)
8. antelope 9. sheepskin, yellow-red
roanoke . . . 6. wampum
Roanoke . . .
city . . 8. Virginia
famed as . . 11. First Colony (1584)
famed for . . 12. Virginia Dare (1st white
child, 1587)
settler . . 16. Sir Walter Raleigh 19. Sir
Richard Grenville
roar . . . 4. bell, blow, boom, rote (surf)
5. brool, laugh, shout 6. bellow, steven
7. ululate 8. cry aloud 9. loud sound
roaring . . . 5. aroar, great 7. booming,
riotous 10. disorderly
Roaring (pert to) . . .
Forties . . 8. Broadway (NYC)
game . . 7. curling (Scot)
Twenties . . 14. Golden Twenties 16. Age
of Red Hot Mamas

roast ... 4. beef, cook 5. cabob, parch
6. assate, banter 7. torrefy 8. ridicule
9. criticize

roasting (pert to) ...
ear .. 4. corn
jack .. 9. smokejack
stick .. 4. spit

rob ... 4. loot, pelf 5. pinch (sl), reave, rifle,
steal, touch 6. pilfer, ravish, snatch,
snitch 7. despoil, pillage, plunder
10. plagiarize

robbed ... 5. stole 6. rubato (Mus)
8. snatched, snitched

robber ... 4. yegg 5. crook (sl), thief
6. bandit, reaver, rifler 7. brigand,
burglar, yeggman 8. pillager
9. despoiler, embezzler, larcenist,
peculator 10. depredator, highwayman,
shoplifter

robber (pert to) ...
grave .. 5. ghoul
high seas .. 6. pirate 7. corsair
9. privateer
highway .. 7. footpad, ladrone
Indian .. 6. dacoit

robber baron ... 4. Fisk 5. Gould

robbery ... 4. reif 5. theft 6. burgle, piracy
7. larceny, pillage, plunder 8. burglary
10. spoliation 11. depredation

robe ... 5. array, cover, dress, tunic
6. invest, mantle 7. costume, garment
8. clerical, vestment

robe (pert to) ...
ancient Roman's .. 4. toga
bishop's .. 6. chimer
camel's hair .. 3. aba
long .. 5. talar
loose .. 5. cymar (symar)
royal .. 6. ermine, purple

robin ... 4. bird, lout, tody 6. thrush
7. bumpkin 8. trimming 9. redbreast
10. toxalbumin

robin (pert to) ...
dipper .. 14. bufflehead duck
runaway .. 7. dewdrop
sandpiper .. 4. knot 5. snipe 9. dowitcher
songbird .. 8. accentor

Robin Bluestring ... 13. Robert Walpole

robinet ... 6. cannon 9. chaffinch

Robin Goodfellow ... 4. Puck 6. sprite
9. hobgoblin

Robin Hood (pert to) ...
famed as .. 6. archer, outlaw, yeoman
followers .. 9. Friar Tuck 10. Little John,
Maid Marian
forest .. 8. Sherwood (Eng)
habit .. 11. robbing rich (for the poor)

Robinson Crusoe's man ... 6. Friday

roborant ... 4. drug 5. tonic 6. bracer
8. pick-me-up 9. stimulant

roborean ... 5. oaken, stout 6. strong

robot ... 9. automaton

Rob Roy ... 5. canoe 6. outlaw (Scot)
15. Robert MacGregor

robust ... 4. hale 5. hardy, lusty, rough,
sound, stout, wally 6. hearty, sinewy,
strong, sturdy 7. healthy 8. muscular,
vigorous

roc ... 4. bird (Arabian Nights) 7. simurgh
(simurg)

rocca ... 4. hold 6. donjon 8. fortress

rock ... 3. orc 4. lull, peak, sway,
trap, tufa, tuff 5. agate, chert, cliff,
quiet, shake, slate, stone 6. basalt,
egeran, gneiss, refuge, schist, teeter
7. diamond, missile 8. dolomite,
porphyry, strength 9. whinstone
10. promontory

rock (pert to) ...
black .. 6. basalt
brittle .. 5. shale
broken .. 4. sand 5. attle
cavity .. 5. druse
chain .. 4. reef
coarse .. 6. psammite, psephite
crystal .. 6. silica
crystalline .. 6. gneiss, schist
decomposed .. 6. gossan
fluid .. 4. lava
fragments .. 5. scree 8. detritus, xenolith
geyser deposit .. 6. sinter
glacial .. 7. moraine
granitelike .. 6. gneiss
granular .. 6. oolite, quartz 7. diorite
10. rockallite
gray .. 5. slate 8. andesite
igneous .. 4. boss, trap 6. basalt
7. peridot
jutting .. 3. tor 4. crag
nodule .. 6. geode
pinnacle .. 4. scar 6. needle
porous .. 4. tufa, tuff
rounded .. 6. rognon
science .. 9. petrology
Sicilian .. 6. Scylla (opp Charybdis)
stratified .. 5. shale
suffix .. 3. ite, yte
volcanic .. 4. tufa 6. basalt, domite,
latite

rock, animal ...
badger .. 4. cony
cavy .. 6. rodent
dassie .. 6. rabbit
goat .. 4. ibex
kangaroo .. 7. wallaby
squirrel .. 11. spermophile

rock, bird ...
blackbird .. 9. ring ouzel
dove .. 9. guillemot 10. rockpigeon
duck .. 9. harlequin
goose .. 9. kelp goose
grouse .. 9. ptarmigan
hawk .. 6. falcon, merlin
hopper .. 7. penguin
lark .. 5. pipit
pigeon .. 10. sand grouse
sandpiper .. 5. piper, snipe
shrike .. 10. rock thrush
starling .. 5. ouzel
swallow .. 10. rock martin

rock, fish ...
bass .. 5. black 7. striped
clam .. 5. borer
cod .. 7. grouper
cook .. 6. wrasse 7. whiting
eel .. 6. gunnel
gurnet .. 8. fortescue
hind .. 7. grouper (spotted)
lobster .. 8. crayfish
salmon .. 7. codfish 9. amberfish
sucker .. 7. lamprey
trout .. 9. greenling

rock, flora . . .
bell . . 9. columbine
brake . . 8. polypody
candytuft . . 8. gold-dust
cedar . . 7. juniper
cranberry . . 8. mountain
elm . . 11. slippery elm
garden . . 6. alpine
geranium . . 8. alumroot
hair . . 6. lichen
lily . . 9. columbine 12. pasqueflower
maple . . 5. sugar
melon . . 10. cantaloupe
shrub . . 9. buckthorn
rocket . . . 5. lance 6. ascend, ascent, fire
at 8. aircraft, firework 9. skyrocket,
spaceship
rocket (famed) . . . 5. Titan 6. Apollo,
Gemini, Saturn 7. Jupiter, Mercury
8. Redstone
Rock of Chickamauga . . . 6. Thomas
(Gen) (Civil War)
rocks . . . 5. money
rocks, on the . . . 7. aground 8. bankrupt,
stranded 10. saxicoline
rocky . . . 4. hard 5. stony 6. rugged
7. sickish 8. obdurate, unsteady
9. unfeeling
Rocky Ford . . . 9. muskmelon
Rocky Mountain . . .
group . . 5. Coast 8. Cascades 12. Sierra
Nevada
park . . 5. Estes
peak . . 6. Elbert 8. McKinley
popular name . . 7. Rockies
range . . 5. Teton, Uinta
rococo . . . 6. florid 7. baroque, bizarre
9. fantastic, grotesque
13. ornamentation
rod . . . 3. gat, gun 4. pole, wand, whip
5. baton, perch, power, scion, staff
7. measure, scepter
rod (pert to) . . .
comb form . . 5. rhabd 6. rhabdo
fibrous . . 5. lytta
flat . . 6. ferula, ferule
grooved . . 4. came (stained glass)
knitting . . 6. needle
meat-holding . . 4. spit
mechanical . . 7. piston
metal . . 7. stemmer
mixing . . 3. rab
pointed . . 4. goat, spit
rodlike . . 9. vergiform
rotating . . 7. spindle
short . . 6. toggle
spinning . . 7. spindle
rodd . . . 8. crossbow, stonebow
rodent . . . 4. cony, hare, paca, vole
5. hutia (jutia), mouse, stoat 6. agouti
(agouty), beaver, gerbil, gopher,
marmot, murine 7. lemming, leveret
8. chipmunk, hedgehog, mongoose,
squirrel 9. guinea pig, porcupine
rodent (pert to) . . .
Andes . . 8. abrocome
aquatic . . 6. beaver 7. muskrat
Belgian . . 9. leporide
burrowing . . 6. marmot 8. sewellel
disease . . 9. tularemia
European . . 4. cony 5. lerot

fur-bearing . . 6. beaver
genus . . 3. Mus 5. Lepus
gnawing . . 3. rat 4. mole
hare . . 6. rabbit
jumping . . 6. jerboa
largest . . 8. capybara (capibara)
migrating . . 7. lemming
Mongoloid . . 3. rat 6. gopher 12. pocket
gopher
mouselike . . 4. vole
rabbitlike . . 4. pika
reference to . . 7. gnawing 8. rosorial
S American . . 4. degu 5. coypu 6. agouti
8. capybara 10. chinchilla
spiny . . 9. porcupine
rodeo . . . 4. show 7. roundup 9. spectacle
11. performance (public)
rodomontade . . . 4. brag, rant 5. boast
7. bluster 8. boastful, boasting,
braggart, bragging
roe . . . 2. ra 3. doe 4. deer, hind, raun
5. coral (lobster) 8. fish eggs
Roentgen, Röntgen (Wilhelm) . . .
famed as . . 9. physicist
famed for . . 5. X-rays 10. Nobel Prize
(1901) 12. Roentgen rays
rogan . . . 4. bowl (wooden) 10. receptacle
(maple sap)
Roger's plane (Will) . . . 9. Winnie May
rogue . . . 3. imp, wag 4. kite 5. cheat,
knave, scamp, shark, tramp 6. beggar,
pirate, rascal 7. corsair, vagrant,
villain 8. elephant, picaroon, vagabond
13. mischief-maker
roguish . . . 3. sly 4. arch 5. pawky
7. knavish 8. espiegle, rascally
10. frolicsome, picaresque
11. mischievous
roguishly . . . 5. slyly 8. impishly, trickily
10. prankishly
roild . . . 5. rough 6. severe 7. riotous
10. frolicsome 12. unmanageable
roil . . . 3. vex 4. foul, roam, romp
5. anger, annoy, horse (Flemish),
muddy 6. fidget, ruffle, wander
7. agitate, disturb 8. irritate
roister . . . 4. brag, rude 5. bully 7. bluster,
boorish, swagger, violent 9. gilravage
roisterer (Hist) . . . 3. mun
roke . . . 3. fog 4. stir 5. moist, smoke,
steam, vapor 8. moisture
roker . . . 3. ray 8. rockling 9. thornback
roky . . . 4. damp 5. foggy, misty, smoky
6. hoarse
role . . . 4. duty, part 6. office 8. capacity,
function 9. character 13. impersonation
roll . . . 3. bun, rob 4. coil, film, food,
furl, list, peli, rota, sway, wind, wrap
5. trill, troll 6. billow, bundle, rotate,
rumble, scroll 8. bankroll, cylinder,
rotation
roll (pert to) . . .
along . . 7. trundle
back . . 6. reduce 8. retrench
bread . . 3. bap
butter . . 3. pat
cloth . . 4. bolt
coins . . 7. rouleau
fish . . 7. rissole
hair . . 3. rat 7. chignon
military . . 5. cadre 6. roster

the bones .. 4. dice 10. shoot craps
tobacco .. 5. cigar
to one side .. 5. lurch
up .. 4. furl 6. bundle 10. accumulate
roller ... 4. wave 5. inker, skate, towel
6. canary, caster, fillet, pigeon, platen
7. bandage, rotator, sirgang 8. cylinder
10. Holy Roller, pulverizer
rolling (pert to) ...
movement .. 6. welter
pin .. 6. roller 8. cylinder
stock .. 7. coaches, engines 8. cabooses,
Pullmans 9. motor cars 11. locomotives
stone .. 8. wanderer
weed .. 10. tumbleweed
rollix ... 4. play 6. frolic 7. rollick
romaine .. 10. cos lettuce
romal ... 5. quirt, thong
Roman ... 5. brave, Latin 6. frugal, honest,
simple 7. Italian
Roman (pert to) ... see also *Rome*
afterpiece (theater) .. 5. exode, farce
8. travesty
alcove .. 8. tablinum
apostle (Bib) .. 4. Neri
assembly .. 5. forum 7. comitia
augur .. 6. auspex
awning .. 8. velarium
barrack, hut .. 6. canaba (cannaba)
basilica .. 7. Lateran
booth, shelter .. 7. taberna
bowl .. 6. patina
boxing glove .. 6. cestus
breastplate .. 6. lorica
bronze .. 3. aes
building .. 5. aedes (worship)
case .. 5. bulla (for amulets)
cathedral .. 7. Lateran
chariot .. 5. essed (esseda)
chest .. 4. cist
circus post .. 4. meta
circus wall .. 5. spina
cistern .. 9. impluvium
citadel .. 3. arx
citizen (nonvoting) .. 8. aerarian
clan .. 4. gens
cloak .. 5. sagum (Mil) 6. abolla 7. planeta
concert hall .. 5. odeum
court (Pope's) .. 5. Curia
cuirass .. 6. lorica
Curia office .. 6. datary 7. dataria
date .. 4. ides 5. nones 7. calends
dish .. 6. patera
division (Polit) .. 5. curia
earthwork (Mil) .. 5. agger
Empire district .. 5. Pagus
era .. 5. Varro
farce .. 5. exode
festival days .. 5. feria 10. feriae Jovi
(festivals of Jupiter)
fish sauce .. 4. alec 5. garum
foot coverage, sock .. 3. udo
galley .. 6. bireme 7. trireme
garment .. 4. toga 5. palla, stole, tunic
general's cloak .. 12. paludamentum
(paludament)
Govt of two men .. 10. duumvirate
Hades .. 5. Orcus 10. lower world
hairpin .. 4. acus
hall (concert) .. 5. odeum
helmet .. 5. galea

highway .. 3. via 4. iter
highway, famed .. 9. Appian Way
hills .. 7. Viminal 8. Aventine, Palatine,
Quirinal 9. Esquiline 10. Capitoline
javelin .. 5. pilum
land (public) .. 4. ager
language .. 5. Latin
law .. 3. jus 4. cern
law, divine .. 3. fas
market day .. 7. nundine
marriage .. 13. confarreation
matron's garment .. 5. stola, stole
meal (chief) .. 4. cena (coena)
military cloak .. 5. sagum
military machine .. 7. terebra
military unit .. 6. legion 7. maniple
money .. 3. aes
ornament (neck) .. 5. bulla
palace .. 7. Lateran
peace .. 3. pax
provisions (free) .. 6. annona
ram (battery) .. 5. aries
religious law .. 3. fas
religious rite .. 5. sacra
road .. 4. iter 6. Appian (paved)
robe .. 4. toga
room .. 3. ala 6. atrium 8. tablinum
seat .. 5. sella
shelter, shop .. 7. taberna
shield .. 6. scutum
soldier's protection .. 7. testudo
spirits (group) .. 5. lares (sing lar),
manes 7. lemures
tablet (writing) .. 7. diptych
temple .. 4. naos 5. cella
tent .. 7. taberna
theater .. 5. odeum
travesty .. 5. exode
vase .. 7. amphora (wine) 8. murrhine
warship .. 6. bireme 7. trireme
Way (famed) .. 6. Appian
wine shop .. 7. taberna
romance ... 5. fancy, novel, story
7. fantasy, fiction, romanza, romaunt
8. idealize 9. falsehood, sentiment
11. imagination
romance (pert to) ...
language .. 6. French 7. Catalan, Italian,
Spanish 9. Provençal 10. Portuguese
ref to .. 8. knightly 10. chivalrous
verse .. 7. sestina
Roman god (of) ...
chief .. 4. Jove 7. Jupiter
dead .. 5. Orcus
fire .. 6. Vulcan
Hades .. 3. Dis 5. Pluto 8. Dispater
households .. 5. Lares 7. Penates
husbandry, animals .. 6. Faunus
love .. 4. Amor 5. Cupid
mirth .. 5. Comus
sun .. 3. Sol
Supreme .. 4. Jove 7. Jupiter
two-faced .. 5. Janus
underworld .. 3. Dis 5. Pluto 8. Dispater
war .. 4. Mars 8. Quirinus
Roman goddess (of) ...
agriculture .. 3. Ops 5. Ceres
beauty .. 5. Venus
burials .. 8. Libitina
childbirth .. 6. Lucina
crops .. 6. Annona

dawn . . 6. Aurora
earth . . 6. Tellus
fertility . . 6. Annona
handicrafts . . 7. Minerva
harvests . . 3. Ops
health . . 7. Minerva
hearth . . 4. Vesta
horses . . 5. Epona
love . . 5. Venus
moon . . 4. Luna 7. Phoebus
mothers, nursing . . 6. Rumina
night . . 3. Nox
peace . . 3. Pax 5. Irene
religion . . 4. Maia
strife . . 9. Discordia
victory (war) . . 6. Vacuna
womanhood . . 4. Juno
Romania . . .
capital . . 9. Bucharest
city . . 4. Cluj, Iasi 7. Ploesti
mountains . . 10. Carpathian
port . . 6. Galati (Galatz)
privileged class . . 5. boyar (boyard)
river . . 6. Danube
Romanian(-born) person . . .
dramatist . . 7. Ionesco
gymnast . . 8. Comaneci (Nadia)
hero . . 7. Michael (the Brave)
king . . 5. Carol
president, dictator . . 9. Ceausescu
violinist . . 6. Enesco
writer . . 6. Wiesel (Elie)
Roman people . . .
author . . 5. Pliny, Varro
biographer . . 5. Nepos
Bishop . . 4. Pope
boy (free birth) . . 8. camillus
Catholic priest . . 8. sacerdos
Catholic Society . . 6. Jesuit
consul . . 6. Scipio
Cupid . . 4. Eros
deity . . 4. faun
Diana . . 7. Artemis
dictator . . 5. Sulla 11. Cincinnatus
diviner . . 5. augur 6. auspex
divinity (chief) . . 4. Jove
Emperor . . 4. Nero, Otto 5. Titus
   7. Maximus 8. Tiberius 11. Constantine
   12. Heliogabalus
Eros . . 5. Cupid
farmer . . 7. colonus
Fates . . 4. Nona 5. Morta 6. Decuma
General . . 5. Sulla, Titus 6. Antony,
   Marius, Scipio
ghosts . . 7. lemures
gladiator . . 7. Samnite 9. retiarius
gladiator trainer . . 7. lanista
governor . . 9. proconsul
guard . . 6. lictor
historian . . 4. Livy 5. Nepos 7. Sallust
   8. Appianus (Appian)
king (1st) . . 7. Romulus
king's adviser (Myth) . . 6. Egeria
magistrate, official . . 5. augur 6. aedile
   (edile), censor, consul 7. praetor
   (pretor), tribune
maiden, betrayer to Sabrines . . 7. Tarpeia
military officer . . 9. proconsul
Naturalist . . 5. Pliny
nun . . 6. vestal
nymph (fountain) . . 6. Egeria

officer . . 6. lictor 8. triumvir (one of
   three)
official of public games . . 6. aedile
   (edile) 7. Asiarch
orator . . 5. Pliny 6. Cicero
palace officer . . 8. palatine
patriot . . 4. Cato
people (anc) . . 7. Sabines 8. Samnites
   9. plebeians 10. patricians
philosopher . . 4. Cato 6. Seneca
   7. Rosmini
physician . . 11. Aesculapius
poet . . 4. Ovid 5. Lucan 6. Horace,
   Vergil 7. Juvenal (satirical)
politician, courtier . . 7. Sejanus
priest . . 5. epulo 8. tresviri (10 in all)
   9. decemviri 10. septemviri
priest, serving a god . . 6. flamen
priestess . . 6. vestal
priests of Faunus . . 7. Luperci
race (conquered) . . 6. Sabine
saint . . 4. Neri
scholar . . 5. Varro
serf . . 6. colona (fem) 7. colonus (male)
slave (befriended lion) . . 9. Androcles
   (Androclus)
soldiers (body of) . . 6. cohort
statesman . . 4. Cato 6. Caesar, Cicero,
   Seneca
Tarquin rulers . . 9. Etruscans
tenant farmer . . 7. colonus
triumvirate, first . . 6. Caesar, Pompey
   7. Crassus
triumvirate, second . . 6. Antony
   7. Lepidus 8. Octavius
troops . . 6. alares
tyrant . . 4. Nero
virgin . . 6. vestal
writer (comic) . . 7. Terence
Romany, Rommany . . . 5. gypsy
   10. mascot blue
Rome . . .
cathedral (world's largest) . . 8. St Peter's
churches . . 7. Lateran 8. Castello,
   Gandolfo
conqueror . . 6. Alaric
founder (legendary) . . 7. Romulus
hills . . 5. Seven 6. Sabine 7. Viminal
   8. Aventine, Palatine, Quirinal
lake . . 4. Nemi
original city . . 12. Roma Quadrata
palace (world's largest) . . 7. Vatican
peak (Capitoline) . . 8. Tarpeian
port (anc) . . 5. Ostia
prairie . . 8. Campagna
river . . 5. Tiber
seat of . . 7. Holy See 11. Vatican City
site, ancient . . 13. Campus Martius
site, founding . . 12. Palatine Hill
street (famed) . . 5. Corso
Romulus (pert to) . . .
brother . . 5. Remus
city site . . 12. Palatine Hill
father . . 4. Mars
founder (Myth) . . 4. Rome
king (1st) . . 4. Rome
mother . . 5. Sylvia
rescued from . . 5. Tiber
suckled by . . 7. she-wolf
ronde . . . 6. script (heavy) 9. round hand
rondeau . . . 4. game, poem 5. rondo

6. rondel
rondel, rondelle . . . 4. poem 5. tower
(Fort) 8. round gem
rondure . . . 9. plumpness, roundness
ronier . . . 7. palmyra
ronin . . . 6. outlaw 7. outcast, samurai
rood . . . 5. cross (holy), goose 7. measure
8. crucifix
roodebok . . . 6. impala 9. duikerbok
roof . . . 3. hip 4. dome, eave, flat, nave, tile
5. cover, gable, slate, spire 6. cupola,
lean-to 7. chopper, gambrel, mansard,
pitched, shingle 8. housetop, thatched
9. penthouse 10. jerkinhead
roof (pert to) . . .
  boards (thin) . . 4. sark
  brain cover . . 4. tela 14. telachorioidea
  frame (raised) . . 7. coaming
  material . . 3. tin 4. tile 5. paper, slate
  6. copper, shakes 7. roofage 8. shingles
  mouth . . 6. palate
  ornament . . 3. epi
  tile . . 7. pantile
  timber . . 6. rafter
  tin (coating) . . 5. terne
  tool . . 3. zax
Roof of the World, Asia . . 6. Pamirs
(The) 9. Bam i Dunya
rook . . . 4. bird, crow, dupe 5. cheat
6. castle 7. defraud, sharper
8. chessman 9. ruddy duck
rookery . . . 4. slum 5. confusion
13. breeding place (rooks, herons,
penguins) 14. breeding ground (seals)
rookie, rooky . . . 6. novice 7. recruit
8. beginner, newcomer
rooky . . . 4. roky 5. foggy
room . . . 3. ala (anc), den 4. aula, cell, hall,
sala, seat, shed 5. attic, lodge, place,
salon, scope, space 6. cellar, leeway,
pantry, parlor, reside 7. chamber,
drawing, laundry, nursery, quarter
8. capacity 9. apartment, storeroom
11. opportunity
room (pert to) . . .
  church (bishop's) . . 4. apse
  convent . . 9. parlatory
  dining . . 7. cenacle, dinette 9. refectory
  harem . . 3. oda
  household . . 5. ewery
  inner . . 3. ben
  large . . 4. aula, hall 7. rotunda, theater
  10. auditorium
  monastery . . 4. cell
  outer . . 3. but
  pantry . . 6. larder 8. cupboard
  prayer . . 7. oratory
  Pueblo Ind ceremonial . . 4. kiva
  Roman . . 6. atrium
  ship's . . 4. brig 5. cabin, salon
  sleeping . . 5. lodge 6. dormer 7. barrack,
  bedroom, chamber 9. dormitory
  tower (bell) . . 6. belfry
roomy . . . 4. airy 5. ample 8. spacious
9. capacious, expansive
10. commodious 11. large-framed
roon . . . 5. shred 6. border 7. darling
8. treasure
roorback, roorbach . . . 3. lie 6. canard
7. lampoon 9. falsehood
roose . . . 5. boast, vaunt 6. praise

Roosevelt . . .
  president, 26th . . 8. Theodore
  president, 32nd . . 8. Franklin
roost . . . 3. bed, sit 4. jouk, pole, rest
5. perch 6. settle 7. lodging, support
rooster . . . 4. cock, male (animal) 5. gallo
7. percher 11. chanticleer 12. fighting
cock
root . . . 4. bulb, word 5. cheer, plant,
radix, tuber 6. source 7. radical 8. take
root 9. establish
root (pert to) . . .
  aromatic . . 9. sassafras
  edible . . 3. oca, yam 4. beet, eddo,
  taro 6. carrot, potato, radish, turnip
  7. parsnip 8. rutabaga
  food (Maori) . . 3. roi
  medicinal . . 4. atis 5. jalep 6. ipecac,
  senega 7. Senegal
  out . . 4. seek 7. extract 9. eliminate,
  eradicate
  perfume . . 5. orris
  pungent . . 6. ginger
  starch . . 7. cassava
  stock . . 7. rhizome
  stringy . . 5. watap (watape)
  taro . . 4. eddo
  word . . 4. etym 6. etymon
rooted . . . 8. habitual 9. implanted
10. deep-seated 11. established,
traditional
rootlet . . . 7. radical, rhizoid, taproot
rope . . . 3. tew, tie, tye 4. bind, cord, line,
rood 5. cable, cigar, lasso, longe, noose,
reata, wanty 6. fasten, halter, hawser,
lariat, string, tether 7. cordage, lanyard,
measure 8. hangman's, inveigle
rope (pert to) . . .
  boat's . . 4. rode 6. hawser 7. painter
  chain . . 3. tye 9. stern fast
  dancer, walker . . 8. balancer
  11. equilibrist, funambulist
  fiber . . 4. bast, hemp, jute 5. sisal
  flag raising . . 7. halyard
  gun carriage . . 8. prolonge
  guy . . 4. stay, vang
  nautical . . 3. tye 4. vang, wapp 6. parrel
  (parral) 7. snotter
  of onions . . 5. reeve
  security device . . 4. butt 5. cleat
  ship's . . 3. tye 4. stay, vang 6. hawser,
  shroud 7. painter, ratline, snotter
  splicer's tool . . 3. fid
  straw, twisted . . 5. sugan (soogan)
  two strand . . 7. marline
  walker . . 11. funambulist
ropery . . . 6. banter 7. roguery
roral . . . 4. dewy, rory 5. roric
rorqual . . . 5. whale 7. finback
Ros . . . 10. Slav rulers (Russ), Varangians
rosary . . . 4. aves 5. beads (prayer)
7. chaplet (of roses), garland 8. devotion
roscoe . . . 3. gat, gun
rose . . . 3. cut (jewelry) 5. color, flush,
Rhoda 6. emblem, flower, nozzle,
symbol, window 7. fixture
rose (pert to) . . .
  apple . . 4. plum 6. cherry 7. jambool
  8. poma rosa
  beetle . . 6. chafer, weevil
  City . . 8. Portland (Oreg)

colored . . 8. alluring 10. auspicious, optimistic
cross . . 6. symbol 11. Rosicrucian 14. cross in a circle
genus . . 4. Rosa 6. Acaena 8. Rosaceae
hiller . . 7. rosella 8. parakeet
moss . . 9. portulaca
of Sharon . . 8. Althea
petal oil . . 4. otto 5. attar
rash . . 7. roseola
under the rose . . 6. secret 7. sub rosa
wild . . 9. eglantine

Rosetta Stone (pert to) . . .
decipherer . . 11. Champollion
famed for . . 11. inscription 13. hieroglyphics
site found . . 4. Nile (1799)
type . . 11. black basalt

roster . . . 4. list, roll, rota 5. slate 8. schedule

rostrum . . . 4. beak, dais, prow 5. snout, stage 6. pulpit 8. platform 9. proboscis

rosy . . . 3. red 4. pink 7. flushed, roseate 8. blooming, blushing 9. rosaceous 10. auspicious, optimistic

rot . . . 3. die 5. decay, spoil 6. blight 7. corrupt, disease, putrefy 8. nonsense 9. decompose 10. degenerate 12. putrefaction 13. decomposition

rota . . . 4. Club (Eng), list, roll 5. court, round (Mus) 6. roster 15. Sacra Romana Rota

rotate . . . 4. roll, spin, turn, whiz 5. recur, wheel 6. gyrate 7. rabatte, revolve, trundle 8. rotiform

rotation . . . 4. spin, turn 5. round 7. turning 8. sequence 10. revolution, succession

rotator . . . 5. rotor 6. muscle 7. whirler 9. carrousel 12. merry-go-round

rotche, rotch . . . 5. goose, rotge 7. dovekie

rote . . . 6. course, custom, system 7. by heart, routine 8. par coeur, practice 9. condition

roti . . . 5. roast 7. roasted

rotor . . . 5. wheel 6. roller, stator 7. rotator, turbine 8. impeller

rotten . . . 3. bad 4. foul, punk 5. doted, fetid 6. putrid, wicked 7. decayed, tainted, unsound 8. depraved, unstable 9. dishonest, offensive, putrefied 10. putrescent, undermined 13. disintegrated

Rotten Row (Hyde Park, London) . . . 12. thoroughfare (equestrian)

rottenstone . . . 6. polish 7. tripoli

rotter . . . 3. cad 7. bounder, shirker, slacker 10. blackguard

rottgoose . . . 5. brant

rotund . . . 3. fat 5. obese, plump, round, stout 6. chubby 7. rounded 8. roly-poly 9. corpulent, spherical

Rotwelsch . . . 5. argot, slang 6. jargon 14. secret language

roué . . . 4. rake, wolf 7. rounder 9. debauchee, libertine

rouge . . . 5. blush, flush 6. polish, redden 7. radical 8. cosmetic

rough . . . 4. hard, rude 5. crude, draft, harsh, raspy, rowdy, seamy, stern

6. broken, choppy, coarse, hoarse, rugged, severe, shaggy 7. boorish, inexact, jarring, jolting, ruffled 8. scabrous, unsmooth 9. imperfect, turbulent 10. incomplete, tumultuous, unfinished 11. approximate

rough (pert to) . . .
avens . . 6. bennet (herb)
cloth . . 5. terry
footed (bird) . . 9. feathered
hair . . 4. shag
hewn . . 6. brutal 10. unpolished 12. uncultivated
house . . 5. cut up 9. rowdiness 10. disorderly, noisy sport
jest (Mus) . . 9. charivari
neck . . 4. boor 5. rowdy, tough
rider . . 9. Roosevelt (Teddy) 10. cavalryman
rock . . 4. crag
shod (to ride) . . 7. trample 8. dominate 9. tyrannize

rough end . . .
hoarse . . 7. raucous
lean . . 6. craggy
ready . . 4. rude 10. unpolished
Ready . . 6. Taylor (Gen Zachary)

roughen . . . 4. chap, shag 8. asperate

roughly . . . 4. or so 6. rudely 7. harshly 8. coarsely, severely, unevenly, vulgarly 9. brusquely 10. unsmoothly 13. approximately

roughness . . . 6. lipper (of the sea) 8. acrimony, asperity, pungency, unfinish 9. gruffness, harshness, vulgarity 10. hoarseness

roughsome . . . 5. rough 6. rustic 7. uncouth

roulade . . . 3. run 8. arpeggio, division, flourish 13. vocal flourish

roulette . . . 3. bas (bet) 4. disk, game 5. wheel 6. roller 8. wagering

rounceval . . . 5. giant, large 6. strong, virago 9. termagant

round . . . 4. beat, bout, rota, rung, turn 5. cycle, orbed, rondo 6. circle, curved, rotate, rotund, series, sphere 7. circuit, routine 8. circular, globular 9. in a circle, spherical 11. cylindrical

round (pert to) . . .
bone . . 3. hip
building . . 7. rotunda
clam . . 6. quahog
fish . . 9. whitefish
head . . 5. Swede 7. Puritan
house . . 5. cabin, coach 6. lockup, prison 10. watch house
of applause . . 7. plaudit
regular . . 4. beat
robin . . 6. angler, letter 7. pancake, request 9. cigarfish
worm . . 4. nema 7. ascarid, Ascaris, eelworm

roundabout . . . 5. about, dance 6. detour, jacket 7. ambient, devious 8. indirect 10. circuitous 13. approximately 14. circumlocution

rounded (pert to) . . .
heap of stone . . 5. cairn
irregularly . . 7. gibbous
leaf . . 6. retuse

molding .. 5. ovolo
projection .. 4. lobe 5. tooth
scalloped .. 7. crenate
Round Table (pert to) ...
knight .. 7. Galahad 8. Lancelot
seating .. 7. knights (King Arthur's)
site .. 7. Camelot
type .. 6. marble
roundup ... 5. rodeo
roup ... 4. cold 6. clamor 7. auction
8. shouting 10. hoarseness
rouse ... 3. hie 4. stir, wake 5. alarm,
raise, start, upset, waken 6. awaken,
bestir, elicit, excite, kindle 7. disturb
9. stimulate
rouser ... 7. stirrer 8. surprise
9. demagogue (demagog) 10. instigator
roussette ... 5. shark 7. dogfish 8. fruit
bat
roust ... 4. roar, stir 5. rouse 6. bellow,
tumult 7. current (tidal), roaring
9. bellowing
roustabout ... 6. lumper 7. laborer
8. handy man 12. longshoreman
rout ... 3. low, mob 4. bray, roar
5. crowd, snort 6. bellow, defeat,
rabble 7. debacle, scatter 8. disperse,
stampede, vanquish 9. agitation,
discomfit, overpower, overthrow 11. put
to flight
route ... 3. way 4. line, path 5. march
6. detour 7. circuit
routh ... 6. plenty 8. abundant
9. abundance, plentiful
routier ... 6. robber 7. brigand 9. free
lance, plunderer
routine ... 3. rut 5. grind, habit, order,
round, troll 6. course, system 7. regular
8. everyday 9. treadmill
rove ... 3. gad 4. flit, part, roam 5. range,
stray 6. maraud, ramble, stroll, swerve,
wander, washer 7. deviate 8. straggle
rover ... 5. nomad 6. bandit, pirate, viking
7. corsair, pilgrim, vagrant 8. marauder,
wanderer
roving ... 8. errantry 9. desultory,
deviative 10. discursive
row ... 3. air, oar 4. file, fuss, live, spat,
tier 5. align, brawl, broil 6. lineup,
paddle, propel, series 7. quarrel, ruction
9. commotion
rowboat ... 3. cog, gig 4. dory 5. canoe,
coble, skiff 6. randan
rowdy ... 5. cutup, rough, tough
7. boorish, ruffian 8. larrikin, plug-ugly
10. boisterous, disorderly
rowdy contention ... 10. donnybrook
rowel ... 4. spur 5. wheel
rowen ... 4. crop (secondary) 5. field
7. stubble 9. aftermath
rowing ... 5. sport 6. randan 7. regatta
8. sculling
rox ... 3. rot 5. decay
royal ... 4. real, rial, riyal, stag, true 5. basil,
noble, regal 6. august, kingly 7. stately
8. imperial, majestic, princely, splendid
9. dignified, sovereign 11. magnificent
royal (pert to) ...
agaric .. 8. mushroom
bay .. 6. laurel
color .. 4. blue 5. smalt

court .. 5. aulic 6. ermine
crest .. 10. fleur-de-lis (Fr)
deer's antler .. 8. tres-tine
fur .. 6. ermine
mace .. 7. scepter (sceptre)
martyr .. 8. Charles I (Eng. 1649)
maundy .. 4. alms
officer .. 7. naperer
rights .. 7. regalia
rock snake .. 6. python
stables .. 4. mews
stars (Astrol) .. 7. Antares, Regulus
9. Aldebaran, Fomalhaut
Royal (pert to) ...
Academy .. 4. Arts (1768)
Arcanum .. 7. Society (1877)
Canadian Mounted Police .. 8. Mounties
16. Northwest Mounted
Castle .. 8. Balmoral
Crown .. 5. tiara
Highlanders .. 10. Black Watch
Highness .. 5. title 6. prince 8. princess
House .. 5. Tudor 6. Stuart, Valois
7. Bourbon, Hanover, Windsor
Oak (Eng Hist) .. 7. lottery 10. Shropshire
Psalmist .. 9. King David
Scot .. 16. Lothian Regiments
royet ... 4. wild 6. unruly 7. romping
11. mischievous
rub ... 4. crux, fret, wipe 6. abrade, polish,
scrape, smooth, stroke 7. burnish,
massage 8. friction, irritate 9. hindrance,
triturate
rub (pert to) ...
away .. 6. abrade
down .. 4. comb 5. curry, groom
7. massage
elbows .. 9. associate 10. fraternize
off .. 5. erase 6. abrade, remove
10. obliterate
out .. 4. kill 5. erase 6. cancel,
efface, excise 7. expunge, wipe out
10. obliterate
wrong way .. 6. ruffle 8. irritate
9. displease 10. antagonize
rub-a-dub ... 6. clamor 7. clatter, pit-a-pat,
rat-a-tat 8. rattatoo 9. drumbeats
Rubáiyát (pert to) ...
author .. 11. Omar Khayyám
stanza form .. 8. quatrain
translator .. 10. Fitzgerald (1859)
rubber ... 4. para 5. stare 6. eraser
7. ebonite, elastic 8. massager,
sight-see 10. caoutchouc
rubber (pert to) ...
city .. 5. Akron
hard .. 7. ebonite
India (pure) .. 10. caoutchouc
plant .. 5. Ficus
ring .. 4. lute 6. gasket
sap .. 5. latex
shoe .. 6. galosh (galoshe)
tree .. 3. ule 7. guayule
wild .. 5. Ceara 6. caucho
rubbish ... 4. junk, ross 5. attle, dross,
stent, trash, waste 6. debris, refuse,
rubble, trashy 8. nonsense, riffraff,
trumpery 9. worthless
rubble ... 5. brash, chalk, stone, trash
7. rubbish 8. nonsense 11. foolishness
rube ... 4. dolt 6. rustic 7. hayseed

rubedity ... 7. redness 9. ruddiness

rubella ... 7. measles, rubeola

rubescent ... 3. red 8. flushing 9. reddening 10. erubescent

rubiator ... 4. rake 5. bully 6. rascal

Rubicon ... 5. river (Caesar's) 9. Fiumicino (modern)

rubicund ... 3. red 4. ruby 5. ruddy 6. florid 7. redness

rubric ... 3. rod 6. paraph, ritual 8. category, red chalk 14. title page in red

rubrics (book of) ... 4. ordo

ruby (pert to) ...
bird .. 11. hummingbird
heraldry .. 5. gules
stained quartz (red) .. 6. Ancona 7. rubasse 9. Mont Blanc
stone .. 3. gem 5. balas 6. spinel
type .. 4. size

ruck ... 3. rut, sit (on eggs) 4. heap, pile, rick 5. cower, crowd, squat, stack 6. crease, crouch, furrow, horses (race), pucker 7. wrinkle 9. multitude 10. generality

ruckus ... 3. ado, row 5. fight 6. rumpus, uproar 7. quarrel, ruction 8. outbreak 9. commotion

rudd ... 3. hue 4. carp, fish 6. redden 7. azurine, redness 10. complexion

rudder ... 4. helm 5. guide

rudder part ... 6. bearding 9. whipstaff

rude ... 3. raw 4. curt 5. rough, rowdy 6. clumsy, coarse, rugged, simple, vulgar 7. boorish, uncouth 8. ignorant, insolent 9. barbarous, inclement, makeshift, turbulent, unlearned, unskilled, untrained 10. boisterous, unpolished 11. impertinent, uncivilized 12. discourteous

rudeness ... 6. ferity 8. curtness 9. impudence, insolence, vulgarity 11. raucousness 12. impertinence

rudiment ... 7. vestige

rudimentary ... 5. basic 7. initial 8. original 9. beginning, elemental, embryonic, vestigial 11. undeveloped

rudimentary digit ... 7. dewclaw

rudiments ... 4. ABCs 6. basics

rue ... 4. rake, Ruta 6. grieve, regret, repent, sorrow 7. afflict, deplore 10. bitterness, compassion, repentance 14. disappointment

ruff ... 3. ree 5. pride, reeve, ruche, trump 6. collar, fringe, rebato 7. sunfish 8. drumbeat 9. sandpiper, vainglory

ruffian ... 4. fish, pimp, thug 5. rowdy, tough 6. brutal, cuttle, pander 8. assassin, paramour, the Devil 9. cutthroat, desperado, murderous, vulgarian

ruffle ... 3. vex 4. fret, roil 5. anger, annoy, frill, jabot 6. edging, muddle, nettle, rumple, tousle 7. agitate, disturb, flounce, fluster, shuffle 8. dishevel, disorder, drumbeat, irritate 9. balayeuse 10. disarrange, discompose

ruffler ... 5. bully 7. boaster, ruffian 8. braggart 9. swaggerer 10. attachment (sewing)

rug ... 3. mat 4. maud, shag 5. Senna,

throw 6. carpet, hooked, petate 7. Chinese, drugget, steamer 8. coverlet, Oriental 9. Samarkand

ruga ... 4. fold 7. wrinkle 8. membrane

rugby ... 5. Fives 6. Rugger, school (Eng) 8. football

rugby term ... 9. scrum half, scrummage

rugged ... 4. rude 5. asper, hardy, harsh, rough, surly 6. craggy, fierce, robust, seamed, shaggy, strong, sturdy 7. austere, crabbed, healthy, uncivil 8. vigorous, wrinkled 9. irregular, not smooth, turbulent 11. substantial

rugged mountain crest ... 5. arête

ruin ... 4. bane, doom, fate, loss 5. blast, havoc, spoil, wrack, wreck 6. defeat 7. debauch, destroy, subvert 8. bankrupt, demolish, downfall 9. perdition 10. desolation, subversion 11. destruction, devastation

ruined ... 4. gone 7. spoiled, wrecked 8. bankrupt, defeated 9. destroyed 11. dilapidated 12. irremediable

ruinous ... 6. deadly 7. baneful, decayed 10. demolished, disastrous, pernicious, submersive, tumbledown 11. destructive

ruins ... 5. relic, wreck 7. remains

rukh ... 6. forest, jungle

rule ... 3. law 4. norm, sway 5. axiom, canon, guide, habit, order, regle, reign 6. decree, govern, manage, method, regime, screed 7. counsel, measure, precept, prevail, regency, regimen 8. dominate, persuade, standard 9. criterion, direction, influence, principle 12. jurisdiction 15. totalitarianism

rule by ...
children .. 9. paedarchy
ecclesiasts .. 9. hierarchy
one .. 8. monarchy
race .. 10. ethnocracy
ten .. 8. decarchy
the mob .. 9. mobocracy
the people .. 9. democracy
tribes .. 9. phylarchy

rule out ... 6. cancel, excise 7. obviate

ruler ... 3. min 4. amir (ameer), czar, emir, lord 5. queen 6. despot, dynast, ferule, gerent, prince, regent, satrap, sultan, tyrant 7. emperor, monarch 8. autocrat, governor, hierarch, measurer 9. potentate

ruling ... 3. law 6. decree 7. average, regnant, statute, verdict 8. decision, reigning 9. governing, prevalent 11. predominant 12. drawing lines

rullion ... 4. shoe 6. sandal

rum ... 3. dye (blue), odd 4. good 5. queer, tafia (taffia) 6. liquor 8. Demon rum

rumal ... 6. fabric 8. kerchief (man's)

Rumania ... see Romania

rumble ... 4. boom, seat (back) 5. rumor 6. murmur, ripple, stir up 9. complaint 11. rolling tone

rumen ... 3. cud 5. tripe 6. gullet, paunch 7. stomach (1st)

ruminant ... 2. ox 3. cow, yak 4. bull, deer, gaur, goat, oryx, zebu 5. bison, camel, eland, gayal, llama, moose,

okapi, sheep, steer 6. alpaca, nilgai,
vicuna, wapiti 7. banteng, buffalo,
caribou, chamois, gemsbok, giraffe
8. antelope, elephant, reindeer,
seladang 9. dromedary, nannygoat,
pronghorn 10. cud-chewing, hartebeest,
meditative, rhinoceros, thoughtful
ruminant (pert to) . . .
  division . . 8. Ungulata 10. Ruminantia
  first stomach . . 5. rumen 6. paunch
  fourth stomach . . 8. abomasum 9. rennet
    bag
  second stomach . . 9. reticulum
  third stomach . . 6. omasum 9. manyplies
    10. psalterium
ruminate . . . 4. chew, muse 6. ponder
  7. reflect 8. consider, meditate
rummage . . . 4. junk 6. litter, search
  7. collect (by search), ransack
rumor, rumour . . . 4. Fama, talk 5. bruit,
  noise, story 6. norate, report 7. hearsay,
  tidings 11. scuttlebutt
rump . . . 4. bone 6. breech, sacrum
  7. meat cut 8. bankrupt, buttocks
  9. remainder
rumpade . . . 3. rob 6. hold up
rumple . . . 4. muss 5. touse 6. crease,
  ruffle, tousle 7. crinkle, crumple, wrinkle
  8. dishevel 10. disarrange
rumpus . . . 3. row 6. fracas, hubbub,
  uproar 9. commotion, confusion
  11. disturbance
rumtytoo . . . 8. ordinary 11. commonplace
run (pert to) . . .
  about . . 5. wagon 6. gadder 8. roadster,
    runagate, vagabond
  after . . 5. chase, fetch, toady 6. pursue
    7. lionize
  aground . . 6. strand 7. founder
  along the edge . . 5. skirt
  away . . 4. bolt, flee 5. elope 6. decamp,
    escape 8. stampede
  before the wind . . 4. scud
  between ports . . 3. ply
  down . . 3. hit 4. find 5. seedy, trace
    7. run over 9. exhausted 11. dilapidated
    12. deteriorated
  out . . 3. end 5. lapse, waste 6. elapse,
    emerge, escape 7. exhaust 8. squander
  over . . 6. browse, exceed, ponder
    7. trample 8. overflow 9. reiterate
  quickly, swiftly . . 4. dart, race, scud
    5. scoot 6. gallop, sprint 7. scuttle
  stocking . . 6. ladder
  through . . 4. stab 6. pierce 7. inspect,
    pervade 8. rehearse, squander, transfix
    11. superabound
  up against . . 4. find 9. encounter,
    stumble on 10. experience
runagate . . . 7. runaway 8. apostate,
  fugitive, renegade, vagabond, wanderer
rundle . . . 4. ball, coil, rung, step 5. round

6. circle, roller, sphere, stream
rune . . . 5. magic 6. secret, symbol
  7. mystery 9. character (anc)
rung . . . 4. step 5. round, spoke, stair,
  tread 6. degree, rundle 7. girdled,
  ratline
runic . . . 5. verse 6. poetic 7. writing
  8. alphabet (anc), Norsemen
runner . . . 3. ski (skee) 4. sled 5. miler,
  racer, stolo 6. stolon 7. tendril
  8. operator, procurer, salesman,
  smuggler, sprinter 9. messenger,
  solicitor
running . . . 7. current, cursive, fleeing,
  flowing, melting 9. advancing,
  prevalent, smuggling 10. continuous
running knot . . . 5. noose
running race . . . 5. relay 6. sprint
running toad . . . 10. natterjack
runt . . . 3. elf 4. chit (letter), wrig 5. dwarf,
  pygmy 6. pigeon 10. diminutive
runway . . . 4. file, ramp 8. airstrip
rupa . . . 4. body, form (visual)
rupee . . . 4. anna, coin 14. money of
  account
rupestrian . . . 14. composed of rock
  15. inscribed on rock
ruption . . . 7. ruction, rupture 8. bursting
rupture . . . 4. rent 5. break, burst 6. hernia,
  injury, rhexis 7. quarrel 9. hostility
  10. disruption, falling out, separating
rural . . . 6. rustic 8. bucolic 8. agrestic,
  pastoral 12. agricultural
rural (pert to) . . .
  deity . . 3. Pan 6. Faunus
  genus . . 6. potato
  life . . 8. pastoral
  poem . . 7. eclogue, georgic
  Spanish . . 9. policeman
  term . . 8. agrestic
Rusa . . . 4. deer 6. sambar
ruse . . . 4. fall, slip, wile 5. fraud, trick
  6. deceit 8. artifice 9. stratagem
  10. subterfuge
rush . . . 3. jet 4. dart, dash, flow, scud
  5. brook, haste, hurry, plant, press,
  scoot, spate, speed, surge 6. charge,
  course, defeat, demand, hasten, runlet,
  sortie 7. cattail, repulse 8. outburst,
  reed mace, stampede 9. attention,
  thronging
rush (pert to) . . .
  forth . . 5. sally
  hour . . 4. peak
  light . . 6. candle, feeble
  nut . . 5. chufa
  Scot . . 5. sprat (herb) 6. Juncus
  toad . . 10. natterjack
  wheat . . 10. couch grass
rusk . . . 5. bread 7. biscuit
rusma . . . 9. quicklime 10. depilatory
Russia . . . see also *Russian*
  Asian part . . 7. Siberia
  capital . . 6. Moscow 9. Petrograd (old)
  citadel . . 7. Kremlin
  city . . 4. Baku, Kiev, Omsk 5. Minsk
    6. Rostov 7. Kharkov 8. Smolensk
    9. Petrograd 10. Sevastopol
    (Sebastopol) 11. Vladivostok 12. St
    Petersburg (Leningrad)
  coal fields . . 6. Donets (Ukraine)

fleet base .. 10. Sevastopol, Stalingrad
former name .. 7. Muscovy
founder .. 4. Ivan 15. Ivan the Terrible
gulf .. 4. Azov
isthmus .. 7. Karelia
lake .. 5. Onega 6. Baykal 7. Aral Sea
    10. Caspian Sea
mountains .. 4. Ural 8. Caucasus
peninsula .. 4. Kola 6. Crimea
resort .. 5. Yalta 6. Crimea
river .. 2. Ob 4. Amur, Lena, Neva,
    Ural 5. Volga 6. Donets 7. Dneiper,
    Yenisei
sea .. 4. Azov 5. Black, White
    6. Baltic 7. Caspian
strait .. 6. Bering
Russian (pert to) ...
antelope .. 5. saiga
aristocratic order .. 4. knez 5. Boyar
assembly .. 4. duma, rada 7. zemstoo
association, guild .. 5. artel
bank .. 4. game
beer, beverage .. 5. kvass, vodka
boat .. 6. baidak (baydak)
braid (trim) .. 8. soutache
calendar (to 1918) .. 6. Julian
cap (peasant) .. 4. aska
carriage .. 6. drosky, troika 9. tarantass
    (tarantas)
cart, wagon .. 6. telega
cathedral .. 5. sober
cloak (fur) .. 5. shuba
council .. 4. duma, rada 6. soviet
dance (rustic) .. 7. ziganka
decree .. 5. ukase
dog (wolfhound) .. 6. borzoi 7. owtchah
dress (peasant) .. 7. sarafan
duke, prince .. 4. knez (kniaz)
edict .. 5. ukase
fur (lamb) .. 7. karakul (karakule)
    9. astrakhan
guild .. 5. artel
hemp .. 4. rine
hut .. 4. isba
leather .. 5. jufti (jufts) 6. Bulgar
    8. shagreen
marsh, lagoon .. 5. liman
massacre .. 6. pogrom
monetary unit .. 5. ruble (rouble)
    6. kopeck (kopek)
musical instrument .. 5. gudok, gusla
    9. balalaika
naval academy .. 6. Frunze
news agency .. 4. Tass
no .. 4. nyet
parliament .. 4. duma
peasant .. 4. Slav 5. kulak 6. muzhik
    (muzjik)
peasant village .. 3. mir
plain (treeless) .. 6. steppe, tundra
police (secret) .. 5. Cheka
pound .. 4. pood
prince, duke .. 4. knez (kniaz)
ruler .. 4. czar (tsar)
satellite .. 7. sputnik
soup (cabbage) .. 5. stchi (shchi)
    6. borsch
stockade .. 5. etape
synod .. 5. sobor
tea urn .. 7. samovar
turnip .. 8. rutabaga

villa .. 5. dacha
wagon (springless) .. 6. telega
wheat .. 5. emmer
whip .. 4. plet (plete) 5. knout
wolfhound .. 6. borzoi
yes .. 2. da
Russian people ...
author .. 5. Gogol, Gorki (Gorky)
    7. Tolstoy (Tolstoi) 8. Turgenev
    10. Dostoevski (Dostoyevsky)
    12. Solzhenitsyn
chess champ (1892) .. 8. Alekhine
composer .. 3. Cui 7. Borodin
    10. Rubenstein, Stravinsky
    12. Tschaikovsky 14. Rimsky-Korsakov
conqueror .. 6. Tatars 7. Mongols
Cossack .. 5. Tatar
czar .. 4. Ivan 13. Peter the Great
duke .. 5. kniaz (knez, knyoz)
empress .. 7. Czarina, Tsarina
General .. 10. Timoshenko
grand duke .. 8. Nicholas
language deviser .. 8. Zamenhof
    9. Esperanto (pseudonym)
leader .. 5. Lenin 6. Stalin 7. Molotov,
    Yeltsin 8. Brezhnev 9. Gorbachev
    10. Khrushchev
little Russian .. 7. Russene (Ruthene)
monk .. 8. Rasputin
people .. 4. Lett, Slav 7. Cossack
    8. Russniak 9. Muscovite, Ruthenian
poet .. 7. Pushkin, Yesenin 9. Pasternak
premier .. 5. Lenin 7. Kosygin, Molotov
    8. Bulganin 10. Khrushchev
saint .. 4. Olga
teacher, monk .. 7. starets
rust ... 3. eat 5. erode 6. aerugo, patina
    7. erosion, oxidize 9. corrosion
rustic ... 4. boor, carl, rube, rude
    5. churl, clown, Damon, rough, rural,
    swain, yokel 6. coarse, simple, sturdy,
    sylvan 7. artless, awkward, boorish,
    bucolic, Corydon, plowboy 8. agrestic,
    pastoral 9. agrestian 10. clodhopper,
    countryman, unpolished
rustic (pert to) ...
lover .. 5. swain
maiden .. 9. Thestylis
peasant .. 4. boor
pipe .. 4. reed
poetic .. 4. carl
verse .. 4. idyl (idyll)
rustle ... 4. flow 5. steal, swish, whisk
    7. crinkle 11. sound softly
rut ... 5. ditch, track 6. furrow, groove,
    strake 7. routine, wrinkle
Ruth (pert to) ...
Book .. 12. Old Testament
country .. 4. Moab
husband .. 4. Boaz
mother-in-law .. 5. Naomi
ruthless ... 5. cruel 8. pitiless 9. merciless
    10. ironfisted
rye ... 5. bread, grain, grass 6. cereal,
    whisky 9. gentleman (gypsy)
rye bread ... 5. black 10. knackebrod
    12. pumpernickel
ryot ... 6. farmer, tenant 7. peasant
Rytina ... 6. dugong, sea cow 7. manatee
    12. Hydrodamalis 14. Steller's sea cow
Ryukyu Islands ... 7. Okinawa

S

S (pert to) ...
  curve . . 4. ogee
  letter . . 10. nineteenth
  shaped . . 7. sigmate, sigmoid
  suffix . . 6. plural
Saal ... 4. hall, room (large)
sabalo ... 6. tarpon 8. milkfish
sabana ... 5. plain 7. plateau, savanna
  (savannah)
sabbat ... 8. assembly (demons), festival
  (orgies)
Sabbatarian ... 9. ritualist 11. Russian
  sect
Sabbath ... 6. Sunday 7. holy day
sabbatical year ... 7. seventh 8. vacation
  14. leave of absence
sabbatism ... 4. rest 9. ritualism
  12. intermission (labor)
Sabbatist (pert to) ...
  devotee of . . 4. cult (Oriental)
  member . . 6. Semite
  named for . . 5. Sabbe (goddess)
  8. Sambathe
saber, sabre (pert to) ...
  bean . . 4. jack
  bill . . 6. curlew
  fish . . 7. cutlass
  knot . . 8. military
  legged (horse) . . 12. sickle-hocked
  Mohammedan . . 8. yataghan (yatagan)
  oriental . . 8. scimitar
  toothed . . 3. cat 5. tiger 12. machairodont
  wing . . 11. hummingbird
sabino ... 5. ahuehuete, rock cedar
sabio ... 4. sage 6. priest 7. wise man
sable ... 4. ebon, pelt 5. black, brush
  6. mammal, marten 8. antelope
  10. mysterious, Russia iron
sabotage ... 6. damage, mayhem
  9. undermine 11. destruction (malicious)
Sabrina ... 10. river nymph 11. River
  Severn
sabuline, sabulous ... 5. sandy 6. gritty
  8. psammous 10. arenaceous
sabutan ... 5. fibre, straw
sac ... 3. bag 4. cyst, sack 5. ascus, bursa,
  pouch, purse, theca 6. cavity, pocket,
  saccus 7. saccule, vesicle 8. sacculus
sacalait ... 7. crappie 8. warmouth
  9. killifish
saccadic ... 5. jerky 9. twitching 11. eye
  movement
saccharine ... 5. sweet 7. honeyed
  10. sweetening
saccos ... 7. tunicle 8. vestment
sacerdocy ... 10. priesthood 13. priestly
  order
sacerdos ... 6. priest
sachem ... 5. chief (Indian) 8. governor
  (Tammany)
sachet ... 3. bag 5. pouch 6. powder
  7. perfume 8. reticule 11. perfumed
  pad
sack ... 3. bag 4. loot, poke, wine 5. ascus,
  bursa, catch, pouch, purse 6. defeat,

ravage, secure 7. pillage, plunder
  8. desolate 9. discharge, dismissal
sack (pert to) ...
  baseball . . 3. bag 4. base
  Bible . . 8. mourning
  but . . 4. butt, cask 8. trombone (anc)
  cloth . . 7. penance, sacking 15. garb of
  penitence
  dress . . 4. robe 6. jacket, sacque
sacrament ... 3. act 4. oath 5. token
  6. pledge, symbol 7. mystery
  8. ceremony, covenant, practice
  9. communion, Eucharist 10. intinction
  (to administer)
Sacramento (pert to) ...
  capital, river . . 10. California
  cat . . 10. horned pout
  pike . . 9. squawfish
  salmon . . 7. quinnat
sacrarium (anc) ... 6. chapel, shrine
  7. oratory 8. sacristy 9. sanctuary,
  synsacrum
sacred ... 4. holy 6. divine 7. blessed
  8. hallowed, reverend 9. dedicated,
  inviolate, religious, venerable
  10. inviolable, sacrosanct
  11. consecrated 13. sanctimonious
sacred (pert to) ...
  bark . . 7. cascara 14. cascara sagrada
  bean . . 11. Indian lotus
  beetle . . 10. scarabaeus
  bird . . 4. ibis
  book . . 5. Bible, Koran
  bo tree . . 3. fig 5. pipal
  bull . . 4. apis, zebu
  chest . . 4. arca 9. reliquary
  comb form . . 5. hagio, hiero
  dialect (Buddh writings) . . 4. Pali
  grove . . 5. Altis (Olympia)
  image . . 4. icon (ikon) 5. Pietà
  instrument . . 4. Urim 7. Thummim
  malady . . 8. epilepsy
  monkey . . 6. baboon, rhesus 8. entellus
  most . . 10. sacrosanct
  music . . 4. hymn 5. chant, motet
  8. oratorio
  river (Ind) . . 6. Ganges (Ganga)
  room . . 8. sacristy
  traffic (in sacred things) . . 6. simony
  weed . . 7. vervain
  wine vessel . . 3. ama
  writ . . 10. Scriptures
sacrifice ... 4. lose, loss 5. offer
  6. give up, victim 8. chiliomb
  (1,000 oxen), hecatomb (100 oxen),
  immolate, libation, oblation, offering
  9. atonement, holocaust, martyrdom,
  privation, surrender 11. crucifixion,
  destruction
sacrificer ... 6. martyr
sacrificial fire ... 5. ignis
sacrilege ... 7. robbery (church)
  9. blasphemy 11. desecration,
  profanation
sacrilegious ... 7. impious 10. irreverent

11. blasphemous, irreligious

sacrosanct . . . 4. holy 6. sacred 8. ironical, most holy

sad . . . 3. bad 4. blue, dark, dire, dull 5. dusky, sorry 6. solemn, somber, triste, wicked 7. doleful, pensive, unhappy 8. dejected, downcast, grievous, pathetic, shameful, terrible 9. cheerless, depressed, sorrowful 10. calamitous, deplorable, depressing, melancholy 11. distressing, unfortunate

saddle . . . 4. meat (cut of), ride, seat 5. cinch, ridge 6. burden 7. harness (part) 8. encumber, straddle

saddle (pert to) . . .
back . . 4. hill 5. ridge
bag . . 7. alforja, pannier
blanket . . 6. corona, tilpah
boot . . 7. gambado
cloth . . 5. cover 7. housing 8. shabrack 9. appendage 10. horsecloth
elephant . . 6. howdah
girth . . 5. cinch
horse . . 5. mount 6. remuda 7. palfrey
light . . 5. pilch 7. pillion
pack . . 7. aparejo
part . . 6. cantle, crutch, pommel 7. stirrup 8. tapadera (tapadero) 9. saddlebow
place behind . . 5. croup
rock . . 6. oyster
strap . . 5. girth 6. latigo

saddler . . . 4. seal 5. horse 6. cozier 7. cobbler, lorimer 8. merchant 9. shoemaker

sadness . . . 5. dolor 6. pathos, sorrow 9. dejection 10. gloominess, melancholy 11. unhappiness 13. sorrowfulness

sad tree . . . 9. hursinghar (dye yield)

safari . . . 4. tour, trip 6. junket 7. caravan, journey 10. expedition, pilgrimage

safe . . . 4. pete (thieves' sl), sane, sure 5. chest, vault 6. closet, secure, unhurt 8. cautious, cupboard, unharmed 9. protected, strongbox 11. trustworthy

safeblower . . . 7. burglar, peteman 8. peterman

safe conduct . . . 4. pass 5. cowle, guard 6. convoy, escort 8. passport 10. precaution, protection

safecracker . . . 4. yegg

safekeeping . . . 4. care 7. custody, storage 10. protection 12. preservation

safety lamp (miner's) . . . 4. Davy

safety rail . . . 9. guardrail

saffron . . . 6. crocus, yellow 10. colchicine

sag . . . 4. bend, hang, reed, rush, sink, wilt 5. drift, droop, sedge, slump 6. weaken 10. depreciate

saga . . . 4. Edda, epic, tale 5. story, witch 6. legend 7. recital, sagaman 9. narrative

Sage . . . 7. goddess, seeress

sagacious . . . 4. sage, wise 5. aware, witty 6. argute, astute, shrewd 7. politic, sapient 9. judicious 10. discerning, farsighted 11. penetrative 13. perspicacious

sagacity . . . 3. ken 6. acumen, wisdom 9. acuteness, quickness 10. shrewdness 11. discernment, penetration 13. judiciousness

sage . . . 4. mint, wise 5. solon 6. astute, Salvia, shrewd 7. sapient 9. counselor, judicious, sagebrush 10. discerning 11. philosopher

Sage (of) . . .
Chelsea . . 7. Carlyle (Thomas)
Concord . . 7. Emerson (Ralph W)
Emporia . . 5. White (Wm Allen)
Ferney . . 8. Voltaire
Monticello . . 9. Jefferson (Thomas)
Pylos . . 6. Nestor

sage (pert to) . . .
Bethlehem . . 9. spearmint
cheese . . 7. Cheddar
chippy . . 14. Brewer's sparrow
cock, hen . . 6. grouse
family . . 4. mint
rose . . 5. alder (yellow)
tea . . 5. tonic

Sagebrush State . . . 6. Nevada

sagene . . . 5. seine 7. measure, network

sagitta . . . 7. otolith 8. keystone (Arch), The Arrow

Sagittarius . . . 6. bowman 9. The Archer 13. constellation

sago (pert to) . . .
palm . . 6. gebang, gomuti
plant . . 10. cuckoopint
product . . 6. starch
tree . . 7. coontie

sagoin . . . 8. marmoset

saguaro . . . 6. cactus, flower

saguing . . . 6. banana

Sahara . . . 5. cocoa (color), leste (wind) 6. desert

sahib . . . 5. title 6. master 9. gentleman

sai . . . 6. monkey 8. capuchin

said . . . 6. stated 7. uttered 9. aforesaid 15. before-mentioned

said to be . . . 7. reputed, rumored 8. reported

saiga . . . 8. antelope

Saigon nickname . . . 14. Paris of the East

sail . . . 3. jib, lug 4. luff, tack 5. craft, float 6. vessel, voyage 8. navigate

sail (pert to) . . .
around . . 14. circumnavigate
close to wind . . 4. luff
end . . 7. yardarm
fish . . 12. basking shark 15. quillback sucker
fore and aft . . 7. spanker
foresail . . 9. spinnaker
part . . 4. clew, yard 5. leech
rope . . 5. sheet 6. earing
secure, lash . . 7. trice up
strings . . 10. reef points
type . . 3. jib, lug, top, try 4. main, reef, stay 6. lateen, mizzen, square 7. topsail 8. mainsail, save-alls 12. mutton-legger

sailboat . . . 4. yawl 5. ketch, skiff, sloop, yacht 7. caravel (caravelle)

sailing term . . . 3. leg, run 4. asea, beat, jibe, scud, tack 5. hoist (sail), point, reach 7. gliding

sailing vessel . . . 4. bark (barque), brig, saic, yawl 5. sloop 7. frigate 8. schooner 10. barkentine (barquentine), windjammer

sailor . . . 3. gob, tar 4. salt, wave 5. middy

6. lascar, matlow 7. mariner, voyager
8. seafarer 10. bluejacket, lobscouser
(sl)

sailor (pert to) . . .
associate at meals . . 8. messmate
clothes . . 11. bell-bottoms
kit . . 8. ditty bag 9. housewife
knot . . 8. geranium
mess tub . . 3. kid
patron saint . . 4. Elmo
song . . 7. chantey 9. barcarole
Saimiri . . . 4. titi 6. monkey 8. squirrel
sain doux . . . 4. lard 6. grease
saint . . . 3. Ste 5. angel 7. apostle, pietist
8. canonize, enshrine, sanctify 10. holy
person 11. godly person
Saint (pert to) . . .
Anthony's fire . . 10. erysipelas
Buddhist . . 5. arhat
Elmo's fire (or light) . . 6. corona, Helena
9. corposant
Esprit . . 9. holy ghost
Francis of Assisi . . 11. il Poverello
13. little poor man
Gaudens . . 8. sculptor
George's flag . . 14. national emblem
Helena's hemlock . . 7. jellica
John Lateran . . 12. Mother Church
John's bread . . 5. carob 9. algarroba
Leger (Eng) . . 9. horse race
Luke's summer . . 12. Indian summer
Martin . . 13. Bishop of Tours
Martin's feast . . 9. Martinmas
Mary-le-Bow . . 15. Cheapside Church
(Cockney area)
Mohammedan . . 3. pir
Patrick's breastplate . . 6. lorica
Paul . . 12. Saul of Tarsus
Paul's Church (London), designer . .
18. Sir Christopher Wren
Peter's dome architect . .
12. Michelangelo
Vitus' dance . . 6. chorea
Saint, patron . . .
children's . . 8. Nicholas (Santa Claus)
desperate person's . . 4. Jude
English . . 6. George
French . . 5. Denis
hospitals . . 9. John of God 10. Juan
Ciudad
Irish . . 7. Patrick
Italian . . 7. Anthony
lawyer's . . 4. Ives
lover's . . 9. Valentine
sailor's . . 4. Elmo
Scottish . . 6. Andrew
Spanish . . 5. James
Welsh . . 5. David
saints (pert to) . . .
biography . . 9. hagiology
11. hagiography
symbol . . 4. halo 6. nimbus
tomb . . 6. shrine
worship of . . 10. hagiolatry
sajou . . 6. monkey 7. sapajou
sake . . . 4. beer 6. motive, reason
7. purpose 8. beverage (rice)
salacious . . . 4. lewd 6. horny (sl)
7. lustful, obscene 8. unchaste
9. lecherous
salad plant, vegetable . . . 4. bibb 5. cress

6. celery, endive 7. cabbage, lettuce,
romaine 10. watercress
salamander . . . 3. eft 4. newt 5. poker
6. triton 7. axolotl, Caudata, urodela
9. fire-eater 10. hellbender 12. pocket
gopher
salary . . . 3. fee, pay 4. hire, wage
5. wages 6. reward 7. stipend 8. pittance
9. allowance, emolument, salt money
(anc) 10. honorarium 12. compensation,
remuneration
salat . . . 6. prayer (facing Mecca)
sale . . . 4. deal, vend 6. barter, demand,
market 7. auction, handsel (1st in
morning) 8. contract 11. black market
salesman . . . 5. agent 6. vendor
7. drummer 9. solicitor
14. representative 18. commercial
traveler
salient . . . 4. bold 6. trench 7. eminent,
jetting, jumping, leaping, obvious
8. bounding, extended 9. prominent
10. noticeable, protruding
11. conspicuous
salient angle . . . 5. arris, Doric
Salientia . . . 5. Anura, frogs, toads
8. Amphibia (tailless)
salient point . . . 7. feature (detail)
saline . . . 5. salty 6. salina 8. solution
10. saliferous
Salinger, J. D. (pert to) . . .
character . . 6. Phoebe 15. Holden
Caulfield
work . . 13. Franny and Zooey 15. Catcher
in the Rye
saliva . . . 7. spittle 8. digester, ptyalism
salivary gland . . 8. racemose
sallow . . . 3. wan 4. gray, pale 5. muddy,
pasty 6. pallid 9. yellowish
sally . . . 4. jest, leap, trip 5. issue, jaunt,
start 6. sortie 7. journey 8. escapade,
outburst 9. witticism
salmagundi . . . 4. hash, olio, stew
6. medley 7. mixture 9. potpourri
10. periodical (old)
salmon . . . 4. fish 5. color 6. orlean,
sauqui 7. annatto, saumont
salmon (pert to) . . .
adult . . 7. gilling
after spawning . . 4. kelt
cured . . 6. kipper
dog . . 4. keta
family . . 10. Salmonidae
female . . 4. raun 6. baggit
genus . . 12. Oncorhynchus
herring . . 8. milkfish
humpbacked . . 5. haddo, holia
kind . . 7. quinnat
landlocked . . 7. kokanee
male . . 3. gib 6. kipper
newly hatched . . 4. pink
second year . . 6. hepper
silver . . 5. coho
small . . 4. peal 6. grilse
third year . . 4. mort
trout . . 5. sewen
young . . 3. fog 4. parr 5. smolt 6. grilse,
samlet 7. essling
Salome (pert to) . . .
Bib . . 6. dancer
father . . 8. Herodias

grandfather .. 5. Herod
opera, by .. 7. Strauss
salon ... 7. gallery 8. New Salon (Paris), Old Salon 9. reception 10. assemblage, exhibition 11. drawing room
Salon del Prado (Madrid) ... 9. promenade
saloon ... 3. bar 4. deck 6. tavern 7. barroom, cantina, gallery 8. dramshop, groggery 11. drawing room
saloop ... 8. hot drink 9. sassafras
salt ... 3. sal 4. cure 5. brine, taste 6. flavor, halite, sailor, saline 8. piquancy 9. seasoning 10. antiseptic, corrective 14. sodium chloride
salt (pert to) ...
acetic acid .. 7. acetate
alkaline .. 5. borax
astringent .. 4. alum
block, rock .. 3. pig
boric acid .. 6. borate
cat .. 4. lump 10. pigeon food
comb form .. 4. sali
cracker .. 7. saltine
dish for .. 10. saltcellar
ethereal .. 5. ester
flat .. 5. playa
lake .. 5. shott (chott)
marsh, pond .. 6. salina
native .. 6. halite
nature of, like .. 6. haloid
of the earth .. 7. the best 10. commonalty
peter, petre .. 5. niter
rock, block .. 3. pig
spring .. 4. lick
tax .. 7. gabelle
tree .. 4. atle (atlee) 5. cedar 7. tamarix 8. tamarisk
working .. 7. halurgy
works .. 7. saltern, saltery 9. salthouse
saltant ... 7. dancing, jumping, leaping 8. bouncing, bounding
salted ... 5. briny, cured 6. corned 7. treated 8. brackish, hardened, seasoned 11. experienced
salty ... 3. reh 5. briny, salic, witty 6. risqué, saline
salubrious ... 4. good 8. salutary 9. healthful, wholesome 10. beneficial
salutary ... 7. healthy 8. curative 9. medicinal 10. salubrious 11. restorative
salutation ... 2. hi 3. ave 4. hail 5. aloha, hello, howdy, skoal 6. curtsy, homage, kowtow, Mizpah (Mizpeh), prosit, salaam (salam) 7. Dear Sir 8. greeting, serenade
salute ... 4. hail, kiss 5. greet 6. homage, signal 7. address
salvage ... 4. save 6. redeem, rescue 10. redemption 11. reclamation
salvation ... 8. soterial 10. liberation, redemption 11. deliverance, soteriology 12. preservation
Salvation Army founder ... 5. Booth
salve ... 3. tip 4. balm, cure 5. allay, quiet 6. anoint, cerate 7. assuage, relieve 8. flattery, medicate, ointment 9. gloss over, lubricate, mitigator 10. medication

salver ... 4. tray 9. flatterer 11. serving dish
salvo ... 6. excuse 7. gunfire, pretext, proviso, quibble, rockets 8. applause 9. discharge, exception 11. projectiles, reservation
Samaria (pert to) ...
capital (anc) .. 6. Israel
deity .. 6. Nibhaz
destroyer .. 6. Romans
founder .. 4. Omri (925 BC)
people .. 9. Assyrians
province of .. 9. Palestine
rebuilder .. 5. Herod (the Great)
Samaritan, good ... 5. aider 6. helper 10. befriender, benefactor 11. helping hand
Sambal (Zambal) **language** ... 4. Tino
sambar (sambur) .. 4. deer, maha, rusa
same ... 2. id 3. ilk, one 4. ibid, idem, self 5. alike, ditto 7. cognate, identic 8. selfsame 9. identical 10. equivalent
sameness ... 6. parity, tedium 7. analogy, oneness 8. identity, monotony 9. alikeness 10. similarity, uniformity 11. equivalence 14. correspondence
Samian (pert to) ...
island .. 5. Samos
Sage .. 10. Pythagoras
sea .. 6. Aegean
ware .. 8. Arretine
samlet ... 4. parr 6. salmon (young)
Samoa ...
anthropologist who studied .. 4. Mead
capital .. 4. Apia
councilor .. 7. faipule
islands .. 8. American
islands, main .. 5. Manua, Upolu 6. Savaii 7. Tutuila
natives .. 10. Polynesian
owl (barn) .. 4. lulu
political council .. 4. fono
town .. 8. Pago Pago
warrior .. 3. toa
samovar ... 3. urn 6. teapot
Samoyed, Samoyede ... 3. dog (Arctic) 8. Siberian
sample ... 4. test 5. model, taste 6. swatch 7. example, pattern 8. specimen
sampler ... 8. original 9. archetype 10. needlework
Samson (pert to) ...
Bib .. 5. judge (Israelite)
death site .. 4. Gaza (Syria)
famed as .. 9. strong man
opera .. 16. Samson and Delilah
tribe .. 3. Dan
wife .. 7. Delilah (betrayer)
Samuel ... 4. Book (Old Test) 5. judge 7. prophet
samurai ... 4. vassal 7. officer
Sana native ... 8. Yemenite
San Andreas rift ... 15. earthquake fault (Calif)
San Antonio mission ... 5. Alamo
sanative ... 7. healing 8. curative, sanatory
Sancho's master ... 10. Don Quixote
Sancta Sanctis ... 20. Holy things for the holy
sanctify ... 5. honor 6. hallow

10. consecrate 11. free from sin

sanctimonious . . . 4. holy 6. sacred
7. saintly 8. affected 12. hypocritical

sanction . . . 4. abet, amen, fiat, okay
6. assent, permit, ratify 7. approve,
condone, endorse, support 8. approval
9. approbate, authority, authorize
11. countenance, endorsement
12. ratification 13. authorization

sanctity . . . 8. holiness 9. godliness,
solemnity 10. sacredness 11. saintliness
13. inviolability

sanctuary . . . 4. bema, fane, holy, naos
5. abbey, barnah, cella, haven 6. priory,
refuge, temple 7. Alsatia, convent,
retreat, shelter 8. cloister 9. monastery
10. penetralia

sanctum . . . 3. den 5. study 6. adytum,
office 7. retreat

sand . . . 4. grit 5. arena, nerve, pluck,
stone

sand (pert to) . . .
applied to body . . 9. arenation
bog . . 4. syrt 9. quicksand
eel . . 4. grig 6. launce
flea . . 6. chigoe, red bug 7. chigger,
  sandboy
fluke . . 7. sand dab 8. flounder
hill, mound . . 4. dene, dune
hog . . 7. laborer (in compressed air)
  8. tunneler (tunneller)
inhabiting . . 11. arenicolous
like (sand) . . 9. arenulous 10. arenaceous
man . . 5. genie
mixture (clay) . . 4. loam 9. sandstone
pear . . 5. Pyrus
submerged bank . . 3. bar 5. hurst, shoal
sugar . . 5. niter
widgeon . . 7. gadwall

sandal . . . 4. boat, shoe, sock 7. talaria

sandpiper . . . 3. ree 4. knot, pume,
ruff, stib 5. stint (long-toed) 6. dunlin
8. pectoral, triddler

sandstone . . . 7. sarsens 8. ganister

Sandwich Islands . . . 6. Hawaii
8. Hawaiian

sandy . . . 6. desert, gritty 7. arenose
8. granular, sabulous, Scotsman
9. sandpiper 10. arenaceous, ring
plover

sane . . . 5. lucid, sound 7. logical
8. rational, sensible 9. practical
10. reasonable

San Francisco Mil Post . . . 8. Presidio

sang . . . 5. blood, sheng 7. chanted,
ginseng, Society

sang-froid . . . 8. coolness 9. cold blood,
composure 11. insouciance

sanguinary . . . 3. ant (slave) 4. gory
5. cruel 6. bloody, yarrow 8. sanguine
9. bloodroot, murderous
12. bloodthirsty

sanguine . . . 4. warm 5. ruddy 6. ardent
7. hopeful 8. blood-red 9. confident
10. optimistic 12. bloodthirsty

sanity . . . 4. wits 6. reason 8. lucidity,
saneness 9. soundness
13. wholesomeness

San Juan Hill . . . 4. Cuba (Battle, 1898)

San Juan Indian . . . 4. Tewa

San Kuo . . . 13. Three Kingdoms (Shu,

Wei, Wu)

San Marino, Europe (pert to) . . .
famed as . . 11. oldest State (Eur)
government . . 8. Republic (smallest)
mountains . . 8. Appenine
site . . 8. Mt Titano

sannup . . . 6. Indian (married male) (opp
of squaw)

Sanskrit (pert to) . . .
college . . 3. tol
dialect . . 4. Pali
drama . . 9. Sakuntala (Shakuntala)
epic . . 8. Ramayana
god . . 4. Kama (Cupid), Vayu (wind)
  5. Indra (Great) 6. Aditya
goddess . . 3. Uma (Splendor) 4. Devi
  (Mother) 5. Aditi, Gauri
human spirit . . 7. jivatma
literature . . 5. sruti (shruti)
period . . 5. Vedic
Phonet (sounds) . . 6. sandhi
poem (epic) . . 11. Race of Raghu,
  Raghuvamsha
poet . . 8. Kalidasa
sacred books . . 4. Veda
soul . . 5. atman
treatise . . 9. Upanishad

Santo Domingo . . . 7. capital (Dominican
Republic)

sap . . . 3. gum 4. boob, dupe, fool, mine,
save, upas 5. drain, fluid, lymph, sapor
6. juices, trench, weaken 7. essence,
schnook 8. unsettle 9. simpleton,
undermine

sapid . . . 5. tasty 7. zestful 8. flavored
9. palatable, toothsome

sapient . . . 4. sage, wise 6. shrewd
7. knowing 8. profound 9. sagacious
10. discerning

sapiutan . . . 4. anoa 6. wild ox

sapodilla . . . 5. chico 6. chicle, zapote
7. nispero 9. naseberry

sapor . . . 5. savor, taste 6. flavor, relish

sapper . . . 5. miner 6. digger 9. excavator

Saracen . . . 4. Arab 5. nomad, pagan
6. Muslim (Moslem) 7. heathen, infidel,
ragwort 9. Moor's head (Her)

Saracen Knight . . . 8. Ruggiero

Sarah (pert to) . . .
bird . . 9. wake-robin
husband . . 7. Abraham
mother of . . 5. Isaac
slave of . . 5. Hagar

sarcasm . . . 4. gibe 5. irony, taunt 6. satire
8. ironical, ridicule

sarcastic . . . 3. dry 6. biting, ironic
7. caustic, cutting, satiric 8. ironical,
sardonic 9. malicious 10. mordacious

sarcophagic . . . 10. sarcophagy 11. flesh-
eating 13. sarcophageous

sarcophagus . . . 5. chest 6. coffin
9. limestone 11. Assian stone, lapis
Assius

sardine . . . 4. bang 7. alewife, anchovy,
herring (young) 8. pilchard

Sardinia, Italy . . .
capital . . 8. Cagliari
island . . 13. Mediterranean
sheep . . 7. mouflon (moufflon)
tower (Prehist) . . 6. nuragh

sardonic . . . 3. dry 6. ironic, morose

7. cynical, satiric **8.** derisive **9.** sarcastic **11.** Rabelaisian

sartor ... **6.** tailor

sash ... **3.** obi **4.** band, belt, benn, tobe **6.** girdle **8.** casement **10.** cummerbund

sash pulley weight ... **5.** mouse

Saskatchewan, Canada ...
capital .. **6.** Regina
city .. **8.** Moose Jaw **9.** Saskatoon

sassaby ... **8.** antelope

sassafras (pert to) ...
nut .. **8.** pichurim
oil of (part) .. **6.** safrol
tea .. **6.** saloop
tree .. **4.** ague

sassy ... **4.** pert **5.** saucy **8.** impudent

Satan ... **5.** Demon, Devil, Eblis, fiend **6.** Belial **7.** Lucifer, Scratch, Tempter **9.** archfiend **14.** Mephistopheles **16.** Prince of Darkness

Satan (pert to) ...
angel (bottomless pit) .. **8.** Apollyon
associate .. **6.** Azazel **9.** Beelzebub
before his fall .. **7.** Lucifer
Jewish .. **8.** Asmodeus
Scottish .. **4.** deil
son .. **3.** Imp (jocular)

satanic ... **5.** cruel **6.** wicked **7.** demonic **8.** devilish, infernal **10.** diabolical

satchel ... **3.** bag **4.** case, etui, grip, sack **5.** cabas **6.** valise

sate ... **4.** cloy, glut **5.** gorge **7.** gratify, satiate, satisfy, surfeit **8.** saturate

sated ... **4.** full **5.** blasé **6.** gorged

satellite ... **4.** Echo, luna, moon **5.** Atlas **6.** comsat, planet **7.** aerosat, Landsat, Sputnik, Telstar **8.** Explorer, follower, Vanguard **9.** companion, dependent

satellite of Jupiter ... **2.** Io (1st) **6.** Europa (2nd) **8.** Callisto, Ganymede

satellite of Saturn ... **4.** Rhea **5.** Dione, Mimas, Titan **6.** Phoebe, Tethys **8.** Hyperion **9.** Enceladus

satellite of Uranus ... **5.** Ariel **6.** Oberon **7.** Titania, Umbriel

satellite's orbit ... **4.** path **14.** geosynchronous

Sati (Egypt) ... **5.** Queen

satiate ... **4.** cloy, glut, sate **5.** gorge **7.** gratify, satisfy, surfeit

satin ... **4.** silk **6.** étoile, fabric, sateen, satiny **9.** satinette **10.** smoothness

satire ... **3.** wit **5.** irony, spoof **6.** parody **7.** lampoon

satiric, satirical ... **3.** dry **6.** bitter, ironic **7.** abusive, caustic, cutting **8.** ironical, poignant **9.** burlesque, sarcastic **11.** reproachful

satisfaction ... **3.** cro **4.** duel **6.** amends **7.** comfort, content, payment, satiety **8.** adequacy, pleasure, reprisal **9.** atonement **10.** recompense, reparation **11.** contentment, fulfillment **12.** compensation, propitiation, remuneration **15.** indemnification

satisfied ... **5.** proud, sated **7.** content, pleased **8.** satiated **9.** contented, convinced, gratified **10.** paid in full

satisfy ... **2.** do **3.** pay **4.** fill, sate, suit **5.** atone, solve **6.** pay off, please, supply **7.** assuage, content, fulfill, gratify,

indulge, requite, satiate **8.** atone for, convince

satrap (anc) ... **5.** ruler **6.** despot, prince **8.** governor, overlord

saturate ... **3.** ret, sop, wet **4.** fill, soak **5.** imbue, souse, steep **6.** drench, seethe **7.** satiate **8.** overfill, permeate **10.** impregnate

saturated ... **4.** full **6.** soaked, sodden

Saturday ... **6.** Samedi **9.** sabbatine **13.** Jewish Sabbath

Saturn (pert to) ...
Astron .. **6.** planet
consort .. **3.** Ops
god of .. **4.** seed
Latin .. **8.** Saturnus
rings .. **7.** moonlet **9.** particles
rings, part .. **4.** ansa
satellite .. **4.** Rhea **5.** Dione, Titan **7.** Iapetus **8.** Hyperion
Temple treasury (State) .. **8.** aerarium

saturnalia ... **4.** orgy **7.** debauch **8.** Festival (of Saturn) **11.** pandemonium

saturnine ... **3.** dismal, gloomy, somber **8.** funereal

satyr ... **4.** faun **5.** deity **7.** demigod, silenus **9.** butterfly, capripede, orangutan

sauce ... **3.** soy **4.** alec, pulp **5.** caper, curry, garum, gravy, pesto **6.** gansel, tahini **7.** catchup (catsup), soubise, Tabasco, veloute **8.** amandine, dressing, marinara **9.** espagnole, insolence, seasoning **11.** beurre blanc **12.** impertinence

saucy ... **4.** bold, pert, vain **5.** brash, cocky, sassy, smart **7.** forward **8.** impudent, malapert **9.** officious **11.** impertinent **13.** disrespectful

Saudi Arabia ...
city .. **5.** Islam
founder .. **7.** Ibn Saud (1913)
gulf .. **7.** Persian
Mohammed's tomb .. **6.** Medina
mosque .. **5.** Kaaba
peninsula .. **7.** Arabian
provinces .. **4.** Asir, Nejd **5.** Hejaz **6.** El Hasa
sea .. **3.** Red
sect .. **6.** Wahabi (Wahabee, Wahhabi)

sauerbraten ... **8.** pot roast

sauger ... **9.** pike perch

Saul (pert to) ...
concubine .. **6.** Rizpah
daughter .. **6.** Michal
father .. **4.** Kish
herdsman .. **4.** Doeg
of Tarsus .. **4.** Paul
uncle .. **3.** Ner
wife .. **7.** Ahinoam
witch of .. **5.** Endor

Sault Ste Marie ... **3.** Soo **6.** rapids **9.** ship canal

saumont ... **6.** salmon

sauna ... **4.** bath (Finnish)

saunter ... **3.** jog, lag, mog **4.** roam, rove, walk **5.** range, stray **6.** dawdle, loiter, lounge, potter, ramble, stroll, wander **8.** ruminate

sauqul ... **6.** salmon

saurian ... **6.** lizard, Sauria **7.** reptile

9. crocodile

sausage . . . 6. banger, salami 7. bologna, chorizo, saveloy 8. kielbasa (kolbasi), rolliche 9. bratwurst, pepperoni 10. knackwurst

sausage-shaped . . . 9. allantoid 10. botuliform

savage . . . 3. att 4. rude, wild 5. brute, cruel, feral, yahoo 6. ferine, fierce, Indian 7. brutish, howling 8. cannibal, pitiless 9. atrocious, barbarian, ferocious, merciless, primitive 11. uncivilized 12. uncultivated

savanna, savannah . . . 5. plain 9. grassland 11. level region

savant . . . 4. sage 6. pundit 7. scholar 9. scientist 10. classicist 12. intellectual, man of letters

save . . . 3. but 4. keep 5. catch, hoard, lay by 6. except, redeem, rescue, scrimp 7. prevent, protect, reserve, salvage 8. conserve 9. economize, excepting, safeguard 10. accumulate

savin, savine . . . 5. cedar 7. juniper 9. evergreen

savior, Saviour . . . 8. Redeemer 9. deliverer, liberator 11. emancipator, Jesus Christ

savoir-faire . . . 4. tact 5. poise, savvy (sl) 7. culture 9. gentility 12. ease of manner, mannerliness

savor, savour . . . 4. odor, zest 5. nidor, sapor, scent, smack, smell, taste 6. flavor, relish 9. degustate

savory, savoury . . . 5. sapid, tasty 7. piquant 8. gustable 9. agreeable 10. appetizing, delightful

saw . . . 3. cut 4. dict 5. adage, maxim 6. cliché, saying, truism 7. noticed, proverb 9. platitude, sentence

saw (kind) . . . 3. jig, rip 4. band, buzz, hack, whip 5. crown, power 7. keyhole 8. crosscut

saw (pert to) . . .
back . . 6. sierra
bill . . 6. motmot 9. merganser
buck . . 8. sawhorse 13. ten-dollar bill
crosscut . . 5. briar
fish . . 3. ray
grass . . 5. sedge
horse . . 4. buck, rack 7. sawbuck
log . . 5. edger
of sawfish . . 5. serra
surgeon's . . 6. trepan (trephine)
teeth . . 5. tines
two-bladed . . 5. stadda

sawmill gate . . . 4. sash

saw-whet . . . 10. Acadian owl

saxhorn . . . 4. tuba 6. althorn 8. bass tuba 9. saxcornet

saxifrage . . . 6. Seseli

Saxon (pert to) . . .
color . . 5. smalt 8. Saxe blue 10. Bremen blue 13. indigo carmine
king . . 6. Egbert 8. Ethelred 14. Alfred the Great
language . . 10. Anglo-Saxon 12. Plattdeutsch
people . . 7. English 9. Sassenach 10. Anglo-Saxon 11. Lowland Scot
serf . . 4. esne

swineherd . . 5. Gurth (Ivanhoe)
warrior . . 5. thane

Saxony capital . . . 7. Dresden 10. Wittenburg (anc)

say . . . 4. aver, cite, tell 5. gnome, speak, state, utter 6. affirm, answer, assert, assume, recite, remark, speech 9. authority 11. declaration 12. conversation

say (pert to) . . .
a blessing . . 5. bensh
again . . 6. repeat 7. restate 9. reiterate
further . . 3. add
no (to) . . 6. negate, refuse 8. prohibit 10. disapprove
one thing, mean another . . 6. palter 7. falsify 9. fluctuate 10. equivocate 12. be capricious
uncle . . 4. cede 9. surrender 10. capitulate 15. throw in the towel

saying . . . 3. dit, mot, saw 4. quip 5. adage, axiom, maxim 6. byword, enigma, phrase, remark 7. proverb 8. aphorism, apothegm 11. declaration

saying, sayings (pert to) . . .
collection of . . 9. gnomology
criterion, party cry . . 10. shibboleth
dogmatic . . 6. dictum
religious . . 5. logia

scab . . . 3. rat 4. sore 5. crust, mange 6. rotter 7. blemish 8. deserter 9. scoundrel 12. incrustation 13. strikebreaker

scabbard . . . 6. sheath 7. holster, pilcher 13. emblem of peace

scabbard fish . . . 7. cutlass 9. frostfish

scaddle . . . 4. cruel, timid 6. fierce 7. nervous 8. skittish, thievish 11. mischievous

scads . . . 4. gobs, wads 5. heaps, money, piles 6. oodles 11. great number 12. considerable

scaffold, scaffolding . . . 5. easel, stage 7. staging, support 8. platform 9. grain loft

scalawag, scallawag . . . 5. scamp 6. rascal 7. sculpin 10. scapegrace

scale . . . 3. hut 4. husk, peel, rate, shed, size 5. climb, crust, flake, gamut 6. ascend, degree, ladder, lamina, rustre (anc armor), series, weight 7. compare, measure 12. incrustation

scale (pert to) . . .
botany . . 5. palea
color . . 10. tintometer
comb form . . 4. cten 5. cteno, lepis
duck . . 9. merganser, sheldrake
fish . . 6. ganoid 8. scabbard
grand . . 4. epic
music . . 3. E la (highest note) 5. gamut, minor 9. chromatic, hexachord 10. tetrachord
slide . . 7. vernier
tail . . 6. rodent
Zool . . 6. scutum

scallop . . . 4. quin 5. crena, notch 7. mollusk 9. serration, shellfish 12. summer squash

scalloped . . . 6. cooked 7. notched 8. invected (Her) 9. crenulate

scalpel . . . 5. knife 6. lancet 7. dissect

8. bistoury

scaly ... 5. flaky 6. crusty, scabby, scurfy 7. leprose 8. squamous

scamp ... 3. imp 5. cheat, knave, rogue 6. rascal, slight 7. bacalao, codfish 8. scalawag, spalpeen 9. scoundrel 15. worthless fellow

scamper ... 3. hie, run 4. dash, race, scud 5. haste 6. hasten 7. brattle 9. hasten off, skedaddle 11. hasty flight

scan ... 3. eye 6. browse, peruse 7. examine 10. scrutinize 11. contemplate 16. recite metrically

scance ... 5. blame, shine 6. glance 7. comment, glitter

scandal ... 5. odium, shame 6. gossip 7. calumny, offense, slander 8. disgrace, ignominy 10. defamation, detraction, opprobrium 11. abomination

scandalous ... 7. wicked 8. libelous, terrible 10. defamatory, slanderous 11. disgraceful, opprobrious

Scandinavia, countries ... see also *Scandinavian* 6. Norway, Sweden 7. Denmark, Iceland

Scandinavian (pert to) ...
alphabetical character .. 4. rune
ash tree .. 10. Yggdrasil
author .. 8. Andersen (Hans C)
bay .. 5. fjord
explorer .. 4. Eric
goblin, brownie .. 5. nisse 6. kobold
god .. 4. Lake, Thor
goose .. 5. nisse
hall of Odin (heroes' souls) .. 8. Valhalla
legend .. 5. Edda, saga
maiden of Odin .. 8. Valkyrie
navigator .. 4. Eric
people .. 4. Dane, Lapp 5. Swede 8. Norseman 9. Norwegian
people, type .. 8. Teutonic
pert to .. 5. runic
plateau .. 5. field
rulers .. 10. Varangians
saga narrator .. 7. sagaman
sea monster (fabled) .. 6. kraken
supernatural being (dwarf or giant) .. 5. troll

scant ... 3. few 5. chary 6. meager, narrow, scarce, slight, sparse 7. slender, sparing 12. parsimonious

scanty ... 4. rare 6. meager (meagre), narrow, scarce, sparse 7. scrimpy 12. insufficient 14. inconsiderable

scapegoat ... 4. goat (Bib) 9. sacrifice 10. substitute

scapegrace ... 5. scamp 8. scalawag (scallawag) 9. reprobate 10. profligate 12. incorrigible

scar ... 3. arr, shy 4. seam, sear 5. cliff, mound 7. blemish 8. cicatrix

scarce ... 4. rare 5. short 6. scanty 7. sparing 8. uncommon 9. deficient 10. infrequent

scarcely ... 6. barely, hardly 7. but just 12. infrequently

scarcity ... 4. lack, want 6. dearth, famine, rarity 7. paucity 8. rareness 11. infrequency 13. insufficiency

scare ... 3. cow 5. alarm, panic 7. startle, terrify 8. affright, frighten

scarecrow ... 4. ogre 5. bogle 6. effigy, goblin, malkin, shewel (sewel) 9. jackstraw 10. frightener 11. hide-and-seek

scarf ... 3. boa, tie 4. sash 5. ascot, cloud, nubia 6. tippet 7. muffler 9. rigolette 10. fascinator

scarf (pert to) ...
bird .. 9. cormorant
broad .. 5. shawl
clerical .. 5. fanon, orale, rabat, stole
feather .. 3. boa
head .. 10. fascinator
Hindu .. 4. sari
India .. 7. dopatta
Mexico .. 6. tapalo
skin .. 7. cuticle 9. epidermis

Scarlet Letter ... 5. novel (Hawthorne)

Scarlet O'Hara's home ... 4. Tara

scarp ... 5. cliff, pitch 7. descent, incline 9. declivity

scary ... 5. eerie, timid, weird 7. ghostly, uncanny 8. alarming 12. easily scared

scat ... 4. hiss 5. burst, smash 6. buffet 7. scatter

scat, scatt (Orkney Isls) ... 3. tax 7. tribute

scathe ... 4. flay, harm, hurt 6. assail, damage, injury, scorch 7. scarify 9. excoriate 10. misfortune

scatter ... 3. sow, ted 4. deal, rout 5. spray, strew 6. dispel, litter, shower, splash, spread 7. bestrew, diffuse, radiate 8. disperse, separate, squander 9. circulate, dissipate 10. disarrange, strew about

scattered ... 4. semé 5. dealt 6. sparse, strewn 8. confused, sparsile, sporadic 9. broadcast, dispersed, separated, sprinkled 10. widespread 11. distributed

scattering ... 3. few 8. Diaspora 10. dispersion, separating 13. dissemination

scatty ... 7. showery

scaup ... 4. duck 8. bluebill 9. blackhead, broadbill

scavenger ... 4. bird 8. organism 10. saprophyte 16. garbage collector

scaw ... 8. headland 10. promontory

scene ... 4. site, view 5. anger, sight, vista 6. locale 7. diorama, picture, tableau

scene (pert to) ...
behind the .. 8. secretly 9. backstage, invisible
inside .. 7. neorama
last .. 6. finale
of action .. 5. arena, stage 6. sphere
of confusion .. 5. babel
of miracle (Bib) .. 4. Cana
opera .. 5. scena
wright .. 6. artist 8. designer (scenery) 9. stageman

scenic ... 8. dramatic 9. panoramic 11. picturesque

scenic (pert to) ...
enigma .. 7. charade
pert to .. 5. stage 7. episode, scenery
representation .. 7. diorama 13. motion picture

scent ... 4. aura, clue, nose, odor

5. aroma, flair, nairn, nidar, smell,
spoor 6. detect 7. perfume 9. fragrance
scented ... 5. olent 6. odored
8. perfumed, smelling 11. odoriferous
scepter, sceptre ... 3. rod 4. mace
5. baton, staff 6. emblem (royal)
8. insignia 11. sovereignty
schedule ... 4. card, list 5. slate
7. program 8. calendar, document
9. catalogue, inventory
scheme ... 3. aim 4. lark, plan, plot
5. cabal 6. device, devise, racket, system
7. complot, concoct, diagram, epitome,
outline, project, purpose 8. artifice,
contrive 9. boomerang 10. conspiracy,
enterprise 11. machination
schemer ... 7. plotter 8. conniver, finagler
9. intriguer
schism ... 4. rent, sect 5. split 6. breach
7. dissent, faction 8. division 10. falling-
out, separation
schismatic ... 7. heretic, sectary
8. apostate 9. dissenter, sectarian
10. factionist
schist ... 4. mica, rock 5. slate
10. hornblende
scholar ... 6. pedant, savant 7. learner,
student 8. disciple 11. philologist
scholarly ... 7. erudite, learned
8. academic, studious 9. philomath
10. scholastic
scholarship ... 5. burse 8. learning
9. education, erudition, knowledge
10. foundation 11. instruction
school ... 4. cult, sect 5. class, drill,
flock, order, teach, train 7. convent,
educate, seminar 8. instruct, seminary
9. institute
school (pert to) ...
book .. 6. primer, reader 7. speller
English .. 4. Eton 6. Oxford 9. Cambridge
French .. 5. ecole, lycée
German .. 6. schule
head, inspector .. 9. scholarch
master .. 7. dominie 9. pedagogue
(pedagog)
ref to .. 10. scholastic
riding .. 6. manège
teacher .. 4. marm
term .. 8. semester
wrestling .. 9. gymnasium, palaestra
(palestra)
school of ...
art .. 4. Dada
divinity .. 8. seminary
Fine Arts .. 9. Wagnerian
fishes .. 5. shoal
philosophers .. 7. Eleatic
philosophy .. 7. Gnostic
seals .. 3. pod
thieves .. 4. gang
whales .. 3. gam, pod
schooner ... 4. boat, brig, tern 5. glass
6. vessel 7. measure, prairie (Hist)
schuit, schuyt ... 5. sloop 6. vessel
7. eelboat
science ... 3. art 5. ology, skill
9. knowledge 11. proficiency
science of ...
agriculture .. 8. agronomy
better living .. 9. euthenics

better working .. 10. ergonomics
breeding .. 8. eugenics
character .. 8. ethology
children's diseases .. 10. pediatrics
(paediatrics)
controversy .. 8. polemics
creatures .. 10. entomology
dining .. 10. aristology
doctrines .. 9. esoterics
ears .. 7. otology
family symbols .. 8. heraldry
forest trees .. 7. silvics (sylvics)
good .. 6. ethics 9. euthenics
10. agathology
government .. 8. politics
happiness .. 11. eudaemonics
healing .. 9. iatrology
health .. 7. hygiene
kissing .. 13. philematology
language .. 9. philology, semantics
11. linguistics
life .. 7. biology 10. entomology
light .. 6. optics
mind .. 10. psychology
moral conduct .. 6. ethics
organism behavior .. 7. ecology
(oecology) 9. bionomics
philosophy .. 6. noesia
reality .. 10. philosophy
reasoning .. 5. logic
rocks .. 9. petrology
sea (the) .. 12. oceanography
self-defense .. 4. judo 7. jujitsu
sound .. 9. acoustics
theology interpretation .. 8. exegesis
12. hermeneutics
verse .. 7. prosody
virtue .. 8. aretaics
words .. 9. semantics
scientific ... 5. exact 8. clinical 9. realistic,
technical 16. precise knowledge
scimiter, scimitar ... 4. snee 5. saber
8. billhook
scintilla ... 4. atom, iota, whit 5. spark,
trace 7. modicum
scintillate ... 5. flash, gleam, spark 7. be
witty, glitter, twinkle 9. coruscate 10. be
eloquent
scion, cion ... 3. son 4. slip 5. graft,
shoot 10. descendant
scold ... 3. jaw, nag 4. carp, rail, rate
5. chide, shrew 6. berate, chider,
rebuke 7. reprove, upbraid 8. admonish
9. reprimand
scolding ... 7. froward 8. reproach,
shrewish 10. upbraiding
12. admonishment, reprimanding
sconce ... 3. top 4. head 5. brain,
mulct, skull 6. screen 7. bulwark,
lantern, redoubt, skelter 11. candlestick,
counterfort
scoop ... 4. bail, beat, lade, news
5. empty, ladle, spoon 6. bucket,
hollow, shovel 8. excavate, gather in
scoop out ... 3. dig 5. gouge 6. chisel,
hollow 7. fashion
scope ... 4. area, room 5. ambit, arena,
range, reach 6. degree, domain
7. compass, freedom, liberty 8. latitude
9. gyroscope, intention, periscope,
telescope 10. microscope

11. stethoscope 12. kaleidoscope, spectroscope

scorch ... 4. burn, char, sear, sere 5. parch, singe, speed 7. shrivel 9. criticize

scordato ... 9. out of tune 14. made discordant

score ... 3. peg, run, sum, tab 4. debt, gain, goal, rate 5. corge, judge, notch, scold, slash, tally 6. berate, furrow, groove, points, reason, twenty 7. account, arrange, scratch 8. incision 9. calculate, tally mark 10. obligation 11. arrangement, composition, orchestrate 12. indebtedness

scoria (volcano) ... 4. lava, slag 5. dross 6. refuse 7. residue

scorn ... 4. defy, geck, mock 5. spurn 6. deride, reject 7. contemn, despise, disdain 8. contempt, derision, disgrace 9. contumely

scornful ... 8. derisive, insolent 10. disdainful 12. contemptuous, contumelious

Scorpio (pert to) ...
  constellation in .. 8. Milky Way
  genus .. 8. Scorpius
  night mansion of .. 4. Mars
  pictured as .. 8. scorpion
  star (brightest) .. 7. Antares
  zodiac sign .. 6. eighth

scorpion ... 4. nepa 7. alacran, scourge (Bib) 8. arachnid, catapult 10. pine lizard, vinaigrier 11. vinegarroon (vinagron) 15. blue-tailed skink

Scot ... 3. Mac 4. Celt, Gael 5. Saxon 6. Sawney 7. bluecap 8. Scotsman 10. Caledonian, Highlander

Scotland ... see also *Scottish*
  capital,. 9. Edinburgh
  city .. 3. Ayr 5. Perth 6. Atholl (Athole), Dundee 7. Glasgow (largest), Renfrew 8. Aberdeen 9. Inverness
  congress (musical) .. 3. Mod
  district .. 6. Argyll, Atholl 10. Midlothian
  famed site .. 9. Trossachs (Lady of the Lake) 10. Loch Lomond 11. Loch Katrine
  firth .. 3. Tay 4. Loch 5. Clyde, Forth, Moray, Tweed
  islands .. 6. Orkney 8. Hebrides, Shetland
  Latin name (anc) .. 9. Caledonia
  moors .. 10. Lochar Moss
  mountain .. 9. Grampians
  poetic name .. 6. Scotia 9. Caledonia
  resort .. 4. Oban
  river .. 3. Ayr, Dee, Tay 5. Afton, Clyde, Forth, Tweed 6. Teviot 7. Deveron
  seaport .. 5. Leith 6. Dundee

Scotland Yard headquarters ...
  6. London 18. Metropolitan Police

Scott, Sir Walter (pert to) ...
  estate .. 10. Abbotsford (Scot)
  famed as .. 4. poet 8. novelist
  novel .. 7. Ivanhoe, Waverly 8. Talisman 10. Kenilworth 14. Quentin Durward
  poem .. 13. Lady of the Lake

Scottish (pert to) ...
  accent .. 4. birr
  alder .. 3. arn
  attendant (hunter's) .. 6. gillie (gilly)

bagpipe music .. 7. pibroch
beret .. 3. tam 11. tam-o'-shanter
bird .. 3. gae (blue) 6. grouse 7. snabbie (snabby) 9. swinepipe
blessing .. 6. rebuke 8. scolding
blood money .. 3. cro 7. galanas
blue .. 6. homage 8. infernal 11. reddish-blue
bluebell .. 8. harebell
boat .. 4. zulu 7. coracle, skaffie
bonnets .. 8. mushroom
brandy .. 6. Athole
breeches .. 5. trews
brier, briar .. 4. rose
broth .. 5. brose
bull, ox .. 4. stot
cake (tea) .. 5. scone
cap .. 3. tam 8. Balmoral 9. Glengarry 11. tam-o'-shanter
carpet .. 13. Kidderminster
cattle .. 8. Aberdeen, Ayrshire
celebration .. 4. kirn (harvest)
child .. 5. bairn 6. scuddy (naked)
church .. 4. kirk
cloth .. 4. kelt 6. tartan
coalfish .. 7. glashan, sillock
court officer .. 5. macer
cup .. 4. tass
dagger (anc) .. 4. dirk
dagger, knife .. 8. skean dhu
dance .. 4. reel 5. fling 9. ecossaise 10. strathspey 13. Highland fling
devil .. 4. deil 6. Hornie
dirge .. 8. coronach (as on bagpipes)
duck .. 4. coot 6. scoter
earth .. 4. eard
elder .. 7. tobacco
elm .. 7. wych-elm
excuse .. 6. sunyie
eye .. 2. ee
family (same) .. 3. ilk
festival .. 3. Mod 7. uphelya (Epiphany)
fish .. 4. sile 7. sillock 8. spalding
fog .. 4. haar
Gaelic .. 4. Erse
ghost .. 6. taisch
girl .. 4. lass 6. lassie, towdie 7. winklot
goblin .. 8. barghest
godmother .. 6. cummer (kimmer)
grandchild .. 2. oy (oye)
grandfather .. 8. gudesire
hill, hillside .. 4. brae 6. strone
icicle .. 7. shoggle
kilt .. 7. filibeg
kiss (stolen) .. 8. smoorich
lake .. 4. loch
language .. 4. Erse 6. Lallan (Lalland)
liquor .. 5. scour 6. Athole 7. whitter
lovage .. 10. sea parsley
money, silver .. 6. siller
nephew .. 6. nepote
New Year's Day .. 7. Cake Day 8. hogmanay
nightingale .. 7. warbler
ox, bullock .. 6. nowt
plaid .. 4. maud 6. tartan
porridge .. 5. brose
pouch, purse (kilt front) .. 7. sporran
pudding .. 6. haggis
reel (fishing) .. 4. pirn
rod, over the door .. 10. willow wand

sausage . . 9. whitehass (whitehawse)
schoolmaster . . 3. dux
shawl (plaid) . . 4. maud
stream, brook . . 4. sike
sweetheart . . 2. jo
sword . . 8. claymore
toad . . 3. ted 4. taed
tobacco . . 5. elder
topaz . . 7. cairngorm
townhall . . 8. tolbooth (tollbooth)
uncle . . 3. eme
village . . 3. rew
waistcoat (under) . . 6. fecket
whirlpool . . 7. swilkie
whisky . . 9. Glenlivet (Glenlivat)
  10. usquebaugh
window . . 7. winnock
youth . . 6. chield (chiel) 7. callant (callan)

Scottish person (pert to) . . .
  author . . 5. Scott 9. Stevenson (Robert Louis)
  biographer, famed . . 7. Boswell
  dynasty . . 6. Stuart
  economist . . 7. Smith (Adam)
  engineer, inventor . . 4. Watt
  geneticist . . 7. Haldane
  king . . 6. Robert (the Bruce)
  physicist . . 7. Maxwell
  poet . . 5. Burns

scoundrel . . . 3. cad 5. cheat, knave, scamp 6. varlet 7. villain 8. scalawag 9. miscreant 10. blackguard 11. rapscallion

scoup . . 3. run 4. leap, skip 7. scamper

scourge . . . 4. bane, flog, lash, whip 6. punish, swinge, switch 8. chastise 10. affliction, infliction, punishment

Scourge of God . . 6. Attila (King of Huns)

Scourge of Princes . . 7. Aretino (It satirist)

scout . . . 3. spy 5. flout, scoff 7. lookout, servant 8. emissary, watchman 9. guillemot 11. reconnoiter 14. razor-billed auk

scow . . 4. acon 6. garvey 7. lighter

scowl . . 5. frown, lower 6. aspect (gloomy), glower 7. wrinkle (brow) 10. sullen look

scraggly . . . 5. rough 6. ragged 7. unkempt 9. irregular

scraggy . . . 4. bony 5. rough 6. meager, rugged, skinny 7. knotted, scrawny, stunted

scram . . . 6. begone, benumb, decamp 7. vamoose

scramble . . . 4. push 5. climb, crowd, crush 6. jostle, strive 7. clamber, scatter 8. struggle

scrap . . . 3. bit, end, ort, rag 4. chip, junk 5. fight, melee, piece, waste 6. morsel, refuse 7. cutting, discard, excerpt, extract, quarrel, remnant 8. fragment, ramentum

scrape . . . 3. row, rub 4. rake, rasp 5. grate, graze, shave 6. abrade, eke out, injure, sclaff 7. collect, scratch 8. economize, obeisance 10. difficulty 11. predicament

scraper . . . 4. harl (wool), tool 6. barber, rasper 7. abrader, fiddler, strigil

8. grattoir

scrappy . . . 9. irregular 10. pugnacious 11. contentious, fragmentary, quarrelsome

scratch . . . 3. mar, rit, rub 4. claw, draw, itch, mark, rake, rist, tear 5. erase 6. cancel, injury, scrape 7. blemish, roughen, scarify 8. scribble, withdraw

scrawl . . . 6. doodle 7. scratch 8. scribble

scrawny . . . 4. lean, poor, thin 5. spare 6. skinny 7. scranny 8. rawboned

scream . . . 3. cry 4. wail, yell 6. shriek, squeal 7. screech

screamer . . . 5. swift (bird) 7. blunder 8. headline

scree . . . 5. stone, talus 6. debris, pebble

screech . . . 3. cry, say 6. outcry, scream, shriek, squeal 7. ululate

screech (pert to) . . .
  hawk . . 10. goatsucker
  martin . . 5. swift
  owl . . 4. barn 5. Scops

screed . . . 4. list, rend, tear 5. shred 6. tirade 7. lecture 8. fragment 12. dissertation

screen . . . 3. net 4. hide, laun, mask, sift, sort, veil 5. arras, blind, cloak, pavis, shade, sieve, spier 6. defend, grille, riddle, sifter, sorter 7. conceal, curtain, protect, reredos, shelter 8. parclose 9. partition, safeguard 10. protection 12. discriminate

screw . . . 3. key 4. coil, turn 5. horse, twist 6. fasten, gimlet, rotate, spiral 7. contort, distort, tighten, turnkey 9. bargainer, propeller, skinflint 10. contortion, thumbscrew

screwlike . . 5. spiral 7. spiroid

scribble . . . 6. doodle, scrawl 7. scratch 8. scrabble

scribe . . . 5. clerk 6. author, jurist, lawyer, penman, writer 8. recorder 10. amanuensis, cuttlefish, journalist 13. bibliographer

scriggle . . . 5. twist 6. squirm 7. wriggle 8. curlicue

scrimmage . . . 3. row 5. fight 6. tussle 8. football (term), practice, skirmish, struggle

scrimp . . . 4. save 5. scant, stint 6. scanty, scrape, sparse 7. sparing 9. economize

scrip . . . 3. bag 4. list 5. money 6. wallet 7. writing 8. document, schedule

script . . . 5. ronde 6. letter 7. writing 8. scenario 10. manuscript, typescript 11. handwriting

scriptural . . . 7. written 8. Biblical, orthodox

scriptural interpreter . . . 7. exegete

scripture . . . 4. writ 5. motto, truth 7. passage, writing 8. document 10. manuscript 11. inscription 13. sacred writing

Scripture, Scriptures . . . 4. text 5. Bible 6. lesson 7. Oracles, passage, Vulgate

Scripture interpretation . . . 8. exegesis 12. hermeneutics

scrivello . . . 4. tusk (elephant's)

scrivener . . . 6. notary, scribe, writer 8. recorder 10. amanuensis

scroll . . . 4. list, roll 5. draft 6. record,

spiral, volute 7. engross, writing
8. document, inscribe, schedule,
streamer 9. parchment

scroll roll ... 8. makimono

scrub ... 3. mop, rub 4. halt, mean, runt,
tree, wash 5. abort, clean, dwarf, scour
6. cancel, drudge, paltry 7. cleanse
8. inferior 10. undersized

scrubby ... 4. base 6. paltry, shabby,
stubby 7. bristly, shrubby, stunted
10. underbrush 13. insignificant

scruff ... 4. nape, scum, slur 5. crust,
dross, scuff 6. refuse 7. surface
8. dandruff

scruple ... 4. coin 5. demur, qualm
6. object, weight 9. small part
10. hesitation 13. unwillingness

scrupulous ... 4. nice 5. exact 6. formal,
proper, strict 8. qualmish 10. fastidious,
meticulous 11. punctilious
13. conscientious

scrutinize ... 3. eye, pry 4. scan 5. probe
7. examine, inspect, observe

scud ... 3. dash, foam, gust, rain, sail,
skim 5. speed 6. clouds, shower

scuffle ... 4. fray 5. melee 6. strive,
tussle 7. contend, contest, shamble,
shuffle 8. struggle

sculduddery ... 9. grossness, obscenity

scull ... 3. oar 4. gull 5. shoal, skate
6. basket, paddle, propel 7. rowboat

scullion ... 4. base 6. menial 7. servant
10. dishwasher, kitchenman

scullog, scullogue ... 6. farmer, rustic
7. laborer

sculp ... 5. carve 7. engrave 8. seal skin
9. engraving, sculpture

sculptor ... 6. artist, carver, imager,
molder 8. chiseler 13. constellation
19. Apparatus Sculptoris (constellation)

sculptor (famed) ... 5. Rodin 7. Cellini,
Phidias 10. Praxiteles 12. Michelangelo,
Saint Gaudens

sculptor's tool ... 6. chisel, graver
9. ébauchoir

sculpture ... 4. form 5. carve, model
6. figure, statue 9. engraving 11. alto-
relievo

scum ... 4. film, foam 5. cover, dross,
froth, scurf, spume 6. refuse, scoria
7. coating 8. riffraff 10. impurities

scup ... 5. bream, porgy

scurrility ... 5. abuse 9. indignity,
obscenity

scurrilous ... 3. low 4. vile 5. gross
6. vulgar 7. abusive 8. indecent,
scurrile 9. insulting 11. foulmouthed,
opprobrious

scurry ... 3. hie 4. dash 5. scoot, speed
6. flurry, hasten 7. scamper, scuttle
9. skedaddle

scurvy ... 4. base, mean 7. disease
12. contemptible, discourteous

scuttle ... 3. hod, run 4. dish, sink
5. haste, scoot 6. basket, hasten, scurry,
shovel 7. octopus, platter 8. hatchway
10. cuttlefish

scutum ... 5. scute 6. shield
13. constellation (Milky Way)
15. Scutum Sobieskii

Scylla (pert to) ...

father .. 5. Nisus
home .. 4. rock (coast of Italy)
lover .. 5. Minos
menace to .. 9. seafarers
Myth .. 7. monster
transformed to .. 7. sea bird

scythe .. 2. sy (sye) 5. swath

scythe handle ... 5. snath, snead

sea ... 3. Red 4. Aral, Azov, Ross, wave
5. Black, brine, China, ocean, swell,
water 6. aequor 7. Caspian 8. seashore
9. Caribbean

sea (pert to) ...
adder .. 8. pipefish 11. stickleback
anemone .. 5. polyp
Antarctic .. 4. Ross
arm .. 4. gulf, meer, mere 5. bayou,
firth 7. estuary
bird .. 3. auk 4. erne (ern), gull, smew,
tern 5. booby, cahow, solan 6. gannet,
petrel, puffin 9. albatross 10. shearwater
comb form .. 3. mer
cow .. 6. dugong, rytina (Steller's),
walrus 7. manatee 8. sirenian
12. hippopotamus
cucumber .. 7. trepang
devil .. 9. angelfish, devilfish
dog .. 4. seal (Her) 6. fogdog, sailor
dragon .. 8. dragonet, sea horse
dread of .. 14. thalassophobia
duck .. 5. eider, scaup 6. scoter
eagle .. 4. erne (ern) 6. osprey
ear .. 7. abalone
eel .. 6. conger
farer .. 3. tar 6. sailor, seaman 7. mariner
foam .. 5. froth 6. sepiolite
10. meerschaum
fowl .. 3. auk 4. gull, tern 6. gannet,
petrel
fox .. 5. shark
god, deity .. 3. Lar 5. Aegir 6. Triton
7. Neptune, Phorcus, Proteus
8. Poseidon
goddess .. 4. Nina 5. Doris 10. Amphitrite
gull .. 3. cob, mew 9. kittiwake
hare .. 7. mollusk
hen .. 4. skua 9. guillemot
hog .. 8. porpoise
holly root .. 6. eryngo (eringo)
ladder .. 6. Jacob's
lion .. 4. seal
mammal .. 4. seal 5. whale 6. dugong
7. manatee 11. bladdernose
mouse .. 4. duck (harlequin) 6. dunlin
7. annelid
nymph .. 5. naiad, siren 6. nereid
7. oceanid
onion .. 6. squill
otter .. 5. kalan
owl .. 6. puffin 8. lumpfish
pig .. 6. dugong 7. dolphin 8. porpoise
pumpkin .. 8. cucumber
quail .. 6. auklet 9. turnstone
raven .. 7. sculpin 9. cormorant
10. squaretail
reference to .. 5. naval 6. marine
7. oceanic, pelagic 8. maritime
9. Neptunian, thalassic
robber .. 6. jaeger, pirate 7. corsair
9. buccaneer, privateer
serpent .. 5. Hydra 8. snake eel

shell .. 5. conch
sickness .. 8. mal de mer 9. naupathia
spider .. 10. spider crab
turtle .. 5. green 9. hawksbill
  10. loggerhead, thalassian
  11. leatherback
unicorn .. 7. narwhal
urchin .. 5. heart 10. echinoderm,
  Spatangina 13. cushionflower
wolf .. 4. seal 6. pirate 9. privateer,
  submarine
sea king ... 3. Ler 5. chief 6. pirate,
  Viking 7. Neptune
seal (pert to) ...
  bearded .. 7. ursuk 6. makluk
  breeding ground .. 7. rookery
  eared .. 5. otary
  flock .. 3. pod
  fur (fem) .. 5. matka (matkah)
  harp (male) .. 7. saddler
  leather .. 3. pin
  limb .. 7. flipper
  skin .. 5. sculp
  type .. 3. fur 7. sea lion 8. elephant,
  pinniped
  young .. 3. pup
sealed instrument .. 6. escrow
seam .. 4. line, load, scar 5. joint, ridge,
  strip 6. burden, groove, stitch, streak,
  suture 7. crevice, stratum 9. horseload
  10. interstice, packsaddle
seaman ... 3. gob, tar 6. sailor, Seabee
  7. mariner
seaman's chapel ... 6. bethel, church
seamark ... 6. beacon 10. lighthouse
seamy ... 5. rough 8. wrinkled
  12. disreputable
séance ... 7. session, sitting 9. treatment
séance holder ... 6. medium
sear, sere ... 3. dry 4. burn, cook
  5. parch 6. braise, scorch, wither
  7. dried up, shrivel 8. deadened,
  withered 9. cauterize 10. threadbare
  11. deteriorate
search ... 4. comb, fish, hunt, look, seek
  5. frisk, ghoom, grope, probe, quest
  6. ferret, forage, survey 7. inquire,
  ransack, rummage, zetetic 9. expiscate
  10. scrutinize 11. investigate
searchlight ... 4. beam 10. flashlight
seashell ... 4. clam 5. conch, snail
  7. scallop
season ... 3. age 4. fall, salt, tide,
  time 5. devil, inure, spice 6. flavor,
  mature 7. qualify 8. accustom, preserve
  11. acclimatize
season (pert to) ...
  Astron .. 5. Aries, Libra 6. Cancer
  11. Capricornus
  Eccl .. 4. Lent 6. Advent, Easter
  7. Trinity 8. Epiphany 9. Christmas
  11. Whitsuntide
  Lent .. 6. carême
  Scot .. 4. sele
  yearly .. 7. Autumn, Spring, Summer,
  Winter
seasonable ... 6. timely 7. apropos
seasoning ... 4. sage, salt 5. spice, thyme
  6. cloves, garlic, pepper 7. mustard,
  paprika 8. allspice, estragon, marjoram,
  rosemary, turmeric 9. condiment

Seasons, goddesses of ...
  justice .. 4. Dike
  order (Universe) .. 5. Horae
  peace .. 6. Eirene
  wise laws .. 7. Eunomia
seat ... 3. pew 4. root, site 5. bench,
  chair, embed, sella, stool 6. settee,
  settle 7. install 9. establish
seat (pert to) ...
  church .. 3. pew 6. sedile
  of justice .. 4. banc
  of self .. 3. ego
  on elephant .. 6. howdah
  outdoor .. 6. exedra
  privileged .. 6. curule
  series (one of) .. 6. gradin (gradine)
seaweed ... 4. kelp 5. algae, dulse, laver,
  varec, wrack 6. Alaria 8. agar-agar
secco ... 3. dry
secern ... 7. secrete 8. separate
  11. distinguish 12. discriminate
Secessionist (S Carolina) ... 5. Rhett
secluded ... 5. aloof, apart 6. hidden,
  lonely, remote, secret 7. private,
  retired 8. debarred, expelled, isolated,
  recessed, retiring, screened, solitary
  9. cloistral, concealed
seclusion ... 7. privacy, retreat 8. solitude
  9. aloofness, exclusion 10. quarantine,
  retirement, separation
second ... 3. aid 4. abet, back, echo,
  time 5. jiffy, trice 6. assist, attend,
  backer, double, moment 7. instant,
  support, sustain 8. inferior 9. assistant,
  encourage, imperfect, prototype,
  reinforce 11. corroborate, subordinate
second (pert to) ...
  childhood .. 6. dotage, dotard 8. senility
  crop .. 5. rowen
  lieutenant .. 9. shavetail
  number .. 6. addend
  person .. 3. you
  rate .. 8. inferior, mediocre
  Republic .. 6. French (1848-52)
  sight .. 6. myopia 7. psychic 9. intuition
  12. clairvoyance
  team .. 5. scrub 9. Yannigans
  thought .. 6. sequel 12. afterthought
  15. reconsideration
secondary ... 4. less 5. minor 6. deputy
  8. inferior, offshoot 9. auxiliary,
  dependent, satellite 10. contingent,
  derivative, second-rate, subsequent,
  substitute 11. subordinate, unessential
  12. nonessential, quill feather
secondary color ... 5. green 6. orange,
  purple
secondary school ... 4. prep 5. lycée
  7. academy 10. Realschule
secrecy ... 4. tile 6. hiding 7. mystery,
  privacy, privity 8. velation 9. reticence,
  seclusion 10. confidence
  11. concealment
secret ... 3. key 4. dern 5. close, inner,
  privy 6. arcane, covert, hidden, mystic,
  occult 7. arcanum, cryptic, mystery,
  private, unknown 8. esoteric, intimate
  (armor), reticent, secluded, skullcap
  9. concealed, recondite, secretive,
  underhand 10. confidence, mysterious
  11. clandestine 12. confidential

13. surreptitious

secret (pert to) ...
agent . . 3. spy 5. scout 6. espier 7. spotter 8. emissary 13. undercover man
council . . 5. by-end, junto 7. purpose
language . . 5. argot 7. dialect
meeting . . 5. tryst
movement . . 7. stealth
name . . 9. cryptonym
place . . 5. cache 6. adytum 7. sanctum 9. sanctuary
society . . 3. hui (Chin) 4. tong 7. Camorra (It)

secretary . . . 4. bird, desk 5. agent 6. scribe 7. officer 8. recorder 9. confidant 10. amanuensis, escritoire

secrete . . . 4. bury, hide, stow 5. exude 7. conceal

secretion (pert to) ...
gland . . 7. hormone
inflammation . . 3. pus
liver . . 4. bile
mammal gland . . 9. lactation
mouth . . 6. saliva
nasal . . 9. secernment
scale, insect . . 3. lac
shrubs . . 4. lerp
whale . . 9. ambergris

secretly . . . 5. aside, slyly 7. sub rosa 8. covertly 9. not openly 13. clandestinely

sect . . . 4. clan, cult, part 5. Alogi (Hist), class, group, order, party 6. essene, school, Yezidi (Kurdish) 9. following, Mennonite 10. shibboleth (Bib) 12. denomination

sectarian . . . 7. heretic 8. partisan 9. dissenter, heterodox 13. nonconformist 14. denominational

section . . . 4. area, part, plot 5. panel, piece, slice, tmema, torso 6. region 7. portion, segment, ternion 8. parabola, surgical 9. paragraph, signature 11. subdivision

secular . . . 3. lay 4. laic 5. civil 6. laical 7. earthly, profane, worldly 8. temporal 9. centuried, temporary

secure . . . 3. fix, get, pin 4. bind, easy, fast, firm, moor, nail, safe, tape 5. fetch, spike, trice (sail) 6. elicit, ensure, fasten, obtain, stable 7. acquire, assured, certain, procure, receive 8. make fast 9. confident, guarantee 10. dependable 11. undisturbed

security . . . 4. bail, gage 5. guard 6. pledge, safety, vadium 7. defense, shelter 8. guaranty 9. guarantee, insurance, stability 10. protection

sedate . . . 4. calm 5. douce, quiet, sober, staid 6. demure, proper, serene, solemn 7. serious, settled 8. composed, decorous 9. dignified, unruffled 11. unobtrusive 13. contemplative, dispassionate

sedative . . . 6. remedy 7. anodyne, bromide, chloral, veronal 8. atropine, barbital, lenitive, soothing 9. calmative, mitigator, paregoric 10. palliative, phenacetin 12. tranquilizer (tranquillizer) 13. phenobarbital

sedent . . . 7. sitting (statue)

sediment . . . 4. lees, silt 5. dregs 7. deposit, grounds, siltage 9. settlings

sedition . . . 4. revolt, strife, tumult 6. treason 9. commotion 10. dissension, turbulence

seditious . . . 7. riotous 8. factious 9. turbulent 11. treasonable 15. insurrectionary

seduce . . . 4. lure 5. decoy, tempt 6. allure, enamor, entice 7. corrupt, mislead 8. inveigle

seducer . . . 7. enticer, tempter 8. Lothario 9. debaucher

seduction . . . 5. charm 10. allurement, corruption, temptation 11. debauchment

sedulous . . . 4. busy 6. steady 8. diligent, untiring 9. assiduous, laborious, unwearied 10. persistent 11. persevering, unremitting

see . . . 3. spy 4. espy, heed, know, look, scry, seat, view 5. visit 6. behold, descry, detect 7. diocese, discern, witness 8. discover, perceive 9. apprehend, interview, visualize 10. comprehend, understand 11. contemplate

seed . . . 3. egg, pip, pit, sow 4. germ 5. grain, ovule, plant, sperm, spore 6. kernel, origin 7. lineage, progeny 8. rudiment 9. beginning 11. descendants

seed (pert to) ...
apple . . 3. pip
aromatic . . 5. anise 7. aniseed, caraway
coat . . 3. pod 4. aril, burr, husk 5. testa 6. carpel 8. pericarp
container, envelope . . 3. bur (burr), pod 6. loment, vessel 7. capsule
edible . . 3. pea 4. bean 5. grain 6. lentil
enclosing soft fruit . . 5. drupe
flower . . 6. pistil
immature . . 5. ovule
lemon, orange, apple . . 3. pip
licorice . . 9. jequerity
medicinal . . 9. flaxseed
Moringa, tropical . . 3. ben
naked (one-seeded fruit) . . 6. achene (akene)
oak . . 5. acorn
one-called . . 6. carpel
part . . 6. tunica
poppy, opium . . 3. maw
underground . . 6. peanut
winged . . 6. samara

seeds (pert to) ...
cocoa . . 5. cacao
feeding on . . 11. granivorous
perfume . . 8. abelmosk
rudiments . . 4. ova 5. eggs, pips, pits 6. ovules, sperms

seedy . . . 5. dingy, lousy, tacky 6. shabby 7. worn out 8. slovenly 10. spiritless 11. spawn-filled 12. bearing seeds

seek . . . 3. beg 4. hunt 5. essay 6. pursue, search 7. explore, solicit 8. endeavor 9. neologize (new words) 11. investigate

seeker . . . 6. prober, tracer 7. pursuer, zetetic 8. aspirant, searcher 9. applicant 10. petitioner

seeker of ...
knowledge . . 10. philonoist

new words . . 9. neologist
pleasure . . 7. epicure 8. hedonist
seem . . . 4. look 6. appear 7. pretend
  8. resemble
seeming . . . 5. guise, quasi 8. apparent,
  illusion, illusory, pretense, specious
  9. befitting
seeming contradiction . . . 7. paradox
seeming truth . . . 14. verisimilitude
seemly . . . 3. fit 4. meet 6. comely,
  decent, proper, suited 7. elegant, fitting
  8. decorous, tasteful 9. expedient
seep . . . 4. leak, ooze 5. exude 6. filter
  8. transude 9. percolate
seer, seeress . . . 5. sibyl 6. oracle, scryer
  7. Phoebad, prophet 8. predictor,
  visionary 10. forecaster, prophetess,
  soothsayer 11. Nostradamus
  14. prognosticator
seesaw . . . 6. teeter, tilter 7. pastime
  8. alternate, crossruff, fluctuate,
  vacillate 11. oscillation 12. teeter-totter
seethe . . . 4. boil, stew, teem 5. be hot,
  steep 6. bubble 7. be angry
segment . . . 3. pip 4. part 5. tmema
  6. cantle 7. portion, section 8. fragment
  12. cross section
segment (pert to) . . .
  botany . . 5. tmema 7. lacinia
  corresponding part . . 7. isomere
  curve . . 3. arc
  shaped . . 5. toric
  Zool . . 6. somite, telson 8. metamere,
    somatome
seine . . . 3. net 5. trawl 6. sagene
  7. dragnet, network
seism . . . 10. earthquake
seize . . . 3. bag, cly, cop, nab, net 4. bind,
  bite, grab, grip, take, trap 5. annex,
  catch, grasp, ravin, reave, usurp,
  wrest 6. arrest, clutch, collar, fasten,
  ravish, snatch 7. capture, embargo,
  grapple 8. distrain 9. apprehend, lay
  hold of 10. confiscate, understand
  11. appropriate
seizin . . . 9. occupancy 10. possession
seizing . . . 6. cord 7. lashing 9. arresting,
  raptorial
seizure . . . 3. fit 4. grip, hold 5. spasm
  6. arrest, attack, frenzy, seizin
  9. ownership 10. convulsion, occupation
  11. manucapture
seladang . . . 4. gaur 6. buffalo
selah (Bib) . . . 4. sign 5. pause
select . . . 3. cull, name, pick, take
  5. elect, elite 6. choice, choose,
  picked 7. appoint, pick out, specify
  9. exclusive, segregate 10. registrate
  11. distinguish, outstanding
selection . . . 5. piece 6. choice 7. analect,
  excerpt, passage 8. collection
  11. appointment
selective . . . 5. draft 8. eclectic
  9. exclusive 10. particular
  14. discriminative
self . . . 3. ego, own 4. same 5. being
  6. person, psyche 7. oneself
  10. individual 11. personality
self (pert to) . . .
  acting . . 9. automatic, voluntary
  assertion . . 6. egoism, vanity

  centered . . 7. selfish 9. egotistic
    10. egocentric 11. independent 12. self-
    absorbed
  comb form . . 4. auto
  complacent . . 13. self-satisfied
  confidence . . 5. poise 6. aplomb
    9. assurance 11. self-reliant
  contained . . 8. reserved 10. controlled,
    sufficient (in itself) 11. independent
    15. uncommunicative
  control . . 8. stoicism 9. restraint
    10. automation, discipline, equanimity,
    temperance
  defense . . 6. karate, jung fu 7. jujitsu
  determination . . 8. autonomy
    12. independence
  enjoyment . . 13. gratification
  esteem . . 5. pride 6. vanity 7. concept,
    ego-trip
  evident . . 5. clear 9. axiomatic
  examination . . 13. introspection,
    introspective
  French . . 3. soi
  love of . . 6. egoism
  ref to . . 8. personal
  reproach . . 7. remorse
  righteous . . 5. pious 9. Pharisaic
    13. sanctimonious 14. holier-than-thou
  same . . 9. identical
  satisfied . . 5. smug 6. jaunty
  Scottish . . 3. sel (sell)
  worship . . 8. idolatry 9. autolatry
selfish . . . 6. grabby (sl) 11. egotistical,
  self-seeking 12. self-centered
sell . . . 4. vend 5. scalp, trade 6. barter,
  market, retail 7. auction, bargain
  8. convince, exchange, persuade
  9. negotiate
sell (out) . . . 6. betray, desert 8. inform
  on 9. victimize
seller . . . 6. dealer, vender, vendor
  7. peddler 8. merchant, salesman
  9. tradesman 10. saleswoman
semantics . . . 8. meanings
  11. semasiology
semblable . . . 4. like 5. alike 7. seeming,
  similar 8. apparent, suitable
  10. ostensible, resembling
  11. conformable
semblance . . . 4. copy, face, form 5. guise,
  image 6. aspect, figure 7. pretext,
  umbrage 8. illusion 10. appearance,
  similarity 11. countenance,
  presumption, resemblance
semeiology, semeiotics . . . 5. signs
  (signaling) 11. diagnostics
  14. interpretation, symptomatology
semester . . . 4. term 6. course, period
Seminole chief . . . 7. Osceola (1804--38)
Semitic (pert to) . . .
  deity . . 4. Baal
  dialect . . 4. Geez
  god (evil) . . 6. Moloch
  language . . 5. Iraqi 6. Syrian 7. Arabian,
    Aramaic 8. Egyptian 11. Palestinian
  people . . 6. Harari , Shagia (Shaiklyeh)
    8. Moabites
semper eadem . . . 13. always the same
  (motto of Queen Elizabeth)
semper fidelis . . . 14. always faithful
semper idem . . . 13. always the same

semper paratus ... 11. always ready
senate .. 5. boule 7. council (Rom)
  8. assembly 11. legislature
  18. administrative body
send ... 4. mail, ship 5. drive, grant,
  issue, speed 6. bestow, convey, export,
  launch, propel 7. forward 8. dispatch,
  transmit 10. commission
send (pert to) ...
  back . . 5. remit 6. remand, return
    11. reverberate
  by different person . . 5. relay
  off . . 5. start 6. launch 7. impulse
    8. dispatch 11. consignment
    13. demonstration
  out . . 4. emit, spew 5. shoot
  out rays . . 7. radiate
  payment . . 5. remit
  to an address . . 7. deliver
Seneca ... 6. Indian 9. Iroquoian
Senegal, Africa ...
  capital . . 5. Dakar
  ebony . . 9. blackwood
  gazelle . . 5. korin
  gum . . 9. gum arabic
  mahogany . . 9. cailcedra
  native . . 10. Senegalese
senescence ... 5. aging 10. growing old
senicide ... 13. killing old men (tribal)
senility ... 6. dotage, old age 8. caducity,
  dementia 10. feebleness
senior ... 4. aine, dean 5. chief, elder
  7. ancient, student 8. superior
senior member ... 5. doyen
sensation ... 5. sense 6. thrill, uproar,
  wonder 7. emotion 8. rhigosis (cold)
  10. perception 12. great success
sensational ... 5. lurid 6. superb
  8. dramatic, exciting 9. emotional
  12. melodramatic
sense ... 4. feel, mind, sane 5. flair, sight,
  smell 7. feeling, meaning 8. sapience
  9. awareness, intuition, sensation,
  sentience 10. perception, understand
  11. discernment, recognition
  12. intelligence
senseless ... 5. inept 6. insane, stupid,
  unwise 7. fatuous, foolish, idiotic,
  inanity 9. illogical, inanimate, insensate,
  unfeeling 11. irrational 11. meaningless,
  purposeless, unconscious
  12. unreasonable 13. unintelligent
sense of ...
  beauty . . 8. aesthete (esthete), tasteful
    9. aesthetic
  dignity . . 5. pride
  distance . . 11. telesthetic
  hearing . . 8. audition 12. auscultation
  humor . . 10. risibility
  sight . . 6. vision
  smell . . 7. osmatic 9. olfaction
  taste . . 6. palate
sense organ ... 3. ear, eye 4. nose, skin
  6. tongue 8. receptor, sensilla
senses ... 4. wits 6. sanity 7. sensory
  9. sensation
sensible ... 4. sane 5. aware, privy,
  sound 7. logical, prudent 8. rational
  9. cognizant, practical, sensitive
  10. reasonable, responsive
  11. intelligent, susceptible

sensitive ... 4. nice, sore 5. acute
  6. pliant, tender, touchy 7. sensory
  8. sensible 9. receptive 10. responsive
  11. susceptible 14. discriminating,
  impressionable
sensitivity ... 9. emotional, hebetated
  (blunted) 11. sensibility 12. irritability
  14. discrimination
sentence ... 4. doom 5. maxim, motto
  6. phrase, remark, saying 7. condemn,
  passage, thought, verdict 8. decision,
  judgment, proposal 9. statement
  12. condemnation
sentence (pert to) ...
  balance . . 7. parison
  clause (concluding) . . 8. apodosis
  concluding . . 8. epilogue (epilog)
  construction . . 6. syntax
  difficult articulation . . 13. tongue twister
  introductory . . 8. protasis
  judicial . . 5. futwa
  pithy . . 5. motto 8. aphorism
  punishment . . 11. year and a day
  subordinate part . . 6. clause, phrase
sententious ... 5. pithy, terse 7. concise,
  laconic 10. aphoristic 13. grandiloquent
sentient ... 4. mind 5. aware 7. feeling
  8. sensible 9. conscious, sensitive
  10. perceptive 13. consciousness
sentiment ... 5. toast 7. emotion, feeling,
  opinion 8. attitude 10. perception,
  sentimento 11. sensibility
  14. sentimentality
sentimental ... 6. loving 7. maudlin,
  mawkish 8. romantic 9. emotional
  13. lackadaisical
sentimental song ... 11. strephonade
sentinel ... 5. guard 6. picket, sentry
  7. vedette (mounted) 8. watchman
  10. lookout man, watchtower
sepad ... 5. think 7. believe, suppose
sepal ... 4. leaf 5. petal
separate ... 4. open, part, shed, sift, sort
  5. alone, apart, sever, space 6. cleave,
  detach, divide, secern, single, sleave,
  sunder, winnow 7. disband, diverge,
  diverse, divided, divorce, isolate
  8. alienate, discrete, distinct, peculiar,
  secluded 9. disjoined, partition,
  segregate, sequester, unrelated
  10. dissociate, particular, respective
  11. disembodied, unconnected
separate (pert to) ...
  Chem . . 11. fractionate
  from others . . 5. aloof 8. isolated
  metal from ore . . 5. smelt
  thread . . 6. sleave
separation ... 6. tmesis 7. divorce
  8. autotomy 9. partition, recession,
  seclusion 10. alienation 11. disjunction,
  segregation 13. sequestration
  14. discontinuance, discrimination
separatist ... 7. heretic, seceder
  8. apostate 9. dissenter 12. secessionist
  13. nonconformist
sepia ... 3. dun, ink 5. color 7. pigment
  10. cuttlebone, cuttlefish
sepiment ... 5. hedge 7. defense
  9. enclosure
Sepiola ... 10. cuttlefish
sepiolite ... 10. meerschaum

503   sepoy / serve

sepoy . . . 7. soldier 9. policeman
seps . . . 6. lizard 7. serpent
sept . . . 4. clan 5. class, seven, tribe
  7. lineage
septic . . . 6. morbid, pyemia (pyaemia)
  8. diseased, infected, poisoned
  9. gangrened, mortified, poisonous
  10. septicemia (blood poison)
sepulcher, sepulchre . . . 4. bury, tomb
  5. crypt, grave, vault 6. entomb
  9. sepulture 10. repository
sepulchral . . . 5. urnal 6. gloomy, hollow
  7. charnel 8. funereal 9. deep-toned
sepulchral (pert to) . . .
  chest . . 4. cist
  mound . . 7. tumulus
  vault . . 6. burial 8. catacomb, monument
  9. interview
sequel . . . 5. issue 6. effect, series, upshot
  7. outcome 8. follow up, sequence,
  sequitur 9. posterity 10. succession
sequela . . . 7. disease (resulting)
  8. adherent 9. inference 10. conclusion
  11. concomitant, consequence
  15. morbid condition
sequence . . . 5. gamut 6. course (usual),
  series, tierce (three cards) 8. straight
  10. succession
sequential . . . 9. deducible, resultant
  10. continuous, succeeding
  11. consecutive
sequestered . . . 6. lonely, secret
  7. private, recluse, retired 8. isolated,
  secluded, solitary, withdraw
  9. concealed, separated
  12. unfrequented
sequitur . . . 9. inference, influence, it
  follows 14. natural sequent
sequoia, Sequoia . . . 4. Park (Calif)
  6. Indian (famed for alphabet) 7. big
  tree, conifer, redwood
seraglio . . . 5. harem, serai 6. zenana
  9. enclosure
serape . . . 5. shawl 7. blanket
seraph . . . 5. angel 6. cherub
seraphic . . . 7. angelic, sublime
  8. cherubic 9. unworldly
Serb . . . 4. Slav 7. Serbian (Servian)
Serbia, Yugoslavia . . .
  church . . 8. Orthodox
  conqueror . . 5. Turks
  hero . . 6. Dushan, Nemaya (1159)
  queen . . 7. Natalie
  Revolutionary . . 7. Chetnik
sere . . . 4. claw, sear, worn 5. talon
  6. effete, yellow 8. withered
  10. desiccated
serenade . . . 4. sing 5. music 8. serenata
  9. charivari, entertain 10. callithump
  11. celebration
serene . . . 4. calm, cool 5. clear, quiet
  6. placid 8. peaceful, serenity, tranquil
  9. collected, unruffled 11. undisturbed
  12. tranquillity (tranquility)
serenity . . . 5. peace 6. repose
  8. calmness, coolness 9. composure
  10. quiescence
serf . . . 4. esne, neif (fem), peon 5. helot,
  slave 6. thrall, vassal 7. captive, villein
series . . . 3. set 4. nest 5. class,
  gamut, group 8. sequence 9. seriation

  10. succession
series, connected . . . 5. chain, suite
  6. catena
series of . . .
  discussions . . 9. symposium
  heroic events . . 4. epos
  meetings . . 7. session
  pictures . . 8. panorama
  races . . 7. regatta
  rings . . 4. coil
  six . . 5. hexad
  steps . . 5. scale
  syllogisms . . 7. sorites
  travels . . 7. odyssey
serious . . . 4. keen 5. grave, serio (comb
  form), sober, staid 6. demure, sedate,
  solemn 7. capital, earnest, weighty,
  zealous 8. resolute 9. important
  10. thoughtful
seriousness . . . 4. zeal 7. gravity
  10. importance 11. earnestness
sermon . . . 4. talk, text 5. psalm 6. homily,
  lesson, preach 7. address, lecture,
  reproof 8. harangue 9. discourse,
  preaching 10. admonition
seron . . . 5. crate 6. hamper 7. boxwood,
  spanner
serotine . . . 3. bat 4. adda 9. late bloom
serpent . . . 3. asp 4. seps (anc) 5. cobra,
  krait, racer, snake
serpent (pert to) . . .
  deity, of good . . 12. agathodaemon
  13. agathos daemon
  fabulous . . 5. Hydra 6. dragon 8. basilisk
  11. amphisbaena
  large . . 3. boa 5. aboma 6. python
  8. jararaca
  monster . . 6. ellops
  Old . . 5. Satan
  semihuman (Hind Myth) . . 4. Naga
  sky (Vedic Myth) . . 3. Ahi
  worshipers (Gnostic) . . 7. Ophites
serpentine . . . 4. wily 5. snaky 6. subtle,
  zigzag 7. sinuous, winding 8. diabolic,
  tempting 9. snakelike 10. circuitous,
  meandering
serpigo . . . 8. ringworm 11. skin disease
serrano . . . 12. squirrelfish
serrate . . . 7. notched, toothed 8. indented
  10. saw-toothed
serried . . . 5. dense 7. compact, concise,
  crowded
serum . . . 4. whey 5. blood, fluid 6. serous
  9. antitoxin
servant . . . 3. gyp 4. bata, cook, maid,
  maty, mozo, serf, syce 5. agent, boots,
  chela, nurse, slave, valet 6. bildar,
  butler, flunky, garçon, gillie (gilly),
  menial, servus, vassal, wallah (walla)
  7. equerry (nobleman's) 8. coistrel,
  domestic, handmaid 9. assistant
  11. chamberlain
servant of God . . . 6. bishop
serve . . . 2. do 3. act, aid 4. deal, help,
  wait 5. avail, cater 6. assist, succor
  7. advance, bestead, forward, further,
  suffice, work for 8. bear arms, fight for
  9. officiate 10. administer, distribute
serve (pert to) . . .
  as accomplice . . 4. abet
  as escort . . 6. squire

food . . 4. wait 5. cater 7. dish out
one's sentence . . 6. do time
religion . . 4. obey 7. worship
server . . 4. tray 6. player, salver
7. acolyte
Servia . . see *Serbia*
service . . . 3. aid, use 4. help, mail,
Mass, rite 5. favor, matin 6. employ,
ritual 7. benefit, nocturn, utility
8. ceremony, evensong, kindness,
ministry 9. servitude 10. attendance,
employment 12. ministration
service tree . . . 4. sorb 5. rowan
serviette . . . 6. napkin
servile . . . 4. mean 6. abject, menial,
minion 7. fawning, slavish 8. cringing,
faithful 9. dependent, parasitic, truckling
10. obsequious, submissive
11. subservient, sycophantic
Servite . . . 9. mendicant 13. Order of
Friars (1233)
servitude . . . 7. bondage, serfdom,
service, slavery 8. servitus 9. vassalage
14. apprenticeship
sesame . . . 3. oil 4. herb 5. benne 7. gingili
(seed), teel oil 8. ajonjoli, sesamine
Sesame, Open . . . 10. magical key
12. magic command (Arab Nights)
sess . . . 4. heap, pile 9. soap frame
session . . . 5. court 6. séance 8. assembly
11. legislature
set . . . 3. lay 4. form, heal, laid, pose, post
5. brood, class, fixed, group, place,
posit, ready, staid, stand 6. adjust,
clique, define, fasten, formal, ossify,
series, settle 7. confirm, congeal,
coterie, station, stiffen 8. regulate,
solidify 9. coagulate, designate,
direction, obstinate, stabilize
10. collection, determined, solidified
11. established, prepared for
set (pert to) . . .
afloat . . 6. launch
against . . 6. oppose 10. antagonize
apart . . 5. allot, elect, taboo 6. exempt
7. isolate, reserve, seclude 8. allocate,
separate 9. segregate, sequester
11. distinguish 13. differentiate
aside . . 4. void 5. annul 6. except, reject
7. abolish, discard, dismiss, earmark,
exclude 8. overrule, postpone
at an angle . . 4. cant
back . . 4. loss 5. check 6. demote,
hinder, recess 7. relapse 8. restrain,
slow down
exclusive . . 5. elect, taboo 6. clique
fire to . . 6. ignite, kindle 7. emblaze,
inflame 8. irritate
firmly . . 5. embed, plant, posit 6. cement,
ossify
forth . . 5. adorn 6. depart, expose, lay
out 7. arrange, commend, display,
enounce, exhibit, explain, expound,
present, promote, propone, publish
8. announce, decorate, indicate,
manifest 9. translate 10. promulgate
11. demonstrate
free . . 6. acquit 7. absolve, release,
unloose 8. liberate 10. emancipate
11. disillusion
off . . 6. incite, offset 7. measure

8. beautify, detonate 9. demarcate,
embellish 11. distinguish
on firm basis . . 9. establish
out . . 4. plot 5. allot, begin 7. arrange
right . . 5. teach 6. adjust, direct, remedy
11. disillusion
up . . 3. rig 4. plan 5. build, cause, erect,
exalt, hoist, print, raise 7. elevate,
finance, install 9. construct, establish
10. inaugurate, prearrange
set (pert to in) . . .
a groove . . 5. dadoe
a row . . 4. tier 5. align, aline, range
columns . . 7. tabular 8. tabulate
from margin . . 6. indent
operation . . 4. move 5. start 6. launch
opposition . . 3. pit
order . . 5. align 6. adjust 7. arrange
set (pert to of) . . .
eight . . 6. ogdoad
friends . . 7. coterie
jeweled ornaments . . 6. parure
laws . . 4. code 8. statutes
on end . . 5. upend 10. topsy-turvy
opinions . . 5. credo
organ pipes . . 5. stops
rules . . 4. code
sheets (paper) . . 5. quire
seta . . 4. hair 5. spine 7. bristle, feather
Seth (pert to) . . .
brother . . 4. Abel, Cain
father . . 4. Adam
son . . 4. Enos
wife . . 8. Nephthys
setting . . . 5. scene 6. locale 8. mounting,
planting 10. background
settle . . . 3. fix, pay 4. nest, root, seat,
sink 5. agree, clear, lodge, order, prove,
quiet, solve 6. assign, assure, decide,
locate, pay off, purify, secure, soothe
7. arrange, clarify, confirm, mediate,
resolve 8. colonize, ensconce, regulate
9. designate, determine, establish,
reconcile 10. strengthen 11. tranquilize
settled . . . 4. paid 5. ended, fixed
6. proved, sedate 7. assured, decided,
located 9. steadfast 10. unchanging
11. established
settled in advance . . . 13. predetermined
settled in mind . . . 10. equanimity
settlement . . . 3. dos 4. camp 6. colony,
hamlet 7. payment 8. fixation, sediment,
showdown 9. community, endowment
10. adjustment 12. colonization,
conciliation, satisfaction
13. determination, establishment
Settlement House . . . 9. Hull House
(Chicago) 10. University (NY)
11. Toynbee Hall (London)
settler . . . 6. Sooner (Okla) 7. pioneer,
planter, Puritan 8. colonist 9. immigrant
settlings . . . 4. lees 5. dregs 8. sediment
10. settlement 12. precipitates
seven (pert to) . . .
angles . . 8. heptagon 9. septangle
arts . . 5. logic, music 7. grammar
8. geometry, rhetoric 9. astronomy
10. arithmetic
comb form . . 5. hepta, septi
days and nights . . 8. sennight
fold . . 8. septuple

gods of happiness .. 5. Ebisu, Hotei
  6. Benten 7. Daikoku, Jurojin
  8. Bishamon 10. Fuku-roku-ju
group .. 6. heptad, septet 8. septuple
  12. septemvirate
Hills .. 4. Rome
languages .. 9. heptaglot
Latin .. 6. septum
number .. 8. hebdomad 9. septenary
Old Test Books (1st seven) ..
  10. Heptateuch
Seas .. 11. world oceans
Stars .. 8. Pleiades
tones .. 10. heptachord, heptatonic
seventy ... 12. septuagenary
seventy-day period ... 12. septuagesima
seventy-year-old ... 14. septuagenarian
sever ... 3. cut, lop 4. part, rend 5. break
  6. behead, cleave, detach, divide,
  except, exempt 7. disjoin 8. accurate,
  disunite, separate 9. interpose,
  segregate 10. decapitate, disconnect,
  dissociate 12. disassociate
several ... 4. many 6. divers, sundry
  7. diverse, various 8. distinct 9. different
  10. respective
severe ... 3. bad 4. dure, hard, keen,
  sore, tart 5. acute, cruel, exact, grave,
  harsh, rigid, snell, sober, stern 6. biting,
  bitter, chaste, sedate, simple, solemn,
  strict, taxing, trying 7. arduous, austere,
  condign, drastic, extreme, intense,
  painful, serious, violent 8. accurate,
  rigorous 9. draconian, strenuous,
  stringent 10. censorious, restrained
severe critic (of Alexandria) ...
  9. Aristarch
severity ... 5. rigor 7. cruelty 8. hardness,
  pungency, violence 9. austerity,
  exactness, gruffness, harshness,
  solemnity, sternness, stiffness
  10. bitterness, difficulty, inclemency,
  simplicity, strictness 12. rigorousness
Seville cathedral tower ... 7. Giralda
Seville orange ... 9. red-yellow 12. bitter
  orange
Sèvres blue ... 5. color 9. bleu de roi,
  porcelain 11. bleu céleste
sew ... 4. mend 5. baste, unite 6. fasten,
  needle, secure, stitch
sewan ... 5. beads, money 6. wampum
sewing ... 6. sutile 8. suturing 9. stitching
  10. needlework
sewing case ... 4. etui
sewing machine inventor ... 9. Elias
  Howe
sexagenarian ... 13. a sixty-year-old
sexagesimal ... 5. sixty
sexes, common to both ... 6. unisex
  7. epicene
sexless ... 6. neuter 7. epicene
sextet, sextette ... 6. sestet 8. six parts
  10. group of six 13. six-line stanza
sexton ... 6. beetle 7. sacrist 9. sacristan
  12. underofficer
sextuplet ... 7. sestole (sestolet) 8. six
  notes
sha ... 5. sheep, urial (oorial)
shabbaeh ... 5. bravo 6. well done
Shabbeth ... 7. Sabbath (Jew)
shabbiness ... 8. baseness, slovenry

  9. seediness
shabby ... 4. base, mean, worn 5. dowdy,
  faded, ratty, seedy, tacky, yucky
  6. grungy, paltry, ragged, scurvy,
  scuzzy, sleazy 7. outworn, shagrag,
  squalid 10. despicable, ragamuffin,
  threadbare 12. contemptible
shack ... 3. coe, hut 4. husk, plug
  5. chase, hutch, tramp 6. shanty
  7. stubble 8. vagabond 9. hibernate
shackle ... 3. tie 4. band, bind, bond,
  gyve, iron, ring 5. chain 6. fetter,
  hobble, hogtie, impede, pinion
  7. manacle, trammel 8. restrain
shackled ... 4. tied 5. bound, gyved
  6. curbed, ironed 7. hobbled 8. fettered,
  hampered, hindered, manacled
  10. restrained
shad ... 4. fish 5. Alosa 7. crappie,
  mojarra
shade ... 3. hue 4. dull, roof, tint, tone,
  veil 5. ghost, tinge, visor 6. awning,
  canopy, darken, degree, follow, nuance,
  screen, shadow, shield, sprite 7. eclipse,
  foliage, parasol, protect, shelter,
  umbrage 10. overshadow, protection
  11. adumbration
shade, affording ... 9. umbratile
shadow ... 3. dim, dog, spy 4. hide,
  tail 5. cloud, image, umbra 6. attend,
  screen 7. blacken, conceal, protect,
  remains 8. follower, hanger-on, illusion,
  penumbra 9. adumbrate, detective
  10. protection
shadow fighting ... 9. sciamachy
shadowless ... 6. ascian
Shadrach (pert to) ...
  enemy .. 14. Nebuchadnezzar
  name once .. 7. Ananias 9. Hannaniah
  one of three Hebrew youths ..
    7. Meshach 8. Abednago, Shadrach
shady ... 4. dark 5. faint, fishy 6. umbral
  7. shadowy 8. deceitful, dishonest,
  underhand 10. indistinct, unreliable
  12. questionable
shaft ... 3. pit, rod 4. axle, fust, mine, orlo
  (part), stem, tige, tole 5. arrow, scape,
  shank, spire, stalk, thill, tower, trunk
  6. column, tongue 7. feather, missile,
  obelisk 8. monument 9. flagstaff
shag ... 3. nap 4. hair, mane, pile
  5. chase, dance 6. follow, rascal
  7. tobacco 9. cormorant, make rough
  10. blackguard
shaggy ... 5. bushy, furry, nappy, rough
  6. ragged 7. hirsute, unkempt, villous
  8. confused (of thought), uncombed
  10. unpolished
shagrag ... 6. ragged, tagrag 7. unkempt
  8. rascally
shake ... 3. jar, jog, wag 4. jolt, rock,
  stir, sway, toze 5. swing, trill 6. dither,
  dodder, quiver, shimmy, shiner,
  weaken 7. agitate, flutter, shingle,
  shudder, tremble, tremolo 8. enfeeble
  10. earthquake
Shakespeare (pert to) ...
  actor .. 4. Ward 7. Gielgud, Olivier,
    Sothern 8. Modjeska
  called .. 10. Bard of Avon
  character, female .. 6. Juliet, Portia

7. Ophelia 9. Cleopatra
character, male . . 5. Romeo, Timon
6. Antony, Hamlet 7. Macbeth, Othello
8. Falstaff
forest . . 5. Arden
river . . 4. Avon
site . . 6. Verona 8. Elsinore
villain . . 4. Iago
wife . . 12. Anne Hathaway
shaky . . 6. infirm, wabbly, wobbly
7. fearful, nervous, unsound 8. agitated,
unsecure 9. tottering, trembling,
uncertain, unsettled 10. precarious,
unreliable 12. questionable
shale . . . 4. rock 5. flake, scale 8. dandruff
Shalimar Gardens . . . 6. Lahore
shallow . . . 5. shoal 6. lagoon (lagune)
7. cursory, trivial 9. depthless, frivolous,
insincere 11. superficial
sham . . . 3. ape 4. fake, hoax, mock
5. dummy, false, fraud, trick 6. deceit,
humbug 7. feigned 8. pretense
9. imitation, imposture, pretended
Shamash (pert to) . . .
centers of worship . . 5. Larsa 6. Sippar
consort . . 3. Aya (Ai)
deity (Babylon) . . 6. sun god
messenger . . 6. Bunene
Sumerian equivalent . . 3. Utu (Utug)
6. Babbar
shame . . . 5. abash 7. mortify 8. disgrace,
dishonor 9. humiliate 11. abomination,
humiliation, impropriety
shameful . . . 4. mean, vile 5. gross
6. wicked 8. flagrant, improper,
indecent, infamous, terrible
9. degrading 10. outrageous,
scandalous 11. disgraceful, ignominious
12. dishonorable, disreputable,
vituperative
shameless . . . 6. arrant, brazen
8. immodest, impudent 9. audacious
10. unblushing 11. brazenfaced
shammer . . . 8. impostor
shanghai . . . 6. abduct, to drug
9. slingshot
shank . . . 3. leg 4. crus, gamb (gambe)
7. meat cut 12. travel on foot
shape . . . 4. bend, form, mold (mould),
plan 5. frame, model 6. adjust,
create, cut out, design, devise,
figure 7. arrange, conform, contour,
develop, fashion, incline 8. phantasm
10. appearance, figuration
11. arrangement
shaped like a . . .
comb . . 9. pectinate
shield . . 7. peltate, scutate
strap, thong . . 6. lorate
urn . . 9. urceolate
shapeless . . . 7. lumpish 8. deformed,
formless 9. amorphous, contorted,
distorted, unshapely
shapely . . . 3. fit 4. neat, trim 6. comely,
gainly 10. well-formed 11. symmetrical
16. well-proportioned
shapes (ornamental, garden) . . . 5. topia
7. topiary
share . . . 3. cut, lot 4. dole, part 5. enter,
quota 6. ration 7. partake, portion
8. take part 9. allowance, apportion

11. co-operative, participate
sharecropper . . . 7. metayer
shark . . . 5. fraud 6. lawyer 8. parasite,
swindler 9. trickster
shark (fish) . . . 4. gata, mako, tope
5. lamia (cub), Rhina 6. Galeos, Galeus,
requin 7. dogfish, tiburon 8. man-
eater, Mustelus, Selachii, sharklet,
Squatina 9. porbeagle 10. Carcharias,
hammerhead 11. Carcharodon,
Galeorhinus
shark-clinger . . . 4. pega 6. remora
sharp . . . 4. acid, curt, edgy, keen, tart
5. acerb, acrid, acute, alert, brisk,
crisp, edged, harsh, quick, smart,
steep, witty 6. abrupt, astute, bitter,
crafty, shrill 7. angular, caustic,
cutting, nipping, painful, pointed,
pungent, sharper 8. incisive, poignant
9. penetrant, sagacious, sarcastic,
trenchant 10. discerning, proficient
11. acrimonious, penetrating, well-
dressed
sharp (pert to) . . .
answer . . 6. retort
blow . . 4. slap
cornered . . 7. angular
edged . . 5. arris
flavor . . 4. tang
make . . 10. caculminate
pointed . . 5. acute
saw . . 8. titmouse
Scot . . 5. snell 6. snelly
sighted . . 4. keen 6. astute 7. lyncean
sound . . 4. ping
Tuesday . . 13. Shrove Tuesday
witted . . 6. shrewd 10. discerning
11. intelligent
sharpen . . . 3. nib, ted 4. edge, hone,
whet 5. grind, point, strop 6. acuate
7. enhance, quicken 9. intensify
10. caculminate
sharper . . . 5. cheat, knave, rogue
6. keener 8. deceiver, swindler
9. trickster
shatter . . . 5. blast, break, crash, smash,
split 8. splinter
shave . . . 3. cut 4. pare 5. cheat, strip
6. cut off 7. swindle, tonsure 9. cut
prices, thin slice
shaver . . . 3. boy, lad 4. tool 5. cheat
6. barber 8. swindler 9. youngster
11. extortioner
shavetail . . . 4. mule 6. ensign
10. lieutenant
shawl . . . 5. manta 6. serape 7. paisley
8. cashmere
Shawnee (pert to) . . .
chief . . 8. Tecumseh
Indian people . . 9. Algonquin
location (present) . . 8. Oklahoma
sheaf . . . 4. kern, omer 6. bundle 7. cluster
11. hyperpencil
shear . . . 3. cut 4. clip, snip, trim 5. sever
6. fleece, remove 7. scissor, whittle
shears . . . 5. lewis 6. forfex 8. secateur
sheatfish . . . 4. wels 7. catfish
sheath . . . 4. case 5. forel (book), glove,
ocrea, theca 6. sleeve, spathe 7. stipule
8. scabbard
sheathe . . . 4. wrap 5. cover, drape

6. encase 7. envelop 8. enshroud

sheave . . . 5. wheel 6. pulley 9. back water, eccentric

shebang . . . 6. affair, boodle, outfit 7. concern 11. contrivance 13. establishment 14. kit and caboodle

she-cat . . 4. elle 9. grimalkin

shed . . . 3. hut 4. abri, cote, lair, molt 5. hovel, scale, spill 6. effuse, hangar, lean-to, slough 7. cottage, diffuse, radiate, shelter

shed (light) . . . 4. glow 7. explain, radiate 10. illuminate

shedding . . . 7. ecdysis (Zool), molting

sheen . . 5. glint, gloss, shine 6. luster 7. glitter, shimmer 8. splendor 9. shininess 10. brightness

sheep . . . 3. ewe, ram, sha, teg, tup 4. buck, lamb, Ovis, zenu 5. bidet, dumba, oudad 6. argali, cosset, gimmer, hogget, mutton, sheder, wether 8. ruminant, shearhog, yeanling 9. blackface

sheep (pert to) . . .
cry . . 3. baa 5. bleat
disease . . 3. coe, gid, rot 4. bane 5. braxy 7. anthrax
faced . . 3. shy 7. bashful 8. sheepish
female . . 3. ewe, teg 6. sheder
flock leader . . 10. bellwether
fold . . 3. ree 4. cote 5. kraal, reeve, stell 6. church
head . . 5. jimmy 8. powsowdy
headed . . 5. silly 6. stupid 12. simpleminded
kidney extract . . 5. renes
laurel . . 6. Kalmia
leg wool . . 4. gare
male . . 3. ram, tup 4. buck 5. heder 6. wether
owner's mark . . 4. smit 6. ruddle
pet . . 6. cosset
sheeplike . . 6. ovine 9. tractable
skin, leather . . 4. pelt, roan 5. basil 7. chamois, diploma 8. woolfell
stealing . . 7. abigest
tick . . 3. ked
wild . . 3. sha 4. Ovis 5. urial 6. aoudad, argali, bharal, nayaur 7. bighorn, mouflon (moufflon) 9. Thian Shan (Marco Polo's)

sheep, breeds . . . 6. Merino, Romney 7. Cheviot, Delaine, Dishley, Karakul, Suffolk, Targhee 8. Cotswold, Dartmoor 9. Kerry Hill, Leicester, Southdown, Teeswater 10. Corriedale, Dorset Horn, Oxford Down, Shropshire 13. Hampshire Down

sheepish . . 3. shy 5. timid 7. bashful 9. chagrined

sheeplike . . . 5. ovine

sheer . . . 4. mere, pure, thin, turn 5. brant, steep, utter 6. abrupt, swerve 7. deviate, unmixed 8. absolute 9. deviation, downright, undiluted 10. completely, diaphanous 11. transparent 13. perpendicular

sheet . . . 4. leaf, rope, sail 5. paper 6. shroud 9. cover with, duodecimo (12-fold), newspaper, sheathing

sheik, sheikh . . . 4. Arab 5. chief 6. prince

shelf . . . 4. berm (berme), reef, sell 5. ledge, shoal 6. mantel 7. stratum 8. postpone, put aside

shell . . . 3. pod 4. boat, bomb, husk 5. conch, crust, shard, shuck 6. cowrie (cowry) 7. bombard, capsule, grenade, missile 8. carapace, exterior, shrapnel 9. cartridge 10. projectile

shell (pert to) . . .
button source . . 5. troca 6. lorica, mucket
cone . . 7. admiral
ear . . 7. abalone
explosive . . 3. dud 4. bomb 7. grenade
fish . . 4. clam, pipi 6. cockle, limpet, mussel, oyster 7. abalone, lobster, mollusk, scallop 8. barnacle 9. trunkfish
fossil . . 8. ammonite
game . . 10. thimblerig 13. sleight of hand
marine . . 6. cowrie (cowry)
money . . 5. hawok, sewan, uhllo (ulo) 6. cowrie, wampum
out . . 4. give 6. expend, pay out
protective . . 6. lorica
ridge . . 4. lira 5. varix
seaweed . . 8. frustule
spiral . . 5. chank, whelk 8. caracole
trumpet (Triton's) . . 5. conch

shelter . . . 3. lee, lee 4. abri, camp, cote, digs, port, roof, shed, skug, tent 5. condo, cover, haven, house, hutch, shack, shade 6. asylum, burrow, dugout, hangar, harbor, refuge, screen, shield 7. defense, hospice, pillbox, protect, retreat 8. mantelet (mantlet), quarters, security 9. coverture, sanctuary 10. protection

sheltered side . . 3. lee 4. alee 7. leeward

shelve . . . 5. slope, table, waive 6. retire 7. dismiss, incline 8. postpone, put aside 10. pigeonhole

Shem (pert to) . . .
brother . . 3. Ham
descendant . . 6. Semite
father . . 4. Noah
son . . 3. Lud 4. Aram, Elam

shenanigan . . . 7. foolery 8. trickery, zaniness 9. horseplay 10. hanky-panky 11. monkeyshine

shend . . . 3. mar 4. harm, ruin 5. spoil 6. injure, revile 7. destroy, stupefy 8. confound, disgrace, reproach

Sheol . . . 4. Hell 5. Aralu, grave, Hades 6. the pit, Toppet 7. Abaddon, Gehenna 10. underworld 11. nether world 14. abode of the dead

shepherd . . . 5. guide 6. direct, escort, feeder, herder, pastor, shadow 8. guardian, herdsman 9. clergyman

shepherd, shepherds (pert to) . . .
band of . . 10. pastoureau
dog . . 5. sheep 6. collie
flute . . 7. musette 9. flageolet
god . . 3. Pan
pipe . . 3. oat 4. reed 7. larigot
spider . . 13. daddy longlegs
staff . . 4. Kent 5. crook

sheriff (pert to) . . .
aide . . 5. posse
deputy . . 6. elisor 7. bailiff
jurisdiction . . 9. bailiwick

sheriffdom .. 10. shrievalty

sherry ... 5. jerez, Xeres 7. oloroso
   8. montilla

Shetland Island (pert to) ...
   fishing grounds (deep-sea) .. 4. haaf
   kingdom of .. 8. Scotland
   land, fee simple .. 4. udal
   promontory .. 4. noup
   Supreme Court Pres .. 4. foud
   viol .. 3. gue

shewbread, showbread (Bib) ... 6. ritual
   10. unleavened

shibboleth (Bib) ... 4. mode 5. habit
   6. saying, slogan 9. criterion,
   watchword 11. peculiarity (speech)

shield ... 3. écu 4. boss, umbo 5. aegis
   (egis), armor, cover, pavis, pelta,
   scute, shade, shell, targe (anc)
   6. defend, scutum, target 7. defense,
   protect, shelter 8. insignia 9. protector
   10. escutcheon, protection

shield (pert to) ...
   Athena's .. 5. aegis (egis)
   bearer .. 8. escudero
   border .. 4. orle 7. bordure
   emblem .. 7. impresa
   French (anc) .. 8. rondache
   heraldry .. 4. enté 6. points
   part .. 4. enté, orle, umbo
   Roman .. 6. scutum
   sacred .. 6. ancile (Rom)
   shaped .. 7. peltate, scutate 8. aspidate

shift ... 3. eddy, fend, jibe, move,
   ruse, stir, tack, veer 5. shunt, smock,
   trick 6. baffle, change, device, rustle
   7. deviate, pretext, quibble 8. artifice,
   mutation, transfer 9. deviation,
   expedient, fluctuate, vacillate
   10. conversion, subterfuge
   12. redistribute 13. transposition

shifty ... 6. crafty, tricky 7. devious,
   evasive, furtive 9. deceitful, makeshift
   10. changeable 11. treacherous

shill, shillaber (circus term) ... 5. decoy
   8. employer, hanger-on 10. accomplice

shilalagh, shillaiah ... 4. club 6. cudgel
   7. sapling

shilly-shally ... 8. hesitate 9. vacillate
   10. hesitation, indecision 11. vacillation

Shiloh ... 4. town (anc) 6. Seilun (modern)
   9. sanctuary (the ark) 10. battle site
   (Tenn)

shimmy ... 5. quake 6. quiver 7. chemise,
   tremble, vibrate 9. jazz dance, vibration

shin ... 5. climb, tibia 6. cnemis 7. foreleg

shindy ... 3. row 4. lark, orgy, riot,
   romp 5. dance, party, revel, spree,
   wince 6. frolic, uproar 7. wassail
   8. carousal 9. commotion, festivity
   11. merrymaking

shine ... 3. ray 4. beam, beek, star
   5. excel, gloss, prank 6. polish
   7. furbish, glisten, glister, glitter,
   radiate, splurge 8. rutilate 9. irradiate

shiner ... 6. bruise 8. black eye
   9. bootblack 10. dollarfish

shingle ... 4. sign, wood 6. hairdo
   7. haircut, overlap 8. chastise, coiffure,
   detritus 9. signboard

shining ... 5. aglow, lucid, nitid, shiny
   6. glossy, lucent 7. beaming, glowing,

radiant 8. luminous, lustrous, nitidous,
   rutilant, splendid 9. refulgent
   10. glistening, glittering 11. illustrious,
   irradiating, resplendent

Shinto (pert to) ...
   adherent .. 9. Shintoist
   cult .. 8. Japanese
   deity .. 8. Hachiman
   temple .. 3. sha 5. jinja (jinsha) 7. yashiro
   temple gateway .. 5. torii
   temple deity .. 5. Jinja (Jinsha)

shiny ... 5. nitid, sleek 6. bright
   7. radiant, shining 8. luminous, nitidous
   9. unclouded

ship ... 3. ark 4. lade, load, send
   5. liner, tramp 6. argosy, vessel
   7. freight, steamer 9. freighter, transport
   10. watercraft

ship (pert to) ...
   abandoned .. 8. derelict
   apparatus .. 5. crane, davit, winch
     7. bollard, capstan 8. windlass
   Argonaut's .. 4. Argo
   armored .. 7. carrack, cruiser
     9. destroyer, submarine
   attendant .. 7. steward
   auxiliary .. 4. dory, life 6. dinghy (dingy),
     tender
   biscuit .. 8. hardtack 10. pilot bread
   cabin .. 6. saloon 9. stateroom
   cargo .. 5. oiler 6. tanker 7. oreboat
     11. supertanker
   deck .. 4. main, poop 5. orlop, upper
   deck, cut down .. 5. razee
   deserter .. 3. rat
   duck shooting .. 4. skag
   flat bottom .. 4. keel 5. barge
   fleet .. 6. armada
   invoice .. 8. manifest
   jail .. 4. brig
   kitchen .. 6. galley 7. caboose
   Levantine .. 4. saic
   loader .. 9. stevedore 12. longshoreman
   Mediterranean .. 5. xebec 6. galiot
     (galliot) 7. polacre
   officer .. 4. mate 6. purser 7. steward
     9. boatswain (bosun)
   one-masted .. 5. sloop
   part .. 4. brig, keel, skeg 5. stern, waist
     6. bridge, rudder 8. binnacle, taffrail
   permit to enter .. 8. pratique
   platform (boarding) .. 9. gangplank
   privateer .. 10. brigantine
   prow .. 5. prore (Poet)
   quarters .. 5. berth 8. steerage
     10. forecastle (fo'c's'le)
   record .. 3. log
   rope .. 4. line 6. hawser 7. halyard,
     lanyard, painter, ratline
   sailing .. 4. bark (barque), dhow, proa,
     saic 5. ketch, sloop, xebec 6. caique,
     cutter, galley, lugger 7. Geordie,
     pinnace, polacre
   side .. 3. lee 4. port 9. starboard
   three-oar bank .. 7. trireme
   twin-hulled .. 9. catamaran
   two-oar bank .. 6. bireme
   Venetian .. 9. frigatoon
   voyage record .. 3. log
   war .. 3. sub 7. cruiser, flattop
     9. destroyer, submarine

11. dreadnaught
window .. 4. port 8. porthole
worm .. 5. borer 6. teredo
ship, famed . . . 4. Nina 5. Maine,
Pinta 6. Bounty 7. Monitor, Titanic
8. Clermont, Half Moon, Merrimac
9. Mayflower 10. Golden Hind, Santa
Maria 12. Constitution (Old Ironsides)
15. Bonhomme Richard
shipment . . . 5. cargo 7. carload
shippage . . . 3. fee 4. levy 8. shipping
shipshape . . . 3. nef (clock) 4. neat, tidy,
trim 7. orderly
shipwreck, cargo overboard . . .
6. jetsam 7. flotsam
shire . . . 5. horse 6. county 8. district,
province 11. subdivision
shirk . . . 4. duck, pike 5. avoid, dodge,
evade, slink 7. goof off 9. fainaigue
(finagle)
shirker . . . 5. piker 6. truant 7. quitter,
slacker 8. embusqué 10. malingerer
shirt . . . 4. polo, sark 6. blouse, camisa,
cilice, skivvy, T-shirt 8. pullover
shiver . . . 5. quake, shake 6. be cold
7. shatter, shudder, tremble, vibrate
8. fragment 11. trepidation
shivering . . . 4. cold 6. creepy 7. nervous,
shaking 8. fragment 9. agitation,
twitching 10. chilliness
shoal . . . 3. bar 4. bank, reef, spit 5. crowd,
flock 6. throng 8. sand bank (shallow)
9. multitude
shock . . . 3. jar 4. blow, heap (grain),
jolt, stun 5. appal, brunt, bushy (hair),
shake, stack, start 6. appall, impact,
offend, stroke, trauma 7. disgust,
horrify, startle, terrify 8. calamity,
frighten, paralyze 9. collision, electrify
10. concussion
shock absorber . . . 7. cushion, snubber
shocking . . . 3. bad 5. awful, lurid
6. horrid 7. ghastly, hideous 8. horrible,
terrible 9. appalling, frightful, offensive,
revolting, startling 10. abominable
shoe (pert to) . . . 4. boot, clog, geta, mule,
pump 5. horse, moyle, sabot, scuff
6. ballet, bootee, brogan, buskin, gillie,
loafer, Oxford, patten, planch (planche)
sandal, secque 7. chopine, rullion,
slipper, sneaker, talaria 8. moccasin,
sabotine, solleret 10. clodhopper
shoe (pert to) . . .
form .. 4. last, tree
grip .. 5. cleat
lace .. 3. tie 5. aglet (aiglet), lacet
6. lacing 7. latchet 8. bootlace
10. shoestring
maker .. 5. sutor 7. cobbler, Crispin
(patron saint) 8. zapatero
part .. 3. cap 4. rand, vamp, welt 6. insole
7. counter 9. inner sole
shoebill, shoebird . . . 5. stork
shoemaker's patron saint . . . 7. Crispin
shogun . . . 5. chief, title (Jap) 6. tycoon
7. shikken
shoneen . . . 4. snob 5. toady
shoot . . . 3. rod 4. bine, dart, film, fine,
hunt, kill, plug, twig, weft 5. bough,
craps, eject, gemma, plant, scion,
snipe, spear, sprig, throw, tuber, vimen

6. branch, sprout, stolon 7. execute,
project 9. discharge 10. descendant,
photograph
shooting (pert to) . . .
fish .. 10. archer fish
iron .. 6. pistol 7. firearm 8. revolver
match .. 3. tir 5. skeet
objective .. 6. target
star .. 5. comet 6. meteor 7. cowslip
shop . . . 4. mart 5. burse, store 6. market,
saloon 7. atelier 8. boutique, emporium
shopping mania . . . 9. oniomania
shore . . . 4. bank, prop 5. beach,
coast, marge, playa 6. rivage, strand
7. support 9. foreshore, waterside
10. run aground, waterfront
shore (pert to) . . .
bird .. 3. ree 5. snipe 6. avocet, curlew,
plover, wading 9. Limicolae
inhabiting .. 8. littoral
pine .. 4. sand 8. tamarack 9. lodgepole
10. hack-me-tack
recess .. 3. bay 4. cove 5. bayou, inlet
short . . . 4. curt, rude 5. brief, brusk,
scant, terse 6. abrupt, scanty 7. curtate,
friable, summary 8. abridged, succinct
12. insufficient
short (pert to) . . .
and pointed .. 5. terse
and stout .. 5. dumpy 6. stocky, stodgy
8. roly-poly, thickset
essay .. 5. tract
legged .. 8. breviped
letter .. 4. chit
lived .. 9. ephemeral
stop .. 5. delay, pause 7. respite
8. interval 9. cessation
shortage . . . 4. want 6. ullage
10. deficiency 13. insufficiency
shorten . . . 3. bob, cut, lop 4. clip, dele,
dock 5. elide 6. lessen, reduce, reef in
7. abridge, curtail 8. condense, contract,
decrease, hold back 9. decurtate
10. abbreviate
shortening a syllable . . . 7. systole
shorthand . . . 5. Gregg 6. Pitman
8. Tironian (Rom) 11. stenography
12. brachygraphy, speed writing
shortly . . . 4. soon 6. curtly, not
far 7. harshly, quickly 8. abruptly
9. presently
shortsighted . . . 4. dull 6. myopic, obtuse
8. purblind 11. nearsighted
Shoshone Indian . . . 3. Ute 4. Hopi
5. Piute 7. Bannock 8. Comanche
shot . . . 4. dram 5. carom, speed 6. birdie,
bullet, gamble, pellet, ruined 7. gunfire,
missile, worn out 8. marksman,
unnerved 9. discharge 10. detonation,
photograph, projectile 11. dilapidated,
vaccination
shoulder . . . 5. carry, shelf 6. épaule
7. meat cut, scapula, support
8. buttress, omoplate
shoulder (pert to) . . .
armor .. 9. épaulière
badge, ornament .. 7. epaulet
blade .. 7. scapula 8. omoplate
comb form .. 3. omo 6. humero
inflammation .. 6. omitis 7. omalgia
of a road .. 4. berm (berme)

reference . . 7. humeral 8. scapular

shout . . . 3. cry 4. call, hoop, hoot, root, yell 5. cheer 7. acclaim 8. applause, laughter

shouting . . . 6. clamor, crying 7. calling, hooting, yelling 9. bellowing

shove . . . 4. push 5. drive, eject, elbow 6. propel, thrust

shovel . . . 4. peel, spud 5. scoop, skeet, spade 7. scooper 8. strockle 10. antler part

show . . . 4. lead 5. movie, prove, revue, teach 6. cinema, escort, evince, reveal 7. betoken, display, divulge, exhibit 8. evidence, indicate, instruct, manifest 11. demonstrate 13. demonstration

show (pert to) . . .
case (glass) . . 7. vitrine
deference . . 3. bow 6. salaam
disapproval . . 3. boo 4. hiss, pout
house . . 4. hall 5. odeum, opera 6. circus 8. coliseum, showboat
musical . . 5. revue
off . . 6. flaunt 10. grandstand
of learning . . 6. pedant
pompous . . 6. parade 7. display, pageant 9. cavalcade 10. exhibition
to a seat . . 5. guide, usher 6. escort 7. conduct
up . . 6. appear, arrive, attend, expose

shower . . . 4. bath, give, rain 6. abound 8. sprinkle

shower of meteorites . . . 6. Leonid (from Leo) 9. Andromede

showing . . .
animal remains . . 6. zootic
care . . 9. attentive, regardful 11. considerate
display . . 10. exhibition 12. presentation
envy . . 9. invidious
first . . 8. premiere
good judgment . . 6. astute 8. sensible

showy . . . 3. gay 4. arty, loud 5. gaudy 6. flashy, garish, sporty, tinsel 7. pompous 8. gorgeous, splendid, striking 9. sumptuous 12. ostentatious 13. grandiloquent

shred . . . 3. rag 4. snip 5. piece, strip 6. sliver, tatter 7. vestige 8. fragment, particle

shrew . . . 3. erd 4. tana 5. satan, scold, Sorex, vixen 6. mammal, migale, tartar 7. Blarina, outcast, villain 9. scoundrel, termagant, Xanthippe

shrewd . . . 3. sly 4. cagy, foxy, sage, wily 5. acute, canny, harsh, sharp, smart, stern 6. artful, astute, biting, clever, crafty 7. cunning, knowing, practic, sapient, subtile 8. shrewish 9. sagacious 10. discerning 11. penetrating, sharp-witted 13. perspicacious

shrewdness . . . 6. acumen 9. smartness 10. craftiness

shriek . . . 3. cry, yip 4. yell 5. laugh 6. holler, outcry, scream 7. screech

shrievalty . . . 7. sheriff (office of)

shrill . . . 4. keen, pipy 5. acute, clear, sharp 6. biting, squeak 7. screech 8. piercing, strident 11. high-pitched, penetrating

shrimp . . . 4. pink 5. dwarf, prawn

7. artemia 8. crevette 10. crustacean

shrine . . . 3. box 4. case, tomb 5. altar, chest 6. chapel, temple 8. monument 9. holy place, reliquary 10. receptacle

shrine (pert to) . . .
ancient . . 4. naos
Buddhist . . 4. tope 5. stupa 9. Amaravati
India . . 6. dagoba (dagaba) 7. chaitya
Mecca . . 5. Kaaba (Caaba) 11. Great Mosque
secret, of goddesses . . 9. anaktoron

shrink . . . 5. cower, parch, quail, rivel, wince 6. blench, cringe, flinch, huddle, recoil 7. dwindle, shrivel 8. contract, draw back 9. constrict 10. depreciate

shrinking . . . 3. coy, shy 5. timid 6. afraid 9. recoiling, sensitive 10. withdrawal 11. contraction

shrivel . . . 3. age, dry 5. parch, wizen 6. shrink, wither 11. deteriorate

shroud . . . 4. cowl, hide, mask, veil, wrap 5. cloak, cover, sheet 6. clothe, screen 7. conceal, curtain, foliage, protect 8. cerement 9. cerecloth 12. graveclothes

Shrove (pert to) . . .
cake . . 7. pancake
Sunday . . 13. Quinquagesima
tide . . 9. pre-Lenten (3 days)
Tuesday . . 9. Mardi gras 10. Pancake Day

shrub . . . 4. bush 5. plant (woody) 6. frutex 8. beverage

shrub (pert to) . . .
Adam's needle . . 5. yucca 9. lady's comb
Arabian tea, narcotic . . 3. kat
aromatic . . 3. tea 4. mint, sage 5. thyme 6. Aralia 7. jasmine (jasmin) 8. lavender, rosemary
Asian . . 5. musky 6. abelmosk
cherry . . 6. Prunus 7. Cerasus 12. laurocerasus
Chinese . . 6. Kerria
climbing . . 5. grape, liana, Vitis 8. Bignonia, clematis 14. trumpet creeper
creeping . . 5. pyxie
dogwood . . 6. aucuba, Cornus
evergreen . . 3. box, yew 4. ilex, moss, titi 5. erica, heath, pyxie, salal, savin 6. laurel, myrtle 7. jasmine, juniper 8. camellia, oleander 9. mistletoe
flowering . . 5. lilac 6. azalea, laurel 7. spiraea, syringa 10. mignonette
fragrant . . see aromatic (above)
Hawaiian . . 5. akala
Mexican . . 7. guayule 9. coyotillo
New Zealand . . 4. tutu 6. myrtle 8. ramarama
ornamental . . 8. hawthorn
parasitic . . 9. mistletoe
pea . . 5. broom
pepper . . 6. kava 8. kavakava
poisonous . . 4. tutu 5. sumac
prickly . . 5. Rubus 6. smilax 8. barberry, dewberry 9. raspberry 10. blackberry
S America . . 6. ceibo
tropical . . 4. sida, titi 5. henna 7. lantana 8. Oacaceae, tamarisk 10. frangipani (frangipane)

shrunken . . . 4. lank, thin 5. dried
6. shrunk, wasted 8. puckered, withered
9. atrophied, shriveled

shudder . . . 4. grue 5. abhor, dread,
quake 6. agrise, loathe, quiver, shiver,
tremor 7. frisson, tremble

shuffle . . . 3. mix 5. scuff, shift 6. huddle,
juggle, riffle 7. confuse, evasion,
quibble, scuffle 10. equivocate 12. walk
slovenly

shuffle off . . . 5. evade, shirk 6. put off
7. push off 10. mosey along (sl)

shun . . . 5. avoid, evade, evite 6. eschew
10. escape from 11. keep clear of
12. cold shoulder

shut . . . 3. bar 4. stop 5. close 7. close
in, exclude 8. prohibit

shut (pert to) . . .
in . . 3. hem 5. embar 6. fenced,
hemmed 7. bottled, confine, impound,
invalid, recluse 8. confined, enclosed
10. surrounded
out . . 3. ban, bar 6. defeat 7. exclude,
lockout, occlude 8. obstruct, preclude,
prohibit
up . . 3. dam, end 4. cage, pent
5. close, mewed, pen in 6. refute
7. confine, enclose 8. conclude,
imprison 9. terminate

shutter . . . 3. lid 4. gate 5. blind 6. screen
7. seclude 8. jalousie 9. diaphragm

shuttle . . . 5. train 6. looper, weaver
7. type bar 9. alternate, vacillate
10. oscillator 11. money drawer

shy . . . 3. coy, mim 4. wary 5. aloof,
dodge, throw, timid 6. demure,
modest, recoil, shrink 7. bashful,
evasive, fearful, quibble, rabbity
8. hesitant, reserved, retiring, secluded,
sheepish, skittish 9. diffident, reluctant,
shrinking 10. shamefaced, unassuming
11. distrustful, unobtrusive

Shylock (pert to) . . .
character in . . 16. Merchant of Venice
coin . . 5. ducat
daughter . . 7. Jessica
famed as . . 6. usurer 11. money lender
12. extortionist
friend . . 5. Tubal

shyness . . . 7. coyness, reserve 8. timidity
10. diffidence 11. bashfulness

Siam . . . 8. Thailand

Siamese (pert to) . . .
group . . 3. Kui, Lao
temple . . 3. wat
twins . . 9. pygopagus (joined at spine)
11. Chang and Eng

sib . . . 4. akin 5. allied 7. kinsman, related
(by blood)

Siberia . . . see also *Siberian*
city . . 7. Irkutsk 11. Novosibirsk
conqueror . . 9. Timafeyev 11. Genghis
Khan
government . . 7. Russian
gulf . . 2. Ob (Arctic)
Mongoloid . . 6. Tartar
mountains . . 4. Ural 5. Altai
people . . 5. Yakut 6. Tartar (Tatar)
7. Samoyed 9. Mongolian
plain . . 6. steppe, tundra
river . . 2. Ob, Om 4. Lena 5. Vitim
6. Abakan 7. Yenisei

squirrel . . 7. miniver

storm . . 5. buran

Siberian (pert to) . . .
antelope . . 5. saiga
hunters, fishers (people) . . 6. Giliak
(Gilyak)
mammal . . 5. sable
sled dog . . 7. Samoyed
squirrel fur . . 7. calaber (calabar)
swamp . . 5. urman
tent . . 4. yurt (yurta)
windstorm . . 5. buran (bura)

sibilate . . . 4. hiss, lisp 8. aspirate

sibling . . . 5. child

Sibyl (Gr) . . . 6. oracle 7. seeress
10. prophetess 13. fortuneteller

Sibylline Books (3) . . . 7. oracles
16. prophetic sayings (BC)

sic . . . 4. thus

siccity . . . 7. aridity, drought, dryness

sice . . . 3. six (dice) 8. sixpence

Sicilian Vespers (pert to) . . .
Bull (anc) . . 8. Phalaris
massacre of . . 6. French (1282)

Sicily . . .
aborigines . . 6. Sicani
anc name . . 7. Trinacria
capital . . 7. Palermo 8. Syracuse (anc)
composer . . 7. Bellini
harbor . . 7. Palermo
port . . 7. Messina
island . . 6. Lipari (group) 11. Pantelleria
river . . 4. Acis
secret society . . 5. Mafia
volcano . . 4. Etna 7. Vulcano 9. Stromboli
whirlpool . . 9. Charybdis

sick . . . 3. ill, sad, wan 4. pale 5. weary
6. sickly, unwell 9. disgusted, nauseated
10. indisposed

sick (pert to) . . .
be . . 3. ail
deathly . . 5. amort 7. à la mort, fatally
10. terminally
flag . . 6. yellow 10. quarantine
headache . . 8. migraine
of . . 7. tired of 8. satiated 9. disgusted
person . . 7. patient 9. aegrotant
terms . . 3. bay 7. hospice 8. syndrome
9. infirmary 10. dispensary 13. intensive
care
worker . . 5. nurse 11. nursekeeper

sicken . . . 4. tire 5. weary 6. impair,
weaken 7. afflict, depress, surfeit
8. languish 10. impoverish

sickly . . . 4. pale, sick, weak 5. faint
6. ailing, feeble, infirm, weakly
7. languid, mawkish 8. diseased
9. unhealthy

Siddhartha, Siddhattha . . . 6. Buddha

side . . . 4. face, team, wall 6. behalf,
border, region 7. faction, lateral,
support, surface 9. declivity

side (pert to) . . .
board . . 5. table 6. buffet 8. dressoir,
whiskers
by side . . 8. parallel
ditch . . 6. escarp
drum . . 5. snare
hog (salted) . . 6. flitch
kick . . 3. pal 7. comrade, partner

9. assistant 11. confederate
left . . 4. port 8. larboard
long . . 7. lateral, oblique, sloping
  8. indirect, slanting
meat . . 5. bacon 8. salt pork
of head . . 6. temple
of triangle . . 3. leg
on the side . . 5. apart
sheltered . . 3. lee 4. alee 8. windless
sidewalk salesman . . 8. pitchman
step . . 4. duck 5. dodge, evade, hedge
  6. astral, starry 7. quibble
view . . 7. profile
ways, wise . . 7. athwart, lateral
  9. laterally, obliquely
whiskers . . 9. sideburns 10. sideboards
windy . . 4. port 9. starboard
sidereal . . 6. astral, starry 7. stellar
  9. celestial
sidero (comb form) . . 4. iron
siderography . . 14. steel engraving
siderology (science of) . . 4. iron
sides, unequal . . 7. scalene
sidle . . 4. cant, edge, skew, tilt 7. advance
  (furtive)
siècle . . 3. age 7. century
siècle d'or . . 9. Golden Age
siege . . 7. besiege 8. assieger 9. besetting
  11. besiegement 12. wearying time
  13. beleaguerment
Siegfried (pert to) . . .
hero of . . 5. opera (Wagner's)
slayer . . 5. Hagen
sword . . 7. Balmung
wife . . 9. Kriemhild
Sierra Leone . . .
capital . . 8. Freetown
lingua franca . . 4. Krio
people . . 5. Mende, Temne
Sierra Nevada fog . . 7. pogonip
Sierra poet . . 13. Joaquin Miller
siesta . . 3. nap 4. lull, rest 6. cat nap,
  midday, snooze 10. forty winks
sieve . . 3. lue 4. bolt, sift, sile 5. purée
  6. bolter, filter, riddle, semmet, sifter,
  sorter, strain 7. dilluer 8. strainer
  9. segregate, separator
sievelike . . 8. cribrate
Sif (Norse), (pert to) . . .
goddess of . . 4. home
wife of . . 4. Thor
sift . . 3. lue 4. bolt 5. sieve 6. dredge,
  filter, riddle, screen, sorter, winnow
  7. refiner 8. cribrate
sigh . . 3. sob 5. mourn, sithe, yearn
  6. bemoan, bewail, exhale, grieve,
  lament 7. deplore 10. lament over
  11. suspiration
sight . . 3. see 4. espy, gaze, view
  5. scene, sense 6. behold, descry,
  vision 7. discern, display 8. aperture
  10. exhibition 11. observation
sight (pert to) . . .
acuteness of . . 7. oxyopia
come into . . 4. loom 5. issue
disorder . . 7. anopsia 8. paropsis
imaginary . . 6. vision
offensive . . 7. eyesore
out of . . 5. range 6. absent 8. vanished
  9. invisible 10. exorbitant
  11. disappeared

second . . 3. ESP 7. psychic
sigil . . . 4. seal 5. image (magic), stamp
  8. sigillum 9. signature 11. endorsement
sigmoid . . . 3. ess 5. curve 9. intestine
sign . . . 3. cue, nod 4. code, hire,
  mark, neon, omen 5. token, trace
  6. emblem, engage, intone, motion,
  notice, signal, symbol 7. endorse,
  execute, insigne, portent, presage,
  symptom, vestige, warning 8. evidence,
  password 9. semaphore, subscribe,
  watchword 10. forerunner, indication,
  underwrite 11. countersign
  13. advertisement, constellation
sign (pert to) . . .
astrological . . 5. Aries 6. Gemini, Pisces,
  Taurus 8. Aquarius 9. Capricorn
  11. Sagittarius
briefly . . 7. initial
by the same . . 8. likewise, moreover
  11. accordingly
diacritical . . 5. tilde 7. cedilla
language . . 11. dactylology
music . . 5. presa
off . . 8. withdraw 10. Yours truly
  11. discontinue
ref to . . 5. semic 7. semeion
representing a word . . 8. logogram
spiritual . . 9. sacrament
up . . 4. join 6. enlist 8. register
zodiac . . see *astrological (above)*
signal . . . 3. cue 4. code, fire, flag,
  sign 5. alarm, flare, token 6. beacon,
  emblem, notify, wigwag 7. eminent,
  lantern, notable, warning 8. striking
  9. memorable, prominent, semaphore,
  watchword 10. lighthouse, remarkable
  11. communicate, conspicuous
  13. extraordinary
signal (pert to) . . .
aviator's . . 5. roger
danger, warning . . 4. bell 5. alert, fusee
flag . . 6. ensign, wigwag
night . . 6. beacon, curlew, pharos
  10. lighthouse
preceding taps . . 6. tattoo
railroad . . 5. fusee 9. semaphore
signature . . . 4. mark, sign, visa (vise)
  5. prima, sigil, stamp 6. signum
  9. autograph 11. endorsement
signed by writer . . . 9. onomatous (opp
  of anonymous)
signet . . . 4. mark, seal 5. sigil, stamp
  9. signature 10. impression
  11. endorsement
significance . . . 6. import, moment,
  weight 7. anagoge, meaning
significant . . . 4. sign 5. token 6. symbol
  7. ominous 8. sinister 9. important,
  momentous 10. expressive, indicative,
  meaningful, portentous, suggestive
  13. consequential
signification . . . 6. import 7. meaning
  10. indication 11. consequence
  12. notification 13. comprehension,
  specification
signify . . . 4. hint, mean, sign 5. imply,
  utter 6. denote, import, matter, signal
  7. betoken, connote, declare, specify
  8. announce, evidence, foreshow,
  indicate, intimate, manifest

11. communicate

signum ... 4. bell (tower), mark, sign
5. cross 9. signature

sika ... 4. deer

sike ... 4. rill 5. brook, ditch, gully
6. ravine, stream, trench

sikhara, sikhra ... 5. tower (pyramidal)

silage ... 4. feed 6. fodder 9. pasturage,
provender

Silas (pert to) ...
Bib .. 7. prophet 8. Silvanus
character .. 4. Wegg
companion of .. 4. Paul (Bib)
novel .. 11. Silas Marner

sile ... 3. fry 4. beam, drip, drop, fall,
flow, pass, pour, sink, skim 5. cheat,
cover, glide, sieve, spawn 6. betray,
filter, strain, stream 7. conceal, deceive,
herring (young), subside 8. strainer

silence ... 3. gag 4. hush, kill, lull, mute,
rest 5. quiet, shush, still, tacet 6. defeat,
muffle 7. confute, repress, secrecy
8. oblivion, preclude, restrain, suppress
9. eliminate, stillness 10. silentness
11. taciturnity 13. noiselessness, tacit
omission

silent ... 3. mum 4. mute, tace 5. quiet,
still, tacet, tacit 8. reserved, reticent,
taciturn 9. soundless 10. speechless
11. unexpressed 15. uncommunicative

silhouette ... 6. shadow 7. contour,
outline, picture, profile 8. delineate,
hourglass

silica ... 4. opal 5. silex

silicate ... 4. mica 8. calamine, wellsite

silk (pert to) ...
ancient .. 6. Mantua, sendal
artificial .. 5. nylon, rayon
Assam .. 4. eria
black .. 5. crape (mourning), crepe
brown .. 4. muga 6. tussah
corded .. 6. faille 7. Ottoman
embroidery thread .. 5. floss 8. arrasene
fiber .. 5. floss
gland .. 9. serictery
gland of .. 7. spiders 9. silkworms
11. insect larva 12. caterpillars
gold .. 4. tash 6. samite 7. brocade
heavy .. 4. crin
kind of .. 5. China, crepe, moiré, ninon,
satin, surah, tabby, tulle 6. pongee,
tobine, tussah 7. taffeta
lining .. 8. sarcenet (sarsenet)
muslin .. 16. mousseline de soie
raw .. 5. marabout
rustle of .. 6. scroop
source .. 6. cocoon
thin, glossy .. 7. alamode
thread (for velvets) .. 4. tram (trame)
unspun .. 6. sleave
upholstery .. 7. tabaret
waste .. 4. noil 6. strass
watered .. 5. moiré
yarn .. 4. tram 7. schappe
yarn size .. 6. denier

silken ... 6. seric, silby, sleek, suave
6. gentle, smooth, tender 7. elegant
8. delicate, lustrous, silklike 9. luxurious
10. effeminate 12. ingratiating

silkworm (pert to) ...
Assam .. 3. eri 4. eria

China .. 6. pernyi 9. Ailanthus
cocoon .. 4. clew
disease .. 7. pebrine
genus (moth) .. 6. Bombyx
India .. 6. tussah
Japan .. 7. yamamai

silky ... 4. soft 5. quiet 6. glossy, smooth
8. delicate 9. sericeous 11. filamentary
12. ingratiating

silky fabric ... 6. barège

sill ... 4. base, beam, seat, sile 5. basis
6. timber 9. threshold 10. foundation

silly ... 3. mad 4. daft, fond 5. anile, apish,
dazed, dense, inane 6. dottle, simple
7. asinine, fatuous, foolish, shallow,
trivial 9. brainless 10. indiscreet
12. simple-minded

silver ... 2. Ag 4. gray 5. metal, money,
plate, white 6. argent 7. bullion
8. argentum, eloquent, metallic, sterling

silver (pert to) ...
alchemy .. 4. luna 6. occamy
alloy .. 6. billon
ball .. 4. pome
coin .. 6. tester
containing .. 5. lunar
German .. 6. albata
gilded .. 7. vermeil
ingots .. 5. sycee
jackal .. 9. silver fox
lace (with gold) .. 6. orris 8. filigree
leaf .. 4. foil 8. hardhack 9. hydrangea,
jewelweed 12. buffalo berry
oak .. 11. flannelbush
tongued .. 7. musical 8. eloquent
uncoined .. 7. bullion

silversides ... 5. smelt 6. minnow
12. silver salmon

Silver State ... 6. Nevada

silverware ... 5. vases 6. dishes
8. flatware 9. ornaments, tableware

silvery ... 7. frosted, musical 8. lustrous,
metallic 9. argentine

simian ... 3. ape 4. monkey 7. apelike

similar ... 4. akin, like, such 5. alike
7. uniform 8. analogic 9. analogous
11. homogeneous

similarity ... 7. analogy 8. likeness
11. homogeneity, resemblance
13. approximation

simile ... 8. allegory, metaphor

simper ... 5. smirk 10. silly smile
13. affected smile

simple ... 4. easy, mere 5. naive
6. dorian, oafish 7. artless 8. innocent
9. ingenuous 10. elementary 11. open
and shut 15. unsophisticated

simpleton ... 3. ass, daw, oaf 4. boob,
dolt, dupe, fool, gaby, gawk, gump,
simp, zang 5. dunce, goose, idiot, ikona,
moron, Simon 6. dawkin,
gander, nitwit 7. half-wit 8. Abderite
9. greenhorn 10. nincompoop
11. Simple Simon

simplicity ... 6. purity 7. modesty, naiveté
9. clearness, ignorance, innocence,
plainness, rusticity 10. homeliness,
humbleness, simpleness 11. gullibility,
informality 13. ingenuousness
14. unaffectedness

simplify ... 7. clarify, explain, expound

9. elucidate, interpret

simply . . . 5. alone, truly 6. barely, easily, merely, purely, really, solely 7. plainly 10. informally

simulate . . . 3. act, ape 4. sham 5. feign 6. affect, assume 7. imitate 11. counterfeit

simulated . . . 4. aped, sham 5. acted 7. assumed, feigned, shammed 9. pretended 10. fictitious

simurgh, simurg (Myth) . . . 3. roc 12. gigantic bird

sin . . . 3. err 4. evil, vice 5. crime, error, guilt, wrong 6. felony, heresy 7. offense 8. iniquity, peccancy 9. deviation 10. immorality, wickedness 11. misdemeanor 13. transgression

Sinai (pert to) . . .
  famed for . . 5. Moses 15. Ten Commandments
  location . . 6. Red Sea 11. Gulf of Aqaba (Akaba)
  mountain (Bib) . . 5. Horeb 6. Serbal 9. Catharine, Umm Shomer

sinapis . . . 7. mustard

sinawa . . . 10. Ceylon hemp

sinay bean . . . 8. rice bean

since . . . 2. as 3. ago, for 4. ergo, gone, past, syne 5. hence, later 7. already, because, whereas 8. inasmuch, until now 9. therefore, thereupon 10. seeing that 11. considering 12. subsequently

sincere . . . 4. open, pure 5. frank 6. candid 7. correct, earnest, genuine, intense, unmixed, upright, zealous 9. authentic, unfeigned, veracious 10. unaffected 11. unvarnished 13. unadulterated 15. straightforward

sincerity . . . 4. zeal 6. candor 7. honesty 10. heartiness 11. genuineness, sincereness

sincerity symbol . . . 8. amethyst

sind . . . 5. rinse 6. drench, quench 7. rinsing

Sind (Ind) . . .
  capital . . 7. Karachi
  ibex . . 8. wild goat
  prince . . 5. ameer

Sindbad's bird . . . 3. roc

Sindbad the Sailor . . . 9. character (Arabian Nights)

sindico . . . 7. trustee 8. assignee, receiver

sine . . . 7. without

sinew . . . 4. thew 5. nerve, power 6. muscle, string, tendon

sinewy . . . 4. firm, wiry 5. thewy, tough 6. brawny, strong 7. fibrose, stringy 8. powerful, vigorous

sinful . . . 3. bad 4. evil 5. wrong 6. wicked 7. vicious 10. iniquitous 11. unrighteous

sing . . . 3. hum, say 4. hymn, lilt 5. carol, chant, croon, yodel 6. intone, warble 7. rejoice 8. proclaim, vocalize 9. celebrate

sing (pert to) . . .
  exultantly . . 4. lilt 7. chortle 10. cheerfully
  jovially . . 5. troll
  off key . . 4. flat
  or whistle . . 7. tweedle
  shrilly . . 4. pipe
  softly . . 5. croon

---

  sorrowfully . . 7. despond 8. complain

Swisslike . . 5. yodel
  with trills . . 6. warble 7. roulade

singe . . . 4. burn, sear 6. scorch 8. discolor

singer . . . 4. bard, bird, diva, poet 5. blues, siren, tenor, torch 6. cantor, hymner 7. caroler, crooner, warbler, yodeler 8. minstrel, songster, vocalist 9. chanteuse, descanter 10. cantatrice, prima donna 11. minnesinger

Singhalese tree . . . 4. poon 5. domba

singing (pert to) . . .
  birds . . 6. Oscine
  canary . . 10. white whale
  fish . . 8. toadfish
  group . . 5. choir 6. chorus
  Memnon . . 9. Amenhotep (statue)
  ref to . . 5. melic

single . . . 3. ace, odd, one 4. lone, only, sole, unit 6. simple, unique 8. sporadic 9. unmarried

single (pert to) . . .
  algebra . . 6. nomial
  comb form . . 3. uni
  odd . . 7. azygous
  racing term . . 4. heat
  tones (one of two) . . 10. monotonous

singleness . . . 5. unity 8. celibacy 9. sincerity, unmarried

singly . . . 4. once, only, solo 5. alone, apart 6. simply 8. uniquely 9. severally 12. individually, particularly, single-handed

singular . . . 3. odd 4. each, rare, sole, unit 5. queer 6. unique 7. eminent, special, strange, unusual 8. peculiar, separate, uncommon 9. eccentric, fantastic, whimsical 10. individual, remarkable, unexampled 11. exceptional 12. unparalleled 13. extraordinary, unprecedented 14. characteristic

singularity . . . 6. oddity 7. oddness, oneness 8. peculiar 11. peculiarity 12. eccentricity 13. individuality 15. distinctiveness

Sinic . . . 7. Chinese, Sinitic

sinister . . . 4. evil, grim, left 7. adverse, corrupt, ominous 8. dishonest, injurious, malicious, underhand 10. disastrous, portentous 11. unfortunate

sinistral . . . 7. baneful 10. left-handed 12. illegitimate, inauspicious (opp of dextral)

sink . . . 3. age, bog, dip, ebb, sag 4. cave, drop, fall, mire, sump 5. drain, droop, lapse, lower, quail 6. cavity, deject, engulf, go down, recede, settle, sicken, weaken 7. decline, depress, descend, despond 8. decrease, diminish, submerge 10. degenerate

sinuous . . . 4. wavy 7. winding 9. deviating, intricate 10. circuitous

Sioux (pert to) . . .
  division . . 5. Teton 6. Santee
  famed as . . 8. warriors
  people . . 3. Oto (Otoe) 4. Crow, Iowa 5. Omaha, Osage 6. Dakota, Plains 9. Winnebago

sip . . . 3. lap, sup 4. gulp 5. drink, quaff, taste 6. tipple

sircar ... 5. ruler 6. master 7. servant 8. province (Mogul) 10. government

sire ... 5. beget

siren ... 5. alarm, Circe, deity, lurer, vixen 7. charmer, enticer, foghorn, Lorelei, mermaid 9. bewitcher, Cleopatra, temptress

Sirenia ... 6. dugong, mammal 7. manatee 14. Steller's sea cow

siriasis ... 9. sunstroke

Sirius ... 4. star 7. Dog Star 10. Canis Major, dog of Orion (Gr Myth)

sissy ... 5. softy 6. prissy, sister 10. effeminate, pantywaist 11. mollycoddle

sister ... 3. kin, nun, sib 5. nurse, soror

sisterhood ... 4. nuns 8. sorority

Sistrurus ... 11. rattlesnake

sit ... 3. fit 4. isle, loll, pose, rest 5. brood, perch, press, roost, squat 6. repose 7. convene 8. incubate

site ... 4. ruin, seat 5. place, scene, venue 6. locale, locate 8. location, position

site of Taj Mahal ... 4. Agra (Ind)

sitting ... 4. seat 5. séance, sedent 7. posture, sessile, session 10. incubation 11. convocation

situated ... 3. lie, set 4. case, seat 5. fixed 6. clutch, placed, plight 9. ensconced, stationed 11. established

situated (pert to) ...
at back .. 6. astern 7. postern 9. posterior
at base .. 5. basal
between folds .. 11. interplical
in middle .. 6. medial, median
on left hand .. 9. sinistrad
on right hand .. 6. dexter

situation ... 3. job 4. case, post 5. place, situs, state 6. office, plight 7. station 8. locality, location, position 9. condition, placement

situation (pert to) ...
approximate .. 11. whereabouts
difficult .. 6. scrape 7. dilemma 8. quandary 9. imbroglio 11. predicament 12. circumstance
doomed .. 7. rattrap
favorable .. 7. vantage
Latin .. 5. situs
perplexing .. 6. strait
three choices .. 8. trilemma

Siva, Shiva (pert to) ...
consort .. 3. Uma 4. Devi
dancer .. 8. Natajara
god, deity .. 8. Hinduism 9. Destroyer
title .. 8. Mahadeva
trident .. 6. trisul (trisula)

six (pert to) ...
balls (Medici) .. 5. palle
dice number .. 4. sice
eyed .. 9. senocular
feet of earth .. 5. grave
fold .. 8. sextuple
footed .. 7. hexaped 9. hexapodal
group .. 5. hexad
lines .. 6. sestet 7. sextain
pence .. 6. bender 7. fiddler
pert to .. 6. senary
pointed figure .. 4. star
square .. 9. hexagonal

sixty, sixties ... 5. cycle, saros 7. numeral

size ... 3. cap 4. area, bulk, pica, pope, pott 5. agate, grade 6. adjust 7. arrange, measure, portion 8. classify 9. magnitude 10. gargantuan 11. measurement

sizzle ... 3. fry 4. hiss 5. speed 7. be angry 10. effervesce

sjambok ... 4. flog, whip

skate ... 3. jag, ray (fish) 4. plug, skim 5. glide, horse, scull, spree

skean ... 4. dirk 6. dagger

skedaddle ... 4. boit, flee, flit 6. scurry 7. run away, scamper

skein ... 3. rap (120 yds), web 4. hank, yarn 6. thread 7. spireme 12. flight of fowl

skelder ... 5. cheat 7. vagrant 9. panhandle

skeleton ... 4. cage 5. bones, frame, mummy 6. sketch 7. contour, diagram, outline 8. thinness 9. framework

skeleton (pert to) ...
at the feast .. 7. kill-joy 10. wet blanket 11. crapehanger
English dialect .. 4. reme
framework .. 5. cadre
in the closet .. 4. evil 6. secret 13. mortification
key .. 6. master
marine animal .. 6. sponge
polyp .. 5. coral

skeptic, sceptic ... 7. doubter, infidel 8. aporetic 10. Pyrrhonist, unbeliever 11. freethinker, irreligious, nullifidian

skeptical, sceptical ... 8. doubtful, doubting 11. incredulous, unbelieving

sketch ... 3. jap, jot 4. draw, idea, limn, plan, skit 5. draft, trace 6. apercu, design 7. diagram, drawing, outline 8. esquisse, treatise 9. delineate 11. delineation, description

sketchy ... 5. rough, vague 10. unfinished

skewer ... 3. pin, rod 5. truss 6. fasten, pierce 9. brochette

skid ... 4. clog, shoe, slip, trig 5. brake, check, slide 7. travois 8. sideslip

skiff ... 4. boat, skim 5. canoe, glide, graze 6. caique 7. rowboat 11. slight touch

skill ... 3. art 5. craft, knack 6. gifted, talent 7. ability, address, aptness, cunning, finesse, mastery 8. aptitude, deftness, facility 9. adeptness, dexterity, expertise, readiness, smartness 10. adroitness, cleverness, proficient 11. proficiency

skilled ... 5. adept 6. expert 7. endowed, trained 8. talented 10. conversant, proficient

skilled (pert to) ...
in government .. 9. statesman
in mechanics .. 5. sloyd
in strategy .. 7. finesse

skillful, skilful ... 3. apt 4. able, deft, fine 6. adroit, clever, crafty, daedal, expert 7. capable 8. artistic, dextrous, tactical 9. daedalian, dexterous, ingenious 10. proficient, well-versed 12. accomplished

skim ... 4. flit, sail, scan, scud 5. glide, graze, scoon, skirr 6. slight 8. pass over

skin ... 4. bark, derm, fell, flay, hide, pare, peel, pelt, rind, scum 5. cheat, cutis, derma, fraud, scalp 6. fleece, lamina, scrape 7. callous, cuticle, defraud, swindle 8. covering, tegument 9. epidermis 10. integument 11. decorticate

skin (pert to) ...
animal .. 4. coat, hide, pelt 7. pellage
animal's neck fold .. 6. dewlap
beaver .. 4. plew
comb form .. 4. derm 5. derma
decoration .. 6. tattoo
destitute of .. 8. apellous
disease .. 4. acne 5. hives, mange, uredo 6. eczema, herpes, tetter 8. ringworm 9. urticaria
drying frame .. 5. herse
dryness .. 7. xerosis
fawnskin (of Dionysus) .. 6. nebris
fold .. 5. plica 6. dewlap
fruit .. 7. epicarp
gobbler's throat .. 3. tar
layer .. 5. cutis, derma
layer, outer .. 7. epicarp
opening .. 4. pore
pert to .. 6. dermal 7. dermoid
piece .. 5. blype
pigment, excess .. 8. melanism
protuberance .. 4. mole, wart
salting bin .. 5. kench
squirrel .. 4. vair
tan .. 3. taw
tanned .. 5. suede
unsheared .. 8. woolfell

skinflint ... 5. cheat, miser 9. bargainer
skink ... 4. adda 6. lizard
skinned ... 6. bested 7. euchred, fleeced
skinned (pert to) ...
dark .. 7. melanic, swarthy
pert to .. 5. bared 7. denuded 8. stripped
slang .. 7. euchred, fleeced
thick .. 9. pachyderm 11. pachydermic
skinny ... 4. lean, thin 5. scant 6. stingy 8. skinlike 9. emaciated, niggardly
skip ... 3. dap 4. gait, jump, leap, omit 5. bound, caper, elide, frisk, salto, vault 6. gambol, lackey, spring 7. abscond 8. ricochet
skipjack ... 3. fop 4. pike 5. saury 6. bonito 7. bounder, parvenu, upstart 8. bluefish, sailboat 9. stripling (conceited) 10. butterfish 14. snapping beetle
skipper ... 5. saury 6. locust, maggot, master, serang 8. skipjack 9. butterfly 11. grasshopper
ski race (obstacle) ... 6. slalom
ski resort ... 4. Vail 5. Aspen
skirling ... 5. trout 6. salmon
skirmish ... 4. fray 5. brush, clash, melee 6. combat 8. conflict, flourish 9. encounter 10. velitation
skirt ... 5. dress, evade, woman 6. border, edging, fringe 8. appendage, baseboard, periphery, petticoat 10. pass around, saddle part
skirt (pert to) ...
armor .. 5. tasse (tace) 7. lamboys
attached to blouse .. 6. peplum

chaser .. 9. libertine 11. philanderer
dance .. 6. ballet
short .. 4. kilt
skit ... 4. joke, play 5. caper 6. parody, shower, sketch
skittish ... 3. coy, shy 5. jumpy 6. fickle, frisky, tricky 7. bashful 8. unstable, volatile 9. excitable 10. capricious 13. irresponsible
skittles ... 4. game, play 8. ninepins 9. enjoyment (not all beer and skittles)
skoal ... 5. toast 10. salutation 11. exclamation 14. pledge of health
skulk ... 4. lurk 5. cower, dodge, hedge, sneak 8. malinger
skull ... 4. bean, head, mind 5. brain 7. cranium, harnpan 8. brain box
skull (pert to) ...
cap .. 6. beanie 7. calotte 9. zucchetto 10. berrettino
cavity .. 5. fossa
measure .. 11. craniometer
monk's .. 6. pileus
operation .. 6. trepan
part .. 4. inion 6. bregma 7. calotte, occiput
ref to .. 5. inial 6. cranic 7. cranial
science of .. 10. craniology
skull and crossbones ... 5. death (symb) 10. danger sign
skunk ... 5. zoril 6. defeat 7. fitchew, polecat, stinker 8. conepate (conepati), zorrillo 9. scoundrel
sky ... 4. blue 5. ether, vault 6. caelum, canopy, heaven, welkin 7. heavens, the blue 8. empyrean 9. firmament 10. blue yonder
sky (pert to) ...
color .. 4. blue 5. azure 7. celeste 8. cerulean
god .. 3. Anu
lark .. 5. pipit 6. Alauda, frolic 7. titlark
light .. 6. window 8. abatjour
lure .. 7. horizon
parlor .. 5. attic 6. garret
pilot .. 8. chaplain 9. clergyman 10. missionary
serpent .. 3. Ahi
slab ... 3. mud 4. tile 5. board, dalle, plank, slime 6. lamina, ledger, pillar (stone), puddle 7. portion 8. monument 9. flagstone
slab (pert to) ...
grave .. 5. stele (stela)
marble .. 5. dalle 6. tablet
slablike .. 6. stelar
slack ... 3. lax 4. lull, slow 5. chaff, inert, let up, loose, shirk, tardy 6. abated, remiss 7. relaxed 8. careless, dilatory, inactive, indolent, sluggish 9. reluctant, secondary 10. diminished, inadequate 11. inattentive
slacken ... 5. abate, delay, relax 6. loosen, reduce, repose, retard 7. let down, relieve 8. hold back
slackening of strained relations ... 7. detente (Internat)
slag ... 4. lava 5. dross 6. cinder, scoria 7. residue 9. recrement 11. agglomerate
slain ... 4. dead 5. fallen, killed 8. murdered 12. assassinated

slake . . . 4. cool, sate 5. abate, allay, slack 6. quench 7. assuage, crumble, hydrate, refresh, relieve, satisfy, slacken 8. decrease, mitigate, moderate 10. extinguish 12. disintegrate

slam . . . 4. bang, blow, give, shut, vole 5. abuse, score 6. impact 9. criticism, criticize

slander . . . 5. belie, libel, smear 6. defame, malign, vilify 7. asperse, blacken, distort, traduce 8. derogate, disgrace, reproach 10. defamation, scandalize 12. misrepresent

slang . . . 4. cant 5. argot 6. jargon, patois 7. hep talk 10. vernacular

slant . . . 4. bend, cant, skew 5. angle, bevel, slope 6. aslant, aspect, biased, glance 7. incline, opinion 8. attitude, occasion 9. obliquely, viewpoint 10. hypotenuse 11. inclination, opportunity

slap . . . 3. hit 4. blow, clap, cuff, snub 5. crack, skelp, sound, twank 6. buffet, rebuff, slight, strike 8. chastise 12. chastisement

slash . . . 3. cut 4. gash, lash, slit 5. marsh, sever 6. attack, reduce, stripe 7. censure, scourge 8. price cut 9. criticize, reduction

slate . . . 4. list, rock 5. color, scold, sculp 6. ballot, enroll, record, roster, tablet, thrash 7. censure, roofing, writing 8. register, schedule, slattern 9. criticize, reprimand

slate (pert to) . . .
ax . . 7. mattock
black . . 4. gray
blue . . 9. Swiss blue
gray . . 7. Russian 9. red-yellow 10. sandy beige 13. oriental pearl
roof . . 3. rag
tool . . 3. zax 7. scantle

slater . . . 6. critic 7. hellier

slattern . . . 4. slut 5. frump, idler, mopsy 6. sloppy 7. trifler, trollop 8. careless, slovenly 9. litterbug

slaughter . . . 4. kill, slay 6. battue, murder, pogrom 7. butcher, carnage, killing 8. butchery, hecatomb, massacre, occision 9. bloodshed 10. butchering 11. destruction

slaughterhouse . . . 8. abattoir, Aceldama, butchery, matadero, shambles 9. stockyard 12. field of blood

Slav . . . 4. Pole, Slav, Sorb, Wend 5. Croat, Czech 6. Slovak 7. Russian, Serbian, Servian 8. Bohemian, Croatian, Moravian 9. Bulgarian

slave . . . 4. boor, esne, peon, serf 5. chela, helot, thane 6. drudge, lascar, minion, thrall, vassal 7. bondman, captive, chattel, enslave, odalisk, servant 8. slave ant 9. bondslave

slave (pert to) . . .
block (selling) . . 7. catasta
born . . 4. neif
comedy (stock name) . . 5. Davus
dealer . . 5. bichy, mango (obs)
Eleusinian (Gr Relig) . . 5. Baubo, lambe
female . . 9. concubine, odalisque (odalisk)

free . . 5. thane (thegn)
fugitive . . 8. marooner
Indian . . 10. Athapascan
The Tempest . . 7. Caliban

slavery . . . 4. bond 7. bondage, service 8. drudgery 9. captivity, servitude, thralldom, vassalage 11. enslavement 12. enthrallment

Slave States . . . 5. Texas 7. Alabama, Florida, Georgia 8. Arkansas, Delaware, Kentucky, Maryland, Missouri, Virginia 9. Louisiana, Tennessee 11. Mississippi 13. North Carolina, South Carolina

slay . . . 4. kill 5. amuse, burke, knock, lynch, smite 6. murder, strike 7. butcher, destroy 9. slaughter 10. annihilate 11. assassinate, destroy life, exterminate

slayer . . . 6. killer 8. criminal, murderer, regicide, vaticide 9. matricide, patricide 10. fratricide, sororicide

sleave . . . 4. sley 5. floss 6. tangle 8. separate 9. floss silk 11. disentangle 13. untwisted silk

sled . . . 4. luge, pung 6. sledge, sleigh, travoy, troika 8. toboggan

sledge . . . 4. sled 6. hammer, sleigh, strike 7. seven-up (game), vehicle

sleep . . . 3. nap, nod 4. dorm, doss, doze, wink 5. death, sopor 6. drowse, snooze, somnus 7. slumber 10. narcolepsy, somnipathy 11. hibernation

sleep (pert to) . . .
comb form . . 5. somni
deep . . 6. stupor 8. lethargy 10. narcolepsy
dreaming stage . . 3. REM
hypnotic . . 10. somnipathy
inducing . . 5. dwale 6. opiate, potion 8. sedative 9. soporific 10. anesthesia, belladonna
insensible . . 4. coma
midday . . 6. siesta
prolonged . . 5. sopor
upon . . 8. consider, postpone

sleeper . . . 3. tie 4. beam 6. rafter, rester, timber 7. Pullman, reposer, support 8. dormouse 9. slumberer 10. slow seller 11. sleeping car

sleeping . . . 4. dead 5. inert 6. asleep, latent 7. dormant 8. dormient, inactive 9. quiescent 10. quiescence 11. inattentive

sleeping (pert to) . . .
pill . . 9. soporific
place . . 3. bed, cot 4. bunk, doss 5. berth, couch 6. pallet 7. cubicle 9. dormitory
sickness . . 6. nagana, tsetse 9. lethargus

sleepwalking . . . 8. neurosis 12. nightwalking, somnambulism

sleepy . . . 4. dull 5. tired 6. drowsy 8. soporose 9. lethargic, somnolent 11. somniferous

sleeve . . . 3. arm 5. gigot (leg-ó-mutton) 10. copper tube 14. British channel

sleigh . . . 4. pung 6. cutter

sleight of hand performer . . . 4. mage 8. magician 14. legerdemainist 15. prestidigitator

slender . . . 4. lank, lean, slim, thin 5. gaunt, lanky, leger, reedy 6. lissom, narrow, svelte 7. gracile, tenuous, trivial, willowy 9. elongated

slender pinnacle . . . 3. epi

sleuth . . . 6. tracer 8. hawkshaw 9. detective, sleuthdog 11. sleuthhound 12. investigator

slice . . . 3. cut, saw 4. gash, slab 5. piece, share, shave 6. rasher, sliver, stroke 7. portion 8. golf term, splinter 12. cross section

slick . . . 4. neat, tidy 5. alert, sleek, smart 6. clever, smooth 8. slippery, unctuous 9. first-rate, lubricate 10. glistening 12. accomplished

slide . . . 3. ski 4. rule, skid, slip, slue 5. chute, clasp, glide, plane (sloping), scoot, skate 6. elapse 7. lantern, slither 8. toboggan 9. avalanche 11. deteriorate

slight . . . 3. cut 4. defy, rare, snub, thin 5. faint, frail, leger, minor, oligo (comb form), scorn, small 6. flimsy, ignore, little, meager 7. disdain, fragile, neglect, nominal, scantly, shallow, trivial 8. contempt, delicate 9. disregard, indignity 10. immaterial 11. unimportant 13. imperceptible, unsubstantial 14. inconsiderable

slight (pert to) . . .
convexity . . 6. camber
sound . . 4. peep
variation . . 6. nuance 7. shading

slightest . . . 5. least 6. barest

slightly (pert to) . . .
damaged paper . . 6. retree
sour . . 8. acescent
tapering . . 6. terete

slim . . . 3. sly 4. lean, mean, thin 5. small, spare 6. adroit, scanty, sparse, svelte 7. slender, tenuous 9. worthless

slime . . . 3. mud 4. ooze 5. filth, gleet 6. mucous

slip . . . 3. err, pew, sin 4. dock, fail, pier, skid, slue 5. boner, cover, error, fault, glide, lapse, slide, strip 6. bungle, elapse 7. blunder, cutting, failure, faux pas, misdeed, mistake, slither 9. youngling 10. pillowslip 12. undergarment 13. transgression

slipknot . . . 5. noose

slipper . . . 4. mule, neap, shoe 5. apron, moyle, Romeo 6. pinson, sandal 7. scuffer 8. babouche (baboosh), covering

slippery . . . 3. sly 4. eely, glib 5. slick 6. crafty, fickle, shifty, tricky, wanton 7. cunning, elusive, evasive 8. unctuous, unstable 9. deceitful, uncertain 10. intangible, precarious, unreliable 11. treacherous 13. untrustworthy

slit . . . 4. kerf 5. cleft, slash, split 6. furrow 7. severed

slither . . . 5. crawl, glide, sidle, slide

sliver . . . 3. cut 5. shred, slice, split 8. fragment, splinter

sloe . . . 3. haw 4. plum

sloe (pert to) . . .
berry . . 7. juniper
bush . . 10. blackthorn
color . . 9. blue-black
fruit (blackthorn) . . 3. haw 4. sloe
gin . . 12. sloe-flavored

slogan . . . 3. cry 5. motto 6. phrase 9. catchword, watchword 10. shibboleth (Bib)

sloop . . . 5. yacht 6. cutter, schuit (schuyt) 7. eelboat

slope . . . 3. dip, lie 4. bank, hade, ramp 5. bevel, scarp, slant, talus 6. calade, decamp, escarp, glacis 7. terrace 9. declivity 10. declension 11. inclination

sloping bank . . . 4. brae 7. terrace

sloth . . . 2. ai 4. pack (bears), pazy, unau 6. acedia, mammal 7. inertia 8. idleness, slowness 9. indolence

slothful . . . 4. lazy 8. inactive, indolent, sluggish

sloth monkey . . . 5. lemur, loris

slough . . . 3. bog 4. husk, mire, molt, shed, skin 5. bayou, swamp 7. channel, discard

sloughing . . . 7. ecdysis, molting 8. shedding 10. discarding

slovenly . . . 5. dowdy, messy, tacky 6. frowzy, sloppy, untidy 8. careless, slattern, slipshod 9. negligent 10. disheveled, disorderly, slatternly

slow . . . 4. dull, late, poky 5. delay, inert, relax 6. boring, hinder, retard, stupid 7. slacken 8. boresome, dilatory, inactive, moderate 9. lingering 20. inch by inch phlegmatic 13. unprogressive

slow (pert to) . . .
action . . 6. dawdle 10. deliberate
adverb . . 10. behindhand
down . . 4. idle 6. retard 8. wind down 10. decelerate
music . . 5. largo, lento, molto, tardo 6. adagio 7. andante 8. lentando 10. lentamento
poke . . 5. snail 7. dawdler
up . . 3. lag 6. retard 7. decline
witted . . 4. dull 6. stupid

sludge . . . 3. mud 4. gunk, mire, ooze 5. slime 8. sediment

slug . . . 3. hit 4. blow, dose 5. Arion, drink, drone, idler, Limax, space, token 6. bullet, loiter, nugget 7. trepang 8. sluggard 9. gastropod

sluggish . . . 4. logy, slow 5. dopey, inert 6. drowsy, stupid, supine 7. dronish, languid 8. dilatory, inactive, indolent, listless, stagnant 9. stagnancy, stupidity, torpidity

sluice . . . 4. race 5. flush 6. drench, stream 7. channel 9. floodgate

slumber . . . 4. doze 5. sleep 6. catnap, drowse, repose, snooze, somnus 14. arms of Morpheus

slump . . . 4. drop, fall 7. decline, descend, dessert, sinkage 9. fall short 10. depreciate, depression

slur . . . 4. blur 5. elide 6. defame, insult, mackle, slight, stigma 7. calumny, traduce 8. disgrace, innuendo, reproach, skim over 9. aspersion, disparage 10. calumniate, stigmatize

slush . . . 3. mud 4. mire, snow 5. slime 14. sentimentality

sly . . . 4. arch, foxy, wary, wily, wink 5. cagey, catty, snaky 6. covert, crafty, feline, shrewd, sneaky, subtle, 7. cunning, furtive 8. craftily

9. underhand 11. mischievous, underhanded 15. surreptitiously

smack ... 3. bit, bop 4. bang, belt, buss, glow, kiss, tang 5. clout, taste 6. strike, vessel, wallop 8. chastise, sailboat

smacking ... 5. brisk 6. lively 7. dashing 8. spanking, vigorous 9. energetic

small ... 3. tot, wee 4. thin, tiny, wisp 5. dwarf, petty 6. humble, little, meager, minute, modest, petite 7. faintly, trivial 8. picayune, trifling 9. miniature, minuscule, thumbnail 10. diminutive, undersized 11. unimportant 13. insignificant 14. contemptuously, inconsiderable

small (pert to) ...
  amount .. 3. dab 4. dram 5. minim 6. morsel 7. modicum 8. pittance
  anvil .. 5. teest
  area .. 6. areola (areole)
  armadillo .. 4. peba
  arms .. 3. bow 5. rifle, sword 6. pistol 7. carbine, grenade
  attractive .. 4. cute 5. dainty
  bomb .. 6. petard 7. grenade
  bottle .. 4. vial 5. phial
  case, handbag .. 4. etui
  comb form .. 5. lepto, micro
  dab .. 3. pat, wad 5. chunk
  deer .. 4. fawn, napu
  delicately .. 6. mignon
  distance .. 3. hop 4. step
  drink .. 3. nip 4. pony, swig
  drum .. 5. bongo, tabor
  field .. 5. croft
  fish .. 3. ide
  flag .. 6. fanion
  fruits .. 10. low growing
  fry .. 4. fish, kids, tots 8. children 10. youngsters
  insect .. 4. flea 5. midge
  island .. 3. ait 4. isle
  lake .. 4. mere, pond
  law .. 5. petit
  minded .. 4. mean 5. petty 6. biased 10. prejudiced, vindictive
  neat .. 6. dapper
  number .. 3. few 7. paucity
  opening .. 4. pore 5. stoma 7. orifice
  ox .. 4. anoa
  part .. 4. iota 6. detail 7. snippet
  particle .. 4. atom, mote 8. molecule
  people .. 5. elves 6. common 7. fairies, midgets, Pygmies
  piece .. 3. mot 4. chip, tate 5. speck 7. driblet, morceau
  post .. 10. paper size
  quantity .. 4. drop, mite 5. trace 7. handful
  rope (Naut) .. 7. marline (marling)
  Scot .. 3. sma, wee
  shield .. 3. écu 5. scutellum
  stream .. 3. run 4. rill 6. rillet
  surface .. 5. facet
  talk .. 6. babble 7. prattle 8. chitchat
  task .. 3. chore 6. odd job
  things .. 3. fry
  tower .. 6. turret 7. minaret
  very .. 3. wee 8. picayune 11. Lilliputian
  world .. 9. microcosm

smallpox ... 7. variola

smaragd ... 7. emerald

smart ... 3. apt 4. chic, perk, posh, trig, trim, wise 5. acute, alert, natty, nifty, quick, sting 6. astute, clever, shrewd, spruce, trendy 7. dashing, painful, pungent, stylish 8. impudent, poignant, pricking 9. competent, ingenious 10. precocious 11. fashionable, intelligent

smash ... 4. blow, mash, pulp, ruin 5. break, crush, drink (spirits), stave, wreck 6. defeat 7. collide, debacle, destroy, failure, shatter, success 8. accident, beverage 9. collision, pulverize

smear ... 3. dab, rub 4. daub, gaum 5. slake, stain, sully 6. anoint, bedaub, defame, defile, grease, malign, smirch, smudge 7. besmear, plaster, pollute, slander 8. besmirch

smear with ...
  egg white .. 5. glair 8. meringue
  mud .. 5. slime
  ointment .. 6. anoint

smell ... 4. odor, olid, reek 5. aroma, fetor, scent, sense, sniff, stink 6. detect 7. perfume 9. fragrance, redolence 10. atmosphere

smell (pert to) ...
  acute .. 8. oxyrhine
  loss of sense of .. 7. anosmia
  offensive .. 3. bad 4. foul, olid 5. fetor 6. stench
  sense of .. 6. osmics 7. osmesis 9. olfaction

smelling salts ... 9. hartshorn 17. ammonium carbonate

smelt ... 4. fish, fuse, melt 6. tomcod 7. scorify 10. silverside

smilax ... 8. catbrier 10. greenbrier

smile ... 4. grin 5. laugh, smirk, sneer 6. simper 8. greeting

smiling ... 5. agrin, merry, riant 6. rident 8. gleaming, grinning

smirch ... 4. blot 5. smear, stain, sully, taint 6. blotch, smutch, stigma, vilify 7. begrime, blacken, blemish, tarnish 8. discolor 10. blackening

smirk ... 4. grin, leer 6. simper

smite ... 4. kill, slap 5. lay low, strike 7. chasten, impress, inflict, trouble 8. chastise

smithy ... 6. forger, stithy 7. farrier 8. smithery 10. blacksmith

smock ... 5. kamis, shift, tunic, woman (obs) 7. chemise 9. philander 11. overgarment

smoke ... 4. burn, cure, floc, fume, pipe 5. cigar, cloud, cubeb, flume, smook, vapor 6. smudge 7. incense, tobacco 8. fumigate, preserve 9. cigarette

smokestack ... 6. funnel 7. chimney 8. fumiduct

smoking apparatus (Orient) ... 7. tabagie 8. narghile (nargile)

smolder, smoulder ... 4. burn 5. choke, smoke 6. smudge 7. smother 9. suffocate

smooth ... 4. comb, ease, even, iron, lene, pave 5. bland, clear, level, plane, press, sleek, slick, suave 6. glossy,

mangle, pacify, urbane 7. uniform
8. hairless, unctuous 10. facilitate,
flattering 12. frictionless, ingratiating

smooth (pert to) . . .
breathing . . 13. spiritus lenis
comb form . . 3. lio
feathers, hair . . 5. preen
hard, transparent . . 6. glassy
phonetically . . 4. lene
tare . . 12. slender vetch
tongued . . 4. glib 5. suave
12. hypocritical

smooth and . . .
soft . . 5. furry, silky, soapy 7. velvety
soothing . . 5. bland
sweet . . 11. mellifluent
white . . 11. alabastrine

smother . . . 4. daub, kill 5. befog, choke,
cover 6. deaden, hush up, muffle, stifle,
welter 7. overlie, smolder 8. suppress
9. suffocate, to blanket 11. exterminate

smudge . . . 4. blot, smut, soil, spot
5. smear, smoke, stain 6. smutch
7. begrime, smolder

smug . . . 4. neat, tidy, trim 5. smart,
suave 6. pilfer 7. correct 9. confident
10. complacent 13. self-satisfied

smuggler . . . 6. runner 9. rumrunner
13. contrabandist

smur . . . 4. mist 5. cloud, smurr 7. drizzle

Smyrna . . 5. Izmir (present name)

Smyrna fig . . 5. eleme (elemi)

Smyrna melon . . 6. casaba

snack . . . 4. nosh

snail . . . 4. slug 5. drone, Helix, Mitra,
whelk 6. Nerita, Triton 7. mollusk
9. gastropod 10. periwinkle

snake . . . 3. asp, ess 4. tree, worm
5. adder, cobra, coral, racer, viper
6. garter, gopher 7. hognose, rattler,
reptile 8. Micrurus, moccasin
9. Heterodon 10. bushmaster,
copperhead, sidewinder
11. cottonmouth, diamondback,
rattlesnake 12. schaapsteker

snake (pert to) . . .
African . . 5. mamba
bird . . 6. darter
black . . 5. racer
cobra . . 3. nag (naga)
comb form . . 5. ophio, ophis 6. herpes
crusher . . 6. python 8. anaconda 14. boa
constrictor
dance . . 4. Hopi 6. ophism
division (serpents) . . 7. Ophidia
9. Serpentes
expert . . 13. herpetologist
fear of . . 13. herpetophobia
Florida . . 8. moccasin
front-fanged . . 5. cobra, mamba 6. elapid
8. Elapinae
garter . . 5. Elaps
genus . . 7. Ophidia
heraldic . . 5. bisse
horned . . 8. cerastes
India . . 5. krait 6. bongar
killer . . 8. mongoose
like . . 7. ophioid 9. colubrine
mouth . . 6. orchid
movement . . 4. coil, drag, wind 5. crawl,
sneak, twist

mythical . . 6. Python (on Mt Parnassus)
nonpoisonous . . 4. king 6. garter, gopher
9. Colubrina
pert to . . 5. ophic 7. anguine 8. viperine
9. colubrine, scoundrel
poisonous . . 3. asp 5. adder, coral
7. rattler 8. moccasin 10. copperhead
11. cottonmouth 13. thanatophidia
python . . 8. anaconda
python deity . . 5. zombi (zombie)
reptilelike . . 9. herpetoid
Russell's viper . . 6. daboia, jessur
sacred . . 6. Shesha
S America . . 5. aboma
sand snake . . 5. Eryx
semihuman, race of . . 4. Naga
shaped . . 9. anguiform
skin . . 6. exuvia
spitting . . 8. ringhals

snaky . . . 3. sly 4. wavy 7. anguine,
sinuous, wriggly 8. spiteful, twisting,
venomous 9. snakelike 10. perfidious,
serpentine 11. treacherous

snaky sisters . . . 6. Erinys 17. snaky-
haired Furies

snap . . . 3. bit 4. bite, flip 5. break, crack,
flick, quick, snarl, thump 6. energy,
fasten, fillip (fingers) 7. bargain, crackle
8. easy task, handcuff, snapshot
9. crispness, fastening, smartness
10. gingersnap, photograph, resilience
11. sharp retort

snapper . . . 4. bean, sesi 5. error, pargo
6. beetle, bonbon, tamure, turtle
7. cracker, grouper 8. fastener, rosefish
9. countfish 10. stitchwort, stringbean,
woodpecker 11. firecracker

snappy . . . 4. cold, fast 5. quick 6. lively,
sudden 7. pungent 8. snappish
9. crackling, energetic

snare . . . 3. beg, gin, net, web 4. lure,
mesh, trap 5. benet, catch, noose, steal
6. entoil, trepan 7. pitfall 9. deception

snark . . . 3. nag 5. snort 6. boojum
8. creature (fabled)

snarl . . . 4. gnar, knot 5. gnarr, growl,
scold, snare 6. tangle 7. confuse,
ensnare, grumble, quarrel 8. complain,
entangle 9. confusion 10. complicate
12. complication

snatch . . . 4. grab, jerk, take 5. catch,
erept, grasp, gripe, pluck, seize, steal,
wrest 6. clutch, kidnap, rescue 7. seizure

sneak . . . 4. lead (game), lurk 5. cower,
creep, knave, slink, snoop 6. coward,
cringe, tattle 7. smuggle 11. furtive
move

sneaking . . . 3. sly 4. mean, poor
6. craven, hidden, paltry, secret
7. furtive 8. cowardly, stealthy
9. dastardly, niggardly, underhand
12. contemptible 13. surreptitious

sneer . . . 4. gibe, jeer, mock 5. fleer,
flout, laugh, scoff, scorn

sneer, expressive . . . 8. sardonic

snell . . . 4. keen 5. acute, eager, quick,
sharp, snood, swift 6. active, biting,
severe 7. caustic, pungent 8. piercing

snicker . . . 5. laugh, neigh, sneer 6. giggle,
nicker, tittle, whinny 7. snigger
8. laughter

sniff . . . 4. nose 5. scent, smell, snuff
6. detect, inhale 7. sniffle 8. sibilate,
smell out 14. show of contempt

snifter . . . 3. nip 4. dram, good 5. drink,
sniff, snort 6. snivel 9. excellent

snip . . . 3. bit, cut 4. clip, snap 5. notch,
piece, shred 8. fragment, particle

snipe (pert to) . . .
eel . . 6. thread
flock . . 4. wisp
game . . 6. godwit
hawk . . 7. harrier
verb . . 7. shoot at 10. sharpshoot

snippy . . . 4. curt, tart 5. brief, sharp
8. snippety, snobbish 11. fragmentary
12. supercilious

snirl . . . 5. gnarl, snare 6. tangle 7. wrinkle

snitch . . . 5. pinch, steal 6. betray, inform,
pilfer, snatch, tattle 8. informer, particle

snob . . . 4. prig 7. cobbler, parvenu
8. bluenose, commoner, courtier
9. sycophant

snobby, snobbish . . . 5. proud 6. uppish
7. haughty 8. arrogant 9. exclusive
11. overbearing

snood . . . 5. snell 6. fillet 7. hairnet

snook . . 4. fish 5. smell 6. robalo, search
9. barracuda

snoop . . . 3. pry 4. nose 5. prowl, sneak
6. meddle 7. meddler 8. busybody
10. sneak thief

snooze . . . 3. nap 4. doze 5. sleep
6. cuddle, nuzzle, siesta 7. snoozle,
snuggle

snore, snoring . . . 4. rale 5. sleep
7. stertor 8. rhonchus, sibilate
10. sibilation, stertorous 15. hoarse
breathing

snort . . . 5. drink, grunt, laugh, snore

snotty . . . 5. dirty, nasty 6. offish,
snooty 7. high-hat 8. offensive
12. contemptible, supercilious

snow . . . 4. firn, neve 5. opium 8. narcotic
12. interference

snow (pert to) . . .
bunting . . 5. finch 9. snowflake
glacial . . 4. firn, neve
grouse, quail . . 9. ptarmigan
house . . 5. igloo
leopard . . 5. ounce
lily . . 6. violet (white)
living in . . 5. nival
mouse . . 4. vole 7. lemming
ref to . . 5. nival
ridges . . 8. sastrugi (zastrugi)
runner . . 3. ski 4. sled
shoe . . 3. pac 7. webfoot
sliding . . 9. avalanche
slope . . 8. glissade

snub . . . 3. cut 5. check, quell, scold
6. cut off, ignore, rebuff, rebuke,
slight 7. neglect, shorten 8. restrain
9. reprimand 10. inhalation

snuff (pert to) . . . 5. scent, smell, sniff
6. draw in, inhale, snoose 7. tobacco
(pulverized), umbrage 10. extinguish,
inhalation

snuff (pert to) . . .
a candle . . 4. snot
box . . 4. mull 9. tabatière
color . . 10. mummy brown

type . . 6. rappee 8. Maccaboy
10. Copenhagen

snug . . . 4. cozy, neat, safe, trim 5. close,
tight 6. secure 7. compact 8. homelike,
reticent 9. concealed, secretive 10. prosperous
11. comfortable

snuggle . . . 6. cuddle, nestle

sny (shipbuilding) . . . 5. curve (of plank)

so . . . 2. as 3. how 4. ergo, thus,
very 5. hence 6. if only 7. because
8. likewise, provided 9. therefore
11. accordingly, in order that
12. consequently

so (pert to) . . .
far . . 3. yet 7. thus far 8. until now
Latin . . 3. sic
so be it . . 4. Amen
to speak . . 8. as it were 12. figuratively

soak . . . 3. dip, sog, sop, wet 4. sock
5. souse, steep 6. drench, imbrue, strike,
tipple 7. extract, immerse 8. drunkard,
macerate, marinate, permeate, saturate
9. percolate 10. overcharge

soap . . . 4. sapo, suds, wash 5. bribe
6. lather 7. bribery 8. cleanser, flattery
9. slush fund

soap (pert to) . . .
box . . 4. dais 5. stage 8. platform
convert to . . 8. saponify
fish . . 10. lizard fish
frame bar . . 4. sess
ingredient . . 3. lye
liniment (camphorated) . . 9. opodeldoc
making . . 14. saponification
mottled . . 8. Eschwege (Eschweg)
opera . . 6. serial 9. broadcast 13. network
   serial
plant . . 5. amole
soft . . 8. flattery

soar . . . 3. fly 4. flit, rise, wing 5. float,
plane 6. ascend, aspire, be high
9. transcend

soaring . . . 6. flight 7. gliding, planing,
winging 8. essorant 9. skyriding
10. ballooning

sob . . . 3. cry 4. bawl, weep 6. boohoo,
simper 7. whimper 9. shed tears

sobeit . . . 4. amen 8. provided

sober . . . 4. calm, cool, dark, sane
5. grave, quiet, staid 6. gentle, sedate,
solemn, somber, subdue, temper
7. chasten, earnest, regular, serious
8. composed, moderate, sensible
9. abstinent, collected, dignified,
temperate 10. abstemious, thoughtful
11. impassioned 13. unintoxicated

sobriety . . . 6. sanity 9. composure,
restraint, soberness 10. abstinence,
moderation, temperance
11. seriousness

sobriquet . . . 5. alias, title 6. byname
7. epithet 8. cognomen, nickname
11. appellation

soccer . . . 19. association football

soccer great . . . 4. Pele

sociable . . . 5. party 7. affable 8. familiar,
friendly, informal 9. reception
10. accessible, gregarious
13. communicative, companionable

social . . . 3. tea 5. party 6. smoker
9. convivial, gathering

13. companionable
social (pert to) . . .
  career . . 5. debut
  class . . 4. clan, sept 5. caste 6. estate
  ethics . . 6. morals 9. standards
    10. principles
  function . . 3. bee, tea 4. ball 5. party
    6. soiree 7. reunion 9. reception
  gathering, men . . 4. stag 6. smoker
  group . . 4. sept 5. tribe 6. ethnos 8. smart
    set 10. upper crust 11. cafe society
    13. kaffeeklatsch
  insect . . 3. ant, bee
  outcast . . 5. leper 6. pariah
  standing . . 6. estate
  system . . 6. regime
socialist . . 3. Red 8. Nihilist 9. anarchist,
  communist 10. Bolshevist
  12. collectivist
society . . 5. union 7. company
  8. alliance, populace 9. community
  10. fellowship 11. association,
  partnership 13. companionship,
  confederation, participation
society (pert to) . . .
  bud . . 3. deb
  Chinese . . 4. Tong
  German . . 6. Verein
  high . . 5. elite 10. upper crust
  Italian . . 5. Mafia (Maffia)
  of Friends . . 7. Quakers
  secret . . 5. lodge, Order
Society Islands . . .
  capital . . 7. Papeete
  chief island . . 6. Tahiti
  site . . 12. South Pacific
Socrates (pert to) . . .
  birthplace . . 6. Athens
  disciple of . . 5. Plato
  famed as . . 7. teacher 11. Grecian sage
  wife . . 9. Xanthippe (Xantippe)
sod . . 4. soil, turf 5. divot, glebe, sward
  7. stratum 10. greensward
soda . . 3. sal 8. beverage 9. saleratus,
  saltpeter
sodden . . 5. drunk, moist, soggy
  6. soaked, stewed, stupid 7. drunken,
  steeped 9. saturated 11. intoxicated
sodium (pert to) . . .
  carbonate . . 4. soda 5. borax, trona
    7. sal soda, saltcat
  chloride . . 3. sal, tar 4. NaCl, salt
  nitrate . . 5. niter
  salicylate . . 8. medicine
  symbol . . 2. Na
sofa . . 5. couch, divan 6. lounge, settee
  7. dos-à-dos 8. causeuse, love seat
  9. davenport, tête-à-tête 12. chesterfield
soft . . 4. easy, limp, weak 5. bland,
  downy, mushy, pulpy 6. dreamy,
  gentle, placid, silken, supple, tender
  7. clement, ductile, lenient, lightly,
  quietly, squashy, velvety 8. flexible,
  gullible, merciful, tranquil 9. temperate,
  tractable 10. effeminate, peacefully
  11. comfortable, sentimental,
  sympathetic 13. compassionate
soft (pert to) . . .
  cancer . . 11. encephaloma
  coal . . 10. bituminous
  food . . 3. pap

  head . . 9. simpleton
  job . . 4. snap 8. sinecure
  mass . . 4. pulp
  music . . 5. dulce, piano
  palate . . 4. cion 5. uvula, velum
  pedal . . 3. ban 4. curb 6. subdue 8. tone
    down
  soap . . 7. blarney 8. blandish, flattery
    9. wheedling
  spoken . . 4. mild 5. suave
soften . . 4. melt, thaw 5. allay, malax,
  relax 6. affect, lenify, pacify, relent,
  soothe, temper, weaken 7. appease,
  assuage, cushion, mollify, relieve
  8. emoliate, enervate, enfeeble,
  macerate, mitigate, modulate
  9. alleviate, meliorate 11. tranquilize
soften (pert to) . . .
  by kneading . . 5. malax
  by soaking . . 8. macerate
  leather . . 5. sammy (sam)
  skins . . 3. taw
  temper . . 6. relent
softening . . 7. lenient 8. emulsive
  9. relenting, relieving, tempering
  10. lightening, mitigating
softening of the brain . . 8. dementia
softhearted . . 4. kind 6. tender
  8. merciful
softly . . 3. low 5. sotto 6. easily, gently
  10. delicately 13. unobtrusively
soggy . . 3. wet 4. damp 5. heavy
  6. soaked, sodden, watery 9. saturated
soil . . 4. clay, daub, dirt, land, loam,
  sand, spot 5. adobe, dirty, earth,
  glebe, gumbo, humus, stain, sully
  6. bedaub, bemire, ground, region,
  smirch, vilify 7. begrime, besmear,
  corrupt, debauch, pollute, tarnish
  8. alluvium 9. bedraggle, bespatter
  11. contaminate 12. fuller's earth
soil (pert to) . . .
  barren . . 4. arid, gall 8. lifeless
  goddess of . . 7. Demeter
  kind of . . 4. clay, lair, loam, malm
    5. adobe, humus
  oneself . . 4. moil
  poetic . . 5. glebe
sojourn . . 4. bide, stay, stop 5. abide
  6. reside 8. abidance, stop over
  11. peregrinate
solace . . 5. allay, amuse, cheer 6. soothe
  7. assuage, comfort, console
  9. alleviate, entertain 10. relaxation
  11. consolation
solan . . 5. goose 6. gannet
solar (pert to) . . .
  deity . . 2. Ra 3. Shu (Su) 6. Helios
  disk . . 4. aten
  exposure . . 9. sunstroke 10. heatstroke
  halo . . 6. nimbus 7. aureole 12. vesica
    piscis
  plexus . . 10. stomach pit
  system . . 6. bodies, planet 15. celestial
    bodies
  system apparatus . . 6. orrery
  year . . 5. epact
soldier . . 3. ant 5. cadet, poilu 6. galoot
  7. fighter, private, regular, trooper,
  veteran, warrior 8. gendarme, servitor
  9. combatant, grenadier, musketeer

11. enlisted man
soldier (pert to) . . .
Algeria . . 6. Zouave
cavalryman . . 6. lancer 7. dragoon, trooper
Croatian . . 5. Croat
field worker . . 6. sapper
flask . . 7. canteen
French . . 5. poilu
Gaelic . . 4. Kern
girl . . 3. WAC (Army)
Gr Myth . . 8. Myrmidon
hireling . . 9. mercenary
Ind (Brit) . . 5. sepoy
Ind (Brit), with own horse . . 8. silladar
Moroccan . . 5. askar
of fortune . . 7. Hessian 9. mercenary 10. adventurer
Prussian . . 5. uhlan
slang . . 6. galoot 7. chicken 8. shackman
soldiers, soldier's . . .
body of . . 5. troop 6. cohort 7. brigade, company, platoon
captured, wounded . . 6. losses
flask . . 7. canteen
Maryland (Rev War) . . 10. macaronies
overcoat . . 6. capote
quarters . . 7. billets 8. barracks
Three . . tales (by Kipling)
vacation . . 4. pass 5. leave 8. furlough
sole . . 3. one 4. base, fish, only 5. alone, slade 6. entire, lonely, single, unique 8. desolate, isolated, solitary, unshared 9. exclusive, unmarried, unmatched 10. underframe
sole (pert to) . . .
cookery . . 8. Marguéry
foot . . 4. vola 6. planta
hand (palm) . . 4. vola
pert to . . 7. plantar
plow . . 5. slade
toward the sole . . 7. plantad
solecism . . . 5. error 7. blunder 9. barbarism, deviation 11. impropriety
solemn . . . 3. sad 5. grave, pious, sober 6. august, devout, formal, gloomy, ritual, silent 7. earnest, serious, stately, sublime 8. funereal 9. dignified 10. ceremonial, devotional 11. ceremonious, reverential 12. awe-inspiring
solemnity . . . 4. pomp 7. dignity, sadness 8. ceremony 9. formality 10. importance
solicit . . . 3. ask, beg 4. lure, seek, tout 5. claim, court, crave, plead 6. accost, demand, invite, obtain 7. beseech, canvass, entreat, implore, request 8. campaign, petition 9. challenge, importune, panhandle, prosecute 10. supplicate
solicitor . . . 6. barker, lawyer 8. attorney 9. canvasser 10. petitioner
solicitude . . . 4. care, coda, heed 7. anxiety, caution, concern 9. attention 11. carefulness 12. apprehension 15. considerateness
solid . . . 4. cone, cube, firm, full, good, hard 5. dense, level, sound, stiff 6. stable, strong 7. uniform 8. complete, resolute, sensible, sterling 9. estimable, unanimous 10. dependable, inflexible

11. homogeneous, responsible, substantial, trustworthy
solid (pert to) . . .
comb form . . 6. stereo
geometrical . . 5. prism
seven-faced . . 11. heptahedron
six-faced . . 4. cube
tapering . . 4. cone 7. pyramid
solidarity . . . 5. unity 10. correality 11. nationality 12. completeness
solidity . . . 5. unity 6. volume 7. density 8. firmness, hardness, solvency, strength 9. solidness, stability 11. compactness 12. completeness 13. dependability 14. substantiality
solidum . . . 4. dado 9. entire sum
soliloquy . . . 6. poem 9. discourse, monologue 16. talking to oneself
solitaire . . . 8. Canfield
solitary . . . 3. one 4. lone, only, sole 5. alone, eremo (comb form) 6. hermit, lonely, single 7. recluse 8. deserted, desolate, lonesome 10. individual 12. unfrequented
solitude . . . 6. desert 7. privacy, retreat 9. aloneness, isolation, seclusion 10. loneliness, wilderness
solo accompaniment . . . 9. obbligato
Solomon (pert to) . . .
author of (reputed) . . 8. Proverbs 9. Canticles 12. Ecclesiastes 15. Wisdom of Solomon
called also . . 8. Koheleth 11. The Preacher
famed as . . 4. sage 7. wise man 12. King of Israel
father . . 5. David
literally . . 9. peaceable
mother . . 9. Bathsheba
Solomon Islands site . . . 9. South Seas
solon . . . 4. sage 8. lawmaker 9. statesman
solstice . . . 5. limit 13. farthest point (from equator)
solution . . . 3. key 6. answer 7. solving 8. analysis 10. denouement, resolution 11. explanation 15. disentanglement
solution (pert to) . . .
alkaline . . 3. lye
saline . . 5. brine
strength . . 5. titer (titre)
Somalia . . .
capital . . 9. Mogadishu
people . . 6. Somali 7. Hamitic
port . . 5. Zeila 6. Bulhar
somber, sombre . . . 3. sad 4. dark 5. grave 6. solemn 7. austere 9. depressed 10. depressing, foreboding, lackluster, melancholy 11. dark-colored, dispiriting
some . . . 3. any, one 5. about 6. plural, suffix 7. several 10. indefinite, more or less 13. approximately
somebody . . . 6. person 7. big name 8. luminary 9. celebrity, personage
somersault . . . 4. flip, leap 8. somerset 9. cartwheel 10. end over end
something . . . 6. object 8. somewhat 9. personage 12. in some degree
something (pert to) . . .
abnormal . . 5. freak 6. mutant 11. monstrosity 12. malformation

else .. 10. irrelevant
extra .. 5. bonus 6. bounty 7. premium
  9. lagniappe
found .. 5. cache, trove 11. serendipity
  13. treasure-trove
frightening .. 7. bugbear
heavy .. 4. onus 9. ponderant
illogical .. 7. alogism
imagined .. 5. story 7. figment
inserted .. 4. gore 5. inset, wedge
like .. 7. related, similar 8. somewhat
similar .. 8. analogue 11. counterpart
small .. 3. dot, jot 4. atom, iota, whit
  5. speck 6. sliver, tittle
soothing .. 7. unction
superfluous .. 5. luxus 6. luxury
unexplained .. 5. poser 7. mystery
unfinished .. 4. quab
somewhat ... 4. part 6. little, partly,
  rather 12. in some degree
somnifacient ... 4. drug 8. hypnotic,
  sedative 9. soporific
somniloquy ... 12. sleep talking
somnolence ... 8. dormancy
  10. drowsiness, sleepiness
somnus ... 5. sleep
Somnus (pert to) ...
  brother .. 4. Mors (Death)
  known also as .. 6. Hypnos
  son of .. 3. Nox (Night)
son, son of (pert to) ...
  a gun .. 5. rogue 6. fellow, wretch
  Anak .. 5. giant
  a Scot .. 3. Mac
  God .. 11. Jesus Christ
  Heaven (China) .. 7. Emperor
  in-law .. 5. gener
  in Trinity .. 6. second (person)
  Jacob .. 4. Levi
  man .. 4. male 6. mortal
  Odin .. 2. Ve
  Odysseus .. 9. Telegonus
  Priam .. 5. Paris
  reference to .. 3. ben 4. fils 5. scion
    6. filial 9. offspring 10. descendant
  Seth .. 4. Enos
  the soil .. 6. farmer 7. peasant
  youngest .. 5. cadet
sonance ... 4. tune 5. sound 7. sonancy
sonant ... 5. sound, tonic, vocal 6. voiced
  8. sounding 9. intonated
song ... 3. air, lay, ode 4. aria, leed, lilt,
  noel, poem, tune 5. carol, chant, ditty,
  melos, troll, verse 6. ballad, melody,
  strain, trifle 7. chantey (chanty), descant
  8. canticle, pittance 9. cabaletta
song (pert to) ...
  after .. 5. epode
  Bib .. 8. canticle 11. Song of Songs
    13. Song of Solomon
  boat, gondolier .. 7. chantey (chanty)
  choral Muse .. 11. Terpsichore
  collection .. 9. anthology 10. cancionero
  college .. 4. glee
  depressing .. 5. blues
  evening .. 6. vesper 8. evensong,
    serenade
  French .. 7. chanson
  funeral .. 5. dirge, elegy 6. lament
    8. threnody 9. epicedium
  gay .. 4. lilt

German .. 4. lied 9. Kunstlied
gypsy .. 10. zingaresca
Italian .. 7. canzone
lament .. 8. threnody
love .. 5. lyric 6. ballad 8. madrigal,
  serenade
merry .. 4. lilt
morning .. 5. matin
mountaineer .. 5. yodel
pert to .. 5. melic
praise .. 5. carol, paean (pean)
sacred .. 4. hymn 5. chant, motet, psalm
  6. anthem
sailor's .. 7. chantey (chanty) 9. barcarole
short .. 7. arietta
simple .. 6. ballad
words .. 6. lyrics
songbird ... 4. lark 5. mavis, robin, veery
  6. canary, oriole, thrush 8. throstle
  11. mockingbird
sonic recorder ... 9. echograph
sonnet ... 4. poem, song 5. verse
sonnet (pert to) ...
  first eight lines .. 5. octet
  last six lines .. 6. sestet
  two quatrains .. 10. Petrarchan
sonorous ... 4. loud 6. tonous 7. ringing
  8. resonant 9. melodious
  10. impressive, resounding
sonsy, sonsie ... 5. buxom, happy
  6. comely 11. good-natured
sontag ... 4. cape 6. jacket
soon ... 3. ere 4. anon 5. early, later
  6. at once 7. betimes, erelong, quickly,
  readily, shortly 8. promptly, speedily
  9. certainly, presently 11. immediately
Sooner State ... 8. Oklahoma
sooner than ... 3. ere 6. before
soot ... 4. smut, stup 5. black, grime,
  smoke 6. carbon, smudge 7. residue
  9. lampblack
soothe ... 3. pet 4. calm, lull 5. allay, quiet
  6. pacify, please, solace 7. assuage,
  compose, mollify, relieve, satisfy
  8. mitigate, palliate 9. alleviate
  11. tranquilize
soother ... 4. balm 5. luller 7. anodyne,
  placebo 8. lenitivo, pacifier, sedative
  9. flatterer
soothing ... 5. balmy, sirup (syrup)
  6. dulcet, gentle 7. calming 8. lenitive,
  sedative 9. appeasing, demulcent
  13. tranquilizing
soothsayer ... 4. seer 5. augur, vatis
  6. mantis 7. diviner, prophet
  8. Chaldean, haruspex 9. Cassandra
  13. praying insect 14. prognosticator
sooty (pert to) ...
  brown .. 6. bister 8. teakwood
  color .. 5. black
  mangabey .. 6. monkey
  pert to .. 9. albatross 10. fuliginous
  petrel .. 7. skimmer 10. shearwater
sophistical ... 8. captious 9. deceptive,
  sophistic
sophistication ... 9. sophistry
  10. corruption, experience
  11. worldliness 13. ungullibility
soporific ... 4. drug 6. drowsy, opiate
  7. anodyne 8. hypnotic, narcotic,
  sedative 11. somniferous 12. sleep

inducer, somnifacient

soprano (operatic) . . . 4. Alda, Bori, Lind,
Pons 5. Calvé, Eames 6. Callas, Steber

sora . . . 4. rail 5. crake

sorcerer . . . 4. mage 5. Magus 6. wizard
7. diviner 8. conjurer, magician
11. necromancer

sorceress . . . 3. hex 5. Circe, lamia,
Medea, witch 6. Gorgon 7. vampire
12. Witch of Endor

sorcery . . . 5. magic, obeah, spell
6. voodoo 8. pishogue 9. diablerie,
diabolism 10. black magic, necromancy,
witchcraft

sordid . . . 3. low 4. base, mean, vile
5. gross 6. filthy, menial 7. ignoble,
servile, squalid 8. sluttish, wretched
10. despicable, slatternly
12. contemptible

sore . . . 4. pain, sair 5. angry, vexed,
wound 6. tender 7. painful 8. abrasion,
inflamed, offended 9. irritated,
vexatious 11. distressing
12. inflammation

soreness . . . 4. ache 5. anger 8. vexation
10. bitterness, tenderness
11. painfulness 12. irritability

sorghum . . . 4. milo 5. durra (dari), grain,
sorgo 6. imphee, shallu 8. feterita

sorority . . . 4. club 7. society
10. fellowship, sisterhood

sorrel . . . 3. oca 4. buck, herb 5. color
(horse), Rumex 7. roselle

Sorrento, Italy (pert to) . . .
anc name . . 9. Sorrentum
famed as . . 6. resort
famed for . . 9. cathedral
site . . 11. Bay of Naples

sorrow . . . 3. rue, woe 4. sigh, teen,
weal 5. dolor, grief, mourn 6. grieve,
lament, misery, repent 7. remorse,
trouble 8. calamity, distress, egrimony,
mourning 9. adversity, penitence
10. affliction, contrition 11. lamentation,
tribulation 12. disconsolate,
wretchedness

sorrowful . . . 3. sad 4. blue 5. drear,
sadly 6. dismal, dolent, dreary,
rueful 7. doleful, grieved, tearful,
unhappy 8. mournful 9. plaintive
10. afflictive, melancholy 11. distressing
12. disconsolate

sorry . . . 3. sad 4. hurt 5. vexed
6. dismal, gloomy, rueful 7. painful,
pitiful, unhappy 8. contrite, grievous,
mournful, penitent, shameful, wretched
9. afflicted, chagrined, mortified,
regretful, repentant, worthless
10. displeased, melancholy
12. disappointed

sort . . . 3. ilk, way 4. cull, kind, rank
5. blend, class, grade, group 6. assort,
manner, nature, strain 7. quality,
species, variety 8. classify, separate
9. character 11. description

sortie . . . 4. raid 5. foray, onset, sally
6. attack, thrust

sottish . . . 4. dull 6. stupid 7. doltish,
drunken, foolish 8. bibulous
9. senseless

sotto (It) . . . 5. below, under

sotto voce . . . 5. aside 8. secretly
9. privately, undertone 14. under the
breath

soubrette . . . 9. lady's maid 10. intrigante
11. maidservant

soudagur . . . 8. merchant 10. shopkeeper

soul . . . 2. ba, ka 3. ego, God 4. life
5. anima 6. pneuma, spirit 7. essence
8. inspirer 9. substance 10. embodiment
15. exemplification, personification

soul (pert to) . . .
beatified . . 6. saint
destiny of . . 8. theodicy
dwelling place . . 2. Po 6. heaven
Egypt . . 2. Ba
Hindu . . 5. atman 7. jivatma
lost . . 9. âme damnée, the damned
maligners . . 7. Harpies
music . . 14. rhythm and blues
personified . . 6. Psyche
transmigration . . 7. rebirth
13. reincarnation

sound . . . 3. bam, cry, hum 4. beep, bong,
hale, honk, rale, ring, sane, test, tone,
toot 5. drone, noise, plumb, probe,
snore, valid, whole 6. intact, report,
report, robust, stable, sturdy 7. feel out,
perfect, resound 8. flawless, reliable,
susurrus 9. undamaged 10. scrutinize
11. trustworthy

sound (pert to) . . .
addition to word end . . 8. paragoge
atonic . . 4. surd
dashing . . 5. swash 6. splash
discordant . . 6. jangle 9. cacophony
drum, beating . . 8. rataplan
explosion . . 4. boom 6. report
fixed . . 5. toned
harsh . . 3. caw 4. bray 5. creak, twang
7. stridor 9. cacophony
insect's . . 5. chirr
loud . . 4. peal 5. blare, clang
low . . 3. hum 4. moan 5. drone
metallic . . 4. ping, ting 5. clank, clink,
twank 6. tinkle
pert to . . 5. tonal 6. sonant 10. acoustical
prosody . . 4. rime (rhyme)
reflected . . 4. echo
sharp . . 3. pop 7. rat-a-tat, tapping
shrill . . 5. reedy
sibilant . . 4. hiss
similar . . 8. assonant
small . . 4. peep 6. rustle
surf . . 4. rote 5. swish
throwing . . 8. abat-sons
trumpet . . 7. clarion
unit . . 7. decibel
warning . . 5. alarm, siren 6. tocsin
whispering . . 8. susurrus
with rhythm . . 5. music

sounding . . . 5. depth, rawin 6. sonant
7. ringing 8. sonation 10. resounding

soundness . . . 5. truth 6. sanity 8. solidity,
solvency, strength 9. integrity, rectitude,
stability 10. heartiness 11. healthiness

soup . . . 3. fog 5. broth, chili, purée
6. bisque, potage, won ton 7. borscht,
chowder, pottage 8. bouillon,
consommé, gazpacho, julienne
10. oyster stew 11. vichyssoise
12. mulligatawny

soupçon ... 5. taste 7. portion 9. suspicion
10. suggestion
soup dish .. 6. tureen
sour ... 3. wry 4. acid, tart 5. acerb,
acrid 6. acetic, bitter, morose, off key,
rancid 7. acetose, acidify, crabbed,
pungent, tainted 8. acescent, embitter
9. acidulous 10. astringent, unpleasant
sour (pert to) ...
  apple.. 9. crab apple
  aspect.. 4. dour, hard 6. sullen
  berry.. 9. cranberry
  bread.. 8. leavened
  cherry.. 7. morello
  stomach.. 4. acor
  turn sour.. 5. prill 6. bleeze
source .. 4. font, germ, mine, rise,
root, seed 5. cause, fount 6. origin,
parent, quarry 8. fountain 9. beginning
10. wellspring 12. fountainhead
source (pert to) ...
  income.. 7. revenue
  insecticides.. 9. sabadilla
  iodine.. 4. kelp
  ipecac.. 4. evea
  metal.. 3. ore 7. bonanza
  opium.. 5. poppy
  rubber.. 3. ule
South Africa ... see also *South African*
  capital.. 8. Cape Town, Pretoria
  city.. 6. Durban 9. Germiston
    12. Johannesburg
  division.. 5. Natal 9. Transvaal 14. Cape
    of Good Hope 15. Orange Free State
  exports.. 4. gold 8. diamonds
  legislature seat location.. 8. Cape Town
  people.. 5. Boers, Zulus 6. Bantus
    7. British 10. Hottentots 11. Afrikanders
    (Dutch)
  river.. 4. Vaal 6. Orange
South African (pert to) ...
  antelope.. 3. gnu 5. eland, oribi, peele
    6. rhebok 7. sassaby
  armadillo.. 4. para
  ass (wild).. 6. quagga
  bird.. 4. taha
  camp.. 6. laager
  Cape ash.. 9. essenhout
  cocktail.. 9. sundowner
  cony.. 3. das
  council.. 4. Raad
  dialect.. 4. Taal 9. Afrikaans
  diamond (blue-white).. 5. jager
  fox.. 4. asse 5. caama
  grass hut.. 8. rondawel (rondavel)
  grassland.. 4. veld (veldt) 8. bushveld
  mountain, hill.. 3. kop
  snake.. 8. eggeater
  tableland.. 5. karoo
  tree (dogwood).. 7. assagai (assegai)
  village.. 5. kraal
  wer.. 4. Boer
  warrior.. 4. impi
  weaverbird.. 4. taha
  whip.. 7. sjambok
South American (pert to) ...
  animal.. 2. ai 4. paca 5. llama, sloth,
    tapir 6. jaguar, tapeti 7. agoura (dog)
    8. anteater 9. armadillo
  armadillo.. 4. apar (apara) 10. pichiciago
    (burrowing)

  arrow poison.. 6. curare (curari)
  balsam.. 4. tolu
  bellbird.. 8. arapunga 9. campanero
  bird.. 4. rara, taha 5. agami, arara,
    chaja, macaw 6. barbet 7. oilbird,
    seriema, tinamou 8. bellbird, boatbill,
    caracara, guacharo, puffbird
  blanket.. 6. serape
  city section.. 6. barrio
  cloth.. 4. crea
  country.. 4. Peru 5. Chile 6. Brazil
    7. Bolivia, Ecuador, Uruguay
    8. Paraguay, Suriname (Surinam)
    9. Argentina, Venezuela
  drink.. 5. assai
  fiber.. 6. yachan
  fish.. 4. paru 7. piranha, scalare
    8. arapaima
  Indian.. 2. Ge (Gesan) 3. Ona 4. Inca
    5. Carib 6. Tapuya
  knife.. 7. machete
  leader.. 7. Franko 7. Pizarro
  liberator.. 7. Bolivar
  mammal.. 5. llama, tapir 6. alpaca
    8. kinkajou 10. chinchilla
  marmoset.. 7. tamarin
  monkey.. 3. sai 4. saki, titi 5. araba
    8. orabassu 9. barrigudo
  mountain range.. 5. Andes
  native.. 5. Carib 6. Arawak
  ostrich.. 4. rhea
  palm.. 5. assai 12. chiquichiqui
  parrot.. 5. macaw
  plains.. 6. llanos, pampas
  plainsman.. 7. llanero
  plant.. 6. ipecac 11. ipecacuanha
  poison.. 6. curare
  river.. 3. Apa 4. Acre, Pará 5. Plata
    6. Amazon, Paraná
  rodent.. 5. coypu 6. agouti (agouty)
    8. capibara, viscacha 10. chinchilla
  snake.. 4. lora 5. aboma 8. anaconda
    10. bushmaster
  stork.. 7. maguari
  tinamou.. 7. tataupa
  toucan.. 7. aracari
  trumpeter.. 5. agami
  tuber.. 3. oca
  vulture.. 6. condor
  weapon.. 4. bola
  wild cat.. 4. eyra
  wind.. 7. pampero
South Carolina ...
  capital.. 8. Columbia
  city.. 8. Beaufort 10. Charleston
    11. Spartanburg
  monument.. 10. Fort Sumter
  mountain.. 9. Blue Ridge, Sassafras
  resort.. 11. Myrtle Beach
  State admission.. 6. Eighth
  State bird.. 4. wren
  State flower.. 9. jessamine
  State motto.. 13. Dum Spiro, Spero
    (While I Breathe, I Hope)
  State nickname.. 8. Palmetto
  State secession.. 5. First (1860)
South Dakota ...
  capital.. 6. Pierre
  city.. 5. Huron 8. Deadwood 9. Rapid
    City 10. Sioux Falls
  Indians.. 5. Brule, Sioux

mine (US largest) . . 9. Homestake
monument . . 10. Crazy Horse, Mt
Rushmore
mountain . . 10. Black Hills, Harney Peak
river . . 5. White 8. Cheyenne, Missouri
State admission . . 8. Fortieth (or
Thirty-ninth)
State bird . . 8. pheasant
State flower . . 12. pasqueflower
State motto . . 21. Under God the People
Rule
State nickname . . 6. Coyote 8. Sunshine
topography . . 8. Bad Lands 10. Black
Hills
southeast wind . . . 5. Eurus
southern . . . 7. austral
Southern (pert to) . . .
Buddhism . . 8. Hinayana
Cross . . 4. Crux 12. Stars and Bars
Crown . . 15. Corona Australis
dish . . 3. yam 4. okra, pone 5. gumbo
7. catfish, hoecake 8. chess pie, ham
hocks 9. cornbread 11. hush puppies
12. chitterlings, turnip greens
shrub . . 8. magnolia, oleander
States . . 5. Dixie 7. Sunbelt
southernmost city . . . 12. Puerto Arenas
(Chile)
South Pole bird . . 4. skua 7. penguin
South Pole constellation . . . 4. Pavo
South Sea . . 12. Pacific Ocean
South Sea Bubble . . . 6. scheme (1720)
10. stock fraud (Eng)
South Wales people . . 7. Silures
southwest wind . . 4. afer
south wind . . . 5. Notus
souvenir . . . 5. relic, token 6. memory,
trophy 7. memento 8. keepsake,
memorial, reminder 11. remembrance
12. recollection, remembrancer
sovereign . . . 5. chief, liege, regal, ruler
6. divine, prince, ruling 7. empress,
monarch, supreme 8. princely, superior,
suzerain 9. effectual, gold piece,
paramount, potentate 11. controlling,
independent
sovereign (pert to) . . .
claim . . 11. seigniorage
coin . . 4. skiv
decree . . 5. arrêt
pardon . . 7. amnesty
petty . . 8. tetrarch
power . . 6. throne
sovereignty . . . 5. realm 6. diadem,
empery, empire 7. dynasty, scepter
(sceptre) 8. dominion 9. supremacy
Soviet, Russian (pert to) . . .
committee . . 9. presidium
farm . . 7. sovkhoz (sovkhose)
government . . 9. Communism, Sovietism
10. Bolshevism
hero . . 5. Lenin
newspaper . . 6. Pravda 8. Izvestia
police, secret service . . 3. KGB
sow . . 3. pig 4. gilt, seed 5. plant
7. implant, scatter 8. disperse, squander
9. broadcast 10. salamander
11. disseminate
sow bug . . 6. slater
sow thistle . . 7. Sonchus
soybean . . 4. Soja 8. soya bean

soybean enzyme . . . 6. urease
spa . . . 3. Ems 4. Bath 5. Baden 6. Bilina
(Bilin), hot tub 7. Jacuzzi (tm)
space . . . 3. gap 4. area, rank, room,
time, void 5. blank, inane, niche, place,
range 6. areola, areole, degree, extent,
vacuum 7. arrange, expanse 8. capacity,
distance, interval 9. concourse, elbow
room
space (pert to) . . .
architectural . . 6. metope 8. pediment
blank . . 5. chasm 6. hiatus, lacuna
botany (leaves) . . 6. areola
environment . . 5. ambit 8. ambiance
larynx . . 7. glottis
occupied . . 6. volume
ref to . . 5. areal, outer 6. cosmos, galaxy,
pulsar 7. heavens, lacunal, spatial
8. galactic, infinity 9. black hole, deep
space
storage . . 4. shed 5. attic, depot 6. cellar,
garage 9. storeroom, warehouse
theory . . 7. plenism
time . . 8. interval
travel . . 4. NASA 7. reentry, swingby
8. time warp
traveler . . 5. alien 6. cyborg 8. aeronaut
9. astronaut, cosmonaut
vehicle . . 6. rocket, Skylab 7. shuttle,
sputnik
void . . 5. chasm 7. inanity
wall . . 5. niche
spacious . . . 5. ample, broad, roomy
9. capacious, expansive, extensive
10. commodious, far and wide,
widespread 13. comprehensive
spadassin . . . 6. bravo 7. duelist
9. swordsman
spade . . . 3. dig, loy 4. spud, stag (3-yr
old), suit (cards) 5. slade 6. shovel
11. playing card
spade (pert to) . . .
bone . . 13. shoulder blade
fish . . 5. porgy 10. paddlefish
foot . . 4. toad
grass . . 4. rush
Irish . . 5. slane
money . . 7. Chinese (early)
peat . . 5. slade
triangular . . 5. didle
spee . . . 6. divine 8. foretell
Spain . . . see also *Spanish*
cape . . 9. Trafalgar
capital . . 6. Madrid
city . . 4. Irun 5. Cadiz, Lorca 6. Malaga
7. Cordoba, Granada, Seville 8. Valencia
9. Barcelona
city cathedral . . 9. Saragossa
islands . . 5. Ceuta 6. Canary 7. Melilla
8. Balearic
kingdom, region . . 4. Léon 6. Aragon,
Basque (Provinces) 7. Castile, Navarre
8. Asturias 9. Catalonia
mountain . . 8. Asturias, Pyrenees
old name . . 6. Iberia
palace . . 8. Escorial
plain, plateau . . 6. Meseta
river . . 4. Ebro, Muga 5. Tagus
span . . . 3. two 4. arch, join, pair, team
6. bridge, extend, length, period (time)
7. breadth, measure, stretch 8. overarch

9. encompass

spangle ... 6. aiglet, sequin 7. glitter, sparkle 8. ornament, zecchino

spaniel ... 5. trasy 6. cocker 8. Brittany, springer

Spanish (pert to) ...
alcazar *(palace)* .. 8. Alhambra
arbor .. 6. ramada
art museum .. 5. Prado
battle .. 6. Armada (1588)
bayonet .. 5. yucca
boat .. 5. aviso 7. galleon (ship)
Christmas .. 7. Navidad
cloak .. 4. capa 5. manta 6. mantle
7. zamarra (zamarro)
corral .. 5. atajo
dance .. 5. tango 6. bolero, gitano
8. fandango, flamenco, saraband
fabric .. 4. crea (cotton) 5. tiraz (silk)
fleet, famed .. 6. Armada
fortress chief .. 4. caid 7. alcaide
friend .. 5. amigo
fruit .. 8. pimiento
game .. 6. pelota 7. jai alai
garment .. 6. serape 8. mantilla
gift holder .. 6. piñata
gold .. 3. oro 8. El Dorado
governor .. 10. gobernador
grass .. 5. spart 7. esparto
gruel .. 5. atole
gypsy .. 7. zincalo
holiday .. 6. fiesta
horse .. 5. genet 6. jennet 7. caballo
hotel .. 6. posada
house .. 4. casa 6. casita
jar .. 4. olla, tina 6. tinaja
knight .. 8. cavalier 9. caballero
lake .. 4. lago
language .. 6. Basque 7. Catalan, Spanish
8. Galician 9. Castilian
light opera .. 8. zarzuela
mausoleum .. 8. Escorial
musical instrument .. 6. atabel, guitar
8. castanet
plant .. 3. aji 8. capsicum
porridge .. 5. atole
promenade .. 5. paseo
raisin .. 4. pasa
river .. 3. ria, rio
road .. 6. camino
room .. 4. sala
shawl .. 5. manta 6. serape
sheep .. 6. merino
sherry .. 5. Xeres 7. oloroso
sorcerer .. 6. brujo
street .. 5. calle
three .. 4. tres
title .. 3. don 5. señor 6. señora 7. hidalgo
8. señorita
trail .. 6. camino
vehicle .. 7. tartana
watch .. 5. reloj
watchtower .. 7. atalaya
watchword .. 6. alerta
watercourse .. 6. arroyo
wind .. 6. solano
window .. 7. ventana
witchcraft .. 8. brujeria
year .. 3. ano

Spanish people ...
architect .. 5. Gaudi 11. Churriguera

artist .. 4. Dali, Goya, Gris, Miró 6. Ribera
7. Murillo 8. Zurbarán 9. Velázquez
(Velásquez)
author .. 9. Cervantes 11. García Lorca,
Pérez Galdos
cellist .. 6. Casals
chaperone .. 6. duenna
composer .. 5. Falla
conqueror .. 6. Cortés (Cortez) 7. Pizarro
dictator, general .. 6. Franco
dramatist .. 9. Echegaray (Nobel Prize
1904)
explorer .. 6. Balboa 11. Ponce de León
gentleman .. 5. señor 8. cavalier
9. caballero
God .. 4. Dios
guitarist .. 7. Segovia
herdsman .. 7. llanero 8. ranchero
hero .. 3. Cid
justice of the peace .. 7. entrada
king .. 7. Alfonso, Charles 9. Ferdinand
lady .. 4. doña 6. señora 8. señorita
letter carrier .. 6. correo
man .. 3. don 6. hombre
missionary .. 5. Serra
monk .. 5. padre
peasant .. 7. paisano
people .. 5. genta
pianist .. 6. Iturbi
pretender to throne .. 6. Carlos (Don)
Queen .. 8. Isabella
singer, tenor .. 7. Domingo (Placido)
soldier .. 8. miquelet
soprano .. 4. Bori (Lucrezia)

spar ... 3. box 4. beam, boom, gaff, mast,
rung, yard 5. sprit, steve 6. timber
7. dispute, quarrel, topmast, yardarm

spare .. 4. lean, thin 5. chary, lanky
6. afford, exempt, frugal, meager,
scanty 7. sparing, surplus 8. preserve
9. duplicate, parsimony 10. economical,
occasional 11. superfluous
12. parsimonious

spare time ... 7. leisure

sparing ... 5. chary 6. frugal, meager,
saving, scanty 7. scrimpy, thrifty
8. merciful, reticent, stinting
9. scrimping 12. parsimonious

spark ... 4. beau, fire, funk 5. aizle, court,
dandy, lover 6. incite 7. diamond,
gallant, glitter, modicum, sparkle
8. humorist 10. sweetheart 11. scintillate

sparkle ... 5. flash, gleam, glint, shine,
trace 7. be smart, be witty, glisten,
glister, glitter, radiate, reflect, spangle,
twinkle 8. be lively 9. coruscate
10. effervesce, illuminate 11. scintillate
13. scintillation

sparkling ... 4. dewy 5. crisp, witty
6. bright, starry 7. shining 8. cheerful,
eloquent, glittery, gorgeous, mousseux
(wine) 9. twinkling 10. glittering,
reflecting 12. effervescent

sparoid fish ... 4. scup 5. porgy 8. sea
bream 10. sheepshead

Sparta, Greece ... see also *Spartan*
capital .. 7. Laconia (anc)
kingdom .. 12. Peloponnesus
river .. 7. Eurotas

spartan ... 5. hardy, stoic 10. courageous
13. uncomplaining

Spartan (pert to) . . .
army division . . 4. mora 6. lochus
cipher writing . . 7. scytale
class (anc) . . 8. perioeci
commander . . 7. lochage
dog . . 10. bloodhound
festival . . 6. Carnea 7. Carneia
king . . 8. Leonidas, Menelaus
lawgiver . . 8. Lycurgus
magistrate . . 5. ephor
native . . 8. Laconian 9. Spartiate
serf . . 5. helot

spasmodic . . . 6. fitful 7. snatchy
9. excitable, irregular 10. convulsive
12. intermittent 13. highly wrought

spasmodic (pert to) . . .
disease . . 5. croup 7. tetanus
inspiration . . 8. hiccough
twitch . . 3. tic

spat . . . 3. row 4. slap, tiff 5. spawn
6. gaiter, oyster, strike 7. dispute,
legging, quarrel 10. oysterseed

spate . . . 4. gush 5. flood 7. freshet, torrent
9. overwhelm, rainstorm 10. waterspout

spatial . . . 5. areal 6. sterical
11. dimensional

spatter . . . 3. wet 4. soil, spot 5. spurt
6. dabble, splash 7. sputter 8. splutter,
sprinkle

spawn . . . 3. ova, roe 4. eggs, germ, seed
7. lay eggs 8. generate 13. numerous
issue

speak . . . 3. say 4. chat, lisp, talk, tell
5. orate, utter 6. reveal 7. address,
chatter, declaim, sputter 8. converse,
proclaim 9. discourse, pronounce
10. articulate 11. tell in words

speak (pert to) . . .
affectedly . . 4. mime 5. mince
against . . 6. oppose
boastfully . . 4. brag 5. vaunt 7. enlarge
10. exaggerate
from memory . . 6. recite
ill of . . 5. decry 8. backbite 9. disparage
noisily . . 4. rant, rime 8. harangue
offhand . . 11. extemporize
slowly . . 5. drawl
softly . . 7. whisper
under breath . . 5. mouth 6. mumble,
murmur, mutter 7. grumble

speaker . . . 5. sayer 6. lisper, orator,
proser 8. lecturer 9. demagogue
10. mouthpiece, prolocutor
11. spellbinder

speaker of languages . . . 8. linguist,
polyglot

speaking (pert to) . . .
generally . . 7. as a rule, roughly 12. in
the long run 13. approximately
of . . 7. apropos 12. incidentally
offhand . . 13. extemporizing
privately . . 7. whisper 9. in one's ear
11. into one's ear
publicly . . 7. oratory 11. declamation
style . . 8. fluently

spear . . . 4. dart, pike, stab 5. catch, lance
6. pierce, weapon 7. javelin, missile
9. penetrate

spear (pert to) . . .
anc Teutons . . 6. framea (fram)
fish . . 3. gig 4. gaff

iron-tipped . . 7. assagai
shaped . . 7. hastate
three-pronged . . 7. trident
two-pronged . . 6. bident

spearfish . . . 6. marlin 9. quillback

special . . . 4. rare 5. extra 6. unique
7. notable, unusual 8. concrete,
detailed, favorite, specific, uncommon
10. individual, noteworthy, particular,
restricted 11. distinctive, exceptional
13. extraordinary

special (pert to) . . .
ability . . 5. forte 6. talent 7. charism
8. charisma
commodity . . 6. leader 7. feature 10. best
seller
edition . . 5. extra
favor . . 9. influence, privilege
train . . 5. flier 7. express 10. cannonball

specialist (pert to) . . .
atomic . . 9. physicist
ear . . 6. aurist 9. otologist
eye . . 7. oculist 15. ophthalmologist
medical . . 6. doctor 7. surgeon
money . . 9. economist

speciality . . . 5. skill 8. aptitude, contract
13. particularity 14. characteristic

specie . . . 4. cash, coin 5. money (hard)

species . . . 4. kind, sort, type 5. class,
genre, genus, group 7. general, isotope,
mankind, variety 8. category, humanity
11. Homo sapiens 12. nomenclature

specific . . . 5. exact, virus 6. remedy
7. limited, precise, special 8. definite,
detailed, explicit, peculiar

specificity . . . 9. haecceity

specify . . . 4. name 5. limit, state
6. define, detail 8. indicate 9. be precise,
designate, enumerate, stipulate

specimen . . . 4. copy 5. model, piece,
taste, token 6. person, sample, swatch
7. example, pattern 14. representative

specious . . . 4. fair 5. showy 7. alleged
8. illusory, pleasing 9. plausible
10. ostensible 12. hypocritical

speck . . . 3. bit, dot, jot, nit 4. blot, iota,
mark, mite, mote, spot, whit 5. fleck,
stain 7. blemish 8. particle 10. sand
darter

speckled . . . 6. menald 7. mottled
9. sprinkled 10. variegated

spectacle . . . 4. show, view 5. scene, sight
6. wonder 7. diorama, display, pageant
8. panorama, spyglass 10. exhibition
14. representation

spectacles . . . 7. glasses

spectator . . . 6. espier, viewer 7. watcher,
witness 8. audience, beholder, kibitzer,
looker-on, observer, onlooker
9. bystander

specter, spectre . . . 4. bogy (bogey,
bogie) 5. ghost, shade, spook 6. idolum,
spirit, wraith 7. eidolon, phantom
8. illusion, phantasm, revenant
10. apparition

spectral . . . 5. eerie (eery) 6. ghosty,
spooky 7. ghostly, phantom
12. apparitional

speculate . . . 5. guess, think 6. gamble,
ponder, wonder 8. consider, meditate,
ruminate, theorize 10. deliberate,

doctrinize, philosophy 11. contemplate
speculative . . . 5. risky 9. uncertain
10. thoughtful 11. inquisitive, theoretical
12. experimental 13. contemplative
speculator . . . 7. lookout, scalper
8. explorer, observer, theorist
12. investigator
speculum . . . 7. diopter 9. reflector
sped . . . 4. hied 5. raced 6. darted,
dashed, let fly 8. galloped, hastened
10. discharged
speech . . . 5. spiel 6. dilogy, orison
7. address, chatter, diction, oration
8. colloquy, harangue, language
9. elocution, utterance 12. conversation
speech (pert to) . . .
abusive . . 6. tirade
blunder . . 8. improper, solecism
comb form . . 4. logo
conclusion . . 10. peroration
conversational . . 13. colloquialism
defective . . 10. disphrasia
difficulty . . 9. baryphony 10. baryphonia
famous . . 9. Philippic (Demosthenes)
goddess . . 3. Vac
hasty . . 7. stammer, stumble, stutter
impediment . . 4. lisp 8. betacism,
    mytecism
intemperate . . 6. tirade
loss of . . 6. alalia 7. aphasia
movements . . 9. vocimotor
parts . . 4. verb 6. adverb 9. adjective
    11. conjunction, preposition
    12. interjection
pompous . . 12. magniloquent
provincial . . 6. patois 7. dialect
set speech (drama) . . 6. rhesis
term . . 6. zeugma 9. syllepsis
understatement . . 7. litotes
vitriolic . . 6. tirade
voiceless . . 7. spirate
without . . 4. mute 6. alogia
world . . 7. Volapük 9. Esperanto
speechless . . . 4. dumb, mute 6. silent
7. aphasic 8. taciturn 9. voiceless
speed . . . 3. fly, hie, run 4. flit, race,
zoom 5. haste, hurry, spurt 6. assist,
go fast, hasten 8. celerity, dispatch,
expedite, promptly, rapidity, velocity
9. posthaste, quickness, swiftness
10. accelerate, expedition, facilitate
12. precipitance
speedily . . . 4. soon 5. apace 6. presto
7. betimes, quickly, rapidly, swiftly
8. promptly 13. expeditiously
speedy . . . 4. fast 5. apace, fleet, hasty,
quick, rapid, swift 6. prompt, racing,
sudden
spell . . . 4. bout, mean, snap, tell, turn
5. charm, magic, relay, shift 6. glamor,
relate, relief, trance 7. explain,
relieve, sorcery, syncope 9. take turns
11. abracadabra 12. entrancement
13. substitute for
spell (pert to) . . .
binder . . 6. orator 7. charmer, spieler
bound . . 4. rapt 9. enchanted
    10. astonished, interested 11. under
    a spell
brief . . 4. snap
in another alphabet . . 13. transliterate

out . . 7. explain, itemize
pretended . . 11. abracadabra
under a spell . . 9. in a trance
    10. hypnotized, mesmerized
with loss of letter . . 7. syncope
spend . . . 3. use 4. pass 5. waste
6. employ, expend, lavish, weaken
7. consume, exhaust 8. disburse,
squander 9. dissipate, sacrifice
10. distribute
spend the summer . . . 8. estivate
(aestivate)
spendthrift . . . 4. daft 6. waster
7. spender, wastrel 8. prodigal
10. profligate, squanderer
Spenser, Edmund (pert to) . . .
character . . 3. Una
famed as . . 4. poet
famed work . . 12. Faerie Queene
poetic stanza . . 10. Spenserian
Spenser's Ireland personified . . .
5. Irene
spent . . . 4. paid 5. weary 6. effete, used
up, wasted 7. worn out 8. consumed,
lavished, tired out 9. exhausted
10. squandered
speos . . . 4. cave, tomb 6. grotto
sphenoid . . . 11. wedge-shaped
sphere . . . 3. orb 4. ball, star 5. arena,
earth, field, glove, orbit, realm,
scope 6. extent, planet 7. circuit,
heavens 8. terrible 10. atmosphere
12. jurisdiction
sphere of . . .
action . . 6. domain
life . . 5. world
making . . 7. orbific
spherical (pert to) . . .
aberration, free from . . 9. aplanatic
geometry . . 10. magnitudes
lune . . 7. portion
magnet . . 8. terrella (terella)
nearly . . 8. obrotund
reference to . . 6. rotund 7. globose
    9. orbicular 15. celestial bodies
ungula . . 5. wedge
sphericity . . . 9. globosity, rotundity,
roundness
sphinx (pert to) . . .
builder (Great Sphinx) . . 6. Khafre (IV
    Dynasty)
Great Sphinx site . . 4. Gaza (Egypt)
Greek myth . . 7. monster (sphinxlike)
reference to . . 9. enigmatic
    11. inscrutable
Zool . . 8. hawk moth
spice . . . 3. dill, herb, mace, sage 5. chili,
clove 6. cassia, nutmeg, pepper,
season, stacte 7. mustard 8. marjoram,
pungency 9. condiment, flavoring,
fragrance, seasoning
spicy . . . 3. hot 4. keen, racy, sexy
5. balmy, natty, smart 6. risqué
7. gingery, peppery, piquant, pungent
8. aromatic, fragrant, spirited
spider . . . 3. cob, pan 5. arain 6. Epeira,
katipo, tripod, trivet 7. pokomoo, retiary,
skillet, spinner 8. arachnid, attercop,
telarian 9. tarantula 10. black widow
spider (pert to) . . .
comb form . . 7. arachno

crab . . 4. Maia (genus)
fly . . 4. tick
genus . . 4. Maia 6. Aranea 7. Agalena, Attidae, Pholcus 9. Drassidae
Gr Myth . . 7. Arachne (Lydian girl)
Latin . . 6. aranea
leaping . . 10. saltigrade
monkey . . 6. ateles, coaita
nest . . 5. nidus
scorpion . . 8. pedipalp
scorpion appendage . . 10. pedipalpus
study of . . 10. araneology
web (anc) . . 8. attercop
weblike . . 9. arachnoid
web-spinning organ . . 9. spinneret
spieler . . . 5. crier 6. barker, talker 7. sharper, speaker 8. lecturer 9. solicitor 10. ballyhooer

spiffy . . . 4. fine, neat 5. smart 8. splendid 9. excellent

spigot . . . 3. peg, tap 5. spile, spout 6. dossil, faucet 7. stopper

spike . . . 3. cob, ear 4. brob, stab, tine, umbo 5. ament, piton, prong, thorn 6. antler, flower, pierce, spadix 7. amentum, dispale, spinule, trenail 10. adulterate 12. tenpenny nail

spikenard . . . 3. phu (Cretan) 4. herb, nard 8. ointment

spile . . . 3. pin, rod 4. plug, tube 5. spill, spout, stake 6. Aralia, spigot

spill . . . 4. blab, fall, shed, slop 5. flosh, waste 6. let out, splash, tumble 7. divulge, scatter 8. downpour, overflow, overture 11. tell secrets

spin . . . 4. birl, fish, reel, ride, turn 5. swirl, twirl, twist, whirl 6. extend, gyrate, rotate 7. prolong, revolve

spinach (wrinkled) . . . 5. savoy

spinal (pert to) . . .
column . . 9. vertebrae
cord . . 4. alba 6. myelon (marrow) 16. medulla oblongata
disease . . 8. myelitis 10. meningitis
muscle (attached) . . 5. psoas

spindle . . . 3. pin, rod 4. axis, axle, hasp 5. pivot, xeres 6. swivel 7. capstan, mandrel

spindle-legged . . . 4. lean 5. lanky 14. spindle-shanked

spindling . . . 4. long 5. gawky, leggy 6. skinny 7. slender 11. ineffectual

spine . . . 3. awn 4. axis, seta 5. chine, ridge, thorn 6. spirit 7. acicula, courage, process 8. backbone, spiculum 9. scoliosis (curvature) 12. spinal column

spinel . . . 5. balas (ruby) 7. mineral 8. spinelle

spineless . . . 4. limp, weak 5. frail 10. weak-willed 12. invertebrate

spinet . . . 5. piano 7. giraffe 8. virginal 10. clavichord 11. couched harp, harpsichord

spinnaker . . . 4. sail

spinner . . . 3. top 4. liar 6. spider, weaver 8. narrator 9. nighthawk 10. goatsucker 11. storyteller 12. whippoorwill

spinning . . . 6. rotary 7. strobic 8. telarian, whirling 9. revolving

spinning device . . . 5. jenny 7. distaff,

---

spindle 8. throstle

spiracle . . . 4. pore, vent 7. orifice 8. aperture, blowhole

spiral . . . 4. coil, curl 5. helix 6. galaxy, volute 7. helical, winding 8. circling, helicoid 9. corkscrew

spire . . . 4. coil, surl 5. tower, twist, whorl 6. ascend, finial, summit 7. steeple

spire finial . . . 3. épi

spirit . . . 3. imp, pep, vim 4. dash, élan, fire, life, mood, pixy, soul 5. demon, devil, fairy, genie, ghost, heart, metal, pluck, Satan, shade, spook, verve 6. animus, breath, energy, fervor, goblin, intent, morale, pneuma, sprite 7. bravery, courage, essence, extract, gremlin, specter 8. spiritus 9. animation 10. enterprise, individual 11. real meaning 12. cheerfulness 13. consciousness

spirit, spirit of (pert to) . . .
avarice . . 6. Mammon
bad . . 6. afreet 7. Amaimon (Amaymon)
Egypt . . 2. ba, ka 3. akh
English folklore . . 2. po
evil . . 4. jinn 5. Aecto, jinni (jinnel) 6. Azazel, Belial, Erinys 7. Tempter (The) 9. Beelzebub
female . . 6. undine 7. banshee
good . . 8. Eudaemon
household . . 5. Lares 15. Lares and Penates
infatuation . . 3. Ate
knights . . 8. errantry
malignant . . 3. Ker
mockery . . 5. Momus
people . . 5. ethos
refined . . 6. elixir
tapping (theory) . . 9. typtology
the age . . 9. Zeitgeist
the air . . 5. Ariel
the sea . . 5. siren 6. Triton 7. mermaid, Neptune 9. Davy Jones

spirited . . . 3. gay 4. gamy, racy 5. brisk, eager, fiery 6. lively, plucky, spunky 7. dashing, fervent 8. eloquent, generous, vigorous 9. audacious, energetic, spiritoso, sprightly 10. mettlesome

spiritless . . . 4. dead, dull, meek 5. amort, vapid 6. gloomy 8. dejected, lifeless, listless 9. depressed, heartless 10. despondent, dispirited

spirits (pert to) . . .
Babylonian . . 5. Igigi
dwelling . . 2. po 5. Hades 7. Elysium
low . . 5. blues, dumps, gloom 8. doldrums
of the dead . . 5. Manes (Rom) 7. lemures 9. chthonian (Gr)

spiritual . . . 4. holy, pure, song 5. pious 6. devout, divine, sacred 7. psychic 8. churchly, internal, platonic, spectral 9. unworldly 10. immaterial 11. disembodied, incorporeal 12. supernatural 14. ecclesiastical, heavenly minded

spiritual (pert to) . . .
affinity . . 8. soul mate
apathy . . 6. acedia
being . . 3. ens 5. angel 6. seraph

darkness.. 4. Hell 5. tamas
director.. 9. confessor
meaning of words.. 7. anagoge
meeting.. 6. séance
shrine.. 6. adytum 7. sanctum

spirt... 3. jet 4. gush 5. flare, spurt
6. squirt

spit... 3. rod 4. rain 5. eject, image,
stick 6. impale, pierce, saliva, skewer,
sputum 7. hissing, spindle, sputter
8. likeness, sprinkle, turnspit
9. exsputory 11. expectorate

spite... 3. vex 4. hate 5. pique, shame,
venom 6. enmity, malice, offend,
rancor, thwart 7. dislike, ill will
8. disgrace, dishonor 9. animosity,
cattiness, humiliate 10. resentment
11. malevolence 12. spitefulness

spiteful... 4. mean 5. catty 7. cattish
8. annoying, venomous 9. malicious,
malignant 10. irritating, vindictive

spittoon... 6. pigdan 8. crachoir,
cuspidor

splash... 3. lap, wet 4. spot 5. spray,
swash 6. blotch, flouse (floush), ripple
7. scatter, spatter, splurge 8. cut a dash,
splatter 9. dashingly 14. ostentatiously

splashboard... 4. gate (false) 5. plank
6. fender, screen 9. dashboard
10. flashboard, flushboard

splay... 3. hem 4. turn 5. adorn, carve,
slant, slope 6. clumsy, expand, spread
7. awkward, display 9. dislocate,
displayed, expansion

spleen... 3. fit 4. fire, mood, whim
5. anger, ardor, freak, gland 6. malice,
temper 7. impulse 9. ill humor
10. low spirits, melancholy, resentment
11. impetuosity

spleen (pert to)...
amarinth.. 4. weed
excision.. 13. splenectomize
reference to.. 6. lienal 7. splenic

splendid... 4. braw, fine 5. grand, regal,
showy 6. costly, superb 7. gallant,
shining, sublime 8. glorious, gorgeous
9. beautiful, brilliant, excellent,
sumptuous 10. brilliance, effulgence
11. illustrious, magnificent

splendor... 4. gite, pomp 5. éclat, glory
6. beauty, luster 7. display 8. grandeur,
radiance, richness 9. pageantry,
showiness 10. brilliance
12. gorgeousness, magnificence,
resplendence

splint... 4. scob, tace 5. brace, plate,
strip 6. fasten, tasset 7. confine

splinter... 4. chip 5. break, broom
6. shiver, sliver 7. shatter 8. fragment
9. matchwood

split... 3. cut, rit 4. chap, open, rend,
rent, rive, tear 5. break, burst, cleft,
crack, laugh, leave (sl), riven, wedge
6. bisect, cleave, cloven, depart (sl),
divide, sunder 7. dispart, divided,
rupture, shatter 8. separate 9. apportion,
partition 10. separation

split (pert to)...
hairs.. 7. quibble 12. discriminate
13. differentiate
into two parts.. 5. bifid 6. cloven

pea.. 3. dal 5. dahll
the difference.. 5. share 7. average
10. compromise 12. go fifty-fifty
up.. 5. cleft 7. disband, divorce
8. separate 9. apportion, partition

spoil... 3. mar, rot 4. loot, prey, ruin,
sack 5. botch, decay, harry 6. coddle,
impair, injure, pamper 7. destroy,
estrepe, louse up (sl), pillage, plunder,
vitiate 9. frustrate

spoliation... 6. rapine 7. pillage
10. plundering, spoliation

spoiled... 3. bad 5. moldy, musty
6. addled, marred, molded, preyed,
rancid, wasted 7. botched, bungled,
decayed, tainted 8. pampered, pillaged
9. plundered 12. deteriorated

spoiler... 6. robber 7. marplot 8. pillager
9. despoiler, plunderer

spoils... 4. loot, prey, swag 5. booty,
perks (sl) 11. perquisites

spoilsport... 7. marplot 10. wet blanket
11. party-pooper

spoke... 3. bar, pin, ray, rod 4. rung,
said 5. check, round, spake, stake
6. radius, speech 7. uttered 9. hindrance
10. impediment

spoke monotonously... 6. droned

spoken... 4. oral 5. parol 9. declaimed,
ideophone (word)

spoliation... 6. rapine 7. pillage
8. ravaging 10. spoliation

sponge... 3. dry, wet 4. bath, swab
5. erase, mooch 6. absorb, animal,
efface, eraser, extort 7. badiaga,
cleanse, sponger, zimocca 8. drunkard,
parasite 9. absorbent, sycophant
10. obliterate, porousness

sponge (pert to)...
Europe.. 7. badiaga
fruit.. 5. luffa (loofah)
Mediterranean.. 7. zimocca
opening.. 7. apopyle
orifice.. 7. osculum
young.. 5. ascon 6. rhagon

sponger... 4. sorn 5. leech 6. cadger
7. moocher 8. parasite 9. scrounger
10. freeloader

sponsor... 5. angel 6. backer, patron
7. finance 9. financier, godparent,
guarantee, guarantor, patronize

sponsorship... 5. aegis (egis) 7. subsidy
8. auspices

spontaneous... 4. free 6. native
8. untaught 9. automatic, voluntary
10. self-acting 11. instinctive,
involuntary

spontoon... 4. club, pike 7. halberd,
pantoon 9. espantoon, truncheon

spoof... 3. guy 4. fool, hoax, joke
5. trick 7. deceive, swindle 8. nonsense
9. deception

spook... 5. ghost 6. spirit, zombie (zombi)
7. specter 8. frighten 9. hobgoblin
10. apparition

spooky... 5. eerie, weird 7. ghostly,
haunted, uncanny 8. spectral

spool... 4. reel, wind 6. bobbin 7. spindle
8. cylinder

spoon... 4. club 5. labis, ladle 6. shovel
7. fish for 8. cochlear, make love,

runcible
spoonbill ... 5. ajaja (ayaya) 9. sandpiper
Spoon River poet ... 7. Masters (E L)
spore (pert to) ...
  capsule, sac .. 5. ascus, theca
    10. sporangium
  cluster .. 5. sorus
  formation .. 6. tetrad
  fruit .. 7. asocarp
sport ... 3. fun, toy 4. game, hunt,
  jest, joke, play, romp, wear 5. dandy,
  mirth 6. banter, flaunt, frolic, gamble,
  racing, skiing 7. contest, gambler,
  jesting, mockery, pastime 8. raillery
  9. amusement, bon vivant, diversion,
  good loser, plaything, sportsman
  10. pleasantry, recreation
  13. entertainment
sport (pert to) ...
  art of (contests) .. 10. agonistics
  cheap .. 5. piker
  of kings .. 6. racing 7. the turf
sportive ... 3. gay 5. merry 7. jocular,
  playful 8. frolicky, playsome 9. facetious
  10. frolicsome
sports ... 5. Rugby, track 6. hockey, jai
  lai, soccer, squash, tennis 7. cricket
  8. baseball, football, la crosse, softball
  9. athletics, palaestra 10. acrobatics,
  gymnastics 11. racquetball
sports attendance ... 4. gate
sports official ... 5. coach, judge
  6. umpire 7. referee 8. linesman
  10. timekeeper
sporty ... 5. rorty, showy 6. dressy,
  flashy
spot ... 3. dot 4. blet, blot, espy, flaw,
  mark, site, soil 5. fleck, place, point,
  speck, stain, taint 6. detect, locate,
  macula, macule, stigma 7. asperse,
  blemish, freckle, observe, speckle,
  splotch 8. discolor, disgrace, locality,
  location, position 9. bespatter, limelight,
  recognize 11. predicament, small
  amount
spot (pert to) ...
  cards .. 3. pip
  fertile .. 5. oasis
  fish .. 7. pinfish
  high .. 4. apex 6. climax
  mineral .. 5. macle
  on the spot .. 3. now 4. here 7. imperil,
    present 8. promptly
  payment .. 4. cash
  secluded .. 6. alcove
  sun .. 6. lucule 7. granule
  wood .. 3. wem
spotless ... 4. pure 5. clean 6. chaste
  8. innocent 9. blameless, faultless,
  unsullied 10. immaculate
  11. unblemished, untarnished
  14. irreproachable
spotted ... 6. espied, marked, soiled
  7. dappled, guttate (droplike), mottled,
  stained, sullied 8. speckled
  9. blemished, sprinkled, tarnished
  11. diversified
spouse ... 4. mate, wife 5. bride
  7. consort, partner 9. companion
  10. better half
spout ... 3. jet, jut, lip 4. dale,

gush, pawn, rant, spew 5. erupt,
spile, spurt 6. pledge, recite, spigot,
squirt, trough 7. chatter, conduit,
declaim 8. downpour, gargoyle (carved)
9. discharge, waterfall 10. waterspout
spouter ... 5. whale 6. geyser 7. oil well,
speaker 9. declaimer 11. speechifier
sprat ... 6. garvie 7. herring 8. sixpence
spray ... 3. jet 4. foam 5. stour, water
6. squirt 7. atomize, flowers, gunfire
8. perfumer, sprinkle 9. spindrift
10. spoondrift
spread ... 3. ted 4. meal 5. bruit, feast,
flare, strew, widen 6. expand, extent,
sprawl, unfurl 7. divulge, radiate, scatter
8. disperse 9. broadcast 11. disseminate
13. advertisement
spread (pert to) ...
  by defamation .. 5. libel
  by report .. 6. norate
  by rumor .. 5. noise
  eagle .. 8. boastful, insignia 9. patriotic
    12. exaggeration
  out .. 3. fan 4. open, span 5. flare
    6. deploy
  over .. 5. cover, smear
  thickly .. 7. slather
  thin .. 4. bray
spree ... 4. lark, orgy, romp 5. binge,
revel 6. bender, frolic, shindy 7. wassail
8. carousal
sprig ... 4. trim, twig 5. scion, shoot,
smart 6. active, spruce 8. ornament
9. youngling
sprightly ... 3. gay 4. airy, pert 5. alive,
brisk, peart 6. blithe, lively 7. briskly,
ghostly 8. vigorous 10. enlivening,
spiritedly 11. incorporeal
spring ... 3. fly, hop, spa 4. dart, font,
jump, leap, well 5. shoot, spurt, vault,
vigor 6. bounce, energy, geyser, origin,
season, source 9. saltation 10. elasticity,
resilience
spring (pert to) ...
  back .. 6. recoil, resile 7. rebound
  of the Muses .. 7. Pierian
  ref to .. 6. vernal
  up .. 4. grow 5. arise, occur 6. appear,
    ascend 9. originate
springing into being ... 9. renascent
springs ... 4. spas 5. baths, fonts 6. resort
(health) 7. thermae
sprinkle ... 3. deg, dot, wet 4. rain
5. bedew, spray, strew, water 6. bedrop,
sparge, spreng 7. baptize, scatter
9. bespatter
sprinkler ... 11. aspergillum (Eccl)
sprinkle with ...
  flour .. 6. dredge
  grit .. 4. sand
  heraldic .. 4. semé
  powder .. 4. dust
  water .. 3. deg
sprint ... 3. run 4. dash, race
sprite ... 3. elf, fay, hob, imp, nix 4. peri
5. fairy, ghost, gnome, pixie, sylph
6. goblin, spirit 7. brownie 9. hobgoblin
10. apparition
sprite (pert to) ...
  fiction .. 5. Ariel
  Irish .. 10. leprechaun

mischievous . . **4.** Puck
ref to . . **6.** elfish

sprocket . . . **5.** tooth, wheel **8.** cylinder (toothed) **10.** projection

sprout . . . **3.** bud, son **4.** cion, grow **5.** scion, shoot, spire, sprit **6.** branch, ratoon, tiller **7.** burgeon, upstart **8.** offshoot **9.** germinate **10.** descendant

spruce . . . **4.** chic, neat, posh, smug, tree, trig, trim **5.** adorn, natty, smart **6.** dapper **7.** finical, smarten **8.** titivate

spruce (pert to) . . .
beverage . . **4.** beer
black . . **7.** yew pine
fir . . **6.** Norway
genus . . **5.** Abies, Picea
Japanese . . **6.** Alcock
type . . **7.** Douglas, hemlock
white . . **8.** épinette

sprue . . . **5.** dross, waste **6.** thrush **7.** disease **8.** psilosis **9.** asparagus

spry . . . **5.** agile, brisk, quick, smart **6.** active, nimble **8.** vigorous **9.** sprightly

spud . . . **5.** drill, knife, spade **6.** dagger, paddle, potato, reamer, shovel

spume . . . **4.** foam, scum **5.** froth

spunky . . . **4.** game **5.** quick, plucky, touchy, spirited **10.** courageous, mettlesome **13.** quick-tempered

spur . . . **3.** egg **4.** goad, move, urge **5.** drive, press, ridge, rowel, spine **6.** calcar, excite, griffe, incite, needle **7.** provoke **8.** stimulus **9.** instigate, stimulate **10.** incitement

spur (pert to) . . .
badge . . **10.** knighthood
fowl . . **5.** quail **9.** partridge
gamecock's . . **4.** gaff **7.** gablock
mountain . . **5.** arête
pert to . . **7.** spicate
railroad . . **5.** track
wheel . . **5.** rowel

spurious . . . **4.** fake, sham **5.** false **6.** pseudo **7.** bastard **10.** adulterate, apocryphal, artificial, fictitious, fraudulent **11.** counterfeit **12.** illegitimate **14.** supposititious

spurious (pert to) . . .
fruit . . **10.** pseudocarp
olive . . **9.** heartwood
rainbow . . **8.** faint arc
wing . . **7.** bastard

spurn . . . **4.** defy **5.** scorn **6.** reject, strike **7.** contemn, disdain

spurt . . . **3.** jet, jut **4.** dash, gush, spew **5.** burst, spout **7.** outpour, upsurge **8.** outbreak

spy . . . **3.** pry, see **4.** espy, note, tout **5.** scout, sneak, snoop, watch **6.** behold, descry, detect, search **7.** examine, snooper **8.** discover, emissary, informer, perceive **10.** scrutinize **11.** reconnoiter

spy (pert to) . . .
city . . **7.** Belgium
in clothing circles . . **4.** keek
Man of . . **14.** paleolithic man
prison . . **4.** mouton

squab . . . **3.** fat **4.** fowl, sofa **5.** piper, plump **6.** fat man, pigeon **7.** cushion **8.** nestling **9.** fledgling

squabble . . . **5.** brawl **6.** bicker, jangle **7.** contend, quarrel, wrangle **10.** disarrange (Print) **13.** collieshangie

squad . . . **4.** team, unit **5.** posse **7.** company

squalid . . . **4.** foul, mean, poor **5.** dirty **6.** filthy, sordid **7.** unclean **8.** slovenly **9.** repellent, repulsive **11.** squalidness **15.** poverty-stricken

squall . . . **3.** cry, row **4.** blow, gale, gust, wail, wind, yell **6.** squawk, squeal **9.** commotion **11.** disturbance

squalor . . . **4.** dirt, mire **5.** filth **8.** slovenry **9.** dirtiness **10.** filthiness **11.** squalidness **16.** unkempt condition

squamate, squamous . . . **5.** scaly **6.** scaled

squander . . . **5.** waste **6.** lavish **7.** scatter **8.** disperse, misspend **9.** dissipate, throw away **10.** run through

squanderer . . . **5.** loser **7.** wastrel

square . . . **4.** even, meal **5.** bribe, plaza **6.** common, honest, settle **7.** exactly, obelisk, old fogy **8.** absolute, cube face, directly, equalize, quadrate **9.** city block, divergent **11.** unequivocal **13.** parallelogram **14.** unsophisticate **15.** straightforward

squash . . . **4.** mash, pepo, pulp **5.** crush, gourd, press **6.** cushaw, refute, simlin, simnel, soften **7.** cymling (cymbling), Hubbard, squeeze **8.** pattypan, suppress **9.** crookneck **10.** extinguish **11.** calabazilla

squat . . . **3.** low **5.** dumpy, pudgy, quash, stoop **6.** crouch, hunker, settle, stubby **7.** sit down **8.** squatter, thickset

squatter . . . **6.** nester (illegal) **7.** pioneer **9.** sandpiper **11.** homesteader

Squatter State . . . **6.** Kansas

squaw . . . **6.** coween, Indian, mahala (mahaly)

squeal . . . **6.** betray, inform **7.** protest, quarrel

squealer . . . **4.** fink **6.** grouse, pigeon, plover **7.** traitor **8.** informer

squeamish . . . **4.** nice **5.** dizzy **6.** dainty, queasy **7.** prudish **8.** overnice, qualmish **9.** nauseated **10.** fastidious, scrupulous

squeeze . . . **3.** hug, jam, nip **4.** cram, crux **5.** crowd, crush, pinch, press, wring **6.** crisis, extort **7.** embrace **8.** compress **9.** constrict, influence **10.** constraint **11.** compression

squeezer, fruit . . . **6.** juicer, reamer

squelch . . . **5.** crush, quash, quell **6.** rebuke, refute, subdue **7.** repress, silence **8.** suppress **10.** disconcert

squib . . . **4.** bomb, fuse, pipe, skit, tube **6.** speech, squirt **7.** explode, lampoon, writing **9.** bespatter **10.** pasquinade **11.** firecracker

squire . . . **4.** beau **5.** court, lover **6.** escort **7.** gallant **8.** henchman, nobleman **9.** attendant, gentleman, landowner

squirm . . . **5.** twist **6.** wiggle, writhe **7.** wriggle

squirrel (pert to) . . .
African . . **5.** xerus
American . . **5.** bunny **7.** assapan **8.** chipmunk **9.** chickaree
American, flying . . **7.** assapan

Asian .. 5. sisel 6. suslik
Austral, flying .. 9. phalanger
burrowing .. 6. gopher
cage .. 9. treadmill
color .. 4. lead
E Ind, flying .. 6. taguan
fish .. 7. serrano
fur (Her) .. 4. vair
genus .. 6. Tamias 7. Sciurus
Java .. 8. jelerang
like .. 8. sciuroid
nest .. 4. dray, drey
shrew .. 4. tana 6. Tupaia
skin .. 4. vair
Spanish .. 7. ardilla
squirrellike mammal ... 8. banxring,
  dormouse
stab ... 4. gore, pang, pink 5. knife, knive,
  lunge, wound 6. attack, injury, pierce,
  thrust 7. poniard, slander 8. puncture,
  stoccado
stability ... 5. poise 7. balance
  8. firmness, strength 9. constancy
  10. permanence, stableness, steadiness
  11. reliability 12. immovability,
  immutability 13. steadfastness
stabilize ... 3. set 5. poise 6. steady
  7. ballast 8. regulate
stable ... 3. mew (Royal) 4. barn, byre,
  firm, safe 5. fixed, solid, sound,
  stall 6. steady, strong 7. durable,
  lasting, paddock, support 8. constant,
  reliable 9. confirmed, permanent,
  steadfast 10. stationary, unwavering
  11. established, trustworthy
stableman ... 5. groom 7. hostler (ostler)
staccato ... 7. détaché 8. ricochet
  12. disconnected
stack ... 4. heap, load, pile, rick 5. mound,
  shock 6. pile up 7. chimney, conduit
  8. quantity
stacked ... 11. accumulated, prearranged
stacked pack, cards ... 8. cold deck
stadium ... 5. stage 6. course, dromos
  8. foot race (anc)
stadium race, start ... 7. aphesis
staff ... 3. rod 4. club, mace, pole
  5. baton, music, stave 7. scepter,
  support 8. caduceus, insignia, pastoral
  9. personnel 10. assistants, associates
staff (pert to) ...
Bacchus .. 7. thyrsus
bearer .. 5. macer
magician's .. 7. rhabdos
marshal's .. 5. baton
member, officer .. 4. aide 7. attaché
mountain climbing .. 10. alpenstock
pastoral .. 5. pedum 7. baculus, crosier
  (crozier)
shepherd's .. 5. crook, pedum
sovereign's .. 7. scepter (sceptre)
stag ... 4. colt, deer (red), hart 5. party,
  royal, spade 7. male fox, pollard
  8. gamecock, informer
stage ... 4. dais, tier 5. arena, phase,
  scene 6. degree 7. display, estrade,
  perform, rostrum 8. platform, scaffold
  9. dramatize, gradation 10. proscenium,
  stagecoach
stage (pert to) ...
call (trumpet) .. 6. sennet

direction .. 5. aside, manet 6. sennet
of disease .. 9. catabasis
of insects .. 5. imago, larva
part .. 5. stair 8. dutchman (patch)
  10. proscenium
scene (side) .. 8. coulisse
scenery .. 3. set
stagger ... 4. reel, stot, stun, sway, walk
  5. lurch 6. excite, totter, zigzag 7. be
  drunk, tremble, vibrate 8. astonish,
  flounder, frighten, titubate, unsettle
  9. alternate, fluctuate
staggering ... 5. areel 9. startling
  10. astounding 11. the staggers
  12. unbelievable
Stagirite, The ... 9. Aristotle
stagnant ... 4. dull, foul 5. inert,
  stale, still 8. inactive, sluggish,
  standing 10. motionless, not flowing
  13. unprogressive
stagnate ... 3. rot 4. dull 5. inert
  8. stagnant, vegetate 10. motionless
staid ... 5. grave, sober 6. demure, sedate,
  solemn 7. serious, settled 8. composed,
  decorous, sensible 9. steadfast
stain ... 3. dye 4. blot, soil, spot, tint
  5. color, paint, smear, sully 6. infamy,
  smudge, stigma 7. blemish, corrupt,
  pigment, tarnish 8. discolor, disgrace,
  dishonor, maculate 9. pollution
  10. stigmatize 11. contaminate
  13. discoloration
stained by decay ... 4. doty
stained glass rod (lead) ... 4. came
stair ... 4. step 5. riser, stage, tread
  6. degree, flight (series)
staircase (pert to) ...
French .. 8. escalier
moving .. 9. escalator
outdoor .. 6. perron
post .. 5. newel
ship's .. 12. companionway
spiral .. 8. caracole
stairs to bath (Ind) ... 4. ghat (ghaut)
stake ... 3. bet, peg, pel, pin 4. ante,
  pale, pile, post, risk, spit 5. sowel,
  teest, wager 6. chance, estate, gamble,
  hazard, picket, pledge 7. finance,
  venture
stale ... 3. old 5. banal, fusty, trite,
  vapid 7. insipid, spoiled 9. hackneyed,
  tasteless 10. flavorless
  11. commonplace
stalemate ... 6. corner 7. impasse
  8. cul-de-sac, deadlock 10. blind alley,
  standstill
stalk ... 4. axis, hunt, risp, stem, walk
  6. pursue, stride 7. pedicel 8. peduncle
  11. reconnoiter
stalk (pert to) ...
cotton, sugar cane .. 6. ratoon
dry .. 3. hay, kex 5. haulm (halm)
flower .. 7. petiole
grain, grass .. 4. culm 5. straw 6. ressum
strawberry .. 4. risp
stalkless ... 7. sessile
stall ... 3. cot, dew 4. crib, fail,
  loge, mire, stop 5. booth, check,
  choir, stick 6. hinder, manger, stable
  7. disgust 9. temporize 10. dillydally
  11. compartment, play for time

12. parking space 13. procrastinate

stalwart . . . 5. brave, stout 6. strong, sturdy 7. valiant 8. partisan, resolute 9. corpulent 10. courageous, unyielding

stamen part . . . 6. anther, pollen 8. filament

stamina . . . 5. pluck, vigor 7. courage 8. backbone, strength 9. endurance, fortitude 12. staying power

stammer . . . 3. haw, hem 4. mant 6. falter 7. stumble, stutter 8. hesitate

stammering . . . 8. psellism

stamp . . . 3. die, dink, form, mark, seal, sign, tool 5. brand, infix, label 6. signet 7. engrave, impress, imprint, postage, trading 8. tressure (tressour) 11. endorsement 14. characteristic

stamp (pert to) . . .
border . . 8. tressure (tressour)
collecting . . 9. philately
collector . . 11. philatelist
madness . . 11. timbromania
paper . . 6. pelure
postage . . 6. timbre
space . . 8. spandrel

stampede . . . 3. run 4. rout, rush 5. panic 6. flight 7. debacle 11. wild scamper

stance . . . 4. pose 7. posture, station 8. position

stanch . . . 5. allay, check, quell 6. steady, strong 7. zealous 8. faithful 9. steadfast 10. extinguish 11. substantial

stanchion . . . 3. bar 4. post, prop 5. brace, piton 6. secure 7. support, upright

stand . . . 4. bear, bier, halt, rack, stop, zarf 5. abide, arise, booth, easel, store, table 6. endure, tripod 7. coaster, étagère, footing, impasse, sustain, taboret 8. attitude, foothold, pedestal, position, tolerate 9. withstand 10. standstill

stand (pert to) . . .
against . . 6. resist
by . . 3. aid 6. defend 7. support 9. be present
cost of . . 5. treat
Eccl . . 4. ambo
for . . 6. permit, typify 9. represent, symbolize
for candles . . 7. epergne 10. candelabra
in . . 6. deputy 10. substitute
it . . 4. bear 5. brook 6. suffer
offish . . 4. cold 5. aloof 8. reserved 10. not cordial
opposite . . 4. face
three-legged . . 6. teapoy, tripod, trivot
up to . . 5. brave 6. resist

standard . . . 3. par 4. flag, norm 5. grade, model, usual 6. ensign 7. average, classic, paragon, precept 8. orthodox 9. customary, principle 13. authoritative

standard (pert to) . . .
battle . . 9. oriflamme (oriflamb)
bearer . . 6. leader 7. officer 10. politician
chem test . . 5. titer (titre)
ensign . . 8. gonfalon, gonfanon
flag (Rom) . . 8. vexillum
of excellence . . 4. idea
of intelligence . . 5. Binet
of light . . 6. carcel
of quantity . . 4. unit
Ottoman Emp . . 4. alem

standerdize . . . 9. calibrate, normalize

standing . . . 4. rank 5. fixed, state 6. at rest, status 7. footing, settled, station, upright 8. duration, prestige 9. permanent 10. durability, reputation

standing (pert to) . . .
long . . 7. durable 8. duration 11. traditional
mode of . . 6. stance
out . . 7. eminent, salient
room only . . 3. SRO
social . . 6. estate, status 8. prestige
upright . . 11. orthostatic

stannum . . . 2. Sn 3. tin

stanza . . . 4. rann, unit 5. stave, verse 6. octave, sestet 7. strophe, triolet (8-lined)

stanza scheme . . . 6. ballad 10. Gray's Elegy, Spenserian

star . . . 3. sun 4. hero, lead 5. actor, shine 6. étoile 7. destiny, fortune 8. asterisk, insignia, ornament 9. emphasize, principal 11. hummingbird 12. heavenly body, luminous body

star (pert to) . . . see also *Stars*
brightest . . 3. Cor, sun 5. Deneb 6. Altair, Lucida, Sirius
Bull's Eye . . 9. Aldebaran
divination . . 9. astrology
Dog . . 4. Sept 6. Sirius 8. Canicula 12. Canis Majoris
evening . . 5. Venus 6. Hesper, Vesper 7. evestar 8. Hesperus
feather . . 9. comatulid
five-pointed . . 9. pentagram, pentalpha
French . . 6. étoile
gazer . . 4. fish 10. astronomer
giant . . 10. Betelgeuse (Betelgeux)
group (fixed) . . 13. constellation
guiding . . 5. Alpha, North 7. Polaris 8. Cynosure, loadstar, lodestar, polestar
large . . 5. Rigel
morning . . 4. Mars 5. Venus 6. Saturn 7. daystar, Jupiter, Mercury 8. Phosphor
North . . 7. Polaris 8. loadstar, lodestar
of Africa . . 15. Cullinan diamond
of Bethlehem (Bib) . . 11. guide of Magi
of the sea . . 11. Maris Stella (Stella Maris)
ornament . . 6. semé
path . . 5. orbit
ref to . . 6. astral, starry 7. sideral, stellar 8. sidereal 9. planatoid
representation . . 6. étoile
shooting . . 5. comet 6. Leonid, meteor
variable . . 4. nova 7. cepheid, R R Lyrae
wars . . 3. SDI

starch . . . 3. vim 4. sago 5. hilum, vigor 6. amidin, energy, farina, fecula 7. cassava 8. glycogen 9. arrowroot, formality, stiffness

starchy . . . 5. stiff 6. formal, viscid 7. amyloid, precise 9. unbending

stare . . . 4. gape, gawk, gaze, look, ogle, peer 5. glare 6. glower, goggle, wonder

starfish . . . 7. asteria 10. echinoderm

stark . . . 4. bare, mere 5. rigid, tense 6. barren, wholly 7. violent 8. absolute, complete, entirely 9. downright, unadorned 10. absolutely

starling . . . 4. myna, sali 6. pastor

Stars (pert to) . . .
  and Bars . . 15. Confederate flag
  belt, tract (luminous) . . 6. Galaxy 8. Milky Way
  circumpolar group . . 5. Draco 6. Dragon
  four (famed) . . 4. Crux 13. Southern Cross
  North Pole group . . 9. Great Bear 10. Little Bear 11. Septentrion
  Ursa Major . . 9. Big Dipper, Great Bear
  Ursa Minor . . 10. Little Bear 12. Little Dipper

start . . . 4. dart, dash, jerk, rush 5. begin, enter, sally 6. broach, origin, twitch 7. get away, startle 8. commence 9. advantage, beginning, departure, originate 10. inaugurate

starting point . . . 4. text (sermon) 7. scratch 9. departure

startle . . . 5. alarm, rouse, scare, shock 6. excite, fright 8. astonish 9. electrify

starve . . . 3. die 4. kill 5. crave 6. famish, perish, scrimp 7. atrophy, destroy 10. be indigent

starved . . . 4. thin 5. empty 6. frozen, hungry 8. famished, ravenous

starwort . . . 5. aster 9. colicroot

stash . . . 5. cache, plant, store 7. lay away 8. hide away

state . . . 3. say 4. aver, case, état, mode, tell 5. utter 6. affirm, allege, assert, plight, recite, remark, report 7. country, declare, expound, express, narrate 8. announce, propound 9. condition, enunciate, postulate, pronounce, territory 10. government, possession 11. body politic 12. circumstance, commonwealth

state (pert to) . . .
  a fact . . 4. aver 5. posit 6. avouch 7. declare
  agitated . . 9. disturbed, perturbed
  disordered . . 9. cluttered
  formally . . 8. propound 9. enunciate, pronounce
  French . . 4. état
  hypnotic . . 6. trance
  ideal . . 6. Utopia
  office . . 8. governor 11. secretariat
  on oath . . 6. depose
  police . . 7. trooper
  reference . . 6. statal
  secret . . 7. arcanum
  specifically . . 6. define 7. itemize 13. particularize
  treasury . . 4. fisc 6. fiscus
  ultimate . . 3. end
  under foreign control . . 12. protectorate
  without proof . . 6. allege

stately . . . 5. grand, largo, lofty, regal, royal 6. august, coldly, kingly 7. haughty, queenly, togated 8. eloquent, imperial, imposing, majestic 9. dignified, grandiose 11. magnificent

statement . . . 4. bill, list 5. audit, dixit 6. dictum, remark, report, resumé 7. account, invoice, premise 8. abstract, proposal, schedule 9. affidavit, assertion, manifesto 10. accounting, expression, recitation 11. declaration

12. announcement, presentation

statement (pert to) . . .
  abridged . . 6. precis, resumé 7. summary 10. abridgment 11. abridgement
  assumed true . . 7. premise
  contradictory . . 7. paradox
  defamatory . . 5. libel
  detailed . . 8. schedule
  dogmatic . . 6. dictum
  introductory . . 5. proem 7. preface, prelude 8. foreword, prologue
  legal . . 11. declaration
  mathematical . . 7. theorem
  of belief . . 5. credo, creed
  of introduction . . 8. prologue
  precise . . 8. aphorism
  self-evident . . 6. truism
  sworn . . 9. affidavit

State nicknames . . .
  Alabama . . 6. Cotton 12. Heart of Dixie, Yellowhammer
  Alaska . . (no official)
  Arizona . . 11. Grand Canyon
  Arkansas . . 17. Land of Opportunity
  California . . 6. Golden
  Colorado . . 10. Centennial
  Connecticut . . 6. Nutmeg
  Delaware . . 5. First
  Florida . . 8. Sunshine
  Georgia . . 5. Peach
  Hawaii . . 5. Aloha
  Idaho . . 3. Gem
  Illinois . . 7. Prairie
  Indiana . . 7. Hoosier
  Iowa . . 7. Hawkeye
  Kansas . . 9. Sunflower
  Kentucky . . 9. Bluegrass
  Louisiana . . 7. Pelican
  Maine . . 8. Pine Tree
  Maryland . . 4. Free 7. Old Line
  Massachusetts . . 3. Bay 9. Old Colony
  Michigan . . 9. Wolverine
  Minnesota . . 6. Gopher 9. North Star
  Mississippi . . 8. Magnolia
  Missouri . . 6. Show Me
  Montana . . 8. Treasure
  Nebraska . . 4. Beef 10. Cornhusker
  Nevada . . 6. Silver 9. Sagebrush
  New Hampshire . . 7. Granite
  New Jersey . . 6. Garden
  New Mexico . . 17. Land of Enchantment
  New York . . 6. Empire
  North Carolina . . 7. Tarheel 8. Old North
  North Dakota . . 5. Sioux 11. Flickertail
  Ohio . . 7. Buckeye
  Oklahoma . . 6. Sooner
  Oregon . . 6. Beaver
  Pennsylvania . . 8. Keystone
  Rhode Island . . 11. Little Rhody
  South Carolina . . 8. Palmetto
  South Dakota . . 6. Coyote 8. Sunshine
  Tennessee . . 9. Volunteer
  Texas . . 8. Lone Star
  Utah . . 7. Beehive
  Vermont . . 13. Green Mountain
  Virginia . . 11. Old Dominion
  Washington . . 9. Evergreen
  West Virginia . . 8. Mountain
  Wisconsin . . 6. Badger
  Wyoming . . 8. Equality

state of . . .

dissension . . 8. scission
disuse . . 9. desuetude
ecstasy . . 6. trance 7. rapture 8. paradise
hostility . . 6. feudal
mind . . 4. mood 5. humor 6. morale
 8. attitude
unconsciousness . . 4. coma 5. faint
state of being . . .
a layman . . 9. laicality
artless . . 7. naiveté
a son . . 7. sonship
a woman . . 10. muliebrity
behindhand . . 9. in arrears
beyond natural laws . . 12. supernatural
complete . . 9. plenitude
confined . . 10. internment
free from error . . 9. inerrancy
married twice, illegally . . 6. bigamy
married twice, legally . . 6. digamy
overfull . . 8. plethora
passive . . 9. stolidity
poison . . 5. toxic 8. toxicity
voiced . . 7. sonancy
worse . . 8. pejority
wrong . . 7. errancy
static . . . 5. inert, noise 6. stable 7. resting
 8. electric, inactive 9. quiescent
 10. stationary 12. atmospherics,
 interference
station . . . 4. fire, post, rank, seat,
 stop 5. berth, depot, place, radio,
 serai 6. health, police 7. calling,
 dignity 8. location, position, prestige
 9. situation 11. institution
stationary . . . 3. set 5. fixed, still 6. stable,
 static, stator 8. immobile 9. immovable
 10. motionless, unchanging
stationery . . . 3. pen 5. paper 6. pencil
 9. onionskin, papeterie 12. writing
 paper
statue . . . 4. bust 5. image 8. acrolith,
 figurine, monument 9. sculpture,
 statuette
statue (pert to) . . .
at Thebes . . 6. Memnon
gigantic . . 8. Colossus
Guildhall (London) . . 3. Gog 5. Magog
holy . . 4. icon (ikon)
male figure (support) . . 7. telamon
part . . 5. socle, trunk 6. plinth
primitive . . 6. xoanon
Pygmalion's . . 7. Galatea
world wonder . . 6. Helios (Rhodes)
status . . . 4. rank 5. class, state 7. station
 8. position, prestige, standing
status symbol . . . 11. swivel chair
statute . . . 3. act, jus, law, lex 5. bylaw,
 canon, edict, title 6. decree, rubric,
 treaty 8. statutum 9. enactment,
 ordinance 10. regulation 11. legislation
staunch, stanch . . . 4. firm, true
 6. hearty 7. devoted 8. faithful,
 resolute 9. steadfast 10. dependable
 11. trustworthy
stave . . . 3. bar, leg 4. fend, pole, rung,
 slat 5. staff, stick 6. cudgel, lathee,
 letter, stanza 7. baculus, support, ward
 off 8. overcome 11. set of verses
stave off . . . 4. fend 7. prevent
 8. postpone
staves, bundle of . . . 5. shook

stay . . . 3. guy, leg, rib 4. prop,
 rely, stop, wait 5. abide, brace,
 cease, check, pause, tarry 6. adhere,
 arrest, linger, remain, retard, status
 7. prevent, respite 8. postpone, restrain
 9. cessation, hindrance 10. impediment
 12. postponement
stead . . . 4. help, lieu 5. place 6. assist,
 behalf 7. replace, service, support
 9. advantage, farmstead, homestead
steadfast . . . 4. firm, true 5. fixed 6. stable
 7. durable, staunch 8. constant, faithful,
 reliable 9. unwinking 10. unchanging,
 unswerving 11. unalterable
steadiness . . . 5. nerve 7. balance
 9. constancy, stability 10. uniformity
 11. reliability
steady . . . 4. firm 5. fixed, grave, sober,
 staid 6. stable, sturdy 7. assured,
 equable, regular, uniform 8. constant,
 resolute 9. incessant, steadfast
 10. invariable, unswerving
 11. unfaltering, unmitigated
 13. uninterrupted
steal . . . 3. cly, cop, gyp, nim, rap,
 rob 4. crib, lift, loot 5. filch, pinch,
 poach, swipe 6. finger, kidnap, pilfer,
 snitch 7. purloin 8. embezzle, peculate
 10. plagiarize 11. appropriate
steal (pert to) . . .
a march on . . 5. evade 7. precede
 10. anticipate 13. gain advantage
away . . 5. creep, slink, sneak
cattle . . 6. rustle
feloniously . . 6. ratten
game . . 5. poach 8. trespass
insane desire to . . 11. kleptomania
nautical . . 7. manavel
stealer . . . 5. crook, thief 6. lifter, pirate
 7. abactor, abigens, filcher, rustler
 8. pilferer 9. embezzler, peculator,
 purloiner 10. pickpocket, plagiarist
 11. biblioklept 12. kleptomaniac
stealthy . . . 3. sly 6. artful, feline,
 secret 7. catlike, cunning, furtive
 11. clandestine
steam . . . 4. boil, fume, heat, mist, reek
 5. force, power, smoke, stufa, vapor
 6. energy, pother (puther) 8. vaporize
 9. evaporate
steam (pert to) . . .
boat . . 5. liner 7. steamer 9. steamship
 11. side-wheeler
jet of . . 5. stufa 8. suffione
organ . . 8. calliope
steamboat cabin (officer's) . . . 5. texas
steamy . . . 5. misty 7. excited 8. vaporous
 9. steamed up
steatite . . . 4. talc 9. soapstone
steed . . . 3. nag 5. horse 6. charger,
 courser, Pegasus (winged)
steel . . . 5. inure 6. harden, smooth
 10. strengthen
steel (pert to) . . .
armor plate . . 4. tace 5. tasse
color . . 4. gray 9. steel blue 12. Prussian
 blue
conversion to . . 10. acieration
India . . 5. wootz 6. wootz steel
metallurgy of . . 9. siderurgy
process . . 8. Bessemer 11. cementation

type . . 6. damask, Toledo 8. Damascus

steep . . . 3. ret, sop 4. brae, buck, high, soak, stew, tall 5. cleve (cleeve), hilly, lofty, scarp, sharp, sheer 6. abrupt, clifty, escarp, imbrue, infuse, seethe 7. extract, extreme 8. elevated, headlong, macerate 9. difficult, excessive, expensive, precipice 10. exorbitant 11. precipitous 13. perpendicular

steeple . . . 5. spire, tower 6. flèche 7. minaret 8. pinnacle

steer . . . 2. ox 3. cow, ply, yaw 4. helm, luff, stot 5. guide, pilot 6. bovina, direct, govern, manage 7. bullock, control, operate

steer clear of . . 4. snub 5. avert, avoid 9. sidetrack, step aside 14. be inhospitable

steer close to wind . . . 4. luff

steeve . . . 4. lade, pack, spar (a) 5. store, stuff 6. freeze

stein . . . 3. mug 4. Toby

stellar . . . 6. astral, starry 7. leading, starlit 8. starlike, stellate 10. theatrical

Steller's sea cow . . . 6. Rytina

stem . . . 3. dam 4. axis, base, cion, corm, prow, root, stop, tige 5. check, shaft, stalk, tuber 6. branch, breast, oppose, scapel, stanch 7. lineage, petiole 8. ancestry, peduncle 9. originate

stem (pert to) . . .
bulblike . . 4. corm, drub
cylinder . . 5. stele
grass . . 4. culm
joint . . 4. cane, node
mushroom . . 5. stipe
plant . . 4. bine
seedling . . 7. tigella (tigelle) 9. hypocotyl
strawberry . . 4. risp
twining . . 7. tendril
underground . . 5. tuber

stemless herb (evergreen) . . . 5. Galax 11. acaulescent

stench . . . 4. odor 5. fetor, smell, stink

stenographer of Cicero . . . 4. Tiro

step . . . 3. pas, way 4. gait, pace, rung 5. dance, grise, phase, riser, stair, stalk, strut, tread 6. degree, stride 7. advance, imprint, measure, process 8. distance, footstep 9. footprint, gradation 10. stepladder

step (pert to) . . .
arrangement of troops . . 7. echelon
clumsy . . 5. stamp
dance . . 3. pas 6. chassé
mincingly . . 6. sashay
mother . . 7. noverca
stately . . 5. stalk
up . . 8. approach 9. intensify 10. accelerate

steppe . . . 5. plain 9. grassland

steps (outdoor flight) . . . 6. perron

stereotyped . . . 5. banal, corny, trite 6. common, old hat 9. hackneyed 11. cut and dried

sterile . . . 4. arid 6. barren 7. useless 8. impotent 9. fruitless 10. unfruitful 11. ineffective, ineffectual 12. unproductive

stern . . . 4. dour, grim, hard, rear, rump

5. harsh 6. gloomy, severe, strict, sullen, unkind 7. austere 8. buttocks, hind part, rigorous 9. harshness, unfeeling 10. strictness, unyielding 11. hardhearted 14. uncompromising

sternutation . . . 8. sneezing

sternutative . . . 7. errhine

stertorous . . . 7. snoring 15. hoarse breathing

stevedore . . . 5. lader 6. loader, stower 7. carrier 8. unloader 12. longshoreman

stew . . . 3. pot 4. boil, cook, food, fret, fume, mess, olio, olla 5. anger, imbue, steep, worry 6. bustle, ragout, seethe, simmer 7. haricot, swelter 8. meat dish 9. Brunswick 10. excitement, hodgepodge 11. predicament

steward . . . 5. agent, reeve 6. seaman, waiter 7. dapifer, erenach, foreman, granger, manager, servant 8. manciple 9. custodian, major-domo, seneschal, treasurer 10. magistrate 11. chamberlain, fiscal agent

Stewart, Stuart sovereigns (last) . . . 4. Anne 5. Henry

stewed fruit . . . 7. compote

stick . . . 3. bar, bat, bow, gad, gum, rod 4. cane, dolt, glue, mast, pogo, ship, stab, wand, wood 5. baton, cling, fagot, paste, shaft, staff, stall, stave, stilt 6. adhere, baffle, ballow, cleave, cohere, mallet, pierce, puzzle, thrust 7. defraud 8. chatwood, revolver, transfix 9. drumstick, persevere 10. matchstick, overcharge 13. stick-in-the-mud

stick (pert to) . . .
bamboo . . 6. lathee (lathi)
bundle . . 5. fagot 6. fasces
crooked . . 5. caman 7. cammock, gambrel
insects . . 5. Emesa
mountain climbing . . 10. alpenstock

sticker . . . 4. burr 5. label, poser, thorn 6. poster, puzzle, weapon 7. bramble 8. adherent

sticky . . . 3. goo 5. gluey, humid, moist, woody 6. clammy, slushy, viscid 7. viscous 8. adhesive 9. difficult, glutinous, tenacious 10. saccharine

stiff . . . 4. dead, hard, hobo, limp, taut 5. harsh, horse, idler, rigid, stark, tense 6. corpse, formal, proper, severe, strict 7. awkward, cadaver, starchy 8. resolute, rigorous, starched 9. dead-drunk, obstinate, unbending 14. uncompromising

stiff-necked . . . 8. stubborn 9. ankylotic, obstinate 11. strait-laced 12. contumacious

stiffness . . . 8. rigidity 9. formality, toughness 10. strictness 11. starchiness

stifle . . . 3. gag 4. stop 5. choke 6. deaden, muffle, quench 7. repress, smother 8. strangle, throttle 9. suffocate 10. extinguish

stigma . . . 4. blot, mark, scar, slur 5. brand, odium, stain, stamp, taint 6. defect 7. blemish 8. disgrace, reproach

stigmatism . . . 7. blemish 10. refraction

(eye)

stigmatize ... 5. brand 6. defame
8. denounce

still ... 3. but, mum, yet 4. calm, even,
lull, moot 5. allay, check, inert, quiet
6. always, hushed, pacify, silent,
soothe, subdue 7. silence, subdued
8. inactive, restrain, suppress, tranquil,
until now 9. quiescent 10. distillery,
motionless, photograph 11. continually
12. nevertheless 15. notwithstanding

still water ... 4. pond, pool 6. lagoon

stilt ... 6. crutch 7. yeguita (black-necked)

stilted ... 6. formal 7. pompous
8. elevated, inflated, on stilts
9. bombastic, inelegant

stimulant ... 3. tea 5. salts, tonic
6. bracer, coffee 7. alcohol 8. caffeine,
stimulus 9. digitalis, sassafras
10. adrenalin, strychnine
11. epinephrine

stimulate ... 3. jog, pep 4. goad, stir,
urge, whet 5. elate, impel, rouse, sting
6. excite, fillip (filip), incite, spur on
7. animate, enliven, quicken, refresh
8. energize, motivate 9. encourage,
instigate, sensitize 10. exhilarate,
invigorate

stimulating ... 4. cool 7. piquant
8. exciting 10. energizing, refreshing

stimulus ... 4. spur 5. sting 6. motive
7. impetus 9. incentive, stimulant

sting ... 4. bite, pain 5. smart 6. offend,
tingle 8. irritate

sting of conscience ... 5. pangs, voice
6. qualms, twinge 11. compunction

sting organ ... 10. nematocyst

stingy ... 4. dree, mean, near 5. close
6. scanty 7. miserly, selfish 8. covetous
9. niggardly 10. avaricious
11. closefisted 12. parsimonious

stinkbird ... 7. hoatzin

stint ... 4. duty, task 5. limit 6. scrimp
7. confine 8. be frugal, restrict 9. be
sparing

stipend ... 3. ann, fee, pay 5. annat,
wages 6. salary 7. annates, pension,
subsidy 9. allowance 12. compensation,
remuneration

stipulate ... 5. agree 6. demand
7. bargain, specify 8. contract, indicate
9. designate, guarantee, postulate

stipulation ... 4. bond 6. clause, demand,
detail 7. compact, proviso 8. contract,
covenant 9. agreement, condition
11. arrangement 13. specification

stir ... 3. ado, mix 4. fuss, jail, move, poke,
roll, to-do 5. budge, churn, rally, rouse,
shake, stoke, waken 6. arouse, awaken,
bestir, bustle, excite, flurry, hubbub,
pother, prison, rustle, tumult 7. agitate,
animate, disturb, inflame, provoke
8. activity, movement 9. commotion
12. penitentiary

stir (pert to) ...
colors (calico) .. 4. teer
fire .. 5. stoke
together .. 3. mix 6. stodge
_up_ .. 3. mix 4. rile, roil 5. anger, awake,
rouse 6. arouse, foment, incite

stirring ... 6. moving 7. rousing

8. bustling, eventful, exciting
9. animating, inspiring 11. stimulating

stirrup ... 4. ring 5. strap 6. saddle
(part), stapes 7. support 8. footrest,
tapadera

stitch ... 3. bit, hem, sew 4. mend, pain
5. baste, piece, ridge 6. suture, tailor
8. particle 9. embroider

stitch (type) ... 3. hem 5. chain, coral,
cross 6. carpet, damask, suture
7. glover's 11. needlepoint, over-and-
over

stitchbird ... 3. ihi 10. honey eater

stithy ... 5. anvil, forge 6. smithy
7. smithery

stoa ... 7. portico 9. colonnade

stoat ... 6. ermine, weasel

stob ... 4. post, stab, stub 5. stake
6. gibbet, pierce

stoccado, stoccata ... 4. stab 6. thrust
(rapier)

stock ... 4. fund, line, race, stem 5. breed,
broth, hoard, store, trunk 6. assets,
cravat, pillar, strain, supply 7. capital,
lineage, provide, rhizome 8. credence,
original 9. livestock, provision, replenish
10. progenitor

stock (pert to) ...
book .. 6. ledger
breeding .. 5. brood
certificate .. 5. scrip 8. document
flower .. 11. gillyflower
hawk .. 15. peregrine falcon
in trade .. 6. assets, supply
11. merchandise
market .. 6. Bourse 8. Exchange 10. Wall
Street
of goods .. 4. line
owl .. 8. eagle owl
payment .. 8. dividend
pile .. 7. reserve 12. accumulation
theater .. 5. plays
type .. 6. common 9. preferred

stockade ... 3. pen 5. étape, pound
6. corral, kennel, laager 7. barrier,
bulwark, parapet, rampart, redoubt
8. palisade 9. barricade, earthwork,
enclosure

stocking ... 4. hose, sock 6. anklet,
argyle 7. bandage, fortune, hosiery
8. seamless 9. livestock 12. bluestocking
15. Leatherstocking (Natty Bumppo)

stocks ... 7. pillory, shackle 10. securities

stoic, stoical ... 7. passive, Spartan
8. enduring 9. impassive 11. unflinching

Stoic School founder ... 4. Zeno

stoker ... 5. firer 6. seaman, teaser
7. fireman, greaser 8. trainman

stolen (pert to) ...
goods receiver .. 5. fence 7. smasher,
swagman
property .. 4. pelf 5. booty, spoil

stolid ... 4. dull, slow 5. beefy 6. stupid
7. adamant, passive 9. impassive,
inanimate 11. inexcitable, unexcitable

stoma ... 4. pore 5. mouth 7. opening,
orifice

stomach ... 3. gut, maw 4. craw, crop,
vell 5. belly, rumen, taste 6. desire,
endure, gaster, paunch 7. abdomen,
gizzard 8. tolerate 10. resentment

stomach (pert to) . . .
  ache . . 5. colic, cramp 7. gullion
    8. rumbling 11. borborygmus
  acidity . . 4. acor
  animal . . 3. maw
  bird . . 4. craw, crop
  comb form . . 6. gaster 7. gastero
  ref to . . 7. gastric, pyloric
  ruminant . . 5. rumen 6. omasum
    8. abomasum, roddikin 9. manyplies,
    reticulum 10. psalterium
stone . . . 3. gem, pit 4. kill, pelt, rock,
  seed 5. agate, block, geode, jewel,
  lapis, shale, slate, spall 6. attack,
  pebble 7. diamond, peridot, sharpen
  8. monument, pavement 9. hailstone,
  sculpture, whetstone 10. gravestone,
  grindstone 12. philosopher's
stone (pert to) . . .
  abrasive . . 5. emery
  Age . . 8. Eolithic 9. Neolithic
    11. Paleolithic
  alchemy . . 6. carmot 12. philosopher's
  arch (top stone) . . 8. keystone
  Bib . . 4. ezel
  broke . . 4. flat 8. strapped
  broken . . 6. rubble
  carved . . 5. cameo 8. intaglio
  chisel . . 4. celt
  cutters' disease . . 9. silicosis
    10. chalicosis
  famed . . 4. Hope, Pitt 5. Mogul, Sancy
  6. Jonker, Orloff, Regent 7. Blarney,
  Rosetta 8. Cullinan, Kohinoor (Kohinur)
  9. Excelsior 10. Great Mogul
  12. Plymouth Rock, Star of Africa
  flat . . 4. flag, slab 5. slate
  fruit . . 3. pip 4. paip, seed 5. cling
  7. putamen 8. endocarp
  gem . . 4. jade, opal, ruby, sard
  5. agate, pearl, topaz 6. garnet, ligure,
  spinel 7. diamond, emerald, peridot
  8. amethyst, sapphire 9. turquoise
  11. alexandrite
  gem cutting . . 6. adamas
  hammer . . 5. kevel
  hard . . 7. adamant 9. chatoyant (cat's-
  eye)
  heap . . 5. cairn
  instrument . . 8. lapideon
  masonry . . 6. ashlar
  medical . . 4. gall 5. renal 7. biliary,
  otolith 8. calculus
  oil . . 4. hone
  ornamental . . 9. scagliola
  pert to . . 7. lithoid
  pillar . . 8. monolith
  pyramid . . 6. benben
  quarry . . 6. latomy
  small . . 6. pebble 8. lapillus
  special . . 3. key, lap, oil, rub 4. curb,
  flag, head, lime, lode, mile, tomb, whet
  5. birth, flint, grave, grind 6. cobble,
  corner 8. stepping
  statue (part wood) . . 8. acrolith
  to dress . . 3. nig
  uncut . . 4. naif
  woman turned to stone by Zeus . .
  5. Niobe
stonecutter (pert to) . . .
  disease of . . 9. silicosis 10. chalicosis

  receptacle . . 7. sebilla
  tool . . 6. eolith
  type . . 6. jadder 7. jeweler 8. lapidary
  worker . . 5. mason
stonecutting art . . 10. stereotomy
stoning, death by . . 10. lapidation
stony . . . 4. cold, hard 5. rigid, rocky
  6. rugged 7. adamant 8. lapidose,
  obdurate, pitiless 9. petrified
  10. inflexible, relentless, unyielding
  15. uncompassionate
stooge . . . 4. foil 5. toady 6. flunky
  7. cat's-paw 8. henchman
stool . . . 4. seat 5. bench 6. pigeon,
  tripod 7. taboret 8. informer
stop . . . 2. ho 3. bar, dam, end 4. balk,
  foil, halt, kill, quit, stay, stem, whoa
  5. avast, block, cease, check, choke,
  close, delay 6. arrest, desist, detain
  7. impasse, prevent, silence 8. preclude,
  swear off 10. standstill 11. discontinue,
  obstruction, punctuation 12. lower the
  boom
stop (pert to) . . .
  close . . 8. obturate
  debate . . 7. cloture
  fermentation . . 4. stum
  gap . . 7. stopper 9. expedient, makeshift
  momentarily . . 5. pause
  nautical . . 5. avast
  organ . . 5. viola 7. gemsbok 8. dulsiana
  seams (boat) . . 4. calk
  short . . 5. pause 7. respite 8. interval
  12. intermission
  unintentional . . 5. stall
  watch . . 5. timer
  with clay . . 3. pug
stopper . . . 4. bung, cork, plug 5. spile
  7. bouchon
storage (pert to) . . .
  bin . . 3. mow 6. loft, shed, silo 7. granary
  8. elevator
  fodder (in silo) . . 6. ensile
  hidden . . 5. cache
  place . . 3. bin 4. barn 5. attic, depot,
  étape 6. cellar, closet 7. arsenal,
  granary 8. cupboard, elevator, magazine
  10. promptuary, repository
stork . . . 4. ibis 6. jabiru 7. Maguari,
  marabou 8. adjutant
storklike . . 8. pelargic
storm . . . 4. blow, fume, fury, rage,
  rain, rave, snow, wind 5. orage
  6. attack, shower, simoom (simoon),
  tumult 7. bluster, disturb, tempest,
  trouble 8. calamity, eruption, outbreak,
  upheaval, violence 9. agitation
  11. disturbance
storm (pert to) . . .
  cold . . 11. northeaster
  evil storm god . . 2. Zu 9. blackbird
  (symb) Hlorrithi
  extreme . . 4. gale 7. cyclone, monsoon,
  tempest, tornado 9. hurricane
  occidental . . 6. wester
  recorder (thunder) . . 11. brontometer
  sand . . 6. tebbad
  snow . . 5. buran
stormy . . . 5. rainy 7. furious, riotous,
  violent 8. agitated 9. inclement,
  turbulent 10. tumultuous

11. tempestuous

story . . . 3. fib, lie 4. hoax, joke, lore, saga, tale, tier, yarn 5. fable, floor 6. gossip, legend, serial 7. mystery, narrate, parable, romance 8. anecdote 9. chronicle, falsehood, tradition

story (pert to) . . .
absurd . . 4. hoax, yarn 6. canard
doleful . . 8. jeremiad
exclusive . . 4. beat, news 5. scoop
part . . 6. serial
short . . 5. conte 7. novella

storyteller . . . 4. liar 5. Aesop 6. fibber 7. relater 9. raconteur

stot . . . 2. ox 4. bull 5. steer 6. bounce 7. paunchy, stammer, stumble, stutter

stout . . . 3. fat 4. bold 5. brave, bulky, burly, hardy, obese, plump 6. fleshy, rotund, stocky, strong 7. haughty, violent 8. forcible, powerful, resolute, thickset 9. corpulent, undaunted 10. courageous, persistent

stoutness . . . 7. courage 8. strength 10. corpulence, embonpoint

stove . . . 4. etna, kiln, oven 5. grate, plate, range 6. heater 7. Coleman, furnace, smelter

stove part . . . 4. oven, pipe 6. burner 7. firebox, griddle

stow . . . 4. cram, hide, mass, pack 5. crowd, lodge, store, stuff 6. steeve 7. arrange, secrete

straddle . . . 5. salvo 6. option 7. astride 8. bestride 9. be neutral, go halfway

straggle . . . 4. rove 6. wander 7. deviate, meander

straight . . . 5. cards, erect, exact, rigid, stern 6. candid, direct, honest 7. correct, exactly, unmixed 8. directly, reliable, sequence, unbroken, vertical 9. authentic 10. horizontal, racing term 11. straightway, undeviating 13. uninterrupted 15. straightforward

straight (pert to) . . .
baseball . . 5. liner
course . . 7. beeline
edge . . 5. ruler
line . . 6. secant 7. enfilade 9. asymptote
Math . . 8. vinculum
out . . 6. candid 9. downright 11. unqualified 13. thoroughgoing 14. uncompromising
shooter . . 11. on the square
way . . 4. anon 8. directly 9. forthwith 11. immediately

straighten . . . 5. align, aline, level, order, plumb 6. tidy up 7. rectify, unravel 11. disentangle

straightforward . . . 5. frank 6. candid, direct, honest 7. sincere 8. outright 9. outspoken 10. forthright 11. undeviating

straightway . . . 4. anon 8. directly 9. downright, forthwith 10. forthright 11. immediately

strain . . . 3. sye, tax, try, tug 4. bend, dash, kind, mood, ooze, race, sort, tone, vein 5. breed, shade, stock, tense, touch 6. filter, melody, overdo, poetry, refine, sprain, streak, stress, strive 7. descent, fatigue, lineage, progeny,

stretch, tension, variety 8. ancestry, endeavor, exertion 9. constrain, overheave, percolate 10. generation

strained . . . 4. taut 5. tense 6. forced 7. intense, labored 8. wrenched 9. stretched 10. farfetched

strainer . . . 4. sile 5. sieve, tamis 6. filter, screen, sifter 8. colander, filterer 17. Hippocrates' sleeve

strait . . . 3. gut 4. neck, need 5. inlet 6. angust, narrow, strict 7. channel, limited 8. rigorous 9. difficult 10. restricted, scrupulous 11. distressful, predicament

Strait . . . 6. Bering 7. Surigao 8. Bosporus 9. Belleisle

Strait of Gibraltar . . . 17. Pillars of Hercules

Straits Settlements . . .
capital, Penang . . 10. Georgetown
capital, Singapore . . 9. Singapore
city . . 7. Malacca
peninsula . . 5. Malay
port . . 4. Prai

strand . . . 3. sea 4. bank, quay 5. beach, shore 6. maroon, thread 7. channel, current 8. filament

strange . . . 3. coy, new, odd, shy 4. rare, xeno (comb form) 5. alien, eerie, novel, queer, timid 6. exotic, quaint 7. curious, erratic, unknown, unusual 8. peculiar, singular, uncommon 9. eccentric, unrelated 10. extraneous, outlandish, tramontane, unfamiliar 12. unaccustomed, unacquainted 13. extraordinary, preternatural

stranger . . . 3. ger 5. alien, guest 7. visitor 8. intruder 9. foreigner, outlander

strangle . . . 5. choke 6. stifle 7. execute, garrote, repress, squeeze 8. suppress, throttle 9. suffocate

strap . . . 3. tie 4. belt, bind, hang, jess, rein, riem, whip 5. leash, strop, thong 6. enarme, latigo, oxreim 7. lanyard (laniard) 8. chastise

strap-shaped . . . 6. lorate 8. ligulate

strass . . . 5. glass, paste 10. silk refuse

strata . . . 6. layers 7. classes 10. formations

stratagem . . . 4. coup, ploy, ruse, trap, wile 5. trick 6. device, gambit 7. finesse 8. artifice

strategy . . . 7. tactics 8. artifice, intrigue, maneuver

stratum . . . 3. bed 4. coat 5. layer

straw . . . 4. stem 5. mulch 6. fodder, sennit, trifle 7. remains, sabutan

straw (pert to) . . .
bid . . 5. fraud 7. auction 9. worthless
coat (Jap peasant) . . 4. mino
color . . 6. flaxen
flower . . 11. everlasting
hat . . 4. baku 5. milan 6. panama
like . . 6. chaffy 15. stramineous
vote . . 5. Roper 6. Gallup

stray . . . 3. err, gad, sin 4. cavy, roam, rove, waif 5. range 6. swerve, wander 7. deviate, digress 8. aberrant, aberrate, go astray 9. wandering 10. occasional

streak . . . 3. roe 4. line, seam, vein 5. fleck, layer, stria 6. groove, strain, strake, stripe

streaked . . . 4. liny 6. banded 7. brindle, striped 8. brindled, striated

stream . . . 3. run 4. burn, flow, rill, sike (syke) 5. brook, creek, river 6. abound, course, rillet, runlet, runnel, throng 7. current, rivulet, torrent 9. streamlet 11. watercourse

stream (pert to) . . .
dry . . 6. arroyo, spruit
gold . . 6. placer
of consciousness . . 8. thoughts 10. psychology 11. abstraction
of forgetfulness . . 5. Lethe
underground . . 3. aar

street . . . 4. road 5. calle 6. avenue 7. highway, roadway 8. chaussée 9. boulevard 12. thoroughfare

street (pert to) . . .
car . . 4. tram
famed . . 4. Beal, Main, Wall 5. Canal 6. Beacon 7. Downing 8. Broadway 9. Peachtree 12. Threadneedle
French . . 3. rue
narrow . . 4. lane 5. alley
show . . 4. peep 5. raree
Spanish . . 5. calle
urchin . . 4. Arab 5. gamin 7. outcast 8. vagabond 11. guttersnipe

Street called Straight (Bib) . . . 8. Damascus

strength . . . 3. vis 4. iron, thew 5. brawn, force, might, nerve, power, rally, sinew, titer, vigor 6. energy, health 7. potency, stamina, sthenia, support 8. firmness 9. endurance, lustiness, stoutness, toughness, vehemence, willpower 10. robustness, stronghold

strengthen . . . 4. grow, prop 5. brace, nerve 6. deepen 7. confirm, fortify, nourish, toughen 8. increase, roborate 9. encourage, intensify, reinforce 10. invigorate 11. consolidate

strengthening . . . 7. bracing 8. roborant 12. invigorating, invigoration

strenuous . . . 6. ardent, severe 7. zealous 8. vigorous 9. difficult, energetic, laborious 11. industrious

strepent . . . 4. loud 5. noisy

streperous . . . 4. loud 5. harsh 7. noisily 9. turbulent 10. boisterous

strepor . . . 5. noise

stress . . . 5. arsis, ictus, labor 6. accent, insist, strain, weight 7. urgency 8. emphasis, exigency, pressure 9. emphasize 10. elasticity, exaggerate 12. exaggeration

stretcher . . . 3. bar, lie 6. litter, racker 9. falsehood

stretch out . . . 6. be long, extend 9. expatiate

strew . . . 3. ted 6. spread 7. diffuse, overlay, scatter 8. disperse 10. distribute 11. disseminate

strown . . . 4. semé 6. littered 9. scattered 12. disseminated

stria . . . 4. line 5. ridge, strip 6. fillet, furrow, groove, hollow, streak, stripe 7. channel 9. striation

stricken . . . 7. smitten, worn out, wounded 8. unnerved 13. incapacitated

strickle . . . 5. rifle 7. pattern 8. template 10. sweepboard 13. striking board

strict . . . 4. hard 5. exact, harsh, rigid, stern 6. severe 7. ascetic, austere, precise 8. accurate, rigorous 9. puritanic, stringent 10. forbidding, inexorable, inflexible, meticulous, relentless, scrupulous 11. strait-laced, undeviating 13. conscientious 14. uncompromising

strict disciplinarian . . . 8. martinet

strict discipline . . . 13. regimentation

stricture . . . 7. binding, censure 9. criticism, narrowing 11. contraction 12. constriction

stride . . . 4. gait, pace, step, walk 8. bestride, progress, straddle, velocity

strident . . . 6. shrill 7. grating, raucous 11. cacophonous

strife . . . 3. war 4. feud 5. fight 6. battle, combat, stasis 7. contest, quarrel 8. conflict, exertion, struggle 9. logomachy 11. altercation

strike . . . 3. hit, pat, rap 4. bump, bunt, slap, swat 5. clout, labor, smite, whack 6. attack, revolt 7. impinge 9. discovery

strike (pert to) . . .
a balance . . 5. weigh 7. average 8. equalize 10. compromise
against . . 7. collide 8. illision
and rebound . . 5. carom (carrom) 9. carambole
breaker . . 4. fink, scab
dumb . . 4. stun
heavily . . 3. lam, ram 4. bash, slam, slog, sock, wham 5. punch, smite
obliquely . . 5. carom 6. glance
out . . 3. fan 4. dele 5. elide, erase 6. cancel, delete 9. eliminate
to and fro . . 5. bandy
with beak . . 4. peck
with fist . . 5. pound, punch
with head . . 4. butt
with weapon . . 5. crunt
with wonder . . 3. awe 7. astound

striking . . . 7. salient 8. dramatic, eloquent, exciting 9. arresting, wonderful 10. noticeable, remarkable, surprising

striking effect . . . 5. éclat

striking part . . . 7. clapper

string . . . 3. ran, set 4. bind, cord 5. lacet, snare, twine 6. fasten, series, thread 10. succession

string (pert to) . . .
alphabet . . 5. knots (for blind)
of beads . . 6. rosary 8. necklace
of horses . . 6. stable
out . . 6. line up 8. lengthen 9. expatiate
pottery . . 13. Schnurkeramik (neolithic)

stringed instrument . . . 4. harp, lute, lyre 5. banjo, piano, recta, viola 6. fiddle, guitar, violin, zither 7. bandore, mandore, ukulele 8. mandolin, psaltery 9. mandolute 11. harpsichord

stringed instrument bridge . . . 5. magas

stringent . . . 4. ropy 5. rigid, tight 6. cogent, severe, strict 10. convincing 11. acrimonious, restrictive

stringy . . . 4. ropy 5. gluey, tough 6. sinewy, viscid 7. fibrous

10. threadlike 11. filamentous

strip . . . 4. bare, belt, live, pare, peel, skin, slat 5. cleat, shred, unrig 6. denude, divest, remove, strake 7. deprive, plunder, pull off, uncloak, uncover, undress 9. dismantle 10. dispossess, impoverish 11. decorticate

strip (pert to) . . .
blubber . . 6. flense
curved . . 5. stave
lead (stained glass) . . 4. came
leather . . 4. welt 5. thong 6. latido 7. belting
narrow . . 4. lath, slat, tape, welt 5. reeve, stave, strap
off skin . . 4. flay
of possessions . . 4. milk 5. bleed, bunko (bunco), shear 6. fleece 7. despoil, swindle 10. dispossess
raised . . 5. ridge
tease dancer . . 8. stripper 9. ecdysiast
wood . . 5. stave 6. reglet, spline

stripe . . . 3. bar, pin 4. band, beat, line, mark, sort, type, wale, weal, welt, whip 5. chalk, strip, vitta 6. streak 7. chevron 8. insignia 9. striation

striped (pert to) . . .
alder . . 11. winterberry
antelope . . 5. bongo
gillyflower . . 9. carnation
longitudinally . . 7. vittate

stripling . . . 3. boy, lad 5. youth 8. juvenile 9. youngster

strive . . . 3. aim, try, tug 4. toil 5. labor 6. battle, buffet, strain 7. compete, contend, emulate 8. endeavor, struggle

strive (pert to) . . .
for . . 3. aim 4. seek
to equal ... 5. rival 6. strain 7. emulate
to overtake . . 5. ensue
with . . 3. vie 7. compete

stroble . . . 4. cone 8. pine cone

strockle . . . 6. shovel

stroke . . . 3. fit, pat, pet, rub 4. beat, blow, coup, flip, line, putt, shot 5. ictus, serif, spasm, trait, whisk 6. caress, fondle 7. illness, solidus

stroll . . . 4. roam, walk 5. range, stray 6. go slow, ramble, wander 7. meander, saunter 8. ambulate 9. promenade 11. perambulate

stroller . . . 5. actor, tramp 6. beggar 7. peddler, vagrant 8. wanderer 9. saunterer 12. perambulator

strolling . . . 7. nomadic 8. rambling 10. meandering 13. perambulation

strong . . . 3. fit, hot 4. able, firm, hale, hard, wiry 5. fetid, hardy, lusty, solid, sound, stout, tough 6. potent, robust, sinewy, stable, sturdy, virile 7. healthy, intense, odorous, tainted 8. accented, forceful, forcible, muscular, resonant, stalwart, vigorous 9. effective, energetic 10. outrageous, persuasive, pronounced, remarkable 11. substantial 12. concentrated

strong (pert to) . . .
drink . . 6. liquor 7. spirits 9. distilled
flavor . . 4. racy 5. acrid 7. pungent
hold . . 4. fort 7. citadel 8. fastness, Fort Knox, fortress, muniment, treasury

man . . 5. Atlas 6. Samson (Sampson)
muscles . . 5. brawn, thewy
music . . 4. loud 5. forte 7. saccade
willed . . 8. resolute 9. obstinate 10. determined
wind . . 7. pampero

stroygood . . . 7. wastrel 11. spendthrift

strubbly . . . 6. untidy 7. unkempt

struck . . . 4. smit 5. smote 7. smitten, swatted 8. shutdown (see also *strike*)

struck (pert to) . . .
an attitude . . 5. posed
out . . 5. deled 6. elided, erased, fanned 7. deleted
with fear . . 6. aghast 7. alarmed
with missiles . . 6. pelted

structure . . . 3. dam 4. dais, form, pier 5. frame, house, jetty, kiosk, stage, tower 6. bridge, make-up, pagoda 7. edifice 8. building, platform 9. formation 10. tabernacle 11. composition 12. constitution, construction

structure (pert to) . . .
calcareous . . 5. coral
conical . . 7. pyramid
crownlike . . 6. corona
filamentous . . 4. hair
human . . 8. physique
monumental . . 5. pylon
roof . . 6. cupola, dormer
tall . . 5. tower 7. steeple 9. campanile
tentlike . . 10. tabernacle

struggle . . . 3. tug, vie 4. cope, wade 5. labor 6. effort, Peniel (Bib), strife, strike, strive, tussle 7. contend, contest, scuffle, wrestle 8. endeavor, flounder, scramble 10. contention, difficulty

strumpet . . . 5. belie 6. harlot 8. harridan 10. prostitute

stub . . . 3. end 4. dock, tail 5. squat, stump 6. coupon, stocky 7. remnant 8. thickset 11. counterfoil

stubble . . . 5. beard, stump 6. arrish 7. bristle 8. eelgrass

stubborn . . . 3. set 4. rude 5. fixed, hardy, rough, tough 6. coarse, mulish, sturdy 7. restive, perverse, resolute, starkish, vigorous 8. obstinate, pigheaded 10. determined, headstrong, inflexible, refractory, unyielding 11. intractable 12. recalcitrant

stuck . . . 4. fast 7. baffled, cohered 8. coherent, stranded (see also *stick*)

stuck-up . . . 4. vain 8. arrogant 9. conceited 10. egocentric 12. supercilious 13. self-important

stud . . . 3. dot, pin 4. boss, knob 5. haras 6. enstar 7. hobnail 8. ornament, stallion 9. studhorse

student . . . 4. co-ed 5. cadet, eleve, plebe, pupil 6. tosher 7. learner, scholar 8. disciple 9. collegian

student of . . .
behavior (human) . . 12. psychologist
birds . . 13. ornithologist
birds' eggs . . 8. oologist
Eton . . 7. Etonian
law . . 8. stagiary
medical . . 6. intern (interne)
military . . 5. cadet, plebe

natural history . . 10. naturalist
navy . . 5. cadet 10. midshipman
Oxford . . 8. commoner
proverbs . . 14. paroemiologist
punishment . . 10. penologist
reptiles . . 13. herpetologist
spiders . . 13. arachnologist
students, advanced group . . . 7. seminar
  13. upperclassmen
studied . . . 5. boned, pored 6. formal
  7. learned, planned, weighed
  8. designed, measured, reasoned
  10. well-versed 11. intentional
  12. premeditated
studio . . . shop 7. atelier, bottega
  8. workshop 11. working room
study . . . 3. con, den 4. bone, muse,
  pore, scan 5. étude, grind, learn, weigh
  7. discuss 6. peruse, ponder 7. analyze,
  examine, pegging, reverie, science,
  subject, thought 8. endeavor, learning,
  treatise 10. discussion, inspection
  11. contemplate 13. contemplation
study of . . .
  animals . . 7. zoology 9. zoography
  bees . . 8. apiology
  birds' eggs . . 6. oology
  disease . . 8. nosology
  fingerprints . . 13. dactylography
  handwriting . . 10. graphology
  insects . . 10. entomology
  man . . 12. anthropology
  mountains . . 7. orology
  old age . . 9. nostology 10. geriatrics
  11. gerontology
  population . . 10. demography, larithmics
  12. demographics
  punishment . . 8. penology
  sacred images . . 9. iconology
  temples . . 7. naology
  words . . 9. etymology 12. lexicography
stuff . . . 3. goo, pad, ram, wad 4. cram, fill,
  stow 5. gorge, trash 6. fabric, matter,
  potion 7. content, element, rubbish,
  satiate 8. marinate, material, nonsense,
  overfill, trumpery 9. principle, substance
  10. gluttonize
stuffiness . . . 7. prudery 8. dullness
  9. obstinacy 10. sullenness, sultriness
  11. pompousness
stuffing . . . 6. lining 7. padding
  8. contents, dressing 9. forcemeat
stuffy . . . 3. fat 4. dull, prim 5. close,
  stout 6. stodgy, sullen, sultry 7. airless,
  pompous, prudish 8. resolute
  9. bombastic, obstinate 10. old-
  fogyish 11. strait-laced 12. conservative
  13. ill-ventilated
stulm . . . 4. adit 7. passage 8. entrance
stumble . . . 3. err 4. fall, trip 5. lurch
  6. boggle, bungle, chance, falter,
  happen 7. blunder, perplex, stagger,
  stammer 8. confound, flounder
stump . . . 4. butt, dare, skeg, snag,
  stab, stub 5. clump, scrab 6. baffle,
  trudge 7. declaim, nonplus 8. platform
  9. challenge, remainder, tortillon
  11. electioneer
stun . . . 4. bowl, daze 5. amaze, daunt
  6. benumb, bruise, deaden 7. astound,
  stupefy, terrify 8. astonish, bewilder

  9. overpower, overwhelm
stunning . . . 8. striking 9. beautiful
  10. astounding, stupefying, terrifying
stunt . . . 4. feat 5. blunt, check, cramp,
  crowl, dwarf, whale (2-yr) 6. hinder
  7. curtail, exploit, shorten
  10. tomfoolery
stunted . . . 7. blunted, checked, dwarfed
  9. curtailed, shortened
stupa . . . 4. tomb 5. mound, tower
  6. shrine 8. monument
stupefied . . . 5. doped 6. aghast,
  sotted 7. drugged, shocked, stunned
  8. benumbed 9. petrified
stupefy . . . 4. daze, dope, drug, numb,
  pall, stun 5. besot, blunt, shock
  6. bedaze, bemuse, muddle 7. astound,
  confuse, petrify, terrify 8. bewilder,
  confound 10. incrassate, make stupid
  11. flabbergast (sl)
stupid . . . 4. clod, dull, dumb 5. blunt,
  crass, dense, inane 6. oafish, obtuse,
  simple, stolid 7. asinine, doltish, foolish,
  witless 8. blockish, Boeotian, gullible
  9. brainless, senseless 11. heavywitted
  13. unintelligent
stupid (pert to) . . .
  grossly . . 7. asinine 9. imbecilic
  person . . 3. ass, oaf 4. clod, coot, dolt,
  loon, lout, nerd 5. goose, klutz, stirk
  7. tomfool 11. gillygaupus
  render . . 8. hebetate
stupidity . . . 7. fatuity 8. dullness,
  hebetude 11. foolishness
  12. indifference 13. foolish remark
stupor . . . 4. coma, daze 5. sleep, sopor
  6. apathy, torpor, trance 8. lethargy,
  neurosis, numbness 9. lassitude
  15. unconsciousness
sturdy . . . 4. firm 5. burly, hardy, lusty,
  stout 6. robust, stable, steady, strong
  8. resolute, stalwart, stubborn, vigorous
  10. courageous, determined, unyielding
  11. substantial
sturgeon . . . 6. beluga, caviar 7. sterlet
  9. Acipenser 10. hackleback
stutter . . . 6. falter 7. stammer
sty . . . 3. pen 4. boil 5. hovel, stair,
  steps, stile 6. ladder, pimple 7. pustule
  8. swelling 9. enclosure
style . . . 3. air, pen, way 4. form, kind,
  mode, name 5. get-up, gusto, trend,
  vogue 6. gnomon, graver, phrase,
  stylus 7. alamode, diction, fashion
  8. elegance 9. execution 10. appearance
  12. characterize, presentation
style (pert to) . . .
  architecture . . 5. Doric, Greek, Ionic,
  Roman 6. Gothic, Norman 7. Italian
  8. Colonial, Georgian 9. Byzantine
  10. Corinthian, Romanesque
  11. Renaissance
  painting . . 5. genre 11. Renaissance
  type . . 6. roman, runic 6. italic
styled . . . 5. named 6. called, termed,
  y-clept (y-cleped) 7. phrased
stylet . . . 5. probe 6. trocar 7. poniard
  8. stiletto 9. specillum
stylish . . . 3. mod 4. chic, cool, neat, tony
  5. nifty, ritzy, sharp, smart, swank 6. chi-
  chi, dressy, jaunty, modish, preppy,

snazzy, trendy 7. alamode, voguish
11. fashionable
styptic . . . 4. alum 10. astringent, tannic
acid 12. constringent
Styx ferryman . . . 6. Charon
suant . . . 4. even 6. demure, smooth,
steady 7. equable, regular
suave . . . 4. oily, smug 5. bland
6. urbane 7. fulsome 8. unctuous
9. agreeable 12. ingratiating, mealy-
mouthed 13. smooth-talking
suavity . . . 7. amenity 8. civility, courtesy,
urbanity 10. gentleness
subdue . . . 3. cow 4. calm, tame
5. allay, crush, lower, quash, quell,
sober 6. disarm, muffle, reduce,
soften 7. conquer, repress, squelch
8. mitigate, overcome, suppress,
surmount, vanquish 9. overpower,
subjugate 11. subordinate
subdued . . . 4. meek, soft 7. muffled,
quelled 8. disarmed, relieved, tempered
9. conquered, toned down 10. made
gentle, subjugated 11. soft colored,
unperturbed
subject . . . 4. text, word 5. cause, prone,
theme, topic 6. matter, motive, submit,
vassal 7. citizen, servant 8. inferior
9. subjugate, substance 10. predispose
11. subordinate 12. part of speech
subjective . . . 6. mental 7. topical
8. fanciful, illusory 9. of the mind
10. nominative 11. introverted
subject of . . .
discourse . . 5. theme, topic
disease . . 4. case 7. patient
lawsuit . . 3. res 7. grounds
sentence . . 4. noun
subject to . . .
abuse . . 6. revile
analysis . . 7. titrate
argument . . 4. moot
change . . 7. mutable 8. amenable
choice . . 8. elective
control . . 7. rulable
death . . 6. mortal
depression . . 5. moody
dislike . . 8. aversion
mistakes . . 7. erratic
outbursts . . 9. irritable
tension . . 8. strained
vassalage . . 5. feoff
sublimation . . . 9. underling
12. underscoring
sublime . . . 4. high 5. grand, great, lofty,
noble, proud 6. refine 7. exalted,
haughty 8. elevated, eloquent,
empyreal, majestic, splendid, upraised,
vaporize 9. beautiful, expletive
11. magnanimous
Sublime Porte . . . 12. Ottoman Court
17. Turkish government
sublimity . . . 4. acme 5. glory 6. beauty
7. majesty 8. grandeur 9. greatness
10. excellence 11. distinction
12. magnificence
submarine . . . 3. sub 4. boat, ship
8. Nautilus, Scorpion, Thresher
11. submersible
submarine eye . . . 9. periscope
submission . . . 5. kneel 8. fatalism,

meekness, patience, yielding
9. deference, obedience, surrender
10. compliance, confession
11. resignation 13. nonresistance
submissive . . . 4. meek, tame 6. humble
7. dutiful, patient 8. obedient, resigned,
uxorious (to wife), yielding 9. compliant
11. acquiescent, conformable
submit . . . 3. bow 4. obey 5. defer,
remit, stoop, yield 6. soften, temper
7. succumb 8. moderate 9. acquiesce,
postulate, surrender 10. condescend
submit to . . . 4. obey 6. endure
11. acknowledge
subordinate . . . 4. exon 5. minor
6. subdue 7. servant, subject 8. inferior,
parergon 9. appendage, assistant,
dependent, secondary 10. collateral,
incidental, submissive 11. subservient
subsequent . . . 5. later 7. ensuing
9. following, postnatal 10. succeeding
11. consecutive
subservient . . . 6. vassal 7. servile, subject
9. assistant, truckling 10. obsequious,
submissive 11. subordinate
12. instrumental
subside . . . 3. ebb 4. bate, fall, lull, sink,
wane 5. abate 6. settle 7. descend,
relapse 8. decrease, languish
9. gravitate 11. deteriorate
subsidiary . . . 8. inferior 9. assistant,
auxiliary, extrinsic, tributary
10. collateral 11. stipendiary
12. nonessential 13. supplementary
subsist . . . 2. be 4. live 5. abide, exist
6. endure, remain 7. prevail, survive
8. continue
subsist on prey . . . 9. rapacious
substance . . . 3. sum 4. gist, meat
5. stuff 6. import, matter, wealth
7. aliment, element, essence, meaning,
purport, summary 8. hardness, material
9. actuality, affluence, solidness
11. consistency
substance (pert to) . . .
absorbent . . 5. fomes
aeriform . . 3. gas 5. argon
amorphous . . 7. ferrite
antitoxic . . 5. serum
aromatic . . 5. myrrh, spice 6. balsam
basic . . 7. element
bitter . . 5. aloes, aloin, linin 7. amarine,
emetine 8. elaterin
brittle . . 5. glass
cleansing, purifying . . 8. depurant
10. abstergent, clarifiant
corrosive . . 4. acid 7. caustic
dissolved . . 6. solute
dissolving . . 9. resolvent
electrical . . 3. ion
elemental . . 5. metal
expanding . . 8. dilatant
fatty . . 5. lipin, suint
ferment . . 7. activator
flocculent . . 4. wool
food . . 7. protein
fruit jellying . . 6. pectin
gelatinous . . 4. agar
hard . . 4. bone 5. ivory 7. adamant
hypnotic . . 4. ural
inflammable . . 6. tinder 7. bitumen

inorganic . . 7. mineral
ipecac root . . 7. emetine
light . . 4. cork
milk curdling . . 6. rennet
moss (Ceylon) . . 4. agar 8. agar-agar
neutralizing . . 6. alkali
resinous . . 3. gum, lac 5. copal 7. shellac
rubberlike . . 5. gutta
soapmaking . . 3. lye
stabilizing . . 7. ballast
sulphur . . 5. hepar
tar . . 6. cresol
unctuous . . 3. fat, oil 7. pinguid
vegetable . . 5. resin, rosin
wax, snow . . 5. cerin 7. suberin
    8. paraffin
whale (perfume) . . 9. ambergris
wood ash . . 6. potash
substantial . . 4. firm, real, true 5. pucka
    (pukka), solid, stout 6. actual, bodily,
    hearty, stable, strong, sturdy 7. genuine
    8. abundant, tangible 9. corporeal,
    essential, important 10. nourishing
    12. considerable
substantiate . . 6. embody, verify
    7. confirm, justify 8. underpin
    9. establish 11. corroborate
substantive . . 4. firm, noun 5. sound
    6. actual, entity 7. pronoun 9. essential
    11. substantial 13. self-contained
substitute . . 5. proxy, vicar 6. deputy,
    ersatz 7. apology, replace 8. exchange,
    nominate, alternate, surrogate
    10. understudy, viceregent
    11. replacement
subterfuge . . 4. ruse 5. blind, trick
    6. refuge 7. evasion, pretext 8. artifice,
    pretense 9. expedient 13. prevarication
subterranean . . 6. hidden, secret
    8. hypogeal, plutonic 10. in the earth
    11. underground
subtile . . 3. sly 4. rare, wily 5. crafty,
    subtle 7. cunning, elusive 9. beguiling
subtle . . 3. sly 4. fine, nice, rare,
    thin 6. artful, clever, crafty, shrewd
    7. cunning, refined, subtile 8. analytic,
    delicate 9. beguiling, designing,
    ingenious 10. mysterious
    14. discriminating
subtle (pert to) . . .
    emanation (invisible) . . 4. aura
       10. atmosphere
    sarcasm . . 5. irony
    variation . . 6. nuance
subtlety . . 6. guile 7. cunning, finesse,
    slyness 8. delicacy, fineness
    9. quodlibet 10. shrewdness
subtraction, terms . . 7. minuend
    9. deduction 10. difference, subtrahend
subversion . . 4. ruin (utter) 9. overthrow
    10. corruption, revolution
    11. destruction
subvert . . 4. ruin 5. evert, upset 6. refute,
    uproot 7. corrupt, destroy, pervert
    8. alienate, overturn 9. overthrow,
    undermine
subvertive . . 8. eversive
subway . . 4. tube 5. train 6. tunnel
    11. underground 18. underground
    railway
succade . . 8. preserve 10. confection

succeed . . . 5. ensue, occur 6. attain,
    follow, thrive 7. achieve, devolve,
    prosper, replace, triumph 8. come next,
    flourish, supplant 10. accomplish
succeeding . . . 4. next 7. ensuing, sequent
    9. following 10. subsequent, successful
    11. in the wake of
success . . . 2. go 3. hit 4. luck 5. elate
    7. fortune, outcome 8. accolade, smash
    hit 10. prosperity 11. consequence
successful . . . 5. lucky 8. thriving
    9. fortunate 10. prosperous, succeeding,
    triumphant 11. flourishing
succession . . . 3. row, run 5. music
    (rhythmic) 6. series 7. dynasty, lineage
    8. sequence 9. posterity
succin . . . 5. amber
succinct . . . 4. curt 5. brief, hasty,
    short, terse 7. compact, concise,
    laconic, summary 10. compressed
    11. compendious, sententious
succor, succour . . . 3. aid 4. abet,
    help 6. brandy (Alpine), relief, rescue
    7. comfort, deliver, relieve, sustain
    8. befriend, mitigate 10. assistance
succulent . . . 3. uva 4. lush 5. juicy,
    pappy, tasty 6. cactus, tender
succumb . . . 3. die 5. faint, yield 6. perish,
    submit 7. give way 8. get tired
such (as) . . . 3. sic 4. like 7. certain,
    similar 8. analogue 9. analogous
suction (as in clicks of Bantu) . . .
    9. implosive
Sudan, Africa . . .
    capital . . 8. Khartoum
    desert . . 6. Libyan, Nubian
    export . . 9. gum arabic
    gazelle . . 4. dama
    gum forests . . 8. Kordofan
    lake . . 4. Chad
    language . . 2. Ga 6. Arabic
    people . . 4. Arab, Sere 5. Fulah (Fula)
       6. Nubian
    Plain . . 6. Gezira
    river . . 8. Blue Nile 9. White Nile
    town . . 5. Segou
sudden . . . 4. rash 5. hasty, swift
    6. abrupt, prompt, speedy 7. violent
    8. headlong 9. impetuous, impromptu,
    impulsive 10. unexpected, unforeseen
    11. precipitate, precipitous
sudden (pert to) . . .
    all of a . . 5. short 6. presto 8. suddenly
    and brilliant . . 8. meteoric
    fear . . 13. consternation
    sally . . 6. sortie
    shock . . 4. jolt
    stroke . . 4. coup, dash
    thrust . . 3. jab 5. lunge
sudor . . . 5. sweat 8. sudation 9. exudation
    12. perspiration
Sudra caste . . . 3. mal (low) 5. palli
sue . . . 3. beg, woo 4. plea, urge
    5. court, plead 6. appeal, pursue
    7. entreat, request 8. continue, petition
    9. prosecute, seek after
suet . . . 6. tallow 8. leaf lard
Suez Canal builder . . . 9. de Lesseps
    (Ferdinand)
suffer . . . 3. let 4. bear, dree 5. admit,
    allow 6. endure, permit, submit

7. undergo 8. tolerate 10. experience

suffer (pert to) . . .
distress . . 5. gripe, groan, smart 6. starve
from heat . . 7. swelter
remorse . . 3. rue
ruin . . 5. wreck

sufferance . . 4. pain 6. misery
9. endurance, passivity 10. permission
11. forbearance

suffering, scene of . . 10. Gethsemane

suffice . . 2. do 5. avail, serve 6. answer
7. appease, content, satisfy
11. sufficiency

sufficiency . . 4. fill 7. ability, conceit
8. adequacy, capacity, validity
9. abundance 10. competency 14. self-
confidence

sufficient . . 3. due, fit 4. enow, full,
good 5. ample, valid 6. enough, plenty
7. suffice 8. adequate 9. qualified
11. responsible 12. satisfactory

suffix, for or denoting . . .
abounding in . . 5. ulent
abundant . . 3. ose
act of . . 3. ure 4. ance, tion
advocate . . 3. ite
alcohol . . 3. ol
being . . 3. ure
capable of . . 3. ile
chemical . . 2. ac 3. ane, ene, ile, ine,
iol, ole, ose 4. alic, idin, itol
diminutive . . 2. el 3. cle, ole, ule 4. ette
disease . . 4. itis
doer . . 4. ator
enzyme . . 3. ase
feminine . . 3. ess
follower . . 3. ist, ite
full of . . 3. ose
geological age . . 4. cene
inflammation . . 4. itis
inhabitants of . . 3. ese 4. ites
jurisdiction . . 3. ric
law . . 2. ee
medicine . . 2. ia 3. oma 4. itis
profession . . 3. eer

suffocate . . 5. burke, choke 6. stifle
7. smother 8. strangle, 'suppress,
throttle 10. asphyxiate, extinguish
12. deprive of air

suffrage . . 4. vote 5. voice 6. assent,
ballot, prayer 7. witness 8. petition
9. franchise 10. assistance 11. right
to vote 12. intercession, supplication

sugar . . 4. cane 5. biose, bribe, candy,
maple, money 6. doctor, season
7. sucrose, sweeten 9. sugarcoat
10. endearment, saccharose,
sweetening 12. carbohydrate,
disaccharide 14. monosaccharide

sugar (pert to) . . .
and molasses . . 6. melada
burnt . . 7. caramel
chemical . . 6. acrose 7. osamine, sucrose
8. fructose 10. saccharose
crude . . 3. gur 5. maple 10. massecuite,
piloncillo
fruit, honey . . 8. levulose
plant . . 7. sorghum
raw . . 5. cassonade, muscovado
sand . . 5. niter
simple . . 6. ketose, triose 7. glucide

substitute . . 5. honey
syrup . . 7. treacle 8. molasses
tree . . 5. maple
without . . 3. sec
wood . . 6. xylose

sugar cane (pert to) . . .
disease . . 5. sereh
pulp, refuse . . 4. marc 7. bagasse
stalk . . 6. ratoon

sugared . . 5. sweet 7. honeyed
9. sweetened 11. mellifluous,
sugarcoated

Sugar Loaf Mt locale . . 3. Rio

suggest . . 4. hint, mean, move 5. imply
6. advise, allude, prompt 7. connote,
inspire, propose 8. indicate, intimate
9. insinuate

suggestion . . 4. clue, hint, idea, plan
5. tinge, trace 6. advice, symbol
7. soupçon 8. proposal 9. hypnotism
10. indication, intimation 11. small
amount, supposition

Suidae . . 5. swine

sui generis . . 6. unique

suit . . 3. fit 4. plea 5. befit, cards,
dress, habit, match, serve, tally
6. adjust, answer, attire, become,
prayer, wooing 7. clothes, comport,
conform, costume, lawsuit, retinue
8. petition, sequence 9. courtship
10. litigation 11. accommodate

suit (pert to) . . .
at law . . 10. litigation
for property . . 6. trover
maker . . 6. sartor, tailor
starter . . 7. relator
the occasion . . 6. timely

suitability . . 7. fitness 9. propriety
10. expedience, timeliness 11. eligibility
13. qualification

suitable . . 3. apt, due, fit, pat 4. meet
6. proper, timely 8. adequate, apposite,
eligible, idoneous 9. accordant,
agreeable, competent, congruent,
congruous, consonant, expedient
10. compatible, consistent
11. appropriate 12. commensurate
13. correspondent

suitably proportioned . . .
13. commensurable

suite . . 3. set 5. music, staff 7. retinue
8. sequence 9. apartment
10. attendance, succession
11. consequence

suitor . . 5. swain, wooer 7. amoroso
10. petitioner 12. party to a suit

sulk . . 3. pet 4. mope, plow, pout
6. furrow

sulky . . 3. gig 4. dull, glum, plow
5. moody, pouty, surly 6. gloomy,
go-cart, sullen 8. carriage 9. obstinate

sullen . . 4. dour, glum, grim, sour
5. cross, gruff, harsh, moody, pouty,
sulky, surly 6. crusty, gloomy, morose
7. austere, cynical, fretful, peevish,
pettish 8. chumpish, churlish, petulant,
spiteful 9. obstinate, saturnine

sully . . 4. foul 5. dirty, smear, stain,
taint 6. defile, smirch, vilify 7. blemish,
corrupt, debauch, disdain, pollute
9. bespatter, denigrate 10. stigmatize

11. contaminate

sulphur (pert to) ...
alchemy .. 7. chibrit
alloy .. 6. niello
butterfly .. 7. clouded 9. cloudless
color .. 6. yellow
comb form .. 5. thion
element .. 11. nonmetallic
reference to .. 7. thionic 9. brimstone

sultan (pert to) ...
decree .. 5. irade
fowls .. 5. breed
home .. 5. serai
Mohammedan State .. 5. ruler 6. prince
  9. sovereign
Turkish ruler .. 6. Caliph 8. Padishah
  13. Grand Seignior
wife .. 7. sultana

sultana ... 4. roll (dessert), wife 5. grape
8. mistress 9. gallinule

sultry ... 3. hot 5. humid, lurid 6. torrid
7. dog days, sensual 10. oppressive,
sweltering

sum ... 3. add, tot 4. loot 5. count,
gross, total, whole 6. amount, number,
result 7. summary 8. addition, quantity
9. aggregate, summarize, summation
12. recapitulate

sum (pert to) ...
forfeited .. 5. dédit
of money .. 6. budget
total .. 8. entirety
unexpended .. 7. savings
up .. 3. tot 5. count 8. perorate

sumac ... 5. Rheus 7. dogwood
8. shadbush 9. squawbush
13. Toxicodendron 14. buckthorn brown

Sumatra ...
harbor .. 6. Padang 9. Palembang
island of .. 16. Malay Archipelago
kingdom .. 5. Achin, Jambi
mountain .. 12. Bukit Barisan
raft (bamboo) .. 5. rakit
river .. 4. Musi 5. Jambi, Rokan 6. Asahan
squirrel shrew .. 4. tana
wildcat .. 4. balu

sumless ... 11. inestimable
12. incalculable 13. unaccountable

summary ... 5. brief, short 6. digest,
prompt, resume 7. epitome 8. abstract
10. compendium 11. abridgement,
enumeration, reiteration
14. recapitulation

summary (pert to) ...
book .. 5. blurb
concise .. 6. précis
of facts .. 7. roundup
of knowledge .. 12. encyclopedia
  (encyclopaedia)
of principles .. 5. creed
of speech .. 5. notes

summer ... 3. été 6. season

summer (pert to) ...
bird .. 7. cuckold, sparrow, tanager,
  wryneck
coot .. 9. gallinule
house .. 6. gazebo 9. belvedere
lilac .. 8. damewort
pert to .. 7. estival
rash .. 11. prickly heat
resort .. 4. camp

squash .. 7. cymling, scallop 9. crookneck

summit ... 3. top 4. acme, apex, knap,
peak 5. crest, crown, knoll, spire
6. height 7. Everest 8. pinnacle
9. fastigium 10. perfection
11. culmination, mountaintop

summon ... 4. call, cite, page, sist
5. evoke 6. call up, demand, elicit,
invite, muster 8. conjure, evocate
8. remember 9. conscript

sumpter ... 4. mule 9. pack horse

sun ... 3. orb, Sol 4. bask 6. Helios
7. Phoebus 12. heavenly body
13. celestial body

sun (pert to) ...
clock .. 6. gnomon (part) 7. sundial
comb form .. 5. helio
crossing the equator .. 7. equinox
disk .. 4. aten
down .. 3. eve 8. twilight
farthest from .. 8. aphelion
fish .. 4. mola, opah 5. bream
god .. 2. Ra 4. Amen, Baal, Lier (Llew)
  6. Apollo, Helios 7. Khepera (Chepera),
  Shamash, Sokaris 8. Hyperion
mock .. 9. parhelion
nearest to .. 10. perihelion
outer layer .. 6. corona
over the equator .. 7. equinox
path .. 4. halo 6. circle 8. ecliptic
pert to .. 5. solar 6. heliac 9. heliology
poetic .. 5. glory, power 6. sunset
  7. daystar, sunrise 8. splendor
satellite .. 6. planet
spot .. 6. facula 7. freckle
squall .. 9. jellyfish
stroke .. 8. siriasis 9. calenture

sundang ... 4. bolo 5. knife

sunder ... 4. part, rend, rive 5. sever, split
6. cleave, divide 7. divorce 8. dissever,
disunite, sejugate

sundry ... 6. divers 7. several, various
8. frequent, manifold, numerous
9. different 10. multiplied
12. multifarious 13. miscellaneous

sunflower ... 8. marigold, rockrose
10. heliotrope

Sunflower State ... 6. Kansas

sunk ... 4. turf 7. baffled, concave,
lowered 8. dejected, overcome
9. depressed (see also *sink*)

sunk fence ... 4. ha-ha (haw-haw)

sunny ... 4. warm 5. clear, merry 6. bright,
sunlit 8. cheerful 9. sparkling, vivacious

sunrise ... 4. dawn

sunset ... 3. eve 4. dusk 7. evening,
sundown 8. twilight

Sunset State ... 6. Oregon 7. Arizona

Sunshine State ... 9. New Mexico
11. South Dakota

supawn ... 4. mush 12. hasty pudding

superabundance ... 5. flood 6. excess,
plenty 7. surplus 8. plethora
10. exuberance 11. superfluity

superabundant ... 4. rank 6. lavish
7. profuse 9. excessive, exuberant,
luxuriant, plentiful 11. overflowing
14. oversufficient

superannuate ... 5. retire 9. antiquate
10. pension off 13. prove obsolete

superb ... 4. rich 5. grand, noble

6. lordly 7. elegant, stately 8. majestic, splendid 9. sumptuous 11. magnificent 13. extraordinary 14. superexcellent

supercilious . . . 5. proud 7. haughty 8. arrogant 9. arbitrary 11. overbearing 12. contemptuous 13. hypercritical

supercilious person . . . 4. snob

superficial . . . 4. glib 6. slight, square 7. cursory, shallow, smatter, surface, trivial 8. apparent, external 9. frivolous, insincere

superfluity . . . 6. excess, luxury, wealth 7. overset 8. frippery 10. redundancy 11. prodigality 14. superabundance

superfluous . . . 4. over 5. luxus, spare 6. excess 7. surplus, useless 8. needless, wasteful 9. redundant 10. inordinate 11. extravagant 12. nonessential 13. superabundant 14. supererogatory

superhuman . . . 6. divine 9. Herculean 12. supernatural 13. extraordinary

superimposed . . . 4. over, upon 5. above 7. covered, layered 8. overlaid 9. overlying

superintend . . . 4. boss 5. guide 6. direct, manage 7. oversee 8. overlook 9. look after, supervise 10. administer, have charge

superintendent . . . 4. boss 7. curator, manager 8. director, overseer 9. inspector, straw boss 10. supervisor 11. chamberlain

superior . . . 4. over, peer 5. above, chief, upper 6. higher, senior 7. exalted, mastery, ranking 8. goodness, priority 9. advantage, paramount, seniority 10. ascendancy, excellence, pre-eminent, surpassing 11. pre-eminence 12. predominancy

superlative . . . 4. acme, best, peak 6. utmost 7. elative, extreme, supreme, the best 8. peerless 9. hyperbole 12. exaggeration

supernatural . . . 5. eerie, magic 6. divine 10. miraculous, superhuman 13. hyperphysical, preternatural

supernatural (pert to) . . .
being . . 3. God 4. atua 5. jinni (jinnee) 7. banshee (banshie), specter (spectre)
event . . 7. miracle
power . . 4. ngai 6. fetish 8. talisman 11. incantation

superscribe . . . 6. direct 7. address (a letter), engrave 8. inscribe

supersede . . . 4. omit 7. replace, succeed 8. displace, make void, supplant

superstition . . . 6. notion, voodoo 8. folklore, idolatry 9. tradition 10. Aberglaube 12. old wives' tale

superstitious . . . 6. goetic 7. magical 10. idolatrous 11. fetishistic (fetichistic)

supervene . . . 5. occur 6. accrue, happen 7. be added 12. be subsequent

supervise . . . 4. boss, read, scan 5. check 6. direct, govern, peruse, revise 7. inspect, oversee 11. superintend

supervisor . . . 4. boss 7. foreman, proctor 9. inspector, straw boss

supine . . . 5. inert, prone 6. abject, drowsy 7. servile, unalert 8. careless, inclined,

indolent, listless, sluggish 9. apathetic, lethargic, recumbent 11. inattentive, indifferent, thoughtless

supplant . . . 5. upset, usurp 6. remove, uproot 7. replace 8. displace, drive out 9. eradicate, extirpate, overthrow, supersede

supple . . . 3. sly 4. bent 5. agile, lithe 6. limber, nimble, pliant 7. fawning, lissome 8. flexible, yielding 9. compliant, resilient 10. obsequious, responsive 11. complaisant

supplement . . . 3. add, eke 5. add to 6. sequel 7. ripieno 8. addition, appendix, complete 9. accessory 10. complement 12. nonessential 13. reinforcement

supplementary, music . . . 7. ripieno

supplicate . . . 3. beg 4. pray 5. crave, plead 6. appeal, obtest 7. beseech, conjure, entreat, implore, solicit 8. petition 9. importune, obsecrate

supplication . . . 4. plea 6. litany, prayer 7. craving 8. entreaty, petition, rogative 11. obtestation 12. solicitation

supplies . . . 6. hoards, relays, stocks, stores 8. estovers, ordnance 9. provender

supply . . . 4. fund, give 5. cache, cater, hoard, relay, stock, store, yield 6. purvey, remuda 7. provide, reserve 9. provision, reservoir 10. administer, contribute

supply (pert to) . . .
food . . 4. feed 5. cater 9. alimental
fuel . . 5. stoke
funds . . 5. endow
horses . . 5. relay
provisions . . 6. purvey

support . . . 3. aid, arm, fid, guy, leg, peg, rib 4. abet, ally, back, base, buoy, limb, mast, prop 5. brace, cleat, shore, spile, stell, strut, tenon 6. backer, pillar, second, uphold 7. bolster, fulcrum, trestle 8. buttress, underlie 9. auxiliary, encourage, reinforce, stanchion 10. assistance, foundation 11. corroborate 12. substantiate 13. corroboration

support (pert to) . . .
anatomy . . 3. rib 5. spine
cannon . . 8. trunnion
coffin . . 4. bier
mast . . 4. bibb
resilient . . 6. spring
three-legged . . 5. easel 6. tripod, trivot
upright . . 8. baluster 9. stanchion
wedge-shaped . . 5. cleat

supporters . . . 6. allies, braces 7. backers, bracers, garters 10. suspenders 15. ministerialists

suppose . . . 3. wis 4. deem, trow 5. allow, imply, judge, opine, think 6. assume, expect, repute 7. presume 8. conclude, consider 9. apprehend, intention 10. conjecture 11. supposition

supposed . . . 8. putative

supposition . . . 2. if 6. theory 7. surmise 8. supposed 9. postulate 10. assumption, conjecture, hypothesis 11. connotation, implication

suppress . . . 4. kill, stop 5. check, crush, elide, quash, quell 6. hush up, muffle, retard, stifle 7. abolish, exclude, oppress, smother 8. hold back, prohibit, restrain, withhold 9. interdict, overpower 10. extinguish

suppression . . . 6. hush up 7. reserve 8. hush-hush 9. overthrow, restraint 10. inhibition

supremacy . . . 5. power 7. control, mastery, primacy 8. dominion 9. influence 10. ascendancy, domination, first place 11. sovereignty 12. championship

supreme . . . 3. top 4. last 5. chief, final 6. divine, ruling 7. crucial, highest 8. foremost, greatest, peerless 9. paramount 10. preeminent

supreme being . . . 3. God 4. Lord 5. Allah, Deity, monad 6. Brahma, Buddha 7. Creator, Jehovah 8. autocrat

surcease . . . 3. end 4. rest, stop 5. defer, delay 6. desist, relief 7. respite 8. drop work, postpone 9. cessation

surd . . . 4. deaf, mute 7. aphonic, radical 9. voiceless

sure . . . 3. yes 4. fast, firm, safe, true 5. bound 6. indeed, secure, stable, steady, strong 7. assured, certain 8. positive, reliable 9. confident, steadfast, unfailing 10. guaranteed, inevitable, infallible 11. trustworthy 12. indisputable 13. incontestable 14. unquestionable

surety . . . 4. bail, bond, fact 6. backer, pledge, safety 7. sponsor 8. security, sureness 9. certainty 10. confidence, engagement

surf . . . 4. foam, rote, wave 5. bathe, spray, surge, swell 7. breaker

surface . . . 4. area, face, orlo, pave, plat, skin 5. facet, meros, facing, patina 7. outside 8. exterior 9. periphery

surface (pert to) . . .
artificial . . 4. rink
front (coin) . . 7. obverse
gem . . 5. facet
geometric . . 6. toroid
medical . . 7. acrotic
toward . . 5. ectad
under . . 6. latent 10. internally
water . . 4. ryme

surfeit . . . 4. cloy, feed, glut, jade, sate 6. excess 7. replete, satiate, satisfy 9. satiation 11. overindulge, superfluity

surge . . . 4. eddy, flow, rush, wave 5. swarm, swell, whirl 6. billow, thrill 7. estuate 8. gurgitate 11. rise and fall

surgeon (pert to) . . .
ancient . . 10. chirurgeon
case (instrument) . . 6. tweeze (tweese)
slang . . 8. sawbones

surgery . . . 7. aciurgy 8. medicine 9. operation, resection

surgery (pert to) . . .
chin . . 11. mentoplasty
ears . . 9. otoplasty
face lift . . 13. rhytidoplasty
14. blepharoplasty (eyelids)
fractures . . 10. agmatology
mouth, lip . . 12. cheiloplasty (chiloplasty)

nose . . 7. nose job 11. rhinoplasty
organ . . 10. transplant
skin . . 12. dermabrasion
vein . . 10. phlebotomy
vertebra . . 11. laminectomy

surgical (pert to) . . .
compress . . 4. swab 5. stupe
counterirritant . . 5. seton
equpment . . 4. X-ray 6. splint 7. CAT scan, scanner 8. iron lung 10. respirator, tomography, tourniquet 11. stethoscope 12. resuscitator
hook . . 9. tenaculum
instrument . . 3. saw 5. fleam, lance, probe 6. catlin, lancet, stylet, trepan, xyster 7. forceps 8. hemostat, keratome, speculum, tweezers
knife . . 7. scalpel
puncture . . 8. céntesis
saw . . 6. trepan
stitch . . 5. seton 6. suture

Suriname (pert to) . . .
capital . . 10. Paramaribo
former name . . 11. Dutch Guiana
mountain . . 10. Tumuc-Humac
toad . . 4. pipa

surly . . . 4. glum, grum, rude 5. gruff 6. abrupt, grumpy, morose, sullen 7. crabbed 8. arrogant, growling 10. ill-natured 11. intractable

surmise . . . 4. deem 5. fancy, guess, judge, opine, think 7. imagine, presume 8. mistrust 9. suspicion 10. assumption, conclusion, conjecture 11. supposition

surmount . . . 3. top 4. pass, rise 5. climb, excel, mount 6. subdue 7. conquer, surpass 8. overcome 9. transcend

surname . . . 6. eponym, family, maiden 7. agnomen 8. cognomen 10. patronymic 11. appellation

surpass . . . 3. cap, top 4. best 5. excel, outdo 6. better, exceed, outvie, outwit 7. outrank, outride 8. go beyond, outrange, outreach, outshine, outsmart, outstrip, surmount 9. transcend

surpassing . . . 12. transcendent

surplice . . . 3. fee 5. cotta, ephod 6. collar 7. pelisse

surplus . . . 4. over, rest 5. epact 6. excess 7. overage, reserve 8. overplus 9. remaining 10. additional, redundancy 11. superfluous

surprise . . . 3. awe 5. alarm, amaze, seize, shock 6. wonder 7. astound, capture, perplex, startle 8. astonish, bewilder, confound, dumfound 9. amazement, dumbfound, overwhelm, surprisal 10. wonderment 11. flabbergast 12. astonishment

surprising . . . 7. amazing 8. striking 9. startling 10. unexpected 11. astonishing, unlooked for 13. extraordinary

surrealism (pert to) . . .
film director . . 6. Buñuel
founder, poet . . 6. Breton
painter . . 4. Dali 5. Ernst 8. Magritte

surrender . . . 4. cede, give 5. yield 6. give up, remise, resign 7. abandon, cession, deliver 8. dedition, remittal 9. extradite 10. relinquish, submission

11. abandonment, divestiture
12. cancellation 14. relinquishment
surreptitious . . . 3. sly 6. hidden, secret
8. stealthy 9. concealed, deceitful
10. fraudulent 11. clandestine
surround . . . 4. gird, isle, wrap 5. beset,
hem in, inarm 6. circle, encase, incase,
invest 7. besiege, enclave, enclose,
envelop, environ 8. encircle, inundate,
overflow 9. encompass 12. circumscribe
14. circumnavigate
surrounding . . . 5. about, beset, midst
7. ambient, setting 9. hemming in,
perioptic 10. encircling, enveloping
11. circumpolar 12. circumjacent
survey . . . 4. plan, poll, scan 5. study,
vista 6. regard, review 7. examine,
inspect, oversee 8. traverse 9. delineate,
determine 10. scrutinize
11. examination, reconnoiter,
superintend 14. reconnaissance
surveying (pert to) . . .
   instrument . . 7. alidade (alidad), transit
      9. stadia rod 10. throdolite
   mathematics . . 7. geodesy
   process . . 13. triangulation
surveyor (pert to) . . .
   helper . . 6. rodman 7. lineman, poleman
   land . . 8. measurer, overseer 9. arpenteur
   measure . . 5. chain
   mine . . 6. dialer
survival . . . 5. relic 9. endurance, outliving
   10. durability
survivor . . . 6. relict 8. outliver, remainer,
   survival 11. joint tenant
susceptibility . . . 3. sense 7. emotion,
   feeling, pliancy 11. sensibility
   12. teachability 13. affectibility,
   vulnerability 14. sentimentality
susceptible . . . 4. easy 6. liable, pliant
   7. exposed, subject 8. sensible
   9. receptive, sensitive, teachable
   10. responsive, vulnerable
   11. softhearted 13. tenderhearted
   14. impressionable
suslik . . . 5. sisel 8. squirrel
   11. spermophile
suspect . . . 4. fear 5. doubt, fancy,
   guess 7. imagine, presume, suppose
   8. distrust, mistrust 9. discredit
   10. disbelieve, suspicious
suspecting . . . 4. wary 8. doubtful,
   doubting 11. incredulous, mistrusting
suspend . . . 4. hang, oust, stay, stop
   5. cease, debar, defer, expel, remit
   6. dangle, depose, recess 7. adjourn,
   pensile 8. intermit, postpone, set aside,
   withhold 9. pretermit
suspended . . . 4. hung 5. inert 6. barred,
   latent 7. abeyant, pendent 8. inactive
   9. pendulous 11. inoperative,
   interrupted
suspenders . . . 4. pegs 5. belts, hooks,
   rings 6. braces, straps 7. gallows,
   garters 8. galluses 9. bretelles
   10. supporters 11. clothespins
suspense . . . 5. pause 7. anxiety
   10. expectancy 11. uncertainty
   12. apprehension, irresolution
   14. indecisiveness
suspension . . . 4. stop 5. delay 7. deposal,

failure, hanging, respite 8. abeyance,
buoyancy 11. withholding
12. intermission, interruption
suspicious . . . 4. fear, hint 5. doubt,
hunch, trace 7. askance, inkling,
soupcon 8. distrust, jealousy, mistrust,
wariness 9. mere trace, misgiving
10. diffidence, intimation, skepticism,
suggestion 11. incredulity, supposition
12. apprehension
Sussex (pert to) . . .
   breed (*Eng*) . . 4. fowl 6. cattle
   kingdom (*anc*) . . 7. English
   land measure . . 4. wist
   land tract (*Downs*) . . 5. laine
   man . . 8. Piltdown (Prehist)
   spaniel . . 6. gun dog
sustain . . . 4. bear, buoy, feed, prop
   5. abide, carry 6. endure, foster, keep
   up, uphold 7. confirm, justify, nourish,
   prolong, support, undergo 8. continue,
   maintain, preserve 9. encourage,
   establish 10. strengthen 11. corroborate
sustained . . . 6. tenuto, upheld
   9. permanent, prolonged, supported
   10. unflagging
suttee . . . 5. widow 9. cremation, sacrifice
   14. self-immolation
suture . . . 5. unite 6. stitch 7. pterion
   12. synarthrosis
swagger . . . 4. brag, gait, walk 5. bluff,
   boast, bully, strut, swell 6. prance
   7. bluster, dashing, roister, stagger,
   stylish 8. domineer 11. braggadocio,
   ostentation 16. ultrafashionable
swain . . . 3. boy, lad 4. beau 5. lover
   6. suitor 7. admirer, gallant, peasant
   8. shepherd 10. countryman
swallow . . . 3. sip 4. gulp 5. drink
   6. absorb, englut, engulf, imbibe,
   ingest, recant 7. consume, engorge,
   retract 8. tolerate 10. bear meekly
swallow (pert to) . . .
   chimney . . 5. swift
   European . . 6. martin
   hawk . . 4. kite
   plover . . 10. pratincole
   sea . . 4. tern
   tail . . 4. coat 9. butterfly
   the anchor . . 10. quit the sea
swamp . . . 3. bog, fen 4. mire, muck,
   sink, slue, sump 5. flood, marsh
   6. deluge, engulf, morass, slough
   7. cienaga, pocosin 8. quagmire,
   submerge 9. everglade, overwhelm
swamp (pert to) . . .
   boggy . . 7. queachy 8. muskeggy
   earth . . 4. muck
   gas . . 6. miasma
   grass . . 5. sedge
   marsh . . 5. slash 8. paludine
   tract . . 10. Everglades
swan . . . 3. cob, pen 4. Olor 5. swear
   6. cygnet, cygnus 7. declare
   9. trumpeter
swan (pert to) . . .
   astronomy . . 6. Cygnus
   flower . . 6. orchid
   goose . . 7. Bewick's, Chinese
   myth (*Hind*) . . 5. hansa
   poem . . 12. Swan of Thames (Pope)

15. Sweet Swan of Avon (Jonson)
star (brightest) . . 5. Deneb
trumpeter . . 4. wild
type . . 4. mute 5. black 8. whooping
   11. black-necked
swap . . . 4. beat 5. trade 6. barter, thrash
   8. exchange 11. give-and-take
sward . . . 3. sod 4. lawn, turf 5. grass
   10. greensward
swarm . . . 3. fry 5. crowd, flock, horde
   6. abound, infest, throng 7. pervade
   9. migration, multitude 10. congregate
   11. aggregation
swarthy . . . 3. dun 4. dark 5. dusky
   8. bistered (bistred), blackish
swashbuckler . . . 5. bravo 6. gascon
   7. ruffian 8. Almanzor 9. blusterer,
   daredevil, swaggerer 10. Drawcansir
swastika (swastica) . . . 6. fylfot, symbol
   (since 1918) 9. gammadion
   10. hakenkreuz
swat . . . 3. bat, hit 5. clout 6. strike 7. hit
   hard
swathe . . . 4. band, bind, wrap 6. enfold
   7. envelop, swaddle
sway . . . 4. bend, bias, rock, rule, veer,
   wave 5. lurch, power, shake, swing,
   waver, wield 6. direct, empire, govern,
   induce, totter, waddle 7. command,
   control, deflect, incline 8. flounder
   9. fluctuate, influence, oscillate, vacillate
   10. ascendancy 11. fluctuation
swayback . . . 8. lordosis
swaying . . . 7. pensile, sagging
   8. swinging, waddling 11. influential,
   oscillating
swear . . . 3. vow 4. oath 5. curse, vouch
   6. adjure, pledge (sacred) 7. confirm,
   declare, promise 10. asseverate,
   deposition 11. bear witness
swear (pert to) . . .
at . . 5. clash (colors), curse 8. disagree
by . . 5. bet on 7. count on 8. take oath
falsely . . 7. perjure
off . . 4. stop 6. eschew, give up
   7. abandon 8. renounce
sweat . . . 4. work 5. exude, grill,
   sudor 6. drudge 7. excrete, ferment
   8. perspire, transude 9. exudation
   10. impatience 11. nervousness
Sweden . . . see also *Swedish*
capital . . 9. Stockholm
city . . 5. Malmö 7. Uppsala (Upsala)
   8. Göteborg
dynasty (1st) . . 8. Ynglings
gulf . . 7. Bothnia
lake . . 6. Vanern 7. Vattern
mountain . . 5. Kölen (Kjölen)
parliament . . 7. Riksdag
peninsula . . 11. Scandinavia
port . . 8. Göteborg 9. Stockholm
river . . 4. Kier 7. Götaalv
sea . . 6. Baltic
university (oldest) . . 7. Uppsula (Upsula,
   1477)
Swedish (pert to) . . .
actress . . 5. Garbo
artist . . 4. Zorn
botanist . . 8. Linnaeus
bread . . 10. knäckebröd
clover . . 6. alsike

dance . . 6. polska
diplomat . . 12. Hammarskjöld (Dag)
dramatist . . 10. Strindberg
explorer . . 5. Hedin
film director . . 7. Bergman (Ingmar)
fir . . 10. Scotch pine
hero (WWII) . . 10. Wallenberg
idiom . . 7. Suecism
manual training . . 5. sloyd (slojd)
northern inhabitants . . 5. Lapps
novelist . . 8. Lagerlöf (Pulitzer prize,
   1909)
opera singer . . 9. Jenny Lind (Swedish
   Nightingale) 7. Nilsson (Birgit)
philosopher . . 10. Swedenborg
religion (State) . . 8. Lutheran
turnip . . 8. rutabaga
sweep . . . 3. oar 4. scan 5. clean, clear,
   cover, curve, glide, strip, surge, swish,
   trail 6. course, vision 7. contour
   8. traverse
sweeping . . . 8. complete, thorough
   9. extensive 12. all-embracing
   13. comprehensive
sweet . . . 5. bonny, candy 10. dolce douce
   5. fresh, spicy 6. dulcet, gentle, sugary,
   syrupy 7. caramel, honeyed, lovable
   8. aromatic, fragrant, luscious, pleasant,
   preserve 9. agreeable, ambrosial,
   melodious, nectarine 10. confection,
   saccharine 11. mellifluous, mellisonant
sweet (pert to) . . .
and fair . . 5. bonny
bread . . 4. food 6. thymus 8. pancreas
   9. ris de veau
brier . . 4. rose 9. eglantine
drink . . 6. nectar
meat . . 4. cake 5. candy 6. comfit, éclair,
   pastry 7. caramel, dessert 8. marzipan
   10. confection
potato . . 3. yam 6. batata
potato, musical . . 7. ocarina
sop . . 4. ates, atta 6. A^nnone 14. Annona
   squamosa
sounding . . 11. mellisonant
wine . . 4. port 5. Lunel
sweetheart . . . 2. jo 3. gra 4. beau, lass
   5. flame, leman, lover, spark, swain
   7. darling 8. dowsabel, honeybun
   (sl), ladylove 9. Amaryllis, inamorata,
   valentine
swell . . . 3. fob, nob 4. grow, rise, surf,
   wave 5. bulge, dandy, grand, heave,
   mound, surge 6. billow, dilate, expand,
   growth, puff up, tiptop 7. distend,
   inflate, stylish 8. increase, protrude
   9. sumptuous 10. aristocrat, prominence
   11. enlargement 12. augmentation
swell (pert to) . . .
ocean . . 4. surf 6. billow, expand, roller
rolling . . 7. seagate
slang . . 3. nob 5. dandy, grand
   9. first-rate
swelled (pert to) . . .
head . . 3. ego 7. conceit 9. cockiness
   14. self-importance
out . . 4. lump, node 5. tumid 6. bulged,
   podded, turgid 9. grandiose
swelling . . . 4. sore 5. bulge, edema
   6. dropsy 8. bombastic 10. distention,
   increasing 12. protuberance

swelter... 4. fret 5. exude, roast, sweat 8. perspire 10. sultry heat

swerve... 4. veer 5. dodge, sheer, shift 6. recoil 7. deflect, deviate 9. deviation, turn aside

swift... 4. bird, fast, racy, reel 5. alert, fleet, hasty, quick, rapid, ready 6. lizard, prompt, speedy, sudden, winged 8. headlong

swift (pert to)...
astronomer.. 5. Lewis (Swift)
bird.. 4. crin 7. chimney
boat.. 7. flyboat 10. Hovercraft
footed.. 5. ariel (gazelle) 7. Mercury
satirist.. 8. Jonathan (Swift)

swiftness... 5. haste, speed 8. celerity, velocity 9. quickness 10. promptness

swimmer... 5. diver 6. bather 7. Cloelia (Tiber Riv), Leander (Hellespont), natator

swimming... 5. crawl 6. natant 7. vertigo 9. dizziness, freestyle, skinny-dip 10. sidestroke 12. breast stroke

swimming (pert to)...
birds.. 9. natatores
bladder.. 10. air bladder (fish)
pert to.. 5. dizzy 7. aquatic 8. natatory
pool.. 4. hole, tank 10. natatorium
sandpiper.. 9. phalarope

swindle... 3. con, gyp 4. dupe, fake, sell 5. bunco, cheat 6. trepan 7. defraud 8. flimflam 9. gold brick

swindler... 3. gyp 5. biter, cheat, crook, knave, rogue, shark 6. gypper 7. sharper 9. defrauder

swindling... 6. estafa

swine... 3. hog, pig, sow, Sus 4. boar 7. Anthony (smallest), peccary 8. slattern 9. scoundrel

swine, breed of... 8. Cheshire, Tamworth 9. Berkshire, Hampshire, razorback, Yorkshire 11. Duroc-Jersey, Poland China 12. Chester-White

swineherd (pert to)...
patron saint.. 7. Anthony
reference to.. 7. sybotic

swinelike... 7. porcine

swing... 4. hang, jazz, jive, lilt, sway 5. shake, trend, waver, wield 6. dangle, manage, rhythm, totter 7. suspend, trapeze, vibrate 8. pendulum, undulate 9. fluctuate, oscillate

swingtree... 11. whippletree

swinish... 5. gross 6. carnal, filthy, greedy 7. beastly, porcine, sensual 8. gluttony

swipe... 4. gulp 5. draft, drink, lever, steal, swape, swath, sweep 6. handle, pilfer, snatch 7. purloin

swipes... 4. beer (Eng sl)

swirl... 4. curl, eddy 5. curve, gurge, surge, twist, whirl, whorl

swirly... 7. knotted, tangled, twisted

Swiss (pert to)... see also *Switzerland*
artist.. 4. Klee
ax (ice).. 6. piolet
bell.. 9. alpenhorn (alphorn)
cabin.. 6. chalet
composer.. 4. Raff
flower, emblem.. 9. edelweiss
herdsman.. 4. senn

hero.. 11. William Tell
language.. 6. French, German 7. Italian 8. Romansch
legislature.. 9. Bundesrat (Bundesrath), Grosse Rat (Grossrat)
mathematician.. 5. Euler
physician, alchemist.. 10. Paracelsus
pine.. 6. arolla
psychologist.. 4. Jung
scientist.. 6. Haller (von)
surgeon.. 6. Kocher (Nobel Prize)
theologian.. 5. Vinet 7. Zwingli
warble.. 5. yodel
warbler.. 7. yodeler (yodeller)
wind.. 4. bise
wine.. 7. Dezaley

switch... 4. lash, turn (on or off), whip 5. shift, shunt 6. change, divert, siding 8. exchange, transfer

switchback (Brit).. 13. roller-coaster

Switzerland (pert to)...
ancient.. 8. Helvetia
canton.. 5. Aarau
capital.. 5. Berne (Bern)
city.. 5. Basel 6. Geneva, Zurich 7. Locarno, Lucerne 8. Lausanne 9. Constance
famed for.. 5. banks (Finan)
lake.. 3. Uri 6. Brienz, Geneva, Zurich 7. Lucerne 8. Maggiore 9. Constance, Neuchâtel 10. Stattersee
mountain.. 4. Alps, Jura 5. Blanc 8. Jungfrau 9. Monte Rosa (peak) 10. Matterhorn
resort.. 7. Urseren, Yverdon
river.. 3. Aar 5. Reuss, Rhine, Rhone
tunnel.. 5. Cenis 7. Gothard, Simplon 11. Loetschberg
university (oldest).. 5. Basel
valley.. 3. Aar

swollen... 5. pursy, tumid 6. turgid 7. bloated, bulbous, bulging, pompous 8. enlarged, inflated, puffed up, varicose 9. bombastic, distended, plethoric, tumescent 11. protuberant

swoon... 3. fit 5. faint, spell 7. ecstasy, syncope 8. languish 10. heavy sleep

swoop... 5. seize, sweep 6. attack, pounce 7. descend

sword (pert to)...
ancient.. 5. estoc 6. glaive
cavalry.. 5. saber (sabre)
curved.. 7. cutlass, Ferrara 8. Claymore, scimitar
fencing.. 4. foil, epee 6. rapier
fine.. 6. Toledo 8. Damascus
handle.. 4. haft, hilt
India.. 5. kukri
like.. 7. xiphoid
Mohammedan's.. 8. scimitar
part.. 5. forte, talon 6. foible
practice.. 5. fence
scabbard tip.. 7. crampit
Scot Highlander's.. 4. dirk
seaman's.. 6. hanger
shaped.. 6. ensate 7. xiphoid (xyphoid) 8. ensiform, gladiate
sheik's.. 4. pata
Siegfried's.. 4. Gram 7. Balmung
Sir Bevis'.. 7. Morglay
Spanish.. 5. bilbo

support . . 7. baldric
two-handed . . 7. espadon
type . . 4. epee, pata 5. blade, degen, estoc, gully, saber 6. barong, creese, parang, rapier 7. cutlass 9. gladiolus
swordfish . . 6. dorado, Dorado (constellation), espada 7. espadon, Xiphias 9. broadbill
sword of . . .
Damocles . . 12. fateful thing
God . . 6. Khaled (Muslim hero)
mercy . . 7. Curtana (pointless)
Sir Bevis . . 7. Morglay (death)
St George . . 7. Askelon
the Cid . . 6. Colada
swordsman . . 6. fencer 7. duelist, epeeist, saberer, sabreur 9. gladiator 11. Beau Sabreur
sworn statement . . . 9. affidavit
sworn to secrecy . . . 5. tiled
sybarite . . . 7. epicure 10. voluptuary 11. luxury lover
sybil (sibil) . . . 4. seer 5. witch 7. seeress 10. prophetess 13. fortuneteller
syce . . . 5. groom
sycophant . . . 5. toady 7. fawning, spaniel 8. hanger-on, informer, parasite 9. charlatan, flatterer, toadeater 10. talebearer
sycophantic . . . 7. fawning, servile, slavish 8. obedient, toadying 10. obsequious 11. bootlicking
syllable . . .
accented . . 5. arsis
by syllable . . 11. syllabation
charm . . 2. om 6. mantra
last . . 6. ultima
last, omission of . . 7. apocope
last but one . . 6. penult
last but two . . 10. antepenult
lengthening of . . 7. ectasis
ref to . . 5. affix 6. prefix, suffix 8. dactylic, syllabic
short . . 4. mora
shortening . . 7. systole
stress . . 5. ictus
table . . 9. syllabary
unaccented . . 4. lene 6. thesis
syllabled, three . . . 7. triseme (3 moras) 11. trisyllabic
syllabus . . . 6. aperçu, digest 8. abstract, synopsis 10. compendium, conspectus
syllogism . . . 7. premise, sorites 9. deduction, reasoning 11. epicheirema (epichirema) 18. deductive reasoning
sylvan, silvan . . . 5. woody 6. groved, rustic, wooded 8. forested 10. forestlike
sylvan deity . . . 3. Pan 4. faun 5. Satyr, Vidar 6. Faunus
symbol . . . 2. om 4. icon, palm, sign, type 5. badge, crest, cross, image, token, totem 6. emblem, ensign, figure, letter, number 9. character (graphic), prototype, trademark 12. abbreviation
symbol (pert to) . . .
authority . . 4. mace
bondage . . 4. yoke
ecclesiastic . . 4. ring
England . . 4. lion
France . . 4. lily
mathematics . . 7. operand

military . . 3. bar 4. star 5. eagle, wings 6. stripe 7. chevron, epaulet (epaulette) 8. caduceus
peace . . 4. dove
power . . 4. mace
prayer figure (anc) . . 5. orant
royal . . 3. rod 5. crown, tiara 6. corona 7. scepter (sceptre)
Tammany Hall . . 5. tiger
tribal . . 5. totem (pole)
victory . . 4. palm
symbol for . . .
arsenic . . 2. As
calcium . . 2. Ca
chromium . . 2. Cr
copper . . 2. Cu
gold . . 2. Au
iron . . 2. Fe
lead . . 2. Pb
neon . . 2. Ne
nickel . . 2. Ni
radium . . 2. Ra
silver . . 2. Ag, Ar
sodium . . 2. Na
tin . . 2. Sn
symbolic, symbolical . . . 7. typical 9. imagerial 10. figurative, relational 11. allegorical, significant 12. emblematical 14. representative
symbolism . . . 7. mystery, writing 9. mysticism, ritualism, symbolics 10. figuration 11. hieroglyphy 14. representation
symmetric, symmetrical . . . 7. orderly, regular, spheral, uniform 8. balanced 10. euphonious
symmetry . . . 5. order 7. balance, euphony, harmony 8. equality 9. congruity 10. conformity, proportion 11. consistency
sympathetic . . . 4. kind 6. humane, tender 7. empathy, pitying 8. dewy-eyed 10. responsive 13. compassionate, understanding
sympathy . . . 4. pity 5. favor 7. consent, harmony, support 8. affinity, interest 9. agreeable, agreement, tolerance 11. sensitivity 13. commiseration, understanding
sympathy, lack of . . . 8. dyspathy 9. antipathy
symphony . . . 6. accord 7. concert, harmony 9. ritornel 9. orchestra 10. consonance 11. composition
symposium . . . 4. book, talk 7. banquet 8. dialogue, tippling 10. collection, discussion 11. compotation
symptom . . . 4. mark, note, omen, sign 5. alarm, token 7. warning 10. indication
synagogue . . . 6. temple 10. tabernacle 12. congregation
synagogue (pert to) . . .
founder (anc) . . 4. Ezra
platform . . 7. almemar
singer . . 6. cantor, chazan (chazzan)
synchronize . . . 5. agree 6. concur 8. coincide 9. harmonize 12. contemporize
syncopation . . . 5. tempo 7. ragtime, syncope
syncope . . . 5. faint, swoon 7. elision

8. fainting, swooning 9. haplology

syndicate . . . 5. chain (journalistic), group, trust 6. cartel, school 7. combine, council 9. committee 10. underworld 11. association 12. organization

synonym . . . 7. antonym, homonym, metonym 8. identity 9. heteronym

synonymous . . . 4. like 5. alike 7. similar 10. equivalent, homonymous

synopsis . . . 6. digest, manual 7. epitome, summary 8. abstract, syllabus 9. statement 10. abridgment (abridgement), compendium, conspectus, tabulation

synthesis . . . 5. logic 11. combination, composition 13. incorporation 14. identification

Syracuse (pert to) . . .
ancient name . . 8. Siracusa
city of . . 6. Sicily
famed for . . 6. battle (BC)
founded by . . 6. Greeks
tyrant of . . 9. Dionysius

Syria, Arab Republic . . . see also *Syrian*
ancient name . . 4. Aram
capital . . 8. Damascus
city . . 4. Hama, Homs 6. Aleppo, Beirut 7. Antioch, Latakia 8. Damascus
language . . 6. Arabic
organization, party . . 5. Baath
river . . 6. Barada, Jordan 7. Orontes 9. Euphrates

Syrian (pert to) . . .
antiquarian . . 11. Syriologist
deity . . 2. El 4. Baal 6. Mammon 7. Resheph
goat . . 6. Angora
grass . . 7. Johnson
leader . . 5. Assad
mallow . . 4. okra
·people . . 7. Ansarie (Ansarieh)
script . . 8. Peshitta (Peshito) 10. estrangelo 11. Syro-Chaldee
sect . . 5. Druse
wind (hot) . . 6. simoom (simoon)

syrinx . . . 4. tomb 6. larynx 7. Panpipe 10. mouthpiece (anc lute) 13. Arcadian nymph

syrup, sirup . . . 4. Karo, sapa 5. maple 6. orgeat 7. dhebbus, glucose, sorghum, treacle 8. molasses 9. grenadine

system . . . 3. ism, way 4. code, plan 5. order 6. regime, theory 8. religio . . universe 9. procedure 10. hypothesis, regularity 11. arrangement, orderliness

system (pert to) . . .
conduct . . 4. code
eating . . 4. diet 7. dietary
geological . . 5. Trias
management . . 6. regime
manual training . . 5. sloyd
mystic . . 6. cabala
numbering . . 7. decimal
pitch (Mus) . . 5. neume
religious . . 4. cult 6. cultus
solar . . 6. planet
weights . . 4. long, troy 5. cubic 6. liquid 11. avoirdupois 12. apothecaries

systematic . . . 4. neat 6. formal 7. orderly, regular 9. organized, schematic 10. methodical

systematics . . . 8. taxonomy 14. classification

systematize . . . 4. code 6. codify 7. arrange 8. classify, organize, regiment 9. catalogue (catalog), formulate

systematized knowledge . . . 7. science

systole (pert to) . . .
correlative . . 8. diastole
medical . . 11. contraction (heart) 14. coming and going
rhyme . . 10. shortening (syllable)

syzygy (pert to) . . .
astronomy . . 7. appulse 11. conjunction
Gnosticism . . 5. aeons (pair)
rhyme . . 11. coupled feet (group)
zoology . . 5. union 7. segment

szlachta . . . 8. nobility (Poland)

szopelka . . . 4. oboe (Russ)

T

T . . . 3. tau (Gr) 6. letter (20th)

tae . . . 6. pagoda

Taal . . . 8. language 9. Afrikaans

taar . . . 10. tambourine

Taaroa . . . 3. God

tab . . . 3. pan, tag 4. bill, cost, flap, loop 5. aglet (aiglet), label, strip 6. eartab, record 7. account, latchet, pendant (pendent) 9. afterpart, appendage, reckoning 10. accounting

tabac . . . 6. brown, snuff 7. tobacco

tabard . . . 4. cape 5. cloak 6. chimer, jacket, mantle

Tabard . . . 3. Inn (Canterbury Tales)

tabatière . . . 8. snuffbox

tabby . . . 3. cat 4. gown, silk 5. dress 6. fabric, gossip 7. old maid, taffeta

tabernacle . . . 4. tent 5. abode, niche 6. church, temple 7. shelter, support 8. enshrine 9. sanctuary 10. habitation

table . . . 4. fare, list, slab 5. board, panel, plate, stand 6. lamina, repast, tablet, teapoy 7. console, plateau, weights 8. postpone, put aside, synopsis, tabulate 9. reference 10. collection 14. multiplication

table (pert to) . . .
calculating . . 6. abacus
centerpiece . . 7. epergne
communion . . 5. altar 8. credence, credenza
contents . . 5. index
cover . . 5. baize, tapis
dish . . 6. tureen

land .. 4. mesa 6. karroo (karoo), plains
    7. plateau
linen .. 6. napery
philosophy .. 13. deipnosophism
salt .. 4. NaCl
talk (versed in) .. 13. deipnosophist
type .. 3. tea 4. turn 6. coffee, gaming
    7. dinette, dresser, gate-leg, kitchen,
    taboret 8. captain's, drop-leaf
tableau ... 5. drama, scene 7. picture
    8. schedule 14. representation
tablet ... 3. pad 4. pill, slab 5. facia, slate,
    stele 6. troche 7. lozenge 8. monument,
    notebook
taboo, tabu ... 3. ban 4. deny 5. debar
    6. forbid 7. embargo 8. disallow,
    prohibit 9. forbidden, interdict,
    proscribe 11. prohibition 12. interdiction
tabulate ... 4. list 6. record 7. tabular
    8. classify, schedule
tabulation ... 7. listing 8. calendar,
    paradigm 12. registration
taccada ... 9. fanflower
tacit ... 6. silent 7. implied 8. unspoken,
    wordless 9. indicated, noiseless
    10. understood
taciturn ... 6. silent 8. reserved, reticent
    9. saturnine
tack ... 4. brad, gear, jibe, join, rope, sail,
    trip 5. baste, lease, route 6. course,
    fasten, secure, staple, tackle 7. clothes
    9. fastening 10. supplement
tackle ... 3. cat, rig 4. gear, tack
    5. davit, seize 6. burton, collar,
    garnet 7. cordage, grapple, harness,
    rigging 8. football (term) 9. encounter,
    equipment, undertake
tacky ... 5. crude, dowdy, seedy
    6. shabby, sticky, untidy 8. adhesive,
    slovenly
tact ... 5. grace, poise, taste 7. address,
    finesse 8. delicacy 9. diplomacy
    10. adroitness, cleverness, discretion
    11. discernment, savoir-faire
    14. discrimination
tadpole ... 4. frog, toad 8. polliwog,
    porwigle 9. youngling
tag ... 3. add, end, rag, tab 4. flap, game,
    loop, name 5. aglet (aiglet), label,
    sheep, strip 6. fasten, follow 7. earmark,
    frazzle, pendant, taglock 9. appendage
    11. aiguillette (ornamental)
Tagalog, Tagal (pert to) ...
    child, servant .. 4. anac, bata
    deity .. 6. Batala
    game (gambling) .. 10. panguingui
    native of .. 5. Luzon 11. Philippines
    peasant .. 3. tao
    race .. 4. Aeta (dwarf) 7. Malayan
Tahiti ...
    arrowroot .. 3. pia
    boat .. 4. pahi
    capital .. 7. Papeete (of all Society Isles)
    food plant .. 4. taro
    god .. 3. oro 6. Taaroa (Supreme)
    old name .. 8. Otaheite
    robe (coronation) .. 4. malo
    woman .. 6. wahine (vahine)
Tai, Thai people ... 4. Laos, Shan
    7. Siamese
tail ... 3. bun, cue, end 4. arse, back,

hair, last, rear 5. cauda, stern 6. follow,
    shadow 7. pendant 8. entailed, streamer
    9. afterpart, appendage, extremity
tail (pert to) ...
    aircraft's .. 9. empennage
    boar's .. 6. wreath
    coin .. 5. verso 7. reverse
    dog's .. 5. plume, stern, twist
    having a .. 7. caudate
    peacock's .. 5. train
    pert to .. 6. caudal 9. coccygeal
    rabbit's .. 4. scut
    rudimentary .. 6. coccyx
    tailrace .. 5. flume 7. channel
tailing ... 5. chaff, waste 6. refuse
tailless ... 6. tenrec (mammal) 7. acaudal,
    anurous, Ranidae 8. acaudate, ecaudate
tailor ... 3. cut, fit 4. form 6. darzee,
    draper, sartor 7. fashion 8. tailleur
tailor (pert to) ...
    goose .. 4. iron 12. pressing iron
    made .. 6. fitted 9. fashioned
    reference to .. 9. sartorial
    twist .. 10. silk thread (stout)
taint ... 3. due, hue 5. color, imbue,
    spoil, stain, sully, tinge 6. defile, infect,
    poison, stigma 7. blemish, corrupt,
    deprave, pollute, vitiate 8. disgrace
    9. denigrate, infection 10. corruption,
    stigmatize 11. contaminate
tainted ... 3. bad 6. soiled 7. stained
    8. diseased 9. corrupted
taintless ... 4. good 5. clean 6. chaste
    8. flawless, innocent
Taiwan ...
    capital .. 6. Taipai
Taj Mahal (pert to) ...
    architecture .. 9. Saracenic
    builder .. 9. Shah-Jahan
    mausoleum site .. 4. Agra
    named for .. 4. wife
take ... 2. go 3. get, win 4. deem,
    doff, gain, shut 5. atone, booty,
    carry, catch, seize, snare, steal,
    usurp 6. accept, borrow, deduce,
    endure, obtain 7. capture, conduct,
    control, detract, receive 8. proceeds,
    receipts, subtract, tolerate 9. apprehend
    11. appropriate
take (pert to) ...
    a chair .. 3. sit
    a direction .. 5. steer
    advantage of .. 4. abuse 6. misuse
    apart .. 8. demolish 11. disassemble
    as one's own .. 5. adopt 6. borrow
    away .. 6. adeem, clear, reave, steal,
    wrest 6. adempt, deduct, remove
    7. deprive, detract, retract 8. derogate,
    subtract, withdraw 11. expropriate
    back .. 6. recant, repeal, return
    by storm .. 5. seize 6. attack
    by stratagem .. 4. trap 8. outsmart
    care of .. 4. mind 5. guard, nurse, serve,
    watch 6. beware 7. support 10. provide
    for
    charge of .. 8. attend to 9. look after
    down .. 4. fell, raze 5. lower, write
    6. humble, record 7. reprove, swallow
    8. emaciate
    first .. 7. pre-empt
    for granted .. 5. infer 6. assume, expect

T

7. believe, presume, suppose

in .. 3. eat, see 4. hear 5. admit, annex,
learn 6. absorb, attend 7. embrace,
include, involve, receive, shorten
9. encompass

notice .. 2. NB 3. see

off .. 5. leave 6. deduct, depart, launch,
parody, remove 8. subtract 9. imitation

on .. 6. hire 6. assume, employ, oppose
9. undertake

out .. 4. dele 5. elide 6. delete, efface
7. expunge

place of .. 8. supplant 9. supersede

the floor .. 5. speak 7. address 9. legislate

to flight .. 4. flee 7. run away, scamper
9. skedaddle

up .. 4. fill, lift 5. adopt, begin, raise
6. absorb, assume, gather, occupy
8. engage in 9. undertake

without authority .. 5. usurp

talapoin ... 6. monkey (guenon)
8. poonghie 12. Buddhist monk

talc ... 6. powder, talcum 7. agalite
8. steatite 9. soapstone

tale .. 3. lai, lay, lie 4. myth, saga, yarn
5. conte, fable, story 6. gossip, legend
7. romance 8. anecdote 9. discourse,
falsehood, narration, narrative
11. declaration 12. conversation

tale (pert to) ...

adventure .. 4. gest

bearer .. 6. gossip 7. blabber, tattler
8. informer 13. scandalmonger

chivalry .. 7. romance

doleful .. 8. jeremiad

fatality .. 5. drama 7. tragedy

symbolic .. 8. allegory

traditional .. 4. saga 8. folktale

talent .. 4. gift 5. dower, flair, forte,
money (anc), skill 6. genius 7. ability,
faculty 8. aptitude, artistry 9. attribute
11. disposition 14. accomplishment

talesman ... 5. juror 8. narrator

talisman ... 4. juju, mojo, tara 5. charm,
karma 6. amulet, fetish, grigri
(greegree), scarab 7. periapt
12. antinganting

talk ... 3. gab, gas, rap, yak, yap 4. blab,
blat, chat, chin, harp, rant, rave
5. lingo, orate, parle, prate, rumor,
speak, spiel, utter 6. babble, confab,
confer, gabble, gossip, jargon, lesson,
speech 7. address, blabber, chatter,
declaim, discuss 8. causerie, chitchat,
colloquy, converse, language, parlance
9. dalliance, discourse 11. communicate
12. conversation

talk (pert to) ...

about .. 5. rumor 6. gossip

affected, pretentious .. 4. cant, rant

ancient .. 5. parle

back .. 4. sass 6. retort 7. riposte
8. feedback, repartee

flattering .. 7. palaver

fluent .. 7. verbose, voluble

idiotically .. 6. drivel

long .. 9. gibberish, rigmarole

loud .. 5. blate

promoting .. 4. hype 8. ballyhoo

running .. 6. patter

silly .. 5. drool 6. drivel, footle 7. blather,

prattle, twaddle

slang .. 3. gab, gas 4. sass 5. spiel

slowly .. 5. drawl

small .. 3. gab 4. chat, chin 7. prattle
8. chitchat

Spanish .. 7. palabra

talkative ... 4. glib 6. fluent 7. verbose,
voluble 9. garrulous 10. loquacious
13. communicative

talker ... 6. gasser, proser, ranter
7. speaker, spieler 10. chatterbox
17. conversationalist

tall .. 4. high, long 5. lofty 6. seemly
7. procere, sky-high 8. towering,
yielding 10. incredible, statuesque
11. exaggerated

tall (pert to) ...

order .. 9. falsehood 10. difficulty

person .. 10. hypermeter

structure .. 7. steeple

talk .. 4. brag 12. exaggeration
14. grandiloquence

tallest known people ... 10. Patagonian

Talleyrand's affair ... 3. XYZ

tallow source ... 4. suet

tally .. 3. run, sum, tab 4. goal,
list, mark 5. agree, check, count,
match, notch, score 6. accord, reckon,
record 7. account, compare, count
up 8. coincide, estimate 9. reckoning
10. bottom line, correspond

Talmud ... 9. Jewish law

Talmud (pert to) ...

academy .. 8. Yeshivah (Yeshiva)

commentary .. 6. Gemara

student .. 5. bahur

text .. 7. Mishnah

talon ... 3. paw 4. claw, fang, nail
6. clutch, finger, pincer

talus ... 5. ankle 8. clubfoot

tamarisk ... 4. atle (atlee) 8. salt tree

tambo ... 3. inn 6. corral, stable, tavern
10. tambourine

tambor ... 6. puffer 8. rockfish

tambour ... 4. desk, drum, lace 5. frame
6. stitch 7. drummer 8. ornament,
stockade 9. embroider

tambourine ... 4. dove, drum, taar
5. daira 7. timbrel 8. minstrel

tambourine effect (Mus) ... 7. travale

tambreet ... 8. duckbill

tamburone ... 4. drum 8. bass drum

tame ... 4. dull, meek, mild 5. inert
6. docile, gentle, humble, subdue
7. crushed, insipid, subdued 8. tone
down 9. tractable 10. cultivated
11. domesticate 12. domesticated

Tamil ... 5. Hindu 8. language (oldest
Dravidian) 9. Dravidian

tamis ... 5. sieve, tammy 8. strainer

Tammany (pert to) ...

Hall .. 14. Democratic Club

man .. 10. politician

officer .. 8. Wiskinky (Wiskinkie)

scandal .. 9. Tweed Ring

Society site .. 11. New York City (1789)

symbol .. 5. tiger

tamper with ... 4. plot 5. alter, bribe
6. meddle, monkey, scheme, tinker
7. falsify 9. influence, interfere

tampion, tampon ... 4. plug 6. tympan

7. stopper, turnpin 9. rhynobyon

tan . . . 3. dun, taw 4. buff, ecru, tent, whip 5. beige, brown, color, tawny 6. rabbit, suntan, thrash 7. sunburn

tanager . . . 4. yeni 5. lindo 7. Piranga, redbird

tanbark . . . 3. oak 7. hemlock

Tancred . . . 6. leader (1st crusade)

Tanganyika . . . see *Tanzania*

tangible . . . 4. real 7. tactile 8. palpable 9. objective, touchable 11. perceptible, substantial

tangle . . . 3. mat, mop 4. kink, shag 5. ravel, snare, snarl, weave 6. entrap, medley, muddle, sleave, tousle 7. ensnare, involve 8. quandary 9. interlock 10. complicate, interweave

tank . . . 3. vat 4. lake, pond, pool 5. basin 6. hot tub 7. cistern, stomach 9. reservoir 11. army vehicle, hard drinker

tanker . . . 4. ship 5. oiler 8. fuel ship

tanner's bath . . . 4. bate

tanning shrub . . . 5. alder, sumac (sumach)

tantalize . . . 3. vex 5. taunt, tease 6. harass, plague 7. torment

tantalum symbol . . . 2. Ta

Tantalus (pert to) . . .
father . . 4. Zeus
father of . . 5. Niobe 6. Pelops
genus of . . 4. ibis
king (*rich*) . . 6. Greece

tantamount . . . 5. equal 9. identical 10. equivalent 13. corresponding

tantara . . . 7. fanfare 9. tantarara 12. trumpet blare

tantrum . . . 3. fit 4. rage 7. caprice 8. tirrivee (tirrivie) 10. conniption

Tanzania, Africa . . .
capital . . 11. Dar es Salaam (Haven of Peace)
famed Mt. . . 11. Kilimanjaro
famed plains . . 9. Serengeti
famed town . . 5. Ujiji (Stanley found Livingstone, 1871)
formerly . . 8. Zanzibar 10. Tanganyika
language . . 7. Swahili
natives . . 5. Bantu

Taoism, names . . . 6. Kwanti, Laotze 7. Yu Hwang

tap . . . 3. dum, hit, hob, rap 4. plug, tamp 5. sound, spile 6. faucet, liquor, siphon, spigot, strike 7. censure, petcock, reprove

tape . . . 3. gin, tie 4. band, wick 5. strip 6. fillet, ribbon, secure 7. bandage, measure 9. recording

taper . . . 4. ream, wick 5. point, snape, spire 6. candle, clerge, narrow 7. conical 8. decrease, diminish 9. acuminate 11. pyramidical

tapering (pert to) . . .
blades . . 6. spires
pert to . . 6. spired, terete 7. conical, pointed 8. fusiform 9. narrowing
piece . . 4. gore 5. miter 6. gusset
pillar . . 7. obelisk
solid . . 4. cone

tapestry . . . 5. arras, tapis 6. Bayeux, dosser 7. Gobelin

tapeworm . . . 6. Taenia

tapeworm (pert to) . . .
embryonic . . 10. oncosphere
like . . 8. taenioid
segment . . 8. strobila

tapioca, source . . . 5. salep 7. cassava (casava)

Tapirus . . . 6. tapirs

tar . . . 3. gob 4. brea, pave, salt 5. black, pitch 6. cresol, maltha, sailor, seaman 7. mariner 8. telegram 10. bluejacket

tarantula . . . 6. spider 7. mygalid 10. wolf spider

tarboosh . . . 3. fez 6. red cap

tardy . . . 3. lag, lax 4. late, slow 5. slack 6. remiss 7. belated, lagging, overdue 8. dilatory 10. behindhand 11. cunctatious

tare . . . 4. weed (Bib) 5. vetch 8. discount 9. allowance, deduction

target . . . 3. aim, tee 4. butt, goal, goat, mark, prey 5. sight 6. object, shield, tassel 8. bull's-eye, ridicule 9. objective

tariff . . . 4. duty, list, rate 6. charge 7. tribute 8. schedule

tariffist . . . 8. advocate 13. protectionist

tarnish . . . 3. dim 4. dull, soil, spot 5. cloud, stain, sully, taint 6. smirch, stigma, vilify 7. blemish, destroy, obscure 8. besmirch, discolor 10. lose luster, stigmatize

taro . . . 3. poi 4. eddo, food, gabi (gabe) 5. cocco, tania (tanier) 12. elephant's-ear

tarot . . . 14. fortunetelling (cards)

tarried . . . 6. waited 7. dallied 8. lingered, remained

tarry . . . 3. lag 4. bide, stay, wait 5. abide, await, dally, delay, pause, stall 6. dawdle, linger, loiter, retard 7. outstay

tarsus . . . 5. ankle 7. segment

tart . . . 4. acid, sour 5. acrid, sharp 6. pastry, severe 7. caustic, pungent, waspish 8. poignant, turnover 10. astringent 11. acrimonious

tartan . . . 4. wool 5. plaid 7. pattern (plaid) 10. Highlander

tartar . . . 5. argol (argal), shrew, valet 12. incrustation

Tartar, Tatar . . . 4. Turk 6. Mongol

Tartar, Tatar (pert to) . . .
domain . . 7. Khanate
horseman . . 7. Cossack
lancer . . 5. uhlan
nobleman . . 5. murza
people . . 2. Hu 3. Hun 6. Mongol
people of . . 6. Turkey 8. Mongolia
title . . 4. Khan

tartarean . . . 5. cruel 7. hellish 8. infernal

Tartarus (Myth) . . . 4. hell 5. Hades 15. infernal regions (Iliad)

Tarzan (pert to) . . .
actor . . 7. Lincoln (Elmo) 11. Weissmuller
creator . . 9. Burroughs (Edgar Rice)
Lord . . 9. Greystoke
mate . . 4. Jane

task . . . 3. job 4. duty, snap, test, toil 5. chore, labor, stent, stint 6. burden, dargue, impost, strain 10. assignment,

employment 11. undertaking
Tasmania (pert to) . . .
  animal (burrowing) . . 6. wombat
  discoverer . . 6. Tasman (1642)
  marsupial . . 9. phalanger
  mountain . . 6. Cradle 9. Ben Lomond
  strait . . 4. Bass
taste . . . 3. sip, sup 4. tang 5. flair,
  sapor, savor, sense, smack, style
  6. liking, palate, relish, sample
  7. soupçon 8. delicacy, elegance,
  fondness, judgment 9. gustation
  10. experience 14. discrimination
  15. aesthetic liking
taste (pert to) . . .
  bite . . 4. nosh 5. snack
  decided . . 8. fondness, penchant
  French . . 7. soupçon
  fundamental . . 4. acid, salt 5. sweet
    6. bitter
  lacking . . 4. rude 5. bland, gross, stale
    10. unpolished
  ref to . . 7. palatal 9. gustatory
  sharp . . 4. acid, tang
tasteless . . . 4. dull, flat 5. vapid 6. vulgar,
  watery 7. insipid 8. lifeless 9. savorless
  10. inartistic
tasty . . . 5. sapid 6. savory 8. saporous,
  tasteful 9. delicious, palatable,
  toothsome
Tatar . . . see *Tartar*
tetouay . . . 9. armadillo
tatter . . . 3. rag 4. tags, tear 5. patch,
  piece, shred 6. ribbon
tatterdemalion . . . 8. gamin 9. ragpicker
  10. ragamuffin
tattle . . . 4. blab, tell 5. prate 6. gossip
  7. chatter, divulge, prattle 8. idle talk,
  inform on
tattler . . . 6. gossip, willet 8. quidnunc,
  redshank, telltale 10. alarm clock,
  talebearer, yellowlegs
tattoo . . . 4. call (drum, bugle), pony,
  scar 13. entertainment
tau . . . 4. ankh, crux, rood 5. cross 6. letter
  (Gr) 7. T-shaped
tau cross . . . 4. ankh 6. symbol 8. crucifix,
  insignia 10. St Anthony's
taunt . . . 4. gibe, jeer, mock, twit 5. sneer,
  tease 6. deride 7. provoke 8. reproach,
  ridicule 9. aggravate
Taurus . . . 4. bull 8. Pleiades
  13. constellation
taut . . . 4. firm, snug, tidy 5. tense, tight
  6. severe, strict 7. nervous 9. distended
tautology . . . 8. pleonasm 10. redundancy,
  repetition
tavern . . . 3. inn, pub 5. hotel 7. barroom,
  cabaret, Gasthof, taberna 8. alehouse,
  Gasthaus, hostelry
taw . . . 4. game, whip 6. marble 7. tanning
tawdry . . . 4. loud 5. cheap, gaudy, showy
  6. garish 8. blatant
tawny, tawney . . . 3. tan 5. dusky, olive,
  tenne 6. tanned 7. jacinth 8. brindled
  9. bullfinch
tax . . . 4. cess, duty, geld, levy, scat
  (scatt), task, toll 5. stent 6. assess,
  burden, custom, excise, impose,
  income, octroi, strain 7. doomage,
  license, tribute 8. exaction, overtire

9. prescribe 10. assessment
tax (pert to) . . .
  ancient . . 3. cro 4. geld 7. galanas
  assessment . . 4. rate 5. ratal 7. doomage
  church . . 5. tithe
  commodity . . 6. octroi
  French history . . 6. taille
  kind . . 5. tithe 6. excise, surtax, taille
    7. boscage 8. auxilium, carucage
    9. surcharge
  liquor . . 6. abkari (abkary)
  pasturage (Shetland Isls) . . 4. scat (scatt)
taxi . . . 3. cab 4. hack
tea . . . 5. dance, party, shrub 6. supper
    8. beverage, function, sociable
    9. collation, reception
tea (pert to) . . .
  cake . . 5. scone
  chemical content . . 6. tannin, theine
    (thein) 8. caffeine
  Chinese . . 5. black, hyson
  Formosa . . 6. oolong
  Ind Ceylon . . 5. pekoe
  infusion . . 6. ptisan, tisane
  Labrador . . 5. Ledum 8. gowiddie
  Paraguay . . 5. yerba
  receptacle . . 5. caddy 8. canister
  table . . 6. teapoy (tepoy)
  type . . 3. cha 4. tsia 5. Assam, black,
    green, hyson, Ledum, oopak, pekoe
    6. oolong 7. cambric 8. gowiddie
  urn . . 3. pot 7. samovar
  weak . . 7. cambric
teach . . . 4. show 5. coach, drill, edify,
  guide, prime, train, tutor 6. direct,
  impart, preach, school 7. educate,
  show how 8. instruct 9. enlighten
  11. demonstrate
teacher . . . 5. coach, guide, rabbi, tutor
  6. doctor, mentor, pastor, pedant, priest,
  pundit, reader, regent, rhetor, scribe
  7. edifier, starets 8. educator, preacher
  9. pedagogue, preceptor 10. instructor
teacher (pert to) . . .
  Alexandrian . . 6. Origen
  Indian . . 4. guru
  Jewish . . 5. rabbi
  Mohammedan . . 3. pir 4. imam 6. mullah
  of the deaf . . 7. oralist
  Russian . . 7. starets
teaching . . . 5. moral 6. docent 7. precept
  8. doctrine 11. instruction
Teaching of the Twelve . . . 10. The
  Didache
team . . . 3. two 4. haul, join, pain, span,
  yoke 5. brood, chain, wagon 7. vehicle
  8. carriage 9. yannigans
teamster . . . 6. carter, driver 7. carrier
Teapot Dome (pert to) . . .
  known as . . 8. Scandals (Teapot Dome)
  leased by . . 4. Fall (Sec'y of Interior)
  lease of . . 8. oil field
  site . . 8. Elk Hills (Wyo)
tear . . . 3. rip 4. rend, rent, rive 5. revel,
  sever, speed, split, spree 6. cleave,
  hasten 7. destroy, shatter, torment
  8. lacerate, separate 10. dilacerate
tear (pert to) . . .
  apart . . 7. disjoin 8. demolish
  asunder . . 10. dilacerate
  down . . 4. rase, raze

limb from limb .. 6. punish 9. dismember
to shreds .. 6. tatter
up .. 3. rip 6. damage
up the roots .. 6. arache
teardrop lace design ... 5. larme
tearful ... 3. sad 7. maudlin, weeping
  9. lachrymal (lacrimal)
tears ... 5. drops (lachrymal), grief, rheum
  6. lament 9. teardrops
tease ... 3. guy, nag, rag, vex 4. twit
  5. annoy, devil, taunt 6. bother,
  harass, heckle, needle, pester, plague
  7. provoke, torment 8. irritate
  9. aggravate, tantalize
teaser ... 4. gull 6. carder, curler, sniper,
  stoker 7. curtain, fireman, problem
  8. pesterer, willower 9. tormentor
  13. advertisement
technical ... 7. skilled, trained 8. specific
  11. specialized 12. professional
technocracy ... 12. organization 17. rule
  by technicians
technology ... 3. art 7. science
  9. technique 10. agrotechny, virtuosity
  11. terminology 12. nomenclature
  13. ethnotechnics
technophobe ... 7. Luddite
techy ... 6. touchy, vexing 7. fretful,
  peevish 8. irascible, irritable, sensitive
tedious ... 3. dry 4. dull 5. bored,
  prosy 6. boring, prolix 7. irksome,
  noxious 11. displeasing, repetitious
  13. uninteresting
tedium ... 5. ennui 7. boredom
  10. melancholy 11. tediousness
teeming ... 4. full 6. aswarm 7. pouring,
  replete 8. crowding, numerous, prolific
  9. abounding 10. productive
  11. overflowing
teeter ... 4. rock 5. waver 6. jiggle, seesaw
  9. alternate, fluctuate, sandpiper,
  vacillate 12. teeter-totter
teeth ... 5. bucks, fangs 6. molars, tushes
  7. canines, ivories 8. grinders, incisors
teeth (pert to) ...
  all alike .. 7. isodont
  cleaning .. 5. brush, floss 10. dentrifice,
  toothpaste
  covering .. 6. enamel
  crustation .. 6. tartar
  destitute of .. 5. morné (Her) 8. edentate
  10. edentulous
  elephant's .. 9. scrivello 11. scrivelloes
  false .. 8. choppers (sl), dentures
  few .. 12. oligodontous
  large .. 8. megadont 9. macrodont
  pointed .. 5. fangs, tusks 6. tushes
  ref to .. 4. pulp 5. molar 6. dental
  7. dentine 8. odontoid
  science .. 10. odontology
teething ... 6. growth 9. dentition,
  odontosis 10. odontogeny
teetotaller ... 3. dry 7. non-user
  9. abstainer, nephalist, Rechabite (Bib)
  11. teetotalist
teg, tag ... 3. doe 5. sheep (young),
  woman 6. fleece (sheep's)
teguexin ... 4. teju 6. lizard
tegument ... 4. bark, coat, skin 5. cover
  6. cortex 10. integument
tekke ... 3. rug 6. carpet 7. convent

  9. monastery
tela ... 6. tissue 8. membrane
Telamon (Gr Myth, pert to) ...
  brother .. 6. Peleus
  companion .. 8. Hercules
  expedition .. 8. boar hunt 10. Argonautic
  male figure .. 6. column 7. support
  son .. 4. Ajax 6. Teucer
telegraph (pert to) ...
  code, inventor .. 5. Morse (Samuel F)
  key .. 6. tapper
  service .. 5. cable 8. dispatch
telephone (pert to) ...
  inventor .. 4. Bell (Alexander)
  term .. 3. PBX 4. buzz, call, dial, hold,
  horn (sl), ring, toll 5. trunk 6. call
  up 7. collect, hotline 8. exchange,
  intercom 10. push-button, videophone
  11. switchboard 12. speakerphone
  14. radiotelephone
telescope ... 4. Lick 6. Yerkes 7. Palomar
  8. Galilean (1609) 9. Gregorian (Scot
  1663)
telescopic ... 9. farseeing
television ... 2. TV 3. box, set 4. tube
  5. telly (Brit) 8. boob tube, idiot box
  11. small screen
television (pert to) ...
  person .. 7. anchor, viewer 7. sponsor
  9. superstar 10. newscaster
  program .. 4. show 6. sitcom 7. variety
  8. newscast 9. docudrama, soap opera
  term .. 3. air 5. audio, bleep, cable,
  rerun 7. channel, minicam 8. telecast
  10. commercial, laugh track
tell ... 3. say 4. talk 5. count, peach, utter
  6. assail, impart, inform, recite, reckon,
  relate, repeat, report, reveal 7. divulge,
  narrate, recount 8. acquaint, disclose,
  rehearse 9. recognize 11. communicate
teller ... 6. banker 8. informer, narrator
  9. describer, informant
telling ... 6. cogent, potent 8. forceful,
  striking 9. affective, narration, pertinent
  11. influential, significant
telltale ... 4. blab, clue, hint 6. bearer,
  device, gossip 7. tattler 8. informer
  9. indicator, informing 10. indication,
  talebearer
tellurian ... 2. Te 7. earthly 11. terrestrial
  12. earth dweller
temerotious, temerarious ... 4. rash
  8. heedless, reckless 10. headstrong
temerity ... 4. gall 5. cheek, nerve
  8. audacity, rashness 10. effrontery
  12. recklessness
temper ... 4. mood 5. humor 6. adjust,
  animus, anneal, attune, dander, harden,
  nature, season, soften 7. assuage,
  mollify, tantrum 8. hardness, mitigate,
  moderate 9. composure 10. equanimity,
  irritation 11. disposition, temperament
temper (pert to) ...
  bad .. 4. fury, rage 5. anger 6. choler,
  spleen
  clay .. 6. puddle
  even .. 4. calm 5. staid 6. sedate
  in a .. 4. huff, rage, stew 5. tizzy
  metal .. 6. anneal, harden 7. toughen
temperament ... 4. mood 6. crasis,
  nature 8. artistic 11. disposition

temperance ... 6. virtue 8. calmness, sobriety 10. abstinence, moderation 11. self-control 13. self-restraint 14. abstemiousness

temperate ... 4. calm, cool 5. sober 8. moderate 10. abstemious, restrained 14. self-controlled

tempered ... 5. angry 6. sedate 8. annealed, disposed, moderate 9. moderated, mollified, qualified

tempest ... 4. gale, wind 5. blast, orage, storm 6. tumult 7. turmoil 9. agitation, commotion, windstorm 10. excitement 12. thunderstorm

Tempest (pert to) ...
Cuban .. 6. bayamo
in a teapot .. 10. triviality 12. exaggeration
The (character) .. 5. Ariel (spirit) 7. Caliban, Miranda 8. Prospero

tempestuous ... 5. windy 6. stormy 7. excited, violent 9. turbulent

temple ... 4. fane, naos 5. cella, ratha, speos 6. aedile, church, pagoda 7. edifice

temple (pert to) ...
Anglo-Ind .. 5. kovil (covil)
approach .. 5. toran (torana)
Assyrian .. 8. ziggurat (anc)
Aztec temple site .. 12. Tenochtitlan
Chinese .. 6. pagoda
Hawaiian .. 5. heiau
Mexico .. 8. teocalli
Muslim .. 6. mosque
part .. 4. naos 5. cella 6. adytum 7. narthex, sanctum 10. penetralia
ref to .. 6. hieron
sanctuary .. 10. penetralia
Shinto .. 3. Sha 5. jinja (jinsha) 7. yashiro

Temple Bar (London) ... 7. gateway

Temple Butte site ... 11. Grand Canyon

Temple of Heaven ... 7. Peiping

Temple of Onias ... 5. Egypt

Temple of Reason ... 9. Notre Dame

Temple of the Sphinx ... 5. Egypt

tempo ... 4. pace, time 5. grave, largo, speed 6. adagio, presto, rhythm 7. allegro, andante 8. moderato 11. synchronism

temporal ... 4. bene, laic 5. civil 7. earthly, secular, worldly 9. ephemeral, temporary 10. transitory 11. present time 13. chronological

temporize ... 5. delay 6. demand, parley 9. negotiate 13. procrastinate

tempt ... 4. lead, lure 5. decoy 6. allure, entice, induce, seduce 7. attract 8. persuade 9. seduction 10. inducement

Tempter, The ... 5. Devil, Satan 7. Evil One 10. Evil Spirit, Old Serpent 14. Prince of Devils

temptress ... 5. siren 7. Delilah (Bib), mermaid 11. enchantress

ten (pert to) ...
ace .. 10. bridge game
Commandments .. 9. Decalogue
dollars .. 7. sawbuck
fold .. 6. denary 7. decuple
footed .. 7. decapod
gallon hat .. 7. Stetson 8. sombrero
geometric figure .. 7. decagon

10. decahedron
measure .. 4. acre, bath 6. decare
number .. 6. decad 7. several
physics .. 3. bel
poetic .. 9. decameter (decametre)
prefix .. 4. deca (deka)
stringed .. 9. decachord
thousand .. 6. myriad
year period .. 6. decade 9. decenniad, decennium

tenable ... 10. defensible 12. maintainable

tenacious ... 5. tough 6. dogged, viscid 7. viscous 8. adhesive, cohesive, sticking, stubborn 9. glutinous, obstinate, retentive 10. persistent 12. pertinacious

tenant ... 4. saer 5. ceile, dreng (drengh) 6. holder, leaser, lessee, renter, vassal 7. cottier, dweller, villein 8. occupant 10. inhabitant

tenant's tribute ... 4. cens

tend ... 4. care, heed, lean, mind, wait 5. nurse, offer, serve, watch 6. attend, manage 7. incline, oversee 8. converge, minister 9. cultivate, gravitate, look after

tendency ... 4. bent, bias, tide 5. drift, drive, trend 6. course, object 7. bearing, leaning 8. aptitude, relation 9. direction, proneness 10. proclivity, propensity 11. disposition, inclination

tender ... 3. bed, pay 4. boat, fond, gift, give, kind, soft, sore 5. offer, young 6. extend, gentle, humane, waiter 7. pitiful, present, rail car 8. delicate, merciful 9. attendant, sensitive 10. effeminate 11. softhearted, sympathetic, warmhearted 12. affectionate 13. compassionate

tender (pert to) ...
animal .. 6. cowboy, herder
farm .. 10. husbandman
feeling .. 9. sentiment
foot .. 4. dude 5. novice 8. newcomer 10. raw recruit
hearted .. 4. kind 8. merciful
horse .. 5. groom 6. ostler 7. hostler
regard .. 4. love 6. tendre
ship .. 7. pinnace
style .. 7. amoroso

tenderloin ... 4. meat 7. brothel 12. city district, vice district

tenderness ... 4. love, pity 8. sympathy 9. affection 10. compassion, gentleness

tending to ...
arouse .. 7. emotive
assist memory .. 8. mnemonic
check .. 10. repressive
clear of guilt .. 11. exculpatory
control .. 10. regulating
drive away .. 9. repellant
evade .. 7. elusory
lateness .. 7. tardive
separate .. 8. divisive
tear .. 10. lacerative
wear away .. 8. abrasive

tendon ... 4. cord, thew 5. sinew 8. ligament 11. aponeurosis

tendril ... 4. coil, curl 5. shoot, sprig 6. branch, cirrus 7. stipule 8. filament

tenet ... 3. ism 4. rule 5. canon, creed,

dogma, maxim 6. belief 7. precept
8. doctrine 9. principle
tenne ... 5. brown, color
Tennessee ...
  battle .. 11. Chattanooga 14. Above the
    Clouds
  capital .. 9. Nashville (Athens of the
    South)
  city .. 7. Memphis 8. Oak Ridge
    9. Knoxville 11. Chattanooga
  first State .. 8. Franklin
  Mts .. 7. Lookout 10. Cumberland, Great
    Smoky 13. Clingman's Dome
  museum .. 9. Hermitage, Parthenon
    12. Atomic Energy (Oak Ridge)
    13. Ancestral Home (Pres Polk)
  park .. 6. Shiloh
  river .. 9. Tennessee
  State admission .. 9. Sixteenth
  State motto .. 16. America At Its Best
  State nickname .. 9. Volunteer
tennis (pert to) ...
  four persons .. 7. doubles
  player .. 6. netman
  score .. 3. ace 4. love (zero) 5. deuce
    (tie)
  series .. 3. set
  site .. 5. court
  stroke .. 3. cut, lob
  term .. 3. ace, lob, net, set 5. serve
    6. hazard 7. receive
  two persons .. 7. singles
tenon ... 3. cog 4. tusk 5. tooth 7. mortise
tenor ... 4. alto (violin), copy, mode,
  tone 5. drift, trend 6. course, intent,
  singer 7. meaning, purport 8. tenoreno
  9. male voice, procedure 10. transcript
tense ... 4. edgy, rapt, taut 5. rigid, tight
  6. intent 7. intense, nervous, stretch
  8. strained 9. stretched 10. breathless
tense (grammar) ... 4. past 6. future
  7. perfect, present 9. preterite
  10. pluperfect 11. past perfect,
  progressive
tensile ... 6. pliant 7. ductile 8. tensible
tension ... 6. strain, stress 7. detente,
  nervous 9. disaccord, stiffness
tent ... 3. hut 4. camp, show 5. cover,
  lodge 6. dossil 7. marquee 8. pavilion
tent (pert to) ...
  covering .. 4. tilt
  Eskimo .. 6. tubik (skin)
  general's .. 10. praetorium (pretorium)
  India .. 4. pawl
  Indian .. 6. tepee, teepee, wigwam
  occupant .. 5. nomad 6. camper 7. tourist
  Russian .. 7. kibitka
  Scottish .. 6. pulpit
  surgical .. 6. screen
  type .. 3. fly, pup 4. bell, wall 6. Sibley
    8. pavilion
tentacle ... 4. hair, palp 6. feeler 7. tendril
tentative ... 7. feeling, testing
  9. makeshift, temporary 10. substitute
  11. making trial, provisional
  12. experimental
tenterhooks ... 6. strain 8. suspense
  10. uneasiness
tenth ... 5. decim, tithe 6. decima 9. organ
  stop
tenth Muse ... 6. Sappho

Tent Maker ... 4. Omar
tenuity ... 6. rarity 7. poverty 8. delicacy,
  subtlety, thinness 9. indigence, unreality
tenuous ... 4. rare, thin 6. subtle
  7. slender 8. delicate, ethereal
  13. unsubstantial
tenure ... 4. term 5. lease 6. socage
  7. holding 10. possession
tepee, teepee ... 4. tent 6. wigwam
tepid ... 4. mild, warm 8. lukewarm
tequila ... 6. liquor 12. century plant
teraphim ... 5. idols 6. images
teras ... 7. monster
tergiversate ... 3. lie 5. evade, shift
  10. apostasize, equivocate
term ... 3. age, end, era 4. date, name,
  time, word 5. epoch, limit, style
  6. estate, period, tenure 7. premise
  8. duration, semester, terminus
  12. nomenclature
term (pert to) ...
  connotation .. 6. intent 11. designation
  death .. 4. doom, mort
  for years .. 10. real estate
  glacial .. 5. stoss
  golf .. 4. hook 5. bogey (bogie), divot,
    eagle, slice 6. birdie
  grammar .. 6. phrase, syntax
    11. phraseology
  logic .. 4. mode 5. major, minor
  of life .. 3. age 5. sands (hourglass)
  Rugby .. 5. scrum
  sea .. 4. ahoy 5. avast, belay
  tennis .. 4. love 5. deuce, serve
termagant ... 5. scold, shrew, vixen
  6. Amazon, virigo 7. furious 8. scolding
  9. turbulent 10. boisterous, tumultuous
  11. quarrelsome
Termagant ... 5. deity 14. imaginary
  being
terminal ... 3. end 4. goal 5. anode,
  depot, final, limit 6. finish 7. limital,
  station 8. desinent, terminus, ultimate
  9. end of life, extremity 10. concluding
  11. desinential, destination, termination
terminal (pert to) ...
  battery .. 5. anode 7. cathode 9. electrode
  leaf .. 8. apiculus
  ornament .. 6. finial
  town (end of line) .. 8. terminus
terminate ... 3. end 4. halt 5. abort,
  cease, close, limit 6. expire, result
  7. end with 8. complete, conclude
termination ... 3. end 4. amen 5. close,
  limit 6. ending, result 7. outcome
  8. terminus 8. desinence 10. completion,
  conclusion, expiration
termite ... 3. ant (white) 4. anay (anai)
  8. Isoptera (Order)
tern ... 4. darr (black), gull 6. Sterna
  (genus) 8. schooner (Naut) 9. threefold
  10. sea swallow
ternary ... 5. three, triad 6. tercet (Poet)
  triple 7. ternion, trinity 9. threefold
ternate ... 4. tern 9. threefold
  12. trifoliolate
terpsichore ... 5. dance 6. dancer
  7. dancing
Terpsichore (Myth) ... 13. Muse of
  dancing
terra ... 5. earth 10. terra firma

terrace ... 4. flaw (marble), mesa, step
  7. balcony, gallery, plateau, portico
  8. platform (earth) 9. colonnade
terrain, terrane ... 4. land 5. tract
  6. region 11. environment
terrapin ... 4. Emys 6. turtle 8. Chelonia,
  Emydinae, tortoise 9. cheloniid
terrapin, turtle (pert to) ...
  color .. 9. grapenuts
  type .. 6. potter, slider 10. red-bellied
    11. diamondback 13. yellow-bellied
  War .. 14. Eighteen Twelve (1812)
terrene ... 4. land 5. earth,
  realm 6. earthy, mortal 7. earthly,
  mundane, worldly
terrestrial planets ... 4. Mars 5. Venus
  7. Mercury
terrible ... 3. bad 4. dire 5. awful
  6. tragic 7. fearful, ghastly, hideous,
  painful 8. dreadful, horrible, terrific
  9. appalling, frightful 10. formidable,
  terrifying, unpleasant
Terrible, The ... 4. Ivan (Russ Czar)
terrier ... 3. fox 4. bull, Skye 5. Cairn,
  Irish, Welsh 6. Boston 8. Airedale,
  Scottish, Sealyham 9. Kerry blue,
  schnauzer 10. Bedlington, Clydesdale
  13. Dandie Dinmont
terrific ... 5. great 6. superb 7. extreme
  8. dreadful, exciting, terrible
  9. appalling, excessive, frightful
  10. tremendous
terrify ... 3. awe, cow 4. stun 5. alarm,
  appal, haunt, scare, shock 6. appall,
  freeze 7. horrify, petrify 8. affright,
  frighten
territory ... 4. area, land 5. banat, field
  6. canton, region 7. country 8. district,
  environs, Pashalic (Pasha's), province
  10. palatinate
terror ... 3. awe 4. fear 5. alarm, dread,
  panic 6. fright, horror 7. hellion, Reign
  of (Hist) 13. consternation
terrorism ... 11. subjugation
  12. intimidation
terse ... 4. curt, neat 5. pithy 6. smooth
  7. compact, concise, laconic, pointed,
  refined 8. succinct 11. sententious
  12. accomplished, epigrammatic
Tertiary period ... 6. Eocene 7. Miocene
  8. Pliocene 9. Oligocene 12. Age of
  Mammals
tertium quid ... 12. third someone
  13. third somewhat
tertulia ... 4. club 5. party 7. meeting
tessellated ... 6. mosaic 9. checkered
tessera ... 3. die 4. cube, tile 5. token
  6. marble, ticket 8. password
  11. certificate
test ... 3. try 4. exam, feel 5. assay,
  proof, prove, taste, tempt, trial
  6. ordeal, sample 7. examine, witness
  8. evidence, standard 9. criterion,
  testimony 10. experience, experiment
  11. examination, performance
  12. authenticate
test (pert to) ...
  fineness .. 3. pyx
  orally .. 7. examine
  ore, value .. 5. assay
  pot .. 8. crucible

severe .. 6. ordeal
testa ... 7. coating 8. covering, tegument
testament ... 3. New, Old 4. will
  8. covenant
testator ... 7. legator, witness 9. testatrix
taster ... 6. canopy, helmet, prover,
  taster 7. assayer, candler, sampler
testify ... 4. avow 6. affirm, depone,
  depose 7. declare, profess, protest
  8. indicate, manifest 11. bear witness
testimonial ... 5. token 7. tribute, warrant
  8. evidence 9. reference 10. compliment
  11. certificate
testimony ... 7. witness 8. evidence
  10. Scriptures 11. affirmation,
  attestation, declaration
testy, tetchy ... 6. touchy 7. fretful,
  peevish 8. petulant, snappish
  9. irascible, obstinate 10. headstrong
tetched in the head ... 9. pixilated
tetrad ... 4. four 7. quartet (quartette),
  quatern 8. foursome 10. quaternion
tetragon ... 4. park 6. square 7. rhombus
  9. courtyard 10. quadrangle
Tetragrammaton ... 7. Jehovah
  12. Supreme Being 14. four consonants
  (unpronounced)
Teuton ... 4. Goth 6. German
Teutonic (pert to) ...
  alphabet character .. 4. rune
  deity .. 2. Er 3. Tiu (Tiwaz), Tyr 4. Frea,
    Odin, Thor 5. Aesir, Bragi, Wodin
    6. Balder, Frigga 7. Forseti 8. Heimdall
  demon .. 3. alp
  giantess .. 4. Norn 11. demigoddess
  goddess .. 3. Eir, Hel, Ran 4. Norn, Urth
    (Urthr), Wyrd
  homicide (tribal) .. 5. morth
  land .. 4. odal
  law .. 5. Salic
  nymph (water) .. 3. nis
  race .. 5. Goths, Jutes 6. Franks, Saxons
    7. Vandals 8. Lombards 10. Norwegians
    13. Scandinavians
  supernatural being .. 5. troll
Teutonic goddess of ...
  death .. 3. Hel, Ran
  healing .. 3. Eir
  peace .. 7. Nerthus
Teutonic god of ...
  justice .. 7. Forseti (Forsete)
  pantheon .. 5. Aesir (group)
  peace .. 6. Balder
  sea .. 5. Aegir
  skill .. 3. Ull (Ullr)
  sky .. 2. Er 3. Tiu (Tiwaz), Tyr
  thunder .. 4. Thor 5. Donar
  war .. 3. Tiu (Tiwaz), Tyr
Texas ...
  birthplace of Pres .. 10. Eisenhower
  capital .. 6. Austin
  cattle .. 8. longhorn
  city .. 4. Waco 6. Dallas, El Paso
    7. Abilene, Denison, Houston
    9. Arlington, Fort Worth, Galveston
    10. San Antonio 13. Corpus Christi
  flags (six) .. 5. Spain 6. France, Mexico
    8. Republic (of Texas) 11. Confederate
    12. United States
  flower .. 10. bluebonnet, yellow rose
  Indian people .. 5. Caddo

monument (Battle).. 10. San Jacinto
police.. 7. Rangers
river.. 3. Red 5. Pecos 9. Rio Grande
shrine, mission.. 5. Alamo
State admission.. 12. Twenty-eighth
State motto.. 6. Friendship
State nickname.. 8. Lone Star
text... 4. book 5. topic, verse 7. passage
  8. libretto, textbook 11. letterpress
textile screw pine... 3. ara
textile shop... 7. mercery
texture... 3. web 4. wale, warp, wooz
  5. grain, weave 6. cobweb, fabric
  7. textile 9. roughness, structure
  10. smoothness
Thailand (Siam), **capital**... 7. Bangkok
Thames River town... 4. Eton
thana... 13. police station
thanador... 7. officer (Hind)
thanatology doctrine... 5. death
thane... 5. baron (anc) 7. servant, warrior
  9. Scots peer
thankless... 7. ingrate 10. ungrateful
  13. unappreciated
thanks... 5. grace 6. prayer 8. gramercy
  9. gratitude 12. appreciation
  14. acknowledgment
Thanks to God... 10. Deo gratias
that (pert to)...
  is.. 2. ie 5. id est
  is to say.. 3. viz 5. to wit 6. namely
  9. videlicit
  pronoun.. 3. who 4. what
thatch (pert to)...
  grass.. 4. rope 6. slough
  hair.. 3. mop 4. crop, mane
  palm.. 5. Sabal 7. Thrinax
  roofing.. 5. reeds, straw 6. rushes
  support.. 6. wattle
thatcher... 7. hellier
thaumaturgy... 5. magic 7. sorcery
  8. wizardry 11. legerdemain
the (pert to)...
  end.. 5. omega 6. thirty
  French.. 2. la, le 3. les
  German.. 3. das, der, die
  Italian.. 2. il, la, le 4. ella
  same.. 4. idem 5. ditto
  Spanish.. 2. el, la 3. las, los
theater, theatre... 5. arena, drama,
  odeum, stage 6. lyceum 8. coliseum
  9. playhouse 12. amphitheater
theater (pert to)...
  actress.. 7. heroine, ingénue
  box.. 4. loge
  curtain.. 4. drop 6. teaser
  district.. 6. Rialto 8. Broadway
  floor (lower).. 7. parquet
  full house.. 3. SRO
  Greek.. 5. odeum (odeon)
  part.. 3. box, pit 4. loge 5. foyer, stage
  7. balcony, gallery, parquet 8. parterre
  9. orchestra 10. proscenium
theatrical... 5. showy, stagy 8. affected,
  dramatic 10. artificial, histrionic
  12. melodramatic
theatrical (pert to)...
  art.. 10. histrionic
  company.. 6. troupe
  machine.. 9. eccyclema
  spectacle.. 5. revue 7. pageant

star.. 4. hero, lead 7. heroine
Theban (pert to)...
  bard.. 6. Pindar
  deity.. 4. Amen (Amon) 6. Amen-Ra
  god.. 5. Ammon (Zeus)
  king.. 5. Laius 7. Amphion, Oedipus
  8. Pentheus
  queen.. 5. Niobe 7. Jocasta
  soothsayer (blind).. 8. Tiresias
  triad.. 3. Mut 6. Amen-Ra, Khonsu
Thebes...
  capital of.. 10. Upper Egypt (anc)
  famed avenue.. 8. Sphinxes
  famed for.. 5. ruins
  location.. 4. Nile
  ruined temple.. 5. Ammon 6. Karnak
  Seven against (one of).. 6. Tydeus
theca... 3. pod 4. case, cell 7. capsule
theft... 6. holdup, piracy 7. larceny,
  robbery 8. burglary, stealing
  10. plagiarism 12. embezzlement
theftlike... 7. piratic 9. piratical
theme... 4. text 5. essay, lemma, motif,
  thema, topic 6. matter, thesis 7. subject
  9. discourse, leitmotiv
then... 3. poi (Mus) 4. also, next,
  when 5. hence 7. besides 8. formerly
  9. therefore 12. subsequently
thence... 4. away 5. hence 9. after that,
  elsewhere, therefore 10. henceforth,
  thereafter
theogamy... 14. marriage of gods
theologian... 5. Arius (Bib) 6. Luther
  7. Abelard, Aquinas, Erasmus
  9. Augustine
theology... 7. irenics 8. canonics, religion
  9. depositum 10. doctrinism
theorem... 3. law 4. rule 5. axiom,
  topic 7. premise 9. principle, statement
  11. proposition
theoretical... 5. ideal 8. academic,
  platonic 11. conjectural, impractical,
  speculative 12. hypothetical, not
  practical
theorize... 6. reason 9. postulate,
  speculate
theory... 3. ism 4. plan 6. scheme
  7. formula, opinion 8. analysis,
  doctrine 10. hypothesis 11. speculation,
  supposition 13. contemplation
theory of...
  evolution.. 9. Darwinism 10. Lamarckism
  13. Spencerianism
  knowledge.. 12. epistemology
  language.. 6. bowwow 8. ding-dong,
  pooh-pooh
  philosophy.. 13. phenomenalism
  relativity.. 8. Einstein
theosophist... 7. Mahatma
theosophy... 4. yoga 6. cabala 7. Nirvana
  8. kamarupa (Kama)
therapeutic... 7. healing 8. curative,
  remedies
therapy... 4. cure 5. faith 9. dietetics,
  medicines, treatment 12. hydrotherapy,
  therapeutics 13. psychotherapy
there... 3. yon 5. ready 6. yonder
  7. thereat, thither 11. at that place
therefore... 2. as, so 4. ergo 5. hence,
  since 6. thence 9. thereupon, to
  that end, wherefore 11. accordingly

12. consequently

thermometer ... 5. Hydra 7. Reaumur
10. Centigrade, Fahrenheit

Thesaurus compiler ... 5. Roget

thesis ... 5. essay, theme, topic 6. accent
7. premise 8. treatise 9. postulate
10. assumption 11. affirmation
12. dissertation

thespian ... 3. art 5. actor 6. player,
tragic 7. actress, Thespis (founder)
8. dramatic

Thessaly, Greece ...
ancient name .. 9. Thessalia
famed for .. 6. horses 8. horsemen
mountain .. 4. Ossa 6. Pelion
native .. 5. Greek 10. Thessalian
town .. 7. Larissa

thew ... 5. brawn, sinew 6. manner,
muscle, virtue 8. strength

they go out ... 6. exeunt

thick ... 4. burr, dull, hazy 5. broad,
bushy, close, crass, dense, gross,
husky, plump, solid, squat 6. coarse,
espeso, stodgy, stupid 7. crowded,
grumous, muffled 8. familiar, friendly,
intimate, numerous, thickset 9. luxuriant
10. indistinct 11. inspissated
12. impenetrable

thicken ... 3. gel 4. clot, curd 5. cloud,
flock 6. curdle, deepen, harden
7. congeal, stiffen 8. increase, solidify
9. intensify 10. incrassate, inspissate,
strengthen

thicket ... 4. bosk, rone 5. copse, grove,
hedge, shola 6. bosket (bosquet)
7. boscage, coppice, spinney
8. brushwood, chaparral 10. underbrush

thickheaded ... 4. dull 5. dense 6. stupid
7. doltish

thickness ... 3. ply 5. layer 7. density
8. diameter, intimacy 10. opaqueness
11. consistency, measurement

thickset ... 5. squat, stout 6. stocky,
stodgy, stubby 14. closely planted

thick-skinned ... 7. callous
11. hardhearted, insensitive,
pachydermic 14. pachydermatous

thick soup ... 6. purée

thief ... 5. scamp 6. ackman, bandit,
looter, pirate, rascal, robber 7. burglar,
filcher, rustler, stealer 8. gangster,
larcener 9. larcenist, scoundrel
10. freebooter, pickpocket, plagiarist

thieves (famed) ... 5. Fagin 9. Robin
Hood 10. Dick Turpin, Jesse James
11. Claude Duval 12. Jonathan Wild
13. Thief of Bagdad

thieves' Latin ... 4. cant 5. slang
12. secret jargon

thigh (pert to) ...
animal's .. 3. ham 4. hock 5. flank
armor plate .. 6. cuisse (cuish)
bone .. 5. femur, ilium
ref to .. 5. groin, meros (merus) 6. crural

thimble ... 3. cap 4. ring 5. cover, watch

thimble (pert to) ...
berry .. 9. raspberry 10. blackberry
eye .. 12. chub mackerel
flower .. 8. foxglove
rig .. 5. cheat 7. swindle 13. sleight of
hand

weed .. 6. clover

thin ... 4. bony, lank, lean, poor, rare,
slim, weak 5. gaunt, lanky, lathy,
reedy, sheer, spare, washy 6. dilute,
meager, rarefy, shrill, sleazy, slinky,
sparse, watery 7. haggard, insipid,
scraggy, scrawny, slender 8. araneous,
rarefied 10. attenuated, diaphanous
11. transparent

thin (pert to) ...
air .. 5. smoke, vapor 6. bubble
and delicate .. 8. araneous
10. diaphanous
and haggard .. 5. gaunt
and withered .. 7. wizened 9. shriveled
fabric .. 8. gossamer
out .. 5. peter
plate, bone .. 6. tegmen
plate, metal .. 4. leaf
plate, Zool .. 6. lamina 7. lamella
skinned .. 6. gentle, tender, touchy
Thin Man's dog .. ● Asta

thine ... 4. tuum

thing ... 3. act, res 4. deed, fact,
idea, unit 5. being, event 6. affair,
entity, gadget, object 7. article, reality
8. anything, creature 9. happening,
situation, something

thing (pert to) ...
added .. 6. insert 8. addendum
9. insertion 10. supplement
assumed .. 7. premise 11. implication
complete .. 4. unit
cursed .. 8. anathema
done .. 5. actum
following .. 6. sequel
found .. 6. trove
hard to classify .. 11. nondescript
huge .. 7. monster
indefinite .. 7. so-and-so 10. thingumbob
(thingumabob) 12. what's-its-name
nonexisting .. 9. nonentity
of little worth .. 6. stiver, trifle 7. trinket
the (thing) .. 7. the rage
unique .. 4. sole

things (pert to) ...
added .. 7. addenda 11. additaments
brought into being .. 9. creations
found, surprise .. 11. serendipity
intricate .. 9. involutes
little .. 16. inconsequentials
moving to and fro .. 7. wigwags
of like nature .. 8. cognates
suitable to eat .. 9. esculents
theoretical .. 7. noumena
to be done .. 6. agenda
to be learned .. 7. lessons
to follow .. 7. sequels 8. sequelae
to sharpen .. 10. whetstones
widely separated .. 8. extremes

think ... 3. wis 4. deem, muse, trow
5. opine 6. reason 7. believe, imagine,
reflect, suppose 8. cogitate, conceive,
meditate 11. contemplate

think (pert to) ...
better of .. 6. repent 10. reconsider
bring to mind .. 6. recall 7. imagine
10. conjecture
logically .. 6. reason
of .. 5. judge 6. intend, recall 8. consider,
remember 9. recollect 10. call to mind

over.. 3. wis 4. mull, muse 5. brood
6. ponder 8. meditate
up.. 6. devise, scheme 7. concoct
thinker, religious freedom...
14. latitudinarian
Thin Man (pert to)...
actor.. 3. Loy (Myrna) 6. Powell (William)
character.. 11. Nick Charles, Nora
Charles
dog.. 4. Asta
thinness... 6. rarity 7. tenuity 8. rareness
11. slenderness
third (pert to)...
comb form.. 3. tri 4. trit
day (Quakers).. 7. Tuesday
estate.. 6. people
figure.. 7. ferison
in number.. 8. tertiary
music.. 6. tierce
ordinal of.. 5. three
person.. 6. escort 7. grammar
8. chaperon
power.. 4. cube
Republic.. 6. French (1871)
thirst... 6. desire, hunger 7. craving,
dryness, longing
this... 4. near 9. the nearer
Thisbe's lover (Bab)... 7. Paramus
thisness... 9. haecceity
thistle (pert to)...
bird.. 9. goldfinch
color.. 6. violet (cobalt)
emblem.. 8. Scotland
genus.. 6. Arnica, Cosmos 7. Carlina
star.. 7. caltrop (caltrap)
thistledown... 6. pappus 12. thistlebeard
thither... 3. yon 5. hence 6. yonder
thong... 4. lash, riem, whip 5. knout,
lorum, quirt, romal, strap 6. lorate
7. amentum, lanyard (laniard)
Thor (pert to)...
father.. 4. Odin
German.. 5. Donar
god of.. 7. thunder
other name.. 9. Hlorrithi
stepson.. 3. Ull (Ullr)·
wife.. 3. Sif
thorax... 5. chest 6. cavity 7. cuirass
8. pectoral 11. breastplate
thorn... 4. bane 5. briar (brier), spine
7. acantha, bramble, prickle
thorn (pert to)...
apple.. 3. haw 6. Datura
back.. 3. ray 4. dorn 5. skate 10. spider
crab 11. stickleback
bill.. 11. hummingbird
comb form.. 5. spini
full of.. 6. briary
letters.. 2. th 3. edh
lizard.. 6. moloch
pert to.. 6. spinal
small.. 7. spinule
thornless... 7. inerm 8. inermous
thorny... 5. sharp, spiny 7. brambly,
prickly 9. acanthoid, bristling, difficult
thorough... 4. full 8. absolute, complete
9. downright, intensive 10. exhaustive
11. painstaking
thoroughfare... 4. road 6. artery,
street 7. highway, parkway, passage,
roadway, thruway 8. arterial, autobahn,

highroad, pent road, turnpike, waterway
9. boulevard, concourse 10. autostrada
thoroughgoing... 4. zeal 7. extreme
9. downright 11. painstaking
thoroughly... 3. all 9. intensive, out-and-
out 11. intensively 18. letter-perfect
thorp, thorpe... 4. dorp, town 6. hamlet
7. village
those (pert to)...
adept at table talk.. 14. deipnosophists
brought to terms.. 11. transigents
in office.. 3. ins
in the stock market.. 5. bears, bulls
7. traders 9. investors
of a habit.. 7. addicts
of the same goal.. 6. rivals
outside a profession.. 5. laity
those who...
read and write.. 9. literates
ridicule.. 8. deriders
verify.. 13. corroborators
work together.. 13. collaborators
thou... 3. tha 7. pronoun 8. thousand
thought... 4. care, heed, idea, view
5. logic 6. deemed, opined 7. anxiety,
opinion 9. attention, cogitated,
reasoning 10. cogitation, meditation,
reflection 11. cerebration
12. deliberation, recollection
13. consideration, ratiocination
thought (pert to)...
continuous.. 10. meditation
deep in.. 10. cogitabund
form.. 6. ideate
laws of.. 7. noetics
reader.. 11. telepathist
thoughtful... 4. kind 5. moody
7. mindful, museful, pensive, prudent,
serious 9. attentive 10. cogitative,
meditative, reflective, ruminative,
solicitous 11. circumspect, considerate
13. contemplative
thoughtless... 4. rash 6. stupid 7. foolish
8. careless, heedless, reckless
9. brainless, impulsive 11. harum-
scarum, inattentive, thought-free
12. unreflecting 13. inconsiderate
thousand... 3. mil 5. mille 7. chiliad
10. ten hundred
Thousand and One Nights...
13. Arabian Nights
thousand men, command of...
11. chiliarchia
thousandth... 9. chiliadal 10. millesimal
thousand years... 7. chiliad 9. millenary
10. millennium
thrall... 4. esne, serf 5. slave 7. bondage,
bondman, captive, slavery 9. thralldom
10. oppression
thrash... 3. lam, tan 4. beat, cave,
drub, flog, whip 5. flail, pound, twist
6. defeat, punish, strike, swinge, thresh
7. belabor, trounce 8. urticate, vanquish
9. pulverize, toss about
thrashing... 7. beating, milling
8. drubbing, flogging, whipping
10. punishment
thread... 4. flax, jute, line, silk, vein, wire,
yarn 5. fiber, floss, linen, lisle, rayon
6. cotton, dacron, sleave 8. arrasene,
filament

thread (pert to) . . .
  ancient . . 4. byss
  a needle . . 5. reeve
  ball . . 4. clew (clue)
  cell . . 5. cnida
  coiled . . 3. cop
  comb form . . 3. nem 4. nema 5. nemat
    6. nemato
  fish . . 7. cutlass 9. threadfin
    11. cobblerfish
  herring . . 11. gizzard shad
  like . . 5. filar 6. filose
  loose . . 4. lint 7. raveled
  medical . . 5. seton
  metal . . 4. wire
  mystery lead . . 4. clue
  shoemaker's (obs) . . 6. lingel (lingle)
  silk . . 5. floss 9. filoselle
  tangle . . 6. sleave
  tape, braid (thread) . . 5. inkle
  tester . . 9. serimeter
  weaving term . . 4. warp, weft, woof
    5. leash
threadbare . . 4. sere, worn 5. trite
  6. shabby
threaten . . . 4. warn 5. curse 6. menace
  7. portend 8. forebode 8. comminate
  10. intimidate 12. anathematize
threatening . . . 4. dark 7. ominous
  8. imminent, lowering, menacing
three (pert to) . . .
  banded armadillo . . 4. apar 5. apara
  comb form . . 3. ter
  dimensional . . 5. bruit, cubic
    12. stereoscopic
  fold . . 4. tern 6. ternal, treble, triple
    7. ternate
  group of . . 4. trio 5. triad 7. triplet
    8. triplets
  hundredth anniversary . .
    13. tercentennial
  in one . . 6. triune 7. trinity 10. The
    Godhead
  legged stand . . 6. teapoy, tripod, trivet
  lined . . 9. trilinear
  masted vessel . . 5. xebec 7. frigate
    8. schooner
  math term . . 2. pi (3.1416)
  prefix . . 3. tri
  R's . . 7. reading, writing 10. arithmetic
  seeded . . 11. trispermous
  sided figure . . 6. trigon 8. triangle
  spot . . 4. trey
  styled . . 10. trystylous
  toed sloth . . 2. ai
Three Kingdoms (Chin) . . . 2. Wu 3. Shu,
  Wei
Three Kings of Cologne . . . 6. Gaspar
  8. Melchior 9. Balthasar 12. Three
  Wise Men
Three Musketeers . . . 5. Athos 6. Aramis
  7. Porthos 9. D'Artagnan (friend)
Three Sisters (Myth) . . . 5. Fates 6. Clotho
  7. Atropos 8. Lachesis
Three Wise Men (Kings of Cologne) . . .
  6. Gaspar 8. Melchior 9. Balthasar
threnody . . . 5. dirge 7. requiem
  8. coronach
threshold . . . 3. eve 4. gate, sill 5. limen
  6. portal 8. doorsill
threw . . . see also *throw* 4. cast 5. flung,

slung 6. bunged, heaved, hurled, pelted,
  tossed 7. pitched
thrice . . . 3. ter, tri 5. fully 6. highly
  10. repeatedly, three times
thrift . . . 7. economy 8. prudence
  9. husbandry 10. providence
  11. thriftiness
thriftless . . . 6. lavish 8. prodigal, wasteful
  11. extravagant, improvident
thrifty . . . 6. frugal, saving 7. careful,
  prudent, sparing 9. provident
  10. economical, forehanded, prosperous
  11. flourishing
thrill . . . 4. tirl 6. dindle, thrush,
  tingle, tremor 7. delight 9. electrify
  10. excitement
thrive . . . 4. grow 5. moise (Eng) 6. batten
  7. prosper, succeed 8. flourish, increase
throat . . . 3. maw 4. crop, neck 5. gular,
  halse, mouth, voice 6. groove,
  gullet, larynx, mutter 7. channel,
  glottis, jugular, orifice, pharynx,
  trachea 9. esophagus 10. passageway
  12. constriction
throb . . . 4. ache, beat, drum, pant 5. pulse
  7. pulsate, vibrate 9. palpitate
throe . . . 4. pang 5. agony 7. anguish
  8. struggle
Throgmorton Street . . . 13. Stock
  Exchange (London)
throne . . . 3. see 4. apse 5. exalt
  8. enthrone 9. royal seat
  11. sovereignty, supreme rank 12. Chair
  of State
throng . . . 4. crew, host, push 5. crowd,
  horde, press, swarm 6. bustle, stress
  7. hurried 9. confusion, multitude
throttle . . . 5. choke, lever, seize 6. throat
  7. garrote 8. strangle, suppress,
  windpipe
through . . . 2. by 3. dia, per 4. into,
  thru 5. ended 7. perpend 8. finished
  9. because of, by means of, completed
throughout . . . 5. about 6. during
  8. thorough 10. completely, everywhere
throw . . . 3. cob, don, lob, peg, shy
  4. bear, cast, hurl, kist, pelt, toss, yerk
  5. chuck, fling, heave, pitch, sling,
  twist, whirl 6. baffle, strike, thwart
  7. discard, project 9. prostrate
throw (pert to) . . .
  a scare . . 7. terrify
  away . . 7. discard 8. handbill, squander
  back . . 5. repel 6. reject, revert
  dice (term) . . 4. sise 7. ambsace
  in the towel . . 4. cede, quit 9. surrender
  into confusion . . 7. disturb, perturb,
    trouble 8. stampede 10. demoralize
  into ecstasy . . 9. enrapture
  into shade . . 7. eclipse
  off . . 4. cast, shed 6. derail, reject
    7. abandon, discard
  out . . 4. emit, lade 5. egest, eject,
    expel 6. bounce 7. discard, project
    9. eliminate
  over . . 4. jilt 5. build 6. give up, refute
    7. abandon, discard 9. eliminate
  overboard . . 8. jettison
  water upon . . 5. douse
throwback . . . 7. setback 9. reversion
  10. misfortune, regression

throwing (pert to) . . .
  rope . . 5. lasso, reata, riata 6. lariat
  science . . 10. ballistics
  stick (anc) . . 6. womera (woomera)
thrum . . . 3. bit, hum 4. drum, tuft 5. strum
  6. fringe, repeat
thrush . . . 5. brown, mavis, robin, veery
  7. disease 8. shagbark, songbird
  9. blackbird
thrush (pert to) . . .
  American . . 5. robin, veery 12. hermit
    thrush
  European . . 5. ouzel (ousel) 6. missel
    7. redwing 11. nightingale
  golden . . 6. oriole
  Hawaiian . . 4. omao
  Ind . . 5. shama
  Scot . . 8. throstle
thrust . . . 3. dig, jab 4. gird, poke,
  push, stab 5. lunge 6. extend, pierce
  7. intrude, obtrude, riposte 8. protrude
  9. interject, interpose
thrust (pert to) . . .
  aside . . 5. shove 7. dismiss 8. brush
    off
  down . . 7. detrude
  fencing term . . 5. lunge 7. allonge,
    riposte 8. estocade
  one's self in . . 5. enter 7. intrude
  out . . 5. eject 6. extend 8. protrude
thug . . . 4. goon, yegg 6. cuttle, gunman
  7. ruffian 8. assassin 9. cutthroat,
  roughneck
thumb . . . 6. pollex, thenar
thumb (pert to) . . .
  a ride . . 9. hitchhike
  bird . . 9. goldcrest
  lady's (herb) . . 9. peachwort, persicary
  mark . . 4. soil 10. impression
    11. fingerprint 14. identification
  nail . . 5. small 8. complete
  over . . 4. skim 6. browse
  part . . 6. thenar
thump . . . 4. bang, beat, blow, drum,
  thud, whip, vent 5. knock, pound
  6. hammer, pummel, strike, thrash
  8. chastise 10. pound along
thunder . . . 4. boom, peal, roar 5. storm
  9. fulminate
thunder (pert to) . . .
  bolt . . 5. speed 6. Caesar 8. surprise
    9. lightning 11. fulmination
  fish . . 4. raad 5. loach 7. catfish (electric)
  god . . 4. Thor 6. Manito
  of applause . . 5. cheer 7. ovation
  peal . . 4. clap 5. crash
  smitten goddess . . 6. Semele 8. Keraunia
thurible . . . 6. censer
thurifer . . . 12. censer bearer
Thursday . . . 4. Thor 8. fifth day 12. god
  of thunder
thus . . . 2. so 3. sic 4. ergo 5. hence
  7. this way 9. therefore 11. for instance
  12. consequently
thwack . . . 3. rap 4. bang, blow, club
  5. crush, knock, whack 6. defeat,
  pommel, strike, thrash 7. belabor
thwart . . . 4. balk, foil 5. block, clash,
  cross, parry, spite 6. defeat, gaffle,
  oppose, outwit 7. oblique, prevent
  8. obstruct, stubborn 9. frustrate,

  interpose 10. across from, disappoint
thymus . . . 5. gland 10. sweetbread
  (lambs, calves)
tiara . . . 5. crown 6. diadem 7. coronet
  8. ornament
Tibbett opera . . . 12. Emperor Jones
  (1932)
tibert . . . 3. cat
Tibet, Asia . . . see also *Tibetan*
  animal . . 3. goa, sus 5. panda
  capital . . 5. Lhasa
  dialect . . 9. Bhutanese
  kingdom . . 5. Nepal
  Mts . . 8. Himalaya 9. Karakoram
  religion . . 5. Lamaism
  river . . 5. Hwang, Indus 7. Yangtze
    11. Brahmaputra
  ruler . . 9. Dalai Lama
Tibetan (pert to) . . .
  beer (barley) . . 5. chang
  deer . . 4. shou
  food (barley) . . 6. tsamba
  gazelle . . 3. goa
  monk, priest . . 4. lama
  ox . . 3. yak
  sheep . . 3. sha 5. urial 6. bharal, nahoor,
    nayaur
  wild ass . . 5. kiang
  wildcat . . 5. manul
tibia . . . 4. bone, shin 5. flute 6. cnemis
Tibur (anc) . . . 6. Tivoli
tiburon . . . 5. shark
Tiburtine . . . 12. Sibyl of Tibur
tic . . . 5. spasm 6. twitch
tick . . . 3. ked, tap 4. beat, mark,
  mite, pest 5. Argas 6. acarid, Ixodes
  7. instant 8. carapato, function, ticktock
  10. pajahuello (pajaroello)
ticket . . . 3. tag 4. note, pass, slip
  5. check, ducat, label, token 6. ballot,
  billet, permit, record 7. license, voucher
  8. document 11. certificate
ticket dealer . . . 7. scalper
tickle . . . 5. amuse 6. thrill, tingle
  7. delight 9. titillate, vellicate
ticklish . . . 5. risky 6. fickle, queasy,
  touchy 7. comical 8. unstable, unsteady
  9. uncertain 10. precarious, unreliable
tidal (pert to) . . .
  creek . . 6. estero 7. estuary
  current . . 8. tiderace
  flood . . 5. eagre
  flow . . 3. ebb 4. bore, neap 5. surge
tidbit, titbit . . . 5. goody 6. morsel
  7. saynete 8. delicacy
tide . . . 3. ebb, rip 4. high, neap, time
  5. drift 6. period, stream 7. current
  8. low water 9. be carried
tide (pert to) . . .
  gate . . 9. floodgate
  go with . . 5. drift, float 7. proceed 13. be
    fashionable
  out with . . 3. ebb 6. recede 8. diminish,
    fade away
  over . . 6. endure 8. surmount 11. live
    through
tidings . . . 4. news, word 6. gospel, report,
  rumors 7. message 10. evangelist
  11. information
tidy . . . 4. neat, trig, trim 5. groom, natty,
  plump 6. spruce 7. orderly 9. shipshape

10. put in order 12. antimacassar, considerable

tie ... 4. bind, bond, draw, even, knot, lash, link 5. ascot, equal, nexus, noose, trice, truss 6. cravat, enlace, fasten, relate, tether 7. confine, necktie, sleeper 8. equality, fastener, restrain, shoelace 10. allegiance, obligation

tie (pert to) ...
off .. 5. belay
ornament .. 3. pin
ready-made .. 4. teck
securely .. 7. trammel
sports .. 8. dead heat
uniting .. 4. bond 5. tache
up .. 4. bind, wrap 5. truss 6. fasten 8. restrain

tier ... 3. row 5. grade, layer 6. series

Tiergarten ... 4. park 16. Zoological Garden

tiff ... 3. sip 4. huff, spat 5. drink 7. dudgeon, quarrel 8. outburst 10. fit of anger

tiffin ... 3. tea 5. brown, lunch 6. repast 8. luncheon

tiger ... 5. bully 6. emblem, savage 9. swaggerer

tiger (pert to) ...
American .. 6. jaguar
bird .. 5. finch 8. amadavat
family .. 3. cat 6. mammal 11. Felis tigris
hunting dog .. 5. dhole
S African .. 7. leopard
Tasmania .. 9. thylacine 13. Tasmanian wolf
wolf .. 5. hyena
young .. 3. cub

tight ... 3. fast, snug, taut, trim 5. alert, close, drunk, tense 6. narrow, stingy 7. exactly, shapely 9. condensed 11. closefisted 12. close-fitting, parsimonious

tight (pert to) ...
fisted .. 5. stingy 12. parsimonious
lipped .. 5. terse 9. secretive
wad .. 5. miser 10. curmudgeon

tighten ... 4. frap, lace 5. brace, tense 6. fasten, tauten 7. squeeze 9. constrict

Tigris River city of ruins ... 7. Nineveh (anc)

til ... 4. tree 6. sesame

tilde ... 4. dash, mark, sign 6. accent, tittle 15. diacritical mark

tile ... 3. red 5. slate 6. domino, mosaic, pament (pamment), tegula 7. ceramic, pantile, tessera 8. pavement

tiler ... 5. thief 6. slater 7. hellier 10. doorkeeper

till ... 3. box 4. farm, plow, tray, when 5. labor, while 6. before, casket, drawer, whilst 7. develop 9. cultivate

tillable ... 6. arable

tiller ... 4. helm 5. stalk 6. farmer, sprout 7. plowman, rancher 8. harrower 10. cultivator, husbandman

tilt ... 3. tip 4. cant, heel, list 5. joust, pitch, slant, slope 6. careen, oliver (hammer), seesaw, unload 7. incline 8. log house 9. tournament 11. altercation

timber ... 3. log 4. beam, tree, wood 6. forest, lumber 7. support 9. underpier

timber (pert to) ...
bend .. 3. sny
building .. 4. sill, stud 5. joist 6. purlin, rafter 8. stringer
convex .. 6. camber
cribs (logging) .. 4. dram
cut .. 6. lumber 7. fallage
decay .. 4. doty (doaty)
end .. 5. tenon
hard, heartwood .. 7. duramen
Naut .. 3. rib 4. bitt, keel, mast, spar, wale 8. sternson
support .. 6. corbel
upright .. 8. puncheon
wolf .. 4. lobo

timbre ... 4. tone 5. clang, crest (Her), miter 7. coronet 9. resonance, tone color

timbrel ... 4. drum 5. tabor 7. sistrum 10. tambourine

time ... 3. age, day, eon, era 4. aeon, date, hour, term, turn, week, year 5. clock, epoch, shift, tempo 6. decade, minute, moment, period, season, second 7. century 8. duration, occasion, schedule 9. fortnight, millenium

time (pert to) ...
accurate .. 10. isochronon
before Christmas .. 6. Advent
before Easter .. 4. Lent
equal .. 10. isochronal
geologic .. 5. azoic
granted .. 4. stay 5. delay 8. reprieve
legal .. 6. usance 11. year and a day
limit .. 8. deadline
long ago .. 4. once, yore 8. formerly
medical .. 3. tid 8. ter in die (three times a day)
of vigor .. 6. heyday
one .. 4. once
present .. 5. nonce 12. contemporary
prior .. 9. antedated 11. retroactive
right .. 3. tid
same .. 3. however 9. meanwhile 10. concurrent 11. synchronous 14. simultaneously
spare .. 7. leisure
waste .. 4. idle, loaf 5. dally 6. loiter
wrong .. 11. anachronism 13. anachronistic

timeless ... 7. ageless, eternal, undated 8. dateless, unending, untimely 9. premature 11. everlasting 12. interminable

timely ... 3. apt, pat 4. soon 5. early 6. prompt 9. opportune 10. seasonably 11. opportunity

timepiece ... 4. dial 5. clock, watch 6. gnomon 8. egg glass, horologe 9. clepsydra, hourglass, metronome 10. isochronon, wristwatch 11. chronometer

times ... 3. ago, eld 4. yore 5. often 10. frequently, yesterdays 11. ups and downs

timid ... 3. shy 4. meek 5. eerie, henny, mousy, pavid, scary 6. afraid, trepid 7. bashful, fearful, nervous, not bold 8. cowardly, retiring, timorous

9. diffident, shrinking 12. fainthearted
13. pusillanimous

timocracy (pert to) . . .
defined by . . 5. Plato
principle . . 11. love of honor
State . . 6. Sparta (anc)

Timon of Athens . . . 5. Cynic (The)
11. misanthrope

timorous . . . 5. timid 6. afraid 7. bashful,
fearful 8. hesitant 9. shrinking

Timothy (pert to) . . .
Bib . . 7. convert 8. Epistles
grass . . 3. hay 10. herd's grass

timpani . . . 11. kettledrums

tin . . . 3. can, pan 5. money, plate
7. element, stannum 8. preserve 10. not
genuine

tin (pert to) . . .
alloy (copper) . . 6. pewter
box . . 7. trummel
coat with . . 5. terne 10. terneplate
comb form . . 6. stanni
extract . . 8. prillion
foil, plate . . 4. tain
mine . . 8. stannary
ref to . . 7. stannic
sheet . . 6. latten
symbol . . 2. Sn

tinamou . . . 5. yutu 7. tataupa 9. partridge

tincture . . . 4. dash 5. color, imbue, myrrh,
tinge, trace 6. iodine 7. extract, vestige
8. solution 9. paregoric, suspicion
10. extraction

tinder . . . 4. punk 5. spunk 6. amadou
9. touchwood

tine . . . 3. nib 5. prong, spike, tooth

tinea . . . 7. sycosis 8. ringworm

tinge . . . 3. dye 4. tint 5. color, imbue,
shade, stain, taint 6. flavor 8. coloring,
tincture 10. suggestion

tingle . . . 4. ring 5. sting 6. dingle, thrill
7. prickle 9. sensation, stimulate

tinkle . . . 5. clink 6. dingle, tingle

tint . . . 3. due, hue 4. tone 5. blush,
color, tinge 6. nuance

tintinnabulum . . . 4. bell 6. tinkle
9. rhymester

tintype . . . 9. ferrotype 12. old-fashioned

tiny . . . 3. wee 4. small, teeny 5. atomic,
infant, minute, petite 9. miniature
10. diminutive 13. infinitesimal

tip . . . 3. cue, end, fee, neb, top 4. apex,
cant, heel, hint, lean, list, tilt 5. crown,
point, slant, spire, upset 6. careen,
inform, summit, tiptop 7. cumshaw,
incline 8. bonamano, gratuity, overturn
9. extremity, overthrow

tip (pert to) . . .
end . . 3. neb
French . . 9. pourboire
Italian . . 8. bonamano
near . . 6. apical
Near East . . 9. baksheesh (bakshish)
scabbard . . 5. chape 7. crampet
(crampette)
slender . . 6. arista
to one side . . 4. list, tile 5. alist 6. careen
up and over . . 4. cant

tippet . . . 4. cape, hood 5. amice, scarf
6. almuce 7. muffler 8. liripipe, palatine
9. comforter

tipple . . . 3. bib, nip, pot, sip 4. suck
5. drink, quaff 6. fuddle, guzzle, liquor,
tumble 7. spirits 8. beverage, overturn

tippler . . . 3. sot 5. souse, toper 7. drinker
9. draftsman

tipster . . . 4. tout 8. dopester 9. informant,
predictor 10. forecaster, speculator

tipsy . . . 4. awry 5. drunk, shaky 6. groggy
7. fuddled, muddled 10. staggering
11. intoxicated

tiptoe . . . 5. alert 6. warily 7. eagerly,
quietly 8. cautious, stealthy
10. cautiously

tirade . . . 6. screed, speech 8. berating
9. philippic

tire . . . 3. fag, lag, rim 4. bore, jade
5. dress, weary 6. attire 7. exhaust,
fatigue

tired . . . 5. bored, jaded, spent, weary
6. aweary

tireless . . . 8. untiring 9. unwearied
10. unwearying 13. indefatigable

tiresome . . . 3. dry 4. dull, tame 6. boring,
prolix 7. irksome, tedious 8. annoying
9. fatiguing, vexatious, wearisome
10. irritating

tissue . . . 4. web 5. bast, tela 5. fiber,
paper 6. fabric 7. culture 8. meshwork

tissue (pert to) . . .
Biol . . 4. bone 5. nerve 6. muscle
8. ganglion 10. epithelium
cell . . 8. meristem
cellular . . 10. epithelium
connecting . . 6. stroma, tendon
8. ligament
decay . . 6. caries
fatty . . 3. fat 4. suet
hardening of . . 9. sclerosis
horny . . 7. keratin
layer . . 7. stratum
lymphoid . . 7. tonsils
nerve . . 8. ganglion
ref to . . 4. tela 5. telar
spinal . . 4. alba
vegetable . . 4. bast 7. endarch
8. meristem
wood . . 6. lignin, lignan

Titan . . . 4. Rhea, Thea 5. Coeus, Creus,
deity, Dione, giant, Theia 6. Phoebe,
Tethys, Themis 7. Cronius, lapetus,
Oceanus 8. Hyperion 9. Mnemosyne

titanic . . . 4. huge 5. great 7. immense
8. colossal, enormous, gigantic

Titan War (Thessaly) . . . 11. Titanomachy

tithe . . . 3. tax 4. part 5. teind, tenth
11. frank pledge

titi . . . 4. monkey 7. sea bird 8. ironwood
9. buckwheat

Titian . . . 3. red 6. artist 7. red hair
9. red-haired

titillate . . . 5. amuse 6. thrill, tickle
7. delight 8. interest

titlark . . . 5. pipit

title . . . 3. sir 4. dame, deed, earl, lord,
name, sire, term, type 5. claim, right
6. knight, madame, squire 7. caption,
epithet, esquire 8. muniment
9. designate 11. appellation, designation

titled member, Stock Exchange . . .
6. orchid (sl)

titmouse . . . 3. mag, tit 4. wren

5. Parus 6. parine, tomtit 7. jacksaw
9. mumruffin

titter ... 5. laugh, te-hee 6. giggle, tee-hee
7. snicker

tittle ... 3. dot, jot 4. iota, mark, whit
5. tilde 6. gossip, tattle 8. particle

tittle-tattle ... 6. gossip 8. idle talk
16. scandalmongering

tittupy ... 3. gay 5. shaky 6. lively
8. prancing, unsteady

titubate ... 4. reel 6. totter 7. stagger,
stammer

titular ... 7. nominal 9. incumbent (of
a title)

Tlingit ... 6. Indian (Alaska)

TNT ... 6. trotol 9. explosive
15. trinitrotoluene

to ... 2. at 4. into, till, unto 5. until
6. toward 7. as far as, thither
11. preposition

to (pert to) ...
  to be.. 4. esse, être
  to-do.. 3. ado 4. fuss, stir 6. bustle
    9. commotion
  to each his own.. 10. suum cuique
  to which.. 7. whereto
  to wit.. 3. viz 6. namely 8. scilicet
    9. videlicet

toad ... 4. agua, Bufo, frog, pipa
6. anuran, peeper 7. crapaud
9. amphibian, Batrachia, spadefoot
10. natterjack

toad (pert to) ...
  eater.. 5. toady 8. hanger-on, parasite
  fish.. 6. puffer, slimer 8. frogfish
  head.. 6. plover (golden)
  lily.. 9. waterlily
  stabber.. 9. jackknife
  tree.. 4. Hyla

toadflax ... 8. flaxweed, ranstead
13. butter-and-eggs

toadstool ... 5. morel 6. fungus
8. mushroom, puffball

toady ... 4. ugly 8. parasite, truckler
9. repulsive, sycophant, toadeater

toast ... 3. tan 4. cook, leep 5. bread,
brede, brown, parch, roast, skoal
6. pledge, sippet 7. drink to 8. cinnamon

tobacco (pert to) ...
  ash.. 6. dottle (dottel)
  Cuban.. 4. capa 6. Vuelta (leaf)
  disease.. 6. calico, mosaic 7. walloon
  English.. 8. bird's-eye
  epithet.. 12. Lady Nicotine
  French.. 7. caporal
  Greek.. 7. Knaster
  hookah smoking.. 7. goracco
  Indian.. 7. uppowoc
  introduced by.. 7. Raleigh (Sir Walter)
  Kentucky.. 6. Burley
  kind.. 4. capa, shag 5. tabac 6. Burley,
    Vuelta 7. caporal, henbane, Latakia,
    perique, Turkish 8. Virginia 9. salvadora
  paste.. 7. goracco
  Persian.. 6. tumbak (tumbaki)
  pipe.. 7. calumet, chibouk (chibouque)
  principle (active).. 8. nicotine
  receptacle.. 4. pipe 7. humidor
  S American.. 8. canaster
  small cut.. 3. cud 4. plug, quid 6. dottle
    (dottel) 7. carotte

Turkish.. 7. Latakia
wrapping.. 9. broadleaf

toboggan ... 4. sled 5. coast, glide
7. coaster 12. sharp decline 14. downhill
course

toby ... 3. dog (Punch's), jug, mug, rob
5. cigar 7. highway, pitcher

tocsin ... 5. alarm 9. alarm bell
13. warning signal

toe ... 3. tae, tip 5. digit 6. dactyl, hallux
7. minimus

toehold ... 7. footing 8. foothold,
purchase

toes, odd-numbered ... 13. perissodactyl

toe the line ... 4. obey

together ... 3. com, con, syn 4. mass,
with 5. union 10. conjointly
11. unanimously 12. coincidently,
concurrently, continuously

toggery ... 3. set 4. garb, togs 5. dress
7. clothes, harness 9. trappings
12. haberdashery

tolerable ... 4. so-so 8. bearable, passable
9. endurable 10. acceptable, fairly well,
sufferable 11. supportable

tolerance ... 8. patience 10. indulgence,
permission

tolerant ... 7. lenient, patient 9. indulgent
10. forbearing, permissive

tolerate ... 4. bear, bide 5. abide, allow,
brook, stand 6. endure, permit, suffer
9. put up with

toll ... 3. due, tax 4. call, duty,
peal, ring 5. knell 6. allure, charge,
custom, entice, impost, invite, strike
7. ringing 8. exaction 10. assessment
12. compensation

Tolypeutes ... 4. apar 9. armadillo

tomahawk ... 3. axe 4. kill 6. attack
7. hatchet

tomb ... 4. cist, lair 5. crypt, grave, speos,
vault 6. shrine 7. mastaba (mastabah),
orruary, tritaph 8. catacomb, cenotaph
9. mausoleum, sepulcher

tombé ... 4. drum

tomboy ... 6. meg 4. romp 5. rowdy
6. hoyden (hoiden), tomrig

tomcat ... 3. gib

tomcod ... 8. bocaccio

tome ... 4. book, opus 5. atlas 6. volume
11. papal letter, publication

tomorrow ... 5. later 6. mañana 9. the
morrow

tonant ... 7. blatant 10. thundering

tone ... 4. mode, mood, note, tang,
tune 5. pitch, reedy, sound, trend,
twang, vigor 6. accent, energy, melody,
nuance, timbre 7. cadence 8. modulate,
monotone, tonology 9. harmonize
10. inflection, intonation, modulation

tone (pert to) ...
  down.. 3. dim 6. mellow, modify, soften
    8. moderate
  lacking.. 5. atony 6. atonal
  quality, color.. 6. timbre
  series.. 5. scale
  single.. 8. monotone
  succession.. 5. melos
  thin.. 7. sfogato
  vibrant.. 5. twang

toneless ... 4. weal 5. stony 6. silent

9. colorless

tonga . . . 7. vehicle (2-wheeled)

Tonga . . . 15. Friendly Islands

tongue . . . 3. gab 4. meat 5. lingo,
speak 6. speech 7. clapper, lingula
8. language, lorriker, parlance
9. utterance

tongue (pert to) . . .
  classical . . 5. Greek, Latin 6. Hebrew
  fish . . 4. sole
  Jesus . . 7. Aramaic
  lash . . 5. scold 8. scolding
  pivoted . . 4. pawl
  reference to . . 7. glossal, lingual
  sacred . . 4. Pali
  shaped . . 9. lingulate
  tied . . 4. mute 8. taciturn
  wagon . . 4. neap, pole

tongueless . . . 4. dumb, mute
10. speechless

tonic . . . 6. bracer, catnip, liquor 7. bracing
8. medicine, remedial, roborant
9. stimulant 10. refreshing
11. corroborant 12. invigorating

tonsil . . . 9. amygdala

tonsorialist . . . 6. barber

tonsured . . . 4. bald 5. shorn 6. shaven
7. clipped 10. baldheaded

too . . . 3. and 4. also, over, very 6. overly
7. besides 8. likewise 9. extremely
11. excessively 12. additionally

too (pert to) . . .
  bad . . 4. alas
  much . . 4. trop 6. excess 7. nimiety
  small . . 13. unappreciable
  soon . . 9. premature

tool . . . 3. axe, saw 4. dupe, file 5. agent
6. device, gadget, puppet 7. engrave,
gimmick, utensil, utility 9. appliance
11. contrivance

tool (type) . . . 2. ax (axe) 3. adz (adze),
awl, bit, hob, hoe, saw, sax, tap 4. file,
jack, pick, tong, vise 5. brush, burin,
drill, knife, lathe, level, plane, punch,
razor, spade 6. chisel, gimlet, hammer,
lifter, peavey (peavy), pliers, reamer,
shears, slater, slicer, square, trepan,
wrench 7. cleaver, mattock, mattoir,
scalpel, spatula 11. screwdriver

tools (pert to) . . .
  category . . 5. power, speed 7. cutlery,
machine, medical 9. precision 11. labor-
saving 12. straightedge
  prehistoric . . 4. celt 6. eolith 9. paleolith
  stone . . 6. banner
  theft of . . 6. ratten

toosh . . . 4. gown (short), robe
9. nightgown

toot . . . 3. pry, spy 4. fool, gaze, peep
5. blare, drink, revel, shout, spree
6. sprout 7. whistle 8. carousal,
eminence, proclaim 9. blow a horn,
elevation

tooth . . . 3. cog 4. dent, fang, snag,
tine, tusk 5. ivory, molar, point,
prong, taste 6. canine, cuspid, wisdom
7. grinder, incisor 8. bicuspid, eyetooth
10. projection

tooth, teeth (pert to) . . .
  ache . . 8. dentagra 9. dentalgia
  comb form . . 5. denti, odont 6. odonto

    7. odontia
  covering . . 6. enamel
  cutting of . . 8. teething 9. dentition
  decay . . 6. caries, cavity 11. saprodontia
  destitute of . . 8. edentate
  irregularity . . 11. odontoloxia
  molar . . 4. wang
  ref to . . 6. dental 7. odontic
  science . . 10. odontology
  Scot . . 3. gam
  socket . . 8. alveolus
  toothlike . . 8. odontoid 9. dentiform

toothless . . . 8. decrepid, edentate

toothsome . . . 5. tasty 9. delicious,
palatable

top . . . 3. cap, fid, lid, tip, toy 4. acme,
apex, pate, roof 5. crest, criss,
crown, excel, mensa, outdo, ridge,
scalp 6. finial, summit, vertex, zenith
7. highest, supreme, surpass, topmost
8. dominate, pinnacle, teetotum
9. uppermost

topaz . . . 3. gem 5. color 7. mineral
11. hummingbird 13. precious stone

tope . . . 4. tomb, wren 5. drink, grove,
shark, stupa, tower 6. guzzle, shrine
7. dogfish

toper . . . 3. sot 4. tope 5. shark 6. barfly,
boozer 7. guzzler, tippler, tosspot
8. drunkard 9. alcoholic, inebriate
12. bacchanalian

tophet, topheth . . . 4. hell 5. chaos
8. darkness

topi, topee . . . 3. cap, hat 8. antelope

topiary . . . 6. garden 9. gardening

topic . . . 4. plot, text 5. theme 6. reason,
remedy 7. subject 8. argument
11. application

topical . . . 5. local 9. temporary
10. thematical

topknot . . . 5. crest, onkos 6. pigeon
8. flounder 9. headdress

topmost . . . 6. apical 7. highest, supreme
8. foremost 9. uppermost

topnotcher . . . 3. ace 4. hero, star
6. tiptop 7. supreme 9. first-rate
11. unsurpassed

topography . . . 7. mapping 8. location
9. surveying 11. description 15. regional
anatomy

topple . . . 3. tip 4. fall, tilt 5. pitch,
upset 6. totter, tumble 8. overturn
9. overthrow 10. somersault

topsail . . . 5. raffe (raffee)

topsy-turvy . . . 8. confused 10. contrarily,
disordered 11. withershins

toque . . . 3. hat 6. monkey (bonnet)
9. headdress

tor . . . 4. crag, peak 5. mound 8. pinnacle

torah, tore . . . 3. law 7. precept 10. Law
of Moses, Pentateuch, revelation

torch . . . 4. lamp 5. blaze, flare, fusee
(fuzee), light 7. lighter, lucigen
8. flambeau 10. flashlight

torero . . . 11. bullfighter

torment . . . 3. rib, vex 4. bait, pain, rack
5. agony, devil, harry, tease, worry
6. badger, harass, harrow, hector,
pester, plague, stir up 7. afflict, anguish,
bedevil, torture 8. distress, vexation
9. suffering, tantalize 10. punishment

11. persecution

torn . . . 4. rent 5. riven, split 6. ripped 7. severed 8. tattered 9. alienated, lacerated (see also *tear*)

tornado . . . 4. wind 7. cyclone, twister 8. blizzard, outburst 9. hurricane, whirlwind, windstorm 12. thunderstorm

toro . . . 4. bull 7. cavalla, cowfish

torpedo . . . 3. ray 4. boat, mine 5. shoot 6. attack, gunman 7. explode 8. fire upon, firework, numbfish 9. crampfish, detonator, submarine

torpid . . . 4. dull, numb 5. inert 6. stupid 7. dormant 8. benumbed, inactive, lifeless, listless, sluggish 9. apathetic, lethargic

torpor . . . 4. coma 6. acedia, apathy, stupor 7. languor 8. dormancy, lethargy 9. inertness 10. inactivity 12. sluggishness 13. insensibility

torque . . . 5. chain 6. collar 7. torsion 8. necklace, ornament

torrefy . . . 5. parch, roast 6. scorch

torrent . . . 5. flood, spate 6. stream 7. current, roaring 8. downpour, outburst

torrential . . . 12. overwhelming

torrid . . . 3. hot 4. arid 7. burning, parched 8. scorched, tropical 10. oppressive, passionate

tortilla cooking dish . . . 5. comal

tortoise . . . 4. emyd, Emys 6. gopher, turtle 7. hicatee 8. Chelonia, matamata 9. ellachick

tortuous . . . 6. spiral 7. devious, sinuous, winding 8. twisting 10. circuitous, roundabout 12. labyrinthine

torture . . . 4. flay, pain, rack 5. agony, twist 6. impale, punish, wrench 7. crucify, distort, torment 10. punishment

tory, Tory . . . 6. bandit, outlaw, Papist 8. loyalist, marauder, partisan, Royalist 11. reactionary 12. Conservative

toss . . . 3. lob 4. cast, flip, hurl 5. bandy, chuck, fling, flirt, heave, pitch, throw 6. billow, thrash 7. disturb 8. flounder, scramble 9. commotion 10. excitement

toss (pert to) . . .
a coin . . 4. flip
and turn . . 6. thrash 8. flounder 9. vacillate
off . . 5. drink 6. tipple 9. dispose of, improvise
out . . 5. eject 8. trick out
together . . 8. scramble

tosspot . . . 3. sot 5. drunk, toper 6. flagon 8. drunkard

tossup . . . 6. gamble 10. even chance 11. uncertainty

tota . . . 6. grivet, monkey

total . . . 3. add, all, sum, tot 5. gross, utter, whole 6. amount, entire 7. perfect, summary 8. absolute, complete, entirety 9. aggregate

totally . . . 5. quite 6. wholly 8. entirely 10. completely

totem . . . 4. pole, post 6. fetish, pillar, symbol

totem pole . . . 3. xat

toto . . . 3. all 4. baby 5. totum

totter . . . 4. reel, rock, sway 5. pitch, shake, waver 6. falter, seesaw 7. stagger 8. titubate 9. fluctuate, vacillate

toucan . . . 4. toco 7. aracari 8. hornbill 13. constellation (opp Southern Cross)

touch . . . 3. dab, tag, tap, tig 4. abut, feel, meet 5. taste, trait 6. adjoin, border 7. contact 9. acuteness

touch (pert to) . . .
acuteness of . . 8. oxyaphia
bound . . 4. abut
closely . . 7. impinge 8. osculate
examine . . 7. palpate
light, lightly . . 3. pat 5. brush 7. attinge, lambent
off . . 4. fire 6. incite
ref to . . 7. tactile, tactual
stone . . 8. basanite 9. criterion 11. Lydian stone
wood . . 4. punk 6. amadou, tinder

touching . . . 6. moving 7. contact, feeling, tangent 8. pathetic 9. affecting, attingent 10. concerning 11. interesting

touchy . . . 4. sore 5. cross, testy 7. peevish 8. ticklish 9. irascible, irritable, sensitive 10. precarious 13. oversensitive

tough . . . 4. hard, wiry 5. hardy, rowdy, stiff 6. robust, sinewy, strong 7. ruffian 8. adhesive, hardened, leathery, stubborn 9. difficult, obstinate, resistant, tenacious 10. unyielding

toupee . . . 3. wig 6. peruke 7. periwig 9. false hair

tour . . . 4. trip 5. shift 6. travel 7. circuit, journey 9. barnstorm, excursion

tourmaline . . . 3. gem 6. schorl 9. rubellite 10. indicolite

tournament . . . 4. tilt 5. games, joust, trial 6. battle 7. contest, regatta, tourney 8. Olympics 9. encounter 11. Turnierfest

tourniquet . . . 6. binder, garrot 7. bandage

tousle, tousel . . . 4. pull, tear 6. rumple, tussle 8. dishevel

tout . . . 3. spy 5. scout, watch 6. praise 7. canvass, lookout, tipster 8. give a tip, informer, smuggler 9. predictor, solicitor

tow . . . 3. tew, tug 4. drag, draw, haul, pull, rope 5. chain 6. hawser 8. cordelle

toward . . . 2. ad, at, to 4. near 5. anent 6. facing 7. forward, towards, willing 8. imminent 9. compliant, headed for 11. approaching

toward (pert to) . . .
blood vessels . . 6. hemad (haemad)
center . . 5. entad 6. inward
direction . . 7. leeward, seaward 8. homeward, landward, windward 9. earthward 10. heavenward
exterior . . 5. ectad
front . . 8. anterior
left . . 3. haw 5. aport 9. sinistrad, sinistral
mouth . . 4. orad
right . . 7. dextrad 9. dextrally
stern . . 3. aft 5. abaft 6. astern

towards . . . 7. ynesche

tower . . . 3. tor 4. boom, silo, soar 5. exalt, pylon, spire, stupa 6. belfry, height, turret, uplift 7. bulwark, defense, elevate, steeple, surpass 8. domineer, fortress 9. campanile 10. stronghold, watchtower

tower (pert to) . . .
astrology. . 7. mansion 14. planetary house
bell. . 9. campanile
chess. . 6. castle
church. . 5. spire 6. belfry, cupola
glacial. . 5. serac
India. . 7. minar 7. sikhara
marker. . 5. pylon
of. . 4. Pisa 5. Babel, Minar 6. Eiffel, Hunger, London 7. silence (dakhma) 10. Kutab Minar
Oriental. . 7. minaret
watch. . 7. mirador

towering . . . 4. high, huge, tall 5. great, lofty 6. Alpine 7. eminent, soaring 11. overweening

towhee . . . 5. finch 7. bunting, chewink

town . . . 4. burg, deme 6. ciudad, hamlet, Podunk, suburb 7. borough, commune, village 8. boom town, township 9. ghost town

townsman . . . 3. cit 7. citizen, oppidan (Eton student) 8. resident 9. selectman

toxic . . . 4. noxious 6. poisoned, venomous, virulent 9. poisonous

toxicology (science of) . . . 7. poisons 9. antidotes

toxology . . . 7. archery

toxophilite . . . 6. archer

toy . . . 3. pet, top 4. doll, hoop, play, whim 5. dally, fancy, flirt 6. bauble, gewgaw, hoople, rattle, trifle 7. cat's paw, trinket 8. flirting 9. plaything 10. knickknack

trace . . . 4. clew (clue), copy, find, hint, mark, nose, seek, sign 5. refer, shade, tinge, track, trail 6. deduce, derive, detect, follow, sketch 7. glimpse, outline, thought, vestige 8. evidence, traverse 9. delineate, footprint 11. investigate, small amount

trachea . . . 4. duct 8. windpipe

tracing . . . 4. copy 6. record 8. ergogram 10. cardiogram 12. reproduction

track . . . 3. rut, way 4. path, rail, slot, spur, wake 6. route, spoor, trail, tread 7. follow, pursue 7. nereite (worm), vestige 8. traverse 9. footprint, spectacle

tract . . . 4. area, plot, zone 5. essay, range 6. estate, region 7. booklet, country, expanse, leaflet, quarter, stretch 8. brochure, district, pamphlet, treatise 9. territory 10. exposition 11. subdivision 12. dissertation

tract (pert to) . . .
arid. . 4. dene 6. desert
boggy, swampy. . 6. morass 10. Everglades
grassland. . 7. prairie
lava. . 8. pedregal
treeless. . 5. llano 6. steppe 7. prairie

tractable . . . 4. easy 6. docile, gentle, pliant 7. ductile 8. amenable, flexible 9. adaptable, compliant, malleable 10. governable 11. conformable

trade . . . 3. buy 4. deal, sell, swap,

wind 5. craft 6. barter, merger, metier 7. bargain, calling, dealing, pursuit, traffic 8. business, commerce, exchange, practice, purchase, vocation 10. handicraft, occupation, profession 11. intercourse

trade-mark, trademark . . . 4. logo 5. brand, label 8. logotype

trader . . . 6. dealer, monger, sutler 8. merchant 9. tradesman 10. shopkeeper

trading association . . . 5. hanse (hansa)

trading station (Mil) . . . 2. PX 4. fort, post

tradition . . . 4. lore, myth 5. usage 6. custom, legend 7. culture 8. folklore 10. convention (established) 12. superstition

traditional . . . 3. old 9. legendary 10. historical 12. conventional, long-standing 15. long-established

traditional tale . . . 4. sage 6. legend

traduce . . . 4. slur 5. abuse, belie 6. debase, defame, malign, vilify 7. asperse, pervert, slander 8. disgrace 10. calumniate

traffic . . . 3. buy 4. sell 5. trade 6. barter, simony (sacred) 8. business, carriage, commerce, dealings 11. familiarity, intercourse

tragedy . . . 6. misery 8. calamity, disaster 10. misfortune

tragic . . . 3. sad 4. dire 5. fatal 8. dramatic, pathetic 10. calamitous, disastrous, fatal event

tragopan . . . 8. pheasant

trail . . . 3. lag 4. drag, hunt, path, slot, spur 5. blaze, piste, route, scent, spoor, trace, track 6. camino, follow 7. draggle 8. be behind, footpath 9. lag behind

Trail (famed) . . . 6. Mormon, Oregon 7. Santa Fe, Spanish 8. Chisholm, El Camino, Heritage 10. Lewis-Clark, Wilderness 11. Appalachian 12. Natchez Trace, Pacific Crest

trail (pert to) . . .
blazer. . 7. pioneer
deer. . 4. slot
mark a. . 5. blaze
marker. . 5. cairn
mountain. . 4. pass
Spanish. . 6. camino

Trail of Tears people . . . 8. Cherokee

train . . . 2. el 4. line, load, tail 5. breed, chain, coach, drill, flier, focus, shape, suite 6. direct, school, series 7. caravan, cortege, educate, retinue 8. accustom, instruct, railroad, rehearse 9. afterpart, entourage, following 10. attendants, conveyance, discipline, line of cars, procession 11. progression, streamliner 13. accommodation

trained mechanic . . . 7. artisan

trainee . . . 6. rookie 7. recruit, student 8. enrollee

traipse . . . 3. gad 5. trail, tramp 6. trudge, wander 8. gadabout

trait . . . 5. habit, touch 6. streak 7. feature, quality 9. lineament, mannerism 11. peculiarity 13. individuality 14. characteristic

traitor ... 3. rat 8. informer, Quisling, turncoat 10. treasonist 13. double-crosser, Judas Iscariot 14. Benedict Arnold

traject ... 3. way 4. sage 5. ferry, route 6. course 7. passage 8. crossing

trajectory ... 5. route 6. rocket 9. celestial 10. fixed orbit

tram ... 3. car 4. limb 5. wagon 7. carrier, railway, tramcar, trolley, vehicle 9. streetcar 10. conveyance

tramontane ... 5. alien 8. polestar 9. foreigner, North Star 11. transalpine

tramp ... 3. bum 4. hike, hobo, hoof, step, walk 5. jaunt, nomad, tread 6. beggar, trudge, wander 7. sponger, traipse, trample, vagrant 8. vagabond 9. sundowner 10. landlouper (landloper), pedestrian 11. bindle stiff 12. foot traveler

trample ... 4. crush, tread 6. bruise, subdue 7. conquer, destroy, run over 9. press down

trance ... 4. coma, doze 5. dream, spell, swoon 6. raptus, stupor 7. amentia, ecstasy, rapture 8. hypnosis 9. catalepsy, enrapture, hypnotize, spellbind

tranchant ... 5. sharp 7. cutting 9. trenchant

tranquil ... 4. calm, cool, easy, mild 5. quiet, still 6. gentle, placid, serene 7. pacific, restful 8. composed, peaceful 9. quiescent 11. undisturbed 13. imperturbable

tranquility ... 3. keg 5. peace, quiet 8. calmness, serenity 9. composure 10. quiescence 12. peacefulness

tranquilize ... 4. calm, lull 5. allay, quiet, still 6. pacify, settle, soothe 7. appease, assuage, compose

transaction ... 4. deal, sale 6. action, affair 7. bargain 8. business 9. discharge, execution 10. proceeding 11. negotiation, performance, proposition 16. buying and selling

transcend ... 3. cap 5. excel, mount 6. ascend, exceed 7. surpass 8. go beyond, outstrip, surmount

transcendent ... 5. above 8. ethereal, heavenly, superior 9. recondite 10. superhuman, surpassing 12. metaphysical, supernatural, transmundane 13. extraordinary 14. transcendental 15. beyond knowledge

transcribe ... 4. copy 5. write 6. record 9. reproduce, translate 10. paraphrase

transcript ... 4. copy 6. record 8. apograph 9. duplicate, imitation 12. reproduction

transfer ... 4. cede, deed, pass, sale 5. grant, shift 6. assign, attorn, change, convey, depute, remove 7. removal 8. alienate, delivery 9. transport 10. conveyance, transcript

transfer (pert to) ...
conveyance (estate) .. 5. lease 6. demise
crown to successor .. 6. demise
design .. 5. decal 12. decalcomania
medical .. 10. transplant

of ownership .. 6. attorn 10. abalienate, alienation, conveyance
of property .. 8. disposal

transfigure ... 5. exalt 6. change 7. glorify 8. idealize 9. irradiate, transform, transmute 12. metamorphose

transfix ... 3. pin 4. hold 5. spear 6. fasten, impale, pierce 9. hold fixed 11. transpierce 14. hold motionless

transform ... 4. turn 5. alter 6. change, revamp 7. convert 9. transmute 10. assimilate 11. transfigure 12. metamorphose, transmogrify 16. transubstantiate

transformation ... 3. wig 6. change 8. mutation 10. conversion, false front 13. metamorphosis, transmutation 17. anthropomorphosis

transgress ... 3. err, sin 5. cross 6. exceed, offend, thwart 7. disobey, infract, violate 8. overstep, trespass 9. break a law

transgression ... 3. sin 5. crime, fault 7. misdeed, offense 8. trespass 9. violation 10. effrontery, infraction 11. lawbreaking 12. infringement 13. nonconformity

transgressor ... 6. sinner 8. offender 9. wrongdoer 10. delinquent, malefactor

transient ... 5. brief 6. lodger 7. flighty 8. fleeting, fugitive, traveler 9. ephemeral, migratory, momentary 10. evanescent, short-lived, transitory

transit ... 6. travel 7. passage 9. metabasis 10. conveyance 12. transference

transition ... 5. shift 7. passage 9. anabolism, evolution, metabasis 10. catabolism (katabolism), conversion, metabolism, modulation 11. transfusion

transitory ... 5. brief, fleet 8. fleeting, temporal 9. ephemeral, temporary, transient 10. evanescent 11. not enduring

transitory things ... 8. ephemera

translate ... 4. read, rede 6. decode, render 7. convert 8. construe, transfer 9. interpret 10. paraphrase

translation ... 4. pony, trot 7. version 9. rendition 10. paraphrase 12. transference 14. interpretation 15. transliteration

translucent ... 6. limpid 8. luminous 11. transparent 14. shining through

transmit ... 4. send 6. convey, render 7. devolve, forward 8. bequeath, hand down, transfer 11. communicate

transmutation ... 9. evolution

transmute ... 6. change 7. convert, resolve 9. transform 11. transfigure 12. metamorphose 16. transubstantiate

transparent ... 4. open 5. clear, gauzy, lucid, sheer 6. bright, candid, glassy, lucent 7. crystal, pellucid, shining 8. luminous, lustrous 9. guileless 10. diaphanous 11. crystalline, perspicuous, translucent, unconcealed

transparent thing ... 4. mica, silk, veil 5. beryl, water 6. quartz, tissue 7. crystal, diamond 8. gossamer 9. isinglass

transport ... 3. dak 4. boat, move, raft, send, ship 5. bring, carry, truck 6. banish, convey, deport, vessel 7. ecstasy, freight, passion, rapture, smuggle 8. carriage, emigrate, entrance, palander, transfer 9. enrapture, troopship

transpose ... 5. shift 6. change, convey, invert 7. convert, reverse 8. transfer 9. rearrange, translate, transmute 11. interchange

transposition of sounds, words ... 10. metathesis, spoonerism

Transvaal (pert to) ...
capital .. 8. Pretoria
city .. 12. Johannesburg
daisy .. 7. gerbera
discovery .. 4. gold, Rand (The)
famed emigration .. 9. great trek (1836)
legislature .. 4. raad
policeman .. 4. zarp
settlers .. 5. Boers
War .. 4. Boer (1899-1902)

transverse ... 6. across 7. oblique, transom 8. diagonal 9. crosswise 10. crosspiece

trap ... 3. gin, net, pat, web 4. cage, door, lure, rock, tipe, tree, weir 5. catch, creel, mouth, snare 6. ambush, corner, device, eelpot, enmesh, recess 7. dragnet, ensnare, pitfall, springe 8. carriage, deadfall, trapping, trickery 9. caparison, road block, stratagem

trapper ... 5. lurer 6. hunter, netter, snarer 7. decoyer

trappings ... 4. gear, tack 5. props 7. scenery 8. wardrobe 9. apparatus, caparison, ornaments 10. horse cloth 13. paraphernalia

trash ... 4. bosh, dirt, junk 5. waste 6. debris, refuse, rubble 7. rubbish 8. nonsense, riffraff, trumpery 10. balderdash

trashy ... 5. cheap, toshy 6. paltry 7. useless 8. rubbishy 9. worthless 11. nonsensical

trauma ... 5. shock, wound 6. injury

travail ... 4. pain, toil 5. agony, labor 7. journey, trouble 9. suffering 11. parturition

trave ... 9. crossbeam

travel ... 2. go 4. fare, move, mush, post, ride, taxi, tour, trek, wend 5. coast 6. motion 7. commute, journey, migrate, sojourn 8. progress, traverse 9. gallivant 11. peregrinate

travel (pert to) ...
equipment .. 7. baggage 9. viaticals
expense .. 8. viaticum
group .. 7. caravan
over obstacles .. 9. roughshod
pert to .. 6. viatic
place to place .. 9. itinerate

traveler, travelers ... 5. farer 6. viator 7. caravan, tourist 8. salesman, wayfarer 9. journeyer

travels ... 7. odyssey 8. journeys 14. peregrinations

traverse ... 4. deny, pass 5. cross 6. refute, thwart 7. athwart, oblique, parados 8. navigate 10. counteract

travesty ... 5. drama 6. parody, satire 7. lampoon 8. disguise 9. burlesque 10. caricature 11. incongruity

tray ... 6. salver, server 7. ashtray, coaster

treacherous ... 5. false, Judas, punic, snaky 8. disloyal, plotting, unstable 9. deceitful, faithless, insidious 10. perfidious, traitorous, unreliable 11. disaffected 13. Machiavellian (Machiavelian), untrustworthy

treachery ... 5. guile 6. deceit 7. perfidy, treason 8. betrayal 10. disloyalty

treacle ... 4. cure 6. remedy 7. claggum, sweeten 8. molasses 10. sweetening

treacle water ... 7. cordial

tread ... 3. rut 4. gait, mark, pace, step, volt, walk 5. crush, stair 6. course 7. conquer, set foot, trample 8. footstep, shoe sole 9. footprint

treadle ... 5. lever, pedal 7. chalaza

tread underfoot ... 5. crush 6. subdue 7. oppress, run over 8. domineer 9. tyrannize

treason ... 7. perfidy 8. betrayal, sedition 9. treachery

treasonable, treasonous ...
10. perfidious, traitorous
11. treacherous

treasure ... 4. fisc (fisk), fund, roon 5. cache, chest, hoard, prize, purse, store, trove, value 6. coffer, fiscus, riches, wealth 7. cherish 8. hold dear 9. exchequer, thesaurus 10. appreciate, depository, repository, storehouse

treasurer ... 6. bursar, purser 7. cashier, curator, officer 8. receiver 9. paymaster 11. chamberlain

Treasure State ... 7. Montana

treasure-trove ... 5. money (hidden) 7. bullion 9. discovery 14. buried treasure

treat ... 4. dose 5. Dutch, feast 6. doctor, handle, regale, repast 7. delight, discuss, process 8. consider 9. discourse, entertain, negotiate 10. manipulate

treat (pert to) ...
improperly .. 4. snub 5. flout, spite 6. insult, misuse, offend 9. humiliate
maliciously .. 5. frame, spite
of morals .. 6. ethics
royally .. 6. regale 9. with honor
silk (for rustle) .. 6. scroop
snobbishly .. 7. high hat, high-hat
surgically .. 7. operate
tenderly .. 6. coddle, pamper
with contempt .. 5. flout, scorn, scout, spurn 7. contemn
with deference .. 7. respect

treatise ... 5. essay, study, tract 6. thesis 7. article 9. discourse 10. discussion 12. dissertation

treatise on ...
forests .. 5. silva
fruit trees .. 6. pomona
language .. 7. grammar
pines .. 7. pinetum

treatment (pert to) ...
application (Med) .. 5. stupe
compassionate .. 5. mercy
harsh .. 5. abuse 8. misusage, severity

ill . . 5. abuse
preparatory . . 8. training 10. ground work, processing
term . . 5. usage 8. addition (to soil), handling
treaty . . 4. mise, pact 6. cartel 7. compact, entente 8. contract 9. agreement 10. convention 11. arrangement, negotiation 12. capitulation 13. understanding
treaty (pert to) . . .
bound nations . . 6. allies
Elm . . 12. Philadelphia (1682)
first draft . . 8. protocol
peace . . 5. truce 6. Pax Dei 9. armistice 10. pax in bella
secret . . 13. the Engagement (1647)
treble . . . 5. three, voice 6. latten, triple 7. soprano 9. threefold 11. high-pitched
treble clef . . . 3. Gee 5. G clef, staff (G clef)
tree . . . 5. plant 6. corner, timber 7. gallows 9. genealogy
tree (pert to) . . . see also *trees*
antidote for snakebite . . 6. cedron
aromatic . . 9. sassafras
bear . . 7. raccoon
cactus . . 7. saguaro
camphor . . 5. kapur
cat . . 9. palm civet
cobra . . 6. mambra
cone-bearing . . 3. fir, yew 5. alder, cedar, larch 7. conifer
dwarf . . 6. bonsai
evergreen fruit . . 5. lemon 6. orange
exudation . . 3. gum, lac, sap
India . . 4. dita 10. devil's tree
lotus . . 4. sadr
mineral (formed on) . . 8. dendrite
of Buddha . . 2. bo
of chastity . . 11. agnus castus
of life . . 10. arbor vitae
of strength . . 3. oak
rain . . 5. saman (zaman) 8. genisaro
resin . . 3. fir 4. pine 6. balsam
sacred (Bib) . . 7. asherah
salt . . 4. atle (atlee) 8. tamarisk
snake . . 4. gimp, lora
sprout . . 5. copse, sprig 7. coppice
sugar . . 5. maple
Texas . . 5. alamo 6. poplar
tiger . . 7. leopard
toad . . 4. hyla
trunk . . 4. bole 5. caber, stock
umbrella . . 5. wahoo
victor's crown . . 6. laurel
worshiper . . 5. dryad, nymph (wood)
trees (pert to) . . .
grove . . 5. copse
plantation . . 6. forest 7. orchard, pinetum
poem . . 6. Kilmer (Joyce)
ref to . . 8. arboreal 9. cacuminal
science . . 7. silvics 12. silviculture
service (rowan) . . 5. sorbs
trefoil . . . 6. clover 8. shamrock 10. black medic, clover leaf (Her)
tregetour (anc) . . . 7. juggler 8. magician
trek . . . 6. travel 7. journey, migrate 10. expedition
trellis . . . 5. arbor 7. lattice, pergola 8. espalier 11. latticework

tremble . . . 5. quake, shake 6. doddle, falter, quaver, quiver, shiver, tatter, thrill, tremor 7. shudder, tremolo, twitter, vibrate 8. be afraid 9. be excited, trepidate
trembling . . . 5. aspen 6. dither, trepid 7. fearful, nervous, quaking, quavery, shaking 9. vibrating
tremendous . . . 3. big 4. huge 5. awful, giant, great 6. superb 8. horrible, powerful, terrific 9. frightful, momentous, monstrous 10. terrifying 13. extraordinary
tremolo . . . 6. quaver 10. fluttering
tremor . . . 5. palsy, quake, shake 6. quiver, thrill 7. tremble 9. vibration
tremulous . . . 5. aspen, quaky, timid 7. excited, fearful, nervous, palsied, shaking, shivery 9. quavering, sensitive, trembling, vibratory 11. palpitating
trench . . . 3. gaw 4. bury, gash, leat, moat 5. canal, carve, ditch, drain, fosse 6. furrow, groove, gutter 7. acequia, intrude 8. aqueduct, encroach, entrench, infringe, trespass 10. excavation 12. entrenchment
trenchant . . . 4. keen 5. acute, sharp 6. biting 7. cutting 8. clear-cut, incisive 11. penetrating
trencherman . . . 5. eater 7. sponger 8. gourmand 9. chowhound 11. gormandizer
trend . . . 4. tone, turn, vein 5. drift, skirt, swing, tenor 6. strike 7. deviate, revolve 8. movement, tendency 9. direction 11. inclination
trepan . . . 3. saw 4. lure, tool 5. snare, trick 6. entrap 7. deceive, swindle 8. deceiver, trephine 9. stratagem, trickster
trepang . . . 10. bêche-de-mer 11. sea cucumber 14. sea caterpillar
trepid . . . 7. quaking 8. timorous 9. trembling
trepidation . . . 4. fear 5. alarm 6. dismay 7. quaking 9. agitation, confusion 10. excitement 11. disturbance, oscillation 12. perturbation 13. consternation
trespass . . . 3. sin 4. tort 5. poach 6. breach, invade, trench 7. intrude, offense 8. encroach, entrench, infringe, overstep 10. infraction, transgress 11. misfeasance 12. infringement 13. transgression
tress . . . 4. curl, hair 5. braid, plait 7. ringlet 10. lock of hair
treasure . . . 4. band 6. border, fillet, ribbon 9. headdress
trestle . . . 5. bench 7. support, viaduct
tret . . . 9. allowance
triad . . . 5. chord, three, trine 7. trinary, trinity 9. trivalent 12. ternary group
trial . . . 2. go 4. bout, case, test 5. venue 6. assize, ordeal 7. attempt, contest, empiric 8. evidence, hardship 9. prolusion, trying out 10. experiment 11. examination, tribulation
triangle . . . 6. trigon 8. virginal 13. constellation
triangle (pert to) . . .

connection . . 5. delta
draw circle within . . 7. escribe
military . . 10. punishment
music instrument . . 10. percussion,
triquetrum (anc)
side . . 3. leg
three acute angles . . 6. oxygon
two equal sides . . 9. isosceles
unequal sides . . 7. scalene
triangular (pert to) . . .
decoration . . 8. pediment, triqueta
muscle . . 7. deltoid
pert to . . 10. trilateral
piece . . 4. gore 5. miter, wedge 6. gusset
sail . . 6. lateen 9. spinnaker
shaped . . 7. deltoid 8. oxygonal
tribal custom . . 7. couvade (childbirth)
tribal symbol . . . 5. totem 6. totem pole
tribe . . . 4. clan, kind, race, sept
5. class, group 6. family 7. company
11. aggregation 14. classification
tribe (pert to) . . .
birds . . 5. flock
head of . . 5. chief 6. sachem 9. patriarch
Israel . . 3. Dan 4. Levi 6. Reuben
migrated . . 5. Aryan
New Zealand . . 3. ati
of Ben . . 5. poets (Ben Jonson)
Tribes, Five Civilized . . . 5. Creek
7. Choctaw 8. Cherokee, Seminole
9. Chickasaw
Tribes, Five Nations (Iroquois) . . .
6. Cayuga, Mohawk, Oneida, Seneca
8. Onondaga
tribulation . . . 5. trial 6. ordeal, sorrow
8. distress 9. suffering
tribunal . . . 3. bar 4. banc, seat 5. bench,
court, curia, forum 9. Areopagus (anc)
tributary . . . 4. fork, vein 6. branch, feeder
8. affluent, effluent, influent 9. auxiliary
11. subordinate 12. contributary
tribute . . . 3. fee, pay, tax 4. cain, duty,
levy, scat 5. allow, grant 6. assign,
bestow, homage, impost, praise,
rental 7. chevage (Hist), ovation,
payment, pension, respect 8. encomium
9. attribute, gratitude 10. allegiance,
contribute, obligation 11. retribution
tricar . . . 8. tricycle 10. motorcycle (with
extra car)
trice . . . 5. jiffy 6. moment 7. instant
9. twinkling
trick . . . 3. fob, gag 4. dido, dupe, feat,
flam, gull, jest, ruse, wile 5. cheat,
child, dodge, fraud, guile, knack, prank,
shift, stunt 6. deceit, delude 7. deceive,
defraud, finesse, pretext 8. artifice,
delusion, flimflam, illusion 9. chicanery,
deception, imposture 10. subterfuge
11. contrivance, legerdemain
trickery . . . 5. fraud, hocus 6. deceit
7. roguery 8. artifice, cheating, trumpery
9. chicanery, deception, duplicity
10. hanky-panky 11. amenability,
legerdemain
trickle . . . 4. drip, drop, flow, leak 7. distill
(distil), dribble, dripple, leakage
tricks . . . 4. shab 5. ruses 7. roguery
10. deceptions
trickster . . . 3. fox 5. cheat, rogue 6. rascal
7. slicker 8. deceiver 12. Artful Dodger

tricky . . . 3. sly 5. snide 6. artful, clever,
crafty, shrewd 7. cunning, devious
8. rascally 9. deceitful 13. Machiavellian
trident . . . 5. curve, spear 6. symbol
7. leister
tried . . . 4. true 6. proved, tested
7. devoted 8. faithful, reliable
11. trustworthy
tries . . . 5. tests 6. assays 8. attempts,
contests
trifle . . . 3. ace, bit, fig, toy 4. doit,
fico, fool, jest 5. dally, fable, straw
6. bauble, dabble, dawdle, doodle,
fiddle, gewgaw, palter, pewter, potter,
wanton 7. dessert, nothing, traneen
8. flimflam, gimcrack, make love
9. bagatelle 10. knickknack, peccadillo,
triviality 11. small amount 12. treat
lightly
trifler . . . 7. dallier, flaneur 8. palterer,
putterer 10. dilettante
trifles . . . 4. toys 6. trivia 7. gewgaws,
palters 8. minutiae, trumpery
trifling . . . 4. idle, mere 5. inane,
petty 6. little 7. trivial 8. badinage,
frippery 9. nugacious 10. immaterial
13. insignificant
trifolium . . . 6. clover 8. shamrock
trig . . . 4. chic, neat, prim, tidy, trim
5. natty, smart 6. lively, spruce
7. precise 10. methodical
trigo . . . 5. wheat
trigon . . . 4. game, harp, lyre (anc)
8. triangle
trigonometry term . . . 4. sine 6. cosine,
secant 7. tangent 8. spherics
10. goniometry
trihoral . . . 11. three-hourly 15. every
three hours
trill . . . 4. move, sing 5. shake, twirl
6. quaver, ripple, warble 7. mordent,
tremolo, trickle, vibrate 8. grupetto
12. pralltriller
trillion . . . 5. trega (comb form) 14. million
million
trim . . . 3. bob, cut, lop 4. chic,
clip, crop, neat, perk, snod, tidy,
trig, whip 5. adorn, natty, nifty,
panel, preen, prune, shear, shrag
6. border, dapper, defeat, punish,
reduce 7. compact, orderly 8. decorate,
ornament 9. embellish, shipshape
10. decoration
trimming . . . 4. gimp, lace 5. braid,
jabot, ruche 6. edging, frieze, fringe,
piping 7. falbala, ruching 8. furbelow,
ornament 9. chicanery, garniture
10. decoration 11. accessories
13. passementerie
trinity . . . 5. three, triad 6. triune
Trinity (Eccl) . . . 7. Godhead (Father,
Son, Holy Ghost) 8. Trimurti
trinket . . . 3. toy 4. gaud, tali (tahli)
5. bijou, jewel 6. bangle, gewgaw,
trifle 7. bibelot 8. gimcrack, ornament
10. knickknack
trip . . . 3. err, run 4. halt, skip, slip,
trap 5. caper, dance, jaunt, speed
6. bungle, cruise, errand, flight, frolic,
voyage 7. journey, misstep, stumble
8. obstruct 9. excursion 10. expedition

triple ... 3. tri 5. trine 6. tercet, treble 9. intensify, threefold 12. three-base hit

triple crown ... 5. tiara (Pope's)

triplet (one of) ... 4. trin

tripletail ... 4. fish, sama 9. berrugate, spadefish

tripod ... 3. cat (6-legged) 5. easel, stand, three 9. trivet

Tripoli, Libya ...
capital of ... 12. Tripolitania
caravan route to ... 5. Wadai 8. Lake Chad, Timbuktu
famed arch to ... 14. Marcus Aurelius
people ... 4. Arab, Turk 6. Berber
ruler ... 3. bey, dey

triptych ... 5. volet (part) 10. altarpiece, writing pad 13. writing tablet (3-part)

trismus ... 7. lockjaw, tetanus 16. gnashing the teeth

trist ... see *tryst*

Tristan and Isolde ... 5. opera (Wagner)

triste ... 3. sad 4. full 6. dismal 10. depressing

tristful ... 3. sad 10. melancholy

tristich group ... 10. three lines 11. three verses (stanza)

Tristram & Iseult ... 4. poem (Arnold)

trite ... 5. banal, corny, petty, stale, vapid 6. betide, cliché, common, jejune 7. bromide 9. hackneyed, well-known 10. threadbare, unoriginal 11. commonplace, stereotyped 13. platitudinous

triton ... 3. eft 4. newt 5. shell, snail 10. salamander

Triton (pert to) ...
art figure ... 7. demigod
Gr Myth ... 10. sea demigod
symbol ... 7. trumpet

triumph ... 3. win 5. exult, glory 6. defeat 8. ceremony (anc), conquest 10. exultation 11. achievement

trivia ... 5. trash 7. trifles 8. trumpery

trivial ... 5. banal, petty, small, trite 6. common, paltry, slight 7. nominal, pipeerly, shallow 8. doggerel, ordinary, trifling 9. frivolous, nugacious 11. commonplace, unimportant 13. insignificant

triviality ... 3. toy 6. bauble, gewgaw, trifle 8. falderal, nugacity 9. bagatelle, frivolity 10. knickknack 14. insignificance

troche ... 4. pill 6. button, rotula, tablet 7. lozenge 8. pastille (pastil) 9. cough drop 10. deer's tines

trochee ... 4. foot (2-syllable) 5. meter 7. choreus

trod ... see *tread*

trogger ... 7. peddler, vagrant

trogon ... 7. quetzal

Troilus (pert to) ...
butterfly genus ... 7. Papilio
legendary hero of ... 7. Chaucer
son of ... 5. Priam

Trojan (pert to) ...
astronomy ... 9. asteroids
epic ... 5. Iliad 6. Aeneid 7. Odyssey
expedition hero ... 4. Ajax 8. Achilles
founder of ... 4. Troy
hero ... 5. Paris 6. Aeneas, Hector

9. Palamedes
horse ... 6. wooden
horse builder ... 5. Epeus
king ... 5. Priam
native ... 6. Dardan
soothsayer ... 7. Helenus
war cause ... 5. Helen (of Troy)
war leader ... 9. Agamemnon
warrior ... 6. Agenor

troll (Myth) ... 5. dwarf, giant, gnome

troll ... 4. bowl, fish, roll, sing 5. angle (fishing), rondo 6. allure, entice, propel 7. revolve, trundle 9. circulate

trolley ... 4. cart, tram 5. truck 6. barrow, sledge 7. tramcar 8. handcart 9. streetcar

trolley, off his ... 4. nuts 5. balmy, batty, daffy, dippy, dotty, goofy 6. cuckoo

trollop ... 5. slump 6. slouch 8. slattern

trombone (pert to) ...
ancient ... 7. sackbut, sambuke
instrument ... 5. brass
mouthpiece ... 5. bocal
popular size ... 5. tenor

troop ... 4. army, band, unit 5. crowd 7. company, march on, ressala 8. quantity, soldiers 9. go forward 10. armed force

troop (pert to) ...
arrangement ... 7. echelon
encampment ... 6. étape
formation ... 4. line
one of ... 7. peltast 8. chasseur
ship ... 9. transport

troops (pert to) ...
assemble ... 6. muster
German ... 6. Panzer
hidden ... 6. ambush
Hungary ... 7. Hussars
mounted ... 7. cavalry
sally ... 6. sortie
term for ... 4. army 5. squad 6. forces 7. battery, militia, phalanx 9. commandos 11. armed forces

trophy ... 3. cup 4. palm 5. award, medal, Oscar, prize 6. reward 7. laurels, memento 8. memorial

tropical (pert to) ...
animal ... 4. eyra 5. araba, coati, potto 6. agouti 7. peccary
bird ... 3. ani 4. tody 5. jalap 6. motmot 7. jacamar
dolphin ... 4. inia
fish ... 4. toro 6. remora, salema
fruit ... 3. fig 4. date 5. guava, mango, papaw 6. banana, papaya
lizard ... 5. agama
rodent ... 6. agouti
tree ... 4. coco, palm 5. balsa, seron 6. sapota 8. tamarind
vine ... 7. cowhage, lantana 14. trumpet creeper

trot ... 3. jog, run 4. gait, pony 5. hurry 7. routine 11. translation

trotting horse ... 6. Morgan 7. Hackney 12. Hambletonian

trottoir (rare) ... 8. footpath, pavement, sidewalk

troubadour ... 4. bard, poet 8. jongleur, minstrel, musician 9. trovatore

trouble ... 3. ado, ail, irk 4. fuss, harm,

stir 5. annoy, grief, worry 6. bother,
effort, grieve, harass, pester, plague,
sorrow 7. agitate, anxiety, concern,
disturb, perturb, torment 8. calamity,
disorder, disquiet, distress, mischief
9. adversity, annoyance, commotion
10. affliction, difficulty, misfortune
11. disturbance 13. inconvenience,
interfere with

troubled ... 6. queasy 7. annoyed,
anxious 8. agitated 9. disturbed
10. distressed

troublemaker ... 8. agitator, gossiper
13. mischief-maker

troublesome ... 5. pesky 8. annoying,
perverse 9. difficult, laborious,
turbulent, vexatious, wearisome
10. bothersome, burdensome,
disturbing, oppressing 11. distressing
12. inconvenient

trough ... 3. bin 4. bosh, bowl, dale,
tank 5. basin, chute, drain, toper
6. coffin, gutter, manger, sluice, trench
7. channel, conduit

trounce ... 4. beat, flog 5. scald 6. indict,
punish, thrash 7. censure, journey

trout ... 4. char, peal 7. oquassa
9. namaycush 11. Dolly Varden

trout (pert to) ...
genus . . 5. Salmo 6. Trutta
lake . . 9. namaycush
Maine . . 7. oquassa
parasite (external) . . 3. sug
ref to . . 11. truttaceous
type . . 3. sea 4. rock 5. brook, brown,
river 7. oquassa, rainbow 8. speckled
9. cutthroat

trovatore ... 10. troubadour

trove ... 4. find 8. treasure (buried)
9. discovery 10. thing found
13. treasure-trove

trow ... 4. boat, hope 5. barge, think,
trust 6. expect 7. believe, suppose
9. catamaran

trowing ... 5. creed 6. belief 7. opinion

Troy, or Ilium ...
capital of . . 5. Troad (anc)
defender . . 6. Aeneas
famed for . . 5. ruins
founder (Myth) . . 4. Ilus (son of Tros),
Tros
king . . 5. Priam 9. Agamemnon
king's wife . . 5. Helen
mountain . . 3. Ida
name, present . . 9. Hissarlik
pert to . . 5. Iliac 6. Trojan
site . . 9. Asia Minor

troy weight ... 5. grain, ounce, pound
11. pennyweight

truant ... 4. idle 7. shirker, trivant, vagrant
8. absentee

truant, to play ... 5. miche

truce ... 5. pause, peace, trève
9. armistice, cessation 10. brief quiet
12. intermission

truck ... 3. van 4. deal, dray, haul
5. bogie, dance, lorry, trade 6. barter,
peddle 7. flatcar, traffic 8. commerce,
exchange, nonsense 9. groceries

truckle ... 4. fawn 5. toady 6. cringe,
submit 7. knuckle

truculent ... 4. base, mean 5. cruel
6. fierce, savage 8. ruthless, scathing
9. barbarous, ferocious 11. destructive

trudge ... 4. pace, plod, slog, walk
5. tramp 6. go slow 7. traipse

true ... 2. so 4. fact, leal, pure, real
6. gospel, honest, lawful 7. certain,
devoted, germane, precise, sincere,
upright 8. faithful, orthodox, reliable,
straight, unerring 9. authentic,
steadfast, veracious, veritable
10. legitimate 11. trustworthy,
unfaltering

true (pert to) ...
blue . . 5. loyal 8. faithful, orthodox
10. man of honor
copy . . 7. estreat
not . . 5. false 10. figurative
poetic . . 4. leal
skin . . 4. derm (suff) 5. derma
to fact . . 7. literal
to life . . 8. lifelike 11. descriptive

truffle ... 5. fungi, tuber 8. earthnut
10. ascus fruit

truism ... 5. axiom, truth 9. platitude
11. commonplace

trull ... 4. girl, lass 5. demon, fiend,
giant, wench 7. trollop 8. strumpet

truly ... 3. yea 4. amen 5. sooth
6. indeed, justly, verily 7. exactly, rightly
8. properly, certainly 10. accurately,
positively, truthfully

trump ... 3. pam 4. card, ruff (cards),
suit 7. surpass 10. good fellow
12. masterstroke

trumpery ... 5. fraud, trash 6. deceit
7. rubbish 8. nonsense

trumpet ... 4. horn 5. blare 6. summon
7. clarion 8. proclaim 9. organ stop
12. elephant's cry 14. wind instrument

trumpet (pert to) ...
blare . . 7. fanfare, tantara
call (stage) . . 6. sennet
creeper . . 6. tacoma
fish . . 7. bellows 10. flutemouth
lily . . 5. calla 7. Bermuda

trumpeter ... 4. bird, fish, swan 5. agami,
perch 6. pigeon 7. whiting 8. musician
9. messenger

truncheon ... 4. club 5. baton, staff
6. cudgel 8. splinter

trunk ... 3. box, log 4. body, bole, pool,
soma, tank 5. chest, stalk, torso 6. coffer
7. railway 8. main stem 9. proboscis
10. lobster pot

trunkfish ... 4. toro 7. cowfish

truss ... 3. tie 4. bind, gird, pack 6. bundle,
fasten 7. support 10. strengthen

trust ... 4. hope, rely, task 5. faith 6. belief,
commit, credit, dartle, depend, estate
7. believe, confide, consign, custody,
entrust, loyalty 8. credence, reliance,
security 9. assurance, syndicate
10. confidence, dependence, give credit,
investment 12. organization

trustee ... 6. bailee 7. sindico 9. fiduciary,
treasurer 10. depository
13. administrator

trustful ... 5. liege 7. reliant 8. trusting
9. confiding, credulous
13. unquestioning

trustworthiness . . . 9. axiopisty
12. trustability 13. dependability
trustworthy . . . 4. safe 5. solid 6. honest
7. certain 8. reliable 9. authentic
10. dependable
trusty . . . 7. convict 8. faithful, prisoner
10. dependable 11. trustworthy
truth . . . 3. tao 4. fact, real 5. sooth (anc)
6. verity 7. honesty, reality 8. fidelity,
veracity 9. constancy, exactness,
orthodoxy, sincerity 11. correctness
14. verisimilitude
truth (pert to) . . .
ancient term . . 5. sooth 6. certes
Chinese Philos . . 3. tao
goddess . . 4. Maat
personified . . 3. Una 4. Maat
ref to . . 6. verily 11. verisimilar
14. verisimilitude
self-evident . . 5. axiom 6. truism
truthful . . . 6. honest 7. veridic
9. veracious, veridical
truthfulness . . . 5. truth 7. honesty
8. accuracy, veracity 13. veraciousness
try . . . 3. do 4. eke 5. annoy,
assay, ettle, prove, taste, trial 6. purify,
refine, render, sample, strive 7. attempt,
contest, torment 8. audition, endeavor,
irritate 9. prosecute, undertake
10. experiment 11. demonstrate,
investigate
trying . . . 7. irksome, painful, tasting
8. annoying, sampling 10. attempting
12. exasperating 13. experimenting
tryst . . . 6. invite, market 7. beguile,
meeting 9. agreement, betrothal
10. engagement, rendezvous
11. appointment 12. meeting place
tsamba . . . 5. flour 6. barley
tsar . . . 4. czar, tzar 6. despot 8. autocrat
tsetse, tsetse fly . . . 4. kivu 8. Glossina,
parasite
tsetse fly disease . . . 6. nagana
16. sleeping sickness
T-shaped . . . 3. tau
tsine . . . 6. wild ox 7. banteng
tsunami . . . 5. wave (tidal)
tuatara, tuatera . . . 7. reptile (iguanalike)
tub . . . 3. hod, keg, kid, soe, tun, vat
4. cask, ship, wash 5. barge, bathe,
bowie, keeve 6. barrel, firkin, piggin,
vessel 7. bathtub, cistern, washtub
9. container, fat person
tuba . . . 6. liquor (palm) 7. helicon,
trumpet (anc) 9. bombardon
10. contrabass 11. bass saxhorn
12. mythical tree
Tubal-cain's father . . . 6. Lamech
Tubal's father . . . 7. Japheth
tube . . . 3. cop 4. bulb, duct, hose, pipe
5. auget, chute, diode 6. siphon, tunnel
7. burette, cannula, conduit, fistula,
matrass, railway, salpinx 8. cylinder,
electron, stenosis 9. spaghetti,
telescope
tuber . . . 3. oca, yam 4. beet, bulb, eddo,
root, taro 5. jalap, salep 6. potato
12. protuberance
tubular . . . 4. pipy 5. round 6. tubate
8. cannular, fistular, tubiform
11. cylindrical

tuck . . . 3. eat, nip 4. cram, fold, poke
5. feast, pinch, pleat, press 7. shorten,
tighten 9. appendage
tucker . . . 3. bib 4. food, meal 5. board
6. ration
Tuesday (pert to) . . .
French . . 5. Mardi
Norse god . . 3. Tyr (Tiu)
Shrove . . 9. Mardi gras
Teutonic . . 10. Martis dies
tufa . . . 4. rock, toph, tuff 5. trass
tuft . . . 4. coma, doss, hair 5. beard,
bunch, clump, crest 6. button, goatee,
pompon, tassel 7. cluster, fetlock
8. aigrette, feathers
tug . . . 3. tow 4. drag, draw, haul, pull,
toil 5. labor 6. drudge, effort, strain,
tussle 7. contend, contest, wrestle
8. struggle
tulip (pert to) . . .
center (World) . . 7. Holland
color . . 6. auburn 9. tulipwood
genus . . 6. Tulipa
Mexican . . 6. orchid
military slang . . 9. explosive
tree . . 6. timber 7. majagua, waratah
type . . 6. Darwin, parrot 7. breeder,
cottage
tumble . . . 4. fall, flop, trip, veer 5. pitch,
spill 6. jumble, rumple, topple, tousle,
wallow 7. stumble 8. collapse, disorder,
flounder, roll over 9. break down,
confusing 10. handspring, somersault
11. precipitate
tumbler . . . 3. dog 4. cart, drum 5. glass
6. Dunker, pigeon, vessel 7. acrobat,
gymnast, tippler, tumbrel 8. lock part
13. contortionist
tumbleweed . . . 6. indigo 7. bugseed,
pigweed, thistle 10. amaranthus
tumbrel, tumbril . . . 4. cart 5. wagon
8. dumpcart 12. cucking stool (Hist)
tumescent, tumid . . . 6. turgid 7. bloated,
bulging, pompous 8. inflated
9. bombastic, disturbed, plethoric
11. protuberant
tumor . . . 4. wen 5. cyst, wart 6. cancer,
goiter, growth, lipoma, struma
7. adenoma, sarcoma 8. ganglion,
swelling 11. excrescence
12. protuberance
tumor, eyelid . . . 9. pladaroma
tumult . . . 3. din, mob 4. fray, riot 5. Babel,
brawl, noise 6. affray, babble, bustle,
émeute, hubbub, uproar 7. bluster,
ferment, turmoil 8. disorder, outbreak,
uprising 9. agitation, commotion,
confusion 10. excitement, turbulence
11. disturbance
tumultuous . . . 4. wild 5. noisy, rough
7. lawless, riotous, violent 8. agitated,
confused 9. disturbed, turbulent
10. boisterous, disorderly, hurly-burly
tumulus . . . 5. mound, stump 6. barrow
7. hillock
tun . . . 3. cup (anc), jar, tub, vat 4. cask,
year (Mayan, 360-day) 5. drink 6. guzzle,
vessel 7. measure
tuna . . . 5. tunny 8. albacore
tune . . . 3. air, key 4. aria, lilt, port, song
5. pitch 6. adjust, melody 7. chorale,

harmony, sonance 9. harmonize
10. adjustment, intonation
tune (pert to) . . .
  correctly . . 3. key
  down . . 6. reduce, soften 8. moderate
  musical instrument . . 6. string
  out of . . 9. dissonant 11. inaccordant
    12. unconforming
tungsten . . . 7. wolfram
Tunisia . . .
  cape . . 3. Bon
  capital . . 5. Tunis
  famed ruins . . 8. Carthage
  gulf . . 5. Gabes
  oasis . . 5. Gafsa
  people . . 5. Arabs 7. Berbers
  resort island . . 6. Djerba
  river . . 8. Medjerda
  ruler . . 3. dey 5. pasha
  seaport . . 4. Sfax 7. Bizorte
tunnel . . . 4. adit, bore, cave, tube 5. drift
  6. burrow, dig out, funnel, subway
  10. excavation, smokestack
tunny . . 4. tuna 8. albacore
tup . . 3. ram 4. beat, butt 5. sheep
  6. mallet 7. cuckold
turban . . . 4. entrée, fillet, Moslem,
  mundil, squash 8. bandanna, seerband
  9. headdress
turbid . . . 4. dark, dull 5. dense, muddy,
  roily 6. cloudy, impure, opaque
  7. clouded, muddled 8. confused,
  feculent, polluted
turbot . . 5. brill 8. flatfish
turbulence . . . 4. fury 6. tumult, uproar
  7. bluster, rioting, turmoil 9. agitation,
  commotion 10. excitement, unruliness
  11. disturbance, impetuosity
  14. tumultuousness
turbulent . . . 4. loud, wild 5. noisy, rough
  6. stormy 7. excited, furious 8. virulent
  10. tumultuous
turf . . . 3. sod 4. peat, slab 5. divot, glebe,
  grass, sward, track 10. race course
turgid . . . 5. tumid 7. bloated, pompous,
  swollen 8. inflated 9. bombastic,
  distended, grandiose, redundant
  12. magniloquent, ostentatious
  13. grandiloquent
Turk . . . 5. Tatar 6. Tartar 7. Osmanli,
  Ottoman 9. Kizilbash
Turkestan people . . . 5. Uzbek (Uzbeg)
turkey . . . 4. fowl 5. poult 7. bustard,
  gobbler, vulture
Turkey . . . see also *Turkish*
  capital . . 6. Angora (anc), Ankara
  city . . 5. Adana, Izmir (Smyrna) 6. Edessa,
    Samsun 7. Scutari 8. Istanbul
    (Constantinople) 10. Adrianople
  founder . . 6. Othman
  mountain . . 6. Ararat
  peninsula . . 9. Anatolian
  river . . 5. Mesta 6. Seyhan
Turkish (pert to) . . .
  army corps . . 4. ordu 8. seraglio
  commander, ruler . . 3. aga (agha), bey
    4. wali 5. pasha 6. atabeg (atabek)
  court (Ottoman) . . 5. Porte 12. Sublime
    Porte
  dignitary . . 5. pasha
  dish (food) . . 5. cabob 6. pilaff (pilau)

  drink . . 4. boza (bozah), raki 5. airan
    6. mastic 9. lion's milk
  dynasty . . 6. seljuk
  emblem . . 8. crescent
  Empire . . 7. Ottoman
  flag . . 4. alem, toug (former)
  harem girl . . 6. kadein (kadine)
  hat, cap . . 3. fez 6. calpac (calpack)
  hospice, inn . . 6. imaret
  infidel . . 6. giaour
  javelin . . 6. jereed (jerid)
  judge . . 4. cadi (kadi)
  minister of state . . 6. vizier
  money of account . . 5. asper
  mosque . . 4. jami
  music . . 8. janizary
  native . . 6. Edesan (anc)
  palace . . 5. serai
  pavilion . . 5. kiosk
  people . . 5. Ersar, Tatar 7. Bashkir,
    Viddhal
  pipe (long-stemmed) . . 7. chibouk
    (chibouque)
  regiment . . 4. alai
  religious war . . 5. jihad (jehad)
  robe . . 6. dolman
  rug . . 5. Melas, Tekke, Yomud, Yuruk
    6. Afghan 8. Turkoman 9. Kurdistan
  ruler . . 3. bey, dey 4. khan 6. sultan
    7. chambul
  sailing vessel . . 4. saic 6. mahone
  sailor . . 9. galiongee (galionji)
  soldier . . 5. nizan, redif 6. Arnaut
    (Arnaout) 8. Janizary 11. bashi-bazouk
  statute . . 8. Tanzimat (1839)
  sultan . . 5. Ahmed, Selim 7. Ilderim,
    Saladin
  sultan's title . . 6. caliph (calif)
  sword . . 8. yataghan (yatagan)
  tambourine . . 5. daira
  tax (from Christians) . . 6. avania
  title . . 3. aga (agha), ali 4. amir (ameer)
  tobacco . . 7. chibouk (chibouque), Latakia
  Turkoman . . 11. tribal group
  veil (double) . . 7. yashmak (yashmac)
  vest . . 6. jelick
  whip, lash . . 7. kurbash
turmeric . . . 3. rea 4. ango, herb 5. olena
  8. curcumin
turmoil . . . 3. ado, din 5. upset, worry
  6. tumult, unrest 7. ferment, tempest,
  trouble 8. disquiet 9. agitation,
  commotion, confusion 10. excitement,
  turbulence 12. perturbation
turn . . . 3. bow, lap 4. bend, deed,
  gyre, roll, slew, slue, spin, tour, veer,
  vert 5. curve, lathe, pivot, quirk,
  round, shift, spell, wheel, whirl, whorl
  6. abvert, change, crisis, gyrate, rotate,
  swivel, zigzag 7. deflect, deviate,
  reverse, revolve 8. aptitude, circuity,
  maneuver, persuade, rotation, tendency
  9. deviation, pirouette, reversion
  11. convolution 12. metamorphose
turn (pert to) . . .
  about . . 9. alternate
  aside, away . . 4. slew, slue 5. avert,
    deter, repel, shunt 6. divert, swerve
    7. deflect, deviate, digress, diverge
  back . . 5. repel 6. coward, revert
    7. evolute, head off, reflect

coat .. 7. traitor 8. apostate, deserter,
renegade
comb form .. 5. tropo
down .. 4. veto 6. refuse, reject 7. decline
gate .. 5. stile 9. turnstile
inside out .. 5. evert 6. invert 7. ransack
inward .. 8. introrse 9. introvert
left .. 3. haw 4. port
of duty .. 5. spell, trick
off .. 5. shunt 7. dismiss, execute
10. extinguish
on axis .. 6. obvert, rotate
one's back upon .. 4. flee, snub 5. avoid
6. ignore, oppose, refuse, reject
on pivot .. 6. swivel
out .. fare, oust 5. array, evert, expel,
track 6. detour, output, siding 7. dismiss
8. assemble, clearing 9. eventuate,
gathering 10. accomplish, extinguish
outward .. 5. evert, splay 8. extrorse
9. extrovert
over .. 3. pie 4. keel, tart 5. sales,
shift, spill 6. assign, pastry 7. capsize
8. hand over, overturn
over a new leaf .. 6. change, reform
over pages .. 4. leaf 5. thumb
over to others .. 4. farm 7. farm out
to left .. 3. haw 4. port
to right .. 3. gee 9. starboard
up .. 4. find, keel 5. occur 6. appear,
arrive 7. be found
upside down .. 4. roll 6. invert, whelve
7. ransack 8. overturn
turned up (nose) .. 9. retroussé
turning .. 6. rotary 7. bending, crooked,
winding 8. rotation, twisting, whirling
9. deviating, deviation 10. circuitous,
revolution 11. convolution, sinistrorse
turning (pert to) ..
left to right .. 9. dextrorse
machine .. 5. lathe
point .. 6. crisis 8. decision, landmark
11. climacteric 13. crucial period
right to left .. 11. sinistrorse
turnip .. 4. neep, rape, root 8. rutabaga
turnip (pert to) ..
large .. 7. Russian, Swedish 8. rutabaga
shaped .. 8. napiform
wild .. 5. navew
Turnix .. 4. bird (3-toed) 5. quail
10. Hemipodius
Turpentine State .. 13. North Carolina
turpentine tree .. 4. pine 6. tarata
9. terebinth
turpid .. 3. low 4. base, vile 8. cowardly
turpitude .. 6. fedity 8. baseness,
vileness 9. decadence, depravity
10. corruption
turquoise .. 3. gem 4. blue 7. mineral,
Turkish
turret .. 4. loom, soar 5. tower
6. cupola (revolving), height 9. structure
10. stronghold, watchtower
turtle (pert to) ..
edible .. 8. terrapin
freshwater .. 4. emyd 8. tortoise
genus .. 8. Emys
hawklike .. 5. carat 9. hawk's-bill
large .. 5. arrau 6. jurara, mamata
largest .. 11. leatherback
ref to .. 9. chelonian

sea .. 10. thalassian
shell .. 8. carapace
snapping .. 6. cooter 8. shagtail
Tuscany ...
birthplace of .. 7. Galileo (Astronomer)
capital .. 8. Florence
city .. 7. Pisa 9. Leghorn
color .. 9. colcothar
famed tower .. 4. Pisa (1174)
island .. 4. Elba (1st exile, Napoleon)
native .. 6. Tuscan
marble .. 7. Carrara
province .. 4. Pisa
river .. 4. Arno 6. Cecina 7. Ombrone
wine .. 7. chianti
tusk .. 4. fang 5. ivory, tooth 6. canine
7. incisor 8. scrivello (elephant's)
Tussaud, Madame's London district ...
8. Waxworks (Museum) 10. Marylebone
tussis ... 5. cough
tussle ... 7. contend, contest, scuffle,
wrestle 8. struggle
tutelage ... 7. nurture 8. teaching,
tutorage 9. oversight, tutorship
11. instruction 12. guardianship
tutelary gods (Rom) ... 5. lares 7. penates
tutor ... 5. coach, teach 6. docent, ground,
mentor, school 7. teacher 8. instruct
9. pedagogue (pedagog), preceptor
twaddle ... 3. rot 6. drivel, gabble
7. chatter, fustian, prattle 8. claptrap,
nonsense 9. absurdity, silly talk
10. flapdoodle 16. trash and nonsense
twang ... 4. tang 5. strum 6. accent
7. dialect 8. pungency
tweak ... 4. jerk, pain 5. pinch 6. snatch,
twitch
tweeg ... 10. hellbender, salamander
tweezers ... 7. pincers 10. instrument
twelfth ... 5. twait, uncia 8. duodenal
9. duodenary
Twelfth Night character ... 5. Viola
6. Olivia, Orsino 7. Sir Toby 8. Malvolio
12. Sir Toby Belch
Twelfthtide ... 8. Epiphany 10. Twelfth-
day
twelve (pert to) ...
amount .. 5. dozen
angles .. 9. dodecagon
prefix .. 5. dodec 6. dodeca
rule of .. 9. dodecarch
series .. 8. dodecade
Twelve, The ... 8. Apostles
twenty (pert to) ...
Anglo-Ind .. 5. carge, score
comb form .. 4. icos 5. icosa, icosi
faces .. 11. icosahedron
pert to .. 7. icosian 8. vicenary
quires .. 4. ream
symbol .. 2. XX
years .. 9. vicennial
twenty-fourth part (gold alloy) ...
5. carat (karat)
twibil (twibill) ... 2. ax (axe) 6. pickax
(pickaxe) 7. mattock 8. battle-ax
(battle-axe)
twice ... 2. bi, di 6. doubly 7. twofold
8. two times
twig ... 4. reis 5. besom, birch, bough
6. branch, sallow, switch, twitch, wattle
twigs, bundle of ... 5. fagot 6. barsom

(sacred)

twilight . . . 3. dim 4. blue, dusk 6. shaded 7. obscure 8. foredawn, gloaming 9. cocklight 10. crepuscule

Twilight of the Gods . . . 8. Ragnarok

twill . . . 3. rib 5. flute, weave 6. fabric 9. tricotine

twilled . . . 3. rep 5. reedy, ridgy, sedgy, serge 6. corded, fluted

twin . . . 3. two 4. dual, mate, pair 5. gemel, macle 6. couple, double 7. didymus, Siamese 8. didymous, matching 9. duplicate, identical 11. counterpart 12. accompanying

Twin Cities (Minn) . . . 6. St Paul 11. Minneapolis

twine . . . 4. bend, coil, turn, wind, wrap 5. braid, snarl, twist, weave 6. enfold, enlace, tangle 7. embrace, enclasp, entwine, wreathe 8. convolve, encircle 9. interlace 10. intertwine, interweave 11. intermingle

twine (pert to) . . .
  color . . 4. dune 7. anamite
  hank of . . 3. ran
  left to right . . 9. dextrorse
  right to left . . 11. sinistrorse
  Scot . . 4. part

twinge . . 4. ache, pain, pang 5. pinch, qualm 6. twitch

twin stars . . . 6. Castor, Pollux

twin stock . . . 4. bees 7. beehive (two colonies)

twirl . . 4. coil, eddy, gyre, spin 5. pitch, querl, twist, whirl 6. gyrate, writhe 7. revolve 8. flourish, rotation 11. convolution

twist . . . 3. cue, ply 4. coil, curl, slew, slub, slue, spin, turn, warp, wind 5. braid, quirk, tweak, wrest 7. contort, deflect, distort, falsify, meander, pervert, wreathe, wriggle 8. convolve 9. insinuate, interlace, prejudice 10. distortion 12. eccentricity, misrepresent

twisted . . . 3. wry 4. awry, cued 5. askew, kinky, torse, wrung 6. warped 7. complex, torqued, tortile, wrested, writhed

twisted cord . . . 7. torsade

twister . . . 3. lie 7. cruller, tornado 8. doughnut 9. dust whirl 10. sand column, somersault, waterspout

twit . . . 4. gibe, josh 5. blame, taunt, tease, tweet 6. banter 7. upbraid 8. reproach, ridicule

twitch . . . 3. nip, tic, tug 4. hurt, jerk, yank 5. pluck, shake, tweak, snatch 9. be excited, quick pull, vellicate 11. contraction

twitter . . . 5. chirp 6. giggle, titter 7. chatter, tremble 9. agitation

two (pert to) . . .
  chambered . . 9. bicameral
  colored . . 9. dichromic
  edged . . 9. ancipital
  faced . . 5. false 6. double 9. deceitful 11. treacherous 12. falsehearted
  fisted . . 6. virile
  fold . . 4. dual, twin 6. binary, double, duplex 8. didymous

  forked . . 6. bident 9. bifurcate 11. dichotomous
  handed . . 7. bimanal 8. bimanous 10. secondhand 12. ambidextrous
  headed . . 9. ancipital 11. dicephalous
  masted ship . . 4. yawl, zulu
  parts . . 3. duo 4. duad, dyad 7. duality
  poetic . . 5. twain
  prefix . . 2. bi, di
  Scot . . 3. twa
  Spanish . . 3. dos
  spot . . 5. deuce
  time . . 7. deceive
  wheeled carriage, chariot . . 3. gig 6. esseda 10. jinrikisha (jinriksha)

Tyche . . . 7. Fortuna 16. goddess of Fortune

tycoon . . . 6. shogun 7. magnate 9. financier 13. industrialist

tyloped . . . 5. camel

tympanum . . . 7. eardrum 9. middle ear 10. water wheel

tympany . . . 6. tympan 7. bombast 9. inflation 10. distention

typal . . . 7. typical 8. symbolic

type . . 2. pi 4. font, form, kind, norm, sign, sort 5. genre, genus, model, print, Roman, token 6. emblem, italic, minion, symbol 7. measure, pattern, species 8. boldface, classify, standard 9. archetype, character 10. transcribe 11. Baskerville 14. characteristic, representative

type (pert to) . . .
  assortment . . 4. font, kern
  block of . . 4. quad 7. quadrat
  bold style . . 4. text
  bridge . . 7. bascule
  classic . . 5. Roman 6. italic 11. black letter (Gothic)
  line . . 4. slug
  measure . . 2. em, en
  mixed . . 2. pi
  mold . . 6. matrix
  perfection . . 7. paragon
  set . . 7. compose
  setter . . 8. linotype, monotype 10. compositor
  size . . 4. norm, pica, ruby 5. agate, canon, pearl 6. minion 7. diamond
  stroke . . 5. serif
  tray . . 6. galley

typewriter (pert to) . . .
  bar . . 6. spacer
  cylinder . . 6. platen, spacer
  type . . 4. pica 5. elite
  type of . . 6. ticker 8. teletype 9. stenotype

typhoon . . . 4. wind 5. storm 7. cyclone

typhus fever . . . 10. tabardillo

typical . . . 4. norm 5. typal 6. normal 7. regular 10. conforming, emblematic, figurative 11. precedental 14. characteristic, representative

typify . . . 6. embody 9. prefigure, represent, symbolize

Tyr (Norse) . . . 3. Tiu 6. sky-god, war-god

tyrannical . . . 5. cruel 6. lordly 8. despotic 9. imperious 10. oppressive 11. domineering

tyrannize . . . 7. oppress 8. domineer

tyranny ... 8. severity 9. despotism
tyrant ... 4. czar, Ivan, Nero, tsar, tzar
6. despot 7. monarch
Tyre ... see also *Tyrian*
capital of .. 9. Phoenicia (anc)
famed for .. 9. purple dye
seaport of .. 7. Lebanon
site .. 9. peninsula 13. Mediterranean
Tyrian (pert to) ...
alphabet .. 7. Moabite
Cynosure .. 9. Ursa Minor
god (Teut) .. 2. Er
king .. 5. Hiram
princess .. 4. Dido (Elissa)

tyro, tiro ... 5. pupil 6. novice 7. amateur
8. beginner, neophyte 9. commencer,
fledgling, greenhorn 10. apprentice
11. abecedarian
Tyrol ...
capital .. 9. Innsbruck
dialect .. 5. Ladin
district .. 8. Trentino
mountain .. 4. Alps 9. Dolomites
province of .. 7. Austria
river .. 4. Isar
tzar, tsar, czar ... 4. king 5. ruler
6. tyrant
tzigane ... 5. gypsy

U

U ... 6. letter (21st)
uang ... 8. beetle
uberous ... 7. copious 8. abundant,
fruitful 9. plentiful
uberty ... 8. plenty 12. fruitfulness
ubiety ... 8. location, position, relation
9. whereness
ubiquity ... 8. doctrine (Luther)
10. everywhere 12. omnipresence
U-boat ... 3. sub 9. submarine
base .. 4. Kiel
Uca ... 11. fiddler crab
Uchean Indian ... 5. Yuchi (Uchee)
udometer ... 9. rain gauge
Uffizi Gallery ... 8. Florence
Uganda (pert to) ...
capital .. 7. Kampala
Falls .. 4. Owen 9. Murchison
lake .. 8. Victoria
lake explorer .. 7. Stanley
mountain .. 9. Ruwenzori 18. Mountains
of the Moon
people .. 5. pygmy
ugly ... 5. cross, surly 6. cranky,
homely 7. crabbed, hideous, vicious
8. gruesome, uncomely, unlovely
9. frightful, loathsome, offensive,
repulsive, unsightly 10. ill-favored, ill-
natured, unpleasant 11. ill-tempered,
quarrelsome 12. disagreeable
uhlan ... 6. lancer 7. militia, soldier
10. cavalryman
uhllo ... 6. wampum 8. currency (shell)
uitlander ... 9. foreigner, outlander
ukase ... 5. edict, order 12. proclamation
Ukraine (pert to) ...
capital .. 4. Kiev 7. Kharkov
legislature .. 4. rada
official name .. 12. Ukrainian SSR
Relig .. 9. Ruthenian 13. Little Russian
scientist .. 10. Bogomolets
sea .. 5. Black
seaport .. 6. Odessa
statesman .. 7. Mazeppa
writer .. 6. Franko
ullage ... 5. dregs 7. deficit, wantage
8. shortage 9. shrinkage 10. deficiency
Ulmas ... 3. elm
ulna ... 4. bone 5. elbow 7. cubitus

ulster ... 8. overcoat
Ulster, to some ... 15. Northern Ireland
ulterior ... 6. future 7. further, remoter,
thither 10. additional, extraneous,
subsequent, succeeding 11. undisclosed
ultima ... 4. last 5. final 8. farthest
10. most remote 12. last syllable
ultimate ... 3. end 4. dire, last 5. final,
telus 6. future, latest, result 7. extreme,
maximum 8. eventful, eventual,
farthest, terminal 9. elemental
10. conclusive, end product
ultimatum ... 5. offer 6. demand
13. ultimate point 14. final objective
ultimo ... 3. ult 9. past month (opp of
proximo)
ultra ... 6. beyond 7. extreme, radical
9. excessive, extremist, fanatical
11. extravagant 14. uncompromising
ultramarine ... 11. blue pigment, lapis
lazuli 12. beyond the sea
ultramontane ... 5. alien 6. beyond
9. foreigner 10. tramontane 13. beyond
the Alps, Roman Catholic
ulu (Esk) ... 5. knife
ululate ... 4. hoot, howl, wail, yelp
6. bellow, lament
Ulysses (pert to) ...
antagonist .. 4. Irus
dog .. 5. Argos
enchantress .. 5. Circe
father .. 7. Laertes
Greek name .. 8. Odysseus
hero .. 7. Odyssey (Homer's)
literally .. 5. hater
son .. 9. Telegonus
wife .. 8. Penelope
umber ... 3. raw 5. brown, burnt
6. shadow, Turkey 8. grayling, umbrette
10. brown earth
umbilicus (pert to) ...
anatomy .. 5. navel
botany .. 5. hilum
geometry .. 5. focus
paleology .. 5. stick (papyrus)
zoology .. 3. pit 10. depression
umbra ... 4. fish 5. ghost, shade
6. shadow 7. phantom, vestige
umbrage ... 5. doubt, pique, shade, trace

6. offend, resent 7. foliage, offense, shelter 8. disfavor 9. semblance, suspicion 10. overshadow, resentment 11. displeasure

umbrella . . . 4. gamp 5. cover, guard, shade 6. chatta, payong, pileus (of a jellyfish) 7. parasol, shelter 9. parachute, sea anchor 11. bumbershoot

umbrella tree . . . 5. bendy 7. dogwood, ginseng 8. magnolia

umbrette . . . 5. bird, fish 5. omber (ombre) 9. hammerkop

umpire . . . 5. judge 7. arbiter, referee 8. mediator 9. moderator 10. arbitrator, negotiator

Umpqua . . . 6. Indian 10. Athapascan

unable . . . 6. cannot 8. helpless, impotent 9. incapable 11. incompetent, inefficient, unqualified 13. incapacitated

Una boat . . . 7. catboat

unabridged . . . 8. complete 11. uncondensed

unaccented . . . 4. lene 6. atonic

unaccountable . . . 7. lawless, strange 9. fantastic 10. mysterious 12. inexplicable, unfathomable 13. irresponsible, unpredictable

unacknowledged . . . 9. anonymous, forgotten, unthanked 10. unrewarded

unadorned . . . 4. bald, bare, form 5. grace, naked, stark 7. austere 13. plain-speaking

unadulterated . . . 4. pure 5. naked 6. honest 7. unmixed 9. unalloyed, undiluted 11. uncorrupted

unaffected . . . 4. naif, real 5. naive, plain 6. simple 7. artless, genuine, natural, sincere 8. informal 9. unaltered, untouched 12. uninfluenced 13. plain-speaking

Unalaska . . . 5. Aleut 9. Eskimauan

unanimous . . . 5. solid 6. agreed, mutual, united 8. agreeing 9. of one mind 10. concordant 11. consentient 12. with one voice

unanimously . . . 7. una voce 12. with one voice

unapproachable . . . 8. reserved 10. unsociable 12. inaccessible

unapt . . . 4. dull, slow 5. inapt 8. backward 10. unskillful, unsuitable 13. inappropriate

unaroused . . . 6. latent 7. dormant 8. inactive 9. unstirred

unaspirated . . . 4. lene 6. smooth

unassuming . . . 3. shy 6. modest 7. genuine, natural 8. informal, retiring 9. diffident 11. undeceptive 14. unostentatious

unau . . . 5. sloth (2-toed)

unavailing . . . 6. futile 8. gainless

unbalanced . . . 6. insane, uneven, unjust 7. unequal 8. deranged, lopsided, one-sided 9. off center 10. disordered

unbecoming . . . 4. rude 5. inept 8. unseemly 10. indecorous, unsuitable 12. unattractive

unbelievable . . . 9. fantastic, untenable 10. incredible, unreliable 11. implausible, unthinkable

13. inconceivable

unbeliever . . . 5. pagan 7. atheist, doubter, heretic, infidel, skeptic 8. agnostic

unbend . . . 4. rest, thaw 5. frese, relax, yield 6. loosen 7. slacken 8. be pliant, unfasten 10. condescend, straighten

unbending . . . 5. rigid, stern, stiff 8. resolute 10. inexorable, inflexible, unyielding

unbiased . . . 4. fair, just 9. impartial 12. free from bias, unprejudiced

unbind . . . 4. free, undo 5. loose, untie 6. loosen 7. absolve, deliver, release 8. dissolve, unfasten

unbound . . . 4. free 5. loose 10. unconfined

unbounded . . . 8. infinite 9. limitless, unchecked, unlimited 10. unconfined 11. measureless 12. uncontrolled, unrestrained

unbridled . . . 4. free 5. loose 7. lawless, violent 10. licentious 12. uncontrolled, unrestrained

unbroken . . . 4. even 5. undug, whole 6. direct, entire, intact, smooth 7. untamed 8. constant, straight, unplowed 10. continuous 13. uninterrupted

uncanny . . . 5. eerie (eery), weird 6. spooky 7. ghostly, strange 8. careless 9. unnatural 10. mysterious

unceasing . . . 6. eterne 7. endless, eternal 9. continual, incessant 11. everlasting

unceremonious . . . 4. curt 5. blunt 6. abrupt, casual 7. offhand 8. informal 14. unconventional

uncertain . . . 4. hazy 5. vague 6. chancy, fickle, fitful, shifty, unsure 7. dubious 8. doubtful, unsteady, variable 9. ambiguous, irregular, undecided 10. changeable, indefinite, irresolute, precarious 11. unequivocal 12. questionable 13. indeterminate, problematical, untrustworthy

uncertainty . . . 5. doubt 6. wonder 7. dubiety 8. suspense 9. dubiosity 10. fickleness, skepticism 12. irresolution 14. precariousness

unchanging . . . 7. eternal, settled, uniform 9. immutable, unvarying 10. invariable, stationary

unchaste . . . 4. lewd 5. bawdy 6. impure 7. obscene 8. immodest

unchecked . . . 4. free 5. loose 7. rampant 9. permanent, unbridled

unchristian . . . 5. pagan 7. heathen, infidel, ungodly 8. barbarous, excessive 11. irreligious, uncivilized

uncivil . . . 4. rude 5. savage 7. ill-bred 8. impolite 9. barbarous 10. indecorous, ungracious 11. ill-mannered, uncivilized 12. discourteous 13. disrespectful

uncivilized . . . 4. rude, wild 5. feral 6. brutal, ferine, savage 8. barbaric 9. primitive, unrefined

uncle . . . 3. eme (yeme), oom

unclean . . . 4. foul, tref, vile 5. dirty 6. filthy, immund, impure 8. polluted, unchaste 11. unwholesome

Uncle Tom's Cabin (pert to) . . .

author.. 5. Stowe (Harriet Beecher)
character.. 5. Topsy 6. Legree 8. Uncle
Tom 9. Little Eva
subject.. 7. slavery

unclose ... 3. ope 4. open 6. reveal
7. expound 8. disclose

uncolored ... 7. genuine 9. colorless
10. achromatic

uncommon ... 3. odd 4. nice, rare
5. novel 6. scarce, unique 7. special,
strange, unusual 8. unwonted
10. infrequent, remarkable
11. exceptional 12. unaccustomed
13. extraordinary

uncommunicative ... 6. silent
8. reserved, reticent 9. secretive
10. unsociable

uncomplaining ... 5. stoic 7. stoical

uncompromising ... 4. firm 5. rigid
6. strict 8. obstinate, unbending
10. inflexible, unyielding
12. conservative, intransigent

unconcerned ... 4. cool, free 8. careless
9. apathetic 10. insouciant
11. indifferent, not involved
13. disinterested

unconditional ... 4. free 8. absolute,
explicit 10. unreserved

unconfined ... 5. loose 9. boundless,
limitless, unlimited 12. unrestrained

unconscious ... 3. out 6. asleep
7. unaware 8. heedless, ignorant,
mindless 9. inanimate, senseless,
unfeeling 10. abstracted, insensible
11. involuntary 12. subconscious

unconstrained ... 4. easy, free 6. candid
7. natural 8. informal 11. spontaneous
12. unrestrained

uncontrolled ... 4. free, wild 5. loose
7. lawless 9. impulsive, irregular,
unmanaged 10. capricious, changeable,
licentious, ungoverned 11. not
governed, unregulated 12. unrestrained

unconventional ... 4. easy 5. outré
6. casual 7. devious, offbeat
8. Bohemian, informal 10. unorthodox
13. unceremonious

uncorrupted ... 8. pristine

uncouth ... 3. odd 4. rude 5. crude
6. clumsy, rustic 7. awkward, boorish,
strange 9. inelegant, unrefined,
untrained 10. outlandish, uncultured,
unpolished

uncover ... 4. bare, open 6. detect,
divest, expose, remove, reveal, unveil
7. divulge, lay bare, take off, undrape
8. disclose, discover

uncovered ... 4. bald, bare, nude, open
7. exposed 8. divested, revealed,
stripped, unveiled 9. décolleté
10. bareheaded 11. unprotected

unction ... 4. balm, rite 6. fervor
7. lanolin, unguent 8. flattery, function
(divine), ointment 10. anointment

unctuous ... 4. oily, smug 5. bland,
fatty, salvy, suave 6. fervid, greasy
7. gushing, pinguid, plastic
10. flattering, oleaginous
12. hypocritical 13. sanctimonious

uncultured ... 7. artless, boorish, uncouth
8. Bohemian 9. unlearned, unrefined

10. Philistine 11. countrified,
undeveloped

undaunted ... 4. bold 5. brave 7. Spartan,
untamed 8. fearless, intrepid, unafraid
9. confident, dauntless 10. courageous,
undismayed 11. persevering,
unconquered

undecided ... 4. moot 7. pending
8. doubtful, wavering 9. uncertain,
unsettled 10. inconstant, irresolute,
unresolved 13. problematical

undependable ... 6. fickle 7. erratic
9. uncertain 13. irresponsible,
untrustworthy

under ... 3. sub 4. alow 5. below, least,
neath, sotto 6. nether 7. beneath
8. guidance 9. lower than 10. subjection,
underneath 11. subordinate

undercover ... 6. secret 7. furtive
11. clandestine, underground
13. surreptitious

underestimate ... 8. belittle, minimize
9. set too low, underrate 10. undervalue

underfong ... 6. entrap 7. ensnare,
receive, sustain 9. undertake
10. circumvent

undergo ... 4. bear, dree, pass 5. shirt
6. endure, suffer 7. sustain
9. undermine 10. experience

underhanded ... 3. sly 4. dern, mean
5. shady 6. covert, crafty, secret,
sneaky 8. sneaking, unfairly 9. deceitful,
dishonest 10. fraudulent 11. clandestine,
short-handed 13. unobtrusively
15. surreptitiously

underling ... 6. menial, minion 7. servant
8. inferior 11. subordinate

underlying ... 5. basic 8. cardinal
11. fundamental

undermine ... 3. sap 4. ruin 5. drain,
erode 6. weaken 7. subvert 8. enfeeble,
excavate

understand ... 3. ken, see 4. know
5. grasp, infer, savvy, sense 6. follow,
reason 7. discern, explain, realize,
signify 8. conceive, perceive
9. apprehend, interpret 10. comprehend

understandable ... 5. clear, lucid
12. intelligible

understanding ... 5. amity, sense
6. accord, reason, treaty 7. compact,
concept, entente, knowing 8. sympathy,
Verstand 9. agreement, intellect,
knowledge, tolerance, unanimity
10. acceptance, accordance, perception
11. discernment, penetration
12. intelligence 13. comprehension

understatement ... 7. litotes

understood ... 5. clear, known, lucid,
tacit 7. assumed, implied, settled
8. implicit 11. traditional

undertake ... 3. try 4. dare 6. accept,
assume, pledge 7. attempt, promise,
reprove 8. contract, covenant, endeavor,
engage in, set about 9. guarantee,
underfong

undertaker ... 5. cerer 6. surety
7. manager, rebuker, sponsor
8. embalmer 9. godfather, mortician
12. entrepreneur

undertaking ... 3. act 4. task 6. cautio

7. calling, project, promise, venture
8. business 9. adventure, guarantee
10. enterprise

undertone ... 4. tone (low) 5. aside
6. murmur 12. subdued color

undertow ... 7. riptide

underworld ... 3. Dis 4. hell 5. Hades,
limbo, Mafia, Orcus, Sheol 6. Erebus,
Tophet 7. Abaddon, Xlbalba 8. Dis
pater, gangland 9. Black Hand,
chthonian, perdition, purgatory

underwrite ... 6. assure, insure 7. finance,
sponsor 8. submit to

underwriter ... 7. insurer 8. endorser
9. financier 10. underclerk 13. Stock
Exchange 14. Lloyd's of London

undesirable condition ... 6. malady

undetermined ... 5. vague 7. dubious
8. not fixed, unproved 9. uncertain,
undecided 10. irresolute

undeveloped ... 5. crude 6. embryo,
latent 8. immature 10. unprepared
11. rudimentary

undignified ... 6. vulgar 8. informal,
infra dig, unworthy 9. inelegant

undine ... 3. nix 5. gnome, sylph 6. vessel
(glass) 9. planetoid 10. salamander

undivided ... 3. one 5. total, whole
6. entire, intact, joined 7. unitary
8. unbroken 9. not shared
10. continuous

undo ... 4. open 5. annul, loose
6. cancel, defeat, foredo, unlash,
unwrap 7. destroy, disjoin, nullify,
release, uncover, unravel 8. unfasten
10. disconnect, invalidate

undoing ... 4. ruin 6. defeat 8. downfall
9. annulment, overthrow
11. destruction, disassembly

undomesticated ... 4. wild 5. feral
6. ferine

undone ... 3. raw 9. neglected
10. defeasible

undue ... 5. wrong 6. unjust 7. extreme
8. improper, not owing 9. excessive
10. exorbitant, immoderate, inordinate,
undeserved, unsuitable 11. unwarranted
13. inappropriate

undulating ... 4. wavy 6. waving
7. aripple, rolling 8. rippling
11. fluctuating 16. rising and falling

undulation ... 4. beat, wave 5. heave,
surge, swell 6. motion, waving
7. tremolo, vibrato 8. waviness
9. pulsation 11. convolution

undying ... 6. eterne 7. ageless, endless,
eternal 8. immortal, unending
9. deathless 11. amaranthine
12. imperishable 14. indestructible

unearth ... 4. find 5. dig up 6. exhume,
expose 7. uncover 8. disclose, discover,
disinter 12. bring to light

unearthly ... 5. eerie (eery), godly, weird
7. awesome, ghostly, strange, uncanny
8. heavenly, terrific 9. appalling,
deathlike 10. mysterious, outlandish
12. preposterous, supernatural
13. preternatural

uneasiness ... 5. worry 6. unrest
7. anxiety, malaise 8. disquiet
10. impatience 11. displeasure,

disquietude, disturbance
12. apprehension

uneasy ... 5. stiff 7. anxious, awkward,
inquiet, restive, worried 8. agitated,
cramping, restless 9. difficult, impatient,
perturbed 10. disquieted, distressed
11. constrained, troublesome

unemotional ... 4. cold 5. stoic 7. stoical
10. phlegmatic

unemployed ... 4. idle, lazy 6. otiose,
unused 7. not used 8. inactive, leisured
11. not invested

unencumbered ... 4. free

unending ... 7. endless, eternal
8. termless, timeless 9. boundless,
perpetual 10. continuous
12. interminable

unequal ... 3. odd 4. odds 5. aniso
(comb form) 6. uneven, unfair, unjust
8. variable 9. disparate, irregular
11. fluctuating, not adequate
12. asymmetrical 16. disproportionate

unequaled ... 7. supreme 8. peerless
9. matchless, nonpareil, unmatched,
unrivaled 10. inimitable, surpassing,
unbeatable, unexcelled 12. unparalleled

unequivocal ... 5. clear, plain 6. candid
7. sincere 8. explicit 9. downright
11. categorical, indubitable

unerring ... 4. sure, true 5. exact 7. certain
8. accurate, virtuous 9. unfailing
10. infallible

unessential ... 8. needless 9. extrinsic
10. irrelevant 11. superfluous,
unimportant 13. insignificant, void of
essence

unethical ... 6. amoral

uneven ... 3. odd 5. erose, rough
6. rugged, unfair, unjust 7. erratic,
unequal, varying 8. not level 10. ill-
matched 11. fluctuating

unexamined ... 7. a priori

unexampled ... 8. peerless 10. unimitated
12. unparalleled 13. extraordinary,
unprecedented

unexpected ... 6. abrupt, sudden
7. unusual 9. inopinate 10. unforeseen
14. not anticipated

unfair ... 4. foul 5. wrong 6. biased,
uneven, unjust 8. unseemly
9. dishonest, unethical 10. not cricket,
unsporting 11. inequitable, unfavorable
12. disingenuous, not equitable

unfaithful ... 6. betray 7. infidel,
traitor 8. apostate, recreant, turncoat
9. faithless 10. inaccurate
12. nonobservant 13. untrustworthy

unfamiliar ... 3. new 7. strange, unknown
8. not known 12. unaccustomed,
unconversant

unfasten ... 4. free, open, undo 5. unbar,
unfix, unpin, untie 6. detach, loosen,
unhook, unlock 7. unloose 8. unbutton
9. disengage

unfavorable ... 3. bad, ill 6. averse
7. adverse, opposed 8. contrary,
untimely 9. repulsive 12. inauspicious

unfeeling ... 4. dull 5. cruel, stoic,
stony 6. brutal, steely, stolid, unkind
7. callous 8. numbness, obdurate
9. apathetic, bloodless, heartless,

inanimate, insensate 10. insensible
11. hardhearted 13. unsusceptible
16. unimpressionable

unfeigned . . . 4. real 7. genuine, natural, sincere 11. undeceptive 14. not counterfeit 15. not hypocritical

unfermented grape juice . . . 4. stum

unfertile . . . 4. arid 6. barren

unfettered . . . 4. free 7. broad 9. liberated, unchained 10. unshackled

unfinished . . . 5. crude, rough 7. sketchy 9. imperfect 10. incomplete 11. uncompleted

unfit . . . 5. inept 6. faulty, not fit, unable 8. disabled 9. untenable 11. handicapped, incompetent, unqualified 12. disqualified

unfledged . . . 4. eyas 5. green 6. callow 8. immature 11. undeveloped 12. not feathered

unflinching . . . 7. staunch 8. resolute, unafraid 9. steadfast 10. unwavering, unyielding 12. not shrinking

unfold . . . 3. ope 4. open 6. evolve, expand, flower, reveal, spread, unfurl 7. develop, display, divulge, evolute, explain, release 8. disclose

unfortunate . . . 3. ill 4. poor 6. wretch 7. hapless, unlucky 8. luckless, untimely 10. calamitous 12. inauspicious, unsuccessful

unfounded . . . 4. idle, vain 8. baseless 9. untenable 10. chimerical 11. unsupported, unwarranted

unfriendly . . . 3. icy 4. cool 7. asocial, hostile, not kind, opposed 8. inimical, unsocial 11. unsociable 12. inhospitable

unfruitful . . . 6. barren, wasted 7. sterile, useless 9. fruitless, infertile 12. unproductive, unprofitable 13. not productive

unfurl . . . 4. open 6. expand, spread, unfold, unroll

ungainly . . . 5. gawky, lanky 6. clumsy, gauche 7. awkward, uncouth 8. bungling 10. cumbersome, ungraceful

ungenteel . . . 6. vulgar 7. ill-bred 8. plebeian 9. inelegant 10. unmannerly

ungentle . . . 4. rude 5. harsh, rough 7. ill-bred 12. discourteous

ungodly . . . 6. sinful, wicked 7. impious 9. atheistic 11. unbelieving

ungovernable . . . 4. wild 6. unruly 9. unbridled 10. disorderly, licentious, rebellious, refractory 12. incorrigible, obstreperous, recalcitrant 13. irrepressible 14. uncontrollable

unguent . . . 4. balm 5. salve 6. cerate, chrism, pomade 7. unction 8. ointment 9. lubricant, unguentum

ungula . . . 4. claw, hoof, nail 6. unguis

ungulate . . . 3. pig 4. deer 5. horse, swine, tapir 6. hoofed 8. elephant, Ungulata 10. rhinoceros 15. hoofed quadruped

unhallowed . . . 6. unholy, wicked 10. desecrated

unhappy . . . 3. sad 6. dismal, woeful 8. dejected, ill-fated, wretched 9. miserable, sorrowful 10. calamitous,

displeased 11. melancholic, unfortunate 12. discontented, unsuccessful

unhealthy . . . 3. ill 4. sick 6. sickly, unsafe 11. unwholesome

unhesitating . . . 4. sure 5. ready 8. implicit, resolute 10. undoubting

unholy . . . 6. wicked 7. impious, profane 8. shocking 10. scandalous, unhallowed

unicellular organism . . . 6. amoeba (ameba)

unicorn . . . 4. reem (Bib), unie 7. monster 8. narwhale 9. monoceros, spike team 10. pursuivant (Her), rhinoceros (one-horned)

uniform . . . 4. even 5. equal 6. livery, outfit, simple, smooth 7. equable, orderly, regular 8. constant, equiform 9. unvarying 10. consistent, invariable, unchanging 11. symmetrical

uniformity . . . 5. order 8. equality, evenness, sameness, symmetry 10. compliance, conformity, smoothness 11. consistency, homogeneity 13. invariability

unify . . . 5. merge, unite 7. combine, make one 8. coalesce 9. integrate 11. consolidate

unimaginative . . . 4. dull 7. literal, prosaic 10. unfanciful

unimpaired . . . 4. free 6. entire, intact 8. unmarred 9. undamaged, unspoiled

unimpressed . . . 6. unawed 7. unmoved 9. unstirred 10. unaffected, uninspired

uninformed . . . 8. ignorant, nescient 9. unknowing 10. unapprized 13. unenlightened, unintelligent

uninhabited . . . 5. empty 6. vacant 8. deserted, desolate, forsaken 9. abandoned, unpeopled 10. unoccupied, untenanted

uninspired . . . 4. dull 6. stodgy 9. uninhaled

unintelligent . . . 4. dumb 5. brute 6. stupid, unwise 7. foolish 8. ignorant 9. senseless

unintentional . . . 7. unmeant 9. unwitting 10. accidental, unintended 11. inadvertent, involuntary, unmeditated 14. unpremeditated

uninterested . . . 5. bored 9. apathetic, impartial, incurious 11. unconcerned 13. disinterested

uninteresting . . . 3. dry 4. arid, drab, dull 6. boring, prolix, stupid 7. humdrum, insipid, prosaic, tedious 8. tiresome 9. colorless 10. unexciting

union . . . 3. one 4. bond 5. joint, unity 6. accord, fusion, league, merger 7. amalgam, entente, liaison, oneness 8. alliance, junction, marriage 9. coalition 10. federation 11. affiliation, association, combination, concurrence, confederacy, conjunction 13. juxtaposition

Union (pert to) . . .
  ensign, British . . 12. three crosses (St Andrew, St George, St Patrick)
  General . . 7. Sherman (Civil War)
  of States . . 6. Empire 12. United States
  of workers . . 5. artel, guild
Union of So Africa . . .

capital . . 8. Cape Town (Legis), Pretoria (Admin)
city . . 6. Durban 9. Germiston 12. Johannesburg
famed Park . . 6. Kruger

Union of Soviet Socialist Republics . . .
   see also *Russia*
anc citadel . . 7. Kremlin
capital . . 6. Moscow
city . . 9. Leningrad
Republics (number) . . 7. fifteen
resort . . 5. Yalta 6. Crimea
river . . 2. Ob 3. Don 4. Lena, Neva, Ural 5. Volga 7. Dnieper
sea . . 4. Aral, Azov 5. Black, White 6. Baltic 7. Caspian
strait . . 6. Bering

unique . . . 3. odd, one 4. rare, sole 5. alone, novel 6. single 7. notable, special, unusual 8. original, peculiar, peerless, singular 9. matchless 12. single-valued 13. extraordinary

unison . . . 5. union 6. accord, assent 7. concord, harmony 9. agreement, unanimity 10. concordant, consonance

unit . . . 3. ace, ane, one 4. item, word 5. digit, group 6. entity 7. measure 8. syllable

unit (pert to) . . .
area (land) . . 3. rod 4. acre 7. hectare
astronomy . . 6. parsec
biology . . 5. idant
electrical . . 3. amp, mho, ohm, rel 4. volt, watt 5. farad, henry, joule 6. ampere, proton 7. coulomb
energy . . 3. erg, rad 5. ergon 6. kilerg 7. quantum
fluidity . . 3. rhe
force . . 4. dyne 5. tonal 7. kinetic
heat . . 3. BTU 5. therm (therme) 7. calorie (calory)
induction . . 5. henry
light . . 3. lux, pyr, rad 5. lumen 6. Hefner
linear . . 3. ell, rod 4. foot, inch, mile, yard 7. furlong
magnetic . . 5. gauss, weber 7. maxwell, oersted
matter . . 5. monad
measure . . 3. are, rod 4. pint 5. maund, meter, stere
military . . 7. brigade, platoon 8. regiment
power . . 2. HP 3. bel 5. dynam, horse
pressure . . 5. barad, barie
reluctance . . 3. rel
resistance . . 3. ohm
speed . . 4. velo
telegraphic . . 4. baud
thermal . . 7. calorie (calory)
velocity . . 4. velo
volume . . 3. ton 4. cord, peck, pint 5. ounce, pound 6. barrel, bushel, gallon 8. hogshead
weight . . 3. ton 5. carat (karat), ounce, pound
wire . . 3. mil
work . . 3. erg 5. ergon, joule 6. kilerg
yarn . . 6. denier

unite . . . 3. fay, tie, wed 4. ally, bind, fuse, join, knit, link, meld, weld 5. annex, graft, marry, merge 6. adhere, cement, concur, mingle,

solder 7. combine, connect 8. coalesce, condense, converge, federate, side with 9. affiliate, associate 10. amalgamate, federalize 11. consolidate, incorporate

unite (pert to) . . .
by freezing . . 8. regelate
by interweaving . . 5. plash 6. pleach, splice
by joints . . 10. articulate
closely . . 11. concentrate
in concordance . . 9. harmonize
timbers . . 6. rabbet

united . . . 3. one, wed 4. knit, tied 5. added 6. allied, banded, joined, linked, merged, welded 7. cohered, grafted, rallied, spliced 8. cemented, clannish 9. concerted, corporate 10. concurrent, corporated

United Provinces . . . 11. (The)
   Netherlands 13. Dutch Republic

United States . . . 9. Etats-Unis

United States . . . see also *American*
artist . . 4. Wood 5. Flagg, Homer, Peale, Ryder, Sloan, Wyeth 6. Benton, Eakins, Hopper, O'Keefe, Stuart, Warhol 7. Bellows, Bingham, Cassatt 8. Rockwell, Whistler 9. Remington 12. Grandma Moses
author . . 3. Ade, Poe 5. Alger, Crane, Harte, James (Henry), Lewis (Sinclair), Stowe, Twain (Clemens) 6. Alcott, Cather, Chopin, Cooper, Ferber, Holmes, Irving, Jewett, London, Lowell, O'Henry (Porter) 7. Dreiser, Ellison, Emerson, Hurston, Thoreau, Whitman 8. Faulkner, Melville, Whittier 9. Hawthorne, Hemingway 10. Fitzgerald, Longfellow, Tarkington
canal . . 4. Erie 6. Panama
capital . . see separate States
composer . . 4. Ives, Kern 5. Foote, Nevin 6. Berlin, Foster 7. Copland, Rodgers 8. Gershwin 9. Bernstein
emblem . . 5. eagle
explorer . . 4. Byrd, Long, Pike 5. Boone, Clark, Lewis, Logan, Perry
Falls . . 7. Niagara 8. Yosemite 9. Multnomah
Indian . . see under *Indian (Am)*
inventor . . 3. Hoe 4. Bell, Howe 5. Fiske, Fitch, Morse 6. Edison, Fulton 7. Whitney
mountain . . 4. Hood 6. Elbert, Helena, Shasta 7. Rainier, Whitney 8. Katahdin, McKinley
naturalist . . 4. Muir 5. Beebe, Seton 7. Thoreau
ornithologist . . 7. Audubon
philosopher . . 5. James
pirate . . 4. Kidd
poet . . 3. Poe 4. Nash 5. Benét, Field, Moore, Wylie 6. Bryant, Holmes, Kilmer, Lanier, Lowell, Millay 7. Whitman 8. Whittier 10. Longfellow

unity . . . 3. one 5. union 6. accord 7. concord, harmony, oneness 8. alliance 9. agreement 10. singleness, uniformity 11. conjunction, unification 12. completeness

universal . . . 3. all 5. local, total, usual, whole 6. cosmic, entire, public

7. general 8. catholic 9. prevalent,
unlimited, well-known 11. widely known
universal (pert to) . . .
   knowledge . . 9. pantology
   language . . 2. Ro 3. Ido 9. Esperanto
   language, written . . 10. pasigraphy
   remedy . . 7. panacea
   solvent . . 8. alkahest
   successor, heir . . 5. heres (haeres)
universe . . 4. olam 5. world 6. cosmos,
system 9. macrocosm 10. Great World
universe, controlling principle . . .
5. logos
unkempt . . . 5. messy, rough 6. frowsy,
shaggy, untidy 7. ruffled, squalid,
tousled, uncouth 9. unrefined
10. disarrayed, disheveled, unpolished
unkind . . . 3. ill 5. cruel, harsh, stern
6. brutal, severe 8. ungenial
9. inclement 10. ungracious, ungrateful
13. unsympathetic 15. uncompassionate
unknowable . . . 6. mystic 8. mystical,
noumenon 9. enigmatic
13. indiscernible 14. unintelligible
15. absolute reality (Kant), ultimate
reality (Spencer)
unknowable object . . . 3. God 7. the
soul 8. noumenon
unknown . . . 7. inconnu, strange
8. stranger 9. anonymous, hereafter,
incognito, unheard of 10. unfamiliar,
unrenowned 12. incalculable
unlawful . . . 7. bastard, illegal, illicit,
lawless 9. irregular 10. contraband
11. unwarranted 12. illegitimate,
unauthorized
unlearned . . . 4. lewd 5. gross 8. ignorant,
untaught 10. illiterate, uneducated
11. instinctive
unleashed . . . 4. free 5. loose 6. untied
8. released 10. unfettered, unshackled,
untethered
unleavened . . . 7. azymous
unleavened bread . . . 4. azym 5. azyme
7. matzoth
unless . . . 4. nisi, save 6. except 7. without
9. except for, excepting 10. except
that
unlettered . . . 8. ignorant 10. illiterate,
uneducated
unlike . . . 6. sundry, uneven 7. dislike,
diverse 9. different, irregular
10. dissimilar, improbable
11. unpromising 12. disagreeable
13. heterogeneous
unlikelihood . . . 11. small chance
13. improbability
unlikeness . . . 8. contrast 13. dissimilarity
unlimited . . . 4. vast 9. boundless,
unbounded, universal 10. unconfined
11. illimitable 12. immeasurable,
unrestricted 13. indeterminate
unload . . . 3. rid 4. dump, sell 5. empty
7. discard, lighten 9. disburden,
discharge, liquidate
unlucky . . . 3. bad, fey, ill 7. infaust
8. ill-fated, untimely 9. ill-omened
11. unfortunate 12. inauspicious, not
favorable
unmannerly . . . 4. rude 7. boorish,
uncivil 8. impolite 10. mannerless

12. discourteous
unmelodious . . . 9. dissonant
11. cacophonous
unmerciful . . . 5. cruel 6. unkind
7. extreme, inhuman 8. pitiless, ruthless
9. heartless, merciless 10. relentless
unmistakable . . . 4. open 5. clear,
plain 6. patent 7. certain, evident,
obvious 8. apparent, distinct, manifest
11. unqualified
unmitigated . . . 4. mere 5. sheer 6. arrant
8. clear-cut, thorough 9. downright
11. not softened, unqualified
unmoved . . . 4. calm, dead, firm 5. inert
6. serene 8. obdurate, unshaken
9. apathetic
unnatural . . . 5. eerie (eery) 7. labored,
strange, uncanny 8. abnormal, affected
9. eccentric, irregular 10. artificial,
factitious
unnecessary . . . 4. fuss 7. useless
8. needless 11. not required,
superfluous, uncalled-for
12. nonessential
unobtrusive . . . 6. modest 8. retiring
11. clandestine
unoccupied . . . 4. idle, void 5. empty
7. not busy 8. deserted 10. unemployed,
untenanted 11. empty-headed,
uninhabited
unorthodox . . . 9. heretical 10. fallacious,
left-handed 14. unconventional
unostentatious . . . 5. quiet 6. lenten,
modest 10. restrained
unparalleled . . . 5. alone 6. unique
8. peerless 9. matchless, unequaled,
unmatched 10. inimitable
13. extraordinary
unpleasant . . . 8. unsavory 9. offensive
10. not amiable, ungracious
11. displeasing, distasteful
12. disagreeable
unpolished . . . 5. bruit, crude, rough
6. coarse, rugged 7. uncouth 8. agrestic,
unpolite 9. inelegant 10. agrestical
11. countrified
unprecedented . . . 3. new 5. novel
10. unexampled, unimitated
13. extraordinary
unprejudiced . . . 4. fair 7. neutral
8. unbiased 9. impartial 10. impersonal
13. dispassionate
unprepared . . . 3. raw 5. unfit 6. unwary
7. unready 9. premature, unskilled
unprepossessing . . . 4. grim, ugly
9. grim-faced 10. ill-looking
unpretentious . . . 6. humble, modest,
simple 7. natural 10. unaffected 11. in
good taste
unprincipled . . . 7. corrupt 9. dishonest
10. fraudulent, perfidious
12. dishonorable, unscrupulous
unprofessional . . . 3. lay 6. laical
7. amateur 9. unskilled 10. amateurish
14. unbusinesslike
unprofitable . . . 6. barren 7. useless
8. gainless 9. fruitless 10. unfruitful
unpropitious . . . 7. adverse, ominous,
opposed 8. untimely 10. disastrous
12. inauspicious
unqualified . . . 5. unfit 6. unable

7. genuine, plenary 8. absolute, complete, unfitted 9. incapable 10. ineligible 11. incompetent 12. not qualified 13. unconditional

unquestionable . . . 7. certain, decided, evident 8. positive 10. undeniable 11. indubitable, irrefutable 12. indisputable 13. unimpeachable

unravel . . . 4. undo 5. feaze, solve 6. unfold, unlace 8. separate 9. disengage 10. disinvolve 11. disentangle

unreal . . . 5. false, ideal 7. fancied 8. fanciful, illusory, spurious 9. fantastic, imaginary, visionary 10. artificial, fictitious 11. imaginative 13. unsubstantial

unreasonable . . . 3. mad 6. absurd, unwise 9. excessive, fanatical, illogical, senseless 10. capricious, exorbitant, immoderate, irrational 11. extravagant, impractical 13. unjustifiable

unrecognizable . . . 3. dim 5. vague 7. blurred, obscure, unclear 9. undefined 10. indistinct 14. unintelligible

unrecognized . . . 6. unsung 7. unknown 13. unappreciated

unrefined . . . 3. raw 4. loud, rude 5. crass, crude, gross, rough 6. coarse, common, earthy, vulgar 7. uncouth 8. inelegant 11. countrified 12. uncultivated

unrefuted . . . 4. true 6. proved 8. undenied 10. unanswered

unrelaxed . . . 4. taut 5. rigid, tense 7. nervous

unrelenting . . . 4. grim, hard, iron 5. stern 6. severe, strict 8. rigorous 9. merciless 10. inexorable, relentless, unyielding

unreliable . . . 6. fickle, unsafe 9. uncertain 10. capricious, changeable 12. undependable 13. irresponsible, untrustworthy 14. tergiversating

unremitting . . . 4. busy 8. constant 9. continual, incessant, perpetual 10. continuous, persistent 11. persevering

unrequited . . . 6. unpaid 9. forgotten, unthanked 10. ungrateful, unrewarded

unreserved, unreservedly . . . 4. free, open 5. frank 6. openly 7. frankly 8. candidly, outright, thorough 9. outspoken 12. unrestricted

unrest . . . 6. bustle 8. disquiet 9. commotion 12. restlessness

unrestrained . . . 3. lax 4. free, wild 5. loose 6. candid, wanton 7. lawless, riotous 9. unbridled, unlimited 10. capricious

unrestricted . . . 4. free, open 9. unlimited 11. extravagant 12. undiminished 13. communicative

unruffled . . . 4. calm, cool 5. still 6. placid, poised, sedate, serene, smooth 9. quiescent, unexcited 10. unaffected 11. undisturbed

unruly . . . 7. lawless 9. fractious, obstinate, turbulent 10. disorderly, licentious, refractory 11. disobedient 12. recalcitrant, ungovernable, unmanageable

unsafe . . . 7. dubious, exposed, unsound 8. insecure, perilous 9. dangerous 10. unreliable 12. undependable

unsatisfactory . . . 8. inferior 10. inadequate, unbearable 11. intolerable 12. insufficient, ungratiating 13. disheartening, unsupportable

unsavory . . . 7. insipid 9. offensive, tasteless 10. unpleasant 11. unpalatable 12. disagreeable

unscrupulous . . . 7. devious 9. dishonest 12. unparticular, unprincipled 13. untrustworthy 16. indiscriminating

unseasonable . . . 8. untimely 9. premature 11. inopportune

unseemly . . . 5. inapt, wrong 6. vulgar 8. improper, indecent 9. inelegant 10. indecorous, solecistic, unbecoming 11. undignified 13. ungrammatical

unseen . . . 6. hidden 8. unheeded, viewless 9. invisible, unnoticed 12. undiscovered

unsettled . . . 4. moot 6. fickle, queasy 8. confused, deranged, restless, unplaced, unproved, unstable 9. ambiguous, disturbed, irregular, uncertain, unquieted 10. irresolute, unoccupied, up in the air 11. unpopulated

unshorn . . . 5. hairy, whole 6. shaggy

unshorn sheep (2nd year) . . . 3. tag, teg

unsightly . . . 4. ugly 8. uncomely, unlovely 9. inelegant, not comely 12. unattractive

unskilled . . . 5. green 6. puisne 8. ignorant, malapert

unskillful . . . 5. inept 7. artless, awkward 9. maladroit 12. unproficient 13. inexperienced

unsophisticated . . . 4. naif, pure, soft 5. green, naïve 6. simple 7. artless, genuine 8. gullible, innocent 9. ingenuous 11. uncorrupted

unsound . . . 4. weak 5. crazy, dotty, risky, shaky 6. addled, fickle 8. impaired, insecure 9. defective, imperfect

unspoken . . . 5. tacit 6. silent 7. implied 9. ineffable, unuttered

unstable . . . 4. weak 5. fickle, fitful, labile, scanty 7. astatic, erratic, flighty, plastic 8. insecure, not solid, ticklish, unsteady 9. ephemeral, irregular, unsettled 10. inconstant, precarious, unreliable 11. fluctuating, vacillating

unsteady . . . 5. dizzy, shaky 6. groggy, wobbly 7. quavery, rickety, unsound 8. titubate, unstable, wavering 9. irregular, uncertain 10. capricious, changeable, flickering, inconstant, precarious 11. fluctuating, ill-balanced, lightheaded, vacillating

unsubstantial . . . 4. airy, rare, slim 5. filmy, light 6. aerial, flimsy, papery 8. illusory 9. illogical, visionary 10. immaterial, intangible, unreliable

unsuitable . . . 5. inept, undue, unfit 8. untimely 10. unbecoming 11. inexpedient 13. inappropriate 14. unsatisfactory

unsullied . . . 4. pure 5. clean 6. chaste

8. innocent, spotless, virginal
10. immaculate

unsure ... 4. weak 5. timid 6. infirm
8. doubtful 10. precarious 11. vacillating

unsweetened ... 3. dry, sec 4. sour, tart
10. unpleasant

unsympathetic ... 6. unkind 7. hostile
8. pitiless 9. heartless 10. intolerant
11. hardhearted 12. unresponsive

untamed ... 4. wild 5. feral 6. savage
9. unsubdued 11. uncivilized

untangle ... 4. free 5. loose, solve
6. sleave 9. extricate 11. disentangle

untenable ... 10. incredible
11. implausible 12. unbelievable,
unreasonable 13. inconceivable

unthinking ... 4. rash 7. puerile
8. careless, heedless 9. impetuous,
impulsive 11. injudicious, instinctive,
involuntary, thoughtless
13. inconsiderate

untidy ... 5. dowdy, messy 6. frowzy,
shabby 8. careless, frumpish, slipshod,
slovenly, unsuited, untimely
10. disheveled

untie ... 4. free 5. loose 6. loosen,
unbind, unknot, unlash 8. unfasten
9. disengage

until now ... 8. hitherto

untiring ... 8. sedulous, tireless
9. unwearied 10. unflagging
13. indefatigable

untold ... 4. vast 8. infinite 9. boundless,
countless 10. uninformed, unrevealed
11. innumerable, unexpressed
12. immeasurable, incalculable,
undetermined

untouched ... 3. new 4. pure 6. intact,
unused 8. pristine, virginal
10. impenitent, unaffected

untoward ... 6. unholy 7. unlucky
8. perverse, stubborn, unseemly
10. indecorous, ungraceful
11. unfavorable, unfortunate
12. unpropitious

untrained ... 4. soft, wild 5. green
8. indocile 9. unskilled, untutored
10. amateurish 11. unpracticed
14. unaccomplished

untrammeled ... 4. free 5. loose
8. not bound 9. unimpeded, unlimited
10. unfettered, unhampered,
unhindered

untransferable ... 11. inalienable

untried ... 3. new 5. fresh, green
8. unproved 9. unhandled
13. inexperienced

untrue ... 5. false, wrong 8. disloyal
9. dishonest, erroneous, incorrect, not
honest 10. fallacious, unfaithful

untrustworthy ... 6. tricky, unsafe
8. slippery 9. deceitful, dishonest,
uncertain 10. perfidious

untruth ... 3. lie 5. error, fable 7. falsity
9. falsehood, treachery 10. disloyalty
11. fabrication 13. faithlessness

unusual ... 3. odd 4. rare 5. novel, queer
6. exotic, quaint, unique 7. strange
8. terrific, uncommon 9. anomalous
10. infrequent, remarkable
11. exceptional 13. extraordinary

unutterable ... 6. sacred, secret
9. ineffable, wonderful 11. unspeakable
13. inexpressible

unvarnished ... 5. plain 6. simple
7. genuine 9. unadorned, unglossed
11. undeceptive 13. unembellished

unvarying ... 7. uniform 8. constant
9. permanent 10. monotonous

unwarranted ... 4. idle, vain 5. undue
7. illegal 8. baseless 9. excessive,
unfounded, untenable 10. exorbitant,
unentitled 11. unjustified

unwary ... 4. rash 7. unaware 8. heedless,
off guard 9. unguarded 10. unwatchful

unwavering ... 4. firm, sure 5. solid
8. constant 9. steadfast 10. unweakened
11. not yielding, persevering

unwelcome ... 8. non grata, unwanted
9. intrusive, uninvited

unwholesome ... 4. evil, sick 6. impure
7. corrupt, immoral, noisome, noxious
9. unhealthy 12. insalubrious

unwieldy ... 5. bulky 6. clumsy
7. awkward, restive 8. ungainly
9. ponderous 10. cumbersome
12. unmanageable 13. insubordinate

unwilling ... 5. loath (loth) 6. averse
9. reluctant 11. disinclined, involuntary

unwilling to prosecute ... 7. nol-pros
13. nolle prosequi

unwise ... 7. foolish 9. impolitic,
imprudent, senseless 10. irrational
11. inexpedient, injudicious

unwonted ... 4. rare 5. unused 7. unusual
8. uncommon 9. not wonted
10. infrequent 12. unaccustomed

unworldly ... 5. eerie (eery), godly, naive,
weird 8. heavenly 9. spiritual, unearthly
10. immaterial 12. supernatural

unyielding ... 3. set 4. firm, hard, iron
5. rigid, stern, stiff 6. strict 7. adamant
8. obdurate, stubborn 9. immovable,
obstinate 10. adamantine, determined,
inexorable, inflexible
14. uncompromising

up (pert to) ...
and coming ... 7. go-ahead 8. hustling
and down ... 6. seesaw, uneven 8. vertical
10. undulating 13. perpendicular
in arms .. 6. at odds 8. prepared
9. resistant
ref to .. 10. at the plate (game)
to .. 4. able, till, unto 5. until 9. cognizant,
competent
to date .. 3. new 6. modern 7. stylish
11. fashionable

upas tree, arrow poison ... 6. antiar

upbraid ... 4. twit 5. blame, chide, scold,
score 6. rebuke 7. reprove 8. admonish,
reproach 9. reprimand 10. put to shame

upheaval ... 5. storm 6. revolt 9. agitation,
cataclysm, elevation 10. convulsion

upheld ... 5. aided 6. backed 7. abetted
8. defended 9. supported, sustained
10. encouraged, maintained

uphill ... 6. upward 7. upgrade
9. ascending, difficult, laborious
10. slantingly

uphold ... 3. aid 4. abet, back, buoy
5. favor, raise 6. defend 7. confirm,
support, sustain 8. maintain, preserve

9. encourage 11. corroborate, countenance, lend support

upkeep . . . 4. cost 6. repair 7. support 11. maintenance

upland . . . 4. wold 5. weald 6. coteau, inland 7. country, plateau 8. highland

uplands . . . 7. country 9. highlands 10. the country

uplift . . . 5. elate, erect, raise 7. elevate, ennoble, glorify, improve 8. upheaval 9. elevation 11. inspiration

upon . . . 2. on 3. sur 4. atop, onto 5. about, above 7. against 9. by means of 10. after which

upon (pert to) . . .
  law . . 3. sur
  prefix . . 3. epi, sur
  that . . 7. whereat 9. whereupon
  which . . 7. whereat
upper . . . 6. higher 8. superior

upper (pert to) . . .
  bed . . 4. bunk
  crust . . 7. society 11. aristocracy 13. highest circle
  end . . 3. tip 4. apex, head
  hand . . 7. mastery 8. dominion 9. advantage, influence 10. preference
  House of Congress . . 6. Senate
  shoe part . . 4. vamp
uppermost . . . 3. top 6. upmost 7. highest, supreme, topmost 8. farthest, foremost 9. outermost

uppish . . . 5. drunk, proud 6. uppity 7. haughty, peevish, stuck-up 8. arrogant, assuming, snobbish 9. high-flown

upright . . . 4. good, just, true 5. erect, moral, piano 6. honest, square 7. endwise, sincere 8. vertical, virtuous 9. equitable, honorable, righteous 13. perpendicular

upright (pert to) . . .
  chair part . . 4. slat
  comb form . . 5. ortho
  posture . . 8. orthotic 11. orthostatic
  slab . . 5. stela
  timber . . 4. jamb, stud
uprising . . . 4. riot 6. ascent, mutiny, revolt 7. sloping 9. acclivity, ascending, rebellion 12. insurrection

uproar . . . 3. din 4. riot, rout 5. noise 6. bedlam, bustle, clamor, fracas, hubbub, outcry, tumult 7. turmoil 8. outbreak 9. commotion, confusion 10. donnybrook, hurly-burly, tintamarre, turbulence 11. pandemonium 12. insurrection

upset . . . 3. irk 4. rile, ruin, stir 6. defeat, refute, topple 7. agitate, capsize, confuse, disturb, fluster, startle, subvert, unnerve 8. distress, overturn, startled, unnerved 9. embarrass, overthrow 10. discompose, disconcert, distressed, frustrated, overturned, refutation, revolution 11. frustration, overwrought

upshot . . . 3. end 5. issue 6. result, sequel 7. outcome 10. conclusion 11. consequence, eventuality, termination 12. consummation

upside down . . . 8. confused, disorder 9. confusion 10. resupinate, topsy-turvy

upsilon (Gr) . . . 5. hyoid, vowel 7. Y-shaped

upstart . . . 4. snob 7. bounder, parvenu 13. social climber

up-to-date . . . 6. modern 7. alamode, topical 8. informed 11. fashionable

upward . . . 2. up 3. ano (comb form) 4. over 5. above, aloft 6. onward 7. skyward 8. upstream 9. ascending

upward movement of vessels . . . 5. scend

ureaus (Egypt Relig) . . . 3. asp 6. symbol 8. symbolic

Ural . . . 5. river 9. mountains

Urania (pert to) . . .
  blue . . 12. independence
  epithet of . . 9. Aphrodite
  genus of . . 5. moths
  Gr Myth . . 4. Muse (Astron)
uranology (study of) . . . 7. heavens 15. celestial bodies

Uranus (pert to) . . .
  astronomy . . 6. planet
  daughter . . 4. Rhea
  father of . . 9. The Titans (12)
  personification of . . 6. heaven
  satellite . . 5. Ariel 6. Oberon 7. Titania, Umbriel
  son . . 6. Cronus
urare, urari . . . 6. curare

urban . . . 5. civic 6. ghetto, polite, uptown 7. oppidan, refined 8. downtown, polished 9. courteous, municipal 12. metropolitan 13. sophisticated

urbane . . . 5. civil, suave 6. polish, polite 7. affable 8. gracious 9. courteous 11. deferential

urbanity . . . 7. amenity 8. civility, courtesy 9. deference

urchin . . . 3. boy, elf, imp, tad 4. arab, brat 5. gamin 6. elfish 8. hedgehog 9. dandiprat, sea urchin, youngster

urge . . . 3. dun, egg, hie, ply, yen 4. abet, coax, goad, prod, push, spur 5. drive, egg on, impel, press 6. advise, compel, dehort, desire, exhort, fillip, hasten, incite, induce 7. animate, entreat, solicit 8. persuade 9. constrain, importune, influence, instigate 10. inducement

urgent . . . 3. hot 5. grave 7. clamant, exigent, instant 8. critical, pressing 9. impelling, important, insistent, necessary 11. importunate

uriel . . . 3. sha 5. sheep 6. oorial

Uriel . . . 9. archangel 10. flame of God (Bib)

Urim and Thummim (Bib) . . . 11. instruments 12. interpreters (Mormon)

urn . . . 3. jar 4. ewer, urna (anc), vase 5. grave, steen 6. vessel 7. pitcher, samovar, vaselet 10. jardiniere

urn-shaped . . . 8. urceolus 9. urceolate

Ursa . . . 4. bear 9. Ursa Major (Great Bear), Ursa Minor (Little Bear)

ursal . . . 7. fur seal

ursuk . . . 11. bearded seal

Ursula . . . 5. Saint 7. she-bear 9. butterfly 15. British princess (legend)

urubu . . . 7. vulture

Uruguay . . .

capital . . 10. Montevideo
city . . 4. Melo 5. Minar 9. Maldonado
estuary . . 5. Plata 12. Rio de la Plata
lake . . 5. Merim
river . . 7. Uruguay
settler . . 5. Cabot (Sebastian, 1527)
university . . 10. Montevideo (1849)
windstorm . . 7. pampero
urus . . 2. ox 3. tur 7. aurochs
usable . . 3. fit 9. practical 10. functional
   11. serviceable, utilitarian
usage . . . 3. use 4. wont 5. habit, ritus
   6. custom, method 7. utility 8. behavior,
   practice 9. treatment 10. convention
use . . . 3. try 5. apply, avail, exert, spend,
   treat, wield 6. employ, expend, occupy
   7. consume, exploit, utilize 8. function
   10. manipulate 11. consumption,
   utilization
use (pert to) . . .
abusive language . . 4. rail
divining rod . . 5. dowse
frugally . . 5. stint
pert to words . . 7. neology, verbose
   8. enallage, pleonasm 9. verbosity
poetry . . 4. vail
refrain from . . 7. boycott
subterfuge . . 7. chicane
up . . 3. eat 7. consume, deplete, exhaust,
   fatigue
useful . . . 4. good 5. utile 7. helpful
   9. practical 10. beneficial, commodious
   11. serviceable, subservient
   12. advantageous, instrumental
usefulness . . . 5. avail, value 6. profit
   7. utility 13. conduciveness
useless . . . 4. idle, null, vain 6. futile,
   otiose 7. of no use 8. bootless,
   hopeless 9. fruitless, worthless 10. fifth
   wheel 11. ineffectual, superfluous
   12. unprofitable 13. unserviceable
   14. good for nothing
uselessness . . . 8. futility 9. inutility
   10. inefficacy
usher . . . 4. lead, page 5. guide 6. escort
   7. chobdar, teacher 9. attendant,
   harbinger, precursor 10. doorkeeper,
   forerunner, inaugurate
uequebaugh . . . 6. whisky 7. cordial
ustion . . . 7. burning 13. cauterization
ustulate . . . 8. scorched 10. discolored
usual . . . 7. average, typical, usitate
   8. everyday, frequent 11. status in
   quo
usurer . . . 5. shark 6. loaner 7. Shylock
   11. moneylender
usurp . . . 4. take 5. seize 6. assume
   8. arrogate 11. appropriate
Utah . . .
capital . . 12. Salt Lake City
city . . 5. Logan, Ogden, Provo
   7. Bingham
dam . . 10. Glen Canyon 12. Flaming
   Gorge
lake . . 6. Powell 9. Great Salt
mountain . . 5. Uinta 7. Wasatch 9. King's
   Peak
name desired . . 7. Deseret
natural wonder . . 4. Zion 5. Bryce
   13. Rainbow Bridge
settled by . . 7. Mormons 12. Brigham

Young 15. Latter-day Saints
State admission . . 10. Forty-fifth
State motto . . 8. Industry
State nickname . . 7. Beehive
utensil . . . 3. mop, pan, pot 4. tool
   5. broom, brush 6. device, ramrod
   7. skillet, sweeper 9. apparatus,
   appliance, implement 10. instrument
utilitarian . . . 5. plain 6. useful
   8. economic 9. practical 10. functional
   12. matter-of-fact
utility . . . 3. use 4. tool 5. avail 6. profit
   7. benefit, service 9. appliance,
   happiness, implement 10. usefulness
utmost . . . 4. best, last 5. final 7. extreme,
   maximum, supreme 8. farthest, greatest
   9. uttermost 11. most distant
Utopia . . . 4. Eden 6. heaven, island
   (imaginary) 7. Erewhon 8. paradise
   9. fairyland, Shangri-La 10. millennium
utopian . . . 5. ideal 6. Edenic 8. Quixotic,
   romantic 9. visionary 10. chimerical,
   idealistic, millennial
utter . . . 3. say 4. emit, pass, tell,
   vent 5. issue, sheer, speak, total,
   voice 6. assert, entire, mumble,
   reveal 7. deliver, divulge, express,
   extreme, publish, unusual
   8. abnormal, absolute, complete, disclose,
   disperse, intonate 9. downright,
   enunciate, out-and-out, pronounce
   10. peremptory 11. unqualified
   13. unconditional
utter (pert to) . . .
harshly . . 3. rap 4. bray
heedlessly . . 4. blat
in devotion . . 4. pray
in slow tone . . 5. drawl
musically . . 6. warble
publicly . . 4. tell 5. voice 7. enounce
softly . . 6. murmur 7. whisper
want . . 9. indigency 11. destitution
with effort . . 5. heave
with impulse . . 9. ejaculate
without voice . . 4. surd 7. spirate
utterance (pert to) . . .
dogmatic . . 8. dictum
gushing . . 8. effusion
rhythmic . . 7. cadence
voice . . 8. phonesis, speaking
   9. phonation 12. articulation
wise . . 6. oracle
utterer of pithy remarks . . . 8. aphorist
utterly . . . 5. fully, stark 7. totally
   8. entirely 10. absolutely, completely
   17. straightforwardly
uttermost . . . 5. final 6. utmost 7. extreme
utu . . . 6. reward 12. compensation,
   satisfaction
uva . . . 5. fruit, grape
uvate . . . 8. conserve (grape)
uvea . . . 4. iris
uxor . . . 4. wife
uxoricide . . . 10. wife murder
Uz (Bib) . . . 8. Job's home
Uzbekistan (pert to) . . .
capital . . 8. Tashkent
city . . 9. Samarkand
formerly part of . . 4. USSR
people . . 5. Uzbek 6. Turkic
Uzziel . . . 5. angel (Paradise Lost)

V

V ... 5. notch 6. letter (22nd), symbol
  14. five-dollar bill
vaagmer ... 8. dealfish (mare of the sea)
Vac (Hind) ... 7. goddess (of speech)
vacant ... 4. free, idle, void 5. blank,
  empty, inane 6. barren, devoid
  7. leisure, vacuous 8. unfilled
  10. disengaged, untenanted
  11. thoughtless 12. unencumbered
  14. expressionless
vacate ... 4. free, quit, void 5. annul,
  empty, leave 6. depart 7. abandon
  8. abdicate, abrogate, evacuate,
  withdraw
vacation ... 4. rest 5. leave 6. outing,
  recess, repeal 7. nonterm, respite
  8. furlough, justitium 10. recreation
  12. intermission 14. leave of absence
vacation place ... 3. spa 4. lake, park
  5. beach 6. forest, resort 9. mountains
vaccination ... 11. inoculation
vaccine (pert to) ...
  discoverer .. 4. Salk 6. Jenner
  protection for .. 5. virus 6. cowpox
  term .. 5. lymph, serum, virus
vacillate ... 4. sway 5. waver 6. dacker
  (daiker), seesaw, teeter, totter 7. flutter,
  stagger 8. hesitate, titubate 9. fluctuate,
  oscillate 13. procrastinate
vacillation ... 5. doubt 8. wavering
  9. faltering, hesitancy 10. fickleness,
  indecision, tibutation 11. oscillation,
  uncertainty 12. irresolution
  14. changeableness 15. procrastination
vacuate ... 5. empty 8. evacuate
vacuous ... 4. dull, void 5. blank, empty
  6. stupid 8. unfilled 9. senseless
  11. empty-headed, thoughtless
  13. unintelligent
vacuum ... 3. gap 4. void 9. emptiness
  11. rarefaction
vade mecum ... 6. manual 8. handbook
vagabond ... 3. bum, vag 4. hobo 5. lorel,
  scamp, tramp 6. beggar, picaro, rascal,
  rodney 7. vagrant, wastrel 8. Bohemian,
  brodyaga, wanderer 10. ne'er-do-well
vagary ... 4. whim 5. caper, fancy, jaunt,
  prank, trick 6. notion, ramble 7. caprice,
  whimsey (whimsy) 9. excursion,
  wandering 10. digression
  13. manifestation
vagrant ... 3. bum 4. hobo 5. rogue,
  tramp 6. roving, truant 7. nomadic,
  prowler, wayward 8. brodyaga,
  vagabond, wanderer 9. desultory,
  deviative, itinerant 10. capricious
vague ... 3. dim 4. dark, hazy 5. loose,
  misty 6. dreamy 7. obscure, shadowy,
  unfixed 8. confused, formless,
  nebulous, not clear 9. ambiguous,
  unsettled, wandering 10. indefinite,
  indistinct, intangible 13. indeterminate
vail ... 3. tip 4. doff (a hat), dole
  5. avail, bribe, yield 6. humble, submit
  7. descend 8. gratuity 10. beneficial

  12. advantageous
vain ... 4. idle 5. empty, proud 6. devoid,
  futile, otiose, snooty 7. foolish, trivial,
  useless 8. arrogant, boastful, nugatory
  9. conceited, fruitless, worthless
  10. unavailing, unrewarded 11. empty-
  headed, overweening, unimportant
  12. vainglorious
vain boasting ... 11. fanfaronade
vainglorious ... 4. vain 7. heroics
  8. boastful 9. gasconade
vain person ... 3. fop 5. dandy
  7. coxcomb 8. popinjay
vair ... 3. fur
vajra (Buddh) ... 7. diamond, trident
  (Indra's) 10. adamantine 11. thunderbolt
valance ... 5. drape 6. border, pelmet,
  ruffle 7. curtain, drapery, hanging
vale ... 4. dale, dell, glen 5. earth, glade,
  world 6. valley
valediction ... 5. adieu 7. address
  8. farewell 11. valedictory
valedictory ... 7. address, oration
  10. apopemptic 11. leave-taking,
  valediction
Valentine (pert to) ...
  romance .. 5. Orson 8. love song
  Saint .. 6. martyr (Rom) 7. holiday
  8. feast day
  State .. 7. Arizona (adm 2/14/1912)
  sweetheart .. 11. one's beloved
valerian ... 4. drug 5. plant 7. panacea
valet ... 3. man 7. Crispin 9. attendant,
  cameriere, chamberer 10. manservant
  11. body servant 16. valet de chambre
valetudinarian ... 6. infirm, shut-in,
  sickly, weakly 7. invalid 11. languishing
Valhalla (Valhall) ... 8. Pantheon (Bavaria)
  10. hall of Odin (Norse Myth)
valiant ... 4. bold, fine 5. brave
  6. heroic, strong, sturdy 7. doughty
  8. intrepid, stalwart, vigorous, virtuous
  9. steadfast 10. chivalrous, courageous
  11. meritorious 12. stouthearted
valid ... 4. good, just, true 5. legal,
  sound 6. cogent, lawful, proved
  7. binding, weighty 9. authentic,
  effective 10. sufficient 11. efficacious
  12. well-grounded
validate ... 6. affirm, attest 7. confirm
  8. legalize 12. substantiate
validity ... 5. force 7. cogency
  9. authority, soundness
  14. substantiality
Valjean (pert to) ...
  discoverer .. 7. Javert
  friend .. 6. Marius
  hero of .. 13. Les Miserables (Victor
  Hugo)
  protégé .. 7. Cosette
valley ... 4. dale, dell, dene, glen, vale,
  wady 5. glade, gully 6. coulee, dingle,
  ravine, trough 10. depression
valley (pert to) ...
  anatomy .. 9. vallecula

circular.. 6. rincon
deep.. 6. canyon
geology.. 5. atrio
India.. 5. dhoon
Jerusalem (near).. 6. Hinnom
   7. Gehenna, Rephaim
moon.. 5. rille
open.. 6. canada
where David killed Goliath.. 4. Elah
   (Bib)
valonia oak ... 6. camata (fruit)
   9. evergreen
valor ... 5. merit, worth 6. virtue
   7. bravery, courage, heroism, prowess
   8. boldness, chivalry 9. gallantry
   11. distinction 12. fearlessness
valuable ... 4. dear 5. asset 6. prized,
   useful, worthy 8. precious 9. estimable,
   treasured 10. worthwhile
value ... 3. par, use 4. rate 5. price,
   prize, worth 6. assess, esteem,
   parity, status 7. apprize (apprise),
   cherish, compute, meaning, respect,
   utility 8. appraise, estimate, evaluate
   9. valuation 10. estimation, excellence,
   importance
value (pert to) ...
   equal.. 6. parity
   least possible.. 5. plack
   nominal.. 3. par
   reduction.. 12. depreciation
valueless ... 4. baff 9. worthless
   10. threepenny 14. good-for-nothing
valve ... 3. tap 4. cock, door, gate
   6. faucet, piston, spigot 7. petcock
vamoose ... 2. go 4. blow, scat 5. leave,
   scram 6. beat it, decamp 7. skiddoo
   9. skedaddle
vamp ... 4. hose, sock 5. flirt, patch, upper
   6. recoct, repair, seduce 7. beguile,
   bewitch, concoct, touch up 9. improvise,
   temptress, transform
vampire ... 3. bat 5. fiend, ghost, lamia,
   witch 6. Alukah 8. bewitcher, sorceress,
   temptress 11. bloodsucker, extortioner
   12. extortionist
van ... 4. lead, wing 5. front, wagon
   6. shovel, summit, winnow 7. vehicle
   9. forefront 10. baggage car 12. advance
   guard
vandal ... 3. Hun 7. wrecker 9. destroyer,
   mutilator, plunderer 10. iconoclast
vandalize ... 3. mar 5. wreck 6. deface
Vandyke ... 5. beard, brown 6. artist,
   collar 7. picture
vane ... 4. cock 11. weathercock,
   weathervane
vanish ... 3. die 4. fade, flee, melt, pass
   6. perish 8. evanesce 9. cease to be,
   disappear
vanity ... 5. pride 6. egoism 7. conceit,
   egotism, falsity 8. futility 9. arrogance,
   emptiness, vainglory 10. hollowness
   11. fatuousness, self-conceit
   12. boastfulness 13. dressing table
vanity case ... 4. etui 6. make-up
   7. compact 9. cosmetics
vanquish ... 3. win 4. beat, best, rout
   5. expel 6. defeat, subdue 7. conquer
   8. confound, overcome, suppress,
   surmount 9. overthrow

vantage ... 4. gain 9. advantage
   10. perquisite 11. opportunity,
   superiority
vapid ... 3. dry 4. dead, dull, flat
   5. inane, stale 7. insipid, prosaic
   8. lifeless 9. pointless, tasteless
   10. spiritless, unanimated 11. indifferent
   13. uninteresting
vapor ... 3. air, fog, gas 4. fume,
   haze, mist 5. brume, cloud, fancy,
   humor, smoke, steam 6. breath,
   bubble 7. halitus 8. humidity, illusion,
   phantasm 9. evaporate 10. exhalation
vaporous ... 4. vain 5. foggy, misty
   6. cloudy, steamy 7. gaseous
   8. ethereal, fanciful, fleeting
   13. unsubstantial
variable ... 6. fickle, fitful, mobile
   7. protean, unequal 8. shifting, unstable,
   unsteady 10. capricious, changeable,
   inconstant
variance ... 3. out 7. dissent 9. deviation,
   disaccord 10. contention, difference
   11. discrepancy 12. disagreement
varied ... 5. mixed 6. daedal, motley
   7. changed, dappled, diverse, mottled,
   piebald, several, various 8. speckled
   9. different 10. variegated 11. diversified
variegated ... 5. pinto 6. daedal, motley,
   varied 7. dappled, diverse, mottled,
   painted 9. different 11. diversified,
   many-colored
variegation ... 7. variety 9. diversity
   10. multicolor
variety ... 4. kind, mode, sort 5. class
   6. change 7. species 9. diversity,
   variation 10. assortment, difference
   13. entertainment
variola ... 6. cowpox 8. smallpox
various ... 4. many 6. divers, sundry
   7. diverse, several 8. manifold, variable
   9. different, many-sided, uncertain
   10. changeable, inconstant, variegated
   11. diversified
varnish ... 4. spar 5. adorn, gloss, japan,
   paint 7. distort, falsify, furbish, lacquer,
   pretext 8. coat over 9. embellish
Varuna (pert to) ...
   art consorts.. 5. Jumna 6. Ganges
   deity.. 6. cosmic (supreme)
   god.. 3. sea
   Vedic equiv.. 3. Avestan Ormazd
   Vedic Relig.. 5. Aditi (fem deity)
vary ... 5. alter, range, shift 6. change,
   differ, modify 7. deviate, dissent,
   diverge 8. disagree 9. alternate,
   diversify, fluctuate, vacillate, variegate
   13. differentiate
vas ... 4. duct 6. pledge, surety, vessel
vascular (pert to) ... 5. hemic (haemic)
   6. vessel (blood, lymph) 7. tubular
   9. vesicular 10. hot-blooded
vase ... 3. jar, urn 4. bowl 5. ascus
   6. vessel 8. ornament 10. cassolette,
   jardiniere
vase (pert to) ...
   covered.. 7. potiche
   Etruscan.. 7. canopic
   Greek.. 5. askos, diota 6. deinos (dinos)
   7. amphora
   Roman.. 8. murrhine

vassal ... 3. man 4. esne, serf 5. helot, liege, slave 6. varlet 7. bondman, servant, servile, subject 9. dependent, feudatory 11. subordinate, subservient 12. feudal tenant

vassalage ... 5. valor 6. fealty 7. courage, enfeoff, prowess, slavery 8. dominion 9. servitude 10. subjection

vast ... 4. huge 5. broad, great, large 6. cosmic, mighty, untold 7. immense, mammoth 8. colossal, enormous, gigantic, spacious 9. cyclopean, extensive 11. far-reaching

vast (pert to) ...
expanse .. 5. ocean 6. desert, empire, region
numbers .. 6. myriad
period .. 3. eon, era 5. cycle
space .. 5. waste 6. boundless, immensity, limitless

vastness ... 6. extent 7. expanse 9. greatness, magnitude

vat ... 3. bac, pit, tub, tun 4. cask, gyle, kier, tank 6. barrel, vessel 7. caldron (cauldron), chessel, cistern, measure, salt pit 8. chessart

Vatican (pert to) ...
chapel .. 7. Sistine
church .. 8. St Peter's
city .. 10. Papal State (Rome)
palace of .. 4. Pope
statuary group .. 7. Laocoon

vaticination ... 8. prophecy 10. prediction 11. prophesying

vault ... 3. sky 4. arch, dome, leap, over, tomb 5. bound, crypt, enbow, groin 6. canopy (of heaven), coffer, curvet, grotto, welkin 10. depository 11. testudinate

vaunt ... 4. brag 5. boast

Vauxhall ... 6. resort 13. London Quarter (Thames) 14. Lambeth Gardens

Veda (pert to) ...
hymns .. 8. Sama-Veda
language .. 13. Vedic Sanskrit
literature .. 6. sacred (most anc)
oldest .. 7. Rig-Veda
prose, poetry (popular) .. 11. Atharva-Veda
ritualistic .. 9. Yajur-Veda

Vedic (pert to) ...
cosmic order .. 4. Rita
dialect .. 4. Pali
god .. 4. Agni 5. Dyaus 6. Aditya, Varuna 7. Savitar
goddess .. 5. Aditi
hymn .. 6. mantra
language .. 4. Pali 8. Sanskrit
sky serpent .. 3. Ahi
text, treatise .. 6. shakha (sakha) 9. Upanishad

veer ... 3. shy, yaw 4. slue, sway, turn 5. alter, shift, sidle 6. career, change, swerve 7. diverge, digress 9. fluctuate

veery ... 6. thrush 13. Wilson's thrush

vegetable ... 3. pea, yam 4. bean, beet, corn, leek, okra 5. onion 6. carrot, celery, lentil, potato, radish, squash, tomato, turnip 7. cabbage, lettuce, parsnip, rhubarb, shallot, spinach (spinage) 8. broccoli, eggplant, rutabaga, scallion 9. artichoke 11. cauliflower

vegetable (pert to) ...
and meat dish .. 4. stew 6. ragout
caterpillar .. 5. aweto
dealer .. 8. huckster 11. greengrocer 12. costermonger
green .. 5. sabzi
herb .. 7. salsify
leafy, salad .. 5. chard 6. endive 7. lettuce, romaine, spinach
oil .. 7. soybean 8. macassar
poison .. 5. abrin
stew .. 11. ratatouille
sugar yielding .. 4. beet

vegetate ... 4. grow, rest 5. exist

vegetation, goddess of ... 5. Ceres

vehemence ... 3. ire 4. fire, fury, rage, zeal 5. anger, ardor 8. violence 9. eloquence 11. impetuosity

vehement ... 3. hot 5. angry, eager, fiery 6. ardent, fervid, heated 7. animose, furious, intense, violent, zealous 8. forceful, vigorous 9. impetuous 10. passionate

vehicle ... 3. ark, bus, cab, car, van, wag 4. auto, cart, dray, hack, jeep, limo (sl), semi, shay, sled, tank 5. buggy, coach, lorry, moped, sulky, tonga, truck, wagon 6. go-cart, hansom, hot rod, jalopy, landau, sleigh, travoy, troika, wheels (sl) 7. caleche, caravan, chariot, clunker (sl), kibitka, minibus, omnibus, phaeton, scooter 8. brougham, carriage, dragster 9. buckboard, dune buggy, limousine 10. automobile, conveyance, jinrikisha (jinriksha), motorcycle 11. convertible

vehicle for oil colors ... 6. megilp (meguilp)

veil ... 3. dim 4. caul, film, mask 5. cloak, cover, orale, shade, velum, volet 6. fannel, masque, screen, shroud, soften 7. conceal, curtain, garment, pretext, secrecy 8. disguise 9. incognito 11. superimpose

veiled ... 5. vague 6. masked, shaded, velate 7. covered 8. shrouded 9. curtained

veiling ... 5. tulle, voile 7. curtain 8. covering 10. obvelation

vein ... 3. rib 4. dash, hilo, lode, mood, tang, vena, wave 5. costa, shade, smack, spice, tinge, touch 6. cavity, streak 7. bonanza, channel, crevice, fissure, mineral, stratum

vein (pert to) ...
arrangement .. 9. neuration
inflammation .. 9. phlebitis
leaf .. 3. rib
ref to .. 5. veiny 6. veinal, venous 7. marbled 8. venulose
small .. 6. venule 7. veinlet
stone .. 6. gangue, matrix 9. lodestuff
without a .. 7. avenous

velar ... 7. palatal, throaty 8. gutteral

veld, veldt ... 6. meadow 8. bushveld 9. grassland, grassveld

velleity ... 4. hope 6. desire 8. volition 9. faint hope 10. slight wish

vellicate ... 3. nip 5. pinch 6. tickle, twitch 9. titillate

vellum . . . 9. parchment 10. manuscript (on parchment)

velocity . . . 4. pace 5. speed 8. celerity, rapidity 9. quickness, swiftness 10. speediness

velocity measure . . . 4. velo

velum . . . 6. palate (soft) 8. membrane

velvet (pert to) . . .
breast . . 6. merganser
cotton . . 9. velveteen
fabric . . 5. panne 6. velure
Japanese . . 6. birodo
knife . . 6. trevet
leaf . . 6. mallow 7. mullein
return . . 4. gain 6. profit
texture . . 4. soft 5. nappy 6. smooth

venal . . . 5. hired 6. venous 7. corrupt, salable (saleable) 8. hireling, vendible 9. mercenary 11. corruptible

vend . . . 4. hawk, sell 5. trade 6. market, peddle 8. dispense 13. publish abroad

vender, vendor . . . 6. seller 7. alienor

vendetta . . . 4. feud 8. bad blood

vendue . . . 4. sale 7. auction

venerable . . . 3. old 4. aged, hoar, sage 5. hoary, olden, title 6. august, sacred 7. ancient, antique, classic, elderly, revered 9. dignified 11. reverential

venerate . . . 4. love 5. adore 6. revere 7. worship

veneration . . . 3. awe 4. fear 5. dulia, piety 6. esteem, latria 7. respect, worship 8. devotion 9. adoration, reverence

Venetian (pert to) . . .
barge . . 9. bucentaur
beach, resort . . 4. Lido
boat . . 4. topo (toppo) 7. gondola
bridge (famed) . . 6. Rialto
magistrate . . 4. doge 7. podesta
medal (New Year's) . . 5. osela (osella)
painter . . 6. Titian 7. Bellini (family), Vecchio 10. Tintoretto
school of . . 8. painting
song . . 9. barcarole
window (Arch) . . 9. Palladian

Venezuela . . .
anc name . . 12. Little Venice
capital . . 7. Caracas
city . . 8. LaGuaira, Valencia 9. Maracaibo 6. Ciudad, Guyana 16. Ciudad Bolivar
copper center . . 4. Aroa
Falls (world's tallest) . . 5. Angel (found 1937)
hero, liberator . . 7. Bolivar
lake . . 9. Maracaibo, Tacarigua
Mt . . 5. Andes 6. Concha, Parima, Sierra 9. Pacaraima
plains . . 6. llanos
river . . 6. Caroni 7. Orinoco
sea . . 9. Caribbean
snake . . 4. lora

vengeance . . . 4. harm 7. revenge 8. reprisal, requital 10. avengement, punishment 11. retaliation, retribution

Vengeance, goddess of (Gr) . . . 3. Ara, Ate 7. Nemesis

Vengeance, god of (Gr) . . . 6. Erinys 7. Alastor

veni, vidi, vici . . . 19. I came, I saw, I conquered (Caesar)

venial . . . 7. trivial 9. excusable, tolerable

10. pardonable 13. insignificant

Venice . . . see also *Venetian*
beach . . 4. Lido
bridge . . 6. Rialto
canal . . 5. Grand 8. Merceria, San Marco
capital of . . 7. Venetia (province)
color . . 4. blue
island . . 6. Rialto
landmark . . 9. Campanile 12. Doges' Palaces 13. Bridge of Sighs
of the North . . 9. Stockholm
river . . 6. Brenta

venison . . . 8. pemmican (pemican)

vennel . . . 4. lane 5. alley, sewer 6. gutter

venom . . . 4. gall 5. spite, virus 6. malice, poison 9. animosity, malignity, virulence

venomous . . . 5. toxic 6. deadly 7. baneful, noxious 8. spiteful, virulent 9. envenomed, malicious, malignant, poisonous, rancorous

vent . . . 3. say 4. exit, hole, slit 5. eject, utter 6. egress, escape, outlet 7. air hole, fissure, opening, publish, release, ventage, volcano 8. aperture, let loose 10. escapement

venta . . . 3. inn

ventilate . . . 3. air, fan 5. utter 6. aerate 7. discuss, publish, refresh 9. oxygenate

ventose . . . 5. windy 9. flatulent 12. cupping glass

ventral . . . 7. sternal 9. abdominal

venture . . . 3. hap, try 4. dare, risk, wage 5. brave, guess, stake 6. be bold, chance, danger, gamble, hazard 7. attempt, presume 8. run a risk 9. adventure, haphazard, speculate 10. enterprise, investment 11. speculation, undertaking

venturesome . . . 4. bold, rash 5. brave, risky 6. daring, heroic 8. fearless, reckless 9. dangerous, foolhardy, venturous 11. adventurous, temerarious 12. enterprising

venturous . . . 4. bold, rash 5. hardy, risky 6. daring 8. fearless 9. dangerous, hazardous 11. temerarious, venturesome

venue . . . 4. bout, site 5. match, onset 6. thrust 7. arrival, assault 9. encounter

Venus (pert to) . . .
astronomy . . 6. planet
church . . 11. Verticordia
goddess . . 7. Victrix 9. Aphrodite
goddess of (Rom) . . 6. Beauty
son . . 5. Cupid
sweetheart . . 6. Adonis
zoology . . 7. mollusk

Venus statue (marble) . . .
Florence . . 8. de Medici
Louvre . . 7. of Arles 8. Genetrix
Melos . . 6. de Milo
Naples . . 7. of Capua
Rome . . 8. Borghese 12. of the Capitol

veracity . . . 5. truth 7. honesty 8. accuracy, trueness 11. correctness 12. truthfulness

veranda, verandah . . . 4. pyal, stoa 5. lanai, porch, stoep 6. loggia, piazza 7. gallery, portico

verb (Gram) . . . 5. rhema 6. action

verbal ... 4. oral 5. wordy 7. literal, verbose 8. verbatim 9. talkative, vocabular

verbal noun ... 6. gerund

verbatim ... 6. orally 7. literal 8. verbally 11. word for word

verbiage ... 4. talk 7. chatter, diction, fustian, wording 8. claptrap 9. prolixity, verbosity, wordiness 10. redundancy

verbose ... 5. wordy 6. prolix 7. diffuse 9. redundant

verbosity ... 10. redundancy

verboten ... 5. taboo (tabu) 9. forbidden 10. prohibited

verdant ... 3. raw 5. color, green 6. unripe 9. evergreen 13. inexperienced 15. unsophisticated

verdelho ... 4. wine (white)

verdict ... 4. word 7. finding, opinion 8. decision, judgment 13. consideration

verdigris ... 4. drug 5. green 6. aerugo 7. deposit (on copper)

verecund ... 6. modest 7. bashful

verge ... 3. lip, rim, top 4. edge, tend, wand 5. brink, limit, marge, range, scope 6. border, emblem, extend, margin 7. incline 9. extremity 10. contiguous 13. circumference

Vergil (pert to) ...
birthplace .. 6. Mantua (It)
called .. 7. Roman Homer
famed as .. 4. poet
friend .. 8. Maecenas
name (last) .. 4. Maro
poem .. 6. Aeneid 8. Eclogues, Georgics
poetic form .. 4. epic 15. heroic hexameter (Aeneid)

verification ... 4. oath, test 8. averment 9. collation 12. confirmation 13. ascertainment

verify ... 4. back, test 5. check, prove 6. affirm, attest, second 7. confirm, support 8. maintain 12. authenticate, substantiate

verily ... 3. yea 4. amen 5. certes 6. truly 6. certes, indeed, in fact, really 9. certainly 10. positively 11. confidently

verisimilitude ... 5. truth 10. likelihood 11. probability, verisimilar

veritable ... 4. real, true 6. actual, gospel, honest 7. genuine 9. authentic

verity ... 4. fact 5. truth 7. honesty, reality 8. veracity

vermilion ... 3. dye, red 7. pigment, vermeil 8. cinnabar

vermin ... 4. lice, mice, rats 5. filth, fleas, flies, moths, worms 7. bedbugs, beetles, insects, spiders, weasels, weevils 8. riffraff, termites 9. parasites 10. centipedes, mosquitoes 11. cockroaches

Vermont ...
capital .. 10. Montpelier
city .. 5. Barre 7. Rutland 10. Burlington 11. Brattleboro
first town .. 10. Fort Dummer
hero .. 10. Ethan Allen
historic group .. 17. Green Mountain Boys
lake .. 9. Champlain
mountain .. 5. Green 7. Taconic
     9. Mansfield
museum .. 9. Shelburne 10. Bennington
product .. 6. marble 10. maple sugar
river .. 5. Otter 11. Connecticut
State admission .. 10. Fourteenth
State motto .. 15. Freedom and Unity
State nickname .. 13. Green Mountain

vernacular ... 5. lingo, local 6. common, jargon, native, patois, vulgar 7. dialect 10. colloquial, indigenous

vernal ... 4. mild, warm 5. fresh 10. springlike

verse ... 4. epic, poem, rime 5. canto, lyric, rhyme, stave, stich 6. poetry, rondel, sonnet, stanza 7. measure, strophe, triolet, trochee 8. limerick

verse (pert to) ...
art .. 10. orthometry
book of .. 5. poesy 9. anthology
devotion .. 8. antiphon
form .. 7. virelay 10. villanelle
Homeric .. 4. epic 6. epopee
Irish .. 4. rann
pause .. 6. cesura 9. diaeresis (dieresis)
romantic .. 7. sestina
satiric .. 6. iambic
scripture .. 4. text
stress .. 5. ictus
term .. 5. ictic, meter 6. accent, poetic, rhythm, scheme 7. cadence 8. eye rhyme, scansion 10. synaeresis (syneresis) 12. alliteration
trivial .. 6. jingle 8. doggerel, limerick

verse (pert to feet) ...
eight .. 9. octameter
four .. 9. tetrameter
one .. 9. monometer
three .. 7. tripody
two .. 7. dimeter

versed ... 5. adept 7. erudite, learned, skilled 8. familiar 9. practiced 10. acquainted, conversant, proficient

versification ... 7. prosody 10. orthometry

versifier ... 4. bard, muse, poet 5. rimer 6. rhymer 7. poetess 8. ballader, eulogist 9. poetaster, rhymester

version ... 7. edition 9. rendition 10. paraphrase 11. translation

version, Bible ... 5. Douay, Greek, Latin 6. Coptic, Geneva, Gothic, Italic (Itala) 7. Aramaic, Bishops, Luther's, Revised, Targums, Vulgate 8. Cranmer's, Georgian, Matthew's, Peshitta, Slavonic 9. Apocrypha, King James, Serampore 10. Pentateuch, Septuagint 11. Alexandrian

vers libra ... 9. free verse

verso (opp of recto) ... 7. reverse 9. back cover 12. left-hand side

versus ... 3. con 7. against 8. contrast, opposite 11. alternative

vertebra, vertebrae ... 4. axis 8. backbone 12. spinal column

vertebrate ... 6. linked 8. well-knit 9. backboned

vertebrates (pert to) ...
division .. 6. somite 10. Vertebrata
feathered .. 5. birds
group .. 4. Aves 7. Amniota

vertex ... 3. top 4. apex 6. summit

11. culmination

vertical ... 5. apeak, erect, plumb, sheer
6. height 7. upright 10. upstanding
13. perpendicular

vertical panel ... 5. stile

verticil ... 5. whorl 6. circle

vertigo ... 5. dinus 6. megrim
9. confusion, dizziness, giddiness
11. disturbance 12. bewilderment

verve ... 3. pep 4. dash, élan 5. vigor
6. energy, fervor, spirit 8. vivacity
9. animation 10. liveliness

vervet ... 6. monkey

very ... 3. eri (comb form) 4. much,
real, très, true 5. truly, utter 6. actual,
in fact, really 7. exactly, genuine
8. absolute, especial, peculiar, truthful
9. extremely, precisely, veracious,
veritable 10. legitimate 11. exceedingly

Very light ... 5. flare 6. signal (Very
system)

vesica ... 7. bladder

vesicate ... 7. blister

vesicle ... 3. sac 4. cyst 5. bulla 6. bubble,
cavity, vessel 7. bladder, blemish,
blister

Vespa ... 4. wasp 6. hornet

vespers ... 6. prayer 7. service
8. ceremony, evensong

vessel ... 3. ark, can, cup, jar, jug, mug,
pod, pot, tub, urn, vas, vat 4. boat,
bowl, dhow, drum, duct, ewer, junk,
olla, olpe, proa, said, seed, ship,
tank, vase, yawl 5. bocal, craft, crock,
cupel, glass, gourd, jorum, ketch,
stein 6. aftaba, aludel, ampule, barrel,
bottle, bucket, caster, cutter, dipper,
firkin, goblet, kettle, picard, retort,
trader, trough 7. catboat, cistern,
coracle, cruiser, frigate, pitcher, psykter,
steamer, tankard, utensil 8. aiguière,
ciborium, decanter, demijohn,
hogshead, schooner 9. alcarraza,
catamaran, privateer, washbasin
10. receptacle 11. earthenware

vessel (pert to) ...
anc .. 3. nef 5. yanky 6. bireme 7. caravel,
galleon, trireme
Arab .. 4. dhow
baptismal .. 4. font 7. piscina
chemist .. 4. etna 6. aludel, beaker,
retort
Columbus .. 7. caravel
cooking .. 9. autoclave
druggist .. 4. vial 5. phial 8. gallipot
Dutch .. 4. koff 5. yanky 6. galiot (galliot)
Eccl .. 3. ama, pyx 4. wine 5. amula
7. stamnos
Hebrides .. 7. birlinn (birling)
heraldry .. 7. lymphad
India .. 6. shibar
Mediterranean .. 5. xebec 6. settee
(setee), tartan 7. polacre
merchant .. 6. argosy 7. baggala
Nile houseboat .. 8. dahabeah
oil-burning .. 7. cresset
part .. 4. deck, keel, prow, skeg 5. brail
8. steerage
sacred .. 3. ama
Scottish .. 6. pourie
Thames (fishing) .. 6. bawley

Venice .. 9. bucentaur
war .. 3. sub 5. Maine 6. corvet
7. carrier, cruiser, felucca, flattop,
Monitor 9. submarine 11. dreadnaught
12. Old Ironsides

vessel (sailing) ... 3. hoy 4. bark, brig,
koff, proa, saic, ship, yawl 5. ketch,
sloop, smack, xebec

vest ... 4. robe 5. endow, gilet 6. invest,
jerkin, linder, weskit 7. furnish, garment
9. waistcoat

vesta ... 5. match

Vesta (Rom) ... 7. goddess (Hearth)
8. asteroid

vestal ... 4. pure 6. chaste 8. virginal

vestige ... 4. mark, sign 5. relic, shred,
tinge, trace, track 7. remains 8. footstep
9. vestigium

vestiture ... 4. garb 5. dress 8. clothing,
covering

vestment ... 3. alb 4. cope, garb, gown,
hood, robe 5. amice, cotta, dress,
ephod, miter, orale, tunic 6. saccos,
tippet 7. cassock, garment, maniple
8. chasuble, crucifix, dalmatic, scapular,
surplice 10. habiliment, omophorion

vestry ... 4. room 5. group (Eccl)
8. sacristy, wardrobe 10. repository

Vesuvius (pert to) ...
Great Eruption (79 AD) .. 6. buried
city .. 7. Pompeii 11. Herculaneum
mountain .. 8. volcanic
site .. 6. Naples

veteran ... 4. long 7. old hand, soldier
8. seasoned 9. practiced
11. experienced

veterinarian ... 7. farrier, surgeon

veto ... 6. forbid 8. negative, prohibit
10. disapprove 12. interdiction

vex ... 3. irk 4. cark, fret, fuss, gall,
miff, rile, roil 5. anger, annoy, harry,
spite, tease, worry 6. bother, harass,
nettle, plague, pother, ruffle 7. agitate,
chagrin, despite, dispute, disturb,
pervert, provoke, torment 8. disquiet,
irritate 9. displease

vexation ... 7. anxiety, chagrin, fatigue,
trouble 8. disquiet, irritate
9. annoyance, weariness 10. affliction,
foreboding, harassment, irritation
11. disturbance 13. mortification

vexatious ... 5. pesky 6. thorny 7. irksome
8. annoying, disturbed, pestilent,
provoking, worrisome 10. afflictive
11. troublesome

vexillum ... 3. web 4. flag 5. cross
6. banner, colors, ensign 7. labarum,
pennant 8. standard 10. Jolly Roger

via ... 2. by 3. way 4. away, road
6. begone 7. by way of, passage,
through

viaduct ... 4. span 6. bridge 7. trestle

vial ... 5. cruet, phial 6. bottle, caster,
castor, vessel 7. ampoule (ampul),
ampulla 9. container

viameter ... 7. measure 8. odometer
12. perambulator

viander ... 4. host 6. vendor

viands ... 4. cate, fare, food 7. viandry
8. victuals 10. provisions

viaticum ... 5. money 8. supplies

9. allowance, last rites **10.** provisions
14. Extreme Unction

viator . . . 8. traveler, wayfarer

vibrant . . . 5. alive 7. pulsing, travale
8. resonant, sonorous, vigorous
9. energetic, thrilling, vibrating
10. resounding

vibrate . . . 4. beat, rock, tirl, whir 5. pulse,
quake, swing, throb, waver 6. dindle,
quaver, quiver, shimmy, shiver, thrill
7. agitate, resound, tremble 8. brandish,
flichter, resonate 9. fluctuate, oscillate

vibration . . . 6. quiver, thrill, tremor
7. flutter, pulsing 9. resonance,
throbbing **11.** oscillation

vibration, music . . . 5. trill 7. sonance,
tremolo, vibrato

vibration measure . . . 9. tonometer

vicar . . . 5. proxy 6. curate, deputy, priest
9. churchman, clergyman **10.** substitute,
vicegerent

vice . . . 3. sin 4. evil 5. crime, fault,
taint 6. defect 7. blemish, stopper
8. iniquity 9. depravity, in place of,
instead of **10.** corruption, substitute,
succeeding, wickedness, wrongdoing
11. viciousness

viceroy . . . 5. nabob 6. satrap 8. governor
9. butterfly

vicinity . . . 6. region 9. proximity
11. propinquity **12.** neighborhood

vicious . . . 3. bad, ill 4. evil, foul, lewd,
mean, ugly, vile 6. faulty, impure,
wicked 7. corrupt, immoral, noxious
8. depraved, spiteful 9. dangerous,
malicious, nefarious, obstinate,
perverted **10.** iniquitous, profligate
11. ill-tempered

vicissitude . . . 6. change 8. mutation,
shifting 9. variation **10.** revolution
11. fluctuation

victim . . . 4. dupe, gull, prey 5. cully
6. sucker 7. patient 8. sufferer

victor . . . 6. captor, master, winner
8. unbeaten 9. conqueror
10. vanquisher

victor fish . . . 3. aku 6. bonito

Victoria, victoria . . . 4. plum 5. cross
(Maltese) 7. goddess 8. asteroid,
carriage **10.** automobile

Victorian . . . 3. era 4. prim 6. stuffy
7. antique, archaic, prudish
10. antiquated **11.** puritanical, strait-
laced

victorious . . . 7. winning 8. unbeaten
9. defeating **10.** conquering, triumphant

victory . . . 7. mastery, success, triumph
8. conquest 9. supremacy

victory (pert to) . . .
at too great cost . . 7. Pyrrhic
Day . . 9. Armistice
goddess . . 4. Nike
hymn . . 9. epinicion (epinikion)
memorial . . 7. trophy
symbol . . 4. palm

Victrola dog (symbol) . . . 6. Nipper

victuals . . . 4. food, grub 6. viands
8. supplies **11.** nourishment

videlicet . . . 3. viz 5. to wit 6. namely
8. scilicet

vie . . . 3. bet 4. cope, life 5. bandy,

stake, wager 6. endure, oppose, strive
7. compare, compete, contend, contest,
emulate 8. struggle 9. challenge

Vienna . . .
artist . . 4. Lieb, Pilz 6. Makart, Zauner
7. Kisling
boulevard (famed) . . **11.** Ringstrasse
capital of . . 7. Austria
Ger name . . 4. Wien
musician . . 5. Gluck, Haydn 6. Czerny,
Mozart 7. Strauss 8. Schubert,
Schumann 9. Beethoven
palace . . **10.** Schönbrunn
park . . 6. Prater
river . . 6. Danube

Vietnam (pert to) . . .
capital . . 5. Hanoi
city . . **13.** Ho Chi Minh City (Saigon)
gulf . . 6. Tonkin
holiday (New Year) . . 3. Tet
historic region . . 5. Annam 6. Tonkin
11. Cochin China
river . . 3. Red 6. Mekong

view . . . 3. aim, end, eye, ken, see 4. look,
scan 5. scene, vista 6. apercu, aspect,
object, regard, survey 7. examine,
glimpse, opinion, outlook, picture
8. attitude, judgment, panorama,
prospect 9. intention **10.** appearance,
perception, scrutinize **11.** contemplate,
expectation **13.** contemplation

vigil . . . 3. eve 4. wake 5. guard, watch
6. patrol 8. watchman 9. keep guard
11. wakefulness **13.** sleeplessness

vigilant . . . 4. agog, wary 5. alert, awake,
aware 6. awatch 7. wakeful 8. cautious,
open-eyed, watchful 9. attentive,
observant, sleepless **11.** circumspect

vigilantes . . . 5. posse 9. committee
(vigilance)

vigor, vigour . . . 3. pep, vim, vir 4. life,
zeal 5. force, power, verve 6. energy,
health 7. potency, stamina, sthenia
8. strength, validity, virility 9. animation,
fraîcheur, vehemence **10.** liveliness

vigorous . . . 4. able, hale, racy, spry
5. eager, frank, fresh, hardy, lusty,
tough 6. potent, robust, strong
7. healthy, zealous 8. athletic, forceful,
spirited, vehement 9. effective,
energetic, sprightly, strenuous
11. efficacious, flourishing

Viking . . . 4. Eric 5. rover 6. pirate
8. Norseman, Northman, sea rover
9. plunderer **12.** Scandinavian

vile . . . 3. bad 4. base, evil, foul, mean
5. cheap, lowly, nasty 6. coarse, filthy,
impure, odious, sinful, sordid, wicked
7. corrupt, debased, ignoble, obscene,
unclean, vicious 8. depraved, infamous
9. degrading, loathsome, nefarious,
repulsive **10.** abominable, disgusting
12. contaminated

vilify . . . 5. abuse, curse, libel 6. debase,
defame, malign, revile 7. asperse,
cheapen, degrade, slander, traduce
8. belittle, disgrace, reproach, vilipend
9. blaspheme, disparage **10.** calumniate,
stigmatize

vilipend . . . 6. slight 7. despise 8. belittle
9. disparage **10.** depreciate, slanderous

12. calumniatory

villa . . . 5. aldea, dacha 9. residence,
villaette 10. villanette

village . . . 3. mir 4. dorp, stad 5. thorp
(thorpe), tract 6. aldeia, castle, hamlet,
pueblo

Village Blacksmith author . . .
10. Longfellow

villain . . . 4. boor, lout, ogre, serf
5. demon, heavy, knave, rogue 6. rascal
7. caitiff 9. miscreant, scoundrel

villainous . . . 3. bad, low 4. base, evil,
mean, vile 6. vulgar, wicked 7. boorish,
knavish 8. criminal, rascally, terrible,
wretched 9. dastardly 10. detestable,
iniquitous 11. scoundrelly
13. objectionable

villous . . . 5. nappy 6. napped, shaggy

vim . . . 3. pep, zip 4. dash, élan, fire,
gimp, kick 5. drive, force, verve, vigor
6. energy, esprit, spirit 8. strength

vinaigre . . . 7. vinegar

vindicate . . . 4. free 5. claim, clear
6. acquit, assert, avenge, defend,
excuse, uphold 7. absolve, justify,
support, sustain 8. maintain
9. exculpate, exonerate

vindication . . . 7. defense

vindictive . . . 7. hostile 8. punitive,
spiteful, vengeful 10. revengeful
11. retaliatory, retributive

vine . . . 3. hop, ivy 4. bine, odal 5. betel,
grape, liana (liene), Vitis 7. cupseed,
trailer 8. clematis, wisteria 9. grapevine
10. chilicothe 11. honeysuckle
12. morning glory

vinegar . . . 4. acid, sour 6. acetum, alegar
8. vinaigre

vinegar (pert to) . . .
acid . . 6. acetic
comb form . . 5. aceto
dregs . . 6. mother
eel . . 4. worm
ester . . 7. acetate
fly . . 5. fruit
preserve in . . 6. pickle 8. marinate
salt . . 7. acetate
spice . . 8. tarragon
tree . . 13. staghorn sumac

Vinegar Joe (Army) . . . 9. Stillwell (Gen)

vinegarroon . . . 8. scorpion, vinagron

vinegary . . . 4. sour, tart 7. acetose,
crabbed, pungent 9. unamiable

vineyard . . . 3. cru 7. Priapus (god of)
10. plantation

vinology (science of) . . . 5. vines
10. grapevines

vinous . . . 4. winy 5. color

vintner . . . 8. merchant (wine)

viol . . . 3. gue 4. rope 5. rebec, ruana
6. vielle 7. quinton, sarinda 9. organ
stop

viola . . . 5. gamba 7. sarangi 9. organ
stop 11. tenor violin

violate . . . 5. abuse, break, wrong 6. defile,
invade, ravage, ravish 7. debauch,
outrage, pollute, profane 8. deflower,
dishonor, mistreat 9. desecrate
10. transgress

violation . . . 7. offense 10. infraction
11. anacoluthon, disturbance,

profanation 12. infringement,
interruption 13. nonobservance,
transgression

violence . . . 5. anger, force 6. unjust
7. assault, cruelty, outrage 8. coercion
9. vehemence 10. roughhouse
11. profanation 12. infringement

violent . . . 4. loud 5. acute, great, rabid,
sharp, vivid 6. fierce, savage, stormy
7. extreme, furious, intense 8. coercive,
vehement 9. turbulent 10. passionate
11. tempestuous

violent (pert to) . . .
Norse folklore . . 8. warriors 9. beserkers
outbreak . . 4. riot 6. tumult, uproar
8. eruption
pain . . 4. pang 5. throe 6. fierce

violet (pert to) . . .
color . . 5. mauve 6. purple 7. blue-red
dye . . 6. archil (orchil)
emblem of . . 7. gravity 8. chastity
genus . . 9. Violaceae
perfume . . 5. irone 6. ionone 9. orrisroot
tip . . 9. butterfly

violin (pert to) . . .
ancient . . 5. rebab, rebec, rocta 12. viola
de gamba
bar . . 4. fret
bass . . 11. violoncello
bow . . 5. arcus
city (famed) . . 7. Cremona (It)
make . . 5. Amati 7. Cremona
10. Guarnerius 12. Stradivarius
maker . . 5. Amati 9. Guarnieri
10. Stradivari
reference to . . 4. pins 5. belly
Scot . . 6. fiddle
small . . 3. kit
tenor . . 4. alto

violinist (famed) . . . 5. Elman, Stern
7. Heifitz, Menuhin

violinist, first . . . 13. concertmaster

viper . . . 3. asp 5. adder, Echis, snake
6. kupper 7. serpent 8. cerastes,
ophidian 9. scoundrel 10. bushmaster

vir . . . 5. vigor

virage . . . 5. scold, shrew, vixen, woman
7. beldame, rullion 9. termagant

Virgil . . . see Vergil

virgin . . . 3. new 4. maid, pure 6. chaste,
maiden, vestal 8. spinster 9. undefiled,
unsullied, untouched 13. unadulterated

virginal . . . 3. new 5. piano (spinet)
6. chaste, ritual 7. natural 8. maidenly
9. unmarried, unsullied

Virginia . . .
bay . . 10. Chesapeake
capital . . 8. Richmond
city . . 7. Norfolk, Roanoke 9. Arlington,
Lexington, Lynchburg 11. Newport
News 12. Hampton Roads
famed sites . . 8. Mt Vernon
10. Monticello 12. Williamsburg
13. Stratford Hall
first white child born . . 12. Virginia
Dare
historic town . . 8. Yorktown
9. Jamestown 10. Appomattox
Indian sachem . . 8. Powhatan
mountain . . 9. Blue Ridge 11. Alleghenies
resort . . 13. Virginia Beach

river . . 4. York 5. James 7. Potomac, Rapidan 12. Rappahannock
settlement (first) . . 9. Jamestown
State admission . . 5. Tenth
State motto . . 17. Sic Semper Tyrannis 19. Thus Always to Tyrants
State nickname . . 11. Old Dominion

Virgin Islands, British . . .
capital . . 8. Road Town
crop . . 9. sugar cane
group . . 7. Leeward
number islands . . 6. thirty

Virgin Islands, United States . . .
capital . . 8. St Thomas 15. Charlotte Amalia (former)
discoverer . . 8. Columbus (1493)
largest . . 6. St John 7. St Croix 8. St Thomas

virginity . . 8. celibacy, chastity 10. maidenhood 12. spinsterhood

Virgin Mary . . 5. Pietà (image) 7. Our Lady 11. Maris Stella, Mother of God 12. Star of the Sea 13. Mother of Jesus

viridity . . 5. youth 7. verdure 9. freshness, greenness 10. grass color

virile . . 4. male 5. manly 8. forceful, powerful, vigorous 9. masculine, masterful

virose . . 5. fetid 8. virulent 9. poisonous 10. malodorous

virtu . . 5. curio 7. antique 8. artistry 12. love of curios 15. artistic quality, study of fine arts

virtual . . 9. essential, potential 10. energizing 12. constructive

virtually . . 7. morally 11. potentially, practically

virtue . . 5. valor, value, worth 6. energy, purity 7. potency, probity 8. chastity, efficacy, goodness, morality 9. godliness, innocence, integrity, rectitude 11. uprightness 13. righteousness

virtue, logic . . 8. aretaics

virtues, cardinal . . . 4. hope 5. faith 7. charity

virtuoso . . . 6. expert 7. scholar 11. connoisseur, philosopher

virtuous . . . 4. good, pure 5. brave, godly, moral 6. chaste, honest, potent 7. upright, valiant 8. valorous 9. righteous 11. efficacious

virulent . . . 5. acrid, rabid 6. deadly, potent 7. noxious 8. venomous 9. animosity, malignant, poisonous 10. infectious, resentment 11. acrimonious

visa, visé . . . 7. endorse 9. signature 11. certificate, endorsement (passport)

visage . . 4. face, look 5. image 11. countenance 14. visible surface

vis-à-vis . . . 4. seat, sofa 8. carriage, opposite 9. encounter 10. face to face

viscera . . 4. guts 6. bowels, vitals 7. insides 8. entrails 10. intestines 11. inside parts

visceral . . . 3. gut 7. enteric 10. intestinal, splanchnic

viscid . . . 4. ropy, waxy 5. slimy 6. sticky

7. viscous 8. adhering, adhesive 9. glutinous

viscosity . . . 8. tenacity 10. stickiness

viscous . . . 4. ropy, sizy 5. gluey, gummy, tarry 6. mucous, sticky, viscid 7. stringy 9. glutinous 10. stickiness

vise . . . 3. jaw 4. tool 5. clamp, winch 6. device 7. squeeze

Vishnu (pert to) . . .
consort . . 3. Sri 7. Lakshim
deity (supreme) . . 6. bhakti 9. preserver
eighth . . 7. Krishna
epithet . . 8. bhagavat
seventh . . 4. Rama
tenth, last incarnation . . 5. Kalki
vehicle . . 6. Garuda

visible . . . 4. open, seen 5. clear 6. extant, in view 7. evident, in sight, obvious 8. apparent, manifest 10. noticeable 11. discernible, perceivable, perceptible

Visigoth king . . . 6. Alaric

vision . . . 3. eye 5. dream, fancy, image, sight 6. glance, mirage 7. glimpse, imagine, specter 8. eyesight 10. apparition

vision (pert to) . . .
comb form . . 4. opto
daylight . . 8. photopia
defect . . 6. anopia, myopia
double . . 8. diplopia
illusory . . 5. image
lacking . . 8. purblind
measure . . 9. optometer
night . . 8. scotopia
science of . . 9. optometry
term . . 5. optic 6. ocular 9. binocular, monocular

visionary . . . 4. aery, airy, seer, wild 5. ideal 6. dreamy, unreal 7. dreamer, Laputan, utopian 8. delusive, idealist, quixotic, romantic 9. fantastic, imaginary 10. chimerical, rhapsodist 11. imaginative, impractical

visit . . 3. see, vis 4. call, chat, go to, slum 5. haunt 6. attend, call on 10. inspection, visitation 12. conversation

visitor . . . 5. guest 6. caller 7. company 8. visitant

visne . . . 5. venue 8. neighbor, vicinage

vison . . . 4. mink

visor, vizor . . . 4. mask 6. vizard 8. disguise 10. camouflage

vista . . . 4. view 5. scene, visto 7. outlook 8. corridor, panorama, prospect

visual . . . 5. optic 6. ocular 11. perceptible

visualize . . . 7. imagine, picture 8. envisage, envision 9. objectify

vital . . . 4. live 5. basic 6. living, mortal, viable 7. animate, exigent, needful, organic 8. inherent, vigorous 9. essential, important, necessary, requisite 10. imperative 11. fundamental 13. indispensable

vital (pert to) . . .
air . . 6. oxygen
force . . 6. energy, spirit 7. neurism 8. bathmism, phrenism 9. theosophy
impulse . . 6. libido 8. instinct
organs . . 6. vitals 7. viscera
records . . 10. demography, statistics
strength . . 7. stamina

vitality ... 3. sap, vim 4. life 5. vigor 8. strength 9. animation, lustiness 10. liveliness

vitals ... 7. insides, viscera 9. internals 11. vital organs (heart, liver, lungs, brain)

vitamin ... 6. biotin, niacin 7. carotin, thiamin 10. riboflavin 11. lactoflavin 12. ascorbic acid

vitellus ... 4. yolk 7. egg yolk

vitiate ... 5. spoil, taint 6. debase, impair, poison, weaken 7. corrupt, deprave, pervert, pollute 10. adulterate, demoralize, invalidate 11. contaminate

vitiated ... 5. pical 6. wicked 7. corrupt, debased, spoiled 9. defective 11. ineffective, invalidated

vitiosity ... 4. vice 6. defect 9. depravity 11. viciousness

vitium ... 5. fault 6. defect

vitric .. 9. glasslike

vitrics .. 9. glassware, glasswork

vitrify ... 5. glaze 13. make into glass

vitriolic ... 4. acid 5. sharp 6. biting, bitter 7. caustic 8. scathing, virulent 11. acrimonious

vituperate ... 5. abuse, curse, scold 6. berate, revile 7. censure

vituperative ... 7. abusive, railing 8. reviling, scolding 10. scurrilous 11. maledictory, opprobrious

vivacious ... 3. gay 4. airy 5. merry 6. active, lively 8. animated, gamesome, spirited, sportive 9. energetic 12. lighthearted

vivacity ... 4. dash, élan, fire, keen, zeal, zest 5. ardor, verve, vigor 6. energy, gaiety (gayety) 9. animation 10. liveliness

Viverra ... 6. civets 9. civet cats

vivers ... 4. food 8. victuals

vix ... 8. scarcely

vixen ... 3. cat, fox 5. scold, shrew, witch 6. virago 9. termagant 12. female animal

viz ... 5. to wit 6. namely 9. videlicet

vizard ... 4. mask 5. guise, visor 8. disguise

viel (vley) ... 5. creek, marsh, swamp

voar ... 6. spring (of the year)

vocabulary ... 5. words 6. jargon 7. diction, lexicon 8. glossary, wordbook 10. dictionary

vocabulist ... 6. writer 13. lexicographer

vocal (pert to) ...
  chink .. 7. glottis
  composition .. 4. aria, song 5. motet 7. cantata
  expression .. 4. oral 9. utterance
  flourish .. 7. roulade
  handicap .. 4. lisp 7. stutter
  sound .. 5. vowel 6. sonant
  statue .. 6. Memnon

vocalist ... 4. alto 5. basso, tenor 6. artist, cantor, singer 7. caroler, crooner, soprano, yodeler 8. songster 10. coloratura, prima donna, songstress

vocalization ... 11. melismatics

vocalize ... 4. sing 5. sound, utter 6. phrase

vocation ... 4. call 5. trade 6. career 7. calling 8. business 10. employment, occupation, profession

vociferous ... 4. loud 5. noisy 7. blatant 8. brawling, strident 9. clamorous, turbulent 11. loudmouthed 12. obstreperous

vogue ... 3. ton 4. mode 5. style 6. custom 7. fashion 8. practice 10. popularity

voice ... 3. say, vox 4. alto, bass, tone, vote, wish 5. rumor, tenor, utter 7. divulge, opinion, soprano 8. announce, falsetto 9. utterance 10. expression 12. articulation

voice (pert to) ...
  box .. 6. larynx
  Greek .. 9. phthongos
  handicap .. 4. lisp 7. stammer, stutter
  loss of .. 7. anaudia, aphonia
  loud .. 12. megalophonic
  phonetics .. 9. affricate
  quality .. 6. timbre (timber)
  quiet .. 5. sotto
  raise .. 6. insist 10. supplicate
  raise against .. 5. decry 6. accuse, object
  singing, above natural .. 8. falsetto
  singing, natural .. 7. dipetto
  stress .. 5. arsis
  with one .. 9. unanimous 12. concurrently

voiced ... 6. sonant, spoken 7. sounded 9. phthongal 11. articulated

voiceless ... 4. dumb, mute, surd 6. atonic, silent 7. spirate 9. not voiced 12. not expressed

void ... 4. idle, lack, null, want 5. abyss, annul, egest, empty 6. devoid, hollow, vacant, vacuum 7. abolish, nothing, nullify, useless 8. evacuate 9. destitute, emptiness 10. unoccupied 11. ineffectual, nonexistent

void of ...
  interest .. 6. jejune 7. insipid
  sense .. 5. inane, silly
  space .. 5. blank 6. vacuum

volaille ... 4. fowl 7. poultry

volant ... 5. agile, light, quick 6. flying, nimble 7. current 8. volatile, volitant

volatile ... 4. airy 5. light 6. fickle, flying, lively, volant 7. alcohol, ammonia, buoyant, flighty, gaseous 8. fleeting, vaporous 9. ephemeral, mercurial 10. capricious, changeable, transitory 11. vaporizable 12. lighthearted

volatile (pert to) ...
  alkali .. 7. ammonia
  flux .. 5. smear
  liquid .. 5. ether 7. alcohol
  oil .. 7. essence, perfume

volcanic (pert to) ...
  glass .. 6. pumice 7. perlite 8. obsidian
  matter .. 2. aa 4. lava, slag, tufa 5. trass 6. pumice 8. lapillus, pahoehoe
  mud .. 5. salse
  orifice of gas issue .. 8. fumarole
  ref to .. 9. excitable, explosive 11. hot-tempered
  rock .. 5. trass 6. dacite 8. tephrite
  saucer .. 6. crater

volcano (pert to) ...
  Africa .. 11. Kilimanjaro
  Alaska .. 6. Katmai 8. Wrangell

Chile . . 6. Lascar
Ecuador . . 8. Cotopaxi
goddess . . 4. Pele (Hawaii)
Guatemala . . 5. Fuego 7. Atitlan
Hawaii . . 8. Mauna Loa
Iceland . . 5. Askja, Hekla
Italy . . 4. Etna 8. Vesuvius 9. Stromboli
Japan . . 4. Fuji 9. Asamayama
Java . . 4. Gede
Mexico . . 12. Popocatepetl
Philippines . . 3. Apo (Mindanao)
Sumatra . . 6. Merapi
United States (mainland) . . 6. Lassen,
  Shasta 7. Rainier
West Indies . . 5. Pelée
vole . . . 6. craber, rodent 8. water rat
  10. field mouse 11. meadow mouse
volée . . . 6. flight, volley
volery (volary) . . . 6. aviary 8. bird cage
volition . . . 4. will 6. choice 11. voluntarily
  13. determination
volley . . . 4. fire 5. blast, salvo, shots
Voltaire volume . . . 7. Candide
voluble . . . 4. glib 6. fluent 8. rotating,
  unstable 9. garrulous, revolving,
  talkative 10. loquacious
volume . . . 4. book, bulk, mass, size, tome
  6. amount 7. compass 8. capacity,
  fullness (fulness) 9. aggregate,
  Decameron 10. crassitude 14. fullness
  of tone
voluntary . . . 4. free 7. prelude, willing
  8. elective, intended, purposed
  9. volunteer, willingly 10. deliberate,
  volitional 11. intentional, spontaneous
  13. not accidental
volunteer . . . 5. offer 6. enlist 7. proffer
  9. be willing, voluntary 11. be of
  service
Volunteer State . . . 9. Tennessee
volute . . . 4. turn 5. whorl 6. cilery (cillery)
  8. rolled up 10. scroll-like
voodoo . . . 5. magic, obeah 6. fetish
  8. sorcerer
voracious . . . 6. greedy, hungry
  8. edacious, esurient, ravening,
  ravenous 9. devouring, rapacious
  10. gluttonous, immoderate, unsatiable
voracity . . . 5. greed 7. edacity 8. gluttony,
  rapacity 9. esurience
vorago . . . 4. gulf 5. abyss
vortex . . . 4. apex, eddy 5. whirl 7. tornado
  8. flatworm 9. whirlpool, whirlwind
  10. waterspout
votary . . . 6. zealot 7. devotee 8. adherent,
  aesthete, follower 9. supporter
  10. enthusiast
vote . . . 3. vow 5. elect, straw 6. ballot,
  choice, ticket 7. declare 8. suffrage
  9. designate 10. plebescite, referendum
vote (pert to) . . .
  group . . 4. bloc
  in . . 5. elect
  of assent . . 6. placet
  plump . . 14. straight ticket
  receptacle . . 8. situla
voter . . . 6. poller 7. elector 8. balloter
  11. constituent
voters . . . 10. electorate
votive . . . 7. devoted 11. consecrated
vouch . . . 4. back 6. affirm, attest,

  depose 7. confirm, declare, promise,
  sponsor, support 8. accredit 9. assertion
  11. attestation, bear witness
vouchsafe . . . 4. give 5. deign 6. accept,
  assure, bestow, permit 7. concede
  9. guarantee 10. condescend
voussoir . . . 8. keystone
vow . . . 3. vum 4. oath 5. swear,
  vouch 6. behest, devote, pledge
  7. declare, promise 8. dedicate
  9. assertion 10. consecrate,
  obligation 11. asseveration
  12. supplication
vowel (pert to) . . .
  change of . . 6. umlaut
  contradiction . . 6. crasis 7. digraph
    9. diphthong
  loss of . . 7. aphesis
  mark . . 6. macron
  point (Heb) . . 5. sere (tsere)
  separate syllables . . 9. diaeresis (dieresis)
  short . . 5. breve
  two, contracted . . 6. crasis
  two, group . . 6. digram 7. digraph
    9. diphthong (dipthong)
  unaspirated . . 4. lene
vowels, none . . . 6. syzygy
vowels in sequence . . . 8. caesious
vox (pert to) . . .
  clandestina . . 7. whisper
  Dei . . 10. Voice of God
  Latin for . . 5. voice
  populi . . 16. voice of the people
voyage . . . 4. trip 6. cruise, travel
  7. journey, passage, passing (sea)
  9. excursion 10. expedition, pilgrimage
  11. undertaking
Vulcan (pert to) . . .
  consort . . 4. Maia
  epithet . . 8. Mulciber
  feast of . . 10. Vulcanalia
  god of . . 4. fire
  Greek . . 10. Hephaestus
  work site . . 4. Etna
vulcanite . . . 7. ebonite
vulcanize . . . 9. rubberize
vulgar . . . 3. low 4. lewd 5. crude,
  gross 6. coarse, common, garish,
  public, ribald 7. boorish, general,
  obscene, profane 8. indecent, ordinary,
  plebeian 9. inelegant, offensive,
  unrefined 10. boisterous, in bad taste,
  rowdydowdy
vulgarian . . . 4. snob 9. pretender
Vulgate . . . 10. Scriptures
vulnerable . . . 6. liable 7. exposed
  8. beatable 9. pregnable, subject
  to 10. expungable 11. conquerable,
  defenseless, susceptible
vulpine . . . 4. foxy 5. artful, crafty,
  tricky 7. cunning, foxlike 9. alopecoid
  10. vulpecular
vult . . . 4. mien 6. aspect 10. expression
  11. countenance
vulture (pert to) . . .
  African . . 8. aasvogel
  American . . 4. aura 5. urubu 6. condor
    13. turkey buzzard
  European . . 7. griffin 11. lammergeier
    (lammergeier)
  king . . 4. papa

large . . 6. condor 11. lammergeier
Mexican . . 8. zopilote
raven . . 9. Corvultur
Spanish . . 9. gallinazo
term . . 5. harpy 9. raptorial 10. bird of

prey, predacious
vulturous . . . 6. lupine 7. wolfish
8. ravenous 9. rapacious
vying . . . 7. emulous 8. rivaling
9. competing 11. competitive

W

W . . . 6. letter (23rd) 7. double U
WAAC . . . 24. Women's Auxiliary Army Corps
waag . . . 6. grivet, monkey
waape . . . 5. canoe
wabber . . . 4. cony 5. daman
wabble . . . see *wobble*
wabby . . . 4. loon (red-throated)
wabe, wabi . . . 5. shrub 8. huisache
wachna . . . 7. codfish
wad . . . 3. pad, ram 4. cram, lump, mass, plug, roll, tuft 5. money, stuff, track 6. bundle, pledge, wealth 7. stopper 8. bankroll
wadding . . . 4. wads 6. lining 7. padding 8. compress, stopping, stuffing
waddle . . . 4. sway 5. mince 6. toddle, wabble, wamble, wobble 10. clumsy gait
waddy, waddie . . . 3. peg 4. beat, club 5. stick 6. attack, cowboy
wade . . . 4. ford, pass 5. study 6. attack, drudge, paddle, plodge 8. struggle
wader . . . 4. coot, ibis, rail 5. crane, heron, snipe, stork 6. jaçana 9. sandpiper, shore bird 11. Grallatores
wadi, wady . . . 5. oasis, river 6. ravine, valley 7. channel 11. watercourse
waeg . . . 9. kittiwake
wafer . . . 4. cake, disk, ring, seal, snap 5. bread 7. biscuit, cracker 10. altar bread
waff . . . 3. wag 4. flap, wave 5. ghost 7. lowborn, vagrant 8. inferior 9. worthless 12. disreputable
waft . . . 4. gust, puff, wave 5. carry, float, whiff 6. beckon, convey, convoy, signal 7. glimpse, pennant 9. beckoning, transport
wag . . . 3. wit 4. card, wave 5. joker, rogue, shake 6. signal, waddle, wiggle 7. farceur, vibrate 8. humorist, jokester 9. oscillate
wagang . . . 5. death 9. departure 11. leave-taking
wage, wages . . . 3. bet, fee, pay, utu 4. hire, levy, pawn, risk 5. fight, incur, stake, yield 6. employ, engage, pledge, reward, salary 7. attempt, contend, hire out, stipend, venture 9. emolument 10. recompense 12. compensation, remuneration
wage insurance . . . 7. chômage
wager . . . 3. bet, bid, vie 4. risk 5. sport, stake 6. gamble, hazard, parlay, pledge 7. venture
waggish . . . 5. droll, merry 7. jesting,

jocular, parlous, roguish 8. humorous, sportive 9. facetious 10. frolicsome 11. mischievous
Wagnerian opera . . . 6. Rienzi 8. Parsifal 9. Lohengrin 10. Tannhauser 15. Gotterdammerung
wagon . . . 3. car, van 4. cart, dray, tram, wain 5. araba, coach, lorry, tonga 6. telega 7. caisson, chariot, vehicle 8. carryall, schooner (prairie) 12. perambulator
wagon (pert to) . . .
canvas-covered . . 15. prairie schooner
lit . . 7. Pullman 11. sleeping car
load . . 6. fother
maker . . 10. wagonsmith, wainwright
on the (*wagon*) . . 8. sworn off, teetotal
part . . 4. neap 5. blade, thill
police . . 3. van 10. Black Maria
sideless . . 6. rolley
wah . . . 5. panda
wahine . . . 4. wife 5. woman 8. mistress 10. sweetheart
wahoo . . . 4. bark, fish, peto 5. shrub 7. rock elm 8. nonsense, tommyrot 9. buckthorn, guarapucu 12. umbrella tree
waif . . . 4. Arab, flag 5. gamin, stray 7. vagrant, wastrel 8. castaway, homeless, wanderer 9. lost sheep
wail . . . 3. cry, sob 4. howl, moan, weep 5. mourn 6. bemoan, grieve, lament 7. deplore, screech, ululate 11. lamentation 14. mournful outcry
wainscot . . . 4. base, ceil, line 5. panel 6. lining 8. paneling (panelling) 9. partition
waist . . . 4. wasp 5. shirt 6. basque, blouse, bodice, dickey, middle, taille 7. corsage, garment 9. garibaldi 12. undergarment
waistcoat . . . 4. vest 5. benjy 6. jacket, jerkin, weskit
wait . . . 4. bide, rest, stay, stop 5. dally, defer, delay, hover, serve, tarry, watch 6. attend, expect, linger, remain 7. observe 8. hesitate, postpone 11. expectation 12. watchfulness
waiter . . . 4. tray 6. garçon, salver, server 7. messboy, messman, servant, steward 8. servitor 9. attendant
wait on . . . 4. help 5. await, cater, serve 6. escort 7. toady to 9. accompany
waive . . . 5. defer, forgo (forego) 6. desert, give up, reject, vacate 7. abandon, cast off, forsake 8. postpone 9. disregard 10. condescend, relinquish

waka . . 5. canoe
Wakashan Indian . . . 6. Nootka 8. Kwakiutl
wake . . . 4. call, stir 5. rouse, track, vigil, waken, watch 6. arouse, awaken, excite, revive 10. death watch
wakeful . . 5. alert 8. restless, vigilant, watchful 9. sleepless, wide-awake
Wake Island . . . 6. Ottori (Jap name)
wake-robin . . . 4. Arum 8. Trillium 9. Anthurium 10. cuckoopint 12. philodendron
wale . . 3. rib 4. welt 5. ridge, wheal 6. stripe
Wales . . . see also *Welsh*
anc . . 7. Cambria
city . . 7. Rhondda, Swansea 8. Hereford, Pembroke 9. Carnarvon
congress of literati . . 10. eisteddfod
deity . . 4. Bran
emblem (floral) . . 4. leek
language . . 7. Cymraeg
mountain . . 7. Snowdon
native . . 5. Cymry (Kymry)
patron saint . . 5. David
port . . 7. Cardiff
river . . 3. Dee, Wye 6. Severn
sea . . 5. Irish
walk . . . 3. mog, pad 4. foot, gait, hike, hoof, pace, path, plod, ramp, step 5. allee, amble, scuff, strut, tramp, tread 6. ramble, sphere, stride, stroll, toddle, travel, trudge 7. conduct, shuffle, traipse 8. ambulate, behavior, frescade, province, sidewalk 9. esplanade, promenade, wandering 10. passageway 11. base on balls, perambulate 13. peregrination
walk (pert to) . . .
a beat . . 6. patrol
about . . 11. perambulate
clumsily . . 5. mince 6. lumber, totter
health . . 14. constitutional
lime-bordered . . 9. tilicetum
proudly . . 5. strut 6. prance
public . . 4. mall 5. arcade 7. alameda 9. esplanade, promenade
wearily . . 4. limp, plod 5. tramp 6. hobble, trudge
with speed . . 10. heel and toe
walking (pert to) . . .
about . . 7. passant (Her) 11. peripatetic
bearlike . . 11. plantigrade
meter . . 9. pedometer
papers . . 7. deposal, the sack 8. mittimus, pink slip 9. discharge, dismissal 10. retirement
wall . . . 4. dado, dike, ha-ha, mure, pier 5. fence, levee, panel, redan 6. escarp, hinder, immure, paries, podium, septum, shut in 7. barrier, defense, enclose, fortify, parapet, rampart 8. espalier, palisade, restrain, stockade 9. barricade, enclosure, encompass, partition, precipice, revetment 13. fortification
wall (pert to) . . .
bracket . . 6. corbel, sconce
creeper . . 4. bird
go to the (wall) . . 4. fail 10. go bankrupt
lining . . 8. wainscot

lizard . . 4. newt 5. gecko
masonry . . 9. revetment
pert to . . 5. mural 8. parietal
recess . . 5. niche 6. alcove
Street . . 9. Manhattan 11. money market, stock market
up . . 6. immure
wallaby . . . 8. kangaroo, Macropus, wallaroo 10. paddymelon
wallah, walla . . 5. agent 6. master, person 7. servant
waller . . 4. wels 9. saltmaker, sheatfish
wallet . . . 3. bag 4. pack, poke, sack 5. purse, 8. billfold, knapsack 10. pocketbook 12. porte-monnaie
walleye . . . 9. exotropia 10. strabismus
wallow . . 4. fade, sail 5. surge 6. grovel, welter, wither 7. debauch, founder, insipid 8. flounder, kommetje, nauseous 9. tasteless
Wall Street org . . . 3. SEC 4. NYSE 6. NASDAQ
walnut . . . 6. bannut
walrus . . . 3. pod (group) 5. morse 6. mammal, sea cat 8. pinniped 9. rosmarine (fable) 10. pinnipedia
Waltonian . . . 6. angler 16. disciple of Walton (Izaak)
wamble . . . 5. twist 6. quiver, ramble, rumble, totter, writhe 7. revolve, stagger, wriggle
wame . . 4. room, womb 5. belly 7. stomach
wampum . . . 4. peag 5. beads, money, uhllo 6. shells 7. jewelry, roanoke 8. ornament 10. wampumpeag
wan . . . 3. dim, sad 4. ashy, dark, pale, sick 5. ashen, black, dusky, faint, lurid 6. dismal, gloomy, pallid, sickly 7. ghastly, languid 9. deathlike, sorrowful 10. lusterless 11. lead-colored
wand . . . 3. rod 4. mace, pole 5. baton, osier, staff, stick (magic) 6. switch, wattle 7. pointer, rhabdos (magic) 8. scepter (sceptre) 8. caduceus 9. horsewhip
wander . . . 3. err, gad 4. moon, rave, roam, rove 5. drift, prowl, range, stray 6. cruise, depart, ramble, stroll, travel 7. digress, meander, saunter, traipse 8. divagate, traverse 9. circulate, itinerate, scamander 11. peregrinate
wanderer . . . 4. Arab, waif 5. gypsy, nomad, rover 6. ranger, roamer, truant 7. migrant, pilgrim, vagrant 9. butterfly, itinerant, straggler 10. covenanter 12. peregrinator
wandering . . . 5. vague 6. astray, errant, roving, vagary 8. aberrant, delirium, straying 9. delirious, deviating, deviation, itinerant 10. circuitous, discursive, journeying 11. noctivigant, perambulant 13. peregrination
wandering (pert to) . . .
bird . . 9. albatross
long . . 7. odyssey
minstrel . . 4. bard 10. troubadour
stars . . 12. seven planets
tattler . . 9. shore bird
votary . . 6. palmer
wanderoo . . . 6. langur, monkey

7. macaque

wand-shaped ... 7. virgate

wane ... 3. age, ebb 4. fail, sink, want
5. abate, peter 6. defect, lessen, recede,
repine 7. decline, grow dim, subside
8. decrease, diminish 10. defervesce
13. deterioration

wanga ... 5. charm, spell 6. voodoo
7. philter, sorcery

wangle ... 4. fake, plot 6. adjust,
juggle, obtain, totter, wiggle 7. finagle
(finaigue), wriggle 8. contrive,
maneuver (manoeuvre) 9. extricate
10. manipulate

want ... 4. lack, miss, need, wish 5. crave
6. dearth, desire, hunger, penury
7. absence, craving, lacking, poverty
8. scarcity, shortage 9. deficient,
indigence, privation 10. inadequacy
11. destitution, requirement

want (of) ...
appetite .. 6. asitia
desire .. 11. inappetence
lacking .. 4. sans 5. out of 7. empty
of, scant of, short of 8. bereft of
10. deprived of
power .. 5. atony
sense (good) .. 5. folly

wanting ... 4. void 5. minus, needy
6. absent, bereft, devoid 7. lacking,
missing, short of, without 9. deficient,
destitute, imperfect

wanting (pert to) ...
be found .. 9. fall short 10. be inferior
confidence .. 11. distrustful
in energy .. 6. atonic
in firmness .. 7. flaccid
in intelligence .. 12. feebleminded

wanton ... 3. gay 4. lewd 5. merry
6. frisky, harlot, unruly 7. immoral,
lustful, wayward 8. flagrant, insolent,
sportive, unchaste 9. dissolute,
merciless 10. capricious, frolicsome,
licentious 11. extravagant
13. undisciplined

wapiti ... 3. elk 4. deer, stag

war ... 5. fight 6. attack, battle 8. conflict

war (pert to) ...
agreement .. 6. cartel
cause of .. 10. casus belli
club .. 4. mace
fleet .. 6. armada
gas .. 8. adamsite
German .. 5. krieg 10. blitzkrieg
god .. 3. Ira, Tyr 4. Ares
goddess .. 5. Bella 6. Ishtar
hating .. 13. misopolemical
hawk .. 5. jingo 7. bailiff
horse .. 5. steed 7. charger 8. partisan
10. campaigner, politician
of words .. 9. logomachy
religious .. 5. jihad (jehad)
vessel, ship .. 3. sub 7. cruiser, frigate
8. corvette (corvet) 9. destroyer,
submarine 11. dreadnought
(dreadnaught)

war bird ... 7. aviator, tanager (scarlet)

warble ... 4. sing 5. carol, trill, yodel
6. quaver 7. twitter, vibrate

warbler ... 4. wren 6. singer 8. blackcap,
grosbeak, redstart, songster 9. beccafico

10. bluethroat 11. whitethroat

ward ... 4. jail, part, rule 5. watch
6. govern, prison 7. custody, keeping
8. district, garrison, guardian,
watchman 9. dependent 10. stronghold
12. guardianship

ward (pert to) ...
division .. 4. army, jail 6. forest
8. hospital
French .. 14. arrondissement
heeler .. 8. henchman 10. politician
off .. 4. fend 5. fence, parry, repel, stave
7. expiate, forfend, prevent

warden ... 5. guard, nazir 6. dizdar
(disdar), jailer, keeper, ranger, sexton
7. alcaide (alcaid), turnkey 8. director,
guardian, official, watchman
9. concierge, custodian 10. gatekeeper

warder ... 6. warden 7. turnkey

wardrobe ... 4. room 6. closet 7. almirah,
apparel, cabinet, clothes 8. costumes
12. clothespress

ware ... 4. sage, wary, wise 5. aware,
china, goods, spend 6. shrewd
7. careful, heedful, pottery, prudent,
seaweed 8. cautious, vigilant
9. cognizant, commodity, conscious,
porcelain 11. commodities,
earthenware, merchandise

warehouse ... 4. silo 5. depot, étape
6. fonduk (fondouk), godown 7. storage
8. entrepôt

warfare ... 7. contest 8. conflict, struggle
11. hostilities 12. armed contest

wariness ... 7. stealth 8. distrust
9. chariness, suspicion

warlock ... 6. wizard 7. monster (Myth)
8. conjuror, magician, sorcerer

warm ... 3. red 4. heat, keen, mild
5. angry, calid, eager, humid, muggy,
tepid, toast 6. ardent, excite, genial,
hearty, heated, torrid 7. clement,
cordial, fervent 8. friendly, generous
10. responsive 11. sympathetic
12. affectionate, enthusiastic 13. near
discovery, near the object (see also
hot)

warm (pert to) ...
bath .. 5. therm
growing .. 9. calescent
hearted .. 4. kind 6. hearty, kindly,
tender 7. cordial 8. friendly, generous
11. sympathetic 12. affectionate
pert to .. 7. thermal
praise .. 8. encomium
room .. 10. tepidarium
springs (Rom) .. 7. thermae

warmblooded ... 6. ardent 9. irascible
13. homoiothermic, quick-tempered
14. haematothermal (hematothermal)

warmed over ... 5. stale, trite
8. rehashed, reheated 9. rechauffé,
twice-told

warmonger ... 4. hawk

warmth ... 4. élan, glow, heat, zeal
5. ardor 7. ardency, thermal 8. fervency
9. animation, eloquency, geniality,
vehemence 10. enthusiasm, excitement
11. calefaction, earnestness

warn ... 4. flag 5. alarm, alert 6. advise,
exhort, inform, notify, remind, signal

7. apprise (apprize), caution, counsel, previse 8. admonish, forebode, threaten 9. reprehend

warning ... 4. bell, omen 5. alarm, alert, radar, siren 6. alarum, beacon, beware, caveat, signal, threat, tocsin 7. blinker, sematic, summons 10. admonition, admonitive 12. caveat emptor

warp ... 4. bend, bias, hurl, sway, turn, wind 5. fling, throw, twist, weave 6. buckle, swerve 7. contort, deflect, distort, pervert 9. fabricate 10. aberration, distortion 12. misinterpret

warp (pert to) ...
cross threads .. 4. woof
threads .. 5. lease 6. stamen
yarn .. 3. abb

warragal, warrigal ... 5. dingo, horse, myall

warrant ... 4. earn, writ 5. order 6. attest, ensure, permit, secure 7. defense, justify, precept, promise, voucher 8. document, guaranty, sanction, security 9. authorize, guarantee, safeguard 10. credential, instrument, protection 11. acknowledge, certificate 13. authorization

warranty ... 4. writ 5. proof 7. promise, warrant 8. guaranty, sanction, security 13. authorization

warrior ... 4. hero, impi 5. brave 6. Amazon 7. fighter, martial, soldier 10. halberdier

warrior (pert to) ...
Bib .. 4. Ehud
female .. 6. Amazon
Indian .. 6. sannup
Roman .. 9. gladiator
Trojan .. 6. Agenor, Hector

Warsaw (pert to) ...
capital .. 6. Poland
river .. 7. Vistula
suburb .. 5. Praga

wary ... 3. shy 5. alert, canny, chary, leery 7. careful, guarded, prudent 8. cautious, discreet, watchful 10. economical 11. circumspect

wash ... 3. lap, pan 4. lave 5. bathe, clean, elute, flush, leach, marsh, paint, purge, rinse, slosh, swash 6. debris, drench, dry bed (river), purify, splash 7. cleanse, immerse, launder, overlay, shampoo 8. ablution 9. lixiviate

wash (pert to) ...
basin .. 4. bowl 6. lavabo
bear .. 7. raccoon
dish .. 11. pied wagtail
for gold .. 3. pan
one's hands of .. 6. give up, refuse 10. relinquish
out .. 4. fade 5. elute, flunk 7. failure, freshet
sale (finance) .. 10. fictitious

washing ... 7. coating 8. ablution 9. drenching

Washington, DC (famed sites) ...
7. Capitol (Bldg), The Mall 8. Pentagon, Treasury 10. Blair House, White House 11. Mount Vernon 12. Ford's Theater (Lincoln Museum), Supreme

Court 14. cherry blossoms 15. Iwo Jima Monument, Lincoln Memorial 16. National Archives, Naval Observatory 17. Jefferson Memorial, Library of Congress 18. Walter Reed Hospital, Washington Monument 19. Unknown Soldier's Tomb 22. Smithsonian Institution 25. Arlington National Cemetery

Washington (State of) ...
capital .. 7. Olympia
city .. 6. Tacoma, Yakima 7. Everett, Seattle, Spokane 10. Bellingham, Walla Walla
dam .. 10. Bonneville 11. Grand Coulee
discoverer .. 4. Gray 9. Vancouver
explorer .. 5. Clark, Lewis 6. Wilkes 7. Fremont
Falls .. 10. Snoqualmie
Fort .. 5. Lewis
lake .. 5. Union 6. Chelan 8. Crescent
mountain .. 7. Rainier 8. Cascades, Olympics
river .. 5. Snake, White 7. Spokane 8. Columbia
Sound .. 5. Puget 7. Rosario
State admission .. 11. Forty-second
State motto .. 4. Al-Ki (By and By)
State nickname .. 9. Evergreen
wind (SW) .. 7. chinook

wasp ... 5. Sphex, vespa, whamp 6. dauber, hornet, Tiphia, vespid 8. Vespidae 12. Hymenopteron, yellow jacket

waspish ... 4. mean 5. cross, testy 6. cranky 7. bearish, peevish, slender 8. choleric, churlish, petulant, snappish, spiteful 9. fractious, irascible, irritable 12. cantankerous

wasp's nest ... 8. vespiary

wassail ... 4. lark, orgy, romp 5. toast 6. frolic, shindy 7. carouse 8. beverage, carousal 9. festivity 10. salutation 11. celebration 12. drinking bout

waste ... 3. eat 4. idle, junk, loss, rind, ross, sack, slag, vain, wear, wild 5. chaff, chips, dross, havoc, spill, trash 6. barren, desert, expend, lavish, ravage, refuse 7. atrophy, exhaust, fritter, rubbish 8. clinkers, demolish, desolate, squander 9. dissipate 10. desolation, diminution 11. destruction, devastation, dissipation, prodigality, uninhabited 12. uncultivated, unproductive 13. unserviceable

waste (pert to) ...
allowance .. 4. tret
away .. 3. age 6. shrink, sicken 7. decline 8. marasmus 11. deteriorate
lay waste .. 4. sack 6. ravage 7. destroy 8. decimate
matter .. 3. ort 4. slag 5. dross 7. clinker
mine .. 3. gob
silk .. 4. knob, noil 6. frison
time .. 4. idle, lazy 5. dally 6. daddle, footle, loiter 10. dillydally

wasted ... 7. haggard 8. phthisic

wasteful ... 6. lavish 10. thriftless 11. extravagant, improvident

wasteland ... 5. heath, marsh, swamp

6. desert, morass 8. badlands 10. barren land, everglades

wasting ... 5. aging 6. awaste 8. marasmic 10. enfeebling 11. consumption, devastating 13. deteriorating

wastrel ... 4. waif 5. idler 8. vagabond 10. profligate 11. spendthrift

watch ... 3. eye, spy 4. espy, heed, mark, mind, tend, time, wake (funeral) 5. guard, vigil 6. ambush, patrol, police, sentry 7. bivouac, lookout, observe 8. horologe, sentinel 9. ambuscade, timepiece, vigilance 11. chronometer, observation, wakefulness

watch (pert to) ...
chain .. 3. fob 6. Albert
face .. 5. bezel
maker .. 10. horologist
military .. 5. perdu (perdue) 6. sentry 7. vedette
stop .. 5. timer
tower .. 6. beacon 7. atalaya, mirador 10. lighthouse
word .. 6. signal 10. shibboleth (Bib) 11. countersign
works .. 10. escapement

watchful ... 3. Ira (Heb) 4. wary 5. alert, aware 7. careful, heedful 8. cautious, open-eyed, vigilant 9. observant, regardful 11. circumspect

watchman ... 5. guard 6. sentry, warder 8. sentinel, watchdog 10. gatekeeper

watchword ... 4. hint, word 6. signal 8. party cry 10. intimation, shibboleth (Bib) 11. countersign

watchworks ... 10. escapement

water ... 3. eau, ice, wet 4. aqua, rain 5. fluid, flume, spray 6. dilute, lagoon, liquid 7. moisten 8. beverage, calendar, irrigate, sprinkle 10. adulterate

water (pert to) ...
baptismal .. 5. laver
bath .. 7. balneum
bird .. 4. coot, loon 5. diver, ouzel 6. dipper 7. pintail, swimmer 9. merganser
bottle .. 4. olla 6. carafe
buffalo .. 2. ox 7. carabao
channel .. 5. canal, flume 6. strait 8. tailrace
chart .. 10. hydrograph
color (art) .. 9. aquarelle
comb form .. 5. hydro 6. hydato
congealed .. 3. ice 4. snow 5. glacé 6. icicle
course .. 4. clow 5. bayou, gorge, gully 6. nullah, ravine, sluice 9. watergate
cow .. 6. sea cow 7. buffalo, manatee
cure .. 10. hydropathy 12. hydrotherapy
deer .. 10. chevrotain
destitute of .. 9. anhydrous
divination by .. 10. hydromancy
eagle .. 6. osprey
element .. 6. oxygen 8. hydrogen
elephant .. 12. hippopotamus
exhibition .. 8. aquacade
fowl .. 7. pelican
gauge (rain) .. 8. udometer
goddess .. 4. Nina 7. Anahita, Anaitis
hare .. 11. swamp rabbit

heater .. 4. etna
history .. 10. hydrognosy
hog .. 8. capybara
hole .. 5. oasis 6. tinaja 7. alberca
jug .. 4. lota (lotah), olla 5. banga 6. hydria, kalpis
lava .. 12. hellgrammite
lily .. 5. lotus 6. Nuphar 7. Nelumbo 8. Nymphaea, Victoria 11. spatterdock
measure .. 10. hydrometer
meter .. 7. Venturi
mineral .. 5. Vichy 6. Shasta 7. Seltzer
monster .. 6. nicker (fabled)
nymph .. 5. naiad 6. undine 7. Oceanid
of oblivion .. 5. Lethe 12. river of Hades
opossum .. 5. yapok (yapock)
pert to .. 7. aqueous 8. hydatoid
plug .. 3. tap 4. cock, cork 5. faucet, spigot 7. hydrant
pocket .. 6. tinaja
rat .. 4. vole 8. vagabond
reddish (with iron) .. 6. riddam
reservoir (underground) .. 6. cenote
rough .. 4. eddy 5. ocean 6. rapids 7. riptide 8. undertow
sapphire .. 6. iolite 10. saphir d'eau
scorpion .. 4. Nepa 7. Ranatra
search for .. 5. dowse
sheet of .. 5. nappe
spirit .. 3. Nix 5. Ariel, Nixie 6. kelpie, nicker, sprite
spout .. 5. spate 8. gargoyle
sprite .. 3. Nix 5. Nixie
stratum .. 7. aquifer
study, science of .. 9. hydrology 11. hydrography
surface .. 4. ryme
swelling .. 5. edema
turkey .. 9. snakebird
vessel .. 3. jug 4. ewer, lota (lotah), pail 5. cruse, flask 6. bottle, bucket, tinaja 7. pitcher, stamnos 8. decanter
wheel .. 5. noria 6. sakieh (sakiyeh) 7. turbine 8. tympanum
without .. 9. anhydrous

watery ... 8. ichorous

Watling Street (London) ... 6. Galaxy 8. Milky Way 9. Roman road

wattle ... 3. rod 4. beat, flog, plat, wand 5. fence, twist, weave, withe 6. barbel, dewlap, hurdle, lappet 8. caruncle 9. boobyalla, loose flap 10. intertwine, interweave 11. skin process 12. native willow

wattlebird ... 4. crow 10. honey eater 11. brush turkey

Wattle Day ... 7. holiday

wave ... 3. ola, sea, wag 4. flap, tide 5. crest, eagre, flood, ridge, surge, swell, tilde 6. beckon, billow, comber, flaunt, hairdo, marcel, ripple, roller, signal 7. breaker, decuman, flutter, tsunami, vibrate 8. brandish, coiffure, flourish, greeting, undulate 9. fluctuate, vibration 10. undulation

waver ... 4. reel, sway, veer 5. demur, quake 6. falter, quiver, totter 7. flicker, flutter, stagger, tremble, vibrate 8. hesitate 9. fluctuate, oscillate, vacillate 12: be indecisive

wavering ... 6. fickle 8. doubtful,

unsteady 9. desultory 10. irresolute

wavy ... 4. onde, undé (undee) 5. curly,
snaky 6. repand, undate 7. billowy,
rolling, sinuous 8. undulant
9. undulated 10. undulatory

wax ... 4. cere, grow 6. candle, cerate,
polish 7. beeswax, cerumen 8. increase,
paraffin 9. lubricant, lubricate
12. zietrisikite (mineral)

wax (pert to) ...
beeswax cells .. 9. honeycomb
beeswax substitute .. 7. ceresin
candle .. 6. cierge
chemical .. 9. adipocere
Chinese .. 4. pela
molded in .. 7. fictile 9. ceroplast
ref to .. 5. ceral
substance .. 5. cerin

way ... 3. via 4. lane, mode, path, plan,
ramp, road 5. alley, habit, means, Milky,
route, track 6. avenue, course, manner,
method, street 7. highway, passage
8. causeway, distance, sidewalk
9. banquette, direction, procedure

way (pert to) ...
astronomy .. 6. Galaxy 8. Milky Way
give .. 5. break, yield 6. weaken
7. despair 10. depreciate
god of .. 6. Hermes
in .. 7. ingress 8. entrance
in a way .. 8. as it were, somewhat
13. theoretically
inclined .. 4. ramp
out .. 4. exit 6. egress, escape
roundabout .. 6. detour

waylay ... 3. rob 5. await, seize
6. ambush, lay for 8. surprise
9. ambuscade

wayward ... 6. unruly 7. erratic, willful
8. perverse, stubborn, untoward
10. capricious, headstrong, refractory
11. disobedient, intractable

weak ... 3. dim, lax, wan 4. pale,
puny, thin, worn 5. faint, frail,
washy 6. dotish, feeble, infirm, sickly,
simple, unwise, watery 7. flaccid,
foolish, fragile, insipid 8. cowardly,
decrepit, fatigued, impotent, wavering
9. enfeebled, exhausted, nerveless,
powerless 10. effeminate 11. debilitated,
ineffective 12. unconvincing

weak (pert to) ...
fish .. 7. totuava 9. gray trout
10. squeteague
hearted .. 6. afraid 7. fearful
12. fainthearted
kneed .. 8. cowardly, yielding
10. irresolute
sister .. 6. coward 8. weakling
11. mollycoddle

weaken ... 3. sap 4. tire 5. break 6. dilute,
impair, lessen, reduce 7. cripple,
disable, exhaust, unnerve 8. enervate
9. undermine 10. debilitate

weakness ... 4. flaw 5. atony, fault
6. defect, foible, liking 7. failing, fatigue,
frailty 8. asthenia, debility 9. cowardice,
impotence, infirmity 10. feebleness,
infirmness 11. decrepitude
12. imperfection 13. powerlessness

weal ... 4. mark, wale, welt 5. ridge,

wheal 6. riches, wealth 7. welfare
9. happiness, well-being
10. commonweal

wealth ... 4. good, weal 5. money
6. assets, mammon, riches 7. capital,
fortune, welfare 8. opulence, property,
treasure 9. abundance, affluence, well-
being 10. prosperity 11. possessions

wealth (pert to) ...
god of .. 6. Plutus
person of .. 6. monied 7. magnate,
opulent 9. plutocrat
pursuit of .. 10. plutomania
study of .. 9. economics, plutology
worship of .. 10. plutolatry

wealthy ... 4. rich 5. ample 8. abundant,
affluent

wealthy (pert to) ...
English slang .. 4. oofy
man .. 5. nabob 10. capitalist
rule by .. 10. plutocracy

wean ... 6. detach 8. alienate, estrange
9. reconcile

weapon ... 3. arm, gat, gun 4. bola, bolo,
celt, club, dart, epee, snee 5. arrow,
knife, lance, rifle, saber (sabre), spear,
sword 6. dagger, musket, pistol, poleax
(poleaxe), rapier 7. bayonet, bazooka,
carbine, gisarme, halberd, machete,
trident 8. battle-ax (battle-axe), catapult,
crossbow, revolver, stiletto, tomahawk
9. derringer, Excalibur 11. blunderbuss

wear ... 3. use 4. bear, fray, fret,
show 5. chafe, weary 7. fatigue
12. disintegrate

wear (pert to) ...
away .. 3. eat, end 5. erode 6. abrade
7. corrode, decline
down .. 4. tire 8. persuade 9. influence
out .. 4. tire 5. waste 7. fatigue

weariness ... 5. ennui 6. tedium
7. boredom, fatigue 9. lassitude

wearisome ... 4. hard 6. boring, dismal,
dreary, tiring 7. irksome, tedious
8. tiresome, toilsome 9. fatiguing,
laborious, vexatious 10. monotonous

weary ... 3. fag, irk, sad 4. bore, jade,
pall, tire, weak 5. bored, spent, tired
6. plague 7. fatigue, languid 9. forjesket

weasel ... 4. stot, vare 5. ratel, stoat
6. ermine, ferret

weasellike ... 4. mink 5. otter, tayra
9. musteline, musteloid

weather (pert to) ...
cock .. 4. vane
glass .. 9. barometer, baroscope
man .. 13. meteorologist
map .. 6. isobar

weave ... 4. mat 4. knit, lace, reel,
spin, sway 5. plait, unite 6. devise,
wattle 7. canelle, entwine, fashion
8. contrive 9. fabricate, interlace,
interwind 10. intertwine, intertwist
11. push one's way

weaver bird ... 4. baya, maya, taha
5. Munia

weaving (pert to) ...
art of .. 4. loom
fabric (rich) .. 3. web 7. brocade, webbing
French .. 5. lisse 8. Jacquard
material .. 5. reeds, twigs 6. raffia

term.. 4. beam, dent, loom, sley 7. shuttle
together.. 7. plexure
weazen (wizen)... 6. shrink, wither 7. shrivel
web... 3. net, ply 4. caul, tela, trap, veil, warp 5. snare 6. tissue 7. network, texture 8. filament, gossamer, membrane, vexillum 12. entanglement
web (pert to)...
footed.. 7. palmate
like.. 4. lacy 5. telar 7. spidery
spinning.. 6. telary 7. retiary
term.. 5. telar
toed.. 11. totipalmate
winged.. 3. bat
work.. 4. maze, mesh 6. tangle 11. Gordian knot
wed... 3. join, mate 5. marry, mated, unite 6. joined 7. espouse, pledged, spliced 13. give in wedlock
wedding... 8. ceremony, espousal, marriage, nuptials
wedding (anniversary)...
1st.. 5. paper
2nd.. 5. straw
3rd.. 5. candy
4th.. 7. leather
5th.. 6. wooden
7th.. 6. floral
10th.. 3. tin
12th.. 5. linen
13th.. 4. lace
15th.. 7. crystal
20th.. 5. china
25th.. 6. silver
30th.. 5. pearl
35th.. 5. coral
40th.. 7. emerald
45th.. 4. ruby
50th.. 6. golden
75th.. 7. diamond
wedding (pert to)...
flower.. 13. orange blossom
proclamation.. 5. banns (bans)
snow.. 4. rice
term.. 7. marital, wedlock 8. marriage, nuptials 9. matrimony 11. espousement
wedge... 3. jam 4. club, shoe 5. cleat, ingot, split 6. sector, wedgie 7. niblick 8. triangle, voussoir 9. machinery
wedge-shaped... 7. cuneate 9. cuneiform (cuniform)
Wednesday... 5. Woden (wise god) 9. fourth day, Woden's Day
wee... 3. bit 4. dock, fine, tiny 5. small, teeny 6. little, minute 10. diminutive, teeny-weeny
weed... 3. bur (burr), hoe, rag 4. loco, milk, sida, tare 5. cigar, flesh, vetch 6. darnel, excise, Jimson, knawel, spurge, tumble 7. allseed, mallows, mustard, ragweed, tobacco 8. plantain, purslane, toadflax 9. cultivate, dandelion 11. undergrowth
weeds... 8. garments (mourning)
week... 8. hebdomad 9. seven days
week (pert to)...
day.. 6. ferial
Eccl.. 4. Holy 7. Passion

of Sundays.. 5. seven 8. hebdomad
of years.. 5. seven
past.. 10. yesterweek
weekly... 5. aweek 10. hebdomadal, periodical 11. publication
weeks, two... 9. fortnight
weel... 4. pooi, trap 6. basket 8. fish trap
ween... 5. think 6. expect 7. believe, imagine, suppose 8. conceive
weep... 3. cry, orp, sob 4. drip, rain, wail 5. exude, mourn 7. blubber, lapwing 9. percolate, shed tears
weeping... 6. crying 7. sobbing 9. festering
weeping (pert to)...
monkey.. 8. capuchin
queen.. 5. Niobe
tree.. 5. cedar 6. spruce, willow
Weeping Philosopher (anc)... 10. Heraclitus
weevil (pert to)...
cotton.. 4. boll
malt.. 4. boud
snout.. 8. curculio
type (other).. 3. pea 4. palm, pine, rice, seed 5. flour
weigh... 4. tare, test 5. hoist, poise, scale 6. ponder, regard 7. balance, be heavy, compare, measure 8. consider, encumber, estimate, ruminate 9. apportion, press hard
weigh down... 4. lade, load 6. burden, hamper 7. ballast, depress, oppress 11. overbalance
weight... 4. load, mass 5. force, power 6. burden, import, moment 7. gravity, tonnage 8. encumber, pressure 9. authority, heaviness, influence 10. importance 11. consequence 12. significance
weight (pert to)...
allowance.. 4. tare, tret 7. scalage
comb form.. 4. baro
gem.. 5. carat (karat)
light.. 6. suttle
system.. 3. net 4. troy 6. metric 10. apothecary 11. avoirdupois
total.. 5. gross
weighty... 3. fat 5. bulky, heavy, hefty, large, obese 6. solemn 7. massive, onerous, serious 8. forcible, powerful 9. corpulent, important, momentous, ponderous 10. burdensome, cumbersome, impressive, oppressive 11. influential 13. authoritative
weir... 3. dam, net 4. bank 5. fence, levee, seine 7. barrier, milldam 9. floodgate
weird... 3. odd 4. omen, wild 5. eerie (eery), queer, scary 6. creepy, spooky 7. awesome, curious, ghostly, macabre, strange, uncanny 8. eldritch 9. deathlike, frightful 10. mysterious, prediction
Weird Sisters (Scot)... 5. Fates
welcome... 4. hail 5. adopt, greet 7. acclaim, accueil 8. grateful, greeting, pleasing 9. agreeable, bienvenue, desirable 10. acceptable, salutation
weld... 5. unite 11. consolidate
welfare... 4. good, weal 5. Salus

(goddess) 9. good cheer 10. prosperity
14. material plenty

welkin . . . 3. air, sky 6. heaven
10. atmosphere

well . . . 3. fit, gay, pit 4. gush, hale, pool
5. aweel, fount, fully 6. easily, gusher,
hearty, justly, kindly, source 7. cistern,
closely 8. artesian, expertly, fountain,
friendly 10. full degree, intimately
11. excellently 12. satisfactory

well (pert to) . . .
being . . 4. weal 7. comfort 8. eucrasia
9. happiness
Bib . . 4. Esek
born . . 5. noble 7. eugenic
bred . . 6. polite 7. genteel, refined
8. cultured, wellborn 9. pedigreed
10. cultivated 11. gentlemanly
12. thoroughbred
comb form . . 4. mene
defined . . 8. distinct 11. distinctive
groomed . . 4. neat 5. sleek 6. soigné
(soignée)
grounded . . 5. valid 7. logical 9. plausible
11. established, substantial 12. well-
informed
gushing . . 8. artesian
heeled . . 4. rich 5. armed 7. moneyed,
wealthy, well-off 8. well-to-do
known . . 6. famous 7. eminent
12. acknowledged
land drain . . 4. sump
lining . . 5. steen
off . . 5. lucky 10. prosperous
oil . . 6. gusher
pole . . 5. sweep
prefix . . 2. eu
timed . . 6. timely 9. opportune
versed . . 7. erudite
watered . . 9. irrigated, irriguous

welsh (welch) . . 5. cheat 6. not pay,
renege 7. swindle 10. shirk out of

Welsh (pert to) . . . see also *Wales*
boat . . 7. coracle
congress of literati . . 10. eisteddfod
fine, for murder . . 7. galanas
god, underworld . . 4. Bran
instrument (reed) . . 7. pibcorn
man . . 5. Taffy 8. Cambrian
onion . . 5. cibal
population . . 6. Cymric
rabbit . . 7. ramekin (ramequin), rarebit
romance collection . . Mabinogion
(Mabinogi)

welt . . 4. mark, wale 5. ridge 6. stripe,
thrash

welter . . . 4. reel, roll, sail, toss 6. grovel,
tumble, wallow 7. stagger 8. flounder,
overturn 9. confusion

wen . . 4. cyst, rune 5. tumor 7. blemish
11. excrescence 12. protuberance

wench . . . 4. doxy, gill, girl 5. child,
squaw, trull, woman 6. damsel,
maiden 7. consort, servant 8. strumpet
11. maidservant

wend . . . 2. go 4. fare, pass 6. depart,
direct, travel 7. circuit, proceed
8. progress

went (pert to) . . . see also *go*
astray . . 6. failed 10. miscarried
away . . 4. left 8. departed

before . . 3. led 8. preceded 9. anteceded
swiftly . . 3. ran 4. sped 6. darted
7. scooted, scudded 8. decamped

wenzel . . . 4. jack (card game) 5. knave

werewolf . . . 6. jaguar 8. uturuncu,
werefolk 11. lycanthrope

wergild . . . 3. cro 4. eric 7. galanas
9. Brehon Law

Wesleyan . . . 9. Methodist 14. Wesley
follower

West African (pert to) . . .
baboon . . 5. drill 8. mandrill
city . . 5. Accra, Dakar
gazelle . . 4. kudu, mohr (mhorr), oryx
lemur . . 5. potto 8. kinkajou
monkey . . 4. mona 6. guenon
native . . 5. Ashanti (Ashantee)
people . . 5. Igara
pepper . . 5. cubeb
tree . . 5. iroko, odoom

West End, London . . . 7. Mayfair
9. Belgravia 11. fashionable
12. aristocratic

Western . . . 9. Hesperian 10. Occidental

Westernmost US . . . 9. Aleutians 11. Attu
islands 12. Cape Wrangell

West Indies . . .
bird . . 4. tody 6. mucaro
boat . . 7. drogher (droger)
chief . . 7. cacique
clingfish . . 6. testar
crop . . 5. sugar 7. bananas
ebony . . 9. cocuswood
fish . . 4. cero, paru, sesi 6. testar
flea . . 6. chigoe
fruit . . 5. papaw (pawpaw)
islands . . 4. Cuba 5. Haiti 6. Cayman,
Virgin 7. Antigua, Bahamas, Leeward
8. Antilles, Windward
liquor . . 5. mobby (mobbie), tafia (taffia)
lizard . . 6. arbalo
magic . . 5. obeah
music . . 7. calypso
owl . . 6. mucaro
resident . . 9. Antillean
rodent . . 6. agouti (agouty)
snuff . . 8. Maccaboy
tea . . 8. goatweed
tortoise . . 7. hicatee
tree . . 4. ausu 5. ebony, papaw 6. bonduc
8. bayberry 9. sapodilla, satinwood
volcano . . 5. Pelée
wood . . 9. cocuswood, sapodilla
10. granadilla

Westminster clock (London) . . . 6. Big
Ben

West Pointer . . . 5. cadet, plebe
8. yearling

West Point motto . . . 16. Duty, Honor,
Country

West Virginia . . .
capital . . 10. Charleston
city . . 5. Logan 8. Wheeling
11. Parkersburg
crop . . 4. coal
mountain . . 10. Spruce Knob
11. Alleghenies
park (famed) . . 12. Harpers Ferry
river . . 4. Ohio 7. Kanawha
11. Monongahela
Springs (resort) . . 8. Berkeley 12. White

Sulphur
State admission.. 11. Thirty-fifth
State motto.. 19. Montani Semper Liberi
  22. Mountaineers Always Free
State nickname.. 8. Mountain
West wind... 8. Favonius, Zephyrus
wet... 4. asop, damp, dank, dewy,
  rain 5. foggy, humid, leach, misty,
  moist, mushy, rainy, soggy, soppy
  6. dampen, drench, soaked, sodden,
  watery 7. moisten 8. sprinkle
wet blanket... 7. kill-joy 8. deadhead
  10. discourage, spoilsport
whale... 3. orc 4. cete, lash, whip
  5. whack 6. beluga, blower, thrash
  7. grampus, ripsack 8. hardhead
  9. zeuglodon 13. sulphur-bottom
whale (pert to)...
Arctic.. 7. narwhal
bird.. 4. gull 6. petrel 9. phalarope
blubber pot.. 6. try-pot
blue.. 8. Sibbaldus
bone.. 6. baleen
carcass.. 5. kreng
constellation.. 5. Cetus
fat.. 7. blubber
food.. 4. brit
gray.. 7. ripsack 8. hardhead
killer.. 4. orca
killer of.. 8. ceticide
legendary.. 9. Mysticeti
monster.. 4. Cete
mustache (legend).. 9. Mysticeti
Order.. 7. Cetacea
ref to.. 5. cetic, sperm 6. baleen
  7. blubber 8. cetacean
school of.. 3. gam, pod
secretion (perfume).. 9. ambergris
small .: 7. grampus
sperm type.. 8. cachalot
study of.. 8. cetology
toothed.. 10. odontocete, zeuglodont
type.. 3. orc 4. blue, orca 5. right, sperm
  6. killer 7. dolphin, rorqual 8. cachalot,
  humpback, porpoise 9. whalebone
wax.. 10. spermaceti
whalebone.. 6. baleen 10. stiffening
young.. 4. calf 9. shorthead
wharf... 4. dock, pier, quay 5. jetty
  6. staith 7. landing
wharf (pert to)...
fish.. 6. cunner
master.. 10. wharfinger
worker.. 9. stevedore
whatnot... 5. thing 6. object
  (nondescript) 7. étagère 10. miscellany
what's what... 4. fact 5. truth 7. reality
  10. what's right
what wonders has God wrought (Arabic
  exclamation)... 9. mashallah
whaup... 6. curlew, outcry 9. scoundrel
wheal... 4. wale, weal, welt 5. whelk
  6. stripe 7. pustule
wheat (pert to)...
beard.. 3. awn
beverage.. 6. zythem
bird.. 4. lark 8. wheatear 9. chaffinch
chaff.. 4. bran
duck.. 7. widgeon 8. baldpate
Europe.. 5. emmer, spelt (speltz)
flour.. 4. atta 5. Hovis

hard.. 5. durum
India.. 4. suji 8. semolina
storage bin.. 4. silo 8. elevator
wheedle... 4. coax, gain 5. tease
  6. banter, cajole, entice 7. blarney,
  flatter 8. blandish, inveigle, persuade
  9. influence
wheel... 3. cam, cog 4. bike, disc, helm,
  ride, roll, rota 5. drive, pivot, rotor,
  rowel, whirl 6. caster, roller, rotate
  7. bicycle, revolve, rotator, torture,
  vehicle 8. tricycle 10. water wheel
wheel (pert to)...
gem-grinding.. 5. skive
hub.. 4. nave
man.. 5. pilot 7. cyclist 8. helmsman,
  pedalist 9. bicyclist
monkey.. 3. gin
part.. 3. rim 5. felly (felloe), spoke
  6. hubcap
pulley.. 6. sheave
shaped.. 8. circular, rotiform
spoke.. 6. radius
spur.. 5. rowel
stopper.. 4. grig 5. sprag
swiveled.. 6. caster
toothed.. 3. cog 4. gear 6. pinion
turbine.. 5. rotor
type.. 3. cog, fly, pin 4. cart, mill, spur
  5. wagon 6. Ferris, paddle 7. balance,
  potter's 9. of fortune
water.. 5. noria 6. sakieh (sakiyeh)
wheels, logging... 7. katydid
wheen... 3. few 5. group 7. several
  8. division, quantity
wheerikins... 10. posteriors
wheetle... 5. chirp 7. whistle
wheeze... 3. gag 4. joke 5. hoose (hooze)
  6. cliché, saying 7. breathe 8. sibilate
  9. witticism 10. sibilation
whelk... 4. acne 5. snail 6. papule,
  pimple 7. pustule
whelp... 3. boy, cub, pup 5. child, puppy,
  tiger, youth 8. give birth, youngling
when... 2. as 3. tho 5. until 6. though
  7. how soon, whereas 8. although,
  whenever 10. how long ago 11. at
  which time
where... 4. here, spot 5. place, there
  7. whither 10. inasmuch as 11. at what
  place, whereabouts
whereas... 5. since
whereby... 7. perquod
whereness... 6. ubiety
whereupon... 4. when 7. on which
  9. upon which 10. after which
wherewithal... 5. means, money
  9. resources
whet... 4. hone 5. grind, point,
  rouse 6. excite 7. quicken, sharpen
  9. intensify, stimulate
whether... 2. if 6. either
whey... 4. curd 5. serum
whiff... 4. blow, fish, gust, odor, puff,
  waft 6. breath, exhale, stanch 7. puff
  out 8. blow away 10. inhalation
while... 2. as 3. yet 4. time 5. until
  7. beguile, interim, whereas 11. space
  of time
whilom... 4. erst, once 5. of old 6. former
  8. sometime 9. erstwhile

whim . . . 3. fad, pun, toy 4. idea
5. fancy, freak 6. megrim, notion,
vagary 7. boutade, caprice, whimsey
(whimsy), widgeon 8. migraine

whimper . . . 3. cry, sob 4. mewl, moan,
pule, weep 5. whine 7. sniffle

whimsey, whimsy . . . 3. wit 4. whim
5. craze, fancy, freak 7. caprice

whimsical . . . 3. fad, odd 4. dish 5. droll,
queer, witty 7. amusing 8. fanciful,
freakish, notional 9. crotchety, eccentric,
fantastic, grotesque 10. capricious

whine . . . 4. moan, pule, wail 6. snivel
7. screech, ululate, whimper 8. complain
12. moaning sound

whinny . . . 4. bray 5. neigh, whine

whip . . . 3. cat, tan 4. beat, crop,
flag, flog, goad, lace, lash, wale
5. birch, froth, quirt, seize, spank,
strap 6. defeat, incite, punish, strike,
swinge, thrash 7. agitate, chabouk
(chabuk), conquer, scourge 8. emulsify,
lambaste 9. bullwhack 10. discipline
11. congressman

whip (pert to) . . .
hand . . 8. dominion 9. advantage,
  influence
mark . . 4. wale, weal, welt
political . . 5. party 11. floor leader
riding . . 4. crop 5. quirt
Russian . . 4. plet (plete) 5. knout
sewing . . 8. overcast
socket . . 5. snead

whir . . . 3. fly 4. burr, buzz, whiz 5. hurry,
swirl, whizz 6. hurtle 7. revolve, vibrate
9. commotion

whirl . . . 4. eddy, reel, spin, tirl, turn
5. twirl 6. circle, gyrate, rotate 7. revelry,
revolve 9. commotion, pirouette, turn
about 10. excitement

whirlpool . . . 4. eddy 6. gurges (Her),
vortex 7. sea puss (sea purse)
9. maelstrom

whirlwind . . . 2. oe (Faroes) 7. cyclone,
tornado, twister, typhoon 9. hurricane,
maelstrom 10. willy-willy

whisk . . . 3. tuft, whip, wist 5. froth,
sweep, swish 6. convey 7. agitate

whiskers . . . 4. chin 5. beard 8. vibrissa
9. sideburns

whisky, whiskey . . . 3. rye 4. corn
6. poteen, redeye 9. moonshine
10. usquebaugh

whisky (pert to) . . .
base . . 3. rye 5. wheat 6. barley
drink . . 4. soda, sour 5. punch, smash
  7. stinger
Insurrection . . 12. Pennsylvania (1794)
Ring . . 10. Conspiracy (1875)
term . . 6. lively 7. flighty

whisper . . . 3. tip 4. blow, buzz 5. rumor
6. breeze, murmur 7. divulge 14. vox
clandestina

whist, game . . . 9. Cavendish
10. Yarborough

whistle . . . 4. hiss, pipe, sing, toot
5. alarm 6. rustle, warble, wheeze
12. interference

whistle (pert to) . . .
duck . . 9. goldeneye
fish . . 8. rockling

pig . . 9. woodchuck
stop . . 12. one-horse town
tree (for boys' whistles) . . 5. maple
  6. willow

whistling (pert to) . . .
coot . . 5. scoter
dick . . 6. thrush
duck . . 6. scoter 9. goldeneye
hawk . . 5. eagle
snipe . . 8. woodcock
sound . . 7. stridor
teal . . 6. scoter 8. tree duck

whit . . . 3. bit, jot 4. atom, iota 5. bodle,
speck 8. particle

white . . . 3. wan 4. milk, pale, snow
5. ashen, chalk, color, happy, ivory,
snowy 6. albino, chalky, chaste, honest,
pallid 7. ivorine, silvery 8. innocent,
platinum 9. alabaster, albescent,
Caucasian, favorable, fortunate,
honorable 11. snow-covered

white (pert to) . . .
admiral . . 9. butterfly
ant . . 4. anay (anai) 7. termite
belly . . 6. pigeon 7. widgeon 14. prairie
  chicken
cat . . 7. catfish
cell . . 9. leucocyte
chub . . 10. spawneater
cloud . . 6. cirrus 7. tendril
coal . . 10. water power
crow . . 7. vulture
curlew . . 4. ibis
devil . . 7. nailrod
elephant . . 6. burden 8. Oriental
ensign . . 12. British naval
fish . . 5. cisco 6. atinga, beluga
  8. menhaden 9. Coregonus 10. white
  whale
grouse . . 9. ptarmigan
growing (hoary) . . 9. canescent
head . . 6. pigeon 9. blue goose 10. surf
  scoter
heat . . 5. anger 13. incandescence
livered . . 6. feeble 8. cowardly
  13. pusillanimous
matter (nerve) . . 4. alba
merganser . . 4. smew
miller . . 11. clothes moth
monk . . 10. Cistercian
mule . . 3. gin 6. whisky (illicit)
  9. moonshine
oak . . 5. roble
of egg . . 5. glair
partridge . . 9. ptarmigan
person . . 9. Caucasian
plague . . 7. disease 8. phthisis
  11. consumption 12. tuberculosis
plantain . . 8. pussytoe
poplar . . 5. aspen
pot . . 7. pudding
pudding . . 7. sausage 9. whitehass
pyrite . . 9. marcasite
shark . . 8. man-eater
throat . . 6. muffet (Eng) 7. warbler
whale . . 6. beluga

White (pert to) . . .
Chapel (Jewish) . . 13. London Quarter
Holland . . 6. turkey
Horse . . 6. emblem (Saxons) 7. carving
House designer . . 5. Hoban

Relig.. 6. Friars 7. Fathers, Sisters 8. Brethren
Rose (Eng).. 6. emblem (House of York)
Sands (N Mex).. 13. proving ground
Squadron.. 4. Navy (US Navy 1883)
Tower.. 13. Tower of London
whiten ... 6. blanch, bleach 8. etiolate 9. whitewash
whitewash ... 5. paint 6. defeat, whiten 7. conceal 9. disinfect, exculpate, gloss over
whither ... 5. where 7. whereto 11. to what place, whereabouts
whiting ... 4. fish 5. chalk 6. tomcod 10. butterfish
whitish ... 4. pale 5. white 9. albescent
whitlow ... 4. herb, sore 5. felon 6. agnail, fetlow 8. hangnail 9. saxifrage 10. paronychia 12. inflammation
Whitsunday ... 9. Pentecost
Whittington, Dick ... 9. Lord Mayor (London)
whittle ... 3. cut, hew 4. gash, hack, pare, trim 5. knife 6. reduce 7. blanket
whiz, whizz ... 3. hum 4. buzz, hiss, pirr, whir, zizz 5. whirr 6. corker, rotate 8. sibilate 10. speed along 12. clever person
who ... 3. wer, wha 5. which 6. person 7. one that, pronoun
whole ... 3. all, sum 4. pure, sole, unit 5. gross, total, uncut, unity 6. entire, intact, mostly, system 7. healthy, perfect 8. absolute, complete, entirety, totality 9. aggregate, generally, unanimous, undivided
whole (pert to) ...
    comb form.. 4. toti, toto
    footed.. 5. frank 8. intimate 9. ingenuous 10. flat-footed
    hearted.. 7. devoted, earnest, sincere 8. complete 10. unreserved 11. unmitigated
    hog.. 8. whole way 12. all or nothing
    note.. 9. semibreve
    number.. 7. integer
    skinned.. 6. unhurt 9. unscathed
    souled.. 7. noble 7. devoted, sincere, zealous 11. noble-minded 12. wholehearted
wholesome ... 4. sane 5. sound 6. hearty, robust 7. healthy 8. salutary, vigorous 9. favorable, healthful 10. beneficial, propitious, salubrious
wholly ... 3. all 4. toto (comb form) 5. fully, quite 6. solely 7. totally 8. entirely, entirety 9. perfectly 10. altogether, completely, thoroughly 11. exclusively
whoop ... 4. call, hoot, urge, yell 5. cheer, shout 6. halloo, hoopee 10. enthusiasm
whooping cough ... 9. pertussis
whoop it up ... 7. be noisy 8. energize 9. make merry 12. create gaiety
whop ... 4. bang, beat, bump, fall, flop, whip 5. knock 6. strike, stroke
whopper ... 3. lie (monstrous) 5. story (false)
whorl ... 4. curl 5. helix, spire 8. flywheel, verticil, volution (shell) 11. fingerprint
wicked ... 3. bad, ill 4. evil, vile 6. guilty,

sinful, unjust 7. heinous, hellish, profane, roguish, ungodly, vicious 8. criminal, depraved, devilish, diabolic, flagrant 9. abandoned, atrocious, malicious, nefarious, perverted 10. diabolical, flagitious, iniquitous, villainous 11. irreligious, mischievous, unrighteous
wickedness ... 3. sin 4. evil 6. Belial (Bib) 7. badness 8. baseness, iniquity 10. sinfulness 13. maliciousness
wicked one ... 5. Demon, Satan 7. Evil One 8. The Devil
wicker (pert to) ...
    basket.. 5. cesta 6. hamper, kipsey 7. pannier
    cradle.. 8. bassinet
    material.. 5. twigs 6. osiers, willow, withes
    ware.. 8. basketry, plaiting
wicket ... 4. arch, door, gate, hoop 6. grille, window 7. grating, guichet, lattice 8. loophole 12. grated window, ticket window
wickiup, wikiup ... 3. hut 7. shelter
Widal's, Widal reaction ... 16. typhoid fever test
widbin ... 7. dogwood 8. woodbine 11. honeysuckle
widdy ... 4. rope (twig) 5. noose, widow, withy 6. halter 7. gallows 11. gallows bird
wide ... 5. ample, broad, large, loose, roomy 6. opened 7. liberal 8. expanded, spacious 9. capacious, distended 13. comprehensive
wide-awake ... 3. hat 4. keen, tern (sooty) 5. alert 7. knowing 8. watchful
wide-eyed ... 5. agog 6. naive 9. amazed 9. surprised
widemouthed ... 4. loud 5. noisy 6. greedy 7. barking 9. devouring
widen ... 4. ream 6. dilate, expand, extend, spread 7. amplify, broaden, enlarge
widespread ... 4. rife 5. broad 7. diffuse, general 8. not local, sweeping 9. dispersed, extensive, prevalent, scattered, universal 13. comprehensive
widgeon ... 4. duck, smee 5. goose 6. Mareca, zuisin 7. poacher 8. baldpate 9. simpleton
widow ... 6. relict 7. bereave, dowager, viduate
widow (pert to) ...
    bird.. 5. finch, Vidua 6. whidah
    cremated.. 6. suttee
    fish.. 5. viuva
    monkey.. 4. titi
    suicide.. 6. suttee
widower ... 6. relict
widow's (pert to) ...
    lock.. 8. hairline 10. widow's peak
    mite.. 4. coin 6. lepton
    portion.. 5. dower
    right.. 5. terce
    weeds.. 8. mourning 9. black veil, widowhood
width ... 5. girth 7. breadth 8. diameter, latitude, wideness
wield ... 3. ply, use 4. cope, deal, rule

5. power, swing **6.** direct, employ, handle, manage **7.** control **8.** brandish **10.** manipulate

wife . . . 4. frau, mate, rani, uxor **5.** bride, mujer **6.** matron, spouse **7.** consort **8.** gudewife (guidwife), helpmate, helpmeet **10.** better half **12.** married woman

wife (pert to) . . .
French . . **5.** femme
killing . . **9.** uxoricide
of a rajah . . **4.** Rani (Ranee)
one . . **8.** monogamy
pert to . . **7.** uxorial
slave's . . **9.** broadwife

wig . . . 4. tête **5.** jasey **6.** peruke, toupee **7.** censure, periwig **8.** seal hood **9.** dignitary

wight . . . 3. man **4.** loud **5.** brave, fairy, swift, witch **6.** active, nimble **7.** valiant **8.** creature, powerful **11.** living being

wigwag . . . 6. signal **8.** to and fro **11.** oscillation

wigwam . . . 4. tent **5.** hogan, tepee **6.** teepee

wild . . . 3. mad **5.** feral, myall, waste, weird **6.** ferine, savage, stormy, unruly **7.** bestial, howling, riotous **8.** aberrant, desolate, dramatic, frenetic, reckless, untilled, wildwood **9.** barbarian, barbarous, ferocious, imprudent, primitive, unbridled, uncertain **10.** boisterous, chimerical, irrational, profligate, tumultuous, unexplored, wilderness **11.** harum-scarum, uncivilized, uninhabited **12.** obstreperous, uncontrolled, uncultivated **14.** uncontrollable

wild (pert to) . . .
alder . . **8.** goutweed
animal . . **3.** gnu **4.** bear, deer, lion, lynx **5.** kiang, moose, tiger **6.** dragon, onager **7.** polecat **8.** antelope **9.** wildebeest
banana . . **5.** papaw (pawpaw)
beasts . . **4.** ziim
buffalo . . **4.** arna **5.** arnee
carrot . . **8.** hilltrot
cat . . **4.** balm, eyra **6.** ocelot **7.** panther
coffee . . **9.** feverroot
crocus . . **12.** pasqueflower
fancy . . **6.** vagary
fowl . . **4.** duck **5.** goose, quail **8.** pheasant **9.** partridge
garlic . . **4.** moly
goat . . **3.** tur **4.** tahr **7.** markhor (markhoor)
gourd . . **7.** pumpkin **11.** calabazilla
growing . . **8.** agrarian
hog . . **4.** boar **5.** razorback **10.** babiroussa
hop . . **6.** bryony
horse . . **6.** tarpan
ibex . . **5.** Capra
Irishman (shrub) . . **10.** tumatakuru
jalap . . **8.** mayapple
mustard . . **8.** charlock
ox . . **3.** yak **4.** anoa
pieplant . . **7.** rhubarb
pineapple . . **7.** pinguin
plum . . **4.** sloe **5.** islay
sheep . . **3.** sha **5.** urial (oorial) **6.** argali
sweet potato . . **7.** manroot

West show . . **5.** rodeo
wildebeest . . . 3. gnu
wilderness . . . 5. waste, wilds **6.** forest **8.** wildwood **9.** confusion **12.** complication

wile . . . 3. art, toy **4.** lure, ruse **5.** fraud, guile, trick **6.** deceit **7.** cunning **8.** artifice, trickery **9.** stratagem

will . . . 4. wish **6.** behest, choice, decree, demise, desire **7.** bequest, command **8.** volition **9.** intention, testament **10.** resolution **11.** disposition, inclination **13.** determination

will (pert to) . . .
appendix . . **7.** codicil
convey . . **6.** demise **7.** bequest
having made . . **7.** testate
maker of . . **8.** testator
power . . **7.** purpose **10.** resolution **13.** determination **14.** strength of mind
proof of . . **7.** probate
to live (Buddh) . . **5.** tanha

willful, wilful . . . 3. mad **4.** rash **5.** heady **7.** wayward **8.** perverse, stubborn **9.** impetuous, obstinate, voluntary **11.** intentional **14.** self-determined

willing . . . 4. free **5.** prone, ready **6.** minded **8.** desirous, disposed, unforced **9.** agreeable, voluntary **10.** consenting, deliberate, ready to act, volitional **11.** intentional **12.** well-disposed

willingly . . . 4. fain, lief **6.** freely, gladly **7.** happily, readily **10.** cheerfully **12.** with pleasure

willow . . . 3. iva **4.** Itea **5.** osier, salix **6.** sallow, teaser

willow (pert to) . . .
basket . . **7.** prickle
genus . . **5.** Salix
green . . **6.** reseda
lark . . **12.** sedge warbler
pattern . . **7.** Nanking **11.** earthenware
twig . . **5.** withe **6.** sallow
wren . . **10.** chiffchaff

willowy . . . 5. lithe **6.** pliant, supple, svelte **7.** slender **8.** flexible, graceful **15.** tall and graceful

Will Rogers' plane . . . 9. Winnie May

wilsome . . . 4. wild **6.** astray, dreary **7.** violent, willful (wilful) **8.** desolate **10.** bewildered

wilt . . . 3. sag **4.** flag, tire **5.** droop, quail **6.** sicken, wither **8.** languish **11.** deteriorate, lose courage, make flaccid

Wilton . . . 3. rug **6.** carpet

wily . . . 3. sly **4.** foxy **5.** canny, smart **6.** artful, astute, crafty, shrews, subtle **7.** cunning **9.** cautelous

wimble . . . 3. awl **4.** bore **5.** auger, brace, scoop, twist **6.** gimlet, pierce **9.** sprightly, whimsical

wimick . . . 3. cry **7.** whimper

wimple . . . 4. fold, veil **7.** meander **8.** covering (head)

win . . . 3. get **4.** earn, gain **5.** to get **6.** attain, defeat, obtain, secure **7.** achieve, acquire, succeed, triumph **8.** be victor, endeavor, vanquish **9.** captivate **10.** accomplish

win (pert to)...
all tricks (game).. 4. slam
by guile.. 8. inveigle
one's spurs.. 10. knighthood
over.. 7. convert 8. convince
persuade.. 10. conciliate

wince.. 4. reel 5. start 6. cringe, flinch,
recoil, shrink 8. draw back, windlass
10. shrink from

wind... 2. oe 3. air 4. bora, coil, gale,
gust, talk, turn, wrap 5. blast, buran,
crank, trade 6. boreal, breath, breeze,
simoom, zephyr 7. chinook, conceit,
cyclone, deviate, etesian, meander,
monsoon, sinuate, sirocco, tempest,
tornado, typhoon 8. convolve, williwaw
9. hurricane, idle words, windstorm
10. instrument

wind (pert to)...
action on land.. 8. eolation
around.. 6. master 8. dominate
9. influence 13. lead by the nose
cloud.. 4. scud
comb form.. 5. anemo
fall.. 7. godsend 8. buckshee, gratuity
flower.. 7. anemone
gauge.. 4. vane 10. anemometer
god.. 4. Adad 6. Aeolus
god of north wind.. 6. Boreas
god of SE wind.. 5. Eurus
instrument.. 3. sax 4. fife, horn
5. flute, organ 6. cornet 7. bassoon,
hautboy, helicon, ocarina 8. clarinet
9. harmonica, saxophone
in the (wind).. 5. drunk 7. sailing
8. imminent 9. happening
into a ball.. 11. agglomerate
personified.. 6. Caurus 7. Caecias
8. Favonius, Zephyrus
ref to.. 7. Aeolian (Eolian)
rose.. 5. poppy
science.. 9. anemology
storm.. 4. gale 7. cyclone, typhoon
9. hurricane
up.. 3. end 7. prepare 8. complete,
conclude
yarn.. 6. windle

wind (type)...
Adriatic (cold).. 4. bora
cold.. 4. bise, bora, puna 7. mistral
8. williwaw
desert.. 6. simoom 7. sirocco
dry.. 9. harmattan
East.. 8. levanter
Egypt.. 7. khamsin (kamsin)
equator.. 5. trade
fierce.. 4. gale 5. buster, squall
7. monsoon 8. blizzard 9. hurricane
gentle.. 4. aura 6. zephyr
Malta (cold).. 7. gregale
Mediterranean.. 6. solano 7. etesian
8. levanter
North.. 6. Boreas
Northwest.. 6. Caurus 7. etesian
Oriental.. 7. monsoon
Peru.. 4. puna
S America.. 4. puna 7. pampero
South.. 6. Auster
Southeast.. 5. Eurus
Southwest.. 7. chinook
Spain.. 6. solano

West (personified).. 8. Favonius
whirl.. 2. oe

windiness... 7. conceit 12. boastfulness

winding... 5. curve, snaky 6. spiral
7. sinuous, twining 8. rambling,
tortuous 9. deviative, meandrous
10. circuitous

windjammer... 6. bugler, talker, vessel
(sailing) 8. bandsman 9. trumpeter

windlass... 4. reel 5. winch 6. windle
7. capstan, machine (hoisting)

windle.. 4. reel 5. winch 6. basket
7. measure, redwing

window (pert to)...
arrangement.. 8. fanlight 12. fenestration
bay.. 5. oriel
dormer, roof.. 5. gable 7. lucarne
8. skylight
frame.. 4. sash
Latin.. 8. fenestra
leading.. 4. came
nautical.. 8. porthole
oval.. 5. oxeye
part.. 4. pane, sash, sill 5. glass
7. shutter
recess.. 6. exedra 9. embrasure
ship's.. 4. port 8. porthole
ticket.. 6. wicket 7. guichet
type.. 4. port 5. gable, oriel 7. eucarne
8. casement, skylight

windpipe... 6. gullet, throat 7. trachea,
weasand

windrow... 5. swath (swathe) 6. furrow

Winds, Father of (Gr)... 8. Astraeus

windward... 5. aloof 6. aweather
9. weatherly

Windy City... 7. Chicago

wine (pert to)...
and honey.. 5. clary, mulse 7. oenomel
Baden.. 8. Ruländer
bag.. 8. wineskin
bibber.. 3. sot 5. toper 7. tippler
8. drunkard
Bordeaux.. 6. claret
bottle.. 6. magnum 8. decanter
cask.. 3. tun
cellar.. 6. bodega
comb form.. 4. oeno
cruet.. 7. burette
cup.. 3. ama 6. goblet 7. chalice
divination by.. 9. oenomancy
dry.. 3. sec
film.. 8. beeswing
French.. 6. Masden, Pontac (Pontacq)
8. muscatel 9. Hermitage
10. Montrachet 12. Saint-Emilion,
Saint-Estèphe
glass.. 6. rummer (Rom)
grower.. 8. vigneron
hater of.. 11. oenophobist
Italian.. 7. Orvieto 8. muscatel
kind.. 4. port 5. Medoc, Rhine, tinta,
Tokay 6. canary, claret, Malaga, sherry
7. Chablis, Madeira 8. Burgundy,
muscatel, sauterne, vermouth
9. champagne
lover of.. 11. oenophilist
maker.. 6. abkari (abkary)
making.. 10. oenopoetic
merchant.. 5. abkar
miracle scene.. 4. Cana (Bib)

palm . . **5.** taree
Persian . . **6.** Shiraz
pitcher . . **4.** olpe **8.** oenochoe
reference to . . **5.** vinic
residue . . **4.** marc
sherry . . **5.** Xeres **7.** Catawba, Moselle, oloroso
shop . . **3.** bar **6.** bistro, bodega
Spain . . **6.** Malaga
sparkling . . **8.** mousseux
study of . . **8.** oenology
sweet . . **5.** lunel
taster . . **10.** oenologist
Tuscan . . **7.** Chianti
white . . **6.** Malaga **8.** Riesling, sauterne, verdelho **12.** Marcobrunner
year . . **7.** vintage
wing . . **3.** ala, arm, fly **6.** convey, flight, member, pinion **7.** faction **8.** addition, dispatch
wing (pert to) . . .
anterior . . **7.** elytron
comb form . . **7.** pterygo
false . . **5.** alula
fish . . **8.** sea robin
footed . . **6.** aliped
Greek . . **6.** pteryx
quill . . **7.** remiges
shaped . . **7.** aliform
tip . . **7.** aileron
winglike . . **4.** alar **7.** pteroid **9.** pterygoid
winged . . . **4.** aile (Her), fast **5.** alate, lofty, rapid, swift **7.** pennate, sublime **9.** aliferous, aligerous
winged (pert to) . . .
boots (of Hermes) . . **7.** talaria
child . . **6.** cherub
fruit . . **6.** samara
monster . . **5.** harpy
Winged Horse (Gr Myth) . . . **7.** Pegasus
Winged Victory . . . **4.** Nike
wingless . . . **7.** apteral, Apteryx, exalate **8.** dealated (dealate)
wink . . . **3.** nap, nod **4.** hint **5.** blink, flash **6.** glance, signal, twitch **7.** flicker, instant, nictate, twinkle **9.** nictation, nictitate, twinkling **10.** palpebrate, periwinkle
winker . . . **3.** eye **7.** blinker, eyelash **8.** blinkard
winking . . . **13.** blepharospasm
winks, forty . . . **3.** nap **6.** catnap **10.** light sleep
winner . . . **3.** ace **6.** earner, reaper, victor **7.** sleeper **8.** bangster **9.** conqueror **11.** breadwinner
winning . . . **7.** gaining, lovable, victory, winsome **8.** alluring, charming **10.** attractive, successful, victorious **11.** acquisition, captivating
winninish, winnonish . . . **6.** salmon (landlocked) **10.** ouananiche
winnock . . . **6.** window
winnow . . . **3.** fan **4.** sift, stir **6.** assort, select, thresh **8.** disperse, separate **9.** eliminate
winsome . . . **3.** gay **5.** bonny, merry **7.** lovable, winning **8.** alluring, charming, cheerful, pleasant **10.** attractive **11.** captivating **12.** lighthearted

winter . . . **4.** bise, snow **5.** hiems **6.** old age, season **8.** coldness
winter (pert to) . . .
beer . . **6.** Schenk
berry . . **4.** Ilex **5.** holly
bloom . . **6.** azalea **10.** witch hazel
bonnet . . **4.** gull
duck . . **7.** pintail **8.** old squaw
fever . . **9.** pneumonia
god . . **5.** Hiems
lettuce . . **6.** endive
mew . . **4.** gull
pert to . . **6.** brumal, hiemal
quarters . . **10.** hibernacle **12.** hibernaculum
sleep . . **11.** hibernation
teal . . **9.** greenwing
Winter Palace (Leningrad) . . . **6.** museum
wipe . . . **3.** dry, mop, rub **5.** cheat, clean, erase **6.** cancel, remove **7.** abolish, defraud **10.** obliterate **11.** exterminate
wire . . . **4.** coil, cord, line, whip **5.** cable, snare **6.** thread **7.** fencing, lametta (gold), netting, reticle **8.** telegram, wirework **9.** cablegram, telegraph **10.** pickpocket **14.** knitting needle
wirepuller . . . **10.** influencer, machinator, politician, strategist
wiry . . . **4.** lean **5.** hardy, stiff, tough **6.** sinewy, strong **7.** stringy **8.** enduring, muscular
wis . . . **5.** think **7.** imagine, suppose
Wisconsin . . .
capital . . **7.** Madison
city . . **6.** Racine **7.** Kenosha, Oshkosh **8.** Green Bay **9.** Fond du Lac, Milwaukee
famed as . . **17.** America's Dairyland
first white man . . **7.** Nicolet (Jean)
lake . . **8.** Michigan, Superior **9.** Winnebago
river . . **7.** St Croix **11.** Mississippi
State admission . . **9.** Thirtieth
State motto . . **7.** Forward
State nickname . . **6.** Badger
wisdom . . . **5.** logos **8.** judgment, learning, sagacity, sapience **9.** erudition, knowledge **10.** discretion, profundity
wisdom god . . . **4.** Nebo (Nabu) **6.** Ganesa (Ganesha)
wisdom goddess . . . **6.** Athena **7.** Minerva (Gr)
wise . . . **3.** hep **4.** sage, sane, wary **5.** aware **6.** shrewd, subtle, versed **7.** erudite, knowing, learned, politic, sapient **8.** discreet, informed, profound **9.** cognizant, expedient, judicious, provident **10.** omniscient **11.** circumspect, enlightened, philosophic **13.** sophisticated
wise (pert to) . . .
councilor . . **6.** mentor, nestor
man . . **4.** sage **5.** solon, witan **6.** nestor, wizard **7.** Solomon
saying . . **4.** rede **5.** adage
Wise Men (three) . . . **6.** Gaspar **8.** Melchior **9.** Balthasar
Wise Men of Greece . . . **5.** Seven
Wise Men of the East . . . **19.** Three Kings of Cologne
wish . . . **4.** care, hope, will, wuss **5.** yearn **6.** aspire, desire, invoke

7. longing, request 8. optative, petition
10. aspiration 11. imprecation

wishbone ... 7. furcula 8. furculum
10. fourchette 12. merry thought

wisp ... 4. floc 5. brush, flock, shred
6. bundle 7. handful 8. fragment

wistful ... 7. longing, pensive 8. desirous,
yearning 9. nostalgic 10. melancholy

wit ... 3. pun, wag 5. humor, sense
6. acumen, esprit, satire, wisdom
7. punster 8. comedian, humorist,
repartee 9. alertness 11. philosopher,
savoir-faire 12. intelligence
13. understanding

wit (to) ... 3. viz 5. truly 6. indeed,
namely, that is 8. scilicet 9. videlicet

witch ... 3. hag, hex 4. baba 5. Circe,
crone, lamia, shrew, vixen 6. cummer,
Hecate (Hekate), Lilith (Lilis), wizard
7. warlock 8. old woman 9. grimalkin,
sorceress 11. witch doctor 12. ugly
old woman

witchcraft ... 5. charm, magic, wanga
7. cunning, hexerei, sorcery 8. brujeria
9. sortilege, voodooism 10. bewitchery,
black magic 11. enchantment
12. invultuation

witch doctor ... 3. hex 6. shaman
9. voodooist, wangateur

witchery ... 5. charm, spell 7. sorcery
8. wizardry 10. allurement, necromancy
11. enchantment, fascination

with (pref) ... 2. co 3. com, con, cum,
mit, syn 4. avec

with ... 5. among 7. jointly 8. together
9. alongside, including 10. hand in
hand 11. association 12. concurrently
13. co-operatively

withal ... 5. still 9. thereupon 10. for all
that

withdraw ... 6. absent, deduct, recall,
recant, recede, remove, repeal, retire,
secede 7. abandon, detract, disavow,
forsake, refrain, regress, retract, retreat,
subside 8. alienate, evacuate, renounce
9. disengage 10. relinquish

withdrawal ... 6. repeal 7. regress,
retiral, retreat 8. escapism 9. departure,
recession, seclusion 10. detachment,
extraction, retraction, separation
11. abandonment, recantation,
resignation

withdrawn ... 7. ingrown 8. detached,
secluded

withe ... 4. band, rope 5. snare 6. halter,
wattle, willow

wither ... 3. age, die, dry 4. fade, sear,
sere, wilt 5. decay, droop, dry up,
wizen 6. blight, shrink 7. shrivel, wrinkle
8. languish 11. deteriorate

withered ... 4. sere 8. shrunken
9. shriveled

withering ... 7. caustic 9. shrinking
10. marcescent 12. contemptuous
13. deteriorating

withhold ... 4. curb, deny 5. check
6. detain, refuse, retain 7. abstain,
prevent, refrain, repress, reserve 8. hold
back, postpone, restrain

within ... 6. at home, during, inside
7. indoors 8. inside of, inwardly 9. inner

side

without ... 4. sans, sine 5. minus
6. beyond, except, lack of, unless
7. lacking, not with 9. absence of,
outwardly 10. externally, out-of-doors

without (pert to) ... see also *absence of*
action .. 8. deedless
animation .. 5. amort
appointment (of day) .. 7. sine die
beginning, or end .. 7. eternal
cause .. 10. unprovoked
connections .. 7. tieless
delay .. 9. summarily
doubt .. 9. sine dubio
ethics .. 8. amoral
exception .. 11. universally
feet .. 4. apod 6. apodal
foliage .. 8. aphylous
friends .. 4. lorn 7. forlorn 8. forsaken
knowledge .. 8. ignorant
mate .. 3. odd
prefix .. 4. ecto
rule .. 8. anarchic
substance .. 5. inane
support .. 7. legless 9. dependent
teeth .. 8. edentate 9. toothless
this .. 7. sine hoc
warning .. 12. out of the blue
wings .. 7. apteral

withstand ... 4. bear, bide, defy, last
5. abide 6. endure, oppose, resist
8. confront 10. contradict

witless ... 3. mad 5. crazy, dazed
6. stupid 7. foolish, unaware 8. heedless
9. brainless, unknowing 10. indiscreet
13. unintelligent

witness ... 3. eye, see 4. know 5. swear,
teste, vouch 6. attend, attest, beheld,
behold, testor 7. observe, testify
8. beholder, deponent, evidence,
observer, onlooker 9. informant,
spectator, subscribe, testimony
11. attestation

witticism ... 3. mot, pun 4. jest,
joke, quip 5. droll, sally, sient
6. repartee 9. wisecrack 10. pleasantry
11. gauloiserie, witty saying

wittingly ... 8. by design 9. knowingly
13. intentionally

witty ... 4. wise 5. comic, droll, sharp
6. clever, facete, jocose, jocund
7. amusing, comical, jocular, knowing
8. humorous 9. facetious, whimsical

wivern, wyvern (Her) ... 6. dragon
(2-legged)

wizard ... 4. mage, sage 6. expert, genius,
Merlin, pellar, shaman 7. magical,
prodigy 8. conjurer, magician, sorcerer
10. Wizard of Oz 11. necromancer,
thaumaturge, witch doctor
13. thaumaturgist

Wizard of the North ... 14. Sir Walter
Scott

wizen ... 3. age, dry 4. thin 6. gullet,
shrink, weazen, wither 7. shrivel
8. windpipe 11. deteriorate

wlo (obs) ... 3. hem 6. fringe

woad ... 3. dye 4. herb 5. tinge 8. dyestuff
10. pastel blue

wobble, wabble ... 4. walk 5. shake,
waver 7. stagger, tremble 8. hobbling

9. fluctuate, oscillate, vacillate

Woden, Wodan (Myth) . . . 3. god (chief)
4. Odin 9. Wednesday (named for
Woden)

woe . . . 4. bale, bane 5. grief 6. misery,
sorrow 7. anguish, trouble 8. anathema
calamity 10. affliction, melancholy,
misfortune

woebegone . . . 3. sad 6. woeful
7. unhappy 8. dejected, desolate
10. dispirited, melancholy

woeful . . . 3. sad 6. paltry 7. direful,
pitiful 8. grievous, mournful, wretched
9. afflicted, miserable, sorrowful,
woebegone 10. deplorable
12. disconsolate

wold . . . 3. lea 4. wood 5. downs, plain,
weald 6. forest, meadow 7. low hill

wolf . . . 4. lobo 5. lupus 6. coyote,
mammal 7. lsegrim 8. werewolf
9. libertine 11. philanderer

wolf fish . . . 6. blenny

wolfhound . . . 6. borzoi

wolflike . . . 6. lupine, thooid

wolverine . . . 4. Gulo 11. Michigander,
Michiganite

Wolverine State . . . 8. Michigan

woman . . . 4. dame, girl, lady, rani, wife
5. adult, begum, gemme, madam,
squaw 6. female 7. distaff 8. feminine,
paramour, senorita 9. womankind
10. sweetheart

woman (pert to) . . .
adviser . . 6. Egeria (Rom Myth)
apartment of . . 3. oda (harem)
8. thalamus
beautiful . . 4. doll 5. filly, pin-up, siren,
sylph, Venus 7. charmer, Zenobia
8. Musidora
bewitching . . 4. peri 5. siren, vixen
7. charmer
celibate . . 7. agapeta
chaser . . 9. libertine 11. philanderer
club (of women) . . 7. sorosis 8. sorority
comb form . . 3. gyn
dignified, elderly . . 7. dowager
dowdy . . 4. drab 5. frump 6. untidy 8. slattern
gossipy . . 3. cat 15. flibbertigibbet
graceful . . 5. sylph 7. slender
gypsy . . 5. romni
hater . . 10. misogynist
hatred of . . 8. misogyny
kept . . 8. mistress 9. concubine
12. demimondaine
killer . . 8. femicide
learned . . 12. bluestocking
loose . . 4. drab 5. whore 6. harlot
7. trollop 10. prostitute 12. streetwalker
lover of . . 11. philogynist
modest (affectedly) . . 5. prude
mythical (ugly) . . 6. Gorgon
noisy . . 9. termagant
of rank . . 4. dame
old . . 5. crone, frump 6. granny 7. carline,
dowager 8. grandame 9. cailleach
ruler . . 9. matriarch
scolding . . 5. shrew 6. virago
socialite . . 5. deb 6. subdeb 9. debutante
13. fashion leader
stately . . 4. lady 6. matron
suffragist . . 8. feminist

vixenish . . 5. shrew 6. virago 8. harridan
weeping . . 5. Niobe
will maker . . 9. testatrix
young, unmarried . . 4. lass 6. damsel
8. spinster 10. demoiselle

womanhood . . . 4. Emer 10. femininity

woman's property (free) . . .
10. parapherna

wonder . . . 3. awe 6. marvel, rarity
7. miracle, prodigy 8. surprise
9. amazement 10. admiration,
wonderment 12. astonishment

wonderful . . . 6. superb, unique
7. amazing, corking, mirific, strange
8. wondrous 9. admirable, marvelous,
mirifical 10. remarkable, surprising
11. astonishing 13. extraordinary

wont . . . 3. use 5. habit, usage 6. custom

woo . . . 3. sue 5. invite 7. beseech,
entreat, solicit

wood . . . 4. tree 5. xylon 6. lignum,
lumber, timber 8. firewood

wood (pert to) . . .
aromatic . . 5. aloes, cedar 8. agalloch
ash . . 6. potash
black . . 5. ebony
block . . 3. nog 4. dook
boring (of insects) . . 8. xylotomy
bundles . . 6. fagots
carving . . 10. xyloglyphy
clearing . . 5. glade
color . . 7. biscuit
comb form . . 4. hylo, xylo 5. ligni, ligno,
xylon
core . . 3. ame
curved strip . . 5. stave
dealer . . 10. xylopolist
deity . . 3. Pan 4. faun 5. Diana, Satyr
7. Silenus 8. Silvanus
eating . . 11. xylophagous
goddess . . 5. Diana
growing on . . 6. fungus 11. xylophilous
growth . . 7. boscage, coppice, thicket
hard . . 3. ash, elm 4. rate, teak 5. ebony,
maple 6. walnut 8. mahogany
inlay . . 9. marquetry
nymph . . 4. moth 5. dryad
overlay . . 6. veneer
resembling . . 6. xyloid
stork . . 4. ibis
strip . . 4. lath, slat 5. sprag, stave
6. batten
touch . . 4. punk 5. spunk (sponk)
9. touchwood
tough, elastic . . 3. ash
tract . . 5. grove 6. forest

woodchuck . . . 6. marmot 9. ground
hog

Woodchuck Day . . . 9. Candlemas

woodcock . . . 5. pewee 6. peewee, shrups
10. woodpecker

wooden (pert to) . . .
container . . 3. box 4. case 6. barrel
horse . . 6. Trojan
Indian . . 15. cigar-store brave
joint . . 5. tenon
made of . . 5. treen
pert to . . 4. dull 6. clumsy, stolid, stupid
8. lifeless 14. expressionless
pin . . 3. fid, nog, peg 5. dowel, spile
pole . . 4. palo

shoe .. 5. sabot 6. patten
stand .. 5. criss
tub .. 3. soe
woodpecker ... 4. chab 5. Picus 6. yaffle,
yukkel (yuckle) 7. flicker, wryneck
8. hickwall 9. sapsucker 10. carpintero,
pickerwood 11. woodknacker
woods (pert to) ...
inhabiting .. 7. nemoral
lover of .. 11. nemophilist
pert to .. 6. sylvan (silvan) 10. sylvestral
sacred (grove) .. 10. Nemorensis
woodwind .. 4. oboe 5. flute 7. bassoon,
piccolo 8. clarinet 9. saxophone
woody ... 6. sylvan, xyloid 8. ligneous
woof ... 3. abb 4. weft 6. fabric 7. filling,
texture
wool ... 3. fur 4. down, hair 5. cloth,
llama, sheep 6. fleece 8. barragan
(barragon)
wool (pert to) ...
card .. 3. tum 4. comb 5. tease
clean .. 7. garnett
cloth .. 5. serge, tweed, yerga 6. angora,
duffel, kersey, satara, tartan, tricot,
vicuña 7. doeskin, flannel, ratteen
8. cashmere 10. broadcloth
comb form .. 4. lani
dead sheep's .. 8. mortling
dryer .. 5. fugal
fat .. 7. lanolin (lanoline)
fatty substance .. 5. suint
garment .. 6. alpaca, linder
implement .. 6. carder, shears, teaser
7. distaff, spindle
inferior, dirty .. 7. cleamer
kind .. 6. alpaca, angora, merino
8. picklock
leg .. 4. gare
reclaimed .. 5. mungo 6. shoddy
reference to .. 5. wooly 6. lanate, lanose
10. flocculent
spun .. 4. yarn
tuft .. 8. floccule 9. flocculus
undyed, natural .. 5. beige
waste .. 3. fud 4. noil
yarn .. 3. abb 7. eis wool
wooly (woolly) ... 5. downy, fuzzy
6. fleecy, lanate 7. blurred 8. confused,
floccose, peronate
word ... 4. news, oath 5. adage,
maxim, parol 6. avowal, remark,
report 7. command, dispute, message,
promise, tidings, vocable 8. acrostic,
password 9. discourse, statement
11. declaration, information
13. communication
word, words (pert to) ...
action .. 4. verb
battle of .. 9. logomachy
blindness .. 6. alexia
book .. 6. Gradus 7. lexicon, speller
8. glossary 9. thesaurus 10. dictionary
contraction .. 9. haplology
deletion at end .. 7. apocope
derivation .. 6. etymon 9. etymology
distinguishing (Bib) .. 10. shibboleth
divine .. 5. Logos
excessive interest .. 10. verbomania
figurative use .. 5. trope
figure of speech .. 7. metonym, paronym

first on walls (Bib) .. 21. mene, mene,
tekel, upharsin
for word .. 8. verbatim 9. literally
hard to pronounce .. 10. jawbreaker
inventor of .. 6. coiner 9. neologist
last syllable .. 6. ultima
last syllable but one .. 6. penult
last syllable omitted .. 7. apocope
law .. 7. by parol 11. word of mouth
letter .. 8. logogram 9. logogriph
11. grammalogue
longest in dictionary ..
28. antidisestablishmentarianism
loss from middle .. 7. syncope
magical .. 6. presto, sesame
meaning .. 9. semantics
misuse .. 11. catachresis, heterophemy,
malapropism
mysterious (Bib) .. 5. selah
new .. 9. neologism
new usage .. 7. neology
of different name for same thing ..
9. heteronym
of honor .. 6. parole 7. promise
of opposite meaning .. 7. antonym
of same derivation .. 7. paronym
of same meaning .. 7. synonym
of same sound .. 7. homonym
of imitation .. 6. echoic 9. onomatope
12. onomatopoeia
play on .. 3. pun
popular .. 6. cliché 8. buzzword
pretentious use .. 10. lexiphanic
puzzle .. 5. rebus 7. anagram 8. acrostic
9. crossword
repetition .. 5. ploce
root .. 6. etymon
same back to front .. 10. palindrome
science .. 10. lexicology
scrambled .. 7. anagram
song hits .. 6. lyrics
substitution .. 5. trope 7. metonym
theory .. 6. bowwow 8. pooh-pooh
The Word (Bib) .. 5. Logos
with loss of vowel at beginning ..
7. aphasia
without vowels .. 6. rhythm, syzygy
with vowels (all) .. 7. eulogia, miaoued,
sequoia 12. ambidextrous
with vowels in sequence .. 8. caesious
wordiness ... 8. pleonasm, verbiage
9. prolixity, verbacity 10. redundance
wording ... 8. phrasing 11. expression
wordless ... 5. tacit 6. silent
wordy ... 6. prolix 7. verbose 9. garrulous
10. long-winded 12. long-drawn-out
work ... 3. gig, job, mix 4. book,
deed, duty, make, opus, plan, task,
to-do, toil 5. chore, ergon, labor,
solve, trade 6. action, Arbeit, create,
effect, effort 7. ferment, operate,
perform, product, travail 8. business,
drudgery, endeavor, function, industry,
struggle 10. accomplish, employment,
engagement, management, occupation,
profession 11. achievement,
performance, undertaking
work (pert to) ...
agreement .. 4. code, pact 8. contract
bag .. 7. tote bag 8. reticule
carelessly .. 5. scamp

clothes.. 8. overalls 9. blue jeans, coveralls, dungarees

comb form .. 3. erg 4. ergo

divine .. 7. miracle, theurgy 9. occult art

hard .. 3. peg, tew 4. char, moil, plug, toil 5. labor, sweat 6. drudge 7. travail 9. lucubrate 18. burn the midnight oil

hate of .. 10. ergophobia

helper .. 3. aid (aide) 9. assistant, paralegal, paramedic

horse .. 4. mule 5. burro

hours .. 9. flexitime (flextime)

household .. 4. char 5. chare

incomplete art .. 7. ébauche

inlay .. 6. mosaic, niello

lover of .. 9. ergophile

measure of .. 9. ergometer

of excellence .. 4. opus 7. classic

out .. 5. solve 7. arrange, develop 9. calculate

over .. 6. recast, rehash, revamp 9. brainwash, influence

shift .. 5. swing 9. graveyard, moonlight

slowly .. 6. potter, putter 7. ca'canny

study of .. 8. ergology

together .. 4. team 9. cooperate 11. collaborate

unit of .. 3. erg 5. ergon, joule

up .. 4. plan 5. rouse 6. excite, incite 7. advance, agitate, develop 10. manipulate

workable .. . 6. pliant 7. operant 8. feasible, operable, solvable 9. practical 11. practicable

worker .. . 3. CPA 5. diver, mason, miner 6. barman, cooper, slater, smithy, tanner, warper, wright 7. analyst, cobbler, glazier, plumber, riveter, sandhog, servant, spinner 8. honeybee, mechanic, strapper 9. carpenter, clinician, machinist, stevedore 10. accountant 11. breadwinner

worker (pert to) ...

fellow .. 5. buddy 8. confrere

group .. 4. crew, gang, team 5. corps, staff 9. personnel

hard .. 6. beaver, drudge, fagger 10. workaholic

head .. 4. boss 7. foreman 8. employer, overseer 14. superintendent

indifferent .. 4. scab 11. scissorbill

migrant .. 4. hobo 6. boomer 7. floater, wetback

workhouse .. . 6. prison 9. almshouse, poorhouse

workman .. . 4. peon 6. coolie, earner 7. artisan, laborer 8. operator, opificer 9. artificer, craftsman, performer

workshop .. . 3. lab 4. mill 5. plant 6. studio 7. atelier, factory 10. laboratory 11. ergasterion

world .. . 5. globe, realm 6. cosmos, domain 7. kingdom, society 8. creation, humanity, universe 9. multitude, the public

world (pert to) ...

external .. 6. nonego

great .. 7. macrocosm

lower .. 5. Hades, Orcus

miniature .. 9. microcosm

of fairies .. 6. faerie (faery)

precreation .. 10. premundane 11. antemundane

reference to .. 7. mundane 11. terrestrial

worldly .. . 7. earthly, mundane, secular, terrene 11. terrestrial 13. materialistic, sophisticated

world's oldest city, still inhabited ... 8. Damascus

world's speech .. . 7. Volapuk 9. universal

worm .. . 3. ess 4. coil, grub, wind 5. borer, tinea 6. blight, insect, maggot, vermin, wretch 8. helminth 9. trematode, vermicule 10. Nemertinea (Nemertina)

worm (pert to) ...

Africa .. 3. loa 6. Guinea

aquatic, marine .. 7. eunicid, lugworm 8. flatworm 9. planarian 13. platyhelminth

arrow .. 7. sagitta

bait .. 9. angleworm, earthworm

bloodsucking .. 5. leech

caddie .. 5. cadew

cotton .. 8. bollworm 10. boll weevil

edible .. 6. palolo

eye-infecting .. 3. loa

genus .. 6. Virmes 7. Ascaris, Filaria 8. Annelida 10. Nemertinea (Nemertina)

grublike .. 5. larva

killer .. 9. vermicide

larva .. 4. army, slug 5. cadew 6. caddis, looper 8. wireworm 11. caterpillar

luminous .. 8. glowworm

marine .. 7. eunicid

measuring .. 6. looper 8. inchworm

parasitic .. 7. Ascaris, Filaria 8. trichina, woodworm 9. trematode 10. Guinea worm 12. enthelmintha

ref to .. 8. anneloid 9. nemertean, nemertine, nemertoid, trematoid

ring .. 5. tinea 7. annelid

round .. 7. ascarid, Ascaris

segmented .. 8. Annelida

ship .. 5. borer 6. teredo

silk .. 4. eria

soft .. 4. grub

study of .. 10. vermeology 13. helminthology

tape .. 6. taenia

track .. 7. nereite 11. helminthite

wire .. 4. lava 9. millepede

worm (type) .. . 3. cut, dew, lug, pin 4. army, boll, eria, flat, glow, inch, ring, ship, silk, slug, tape, wire, wood 5. angle, earth, larva, leech, round, tinea 6. marine 9. measuring, parasitic

wormlike .. . 7. vermian 11. helminthoid

wormy .. . 6. earthy, humble, rotten 8. crawling 9. groveling

worn .. . 3. old 4. sere, used 5. stale, trite 7. abraded, haggard 8. attrited, tattered, weakened 9. exhausted, hackneyed 10. secondhand 11. commonplace

worn-out .. . 4. used 5. jaded, passé, seedy, spent, trite 6. shabby, used up 7. haggard 8. consumed, fatigued, impaired, tired out 9. enfeebled, exhausted 10. threadbare

worried .. . 5. cared, fazed 6. stewed 7. annoyed, anxious, fearful, fretted

8. troubled 9. perturbed

worry . . . 3. nag, rux, vex 4. care, cark, faze, fret, stew 5. annoy, brood, harry 6. bother, harass, pester, plague, pother 7. anxiety, bedevil, concern, perturb, torment, trouble 8. distress 9. annoyance 10. harassment, uneasiness

worship . . . 5. adore, honor, serve 6. bhakti, homage, revere 7. idolize, liturgy, respect 8. blessing, devotion, idolatry, venerate 9. adoration, deference, reverence 10. veneration

worship (pert to) . . .
form of . . 6. preces, ritual 7. liturgy
house of . . 6. chapel, church, mosque, shrine 9. cathedral, synagogue 10. tabernacle
object of . . 4. icon, idol 5. totem 6. fetish
place of . . 5. altar
system of . . 4. cult 6. cultus, fetish, ritual 8. doctrine

worshiper . . . 6. adorer, bhakti, votary 8. disciple, idolater 10. ignicolist 12. iconomachist

worshipful . . . 6. devout 7. notable 8. esteemed 9. honorable, venerable 13. distinguished

worship of . . .
a god . . 9. theolatry
angels . . 5. dulia
genii . . 10. geniolatry
god . . 6. latria (RCCh)
idols . . 8. idolatry
images . . 10. iconolatry
nature . . 11. physiolatry
one god . . 9. monolatry
snakes . . 10. ophiolatry
soul . . 7. animism
sun . . 10. heliolatry
the mob . . 9. mobolatry

worst . . . 3. bad 4. beat, evil 6. defeat, wicked 7. harmful 8. inferior 10. calamitous, pernicious, unpleasant 12. disagreeable

worsted . . . 4. yarn 6. crewel 7. genappe

worth . . . 5. merit, price, value 6. desert, repute, riches, stiver, wealth 8. eminence, meriting, property 9. deserving 10. excellence, importance, usefulness

worthless . . . 3. bad, ort 4. base, evil, mean, raca (Bib), vile 6. futile, nought (naught), paltry 7. fustian, useless 8. nugatory, rubbishy, unworthy 9. valueless 11. undeserving 14. good-for-nothing

worthwhile . . . 6. useful 7. gainful 9. expedient, well-spent 10. invaluable, profitable

worthy . . . 3. fit 7. merited 8. eligible, valuable 9. celebrity, competent, deserving, estimable, excellent, honorable, qualified, reputable 11. meritorious

worthy of . . . 8. credible, meriting 9. deserving 10. entitled to

wound . . . 3. cut 4. gore, harm, hurt, pain, rist, scar, sore, stab 5. stab 6. breach, damage, grieve, injury, lesion, offend, trauma 8. distress 9. detriment

wound (pert to) . . .
discharge . . 5. ichor 6. sanies
dressing . . 7. bandage, pledget
mark . . 4. scab, scar, welt 7. blister

woven . . . 4. spun 10. fabricated

wow . . . 4. howl, rave, wail 5. whine

wrack . . . 4. kelp, rack, ruin 5. tease, trash, weeds, wreck 6. refuse 7. seaweed 8. eelgrass, wreckage 9. shipwreck 11. destruction

wraith . . . 4. food 5. ghost, spook 8. illusion 10. apparition 12. Doppelgänger, doubleganger

wrangle . . . 4. herd, spar 5. argue, brawl 6. bicker, debate 7. contend, dispute, quarrel 8. haggling 9. altercate, bickering 11. altercation, controversy 12. disagreement

wrangler . . . 6. cowboy 7. debater, student (Cambridge, Eng) 8. herdsman, opponent 9. combatant, disputant 10. antagonist

wrangling . . . 11. belligerent, contentious

wrap . . . 3. rug 4. cape, cere, furl, roll, wind 5. cloak, gange 6. afghan, encowl, enfold, swathe 7. blanket, conceal, package 8. covering, enshroud, enswathe, envelope 9. encompass

wrapped up . . . 7. bound up, selfish 8. absorbed, included, involved 9. dependent, devoted to, engrossed 11. inseparable

wrapper . . . 4. gown 5. cerer 6. fardel, kimono, tillot 7. garment, pelisse 8. envelope, peignoir

wrapping . . . 6. charta 7. wrapper 8. cerement, covering 9. parchment

wrasse . . . 4. fish 6. ballan, cunner, Labrus 7. seawife 11. peacock fish

wrath . . . 3. ire 4. fury, grim, rage 5. anger 6. choler 7. passion 8. violence 10. turbulence 11. indignation 12. exasperation

wrathful . . . 3. mad 5. angry, irate 6. ireful, raging 7. angered 8. incensed 9. indignant, malignant 10. passionate

wreak . . . 4. do to 5. avenge 7. gratify, indulge, inflict 13. bring down upon

wreath . . . 3. lei 4. band, orle 5. crown, torse (Her), whorl 6. anadem, circle, corona, laurel, trophy 7. coronet, festoon, garland, lresine 8. encircle

wreathe . . . 4. coil, wind 5. crown, twine, twist 7. entwine 8. decorate, encircle 9. interlace 10. twist about

wreck . . . 4. raze, ruin, undo 5. crash, smash 6. jalopy 7. destroy, disable 8. accident, demolish, derelict 9. shipwreck 10. broken form 11. disassemble, The Hesperus

wreckage . . . 5. ruins 6. jetsam 7. flotsam 8. driftage

wrench . . . 4. jerk, pipe, pull, tear 5. twist, wrest 6. sprain, twinge 7. distort 8. crescent, distress

wrench, type of . . . 3. box, pin 5. wramp 6. monkey 7. spanner 8. carriage, Stillson 9. alligator

wrest . . . 4. rend, turn 5. exact, force, seize, twist, wring 6. elicit, extort, wrench 7. distort, extract, pervert, wrestle 8. misapply

wrestle ... 3. tug 6. squirm, tussle
7. contend, grapple, scuffle, wriggle
8. struggle 9. throw down 10. twist
about 11. come to grips

wrestling school ... 9. palaestra
(palestra)

wretch ... 3. dog 5. miser, ronin
6. outlaw, pariah 7. caitiff, cullion,
outcast 8. derelict, sufferer 9. miscreant
10. base person 11. offscouring,
rapscallion 14. good-for-nothing
16. pitiable creature

wretched ... 3. sad 4. base, mean
6. dismal, paltry, woeful 7. baleful,
forlorn, squalid, unhappy, very bad
8. grievous 9. execrable, miserable
10. despicable, distressed
12. contemptible, disreputable

wretchedness ... 6. misery 8. distress,
meanness, poorness 10. paltriness
11. unhappiness 13. penuriousness

wriggle ... 5. twist 6. squirm, writhe
7. meander

wriggle out of ... 4. turn, wind 5. dodge,
snake, twist 6. squirm, writhe 8. slip
away 10. crawl out of 11. squirm out
of 13. find a loophole

wring ... 4. twist, wrest 6. extort, wrench
7. extract, torture, wrestle 8. compress,
convolve 9. cause pain 10. contortion,
extraction

wrinkle ... 3. fad 4. fold, idea, ruga,
seam 5. crimp, knack, ridge, rivel
6. crease, furrow, pucker, rimple, ripple,
rumple 7. crinkle, novelty 8. contract
9. corrugate 11. corrugation 12. clever
notion

wrinkled ... 4. aged 5. savoy 6. rugate,
rugose, rugous 7. creased 8. crinkled,
crumpled, furrowed, puckered, rugulose
9. shriveled 10. contracted, corrugated

wrinkles ... 5. rugae

wrist ... 5. joint 6. carpal, carpus 8. os
magnum 9. capitatum

writ ... 5. breve, tales 6. capias, elegit,
venire 7. process 8. detainer, document,
mittimus, replevin, subpoena
10. certiorari, instrument 11. fieri facias

writ (pert to) ...
common law .. 11. fieri facias
court .. 7. summons 8. subpoena
execution .. 6. elegit
jury .. 5. tales 6. venire
law .. 4. capo, pone 5. breve, error
6. capias, elegit 7. mandate, process,
warrant 8. citation 10. certiorari

write ... 3. pen 5. draft, trace 6. decree,
depict, draw up, enroll, indite, record,
scrive 7. compose, scriven 8. inscribe,
scribble 11. communicate

write (pert to) ...
carelessly .. 6. scrawl 8. scrabble,
scribble
in large hand .. 7. engross
off .. 4. drop 6. cancel, deduct, repeal
out .. 6. record 9. spill out 12. put in
writing
poetry .. 7. versify
up .. 6. record, report 7. article
9. publicize 11. press report

writer ... 4. hack, poet 6. author, penman,
penner, scribe 7. elegist, glosser,
hymnist 8. annalist, composer, lyricist,
novelist, parodist, scriptor 9. annotator,
columnist, scrivener 10. chronicler,
journalist 13. correspondent

writer's afterthoughts ... 7. addenda

writhe ... 4. bend, coil, curl, wind 5. twist,
wring 6. squirm 7. contort, distort,
wriggle

writing ... 4. book, poem 6. script
7. article, epistle 8. covenant, document,
makimono 10. expression, penmanship,
profession 11. chirography,
composition, handwriting, inscription,
publication

writing (pert to) ...
alternate .. 13. boustrophedon
ancient characters .. 7. cuneiform
ancient manuscript .. 6. uncial
cipher .. 12. cryptography
instrument .. 3. pen 5. quill 6. stylus
italic .. 7. cursive
mania for .. 11. graphomania
material .. 3. pad 5. paper, slate 6. tablet
9. parchment 10. stationery
omission of a letter .. 8. lipogram
10. lipography
pert to .. 7. scribal
record .. 3. log 5. album, diary
script .. 5. ronde
scroll .. 8. makimono
scroll hanging .. 8. kakemono
secret .. 4. code 10. cryptogram
12. cryptography
unrhymed .. 5. prose

writings, sacred ... 5. Bible, Koran
6. Psalms, Talmud 9. Testament (Old,
New) 10. Scriptures

written (pert to) ...
agreement .. 6. cartel
characters .. 6. script
it is .. 8. it must be 10. in the books,
in the cards 12. the die is cast
law .. 10. legislated
law, unwritten .. 6. common
memo .. 5. scrip

wrong ... 3. bad, off, out, sin 4. awry,
evil, harm, side, tort, vice 5. amiss,
cheat, crime, false, malum, unfit
6. faulty, injure, injury, seduce, sinful,
unjust, wicked 7. defraud, immoral,
misdeed, offense 8. improper, iniquity,
mistaken 9. erroneous, incorrect,
injustice, violation 10. inaccurate,
iniquitous 11. impropriety, inexpedient,
malfeasance, misfeasance
12. illegitimate

wrong (pert to) ...
go (wrong) .. 3. err 4. fail 5. lapse
8. go astray, go to ruin 9. backslide
10. misbelieve 11. go to the dogs
in the .. 6. guilty 7. at fault, in error
8. mistaken 9. violation
law .. 4. tort 5. crime, malum
name .. 8. misnomer
nor right (neither) .. 7. neutral
11. adiaphorous
prefix .. 3. mis
side of .. 5. shady
way .. 5. amiss 6. astray 10. out of

place
wrongdoer . . . 6. sinner 8. criminal,
evildoer, violator 10. malefactor,
trespasser 12. transgressor
wroth . . . 3. mad 5. angry, irate 7. violent
8. incensed, wrathful 9. turbulent,
wrought up 11. exasperated
wrought . . . 4. made 6. formed, shaped,
worked 9. decorated, fashioned,
processed 10. elaborated,
ornamented 11. embroidered
12. manufactured
wrought up . . . 4. agog 5. angry, eager
7. excited 9. disturbed, stirred up
wry . . . 4. awry 6. biased, swerve, turned
7. crooked, twisted 9. contorted
wryneck . . . 4. Jynx, weet 5. loxia
9. snakebird 11. torticollis
Württemberg, Germany . . .
capital . . 9. Stuttgart
city . . 3. Ulm 9. Esslingen, Heilbronn,
Hohenheim
lake . . 9. Constance
river . . 6. Danube, Neckar

Wyandot . . . 6. Indian (Iroquois)
Wyandotte . . . 4. cave, city, fowl
Wycliff (Wyclif), **John** (pert to) . . .
birthplace . . 9. Yorkshire (Eng)
disciple . . 4. Huss
remains cast into . . 10. Swift River
translator of . . 5. Bible
Wyoming . . .
capital . . 8. Cheyenne
city . . 4. Cody 6. Casper 7. Big Horn,
Laramie 8. Cheyenne, Sheridan
historic site . . 11. Fort Laramie
17. Buffalo Bill Center
mountain . . 6. Tetons 7. Rockies
11. Gannett Peak
park . . 10. Grand Teton 11. Yellowstone
river . . 4. Wind 6. Platte 7. Big Horn
river source . . 8. Colorado, Columbia,
Missouri
State admission . . 11. Forty-fourth
State bird . . 10. meadowlark
State flower . . 16. Indian paintbrush
State motto . . 11. Equal Rights
Woman Suffrage . . 10. First State

X

X . . . 3. ten 5. error 6. letter (24th), symbol
7. unknown
xanthic . . . 6. cyanic, yellow
Xanthippe, wife of . . . 8. Socrates
xanthoma . . . 9. xanthosis 11. skin disease
13. yellow patches
xanthos . . . 6. yellow
Xanthué (pert to) . . .
ancient site . . 7. marbles (Xanthian)
placed now . . 13. British Museum
xebec . . . 7. vessel 8. corsair
xen, xeno (comb form) . . . 7. foreign
8. stranger
xenium . . . 4. gift 7. present (official)
Xenocrates (Gr) . . . 11. philosopher
xenogamy . . . 18. cross-fertilization
xenophobic . . . 9. strangers (afraid of)
12. chauvinistic
Xenophon's historic tale . . . 8. Anabasis
xenophthalmia . . . 11. foreign body (eye)
14. conjunctivitis
Xenopus . . . 5. toads
Xenorhynchus . . . 6. storks
Xenurus . . . 7. tatouay 10. armadillos
Xeres . . . 5. jerez 6. sherry
xerophagy . . . 4. Fast (Lenten)
xerotes . . . 7. dryness (body)
Xerox (tm) . . . 4. copy 9. duplicate,
replicate, reproduce
Xerus . . . 9. squirrels

Xerxes (pert to) . . .
crossing of . . 10. Hellespont
destroyer of . . 8. Athens (BC)
king of . . 6. Persia
xibalba . . . 10. underworld
Xinca . . . 6. Indian, Jincan
Xipe, Xipe-totec . . . 11. god of sowing
Xiphias . . . 5. comet (sword-shaped)
6. Dorado (constellation) 9. swordfish
xiphoid . . . 4. bone 8. ensiform
9. swordlike 12. xiphisternum
Xiphopagus . . . 7. monster (twinlike)
Xiphosura . . . 8. king crab
Xiuhtecutli . . . 7. fire god (Aztec)
Xmas . . . 9. Christmas
X ray (pert to) . . .
measure . . 3. rad 11. quantimeter
named . . 12. Roentgen rays
type . . 7. CAT scan 8. tomogram
9. myelogram 11. arteriogram
xyloglyphy . . . 11. wood carving (art)
xylography . . . 13. wood engraving
xyloid . . . 5. woody 8. ligneous, woodlike
xylomancy, divination by . . . 4. wood
10. wood pieces
xylophone . . . 5. saron 7. gambang,
marimba 8. gamelang (gamelan),
gigelira, sticcado
xyrid . . . 4. iris 5. Xyris
xystus, xyst (Gr) . . . 16. portico colonnade

Y

-y pl ... 3. -ies

Y ... 4. tube 5. curve, track 6. letter
(25th), prefix, suffix

yabber ... 4. talk 6. jabber

yabby, yabbie ... 8. crayfish

yaboa ... 10. night heron

yabu, yaboo ... 4. pony

yacht ... 4. boat, race, sail, ship

yaffle ... 6. armful 7. handful
10. woodpecker

yahoo ... 4. lout, rube 5. brute

Yahoo (pert to) ...
   represented by .. 10. Houyhnhnms
   (horses of reason)
   tale .. 16. Gulliver's Travels

yakalo, yakattalo ... 8. creature
   10. crossbreed (yak, cattle)

yakka ... 4. work 5. labor

yaksha ... 4. ogre 5. demon, dryad, fairy,
   gnome, jinni 6. Kubera (Chief), spirit
   7. tree-god 13. guardian angel

Yale (pert to) ...
   college .. 8. New Haven
   color .. 4. blue 7. Rameses
   founded at .. 8. Saybrook
   founder .. 9. Elihu Yale
   graduate .. 9. Yalensian

Yalta Conference ... 6. Crimea (1945)

yam (pert to) ...
   Fiji .. 6. uviyam 8. white yam
   Hawaiian .. 3. hoi
   reference to .. 5. tuber 6. igname
   Scot .. 6. potato
   tropical .. 8. cush-cush
   US .. 11. sweet potato

yamstchik ... 7. postboy 8. coachman
   9. postilion

yang ... 4. good, male 6. bright (opp of
   yin)

yang-kin ... 8. dulcimer

yank ... 4. jerk, pull 6. Yankee

Yankee ... 12. New Englander

Yannigans ... 9. scrub team (baseball)

Yao ... 6. Indian 9. aborigine

yap ... 3. cur, dog, gab 4. bark, talk, yell,
   yelp 6. jabber 7. bumpkin, hoodlum
   8. easy mark 9. greenhorn

yapok, yapock ... 6. monkey 7. opossum

yapp ... 11. bookbinding

yapster ... 3. dog

Yaqui ... 6. Indian

yard ... 3. rae (sail) 4. lawn, spar,
   wand 5. garth, stick, verge 6. campus
   7. confine, enclose, measure
   9. courtyard, curtilage, enclosure,
   yardstick 10. playground

yarn ... 3. abb, cop 4. hank, joke, tale
   5. fiber, skein, story 6. caddis, crewel,
   spinel, thread 7. genappe 9. falsehood

yarn (pert to) ...
   clew .. 4. ball
   holder .. 3. cop
   measure .. 4. hank, hasp 5. skein
   7. spangle
   size .. 6. denier

winder .. 10. yarnwindle

yashiro ... 3. sha 6. temple (Shinto)

yashmak ... 4. veil (double)

yati ... 7. ascetic, devotee

yaw ... 4. sail, tack 5. steer, tumor
   7. deviate 9. deviation

yewl ... 4. boat, howl, wail, yell, yowl
   5. ketch 9. jolly boat

yawn ... 3. gap 4. gape 5. chasm, mouth
   7. opening, stretch 8. open wide,
   oscitate 12. seek greedily

yaws ... 9. frambesia

yawweed ... 5. shrub 7. rhubarb 12. wild
   mulberry

Yazoo (pert to) ...
   Fraud .. 9. land grant (1795)
   Indian .. 11. Mississippi
   river .. 11. Mississippi

yclept, ycleped ... 5. named 6. called,
   styled

year (pert to) ...
   after year .. 10. constantly, repeatedly
   11. over and over
   book .. 7. almanac
   division of .. 6. season 8. semester
   9. trimester
   Latin .. 5. annus
   of mourning .. 11. annus luctus
   of our Lord .. 10. Anno Domini 11. annus
   Domini, year of grace
   of thirteen months (384 days) ..
   10. embolismic
   of travel .. 10. sabbatical, Wanderjahr
   14. leave of absence
   old (Zool) .. 10. annotinous
   pert to .. 5. epact
   quarter .. 5. raith
   record .. 5. annal 8. calendar

yearly (pert to) ...
   church income .. 7. annates
   payment .. 4. cens
   recurring .. 6. annual 7. etesian
   8. annually

yearn for ... 3. yen 4. ache, hope, itch,
   long, pine, sigh, wish 6. desire, hanker

yearning ... 3. yen 4. wish 5. eager
   7. anxious, longing 9. hankering,
   nostalgia 10. tenderness 11. languishing
   12. homesickness

years (pert to) ...
   adolescent .. 4. teen
   ago .. 4. ages 9. long since 10. days
   of yore, yesteryear
   eight .. 9. octennial
   fifteen .. 9. indiction
   five .. 6. pentad 7. lustrum
   hundred .. 7. centenary 10. centennial
   ten .. 6. decade 9. decennary
   thousand .. 7. chiliad 10. millennium
   two .. 8. biennial, biennium

yeast ... 4. barm, foam, koji 5. froth
   6. leaven 7. anamite, ferment
   9. agitation

yeasty ... 5. foamy, light, spumy 6. frothy
   8. restless 9. frivolous, leavening

yegg ... 5. thief, tramp 6. robber
7. burglar, yeggman 8. criminal
10. safeblower 11. safebreaker,
safecracker

yell ... 3. cry 4. howl, roar, wail, yowl
5. cheer, shout 6. outcry, scream, shriek

yelling ... 7. bawling 8. shouting, strident
9. clamorous 11. full of yells

yellow ... 3. dun, sil 4. buff, cuir, deer,
ecru, flax, gull, mean, nude, yolk
5. amber, beige, color, cream, grège,
jaune, lemon, maize, ocher (ochre),
straw, taupe, topaz, twine 6. bisque,
butter, canary, Cassel, chrome, citron,
creamy, flaxen, golden, mimosa,
sallow, Seasan 7. anamite, annatto,
aureate, egg yolk, envious, etiolin,
jealous, jonquil, saffron, sulphur,
xanthic, xanthin 8. cowardly, ocherous,
primrose, recreant 9. champagne,
dandelion, flavicant, goldenrod,
jaundiced, lutescent, sunflower
10. flavescent, melancholy
11. treacherous

yellow (pert to) ...
brown .. 3. dun 5. straw 6. manila
coloring .. 7. xanthic 8. xanthine
comb form .. 5. luteo
dyestuff .. 5. morin 7. annatto 8. luteolin
golden .. 2. or (Her) 4. gild, gilt
green .. 5. olive 8. tarragon
10. chartreuse, serpentine
herb .. 3. iva
jacket .. 4. wasp
medical .. 7. icterus 8. jaundice
11. xanthoderma
mustard .. 8. charlock
ocher, ochre .. 3. sil
pert to .. 7. xanthic
pigment .. 8. etiolin 8. orpiment
race .. 9. Mongolian
red .. 4. roan 5. aloma, sandy 6. bisque,
dorado, orange 7. annatto, nacarat
sensational .. 5. press 7. journal

yellow fever mosquito ... 12. Aëdes
aegypti

yellowhammer ... 4. yite 5. ammer, finch,
skite 6. gladdy 7. flicker 10. woodpecker
13. yellow bunting

Yellowhammer State ... 7. Alabama

yellow jacket ... 4. wasp 8. eucalypt

Yellowstone Park geyser ... 11. Old
Faithful

yelp ... 3. cry, yip 4. bark, yell 5. shout
6. outcry, shriek, squeal 7. ululate
8. complain 9. criticize

yelper ... 8. redshank 10. yellowlegs
11. hunting call

yeme ... 4. heed 5. guard 6. govern,
regard

Yemen (pert to) ...
archeology site .. 4. Sana 5. Marib
Bib kingdom .. 5. Sheba (Saba)
capital .. 4. Sana
citadel .. 5. Damar
division of .. 7. Arabia
plateau .. 7. El Jebel
port .. 5. Mocha 7. Hodeida, Loheiya
ruler .. 4. Imam
sea .. 3. Red

yemochik ... see *yamstchik*

yen ... 4. coin, urge 5. yearn 6. desire,
hanker 7. longing

yeoman ... 4. exon 5. clerk 6. butler,
seaman 8. retainer 9. assistant,
attendant 10. freeholder 11. subordinate
12. petty officer

yep ... 3. yes 4. bold 5. alert, smart
6. active 8. vigorous

yerba ... 4. herb, maté 5. plant
11. Paraguay tea

yes ...
English .. 3. aye, yea, yep 5. uh-huh
6. assent 11. affirmation
French .. 3. oui
German .. 2. ja
Italian, Spanish .. 2. si
Russian .. 2. da

yes man ... 5. toady

yesterday ... 6. yester 7. the past
10. days gone by, heretofore, yesteryear
11. bygone times

yet ... 3. but 5. still 6. algate 7. besides,
however 10. eventually 11. nonetheless
15. notwithstanding

yeti ... 17. Abominable Snowman

yew ... 5. green, Taxus 7. conifer, hemlock
9. evergreen

Yiddish ... 6. Jewish 12. Judaeo-German
(Judeo-German)

yield ... 3. bow, net 4. bear, bend,
cede, crop, give, lose, obey, vail
5. admit, allow, defer, grant, stoop,
waive 6. accede, afford, comply, give
up, relent, render, reward, soften,
submit 7. concede, consent, produce,
provide, requite, revenue, succumb
9. acquiesce, surrender
10. capitulate, relinquish
11. acknowledge

yielding ... 4. meek, soft 6. pliant, supple
7. bearing 8. flexible 9. compliant,
deference, producing, tractable
10. compliance, manageable,
submissive

Yigdal ... 4. poem (Jew Relig)

yili-caup ... 6. ale cup

yin ... 4. dark, evil (opp of yang)

Ymir, Ymer (pert to) ...
blood of .. 3. sea
bones of .. 9. mountains
brains of .. 6. clouds
flesh of .. 5. earth
killed by .. 2. Ve 4. Odin, Vili
Norse Myth .. 3. God 13. rime-cold
giant (body-shaped world)

yodel, yodle ... 4. call, sing (falsetto)
5. carol, chant 6. warble

yoga (pert to) ...
follower of .. 4. yogi (yogin) 5. fakir
7. ascetic 9. occultist
objective .. 16. mental discipline
stages .. 5. jnana, karma 6. bhakti
trance .. 6. dhyana 7. dharana, samadhi

yoke ... 3. two 4. join, link, pair, span,
team 5. frame, marry 6. cangue,
couple, inspan 7. bondage, enclave,
harness, oppress, pillory, shackle,
slavery 9. associate, servitude

yoked ... 6. united 7. coupled 9. conjugate

yokel ... 3. oaf 4. boor, clod, hick,
lout, rube 6. rustic 7. bumpkin,

hayseed, plowboy 8. abderite (anc), gullible 9. simpleton 10. countryman, slow-witted

yokemate . . . 4. mate 6. fellow, spouse 7. partner 9. companion

yolked (egg) . . . 6. yellow 8. lecithal, vitellus

Yom Kippur (Jew) . . . 7. fast day 14. Day of Atonement

Yom Teruah (Jew) . . . 15. Feast of Trumpets

Yom Tob, or Tov (Jew) . . . 8. festival

yon, yonder . . . 4. away 6. beyond 7. distant, thither 11. at a distance

yore . . . 5. of old, olden 6. before 9. in old time, long since

young . . . 3. fry, new 4. tyro 5. brood, fresh, green 6. litter, novice, tender 7. pliable 8. childish, immature, juvenile, youthful 9. offspring, succulent 13. inexperienced

young (pert to) . . .
bear, fox . . 3. cub
birds . . 5. brood
calf (motherless) . . 5. dogie
hare . . 7. leveret
herring . . 4. brit
horse . . 4. colt, foal
oyster . . 4. spat
pigeon . . 5. piper

youngling . . . 5. youth 6. novice 8. beginner, neophyte

youngster . . . 3. boy, kid, lad, pup, tad 4. baby, lass, tike 5. child, youth 6. filius, shaver, urchin 7. Aladdin (Arab Nights) 8. teenager 9. fledgling, stripling

younker . . . 5. child, youth 6. knight 7. gallant 8. nobleman 9. stripling

youth goddess . . . 4. Hebe

yo-yo . . . 3. top, toy

Ypres, Belgium . . .
famed for . . 7. Battles (WWI)

lace . . 12. Valenciennes
province of . . 8. Flanders
ruins rebuilt . . 9. Cloth Hall 15. Gothic Cathedral (St Martin)

ypsiliform, shape of . . . 7. letter T (Gr)

yu (Chin) . . . 4. jade

Yucatan, Cent America . . .
anc domain of . . 5. Mayas
capital . . 6. Mérida
city . . 5. Sisal
peninsula of . . 6. Mexico

yucca (pert to) . . .
called . . 11. Adam's needle
family . . 9. Liliaceae
native of . . 7. America
species . . 9. bear grass
State flower of . . 9. New Mexico

Yugoslavia . . .
capital . . 8. Belgrade
former leader . . 4. Tito (Communist)
river . . 5. Drava, Drina 6. Danube
sea . . 8. Adriatic

yukkel . . . 7. flicker 10. woodpecker

Yukon . . .
famed for . . 4. gold (mining)
ocean . . 6. Arctic
river . . 5. Lewes, Yukon
territory of . . 6. Canada
town . . 10. Whitehorse

Yule . . . 4. Noel 8. Nativity (Feast of the), yuletide 9. Christmas 13. Christmastide

Yule (pert to) . . .
plant . . 5. holly 9. mistletoe
good cheer . . 11. wassail bowl

Yuma (Ariz) . . . 4. city 9. Talkepaia (Indian)

yun . . . 10. Laos people (tattooed)

Yunca . . . 6. Indian (Peru)

Yurma . . . 6. Indian (Brazil)

Yurok . . . 6. Indian (Calif)

yurt, yurta . . . 4. tent (Siberia)

Yuruk . . . 10. Turkish rug

yutu . . . 7. tinamou

Yuzen birodo . . . 6. velvet (designed)

Z

Z . . . 3. end, zed, zee 5. omega 6. izzard, letter (26th)

zac . . . 4. ibex

zacate . . . 7. herbage 9. rice grass

Zacchaeus, Zaccheus . . . 4. pure 8. innocent, publican (Bib)

Zachariah, Zacharias (Bib) . . .
father . . 9. Barachias
father of . . 14. John the Baptist
literally . . 21. Jehovah hath remembered

Zadkiel (Jew) . . . 5. angel (of planet Jupiter)

zaftig . . . 5. buxom 7. shapely

Zagreus . . . 3. god 8. Dionysus (identified with)

Zaire, Africa . . .
capital . . 8. Kinshasa
formerly . . 12. Belgian Congo
river . . 4. Uele 5. Kasai, Zaire (Congo)

zaman, zamang . . . 8. rain tree

Zambia, Africa . . .
capital . . 6. Lusaka
formerly . . 16. Northern Rhodesia
wealth . . 6. copper (3rd largest)

Zamenhof, inventor of . . . 9. Esperanto

zampogna . . . 7. bagpipe, panpipe

zanja . . . 5. canal, gully 6. arroyo

zany . . . 3. wag, wit 4. dolt, fool 5. clown, crazy, goofy, kooky, nutty 6. madcap, sawney 7. acrobat, bonkers, buffoon, idiotic 8. clownish 9. simpleton 10. lieutenant, mountebank 11. merry-andrew

Zanzibar, Africa . . . see *Tanzania*

zap . . . 4. slay, stun 5. smite 6. strike

zapatero . . . 7. boxwood, cobbler, dogwood

zarf . . . 9. cup holder (Levant)

zati ... 6. monkey (bonnet)

zeal ... 5. ardor, piety 6. desire, fervor
7. passion 8. devotion 9. eagerness
10. enthusiasm, fanaticism

zealot ... 4. sect 5. bigot, freak (sl)
6. votary 7. devotee, faddist, fanatic,
pietist 9. partisan 10. enthusiast

zealous ... 5. eager, pious 6. ardent,
fervid 7. devoted, fervent 9. phrenetic
11. industrious

zebra (pert to) ...
ally .. 6. quagga
Burchell's .. 4. dauw (nonstriped legs)
hybrid .. 8. zebrinny
insect .. 7. butterfly
ref to .. 7. zebrine, zebroid

zebrawood ... 5. shrub 7. araroba
10. marblewood

zebu ... 2. ox 5. zebus (group) 6. cattle
12. Brahmany bull (sacred)

zecchino ... 6. sequin (chequeen)

Zechariah (Bib) ... 7. prophet 12. King
of Israel

zed ... 7. letter Z (Brit)

zeekoe ... 12. hippopotamus

zeism ... 8. pellagra 11. morbid state

zemi ... 4. holy (Peru) 5. huaca (huaco)
6. fetish, sacred, spirit (magic)

Zemzem ... 10. sacred well (Mecca)

Zen ... 12. Buddhist sect

zenana ... 5. harem, serai 7. mission
8. seraglio

Zenda, Prisoner of ... 9. Ruritania

Zend-Avesta ... 10. sacred text
(Zoroastrian)

zenith ... 3. top 4. acme, apex, blue,
peak 6. apogee, climax, summit, vertex
11. culmination 14. greatest height
(opp of nadir)

Zeno ... 5. Stoic 11. philosopher (Gr)

zenography, study of ... 7. Jupiter
(planet)

zenu ... 5. sheep

zephyr ... 5. shawl 6. breath, breeze

zero ... 3. nil 4. hour 5. zilch 6. cipher,
nought (naught) 7. nothing, nullity
11. temperature

zest ... 4. tang 5. gusto, savor 6. flavor,
relish 8. membrane (fruit), piquancy,
pungency 9. eagerness 10. enthusiasm

Zeus (pert to) ...
attendant .. 4. Nike
consort .. 6. Europa
brother of .. 5. Hades 8. Poseidon
deity .. 7. supreme 12. father of gods
father .. 6. Cronus
games in his honor .. 6. Nemean
8. Olympian
messenger .. 4. Iris 6. Hermes
mother .. 4. Rhea
oracle .. 6. Dodona
Roman .. 7. Jupiter
sister .. 4. Hera
son .. 4. Ares 5. Argus 6. Apollo, Hermes
7. Perseus 8. Dionysus, Hercules,
Tantalus
temple (Athens) .. 8. Olympium

ziara, ziarat ... 4. tomb (Muslim saint)
6. shrine

zibet, zibeth ... 5. civet

ziganka ... 5. dance (rustic)

zigeuner ... 5. gypsy 7. czigany, Zincalo,
zingaro

ziggurat ... 11. temple tower 12. Tower
of Babel (Bib)

zigzag ... 5. turns 6. angles 7. stagger
8. flexuous, wavering 9. alternate

zillion ... 4. many 9. countless

Zimbabwe ...
capital .. 6. Harare
Falls .. 8. Victoria
Falls discoverer .. 11. Livingstone (1855)
formerly .. 8. Rhodesia
people .. 7. Bantu

zinc (pert to) ...
alloy .. 5. bidri 7. paktong
alloy with copper .. 6. oroide
crude .. 7. tutenag (tutenague)
slabs .. 6. solder 7. spelter
symbol .. 2. Zn

zing ... 3. pep, vim, zip 5. vigor 6. energy,
spirit, thrill 10. enthusiasm

zingaresca (gypsy) ... 4. song 5. dance

zingaro ... 5. gypsy

Zion (pert to) ... 4. hill (Jerusalem)
10. Israelites 12. chosen people

zip ... 4. zing 5. close, speed 6. energy
8. pungency 10. sibilation

zizith ... 7. fringes (Bib), tassels

zoanthropy ... 9. monomania
15. changed to animal (belief)

zobo ... 6. hybrid 10. zebu and yak

zodiac ... 4. belt, zone 5. stars 7. circuit

zodiac signs (twelve) ... 3. Leo 5. Aries,
Libra, Virgo 6. Cancer, Gemini,
Pisces, Taurus 7. Scorpio 8. Aquarius
9. Capricorn 11. Capricornus, Sagittarius

zoetic ... 5. vital 6. living 7. organic

zombie, zombi ... 6. corpse, voodoo

zone ... 4. area, band, belt, isle,
path 5. Canal, clime, girth, tract
6. assise, circle, course, Frigid, region,
Torrid 7. stratum 8. cincture, latitude
9. Temperate

zoo ... 9. menagerie 10. collection
12. animal garden

zoo, zo (comb form) ... 6. animal

zoologist ... 9. biologist, scientist

zoology, science of ... 7. animals

zoology branches ... 8. taxonomy
9. bionomics, phylogeny
10. embryology, entomology
11. herpetology, ornithology

zoom ... 4. lens, rise 5. climb

zoopathology, science of ... 8. diseases
(animal) 11. zoonosology

zoophilist ... 11. animal lover

zoophobia ... 13. fear of animals

zoophyte ... 5. coral 6. sponge 10. sea
anemone

zootomy ... 13. animal anatomy
16. animal dissection

zootrophy ... 13. animal rearing

zoril, zorillo ... 5. skunk 7. polecat

Zoroaster, Zarathustra ... 7. Persian
8. reformer (Relig)

Zoroastrianism (pert to) ...
adherence to .. 5. Parse (Parsee)
doctrine .. 7. dualism 11. good and evil
evil spirit .. 4. deva 7. Ahriman
fire worshiper .. 6. Gheber
founder .. 9. Zoroaster

literature . . **6.** Avesta
lord of creation . . **6.** Ormazo
religion of . . **6.** Persia (anc)
zoster . . . **4.** zona **6.** girdle **8.** shingles
(Med) **12.** herpes zoster
Zouave . . . **4.** Zu-Zu **8.** chasseur
11. infantryman
Zu (Bab Myth) . . . **8.** storm god (evil)
9. blackbird (symbol)
Zuider Zee (pert to) . . .
gulf . . **8.** North Sea
Netherlands . . **4.** dike **7.** highway
present name . . **9.** Ijsel Lake, Ijselmeer
zuisin . . . **7.** widgeon
Zulu (pert to) . . .
army . . **4.** impi
boy . . **6.** umfaan
conference . . **6.** indaba
marauders . . **4.** Viti
people . . **6.** Santus **7.** Kaffirs

spear . . **7.** assagai (assegai)
Zululand capital . . . **6.** Eshowe
Zuñi (pert to) . . .
famed for . . **19.** Seven Cities of Cibola
(Myth)
Indian . . **4.** Hopi **6.** Ashivi
kingdom of Cibola . . **16.** gold-paved
streets (Myth)
zwieback . . . **4.** rusk **7.** biscuit (toasted)
Zwinger . . . **6.** palace (Dresden)
zygal . . . **7.** H-shaped
zygodactyl (zygodactyle) . . . **8.** yoke-toed
10. paired toes
zygon . . . **5.** bench **6.** thwart **9.** brain
part
zygous . . . **5.** yoked **6.** paired
zymology (science of) . . .
12. fermentation
zymosis . . . **12.** fermentation
zythum . . . **4.** beer (anc Egypt)

TABLES

BOOKS OF THE BIBLE

Old Testament Books and Abbreviations

Book, Letter Count	Abbreviation
Genesis 7	Gen
Exodus 6	Exod
Leviticus 9	Lev
Numbers 7	Num
Deuteronomy 11	Deut
Joshua 6	Josh
Judges 6	Judg
Ruth 4	Ruth
1 Samuel 6	1 Sam
2 Samuel 6	2 Sam
1 Kings 5	1 Kings
2 Kings 5	2 Kings
1 Chronicles 10	1 Chron
2 Chronicles 10	2 Chron
Ezra 4	Ezra
Nehemiah 8	Neh
Esther 6	Esther
Job 3	Job
Psalms 6	Psalms
Proverbs 8	Proverbs
Ecclesiastes 12	Eccles
Song of Solomon 13	Song of Sol
Isaiah 6	Isa
Jeremiah 8	Jer
Lamentations 12	Lam
Ezekiel 7	Ezek
Daniel 6	Dan
Hosea 5 (Osee)	Hos
Joel 4	Joel
Amos 4	Amos
Obadiah 7	Obad
Jonah 5	Joh
Micah 4	Mic
Nahum 5	Nah
Habakkuk 8	Hab
Zephaniah 9	Zeph
Haggai 6	Hag
Zechariah 9	Zech
Malachi 7	Mal

New Testament Books and Abbreviations

Book, Letter Count	Abbreviation
Matthew 7	Matt
Mark 4	Mark
Luke 4	Luke
John 4	John
Acts of the Apostles 17	Acts
Romans 6	Rom
1 Corinthians 11	1 Cor
2 Corinthians 11	2 Cor
Galatians 9	Gal
Ephesians 9	Eph
Philippians 11	Phil
Colossians 10	Col
1 Thessalonians 13	1 Thess
2 Thessalonians 13	2 Thess
1 Timothy 7	1 Tim
2 Timothy 7	2 Tim
Titus 5	Titus
Philemon 8	Philem
Hebrews 7	Heb
James 5	James
1 Peter 5	1 Pet
2 Peter 5	2 Pet
1 John 4	1 John
2 John 4	2 John
3 John 4	3 John
Jude 4	Jude
Revelation 10	(Apocalypse) Rev

Books of the Apocrypha and Abbreviations

Book, Letter Count	Abbreviation
1 Esdras 6	1 Esd
2 Esdras 6	2 Esd
Tobit 5	Tob
Judith 6	Jth
Rest of Esther 12	Rest of Esther
Wisdom of Solomon 15	Wisd of Sol
Ecclesiasticus 14	Ecclus
Baruch 6	Bar
Song of the Three Holy Children 26	Song of Three Children
Susanna 7	Sus
Bel and the Dragon 15	Bel and Dragon
Manasseh 8	Man
1 Maccabees 9	1 Macc
2 Maccabees 9	2 Macc

Books of the Bible by Letter Count

3. Job 4. Acts (of the Apostles), Amos, Ezra, Joel, John, Jude, Luke, Mark, Osee, Ruth 5. Hosea, James, Jonah, Kings, Micah, Nahum, Peter, Titus, Tobit 6. Baruch, Daniel, Esdras, Esther, Exodus, Haggai, Isaiah, Joshua, Judges, Judith, Psalms, Romans, Samuel 7. Ezekiel, Genesis, Hebrews, Malachi, Matthew, Numbers, Obadiah, Susanna, Timothy 8. Habakkuk, Jeremiah, Manasseh, Nehemiah, Philemon, Proverbs 9. Ephesians, Galatians, Leviticus, Maccabees, Zechariah, Zephaniah 10. Apocalypse, Chronicles, Colossians, Revelation 11. Corinthians, Deuteronomy, Philippians 12. Ecclesiastes, Lamentations, Rest of Esther 13. Song of Solomon, Thessalonians 14. Ecclesiasticus 15. Bel and the Dragon, Wisdom of Solomon 17. Acts of the Apostles 26. Song of the Three Holy Children

CHEMICAL ELEMENTS

Listed by atomic number, name, letter count, and symbol.

Atomic Number	Element, Letter Count	Symbol	Atomic Number	Element, Letter Count	Symbol
1	hydrogen 8	H	58	cerium 6	Ce
2	helium 6	He	59	praseodymium 12	Pr
3	lithium 7	Li	60	neodymium 9	Nd
4	beryllium 9	Be	61	promethium 10	Pm
5	boron 5	B	62	samarium 8	Sm
6	carbon 6	C	63	europium 8	Eu
7	nitrogen 8	N	64	gadolinium 10	Gd
8	oxygen 6	O	65	terbium 7	Tb
9	fluorine 8	F	66	dysprosium 10	Dy
10	neon 4	Ne	67	holmium 7	Ho
11	sodium 6	Na	68	erbium 6	Er
12	magnesium 9	Mg	69	thulium 7	Tm
13	aluminum 8	Al	70	ytterbium 9	Yb
14	silicon 7	Si	71	lutetium 8	Lu
15	phosphorus 10	P	72	hafnium 7	Hf
16	sulfur 6	S	73	tantalum 8	Ta
17	chlorine 8	Cl	74	tungsten 8	W
18	argon 5	Ar	75	rhenium 7	Re
19	potassium 9	K	76	osmium 6	Os
20	calcium 7	Ca	77	iridium 7	Ir
21	scandium 8	Sc	78	platinum 8	Pt
22	titanium 8	Ti	79	gold 4	Au
23	vanadium 8	V	80	mercury 7	Hg
24	chromium 8	Cr	81	thallium 8	Tl
25	manganese 9	Mn	82	lead 4	Pb
26	iron 4	Fe	83	bismuth 7	Bi
27	cobalt 6	Co	84	polonium 8	Po
28	nickel 6	Ni	85	astatine 8	At
29	copper 6	Cu	86	radon 5	Rn
30	zinc 4	Zn	87	francium 8	Fr
31	gallium 7	Ga	88	radium 6	Ra
32	germanium 9	Ge	89	actinium 8	Ac
33	arsenic 7	As	90	thorium 7	Th
34	selenium 8	Se	91	protactinium 12	Pa
35	bromine 7	Br	92	uranium 7	U
36	krypton 7	Kr	93	neptunium 9	Np
37	rubidium 8	Rb	94	plutonium 9	Pu
38	strontium 9	Sr	95	americium 9	Am
39	yttrium 7	Y	96	curium 6	Cm
40	zirconium 9	Zr	97	berkelium 9	Bk
41	niobium 7	Nb	98	californium 11	Cf
42	molybdenum 10	Mo	99	einsteinium 11	Es
43	technetium 10	Tc	100	fermium 7	Fm
44	ruthenium 9	Ru	101	mendelevium 11	Md
45	rhodium 7	Rh	102	nobelium 8	No
46	palladium 9	Pd	103	lawrencium 10	Lr
47	silver 6	Ag	104	rutherfordium 13	Rf
48	cadmium 7	Cd	105	hahnium 7	Ha
49	indium 6	In			
50	tin 3	Sn			
51	antimony 8	Sb			
52	tellurium 9	Te			
53	iodine 6	I			
54	xenon 5	Xe			
55	cesium 6	Cs			
56	barium 6	Ba			
57	lanthanum 9	La			

Chemical Elements by Letter Count

3. tin 4. gold, iron, lead, neon, zinc 5. argon, boron, radon, xenon 6. barium, carbon, cerium, cesium, cobalt, copper, curium, erbium, helium, indium, iodine, nickel, osmium, oxygen, radium, silver, sodium, sulfur 7. arsenic, bismuth, bromine, cadmium, calcium, fermium, gallium, hafnium, hahnium, holmium, iridium, krypton, lithium, mercury, niobium, rhenium, rhodium, silicon, terbium, thorium, thulium, uranium, yttrium 8. actinium, aluminum, antimony, astatine, chlorine, chromium, europium, fluorine, francium, hydrogen, lutetium, nitrogen, nobelium, platinum, polonium, rubidium, samarium, scandium, selenium, tantalum, thallium, titanium, tungsten, vanadium 9. americium, berkelium, beryllium, germanium, lanthanum, magnesium, manganese, neodymium, neptunium, palladium, plutonium, potassium, ruthenium, strontium, tellurium, ytterbium, zirconium 10. dysprosium, gadolinium, lawrencium, molybdenum, phosphorus, promethium, technetium 11. californium, einsteinium, mendelevium 12. praseodymium, protactinium 13. rutherfordium

CHIEF JUSTICES OF THE U.S. SUPREME COURT IN CHRONOLOGICAL ORDER

Name, Letter Count	Term	Name, Letter Count	Term
Jay, John 3	1789-95	White, Edward 5	1910-21
Rutledge, John 8	1795	Taft, William 4	1921-30
Ellsworth, Oliver 9	1796-1800	Hughes, Charles 6	1930-41
Marshall, John 8	1801-35	Stone, Harlan 5	1941-46
Taney, Roger 5	1836-64	Vinson, Frederick 6	1946-53
Chase, Salmon 5	1864-73	Warren, Earl 6	1953-69
Waite, Morrison 5	1874-88	Burger, Warren 6	1969-86
Fuller, Melville 6	1888-1910	Rehnquist, William 9	1986-

Chief Justices by Letter Count

3. Jay 4. Taft 5. Chase, Stone, Taney, Waite, White 6. Burger, Fuller, Hughes, Vinson, Warren 8. Marshall, Rutledge 9. Ellsworth, Rehnquist

FAMOUS NAMES IN CROSSWORD PUZZLES

Listed alphabetically, with letter count and identification.

Aalto, Alvar 5 (Finnish architect)

Adams, John Quincy 5 (U.S. president)

Alcott, Louisa May 6 (U.S. writer)

Alexander, Grover Cleveland 9 (U.S. baseball player)

Amin, Idi 4 (Ugandan leader)

Angelico, Fra 8 (Italian painter)

Angelou, Maya 7 (U.S. poet)

Antony, Marc 6 (Roman general)

Arnaz, Desi 5 (U.S. actor & producer)

Astor, John Jacob 5 (U.S. fur trader & financier)

Attucks, Crispus 7 (American Revolution figure)

Auden, W(ystan) H(ugh) 5 (English poet)

Baer, Max 4 (U.S. boxer)

Barnes, Djuna 6 (novelist)

Beiderbecke, Bix 11 (U.S. jazz musician)

Belloc, Hilaire 6 (English writer)

Ben-Gurion, David 9 (Israeli leader)

Benton, Thomas Hart 6 (U.S. painter)

Berg, Alban 4 (Austrian composer)

Bierce, Ambrose 6 (U.S. satirical writer)

Bombeck, Erma 7 (U.S. humorist)

Borges, Jorge Luis 6 (Argentine writer)

Borglum, Gutzon 7 (U.S. sculptor)

Bourke-White, Margaret 11 (U.S. photographer)

Boutros-Ghali, Boutros 12 (Egyptian diplomat)

Bragg, Braxton 5 (U.S. Confederate general)

Brecht, Bertolt 6 (German dramatist)

Bryan, William Jennings 5 (U.S. politician)

Bryant, William Cullen 6 (U.S. writer)

Burne-Jones, Edward 10 (English painter)

Burroughs, Edgar Rice 9 (U.S. writer)

Cabell, James Branch 6 (U.S. novelist)

Cannon, Dyan 6 (U.S. actress)

Capote, Truman 6 (U.S. writer)

Carey, Mariah 5 (U.S. popular singer)

Caruso, Enrico 6 (Italian operatic singer)

Carver, George Washington 6 (U.S. inventor)

Casals, Pablo 6 (Spanish cellist)

Castro, Fidel 6 (Cuban leader)

Chanel, Coco 6 (French fashion designer)

Chaplin, Oona 7 (daughter of Charlie Chaplin)

Charles, Ezzard 7 (U.S. boxer)

Clemens, Samuel Langhorne 7 (U.S. writer)

Coca, Imogene 4 (U.S. comedienne)

Cooper, James Fenimore 6 (U.S. writer)

Copland, Aaron 7 (U.S. composer)

Crane, Hart 5 (U.S. poet)

Cronyn, Hume 5 (actor)

Cummings, E(dward) E(stlin) 8 (U.S. poet)

Cunningham, Merce 10 (U.S. choreographer)

Dahl, Arlene 4 (U.S. actress)

Dali, Salvador 4 (Spanish artist)

Dare, Virginia 4 (first English person born in America)

Davis, Jefferson 5 (U.S. Confederate leader)

Davis, Miles 5 (U.S. jazz musician)

de la Renta, Oscar 9 (fashion designer)

Derek, Bo 5 (U.S. actress)

Dinesen, Isak 7 (Danish writer)

Dior, Christian 4 (French fashion designer)

Doyle, Arthur Conan 5 (English writer)

Du Bois, W(illiam) E(dward) B(urghardt) 6 (U.S. writer & civil rights leader)

Dulles, John Foster 6 (U.S. diplomat)

Dunbar, Paul Laurence 6 (U.S. poet)

Duns Scotus, John 10 (Scottish theologian)

Eban, Abba 4 (Israeli leader)

Edison, Thomas Alva 6 (U.S. inventor)

Fawkes, Guy 6 (English conspirator)

Ferrari, Enzo 7 (Italian car designer & manufacturer)

Gandhi, Indira 6 (Indian leader)

Gandhi, Rajiv 6 (Indian leader)

Gardner, Erle Stanley 7 (U.S. writer)

Gerry, Elbridge 5 (U.S. jurist)

Gilman, Charlotte Perkins 6 (U.S. writer)

Hammer, Armand 6 (U.S. businessman)

Havel, Vaclav 5 (Czech writer & politician)

Helmsley, Leona 8 (U.S. businesswoman)

Hendrix, Jimi 7 (U.S. musician)

Henie, Sonja 5 (skater)

Hilton, Conrad 6 (U.S. businessman)

Holmes, Oliver Wendell 6 (U.S. jurist)

Howells, William Dean 7 (U.S. writer)

Hubbard, L. Ron 7 (U.S. writer)

Huie, William Bradford 4 (U.S. writer)

Kemal Atatürk 5 (Turkish leader)

Kent, Rockwell 4 (U.S. artist)

Keynes, John Maynard 6 (English economist)

Khrushchev, Nikita 10 (Soviet leader)

Kierkegaard, Søren 11 (Danish philosopher)

Lajoie, Nap(oleon) 6 (U.S. baseball player)

Lévi-Strauss, Claude 11 (French anthropologist)

Lewis, C(live) S(taples) 5 (English writer)

Lewis, Meade Lux 5 (U.S. jazz musician)

Lewis, Meriwether 5 (U.S. explorer)

Limbaugh, Rush 8 (U.S. radio/TV personality)

Lincoln, Elmo 7 (actor)

Mather, Cotton 6 (American clergyman & writer)

Mather, Increase 6 (American clergyman & writer)

Maupassant, Guy de 10 (French writer)

Meir, Golda 4 (Israeli leader)

Midler, Bette 6 (U.S. singer & actress)

Mies van der Rohe, Ludwig 14 (U.S. architect)

Miró, Joan 4 (Spanish artist)

Monk, Thelonious 4 (U.S. jazz musician)

Morton, Jelly Roll 6 (U.S. jazz musician)

Murphy, Audie 6 (U.S. war hero & actor)

Nasby, Petroleum V. 5 (U.S. humorist)

Negri, Pola 5 (actress)

Nin, Anaïs 3 (diarist)

O'Connor, Sandra Day 7 (U.S. jurist)

O'Neal, Shaquille 5 (U.S. basketball player)

Oates, Joyce Carol 5 (U.S. writer)

Odets, Clifford 5 (U.S. dramatist)

Olds, Ransom 4 (U.S. inventor)

Omar Khayyam 11 (Persian poet)

Oswald, Lee Harvey 6 (U.S. assassin)

Ozawa, Seiji 5 (conductor)

Parrish, Maxfield 7 (U.S. artist)

Parsons, Talcott 7 (U.S. sociologist)

Pascal, Blaise 6 (French philosopher)

Peacock, Thomas Love 7 (English writer)

Pei, I. M. 3 (U.S. architect)

Piaf, Edith 4 (French singer)

Picasso, Pablo 7 (Spanish artist)

Pike, Zebulon 4 (U.S. explorer)

Plath, Sylvia 5 (U.S. poet)

Poe, Edgar Allan 3 (U.S. writer)

Pollock, Jackson 7 (U.S. artist)

Pol Pot 6 (Cambodian leader)

Pound, Ezra 5 (U.S. poet & critic)

Powell, Adam Clayton 6 (U.S. politician)

Powys, John Cowper 5 (English writer)

Presley, Elvis Aron 7 (U.S. singer & actor)

Rand, Ayn 4 (U.S. writer)

Rembrandt van Rijn 16 (Dutch artist)

Ride, Sally 4 (U.S. astronaut)

Roberts, Oral 7 (U.S. evangelist)

Rockne, Knute 6 (U.S. football coach)

Rose, Axl 4 (U.S. singer)

Rushdie, Salman 7 (writer)

Saarinen, Eero 8 (Finnish architect)

Sackville-West, Vita 13 (English writer)

Sartre, Jean-Paul 6 (French writer & philosopher)

Savalas, Telly 7 (U.S. actor)

Shelley, Percy Bysshe 7 (English poet)

Sherman, William Tecumseh 7 (U.S. Union general)

Sommer, Elke 6 (actress)

Sousa, John Philip 5 (U.S. composer)

Speaker, Tris 7 (U.S. baseball player)

Spenser, Edmund 7 (English poet)

Stanton, Elizabeth Cady 7 (U.S. reformer)

Stevenson, Robert Louis 9 (Scottish writer)

Stowe, Harriet Beecher 5 (U.S. writer)

Strachey, Lytton 8 (English writer)

Stravinsky, Igor 10 (Russian composer)

Synge, John Millington 5 (Irish dramatist)

Tharp, Twyla 5 (U.S. choreographer)

Toklas, Alice B. 6 (U.S. writer)

Torme, Mel 5 (U.S. singer)

Vaughan Williams, Ralph 15 (English composer)

Washington, Booker T. 10 (U.S. educator & reformer)

Washington, Denzel 10 (U.S. actor)

Weaver, Sigourney 6 (U.S. actress)

Webber, Andrew Lloyd 6 (English composer)

Williams, William Carlos 8 (U.S. poet)

Winfrey, Oprah 7 (U.S. TV personality)

Wodehouse, P(elham) G(renville) 9 (English writer)

Wright, Frank Lloyd 6 (U.S. architect)

Yeats, William Butler 5 (Irish writer)

NATIONS OF THE WORLD

Listed alphabetically by nation, with letter counts.

Nation	Capital	Currency
Afghanistan 11	Kabul 5	afghani 7
Albania 7	Tirana 6	lek 3
Algeria 7	Algiers 7	dinar 5
Andorra 7	Andorra la Vella 14	franc 5, peseta 6
Angola 6	Luanda 6	kwanza 6
Antigua and Barbuda 17	St. John's 7	dollar 6
Argentina 9	Buenos Aires 11	peso 4
Armenia 7	Yerevan 7	dram 4
Australia 9	Canberra 8	dollar 6
Austria 7	Vienna 6	schilling 9
Azerbaijan 10	Baku 4	manat 5
Bahamas 7	Nassau 6	dollar 6
Bahrain 7	Manama 6	dinar 5
Bangladesh 10	Dhaka 5 (Dacca)	taka 4
Barbados 8	Bridgetown 10	dollar 6
Belarus 7	Minsk 5	ruble 5
Belgium 7	Brussels 8	franc 5
Belize 6	Belmopan 8	dollar 6
Benin 5	Porto Novo 9	franc 5
Bhutan 6	Thimphu 7	ngultrum 8
Bolivia 7	La Paz 5, Sucre 5	boliviano 9
Bosnia and Herzegovina 20 (Hercegovina)	Sarajevo 8	dinar 5
Botswana 8	Gaborone 8	pula 4
Brazil 6	Brasília 8	real 4
Brunei 6	Bandar Seri Begawan 17	dollar 6
Bulgaria 8	Sofia 5	lev 3
Burkina Faso 11	Ouagadougou 11	franc 5
Burundi 7	Bujumbura 9	franc 5
Cambodia 8	Phnom Penh 9	riel 4
Cameroon 8	Yaoundé 7	franc 5
Canada 6	Ottawa 6	dollar 6
Cape Verde 9	Praia 5	escudo 6
Central African Republic 22	Bangui 6	franc 5
Chad 4	N'Djamena 8	franc 5
Chile 5	Santiago 8	peso 4
China 5	Beijing 7 (Peking, Peiping)	yuan 4
Colombia 8	Bogotá 6	peso 4
Comoros 7	Moroni 6	franc 5
Congo 5	Brazzaville 11	franc 5
Costa Rica 9	San José 7	colón 5
Croatia 7	Zagreb 6	kuna 4
Cuba 4	Havana 6	peso 4
Cyprus 6	Nicosia 7	pound 5
Czech Republic 13	Prague 6	koruna 6
Denmark 7	Copenhagen 10	krone 5
Djibouti 8	Djibouti 8	franc 5
Dominica 8	Roseau 6	dollar 6
Dominican Republic 17	Santo Domingo 12	peso 4
Ecuador 7	Quito 5	sucre 5
Egypt 5	Cairo 5	pound 5
El Salvador 10	San Salvador 11	colón 5
Equatorial Guinea 16	Malabo 6	franc 5
Eritrea 7	Asmara 6	birr 4
Estonia 7	Tallinn 7	kroon 5
Ethiopia 8	Addis Ababa 10	birr 4
Fiji 4	Suva 4	dollar 6

Nation	Capital	Currency
Finland 7	Helsinki 8	markka 6
France 6	Paris 5	franc 5
Gabon 5	Libreville 10	franc 5
Gambia 6	Banjul 6	dalasi 6
Georgia 7	Tbilisi 7	lari 4
Germany 7	Berlin 6	deutsche mark 12
Ghana 5	Accra 5	cedi 4
Greece 6	Athens 6	drachma 7
Grenada 7	St. George's 9	dollar 6
Guatemala 9	Guatemala City 13	quetzal 7
Guinea 6	Conakry 7	franc 5
Guinea-Bissau 12	Bissau 6	peso 4
Guyana 6	Georgetown 10	dollar 6
Haiti 5	Port-au-Prince 12	gourde 6
Honduras 8	Tegucigalpa 11	lempira 7
Hungary 7	Budapest 8	forint 6
Iceland 7	Reykjavik 9	króna 5
India 5	New Delhi 8	rupee 5
Indonesia 9	Jakarta 7	rupiah 6
Iran 4	Tehran 6 (Teheran)	rial 4
Iraq 4	Baghdad 7 (Bagdad)	dinar 5
Ireland 7	Dublin 6	pound 5 (punt)
Israel 6	Jerusalem 9	shekel 6
Italy 5	Rome 4	lira 4
Ivory Coast 10	Yamoussoukro 12	franc 5
Jamaica 7	Kingston 8	dollar 6
Japan 5	Tokyo 5	yen 3
Jordan 6	Amman 5	dinar 5
Kazakhstan 10	Alma-Ata 7 (Almaty)	tenge 5
Kenya 5	Nairobi 7	shilling 8
Kiribati 8	Tarawa 6	dollar 6
Korea, North 10	Pyongyang 9	won 3
Korea, South 10	Seoul 5	won 3
Kuwait 6	Kuwait 6 (Kuwait City)	dinar 5
Kyrgyzstan 10 (Kirghizstan)	Bishkek 7	som 3
Laos 4	Vientiane 9	kip 3
Latvia 6	Riga 4	lats 4
Lebanon 7	Beirut 6	pound 5
Lesotho 7	Maseru 6	loti 4
Liberia 7	Monrovia 8	dollar 6
Libya 5	Tripoli 7	dinar 5
Liechtenstein 13	Vaduz 5	franc 5
Lithuania 9	Vilnius 7	litas 5
Luxembourg 10	Luxembourg 10	franc 5
Macedonia 9	Skopje 6	denar 5
Madagascar 10	Antananarivo 12	franc 5
Malawi 6	Lilongwe 8	kwacha 6
Malaysia 8	Kuala Lumpur 11	ringgit 7
Maldives 8	Malé 4	rufiyaa 7
Mali 4	Bamako 6	franc 5
Malta 5	Valletta 8	lira 4
Marshall Islands 15	Dalap-Uliga-Darrit 16	dollar 6
Mauritania 10	Nouakchott 10	ouguiya 7
Mauritius 9	Port Louis 9	rupee 5
Mexico 6	Mexico City 10	peso 4
Micronesia 10	Palikir 7	dollar 6
Moldova 7	Kishinev 8	leu 3
Monaco 6	Monaco 6	franc 5
Mongolia 8	Ulan Bator 9	tugrik 6

Nation	Capital	Currency
Morocco 7	Rabat 5	dirham 6
Mozambique 10	Maputo 6	metical 7
Myanmar 7	Yangon 6 (Rangoon)	kyat 4
Namibia 7	Windhoek 8	dollar 6
Nauru 5	—	dollar 6
Nepal 5	Katmandu 8 (Kathmandu)	rupee 5
Netherlands 11	Amsterdam 9	guilder 7
New Zealand 10	Wellington 10	dollar 6
Nicaragua 9	Managua 7	córdoba 7
Niger 5	Niamey 6	franc 5
Nigeria 7	Abuja 5	naira 5
Norway 6	Oslo 4	krone 5
Oman 4	Muscat 6	rial 4
Pakistan 8	Islamabad 9	rupee 5
Palau 5	Koror 5	dollar 6
Panama 6	Panama City 10	balboa 6
Papua New Guinea 14	Port Moresby 11	kina 4
Paraguay 8	Asunción 8	guaraní 7
Peru 4	Lima 4	sol 3
Philippines 11	Manila 6	peso 4
Poland 6	Warsaw 6	zloty 5
Portugal 8	Lisbon 6	escudo 6
Qatar 5	Doha 4	riyal 5
Romania 7	Bucharest 9	leu 3
Russia 6	Moscow 6	ruble 5
Rwanda 6	Kigali 6	franc 5
San Marino 9	San Marino 9	lira 4
São Tomé and Príncipe 18	São Tomé 7	dobra 5
Saudi Arabia 11	Riyadh 6	riyal 5
Senegal 7	Dakar 5	franc 5
Seychelles 10	Victoria 8	rupee 5
Sierra Leone 11	Freetown 8	leone 5
Singapore 9	Singapore 9	dollar 6
Slovakia 8	Bratislava 10	koruna 6
Slovenia 8	Ljubljana 9	tolar 5
Solomon Islands 14	Honiara 7	dollar 6
Somalia 7	Mogadishu 9	shilling 8
South Africa 11	Pretoria (administrative) 8	rand 4
Spain 5	Madrid 6	peseta 6
Sri Lanka 8	Colombo 7	rupee 5
St. Kitts and Nevis 15	Basseterre 10	dollar 6
St. Lucia 7	Castries 8	dollar 6
St. Vincent and the Grenadines 25	Kingstown 9	dollar 6
Sudan 5	Khartoum 8	pound 5
Suriname 8	Paramaribo 10	guilder 7
Swaziland 9	Mbabane 7	lilangeni 9
Sweden 6	Stockholm 9	krona 5
Switzerland 11	Bern 4	franc 5
Syria 5	Damascus 8	pound 5
Taiwan 6	Taipei 6	dollar 6
Tajikistan 10 (Tadzhikistan)	Dushanbe 8	ruble 5
Tanzania 8	Dodoma 6	shilling 8
Thailand 8	Bangkok 7	baht 4
Togo 4	Lomé 4	franc 5
Tonga 5	Nukualofa 9	pa'anga 5
Trinidad and Tobago 17	Port-of-Spain 11	dollar 6
Tunisia 7	Tunis 5	dinar 5
Turkey 6	Ankara 6	lira 4
Turkmenistan 12	Ashkhabad 9	manat 5

Nation	Capital	Currency
Tuvalu 6	Fongafale 9	dollar 6
Uganda 6	Kampala 7	shilling 8
Ukraine 7	Kiev 4	hryvnia 7
United Arab Emirates 18	Abu Dhabi 8	dirham 6
United Kingdom 13	London 6	pound 5
United States 12	Washington (DC) 10	dollar 6
Uruguay 7	Montevideo 10	peso 4
Uzbekistan 10	Tashkent 8	som 3
Vanuatu 7	Vila 4	vatu 4
Vatican City 11	—	lira 4
Venezuela 9	Caracas 7	bolívar 7
Vietnam 7	Hanoi 5	dong 4
Western Samoa 12	Apia 4	tala 4
Yemen 5	Sana 4 (Sanaa)	rial 4
Yugoslavia 10	Belgrade 8	dinar 5
Zaire 5	Kinshasa 8	zaire 5
Zambia 6	Lusaka 6	kwacha 6
Zimbabwe 8	Harare 6	dollar 6

SELECTED NOBEL PRIZE WINNERS

Listed alphabetically with letter count, prize category, and year.

Addams, Jane 6 (Peace) 1931
Agnon, Samuel 5 (Literature) 1966
Aleixandre, Vicente 10 (Literature) 1977
Alfven, Hannes 6 (Physics) 1970
Alvarez, Luis 7 (Physics) 1968
Andric, Ivo 6 (Literature) 1961
Angell, Sir Norman 6 (Peace) 1933
Appleton, Sir Edward 8 (Physics) 1947
Arafat, Yasir 6 (Peace) 1994
Arias Sánchez, Oscar 12 (Peace) 1987
Arrhenius, Svante 9 (Chemistry) 1903
Asturias, Miguel 8 (Literature) 1967
Aung San Suu Kyi 13 (Peace) 1991
Banting, Sir Frederick 7 (Physiology or
  Medicine) 1923
Bardeen, John 7 (Physics) 1956
Becker, Gary 6 (Economics) 1992
Beckett, Samuel 7 (Literature) 1969
Becquerel, Antoine Henri 9 (Physics) 1903
Begin, Menachem 5 (Peace) 1978
Bellow, Saul 6 (Literature) 1976
Benavente, Jacinto 9 (Literature) 1922
Bergson, Henri 7 (Literature) 1927
Bethe, Hans 5 (Physics) 1967
Bjornson, Bjornsterne 8 (Literature) 1903
Bloch, Felix 5 (Physics) 1952
Bohr, Niels 4 (Physics) 1922
Böll, Heinrich 4 (Literature) 1972
Borlaug, Norman 7 (Peace) 1970
Born, Max 4 (Physics) 1954
Brandt, Willy 6 (Peace) 1971
Brattain, Walter 8 (Physics) 1956
Braun, Karl (Carl) 5 (Physics) 1909
Briand, Aristide 8 (Peace) 1926
Brodsky, Joseph 7 (Literature) 1987
Buchanan, James 8 (Economics) 1986
Buchner, Eduard 7 (Chemistry) 1907
Buck, Pearl 4 (Literature) 1938
Bunche, Ralph 6 (Peace) 1950
Bunin, Ivan 5 (Literature) 1933
Butenandt, Adolf 9 (Chemistry) 1939
Butler, Nicholas Murray 6 (Peace) 1931
Camus, Albert 5 (Literature) 1957
Canetti, Elias 7 (Literature) 1981
Carducci, Giosue 8 (Literature) 1906
Carrel, Alexis 6 (Physiology or Medicine)
  1912
Cassin, René 6 (Peace) 1968
Cela, Camilo José 4 (Literature) 1989
Chadwick, Sir James 8 (Physics) 1935
Chain, Ernst 5 (Physiology or Medicine)
  1945
Chamberlain, Sir J. Austen 11 (Peace)
  1925
Chandrasekhar, Subrahmanyan 13
  (Physics) 1983
Cherenkov, Pavel 9 (Physics) 1958
Churchill, Sir Winston 9 (Literature) 1953

Compton, Arthur 7 (Physics) 1927
Corrigan, Mairead 8 (Peace) 1976
Crick, Francis 5 (Physiology or Medicine)
  1962
Cronin, James 6 (Physics) 1980
Curie, Marie 5 (Chemistry) 1911
Curie, Marie 5 (Physics) 1903
Curie, Pierre 5 (Physics) 1903
Dalai Lama 9 (Peace) 1989
Dawes, Charles 5 (Peace) 1925
de Broglie, Prince Louis-Victor 9 (Physics)
  1929
de Klerk, F.W. 7 (Peace) 1993
Delbrück, Max 8 (Physiology or Medicine)
  1969
Deledda, Grazia 7 (Literature) 1926
Dirac, Paul 5 (Physics) 1933
Eccles, Sir John 6 (Physiology or
  Medicine) 1963
Echegaray, Jose 9 (Literature) 1904
Ehrlich, Paul 7 (Physiology or Medicine)
  1908
Einstein, Albert 8 (Physics) 1921
Eliot, T.S. 5 (Literature) 1948
Elytis, Odysseus 6 (Literature) 1979
Enders, John 6 (Physiology or Medicine)
  1954
Erlanger, Joseph 8 (Physiology or
  Medicine) 1944
Esquivel, Adolfo Pérez 8 (Peace) 1980
Eucken, Rudolf 6 (Literature) 1908
Faulkner, William 8 (Literature) 1949
Fermi, Enrico 5 (Physics) 1938
Feynman, Richard 7 (Physics) 1965
Fischer, Emil 7 (Chemistry) 1902
Fischer, Ernst 7 (Chemistry) 1973
Fleming, Sir Alexander 7 (Physiology or
  Medicine) 1945
Florey, Sir Howard 6 (Physiology or
  Medicine) 1945
France, Anatole 6 (Literature) 1921
Franck, James 6 (Physics) 1925
Friedman, Milton 8 (Economics) 1976
Galsworthy, John 10 (Literature) 1932
García Márquez, Gabriel 13 (Literature)
  1982
Gell-Mann, Murray 8 (Physics) 1969
Gide, André 4 (Literature) 1947
Gjellerup, Karl 9 (Literature) 1917
Glashow, Sheldon 7 (Physics) 1979
Golding, William 7 (Literature) 1983
Golgi, Camillo 5 (Physiology or Medicine)
  1906
Gorbachev, Mikhail 9 (Peace) 1990
Gordimer, Nadine 8 (Literature) 1991
Grignard, Victor 8 (Chemistry) 1912
Haber, Fritz 5 (Chemistry) 1918
Hahn, Otto 4 (Chemistry) 1944

Hammarskjöld, Dag 12 (Peace) 1961
Hamsun, Knut 6 (Literature) 1920
Hauptmann, Gerhart 9 (Literature) 1912
Heaney, Seamus 6 (Literature) 1995
Heisenberg, Werner 10 (Physics) 1932
Hemingway, Ernest 9 (Literature) 1954
Hertz, Gustav 5 (Physics) 1925
Hesse, Hermann 5 (Literature) 1946
Heyse, Paul 5 (Literature) 1910
Hull, Cordell 4 (Peace) 1945
Jensen, Johannes 6 (Literature) 1944
Jiménez, Juan 7 (Literature) 1956
Johnson, Eyvind 7 (Literature) 1974
Joliot-Curie, Frederic 11 (Chemistry) 1935
Joliot-Curie, Irene 11 (Chemistry) 1935
Josephson, Brian 9 (Physics) 1973
Kapitsa, Pyotr 7 (Physics) 1978
Karlfeldt, Erik 9 (Literature) 1931
Kawabata, Yasunari 8 (Literature) 1968
Kellogg, Frank 7 (Peace) 1929
King, Martin Luther, Jr. 4 (Peace) 1964
Kipling, Rudyard 7 (Literature) 1907
Kissinger, Henry 9 (Peace) 1973
Koch, Robert 4 (Physiology or Medicine) 1905
Krebs, Sir Hans 5 (Physiology or Medicine) 1953
Lagerkvist, Pär 10 (Literature) 1951
Lagerlöf, Selma 8 (Literature) 1909
Landsteiner, Karl 11 (Physiology or Medicine) 1930
Lawrence, Ernest 8 (Physics) 1939
Laxness, Halldor 7 (Literature) 1955
Le Duc Tho 8 (Peace) 1973
Leontief, Wassily 8 (Economics) 1973
Lewis, Sinclair 5 (Literature) 1930
Lorentz, Hendrik 7 (Physics) 1902
Lorenz, Konrad 6 (Physiology or Medicine) 1973
Luthuli, Albert 7 (Peace) 1960
MacBride, Sean 8 (Peace) 1974
Maeterlinck, Maurice 11 (Literature) 1911
Mahfouz, Naguib 7 (Literature) 1988
Mandela, Nelson 7 (Peace) 1993
Mann, Thomas 4 (Literature) 1929
Marconi, Guglielmo 7 (Physics) 1909
Marshall, George 8 (Peace) 1953
Martin du Gard, Roger 12 (Literature) 1937
Martinson, Harry 9 (Literature) 1974
Mauriac, François 7 (Literature) 1952
McClintock, Barbara 10 (Physiology or Medicine) 1983
McMillan, Edwin 8 (Chemistry) 1951
Medawar, Peter 7 (Physiology or Medicine) 1960
Menchú, Rigoberta 6 (Peace) 1992
Michelson, Albert 9 (Physics) 1907
Millikan, Robert 8 (Physics) 1923
Miłosz, Czeslaw 6 (Literature) 1980
Mistral, Frederic 7 (Literature) 1904

Mistral, Gabriela 7 (Literature) 1945
Mommsen, Theodor 7 (Literature) 1902
Monod, Jacques 5 (Physiology or Medicine) 1965
Montale, Eugenio 7 (Literature) 1975
Morrison, Toni 8 (Literature) 1993
Mössbauer, Rudolf 9 (Physics) 1961
Mother Teresa 12 (Peace) 1979
Myrdal, Alva 6 (Peace) 1982
Myrdal, Gunnar 6 (Economics) 1974
Nansen, Fridtjof 6 (Peace) 1922
Neruda, Pablo 6 (Literature) 1971
Noel-Baker, Philip 9 (Peace) 1959
O'Neill, Eugene 6 (Literature) 1936
Oe, Kenzaburo 2 (Literature) 1994
Ostwald, Wilhelm 7 (Chemistry) 1909
Pasternak, Boris 9 (Literature) 1958
Pauli, Wolfgang 5 (Physics) 1945
Pauling, Linus 7 (Chemistry) 1954
Pauling, Linus 7 (Peace) 1962
Pavlov, Ivan 6 (Physiology or Medicine) 1904
Paz, Octavio 3 (Literature) 1990
Pearson, Lester 7 (Peace) 1957
Penzias, Arno 7 (Physics) 1978
Peres, Shimon 5 (Peace) 1994
Perse, Saint-John 5 (Literature) 1960
Pirandello, Luigi 10 (Literature) 1934
Pire, Dominique Georges 4 (Peace) 1958
Planck, Max 6 (Physics) 1918
Pontoppidan, Henrik 11 (Literature) 1917
Prudhomme, René 9 (Literature) 1901
Quasimodo, Salvatore 9 (Literature) 1959
Rabi, Isidor 4 (Physics) 1944
Rabin, Yitzhak 5 (Peace) 1994
Ramsay, Sir William 6 (Chemistry) 1904
Reymont, Wladyslaw 7 (Literature) 1924
Robles, Alfonso Garcia 6 (Peace) 1982
Roentgen (Röntgen), Wilhelm 8 (Physics) 1901
Rolland, Romain 7 (Literature) 1915
Roosevelt, Theodore 9 (Peace) 1906
Root, Elihu 4 (Peace) 1912
Ross, Sir Ronald 4 (Physiology or Medicine) 1902
Rotblat, Joseph 7 (Peace) 1995
Rubbia, Carlo 6 (Physics) 1984
Russell, Bertrand 7 (Literature) 1950
Rutherford, Ernest 10 (Chemistry) 1908
Sachs, Nelly 5 (Literature) 1966
Sadat, Anwar 5 (Peace) 1978
Sakharov, Andrei 8 (Peace) 1975
Salam, Abdus 5 (Physics) 1979
Samuelson, Paul 9 (Economics) 1970
Sanger, Frederick 8 (Chemistry) 1980
Sartre, Jean-Paul 6 (Literature) 1964
Sato, Eisaku 6 (Peace) 1974
Schrödinger, Erwin 11 (Physics) 1933
Schweitzer, Albert 10 (Peace) 1952
Seaborg, Glenn 7 (Chemistry) 1951

PULITZER PRIZE WINNERS FOR FICTION

Listed alphabetically, with letter count, year, and title of work.

Agee, James 4 (1958) *A Death in the Family*

Barnes, Margaret 6 (1931) *Years of Grace*

Bellow, Saul 6 (1976) *Humboldt's Gift*

Bromfield, Louis 9 (1927) *Early Autumn*

Buck, Pearl 4 (1932) *The Good Earth*

Butler, Robert Olen 6 (1993) *A Good Scent from a Strange Mountain*

Cather, Willa 6 (1923) *One of Ours*

Cheever, John 7 (1979) *The Stories of John Cheever*

Cozzens, James 7 (1949) *Guard of Honor*

Davis, Harold 5 (1936) *Honey in the Horn*

Drury, Allen 5 (1960) *Advise and Consent*

Faulkner, William 8 (1955) *A Fable*

Faulkner, William 8 (1963) *The Reivers*

Ferber, Edna 6 (1925) *So Big*

Flavin, Martin 6 (1944) *Journey in the Dark*

Glasgow, Ellen 7 (1942) *In This Our Life*

Grau, Shirley Ann 4 (1965) *The Keepers of the House*

Guthrie, A.B., Jr. 7 (1950) *The Way West*

Hemingway, Ernest 9 (1953) *The Old Man and the Sea*

Hersey, John 6 (1945) *A Bell for Adano*

Hijuelos, Oscar 8 (1990) *The Mambo Kings Play Songs of Love*

Johnson, Josephine 7 (1935) *Now in November*

Kantor, MacKinlay 6 (1956) *Andersonville*

Kennedy, William 7 (1984) *Ironweed*

La Farge, Oliver 7 (1930) *Laughing Boy*

Lee, Harper 3 (1961) *To Kill a Mockingbird*

Lewis, Sinclair 5 (1926) *Arrowsmith*

Lurie, Alison 5 (1985) *Foreign Affairs*

Mailer, Norman 6 (1980) *The Executioner's Song*

Malamud, Bernard 7 (1967) *The Fixer*

Marquand, John 8 (1938) *The Late George Apley*

McMurtry, Larry 8 (1986) *Lonesome Dove*

McPherson, James Alan 9 (1978) *Elbow Room*

Michener, James 8 (1948) *Tales of the South Pacific*

Miller, Caroline 6 (1934) *Lamb in His Bosom*

Mitchell, Margaret 8 (1937) *Gone with the Wind*

Momaday, N. Scott 7 (1969) *House Made of Dawn*

Morrison, Toni 8 (1988) *Beloved*

O'Connor, Edwin 7 (1962) *The Edge of Sadness*

Peterkin, Julia 8 (1929) *Scarlet Sister Mary*

Poole, Ernest 5 (1918) *His Family*

Porter, Katherine Anne 6 (1966) *The Collected Stories of Katherine Anne Porter*

Proulx, E. Annie 6 (1994) *The Shipping News*

Rawlings, Marjorie Kinnan 8 (1939) *The Yearling*

Richter, Conrad 7 (1951) *The Town*

Shaara, Michael 6 (1975) *The Killer Angels*

Shields, Carol 7 (1995) *The Stone Diaries*

Sinclair, Upton 8 (1943) *Dragon's Teeth*

Smiley, Jane 6 (1992) *A Thousand Acres*

Stafford, Jean 7 (1970) *Collected Stories*

Stegner, Wallace 7 (1972) *Angle of Repose*

Steinbeck, John 9 (1940) *The Grapes of Wrath*

Stribling, T.S. 9 (1933) *The Store*

Styron, William 6 (1968) *The Confessions of Nat Turner*

Tarkington, Booth 10 (1919) *The Magnificent Ambersons*

Tarkington, Booth 10 (1922) *Alice Adams*

Taylor, Peter 6 (1987) *A Summons to Memphis*

Taylor, Robert 6 (1959) *The Travels of Jaimie McPheeters*

Toole, John Kennedy 5 (1981) *A Confederacy of Dunces*

Tyler, Anne 5 (1989) *Breathing Lessons*

Updike, John 6 (1982) *Rabbit is Rich*

Updike, John 6 (1991) *Rabbit at Rest*

Walker, Alice 6 (1983) *The Color Purple*

Warren, Robert Penn 6 (1947) *All the King's Men*

Welty, Eudora 5 (1973) *The Optimist's Daughter*

Wharton, Edith 7 (1921) *The Age of Innocence*

Wilder, Thornton 6 (1928) *The Bridge of San Luis Rey*

Wilson, Margaret 6 (1924) *The Able McLaughlins*

Wouk, Herman 4 (1952) *The Caine Mutiny*

SHAKESPEARE'S PLAYS AND CHARACTERS

Listed by play, with characters by letter count.

Comedies

All's Well That Ends Well . . . 8. Parolles (Paroles)

As You Like It . . . 5. Arden (forest), Celia 6. Jaques 7. Orlando 8. Rosalind 10. Touchstone (fool)

The Comedy of Errors . . . 7. Ephesus (setting)

Cymbeline . . . 6. Imogen 9. Cymbeline

Love's Labour's Lost . . . 7. Navarre (setting) 10. Holofernes

Measure for Measure . . . 6. Angelo, Vienna (setting) 7. Claudio 8. Isabella

The Merchant of Venice . . . 5. Tubal 6. Portia 7. Antonio (the merchant), Jessica, Shylock (villain)

The Merry Wives of Windsor . . . 6. Pistol 7. Quickly (Mistress), Windsor (setting) 8. Falstaff (Sir John)

A Midsummer Night's Dream . . . 4. Puck (Robin Goodfellow) 6. Athens (setting), Bottom (Nick), Helena, Hermia, Oberon (Fairy King) 7. Titania (Fairy Queen) 8. Lysander 9. Demetrius

Much Ado About Nothing . . . 7. Messina (setting) 8. Beatrice, Benedick

Pericles, Prince of Tyre

The Taming of the Shrew . . . 5. Padua (setting) 9. Katherina (Kate), Petruchio

The Tempest . . . 5. Ariel (fairy) 7. Caliban (ogre), Miranda 8. Prospero

Troilus and Cressida . . . 4. Troy (setting) 7. Troilus 8. Cressida, Pandarus

Twelfth Night . . . 5. Belch (Sir Toby), Feste (fool), Viola 6. Olivia, Orsino (duke) 7. Illyria (setting) 8. Malvolio 9. Aguecheek (Sir Andrew)

The Two Gentlemen of Verona . . . 5. Julia 7. Proteus 9. Valentine

The Two Noble Kinsmen

The Winter's Tale . . . 7. Leontes, Perdita 8. Hermione 9. Autolycus (thief)

Tragedies

Antony and Cleopatra . . . 6. Antony (Mark) 7. Octavia 8. Charmian, Octavius (Caesar) 9. Cleopatra, Enobarbus 10. Mark Antony

Coriolanus . . . 8. Volumnia 10. Coriolanus

Hamlet . . . 6. Hamlet (prince) 7. Denmark (setting), Horatio, Laertes, Ophelia 8. Claudius (uncle), Elsinore (castle), Gertrude (queen), Polonius 11. Rosencrantz 12. Guildenstern

Julius Caesar . . . 6. Antony (Mark), Brutus, Portia 7. Cassius 9. Calpurnia 10. Mark Antony 12. Julius Caesar

King Lear . . . 4. Lear 5. Edgar, Regan 6. Edmund 7. Goneril 8. Cordelia

Macbeth . . . 6. Banquo, Duncan (king) 7. Macbeth, Macduff 9. Inverness (castle) 11. Lady Macbeth

Othello . . . 4. Iago (villain) 6. Cassio, Cyprus (setting), Emilia, Venice (setting) 7. Othello (the Moor) 9. Desdemona

Romeo and Juliet . . . 5. Romeo 6. Juliet, Mantua (setting), Tybalt (Juliet's cousin), Verona (setting) 7. Capulet (Juliet's family) 8. Laurence (Friar), Mercutio, Montague (Romeo's family)

Timon of Athens

Titus Andronicus

Histories

Henry IV, Parts 1, 2 . . . 3. Hal (Prince) 6. Pistol 7. Hotspur, Quickly (Mistress) 8. Falstaff (Sir John)

Henry V

Henry VI, Parts 1, 2, 3

Henry VIII

King John

Richard II

Richard III

PRESIDENTS AND FIRST LADIES OF THE UNITED STATES

Listed chronologically by term, with letter count and first names of first ladies.

Name	Term	First Lady
Washington, George 10	1789-97	Martha
Adams, John 5	1797-1801	Abigail
Jefferson, Thomas 9	1801-09	Martha
Madison, James 7	1809-17	Dorothea (Dorothy, Dolley)
Monroe, James 6	1817-25	Elizabeth (Eliza)
Adams, John Quincy 5	1825-29	Louisa
Jackson, Andrew 7	1829-37	Rachel
Van Buren, Martin 8	1837-41	Hannah
Harrison, William Henry 8	1841	Anna
Tyler, John 5	1841-45	Letitia; Julia
Polk, James Knox 4	1845-49	Sarah
Taylor, Zachary 6	1849-50	Margaret
Fillmore, Millard 8	1850-53	Abigail
Pierce, Franklin 6	1853-57	Jane
Buchanan, James 8	1857-61	—
Lincoln, Abraham 7	1861-65	Mary Todd
Johnson, Andrew 7	1865-69	Eliza
Grant, Ulysses S. 5	1869-77	Julia
Hayes, Rutherford B. 5	1877-81	Lucy
Garfield, James A. 8	1881	Lucretia
Arthur, Chester A. 6	1881-85	Ellen
Cleveland, Grover 9	1885-89	Frances
Harrison, Benjamin 8	1889-93	Caroline
Cleveland, Grover 9	1893-97	Frances
McKinley, William 8	1897-1901	Ida
Roosevelt, Theodore (Teddy) 9	1901-09	Edith
Taft, William Howard 4	1909-13	Helen
Wilson, Woodrow 6	1913-21	Ellen; Edith
Harding, Warren G. 7	1921-23	Florence
Coolidge, Calvin 8	1923-29	Grace
Hoover, Herbert 6	1929-33	Lou
Roosevelt, Franklin Delano 9	1933-45	Anna Eleanor
Truman, Harry S 6	1945-53	Bess
Eisenhower, Dwight D. 10	1953-61	Mamie
Kennedy, John Fitzgerald 7	1961-63	Jacqueline
Johnson, Lyndon Baines 7	1963-69	Claudia (Lady Bird)
Nixon, Richard Milhous 5	1969-74	Thelma (Pat)
Ford, Gerald R. 4	1974-77	Elizabeth (Betty)
Carter, Jimmy (James Earl, Jr.) 6	1977-81	Rosalynn
Reagan, Ronald 6	1981-89	Anne (Nancy)
Bush, George 4	1989-93	Barbara
Clinton, Bill (William Jefferson) 7	1993-	Hillary Rodham

Presidents of the United States by Letter Count

4. Bush, Ford, Polk, Taft 5. Adams (John and John Quincy), Grant, Hayes, Nixon, Tyler
6. Arthur, Carter, Hoover, Monroe, Pierce, Reagan, Taylor, Truman, Wilson 7. Clinton,
Harding, Jackson, Johnson (Andrew and Lyndon Baines), Kennedy, Lincoln, Madison 8.
Buchanan, Coolidge, Fillmore, Garfield, Harrison (Benjamin and William Henry),
McKinley, Van Buren 9. Cleveland, Jefferson, Roosevelt (Franklin Delano and Theodore)
10. Eisenhower, Washington

STATES OF THE UNITED STATES

Listed alphabetically, with number counts for states and capitals.

State	Capital
Alabama 7	Montgomery 10
Alaska 6	Juneau 6
Arizona 7	Phoenix 7
Arkansas 8	Little Rock 10
California 10	Sacramento 10
Colorado 8	Denver 6
Connecticut 11	Hartford 8
Delaware 8	Dover 5
Florida 7	Tallahassee 11
Georgia 7	Atlanta 7
Hawaii 6	Honolulu 8
Idaho 5	Boise 5
Illinois 8	Springfield 11
Indiana 7	Indianapolis 12
Iowa 4	Des Moines 9
Kansas 6	Topeka 6
Kentucky 8	Frankfort 9
Louisiana 9	Baton Rouge 10
Maine 5	Augusta 7
Maryland 8	Annapolis 9
Massachusetts 13	Boston 6
Michigan 8	Lansing 7
Minnesota 9	St. Paul 6
Mississippi 11	Jackson 7
Missouri 8	Jefferson City 13
Montana 7	Helena 6
Nebraska 8	Lincoln 7
Nevada 6	Carson City 10
New Hampshire 12	Concord 7
New Jersey 9	Trenton 7
New Mexico 9	Santa Fe 7
New York 7	Albany 6
North Carolina 13	Raleigh 7
North Dakota 11	Bismarck 8
Ohio 4	Columbus 8
Oklahoma 8	Oklahoma City 12
Oregon 6	Salem 5
Pennsylvania 12	Harrisburg 10
Rhode Island 11	Providence 10
South Carolina 13	Columbia 8
South Dakota 11	Pierre 6
Tennessee 9	Nashville 9
Texas 5	Austin 6
Utah 4	Salt Lake City 12
Vermont 7	Montpelier 10
Virginia 8	Richmond 8
Washington 10	Olympia 7
West Virginia 12	Charleston 10
Wisconsin 9	Madison 7
Wyoming 7	Cheyenne 8

NOTES

NOTES